MAJOR ♦
20th- ♦
CENTURY ♦
WRITERS ♦

MAJOR 20th-CENTURY WRITERS

A Selection of Sketches from
Contemporary Authors

Contains more than one thousand entries on the
most widely studied twentieth-century writers,
all originally written or updated for this set.

Second Edition

Kathleen Wilson, Editor

Volume 5: Sh-Z

GALE

DETROIT • LONDON

STAFF

Kathleen Wilson, *Project Manager*

James E. Person, Jr., *Senior Editor*
Kathy D. Darrow, *Manuscript Editor*
Craig E. Hutchinson, *Assistant Manuscript Editor*
Aarti D. Stephens, *Managing Editor*

Bonnie E. Burns, Edith S. Davis, Carol Dell'Amico, George Delury, Sarah Madsen Hardy,
Katherine Hasal, Blaine Howard, Erik Huber, Jean Leverich, Maarten Reilingh,
Judith C. Reveal, Kathleen Savory, Robert E. Schnakenberg,
Kelly Winters, Robert E. Winters, *Sketchwriters*

Nicholas Assendelft, Karen C. Branstetter, Rebecca C. Condit, Karen J. Hansen,
Daniel J. Harvey, Wyn A. Hilty, John Kane, Jill Kushner, Patricia A. Onorato, Carol Page,
Debra M. Reilly, Bohdan R. Romaniuk, Molly C. Stephanou, Lisa A. Wroble, *Proofreaders*

Victoria Cariappa, *Research Manager*
Tamara C. Nott, Tracie A. Richardson, Norma Sawaya, Cheryl Warnock, *Research Associates*

Mary Beth Trimper, *Production Director*
Deborah Milliken, *Production Assistant*
Gary Leach, *Graphic Artist*

ISBN 0-8103-8450-7 (Set)
ISBN 0-7876-2958-8 (Volume 5)

Library of Congress Cataloging-in-Publication Data

Major 20-century writers : a selection of sketches from contemporary
authors / Kathleen Wilson, editor. -- 2nd ed.
    p.   cm.
   1st edition edited by Bryan Ryan.
   Includes bibliographical references and indexes.
    ISBN 0-8103-8450-7 (set). -- ISBN 0-8103-8451-5 (v. 1). -- ISBN
0-8103-8452-3 (v. 2). -- ISBN 0-8103-8453-1 (v. 3). --
ISBN 0-8103-8454-X (v. 4). -- ISBN 0-7876-2958-8 (v. 5).
    1. Literature, Modern--20th century--Bio-bibliography.   I. Wilson,
Kathleen, 1968-   .   II. Ryan, Bryan. Major 20th-century writers.
III. Title: Major twentieth-century writers.
   PN771.M27   1998
   809'.04
   [B]--DC21   98-39995
                                                            CIP
                                                            r98

10 9 8 7 6 5 4 3 2 1

Contents

Introduction

An Important Information Source on Twentieth-Century Literature and Culture

Major Twentieth-Century Authors (*MTCW*) provides students, educators, librarians, researchers, and general readers with a concise yet comprehensive source of biographical and bibliographical information on more than 1,000 of the most influential authors of the century. Based on Gale's award-winning *Contemporary Authors* series, *MTCW* gives users a one-stop resource for information on the figures who have shaped literature in the past 100 years.

New to This Edition

MTCW, second edition, includes sketches on over 1,000 authors. Over 20 percent of these authors are new to this edition, evidencing Gale's commitment to identifying emerging and important writers of recent eras and of many cultures. In addition, sketches on authors who appeared in the first edition of *MTCW* have been updated to include information on their lives and works through 1998.

Who Is a "Major" Author?

In the interests of winnowing the massive list of published world authors to a number that could fit within these five volumes, the editors enlisted the expert guidance of ten advisers, professionals in library science and literature, whose input resulted in informal inclusion criteria. Of no doubt was that *MTCW* would need to include prominent novelists, poets, short story writers, and playwrights who have had at least part of their oeuvre published in English. It was also evident that *MTCW* would have to include writers of all nationalities, ethnicities, and genres, including children's literature and literary criticism. Perhaps not as obvious, advisors believed that authors must have had a significant portion of their writings first published in the twentieth century. This eliminates writers like Mark Twain, who lived until 1910, but includes the French Symbolist Remy de Gourmont, who lived until 1915. Secondly, the editors decided to focus on those who have made writing literature their primary occupation. Therefore, figures such as Adolf Hitler, well known as the author of *Mein Kampf,* have been excluded. Journalists, screenwriters, reporters, and television writers have also been excluded unless their work has been collected into significant, book-length publications. The most spirited debate between the editors and advisors involved choosing between writers who are popular and those whose popularity may not be as broad but whose critical reputations cannot be denied. Although it is hard to determine the eventual reputation of many of today's popular writers, there can be no doubt that their works are known and appreciated by millions, thus conferring upon them the status of "major" author. Lastly, though the primary focus of *MTCW* is writers of fiction, the editors and advisors agreed that authors of the major nonfiction works of the twentieth century should be represented. Therefore, *MTCW* includes writers such as Sigmund Freud, whose writings have had a profound influence on both science and art during the twentieth century, and Martin Luther King, Jr., whose essays and speeches have had a major impact on society and politics over the course of the last several decades.

How Authors Were Chosen for *MTCW*

A preliminary list of authors was sent to an advisory board of librarians, teaching professionals, and writers in both the United States and Great Britain. In consultation with the editors, the list was narrowed to 1,000 authors. Writers who were in the first edition of *MTCW* were not automatically chosen for the second edition. For information about our advisory board for the second edition of *MTCW,* please see p. ix.

Broad Coverage in a Single Source

MTCW provides coverage of the most influential writers of our time, including:

- *Novelists and short story writers:* James Baldwin, Saul Bellow, William Faulkner, Ellen Glasgow, James Joyce, Franz Kafka, C. S. Lewis, Flannery O'Connor, Carlos Fuentes, George Orwell, Eudora Welty, and Edith Wharton, among many others.

- *Dramatists:* Samuel Beckett, Tony Kushner, Bertolt Brecht, Eugene O'Neill, Wendy Wasserstein, and Tennessee Williams, and many more.

- *Poets:* W. H. Auden, Joseph Brodsky, T. S. Eliot, Robert Frost, Howard Nemerov, Charles Simic, Rainer Maria Rilke, and William Butler Yeats, among many others.

- *Contemporary literary figures:* Martin Amis, Maya Angelou, Wendell Berry, Amy Tan, Don DeLillo, Laura Esquivel, Gabriel Garcia Marquez, Nadine Gordimer, Leslie Marmon Silko, Maxine Hong Silko, Madeleine L'Engle, Toni Morrison, V. S. Naipaul, Jeanette Winterson, Joyce Carol Oates, and Thomas Pynchon, among many more.

- *Genre writers:* Ray Bradbury, Agatha Christie, Tom Clancy, Stephen King, Anne Rice, Anne Rivers Siddons, Georges Simenon, J. R. R. Tolkien, and P. G. Wodehouse, among many others.

- *Twentieth-century thinkers:* Hannah Arendt, Bruno Bettelheim, Albert Einstein, Mohandas Gandhi, Russell Kirk, Margaret Mead, Jean-Paul Sartre, and Aleksandr Solzhenitsyn, among many more.

How Entries Are Organized

Each entry begins with a series of rubrics that outline the writer's personal history, including information on the author's birth, death, family life, education, career, memberships, and awards. The *Writings* section lists all known first editions of the author's works, along with the publisher and year published. In some cases, this section may be further divided with helpful subheadings, such as *Plays* or *Mysteries,* in an effort to group like publications together for the user's convenience. The *Sidelights* section provides a critical overview of the author's reception among critics and readers, and the *Biographical/Critical Sources* section provides a useful list of books, feature articles, and reviews in which the writer's work has been treated. This section includes citations for all material quoted in the *Sidelights* essay.

Other helpful sections include *Adaptations,* listing film and television versions of an author's works and information on collections of the author's papers.

Using the Indexes

MTCW includes a Nationality/Ethnicity index as well as a Subject/Genre index. More than 60 nations are represented in the Nationality index, reflecting the international scope of this set and the multinational status of many authors. The Subject/Genre index covers over 25 genres and subject areas of fiction and nonfiction frequently referenced by educators and students, including Holocaust literature, environmental issues, and science fiction/science fantasy literature.

Citing *MTCW*

Students writing papers who wish to include references to information found in *MTCW* may cite sources in their bibliographies using the following format. Teachers adhering to other bibliographic formats may request that their students alter the citation below, which should serve only as a guide:

"Margaret Atwood." *Major Twentieth-Century Writers,* 2nd edition. Ed. Kathleen Wilson. Vol. 1. Detroit: Gale, 1999, pp. 159-64.

Comments are Appreciated

Major Twentieth-Century Writers is intended to serve as a useful reference tool for a wide audience, so your comments about this work are encouraged. Suggestions of authors to include in future editions of *MTCW* are also welcome. Send comments and suggestions to The Editor, *Major Twentieth-Century Writers,* Gale Research, 27500 Drake Road, Farmington Hills, MI 48331-3535. Or, call toll-free at 1-800-347-GALE.

Advisory Board

In preparation for the first edition of *Major Twentieth-Century Writers (MTCW)*, the editors of *Contemporary Authors* conducted a telephone survey of librarians and mailed a print survey to more than four thousand libraries to help determine the kind of reference resource libraries wanted. Once it was clear that a comprehensive, yet affordable source of information on twentieth-century writers was needed to serve small and medium-sized libraries, a wide range of resources was consulted: national surveys of books taught in American high schools and universities; British secondary school syllabi; reference works such as the *New York Public Library Desk Reference, Reading Lists for College-Bound Students: The Books Most Recommended by America's Top Colleges, The List of Books,* E. D. Hirsch's *Cultural Literacy,* and volumes in Gale's Literary Criticism Series and *Dictionary of Literary Biography*. From these resources and with the advice of an international advisory board, the author list for the first edition of *MTCW* was finalized, the sketches edited, and the volume published.

For the second edition, the editors submitted a preliminary author list based largely upon a list of authors included in the first edition. This list was sent to an advisory board of librarians, authors, and teaching professionals in both the United States and Great Britain. In addition to vetting the existing list, the advisors suggested other writers who had not appeared in the first edition. Recommendations made by the advisors ensure that authors from all nations and genres are represented. The ten-member advisory board includes the following individuals, whom the editors wish to thank for sharing their expertise:

- **Robert Bibbee,** Chief of the Literature and Language Division, Chicago Public Library, Harold Washington Library Center, Chicago, Illinois.

- **Michael Burgess,** Head of Technical Services and Collection Development, John M. Pfau Library, California State University, San Bernardino, California.

- **Mary Ann Capan,** Associate Professor and Young Adult and Children's Literature Specialist in the Elementary Reading Department, Western Illinois University, Macomb, Illinois.

- **Eleanor Dore,** Chief of the Language and Literature Division, District of Columbia Public Library, Washington, D.C.

- **Rebecca Havenstein-Coughlin,** Department Head, Adult Services, Canton Public Library, Canton, Michigan.

- **Marcia Pankake,** Professor and Bibliographer in English and American Literature, Meredith Wilson Library, University of Minnesota, Minneapolis, Minnesota.

- **Janice Schuster,** Head of Public Services, Phillips Memorial Library, Providence College, Providence, Rhode Island.

- **Brian Stableford,** literary critic and writer of speculative fiction, Reading, England.

- **Darlene Ursel,** reference librarian at the Plymouth District Library, Plymouth, Michigan.

- **Hope Yelich,** reference librarian at the Earl Gregg Swem Library, The College of William and Mary, Williamsburg, Virginia.

Major 20th-Century Authors

VOLUME 1: A-Ce

Abbey, Edward 1927-1989
Abe, Kobo 1924-1993
Abrahams, Peter 1919-
Abse, Dannie 1923-
Achebe, Chinua 1930-
Ackroyd, Peter 1949-
Adams, Alice 1926-
Adams, Douglas 1952-
Adams, Henry 1838-1918
Adams, Richard 1920-
Adler, Mortimer J. 1902-
Agee, James 1909-1955
Agnon, S. Y. 1888-1970
Aiken, Conrad 1889-1973
Akhmatova, Anna 1888-1966
Albee, Edward 1928-
Aldiss, Brian W. 1925-
Alegria, Claribel 1924-
Aleixandre, Vicente 1898-1984
Alexie, Sherman 1966-
Algren, Nelson 1909-1981
Allen, Paula Gunn 1939-
Allende, Isabel 1942-
Allingham, Margery 1904-1966
Allison, Dorothy E. 1949-
Alvarez, Julia 1950-
Amado, Jorge 1912-
Ambler, Eric 1909-
Amichai, Yehuda 1924-
Amichai, Yehudah
   See Amichai, Yehuda
Amis, Kingsley 1922-1995
Amis, Martin 1949-
Ammons, A. R. 1926-
Anand, Mulk Raj 1905-
Anaya, Rudolfo A. 1937-
Anderson, Maxwell 1888-1959
Anderson, Poul 1926-
Anderson, Sherwood 1876-1941
Angelou, Maya 1928-

Anouilh, Jean 1910-1987
Anthony, Piers 1934-
Apollinaire, Guillaume 1880-1918
Aragon, Louis 1897-1982
Arenas, Reinaldo 1943-1990
Arendt, Hannah 1906-1975
Arias, Ron 1941-
Arnow, Harriette Simpson 1908-1986
Artaud, Antonin 1896-1948
Ashbery, John 1927-
Ashton-Warner, Sylvia 1908-1984
Asimov, Isaac 1920-1992
Asturias, Miguel Angel 1899-1974
Atwood, Margaret 1939-
Auden, W. H. 1907-1973
Auster, Paul 1947-
Ayckbourn, Alan 1939-
Ayer, A. J. 1910-1989
Azuela, Mariano 1873-1952
Babel, Isaak 1894-1941
Bachman, Richard
   See King, Stephen
Bainbridge, Beryl 1933-
Baker, Russell 1925-
Baldwin, James 1924-1987
Ballard, J. G. 1930-
Bambara, Toni Cade 1939-
Banks, Russell 1940-
Baraka, Amiri 1934-
Barker, Clive 1952-
Barnes, Djuna 1892-1982
Barnes, Julian 1946-
Barrie, J. M. 1860-1937
Barthelme, Donald 1931-1989
Barthes, Roland 1915-1980
Bates, H. E. 1905-1974
Baum, L. Frank 1856-1919
Baxter, Charles 1947-
Beagle, Peter S. 1939-
Beattie, Ann 1947-

Beauchamp, Kathleen Mansfield
   1888-1923
Beauvoir, Simone de 1908-1986
Beckett, Samuel 1906-1989
Beerbohm, Max 1872-1956
Behan, Brendan 1923-1964
Bell, Madison Smartt 1957-
Belloc, Hilaire 1870-1953
Bellow, Saul 1915-
Bely, Andrey
   See Bugayev, Boris Nikolayevich
Benavente, Jacinto 1866-1954
Benchley, Peter 1940-
Benet, Stephen Vincent 1898-1943
Bennett, Alan 1934-
Bennett, Arnold 1867-1931
Berendt, John 1939-
Berger, Thomas 1924-
Bergman, Ingmar 1918-
Berry, Wendell 1934-
Berryman, John 1914-1972
Betjeman, John 1906-1984
Bettelheim, Bruno 1903-1990
Binchy, Maeve 1940-
Bioy Casares, Adolfo 1914-
Bishop, Elizabeth 1911-1979
Biyidi, Alexandre 1932-
Black Elk 1863-1950
Blair, Eric 1903-1950
Blais, Marie-Claire 1939-
Bland, Edith Nesbit
   See Nesbit, E.
Blixen, Karen 1885-1962
Bloch, Robert 1917-1994
Block, Lawrence 1938-
Bloom, Harold 1930-
Blount, Roy, Jr. 1941-
Blume, Judy 1938-
Bly, Robert 1926-
Boell, Heinrich 1917-1985

Bogan, Louise 1897-1970
Boland, Eavan 1944-
Bonnefoy, Yves 1923-
Bontemps, Arna 1902-1973
Borges, Jorge Luis 1899-1986
Bowen, Elizabeth 1899-1973
Bowles, Paul 1910-
Boyle, Kay 1902-1992
Boyle, T. Coraghessan 1948-
Bradbury, Edward P.
Bradbury, Malcolm 1932-
Bradbury, Ray 1920-
Bradley, Marion Zimmer 1930-
Brecht, Bertolt 1898-1956
Breslin, James 1930-
Breslin, Jimmy
    See Breslin, James
Breton, Andre 1896-1966
Brink, Andre 1935-
Brittain, Vera 1893(?)-1970
Brodsky, Iosif
    Alexandrovich 1940-1996
Brodsky, Joseph
    See Brodsky, Iosif Alexandrovich
Brooke, Rupert 1887-1915
Brookner, Anita 1928-
Brooks, Cleanth 1906-1994
Brooks, Gwendolyn 1917-
Brophy, Brigid 1929-1995
Brown, Dee 1908-
Brown, Rita Mae 1944-

Brown, Sterling Allen 1901-1989
Brownmiller, Susan 1935-
Bruchac, Joseph III 1942-
Brunner, John 1934-1995
Bryher
    See Ellerman, Annie Winifred
Buber, Martin 1878-1965
Buchan, John 1875-1940
Buchwald, Art 1925-
Buck, Pearl S. 1892-1973
Buckley, William F., Jr. 1925-
Buechner, Frederick 1926-
Buero Vallejo, Antonio 1916-
Bugayev, Boris
    Nikolayevich, 1880-1934
Bukowski, Charles 1920-1994
Bulgakov, Mikhail 1891-1940
Bullins, Ed 1935-
Burgess, Anthony
    See Wilson, John Burgess
Burke, Kenneth 1897-1993
Burroughs, Edgar Rice 1875-1950
Burroughs, William S. 1914-1997
Butler, Octavia E. 1947-
Butler, Robert Olen 1945-
Butor, Michel 1926-
Byatt, A. S. 1936-
Cabell, James Branch 1879-1958
Cabrera Infante, G. 1929-
Caldicott, Helen 1938-
Caldwell, Erskine 1903-1987

Caldwell, Taylor 1900-1985
Calisher, Hortense 1911-
Callaghan, Morley
    Edward 1903-1990
Calvino, Italo 1923-1985
Campbell, Bebe Moore 1950-
Campbell, Joseph 1904-1987
Campbell, Roy 1901-1957
Camus, Albert 1913-1960
Canetti, Elias 1905-1994
Capek, Karel 1890-1938
Capote, Truman 1924-1984
Card, Orson Scott 1951-
Cardenal, Ernesto 1925-
Carey, Peter 1943-
Carr, John Dickson 1906-1977
Carroll, James P. 1943-
Carruth, Hayden 1921-
Carson, Rachel 1907-1964
Carter, Angela 1940-1992
Cartland, Barbara 1901-
Carver, Raymond 1938-1988
Cary, Joyce 1888-1957
Casares, Adolfo Bioy
    See Bioy Casares, Adolfo
Castellanos, Rosario 1925-1974
Cather, Willa Sibert 1873-1947
Catton, Bruce 1899-1978
Cavafy, C. P. 1863-1933
Cela, Camilo Jose 1916-
Cesaire, Aime 1913-

VOLUME 2: Ch-G

Challans, Mary 1905-1983
Chandler, Raymond 1886-1959
Char, Rene 1907-1988
Chase-Riboud, Barbara 1939-
Chavez, Denise 1948-
Cheever, John 1912-1982
Chesnutt, Charles W. 1858-1932
Chesterton, G. K. 1874-1936
Ch'ien, Chung-shu 1910-
Childress, Alice 1920-1994
Chomsky, Noam 1928-
Christie, Agatha 1890-1976
Churchill, Winston 1874-1965
Ciardi, John 1916-1986
Cisneros, Sandra 1954-
Cixous, Helene 1937-
Clancy, Thomas L. 1947-
Clancy, Tom

    See Clancy, Thomas L.
Clark, John Pepper 1935-
Clark, Kenneth 1903-1983
Clark, Mary Higgins 1929-
Clarke, Arthur C. 1917-
Clarke, Austin C. 1934-
Clavell, James 1925-1994
Cleary, Beverly 1916-
Cleaver, Eldridge 1935-1998
Clifton, Lucille 1936-
Clutha, Janet Paterson Frame 1924-
Cocteau, Jean 1889-1963
Codrescu, Andrei 1946-
Coetzee, J. M. 1940-
Colette 1873-1954
Comfort, Alex 1920-
Commager, Henry Steele 1902-
Commoner, Barry 1917-

Compton-Burnett, I. 1884-1969
Conan Doyle, Arthur
    See Doyle, Arthur Conan
Conde, Maryse 1937-
Condon, Richard 1915-1996
Connell, Evan S., Jr. 1924-
Connolly, Cyril 1903-1974
Conrad, Joseph 1857-1924
Conroy, Pat 1945-
Cookson, Catherine 1906-
Cooper, Susan 1935-
Coover, Robert 1932-
Cormier, Robert 1925-
Cornwell, David 1931-
Cornwell, Patricia 1956-
Corso, Gregory 1930-
Cortazar, Julio 1914-1984
Cousins, Norman 1915-1990

Coward, Noel 1899-1973
Cowley, Malcolm 1898-1989
Cox, William Trevor 1928-
Cozzens, James Gould 1903-1978
Crane, Hart 1899-1932
Creeley, Robert 1926-
Crews, Harry 1935-
Crichton, Michael 1942-
Cruz, Victor Hernandez 1949-
Cullen, Countee 1903-1946
Cummings, E. E. 1894-1962
Dahl, Roald 1916-1990
Danticat, Edwidge 1969-
Dario, Ruben 1867-1916
Darwish, Mahmud 1942-
Davies, Robertson 1913-1995
Davis, Ossie 1917-
Day Lewis, C. 1904-1972
de Beauvoir, Simone
    See Beauvoir, Simone de
de Gourmont, Remy
    See Gourmont, Remy de
Deighton, Len
    See Deighton, Leonard Cyril
Deighton, Leonard Cyril 1929-
de la Mare, Walter 1873-1956
Delany, Samuel R. 1942-
DeLillo, Don 1936-
de Man, Paul 1919-1983
Derrida, Jacques 1930-
Desai, Anita 1937-
de Vries, Peter 1910-1993
Dexter, Colin 1930-
Dick, Philip K. 1928-1982
Dickey, James 1923-1997
Didion, Joan 1934-
Dillard, Annie 1945-
Dinesen, Isak
    See Blixen, Karen
Disch, Thomas M. 1940-
Disch, Tom
    See Disch, Thomas M.
Doctorow, E. L. 1931-
Donleavy, J. P. 1926-
Donoso, Jose 1924-1996
Doolittle, Hilda 1886-1961
Dorris, Michael 1945-1997
Dos Passos, John 1896-1970
Dove, Rita 1952-
Doyle, Arthur Conan 1859-1930
Doyle, Conan
    See Doyle, Arthur Conan
Doyle, Roddy 1958-
Drabble, Margaret 1939-

Dreiser, Theodore 1871-1945
D'Souza, Dinesh 1961-
Du Bois, W. E. B. 1868-1963
Duerrenmatt, Friedrich 1921-1990
du Maurier, Daphne 1907-1989
Duncan, Robert 1919-1988
Dunn, Katherine 1945-
Dunsany, Edward John Moreton
    Drax Plunkett 1878-1957
Dunsany, Lord
    See Dunsany, Edward John
    Moreton Drax Plunkett
Durang, Christopher 1949-
Durant, Will 1885-1981
Duras, Marguerite 1914-1996
Durrell, Lawrence 1912-1990
Dworkin, Andrea 1946-
Eagleton, Terence 1943-
Eagleton, Terry
    See Eagleton, Terence
Eco, Umberto 1932-
Ehrenreich, Barbara 1941-
Einstein, Albert 1879-1955
Ekwensi, Cyprian 1921-
Eliot, T. S. 1888-1965
Elkin, Stanley L. 1930-1995
Ellerman, Annie Winifred
    1894-1983
Ellis, Alice Thomas
    See Haycraft, Anna
Ellis, Bret Easton 1964-
Ellison, Harlan 1934-
Ellison, Ralph 1914-1994
Ellmann, Richard 1918-1987
Ellroy, James 1948-
El-Shabazz, El-Hajj Malik
    See Little, Malcolm
Elytis, Odysseus 1911-1996
Emecheta, Buchi 1944-
Empson, William 1906-1984
Endo, Shusaku 1923-1996
Erdrich, Louise 1954-
Erikson, Erik H. 1902-1994
Esquivel, Laura 1951(?)-
Esslin, Martin 1918-
Estleman, Loren D. 1952-
Fair, A. A.
    See Gardner, Erle Stanley
Faludi, Susan 1959(?)-
Farrell, James T. 1904-1979
Fast, Howard 1914-
Faulkner, William 1897-1962
Ferber, Edna 1887-1968
Ferlinghetti, Lawrence 1919(?)-

Ferre, Rosario 1942-
Fiedler, Leslie A. 1917-
Fisher, M. F. K. 1908-1992
Fitzgerald, F. Scott 1896-1940
Fitzgerald, Penelope 1916-
Fleming, Ian 1908-1964
Fo, Dario 1926-
Foote, Shelby 1916-
Forche, Carolyn 1950-
Ford, Ford Madox 1873-1939
Ford, Richard 1944-
Forster, E. M. 1879-1970
Forsyth, Frederick 1938-
Foucault, Michel 1926-1984
Fowles, John 1926-
France, Anatole
    See Thibault, Jacques Anatole
    Francois
Francis, Dick 1920-
Frank, Anne 1929-1945
Franklin, Miles 1879-1954
Fraser, Antonia 1932-
Fraser, George MacDonald 1925-
Frayn, Michael 1933-
French, Marilyn 1929-
Freud, Sigmund 1856-1939
Friedan, Betty 1921-
Friedman, Milton 1912-
Frisch, Max 1911-1991
Frost, Robert 1874-1963
Fry, Christopher 1907-
Frye, Northrop 1912-1991
Fuentes, Carlos 1928-
Fuller, R. Buckminster 1895-1983
Fussell, Paul 1924-
Gaddis, William 1922-
Gaines, Ernest J. 1933-
Galbraith, John Kenneth 1908-
Gallant, Mavis 1922-
Galsworthy, John 1867-1933
Gandhi, Mahatma
    See Gandhi, Mohandas
    Karamchand
Gandhi, Mohandas Karamchand
    1869-1948
Garcia Lorca, Federico 1898-1936
Garcia Marquez, Gabriel 1928-
Gardner, Erle Stanley 1889-1970
Gardner, John, Jr. 1933-1982
Garner, Alan 1934-
Garnett, David 1892-1981
Gass, William H. 1924-
Gasset, Jose Ortega y
    See Ortega y Gasset, Jose

Gates, Henry Louis, Jr. 1950-
Geisel, Theodor Seuss 1904-1991
Genet, Jean 1910-1986
Gibbons, Kaye 1960-
Gibran, Kahlil 1883-1931
Gibson, William 1948-
Gibson, William 1914-
Gide, Andre 1869-1951
Gilchrist, Ellen 1935-
Gill, Brendan 1914-1997
Gilman, Charlotte Perkins
    1860-1935
Ginsberg, Allen 1926-1997
Ginzburg, Natalia 1916-1991
Giovanni, Nikki 1943-

Glasgow, Ellen, 1873-1945
Gluck, Louise 1943-
Godoy Alcayaga, Lucila 1889-1957
Godwin, Gail 1937-
Golding, William 1911-1993
Gordimer, Nadine 1923-
Gordon, Caroline 1895-1981
Gorky, Maxim
    See Peshkov, Alexei Maximovich
Gould, Stephen Jay 1941-
Gourmont, Remy de 1858-1915
Goytisolo, Juan 1931-
Grahame, Kenneth 1859-1932
Grass, Guenter 1927-
Graves, Robert 1895-1985

Gray, Alasdair 1934-
Gray, Francine du Plessix 1930-
Gray, Spalding 1941-
Greeley, Andrew M. 1928-
Green, Julien 1900-1998
Greene, Graham 1904-1991
Greer, Germaine 1939-
Grey, Zane 1872-1939
Grigson, Geoffrey 1905-1985
Grisham, John 1955-
Grumbach, Doris 1918-
Guare, John 1938-
Guest, Judith 1936-
Guterson, David 1956-

VOLUME 3: H-Ma

Haggard, H. Rider 1856-1925
Hailey, Arthur 1920-
Halberstam, David 1934-
Hale, Janet Campbell 1947-
Haley, Alex 1921-1992
Hall, Donald 1928-
Hall, Radclyffe 1886-1943
Hamilton, Clive
    See Lewis, C. S.
Hamilton, Virginia 1936-
Hammett, Dashiell 1894-1961
Handke, Peter 1942-
Hansberry, Lorraine 1930-1965
Hardwick, Elizabeth 1916-
Hardy, Thomas 1840-1928
Hamson, Knut
    See Pedersen, Knut
Harjo, Joy 1951-
Hartley, L. P. 1895-1972
Hasek, Jaroslav 1883-1923
Havel, Vaclav 1936-
Hawkes, John 1925-
Hawking, S. W.
    See Hawking, Stephen W.
Hawking, Stephen W. 1942-
Haycraft, Anna
Hayden, Robert E. 1913-1980
Hayek, F. A. 1899-1992
H. D.
    See Doolittle, Hilda
Head, Bessie 1937-1986
Heaney, Seamus 1939-
Hebert, Anne 1916-
Heidegger, Martin 1889-1976

Heinlein, Robert A. 1907-1988
Heller, Joseph 1923-
Hellman, Lillian 1906-1984
Helprin, Mark 1947-
Hemingway, Ernest 1899-1961
Hempel, Amy 1951-
Henley, Elizabeth Becker 1952-
Henry, O.
    See Porter, William Sydney
Herbert, Frank 1920-1986
Herriot, James 1916-1995
Hersey, John 1914-1993
Hesse, Hermann 1877-1962
Heyer, Georgette 1902-1974
Heyerdahl, Thor 1914-
Hiassen, Carl 1953-
Hibbert, Eleanor Alice Burford
    1906-1993
Highsmith, Patricia 1921-1995
Highway, Tomson 1951-
Hijuelos, Oscar 1951-
Hillerman, Tony 1925-
Himes, Chester 1909-1984
Hinojosa, Rolando 1929-
Hinton, S. E. 1950-
Hiraoka, Kimitake 1925-1970
Hoban, Russell 1925-
Hochhuth, Rolf 1931-
Hodgson, William Hope 1877-1918
Hoeg, Peter 1957-
Hoffman, Alice 1952-
Holroyd, Michael 1935-
Hooks, Bell
    See Watkins, Gloria

Hope, A. D. 1907-
Hopley-Woolrich, Cornell George
    1903-1968
Horgan, Paul 1903-1995
Housman, A. E. 1859-1936
Howard, Maureen 1930-
Howe, Irving 1920-1993
Howells, W. D.
    See Howells, William Dean
Howells, William Dean 1837-1920
Hoyle, Fred 1915-
Hubbard, L. Ron 1911-1986
Hueffer, Ford Madox
    See Ford, Ford Madox
Hughes, Langston 1902-1967
Hughes, Ted 1930-
Hurston, Zora Neale 1903-1960
Huxley, Aldous 1894-1963
Hwang, David Henry 1957-
Infante, G. Cabrera
    See Cabrera Infante, G.
Inge, William 1913-1973
Ionesco, Eugene 1912-1994
Irving, John 1942-
Isaacs, Susan 1943-
Isherwood, Christopher 1904-1986
Ishiguro, Kazuo 1954-
Jackson, Shirley 1919-1965
Jakes, John 1932-
James, Henry 1843-1916
James, P. D.
    See White, Phyllis Dorothy James
Jarrell, Randall 1914-1965
Jeffers, Robinson 1887-1962

Jhabvala, Ruth Prawer 1927-
Jimenez, Juan Ramon 1881-1958
Johnson, Charles 1948-
Johnson, James Weldon 1871-1938
Johnson, Pamela Hansford
    1912-1981
Jones, Gayl 1949-
Jones, LeRoi
    See Baraka, Amiri
Jong, Erica 1942-
Joyce, James 1882-1941
Jung, C. G. 1875-1961
Justice, Donald 1925-
Kael, Pauline 1919-
Kafka, Franz 1883-1924
Kantor, MacKinlay 1904-1977
Kaufman, George S. 1889-1961
Kawabata, Yasunari 1899-1972
Kaye, M. M. 1909-
Kazantzakis, Nikos 1883(?)-1957
Keillor, Garrison
    See Keillor, Gary
Keillor, Gary 1942-
Keneally, Thomas 1935-
Kennedy, William 1928-
Kerouac, Jack
    See Kerouac, Jean-Lous Lebris de
Kerouac, Jean-Louis Lebris de
    1922-1969
Kesey, Ken 1935-
Keyes, Daniel 1927-
Keynes, John Maynard 1883-1946
Kienzle, William X. 1928-
Kincaid, Jamaica 1949-
King, Martin Luther Jr. 1929-1968
King, Stephen 1947-
Kingsolver, Barbara 1955-
Kingston, Maxine Hong 1940-
Kinnell, Galway 1927-
Kinsella, Thomas 1928-
Kinsella, W. P. 1935-
Kinsey, Alfred 1894-1956
Kipling, Rudyard 1865-1936
Kirk, Russell 1918-1994
Kizer, Carolyn 1925-
Knight, Etheridge 1931(?)-1991
Knowles, John 1926-
Koch, Kenneth 1925-
Koestler, Arthur 1905-1983
Kogawa, Joy Nozomi 1935-
Kosinski, Jerzy 1933-1991
Kueng, Hans 1928-
Kumin, Maxine 1925-
Kundera, Milan 1929-

Kung, Hans
    See Kueng, Hans
Kunitz, Stanley 1905-
Kushner, Tony 1956-
Lagerkvist, Paer 1891-1974
Lagerkvist, Par
    See Lagerkvist, Paer
Lagerloef, Selma 1858-1940
La Guma, Alex 1925-1985
Lamming, George 1927-
L'Amour, Louis 1908-1988
Lampedusa, Giuseppe Tomassi di
    1896-
Lardner, Ring W. 1885-1933
Larkin, Philip 1922-1985
Lasch, Christopher 1932-1994
Laurence, Margaret 1926-1987
Lawrence, D. H. 1885-1930
Laye, Camara 1928-1980
Layton, Irving 1912-
Leacock, Stephen 1869-1944
Leavis, F. R. 1895-1978
Leavitt, David 1961-
Le Carre, John
    See Cornwell, David
Lee, Harper 1926-
Le Guin, Ursula K. 1929-
Lchmann, Rosamond 1901-
Leiber, Fritz 1910-1992
L'Engle, Madeleine 1918-
Leonard, Elmore 1925-
Leonov, Leonid 1899-1994
Leseig, Theo.
    See Geisel, Theodore Seuss
Lessing, Doris 1919-
Levertov, Denise 1923-1997
Levi, Primo 1919-1987
Levin, Ira 1929-
Levi-Strauss, Claude 1908-
Lewis, C. Day
    See Day Lewis, C.
Lewis, C. S. 1898-1963
Lewis, Sinclair 1885-1951
Lewis, Wyndham 1882(?)-1957
Leyner, Mark 1956-
Liebling, A. J. 1904-1963
Lindbergh, Anne Morrow 1906-
Lippmann, Walter 1889-1974
Little, Malcolm 1925-1965
Lively, Penelope 1933-
Llosa, Mario Vargas
    See Vargas Llosa, Mario
Lodge, David 1935-
London, Jack

    See London, John Griffith
London, John Griffith 1876-1916
Loos, Anita 1893-1981
Lorca, Federico Garcia
    See Garcia Lorca, Federico
Lorde, Audre 1934-1992
Lorenz, Konrad Zacharias
    1903-1989
Lovecraft, H. P. 1890-1937
Lowell, Amy 1874-1925
Lowell, Robert 1917-1977
Lowry, Lois 1937-
Lowry, Malcolm 1909-1957
Ludlum, Robert 1927-
Lukacs, George
    See Lukacs, Gyorgy
Lukacs, Gyorgy 1885-1971
Lustbader, Eric Van 1946-
Maas, Peter 1929-
MacDonald, John D. 1916-1986
MacInnes, Colin 1914-1976
MacInnes, Helen 1907-1985
MacKinnon, Catharine A. 1946-
MacLeish, Archibald 1892-1982
MacLennan, Hugh 1907-1990
MacLeod, Alistair 1936-
MacNeice, Louis 1907-1963
Madhubuti, Haki R. 1942-
Mahfouz, Naguib 1911(?)-
Mailer, Norman 1923-
Maillet, Antonine 1929-
Malamud, Bernard 1914-1986
Malcolm X
    See Little, Malcolm
Malouf, David 1934-
Malraux, Andre 1901-1976
Mamet, David 1947-
Manchester, William 1922-
Mandelstam, Osip 1891(?)-1938(?)
Mann, Thomas 1875-1955
Mansfield, Katherine
    See Beauchamp, Kathleen
    Mansfield
Mao Tse tung 1893-1976
Marcel, Gabriel Honore
    1889-1973
Marquand, John P. 1893-1960
Marquez, Gabriel Garcia
    See Garcia Marquez, Gabriel
Marsh, Ngaio 1899-1982
Marshall, Paule 1929-
Martinez, Jacinto Benavente y
    See Benavente, Jacinto
Masefield, John 1878-1967

Maslow, Abraham H. 1908-1970
Mason, Bobbie Ann 1940-
Masters, Edgar Lee 1868-1950
Mathabane, Mark 1960-

Matthiessen, Peter 1927-
Maugham, W. Somerset 1874-1965
Maupin, Armistead 1944-
Mauriac, Francois 1885-1970

Maurois, Andre 1885-1967
Mayakovsky, Vladimir 1893-1930

VOLUME 4: Mc-Se

McCaffrey, Anne 1926-
McCarthy, Charles, Jr. 1933-
McCarthy, Cormac
    See McCarthy, Charles, Jr.
McCarthy, Mary 1912-1989
McCullers, Carson 1917-1967
McCullough, Colleen 1938-
McEwan, Ian 1948-
McInerney, Jay 1955-
McKay, Claude
    See McKay, Festus Claudius
McKay, Festus Claudius 1889-1948
McLuhan, Marshall 1911-1980
McMillan, Terry 1951-
McMurtry, Larry 1936-
McNally, Terrence 1939-
McPhee, John 1931-
McPherson, James Alan 1943-
Mead, Margaret 1901-1978
Mencken, H. L. 1880-1956
Mendez, Miguel 1930-
Menninger, Karl 1893-1990
Merrill, James 1926-1995
Merton, Thomas 1915-1968
Merwin, W. S. 1927-
Metalious, Grace 1924-1964
Michener, James A. 1907(?)-1997
Millar, Kenneth 1915-1983
Millay, Edna St. Vincent 1892-1950
Miller, Arthur 1915-
Miller, Henry 1891-1980
Millett, Kate 1934-
Millhauser, Steven 1943-
Milne, A. A. 1882-1956
Milosz, Czeslaw 1911-
Mishima, Yukio
    See Hiraoka, Kimitake
Mistral, Gabriela
    See Godoy Alçayaga, Lucila
Mitchell, Margaret 1900-1949
Mofolo, Thomas 1875(?)-1948
Momaday, N. Scott 1934-
Montgomery, L. M. 1874-1942
Moorcock, Michael 1939-
Moore, Brian 1921-

Moore, Marianne 1887-1972
Morante, Elsa 1918-1985
Moravia, Alberto 1907-1990
Morris, Wright 1910-
Morrison, Toni 1931-
Morrow, James 1947-
Mortimer, John 1923-
Mosley, Walter 1952-
Mowat, Farley 1921-
Mphahlele, Ezekiel 1919-
Muggeridge, Malcolm 1903-1990
Mukherjee, Bharati 1940-
Munro, Alice 1931-
Munro, H. H. 1870-1916
Murdoch, Iris 1919-
Musil, Robert 1880-1942
Myers, Walter Dean 1937-
Nabokov, Vladimir 1899-1977
Naipaul, Shiva 1945-1985
Naipaul, V. S. 1932-
Narayan, R. K. 1906-
Nash, Ogden 1902-1971
Naylor, Gloria 1950-
Nemerov, Howard 1920-1991
Neruda, Pablo 1904-1973
Nesbit, E. 1858-1924
Ngugi Wa Thiong'o 1938-
Nin, Anais 1903-1977
Niven, Laurence Van Cott 1938-
Norway, Nevil Shute 1899-1960
Oates, Joyce Carol 1938-
Oates, Stephen B. 1936-
O'Brian, Patrick 1914-
O'Brien, Edna 1936-
O'Brien, Tim 1946-
O'Casey, Sean 1880-1964
O'Connor, Flannery 1925-1964
Odets, Clifford 1906-1963
Oe, Kenzaburo 1935-
O'Faolain, Sean 1900-1991
O'Flaherty, Liam 1896-1984
O'Hara, Frank 1926-1966
O'Hara, John 1905-1970
Okigbo, Christopher 1932-1967
Okri, Ben 1959-

Olds, Sharon 1942-
Olsen, Tillie 1912-
Olson, Charles 1910-1970
Ondaatje, Michael 1943-
O'Neill, Eugene 1888-1953
Onetti, Juan Carlos 1909-1994
Ortega y Gasset, Jose 1883-1955
Orton, Joe
    See Orton, John Kingsley
Orton, John Kingsley 1933-1967
Orwell, George
    See Blair, Eric
Osborne, John 1929-1994
Owen, Wilfred 1893-1918
Oz, Amos 1939-
Ozick, Cynthia 1928-
Paglia, Camille 1947-
Paley, Grace 1922-
Parker, Dorothy 1893-1967
Parks, Gordon 1912-
Pasternak, Boris 1890-1960
Paton, Alan 1903-1988
Pauling, Linus 1901-1994
Paz, Octavio 1914-1998
p'Bitek, Okot 1931-1982
Pedersen, Knut 1859-1952
Percy, Walker 1916-1990
Percy, William Alexander
    1885-1942
Perelman, S. J. 1904-1979
Peretti, Frank E. 1951-
Peshkov, Alexei Maximovich
    1868-1936
Phillips, Caryl 1958-
Phillips, Jayne Anne 1952-
Piaget, Jean 1896-1980
Piercy, Marge 1936-
Pinsky, Robert 1940-
Pinter, Harold 1930-
Pirandello, Luigi 1867-1936
Pirsig, Robert M. 1928-
Plath, Sylvia 1932-1963
Plimpton, George 1927-
Pohl, Frederik 1919-
Pollitt, Katha 1949-

Popper, Karl R. 1902-1994
Porter, Katherine Anne 1890-1980
Porter, William Sydney 1862-1910
Potok, Chaim 1929-
Potter, Beatrix 1866-1943
Pound, Ezra 1885-1972
Powell, Anthony 1905-
Powys, John Cowper 1872-1963
Priestley, J. B. 1894-1984
Pritchett, V. S. 1900-1997
Prokosch, Frederic 1908-
Proulx, E. Annie 1935-
Proust, Marcel 1871-1922
Puig, Manuel 1932-1990
Puzo, Mario 1920-
Pyle, Ernie 1900-1945
Pym, Barbara 1913-1980
Pynchon, Thomas 1937-
Queneau, Raymond 1903-1976
Quindlen, Anna 1953-
Quoirez, Francoise 1935-
Rand, Ayn 1905-1982
Ransom, John Crowe 1888-1974
Rao, Raja 1909-
Rattigan, Terence 1911-1977
Rawlings, Marjorie Kinnan
    1896-1953
Reed, Ishmael 1938-
Remarque, Erich Maria
    1898-1970
Renault, Mary
    See Challans, Mary

Rendell, Ruth 1930-
Rexroth, Kenneth 1905-1982
Rhys, Jean 1890(?)-1979
Rice, Anne 1941-
Rice, Elmer 1892-1967
Rich, Adrienne 1929-
Richards, I. A. 1893-1979
Richler, Mordecai 1931-
Richter, Conrad 1890-1968
Rilke, Rainer Maria 1875-1926
Robbe-Grillet, Alain 1922-
Robbins, Harold 1916-1997
Robbins, Thomas Eugene 1936-
Robbins, Tom
    See Robbins, Thomas Eugene
Robinson, Edwin Arlington
    1869-1935
Roethke, Theodore 1908-1963
Rogers, Will 1879-1935
Rossner, Judith 1935-
Roth, Henry 1906-1995
Roth, Philip 1933-
Rozewicz, Tadeusz 1921-
Rukeyser, Muriel 1913-1980
Rule, Ann 1935-
Rulfo, Juan 1918-1986
Runyon, Damon 1884(?)-1946
Rushdie, Salman 1947-
Russell, Bertrand 1872-1970
Sabato, Ernesto 1911-
Sachs, Nelly 1891-1970
Sacks, Oliver 1933-

Sackville-West, V. 1892-1962
Sagan, Carl 1934-1996
Sagan, Francoise
    See Quoirez, Francoise
Said, Edward W. 1935-
Saint-Exupery, Antoine de
    1900-1944
Saki
    See Munro, H. H.
Salas, Floyd Francis 1931-
Salinger, J. D. 1919-
Sanchez, Sonia 1934-
Sandburg, Carl 1878-1967
Sandoz, Mari 1896-1966
Saroyan, William 1908-1981
Sarraute, Nathalie 1900-
Sarton, May 1912-1995
Sartre, Jean-Paul 1905-1980
Sassoon, Siegfried 1886-1967
Sayers, Dorothy L. 1893-1957
Schaeffer, Susan Fromberg 1941-
Schlesinger, Arthur M., Jr. 1917-
Schulz, Bruno 1892-1942
Schwartz, Delmore 1913-1966
Schwartz, Lynne Sharon 1939-
Seifert, Jaroslav 1901-1986
Sendak, Maurice 1928-
Senghor, Leopold Sedar 1906-
Seth, Vikram 1952-
Seuss, Dr.
    See Geisel, Theodore Seuss
Sexton, Anne 1928-1974

VOLUME 5: Sh-Z

Shaffer, Peter 1926-
Shange, Ntozake 1948-
Shapiro, Karl 1913-
Shaw, Bernard
    See Shaw, George Bernard
Shaw, George Bernard 1856-1950
Shaw, Irwin 1913-1984
Sheed, Wilfrid 1930-
Sheldon, Sidney 1917-
Shepard, Sam 1943-
Shiel, M. P. 1865-1947
Shields, Carol 1935-
Shilts, Randy 1951-1994
Shirer, William L. 1904-1993
Sholokhov, Mikhail 1905-1984
Shute, Nevil
    See Norway, Nevil Shute

Siddons, Anne Rivers 1936-
Silko, Leslie Marmon 1948-
Sillitoe, Alan 1928-
Silverberg, Robert 1935-
Silverstein, Shel 1932-
Simenon, Georges 1903-1989
Simic, Charles 1938-
Simon, Neil 1927-
Simpson, Louis 1923-
Sinclair, Upton 1878-1968
Singer, Isaac Bashevis 1904-1991
Sitwell, Dame Edith 1887-1964
Skinner, B. F. 1904-1990
Skvorecky, Josef 1924-
Smith, Clark Ashton 1893-1961
Smith, Florence Margaret
    1902-1971

Smith, Martin Cruz 1942-
Smith, Rolando Hinojosa
    See Hinojosa-Smith, Rolando
Smith, Stevie
    See Smith, Florence Margaret
Smith, Wilbur 1933-
Snodgrass, W. D. 1926-
Snow, C. P. 1905-1980
Snyder, Gary 1930-
Solzhenitsyn, Aleksandr 1918-
Sontag, Susan 1933-
Soto, Gary 1952-
Soyinka, Wole 1934-
Spark, Muriel 1918-
Spender, Stephen 1909-1995
Spiegelman, Art 1948-
Spillane, Frank Morrison 1918-

Spillane, Mickey
   See Spillane, Frank Morrison
Spock, Benjamin 1903-1998
Stafford, Jean 1915-1979
Stead, Christina 1902-1983
Steel, Danielle 1947-
Stegner, Wallace 1909-1993
Stein, Gertrude 1874-1946
Steinbeck, John 1902-1968
Steinem, Gloria 1934-
Steiner, George 1929-
Stephen, Virginia
   See Woolf, Virginia
Stevens, Wallace 1879-1955
Stewart, J. I. M. 1906-1994
Stine, Jovial Bob
   See Stine, R. L.
Stine, R. L. 1943-
Stone, Irving 1903-1989
Stoppard, Tom 1937-
Strachey, Lytton 1880-1932
Straub, Peter 1943-
Strindberg, August 1849-1912
Sturgeon, Theodore 1918-1985
Styron, William 1925-
Susann, Jacqueline 1921-1974
Suzuki, Daisetz Teitaro 1870-1966
Swenson, May 1919-1989
Swift, Graham 1949-
Szymborska, Wislawa 1923-
Tagore, Rabindranath 1861-1941
Talese, Gay 1932-
Tan, Amy 1952-
Tanizaki, Jun'ichiro 1886-1965
Tarkington, Booth 1869-1946
Tate, Allen 1899-1979
Taylor, A. J. P. 1906-1990
Taylor, Peter 1917-1994
Terkel, Louis 1912-
Terkel, Studs
   See Terkel, Louis
Theroux, Paul 1941-
Thibault, Jacques Anatole Francois 1844-1924
Thomas, D. M. 1935-
Thomas, Dylan 1914-1953
Thomas, Joyce Carol 1938-
Thomas, Lewis 1913-1993
Thompson, Francis Clegg
Thompson, Hunter S. 1939-
Thurber, James 1894-1961
Tillich, Paul 1886-1965
Toffler, Alvin 1928-

Toland, John 1912-
Tolkien, J. R. R. 1892-1973
Tonson, Jacob
   See Bennett, Arnold
Toole, John Kennedy 1937-1969
Toomer, Jean 1894-1967
Tournier, Michel 1924-
Trakl, Georg 1887-1914
Tremblay, Michel 1942-
Trevor, William
   See Cox, William Trevor
Trillin, Calvin 1935-
Trilling, Diana 1905-1996
Trilling, Lionel 1905-1975
Tsvetaeva, Marina 1892-1941
Tuchman, Barbara W. 1912-1989
Turow, Scott 1949-
Tutuola, Amos 1920-1997
Tyler, Anne 1941-
Tynan, Kenneth 1927-1980
Tzara, Tristan 1896-1963
Uchida, Yoshiko 1921-1992
Unamuno, Miguel de 1864-1936
Undset, Sigrid 1882-1949
Updike, John 1932-
Uris, Leon 1924-
Ustinov, Peter 1921-
Valery, Paul 1871-1945
Van Doren, Mark 1894-1972
Vargas Llosa, Mario 1936-
Vendler, Helen 1933-
Vian, Boris 1920-1959
Vidal, Gore 1925-
Vizenor, Gerald 1934-
Vollmann, William T. 1959-
Vonnegut, Kurt 1922-
Wain, John 1925-1994
Wakoski, Diane 1937-
Walcott, Derek 1930-
Walker, Alice 1944-
Walker, Margaret 1915-
Wallace, David Foster 1962-
Wallace, Irving 1916-1990
Wallant, Edward Lewis 1926-1962
Walpole, Hugh 1884-1941
Wambaugh, Joseph 1937-
Warner, Sylvia Ashton
   See Ashton-Warner, Sylvia
Warner, Sylvia Townsend 1893-1978
Warren, Robert Penn 1905-1989
Wasserstein, Wendy 1950-
Waterhouse, Keith 1929-

Watkins, Gloria 1952-
Waugh, Evelyn 1903-1966
Weil, Simone 1909-1943
Weldon, Fay 1931-
Wells, H. G. 1866-1946
Welty, Eudora 1909-
West, Jessamyn 1902-1984
West, Morris L. 1916-
West, Nathanael 1903-1940
West, Paul 1930-
West, Rebecca 1892-1983
West, V. Sackville
   See Sackville-West, V.
Westlake, Donald E. 1933-
Wharton, Edith 1862-1937
White, E. B. 1899-1985
White, Edmund 1940-
White, Phyllis Dorothy James 1920-
White, Theodore H. 1915-1986
Whitney, Phyllis A. 1903-
Wideman, John Edgar 1941-
Wiesel, Elie 1928-
Wilbur, Richard 1921-
Wilder, Laura Ingalls 1867-1957
Wilder, Thornton 1897-1975
Williams, Tennessee 1911-1983
Williams, William Carlos 1883-1963
Wilson, A. N. 1950-
Wilson, Angus 1913-1991
Wilson, August 1945-
Wilson, Edmund 1895-1972
Wilson, Edward O. 1929-
Wilson, John Burgess 1917-1993
Winterson, Jeanette 1959-
Wittgenstein, Ludwig 1889-1951
Wodehouse, P. G. 1881-1975
Wolfe, Gene 1931-
Wolfe, Thomas 1900-1938
Wolfe, Thomas Kennerly, Jr. 1930-
Wolfe, Tom
   See Wolfe, Thomas Kennerly, Jr.
Wolff, Tobias 1945-
Woodiwiss, Kathleen E. 1939-
Woolf, Virginia 1882-1941
Wouk, Herman 1915-
Wright, Charles 1935-
Wright, James 1927-1980
Wright, Judith 1915-
Wright, Richard 1908-1960
Yeats, William Butler 1865-1939
Yourcenar, Marguerite 1903-1987
Zelazny, Roger 1937-1995
Zindel, Paul 1936-

Sh–Sz

SHAFFER, Peter (Levin) 1926-
(Peter Anthony, a joint pseudonym)

PERSONAL: Born May 15, 1926, in Liverpool, England; son of Jack (a real estate agent) and Reka (Fredman) Shaffer. *Education:* Trinity College, Cambridge, B.A., 1950. *Politics:* Conservative anarchist. *Religion:* Humanist. *Avocational interests:* Music, architecture.

ADDRESSES: Home—173 Riverside Dr., New York, NY 10024-1615. *Office*—The Lantz Office, 888 7th Ave., Ste 2500, New York, NY 10010-6000. *Agent*—c/o McNaughton-Lowe Representation, 200 Fulham Road, SW10, England.

CAREER: Playwright and critic. Worked in the New York Public Library, New York City, 1951-54, and for Boosey & Hawkes (music publishers), London, England, 1954-55; literary critic for *Truth,* 1956-57; music critic for *Time and Tide,* 1961-62. *Wartime service:* Served as a conscript in coal mines in England, 1944-47.

MEMBER: Royal Society of Literature (fellow), Dramatists Guild, Garrick Club (London).

AWARDS, HONORS: Evening Standard Drama Award, 1958, and New York Drama Critics Circle Award, 1960, both for *Five Finger Exercise;* Antoinette Perry Award (Tony) for Best Play, Outer Critics Circle Award, and New York Drama Critics Circle Award, all 1975, all for *Equus;* Tony Award, 1980, and best play of the year award from *Plays and Players,* both for *Amadeus;* New York Film Critics Circle Award, 1984, Los Angeles Film Critics Association Award, 1984, and Academy Award of Merit (Oscar) from the Academy of Motion Picture Arts and Sciences, 1985, all for screenplay adaptation of *Amadeus;* named Commander of the British Empire, 1987; *Evening Standard* Drama Award for Best Comedy, 1988, for *Lettice and Lovage: A Comedy;* Hamburg Shakespeare Prize, 1989; William Ingo Award for Distinguished Achievement in the American Theatre, 1992.

WRITINGS:

PLAYS

Five Finger Exercise (produced on the West End at the Comedy Theatre, July 16, 1958; produced on Broadway at the Music Box Theater, December 2, 1959; also see below), Hamish Hamilton, 1958, Harcourt, 1959.

The Private Ear [and] *The Public Eye* (two one-acts; produced on the West End at the Globe Theatre, May 10, 1962; produced on Broadway at the Morosco Theatre, October 9, 1963; also see below), Hamish Hamilton, 1962, Stein & Day (Briarcliff Manor, NY), 1964.

The Merry Rooster's Panto, produced on the West End at Wyndham's Theatre, December, 1963.

The Royal Hunt of the Sun: A Play Concerning the Conquest of Peru (produced by the National Theatre Co. at the Chichester Festival, July 7, 1964; produced on Broadway at the ANTA Theatre, October 26, 1965), Samuel French (London), 1964, Stein & Day, 1965.

A Warning Game, produced in New York City, 1967.

Black Comedy (one-act; produced by the National Theatre Co. at the Chichester Festival, July 27, 1965, [also see below], produced on Broadway at the Ethel Barrymore Theatre with *White Lies* [also see below], February 12, 1967; produced on the West End at the Lyric Theatre as *Black Comedy* [and] *The White Liars* [also see below], 1968), Samuel French, 1967.

The White Liars, Samuel French, 1967.

Black Comedy [and] *White Lies,* Stein & Day, 1967, published in England as *The White Liars* [and] *Black Comedy,* Hamish Hamilton, 1968.

It's about Cinderella, produced in London, 1969.

Equus (produced by the National Theatre Co. on the West End at the Old Vic Theatre, July 26, 1973; produced on Broadway at the Plymouth Theater, October 24, 1974; also see below), Deutsch, 1973, Samuel French, 1974.

Shrivings (three-act; produced on the West End at the Lyric Theatre as *The Battle of Shrivings,* February 5, 1970; also see below), Deutsch, 1974.

Equus [and] *Shrivings,* Atheneum (New York City), 1974.

Three Plays (contains *Five Finger Exercise, Shrivings,* and *Equus*), Penguin (New York City), 1976.

Four Plays, Penguin, 1981.

Amadeus (produced on the West End by the National Theatre Co. at the Olivier Theatre, November 2, 1979; produced on Broadway at the Broadhurst Theater, December 17, 1980; also see below), Deutsch, 1980, Harper (New York City), 1981.

Collected Plays of Peter Shaffer, Crown, 1982.

Yonadab: The Watcher, produced on the West End by the National Theatre Co. at the Olivier Theatre, December 4, 1985, published as *Yonadab: A Play,* Harper, 1988.

Lettice and Lovage: A Comedy (produced on the West End at the Globe Theatre, 1987; produced on Broadway at the Ethel Barrymore Theater, March 25, 1990), HarperCollins, 1990.

The Gift of the Gorgon: A Play (produced at the Barbican, 1992), Pantheon Books (New York City), 1994.

NOVELS; WITH BROTHER, ANTHONY SHAFFER

(Under joint pseudonym Peter Anthony) *Woman in the Wardrobe*, Evans Brothers, 1951.

(Under joint pseudonym Peter Anthony) *How Doth the Little Crocodile?* Evans Brothers, 1952, published under names Peter Shaffer and Anthony Shaffer, Macmillan (New York City), 1957.

Withered Murder, Gollancz, 1955, Macmillan, 1956.

SCREENPLAYS

(With Peter Brook) *Lord of the Flies*, Walter Reade, 1963.

The Pad (and How to Use It) (adaptation of *The Private Ear*), Universal, 1966.

Follow Me! Universal, 1971.

The Public Eye (based on Shaffer's play of the same title), Universal, 1972.

Equus (based on Shaffer's play of the same title), United Artists, 1977.

Amadeus (based on Shaffer's play of the same title), Orion Pictures, 1984.

OTHER

The Salt Land (television play), Independent Television Network, 1955.

The Prodigal Father (radio play), British Broadcasting Corp., 1955.

Balance of Terror (television play), British Broadcasting Corp., 1957.

(Editor) *Elisabeth Frink Sculpture: Catalogue Raisonne*, Trafalger Square, 1988.

Whom Do I Have the Honor of Addressing? Deutsch, 1990.

Contributor of articles to periodicals, including *Theatre Arts, Atlantic, Encore,* and *Sunday Times.*

MEDIA ADAPTATIONS: Five Finger Exercise was filmed by Columbia in 1962; *The Royal Hunt of the Sun: A Play Concerning the Conquest of Peru* was filmed by CBS's Cinema Center Films.

SIDELIGHTS: "Whatever else Peter Shaffer may lack, it isn't courage, it isn't derring-do. His plays traverse the centuries and the globe, raising questions that have perplexed minds from Job to Samuel Beckett," Benedict Nightingale writes in the *New York Times.* Shaffer examines the conflict between atheism and religion in *The Royal Hunt of the Sun: A Play Concerning the Conquest of Peru;* the nature of sanity and insanity in modern society in *Equus;* the role of genius in *Amadeus;* and Old Testament ethics in *Yonadab: The Watcher.* These epic plays are always a visual spectacle, but some critics feel that Shaffer's spectacles mask superficial stories. *Newsweek* contributor Jack Kroll characterizes the typical Shaffer play as "a large-scale, large-voiced treatment of large themes, whose essential superficiality is masked by a skillful theatricality reinforced by . . . extraordinary acting." Despite such criticism, Shaffer's plays are enormously popular— both *Equus* and *Amadeus* had Broadway runs of more than one thousand performances each.

Shaffer's first major success was *The Royal Hunt of the Sun,* based on Francisco Pizarro's sixteenth-century expedition to the Inca Empire of Peru. To force the Inca people to give him the gold

he desired, Pizarro took their leader, Atahuallpa, prisoner. But Atahuallpa refused to concede defeat and the resulting battle between Pizarro's forces and the Inca Indians proved disastrous for his people. In the ensuing battle, Atahuallpa is killed. But Pizarro had befriended the Inca leader. When Atahuallpa dies, Pizarro renounces Catholicism to adopt the Inca religion.

The Royal Hunt of the Sun is considered unique because of its historical subject and its stylized theatrical techniques, including mime and adaptations of Japanese Kabuki theater. To enhance the visual spectacle of the play, Shaffer specified that the Indians wear dramatic Inca funeral masks during Atahuallpa's death scene; many in the audience later claimed to have seen the masks change expression during the production. "They hadn't, of course," Shaffer told Richard Schickel in *Time.* "But the audience invested so much emotion in the play that it looked as if they had."

Despite this positive emotional response from audiences, some critics feel the play's language and theatrical devices are not effective. *Drama*'s Ronald Hayman thinks that Shaffer borrows from so many different traditions and uses so many theatrical devices that "instead of unifying to contribute to the same effect, the various elements make their effects separately and some of them are superfluous and distracting." Warren Sylvester Smith in the *Dictionary of Literary Biography* indicates that the language "sometimes fail[s] to achieve the magnitude of the characters or to match the scope of the events." And Hayman faults the dialogue for being "lustreless, tumbling into cliches and even pleonasms like 'trapped in time's cage' when nothing less than poetry would take the strain Shaffer is putting on it."

But other critics, and many playgoers, had a more generous response to *The Royal Hunt of the Sun.* These reviewers mention that the elaborate sets and costumes, the epic story, and the innovative rendition of history were exciting additions to the contemporary dramatic scene. John Russell Taylor writes in *Peter Shaffer* that as a "piece of sheer theatrical machinery the play is impeccable." He concludes that *The Royal Hunt of the Sun* is "at once a spectacular drama and a thinkpiece."

In Shaffer's 1973 play, *Equus,* he confronts the question of sanity in the modern world. Despite its morbid focus, *Equus* was so well-liked that the opening-night Broadway audience gave it a five-minute standing ovation. "It's never happened to me before," Shaffer told Schickel. "I cry every time I think about it." *Equus* is based on a newspaper report of a boy who blinded several horses in a north England stable. The play revolves around psychiatrist Martin Dysart's treatment of the boy, Alan Strang, for the offense he committed.

During his examination of the boy, Dysart discovers that Strang is a pagan who believes that horses are gods. Therefore, when a stable girl attempts to seduce him in front of the horses, Strang is impotent. In frustrated rage that they have seen his failure, Strang blinds the horses. Dysart tries to treat him in a conventional manner, but eventually finds that he prefers Strang's primitive passion to his own rational, controlled personality. Brendan Gill notes in the *New Yorker* that Dysart "poses questions that go beyond the sufficiently puzzling matter of the boy's conduct to the infinitely puzzling matter of why, in a world charged with insanity, we should seek to 'cure' anyone in the name of sanity."

Equus brought complaints from some reviewers who argue that it superficially portrays insanity and psychoanalysis. *Equus,* John Simon suggests in *New York,* "falls into that category of worn-out whimsy wherein we are told that insanity is more desirable, admirable, or just saner than sanity." *Commentary* contributor Jack Richardson states that *Equus* seems to be a "perfect case-study in the mediocrity of insight necessary nowadays for a play to enjoy a popular reputation for profundity." Simon concludes that no "amount of external embellishment can overcome the hollowness within."

Shaffer's next play, *Amadeus,* is based on the life of eighteenth-century composer Wolfgang Amadeus Mozart. Richard Christiansen of the *Chicago Tribune* believes that the characters in *Amadeus* and *Equus* are similar, remarking that "here again, as in 'Equus,' an older, learned man of the world is struck and amazed by the wild inspiration of a much younger man who seemingly is possessed with divine madness." The older man in *Amadeus* is Antonio Salieri, portrayed as a second-rate composer who is consumed by jealousy because of the young Mozart's greater talent.

Shaffer became interested in the rivalry between Mozart and Salieri upon reading material about Mozart's mysterious death. Shaffer at first suspected that Salieri may have murdered the composer, but further research proved this to be wrong. "But by then the cold eyes of Salieri were staring at me," Shaffer tells Roland Gelatt in the *Saturday Review.* "The conflict between virtuous mediocrity and feckless genius took hold of my imagination, and it would not leave me alone."

In *Amadeus,* Salieri has made a bargain with God. He is to remain pious in return for being made the most popular composer of his time. As court composer in Vienna, Salieri is satisfied that his bargain with God has been kept. But then Mozart arrives at the court, playing music Salieri considers to be the finest he has ever heard. And in contrast to Salieri's piety, Mozart is a moral abomination—a bastard, a womanizer, and an abrasive man with a scatological sense of humor. Salieri feels cheated and angry, and begins to sabotage Mozart's budding career by spreading rumors about him. These rumors, along with Mozart's contentious personality, serve to ostracize him from polite society and cause him to lose his pupils. Eventually Mozart becomes ill and dies, and the play asks whether he was killed by Salieri or died from natural causes.

"*Amadeus* . . . is about the ravaging of genius by mediocrity," Robert Brustein writes in the *New Republic.* Some critics believe Shaffer handled his material in much the same manner, charging him with a superficial portrayal of Mozart's life. Brustein argues that "at the same time that the central character—a second-rate kapellmeister named Antonio Salieri—is plotting against the life and reputation of a superior composer named Wolfgang Amadeus Mozart, a secondary playwright named Peter Shaffer is reducing this genius, one of the greatest artists of all time, to the level of a simpering, braying ninny."

Despite complaints from reviewers, audiences received *Amadeus* enthusiastically, and it played in many European cities. Bernard Levin, writing in the London *Times,* sums up the feelings of many theatergoers by writing that "those who go to [*Amadeus*] prepared to understand what it is about will have an experience that far transcends even its considerable value as drama." Impressed with the play's serious intentions, Gelatt writes that "*Amadeus* gives heartening evidence that there is still room for the play of ideas." Perhaps Shaffer's most famous work is the screenplay adaptation of *Amadeus,* written in collaboration with director Milos Forman and producer Saul Zaentz. This 1984 film won several Academy

Awards, including best screenplay adaptation and best picture of the year.

Amadeus was filmed with Shaffer's characteristic visual spectacle in the centuries-old cathedrals and churches of Prague, Czechoslovakia. Geoff Brown comments in the London *Times* on the ambience of the production, writing that "so many films lie on the screen today looking shrivelled or inert; *Amadeus* sits there resplendent, both stately and supple, a compelling, darkly comic story of human glory and human infamy."

In December of 1985, Shaffer's play *Yonadab: The Watcher* opened to mixed reviews. Based on the Old Testament account of King David's reign in ancient Jerusalem, the play focuses on court hanger-on Yonadab, who believes an ancient superstition that incest committed between members of the royal family promotes wisdom in government. He convinces Amnon, King David's son, to rape his own sister, Tamar. Commenting on the strikingly different subject matter of this play, Shaffer tells Higgins: "I never want to repeat myself, so it is essential to come up in a different place every time."

Although some critics express many of the same complaints about *Yonadab: The Watcher* that they have about previous Shaffer plays—historical inaccuracies, superficial treatment of theme, lack of character development—Shaffer remains undaunted. Dan Sullivan reports in the *Los Angeles Times* that Shaffer told Associated Press's Matt Wolf: "Audiences are very excited by the play; that's the main thing."

Audience reaction to 1987's *Lettice and Lovage: A Comedy* was also positive. Wolf writes in the *Chicago Tribune* that the play, "an overtly commercial, out-and-out comedy," was winning "nightly bravos and may even get an award or two." Shaffer wrote the play as a gift for actress Maggie Smith, who starred in his earlier work *Black Comedy* and plays the lead role of Lettice.

The fact that audiences are excited by Shaffer's plays is a testament to his popularity and staying power. Smith concludes that though Shaffer is sometimes slighted by critics, "none of [his] imputed failings has inhibited the lines at the box office or deterred serious theatergoers from expressing gratitude for the revitalization [he] has brought to contemporary drama."

BIOGRAPHICAL/CRITICAL SOURCES:

BOOKS

Brustein, Robert, *The Third Theatre,* Knopf, 1969.
Contemporary Literary Criticism, Gale (Detroit), Volume 5, 1976; Volume 14, 1980; Volume 18, 1981; Volume 37, 1986.
Dictionary of Literary Biography, Volume 13: *British Dramatists since World War II,* Gale, 1982.
Lumley, Frederick, *New Trends in Twentieth-Century Drama,* Oxford University Press, 1967.
McCrindle, J. F., editor, *Behind the Scenes,* Holt, 1971.
Taylor, John Russell, *Anger and After,* Methuen, 1962.
Taylor, John Russell, *Peter Shaffer,* Longman, 1974.

PERIODICALS

America, October 13, 1984.
Chicago Tribune, March 7, 1983; September 19, 1984; November 15, 1987.
Classical and Modern Literature, summer, 1995, p. 345.
Commentary, February, 1975.
Commonweal, April 25, 1975.
Drama, autumn, 1970; January, 1980.

Film Comment, September/October, 1984; January/February, 1985.

Globe and Mail (Toronto), June 13, 1987.

Guardian, August 6, 1973.

Harper's, July, 1981.

Hudson Review, summer, 1967.

Listener, February 12, 1970; December 12, 1985.

Los Angeles Times, December 10, 1982.

Modern Drama, September, 1978; March, 1985.

Monthly Film Bulletin, January, 1985.

Nation, February 27, 1967; January 17, 1981.

National Review, October 19, 1984.

New Leader, February 27, 1967.

New Republic, January 17, 1981; October 22, 1984.

New Statesman, February 13, 1970.

Newsweek, February 20, 1967; November 4, 1974; December 29, 1980.

New York, November 11, 1974; September 24, 1984.

New Yorker, February 25, 1967; November 4, 1974; March 10, 1980; December 29, 1980.

New York Times, September 29, 1968; December 23, 1979; December 18, 1980; September 16, 1984; September 19, 1984; December 22, 1985; February 13, 1987; March 26, 1990.

New York Times Magazine, August 17, 1973; October 25, 1974; October 27, 1974; April 13, 1975.

Observer, February 25, 1968; December 8, 1985.

Partisan Review, spring, 1966.

Punch, February 28, 1968.

Saturday Review, February 25, 1967; February, 1981.

South Atlantic Quarterly, autumn, 1980.

Spectator, March 1, 1968.

Time, November 11, 1974; December 29, 1980.

Times (London), January 9, 1985; January 18, 1985; November 28, 1985; December 6, 1985; November 17, 1988.

Washington Post, July 5, 1979; November 9, 1980; November 13, 1980; November 23, 1980; March 26, 1990.

*   *   *

SHANGE, Ntozake 1948-

PERSONAL: Original name Paulette Linda Williams; name changed in 1971, pronounced "En-to-zaki Shong-gay"; born October 18, 1948, in Trenton, NJ; daughter of Paul T. (a surgeon) and Eloise (a psychiatric social worker and educator) Williams; married second husband, David Murray (a musician), July, 1977 (divorced); children: Savannah. *Education:* Barnard College, B.A. (with honors), 1970; University of Southern California, Los Angeles, M.A., 1973, and graduate study. *Avocational interests:* Playing the violin.

ADDRESSES: Home—231 North Third St., No. 119, Philadelphia, PA 19106. *Office*—Department of Drama, University of Houston, University Park, 4800 Calhoun Rd., Houston, TX 77004; c/o St. Martins Press, 175 5th Ave, New York, NY 10010-7703.

CAREER: Writer, performer, and teacher. Faculty member in women's studies, California State College, Sonoma Mills College, and the University of California Extension, 1972-75; associate professor of drama, University of Houston, beginning in 1983; artist in residence, New Jersey State Council on the Arts; creative writing instructor, City College of New York. Lecturer at Douglass College, 1978, and at many other institutions, such as

Yale University, Howard University, Detroit Institute of Arts, and New York University. Dancer with Third World Collective, Raymond Sawyer's Afro-American Dance Company, Sounds in Motion, West Coast Dance Works, and For Colored Girls Who Have Considered Suicide (Shange's own dance company); has appeared in Broadway and off-Broadway productions of her own plays, including *For Colored Girls Who Have Considered Suicide/When the Rainbow Is Enuf* and *Where the Mississippi Meets the Amazon.* Director of several productions including *The Mighty Gents,* produced by the New York Shakespeare Festival's Mobile Theatre, 1979, *A Photograph: A Study in Cruelty,* produced in Houston's Equinox Theatre, 1979, and June Jordan's *The Issue* and *The Spirit of Sojourner Truth,* 1979. Has given many poetry readings.

MEMBER: Actors Equity, National Academy of Television Arts and Sciences, Dramatists Guild, PEN American Center, Academy of American Poets, Poets and Writers Inc., Women's Institute for Freedom of the Press, New York Feminist Arts Guild, Writers' Guild.

AWARDS, HONORS: NDEA fellow, 1973; Obie Award, Outer Critics Circle Award, Audience Development Committee (Audelco) Award, Mademoiselle Award, and Tony, Grammy, and Emmy award nominations, all 1977, all for *For Colored Girls Who Have Considered Suicide/When the Rainbow Is Enuf;* Frank Silvera Writers' Workshop Award, 1978; *Los Angeles Times* Book Prize for Poetry, 1981, for *Three Pieces;* Guggenheim fellowship, 1981; Medal of Excellence, Columbia University, 1981; Obie Award, 1981, for *Mother Courage and Her Children;* Nori Eboraci Award, Barnard College, 1988; Lila Wallace-Reader's Digest Fund annual writer's award, 1992; Paul Robeson Achievement Award, 1992; Arts and Cultural Achievement Award, National Coalition of 100 Black Women, Inc. (Pennsylvania chapter), 1992; Living Legend Award, National Black Theatre Festival, 1993; Claim Your Life Award, WDAS-AM/FM, 1993; Monarch Merit Award, National Council for Culture and Art, Inc.; Pushcart Prize.

WRITINGS:

For Colored Girls Who Have Considered Suicide/When the Rainbow Is Enuf: A Choreopoem (first produced in New York City at Studio Rivbea, July 7, 1975; produced off-Broadway at Anspacher Public Theatre, 1976; produced on Broadway at Booth Theatre, September 15, 1976), Shameless Hussy Press (San Lorenzo, CA), 1975, revised edition, Macmillan (New York City), 1976.

Sassafrass (novella), Shameless Hussy Press, 1976.

Melissa & Smith, Bookslinger (St. Paul, MN), 1976.

A Photograph: A Study of Cruelty (poem-play), first produced off-Broadway at Public Theatre, December 21, 1977, revised edition, *A Photograph: Lovers in Motion* (also see below), produced in Houston, TX, at the Equinox Theatre, November, 1979.

(With Thulani Nkabinde and Jessica Hagedorn) *Where the Mississippi Meets the Amazon,* first produced in New York City at Public Theatre Cabaret, December 18, 1977.

Natural Disasters and Other Festive Occasions (prose and poems), Heirs International (San Francisco, CA), 1977.

Nappy Edges (poems), St. Martin's (New York City), 1978.

Boogie Woogie Landscapes (play; also see below; first produced in New York City at Frank Silvera Writers' Workshop, June, 1979, produced on Broadway at the Symphony Space Theatre, produced in Washington, DC, at the Kennedy Center), St. Martin's, 1978.

Spell #7: A Geechee Quick Magic Trance Manual (play; also see below), produced on Broadway at Joseph Papp's New York Shakespeare Festival Public Theater, July 15, 1979.

Black and White Two Dimensional Planes (play), first produced in New York City at Sounds in Motion Studio Works, February, 1979.

(Adapter) Bertolt Brecht, *Mother Courage and Her Children,* first produced off-Broadway at the Public Theatre, April, 1980.

Three Pieces: Spell #7; A Photograph: Lovers in Motion; Boogie Woogie Landscapes (plays), St. Martin's, 1981.

A Photograph: Lovers in Motion, Samuel French (New York City), 1981.

Spell #7: A Theatre Piece in Two Acts, Samuel French, 1981.

Sassafrass, Cypress & Indigo: A Novel, St. Martin's, 1982.

Three for a Full Moon [and] *Bocas,* first produced in Los Angeles, CA, at the Mark Taper Forum Lab, Center Theatre, April 28, 1982.

(Adapter) Willy Russell, *Educating Rita* (play), first produced in Atlanta, GA, by Alliance Theatre Company, 1982.

A Daughter's Geography (poems), St. Martin's, 1983.

See No Evil: Prefaces, Essays and Accounts, 1976-1983, Momo's Press (San Francisco, CA), 1984.

From Okra to Greens: Poems, Coffee House Press, 1984.

From Okra to Greens: A Different Kinda Love Story; A Play with Music and Dance (first produced in New York City at Barnard College, November, 1978), Samuel French, 1985.

Betsey Brown: A Novel, St. Martin's, 1985.

(Author of foreword) Mapplethorpe, Robert, *The Black Book,* St. Martin's, 1986.

Three Views of Mt. Fuji (play), first produced at the Lorraine Hansberry Theatre, June, 1987, produced in New York City at the New Dramatists, October, 1987.

Ridin' the Moon in Texas: Word Paintings (responses to art in prose and poetry), St. Martin's, 1987.

(Contributor) Jules Feiffer, *Selected from Contemporary American Plays: An Anthology,* Literacy Volunteers of New York City, 1990.

The Love Space Demands: A Continuing Saga, St. Martin's, 1991.

Three Pieces, St. Martin's, 1992.

I Live in Music (poem), edited by Linda Sunshine, illustrated by Romare Bearden, Stewart, Tabori & Chang (New York City), 1994.

Liliane: Resurrection of the Daughter (fiction), St. Martin's, 1994.

Whitewash, illustrated by Michael Sporn, Walker (New York City), 1997.

If I Can Cook You Know God Can, Beacon Press, 1998.

Also author of *Some Men* (poems in a pamphlet that resembles a dance card), 1981. Author of the play *Mouths* and the operetta *Carrie,* both produced in 1981. Has written for a television special starring Diana Ross, and appears in a documentary about her own work for WGBH-TV (Boston). Work represented in several anthologies, including *"May Your Days Be Merry and Bright" and Other Christmas Stories by Women,* edited by Susan Koppelman, Wayne State University Press (Detroit, MI), 1988; *New Plays for the Black Theatre,* edited by Woodie King, Jr., Third World Press (Chicago, IL), 1989; *Breaking Ice: An Anthology of Contemporary African American Fiction,* edited by Terry McMillan, Penguin Books (New York City), 1990; *Yellow Silk: Erotic Arts and Letters,* edited by Lily Pond and Richard Russo, Harmony Books (New York City), 1990; *Daughters of Africa: An International Anthology,* edited by Margaret Bushby, Pantheon (New York City), 1992; *Erotique Noire—Black Erotica,*

edited by Miriam DeCosta-Willis, Reginald Martin, and Roseann P. Bell, Anchor (New York City), 1992; *Resurgent: New Writing by Women,* edited by Lou Robinson and Camille Norton, University of Illinois Press (Champaign, IL), 1992; and *Wild Women Don't Wear No Blues: Black Women Writers on Love, Men and Sex,* edited by Marita Golden, Doubleday (New York City), 1993. Author of preface to *Plays by Women, Book Two: An International Anthology,* Ubu Repertory Theater Publications (New York City), 1994. Contributor to periodicals, including *Black Scholar, Third World Women, Ms.,* and *Yardbird Reader.*

MEDIA ADAPTATIONS: A musical-operetta version of Shange's novel *Betsey Brown* was produced by Joseph Papp's Public Theater in 1986.

SIDELIGHTS: Born to a surgeon and an educator, Ntozake Shange—originally named Paulette Williams—was raised with the advantages available to the black middle class. But one by one, the roles she chose for herself—including war correspondent and jazz musician—were dismissed as "no good for a woman," she told Stella Dong in a *Publishers Weekly* interview. She chose to become a writer because "there was nothing left." Frustrated and hurt after separating from her first husband, Shange attempted suicide several times before focusing her rage against the limitations society imposes on black women. While earning a master's degree in American Studies from the University of Southern California, she reaffirmed her personal strength based on a self-determined identity and took her African name, which means "she who comes with her own things" and she "who walks like a lion." Since then she has sustained a triple career as an educator, a performer/director in New York and Houston, and a writer whose works draw heavily on her experiences and the frustrations of being a black female in America. "I am a war correspondent after all," she told Dong, "because I'm involved in a war of cultural and esthetic aggression. The front lines aren't always what you think they are."

Though she is an accomplished poet and an acclaimed novelist, Shange became famous for her play *For Colored Girls Who Have Considered Suicide/When the Rainbow Is Enuf.* A unique blend of poetry, music, dance and drama called a "choreopoem," it was still being produced around the country more than ten years after it "took the theatre world by storm" in 1975. Before it won international acclaim, *For Colored Girls,* notes Jacqueline Trescott in the *Washington Post,* "became an electrifying Broadway hit and provoked heated exchanges about the relationships between black men and women. . . . When [it] debuted, [it] became the talk of literary circles. Its form—seven women on the stage dramatizing poetry—was a refreshing slap at the traditional, one-two-three-act structures." Whereas plays combining poetry and dance had already been staged by Adrienne Kennedy, Mel Gussow of the *New York Times* states that "Miss Shange was a pioneer in terms of her subject matter: the fury of black women at their double subjugation in white male America."

However privileged her childhood might have seemed, Shange felt that she was "living a lie." As she explained to *Newsday* reviewer Allan Wallach: "[I was] living in a world that defied reality as most black people, or most white people, understood it—in other words, feeling that there was something that I could do, and then realizing that nobody was expecting me to do anything because I was colored and I was also female, which was not very easy to deal with."

Writing dramatic poetry became a means of expressing her dissatisfaction with the role of black women in society. She and a group of friends, including various musicians and the choreographer-dancer Paula Moss, would create improvisational works comprised of poetry, music, and dance, and they would frequently perform them in bars in San Francisco and New York. When Moss and Shange moved to New York City, they presented *For Colored Girls* at a Soho jazz loft, the Studio Rivbea. Director Oz Scott saw the show and helped develop the production as it was performed in bars on the Lower East Side. Impressed by one of these, black producer Woodie King, Jr., joined Scott to stage the choreopoem off-Broadway at the New Federal Theatre, where it ran successfully from November, 1975, to the following June. Then Joseph Papp became the show's producer at the New York Shakespeare Festival's Anspacher Public Theatre. From there, it moved to the Booth Theatre uptown. "The final production at the Booth is as close to distilled as any of us in all our art forms can make it," Shange says of that production in the introduction to *For Colored Girls,* published in 1976. "The cast is enveloping almost 6,000 people a week in the words of a young black girl's growing up, her triumphs and errors, [her] struggle to be all that is forbidden by our environment, all that is forfeited by our gender, all that we have forgotten."

In *For Colored Girls,* poems dramatized by the women dancers recall encounters with their classmates, lovers, rapists, abortionists, and latent killers. The women survive the abuses and disappointments put upon them by the men in their lives and come to recognize in each other, dressed in the colors of Shange's personal rainbow, the promise of a better future. As one voice, at the end, they declare, "i found god in myself / and i loved her / . . . fiercely." To say this, remarks Carol P. Christ in *Diving Deep and Surfacing: Women Writers on Spiritual Quest,* is "to say . . . that it is all right to be a woman, that the Black woman does not have to imitate whiteness or depend on men for her power of being." "The poetry," says Marilyn Stasio in *Cue,* "touches some very tender nerve endings. Although roughly structured and stylistically unrefined, this fierce and passionate poetry has the power to move a body to tears, to rage, and to an ultimate rush of love."

While some reviewers are enthusiastic in their praise for the play, others are emphatically negative. "Some Black people, notably men, said that . . . Shange broke a taboo when her *For Colored Girls* . . . took the theatre world by storm," Connie Lauerman reports in the *Chicago Tribune.* "[Shange] was accused of racism, of 'lynching' the black male." But the playwright does not feel that she was bringing any black family secrets to light. She told Lauerman, "Half of what we discussed in *For Colored Girls* about the dissipation of the family, rape, wife-battering and all that sort of thing, the U.S. Census Bureau already had. . . . We could have gone to the Library of Congress and read the Census reports and the crime statistics every month and we would know that more black women are raped than anyone else. We would know at this point that they think 48 per cent of our households are headed by single females. . . . My job as an artist is to say what I see."

"Shange's poems aren't war cries," Jack Kroll writes in a *Newsweek* review of the Public Theatre production of *For Colored Girls.* "They're outcries filled with a controlled passion against the brutality that blasts the lives of 'colored girls'—a phrase that in her hands vibrates with social irony and poetic beauty. These poems are political in the deepest sense, but there's no dogma, no sentimentality, no grinding of false mythic axes." Critic Edith Oliver of the *New Yorker* remarks: "The evening grows in dramatic power, encompassing, it seems, every feeling and experience a woman has ever had; strong and funny, it is

entirely free of the rasping earnestness of most projects of this sort. The verses and monologues that constitute the program have been very well chosen—contrasting in mood yet always subtly building."

Reviews of Shange's next production, *A Photograph: A Study of Cruelty,* were less positive, although critics were generally impressed with the poetic quality of her writing. "Miss Shange is something besides a poet but she is not—at least not at this stage—a dramatist," Richard Eder declares in a *New York Times* review. "More than anything else, she is a troubadour. She declares her fertile vision of the love and pain between black women and black men in outbursts full of old malice and young cheerfulness. They are short outbursts, song-length; her characters are perceived in flashes, in illuminating vignettes."

Shange's next play, *Spell #7: A Geechee Quick Magic Trance Manual,* more like *For Colored Girls* in structure, elicits a higher recommendation from Eder. Its nine characters in a New York bar discuss the racism black artists contend with in the entertainment world. At one point, the all-black cast appears in overalls and minstrel-show blackface to address the pressure placed on the black artist to fit a stereotype in order to succeed. "That's what happens to black people in the arts no matter how famous we become. . . . Black Theatre is not moving forward the way people like to think it is. We're not free of our paint yet," Shange told Claudia Tate in *Black Women Writers at Work.* "On another level, *Spell #7* deals with the image of a black woman as a neutered workhorse, who is unwanted, unloved, and unattended by anyone," notes Elizabeth Brown in the *Dictionary of Literary Biography.* "The emphasis is still on the experiences of the black woman but it is broadened and deepened, and it ventures more boldly across the sexual divide," Eder writes in the *New York Times.* Don Nelson, writing in the *New York Daily News,* deems the show "black magic. . . . The word that best describes Shange's works, which are not plays in the traditional sense, is power."

Shange's poetry books, like her theater pieces, are distinctively original. *Nappy Edges,* containing fifty poems, is too long, says Harriet Gilbert in the *Washington Post Book World;* however, she claims, "nothing that Shange writes is ever entirely unreadable, springing, as it does, from such an intense honesty, from so fresh an awareness of the beauty of sound and of vision, from such mastery of words, from such compassion, humor and intelligence." Alice H. G. Phillips relates in the *Times Literary Supplement,* "Comparing herself to a jazzman 'takin' a solo,' she lets go with verbal runs and trills, mixes in syncopations, spins out evocative hanging phrases, variations on themes and refrains. Rarely does she come to a full stop, relying instead on line breaks, extra space breaking up a line, and/or oblique strokes. . . . She constantly tries to push things to their limit, and consequently risks seeming overenthusiastic, oversimplistic or merely undisciplined. . . . But at its best, her method can achieve both serious humour and deep seriousness."

In her poetry, Shange takes many liberties with the conventions of written English, using nonstandard spellings and punctuation. Some reviewers feel that these innovations present unnecessary obstacles to the interested readers of *Nappy Edges, A Daughter's Geography,* and *From Okra to Greens: Poems.* Explaining her "lower-case letters, slashes, and spelling" to Tate, she said that "poems where all the first letters are capitalized" bore her; "also, I like the idea that letters dance. . . . I need some visual stimulation, so that reading becomes not just a passive act and more than an intellectual activity, but demands rigorous participation." Her idiosyncratic punctuation assures her "that the reader is not in control of the process." She wants her words in print to engage the reader in a kind of struggle, and not be "whatever you can just ignore." The spellings, she said, "reflect language as I hear it. . . . The structure is connected to the music I hear beneath the words."

Shange's rejection of standard English serves deeper emotional and political purposes as well. In a *Los Angeles Times Book Review* article on Shange's *See No Evil: Prefaces, Essays and Accounts, 1976-1983,* Karl Keller relates, "[Shange] feels that as a black performer/playwright/poet, she has wanted 'to attack deform n maim the language that i was taught to hate myself in. I have to take it apart to the bone.'" Speaking to Tate, Shange declared, "We do not have to refer continually to European art as the standard. That's absolutely absurd and racist, and I won't participate in that utter lie. My work is one of the few ways I can preserve the elements of our culture that need to be remembered and absolutely revered."

Shange takes liberties with the conventions of fiction writing with her first full-length novel, *Sassafrass, Cypress & Indigo.* "The novel is unusual in its form—a tapestry of narrative, poetry, magic spells, recipes and letters. Lyrical yet real, it also celebrates female stuff—weaving, cooking, birthing babies," relates Lauerman. Its title characters are sisters who find different ways to cope with their love relationships. Sassafrass attaches herself to Mitch, a musician who uses hard drugs and beats her; she leaves him twice, but goes back to him for another try. To male readers who called Mitch a "weak" male character, Shange replied to Lauerman, "[He] had some faults, but there's no way in the world you can say [he wasn't] strong. . . . I think you should love people with their faults. That's what love's about." Cypress, a dancer in feminist productions, at first refuses to become romantically involved with any of her male friends. Indigo, the youngest sister, retreats into her imagination, befriending her childhood dolls, seeing only the poetry and magic of the world. The music she plays on her violin becomes a rejuvenating source for her mother and sisters. "Probably there is a little bit of all three sisters in Shange," Lauerman suggests, "though she says that her novel is not autobiographical but historical, culled from the experiences of blacks and from the 'information of my feelings'."

Critics agree that Shange's poetry is more masterfully wrought than her fiction, yet they find much in the novel to applaud. Writes Doris Grumbach in the *Washington Post Book World,* "Shange is primarily a poet, with a blood-red sympathy for and love of her people, their folk as well as their sophisticated ways, their innocent, loving goodness as much as their lack of immunity to powerful evil. . . . But her voice in this novel is entirely her own, an original, spare and primary-colored sound that will remind readers of Jean Toomer's *Cane.*" In Grumbach's opinion, "Whatever Shange turns her hand to she does well, even to potions and recipes. A white reader feels the exhilarating shock of discovery at being permitted entry into a world she couldn't have known" apart from the novel.

In *The Love Space Demands,* a choreopoem published in 1991, Shange returns to the blend of music, dance, poetry and drama that characterized *For Colored Girls Who Have Considered Suicide.* "I've gone back to being more like myself," Shange explains to *Voice Literary Supplement* interviewer Eileen Myles. "I'm working on my poetry with musicians and dancers like I originally started." Described by Myles as "a sexy, discomfiting,

energizing, revealing, occasionally smug, fascinating kind of book," *The Love Space Demands* includes poems on celibacy and sexuality, on black women's sense of abandonment by black men, on a crack-addicted mother who sells her daughter's virginity for a hit and a pregnant woman who swallows cocaine, destroying her unborn child, to protect her man from arrest. The lead poem of the book, "irrepressibly bronze, beautiful & mine," was inspired by Robert Mapplethorpe's photographs of black and white gay men. The artist's task, Shange tells Myles, is "to keep our sensibilities alive. . . . To keep people alive so they know they can feel what is happening as opposed to simply trying to fend it off." "I would rather you not think about how the poem's constructed but simply be in it with me," she adds. "That's what it's for, not for the construction, even for the wit of it. It's for actual, visceral responses."

Shange's 1994 novel, *Liliane: Resurrection of the Daughter,* again finds the author exploring the issues of race and gender in contemporary America. The protagonist, Liliane Lincoln, undergoes psychoanalysis in an attempt to better understand the events of her life, particularly her mother's decision to abandon Liliane and her father for a white man when Liliane was a child. In the course of Liliane's monologues, we see her form brief, sexual relationships with men; mourn the deaths of her childhood friends; and travel around the globe seeking artistic inspiration and life wisdom. As Clarence Major notes in the *Washington Post Book World,* the story is presented "through 12 monologue-performance pieces narrated in turn by [Liliane] and her friends and lovers." Shange "offers a daring portrait of a black woman artist recreating herself out of social and psychological chaos," remarks Kelly Cherry in the *Los Angeles Times Book Review.* Cherry adds, ". . . Shange has written a novel that manages to be both risky and stylish." While some reviewers praised the author for her lush and unusual prose, others felt that Shange's stylistic density occasionally "up-ends the narrative," in the words of *New Statesman & Society* reviewer Andrea Stuart. Nevertheless, comments Valerie Sayers in the *New York Times Book Review,* the book "is a dense, ambitious, worthy song." And Major concludes, "A standing ovation for Ntozake Shange. This is her finest work of fiction so far."

"In the tradition of M. F. K. Fisher," according to the publisher, *If I Can Cook You Know God Can* is a "generous banquet" of essays steeped in "lyrical originality and musical patois." These conversational essays take the reader to the tables of African Americans, Nicaraguans, Londoners, Barbadoans, Brazilians, and Africans. Recipes range from the traditional, like collard greens, to the exotic, like turtle eggs and feijoada. As *Booklist* notes, the recipes are interwoven with a "fervent, richly impassioned chronicle of African American experience" that examines political turmoil and relates "how connections are made beyond issues of class or skin color."

BIOGRAPHICAL/CRITICAL SOURCES:

BOOKS

Betsko, Kathleen, and Rachel Koenig, editors, *Interviews with Contemporary Women Playwrights,* Beech Tree Books, 1987.
Christ, Carol P., *Diving Deep and Surfacing: Women Writers on Spiritual Quest,* Beacon Press (Boston, MA), 1980.
Contemporary Literary Criticism, Gale (Detroit), Volume 8, 1978; Volume 25, 1983; Volume 38, 1986.

Dictionary of Literary Biography, Volume 38: *Afro-American Writers after 1955: Dramatists and Prose Writers,* Gale, 1985.

Lester, Neal A., *Ntozake Shange: A Critical Study of the Plays,* Garland (New York), 1995.

Olaniyan, Tejumola, *Scars of Conquest/Masks of Resistance: The Invention of Cultural Identities in African-American, and Caribbean Drama,* Oxford University Press (New York), 1995.

Squier, Susan Merrill, editor, *Women Writers and the City: Essays in Feminist Literary Criticism,* University of Tennessee Press (Knoxville, TN), 1984.

Tate, Claudia, editor, *Black Women Writers at Work,* Continuum (New York City), 1983.

PERIODICALS

African American Review, spring, 1992; summer, 1992.
American Black Review, September, 1983; March, 1986.
Black American Literature Forum, summer, 1981; fall, 1990.
Black Scholar, March, 1979; March, 1981; December, 1982; July, 1985; winter, 1996, p. 68; summer, 1996, p. 67.
Booklist, April 15, 1987; May 15, 1991; January 1, 1998.
Chicago Tribune, October 21, 1982.
Chicago Tribune Book World, July 1, 1979; September 8, 1985.
Christian Science Monitor, September 9, 1976; October 8, 1982; May 2, 1986.
Cue, June 26, 1976.
Detroit Free Press, October 30, 1978.
Entertainment Weekly, March 10, 1995, p. 65.
Essence, November, 1976; May, 1985; June, 1985; August, 1991.
Horizon, September, 1977.
Kliatt Young Adult Paperback Book Guide, January, 1989.
Library Journal, May 1, 1987.
Los Angeles Times, October 20, 1982; June 11, 1985; July 28, 1987.
Los Angeles Times Book Review, August 22, 1982; October 20, 1982; January 8, 1984; July 29, 1984; June 11, 1985; July 19, 1987; December 18, 1994, p. 12.
Mother Jones, January/February, 1995, p. 69.
Ms., September, 1976; December, 1977; June, 1985; June, 1987.
Newsday, August 22, 1976.
New Statesman, October 4, 1985.
New Statesman & Society, May 19, 1995, p. 37.
Newsweek, June 14, 1976; July 30, 1979.
New York Daily News, July 16, 1979.
New Yorker, June 14, 1976; August 2, 1976; January 2, 1978.
New York Times, June 16, 1976; December 22, 1977; June 4, 1979; June 8, 1979; July 16, 1979; July 22, 1979; May 14, 1980; June 15, 1980.
New York Times Book Review, June 25, 1979; July 16, 1979; October 21, 1979; September 12, 1982; May 12, 1985; April 6, 1986; January 1, 1995, p. 6; October 15, 1995, p. 36; February 25, 1996, p. 32.
New York Times Magazine, May 1, 1983.
Publishers Weekly, May 3, 1985; November 14, 1994, p. 65; January 1, 1996, p. 69.
Saturday Review, February 18, 1978; May/June, 1985.
Time, June 14, 1976; July 19, 1976; November 1, 1976.
Times (London), April 21, 1983.
Times Literary Supplement, December 6, 1985; April 15-21, 1988.
Variety, July 25, 1979.
Village Voice, August 16, 1976; July 23, 1979; June 18, 1985.
Voice Literary Supplement, August, 1991; September, 1991.
Washington Post, June 12, 1976; June 29, 1976; February 23, 1982; June 17, 1985.
Washington Post Book World, October 15, 1978; July 19, 1981; August 22, 1982; August 5, 1984; February 5, 1995, p. 4.
Wilson Library Bulletin, October, 1990.
World Literature Today, summer, 1995, p. 584.

*   *   *

SHAPIRO, Karl (Jay) 1913-

PERSONAL: Born Carl Shapiro November 10, 1913, in Baltimore, MD; name legally changed to Karl Shapiro in 1920; son of Joseph (in business) and Sarah (Omansky) Shapiro; married Evalyn Katz (a secretary), March 25, 1945 (divorced, January, 1967); married Teri Kovach, July 31, 1967 (died, July, 1982); married Sophie Wilkins, April 25, 1985; children: (first marriage) Katharine, John Jacob, Elizabeth (deceased). *Education:* Attended University of Virginia, 1932-33, Johns Hopkins University, 1937-39, and Enoch Pratt Library School, 1940. *Politics:* Republican. *Religion:* Unaffiliated.

ADDRESSES: Home—904 Radcliffe Dr., Davis, CA 95616.

CAREER: Library of Congress, Washington, DC, consultant in poetry, 1946-47; Johns Hopkins University, Baltimore, MD, associate professor of writing, 1947-50; *Poetry,* Chicago, IL, editor, 1950-56; University of Nebraska, Lincoln, professor of English, 1956-66; University of Illinois at Chicago Circle, professor of English, 1966-68; University of California, Davis, professor of English, 1968-85. Lecturer in India, summer of 1955, for U.S. Department of State. Visiting professor or lecturer at University of Wisconsin, 1948, Loyola University, 1951-52, Salzburg Seminar in American Studies, 1952, University of California, 1955-56, and University of Indiana, 1956-57. Member, Bollingen Prize Committee, 1949. *Military service:* U.S. Army, 1941-45.

MEMBER: National Institute of Arts and Letters, American Academy of Arts and Sciences (honorary), Phi Beta Kappa, PEN.

AWARDS, HONORS: Fellow in American Letters, Library of Congress; Jeanette S. Davis Prize and Levinson prize, both from *Poetry* in 1942; *Contemporary Poetry* prize, 1943; American Academy of Arts and Letters grant, 1944; Pulitzer Prize in poetry, 1945, for *V-Letter and Other Poems;* Shelley Memorial Prize, 1946; Guggenheim Foundation fellowships, 1944, 1953; Kenyon School of Letters fellowship, 1956-57; Eunice Tietjens Memorial Prize, 1961; Oscar Blumenthal Prize, *Poetry,* 1963; Bollingen Prize, 1968; Robert Kirsch Award L.A. Times, 1989; Charity Randall Citation, 1990; Library of Congress fellowship.

WRITINGS:

English Prosody and Modern Poetry, Johns Hopkins Press, 1947.
A Bibliography of Modern Prosody, Johns Hopkins Press, 1948.
(Editor with Louis Untermeyer and Richard Wilbur) *Modern American and Modern British Poetry,* Harcourt, 1955.
(Author of libretto) *The Tenor* (opera; music by Hugo Weisgall), Merion Music, 1956.
(Editor) *American Poetry* (anthology), Crowell, 1960.
(Editor) *Prose Keys to Modern Poetry,* Harper, 1962.
(With Robert Beum) *Prosody Handbook,* Harper, 1965.
Edsel (novel), Geis, 1970.
(Editor with Robert Phillips) *Letters of Delmore Schwartz,* Ontario Review Press/Persea Books, 1984.

The Younger Son: Poet; An Autobiography in Three Parts; The Youth and War Years of a Distinguished American Poet, Algonquin Books, 1988.

Reports of My Death: An Autobiography, Algonquin Books, 1990.

POETRY

Poems, Waverly, 1935.

(Contributor) *Five Young American Poets,* New Directions, 1941.

Person, Place, and Thing, Reynal, 1942.

The Place of Love, Comment Press, 1942.

V-Letter and Other Poems, Reynal, 1944.

Essay on Rime, Secker & Warburg, 1945.

Trial of a Poet and Other Poems, Reynal, 1947.

(Contributor) *Poets at Work,* Harcourt, 1948.

Poems: 1940-1953, Random House, 1953.

The House, privately printed, 1957.

Poems of a Jew, Random House, 1958.

(Editor) *American Poetry,* Cromwell, 1960.

The Bourgeois Poet, Random House, 1964.

Selected Poems, Random House, 1968.

White-Haired Lover, Random House, 1968.

Adult Book Store, Random House, 1976.

Collected Poems: 1948-1978, Random House, 1978.

Love and War, Art and God, Stuart Wright, 1984.

Adam and Eve, edited by John Wheatcroft, Press Alley, 1986.

New and Selected Poems, 1940-1986, University of Chicago Press, 1987.

Old Horsefly, Northern Lights, 1992.

The Wild Card: Selected Poems, Early and Late, University of Illinois, 1998.

LITERARY CRITICISM

Beyond Criticism, University of Nebraska Press, 1953, published as *A Primer for Poets,* 1965.

In Defense of Ignorance, Random House, 1960.

(With James E. Miller, Jr. and Beatrice Slote) *Start It with the Sun: Studies in Cosmic Poetry,* University of Nebraska Press, 1960.

(With Ralph Ellison) *The Writer's Experience,* Library of Congress, 1964.

Randall Jarrell, Library of Congress, 1967.

To Abolish Children and Other Essays, Quadrangle Books, 1968.

The Poetry Wreck: Selected Essays, 1950-1970, Random House, 1975.

OTHER

Also author of screenplay "Karl Shapiro's America," 1976. Work appears in anthologies. Contributor of articles, poetry, and reviews to *Partisan Review, Poetry, Nation, Saturday Review,* and other periodicals. Editor, *Poetry,* 1950-56, *Newberry Library Bulletin,* 1953-55, and *Prairie Schooner,* 1956-66.

SIDELIGHTS: Karl Shapiro's poetry received early recognition, winning a number of major poetry awards, including the Pulitzer prize, during the 1940s. Strongly influenced by the traditionalist poetry of W. H. Auden, Shapiro's early work is "striking for its concrete but detached insights," Alfred Kazin writes in *Contemporaries.* "It is witty and exact in the way it catches the poet's subtle and guarded impressions, and it is a poetry full of clever and unexpected verbal conceits. It is a very professional poetry—supple [and] adaptable." Stephen Stepanchev notes in *American Poetry since 1945: A Critical Survey* that Shapiro's poems "found impetus and subject matter in the public crises of the 1940's [and all] have their social meaning."

In the poetry of both Whitman, which he memorized in his youth, and the Beat poets, Shapiro found a confirmation of his own idea of feeling over form. In his collection *The Bourgeois Poet,* Shapiro broke with his traditional poetic forms in favor of the free verse of Whitman and the Beats. Critics observed that the new poems also contained insights and an apocalyptic tone that was shocking compared to other poetry being published at that time. Writing in *American Poets from the Puritans to the Present,* Hyatt H. Waggoner finds *The Bourgeois Poet* "a work of greater poetic integrity than any of Shapiro's earlier volumes."

Person, Place and Thing, containing poems that had won the Levinson prize when published in *Poetry* magazine, was applauded by the critics. Directly confronting subjects such as love, the history of the South in which Shapiro grew up an outsider, or the war in the South Pacific in which he served as a medical corps clerk, the poems were received as palpable "attacks." His most frequent target in the poems, relates Ross Labrie in the *Dictionary of Literary Biography,* was the "dehumanized technocracies" that fostered urban decadence and sent men and women to war without regard for their worth as persons. In a *Poetry* review of a later book, *Love & War, Art & God,* David Wojahn comments that social criticism has always been part of Shapiro's work. Wojahn writes, "From the very beginning, Shapiro identified himself as an iconoclast, and his outsider's role extended beyond his attacks on social injustice. At a time before it was fashionable to do so, he proudly proclaimed his Jewishness and set himself against the main trends of Modernism." Coming of age in the United States had much to do with his development as an iconoclast. In his introduction to *The Poems of a Jew,* he wrote, "As a third generation American I grew up with the obsessive idea of personal liberty which engrosses all Americans except the oldest and richest families." In a *Paris Review* interview, Shapiro explained how being both a Jew and a poet also partly accounts for his point of view as an "outsider": "I've always had this feeling—I've heard other Jews say—that when you can't find any other explanation for the Jews, you say, 'Well, they are poets.'. . . The poet is in exile whether he is or he is not. Because of what everybody knows about society's idea of the artist as a peripheral character and a potential bum. Or a troublemaker. . . . I always thought of myself as being both in and out of society at the same time. Like the way most artists probably feel in order to survive—you have to at least pretend that you are 'seriously' in the world. Or actually perform in it while you know that in your own soul you are not in it at all."

Shapiro published the Pulitzer prize-winning volume *V-Letter and Other Poems* in 1944 while serving with the U.S. Army in New Guinea. V-letters were letters written by American soldiers and microfilmed by censors before delivery to the United States. The poems recreate the tension between the intensity of wartime experiences and a sense of detachment from events that many soldiers felt while trying to conduct their personal lives over the obstacles of distance and the added obstacle of the censors. Though he appreciated what the award would do to establish his career as a writer, Shapiro felt more honored when he found out that copies of *V-Letter and Other Poems* had been placed in all U.S. Navy ship libraries.

In 1988 Shapiro published the first volume in a planned three-volume autobiography. This first volume, titled *The Younger Son,* details Shapiro's childhood and early manhood, including his World War II experience and the beginnings of his literary career. While "the poet," as Shapiro refers to himself throughout the volume, divulges little information about his relationship with his parents and the experiences of his youth, he is more expansive when discussing his wartime tour of duty, when he managed a prodigious poetic output while caring for wounded soldiers. He arrived home in 1945, having just been awarded the Pulitzer Prize for *V-Letter.* Commenting on the author's use of the third-person in the book and the resulting detachment from his life that is implied, *Sewanee Review* contributor David Miller notes that "The mood is an eerie one of diminishment and distance." However, Miller concludes that "*The Younger Son* is beautifully styled, honest, and fascinating."

Shapiro continued his autobiography with 1990's *Reports of My Death,* the title referring to inaccurate media reports in the 1980s that Shapiro had committed suicide. The volume covers the period between 1945, when Shapiro returned home from World War II, and 1985, chronicling in the process Shapiro's literary development; his stints as editor of *Poetry* and *Prairie Schooner;* his controversial decision to vote against Ezra Pound as recipient of the first Bollingen Prize for poetry; and his gradual fading from the literary limelight during the 1970s and 1980s. Again referring to himself in the third person, Shapiro openly discusses his numerous extramarital affairs, his disgust with the American literary scene, and his frustration at being dropped from the prestigious *Oxford Book of American Verse.* "Shapiro has written a beautiful book, not only tracing the long career of 'the poet' but doing so in dreamy, mellifluous sentences that sometimes left me feeling euphoric," remarks Morris Dickstein in the *Washington Post Book World.* Several critics expressed disappointment with Shapiro's decision not to date important events and not to identify people who figure prominently in his story. *World Literature Today* critic John Boening avers that "such indirectness may make the book rough going for future generations." Nevertheless, Chicago *Tribune Books* reviewer Larry Kart declares that Shapiro's two volumes of autobiography "not only rank with Shapiro's finest poetic achievements but also will come to occupy . . . a high place in the canon of American autobiography."

Examining Shapiro's career as a whole in the *Small Press Review,* Leo Connellan remarks, "Poets owe Karl Shapiro, first for creating a sound and music in language that no other poet has surpassed." Secondly, Shapiro has helped to support the work of new poets by including their works in textbook anthologies. *New York Times* contributor Laurence Leiberman sees Shapiro as one of "a generation of poets who . . . wrote a disproportionate number of superbly good poems in early career, became decorated overnight with honors . . . and spent the next twenty-odd years trying to outpace a growing critical notice of decline." Leiberman judges *The Bourgeois Poet* to be Shapiro's attempt to "recast the poetic instrument to embody formerly intractable large sectors of [his life]" and to win "a precious freedom to extend the limits of [his art]." Leiberman sees the two styles in Shapiro's poetry, the traditionalist and free verse, enhancing each other. He believes that Shapiro's "future work stands an excellent chance of merging the superior qualities of two opposite modes: the expressiveness of candid personal confession and the durability of significant form."

BIOGRAPHICAL/CRITICAL SOURCES:

BOOKS

Bartlett, Lee, *Karl Shapiro: A Descriptive Bibliography,* Garland Publishing, 1979.
Contemporary Authors Autobiography Series, Volume 6, Gale (Detroit), 1987.
Contemporary Literary Criticism, Gale, Volume 4, 1975; Volume 8, 1978; Volume 15, 1980; Volume 53, 1989.
Dictionary of Literary Biography, Volume 48: *American Poets, 1880-1945, Second Series,* Gale, 1986.
Jarrell, Randall, *The Third Book of Criticism,* Farrar, Straus, 1969.
Kazin, Alfred, *Contemporaries,* Little, Brown, 1962.
Nemerov, Howard, *Poetry and Fiction,* Rutgers University Press, 1963.
Rosenthal, M. L., *The Modern Poets: A Critical Introduction,* Oxford University Press, 1960.
Scannell, Vernon, *Not without Glory,* Woburn Press, 1976.
Spears, Monroe K., *Dionysus and the City,* Oxford University Press, 1970.
Stepanchev, Stephen, *American Poetry since 1945: A Critical Survey,* Harper, 1965.
Waggoner, Hyatt H., *American Poets from the Puritans to the Present,* Houghton, 1968.
White, William, *Karl Shapiro: A Bibliography,* Wayne State University Press, 1960.

PERIODICALS

America, January 7, 1989, p. 14.
Book World, July 28, 1968.
Carleton Miscellany, spring, 1965.
Christian Science Monitor, July 3, 1968.
College English, February, 1946.
Commonweal, September 19, 1958; January 20, 1960; October 4, 1968.
Esquire, April, 1968.
Harper's, August, 1964.
Hollins Critic, December, 1964.
Hudson Review, autumn, 1975; summer, 1988.
Kenyon Review, winter, 1946.
Los Angeles Times, July 7, 1968.
Nation, July 5, 1958; September 24, 1960; August 24, 1964; November 11, 1978.
New Republic, November 24, 1958.
New Yorker, November 7, 1964.
New York Times, July 29, 1968; January 6, 1969; October 4, 1971.
New York Times Book Review, September 7, 1958; May 8, 1960; July 14, 1968; August 18, 1968; July 25, 1976; March 31, 1985; November 27, 1988, p. 23; May 13, 1990, p. 25.
Paris Review, spring, 1986.
Partisan Review, winter, 1969.
Poetry, June, 1965; April, 1969; July, 1969; February, 1970; June, 1985.
Prairie Schooner, winter, 1965.
Publishers Weekly, March 2, 1990, p. 67.
Saturday Review, September 27, 1958; April 15, 1978.
Sewanee Review, winter, 1965; April, 1989, p. 283.
Southern Review, winter, 1973.
Time, August 2, 1968.
Tribune Books (Chicago), October 30, 1988; July 15, 1990, p. 3.
Village Voice, March 29, 1976.
Virginia Quarterly Review, winter, 1969.
Wall Street Journal, July 7, 1976.
Washington Post, January 4, 1980; December 9, 1988.
Washington Post Book World, July 1, 1990, p. 1.
Western Review, spring, 1954.
World Literature Today, winter, 1992, p. 139.
Yale Review, winter, 1954; June, 1975.

SHAW, Bernard
See SHAW, George Bernard

*   *   *

SHAW, G. Bernard
See SHAW, George Bernard

*   *   *

SHAW, George Bernard 1856-1950
(G. B. S., Bernard Shaw, G. Bernard Shaw,
Corno di Bassetto)

PERSONAL: Born July 26, 1856, in Dublin, Ireland; died November 2, 1950, in Ayot Saint Lawrence, Hertfordshire, England; son of George Carr (an agricultural merchant) and Lucinda Elizabeth (a singer, musician, and music teacher; maiden name, Gurly) Shaw; married Charlotte Francis Payne-Townshend, 1898 (died, September, 1943). *Education:* Attended Central Model Boys' School, 1868, and English Scientific and Commercial Day School, 1869.

CAREER: Playwright, novelist, essayist, critic, and lecturer. Cashier for a land agent in Dublin, Ireland, 1871-76; writer and commercial laborer, c. 1876-85; public speaker and lecturer, beginning 1883; cofounder of Fabian Society, 1884; helped establish, with Sidney and Beatrice Webb, the London School of Economics, 1895; vestryman and borough councilor in London, 1897-1903.

MEMBER: Society of Authors, Playwrights, and Composers, Fabian Society (member of executive committee, 1885-1911), British Interplanetary Society, Royal Automobile Club, Burlington Fine Arts Club.

AWARDS, HONORS: Nobel Prize for literature from the Swedish Academy, 1925; Irish Academy of Letters Medal, 1934; Academy Award (Oscar), Academy of Motion Picture Arts and Sciences, 1938, for screenplay of *Pygmalion.*

WRITINGS:

PLAYS—INDIVIDUAL WORKS; UNDER NAME BERNARD SHAW, EXCEPT AS NOTED

Widowers' Houses (produced in London at the Royalty Theatre, December 9, 1892), Henry, 1893, Brentano's, 1913.
The Gadfly; or, The Son of the Cardinal, produced in Bayswater at the Bijou Theatre, March, 1898.
The Man of Destiny produced in Croydon at the Grand Theatre, July 1, 1897, produced in London at the Royal Court Theatre, June 4, 1907.
How He Lied to Her Husband, produced in New York at the Berkeley Lyceum Theatre, September 26, 1904, produced in London at the Royal Court Theatre, February 28, 1905.
Passion, Poison, and Petrifaction; or, The Fatal Gazogene (produced in London at the Theatrical Garden Party, Regent's Park, July 14, 1905), H. B. Clafin, 1905.
Man and Superman (produced in London at the Royal Court Theatre, May 21, 1905; revised version, including *Don Juan in Hell,* produced in Edinburgh at the Lyceum Theatre, June 11, 1915 [also see below]; revised version produced in London at the Regent Theatre, October 23, 1925), University Press, 1903, reprinted with introduction and notes by A. C.

Ward, Longman, 1947, reprinted with introduction by Lewis Casson, illustrated by Charles Mozley, Heritage Press, 1962.
You Never Can Tell (produced in London at the Royalty Theatre, November 26, 1899), Constable, 1906, Brentano's, 1913, reprinted with introduction by Margery M. Morgan, Hicks Smith, 1967.
The Interlude at the Playhouse, produced in London at the Playhouse Theatre, January 28, 1907.
Don Juan in Hell (from *Man and Superman*), produced in London at the Royal Court Theatre, June 4, 1907.
The Doctor's Dilemma (produced in London at the Royal Court Theatre, November 20, 1906), Constable, 1908, Brentano's, 1911, revised with preface, 1913, Dodd, 1941, reprinted with an introduction and notes by Ward, Longman, 1957.
(Under name George Bernard Shaw) *The Admirable Bashville; or, Constancy Unrewarded* (based on Shaw's novel *Cashel Byron's Profession;* produced in London at the Imperial Theatre, June 7, 1903), Brentano's, 1909.
Captain Brassbound's Conversion (produced in London at the Strand Theatre, December 16, 1900), Constable, 1906, Brentano's, 1913.
The Devil's Disciple (produced in Albany, NY, at Hermanus Bleecker Hall, October 1, 1897, produced in London at the Savoy Theatre, October 14, 1907), Constable, 1906, Brentano's, 1913, reprinted with an introduction and notes by Ward, Longman, 1958, reprinted with illustrations by Leonard Everett Fisher, F. Watts, 1967.
The Shewing-up of Blanco Posnet (produced in Dublin at the Abbey Theatre, August 25, 1909, produced in London at the Everyman Theatre, March 14, 1921), Brentano's, 1909.
Press Cuttings (produced in Manchester at the Gaiety Theatre, September 27, 1909), Brentano's, 1909.
Misalliance, produced in London at the Duke of York's Theatre, February 23, 1910.
The Dark Lady of the Sonnets, produced in London at the Haymarket Theatre, November 24, 1910.
Fanny's First Play, produced in London at the Little Theatre, April 19, 1911.
Arms and the Man (produced in London at the Avenue Theatre, April 21, 1894), Brentano's, 1913, reprinted with introduction by Ward, Longman, 1956, reprinted with introduction by Louis Kronenberger, Bantam, 1960, authoritative edition with critical material and introduction by Henry Popkin, Avon, 1967, revised edition with introduction and notes by Louis Crompton, Bobbs-Merrill, 1969, definitive text edition, Penguin, 1977.
Candida (produced in Aberdeen at Her Majesty's Theatre, July 30, 1897, produced in London at the Royal Court Theatre, April 26, 1904), Brentano's, 1913, reprinted with an introduction and notes by Ward, Longman, 1956.
Mrs. Warren's Profession (produced in London at the New Lyric Club, January 5, 1902), Brentano's, 1913 (also see below).
John Bull's Other Island (produced in London at the Royal Court Theatre, November 1, 1904), Brentano's, 1913.
The Philanderer (produced in London at the New Stage Club, Applegate Institute, February 20, 1905, produced in London at the Royal Court Theatre, February 5, 1907), Brentano's, 1913.
Major Barbara (produced in London at the Royal Court Theatre, November 28, 1905), Brentano's, 1913, Dodd, 1941, reprinted with introduction and notes by Ward, Longman, 1958, revised edition edited by Elizabeth T. Forter, Appleton-Century-Crofts, 1971.

Caesar and Cleopatra (produced in Berlin at the Neues Theatre, March 31, 1906, produced in New York at the New Amsterdam Theatre, October 30, 1906, produced in London at the Savoy Theatre, November 25, 1907), Brentano's, 1913, revised edition edited by Forter, Appleton-Century-Crofts, 1965.

Great Catherine, produced in London at Vaudeville Theatres, November 18, 1913.

Getting Married (produced in London at the Haymarket Theatre, May 12, 1908), Brentano's, 1913, Players Press (Studio City, CA), 1995.

Pygmalion (also see below; produced in Siegfried Trebitsch's German translation in Vienna at the Hofburg Theatre, October 16, 1913; produced in English in London at His Majesty's Theatre, April 11, 1914), German translation by Trebitsch, S. Fischer, 1913, English-language edition first published in 1920, reprinted with an introduction by Ward, Longman, 1957, definitive text edition, illustrated by Feliks Topolski, Penguin, 1982.

The Music-Cure, produced in London at the Little Theatre, January 28, 1914.

Overruled (produced in London at the Duke of York's Theatre, October 14, 1912), Constable, 1915.

The Inca of Perusalem, produced in Birmingham at the Repertory Theatre, October 7, 1916, produced in London at the Criterion Theatre, December 16, 1917.

Augustus Does His Bit, produced in London at the Royal Court Theatre, January 21, 1917.

Annajanska, the Wild Grand Duchess, produced in London at the London Coliseum, January 21, 1918.

O'Flaherty, V. C., produced in New York at the 39th Street Theatre, June 21, 1920, produced in London at the Lyric Theatre, Hammersmith, December 19, 1920.

Back to Methuselah (produced in New York at the Garrick Theatre, February 27, 1922, produced in London at the Royal Court Theatre, February 18, 1924), Brentano's, 1921, revised edition with a postscript, Oxford University Press, 1946, definitive text edition, Penguin, 1977, reprinted as *Back to Methuselah: A Metabiological Pentateuch,* Penguin, 1988.

Jitta's Atonement (adapted from Siegfried Trebitsch's *Frau Gittas Suehne*), produced in Washington, DC, at the Shubert Theatre, January 8, 1923, produced in New York at the Comedy Theatre, January 17, 1923, produced in London at the Arts Theatre, April 30, 1930.

Saint Joan (produced in New York at the Garrick Theatre, December 28, 1923, produced in London at the New Theatre, March 26, 1924), Brentano's, 1923, revised edition edited and with an introduction and notes by Stanley Weintraub, Bobbs-Merrill, 1971.

The Glimpse of Reality, produced in London at the Arts Theatre Club, November 20, 1927.

The Fascinating Foundling, produced in London at the Arts Theatre Club, January 28, 1928.

The Apple Cart (produced in Warsaw at the Teatr Polski, June 14, 1929, produced in Malvern at the Malvern Theatre Festival, August 19, 1929, produced in London at the Queen's Theatre, September 17, 1929), Constable, 1930, Brentano's, 1931.

Too True to Be Good, produced in Boston at the National Theatre, February 29, 1932, produced in New York at the Guild Theatre, April 4, 1932.

On the Rocks, produced in London at the Winter Garden Theatre, November 25, 1933.

Village Wooing, produced in Dallas at the Little Theatre, April 16, 1934, produced in Tunbridge Wells at the Pump Room, May 1, 1934.

(With Jean Froissart and Auguste Rodin) *The Six of Calais* (produced in London at the Open Air Theatre, Regent's Park, July 17, 1934), privately printed, 1934.

The Simpleton of the Unexpected Isles, produced in New York at the Guild Theatre, February 18, 1935.

The Millionairess, produced in Vienna at the Akademie Theatre, January 4, 1936, produced in Melbourne at the King's Theatre, March 7, 1936.

Cymbeline Refinished (produced in London at the Embassy Theatre, Swiss Cottage, November 16, 1937), privately printed, 1937.

Geneva (produced in Malvern at the Festival Theatre, August 1, 1938, produced in London at the Saville Theatre, November 22, 1938), Constable, 1939.

In Good King Charles's Golden Days (produced in Malvern at the Festival Theatre, August 12, 1939, produced in London at the Streatham Hill Theatre, April 15, 1940), illustrated by Topolski, Constable, 1939.

Buoyant Billions (produced in Zurich at the Schauspielhaus, October 21, 1948, produced in Malvern at the Festival Theatre, August 13, 1949), Constable, 1949.

Shakes Versus Shav (puppet play), produced in Malvern at the Waldo Lanchester Marionette Theatre, Lyttleton Hall, August 9, 1949, produced in Battersea Park at the Riverside Theatre, June 10, 1951.

Farfetched Fables, produced in London at the Watergate Theatre, September 6, 1950.

Androcles and the Lion (produced in Berlin at Kleines Theatre, November 25, 1912, produced in London at St. James's Theatre, September 1, 1913), Penguin, 1951, reprinted with an introduction and notes by Ward, Longman, 1957.

Why She Would Not, produced in New York by the Shaw Society of America at the Grolier Club, January 21, 1957.

Heartbreak House (produced in New York at the Garrick Theatre, November 10, 1920, produced in London at the Royal Court Theatre, October 18, 1921), Penguin, 1964; published as *Heartbreak House: A Fantasia in the Russian Manner on English Themes,* Signet, 1996.

LETTERS, CONVERSATIONS, AND DIARIES; UNDER NAME BERNARD SHAW, EXCEPT AS NOTED

(Under name George Bernard Shaw) *Table-Talk of G. B. S.: Conversations on Things in General Between George Bernard Shaw and His Biographer,* compiled and edited by Archibald Henderson, Harper, 1925.

Ellen Terry and Bernard Shaw: A Correspondence, edited by Christopher St. John, Putnam, 1931, reprinted with illustrations, Theatre Arts Books, 1969.

(Under name George Bernard Shaw) *Some Unpublished Letters of George Bernard Shaw,* edited by Julian Park, [Buffalo], 1939.

Florence Farr, Bernard Shaw, and W. B. Yeats, edited by Clifford Bax, Cuala Press, 1941, Dodd, 1942.

Bernard Shaw and Mrs. Patrick Campbell: A Correspondence, edited by Alan Dent, Knopf, 1952.

Advice to a Young Critic, and Other Letters, notes and introduction by E. J. West, Crown, 1955.

Bernard Shaw's Letters to Harley Granville Barker, edited by C. B. Purdom, Phoenix, 1956, Crown, 1957.

To a Young Actress: The Letters of Bernard Shaw to Molly Tompkins, edited with an introduction by Peter Tompkins, Potter, 1960.

Collected Letters, four volumes, edited by Dan H. Laurence, Volume 1: *1874-1897,* Dodd, 1965, Volume 2: *1898-1910,* Dodd, 1965, Volume 3: *1911-1925,* Viking, 1985, Volume 4: *1926-1950,* Viking, 1988.

Bernard Shaw and Alfred Douglas: A Correspondence, edited by Mary Hyde, Ticknor & Fields, 1982.

The Playwright and the Pirate: Bernard Shaw and Frank Harris, a Correspondence, edited with an introduction by Weintraub, Pennsylvania State University Press, 1982.

Agitations: Letters to the Press, 1875-1950, edited by James Rambeau and Laurence, Ungar, 1985.

Bernard Shaw's Letters to Siegfried Trebitsch, edited by Samuel A. Weiss, Stanford University Press, 1986.

Bernard Shaw: The Diaries, 1885-1897, edited and annotated by Weintraub, transliterated from shorthand notation by Stanley Rypins, additional transliterations and transcriptions by Blanche Patch, Pennsylvania State University Press, 1986.

Dear Mr. Shaw: Selections From Bernard Shaw's Postbag, edited by Vivian Elliot, Bloomsbury, 1988.

Theatrics, edited by Dan Laurence, University of Toronto Press (Buffalo), 1995.

Bernard Shaw and H. G. Wells, edited by J. Percy Smith, University of Toronto Press (Toronto), 1995.

Bernard Shaw and Gabriel Pascal, edited by Bernard F. Dukore, University of Toronto Press, 1996.

COLLECTIONS; UNDER NAME BERNARD SHAW

Plays: Pleasant and Unpleasant, two volumes, Stone, 1898.

Three Plays for Puritans, Stone, 1901, abridged edition published as *Two Plays for Puritans,* illustrated by George Him, Heritage Press, 1966).

The Wisdom of Bernard Shaw (passages from Shaw's works), selected by Charlotte F. Shaw, Brentano's, 1913.

The Socialism of Shaw, edited with an introduction by James Fuchs, Vanguard Press, 1926.

The Works of Bernard Shaw, Collected Edition, thirty volumes, Constable, 1930-1932, revised edition published as *The Works of Bernard Shaw, Ayot St. Lawrence Edition,* Wise, 1931-1932, enlarged edition published as *Standard Edition of the Works of Bernard Shaw,* thirty-six volumes, Constable, 1947-1952.

The Complete Plays of Bernard Shaw, Constable, 1931.

Major Critical Essays, Constable, 1932, reprinted as *Major Critical Essays: The Quintessence of Ibsenism, the Perfect Wagnerite, the Sanity of Art,* Penguin, 1986; Dover Publications (New York), 1994.

Short Stories, Scraps and Shavings, illustrated by John Farleigh, Dodd, 1934, published as *The Black Girl in Search of God, and Some Lesser Tales,* Penguin, 1964.

Three Plays: Too True to Be Good, Village Wooing, and On the Rocks, Dodd, 1934.

Prefaces, Constable, 1934, reprinted as *Prefaces by Bernard Shaw,* Reprint Services, 1988.

Nine Plays, Dodd, 1935.

Six Plays (a companion to *Nine Plays*), Dodd, 1941.

Selected Novels, introduction by Arthur Zeiger, Caxton House, 1946.

Selected Plays (includes prefaces), Dodd, 1948-1957.

Plays and Players: Essays on the Theatre, selected with an introduction by Ward, Oxford University Press, 1952.

Selected Prose, selected by Diarmuid Russell, Dodd, 1952.

Selected Plays and Other Writings, introduction by William Irvine, Rinehart, 1956.

The Illusions of Socialism, Together with Socialism: Principles and Outlook, Shaw Society, 1956.

Shaw's Dramatic Criticism: 1895-1898 (selections from the author's contributions to *Saturday Review*), edited by John F. Matthews, Hill & Wang, 1959.

A Prose Anthology, selected with introduction and notes by H. M. Burton, preface by Ward, Fawcett, 1959.

Selected Nondramatic Writings of Bernard Shaw, edited by Laurence, Houghton, 1965.

Bernard Shaw: Selections of His Wit and Wisdom, compiled by Caroline Thomas Harnsberger, Follett, 1965.

The Complete Prefaces of Bernard Shaw, Hamlyn Publishing, 1965.

Bernard Shaw's Ready-Reckoner, edited with an introduction by N. H. Leigh-Taylor, Random House, 1965.

Four Plays, foreword and introduction by Paul Kozelka, Washington Square Press, 1965.

Selected One-Act Plays, Penguin, 1965.

Seven Plays With Prefaces and Notes, Dodd, 1966.

Three Shorter Plays, Heinemann Educational, 1968.

Bernard Shaw's Plays, edited by Warren Sylvester Smith, Norton, 1970.

The Bodley Head Bernard Shaw, seven volumes (includes *A Passion Play*), Bodley Head, 1970, Reinhardt, 1970-1974, published as *Collected Plays With Their Prefaces,* Dodd, 1975.

The Road to Equality: Ten Unpublished Lectures and Essays, 1884-1918, introduction by Crompton, edited by Crompton and Hilayne Cavanaugh, Beacon Press, 1971.

Collected Music Criticism, Vienna House, 1973.

The Portable Bernard Shaw, edited with an introduction by Weintraub, Penguin, 1977.

The Collected Screenplays of Bernard Shaw, edited by Bernard F. Dukore, University of Georgia Press, 1980.

Selected Plays, preface by Rex Harrison, introductory essay by David Bearinger, Dodd, 1981.

Selected Short Plays, Viking Penguin, 1988.

Monologues from George Bernard Shaw, edited by Ian Michaels, Dramaline Publications, 1988.

Unpublished Shaw, edited by Dan H. Laurence and Margot Peters, Pennsylvania State University Press, 1996.

Selected Plays of George Bernard Shaw, introduction by Alfred Kazin, Vintage Books, 1999.

Facsimile editions of plays published as *Early Texts: Play Manuscripts in Facsimile,* twelve volumes, edited by Laurence, Garland, 1981.

OTHER; UNDER NAME BERNARD SHAW, EXCEPT AS NOTED

Cashel Byron's Profession (novel), Harper, 1886, revised edition, Stone, 1901, reprinted alone with preface by Harry T. Moore, edited with an introduction by Weintraub, Southern Illinois University Press, 1968, definitive text edition edited by Laurence, Penguin, 1979.

An Unsocial Socialist (novel), Lowry, 1887, Brentano's, 1900.

(Editor) *Fabian Essays in Socialism,* Fabian Society, 1889.

The Quintessence of Ibsenism, Tucker, 1891, enlarged edition, Brentano's, 1913, 3rd edition, Constable, 1922, revised enlarged edition published as *Shaw and Ibsen: Bernard Shaw's The Quintessence of Ibsenism and Related Writings,* edited by J. L. Wisenthal, University of Toronto Press, 1979.

The Perfect Wagnerite, G. Richards, 1898, Stone, 1899.

(Editor) *Fabianism and the Empire: A Manifesto by the Fabian Society,* G. Richards, 1900.

Love Among the Artists (novel), Stone, 1900.

The Common Sense of Municipal Trading, Constable, 1904, revised edition with preface, A. C. Fifield, 1908, John Lane, 1911.

The Author's Apology From Mrs. Warren's Profession: The Tyranny of Police and Press, introduction by John Corbin, Brentano's, 1905 (also see above).

The Irrational Knot (novel), Brentano's, 1905.

(Under name G. Bernard Shaw) *An Essay on Going to Church,* J. W. Luce, 1905.

(Under name G. Bernard Shaw) *Dramatic Opinions and Essays,* with a word by James Huneker, Brentano's 1906, reprinted (under name Bernard Shaw) with an apology by Shaw, 1907.

The Sanity of Art, Tucker, 1908.

Socialism and Superior Brains, John Lane, 1910.

Peace Conference Hints, Constable, 1919.

Imprisonment, Brentano's, 1925, published as *The Crime of Imprisonment,* illustrated by William Gropper, Greenwood Press, 1946.

Translations and Tomfooleries, Brentano's, 1926.

The Intelligent Woman's Guide to Capitalism and Socialism, Brentano's, 1928, reprinted with an introduction by Susan Moller Okin, Transaction Books, 1984, published as *The Intelligent Woman's Guide to Socialism, Capitalism, Sovietism, and Fascism,* Penguin, 1965.

Bernard Shaw and Karl Marx: A Symposium, 1884-1889, Georgian Press, 1930, Norwood, 1978.

Immaturity (novel), Constable, 1931.

What I Really Wrote About the War (includes "Common Sense About the War"), Constable, 1931, Brentano's, 1932.

Doctor's Delusions, Crude Criminology, and Sham Education, Constable, limited edition, 1931, revised standard edition, 1932.

Pen Portraits and Reviews, Constable, 1932.

Essays in Fabian Socialism, Constable, 1932.

Our Theatres in the Nineties, Constable, 1932.

The Adventures of the Black Girl in Her Search for God, Constable, 1932, Dodd, 1933.

Music in London, 1890-1894 (criticisms originally published in *World*), Constable, 1932.

(Under name George Bernard Shaw) *American Boobs,* E. O. Jones, 1933, published as *The Future of Political Science in America,* Dodd, 1933 (published in England as *The Politicial Madhouse in America and Nearer Home,* Constable, 1933).

William Morris As I Knew Him, Dodd, 1936.

London Music in 1888-1889 as Heard by Corno di Bassetto, Dodd, 1937.

(With others) *Pygmalion* (screenplay; based on his play), Metro-Goldwyn-Mayer, 1938; Dover Publications (New York), 1994.

Shaw Gives Himself Away: An Autobiographical Miscellany, Gregynog Press, 1939.

(With Anatole de Grunwald) *Major Barbara* (screenplay; based on his play), United Artists, 1941.

Everybody's Political What's What, Dodd, 1944.

(With Marjorie Deans and W. P. Lipscomb) *Caesar and Cleopatra* (screenplay; based on his play), Eagle-Lion, 1946.

Sixteen Self Sketches, Dodd, 1949.

Shaw on Vivisection, compiled and edited by G. H. Bowker, Allen & Unwin, 1949, published as *Are Doctors Really Inhuman?,* Fridtjof-Karla, 1957.

Shaw on Music, selected by Eric Bentley, Doubleday, 1955; Applause (New York), 1995.

My Dear Dorothea: A Practical System of Moral Education for Females, Embodied in a Letter to a Young Person of That Sex (novel), illustrated by Clare Winsten, with a note by Stephen Winsten, Phoenix, 1956, Vanguard Press, 1957.

Shaw on Theatre, edited by E. J. West, Hill & Wang, 1958.

An Unfinished Novel, edited by Weintraub, Dodd, 1958.

How to Become a Musical Critic, edited by Laurence, Hart-Davis, 1960, Hill & Wang, 1961.

Platform and Pulpit, edited by Laurence, Hill & Wang, 1961.

Shaw on Shakespeare, Dutton, 1961, edited with an introduction by Edwin Wilson, Books for Libraries Press, 1971.

G. B. S. on Music, foreword by Alec Robertson, Penguin, 1962.

The Matter With Ireland, edited with an introduction by David H. Greene and Laurence, Hill & Wang, 1962.

(Under name George Bernard Shaw) *On Language,* edited with an introduction and notes by Abraham Tauber, foreword by James Pitman, Philosophical Library, 1963.

Religious Speeches, edited by Smith, foreword by Arthur N. Nethercot, Pennsylvania State University Press, 1963.

(Under name George Bernard Shaw) *The Rationalization of Russia,* edited with an introduction by Harry M. Geduld, Indiana University Press, 1964.

Shaw on Religion, edited with an introduction and notes by Smith, Dodd, 1967.

Shaw: An Autobiography, 1856-1898, compiled and edited by Weintraub, Weybright & Talley, 1969.

Shaw: An Autobiography; The Playwright Years, 1898-1950, compiled and edited by Weintraub, Weybright & Talley, 1970.

Practical Politics: Twentieth-Century Views on Politics and Economics, edited by Lloyd J. Hubenka, University of Nebraska Press, 1976.

The Great Composers: Reviews and Bombardments, edited with an introduction by Crompton, University of California Press, 1978.

(Presumed author) *Lady, Wilt Thou Love Me?* (eighteen love poems to Ellen Terry attributed to Bernard Shaw), edited with introduction and notes by Jack Werner, Stein & Day, 1980.

Shaw's Music, three volumes, edited by Laurence, Dodd, 1981.

Shaw on Dickens, edited with introduction by Laurence and Martin Quinn, Ungar, 1985.

Shaw on Photography: Essays and Photographs, edited by Bill Jay and Margaret Moore, 1989.

Shaw on the London Art Scene 1885-1950, edited by Weintraub, 1990.

Sheffielder (social commentary), Alan Sutton, 1993.

Bernard F. Dukore, editor, *Not Bloody Likely!: And Other Quotations from Bernard Shaw,* Columbia University Press, 1996.

Bernard F. Dukore, editor, *Bernard Shaw on Cinema,* Southern Illinois University Press, 1997.

Reviewer, *Pall Mall Gazette,* 1885-88; music critic, *Dramatic Review,* 1886; art critic, 1886-89, and music critic, 1890-94, under name G. B. S., for *World*; music critic under pseudonym Corno di Bassetto, London *Star,* 1888-90; drama critic, *Saturday Review,* 1895-98. Contributor to newspapers and periodicals, including *Daily Telegraph* and *Daily Sketch.*

MEDIA ADAPTATIONS: Among the films adapted from Shaw's plays are *Arms and the Man,* 1932 and 1962; *Major Barbara,* 1941; *Caesar and Cleopatra,* 1946; *Androcles and the Lion,* 1952;

Saint Joan, 1957 and 1994; *The Doctor's Dilemma,* 1958; *The Devil's Disciple,* 1959; *The Millionairess,* 1960; *Mrs. Warren's Profession,* 1960; and *Great Catherine,* 1968. *Pygmalion,* was also adapted as the stage musical *My Fair Lady,* which was adapted for film in 1964; *The Devil's Disciple,* was recorded for sound cassette in 1994 by L.A. Theatre Works.

SIDELIGHTS: George Bernard Shaw has earned almost universal recognition as the chief English-speaking dramatist of the modern age, second only to William Shakespeare in his contribution to the British theatrical tradition. "One after another," H. W. Nevinson wrote in a 1929 *New Leader,* "his plays and the prefaces to his plays have laid bare the falsities and hypocrisies and boastful pretensions of our . . . time. I can think of no modern prophet who has swept away so much accepted rubbish and cleared the air of so much cant." A great innovator, Shaw invented the theater of ideas, turned the stage into a forum for moral instruction, altered outmoded and unrealistic theatrical conventions, and paved the way for later symbolist drama and the theater of the absurd. As such, he is credited with returning intellect to the theater. As Joseph Knight wrote in *Athenaeum* in 1907, before Shaw had even written his masterpieces: "Mr. Shaw is the playwright who has put new brains into the theatre, and ruthlessly taxed the brains of his audiences. He it is who has shown that it is possible to have an intellectual drama even in England, and an intellectual drama that shall be amusing." According to Archibald Henderson in *European Dramatists,* "Back of all surface manifestations lies the supreme conviction of Shaw that the theatre of today, properly utilized, is an instrumentality for the molding of character and the shaping of conduct no whit inferior to the Church and the School."

Shaw's own career in the theater developed in four phases. In the initial period—from 1892 to 1902—his plays appeared in suburban and matinee performances in England and won wider audiences only through publication. During the second period, running from 1903 to the eve of World War I, Shaw secured a place in the London theater, scoring successes at the Royal Court Theatre and in the commercial West End. The third phase began in 1914 with intense public disapproval of his "Common Sense About the War" but took a turn in 1923 with public adulation for *Saint Joan* and peaked in 1925 with Shaw receiving the Nobel Prize for literature. In the final stage, which extended from 1929 to his death, Shaw became preoccupied with political issues, and he alienated many people with his often controversial views on European dictators.

The plays of Shaw's first period were criticized on several counts. One common charge was that they were not really plays at all. Arnold Bennett, writing for *Academy,* felt that Shaw's works were "decidedly not drama" even if they included "amusing and edifying dialogue." Another charge that critics frequently leveled at Shaw concerned the supposed heartlessness of his approach to life and the ostensibly inhuman nature of his characters. Responding to *Arms and the Man,* Archer commented in the *World,* "To look at nothing but the seamy side may be to see life steadily, but is not to see it whole. As an artist, Mr. Shaw suffers from this limitation; and to this negative fault, if I may call it so, he superadds a positive vice of style." Further, Archer criticized Shaw for his "peculiar habit of straining all the red corpuscles out of the blood of his personages. They have nothing of human nature except its pettinesses; they are devoid alike of its spiritual and its sensual instincts."

During the playwright's second phase, some critics expressed greater understanding of Shaw's methods. In 1900, reviewing

Captain Brassbound's Conversion in the *World,* Archer ridiculed theater managers' failures to realize that Shaw's plays could be commercially successful in West End theaters. Archer contended that audiences enjoyed Shaw's plays thoroughly despite the disapproval of drama critics. Max Beerbohm, reviewing the published volume *Man and Superman* for *Saturday Review* in 1903, also blamed theater managers for the commercial failure of Shaw's plays. "It is only the theatrical managers," he wrote, "who stand between him and the off-chance of a real popular success."

Man and Superman was an important turning point in Shavian drama, presenting for the first time a coherent statement—in the *Don Juan in Hell* interlude—of Shaw's ideal of the "Life Force." To the consternation of Shaw's socialist friends, the play treats Fabianism comically, satirizing socialist movements among the brigands and commenting—specifically in the *Revolutionist's Handbook* appended to the public version of the play—that Fabianism is one of socialism's failed experiments. In *The Bishop of Everywhere,* Warren Sylvester Smith declared that the play's "subject is simply: *The Life Force, acting through the will of woman, subdues man to its purpose, and thereby moves the race to its next higher level.* That is the subject that gives unity to the play, even though it proves somewhat limiting to its philosophical development." Smith agreed with Alfred Turco, Jr., who in *Shaw's Moral Vision* noted that *Man and Superman* is the culmination of Shaw's career, "the first play in which Shaw's belief in the possibility of an *effective* idealism is presented with real conviction."

More important to Shaw's popular success were the 1904-1907 seasons of the Royal Court Theatre, which began its association with Shaw with six matinee performances of *Candida* in April and May of 1904. Following the popularity of the matinees, the Royal Court performed *John Bull's Other Island* in November of 1904, launching Shaw's stage career in England. The play drew large audiences and favorable responses, and it was given a command performance for King Edward VII. Subsequent performances of Shaw's plays at the Royal Court included *Man and Superman, Major Barbara, The Doctor's Dilemma, Captain Brassbound's Conversion, The Philanderer, The Man of Destiny,* and *Don Juan in Hell.* Of 988 performances during the years 1904 to 1907 at the Royal Court, 701 were of plays by Shaw. These productions clearly established the viability of Shaw's work in performance and attracted a larger theater-going audience to his plays.

The third phase of Shaw's dramatic career—the years 1914 to 1925—saw him fall to the lowest point of his popularity only to rise again to the height of international fame. When World War I broke out in August of 1914, Shaw turned down several remunerative offers and withdrew to write "Common Sense About the War," collected in the 1931 publication *What I Really Wrote About the War.* When "Common Sense" first appeared in November, 1914, it sold more than seventy-five thousand copies and managed to alienate practically everyone with its contention that England must bear its share of responsibility for a war that would be ruinous for all parties. Shaw's stance was so disturbing to superpatriots that he found himself unwanted even at the Dramatists' Club, where he was the most eminent member. The essay proved extremely damaging to Shaw's reputation, destroying a popularity that his best efforts had taken more than two decades to establish.

Eventually the British government realized the accuracy of Shaw's farsightedness, and by 1917 he was invited to Flanders to report from the front for the *Daily Sketch.* As T. S. Eliot commented in *Dial,* "It might have been predicted that what he said then would not seem so subversive or blasphemous now. The public has accepted Mr. Shaw not by recognizing the intelligence of what he said then, but by forgetting it." By the close of World War I in 1918, Shaw had emerged as virtually the only public figure who had seen the folly of the war from its inception, and from his wartime experiences grew his greatest plays.

Still, Shaw drew what some critics consider his three greatest plays—*Heartbreak House, Back to Methuselah,* and *Saint Joan*—from the crucible of his 1914-1918 experiences. In *Shakes Versus Shav,* Shaw explicitly identified *Heartbreak House* as his "King Lear." Begun during the war and performed in 1920, *Heartbreak House* examines the prewar spiritual impoverishment that made World War I inevitable. Shaw's most ambitious work, *Back to Methuselah,* is a five-part cycle that dramatizes the workings of Creative Evolution as a solution to man's propensity for self-slaughter.

Neither *Heartbreak House* nor *Back to Methuselah* received enthusiastic responses. But *Saint Joan,* which concerns the religious martyr Joan of Arc, restored Shaw to the highest place in public esteem. As Alexander Woolcott commented in the *New York Herald,* "for most of those who see *Saint Joan* this will be their image of her." For J. I. M. Stewart, Joan "at last" revealed Shaw's capability to create a real human being. Instead of ending the play with Joan's execution, which would impress upon an audience the inevitability of tragedy, Shaw provided an epilogue that presents Joan ultimately triumphant over the religious and secular forces that combined to oppose her. Despite her canonization, however, Joan is once again vilified, revealing the paradox that humanity fears and even kills its saints and heroes for the very qualities that ennoble them. Such rejection, Shaw suggests, will continue until saintly and heroic qualities become universal among humankind.

When Shaw won the Nobel Prize in 1925, he reportedly joked that it was in recognition of his not having written a play for that year. He then refused the prize money, suggesting that it fund an Anglo-Swedish literary foundation, which it ultimately did. After *Saint Joan,* Shaw wrote no plays for six years. From 1923 to 1928 he worked on *The Intelligent Woman's Guide to Capitalism and Socialism,* and when he returned to writing plays, he gave most of them a political bent. His 1929 work *The Apple Cart,* drawing its ideas from *The Intelligent Woman's Guide,* contrasts the ineptitude of popular leaders with the superiority of a competent aristocrat, thus alienating those who regarded Shaw's elevation of King Magnus as a direct attack on parliamentary government.

In *Too True to Be Good,* written in 1932, Shaw takes an absurdist stance toward several aspects of the British military presence in other lands, while *On the Rocks* predicts the collapse of parliamentary democracy in the face of overwhelming economic problems. In *Geneva,* Shaw presents a ridiculously futile League of Nations trying to control thinly disguised caricatures of Benito Mussolini, Adolf Hitler, and Francisco Franco, suggesting that his sympathy for "benevolent" despots lingered until the eve of World War II.

Between the end of World War II and his death in 1950, Shaw seemed to write in the spirit of his comment "as long as I live I must write" (from his preface to the published edition of *Buoyant Billions*), returning to earlier concerns in his grappling for something to convey. *Buoyant Billions* reworks the themes of the 1936 play *The Millionairess, Farfetched Fables* takes a post-atomic view of the future, *Shakes Versus Shav* provides a

discussion between Shakespearean and Shavian puppets on their relative merits, and *Why She Would Not* employs the "born boss" and duel-of-sex themes that Shaw had used earlier. These last plays failed to match the success of Shaw's greater works, but at his death he was still considered a premier dramatist.

Although some critics contend that Shaw's acceptance as a major playwright was much more gradual than it should have been, his many contributions to the theater are undeniable. By insisting that the theater provide moral instruction, for instance, he invented the theater of ideas, which ranks as one of his greatest achievements. He also created his own genre—serious farce—by inverting melodramatic conventions and using the techniques of comedy to advance serious views on human conduct, social institutions, and political systems. Ronald Peacock described this in *The Poet in the Theatre* as a "remarkable feat." Maxwell Anderson expressed equally great praise for Shaw in *Off Broadway* when he wrote, "The worth of his work lies in this—that in expounding, defending, attacking, and laying bare all the conceivable aspects of belief and all the possible motives for action he has irradiated almost the whole of a century with the unquenchable wildfire of an extraordinary brain."

BIOGRAPHICAL/CRITICAL SOURCES:

BOOKS

Anderson, Maxwell, *Off Broadway: Essays About the Theater,* William Sloane, 1947.

Berst, Charles A., *Pygmalion: Shaw's Spin on Myth and Cinderella,* Twayne, 1995.

Berst, Charles A., editor, *Shaw and Religion,* Pennsylvania State University Press, 1981.

Black, Martha Fodaski, *Shaw and Joyce: The Last Word in Stolentelling,* University Press of Florida, 1995.

Bloom, Harold, editor, *George Bernard Shaw's "Pygmalion,"* Chelsea House, 1988.

Bryan, George (with Wolfgang Mieder), *The Proverbial Shaw: An Index to Proverbs in the Works of George Bernard Shaw,* Greenwood Press, 1994.

Chesterton, G. K., *George Bernard Shaw,* John Lane, 1909.

Davis, Tracy, *George Bernard Shaw and the Socialist Theatre,* Greenwood Press, 1994.

Dictionary of Literary Biography, Volume 10: *Modern British Dramatists, 1940-1945,* Gale, 1982.

Dietrich, Richard, *Bernard Shaw's Novels: Portraits of the Artist as Man and Superman,* University Press of Florida, 1996.

Gibbs, A. M., *Heartbreak House: Preludes of Apocalypse,* Twayne, 1994.

Gibbs, A. M., editor, *Shaw: Interviews and Recollections,* University of Iowa Press, 1990.

Henderson, Archibald, *European Dramatists,* Appleton, 1926.

Holroyd, Michael, *Bernard Shaw,* Chatto & Windus, Volume 1: *1856-1898: The Search for Love,* 1988, Volume 2: *1898-1918: The Pursuit of Power,* 1989, Volume 3: *1918-1950: The Lure of Fantasy,* 1991.

Holroyd, Michael, editor, *The Genius of Shaw,* Holt, Rinehart, 1979.

Innes, Christopher D., editor, *The Cambridge Companion to George Bernard Shaw,* Cambridge University Press, 1998.

Linscott, Gillian, *Stage Fright,* Curley Large Print (Hampton, NH), 1994.

Peacock, Ronald, *The Poet in the Theatre,* Harcourt, 1946, revised edition, Hill & Wang, 1960.

Peters, Sally, *Bernard Shaw: The Ascent of the Superman,* Yale University Press (New Haven), 1996.

Shaw: The Annual of Bernard Shaw Studies, Pennsylvania State University Press, 1981–.

Silver, Arnold, *Bernard Shaw: The Darker Side,* Stanford University Press, 1982.

Smith, Warren Sylvester, *The Bishop of Everywhere,* Pennsylvania State University Press, 1982.

Stewart, J. I. M., *Eight Modern Writers,* Clarendon Press, 1963.

Turco, Alfred, Jr., *Shaw's Moral Vision: The Self and Salvation,* Cornell University Press, 1976.

Twentieth-Century Literary Criticism, Gale, Volume 3, 1980; Volume 9, 1983; Volume 21, 1986; Volume 46, 1993.

Weintraub, Rodelle, editor, *Fabian Feminist: Bernard Shaw and Women,* Pennsylvania State University Press, 1977.

Weintraub, Stanley, *Shaw's People: Victoria to Churchill,* Pennsylvania State University Press, 1996.

PERIODICALS

Academy, February 9, 1901, p. 127.
Athenaeum, July 27, 1907, p. 107.
Dial, October, 1921.
English Review, September, 1931.
New Leader, August 23, 1929.
New Statesman, July 9, 1921.
New York Herald, December 29, 1923, p. 3.
Saturday Review (London), February 1, 1902; September 12, 1903.
Shaw Review.
Time, July 24, 1995, p. 66
Times Literary Supplement, June 24, 1988.
Vanity Fair, September, 1991, p. 214.
World (London), April 25, 1894, p. 22; December 26, 1900, p. 25.

* * *

SHAW, Irwin 1913-1984

PERSONAL: Born February 27, 1913, in New York, NY; died May 16, 1984, in Davos, Switzerland; buried in Klosters, Switzerland; son of William and Rose (Tompkins) Shaw; married Marian Edwards, October 13, 1939 (divorced, 1970; remarried, 1982); children: Adam. *Education:* Brooklyn College (now Brooklyn College of the City University of New York), B.A., 1934.

CAREER: Novelist and playwright. Script writer for the *Andy Gump* and *Dick Tracy* radio shows, 1934-36; *New Republic,* Washington, DC, drama critic, 1947-48; New York University, New York City, instructor in creative writing, 1947-48. *Military service:* U.S. Army, 1942-45; became warrant officer.

AWARDS, HONORS: O. Henry Awards, 1944, for "Walking Wounded" (first prize), and 1945, for "Gunner's Passage" (second prize); National Institute of Arts and Letters grant, 1946; *Playboy* Award, 1964, 1970, and 1979; Brooklyn College, honorary doctorate.

WRITINGS:

NOVELS

The Young Lions, Random House, 1948.
The Troubled Air, Random House, 1950.
Lucy Crown, Random House, 1956.
Two Weeks in Another Town, Random House, 1960.
Voices of a Summer Day, Delacorte, 1965.
Rich Man, Poor Man, Delacorte, 1970.

Evening in Byzantium, Delacorte, 1973.
Nightwork, Delacorte, 1975.
Beggarman, Thief, Delacorte, 1977.
The Top of the Hill (also see below), Delacorte, 1979.
Bread upon the Waters, Delacorte, 1981.
Acceptable Losses, Arbor House, 1982.

PLAYS

Bury the Dead (one-act; produced on Broadway, 1936), Random House, 1936.

Siege, produced on Broadway, 1937.

The Gentle People: A Brooklyn Fable (produced on Broadway, 1939; produced in London, 1939), Random House, 1939.

Quiet City, produced on Broadway, 1939.

Retreat to Pleasure, produced on Broadway, 1940.

Sons and Soldiers (produced on Broadway, 1943), Random House, 1944.

The Assassin (produced on Broadway, 1945; produced in London, 1945), Random House, 1946.

(With Peter Viertel) *The Survivors* (produced on Broadway, 1948), Dramatists Play Service, 1948.

(Adaptor) Marcel Achard, *Patate,* produced in New York City, 1958.

Children from Their Games (produced on Broadway, 1963), Samuel French, 1962.

A Choice of Wars, produced in Salt Lake City, UT, 1967.

The Shy and Lonely (one-act), produced in Los Angeles; produced with *Sailor Off the Bremen* (based on Shaw's story; also see below) by William Kramer under joint title *I, Shaw,* in New York City at the Jewish Repertory Theatre, February 19, 1986.

STORY COLLECTIONS

Sailor Off the Bremen and Other Stories, Random House, 1939.
Welcome to the City and Other Stories, Random House, 1942.
Act of Faith and Other Stories, Random House, 1946.
Mixed Company: Collected Short Stories, Random House, 1950.
Tip on a Dead Jockey and Other Stories, Random House, 1957.
Selected Short Stories, Modern Library, 1961.
In the French Style (screenplay and stories; also see below), MacFadden, 1963.
Love on a Dark Street and Other Stories, Delacorte, 1965.
Short Stories, Random House, 1966.
Retreat and Other Stories, New English Library, 1970.
Whispers in Bedlam: Three Novellas, Weidenfeld & Nicolson, 1972.
God Was Here, But He Left Early, Arbor House, 1973.
Short Stories: Five Decades, Delacorte, 1978.

SCREENPLAYS

The Big Game, RKO, 1936.
Commandos Strike at Dawn, Columbia, 1942.
(With Daniel Fuchs and Jerry Wald) *The Hard Way,* Warner Bros., 1942.
(With Sidney Buchman) *Talk of the Town,* RKO, 1942.
(With Chester Erskine and David Shaw) *Take One False Step,* Universal, 1949.
I Want You, RKO, 1951.
Act of Love, United Artists, 1953.
Fire Down Below, Columbia, 1957.
Desire under the Elms, Paramount, 1958.
(With Rene Clement) *This Angry Age,* Columbia, 1958.
The Big Gamble, Twentieth Century-Fox, 1961.
In the French Style, Columbia, 1963.
Survival 1967, United Film, 1968.

Also author, with Charles Schnee, of *Easy Living,* 1949, and, with others, of *Ulysses,* 1955.

OTHER

Report on Israel, Simon & Schuster, 1950.
In the Company of Dolphins (travel book), Geis, 1964.
Paris! Paris! Harcourt, 1977.
The Top of the Hill (television script; based on the novel of the same title), WPIX-TV (New York City), February 6-7, 1980.
(Author of text) *Paris/Magnum: Photographs, 1935-1981,* Harper, 1981.

Contributor to *New Yorker, Esquire, Yale Review* and other publications.

SIDELIGHTS: During a writing career spanning four decades, the late Irwin Shaw practiced his natural storytelling talent in a host of genres. At age 23, Shaw saw his play *Bury the Dead* become a Broadway hit. His short stories are ranked among the very best produced by writers of his generation; *Newsweek* called him "a master of the short story." *The Young Lions* established him as one of the major novelists of the 1950s while his later novels, although critically snubbed, sold in the millions of copies.

Shaw began his career at the age of 21 as a radio script writer on the "Andy Gump" and "Dick Tracy" shows, two popular radio programs of the 1930s. For three years he wrote nine serial episodes a week. This led to a stint as a film writer in Hollywood, but Shaw soon grew dissatisfied with the film industry and returned to New York City. In 1935 a contest sponsored by the New Theatre League caught his attention, and Shaw wrote a one-act play for the competition. Though his entry did not win, it was produced on Broadway at the Ethel Barrymore Theatre in 1936.

A searing antiwar play, *Bury the Dead* is set during "the second year of the war that is to begin tomorrow night," as Shaw explained in the text. It concerns a group of dead soldiers who refuse to be buried. They argue that they never had a chance to finish their lives. The play ends with the soldiers walking off the stage, ignoring the pleas of their family and commanding officers to stay and be buried. Stark Young of the *New Republic* thought *Bury the Dead* "presents the finest image that has appeared in our theatre this year. . . . When these six dead men arise from their graves and refuse to be buried, the imagination is shocked and caught by the sheer sight of them. . . . As theatre image this motif ranks with the entrance of Oedipus with his blinded eyes, in Sophocles' play, with the sleep-walking scene in 'Macbeth,' with Lear in the storm, with, that is, such consummations of action, the visual and the idea as are rare even in first-rank drama."

Bury the Dead was an immediate success. Because it reflected the antiwar rhetoric of the Popular Front of the time it also became, a writer for the London *Times* recounted, "one of the radically chic events of the 1930s." Joseph Wood Krutch, reviewing the play for the *Nation,* called it "incomparably the best of the left-wing dramas seen this year." But Shaw was later to disavow the work's pacifism. Jack Jones and William Tuohy of the *Los Angeles Times* quoted him, explaining: "I'm not a pacifist. I don't believe you can be. Lie down and let people walk over you? Some wars have to be fought." Although Shaw devoted the next few years to writing plays, and had new works produced until the 1960s, he never again enjoyed such a popular success as *Bury the Dead.*

But in another field of writing he gained lasting critical acceptance. During the late 1930s, Shaw began to contribute short stories to such magazines as the *New Yorker* and *Esquire.* His first collection, *Sailor Off the Bremen and Other Stories,* appeared in 1939 and established his reputation as a short story writer. Shaw's stories, Walter W. Ross explained in the *Dictionary of Literary Biography Yearbook: 1984,* are what "many critics regard as his best work." As Hubert Saal maintained in the *Saturday Review,* "Shaw's high place among contemporary writers rests largely on his short stories."

Shaw's ability to create believable characters was cited by several critics as another strength of his short stories. Robert Cromie, writing in the *Saturday Review,* thought that Shaw "has the gift of all great storytellers: when he's really swinging, he creates characters as genuine as that odd couple across the street, the curious patrons of the corner bar, the tragic figures from the headlines. They are individuals who walk into the living room of your mind, ensconce themselves, and refuse to be dislodged." Also writing in *Saturday Review,* William Peden believed that "Shaw's power lies in his ability to capture the essence of a character by the revealing statement, gesture, or thought. . . . Shaw's people seem wonderfully alive, even when the author descends to caricature and burlesque. Like Dickens, Mr. Shaw has created, prodigally, a crowded gallery of memorable people."

A continuing theme of Shaw's short fiction was war and violence. Peden believed that Shaw's "best-known and most memorable stories are those directly or indirectly connected with war and the effect of war, violence, and intolerance." Willie Morris, in an article for the *Washington Post,* agreed with this assessment: "The war molded [Shaw] irrevocably and inspired many of his most enduring stories." One such story is "Sailor Off the Bremen," in which an American athlete fights a Nazi sailor who has attacked his communist brother. Their fight becomes "a graphic dramatization on a small scale of the clash between the forces of Teutonic fascism and communism," Ross wrote in the *Dictionary of Literary Biography.*

War and violence also provided the impetus for Shaw's first novel, *The Young Lions,* published in 1948. Following the lives of three young soldiers—two Americans, Michael Whitacre and Noah Ackerman, and a German, Christian Diestl—during World War II, the novel brings the three men together at a concentration camp at the close of the war. There, Whitacre "finds meaning beyond all the bloodshed which has consumed his life for the last four years. He realizes if struggle and sacrifice will bring about the survival of a few men of decency, then all their hardships have been worth the cost," Ross explained in the *Dictionary of Literary Biography.* John Lardner of the *New Yorker* found the novel's climax to be "particularly well and movingly written," and called Shaw "one of the most skillful storytellers extant." In the *Saturday Review of Literature,* Lee Rogow called *The Young Lions* "a fine, full, intelligent book, packed with wonderful talk and crackling writing."

Publication of *The Young Lions* marked a turning point in Shaw's career. The book was praised by the critics of the time and is still held in high esteem today. Bart Barnes of the *Washington Post* explained that it was "hailed as one of the most important novels to come out of the war." Writing in the *Times Literary Supplement,* William Boyd described *The Young Lions* as "one of the few genuinely praiseworthy 'big' novels to come out of the Second World War," while Morris called it "the finest novel of the European theater." But perhaps more important to Shaw's later career was the book's financial success. *The Young Lions* made the best-seller lists and was adapted as a movie. "It enabled Shaw," Ross reported in the *Dictionary of Literary Biography Yearbook: 1984,* "to rise above a hand-to-mouth existence as a struggling author." Because of the lucrative rewards available in the genre, Shaw devoted most of his remaining years to writing novels. As Richard Haver Costa stated in the *Dictionary of Literary Biography Yearbook: 1984,* the success of *The Young Lions* "convinced him that only in the novel could he find the passport to economic self-sufficiency."

The Troubled Air, Shaw's second novel, concerns a radio station director who must investigate press charges that five of his employees are Communist agents. He is caught between the right-wing attackers who demand dismissal of the employees because of their political beliefs and the left-wingers who defend the accused regardless of their actual activities. The novel demonstrated, Stephen Stepanchev wrote in the *Nation,* that "radicalism is no longer fashionable on the air waves and can, as a matter of fact, spin careers downward to economic ruin and suicide." A London *Times* writer reported that *The Troubled Air* "was disliked by some because Shaw did not find Communism perfect, but it remains his most psychologically convincing" novel. Writing in the *New York Herald Tribune Book Review,* Milton Rugoff found *The Troubled Air* to be "Shaw at his characteristic best, seizing passionately on a vital social issue and presenting it with a firm grasp not only of the intellectual and moral values but of the many kinds of human beings it involves."

Soon after publishing *The Troubled Air* in 1950, Shaw left the United States to live in Europe. As Ross quoted Shaw's explanation in the *Dictionary of Literary Biography Yearbook: 1984,* "America was not a good place to live in then." Shaw continued to write about Americans, however, and in the years to follow he produced a string of popular best-sellers. Speaking to the *Paris Review* about his decision to live in Europe, Shaw stated: "The charge that I've become less American is ridiculous. . . . I think I gained a whole lot of insight by living in Europe."

Shaw's novels after *The Troubled Air* often concern a large cast of characters in a host of exotic locales and occupy what R. V. Cassill described in the *Chicago Tribune Book World* as "the borderland where serious art and commercial sentimentalities blur comfortably." Few of these novels received kind reviews from the critics. Speaking of *The Top of the Hill,* for example, Curt Suplee of the *Washington Post* complained that "nearly 1,000 trees have already fallen to provide the paper for Irwin Shaw's new novel. By any literary standard, those trees have died in vain." Stanley Kauffmann of the *Chicago Tribune Book World* called "writers like Shaw . . . retailers of the serious" who offer "pasteurized social-historical insight [and] tragedy 'worked' for easy pathos." But other critics praised Shaw's continued ability to create worthwhile, entertaining stories. Among these reviewers, Charles Champlin of the *Los Angeles Times* believed Shaw to be "a strong storyteller first and always. . . . Shaw's writing, whether unabashedly commercial or more intensely personal, reveals his knowledge of time, place, character and history, and the artist's sure control of his materials." Mark Goodman of *Time* commented that Shaw had the "ability to create a bestseller with moral resonance."

Undoubtedly Shaw's most successful novel was the 1970 best-seller *Rich Man, Poor Man,* which has sold well over six million copies and was made into the first television mini-series. As Barnes recounted, "it is generally credited with inspiring the television craze for mini-series based on novels that continues today." The novel tells the saga of the Jordache family, descended from a New York baker, and ranges over the whole of American

society. As W. G. Rogers maintained in the *New York Times Book Review,* "this is the dawn-to-dusk, 1940's-to-1970's, success-to-failure, poor-to-rich spectrum."

Though the novel was extremely popular, its critical reception was as cold as that given to previous Shaw efforts. Christopher Lehmann-Haupt of the *New York Times* simply called *Rich Man, Poor Man* "bad, bad." John Leggett of the *Saturday Review* allowed that "along with nearly everyone else, I was, and am, in awe of Irwin Shaw. . . . He is the kind of craftsman—sincere, knowledgeable, unassuming—that I am drawn to and want to see confirmed as one of our great writers. It is my agonizing duty to report that *Rich Man, Poor Man* does not redeem his long-standing promise." Rogers stated that "few of our younger technicians can beat Irwin Shaw's expertise. . . . His pace doesn't slacken for chapter after chapter. Incidents lead to incidents—and they are uncommonly appealing. . . . 'Rich Man, Poor Man' is exciting reading. It's a book you can't put down. Once you do, it wouldn't occur to you to pick it up again."

Upon Shaw's death in 1984, Barnes described him as "one of the most prolific of contemporary American authors [and one] whose novels, short stories and plays portrayed a kaleidoscope of the human experience." Shaw's books have sold over fourteen million copies and have been translated into 28 languages. Several of his novels have been adapted as popular movies and television programs. But despite his commercial success, Shaw's critical reputation is still mixed. His early short stories are highly regarded but many critics, Ross explained in the *Dictionary of Literary Biography Yearbook: 1984,* believe that Shaw "decided he could earn big money writing bestsellers and traded his integrity as a writer for slick novels."

But this judgement is belied by Gay Talese. Writing in the *Washington Post,* Talese stated that Shaw "deserved kinder treatment than he got from the book critics, but their resentment of him had less to do with his work than with the way he lived. Irwin Shaw enjoyed living—in a way so few writers do. He was an outdoor man in an indoor sport, and his international fame served to inspire envy and some cruelty in critics. Irwin accepted this, and he left behind a body of work any good writer should envy." Also writing in the *Washington Post,* Jonathan Yardley described Shaw as "a professional writer with standards. His short stories (at which he was best) and novels were intended, without embarrassment, to entertain, and this they often did very well. . . . He seems always to have believed that he was writing for intelligent people; his prose was clean, literate and polished, and he usually had something interesting to say. He was certainly a 'popular' writer, but he could hold his head high in polite company and indeed was reversed, as a personal and professional example, by many writers with larger literary reputations than his own." Morris believed Shaw to be "the author of . . . many of the finest short stories in the English language" and a "worldly and profoundly sensitive American writer, one of our great ones." Speaking to the *Miami Herald,* Shaw once explained his goal as a writer: "Starting with the first minute I got my first paycheck, my object was to be an absolute pro. What does that mean? A man who does hard things and makes them look easy. Who doesn't get rattled, who knows what to do, when to do it, who takes his time."

BIOGRAPHICAL/CRITICAL SOURCES:

BOOKS

Aldridge, John W., *After the Lost Generation,* Noonday, 1951.
Contemporary Literary Criticism, Gale (Detroit), Volume 7, 1977; Volume 23, 1983; Volume 34, 1985.

Dictionary of Literary Biography, Volume 7: *American Novelists since World War II, Second Series,* Gale, 1980.

Dictionary of Literary Biography Yearbook: 1984, Gale, 1985.

Eisinger, Chester E., *Fiction of the Forties,* University of Chicago Press, 1963.

Giles, James R., *Irwin Shaw: A Study of the Short Fiction,* Twayne Publishers, 1991.

Lewis, Allan, *American Plays and Playwrights of the Contemporary Theatre,* Crown, 1965.

Newquist, Roy, *Counterpoint,* Rand McNally, 1964.

PERIODICALS

Atlantic Monthly, November, 1948; February, 1960; February, 1973.

Chicago Tribune Book World, March 7, 1965; September 27, 1970; November 4, 1979; August 30, 1981; November 7, 1982; December 26, 1982.

Commentary, July, 1956.

Commonweal, March 18, 1960; April 23, 1965.

Detroit News, September 6, 1981; September 12, 1982.

Esquire, October, 1975.

Los Angeles Times, August 28, 1981.

Los Angeles Times Book Review, September 26, 1982; January 9, 1983.

Nation, May 6, 1936; October 9, 1948; June 23, 1951.

National Review, February 16, 1979; October 23, 1995, p. 61.

New Republic, May 13, 1936; February 2, 1942.

New Statesman, August 7, 1981.

Newsweek, November 5, 1962; November 3, 1975.

New Yorker, October 2, 1948; October 20, 1975; November 14, 1977; December 24, 1979.

New York Herald Tribune, January 25, 1942; October 22, 1945.

New York Herald Tribune Book Review, June 10, 1951.

New York Times, October 22, 1945; January 26, 1948; March 9, 1965; September 27, 1970; January 15, 1973; March 28, 1973; September 18, 1975; March 15, 1977; October 17, 1977; October 30, 1979; June 1, 1981; August 29, 1981; September 28, 1982; February 17, 1983.

New York Times Book Review, August 25, 1946; February 28, 1965; October 4, 1970; February 4, 1973; April 1, 1973; June 9, 1974; September 7, 1975; October 23, 1977; November 12, 1978; February 10, 1980; July 13, 1980; August 23, 1981; October 3, 1982.

Paris Review, number 1, 1953; spring, 1979.

Saturday Review, November 18, 1950; June 9, 1951; March 31, 1956; August 3, 1957; March 6, 1965; October 2, 1965; October 17, 1970; August, 1981.

Saturday Review of Literature, September 2, 1939; October 2, 1948; February 12, 1949.

Time, December 29, 1975; November 6, 1978.

Times Literary Supplement, October 28, 1965; December 8, 1972; April 22, 1977; November 25, 1977; July 31, 1981.

Washington Post, December 11, 1979; August 27, 1981; November 19, 1982; May 18, 1984; May 21, 1984.

Washington Post Book World, April 22, 1973; November 5, 1978; December 3, 1978.

*   *   *

SHEED, Wilfrid (John Joseph) 1930-

PERSONAL: Born December 27, 1930, in London, England; came to the United States in 1940; son of Francis Joseph (an author and publisher) and Maisie (an author and publisher; maiden name Ward) Sheed; married Miriam Ungerer; children: Elizabeth Carol, Francis, Marion. *Education:* Lincoln College, Oxford, B.A. 1954, M.A., 1957. *Religion:* Roman Catholic. *Avocational interests:* Baseball, softball, boxing.

ADDRESSES: Home—Stock Farm Lane, Sag Harbor, NY 11963. *Agent*—Lantz-Donadio, 111 West 57th St., New York, NY 10019.

CAREER: Jubilee, New York City, movie reviewer, 1959-61, associate editor, 1959-66; *Commonweal,* New York City, drama critic and book editor, 1964-71; *Esquire,* New York City, movie critic, 1967-69; *New York Times,* New York City, columnist, 1971–. Visiting lecturer in creative arts, Princeton University, 1970-71; Book-of-the-Month Club judge, 1972–; reviewer for numerous publications.

MEMBER: PEN, Authors Guild.

AWARDS, HONORS: National Book Award nomination, 1966, for *Office Politics,* and 1971, for *Max Jamison;* best fiction book of 1970 citation from *Time* magazine, 1971, for *Max Jamison;* Guggenheim fellowship and National Institute and American Academy award in literature, both 1971.

WRITINGS:

FICTION

Joseph (juvenile), Sheed, 1958.

A Middle Class Education: A Novel, Houghton (Boston), 1960.

The Hack (novel), Macmillan (New York City), 1963.

Square's Progress: A Novel, Farrar, Straus (New York City), 1965.

Office Politics: A Novel, Farrar, Straus, 1966.

The Blacking Factory & Pennsylvania Gothic: A Short Novel and a Long Story, Farrar, Straus, 1968.

Max Jamison: A Novel, Farrar, Straus, 1970, published as *The Critic: A Novel,* Weidenfeld & Nicolson (London), 1970.

People Will Always Be Kind (novel), Farrar, Straus, 1973.

Transatlantic Blues (novel), Dutton (New York City), 1978.

The Boys of Winter (novel), Knopf (New York City), 1987.

NONFICTION

(Editor) G. K. Chesterton, *Essays and Poems,* Penguin, 1958.

The Morning After: Selected Essays and Reviews, Farrar, Straus, 1971.

Three Mobs: Labor, Church, and Mafia, Sheed, 1974.

Muhammad Ali: A Portrait in Words and Photographs, New American Library, 1975.

(Author of introduction) James Thurber, *Men, Women and Dogs,* Dodd, 1975.

The Good Word & Other Words, Dutton, 1978.

Clare Boothe Luce, Thorndike Press, 1982.

Frank & Maisie: A Memoir with Parents, Simon & Schuster (New York City), 1985.

(Editor) *Sixteen Short Novels,* Dutton, 1986.

(Author of text) *The Kennedy Legacy: A Generation Later,* Viking, 1988.

Essays in Disguise, Random House (New York City), 1990.

(With John Weiss) *The Face of Baseball,* Thomasson-Grant (Charlottesville, VA), 1990.

Baseball and Lesser Sports, HarperCollins (New York City), 1991.

My Life as a Fan, Simon & Schuster, 1993.

In Love with Daylight: A Memoir of Recovery, Simon & Schuster, 1995.

OTHER

Also author of *Vanishing Species of America,* 1974. Contributor to numerous periodicals, including *New York Times Book Review, Esquire, Sports Illustrated,* and *Commonweal.*

SIDELIGHTS: Novelist and critic Wilfrid Sheed has been a prominent man of letters in the United States for over four decades. *Time* correspondent John Skow calls Sheed "almost certainly the best American reviewer of books," an elegant writer who is also "a novelist of wit and intelligence." Sheed, who was raised both in England and the United States, is often cited as an essayist who is penetrating but not pompous—"an acute and twinkling observer, adept at both irony and slapstick farce, compassionate to a fault and a most clever and accomplished stylist," to quote Eliot Fremont-Smith in the *New York Times.* The author may be slightly better known for his reviews, but he has also penned almost a dozen works of fiction, many of which draw upon his personal experiences from childhood to maturity. *Washington Post Book World* columnist Jonathan Yardley finds Sheed "a novelist of depth, complexity and compassion. . . . Sheed gets better with each new novel, and there are few writers of whom that can be said." All of Sheed's works share two essential components, according to his critics: they display finely-wrought prose and subtle, ironic humor. In *Newsweek,* Peter S. Prescott contends that Sheed "is a very funny man, but (especially in recent years) his wit has been used in the service of humaneness, a kind of domestic service to the family of man."

Sheed may have seemed destined for a literary life from his birth. Four years before he was born his parents, Frank Sheed and Maisie Ward Sheed, established the prestigious publishing firm of Sheed & Ward, "one of the most respected religious publishers in the world," according to Walter W. Ross III in the *Dictionary of Literary Biography.* Thus, Sheed and his sister grew up surrounded by the important Catholic writers and thinkers of their day; both children were encouraged to excel in their studies and to enjoy vigorous exercise. When Sheed was nine World War II erupted, and the family moved to the United States, settling in Torresdale, Pennsylvania. Sheed spent his early teen years there, fascinated by American sports, especially baseball. His own budding athletic talent was squelched abruptly at fourteen when he contracted the dreaded polio, an event that shadowed the rest of his youth.

Several of Sheed's best known novels, including *Office Politics, The Hack, Max Jamison,* and *The Boys of Winter,* deal with the wry and sometimes sordid worlds of journalism and publishing. According to John Blades in a Chicago *Tribune Books* review, Sheed "comes from a publishing family, and few writers cover the territory so confidently, or write about it with so much vim and vitriol, such malicious afore-and afterthought." For instance, *Office Politics,* which was nominated for the National Book Award in 1966, analyzes a vicious power struggle that ensues among members of a magazine staff after the editor-in-chief becomes ill. In an essay for *Wisconsin Studies in Contemporary Literature,* Richard Lehan writes that *Office Politics* "uses the drab world of New York City to intensify the drab, sordid, meaningless routine that turns young men into cynics and romantic expectation into despair." *New York Times* commentator Charles Poore suggests that Sheed "has a splendid gift for dramatizing the search-and-destroy diabolism of outrageous fortune. His characters are multidimensional without hazing off into the pretentiously symbolic."

Not every reviewer finds Sheed's characters so multidimensional. In a *New York Review of Books* essay, Robert Towers contends that Sheed's novels "read more like demonstrations than imaginative works of fiction. . . . His novels seem stronger in documentation than in invention and regularly give the *appearance* of autobiography only slightly transmuted—even when the characters and their circumstances are obviously 'made up.' They have trouble progressing beyond their initial premise or situation into a freely moving story, with the result that their denouements are often unconvincing . . . or melodramatic." *Village Voice* contributor James Wolcott likewise sees Sheed's fiction as working in a "self-created void: the characters are store-window mannequins, the scenery consists of painted back-drops. Nothing is at stake, no giddy risks are taken, so the jokes become only curlicues in his elegant doodling." Other critics have responded warmly to Sheed's work. A *Time* reviewer writes: "Sheed constructs a bright, cutting prose from the dross of everyday slang. He wields that prose with a subtle ear for speech rhythms and a sardonic eye for the tell-tale gesture. . . . His protagonists are ordinary guys desperately trying to fend off the world's idiocies and evils long enough to define themselves and do the decent thing. They rarely succeed completely." In the *New Republic,* Yardley maintains that Sheed has moved "toward a fiction which, while the dazzle remains, has gained measurably in depth and subtlety. . . . Even at his darkest, he is a joy to read. His wit and perceptiveness are marvelous. . . . It is a measure of his achievement that we only rarely feel that the glitter is for its own sake."

Max Jamison, published in 1970, is one of Sheed's most successful novels. In another case of thinly veiled autobiography, the book spotlights a Broadway theatre critic whose life is consumed by his work. *Saturday Review* correspondent Robert Cromie calls it "a darkly engaging book, which may be read purely as entertainment, or, as I am sure Sheed intended it should, as a sympathetic, occasionally ribald, always engrossing portrait of a tragi-comic man, mired in a profession he no longer respects or truly enjoys, a man doomed to boredom and despair, with only an occasional slight flash of pleasure in prospect to keep him alive until the fall of the final curtain." *Max Jamison* also received a nomination for the National Book Award and has been generally well-received by critics. *Commonweal* essayist David Lodge finds in the work "impressive evidence of the mature poise and skill Wilfrid Sheed has achieved as a novelist," and a *National Observer* contributor calls the book "one of the most unhappily accurate accounts of a critic's day-to-day life ever committed to paper." In a *New Republic* review, Yardley finds the unhappy Max "nonetheless a curiously admirable character for whom, in the end, one grieves. His pomposity is maddening, but in his insistence upon 'standards' there is an old-fashioned deference to tradition which one must honor; he is a man of genuine if dubiously exercised integrity. For all his stiffness, his infuriating withdrawal from the turmoil and pain of life, he inspires sadness and sympathy."

Transatlantic Blues, Sheed's 1978 novel, concerns the travails of a continent-hopping television personality with roots in England and the United States. *New York Times Book Review* correspondent Julian Moynahan finds the work "fictional autobiography structured as a general confession in the old Catholic sense of the term. . . . It turns out to be a tale of growing up between two countries and is one we have been waiting for from Wilfrid Sheed. . . . That isn't, of course, to pretend that the book is Sheed's own confession." According to Walter Clemons in *Newsweek, Transatlantic Blues* "is a rich mess of a novel, the funniest and freest Sheed has written. The miserable [protagonist]

Chatworth is endowed with a ripped-open version of a transatlantic style Sheed has made his own, in which Oxonian clarity joins with American lowdown colloquial. . . . Chatworth's confessional prose is rawer and speedier, edgier and more combative than anything we have heard from Sheed before. At full throttle it is exciting and explosively funny." Many observers have found Sheed's use of first-person narration in the book more conducive to his humor and prose style. *Critic* essayist Laurence P. Smith calls the book "clearly Sheed's finest novel to date. . . . His voice seems less coldly detached, revealing an emotional concern for his characters that his sardonic, cutting style has often obscured. *Transatlantic Blues* is a novel filled with so much humor that the temptation is to speak of nothing else. It is rich in the irony, parody, satire and witty verbal gymnastics that have earned Sheed his reputation as a leading novelist of manners. Yet his vision is the entire sad human predicament. . . . It is humor with a serious purpose." Smith elaborates: "Between the laughs are the leads, the themes and insights which help to explain the chaos within every man. Tear-washed eyes, from laughter or grief, may offer the clearest view of the truth, or at least of one's own soul."

Nine years separate the publication dates of *Transatlantic Blues* and *The Boys of Winter,* a tragi-comic novel about struggling authors and their editors set in the rural reaches of Long Island. As Herbert Gold notes in the *New York Times Book Review,* the subject of the tale "is not so much the life of literature as careerism—also sex and softball—in an exurban Long Island colony." Sheed makes forays into the jealousies between competing fiction writers, the vagaries of the book business, and the macho antics of grown men let loose on a softball diamond. Gold writes that *The Boys of Winter* "brings Grub Street to contemporary times and the exurbs—and it's funny. Finally it does the satirist's good work of demolition, but it also, alas, tells much of the truth about literary politicking. . . . The gloomy conditions of publishing are not rubbed in our faces, and the implications are among the subtexts adroitly not emphasized. There is a nostalgia for times when the Word really did seem haunted and holy." *Los Angeles Times Book Review* contributor Art Seidenbaum concludes: "Anyone unfortunate enough to earn or learn a living in the book business will relish the back-biting behind the back-slapping in this artful novel about the wiles of writers, editors, publishers and hangers-on. Every character, as a matter of fiction, is a hanger-on here, trying to survive over somebody else's live body."

Sheed began his career as a critic writing reviews for popular periodicals, and even now he prefers a more colloquial and less academic style for his criticism—and a popular rather than academic forum. "The ideal critic, after all, is not an Aristotle or Solon or Lionel Trilling, stuffing laws down the artists' and readers' throats;" writes Mitchell S. Ross in the *Chicago Tribune Book World,* "he is a stimulator, even an agitator, whose first responsibility is to rouse his readers and irritate the cogitative cells, a task at which Sheed succeeds brilliantly. . . . His is the sort of critic who makes the ordinary labels of reviewers seem trivial—which is to say, the only kind of critic who really counts. . . . If this is not criticism, then nothing being written today is worthy of that great classification." Sheed's essays and reviews have appeared in such disparate places as *Sports Illustrated, Life, Esquire,* and the *New York Times Book Review.* The best of them are collected in two works, *The Morning After: Selected Essays and Reviews* and *The Good Word and Other Words.* Morris Freedman describes Sheed's criticism in the *New Republic:* "Mr. Sheed writes to order, mostly pithy essays on

movies, plays or books, in the pages of [magazines]. The formal demands of this occasional writing, like those of the heroic couplet itself, force a concentration on the epigram, the compact summation, the striking generalization. . . . To this highly professional skill Sheed fortunately brings the restraint of common sense, balance and, most importantly, a sense of responsibility." George Stade puts it another way in the *New York Times Book Review.* "The bright, quick sentences flash through the reader's head, depositing pictures and patterns that only fade behind the rush of new ones, the sequence and sum by no means altogether without subtlety," Stade comments. ". . .Sheed is not the kind of bullying guide who in a fit of naive vanity wants to put the skeptical tourist in his place. There are no significant pauses before dark solemnities or pointed gestures toward an ineffable murk."

Drawing on the love of baseball that found its way into such fictional works as *The Boys of Winter,* Sheed has also written several nonfictional works on that subject. *Baseball and Lesser Sports,* a collection of essays on the game, is dedicated to Roger Angell, who writes on baseball for the *New Yorker.* Covering a wide variety of baseball personalities—not only players but notable fans such as David Halberstam as well—Sheed "has added a new perspective" as a foreign-born fan, according to *New York Times Book Review* critic Roberto Gonzalez Echevarria. Sheed "contributes a distancing element that lets him see himself and the game in a context broader than that of an ordinary American childhood, and from a viewpoint that is something like a split vision," notes Echevarria. For Sheed, memories of baseball combine with those of his personal battle with debilitating polio, a battle that he ultimately won but that ended his dreams of participating in his favorite sport as anything but a fan. In 1993's *My Life as a Fan: A Memoir,* Sheed provides readers with both his manner of reconciling his non-participant status within the game and an unsentimental but entrancing account of the history of America's favorite pastime. Beginning his history in 1941, the year Sheed and his family immigrated to the United States to escape the German *Blitzkreig,* his travels through baseball's colorful past include such moments as the 1947 World Series, the Dodgers' move to Los Angeles in 1957, and his continuing concern over both the New York Mets and the future of the game.

In recent years Sheed has added full-length biographies to his list of publications. Both *Clare Boothe Luce* and *Frank and Maisie: A Memoir with Parents* are intimate accounts of their subjects, less scholarly than personal. In a *Chicago Tribune Book World* review of *Clare Boothe Luce,* Ronald Steel finds the work "a brilliantly written pastiche," adding: "Sheed is a masterly prose stylist, as addictive as chocolates, and as biting at one-liners as the lady herself. . . . Although he doesn't unveil what makes Clare tick, he does make her human. And in doing so he shows one way that an intelligent and ambitious woman made it in America in the days before affirmative action." Likewise, *New York Times* contributor John Gross notes that in *Frank and Maisie* Sheed "has not attempted to provide a full-scale portrait of his parents. Instead, he has written an account of what it was like to grow up as one of their two children. . . . But the book is Frank and Maisie's, beyond a doubt, and a very eloquent memorial to them it is—both entertaining and deeply felt, full of wry insights into the contradictions of human nature, a demonstration (if one is needed) that love and what in the end can only be called filial piety are no barrier to the incisiveness that readers of Mr. Sheed's novels and journalism have come to expect of him."

Sheed wrote 1995's *In Love with Daylight: A Memoir of Recovery* with a different subtitle in mind; he expected that it would be published after his death. The work is a full and open expression of his encounter with three separate and potentially fatal illnesses. Polio struck in 1945; depression and its attendant drug and alcohol addiction would follow in the mid-1980s, when the novelist was in his fifties. A tortuous year-long stay in a sanatorium, during which time Sheed was put on a variety of antidepressants, did little to help the recovery. The diagnosis of cancer in 1991 forced him to come to terms with his own self-destructive impulses; the battle for his body joined that for his mind. "Sheed proves that the greatest enemy of life is capitulation," notes Thomas Curwen in *People*, "yet he also knows that loving it too much has a price as well." Robert Stone comments in the *New York Review of Books* that Sheed's loosely interpreted Catholicism and the early bout with polio helped to inform the attitude that enabled him to overcome his tragic later circumstances. "*In Love with Daylight*'s account and its style, aphoristic, forthright, humorous, and irascible" Stone writes, "will provide the stuff of a few useful arguments for anyone who has experienced addiction-depression at close quarters, from the inside or the outside." Sherwin B. Nuland agrees in the *New York Times Book Review*, writing that, "Like all the finest narrators of illness, Mr. Sheed teaches as he tells. . . . When serious depressions lift, those who experienced them can no longer call up or even imagine their painful despair, but Mr. Sheed's account is as close to the reality of those forlorn days as one can reasonably be expected to come."

Sheed is quoted on his occupation in the *Dictionary of Literary Biography*. "Circumstances have obliged me to do a good deal of reviewing (the last refuge of the light essayist): books, plays, etc.," he said. "I find this work painful, but it serves a couple of selfish purposes. It enables me to work out various aesthetic ideas, while unloading my little burden of didacticism in a safe place; and it gives me a certain thin-lipped benignity towards my own critics, when they turn the cannon round and aim it in my direction." Sheed told the *New York Times Book Review* that, as an experience, "fiction is more rewarding, even if it dumps you out of a flying door into a mudbath. But, whatever the word on that, one's nonfiction gains tremendously from having known the pressure, just as a political commentator would gain from running for office. Whatever you can still do when you can't be fastidious is your essence."

BIOGRAPHICAL/CRITICAL SOURCES:

BOOKS

Contemporary Literary Criticism, Gale (Detroit), Volume 2, 1973; Volume 4, 1975; Volume 10, 1979.
Dictionary of Literary Biography, Volume 6: *American Novelists since World War II, Second Series*, Gale, 1980.

PERIODICALS

Atlantic Monthly, May, 1973; March, 1978.
Chicago Tribune Book World, December 17, 1978; February 7, 1982.
Commonweal, January 24, 1969; May 8, 1970; June 24, 1977; April 14, 1978.
Critic, summer, 1978; December, 1978.
Horizon, autumn, 1971.
Life, April 18, 1969.
Los Angeles Times, October 30, 1985.
Los Angeles Times Book Review, July 19, 1987; August 28, 1988; July 18, 1993, p. 9.
Nation, December 20, 1971; February 20, 1982.

National Observer, October 28, 1968; May 11, 1970.
National Review, February 9, 1971; November 1, 1993, p. 76.
New Republic, May 23, 1970; October 2, 1971; May 5, 1973; January 21, 1978.
Newsweek, October 4, 1971; January 16, 1978; February 22, 1982; August 24, 1987.
New Yorker, November 30, 1968; March 13, 1978; December 9, 1985.
New York Review of Books, May 17, 1973; October 30, 1975; January 26, 1978; November 8, 1979; April 1, 1982; May 8, 1986; April 6, 1995, pp. 4-5.
New York Times, August 23, 1965; September 19, 1968; May 7, 1970; April 11, 1973; September 15, 1975; January 13, 1978; December 21, 1978; February 10, 1982; October 15, 1985; July 30, 1987; February 26, 1990; May 10, 1993.
New York Times Book Review, August 22, 1965; September 8, 1968; May 3, 1970; October 10, 1971; April 8, 1973; September 21, 1975; January 15, 1978; January 21, 1979; February 21, 1982; November 10, 1985; August 2, 1987; March 18, 1990; June 2, 1991; Juen 20, 1993; March 5, 1995.
People Weekly, August 31, 1987; May 8, 1995, p. 43.
Publishers Weekly, February 6, 1978; May 10, 1991, p. 254; January 9, 1995, pp. 49-50.
Saturday Review, September 4, 1965; September 14, 1968; June 6, 1970; January 20, 1979; July, 1982.
Spectator, January 26, 1974.
Sports Illustrated, November 11, 1968.
Time, September 20, 1968; January 6, 1975; September 8, 1975; January 27, 1978; December 25, 1978; February 22, 1982; November 18, 1985; August 3, 1987.
Times Literary Supplement, November 4, 1965; February 9, 1967; August 14, 1969; July 31, 1970; January 18, 1974; November 23, 1979; October 1, 1982; May 30, 1986.
Tribune Books (Chicago), July 19, 1987; July 4, 1993.
Village Voice, August 26, 1971; January 23, 1978.
Washington Post Book World, January 7, 1968; September 22, 1968, April 29, 1973; February 5, 1978; December 24, 1978; February 14, 1982; January 5, 1986; August 19, 1987; October 16, 1988; February 18, 1990, p. 9.
Wisconsin Studies in Contemporary Literature, summer, 1967.

*　　*　　*

SHELDON, John
See BLOCH, Robert (Albert)

*　　*　　*

SHELDON, Sidney 1917-

PERSONAL: Born February 11, 1917, in Chicago, IL; son of Otto (a salesman) and Natalie (Marcus) Sheldon; married Jorja Curtright (an actress), March 28, 1951 (died, 1985); married Alexandra Kostoff, 1989; children: Mary Sheldon Dastin. *Education:* Attended Northwestern University, 1935-36. *Religion:* Church of Religious Science.

ADDRESSES: Home—Bel Air, CA. *Office*—c/o Press Relations, William Morrow, 1350 Avenue of the Americas, New York, NY 10016-4702.

CAREER: Writer. Former script reader for Universal and Twentieth Century-Fox Studios; creator, producer, and writer of television shows, Los Angeles, CA, 1963–, including *The Patty Duke Show, I Dream of Jeannie, Nancy,* and *Hart to Hart. Military service:* U.S. Army Air Forces, 1941.

MEMBER: Freedom to Read Foundation.

AWARDS, HONORS: Academy Award for best original screenplay, Academy of Motion Picture Arts and Sciences, 1948, for *The Bachelor and the Bobby-Soxer;* Screen Writers' Guild Award for best musical of the year, 1948, for *Easter Parade,* and 1950, for *Annie Get Your Gun;* Tony Award, 1959, for book of *Redhead;* Emmy Awards for *I Dream of Jeannie;* Edgar Allan Poe Award for best first mystery novel, Mystery Writers of America, and *New York Times* citation for best first mystery novel, both 1970, both for *The Naked Face;* recipient of a star on the Hollywood Walk of Fame.

WRITINGS:

NOVELS

The Naked Face, Morrow, 1970.
The Other Side of Midnight, Morrow, 1974.
A Stranger in the Mirror, Morrow, 1976.
Bloodline, Morrow, 1977.
Rage of Angels, Morrow, 1980.
Master of the Game, Morrow, 1982.
If Tomorrow Comes, Morrow, 1985.
Windmills of the Gods, Morrow, 1987.
The Sands of Time, Morrow, 1988.
Sheldon Boxed Set: Bloodline, A Stranger in the Mirror, Rage of Angels, Warner Books, 1988.
Memories of Midnight, Morrow, 1990.
The Doomsday Conspiracy, Morrow, 1991.
The Stars Shine Down, Morrow, 1992.
Sidney Sheldon: Three Complete Novels, Random House, 1992.
Nothing Lasts Forever: The New Novel, Morrow, 1994.
Morning, Noon, and Night, Morrow, 1995.
The Best Laid Plans, William Morrow, 1997.

PLAYS

(Adaptor with Ben Roberts) *The Merry Widow* (operetta), first produced on Broadway, August 4, 1943.
Jackpot, first produced on Broadway, January 13, 1944.
(With Roberts and Dorothy Kilgallen) *Dream with Music,* first produced on Broadway, May 18, 1944.
(With Ladislaus Bush-Fekete and Mary Helen Fay) *Alice in Arms,* first produced on Broadway, January 31, 1945.
(With Dorothy and Herbert Fields, and David Shaw) *Redhead* (musical), first produced on Broadway, February 5, 1959.
Roman Candle, first produced on Broadway, February 3, 1960.

Also author of *Gomes,* produced in London.

SCREENPLAYS

(Author of story with Roberts) *Borrowed Hero,* Monogram, 1941.
(With Jack Natteford) *Dangerous Lady,* Producers Releasing Corp., 1941.
(Author of story with Roberts) *Gambling Daughters,* Producers Releasing Corp., 1941.
(With Roberts) *South of Panama,* Producers Releasing Corp., 1941.
(Author of story with Roberts) *Fly by Night,* Paramount, 1942.
She's in the Army, Monogram, 1942.
(With Roberts) *The Carter Case,* Republic, 1947.
The Bachelor and the Bobby-Soxer, RKO, 1947.

(With Albert Hackett and Frances Goodrich) *Easter Parade* (musical), Metro-Goldwyn-Mayer, 1948.
Annie Get Your Gun (adapted from the musical by Irving Berlin), Metro-Goldwyn-Mayer, 1950.
Nancy Goes to Rio, Metro-Goldwyn-Mayer, 1950.
(With Dorothy Cooper) *Rich, Young, and Pretty* (musical), Metro-Goldwyn-Mayer, 1951.
No Questions Asked, Metro-Goldwyn-Mayer, 1951.
Three Guys Named Mike, Metro-Goldwyn-Mayer, 1951.
Just This Once, Metro-Goldwyn-Mayer, 1952.
(With Herbert Baker and Alfred L. Levitt, and director) *Dream Wife,* Metro-Goldwyn-Mayer, 1953.
Remains to Be Seen, Metro-Goldwyn-Mayer, 1953.
You're Never Too Young, Paramount, 1955.
Anything Goes (adapted from the musical by Cole Porter), Paramount, 1956.
Pardners, Paramount, 1956.
(And director and producer with Robert Smith) *The Buster Keaton Story,* Paramount, 1957.
All in a Night's Work, Paramount, 1961.
Billy Rose's Jumbo (also titled *Jumbo*), Metro-Goldwyn-Mayer, 1962.
(With Preston Sturges) *The Birds and the Bees,* Paramount, 1965.

OTHER

(With Mary Sheldon) *The Adventures of Drippy, the Runaway Raindrop* (juvenile), illustrated by Alexandra Sheldon, Dove Kids (West Hollywood, CA), 1996.

Also author of a children's book, published in Japan. Author of more than 250 scripts, occasionally under a pseudonym, for *The Patty Duke Show,* 1963-66, and *I Dream of Jeannie,* 1965-70.

The Other Side of Midnight was made into a film by Twentieth Century-Fox in 1977; *Bloodline* was filmed by Paramount in 1979, and was re-edited by Sheldon and shown as an ABC miniseries in 1982; *Rage of Angels,* for which Sheldon served as executive producer, became an NBC miniseries in 1983, and inspired a 1986 sequel which Sheldon also produced; CBS broadcast miniseries adaptations of *Master of the Game* in 1984, *If Tomorrow Comes* in 1986, and *Windmills of the Gods* in 1988; *The Naked Face* was filmed by Cannon in 1985; *The Sands of Time* has been optioned.

SIDELIGHTS: At age fifty, at the top of his profession as a film and television producer of hits like *I Dream of Jeannie,* Sidney Sheldon had no hint of another, even more successful career ahead of him. "[Novels] never occurred to me," Sheldon told *Detroit News* reporter Ruth Pollack Coughlin. "I wasn't a novelist. I was writing for motion pictures and television and Broadway. For me, writing novels was an unnatural next step." Why then, would the winner of Oscar, Tony, and Emmy Awards turn to fiction? The author explained his decision to Sarah Booth Conroy of the *Washington Post:* "I got an idea that was so introspective I could see no way to do it as a television series, movie or Broadway play, because you had to get inside the character's mind. With much trepidation, I decided I'd try a novel." The result was *The Naked Face,* which despite winning awards as the best first mystery novel of the year, initially sold only 17,000 copies. "I was horrified," Sheldon told Conroy, "because 20 million people watched [I Dream of] *Jeannie.*" Nevertheless, Sheldon persisted in his efforts, and his next work, *The Other Side of Midnight,* sold over three million copies in paperback. Since then, Sheldon has published seven more million-selling novels, and is now considered one of the best-selling writers in the world, with books in print in thirty-nine countries.

The typical Sheldon potboiler features a beautiful and determined heroine enacting revenge on her enemies; as Conroy describes, in Sheldon's novels "the beautiful but often poor and pure heroines are raped, sodomized and defrauded, and go on to avenge themselves by questionable, often illegal, but ingenious methods." These works, with their rapid momentum and mass appeal, "evidently satisfy . . . everyone except most literary critics, who regard popularity and quality as incompatible," *Los Angeles Times* arts editor Charles Champlin comments. Indeed, Sheldon's work has not fared well with critics, who often fault his plots and characters as unbelievable, and his prose as "staccato [and] lackluster," as *New York Times Book Review* contributor Mel Watkins states.

Some reviewers, however, find some merit in Sheldon's work; as Carol E. Rinzler notes in the *Washington Post,* "there aren't a whole lot of writers around who can be depended on to produce good junk reading time after time; Sheldon is one of the few." *Washington Post* reviewer Joseph McLellan similarly observes that in *Rage of Angels* "craftsmanship is the keynote, as a matter of fact, in this novel that ticks along like an intricate, beautifully designed piece of clockwork, full of characters and incidents that are usually interesting even if they are slightly unreal." "Although this may be literary junk food," *New York Times Book Review* contributor Robert Lekachman comments, "it is hard to put down once you get started. . . . Sheldon's smooth, serviceable, if unmemorable, prose carries one along, much like the movie serials of the Great Depression."

Windmills of the Gods, published in 1987, received similarly mixed reviews. Rory Quick, writing for *Washington Post Book World,* notes that "When it comes to novels, Sidney Sheldon is living proof that 'quality trash' is not an oxymoron. Sheldon may not be the Colossus of American letters, but he's clearly the Midas." Quick welcomed the publication of *Windmills,* stating that "Sheldon's position as America's trashmeister remains secure." A *Time* reviewer offers the opinion that "The Sheldon brand name guarantees a predictable mix of global gore and paperback psychopathology."

Other critics however, greeted the effort with less enthusiasm. "*Windmills* is a mercifully quick read, an ideal airplane book," writes Daniel Akst in the *Los Angeles Times Book Review.* However, he offers this suggestion: "Readers who are not behind bars, stranded on a desert island, or accepting money to read this book are urged to skip ruthlessly, and then to atone by contemplating the gratuitous martyring of trees that went into it." *New York Times Book Review* critic Susan Spano Wells is even more blunt: "The grand master of commercial fiction seems to be coasting."

Sheldon's next novel, *The Sands of Time,* fared somewhat better with critics. The tale follows four Catholic nuns whose calm is broken when their Spanish convent is leveled by a military leader who believes the sisters are sheltering Basque separatists. Joyce Slater of *Chicago Tribune Books* calls Sheldon "a storyteller in the oldest, best tradition," specifically praising his "unrelenting" action as well as the background on the convent and the nuns themselves. A critic for the *Los Angeles Times Book Review* notes that "One sometimes has the feeling that Sidney Sheldon could start out with four Cub Scouts, a dog named Spot and a West Los Angeles bag lady and, somehow, turn it into a torrid suspense novel." The critic concludes, "The man tells a whale of a story."

David Murray, in a review for the *New York Times Book Review,* feels differently, calling the effort "a literary version of painting by numbers" and stating that "Being Sidney Sheldon means never having to say you're writing."

After branching out to science fiction (albeit with a commercial touch) with *The Doomsday Conspiracy,* Sheldon returned to more conventional commercial fiction with *The Stars Shine Down* (1992), *Nothing Lasts Forever: The New Novel* (1994), and *Morning, Noon, and Night* (1995). While these works were generally acknowledged by critics to be appealing to Sheldon's core fans, several critics broached the topic of his reduced ability to charm new fans with his somewhat tired prose. "For diehard Sheldon fans, this will probably do the trick. But it won't win any new converts," states a *Kirkus Reviews* critic of *Nothing Lasts Forever.* A *Publishers Weekly* reviewer finds that *Morning, Noon, and Night* "isn't Sheldon's finest. . . . But his plot hooks remain sharp and it's the rare fan who's not going to be ensnared once again by this perennially bestselling author."

The protagonist of *Stars Shine Down* hearkens back to Sheldon's earlier, edgier heroines, according to a critic for *Kirkus Reviews.* However, she's not enough to overcome "an annoying tendency to speak in overwrought cliches," remarks a *Publishers Weekly* critic, a criticism also leveled at *Nothing Lasts Forever* by another *Publishers Weekly* critic. "Banal prose is built on a banal plot," writes an *Entertainment Weekly* reviewer of *Morning, Noon, and Night.* The reviewer concludes, "Sheldon's twist ending might come as a surprise to someone who's never read a book before."

Several reviewers praised Sheldon's previous work but posited that he may be running out of steam. "Sidney Sheldon is living proof of how one keeps on keeping on," writes Slater, "but perhaps he should have stopped short of *The Stars Shine Down.*" And from *People*'s reviewer on *Nothing Lasts Forever:* "Sheldon is on cruise control in this crass enterprise."

Because of their brisk pace, Sheldon's novels are often characterized as being "less like a book than like a movie," according to *New York Times* writer Janet Maslin, a description their author refutes: "I am accused constantly of writing books as movies," Sheldon told Paul Rosenfield of the *Los Angeles Times.* "But it just isn't true. What's true is that I write visually. It's my training from movies and TV." Sheldon does, however, strive for a captivating effect in his books: "I have this goal," the author remarked to Rosenfield. "And it's for a reader to not be able to go to sleep at night. I want him to keep reading another four pages, then one more page. The following morning, or night, he's anxious to get back to the book."

BIOGRAPHICAL/CRITICAL SOURCES:

PERIODICALS

Booklist, September 15, 1992, p. 101; August, 1995, p 1911.
Chatelaine, March, 1989, p. 12.
Cosmopolitan, February, 1987, pp. 238-46; June, 1987, pp. 152-54; November, 1988, p. 48; December, 1988, pp. 226-30; October, 1991, p. 48; November, 1992, pp. 267-77.
Detroit News, February 8, 1987.
Entertainment Weekly, October 6, 1995, p. 58.
Esquire, July, 1989, pp. 82-89.
Fortune, December 30, 1991, pp. 136-38.
Kirkus Reviews, July 1, 1991, p. 822; August 1, 1992, p. 945; June 15, 1994, p. 802; July 1, 1995, p. 894.
Library Journal, March 1, 1987, p. 94; July, 1994, p. 130.
Los Angeles Times, October 3, 1982; March 12, 1987.

Los Angeles Times Book Review, February 8, 1987; September 18, 1988; September 15, 1991, p. 6; August 21, 1994, p. 13.

New Statesman & Society, September 6, 1991, p. 35.

Newsweek, June 13, 1977.

New Yorker, July 11, 1977.

New York Times, July 24, 1947; July 1, 1948; July 22, 1979.

New York Times Book Review, January 27, 1974; May 2, 1976; February 19, 1978; August 29, 1982; March 10, 1985; February 8, 1987; January 8, 1989; October 15, 1995, p. 20.

People Weekly, January 23, 1989, pp. 27-28; October 8, 1990, pp. 23-24; September 16, 1991, p. 31; August 29, 1994, p. 32.

Publishers Weekly, September 23, 1988, p. 58; November 25, 1988; May 5, 1989, p. 52; April 6, 1990, p. 94; September 6, 1991, p. 78; August 24, 1992, p. 62; July 11, 1994, pp. 61-62; July 17, 1995, p. 219.

Time, June 20, 1977; February 23, 1987, p. 78; October 15, 1990, p. 86.

Tribune Books (Chicago), December 25, 1988; October 25, 1992.

Washington Post, July 12, 1982; February 19, 1985; December 6, 1988.

Washington Post Book World, February 18, 1979; February 22, 1987.

Writer, March, 1988, p. 7.

*   *   *

SHEPARD, Sam(uel) 1943-

PERSONAL: Given name Samuel Shepard Rogers VII; born November 5, 1943, in Fort Sheridan, IL; son of Samuel Shepard (a teacher and farmer) and Elaine (Schook) Rogers; married O-Lan Johnson Dark (an actress), November 9, 1969 (divorced); currently living with Jessica Lange (an actress and film producer); children: (first marriage) Jesse Mojo; (with Lange) Hannah Jane, Samuel Walker. *Education:* Attended Mount Antonio Junior College, CA, 1960-61. *Avocational interests:* Polo, rodeo.

ADDRESSES: Office—International Creative Management, 8942 Wilshire Blvd., Beverly Hills, CA 90211-1934. *Agent*—Toby Cole, 234 West 44th St., New York, NY 10036.

CAREER: Writer, 1964–. Conley Arabian Horse Ranch, Chino, CA, stable hand, 1958-60; Bishop's Company Repertory Players (touring theater group), actor, 1962-63; Village Gate, New York City, busboy, 1963-64. Rock musician (drums and guitar) with Holy Modal Rounders, 1968-71; playwright in residence at Magic Theatre, San Francisco, CA, 1974-84; actor in feature films, including *Days of Heaven,* 1978, *Resurrection,* 1980, *Raggedy Man,* 1981, *Frances,* 1982, *The Right Stuff,* 1983, *Country,* 1984, *Fool for Love,* 1985, and *Crimes of the Heart,* 1986, *Baby Boom,* 1987, *Steel Magnolias,* 1989, *The Hot Spot,* 1990, *Defenseless,* 1991, *Voyager,* 1991, *Thunderheart,* 1992, *The Pelican Brief,* 1993; *Silent Tongue,* 1994; director of feature film *Far North,* 1988.

MEMBER: American Academy and Institute of Arts and Letters, 1992.

AWARDS, HONORS: Obie Awards from *Village Voice* for best plays of the off-Broadway season, 1966, for *Chicago, Icarus's Mother,* and *Red Cross,* 1967, for *La Turista,* 1968, for *Forensic and the Navigators* and *Melodrama Play,* 1973, for *The Tooth of Crime,* 1975, for *Action,* 1977, for *Curse of the Starving Class,* 1979, for *Buried Child,* and 1984, for *Fool for Love;* grant from University of Minnesota, 1966; Rockefeller foundation grant and

Yale University fellowship, 1967; Guggenheim foundation memorial fellowships, 1968 and 1971; National Institute and American Academy award for literature, 1974; Brandeis University creative arts award, 1975-76; Pulitzer Prize for drama, 1979, for *Buried Child;* Academy Award for best supporting actor nomination from Academy of Motion Picture Arts and Sciences, 1984, for *The Right Stuff;* Golden Palm Award from Cannes Film Festival, 1984, for *Paris, Texas;* New York Drama Critics' Circle Award, 1986, for *A Lie of the Mind;* Theater Hall of Fame, 1994.

WRITINGS:

PLAYS

Cowboys (one-act), first produced off-off-Broadway at St. Mark Church in-the-Bowery, October 16, 1964.

The Rock Garden (one-act; also see below), first produced off-off-Broadway at St. Mark Church in-the-Bowery, October 16, 1964.

4-H Club (one act; also see below), first produced off-Broadway at Cherry Lane Theatre, 1965.

Up to Thursday (one-act), first produced off-Broadway at Cherry Lane Theatre, February 10, 1965.

Dog (one-act), first produced off-Broadway at La Mama Experimental Theatre Club, February 10, 1965.

Chicago (one-act; also see below), first produced off-off-Broadway at St. Mark Church in-the-Bowery, April 16, 1965.

Icarus's Mother (one-act; also see below), first produced off-off-Broadway at Caffe Cino, November 16, 1965.

Fourteen Hundred Thousand (one-act; also see below), first produced at Firehouse Theater, Minneapolis, MN., 1966.

Red Cross (one-act; also see below), first produced off-Broadway at Martinique Theatre, April 12, 1966.

La Turista (two-act; first produced off-Broadway at American Place Theatre, March 4, 1967; also see below), Bobbs-Merrill, 1968.

Cowboys #2 (one-act; also see below), first produced off-Broadway at Old Reliable, August 12, 1967.

Forensic and the Navigators (one-act; also see below), first produced off-off-Broadway at St. Mark Church in-the-Bowery, December 29, 1967.

(Contributor) *Oh! Calcutta!,* first produced on Broadway at Eden Theatre, 1969.

The Unseen Hand (one-act; also see below), first produced off-Broadway at La Mama Experimental Theatre Club, December 26, 1969.

Holy Ghostly (one-act; also see below), first produced in New York, NY, 1970.

Operation Sidewinder (two-act; first produced off-Broadway at Vivian Beaumont Theatre, March 12, 1970; also see below), Bobbs-Merrill, 1970.

Shaved Splits (also see below), first produced off-Broadway at La Mama Experimental Theatre Club, July 29, 1970.

Mad Dog Blues (one-act; also see below), first produced off-off-Broadway at St. Mark Church in-the-Bowery, March 4, 1971.

(With Patti Smith) *Cowboy Mouth* (also see below), first produced at Transverse Theatre, Edinburgh, Scotland, April 2, 1971, produced off-Broadway at American Place Theatre, April 29, 1971.

Back Bog Beast Bait (one-act; also see below), first produced off-Broadway at American Place Theatre, April 29, 1971.

The Tooth of Crime (two-act; also see below), first produced at McCarter Theatre, Princeton, NJ, 1972, produced off-off-Broadway at Performing Garage, March 7, 1973.

Blue Bitch (also see below), first produced off-off-Broadway at Theatre Genesis, February, 1973.

(With Megan Terry and Jean-Claude van Itallie) *Nightwalk* (also see below), first produced off-off-Broadway at St. Clement's Church, September 8, 1973.

Geography of a Horse Dreamer (two-act; also see below), first produced at Theatre Upstairs, London, England, February 2, 1974.

Little Ocean, first produced at Hampstead Theatre Club, London, England, March 25, 1974.

Action (one-act; also see below), first produced off-Broadway at American Place Theatre, April 4, 1975.

Killer's Head (one-act; also see below), first produced off-Broadway at American Place Theatre, April 4, 1975.

Angel City (also see below), first produced at Magic Theatre, San Francisco, CA, 1976.

Curse of the Starving Class (two-act; also see below), first produced off-Broadway at Newman/Public Theatre, March, 1978.

Buried Child (two-act; also see below), first produced off-Broadway at Theatre of the New City, November, 1978.

Seduced (also see below), first produced off-Broadway at American Place Theatre, February 1, 1979.

Suicide in B-flat (also see below), first produced off-off-Broadway at Impossible Ragtime Theatre, March 14, 1979.

Tongues, first produced at Eureka Theatre Festival, CA, 1979, produced off-off-Broadway at The Other Stage, November 6, 1979.

Savage/Love, first produced at Eureka Theater Festival, CA, 1979, produced off-off-Broadway at The Other Stage, November 6, 1979.

True West (two-act; first produced off-Broadway at Public Theatre, December 23, 1980), Doubleday, 1981.

(Also director of original production) *Fool for Love* (one-act; also see below), first produced at Magic Theatre, San Francisco, 1983, produced off-Broadway by Circle Repertory Company, May 27, 1983.

The Sad Lament of Pecos Bill on the Eve of Killing His Wife (one-act; also see below), first produced off-Broadway at La Mama Experimental Theatre Club, September 25, 1983.

Superstitions (one-act), first produced off-Broadway at La Mama Experimental Theatre Club, September 25, 1983.

(Also director of original production) *A Lie of the Mind* (three-act; first produced off-Broadway at Promenade Theatre, December, 1985), published with *The War in Heaven* (also see below), New American Library, 1987.

Hawk Moon, produced in London, 1989.

States of Shock, produced in New York, 1991.

Simpatico, Dramatists Play Service (New York City), 1995.

PLAY COLLECTIONS

Five Plays by Sam Shepard (contains *Icarus's Mother, Chicago, Melodrama Play, Red Cross,* and *Fourteen Hundred Thousand*), Bobbs-Merrill, 1967.

The Unseen Hand and Other Plays (contains *The Unseen Hand, 4-H Club, Shaved Splits, Forensic and the Navigators, Holy Ghostly,* and *Back Bog Beast Bait*), Bobbs-Merrill, 1971.

Mad Dog Blues and Other Plays (includes *Mad Dog Blues, The Rock Garden, Cowboys #2, Cowboy Mouth, Blue Bitch,* and *Nightwalk*), Winter House, 1972.

The Tooth of Crime [and] *Geography of a Horse Dreamer,* Grove, 1974.

Angel City, Curse of the Starving Class and Other Plays (includes *Angel City, Curse of the Starving Class, Killer's Head,* and *Action*), Urizen Books, 1976.

Buried Child, Seduced, Suicide in B-flat, Urizen Books, 1979.

Four Two-Act Plays by Sam Shepard (contains *La Turista, The Tooth of Crime, Geography of a Horse Dreamer,* and *Operation Sidewinder*), Urizen Books, 1980.

Chicago and Other Plays, Urizen Books, 1981.

The Unseen Hand and Other Plays, Urizen Books, 1981.

Seven Plays by Sam Shepard, Bantam, 1981.

Fool for Love [and] *The Sad Lament of Pecos Bill on the Eve of Killing His Wife,* City Lights Books, 1983.

Fool for Love and Other Plays, Bantam, 1984.

The Unseen Hand and Other Plays, Bantam, 1986.

SCREENPLAYS

(With Michelangelo Antonioni, Tonino Guerra, Fred Graham, and Clare Peploe) *Zabriskie Point* (produced by Metro-Goldwyn-Mayer, 1970), Cappelli (Bologna, Italy), 1970, published with Antonioni's *Red Desert,* Simon & Schuster, 1972.

(With L. M. Kit Carson) *Paris, Texas,* Twentieth Century-Fox, 1984.

Fool for Love (based on Shepard's play of the same title), Golan Globus, 1985.

Also author, with Robert Frank, of *Me and My Brother,* and with Murray Mednick, of *Ringaleerio.*

OTHER

Hawk Moon: A Book of Short Stories, Poems, and Monologues, Black Sparrow Press, 1973.

Rolling Thunder Logbook, Viking, 1977.

Motel Chronicles, City Lights Books, 1982.

(With Joseph Chaikin) *The War in Heaven* (radio drama; first broadcast over WBAI in January, 1985), published with *A Lie of the Mind,* New American Library, 1987.

Joseph Chaikin and Sam Shepard: Letters and Texts 1972-1984, edited by Barry V. Daniels, New American Library, 1989.

Cruising Paradise: Tales, Knopf (New York City), 1996.

MEDIA ADAPTATIONS: Fourteen Hundred Thousand was filmed for NET Playhouse, 1969; *Blue Bitch* was filmed by the British Broadcasting Corporation (BBC), 1973; *True West* was filmed for the Public Broadcasting Service (PBS) series American Playhouse.

SIDELIGHTS: Sam Shepard has devoted more than two decades of his life to a highly eclectic—and critically acclaimed—career in the performing arts. Considered the preeminent literary playwright of his generation, he is an author whose prolific output and imaginative intensity consistently outpace his contemporaries. Throughout his career Shepard has never confined himself merely to pen and paper; he has also directed plays of his authorship, played drums and guitar in rock bands and jazz ensembles, and acted in major feature films. He is perhaps best known to the American public for his movie appearances, including leading roles in *The Right Stuff* and *Country,* but acting is a sideline for the man *Newsweek*'s Jack Kroll calls "the poet laureate of America's emotional Badlands." Despite his success in Hollywood, Shepard is first and foremost a playwright whose dramas explore mythic images of modern America in the nation's own eccentric vernacular.

Shepard established himself by writing numerous one-act plays and vignettes for the off-off-Broadway experimental theater. Although his audiences have grown and his plays have been widely produced in America and abroad, he has not yet staged a production on Broadway. *New Republic* contributor Robert Brustein, who finds Shepard "one of our most celebrated writers," contends that the lack of attention from Broadway "has not limited Shepard's powers." Indeed, continues Brustein, "unlike those predecessors who wilted under such conditions, Shepard has flourished in a state of marginality. . . . Shepard's work has been a model of growth and variety." From his early surreal one-acts to his more realistic two-and three-act plays, Shepard has placed stress on artistic integrity rather than on theatrical marketability. As a result, contends Kroll, Shepard's plays have "overturned theatrical conventions and created a new kind of drama filled with violence, lyricism and an intensely American compound of comic and tragic power." The numerous awards Shepard has received for his work stand as evidence of his plays' extraordinary originality; Shepard has won more than ten Obie Awards for best off-Broadway plays, a Pulitzer Prize for *Buried Child,* and a prestigious New York Drama Critics' Circle Award in 1986 for *A Lie of the Mind. Plays and Players* magazine contributor Richard A. Davis comments that Shepard has both "a tremendous ability to make words bring the imagination of an audience to life" and "a talent for creating with words alone extremely believable emotional experiences."

While Shepard's subjects—nostalgia, power struggles, family tensions—may seem simple and quintessentially American at a cursory glance, his plays remain "extraordinarily resistant to thematic exegesis," according to Richard Gilman in his introduction to *Seven Plays by Sam Shepard.* Gilman finds the standard critical vocabulary inadequate for the assessment of Shepard's work because the dramatist "slips out of all the categories" and seems to have come "out of no literary or theatrical tradition at all but precisely for the breakdown or absence—on the level of art if not of commerce—of all such traditions in America." Gilman further comments that a number of the plays "seem like fragments, chunks of various sizes thrown out from some mother lode of urgent and heterogeneous imagination in which [Shepard] has scrabbled with pick, shovel, gun-butt and hands. The reason so many of them seem incomplete is that they lack the clear boundaries as artifact, the internal order, the progress toward a denouement . . . and the consistency of tone and procedure that ordinarily characterize good drama. . . . Another difficulty is that we tend to look at all plays for their single 'meanings' or ruling ideas but find this elusive in Shepard and find, moreover, his plays coalescing, merging into one another in our minds."

In *American Dreams: The Imagination of Sam Shepard,* Michael Earley also remarks that Shepard "seems to have forged a whole new kind of American play that has yet to receive adequate reckoning." Earley calls the playwright "a true American primitive, a literary naif coursing the stage of American drama as if for the first time" who brings to his work "a liberating interplay of word, theme and image that has always been the hallmark of the romantic impulse. His plays don't work like plays in the traditional sense but more like romances, where the imaginary landscape (his version of America) is so remote and open that it allows for the depiction of legend, adventure, and even the supernatural. . . . Even though Shepard is one of our most modernist playwrights . . . what he more keenly resembles is a transcendentalist or new romantic whose 'innocent eye' wonders at all it surveys and records experience without censure." *Partisan Review* contributor Ross Wetzsteon contends that viewers respond to Shepard's plays "not by interpreting their plots or analyzing their characters or dissecting their themes, but simply by experiencing their resonance. . . . Shepard's arias seek to soar

into a disembodied freedom, to create emotions beyond rational structure, to induce in both player and audience a trancelike state of grace."

Shepard was born in Fort Sheridan, Illinois, on November 5, 1943, and was given the name his forebears had used for six generations—Samuel Shepard Rogers. His father was a career army officer, so as a youngster Shepard moved from base to base in the United States and even spent some time in Guam. When Shepard's father retired from the service, the family settled on a ranch in Duarte, California, where they grew avocados and raised sheep. Although the livelihood was precarious, Shepard enjoyed the atmosphere on the ranch and liked working with horses and other animals. Influenced by his father's interest in Dixieland jazz, Shepard gravitated to music; he began to play the drums and started what *Dictionary of Literary Biography* contributor David W. Engel calls "his lifelong involvement with rock and roll music and its subculture." He graduated from Duarte High School in 1960 and spent one year studying agricultural science at the local junior college, but his family situation deteriorated as his father began drinking excessively. Shepard fled the "hysterical" family scene by joining a touring theatrical group called the Bishop's Company Repertory Players. At the age of nineteen, he found himself in New York City, determined to seek his fortune with only a few months' acting experience to his credit.

By chance, Shepard encountered a high school friend in New York, Charles Mingus, Jr., son of the renowned jazz musician. Mingus found Shepard a job at The Village Gate, a jazz club, and the two young men became roommates. While working at The Village Gate, Shepard met Ralph Cook, founder of the off-off-Broadway company Theatre Genesis. Cook encouraged Shepard to write plays, and Shepard obliged him by producing *Cowboys* and *The Rock Garden,* two one-acts that became part of the first Theatre Genesis show at St. Mark Church in-the-Bowery. Though Engel notes that most of the critics regarded Shepard's first two works as "bad imitations of Beckett," the *Village Voice* columnist "gave the plays a rave review." Shepard began to turn out one-act pieces in rapid fashion; many of them were performed off-off-Broadway, and they attracted a cult following within that theatrical circuit. Shepard also continued his association with jazz and rock music, incorporating the rhythms into his dialogue and including musical riffs in the scripts.

Some critics have dismissed Shepard's early work as undisciplined, obscure, and lacking in sufficient self-awareness. For instance, *Massachusetts Review* essayist David Madden finds the plays "mired in swampy attitudes toward Mom and Dad. Their main line of reasoning seems to be that if Mom and Dad's middle class values are false, that if they and the institutions they uphold are complacent and indifferent, the only alternative is some form of outlaw behavior or ideology." Other national drama critics have evaluated the one-act plays quite differently. In the *New York Review of Books,* Robert Mazzocco writes: "If one is content to follow this hard-nosed, drug-induced, pop-flavored style, this perpetual retuning of old genres and old myths, one encounters, finally, a profuse and unique panorama of where we are now and where we have been." *Journal of Popular Culture* contributor George Stambolian declares that Shepard "is in fact showing to what extent the mind, and particularly the modern American mind, can become and has become entrapped by its own verbal and imaginative creations." And according to Clive Barnes, Shepard "is so sweetly unserious about his plays, and so desperately serious about what he is saying. . . . There is more in them than meets the mind. They are very easy to be funny about, yet they linger oddly in the imagination." In his own assessment of his first plays, Shepard told *New York* he thinks of them as "survival kits, in a way. They were explosions that were coming out of some kind of inner turmoil in me that I didn't understand at all. There are areas in some of them that are still mysterious to me."

Shepard's first major production, *Operation Sidewinder,* premiered at the Vivian Beaumont Theatre on March 12, 1970. Engel describes the two-act play as "an excellent example of how [Shepard] combines the roles of poet, musician, and playwright." Set in the Hopi Indian country of the American Southwest, *Operation Sidewinder* follows the attempts of many different factions of American society to control a huge mechanical rattlesnake originally designed to trace unidentified flying objects. Air force commandos, Hopi snake-worshippers, black power activists, and even a beautiful but foolish blonde named Honey try to use the computerized sidewinder for their own ends. Engel notes that the "playful and satiric action is amplified by Shepard's production techniques. He assaults the senses of the audience by the use of intense sound and lights, and by various chants and songs." Shepard himself helped to provide the music in the play by performing with a rock band, the Holy Modal Rounders. Although Engel claims that "the psychological resonance of stylized production, and not its sociological satire, is Shepard's aim," critics have found the work overly moralistic and stylistically confusing. "The difficulty of the play is in the writing," Barnes states in his *New York Times* review. "The symbolic progression, while clearly charting the progress to atomic holocaust, is altogether too symbolic." Kroll maintains that the play's energy "has congealed in a half-slick pop machine with the feel of celluloid and the clackey sound of doctrinaire contemporaneity." Martin Gottfried offers a different assessment of the play in *Women's Wear Daily.* "Everything about Sam Shepard's *Operation Sidewinder* is important to our theatre," writes Gottfried. "More than any recent major production, it is built upon exactly the style and the mentality energizing the youth movement in America today."

The Tooth of Crime, first produced in 1972, further strengthened Shepard's literary reputation. A two-act study of rock-and-roll stars who fight to gain status and "turf," the play "depicts a society which worships raw power," in Engel's words. London *Times* reviewer Irving Wardle writes of the work: "Its central battle to the death between an aging superstar and a young pretender to his throne is as timeless as a myth . . . and . . . has proved a durably amazing reflection of the West Coast scene. If any classic has emerged from the last 20 years of the American experimental theatre, this is it." "Moving freely from gangster movies of the 40's to punk rock of the 70's, Mr. Shepard speaks in a language that is vividly idiomatic," Mel Gussow claims in the *New York Times.* "The imagery is visceral and sexual, a necromantic view of a rapacious society where, for an achiever, there is no acceptable alternative to being on top of the charts." Mazzocco calls *The Tooth of Crime* "undoubtedly the quintessential Shepard play" and "a dazzlingly corrosive work . . . one of the most original achievements in contemporary theater. It is also the play that best illustrates the various facets—at once highly eclectic and highly singular—of [Shepard's] genius."

The Tooth of Crime also proved to be a stylistic departure from previous Shepard plays. *Modern Drama* critic Charles R. Bachman contends that the work "utilizes . . . the traditional dramatic values of taut, disciplined structure, vivid and consistent characterization, and crescendo of suspense." More recently these criteria have come to play more prominent roles in Shepard's work, although the transition from modernist to traditional style has hardly been either abrupt or thorough. According to Richard L. Homan in *Critical Quarterly,* Shepard has learned "to express the outrage, which gave rise to the experimental theatre, in plays which work through realistic conventions to challenge our everyday sense of reality."

Buried Child and *A Lie of the Mind*—separated by seven years of the playwright's career—both traverse the psychological topography of disturbed families. In *Buried Child,* notes *Washington Post* contributor David Richards, Shepard "delivers a requiem for America, land of the surreal and home of the crazed. . . . Beyond the white frame farmhouse that contains the evening's action, the amber waves of grain mask a dark secret. The fruited plain is rotting and the purple mountain's majesty is like a bad bruise on the landscape." The action in *Buried Child* unfolds when son Vince arrives at his midwestern farm home after a long absence. He is confronted with a dangerously unbalanced cast of relatives who harbor secrets of incest and murder. As Richard Christiansen points out in the *Chicago Tribune,* the Pulitzer Prize-winning play is "a Norman Rockwell portrait created for Mad Magazine, a scene from America's heartland that reeks with 'the stench of sin.'" Similarly, the 1985 play *A Lie of the Mind* presents a tale of "interior domestic violence, the damage that one does to filial, fraternal and marital bonds—and the love that lingers in the air after the havoc has run its natural course," according to Gussow. In that work, two families are galvanized into violence by the near-fatal beating a jealous husband administers to his wife. Gussow calls the drama "a play of penetrating originality" while noting that it "follows a clear naturalistic plotline, with characters who behave like normal, irrational human beings." *A Lie of the Mind* won the New York Drama Critics' Circle Award for best new off-Broadway play of 1985, and Shepard himself directed the original production.

Shepard also directed his 1983 play *Fool for Love*—probably his best-known work. The one-act piece has been produced for stage and has also been made into a feature film in which Shepard performed the starring role. *Fool for Love* charts a course of alternating submission and rejection between two lovers who may also be half-brother and half-sister. New York *Daily News* critic Douglas Watt maintains that the ninety minute non-stop drama "is Sam Shepard's purest and most beautiful play. An aching love story of classical symmetry, it is . . . like watching the division of an amoeba in reverse, ending with a perfect whole." *Fool for Love,* writes *New York Times* reviewer Frank Rich, "is a western for our time. We watch a pair of figurative gunslingers fight to the finish—not with bullets, but with piercing words that give ballast to the weight of a nation's buried dreams. . . . As Shepard's people race verbally through the debris of the West, they search for the identities and familial roots that have disappeared with the landscape of legend." In the *New Republic,* Brustein finds "nothing very thick or complicated about either the characters or the plot" and a lack of resolution to the play's ending. The critic concludes nevertheless that *Fool for Love* is "not so much a text as a legend, not so much a play as a scenario for stage choreography, and under the miraculous direction of the playwright, each moment is rich with balletic nuances." Clive Barnes concludes in the *New York Post* that the drama "moves with a deathless effortlessness through planes of meaning. Everything . . . is always what it seems but then a little bit more."

Shepard's film work has not been confined to his 1985 appearance in *Fool for Love.* Since 1978 he has taken a major movie role each year and has, despite his discomfort with the image, assumed a certain matinee idol status. "Shepard did not become famous by writing plays," declares Stephen Fay in *Vogue.* "Like it or not, acting [has] made him a celebrity." Shepard does *not* like to be considered a screen celebrity; his attitude toward film work is ambivalent, and the public scrutiny has driven him into near-seclusion. He told *New York:* "There's a definite fear about being diminished through film. It's very easy to do too much of it, to a point where you're lost. Image-making is really what film acting is about. It's image-making, as opposed to character-making, and in some cases it's not true." *Film Comment* essayist David Thomson contends, however, that Shepard's long-standing fascination with movies lures him into that sort of work. "His sternness wants to be tested against their decadence," writes Thomson. "His restraint struggles to reconcile a simultaneous contempt and need for movies. The uneasiness hovers between passion and foolishness, between the lack of skill and a monolith of intractability." Some critics, including *Washington Post* correspondent Harry Haun, maintain that Shepard's disdain for Hollywood publicity is a calculated device to strengthen his personal mystique. "He chooses to hide out from the world on the silver screen," notes Haun. "That fine irony is the stuff that animates many a Shepard work. He is The Recluse as Superstar, the man who has arrived on his own terms, carefully sculpting a special myth for himself."

In 1983, German director Wim Wenders commissioned Shepard to write a screenplay based loosely on the playwright's book *Motel Chronicles.* The resulting work, *Paris, Texas,* was a unanimous winner of the Golden Palm Award at the 1984 Cannes Film Festival. The film recasts many of Shepard's central concerns—broken families, the myth of the loner, and the elegy for the old West—in a story of reunion between a father and a son. In *People* magazine, Peter Travers calls *Paris, Texas* the "most disturbing film ever about the roots of family relationships. Shepard's words and Wenders' images blend in a magical poetry." *New York* reviewer David Denby finds the film "a lifeless art-world hallucination—a movie composed entirely of self-conscious flourishes," but most other critics praise the work. In the *Los Angeles Times,* Sheila Benson, for one, writes: "This is a deeply affecting film about family, separation, loss and a man's last act of repentence. . . . Its beautiful parable about rootlessness has gone deep into our unconscious."

BIOGRAPHICAL/CRITICAL SOURCES:

BOOKS

Auerbach, Doris, *Sam Shepard, Arthur Kopit, and the Off Broadway Theater,* Twayne, 1982.
Contemporary Literary Criticism, Gale (Detroit), Volume 4, 1975; Volume 6, 1976; Volume 17, 1981; Volume 34, 1985; Volume 41, 1987; Volume 44, 1987.
DeRose, David J., *Sam Shepard,* Twayne, 1992.
Dictionary of Literary Biography, Volume 7: *Twentieth-Century American Dramatists,* Gale, 1981.
Drama Criticism, Gale, Volume 5, 1995.
Graham, Laura, *Sam Shepard: Theme, Image, and the Director,* Lang (New York), 1995.
Hart, Lynda, *Sam Shepard's Metaphorical Stages,* Greenwood Press, 1987.
King, Kimball, *Ten Modern American Playwrights,* Garland, 1982.
King, Kimball, *Sam Shepard: A Case Book,* Garland, 1988.
Marranca, Bonnie, editor, *American Dreams: The Imagination of Sam Shepard,* Performing Arts Journal Publications, 1981.

Mottram, Ron, *Inner Landscapes: The Theater of Sam Shepard,* University of Missouri Press, 1984.
Oumano, Ellen, *Sam Shepard: The Life and Work of an American Dreamer,* St. Martin's Press, 1986.
Patraka, Vivian M., and Siegel, Mark, *Sam Shepard,* Boise State University, 1985.
Rosen, Carol, *Sam Shepard,* St. Martin's Press, 1997.
Shewey, Don, *Sam Shepard,* Dell, 1985.
Trussler, Simon, *File on Shepard,* Methuen, 1989.
Wade, Leslie A., *Sam Shepard and the American Theatre,* Greenwood, 1997.

PERIODICALS

American Film, October, 1984.
Chicago Tribune, December 15, 1978; December 7, 1979; July 2, 1980; April 23, 1982; December 16, 1985; December 18, 1985.
Christian Science Monitor, June 9, 1983.
Commonweal, June 14, 1968; May 8, 1970; November 30, 1984; July 12, 1991.
Critical Quarterly, spring, 1982.
Drama, winter, 1965; spring, 1969; autumn, 1973; summer, 1976.
Esquire, February, 1980; November, 1988.
Film Comment, November-December, 1983; June, 1984.
Globe and Mail (Toronto), December 21, 1985.
Hudson Review, spring, 1979; spring, 1984.
Interview, September, 1988.
Journal of Popular Culture, spring, 1974.
Los Angeles Magazine, March, 1988.
Los Angeles Times, May 12, 1982; February 12, 1983; October 1, 1983; December 12, 1983; March 14, 1984; November 16, 1984; September 25, 1985; December 6, 1985; January 25, 1986; April 11, 1986; August 11, 1986.
Massachusetts Review, autumn, 1967.
Modern Drama, December, 1976; March, 1979; March, 1981.
Ms., November, 1984.
Nation, February 21, 1966; April 4, 1966; March 30, 1970; March 26, 1973; May 3, 1975; January 10, 1976; February 24, 1979; January 31, 1981; October 27, 1984; December 29, 1984-January 5, 1985; January 11, 1986; February 22, 1986.
New Leader, April 10, 1967.
New Republic, April 21, 1973; April 8, 1978; January 31, 1981; June 27, 1983; October 29, 1984; December 3, 1984; December 23, 1985; September 29, 1986; February 2, 1987; November 28, 1988; July 15, 1995, p. 27.
New Statesman, August 24, 1984; October 12, 1984; March 1, 1985; July 4, 1986; October 30, 1987; February 9, 1990; September 6, 1991.
Newsweek, March 23, 1970; January 5, 1981; June 6, 1983; October 1, 1984; November 19, 1984; November 11, 1985; December 16, 1985.
New York, November 27, 1978; February 19, 1979; June 13, 1983; December 5, 1983; October 15, 1984; November 19, 1984; December 9, 1985; May 27, 1991; May 13, 1996, p. 64.
New Yorker, May 11, 1968; March 21, 1970; March 17, 1973; May 5, 1975; December 22, 1975; November 29, 1982; October 1, 1984; September 2, 1985; January 27, 1986; December 15, 1986; June 3, 1991; April 22, 1996, p. 84; May 27, 1996, p. 138.
New York Review of Books, April 6, 1967; May 9, 1985.
New York Times, February 11, 1965; April 13, 1966; May 28, 1968; April 13, 1969; March 15, 1970; April 2, 1970; March 8, 1971; June 28, 1971; March 7, 1973; September 17, 1977; March 3, 1978; April 28, 1978; November 7, 1978; Decem-

ber 10, 1978; February 2, 1979; March 4, 1979; March 14, 1979; April 17, 1979; June 3, 1979; February 7, 1980; March 12, 1980; December 24, 1980; November 9, 1981; January 6, 1982; October 18, 1982; March 2, 1983; May 27, 1983; June 5, 1983; September 20, 1983; September 25, 1983; May 27, 1983; January 29, 1984; September 28, 1984; September 30, 1984; November 9, 1984; November 14, 1984; November 18, 1984; November 22, 1984; November 29, 1984; November 30, 1984; August 15, 1985; October 1, 1985; October 4, 1985; November 14, 1985; December 1, 1985; December 15, 1985; January 12, 1986; January 21, 1986; April 13, 1986; May 17, 1996, p. B12; June 16, 1996, p. H5.

New York Times Book Review, June 23, 1996, p. 23.

Partisan Review, Volume XLI, number 2, 1974; Volume XLIX, number 2, 1982.

People Weekly, December 26, 1983; January 2, 1984; October 15, 1984; November 5, 1984; December 9, 1985; January 6, 1986.

Plays and Players, June, 1970; October-November, 1971; April, 1974; May, 1974; November, 1974; April, 1979.

Rolling Stone, August 11, 1977; December 18, 1986; February 24, 1994.

Time, November 27, 1972; June 6, 1983; October 8, 1984; August 12, 1985; December 2, 1985; December 16, 1985; May 20, 1996, p. 77.

Times (London), September 24, 1983; September 26, 1983; October 6, 1984; January 7, 1986.

Times Literary Supplement, November 24, 1978; March 1, 1985.

Variety, September 14, 1988; May 20, 1991; February 8, 1993; September 19, 1994.

Village Voice, April 4, 1977; August 15, 1977; February 12, 1979.

Vogue, February, 1984; February, 1985.

Washington Post, January 14, 1979; June 2, 1979; March 5, 1983; April 22, 1983; October 23, 1983; April 12, 1985; October 15, 1985; May 1, 1986; September 12, 1986.

Women's Wear Daily, March 13, 1970; May 27, 1983.

*　　*　　*

SHEPHERD, Michael
See LUDLUM, Robert

*　　*　　*

SHIEL, M(atthew) P(hipps) 1865-1947
(Gordon Holmes, a joint pseudonym)

PERSONAL: Born July 21, 1865, in Plymouth, Montserrat, West Indies; died February 14, 1947, in Chichester, England; son of Matthew Dowdy (a shipowner, storekeeper, and Methodist lay preacher) and Priscilla Ann (Blake) Shiel; married Carolina Garcia Gomez, 1898 (died, 1902); married Lydia Gerald Newson, c. 1918 (separated, 1929); children: two daughters. *Education:* Attended Harrison College, King's College, studied at St. Bartholomew's Hospital, London.

CAREER: Novelist, short story writer, essayist, poet, and translator. Taught mathematics at a school in Devonshire, c. 1888-89, International Congress of Hygiene and Demography interpreter; worked in British Censor's Office during World War I. Granted Civil List pension, 1938.

WRITINGS:

SCIENCE FICTION NOVELS

(With W. T. Stead) *The Rajah's Sapphire,* Ward Lock (London), 1896.

Shapes in the Fire: Being a Mid-Winter's Night Entertainment in Two Parts and an Interlude, Lane (London), Roberts (Boston, MA), 1896.

The Yellow Danger: The World of the World's Greatest War, Richards (London), 1898, Fenno (New York City), 1899.

The Purple Cloud, Chatto and Windus (London), 1901, revised edition, Gollancz (London), 1929, Vanguard Press (New York City), 1930.

The Lord of the Sea, Richards (London), 1901, Stokes (New York City), 1901, revised edition, Knopf (New York City), 1924, Gollancz (London), 1929.

The Yellow Wave, Ward Lock (London), 1905.

The Last Miracle, Laurie (London), 1906, revised edition, Gollancz (London), 1929.

The Isle of Lies, Laurie (London), 1909.

The Dragon, Richards (London), 1913, Clode (New York City), 1914, revised edition published as *The Yellow Peril,* Gollancz (London), 1929.

This above All, Vanguard Press (New York City), 1933, published as *Above All Else,* Cole (London), 1943.

The Young Men Are Coming! Allen and Unwin (London), 1937, Vanguard Press (New York City), 1937.

SCIENCE FICTION SHORT STORIES

The Pale Ape and Other Pulses, Laurie (London), 1911.

Xelucha and Others, Arkham House (Sauk City, WI), 1975.

Prince Zaleski and Cummings King Monk, 1895, Mycroft and Moran (Sauk City, WI), 1977.

The Empress of the Earth, 1898; The Purple Cloud, 1901; "Some Short Stories": Offprints of the Original Editions, Reynolds Morse Foundation (Cleveland, OH), 1979.

The New King, Plus an Unpublished Dialog with Cummings King Monk Omitted from The Pale Ape of 1911, Reynolds Morse Foundation (Cleveland, OH), 1980.

OTHER NOVELS

Contraband of War, Richards (London), 1899, revised edition, Pearson (London), 1914, Gregg Press (Ridgewood, New Jersey), 1968.

Cold Steel (historical romance) Richards (London), 1899, Brentano's (New York), 1900, revised edition, Gollancz (London), 1929, Vanguard Press (New York), 1929.

The Man-Stealers (historical romance) Hutchinson (London), 1900, Lippincott (Philadelphia), 1900, revised edition, Hutchinson, 1927.

The Weird o'It, Richards (London), 1902.

Unto the Third Generation, Chatto and Windus (London), 1903.

The Evil That Men Do, Ward Lock (London), 1904.

The Lost Viol, Clode (New York City), 1905, Ward Lock (London), 1908.

The White Wedding, Laurie (London), 1908.

This Knot of Life, Everett (London), 1909.

Children of the Wind, Laurie (London), 1923.

Dr. Krasinski's Secret, Vanguard Press (New York City), 1929, Jarrolds (London), 1930.

The Black Box, Vanguard Press (New York), 1930, Richards (London), 1931.

Say Au R'voir but Not Goodbye, Benn (London), 1933.

NOVELS; AS GORDON HOLMES (WITH LOUIS TRACY)

The Late Tenant, Clode (New York City), 1906, Cassell (London), 1907.

By Force of Circumstances, Clode (New York City), 1909, Mills and Boon (London), 1910.

The House of Silence, Clode (New York City), 1911, published as *The Silent House,* Nash (London), 1911.

SHORT STORIES

Prince Zaleski, Lane (London), 1895, Roberts (Boston), 1895.

How the Old Woman Got Home, Richards (London), 1927, Vanguard Press (New York City), 1928.

Here Comes the Lady, Richards (London), 1928.

The Invisible Voices, with John Gawsworth, Richards (London), 1935, Vanguard Press (New York City), 1936.

The Best Short Stories of M. P. Shiel, edited by John Gawsworth, Gollancz (London), 1948.

OTHER

(Editor) *An American Emperor: The Story of the Fourth Empire of France,* by Louis Tracy, Putnam (New York City), 1897, Pearson (London), 1897.

(Translator) *The Hungarian Revolution: An Eyewitness's Account,* by Charles Henry Schmitt, Worker's Socialist Federation, 1919.

Richard's Shilling Selections from Edwardian Poets—M. P. Shiel, edited by John Gawsworth, Richards (London), 1936.

Science, Life, and Literature, Williams and Norgate (London), 1950.

The New King, Reynolds Morse Foundation (Cleveland, OH), 1980.

The Works of M. P. Shiel, four volumes, edited by A. Reynolds Morse, Reynolds Morse Foundation, 1980.

Also author of the unpublished work *Jesus,* a translation and reinterpretation of the Gospels, of which only fragments of manuscript have been found.

MEDIA ADAPTATIONS: *The Purple Cloud* was adapted as a motion picture with the title *The World, the Flesh and the Devil,* 1958.

SIDELIGHTS: A prolific and popular writer at the turn of the century, M. P. Shiel published in many genres producing essays and poems, detective stories and works of horror in the tradition of Edgar Allan Poe as well as the science fiction and fantasy tales for which he is primarily remembered today. As was often the case in that period, much of his work appeared in serial form in popular magazines before being published in the form of novels or collections of short stories. Shiel is best known for his science fiction novel *The Purple Cloud* (1901) and for his role in popularizing the racist concept of the "Yellow Peril"—the belief that the peoples and cultures of the Orient posed an intrinsic threat to the survival of Western civilization. Modern-day discussions of Shiel's work usually focus on his erudite and idiosyncratic use of language and on the racist tenor of the ideas embodied in his writings. In his study *Explorers of the Infinite,* Sam Moskowitz documents the author's insistent racism, misogyny, and anti-Semitism as well as "his almost paranoid vilification of organized religion." While conceding the existence of "honest flashes of power and brilliance" in Shiel's works, Moskowitz concludes, "It would have to be admitted that, in the psychiatrist's vernacular, the man had a 'problem.'" On the other hand, A. Reynolds Morse, who edited a collection of Shiel's works in 1980, has portrayed the author as a master stylist, citing his "profound knowledge, his

immense vocabulary, his liquid light-bubbling poetic narrative, [and] his vast vivid imaginings."

Shiel wrote his first book-length story, *The Rajah's Sapphire,* in collaboration with journalist W. T. Stead for serial publication in a new journal, the *Daily Paper,* in 1893. The *Paper* folded after its first issue, but Shiel's story appeared in book form in 1896. Shiel's next venture was a collection of detective stories, *Prince Zaleski.* The protagonist of the stories, the "Prince" of the title, is a mysterious figure who lives a solitary life in Oriental splendor attended only by his black manservant, Ham. Zaleski brings his encyclopedic knowledge and phenomenal powers of reason to bear on mysteries brought to his attention by the narrator. A critic writing for a contemporary British magazine, the *Athenaeum,* described the Prince Zaleski stories as "a combination of the mysterious terror inspired by Poe's tales and of the sensational amazement which Mr. Sherlock Holmes's extraordinary perspicacity provokes." These stories, the critic added, "have distinctly the faculty of creating a creepy feeling and of making the reader feel genuinely uncomfortable."

The author's next book, *Shapes in the Fire: Being a Mid-Winter's Night Entertainment in Two Parts and an Interlude* (1896), was a work of horror in the manner of Poe. Shiel was then convinced by his friend Louis Tracy, a well-known author of adventure stories with whom he would later coauthor several books, to produce a "future-war" story—a tale imagining a war between Britain and would-be invaders at some time in the near future. The turn of the century was a period of intense rivalries among the European countries, which were competing against each other and against Japan for economic supremacy and control over colonies. A persistent awareness of the possibility of war—a conflict which would eventually materialize in what would become known as World War I—was one factor contributing to British fascination with this subject. Shiel's first contribution to the genre was *The Yellow Danger: The World of the World's Greatest War* (1898), in which Europe is invaded by the "yellow hordes" of Asia led by the "evil genius" Dr. Yen How. In the end, Western civilization is saved through the heroic efforts of a British sailor, John Hardy, who engineers the drowning of several million invaders and the infection with cholera of several million others. A critic for *Bookman,* reviewing the novel at the time of its publication, described it and its author as "marvelous": "[Shiel's] audacity is splendid. He foretells the future—a ghastly vision. . . . He slaughters not regiments, but races; he blows up not ships, but fleets. He harrows our very souls with prophecies of horror."

Shiel would revisit the "yellow peril" theme repeatedly in subsequent books, including *The Yellow Wave* (1905) and *The Dragon* (1913). His next contribution to the future-war genre, however, *The Lord of the Sea* (1901), had a somewhat different slant. In this story, which would prove to be the author's most controversial work, large numbers of Jews have fled to England to escape violent persecution in mainland Europe. In England, their usurious money-lending quickly gains them control over land ownership, and the native English population is reduced to virtual serfdom. The hero of the story is an English farmer and blacksmith, John Hogarth, who finds a meteorite full of diamonds and uses his newfound wealth to build a series of giant floating fortresses. His ensuing control of the seaways as "King Richard, Lord of the Sea" gives him the power to force a reform of European land ownership and to banish the Jews to their original home in Palestine. Overthrown through treachery, the former King Richard discovers that he is himself of Jewish descent and travels to Palestine, where he is revealed to be the long-awaited Messiah.

One of Shiel's most popularly successful novels, *The Lord of the Sea* attracts attention today in part because of its eerie prediction of the establishment of a Jewish state in Palestine a full forty-seven years before the creation of the state of Israel in 1948. Of greater concern to modern critics, however, is the way in which, as C. J. Keep stated in the *Dictionary of Literary Biography,* the novel "capitalizes on the widespread anti-Semitism of the day." Shiel's blatant use of negative stereotypes about Jews has led at least one critic, Sam Moskowitz, to compare *The Lord of the Sea* to Adolf Hitler's *Mein Kampf* (1924). "It can scarcely be emphasized," wrote Moskowitz in his book *Explorers of the Infinite,* "that the only difference between [Shiel's] method and the Nazis' rests in the fact that he would have permitted the Jews to emigrate with their lives."

The Yellow Danger and *The Lord of the Sea* also exemplify another common theme of Shiel's writing, that of the "overman" or *ubermensch,* a superior individual whose outstanding qualities afford him a natural and, in the author's view, permissible dominance over others. The concept has its origin in the writings of the nineteenth-century German philosopher Friedrich Nietzsche. According to Keep, however, Shiel's vision differs from that of Nietzsche in that Shiel's overman must place himself at the service of the common good. Shiel expanded on the theme of the overman in his most acclaimed novel, *The Purple Cloud* (1901), conceived as the second book in a trilogy that also included *The Lord of the Sea* and *The Last Miracle* (1906).

The protagonist of *The Purple Cloud* is a doctor, Adam Jeffson, who is torn between good and evil impulses. Sole survivor of a polar expedition in the course of which he has murdered several of his fellows, Jeffson returns to civilization to discover that during his absence at the North Pole the rest of humanity appears to have been completely exterminated by a cloud of purple gas emanating from the interior of the earth. Jeffson wanders the deserted earth amusing himself by destroying large cities until he encounters a young woman, Leda, who has also escaped death. Although initially he behaves brutally towards the woman, eventually the forces of good win out and the two join in marriage, ending the story on a note of hope for the restoration of humankind. Writing in *London Magazine,* J. Maclaren-Ross commented that *The Purple Cloud* contains "some of Shiel's most magnificent scenes and set-pieces." He added that the book "illustrates one of [Shiel's] greatest strengths: the ability to buttress his situations with selective and specific detail which—despite the melodramatic plots, missing wills, lost heiresses, hidden treasures, etc.—causes the reader to suspend disbelief." Admired by such noted and diverse writers as H. G. Wells, James Barrie, Raymond Chandler, and H. P. Lovecraft, *The Purple Cloud* is generally considered a classic of early science fiction and fantasy.

Shiel continued to publish prolifically until the outbreak of World War I, but he published nothing between 1913 and 1923. Little is known of his life during this period; he worked in the British Censor's Office during the early years of the war, but the end of the war found him living in Italy. His next published work was *Children of the Wind* (1923), an adventure set in South Africa, followed by the mystery story *How the Old Woman Got Home* (1927). He published several other titles in the late 1920s and early 1930s, at the same time as the republication of several of his earlier books created a brief revival in his popularity. The last of his books published during his lifetime was *The Young Men Are Coming!* (1937), a science fiction work about a cataclysmic struggle between supporters of science and supporters of religion. The proponents of science ultimately prevail with the help of a superior alien intelligence known as the Cosmic Egg which their leader has encountered on one of the moons of Jupiter after being abducted by aliens.

Writing in the *Dictionary of Literary Biography,* C. J. Keep suggested that for the modern-day reader the value and the pleasure of Shiel's work lies in "the ways in which his texts take up and transform the dominant ideological currents of their age." Keep also suggested that Shiel's frank expression of the ideology of his time may be one reason for his lack of popularity today. "To read Shiel today," Keep wrote, "is to struggle with the fact that people of his evident skill and intelligence once harbored the same theories that contributed to the Holocaust. Shiel, in short, represents much of that which modern readers would rather forget, and it is thus hardly surprising that, despite his abilities as a storyteller and a prose stylist, he too has been largely forgotten."

BIOGRAPHICAL/CRITICAL SOURCES:

BOOKS

Aldiss, Brian, *Trillion Year Spree,* Paladin, 1988, pp. 181-82.
Dictionary of Literary Biography, Volume 153, Gale (Detroit), 1995, pp. 268-77.
Lovecraft, H. P., *Supernatural Horror in Literature,* Dover, 1973, pp. 77-78.
Morse, A. Reynolds, editor, *Shiel in Diverse Hands,* Morse, 1980.
Morse, A. Reynolds, editor, *The Works of M. P. Shiel,* four volumes, Morse, 1980.
Morse, A. Reynolds, *The Works of M. P. Shiel: A Study in Bibliography,* Fantasy, 1948.
Moskowitz, Sam, *Explorers of the Infinite,* World, 1963, pp. 142-56.
Ransome, Arthur, *Bohemia in London,* Chapman and Hall, 1907, pp. 247-56.
Stableford, Brian, *Scientific Romance in Britain 1890-1950,* Fourth Estate, 1985, pp. 75-84, 175-78.
Twentieth-Century Literature Criticism, Volume 8, Gale, 1982, pp. 357-65.
Twentieth-Century Science Fiction Writers, St. James Press, 1991, pp. 842-43.

PERIODICALS

Athenaeum, March 23, 1895, pp. 375-76.
Bookman, September, 1898, pp. 169-70.
London Magazine, volume 4, number 6, September, 1964, pp. 76-84.
New York Herald Tribune Books, May 4, 1930, p. 14.
New York Times Book Review, April 8, 1945, pp. 3, 27.
Times Literary Supplement, June 26, 1981, p. 26.

*   *   *

SHIELDS, Carol 1935-

PERSONAL: Born June 2, 1935, in Oak Park, IL; daughter of Robert E. and Inez (Selgren) Warner; married Donald Hugh Shields (a professor), July 20, 1957; children: John, Anne, Catherine, Margaret, Sara. *Education:* Hanover College, B.A., 1957; University of Ottawa, M.A., 1975. *Politics:* New Democratic Party. *Religion:* Quaker.

ADDRESSES: Home—701-237 Wellington Crescent, Winnipeg, Manitoba, Canada, R3M OA1. *Agent*—Bella Pomer, 22 Shallmar Blvd., Toronto, Ontario, Canada.

CAREER: Canadian Slavonic Papers, Ottawa, Ontario, editorial assistant, 1972-74; writer, 1974–; University of Manitoba, professor, 1980–.

MEMBER: Writers' Union of Canada, Writers Guild of Manitoba, PEN.

AWARDS, HONORS: Winner of young writers' contest sponsored by Canadian Broadcasting Corp. (CBC), 1965; Canada Council grants, 1972, 1974, 1976; fiction prize from Canadian Authors Association, 1976, for *Small Ceremonies;* CBC Prize for Drama, 1983; National Magazine Award, 1984, 1985; Arthur Ellis Award, 1988; Marian Engel Award, 1990; Governor General's Award for English-language fiction and National Book Critics Circle Award for fiction, 1994, and Pulitzer Prize for fiction, 1995, all for *The Stone Diaries.* Honorary doctorate, University of Ottawa, 1995.

WRITINGS:

Others (poetry), Borealis Press, 1972.
Intersect (poetry), Borealis Press, 1974.
Susanna Moodie: Voice and Vision (criticism), Borealis Press, 1976.
Small Ceremonies (novel), McGraw, 1976.
The Box Garden (novel), McGraw, 1977.
Happenstance (novel), McGraw, 1980, Penguin (New York City), 1994.
A Fairly Conventional Woman (novel), Macmillan (Toronto, Canada), 1982.
Various Miracles (short stories), Stoddart (Don Mills, Canada), 1985, Penguin (New York City), 1989.
Swann: A Mystery (novel), General, 1987, Viking (New York City), 1989.
The Orange Fish (short stories), Random House (Toronto, Canada), 1989, Viking (New York City), 1990.
Departures and Arrivals, Blizzard, 1990.
(With Blanche Howard) *A Celibate Season* (novel), Coteau (Regina, Canada), 1991.
The Republic of Love (novel), Viking (New York City), 1992.
Coming to Canada (poetry), Carleton University Press (Ottawa, Canada), 1992.
The Stone Diaries (novel), Random House, 1993, Viking, 1994.
Thirteen Hands (drama), 1994.
(With Catherine Shields) *Fashion, Power, Guilt, and the Charity of Families,* Blizzard (Winnipeg), 1995.
Larry's Party (novel), Viking, 1997.

Author of *The View,* 1982, *Women Waiting,* 1983, and *Face Off,* 1987. Also author with D. Williamson of *Not Another Anniversary,* 1986.

SIDELIGHTS: Carol Shields has had two distinct phases in her writing career. Her first four novels, *Small Ceremonies* (1976), *The Box Garden* (1977), *Happenstance* (1980), and *A Fairly Conventional Woman* (1982), are portrayals of everyday life. Her heros and heroines struggle to define themselves and make human connections in their close relationships. Kathy O'Shaughnessy wrote in *Observer Review* that "*Small Ceremonies* is a novel of ideas: about privacy, knowledge of others, about how we perceive each other, and are perceived by others," while *London Review of Books* writer Peter Campbell, in a review of *Happenstance,* stated that "Shields writes well about decent people, and her resolutions are shrewder than those in the self-help books."

The next phase of Shields's career is marked by risk taking. With her first short story collection, *Various Miracles* (1985), Shields began to experiment more with form by using a variety of voices. She continued, however, to portray ordinary people in everyday situations. *Books Magazine* writer Andrea Mynard asserted that Shields's "robust realism is typical of the growing sorority of Canadian writers, including Margaret Atwood and Alice Munro, who have been gaining a strong reputation. . . . In her accessibly simple and lucid style, Carol intelligently grasps the minutiae of everyday life and illuminates the quirks of human nature. Her observations of contemporary dilemmas are brilliant."

In *Swann: A Mystery* (1987) Shields continued her experimentation by using four distinct voices to tell the story. In this novel she also developed a theme seen in her other work, that of the mysterious nature of art and creation. *Swann,* noted Danny Karlin in *London Review of Books,* "is a clever book, self-conscious about literature, fashionably preoccupied with questions of deconstruction, of the 'textuality' of identity, of the powers and powerlessness of language. This impression is confirmed by its confident and playful manipulation of different narrative modes." Some critics, however, castigated what they considered Shields's simple characterizations. *New York Times Book Review* writer Josh Robins noted that "the characters remain too one-dimensional, often to the point of caricature, to support sporadic attempts at psychological portraiture."

Shields took another risk by attempting the genre of the romance novel in *The Republic of Love* (1992), but she made the form her own by making her main characters wade through the coldness and problems of the twentieth century before reaching the happy ending. "Shields has created a sophisticated [romance] story," stated *Books in Canada* writer Rita Donovan. "And the 'happy ending,' so traditional to the romance novel, is here refurbished, updated, and—most happily—earned."

Shields's early novels were popular but not taken seriously by critics. Some critics argue that in the early part of her career Shields was underestimated as a stylist and her works were dismissed as being naturalistic. Critics generally praised Shields when she began experimenting more with form. Some of her risks were considered failures, however, as in the case of the last section of *Swann,* in which she attempted to bring all four voices together in a screenplay form.

The Stone Diaries (1993) is the fictional biography of Daisy Goodwill Flett, whose life spans eight decades and includes time spent in both Canada and the United States. Written in both the first and third person, the story begins with her birth in 1905 in rural Manitoba, Canada. Daisy's mother, extremely obese and unaware that she is pregnant, dies moments later. Unable to care for his daughter, Cuyler Goodwill convinces his neighbor Clarentine Flett to raise the child. Soon afterward, Clarentine leaves her husband and, taking Daisy with her, travels to Winnipeg, where she moves in with her son, Barker. Cuyler later takes Daisy to Bloomington, Indiana, where he has become a highly successful stonecarver. There, Daisy marries a wealthy young man who dies during their honeymoon. In 1936 she marries Barker, who has become renowned for his agricultural research, and resettles in Canada. In her role as wife and mother, Daisy appears quiet and content, but after her husband dies, she takes over a gardening column for the *Ottawa Recorder,* writing as Mrs. Greenthumb. Her joy—she finds the work incredibly meaningful and fulfilling—is short-lived however, as the editor decides to give the column to a staff writer despite Daisy's protests. She eventually recovers from the disappointment and lives the remainder of her life in Sarasota, Florida, where she amuses herself playing bridge.

Critical reaction to *The Stone Diaries,* which won the Governor General's Award, the National Book Critics Circle Award, and the Pulitzer Prize, and was also short-listed for the Booker Prize, has been overwhelmingly favorable. Commentators have praised Shields for exploring such universal problems as loneliness and lost opportunities and for demonstrating that all lives are significant and important no matter how banal and confined they appear. Others have lauded the novel as a brilliant examination of the divergence between one's inner and outer self, and of the relations between fiction, biography, and autobiography. Allyson F. McGill wrote in *Belles Lettres,* "Shields and Daisy challenge us to review our lives, to try and see life honestly, even while 'their' act of authorship only reveals how impossible it is to see and speak objective truth," while a *Canadian Forum* reviewer noted that "Shields demonstrates there are no small lives, no lives out of which significance does not shine. She makes us aware that banality, ultimately, is in the eye of the beholder."

Shields's follow-up to *The Stone Diaries* is *Larry's Party,* published in 1997. Shields structured the novel thematically; each chapter covers a different area of Larry's life, for instance his friends and children. However, readers can follow Larry as he grows from an awkward adolescent to a somewhat settled, typical middle-aged white male. What is not typical about Larry is his job—he builds elaborate mazes out of shrubbery. And these, according to Michiko Kakutani of the *New York Times,* "become a metaphor for the path his own life has taken, full of twists and turns and digressions. They also become a metaphor for Ms. Shields's own looping narrative, a narrative that repeatedly folds back on itself to gradually disclose more and more details about Larry's past." Commentators have remarked that in *Larry's Party,* Shields portrays the Everyman, much as she portrayed the Everywoman in The Stone Diaries. Linnea Lannon wrote in the *Detroit Free Press,* "Shields gives us Larry Weller, a man who seems as average as any, but under her scrutiny, more fascinating than you might reasonably expect."

While Shields has been a leading author in Canada for numerous years, she began to attract an international following in the early 1990s, particularly following the American publication of *The Stone Diaries.* Many of her early novels have recently been re-released in the United States and England to much popular and critical acclaim.

BIOGRAPHICAL/CRITICAL SOURCES:

PERIODICALS

Belles Lettres, spring, 1991, p. 56; summer, 1992, p. 20; fall, 1994, pp. 32, 34.
Books in Canada, October, 1979, pp. 29-30; May, 1981, pp. 31-32; November, 1982, pp. 18-19; October, 1985, pp. 16-17; October, 1987, pp 15-16; May, 1989, p. 32; January/February, 1991, pp. 30-31; April, 1992, p. 40; February, 1993, pp. 51-52; September, 1993, pp. 34-35; October, 1993, pp. 32-33.
Books in Review, summer, 1989, pp. 158-60.
Books Magazine, November/December, 1994, p. 12.
Canadian Forum, July, 1975, pp. 36-38; November, 1993, pp. 44-45; January/February, 1994, pp. 44-45.
Canadian Literature, summer, 1989, pp. 158-60; autumn, 1991, pp. 149-50; spring, 1995.
Christian Science Monitor, December 7, 1990, pp. 10-11.

Detroit Free Press, September 7, 1997.
Kirkus Reviews, May 1, 1976, p. 559.
London Review of Books, September 27, 1990, pp. 20-21; March 21, 1991, p. 20; May 28, 1992, p. 22; September 9, 1993, p. 19.
Los Angeles Times Book Review, August 20, 1989, p. 2; April 17, 1994, pp. 3, 7.
Maclean's, October 11, 1993, p. 74.
New Statesman and Society, August 20, 1993, p. 40.
New York, March 7, 1994.
New York Times, July 17, 1989, p. C15; May 10, 1995; August 26, 1997.
New York Times Book Review, August 6, 1989, p. 11; August 12, 1990, p. 28; March 14, 1992; March 1, 1992, pp. 14, 16; March 27, 1994, pp. 3, 14.
Observer Review, February 19, 1995, p. 19.
Publishers Weekly, February 28, 1994.
Quill and Quire, January, 1981, p. 24; September, 1982, p. 59; August, 1985, p. 46; May, 1989, p. 20; August, 1993, p. 31.
Scrivener, spring, 1995.
Spectator, March 21, 1992, pp. 35-36; September 24, 1994, p. 41.
Times Literary Supplement, August 27, 1993, p. 22; February 17, 1995.
West Coast Review, winter, 1988, pp. 38-56, pp. 57-66.
Women's Review of Books, May, 1994, p. 20.

*   *   *

SHILTS, Randy 1951-1994

PERSONAL: Born August 8, 1951, in Davenport, IA; died of complications from acquired immune deficiency syndrome (AIDS), February 17, 1994, in Guerneville, CA; son of Bud (a salesman) and Norma (a homemaker) Shilts. *Education:* University of Oregon, B.S., 1975.

ADDRESSES: Office—San Francisco Chronicle, 901 Mission St., San Francisco, CA 94103. *Agent*—Fred Hill, 2237 Union St., San Francisco, CA 94123.

CAREER: Journalist. KQED, San Francisco, CA, reporter, 1977-80; KTVU, Oakland, CA, reporter, 1979-80; *San Francisco Chronicle,* San Francisco, staff reporter, 1981-87, national correspondent, 1988-94.

AWARDS, HONORS: Winner of numerous journalism awards while attending University of Oregon; Media Alliance Award for outstanding nonfiction author and Gay Academic Union Award for outstanding journalist, both 1982; special citations from San Francisco Board of Supervisors, 1982 and 1987; Silver Medal, Commonwealth Club, 1987, for best nonfiction author of the year; Outstanding Communicator Award from Association for Education in Journalism and Mass Communication, 1988; special citation from the office of San Francisco mayor, 1988; Outstanding Achievement Award from Parents and Friends of Lesbians and Gays, 1988; named outstanding author by the American Society of Journalists and Authors, 1988.

WRITINGS:

The Mayor of Castro Street: The Life and Times of Harvey Milk, St. Martin's (New York City), 1982.
And the Band Played On: Politics, People, and the AIDS Epidemic, St. Martin's, 1987, new edition, Penguin (New York City), 1988.

Conduct Unbecoming: Gays and Lesbians in the U.S. Military, Vietnam to the Persian Gulf, St. Martin's, 1993.

Contributor of articles to periodicals, including *Christopher Street, Washington Post, New West, Village Voice, Advocate, Columbia Journalism Review, Los Angeles Herald Examiner, San Francisco Examiner,* and *San Francisco Chronicle.*

MEDIA ADAPTATIONS: The Mayor of Castro Street has been optioned by Cineplex-Odeon to be a theatrical feature; *And the Band Played On* was released on audiotape in 1988 by Simon & Schuster, and was adapted into a film by Home Box Office (HBO) in 1993.

SIDELIGHTS: Randy Shilts, the first openly gay establishment journalist in California, gained national attention in 1982 with the release of his first book, *The Mayor of Castro Street: The Life and Times of Harvey Milk.* Following the success of his debut effort, Shilts continued to write, publishing two similarly acclaimed journalistic works. *And the Band Played On: Politics, People, and the AIDS Epidemic,* a chronicle of the early growth and spread of AIDS, was released in 1987, and *Conduct Unbecoming: Gays and Lesbians in the U.S. Military,* the last book written by Shilts before his death in 1994, appeared in 1993.

Ostensibly a biography of gay leader Harvey Milk, the San Francisco supervisor assassinated on November 27, 1978, with Mayor George Moscone, in City Hall, Shilts' *The Mayor of Castro Street* is also a comprehensive history of the homosexual movement in San Francisco. As observed by *Los Angeles Times* staff writer Elizabeth Mehren, "*The Mayor of Castro Street* is how San Francisco Supervisor Harvey Milk . . . liked to be known. *The Life and Times of Harvey Milk* is what Shilts endeavors to recount."

Milk, a former high-school athlete and Barry Goldwater campaign worker, moved to San Francisco in 1972. Using his camera shop on Castro Street as a base of operations and an unofficial community center, he entered local politics at the age of forty-three. His politics, a blend of fiscal conservatism and civil rights reform, intrigued many, but it was his dramatic delivery and theatrical presentation that brought him broad attention. After a series of defeats, Milk's populist views were appealing enough to elect him supervisor of his district. He thus became the first openly gay elected official of any major city in the country, and with his influence in various unions, his power eventually extended far beyond his post.

According to Shilts, Milk predicted his own assassination several times, forecasting that he would not live to be fifty. The fulfillment of that prophecy came just a few days short of his forty-ninth birthday at the hands of Dan White, a fellow city supervisor and former police officer. White, who was the only board member to cast a ballot against Milk's local gay rights bill, quit his supervisor's job shortly after the bill passed, fully expecting Mayor Moscone to reappoint him. When Moscone instead yielded to Milk's pressure to appoint someone else, White retaliated by crawling through a basement window at City Hall and shooting Milk and Moscone to death in their offices. A jury found White guilty on two charges of manslaughter, for which he was sentenced to seven-and-a-half years in prison. He was released in 1984, just five years into his prison term. In 1985, he committed suicide.

The Mayor of Castro Street received high praise from critics and readers alike for its account of the San Francisco gay community's relationship to local politics. Mehren dubbed it "one of the first

avowedly gay nonfiction books to be accepted—embraced, even—by the mainstream press and public." A critic in *Chicago Tribune Book World* hailed Shilts's book as "remarkable," calling it "a biography, a history of the Castro Street gay community and a story of big-city politics that, for all of its complexity, is as readable as a good novel." Christopher Schemering commented in the *Washington Post Book World,* "In addition to a no-holds-barred character study and a history of the local gay movement, *The Mayor of Castro Street* functions equally well as an investigative piece on the mechanics of big-city government in all of its expedient, back-biting splendor." Shilts, claimed Schemering, "pulls off this threefold stunt admirably, juggling his themes, irreverently reporting on how they have clashed and played off one another, and often just standing back to watch the fireworks." A *Kirkus Reviews* writer complimented Shilts's skill in "balancing the public Harvey Milk with an account of his private life without being lurid" and declared Shilts's "account of the emergence of San Francisco as a gay mecca—and the accompanying rise in gays' political clout" first-rate.

Five years later Shilts published his second book, *And the Band Played On: Politics, People and the AIDS Epidemic,* described by a *Kirkus Reviews* writer as "a massive, ominous, compelling book that tells the most definitive story of the AIDS crisis in America to date." In *And the Band Played On,* Shilts chronicles the early spread—in the late 1970s and early 1980s—of human immunodeficiency virus (HIV), a semen-and blood-transmitted virus that destroys the body's ability to fight infection and leads to AIDS. In addition to tracing the history of AIDS, the book also provides details of the initial failure of society to comprehend and curb the deadly virus. This failure is attributed to a slow government response, lack of attention from the news media, foot-dragging by scientists and government health officials, and the reluctance of the gay community to accept the changes in lifestyle necessary for prevention. These factors allowed AIDS to rage out of control in its early years. In the book, Shilts argues that by the time America "paid attention to the disease it was too late to do anything about it." The epidemic, he insists, "was allowed to happen by an array of institutions, all of which failed to perform their appropriate tasks to safeguard the public health."

The story of the epidemic is recounted through the experiences of both obscure and well-known patients, the few physicians and researchers who tried to sound early alarms, their political allies and foes—from San Francisco City Hall to Congress—and the scientific infighting that long delayed reliable identification of the AIDS virus. One of the most notable characters in the book is the French-Canadian airline steward Gaetan Dugas, who scientists suspect brought HIV to the United States after having contracted it in Europe through sexual contacts with Africans. Calling Dugas "Patient Zero," researchers for the federal Centers for Disease Control retraced his sexual activity as he traveled through North America. Forty of the first 248 cases of AIDS could be traced to him; the first cases in New York and Los Angeles were linked to him; and as early as 1982, eleven AIDS cases could be traced from a single partner of Dugas, who remained sexually active after his diagnosis until his death in 1984.

The book concludes with movie star Rock Hudson's widely publicized death from AIDS in 1985, a watershed in the nation's awareness of the crisis. In a new last chapter added to the 1988 Penguin paperback edition of the book, however, Shilts reports that, even after AIDS had become "infinitely more respectable as a cause and subject of discussion" and "it was clear that most Americans wanted to respond compassionately to the problem," what remained "most noteworthy about AIDS in America during 1987 and 1988 was how, in Congress, in the White House, at the National Institutes of Health and in the media, very little had fundamentally changed. The band still played on."

Like the earlier work on Harvey Milk, *And the Band Played On* elicited a chorus of critical hurrahs. Christopher Lehmann-Haupt hailed *And the Band Played On* in the *New York Times* as "a heroic work of journalism in what must rank as one of the foremost catastrophes of modern history." *Newsweek* contributor Jim Miller concurred, recommending "Shilts's impassioned and path-breaking piece of investigative journalism" as "essential reading" for anyone interested in understanding the roots of "the greatest health crisis of the 20th century." Several reviewers judged Shilts's volume as one of the best nonfiction books of 1987, among them *Publishers Weekly* editor Genevieve Stuttaford and *Los Angeles Times* reviewer Carolyn See. See designated *And the Band Played On* her favorite nonfiction book of 1987, applauding "Shilts' marvelously researched tales of greed, vanity, theft, deceit—set against individual examples of great courage and heroism" as "by far the most important work in years."

In contrast to the backlash from certain members of the gay community who felt betrayed by Shilts' criticism of their role in the epidemic, many reviewers were enthusiastic about the book's examination of society's reluctance to confront the virus early in its history. In her review for *Tribune Books,* Jean Latz Griffin called Shilts' book "a painstakingly detailed history—well documented and fairly presented—of America's failure to deal with AIDS." She continued, "The culprits Shilts castigates are many— the Reagan administration, the federal scientific and health agencies, the blood-banking industry, feuding scientists, the media, some gay leaders." Similarly, *Los Angeles Times Book Review* contributor Woodrow Myers, Jr., declared *And the Band Played On* "the best job thus far of cataloguing the fear and the denial that have accompanied the intrusion of the human immunodeficiency virus into American life."

Shilts' third book, *Conduct Unbecoming: Gays and Lesbians in the U.S. Military,* is an exposure of the discrimination, hostility, and mistreatment suffered by many homosexuals within the military hierarchy. In the *Los Angeles Times Book Review,* Robert Dawldoff explained that "in case after case, Shilts shows malicious prosecution, vicious and brutal abuse of individuals, rights and careers, and what amounts to systematized torture as part of a witch hunt." John D'Emilio in the *Nation* offered a similar interpretation: "Shilts demonstrates that the military has, in fact, taken the lead in perfecting techniques for mass persecution, in indoctrinating millions of young Americans in an ideology of hatred and in defining homophobia."

In the book, Shilts explains the apparent and ironic willingness of the military establishment to overlook or ignore homosexuality during times of national crisis. According to *Time* reviewer R. Z. Sheppard, Shilts argues two main points in his documentary· "First, that homosexuals can soldier as well as heterosexuals, and, second, that the military has always been more concerned with appearances than with reality." Sheppard continued, citing two facts that the book attempts to document using interviews and government statistics: "Homosexuals become less unbecoming in time of war when every able body is needed; and harassment, intimidation and administrative discharges for gays and lesbians increase when the shooting stops."

Conduct Unbecoming also argues that the military, often thought of as a reflection of society, has played a major role in the creation and maintenance of negative social attitudes with regards to homosexuality. D'Emilio identified this argument, writing that the military "no longer just reflects the prejudices of American society. Rather, according to Shilts, it has become the main bastion of homophobic terrorism." Dawldoff explained that Shilts' ultimate plea is for American society to realize a way to resist such terrorism: "*Conduct Unbecoming* lays it all out for us, leaving little to the imagination except how this country will manage to salvage its honor from the betrayal of all of the thousands of lesbian and gay soldiers."

Following his death in 1994, Shilts was lauded as an important journalist and influential writer who helped to bring world-wide attention to the AIDS epidemic. In Shilts' *Chicago Tribune* obituary notice, Larry Kramer, playwright and founder of the militant AIDS-activist group ACT UP, said that Shilts "did more to educate the world about AIDS than any single person." Dave Ford of the San Francisco AIDS Foundation explained in the obituary that Shilts "was disliked in some quarters of the gay community for his politics and some of the reporting he did. But I think the key thing about him was that he was a reporter from start to finish."

BIOGRAPHICAL/CRITICAL SOURCES:

PERIODICALS

Best Sellers, April, 1982.
Chicago Tribune Book World, February 13, 1983.
Commonwealth, May 21, 1993, p. 6.
Detroit News, October 18, 1987.
Economist, December 5, 1987.
Film Comment, December, 1984.
Kirkus Reviews, January 1, 1982; September 1, 1987.
Library Journal, April 15, 1993, p. 107.
Los Angeles Times, March 25, 1982; October 9, 1987.
Los Angeles Times Book Review, March 7, 1982; December 6, 1987; January 3, 1988; May 2, 1993, p. 4.
Nation, November 7, 1987; December 26, 1987; June 7, 1993, p. 806.
National Review, December 4, 1987.
Newsweek, October 19, 1987.
New York Times, October 7, 1987; October 26, 1987; October 31, 1987; April 21, 1993, p. C20.
New York Times Book Review, November 8, 1987.
Observer (London), March 6, 1988; May 2, 1993, p. 58.
Publishers Weekly, March 19, 1982; September 11, 1987.
Time, October 19, 1987; March 1, 1993, p. 9; May 24, 1993, p. 76.
Tribune Books (Chicago), October 18, 1987; May 30, 1993, p. 5.
Village Voice, March 23, 1982.
Voice Literary Supplement, October, 1987.
Washington Post Book World, April 2, 1982.

*   *   *

SHIRER, William L(awrence) 1904-1993

PERSONAL: Surname is pronounced *Shy*-rer; born February 23, 1904, in Chicago, IL; died December 28, 1993, in Boston, MA; son of Seward Smith (a lawyer) and Josephine (Tanner) Shirer; married Theresa Stiberitz, January 30, 1931 (divorced, 1970); married Irina Lugovskaya; children: Eileen Inga, Linda Elizabeth. *Education:* Coe College, B.A., 1925; College de France, Paris, courses in European history, 1925-27. *Politics:* Independent. *Religion:* Presbyterian. *Avocational interests:* Walking, sailing, attending the theater and ballet, listening to symphonic and chamber music.

ADDRESSES: Agent—Don Congdon, Harold Matson Co., Inc., 276 Fifth Ave., New York, NY 10001.

CAREER: Chicago Tribune, Paris edition, reporter in Paris, France, 1925-27, foreign correspondent in Paris, London, Geneva, Rome, Dublin, Vienna, and Prague, 1927-29, chief of Central European bureau in Vienna, 1929-32; European correspondent for Paris edition of *New York Herald,* 1934; Universal News Service, foreign correspondent in Berlin, 1935-37; Columbia Broadcasting System (CBS), continental representative in Vienna, 1937-38, and in Prague and Berlin, 1938-40, war correspondent, 1939-45, radio commentator in the United States, 1941-47; radio commentator for Mutual Broadcasting System, 1947-49; full-time writer, 1950-93. Columnist for *New York Herald Tribune* and its syndicate, 1942-48.

MEMBER: Authors Guild (president, 1953-57), PEN, Council on Foreign Relations, Foreign Policy Association, Phi Beta Kappa, Tau Kappa Epsilon, Century Club.

AWARDS, HONORS: Headliners Club Award, 1938, for coverage of the Austrian Anschluss, and 1941, for general excellence in radio reporting; Litt.D., Coe College, 1941; Chevalier, Legion d'Honneur; George Foster Peabody Award, 1947; Wendell Willkie One World Award, 1948; National Book Award and Sidney Hillman Foundation Award, both 1961, both for *The Rise and Fall of the Third Reich: A History of Nazi Germany.*

WRITINGS:

Berlin Diary: The Journal of a Foreign Correspondent, 1934-1941 (Book-of-the-Month Club selection), Knopf (New York City), 1941.
End of a Berlin Diary, Knopf, 1947.
The Traitor (novel), Farrar, Straus (New York City), 1950.
Midcentury Journey: The Western World through Its Years of Conflict (Literary Guild selection), Farrar, Straus, 1952.
Stranger Come Home (novel), Little, Brown (Boston), 1954.
The Challenge of Scandinavia: Norway, Sweden, Denmark, and Finland in Our Time, Little, Brown, 1955.
The Consul's Wife (novel), Little, Brown, 1956.
The Rise and Fall of the Third Reich: A History of Nazi Germany (Book-of-the-Month Club selection), Simon & Schuster (New York City), 1960, reprinted with a new afterword by the author, 1990.
The Rise and Fall of Adolf Hitler (juvenile), Random House (New York City), 1961 (published in England as *All about the Rise and Fall of Adolf Hitler,* W. H. Allen [London], 1962).
The Sinking of the Bismarck (juvenile), Random House, 1962 (published in England as *All about the Sinking of the Bismarck,* W. H. Allen, 1963).
The Collapse of the Third Republic: An Inquiry into the Fall of France in 1940 (Book-of-the-Month Club selection), Simon & Schuster, 1969.
Twentieth-Century Journey: A Memoir of a Life and the Times, Volume I: *The Start, 1904-1930,* Simon & Schuster, 1976; Volume II: *The Nightmare Years, 1930-1940,* Little, Brown, 1984; Volume III: *A Native's Return, 1945-1988,* Little, Brown, 1990.
Gandhi: A Memoir, Simon & Schuster, 1980.
An August to Remember: A Historian Remembers the Last Days of World War II and the End of the World that Was (limited edition), Thornwillow Press (New York City), 1986.

Love and Hatred: The Troubled Marriage of Leo and Sonya Tolstoy, Simon & Schuster, 1994.

Contributor to *Harper's, Atlantic, Reader's Digest, Look,* and other publications.

SIDELIGHTS: In the summer of 1925, twenty-one-year-old William L. Shirer left his home in Cedar Rapids, Iowa, and set out for Paris on what was intended to be one last youthful fling before settling into a stateside job in the fall. Having borrowed $200 (enough money, he figured, to last him about two months) from his uncle and the president of his alma mater, Coe College, the young man proceeded to work his way across the Atlantic on a cattle boat, arriving in the French capital with dreams of becoming a writer of fiction and poetry. Shirer found his new life to be far more "intellectually stimulating and less personally restrictive" than his life had been in the United States, reports Alice Henderson in the *Dictionary of Literary Biography,* and he soon decided to try his luck at obtaining a newspaper job in Paris. But editors of two major American newspapers with Paris editions, the *New York Herald* and the *Chicago Tribune,* could offer him little encouragement; hundreds of other job-seeking men and women had been there before him, all with similar stories and requests.

Resigned to the prospect of having to return to what he called the land of "Prohibition, fundamentalism, puritanism, Coolidgeism, [and] Babbitry" when his money ran out, Shirer vowed to make the most of his remaining time in Paris. On the morning of his last day in the city, after a particularly lively farewell night on the town, he awoke to discover a note from the editor of the *Chicago Tribune* asking him to report to the newspaper office that very evening for a possible job. Thus, at 9 o'clock, Shirer found himself at the *Tribune* copy desk sitting next to a fellow expatriate-turned-copywriter, James Thurber.

Until December of 1940, Shirer roamed from one European capital to another as a foreign correspondent, first for the *Tribune* and subsequently for the Paris edition of the *New York Herald,* the Universal News Service, and the Columbia Broadcasting System. He spent much of this time in Vienna, Berlin, and Prague, reporting on Hitler and the Nazis during crucial phases of their rise to power. His observations of these tumultuous years formed the basis of two voluminous best-sellers, each one a blend of journalism and history: *Berlin Diary: The Journal of a Foreign Correspondent, 1934-1941* and *The Rise and Fall of the Third Reich: A History of Nazi Germany.*

Berlin Diary was Shirer's first book. It opens on January 11, 1934, when the author was vacationing in Spain, and ends on December 13, 1940, as he was on board a ship heading back to America. Published in mid-1941, the book met with a great deal of praise, as in this *Saturday Review of Literature* article by W. L. White: "[*Berlin Diary*] is the best book on Germany in many years, and it will be many more before a better one can be written. . . . [The author] is gifted with an eye for significant detail. . . . I have yet to find anyone who picked the book up who was able to put it down unfinished." Joseph Barnes of *New York Herald Tribune Books* likewise observed that *Berlin Diary* "is the most important and exciting book written out of Germany since long before the war began. This is, first of all, an absorbing book. Most of it reads like the scenario of a partly forgotten but important nightmare, written down with footnotes."

Only a few reviewers had less positive assessments of *Berlin Diary.* The *Catholic World* critic, for instance, despite calling the book "a vivid picture deftly drawn," felt that "judicious readers will be wary about accepting [Shirer's] implications and deductions." The lack of material on subjects "not in the headlines" prompted *Commonweal* reviewer Max Fischer to "seriously question [the book's] quality." Continued Fischer: "Mr. Shirer is just the typical newspaperman, whose interests are restricted to his profession. I admit he is an excellent reporter, but his book seems to me rather sterile."

After the publication of *Berlin Diary,* Shirer continued his career in radio and newspaper reporting until being inexplicably blacklisted during the McCarthy era. "I became unemployable," he told the *New York Times Book Review.* "I was broke, with two kids in school. Some of my friends were editors and would pay me for a piece, but nothing was ever published. I then decided I would speak my piece on the lecture trail. I spent almost five years when my sole income was from these one-night stands at universities. They were almost the only place in the country that still had some sort of respect for freedom of speech."

Being blacklisted did, however, give Shirer the time he needed to research and write the book many regard as his best, the massive, 1,245-page *The Rise and Fall of the Third Reich.* "The work of a newspaperman, not a university scholar," as the author described it, *The Rise and Fall of the Third Reich* took Shirer ten years to complete; among his major sources were his own reports on events of the era, transcripts of the Nuremberg Trial, diaries, and a wealth of captured German documents. The result, noted G. A. Craig in the *New York Herald Tribune Book Review,* is "a book that will please [Shirer's] admirers, make him many new ones, and perhaps, by the force of its narrative, help restore the perspective of a generation which, in its preoccupation with present world dangers, has forgotten how desperate our situation seemed when Hitler's monstrous tyranny was at the height of its power. . . . Mr. Shirer's own intense interest in his subject has been reflected in his writing: and this and his excellent taste in anecdotes and striking details make this an immensely readable book."

Many critics marveled at the author's ability to organize and present a vast array of basically familiar material in such an attention-riveting fashion. As Bernard Levin reported in *Spectator,* Shirer took the available information "and sifted and kneaded it until it takes on a new, clear, polished aspect." Though the *New York Times Book Review* essayist H. R. Trevor-Roper would like to have seen Shirer cover certain topics in greater detail or with more skill, he decided that such criticism is "trivial" when one considered "the greatness of his achievement" in bringing together the memories of living witnesses and historical truth. "This is a splendid work of scholarship," Trevor-Roper added, "objective in method, sound in judgment, inescapable in its conclusions." In short, declared Alan Bullock in his *Guardian* review, "neither Mr. Shirer nor the reader has any reason to regret the five years' hard work he put into writing [*The Rise and Fall of the Third Reich*]. . . . There are half a dozen books on Nazi Germany which I should rate higher as historical studies of particular aspects, but I can think of none which I would rather put in the hands of anyone who wanted to find out what happened in Germany between 1930 and 1945, and why the history of those years should never be forgotten."

Both Naomi Bliven in the *New Yorker* and Telford Taylor in the *Saturday Review* were pleased to note that despite Shirer's obvious hatred of Hitler and Nazism, he did not try to moralize. Bliven, for example, pointed out that Shirer "knew a great deal about the Nazis before he began his researches; he was, in fact, an

expert—a man who knows so much that he knows how much more there is to know. His book is a judicious blend of several kinds of knowledge. . . . [The result is] a literary scale model of an era. And while it is impossible to write a book about Nazi Germany without writing a book against Nazi Germany, Mr. Shirer neither moralizes nor argues but simply presents." Taylor made a similar assessment, stating: "Some history is Olympian and objective; this is personal and passionate. . . . Passionately written as it is, [*The Rise and Fall of the Third Reich*] is rarely marred by prejudice. For the most part, the diction is restrained and poised, and the judgments tempered and well-supported. The level of factual accuracy is high. . . . Mr. Shirer is a journalist, and his book carries the marks of his profession at its best."

The challenges of old age did little to diminish Shirer's writing habits. Beginning in 1976 and stretching to 1990, he published a three-volume autobiography entitled *Twentieth Century Journey: A Memoir of a Life and the Times.* The first volume, *The Start, 1904-1930,* concerns his Midwestern youth and his early career work in Paris. The second installment, *The Nightmare Years, 1930-1940,* covers his work as a foreign correspondent for print and radio, and the final volume, *A Native's Return, 1945-1988,* chronicles his years of disappointment and difficulty as a blacklisted journalist, as well as his triumph with the publication of *The Rise and Fall of the Third Reich.* Shirer told the *New York Times* that his voluminous memoir offers "one man's journey through the 20th century, a time that saw more changes on the planet than in the previous 1,900 years." He added: "Luck, of fate, or God, or whatever it is that determines the extent of our lives, allowed me to live through most of this tumultuous 20th century and through a sizable chunk of our country's existence."

New York Times Book Review correspondent Alan Brinkley observed that Volume III of *Twentieth Century Journey* provides evidence that "Shirer's preoccupation with Germany is not just a reflection of his fascination with the Nazi past. It is also a reflection of his own difficulties in coming to terms with the America he encountered when he returned home in 1945." The key difficulty, according to Brinkley, was the widespread high level of anti-Communist concern that resulted in Shirer's firing by CBS in 1947 and his being blacklisted for the next fifteen years, even though there was no indication that Shirer had Communist leanings. The author's long-lived resentment is clear, Brinkley noted. In the *Christian Science Monitor,* Gregory M. Lamb concluded of the same work: "Shirer largely succeeds in making the pages fly by. And while the book builds to no great single dramatic climax or tidy conclusion (how many real lives do?), it tugs the reader along by inches: a vignette of a famous friend here, a scrap of diary there, a reminiscence followed by an observation. No clever word play here: This is storytelling that puts the story first, whether small or great, artful in its lack of artifice."

A long fascination with the life and works of Leo Tolstoy led Shirer to his last major project, a book-length study of Tolstoy's tumultuous marriage and his ultimate escape from it. *Love and Hatred: The Troubled Marriage of Leo and Sonya Tolstoy* was published in mid-1994, several months after Shirer's death. Using the extensive diary entries of both Leo and Sonya Tolstoy, some of which had not been available to American scholars before, Shirer explored the many forces, both internal and external, that contributed to the acrimony in the Tolstoy household. *Christian Science Monitor* correspondent Merle Rubin noted that Shirer "completed the book in his 89th year, aided in this ambitious endeavor by his Russian-born wife, who translated the diaries for him. Drawing on these and other sources, Shirer has constructed a vividly close-up, year-by-year, sometimes day-by-day, account of a marriage that was a lot more like war than peace."

Spectator reviewer James Buchan called *Love and Hatred* "an efficient, literate, cautious and unobtrusive account," adding: "Shirer knows it is unwise to distribute blame within a marriage. One comes away with fresh admiration at the professionalism of American reporters of the heroic era." Likewise, *New Yorker* correspondent Francine du Plessix Gray noted: "This is the first work in English to focus exclusively on the last decades of the Tolstoys' marriage . . . and its closing chapters are the most powerful to date on the writer's extraordinary end." The book also is more sympathetic to Sonya than were previous accounts, she observed. While finding some of the work "shallow" and "slipshod," Du Plessix Gray concluded that, in its best moments, "Shirer's book is a marvelous commentary on the toll of genius: on its possessors; on the ill-fated persons called to be their helpmates; on the dreadful frailty of their marriages; and on the lucid opacity that needs to be preserved in all marital unions."

Determined to finish his Tolstoy book before he died, despite severe heart problems, Shirer completed his task and dedicated *Love and Hatred* to his wife and his cardiologist. He died in Boston on December 28, 1993.

BIOGRAPHICAL/CRITICAL SOURCES:

BOOKS

Contemporary Authors New Revisions Series, Volume 55, Gale (Detroit), 1997.
Dictionary of Literary Biography, Volume 4, Gale, 1980.

PERIODICALS

American Scholar, summer, 1995, pp. 464-67.
Atlantic Monthly, September, 1941; December, 1960; December, 1969.
Books, June 22, 1941.
Catholic World, October, 1941.
Christian Science Monitor, June 30, 1941; October 20, 1960; April 20, 1990, p. 14; August 17, 1994, p. 13.
Commonweal, August 1, 1941.
Guardian, November 11, 1960.
Los Angeles Times, February 3, 1980.
Nation, July 19, 1941; October 29, 1960.
National Review, November 26, 1976.
New Republic, June 30, 1941; November 14, 1960; February 12, 1977.
New Statesman, November 5, 1960.
Newsweek, January 28, 1980.
New Yorker, June 21, 1941; October 29, 1960; September 27, 1976; August 8, 1994, pp. 76-81.
New York Herald Tribune Book Review, October 16, 1960.
New York Herald Tribune Books, June 22, 1941.
New York Times, June 22, 1941; September 11, 1976; January 7, 1980; January 13, 1990, p. 18; February 3, 1990, p. 19.
New York Times Book Review, October 16, 1960; November 9, 1969; October 10, 1976, p. 2; July 24, 1977, p. 3; January 20, 1980; January 21, 1990, p. 15; July 24, 1994, p. 7.
Saturday Review, October 15, 1960; August 21, 1976; January 19, 1980.
Saturday Review of Literature, June 28, 1941.
Spectator, October 3, 1941; November 18, 1960; August 6, 1994, pp. 26-27.
Time, October 27, 1941; October 17, 1960; November 21, 1969.
Times Literary Supplement, December 2, 1960.
Wall Street Journal, February 8, 1990, p. A14.

Washington Post, January 29, 1980.
Washington Post Book World, November 9, 1969.

*   *   *

SHOLOKHOV, Mikhail (Aleksandrovich) 1905-1984

PERSONAL: Surname is pronounced *Shaw-loh-khoff;* born May 24, 1905, in Kruzhlino, Russia; died February 21 (some sources say February 20), 1984, in Veshenskaya, Rostov-on-Don, after a long illness; buried in Veshenskaya; son of Aleksander Mikhailo-vich (a farmer, cattle buyer, clerk, and owner of a power mill) and Anastasiya Danilovna (Chernikova) Sholokhov; married Maria Petrovna Gromoslavskaya (a teacher), 1923; children: four. *Education:* Attended public schools in Voronezh; studied under Ossip Brik and Viktor Shklovsky. *Politics:* Communist. *Avocational interests:* Fishing, hunting, breeding cattle.

ADDRESSES: Home—Stanitsa Veshenskaya, Rostov Region, Russia. *Office*—Union of Soviet Writers, Ulitsa Vorovskogo 52, Moscow, Russia.

CAREER: Writer. Held a variety of jobs, including teacher, laborer, musician, playwright, actor, and journalist; worked as a war correspondent during World War II. Elected Deputy to the Supreme Soviet, 1937; member of Communist Party of Soviet Union Central Committee and of Committee for Defense of Peace. *Military service:* Red Army, c. 1920-22, served in various capacities, including journalist, freight handler, food inspector, mason, and machine gunner.

MEMBER: Academy of Sciences of the U.S.S.R., Union of Soviet Writers.

AWARDS, HONORS: Stalin Prize, 1941, for *Tikhii Don;* Nobel Prize for literature, 1965; named Hero of Socialist Labor, 1967; received Order of Lenin eight times.

WRITINGS:

IN ENGLISH TRANSLATION

Donskie rasskazy (short stories), [Moscow], 1925, translation by H. C. Stevens published as *Tales From the Don,* Putnam, 1961, published as *Tales of the Don,* Knopf, 1962.
Tikhii Don (novel; title means "The Quiet Don"), Volumes 1-3 serialized in *Oktiabr,* 1928-32, Volume 4 serialized in *Novyi Mir,* 1937-40, revised Russian edition of Volumes 1-4 published in 1953' translation of Volumes 1-2 by Stephen Garry published as *And Quiet Flows the Don,* Putnam, 1934; translation of Volumes 3-4 by Garry published as *The Don Flows Home to the Sea,* Putnam, 1940, Knopf, 1941; translation of Volumes 1-4 published as *The Silent Don,* Knopf, 1941.
Podniataia tselina (novel), Volume 1 published serially in *Novyi Mir,* 1932, revised Russian edition, 1953, Volume 2 published serially in *Pravda, Ogonyok,* and *Oktiabr,* 1955-60; translation of Volume 1 by Garry published as *Seeds of Tomorrow,* Knopf, 1935 (published in England as *Virgin Soil Upturned,* Putnam, 1935); translation of Volume 2 by Stevens published as *Harvest on the Don,* Putnam, 1960, Knopf, 1961.
Nauka nenavisti, [Moscow], 1942, translation published as *Hate,* Foreign Languages Publishing House, 1942.
Oni srazhalis' za rodinu (novel), Volume 1, [Moscow], 1943, translation published as *They Fought for Their Country* in

Soviet Literature, July and August, 1959, excerpts from Volume 2 published in *Pravda,* 1969.

Sobranie sochinenii (collected works), eight volumes, Goslitzdat (Moscow), 1956-60, translation published as *Collected Works in Eight Volumes,* State Mutual Book, 1985.

Sud'ba cheloveka, [Moscow], 1957, translation by Robert Daglish published as *The Fate of a Man,* Foreign Languages Publishing House, 1957, published as *The Fate of Man,* Von Nostrand, 1960, translation by Stevens contained in *One Man's Destiny, and Other Stories, Articles, and Sketches* (also see below), Knopf, 1967.

Slovo o rodine (title means "A Word on Our Country"), [Moscow], 1965, translation by Stevens contained in *One Man's Destiny, and Other Stories, Articles, and Sketches,* Knopf, 1967.

Early Stories (contains "The Birthmark," "The Herdsman," "The Bastard," "The Azure Steppe," "The Foal," "Alien Blood"), translation by Daglish and Yelena Oltshuler, Progress Publishers, 1966.

Fierce and Gentle Warriors (short stories; contains "The Colt," "The Rascal," "The Fate of a Man"), translation by Miriam Morton, Doubleday, 1967.

Selected Tales From the Don (biography in English; stories in Russian), introduction and notes by C. G. Bearne, Pergamon Press, 1967.

Po veleniiu dushi, [Moscow], 1970, translation by Olga Shartse published as *At the Bidding of the Heart,* Progress Publishers, 1973.

Stories (includes "The Fate of a Man"), Progress Publishers, 1975.

OTHER

Nakhalenok, 1925, reprinted, [Moscow], 1967.

Lazorevaya Steppe (short stories; title means "The Azure Steppe"), [Moscow], 1925.

Sbornik statei, Izdvo Leningradskogo Universiteta, 1956.

Rannie rasskazy, Sovetskaia Rossia, 1961.

Plesums, romans, [Riga], 1961.

Put'dorozhen'ka, Molodaia Gvardiia, 1962.

Izbrannoe, Molodaia Gvardiia, 1968.

Rossiia v serdtse, [Moscow], 1975.

(With others) *Slovo k molodym* (addresses, essays, and lectures), [Moscow], 1975.

Quiet Flows the Don, Carroll and Graf Publishers (New York City), 1997.

MEDIA ADAPTATIONS: The Quiet Don, Virgin Soil Upturned, and "The Fate of a Man" have all been produced as motion pictures. Ivan Dzerzhinsky has written operas based on *The Quiet Don* and *Virgin Soil Upturned. Virgin Soil Upturned* has also been dramatized as a four-act play.

SIDELIGHTS: Few writers have been more revered by Soviet officials than Mikhail Sholokhov. *The Quiet Don,* his epic about life in a Cossack village from 1912 to 1922, and *Virgin Soil Upturned,* his story of the collectivization of agriculture, are part of the curriculum in all Soviet schools. Sholokhov has been showered with honors by the Communist regime, including the Stalin Prize and the Order of Lenin. In 1955 his fiftieth birthday was declared a national celebration. But Sholokhov's fame extended far beyond the borders of the Soviet Union. His works have been translated into more than forty languages and have sold millions of copies. In recognition of "the artistic power and integrity with which, in his epic of the Don, Sholokhov has given expression to the history of the Russian people," the Swedish Academy awarded him the Nobel Prize for literature in 1965.

Despite these laurels, in the 1960s Sholokhov came under increasing attack by liberal Russian intellectuals and Western observers. Some critics accused him of being nothing more than an apologist for Communism. Others suggested that *The Quiet Don* was plagiarized. Although there has been a tendency to portray Sholokhov in black-and-white terms, he was, as Alexander Werth pointed out, "an extremely puzzling man." Sholokhov ardently defended the concept of socialist realism, which holds that the purpose of art is to glorify socialism, even though his own work was not always acceptable to government censors. He repeatedly declared his loyalty to the Soviet regime, but on occasion criticized authorities.

If this "extremely puzzling man" is ever to be understood, an examination of his background is essential. He was born on a farm not far from the river Don. This region was dominated by the Cossacks, a privileged group of people who were required to serve in the Russian Army and who were often used by the czar to suppress revolutionary movements. Sholokhov's father, Alexander Mikhailovich Sholokhov, was an "outlander" whose family had moved to Veshenskaya from the Ryazan region near Moscow. His mother, Anastasiya Danilovna Chernikova, was half-Turkish and half-Cossack. While working as a maid in the Sholokhov household, she met and fell in love with the young Alexander Mikhailovich. When she discovered she was pregnant, the older Sholokhovs were so dismayed by the prospect of their son wedding a peasant that they quickly married the servant girl off to an elderly Cossack officer. Not one to be thwarted by his parents, Alexander Mikhailovich collected his inheritance, purchased his own house, and hired Anastasiya Danilovna as his servant.

Since her legal husband was a Cossack, when she gave birth to Mikhail in 1905, he inherited all the rights and privileges of the Cossacks. When the old man died in 1912, however, Anastasiya Danilovna and Alexander Mikhailovich were officially married. This act meant that Mikhail lost his Cossack status. "What problems this may have caused a seven-year-old boy we do not know," D. H. Stewart noted in *Mikhail Sholokhov: A Critical Introduction,* "though echoes of traumatic discomfiture can be detected in Sholokhov's early stories about children. The crucial fact is that Sholokhov lacked full Cossack status."

In 1922 Sholokhov went to Moscow to resume his education. While he was in that city he came under the tutelage of writers Ossip Brik and Viktor Shklovsky, and his essays and short stories began to appear in print. He returned to Veshenskaya in 1923 to marry Maria Gromoslavskaya, the daughter of a clerk in a Cossack regiment. After living for a short time in Moscow, Sholokhov and his wife settled down in the Don Region, where he lived until his death in 1984. Sholokhov found living on his native turf to be much more conducive to his writing than big-city life. He distrusted the urban intellectuals whom he had met in Moscow; besides, he had already determined that his literary creations would deal with the people of the Don Region. "I wanted," he later recalled, "to write about the people among whom I was born and whom I knew."

This regional interest is reflected in his first two books, *Tales of the Don* and *The Azure Steppe,* both of which were published in 1925. In retrospect, some critics discerned in these short story collections the same qualities that distinguish Sholokhov's subsequent work. For instance, Marc Slonim remarked in *Modern Russian Literature: From Chekhov to the Present,* " 'Tales of the Don' contains all the elements that later made Sholokhov a master of representational narrative; tense dramatic plots, fresh landscape, catching humor and a racy, uninhibited popular idiom. It is true that they are lacking in depth and character portrayal, but these primitive stories about primitive men are interesting as a document of an unsettled time, and they offer revealing material about the origins of an important Soviet writer." Commenting on the stories in *The Azure Steppe,* Ernest J. Simmons declared in *Russian Fiction and Soviet Ideology: Introduction to Fedin, Leonov, and Sholokhov,* that "we see in embryo in these early tales the future powerful psychological realist as he creates characters and bold, dramatic situations."

In October of 1925, when he was only twenty-one, Sholokhov began writing his masterpiece, *The Quiet Don,* a work that took him nearly fourteen years to complete. From 1925 to 1930 he worked on *The Quiet Don* almost constantly. In order to collect material for his book, he examined documents in the archives in Moscow and Rostov, listened to the tales of his Don Cossack neighbors, and read newspapers from the czarist era. The first two segments of *The Quiet Don* were published serially in *Oktiabr* in 1928 and 1929. Because of objections by Communist officials that the book was not sufficiently proletarian in outlook, publication ceased in April of 1929. It did not resume until 1932, when Sholokhov gained full membership into the Communist party. At this time the novelist became increasingly involved with public affairs. This new demand on his time, coupled with further censorship problems, delayed the publication of the final installment of *The Quiet Don* until 1940. *The Quiet Don* was published in English in two parts: *And Quiet Flows the Don* and *The Don Flows Home to the Sea.*

Sholokhov's epic portrays the life of the Don Cossacks during World War I and the Bolshevik Revolution. Because of the book's huge cast of characters and panoramic sweep, some critics have termed it "Tolstoyan." The central figure in the story is Gregor Melekhov, a young Cossack so beset by conflicting loyalties that he comes to believe that all is meaningless. Most Western critics feel that *The Quiet Don* demonstrates the principle of historical inevitability, in which people must either adapt to or be destroyed by historical forces. Rufus W. Mathewson, for instance, commented in *The Positive Hero in Russian Literature* that the theme of *The Quiet Don* is that "private moral judgment is sometimes irrelevant to the higher struggles of historical forces, and . . . in this fact there is genuine human tragedy."

One of the most striking characteristics of *The Quiet Don* is its dispassionate objectivity. Sholokhov's allegiance to the Communist party, Slonim pointed out, "did not affect his artistic integrity and his objectivity in description. . . . *The Quiet Don* told a story of nation-wide significance. . . . Sholokhov never subordinated these stories to his political ideas, never used his plot to drive a point home." Writing in *Introduction to Russian Realism,* Simmons also remarked upon the lack of political posturing in *The Quiet Don:* "*The Quiet Don* . . . represents with near perfection that fusion of traditional Russian realism with Soviet socialist realism, and was written by a Communist who, because of his artistic integrity, all but refused to sacrifice either the logic of his design or—in the Tolstoyan sense—the truth of his hero to extraneous demands of Party doctrine. If there is any point in the old cliche that all literature is propaganda, but not all propaganda is literature, then it may be said that propaganda is brilliantly sublimated in *The Quiet Don.*"

Between the publication of the third and fourth volumes of *The Quiet Don,* Sholokhov began work on *Virgin Soil Upturned.* This novel tells the story of the efforts to organize collective farming in

the Cossack village of Gremyachy Log. Sholokhov had witnessed both the virtues and the drawbacks of this system in his own village of Veshenskaya. In 1933 he became so incensed at some of the injustices perpetrated against the Cossack farmers that he wrote a letter of complaint to Stalin. Later, in 1937 and 1938, he displayed a similar courage when he helped reinstate some local Communist officials who had been wrongfully convicted.

In Volume I of *Virgin Soil Upturned,* as in his personal life, Sholokhov had the courage to point out both the pros and cons of collective farming. A critic for the *Saturday Review* wrote that in this book, "the artist in Sholokhov triumphs over the propagandist, for not only are we presented with the wonderfully sympathetic picture of the Cossacks' love for their land and their fierce determination to acquire it for themselves, but the absurdities of the whole Soviet mechanising system and the stupidities of its officials are relentlessly exposed with an audacity that is almost incredible." The explanation for Sholokhov's audacity, Mihajlo Mihajlov observed in *Russian Themes,* "lies in the fact that Sholokhov had been dedicated to the Party heart and soul all his life and was a true believer in Communism, just like the people who crucified Russia, and he could therefore allow himself to depict reality much more truthfully than those who did not share his belief. He described reality honestly because he believed that in spite of all sacrifices the imposed collectivization would benefit Russia in the long run."

In Volume II of *Virgin Soil Upturned* (published in the United States as *Harvest on the Don*), the propaganda is much more overt. More than twenty-five years elapsed between the publication of the first and second volumes, and rumors circulated that the reason for the long delay in publication was that Sholokhov had been fighting with Communist censors about the conclusion of the novel. When the final installment of *Virgin Soil Upturned* appeared in *Pravda* in February of 1960, Sholokhov denied that he had changed the ending to conform with the party line. Many American critics, however, complained about the book's rigid adherence to Communist dogma, and several felt that he had let ideological considerations take precedence over artistic integrity. Anthony West asserted in the *New Yorker* that "it is all too clear in 'Harvest on the Don' that Sholokhov's gifts have been eroded by a lifetime in a literary world ruled by the inevitably second-rate utilitarian aesthetics that foster this kind of thing. His intuitive grasp of what writing can and should be . . . has deserted him, and he now alternates uneasily between broad vulgarities and parodies of the official style."

In *They Fought for Their Country,* Sholokhov set out to give a fictional account of the Soviet people's valiant struggles during the German invasion of World War II. Sholokhov had ample opportunity to observe the war effort, for he served as a correspondent on the front lines. Volume I of *They Fought for Their Country,* published in 1943, describes the Russian retreat in the Don area. Further installments of the novel were not published until 1969, when excerpts began to appear in *Pravda.* At that time it was announced that Volume II would be published shortly, but it has never appeared. The excerpts in *Pravda* contained an unfavorable depiction of Stalin's capacity as a wartime leader, and some observers believe that the complete book was never published because of this negative portrait.

Another reason for Sholokhov's relative silence in the past four decades was censorship problems. Despite his avowal that he was "first and foremost a Communist," Sholokhov often quarreled with censors when they attempted to inject political messages into his literary work. In the 1930s he was compelled by censors to make many revisions in the original text of *The Quiet Don.* In an edition that was published in 1953, the novel was revised extensively to adhere more closely to the Communist party line. It is not clear whether this bowdlerized version was prepared with the approval of Sholokhov, however. In 1956, after Stalin's death, a new edition of *The Quiet Don* came out, similar in nearly every way to the original. As mentioned previously, there are also reports that Sholokhov had difficulties getting *Harvest on the Don* and *They Fought for Their Country* past government censors.

Whatever difficulties Sholokhov may have had with censors in private, publicly he stoutly denied allegations that he had to alter his work. In 1965, when asked about literary freedom in the Soviet Union, he asserted: "No one is being prevented from writing anything he wants to. The only problem is how to write it and for what purpose. There is a way of writing everything honestly. I stand for those writers who look honestly into the face of Soviet power and publish their works here and not abroad." Although there is evidence that Sholokhov often chafed under the bonds of socialist realism, he publicly averred that he was a supporter of that doctrine. In his Nobel Prize acceptance speech, he extolled socialist realism because "it expresses a philosophy of life that accepts neither a turning away from the world nor a flight from reality, a philosophy that enables one to comprehend goals that are dear to the hearts of millions of people and to light up their path in the struggle."

Sholokhov's criticism of his fellow writers aroused the anger of many literary figures on both sides of the Iron Curtain. After his attack on Sinyavsky and Daniel, Soviet writer Lydia Chukovskaya wrote a scathing open letter to him in which she accused him of literary sterility. In an even more vociferous attack, Solzhenitsyn denounced Sholokhov as a plagiarist. Specifically, he charged that *The Quiet Don* was actually written by Fyodor Kryukov, a Cossack who had served with the Whites during the Civil War. After Kryukov died in 1920, Solzhenitsyn maintained, Sholokhov got his hands on the manuscript, added some sections sympathetic to the Communist cause, and then passed it off as his own.

Solzhenitsyn's charges are nothing new. Rumors began circulating that Sholokhov plagiarized *The Quiet Don* as early as 1928. In 1977 Roy Medvedev wrote a study of the case, *Problems in the Literary Biography of Mikhail Sholokhov.* Among the arguments that Medvedev cites as evidence that Sholokhov was not the sole author of *The Quiet Don* are his young age when he began writing the novel, the low level of his succeeding work, and the humanism displayed in *The Quiet Don* (which Medvedev thinks Sholokhov has never personally demonstrated). Other commentators have suggested that Sholokhov may have used Kryukov's manuscript as source material, but that he reworked it into his own novel. It is unlikely that the issue will ever be resolved. The original manuscript of the book was destroyed during a German bombing raid in World War II, so it can provide no clues for investigators. Sholokhov always dismissed charges of plagiarism as nonsense.

BIOGRAPHICAL/CRITICAL SOURCES:

BOOKS

Alexandrova, Vera, *A History of Soviet Literature,* translated by Mina Ginsburg, Doubleday, 1963.
Carlisle, Olga, *Voices in the Snow,* Random, 1962.
Contemporary Literary Criticism, Gale (Detroit), Volume 7, 1977; Volume 15, 1980.
Ermolaev, Herman, *Mikhail Sholokhov and His Art,* Princeton University Press, 1983.

Hayward, Max, and Edward L. Crowley, editors, *Soviet Literature in the Sixties,* Praeger, 1964.
Klimenko, Michael, *World of Young Sholokhov: Vision of Violence,* Christopher Publishing House, 1972.
Mathewson, Rufus W., Jr., *The Positive Hero in Russian Literature,* Columbia University Press, 1958, 2nd edition, Stanford University Press, 1975.
Medvedev, Roy A., *Problems in the Literary Biography of Mikhail Sholokhov,* Cambridge University Press, 1977.
Mihajlov, Mihajlo, *Russian Themes,* Farrar, Straus, 1968.
Muchnic, Helen, *From Gorky to Pasternak,* Random, 1961.
Muchnic, *Russian Writers: Notes and Essays,* Random House, 1971.
Mukerjee, G., *Mikhail Sholokhov: A Critical Introduction,* Northern Book Centre (New Delhi), 1992.
Simmons, Ernest J., *Russian Fiction and Soviet Ideology: Introduction to Fedin, Leonov, and Sholokhov,* Columbia University Press, 1958.
Simmons, *Introduction to Russian Realism,* Indiana University Press, 1965.
Slonim, Marc, editor, *Modern Russian Literature: From Chekhov to the Present,* Oxford University Press, 1953.
Stewart, D. H., *Mikhail Sholokhov: A Critical Introduction,* University of Michigan Press, 1967.

PERIODICALS

Atlantic Monthly, March, 1961.
Christian Science Monitor, November 20, 1935; February 23, 1961.
Columbia University Forum, winter, 1961.
Commonweal, May 11, 1962; October 20, 1967.
London Magazine, April, 1967.
Nation, July 11, 1934; August 16, 1941.
New Republic, August 15, 1934; December 25, 1935; August 18, 1941; May 8, 1961.
New Statesman, October 29, 1960; May 6, 1977.
New Yorker, August 9, 1941; April 29, 1961.
New York Herald Tribune, July 3, 1934.
New York Review of Books, June 15, 1967.
New York Times, November 10, 1935; August 3, 1941; March 4, 1962; October 16, 1965; December 1, 1965; December 10, 1965; December 11, 1965; April 2, 1966; May 27, 1969; June 25, 1970.
New York Times Book Review, February 19, 1961; March 4, 1962; March 5, 1967; August 20, 1967.
Observer Review, February, 1967.
Russian Review, April, 1957.
Saturday Review, October 26, 1935; February 18, 1961; February 24, 1962; June 17, 1967.
Saturday Review of Literature, July 7, 1934; August 9, 1941.
Spectator, April 6, 1934; October 11, 1935; October 18, 1940.
Time, February 24, 1961; September 16, 1974.
Times Literary Supplement, April 5, 1934; October 5, 1940; November 4, 1960; December 1, 1961; February 16, 1967.
World Literature Today, winter, 1978.
Yale Review, autumn, 1941.

*   *   *

SHUTE, Nevil
See NORWAY, Nevil Shute

SIDDONS, (Sybil) Anne Rivers 1936-

PERSONAL: Born January 9, 1936, in Atlanta, GA; daughter of Marvin (an attorney) and Katherine (a secretary; maiden name, Kitchens) Rivers; married Heyward L. Siddons (a business partner and creative director), 1966; children: (stepsons) Lee, Kemble, Rick, David. *Education:* Auburn University, B.A.A., 1958; attended Atlanta School of Art, c. 1958. *Avocational interests:* Swimming, cooking, reading, cats.

ADDRESSES: Home—3767 Vermont Rd. N.E., Atlanta, GA 30319; and (summer) Osprey Cottage, Brooklin, ME 04616.

CAREER: Worked in advertising with Retail Credit Co., c. 1959, Citizens & Southern National Bank, 1961-63, Burke-Dowling Adams, 1967-69, and Burton Campbell Advertising, 1969-74; full-time writer, 1974–. Member of governing board, Woodward Academy; member of publications board and arts and sciences honorary council, Auburn University, 1978-83.

MEMBER: Chevy Chase Club, Every Saturday Club, Ansley Golf Club.

AWARDS, HONORS: Alumna achievement award in arts and humanities, Auburn University, 1985; Honorary Doctorate in Humanities, Oglethorpe University, 1991.

WRITINGS:

NOVELS

Heartbreak Hotel, Simon & Schuster (New York City), 1976.
The House Next Door (horror), Simon & Schuster, 1978.
Fox's Earth, Simon & Schuster, 1980.
Homeplace, Harper (New York City), 1987.
Peachtree Road, Harper, 1988.
King's Oak, HarperCollins (New York City), 1990.
Outer Banks, HarperCollins, 1991.
Colony, HarperCollins, 1992.
Hill Towns, HarperCollins, 1993.
Downtown, HarperCollins, 1994.
Fault Lines, HarperCollins, 1995.
John Chancellor Makes Me Cry (essays), Doubleday, 1975.
Go Straight on Peachtree (nonfiction guide book), Dolphin Books (New York City), 1978.
Heartbreak Hotel, Beeler Large Print (Hampton Falls, NH), 1996.
Up Island, HarperCollins, 1997.
Low Country, HarperCollins, 1998.

Contributor to *Gentleman's Quarterly, Georgia, House Beautiful, Lear's, Reader's Digest, Redbook,* and *Southern Living.* Senior editor, *Atlanta,* 1964-67.

MEDIA ADAPTATIONS: Heartbreak Hotel was adapted as the film *Heart of Dixie,* Orion Pictures, 1989.

SIDELIGHTS: Novelist Anne Rivers Siddons identifies herself as an author of the South—an author of Atlanta in particular. "Everything I know and do is of here, of the South," she says in an interview in *Southern Living.* Her novels are most often concerned with the lives of Southern women; later books have occasionally seen these characters transplanted to other locales. Reviewer Michael Skube has called Siddons "Atlanta's best known writer."

Siddons's first book, *John Chancellor Makes Me Cry,* chronicles one year of her life in Atlanta, humorously reflecting on the frustrations and joys of life—serving jury duty, hosting parties, and taking care of a husband suffering with the flu. The author's style in *John Chancellor Makes Me Cry* has been favorably compared to that of Erma Bombeck, whose own review of the book praises Siddons: "She is unique. She's an original in her essays that combine humor, intimacy and insight into a marriage." Bombeck finds the most "poignant and very real" chapter to be the one describing "the month [Siddons's] husband lost his job, her Grandmother died, a Siamese cat they were keeping for a friend was hit by a car, their house was burgled and their Persian cat contracted a $50-a-week disease."

Siddons turned to fiction with her first novel, *Heartbreak Hotel,* the story of a young Southern woman who must choose between her two suitors and the very different lifestyles they represent. Katha Pollitt asserts: "The author dissects the 1950's, Southern style, with a precision that is anything but nostalgic; and yet somehow the very wealth of detail she provides makes *Heartbreak Hotel* a good-natured rather than an angry look backward. . . . This is a marvelously detailed record of a South as gone with the wind as Scarlett O'Hara's."

The House Next Door, Siddons's tale of an affluent couple whose lives are changed by the mysterious evils occurring in a neighboring house, was praised by Stephen King. In his critique on the horror genre, *Stephen King's Danse Macabre,* King devoted an entire chapter to an analysis of *The House Next Door,* comparing it to Shirley Jackson's *Haunting of Hill House.* Siddons, in an interview in *Publishers Weekly,* calls the book "something of a lark. It's different from anything I've ever written, or probably ever will. But I like to read occult, supernatural stories. Some of the world's great writers have written them, and I guess I wanted to see what I could do with the genre."

Later novels, such as *Homeplace* and *Peachtree Road,* won greater favor with critics and became best-sellers. Notes Bob Summers in *Publishers Weekly, Homeplace* "struck a national chord" with its account of an independent Southern-born woman returning home after more than twenty years. *Peachtree Road* is Siddons's "love letter to Atlanta," according to *Chicago Tribune* contributor Joyce Slater. "Siddons does an admirable job of tracing the city's rebirth after World War II without idealizing it." Slater concludes: *Peachtree Road* is Siddons's "most ambitious [book] to date."

Siddons's first novel set outside the South, *Colony,* is the saga of the family of a Carolinian woman who has been transplanted by marriage into the Brahmin milieu of a coastal Maine retreat. As a young bride, heroine Maude Gascoigne detests her new summer home and its people, but with the passing decades she grows to love it enough to fight hard to pass it on to her granddaughter. Joan Mooney, writing in the *New York Times Book Review,* calls Maude "a match for anything that's thrown her way—and plenty is." Others have also praised Siddons's development of character in *Colony:* a reviewer for *Publishers Weekly* describes the novel as "a page-turner by virtue of realistic characters who engage the reader's affection and concern," though *Booklist's* Denise Blank observes that "although her verbal artistry cannot be denied, Siddons never quite captures the feel of a place or a person—one is left with the impression of a very pretty painting that looks much like other very pretty paintings."

In her next novel, *Hill Towns,* Siddons again sends a Southern woman into new territory, this time even farther afield. Cat Gaillard suffers from what *Chicago Tribune* reviewer Joyce R. Slater terms "reverse acrophobia": she is only comfortable at heights that allow her to see for miles around her. She is also agoraphobic and is finally lured from an hermetic existence in her

Appalachian lookout by an invitation to a wedding in Italy. Rome, Venice, and Tuscany have the expected loosening effect on Cat, though she and her husband "will not be corrupted by decadent Europeans, but by their fellow countrymen altered by extended sojourns abroad," according to Elaine Kendall in the *Los Angeles Times*. Among these are a famous expatriate painter and his wife, who work their separate wiles on Cat and her husband, Joe. Yet Cat pulls back from the brink: in the words of Slater, "Italy and the charismatic painter, Sam Forrest, are nearly Cat's undoing. Nearly."

Many reviewers identify Siddons's greatest strength in this book as her creation of character. Writing for the *Washington Post*, Natalie Danford says that the author's "portrayals of people, . . . are often stunning." Slater too praises Siddons in this regard, writing that she "sensitively describes the confusion of a woman who opts to travel from an existence of academic, almost Elysian perfection to one of the steamiest, most chaotic cities in the world."

Downtown, Siddons's 1994 novel set in the mid-sixties, is admittedly autobiographical. The circumstances that surround its main character, Smoky O'Donnell, a 26-year-old ingenue with the dream and drive to succeed as a writer for Atlanta's trendiest magazine, mirror those of Siddons's own past. As a writer for *Downtown* magazine, Smoky sees the up and down sides of Atlanta life at a time when "promises . . . hung in the bronze air like fruit on the eve of ripeness." For Smoky some of these promises are kept, but others, such as the promise that brightens within her growing awareness of the civil rights movement, are shot down as the decade approaches its close.

Critical reaction to *Downtown* has been mixed. The reviewer for *Publishers Weekly* writes of being "disappointed in [Siddons's] uninspired and often pretentious story line," and Jean Hanff Korelitz complains in the *Washington Post Book World* that Smoky's "responses are so predictable and her path to adulthood so well-worn that we can't escape feeling that we have already read this novel, that only the names and locations have been changed." Both reviewers nevertheless write favorably of Siddons's evocation of the ambience of Atlanta in the 1960s.

In a 1994 interview for the *Atlanta Journal & Constitution*, Siddons hints that she was finished writing about Atlanta, although she toyed with the possibility of setting a future book in the nearby affluent enclave of Cobb County. But though she may take her novels out of the South, she doesn't believe she will ever take the South out of her novels. In *Southern Living* Siddons comments: "I have found I can move anywhere in my fiction. If I take it from the point of view of a Southerner traveling there, it's still an honest point of view."

BIOGRAPHICAL/CRITICAL SOURCES:

BOOKS

King, Stephen, *Stephen King's Danse Macabre*, Everest House, 1981.

PERIODICALS

Atlanta Journal & Constitution, October 9, 1988; July 14, 1991, p. N8; June 26, 1992, p. P1; June 28, 1992, p. N9; June 5, 1994, pp. M1, N10.
Booklist, May 1, 1987, p. 948; July, 1988, p. 1755; August, 1990, p. 2123; June 1, 1991, p. 1843; November 15, 1991, p. 638; April 15, 1992, p. 1643; March 15, 1993, p. 1369; May 1, 1993, p. 1548; February 15, 1994, p. 1100; May 15, 1994, p. 1645.
Book World, July 28, 1991, p. 1; June 12, 1994, p. 8.
Chicago Tribune, June 14, 1987; November 11, 1988; July 25, 1993, p. 6.
Chicago Tribune Book World, June 28, 1981.
Christian Science Monitor, July 1, 1994, p. 10.
Kirkus Reviews, April 1, 1987, p. 510; August 1, 1988, p. 1093; August 1, 1990, p. 1038; June 1, 1991, p. 692; May 1, 1992, p. 564; April 15, 1993, p. 484; May 1, 1994, p. 587.
Kliatt, spring, 1985, p. 18; July, 1994, p. 89; January, 1995, p. 52; March, 1995, p. 53.
Library Journal, June 15, 1975; April 1, 1987, p. 165; August, 1990, p. 145; October 1, 1991, p. 159; September 15, 1992, p. 108; August, 1993, p. 178; October 15, 1993, p. 110; June 15, 1994, p. 97; November 15, 1994, p. 106.
Locus, January, 1990, p. 52.
Los Angeles Times, September 3, 1993, p. E6.
Los Angeles Times Book Review, September 18, 1988, p. 10; September 16, 1990, p. 8; August 4, 1991, p. 3; October 3, 1993, p. 8; July 10, 1994, p. 14.
New York Times, September 16, 1989.
New York Times Book Review, April 13, 1975; September 12, 1976; October 23, 1977; December 10, 1978; August 30, 1987, p. 20; August 14, 1988, p. 26; January 1, 1989, p. 14; November 4, 1990, p. 33; August 2, 1992, p. 20.
Publishers Weekly, May 1, 1987, p. 55; August 5, 1988, p. 72; November 18, 1988; November 3, 1989, p. 88; February 2, 1990, p. 50; August 3, 1990, p. 62; May 31, 1991, p. 61; March 30, 1992, pp. 21-26; May 18, 1992, p. 57; May 25, 1992, p. 51; May 24, 1993, p. 67; May 23, 1994, pp. 76-77.
Southern Living, October, 1987, p. 96; March, 1991, p. 118; December, 1991, p. 83; September, 1994, p. 100.
Tribune Books (Chicago), June 14, 1987, p. 7; November 25, 1990, p. 4; July 25, 1993, p. 6.
Washington Post, August 3, 1987; July 28, 1991, p. July 13, 1993, p. E2.
Washington Post Book World, July 28, 1991, p. 1; June 12, 1994, p. 8.
Woman's Journal, February, 1995, p. 13.

*   *   *

SILKO, Leslie Marmon 1948-

PERSONAL: Born March 5, 1948, in Albuquerque, NM; daughter of Lee H. Marmon (a photographer); children: two sons. *Education:* University of New Mexico, received B.A. (summa cum laude), 1969.

ADDRESSES: Home—8000 West Camireo Del Certo, Tucson, AZ 85705.

CAREER: Associated with University of New Mexico, Albuquerque; assistant professor of English at University of Arizona, Tucson; writer.

AWARDS, HONORS: Grant from National Endowment for the Arts and poetry award from *Chicago Review*, both 1974; Pushcart Prize for poetry, 1977; John D. and Catherine T. MacArthur Foundation grant, 1983.

WRITINGS:

Laguna Woman: Poems, Greenfield Review Press, 1974.
Ceremony (novel), Viking, 1977.
Storyteller (poems and stories), Seaver Books, 1981.

(With James A. Wright) *With the Delicacy and Strength of Lace: Letters Between Leslie Marmon Silko and James Wright,* Graywolf Press, 1985.

Almanac of the Dead (novel), Simon & Shuster, 1991.

Sacred Water: Narratives and Pictures (autobiography), Flood Plain (Tucson, AZ), 1993.

Yellow Woman and a Beauty of the Spirit: Essays on Native American Life Today, Simon & Schuster, 1996.

Gardens in the Dunes (novel), Simon & Schuster, 1998.

Author of stories, including "Lullaby," "Yellow Woman," and "Tony's Story." Work represented in anthologies, including *The Man to Send Rainclouds,* Viking, 1974. Contributor to periodicals, including *New York Times Book Review.*

SIDELIGHTS: Leslie Marmon Silko has earned acclaim for her writings about Native Americans. She first received substantial critical attention in 1977 with her novel *Ceremony,* which tells of a half-breed war veteran's struggle for sanity after returning home from World War II. The veteran, Tayo, has difficulties adjusting to civilian life on a New Mexico Indian reservation. He is haunted by his violent actions during the war and by the memory of his brother's death in the same conflict. Deranged and withdrawn, Tayo initially wastes away on the reservation while his fellow Indian veterans drink excessively and rail against racism.

After futilely exploring Navajo rituals in an attempt to discover some sense of identity, Tayo befriends a wise old half-breed, Betonie, who counsels him on the value of ceremony. Betonie teaches Tayo that ceremony is not merely formal ritual but a means of conducting one's life. With the old man's guidance, Tayo learns that humanity and the cosmos are aspects of one vast entity, and that ceremony is the means to harmony within that entity.

With its depiction of life on the Indian reservation and its exploration of philosophical issues, *Ceremony* established Silko as an important artist from the American Indian community. Charles R. Larson, writing in *Washington Post Book World,* called *Ceremony* a novel "powerfully conceived" and attributed much of the book's success to Silko's incorporation of Indian elements. "Tayo's experiences may suggest that *Ceremony* falls nicely within the realm of American fiction about World War II," Larson wrote. "Yet Silko's novel is also strongly rooted within the author's own tribal background and that is what I find especially valuable here." Similarly, Frank MacShane wrote in the *New York Times Book Review* that Silko skillfully incorporates aspects of Indian storytelling techniques into *Ceremony.* "She has used animal stories and legends to give a fabulous dimension to her novel," he declared. MacShane added that Silko was "without question . . . the most accomplished Indian writer of her generation."

Some critics considered *Ceremony* a powerful confirmation of cosmic order. Elaine Jahner, who reviewed the novel for *Prairie Schooner Review,* wrote that the book "is about the power of timeless, primal forms of seeing and knowing and relating to all of life." She observed that the Indian custom of communal storytelling provided the novel with both theme and structure and added that Tayo eventually "perceives something of his responsibilities in shaping the story of what human beings mean to each other." And Peter G. Beidler focused on the importance of storytelling in *Ceremony* by writing in *American Indian Quarterly* that the novel is both "the story of a life [and] the life of a story." Beidler called *Ceremony* "a magnificent novel" that "brings life to human beings and makes readers care about them."

After the publication of *Ceremony* in 1977, Silko received greater recognition for her earlier short stories. Among her most noteworthy stories were "Lullaby," "Yellow Woman," and "Tony's Story." "Lullaby" is an old woman's recollection of how her children were taken away for education and how they returned to a culture that no longer seemed familiar or comfortable. Writing in the *Southwest Review,* Edith Blicksilver called "Lullaby" Silko's "version of the Native American's present-day reality." "Yellow Woman" concerns a Navajo woman who is abducted by a cattle ranger whom she suspects to be the embodiment of a spirit. In *MELUS,* A. LaVonne Ruoff wrote that "'Yellow Woman' is based on traditional abduction tales, [but] it is more than a modernized version." Ruoff attributed the difference to Silko's emphasis on "the character's confusion about what is real and what is not." "Tony's Story" is about an Indian who kills a vicious policeman. In *MELUS,* Ruoff noted Silko's ability to equate the murder with the Pueblo exorcism ritual. "Tony's Story," Ruoff declared, "deals with the return to Indian ritual as a means of coping with external forces."

Some of Silko's stories were included in the anthology *The Man to Send Rainclouds,* which derives its title from Silko's humorous tale of conflict between a Catholic priest and Pueblo Indians during an Indian funeral. Silko also included some of her early stories in her 1981 collection *Storyteller,* which features her poetry as well. In the *New York Times Book Review,* N. Scott Momaday called *Storyteller* "a rich, many-faceted book." Momaday acknowledged Silko's interests in ritual and the Indian storytelling tradition and her ability to portray characters and situations. "At her best," Momaday contended, "Leslie Silko is very good indeed. She has a sharp sense of the way in which the profound and the mundane often run together." James Polk gave similar praise in *Saturday Review* when he wrote that Silko's "perceptions are accurate, and her style reflects the breadth, the texture, the mortality of her subjects."

In 1983 Silko received an award from the prestigious MacArthur Foundation for her small but influential body of work. The award—for $176,000—was particularly appreciated by Silko, who produced most of her writings while also working as an English professor. Acknowledging her cash prize, she told *Time* that she was now "a little less beholden to the everyday world." Indeed, Silko used that money to work on an epic novel, *Almanac of the Dead,* that eventually took ten years to complete. Published in 1991, the novel "ranges over five centuries of the struggle between Native Americans and Europeans and focuses upon a half-breed Tucson family voyaging to Africa and Israel," noted John Domini in the *San Francisco Review of Books.* In addition to its wide scope, the novel contains a multitude of original, colorful characters. As *Bloomsbury Review* contributor M. Annette Jaimes explained, "Throughout the book, this entire wondrous and seedy spectrum of humanity parades itself endlessly across the knotted tightrope of a world gone hopelessly, splendidly, and quite believably mad."

Some reviewers of *Almanac of the Dead* felt that this array of characters was the novel's weakest aspect: Writing in the *Los Angeles Times Book Review,* Paul West remarked that the author's "myth remains unforgettable, whereas her characters—too many, introduced too soon and then abandoned for long stretches—remain invisible and forgettable." Silko herself acknowledged that she experimented with characterization in the novel. In an interview with Linda Niemann for the *Women's Review of Books,* Silko commented: "I was trying to give history a character. It was as if native spirits were possessing me, like a spell. . . . I knew I was breaking rules about not doing characters in the traditional way, but this other notion took over—and I couldn't tell you rationally why. I knew it was about time and about old notions of history, and about narrative being alive." While West called the book "an excellent work of myth and a second-rate novel," Jaimes concluded, "*Almanac* must be ranked as a masterpiece."

BIOGRAPHICAL/CRITICAL SOURCES:

BOOKS

Allen, Paula Gunn, editor, *Studies in American Indian Literature: Critical Essays and Course Designs,* Modern Language Association of America, 1983, pp. 127-33.

Contemporary Literary Criticism, Gale (Detroit), Volume 23, 1983; Volume 74, 1993.

Dictionary of Literary Biography, Volume 143: *American Novelists since World War II, Third Series,* Gale, 1994; Volume 175: *Native American Writers of the United States,* Gale, 1997.

Jaskoski, Helen, *Leslie Marmon Silko: A Study of the Short Fiction,* Twayne, 1998.

Native North American Literature, Gale, 1994.

Patraka, Vivian, and Louise A. Tilly, editors, *Feminist Re-Visions: What Has Been and Might Be,* University of Michigan Press, 1983, pp. 26-42.

Rand, Naomi R., *Silko, Morrison, and Roth: Studies in Survival,* P. Lang, 1998.

Salyer, Gregory, *Leslie Marmon Silko,* Twayne, 1997.

Scholer, Bo, editor, *Coyote Was Here: Essays on Contemporary Native American Literary and Political Mobilization,* Seklos, 1984, pp. 116-23.

Seyerstad, Per, *Leslie Marmon Silko,* Boise State University, 1980, pp. 45-50.

Velie, Alan R., *Four American Indian Literary Masters: N. Scott Momaday, James Welch, Leslie Marmon Silko, and Gerald Vizenor,* University of Oklahoma Press, 1982, pp. 106-21.

PERIODICALS

American Indian Quarterly, winter, 1977-78; fall, 1988, pp. 313-28; fall, 1990, pp. 367-77; spring, 1990, pp. 155-59.

Arizona Quarterly, spring, 1988, pp. 86-94.

Bloomsbury Review, April/May, 1992, p. 5.

Booklist, February 15, 1996, p. 988.

Chicago Tribune, December 1, 1991, p. 30.

Critique, spring, 1983, pp. 158-72.

Denver Quarterly, winter, 1980, pp. 22-30.

Harper's, June, 1977.

Los Angeles Times, January 13, 1992, pp. E1, E3.

Los Angeles Times Book Review, January 4, 1987; February 2, 1992, p. 8.

MELUS, winter, 1978; summer, 1981; winter, 1983, pp. 37-48; spring, 1985, pp. 25-36, 65-78; spring, 1988, pp. 83-95; summer, 1993, pp. 47-60.

Ms., July, 1981.

New Leader, June 6, 1977.

Newsweek, July 4, 1977, pp. 73-74; November 18, 1991, p. 84.

New York Times, May 25, 1981.

New York Times Book Review, June 12, 1977; May 24, 1981; December 22, 1991, p. 6.

Prairie Schooner Review, winter, 1977-78.

San Francisco Review of Books, fall, 1992, p. 18.

Saturday Review, May, 1981.

Southwest Review, spring, 1979.

Time, August 8, 1983.

Voice Literary Supplement, November, 1991, pp. 17-18.

Washington Post Book World, April 24, 1977.

Western American Literature, February, 1994, pp. 301-12.

Women's Review of Books, July, 1992, p. 10.

*   *   *

SILLITOE, Alan 1928-

PERSONAL: Born March 4, 1928, in Nottingham, England; son of Christopher (a tannery laborer) and Sabina (Burton) Sillitoe; married Ruth Fainlight (a poet, writer, and translator), November 19, 1959; children: David Nimrod, Susan (adopted). *Education:* Left school at the age of fourteen. *Avocational interests:* Travel, shortwave radio.

ADDRESSES: Home—c/o Savage Club, 1 Whitehall Place, London, SW1A 2HD, England. *Agent*—Sheil and Associates, 14 Ladbroke Terrace, London W11 3PG, England.

CAREER: Worked in a bicycle plant, in a plywood mill, and as a capstan-lathe operator; air traffic control assistant, 1945-46; freelance writer, 1948–. *Military service:* Royal Air Force, radio operator in Malaya, 1946-49.

MEMBER: Society of Authors, Royal Geographical Society (fellow), Writers Action Group, Savage Club.

AWARDS, HONORS: Author's Club prize, 1958, for *Saturday Night and Sunday Morning;* Hawthornden Prize for Literature, 1960, for *The Loneliness of the Long-Distance Runner;* honorary fellow, Manchester Polytechnic, 1977; honorary doctorates, Nottingham Polytechnic, 1990, and Nottingham University, 1994.

WRITINGS:

POEMS

Without Beer or Bread, Outpost Publications (London), 1957.

The Rats and Other Poems, W. H. Allen (London), 1960.

A Falling Out of Love and Other Poems, W. H. Allen, 1964.

Shaman and Other Poems, Turret Books (London), 1968.

Love in the Environs of Voronezh and Other Poems, Macmillan (London), 1968, Doubleday (New York City), 1969.

(Contributor) *Poems* [by] *Ruth Fainlight, Ted Hughes, Alan Sillitoe,* Rainbow Press (London), 1971.

Canto Two of the Rats, Ithaca (London), 1973.

Storm: New Poems, W. H. Allen, 1974.

Barbarians and Other Poems, Turret Books, 1974.

(With wife, Ruth Fainlight) *Words Broadsheet Nineteen,* Words Press (Bramley, Surrey), 1975.

Snow on the North Side of Lucifer, W. H. Allen, 1979.

More Lucifer, Booth (Knotting, Bedfordshire), 1980.

Israel: Poems on a Hebrew Theme, Steam Press (London), 1981.

Sun before Departure, Grafton & Co. (London), 1984.

Tides and Stone Walls, Grafton & Co., 1986.

Collected Poems, HarperCollins (London), 1993.

NOVELS

Saturday Night and Sunday Morning (also see below), W. H. Allen, 1958, Knopf (New York City), 1959, revised edition, with an introduction by the author and commentary and notes by David Craig, Longmans, Green (London), 1968, new edition, HarperCollins, 1995.

The General (also see below), W. H. Allen, 1960, Knopf, 1961.

Key to the Door, W. H. Allen, 1961, Knopf, 1962.

The Death of William Posters (first volume of trilogy), Knopf, 1965.

A Tree on Fire (second volume of trilogy), Macmillan, 1967, Doubleday, 1968.
A Start in Life, W. H. Allen, 1970, Scribner (New York City), 1971.
Travels in Nihilon, W. H. Allen, 1971, Scribner, 1972.
The Flame of Life (third volume of trilogy), W. H. Allen, 1974.
The Widower's Son, W. H. Allen, 1976, Harper (New York City), 1977.
The Storyteller, W. H. Allen, 1979, Simon & Schuster (New York City), 1980.
Her Victory, F. Watts (New York City), 1982.
The Lost Flying Boat, Little, Brown (New York City), 1983.
Down from the Hill, Granada, 1984.
Life Goes On (sequel to *A Start in Life*), Grafton & Co., 1985.
Out of the Whirlpool, Hutchinson (London), 1987.
The Open Door, HarperCollins, 1988.
Last Loves, HarperCollins, 1989, Chivers (Boston), 1991.
Leonard's War: A Love Story, HarperCollins, 1991.
Snowstop, HarperCollins, 1994.

SHORT STORIES

The Loneliness of the Long-Distance Runner (also see below), W. H. Allen, 1959, Knopf, 1960, bound with *Sanctuary,* by Theodore Dreiser, and related poems, edited by Roy Bentley, Book Society of Canada, 1967.
The Ragman's Daughter and Other Stories, W. H. Allen, 1961, Knopf, 1964.
Guzman Go Home and Other Stories, Macmillan, 1968, Doubleday, 1969.
A Sillitoe Selection, Longmans, Green, 1968.
Men, Women and Children, W. H. Allen, 1973, Scribner, 1974.
The Second Chance and Other Stories, Simon & Schuster, 1981.
The Far Side of the Street: Fifteen Short Stories, W. H. Allen, 1988.
Collected Stories, HarperCollins, 1995.

PLAYS

Saturday Night and Sunday Morning (screenplay; based on novel of same title), Continental, 1960.
The Loneliness of the Long-Distance Runner (screenplay; based on short story of same title), Continental, 1961.
(Translator and adapter with Ruth Fainlight) Lope de Vega, *All Citizens Are Soldiers* (two acts; first produced at Theatre Royal, Stratford, London, 1967), Macmillan, 1969, Dufour (Chester Springs, PA), 1970.
Counterpoint (screenplay, based on novel *The General*), Universal, 1968.
Three Plays: The Slot Machine, The Interview, Pit Strike (*The Slot Machine,* first produced as *This Foreign Field* in London at Round House, 1970; *Pit Strike,* produced by British Broadcasting Corporation, 1977; *The Interview,* produced at the Almost Free Theatre, 1978), W. H. Allen, 1978.

JUVENILE

The City Adventures of Marmalade Jim, Macmillan, 1967.
Big John and the Stars, Robson Books (London), 1977.
The Incredible Fencing Fleas, Robson Books, 1978.
Marmalade Jim on the Farm, Robson Books, 1979.
Marmalade Jim and the Fox, Robson Books, 1985.

TRAVEL

Road to Volgograd, Knopf, 1964.
The Saxon Shore Way, Hutchinson, 1983.
Nottinghamshire (photography by David Sillitoe), Grafton & Co., 1987.

Leading the Blind: A Century of Guide Book Travel, 1815-1914, Picador, 1995, Papermac (London), 1996.
(Author of introduction) Arnold Bennett, *Riceyman Steps,* Pan Books, 1964.
(Author of introduction) Bennett, *The Old Wives' Tale,* Pan Books, 1964.
Raw Material (memoir), W. H. Allen, 1972, Scribner, 1973.
Mountains and Caverns: Selected Essays, W. H. Allen, 1975.
Down to the Bone (collection), Wheaton (Exeter), 1976.
Day Dream Communique, Sceptre (Knotting, Bedfordshire), 1977.
Every Day of the Week: An Alan Sillitoe Reader, W. H. Allen, 1987.
The Far Side of the Street, W. H. Allen, 1990.
Life without Armor (autobiography), Macmillan, 1995.

Also author of film script *Che Guevara,* 1968.

MEDIA ADAPTATIONS: Sillitoe's short story "The Ragman's Daughter" was produced as a film in 1972.

SIDELIGHTS: "I was twenty years old when I first tried to write, and it took ten years before I learned how to do it," remarked Alan Sillitoe in reference to *Saturday Night and Sunday Morning,* the novel that catapulted the thirty-year-old self-educated Briton into the literary limelight. Described by the *New Yorker*'s Anthony West as a "brilliant first book," *Saturday Night and Sunday Morning* broke new ground with its portrayal of "the true robust and earthy quality characteristic of English working-class life." Only one year later, Sillitoe was again the center of critical attention, this time for "The Loneliness of the Long-Distance Runner," the title novella in a collection of short stories that also contained some frank representations of working-class life in Britain. Although he has since written numerous novels and short stories, as well as several poems and plays, Sillitoe has almost always been evaluated in terms of these first two works. Both, in fact, are the focus of a debate that has yet to be resolved: is Alan Sillitoe a traditionalist, a sentimental throwback to writers of an earlier age, or is he a genuine "revolutionary," an Angry Young Man of the modern age?

Sillitoe populates his rather grim world with factory workers, shop girls, and other types not often depicted from the inside in English literature. Whether they are at home, at work, or relaxing in the pubs, these characters reveal themselves to be "unfamiliar with the great world of London or country houses or what is called high culture," says the *Chicago Tribune Book World*'s Kendall Mitchell. "And they don't care—they have their lives to live, their marriages to make and wreck, their passions to pursue." "The cumulative impression of Sillitoe's people," notes Charles Champlin in the *Los Angeles Times,* "is of their strength and will to survive, however forces beyond their control blunt their prospects."

John W. Aldridge expands on this idea in the book *Time to Murder and Create: The Contemporary Novel in Crisis,* but suggests that Sillitoe's belief in the power of fate hinders rather than helps the reader to understand his characters and their motivations. States the critic: "To the extent that his people are the victims of their economic situation, they are people without the power of moral freedom. And to the extent that they are unfree, and lack even the opportunity to be enticed to choose freedom and to be damned by it, they are grossly oversimplified as fictional characters." Aldridge continues, "Hence, nothing they think is interesting, nothing they do is finally worth doing, and nothing they want will in the end be of any value whatever to them. There can be no doubt that one may be impressed by this and frequently moved to compassion. But one is emphatically not moved to understanding."

Yet as even Aldridge admits, Sillitoe is a master at presenting his material in such a way that compassion, and not disgust, is what many readers feel for his rough-edged characters. Several critics, including the *Washington Post*'s Daniel O'Neill, credit the author with an "ability to blend cold-blooded rendering of the exterior world with insightful and sensitive representation of the inner workings of the characters' minds." According to Max Cosman of *Commonweal*, "such is Mr. Sillitoe's interest in his fellow man and such [is] his skill in compelling attention, that ignoble, or subnormal as his Nottinghamites are, they can [bring] forth compassion even in the midst of disapproval."

Others, however, feel that this emphasis on compassion makes Sillitoe less an Angry Young Man with a special talent for describing the plight of the proletariat than a sentimentalist who idealizes the lives of his working-class heroes. Though the *New Republic*'s Irving Howe is pleased by the lack of romanticization, "moral nagging [and] political exhortation" in *Saturday Night and Sunday Morning,* for instance, he nevertheless concludes that "in its hard-headed and undeluded way it is not quite free from sentimentality." *New York Review of Books* contributor Stanley Kauffmann is especially critical of what he feels is Sillitoe's mishandling of pathos, pointing out that "often he appeals for sympathy with music-hall blatancy." David Boroff of the *Saturday Review* agrees that Sillitoe is "sometimes betrayed by his own sentimentality," as does a *Times Literary Supplement* critic, who suggests that such lapses may stem not from the author's attitude toward his subject but from "the difficulties presented by the use of a fictitious narrator who is not supposed to be as articulate or as sophisticated as the writer himself."

A *Times Literary Supplement* critic is especially impressed by Sillitoe's "integrity of style that never falsifies the writer's role—which is why, for instance, he refuses to go on 'like a penny-a-liner to force an ending' if inspiration stops before he knows what to do with the character he has created. There may not even *be* an ending to a Sillitoe story." John Updike notices this same feature in Sillitoe's writing, pointing out in a *New Republic* article that his stories "have a wonderful way of going on, of not stopping short . . . that lifts us twice, and shows enviable assurance and abundance in the writer."

P. H. Johnson of the *New Statesman* also regards Sillitoe as "highly gifted technically: he is an excellent story-teller, and his style is perfectly adapted to his subject-matter; he has literary tact and a sense of design." The *Saturday Review*'s James Yaffe reports that among Sillitoe's "many wonderful qualities" are "a fluent, often brilliant command of language, an acute ear for dialect, [and] a virtuoso ability to describe the sight, sound, and smell of things."

Allen R. Penner of *Contemporary Literature* sees traces of an old-fashioned literary tradition in Sillitoe's works—but with a modern twist. Explains Penner: "'The Loneliness of the Long-Distance Runner' . . . is written in a tradition in English fiction which dates at least from Elizabethan times, in . . . the rogue's tale, or thief's autobiography." In his opinion, Sillitoe "has reversed the formula of the popular crime tale of fiction, wherein the reader enjoys vicariously witnessing the exploits of the outlaw and then has the morally reassuring pleasure of seeing the doors of the prison close upon him in the conclusion. Sillitoe begins his tale in prison, and he ends it before the doors have opened again, leaving us with the unsettling realization that the doors will indeed open and that the criminal will be released unreformed." This emphasis on unrepentant rebellion, says Penner, proves that "Sillitoe was never, really, simply an 'angry young man.' His hostility was not a transitory emotion of youth, but a permanent rancor well grounded in class hatred. 'The Loneliness of the Long-Distance Runner' contains the seeds of the revolutionary philosophy which would eventually attain full growth in his works."

On the other hand, some critics see nothing but youthful anger in Sillitoe's writings. Commenting in the *New York Times Book Review,* Malcolm Bradbury notes that "if the heroes of some . . . English novels are angry young men, Mr. Sillitoe is raging; and though he doesn't know it, he is raging for much the same reasons." Champlin remarks that Sillitoe's emergence was "a sharp signaling of an end to quiet acceptance of the way things are. It was a protest, fueled by the war, against the stratified status quo. . . . Unlike some of Britain's angry young men who have matured and prospered into more conservative postures, Sillitoe remains the poet of the anonymous millions in the council flats and the cold-water attached houses, noting the ignored, remembering the half-forgotten."

Though John R. Clark of the *Saturday Review* also sees Sillitoe as an Angry Young Man, he feels that "his anger and fictions have altered with time. In [his] early work there was something single-minded and intense in the actions and scenes, particularly in the shorter novels." On the other hand, "Later novels reveal a broader social and political horizon. Sillitoe's characters not only privately rebel but become dedicated to larger 'movements.'"

Prairie Schooner contributor Robert S. Haller rejects the notion that Sillitoe is an Angry Young Man. "If this title is justified for any writers," he begins, "it would be so for [those] men with university training who wanted room at the top but who resented the moral and aesthetic cost of getting there. But it hardly applies to Sillitoe [and others] who are authentically of the working class, self-educated, and uninterested in the matter of rising to the upper classes. . . . Anger is the resentment of frustrated ambition; neither Sillitoe nor his early heroes see in established values and styles anything to aspire to."

Some thirty years after the publication of *Saturday Night and Sunday Morning* and its sequel, *Key to the Door,* Sillitoe returned to the characters introduced in those books. *The Open Door* centers on Brian Seaton, the older brother of *Saturday Night*'s protagonist Arthur Seaton. Brian is "the most closely autobiographical of Sillitoe's characters," according to *World Literature Today* reviewer William Hutchings. Like the author, Brian escapes his working-class home town by joining the army and serving as a radio operator in Malaya. Also like Sillitoe, Brian discovers upon his return to England that he has contracted tuberculosis. "His illness dominates the first two thirds of the novel, as . . . Brian gains a heightened awareness of his own mortality," relates Hutchings. Parallels to Sillitoe's life continue as Brian uses his convalescence to read voraciously and to realize his ambition to become a writer. Hutchings finds that together, *Key to the Door* and *The Open Door* "constitute an extraordinarily intimate fictional 'portrait of the artist as a young man.'" Brian Morton also comments very favorably on the book, writing in *Times Literary Supplement* that "*The Open Door* is an extraordinary, almost symphonic development of deceptively familiar materials, and confirms [Sillitoe's] standing as one of Britain's most powerful and sophisticated fiction-writers."

In 1995, Sillitoe published the memoir *Life without Armour,* relating in nonfiction form the story of his childhood, his military service, his struggle with tuberculosis, and his eventual triumph as a writer. Ironically, his illness provided the means for him to realize his artistic dreams, as his small disability pension made it possible for him to support himself in the days before his writing sold. Several reviewers note that the autobiography's early sections are its best; John Melmoth notes in *Times Literary Supplement* that "the squalor of [Sillitoe's] upbringing is captured with a novelistic verve that later sections of the book fail to match. Deprivation makes good copy; hard work and dedication—as ever—write white." Nicholas Wollaston finds the author's life story inspirational, and comments that it is "the more impressive for being told in a simple, almost biblical voice. . . . There was iron in his soul as faith and energy drove him on, fighting solitude and publishers' indifference."

In his *Nation* interview, Sillitoe declared his opinion that "a writer never stands still. When you are young, everything is simple, but I am not young any more, [which] means that I am leaving a lot of simplicities behind. Basic beliefs stay, but things now look more complex." In short, concludes Sillitoe, "Each individual has to make a choice: either to accept this society or stand up against it. . . . In this country, as in any other, a writer is liked if he is loyal to the system. But it is the writer's duty in a sense to be disloyal. In the modern world, he is one of the few people who are listened to, and his primary loyalty should be to his integrity and to his talent. He can speak up in many ways; the best way is to write a book."

BIOGRAPHICAL/CRITICAL SOURCES:

BOOKS

Aldridge, John W., *Time to Murder and Create: The Contemporary Novel in Crisis,* McKay, 1966.

Hanson, Gillian Mary, *Understanding Alan Sillitoe,* University of South Carolina Press, 1998.

Hitchcock, Peter, *Working-Class Fiction in Theory and Practice: A Reading of Alan Sillitoe,* University of Rochester Press, 1989.

PERIODICALS

Books and Bookmen, December, 1973, pp. 42-46.
Chicago Tribune Book World, October 26, 1980; August 31, 1981.
Commonweal, September 4, 1959; April 29, 1960; March 27, 1964.
Contemporary Literature, Volume X, number 2, 1969; October, 1987, p. 214.
Globe and Mail (Toronto), September 7, 1985.
Listener, November 11, 1982, p. 27.
Literature-Film Quarterly, number 3, 1981, pp. 161-88.
London Review of Books, November 17, 1983, pp. 12-13; December 5, 1985, pp. 22-23; December 20, 1985, pp. 19-20.
Los Angeles Times, October 1, 1980; April 21, 1981.
Los Angeles Times Book Review, November 21, 1982.
Nation, January 27, 1969.
New Republic, August 24, 1959; May 9, 1960.
New Statesman, October 3, 1959.
New Statesman & Society, March 10, 1989, p. 36; July 21, 1995, p. 39.
New Yorker, September 5, 1959; June 11, 1960.
New York Review of Books, March 5, 1964.
New York Times Book Review, August 16, 1959; April 10, 1960; December 14, 1969, pp. 44-45; September 28, 1980; April

19, 1981, pp. 6, 25; December 12, 1982, pp. 15, 28; April 24, 1988, p. 34.
Observer, February 26, 1989, p. 47; May 13, 1990, p. 58; September 29, 1991, p. 61; July 23, 1995, p. 14.
Prairie Schooner, winter, 1974-75, pp. 151-58.
San Francisco Chronicle, November 29, 1959; May 1, 1960.
Saturday Review, September 5, 1959; April 16, 1960; January 25, 1964; November 22, 1969, p. 86; October 16, 1971.
Sewanee Review, summer, 1975.
Spectator, September 25, 1959.
Studies in Short Fiction, number 4, 1966-67, pp. 350-51; winter, 1975, pp. 9-14.
Studies in the Novel, winter, 1973, pp. 469-82.
Time, April 18, 1960.
Times (London), November 10, 1983; November 15, 1984; October 10, 1985; February 23, 1989, p. 19.
Times Educational Supplement, July 4, 1993, p. 10; July 7, 1995, p. 12.
Times Literary Supplement, October 2, 1959; October 24, 1968, p. 1193; October 19, 1973; January 15, 1981; January 23, 1981, p. 76; October 15, 1982; November 11, 1983; November 16, 1984, p. 1301; June 7, 1985; December 6, 1985, p. 1407; April 7, 1989, p. 364; October 11, 1991, p. 24; May 18, 1990, p. 535; May 14, 1993, p. 23; August 12, 1994, p. 24; August 18, 1995, p. 22.
Washington Post, June 2, 1981; December 10, 1982; April 13, 1988, p. 8.
Washington Post Book World, October 26, 1980.
World Literature Today, summer, 1990, p. 465; spring, 1991, pp. 304-5.
Yale Review, September, 1959.

*   *   *

SILVERBERG, Robert 1935-
(T. D. Bethlen, Walker Chapman, Dirk Clinton, Roy Cook, Walter Drummond, Dan Eliot, Don Elliott, Franklin Hamilton, Paul Hollander, Ivar Jorgenson, Calvin M. Knox, Dan Malcolm, Webber Martin, Alex Merriman, David Osborne, George Osborne, Lloyd Robinson, Eric Rodman, Lee Sebastian, Hall Thornton, Richard F. Watson; Gordon Aghill, Ralph Burke, Robert Randall, Ellis Robertson, joint pseudonyms; Robert Arnette, Alexander Blade, Richard Greer, E. K. Jarvis, Warren Kastel, Clyde Mitchell, Leonard G. Spencer, S. M. Tenneshaw, Gerald Vance, house pseudonyms)

PERSONAL: Born January 15, 1935, in New York, NY; son of Michael (an accountant) and Helen (Baim) Silverberg; married Barbara H. Brown (an engineer), August 26, 1956 (separated, 1976; divorced, 1986); married Karen L. Haber, 1987. *Education:* Columbia University, B.A., 1956.

ADDRESSES: Home—P.O. Box 13160, Station E, Oakland, CA 94661-0160. *Agent*—Ralph Vicinanza, 111 Eighth Ave., No. 1501, New York, NY 10011.

CAREER: Writer, 1956–; president, Agberg Ltd., 1981–.

MEMBER: Science Fiction Writers of America (president, 1967-68), Hydra Club (chairman, 1958-61).

AWARDS, HONORS: Hugo Awards, World Science Fiction Convention, 1956, for best new author, 1969, for best novella *Nightwings,* 1987, for best novella, *Gilgamesh in the Outback,* and 1990, for best novella, *Enter a Soldier; Later: Enter Another; New York Times* best hundred children's books citation, 1960, for *Lost Race of Mars;* Spring Book Festival Awards, *New York Herald Tribune,* 1962, for *Lost Cities and Vanished Civilizations,* and 1967, for *The Auk, the Dodo, and the Oryx: Vanished and Vanishing Creatures;* National Association of Independent Schools award, 1966, for *The Old Ones: Indians of the American Southwest;* Guest of Honor, World Science Fiction Convention, 1970; Nebula Awards, Science Fiction Writers of America, 1970, for story "Passengers," 1972, for story "Good News from the Vatican," 1972, for novel *A Time of Changes,* 1975, for novella *Born with the Dead,* and 1986, for novella *Sailing to Byzantium;* John W. Campbell Memorial Award, 1973, for excellence in writing; Jupiter Award, 1973, for novella *The Feast of St. Dionysus;* Prix Apollo, 1976, for novel *Nightwings;* Milford Award, 1981, for editing; Locus Award, 1982, for fantasy novel *Lord Valentine's Castle.*

WRITINGS:

SCIENCE FICTION

Master of Life and Death (also see below), Ace Books, 1957.
The Thirteenth Immortal (bound with *This Fortress World* by J. E. Gunn), Ace Books, 1957.
Invaders from Earth (bound with *Across Time* by D. Grinnell), Ace Books, 1958, published separately, Avon, 1968, published as *We, the Marauders* (bound with *Giants in the Earth* by James Blish under joint title *A Pair in Space*), Belmont, 1965.
Stepsons of Terra (bound with *A Man Called Destiny* by L. Wright), Ace Books, 1958, published separately, 1977.
The Planet Killers (bound with *We Claim These Stars!* by Poul Anderson), Ace Books, 1959.
Collision Course, Avalon, 1961.
Next Stop the Stars (story collection) [and] *The Seed of Earth* (novel), Ace Books, 1962, each published separately, 1977.
Recalled to Life, Lancer Books, 1962.
The Silent Invaders (bound with *Battle on Venus* by William F. Temple), Ace Books, 1963, published separately, 1973.
Godling, Go Home! (story collection), Belmont, 1964.
Conquerors from the Darkness, Holt, 1965.
To Worlds Beyond: Stories of Science Fiction, Chilton, 1965.
Needle in a Timestack (story collection), Ballantine, 1966, revised edition, Ace Books, 1985.
Planet of Death, Holt, 1967.
Thorns, Ballantine, 1967.
Those Who Watch, New American Library, 1967.
The Time-Hoppers, Doubleday, 1967.
To Open the Sky (story collection), Ballantine, 1967.
Hawksbill Station, Doubleday, 1968, published as *The Anvil of Time,* Sidgwick & Jackson (London), 1968.
The Masks of Time, Ballantine, 1968, published as *Vornan-19,* Sidgwick & Jackson, 1970.
Dimension Thirteen (story collection), Ballantine, 1969.
The Man in the Maze, Avon, 1969.
Nightwings, Avon, 1969.
(Contributor) *Three for Tomorrow: Three Original Novellas of Science Fiction,* Meredith Press, 1969.
Three Survived, Holt, 1969.
To Live Again, Doubleday, 1969.
Up the Line, Ballantine, 1969, revised edition, 1978.

The Cube Root of Uncertainty (story collection), Macmillan, 1970.
Downward to the Earth, Doubleday, 1970.
Parsecs and Parables: Ten Science Fiction Stories, Doubleday, 1970.
A Robert Silverberg Omnibus (contains *Master of Life and Death, Invaders from Earth,* and *The Time-Hoppers*), Sidgwick & Jackson, 1970.
Tower of Glass, Scribner, 1970.
Moonferns and Starsongs (story collection), Ballantine, 1971.
Son of Man, Ballantine, 1971.
A Time of Changes, New American Library, 1971.
The World Inside, Doubleday, 1971.
The Book of Skulls, Scribner, 1972.
Dying Inside, Scribner, 1972, recorded by the author, Caedmon, 1979.
The Reality Trip and Other Implausibilities (story collection), Ballantine, 1972.
The Second Trip, Doubleday, 1972.
(Contributor) *The Day the Sun Stood Still,* Thomas Nelson, 1972.
Earth's Other Shadow: Nine Science Fiction Stories, New American Library, 1973.
(Contributor) *An Exaltation of Stars: Transcendental Adventures in Science Fiction,* Simon & Schuster, 1973.
(Contributor) *No Mind of Man: Three Original Novellas of Science Fiction,* Hawthorn, 1973.
Unfamiliar Territory (story collection), Scribner, 1973.
Valley beyond Time (story collection), Dell, 1973.
Born with the Dead: Three Novellas about the Spirit of Man, Random House, 1974.
Sundance and Other Science Fiction Stories, Thomas Nelson, 1974.
The Feast of St. Dionysus: Five Science Fiction Stories, Scribner, 1975.
The Stochastic Man, Harper, 1975.
The Best of Robert Silverberg, Volume 1, Pocket Books, 1976, Volume 2, Gregg, 1978.
Capricorn Games (story collection), Random House, 1976.
Shadrach in the Furnace, Bobbs-Merrill, 1976.
The Shores of Tomorrow (story collection), Thomas Nelson, 1976.
The Songs of Summer and Other Stories, Gollancz, 1979.
Lord Valentine's Castle, Harper, 1980.
The Desert of Stolen Dreams, Underwood-Miller, 1981.
A Robert Silverberg Omnibus (contains *Downward to the Earth, The Man in the Maze,* and *Nightwings*), Harper, 1981.
Majipoor Chronicles, Arbor House, 1982.
World of a Thousand Colors (story collection), Arbor House, 1982.
Valentine Pontifex (sequel to *Lord Valentine's Castle*), Arbor House, 1983.
The Conglomeroid Cocktail Party (story collection), Arbor House, 1984.
Sailing to Byzantium, Underwood-Miller, 1985.
Tom O'Bedlam, Donald I. Fine, 1985.
Beyond the Safe Zone: Collected Short Fiction of Robert Silverberg, Donald I. Fine, 1986.
Star of Gypsies, Donald I. Fine, 1986.
At Winter's End, Warner, 1988.
Born with the Dead (bound with *The Saliva Tree* by Brian W. Aldiss), Tor Books, 1988.
To the Land of the Living, Gollancz, 1989.
(With wife, Karen Haber) *The Mutant Season,* Foundation/Doubleday, 1989.
The New Springtime, Warner, 1990.

In Another Country: Vintage Season, Tor Books, 1990.
(With Isaac Asimov) *Nightfall,* Doubleday, 1990.
Time Gate II, Baen Books, 1990.
The Face of the Waters, Bantam, 1991.
(With Asimov) *Child of Time,* Gollancz, 1991.
(With Asimov) *The Ugly Little Boy,* Doubleday, 1992.
The Collected Stories of Robert Silverberg, Volume 1: Secret Sharers, Bantam, 1992, published in 2 volumes, Grafton (London), 1992.
(With Asimov) *The Positronic Man,* Doubleday, 1993.
Kingdoms of the Wall, Bantam, 1993.
Hot Sky at Midnight, Bantam, 1994.
The Mountains of Majipoor, Bantam, 1995.
Sorcerers of Majipoor, HarperPrism, 1996.
Starborne, Bantam, 1996.

JUVENILE FICTION

Revolt on Alpha C, Crowell, 1955.
Starman's Quest, Gnome Press, 1959.
Lost Race of Mars, Winston, 1960.
Regan's Planet, Pyramid Books, 1964, revised edition published as *World's Fair, 1992,* Follett, 1970.
Time of the Great Freeze, Holt, 1964.
The Mask of Akhnaten, Macmillan, 1965.
The Gate of Worlds, Holt, 1967.
The Calibrated Alligator and Other Science Fiction Stories, Holt, 1969.
Across a Billion Years, Dial, 1969.
Sunrise on Mercury and Other Science Fiction Stories, Thomas Nelson, 1975.
(Editor with Charles G. Waugh and Martin H. Greenberg) *The Science Fictional Dinosaur,* Avon, 1982.
Project Pendulum, Walker, 1987.
Letters from Atlantis, Macmillan, 1990.

NONFICTION

First American Into Space, Monarch, 1961.
Lost Cities and Vanished Civilizations, Chilton, 1962.
Empires in the Dust: Ancient Civilizations Brought to Light, Chilton, 1963.
The Fabulous Rockefellers: A Compelling, Personalized Account of One of America's First Families, Monarch Books, 1963.
Akhnaten: The Rebel Pharaoh, Chilton, 1964.
(Editor) *Great Adventures in Archaeology,* Dial, 1964.
Man before Adam: The Story of Man in Search of His Origins, Macrae Smith, 1964.
The Great Wall of China, Chilton, 1965, published as *The Long Rampart: The Story of the Great Wall of China,* 1966.
Scientists and Scoundrels: A Book of Hoaxes, Crowell, 1965.
Bridges, Macrae Smith, 1966.
Frontiers in Archaeology, Chilton, 1966.
The Auk, the Dodo, and the Oryx: Vanished and Vanishing Creatures, Crowell, 1967.
Light for the World: Edison and the Power Industry, Van Nostrand, 1967.
Men Against Time: Salvage Archaeology in the United States, Macmillan, 1967.
Mound Builders of Ancient America: The Archaeology of a Myth, New York Graphic Society, 1968.
The Challenge of Climate: Man and His Environment, Meredith Press, 1969.
The World of Space, Meredith Press, 1969.
If I Forget Thee, O Jerusalem: American Jews and the State of Israel, Morrow, 1970.

The Pueblo Revolt, Weybright & Talley, 1970.
Before the Sphinx: Early Egypt, Thomas Nelson, 1971.
Clocks for the Ages: How Scientists Date the Past, Macmillan, 1971.
To the Western Shore: Growth of the United States, 1776-1853, Doubleday, 1971.
The Longest Voyage: Circumnavigators in the Age of Discovery, Bobbs-Merrill, 1972.
The Realm of Prester John, Doubleday, 1972.
(Contributor) *Those Who Can,* New American Library, 1973.
Drug Themes in Science Fiction, National Institute on Drug Abuse, 1974.
(Contributor) *Hell's Cartographers: Some Personal Histories of Science Fiction Writers,* Harper, 1975.

JUVENILE NONFICTION

Treasures beneath the Sea, Whitman Publishing, 1960.
Fifteen Battles That Changed the World, Putnam, 1963.
Home of the Red Man: Indian North America before Columbus, New York Graphic Society, 1963.
Sunken History: The Story of Underwater Archaeology, Chilton, 1963.
The Great Doctors, Putnam, 1964.
The Man Who Found Nineveh: The Story of Austen Henry Layard, Holt, 1964.
Men Who Mastered the Atom, Putnam, 1965.
Niels Bohr: The Man Who Mapped the Atom, Macrae Smith, 1965.
The Old Ones: Indians of the American Southwest, New York Graphic Society, 1965.
Socrates, Putnam, 1965.
The World of Coral, Duell, 1965.
Forgotten by Time: A Book of Living Fossils, Crowell, 1966.
To the Rock of Darius: The Story of Henry Rawlinson, Holt, 1966.
The Adventures of Nat Palmer: Antarctic Explorer and Clipper Ship Pioneer, McGraw, 1967.
The Dawn of Medicine, Putnam, 1967.
The Morning of Mankind: Prehistoric Man in Europe, New York Graphic Society, 1967.
The World of the Rain Forest, Meredith Press, 1967.
Four Men Who Changed the Universe, Putnam, 1968.
Ghost Towns of the American West, Crowell, 1968.
Stormy Voyager: The Story of Charles Wilkes, Lippincott, 1968.
The World of the Ocean Depths, Meredith Press, 1968.
Bruce of the Blue Nile, Holt, 1969.
Vanishing Giants: The Story of the Sequoias, Simon & Schuster, 1969.
Wonders of Ancient Chinese Science, Hawthorn, 1969.
Mammoths, Mastodons, and Man, McGraw, 1970.
The Seven Wonders of the Ancient World, Crowell-Collier, 1970.
(With Arthur C. Clarke) *Into Space: A Young Person's Guide to Space,* Harper, revised edition, 1971.
John Muir: Prophet among the Glaciers, Putnam, 1972.
The World within the Ocean Wave, Weybright & Talley, 1972.
The World within the Tide Pool, Weybright & Talley, 1972.

EDITOR; SCIENCE FICTION

Earthmen and Strangers: Nine Stories of Science Fiction, Duell, 1966.
Voyagers in Time: Twelve Stories of Science Fiction, Meredith Press, 1967.
Men and Machines: Ten Stories of Science Fiction, Meredith Press, 1968.
Dark Stars, Ballantine, 1969.

Tomorrow's Worlds: Ten Stories of Science Fiction, Meredith Press, 1969.

The Ends of Time: Eight Stories of Science Fiction, Hawthorn, 1970.

Great Short Novels of Science Fiction, Ballantine, 1970.

The Mirror of Infinity: A Critics' Anthology of Science Fiction, Harper, 1970.

The Science Fiction Hall of Fame, Doubleday, Volume 1, 1970, published in two volumes, Sphere (London), 1972.

Worlds of Maybe: Seven Stories of Science Fiction, Thomas Nelson, 1970.

Alpha, Volumes 1-6, Ballantine, 1970-76, Volumes 7-9, Berkley, 1977-78.

Four Futures, Hawthorn, 1971.

Mind to Mind: Nine Stories of Science Fiction, Thomas Nelson, 1971.

The Science Fiction Bestiary: Nine Stories of Science Fiction, Thomas Nelson, 1971.

To the Stars: Eight Stories of Science Fiction, Hawthorn, 1971.

Beyond Control: Seven Stories of Science Fiction, Thomas Nelson, 1972.

Invaders from Space: Ten Stories of Science Fiction, Hawthorn, 1972.

Chains of the Sea: Three Original Novellas of Science Fiction, Thomas Nelson, 1973.

Deep Space: Eight Stories of Science Fiction, Thomas Nelson, 1973.

Other Dimensions: Ten Stories of Science Fiction, Hawthorn, 1973.

Three Trips in Time and Space, Hawthorn, 1973.

Infinite Jests: The Lighter Side of Science Fiction, Chilton, 1974.

Mutants: Eleven Stories of Science Fiction, Thomas Nelson, 1974.

Threads of Time: Three Original Novellas of Science Fiction, Thomas Nelson, 1974.

Windows into Tomorrow: Nine Stories of Science Fiction, Hawthorn, 1974.

(With Roger Elwood) *Epoch,* Berkley, 1975.

Explorers of Space: Eight Stories of Science Fiction, Thomas Nelson, 1975.

The New Atlantis and Other Novellas of Science Fiction, Warner Books, 1975.

Strange Gifts: Eight Stories of Science Fiction, Thomas Nelson, 1975.

The Aliens: Seven Stories of Science Fiction, Thomas Nelson, 1976.

The Crystal Ship: Three Original Novellas of Science Fiction, Thomas Nelson, 1976.

Earth Is the Strangest Planet: Ten Stories of Science Fiction, Thomas Nelson, 1977.

Galactic Dreamers: Science Fiction as Visionary Literature, Random House, 1977.

The Infinite Web: Eight Stories of Science Fiction, Dial, 1977.

Triax: Three Original Novellas, Pinnacle, 1977.

Trips in Time: Nine Stories of Science Fiction, Thomas Nelson, 1977.

Lost Worlds, Unknown Horizons: Nine Stories of Science Fiction, Thomas Nelson, 1978.

The Androids Are Coming: Seven Stories of Science Fiction, Elsevier-Nelson, 1979.

(With Greenberg and Joseph D. Olander) *Car Sinister,* Avon, 1979.

(With Greenberg and Olander) *Dawn of Time: Prehistory through Science Fiction,* Elsevier-Nelson, 1979.

The Edge of Space: Three Original Novellas of Science Fiction, Elsevier-Nelson, 1979.

(With Greenberg) *The Arbor House Treasury of Great Science Fiction Short Novels,* Arbor House, 1980.

(With Greenberg) *The Arbor House Treasury of Modern Science Fiction,* Arbor House, 1980.

Randall Garrett, *The Best of Randall Garrett,* Pocket Books, 1982.

The Nebula Awards, Arbor House, 1983.

(With Greenberg) *The Arbor House Treasury of Science Fiction Masterpieces,* Arbor House, 1983.

(With Greenberg) *The Fantasy Hall of Fame,* Arbor House, 1983.

(With Greenberg) *The Time Travelers: A Science Fiction Quartet,* Donald I. Fine, 1985.

(With Greenberg) *Neanderthals,* New American Library, 1987.

Robert Silverberg's Worlds of Wonder, Warner, 1987.

(With Greenberg) *The Mammoth Book of Fantasy All-Time Greats,* Robinson, 1988.

Worlds Imagined: Fifteen Short Stories, Crown, 1989.

(With Haber) *Universe 1,* Foundation/Doubleday, 1990.

(With Haber) *Universe 2,* Bantam Books, 1992.

Alfred Bester, *Virtual Unrealities: The Short Fiction of Alfred Bester,* Vintage, 1997.

EDITOR; "NEW DIMENSIONS" SERIES

New Dimensions, Volumes 1-5, Doubleday, 1971-75, Volumes 6-10, Harper, 1976-80 (with Marta Randall), Volumes 11-12, Pocket Books, 1980-81.

The Best of New Dimensions, Pocket Books, 1979.

UNDER PSEUDONYM WALKER CHAPMAN

The Loneliest Continent: The Story of Antarctic Discovery, New York Graphic Society, 1964.

(Editor) *Antarctic Conquest: The Great Explorers in Their Own Words,* Bobbs-Merrill, 1966.

Kublai Khan: Lord of Xanadu, Bobbs-Merrill, 1966.

The Golden Dream: Seekers of El Dorado, Bobbs-Merrill 1967, published as *The Search for El Dorado,* 1967.

UNDER PSEUDONYM DON ELLIOTT

Flesh Peddlers, Nightstand, 1960.

Passion Trap, Nightstand, 1960.

Backstage Sinner, Nightstand, 1961.

Lust Goddess, Nightstand, 1961.

Sin Cruise, Nightstand, 1961.

Kept Man, Midnight, 1962.

Shame House, Midnight, 1962.

Sin Hellion, Ember, 1963.

Sin Servant, Nightstand, 1963.

Beatnik Wanton, Evening, 1964.

Flesh Bride, Evening, 1964.

Flesh Prize, Leisure, 1964.

Flesh Taker, Ember, 1964.

Sin Warped, Leisure, 1964.

Switch Trap, Evening, 1964.

Nudie Packet, Idle Hour, 1965.

The Young Wanton, Sundown, 1965.

Depravity Town, Reed, 1973.

Jungle Street, Reed, 1973.

Summertime Affair, Reed, 1973.

Also author of eighty other novels, 1959-65, under pseudonyms Dan Eliot and Don Elliott.

OTHER

(With Randall Garrett, under joint pseudonym Robert Randall) *The Shrouded Planet,* Gnome Press, 1957, published under names Robert Silverberg and Randall Garrett, Donning, 1980.

(Under pseudonym Calvin M. Knox) *Lest We Forget Thee, Earth,* Ace Books, 1958.

(Under pseudonym David Osborne) *Aliens from Space,* Avalon, 1958.

(Under pseudonym Ivar Jorgenson) *Starhaven,* Avalon, 1958.

(Under pseudonym David Osborne) *Invisible Barriers,* Avalon, 1958.

(With Randall Garrett, under joint pseudonym Robert Randall) *The Dawning Light,* Gnome Press, 1959, published under names Robert Silverberg and Randall Garrett, Donning, 1981.

(Under pseudonym Calvin M. Knox) *The Plot against Earth,* Ace Books, 1959.

(Under pseudonym Walter Drummond) *Philosopher of Evil,* Regency Books, 1962.

(Under pseudonym Walter Drummond) *How to Spend Money,* Regency Books, 1963.

(Under pseudonym Franklin Hamilton) *1066,* Dial, 1963.

(Under pseudonym Calvin M. Knox) *One of Our Asteroids Is Missing,* Ace Books, 1964.

(Under pseudonym Paul Hollander) *The Labors of Hercules,* Putnam, 1965.

(Under pseudonym Franklin Hamilton) *The Crusades,* Dial, 1965.

(Under pseudonym Lloyd Robinson) *The Hopefuls: Ten Presidential Candidates,* Doubleday, 1966.

(Under pseudonym Roy Cook) *Leaders of Labor,* Lippincott, 1966.

(Under pseudonym Lee Sebastian) *Rivers,* Holt, 1966.

(Under pseudonym Franklin Hamilton) *Challenge for a Throne: The Wars of the Roses,* Dial, 1967.

(Under pseudonym Lloyd Robinson) *The Stolen Election: Hayes versus Tilden,* Doubleday, 1968.

(Under pseudonym Paul Hollander) *Sam Houston,* Putnam, 1968.

(Under pseudonym Lee Sebastian) *The South Pole,* Holt, 1968.

Robert Silverberg Reads "To See the Invisible Man" and "Passengers" (recording), Pelican Records, 1979.

Lord of Darkness (fiction), Arbor House, 1983.

Gilgamesh the King (fiction), Arbor House, 1984.

Reflections and Refractions: Thoughts on Science-Fiction, Science, and Other Matters, Underwood Books (Grass Valley, CA), 1997.

Contributor, sometimes under pseudonyms, to *Omni, Playboy, Amazing Stories Science Fiction, Fantastic Stories Science Fiction, Magazine of Fantasy and Science Fiction,* and other publications.

SIDELIGHTS: Robert Silverberg is among the best-known contemporary science-fiction writers in the United States. A prolific author, he has won the field's prestigious Nebula and Hugo awards and has received more award nominations for his work than any other writer in the genre. Interestingly, despite his prominence in the field, Silverberg's science fiction makes up only a portion of his total production—indeed, he has even left the field entirely to work in other genres on two separate occasions. Much of Silverberg's work has been nonfiction, reflecting his interests in such varied topics as archaeology, conservation, history, and the natural sciences. He has received awards for several of these nonfiction books—his *Mound Builders of Ancient*

America: The Archaeology of a Myth has even been hailed as one of the standard works on the subject. Still, this considerable success in the nonfiction field is consistently overshadowed by his continuing popularity among science-fiction fans. As George R. R. Martin, writing in the *Washington Post Book World,* admits, Silverberg "is best known and best regarded for his work within science fiction."

During the 1950s, Silverberg produced hundreds of stories for the science fiction magazines. His production was so high that he was obliged to publish much of this work under a host of pseudonyms. Silverberg recalled that time to Charles Platt in *Dream Makers: The Uncommon People Who Write Science Fiction:* "I was courted by editors considerably back then, because I was so dependable; if they said, 'Give me a story by next Thursday,' I would." These early stories, George W. Tuma characterizes in the *Dictionary of Literary Biography* as "conform[ing] closely to the conventions of science fiction: alien beings, technological gadgetry, standard plot devices, confrontations between [Earthlings] and extraterrestrial beings, and so forth." Among these early works were *Master of Life and Death* and *The Shrouded Planet,* both published in 1957.

During the 1960s, Silverberg maintained a rapid writing pace, publishing nearly two million words per year, not only juvenile nonfiction works but science-fiction novels such as 1963's *The Silent Invaders* and the highly praised *Collision Course,* sci-fi short stories, and rewrites of many of his earlier novels. He told Jeffrey M. Elliot that he managed to write so much due to intense concentration. "I concentrated on a point source and the words just came out right," the author recalled. Barry M. Malzberg in the *Magazine of Fantasy and Science Fiction* allows that "the man is prolific. Indeed, the man may be, in terms of accumulation of work per working year, the most prolific writer who ever lived."

But the years of prolific writing finally ended in the mid-1960s. Silverberg would later cite two factors for the slowdown in his production at that time. The first was a hyperactive thyroid gland, brought on by prolonged overwork, which forced him in 1966 to slow his working pace considerably. The second factor was a fire in early 1968 at Silverberg's New York City home. This fire, he wrote in *Contemporary Authors Autobiography Series (CAAS),* "drained from me, evidently forever, much of the bizarre energy that had allowed me to write a dozen or more significant books in a single year."

Despite a drop in production, the late 1960s would find the author embarking on a more experimental type of science-fiction writing. In fact, it is the work from this period that most observers credit as the beginning of his serious fiction in the genre. Thomas D. Clareson, although noting in his book *Robert Silverberg* that "from the beginning, he was a skilled storyteller," nonetheless marks 1969 to 1976 as the period when Silverberg "conducted his most deliberate experiments and attained the most consistent command of his material." Malzberg claims that "in or around 1965 Silverberg put his toys away and began to write literature." 1967's *Thorns* has been cited as the author's transitional work through its focus on not only the physical universe but the inner, psychic universe as reflected by philosophical, psychological, and social elements. In the novel, human protagonist Minner Burris has been physically altered to conform to beings on the planet Manipol. On Manipol, while now accepted for his appearance, Burris is emotionally isolated from native Manipolians due to his social, cultural, and psychological differences. Eventually returning to Earth, he finds himself rejected due to his unusual appearance. Burris's resulting alienation from human society is contrasted with that of other characters, whose circumstances have set them apart while their inner natures continue to need the contact of fellow humans.

His experiments with style and narrative structure continued into the 1970s, as Silverberg sought to extend the range of science fiction. "Having already proved that he could write every kind of s.f. story at least as well as anyone else," Gerald Jonas comments in the *New York Times Book Review,* "Silverberg set out . . . to stretch both the genre and himself." In 1971's *Son of Man,* for example, the story is told as a series of bizarre adventure sequences set on "not the physical planet Earth but the Earth of human perception—the model world of the mind," as Brian Stableford relates in *Masters of Science Fiction.* Clay, the novel's aptly named protagonist, time-shifts to the future, where he meets up with several species of humanoids that have evolved in differing directions. In this future world, communication between beings involves sexual contact, and Clay eventually experiences unity and transcendence through understanding the heightened significance of physical union. Sandra Miesel, writing in *Extrapolation,* calls *Son of Man* a "sensuous, didactic, and witty novel" in which "the dream fantasy is stretched to the breaking point."

For the next four years Silverberg wrote no new science fiction. Instead, he devoted his time to the garden of his California home. "I had had my career," the author recalled in *CAAS.* "Now I had my garden." But in 1978 he was pushed back into the field after he and his first wife separated and she required a house of her own. To raise the necessary money, Silverberg decided to write "one last book." The result was *Lord Valentine's Castle,* a massive novel that set a record when it was offered to publishers at auction. Harper & Row paid the largest sum ever given for a science fiction novel—$127,500—and Silverberg was a writer again.

In *Lord Valentine's Castle* Silverberg mixes elements from science fiction and heroic fantasy. The science fiction elements include a far future setting, the imaginary planet of Majipoor, and a host of exotic alien life forms. But the plot—a quest by the exiled prince of a distant planet that allows him to regain the throne of Majipoor, right the ancient wrong of dispossession committed against the planet's original inhabitants, the primitive Metamorph peoples, and rejuvenate his own self-confidence—is common to the fantasy genre. The clever combination of genre elements was praised by Jack Sullivan in the *New York Times Book Review.* Sullivan calls *Lord Valentine's Castle* "an imaginative fusion of action, sorcery and science fiction, with visionary adventure scenes undergirded by scientific explanations." In his book *Robert Silverberg,* Clareson states that "whatever else it does, *Lord Valentine's Castle* demands that its readers re-examine the relationship between science fiction and fantasy, for in this narrative Silverberg has fused the two together."

The rich diversity of the planet Majipoor was remarked upon by several reviewers, including Patrick Parrinder of the *Times Literary Supplement.* "Silverberg's invention," Parrinder writes, "is prodigious throughout. The early sections . . . are a near-encyclopaedia of unnatural wonders and weird ecosystems. I suspect this book breaks all records in the coinage of new species." John Charnay of the *Los Angeles Times Book Review,* although believing the book "lacks depth of dialogue and emotion to match the grandeur of scenery and plot," still finds that "Silverberg's inventiveness is intriguing."

With *Valentine Pontifex,* Silverberg did what he had once owed he would never do: write a sequel to *Lord Valentine's Castle.* Colin Greenland of the *Times Literary Supplement,* who had maintained that *Lord Valentine's Castle* was a weak novel that "satisfied readers' wishes for a great big safe world where nice things flourish and evil succumbs to forgiveness," sees Silverberg's sequel as an "act of conscience for *Lord Valentine's Castle.*" In *Valentine Pontifex,* Lord Valentine, now restored to his position as ruler of Majipoor, faces opposition from the Piurivars, an aboriginal race dispossessed years before by Earthling colonists. The Piurivars release plagues and deadly bio-engineered creatures upon the humans. Finding that "the lazy pace through time and space" found in *Lord Valentine's Castle* gives way in this novel "to a dance of conflicting emotions and political intrigue," a reviewer for the *Voice Literary Supplement* reviewer sees *Lord Valentine's Castle, Majipoor Chronicles,* and *Valentine Pontifex* as related works forming a loose trilogy that "becomes a whole in a way that the form rarely achieves."

In the years since his return from self-imposed "early retirement," Silverberg has continued his work in the genre with both novels and short stories that expand upon his view of future worlds. Among his more recent novels are 1988's *At Winter's End,* the following year's *To the Land of the Living,* which he coauthored with his second wife, author Karen Haber, and *Kingdoms of the Wall,* which Silverberg published in 1993. Compared by one reviewer to the works of nineteenth-century fantasy writer Lord Dunsany, the novel follows the pilgrimage of a group of young alien beings to the summit of a daunting mountain range called Kosa Saag—the Wall—there to learn from the gods who live at that great height. Traditionally, few pilgrims have ever returned from this annual trip, and none have ever returned sane. On the way, the group passes through numerous "worlds" at different levels of its ascent, at one point coming across a space traveler—an "Irtiman" (Earthman)—who has been stranded on their planet; he is weak from hunger and eventually dies. Finally nearing the summit, the surviving members of the group are tempted to end their quest when they discover a land of magic where they can remain perpetually young. *Analog* reviewer Tom Easton views Silverberg's tale as social allegory: "He is . . . hinting that those who persevere despite all the pressures upon them to conform do not find the satisfaction they crave. In fact, if they ever reach the goal of their quest, they are crashingly disillusioned," Easton writes.

The Conglomeroid Cocktail Party, released in 1984, collects several short stories from the early 1980s that a *Science Fiction Chronicle* critic terms "very slick, very polished, and often [focusing on] substantial matters, but at the same time . . . perfunctory." However, Stan Gebler Davies disagrees in *Punch,* praising Silverberg's ability to portray time travel realistically. Citing such included works as "Needles in a Timesack" and "Jennifer's Lover," Davies notes that "Silverberg is hooked on time-travel and comes as near as any writer to getting away with it." And with the publication of the first part of *The Collected Stories of Robert Silverberg* in 1992, Silverberg devotees are able to sample twenty-four of his most critically acclaimed short stories of the 1980s. In addition to the Nebula-award-winning novella *Sailing to Byzantium* and *Enter a Soldier; Later: Enter Another,* a Hugo winner, are lesser-known but equally well-written works, each prefaced by the author's own introduction, which puts the story into the context of the author's total oeuvre. "The end result," notes Gary K. Wolfe in *Locus,* "is not only a good lesson in craft and style, but a clear picture of a highly professional writer who knows exactly what he's doing—even when he plays it safe." James Sallis agrees in a *Los Angeles Times Book Review* piece; of Silverberg he comments that "This man who speaks so insistently of simple craftsmanship again and again delivers, surreptitiously and a little abashedly, it seems, a rare kind of art."

Over a professional writing career spanning several decades, Silverberg has produced an immense body of original fiction in several genres, authored numerous nonfiction works, and edited several highly praised collections, such as 1992's shared-world anthology titles *Murasaki,* featuring work by writers Frederik Pohl, Nancy Kress, and Pohl Anderson. Commenting on Silverberg's diversity, Martin writes that "few writers, past or present, have had careers quite as varied, dramatic, and contradictory as that of Robert Silverberg." As a writer of nonfiction, Silverberg has enjoyed particular success. But as a writer of science fiction, he is among a handful of writers who have helped to shape the field into what it is today. He is, Elliot declares, "a titan in the science fiction field." "Few science fiction readers," Elliot goes on, "have not been enriched and inspired by his contributions to the genre, contributions which reflect his love of the field and his deep respect for its readers." Silverberg's contributions to the field, Clareson writes in the *Magazine of Fantasy and Science Fiction,* are of predictably high quality: "He will tell a good story, he will fuse together content and form, and he will add to our perception of the human condition."

BIOGRAPHICAL/CRITICAL SOURCES:

BOOKS

Clareson, Thomas D., editor, *Voices for the Future: Essays on Major Science Fiction Writers,* Volume 2, Bowling Green State University Popular Press, 1979.

Clareson, Thomas D., *Robert Silverberg,* Starmont House, 1983.

Clareson, Thomas D., *Robert Silverberg: A Primary and Secondary Bibliography,* G. K. Hall, 1983.

Contemporary Authors Autobiography Series, Volume 3, Gale (Detroit), 1986.

Contemporary Literary Criticism, Volume 7, Gale, 1977.

Dictionary of Literary Biography, Volume 8: *Twentieth-Century American Science Fiction Writers,* Gale, 1981.

Elliot, Jeffrey M., *Science Fiction Voices #2,* Borgo Press, 1979.

Magill, Frank N., editor, *Survey of Science Fiction,* Salem Press, 1979.

Platt, Charles, *Dream Makers: The Uncommon People Who Write Science Fiction,* Berkley, 1980.

Rabkin, Eric S., and others, editors, *No Place Else,* Southern Illinois University Press, 1983.

Schweitzer, Darrell, editor, *Exploring Fantasy Worlds: Essays on Fantastic Literature,* Borgo Press, 1985.

Stableford, Brian M., *Masters of Science Fiction,* Borgo Press, 1981.

Staircar, Tom, editor, *Critical Encounters II,* Ungar, 1982.

Walker, Paul, *Speaking of Science Fiction: The Paul Walker Interviews,* Luna Press, 1978.

PERIODICALS

Analog Science Fiction/Science Fact, November, 1979; December, 1990; August, 1993, p. 162; July, 1994, p. 306.

Atlantic Monthly, April, 1972.

Booklist, September 1, 1992; April 1, 1997.

Extrapolation, summer, 1979; winter, 1980; winter, 1982.

Locus, March 1992, p. 60; April, 1992, p. 15; October, 1992, p. 33; January, 1993, pp. 22-23; February, 1994, p. 27.

Los Angeles Times Book Review, May 18, 1980; April 18, 1986; September 13, 1987; January 10, 1993.

Magazine of Fantasy and Science Fiction, April, 1971; April, 1974; May, 1988.

New Statesman, June 18, 1976.

New York Times Book Review, May 9, 1965; November 3, 1968; March 5, 1972; August 24, 1975; August 3, 1980; August 4, 1985; November 23, 1986; July 24, 1988; December 31, 1989; May 13, 1990; December 9, 1990; May 3, 1992, p. 38; March 14, 1993; November 14, 1993; March 13, 1994 p. 30; June 30, 1996, p. 28.

Publishers Weekly, January 27, 1997; June 16, 1997.

Punch, March 6, 1985, p. 54.

Rapport, Volume 18, number 2, 1994, p. 19.

Science Fiction Chronicle, January, 1985; May, 1985.

Times (London), November 19, 1988; August 2, 1990.

Times Literary Supplement, June 12, 1969; March 15, 1974; November 7, 1980; August 3, 1984; January 2, 1987.

Tribune Books (Chicago), December 30, 1990.

Voice Literary Supplement, December, 1983.

Voice of Youth Advocates, August, 1993, pp. 170-71; June, 1993, p. 104.

Washington Post Book World, February 28, 1982; May 8, 1983; September 28, 1986; September 27, 1987; May 27, 1990; March 28, 1993, p. 9.

*   *   *

SILVERSTEIN, Shel(by) 1932-
(Uncle Shelby)

PERSONAL: Born in Chicago, IL; divorced; children: one daughter.

ADDRESSES: Office—c/o Grapefruit Productions, 106 Montague St., Brooklyn, NY 11201.

CAREER: Cartoonist, composer, lyricist, folksinger, writer, and director. *Playboy,* Chicago, IL, writer and cartoonist, 1956–. Appeared in film, *Who Is Harry Kellerman and Why Is He Saying Those Terrible Things about Me?,* 1971. *Military service:* Served with U.S. forces in Japan and Korea during 1950s; cartoonist for Pacific *Stars and Stripes.*

AWARDS, HONORS: New York Times Outstanding Book Award, 1974, Michigan Young Readers' Award, 1981, and George G. Stone Award, 1984, all for *Where the Sidewalk Ends: The Poems & Drawings of Shel Silverstein; School Library Journal* Best Books Award, 1981, Buckeye Award, 1983 and 1985, George G. Stone Award, 1984, and William Allen White Award, 1984, all for *A Light In the Attic;* International Reading Association's Children's Choice Award, 1982, for *The Missing Piece Meets the Big O.*

WRITINGS:

SELF-ILLUSTRATED

Now Here's My Plan: A Book of Futilities, foreword by Jean Shepherd, Simon & Schuster (New York City), 1960.

Uncle Shelby's ABZ Book: A Primer for Tender Young Minds (humor), Simon & Schuster, 1961.

Playboy's Teevee Jeebies (drawings), Playboy Press (Chicago), 1963.

Uncle Shelby's Story of Lafcadio, the Lion Who Shot Back (juvenile), Harper (New York City), 1963.

The Giving Tree (juvenile), Harper, 1964.

Uncle Shelby's Giraffe and a Half (verse; juvenile), Harper, 1964, published in England as *A Giraffe and a Half*, J. Cape (London), 1988.

Uncle Shelby's Zoo: Don't Bump the Glump! (verse; juvenile), Simon & Schuster, 1964.

(Under pseudonym Uncle Shelby) *Who Wants a Cheap Rhinoceros!* Macmillan (New York City), 1964.

More Playboy's Teevee Jeebies: Do-It-Yourself Dialog for the Late Late Show (drawings), Playboy Press, 1965.

Where the Sidewalk Ends: The Poems & Drawings of Shel Silverstein (poems), Harper, 1974.

The Missing Piece (juvenile), Harper, 1976.

Different Dances (drawings), Harper, 1979.

A Light in the Attic (poems), Harper, 1981.

The Missing Piece Meets the Big O (juvenile), Harper, 1981.

(With Cherry Potts) *Poetry Galore and More,* Upstart Library, 1993.

Falling Up: Poems and Drawings, HarperCollins, 1996.

PLAYS

The Lady or the Tiger Show (one-act; from the short story by Frank Stockton), first produced in New York City at Ensemble Studio Theatre, May, 1981.

(And director) *Gorilla,* first produced in Chicago, 1983.

Wild Life (contains *I'm Good to My Doggies, Nonstop, Chicken Suit Optional,* and *The Lady or the Tiger Show*), first produced in New York City, 1983.

Remember Crazy Zelda? first produced in New York City, 1984.

The Crate, first produced in New York City, 1985.

The Happy Hour, first produced in New York City, 1985.

One Tennis Shoe, first produced in New York City, 1985.

Little Feet, first produced in New York City, 1986.

Wash and Dry, first produced in New York City, 1986.

The Devil and Billy Markham (drama; produced in New York City at Lincoln Center, December, 1989, with David Mamet's *Bobby Gould in Hell* under the collective title *Oh, Hell*) published in *Oh, Hell!: Two One-Act Plays,* Samuel French (New York City), 1991.

(Contributor) Billy Aronson, editor, *The Best American Short Plays 1992-1993: The Theatre Annual since 1937,* Applause (Diamond Bar, CA), 1993.

OTHER

(Contributor) Myra Cohn Livingston, editor, *I Like You, If You Like Me: Poems of Friendship,* Margaret McElderry Books (New York City), 1987.

(With David Mamet) *Things Change* (screenplay), Grove Press (New York City), 1988.

Also composer and lyricist of songs, including "A Boy Named Sue," "One's on the Way," "The Unicorn," "Boa Constrictor," "So Good to So Bad," "The Great Conch Train Robbery," and "Yes, Mr. Rogers." Albums of Silverstein's songs recorded by others include *Freakin' at the Freakers Ball,* Columbia, 1972; *Sloppy Seconds,* Columbia, 1972; *Dr. Hook,* Columbia, 1972; and *Bobby Bare Sings Lullabys, Legends, and Lies: The Songs of Shel Silverstein,* RCA Victor, 1973. Albums of original motion picture scores include *Ned Kelly,* United Artists, 1970, and *Who Is Harry Kellerman and Why Is He Saying Those Terrible Things about Me?* Columbia, 1971. Other recordings include *Drain My Brain,* Cadet; *Dirty Feet,* Hollis Music, 1968; *Shel Silverstein: Songs and Stories,* Casablanca, 1978; *The Great Conch Train Robbery,* 1980; and *Where the Sidewalk Ends,* Columbia, 1984. *The Giving Tree* has been translated into French.

SIDELIGHTS: Shel Silverstein is best known for his collections of children's poetry *Where the Sidewalk Ends: The Poems & Drawings of Shel Silverstein* and *A Light in the Attic,* both of which enjoyed extended stays on the *New York Times* Bestseller List. Silverstein is also the author of the children's classic *The Giving Tree.* In addition to his writings for children, Silverstein has served as a longtime *Playboy* cartoonist, has written several plays for adults, and has penned and recorded such country and novelty songs as Johnny Cash's "A Boy Named Sue."

Silverstein's talents were well-developed when he joined the U.S. armed forces in the 1950s. Stationed in Japan and Korea, he worked as a cartoonist for the Pacific edition of the military newspaper *Stars and Stripes.* After leaving the military, Silverstein became a cartoonist for *Playboy* in 1956, and his work for that magazine resulted in such collections as *Playboy's Teevee Jeebies* and *More Playboy's Teevee Jeebies: Do-It-Yourself Dialog for the Late Late Show.*

Silverstein's career as a children's author began with the 1963 publication of *Uncle Shelby's Story of Lafcadio, the Lion Who Shot Back.* In a *Publishers Weekly* interview, he confided to Jean F. Mercier: "I never planned to write or draw for kids. It was Tomi Ungerer, a friend of mine, who insisted . . . practically dragged me, kicking and screaming, into (editor) Ursula Nordstrom's office. And she convinced me that Tomi was right, I could do children's books." *Lafcadio* concerns a lion who obtains a hunter's gun and practices until he becomes a good enough marksman to join a circus. A *Publishers Weekly* reviewer called the book "a wild, free-wheeling, slangy tale that most children and many parents will enjoy immensely."

Although *Lafcadio* and *Uncle Shelby's Giraffe and a Half* met with moderate success, it was not until *The Giving Tree* that Silverstein first achieved widespread fame as a children's writer. The story of a tree that sacrifices its shade, fruit, branches, and finally its trunk to a little boy in order to make him happy, *The Giving Tree* had slow sales initially, but its audience steadily grew. As Richard R. Lingeman reported in the *New York Times Book Review,* "Many readers saw a religious symbolism in the altruistic tree; ministers preached sermons on *The Giving Tree;* it was discussed in Sunday schools." Despite its popularity as a moral or fable, the book was on occasion attacked by feminist critics for what they perceived as its inherent sexism; Barbara A. Schram noted in *Interracial Books for Children:* "By choosing the female pronoun for the all-giving tree and the male pronoun for the all-taking boy, it is clear that the author did indeed have a prototypical master/slave relationship in mind . . . How frightening that little boys and girls who read *The Giving Tree* will encounter this glorification of female selflessness and male selfishness."

In 1974 Silverstein published the collection of poems titled *Where the Sidewalk Ends.* Earning Silverstein favorable comparisons to Dr. Seuss and Edward Lear, *Where the Sidewalk Ends* contained such humorous pieces as "Sarah Cynthia Sylvia Stout / Would Not Take the Garbage Out," "Dreadful," and "Band-Aids." The collection and its 1981 successor, *A Light in the Attic,* continue to be popular with both children and adults; *Publishers Weekly* called the latter book "a big, fat treasure for Silverstein devotees, with trenchant verses expressing high-flown, exhilarating nonsense as well as thoughts unexpectedly sober and even sad."

Silverstein's 1976 *The Missing Piece,* like *The Giving Tree,* has been subject to varying interpretations. The volume chronicles the adventures of a circle who, lacking a piece of itself, goes along singing and searching for its missing part. But after the circle finds the wedge, he decides he was happier on the search—without the missing wedge—than he is with it. As Anne Roiphe explained in the *New York Times Book Review, The Missing Piece* can be read in the same way as "the fellow at the singles bar explaining why life is better if you don't commit yourself to anyone for too long— the line goes that too much togetherness turns people into bores— that creativity is preserved by freedom to explore from one relationship to another. . . . This fable can also be interpreted to mean that no one should try to find all the answers, no one should hope to fill all the holes in themselves, achieve total transcendental harmony or psychic order because a person without a search, loose ends, internal conflicts and external goals becomes too smooth to enjoy or know what's going on. Too much satisfaction blocks exchange with the outside." Silverstein published a sequel, *The Missing Piece Meets the Big O,* in 1981. This work is told from the missing piece's perspective, and as in the original, the book's protagonist discovers the value of self-sufficiency.

Since 1981, Silverstein has concentrated on writing plays for adults. One of his best known, *The Lady or the Tiger Show,* has been performed on its own and with other one-act works collectively entitled *Wild Life.* Updating a short story by American novelist and fiction writer Frank Stockton, *The Lady or the Tiger Show* concerns a game show producer willing to go to extreme lengths to achieve high ratings. Placed in a life-or-death situation, the contestant of the show is forced to choose between two doors; behind one door lies a ferocious tiger, while the girl of his dreams is concealed behind the other. The play was characterized in *Variety* as "a hilarious harpooning of media hype and show biz amorality."

With *Falling Up,* Silverstein returned to poetry for children (and adults) after a fifteen-year absence. This collection of 140 poems with drawings ranges in subject matter "from tattoos to sun hats to God to—no kidding—a garden of noses," wrote Susan Stark in the *Detroit News. Publishers Weekly* called the poems "vintage Silverstein," a work "cheeky and clever and often darkly subversive," focusing on the unexpected. Judy Zuckerman reported in the *New York Times Book Review,* "Mr. Silverstein's expressive line drawings are perfectly suited to his texts, extending the humor, and sometimes the strangeness of his ideas."

Silverstein has also collaborated with American playwright, scriptwriter, director, and novelist David Mamet on several projects. The two cowrote the screenplay for Mamet's 1988 film *Things Change,* which starred Joe Mantegna and Don Ameche. Silverstein's play *The Devil and Billy Markham* and Mamet's *Bobby Gould in Hell* have also been published and produced together under the collective title *Oh, Hell.* Performed as a monologue, *The Devil and Billy Markham* relates a series of bets made between Satan and a Nashville songwriter and singer. Although the work received mixed reviews, William A. Henry III noted in *Time* that "Silverstein's script, told in verse with occasional bursts of music, is rowdy and rousing and raunchily uproarious, especially in a song about a gala party where saints and sinners mingle."

BIOGRAPHICAL/CRITICAL SOURCES:

BOOKS

Children's Literature Review, Volume 5, Gale (Detroit), 1983, pp. 208-13.
Twentieth-Century Children's Writers, 3rd edition, St. James Press (Detroit), 1989, pp. 886-87.

PERIODICALS

Book Week, March 21, 1965.
Detroit News, November 4, 1979; May 1, 1996.
Interracial Books for Children, Volume 5, number 5, 1974.
Nation, January 29, 1990, pp. 141-44.
New Republic, January 29, 1990, pp. 27-28.
Newsweek, December 7, 1981.
New York, May 30, 1983, p. 75; December 18, 1989, pp. 105-7.
New Yorker, November 14, 1988, p. 89; December 25, 1989, p. 77.
New York Times, May 29, 1981; October 11, 1981.
New York Times Book Review, September 24, 1961; September 9, 1973; November 3, 1974; May 2, 1976; April 30, 1978; November 25, 1979; November 8, 1981; March 9, 1986, pp. 36-37; May 19, 1996, p. 29.
People Weekly, August 18, 1980.
Publishers Weekly, October 28, 1963; February 24, 1975; September 18, 1981; April 29, 1996.
Saturday Review, November 30, 1974; May 15, 1976.
Time, December 18, 1989, p. 78.
Variety, May 11, 1983, p. 112; December 13, 1989, p. 89.
Washington Post Book World, April 12, 1981.
Wilson Library Bulletin, November, 1987, p. 65.

*   *   *

SIM, Georges
  See SIMENON, Georges (Jacques Christian)

*   *   *

SIMENON, Georges (Jacques Christian) 1903-1989 (Bobette, Christian Brulls, Germain d'Antibes, Jacques Dersonnes, Georges d'Isly, Luc Dorsan, Jean Dorsange, Jean Dossage, Jean du Perry, Georges Martin Georges, Gom Gut, Kim, Plick et Plock, Georges Sim, Gaston Vialis, G. Violis)

PERSONAL: Born February 13, 1903, in Liege, Belgium; died September 4, 1989, in Lausanne, Switzerland; cremated and ashes spread outside his home in Lausanne, Switzerland; son of Desire (an insurance clerk) and Henriette (Brull) Simenon; married Regine Renchon, March 24, 1923 (divorced, June 21, 1950); married Denyse Ouimet, June 22, 1950 (separated, c. 1970); children: (first marriage) Marc; (second marriage) Jean, Marie-Georges (deceased), Pierre. *Education:* Graduated from College Saint-Servais, Liege, Belgium.

CAREER: Worked as a baker's apprentice and bookstore clerk in Liege, Belgium; *Liege Gazette,* Liege, began as police reporter, became comic columnist; went to Paris, 1922, and became fulltime writer of pulp fiction under various pseudonyms; traveled in Europe during late 1920s on his yacht, *Ostrogot;* wrote first "Maigret" novel while in the Netherlands, 1931, and produced nineteen "Maigret" mysteries, 1931-33; abandoned "Maigret" character, 1933, turned to psychological novels, 1933-73; continued "Maigret" series, 1940; came to the United States following World War II and traveled and lived in the United States and Canada; moved to Switzerland, 1955; retired from writing novels, 1973, to write nonfiction and his diaries. *Wartime service:* Worked with refugees in Vichy, France, during World War II.

MEMBER: Acadame Royale de Langue et Litterature Francaise (Brussels), American Academy of Arts and Letters, Mystery Writers of America (former president).

AWARDS, HONORS: Grand Master Award, Mystery Writers of America, 1965.

WRITINGS:

"MAIGRET" SERIES NOVELS

Pietr-le-Letton, Fayard, 1931, translation published as *The Strange Case of Peter the Lett,* Covici-Friede, 1933, translation by Anthony Abbott published as *The Case of Peter the Lett* in *Inspector Maigret Investigates,* Hurst & Blackett, 1934, translation by Daphne Woodward published as *Maigret and the Enigmatic Lett,* Penguin, 1963.

Au rendez-vous des terre-neuvas, Fayard, 1931, translation by Margaret Ludwig published as *The Sailors Rendezvous* in *Maigret Keeps a Rendezvous,* George Routledge, 1940, Harcourt, 1941.

Le Charretier de la "Providence," Fayard, 1931, translation published as *The Crime at Lock 14* [with] *The Shadow on the Courtyard,* Covici-Friede, 1934, translation by Robert Baldick published as *Maigret Meets a Milord,* Penguin, 1963.

Le Chien jaune, Fayard, 1931, translation by Geoffrey Sainsbury published as *A Face for a Clue,* George Routledge, 1939, Harcourt, 1940.

La Danseuse du Gai-Moulin, Fayard, 1931, translation by Sainsbury published as *At the Gai-Moulin,* Harcourt, 1940, published as *At The Gai-Moulin* [with] *A Battle of Nerves,* Penguin, 1951.

M. Gallet decede, Fayard, 1931, translation published as *The Death of Monsieur Gallet,* Covici-Friede, 1932, translation by Abbott published as *The Death of M. Gallet* in *Introducing Inspector Maigret,* Hurst & Blackett, 1933, translation by Margaret Marshall published as *Maigret Stonewalled,* Penguin, 1963.

La Nuit du carrefour, Fayard, 1931, translation published as *The Crossroad Murders,* Covici-Friede, 1933, translation by Abbot published as *The Crossroad Murders* in *Inspector Maigret Investigates,* Hurst & Blackett, 1933, published as *La Nuit de carrefour,* edited and adapted by P. W. Packer, Oxford University Press, 1935, translation by Baldick published as *Maigret at the Crossroads,* Penguin, 1963.

Le Pendu de Saint-Phiolien, Fayard, 1931, translation by Abbot published as *The Crime of Inspector Maigret,* Covici-Friede, 1933, published as *The Crime of Inspector Maigret* in *Introducing Inspector Maigret,* Hurst & Blackett, translation by Tony White published as *Maigret and the Hundred Gibbets,* Penguin, 1963, published as *Maigret et le Pendu de Saint-Pholien,* edited by Geoffrey Goodall, St. Martin's, 1965.

Un Crime en Hollande, Fayard, 1931, translation by Sainsbury published as *A Crime in Holland,* Harcourt, 1940, published as *A Crime in Holland* [with] *A Face for a Clue,* Penguin, 1952.

La Tete d'un homme (L'Homme de la Tour Eiffel), Fayard, 1931, translation by Sainsbury published as *A Battle of Nerves* in *The Patience of Maigret,* George Routledge, 1939, Harcourt, 1940.

L'Affaire Saint Fiacre, Fayard, 1932, translation by Ludwig published as *The Saint-Fiacre Affair* in *Maigret Keeps a Rendezvous,* George Routledge, 1940, Harcourt, 1941, translation by Baldick published as *Maigret Goes Home,* Penguin, 1967, Thorndike, 1993.

Chez les Flamands, Fayard, 1932, translation by Sainsbury published as *The Flemish Shop,* George Routledge, 1940, Harcourt, 1941.

Le Fou de Bergerac, Fayard, 1932, translation by Sainsbury published as *The Madman of Bergerac* in *Maigret Travels South,* Harcourt, 1940.

La Guinguette a deux sous, Fayard, 1932, translation by Sainsbury published as *Guinguette by the Seine* in *Maigret to the Rescue,* George Routledge, 1940, Harcourt, 1941.

Liberty Bar, Fayard, 1932, translation by Sainsbury published as *Liberty Bar* in *Maigret Travels South,* Harcourt, 1940.

L'Ombre Chinoise, Fayard, 1932, translation published as *The Shadow in the Courtyard* [with] *The Crime at Lock 14,* Covici-Friede, 1934, published in England as *The Shadow in the Courtyard* in *The Triumph of Inspector Maigret,* Hurst & Blackett, 1934, translation by Jean Stewart published as *Maigret Mystified,* Penguin, 1965.

Le Port des brumes, Fayard, 1932, translation by Stuart Gilbert published as *Death of a Harbormaster* in *Maigret and M. L'Abbe,* George Routledge, 1941, Harcourt, 1942.

L'Ecluse no. 1, Fayard, 1933, translation by Ludwig published as *The Lock at Charenton* in *Maigret Sits It Out,* Harcourt, 1941.

Maigret, Fayard, 1934, translation by Ludwig published as *Maigret Returns* in *Maigret Sits It Out,* Harcourt, 1941.

Cecile est morte (also see below), Gallimard, 1942, translation by Eileen Ellenbogen published as *Maigret and the Spinster,* Harcourt, 1977.

Maigret et les Caves du Majestic (also see below), [France], 1942, translation by Caroline Hiller published as *Maigret and the Hotel Majestic,* Hamish Hamilton, 1977.

La Maison du juge (also see below), [France], c. 1942, translation by Ellenbogen published as *Maigret in Exile,* Hamish Hamilton, 1978.

Felice est la, Gallimard, 1944, translation by Ellenbogen published as *Maigret and the Toy Village,* Hamish Hamilton, 1978.

L'Inspector Cadavre, Gallimard, 1944, translation by Thomson published as *Maigret's Rival,* Hamish Hamilton, 1978.

Signe Picpus, Gallimard, 1944, translation by Sainsbury published as *Maigret and the Fortuneteller,* Harcourt, 1989.

Maigret a New York, Presses de la Cite, 1947, translation by Adrienne Foulke published as *Maigret in New York's Underworld,* Doubleday, 1955, published as *Inspector Maigret in New York's Underworld,* New American Library, 1956.

Maigret se fache, Presses de la Cite, 1947.

La Pipe de Maigret, Presses de la Cite, 1947, translation by Stewart published as *Maigret's Pipe,* Harcourt, 1985.

Maigret et son morte, Presses de la Cite, 1948, translation by Stewart published as *Maigret's Dead Man,* Doubleday, 1964, published as *Maigret's Special Murder,* Hamish Hamilton, 1964

Les Vacances de Maigret, Presses de la Cite, 1948, translation by Sainsbury published as *Maigret on Holiday,* Routledge & Kegan Paul, 1950, published as *No Vacation for Maigret,* Doubleday, 1953.

Maigret chez le coroner, Presses de la Cite, 1949, translation by Francis Keene published as *Maigret at the Coroner's,* Harcourt, 1980, published in England as *Maigret and the Coroner,* Hamish Hamilton, 1980.

Maigret et la vieille dame, Presses de la Cite, 1949, translation by Robert Brain published as *Maigret and the Old Lady,* Hamish Hamilton, 1958.

Mon ami Maigret, Presses de la Cite, 1949, translation by Nigel Ryan published as *My Friend Maigret,* Hamish Hamilton, published as *The Methods of Maigret,* Doubleday, 1957.

La Premier Enquette de Maigret, 1913, Presses de la Cite, 1949, translation by Robert Brain published as *Maigret's First Case,* Hamish Hamilton, 1965.

L'Amie de Mine Maigret, Presses de la Cite, 1950, translation by Helen Sebba published as *Madame Maigret's Own Case,* Doubleday, 1959, published as *Madame Maigret's Friend* (also see below), Hamish Hamilton, 1960.

Les Petits Cochons sans queues, Presses de la Cite, 1950, published as *Maigret et les petits cochons sans queues,* 1957.

Les Memoires de Maigret, Presses de la Cite, 1951, translation by Stewart published as *Maigret's Memoires,* Hamish Hamilton, 1963, Harcourt, 1985.

Maigret en mueble, Presses de la Cite, 1951, translation by Robert Brain published as *Maigret Takes a Room,* Hamish Hamilton, 1960, published as *Maigret Rents a Room,* Doubleday, 1961.

Maigret et la grande perche, Presses de la Cite, 1951, translation by J. Maclaren-Ross published as *Maigret and the Burglar's Wife,* Hamish Hamilton, 1955, published as *Inspector Maigret and the Burglar's Wife,* Doubleday, 1956.

Maigret, Longnon et les gangsters, Presses de la Cite, 1952, translation by Louise Varese published as *Maigret and the Killers,* Doubleday, 1954, published as *Maigret and the Gangsters,* Hamish Hamilton, 1974.

Le Revolver de Maigret, Presses de la Cite, 1952, translation by Ryan published as *Maigret's Revolver,* Doubleday, 1956.

Maigret et l'homme du banc, Presses de la Cite, 1953, translation by Ellenbogen published as *Maigret and the Man on the Bench,* Harcourt, 1975 (published in England as *Maigret and the Man on the Boulevard,* Hamish Hamilton, 1975).

Maigret a peur, Presses de la Cite, 1953, translation by Margaret Duff published as *Maigret Afraid,* Hamish Hamilton, 1961, Harcourt, 1983, published as *Maigret se trompe,* Presses de la Cite, 1953, French & European Publications, 1990, translation by Alan Hodge published as *Maigret's Mistake* in *Maigret Right and Wrong,* Hamish Hamilton, 1957, published as *Maigret's Mistake,* Harcourt, 1988.

Maigret a l'ecole, Presses de la Cite, 1954, translation by Woodward published as *Maigret Goes to School,* Hamish Hamilton, 1957, Thorndike, 1994.

Maigret chez le ministre, privately printed, 1954, translation by Moura Budberg published as *Maigret and the Calame Report,* Harcourt, 1969 (published in England as *Maigret and the Minister,* Hamish Hamilton, 1969).

Maigret Right and Wrong (contains *Maigret in Montmarte,* translation by Woodward; also see below), Hamish Hamilton, 1954.

Maigret et la jeune morte, Presses de la Cite, 1954, translation by Woodward published as *Inspector Maigret and the Dead Girl,* Doubleday, 1955 (published in England as *Maigret and the Young Girl,* Hamish Hamilton, 1955).

Maigret et le corps sans tete, privately printed, 1955, translation by Ellenbogen published as *Maigret and the Headless Corpse,* Hamish Hamilton, 1967, Harcourt, 1968.

Maigret tend un piege, Presses de la Cite, 1955, translation by Woodward published as *Maigret Sets a Trap,* Hamish Hamilton, 1965, G. K. Hall, 1990.

Un Echec de Maigret, Presses de la Cite, 1956, translation by Woodward published as *Maigret's Failure,* Hamish Hamilton, 1962.

Inspector Maigret and the Strangled Stripper (originally published as *Maigret au "Picratts,"* Presses de la Cite), translation by Cornelia Schaffer, Doubleday, 1956, published as *Maigret at Montmartre,* Harcourt, 1989.

Maigret s'amuse, Presses de la Cite, 1957, translation by Richard Brain published as *Maigret's Little Joke,* Hamish Hamilton, 1957, published as *None of Maigret's Business,* Doubleday, 1958.

Maigret voyage, Presses de la Cite, 1958, translation by Stewart published as *Maigret and the Millionaires,* Harcourt, 1974.

Les Scrupules de Maigret, Presses de la Cite, 1959, translation by Robert Eglesfield published as *Maigret Has Scruples,* Hamish Hamilton, 1959, Harcourt, 1988, published as *Maigret Has Scruples* in *Versus Inspector Maigret,* Doubleday, 1960, published as *Maigret Has Scruples* [with] *Maigret and the Reluctant Witness,* Ace Books, 1962.

Une Confidence de Maigret, Presses de la Cite, 1959, translation by Lyn Moir published as *Maigret Has Doubts,* Hamish Hamilton, 1968, Harcourt, 1982.

Maigret et les temoins recalcitrants, Presses de la Cite, 1959, French & European Publications, 1990, translation by Woodward published as *Maigret and the Reluctant Witness* in *Versus Inspector Maigret,* Doubleday, 1960.

Maigret aux assises, Presses de la Cite, 1960, translation by Robert Brain published as *Maigret in Court,* Hamish Hamilton, 1961, Avon, 1988.

Maigret et les vieillards, Presses de la Cite, 1960, translation by Eglesfield published as *Maigret in Society,* Hamish Hamilton, 1962.

Maigret et le voleur paresseux, Presses de la Cite, 1961, translation by Woodward published as *Maigret and the Lazy Burglar,* Hamish Hamilton, 1963.

Maigret et les braves gens, Presses de la Cite, 1962, translation by Helen Thomson published as *Maigret and the Black Sheep,* Harcourt, 1976.

Maigret et le client du samedi, Presses de la Cite, 1962, translation by White published as *Maigret and the Saturday Caller,* Hamish Hamilton, 1964.

Maigret et l'inspecteur malgracieux, Presses de la Cite, 1962.

La Colere de Maigret, Presses de la Cite, 1963, translation by Eglesfield published as *Maigret Loses His Temper,* Hamish Hamilton, 1965, Harcourt, 1974.

Maigret et le clochard, Presses de la Cite, 1963, translation by Stewart published as *Maigret and the Bum,* Harcourt, 1973 (published in England as *Maigret and the Dosser,* Hamish Hamilton, 1973).

Maigret et le fantome, Presses de la Cite, 1964, translation by Ellenbogen published as *Maigret and the Apparition,* Harcourt, 1976, published in England as *Maigret and the Ghost,* Hamish Hamilton, 1976.

Maigret se defend, Presses de la Cite, 1964, translation by Alistair Hamilton published as *Maigret on the Defensive* (also see below), Hamish Hamilton, 1966, Avon, 1987.

La Patience de Maigret, Presses de la Cite, 1965, translation by Hamilton published as *The Patience of Maigret* (also see below), Hamish Hamilton, 1966, published as *Maigret Bides His Time,* Harcourt, 1985.

Maigret et l'affair Nahour, Presses de la Cite, 1966, translation by Hamilton published as *Maigret and the Nahour Case,* Hamish Hamilton, 1967, Harcourt, 1986.

Le Voleur de Maigret, Presses de la Cite, 1967, translation by Ryan published as *Maigret's Pickpocket* (also see below), Harcourt, 1968, published as *Maigret and the Pickpocket,* 1985.

L'Ami d'enfance de Maigret, Presses de la Cite, 1968, translation by Ellenbogen published as *Maigret's Boyhood Friend,* Harcourt, 1970.

Maigret a Vichy, Presses de la Cite, 1968, translation by Ellenbogen published as *Maigret in Vichy,* Harcourt, 1969 (published in England as *Maigret Takes the Waters* [also see below], Hamish Hamilton, 1969).

Maigret hesite, Presses de la Cite, 1968, translation by Moir published as *Maigret Hesitates* (also see below), Harcourt, 1970.

Maigret et le tueur, Presses de la Cite, 1969, translation by Moir published as *Maigret and the Killer* (also see below), Harcourt, 1971, published as *Le Meurtre d'un etudiant,* edited by Frederick Ernst, Holt, 1971.

La Folle de Maigret, Presses de la Cite, 1970, translation by Ellenbogen published as *Maigret and the Madwoman,* Harcourt, 1972.

Maigret et le marchand de vin, Presses de la Cite, 1970, translation by Ellenbogen published as *Maigret and the Wine Merchant,* Harcourt, 1971.

Maigret et l'homme tout seul, Presses de la Cite, 1971, translation by Ellenbogen published as *Maigret and the Loner,* Harcourt, 1975.

Maigret et l'indicateur, Presses de la Cite, 1971, translation by Moir published as *Maigret and the Informer,* Harcourt, 1972 (published in England as *Maigret and the Flea,* Hamish Hamilton, 1972).

Maigret et Monsieur Charles, Presses de la Cite, 1972, translation by Marianne A. Sinclair published as *Maigret and Monsieur Charles,* Hamish Hamilton, 1973.

Maigret on the Riviera (originally published in France, 1940), translation by Sainsbury, Harcourt, 1988.

NOVELS

Le Relais d'Alsace, Fayard, 1931, translation by Gilbert published as *The Man From Everywhere* in *Maigret and M. Labbe,* George Routledge, 1941, Harcourt, 1942, published as *The Man from Everywhere* [with] *Newhaven-Dieppe,* Penguin, 1952.

Le Passageur du "Polarlys," Fayard, 1932, translation by Gilbert published as *The Mystery of the 'Polarlys'* in *Two Latitudes,* George Routledge, 1942, Harcourt, 1943, translation by Victor Kosta published as *Danger at Sea* in *On Land and Sea,* Hanover House, 1954.

Les Treize Coupables, Fayard, 1932.

Les Treize Enigmes, Fayard, 1932.

Les Treize Mysteries, Fayard, 1932.

L'Ane rouge, Fayard, 1933, translated by Stewart published as *The Nightclub,* Harcourt, 1979.

Le Coup de lune, Fayard, 1933, translation by Gilbert published as *Tropic Moon,* George Routledge, 1942, Harcourt, 1943, published as *Tropic Moon,* Berkeley, 1958.

Les Fiancailles de M. Hire, Fayard, 1933, translation by Woodward published as *Mr. Hire's Engagement* in *The Sacrifice,* Hamish Hamilton, 1958.

Les Gens d'en face, Fayard, 1933, translation by Sainsbury published as *The Window Over the Way* [with] *The Gendarme's Report,* Routledge & Kegan Paul, 1951, translation by Kosta published as *Danger Ashore* in *On Land and Sea,* Hanover House, 1954, translation by Baldick published as *The Window over the Way,* Penguin, 1966.

Le Haut-mal, 1933, translation by Gilbert published as *The Woman in the Grey House,* George Routledge, 1942, Harcourt, 1944.

La Maison du Canal, Fayard, 1933, translation by Sainsbury published as *The House by the Canal* [with] *The Ostenders,* Routledge & Kegan Paul, 1952.

Les Suicides, Nouvelle Revue Francaise, 1934, translation by Gilbert published as *One Way Out* in *Escape in Vain,* George Routledge, 1943, Harcourt, 1944.

L'Homme de Londres, Fayard, 1934, translation by Gilbert published as *Newhaven-Dieppe* in *Affairs of Destiny,* George Routledge, 1942, Harcourt, 1944, published as *Newhaven-Dieppe* [with] *The Man From Everywhere,* Penguin, 1952.

La Locataire, Nouvelle Revue Francaise, 1934, translation by Gilbert published as *The Lodger* in *Escape in Vain,* George Routledge, 1943, Harcourt, 1944, published as *The Lodger,* Harcourt, 1983.

Les Clients d'Avrenos, Nouvelle Revue Francaise, 1935.

Les Pitard, Nouvelle Revue Francaise, 1935, translation by Sainsbury published as *A Wife at Sea* [with] *The Murderer,* Routledge & Kegan Paul, 1949.

Quartier Negre, Nouvelle Revue Francaise, 1935.

Les Demoiselles de Concarneau, Nouvelle Revue Francaise, 1936, translation by Gilbert published as *The Breton Sisters* in *Havoc by Accident,* Harcourt, 1943.

L'Evade, Nouvelle Revue Francaise, 1936, translation by Sainsbury published as *The Disintegration of J.P.G.,* George Routledge, 1937.

Long cours, Nouvelle Revue Francaise, 1936, translation by Ellenbogen as *The Long Exile,* Harcourt, 1983.

45 a l'hombre, Nouvelle Revue Francaise, 1936.

L'Assassin, Nouvelle Revue Francaise, 1937, translation by Sainsbury published as *The Murderer* [with] *A Wife at Sea,* Routledge & Kegan Paul, 1947, published as *The Murderer,* Harcourt, 1986.

Le Blanc a lunettes, Nouvelle Revue Francaise, 1937, translation by Gilbert published as *Tatala,* in *Havoc by Accident,* Harcourt, 1943.

Faubourg, Nouvelle Revue Francaise, 1937, translation by Gilbert published as *Home Town* in *On the Danger Line,* Harcourt, 1944.

Le Testament Donadieu, Nouvelle Revue Francaise, 1937, translation by Gilbert published as *The Shadow Falls,* Harcourt, 1945, and as *Donadieu's Will,* Harcourt, 1991.

Ceux de la soif, Nouvelle Revue Francaise, 1938.

Chemin sans issue, Nouvelle Revue Francaise, 1938, translation by Gilbert published as *Blind Alley,* Reynal & Hitchcock, 1946, published as *Blind Alley* in *Lost Moorings,* George Routledge, 1946.

Le Cheval blanc, Nouvelle Revue Francaise, 1938, translated by Norman Denny as *The White Horse Inn,* Harcourt, 1980.

L'Homme qui regardait passer les trains, Nouvelle Revue Francaise, 1938, translation by Gilbert published as *The Man Who Watched the Trains Go By,* Musson, 1942, Reynal & Hitchcock, 1946.

La Marie du port, Nouvelle Revue Francaise, 1938.

La Mauvaise Etoile, Nouvelle Revue Francaise, 1938.

Monsieur La Souris, Nouvelle Revue Francaise, 1938, translation by Sainsbury published as *Monsieur La Souris* [with] *Poisoned Relations,* Routledge & Kegan Paul, 1950, translation by Baldick published as *The Mouse,* Penguin, 1966.

Les Rescapes du "Telmaque," Nouvelle Revue Francaise, 1938, translation by Gilbert published as *The Survivors* [with] *Black Rain,* Routledge & Kegan Paul, 1949, published as *The Survivors,* Harcourt, 1985.

Les Soeurs Lacroix, Nouvelle Revue Francaise, 1938, translation by Sainsbury published as *Poisoned Relations* [with] *Monsieur La Sours,* Routledge & Kegan Paul, 1950.

Le Suspect, Nouvelle Revue Francaise, 1938, translation by Gilbert published as *The Green Thermos* in *On the Danger Line,* Harcourt, 1944, and as *The Suspect,* Harcourt, 1991.

Touriste de bananes (ou, Les Dimanches de Tahiti), Nouvelle Revue Francaise, 1938, translation by Gilbert published as *Banana Tourist* in *Lost Moorings,* George Routledge, 1946.

Les Trois Crimes de mes amis, Nouvelle Revue Francaise, 1938.

Le Bourgmestre de Furnes, Nouvelle Revue Francaise, 1939, translation by Sainsbury published as *The Bourgomaster of Furnes,* Routledge & Kegan Paul, 1952.

Chez Krull, Nouvelle Revue Francaise, 1939, translation by Woodward published as *Chez Krull,* Hamish Hamilton, 1955, published as *Chez Krull,* New English Library, 1966.

Le Coup de vague, Nouvelle Revue Francaise, 1939.

Les Inconnus dans la maison, Nouvelle Revue Francaise, 1940, translation by Sainsbury published as *Strangers in the House,* Routledge & Kegan Paul, 1951, Doubleday, 1954.

Malempin, Nouvelle Revue Francaise, 1940, translation by Isabel Quigly published as *The Family Lie,* Hamish Hamilton, 1978.

Bergelon, Nouvelle Revue Francaise, 1941, translation by Ellenbogen published as *The Delivery,* Harcourt, 1981.

Cour d'Assises, Nouvelle Revue Francaise, 1941, translation by Sainsbury published as *Justice* [with] *A Chit of a Girl,* Routledge & Kegan Paul, 1949, published as *Justice,* Harcourt, 1983.

Il pleut bergere, Nouvelle Revue Francaise, 1941, translation by Sainsbury published as *Black Rain,* Reynal & Hitchcock, 1947, published as *Black Rain* [with] *The Survivors,* Routledge & Kegan Paul, 1949.

La Maison des sept jeunes filles, Gallimard, 1941.

L'Outlaw, Gallimard, 1941, translation by Howard Curtis published as *The Outlaw,* Harcourt, 1986.

Le Voyageur de la Toussaint, Nouvelle Revue Francaise, 1941, translation by Sainsbury published as *Strange Inheritance,* Routledge & Kegan Paul, 1970.

Les Fantomes du chapelier, Presses de la Cite, 1941, translation by Ryan published as *The Hatter's Ghost* in *The Judge and the Hatter,* Hamish Hamilton, 1956, translation by Willard Trask published as *The Hatter's Phantoms,* Harcourt, 1976.

Le Fils Cardinaud, Gallimard, 1942, translation by Richard Brain published as *Young Cardinaud* in *The Sacrifice,* Hamish Hamilton, 1956, published as *Young Cardinaud,* New English Library, 1966.

Oncle Charles s'est enferme, Nouvelle Revue Francaise, 1942, translation published as *Uncle Charles Has Locked Himself In,* Harcourt, 1987.

La Verite sur Bebe Donge, Nouvelle Revue Francaise, 1942, translation by Sainsbury published as *The Trial of Bebe Donge,* Routledge & Kegan Paul, 1952, translation by Varese published as *I Take This Woman* in *Satan's Children,* Prentice-Hall, 1953, and as *The Truth about Bebe Donge,* Harcourt, 1992.

La Veuve couderc, Nouvelle Revue Francaise, 1942, translation by Robert J. P. Hewitton (under pseudonym John Petrie) published as *Ticket of Leave,* Routledge & Kegan Paul, 1954, published as *The Widow* [with] *Magician,* Doubleday, 1955.

La Rapport du gendarme, Nouvelle Revue Francaise, 1944, translation by Sainsbury published as *The Gendarme's Report* [with] *Window Over the Way,* Routledge & Kegan Paul, 1951.

L'Aine des ferchaux, Gallimard, 1945, translation by Sainsbury published as *Magnet of Doom,* George Routledge, 1948, published as *The First Born,* Reynal & Hitchcock, 1949.

Le Fenetre des Rouet, Editions de la Jeune Parque, 1945, translation by Hewitton (under pseudonym John Petrie) published as *Across the Street,* Routledge & Kegan Paul, 1954.

La Fuite de Monsieur Monde, Editions de la Jeune Parque, 1945, translation by Stewart published as *Monsieur Monde Vanishes,* Hamish Hamilton, 1967, Harcourt, 1977.

Je me souviens, Presses de la Cite, 1945.

Trois Chambres a Manhattan, Presses de la Cite, 1945, translation by Lawrence G. Blochman published as *Three Beds in Manhattan,* Doubleday, 1964.

Le Cercle des Mahe, Gallimard, 1946.

Les Noces de Poitiers, Gallimard, 1946, translation by Ellenbogen published as *The Couple from Poitiers,* Harcourt, 1985.

Au Bout du rouleau, Presses de la Cite, 1947.

Le Clan des Ostendais, Gallimard, 1947, translation by Sainsbury published as *The Ostenders* [with] *The House by the Canal,* Routledge & Kegan Paul, 1952.

Lettre a mon juge, Presses de la Cite, 1947, translation by Varese published as *Act of Passion,* Prentice-Hall, 1952.

Le Passager clandestin, Editions de la Jeune Parque, 1947, translation by Ryan published as *The Stowaway,* Hamish Hamilton, 1957.

Le Bilan maletras, Gallimard, 1948, translation by Emily Read published as *The Reckoning,* Harcourt, 1984.

Le Destin des Malou, Presses de la Cite, 1948, translation by Dennis George published as *The Fate of the Malous,* Hamish Hamilton, 1962.

La Jument perdu, Presses de la Cite, 1948.

La Neige etait sale, Presses de la Cite, 1948, translation by Varese published as *The Snow Was Black,* Prentice-Hall, 1950, translation by Hewitton (under pseudonym John Petrie) published as *The Stain on the Snow,* Routledge & Kegan Paul, 1953.

Pedigree, Presses de la Cite, 1948, translation by Baldick published under same title, Hamish Hamilton, 1962.

Le Fond de la bouteille, Presses de la Cite, 1949, translation by Schaffer published as *The Bottom of the Bottle* in *Tidal Wave,* Doubleday, 1954 (published in England as *The Bottom of the Bottle,* Hamish Hamilton, 1977).

Les Quatre Jours du pauvre homme, Presses de la Cite, 1949, translation by Varese published as *Four Days in a Lifetime* in *Satan's Children,* Prentice-Hall, 1953, published as *Four Days in a Lifetime,* Hamish Hamilton, 1977.

L'Enterrement de Monsieur Bouvet, Presses de la Cite, 1950, translation by Eugene MacCowan published as *The Burial of Monsieur Bouvet* in *Destinations,* Doubleday, 1955, published as *Inquest on Bouvet,* Hamish Hamilton, 1958.

Un Nouveau dans la ville, Presses de la Cite, 1950.

Tante Jeanne, Presses de la Cite, 1950, translation by Sainsbury published as *Aunt Jeanne,* Routledge & Kegan Paul, 1953.

Les Volets verts, Presses de la Cite, 1950, translation by Varese published as *The Heart of a Man,* Prentice-Hall, 1951 (published in England as *The Heart of a Man,* Hamish Hamilton, 1955).

Marie qui louche, Presses de la Cite, 1951, translation by Varese published as *The Girl with a Squint,* Harcourt, 1978.

Le Temps d'Anais, Presses de la Cite, 1951, translation by Varese published as *The Girl in His Past,* Prentice-Hall, 1952.

Une Vie comme neuve, Presses de la Cite, 1951, translation by Joanne Richardson published as *A New Lease on Life,* Doubleday, 1963.

Les Freres Rico, Presses de la Cite, 1952, translation by Ernst Pawel published as *The Brothers Rico* in *Tidal Wave,* Doubleday, 1954 (published in England as *The Brothers Rico* in *Violent Ends,* Hamish Hamilton, 1964).

La Morte de Belle, Presses de la Cite, 1952, translation by Varese published as *Belle* in *Tidal Wave,* Doubleday, 1954 (published in England as *Belle* in *Violent Ends,* Hamish Hamilton, 1954).

Antoine et Julie, Presses de la Cite, 1953, translation by Sebba published as *Magician* [with] *The Widow,* Doubleday, 1955, published as *Magician,* Berkeley, 1956 (published in England as *The Magician,* Hamish Hamilton, 1974).

L'Escalier de fer, Presses de la Cite, 1953, translation by Ellenbogen published as *The Iron Staircase,* Hamish Hamilton, 1963, Harcourt, 1977.

Feux Rouges, Presses de la Cite, 1953, translation by Denny published as *The Hitchhiker* in *Destinations,* Doubleday, 1955, published as *Red Lights* in *Danger Ahead,* Hamish Hamilton, 1955, published as *The Hitchhiker,* Signet, 1957.

Crime impuni, Presses de la Cite, 1954, translation by Varese published as *Fugitive,* Doubleday, 1955, translation by White published as *Account Unsettled,* Hamish Hamilton, 1962.

Le Grand Bob, Presses de la Cite, 1954, translation by Eileen Lowe published as *Big Bob,* Hamish Hamilton, 1969.

L'Horloger d'Everton, Presses de la Cite, 1954, French & European Publications, 1992, translation by Denny published as *The Watchmaker of Everton* in *Danger Ahead,* Hamish Hamilton, 1955, published as *The Watchmaker of Everton* [with] *Witnesses,* Doubleday, 1956.

Les Temoins, privately printed, 1954, translation by Budberg published as *Witnesses* [with] *The Watchmaker of Everton,* Doubleday, 1956 (published in England as *The Witnesses* in *The Judge and the Hatter,* Hamish Hamilton, 1956).

La Boule noire, Presses de la Cite, 1955.

Les Complices, Presses de la Cite, 1955, translation by Bernard Frechtman published as *The Accomplices* [with] *The Blue Room,* Harcourt, 1964, published as *The Accomplices,* Hamish Hamilton, 1966, Harcourt, 1977.

En Case de malheur, Presses de la Cite, 1956, translation by Sebba published as *In Case of Emergency,* Doubleday, 1958.

Le Fils, Presses de la Cite, 1957, translation by Woodward published as *The Son,* Hamish Hamilton, 1958.

Le Negre, Presses de la Cite, 1957, translation by Sebba published as *The Negro,* Hamish Hamilton, 1959.

Le Petit Homme d'Arkhangelsk, Presses de le Cite, 1957, translation by Ryan published as *The Little Man From Arkangel,* Hamish Hamilton, 1957, published as *The Little Man From Arkangel* [with] *Sunday,* Harcourt, 1966.

Le Passage de la Ligne, Presses de la Cite, 1958.

Le President, Presses de la Cite, 1958, translation by Woodward published as *The Premier,* Hamish Hamilton, 1961, published as *The Premier* [with] *The Train,* Harcourt, 1966.

Strip-Tease, Presses de la Cite, 1958, translation by Robert Brain published as *Striptease,* Hamish Hamilton, 1959.

Dimanche, Presses de la Cite, 1959, translation by Ryan published as *Sunday,* Hamish Hamilton, 1960, published as *Sunday* [with] *The Little Man From Arkangel,* Harcourt, 1966.

La Vieille, Presses de la Cite, 1959.

L'Ours en pluche, Presses de la Cite, 1960, translation by John Clay published as *Teddy Bear,* Hamish Hamilton, 1971, Harcourt, 1972.

Le Veuf, Presses de la Cite, 1960, translation by Baldick published as *The Widower,* Hamish Hamilton, 1961.

Betty, Presses de la Cite, 1961, translation by Hamilton published as *Betty,* Harcourt, 1975.

Le Train, Presses de la Cite, 1961, translation by Baldick published as *The Train,* Hamish Hamilton, 1964, published as *The Train* [with] *The Premier,* Harcourt, 1966.

Les Autres, Presses de la Cite, 1962, 1992, translation by Hamilton published as *The House on Quai Notre Dame,* Harcourt, 1975 (published in England as *The Others,* Hamish Hamilton, 1975).

La Porte, Presses de la Cite, 1962, translation by Woodward published as *The Door,* Hamish Hamilton, 1964.

Les Anneaux de Bicetre, Presses de la Cite, 1963, translation by Stewart published as *The Patient,* Hamish Hamilton, 1963, published as *The Bells of Bicetre,* Harcourt, 1964.

La Chambre bleue, Presses de la Cite, 1964, translation by Ellenbogen published as *The Blue Room* [with] *The Accomplices,* Harcourt, 1964, published as *The Blue Room,* Hamish Hamilton, 1965.

L'Homme au petit chien, Presses de la Cite, 1964, translation by Stewart published as *The Man with the Little Dog,* Hamish Hamilton, 1965, Harcourt, 1989.

Le Petit Saint, Presses de la Cite, 1965, translation by Frechtman published as *The Little Saint,* Harcourt, 1965.

Le Train de Venise, Presses de la Cite, 1965, translation by Hamilton published as *The Venice Train,* Harcourt, 1974.

Le Confessional, Presses de la Cite, 1966, translation by Stewart published as *The Confessional,* Hamish Hamilton, 1967, Harcourt, 1968.

La Mort d'Auguste, Presses de la Cite, 1966, translation by Frechtman published as *The Old Man Dies,* Harcourt, 1967.

Le Chat, Presses de la Cite, 1967, translation by Frechtman published as *The Cat,* Harcourt, 1967.

Le Demenagement, Presses de la Cite, 1967, translation by Christopher Sinclair-Stevenson published as *The Move,* Harcourt, 1968 (published in England as *The Neighbors,* Hamish Hamilton, 1968).

La Main, Presses de la Cite, 1968, translation by Budberg published as *The Man on the Bench in the Barn,* Harcourt, 1970.

La Prison, Presses de la Cite, 1968, translation by Moir published as *The Prison,* Harcourt, 1969.

Il y a encore des noisetiers, Presses de la Cite, 1969.

Novembre, Presses de la Cite, 1969, translation by Stewart published as *November,* Harcourt, 1970.

Le Riche Homme, Presses de la Cite, 1970, translation by Stewart published as *The Rich Man,* Harcourt, 1971.

Le Cage de verre, Presses de la Cite, 1971, translation by Antonia White published as *The Glass Cage,* Harcourt, 1973.

La Disparition d'Odile, Presses de la Cite, 1971, translation by Moir published as *The Disappearance of Odile,* Harcourt, 1972.

Les Innocents, Presses de la Cite, 1972, translation by Ellenbogen published as *The Innocents,* Hamish Hamilton, 1973, Harcourt, 1974.

The Rules of the Game, translation by Curtis, Harcourt, 1988.

UNDER PSEUDONYM GEORGES SIM

Au pont des arches (title means "Aboard the Ark"), Benard (Liege), 1921.

Les Ridicules (title means "The Ridiculous Ones"), Benard, 1921.

Les Larmes avant le bonheur (title means "Tears Before Happiness"), Ferenczi, 1925.

Le Feu s'eteint (title means "The Fire Is Out"), Fayard, 1927.

Les Voleurs de bavires (adventure; title means "The Ship Robbers"), Tallindier, c. 1927.

Defense d'aimer (title means "Defense of Loving"), Ferenczi, 1927.

Le Cercle de la soif (adventure; title means "The Circle of Thirst"), Ferenczi, 1927, published as *Le Cercle de la mort* (title means "The Circle of Death"), 1933.

Paris-Leste, Editions Paris-Plaisirs, 1927.

Un Monsieur libidineux (title means "A Libidinous Gentleman"), Editions Prima, 1927.

Les Coeurs perdus (title means "The Lost Hearts"), Tallandier, 1928.

Le Secret des Lamas (adventure; title means "The Secret of the Lamas"), Tallandier, 1928.

Les Maudits du Pacifique (adventure; title means "The Damned of the Pacific"), Tallandier, 1928.

Le Monstre blanc de la terre de feu (title means "The White Monster of the Land of Fire"), Ferenczi, 1928, published (under pseudonym Christian Brulls) as *L'Ile de la desolation* (title means "Desolation Island"), 1933.

Miss Baby, Fayard, 1928.

Le Semeur de larmes (title means "Sower of Tears"), Ferenczi, 1928.

Le Roi des glaces (adventure), Tallandier, 1928.

Le Sousmarin dans la foret (title means "The Submarine in the Forest"), Tallandier, 1928.

La Maison sans soleil (title means "The House without Sunshine"), Fayard, 1928.

Aimer d'amour (title means "In Love With Love"), Ferenczi, 1928.

Songes d'ete (title means "Summer Dreams"), Ferenczi, 1928.

Le Lac d'angoisse (adventure; title means "The Lake of Agony"), Ferenczi, 1928, published (under pseudonym Christian Brulls) as *Le Lac des esclaves* (title means "The Lake of the Slaves"), 1933.

Le Sang des gitanes (title means "The Blood of the Gipsies"), Ferenczi, 1928.

Chair de beaute (title means "Beautiful Flesh"), Fayard, 1928.

Les Memoires d'un prostitute (title means "Memoirs of a Prostitute"), Editions Prima, 1929.

En Robe de mariee, Tallandier, 1929.

La Panthere borgne (adventure; title means "The Blind Panther"), Tallandier, 1929.

La Fiancee aux mains de glace (title means "The Fiancee and the Sea of Ice"), Fayard, 1929.

Les Bandits de Chicago (adventure; title means "The Outlaws of Chicago"), Fayard, 1929.

L'Ile des hommes roux (adventure; title means "The Island of the Red Men"), Tallandier, 1929.

Le Roi du Pacifique (adventure; title means "The King of the Pacific"), Ferenczi, 1929, abridged edition published as *Le Bateau d'or* (title means "The Boat of Gold"), Ferenczi, 1955.

Le Gorille-Roi (title means "The Gorilla King"), Tallandier, 1929.

Les Contrabaniers de l'alcool (adventure; title means "The Rum Runners"), Fayard, 1929.

La Femme qui tue (title means "The Dead Woman"), Fayard, 1929.

Destinees (title means "Destinies"), Fayard, 1929.

L'Ile des maudits (adventure; title means "Island of the Damned"), Ferenczi, c. 1929, abridged edition published as *Naufrage du "Pelican"* (title means "The Shipwreck of the Pelican"), 1933.

La Femme en deuil (title means "The Wife in Mourning"), Tallandier, 1929.

L'Oeil de l'Utah (adventure; title means "The Eye of Utah"), Tallandier, 1930.

L'Homme qui tremble (adventure; title means "The Shaky Man"), Fayard, 1930.

Nez d'argent (adventure; title means "The Scent of Money"), Ferenczi, 1930, abridged edition published as *Le Paria des bois sauvages* (title means "The Outcast of the Wild Woods"), 1933.

Mademoiselle Million (title means "Miss Million"), Fayard, 1930, published as *Les Ruses de l'amour* (title means "The Tricks of Love"), 1954.

Le Pecheur de bouees (adventure; title means "The Fisherman of the Buoys"), Tallandier, 1930.

Le Chinois de San-Francisco (title means "The Chinese of San Francisco"), Tallandier, 1930.

La Femme 47 (title means "The Woman 47"), Fayard, 1930.

Katia, Acrobate (title means "Katia, Acrobat"), Fayard, 1931.

L'Homme a la cigarette (title means "The Man with the Cigarette"), Tallandier, 1931.

L'Homme de poire (title means "The Victim"), Fayard, 1931.

Les Errants (title means "The Ramblers"), Fayard, 1931.

La Maison de l'inquietude (crime novel; title means "The House of Anxiety"), Tallandier, 1932.

L'Epave (title means "The Slave"), Fayard, 1932.

Matricule 12 (crime novel; title means "Ledger 12"), Tallandier, 1932.

La Fiance du diable (title means "The Devil's Intended"), Fayard, 1932.

La Femme rousse (crime novel; title means "The Redheaded Woman"), Tallandier, 1933.

Le Chateau des sables rouges, Tallandier, 1933.

Le Yacht fantome (adventure; title means "The Phantom Yacht"; originally published [under pseudonym Christian Brulls] as *Le Desert du froid qui tue* [title means "The Loneliness as Cold as Death"], Ferenczi, 1928), Ferenczi, 1933.

Deuxieme Bureau (crime novel; title means "Second Bureau"), Tallandier, 1933.

Les Nains des cataractes (adventure), Tallandier, 1954.

NOVELS UNDER PSEUDONYM JEAN du PERRY

Le Roman d'une dactylo (title means "The Romance of a Typist"), Ferenczi, 1924.

Amour d'exile (title means "Love of an Exile"), Ferenczi, c. 1924.

L'Oiseau blesse (title means "The Wounded Bird"), Ferenczi, 1925.

L'Heureuse fin (title means "Precious Happiness"), Ferenczi, 1925.

Pour la sauver (title means "For the Rescue"), 1925.

Ceux qu'on avait oubles . . . , [France], 1925.

Pour qu'il soit heureux, [France], 1925.

Amour Afrique (title means "African Love"), [France], 1925.

A l'assaut d'un coeur (title means "Assault on a Heart"), [France], 1925.

L'Orgueil d'aimer (title means "The Pride of a Lover"), [France], 1926.

Celle qui est aimee (title means "One Who is Loved"), [France], 1926.

Les Yeux qui ordonnent (title means "The Commanding Eyes"), [France], 1926.

Que ma mere l'ignore (title means "What My Mother Didn't Know"), [France], 1926.

De la rue au bonheur (title means "On the Street of Happiness"), [France], 1926.

Un Peche de jeunesse (title means "A Sin of Youth"), [France], 1926.

Lili Tristesse (title means "Lili Sadness"), [France], 1927.

Un Tout petit coeur (title means "Every Little Heart"), Editions du Livre National, 1927.

Le Fou d'amour (title means "The Madman of Love"), [France], 1928.

Coeur Exalte (title means "Exalted Heart"), [France], 1928.

Trois Coeurs dans la tempete (title means "Three Hearts in a Storm"), [France], 1928.

Les Amants de la mansarde (title means "The Attic Lovers"), [France], 1928.

Un Jour de soleil (title means "A Sunny Day"), [France], 1928.

La Fille de l'autre (title means "The Other's Daughter"), [France], 1929.

L'Amour et l'argent (title means "Love and Money"), [France], 1929.

Coeur de poupee (title means "The Heart of a Doll"), [France], 1929.

Une Femme a tue (title means "A Wife to Murder"), [France], 1929.

Deux Coeurs de femme (title means "Two Hearts of a Woman"), [France], 1929.

L'Epave d'amour (title means "The Wreckage of Love"), [France], 1929.

Le Mirage de Paris (title means "The Illusion of Paris"), [France], 1929.

Celle qui passe (title means "Those Who Pass"), [France], 1930.

Petite Exile (title means "Little Exile"), [France], 1930.

Les Amants de malheur (title means "Lovers of Trouble"), [France], 1930.

La Femme ardente (title means "The Passionate Woman"), [France], 1930.

La Porte close (title means "The Closed Door"), [France], 1930.

Le Poupee brisee (title means "The Broken Doll"), [France], 1930.

Pauvre Amante (title means "Poor Lover"), [France], 1931.

Le Reve qui meurt (title means "The Murderous Dream"), F. Rouff, 1931.

Marie-Mystere (title means "Mysterious Marie"), Fayard, 1931.

NOVELS UNDER PSEUDONYM GEORGES MARTIN GEORGES

L'Orgueil qui meurt (title means "The Pride That Murdered"), Editions du Livre National, 1925.

Un Soir de veritage (title means "An Evening of Truth"), Ferenczi, 1928.

Brin d'amour (title means "Quality of Love"), Ferenczi, 1928.

Les Coeurs vides (title means "The Empty Hearts"), Ferenczi, 1928.

Cabotine . . . , Ferenczi, 1928.

Amier, Mourir (title means "To Love, To Murder"), Ferenczi, 1928.

Voleuse d'amour (title means "The Thief of Love"), Ferenczi, 1929.

Une Ombre dans la nuit (title means "A Shadow in the Night"), Ferenczi, 1929.

Nuit de Paris (title means "Parisian Night"), Ferenczi, 1929.

Un Nid d'amour (title means "A Love Nest"), Ferenczi, 1930.

Bobette, mannequin (title means "Bobette, Model"), Ferenczi, 1930.

La Puissance du souvenir (title means "The Power to Remember"), Ferenczi, 1930.

Le Bonheur de Lili (title means "Lili's Happiness"), Ferenczi, 1930.

Le Double Vie (title means "The Double Life"), Ferenczi, 1931.

NOVEL UNDER PSEUDONYM GEORGES d'ISLY

Etoile de cinema (title means "Movie Star"), F. Rouff, 1925.

NOVELS UNDER PSEUDONYM CHRISTIAN BRULLS

La Pretresse des vaudoux (adventure; title means "The Voodoo Priestess"), Tallandier, 1925.

Nox l'insaissable (crime novel), Ferenczi, 1926.

Se Ma Tsien, le sacrificateur (adventure), Tallandier, 1926.

Mademoiselle X . . . (title means "Miss X"), Fayard, 1928.

Annie, danseuse (title means "Annie, Dancer"), Ferenczi, 1928.

Dolorosa (title means "Delores"), Fayard, 1928.

Les Adolescents passionnes (title means "The Passionate Teenagers"), Fayard, 1929.

L'Amant sans nom (title means "The Nameless Lover"), Fayard, 1929.

Un Drame au Pole Sud (adventure; title means "A Drama at the South Pole"), Fayard, 1929.

Les Pirates du Texas (adventure; title means "The Texas Pirates"), Ferenczi, 1929, published as *La Chasse au whiskey* (title means "The Shot of Whiskey"), 1934.

Capitan S.O.S. (adventure; title means "Captain S.O.S."), Fayard, 1929.

Jacques d'Antifer, roi des Iles du Vent (adventure; title means "Jacques d'Antifer, King of the Windy Islands"), [France], 1930, published as *L'Heritier du Corsaire*, 1934.

L'Inconnue (title means "The Stranger"), Fayard, 1930.

Train de nuit (title means "Night Train"), Fayard, 1930.

Pour venger son pere (title means "To Avenge One's Father"), Ferenczi, 1931.

La Maison de la haine (title means "The House of Hatred"), Fayard, 1931.

La Maison des disparus, Fayard, 1931.

Les Forcats de Paris (title means "The Convicts of Paris"), Fayard, 1932.

La Figurante (title means "The Figurehead"), Fayard, 1932.

Fievre (title means "Fever"), Fayard, 1932.

Le Lac des esclaves (title means "The Lake of the Slaves"; originally published [under pseudonym Georges Sim] as *Le Lac d'angoisse* [title means "The Lake of Agony"], 1928), Ferenczi, 1933.

L'Evasion (title means "The Escape"), Fayard, 1934.

L'Ils empoisonne (adventure; title means "The Poisoned Island"), Ferenczi, 1937.

Seul parmi les gorilles (adventure; title means "Alone Among the Gorillas"), Ferenczi, 1937.

NOVELS UNDER PSEUDONYM GOM GUT

Un Viol aux q'uat'z arts, Prima, 1925.

Perversites frivotes, Prima, 1925.

Au grand 13, Prima, 1925.

Plaisirs charnes, Prima, 1925.

Aux vingt-huit negresses, Prima, 1925.

La Noche a Montmartre, Prima, 1925.

Liquettes au vent, Prima, 1926.

Une Petite tres sensuelle, Prima, 1926.

Orgies bourgoise, Prima, 1926.

L'Homme aux douze etreintes, Prima, 1927.

Entreintes passionnees, Prima, 1927.

Une Mome dessalee, Prima, 1927.

L'Amant fantome, Prima, 1928.

L'Amour a Montparnasse, Prima, 1928.

Les Distractions d'Helene, Prima, 1928.

NOVELS UNDER PSEUDONYM PLICK ET PLOCK

Voluptueues Etreintes, Prima, 1925.
Le Cheri de Tantine, Prima, 1925.

NOVELS UNDER PSEUDONYM LUC DORSAN

Histoire d'un pantalon, Prima, 1926.
Nini violce, Prima, 1926.
Nichonnette, Prima, 1926.
Memoires d'un vieux suiveur, Prima, 1926.
Nuit de noces, doubles noces, les noces ardents, Prima, 1926.
Le Pucelle de Benouville, Prima, Ferenczi, 1928.

UNDER PSEUDONYM BOBETTE

Bobette et ses satyres, Ferenczi, 1928.

UNDER PSEUDONYM KIM

Un Petit Poison, Ferenczi, 1928.

NOVELS UNDER PSEUDONYM JACQUES DERSONNES

Un Seul Basier (title means "A Single Kiss"), Ferenczi, 1928.
La Merveilleuse Adventure (title means "The Marvelous Adventure"), Ferenczi, 1929.
Les Etapes du Mensonge, Ferenczi, 1930.
Baisers mortels (title means "Deadly Kisses"), Ferenczi, 1930.
Victime de son fils (title means "Victim of His Son"), Ferenczi, 1931.

NOVELS UNDER PSEUDONYM JEAN DORSANGE

L'Amour meconnu (title means "Misunderstood Love"), Ferenczi, 1928.
Celle qui revient, Ferenczi, 1929.
Coeur de jeune fille (title means "Heart of a Young Girl"), Ferenczi, 1930.
Soeurette (title means "Little Sister"), Ferenczi, 1930.
Les Chercheurs de bonheur (title means "The Fortune Hunters"), Ferenczi, 1930.

NOVELS UNDER PSEUDONYM GASTON VIALIS

Un Petit Corps blesse (title means "A Small Wounded Body"), Ferenczi, 1928.
Hair a force d'amier (title means "Hate and the Power of Love"), Ferenczi, 1928.
Le Parfum du passe (title means "The Perfume of the Past"), Ferenczi, 1929.
Lili-sourire (title means "Smile, Lili"), Ferenczi, 1930.
Folie d'un soir (title means "Madness of an Evening"), Ferenczi, 1930.
Ame de jeune fille (title means "Soul of a Young Girl"), Ferenczi, 1931.

NOVELS UNDER PSEUDONYM GERMAIN d'ANTIBES

Helas! (title means "Alas!"), Ferenczi, 1929.

NOVELS UNDER PSEUDONYM JEAN DOSSAGE

Les Deux Maitresses (title means "The Two Mistresses"), Ferenczi, 1929.

NOVELS UNDER PSEUDONYM G. VIOLIS

Trop belle pour elle! (title means "Very Good for Her!"), Ferenczi, 1929.

SHORT STORIES AND OMNIBUS VOLUMES

Les Sept Minutes (short stories; title means "The Seven Minutes"), Nouvelle Revue Francaise, 1938.

Maigret revient (title means "Maigret Returns"), Nouvelle Revue Francaise, 1942.
Le Petit Docteur (short stories), Nouvelle Revue Francaise, 1943, translation by Stewart published as *The Little Doctor,* Harcourt, 1978.
Les Nouvelles Enquetes de Maigret (short stories; title means "The New Cases of Maigret"), Nouvelle Revue Francaise, 1944.
Les Dossiers de l'agence O (short stories; title means "The Files of the O Agency"), Nouvelle Revue Francaise, 1945.
Un Noel de Maigret (short stories), Presses de la Cite, 1951, translation by Stewart published as *Maigret's Christmas: Nine Stories,* Hamish Hamilton, 1976, Harcourt, 1977.
Omnibus Simenon (collection of novels), ten volumes, Gallimard, 1951-52.
Les Tournants dangereux (four novellas), Appleton, 1953.
Le Bateau d'Emile (short stories; title means "Emile's Boat"), Gallimard, 1954.
The Short Cases of Inspector Maigret (short stories), Doubleday, 1959.
Le Commissaire Maigret et L'Inspecteur Malchanceaux (four novellas; title means "Commissioner Maigret and Inspector Malchanceaux," Doubleday, 1959, *Maigret et l'Inspector Malchanceux, On ne tue pas les pauvres types,* and *Le Temoingnage de l'enfant de choeur*), Presses de la Cite, 1947.
A Maigret Omnibus, Hamish Hamilton, 1962, published as *Five Times Maigret,* Harcourt, 1964.
La Rue aux trois poussins (short stories), Presses de la Cite, 1963, bound with *Le Mari de Melie,* EMC Publications, 1986.
A Maigret Quartet, Hamish Hamilton, 1964.
The Second Maigret Omnibus, Hamish Hamilton, 1964, published as *Maigret Cinq,* Harcourt, 1965.
A Simenon Omnibus, Hamish Hamilton, 1965.
Trois Nouvelles (title means "Three New Works"), edited by Frank W. Lindsay and Anthony M. Nazzano, Appleton, 1966.
Les Enquetes du Commissaire Maigret (title means "The Cases of Commissioner Maigret"), Presses de la Cite, Volume 1, 1966, Volume 2, 1967.
An American Omnibus, Harcourt, 1967.
Ouevres completes (title means "Complete Works"), compiled by Gilbert Sigaux, Editions Rencontre (Lausanne), seventy-two volumes, 1967-73.
Ouevres Completes Maigret (title means "Complete Maigret"), compiled by Sigaux, Editions Rencontre, twenty-five volumes, 1967-70.
Maigret Triumphant, Hamish Hamilton, 1969.
The Simenon Omnibus, thirteen volumes, Penguin, 1970-78.
Choix de Simenon (textbook edition; short stories; title means "Choice Simenon"), edited by Frank W. Lindsay and Anthony M. Nazzaro, Appleton, 1972.
A Maigret Trio: Maigret's Failure, Maigret in Society, and Maigret and the Lazy Burglar, Harcourt, 1973.
La Piste du Hollandais (short stories), Presses de la Cite, 1973.
Maigret: A Fifth Omnibus, Hamish Hamilton, 1973.
Maigret Victorious, Hamish Hamilton, 1975.
Complete Maigret Short Stories, two volumes, Hamish Hamilton, 1976, Harcourt, 1977.
Maigret and the Mad Killers, Doubleday, 1980.

DIARIES

Des Traces de pas, Presses de la Cite, 1975.
Vent du nord, vent du sud, Presses de la Cite, 1976.

Les Petits Hommes (title means "The Little Men"), Presses de la Cite, 1976.

De la cave au grenier, Presses de la Cite, 1977.

A l'abri de notre arbre, Presses de la Cite, 1977.

Un Banc au soleil, Presses de la Cite, 1977.

Tant que je suis vivant, Presses de la Cite, 1978.

Vacances obligatoires, Presses de la Cite, 1978.

A quoi bon jurer? Presses de la Cite, 1979.

Au-dela de ma port-fenetre, Presses de la Cite, 1979.

Je suis reste un enfant de choeur, Presses de la Cite, 1979.

Point-virgule, Presses de la Cite, 1979.

Les Libertes qu'il nous reste, Presses de la Cite, 1980.

On dit que j'ai soixante-quinze ans, Presses de la Cite, 1980.

Le Prix d'un homme, Presses de la Cite, 1980.

Quand vient le froid, Presses de la Cite, 1980.

Le Femme endormie, Presses de la Cite, 1981.

Jour et Nuit, Presses de la Cite, 1981.

Memoires intimes, Presses de la Cite, 1981, translation by Harold J. Salemson published as *Intimate Memoires,* Harcourt, 1984.

OTHER

Lone Cours dur les rivieres et canaux (illustrated nonfiction), Editions Dynamo (Liege), 1952.

Le Roman de l'homme (lectures and essays), Presses de la Cite, 1959, translation by Frechtman published as *The Novel of Man,* Harcourt, 1964.

La Femme en France (illustrated nonfiction; title means "The Woman in France"), Presses de la Cite, 1960.

Entretien avec Roger Stephanie (interview), Radio Television Francaise, 1963.

Ma Conviction profonde (unedited writings), Callier, 1963.

Le Paris de Simenon (illustrated nonfiction), Tehou, 1969, translation published as *Simenon's Paris,* Dial, 1970.

Quand j'etais vieux (autobiography), translation by Helen Eustis published as *When I Was Old,* Harcourt, 1971.

Lettre a ma mere (autobiography), Presses de la Cite, 1974, translation by Ralph Manheim published as *Letter to My Mother,* Harcourt, 1976.

Un Homme comme un autre (biography; title means "A Man Like Any Other"), Presses de la Cite, 1975.

(With Francis Lacassin and Sigaux) *A la decouverte de la France,* Union General d'Editions, 1976.

(With Lacassin and Sigaux) *A la recherche de l'homme nu,* Union General d'Editions, 1976.

Lettres sur Balzac: Correspondance avec Andrae Jeannot, Les Amis de Georges Simenon (Bruxelles, Belgium), 1994.

The Centre d'Etudes Georges Simenon in Liege, Belgium, and the Simenon Center at Drew University have preserved collections of Simenon's papers.

MEDIA ADAPTATIONS: Approximately two dozen films and television shows have been produced based on Simenon's books, including the 1983 film *L'Etoile du Nord,* written by Jean Aurenche and directed by Pierre Granier-Deferre, which is based on the novel, *La Locataire.*

SIDELIGHTS: Georges Simenon was one of the world's most prolific writers, having produced novels, stories, and other works numbering in the hundreds over a span of five decades. Although he wrote exclusively in French, his work is available worldwide in more than forty languages. It has been said that at the peak of his writing career, when he was regularly producing four or more books per year, a new Simenon translation was appearing somewhere in the world on the average of once every three days.

But of all his writing, he was best known as the creator and chronicler of the cases of his detective, Inspector Jules Maigret.

Simenon was born in Liege, Belgium, where as a youth he was already determined to become a writer of some sort. His schooling was cut short as a result of the death of his father. Accordingly, he was apprenticed to a pastry chef to learn a trade. Simenon abandoned his apprenticeship after one year, and at the age of seventeen he began his career as a writer by taking a newspaper job with the *Leige Gazette* as an assistant night police reporter. His writing began in earnest. At the age of seventeen he published his first novel, *Au pont des arches* ("Aboard the Ark").

In 1925 Simenon left Belgium for Paris to concentrate on a career as a full-time writer of fiction. His early attempts met with rejection and led him to consult Sidonie-Gabrielle Colette, the renowned novelist, who was at that time the editor of *Le Matin.* Colette, too, rejected Simenon's material for publication and suggested that his writing was too literary for the mass market. She advised him to simplify and clarify his writing. Simenon's efforts in this direction resulted in the development of his skills as a storyteller of the first rank. He began writing pulp fiction at the rate of eighty pages per day. Simenon published hundreds of books and stories under various pseudonyms during the next several years and soon found that he was able to afford such luxuries as a chauffeur-driven car and, finally, a yacht, the *Ostrogot.*

In 1929, while traveling throughout Europe aboard his yacht, Simenon wrote *The Strange Case of Peter the Lett,* which was the first novel to feature Inspector Maigret. Simenon's creation of Inspector Maigret represented a departure from the conventional portrayal of a super-sleuth. When Simenon presented his first Maigret manuscript to the editors at Fayard, his sometime publishers, they were doubtful of the novel's chances for success with the reading public. Trudee Young wrote: "They [the Maigrets] were not like other detective novels. The main character, Inspector Maigret—a heavy-set, pipe-smoking detective—did not use scientific means to solve his cases, only his intuition; there were no love affairs; there were no truly good guys and bad guys; and, finally, the story ended neither bad nor good."

Simenon's Inspector Maigret is a real police officer, unlike Sherlock Holmes, consulting detective, or Hercule Poirot, Agatha Christie's eccentric Belgian detective. Although Maigret rose through the ranks of the Paris Police Department, he is, in many of the novels, the highest ranking working policeman in France. His actual position is chief superintendent, in charge of the homicide division of the police judiciaire, but he is generally demoted in translation and referred to as "Inspector." Because of his high official position, Maigret is often photographed and quoted in the Parisian press. He is, despite his personal modesty, a very well known personage.

Maigret also differs from most famous fictional crime fighters (particularly his American counterparts) in that he rarely carries a gun, rarely throws a punch or takes one, and hardly ever is involved in a chase either on foot or in a car. In fact, Maigret does not know how to drive. Although in the later novels he owns a car, his wife, Madame Maigret, drives him to Meung-sur-Loire for quiet weekends at their country house. If to all outward appearances Maigret is an ordinary man, of ordinary habits and tastes (although while on a case, he can and does consume inordinate amounts of alcohol), the opposite is true of his abilities and methods as a policeman. Maigret's outstanding traits are his unerring intuition, his compassion for both victim and murderer, and his extraordinary patience. While investigating a murder, Maigret spends hours, and more often days, in watchful waiting—seeking insights into the lives and minds of both the victim and his assassin. Only when he finally and thoroughly understands the reasons why the crime came to be committed does he arrest his suspect.

Attesting to the uniqueness of Simenon's mystery fiction, novelist and critic Julian Symons wrote in his *Mortal Consequences: A History—From the Detective Story to the Crime Novel:* "The Maigret stories stand quite on their own in crime fiction, bearing little relation to most of the other work done in the field. (Simenon is not much interested in crime stories and has read few of them). . . . There are no great feats of ratiocination in them and the problems they present are human as much as they are criminal. . . . Maigret's detached sympathy becomes our own, and like him we do not care to dig too deeply into the roots of crime. . . . Simenon is an undoubted master of the crime story, but his mastery rests primarily in the creation of Jules Maigret."

As much as Maigret is admired and enjoyed by readers of crime fiction, Simenon himself has not always been one of the Inspector's fans. After completing nineteen Maigret novels, Simenon gave up the series for a number of years to concentrate on writing more serious novels, which he termed *romans-crise,* or novels of crisis. His serious novels focus on the psychological motivations of the characters as they approach and experience a crisis in their lives. These novels, like the Maigrets, often involve crime—not the solution of crime, as in the Maigrets—but rather, in the examination of the events in the lives and psyches of the characters which lead them inexorably and inevitably to commit a crime—usually murder. Edward Galligan wrote, "The serious novels are individually more complex and as a group more varied than the Maigrets. They deal with characters from all walks of life, though usually with a preference for those who are in or who have come from obscure positions in society. The novels are set in all sorts of places, for Simenon has traveled widely and has lived for extended periods in a number of different countries, including the United States. And they confront, in one way or another, all of the fundamental problems in individual lives. There are very few descriptive generalizations to be made about them which are both valid and useful. They are short. . . . They nearly all involve acts of violence . . . because they are concerned with people who are driven to their limits."

Although Simenon "attempted to persuade critics and publishers that he should be taken seriously as an author of *romans serieux,*" observed *Dictionary of Literary Biography* contributor Catharine Savage Brosman, "sales figures suggest that the Maigret series and a few other books in the same vein have the most appeal, and his fame continues to rest principally on them." As Brosman later explained, "His serious novels do not offer wisdom or illumination, and, despite the strong characterization, the reader does not enter into their world. . . . In the detective mode, however, his work sets the standard, rather than following it." Andre Gide, an admirer and long-time critical correspondent of Simenon, nevertheless asserted that there is a "profound psychological and ethical interest" in all of Simenon's books. Gide stated, "This is what attracts and holds me in him. He writes for 'the vast public,' to be sure, but delicate and refined readers find something for them too as soon as they begin to take him seriously. He makes one reflect; and this is close to being the height of art; how superior he is in this to those heavy novelists who do not spare us a single commentary! Simenon sets forth a particular fact, perhaps of general interest; but he is careful not to generalize; that is up to the reader."

Simenon's desire to be known as an earnest novelist was tempered by his lack of self-confidence as a writer and his distrust of the intellectual community. He therefore formed "a theory of the 'semi-literary' novel, or, more earthily, 'semi-alimentary,'" Stanley G. Eskin related, in *Dictionary of Literary Biography Yearbook: 1989.* "The theory was that he wrote pulps to make money, was aiming at 'straight' novels but felt insecure about 'high' literature, and took up the detective story as a midway step." In an article entitled "Simenon on Simenon" for the *Times Literary Supplement,* Simenon illuminated the man behind the writer who believed that humility was the grandest virtue one could hope to possess. "Simenon," he wrote of himself, "is truly a modest man. He knows his own limitations and does not make for himself the claims that have sometimes been made for him by some of his more florid admirers. He describes himself as a craftsman, has a healthy distrust of intellectuals, of *belle-lettriens,* of literary occasions and intellectual conversations, feels ill at ease at social functions, and is quite unambitious in conventional terms: recognition, decorations, and so on. He can, it is true, well afford to be."

After producing over five hundred novels and novellas, Simenon retired from writing fiction in 1974, devoting himself to nonfiction and the taping of his diaries, which were then transcribed and published. In 1978, the author suffered the greatest tragedy in his life when his daughter, Marie-Georges, whom he called Marie-Jo, committed suicide in her apartment. Devastated by his loss, Simenon felt the need to write about it; the result was his lengthy *Intimate Memoirs,* which begins with the discovery of Marie-Jo's body and is reminiscent of the openings of one of the author's Maigret novels. "Simenon," wrote Leslie Garis in a *New York Times Magazine* interview with the author, "using the insightful probing into human character and clear-eyed equilibrium that have always distinguished his best work, applied his skills to unravelling the causes of her death."

BIOGRAPHICAL/CRITICAL SOURCES:

BOOKS

Assouline, Pierre, *Simenon: A Biography,* Knopf, 1997.

Becker, Lucille Frackman, *Georges Simenon,* Twayne, 1977.

Benstock, Bernard, editor, *Art in Crime Writing: Essays on Detective Fiction,* St. Martin's, 1983.

Brophy, Brigid, *Don't Never Forget: Collected Views and Reviews,* Holt, 1966.

Contemporary Literary Criticism, Gale (Detroit), Volume 1, 1973; Volume 2, 1974; Volume 3, 1975; Volume 8, 1978; Volume 18, 1981; Volume 47, 1988.

Dictionary of Literary Biography, Volume 72: *French Novelists, 1930-1960,* Gale, 1988.

Dictionary of Literary Biography Yearbook: 1989, Gale, 1990.

Gide, Andre, *The Journals of Andre Gide,* Volume 4: *1938-1949,* translated by Justin O'Brien, Knopf, 1951.

Marnham, Patrick, *The Man Who Wasn't Maigret: A Portrait of Georges Simenon,* Harcourt Brace (San Diego), 1994.

Mauriac, Claude, *The New Literature,* translated by Samuel I. Stone, Braziller, 1959.

Moore, Harry T., *Twentieth Century French Literature since World War II,* Southern Illinois University Press, 1966.

Narcejac, Thomas, *The Art of Simenon,* translated by Cynthia Rowland, Routledge & Kegan Paul, 1952.

Penzler, Otto, *The Private Lives of Private Eyes, Spies, Crime Fighters and Other Good Guys,* Grosset, 1977.
Symons, Julian, *Mortal Consequences: A History—From the Detective Story to the Crime Novel,* Harper, 1972.
Young, Trudee, *Georges Simenon,* Scarecrow, 1976.

PERIODICALS

Armchair Detective, January, 1971; October, 1977; winter, 1980.
Chicago Tribune Book World, December 25, 1983; July 1, 1984.
Globe and Mail (Toronto), November 23, 1985.
Life, May 9, 1969.
Listener, February 17, 1983.
Los Angeles Times, February 27, 1981.
Los Angeles Times Book Review, May 24, 1981; July 2, 1983; June 24, 1984; August 5, 1984; November 18, 1984; April 10, 1988; September 9, 1990.
National Review, June 23, 1972; April 30, 1976; December 10, 1976.
New Republic, March 4, 1940; March 10, 1941.
New Statesman, March 5, 1965; October 17, 1969; June 27, 1980; October 21, 1983.
New Statesman and Nation, February 10, 1940; May 25, 1940; August 13, 1955.
Newsweek, April 27, 1970; February 19, 1973; January 9, 1984; June 25, 1984.
New Yorker, January 24, 1953; January 17, 1970; April 7, 1975; April 24, 1978; April 2, 1979; June 28, 1982; January 17, 1983; December 23, 1985.
New York Review of Books, October 12, 1978.
New York Times, December 12, 1980; June 27, 1984; September 4, 1989.
New York Times Book Review, September 4, 1932; February 5, 1933; March 4, 1934; October 11, 1953; July 11, 1954; November 28, 1954; January 27, 1957; August 25, 1957; June 20, 1965; August 18, 1968; March 16, 1969; August 8, 1971; February 25, 1973; November 4, 1973; November 24, 1974; August 4, 1975; November 21, 1976; May 22, 1977; July 1, 1979; May 30, 1982; October 10, 1983; July 1, 1984.
New York Times Magazine, April 22, 1984.
Publishers Weekly, November 13, 1978; January 24, 1986.
Saturday Review, February 21, 1953.
Spectator, June 13, 1941; October 3, 1941; March 23, 1951.
Time, March 14, 1969; June 18, 1984.
Times (London), August 21, 1984; August 22, 1984.
Times Literary Supplement, December 14, 1940; November 25, 1960; July 29, 1983; August 12, 1988.
Tribune Books (Chicago), April 24, 1988; July 2, 1989; September 3, 1989.
Washington Post, September 17, 1972.
Washington Post Book World, September 27, 1970; May 18, 1980; January 18, 1981.

*   *   *

SIMIC, Charles 1938-

PERSONAL: Born May 9, 1938, in Belgrade, Yugoslavia; came to United States in 1954, naturalized citizen 1971; son of George (an engineer) and Helen (Matijevic) Simic; married Helene Dubin (a designer), October 25, 1965; children: Anna, Philip. *Education:* New York University, B.A., 1967. *Religion:* Eastern Orthodox.

ADDRESSES: Home—P.O. Box 192, Strafford, NH 03884-0192. *Office*—Department of English, University of New Hampshire, Durham, NH 03824.

CAREER: Aperture (photography magazine), New York City, editorial assistant, 1966-69; University of New Hampshire, Durham, associate professor of English, 1974–. Visiting assistant professor of English, State University of California, Hayward, 1970-73, Boston University, 1975, and Columbia University, 1979. *Military service:* U.S. Army, 1961-63.

AWARDS, HONORS: PEN International Award for translation, 1970; Guggenheim fellowship, 1972-73; National Endowment for the Arts fellowship, 1974-75, and 1979-80; Edgar Allan Poe Award from American Academy of Poets, 1975; National Institute of Arts and Letters and American Academy of Arts and Letters Award, 1976; National Book Award nomination, 1978, for *Charon's Cosmology;* Harriet Monroe Poetry Award from University of Chicago, Di Castignola Award from Poetry Society of America, 1980, and PEN Translation award, all 1980; Fulbright travelling fellowship, 1982; Ingram Merrill fellowship, 1983-84; MacArthur Foundation fellowship, 1984-89; Pulitzer Prize nominations, 1986 and 1987; Pulitzer Prize, 1990, for *The World Doesn't End;* finalist for National Book Award in poetry, 1996, for *Walking the Black Cat.*

WRITINGS:

POETRY

What the Grass Says, Kayak, 1967.
Somewhere among Us a Stone Is Taking Notes, Kayak, 1969.
Dismantling the Silence, Braziller, 1971.
White, New Rivers Press, 1972, revised edition, Logbridge-Rhodes, 1980.
Return to a Place Lit by a Glass of Milk, Braziller, 1974.
Biography and a Lament, Bartholemew's Cobble, 1976.
Charon's Cosmology, Braziller, 1977.
Brooms: Selected Poems, Edge Press, 1978.
School for Dark Thoughts, Banyan Press, 1978, sound recording of same title published by Watershed Tapes (Washington, DC), 1978.
Classic Ballroom Dances, Braziller, 1980.
Austerities, Braziller, 1982.
Shaving at Night, Meadow, 1982.
Weather Forecast for Utopia and Vicinity, Station Hill Press, 1983.
The Chicken without a Head: A New Version, Trace, 1983.
Selected Poems 1963-1983, Braziller, 1985.
Unending Blues, Harcourt, 1986.
The Best of Intro, edited by William H. Gass, Associated Writing Programs, 1986.
Nine Poems, Exact Change, 1989.
The World Doesn't End, Harcourt, 1989.
The Book of Gods and Devils, Harcourt, 1990.
Horse Has Six Legs: Contemporary Serbian Poetry, Graywolf Press, 1992.
Hotel Insomnia, Harcourt, 1992.
A Wedding in Hell: Poems, Harcourt, 1994.
Frightening Toys, Faber & Faber, 1995.
Walking the Black Cat: Poems, Harcourt, 1996.
Displaced Person, New Directions, 1996.

ESSAYS AND INTERVIEWS

The Uncertain Certainty: Interviews, Essays, and Notes on Poetry, University of Michigan Press, 1985.

Wonderful Words, Silent Truth, University of Michigan Press, 1990.

Dime-Store Alchemy: The Art of Joseph Cornell, Ecco, 1992.

The Unemployed Fortune-Teller: Essays and Memoirs, University of Michigan Press, 1994.

Orphan Factory: Essays and Memoirs, University of Michigan Press, 1997.

TRANSLATOR

Ivan V. Lalic, *Fire Gardens,* New Rivers Press, 1970.

Vasko Popa, *The Little Box: Poems,* Charioteer Press, 1970.

Four Modern Yugoslav Poets: Ivan V. Lalic, Branko Miljkovic, Milorad Pavic, Ljubomir Simovic, Lillabulero, 1970.

(And editor with Mark Strand) *Another Republic: 17 European and South American Writers,* Viking, 1976.

Key To Dream, According to Djordje, Elpenor, 1978.

Popa, *Homage to the Lame Wolf Selected Poems,* Field, 1979.

(With Peter Kastmiler) Slavko Mihalic, *Atlantis,* Greenfield Review Press, 1983.

(With others) Henri Michaux, *Translations: Experiments in Reading,* OARS, 1983.

Tomaz Salamun, *Selected Poems of Tomaz Salamun,* Viking, 1987.

Lalic, *Roll Call of Mirrors,* Wesleyan University Press, 1987.

(Editor) Ristovic, Aleksandar, *Some Other Wine or Light,* introduction by Charles Simic, Charioteer Press, 1989.

Janevski, Slavko, *The Bandit Wind,* Dryand, 1991.

Tadic, Nicola, *Night Mail: Selected Poems,* Oberlin College Press, 1992.

Jovanovski, Meto, *Faceless Men and Other Macedonian Stories,* Dufour, 1993.

EDITOR

The Essential Campion, introduction by Charles Simic, Ecco, 1988.

Lehman, David, *The Best American Poetry, 1992,* Collier, 1992.

The Horse Has Six Legs: An Anthology of Serbian Poetry, Graywolf, 1992.

OTHER

Contributor to anthologies, including *The Young American Poets,* Follett, 1968; *The Contemporary American Poets,* World Publishing, 1969; *Major Young American Poets,* World Publishing, 1971; *America a Prophesy,* Random House, 1973; *Shake the Kaleidoscope: A New Anthology of Modern Poetry,* Pocket Books, 1973; *The New Naked Poetry,* Bobbs-Merrill, 1976; *The American Poetry Anthology,* Avon, 1976; *A Geography of Poets,* Bantam, 1979; *Contemporary American Poetry, 1950-1980,* Longman, 1983; *The Norton Anthology of Poetry,* Norton, 1983; *Harvard Book of American Poetry,* Harvard University Press, 1985; and *The Harper American Literature,* Volume 2, Harper, 1987. Author of introductions, *Homage to a Cat: As It Were: Logscapes of the Lost Ages,* by Vernon Newton, Northern Lights, 1991, and *Prisoners of Freedom: Contemporary Slovenian Poetry,* edited by Ales Debeljak, Pedernal, 1992.

SIDELIGHTS: Charles Simic, a native of Yugoslavia who immmigrated to America in his teens, has been hailed as one of the finest of America's younger generation of poets. Simic's work has won numerous prestigious awards, among them the coveted MacArthur foundation "genius grant." Although he writes in English, Simic draws heavily upon Eastern European tradition—and his own experiences of war-torn Belgrade—to compose poems about the physical and spiritual poverty of modern life. *Hudson Review* contributor Liam Rector notes that the author's

work "has about it a purity, an originality unmatched by many of his contemporaries."

Simic spent his formative years in Belgrade. His early childhood coincided with the Second World War; several times his family members evacuated their home on foot to escape indiscriminate bombing. The atmosphere of violence and desperation continued after the war as well. Simic's father left the country for work in America, and his mother tried several times to follow, only to be turned back at the border by Yugoslavian authorities. In the meantime, young Simic was growing up in Belgrade, where he was considered a below-average student and a minor troublemaker.

When Simic was fifteen, his mother finally arranged for the family to travel to Paris. After a year spent studying English in night school and attending French public schools during the day, Simic sailed for America and reunion with his father. He entered the United States at New York City and then moved with his family to Chicago, where he enrolled in high school.

Simic's first poems were published in 1959, when he was twenty-one. Between that year and 1961, when he entered the service, he churned out a number of poems, most of which he has since destroyed. Simic finally earned his Bachelor's degree in 1966. His first full-length collection of poems, *What the Grass Says,* was published the following year. In a very short time, Simic's work—original poetry in English and translations of important Yugoslavian poets—began to attract critical attention. In *The American Moment: American Poetry in the Mid-Century,* Geoffrey Thurley notes that the substance of Simic's earliest verse is that its material referents—"are European and rural rather than American and urban. . . . The world his poetry creates—or rather with its brilliant semantic evacuation decreates—is that of central Europe—woods, ponds, peasant furniture." *Voice Literary Supplement* reviewer Matthew Flamm also contends that Simic was writing "about bewilderment, about being part of history's comedy act, in which he grew up half-abandoned in Belgrade and then became, with his Slavic accent, an American poet."

Simic's work defies easy categorization. Some poems reflect a surreal, metaphysical bent and others offer grimly realistic portraits of violence and despair. *Hudson Review* contributor Vernon Young maintains that memory—a taproot deep into European folklore—is the common source of all of Simic's poetry. "Simic, a graduate of NYU, married and a father in pragmatic America, turns, when he composes poems, to his unconscious and to earlier pools of memory," the critic writes. "Within microcosmic verses which may be impish, sardonic, quasi-realistic or utterly outrageous, he succinctly implies an historical montage." Young elaborates: "His Yugoslavia is a peninsula of the mind. . . . He speaks by the fable; his method is to transpose historical actuality into a surreal key. . . . [Simic] feels the European yesterday on his pulses."

Childhood experiences of war, poverty, and hunger lie behind a number of Simic's poems. *Georgia Review* correspondent Peter Stitt claims that the poet's most persistent concern "is with the effect of cruel political structures upon ordinary human life. . . . The world of Simic's poems is frightening, mysterious, hostile, dangerous." Thurley too declares that Simic "creates a world of silence, waiting for the unspeakable to happen, or subsisting in the limbo left afterwards. . . . The dimension of menace in Simic becomes metaphysics in itself." Simic tempers this perception of horror with gallows humor and an ironic self-awareness. Stitt claims: "Even the most somber poems . . . exhibit a liveliness of style and imagination that seems to re-create, before our eyes, the possibility of light upon the earth. Perhaps a better way of expressing this would be to say that Simic counters the darkness of political structures with the sanctifying light of art."

Critics find Simic's style particularly accessible, a substantial achievement for an author for whom English is a second language. According to Shaw, the "exile's consciousness still colors [Simic's] language as well as his view of existence. Having mastered a second language, Simic is especially aware of the power of words, and of the limits which words grope to overcome. His diction is resolutely plain: as with the everyday objects he writes about, he uncovers unexpected depth in apparently commonplace language." In the *New Letters Review of Books,* Michael Milburn writes: "Charles Simic is a poet of original vision. . . . Simic practically taunts the reader with a familiarity bordering on cliche. He seems to challenge himself to write as plainly as possible, while still producing works of freshness and originality. [His works] literally beckon us off the street and into a world that at first looks indistinguishable from our own. . . . But a brilliant method lies behind Simic's plainness. . . . Casual, unobtrusive language expresses the most fantastic images." Milburn concludes that the poet "mines ingredients of language and experience that readers may take for granted, and fuses them in a singular music."

BIOGRAPHICAL/CRITICAL SOURCES:

BOOKS

Contemporary Authors Autobiography Series, Volume 4, Gale (Detroit), 1986.
Contemporary Literary Criticism, Gale, Volume 6, 1976; Volume 9, 1978; Volume 22, 1982; Volume 49, 1988; Volume 68, 1991.
Stitt, Peter, *Uncertainty and Plentitude: Five Contemporary Poets,* University of Iowa Press, 1997.
Thurley, Geoffrey, *The American Moment: American Poetry in the Mid-Century,* St. Martin's, 1978.
Weigl, Bruce, editor, *Charles Simic: Essays on the Poetry,* University of Michigan Press (Ann Arbor), 1996.

PERIODICALS

America, January 13, 1996, p. 18.
Antioch Review, spring, 1977.
Boston Review, March/April, 1981; April, 1986.
Chicago Review, Volume 48, number 4, 1977.
Chicago Tribune Book World, June 12, 1983.
Choice, March, 1975.
Georgia Review, winter, 1976; summer, 1986.
Hudson Review, spring, 1981; autumn, 1986.
Los Angeles Times Book Review, March 16, 1986; December 7, 1986.
New Boston Review, March/April, 1981.
New Letters Review of Books, spring, 1987.
New Republic, January 24, 1976; March 1, 1993, p. 28.
New Yorker, December 21, 1992, p. 130; June 28, 1993, p. 74.
New York Times, May 28, 1990.
New York Times Book Review, March 5, 1978; October 12, 1980; May 1, 1983; January 12, 1986; October 18, 1987; March 21, 1993, p. 14.
Ploughshares, Volume 7, number 1, 1981.
Poetry, December, 1968; September, 1971; March, 1972; February, 1975; November, 1978; July, 1981; October, 1983; July, 1987; April, 1996, p. 33.
Poetry Review, June, 1983.

Publishers Weekly, November 2, 1990; September 21, 1992, p. 78; August 25, 1997, p. 54.
Village Voice, April 4, 1974; February 28, 1984.
Virginia Quarterly Review, spring, 1975.
Voice Literary Supplement, December, 1986.
Washington Post, April 13, 1990.
Washington Post Book World, November 2, 1980; April 13, 1986; May 7, 1989.

*   *   *

SIMON, (Marvin) Neil 1927-

PERSONAL: Born July 4, 1927, in Bronx, NY; son of Irving (a garment salesman) and Mamie Simon; married Joan Baim (a dancer), September 30, 1953 (died, 1973); married Marsha Mason (an actress), 1973 (separated, 1983); married Diana Lander, 1986; children (first marriage) Ellen, Nancy. *Education:* Attended New York University, 1946, and University of Denver.

ADDRESSES: Office—c/o G. Da Silva, 616 Highland Ave., Manhttan Beach, CA, 90266-5646.

CAREER: Playwright. Owner of the Eugene O'Neill Theatre, New York City. Warner Brothers, Inc., New York City, mail room clerk, 1946; Columbia Broadcasting System, New York City, comedy writer for Goodman Ace, late 1940s; comedy writer for *The Phil Silvers Arrow Show,* NBC-TV, 1948, *The Tallulah Bankhead Show,* NBC-TV, 1951, *The Sid Caesar Show,* NBC-TV, 1956-57, *The Phil Silvers Show,* CBS-TV, 1958-59, *The Gary Moore Show,* CBS TV, 1959-60, for *The Jackie Gleason Show* and *The Red Buttons Show,* both CBS-TV, and for NBC-TV specials. *Military service:* U.S. Army Air Force Reserve; sports editor of *Rev-Meter,* the Lowry Field (Colorado) base newspaper, 1946.

MEMBER: Dramatists Guild, Writers Guild of America.

AWARDS, HONORS: Academy of Television Arts and Sciences Award (Emmy), 1957, for *The Sid Caesar Show,* and 1959, for *The Phil Silvers Show;* Antoinette Perry Award (Tony) nomination, 1963, for *Little Me* and *Barefoot in the Park,* 1968, for *Plaza Suite,* 1969, for *Promises, Promises,* 1970, for *Last of the Red Hot Lovers,* 1972, for *The Prisoner of Second Avenue,* and 1987, for *Broadway Bound;* Tony Award, 1965, for best playwright, 1985, for *Biloxi Blues,* and 1991, for *Lost in Yonkers;* Writers Guild Award nomination, 1967, for *Barefoot in the Park; Evening Standard* Drama Award, 1967, for *Sweet Charity;* Sam S. Shubert Foundation Award, 1968; Academy of Motion Picture Arts and Sciences Award (Oscar) nomination, 1968, for *The Odd Couple;* Writers Guild Screen Award, 1969, for *The Odd Couple,* 1970, for *Last of the Red Hot Lovers,* 1971, for *The Out-of-Towners,* and 1972, for *The Trouble with People;* named Entertainer of the Year, *Cue* magazine, 1972; Writers Guild Laurel Award, 1975; L.H.D., Hofstra University, 1981; New York Drama Critics Circle Award, 1983, for *Brighton Beach Memoirs;* elected to the Theater Hall of Fame, Uris Theater, 1983; L.H.D., Williams College, 1984; a Neil Simon tribute show was held at the Shubert Theater, March 1, 1987; the Neil Simon Endowment for the Dramatic Arts has been established at Duke University; Pulitzer Prize for drama, 1991, for *Lost in Yonkers.*

WRITINGS:

PUBLISHED PLAYS

(With William Friedberg) *Adventures of Marco Polo: A Musical Fantasy* (music by Clay Warnick and Mel Pahl), Samuel French, 1959.

(Adaptor with Friedberg) *Heidi* (based on the novel by Johanna Spyri; music by Warnick), Samuel French, 1959.

(With brother, Danny Simon) *Come Blow Your Horn* (also see below; first produced in New Hope, Pa., at the Bucks County Playhouse, August, 1960; produced on Broadway at the Brooks Atkinson Theatre, February 22, 1961; produced on the West End at the Prince of Wales Theatre, February 17, 1962), Doubleday, 1963.

Barefoot in the Park (also see below; first produced, under title *Nobody Loves Me,* in New Hope, PA, at the Bucks County Playhouse, 1962; produced on Broadway at the Biltmore Theatre, October 23, 1963; produced on the West End, 1965), Random House, 1964.

The Odd Couple (also see below; first produced on Broadway at the Plymouth Theatre, March 10, 1965; produced on the West End at the Queen's Theatre, October 12, 1966; revised version first produced in Los Angeles at the Ahmanson Theatre, April 6, 1985; produced on Broadway at the Broadhurst Theatre, June, 1985), Random House, 1966.

Sweet Charity (musical; based on the screenplay "*The Nights of Cabiria*" by Federico Fellini; music and lyrics by Cy Coleman and Dorothy Fields; first produced on Broadway at the Palace Theatre, January 29, 1966; produced on the West End at the Prince of Wales Theatre, October 11, 1967), Random House, 1966.

The Star-Spangled Girl (also see below; first produced on Broadway at the Plymouth Theatre, December 21, 1966), Random House, 1967.

Plaza Suite (also see below; three one-acts entitled "Visitor from Hollywood," "Visitor from Mamaroneck," and "Visitor from Forest Hills"; first produced on Broadway at the Plymouth Theatre, February 14, 1968; produced on the West End at the Lyric Theatre, February 18, 1969), Random House, 1969.

Promises, Promises (also see below; musical; based on the screenplay *The Apartment* by Billy Wilder and I.A.L. Diamond; music by Burt Bacharach; lyrics by Hal David; first produced on Broadway at the Shubert Theatre, December 1, 1968; produced on the West End at the Prince of Wales Theatre, October 2, 1969), Random House, 1969.

Last of the Red Hot Lovers (also see below; three-act; first produced in New Haven at the Shubert Theatre, November 26, 1969; produced on Broadway at the Eugene O'Neill Theatre, December 28, 1969; produced in London, 1979), Random House, 1970.

The Gingerbread Lady (also see below; first produced in New Haven at the Shubert Theatre, November 4, 1970; produced on Broadway at the Plymouth Theatre, December 13, 1970; produced in London, 1974), Random House, 1971.

The Prisoner of Second Avenue (also see below; first produced in New Haven at the Shubert Theatre, October 12, 1971; produced on Broadway at the Eugene O'Neill Theatre, November 11, 1971), Random House, 1972.

The Sunshine Boys (also see below; first produced in New Haven at the Shubert Theatre, November 21, 1972; produced on Broadway at the Broadhurst Theatre, December 20, 1972; produced in London, 1975), Random House, 1973.

The Good Doctor (also see below; musical; adapted from stories by Anton Chekhov; music by Peter Link; lyrics by Simon; first produced on Broadway at the Eugene O'Neill Theatre, November 27, 1973), Random House, 1974.

God's Favorite (also see below; first produced on Broadway at the Eugene O'Neill Theatre, December 11, 1974), Random House, 1975.

California Suite (also see below; first produced in Los Angeles, April, 1976; produced on Broadway at the Eugene O'Neill Theatre, June 30, 1976; produced in London, 1976), Random House, 1977.

Chapter Two (also see below; first produced in Los Angeles, 1977; produced on Broadway at the Imperial Theatre, December 4, 1977; produced in London, 1981), Random House, 1979.

They're Playing Our Song (musical; music by Marvin Hamlisch; lyrics by Carol Bayer Sager; first produced in Los Angeles, 1978; produced on Broadway at the Imperial Theatre, February 11, 1979; produced in London, 1980), Random House, 1980.

I Ought to Be in Pictures (also see below; first produced in Los Angeles, 1980; produced on Broadway at the Eugene O'Neill Theatre, April 3, 1980; produced in London at the Offstage Downstairs, December, 1986), Random House, 1981.

Fools (first produced on Broadway at the Eugene O'Neill Theatre, April, 1981), Random House, 1982.

Brighton Beach Memoirs (also see below; first produced in Los Angeles at the Ahmanson Theatre, December, 1982; produced on Broadway at the Alvin Theatre, March 27, 1983), Random House, 1984.

Biloxi Blues (also see below; first produced in Los Angeles at the Ahmanson Theatre, December, 1984; produced on Broadway at the Neil Simon Theatre, March, 1985), Random House, 1986.

Broadway Bound (first produced at Duke University, October, 1986; produced on Broadway at the Broadhurst Theatre, December, 1986), Random House, 1987.

Rumors (first produced in San Diego in the Old Globe Theater in 1988), 1990.

Lost in Yonkers (first produced in 1991), Random House, 1992.

Jake's Women (first produced in 1992), Random House, 1994.

London Suite, S. French, 1996.

OMNIBUS COLLECTIONS

The Comedy of Neil Simon (contains *Come Blow Your Horn, Barefoot in the Park, The Odd Couple, The Star-Spangled Girl, Promises, Promises, Plaza Suite,* and *Last of the Red Hot Lovers*), Random House, 1971, published as *The Collected Plays of Neil Simon,* Volume 1, New American Library, 1986.

The Collected Plays of Neil Simon, Volume 2 (contains *The Sunshine Boys, Little Me* [also see below], *The Gingerbread Lady, The Prisoner of Second Avenue, The Good Doctor, God's Favorite, California Suite,* and *Chapter Two*), Random House, 1979.

The Collected Plays of Neil Simon, Random House, 1992.

Neil Simon Monologues: Speeches from the Works of America's Foremost Playwright, edited by Roger Karshner, Dramaline (Rancho Mirage, California), 1996.

UNPUBLISHED PLAYS

(Contributor of sketches) *Tamiment Revue,* first produced in Tamiment, PA, 1952-53.

(Contributor of sketches, with D. Simon) *Catch a Star!* (musical revue), first produced on Broadway at the Plymouth Theatre, November 6, 1955.

(Contributor of sketches, with D. Simon) *New Faces of 1956,* first produced on Broadway at the Ethel Barrymore Theatre, June 14, 1956.

(Adaptor) *Little Me* (musical; based on the novel by Patrick Dennis), music by Coleman, first produced on Broadway at the Lunt-Fontanne Theatre, November 17, 1962, produced on the West End at the Cambridge Theatre, November 18, 1964.

(Contributor of sketch) *Broadway Revue* (satirical musical revue), first produced in New York City at the Karmit Bloomgarden Theatre, November, 1968.

(Editor of book for musical) *Seesaw* (based on *Two for the Seesaw* by William Gibson), first produced on Broadway, March 18, 1973.

SCREENPLAYS

(With Cesare Zavattini) *After the Fox,* United Artists, 1966.

Barefoot in the Park (based on Simon's play of the same title), Paramount, 1967.

The Odd Couple (based on Simon's play of the same title), Paramount, 1968.

The Out-of-Towners, Paramount, 1970.

Plaza Suite (based on Simon's play of the same title), Paramount, 1971.

Last of the Red Hot Lovers (based on Simon's play of the same title), Paramount, 1972.

The Heartbreak Kid (based on short story by Bruce Jay Friedman), Twentieth Century-Fox, 1972.

The Sunshine Boys (based on Simon's play of the same title), Metro-Goldwyn-Mayer, 1974.

The Prisoner of Second Avenue (based on Simon's play of the same title), Warner Bros., 1975.

Murder by Death, Columbia, 1976.

The Goodbye Girl, Warner Bros., 1977.

The Cheap Detective, Columbia, 1978.

California Suite (based on Simon's play of the same title), Columbia, 1978.

Chapter Two (based on Simon's play of the same title), Columbia, 1979.

Seems Like Old Times, Columbia, 1980.

Only When I Laugh, Columbia, 1981.

I Ought to Be in Pictures (based on Simon's play of the same title), Twentieth Century-Fox, 1982.

Max Dugan Returns, Twentieth Century-Fox, 1983.

(With Ed. Weinberger and Stan Daniels) *The Lonely Guy,* Universal, 1984.

The Slugger's Wife, Columbia, 1985.

Brighton Beach Memoirs (based on Simon's play of the same title), Universal, 1986.

Biloxi Blues (based on Simon's play of the same title), Universal, 1988.

Lost in Yonkers (based on Simon's play of the same title), 1993.

OTHER

The Trouble with People (television script), National Broadcasting Co., 1972.

(Coauthor) *Happy Endings* (television script), 1975.

Laughter on the 23rd Floor (television script), Random House (New York), 1995.

Rewrites (biography), Simon & Schuster (New York), 1996.

MEDIA ADAPTATIONS: Come Blow Your Horn was filmed by Paramount in 1963; *Sweet Charity* was filmed by Universal in 1969; *The Star-Spangled Girl* was filmed by Paramount in 1971; *Barefoot in the Park* was adapted as a television series by American Broadcasting Co. in 1970; *The Odd Couple* was adapted as a television series by ABC in 1970-75, and as *The New Odd Couple,* ABC, in 1982-83.

SIDELIGHTS: For some thirty years, Neil Simon's comedies have dominated the Broadway stage and have been adapted as popular Hollywood films as well. As David Richards explains in the *Washington Post,* Simon's comedies have always run "forever on Broadway and made him pots of money, after which they were turned into movies that made him pots more." Such plays as *Barefoot in the Park, The Odd Couple, Plaza Suite, The Prisoner of Second Avenue, The Sunshine Boys,* and the autobiographical trilogy of *Brighton Beach Memoirs, Biloxi Blues,* and *Broadway Bound,* have ensured Simon a position as "one of America's most popular and prolific playwrights" and "the most formidable comedy writer in American theatre," as Sheila Ennis Geitner reports in the *Dictionary of Literary Biography.*

Even though Simon's plays are often "detonatingly funny," as a critic for *Time* claims, in recent years they have grown more serious too, confronting issues of importance, the humor developing naturally from the characters and their interactions. With these plays, Simon has gained a new respect for his work. "Simon's mature theatre work," Robert K. Johnson writes in his *Neil Simon,* "combines comedy with moments of poignance and insight." Speaking of the Tony Award-winning *Biloxi Blues,* Frank Rich of the *New York Times* argues that in this play Simon "at last begins to examine himself honestly, without compromises, and the result is his most persuasively serious effort to date." In his review of the same play, Clive Barnes of the *New York Post* calls it "a realistic comedy of the heart" and allows that it "is funny, often heartrendingly funny, but nowadays Simon will not compromise character for a laugh."

Simon began his career as a radio writer in the 1940s. He and his brother Danny Simon worked as a team, writing comedy sketches for radio personality Goodman Ace. In the 1950s, the pair graduated to television, working with such popular entertainers as Sid Caesar, Phil Silvers, and Jackie Gleason, and with such other writers as Mel Brooks and Woody Allen. But after some ten years in the business, Simon wanted out. "I hated the idea of working in television and having conferences with network executives and advertising executives who told you what audiences wanted and in what region they wanted it," Simon tells the *New York Times Magazine.* With the success of his play *Come Blow Your Horn,* written with Danny, Simon was finally able to leave television and devote his efforts to the stage. He has never regretted the move. As he tells Richards, "I would rather spend my nights writing for an audience of 1,000, than an audience of 14 million."

Since the initial success of *Come Blow Your Horn,* which ran for eighty-four weeks on Broadway, Simon has seldom had a disappointing reception to his work. His second play, *Barefoot in the Park,* ran for over 1,500 performances on Broadway; *The Odd Couple* for over 900 performances; *Plaza Suite* for over 1,000 performances; and *Last of the Red Hot Lovers* and *The Prisoner of Second Avenue* ran for over 700 performances each. Richards notes that "all but a handful of Simon's plays" have made a profit, while Simon is reputedly "the richest playwright alive and arguably the richest ever in the history of the theater." "Most of Simon's plays . . . ," Richard Christiansen remarks in the *Chicago Tribune,* "have been good box office. [And] he still holds the record for having the most plays running simultaneously on Broadway (four)." Speaking of Simon's phenomenal career, Christine Arnold of the *Chicago Tribune* calls him "America's most successful playwright, more prolific and far less troubled than Tennessee Williams, more popular than Eugene O'Neill or Lanford Wilson or Sam Shepard. Critics may dismiss or embrace his work, but they cannot dispute his genius for creating plays that resonate for vast audiences."

Simon's plays usually focus on the members of one family or on a small group of friends, and often concern the more disruptive problems of modern life: divorce, urban crime and congestion, conflicts between children and parents, infidelity. These conflicts occur in a closed environment: an apartment or the family home. "Many of my plays [deal] with people being dumped together in a confined space, physically and emotionally," Leslie Bennetts quotes Simon as explaining, in the *New York Times*. He uses this confined space with expert skill. David Kehr of the *Chicago Tribune* claims that Simon has "a kind of genius—a genius for stagecraft, the art of getting characters on and off a stage as unobtrusively as possible and of finding plausible, natural excuses for restricting a whole range of dramatic action to the confines of a single set. As a master of logistics, Simon is without peer."

Although Simon's plays are often concerned with domestic troubles, they nonetheless find humor in these painful situations. In his critique of *The Odd Couple* for the *Saturday Review,* Henry Hewes explains that Simon "makes comic cadenzas out of our bleats of agony." Simon's characters, Hewes maintains, "are blissfully unhappy but the pain of what they do to each other and to themselves is exploded into fierce humor." In his analysis of what makes Simon's plays funny, T. E. Kalem of *Time* finds that "the central aspect of his plays is that the central characters are not funny at all. They never laugh, and they are frequently utterly miserable. . . . Why does the audience laugh? Two reasons suggest themselves. The first is the catharsis of relief—thank God, this hasn't happened to me. The second is to ward off and suppress anxiety—by God, this might happen to me." Speaking to Paul D. Zimmerman of *Newsweek,* Simon explains: "My view is 'how sad and funny life is.' I can't think of a humorous situation that does not involve some pain. I used to ask, 'What is a funny situation?' Now I ask, 'What is a sad situation and how can I tell it humorously?'"

In her *Neil Simon: A Critical Study,* Edythe M. McGovern argues that in his early plays Simon also advocates compromise and moderation. In *Barefoot in the Park,* for instance, a newly-married couple are opposites: she is spontaneous; he is overly-careful. Their different outlooks on life threaten to pull them apart. But by play's end, they have moderated their behavior so that they can live comfortably together. "Simon," McGovern writes, "has made a point here regarding the desirability of following a middle course in order to live pleasurably without boredom, but with a sensible regard for responsibility."

The same theme is returned to in *The Odd Couple,* in which two divorced male friends share an apartment, only to find that the disagreeable personality traits which led them to get divorces also make their living together impossible. They are "two rather nice human beings who will never be able to communicate with one another simply because each man has a completely different way of viewing the world and is committed to what amounts to an extreme position with no intention of compromise," as McGovern explains. Their unyielding attitudes lead to an angry confrontation and eventual break. In showing the consequences of their inability to compromise, Simon again argues for "a middle course rather than an extremely polarized position," McGovern writes. Speaking of Simon's handling of such important themes in his comedies, McGovern claims that "to Neil Simon, . . . the comic

form provides a means to present serious subjects so that audiences may laugh to avoid weeping."

For many years, Simon was taken less than seriously even by critics who enjoyed his work. A *Time* reviewer, for example, once claimed that "Santa Claus is just an alias for Neil Simon. Every year just before Christmas, he loads up packets of goodies and tosses two unbridled hours of laughter to Broadway audiences." Johnson notes that many people saw Simon as "a sausage grinder turning out the same pleasing 'product' over and over again. The 'product' is a play or movie realistic in style and featuring New Yorkers who spout a lot of funny lines." Geitner remarks that Simon's reputation as "the most formidable comedy writer in American theatre . . . prevented his being considered a serious dramatist by many critics."

With the production of the trilogy *Brighton Beach Memoirs, Biloxi Blues,* and *Broadway Bound* in the 1980s, however, critical opinion about Simon's work has improved enormously. Speaking of the critical reception of *Brighton Beach Memoirs,* Richards explains that "the critics, who have sometimes begrudged the playwright his ability to coin more funny lines per minute than seems humanly possible, have now decided that he has a very warm heart." And *Biloxi Blues,* his twenty-first Broadway play, won Simon in 1985 his first Tony Award for best drama. (He had twenty years earlier won the Tony for best playwright.)

The trilogy is based on Simon's own childhood and youth in the 1930s and 1940s, although he tells Charles Champlin of the *Los Angeles Times:* "I hate to call it autobiographical, because things didn't necessarily happen, or happen to me. It's an Impressionist painting of that era and that place. But there are bits and pieces of me in several of the characters." *Broadway Bound* is close enough to the truth, however, for William A. Henry III of *Time* to report that both Simon "and his brother Danny have wept openly while watching it in performance."

Brighton Beach Memoirs is set in the Brooklyn of 1937 and tells of a Jewish family, the Jeromes, and their financial troubles during the Depression. When an aunt loses her job, she and her son move in with the Jeromes, and the family, now seven people in a cramped house, must survive their financial crisis and the aggravatingly close proximity to each other. Rich explains that "Simon uses the family's miseries to raise such enduring issues as sibling resentments, guilt-ridden parent-child relationships and the hunger for dignity in a poverty-stricken world." Simon's alter ego is the family's teenage son, Eugene, who comments on his family's problems in asides to the audience. Eugene, Richards explains, "serves as the play's narrator and [his] cockeyed slant on the family's tribulations keeps the play in comic perspective."

The play has earned Simon some of the best reviews of his career. Brown writes that *Brighton Beach Memoirs* has "plenty of laughs," but "Simon avoids the glib, tenderly probing the often-awkward moments where confused emotions cause unconscious hurts. . . . Simon's at his best, finding the natural wit, wisecracking and hyperbole in the words and wisdom of everyday people." Barnes finds *Brighton Beach Memoirs* to be "a very lovely play." He continues: "I am certain—if the kids of our academic establishment can get off their pinnacles and start taking Simon as seriously as he deserves—*Brighton Beach Memoirs* will become a standard part of American dramatic literature."

Eugene Jerome joins the Army in *Biloxi Blues,* the second play of the trilogy. The story follows Eugene through his ten weeks of basic training in Biloxi, Mississippi. During this training, one recruit is jailed for his homosexuality; one comes into constant conflict with his superior officers; and Eugene faces anti-Semitic insults from another soldier. Eugene, an aspiring writer, records these events faithfully in his diary, learning to examine his life and the lives of his friends honestly, and developing personal values in the process. Eugene's dream of becoming a writer is greatly furthered when he is assigned to work on an Army newspaper instead of being sent to the front, a fortunate turn of events that nonetheless makes him feel guilty.

The story of Eugene Jerome continues in *Broadway Bound,* in which Eugene and his older brother, Simon, become comedy writers, leave home, and take jobs with a major network radio show. The breakup of their parents' marriage, the family's resistance to their new profession, and Eugene's realization that life does not enjoy the happy endings found in art form the basis of the plot. Danny Simon tells Nina Darnton of the *New York Times* that *Broadway Bound* "is the closest in accuracy" of the three autobiographical plays.

Eugene's mother is the primary character in *Broadway Bound.* "Through much of the comedy," Christiansen notes, "she has been the needling, nagging Jewish mother who gets the old, familiar laughs. But by the end of the play, with her personal life a shambles, she has turned into a creature of great sorrow and weariness, as well." After recounting to Eugene the story of how she once danced with actor George Raft—an exhilarating and romantic moment she still recalls fondly—Eugene asks his mother to dance with him. "In this," *Newsweek*'s Jack Kroll observes, "perhaps the most delicate and highly charged moment in any Simon play, we feel the waste of a woman's unlived life and the shock of a young man who feels in his arms the repressed rhythm of that life." Eugene "sees that behind his mother's depressed exterior," Mel Gussow comments in the *New York Times,* "is the heart of a once vibrant and hopeful young woman; she is someone who has been defeated by the limits she has imposed on her life."

According to Sylvie Drake of the *Los Angeles Times, Broadway Bound* is the third and best and final segment of Simon's semiautobiographical trilogy. . . . There is plenty of comedy left, but of a different order. The one-liners are gone, replaced by a well-timed visceral humor that is coated in melancholy." Drake concludes that *Broadway Bound* is Simon "not only at his finest, but at his most personal and complex." Similarly, although he sees some flaws in *Broadway Bound,* Rich admits that it "contains some of its author's most accomplished writing to date—passages that dramatize the timeless, unresolvable bloodlettings of familial existence as well as the humorous conflicts one expects." And Holly Hill, writing for the London *Times,* believes that Eugene's mother "is the most masterful portrait Neil Simon has ever drawn."

Although primarily known for his plays, Simon also has written a score of popular films. These include the screen adaptations of many of his own hit plays—including *Barefoot in the Park, The Odd Couple,* and *The Sunshine Boys*—as well as such original screenplays as *The Cheap Detective, Murder by Death,* and *The Goodbye Girl.* Simon's best screen work is found in films where he creates a desperate situation, Vincent Canby argues in the *New York Times.* Simon's "wisecracks define a world of mighty desperation," Canby writes, "in which every confrontation, be it with a lover, a child, a husband, a friend or a taxi driver, becomes a last chance for survival. When he writes a work in which the desperation is built into the situations, Mr. Simon can be both immensely funny and surprisingly moving."

"Writing is an escape from a world that crowds me," Simon tells John Corry of the *New York Times.* "I like being alone in a room. It's almost a form of meditation—an investigation of my own life." He explains to Henry how he begins a play: "There's no blueprint per se. You just go through the tunnels of your mind, and you come out someplace." Simon admits to Zimmerman that the writing process still frightens him. "Every time I start a play," he explains, "I panic because I feel I don't know how to do it. . . . I keep wishing I had a grownup in the room who would tell me how to begin." Accepting his success as a writer has also been difficult. "I was depressed for a number of years," Simon tells Corry. The opening of a new play always filled him with guilt. It took psychoanalysis, and a consultation with his second wife's swami, before Simon learned to enjoy his accomplishments.

BIOGRAPHICAL/CRITICAL SOURCES:

BOOKS

Contemporary Literary Criticism, Gale (Detroit), Volume 6, 1976; Volume 9, 1979; Volume 31, 1985; Volume 39, 1986.
Dictionary of Literary Biography, Volume 7: *Twentieth-Century American Dramatists,* Gale, 1981.
Johnson, Robert K., *Neil Simon,* Twayne, 1983.
Kerr, Walter, *Thirty Plays Hath November,* Simon & Schuster, 1969.
Konas, Gary, *Neil Simon: A Casebook,* Garland, 1997.
McGovern, Edythe M., *Neil Simon: A Critical Study,* Ungar, 1979.
Monaco, James, *American Film Now,* Oxford University Press, 1979.
Simon, John, *Uneasy Stages: A Chronicle of the New York Theater, 1963-73,* Random House, 1975.

PERIODICALS

America, May 20, 1961; May 29, 1965; April 1, 1989.
Chicago Tribune, March 26, 1982; April 7, 1986; November 2, 1986; December 31, 1986; August 23, 1989.
Christian Science Monitor, January 17, 1970; November 11, 1970.
Commonweal, November 15, 1963; April 2, 1965; October 9, 1992.
Life, April 9, 1965; March 6, 1970; May 7, 1971.
Los Angeles Times, December 5, 1982; December 11, 1982; August 24, 1984; December 15, 1984; April 6, 1985; April 8, 1985; December 6, 1986; December 25, 1986; March 25, 1988; November 19, 1988; November 23, 1988; August 19, 1989; September 8, 1989; March 10, 1990; April 7, 1990.
Nation, March 4, 1968; July 3, 1976.
National Observer, November 20, 1971.
New Republic, January 16, 1971.
New Statesman, November 1, 1974.
Newsweek, January 9, 1967; February 26, 1968; February 2, 1970; November 23, 1970; December 10, 1973; April 26, 1976; February 26, 1979; April 14, 1980; April 20, 1981; December 15, 1986; March 4, 1991; March 15, 1993; December 6, 1993.
New York, January 13, 1975; April 11, 1983; March 29, 1985.
New Yorker, January 10, 1970; December 23, 1974; March 11, 1991; March 15, 1993; December 20, 1993.
New York Post, December 22, 1966; November 12, 1971; April 7, 1981; March 28, 1983; March 29, 1985.
New York Times, August 4, 1968; December 2, 1968; December 31, 1969; November 17, 1971; December 9, 1973; December 12, 1974; December 22, 1974; December 1, 1977; June 23,

1978; December 22, 1978; December 19, 1980; March 23, 1981; April 5, 1981; April 7, 1981; April 12, 1981; September 23, 1981; March 25, 1983; March 27, 1983; March 28, 1983; April 3, 1983; March 29, 1985; April 1, 1985; April 7, 1985; April 16, 1985; June 9, 1985; August 29, 1986; November 30, 1986; December 5, 1986; December 14, 1986; December 25, 1986; December 26, 1986; January 8, 1987; January 25, 1987; August 17, 1987; December 9, 1987; March 25, 1988; April 15, 1988; November 13, 1988; November 18, 1988.

New York Times Book Review, September 29, 1996, p. 13.

New York Times Magazine, March 7, 1965; March 22, 1970; May 26, 1985.

People Weekly, October 9, 1995, p. 83.

Saturday Review, March 27, 1965.

Time, November 1, 1963; January 12, 1970; January 15, 1973; December 23, 1974; April 8, 1985; December 15, 1986; November 28, 1988; April 8, 1991; May 24, 1993; December 6, 1993.

Times (London), April 20, 1983; April 10, 1985; December 4, 1986; January 3, 1987; June 4, 1987.

Times Literary Supplement, January 17, 1997, p. 13.

Washington Post, January 13, 1970; February 9, 1971; April 10, 1983; December 14, 1984; April 6, 1985; July 16, 1985; June 12, 1986; September 12, 1986; October 19, 1986; December 25, 1986; December 26, 1986; March 25, 1988.

World Journal Tribune, December 22, 1966.

*   *   *

SIMPSON, Harriette
See ARNOW, Harriette (Louisa) Simpson

*   *   *

SIMPSON, Louis (Aston Marantz) 1923-

PERSONAL: Born March 27, 1923, in Kingston, Jamaica, British West Indies; son of Aston and Rosalind (Marantz) Simpson; married Jeanne Rogers, 1949 (divorced, 1954); married Dorothy Roochvarg, 1955 (divorced, 1979); married Miriam Butensky Bachner, 1985; children: (first marriage) Matthew; (second marriage) Anne, Anthony. *Education:* Columbia University, B.S., 1948, M.A., 1950, Ph.D., 1959.

ADDRESSES: Home—186 Old Field Rd., Setauket, New York, NY 11733-1636.

CAREER: Bobbs-Merrill Publishing Co., New York City, editor, 1950-55; Columbia University, New York City, instructor in English, 1955-59; University of California, Berkeley, 1959-67, began as assistant professor, became professor of English; State University of New York at Stony Brook, professor of English and comparative literature, 1967-91, distinguished professor 1991–. Has given poetry readings at colleges and poetry centers throughout the United States and Europe and on television and radio programs in New York, San Francisco, and London. *Military service:* U.S. Army, 1943-46; became sergeant; awarded Bronze Star with oak leaf cluster, Purple Heart (twice), Presidential Unit Citation.

MEMBER: American Academy in Rome.

AWARDS, HONORS: Fellowship in literature (Prix de Rome) at American Academy in Rome, 1957; *Hudson Review* fellowship, 1957; Columbia University, distinguished alumni award, 1960, Medal for Excellence, 1965; Edna St. Vincent Millay Award, 1960; Guggenheim fellowship, 1962, 1970; American Council of Learned Societies grant, 1963; Pulitzer Prize for poetry, 1964, for *At the End of the Open Road;* American Academy of Arts and Letters award in literature, 1976; D.H.L., Eastern Michigan University, 1977; Institute of Jamaica, Centenary Medal, 1980; Jewish Book Council, Award for Poetry, 1981; Elmer Holmes Bobst Award, 1987; Hampden Sydney College, D.Litt., 1990.

WRITINGS:

The Arrivistes: Poems, 1940-49, Fine Editions, 1949.
Good News of Death and Other Poems, Scribner, 1955.
(Editor with Donald Hall and Robert Pack) *New Poets of England and America,* Meridian, 1957.
A Dream of Governors (poems), Wesleyan University Press, 1959.
Riverside Drive (novel), Atheneum, 1962.
James Hogg: A Critical Study, St. Martin's, 1962.
At the End of the Open Road (poems), Wesleyan University Press, 1963.
(Contributor) Thom Gunn and Ted Hughes, editors, *Five American Poets,* Faber, 1963.
Selected Poems, Harcourt, 1965.
(Editor) *An Introduction to Poetry,* St. Martin's, 1967, 2nd edition, 1972.
Adventures of the Letter I (poems), Harper, 1972.
North of Jamaica (autobiography), Harper, 1972, published as *Air with Armed Men,* London Magazine Editions, 1972.
Three on the Tower: The Lives and Works of Ezra Pound, T. S. Eliot and William Carlos Williams, Morrow, 1975.
Searching for the Ox (poems), Morrow, 1976.
The Invasion of Italy (limited edition), Main Street Inc., 1976.
A Revolution in Taste: Studies of Dylan Thomas, Allen Ginsberg, Sylvia Plath and Robert Lowell, Macmillan, 1978.
Out of Season (limited edition), Deerfield Press, 1979.
Caviare at the Funeral, F. Watts, 1980.
A Company of Poets, University of Michigan Press, 1981.
The Best Hour of the Night, Ticknor & Fields, 1983.
The Character of the Poet, University of Michigan Press, 1986.
Collected Poems, 1988.
Selected Prose, Paragon House, 1989.
Wei Wei and Other Friends, Typographeum, 1990.
In the Room We Share, Paragon House, 1990.
Jamaica Poems (limited edition), Press of Appletree Alley, 1993.
The King My Father's Wreck (memoir), Story Line Press, 1994.
Ships Going into the Blue: Essays and Notes on Poetry, University of Michigan Press (Ann Arbor), 1994.
There You Are: Poems, Story Line (Brownsville, OR), 1995.
(Editor) *Modern Poets of France: A Bilingual Anthology,* Story Line Press, 1997.

SIDELIGHTS: Jamaican-born poet and educator Louis Simpson, author of poetry collections that include the Pulitzer Prize-winning *At the End of the Open Road, Searching for the Ox,* and *There You Are,* is noted for simple, controlled verses that reveal hidden layers of meaning. Critic Yohma Gray writes in praise of the poet's ability to make his readers heed that which usually passes undiscerned. "Even in the most mundane experience there is a vast area of unperceived reality," the critic notes, "and it is Louis Simpson's kind of poetry which brings it to our notice. It enables us to see things which are ordinarily all about us but which we do not ordinarily see; it adds a new dimension to our sensational perception, making us hear with our eyes and see with our ears." Gray maintains that poetry seeks the same goal as religious belief: "to formulate a coherent and significant meaning for life. The poetry of Louis Simpson offers us that meaning."

In a discussion of Simpson's early poetry, Gray comments that the author "never departs from traditional form and structure and yet he never departs from contemporary themes and concerns." Gray describes one poem, for example, in which Simpson "handles a modern psychological situation in the delicate cadence of seventeenth-century verse." Ronald Moran makes a similar comment in regard to *The Arrivistes,* Simpson's first book. Moran finds that Simpson often sounds "like an Elizabethan song-maker or like a Cavalier poet." Gray argues that this juxtaposition of traditional form (ordered meter and rhyme) and modern subjects emphasizes, particularly in the poems about the world wars, the chaotic quality and the tensions of contemporary life. Gray finds that Simpson neither complains nor moralizes about modern problems; rather he clarifies difficulties and presents rational insights.

After 1959, the publication date of *A Dream of Governors,* there was a perceived change in Simpson's work; reviewer Stephen Stepanchev contends that it changed for the better. Notes Stepanchev: "The prosaism of his early work—which required metrics and rhyme in order to give it character as verse—now gave way to rich, fresh, haunting imagery. His philosophical and political speculations achieved a distinction and brilliance that they had lacked before." A *Chicago Review* critic had more cautious praise for the shift in Simpson's poetry, writing that, "*A Dream of Governors* has wit, sophistication, perceptiveness, intelligence, variety, and knowingness, but it comes perilously close to being a poetry of chic." The reviewer goes on to say that this early work lacks a depth of feeling. However, he continues, "*At the End of the Open Road* (1963) . . . is a different story entirely. Simpson has found the secret of releasing the meaning and power of his themes. . . . It is not that his stanzas . . . are becoming more flexible and experimental: this in itself does not mean very much. . . . What is more fundamental, it seems to me, is that greater stylistic flexibility should be the sign of growth in the character and thought of the speaker. Simpson is becoming more able to be a part of what he writes about, and to make what he writes about more a part of him."

Not all critics appreciated the change in Simpson's verse. In a review of 1965's *Selected Poems,* which contains twelve new poems in addition to selections of earlier work, Harry Morris states that "Simpson's first three volumes are better" than his new poetry. Morris believes that Simpson's "new freedoms" have not helped him convey his themes more effectively. T. O'Hara, in a critique of *Adventures of the Letter I,* also questions Simpson's new manner: "What has happened to Louis Simpson's energy? . . . It almost appears that success has mellowed the tough poetic instinct that once propelled him, for this present collection barely flexes a muscle." Yet Marie Borroff, speaking of the same book, avows that "when the remaining decades of the twentieth century have passed ignominiously into history along with the 1960's, these stanzas and other gifts will remain to us." And Christopher Hope deems *Adventures* "a work of pure, brilliant invention."

Critical dissent continued in reviews of *Searching for the Ox.* Derwent May finds the quiet, reflective mood of the poems attractive. Nikki Stiller, on the other hand, feels that "Louis Simpson's work now suggests too much comfort: emotional, physical, intellectual. He has stopped struggling, it seems, for

words, for rhythms, for his own deepest self." Yet in contrast to this, Peter Stitt remarks that *Searching for the Ox* "is a tremendously refreshing book. . . . The style in which [the poems] are written presents us with no barriers—it is plain, direct and relaxed. Moreover, the poems tell a story, or stories, in which we can take a real interest."

Simpson occasionally ventures from verse into other genres: novel, autobiography, and literary critical study. Robert Massie writes of the poet's 1962 novel *Riverside Drive* in the *New York Times Book Review:* "Into fragments of dialogue, [Simpson] packs more meaning and drama than many novelists can bring off in a chapter. . . . As novels go, *Riverside Drive* is not a tragedy to shake the Gods—but it should stir most of its readers. From the first chapter to the last, it has the ring of truth." Concerning Simpson's literary critical study *A Revolution in Taste,* Paul Zweig comments that the author "has provided a series of engaging portraits of poets whom he presents less as cultural exemplars than as individuals struggling, as Baudelaire wrote, to absolve the pain of their lives with the grace of an enduring poem. It is the life narrowing intensely and heatedly into the act of writing that interests Simpson, the life pared to the poem. And this has enabled him to write a series of compact literary biographies that have the pithiness of a 17th-century 'character' and a literary good sense that reminds me of [Samuel] Johnson's 'Lives of the Poets.'"

In the 1990s, Simpson published two more volumes of poetry, *In the Room We Share* and *There You Are. In the Room We Share,* writes Stephen Dobyns in the *New York Times Book Review,* is noteworthy for the clarity of its language; the language is so simple and unadorned, says Dobyns, that "one good shove would tumble it into banality." The book begins with poems about Simpson's mother, a Russian immigrant who came to New York and then travelled on to Jamaica, where Simpson was born. The book ends with a forty-page section of Simpson's diary recording two weeks in June, 1988, when Simpson's mother broke her leg and stayed with him. "I believed . . . that [writing] should show the poetry in common things," Simpson writes, and the poems are full of common things: friends and neighbors, work, time in the army. *There You Are,* Simpson's thirteenth book of poems, shows him as "a mature writer with a mature voice," according to Sima Rabinowitz of the *Hungry Mind Review.* the poems, Rabinowitz writes, are "typically and brilliantly matter-of-fact," making the ultra-serious, the exceptions, and the truly horrific accessible and even ordinary: "The intensity of Simpson's poems create is a subtle sensation, created almost, paradoxically, out of a lack of urgency."

Simpson has also written several volumes of autobiography, including 1972's *North of Jamaica* and *The King My Father's Wreck,* published in 1994. The latter work recounts the poet's early years in Jamaica and his transition to adulthood and literary maturity through a selection of essays. Focusing on specific images from his past—his mother's disappearance from home when he was a young boy, his excitement at the prospect of becoming a U.S. citizen, a dissatisfying job working as an editor for a publishing house, the experiences he encountered in the armed forces during World War II that led to later protestations over the conflict in Vietnam, returning a book to his Jamaican school sixty years after borrowing it—*The King My Father's Wreck* is written in the same spare style that is characteristic of Simpson's verse. The poet's "insistent voice" imbues his reminiscences with "more dramatic emotional topography than most," comments a *Publishers Weekly* reviewer, thereby "rewarding adventurous readers."

BIOGRAPHICAL/CRITICAL SOURCES:

BOOKS

Contemporary Literary Criticism, Gale (Detroit), Volume 4, 1975; Volume 7, 1977; Volume 9, 1978; Volume 32, 1985.

Hungerford, Edward, editor, *Poets in Progress: Critical Prefaces to Thirteen Modern American Poets,* Northwestern University Press, 1967.

Lensing, George S., and Ronald Moran, *Four Poets and the Emotive Imagination,* Louisiana State University Press (Baton Rouge), 1976.

Moran, Ronald, *Louis Simpson,* Twayne, 1972.

Stepanchev, Stephen, *American Poetry since 1945,* Harper, 1965.

PERIODICALS

American Poetry Review, January-February 1979.
Best Sellers, June 15, 1972.
Chicago Review, Volume XIX, number 1, 1966.
Harper's, October 1965.
Hudson Review, autumn, 1995, p. 499.
Hungry Mind Review, November 1, 1995.
Listener, November 25, 1976.
London Magazine, February-March 1977.
Los Angeles Times Book Review, April 30, 1995, p. 13.
New Statesman, January 31, 1964.
New York Herald Tribune Book Review, November 15, 1959; May 13, 1962.
New York Times Book Review, September 27, 1959; May 13, 1962; May 9, 1976; December 17, 1978; September 2, 1990.
New York Times Magazine, May 2, 1965.
Parnassus, January, 1996, p. 138.
Poetry, April 1960.
Publishers Weekly, October 24, 1994, p. 58.
Saturday Review, May 21, 1960.
Saturday Review/World, April 3, 1976.
Sewanee Review, spring, 1969; January, 1996, p. 142.
Time, May 18, 1962.
Times Literary Supplement, June 9, 1966; January 4, 1980.
Washington Post Book World, March 5, 1995, p. 12.
World Literature Today, summer, 1995, p. 594.
Yale Review, March 1964; October 1972.

*   *   *

SINCLAIR, Emil
See HESSE, Hermann

*   *   *

SINCLAIR, Upton (Beall) 1878-1968
(Clarke Fitch, Frederick Garrison, Arthur Stirling)

PERSONAL: Born September 20, 1878, in Baltimore, MD; died November 25, 1968, in Bound Brook, NJ; son of Upton Beall (a traveling salesman) and Priscilla (Harden) Sinclair; married Meta H. Fuller, 1900 (divorced, 1913); married Mary Craig Kimbrough (a poet), April 21, 1913 (died April 26, 1961); married Mary Elizabeth Willis, October 14, 1961 (died December 18, 1967); children: (first marriage) David. *Education:* City College (now City College of the City University of New York), A.B., 1897;

graduate studies at Columbia University, 1897-1901. *Politics:* Formerly Socialist, then left-wing Democrat.

CAREER: Supported himself while an undergraduate by writing jokes, light verse, short stories, and other commissioned works for comic papers and adventure magazines; wrote nearly one hundred pseudonymous "dime novels" while attending graduate school; full-time writer, 1898-1962. Founder, Intercollegiate Socialist Society (now League for Industrial Democracy), Helicon Home Colony, Englewood, NJ, 1906, and EPIC (End Poverty in California) League, 1934; assisted U.S. Government in investigation of Chicago stock yards, 1906; established theater company for performance of socialist plays, 1908. Socialist candidate for U.S. House of Representatives from New Jersey, 1906, and from California, 1920, for U.S. Senate from California, 1922, and for governor of California, 1926 and 1930; Democratic candidate for governor of California, 1934. Occasional lecturer.

MEMBER: Authors League of America (founder), American Institute of Arts and Letters, American Civil Liberties Union (founder of Southern California chapter).

AWARDS, HONORS: Nobel Prize for literature nomination, 1932; Pulitzer Prize, 1943, for *Dragon's Teeth;* New York Newspaper Guild Page One Award, 1962; United Auto Workers Social Justice Award, 1962.

WRITINGS:

NOVELS

Springtime and Harvest: A Romance, Sinclair Press, 1901, published as *King Midas,* Funk, 1901, 2nd edition, Heinemann, 1906.
The Journal of Arthur Stirling, revised and condensed edition, Appleton, 1903, new edition, Heinemann, 1907.
Prince Hagen: A Phantasy, L. C. Page and Co., 1903.
Manassas: A Novel of the War, Macmillan, 1904, revised edition published as *Theirs Be the Guilt: A Novel of the War between the States,* Twayne, 1959.
The Jungle, Doubleday, 1906, unabridged edition, Doubleday, 1988, Barnes and Noble, 1995.
A Captain of Industry, Being the Story of a Civilized Man, The Appeal to Reason, 1906.
The Overman, Doubleday, Page and Co., 1907.
The Moneychangers, B. W. Dodge and Co., 1908.
The Metropolis, Moffat, Yard and Co., 1908.
Samuel the Seeker, B. W. Dodge and Co., 1910.
Love's Pilgrimage, M. Kennerley, 1911.
The Millennium: A Comedy of the Year 2000, Laurie, 1912.
Damaged Goods (novelization of play "Les Avaries" by Eugene Brieux), Winston, 1913, published as *Damaged Goods: A Novel about the Victims of Syphilis,* Haldeman-Julius Publications, 1948.
Sylvia, Winston, 1913.
Sylvia's Marriage, Winston, 1914.
King Coal, Macmillan, 1917.
Jimmie Higgins, Boni & Liveright, 1919.
100%: The Story of a Patriot (also see below), privately printed, 1920 (published in England as *The Spy,* Laurie, 1920).
They Call Me Carpenter: A Tale of the Second Coming, Boni & Liveright, 1922.
Oil! A. & C. Boni, 1927, four-act play adaptation, privately printed, 1929.
Boston: A Documentary Novel of the Sacco-Vanzetti Case, A. & C. Boni, 1928 (published in England as *Boston: A Novel,* Laurie, 1929), condensed edition published as *August 22,*

Award Books, 1965 (published in England as *Boston: August 22,* Heinemann, 1978).

Mountain City, A. & C. Boni, 1930.

Peter Gudge Becomes a Secret Agent (excerpted from *100%*), State Publishing House, 1930.

Roman Holiday, Farrar & Rinehart, 1931.

The Wet Parade, Farrar & Rinehart, 1931.

Co-op: A Novel of Living Together, Farrar & Rinehart, 1936.

The Gnomobile: A Gnice Gnew Gnarrative with Gnonsense, but Gnothing Gnaughty (juvenile), Farrar & Rinehart, 1936.

No Pasaran! (They Shall Not Pass): A Story of the Battle of Madrid, Laurie, 1937.

Little Steel, Farrar & Rinehart, 1938.

Our Lady, Rodale Press, 1938.

Limbo on the Loose: A Midsummer Night's Dream, Haldeman-Julius Publications, 1948.

Marie and Her Lover, Haldeman-Julius Publications, 1948.

Another Pamela; or, Virtue Still Rewarded, Viking, 1950.

What Didymus Did, Wingate, 1954, published as *It Happened to Didymus,* Sagamore Press, 1958.

Cicero: A Tragedy of Ancient Rome, privately printed, 1960.

Affectionately Eve, Twayne, 1961.

The Coal War: A Sequel to King Coal, edited by John Graham, Colorado Associated University Press, 1976.

POLITICAL, SOCIAL, AND ECONOMIC STUDIES

The Industrial Republic: A Study of the America of Ten Years Hence, Doubleday, Page and Co., 1907.

(With Michael Williams) *Good Health and How We Won It, with an Account of the New Hygiene,* F. A. Stokes, 1909.

The Fasting Cure, M. Kennerley, 1911.

The Profits of Religion: An Essay in Economic Interpretation, privately printed, 1918, Vanguard, 1927.

The Brass Check: A Study of American Journalism, privately printed, 1919, 11th edition, 1936.

The Book of Life, Mind and Body, Macmillan, 1921, 4th edition, privately printed, 1926.

The Goose-Step: A Study of American Education, privately printed, 1923, revised edition, Haldeman-Julius Publications, 1923.

The Goslings: A Study of the American Schools, privately printed, 1924.

Mammonart: An Essay in Economic Interpretation, privately printed, 1925.

Letters to Judd, An American Workingman, privately printed, 1926, revised edition published as *This World of 1949 and What to Do about It: Revised Letters to a Workingman on the Economic and Political Situation,* Haldeman-Julius Publications, 1949.

The Spokesman's Secretary, Being the Letters of Mame to Mom, privately printed, 1926.

Money Writes! A. & C. Boni, 1927.

Upton Sinclair Presents William Fox, privately printed, 1933.

The Way Out. What Lies Ahead for America, Farrar & Rinehart, 1933.

I, Governor of California, and How I Ended Poverty: A True Story of the Future, Farrar & Rinehart, 1933.

The Lie Factory Starts, End Poverty League, 1934.

The EPIC Plan for California, Farrar & Rinehart, 1934.

EPIC Answers: How to End Poverty in California, End Poverty League, 1934, 2nd edition, 1935.

I, Candidate for Governor, and How I Got Licked, Farrar & Rinehart, 1935 (published in England as *How I Got Licked and Why,* Laurie, 1935).

We, People of America, and How We Ended Poverty: A True Story of the Future, National EPIC League, 1935, republished, University of California Press, 1994.

The Flivver King: A Story of Ford-America, Haldeman-Julius Publications, 1937, published in England as *The Flivver King: A Novel of Ford-America,* Laurie, 1938.

(With Eugene Lyons) *Terror in Russia?: Two Views,* Richard R. Smith, 1938.

Your Million Dollars, privately printed, 1939 (published in England as *Letters to a Millionaire,* Laurie, 1939).

Expect No Peace! Haldeman-Julius Publications, 1939.

What Can Be Done about America's Economic Troubles, privately printed, 1939.

Telling the World, Laurie, 1940.

The Cup of Fury, Channel Press, 1956.

PLAYS

Plays of Protest (includes *The Naturewoman, The Machine, The Second-Story Man,* and *Prince Hagen*), M. Kennerley, 1912.

Hell: A Verse Drama and Photo-Play, privately printed, 1923.

Singing Jailbirds: A Drama in Four Acts, privately printed, 1924.

Bill Porter: A Drama of O. Henry in Prison, privately printed, 1925.

Depression Island, Laurie, 1935.

Wally for Queen!: The Private Life of Royalty, privately printed, 1936.

Marie Antoinette, Vanguard, 1939.

A Giant's Strength, Laurie, 1948.

The Enemy Had It Too (three-act), Viking, 1950.

JUVENILE NOVELS; UNDER PSEUDONYM CLARKE FITCH

Courtmartialed, Street & Smith, 1898.

Saved by the Enemy, Street & Smith, 1898.

Wolves of the Navy; or, Clif Faraday's Search for a Traitor, Street & Smith, 1899.

A Soldier Monk, Street & Smith, 1899.

A Soldier's Pledge, Street & Smith, 1899.

Clif, the Naval Cadet; or, Exciting Days at Annapolis, Street & Smith, 1903.

From Port to Port; or, Clif Faraday in Many Waters, Street & Smith, 1903.

The Cruise of the Training Ship; or, Clif Faraday's Pluck, Street & Smith, 1903.

A Strange Cruise; or, Clif Faraday's Yacht Chase, Street & Smith, 1903.

"LANNY BUDD" SERIES; NOVELS

World's End, Viking, 1940.

Between Two Worlds, Viking, 1941.

Dragon's Teeth, Viking, 1942.

Wide Is the Gate, Viking, 1943.

Presidential Agent, Viking, 1944.

Dragon Harvest, Viking, 1945.

A World to Win, 1940-1942, Viking, 1946.

Presidential Mission, Viking, 1947.

One Clear Call, Viking, 1948.

O Shepherd, Speak, Viking, 1949.

The Return of Lanny Budd, Viking, 1953.

OTHER

(Under pseudonym Frederick Garrison) *Off for West Point; or, Mark Mallory's Struggle,* Street & Smith, 1903.

(Under Garrison pseudonym) *On Guard; or, Mark Mallory's Celebration,* Street & Smith, 1903.

(Editor) *The Cry for Justice: An Anthology of the Literature of Social Protest,* Winston, 1915, revised edition, Lyle Stuart, 1963; published as *The Cry for Justice: An Anthology of the Great Social Protest Literature of All Time,* Barricade Books (New York), 1996.

Mental Radio, A. & C. Boni, 1930 (published in England as *Mental Radio: Does It Work, and How?* Laurie, 1930), revised edition, C. C. Thomas, 1962.

American Outpost: A Book of Reminiscences, Farrar & Rinehart, 1932, published in England as *Candid Reminiscences: My First Thirty Years,* Laurie, 1932.

The Book of Love, Laurie, 1934.

An Upton Sinclair Anthology, compiled by I. O. Evans, Farrar & Rinehart, 1934, revised edition, Murray & Gee, 1947.

What God Means to Me: An Attempt at a Working Religion, privately printed, 1935, Farrar & Rinehart, 1936.

A Personal Jesus: Portrait and Interpretation, Evans Publishing Co., 1952, 2nd edition published as *The Secret Life of Jesus,* Mercury Books, 1962.

My Lifetime in Letters, University of Missouri Press, 1960.

Autobiography, Harcourt, 1962.

(Author of foreword) Morton T. Kelsey, *Tongue Speaking,* Doubleday, 1964.

Sinclair's personal papers, books, manuscripts, and other materials are housed in the Lilly Library at Indiana University.

MEDIA ADAPTATIONS: Several films have been based on books by Sinclair, including *The Adventurer,* U.S. Amusement Corp., 1917, *The Money Changers,* Pathe Exchange, 1920, *Marriage Forbidden,* Criterion, 1938, and *The Gnome-Mobile,* Walt Disney Productions, 1967.

SIDELIGHTS: "He was a man with a cause, and his weapon was an impassioned pen." With these words, a *National Observer* reporter summed up the life of Upton Sinclair, one of the twentieth century's foremost novelists, journalists, and pamphleteers. A "muckraker" whose motto was the same as that of American reformer Wendell Phillips—"If anything can't stand the truth, let it crack"—Sinclair spent most of his ninety years engaged in what William A. Bloodworth, Jr., in the *Dictionary of Literary Biography* calls "idealistic opposition to an unjust society." Time and time again, in books like the international bestseller *The Jungle* (a graphic portrayal of the wretched lives of workers in Chicago's meat-packing plants), the socialist crusader set out to reveal what he described as "the breaking of human hearts by a system which exploits the labor of men and women for profits."

In addition to zeal, Sinclair was noted for his morally simple view of history, a view that is especially evident in the "Lanny Budd" novels. This eleven-volume series, begun in 1940 and completed in 1953, traces the political history of the Western world from 1913 to 1950. It describes historical change in terms of international conspiracy and conflict, primarily between the forces of progress (socialism and communism) and the forces of oppression (fascism). As the series moves forward in time, however, America of the 1930s and 1940s takes up the cause of progress to do battle with both fascism and Soviet-style communism. (Sinclair enthusiastically supported Franklin Roosevelt and abhorred Stalinism.)

In his book *Sketches in Criticism,* Van Wyck Brooks presents a more pointed assessment of Sinclair's characters. It is hardly surprising, he says, that "Sinclair should be popular with the dispossessed: they who are so seldom flattered find in his pages a land of milk and honey. Here all the workers wear haloes of pure golden sunlight and all the capitalists have horns and tails; socialists with fashionable English wives invariably turn yellow at the appropriate moment, and rich men's sons are humbled in the dust, winsome lasses are always true unless their fathers have money in the bank, and wives never understand their husbands, and all those who are good are also martyrs, and all those who are patriots are also base. Mr. Sinclair says that the incidents in his books are based on fact and that his characters are studied from life. . . . But Mr. Sinclair, like the rest of us, has seen what he wanted to see and studied what he wanted to study; and his special simplification of the social scene is one that almost inevitably makes glad the heart of the victim of our system."

Sinclair's strong identification with "the masses" is most often attributed to the circumstances of his youth. He was born into an aristocratic but impoverished Southern family whose financial difficulties dated back to the Civil War era. His father, Upton Beall, a traveling salesman who turned to alcohol to cope with the unaccustomed pressures of having to work for a living, rarely made enough money to provide Upton and his mother with some measure of comfort. This life of genteel hardship contrasted sharply with that of Priscilla Sinclair's wealthy Baltimore relatives; it was a difference that disturbed young Sinclair, who could not understand why some people were rich and others poor. (Many years later, at the age of eighty-five, he remarked at a gathering held in his honor that he still did not understand.)

A sickly but precocious child, Sinclair entered New York's City College at the age of fourteen. Determined to become financially independent from his unreliable father, he immediately began submitting jokes, riddles, poems, and short stories to popular magazines; by the time he graduated, Sinclair was selling full-length adventure novels (which appeared under various pseudonyms) to Street & Smith, one of the day's foremost publishers of pulp fiction. During this period, the teenager learned to write quickly, prolifically, and with a minimum of effort, turning out an average of six to eight thousand words per day, seven days per week.

Once in contact with members of the socialist movement, Sinclair began studying philosophy and theoretics in earnest and was soon invited to contribute articles to major socialist publications. In late 1904, Fred D. Warren, editor of the magazine *Appeal to Reason,* approached Sinclair and challenged him to write about the "wage slaves" of industry in the same way he had written about the "chattel slaves" on the Southern plantations of *Manassas.* Encouraged by his editor at Macmillan, Sinclair accepted Warren's challenge and took as his starting point an article he had worked on that very summer dealing with an unsuccessful strike in the Chicago meat-packing industry. Thus in November, 1904, having moved his wife and son to a small New Jersey farm he had bought with the five-hundred dollar advance he received for his novel-to-be, *The Jungle,* Sinclair set out for Chicago, promising to "shake the popular heart and blow the roof off of the industrial tea-kettle." It was, notes Bloodworth in his study *Upton Sinclair,* a trip that "made a traumatic, life-long impression on him." Explains the critic: "What World War I meant to Ernest Hemingway, what the experiences of poverty and crime meant to Jack London, the combination of visible oppression and underlying corruption in Chicago in 1904 meant to Upton Sinclair. *This* kind of evidence, *this* kind of commitment to social justice became the primal experience of his fiction. For at least the next four decades, . . . Sinclair would continually retell the story of what happened to him in Chicago."

Sinclair's investigative work for *The Jungle* took seven weeks, during which time the young man talked with workers and visited packing plants, both on an official basis and in disguise. "I sat at night in the homes of the workers, foreign-born and native, and they told me their stories, one after one, and I made notes of everything," he once recalled. "In the daytime I would wander about the yards, and their friends would risk their jobs to show me what I wanted to see."

Sinclair fashioned his story around the experiences of Jurgis Rudkus, a fictional Lithuanian immigrant who arrives in Chicago with his family "expecting to achieve the American dream," Bloodworth writes. "Instead," the critic continues, "their life becomes a nightmare of toil, poverty, and death. . . . [Rudkus] not only sees his father, wife, and son die, but he is also brutalized by working conditions in the Chicago packing houses and exploited by corrupt politics." To dramatize his story of pain and oppression, Sinclair included some unpleasant passages on the meat-packing process itself, focusing on the diseased and chemically-tainted condition of the products manufacturers were offering to the American public.

Sinclair completed *The Jungle* in late 1905. Though a serialized version in *Appeal to Reason* had begun to attract attention as early as the summer of that year, the book version caused officials at Macmillan and four other companies the author approached to balk at the idea of publishing potentially libelous material. Eventually, however, after sending investigators to Chicago to check out Sinclair's facts, the firm of Doubleday, Page and Company agreed to bring out *The Jungle.*

The book appeared early in 1906 and, in an ironic twist of fate, was promoted not as a socialist novel, but as an expose of "the flagrant violations of all hygienic laws in the slaughter of diseased cattle . . . and in the whole machinery of feeding a nation." Published at a time of growing public outcry against contaminated food, *The Jungle* shocked and infuriated Americans; it was, in fact, this widespread revulsion that made the book a best seller and its author a world-famous writer. (Well aware of the real reason for *The Jungle*'s success, Sinclair once remarked, "I aimed at the public's heart, and by accident I hit it in the stomach.") Observes Alfred Kazin in his book *On Native Grounds:* "*The Jungle* attracted attention because it was obviously the most authentic and most powerful of the muckraking novels. The romantic indignation of the book gave it its fierce honesty, but the facts in it gave Sinclair his reputation, for he had suddenly given an unprecedented social importance to muckraking. The sales of meat dropped, the Germans cited the book as an argument for higher import duties on American meat, Sinclair became a leading exponent of the muckraking spirit to thousands in America and Europe, and met with the President. No one could doubt it, the evidence was overwhelming: here in *The Jungle* was the great news story of a decade written out in letters of fire."

While few reviewers dispute the remarkable emotional impact of *The Jungle,* many believe its "letters of fire" do not constitute great literature. Its plot and characterization have come under particularly heavy fire in the years since 1906. *Bookman*'s Edward Clark Marsh, for instance, finds it "impossible to withhold admiration of Mr. Sinclair's enthusiasm" as he describes the "intolerable" conditions in Packingtown. But "when [the author] betakes himself to other scenes, and attempts to let his characters breathe the air of a more familiar life," continues the critic, "it is impossible not to recognize his ignorance." Furthermore, declares Marsh, "we do not need to be told that thievery, and prostitution,

and political jobbery, and economic slavery exist in Chicago. So long as these truths are before us only as abstractions they are meaningless."

Several reviewers were disappointed with the book's ending, especially the abrupt switch from fiction to political rhetoric that occurs when Jurgis is "converted" to socialism. Writing in *The Strenuous Age in American Literature,* Grant C. Knight observes that the final section "is uplifting but it is also artificial, an arbitrary re-channelling of the narrative flow, a piece of rhetoric instead of a logical continuation of story." Walter B. Rideout accepts the notion of a religious-like conversion to socialism as being "probable enough," but declares that from that point onward *The Jungle* becomes "intellectualized" as political philosophy supplants Jurgis as the novel's focus. In short, notes Bloodworth, Sinclair failed to "carry out his intentions of a heart-breaking story with imminent Socialism. Instead, he settled for an uneven story dealing mainly with proletarian experience until the last four chapters, which switch disturbingly to the Socialist movement, its leaders, and its ideas."

Some critics regard this ending not so much as a demonstration of Sinclair's lack of literary skill as a confirmation of his elitism and essentially nineteenth-century liberal (rather than socialist) bent. Like several of his colleagues, Rideout finds that Sinclair had more in common with someone like Charles Dickens than with most other socialist writers, observing that the two men championed not "blood and barricades, but . . . humanitarianism and brotherly love." Hicks, commenting in his book *The Great Tradition,* maintains Sinclair's socialism "has always been of the emotional sort, a direct response to his own environment, and, as a result of his failure to undergo an intense intellectual discipline, he has never eradicated the effects of his bourgeois upbringing. Though his aim has been socialistic, his psychology has remained that of the liberal. Therefore, whether he realizes it or not, he is always writing for the middle class, trying to persuade his fellows to take their share of the burden of humanity's future, to pity the poor worker and strive for his betterment." Bloodworth also believes that Sinclair's socialism "had an obvious middle-class bias to it. Although he spoke *for* the lowest working classes, he spoke *to* a much wider audience in *The Jungle.* . . . [In the last few chapters of the novel] Sinclair's attitudes towards his protagonist and the lower social class he represents seem to take on qualities of paternalism and condescension. . . . The overcoming of capitalism that the orator speaks of does not really seem to be the task of the working class. The responsibilities fall mainly on the shoulders of men like himself—articulate, educated, even wealthy spokesmen." Brooks, noting that Sinclair fosters "the emotion of self-pity" among members of the working class because he chooses to depict "the helplessness, the benightedness, [and] the naivete of the American workers' movement," wonders how the author expects such an inept group to master their own fate and advance the cause of socialism.

Never again did Sinclair write a novel with quite the impact of *The Jungle.* In fact, Bloodworth contends, the success of this one book "virtually guaranteed that the rest of [Sinclair's] career would be anticlimactic." In the book *Sixteen Authors to One,* David Karsner expands on this idea, stating: "I cannot help but feel that *The Jungle* gave Sinclair a bad start by making him famous before he had reached his maturity as an artist. It chained him to propaganda and placed him in the literary pulpit where [he continued to preside] over our social morals and economic manners. . . . The true artist does not address his readers from a rostrum."

"Sinclair originated *none* of the ideas for which he propagandized, nor did he claim to have," observes Leon Harris in his book *Upton Sinclair: American Rebel.* "But he convinced millions of people all over the world of them. Other of his contemporary muckrakers played a greater role than he in effecting particular social change. But not one of them approached his total influence in regard to all the ideas he advocated. In the variety of his work and in his incomparable success in having it widely reprinted, discussed, attacked, and kept in print, Sinclair outweighed all other individual muckrakers."

BIOGRAPHICAL/CRITICAL SOURCES:

BOOKS

Blinderman, Abraham, editor, *Critics on Upton Sinclair,* University of Miami Press, 1975.
Bloodworth, William A., Jr., *Upton Sinclair,* Twayne, 1977.
Brooks, Van Wyck, *Sketches in Criticism,* Dutton, 1932.
Contemporary Literary Criticism, Gale (Detroit), Volume 1, 1973; Volume 9, 1979; Volume 15, 1980.
Cowley, Malcolm, editor, *After the Genteel Tradition: American Writers since 1910,* Norton, 1937, published as *After the Genteel Tradition: American Writers 1910-1930,* Southern Illinois University Press, 1964.
Dell, Floyd, *Upton Sinclair: A Study in Social Protest,* Doubleday, 1927.
Dictionary of Literary Biography, Volume 9: *American Novelists, 1910-1945,* Gale, 1981.
Harris, Leon, *Upton Sinclair: American Rebel,* Crowell, 1975.
Hicks, Granville, *The Great Tradition,* revised edition, Biblo & Tannen, 1967.
Karsner, David, *Sixteen Authors to One,* Books for Libraries, 1968.
Kazin, Alfred, *On Native Grounds: An Interpretation of Modern American Prose Literature,* Harcourt, 1942.
Knight, Grant C., *The Strenuous Age in American Literature,* University of North Carolina Press, 1954.
Rideout, Walter B., *The Radical Novel in the United States 1900-1954: Some Interrelations of Literature and Society,* Harvard University Press, 1956.
Scott, Ivan, *Upton Sinclair: The Forgotten Socialist,* University Press of America (Lanham, MD), 1996.
Yoder, John A., *Upton Sinclair,* Ungar, 1975.

PERIODICALS

American Heritage, September-October, 1988, p. 34.
Atlantic Monthly, August, 1946.
Chicago Tribune, April 16, 1932.
Christian Century, October 19, 1932.
College English, January, 1943; December, 1959.
Critic, December, 1962-January, 1963.
Harper's, March, 1961.
Monthly Review, December, 1991, p. 58.
Nation, February 4, 1931; April 13, 1932.
New Republic, October 7, 1931; June 22, 1932; February 24, 1937; June 24, 1940; January 11, 1943; September 29, 1958; December 1, 1962.
New Yorker, June 26, 1995, p. 66.
New York Times, March 3, 1906; June 16, 1906; August 22, 1988.
New York Times Book Review, May 13, 1962.
Saturday Review, March 3, 1928; August 28, 1948.
Saturday Review of Literature, May 7, 1932.
Spectator, July 9, 1932.
Time, December 14, 1962.
Vanity Fair, August, 1991, p. 176.

SINGER, Isaac
See SINGER, Isaac Bashevis

*   *   *

SINGER, Isaac Bashevis 1904-1991
(Isaac Bashevis, Isaac Warshofsky)

PERSONAL: Born July 14, 1904, in Radzymin, Poland; immigrated to United States, 1935, naturalized citizen, 1943; died after several strokes, July 24, 1991, in Surfside, Florida; buried Beth-El Cemetery, New York; son of Pinchos Menachem (a rabbi and author) and Bathsheba (Zylberman) Singer; married first wife, Rachel (divorced); married Alma Haimann, February 14, 1940; children: (first marriage) Israel Zamir. *Education:* Attended Tachkemoni Rabbinical Seminary, Warsaw, Poland, 1920-27. *Religion:* Jewish.

CAREER: Novelist, short story writer, children's author, and translator. *Literarishe Bletter,* Warsaw, Poland, proofreader and translator, 1923-33; *Globus,* Warsaw, associate editor, 1933-35; *Jewish Daily Forward,* New York City, member of staff, 1935-91. Founder of the literary magazine *Svivah.* Appeared in *Isaac in America* and *The Cafeteria* (based on one of his short stories), both Direct Cinema Limited Associates, both 1986.

MEMBER: Jewish Academy of Arts and Sciences (fellow), National Institute of Arts and Letters (fellow), Polish Institute of Arts and Sciences in America (fellow), American Academy of Arts and Sciences, PEN.

AWARDS, HONORS: Louis Lamed Prize, 1950, for *The Family Moskat,* and 1956, for *Satan in Goray;* National Institute of Arts and Letters and American Academy award in literature, 1959; Harry and Ethel Daroff Memorial Fiction Award, Jewish Book Council of America, 1963, for *The Slave;* D.H.L., Hebrew Union College, 1963; Foreign Book prize (France), 1965; National Council on the Arts grant, 1966; *New York Times* best illustrated book citation, 1966, Newbery Honor Book Award, 1967, International Board on Books for Young People honor list, 1982, *Horn Book* "Fanfare" citation, and American Library Association (ALA) notable book citation, all for *Zlateh the Goat and Other Stories;* National Endowment for the Arts grant, 1967; *Playboy* magazine award for best fiction, 1967; Newbery Honor Book Award, 1968, for *The Fearsome Inn;* Bancarella Prize, 1968, for Italian translation of *The Family Moskat;* Newbery Honor Book Award, 1969, ALA notable book citation, and *Horn Book* honor list citation, all for *When Schlemiel Went to Warsaw and Other Stories;* Brandeis University Creative Arts Medal for Poetry-Fiction, 1970; National Book Award for children's literature, 1970, and ALA notable book citation, both for *A Day of Pleasure;* Sydney Taylor Award, Association of Jewish Libraries, 1971; Children's Book Showcase Award, Children's Book Council, 1972, for *Alone in the Wild Forest;* D.Litt., Texas Christian University, 1972, Colgate University, 1972, Bard College, 1974, and Long Island University, 1979; Ph.D., Hebrew University, Jerusalem, 1973; National Book Award for fiction, 1974, for *A Crown of Feathers and Other Stories;* Agnon Gold Medal, 1975; ALA notable book citation, 1976, for *Naftali the Storyteller and His Horse, Sus, and Other Stories;* Nobel Prize for Literature, 1978; Kenneth B. Smilen/ *Present Tense* Literary Award, *Present Tense* magazine, 1980, for *The Power of Light;* *Los Angeles Times* fiction prize nomination, 1982, for *The Collected Stories of Isaac Bashevis Singer;* *New York Times* outstanding book citation, and

Horn Book honor list citation, both 1982, Parents' Choice Award, Parents' Choice Foundation, 1983, and ALA notable book citation, all for *The Golem; New York Times* notable book citation, and ALA notable book citation, both 1984, both for *Stories for Children;* Handel Medallion, 1986; PEN/Faulkner Award nomination, 1989, for *The Death of Methuselah and Other Stories;* Gold Medal for Fiction, American Academy and Institute of Arts and Letters, 1989; *Mazel and Shlimazel; or, The Milk of a Lioness* and *The Wicked City* received ALA notable book citations.

WRITINGS:

NOVELS; ORIGINALLY IN YIDDISH

Der Satan in Gorey, [Warsaw], 1935, translation by Jacob Sloan published as *Satan in Goray,* Noonday, 1955.

(Under name Isaac Bashevis) *Di Familie Mushkat,* two volumes, [New York], 1950, translation by A. H. Gross published under name Isaac Bashevis Singer as *The Family Moskat,* Knopf, 1950.

The Magician of Lublin, translation by Elaine Gottlieb and Joseph Singer, Noonday, 1960.

The Slave (also see below), translation by author and Cecil Hemley, Farrar, Straus, 1962.

The Manor, translation by Gottlieb and J. Singer, Farrar, Straus, 1967.

The Estate, translation by Gottlieb, J. Singer, and Elizabeth Shub, Farrar, Straus, 1969.

Enemies: A Love Story (first published in *Jewish Daily Forward* under title *Sonim, di Geshichte fun a Liebe,* 1966; also see below), translation by Aliza Shevrin and Shub, Farrar, Straus, 1972.

Shosha (also see below), Farrar, Straus, 1978.

Reaches of Heaven: A Story of the Baal Shem Tov, Farrar, Straus, 1980.

Isaac Bashevis Singer, Three Complete Novels (includes *The Slave, Enemies: A Love Story,* and *Shosha*), Avenel Books, 1982.

The Penitent, Farrar, Straus, 1983.

The King of the Fields, limited edition, Farrar, Straus, 1988.

Scum, translation by Rosaline D. Schwartz, Farrar, Straus, 1991.

Meshugah, translation by Nili Wachtel, Farrar, Straus, 1994.

Shadows on the Hudson, translation by Joseph Sherman, Farrar, Straus, 1998.

SHORT STORY COLLECTIONS; ORIGINALLY IN YIDDISH

Gimpel the Fool and Other Stories, translation by Saul Bellow and others, Noonday, 1957.

The Spinoza of Market Street and Other Stories, translation by Gottlieb and others, Farrar, Straus, 1961.

Short Friday and Other Stories, translation by Ruth Whitman and others, Farrar, Straus, 1964.

Selected Short Stories, edited by Irving Howe, Modern Library, 1966.

The Seance and Other Stories, translation by Whitman, Roger H Klein, and others, Farrar, Straus, 1968.

A Friend of Kafka and Other Stories, translation by the author and others, Farrar, Straus, 1970.

An Isaac Bashevis Singer Reader, Farrar, Straus, 1971.

A Crown of Feathers and Other Stories, translation by the author and others, Farrar, Straus, 1973.

Passions and Other Stories, Farrar, Straus, 1975.

Old Love and Other Stories, Farrar, Straus, 1979.

The Collected Stories of Isaac Bashevis Singer, Farrar, Straus, 1982.

The Image and Other Stories, Farrar, Straus, 1985.

Gifts, Jewish Publication Society of America, 1985.

The Death of Methuselah and Other Stories, Farrar, Straus, 1988.

JUVENILE; ORIGINALLY IN YIDDISH; TRANSLATION BY SINGER AND ELIZABETH SHUB

Mazel and Shlimazel; or, The Milk of a Lioness, illustrated by Margot Zemach, Harper, 1966.

Zlateh the Goat and Other Stories, illustrated by Maurice Sendak, Harper, 1966.

The Fearsome Inn, illustrated by Nonny Hogrogian, Scribner, 1967.

When Schlemiel Went to Warsaw and Other Stories (also see below), illustrated by Zemach, Farrar, Straus, 1968.

Elijah the Slave: A Hebrew Legend Retold, illustrated by Antonio Frasconi, Farrar, Straus, 1970.

Joseph and Koza; or, The Sacrifice to the Vistula, illustrated by Symeon Shimin, Farrar, Straus, 1970.

Alone in the Wild Forest, illustrated by Zemach, Farrar, Straus, 1971.

The Topsy-Turvy Emperor of China, illustrated by William Pene du Bois, translated by Singer and Elizabeth Shub, Harper, 1971.

The Wicked City, illustrated by Leonard Everett Fisher, Farrar, Straus, 1972.

The Fools of Chelm and Their History, illustrated by Uri Shulevitz, Farrar, Straus, 1973.

Why Noah Chose the Dove, illustrated by Eric Carle, Farrar, Straus, 1974.

A Tale of Three Wishes, illustrated by Irene Lieblich, Farrar, Straus, 1975.

Naftali the Storyteller and His Horse, Sus, and Other Stories (also see below), illustrated by Zemach, Farrar, Straus, 1976.

The Power of Light: Eight Stories for Hanukkah (also see below), illustrated by Lieblich, Farrar, Straus, 1980.

The Golem, limited edition, illustrated by Shulevitz, Farrar, Straus, 1982.

Stories for Children (includes stories from *Naftali the Storyteller and His Horse, Sus, and Other Stories, When Schlemiel Went to Warsaw and Other Stories,* and *The Power of Light*), Farrar, Straus, 1984.

AUTOBIOGRAPHY; ORIGINALLY IN YIDDISH; UNDER PSEUDONYM ISAAC WARSHOFSKY

Mayn Tatn's Bes-din Shtub, [New York], 1956, translation by Channah Kleinerman-Goldstein published under name Isaac Bashevis Singer as *In My Father's Court,* Farrar, Straus, 1966.

A Day of Pleasure: Stories of a Boy Growing Up in Warsaw (juvenile), translation by author and Shub, photographs by Roman Vishniac, Farrar, Straus, 1969.

A Little Boy in Search of God: Mysticism in a Personal Light (also see below), illustrated by Ira Moskowitz, Doubleday, 1976.

A Young Man in Search of Love (also see below), translation by J. Singer, Doubleday, 1978.

Lost in America (also see below), translation by J. Singer, paintings and drawings by Raphael Soyer, Doubleday, 1981.

Love and Exile: The Early Years: A Memoir (includes *A Little Boy in Search of God: Mysticism in a Personal Light, A Young Man in Search of Love,* and *Lost in America*), Doubleday, 1984.

PLAYS; ORIGINALLY IN YIDDISH

The Mirror (also see below), produced in New Haven, CT, 1973.

(With Leah Napolin) *Yentl, the Yeshiva Boy* (adaptation of a story by Singer; produced on Broadway, 1974), Samuel French, 1978.

Schlemiel the First, produced in New Haven, 1974.

(With Eve Friedman) *Teibele and Her Demon* (produced in Minneapolis at Guthrie Theatre, 1978, produced on Broadway, 1979), Samuel French, 1984.

A Play for the Devil (based on his short story "The Unseen"), produced in New York City at the Folksbiene Theatre, 1984.

TRANSLATOR INTO YIDDISH

Knut Hamsun, *Pan,* Wilno (Warsaw), 1928.

Hamsun, *Di Vogler* (title means "The Vagabonds"), Wilno, 1928.

Gabriele D'Annunzio, *In Opgrunt Fun Tayve* (title means "In Passion's Abyss"), Goldfarb (Warsaw), 1929.

Karin Michaelis, *Mete Trap,* Goldfarb, 1929.

Stefan Zweig, *Roman Rolan* (title means "Romain Rolland"), Bikher (Warsaw), 1929.

Hamsun, *Viktorya* (title means "Victoria"), Wilno, 1929.

Erich Maria Remarque, *Oyfn Mayrev-Front Keyn Nayes* (title means "All Quiet on the Western Front"), Wilno, 1930.

Thomas Mann, *Der Tsoyberbarg* (title means "The Magic Mountain"), four volumes, Wilno, 1930.

Remarque, *Der Veg oyf Tsurik* (title means "The Road Back"), Wilno, 1930.

Moshe Smilansky, *Araber: Folkstimlekhe Geshikhtn* (title means "Arabs: Stories of the People"), Farn Folk (Warsaw), 1932.

Leon S. Glaser, *Fun Moskve biz Yerusholayim* (title means "From Moscow to Jerusalem"), Jankowitz, 1938.

OTHER

(Editor with Elaine Gottlieb) *Prism 2,* Twayne, 1965.

Visit to the Rabbinical Seminary in Cincinnati, [New York], 1965.

(With Ira Moscowitz) *The Hasidim: Paintings, Drawings, and Etchings,* Crown, 1973.

Nobel Lecture, Farrar, Straus, 1979.

The Gentleman from Cracow; The Mirror, illustrated with water colors by Raphael Soyer, introduction by Harry I. Moore, Limited Editions Club, 1979.

Isaac Bashevis Singer on Literature and Life, University of Arizona Press, 1979.

The Meaning of Freedom, United States Military Academy, 1981.

My Personal Conception of Religion, University of Southwestern Louisiana Press, 1982.

One Day of Happiness, Red Ozier Press, 1982.

Remembrances of a Rabbi's Son, translated by Rena Borrow, United Jewish Appeal-Federation Campaign, 1984.

(With Richard Burgin) *Conversations with Isaac Bashevis Singer,* Farrar, Straus, 1986.

The Safe Deposit and Other Stories about Grandparents, Old Lovers and Crazy Old Men ("Masterworks of Modern Jewish Writing" series), edited by Kerry M. Orlitzky, Wiener, Markus, 1989.

The Certificate, Farrar, Straus, 1992.

Singer's works are housed in the Elman Collection, Arents Research Library, Syracuse University, and at the Butler Library, Columbia University.

MEDIA ADAPTATIONS: Zlateh the Goat and Other Stories was adapted into a film by Weston Woods, 1973, and broadcast on the National Broadcasting Company (NBC-TV), 1973; *The Magician of Lublin* was adapted into a film starring Alan Arkin, produced by Menahem Golan, 1978; *Gimpel the Fool* was adapted for the stage by David Schechter and produced by the Bakery Theater

Cooperative of New York, 1982; *Yentl, the Yeshiva Boy* was adapted into the movie *Yentl,* by Barbara Streisand, Metro-Goldwyn-Mayer/United Artists, 1983; *Enemies: A Love Story* was adapted into a film by Paul Mazursky and Roger L. Simon and released by Twentieth Century-Fox, 1989.

SIDELIGHTS: Widely proclaimed to be one of the foremost writers of Yiddish literature, Isaac Bashevis Singer stood clearly outside the mainstream and basic traditions of both Yiddish and American literature. Singer's writing proved difficult to categorize, with critics attaching to him various and sometimes contradictory labels in an attempt to define his work. He was called a modernist, though he personally disliked most contemporary fiction. He was also accused of being captivated by the past, of writing in a dying language despite his English fluency, of setting his fiction in a world that no longer exists: the *shtetls* (Jewish villages) of Eastern Europe which were destroyed by Hitler's campaign against the Jews. And despite the attention called to the mysticism, the prolific presence of the supernatural, and the profoundly religious nature of his writing, Singer was called both a realist and a pessimist. Undeniably a difficult author to place in critical perspective, Singer addressed himself to the problems of labeling his work in an interview with Cyrene N. Pondrom for *Contemporary Literature:* "People always need a name for things, so whatever you will write or whatever you will do, they like to put you into a certain category. Even if you would be new, they would like to feel that a name is already prepared for you in advance. . . . I hope that one day somebody will find a new name for me, not use the old ones."

More than with most writers, the key to Singer's work lies in his background, in his roots in the Polish Yiddish-speaking Jewish ghettos. "I was born with the feeling that I am part of an unlikely adventure, something that couldn't have happened, but happened just the same," Singer once remarked to a *Book Week* interviewer. Born in a small Polish town, his father was a Hassidic rabbi and both his grandfathers were also rabbis. Visiting his maternal grandfather in Bilgoray as a young boy, Singer learned of life in the *shtetl,* which would become the setting of much of his later work. The young Singer received a basic Jewish education preparing him to follow his father and grandfathers' steps into the rabbinical vocation; he studied the Torah, the Talmud, the Cabala, and other sacred Jewish books. An even stronger influence than his education and his parents' orthodoxy was his older brother, the novelist I. J. Singer, who broke with the family's orthodoxy and began to write secular stories. Attempting to overcome the influence of his brother's rationalism and to strengthen the cause of religion, his parents told him stories of *dybbuks* (wandering souls in Jewish folklore believed to enter a human body and control its actions, possessions, and other spiritual mysteries). Singer once commented that he was equally fascinated by both his parents' mysticism and his brother's rationalism. Although he was eventually to break from both traditions, this dualism characterizes his writing.

Singer's desire to become a secular writer caused a painful conflict within himself and with his family; it represented a break from traditional ways. Eventually, Singer rejected his parents' orthodoxy, although not their faith in God. He joined his brother in Warsaw and began working for the Hebrew and Yiddish press and also began to publish stories. At first he wrote in Hebrew but switched to Yiddish because he felt that Hebrew was a dead language (this was before its revival as the national language of Israel). Feeling that the Nazis would certainly invade Poland, Singer followed his brother to the United States where he began to write for the *Jewish Daily Forward*. Here he wrote fiction under the name Isaac Bashevis and nonfiction under the pseudonym Isaac Warshofsky. Most of Singer's stories appeared first in the *Jewish Daily Forward* in their original Yiddish; the novels appeared in serialized form.

Aside from believing that he must write in his native tongue, Singer also believed that the function of his fiction should be entertainment. "I never thought that my fiction—my kind of writing—had any other purpose than to be read and enjoyed by the reader," he commented to Sanford Pinsker in *The Schlemiel as Metaphor: Studies in the Yiddish and American Jewish Novel*. "I never sit down to write a novel to make a better world or to create good feelings towards the Jews or for any other purpose," he continued. "I knew this from the very beginning, that writing fiction has no other purpose than to give enjoyment to a reader. . . . I consider myself an entertainer. . . . I mean an entertainer of good people, of intellectual people who cannot be entertained by cheap stuff. And I think this is true about fiction in all times."

Over the course of his career, Singer established himself as a renowned storyteller. Considered to be a master of the short story, it was his most effective and favorite genre because, as he once explained, it was more possible to be perfect in the short story than in a longer work. Also Singer did not think that the supernatural, which was his main element, lent itself well to longer, novelistic writing. Singer's style in the short story was simple, spare, and in the tradition of the spoken tale. In his *Commentary* interview, Singer remarked: "When I tell a story, I tell a story. I don't try to discuss, criticize, or analyze my characters." For Singer, his special stories, the ones that belonged to him, were placed for the most part in the nineteenth-and early twentieth-century *shtetl*. He was criticized for his overuse of this setting, with some critics suggesting that he was not effective in any other surrounding. In an interview for the *Atlantic* Singer told Lance Morrow: "I prefer to write about the world which I knew, which I know, best. This is Bilgoray, Lublin, the Jews of Kreshev. This is enough for me. I can get from these people art. I don't need to go to the North Pole and write a novel about the Eskimos who live in that neighborhood. I write about the things where I grew up, and where I feel completely at home."

Even Singer's children's stories are placed in the setting of his childhood home. And although he did not start writing for children until 1966, Singer claimed in *Top of the News:* "Children are the best readers of genuine literature. Grownups are hypnotized by big names, exaggerated quotes, and high pressure advertising. Critics who are more concerned with sociology than with literature have persuaded millions of readers that if a novel doesn't try to bring about a social revolution, it is of no value," he continued. "But children do not succumb to this kind of belief. . . . In our epoch, when storytelling has become a forgotten art and has been replaced by amateurish sociology and hackneyed psychology, the child is still the independent reader who relies on nothing but his own taste. Names and authorities mean nothing to him. Long after literature for adults will have gone to pieces, books for children will constitute that last vestige of storytelling, logic, faith in the family, in God and in real humanism."

Most of Singer's children's books are collections of short stories in which "religion and custom dominate life and a rich folktale tradition abounds," described Sylvia W. Iskander in the *Dictionary of Literary Biography*. A number of his stories are set in the humorous Polish city of Chelm—a town that Yiddish people view as a place of fools. And they also include *schlemiel* (eternal loser) characters, who naturally reside in the city of Chelm. They are essentially fools, but are portrayed as being charming and engaging, as is the city itself. Aside from these humorous and silly tales, Singer also wrote about animals and such supernatural beings as witches, goblins, devils, and demons. "Certainly the union of stories by a Nobel laureate storyteller with illustrations by some of the finest artists in the field of children's literature has produced outstanding books," concluded Iskander. "But it is the content of the stories—the combination of folklore, fairy tale, religion, and imagination—that makes Singer's books unique and inimitable."

Three of Singer's novels have been published posthumously: *Scum, The Certificate,* and *Meshugah*. A *dybbuk* and Polish Jewry figure in *Scum,* which concerns one Max Barabander, who has returned to Warsaw from Argentina in 1906, some twenty years after leaving. Because of shady dealings, he now is a wealthy man, but he is impotent after the sudden death of his teenage son and his wife's isolation. In Warsaw he becomes a womanizer, convinced he is possessed by a dybbuk, and a master of language. "There is, as Singer warns, little of God's wisdom and mercy in this book, but the display of human perversity and sheer cussedness is enthralling," Paul Gray remarked in *Time.*

Kenneth Turan stated in the *Los Angeles Times Book Review* that *The Certificate* "is a mildly engaging piece of work, more fictionalized memoir than anything else." The protagonist is unpublished writer David Bendinger, whose father is a rabbi and brother is a writer, aspects of Singer's own life. After four years in the country, Bendinger returns to Warsaw seeking a certificate from the British government that will allow him to immigrate to Palestine. Through Bendinger's relationships with three very different women, Singer subtly criticizes the Zionists, Communists, and the religious Jewish community and reveals Bendinger's anxieties. "It is impossible not to feel the charm of this book, which may be the most Jewish of all Singer's works. The warmest and the saddest too," remarked Chicago *Tribune Books* reviewer Elie Wiesel. "With a lesser writer, the revelation that entire episodes and specific personal details in his fiction were lifted intact from his life would be damning, and would detract from the work. But Singer is the most magical of writers, transforming reality into art with seemingly effortless sleight of hand," commented Lore Dickstein of the *New York Times Book Review.*

Originally titled *Lost Souls, Meshugah* (Yiddish for "crazy") describes the encounters that Polish exile Aaron Greidinger has with Holocaust survivors in early-1950s Manhattan. "The various survivors, all mourning loved ones, are indeed 'lost souls,' subject to melancholy, poisonous dreams and thoughts of suicide," Joel Conarroe pointed out in the *New York Times Book Review.* He added, "As for the concept of *meshugah,* Singer weaves into his narrative references to the innate craziness not only of his high strung men and women, but of the mad events that have shaped their behavior." George Packer commented in *Washington Post Book World* that in *Meshugah* Singer uses his "familiar bag of tricks: love triangles and quadrangles, sudden reversals from disaster to fulfillment and back, relentless questions about good and evil." However, concluded Packer, "the concoction lacks Singer's customary zest." According to Mark Shechner of the Chicago *Tribune Books,* the previously serialized story "is reminiscent of daytime television" because it is episodic and contains licentiousness and pathos. However, stressed Shechner, "Its licentiousness, far from being a commercial pandering to the market, is a tragic metaphysics, warranted by the apocalypses of the 20th Century."

BIOGRAPHICAL/CRITICAL SOURCES:

BOOKS

Allison, Alida, *Isaac Bashevis Singer: Children's Stories and Memoirs,* Twayne (New York City), 1996.

Biletzky, Israel Ch., *God, Jew, Satan in the Works of Isaac Bashevis-Singer,* University Press of America (Lanham, MD), 1995.

Children's Literature Review, Volume 1, Gale (Detroit), 1976.

Concise Dictionary of American Literary Biography: The New Consciousness, 1941-1968, Gale, 1987.

Contemporary Literary Criticism, Gale, Volume 1, 1973; Volume 3, 1975; Volume 6, 1976; Volume 9, 1978; Volume 11, 1979; Volume 15, 1980; Volume 23, 1983; Volume 38, 1986.

Dictionary of Literary Biography, Gale, Volume 6: *American Novelists since World War II,* 1980; Volume 28: *Twentieth-Century American-Jewish Fiction Writers,* 1984; Volume 52: *American Writers for Children since 1960: Fiction,* Gale, 1986.

Farrell, Grace, editor, *Critical Essays on Isaac Bashevis Singer,* Hall (New York City), 1996.

Gibbons, Frances Vargas, *Transgression and Self-Punishment in Isaac Bashevis Singer's Searches,* P. Lang (New York City), 1995.

Goran, Lester, *The Bright Streets of Surfside: The Memoir of a Friendship with Isaac Bashevis Singer,* Kent State University Press (Kent, OH), 1994.

Hada, Janet, *Isaac Bashevis Singer: A Life,* Oxford University Press (New York City), 1997.

Pearl, Lila (illustrated by Donna Ruff), *Isaac Bashevis Singer: The Life of a Storyteller,* Jewish Publication Society (Philadelphia), 1994.

Pinsker, Sanford, *The Schlemiel as Metaphor: Studies in the Yiddish and American Jewish Novel,* Southern Illinois University Press, 1971.

Ran-Moseley, Fay, *The Tragicomic Passion: A History and Analysis of Tragicomedy and Tragicomic Characterization in Drama, Film, and Literature,* Lang (New York City), 1994.

Telushkin, Dvorah, *Master of Dreams: A Memoir of Isaac Bashevis Singer,* Morrow (New York City), 1997.

Wirth-Nesher, Hana, *City Codes: Reading the Modern Urban Novel,* Cambridge University Press (New York City), 1996.

Zamir, Israel, and Barbara Harshav, *Journey to My Father, Isaac Bashevis Singer,* Little, Brown (New York City), 1995.

PERIODICALS

Atlantic Monthly, August, 1962; January, 1965; July, 1970; January, 1979.
Book Week, July 4, 1965.
Chicago Tribune, October 25, 1980; June 23, 1987; July 25, 1991.
Chicago Tribune Book World, July 12, 1981; March 21, 1982; November 6, 1983; July 21, 1985.
Christian Science Monitor, October 28, 1967; September 5, 1978; September 18, 1978.
Commentary, November, 1958; October, 1960; November, 1963; February, 1965; February, 1979; November, 1991; December, 1992.
Contemporary Literature, winter, 1969; summer, 1969.
Critical Quarterly, spring, 1976.
Detroit Free Press, July 25, 1991.

Globe & Mail (Toronto), May 3, 1980; November 23, 1985; June 13, 1988.
Horn Book, September/October, 1991, p. 654.
Hudson Review, winter, 1966-67; spring, 1974.
Library Journal, March 1, 1994, p. 120.
London Review of Books, October 24, 1991, p. 17.
Los Angeles Times, November 8, 1978; December 28, 1981; November 18, 1983; March, 18, 1984; December 4, 1986; December 12, 1989.
Los Angeles Times Book Review, November 16, 1980; August 16, 1981; May 2, 1982; February 6, 1983; December 9, 1984; August 25, 1985; May 1, 1988; April 14, 1991; January 3, 1993, p. 7.
Nation, November 19, 1983.
New Republic, November 24, 1958; January 2, 1961; November 13, 1961; June 18, 1962; November 3, 1973; October 25, 1975; September 16, 1978; October 21, 1978.
Newsweek, June 26, 1972; November 12, 1973; April 12, 1982; September 26, 1983; August 5, 1991.
New Yorker, August 17, 1981; December 21, 1992.
New York Review of Books, April 22, 1965; February 7, 1974; December 7, 1978.
New York Times, October 30, 1966; January 29, 1967; July 10, 1978; July 22, 1978; December 9, 1978; October 17, 1979; December 5, 1979; December 16, 1979; December 17, 1979; April 19, 1980; June 15, 1982; November 30, 1982; September 22, 1983; October 7, 1984; November 7, 1984; October 30, 1985; November 17, 1985; June 24, 1986; September 28, 1986; November 8, 1986; July 6, 1987; April 12, 1988; May 18, 1989; July 30, 1989; December 10, 1989; December 13, 1989; April 9, 1991; July 26, 1991; May 30, 1996, p. B3.
New York Times Book Review, December 29, 1957; June 26, 1960; October 22, 1961; June 17, 1962; November 15, 1964; October 8, 1967; June 25, 1972; November 4, 1973; November 2, 1975; April 30, 1978; July 23, 1978; October 28, 1979; January 18, 1981; June 21, 1981; January 31, 1982; March 21, 1982; November 14, 1982; September 25, 1983; November 11, 1984; June 30, 1985; October 27, 1985; October 16, 1988; November 1, 1992, p. 7; April 10, 1994, p. 9; May 30, 1996, p. C13.
School Library Journal, September, 1991; June, 1996, p. 124.
Sewanee Review, fall, 1974.
Time, October 20, 1967; September 21, 1970; October 27, 1975; November 3, 1975; June 15, 1981; April 5, 1982; October 17, 1983; October 28, 1984; July 15, 1985; May 2, 1988; March 25, 1991, p. 70; August 5, 1991.
Top of the News, November, 1972.
Tribune Books (Chicago), April 10, 1988; November 6, 1988; June 7, 1992, p. 2; November 1, 1992, p. 6; May 8, 1994, p. 5.
Washington Post, October 6, 1978; October 16, 1979; October 26, 1979; November 4, 1981; September 17, 1984; July 26, 1991.
Washington Post Book World, November 30, 1980; June 28, 1981; March 28, 1982 (interview); November 7, 1982; July 7, 1985; September 21, 1986; October 23, 1988; April 3, 1994, p. 9.

*   *   *

SINJOHN, John
See GALSWORTHY, John

SIRIN, V.
See NABOKOV, Vladimir (Vladimirovich)

*   *   *

SITWELL, Dame Edith (Louisa) 1887-1964

PERSONAL: Born September 7, 1887, in Scarborough, Yorkshire, England; died December 9, 1964, in London, England; daughter of Sir George Reresby and Lady Ida Emily Augusta (Denison) Sitwell. *Education:* Privately educated. *Religion:* Roman Catholic convert, 1955.

CAREER: Writer. Visiting professor, Institute of Contemporary Arts, 1957.

MEMBER: Royal Society of Literature (fellow; vice-president, 1958), American Institute of Arts and Letters (honorary associate).

AWARDS, HONORS: Benson Medal, Royal Society of Literature, 1934; created Dame, Commander Order of the British Empire, 1954 (the first poet to be so honored); William Foyle Poetry Prize, 1958, for *Collected Poems;* with Robert Lowell and W. H. Auden, shared Guiness Poetry Award, 1959; Litt.D., University of Leeds, 1948; D.Litt., University of Durham, 1948, Oxford University, 1951, University of Sheffield, 1955, University of Hull, 1963.

WRITINGS:

The Mother and Other Poems, Basil Blackwell, 1915.
(With brother, Osbert Sitwell) *Twentieth Century Harlequinade and Other Poems,* Basil Blackwell, 1916.
Clown's Houses (poems), Longmans, Green, 1918.
The Wooden Pegasus (poems), Basil Blackwell, 1920.
Facade (poems), Favil Press, 1922, new edition with introduction by Jack Lindsay, Duckworth, 1950.
Bucolic Comedies (poems), Duckworth, 1923.
The Sleeping Beauty (poems), Duckworth, 1924.
(With brothers Osbert and Sacheverell Sitwell) *Poor Young People* (poems), Fleuron, 1925.
(Author of introduction) Ann Taylor, *Meddlesome Matty and Other Poems for Infant Minds,* John Lane, 1925.
Poetry and Criticism, L. and V. Woolf, 1925, Holt, 1926, Folcroft Press, 1969.
Troy Park (poems), Duckworth, 1925.
Elegy on Dead Fashion, Duckworth, 1926.
Twelve Poems, E. Benn, 1926.
Rustic Elegies, Knopf, 1927.
Popular Song (poems), Faber and Gwyer, 1928.
Five Poems, Duckworth, 1928.
Gold Coast Customs (poems), Duckworth, 1929.
Alexander Pope, Cosmopolitan Book Corp., 1930.
The Collected Poems of Edith Sitwell, Duckworth, 1930, Vanguard, 1968.
(Editor) *The Pleasures of Poetry: A Critical Anthology,* Duckworth, Volume 1: *First Series, Milton and the Augustan Age,* 1930, Volume 2: *Second Series, The Romantic Revival,* 1931, Volume 3: *Third Series, The Victorian Age,* 1932, Norton, 1934.
Children's Tales from the Russian Ballet, [London], 1930.
Epithalamium, Duckworth, 1931.
Jane Barston, 1719-1746, Faber, 1931.
In Spring (poems), privately printed, 1931.

Bath, Faber, 1932, new edition, 1948, 2nd edition, International Specialized Books, 1984.
(Author of introductory essay to translation by Helen Rootham) Rimbaud, *Prose Poems from Les Illuminations,* Faber, 1932.
Five Variations on a Theme, Duckworth, 1933.
The English Eccentrics, Houghton, 1933, revised and enlarged edition, Vanguard, 1957, abridged edition, Arrow Books, 1960.
Aspects of Modern Poetry, Duckworth, 1934, Scholarly Press, 1972.
Selected Poems, Duckworth, 1936.
Some Recent Developments in English Literature, University of Sydney, 1936.
Victoria of England, Houghton, 1936, revised edition, Faber, 1949.
(Author of introductory essay) Sacheverell Sitwell, *Collected Poems,* Duckworth, 1936.
I Live Under a Black Sun (novel), Gollancz, 1937, Doubleday, Doran, 1938, new edition, Lehmann, 1948.
(With O. and S. Sitwell) *Trio: Dissertations on Some Aspects of National Genius,* Macmillan, 1938, published as *Triad of Genius,* British Book Centre, 1953.
(Editor) *Edith Sitwell's Anthology,* Gollancz, 1940.
Poems New and Old, Faber, 1940.
(Editor) *Look! The Sun,* Gollancz, 1941.
English Women, Collins, 1942.
Street Songs, Macmillan, 1942.
A Poet's Notebook, Macmillan, 1943, Little, Brown, 1950.
Green Song and Other Poems, Macmillan, 1944, Vanguard, 1946.
(Compiler) *Planet and Glow-Worm: A Book for the Sleepless,* Macmillan, 1944.
The Song of the Cold (poems), Macmillan, 1945, Vanguard, 1948.
Fanfare for Elizabeth, Macmillan, 1946, Dufour, 1989.
The Shadow of Cain (blank verse), Lehmann, 1947.
A Notebook of William Shakespeare, Macmillan, 1948, Beacon, 1961.
The Canticle of the Rose: Selected Poems, 1920-1947, Macmillan, 1949, Vanguard, 1949.
(Author of foreword) Charles Henri Ford, *Sleep in a Nest of Flames,* New Directions, 1949.
(Compiler) *A Book of the Winter* (poems and prose), Macmillan, 1950, Vanguard, 1951.
Poor Men's Music, Fore Publications, 1950.
(Editor) *The American Genius,* Lehmann, 1951.
Facade: An Entertainment with Poems by Edith Sitwell, with music by William Turner Walton (performed in 1922), Oxford University Press, 1951.
(Compiler) *A Book of Flowers,* Macmillan, 1952.
Gardeners and Astronomers: New Poems, Vanguard, 1953.
Collected Poems, Vanguard, 1954.
(Editor) *The Atlantic Book of British and American Poetry,* Little, Brown, 1958.
(Author of introduction) Jose Garcia Villa, *Selected Poems and New,* McDowell, Oblensky, 1958.
(Editor) Algernon Charles Swinburne, *Swinburne: A Selection,* Harcourt, 1960.
Edith Sitwell (poems), Vista Books, 1960.
The Queens and the Hive, Little, Brown, 1962.
The Outcasts (poems), Macmillan, 1962.
Music and Ceremonies (poems), Vanguard, 1963.
Taken Care Of (autobiography), Atheneum, 1965.
Selected Poems, compiled with an introduction by John Lehmann, Macmillan, 1965.

Selected Letters, 1919-1964, edited by Lehmann and Derek Parker, Macmillan, 1970, Vanguard, 1971.

Facade and Other Poems, 1920-1935, Duckworth, 1971.

Edith Sitwell: A Fire of the Mind, An Anthology, compiled by Elizabeth Salter and Allanah Harper, Joseph, 1976.

The Early Unpublished Poems of Edith Sitwell, edited by Gerald W. Morton and Karen P. Helgeson, P. Lang (New York), 1994.

Editor of *Wheels,* an annual anthology of modern verse, 1916-21.

SIDELIGHTS: In the introduction to *The Canticle of the Rose* British poet Dame Edith Sitwell wrote: "At the time I began to write, a change in the direction, imagery and rhythms in poetry had become necessary, owing to the rhythmical flaccidity, the verbal deadness, the dead and expected patterns, of some of the poetry immediately preceding us." Her early work was often experimental, creating melody, using striking conceits, new rhythms, and confusing private allusions. Her efforts at change were resisted, but, as the *New Statesman and Nation* observed, "losing every battle, she won the campaign," and emerged the high priestess of twentieth-century poetry.

The London *Times* stated in 1955 that "she writes for the sake of sound, of color, and from an awareness of God and regard for man." She believed that "Poetry is the deification of reality, and one of its purposes is to show that the dimensions of man are, as Sir Arthur Eddington said, 'half way between those of an atom and a star.'" An admiring critic, John Lehmann, author of *Edith Sitwell* and *A Nest of Tigers: The Sitwells in Their Times,* admitted that "her tendency has always been rather to overwork her symbolism; by a certain overfluid quality in her imagination to make the use of the symbols sometimes appear confused and indiscriminate." This Baroque quality has its admirers, however. Babette Deutsch in *Poetry in Our Time* wrote: "like the medieval hangings that kept the cold away from secular kings and princes of the Church, the finest of [Dame Edith's] poems have a luxurious beauty that serves to grace the bareness, to diminish the chill of this bare, cold age." Writing in the London *Times,* Geoffrey Elborn commented that Sitwell's best work was written in the 1920s, collected in the volumes *Bucolic Comedies, The Sleeping Beauty,* and *Troy Park.* "These . . . [were] written with a highly individual use of language still unsurpassed for its peculiar, inimitable artifice. Far from being trivial, these early poems by one 'a little outside life' should now find a greater acceptance in an era more concerned with Sitwell's concepts than her own age, earning her the deserved and secure reputation for which she herself so earnestly but recklessly fought."

The *New Statesman and Nation* has said that Sitwell's place in poetry is "roughly commensurate with that of Christina Rossetti in the previous century," and insists on the primacy of her personality. The sister of Osbert and Sacheverell was indeed not to be trifled with. Says Sacheverell: "She was always determined to be remarkable and she has succeeded." The *New Statesman and Nation* described her thus: "great rings load the fingers, the hands are fastidiously displayed, the eye-sockets have been thumbed by a master, the eyes themselves haunt, disdain, trouble indifference, and the fashions are century-old with a telling simplification." At times, and perhaps not unintentionally, she looked like a Tudor monarch. The author of a study of Elizabeth I, she once remarked: "I've always had a great affinity for Queen Elizabeth. We were born on the same day of the month and about the same hour of the day and I was extremely like her when I was young." Dame Edith always insisted that she was no eccentric: "It's just that I am more alive than most people."

Her outspoken manner and rebellion against accepted modes of behavior led to encounters with such as Wyndham Lewis and Geoffrey Grigson. When *Facade* was first performed in London in 1922, the response of the audience and of critics was derisive and indignant. Dame Edith recalled: "I had to hide behind the curtain. An old lady was waiting to beat me with an umbrella." (In 1949 the work was enthusiastically received in New York.) She remained wonderfully candid. On a visit to America she revealed that her most serious objection to certain Beat poets was that they smelled bad, and found she liked the late Marilyn Monroe, "largely because she was ill treated. She was like a sad ghost."

Robert K. Martin summed up Sitwell's literary career in *Dictionary of Literary Biography:* "Sitwell's reputation has suffered from the exceptional success of *Facade,* which was often treated as if it were the only work she had ever written. Inadequate attention has been paid to her development as a social poet, as a religious poet, and as a visionary. Her career traces the development of English poetry from the immediate post-World War I period of brightness and jazzy rhythms through the political involvements of the 1930s and the return to spiritual values after World War II. Her technique evolved, and, although she always remained a poet committed to the exploration of sound, she came to use sound patterns as an element in the construction of deep philosophic poems that reflect on her time and on man's condition. Edith Sitwell needs to be remembered not only as the bright young parodist of *Facade,* but as the angry chronicler of social injustice, as a poet who has found forms adequate to the atomic age and its horrors, and as a foremost poet of love. Her work displays enormous range of subject and of form. With her contemporary [T. S.] Eliot she remains one of the most important voices of twentieth-century English poetry."

BIOGRAPHICAL/CRITICAL SOURCES:

BOOKS

Bogan, Louise, *Selected Criticism,* Noonday, 1955.

Bradford, Sarah, *The Sitwells and the Arts of the 1920s and 1930s,* University of Texas Press, 1996.

Brophy, James, *Edith Sitwell,* Southern Illinois University Press, 1968.

Cevasco, G. A., *The Sitwells: Edith, Osbert, and Sachervell,* Twayne, 1987.

Contemporary Literary Criticism, Gale (Detroit), Volume 2, 1974; Volume 9, 1978; Volume 67, 1992.

Daiches, David, *Poetry and the Modern World,* University of Chicago Press, 1940, pp. 85-89.

Deutsch, Babette, *Poetry in Our Time,* Columbia University Press, 1956, pp. 220-28.

Dictionary of Literary Biography, Volume 20: *British Poets, 1914-1945,* Gale, 1983.

Fifoot, Richard, *A Bibliography of Edith, Osbert, and Sacheverell Sitwell,* Hart/Davis, 1963, revised, Archon, 1971.

Glendinning, Victoria, *Edith Sitwell: A Unicorn among Lions,* Knopf, 1981.

Lehmann, John, *Edith Sitwell,* Longmans, Green, 1952.

Lehmann, John, *A Nest of Tigers: The Sitwells in Their Times,* Little, Brown, 1968.

Megroz, R. L., *The Three Sitwells,* Doran, 1927.

Mills, Ralph J., Jr., *Edith Sitwell: A Critical Essay,* Eerdmans, 1966.

Moore, Marianne, *A Marianne Moore Reader,* Viking, 1965, pp. 210-15.

Pearson, John, *Facades: Edith, Osbert and Sacheverell Sitwell,* Macmillan, 1978; also published as *The Sitwells: A Family Biography,* Harcourt, Brace, 1979.

Pinto, Vivian de Sola, *Crisis in English Poetry: 1880-1940,* Hutchinson, 1967, pp. 190-93, 205-8.

Poetry Criticism, Gale, Volume 3, 1991.

Salter, Elizabeth, *The Last Years of a Rebel: A Memoir of Edith Sitwell,* Houghton, 1967.

Singleton, Geoffrey, *Edith Sitwell: The Hymn to Life,* Fortune Press, 1960.

Villa, Jose Garcia, *A Celebration for Edith Sitwell,* New Directions, 1948.

PERIODICALS

Agenda, autumn, 1983, pp. 57-68.
Comparative Literature, summer, 1955, pp. 240-51.
Contemporary Review, February, 1959, pp. 120-23.
Criticism, winter, 1967.
Encounter, May, 1966.
Hudson Review, autumn, 1954, pp. 445-53.
Life, January 4, 1963.
Life and Letters, January, 1950, pp. 39-52.
Listener, November 30, 1978, pp. 731-32.
London Magazine, September, 1970.
Nation, June 7, 1965.
New Republic, April 24, 1965.
New Statesman and Nation, January 23, 1954.
New York Times, December 10, 1964.
Observer, April 4, 1965.
Spectator, November 10, 1950, p. 472.
Time, December 18, 1964.
Times (London), September 7, 1987.
Vogue, July, 1960.

*   *   *

SKINNER, B(urrhus) F(rederic) 1904-1990

PERSONAL: Born March 20, 1904, in Susquehanna, PA; died of leukemia, August 18, 1990, in Cambridge, MA; buried Mt. Auburn Cemetery, MA; son of William Arthur (an attorney) and Grace (Burrhus) Skinner; married Yvonne Blue, November 1, 1936; children: Julie Skinner Vargas, Deborah Skinner Buzan. *Education:* Hamilton College, A.B., 1929; Harvard University, M.A., 1930, Ph.D., 1931.

ADDRESSES: Home—11 Old Dee Rd., Cambridge, MA 02138. *Office*—William James Hall, Harvard University, Cambridge, MA 02138.

CAREER: Harvard University, Cambridge, MA, research fellow with National Research Council, 1931-32, junior fellow in Harvard Society of Fellows, 1933-36; University of Minnesota, Minneapolis, instructor, 1936-37, assistant professor, 1937-39, associate professor of psychology, 1939-45; Indiana University, Bloomington, professor of psychology and department chairman, 1945-48; Harvard University, Cambridge, William James Lecturer, 1947, professor of psychology, 1948-57, Edgar Pierce Professor of Psychology, 1958-74, professor emeritus, 1974-90. Lecturer. Conducted war research for the Office of Scientific Research and Development, 1942-43.

MEMBER: American Psychological Association, American Association for the Advancement of Science, Society of Experimental Psychologists, National Academy of Sciences, American Philosophical Society, American Academy of Arts and Sciences, Royal Society of Arts (fellow), British Psychological Society, Spanish Psychological Society, Swedish Psychological Society, Phi Beta Kappa, Sigma Xi.

AWARDS, HONORS: Howard Crosby Warren Medal, 1942; Guggenheim fellow, 1944-45; National Institute of Mental Health career grant; American Psychological Association award, 1958; National Medal of Science, 1968; American Psychological Association gold medal, 1971; Joseph P. Kennedy, Jr. Foundation award, 1971; Humanist of the Year award, American Humanist Society, 1972; Creative Leadership in Education Award, New York University, 1972; American Educational Research Association award, 1978; National Association for Retarded Citizens first annual award, 1978; Award for Excellence in Psychiatry, Albert Einstein School of Medicine, 1985; President's Award, New York Academy of Science, 1985; American Psychology Association, Lifetime Achievement Award, 1990. Honorary degrees from many universities and colleges, including Sc.D., University of Chicago, 1967, University of Exeter, 1969, and McGill University, 1970; Litt.D., Ripon College, 1961; LH.D., Rockford College, 1971; L.L.D., Ohio Wesleyan University, 1971.

WRITINGS:

(Editor with father, William A. Skinner) *A Digest of Decisions of the Anthracite Board of Conciliation,* [Scranton, PA], 1928.

Behavior of Organisms: An Experimental Analysis, Appleton-Century-Croft, 1938.

(With others) *Current Trends in Psychology* (lectures), University of Pittsburgh Press, 1947.

Walden Two (novel), Macmillan, 1948, revised edition, Macmillan (London), 1969, published with introduction by Skinner, Macmillan, 1976.

Science and Human Behavior, Macmillan, 1953.

(Editor with Peter B. Dews) *Techniques for the Study of Behavioral Effects of Drugs,* Annals of the New York Academy of Sciences, 1956.

(With C. B. Ferster) *Schedules of Reinforcement,* Prentice-Hall, 1957.

Verbal Behavior, Prentice-Hall, 1957.

(Editor) *Cumulative Record: A Selection of Papers,* Prentice-Hall, 1959, 3rd edition, 1972.

(With James G. Holland) *The Analysis of Behavior: A Program for Self-Instruction,* McGraw, 1961.

Teaching Machines, Freeman, 1961.

(With others) *Understanding Maps: A Programmed Text,* Allyn, 1964.

(With Sue-Ann Krakower) *Handwriting with Write and See* (patented method of teaching writing), Lyons & Carnahan, 1968.

The Technology of Teaching, Prentice-Hall, 1968.

Earth Resources (textbook), Prentice-Hall, 1969, 2nd edition, 1976.

Contingencies of Reinforcement: A Theoretical Analysis, Prentice-Hall, 1969.

(With Arnold J. Toynbee and others) *On the Future of Art* (lectures), Viking, 1970.

Beyond Freedom and Dignity, Knopf, 1971.

About Behaviorism, Knopf, 1974.

Particulars of My Life (also see below; autobiography), Knopf, 1976.

Reflections on Behaviorism and Society, Prentice-Hall, 1978.
The Shaping of a Behaviorist: Part Two of an Autobiography (also see below), Knopf, 1979.
Notebooks, edited by Robert Epstein, Prentice-Hall, 1981.
Skinner for the Classroom: Selected Papers, edited by Robert Epstein, Research Press (Champaign, IL), 1982.
A Matter of Consequences: Part Three of an Autobiography (also see below), Knopf, 1983.
(With Margaret E. Vaughn) *Enjoy Old Age: A Program of Self Management,* Norton, 1983, published in England as *How to Enjoy Your Old Age,* Sheldon Press, 1985.
Particulars of My Life [and] *The Shaping of a Behaviorist* [and] *A Matter of Consequences* (three-book set), New York University Press, 1984.
Upon Further Reflection, Prentice-Hall, 1987.
The Selection of Behavior: The Operant Behaviorism of B. F. Skinner: Comments and Consequences, edited by A. Charles Catania and Steven Harnad, Cambridge University Press, 1988.
Recent Issues in the Analysis of Behavior, Merrill, 1989.

SIDELIGHTS: An influential and controversial figure in modern psychology, B. F. Skinner was "the most famous of behaviorist psychologists," Harold Kaplan once stated in *Commentary.* Writing in *Behavioral and Brain Sciences,* Joseph M. Scandura called Skinner "contemporary behaviorism personified." His belief that people are controlled solely by external factors in the environment—specifically, that rewarded behavior is encouraged and unrewarded behavior is extinguished—and his rejection of the human individual as an autonomous being capable of independent, self-willed action made Skinner notorious among many of his colleagues. His supporters maintained, however, that Skinner made an important contribution to behaviorism and that his insights could be used to improve society radically.

Behaviorism, Daniel Goleman explained in the *New York Times,* "holds that people act as they do because of the rewards and punishments—positive and negative reinforcements—they have received. The mind and such things as memory and perception cannot be directly observed, and so . . . are unworthy of scientific study." "From the 1930s to the 1960s," Goleman reported, "behaviorism dominated academic psychology." The ideas and findings of behaviorism had a tremendous impact on such areas as drug and alcohol rehabilitation where the chief concern is behavior modification. Skinner stood out from most other behaviorists in that he not only dismissed the scientific analysis of human consciousness but also believed that "feelings and mental processes are just the meaningless byproducts of [the] endless cycle of stimulus and response," John Leo wrote in *Time.* As Skinner explained in *A Matter of Consequences,* the third volume of his autobiography, "I . . . do not think feelings are important. Freud is probably responsible for the current extent to which they are taken seriously." Skinner also advocated the use of "behavioral technology" to restructure society. He suggested that the same techniques that successfully train laboratory animals could be used to control man's negative behavior and thereby eliminate such social ills as crime, poverty, and war. Because his critics saw a totalitarian danger in his suggestions for social change, they called Skinner "politely, a social engineer; less politely, a neo-fascist," Elizabeth Mehren wrote in the *Los Angeles Times.* Despite such criticism, "Skinner . . . influenced everything from crib toys for babies to inventory management systems in industry," Webster Schott wrote in the *Washington Post Book World.*

Skinner's interest in psychology began in the 1920s. A college English major who for a time nurtured literary aspirations, he eventually shifted his focus to the scientific exploration of human behavior. Skinner's behaviorist beliefs were derived from a series of laboratory experiments he conducted using rats and pigeons during the 1930s and 1940s. By rewarding his test animals whenever they performed desired behavior—a process he called positive reinforcement—Skinner succeeded in training them to do a number of difficult tasks. His pigeons could play Ping-Pong, dance, walk in figure eights, and distinguish between colors. He taught rats to push buttons, pull strings, and push levers to receive food and drink. These experiments convinced Skinner that behavior control could be achieved through the manipulation of environmental stimuli. The special environment in which Skinner's animals were trained—an enclosed, soundproof box equipped with buttons, levers, and other training devices—was "a marvelous tool for conditioning animals," John Langone pointed out in *Discover.* Widely used by other researchers, this training environment became known as the Skinner Box.

Convinced that the techniques used on his pigeons and rats could work on human beings as well, Skinner built a training box for children in 1943. Called the Air-Crib by Skinner, but popularly dubbed the "baby box" by the media, the device was "nothing more than an elaborate, insulated, glassed-in crib with the temperature carefully controlled," Langone reported. It was designed to provide a child with "a very comfortable, stimulating environment," Skinner told Lawrence Meyer in the *Washington Post.* Skinner used the box for two and a half years while raising his daughter Deborah. When his account of the child-rearing experiment was published in the *Ladies' Home Journal,* it sparked a national controversy. Skinner was accused of carrying out monstrous experiments on his own children. He was attacked in newspaper editorials and featured on radio shows and in newsreels. His daughter suffered no ill effects from the experiment, grew up normally, and had a good relationship with her father. Nonetheless, Skinner's attempt to market the "baby box" under the name "Heir Conditioner" was a failure.

In 1948, Skinner speculated on how the findings from his laboratory work and his experiment with his daughter's upbringing could be applied to the structuring of society. In his novel *Walden Two,* he portrayed a behaviorist society in which positive and negative reinforcements were built into the social structure. The novel's plot revolved around a tour of the community taken by two college professors. As T. Morris Longstreth reported in the *Christian Science Monitor,* the community was conceived as "a sort of managed democracy." Children, raised in communal nurseries, were taught to think and learn instead of called upon to memorize specific facts. Theology and history were suppressed. All members of the society encouraged social harmony by practicing positive reinforcement for approved behavior. "One can admire much of this and only marvel that such large adjustments in human nature are to be bought at such a cheap price," Longstreth commented. Tabitha M. Powledge pointed out in *Nation* that in *Walden Two* "ideal social behavior is shaped by gentle means for good ends; the fascist dystopia which is equally possible from such techniques seems not to trouble [Skinner]." In his review of the novel for the *New York Times Book Review,* Charles Poore wondered "why anyone should want to spend his days in this antiseptic elysium," but allowed that the book was "a brisk and thoughtful foray in search of peace of mind, security, and a certain amount of balm for burnt-fingered moderns." Mehren described *Walden Two* as "a kind of behavioristic book of the Bible: a road map to a future in which free will would recede to the positive and negative reinforcements of culture and the environment." Speaking to *Psychology Today,* Skinner expressed some reservations about the book. "If I were to rewrite *Walden Two,*" he explained, "I would have more in it about the nitty-gritty conditions of our incentive systems. I was counting on everybody being willing to give four hours a day in exchange for the privilege of living in the community. That's Marx, and I don't think it really works. I would change *Walden Two*'s education. . . . I dealt too timidly with sex. . . . Also, *Walden Two* has no criminals, no psychotics, no retardates—I would do something about them now."

Where Skinner spoke fictionally about a new society in *Walden Two,* in *Beyond Freedom and Dignity,* described by Kaplan as "the culminating book of [Skinner's] career," he openly argued for radical social change based on behaviorist findings. "Almost all our major problems involve human behavior, and they cannot be solved by physical and biological technology alone. What is needed is a technology of behavior," Skinner asserted in the book. This proposed technology of behavior would utilize our knowledge about "the interaction between organism and environment" to design a society capable of altering man's destructive behavior through a system of positive and negative reinforcements. But before this could come about, Skinner maintained, the belief in an autonomous, self-directed individual and the related concepts of freedom and dignity must be discarded. Freedom and dignity, Skinner wrote, "are the possessions of the autonomous man of traditional theory, and they are essential to practices in which a person is held responsible for his conduct and given credit for his achievements. A scientific analysis shifts both the responsibility and the achievement to the environment."

Reaction to *Beyond Freedom and Dignity* was divided. Those critics opposed to Skinner's ideas thought his denial of human autonomy and his plans for social manipulation were incorrect and possibly dangerous. Writing in *National Review,* Michael S. Gazzinaga stated: "No one denies reinforcement is an important controlling influence on our behavior. Skinner is correct to say we could order our society a little more logically than we do. But to extend the limited benefits of the obvious to a new world-view that eliminates concepts such as free will is both pretentious and incredibly naive." Kaplan called Skinner's proposals "nothing less than a bid for power by a new leader class, called, in [Skinner's] words, the 'technologists of behavior.'" Skinner "knows almost nothing about human beings," Robert Claiborne charged in a review of the volume for *Book World,* an opinion echoed by Richard Sennett, who claimed in the *New York Times Book Review* that Skinner "appears to understand so little, indeed to care so little, about society itself that the reader comes totally to distrust him."

But those who found value in *Beyond Freedom and Dignity* pointed to its basic insight that man's behavior is shaped by his environment, although some critics disagreed with Skinner's conclusions based on that insight. As Michael Novak wrote in *Beyond the Punitive Society: Operant Conditioning, Social and Political Aspects* (edited by Harvey Wheeler), "few question the technical validity of his laboratory work, or even the technically expressed theory interpreting it. Many do question Professor Skinner's extrapolation therefrom." In another article in *Beyond the Punitive Society,* Karl H. Pribram argued that because of information omitted from the book, such as evidence that the human brain is modified by experience, Skinner's conclusions were not entirely correct. "Designs of cultures, therefore, cannot, in and of themselves, completely specify behavior," Pribram

wrote. But there was "much good in the book," Pribram maintained, including "a good case for . . . behavioral technology." Pribram also admired "Skinner's contributions to our knowledge of the environmental contingencies that lead to reinforcement." W. F. Day, writing in *Contemporary Psychology,* stated that Skinner's "frontal attack on what he calls the concept of autonomous man" was essentially correct. We do "incalculable damage . . . to ourselves, to those we love, and to those others for whom we want to assume some responsibility when we base our social decisions on the model of autonomous man," Day declared. Gerald Marwell countered critics who saw Skinner's suggestions as totalitarian. In a *Contemporary Sociology* article, Marwell contended that what Skinner proposed was a society in which those who were controlled would have power over society's control mechanisms. Skinner "asserts that social control over populations will be exercised by someone. The choice which remains is only *who* shall control and by what means," Marwell explained.

The questions raised in *Beyond Freedom and Dignity* continued to be addressed in Skinner's three volumes of autobiography—*Particulars of My Life, The Shaping of a Behaviorist,* and *A Matter of Consequences.* Each of these books covered a particular period in Skinner's career. The first traced his childhood and education; the second addressed his years of research during the 1930s and 1940s; the third chronicled his later life as one of the leading psychologists in the country. Skinner's approach to autobiography reflected his beliefs about behavior and motivation. As he explained in *A Matter of Consequences:* "I have tried to report my life *as it was lived.* . . . I have seldom mentioned later significances. When I first bent a wire in the shape of a lever to be pressed by a rat, I was making the prototype of many thousands of levers, but did not know it then, and mentioning it would have been a mistake." This approach led Christopher Lehmann-Haupt in the *New York Times* to complain that "instead of reflecting on or trying to pick out and organize whatever shaped him as a behaviorist, Mr. Skinner simply slogs his way chronologically through the years." But Eugene Kennedy wrote in the *Chicago Tribune Book World* that *The Shaping of a Behaviorist* "opens to us the life of a genius."

The publication of the autobiographies gave critics the opportunity to appraise Skinner's contributions to his field. Schott suggested that "Skinner has been working at what scientists everywhere work at: meaning. Except he has devoted his life to the refinement of what precedes meaning—observation and description." In the Toronto *Globe and Mail,* Andrew Nikiforuk held that Skinner had "long argued that a scientific analysis of human behavior need not slight the dignity of mankind. Behaviorism, he says, examines what people do and why they do it, points to conditions that can be changed and shows the inadequacies of other views."

BIOGRAPHICAL/CRITICAL SOURCES:

BOOKS

Bjork, Daniel W., *B. F. Skinner: A Life,* American Psychological Association, 1997.
Chomsky, Noam, *For Reasons of State,* Pantheon, 1973.
Epstein, Robert, *Cognition, Creativity and Behavior: Selected Essays,* Praeger (Westport, CT), 1996.
Koestler, Arthur, *The Ghost in the Machine,* Hutchinson, 1967.
Nye, Robert D., *Three Psychologies: Perspectives from Freud, Skinner, and Rogers,* Brooks/Cole (Pacific Grove, CA), 1995.

Richel, Marc N., *B. F. Skinner: A Reappraisal,* Psychology Press, 1995.

Smith, Laurence D. (with William Ray Woodward), *B. F. Skinner and Behaviorism in American Culture,* Lehigh University Press (Bethlehem, PA), 1996.

Todd, James T. (with Edward K. Morris), *Modern Perspectives on B. F. Skinner and Contemporary Behaviorism,* Greenwood (Westport, CT), 1995.

Wheeler, Harvey, editor, *Beyond the Punitive Society: Operant Conditioning, Social and Political Aspects,* W. H. Freeman, 1973.

Wiener, Daniel N., *B. F. Skinner: Benign Anarchist,* Allyn and Bacon (Boston), 1996.

PERIODICALS

American Journal of Sociology, September, 1980.
Atlantic Monthly, February, 1995, p. 88.
Behavioral and Brain Sciences, December, 1984.
Book World, October 10, 1971.
Chicago Tribune Book World, May 20, 1979.
Christian Science Monitor, June 24, 1948.
Commentary, February, 1972.
Contemporary Psychology, September, 1972; September, 1979.
Contemporary Sociology, January, 1972.
Discover, September, 1983.
Economist, December 5, 1992, p. 90.
Globe and Mail (Toronto), March 10, 1984.
Journal of Individual Psychology, Volume 26, 1970.
Journal of the Experimental Analysis of Behavior, May, 1969; March, 1971.
Los Angeles Times, September 22, 1982.
Los Angeles Times Book Review, October 9, 1983.
Nation, July 28-August 4, 1979.
National Review, November 5, 1971; November 22, 1974.
New Republic, October 16, 1971; June 1, 1974; August 4, 1979.
New Yorker, October 9, 1971.
New York Review of Books, December 30, 1971.
New York Times, June 6, 1979; August 25, 1987; September 13, 1987.
New York Times Book Review, June 13, 1948; October 24, 1971; July 14, 1974; May 20, 1979; January 1, 1984.
Psychology Today, September, 1983.
Saturday Review, October 9, 1971.
Science, June 8, 1979.
Time, October 10, 1983.
Times Literary Supplement, February 29, 1975; December 4, 1981.
Washington Post, August 24, 1982.
Washington Post Book World, July 8, 1979.

*   *   *

SKVORECKY, Josef (Vaclav) 1924-

PERSONAL: Surname pronounced "*Shquor*-et-skee"; born September 27, 1924, in Nachod, Czechoslovakia; immigrated to Canada, 1969; son of Josef Karel (a bank clerk) and Anna Marie (Kurazova) Skvorecky; married Zdena Salivarova (a writer and publisher), March 31, 1958. *Education:* Charles University, Prague, Ph.D., 1951. *Politics:* Christian democrat. *Religion:* Roman Catholic. *Avocational interests:* Film, jazz (Skvorecky plays the saxophone), American folklore.

ADDRESSES: Home—487 Sackville St., Toronto, Ontario, Canada M4X 1T6M. *Agent*—Janice Whitford, Westwood Creative Artists, 94 Harbord St., Toronto, Ontario, Canada M5S 1G6.

CAREER: Odeon Publishers, Prague, Czechoslovakia, editor of Anglo-American department, 1953-56; *World Literature Magazine,* Prague, assistant editor-in-chief, 1956-59; freelance writer in Prague, 1963-69; University of Toronto, Erindale College, Mississawga, Ontario, special lecturer in English and Slavic drama, 1969-71, writer-in-residence, 1970-71, associate professor, 1971-75, professor of English, 1975-90, professor emeritus, 1990–. 68 Publishers, founder and editor-in-chief, 1972–. *Military service:* Czechoslovak Army, 1951-53.

MEMBER: International PEN, International Association of Crime Writers, Authors Guild, Authors League of America, Mystery Writers of America, Royal Society of Canada (fellow), Crime Writers of Canada, Canadian Writers Union, Czechoslovak Society of Arts and Letters (honorary member), Order of Canada.

AWARDS, HONORS: Literary Award of Czechoslovakian Writers Union, 1968; Neustadt International Prize for Literature, 1980; Guggenheim fellowship, 1980; Silver Award for Best Fiction Publication in Canadian Magazines of 1980, 1981; nominated for the Nobel Prize in literature, 1982; Governor General's Award for Best Fiction, 1985, for *The Engineer of Human Souls;* City of Toronto Book Award 1985; Echoing Green Foundation Literature Prize, 1985; D.H.L., State University of New York, 1986, Masaryk University, Brno, 1991, University of Calgary, 1992, University of Toronto, 1992, and McMaster University, Hamilton, 1993; Czechoslovak Order of the White Lion, 1990; Order of Canada, appointed member, 1992; Chevalier de L'ordre des Arts te des Lattres, Republique Francaise, 1996.

WRITINGS:

Zbabelci (novel), Ceskoslovensky spisovatel (Prague), 1958, 4th edition, Nase vojsko (Prague), 1968, translation by Jeanne Nemcova published as *The Cowards,* Grove, 1970.

Legenda Emoke (novel; title means "The Legend of Emoke"), Ceskoslovensky spisovatel, 1963, 2nd edition, 1965.

Sedmiramenny svicen (stories; title means "The Menorah"), Nase vojsko, 1964, 2nd edition, 1965.

Napady ctenare detektivek (essays; title means "Reading Detective Stories"), Ceskoslovensky spisovatel, 1965.

Ze zivota lepsi spolecnosti (stories; title means "The Life of Better Society"), Mlada fronta (Prague), 1965.

Babylonsky pribeh (stories; title means "A Babylonian Story"), Svovodne Slovo (Prague), 1965.

Smutek porucika Boruvka (stories), Mlada fronta, 1966, translation published as *The Mournful Demeanor of Lieutenant Boruvka,* Gollancz, 1974.

Konec nylonoveho veku (novel; title means "The End of the Nylon Age"), Ceskoslovensky spisovatel, 1967.

O nich—o nas (essays; title means "About Them—Which Is about Us"), Kruh (Hradec Kralove), 1968.

(With Evald Schorm) *Fararuv Konec* (novelization of Skvorecky's filmscript "Konec farare"; title means "End of a Priest"; also see below), Kruh, 1969.

Lvice (novel), Ceskoslovensky spisovatel, 1969, translation published as *Miss Silver's Past,* Grove, 1973.

Horkej svet: Povidky z let, 1946-1967 (title means "The Bitter World: Selected Stories, 1947-1967"), Odeon (Prague), 1969.

Tankovy prapor (novel; title means "The Tank Corps"), 68 Publishers (Toronto), 1971.

All the Bright Young Men and Women: A Personal History of the Czech Cinema, translation from the original Czech by Michael Schonberg, Peter Martin Associates, 1971.

Mirakl, 68 Publishers, 1972, translation by Paul Wilson published as *The Miracle Game,* Knopf, 1991.

Hrichy pro patera Knoxe (novel), 68 Publishers, 1973, translation by Kaca Polackova-Henley published as *Sins for Father Knox,* Norton, 1989.

Prima Sezona (novel), 68 Publishers, 1974, translation published as *The Swell Season,* Ecco, 1986.

Konec porucika Boruvka (novel), 68 Publishers, 1975, translation published as *The End of Lieutenant Boruvka,* Norton, 1990.

Pribeh inzenyra lidskych dusi (novel), 68 Publishers, 1977, translation published as *The Engineer of Human Souls: An Entertainment of the Old Themes of Life, Women, Fate, Dreams, the Working Class, Secret Agents, Love, and Death,* Knopf, 1984.

The Bass Saxophone, translation from the original Czech by Kaca Polackova-Henley, Knopf, 1979.

Navrat porucika Boruvka (novel), 68 Publishers, 1980, translation published as *The Return of Lieutenant Boruvka,* translation by Wilson, Norton, 1991.

Jiri Menzel and the History of the "Closely Watched Trains" (comparative study), University of Colorado Press, 1982.

Scherzo capriccioso (novel), 68 Publishers, 1984, translation published as *Dvorak in Love,* Knopf, 1986.

Talkin' Moscow Blues (essays), Ecco, 1990.

Nevesta z Texasu (novel), 68 Publishers, 1992, published as *The Bride of Texas,* Knopf, 1996.

Republic of Whores: A Fragment from the Time of the Cults, translation by Wilson, Ecco Press, 1994.

The Bass Saxophone: Two Novellas (includes the memoir *Red Music,* and the novellas *The Bass Saxophone* and *Emoke*), Ecco Press, 1994.

Headed for the Blues: A Memoir, translated by Kaca Polackova-Henley, Ecco Press, 1996.

EDITOR

Selected Writings of Sinclair Lewis, Odeon, 1964-69.

(With P. L. Doruzka) *Tvar jazzu* (anthology; title means "The Face of Jazz"), Statni hudebni vydavatelstvi (Prague), Part 1, 1964, Part 2, 1966.

Collected Writings of Ernest Hemingway, Odeon, 1965-69.

Three Times Hercule Poirot, Odeon, 1965.

(With Doruzka) *Jazzova inspirace* (poetry anthology; title means "The Jazz Inspiration"), Odeon, 1966.

Nachrichten aus der CSSR (title means "News from Czechoslovakia"), translation from the original Czech by Vera Cerna and others, Suhrkamp Verlag (Frankfurt), 1968.

OTHER

Ze zivota ceskae spolecnosti, 68 Publishers, 1985.

(Author of afterword) Lustig, Arnost, *Indecent Dreams,* Northwestern University Press, 1990.

(Author of introduction) Hrabal, Bohumil, *The Little Town where Time Stood Still,* Pantheon, 1993.

Pribech newspesneno saxofonisty: vlastni zivotopis = Dichtung und Wahrheit, Bla izkaasetkani (Prague), 1994.

Pribehy o Lize a mladem Wertherovi a jine povidky, Ivo Zelez nay (Prague), 1994.

Also author of movie screenplays, including "Zlocin v divci skole" (title means "Crime in a Girl's School"), 1966; "Zlocin v santanu" (title means "Crime in a Night Club"), 1968; "Konec farare" (title means "End of a Priest"), 1969; "Flirt se slecnou

Stribrnou" (title means "Flirtations with Miss Silver"), 1969; and "Sest cernych divek" (title means "Six Brunettes"), 1969. Author of scripts for television programs. Author of prefaces and introductions to Czech and Slovak editions of the works of Saul Bellow, Bernard Malamud, Stephen Crane, Rex Stout, Dorothy Sayers, Charles Dickens, Sinclair Lewis, and others. Translator of numerous books from English to Czech, including the works of Ray Bradbury, Henry James, Ernest Hemingway, William Faulkner, Raymond Chandler, and others.

MEDIA ADAPTATIONS: Tankovy prapor was produced as a feature film by BONTON Co. in Prague, 1991; several other works have been produced as films for Czech television.

SIDELIGHTS: "In his native country, Josef Skvorecky is a household word," fellow Czech author Arnost Lustig tells the *Washington Post.* Skvorecky wrote his first novel, *The Cowards,* in 1948 when he was twenty-four. Not published until 1958, the book caused a flurry of excitement that led to "firings in the publishing house, ragings in the official press, and a general purge that extended eventually throughout the arts," according to Neal Ascherson in the *New York Review of Books.* The book was banned by Czech officials one month after publication, marking "the start of an incredible campaign of vilification against the author," a *Times Literary Supplement* reviewer reports. Skvorecky subsequently included a "cheeky and impenitent Introduction," Ascherson notes, in the novel's 1963 second edition. "In spite of all the suppression," the *Times Literary Supplement* critic explains, "*The Cowards* became a milestone in Czech literature and Joseph Skvorecky one of the country's most popular writers." Formerly a member of the central committees of the Czechoslovak Writers' Union and the Czechoslovak Film and Television Artists, Skvorecky chose exile and immigrated to Canada in 1969 following the Soviet invasion of his country.

Ascherson explains why *The Cowards* caused so much controversy: "It is not at all the sort of mirror official Czechoslovakia would wish to glance in. A recurring theme is . . . pity for the Germans, defeated and bewildered. . . . The Russians strike [the main character] as alluring primitives (his use of the word 'Mongolian' about them caused much of the scandal in 1958)." The *Times Literary Supplement* writer adds, "The novel turned out to be anti-Party and anti-God at the same time; everybody felt himself a victim of the author's satire." Set in a provincial Bohemian town, the story's events unfold in May, 1945, as the Nazis retreat and the Russian army takes control of an area populated with "released prisoners of war, British, Italian, French and Russian (Mongolians, these, whom the locals do not find very clean), and Jewish women survivors from a concentration camp," writes Stuart Hood in the *Listener.* The narrator, twenty-year-old Danny Smiricky, and his friends—members of a jazz band—observe the flux of power, human nature, and death around them while devoting their thoughts and energies to women and music. "These are, by definition, no heroes," states Hood. "They find themselves caught up in a farce which turns into horror from one minute to the next." The group may dream of making a bold move for their country, but, as Charles Dollen notes in *Best Sellers,* "they never make anything but music."

Labeled "judeonegroid" (Jewish-Negro) and suppressed by the Nazis, their jazz is, nonetheless, political. To play blues or sing scat is to stand up for "individual freedom and spontaneity," states Terry Winch in *Washington Post Book World.* "In other words, [jazz] stood for everything the Nazis hated and wanted to crush." Skvorecky, like his narrator, was a jazz musician during the Nazi "protectorate." The author wields this music as a "goad, the 'sharp thorn in the sides of the power-hungry men, from Hitler to Brezhnev,'" Saul Maloff declares in the *New York Times Book Review*. Described as a "highly metaphorical writer" by Winch, Skvorecky often employs jazz "in its familiar historical and international role as a symbol (and a breeding-ground) of anti-authoritarian attitudes," according to Russell Davies, writing in the *Times Literary Supplement*.

Skvorecky follows the life of the semi-autobiographical character Danny Smiricky in *Tankovy prapor* ("The Tank Corps"), *The Republic of Whores: A Fragment from the Time of the Cults*, *The Miracle Game*, *The Bass Saxophone*, and *The Engineer of Human Souls: An Entertainment of the Old Themes of Life, Women, Fate, Dreams, the Working Class, Secret Agents, Love, and Death*. *The Republic of Whores*, which originally appeared in 1971, portrays Danny as a conscript in a Czechoslovakian tank division during the 1950s. This bitter satire exposes the hypocrisy and incompetence of the East Bloc military through Skvorecky's depiction of sadistic officers, idiotic interrogations, mock battles, habitual drunkenness, and sexual liaisons. "Mr. Skvorecky has made a reputation as one of the pre-eminent writers of postwar Europe. For him to have composed such a scathing fictional indictment of the Soviet military system while he was still within its jurisdiction was an act of considerable courage," writes James McManus in the *New York Times Book Review*. John-Paul Flintoff notes in the *Times Literary Supplement*, "hard-boiled cynicism is not confined to the army, according to Skvorecky. The whole of Czechoslovakia is the same—nobody really cares about anything—hence the insistent reference to whoredom, in the (translator's) title and in the text."

Skvorecky builds on this theme in *The Miracle Game*. The novel opens in 1948 in a provincial Czechoslovakian town under Stalinist rule where Danny has secured employment as a teacher at a girl's school. While Danny is bedridden with gonorrhea and characteristically absent, a local priest claims that a statue of Saint Joseph has miraculously moved. Despite the unequivocal rejection of his claim by Communist authorities, the priest insists on the reality of the miracle until he is eventually tortured and killed by the police. In 1968, twenty years later, Danny returns to the place of this tragic mystery to investigate the veracity of the priest's sighting and to determine if it may have been a prank or a Communist rouse to discredit the church. "Danny is a self-described 'misguided counter-revolutionary of minor importance, re-educable, the author of librettos for musical comedies, of detective novels and comedy films, fearing God less than he feared the world, a skeptic,'" notes David Rieff in *Washington Post Book World*. "In the end," Rieff adds, "Danny both solves the riddle and lets the mystery stand. 'Every idea brought into fruition is awful,' he reflects somberly, even a miracle.'"

The Miracle recounts life during the dark years of Soviet hegemony over Czechoslovakia and alludes to the then unforeseeable possibility of change. Stephanie Strom notes in the *New York Times Book Review*, "Josef Skvorecky began writing *The Miracle* when it seemed that a bloodless revolution installing a liberal intellectual at the helm of his native Czechoslovakia would require a miracle." Describing the significance of the miraculous statue in the novel, *New York Times Book Review* contributor Angela Carter observes, "The statue, freshly painted in bright greens, blues and pinks by a devout toy maker, is an image of innocence, of faith, perhaps even hope, which emerges battered but unbowed from the long winter of Communist oppression and survives even the brutal suppression of the Prague Spring, in

1968, when, for a brief moment, it looked as if the system might renew itself." However, this hope vanished when Soviet tanks rolled into Czechoslovakia in 1968 to support the Communist Party. "The novel teems with well-drawn figures, from jazzmen to schoolgirls, intellectuals to priests, pious old ladies to true Communist believers," writes Peter Sherwood in the *Times Literary Supplement*. "None the less," Sherwood adds, "its high points are the manic set-pieces which encapsulate in all its painful absurdity life behind the Iron Curtain in the early 1950s and for far too long thereafter."

The Bass Saxophone contains a memoir and two novellas first published individually in Czechoslovakia during the 1960s. Like *The Cowards*, the memoir *Red Music*, observes Maloff, "evokes the atmosphere of that bleak time [during World War II], the strange career of indigenous American music transplanted abroad to the unlikeliest soil." Although it is only a "brief preface to the stories," Winch maintains that the memoir "in some ways is the more interesting section" of the book. Davies believes that the "short and passionate essay" shows how, "since [the jazz enthusiast in an Iron Curtain country] has sorrows other than his own to contend with, the music must carry for him not just a sense of isolation and longing but a bitterly practical political resentment."

Emoke, the novella that follows, is "fragile, lyrical, 'romantic'" and, like its title character, "fabulous: precisely the materials of fable," comments Maloff. Davies adds that "in its poetic evocation of Emoke, a hurt and delicate creature with an array of spiritual cravings, . . . the story has a . . . depth of soul and concern." Winch, however, feels the woman "is not a vivid or forceful enough character to bear the burden of all she is asked to represent." The three critics believe that the title novella, *The Bass Saxophone*, is more successful, "perhaps because music, Skvorecky's real passion, is central to the narrative," Winch explains. Here, writes Davies, "music . . . emerges as a full symbolic and ideological force," whereas in *Emoke* it was "a mere undercurrent." The story of a boy playing music while under Nazi rule, claims Maloff, is "sheer magic, a parable, a fable about art, about politics, about the zone where the two intersect." Writing in the *Atlantic Monthly*, Benjamin De Mott calls *The Bass Saxophone* "an exceptionally haunting and restorative volume of fiction, a book in which literally nothing enters except the fully imagined, hence the fully exciting."

The Engineer of Human Souls is divided into seven long chapters named after American authors whom Danny discusses in class. Through commentary on major literary figures such as Mark Twain, Edgar Allan Poe, and Nathaniel Hawthorne, Skvorecky illustrates Danny's frustration over his students' misunderstanding of great literature, which uncomfortably recalls for him the uniformity and intolerance of the Communists. As Anthony Burgess notes in an *Observer* review, Danny's "students have no sense of history; for them the past contains events like the deaths of James Dean and Janis Joplin. Their response to art is glibly ideological, and Smiricky hears in their wretched little slogans the voices of his country's oppressors." According to Richard Eder in the *Los Angeles Times Book Review*, "Skvorecky calls *The Engineer of Human Souls* an entertainment. It is, in places, so entertaining that it would be dangerous to read it without laughing aloud; in other places it is sad or dismaying. What he has really written, though, is an epic of his country and its exiles." Though some critics find shortcomings in the novel's amorphous plot and narrative meanderings, as Burgess notes, acclaimed Czechoslovakian novelist Milan Kundera regards *The Engineer of Human Souls* as "a magnum opus."

In his next novel, *Dvorak in Love,* Skvorecky builds on the theme of music which is maintained throughout the Smiricky books. *Dvorak in Love* is a fictionalized account of Skvorecky's compatriot, composer Antonin Dvorak, and his visit to New York City. The life of Dvorak, whose music was influenced by black folk music and jazz, provided the author with the perfect subject for discussing the synthesis "of the two dominant musical cultures of our time—the classical European tradition . . . and the jazzy American tradition," as William French put it in a *Globe and Mail* review. Although some reviewers like Barbara Black have found the narrative structure of the opening chapters of *Dvorak in Love* too complicated to enjoy, the author's characteristic humor later enlivens the story. "Best of all" in this book, remarks Black, "Skvorecky celebrates Dvorak and the musical trail he blazed."

Skvorecky has also produced a series of detective stories featuring Lieutenant Josef Boruvka, a painfully sensitive Prague police officer whose ardent humanism is nearly a professional liability. He dislikes guns, disapproves of the death penalty, and carefully solves crimes, though not without experiencing deep sadness for the captured perpetrators. *The Mournful Demeanor of Lieutenant Boruvka* introduces the melancholic Boruvka through twelve interrelated stories centered around diverse themes including music, ballet, science, and mountain climbing. "Skvorecky's undeniable qualities as a fiction writer shine throughout the stories," writes Alberto Manguel in *Books in Canada,* though Manguel contends that the stories lack enough convincing mystery to represent effective detective fiction. Citing elements of parody in Skvorecky's mysteries, Stewart Lindh observes in the *Los Angeles Time Book Review,* "lurking at the side of every story is the following question: How can a detective find truth in a society concealing it? He can't." Summarizing Skvorecky's message, Lindh concludes, "[Boruvka] lives in a society that itself is guilty of a monstrous crime: the murder of truth."

Sins for Father Knox is a volume of ten detective stories in which Skvorecky deliberately sets out to violate the ten commandments of crime fiction writing as set down by Monsignor Ronald Knox, who lived between 1888 and 1957. Among his cardinal rules, Knox proclaims that no more than one secret chamber or passage should exist in the story, the detective must not have committed the crime himself, and no previously unknown poisons should figure into the plot. Only two of the stories involve Lieutenant Boruvka, while the remainder feature Prague nightclub singer Eve Adam as she tours the Western world and solves crimes that leave the local police befuddled. D. J. Enright comments in the *New York Review of Books,* "In each tale the reader is challenged to spot both the guilty party and the commandment broken. Some of the mysteries are tricky in the extreme." Though praising the compelling characters, *Los Angeles Times Book Review* contributor Ross Thomas finds the Father Knox premise and cryptic formulas "tedious and opaque." Comparing the volume to an excursion on the Orient Express, Michael Dibdin concludes in *Observer* that the stories represent "an elaborately unconvincing blend of parody and pastiche which will delight those nostalgic for the days before the detective story was gentrified into crime fiction."

Skvorecky turned to historical fiction in the 1990s with *The Bride of Texas,* a novel that recounts the adventures of Czechoslovakian immigrants who served in the Union army during the American Civil War. The story opens near the end of the war with Czech troops assisting General William Tecumseh Sherman in his destructive campaign through the South. Inspired by his own research into the lives of actual immigrant troops, Skvorecky's complex subplots and flashbacks describe the lives of numerous characters in Europe and America before the war. "Mr. Skvorecky notes that nearly all of the characters here, including all but one of the Czech soldiers in the 26th Wisconsin, actually existed," writes Verlyn Klinkenborg in the *New York Times Book Review.* "Yet," Klinkenborg continues, "*The Bride of Texas* is pure, exalted romance generated by the forces we think of as constituting history itself." The romantic element of the novel centers primarily around Moravian Lida Toupelik, a Czech immigrant who is forced by her lover's disapproving father to emigrate to the U.S. where she marries the son of a plantation owner in Texas.

Commenting on Skvorecky's historical portrayal of the war, Donald McCraig writes in *Washington Post Book World,* "His view of the war is the standard Northern view and unexceptional." Noting the difficulty of keeping track of the many plots and characters in the novel, McCraig adds, "Page by page, anecdote by anecdote, Skvorecky is a fine writer, but his structure betrays his story." According to *Quill and Quire* reviewer Carol Toller, "Skvorecky has an obvious passion for U.S. history and the motley assortment of characters that have shaped it. But ultimately, his exhaustive research is as frustrating as it is enlightening: the novel's romantic tale seems overburdened by the weight of historical facts and figures heaped so liberally upon it." However, *Booklist* reviewer Donna Seaman praises the novel as "a colossal feat of imagination and cerebration . . . often hilarious and consistently engrossing." *Publishers Weekly* similarly concludes, "Skvorecky's stunning novel shows us the Civil War, race relations, slavery and melting-pot America in a fresh and often startling light."

BIOGRAPHICAL/CRITICAL SOURCES:

BOOKS

Contemporary Authors Autobiography Series, Volume 1, Gale (Detroit), 1984.
Contemporary Literary Criticism, Gale, Volume 15, 1980; Volume 39, 1986; Volume 63, 1991.
Solecki, Sam, editor, *The Achievement of Josef Skvorecky,* University of Toronto Press, 1994.
Solecki, Sam, *Prague Blues: The Fiction of Josef Skvorecky,* ECW Press, 1990.

PERIODICALS

Atlantic Monthly, March, 1979.
Best Sellers, November 1, 1970.
Booklist, December 15, 1995, p. 668.
Books in Canada, May, 1981, p. 40; February, 1983, pp. 13-14; November, 1986, pp. 17-18; June-July, 1987, p. 13; October, 1988, pp. 31-32; December, 1989, p. 9; June-July, 1990, pp. 24-26.
Canadian Forum, November, 1977, pp. 40-41; December-January, 1982-83, p. 40; August-September, 1984; April, 1994, p. 40.
Chicago Tribune, June 9, 1987.
Chicago Tribune Book World, August 12, 1984; March 1, 1987.
Chicago Tribune Review, July 19, 1992, p. 8; August 21, 1994, p. 1; February 18, 1996, p. 6.
Encounter, July-August, 1985.
Globe and Mail (Toronto), November 25, 1986; November 29, 1986; June 25, 1988; November 24, 1990.
Library Journal, July, 1970; February 1, 1996, p. 100.

Listener, October 8, 1970; March 11, 1976; August 17, 1978.
Los Angeles Times Book Review, July 1, 1984, p. 1; February 15, 1987, pp. 3, 8; August 23, 1987, p. 13; June 12, 1988; February 26, 1989, p. 1; May 10, 1991, p. 7.
Maclean's, December 31, 1990, p. 47; December 4, 1995, p. 76.
Nation, August 4, 1984; March 25, 1991, p. 381.
New Republic, August 27, 1984.
New Statesman, October 2, 1970, p. 426; February 5, 1988, p. 33.
New Statesman & Society, March 1, 1991, p. 37.
Newsweek, August 13, 1984.
New York Review of Books, November 19, 1970, p. 45; April 5, 1973, pp. 34-35; September 27, 1984; May 18, 1989, p. 37; April 11, 1991, pp. 45-46.
New York Times, July 23, 1984; August 9, 1984; January 31, 1987, p. 13.
New York Times Book Review, September 21, 1975, p. 38; January 14, 1979, pp. 7, 35; November 25, 1979, p. 46; August 19, 1984; January 12, 1986; February 22, 1987; September 6, 1987, p. 16; March 12, 1989, p. 24; February 18, 1990, p. 14; February 10, 1991, p. 1; March 10, 1991, p. 21; July 19, 1992, p. 32; August 28, 1994, p. 9; December 15, 1995, p. 32; January 21, 1996, p. 14.
Observer (London), March 3, 1985, p. 26; January 3, 1988, p. 23; May 7, 1989, p. 44; February 10, 1991, p. 54; May 8, 1994, p. 17.
Publishers Weekly, June 22, 1984; December 4, 1995, p. 53.
Quill and Quire, May, 1984, p. 30; November, 1988, p. 18; October, 1989, p. 23; September, 1990, pp. 60-61; December, 1995.
Sewanee Review, winter, 1993, pp. 107-15.
Time, July 30, 1984.
Times Literary Supplement, October 16, 1970; June 23, 1978; August 12, 1983; March 8, 1985, p. 256; January 23, 1987; November 30, 1990, p. 1300; March 8, 1991, p. 19; May 13, 1994, p. 20.
Washington Post, December 4, 1987.
Washington Post Book World, July 29, 1984; March 29, 1987; April 16, 1989, p. 8; February 17, 1991, p. 6; March 3, 1996, p. 8.
World Literature Today, autumn, 1978; summer, 1979, p. 524; autumn, 1985, p. 622; summer, 1986, p. 489; autumn, 1987, pp. 652-53; summer, 1991, pp. 511-12.

*   *   *

SMILEY, Jane (Graves) 1949-

PERSONAL: Born September 26, 1949, in Los Angeles, CA; daughter of James Laverne (in U.S. Army) and Frances Nuelle (a writer; maiden name, Graves) Smiley; married John Whiston, September 4, 1970 (divorced November, 1975); married William Silag (an editor), May 1, 1978 (divorced February, 1986); married Stephen Mortensen (a screenwriter), July 25, 1987; children: (second marriage) Phoebe Graves Silag, Lucy Gallagher Silag; (third marriage) Axel James Mortensen. *Education:* Vassar College, B.A., 1971; University of Iowa, M.A., 1975, M.F.A., 1976, Ph.D., 1978. *Politics:* "Skeptical." *Religion:* "Vehement agnostic." *Avocational interests:* Cooking, swimming, playing piano, quilting.

ADDRESSES: Office—Department of English, Iowa State University, 201 Ross, Ames, IA 50011-1401. *Agent*—Molly Friedrich, Aaron Priest Agency, 122 East 42nd St., New York, NY 10168.

CAREER: Iowa State University, Ames, professor of English, 1981-90, distinguished professor of English, 1992–. Visiting assistant professor at University of Iowa, 1981, 1987.

MEMBER: Authors Guild, Authors League of America, Screenwriters Guild.

AWARDS, HONORS: Fulbright fellowship, 1976-77; grants from National Endowment for the Arts, 1978 and 1987; Friends of American Writers Prize, 1981, for *At Paradise Gate;* O. Henry awards, 1982, 1985, and 1988; National Book Critics Circle Award nomination, 1987, for *The Age of Grief* and 1995 for *Moo;* Pulitzer Prize, National Book Critics Circle Award, and Heartland Award, all 1991, all for *A Thousand Acres;* Midland Authors Award, 1992.

WRITINGS:

Barn Blind (novel), Harper (New York City), 1980.
At Paradise Gate (novel), Simon & Schuster (New York City), 1981.
Duplicate Keys (mystery novel), Knopf (New York City), 1984.
The Age of Grief (story collection), Knopf, 1987.
Catskill Crafts: Artisans of the Catskill Mountains (nonfiction), Crown (New York City), 1987.
The Greenlanders (novel), Knopf, 1988.
Ordinary Love and Good Will (novellas), Knopf, 1989.
The Life of the Body (short story), Coffee House Press (Minneapolis), 1990.
A Thousand Acres (novel), Knopf, 1991.
(With others) *The True Subject: Writers on Life and Craft,* Graywolf Press (St. Paul), 1993.
Moo (novel), Knopf, 1995.
(Author of introduction) Keene, Carolyn, *Nancy's Mysterious Letter,* Applewood Books, 1996.
The All-True Travels and Adventures of Lidie Newton (novel), Knopf, 1998.

SIDELIGHTS: Even before her Pulitzer Prize-winning novel *A Thousand Acres,* Jane Smiley's fiction has shared a concern for families and their troubles. As Joanne Kaufman remarks in *People,* Smiley "has an unerring, unsettling ability to capture the rhythms of family life gone askew." Smiley also possesses what Jane Yolen in the *Washington Post* calls a "spare, yet lyric" prose. In addition, Yolen finds Smiley to be "a true storyteller."

The theme of family life was present in Smiley's first book, *Barn Blind,* a "pastoral novel of smooth texture and—like the Middle Western summer in which it is set—rich, drowsy pace," as Michael Malone describes it in the *New York Times Book Review.* The story revolves around Kate Karlson, a rancher's wife, and her strained relationships with her four teenaged children. "Smiley handles with skill and understanding the mercurial molasses of adolescence, and the inchoate, cumbersome love that family members feel for one another," according to Malone.

In her next book, *At Paradise Gate,* Smiley looked again at conflict between family members. In this story, elderly Anna Robinson faces the imminent death of her husband, Ike. The couple have had a rough marriage; Ike is an emotionally cold and violent person. When Anna's three daughters arrive to visit their dying father, old sibling rivalries are revived, tensions between the parents are renewed, and Anna must confront the failures and triumphs of her life. The story, explains Valerie Miner in the *New York Times Book Review,* "is not so much about Ike's death as about Anna's life—a retrospective on her difficult past and a resolution of her remaining years." *At Paradise Gate,* Susan

Wood maintains in the *Washington Post,* "is a sensitive study of what it means to grow old and face death, and of the courage to see clearly what one's life has meant."

Smiley took a different tack with *Duplicate Keys,* a mystery novel set in Manhattan; and yet even in this book her concern for family relations holds firm. Laura Marcus of the *Times Literary Supplement* calls *Duplicate Keys* a story about "marriages, affairs, friendships, growing up and growing older. . . . Smiley demonstrates a considerable sensitivity in the treatment of love and friendship." Lois Gould in the *New York Times Book Review* calls the book only incidently a mystery. "More important and far more compelling," Gould notes, "is the anatomy of friendship, betrayal, the color of dusk on the Upper West Side, the aroma of lilacs in Brooklyn's Botanic Garden, of chocolate tortes at Zabar's, and the bittersweet smell of near success that is perhaps the most pungent odor in town." Alice Cromie in the *Chicago Tribune Book World* concludes that *Duplicate Keys* is "a sophisticated story of friendships, loves, jealousies, drugs, celebrities and life in the fastest lane in Manhattan."

In 1987 Smiley published *The Age of Grief,* a collection of five stories and a novella, focusing on the joys and sorrows of married life. The title novella, according to Kaufman, "is a haunting view of a marriage from the inside, a tale told by a betrayed husband full of humor and sadness and sound and quiet fury." Michiko Kakutani, writing in the *New York Times,* finds that the novella "opens out, organically, from a comic portrait . . . into a lovely and very sad meditation on the evanescence and durability of love." Speaking of the book as a whole, Roz Kaveney writes in the *Times Literary Supplement* that "one of the major strengths of this quiet and unflashy collection . . . is that in [Smiley's] stories things actually do happen. These events are entirely in keeping with her strong vein of social realism, but they have too a quality of the unpredictable, a quality which gives an uninsistent but pervasive sense of the pain and surprise which lie beneath even the most conventional of lives." Anne Bernays, in her review for the *New York Times Book Review,* concludes: "The stories are fine; the novella is splendid." John Blades in the *Chicago Tribune* finds that Smiley "speaks most confidently and affectingly [about] the delicate mechanics of marriage and family life, the intricate mysteries of love."

In 1988 Smiley published *The Greenlanders,* a "prodigiously detailed, haunting novel," as Howard Norman describes it in the *New York Times Book Review.* A 500-page historical novel set in fourteenth-century Greenland, the novel took Smiley five years to research and write. *The Greenlanders* is "a sprawling, multigenerational, heroic Norse narrative," according to Richard Panek in *Tribune Books.* Based on old Viking sagas and, in particular, on surviving accounts of the colonies the Vikings established in Greenland, the story blends fact and fiction to create a modern novel with a traditional flavor. As Norman explains, the book "employs a 'folkloristic' mode—with its stories overlapping other stories, folded into yet others." The technique, Yolen finds, presents "more than an individual's story. It is the community's story, the land's." By telling the community's story, Smiley contrasts the tragic failure of the Greenland colonies to survive with our contemporary society and its problems. "The result," Panek writes, "is a novel that places contemporary conflicts into the context of the ages."

As in her other novels, Smiley also focuses on family relations in *The Greenlanders,* tracing the effects of a curse on several generations of the Gunnarsson family, well-to-do farmers in Greenland. "Family matters . . .," Yolen states, "become both the focus and the subtext of the novel: the feuds, the curses, the marriages, the passions and the brutal deaths." Norman notes the complexity of the novel, citing the "hundreds of episodes and tributary episodes: the seasonal seal hunts and rituals, the travels over hazardous yet awe-inspiring terrain, the births and deaths. . . . Given the vast template of History, it is impressive how Ms. Smiley is able to telescope certain incidents, unravel personalities in a few paragraphs, [and] delve into a kind of folkloric metaphysics." Norman concludes that Smiley "is a diverse and masterly writer."

After the publication of the novellas *Ordinary Love and Good Will,* and a short story, *The Life of the Body,* Smiley published *A Thousand Acres.* The subtle account of a family's disintegration emerges through a painstakingly detailed portrait of Midwestern farm life, just before much of it was lost during the wave of foreclosures in the 1980s. Donna Rifkind comments in her *Washington Post* review that the novel "has all the stark brutality, if not the poetic grandeur, of a Shakespearean tragedy."

The correlation to Shakespeare is no accident, as Smiley admits that the novel is a deliberate recasting of *King Lear,* the Elizabethan playwright's drama of an aged king bordering on madness and conspired against by three daughters plotting to take control of his kingdom. Reinterpreting the motivations of the daughters through a more jaundiced view of patriarchal control and feminine subjugation, Smiley puts the character of Lear's eldest daughter, Goneril in Shakespeare's work, now Ginny in her own, at the center of her family narrative. "Her feminist re-writing of Shakespeare's plot replaces the incomprehensibly malign sisters with real women who have suffered incomprehensible malignity," notes Diane Purkiss in a review for the *Times Literary Supplement.* "In giving Goneril a voice, Smiley joins the distinguished line of women's writers who have written new parts for Shakespeare's women."

For Jack Fuller, reworking the plot of *King Lear* has its dangers. "The large risk that Smiley runs, of course, is using the Lear story so explicitly," Fuller notes in Chicago *Tribune Books.* "It could have turned the book into a kind of precious exercise or a literary curiosity. But Smiley avoids this by the mounting brilliance of her close observations and delicate rendering of human behavior."

Through Ginny's eyes, Smiley shows the deleterious impact of her father Larry's decision to divide his multimillion dollar farm among his three daughters, who include the embittered Rose and the emotionally distant Caroline. As the divided enterprise deteriorates, marriages fall apart and family relationships are crippled by suspicion and betrayal. Describing *A Thousand Acres* as "powerful" and "poignant," Ron Carlson writes in the *New York Times Book Review* that "Ms. Smiley brings us in so close that it's almost too much to bear. She's good in those small places, with nothing but the family, pulling tighter and tighter until someone has to leave the table, leave the room, leave town."

As the Cook family saga unfolds, Smiley gently yet skillfully reveals her feminist and environmentalist sympathies. "In *A Thousand Acres,* men's dominance of women takes a violent turn, and incest becomes an undercurrent in the novel," writes Martha Duffy in *Time.* "The magic of [the novel] is that it deals so effectively with both the author's scholarship and her dead-serious social concerns in an engrossing piece of fiction."

In her next work, *Moo,* Smiley leaves the strains of family relationships to poke some fun at campus life, which she explores at the fictitious Midwestern agricultural college, nicknamed Moo U. *Moo* received mixed reactions from reviewers. While critics found moments of brilliance in the work, some considered it flawed. In a review appearing in *Washington Post Book World,* the writer compares *Moo* with another satire of academia, *Pictures from an Institution* by Randall Jarrell. "Stylistically, [Smiley] employs a prose and tone reminiscent of the dry, ironic, distanced manner Jarrell so masterfully adopted. . . . When it comes down to the essential business of satire, though, Smiley is ill-equipped to follow in Jarrell's train. This is not because she lacks humor but because, more tellingly, she lacks malice." While commenting that Smiley wields a "considerable wit" and "provocative intelligence," Richard Eder's review in the *Los Angeles Times Book Review* takes the novel to task for being "a playful takeoff on too many things, all crowded together and happening at once." In contrast *New York Review of Books'* Cathleen Schine finds *Moo* a social comedy closer to Anthony Trollope's work than Jarrell's satire. Schine notes, "Smiley subverts satire, making it sweeter and ultimately more pointed. She has written a generous and, therefore, daring book. . . . Smiley has transformed the genre by embracing a different tradition altogether. . . . Jane Smiley has created what modern novel readers have until now been able only to dream about, that elusive, seemingly impossible thing: a fresh literary, modern twentieth-century nineteenth-century novel." A reviewer for *Publishers Weekly* offers praise for the work, writing that in *Moo* "Smiley delivers a surprising tour de force, a satire of university life that leaves no aspect of contemporary academia unscathed." Joanne Wilkinson sounds a similar positive note in her review for *Booklist* in her appreciation of the novel's ending. She writes, "Smiley's great gift here is the way she gently skewers any number of easily recognizable campus fixtures . . . while never failing to show their humanity."

BIOGRAPHICAL/CRITICAL SOURCES:

BOOKS

Contemporary Literary Criticism, Volume 76, Gale (Detroit), 1993.
Sheldon, Barbara H., *Daughters and Fathers in Feminist Novels,* P. Lang, 1997.

PERIODICALS

Belles Lettres, summer, 1992, pp. 36-38.
Booklist, February 1, 1995, p. 971; November 1, 1995, p. 453.
Chicago Tribune, November 6, 1987; November 24, 1991.
Chicago Tribune Book World, July 8, 1984.
London Review of Books, November 19, 1992; October 19, 1995, p. 38.
Los Angeles Times Book Review, March 18, 1984; October 18, 1987; April 2, 1995, pp. 3, 8.
Nation, May 8, 1995, p. 638.
New Leader, March 13, 1995, p. 18.
New Statesman, June 9, 1995, p. 37.
New York Review of Books, August 10, 1995, pp. 38-39.
New York Times, August 26, 1987.
New York Times Book Review, August 17, 1980; November 22, 1981; April 29, 1984; September 6, 1987; May 15, 1988; November 3, 1991; April 2, 1995, p. 1; April 5, 1998, p. 10.
People Weekly, January 18, 1988; April 24, 1995, p. 29; January 15, 1996, p. 35.
Publishers Weekly, April 1, 1988; February 6, 1995, pp. 75-76.
Time, November 11, 1991; April 17, 1995, p. 68.
Times (London), February 4, 1988.
Times Literary Supplement, August 24, 1984; March 18, 1988; October 30, 1992.

Tribune Books (Chicago), April 3, 1988; November 3, 1991.
Washington Post, October 27, 1981; May 13, 1988; October 27, 1991.
Washington Post Book World, March 26, 1995.
Yale Review, October, 1995, p. 135.

*   *   *

SMITH, Clark Ashton 1893-1961

PERSONAL: Born January 13, 1893, in Long Valley, CA; died August 14, 1961, in Pacific Grove, CA; son of Timeus and Mary Frances (Gaylord) Smith; married Carolyn Jones Dorman, 1954.

CAREER: Writer of fiction and essays; poet; journalist; painter and sculptor; also performed odd jobs and manual labor.

WRITINGS:

SHORT STORIES

The Double Shadow and Other Fantasies, privately printed, 1933.
Out of Space and Time, Arkham House, 1942.
Lost Worlds, Arkham House, 1944.
Genius Loci, and Other Tales, Arkham House, 1948.
The Abominations of Yondo, Arkham House, 1960.
Tales of Science and Sorcery, Arkham House, 1964.
Other Dimensions, Arkham House, 1970.
Zothique, introduction by Lin Carter, Ballantine, 1970.
Xiccarph, introduction by Carter, Ballantine, 1972.
The Last Incantation, introduction by Donald Sidney-Fryer, Pocket Books, 1982.
A Rendezvous in Averoigne: Best Fantastic Tales of Clark Ashton Smith, introduction by Ray Bradbury, illustrated by Jeffrey K. Potter, Arkham House, 1988.

Contributor of short stories to magazines, including *The Black Cat, The Overland Monthly, Weird Tales, Amazing Stories, Magic Carpet, Fantastic Universe, Stirring Science Stories, Wonder Stories,* and *Fantasy and Science Fiction.*

POETRY

The Star-Treader and Other Poems, A. M. Robertson, 1912.
Odes and Sonnets, Book Club of California, 1918.
Ebony and Crystal: Poems in Verse and Prose, privately printed, 1922.
Sandalwood, privately printed, 1925.
Nero and Other Poems, Futile Press, 1937.
The Dark Chateau, and Other Poems, Arkham House, 1951.
Spells and Philtres, Arkham House, 1958.
The Hill of Dionysus, a Selection, [Pacific Grove, CA], 1962.
Poems in Prose, illustrated by Frank Utpatel, Arkham House, 1964.
Selected Poems, introduction by Benjamin DeCasseres, Arkham House, 1971.

OTHER

Planets and Dimensions: Collected Essays of Clark Ashton Smith, edited and with an introduction by Charles K. Wolfe, Mirage Press, 1973.
The Black Book of Clark Ashton Smith (Smith's notebook and biographical essays), illustrated by Andrew Smith, Arkham House, 1979.
Strange Shadows: The Uncollected Fiction and Essays of Clark Ashton Smith, edited by Steve Behrends, Donald Sidney-Fryer, and Rah Hoffman, introduction by Robert Bloch, Greenwood Press, 1989.

The Devil's Notebook: Collected Epigrams and Pensees of Clark Ashton Smith, compiled by Sidney-Fryer, edited with an introduction by Don Herron, Starmount House, 1990.

Also translator of *Flowers of Evil* by Charles Baudelaire, illustrated by Jacob Epstein, published by Limited Editions Club of New York. Contributor of column to, and part-time night editor of, the *Auburn Journal.* Poetry, prose, and artwork published in chapbooks, including *Grotesques and Fantastiques* (previously unpublished drawings and poems), Gerry de la Ree, 1973, and *Klarkash-ton and Monstro Ligriv* (previously unpublished poems and art by Smith and Virgil Finlay), Gerry de la Ree, 1974.

SIDELIGHTS: Clark Ashton Smith is recognized by many critics of fantasy and science fiction as one of the foremost authors in the genre known as "weird fiction." H. P. Lovecraft, an acclaimed horror writer himself, defined a "true weird tale" in his essay "Supernatural Horror in Literature" as "something more than secret murder, bloody bones, or a sheeted form clanking chains according to rule. A certain atmosphere of breathless and unexplainable dread of outer, unknown forces must be present." Locating his stories in such mythical lands as Zothique (a futuristic realm where magic has replaced science), Smith distinguished his prose from the formulaic pulp stories of the day by fashioning fantastic plots and bizarre imagery out of poetic, and sometimes archaic, language. Writing in a tradition which traces its roots back to the works of Edgar Allan Poe and other nineteenth-century writers of the macabre, Smith and fellow contributors Lovecraft and Robert E. Howard (creator of Conan the Barbarian) defined the "golden age" of the pulp magazine *Weird Tales* during the 1930s. Although the works of Lovecraft and Howard are still widely appreciated by readers of horror and fantasy literature—tales by both authors have been adapted into films—Smith's stories, despite their critical acclaim, are known only to a smaller and more specialized audience. "Of these three gifted men (who were all good friends and correspondents although I do not believe they ever actually met), it is Clark Ashton Smith alone who has yet to achieve the wide recognition his artistry so richly deserves," observed Lin Carter in his introduction to Smith's paperback anthology *Zothique.*

Born in Long Valley, California, in 1893, Smith never ranged far from the place of his birth. Although his formal education ended at grammar school, he continued to read and write stories and poems with the intention of devoting his life to literature, specifically poetry. "While his withdrawal from the normal schoolboy milieu may or may not have made him a better poet, it also, probably, contributed to his later frustrating difficulties in making a living," L. Sprague de Camp pointed out in *Literary Swordsmen and Sorcerers.* During his writing career, Smith was sometimes forced to cut wood and pick fruit to make ends meet. In a quote published in *Literary Swordsmen and Sorcerers,* Smith described his struggle with poverty: "If I work for a living, I will have to give up my art. I've not the energy for both. And I hardly know what I could do—I'm 'unskilled labor' at anything except drawing and poetry. . . . Nine hours of work on week days leaves me too tired for any mental effort." Smith also suffered from ill health during his twenties and thirties, but he would improve physically by the late 1920s, finding the energy from 1929 to 1936 to complete more than one hundred short stories.

Smith had his first short stories published in the general fiction magazine *The Black Cat* in 1910; they were, according to de Camp in *Literary Swordsmen and Sorcerers,* "undistinguished tales of oriental adventure." By 1912, however, Smith's poetry

met with some success and he was encouraged to contact George Sterling, one of his favorite poets and the leader of an artists' colony in Carmel, California. Sterling, a protege of author and journalist Ambrose Bierce, wrote poems reminiscent of French "Decadent" literature, a pessimistic movement that acknowledged the inevitability of moral decline and exulted unrepentingly in it. According to Brian Stableford in *The Second Dedalus Book of Decadence: The Black Feast,* Sterling's verse (the poem "A Wine of Wizardry," for example) "placed morbid meditations on destiny within a peculiar cosmic perspective." A friendship developed between Smith and Sterling—with the older poet serving as a mentor—that continued until Sterling's suicide in 1926. After Sterling introduced Smith to the writings of prominent Decadent author Charles Baudelaire, the champion and translator of Poe into French during the mid-nineteenth century, Smith, in turn, later learned French and translated Baudelaire's poems into English. Sterling also served as the subject for one of Smith's numerous essays, many of which dealt with authors Smith deemed influential.

Smith's stories are clearly identifiable by his unique writing style; in the introduction to *Zothique,* Carter noted, "The short stories of Clark Ashton Smith are very much his own, and nothing quite like them has been written in America, at least since Poe." Various critics have observed the influence on Smith's fiction of Sterling, Bierce, and French author Gustave Flaubert (notably the novels *Salammbo* and *Tentation de Saint Antoine*). English author William Beckford's gothic novel *Vathek* as well as the fantasies of Irish writer Lord Dunsany and supernatural stories by Lovecraft have also been cited as important references in the formation of Smith's prose. Gahan Wilson commented in the *Magazine of Fantasy and Science Fiction* that Smith's stories "were beautifully constructed, full of lovely images and absolutely sumptuous English." Smith's penchant for choosing obscure and archaic words, de Camp suggested in *Literary Swordsmen and Sorcerers,* stemmed from the author's self-educational technique; he would "read an unabridged dictionary through, word for word, studying not only the definitions of the words but also their derivations from ancient languages. Having an extraordinary eidetic memory, he seems to have retained most or all of it."

The settings of most of Smith's stories can be divided into several different worlds. In addition to the continent of Zothique, he created the locales of Hyperborea (an arctic land of ancient Earth), Poseidonis (Atlantis), Averoigne (medieval France), and Xiccarph (a region on the planet Mars). Many of Smith's fictional heroes find themselves transported from one world to another via space travel, enchantment, or a portal to another dimension. In the story "City of the Singing Flame," the narrator discovers an invisible gateway in the rugged California countryside that leads to an alien realm. Joining other creatures of all description who are drawn to a strange monolithic city by a flame that radiates mesmerizing music, the narrator witnesses—several times—the voluntary sacrifice of certain pilgrims. "The narrator , , , ends the tale by saying that he will return to the City and immolate himself in the Flame, that he might merge with the unearthly beauty and music that he had sampled and lost," Steve Behrends informed in *Studies in Weird Fiction.* Two prominent, award-winning science fiction authors have both credited "City of the Singing Flame" as a major source of inspiration. In the introduction to Smith's *A Rendezvous in Averoigne: Best Fantastic Tales of Clark Ashton Smith,* Ray Bradbury recalled that "City" and "Master of the Asteroid" were the two tales that "more than any others I can remember had everything to do with my decision, while in the seventh grade, to become a writer." And in a letter published in *Emperor of*

Dreams: A Clark Ashton Smith Bibliography, Harlan Ellison related that "City of the Singing Flame" specifically influenced his career when he discovered an anthology containing the story in his high school library. (Ellison was so impressed, he admitted in the letter that he stole the volume, writing, "I own it to this day.") Ellison further commented, "I owe the greatest of debts to Clark Ashton Smith, for he truly opened up the universe for me."

The theme of loss has appeared frequently in Smith's fiction. Behrends explained, "Smith created scores of situations in which individuals lose the things closest to their hearts, and live on only to regret their loss and to contrast their fallen state with the glory they once knew. He gave his characters the capacity to realize the extent of their loss, and to express the pain they felt." The story "The Last Incantation," according to Behrends, "contains some of Smith's finest descriptions of the emotions of loss." The plot concerns the elderly wizard Malgyris who uses magic to bring a lover, long dead, back to life. "But, once she is back, he learns with disappointment how different from his memories of her she now seems. He is disillusioned to learn that what he cannot call back is his own youth with all its idealism," stated Douglas Robillard in *Supernatural Fiction Writers.*

Among Smith's Martian stories is "The Vaults of Yoh-Vombis," about an archaeological expedition that discovers an ancient tomb in the planet's unexplored wastelands. As the archaeologists venture into the ruins of Yoh-Vombis, unaccompanied by their reluctant Martian guides, they encounter a mummified being in an inner vault whose head is covered with a mysterious black cowl; the cowl, in fact, is a brain-feeding leech-like creature. By suddenly attaching itself to the head of an expedition member, the creature controls its host and frees others of its kind. Although the story is ostensibly science fiction, Carter, writing in the introduction to Smith's paperback anthology *Xiccarph,* perceives it as a superior hybrid of genres: "Read the tale and savor the prose style: this rich, bejeweled, exotic kind of writing is the sort we most often think of as being natural to the heroic fantasy tale of magic kingdoms and fabulous eras of the mysterious past. Finally, read the story straight through and notice the actual plot. As you will find, it is precisely the sort of thing we call weird or horror fiction." Donald Sidney-Fryer stated in the introduction to Smith's paperback anthology *The Last Incantation* that "The Vaults of Yoh-Vombis" is "one of the most purely horrific stories that Smith ever created" and has "obvious parallels with such Lovecraftian masterpieces as 'The Color Out of Space' and 'The Shadow Out of Time,' as well as with such a recent 'Lovecraftian' film as *Alien.*"

Smith abruptly ceased to write fiction after the deaths of his parents (his mother died in September of 1935, his father in December of 1937). Although he would write the occasional story, "the tales actually completed after 1937 could be counted on the fingers of two hands," de Camp remarked in *Literary Swordsmen and Sorcerers.* Having also shown a flair for the visual arts throughout his life, Smith turned more to rendering his fantastic visions in paintings and sculptures. Eleanor Fait reported in a December, 1941, article in the *Sacramento Union* that Smith started sculpting out of native rock in 1935. "Visiting his uncle who owned a copper mine . . . he picked up a piece of talc, took it home, and casually carved it into a figure one day. Pleased by the result, since then, he has done more than two hundred pieces."

BIOGRAPHICAL/CRITICAL SOURCES:

BOOKS

Behrends, Steve, Donald Sidney-Fryer, and Rah Hoffman, editors, *Strange Shadows: The Uncollected Fiction and Essays of Clark Ashton Smith,* Greenwood Press, 1989.

Behrends, Steve, *Clark Ashton Smith,* Starmont House (Mercer Island, WA), 1990.

Bleiler, E. F., editor, *Supernatural Fiction Writers,* Scribner, 1985.

de Camp, L. Sprague, *Literary Swordsmen and Sorcerers,* Arkham House, 1976.

Long, Frank Belknap, *Howard Phillips Lovecraft: Dreamer on the Nightside,* Arkham House, 1975.

Lovecraft, H. P., *Dagon and Other Macabre Tales,* Arkham House, 1965.

Sidney-Fryer, Donald, *Emperor of Dreams: A Clark Ashton Smith Bibliography,* Donald M. Grant, 1978.

Stableford, Brian, editor, *The Second Dedalus Book of Decadence: The Black Feast,* Dedalus, 1992.

PERIODICALS

Magazine of Fantasy and Science Fiction, July, 1971, pp. 73-76.
Sacramento Union, December 21, 1941.
Studies in Weird Fiction, August 1, 1986, pp. 3-12.

* * *

SMITH, Florence Margaret 1902-1971
(Stevie Smith)

PERSONAL: Born September 20, 1902, in Hull, Yorkshire, England; died of a brain tumor, March 7, 1971; daughter of Charles Ward (a shipping agent) and Ethel Rachel (Spear) Smith. *Education:* Attended high school in Palmers Green, London, and North London Collegiate School.

CAREER: Newnes Publishing Co., London, England, secretary, 1923-53; writer and broadcaster. Gave poetry readings for British Broadcasting Corp. radio and television; read and sang poems set to music (based on plainsong and folk music) at festivals in London, Edinburgh, Stratford on Avon, and elsewhere in England. Member of literature panel of Arts Council.

AWARDS, HONORS: Cholmondeley Poetry Award, 1966; Queen's Gold Medal for Poetry, 1969.

WRITINGS:

POETRY; UNDER NAME STEVIE SMITH; SELF-ILLUSTRATED

A Good Time Was Had by All, J. Cape, 1937.
Tender Only to One, J. Cape, 1938.
Mother, What is Man?, J. Cape, 1942.
Harold's Leap, Chapman & Hall, 1950.
Not Waving but Drowning, Deutsch, 1957.
Selected Poems (also see below), Longmans, Green, 1962, New Directions, 1964.
The Frog Prince and Other Poems (also see below), Longmans, Green, 1966.
(With Edwin Brock and Geoffrey Hill) *Penguin Modern Poets 8,* Penguin, 1966.
The Best Beast, Knopf, 1969.
Two in One (includes *Selected Poems* and *The Frog Prince and Other Poems*), Longman, 1971.
Scorpion and Other Poems, Longman, 1972.
Collected Poems, A. Lane, 1975, Oxford University Press, 1976.

OTHER; UNDER NAME STEVIE SMITH

Novel on Yellow Paper; or, Work It out for Yourself, J. Cape, 1936, Morrow, 1937, New Directions (New York), 1994.
Over the Frontier (novel), J. Cape, 1938.
The Holiday (novel), Chapman & Hall, 1949.
Some Are More Human than Others (drawings and captions), Gaberbocchus, 1958.
(Editor) *T. S. Eliot: A Symposium for His 70th Birthday,* Hart-Davis, 1958.
(Editor) *The Poet's Garden,* Viking, 1970 (published in England as *The Batsford Book of Children's Verse,* Batsford, 1970).
Me Again: Uncollected Writings of Stevie Smith, edited by Jack Barbera and William McBrien, Virago, 1981, Farrar, Straus, 1982.
A Very Pleasant Evening with Stevie Smith: Selected Short Prose, New Directions (New York), 1995.

MEDIA ADAPTATIONS: Smith recorded, with three other poets, a reading of her own poems, "The Poet Speaks," Arco, 1965; a recorded poetry reading was released by Marwell Press, 1966; and she recorded her poems for Listener Records, 1967.

SIDELIGHTS: Calling Florence Margaret (Stevie) Smith's *Not Waving but Drowning* "the best collection of new poems to appear in 1957," *Poetry* contributor David Wright observed that "as one of the most original women poets now writing [Stevie Smith] seems to have missed most of the public accolades bestowed by critics and anthologists. One reason may be that not only does she belong to no 'school'—whether real or invented as they usually are—but her work is so completely different from anyone else's that it is all but impossible to discuss her poems in relation to those of her contemporaries." "Without identifying itself with any particular school of modern poetics," Linda Rahm Hallett similarly noted in the *Dictionary of Literary Biography,* "[Smith's] voice is nevertheless very much that of what she once called the 'age of unrest' through which she lived." Combining a deceptively simple form and mannered language with serious themes, Smith was able "both to compass the pity and terror of her themes and to respond to them with rueful courage and humour," a *Times Literary Supplement* reviewer remarked.

Smith's "seemingly light verse," stated Hallett, contains a "sometimes disconcerting mixture of wit and seriousness . . . , making her at once one of the most consistent and most elusive of poets." "We say that her poetry is childlike, everyone is charmed, delighted," Jerome McGann explained in *Poetry.* "She goes self-consciously to Blake, to nursery rhymes, to naive ballad forms, and offers us afterwards imaginary gardens with real toads in them." Smith's writings, however, frequently demonstrate a fascination with death and explore "the mysterious, rather sinister reality which lurks behind appealing or innocent appearances," Hallett described. As a result, Wright commented, "the apparent geniality of many of her poems is in fact more frightening than the solemn keening and sentimental despair of other poets, for it is based on a clear-sighted acceptance, by a mind neither obtuse nor unimaginative, but sharp and serious, innocent but far from naive, and because feminine having a bias towards life and survival, of the facts as they are and the world as it is."

Contributing to the deceptive quality of the poet's work is her language, which the *Times Literary Supplement* reviewer termed "Smith's most distinctive achievement." The critic elaborated: "The cliches, the excesses, the crabbed formalities of this speech are given weight by the chillingly amusing or disquieting elements; by the sense of a refined, ironic unhappiness underlying the poems; and by the variety of topics embraced by the poet's three or four basic and serious themes." Although the writer found some of Smith's work "indulgent, even trivial . . . it ought at last to be recognized that Miss Smith's is a purposeful and substantial talent. From below the surface oddness, her personal voice comes out to us as something questing, discomfiting, compassionate." Smith's "highly individualistic poetic style [was] vulnerable to shifts in critical taste and to the charges of eccentricity, a charge which Smith risked, and in a sense even flirted with, throughout her career," Hallett concluded. "However, the integrity with which she adhered to her own style earned Stevie Smith a considerable amount of respect, and, more than ten years after her death, her reputation with both readers and fellow poets is deservedly high."

BIOGRAPHICAL/CRITICAL SOURCES:

BOOKS

Barbera, Jack, and William McBrien, *Stevie: A Biography of Stevie Smith,* Oxford University Press, 1986.
Bedient, Calvin, *Eight Contemporary Poets,* Oxford University Press, 1974, pp. 139-58.
Civello, Catherine A., *Patterns of Ambivalence: The Fiction and Poetry of Stevie Smith,* Camden House, 1997.
Contemporary Literary Criticism, Gale (Detroit), Volume 3, 1975; Volume 8, 1980; Volume 25, 1983; Volume 44, 1987.
Dictionary of Literary Biography, Volume 20, Gale, 1983.
Dick, Kay, *Ivy and Stevie,* Duckworth, 1971.
Orr, Peter, editor, *The Poet Speaks,* Routledge, 1966, pp. 225-31.
Severin, Laura, *Stevie Smith's Resistant Antics,* University of Wisconsin Press, 1997.

PERIODICALS

Critical Quarterly, 1986, pp. 41-55.
Grand Street, autumn, 1981.
London Times, November 19, 1981.
New Leader, September 18, 1989, p. 16.
Poetry, August, 1958; March, 1965; December, 1970.
Spectator, August 30, 1969.
Times (London), November 19, 1981.
Times Literary Supplement, January 19, 1967; July 14, 1972, p. 820.

*   *   *

SMITH, Martin
See SMITH, Martin Cruz

*   *   *

SMITH, Martin Cruz 1942-
(Martin Smith, Martin Quinn, Simon Quinn, Nick Carter, Jake Logan)

PERSONAL: Original name, Martin William Smith; born November 3, 1942 in Reading, PA; son of John Calhoun (a musician) and Louise (a jazz singer and Native American rights leader; maiden name, Lopez) Smith; married Emily Arnold (a chef), June 15, 1968; children: Ellen Irish, Luisa Cruz, Samuel Kip. *Education:* University of Pennsylvania, B.A., 1964.

ADDRESSES: Home—240 Cascade Dr., Mill Valley, CA 94941. *Agent*—c/o Knox Burger Associates Ltd., 39 1/2 Washington Sq. S., New York, NY 10012.

CAREER: Writer. Worked for local television stations, newspapers, and as a correspondent for Associated Press; *Philadelphia Daily News,* Philadelphia, PA, reporter, 1965; Magazine Management, New York City, 1966-69, began as writer, became editor of *For Men Only.*

MEMBER: Authors League of America, Authors Guild.

AWARDS, HONORS: Edgar Award nomination, Mystery Writers of America, 1972, for *Gypsy in Amber;* 1976, for *The Midas Coffin;* 1978, for *Nightwing;* and 1982, for *Gorky Park;* Gold Dagger, Crime Writers Association, 1982.

WRITINGS:

NOVELS

Nightwing (also see below), Norton, 1977.
The Analog Bullet, Belmont-Tower, 1978.
Gorky Park, Random House, 1981.
Stallion Gate, Random House, 1986.
Polar Star, Random House, 1989.
Red Square, Random House, 1992.
Rose, Random House, 1996.

NOVELS; UNDER NAME MARTIN SMITH

The Indians Won, Belmont-Tower, 1970.
Gypsy in Amber, Putnam, 1971.
Canto for a Gypsy, Putnam, 1972.

NOVELS; UNDER PSEUDONYM SIMON QUINN

His Eminence, Death, Dell, 1974.
Nuplex Red, Dell, 1974.
The Devil in Kansas, Dell, 1974.
The Last Time I Saw Hell, Dell, 1974.
The Midas Coffin, Dell, 1975.
Last Rites for the Vulture, Dell, 1975.
The Human Factor (movie novelization), Dell, 1975.

NOVELS; UNDER HOUSE PSEUDONYM JAKE LOGAN

North to Dakota, Playboy Press, 1976.
Ride for Revenge, Playboy Press, 1977.
Slocum Bursts Out, Berkley, 1990.
Slocum, No. 150: Trail of Death, Berkley, 1991.
Slocum, No. 154: Slocum's Standoff, Berkley, 1991.
Slocum, No. 155: Death Council, Berkley, 1991.
Slocum, No. 156: Timber King, Berkley, 1992.
Slocum, No. 157: Railroad Baron, Berkley, 1992.
Slocum, No. 158: River Chase, Berkley, 1992.
Slocum, No. 159: Tombstone Gold, Berkley, 1992.
Slocum, No. 163: Slocum and the Bushwackers, Berkley, 1992.
Slocum, No. 165: San Angelo Shootout, Berkley, 1992.
Slocum, No. 166: Blood Fever, Berkley, 1992.
Revenge at Devil's Tower, Berkley, 1993.
Ambush at Apache Rocks, Berkley, 1993.
Slocum, No. 167: Helltown Trail, Berkley, 1993.
Slocum, No. 168: Sheriff Slocum, Berkley, 1993.
Slocum, No. 169: Virginia City Showdown, Berkley, 1993.
Slocum, No. 170: Slocum and the Forty Thieves, Berkley, 1993.
Slocum, No. 171: Powder River Massacre, Berkley, 1993.
Slocum, No. 173: Slocum and the Tin Star Swindle, Berkley, 1993.
Slocum, No. 174: Slocum and the Nightriders, Berkley, 1993.
Slocum, No. 176: Slocum at Outlaw's Haven, Berkley, 1993.
Pikes Peak Shoot-Out, Berkley, 1994.
Slocum and the Cow Town Kill, Berkley, 1994.
Slocum and the Gold Slaves, Berkley, 1994.
Slocum and the Invaders, Berkley, 1994.

Slocum and the Mountain of Gold, Berkley, 1994.
Slocum and the Phantom Gold, Berkley, 1994.
Slocum, No. 179: Slocum and the Buffalo Soldiers, Berkley, 1994.
Ghost Town, Berkley, 1994.
Blood Trail, Berkley, 1994.

UNDER PSEUDONYM MARTIN QUINN

The Adventures of the Wilderness Family (movie novelization), Ballantine, 1976.

OTHER

(Under name Martin Cruz Smith, with Steve Shagan and Bud Shrake) *Nightwing* (screenplay; based on novel of same title), Columbia, 1979.

Also author of several other genre novels under various pseudonyms, including Nick Carter. Contributor of stories to *Male, Stag,* and *For Men Only* and of book reviews to *Esquire. Gorky Park* has been translated into Russian.

MEDIA ADAPTATIONS: Gorky Park, starring William Hurt and Lee Marvin, was released by Orion Pictures, 1983.

SIDELIGHTS: In 1972, Martin William Smith, better known to his readers as Martin Cruz Smith, approached his publisher, G. P. Putnam's Sons, with an idea for a different sort of mystery. Inspired by a *Newsweek* review of *The Face Finder,* a nonfiction book recounting the efforts of Soviet scientists to reconstruct faces from otherwise unidentifiable human remains, Smith outlined a plot involving a partnership between a Soviet detective and his American counterpart as they attempt to solve an unusual murder. (As the author later revealed in the *Washington Post,* his original inclination was to portray a sort of "Butch Cassidy and the Sundance Kid, but one [partner would be] Russian.") Putnam's liked Smith's proposal and agreed to pay him a $15,000 advance.

For the next five years, Smith eked out a living writing several dozen paperback novels, often under one of his various pseudonyms. ("I didn't want to be associated with those books," he told *Newsweek's* Peter S. Prescott.) Whenever he had accumulated enough to live on for awhile, he did research for his murder mystery; in 1973, he even managed to make a trip to Moscow where he spent almost a week wandering through the city jotting down notes on how it looked and sketching scenes he hesitated to photograph. Later denied permission for a return visit, Smith instead spent hours pumping various Russian emigres and defectors for details about life in the Soviet Union "on everything from the quality of shoes . . . to whether a ranking policeman would have to be a member of the Communist Party," as Arthur Spiegelman of the *Chicago Tribune* noted. "I would write a scene and show it to one of my Russian friends," Smith recalled. "If he would say that some Russian must have told me that, then I knew it was OK."

The result of eight years of research and writing, *Gorky Park* chronicles the activities of homicide detective Arkady Renko as he investigates a bizarre murder. Three bullet-riddled bodies—two men and a woman—have been discovered frozen in the snow in Moscow's Gorky Park, their faces skinned and their fingertips cut off to hinder identification. Renko immediately realizes that this is no ordinary murder; his suspicions are confirmed when agents of the KGB arrive on the scene. But instead of taking over the investigation, the KGB suddenly insists that Renko handle the affair. From this point on, the main plot is complicated by an assortment of sub-plots and a large cast of characters, including a greedy American fur-dealer, a visiting New York City police detective who suspects one of the murder victims might be his radical brother, and a dissident Siberian girl with whom Renko falls in love. Before the end of the story, the detective has tracked the killer across two continents and has himself been stalked and harassed by the KGB, the CIA, the FBI, and the New York City police department.

Critics praised the novel for Smith's ability to portray exceptionally vivid Russian scenes and characters. A review by Peter Andrews in the *New York Times Book Review* was typical. "Just when I was beginning to worry that the large-scale adventure novel might be suffering from a terminal case of the Folletts," he wrote, "along comes *Gorky Park* . . . , a book that reminds you just how satisfying a smoothly turned thriller can be." The *Washington Post Book World*'s Peter Osnos compared Smith to John le Carre, maintaining that "*Gorky Park* is not at all a conventional thriller about Russians. It is to ordinary suspense stories what John le Carre is to spy novels. The action is gritty, the plot complicated, the overriding quality is intelligence. You have to pay attention or you'll get hopelessly muddled. But staying with this book is easy enough since once one gets going, one doesn't want to stop." Perhaps because he is the protagonist, the character of Arkady Renko seems to have impressed reviewers the most, though Osnos, among others, pointed out that Smith avoids making *any* of his characters into the "sinister stick figures" common in other novels about the Soviets. The *New Republic*'s Tamar Jacoby regarded the detective as an "unusual and winning . . . moral hero without a trace of righteousness, an enigmatic figure as alluring as the mystery he is trying to solve. . . . Smith sees to it that there is nothing easy or superior about the moral insight that Arkady earns."

In 1986, Smith published *Stallion Gate,* setting his fiction among the scientists and military personnel of the Manhattan Project, those men and women who gathered near Los Alamos, New Mexico, to develop and test the first atom bomb. "Where *Gorky Park*'s subject was Russian," wrote Stephen Pickles in the *Spectator,* "in this novel Martin Cruz Smith turns to something very American, taking on one of the 20th century's most crucial historical moments." Yet, even with this more familiar setting, Smith recognized the need to investigate his subject in order to reanimate the now famous scientists and to reconstruct the historical setting. Explained Pickles, Smith "researched the subject for 18 months, interviewing survivors and anyone who knew or worked with those involved with the Manhattan Project."

Though closer to home, the backdrop for Smith's novel of intrigue gives it an alien quality much as Moscow colored *Gorky Park.* Set in the desert, the novel blends native Indian allusions with modern, even futuristic images of scientists and their work. At the test site are J. Robert Oppenheimer, Edward Teller, Enrico Fermi, Brigadier General Leslie Groves, Harry Gold, and Klaus Fuchs. In a review of *Stallion Gate* for *Time,* R. Z. Sheppard observed that Smith "shapes images that contain haunting affinities: wild horses and Army jeeps; rattlesnakes and coils of electrical cable; the lustrous surfaces of ceremonial pottery and the polished plutonium core of the atom bomb." "Through the Indians, the author develops a magical dimension within the story," added Pickles.

Smith resumed the adventures of *Gorky Park*'s hero, Russian inspector Arkady Renko, in two novels: 1989's *Polar Star,* and *Red Square,* published in 1992. Readers last saw Renko at the end of *Gorky Park* returning from America to his homeland, Russia. Upon his arrival, however, he is imprisoned in a mental hospital, escapes to Siberia, and lands a job as a second-class seaman on the Russian fishing ship *Polar Star,* bound for the Bering Sea. Once out to sea, the fishing nets haul in a dead body identified as crew member Zina Patiashvili. Renko is then ordered to investigate whether Patiashvili's death was suicide or murder.

Reviews of *Polar Star* were largely favorable; Robert Stuart Nathan's comments in the *New York Times Book Review* were typical. "The novel opens with a Conradian evocation of a ship at sea," he proclaimed, "and immediately we are reminded of just how skilled a storyteller Mr. Smith is, how supple and commanding his prose." Reid Beddow, in the *Washington Post Book World,* labeled the characterization of Renko as "terrific," adding that "Martin Cruz Smith writes the most inventive thrillers of anyone in the first rank of thriller-writers." Smith's descriptive settings in *Polar Star* were also singled out for critical acclaim. Although some reviewers noted that the setting has a tendency to overpower the plot, Allen J. Hubin of *Armchair Detective* asserted that the book is "filled with graphic images and cinematic sequences, involving the ship and the frigid, ice-filled expanses of the Bering Sea." Likewise, T. J. Binyon, in the *Times Literary Supplement,* remarked that "Martin Cruz Smith does a magnificent job on the background," calling the work "wholly absorbing."

In Smith's 1992 novel *Red Square,* Renko operates in post-Communist Russia, a Moscow quite different, but every bit as threatening, as that of *Gorky Park.* In *Red Square,* Renko faces a new threat—the corrupt "Chechen" mafia of Moscow. As black markets flourish in this new capitalist atmosphere, Renko seeks to solve the murder of his informant Rudy, who turns out to have had connections with the mob. Reviewers such as Francis X. Clines in *New York Times Book Review* praised the work, focusing on Smith's finely detailed settings: "The great virtue of the book is its narrative rendering of the sleazy, miasmic environment of *fin-de-Communisme* Moscow . . . that slouching, unworkable 'Big Potato,' as its citizens call it." Other reviewers praised Smith's expert characterization. A *Washington Post Book World* critic welcomed back Smith's much-loved hero, Renko, as "an immensely complex and likeable man. Here his qualities stand out even more luminously." The critic added that Martin Cruz Smith's *Red Square* "is as good popular fiction should be, a novel that proceeds on many levels."

In *Rose,* published in 1996, Smith departed from Russia for an altogether different setting: 1870s Victorian England. The plot features Jonathan Blair, an engineer and explorer recently returned from Africa who journeys to the Lancashire town of Wigan to investigate a mystery. Wigan is a gritty, coal-mining town, and Blair sets about determining the whereabouts of the local curate, who has not been seen since the day when a mining accident killed seventy-six people. In attempting to discover what happened to the man, Blair finds himself bewitched by the "pit girls"—local women who work in the mines-and in conflict with several male miners. In particular, one pit girl, Rose, eventually comes to play a large role in the mystery—and in Blair's life as well. Reviewing the book in the *Washington Post Book World,* Bruce Cook praised the author's command of historical details in telling his story and noted that "This novel is blessed with the sort of strong narrative line that makes it a joy to read, yet it is about a good deal more than plot." While remarking that Smith's dialogue sometimes betrays a modern tone, *New York Times Book Review* contributor Eugen Weber declared that "Smith's tale is smartly told, engaging and worth reading."

BIOGRAPHICAL/CRITICAL SOURCES:

BOOKS

Contemporary Authors, Volume 23, Gale (Detroit), 1988.

PERIODICALS

Armchair Detective, fall, 1990, pp. 422-23.
Booklist, March 15, 1996.
Books Magazine, April, 1996, p. 14.
Chicago Tribune, March 25, 1981; July 19, 1992, p. 9.
Chicago Tribune Book World, April 19, 1981; May 11, 1986.
Library Journal, June 1, 1996.
London Review of Books, September 4, 1986, pp. 18-19; December 7, 1989, p. 19.
Los Angeles Times Book Review, April 19, 1981; May 11, 1986; June 24, 1990.
Maclean's, May 4, 1981, p. 56.
Nation, April 4, 1981, pp. 406-7.
New Republic, May 9, 1981, pp. 37-38.
Newsweek, April 6, 1981; May 25, 1981; April 14, 1986; September 14, 1992, p. 70.
New Yorker, April 6, 1981, pp. 181-82.
New York Times, March 19, 1981; October 12, 1992, p. C20; May 1, 1996, p. B2.
New York Times Book Review, April 5, 1981; May 3, 1981; May 4, 1986; July 16, 1989, pp. 33-34; July 15, 1990, p. 32; October 18, 1992, pp. 45-46; June 16, 1996, p. 50.
People Weekly, June 3, 1996, p. 35.
Playboy, December, 1992, p. 34.
Saturday Review, April, 1981, pp. 66-67.
Spectator, July 5, 1986, p. 30.
Time, March 30, 1981; May 12, 1986; November 16, 1992, p. 98; June 3, 1996, p. 73.
Times Literary Supplement, June 5, 1981; December 8, 1989, p. 1369.
Wall Street Journal, May 18, 1981, p. 26; May 29, 1996, p. A16.
Washington Post Book World, March 29, 1981; April 30, 1986; July 2, 1989, p. 5; November 1, 1992, p. 3; May 5, 1996, p. 1.
West Coast Review of Books, 1986, p. 25.

*   *   *

SMITH, Rolando (R.) Hinojosa
    See HINOJOSA(-SMITH), Rolando (R.)

*   *   *

SMITH, Rosamond
    See OATES, Joyce Carol

*   *   *

SMITH, Stevie
    See SMITH, Florence Margaret

*   *   *

SMITH, Wilbur (Addison) 1933-

PERSONAL: Born January 9, 1933, in Broken Hill, Northern Rhodesia (now Zambia); son of Herbert James and Elfreda

(Lawrence) Smith; married Jewell Slabbert, August 28, 1964; married second wife, Danielle Thomas, February 1971; children: two sons and one daughter. *Education:* Rhodes University, Bachelor of Commerce, 1954. *Avocational interests:* Fishing and wildlife conservation.

ADDRESSES: Home—Sunbird Hill, 34 Klaassens Road, Constantia 7800, South Africa. *Agent*—Charles Pick Consultancy, Flat 3, 3 Bryanston Place, London W1H 7FN, England.

CAREER: Affiliated with Goodyear Tire & Rubber Co., Port Elizabeth, South Africa, 1954-58, and H. J. Smith & Son, Ltd., Salisbury, Rhodesia (now Zimbabwe), 1958-63; full-time writer, 1964–.

MEMBER: Chartered Institute of Secretaries, South African Wildlife Society (trustee), Friends of Conservation (trustee), Rhodesian Wildlife Conservation Association, British Sub Aqua Club.

WRITINGS:

When the Lion Feeds, Viking, 1964.
The Train from Katanga, Viking, 1965, published in England as *The Dark of the Sun,* Heinemann, 1965.
Shout at the Devil, Coward, 1968.
Gold Mine, Doubleday, 1970.
The Diamond Hunters, Heinemann, 1971, Doubleday, 1972.
The Sunbird, Heinemann, 1972, Doubleday, 1973.
Eagle in the Sky, Doubleday, 1974.
Eye of the Tiger, Doubleday, 1974.
Cry Wolf, Doubleday, 1975.
A Sparrow Falls, Doubleday, 1976.
Hungry as the Sea, Doubleday, 1977.
Wild Justice, Doubleday, 1978.
A Falcon Flies, Doubleday, 1979, published in England as *Flight of the Falcon,* Doubleday, 1982.
Men of Men, Doubleday, 1980.
The Delta Decision, Doubleday, 1981.
The Angels Weep, Doubleday, 1983.
The Leopard Hunts in Darkness, Doubleday, 1984.
The Burning Shore, Doubleday, 1985.
Power of the Sword, Little, Brown, 1986.
Rage, Little, Brown, 1987.
The Courtneys, Little, Brown, 1988.
A Time to Die, Random House, 1989.
Golden Fox, Random House, 1990.
Elephant Song, Random House, 1991.
The Sound of Thunder, Fawcett, 1991.
River God, St. Martin's (New York City), 1994.
The Seventh Scroll, St. Martin's, 1995.
Birds of Prey, St. Martin's, 1997.

Writer for British Broadcasting Corporation programs.

MEDIA ADAPTATIONS: The Dark of the Sun was filmed by Metro-Goldwyn-Mayer and released in 1968; *Gold Mine* was filmed by Hemdale and released in 1974; the film rights to *Leopard Hunts in Darkness* have been purchased by Sylvester Stallone, as have the film rights of two of Smith's other novels.

SIDELIGHTS: Wilbur Smith's three related novels *A Falcon Flies, Men of Men,* and *The Angels Weep* are concerned with the European conquest of what is now Zimbabwe. In this trilogy, the Ballantynes, a fictional family, challenge the historical figure, Cecil Rhodes, who amassed a fortune in South Africa and after whom both the nation of Rhodesia and Rhodes scholarships were named. The *Washington Post*'s Richard Harwood, reviewing *Men of Men,* compared Smith favorably to other historical thriller writers: "Wilbur Smith is more artful than John Jakes and less pedantic than James Michener but the genre is the same." Roger Manvell, who reviewed *A Falcon Flies* for *British Book News,* praised Smith for the detail of this work; he observed: "The author, who seems to possess an unrivalled knowledge of his subject, writes with an impressive authenticity, as if he had himself taken part in these varied actions a century and more ago."

Some critics fault Smith's novels for weak characterization and improbable plot development. The *Washington Post*'s Philip Smith complained of "too many grating cliches and stereotypes" in *Rage,* Smith's novel about three generations of a diamond-mining family in South Africa. Rob Nixon, writing in the *Voice Literary Supplement,* criticized Smith for championing colonialism: "At a time when anti-apartheid literature crowds the shelves, *A Time To Die* serves as a reminder that a considerable audience remains for writing that glamorizes South African racism." Similarly, Andrew Jaffe charged Smith with "playing politics" and using *A Time To Die* as a vehicle for demonstrating how the American and European perspective on black leadership is too simplistic.

River God, like Smith's other novels, also takes place in Africa, but it is the Africa of Egypt in 2000 B.C. A tale of fictional pharaohs and eunuchs, *River God* concerns the warrior Tanus, and a young woman who loves him, Lostris, whose father conspires to have her married off to the pharaoh instead. Complete with battles involving thousands of soldiers, descriptions of resplendent palaces, and crowds of hundreds of thousands of people on the banks of the Nile greeting their pharaoh, the book was hailed as "compulsively readable" by a *Publishers Weekly* reviewer. Similarly, Brian Jacomb of *Washington Post Book World* declared it a "majestic novel, one filled to overflowing with passion, rage, treachery, barbarism, prolonged excitement and endless passages of sheer, exquisite color."

Smith followed *River God* with a sequel, *The Seventh Scroll.* Set in the present, the novel is the story of an adventurous search for the tomb of the Pharaoh Mamose, husband of Lostris. At the story's opening, Egyptologist Royan Al Simma and her husband, Duraid, have discovered a scroll from the tomb of Lostris that purports to tell the location of Mamose's tomb. However, Duraid is murdered by a rival. Royan then teams up with Sir Nicholas Quenton-Harper, a wealthy collector mourning the deaths of his wife and child. The two battle villainous rivals, booby traps, and other dangerous events in a race to find the tomb. A *Publishers Weekly* reviewer called the novel "intoxicating."

Set in 1667, the novel *Birds of Prey* chronicles the adventures of Sir Francis Courteney, a pirate, and his son, Hal, on a journey from the Cape of Good Hope off the southern tip of Africa to the Great Horn of Ethiopia. Complications arise when the lusty crew of buccaneers attempts to seize one of the treasure laden galleons of the Dutch East India Company. In due course, the pirates are captured, Sir Francis executed, and Hal is forced to assume command. "Fans of Smith's previous work will not be disappointed," enthused Kathleen Hughes, a reviewer for *Booklist.* She called *Birds of Prey* a "meticulously researched, exhaustive adventure saga." A critic for *Publishers Weekly* praised Smith for his handling of the action sequences and his use of terse paragraphs to sustain plot momentum.

Smith is a masterful enough storyteller that many of his critics are quick to acknowledge his strengths. Writing in the *Washington Post Book World,* Bruce VanWyngarden began: "*Power of the Sword* is a sort of 'Out of Africa' for the bodice-ripper set." Although he criticized the novel for being formulaic and overly romanticized, VanWyngarden also noted, "The book's principal strengths lie in the author's considerable storytelling talents and his compelling way with action sequences. Smith writes with real panache about fighting and riding and shooting and bleeding." Of *The Leopard Hunts in Darkness,* Thomas Gifford of the *Washington Post* concluded: "The politics may be simplistic, the macho-man number may wear thin. But Smith does this better than most and it all adds up to a helluva couple days' read, if you're in the mood."

BIOGRAPHICAL/CRITICAL SOURCES:

BOOKS

Contemporary Authors New Revision Series, Volume 46, Gale (Detroit), 1995.
Contemporary Literary Criticism, Volume 33, Gale, 1985.

PERIODICALS

Booklist, April 15, 1997.
British Book News, August, 1980.
Guardian Weekly, August 19, 1990.
Library Journal, May 1, 1997.
Listener, April 4, 1974.
Los Angeles Times Book Review, November 22, 1987; April 8, 1990.
New Statesman, October 20, 1972.
New York Times Book Review, October 25, 1970; April 23, 1972; July 29, 1973; May 30, 1976; September 4, 1977; February 24, 1980; April 26, 1981.
Publishers Weekly, December 6, 1993; March 20, 1995, p. 42; May 1, 1995, p. 38; May 12, 1997.
Spectator, July 6, 1991.
Times (London), April 30, 1981; June 16, 1990.
Tribune Books (Chicago), April 21, 1991; February 16, 1992.
Voice Literary Supplement, July/August, 1990.
Virginia Quarterly Review, winter 1978; summer 1992.
Washington Post, August 3, 1983; August 4, 1984; October 7, 1985; September 20, 1986; October 9, 1987.
Washington Post Book World, September 20, 1986; February 24, 1994.

*   *   *

SNODGRASS, W(illiam) D(e Witt) 1926-
(S. S. Gardons)

PERSONAL: Born January 5, 1926, in Wilkinsburg, PA; son of Bruce DeWitt (an accountant) and Jesse Helen (Murchie) Snodgrass; married Lila Jean Hank, June 6, 1946 (divorced, December, 1953); married Janice Marie Ferguson Wilson, March 19, 1954 (divorced August, 1966); married Camille Rykowski, September 13, 1967 (divorced, 1978); married Kathleen Ann Brown, June 20, 1985; children: (first marriage) Cynthia Jean; (second marriage) Kathy Ann Wilson (stepdaughter), Russell Bruce. *Education:* Attended Geneva College, 1943-44, 1946-47; University of Iowa, B.A., 1949, M.A., 1951, M.F.A., 1953. *Avocational interests:* "My wife and I spend roughly half our year in San Miguel de Allende, Mexico."

ADDRESSES: Home—RD 1 Box 51, Erieville, NY 13061-9801; c/o Border Crossings, 5912 San Bernardo, Laredo, TX 78014.

CAREER: Worked as hotel clerk and hospital aide in Iowa; Cornell University, Ithaca, NY, instructor in English, 1955-57; University of Rochester, Rochester, NY, instructor, 1957-58; Wayne State University, Detroit, MI, assistant professor of English, 1959-68; Syracuse University, Syracuse, NY, professor of English and speech, 1968-77; Old Dominion University, Norfolk, VA, visiting professor, 1978-79; University of Delaware, Newark, distinguished professor, 1979-80, distinguished professor of creative writing and contemporary poetry, 1980-94, distinguished professor emeritus, 1994–. Leader of poetry workshop, Morehead Writers' Conference, 1955, Antioch Writers' Conference, 1958, 1959, and Narrative Poetry Workshop, State University of New York at Binghamton, 1977. Lectures and gives poetry readings. *Military service:* U.S. Navy, 1944-46.

MEMBER: National Institute of Arts and Letters, Academy of American Poets (fellow), PEN, Dramatists Guild.

AWARDS, HONORS: Ingram Merrill Foundation Award, 1958; *Hudson Review* fellowship in poetry, 1958-59; Longview Foundation Literary Award, 1959; Poetry Society of America citation, 1960; National Institute of Arts and Letters grant, 1960; Pulitzer Prize for poetry, 1960, British Guinness Award, 1961, both for *Heart's Needle;* Yaddo resident award, 1960, 1961, 1965; Ford Foundation grant, 1963-64; Miles Poetry Award, 1966; National Endowment for the Arts grant, 1966-67; Guggenheim fellowship, 1972; Bicentennial medal from College of William and Mary, 1976; centennial medal from government of Romania, 1977; honorary doctorate of letters, Allegheny College, 1991; first prize for translations of Romanian letters, Colloquium of Translators and Editors, Siaia, Romania, 1995.

WRITINGS:

Heart's Needle (poetry), Knopf, 1959.
(Translator with Lore Segal) Christian Morgenstern, *Gallows Songs,* University of Michigan Press, 1967.
After Experience (poetry), Harper, 1967.
(Under pseudonym S. S. Gardons) *Remains: A Sequence of Poems,* Perishable Press, 1970, revised edition published as W. D. Snodgrass, BOA Editions, 1985.
In Radical Pursuit (critical essays), Harper, 1975.
(Translator) *Six Troubadour Songs,* Burning Deck Press, 1977.
The Fuehrer Bunker: A Cycle of Poems in Progress (poetry; also see below), BOA Editions, 1977, revised edition published as *The Fuehrer Bunker: The Complete Cycle: Poems,* BOA Editions, 1995.
(Translator from the Hungarian) *Traditional Hungarian Songs,* Seluzicki Fine Books, 1978.
If Birds Build with Your Hair (poetry), Nadja Press, 1979.
The Boy Made of Meat (poetry), William B. Ewert, 1982.
Six Minnesinger Songs, Burning Deck, 1983.
D. D. Byrde Calling Jennie Wrenne, William B. Ewert, 1984.
Heinrich Himmler: Platoons and Files, Pterodactyl Press, 1985.
A Colored Poem (poetry), Brighton Press, 1986.
The House the Poet Built (poetry), Brighton Press, 1986.
A Locked House (poetry), William B. Ewert, 1986.
Selected Poems, 1957-1987, Soho Press, 1987.
(With DeLoss McGraw) *W. D.'s Midnight Carnival,* Artra, 1988.
The Death of Cock Robin: Poems by W. D. Snodgrass, Paintings by DeLoss McGraw, University of Delaware Press, 1989.
To Shape a Song (poetry), Nadja Press, 1989.
Snow Songs (poetry), Nadja Press, 1992.
Each in His Season (poetry), BOA Editions, 1993.
Spring Suite (poetry), Nadja Press, 1994.
(Translator) Mihai Eminescu, *Star and Other Poems,* Ewert, 1990.

The Fuehrer Bunker: The Complete Cycle, BOA Editions, 1995. *Selected Translations,* BOA Editions, 1998.

Also author, sometimes under pseudonym S. S. Gardons, of fourteen limited fine press editions, including *Syracuse Poems,* 1969, Syracuse University, 1969; *These Trees Stand,* Carol Joyce, 1981; *The Boy Made of Meat: A Poem,* William B. Ewert, 1983; *The Kinder Capers: Poems,* Nadja, 1986; *Autumn Variations,* Nadja Press, 1990; and the translations *Antonio Vivaldi: The Four Seasons,* Tarq, 1984 (also published in the *Syracuse Scholar*), and *Star and Other Poems,* by Mihai Eminescu, W. B. Ewert, 1990.

PLAYS

(Translator) Max Frisch, *Biederman and the Firebugs,* produced at the Regent Theatre, Syracuse University, Syracuse, NY, 1966.
The Fuehrer Bunker (play; adaptation of book of poetry of the same title), produced at River Playhouse, Old Dominion University, Norfolk, VA, 1978, then off-Broadway at American Place Theatre, 1981, later at Eastern Michigan University, Ypsilanti, MI, 1987.
Dr Joseph Goebbels, 22 April 1945, produced at West Gate Theatre, NY, 1981.

MEDIA ADAPTATIONS: Several of Snodgrass's song translations have been performed by early music groups, including the Waverley Consort, Columbia Collegium (New York City), Persis Ensor (Boston), and the Antiqua Players (Pittsburgh).

SIDELIGHTS: W. D. Snodgrass is often credited with being one of the founding members of the "confessional" school of poetry, even though he dislikes the term confessional and does not regard his work as such. Nevertheless, his Pulitzer Prize-winning first collection, *Heart's Needle,* has had a tremendous impact on that particular facet of contemporary poetry. "Like other confessional poets, Snodgrass is at pains to reveal the repressed, violent feelings that often lurk beneath the seemingly placid surface of everyday life," David McDuff observes in *Stand.* The style was imitated and, in some cases, surpassed by other poets. This fact leads *Yale Review*'s Laurence Lieberman to comment that a later book, *After Experience,* reveals "an artist trapped in a style which . . . has reached a dead end," because the group style had taken a different direction than Snodgrass's own. However, later works by Snodgrass show him widening his vision to apply the lessons of self-examination to the problems of twentieth-century Western culture. His poems also present, beyond the direct statement and sentimentality common to confessional poetry, an inclusiveness of detail and variety of technique aimed to impact the reader's subconscious as well as conscious mind.

Regarding Snodgrass's translation (with Lore Segal) of Christian Morgenstern's *Gallows Songs,* Louise Bogan writes in *New Yorker:* "German . . . here takes on a demonic life of its own. . . . To translate Morgenstern is a very nearly impossible task, to which the present translators have faced up bravely and well." Even though some critics may not agree with Bogan— Hayden Carruth of *Poetry* calls the translation "dreadful"—*Books Abroad*'s Sidney Rosenfeld finds that in spite of its possible shortcomings, *Gallows Songs* opens "a door into the world of Christian Morgenstern and impart[s] to the English reader some sense of the playfully profound genius that enlivens it."

Paul Gaston points out that Snodgrass's critical essays and translations help develop his talents and prevent him from reaching the complete dead end of Lieberman's prediction. "These endeavors," writes Gaston in his book *W. D. Snodgrass,* "reveal a poet intent on carefully establishing his creative priorities and perfecting his language." He continues, "Snodgrass's criticism gives the impressions of a mind reaching beyond the pleasures of cleverness to the hard-won satisfactions of wisdom." And finally, "[His] work with translations . . . has encouraged the increasing linguistic, metrical, and structural diversity of his own work."

This diversity is apparent in Snodgrass's third volume of original poetry, *The Fuehrer Bunker,* which uses dramatic monologues to recreate what was said by the men and women who shared Hitler's bunker from April 1 to May 1, 1945. "In these poems," writes Gertrude M. White in *Odyssey: A Journal of the Humanities,* "we are overhearing people talking to themselves, each character speaking in a verse form expressive of his or her personality, revealing who and what they are with a dramatic power that carries conviction almost against our will." Robert Peters, writing in the *American Book Review,* believes that the volume is "a rare example of ambitious, on-going verse sculpture. . . . It will be around for a long time to inspire writers who've come to realize the sad limitations of the locked-in, private, first lesson, obsessional poem."

However, the subject matter of the poems troubles critic Laurence Goldstein, who fears that the writer's choice of subject overwhelms the artistry of the writing. Goldstein, writing for the *Southern Review,* believes that writing about Nazism in the way that Snodgrass does in *The Fuehrer Bunker* violates the poetic aesthetic. "When a poet as skilled in sweet rhetoric as Snodgrass," Goldstein declares, "who can charm and disarm his audience at will, presents twenty-two dramatic monologues spoken by the most despised Nazis, nothing less than ultimate questions about the enterprise of contemporary poetry loom before us." "Is there a shameless sensationalism involved in trying to change belief on *that* dreadful subject?" the critic asks. "Shouldn't the poet pass by the Medusa head of *that* modern horror lest he petrify, or worse entertain, himself and his readers by staring at vipers?" *The Fuehrer Bunker,* which was first published as a work in progress in 1977, was finally released as a completed cycle of poems in 1995. Critics who reviewed the revised edition recognized its power, but their conclusions differed from Goldstein's fears. Frank Allen writes in *Library Journal* that "to hear these voices imaginatively re-created is purgative," while *Booklist* contributor Elizabeth Gunderson calls it "an astonishing work that lets us see with clarity the fall of the Third Reich—and wonder."

Snodgrass's collection *Each in His Season* also raised questions among critics. *New York Times Book Review* contributor Bruce Bennett calls the work "a large-scale, free-wheeling roller coaster of a book," adding that the poet "displays his life and art in often contradictory guises." A *Publishers Weekly* reviewer dismisses the volume, declaring that it "is almost completely stripped of content, with a few notable exceptions." William Pratt, writing in *World Literature Today,* declares that "*Each in His Season* does no credit to W. D. Snodgrass or to any of his models." A reviewer for *Poetry* magazine offers a different assessment, asserting that "among the major poets of his generation it would be difficult to find a wittier or more exuberant writer—or one more committed to the making of verbal music." "If Snodgrass is not always convincing as plaintiff or prosecutor," the critic concludes, "he is both pleasing and persuasive in his role as lyric poet, the 'robin with green face,' singing exquisitely of 'all things vile and ugly.'"

BIOGRAPHICAL/CRITICAL SOURCES:

BOOKS

Contemporary Authors New Revision Series, Volume 36, Gale (Detroit), 1992.
Contemporary Literary Criticism, Gale, Volume 2, 1974; Volume 6, 1976; Volume 10, 1979; Volume 18, 1981; Volume 68, 1991.
Gaston, Paul, *W. D. Snodgrass,* Twayne, 1978.
Haven, Steven, *The Poetry of W. D. Snodgrass: Everything Human,* University of Michigan Press, 1993.
Hungerford, Edward, editor, *Poets in Progress,* revised edition, Northwestern University Press, 1967.
Phillips, Robert, *The Confessional Poets,* Southern Illinois University Press, 1973, pp. 45-72.
Raisor, Philip, *Tuned and Under Tension: The Recent Poetry of W. D. Snodgrass,* University of Delaware Press, 1998.
Rosenthal, M. L., *The New Poets,* Oxford University Press, 1967.
Spires, Elizabeth, *W. D. Snodgrass, An Interview,* Northouse & Northouse (Dallas), 1988.

PERIODICALS

American Book Review, December, 1977.
American Poetry Review, July-August, 1990, pp. 38-46.
Booklist, March 15, 1995, p. 1303.
Book World, April 14, 1968.
Detroit Free Press, June 6, 1965.
Kenyon Review, summer, 1959.
Library Journal, April 1, 1995, p. 99.
Literary Times, April, 1965.
London Magazine, March, 1969.
Los Angeles Times Book Review, August 2, 1987; November 1, 1987; January 3, 1988.
Massachusetts Review, spring, 1975.
Nation, September 16, 1968.
New Republic, June 15, 1968; February 15, 1975.
New Yorker, October 24, 1959.
New York Times, March 30, 1968; June 3, 1981.
New York Times Book Review, April 28, 1968; September 13, 1987, p. 52; April 17, 1994, pp. 20-21.
Observer Review, December 15, 1968.
Odyssey: A Journal of the Humanities, April, 1979.
Papers on Language & Literature, summer, 1977; fall, 1977, pp. 401-12.
Poetry, November, 1959; September, 1968; November, 1994, pp. 97-101.
Publishers Weekly, June 12, 1987, p. 79; August 9, 1993, p. 471.
Salmagundi, spring, 1972; spring, 1973; summer, 1973; spring/summer, 1988, pp. 176-204.
Shenandoah, summer, 1968.
Southern Review, winter, 1988, pp. 100-14; January, 1990, pp. 65-80.
Southwest Review, summer, 1975.
Stand, autumn, 1988.
Tri-Quarterly, spring, 1960.
Western Humanities Review, winter, 1970.
World Literature Today, spring, 1994, p. 375.
Yale Review, autumn, 1968.

SNOW, C(harles) P(ercy) 1905-1980

PERSONAL: Born October 15, 1905, in Leicester, England; died of a perforated ulcer, July 1, 1980, in London, England; son of William Edward (an organist and shoe factory clerk) and Ada Sophia (Robinson) Snow; married Pamela Hansford Johnson (a novelist and critic), July 14, 1950 (died June 18, 1981); children: Philip Charles Hansford. *Education:* University College, Leicester, B.Sc. (London; first class honours in chemistry), 1927, M.Sc. (London; physics), 1928; Christ's College, Cambridge, Ph.D. (physics), 1930.

CAREER: Cambridge University, Christ's College, Cambridge, England, fellow, 1930-50, tutor, 1935-45; British Civil Service, London, England, commissioner, 1945-60; English Electric Co. Ltd., London, physicist and director of scientific personnel, 1944-47, director, 1947-64; British Ministry of Technology, London, parliamentary under-secretary, 1964-66. Writer, 1932-80. Director, Educational Film Centre Ltd., 1961-64; member of board of directors, London bureau, University of Chicago Press; member, Arts Council, 1971-80. Rede Lecturer, Cambridge University, 1959; Godkin Lecturer, Harvard University, 1960; Regent's Professor of English, University of California, Berkeley, 1960. Rector, St. Andrews University, 1962-64; fellow, Morse College, Yale University, 1962. Member of Royal College of Malta Commission, 1956-60. *Wartime service:* British Ministry of Labour, director of technical personnel, 1942-45.

MEMBER: Royal Society of Literature (fellow), American Academy of Arts and Sciences—National Institute of Arts and Letters (honorary member), Society for European Culture, British Migraine Association (president, 1965), Library Association (president, 1961), H. G. Wells Society (vice-president, 1964); Savile Club, Athenaeum Club, and Marylebone Cricket Club (all London); Century Club (New York).

AWARDS, HONORS: Commander, Order of the British Empire, 1943, for services to the Ministry of Labour; British Annual of Literature medal, 1949, for *Time of Hope;* James Tait Black Memorial Prize, Edinburgh University, 1955, for *The Masters* and *The New Men;* knighted, 1957; created life peer Baron Snow of Leicester, 1964; Diamond Jubilee medal, Catholic University of America, 1964; Centennial Corporation award, Albert Einstein Medical Center, 1965; resolution of esteem, Congressional Committee on Science and Aeronautics, 1966; Centennial Engineering medal, Pennsylvania Military College, 1966; Cambridge University, extraordinary fellow of Churchill College and honorary fellow of Christ's College, both 1966; honorary fellow, Hatfield Polytechnic College, and York University, Toronto, both 1967; award for creative leadership in education, School of Education, New York University, 1969; International Dimitrov Prize, Bulgaria, 1980. Recipient of honorary doctorates and other academic awards from American, Canadian, English, Scottish, and Soviet universities, colleges, and academies.

WRITINGS:

NOVELS

Death under Sail (mystery), Doubleday, 1932, revised edition, Heinemann, 1959.
New Lives for Old (science fiction; published anonymously), Gollancz, 1933.
The Search, Gollancz, 1934, Bobbs-Merrill, 1935, revised edition, Macmillan (London), 1959.
The Malcontents, Scribner, 1972.
In Their Wisdom, Scribner, 1974.

A Coat of Varnish (mystery), Scribner, 1979.

Also author of unpublished novels, *Youth Searching* and *The Devoted.*

NOVELS; "STRANGERS AND BROTHERS" CYCLE

Strangers and Brothers, Faber, 1940, Scribner, 1960, published as *George Passant,* Penguin, 1973.
The Light and the Dark, Faber, 1947, Macmillan, 1948.
Time of Hope, Faber, 1949, Macmillan, 1950.
The Masters (British Book Society selection), Macmillan, 1951.
The New Men, Macmillan (London), 1954, Scribner, 1955.
Homecoming, Scribner, 1956 (published in England as *Homecomings,* Macmillan, 1956).
The Conscience of the Rich, Scribner, 1958.
The Affair (British Book Society and Book-of-the-Month Club selection), Scribner, 1960.
Corridors of Power, Scribner, 1964.
The Sleep of Reason (Book-of-the-Month Club selection), Macmillan (London), 1968, Scribner, 1969.
Last Things (Book-of-the-Month Club selection), Scribner, 1970.
Strangers and Brothers: Omnibus Edition, Volume 1: *Time of Hope, George Passant, The Conscience of the Rich, The Light and the Dark,* Volume 2: *The Masters, The New Men, Homecomings, The Affair,* Volume 3: *Corridors of Power, The Sleep of Reason, Last Things,* Scribner, 1972.

ESSAYS, ADDRESSES, AND LECTURES

The Two Cultures and the Scientific Revolution (Rede Lecture), Cambridge University Press, 1959, expanded edition published as *The Two Cultures: And a Second Look,* 1963, New American Library, 1964.
The Moral Un-Neutrality of Science, [Philadelphia], 1961.
Science and Government (Godkin Lectures), Harvard University Press, 1961.
Recent Thoughts on the Two Cultures, Birkbeck College, University of London, 1961.
A Postscript to "Science and Government," Harvard University Press, 1962.
On Magnanimity (Rector's Address), St. Andrews University, 1962.
The State of Siege (John Findlay Greene Foundation Lectures), Scribner, 1969.
Kinds of Excellence (Kenneth Aldred Spencer Lecture), University of Kansas Libraries, 1970.
Public Affairs (lectures; includes "The Two Cultures: And a Second Look," "The Moral Un-Neutrality of Science," "Science and Government," "The State of Siege," and "The Case of Leavis and the Serious Case"), Scribner, 1971.

Also contributor to *Essays and Studies* of the English Association, 1961.

CRITICISM

Richard Aldington: An Appreciation, Heinemann, 1938.
The English Realistic Novel, Modern Language Teachers' Association of Sweden, 1957.
Variety of Men (biographies and reminiscences), Scribner, 1967.
Trollope: His Life and Art, Scribner, 1975 (published in England as *Trollope,* Macmillan, 1975).
The Realists: Eight Portraits, Scribner, 1978 (published in England as *The Realists: Portraits of Eight Novelists— Stendhal, Balzac, Dickens, Dostoevsky, Tolstoy, Galdos, Henry James, Proust,* Macmillan, 1978).
The Physicists: A Generation That Changed the World (history), Little, Brown, 1981.

PLAYS

The Ends of the Earth, televised by British Broadcasting Corp., 1949, produced on stage as *Views over the Park,* in Hammersmith at Lyric Theatre, 1950.

(With wife, Pamela Hansford Johnson) *The Supper Dance,* Evans Brothers, 1951.

(With Johnson) *Family Party,* Evans Brothers, 1951.

(With Johnson) *Spare the Rod,* Evans Brothers, 1951.

(With Johnson) *To Murder Mrs. Mortimer,* Evans Brothers, 1951.

(With Johnson) *Her Best Foot Forward,* Evans Brothers, 1951.

(With Johnson) *The Pigeon with the Silver Foot: A Legend of Venice* (one act), Evans Brothers, 1951.

The Young and Antient Men: A Chronicle of the Pilgrim Fathers, BBC-TV, 1952.

(Adapter with Johnson, and author of introduction) Georgi Dzhagarov, *The Public Prosecutor* (produced in London at Hampstead Theatre Club, 1967), translated from the Bulgarian by Marguerite Alexieva, University of Washington, 1969.

Also author of unproduced play, "Nights Ahead," and, with William Gerhardi, of play *The Fool of the Family.*

OTHER

(Editor with Johnson) *Winter's Tales 7: Stories from Modern Russia,* St. Martin's, 1961, published as *Stories from Modern Russia,* 1962.

(Author of introduction) Arnold A. Rogow, *The Jew in a Gentile World,* Macmillan, 1961.

(Author of preface) Jessica Brett Young, *Francis Brett Young: A Biography,* Heinemann, 1962.

C. P. Snow: A Spectrum—Science, Criticism, Fiction (selections from novels, speeches, and articles), edited by Stanley Weintraub, Scribner, 1963.

(Author of introduction) Charles Reznikoff, *By the Waters of Manhattan: Selected Verse,* New Directions, 1962.

(Author of preface) Ronald Millar, *The Affair, The New Men and The Masters* (three plays based on Snow's novels of the same titles), Macmillan (London), 1964.

(Author of introduction) John Holloway, *A London Childhood,* Routledge & Kegan Paul, 1966, Scribner, 1967.

(Author of foreword) G. H. Hardy, *A Mathematician's Apology,* Cambridge University Press, 1967.

(Author of introduction) Sir Arthur Conan Doyle, *The Case-Book of Sherlock Holmes,* Murray & Cape, 1974.

The Role of Personality in Science (sound recording; read by the author), J. Norton Publishers, 1974.

The Two Cultures of C. P. Snow: A Contemporary English Intellectual Discusses Science and the State of Man (sound recording), Center for Cassette Studies, 1975.

Also contributor of many scientific papers, primarily on infra-red investigation of molecular structures, to *Proceedings of the Royal Society,* 1928-29, 1930-32, and 1935. Contributor of weekly articles on Cambridge cricket to *The Cricketer,* summers, 1937-39. Editor, "Cambridge Library of Modern Science" series, beginning 1931. Contributor to periodicals, including *New Statesman, Nation, Look, Sunday Times, Financial Times,* and *Science.* Editor, *Discovery,* 1938-40.

MEDIA ADAPTATIONS: Sir Ronald Millar adapted several of Snow's novels as plays, including *The Affair,* a three-act play produced in London at the Strand Theatre in 1961-62, and published by Scribner in 1962; it also opened in Boston at the Henry Miller Theater on September 6, 1982. *The New Men* was first produced in Brighton at the Theatre Royal in 1962, but later

that year it moved to London, where it was produced at the Strand Theatre. *The Masters: A Play* was first produced in London at the Savoy Theatre on May 29, 1963, and published by Samuel French in 1964. These three were also published by Macmillan of London in one volume under the title *The Affair, The New Men and The Masters* in 1964. Other Millar versions include *The Case in Question: A Play,* an adaptation of *In Their Wisdom,* produced at the Theatre Royal in Haymarket in 1975, and published by Samuel French in the same year, and *A Coat of Varnish: A Play in Two Acts,* produced at the Theatre Royal in Haymarket in 1982, and published by Samuel French in 1983. Arthur and Violet Ketels adapted *Time of Hope* to the stage; it was produced in Philadelphia in 1963.

SIDELIGHTS: C. P. Snow was "an attentive observer of life in three disparate worlds—the world of science, the world of literature, and the world of government and administration—and to some extent a participant in all of them," according to Arthur C. Turner in the *New York Times Book Review.* Alan Gardner in *Saturday Review* further characterized him as possessing "the intellect of a professor; the confidence of a soothsayer; the erudition of a top-flight statesman; the devil-may-care approach of a warm-blooded novelist; and the hardsell technique of a successful businessman." "In truth," Gardner concluded, he was "all these things." Trained as a scientist, Snow achieved success as an administrator and novelist, and became "a household word in many places and [had] a celebrity achieved by few writers after Shaw and Hemingway," stated *New Yorker* contributor George Steiner. "All of his life," announced a reporter for the *National Observer,* "[was] spent combining and understanding the interactions of science, art, and government, and he [became] an accepted master in all three disciplines."

Snow began his career as a scientist through necessity rather than by choice. The second of four sons born to parents of low income, Snow's education was limited to what he could afford. In order to attend college at all he required financial aid, and at that time the only assistance available to students from his background was in the sciences. So, in 1925, he enrolled in the newly created department of physics and chemistry at Leicester University College. As his brother Philip Snow stated in his *Stranger and Brother: A Portrait of C. P. Snow,* "It would not have been possible to do this from the school's Arts side to which, he told me, he would have otherwise transferred as early as he could."

Although Snow proved to be a first-rate student of theory, professors soon realized that in handling laboratory equipment he was less than adept. Nonetheless, he won another scholarship to Cambridge University, based on his performance at Leicester. Soon after he received his Ph.D. he was elected a fellow of Christ's College, "which meant that he might hope to find a permanent place at the University: among scientists he was beginning to be spoken of . . . as a bright young man," wrote William Cooper in his study *C. P. Snow.* In 1933, however, "a piece of research that went wrong through oversight" helped convince Snow that his true vocation lay elsewhere, stated Cooper. Philip Snow further suggested that his brother's awkwardness in the laboratory "was the real reason for his abandoning scientific research, especially as some of his technical predictions turned out to be false."

Snow's horizons expanded during the 1940s. At the onset of the Second World War, he left Cambridge for government service. He was approached by a branch of the Royal Society to assist in recruiting other scientists for Britain's war effort, a function later assumed by the Ministry of Labour. During the war, Cooper stated, Snow's "chief role was to exercise personal judgement on how individual scientists might best be employed, in research, in government research establishments or industry, or as technical officers in the Armed Forces; and to plan how the number of scientists and engineers in the country might be increased." Snow continued in this line of work as a commissioner for scientific appointments in the civil service after the war. From 1945 until 1960, said Cooper, he "participated in all the major appointments of scientists to the government service; and he acted as an essential point of reference in questions of official policy relating to scientific manpower and technological education." For his services in these areas, a knighthood was conferred upon him in 1957. In 1964 he was awarded a life peerage to enable him to serve the government in the House of Lords as parliamentary secretary to the newly formed Ministry of Technology.

In *The Two Cultures and the Scientific Revolution* Snow highlighted two weaknesses in modern thought which he saw as ultimately disastrous for Western civilization. Snow's first thesis suggested that scientists and other educated people can no longer communicate effectively with each other; scientists tend to regard literature as unproductive, while literary thinkers see science as incomprehensible. According to Cooper, Snow felt that this condition "is in any case intellectually and socially undesirable," and "in the case of a country in the particular situation that [Great Britain] is in, it could in a short time be catastrophic." Why? Because what Snow labelled the "scientific revolution"—the industrial application of electronics, the peaceful use of atomic energy, and the expansion of robotics and automation—will change the world to an even greater extent than did the industrial revolution of the nineteenth century. Snow argued, said Cooper, that this lack of communication between scientists and non-scientists would lead to disaster; he stated that "the splintering of a culture into an increasing number of fragments, between which communication becomes less and less possible, inevitably leads to attrition and decay." A way to change this situation, Snow suggested, is through educational reforms which stress sciences and mathematics in the elementary levels and the humanities in the higher grades.

Snow's second thesis, according to Cooper, was that this lack of communication between scientists and others "obscures the existence of the major gap in the world today, namely that between the countries which are technologically advanced and the rest—major because it is a more deep-seated cause of possible world conflict than any other." Snow saw the contrast between the poverty of the undeveloped Third World nations and the wealth of the Western powers as a threat to world peace. He believed that "the prime social task of the advanced countries, for the sake of their own continued peaceful existence if no one else's, is to reduce the gap. This can only be done by helping the less advanced countries to industrialize as rapidly as possible," declared Cooper. In order for Western civilization to survive, Snow suggested, the entire world must be advanced to their level. "It is technically possible to carry out the scientific revolution in India, Africa, South-east Asia, Latin America, the Middle East, within fifty years," Snow stated in his lecture. "There is no excuse for western man not to know this. And not to know that this is the one way out through the three menaces which stand in our way—H-bomb war, over-population, the gap between the rich and the poor. This is one of the situations where the worst crime is innocence." Snow concluded, "We have very little time. So little that I dare not guess at it."

Reaction to Snow's thesis varied. It impressed a variety of people ranging from then-Senator John F. Kennedy to Bertrand Russell to the Russian ambassador to Britain. What Charles Snow had to say, Philip Snow declared, "had long been obvious to thinking people but nothing was being done about it. . . . his honest account of the lack of communication between scientists and non-scientists on everyday and more critically important levels aroused the deepest feelings of anxiety. Many found the truth unpalatable, and books and articles—from the highly commendatory to unwarrantably vituperative—came pouring out." Philip Snow quotes Kennedy as calling *The Two Cultures and the Scientific Revolution* "one of the most provocative discussions that I have ever read of this intellectual dilemma which at the same time is of profound consequence to our public policy." The greatest assault came from F. R. Leavis, whose vitriolic attack was published in the *Spectator* in 1962. Leavis's onslaught, which included personal slights on Snow's character, "seemed to do Snow little professional harm at first, but it has had some destructive effects in later years," said Russell Davies in the *New York Review of Books*. "For one thing, Leavis was abominably rude to Snow, who accepted this with a kind of stolid disgust," Davies continued, "and the result has been that ever since, many British critics and less-than-critics have been able to disparage Snow freely, happy in the knowledge that he has suffered worse." Snow finally responded to Leavis's criticisms in an article in the *Times Literary Supplement* in 1970.

Snow addressed his critics in what is generally regarded as his greatest work, the eleven books that make up the cycle called "Strangers and Brothers." In these novels, declared Douglas Hill of the Toronto *Globe and Mail*, the author examined "the world of public affairs, the academic, scientific and political arenas judged as moral testing grounds." Snow first conceived of a sequence of interrelated novels early in 1935. Philip Snow remarked, "It was to take him five years to plan the sequence in general and to produce, as his next book after *The Search* in 1934, the first of the 'Strangers and Brothers' series, initially entitled *Strangers and Brothers* [published in 1940] and later changed to *George Passant*. This was to be followed by *The Conscience of the Rich*, *The Masters*, and *Time of Hope*."

Snow's program was interrupted by the war, and later volumes in the sequence were delayed because of his work for the government. However, he kept the idea alive, and by the war's end had a firm idea of what the sequence should be. Philip Snow quoted from a note written by his brother in 1945: "Each of the novels [in the 'Strangers and Brothers' sequence] will be intelligible if read separately, but the series is planned as one integral work of art and I should like it so considered and so judged. The work has two explicit intentions—first to carry out an investigation into human nature . . . through a wide variety of characters, major and minor, second, to depict a number of social backgrounds in England in the period 1920-50 from the dispossessed to Cabinet Ministers. For each major character, the narrator is occupied with the questions: How much of his fate is due to the accident of his class and time? and how much to the essence of his nature which is unaffected by class and time?" "All the social backgrounds are authentic," Snow concluded. "I have lived in most of them myself; and the one or two I have not lived in I know at very close second-hand."

Readers familiar with Snow's life and career detected many elements from the author's experiences in his novels. Philip Snow pointed out that Snow based many of his characters on people he had known. Many readers identified Lewis Eliot, the narrator of the entire sequence, with Snow himself; one reason for this was because Eliot was born in 1905, the same year as Snow. *Dictionary of Literary Biography* contributor David Shusterman commented, "Though dissimilarities exist between the author and his narrator—the main one being that Lewis Eliot is a lawyer—there are some striking similarities. The chief of these is that the narrator becomes a member of the Labour party and lives securely, for the most part, within the establishment." In one case, at least, fiction anticipated life. In the novel *Corridors of Power* Eliot was chosen by defense minister Roger Quaife as his closest political associate; the year the book was published, Snow himself joined Harold Wilson's government. However, some critics have questioned how closely Snow and Eliot should be identified. "Though it may be unwise to assert that Eliot's reactions throughout the sequence are Snow's, nevertheless many readers of the sequence have made this assertion," declared Shusterman. "Certainly there is not much evidence, except of the most superficial kind, that the two are very different."

The character of Lewis Eliot is one of the factors that ties these novels together. According to Cooper, the structure of the sequence is basically simple; the accounts trace "the life-story of the narrator, Lewis Eliot, in terms of alternation between what Snow himself [called] 'direct experience' and 'observed experience.'" In some of the novels, the actions of the narrator Lewis Eliot himself were emphasized; this was what Snow called "direct experience." In other books, Eliot functioned as an interested third party, observing the actions of the featured characters and commenting on them. This was what Snow called "observed experience." Cooper continued, "The design of the sequence is continuously cyclical. With *Time of Hope* Lewis Eliot first of all tells his own story over a certain period of time and then, in the next five novels, the stories of some of his friends during more or less the same period. . . . With *Homecomings* Lewis begins a second similar cycle over a later period. And *Last Things,* again a novel of 'direct experience,' draws the whole work together."

Part of the reason Snow's novels differ from most modern literary works is that they are intended to be didactic rather than artistic. Alfred Kazin suggested that Snow was reactionary in the form his novels took because his interest was not in the book itself, but in the questions and ideas raised by it: "Snow, in opposing his work to the formal esthetic of [Virginia] Woolf and Joyce, has also saved himself from artistic risks and demands in which he is not interested." Peter Fison, writing in *Twentieth Century,* declared, "[To] blame Snow's style for lacking virtues which are not only irrevelant but would be completely out of place in the character of his work is . . . inadequate." Frederick R. Karl stated in *The Politics of Conscience: The Novels of C. P. Snow,* "In short, Snow is that phenomenon among twentieth-century novelists: a serious moralist concerned with integrity, duty, principles, and ideals. . . . His novelistic world is not distorted or exaggerated; his work rests not on artistic re-creation but on faithful reproduction, careful arrangement, and common-sensical development of character and situation." In short, Karl maintained, "Snow has attempted in his modest way to bring fiction back to a concern with commonplace human matters without making the novel either journalistic, naturalistic, or prophetic."

On one level, Snow's novels concern people faced with old questions in the new world of the twentieth century. *Strangers and Brothers* is, as Robert K. Morris described it in *Continuance and Change: The Contemporary British Novel Sequence,* the "most sustained attempt at codifying fictionally the dilemmas and directions of our age." "Specifically, Snow asks," stated Karl, "what is man like in the twentieth century? how does a good man live in a world of temptations? how can ambition be reconciled with conscience? what is daily life like in an age in which all things are uncertain except one's feelings?" But Snow also used the sequence to describe the placement and use or abuse of power in twentieth-century society. His depiction of the workings of power politics, stated G. S. Fraser (a contributor to *The Politics of Twentieth-Century Novelists*), deal "with centrally important questions of 'pure' politics, in the sense that I have defined that: the relationships between knowledge and power (or knowledge and charisma), between expedience and justice, between one's affection for a certain person, say, and one's perception that another person, for whom one has little affection, is the better man for a certain job." Snow's novels, he declared, "are at least unique in modern fiction in giving us a dry but accurate notion of how we are ruled and some quite deep insights into the consciences of our rulers."

On another level, *Strangers and Brothers* is about relations between people. Cooper declared, "In content [the cycle] is essentially a personal story—the story of a man's life, through which is revealed his psychological and his moral structure—yet by extension and implication it is an enquiry into the psychological and moral structure of a large fraction of the society of our times." Philip Snow cited a letter C. P. Snow wrote to Mrs. Maryke Lanius in 1961, reading in part: "The phrase Strangers and Brothers is supposed to represent the fact that in part of our lives each person is alone (each of us lives in isolation and in such parts of the individual life we are all strangers) and in part of our lives, including social activities, we can and should feel for each other like brothers." Snow continued, "Socially I am optimistic and I believe that men are able to grapple with their social history. That is, the brothers side of the overall theme contains a completely definite hope. But some aspects of the individual life do not carry the same feeling. Have you ever seen anyone you love die of disseminated sclerosis? This is the strangers part of the thing. I don't believe we subtract from our social optimism if we see the individual tragedies with clear eyes. On the contrary, I believe we strengthen ourselves for those tasks which are within our power."

Snow's tasks were for the most part finished by 1970. He left government service in 1966 and returned to writing full-time, completing the "Strangers and Brothers" sequence with *Last Things.* Between lectures and addresses he continued to attend debates in the House of Lords, and completed three novels and several works of nonfiction. As the sixties and seventies progressed, however, his optimism began to fade. "The Vietnam war, antagonism between Russia and America, the unsettled state of the Third World were all causes for concern," declared Philip Snow, and attacks of what, at the time, was believed to be migratory arthritis also contributed to his depression. Snow's health worsened and he died in 1980 of a massive hemorrhage precipitated by a perforated gastric ulcer. His last book, *The Physicists,* a series of biographical sketches, was published posthumously.

BIOGRAPHICAL/CRITICAL SOURCES:

BOOKS

Boytinck, Paul, *C. P. Snow: A Reference Guide,* G. K. Hall, 1980.
Bradbury, Malcolm, *Possibilities: Essays on the State of the Novel,* Oxford University Press, 1973.
Burgess, Anthony, *The Novel Now: A Guide to Contemporary Fiction,* Norton, 1967.

Contemporary Literary Criticism, Gale (Detroit), Volume 1, 1973; Volume 4, 1975; Volume 6, 1976; Volume 9, 1978; Volume 13, 1980; Volume 19, 1981.

Cooper, William (pseudonym of Harry Summerfield Hoff), *C. P. Snow,* Longmans, Green, 1959.

Davis, Robert Gorham, *C. P. Snow,* Columbia University Press, 1965.

De La Mothe, John, *C. P. Snow and the Struggle of Modernity,* McGill Queens University Press, 1992.

Dictionary of Literary Biography, Volume 15: *British Novelists, 1930-1959,* Gale, 1983.

Greacen, Robert, *The World of C. P. Snow,* London House & Maxwell, 1963.

Halperin, John, *C. P. Snow: An Oral Biography; Together with a Conversation with Lady Snow (Pamela Hansford Johnson),* St. Martin's, 1983.

Karl, Frederick R., *The Politics of Conscience: The Novels of C. P. Snow,* Southern Illinois University Press, 1963.

Kazin, Alfred, *Contemporaries,* Little, Brown, 1962.

Morris, Robert K., *Continuance and Change: The Contemporary British Novel Sequence,* Southern Illinois University Press, 1972.

Panichas, George A., editor, *The Politics of Twentieth-Century Novelists,* Hawthorne, 1971.

Ramanthan, Suguna, *The Novels of C. P. Snow,* Macmillan (London), 1978.

Raymond, John, editor, *The Baldwin Age,* Eyre & Spottiswoode, 1960.

Schusterman, David, *C. P. Snow,* Twayne, 1975.

Snow, Philip, *Stranger and Brother: A Portrait of C. P. Snow,* Macmillan, 1982, Scribner, 1983.

Snow, Philip, *A Time of Renewal: Clusters of Characters, C. P. Snow and Coups,* Harvill Press, 1997.

Symons, Julian, *Critical Occasions,* Hamish Hamilton, 1966.

Thale, Jerome, *C. P. Snow,* Oliver & Boyd, 1964.

Wain, John, *Essays on Literature and Ideas,* St. Martin's, 1963.

Weintraub, Stanley, editor, *C. P. Snow: A Spectrum—Science, Criticism, Fiction,* Scribner, 1963.

PERIODICALS

AB Bookman's Weekly, August 11, 1980.

Atlantic Monthly, February, 1955; April, 1958; June, 1960; November, 1964; February, 1969; September, 1970; June, 1972; December, 1974; January, 1980.

Bookseller, July 17, 1980.

Chicago Tribune, July 3, 1980.

Chicago Tribune Book World, November 11, 1979; September 20, 1981.

Choice, April, 1970; February, 1985.

Christian Science Monitor, January 13, 1955; October 11, 1956; February 27, 1958; May 12, 1960; September 29, 1960; September 17, 1964; May 4, 1967; January 16, 1969; August 27, 1970.

Detroit News, May 30, 1972.

Economist, November 21, 1970.

Financial Times (London), July 12, 1980.

Globe and Mail (Toronto), March 31, 1984.

Guardian, April 14, 1960; July 2, 1980.

Harper's Magazine, February, 1969.

Life, April 7, 1961; May 5, 1967; January 17, 1969.

Listener, October 31, 1968; October 10, 1974; September 13, 1979.

Los Angeles Times, October 18, 1981.

Los Angeles Times Book Review, June 28, 1987.

Nation, December 8, 1956; March 15, 1958; June 25, 1960; July 17, 1967; December 9, 1968; April 28, 1969; May 29, 1972.

National Observer, November 18, 1968; January 13, 1969.

National Review, October 6, 1964; May 22, 1967; February 25, 1969; June 8, 1979; June 13, 1980.

New Republic, February 23, 1948; October 8, 1956; June 2, 1958; April 11, 1960; May 30, 1960; April 13, 1963; November 28, 1964; May 27, 1967; February 1, 1969; November 27, 1971; October 25, 1975; December 16, 1978.

New Statesman, October 6, 1956; March 29, 1958; June 6, 1959; April 16, 1960; March 6, 1964; November 6, 1964; May 26, 1967; November 1, 1968; September 19, 1969; October 30, 1970; October 29, 1971; July 7, 1972; October 18, 1974; November 3, 1978; September 14, 1979; October 10, 1980.

Newsweek, September 14, 1964; April 24, 1967; August 17, 1970; July 14, 1980.

New Yorker, November 3, 1956; May 10, 1958; May 28, 1960; December 16, 1961; November 7, 1964; May 27, 1967; July 12, 1969; May 13, 1972; January 13, 1975; November 20, 1978; November 26, 1979.

New York Review of Books, November 5, 1964; August 3, 1967; March 11, 1971; September 21, 1972; February 21, 1980; December 17, 1981.

New York Times, February 29, 1948; July 16, 1950; December 16, 1951; January 9, 1955; October 7, 1956; February 23, 1958; February 11, 1969; April 26, 1972; May 7, 1972; October 30, 1972; October 17, 1979; July 2, 1980.

New York Times Book Review, January 3, 1960; May 8, 1960; September 25, 1960; September 13, 1964; April 23, 1967; January 19, 1969; August 23, 1970; December 6, 1970; December 26, 1971; May 7, 1972; October 27, 1974; December 2, 1979; March 22, 1981; July 12, 1981; December 27, 1981.

Observer, July 6, 1980; September 15, 1980.

Partisan Review, Volume 30, 1963.

Publishers Weekly, November 30, 1959; April 14, 1969; July 25, 1980.

Saturday Review, November 3, 1951; January 8, 1955; October 13, 1956; February 22, 1958; May 7, 1960; October 1, 1960; March 4, 1961; March 4, 1964; September 12, 1964; October 23, 1965; November 26, 1966; December 17, 1966; April 1, 1967; May 27, 1967; January 11, 1969; August 22, 1970; December 25, 1971; May 27, 1972; June 17, 1972; January 11, 1975; January 6, 1979; August, 1980.

Spectator, May 14, 1954; September 14, 1956; April 11, 1958; August 7, 1959; April 15, 1960; March 9, 1962; June 16, 1967; November 15, 1968; November 7, 1970; July 8, 1972; December 5, 1981.

Sunday Times (London), July 6, 1980.

Time, October 8, 1956; May 16, 1960; April 20, 1962; September 18, 1964; January 3, 1969; January 10, 1969; August 24, 1970; June 12, 1972; November 25, 1974; July 14, 1980; October 12, 1981.

Times (London), July 2, 1980; July 11, 1980; September 15, 1980; September 26, 1980.

Times Educational Supplement, July 11, 1980; August 22, 1980; March 26, 1982.

Times Literary Supplement, November 8, 1947; July 20, 1951; May 7, 1954; September 7, 1956; March 28, 1958; August 15, 1958; April 15, 1960; November 5, 1964; May 18, 1967; October 31, 1968; July 3, 1969; July 9, 1970; October 23, 1970; November 19, 1971; June 30, 1972; December 25, 1972; October 11, 1974.

Twentieth Century, March, 1960; June, 1960.

Voice Literary Supplement, March, 1982.

Vogue, March 1, 1961.

Washington Post, November 24, 1971; December 6, 1978; July 3, 1980.

Washington Post Book World, January 5, 1969; August 23, 1970; May 7, 1972; September 17, 1972; November 19, 1978; November 18, 1979; March 15, 1981; October 4, 1981; September 26, 1982; July 12, 1987.

Yale Review, spring, 1955; June, 1960; spring, 1969.

*   *   *

SNOW, Frances Compton
See ADAMS, Henry (Brooks)

*   *   *

SNYDER, Gary (Sherman) 1930-

PERSONAL: Born May 8, 1930, in San Francisco, CA; son of Harold Alton and Lois (Wilkie) Snyder; married Alison Gass, 1950 (divorced, 1951); married Joanne Kyger (a poet), 1960 (divorced, 1964); married Masa Uehara, August 6, 1967 (divorced); married Carole Koda, April 28, 1991; children: (third marriage) Kai, Gen. *Education:* Reed College, B.A. (in anthropology and literature), 1951; attended Indiana University, 1951; University of California, Berkeley, graduate study in Oriental languages, 1953-56. *Politics:* Radical. *Religion:* Buddhist of the Mahayana-Vajrayana line.

CAREER: Poet and translator, 1959–. Worked as seaman, logger, trail crew member, and forest lookout, 1948-56; lecturer at University of California, Berkeley, 1964-65; professor at University of California, Davis, 1985–. Visiting lecturer at numerous universities and writing workshops. Member of United Nations Conference on the Human Environment, 1972; former chair of California Arts Council.

MEMBER: American Academy and Institute of Arts and Letters.

AWARDS, HONORS: Scholarship from First Zen Institute of America, 1956, for study in Japan; National Institute and American Academy poetry award, 1966; Bollingen Foundation grant, 1966-67; Frank O'Hara Prize, 1967; Levinson Prize from *Poetry* magazine, 1968; Guggenheim fellowship, 1968-69; Pulitzer Prize in poetry, 1975, for *Turtle Island;* Bollingen Prize for Poetry, 1997.

WRITINGS:

POETRY

Riprap (also see below), Origin Press, 1959.

Myths & Texts, Totem Press, 1960.

Riprap & Cold Mountain Poems (the *Cold Mountain* poems are Snyder's translations of poems by Han-Shan), Four Seasons Foundation, 1965.

Six Sections from Mountains and Rivers without End, Four Seasons Foundation, 1965, revised edition published as *Six Sections from Mountains and Rivers without End, Plus One,* 1970.

A Range of Poems (includes translations of the modern Japanese poet, Miyazawa Kenji), Fulcrum (London), 1966.

Three Worlds, Three Realms, Six Roads, Griffin Press, 1966.

The Back Country, New Directions, 1968.

The Blue Sky, Phoenix Book Shop, 1969.

Regarding Wave, New Directions, 1970.

Manzanita, Kent State University Libraries, 1971.

Plute Creek, State University College at Brockport, 1972.

The Fudo Trilogy: Spel against Demons, Smokey the Bear Sutra, The California Water Plan (also see below), illustrated by Michael Corr, Shaman Drum, 1973.

Turtle Island, New Directions, 1974.

All in the Family, University of California Library, c. 1975.

Smokey the Bear Sutra (chapbook), 1976.

Songs for Gaia, illustrated by Corr, Copper Canyon, 1979.

True Night (limited edition), Bob Giorgio, 1980.

Axe Handles, North Point Press, 1983.

Good Wild Sacred, Five Seasons Press, 1984.

Left Out in the Rain: New Poems 1947-1986, North Point Press, 1986.

The Fates of Rocks and Trees: Two Poems (limited edition), James Linden, 1986.

No Nature: New and Selected Poems, Pantheon, 1992.

North Pacific Lands and Waters; A Further Six Sections (limited edition), Brooding Heron Press, 1993.

Mountains and Rivers without End, Counterpoint (Washington, DC), 1996.

PROSE

Earth House Hold: Technical Notes and Queries to Fellow Dharma Revolutionaries (essays), New Directions, 1969.

(Contributor) *Ecology: Me,* Moving On, 1970.

The Old Ways: Six Essays, City Lights, 1977.

On Bread & Poetry: A Panel Discussion between Gary Snyder, Lew Welch and Philip Whalen, edited by Donald M. Allen, Grey Fox, 1977.

He Who Hunted Birds in His Father's Village (undergraduate thesis), preface by Nathaniel Tarn, Grey Fox, 1979.

The Real Work: Interviews & Talks, 1964-1979, edited with introduction by Scott McLean, New Directions, 1980.

Passage through India (autobiography), Grey Fox, 1983.

The Practice of the Wild, Farrar, Straus, 1990.

A Place in Space: Ethics, Aesthetics, and Watersheds (new and selected prose), Counterpoint (Washington, DC), 1995.

OTHER

(Editor with Kanetsuki Gutetsu) *The Wooden Fish: Basic Sutras and Gathas of Rinzai Zen,* First Zen Institute of America in Japan, 1961.

The New Religion (sound recording), Big Sur Recordings, 1967.

Contributor to numerous periodicals, including *Janus, Evergreen Review, Black Mountain Review, Yugen, Chicago Review, Jabberwock, San Francisco Review, Big Table, Origin, Kulchur, Journal for the Protection of All Beings, Nation, City Lights Journal, Yale Literary Magazine, Beloit Poetry Journal,* and *Poetry.* The University of California, Davis, holds a collection of Snyder's manuscripts.

SIDELIGHTS: Gary Snyder is one of the rare modern poets who has bridged the gap between popular appeal and serious academic criticism. Snyder began his career in the 1950s as a noted member of the "Beat Generation," and since then he has explored a wide range of social and spiritual matters in both poetry and prose. Snyder's work blends physical reality—precise observations of nature—with inner insight received primarily through the practice of Zen Buddhism. *Southwest Review* essayist Abraham Rothberg notes that the poet "celebrates nature, the simple, the animal, the sexual, the tribal, the self. . . . He sees man as an indissoluble part of the natural environment, flourishing when he accepts and adapts to that natural heritage, creating a hell on earth and within himself when he is separated from it by his intellect and its technological and societal creations." While Snyder has gained the attention of readers as a spokesman for the preservation of the natural world and its earth-conscious cultures, he is not simply a "back-to-nature" poet with a facile message. In *American Poetry in the Twentieth Century,* Kenneth Rexroth observes that although Snyder proposes "a new ethic, a new esthetic, [and] a new life style," he is also "an accomplished technician who has learned from the poetry of several languages and who has developed a sure and flexible style capable of handling any material he wishes." According to Charles Altieri in *Enlarging the Temple: New Directions in American Poetry during the 1960s,* Snyder's achievement "is a considerable one. Judged simply in aesthetic terms, according to norms of precision, intelligence, imaginative play, and moments of deep resonance, he easily ranks among the best poets of his generation. Moreover, he manages to provide a fresh perspective on metaphysical themes, which he makes relevant and compelling."

Snyder's emphasis on metaphysics and his celebration of the natural order remove his work from the general tenor of Beat writing. *Dictionary of Literary Biography* contributor Dan McLeod explains that while authors such as Allen Ginsberg and Neal Cassady "represented in their different ways rather destructive responses to the alienation inherent in modern American technocracy, the example of Snyder's life and values offered a constructive, albeit underground, alternative to mainstream American culture." No less searing in his indictments of Western values than the other Beat writers, Snyder has proposed "a morality that is unharmful, that tends toward wholeness. An ethics not of the trigger or fist, but of the heart," to quote *New Republic* reviewer Timothy Baland. Snyder has looked to the Orient and to the beliefs of American Indians for positive responses to the world, and he has tempered his studies with stints of hard physical labor as a logger and trail builder. In the *Southwest Review,* Roger Jones calls Snyder "one of the century's *healthiest* writers," a poet who "perceives man as completely situated within the schemes of natural order, and sees as a necessity man's awareness that he is as real and as whole as the world—a perception muddled by the metaphysical notion of the world as a mere stage for the enactment of our eternal destinies." Charles Molesworth elaborates on this premise in his work *Gary Snyder's Vision: Poetry and the Real Work.* Molesworth sees Snyder as "a moral visionary who is neither a scourge nor a satirist; . . . he has spoken as a prophet whose 'tribe' is without definite national or cultural boundaries."

In the autumn of 1952 Snyder moved to the San Francisco Bay area in order to study Oriental languages at Berkeley. He was already immersed in Zen Buddhism and had begun to write poetry about his work in the wilderness. McLeod contends that the four years Snyder spent in San Francisco "were of enormous importance to his . . . growth as a poet." He became part of a community of writers, including Philip Whalen, Allen Ginsberg, and Jack Kerouac, who would come to be known as the Beat Generation and who would be heralded as the forerunners of a counterculture revolution in literature. The literary fame of the Beat Generation was launched with a single event: a poetry reading in October of 1955 at San Francisco's Six Gallery. While it is Ginsberg's poem "Howl" that is best remembered from that evening, Snyder also participated, reading his poem "The Berry Feast."

If Snyder was influenced by his antisocial contemporaries, he also exerted an influence on them. Kerouac modeled his character Japhy Ryder in *The Dharma Bums* on Snyder, and the poet encouraged his friends to take an interest in Eastern philosophy as an antidote to the ills of the West. McLeod notes, however, that although "he is clearly one of its major figures, Snyder was out of town when the Beat movement was most alive on the American scene." Having been awarded a scholarship by the First Zen Institute of America, Snyder moved to Japan in 1956 and stayed abroad almost continuously for the next twelve years. Part of that time he lived in an ashram and devoted himself to strenuous Zen study and meditation. He also travelled extensively, visiting India and Indonesia, and even venturing as far as Istanbul on an oil tanker, the *Sappa Creek.* His first two poetry collections, *Riprap* and *Myths & Texts,* were published in 1959 and 1960. After returning to the United States, Snyder built his own house—along the Yuba River in the northern Sierra Nevada mountains—where he has lived since.

Snyder's early poems represent a vigorous attempt to achieve freedom from the "establishment" mores of urban America. *Sagetrieb* contributor Thomas Parkinson describes the works as moments in which "action and contemplation become identical states of being, and both states of secular grace. From this fusion wisdom emerges, and it is not useless but timed to the event. The result is a terrible sanity, a literal clairvoyance, an innate decorum." The poems in *Riprap* and *Myths & Texts* are miniature narratives captured from the active working life of the author; Rothberg contends that in them Snyder wants "to be considered a poet of ordinary men, writing in a language shaped in their idiom." Audiences responded to Snyder's portrayals of the vigorous backwoods visionary whose joy flows from physical pursuits and contemplation of the wild world. In the *Los Angeles Times Book Review,* Schuyler Ingle writes: "I could sense [Snyder] in his lines, all long-haired and denim-clad, laced-up high-top logger boots. He was an educated, curious man comfortable with his own sexuality." Rothberg too detects the education underlying the hardier roles. According to the critic, Snyder "cannot quite conceal the intellect or learning in his work, which everywhere reveals his considerable knowledge of anthropology, linguistics, Zen Buddhism, history, and other arcane lore."

It is not surprising that Snyder draws on the traditions of oral literature—chants, incantations, and songs—to communicate his experiences. *Denver Quarterly* contributor Kevin Oderman observes that the poet "writes out of a tradition of self-effacement, and his yearnings are for a communal poetry rooted in place." Scott McLean also addresses this idea in his introduction to Snyder's *The Real Work: Interviews & Talks, 1964-1979.* "All of Gary Snyder's study and work has been directed toward a poetry that would approach phenomena with a disciplined clarity that would then use the 'archaic' and the 'primitive' as models to once again see this poetry as woven through all the parts of our lives," McLean writes. "Thus it draws its substance and forms from the broadest range of a people's day-to-day lives, enmeshed in the facts of work, the real trembling in joy and grief, thankfulness for good crops, the health of a child, the warmth of the lover's touch. Further, Snyder seeks to recover a poetry that could sing and thus relate us to: magpie, beaver, a mountain range, binding us to all these other lives, seeing our spiritual lives as bound up in the rounds of nature." McLean concludes that in terms of the human race's future, "Snyder's look toward the primitive may vouchsafe one of the only real alternative directions available." Addressing specifically the poetry, Jones admits in *Southwest Review* that Snyder's shamanistic role is an important one for modern letters "as poetry seems to base itself less in sound than in the medium of print."

Many of Snyder's poems aim specifically at instilling an ecological consciousness in his audience. Jones observes that the poet advocates "peaceful stewardship, economy, responsibility with the world's resources, and, most importantly, sanity—all still within the capabilities of modern societies, and bound up in the perception of the world and its life-sources as a glorious whole." This theme pervades Snyder's 1974 Pulitzer Prize-winning volume, *Turtle Island,* a work in which the poet manages "to locate the self ecologically in its actions and interactions with its environment, to keep it anchored to its minute-by-minute manifestations in (and as a part of) the physical world," to quote Robert Kern in *Contemporary Literature.* According to Julian Gitzen, writing in *Critical Quarterly,* Snyder assumes that "while man neither individually nor as a species is essential to nature . . . nature is essential to the existence of all men. Consideration for our own welfare demands that we abandon efforts to dominate nature and assume instead an awareness of our subjection to natural law. . . . Snyder repeatedly seeks to impress upon his readers the awesome immensity of space, time, energy, and matter working together to generate a destiny beyond the reach of human will." Some critics, such as *Partisan Review* contributor Robert Boyers, find Snyder's commitment "programmistic and facile," a simplistic evocation of the "noble savage" as hero. Others, including *New York Times Book Review* correspondent Herbert Leibowitz, applaud the poet's world view. "Snyder's sane housekeeping principles desperately need to become Government and corporate policy," Leibowitz writes. "He is on the side of the gods."

Not all reviewers feel that Snyder's more recent poetry scales the heights he reached with *Turtle Island.* Reviewing *No Nature,* a collection of old and new poems published in 1992, David Barber comments in *Poetry* that "the vigor and output of Snyder's poetry has clearly been on the wane over the last 20 years. . . . The poet who was formerly adept at elucidating intimations now seems to be content with simply espousing positions." However, Richard Tillinghast, writing in the *New York Times Book Review,* avers that Snyder possesses "a command of geology, anthropology and evolutionary biology unmatched among contemporary poets," adding that "there is an understated majesty about the ease with which Mr. Snyder puts the present into perspective." Both Tillinghast and Barber in particular commend Snyder's evocation of the subject of work. Notes Barber, "Few contemporary poets have written with such authentic incisiveness about the particulars of work and the rhythms of subsistence, and done so without succumbing to class-rooted righteousness or rural nostalgia."

One project that spanned much of the poet's career—a long poem, *Mountains and Rivers without End,* titled after a Chinese sideways scroll painting—was finally published in 1996 to glowing praise from critics. As Bob Steuding claims, "one finds directness and simplicity of statement, clarity and brilliance of mind, and profundity and depth of emotional range. In these instances, Snyder's is a poetry of incredible power and beauty." Similarly, a *Publishers Weekly* reviewer comments that *Mountains and Rivers without End* "is a major work by a venerable master of post-[World War II] American poetry."

In addition to his many volumes of verse, Snyder has published books of prose essays and interviews that can be read "not only as partial explanation of the poetry but as the record of an evolving mind with extreme good sense in treating the problems of the

world," according to Parkinson. Snyder's prose expands his sense of social purpose and reveals the series of interests and concerns that have sparked his creative writing. In *The Practice of the Wild,* published in 1990, Snyder muses on familiar topics such as environmental concerns, Native American culture, ecofeminism, language, and mythology. Praising the author's "exquisite craftsmanship and new maturity in style," Michael Strickland in the *Georgia Review* notes, "Any serious consideration of Snyder's work, whether critical text or classroom study, must now include *The Practice of the Wild.*" Environmental writer Bill McKibben, commenting in the *New York Review of Books,* concurs, stating that the collection represents Snyder's "best prose work so far."

A Place in Space: Ethics, Aesthetics, and Watersheds, characterized by a reviewer for *Nature and Ecology* as a "grand summation of a life's work," is a collection of essays written over forty years, including thirteen new essays written since the publication of *The Practice of the Wild.* The book, which displays Snyder's playful and subtle intellect, also reiterates his ecological ethic. As a critic for *Booklist* notes, Snyder analyzes humanity's troubled relationship with the earth from this ecological perspective, incorporating his views as a Buddhist, an environmentalist, and a poet, and encourages readers to expand their own concept of community to include all life forms. The critic calls the essays "bracingly pragmatic and unerringly spiritual." A reviewer for the *New York Times Book Review* agrees, saying that "no one has written so forcefully against urban sprawl, pollution, and mechanization."

Critics and general readers alike have responded to Snyder's "new set of cultural possibilities." Steuding proposes that the writer's work "truly influences one who reads him thoroughly to 'see' in a startling new way. Presenting the vision of an integrated and unified world, this heroic poetic effort cannot but help to create a much needed change of consciousness." Writing in *Western Humanities Review,* Robert Mezey notes that Snyder "has a compelling vision of our relationship with this living nature, which is our nature, what it is and what it must be if we/nature survive on this planet, and his art serves that vision unwaveringly." According to Halvard Johnson in the *Minnesota Review,* the "unique power and value of Snyder's poetry lies not simply in clearly articulated images or in complex patterns of sound and rhythm, but rather in the freedom, the openness of spirit that permits the poems simply to be what they are, what they can be. . . . They respond to the rhythms of the world." Molesworth offers perhaps the most succinct appraisal of Gary Snyder's poetic vision. "Snyder has built a place for the mind to stay and to imagine more far-reaching harmonies while preserving all the wealth of the past," Molesworth concludes. "This, of course, is the world of his books where he is willing and even eager to give us another world both more ideal and more real than our own. The rest of the work is ours."

BIOGRAPHICAL/CRITICAL SOURCES:

BOOKS

Almon, Bert, *Gary Snyder,* Boise State University Press, 1979.
Altieri, Charles, *Enlarging the Temple: New Directions in American Poetry during the 1960s,* Bucknell University Press, 1979.
Contemporary Literary Criticism, Gale (Detroit), Volume 1, 1973; Volume 2, 1974; Volume 5, 1976; Volume 9, 1978; Volume 32, 1985.
Cook, Bruce, *The Beat Generation,* Scribner, 1971.
Dictionary of Literary Biography, Gale, Volume 5: *American Poets since World War II, First Series,* 1980; Volume 16:

The Beats: Literary Bohemians in Postwar America, 1983; Volume 165: *American Poets since World War II, Fourth Series,* 1996.

Faas, Ekbert, editor, *Towards a New American Poetics: Essays & Interviews,* Black Sparrow Press, 1978.

Leary, Paris, and Robert Kelly, editors, *A Controversy of Poets,* Doubleday, 1965.

McCord, Howard, *Some Notes to Gary Snyder's "Myths & Texts,"* Sand Dollar, 1971.

McNeill, Katherine, *Gary Snyder,* Phoenix, 1980.

Molesworth, Charles, *Gary Snyder's Vision: Poetry and the Real Work,* University of Missouri Press, 1983.

Rexroth, Kenneth, *Assays,* New Directions, 1961.

Rexroth, Kenneth, *American Poetry in the Twentieth Century,* Herder & Herder, 1971.

Schuler, Robert Jordan, *Journeys toward the Original Mind: The Long Poems of Gary Snyder,* Lang (New York), 1994.

Steuding, Bob, *Gary Snyder,* Twayne, 1976.

PERIODICALS

American Poetry Review, November, 1983.

American West, January-February, 1981; Volume 25, August, 1988, p. 30.

Booklist, September 15, 1996, p. 205.

Contemporary Literature, spring, 1977.

Critical Quarterly, winter, 1973.

Criticism, spring, 1977.

Denver Quarterly, fall, 1980.

Epoch: A Magazine of Contemporary Literature, fall, 1965.

Georgia Review, summer, 1992, p. 382.

Iowa Review, summer, 1970.

Journal of Modern Literature, Volume 2, 1971-72.

Kansas Quarterly, spring, 1970.

Kirkus Reviews, July 1, 1995, p. 933.

Library Journal, October 1, 1995, p. 83; April 1, 1997, p. 95.

Los Angeles Times, November 28, 1986.

Los Angeles Times Book Review, July 1, 1979; November 23, 1980; November 13, 1983; December 28, 1986.

Minnesota Review, fall, 1971.

Nation, September 1, 1969; November 19, 1983.

Nature and Ecology, June 1, 1997.

New Republic, April 4, 1970; March 24, 1997, p. 38.

New Statesman, November 4, 1966.

New York Review of Books, January 22, 1976; April 11, 1991, p. 29.

New York Times Book Review, May 11, 1969; June 8, 1969; March 23, 1975; December 27, 1992, p. 2.

New York Times Magazine, October 6, 1996, p. 62.

Partisan Review, summer, 1969; winter, 1971-72.

Poetry, June, 1971; June, 1972; September, 1984; June, 1994, p. 167.

Prairie Schooner, winter, 1960-61.

Progressive, November, 1995, p. 28.

Publishers Weekly, August 17, 1990, p. 62; August 10, 1992, p. 58; July 31, 1995, p. 62; August 26, 1996, p. 94; November 4, 1996, p. 47.

Sagetrieb, spring, 1984.

Saturday Review, October 11, 1969; April 3, 1971.

Southern Review, summer, 1968.

Southwest Review, spring, 1971; winter, 1976; spring, 1982.

Spectator, December 25, 1971.

Tamkang Review, spring, 1980.

Times Literary Supplement, December 24, 1971; May 30, 1980; February 21, 1997, p. 12.

Village Voice, November 17, 1966; May 1, 1984.

Washington Post Book World, December 25, 1983.

Western American Literature, fall, 1968; spring, 1980; fall, 1980; spring, 1981.

Western Humanities Review, spring, 1975.

Whole Earth Review, winter, 1988, p. 22; spring, 1991, p. 80; spring, 1996, p. 74.

World Literature Today, summer, 1984.

*   *   *

SOFTLY, Edgar
    See LOVECRAFT, H(oward) P(hillips)

*   *   *

SOFTLY, Edward
    See LOVECRAFT, H(oward) P(hillips)

*   *   *

SOLO, Jay
    See ELLISON, Harlan (Jay)

*   *   *

SOLWOSKA, Mara
    See FRENCH, Marilyn

*   *   *

SOLZHENITSYN, Aleksandr (Isayevich) 1918-

PERSONAL: Surname is pronounced "sohl-zhe-*neet*-sin"; born December 11, 1918, in Kislovodsk, Russia; immigrated to the United States, 1976; father was an artillery officer in World War I; mother was a typist and stenographer; married Natalya Reshetov-skaya (a professor and research chemist), April 27, 1940 (divorced), remarried, 1956 (divorced, 1972); married Natalya Svetlova (a mathematics teacher), April, 1973; children: (from third marriage) Yermolai, Ignat, Stephan (sons); Dmitri Turni (stepson). *Education:* Moscow Institute of History, Philosophy and Literature, correspondence course in philology, 1939-41; University of Rostov, degree in mathematics and physics, 1941. *Avocational interests:* Photography, bicycling, hiking, gardening.

ADDRESSES: Home—Moscow, Russia. *Agent*—c/o Farrar, Straus, & Giroux, 19 Union Square West, New York, NY 10003; c/o YMCA Press, 11 rue de la Montagne Sainte-Genevieve, 75005 Paris, France.

CAREER: Writer. First Secondary School, Morozovka, Rostov, USSR (now Russia), physics teacher, 1941; arrested 1945, while serving as commander in Soviet Army; sent to Greater Lubyanka Prison, Moscow, 1945; convicted of anti-Soviet actions and sentenced to eight years in prison; sent to Butyrki Prison, Moscow, and worked in construction, 1946; transferred to Marfino Prison and worked as mathematician in radio and telephone communications research, 1947-50; sent to Ekibastuz labor camp in Kazakhstan in Asian U.S.S.R., and worked as bricklayer and carpenter, 1950-53; released from prison, 1953;

exiled to Kok-Terek in Kazakhstan and worked as mathematics teacher; released from exile, 1956; teacher of mathematics and physics in Riazan, U.S.S.R., until early 1960s; banned from teaching and exiled from Moscow; arrested, 1974; sent to Lefortovo Prison and charged with treason, 1974; exiled from U.S.S.R., 1974-94. Lecturer; moderator of *A Meeting with Solzhenitsyn* (talk show), No. 1 (Russian state television channel), 1994-95. *Military service:* Soviet Army, 1941-45; became captain of artillery unit; decorated twice; stripped of rank and decorations when arrested (see above).

MEMBER: American Academy of Arts and Sciences, Russian Academy of Sciences, Hoover Institute on War, Revolution and Peace (honorary).

AWARDS, HONORS: Nominated for Lenin Prize, 1964; Prix du Meilleur Livre Etranger (France), 1969, for *The First Circle* and *Cancer Ward;* Nobel Prize for Literature, 1970; Freedoms Foundation Award, Stanford University, 1976; Templeton Prize for Progress in Religion, Templeton Foundation, 1983; Russian State Literature Prize, 1990; Medal of Honor for Literature, National Arts Club, 1993. Honorary degrees from various institutions, including Harvard University, 1978, and Holy Cross, 1984.

WRITINGS:

Odin den' Ivana Denisovicha (novella; first published in *Novy Mir,* 1962), Flegon Press (London), 1962, translated by Ralph Parker as *One Day in the Life of Ivan Denisovich,* Dutton, 1963.

Dlya polzy'dela (novella; first published in *Novy Mir,* 1963), Russian Language Specialties, 1963, translated by David Floyd and Max Hayward as *For the Good of the Cause,* Praeger, 1964.

Sluchay na stantsii Krechetovka [i] Matrenin dvor (novellas; titles mean "An Incident at Krechetovka Station" and "Matryona's House"; first published in *Novy Mir,* 1963), Flegon Press, 1963, translated by Paul W. Blackstock as *We Never Make Mistakes,* University of South Carolina Press, 1963.

"Ztiudy i Krokhotnye Rasskazy" (short story; first published in *Grani* [Frankfurt], 1964), published as *Krokhotnye Rasskazy,* Librarie des Cinq Continents (Paris), 1970.

Sochininiia (selected works), [Frankfurt], 1966.

V kruge pervom (novel), Harper, 1968, translated by Thomas P. Whitney as *The First Circle,* Harper, 1968.

Rakovyl korpus (novel), Bodley Head, 1968, translated by Nicholas Bethell and David Burg as *Cancer Ward* (two volumes), Bodley Head, 1968-69, published as *The Cancer Ward,* Farrar, Straus, 1969.

Olen'i shalashovka (play), Flegon Press, 1968, translated by Bethell and Burg as *The Love Girl and the Innocent,* Farrar, Straus, 1969.

Svecha na vetru (play), Flegon Press, 1968, translated by Keith Armes and Arthur Hudgins as *Candle in the Wind,* University of Minnesota Press, 1973.

Les Droits de l'ecrivain (title means "The Rights of the Writer"), Editions du Seuil (Paris), 1969.

Krasnoe koleso (multi-volume novel; title means "The Red Wheel"), Volume 1: *Avgust chetyrnadtsatogo,* Flegon Press, 1971, translated by Michael Glenny as *August 1914,* Farrar, Straus, 1972, revised edition, YMCA Press (Paris), 1983, translated by Harry Willetts, Farrar, Straus, 1989; Volume 2: *Oktyabr' shestnadtsatogo,* YMCA Press, 1984, translated by Willetts as *October 1916,* Farrar, Straus, c. 1985; Volume 3:

Mart semnadtsatogo, YMCA Press, 1986; Volume 4: *Aprel' semnadtsatogo,* YMCA Press, 1991.

Stories and Prose Poems by Aleksandr Solzhenitsyn, translated by Glenny, Farrar, Straus, 1971.

Six Etudes by Aleksandr Solzhenitsyn, translated by James G. Walker, College City Press, 1971.

Nobelevskara lektsira po literature, YMCA Press, 1972, English translation by F. D. Reeve published as *Nobel Lecture by Aleksandr Solzhenitsyn,* Farrar, Straus, 1972.

A Lenten Letter to Pimen, Patriarch of All Russia, translated by Theofanis G. Staurou, Burgess, 1972.

Arkhipelag Gulag, 1918-1956: Op 'bit khudozhestvennopo issledovaniia, YMCA Press, 1973, translated as *The Gulag Archipelago, 1918-1956: An Experiment in Literary Investigation,* Harper, Volume 1, translated by Thomas P. Whitney, 1974, Volume 2, translated by Whitney, 1976, Volume 3, translated by Willetts, 1979.

Mir i nasilie (title means "Peace and Violence"), [Frankfurt], 1974.

Prusskie nochi: pozma napisappaja v lagere v 1950 (title means "Prussian Nights: Epic Poems Written at the Forced Labor Camp, 1950"), YMCA Press, 1974.

Pis'mo vozhdram Sovetskogo Soruza, YMCA Press, 1974, translated by Hilary Sternberg as *Letter to the Soviet Leaders,* Harper, 1974.

(And photographer with others) *Solzhenitsyn: A Pictorial Autobiography,* Farrar, Straus, 1974.

Bodalsra telenok s dubom, YMCA Press, 1975, translated as *The Oak and the Calf,* Association Press, 1975, translated by Willetts as *The Oak and the Calf: Sketches of Literary Life in the Soviet Union,* Harper, 1980.

Lenin v Tsiurikhe, YMCA Press, 1975, translated by Willetts as *Lenin in Zurich,* Farrar, Straus, 1976.

Amerikanskie rechi (title means "American Speeches"), YMCA Press, 1975.

(With others) *From under the Rubble,* translated by Michael Scammell, Little, Brown, 1975, published as *From under the Ruins,* Association Press, 1975.

(With others) *Detente: Prospects for Democracy and Dictatorship,* Transaction Books, 1975.

Warning to the West, Farrar, Straus, 1976.

A World Split Apart (commencement address), Harper, 1979.

The Mortal Danger, Harper, 1981.

Victory Celebrations: A Comedy in Four Acts [and] *Prisoners: A Tragedy* (plays), translated by Helen Rapp and Nancy Thomas, Bodley Head, 1983.

Rasskazy (short stories), Sovremennik, 1990.

Kak nam obustroit' Rossiiu, YMCA Press, 1990, translated as *Rebuilding Russia: Reflections and Tentative Proposals,* Farrar, Straus, 1991.

Les Invisibles, Fayard, 1992, translated as *Invisible Allies,* Counterpoint, 1995.

The Russian Question Toward the End of the Century, Farrar, Straus, 1995.

Also author of unpublished works, including "The Right Hand" (story), "The Light That Is in You" (play), "The Tanks Know the Truth" (screenplay), "Feast of the Victors" (play). Contributor to periodicals, including *New Leader.*

MEDIA ADAPTATIONS: The Love Girl and the Innocent was adapted for the stage by Paul Avila Mayer as *A Play by Aleksandr Solzhenitsyn,* 1970.

SIDELIGHTS: Very rarely does an author burst so dramatically upon the world as the Russian Aleksandr Solzhenitsyn, who became famous seemingly overnight with the publication of his novella *One Day in the Life of Ivan Denisovich.* The first published Soviet work of its kind, the novella centers on the concentration camps in which millions died under dictator Joseph Stalin. *Ivan Denisovich,* which initially seemed to signal the beginning of relaxed Soviet censorship, instead contributed to the political demise of Premier Nikita Khrushchev, who supported de-Stalinization before being deposed in 1964. There followed a decade of creativity and conflict for Solzhenitsyn. Ultimately, this was to the chagrin of Soviet authorities, who deported him in 1974.

The paradoxes of Solzhenitsyn's life began very early. He never knew his father, who died in a hunting accident before Solzhenitsyn was born, and his mother, daughter of a wealthy landowner, was denied sufficient employment by the Soviet government. Thus mother and son lived in relative squalor from 1924 to 1936. Young Solzhenitsyn was a child of his era: the parades and speeches of the Pioneers, the Soviet equivalent of the Boy Scouts, had an effect on him, and he later joined the Communist Youth League. In *Solzhenitsyn: A Biography,* Michael Scammell quotes him as saying of this period: "Inside me I bore this social tension—on one hand, they used to tell me everything at home, and on the other, they used to work on our minds at school. And so this collision between two worlds gave birth to such social tensions within me that it somehow defined the path I was to follow for the rest of my life."

Perhaps it was such conflict that prompted Solzhenitsyn to begin writing in his youth. He had some sense of his literary ambition by the age of nine, and before he was eighteen he resolved to write a major novel about the Revolution. But he regrets that his literary education was haphazard and that he read little Western literature. Yet his aestheticism breaks out even in the most adverse conditions. After he was arrested in 1945 and sent to Moscow's notorious Lubyanka prison, which had a relatively good library, he read otherwise unobtainable works by such authors as Yevgeny Zamyatin, the great Soviet prose writer of the 1920s, and American novelist John Dos Passos, whose expressionist style later influenced Solzhenitsyn's own writing.

Solzhenitsyn turned to poetry in the years 1946 to 1950, when he was interred just outside of Moscow at a *sharashka,* or special prison. This was a unique creation of Stalinism—a high-level research institute in which all the scientists and technicians were prisoners. Because everything he wrote was subject to constant inspection, Solzhenitsyn composed poetry in his head and kept his memory precise by repeating certain portions of his verse each day. He continued to compose what was essentially oral poetry during the years 1950-1953, which he spent in a Central Asian concentration camp in Ekibastuz, Kazakhstan.

In March of 1953 Solzhenitsyn was released from the concentration camp and sent into exile in Kok-Terek in Central Asia, where he taught mathematics and physics in a secondary school. In Kok-Terek, he had pen and paper and wrote down both a long poem and some plays. He also began making notes for a novel. Freed from exile in April of 1956, he returned to central Russia, and, in September of the following year, took a position as a teacher of physics and astronomy in the city of Ryazan.

Ivan Denisovich presents a day in the life of a simple prisoner who wants only to serve out his sentence with a certain integrity. Solzhenitsyn's strategy was to reverse the usual procedure of

Socialist Realism, which imposed thoughts and feelings on its readers, and thus he rendered his tale in an ironic, understated, elliptical manner. His purpose with this sparse style was to elicit feelings, rather than impose them, as the official propaganda had done for so long. As Luellen Lucid explains in *Twentieth Century Literature,* Solzhenitsyn's *Ivan Denisovich* "deals in an allegorical manner with the reversal of the individual from citizen to political prisoner. The Soviet prison camp serves as a microcosm of the society at large," further notes the critic, "and metaphorically represents the repressive atmosphere which characterizes Soviet governance." During the course of one twenty-four hour period, readers share the dehumanizing existence within a Soviet prison camp; the novel's reading is an experience that is not easily forgotten.

With *Ivan Denisovich* Solzhenitsyn realized considerable success. The issue of *Novy Mir* in which the story appeared sold out immediately, and editor Tvardovsky kept asking Solzhenitsyn for new works. In 1963, Solzhenitsyn published three more stories in *Novy Mir:* "Matryona's House," a story about the quiet dignity of an elderly woman who had been his landlady; "Incident at Kochetovka Station," about an over-zealous young officer who turns an innocent man over to the secret police; and "For the Good of the Cause," which involves the abuse of power by local party officials.

The First Circle—the manuscript of which was confiscated by police during the raid on the author's archive that led to his expulsion from the U.S.S.R.—begins outside a prison with Innokenty Volodin, an idealistic young diplomat who makes a telephone call to the American Embassy, a call that eventually results in his arrest and imprisonment in a *sharashka.* The principal prisoners are Lev Rubin, a Jew and a dedicated Communist; Dmitry Sologdin, an engineer and idiosyncratic spiritual teacher; and Gleb Nerzhin, a scientist and aspiring writer. At the end of the novel, Nerzhin is taken away to a far more difficult camp, Sologdin is about to gain a pardon, and Rubin is kept behind. In the novel, "Solzhenitsyn examines both the omnipresence of lying as a demonstrable feature of Soviet society and as a metaphysical, demonic device," according to David M. Halperin in an article published in *Alexandr Solzhenitsyn: Critical Essays and Documentary Materials.* "By uniting these two aspects of the Lie, he has effectively forged his central metaphor—Hell; for it is from Stalin just as from the devil that lies emanate to poison a whole society." With *The First Circle* Solzhenitsyn countered stifling Socialist Realism by relating his work to both Russian classics and Western culture. The three principal prisoners each correspond to the siblings of Dostoyevsky's *Brothers Karamazov,* while the Stalinist *sharashka*—and the title itself—recall the first circle of hell in Dante's *Inferno.*

Like *The First Circle, Cancer Ward* presents an isolated environment. The latter novel, drawing a parallel between the hospital and Soviet society, thus constitutes another meditation on the human condition. The work's principal protagonists present two extremes, yet their illness makes them draw back into themselves instead of widening their sympathies and understanding. Pavel Rusanov, a bureaucrat with connections to the secret police, expects special treatment and deference, while Oleg Kostoglotov, a former camp inmate, tolerates no elitism. Both benefit from their treatment, but each leaves the hospital with unchanged attitudes.

Citing the influence of Chekhov's short story "Ward 6," wherein a sane doctor is imprisoned in a ward for the mentally dysfunctional as a symbol of the corruption of the Soviet state, reviewer Jeffrey

Meyers calls *Cancer Ward* "the most complete and accurate fictional account of the nature of disease and its relation to love." Its author uses his personal military experience as "a metaphor for both the invasion of the hostile disease and the victim's desperate battle against it," aligning the progress of the disease with the gradual dehumanization that occurs in a prison camp, as well as with the spread of Stalinism, continues the critic in his *Twentieth Century Literature* review. "The remission of Kostoglotov's disease in the spring of 1955 coincides with the political thaw that began to take place . . . after the death of Stalin," Meyers concludes, adding that "Kostoglotov's life shows that dictators, party officials, police, guards, and prisoners are all trapped in the vast prison of Russia. There is no escape from cancer, despite periods of remission, just as there is no escape from the legacy of Stalinism, despite the political thaw."

Most Western critics agree that Solzhenitsyn's most important work of nonfiction is *The Gulag Archipelago,* a detailed account of Stalinist repression. *Gulag* is predicated on the fact that arrest and torture were everyday practices in the Soviet Union. Solzhenitsyn proceeds as a scientist might, creating a taxonomy of arrests and tortures. In one passage, he even invites readers to participate with him in deciding which forms of torture belong in which categories. He makes his narrative vivid and direct. Again and again, he speaks of his own experiences, such as his arrest and confinement in different prisons and concentration camps. He also includes many personal narratives, replete with horrifying detail from other victims of arbitrary violence.

Solzhenitsyn's most famous work "is not only a report, a record for history," according to Alla Braithwaite in the *Month*. His "mood is one of reflection about his data but also of confession." Likening the work to Augustine's *Confessions,* the critic contends that the Russian author "recognizes that wickedness is not simply an individual phenomenon. He confesses the sins of his people as well as the nation. Confession is salutary and necessary. There can be no healing without it." As Solzhenitsyn writes in *Gulag,* "Only through repentance of a multitude of people can the air and soil of Russia be cleansed, so that a new, healthy national life can grow up."

Within the pages of *Gulag* Solzhenitsyn repeatedly finds all Russians—including himself—accountable for the horrors of Stalinism. "We didn't love freedom enough," he writes at one point. "We purely and simply deserved everything that happened afterward." He also observes that "the line dividing good and evil cuts through the heart of every human being." A lesson of *Gulag,* then, is that to divide the world into good and evil is itself a fallacy and evil.

Solzhenitsyn wrote *Gulag* between 1964 and 1968. Through intermediaries, he sent the manuscript to Paris, where it was published on December 28, 1973. A few months later he was expelled from the Soviet Union. The period that extended from the early 1960s through publication of *Gulag* and its author's subsequent exile from Russia would later be documented by Solzhenitsyn in *Invisible Allies*. A section omitted from the 1975 publication of his memoir *The Oak and the Calf, Invisible Allies* was finally published after the fall of communism lifted any threat of Soviet retaliation against persons still living in the Soviet Union. Like its parent volume, the memoir addresses the questions of many Western readers: With the constant harassment by government authorities and the surveillance of state security, how was the writer able to complete his work? Who helped him type manuscripts (*The First Circle* was, by this account, retyped nine

separate times), edit, microfilm, and smuggle his texts to the West for publication? Solzhenitsyn mentions more than a hundred individuals who helped him, several of which, including typist Elizaveta Voronyanskaya, lost their lives as a result. The work also provides another glimpse of the inner character of its reclusive author. "Solzhenitsyn emerges as a person whose deepest identity is that of a former political prisoner," notes *Washington Post Book World* reviewer Lars T. Lih. For Solzhenitsyn, "the world is cleanly divided into the good versus those who helped the communists." While the writer's aversion to communism is clearly manifested, "his religiosity and his 'love of Russia' come across as somewhat pale, almost an affectation," Lih continues. Western readers "cannot help being moved by Solzhenitsyn's uncompromising defiance," notes the critic. "Those who are tempted to make an icon of him must deal with his unabashed disdain for Westerners in general, whom he regards as all petty and hard hearted, except for a few whose contact with Russians allows them temporarily to rise above themselves."

In 1970 Solzhenitsyn received the Nobel Prize for literature, but he had only just begun what he thought of as his life's work—a multi-volume novel to be known as *The Red Wheel.* Much of *August 1914,* the first volume in the series, centers on the battle of Tannenberg, which is filtered through the eyes of two important characters in the entire *Red Wheel:* Colonel Georgy Vorotyntsev, a graduate of the Russian equivalent of West Point, and Arseny Blagodaryov, an enlisted man whom Vorotyntsev befriends. Vorotyntsev and Blagodaryov see various kinds of action, ultimately serving with a group of Russian soldiers who are surrounded by advancing German troops and who succeed in breaking through enemy lines.

Partly due to its narrative complexity, *August 1914* received mixed responses from critics—Irving Howe would deem it a "swollen and misshapen book" in his *New York Times Book Review* article—and charges of anti-Semitism were even brought against the author. Many parallels were also drawn with Tolstoy's masterwork *War and Peace.* Likening Solzhenitsyn's ambitious project, of which *August 1914* is a part, to a geological formation, Geoffrey A. Hosking notes of the novel that its author's intent is to illustrate "why [the U.S.S.R.'s] economic growth took place in a lopsided and debilitating manner, why Siberia remained relatively undeveloped, and above all why Russians started disembowelling each other in great numbers. The root of all this," Solzhenitsyn concluded, was the Russian Revolution of 1917. "His narrative and historical method is to take the decisive turning-points and explain them from all sides," continues Hosking in his *Times Literary Supplement* piece. "The result . . . is [what] he describes as a 'dense, all-round exposition of the events of a brief time span.'"

The second *Red Wheel* volume, *October 1916* (currently available only in a Russian-language edition) is approximately twice as long as *August 1914* and contains proportionately more characters, thereby creating a society in all its intriguing variety. If *August 1914* is a war novel, then *October 1916* is a peace novel. It presents very little military action but emphasizes the effect of the war on the home front. Among the various storylines is one involving Vorotyntsev, who is married but nonetheless falls in love with a woman professor at Petrograd University.

The Russian-language publication of *March 1917* in 1986 and 1987 marked another major change in the emphasis of *The Red Wheel.* In this extraordinarily long volume—it occupies four books and runs to well over two thousand pages—the fictional characters all but disappear. There are a few isolated chapters on Vorotyntsev in Moscow, but virtually all the action takes place in revolutionary Petrograd, and virtually all the characters are historical ones. Politicians such as Pavel Milyukov and Vasily Maklakov connive and deal, generals consult each other, and members of the imperial family convey their uncertainty and anxiety. There are scenes of public confusion and domestic tranquility. Solzhenitsyn minutely details various episodes, describing weather and clothing as well as actions and emotions. He therefore allows his readers to experience what happens when a society slowly but inexorably falls apart.

In 1974 Solzhenitsyn was exiled from Russia, having run afoul of the communist authorities one time too many. He spent the next two decades living and writing in relative seclusion in rural Vermont, though his few public pronouncements on both the evils of communism and the spiritual emptiness of the West raised periodic storms of controversy. After twenty years in exile, Solzhenitsyn returned to his homeland in May of 1994. Viewing Russia's troubled past from an altered perspective after the fall of communism, he attempted to grapple with the problems of its future in 1995's *The Russian Question at the End of the Twentieth Century*. Viewing the roots of the country's downfall as 1) expanding beyond the natural boundaries delineated by the Black Sea and the Pacific and Arctic Oceans, and 2) the process of gradual Westernization that began during the reign of Peter Romanov (Solzhenitsyn refuses to augment the stature of this eighteenth-century Russian leader through use of his time-honored status as "the Great"), he proposes reuniting the three major Slavic areas—Russia, the Ukraine, and Belarus—and seeks to reaffirm what he describes as the traditional Russian mindset: simple wants, fatalism, humility, compassion, and what the writer characterizes as "a trusting resignation." "Solzhenitsyn's fundamental reproach to [Western civilization's] clumsy, myriad lords is that they are bad, improvident imperialists. And he himself is provident, that's the whole difference," writes Tatyana Tolstaya in a review of *The Russian Question* in the *New York Review of Books*. "That wasn't the way to make war, those weren't the people to hang out with, to believe. If they'd listened to him, everything would have been different." While acknowledging the noted writer's contributions to the downfall of communism, Tolstaya opines that his political views have become outdated, his dwindling numbers of still-enthusiastic followers inviting comparison with "religious zealots" in their continued support of his separatist notions of withdrawing from the global society that many see as the planet's inevitable future. "It is not the text that is extolled," the critic maintains of the aging Solzhenitsyn's more recent works, "but the author, may his name live in glory throughout the ages, Amen."

BIOGRAPHICAL/CRITICAL SOURCES:

BOOKS

Allaback, Steven, *Alexander Solzhenitsyn,* Taplinger, 1978.
Barker, Francis, *Solzhenitsyn: Politics and Form,* Barnes & Noble, 1977.
Carter, Stephen, *The Politics of Solzhenitsyn,* Macmillan, 1977.
Contemporary Literary Criticism, Gale (Detroit), Volume 1, 1973; Volume 2, 1974; Volume 4, 1975; Volume 7, 1977; Volume 9, 1978; Volume 10, 1979; Volume 18, 1981; Volume 26, 1983; Volume 34, 1985; Volume 78, 1994.
Curtis, James M., *Solzhenitsyn's Traditional Imagination,* University of Georgia Press, 1984.

Dunlop, John B., and others, editors, *Solzhenitsyn in Exile: Critical Essays and Documentary Materials,* Hoover Institution Press, 1985.
Ericson, Edward E., *Solzhenitsyn: The Moral Vision,* Eerdmans, 1982.
Fiene, Donald M., *Alexander Solzhenitsyn: An International Bibliography of Writings By and About Him, 1962-1973,* Ardis, 1973.
Flegon, A., *Alexander Solzhenitsyn: Myth and Reality,* Flegon Press, 1986.
Kelly, Donald R., *The Solzhenitsyn-Sakharov Dialogue: Politics, Society, and the Future,* Greenwood Press, 1982.
Krasnov, Vladislav, *Solzhenitsyn and Dostoevsky: A Study in the Polyphonic Novel,* Prior, 1980.
Pontuso, James F., *Solzhenitsyn's Political Thought,* University Press of Virginia, 1990.
Scammell, Michael, *Solzhenitsyn: A Biography,* Norton, 1984.
Scammell, Michael, editor, *The Solzhenitsyn Files: Secret Soviet Documents Reveal One Man's Fight against the Monolith,* Edition q (Chicago), 1995.

PERIODICALS

America, November 16, 1996, p. 112.
American Spectator, October, 1995, p. 70; February, 1996, p. 64.
Atlantic Monthly, January, 1996, p. 112.
Booklist, December 15, 1997, p. 666.
Forbes, May 9, 1994, pp. 10, 118.
Journal of Contemporary History, September 1991, pp. 611-36.
Listener, May 26, 1983, pp. 2-4.
Modern Age, spring/summer 1984, pp. 215-21; fall 1989, pp. 294-310; spring 1995, pp. 233-40.
Month, May, 1990, pp. 179-85.
Nation, October 7, 1968; February 17, 1992, pp. 202-5.
National Review, October 15, 1976; September 23, 1991; September 26, 1994, p. 78; April 8, 1996, p. 62.
New Leader, December 18, 1995, p. 16.
New Perspectives Quarterly, fall 1991; spring 1994.
New Republic, May 11, 1963; August 28, 1989, pp. 33-37; June 29, 1992.
New Statesman, December 8, 1995, p. 28.
New Yorker, August 14, 1971; February 14, 1994, p. 64.
New York Review of Books, December 19, 1968; December 21, 1989, pp. 11-13; November 24, 1991; February 7, 1993; October 19, 1995, p. 7.
New York Times Book Review, September 15, 1968; September 10, 1972; March 3, 1974; July 2, 1989, pp. 1, 17-18; January 7, 1996, p. 14; October 6, 1996, p. 111.
Saturday Review, August 23, 1975.
Solzhenitsyn Studies.
Soviet Studies, October 1982, pp. 601-15.
Times Literary Supplement, February 3, 1984, pp. 99-100; January 26, 1996, p. 3.
Twentieth Century Literature, December, 1977, pp. 498-517; spring 1983, pp. 54-68.
Washington Post Book World, February 16, 1992, p. 7; December 31, 1995, pp. 1, 10.

*   *   *

SOMERS, Jane
See LESSING, Doris (May)

SONTAG, Susan 1933-

PERSONAL: Born January 16, 1933, in New York, NY; married Philip Rieff (a professor of sociology), 1950 (divorced, 1958); children: David. *Education:* Attended University of California, Berkeley, 1948-49; University of Chicago, B.A., 1951; Harvard University, M.A. (English), 1954, M.A. (philosophy), 1955, Ph.D. candidate, 1955-57; St. Anne's College, Oxford, graduate study, 1957.

ADDRESSES: Office—The Wylie Agency, 250 W. 57th St., Suite 2114, New York, NY 10107.

CAREER: University of Connecticut, Storrs, instructor in English, 1953-54; *Commentary,* New York City, editor, 1959; lecturer in philosophy, City College (now City College of the City University of New York), New York City, and Sarah Lawrence College, Bronxville, NY, 1959-60; Columbia University, New York City, instructor in department of religion, 1960-64; Rutgers University, New Brunswick, NJ, writer-in-residence, 1964-65. Novelist, short-story writer, critic, and essayist. Director of motion pictures *Duet for Cannibals,* 1969, *Brother Carl: A Filmscript,* 1971, and *Promised Lands,* 1974.

MEMBER: PEN American Center (president, 1987-89), American Academy of Arts and Letters, American Academy of Arts and Sciences (elected 1993).

AWARDS, HONORS: Fellowships from American Association of University Women, 1957, Rockefeller Foundation, 1966, 1974, Guggenheim Memorial Foundation, 1966, 1975, MacArthur Foundation, 1990-95; George Polk Memorial Award, 1966, for contributions toward better appreciation of theater, motion pictures, and literature; National Book Award nomination, 1966, for *Against Interpretation, and Other Essays;* Brandeis University Creative Arts Award, 1975; National Institute and American Academy award for literature, 1976; National Book Critics Circle prize for criticism, 1978, for *On Photography;* named Officier de l'Ordre des Arts et des Lettres, France, 1984; Malaparte Prize, 1992.

WRITINGS:

NONFICTION

Against Interpretation, and Other Essays, Farrar, Straus, 1966.
Styles of Radical Will, Farrar, Straus, 1969.
Trip to Hanoi, Farrar, Straus, 1969.
(Contributor) Douglas A. Hughes, editor, *Perspectives on Pornography,* St. Martin's, 1970.
(Author of introduction) Dugald Stermer, compiler, *The Art of Revolution,* McGraw-Hill, 1970.
(Author of introduction) E. M. Cioran, *The Temptation to Exist,* translated by Richard Howard, Quadrangle, 1970.
(Editor and author of introduction) *Antonin Artaud: Selected Writings,* Farrar, Straus, 1976.
On Photography, Farrar, Straus, 1977.
Illness as Metaphor, Farrar, Straus, 1978.
Under the Sign of Saturn, Farrar, Straus, 1980.
(Editor and author of introduction) *A Barthes Reader,* Farrar, Straus, 1982.
A Susan Sontag Reader, introduction by Elizabeth Hardwick, Farrar, Straus, 1982.
(With Cesare Colombo) *Italy: One Hundred Years of Photography,* Alinari, 1988.
AIDS and Its Metaphors, Farrar, Straus, 1989.
Cage-Cunningham-Johns: Dancers on a Plane, Knopf, 1990.

(Author of introduction) Danilo Kies, editor, *Homo Poeticus: Essays and Interviews,* Farrar, Straus, 1995.
(Contributor) Michael Auping et al., *Howard Hodgkin Paintings,* Harry N. Abrams Publishers in association with The Modern Art Museum of Forth Worth, 1995.
(Author of introduction) *Photographs from Storyville, the Red-Light District of New Orleans,* J. Cape (London), 1996.
(With Robert Wilson and Vittorio Santoro) *Rwwm: On Robert Wilson's Production Site Watermill,* Distributed Art, 1997.
(With Mikhail Lemkhin and Czeslaw Milosz) *Fragments: Joseph Brodsky, Leningrad,* Farrar, Straus, 1998.

FICTION

The Benefactor (novel), Farrar, Straus, 1963.
Death Kit (novel), Farrar, Straus, 1967.
I, etcetera (short stories), Farrar, Straus, 1978.
The Volcano Lover: A Romance (novel), Farrar, Straus, 1992.

SCREENPLAYS

Duet for Cannibals (produced by Sandrew Film & Teater AB [Sweden], 1969), Farrar, Straus, 1970.
Brother Carl: A Filmscript (produced by Sandrew Film & Teater AB and Svenska Filminstitutet [Sweden], 1971), Farrar, Straus, 1974.

OTHER

Alice in Bed: A Play in Eight Scenes (play), Farrar, Straus, 1993.
The Way We Live Now, Farrar, Straus, 1991.
Conversations with Susan Sontag, edited by Leland A. Poague, University Press of Mississippi (Jackson), 1995.

Also author of *Literature* (monograph), 1966; and the screenplays *Promised Lands,* 1974 and *Unguided Tour,* 1983. Contributor to *Great Ideas Today,* 1966; also contributor of short stories, reviews, essays, and articles to numerous periodicals, including *Atlantic Monthly, American Review, Playboy, Partisan Review, Nation, Commentary, Harper's,* and *New York Review of Books.*

SIDELIGHTS: Susan Sontag is an American intellectual whose works on modernist writing and Western culture form an important critical canon. Considered "one of the few bold and original minds to be found among the younger critics," to quote *Partisan Review* contributor William Phillips, Sontag has penned controversial essays on topics ranging from "camp" to cancer, encompassing her views on literature, plays, film, photography, and politics. Though best known for her nonfiction, the author has also written novels and short stories and has written and directed several films; in an introduction to *A Susan Sontag Reader,* Elizabeth Hardwick calls Sontag a "foraging pluralist" who is attracted to "waywardness," "outrageousness," and "the unpredictable, along with extremity." *New York Times Book Review* correspondent David Bromwich notes that her "subjects bear witness to Miss Sontag's range as well as her diligence. She keeps up—appears, at times, to do the keeping-up for a whole generation. . . . From ground to summit, from oblivion to oblivion, she covers the big movements and ideas and then sends out her report, not without qualms. For the art she most admires, an inward and recalcitrant art, exists in tension with her own role as its advocate." According to Susan Walker in the *Dictionary of Literary Biography,* Sontag's career as a writer "has been marked by a seriousness of pursuit and a relentless intelligence that analyzes modern culture on almost every possible level: artistic, philosophical, literary, political, and moral. . . . Sontag has produced a stimulating and varied body of work which entertains the issues of art while satisfying the rigors of her own intellect."

Sontag has been a shaper of contemporary criticism through her call for a new formal aestheticism. Michiko Kakutani observes in the *New York Times* that Sontag argues "that art and morality have no common ground, that it is style, not content, that matters most of all." Likewise, *Saturday Review* contributor Edward Grossman suggests that Sontag takes "distinctions between art and science, between high and low, to be largely, though not entirely, false and irrelevant," and she also dismisses the "old, mainly literary notion that art is the criticism of life." According to Stanley Aronowitz in the *Voice Literary Supplement*, Sontag's reactions "against the dessication of literature by sociology," seen especially in her works *Against Interpretation, and Other Essays* and *Styles of Radical Will,* have offered "a liberating vision." Although her ideas have evolved over the more than twenty years she has been writing, Sontag is still deeply involved in aesthetic awareness and is an advocate of sensuous perception of the arts. *Commentary* essayist Alicia Ostriker notes, however, that as an author, Sontag "is distinguished less by a decided or passionate point of view. . . than by an eagerness to explore anything new." Ostriker concludes: "Sensitive people are a dime a dozen. The rarer gift Miss Sontag has to offer is brains."

As a young critic writing for *Partisan Review, Harper's,* the *Nation* and the *New York Review of Books,* Sontag became known as a champion of European artists and thinkers. *Chicago Tribune Book World* contributor Seymour Krim writes: "Although she was reared in Arizona and California, . . . Sontag has been much more at home with modern Europe than with this country. She made this plain . . . when she gave us fresh studies of such people as Simone Weil, Camus, Sartre, Marxist critic Georg Lukacs, Nathalie Sarraute, Eugene Ionesco, etc. In Sontag's hands the distant and blurred became sharp and immediate, and [she] . . . is a trail-blazer of what might be called America's new cultural internationalism." In a *New Republic* review, Leo Braudy states that Sontag's particular polemic has been "to celebrate the leopards in the temple of literature, not those cool and calm consciousnesses . . . who abided all questions and saw life whole, but those whose own derangement allowed them to explode the lies of order so that better forms might be discovered. In her criticism she labors to turn even the most self-isolating, uncompromising, and personally outrageous of such figures . . . into humane teachers, whose flame, all the brighter for being trimmed, she will pass on to future generations." With a tone of "eminent rationality," to quote Wendy Lesser in *Threepenny Review,* Sontag has acquainted readers with "the artist as exemplary sufferer" and with "the fragmentation, exaggeration, morbidity, and lunacy with which art has responded to the modern world."

From case studies of neglected artists, Sontag moved to theoretical essays on the aims of modern art and the relationship between art and criticism. Her works "encourage, in art and criticism, . . . respect for sensuous surfaces, for feeling, for form, for style," according to Ostriker. A *Times Literary Supplement* reviewer observes that in *Against Interpretation, and Other Essays,* Sontag "is tired of interpretive criticism and mimetic art. . . . She proposes instead an art which is joyously itself and a criticism which enthusiastically dwells on the fact." John S. Peterson elaborates in the *Los Angeles Times:* "Sontag has argued that critical interpretation tends to be stifling and reactionary, and that the job of the critic is not to assign 'meanings' but to show how a work of art is what it is. Her own writings [are] not to be regarded as criticism, strictly speaking, but as case studies for an aesthetic, a theory of her own sensibility." *Nation* essayist Robert Sklar suggests that Sontag makes this aesthetic criticism a form of philosophical inquiry: "Art, particularly the language arts, are

themselves caught in the trap of consciousness. When consciousness as we know it is destroyed, art as we know it will also come to an end—art as expression or representation, art as truth and beauty. The 'minimal art' of our own time, in painting, sculpture, the new novel, already aims, in this sense, at the abolition of art." Sklar concludes that Sontag's "form of prophecy and critical insight, this mode of radical will, can be extremely clarifying and stimulating for the willing reader."

Against Interpretation, and Other Essays and *Styles of Radical Will,* both published in the 1960s, assured Sontag a wide and controversial reputation. In the *Atlantic Monthly,* Hilton Kramer describes how the American intellectual community reacted to her works: "Sontag seemed to have an unfailing faculty for dividing intellectual opinion and inspiring a sense of outrage, consternation, and betrayal among the many readers—especially older readers—who disagreed with her. And it was just this faculty for offending respectable opinion that, from the outset, was an important part of her appeal for those who welcomed her pronouncements. She was admired not only for what she said but for the pain, shock, and disarray she caused in saying it. Sontag thus succeeded in doing something that is given to very few critics to achieve. She made criticism a medium of intellectual scandal, and this won her instant celebrity in the world where ideas are absorbed into fashions and fashions combine to create a new cultural atmosphere." Phillips contends that since Sontag was taken as a spokesperson for "The New," she was perceived "as someone to take a stand for or against. Hence, as with so many of the younger writers, the reactions to her have fallen into the stereotypes of polarization. But because she is so articulate and takes all questions as her theoretical province, because her writing has political as well as literary implications, the polarization is both sharper and more distorting. Susan Sontag is both an exponent and a victim of the new polarization; an exponent in that she doesn't go in for modulation and adjustment, a victim because her concern with speculative and literary problems often falls outside the prevailing left-right fashions."

A near-fatal case of cancer interrupted Sontag's career in the early 1970s, but as she recovered she wrote two of her best-known works, *On Photography* and *Illness as Metaphor.* In the *Washington Post Book World,* William McPherson describes *On Photography* as "a brilliant analysis of the profound changes photographic images have made in our way of looking at the world, and at ourselves over the last 140 years. . . . *On Photography* merely describes a phenomenon we take as much for granted as water from the tap, and how that phenomenon has changed us—a remarkable enough achievement, when you think about it." William H. Gass offers even stronger praise for the National Book Critics Circle prize-winning work in the *New York Times Book Review.* Every page of *On Photography,* writes Gass, "raises important and exciting questions about its subject and raises them in the best way. In a context of clarity, skepticism and passionate concern, with an energy that never weakens but never blusters, and with an admirable pungency of thought and directness of expression that sacrifices nothing of subtlety or refinement, Sontag encourages the reader's cooperation in her enterprise. . . . The book understands exactly the locale and the level of its argument." *Time* columnist Robert Hughes expresses a similar opinion. "It is hard to imagine any photographer's agreeing point for point with Sontag's polemic," Hughes concludes. "But it is a brilliant, irritating performance, and it opens window after window on one of the great *faits accomplis* of our culture. Not many photographers are worth a thousand of her words."

Illness as Metaphor is not an autobiographical account of Sontag's own experience with cancer, but rather an examination of the cultural myths that have developed around certain diseases, investing them with meaning beyond mere human debilitation. *New Republic* contributor Edwin J. Kenney, Jr. calls the book "a critical analysis of our habitual, unconscious, and even pathological ways of conceptualizing illness and of using the vocabulary of illness to articulate our feelings about other crises, economic, political, and military. Sontag is seeking to go behind the language of the mind to expose and clarify the assumptions and fears the language masks; she wants to liberate us from the terrors that issue not from disease itself, but from our ways of imagining it." Braudy writes: "In *Illness as Metaphor* [Sontag] condemns the way we have used metaphoric language to obscure and mystify the physical and material world, turning diseases into imagery, metamorphosing the final reality of bodily decay and death into the shrouded fantasies of moral pollution and staining sin." Writing in the *Atlantic Monthly*, Benjamin DeMott claims that the work "isn't conceived as an act of conversion. It presents itself as an attack on some corrupt uses of language. In a series of ten meditations on the human failure to grasp that sickness is not a metaphor, not a sign standing in for something else, not a symbol of a moral or cultural condition, Miss Sontag develops the thesis that it is therefore wrong to use sickness as a means of interpreting the character of either individuals or nations."

Sontag's novels, *The Benefactor* and *Death Kit,* have received mixed reviews. Both works "emphasize fiction as a construct of words rather than as a mimesis," to quote Leon S. Roudiez's appraisal in *World Literature Today.* In a *New Republic* piece, Stanley Kauffmann calls *The Benefactor* "a skillful amalgam of a number of continental sources in fiction and thought" and adds that it contains "a good deal of well fashioned writing." Kauffmann maintains, however, that the book "remains a neat knowledgeable construct, reclining on the laboratory table." Conversely, Alfred Kazin feels that the novel "works because its author really sees the world as a series of propositions *about* the world. Her theoreticalness consists of a loyalty not to certain ideas but to life as the improvisation of ideas. She is positive only about moving on from those ideas, and this makes her an interesting fantasist about a world conceived as nothing but someone thinking up new angles to it." *New York Review of Books* essayist Denis Donoghue finds *Death Kit* "an extremely ambitious book," but notes that it is "undermined by the fact that its ideas never become its experience: the ideas remain external, like the enforced correlation of dream and act in *The Benefactor.*" Maureen Howard, on the other hand, praises *Death Kit* in a *Saturday Review* column. "The writing is vigorous, the plot highly imaginative," Howard claims. "*Death Kit . . .* is about the endless and insane demands put upon us to choose coherence and life over chaos and death."

Some critics express reservations about Sontag's work, most notably about her critical stance and her highly erudite presentations. For instance, writing in the *Nation,* Walter Kendrick claims that the author's "eminence in American letters is disproportionate to the quality of her thought" because "she perpetuates a tradition of philosophical naivete that has always kept America subservient to Europe and that surely should have run its course by now." *Saturday Review* correspondent James Sloan Allen calls Sontag "a virtuoso of the essay, the Paganini of criticism," who "has often overwhelmed her subjects and intimidated her readers with intellectual pyrotechniques, pretentious erudition, and cliquish hauteur. Lacking has been the quality of mind that deals in modern but sure understanding rather than bravura." Donoghue

offers a similar opinion in the *New York Times Book Review:* "Her mind is powerful rather than subtle; it is impatient with nuances that ask to be heard, with minute discriminations that, if entertained, would impede the march of her argument." In his book *The Confusion of Realms,* Richard Gilman states that while Sontag's essays are "true extensions of our awareness," they nevertheless reveal that beneath the "clean-functioning, superbly armed processes of her thought exists a confused, importunate, scarcely acknowledged desire that culture, the culture she knows so much about, be other than it is in order for her to be other than she is."

"Thinking about Susan Sontag in the middle of her career is to feel the happiness of more, more, nothing ended," writes Hardwick. Indeed, although a compendium of her work was published in 1982 as *A Susan Sontag Reader,* the author continues to write, especially fiction. In the *Village Voice,* Kendrick suggests that Sontag is engaged in the lifetime project of "making a multifaceted creative and critical presence of herself." She undertakes this task with very exacting standards, as she told the *New York Times Book Review:* "Of course, I want readers, and I want my work to matter. Above all I don't just want the work to be good enough to last, I want it to *deserve* survival. That's a very great ambition because one knows that 99.9 percent of everything that's written at any given time is not going to last." Still in her fifties, Sontag remains a prominent figure in the American literary community; her presence in the intellectual world is felt through speeches as well as writings. Reflecting on her accomplishments in the *Threepenny Review,* Sontag once said, "What readers do with it, whether I am (as I hope) making work which will last— my part ends with my doing the best I can."

BIOGRAPHICAL/CRITICAL SOURCES:

BOOKS

Contemporary Literary Criticism, Gale (Detroit), Volume 1, 1973; Volume 2, 1974; Volume 10, 1979; Volume 13, 1980; Volume 31, 1985.

Dictionary of Literary Biography, Gale, Volume 2: *American Novelists since World War II,* 1978; Volume 67: *Modern American Critics since 1955,* 1988.

Gilman, Richard, *The Confusion of Realms,* Random House, 1970.

Kazin, Alfred, *Bright Book of Life: American Novelists and Storytellers from Hemingway to Mailer,* Little, Brown, 1973.

Kennedy, Liam, *Susan Sontag: Mind as Passion,* Manchester University Press (Manchester, UK), 1995.

Sayres, Sohnya, *Susan Sontag: The Elegaic Modernist,* Routledge, 1990.

Smith, Sharon, *Women Who Make Movies,* Hopkinson & Blake, 1975.

Solotaroff, Theodore, *The Red Hot Vacuum,* Atheneum, 1970.

Vidal, Gore, *Reflections upon a Sinking Ship,* Little, Brown, 1969.

PERIODICALS

Antioch Review, spring, 1978.

Atlantic Monthly, September, 1966; November, 1978; September, 1982; November, 1992, p. 162.

Best Sellers, April, 1979.

Chicago Tribune Book World, December 10, 1978; October 19, 1980; January 9, 1983.

College English, February, 1986.

Commentary, June, 1966.

Commonweal, February 3, 1978.

Detroit News, January 15, 1967.

Encounter, November, 1978.

Esquire, July, 1968; February, 1978.

Harper's, January, 1979; February, 1983.

Hudson Review, autumn, 1969; summer, 1983; spring, 1993, pp. 247-55.

Library Journal, July, 1993, p. 82.

Los Angeles Times, December 22, 1980.

Los Angeles Times Book Review, November 19, 1978; December 12, 1982.

Ms., March, 1979.

Nation, October 2, 1967; March 24, 1969; June 2, 1969; October 23, 1982; May 1, 1989, p. 598; October 5, 1992, pp. 365-68.

New Republic, September 21, 1963; February 19, 1966; September 2, 1967; May 3, 1969; January 21, 1978; July 8, 1978; November 25, 1978; November 29, 1980; December 26, 1988, pp. 28-33.

New Statesman, March 24, 1967.

Newsweek, December 5, 1977; June 12, 1978; October 11, 1982.

New Yorker, May 31, 1993, pp. 142-49.

New York Review of Books, June 9, 1966; September 28, 1967; March 13, 1969; July 20, 1978; January 25, 1979; November 6, 1980.

New York Times, August 18, 1967; February 4, 1969; May 2, 1969; October 3, 1969; November 14, 1977; January 30, 1978; June 1, 1978; November 11, 1978; October 13, 1980; November 11, 1980.

New York Times Book Review, September 8, 1963; January 23, 1966; August 27, 1967; July 13, 1969; February 13, 1972; December 18, 1977; July 16, 1978; November 26, 1978; November 23, 1980; September 12, 1982; October 24, 1982; January 22, 1989, p. 11; March 1, 1992, p. 20.

Partisan Review, summer, 1968; Volume 36, number 3, 1969.

Psychology Today, July, 1978.

Publishers Weekly, October 22, 1982.

Salmagundi, fall, 1975.

Saturday Review, February 12, 1966; August 26, 1967; May 3, 1969; December 10, 1977; October 28, 1978; October, 1980.

Sewanee Review, summer, 1974.

Spectator, March 17, 1979.

Threepenny Review, fall, 1981.

Time, August 18, 1967; December 26, 1977; January 27, 1986.

Times Literary Supplement, March 16, 1967; April 25, 1967; January 8, 1970; March 17, 1978; November 23, 1979; December 10, 1982.

Tri-Quarterly, fall, 1966.

Variety, April 29, 1996, p. 150.

Village Voice, August 31, 1967; October 15-21, 1980.

Voice Literary Supplement, November, 1982.

Washington Post, March 16, 1982.

Washington Post Book World, February 5, 1978; June 25, 1978; December 17, 1978; October 26, 1980.

World Literature Today, spring, 1983; autumn, 1992, p. 723.

*   *   *

SOTO, Gary 1952-

PERSONAL: Born April 12, 1952, in Fresno, CA; son of Manuel and Angie (Trevino) Soto; married Carolyn Sadako Oda, May 24, 1975; children: Mariko Heidi. *Education:* California State University, Fresno, B.A., 1974; University of California, Irvine, M.F.A., 1976. *Avocational interests:* Karate, reading, Aztec dancing, travel.

ADDRESSES: Home—43 The Crescent, Berkeley, CA 94708.

CAREER: University of California, Berkeley, assistant professor 1979-85; associate professor of English and ethnic studies, 1985-92, part-time senior lecturer in English department, 1992-93; University of Cincinnati, Elliston Poet, 1988; Wayne State University, Martin Luther King/Cesar Chavez/Rosa Parks Visiting Professor of English, 1990; full-time writer, 1993–.

AWARDS, HONORS: Academy of American Poets Prize, 1975; *Discovery/The Nation* prize, 1975; United States Award, International Poetry Forum, 1976, for *The Elements of San Joaquin;* Bess Hokin Prize from *Poetry,* 1978; Guggenheim fellowship, 1979-80; National Endowment for the Arts fellowships, 1981 and 1991; creative writing fellowship, National Education Association, 1982; Levinson Award, *Poetry,* 1984; American Book Award, Before Columbus Foundation, 1985, for *Living up the Street;* California Arts Council fellowship, 1989; Best Book for Young Adults citation, American Library Association, 1990, Beatty Award, California Library Association, 1991, and Reading Magic Award, *Parenting* magazine, all for *Baseball in April, and Other Stories;* George G. Stone Center Recognition of Merit, Claremont Graduate School, 1993; Carnegie Medal, 1993; National Book Award and *Los Angeles Times* Book Prize nominations, both 1995, both for *New and Selected Poems.*

WRITINGS:

The Elements of San Joaquin (poems), University of Pittsburgh Press (Pittsburgh), 1977.

The Tale of Sunlight (poems), University of Pittsburgh Press, 1978.

Fathers Is a Pillow Tied to a Broom, Slow Loris (Pittsburgh), 1980.

Where Sparrows Work Hard (poems), University of Pittsburgh Press, 1981.

Black Hair (poems), University of Pittsburgh Press, 1985.

Living up the Street: Narrative Recollections (prose memoirs), Strawberry Hill (San Francisco, CA), 1985.

Small Faces (prose memoirs), Arte Publico (Houston, TX), 1986.

The Cat's Meow, illustrated by Carolyn Soto, Strawberry Hill, 1987.

Lesser Evils: Ten Quartets (memoirs and essays), Arte Publico, 1988.

(Editor) *California Childhood: Recollections and Stories of the Golden State,* Creative Arts Book Company (Berkeley, CA), 1988.

A Fire in My Hands (poems), Scholastic (New York City), 1990.

A Summer Life (autobiography), University Press of New England (Hanover, NH), 1990.

Baseball in April and Other Stories (short stories), Harcourt (San Diego, CA), 1990.

Who Will Know Us? (poems), Chronicle Books (San Francisco, CA), 1990.

Home Course in Religion (poems), Chronicle Books, 1991.

Taking Sides, Harcourt, 1991.

Neighborhood Odes, Harcourt, 1992.

Pacific Crossing, Harcourt, 1992.

The Skirt, Delacorte (New York City), 1992.

Too Many Tamales (picture book), Putnam (New York City), 1992.

(Editor) *Pieces of the Heart: New Chicano Fiction,* Chronicle Books, 1993.

Local News (short stories), Harcourt, 1993.

The Pool Party, Delacorte, 1993 (also see below).

Crazy Weekend, Scholastic, 1994.

Jesse, Harcourt, 1994.

Boys at Work, Delacorte, 1995.
Canto Familiar/Familiar Song (poetry), Harcourt, 1995.
The Cat's Meow, Scholastic, 1995.
Chato's Kitchen, Putnam, 1995.
(Editor) *Everyday Seductions,* Ploughshare Press (Sea Bright, NJ), 1995.
New and Selected Poems, Chronicle Books, 1995.
Summer on Wheels, Scholastic, 1995.
The Old Man and His Door, Putnam, 1996.
Snapshots of the Wedding, Putnam, 1996.
Off and Running (juvenile), illustrated by Eric Velasquez, Delacorte (New York City), 1996.
Buried Onions, Harcourt (San Diego), 1997.
Novio Boy (play), Harcourt, 1997.
Junior College: Poems, Chronicle Books (San Francisco), 1997.
Petty Crimes, Harcourt, 1998.
Bushy Mustache, Knopf (New York City), 1998.
Chato and the Party Animals, Putnam, 1998.

SHORT FILMS

The Bike, Gary Soto Productions, 1991.
The Pool Party, Gary Soto Productions, 1993.
Novio Boy, Gary Soto Productions, 1994.

SIDELIGHTS: Gary Soto is an American poet and prose writer influenced by his working-class Mexican-American background. Born in Fresno, California, in the agricultural San Joaquin Valley, he worked as a laborer during his childhood. In his writing, as Raymund Paredes noted in the *Rocky Mountain Review,* "Soto establishes his acute sense of ethnicity and, simultaneously, his belief that certain emotions, values, and experiences transcend ethnic boundaries and allegiances." Many critics have echoed the assessment of Patricia De La Fuente in *Revista Chicano-Requena* that Soto displays an "exceptionally high level of linguistic sophistication."

In his first volume of poetry, *The Elements of San Joaquin,* Soto offers a grim portrait of Mexican-American life. His poems depict the violence of urban life, the exhausting labor of rural life, and the futility of trying to recapture the innocence of childhood. In the book *Chicano Poetry* Juan Bruce-Novoa likened Soto's poetic vision to T. S. Eliot's bleak portrait of the modern world, *The Waste Land.* Soto uses wind-swept dust as a dominant image, and he also introduces such elements as rape, unflushed toilets, a drowned baby, and, as Bruce-Novoa quotes him, "men / Whose arms / Were bracelets / Of burns." Soto's skill with the figurative language of poetry has been noted by reviewers throughout his career, and in *Western American Literature* Jerry Bradley praised the metaphors in *San Joaquin* as "evocative, enlightening, and haunting." Though unsettled by the negativism of the collection, Bruce-Novoa felt the work "convinces because of its well-wrought structure, the craft, the coherence of its totality." Moreover, he thought, because it brings such a vivid portrait of poverty to the reading public, *San Joaquin* is "a social as well as a literary achievement."

Many critics have also observed that Soto's writing transcends social commentary. Bruce-Novoa said that one reason why the author's work has "great significance within Chicano literature" is because it represents "a definite shift toward a more personal, less politically motivated poetry." As Alan Williamson suggested in *Poetry,* Soto avoids either idealizing the poor for their oppression or encouraging their violent defiance. Instead, he focuses on the human suffering that poverty engenders. When Peter Cooley reviewed Soto's second volume of poetry, *The Tale of Sunlight,* in

Parnassus, he praised the author's ability to temper the bleakness of *San Joaquin* with "imaginative expansiveness." The poems in *Sunlight,* many of which focus on a child named Molina or on the owner of a Hispanic bar, display both the frustrations of poverty and what Williamson called "a vein of consolatory fantasy which passes beyond escapism into a pure imaginative generosity toward life." Williamson cited as an example "the poem in which an uncle's gray hair is seen as a visitation of magical butterflies."

In the poems of *Black Hair,* Soto focuses on his friends and family. He portrays fondly the times he shared with his buddies as an adolescent and the more recent moments he has spent with his young daughter. Some critics, such as David Wojahn in *Poetry,* argued that Soto was moving away from his strengths as a writer. While acknowledging that "by limiting his responses to a naive aplomb, Soto enables himself to write with a freshness that is at times arresting," Wojahn considered the work "a disappointment." He praised *San Joaquin* and *Tale of Sunlight* as "thematically urgent . . . and ambitious in their scope" and said that "compared to them, *Black Hair* is a distinctly minor achievement." Others, such as Ellen Lesser in *Voice Literary Supplement,* were charmed by Soto's poetic tone, "the quality of the voice, the immediate, human presence that breathes through the lines." Lesser contended that Soto's celebration of innocence and sentiment is shaded with a knowledge of "the larger, often threatening world." In the *Christian Science Monitor,* Tom D'Evelyn hailed Soto's ability to go beyond the circumstances of his own life and write of "something higher," concluding, "Somehow Gary Soto has become not an important Chicano poet but an important American poet. More power to him."

When Soto discusses American racial tensions in the prose collections *Living up the Street: Narrative Recollections* and *Small Faces,* he uses vignettes drawn from his own childhood. One vignette shows the anger the author felt upon realizing that his brown-skinned brother would never be considered an attractive child by conventional American standards. Another shows Soto's surprise at discovering that, contrary to his family's advice to marry a Mexican, he was falling in love with a woman of Japanese ancestry. In these deliberately small-scale recollections, as Paredes noted, "it is a measure of Soto's skill that he so effectively invigorates and sharpens our understanding of the commonplace." With these volumes Soto acquired a solid reputation as a prose writer as well as a poet; *Living up the Street* earned him an American Book Award.

Soto's autobiographical prose continued with *Lesser Evils: Ten Quartets* and *A Summer Life.* The first of these, as Soto explained in an unpublished 1988 interview, reflects the author's experience with Catholicism—in the same interview Soto declared himself a reconciled Catholic. *A Summer Life* consists of thirty-nine short essays. According to Ernesto Trejo in the *Los Angeles Times Book Review,* these pieces "make up a compelling biography" of Soto's youth. As he had done in previous works, Soto here "holds the past up to memory's probing flashlight, turns it around ever so carefully, and finds in the smallest of incidents the occasion for literature." Writing in the *Americas Review,* Hector Torres compared *A Summer Life* with Soto's earlier autobiographical texts and asserted that the later book "moves with greater stylistic elegance and richer thematic coherence."

During the early 1990s Soto turned his attentions in a new direction: children's literature. A first volume of short stories for young readers, *Baseball in April and Other Stories,* was published in 1990. The eleven tales depict Mexican-American boys and girls as they enter adolescence in Hispanic California neighborhoods. In the *New York Times Book Review,* Roberto Gonzalez Echevarria called the stories "sensitive and economical." Echevarria praised Soto: "Because he stays within the teenagers' universe . . . he manages to convey all the social change and stress without bathos or didacticism. In fact, his stories are moving, yet humorous and entertaining." In the *Americas Review,* Torres suggested that *Baseball in April* was "the kind of work that could be used to teach high school and junior high school English classes."

One of Soto's juvenile characters, a boy named Lincoln Mendoza, appears as a protagonist in two works: *Taking Sides* and *Pacific Crossing.* As a Mexican-American eighth-grader in *Taking Sides,* Lincoln is confronted with challenges and insecurities when he and his mother move from San Francisco's Mission District to a predominantly Anglo suburb. He works to keep his heritage intact in his new environment. *Pacific Crossing* finds Lincoln and one of his friends facing cultural challenges in another context: they embark on a voyage to Japan as exchange students. Writing in the *Multicultural Review,* Osbelia Juarez Rocha called *Pacific Crossing* "cleverly crafted" and "entertaining."

Soto has also written poetry for younger readers, most notably the volumes *A Fire in My Hands* and *Neighborhood Odes,* both of which focus on growing up in the Mexican neighborhoods of California's Central Valley. Soto has ventured as well into the arena of children's picture books. *Too Many Tamales* depicts the story of Maria, a young girl who misplaces her mother's wedding ring in tamale dough while helping to prepare a Christmastime feast. Maria—with her cousins' help—embarks on a futile effort to recover the ring by consuming vast quantities of tamales. *Chato's Kitchen* introduces a cat whose efforts to entice the local "ratoncitos"—little mice—lead him to prepare abundant portions of fajitas, frijoles, enchiladas, and other foods.

In a 1989 volume of the *Dictionary of Literary Biography,* Hector Torres declared: "Soto's consistent attention to the craft of writing and his sensitivity to his subject matter have earned him an indisputable place in American and Chicano literature." Torres noted that critical response to Soto's work has been "overwhelmingly positive." He attributed that respect and admiration to Soto's ability to represent his experience "in a manner that shows his talent at creating poetry and prose that, through simple and direct diction, expresses the particulars of everyday life and simultaneously contains glimpses of the universal."

BIOGRAPHICAL/CRITICAL SOURCES:

BOOKS

Bruce-Novoa, Juan, *Chicano Poetry: A Response to Chaos,* University of Texas Press (Austin), 1982.
Contemporary Authors, Volume 119, Gale (Detroit), 1986.
Contemporary Literary Criticism, Gale, Volume 32, 1985; Volume 80, 1994.
Dictionary of Literary Biography, Volume 82: *Chicano Writers,* Gale, 1989.

PERIODICALS

American Book Review, July-August, 1982.
Americas Review, spring, 1991, pp. 111-15.
Christian Science Monitor, March 6, 1985.
Denver Quarterly, summer, 1982.
Los Angeles Times Book Review, August 5, 1990, pp. 1, 9.
Multicultural Review, June 1993, pp. 76, 78.
Nation, June 7, 1993, pp. 772-74.
NEA Today, November, 1992, p. 9.
New York Times Book Review, May 20, 1990, p. 45.
Parnassus, fall-winter, 1979.
Poetry, March, 1980, June, 1985.
Publishers Weekly, March 23, 1992, p. 74; April 12, 1993, p. 64; August 16, 1993, p. 103; February 6, 1995, pp. 84-85.
Revista Chicano-Riquena, summer, 1983.
Rocky Mountain Review, Volume 41, numbers 1-2, 1987.
San Francisco Review of Books, summer, 1986.
Voice Literary Supplement, September, 1985.
Western American Literature, spring, 1979.

* * *

SOYINKA, Wole 1934-

PERSONAL: Name is pronounced "*Woh*-leh Shaw-*yin*-ka"; given name, Akinwande Oluwole; born July 13, 1934, in Isara, Nigeria; son of Ayo (a headmaster) and Eniola Soyinka; married; four children. *Education:* Attended University of Ibadan; University of Leeds, B.A. (with honors), 1959. *Religion:* "Human liberty."

ADDRESSES: Office—PO Box 935, Abeokuta, Ogun, Nigeria. *Agent*—Greenbaum, Wolff & Ernst, 437 Madison Ave., New York, NY 10022.

CAREER: Playwright, poet, and novelist. University of Ibadan, Nigeria, research fellow in drama, 1960-61, chairman of department of theater arts, 1967-71; University of Ife, professor of drama, 1972; Cambridge University, Cambridge, England, fellow of Churchill College, 1973-74; University of Ife, chairman of department of dramatic arts, 1975-85. Director of own theater groups, Orisun Players and 1960 Masks, in Lagos and Ibadan, Nigeria, and Unife Guerilla theater, Ife-Ife, 1978. Visiting professor at University of Sheffield, 1974, University of Ghana, 1975, Cornell University, 1986, and Yale University, 1979-80. Goldwin Smith professor for African Studies and Theater Arts, Cornell University, 1988–. Director of plays and actor on stage, film and radio.

MEMBER: International Theatre Institute (president), Union of Writers of the African Peoples (secretary-general), African Academy of Sciences.

AWARDS, HONORS: Rockefeller Foundation grant, 1960; John Whiting Drama Prize, 1966; Dakar Negro Arts Festival award, 1966; *New Statesman* Jock Campbell Award, *New Statesman,* 1968, for *The Interpreters;* Nobel Prize in Literature, 1986; Leopold Sedan Senghor Award, 1986; Enrico Mattei Award for Humanities, 1986; named Commander of the Federal Republic of Nigeria by General Ibrahim Babangida, 1986; named Commander of the French Legion of Honor, 1989; named Commander of Order of the Italian Republic, 1990; D.Litt., Yale University, University of Leeds, 1973, University of Montpellier, France, and University of Lagos; Prisoner of Conscience Prize, Amnesty International.

WRITINGS:

POETRY

Idanre and Other Poems, Methuen, 1967, Hill & Wang, 1969.
Poems from Prison, Rex Collings, 1969, expanded edition published as *A Shuttle in the Crypt,* Hill & Wang, 1972.
(Editor and author of introduction) *Poems of Black Africa,* Hill & Wang, 1975.
Ogun Abibiman, Rex Collings, 1976.

Mandela's Earth and Other Poems, Methuen, 1990.

PLAYS

The Invention, first produced in London at Royal Court Theatre, 1955.

A Dance of the Forests (also see below; first produced in London, 1960), Oxford University Press, 1962.

The Lion and the Jewel (also see below; first produced at Royal Court Theatre, 1966), Oxford University Press, 1962.

Three Plays (includes *The Trials of Brother Jero* [also see below], one-act, produced off-Broadway at Greenwich Mews Playhouse, November 9, 1967; *The Strong Breed* [also see below], one-act, produced at Greenwich Mews Playhouse, November 9, 1967; and *The Swamp Dwellers* [also see below]), Mbari Publications, 1962, Northwestern University Press, 1963.

Five Plays: A Dance of the Forests, The Lion and the Jewel, The Swamp Dwellers, The Trials of Brother Jero, The Strong Breed, Oxford University Press, 1964.

The Road (produced in Stratford, England, at Theatre Royal, 1965), Oxford University Press, 1965.

Kongi's Harvest (also see below; produced off-Broadway at St. Mark's Playhouse, April 14, 1968), Oxford University Press, 1966.

Rites of the Harmattan Solstice, produced in Lagos, 1966.

Three Short Plays, Oxford University Press, 1969.

The Trials of Brother Jero, Oxford University Press, 1969, published with *The Strong Breed* as *The Trials of Brother Jero and The Strong Breed: Two Plays,* Dramatists Play Service, 1969.

Kongi's Harvest (screenplay), produced by Calpenny-Nigerian Films, 1970.

Madmen and Specialists (two-act; produced in Waterford, Conn., at Eugene O'Neill Memorial Theatre, August 1, 1970), Methuen, 1971, Hill & Wang, 1972.

(Contributor) *Palaver: Three Dramatic Discussion Starters* (includes *The Lion and the Jewel*), Friendship Press, 1971.

Before the Blackout (revue sketches; also see below), Orisun Acting Editions, 1971.

(Editor) *Plays from the Third World: An Anthology,* Doubleday, 1971.

The Jero Plays: The Trials of Brother Jero, and Jero's Metamorphosis, Methuen, 1973.

(Contributor) *African Theatre: Eight Prize Winning Plays for Radio,* Heinemann, 1973.

Camwood on the Leaves, Methuen, 1973, published with *Before the Blackout* as *Camwood on the Leaves and Before the Blackout: Two Short Plays,* Third Press, 1974.

(Adapter) *The Bacchae of Euripides: A Communion Rite* (first produced in London at Old Vic Theatre, August 2, 1973), Methuen, 1973, Norton, 1974.

Collected Plays, Oxford University Press, Volume 1: *A Dance of the Forests, The Swamp Dwellers, The Strong Breed, The Road, The Bacchae,* 1973, Volume 2: *The Lion and the Jewel, Kongi's Harvest, The Trials of Brother Jero, Jero's Metamorphosis, Madmen and Specialists,* 1974.

Death and the King's Horseman (produced at University of Ife, 1976; produced in Chicago at Goodman Theatre, 1979; produced in New York at Vivian Beaumont Theatre, March, 1987), Norton, 1975.

Opera Wonyosi (light opera; produced in Ife-Ife, 1977), Indiana University Press, 1981.

Priority Projects, revue; produced on Nigeria tour, 1982.

A Play of Giants (produced in New Haven, CT, 1984), Methuen, 1984.

Six Plays, Methuen, 1984.

Requiem for a Futurologist (produced in Ife-Ife, 1983), Rex Collings, 1985.

From Zia, with Love; and A Scourge of Hyacinths, Methuen, 1992.

The Beatification of Area Boy: A Lagosian Kaleidoscope, Methuen, 1995.

Also author of television script, "Culture in Transition."

OTHER

The Interpreters (novel), Deutsch, 1965.

(Translator) D. O. Fagunwa, *The Forest of a Thousand Daemons: A Hunter's Saga* (novel), Nelson, 1967, Humanities, 1969.

(Contributor) D. W. Jefferson, editor, *The Morality of Art,* Routledge & Kegan Paul, 1969.

(Contributor) O. R. Dathorne and Wilfried Feuser, editors, *Africa in Prose,* Penguin, 1969.

The Man Died: Prison Notes of Wole Soyinka, Harper, 1972, 2nd edition, Rex Collings, 1973.

Season of Anomy (novel), Rex Collings, 1973.

Myth, Literature and the African World (essays), Cambridge University Press, 1976.

Ake: The Years of Childhood (autobiography), Random House, 1981.

Art, Dialogue, and Outrage (essays), New Horn, 1988.

Isara: A Voyage around "Essay," (biography of the author's father), Random House, 1989.

Ibadan: The Penkelemes Years: A Memoir, Spectrum Books (Ibadan), 1994.

The Open Sore of a Continent: A Personal Narrative of the Nigerian Crisis, Oxford University Press, 1996.

Early Poems, Oxford University Press, 1997.

The Essential Soyinka: A Reader, Pantheon, 1998.

The Burden of Memory, the Muse of Forgiveness (essays), Oxford University Press, 1998.

Coeditor, *Black Orpheus,* 1961-64; editor, *Transition* (now *Ch'Indaba*), 1974-76.

SIDELIGHTS: Many critics consider Wole Soyinka Africa's finest writer. The Nigerian playwright's unique style blends traditional Yoruban folk-drama with European dramatic form to provide both spectacle and penetrating satire. Soyinka told *New York Times Magazine* writer Jason Berry that in the African cultural tradition, the artist "has always functioned as the record of the mores and experience of his society." His plays, novels, and poetry all reflect that philosophy, serving as a record of twentieth-century Africa's political turmoil and its struggle to reconcile tradition with modernization. Eldred Jones states in his book *Wole Soyinka* that the author's work touches on universal themes as well as addressing specifically African concerns. "The essential ideas which emerge from a reading of Soyinka's work are not specially African ideas, although his characters and their mannerisms are African. His concern is with man on earth. Man is dressed for the nonce in African dress and lives in the sun and tropical forest, but he represents the whole race."

As a young child, Soyinka was comfortable with the conflicting cultures in his world, but as he grew older he became increasingly aware of the pull between African tradition and Western modernization. Ake, his village, was mainly populated with people from the Yoruba tribe, and was presided over by the *ogboni,* or tribal elders. Soyinka's grandfather introduced him to the pantheon of

Yoruba gods and to tribal folklore. His parents were key representatives of colonial influences, however; his mother was a devout Christian convert and his father acted as headmaster for the village school established by the British. When Soyinka's father began urging Wole to leave Ake to attend the government school in Ibadan, the boy was spirited away by his grandfather, who administered a scarification rite of manhood. Soyinka was also consecrated to the god Ogun, ruler of metal, roads, and both the creative and destructive essence. Ogun is a recurring figure in Soyinka's work and has been named by the author as his muse.

Ake: The Years of Childhood, Soyinka's account of his first ten years, stands as "a classic of childhood memoirs wherever and whenever produced," states *New York Times Book Review* contributor James Olney. Numerous critics have singled out Soyinka's ability to recapture the changing perspective of a child as the book's outstanding feature; it begins in a light tone but grows increasingly serious as the boy matures and becomes aware of the problems faced by the adults around him. The book concludes with an account of a tax revolt organized by Soyinka's mother and the beginnings of Nigerian independence. "Most of 'Ake' charms; that was Mr. Soyinka's intention," writes John Leonard of the *New York Times.* "The last 50 pages, however, inspire and confound; they are transcendent."

Soyinka published some poems and short stories in *Black Orpheus,* a highly regarded Nigerian literary magazine, before leaving Africa to attend the University of Leeds in England. There his first play was produced. *The Invention* is a comic satire based on a sudden loss of pigment by South Africa's black population. Unable to distinguish blacks from whites and thus enforce its apartheid policies, the government is thrown into chaos. "The play is Soyinka's sole direct treatment of the political situation in Africa," notes Thomas Hayes in the *Dictionary of Literary Biography Yearbook: 1986.* Soyinka returned to Nigeria in 1960, shortly after independence from colonial rule had been declared. He began to research Yoruba folklore and drama in depth and incorporated elements of both into his play *A Dance of the Forests.*

A Dance of the Forests was commissioned as part of Nigeria's independence celebrations. In his play, Soyinka warned the newly independent Nigerians that the end of colonial rule did not mean an end to their country's problems. It shows a bickering group of mortals who summon up the *egungun* (spirits of the dead, revered by the Yoruba people) for a festival. They have presumed the *egungun* to be noble and wise, but they discover that their ancestors are as petty and spiteful as any living people. "The whole concept ridicules the African viewpoint that glorifies the past at the expense of the present," suggests John F. Povey in *Tri-Quarterly.* "The sentimentalized glamour of the past is exposed so that the same absurdities may not be reenacted in the future. This constitutes a bold assertion to an audience awaiting an easy appeal to racial heroics." Povey also praises Soyinka's skill in using dancing, drumming, and singing to reinforce his theme: "The dramatic power of the surging forest dance [in the play] carries its own visual conviction. It is this that shows Soyinka to be a man of the theatre, not simply a writer."

Soyinka was well established as Nigeria's premier playwright when in 1965 he published his first novel, *The Interpreters.* The novel allowed him to expand on themes already expressed in his stage dramas and to present a sweeping view of Nigerian life in the years immediately following independence. Essentially plotless, *The Interpreters* is loosely structured around the informal discussions among five young Nigerian intellectuals. Each has been educated in a foreign country and returned hoping to shape Nigeria's destiny. They are hampered by their own confused values, however, as well as the corruption they encounter everywhere. Some reviewers liken Soyinka's writing style in *The Interpreters* to that of James Joyce and William Faulkner. Others take exception to the formless quality of the novel, but Eustace Palmer asserts in *The Growth of the African Novel:* "If there are reservations about the novel's structure, there can be none about the thoroughness of the satire at society's expense. Soyinka's wide-ranging wit takes in all sections of a corrupt society—the brutal masses, the aimless intellectuals, the affected and hypocritical university dons, the vulgar and corrupt businessmen, the mediocre civil servants, the illiterate politicians and the incompetent journalists. [The five main characters are all] talented intellectuals who have retained their African consciousness although they were largely educated in the western world. Yet their western education enables them to look at their changing society with a certain amount of detachment. They are therefore uniquely qualified to be interpreters of this society. The reader is impressed by their honesty, sincerity, moral idealism, concern for truth and justice and aversion to corruption, snobbery and hypocrisy; but anyone who assumes that Soyinka presents all the interpreters as models of behaviour will be completely misreading the novel. He is careful to expose their selfishness, egoism, cynicism and aimlessness. Indeed the conduct of the intellectuals both in and out of the university is a major preoccupation of Soyinka's in this novel. The aimlessness and superficiality of the lives of most of the interpreters is patent."

Neil McEwan points out in *Africa and the Novel* that for all its seriousness, *The Interpreters* is also "among the liveliest of recent novels in English. It is bright satire full of good sense and good humour which are African and contemporary: the highest spirits of its author's early work. . . . Behind the jokes of his novel is a theme that he has developed angrily elsewhere: that whatever progress may mean for Africa it is not a lesson to be learned from outside, however much of 'modernity' Africans may share with others." McEwan further observes that although *The Interpreters* does not have a rigidly structured plot, "there is unity in the warmth and sharpness of its comic vision. There are moments which sadden or anger; but they do not diminish the fun." Palmer notes that *The Interpreters* notably influenced the African fiction that followed it, shifting the focus "from historical, cultural and sociological analysis to penetrating social comment and social satire."

The year *The Interpreters* was published, 1965, also marked Soyinka's first arrest by the Nigerian police. He was accused of using a gun to force a radio announcer to broadcast incorrect election results. No evidence was ever produced, however, and the PEN writers' organization launched a protest campaign, headed by William Styron and Norman Mailer. Soyinka was released after three months. He was next arrested two years later, during Nigeria's civil war. Soyinka was completely opposed to the conflict, and especially to the Nigerian Government's brutal policies toward the Ibo people who were attempting to form their own country, Biafra. He traveled to Biafra to establish a peace commission composed of leading intellectuals from both sides; when he returned, the Nigerian police accused him of helping the Biafrans to buy jet fighters. Once again he was imprisoned. This time Soyinka was held for more than two years, although he was never formally charged with any crime. Most of that time he was kept in solitary confinement. When all of his fellow prisoners were vaccinated against meningitis, Soyinka was passed by; when he developed serious vision problems, they were ignored by his jailers. He was denied reading and writing materials, but he manufactured his own ink and began to keep a prison diary, written on toilet paper, cigarette packages and in between the lines of the few books he secretly obtained. Each poem or fragment of journal he managed to smuggle to the outside world became a literary event and a reassurance to his supporters that Soyinka still lived, despite rumors to the contrary. He was released in 1969 and left Nigeria soon after, not returning until a change of power took place in 1975.

Published as *The Man Died: Prison Notes of Wole Soyinka,* the author's diary constitutes "the most important work that has been written about the Biafran war," believes Charles R. Larson, contributor to *Nation.* "'The Man Died' is not so much the story of Wole Soyinka's own temporary death during the Nigerian Civil War but a personified account of Nigeria's fall from sanity, documented by one of the country's leading intellectuals." Gerald Weales's *New York Times Book Review* article suggests that the political content of *The Man Died* is less fascinating than "the notes that deal with prison life, the observation of everything from a warder's catarrh to the predatory life of insects after a rain. Of course, these are not simply reportorial. They are vehicles to carry the author's shifting states of mind, to convey the real subject matter of the book; the author's attempt to survive as a man, and as a mind. The notes are both a means to that survival and a record to it." Larson underlines the book's political impact, however, noting that ironically, "while other Nigerian writers were emotionally castrated by the war, Soyinka, who was placed in solitary confinement so that he wouldn't embarrass the government, was writing work after work, books that will no doubt embarrass the Nigerian Government more than anything the Ibo writers may ever publish." A *Times Literary Supplement* reviewer concurs, characterizing *The Man Died* as "a damning indictment of what Mr. Soyinka sees as the iniquities of wartime Nigeria and the criminal tyranny of its administration in peacetime."

In spite of its satire, most critics had found *The Interpreters* to be ultimately an optimistic book. In contrast, Soyinka's second novel expresses almost no hope for Africa's future, says John Mellors in *London Magazine:* "Wole Soyinka appears to have written much of *Season of Anomy* in a blazing fury, angry beyond complete control of words at the abuses of power and the outbreaks of both considered and spontaneous violence. . . . The plot charges along, dragging the reader (not because he doesn't want to go, but because he finds it hard to keep up) through forest, mortuary and prison camp in nightmare visions of tyranny, torture, slaughter and putrefaction. The book reeks of pain. . . . Soyinka hammers at the point that the liberal has to deal with violence in the world however much he would wish he could ignore it; the scenes of murder and mutilation, while sickeningly explicit, are justified by . . . the author's anger and compassion and insistence that bad will not become better by our refusal to examine it."

Like *Season of Anomy,* Soyinka's postwar plays are considered more brooding than his earlier work. *Madmen and Specialists* is called "grim" by Martin Banham and Clive Wake in *African Theatre Today.* In the play, a doctor returns from the war trained as a specialist in torture and uses his new skills on his father. The play's major themes are "the loss of faith and rituals" and "the break-up of the family unit which traditionally in Africa has been the foundation of society," according to Charles Larson in the *New York Times Book Review.* Names and events in the play are fictionalized to avoid censorship, but Soyinka has clearly "leveled a wholesale criticism of life in Nigeria since the Civil War: a

police state in which only madmen and spies can survive, in which the losers are mad and the winners are paranoid about the possibility of another rebellion. The prewar corruption and crime have returned, supported by the more sophisticated acts of terrorism and espionage introduced during the war."

In *Isara: A Voyage around "Essay,"* Soyinka provides a portrait of his father, Akinyode Soditan, as well as "vivid sketches of characters and culturally intriguing events that cover a period of 15 years," Charles Johnson relates in the *Washington Post.* The narrative follows S. A., or "Essay," and his classmates through his years at St. Simeon's Teacher Training Seminary in Ilesa. Aided by documents left to him in a tin box, Soyinka dramatizes the changes that profoundly affected his father's life. The Great Depression that brought the Western world to its knees during the early 1930s was a time of economic opportunity for Africans. The quest for financial gain transformed African culture, as did Mussolini's invasion of Ethiopia and the onset of World War II. More threatening was the violent civil war for the throne following the death of their king. An aged peacemaker named Agunrin resolved the conflict by an appeal to the people's common past. "As each side presents its case, Agunrin, half listening, sinks into memories that unfold his people's collective history, and finally he speaks, finding his voice in a scene so masterfully rendered it alone is worth the price of the book," Johnson claims. The book is neither a strict biography nor a straight historical account. However, "in his effort to expose Western readers to a unique, African perspective on the war years, Soyinka succeeds brilliantly," Johnson comments. *New York Times* reviewer Michiko Kakutani writes that, in addition, "Essay emerges as a high-minded teacher, a mentor and companion, blessed with dignity and strong ideals, a father who inspired his son to achievement."

In his most recent work, *The Open Sore of a Continent: A Personal Narrative of the Nigerian Crisis,* Soyinka takes an expansive and unrestrained look at Nigeria's dictatorship. A collection of essays originally delivered as lectures at Harvard, *The Open Sore* questions the corrupt government, the ideas of nationalism, and international intervention. The book begins with the execution of Ken Saro-Wiwa. For Soyinka, his death, along with the annulment of the recent elections, signals the disintegration of the state. According to Robert Kaplan in the *New York Times Book Review,* Soyinka "uses these harsh facts to dissect, then reinvent not just Nigeria but the concept of nationhood itself."

Soyinka's work is frequently described as demanding but rewarding reading. Although his plays are widely praised, they are seldom performed, especially outside of Africa. The dancing and choric speech often found in them are unfamiliar and difficult for non-African actors to master, a problem Holly Hill notes in her London *Times* review of the Lincoln Center Theatre production of *Death and the King's Horseman.* She awards high praise to the play, however, saying it "has the stateliness and mystery of Greek tragedy." When the Swedish Academy awarded Soyinka the Nobel Prize in Literature in 1986, its members singled out *Death and the King's Horseman* and *A Dance of the Forests* as "evidence that Soyinka is 'one of the finest poetical playwrights that have written in English,'" reports Stanley Meisler of the *Los Angeles Times.*

BIOGRAPHICAL/CRITICAL SOURCES:

BOOKS

Adelugba, Dapo, *Wole Soyinka: A Birthday Letter, and Other Essays,* University of Ibadan, 1984.

Adelugba, Dapo, editor, *Before Our Very Eyes: Tribute to Wole Soyinka,* Spectrum, 1987.

Adeniran, Tunde, *The Politics of Wole Soyinka,* Fountain, 1994.

Bamikunle, Aderemi, *Introduction to Soyinka's Poetry: Analysis of A Shuttle in the Crypt,* Ahmadu Bello University Press, 1991.

Banham, Martin, and Clive Wake, *African Theatre Today,* Pitman Publishing, 1976.

Banham, Martin, *Wole Soyinka's "The Lion and the Jewel,"* Rex Collings, 1981.

Black Literature Criticism, Gale (Detroit), 1992.

Chinweizu, Onwuchekwa Jemie, and others, *Toward the Decolonization of African Literature,* Routledge, 1985, pp. 163-238.

Coger, Greta M. K., *Index of Subjects, Proverbs, and Themes in the Writings of Wole Soyinka,* Greenwood, 1988.

Contemporary Literary Criticism, Gale, Volume 3, 1975; Volume 5, 1976; Volume 14, 1980; Volume 36, 1986; Volume 44, 1987.

Dictionary of Literary Biography, Volume 125: *Twentieth-Century Caribbean and Black African Writers, Second Series,* Gale, 1993.

Dictionary of Literary Biography Yearbook: 1986, Gale, 1987, pp. 3-18.

Drama Criticism, Volume 2, Gale, 1992.

Dunton, C. P., *Notes on "Three Short Plays,"* Longman, 1982.

Etherton, Michael, *The Development of African Drama,* Hutchinson, 1982, pp. 242-84.

Fraser, Robert, *West African Poetry: A Critical History,* Cambridge University Press, 1986, pp. 231-50, 265-70, 295-300.

Gakwandi, Shatto Arthur, *The Novel and Contemporary Experience in America,* Heinemann, 1977, pp. 66-86.

Gates, Henry Louis, Jr., and K. A. Appiah, editors., *Wole Soyinka: Critical Perspectives Past and Present,* Amistad, 1996.

Gibbs, James, *Wole Soyinka,* Macmillan, 1986.

Gibbs, James, Ketu Katrak, and Henry Gates, Jr., editors, *Wole Soyinka: A Bibliography of Primary and Secondary Sources,* Greenwood Press, 1986.

Herdeck, Donald E., *Three Dynamite Authors: Derek Walcott (Nobel 1992), Naguib Mahfouz (Nobel 1988), Wole Soyinka (Nobel 1986): Ten Bio-Critical Essays from Their Works As Published by Three Continents Press,* Three Continents Press (Colorado Springs), 1995.

Jones, Eldred, *Wole Soyinka,* Twayne, 1973 (published in England as *The Writings of Wole Soyinka,* Heinemann, 1973), revised, Currey, 1988.

Katrak, Ketu, *Wole Soyinka and Modern Tragedy: A Study of Dramatic Theory and Practice,* Greenwood Press, 1986.

Lindfors, Bernth, and James Gibbs, editors, *Research on Wole Soyinka,* Africa World, 1992.

Maduakor, Obi, *Wole Soyinka: An Introduction to His Writing,* Garland, 1986.

Maja-Pearce, Adewale, editor, *Wole Soyninka: An Appraisal,* Heinemann, 1994.

McEwan, Neil, *Africa and the Novel,* Humanities Press, 1983.

Moore, Gerald, *Wole Soyinka,* Africana Publishing, 1971.

Morell, Karen L., editor, *In Person—Achebe, Awoonor, and Soyinka at the University of Washington,* African Studies Program, Institute for Comparative and Foreign Area Studies, University of Washington, 1975.

Omotoso, Kole, *Achebe Or Soyinka: A Study in Contrasts,* Zell (London), 1996.

Palmer, Eustace, *The Growth of the African Novel,* Heinemann, 1979.

Parsons, E. M., editor, *Notes on Wole Soyinka's "The Jero Plays,"* Methuen, 1982.

Quayson, Ato, *Strategic Transformations in Nigerian Writing: Orality and History in the Work of Rev. Samuel Johnson, Amos Tutuola, Wole Soyinka, and Ben Okri,* Indiana University Press, 1997.

Wilkinson, Jane, *Talking with African Writers,* Currey, 1992, pp. 90-108.

World Literature Criticism, Gale, 1992.

Wright, Derek, *Wole Soyinka Revisited,* Twayne, 1993.

PERIODICALS

African American Review, spring, 1996, p. 99.

Black Orpheus, March, 1966.

Chicago Tribune Book World, October 7, 1979.

Christian Science Monitor, July 31, 1970; August 15, 1970.

Commonweal, February 8, 1985.

Commonwealth Essays and Studies (special on Wole Soyinka), spring, 1991.

Detroit Free Press, March 20, 1983; October 17, 1986.

Detroit News, November 21, 1982.

Globe and Mail (Toronto), June 7, 1986; January 6, 1990.

London Magazine, April/May, 1974.

Los Angeles Times, October 17, 1986.

Los Angeles Times Book Review, October 15, 1989.

Nation, October 11, 1965; April 29, 1968; September 15, 1969; November 10, 1969; October 2, 1972; November 5, 1973; May 27, 1996, p. 31.

New Perspectives, summer, 1994, p. 61.

New Republic, October 12, 1974; May 9, 1983; December 18, 1995, p. 12.

New Statesman, December 20, 1968.

Newsweek, November 1, 1982.

New Yorker, May 16, 1977.

New York Review of Books, July 31, 1969; October 21, 1982.

New York Times, November 11, 1965; April 19, 1970; August 11, 1972; September 23, 1982; May 29, 1986; May 31, 1986; June 15, 1986; October 17, 1986; November 9, 1986; March 1, 1987; March 2, 1987; November 3, 1989; August 26, 1996, p. 26.

New York Times Book Review, July 29, 1973; December 24, 1973; October 10, 1982; January 15, 1984; November 12, 1989; May 15, 1994, p. 24; August 11, 1996.

New York Times Magazine, September 18, 1983.

Publishers Weekly, June 3, 1996.

Time, October 27, 1986; December 5, 1994, p. 29.

Times (London), October 17, 1986; April 6, 1987; March 15, 1990.

Times Literary Supplement, April 1, 1965; June 10, 1965; January 18, 1968; December 31, 1971; March 2, 1973; December 14, 1973; February 8, 1974; March 1, 1974; October 17, 1975; August 5, 1977; February 26, 1982; September 23, 1988; March 22-29, 1990; February 24, 1995.

Tribune Books (Chicago), November 19, 1989; Jule 31, 1994.

Tri-Quarterly, fall, 1966.

Washington Post, October 30, 1979; October 17, 1986; November 10, 1989.

World Literature Today, winter, 1977; autumn, 1981; summer, 1982.

SPARK, Muriel (Sarah) 1918-
(Evelyn Cavallo)

PERSONAL: Born February 1, 1918, in Edinburgh, Scotland; daughter of Bernard and Sarah Elizabeth Maud (Uezzell) Camberg; married S. O. Spark, 1937 (divorced); children: Robin (son). *Education:* Attended Heriot Watt College, c. 1944. *Religion:* Roman Catholic. *Avocational interests:* Reading, travel.

ADDRESSES: Home—Italy. *Agent*—c/o David Higham Associates Ltd., 5-8 Lower John Street, Golden Square W1R 4HA, England.

CAREER: Writer. Employed in the Political Intelligence Department of the British government's Foreign Office, 1944-45; affiliated with *Argentor* (jewelry trade magazine); general secretary, Poetry Society, 1947-49; founder, *Forum* (literary magazine), and editor of *Poetry Review,* 1949; part-time editor, Peter Owen Ltd. (publishing company).

MEMBER: PEN, American Academy and Institute of Arts and Letters (honorary member), Society of Authors, Authors Guild, Royal Society of Edinburgh.

AWARDS, HONORS: Observer short story prize, 1951, for "The Seraph and the Zambesi"; Prix Italia, 1962, for radio play adaptation of *The Ballad of Peckham Rye;* Yorkshire Post Book of the Year Award, 1965, and James Tait Black Memorial Prize, 1966, both for *The Mandelbaum Gate;* Order of the British Empire, 1967; D.Litt., University of Strathclyde, 1971, and University of Edinburgh, 1989; Booker McConnell Prize nomination, 1981, for *Loitering with Intent;* Scottish Book of the Year Award, 1987, for *The Stories of Muriel Spark;* First Prize, F.N.A.C. La Meilleur Recueil des Nouvelles Etrangeres, 1987, for the Editions Fayard translation of *The Stories of Muriel Spark;* Officier de l'Ordre des Arts et des Lettres, France, 1988; Ingersoll T. S. Eliot Award, 1992; Dame, Order of the British Empire, 1993; Commandeur de l'Ordre des Arts et des Lettres, France, 1996; David Cohen British Literature Prize, 1997.

WRITINGS:

FICTION

The Comforters (also see below), Lippincott, 1957.
Robinson, Lippincott, 1958.
The Go-Away Bird and Other Stories (short stories), Macmillan (London), 1958, Lippincott, 1960.
Memento Mori (also see below), Lippincott, 1959.
The Ballad of Peckham Rye (also see below), Lippincott, 1960.
The Bachelors, Macmillan (London), 1960, Lippincott, 1961.
Voices at Play (short stories and radio plays), Macmillan (London), 1961, Lippincott, 1962.
The Prime of Miss Jean Brodie (also see below), Macmillan (London), 1961, Lippincott, 1962.
A Muriel Spark Trio (contains *The Comforters, Memento Mori,* and *The Ballad of Peckham Rye*), Lippincott, 1962.
The Girls of Slender Means (also see below), Knopf, 1963.
The Mandelbaum Gate, Knopf, 1965.
Collected Stories 1 (short stories), Macmillan (London), 1967, Knopf, 1968.
The Public Image, Knopf, 1968.
The Very Fine Clock (juvenile), Knopf, 1968.
The Driver's Seat, Knopf, 1970.
The French Window (juvenile), Macmillan (London), 1970.
Not to Disturb, Macmillan (London), 1971, Viking, 1972.
The Hothouse by the East River, Viking, 1973.

The Abbess of Crewe (also see below), Viking, 1973.
The Takeover, Viking, 1976.
Territorial Rights, Coward, 1979.
Loitering with Intent, Coward, 1981.
Bang-Bang You're Dead and Other Stories, Granada, 1982.
The Only Problem, Coward, 1984, Franklin Library, 1984.
The Stories of Muriel Spark, Dutton, 1985.
A Far Cry from Kensington, Houghton, 1988.
Symposium, Houghton, 1990.
The Novels of Muriel Spark (selections), Houghton, 1995.
Reality and Dreams, Constable, 1996.
Open to the Public: New and Collected Stories, New Directions (New York City), 1997.

Also author of *The Small Telephone* (juvenile), 1993.

POETRY

The Fanfarlo and Other Verse, Hand and Flower Press, 1952.
Collected Poems 1, Macmillan (London), 1967, Knopf, 1968, published as *Going Up to Sotheby's and Other Poems,* Granada, 1982.

NONFICTION

Child of Light: A Reassessment of Mary Wollstonecraft Shelley, Tower Bridge Publications, 1951, revised edition published as *Mary Shelley,* Dutton, 1987.
Emily Bronte: Her Life and Work, P. Owen, 1953.
John Masefield, Nevill, 1953.
The Essence of the Brontes, P. Owen (Chester Springs, PA), 1993.

EDITOR

(And author of introduction) *A Selection of Poems by Emily Bronte,* Grey Walls Press, 1952.
(With Derek Stanford) *My Best Mary: The Letters of Mary Shelley,* Wingate, 1953.
The Letters of the Brontes: A Selection, University of Oklahoma Press, 1954, published in England as *The Bronte Letters,* Nevill, 1954.
(With Stanford) *Letters of John Henry Newman,* P. Owen, 1957.

Also edited with others *Tribute to Wordsworth,* 1950. Review editor, *European Affairs,* 1949-50.

OTHER

Doctors of Philosophy (play; produced in London, 1962), Macmillan (London), 1963, Knopf, 1966.
Curriculum Vitae: Autobiography, Houghton, 1993.

Also author of radio plays *The Party through the Wall,* 1957, *The Interview,* 1958, *The Dry River Bed,* 1959, *The Ballad of Peckham Rye,* 1960, and *The Danger Zone,* 1961. Contributor of short stories and poems to the *New Yorker,* and of poems, articles, and reviews to magazines and newspapers, occasionally under the pseudonym Evelyn Cavallo.

MEDIA ADAPTATIONS: Several of Muriel Spark's novels have been adapted for the stage, film, and television. A dramatization of *Memento Mori* was produced on stage in 1964 and a version was televised by British Broadcasting Corporation (BBC) in 1992. Jay Presson Allen's dramatization of *The Prime of Miss Jean Brodie,* published by Samuel French in 1969, was first produced in Torquay, England, at the Princess Theatre beginning April 5, 1966, then in Boston at the Colonial Theatre from December 26, 1967, to January 6, 1968, and finally on Broadway at the Helen Hayes Theatre beginning January 9, 1968. Allen also wrote the screenplay for the 1969 film version of the same novel, a Twentieth Century-Fox production starring Maggie Smith. John

Wood's dramatization of *The Prime of Miss Jean Brodie* was produced in London at Wyndham's Theatre in 1967, and on Broadway in 1968; a six-part adaptation of the novel appeared on public television in England in 1978 and in the United States in 1979. *The Driver's Seat* was filmed in 1972, and in 1974 *The Girls of Slender Means* was adapted for BBC television. *The Abbess of Crewe* was filmed and released in 1976 under the title *Nasty Habits.*

SIDELIGHTS: Often described as one of the best, yet one of the most unappreciated, of today's novelists, Muriel Spark puzzles those readers and critics who have an affinity for labels and categories. Explains Richard Sullivan in *Book World:* "For those who take comfort in instant classification Muriel Spark keeps posing a mischievous problem. She's elusive. There is no question about her quality: her work to date has demonstrated it. . . . Yet she doesn't fit neatly into any pigeonhole. . . . She is—and probably without bothering in the least about it, prefers to be—an original."

Spark had already achieved some recognition as a critic and poet when she entered what was virtually her first attempt at fiction, the short story "The Seraph and the Zambesi," in a 1951 Christmas writing contest sponsored by the London *Observer.* The fanciful tale of a troublesome angel who bursts in on an acting troupe staging a holiday pageant on the banks of Africa's Zambesi River, "The Seraph and the Zambesi" won top honors in the competition and attracted a great deal of attention for its unconventional treatment of the Christmas theme. Several other stories set in Africa and England followed; soon Spark's successes in fiction began to overshadow those in criticism and poetry.

With financial and moral support from author Graham Greene, Spark struggled for nearly three years to sort out the aesthetic, psychological, and religious questions raised by her conversion and her attempt at writing longer fiction. Drawing on the tenets of her new faith, which she believes is especially "conducive to individuality, to finding one's own individual point of view," the young writer formulated her own theory of the novel. According to Frank Kermode in his book *Continuities,* this theory suggests that "a genuine relation exists between the forms of fiction and the forms of the world, between the novelist's creation and God's." In essence, Spark sees the novelist as very God-like—omniscient and omnipotent, able to manipulate plot, character, and dialogue at will. Viewed in this light, Kermode and others contend, Spark's first novel, *The Comforters,* is obviously "an experiment designed to discover whether . . . the novelist, pushing people and things around and giving 'disjointed happenings a shape,' is in any way like Providence."

Because Spark's Catholicism figures so prominently in *The Comforters* and subsequent works, it is "much more than an item of biographical interest," in the opinion of Victor Kelleher. Comments Kelleher in *Critical Review:* "Spark does not stop short at simply bringing the question of Catholicism into her work; she has chosen to place the traditionally Christian outlook at the very heart of everything she writes. . . . [Her tales proclaim] the most basic of Christian truths: that all man's blessings emanate from God; that, in the absence of God, man is nothing more than a savage." Catharine Hughes makes a similar assessment of Spark's religious sentiment in an article in *Catholic World.* Observes the critic: "[Spark satirizes] humanity's foibles and incongruities from a decidedly Catholic orientation. One is conscious that she is a writer working within the framework of some of Christianity's greatest truths; that her perspective, which takes full cognizance of

eternal values, is never burdened by a painful attempt to inflict them upon others."

At first glance, however, Spark's novels do not seem to reflect her strong religious and moral preoccupations. In terms of setting, for example, the author usually chooses to locate her modern morality tales in upper-class urban areas of England or Italy. Her "fun-house plots, full of trapdoors, abrupt apparitions, and smartly clicking secret panels," as John Updike describes them in a *New Yorker* article, focus on the often bizarre behavior of people belonging to a small, select group: elderly men and women linked by long-standing personal relationships in *Memento Mori;* unmarried male and female residents of the same London district in *The Bachelors;* students and teachers at a Scottish girls' school in *The Prime of Miss Jean Brodie;* servants on a Swiss estate in *Not to Disturb;* guests at a pair of neighboring Venetian hotels in *Territorial Rights.* The "action" in these stories springs from the elaborate ties Spark concocts between the members of each group—ties of blood, marriage, friendship, and other kinds of relationships. Commenting in her study of the author titled *Muriel Spark,* critic Patricia Stubbs observes that the use of such a technique reflects Spark's fascination with "the way in which the individual varies in different settings, or different company." "By taking this restricted group of protagonists," explains Stubbs, "[Spark] is able to create multiple ironies, arising from their connecting and conflicting destinies: by her selection of such a restricted canvas, she can display the many facets of her creatures' personalities, and the different roles which they, or society, decree they should play."

In the tradition of the intellectual novelist, Spark avoids florid descriptions of the physical world, preferring instead to concentrate on dialogue, on "the play of ideas and experiences upon the mind, and the interplay of minds upon each other," in Joseph Hynes's words. Her characterizations are quick, sharp, and concise; in a *New Statesman* article, for instance, Walter Allen writes that the author "pins [her types] to the page quivering in their essential absurdity." As a result, says *Newsweek* reviewer Raymond A. Sokolov, "a [typical Spark] character is born, with a deft flick of the author's wrist, in an effortless few pages."

Spark teams her technical virtuosity with an elegant, acerbic wit and condescending attitude that most readers find highly entertaining. As Melvin Maddocks declares in *Life:* "Reading a Muriel Spark novel remains one of the minor pleasures of life. Like a perfect hostess, she caters to our small needs. In the manner available to only the best British novelists, she ordains a civilized atmosphere—two parts what Evelyn Waugh called creamy English charm, one part acid wit. She peoples her scene discriminatingly, showing a taste for interesting but not overpowering guests. . . . As the evening moves along, she has the good sense to lower the drawing-room lights and introduce a pleasantly chilling bit of tension—even violence—just to save us all, bless her, from the overexquisite sensibilities of the lady novelist."

The 1990 best seller *Symposium* demonstrates the qualities to which Maddocks refers. It centers on Margaret Demien, a character whose wealthy mother-in-law dies while Margaret is away at a dinner party. Appearing to all as virtuous at first, Margaret openly expresses a more sinister intent. She is also connected to other mysterious deaths, so that when the guests receive news of the older woman's death, Margaret is a suspect. Peter Parker comments in the *Listener,* "This is a marvelous premise for a novel, and, as one would expect, Spark makes the most of opportunities for dark comedy. Against Margaret's wilful attempt to become an instrument of evil is set an example of casual wickedness that unwittingly leads to mortal sin and provides the novel with a terrific final chapter. The book's epigraphs, taken from *Symposia* of Lucian and Plato, supply hints both of the book's resolution and of Spark's fictional method." The epigraphs also provide clues about the five couples at the dinner party, who in some ways represent the varieties of love Plato defined. "But the real philosophical dialogue in *Symposium* is not about love nor is it explicitly argued. Rather, it takes place almost between the lines and concerns the mysteries of evil and suffering, destiny and predestination, guilt and intention," Nina King relates in a *Washington Post Book World* review. A *Publishers Weekly* reviewer comments, "Spark's exquisitely balanced tone proves that the richest comedy is that which explores the darkest themes."

Yet, as Barbara Grizzuti Harrison reminds readers in a *New York Times Book Review* article, Spark is at heart "a profoundly serious comic writer whose wit advances, never undermines or diminishes, her ideas." This sentiment is shared by Harrison's fellow *New York Times Book Review* critic Leonard Graver, who writes: "Sinister metaphysical farce has always been one of Muriel Spark's specialties. . . . [But] lurid entertainment is only part of [her] intention. She has always been a novelist who wishes to tease readers into serious thought. . . . [Her work] has the cleverness to entertain and the intelligence to provoke thought." Spark once explained to *Contemporary Authors* that the intent behind her "mischief" is to make a lasting impression on her readers: "Satire is far more important, it has a more lasting effect, than a straight portrayal of what is wrong. I think that a lot of the world's problems should be ridiculed, but ridiculed properly rather than, well, wailed over. People go to the theater, for instance, to see a play about some outrage or other, and then they come away feeling that they've done something about it, which they haven't. But if these things are ridiculed, it sticks and the perpetrators stop doing it. . . . I do believe in satire as a very, very potent art form."

Despite all that has been written about her and her fiction, Muriel Spark remains an enigma to most critics, concerning herself as she does "with matters beyond reality, with forces that do not lend themselves to facile explanations," according to Florence Rome in the *Chicago Tribune Book World*. Described by Sybille Bedford in the *Saturday Review* as "an artist, a serious—and most accomplished—writer, a moralist engaged with the human predicament, wildly entertaining, and a joy to read," Spark has nevertheless, in Stubbs's opinion, "succeeded triumphantly in evading classification." Updike, too, contends that Spark possesses a truly exceptional talent—a talent that without a doubt makes her an unclassifiable "original." In fact, he declares in the *New Yorker*, Spark "is one of the few writers of the language on either side of the Atlantic with enough resources, daring, and stamina to be altering, as well as feeding, the fiction machine."

Spark produced *Curriculum Vitae: An Autobiography* in 1993, at the age of 75, partly to correct critical misunderstandings and inaccuracies about her life, and partly to put together the facts about her life and her fiction. "So many strange and erroneous accounts of parts of my life have been written since I became well known," *New Leader* contributor Hope Hale Davis quotes the author as saying, "that I felt it time to put the record straight." *Curriculum Vitae* covers the first thirty-nine years of Spark's life, up to the publication of her first novel *The Comforters*. It tells of her childhood in Edinburgh, daughter of a Jewish father and a Protestant English mother (whose accent mortified her daughter

on more than one occasion). Spark also tells of her years at Gillespie's, where she studied under Christina Day, who later served as the model for the title character in *The Prime of Miss Jean Brodie*. Unlike the fictional Brodie, however, Spark declares, Day would never have manipulated her charges in an attempt to seduce a fellow teacher. *Curriculum Vitae* covers Spark's time spent caring for her bedridden English grandmother; her unhappy marriage to and seven years in Northern Rhodesia with the mentally disturbed Sydney O. Spark, who fathered her son Robin; her war years in the propaganda wing of the British government; and her emergence as a powerful writer of fiction. "In her own fashion, reticent when she chooses but always free of invention," states Helen Bevington in the *New York Times Book Review*, "Muriel Spark succeeds in her mission: she puts the record straight. With nearly half her life yet to consider, she will, I hope, tell us the rest of it."

BIOGRAPHICAL/CRITICAL SOURCES:

BOOKS

Contemporary Authors New Revision Series, Gale (Detroit), Volume 12, 1984; Volume 36, 1992.
Contemporary Literary Criticism, Gale, Volume 2, 1974; Volume 3, 1975; Volume 5, 1976; Volume 8, 1978; Volume 13, 1980; Volume 18, 1981; Volume 40, 1987.
Dictionary of Literary Biography, Volume 15: *British Novelists, 1930-1959,* Gale, 1983.
Edgecombe, Rodney Stenning, *Vocation and Identity in the Fiction of Muriel Spark,* University of Missouri Press, 1990.
Enright, D. J., *Man Is an Onion: Reviews and Essays,* Chatto & Windus, 1972.
Hynes, Joseph, editor, *Critical Essays on Muriel Spark,* G. K. Hall (New York City), 1992.
Kemp, Peter, *Muriel Spark,* Elek, 1974, Barnes & Noble, 1975.
Kermode, Frank, *Continuities,* Random House, 1968.
Malkoff, Karl, *Muriel Spark,* Columbia University Press, 1968.
Pearlman, Mickey, *Re-inventing Reality: Patterns and Characteristics in the Novels of Muriel Spark,* Lang (New York), 1996.
Randisi, Jennifer Lynn, *On Her Way Rejoicing: The Fiction of Muriel Spark,* Catholic University of America Press (Washington, DC), 1991.
Sproxton, Judy, *The Women of Muriel Spark,* St. Martin's Press (New York City), 1992.
Sproxton, Judy, *Muriel Spark,* St. Martin's Press, 1994.
Stubbs, Patricia, *Muriel Spark,* Longman, 1973.
Whittaker, Ruth, *The Faith and Fiction of Muriel Spark,* Macmillan (London), 1978.

PERIODICALS

America, February 12, 1994, p. 26.
Book World, September 29, 1968; November 23, 1969; June 6, 1993.
Catholic World, August, 1961
Chicago Tribune, February 13, 1990.
Chicago Tribune Book World, April 29, 1973; May 24, 1981; November 3, 1985.
Christian Science Monitor, November 14, 1968; May 18, 1993.
Commonweal, August 23, 1957; September 18, 1959; February 23, 1962; December 3, 1965; January 14, 1966; May 21, 1993.
Critical Review, number 18, 1976.
Detroit News, June 21, 1981; July 8, 1984; December 5, 1990.
Life, October 11, 1968.
Listener, December 7, 1967; September 24, 1970; September 20, 1990.

London Magazine, July, 1968.
Los Angeles Times, July 14, 1968; July 26, 1984; July 29, 1987; July 14, 1988.
Los Angeles Times Book Review, February 2, 1990; May 16, 1993.
Ms., May, 1976.
New Leader, November 30, 1970; July 30, 1979; May 17, 1993.
New Republic, January 29, 1962.
New Statesman, July 5, 1958; March 28, 1959; March 5, 1960; October 15, 1960; November 3, 1961; September 27, 1963; September 25, 1970; March 2, 1973; April 27, 1979.
New Statesman and Nation, February 23, 1957.
Newsweek, October 21, 1968; November 30, 1970; May 18, 1981; July 2, 1984; September 16, 1985.
New Yorker, June 13, 1959; August 27, 1960; September 30, 1961; September 14, 1963; January 27, 1968; June 8, 1981.
New York Review of Books, October 28, 1965; December 19, 1968; November 28, 1974; November 11, 1976.
New York Times, September 1, 1957; October 19, 1958; March 29, 1972; November 26, 1974; October 7, 1976; May 19, 1979; May 28, 1981; June 26, 1984; September 18, 1985; July 20, 1987; May 16, 1993; May 16, 1997.
New York Times Book Review, May 17, 1959; August 28, 1960; September 29, 1968; March 26, 1972; October 3, 1976; May 20, 1979; May 31, 1981; July 15, 1984; October 20, 1985; September 6, 1987; July 31, 1988; November 25, 1990; May 16, 1993.
Observer (London), July 18, 1993.
Publishers Weekly, October 26, 1990.
Time, August 15, 1960; January 19, 1962; January 13, 1967; November 1, 1968; October 26, 1970; June 11, 1979; July 6, 1981; July 16, 1984.
Times (London), September 6, 1984; April 16, 1987.
Times Literary Supplement, June 27, 1958; March 4, 1960; October 11, 1960; November 3, 1961; October 25, 1963; October 14, 1965; September 25, 1970; May 22, 1981.
Washington Post Book World, October 3, 1976; June 24, 1979; May 24, 1981; September 29, 1985; August 23, 1987; November 25, 1990.

* * *

SPAULDING, Douglas
    See BRADBURY, Ray (Douglas)

* * *

SPAULDING, Leonard
    See BRADBURY, Ray (Douglas)

* * *

SPENCE, J. A. D.
    See ELIOT, T(homas) S(tearns)

* * *

SPENCER, Leonard G.
    See SILVERBERG, Robert

SPENDER, Stephen (Harold) 1909-1995

PERSONAL: Born February 28, 1909, in London, England; died July 16, 1995, in London; son of Edward Harold (a journalist and lecturer) and Violet Hilda (Schuster) Spender; married Agnes Marie Pearn, 1936 (divorced); married Natasha Litvin (a pianist), 1941; children: (second marriage) Matthew Francis, Elizabeth. *Education:* Attended University College, Oxford, 1928-30.

CAREER: Writer. Elliston Chair of Poetry, University of Cincinnati, 1953; Beckman Professor, University of California, 1959; visiting lecturer, Northwestern University, 1963; Clark lecturer, Cambridge University, 1966; Mellon lecturer, Washington, DC, 1968; Northcliffe lecturer, University of London, 1969; visiting professor at University of Connecticut, 1968-70, University of Florida, 1976, Vanderbilt University, 1979, and University of South Carolina, 1981; University of London, University College, London, England, professor of English, 1970-77, professor emeritus, 1977-95.

Counselor in Section of Letters, UNESCO, 1947. Fellow of Institute of Advanced Studies, Wesleyan University, 1967. Consultant on poetry in English, Library of Congress, Washington, DC, 1965. *Military service:* National Fire Service, fireman, 1941-44.

MEMBER: PEN International (president, English Centre, beginning in 1975); American Academy of Arts and Letters and National Institute for Arts and Letters (honorary), Phi Beta Kappa, Beefsteak Club.

AWARDS, HONORS: Commander of the British Empire, 1962; Queen's Gold Medal for Poetry, 1971; named Companion of Literature, 1977; knighted by Queen Elizabeth II, 1983; *Los Angeles Times* Book Award in poetry nomination for *Collected Poems, 1928-1985,* 1986; honorary fellow, University College, Oxford; D.Litt. from University of Montpelier, Cornell University, and Loyola University.

WRITINGS:

POETRY

Nine Experiments: Being Poems Written at the Age of Eighteen, privately printed, 1928.
Twenty Poems, Basil Blackwell (Oxford, England), 1930.
Poems, Faber (London), 1933, Random House (New York City), 1934.
Perhaps (limited edition), privately printed, 1933.
Poem (limited edition), privately printed, 1934.
Vienna, Faber, 1934.
At Night, privately printed, 1935.
The Still Centre, Faber, 1939.
Selected Poems, Random House, 1940.
I Sit by the Window, Linden Press (New York City), c. 1940.
Ruins and Visions: Poems, 1934-1942, Random House, 1942.
Poems of Dedication, Random House, 1947.
Returning to Vienna, 1947: Nine Sketches, Banyan Press (Chicago), 1947.
The Edge of Being, Random House, 1949.
Sirmione Peninsula, Faber, 1954.
Collected Poems, 1928-1953, Random House, 1955, revised edition published as *Collected Poems, 1928-1985,* Faber, 1985.
Inscriptions, Poetry Book Society (London), 1958.
Selected Poems, Random House, 1964.

The Generous Days: Ten Poems, David Godine (Boston), 1969, enlarged edition published as *The Generous Days,* Faber, 1971.

Descartes, Steam Press (London), 1970.

Art Student, Poem-of-the-Month Club (London), 1970.

Recent Poems, Anvil Press Poetry (London), 1978.

Dolphins, St. Martin's (New York City), 1994.

PLAYS

Trial of a Judge: A Tragedy in Five Acts (first produced in London at Rupert Doone's Group Theatre on March 18, 1938), Random House, 1938.

(Translator and adapter with Goronwy Rees) *Danton's Death* (first produced in London, 1939; adaptation of a play by Georg Buechner), Faber, 1939.

To the Island, first produced at Oxford University, 1951.

(Adapter) *Lulu* (adaptation from plays by Frank Wedekind; also see below), produced in New York, 1958.

(Translator and adapter) *Mary Stuart* (adaptation of a play by Johann Christoph Friedrich von Schiller; produced on the West End at Old Vic, 1961; produced on Broadway at Vivian Beaumont Theatre, November 11, 1971), Faber, 1959.

(Translator and adapter) *The Oedipus Trilogy—King Oedipus, Oedipus at Colonos, Antigone: A Version by Stephen Spender* (three-act play; revision of play produced at Oxford Playhouse, 1983), Faber, 1985.

ESSAYS

The Destructive Element: A Study of Modern Writers and Beliefs, J. Cape (London), 1935, Houghton (Boston), 1936.

Forward from Liberalism, Random House, 1937.

The New Realism: A Discussion, Hogarth (London), 1939, Folcroft, 1977.

Life and the Poet, Secker & Warburg (London), 1942, Folcroft, 1974.

European Witness, Reynal, 1946.

(Contributor) Richard H. Crossman, editor, *The God That Failed: Six Studies in Communism,* Harper, 1950.

Learning Laughter, Weidenfeld & Nicolson (London), 1952, Harcourt, 1953.

The Creative Element: A Study of Vision, Despair, and Orthodoxy among Some Modern Writers, Hamish Hamilton (London), 1953, Folcroft, 1973.

The Making of a Poem, Hamish Hamilton, 1955, Norton, 1962.

The Imagination in the Modern World: Three Lectures, Library of Congress (Washington, DC), 1962.

The Struggle of the Modern, University of California Press (Berkeley, CA), 1963.

Chaos and Control in Poetry, Library of Congress, 1966.

The Year of the Young Rebels, Random House, 1969.

Love-Hate Relations: A Study of Anglo-American Sensibilities, Random House, 1974.

Eliot, Fontana, 1975, published as *T. S. Eliot,* Viking, 1976.

Henry Moore: Sculptures in Landscape, Studio Vista (London), 1978, C. N. Potter, 1979.

The Thirties and After: Poetry, Politics, People, 1933-1970, Random House, 1978.

(Contributor) *America Observed,* C. N. Potter, 1979.

(With David Hockney) *China Diary* (travel guide), with illustrations by Hockney, Thames & Hudson, 1982.

In Irina's Garden with Henry Moore's Sculpture, Thames & Hudson, 1986.

EDITOR

W. H. Auden, *Poems,* privately printed, 1928.

(With Louis MacNeice) *Oxford Poetry 1929,* Basil Blackwell, 1929.

(With Bernard Spencer) *Oxford Poetry 1930,* Basil Blackwell, 1930.

(With John Lehmann and Christopher Isherwood) *New Writing, New Series I,* Hogarth, 1938.

(With Lehmann and Isherwood) *New Writing, New Series II,* Hogarth, 1939.

(With Lehmann and author of introduction) *Poems for Spain,* Hogarth, 1939.

Spiritual Exercises: To Cecil Day Lewis (poems), privately printed, 1943.

(And author of introduction) *A Choice of English Romantic Poetry,* Dial, 1947.

(And author of introduction) Walt Whitman, *Selected Poems,* Grey Walls Press (London), 1950.

Martin Huerlimann, *Europe in Photographs,* Thames & Hudson, 1951.

(With Elizabeth Jennings and Dannie Abse) *New Poems 1956: An Anthology,* M. Joseph (London), 1956.

(And author of introduction) *Great Writings of Goethe,* New American Library, 1958.

(And author of introduction) *Great German Short Stories,* Dell, 1960.

(And author of introduction) *The Writer's Dilemma,* Oxford University Press, 1961.

(With Irving Kristol and Melvin J. Lasky) *Encounters: An Anthology from the First Ten Years of "Encounter" Magazine,* Basic Books, 1963.

(With Donald Hall) *The Concise Encyclopedia of English and American Poets and Poetry,* Hawthorn, 1963, revised edition, Hutchinson, 1970.

(And author of introduction) *A Choice of Shelley's Verse,* Faber, 1971.

(And author of introduction) *Selected Poems of Abba Kovne* [and] *Selected Poems of Nelly Sachs,* Penguin, 1971.

The Poems of Percy Bysshe Shelley, Limited Editions Club (Cambridge), 1971.

D. H. Lawrence: Novelist, Poet, Prophet, Harper, 1973.

W. H. Auden: A Tribute, Macmillan, 1975.

Herbert List: Junge Maenner, Twin Palms, 1988.

Hockney's Alphabet, Random House/American Friends of AIDS Crisis Trust, 1991.

TRANSLATOR

(And author of introduction and, with J. B. Leishman, commentary) Rainer Maria Rilke, *Duino Elegies* (bilingual edition), Norton, 1939, 4th edition, revised, Hogarth, 1963.

(With Hugh Hunt) Ernst Toller, *Pastor Hall* (three-act play), John Lane, 1939; also bound with *Blind Man's Buff* by Toller and Denis Johnson, Random House, 1939.

(With J. L. Gili) Federico Garcia Lorca, *Poems,* Oxford University Press, 1939.

(With Gili) *Selected Poems of Federico Garcia Lorca,* Hogarth, 1943.

(With Frances Cornford) Paul Eluard, *Le Dur desir de Durer,* Grey Falcon Press, 1950.

(And author of introduction) Rilke, *The Life of the Virgin Mary (Das Marien-Leben)* (bilingual edition), Philosophical Library, 1951.

(With Frances Fawcett) Frank Wedekind, *Five Tragedies of Sex,* Theatre Arts, 1952.

(With Nikos Stangos) C. P. Cavafy, *Fourteen Poems,* Editions Electo, 1977.

Wedekind, *Lulu Plays and Other Sex Tragedies,* Riverrun, 1979.

OTHER

The Burning Cactus (short stories), Random House, 1936.

The Backward Son (novel), Hogarth, 1940.

(With William Sansom and James Gordon) *Jim Braidy: The Story of Britain's Firemen,* Lindsay Drummond, 1943.

(Author of introduction and notes) *Botticelli,* Faber, 1945, Pitman (London), 1948.

(Author of introduction) Patrice de la Tour du Pin, *The Dedicated Life in Poetry* [and] *The Correspondence of Laurent de Cayeux,* Harvill Press, 1948.

World within World: The Autobiography of Stephen Spender, Harcourt, 1951, reprinted with an introduction by the author, St. Martin's, 1994.

Engaged in Writing, and The Fool and the Princess (short stories), Farrar, Straus (New York City), 1958.

(With Nicholas Nabokov) *Rasputin's End* (opera), Ricordi (Milan), 1963.

(Contributor with Patrick Leigh Fermor) *Ghika: Paintings, Drawings, Sculpture,* Lund, Humphries, 1964, Boston Book and Art Shop, 1965.

(Reteller) *The Magic Flute: Retold* (juvenile; based on the opera by Mozart), Putnam, 1966.

(Author of introduction) *Venice,* Vendome, 1979.

Letters to Christopher: Stephen Spender's Letters to Christopher Isherwood, 1929-1939, with "The Line of the Branch"—Two Thirties Journals, Black Sparrow (Santa Barbara, CA), 1980.

(Author of introduction) *Herbert List: Photographs, 1930-1970,* Thames & Hudson, 1981.

(Contributor) Martin Friedman, *Hockney Paints the Stage,* Abbeville Press, 1983.

The Journals of Stephen Spender, 1939-1983, Random House, 1986.

The Temple (novel), Grove, 1988.

(Author of preface) David Finn, *Evocations of "Four Quartets,"* Black Swan, 1991.

(Translator with others) *Selected Poems by Rilke,* Knopf (New York City), 1996.

Editor, with Cyril Connolly, of *Horizon,* 1939-41; coeditor, with Melvin J. Lasky, 1953-66, and corresponding editor, 1966-67, *Encounter;* cofounder of *Index on Censorship* (bimonthly magazine). Contributor to numerous anthologies.

SIDELIGHTS: Stephen Spender was a member of the generation of British poets who came to prominence in the 1930s, a group—sometimes referred to as the Oxford Poets—that included W. H. Auden, Christopher Isherwood, C. Day Lewis, and Louis MacNeice. In *World within World: The Autobiography of Stephen Spender* the author speculated that the names of the members of the group became irreversibly linked in the minds of critics for no other reason than having their poems included in the same important poetic anthologies of the early thirties. However, in *The Angry Young Men of the Thirties* Elton Edward Smith found that the poets had much more in common and stated that they shared a "similarity of theme, image, and diction." According to Smith, the poets also all rejected the writing of the immediately preceding generation. Gerald Nicosia reached the same conclusion in his *Chicago Tribune Book World* essay on Spender's work. "While preserving a reverence for traditional values and a high standard of craftsmanship," Nicosia wrote, "they turned away from the esotericism of T. S. Eliot, insisting that the writer stay in touch with the urgent political issues of the day and that he speak in a voice whose clarity can be understood by all." Comparing the older and younger generations of writers, Smith noted that while the poets of the 1920s focused on themes removed from reality, "the poets of the 1930s represented a return to the objective world outside and the recognition of the importance of the things men do together in groups: political action, social structure, cultural development."

Spender's name was most frequently associated with that of W. H. Auden, perhaps the most famous poet of the thirties; yet some critics, including Alfred Kazin and Helen Vendler, found the two poets dissimilar in many ways. In the *New Yorker,* for example, Vendler observed that "at first [Spender] imitated Auden's self-possessed ironies, his determined use of technological objects. . . . But no two poets can have been more different. Auden's rigid, brilliant, peremptory, categorizing, allegorical mind demanded forms altogether different from Spender's dreamy, liquid, guilty, hovering sensibility. Auden is a poet of firmly historical time, Spender of timeless nostalgic space." In the *New York Times Book Review* Kazin similarly concluded that Spender "was mistakenly identified with Auden. Although they were virtual opposites in personality and in the direction of their talents, they became famous at the same time as 'pylon poets'— among the first to put England's gritty industrial landscape of the 1930's into poetry."

The term "pylon poets" refers to "The Pylons," a poem by Spender which many critics described as typical of the Auden generation. The much-anthologized work, included in one of Spender's earliest collections, *Poems,* as well as in his compilation of a lifetime's accomplishments, *Collected Poems, 1928-1985,* is characteristic of the group's imagery and also reflects the political and social concerns of its members. Smith recognized that in such a poem "the poet, instead of closing his eyes to the hideous steel towers of a rural electrification system and concentrating on the soft green fields, glorifies the pylons and grants to them the future. And the nonhuman structure proves to be of the very highest social value, for rural electrification programs help create a new world of human equality."

The decade of the thirties was marked by turbulent events that would shape the course of history: the world-wide economic depression, the Spanish Civil War, and the beginnings of the Second World War. Seeing the established world crumbling around them, the writers of the period sought to create a new reality to replace the old, which in their minds had become obsolete. According to D. E. S. Maxwell, commenting in his *Poets of the Thirties,* "the imaginative writing of the thirties created an unusual *milieu* of urban squalor and political intrigue. This kind of statement—a suggestion of decay producing violence and leading to change—as much as any absolute and unanimous political partisanship gave this poetry its marxist reputation. Communism and 'the communist' (a poster-type stock figure) were frequently invoked." For a time Spender, like many young intellectuals of the era, was a member of the Communist party. "Spender believed," Smith noted, "that communism offered the only workable analysis and solution of complex world problems, that it was sure eventually to win, and that for significance and relevance the artist must somehow link his art to the Communist diagnosis." Smith described Spender's poem, "The Funeral" (included in *Collected Poems: 1928-1953* but omitted from the 1985 revision of the same work), as "a Communist elegy" and observed that much of Spender's other works from the same early period as "The Funeral," including his play, *Trial of a Judge: A Tragedy in Five Acts,* his poems from *Vienna,* and his essays in *The Destructive*

Element: A Study of Modern Writers and Beliefs and *Forward from Liberalism* deal with the Communist question.

Spender continued to write poetry throughout his life, but it came to consume less of his literary output in later years than it did in the 1930s and 1940s. The last collection of poems published before his death was *Dolphins*. "To find him still reaching out at 85—the same age as [English novelist and poet Thomas] Hardy was when he published his last poems—is confirmation of the old truism that feeling is not an optional extra of humans but bred in the bone," commented William Scammell in the *Spectator*. In the title piece, Spender turns his attention to those creatures of the sea which have captivated poets for centuries. "For him, their movements constitute a kind of scripture, communicating at an ontological level beyond merely human speech," observed Peter Firchow in *World Literature Today*. "Their message is utterly simple, the simplest and most basic of all: 'I AM.'" For several critics, these two words spoke volumes about Spender's poetry. In a *Times Literary Supplement* review, Julian Symons explained, "If Stephen Spender ever intended to create a poetry of 'direct social function,' the idea was long ago abandoned in favour of a concern to express in verse his own true beliefs and attitudes, about which he remains permanently uncertain."

Firchow found that most of the poems in *Dolphins* did not live up to the high standards that Spender had set in his previous work, but the reviewer did admit that "two long autobiographical poems, 'A First War Childhood' and 'Wordsworth,' come close." Symons praised Spender's long poem about the life of Arthur Rimbaud. "The sequence is successful in part because Spender can have found no difficulty in imagining himself both Rimbaud and [Paul] Verlaine, in part because of his strong dramatic sense," wrote the reviewer. "Yet the most striking poem here records not the insight of the witness, but the anguish of the absentee," observed Boyd Tonkin in the *New Statesman and Society*. "'History and Reality' pays homage to the Jewish, Catholic and quasi-Marxist thinker Simone Weil, who starved herself in solidarity with Hitler's victims."

The past often became the subject of Spender's writing in the eighties. Particularly *The Journals of Stephen Spender, 1939-1983, Collected Poems, 1928-1985,* and *Letters to Christopher: Stephen Spender's Letters to Christopher Isherwood, 1929-1939, with "The Line of the Branch"—Two Thirties Journals* placed a special emphasis on autobiographical material that reviewers found revealed Spender as both an admirable personality and a notable writer. In a *New York Times Book Review* commentary by Samuel Hynes on the collection of Spender's letters, for instance, the critic expressed his belief that "the person who emerges from these letters is neither a madman nor a fool, but an honest, intelligent, troubled young man, groping toward maturity in a troubled time. And the author of the journals is something more; he is a writer of sensitivity and power." Discussing the same volume in the *Times Literary Supplement* Philip Gardener noted, "If, since the war, Spender's creative engine has run at less than full power, one remains grateful for his best work, the context of which is fascinatingly provided by these letters and journals."

One of Spender's earliest published works of autobiography, *World within World,* came to be emblematic of the author's candor, commitment to honesty, and longevity. First published in 1951, the book created a stir for Spender's frank disclosure of a homosexual relationship he had had at around the time of the Spanish Civil War. The relationship ended when Spender married. Spender's ex-lover then ran off to fight in Spain; Spender ended

up going after him to try to get him out of the country. The book earned a second life when it became the subject of another controversy in the 1990s. In 1993, American writer David Leavitt published his novel *While England Sleeps,* in which a writer has a homosexual affair that follows many of the events of Spender's life but adds more explicit sexual detail. Feeling his integrity and his literary license threatened, Spender accused Leavitt of plagiarism. He also filed a lawsuit in British courts to stop the British publication of the book, charging the American novelist with copyright infringement and violation of a British law that assures authors the right to control adaptations of their work. In 1994, Leavitt and his publisher, Viking Penguin, agreed to a settlement that would withdraw the book from publication; Leavitt made changes to *While England Sleeps* for a revised edition.

During this period of intense attention focused on *World within World,* St. Martin's reprinted the autobiography with a new introduction by Spender. As a result, many readers were afforded the opportunity to discover or rediscover Spender's work. "With the passage of time," commented Eric Pace in a *New York Times* obituary, "'World within World' has proved to be in many ways Sir Stephen's most enduring prose work because it gives the reader revealing glimpses of its author, Auden and Mr. Isherwood and of what it was like to be a British poet in the 1930's."

BIOGRAPHICAL/CRITICAL SOURCES:

BOOKS

David, Hugh, *Stephen Spender: A Portrait with Background,* Heinemann (London), 1992.
Maxwell, D. E. S., *Poets of the Thirties,* Barnes & Noble, 1969.
Smith, Elton Edward, *The Angry Young Men of the Thirties,* Southern Illinois University Press, 1975.
Sternlicht, Sanford, *Stephen Spender,* Twayne Publishers, 1992.

PERIODICALS

American Scholar, winter, 1988, p. 148.
Boston Globe, November 12, 1993, p. 45.
Chicago Tribune Book World, January 12, 1986.
New Republic, September 23, 1978; August 1, 1988, p. 52.
New Statesman and Society, February 26, 1988, p. 22; February 25, 1994, p. 41.
New Yorker, November 10, 1986; February 28, 1994, p. 72; January 8, 1996, p. 58.
New York Review of Books, January 25, 1979; April 24, 1986.
New York Times, February 17, 1994, p. C24; February 20, 1994, sec. 4, p. 14.
New York Times Book Review, February 1, 1981; January 26, 1986; September 11, 1988, p. 20; September 4, 1994, p. 10.
New York Times Magazine, April 3, 1994, p. 36.
People Weekly, December 25, 1995, p. 166.
Publishers Weekly, February 21, 1994, p. 10; March 20, 1995, p. 16.
Spectator, February 26, 1994, p. 37.
Times Literary Supplement, April 17, 1981; February 18, 1994, p. 10.
Washington Post, February 17, 1994, p. A1; October 26, 1993, p. F1.
Washington Post Book World, January 12, 1986.
World Literature Today, spring, 1995, p. 367.

SPIEGELMAN, Art 1948-
(Joe Cutrate, Al Flooglebuckle, Skeeter Grant)

PERSONAL: Born February 15, 1948, in Stockholm, Sweden; immigrated to United States; naturalized citizen; son of Vladek (in sales) and Anja (Zylberberg) Spiegelman; married Francoise Mouly (a publisher), July 12, 1977; children: Nadja Rachel, Dashiell Alan. *Education:* Attended Harpur College (now State University of New York at Binghamton), 1965-68.

ADDRESSES: Agent—Deborah Karl, 52 West Clinton Ave., Irvington, NY 10533.

CAREER: Freelance artist and writer, 1965–; Topps Chewing Gum, Inc., Brooklyn, NY, creative consultant, artist, designer, editor, and writer for novelty packaging and bubble gum cards and stickers, including Wacky Packages and Garbage Pail Kids, 1966-89; artist and contributing editor to the *New Yorker,* 1991–. Instructor in studio class on comics, San Francisco Academy of Art, 1974-75; instructor in history and aesthetics of comics at New York School of Visual Arts, 1979-87.

MEMBER: PEN.

AWARDS, HONORS: Annual *Playboy* Editorial Award for best comic strip and Yellow Kid Award (Italy) for best comic strip author, both 1982; Regional Design Award, *Print* magazine, 1983, 1984, and 1985; Joel M. Cavior Award for Jewish Writing, and National Book Critics Circle nomination, both 1986, both for *Maus: A Survivors Tale, My Father Bleeds History;* Inkpot Award, San Diego Comics Convention, and Stripschappenning Award (Netherlands) for best foreign comics album, both 1987; Special Pulitzer Prize, for both *Maus: A Survivors Tale, My Father Bleeds History* and *Maus: A Survivors Tale II, and Here My Troubles Began;* National Book Critics Circle award, *Los Angeles Times* book prize, and Before Columbus Foundation Award, both 1992, both for *Maus: A Survivors Tale II, and Here My Troubles Began;* Spiegelman also received a Guggenheim fellowship for his work on *Maus.*

WRITINGS:

COMICS

The Complete Mr. Infinity, S. F. Book Co. (New York City), 1970.
The Viper Vicar of Vice, Villainy, and Vickedness, privately printed, 1972.
Zip-a-Tune and More Melodies, S. F. Book Co., 1972.
(Compiling editor with Bob Schneider) *Whole Grains: A Book of Quotations,* D. Links (New York City), 1972.
Ace Hole, Midget Detective, Apex Novelties (New York City), 1974.
Language of Comics, State University of New York at Binghamton, 1974.
(Contributor) Don Donahue and Susan Goodrich, editors, *The Apex Treasury of Underground Comics,* D. Links, 1974.
Breakdowns: From Maus to Now, an Anthology of Strips, Belier Press (New York City), 1977.
Work and Turn, Raw Books (New York City), 1979.
Every Day Has Its Dog, Raw Books, 1979.
Two-Fisted Painters Action Adventure, Raw Books, 1980.
(Contributor) Nicole Hollander, Skip Morrow, and Ron Wolin, editors, *Drawn Together: Relationships Lampooned, Harpooned, and Cartooned,* Crown (New York City), 1983.
Maus: A Survivors Tale, My Father Bleeds History, Pantheon (New York City), 1986.

(Editor) Francoise Mouly, *Raw: The Graphic Aspirin for War Fever,* Raw Books & Graphics, 1986.
(Editor with Mouly, and contributor) *Read Yourself Raw: Comix Anthology for Damned Intellectuals,* Pantheon, 1987.
(Editor with Mouly, and contributor) Mark Beyer, *Agony, Raw,* Pantheon, 1987.
(Editor with Mouly, and contributor), Gary Panter, *Jimbo: Adventures in Paradise,* Pantheon, 1988.
(With Mouly) *Jimbo: Adventures in Paradise,* Pantheon, 1988.
Raw: Open Wounds from the Cutting Edge of Commix, No. 1, Penguin (New York City), 1989.
Raw, No. 2, edited by Mouly, Penguin, 1990.
(Contributor) *The Complete Color Polly and Her Pals, Vol. 1: The Surrealist Period, 1926-1927,* Remco Worldservice Books (New York City), 1990.
(Editor with Mouly and R. Sikoryak) *Warts and All/Drew Friedman and Josh Alan Friedman,* Penguin, 1990.
Maus: A Survivors Tale II, and Here My Troubles Began, Pantheon, 1991.
Raw 3: High Culture for Lowbrows, Viking (New York City), 1991.
(Editor with R. Sikoryak) Charles Burns, *Skin Deep: Tales of Doomed Romance,* Penguin, 1992.
The Complete Maus (CD-ROM), Voyager (New York City), 1994.
(Illustrator) Joseph Moncura March, *The Wild Party: The Lost Classic,* Pantheon, 1994.
Open Me, I'm a Dog (children's book), HarperCollins (New York City), 1996.
(Author of introduction) Bob Adelman, editor, *Tijuana Bibles: Art and Wit in America's Forbidden Funnies, 1930s-1950s,* Simon & Schuster (New York City), 1997.

Also contributor to numerous underground comics. Editor of *Douglas Comix,* 1972; editor, with Bill Griffith, and contributor, *Arcade, the Comics Revue,* 1975-76; founding editor, with Mouly, and contributor, *Raw,* 1980–.

Contributing editor and artist, *New Yorker,* 1992–.

SIDELIGHTS: "*Maus: A Survivors Tale, My Father Bleeds History* is among the remarkable achievements in comics," wrote Dale Luciano in the *Comics Journal.* The comic, an epic parable of the Holocaust that substitutes mice and cats for human Jews and Nazis, marks a zenith in Art Spiegelman's artistic career. Prior to the *Maus* books, Spiegelman made a name for himself on the underground comics scene. He has been a significant presence in graphic art since his teen years, when he wrote, printed, and distributed his own comics magazine. In the early 1980s Spiegelman and his wife, Francoise Mouly, produced the first issue of *Raw,* an underground comics (or as Spiegelman and Mouly refer to them, "comix") anthology that grew into a highly respected alternative press by the middle of the decade. It was not until the publication of the first *Maus* collection in 1986, however, that a wide range of readers became aware of Spiegelman's visionary talent and his considerable impact on the realm of comics.

Maus starts with Spiegelman, representing himself as a humanoid mouse, going to his father, Vladek, for information about the Holocaust. As Vladek's tale begins, he and his wife, Anja, are living in Poland with their young child, Richieu, at the outset of World War II. The Nazis, as cats, have overrun much of Eastern Europe, and their oppression is felt by everyone, especially the Jews/mice. The story recalls Vladek's service in the Polish army and subsequent incarceration in a German war prison. As he returns to Anja and his home, the Nazi "Final Solution"—to exterminate the entire Jewish race—is well underway. There is much talk of Jews being rounded up and shipped off to the camps, where they are either put to strenuous work or put to death. Vladek and Anja's attempt to flee is thwarted and they are sent to Auschwitz, Poland, site of one of the most notorious camps. As the first book of *Maus* concludes, Richieu has been taken from his parents by the Nazis—never to be seen again—and Vladek and Anja are separated and put in crowded train cars for shipment to Auschwitz.

As the second volume, *And Here My Troubles Began,* opens, Art and his wife, Francoise, are visiting Vladek at his summer home in the Catskills. During the visit Art and his father resume their discussion. Vladek recounts how he and Anja were put in separate camps, he in the Auschwitz facility, she in the neighboring Birkenau. The horrors and inhumanity of concentration camp life are related in graphic detail. Vladek recalls the discomfort of cramming three or four men into a bunk that is only a few feet wide and the ignominy of scrounging for any scrap of food to sate his unending hunger. His existence at Auschwitz is marked by agonizing physical labor, severe abuse from the Nazis, and the ever present fear that he—or Anja—may be among the next Jews sent to the gas chambers. Despite these overwhelming incentives to abandon hope, Vladek is bolstered by his clandestine meetings with Anja and the discovery of supportive allies among his fellow prisoners. In an encounter with a former priest, Vladek is told that the numerals in his serial identification, which the Nazis tattooed upon their victims, add up to eighteen, a number signifying life.

Vladek manages to hold on through several harrowing incidents, including a bout with typhus. As the war ends and the Allied troops make their way toward Auschwitz, Vladek and some fellow prisoners flee the camp and eventually make their way to safety. In the haste of his escape, however, Vladek loses contact with Anja and does not know if she is alive. Their reunion marks a happy point in Vladek's tale. As the book continues Vladek and Anja desperately search orphanages in Europe for Richieu, to no avail. They eventually immigrate to Sweden, where Art is born, and from there the family moves to America. However, the horrors of the war have scarred Anja permanently, and in 1968 she commits suicide. The book concludes with Art visiting Vladek just before his death in 1982.

Although *Maus* is essentially the story of Vladek and Anja's ordeal, Spiegelman has stated that *Maus* is, in part, "a meditation on my own awareness of myself as a Jew." There are deeply personal passages depicting conversations between Art and his psychiatrist, Pavel, who, like Vladek, survived the Nazi's attempted purge. Their conversation ranges from Anja's suicide to the guilt that Art feels for being successful in light of his father's tribulation. As much as *Maus* serves as a piece of edifying literature, it also provided its creator with an opportunity to confront his personal demons. As Spiegelman wrote in an article in the *Village Voice, Maus* was motivated "by an impulse to look dead-on at the root cause of my own deepest fears and nightmares."

A good deal of discussion has arisen since the publication of the *Maus* books, much of it regarding Spiegelman's use of animals in the place of humans. When the story originated, Spiegelman made no mention of Jews or Nazis. The protagonists were mice, persecuted because they were "Maus." Likewise, the antagonists were cats, or "Die Katzen," and they chased the mice, although "chasing" the mice meant rounding them up in camps for work,

torture, and extermination. The closest the strip comes to an outright identification with the Holocaust is in the name of the concentration camp, "Mauschwitz." As Spiegelman began the expanded version however, he found that he had to write in terms of "Jews" and "Nazis" when going into detail. Spiegelman decided to maintain his characters as animals, however, citing a fear that using human characters would turn the work into a "corny" plea for sympathy. He explained to Joey Cavalieri in *Comics Journal,* "To use these ciphers, the cats and mice, is actually a way to allow you past the cipher at the people who are experiencing it. So it's really a much more direct way of dealing with the material."

Luciano agreed with Spiegelman's reasoning in his description of *Maus:* "By making the characters cats and mice, the result is that the characters *human* qualities are highlighted all the more, to an inexplicably poignant effect." "By relating a story of hideous inhumanity in non-human terms," declared *Los Angeles Times Book Review* contributor James Colbert, " 'Maus' and 'Maus II" allow us as readers to go outside ourselves and to look objectively at ourselves and at otherwise unspeakable events." Luciano continued, "The situations recalled and acted-out in *Maus* place the characters in a variety of delicate situations: they express themselves with a simplicity and candor that is unsettling because it is so accurately *human.*" "And while the presentation is enormously effective (and while the events Mr. Spiegelman relates are factually accurate, in most ways a memoir)," Colbert concluded, "the fact is, too that these events did not take place among mice, cats and dogs. That is fiction—and it is fiction of the very highest order."

Full recognition of *Maus*'s seminal status came in 1992, when Spiegelman received a special Pulitzer Prize for the work. The event marked a change in his working status—he joined the prestigious *New Yorker* magazine as a contributing editor and artist the same year—and launched another round of *Maus* commentary from critics. A special exhibition, entitled "Art Spiegelman: The Road to Maus" and featuring the artist's sketches and stories used in the composition of the work, opened at the Galerie St. Etienne toward the end of the year. In this exhibition, and in the CD-ROM of the work that appeared in 1994, Spiegelman shows how the work evolved both out of his relationship with his father and his own need to understand himself. "Art Spiegelman's 'Maus' books go a step further than many Holocaust memoirs," wrote April Austin in the *Christian Science Monitor,* "because they portray the difficulties of *living with* a Holocaust survivor. Spiegelman achieves this by writing himself . . . into the stories, breaking into his mouse-father's narrative with descriptions of their present-day conversations."

Spiegelman's appointment as contributing artist at the *New Yorker* sparked some controversy among critics who were taken aback by the graphic content of his illustrations. The artist, working with editor-in-chief Tina Brown, helped create a new style for the magazine that alienated some readers. "In case you hadn't noticed or are one of the New Yorker traditionalists who refuse to pick up the magazine these days," declared Sean Mitchell in the *Los Angeles Times,* "it now contains comic strips by Spiegelman, Edward Sorel and other artists who once toiled mainly in the pages of the nation's 'underground' and alternative media. The truth is, they are—many of them, anyway—comic strips of a high order." Spiegelman kindled controversy with a Valentine's Day cover showing a Hasidic Jewish man embracing a black woman. "Spiegelman has become one of the New Yorker's most sensational artists," the critic continued, "in recent years drawing covers that are meant not just to be plainly understood but also to reach up and tattoo your eyeballs with images once unimaginable in the magazine of old moneyed taste." Spiegelman covers have also included depictions of a naked press corps reviewing a fashion show model in spiked heels.

The artist views this change not as an escape from the *New Yorker*'s traditions, but as a return to them. "In its Ross days," he told Mitchell, "it was a kind of live wire—like Peter Arno's cartoons were pretty hot for their moment. Charles Addams was considered rather morbid. It wasn't all those cartoons about businessmen in suits talking to each other over martinis." Spiegelman showed his respect for the magazine's editorial staff in his illustrations to journalist Joseph Moncure March's long 1920s poem *The Wild Party*. The mildly pornographic poem tells about the life of a showgirl and about a party that ends in a murder. Spiegelman refers to March's work as "a lost nugget of the noir genre," according to *Boston Globe* contributor Joseph P. Kahn. It was excerpted in the *New Yorker* and marked the kind of changes that Spiegelman helped bring about.

BIOGRAPHICAL/CRITICAL SOURCES:

Witek, Joseph, *Comic Books as History: The Narrative Art of Jack Jackson, Art Spiegelman, and Harvey Pekar,* University Press of Mississippi (Jackson), 1989.

PERIODICALS

Boston Globe, November 23, 1994, p. 25.
Christian Science Monitor, December 14, 1992, p. 14.
Comics Journal, August, 1981, pp. 98-125; December, 1986, pp. 43-45; April, 1989, pp. 110-17.
Commonweal, December 5, 1997, p. 20.
Los Angeles Times, December 18, 1994, p. 7.
Los Angeles Times Book Review, November 8, 1992, p. 2.
New York Times, February 11, 1994, p. D17.
New York Times Book Review, November 3, 1991, pp. 1, 35-36.
Publishers Weekly, April 26, 1991; January 31, 1994, pp. 26-27; October 10, 1994, p. 61.
Rolling Stone, November 20, 1986, pp. 103-6, 146-48.
Times Educational Supplement, December 2, 1994, p. 7.
Village Voice, June 6, 1989, pp. 21-22.

*   *   *

SPILLANE, Frank Morrison 1918-
(Mickey Spillane)

PERSONAL: Born March 9, 1918, in Brooklyn, NY; son of John Joseph (a bartender) and Catherine Anne Spillane; married Mary Ann Pearce, 1945 (divorced); married Sherri Malinou, November, 1965 (divorced); married Jane Rodgers Johnson, October, 1983; children: (first marriage) Kathy, Mark, Mike, Carolyn; (third marriage; stepdaughters) Britt, Lisa. *Education:* Attended Kansas State College (now University). *Religion:* Converted to Jehovah's Witnesses in 1952.

ADDRESSES: Home—Murrells Inlet, Myrtle Beach, SC.

CAREER: Writer of mystery and detective novels, short stories, books for children, comic books, and scripts for television and films. Spillane, with producer Robert Fellows, formed an independent film company in Nashville, TN, called Spillane-Fellows Productions, which filmed features and television productions, 1969. Creator of television series, *Mike Hammer,* 1984-87. Actor; has appeared in over 110 commercials for Miller Lite Beer.

Military service: U.S. Army Air Force; taught cadets and flew fighter missions during World War II; became captain.

AWARDS, HONORS: Junior Literary Guild Award, 1979, for *The Day the Sea Rolled Back;* Lifetime Achievement Award, 1983, and short story award, 1990, both from Private Eye Writers of America; Grand Master Award, Mystery Writers of America, 1995.

WRITINGS:

UNDER NAME MICKEY SPILLANE; CRIME NOVELS

I, the Jury (also see below), Dutton (New York City), 1947.
Vengeance Is Mine! (also see below), Dutton, 1950.
My Gun Is Quick (also see below), Dutton, 1950.
The Big Kill (also see below), Dutton, 1951.
One Lonely Night, Dutton, 1951.
The Long Wait, Dutton, 1951.
Kiss Me, Deadly (also see below), Dutton, 1952.
The Deep, Dutton, 1961.
The Girl Hunters (also see below), Dutton, 1962.
Me, Hood! Corgi (London), 1963, New American Library, 1969.
Day of the Guns, Dutton, 1964.
The Snake, Dutton, 1964.
The Flier, Corgi, 1964.
Bloody Sunrise, Dutton, 1965.
The Death Dealers, Dutton, 1965.
Killer Mine, Corgi, 1965.
The Twisted Thing, Dutton, 1966, published as *For Whom the Gods Would Destroy,* New American Library, 1971.
The By-Pass Control, Dutton, 1967.
The Delta Factor, Dutton, 1967.
Body Lovers, New American Library, 1967.
Survival: Zero, Dutton, 1970.
Tough Guys, New American Library, 1970.
The Erection Set, Dutton, 1972.
The Last Cop Out, New American Library, 1973.
Mickey Spillane: Five Complete Mike Hammer Novels (contains *I, the Jury, Vengeance Is Mine!, My Gun Is Quick, The Big Kill,* and *Kiss Me, Deadly*), Avenel Books (New York City), 1987.
The Hammer Strikes Again: Five Complete Mike Hammer Novels (contains *One Lonely Night, The Snake, The Twisted Thing, The Body Lovers,* and *Survival: Zero*), Avenel Books, 1989.
The Killing Man, Dutton, 1989.
Black Alley, Dutton, 1996.

Also author of *Return of the Hood.*

OTHER

(With Robert Fellows and Roy Rowland) *The Girl Hunters* (screenplay; based on Spillane's novel of the same title and starring Spillane in role of Mike Hammer), Colorama Features, 1963.
The Day the Sea Rolled Back (children's book), Windmill Books (New York City), 1979.
The Ship That Never Was (children's book), Bantam (New York City), 1982.
Tomorrow I Die (short stories), Mysterious Press, 1984.
(Editor with Max Allan Collins) *Murder Is My Business,* Dutton, 1994.

Also author of *The Shrinking Island.* Creator and writer of comic books, including *Mike Danger.* Author of several television and movie screenplays. Contributor of short stories to magazines.

MEDIA ADAPTATIONS: I, the Jury was filmed in 1953 by United Artists; a remake of *I, the Jury* was filmed in 1981 by Twentieth Century-Fox; *The Long Wait* was filmed in 1954, *Kiss Me, Deadly* in 1955, and *My Gun Is Quick* in 1957, all by United Artists; *The Delta Factor* was filmed in 1970 by Colorama Features. *Mickey Spillane's Mike Hammer,* a television series based on Spillane's mystery novels and his character, Mike Hammer, was produced by Revue Productions, distributed by MCA-TV, and premiered in 1958; another television series based on Spillane's writings, *Mike Hammer,* starring Stacey Keach, was produced and broadcasted from 1984-87. "That Hammer Guy" was produced on radio, 1953.

SIDELIGHTS: Frank Morrison Spillane, known by his readers as Mickey Spillane, started his writing career in the early 1940s scripting comic books for Funnies, Inc. Spillane made the switch from comic books to novels in 1946 when, needing $1,000 to buy a parcel of land, he decided the easiest and quickest way to earn the money was to write a novel. Three weeks later, he sent the finished manuscript of *I, the Jury* to Dutton. Although the editorial committee questioned its good taste and literary merit, they felt the book would sell. *I, the Jury* did indeed sell—well over eight million copies have been sold to date. In addition to buying the property, Spillane was able to construct a house on the site as well. This book would be the start of a long and prolific career during which, as Julie Baumgold points out in *Esquire,* Spillane "sold two hundred million books and became the most widely read and fifth most translated writer in the world." All those books have made Spillane famous, wealthy, and a personality in his own right.

I, the Jury did sell, because it pleased the public, not because it won critical acclaim. *San Francisco Chronicle* critic Anthony Boucher finds the book a "vicious . . . glorification of force, cruelty, and extra-legal methods." A critic for the *Saturday Review* criticizes *I, the Jury* for its "lurid action, lurid characters, lurid plot, lurid finish." These responses reflect the time in which the book was published, 1947, and the belief that the world depicted in the book was only a small, dirty fringe on mainstream America, a fringe that Spillane was exploiting for its shock effect. Yet, as Frederic D. Schwarz, writing in *American Heritage,* notes *I, the Jury* may represent one of the first signs of recognition of "the darker side of postwar America." Schwarz pairs the July, 1947 publication of Spillane's first novel with an event that occurred on July 4 of that year. Hundreds of motorcyclists and their followers overwhelmed the town of Hollister, California, trashing it in a weekend of biker wildness. As Schwarz points out, "The incident formed the basis for a 1954 movie, *The Wild One,*" starring Marlin Brando. Both the biker's rampage and *I, the Jury,* according to Schwarz, "reflect a violent nature of the era." Spillane, who Baumgold observes lives under the motto "A Wild Man Proper," has always dismissed the charges of sensationalizing. As Schwarz quotes him, "I don't really go for sex and violence unless it's necessary."

Not only did *I, the Jury* introduce Spillane to the book-buying public, but it also gave birth to the character, Mike Hammer, a 6-foot, 190-pound, rough and tough private investigator. Spillane's next several novels recorded the action-packed adventures of Hammer as he drank, fought, and killed his way through solving mystery after mystery. While Hammer is not featured in all of Spillane's mysteries, he is undoubtedly the most popular of Spillane's leading men. Art Harris describes Hammer in the *Washington Post:* "There was no one like Hammer. Sam Spade was tame. Never before had a private eye spilled blood on such a vast scale. He shot quick, punched hard, fought off beautiful

women and always got the bad guys. Mobsters got it. Commies got it. And if a woman deserved it, well, she got it, too."

In 1952 Spillane began a nine year break from writing mystery novels. Some people have attributed this hiatus to his religious conversion to the sect of Jehovah's Witnesses, while others feel that Spillane earned enough money from his writings and by selling the film rights to several of his books to live comfortably, enjoying life in his new beach home on Murrells Inlet located in Myrtle Beach, South Carolina. Although he stopped writing mysteries, Spillane wrote short stories for magazines and scripts for television and films. He also appeared on a number of television programs, often performing in parodies of his tough detective characters.

Spillane reappeared on the publishing scene in 1961 with his murder mystery *The Deep* and in the following year Mike Hammer returned to fight crime in *The Girl Hunter.* The public was ecstatic—buying copies of the novel as soon as they were placed on the shelf. Reviewers seemed to soften their criticism somewhat at Hammer's return. For example, Boucher writes in his review of *The Girl Hunter* that "Spillane's rough tough Mike Hammer has been away for so long . . . that it's possible for even an old enemy of his, like me, to view him afresh and recognize that he does possess a certain genuine vigor and conviction lacking in his imitators."

Many of Spillane's later books also were somewhat praised by critics. For example, a reviewer for the *Times Literary Supplement* remarks: "Nasty as much of it is, [*The Deep*] has a genuine narrative grip; and there is a certain sociological conscience at work in the presentation of the street which has bred so much crime and an unusual perception in the portrait of an old Irish patrol officer." And Newgate Callendar comments in the *New York Times Book Review* that "editorials were written condemning [Spillane's novels], and preachers took to the pulpit. But things have changed, and one reads Spillane's . . . *The Erection Set* with almost a feeling of sentimental *deja vu.* The sex, sadism and assorted violence remain. Basically, what the Spillane books are about is the all-conquering hero myth. We all like to escape into a fantasy world to identify with the figure who is all-knowing, all-powerful, infinitely virile, sending off auras of threat in solar pulsations."

Spillane followed *The Erection Set* with *The Last Cop Out* and then came another hiatus in his publication of crime novels. During this time, Spillane's publisher dared him to write a children's book. A number of editors at the company felt he could never change his style of writing in order to appeal or be acceptable to a much younger, more impressionable audience. Not one to back down from a challenge, Spillane produced *The Day the Sea Rolled Back* in 1979 and three years later, *The Ship That Never Was.* In general, reviewers have praised the books for their suspense and clean-cut high adventure. For example, a critic for the *Washington Post Book World* notes: "Yes, Mickey Spillane has written a kids' book, and quite an entertaining one too. As you might expect there's plenty of suspense, but violence is held in the wings; Spillane has trimmed his sails a bit for the young set."

In 1989, Spillane published his first Mike Hammer novel since 1970. In this return of Mike Hammer, *The Killing Man,* the detective returns to his office to find his secretary (and the unrecognized love of his life), Velda, unconscious on the floor and a dead man at his desk. True to form, Hammer sets out to bring the perpetrator to his own special brand of justice. Mickey Friedman, writing in the *New York Times Book Review,* maintains that "the book is a limp performance; the author makes no attempt to revitalize ingredients that are shopworn by now, and the book seems more like a ritual than a novel."

The year 1996 saw the publication of Spillane's thirteenth Mike Hammer novel, *Black Alley.* Hammer has just emerged from a coma, having been shot and put at the brink of death by gangsters. As with his first novel, *I, the Jury,* this book begins with the death of one of Hammer's military buddies. He sets off in search of his friend's murderer and billions in dirty mob money. The plot is familiar, but as a *Publishers Weekly* contributor writes, "Spillane's hard-boiled hero has softened with time; he finally tells Velda how he really feels about her—but, on doctor's orders, he refrains from consummation." *Forbes* magazine's Steve Forbes finds much to reward the reader in *Black Alley.* He observes, "The action never lets up as the tough, street-smart Hammer grapples with intense physical pain, revenue-hungry federal agents, cold-blooded gangsters, a recovering-alcoholic physician and a determined get-him-to-the-altar secretary."

Spillane's audience has been very loyal to his Mike Hammer character and his other mystery novels. This loyalty and Spillane's ability to give his readers what they want accounts for hundreds of millions of books sold. It also accounts for the fact that seven of his books are still listed among the top fifteen all-time fiction best sellers published in the last fifty years. "I'm the most translated writer in the world, behind Lenin, Tolstoy, Gorki, and Jules Verne," Spillane said to Art Harris of the *Washington Post.* "And they're all dead." Spillane went on to declare: "I have no fans. You know what I got? Customers. And customers are your friends." In 1984 Spillane shared these thoughts with the *Washington Post:* "I'm 66. . . . If you're a singer, you lose your voice. A baseball player loses his arm. A writer gets more knowledge, and if he's good, the older he gets, the better he writes. They can't kill me. I still got potential." Or as Baumgold comments in *Esquire,* "Mickey Spillane still has a few good surprise endings left."

BIOGRAPHICAL/CRITICAL SOURCES:

BOOKS

Collins, Max Allan, and James L. Traylor, *One Lonely Knight: Mickey Spillane's Mike Hammer,* Popular Press (Bowling Green, OH), 1984.
Contemporary Literary Criticism, Gale (Detroit), Volume 3, 1975; Volume 13, 1980.
St. James Guide to Crime and Mystery Writers, 4th edition, St. James Press (Detroit), 1996.
Van Dover, J. Kenneth, *Murder in the Millions: Erle Stanley Gardner, Mickey Spillane, and Ian Fleming,* Ungar (New York City), 1984.

PERIODICALS

American Heritage, July-August, 1997, p. 98.
Chicago Tribune, April 18, 1986.
Chicago Tribune Magazine, April 8, 1984.
Detroit Free Press, June 11, 1967; March 23, 1969.
Detroit News, September 14, 1967.
Entertainment Weekly, December 16, 1994, p. 63.
Esquire, August, 1995, p. 132.
Forbes, December 16, 1996, p. 26.
Interview, December, 1990, p. 48.
New York Times, November 11, 1951; October 26, 1952.
New York Times Book Review, October 14, 1962; February 27, 1966; August 13, 1967; February 27, 1972; May 20, 1973; October 15, 1989, p. 43.

People Weekly, July 28, 1986.
Publishers Weekly, May 15, 1967; September 22, 1989, p. 41; September 2, 1996, p. 11; October 7, 1996, p. 32.
San Francisco Chronicle, August 3, 1947, p. 19.
Saturday Review, May 29, 1965; September 27, 1970; March 25, 1972; April 7, 1973.
Times Literary Supplement, November 10, 1961; September 19, 1980.
Voice Literary Supplement, July, 1988.
Washington Post, October 24, 1984.
Washington Post Book World, May 10, 1981.
Writer's Digest, September, 1976.

                                *   *   *

SPILLANE, Mickey
    See SPILLANE, Frank Morrison

                                *   *   *

SPOCK, Benjamin (McLane) 1903-1998

PERSONAL: Born May 2, 1903, in New Haven, CT; died March 15, 1998, in San Diego, CA; son of Benjamin Ives and Mildred Louise (Stoughton) Spock; married Jane Davenport Cheney, June 25, 1927 (marriage dissolved, 1975); married Mary Morgan Councille, October 24, 1976; children: (first marriage) Michael, John Cheney; (second marriage) one stepdaughter. *Education:* Yale University, B.A., 1925; Yale Medical School, student, 1925-27; Columbia University, College of Physicians and Surgeons, M.D., 1929.

ADDRESSES: Home—P.O. Box 1268, Camden, ME 04843-1268.

CAREER: Presbyterian Hospital, New York City, intern in medicine, 1929-31; New York Nursery and Child's Hospital, service in pediatrics, 1931-32; New York Hospital, service in psychiatry, 1932-33, assistant attending pediatrician, 1933-47; practice in pediatrics, New York City, 1933-44 and 1946-47; Cornell University, Medical College, New York City, instructor in pediatrics, 1933-47; New York City Health Department, consultant in pediatric psychiatry, 1942-47; Mayo Clinic, Rochester, MN, consultant in psychiatry, 1947-51; Mayo Foundation for Medical Education and Research, Rochester, associate professor of psychiatry, 1947-51; University of Pittsburgh, Pittsburgh, PA, professor of child development, 1951-55; Western Reserve University (now Case Western Reserve University), Cleveland, OH, professor of child development, 1955-67. Presidential candidate, People's Party, 1972. Lecturer and writer "for peace and justice." *Military service:* United States Naval Reserve, lieutenant commander, Medical Corps, 1944-46.

MEMBER: National Committee for a Sane Nuclear Policy (SANE), National Conference for a New Politics (NCNP; member of executive board, 1967-98).

AWARDS, HONORS: Olympic Gold Medal for rowing, Paris, 1924; Family Life Book Award, 1963, for *Problems of Parents;* Thomas Paine Award, National Emergency Civil Liberties Committee, 1968. Honorary degrees from University of Durham, Yale University, and University of Hartford.

WRITINGS:

The Common Sense Book of Baby and Child Care, Duell, Sloan and Pearce, 1946, published as *The Pocket Book of Baby and Child Care,* Pocket Books, 1949, 2nd edition published as *Baby and Child Care,* 1957, revised edition with Michael B. Rothenberg published as *Dr. Spock's Baby and Child Care: Fortieth Anniversary Edition,* Dutton, 1985, published as *Dr. Spock's Baby and Child Care,* 6th edition, fully revised and updated for the 1990s, Pocket Books (New York City), 1992.

(With John Reinhart) *A Baby's First Year,* Duell, Sloan and Pearce, 1955.

(With Miriam F. Lowenberg) *Feeding Your Baby and Child,* Duell, Sloan and Pearce, 1955.

Dr. Spock Talks with Mothers: Growth and Guidance, Houghton, 1961.

On Being a Parent . . . of a Handicapped Child, National Society for Crippled Children and Adults (Chicago), 1961.

Problems of Parents, Houghton, 1962.

Prejudice in Children: A Conversation with Dr. Spock, Anti-Defamation League of B'nai B'rith (New York City), 1963.

(With M. O. Lerrigo) *Caring for Your Disabled Child,* Macmillan, 1965.

(With J. Darnell Barnard and Celia Stendler) *Macmillan Science Series* (science textbooks, grades 1-9; nine volumes), Books 1-6: *Science for Tomorrow's World,* Book 7: *Science: A Search for Evidence,* Book 8: *Science: A Way to Solve Problems,* Book 9: *Science: A Key to the Future,* Macmillan, 1966–.

(With Mitchell Zimmerman) *Dr. Spock of Vietnam,* Dell, 1968.

Decent and Indecent: Our Personal and Political Behavior, McCalls Publishing, 1970, revised edition, Fawcett World Library, 1971.

A Teenager's Guide to Life and Love, Simon & Schuster, 1970 (published in England as *A Young Person's Guide to Life and Love,* Bodley Head, 1971).

Raising Children in a Difficult Time, Norton, 1974 (published in England as *Bringing Up Children in a Difficult Time,* Bodley Head, 1974).

Dr. Spock on Parenting: Sensible Advice from America's Most Trusted Child-Care Expert, Simon & Schuster, 1988.

Spock on Spock: A Memoir of Growing Up with the Century, edited by wife, Mary Morgan, Pantheon, 1989.

A Better World for Our Children: Rebuilding American Family Values, National Press Books (Washington, DC), 1994.

SOUND RECORDINGS

Women's Lib, Politics and Children (cassette) Encyclopedia Americana/CBS News Audio Resource Library, 1973.

(With Claude Steiner) *Children, Parents and Education,* Big Sur Recordings, 1975.

(With Steiner) *Power: Abuses and Uses,* Big Sur Recordings, 1975.

(With Steiner) *I.A. Demonstrations* (cassette), Big Sur Recordings, 1975.

(With Steiner) *Views on Political Movements* (cassette), Big Sur Recordings, 1975.

SIDELIGHTS: Benjamin Spock is the author of *Dr. Spock's Baby and Child Care,* which has sold twenty-eight million copies since its first printing in 1946. The book has been published in some thirty languages, including Catalan, Russian, and Urdu. *Baby and Child Care* has changed with the times. According to a *Parade* reviewer, the latest edition ". . . contains a section on working mothers, pays more attention to male participation in child-

rearing, avoids sexual stereo-typing, even updates baby formulas." A *Washington Post* columnist agrees: "Spock has changed—somewhat. . . . He plans to keep recommending that infants receive constant parental care, but will no longer specify which parent should curtail his career to supply it. . . . He'll continue to state that sexual identity is necessary to mental health, but no longer suggest that it be re-enforced through the selection of toys and clothes." Spock was, however, angered and appalled at the growing attitude that child raising is burdensome and unfulfilling work. He told a *New York Times* reporter, "If our society can get it through its noodle that rearing children is exciting and creative work, we'll have accomplished something useful."

With regard to child rearing, many people blame Spock for the restlessness and rebellion in today's youth. *Newsweek* states: "It has been commonplace during the past couple of decades to speak of our children as the Spock Generation. . . . What we really seem to say when we speak of the Spock Generation is that America's children have been nurtured indulgently and permissively." A three-year study of 1,000 students at the University of California, Berkeley and San Francisco State University was conducted by psychologists M. Brewster Smith, Norma Haan and Jeanne H. Block to test the relationship of parental guidance to social involvement and unrest. Many of the students involved in the study had been jailed for participation in demonstrations. According to *Newsweek* the psychologists found that those students actively involved in demonstrations "described their parents as being more permissive and less authoritarian than did the other, uninvolved students. These parents had a close relationship with their children and avoided imposing flat prohibitions and arbitrary punishments on them." Then the psychologists "concluded—quite approvingly—'that the emergence of a dedicated spontaneous generation concerned with humanitarian values and personal authenticity is a triumph of Spockian philosophy.'"

Spock himself was involved in demonstrations against the Vietnam War and was indicted by a Federal Grand Jury on January 5, 1968, for conspiring to counsel American youths to avoid the draft. He was later acquitted on appeal of his case. When questioned about his involvement, Spock said, "What is the use of physicians like myself trying to help parents to bring up children, healthy and happy, to have them killed in such numbers for a cause that is ignoble?"

Reviewing *Decent and Indecent,* a *Time* reporter writes: "Spock's most useful perception, perhaps, is his understanding that man in the 20th century has indulged in such an orgy of self-depreciation that he grows violent in self-revulsion. There is, mourns Spock, 'an unprecedented loss of belief in man's worthiness.' Art becomes grotesquerie, music a concert where the players splinter their instruments in a convulsion that suggests strychnine poisoning. 'This represents emotional regression all the way back to the one-to-two-year-old level,' Spock writes briskly, 'when the child in a spell of anger wants to antagonize and mess and destroy on a titanic scale.' What troubles the doctor is that such impulses escape the nursery; fathers and mothers, artists, politicians, scientists and generals—all of them go around breaking things. Medicine cannot cope with civilization as tantrum."

At the age of ninety one, Spock published his thoughts on what he considers the decline of American family life and his ideas for reversing the trend. The book, *A Better World for Our Children: Rebuilding American Family Values,* is considered by Spock to be "his political testament" according to Jerry Adler in *Newsweek.* Adler quotes Spock as saying "I felt the situation was getting worse and worse. I couldn't keep putting it off, because pretty soon I'll be dead." While the term "family values" in the title bespeaks views of the religious right, Spock continues to hold his own brand of conservative liberalism in both child- and "society-raising." He decries a culture that touts competition and undermines solid ethical values and offers suggestions for families and individuals such as eating together and running for political office.

When Spock died of natural causes at the age of ninety-four, President Clinton, a member himself of the "Spock generation," said that "for half a century Dr. Spock guided parents across the country and around the world in their most important job—raising their children. As a pediatrician, writer, and teacher, Dr. Spock offered sage advice and gentle support to generations of families, and taught all of us the importance of respecting children." At the time of his death, *The Common Sense Book On Baby and Child Care* had sold almost fifty million copies around the world. In spite of this success, during his last months his wife made public pleas for contributions to offset the costs of his health care (he suffered from pneumonia and numerous strokes). But Spock remained optimistic, and prepared yet another revised edition of his classic book to be published in 1998, the year of his death. In an obituary in the *Boston Globe,* John Powers eulogized that "Spock seemed to know everything that could go wrong with children from infancy through adolescence and he explained it in simple English. . . . Spock had it all spelled out and indexed for groggy eyes and trembling fingers."

BIOGRAPHICAL/CRITICAL SOURCES:

BOOKS

Bloom, Lynn Z., *Dr. Spock: Biography of a Conservative Radical,* Bobbs-Merrill, 1972.
Kaye, Judith, *The Life of Benjamin Spock,* Twenty-first Century Books (New York City), 1993.
Maier, Thomas, *Doctor Spock: An American Life,* Harcourt Brace, 1998.
Mitford, Jessica, *The Trial of Dr. Spock,* Knopf, 1969.

PERIODICALS

Best Sellers, January 15, 1971.
Boston Globe, March 17, 1998.
Christian Century, October 22, 1969.
Detroit News, October 3, 1971; January 31, 1990.
Esquire, February, 1969; May, 1970; December, 1983.
Harper's, May, 1968.
Kirkus Reviews, August 1, 1994, p. 1069.
Library Journal, November 1, 1994.
Life, May 17, 1968; September 12, 1969.
Los Angeles Times, November 3, 1989; November 22, 1989.
Nation, March 11, 1968; October 13, 1969.
National Observer, June 17, 1968; July 2, 1968.
New Republic, February 7, 1970.
Newsweek, September 23, 1968; September 15, 1969; February 2, 1970; May 3, 1976; July 3, 1978; March 4, 1985; October 24, 1994, p. 84.
New Yorker, May 20, 1996, p. 82.
New York Times, December 14, 1968; August 6, 1969; January 28, 1970; November 3, 1970; March 1, 1985; December 30, 1989; March 17, 1997.
New York Times Book Review, February 16, 1969; March 15, 1970; November 5, 1989.
Parade, March 14, 1976.
People Weekly, May 13, 1985.

Publishers Weekly, November 2, 1984; August 15, 1994, p. 20; August 29, 1994, p. 76.
Time, February 16, 1970; November 16, 1970; April 8, 1985.
Times (London), May 2, 1988.
Washington Post, September 24, 1971; December 4, 1971; October 22, 1989; November 27, 1989; March 18, 1998.

*   *   *

S. S.
  See SASSOON, Siegfried (Lorraine)

*   *   *

STACY, Donald
  See POHL, Frederik

*   *   *

STAFFORD, Jean 1915-1979

PERSONAL: Born July 1, 1915, in Covina, CA; died March 26, 1979, in White Plains, NY; buried in Greenriver Cemetery, East Hampton, NY; daughter of John Richard (a writer of westerns under pseudonym Jack Wonder) and Mary (McKillop) Stafford; married Robert Lowell (a poet), April 2, 1940 (divorced, 1948); married Oliver Jensen (a writer), January 28, 1950 (divorced, 1953); married A. J. Liebling (a columnist for the *New Yorker*), April, 1959 (died, 1963). *Education:* University of Colorado, B.A. and M.A., 1936; Heidelberg University, additional study, 1936-37. *Politics:* Democrat.

CAREER: Novelist and short story writer. Stephens College, Columbia, MO, instructor, 1937-38; Queens College (now Queens College of the City University of New York), lecturer, 1945; Columbia University, New York City, adjunct professor, 1967-69. Secretary, *Southern Review,* 1940-41. Fellow, Center for Advanced Studies, Wesleyan University, 1964-65.

MEMBER: Cosmopolitan Club (New York).

AWARDS, HONORS: Mademoiselle's merit award, 1944; National Institute of Arts and Letters grant in literature, 1945; Guggenheim fellowships in Fiction, 1945, 1948; National Press Club Award, 1948; O. Henry Memorial Award, 1955, for best short story of the year; Ingram-Merrill grant, 1969; Chapelbrook grant, 1969; Pulitzer Prize, 1970, for *The Collected Stories of Jean Stafford.*

WRITINGS:

Boston Adventure (novel), Harcourt (New York City), 1944.
The Mountain Lion (novel), Harcourt, 1947.
The Catherine Wheel (novel), Harcourt, 1952.
Children Are Bored on Sunday (short stories), Harcourt, 1953.
The Interior Castle (short stories), Harcourt, 1953.
(With others) *New Short Novels,* Ballantine (New York City), 1954.
(With others) *Stories,* Farrar, Straus (New York City), 1956, published as *A Book of Stories,* Gollancz (London), 1957.
Elephi: The Cat with the High I.Q. (juvenile), Farrar, Straus, 1962.
The Lion and the Carpenter and Other Tales from the Arabian Nights Retold (juvenile), Macmillan (New York City), 1962.
Bad Characters (short stories), Farrar, Straus, 1966.

A Mother in History (based on interviews with the mother of Lee
  Harvey Oswald), Farrar, Straus, 1966.
Selected Stories, New English Library (London), 1966.
The Collected Stories of Jean Stafford, Farrar, Straus, 1969.

Also author of an unfinished novel. Contributor of articles and
stories to *New Yorker, Vogue, Harper's Bazaar, Library Journal,
Mademoiselle, Holiday, Horizon, Reporter, New Republic,* and
other magazines.

SIDELIGHTS: Novelist and short story writer Jean Stafford was
noted both for her precise prose style and for her unconventional
portraits of alienated female adolescence, often set in the
American West. Throughout her tumultuous career, Stafford
experienced great success, as well as tragedy, despair, and failure.
She wrote in many genres, but one constant throughout her work
is the use of classic themes of American literature—such as nature
versus civilization, individualism, and coming of age—which
Stafford comments upon from a woman's point of view. In the
Dictionary of Literary Biography Jeanette Mann wrote that
Stafford's "contribution to American letters is in the truths she has
told about the lives of women and the West—and in the sureness
of the telling."

The facts of Stafford's biography do much to illuminate the use of
her chosen themes, as well as the dramatic and often tragic turns
of her narratives. Stafford was the youngest of four children, born
in Covina, California, where she lived in middle-class comfort
until age six. Then her father, who had inherited wealth, lost his
entire fortune due to poor investments in the stock market, and the
family was forced to move to Boulder, Colorado. Stafford's
family never again enjoyed financial stability. Her father had
published a pulp western novel, *When Cattle Kingdom Fell,*
before Stafford's birth, and after the family moved he returned to
writing full time, though he never sold another novel. The family
took in local sorority girls as boarders to support themselves.
Individualistic and tomboyish, Stafford grew up exasperated with
her father and alienated from her conventionally feminine mother
and older sisters. She was close only with her brother Dick. Her
family's riches to rags story surfaces in Stafford's many portrayals
of the contrast between social classes, and the rigid gender roles in
her family are also frequently explored as a fictional theme.
Stafford's own coming of age is also reflected in much of her
writing.

Stafford went to the University of Colorado on a scholarship,
majored in English and graduated cum laude. She was reportedly
a fragile and innocent young woman when she started college, but
Stafford soon befriended and moved in with Lucy McKee and
Andrew Cooke, two sophisticated, bohemian law students, who
introduced her to their unorthodox lifestyle of heavy drinking and
sexual experimentation. In Stafford's senior year, Lucy committed
suicide in her presence. This profound loss had a powerful impact
on Stafford, appearing thematically in her writing and also
contributing to her periods of writer's block.

A few years after college, Stafford became involved with poet
Robert Lowell. He proposed to her despite his genteel Boston
family's disapproval, but she hesitated to give an answer. Only
days later, she and Lowell were in a serious car accident. He, who
was driving drunk, was unhurt, but she sustained painful and
disfiguring injuries to the head and face. Themes of beauty and
disfigurement appear in several of her stories. Shortly after her
recovery, Stafford accepted Lowell's proposal. They were married
in 1940.

Stafford's six-year marriage to Lowell was stressful and unhappy.
However, these were artistically productive years for her. In 1944
she published her first novel, *Boston Adventure,* a marketable
novel of manners. In it, the young heroine, Sonie Marburg,
escapes from her immigrant family and the dreary working-class
town where she was raised and goes to work for a wealthy and
cultured lady from Boston. However, in this new sophisticated
milieu she finds herself just as entrapped, and the novel concludes
tragically. *Boston Adventure* was by all measures highly successful. It was a bestseller in 1944 and garnered strong reviews. While
some critics found the writing over-wrought and the plot
melodramatic, most praised the book as the harbinger of an
extremely promising career. In 1944 Howard Mumford Jones
wrote in the *Saturday Review of Literature,* "The book is bigger
than its mistakes. . . . American letters have been enriched by a
unique, vigorous, and remarkable artist."

Over the next several years, as Stafford's marriage to Lowell
collapsed, she grieved the death of her brother Dick, and was
hospitalized for a nervous breakdown, Stafford wrote her second
and most highly acclaimed novel, *The Mountain Lion.* Loosely
based on the childhoods of Stafford and her brother, *The
Mountain Lion* tells the double coming-of-age story of two
unconventional adolescents, Molly and Ralph Fawcett. They
spend summers at their grandfather's ranch, which at first seems
to offer a liberating alternative to the town where they are
outcasts. However, at the ranch, Molly and Ralph drift apart, as
Ralph shifts alliance to his ruggedly individualistic cowboy uncles
and the introverted young Molly becomes more and more isolated.
In a climactic and symbolic conclusion, Ralph accidentally shoots
and kills Molly while out hunting for a mountain lion.

The Mountain Lion was not a bestseller and again financial
difficulties beset Stafford. She began to write short stories,
publishing them in the *New Yorker.* She supplemented her income
by writing journalistic pieces and also lived off the advance for a
novel based on Lucy McKee's suicide. The novel was never
completed, but a piece of it appeared much later as the acclaimed
short story "In the Snowfall." Stafford published her third novel,
The Catherine Wheel, in 1952. It is again a double story—this
time of a lovelorn middle-aged woman and the twelve-year-old
boy who is her charge. The two characters' worlds remain
disconnected and hopelessly alienated from each other. Again, the
novel ends with a highly symbolic tragedy.

Stafford's work as a prolific writer of short stories overshadows
her accomplishments as a novelist. In 1969 *The Collected Stories
of Jean Stafford* was published and won a Pulitzer Prize. In the
New Criterion, Bruce Bawer characterized the collection as "one
of the finest moments of the American short story . . . witty,
luminous, and impeccably crafted." Despite the accolades this
book brought her, Stafford's later years were plagued by heavy
drinking and unproductive writing. Stafford had married twice
more, but lived out her last fifteen years alone. She died in 1979
of a stroke and left her entire estate to her cleaning woman.

Ironically, the praise Stafford earned for her elegant, well-wrought
prose has not always served her well. In *Essays in Literature*
Barbara White wrote: "Although her novels were very well
reviewed and her *Collected Stories* (1969) won a Pulitzer Prize,
Stafford is not well known. . . . It may be that critics have been
diverted by her reputation as a writer of 'well-made' short stories.
At any rate, Stafford is an important novelist whose work has been
undeservedly neglected." The comparison critics make between
Stafford's craft and that of illustrious modern storytellers like

Henry James, Anton Checkov, James Joyce, and Eudora Welty is double-edged. While Stafford is judged to be the lesser writer in such comparisons, as Bawer noted, "The fact that one is compelled to speak of Stafford in the company of such masters is to acknowledge that her achievement in the genre is of a very high order indeed."

More recently, critics have begun to appreciate the cultural commentary that Stafford's special perspective as a woman writer of the American West allows. Since her death, scholars have become more interested in how Stafford's work both fits into and re-imagines American and Western regional literary traditions, and in how she portrays the struggle for female identity in the face of the limitations presented by these traditions. In an analysis of *The Mountain Lion* in a *Denver Quarterly* article, Melody Graulich argued: "Ralph can choose membership in either world; he can be, in effect, Huck Finn or Tom Sawyer. . . . Stafford suggests that girls cannot escape stereotyped women's roles, that the young female rebel should give up on the possibility of becoming Huckleberry Finn." In her 1982 overview of Stafford's career, White suggested that Stafford's unusual subject matter—as well as her fine writing style—should single her out as an important writer worthy of greater critical attention: "Her fiction is not, as the label 'well-made' can imply, detached from broad social concerns. It has much to say about cherished American myths."

BIOGRAPHICAL/CRITICAL SOURCES:

BOOKS

Auchincloss, Louis, *Pioneers and Caretakers: A Study of Nine American Women Novelists,* University of Minneapolis Press, 1965, pp. 152-60.
Avila, Wanda, editor, *Jean Stafford: A Comprehensive Bibliography,* Garland, 1983.
Contemporary Literary Criticism, Gale (Detroit), Volume 4, 1975; Volume 7, 1977; Volume 19, 1981; Volume 68, 1991.
Dictionary of Literary Biography, Gale, Volume 2: *American Novelists since World War II, First Series,* 1978; Volume 173: *American Novelists since World War II, Fifth Series,* 1996.
Goodman, Charlotte Margolis, *Jean Stafford: The Savage Heart,* University of Texas Press, 1990.
Hassan, Ihab, *Radical Innocence: Studies in the Contemporary American Novel,* Princeton University Press, 1961, pp. 70-72, 100.
Hulbert, Ann, *The Interior Castle: The Art and Life of Jean Stafford,* Knopf, 1992.
Roberts, David, *Jean Stafford: A Biography,* Little, Brown, 1988.
Roberts, David, *Jean Stafford: The Life of a Writer,* St. Martin's, 1989.
Ryan, Maureen, *Innocence and Estrangement in the Fiction of Jean Stafford,* Louisiana State University Press, 1987.
Twentieth-Century Western Writers, 2nd edition, St. James Press, 1991.
Walsh, Mary Ellen Williams, *Jean Stafford,* Twayne, 1985.
Wilson, Mary Ann, *Jean Stafford: A Study of the Short Fiction,* Twayne, 1995.

PERIODICALS

American Heritage, October, 1992, p. 109.
Denver Quarterly, spring, 1983, pp. 28-55.
Economist, October 24, 1992, p. 102.
Essays in Literature, fall, 1982, pp. 194-210.
Harper's, June, 1983, pp. 57-59.
Kenyon Review, spring, 1987, pp. 1-8; fall, 1994, pp. 104-19.
Massachusetts Review, spring, 1979, pp. 117-25.
Nation, February 9, 1952, pp. 136-37.
New Criterion, November, 1988, pp. 61-72.
New Republic, October 31, 1964; May 10, 1975, pp. 22-25.
Newsweek, April 9, 1979.
New York Times, August 26, 1973, p. 104; March 28, 1979.
New York Times Book Review, October 11, 1964; February 16, 1969; March 4, 1973.
Novel, fall, 1983, pp. 28-43.
Saturday Review, May 9, 1953.
Saturday Review of Literature, September 23, 1944, p. 10; March 1, 1947.
Sewannee Review, fall, 1985, pp. 584-96; summer, 1990, pp. 333-49.
Shenandoah, summer, 1979, pp. 65-76; fall, 1979 (special issue on Jean Stafford); winter, 1983, pp. 79-95.
South Atlantic Quarterly, fall, 1962, pp. 484-91; spring, 1986, 123-33.
Southern Quarterly, summer, 1990, pp. 25-34.
Southern Review, winter, 1993, pp. 58-66.
Southwest Review, summer, 1987, 389-403.
Time, April 9, 1979.
Voice Literary Supplement, June, 1992, pp. 31-32.
Virginia Quarterly Review, spring, 1986, pp. 213-36.
Washington Post, March 29, 1979.
Western American Literature, August, 1986, pp. 261-70; August, 1986, pp. 99-109; November, 1986, pp. 195-205; August, 1988, pp. 128-39.

*   *   *

STAINES, Trevor
See BRUNNER, John (Kilian Houston)

*   *   *

STANCYKOWNA
See SZYMBORSKA, Wislawa

*   *   *

STANTON, Schuyler
See BAUM, L(yman) Frank

*   *   *

STARK, Richard
See WESTLAKE, Donald E(dwin)

*   *   *

STAUNTON, Schuyler
See BAUM, L(yman) Frank

STEAD, Christina (Ellen) 1902-1983

PERSONAL: Born July 17, 1902, in Rockdale, Sydney, New South Wales, Australia; died March 31, 1983, in Sydney, Australia; daughter of David George (a naturalist) and Ellen (Butters) Stead; married William James Blake, 1952 (an author; surname originally Blech; died, 1968). *Education:* Attended Teachers' College, Sydney University, received teacher's certification.

CAREER: Novelist, short story writer, editor, and translator. Worked as a public school teacher, a teacher of abnormal children, and a demonstrator in the psychology laboratory of Sydney University, all in Australia; grain company clerk, London, England, 1928-29; bank clerk in Paris, France, 1930-35; senior writer for Metro-Goldwyn-Mayer, 1943; instructor in Workshop in the Novel, New York University, 1943-44; Australian National University, Canberra, fellow in creative arts, 1969.

AWARDS, HONORS: Aga Khan Prize, *Paris Review,* 1966; Arts Council of Great Britain grant, 1967; first recipient of Patrick White Award, 1974; honorary member, American Academy and Institute of Arts and Letters, 1982; Victorian Fellowship, Australian Writers Awards, 1986, for *An Ocean of Story;* Premiere's Award for Literature, Premiere of New South Wales, Australia; several times nominated for the Nobel Prize.

WRITINGS:

NOVELS

Seven Poor Men of Sydney, Appleton, 1935.
The Beauties and Furies, Appleton, 1936.
House of All Nations, Simon & Schuster, 1938.
The Man Who Loved Children, Simon & Schuster, 1940, reprinted with introduction by Randall Jarrell, Holt, 1965.
For Love Alone, Harcourt, 1944.
Letty Fox: Her Luck, Harcourt, 1946.
A Little Tea, a Little Chat, Harcourt, 1948.
The People with the Dogs, Little, Brown, 1952.
Dark Places of the Heart, Holt, 1966 (published in England as *Cotters' England,* Secker & Warburg, 1966).
The Little Hotel, Angus & Robertson, 1973, Holt, 1975.
Miss Herbert (the Suburban Wife), Random House, 1976.
I'm Dying Laughing: The Humorist, Holt, 1987.

STORIES

The Salzburg Tales, Appleton, 1934.
The Puzzleheaded Girl (four novellas), Holt, 1967.
An Ocean of Story (uncollected stories), edited by R. G. Geering, Viking, 1986.

OTHER

(Contributor) *The Fairies Return,* P. Davies, 1934.
(Editor with husband, William J. Blake) *Modern Women in Love,* Dryden Press, 1946.
(Editor) *South Sea Stories,* Muller, 1955.
(Translator) Fernand Gigon, *Colour of Asia,* Muller, 1955.
(Translator) Jean Giltene, *The Candid Killer,* Muller, 1956.
(Translator) August Piccard, *In Balloon and Bathyscape,* Cassell, 1956.
A Christina Stead Reader, selected by Jean B. Read, Random House, 1978.
Christina Stead, Selected Fiction and Nonfiction, edited by R. G. Geering and A. Segerberg, University of Queensland Press (St. Lucia, Queensland, Australia), 1994.

Contributor of short stories to *Southerly, Kenyon Review,* and *Saturday Evening Post,* and of reviews to various papers. Stead's novels have been translated into foreign languages.

SIDELIGHTS: Australian-born novelist and short story author Christina Stead—whose work went unregarded for a large part of her life—is considered by many critics to be one of the most gifted writers of the twentieth century. "To open a book, any book, by Christina Stead and read a few pages," Angela Carter wrote in the *London Review of Books,* "is to be at once aware that one is in the presence of greatness." Stead's novel *The Man Who Loved Children,* which depicts a boisterous, often cruel family led by an idealist father, is generally regarded as her masterpiece.

Stead was born in 1902, the daughter of a prominent naturalist. Her mother passed away when Stead was two years old. At the age of 26, Stead left Australia for England, working as a clerk until her health failed her the following year. With her companion William J. Blake (the couple was married in 1952), she then traveled over Europe, living in such cities as Brussels, Antwerp, and Basel. During World War II she and Blake lived in the United States, where Stead worked for a time—unhappily—as a screenwriter for Metro-Goldwyn-Mayer. The couple returned to Europe at war's end.

In 1934 Stead published her first book, a collection of short stories entitled *The Salzburg Tales.* Based on Stead's idea that every fairy tale has a modern equivalent, *The Salzburg Tales* display a matter-of-fact Gothic quality which Stead would later employ in her realistic novels of modern family life. These early stories are, Carter stated, "glittering, grotesque short fictions, parables and allegories. . . . contrived with a lush, jewelled exquisiteness of technique." Writing in *Southerly,* Michael Wilding found the same collection to be "running riot" with "adolescent-like fantasy and whimsy."

During the 1930s Stead published several novels set in her native Australia, including *Seven Poor Men of Sydney,* a tale of an impoverished fishing community. Her biggest critical and financial success, however, came with the publication of *House of All Nations,* an 800-page epic novel tracing the decline and final collapse of a Swiss banking house. The novel's myriad characters, its behind-the-scenes look at currency manipulations, and the glamorous lifestyles it depicted guaranteed the story a wide and appreciative audience. R. G. Geering, writing in *Christina Stead,* found *House of All Nations* to be "Stead's greatest intellectual achievement—its knowledge of the workings of international finance and its revelation of the fraud, the ruthlessness, the energy, the sheer luck, and the genius that go into money-making, are by any standards remarkable." Writing in *New Statesman,* Elaine Feinstein claimed that *House of All Nations,* "for all its flaws, marks out an extraordinary terrain of avarice with as much passion as other novelists have given to the violence of sexual love."

Stead followed *House of All Nations* with a quite different novel, *The Man Who Loved Children,* the story of a self-centered man, his suffering wife, and their young daughter. Writing in her study *Christina Stead,* Joan Lidoff found that "at the heart of Christina Stead's fiction echoes the persistent moral issue: egotism. She sees everyone striving by subtle or overt manipulations to subordinate others to his or her own needs and desires, trying to take as much while giving as little as possible. In her 1940 masterpiece, *The Man Who Loved Children,* Stead criticizes this ongoing struggle between competing egoisms, not only in her characterization and analysis, but in the very form of her fiction.

This novel takes as protagonist no single hero, but an entire family." In contrast, Dorothy Green claimed in *The Australian Experience: Critical Essays on Australian Novels:* "Stead has created what is extremely rare in modern literature: three archetypal characters who have a life of their own, independent of their author."

When first published in 1940 *The Man Who Loved Children* was both a critical and popular failure. For years, it led an underground existence, read and admired by only a few. But in 1965, Randall Jarrell arranged a reprint of the novel which brought it to the attention of the reading public. In his introduction to the reprint Jarrell proclaimed: "[*The Man Who Loved Children*] seems to me as plainly good as *Crime and Punishment* and *Remembrance of Things Past* and *War and Peace* are plainly great. I call it a good book, but it is a better book, I think, than most of the novels people call great; perhaps it would be fairer to call it great. It has one quality that, ordinarily, only a great book has: it makes you a part of one family's immediate existence as no other book quite does. One reads the book, with an almost ecstatic pleasure of recognition. You get used to saying, 'Yes, that's the way it is'; and you say many times, but can never get used to saying, 'I didn't know *anybody* knew that. Henny, Sam, Louie, and the children are entirely real to the reader, and reality is rare in novels."

Some critics compared Stead's approach in *The Man Who Loved Children* to that used by certain writers of the nineteenth century. Christopher Ricks wrote: "In its sense of growth and of generations, in its generality and specificity, above all in the central place which it accords to feelings of indignation and embarrassment, *The Man Who Loved Children* is in the best tradition of the nineteenth-century novel. . . . Like George Meredith at his best, [Stead] is fascinated by the way we speak to ourselves in the privacy of our skulls, and she is able to remind us of what we would rather forget—that we are all continually employing, to ourselves and to others, a false rhetoric, overblown, indiscriminately theatrical, and yet indisputably ours."

The novel's grimly domestic focus caught the attention of other critics. Carter noted that the book's "single-minded intensity of its evocation of domestic terror gives it a greater artistic cohesion than Stead's subsequent work, which tends towards the random picaresque. And Stead permits herself a genuinely tragic resolution." Similarly, Green stated that *The Man Who Loved Children* "presents the observer with the spectacle of a struggle for survival in a habitat which is too small and too impoverished for the 'fighting fish' it contains." Eleanor Perry remarked that the novel is "not a slice of life. It is life," while Jose Yglesias of the *Nation* proclaimed *The Man Who Loved Children* "a funny, painful, absorbing masterpiece, obviously the work of a major writer."

BIOGRAPHICAL/CRITICAL SOURCES:

BOOKS

Contemporary Literary Criticism, Gale (Detroit), Volume 2, 1975; Volume 5, 1976; Volume 8, 1978; Volume 32, 1985.
Geering, R. G., *Christina Stead,* Twayne, 1969.
Gribble, Jennifer, *Christina Stead,* Oxford University Press (Melbourne, New York City), 1994.
Lidoff, Joan, *Christina Stead,* Ungar, 1982.
Ransome, W. S., editor, *The Australian Experience: Critical Essays on Australian Novels,* Australian National University, 1974, pp. 174-208.
Rowley, Hazel, *Christina Stead: A Biography,* Holt (New York), 1994.

PERIODICALS

Atlantic Monthly, March, 1965; June, 1965; August, 1976.
Chicago Tribune Book World, December 24, 1978, Section 7, p. 1.
Christian Science Monitor, December 28, 1967.
London Magazine, November, 1967, pp. 98-100; June, 1968, pp. 112-13.
London Review of Books, September 16, 1982, pp. 11-13.
Los Angeles Times, May 19, 1986.
Los Angeles Times Book Review, October 4, 1987, p. 12; November 8, 1987, p. 11.
Nation, April 5, 1965; October 24, 1966; April 26, 1975, pp. 501-3.
New Leader, September 29, 1975, pp. 21-22.
New Republic, September 9, 1967, pp. 30-31; February 24, 1979, pp. 36-37.
New Statesman, June 14, 1974, p. 856; August 21, 1981, pp. 21-22.
New Yorker, August 18, 1975; August 9, 1976.
New York Review of Books, June 17, 1965; December 15, 1966; September 28, 1967; June 26, 1975.
New York Times Book Review, December 10, 1967; May 11, 1975; February 4, 1979, p. 9; March 15, 1981, p. 35; May 25, 1986, p. 7; August 23, 1987, p. 28; September 20, 1987, p. 26.
Observer (London), July 25, 1982, p. 31.
Saturday Review, April 10, 1965; May 31, 1975.
Southerly (Sydney), 1962; Volume 27, number 1, 1967, pp. 20-33.
Stand, Volume 10, number 1, 1968, pp. 30-37.
Times (London), January 12, 1985; April 24, 1986.
Times Literary Supplement, September 25, 1981, p. 1110; May 16, 1986, p. 535; April 24, 1987, p. 435.
Tribune Books (Chicago), October 4, 1987, p. 3.
Virginia Quarterly Review, winter, 1968.
Washington Post Book World, June 1, 1975, pp. 1-2; May 25, 1986, p. 6; August 2, 1987, p. 12; December 20, 1987, p. 9.

*   *   *

STEEL, Danielle (Fernande) 1947-

PERSONAL: Born August 14, 1947, in New York, NY; daughter of John and Norma (Stone) Schuelein-Steel; married second husband, 1977 (divorced); married third husband, John Traina (in business); children: (first marriage) one daughter; (second marriage) one son; (third marriage) two stepsons, four daughters, one son. *Education:* Educated in France; attended Parsons School of Design, 1963, and New York University, 1963-67. *Religion:* Christian Scientist.

ADDRESSES: Home—P.O. Box 1637, New York, NY 10156-1637. *Agent*—Morton L. Janklow Associates, Inc., 598 Madison Ave., New York, NY 10022-1614. *Office*—c/o Dell Publishing Co., 1540 Broadway, New York, NY 10036.

CAREER: Supergirls, Ltd. (public relations firm), New York, vice president of public relations, 1968-71; Grey Advertising, San Francisco, CA, copywriter, 1973-74; has worked at other positions in public relations and advertising; writer.

WRITINGS:

NOVELS

Going Home, Pocket Books, 1973.
Passion's Promise, Dell, 1977.

The Promise (based on a screenplay by Garry Michael White), Dell, 1978.
Now and Forever, Dell, 1978.
Season of Passion, Dell, 1979.
Summer's End, Dell, 1979.
The Ring, Delacorte, 1980.
Loving, Dell, 1980.
Remembrance, Delacorte, 1981.
Palomino, Dell, 1981.
To Love Again, Dell, 1981.
Crossings, Delacorte, 1982.
Once in a Lifetime, Dell, 1982.
A Perfect Stranger, Dell, 1982.
Changes, Delacorte, 1983.
Thurston House, Dell, 1983.
Golden Moments, Charnwood Publishers, 1983.
Full Circle, Delacorte, 1984.
Secrets, Delacorte, 1985.
Family Album, Delacorte, 1985.
Wanderlust, Delacorte, 1986.
Fine Things, Delacorte, 1987.
Kaleidoscope, Delacorte, 1987.
Zoya, Delacorte, 1988.
The Long Road Home, Delacorte, 1988.
Star, Delacorte, 1989.
Daddy, Delacorte, 1989.
Message from Nam, Delacorte, 1990.
Heartbeat, Delacorte, 1991.
No Greater Love, Delacorte, 1991.
Mixed Blessings, Delacorte, 1992.
Jewels, Delacorte, 1992.
Vanished, Delacorte, 1993.
The Gift, Delacorte, 1994, Spanish-language version with Maria Jose Rodellar published as *El Regalo,* 1994.
Accident, Delacorte, 1994.
Wings, Delacorte, 1994.
Five Days in Paris, Delacorte, 1995.
Lightning, Delacorte, 1995.
Days of Shame, Delacorte, 1996.
Malice, Delacorte, 1996.
Silent Honor, Delacorte, 1996.
The Wedding, Delacorte, 1996.
The Ranch, Delacorte, 1997.
Special Delivery, Delacorte, 1997.
The Ghost, Delacorte, 1997.
The Long Road Home, Delacorte, 1998.
The Klone and I: A High-Tech Love Story, Delacorte, 1998.

JUVENILE

Amando, Lectorum Publications, 1985.
Martha's Best Friend, Delacorte, 1989.
Martha's New Daddy, Delacorte, 1989.
Martha's New School, Delacorte, 1989.
Max and the Baby-Sitter, Delacorte, 1989.
Max's Daddy Goes to the Hospital, Delacorte, 1989.
Max's New Baby, Delacorte, 1989.
Martha's New Puppy, Delacorte, 1990.
Max Runs Away, Delacorte, 1990.
Max and Grandma and Grandpa Winky, Delacorte, 1991.
Martha and Hilary and the Stranger, Delacorte, 1991.
Freddie's Trip, Dell, 1992.
Freddie's First Night Away, Dell, 1992.
Freddie's Accident, Dell, 1992.
Freddie and the Doctor, Dell, 1992.

OTHER

Love Poems: Danielle Steel (poetry), Dell, 1981, abridged edition, Delacorte, 1984.
(Coauthor) *Having a Baby* (nonfiction), Dell, 1984.

MEDIA ADAPTATIONS: Now and Forever was adapted into a movie and released by Inter Planetary Pictures in 1983; *Crossings* was made into an ABC-TV miniseries in 1986; NBC made television movies from *Kaleidoscope* and *Fine Things* in 1990, and aired *Changes, Daddy,* and *Palomino* in 1991; *Mixed Blessings* aired on television in 1998; a miniseries called *Danielle Steel's "Zoya"* aired in 1996; several of Steel's other novels, including *Wanderlust* and *Thurston House,* have also been optioned for television films and miniseries; *The Ghost* has been optioned for film. *The Ranch* has been recorded and released by Bantam Books Audio, 1997.

SIDELIGHTS: After producing a score of romance novels, which have been generally dismissed by critics but almost always embraced by readers, Danielle Steel has distinguished herself as nothing less than "a publishing phenomenon," Jacqueline Briskin reports in the *Los Angeles Times Book Review.* Since the publication of her first hardcover in 1980, Steel has consistently hit both hardback and paperback best-seller lists; there are reportedly over 125 million of her books in print. Her popularity has also spilled over into television, where film versions of her books appear regularly, garnering good ratings each time.

Steel's fiction is peopled by women in powerful or glamorous positions; often they are forced to choose the priorities in their lives. Thus in *Changes* a New York anchorwoman who weds a Beverly Hills surgeon must decide whether her career means more to her than her long-distance marriage does. *Jewels* tells of the struggles of an American born noblewoman, the Duchess of Whitfield, to find peace and raise her children in pre-World War II Europe. And while reviewers seldom express admiration for the style of romantic novelists in general—*Chicago Tribune Book World* critic L. J. Davis claims that *Changes* is written in "the sort of basilisk prose that makes it impossible to tear your eyes from the page even as your brain is slowly [turning] to stone"—some reviewers, such as a *Detroit News* writer, find that the author's "flair for spinning colorful and textured plots out of raw material . . . is fun reading. The topic [of *Changes*] is timely and socially relevant." Toronto *Globe & Mail* contributor Peggy Hill similarly concludes about 1988's *Zoya:* "Steel has the ability to give such formula writing enough strength to not collapse into an exhausted state of cliche. *Zoya* is a fine example of that achievement."

In addition to her trademark romances, Steel also confronts serious issues in her books. *Mixed Blessings* looks at issues of infertility in a work that a *Rapport* reviewer calls "not only well written but extremely well researched." "On the whole," the reviewer concludes, "*Mixed Blessings* is definitely one of Steel's all-time best books." *Vanished* confronts the problem of kidnapped children in a story "set mainly in 1930's Manhattan," declares a *Kirkus Reviews* contributor. "The questions Steel raises about the tug-of-wars between guilt and responsibility . . . are anything but simple," states Stuart Whitwell in *Booklist.* "The author of *Mixed Blessings* keeps her secrets well," states a *Publishers Weekly* reviewer, "and . . . presents a strong portrait of a tormented young woman moving toward stability."

In *Accident* Steel offers a story about the stresses placed on a family after a serious car accident lands a couple's teenaged daughter in the hospital with a brain injury. Romance reenters protagonist Page Clark's life when she falls for the Norwegian divorced father of her daughter's friend—this after having learned that her husband has been having an affair with another woman. "Steel's good intentions—to show the resilience of the human spirit in the face of insurmountable odds—are obscured by her prose," states Joyce R. Slater in the *Chicago Tribune.* "The ending is predictable but pleasant," declares a *Publishers Weekly* contributor, "bound to delight Steel's fans." *Malice* is the story of Grace Adams's attempts to deal with her self-defense murder of her abusive father, while *The Gift* tells how a 1950s family slowly comes to accept the death of their youngest daughter and welcomes an unmarried expectant mother into their fold. "The narrative," states a critic in a *Publishers Weekly* review of *The Gift,* has well-meaning characters, uplifting sentiments and a few moments that could make a stone weep. A *Rapport* reviewer asserts that the most significant part of the story is "the affirmation of the grand design of tragedy and its transcendent message of purpose." As Steel revealed in an interview with *Contemporary Authors,* "I want to give [readers] entertainment and something to think about."

BIOGRAPHICAL/CRITICAL SOURCES:

BOOKS

Bane, Vickie L., *The Lives of Danielle Steel: The Unauthorized Biography of America's #1 Best-Selling Author,* St. Martin's (New York City), 1994.
Contemporary Authors New Revision Series, Gale (Detroit), Volume 19, 1987; Volume 36, 1992.

PERIODICALS

Booklist, April 1, 1992, p. 1413; October 15, 1992, p. 380; June 1 & 15, 1993, p. 1735; October 15, 1994, pp. 372-73; April 15, 1995, p. 1453; October 15, 1995, p. 364; March 1, 1996, p. 1077.
Books, July, 1992, p. 18.
Chicago Tribune, September 26, 1993, pp. 6-7; March 27, 1994, p. 4.
Chicago Tribune Book World, August 28, 1983.
Detroit Free Press, December 1, 1989.
Detroit News, September 11, 1983.
Globe & Mail (Toronto), July 9, 1988.
Kirkus Reviews, October 1, 1992, p. 1212; June 1, 1993, p. 685; January 1, 1994, p. 16; April 15, 1994, p. 504; September 15, 1994, p. 1225; April 1, 1995, p. 422; October 1, 1995, pp. 1377-78; March 1, 1996, pp. 328-29.
Library Journal, September 1, 1993; October 15, 1993; October 15, 1994, p. 89.
Los Angeles Times, January 6, 1988.
Los Angeles Times Book Review, April 14, 1985.
New York Times Book Review, September 11, 1983; August 19, 1984; March 3, 1985; July 9, 1995, p. 21.
People Weekly, October 3, 1994, p. 43.
Publishers Weekly, March 30, 1992, p. 88; October 26, 1992, pp. 55-56; June 7, 1993, p. 52; January 10, 1994, p. 41; May 23, 1994, p. 76; October 10, 1994, p. 60; December 12, 1994, p. 17; February 13, 1995, p. 21; May 1, 1995, p. 41; October 16, 1995, p. 44; March 25, 1996, p. 63; June 16, 1997.
Rapport, Volume 17, number 3, 1993, p. 23; Volume 18, number 1, 1994, p. 26; Volume 18, number 3, 1994, p. 23.
Time, November 25, 1985.
Washington Post Book World, July 3, 1983; March 3, 1985.

STEGNER, Wallace (Earle) 1909-1993

PERSONAL: Born February 18, 1909, in Lake Mills, IA; died, April, 1993; son of George H. and Hilda (Paulson) Stegner; married Mary Stuart Page, September 1, 1934; children: Stuart Page. *Education:* University of Utah, B.A., 1930; additional study at University of California, 1932-33; State University of Iowa, M.A., 1932, Ph.D., 1935.

CAREER: Augusta College, Rock Island, IL, instructor in English, 1933-34; University of Utah, Salt Lake City, instructor, 1934-37; University of Wisconsin—Madison, instructor, 1937-39; Harvard University, Cambridge, MA, Briggs-Copeland Instructor of Composition, 1939-45; Stanford University, Stanford, CA, professor of English, 1945-93; Jackson Eli Reynolds Professor of Humanities, 1969-71, director of creative writing program, 1946-71; University of Toronto, Toronto, Ontario, Bissell Professor of Canadian-U.S. Relations, 1975.

Writer-in-residence, American Academy in Rome, 1960; Phi Beta Kappa visiting scholar, 1960-61; Tanner Lecturer, University of Utah, 1980. Assistant to the Secretary of the Interior, 1961; National Parks Advisory Board, member, 1962-66, and chairman, 1965-66.

MEMBER: American Academy of Arts and Sciences, American Institute and Academy of Arts and Letters, American Antiquarian Society, Phi Beta Kappa.

AWARDS, HONORS: Little, Brown Prize, 1937, for *Remembering Laughter;* O. Henry Award, 1942, 1950, and 1954; Houghton-Mifflin Life-in-America Award and Anisfield-Wolfe Award, both 1945, both for *One Nation;* Guggenheim fellow, 1950 and 1959; Rockefeller fellow, 1950-51, to conduct seminars with writers throughout the Far East; Wenner-Gren Foundation grant, 1953; Center for Advanced Studies in the Behavioral Sciences fellow, 1955-56; Blackhawk Award, 1963, for *Wolf Willow;* Commonwealth Club gold medal, 1968, for *All the Little Live Things;* D.Litt., University of Utah, 1968; D.F.A., University of California, 1969, and Utah State University, 1972; National Endowment for the Humanities senior fellow, 1972; Pulitzer Prize, 1972, for *Angle of Repose;* D.L., University of Saskatchewan, 1973; National Book Award for fiction, 1977, for *The Spectator Bird;* D.H.L., University of Santa Clara, 1979; Robert Kirsch Award, *Los Angeles Times,* 1980; Montgomery fellow, Dartmouth College, 1980; has also received five Commonwealth Club medals; D.Litt., University of Wisconsin, 1986, and Montana State University, 1987.

WRITINGS:

NOVELS

Remembering Laughter, Little, Brown, 1937.
The Potter's House, Prairie Press, 1938.
On a Darkling Plain, Harcourt, 1940.
The Big Rock Candy Mountain, Duell, 1943.
Second Growth, Houghton, 1947.
The Preacher and the Slave, Houghton, 1950, published as *Joe Hill: A Biographical Novel,* Doubleday, 1969.
A Shooting Star, Viking, 1961.
All the Little Live Things, Viking, 1967.
Angle of Repose, Doubleday, 1971.
Fire and Ice, Duell, 1971.
The Spectator Bird, Doubleday, 1976.
Recapitulation, Doubleday, 1979.
Crossing to Safety, Random House, 1987.

STORY COLLECTIONS

The Women on the Wall, Houghton, 1948.
The City of the Living and Other Stories, Houghton, 1956.
Where the Bluebird Sings to the Lemonade Springs: Living and Writing in the West (short stories and essays), Viking, 1992.
Collected Stories of Wallace Stegner, Random House, 1994.

ESSAY COLLECTIONS

The Sound of Mountain Water: The Changing American West, Doubleday, 1969.
One Way to Spell Man, Doubleday, 1982.

EDITOR

(With others) *An Exposition Workshop: Readings in Modern Controversy,* Little, Brown, 1939.
(With others) *Readings for Citizens at War,* Harper, 1941.
(With Richard Scowcroft and Boris Ilyin) *The Writer's Art: A Collection of Short Stories,* Heath, 1950.
This Is Dinosaur: Echo Park and Its Magic Rivers, Knopf, 1955.
J. W. Powell, *The Exploration of the Colorado River of the West,* University of Chicago Press, 1957.
(With wife, Mary Stegner) *Great American Short Stories,* Dell, 1957.
Selected American Prose, 1841-1900: The Realistic Movement, Rinehart, 1958.
Mark Twain, *The Adventures of Huckleberry Finn,* Dell, 1960.
Bret Harte, *The Outcasts of Poker Flat,* New American Library, 1961.
Powell, *Report on the Lands of the Arid Region of the United States,* Harvard University Press, 1962.
(With others) *Modern Composition,* four volumes, Holt, 1964.
The American Novel: From James Fenimore Cooper to William Faulkner, Basic Books, 1965.
A. B. Guthrie, Jr., *The Big Sky,* Houghton, 1965.
(With others) *Twenty Years of Stanford Short Stories,* Stanford University Press, 1966.
Nathaniel Hawthorne, *Twice-Told Tales,* Heritage Press, 1967.
The Letters of Bernard DeVoto, Doubleday, 1975.

Editor, with Richard Scowcroft, of *Stanford Short Stories* (annual), Stanford University Press, 1946-68. West Coast editor, Houghton-Mifflin Co., 1945-53; editor-in-chief, *American West Magazine,* 1966-68.

OTHER

Mormon Country, Duell, 1941.
(With the editors of *Look* magazine) *One Nation,* Houghton, 1945.
The Writer in America (lectures), Hokuseido Press (Tokyo), 1951, Folcroft Press, 1969.
Beyond the Hundredth Meridian: John Wesley Powell and the Second Opening of the West, with an introduction by Bernard DeVoto, Houghton, 1954.
Wolf Willow: A History, a Story, and a Memory of the Last Plains Frontier, Viking, 1962.
The Gathering of Zion: The Story of the Mormon Trail, McGraw 1964.
Teaching the Short Story, Department of English, University of California, Davis, 1965.
Discovery!: The Search for Arabian Oil, Middle East Export Press, 1971.
Variations on a Theme of Discontent, Utah State University Press, 1972.
Robert Frost and Bernard DeVoto, Association of the Stanford University Libraries, 1974.

The Uneasy Chair: A Biography of Bernard DeVoto, Doubleday, 1974.
(Author of foreword) Ansel Adams, *Images, 1923-1974,* New York Graphic Society, 1974.
(With son, Stuart Page Stegner, and Eliot Porter) *American Places,* Dutton, 1981.
(With Richard Etulain) *Conversations with Wallace Stegner on Western History and Literature,* University of Utah Press, 1983, revised edition, University of Utah Press (Salt Lake City), 1990, published as *Stegner: Conversations on History and Literature,* revised edition, with a new foreword by Stewart L. Udall, University of Nevada Press (Reno), 1996.
The American West As Living Space, University of Michigan Press, 1987.
Marking the Sparrow's Fall: The Best of Wallace Stegner, edited by Page Stegner, H. Holt, 1998.

MEDIA ADAPTATIONS: Angle of Repose was adapted as an opera by Andrew Imbrie and Oakley Hall and produced by the San Francisco Opera Company in 1976.

SIDELIGHTS: The American West figured prominently in the writings of Wallace Stegner for five decades. He wrote two major works on the history of the Mormons, a biography of Western explorer John Wesley Powell, and a remembrance of the plains of Saskatchewan where he spent his boyhood. His novel *The Big Rock Candy Mountain* ranges over North Dakota, Washington, Minnesota, and Saskatchewan and concerns "that place of impossible loveliness that pulled the whole nation westward," as Stegner wrote in the book. The Pulitzer Prize-winning *Angle of Repose* concerns a professor in California who writes a book about his grandmother, an illustrator and writer of the old West.

Stegner was born in Iowa and raised in Utah, North Dakota, Washington, Montana, Wyoming, and Saskatchewan. After graduating from the University of Utah in 1930, he went to the State University of Iowa for his graduate degrees. He taught at the University of Utah, the University of Wisconsin—Madison, and Harvard University before moving to Stanford University in California, where Stegner was a professor of English for 26 years. During his years at Stanford, Stegner "founded and orchestrated one of the country's most prestigious writing programs," as James D. Houston stated in the *Los Angeles Times Book Review.* Merrill and Lorene Lewis, in their study *Wallace Stegner,* maintained that Stegner's "success as a teacher of creative writing, as well as his success as a writer, has given him opportunities and honors that not many regional writers have obtained. He has had access to major libraries for research; he has had the opportunity to travel and the leisure to write."

A book contest sponsored by the publishing house of Little, Brown in 1936 first prompted Stegner to try his hand at writing a novel. *Remembering Laughter,* his entry in the contest, won the top prize of $2,500 and was published in 1937. Over the next five years Stegner was to publish three more novels—*The Potter's House, On a Darkling Plain,* and *Fire and Ice.* All of these early novels are short, novella-length works and explore the relationships between individuals and their communities. *Remembering Laughter,* for instance, concerns a love triangle between a farmer, his wife, and his wife's sister. When the sister becomes pregnant, the truth about the child's parentage is kept secret for fear of the puritanical reaction of the community. *On a Darkling Plain* tells the story of Edwin Vickers, a disabled soldier who becomes a farmer on the Saskatchewan prairie. Though seeking self-sufficient isolation from others, Vickers is drawn back into the community when an outbreak of influenza threatens the local town and he must go to the aid of his neighbors. *Fire and Ice* concerns a college student who works untiringly for the campus branch of the Young Communist League. His devotion to party discipline is undone, however, when an outburst of drunken violence forces him to leave town. The Lewises saw this novel as a sign of Stegner's "rejection of closed systems" and indicative of his "early conservatism regarding any ready-made radical political or utopian economic solutions to human inequities. . . . The portrayal of the self-destructiveness of Calvinism in *Remembering Laughter,* the failure of isolationist Thoreauvian individualism in *On a Darkling Plain* both indicate, too, that Stegner expects the human lot to be a complex one, without formulas for success."

With the publication of *The Big Rock Candy Mountain* in 1942 Stegner achieved his first popular and critical success. A much longer and more fully developed novel than its predecessors, *The Big Rock Candy Mountain* "confirmed Stegner's place as an important American writer," as Richard H. Simpson stated in the *Dictionary of Literary Biography*. It chronicles the lives of Bo Mason, his wife Elsa, and their two sons from 1906 to 1942. The family history is one of continuous travel across the American and Canadian West as Bo, convinced that there is a place where opportunity awaits him, seeks to make his fortune. The Lewises explained that *The Big Rock Candy Mountain* is "more than the dream of the bitch goddess Success. It is the 'dream of taking from life exactly what you wanted,' and the quest for the Promised Land."

Critics particularly praised Stegner's handling of character and his evocation of the hardships of Western life. Milton Rugoff of the *New York Herald Tribune Weekly Book Review* believed that "who Bo Mason was and he did and how he lived Wallace Stegner conveys to us a vividness and a fullness hardly less than that with which we know our own fathers." Edward Weeks of the *Atlantic Monthly* spoke of "the ever deepening sympathy which [he feels] for the man and wife" of the story. Commenting on Stegner's ability to recreate Western life, Joseph Warren Beach of the *New York Times Book Review* wrote that "Stegner has felt the spell of mountain and prairie, of drought, flood and blizzard; he can write of moving accidents and hairbreadth escapes which give us the feel of frontier life better than phrases about the stars and seasons." Orville Prescott, writing in the *Yale Review,* concluded that *The Big Rock Candy Mountain* "is a sound, solid, intelligent, interesting novel, a good story and an excellent interpretation of an important phase of American life." Robert Canzoneri of the *Southern Review* called *The Big Rock Candy Mountain* "a once-in-a-lifetime book."

Stegner was not to enjoy another such success until *A Shooting Star* in 1961, a book that was a Literary Guild selection and sold over 150,000 copies. Sabrina Castro, the novel's troubled protagonist, "is Stegner's first strong and rebellious woman," Kerry Ahearns wrote in the *Western Humanities Review*. Sabrina's infidelity and the resultant breakup of her marriage, her mother's strength and compassion during her trials, and the efforts of the two women to insure that the development of the family's land will include a city park, are what the Lewises called Stegner's "old themes of familial and community concern." Simpson found Sabrina's mother to be "portrayed with skill," and believed that Stegner's "skillful portrait of this woman may serve as an example of one of his important achievements as a writer: throughout his career, Stegner has intelligently explored the experience of women." Writing in *Commonweal,* Martin Tucker maintained that "the ever-radiant undercurrent of compassion, of the idea that

everyone needs love-and-understanding, and that the only way to get it is to start giving it, streaks through the book and cannot fail to make it a moving experience."

In 1972 Stegner won the Pulitzer Prize for his novel *Angle of Repose,* a work Houston explained is now "recognized as a masterpiece." The story is set in California and concerns a retired history professor, Lyman Ward, who is editing the papers of his grandmother, a writer and illustrator of the nineteenth century. Ward has taken on this project so that he can forget his health and marital problems. Because he has lost a leg to a degenerative disease, Ward's wife has left him. As he imagines the lives of his grandparents through his grandmother's letters, Ward reflects upon his own life, and so Stenger "manages to bring past and present together in a brilliant fabric of memory interwoven with intuition," as Fred Rotondaro wrote in *Best Sellers*.

Ward's grandparents embody the tensions of America itself. His grandmother is Eastern, cultured, and genteel; his grandfather is a Western mining engineer and a rugged pioneer. "The relationship that emerges is one of complex unease," Janet Burroway remarked in the *New Statesman*. "Neither East nor West is the true region of [Stegner's] novel," Glendy Culligan explained in the *Saturday Review,* "but rather the human soul and the tension between its poles."

Through his investigation of his grandparents' lives, Ward finally comes to an understanding of his own life. "From them," Culligan wrote, "he learns that 'wisdom is knowing what you have to accept." This sense of tranquility is reflected in the novel's title, Burroway explained: "Peace-seeking in the poisoned American West is a recurrent theme of Wallace Stegner's novels. He seems now to have found its ideal image in *Angle of Repose,* the geological term for the slope at which rocks cease to roll." William Abrahams of the *Atlantic Monthly* saw Stegner as using family history to create an ultimately personal statement. *Angle of Repose,* he wrote, "is neither the predictable historical-regional Western epic, nor the equally predictable four-decker family saga. . . . For all the breadth and sweep of the novel, it achieves an effect of intimacy, hence of immediacy, and, though much of the material is 'historical,' an effect of discovery also, of experience newly minted rather than a pageantlike re-creation."

Ahearns believed that *Angle of Repose* represents a culmination for Stegner. "That this novel," she wrote, "is his most ambitiously and perfectly crafted only hints at how fully it grew from the thinking and experience most moving to him over the years. The story of the Ward family has the scope of an epic and the control of a lyric because it draws together all the threads of Stegner's thinking about the West and about that final man-woman judgment." Similarly, Simpson found that *Angle of Repose* "brings some of the most important elements of Stegner's work into sharp relief," including "his enduring concern with the family, especially the subtle shadings of emotional relations between parents and children, husbands and wives."

The Spectator Bird concerns another search of the past. Joe Allston is a seventy-year-old literary agent who lives in California. A chance postcard from an old friend moves him to read over his journal of a trip he made to Denmark some twenty years earlier, looking for his family's roots. The journal is a gothic tale that even includes Danish writer Isak Dinesen as a character. While reading the journal, Allston seeks some answers to his life. He wants to know "how to live and grow old inside a head I'm contemptuous of, in a culture I despise." David Dillon of *Southwest Review* described Allston as "a sardonic commentator on his own professional failures and geriatric disorders, hostile critic of contemporary fiction, sexual liberation, and anything connected with youth culture, [and] thinks of himself as a spokesman for traditional ethical and social values but acts like someone on the lam from life."

Although the *Saturday Review* critic found *The Spectator Bird* "a disappointment" because Stegner "simply refused to exploit the dramatic tension to be found in the life his protagonist looks back on," P. L. Adams of the *Atlantic Monthly* disagreed. "The tale," Adams wrote, "can be interpreted in several ways, but regardless of interpretation, it is consistently elegant and entertaining reading, with every scene adroitly staged and each effect precisely accomplished." *The Spectator Bird* received a National Book Award for fiction in 1977.

Stegner's concern with the influence of the past on the present and with a personal and societal sense of identity is most obvious is his nonfiction books, many of which deal with Western history and historical figures. In his essay "On the Writing of History," included in *The Sound of Mountain Water: The Changing American West,* Stegner defined the best history writing as a branch of literature, combining historical fact with the narrative prose of fiction. The proper blending of history and fiction "should help to unveil those continuities between past and present which have remained obscure," as Forrest G. Robinson and Margaret G. Robinson explained in their study, *Wallace Stegner.* Speaking to Dillon in the *Southwest Review,* Stegner explained his attraction to the writing of history: "I think to become aware of your life, to examine your life in the best Socratic way, is to become aware of history and of how little history is written, formed, and shaped. I also think that writers in a new tradition, in a new country, invariably, by a kind of reverse twist of irony, become hooked on the past, which in effect doesn't exist and therefore has to be created even more than the present needs to be created."

Having lived in Salt Lake City and attended the University of Utah, Stegner was naturally drawn to write about the region and the people who live there. His first nonfiction book was *Mormon Country,* an account of the geography of Utah and a short history of the Mormons who settled it. Stegner's "process of fusing personal experience with historical fact . . . took its first important nonfictional expression in *Mormon Country,*" the Robinsons maintained. Combining fiction, straight historical narrative, and personal anecdotes, the book examines a central feature of Mormon life and one of Stegner's primary concerns—the sense of community. The Mormon community, achieved by strict discipline imposed by a theocratic religion, was in stark contrast to the rugged individualism of non-Mormon pioneers. But the stability of Mormon society earned Stegner's admiration. The Robinsons found that his account of Mormon life is therefore biased, ignoring the drawbacks of Mormon culture and exaggerating the faults of other ways of life.

In his second book on the Mormons, *The Gathering of Zion: The Story of the Mormon Trail,* Stegner achieves an impartiality about his subject, according to the Robinsons. As he states in the book, Stegner is writing "as a non-Mormon but not a Mormon-hater." The book tells the story of the Mormon Trail, the long and arduous journey the Mormons underwent from Illinois to Utah from 1846 to 1869. Based on journals kept by the participants, Stegner's account achieves an "understanding of the eminently human pioneers," D. L. Morgan wrote in the *Saturday Review.* G. M. Greesley of *Library Journal* believed that Stegner's account is

so vivid that "the reader can almost hear the wail of the undernourished infant and the creak of wagons." It is, R. A. Billington wrote in *Book Week,* "the best single volume to appear on the Mormon migration. . . . [Stegner's] sensitivity to human beings and his ability to understand the spirit motivating the oft-persecuted Latter Day Saints allow him insights missed by earlier writers."

The nineteenth-century Western explorer and naturalist John Wesley Powell is the subject of Stegner's biography *Beyond the Hundredth Meridian: John Wesley Powell and the Second Opening of the West.* Powell led the first expeditions on the Green and Colorado Rivers and conducted some of the earliest geological surveys of the West. "Ethnology and Indian policies, public land policy and the structure of government science stem back to his trail blazing efforts," the *Kirkus* reviewer explained. Stegner sees Powell, he writes in the book, as "the personification of an ideal of public service that seems peculiarly a product of the American experience."

Critical reaction to *Beyond the Hundredth Meridian* was favorable. The *New Yorker* reviewer called it "an important book and, what is more, an exciting one." Mari Sandoz of *Saturday Review* found it "a complex story, but no man is better fitted by understanding and artistry to tell it than Wallace Stegner." J. H. Jackson of the *San Francisco Chronicle* believed the book to have "a fine chance to qualify either as biography or history when the 1954 Pulitzer awards are made next spring." The Robinsons, looking back on the book in 1977, found it to be "the longest, the most scholarly, perhaps the best written, and certainly the most valuable of Stegner's contributions to historical nonfiction."

In his essay collections *The Sound of Mountain Water* and *One Way to Spell Man* Stegner writes of the history and geography of the West, reflects on being a Western writer, and examines the culture and literature of the region. Though the essays collected in these two books were written over a period of several decades, Stegner's concerns remain remarkably consistent. One such concern is his fervent environmentalism. "We need," he writes in *The Sound of Mountain Water,* "wilderness preserved—as much as is still left, and as many kinds—because it was the challenge against which our character as a people was formed." Another of Stegner's continuing concerns was the need for a moral reference in American society. He "speaks of the survival of a lifelong essential code of conduct and esthetics, the belief in conscience and in American pride," Karl Shapiro explained in the *Chicago Tribune Book World.* Speaking of *One Way to Spell Man,* Vance Bourjaily wrote in the *New York Times Book Review* that the book contains "the attitudes and beliefs of a humane and civilized man who is both an artist and a Westerner."

BIOGRAPHICAL/CRITICAL SOURCES:

BOOKS

Arthur, Anthony, editor, *Critical Essays on Wallace Stegner,* 1982.

Benson, Jackson J., *Wallace Stegner: His Life and Work,* Viking (New York), 1996.

Contemporary Literary Criticism, Volume 9, Gale, 1978.

Cook-Lynn, Elizabeth, *Why I Can't Read Wallace Stegner and Other Essays: A Tribal Voice,* University of Wisconsin Press (Madison), 1997.

Dourgarian, James M., editor, *Wallace Earle Stegner, 1909-1993,* J. M. Dourgarian (Walnut Creek, CA), 1994.

Hepworth, James R., and Nancy Colberg, *Wallace Stegner: A Descriptive Bibliography,* Confluence, 1990.

Lewis, Merrill, and Lorene Lewis, *Wallace Stegner,* Boise State College, 1972.

Meine, Curt, *Wallace Stegner and the Continental Vision: Critical Essays and Commentary,* Island Press, 1997.

Rankin, Charles E., editor, *Wallace Stegner: Man and Writer,* University of New Mexico Press (Albuquerque), 1996.

Robinson, Forrest G., and Margaret G. Robinson, *Wallace Stegner,* Twayne, 1977.

Stegner, Page, editor, *The Geography of Hope: A Tribute to Wallace Stegner,* Sierra Club Books (San Francisco), 1996.

PERIODICALS

Atlantic Monthly, November, 1943, p. 128; April, 1971; June, 1976.

Best Sellers, April 1, 1971.

Bloomsbury Review, July-August, 1990, p. 5.

Book Week, October 3, 1943; January 10, 1965.

Chicago Tribune Book World, April 4, 1982.

Christian Science Monitor, November 16, 1967; February 12, 1979.

College English, December, 1958.

Commonweal, July 14, 1961; November 6, 1987, pp. 630-31.

Kirkus Reviews, March 1, 1954, p. 184.

Library Journal, October 1, 1964; April 1, 1971.

Los Angeles Times, June 7, 1992, p. M3.

Los Angeles Times Book Review, March 25, 1979; November 23, 1980; November 1, 1981; March 7, 1993, p. 12.

New Republic, August 20, 1990, pp. 38-40.

New Statesman, May 1961; September 17, 1971.

New Yorker, October 2, 1943, p. 86; September 25, 1954; June 5, 1971; June 21, 1976.

New York Herald Tribune Weekly Book Review, October 3, 1943, p. 3.

New York Times, July 27, 1967; March 24, 1971; February 24, 1979.

New York Times Book Review, September 26, 1943, p. 4; October 28, 1962; February 10, 1974; May 30, 1982.

San Francisco Chronicle, September 12, 1954.

Saturday Review, September 11, 1954; May 20, 1961; December 1, 1962; January 16, 1965; March 20, 1971; May 15, 1976.

Saturday Review of Literature, October 2, 1943, p. 11.

Sewanee Review, winter, 1962.

Smithsonian, April, 1990, p. 212.

South Dakota Review, spring, 1971.

Southern Review, autumn, 1973.

Southwest Review, summer, 1976; spring, 1977.

Time, July 12, 1976.

Times Literary Supplement, April 26, 1963.

Washington Post, April 15, 1993, pp. C1-C2.

Washington Post Book World, May 2, 1982.

Western Humanities Review, spring, 1977; May, 1983, pp. 52-53.

Yale Review, winter, 1944; spring, 1968.

*   *   *

STEIN, Gertrude 1874-1946

PERSONAL: Born February 3, 1874, in Allegheny, PA; died of cancer, July 27, 1946, in the American Hospital at Neuilly-sur-Seine, France; daughter of Daniel and Amelia (Keyser) Stein. *Education:* Radcliffe College, Harvard University, B.A., 1897; attended Johns Hopkins Medical School, 1897-1901. *Avocational interests:* Collecting postimpressionist art.

CAREER: Poet, short story writer, novelist, literary experimentalist.

AWARDS, HONORS: Medal of French Recognition from the French government, for services during the Second World War.

WRITINGS:

Three Lives: Stories of the Good Anna, Melanctha, and the Gentle Lena, Grafton Press, 1909.

Portrait of Mabel Dodge at the Villa Curonia, Privately printed, 1912.

Tender Buttons: Objects, Food, Rooms, Claire Marie, 1914.

Geography and Plays, Four Seas, 1922.

The Making of Americans: Being a History of a Family's Progress, Contact Editions (Paris), 1925, published as *The Making of Americans: The Hersland Family,* Harcourt, 1934.

Composition as Explanation, Hogarth, 1926.

Useful Knowledge, Payson & Clarke, 1928.

An Acquaintance with Description, Seizin Press, 1929.

Lucy Church, Amiably, Imprimerie Union, 1930.

How to Write, Plain Edition, 1931, originally entitled *Grammar, Paragraphs, Sentences, Vocabulary, Etcetera.*

Before the Flowers of Friendship Faded Friendship Faded, Plain Edition, 1931.

Operas and Plays, Plain Edition, 1932.

The Autobiography of Alice B. Toklas, Harcourt, 1933.

Matisse, Picasso and Gertrude Stein, Plain Edition, 1933.

Portraits and Prayers, Random House, 1934.

Lectures in America, Random House, 1935.

Narration, University of Chicago Press, 1935.

The Geographical History of America; or, The Relation of Human Nature to the Human Mind, Random House, 1936, paperback edition, Johns Hopkins University Press (Baltimore), 1995.

Everybody's Autobiography, Random House, 1937.

Picasso, Floury, 1938, English translation by Alice B. Toklas, Scribner, 1939.

The World . . . Is Round, W. R. Scott, 1939.

Paris France, Scribner, 1940.

What Are Masterpieces?, Conference Press, 1940.

Ida, a Novel, Random House, 1941.

Wars I Have Seen, Random House, 1945.

Brewsie and Willie, Random House, 1946.

In Savoy; or, Yes Is for a Very Young Man, a Play of the Resistance in France, Pushkin Press, 1946.

Selected Writings of Gertrude Stein, edited by Carl Van Vechten, Random House, 1946.

Four in America, Yale University Press, 1947.

The Gertrude Stein First Reader & Three Plays, M. Fridberg (London), Houghton, 1948.

Blood on the Dining-Room Floor, Banyan Press, 1948.

Last Operas and Plays, edited by Van Vechten, Rinehart, 1949, paperback edition, Johns Hopkins University Press (Baltimore), 1995.

Things As They Are, A Novel in Three Parts, Banyan Press, 1950.

The Yale Edition of the Unpublished Writings of Gertrude Stein, edited by Van Vechten, Yale University Press, Volume 1: *Two: Gertrude Stein and Her Brother, and Other Early Portraits, 1906-12,* 1951, Volume 2: *Mrs. Reynolds and Five Earlier Novelettes,* 1952, Volume 3: *Bee Time Vine, and Other Pieces, 1913-1927,* 1953, Volume 4: *As Fine as Melanctha, 1914-1930,* 1954, Volume 5: *Painted Lace, and Other Pieces, 1914-1937,* 1955, Volume 6: *Stanzas in Meditation, and Other Poems, 1929-1933,* 1956, Volume 7:

Alphabets and Birthdays, 1957, Volume 8: *A Novel of Thank You,* 1958.

Selected Writings, edited by Van Vechten, Modern Library, 1962.

Gertrude Stein's America, edited by Gilbert A. Harrison, R. B. Luce, 1965.

Writings and Lectures 1911-1945, edited by Patricia Meyerowitz, Owen, 1967.

Gertrude Stein on Picasso, edited by Edward Burns, Liveright (in cooperation with the Museum of Modern Art), 1970.

Selected Operas and Plays of Gertrude Stein, edited by John Malcolm Brinnin, University of Pittsburgh Press, 1970.

Fernhurst, Q.E.D., and Other Early Writings, Liveright, 1971.

Look at Me Now and Here I Am; Writings and Lectures 1909-45, edited by Meyerowitz, Penguin, 1971.

Matisse, Picasso, and Gertrude Stein, with Two Shorter Stories, Something Else Press, 1972.

The Previously Uncollected Writings of Gertrude Stein, edited by Robert Bartlett Haas, Black Sparrow Press, Volume 1: *Reflection on the Atomic Bomb,* 1973, Volume 2: *How Writing Is Written,* 1974.

Dear Sammy: Letters from Gertrude Stein and Alice B. Toklas, edited by Samuel M. Steward, Houghton, 1977.

A Novel of Thank You (originally published in 1958 by Yale University Press as volume 8 of "The Yale Edition of the Unpublished Writings of Gertrude Stein"), Dalkey Archive Press (Normal, IL), 1994.

Stanzas in Mediation (originally published in 1958 by Yale University Press as volume 6 of "The Yale Edition of the Unpublished Writings of Gertrude Stein"), Sun & Moon Press (Los Angeles), 1994.

Mirrors of Friendship: The Letters of Gertrude Stein and Thornton Wilder, edited by Edward M. Burns, Ulla E. Dydo, and William Rice, Yale University Press, 1996.

A History of Having a Great Many Times not Continued to Be Friends: The Correspondence between Mabel Dodge and Gertrude Stein, 1911-1934, edited by Patricia R. Everett, University of New Mexico Press, 1996.

Gertrude Stein: Writings 1903-1932, edited by Catharine R. Stimpson and Harriet Chessman, Library of America, 1998.

Gertrude Stein: Writings 1932-1946, edited by Catharine R. Stimpson and Harriet Chessman, Library of America, 1998.

LIBRETTOS; MUSIC BY VIRGIL THOMSON

Four Saints in Three Acts; An Opera to Be Sung (first produced at the Wadsworth Atheneum in Hartford, Connecticut, February, 1934), Random House, 1934.

Capital, Capitals; For Four Men and a Piano, [New York], 1947.

The Mother of Us All (first produced at Columbia University in 1947), Music Press, 1947.

Preciosilla; For Voice and Piano, G. Schirmer, 1948.

OTHER

Contributor to *The Collectors: Dr. Claribel and Miss Etta Cone; with a Portrait by Gertrude Stein,* by Barbara Pollack, Bobbs-Merrill, 1962. Also contributor of two articles to the Harvard *Psychological Review,* 1896 and 1898.

SIDELIGHTS: From the time she moved to Paris, France in 1903 until her death in Neuilly-sur-Seine in 1946, American writer Gertrude Stein was a central figure in the Parisian art world. An advocate of the avant garde, Stein helped shape an artistic movement that demanded a new form of expression and a conscious break with the past. The salon she shared with Alice B. Toklas, her lifelong companion and secretary, at 27 rue de Fleurus became a gathering place for the "new moderns," as the talented

young artists supporting this movement came to be called. Among those whose careers she helped launch were painters Henri Matisse, Juan Gris, and Pablo Picasso. What these creators achieved in the visual arts, Stein attempted in her writing. A bold experimenter and self-proclaimed genius, she rejected the linear, time-oriented writing characteristic of the nineteenth century for a spatial, process-oriented, specifically twentieth-century literature. The results were dense poems and fictions, often devoid of plot or dialogue, which yielded memorable phrases ("Rose is a rose is a rose") but not commercially successful books. In fact, her only bestseller, *The Autobiography of Alice B. Toklas,* a memoir of Stein's life written in the person of Alice B. Toklas, was a standard narrative, conventionally composed.

Though commercial publishers slighted her experimental writings and critics dismissed them as incomprehensible, Stein's theories did interest some of the most talented writers of the day. During the years between World War I and World War II, a steady stream of expatriate American and English writers, whom Stein dubbed "the Lost Generation," found their way to her soirees. Ernest Hemingway, F. Scott Fitzgerald, and Sherwood Anderson were among those exposed to her literary quest for what she called an "exact description of inner and outer reality." Whether or not Stein influenced these and other major modern writers—including James Joyce, whose masterpiece of modernist writing, *Ulysses,* was composed after his exposure to Stein—remains an issue of some contention. Critics do agree, however, that whatever her influence, her own work, and particularly her experimental writing, is largely neglected. As Edmund Wilson noted in *Axel's Castle,* "Most of us balk at her soporific rigmaroles, her echolaliac incantations, her half-witted-sounding catalogues of numbers; most of us read her less and less. Yet, remembering especially her early work, we are still always aware of her presence in the background of contemporary literature."

Born in Allegheny, Pennsylvania, in 1874, Stein moved frequently and was exposed to three different languages before mastering one. When she was six months old, her parents took her and her two older brothers, Michael and Leo, abroad for a five-year European sojourn. Upon their return, they settled in Oakland, California, where Stein grew up. At eighteen, she followed her brother Leo to Baltimore; while he attended Harvard, she enrolled in the Harvard Annex (renamed Radcliffe College before she graduated). At this time Stein's primary interest was the study of psychology under noted psychologist William James. With his encouragement, she published two research papers for the Harvard *Psychological Review* ("Normal Motor Automatism," 1896, and "Cultivated Motor Automatism," 1898) and enrolled in the Johns Hopkins Medical School. After failing several courses, Stein quit the program without taking a degree. Instead she followed Leo first to London, and then to Paris, where he had settled early in 1903 to pursue a career as an artist. "Paris was the place," Stein is quoted in *Gertrude Stein's America,* "that suited us who were to create the twentieth century art and literature."

As soon as she arrived, Stein submerged herself in the bohemian community of the avant-garde, described by her brother Leo as an "atmosphere of propaganda." With guidance from her eldest brother Michael—an art collector who lived just a few blocks away—Stein began to amass a modern art collection of her own. She also, at age twenty-nine, dedicated herself in earnest to her writing.

Stein published her first—and some say her best—book in 1909. *Three Lives* is comprised of three short tales, each of which investigates the essential nature of its main character. Of these, "Melanctha," the portrait of a young mulatto girl who suffers an unhappy affair with a black doctor, has been particularly singled out for praise. A reworking of an autobiographical story Stein wrote about an unhappy lesbian affair, the story "attempts to trace the curve of a passion, its rise, its climax, its collapse, with all the shifts and modulations between dissension and reconciliation along the way," Mark Schorer wrote in *The World We Imagine.* James R. Mellow, writing in the *Dictionary of Literary Biography,* commended it as "one of the earliest and most sensitive treatments of Negro experience," attributing much of its success to "the racy, almost vernacular style of the dialogue."

In a critique of *The Making of Americans,* Katherine Anne Porter compared the experience of reading the book to walking into "a great spiral, a slow, ever-widening, unmeasured spiral unrolling itself horizontally. The people in this world appear to be motionless at every stage of their progress, each one is simultaneously being born, arriving at all ages and dying. You perceive that it is a world without mobility, everything takes place, has taken place, will take place; therefore nothing takes place, all at once," she wrote in *The Collected Essays and Occasional Writings of Katherine Anne Porter.* Porter maintained that such writing was not based upon moral or intellectual judgments but simply upon Stein's observations of "acts, words, appearances giving her view; limited, personal in the extreme, prejudiced without qualification, based on assumptions founded in the void of pure unreason." In his *I Hear America,* Vernon Loggins described Stein's language as "thought in the nude—not thought dressed up in the clothes of time-worn rhetoric." Schorer also noted her process-oriented approach: "Her model now is Picasso in his cubist phase and her ambition a literary plasticity divorced from narrative sequence and consequence and hence from literary meaning. She was trying to transform literature from a temporal into a purely spatial art, to use words for their own sake alone."

Stein carried this technique even further in *Tender Buttons: Objects, Food, Rooms,* which appeared in 1914. Published at her own expense, the book contains passages of automatic writing and is configured as a series of paragraphs about objects. Devoid of logic, narration, and conventional grammar, it resembles a verbal collage. "*Tender Buttons* is to writing . . . , exactly, what cubism is to art," wrote W. G. Rogers in his *When This You See Remember Me: Gertrude Stein in Person.* "Both book and picture appeared in, belong to, can't be removed from our time. That particular quality in them which is usually ridiculed, the disparate, the dispersed, the getting onto a horse and riding off in all directions, the atomization of their respective materials, the distorted vision, all that was not imagined but rather drawn out of their unique age. If the twentieth century makes sense, so do Stein and Picasso." Despite its inaccessibility, Rogers called *Tender Buttons* "essential, for here is the kind of Stein that launched a thousand jibes; this represents the big break with the sort of books to which we had been accustomed, and once you have succumbed to it, you can take anything, you have become a Stein reader."

Stein explained the theory behind her techniques in *Composition as Explanation,* published in 1926. But even those critics who understood her approach were largely skeptical of her ability to reduce language to abstraction and still use it in a way that had meaning to anyone beyond herself. As Alfred Kazin noted in the *Reporter,* "she let the stream of her thoughts flow as if a book were only a receptacle for her mind. . . . But the trouble with these pure thinkers in art, criticism, and psychology is that the mind is always an instrument, not its own clear-cut subject matter." When Stein did embrace conventional subjects, as she did in her memoir, *The Autobiography of Alice B. Toklas,* she was a resounding success.

Published in 1933, *The Autobiography of Alice B. Toklas* recounts Stein's experiences in the colorful art world of Paris between the world wars. It was written by Stein from Toklas's point of view, a technique that "enables Miss Stein to write about herself while pretending she is someone dearly devoted to herself," in the words of *New Outlook* contributor Robert Cantwell. Notwithstanding the enormous egotism behind the endeavor, readers flocked to the publication (which was to be Stein's only bestseller), fascinated by the vivid portrait of a genuinely creative world. As Ralph Thompson noted in *Current History,* "The style is artful, consciously naive, at times pompous, but it is never boring or obscure, and is often highly amusing. *The Autobiography of Alice B. Toklas* should convince even the most skeptical that Miss Stein is gifted and has something to say."

In addition to writing books, Stein also contributed librettos to several operas by Virgil Thompson, notably *Four Saints in Three Acts* and *The Mother of Us All.* The year after her autobiography appeared, Stein returned to the United States to celebrate the successful staging of *Four Saints* at the Wadsworth Atheneum in Hartford, Connecticut, and conduct a lecture tour. Though she had been absent for thirty years, Stein was treated royally and her return was front page news in the major daily papers. She described her six-month visit in a second memoir, *Everybody's Autobiography,* published in 1937. Her tour completed, Stein returned to France where she remained for the rest of her life, though she moved from Paris to an unoccupied village near the Swiss border during the Second World War. Many of her later writings took the war as a subject, notably the 1946 publication *Brewsie and Willie,* which sought to capture the life of common American soldiers through their speech.

Remembered today largely as an interesting personality, whose works are seldom read, Gertrude Stein nonetheless has left her stamp upon modern literature. As John Ashbery concluded in *ARTnews,* "Her structures may be demolished; what remains is a sense of someone's having built."

BIOGRAPHICAL/CRITICAL SOURCES:

BOOKS

Caramallo, Charles, *Henry James, Gertrude Stein, and the Biographical Act,* University of North Carolina Press (Chapel Hill), 1996.

Concise Dictionary of Literary Biography, 1917-1929, Gale (Detroit), 1989.

Dickie, Margaret, *Stein, Bishop, and Rich: Lyrics of Love, War, and Peace,* University of North Carolina Press, 1997.

Dictionary of Literary Biography, Gale, Volume 4: *American Writers in Paris, 1920-1939,* 1980, Volume 54: *American Poets, 1880-1945, Third Series,* 1987.

Everett, Patricia R., *A History of Having a Great Many Times Not Continued To Be Friends: The Correspondence Between Mabel Dodge and Gertrude Stein, 1911-1934,* University of New Mexico Press (Albuquerque), 1996.

Kaufmann, Michael, *Textual Bodies: Modernism, Postmodernism, and Print,* Bucknell University Press (Lewisburg, PA), 1994.

Loggins, Vernon, *I Hear America . . . Literature in the United States since 1900,* Crowell (New York City), 1937.

Moore, George B., *The Unfinished Aesthetic: Gertrude Stein and The Making of Americans,* Peter Lang (New York City), 1998.

Moore, George B., *Gertrude Stein's The Making of Americans: Repetition and the Emergence of Modernism,* Peter Lang, 1997.

Perelman, Bob, *The Trouble with Genius: Reading Pound, Joyce, Stein, and Zukofsky,* University of California Press (Berkeley and Los Angeles), 1994.

Porter, Katherine Anne, *The Collected Essays and Occasional Writings of Katherine Anne Porter,* Delacorte Press (New York City), 1970.

Riddel, Joseph N., *The Turning Word: American Literary Modernism and Continental Theory,* edited by Mark Bauerlein, University of Pennsylvania Press (Philadelphia), 1996.

Rogers, W. G., *When This You See Remember Me: Gertrude Stein in Person,* Rinehart & Co., 1948.

Schorer, Mark, *The World We Imagine: Selected Essays,* Farrar, Straus (New York City), 1968.

Simon, Linda, *Gertrude Stein Remembered,* University of Nebraska Press (Lincoln), 1994.

Stendhal, Renate, editor, *Gertrude Stein: In Words and Pictures: A Photobiography,* Algonquin Books of Chapel Hill, 1994.

Twentieth-Century Literary Criticism, Gale, Volume 1, 1978; Volume 6, 1982; Volume 28, 1988.

Wagner-Martin, Linda, *Favored Strangers: Gertrude Stein and Her Family,* Rutgers University Press (New Brunswick), 1995.

Watts, Linda S., *Rapture Untold: Gender, Mysticism, and the 'Moment of Recognition' in Works by Gertrude Stein,* Lang (New York City), 1996.

Welch, Lew (with Eric Paul Shaffer), *How I Read Gertrude Stein,* Grey Fox Press (San Francisco), 1994.

Wilson, Edmund, *Axel's Castle: A Study in the Imaginative Literature of 1870-1930,* Scribner (New York City), 1931.

Wineapple, Brenda, *Sister Brother: Gertrude and Leo Stein,* Putnam (New York City), 1996.

PERIODICALS

ARTnews February, 1971.
Current History, January, 1934.
Library Journal, September 15, 1995, p. 58.
New Outlook, October, 1933.
New York Times Book Review, June 2, 1996, p. 29.
Opera News, January 6, 1996, p. 10.
People Weekly, February 12, 1996, p. 127.
Reporter, February 18, 1960.
Writer, October, 1995, p. 7.
Writer's Digest, February, 1996, p. 12.

*　　　*　　　*

STEINBECK, John (Ernst) 1902-1968
(Amnesia Glasscock)

PERSONAL: Born February 27, 1902, in Salinas, CA, died December 20, 1968, of heart disease, in New York, NY; buried in Salinas; son of John Ernst (a county treasurer) and Olive (a schoolteacher; maiden name, Hamilton) Steinbeck; married Carol Henning, 1930 (divorced, 1943); married Gwyn Conger (a writer, singer, and composer), March 29, 1943 (divorced, 1948); married Elaine Scott, December 29, 1950; children: (second marriage) Tom, John. *Education:* Stanford University, special student, 1919-25.

CAREER: Variously employed as hod-carrier, fruit-picker, apprentice painter, laboratory assistant, caretaker, surveyor, and reporter; writer. Foreign correspondent in North Africa and Italy for *New York Herald Tribune,* 1943; correspondent in Vietnam for *Newsday,* 1966-67. Special writer for U.S. Army Air Forces, during World War II.

AWARDS, HONORS: General Literature Gold Medal, Commonwealth Club of California, 1936, for *Tortilla Flat,* 1937, for *Of Mice and Men,* and 1940, for *The Grapes of Wrath;* New York Drama Critics Circle Award, 1938, for play, *Of Mice and Men;* Pulitzer Prize, 1940, for *The Grapes of Wrath;* Academy Award nomination for best original story, Academy of Motion Picture Arts and Sciences, 1944, for *Lifeboat,* and 1945, for *A Medal for Benny;* Nobel Prize for literature, 1962; Paperback of the Year Award, Best Sellers, 1964, for *Travels with Charley: In Search of America.*

WRITINGS:

NOVELS

Cup of Gold: A Life of Henry Morgan, Buccaneer, Robert McBride, 1929.
The Pastures of Heaven, Viking, 1932, new edition, 1963.
To a God Unknown, Viking, 1933.
Tortilla Flat, Viking, 1935, illustrated edition, 1947.
In Dubious Battle, Viking, 1936, new edition, 1971.
Of Mice and Men (also see below; Book-of-the-Month Club selection), Viking, 1937.
The Red Pony (also see below), Covici, Friede, 1937.
The Grapes of Wrath, Viking, 1939, published with introduction by Carl Van Doren, World Publishing, 1947, revised edition, edited by Peter Lisca, 1972, 2nd edition, updated by Kevin Hearle, Penguin Books (New York), 1996, edited by Peter Lisca, with criticism, Penguin, 1997.
The Forgotten Village (also see below), Viking, 1941.
The Moon Is Down (also see below), Viking, 1942.
Cannery Row, Viking, 1945, new edition, 1963, published with manuscript, corrected typescript, corrected galleys, and first edition, Stanford Publications Service, 1975.
The Wayward Bus (Book-of-the-Month Club selection), Viking, 1947.
The Pearl (also see below), Viking, 1947.
Burning Bright: A Play in Story Form (also see below), Viking, 1950.
East of Eden, Viking, 1952.
Sweet Thursday, Viking, 1954.
The Short Reign of Pippin IV: A Fabrication (Book-of-the-Month Club selection), Viking, 1957.
The Winter of Our Discontent, Viking, 1961.

SHORT STORIES

Saint Katy the Virgin (also see below), Covici, Friede, 1936.
Nothing So Monstrous, Pynson Printers, 1936.
The Long Valley (contains fourteen short stories, including "The Red Pony," "Saint Katy the Virgin," "Johnny Bear," and "The Harness"), Viking, 1938, published as *Thirteen Great Short Stories from the Long Valley,* Avon, 1943, published as *Fourteen Great Short Stories from the Long Valley,* Avon, 1947.
How Edith McGillicuddy Met R. L. S., Rowfant Club (Cleveland), 1943.
The Crapshooter, Mercury Publications (New York), 1957.

PLAYS

(With George S. Kaufman) *Of Mice and Men: A Play in Three Acts* (based on novel of same title; first produced on Broadway at The Music Box Theatre, November 23, 1937),

Viking, 1937, published in *Famous American Plays of the Nineteen Thirties,* edited by Harold Clurman, Dell, 1980.

The Moon Is Down: Play in Two Parts (based on novel of same title; first produced on Broadway at Martin Beck Theatre, April 7, 1942), Dramatists Play Service, 1942.

Burning Bright: Play in Three Acts (based on novel of same title; first produced on Broadway at Broadhurst Theatre, October 18, 1950), acting edition, Dramatists Play Service, 1951.

SCREENPLAYS

Forgotten Village (based on novel of same title), independently produced, 1939.

Lifeboat, Twentieth Century-Fox, 1944.

A Medal for Benny, Paramount, 1945 (published in *Best Film Plays—1945,* edited by John Gassner and Dudley Nichols, Crown, 1946).

The Pearl (based on novel of same title), RKO, 1948.

The Red Pony (based on novel of same title), Republic, 1949.

Viva Zapata! (produced by Twentieth Century-Fox, 1952), edited by Robert E. Morsberger, Viking, 1975.

OMNIBUS VOLUMES

Steinbeck, edited by Pascal Covici, Viking, 1943, enlarged edition published as *The Portable Steinbeck,* 1946, revised edition, 1971, published in Australia as *Steinbeck Omnibus,* Oxford University Press, 1946.

Short Novels: Tortilla Flat, The Red Pony, Of Mice and Men, The Moon Is Down, Cannery Row, The Pearl, Viking, 1953, new edition, 1963.

East of Eden [and] *The Wayward Bus,* Viking, 1962.

The Red Pony, Part I: The Gift [and] *The Pearl,* Macmillan (Toronto), 1963.

The Pearl [and] *The Red Pony,* Viking, 1967.

Cannery Row [and] *Sweet Thursday,* Heron Books, 1971.

To a God Unknown [and] *The Pearl,* Heron Books, 1971.

Of Mice and Men [and] *Cannery Row,* Penguin (Harmondsworth, England), 1973, Penguin (New York), 1978.

The Grapes of Wrath [and] *The Moon Is Down* [and] *Cannery Row* [and] *East of Eden* [and] *Of Mice and Men,* Heinemann, 1976.

John Steinbeck, 1902-1968 (contains *Tortilla Flat, Of Mice and Men,* and *Cannery Row*), limited edition, Franklin Library, 1977.

The Short Novels of John Steinbeck (contains *Tortilla Flat, The Red Pony, Of Mice and Men, The Moon Is Down, Cannery Row,* and *The Pearl*), introduction by Joseph Henry Jackson, Viking, 1981.

Novels and Stories, 1932-1937, Library of America (New York), 1994.

The Grapes of Wrath & Other Writings, 1938-1941 (contains *The Long Valley, The Grapes of Wrath, The Log from the Sea of Cortez,* and *The Harvest Gypsies*), Library of America (New York), 1996.

OTHER

Their Blood Is Strong (factual story of migratory workers), Simon J. Lubin Society of California, 1938, published as *The Harvest Gypsies: On the Road to the Grapes of Wrath,* Heyday, 1988.

A Letter to the Friends of Democracy, Overbrook Press, 1940.

(With Edward F. Ricketts) *Sea of Cortez* (description of expedition to Gulf of California), Viking, 1941, published as *Sea of Cortez: A Leisurely Journal of Travel,* Appel, 1971, revised edition published as *The Log from the "Sea of Cortez": The Narrative Portion of the Book, "Sea of Cortez,"* Viking, 1951.

Bombs Away: The Story of a Bomber Team (account of life and training in U.S. Army Air Forces), Viking, 1942.

A Russian Journal (description of tour to Russia), photographs by Robert Capa, Viking, 1948.

Once There Was a War (collection of dispatches and anecdotes from World War II), Viking, 1958.

Travels with Charley: In Search of America, Viking, 1962.

Letters to Alicia (collection of newspaper columns written as a correspondent in Vietnam), [Garden City, NJ], 1965.

America and Americans (description of travels in United States), Viking, 1966.

Journal of a Novel: The "East of Eden" Letters, Viking, 1969.

Steinbeck: A Life in Letters (collection of correspondence), edited by wife, Elaine Steinbeck, and Robert Wallsten, Viking, 1975.

The Acts of King Arthur and His Noble Knights: From the Winchester Manuscripts of Thomas Malory and Other Sources, edited by Chase Horton, Farrar, Straus, 1976.

The Collected Poems of Amnesia Glasscock (poems published by Steinbeck under pseudonym Amnesia Glasscock in *Monterey Beacon,* January-February, 1935), Manroot Books (San Francisco), 1976.

Letters to Elizabeth: A Selection of Letters from John Steinbeck to Elizabeth Otis, edited by Florian J. Shasky and Susan F. Kiggs, Book Club of California (San Francisco), 1978.

Working Days: The Journals of the Grapes of Wrath, edited by Robert DeMott, Penguin, 1989.

Short stories and short novels have appeared in numerous anthologies. Author of syndicated column written during tour of Vietnam, 1966-67. Contributor of numerous short stories, essays, and articles to popular magazines and periodicals.

MEDIA ADAPTATIONS: Several of Steinbeck's works have been adapted for films, the stage, and television. *The Grapes of Wrath,* with Henry Fonda, was filmed by Twentieth Century-Fox in 1940. *Of Mice and Men,* starring Burgess Meredith and Lon Cheney, was produced by United Artists in 1939, in 1970 it premiered as an opera, adapted by Carlisle Floyd, at the Seattle Opera House, and was also adapted as a teleplay by E. Nick Alexander. *Tortilla Flat,* featuring Spencer Tracy, was filmed by Metro-Goldwyn-Mayer in 1942. *The Moon is Down,* produced by Twentieth Century-Fox in 1943, starred Sir Cedric Hardwicke and Lee J. Cobb. *East of Eden,* with James Dean and Jo Van Fleet, who won an Oscar for her performance, was filmed by Warner Brothers in 1954, and was later made into a television mini-series; it was also adapted into a musical, *Here's Where I Belong,* which opened at the Billy Rose Theatre in 1968. *Pipe Dream,* a 1955 musical adapted by Oscar Hammerstein II, with music by Richard Rogers, was based on Steinbeck's *Sweet Thursday.* Twentieth Century-Fox produced *The Wayward Bus* in 1957. The National Broadcasting Co. has produced the following works for television: *America and Americans,* 1967, and *Travels with Charley,* 1968, both narrated by Henry Fonda; "The Harness," a story from *The Pastures of Heaven,* was televised in 1971 and featured Lorne Greene; *The Red Pony,* starring Henry Fonda and Maureen O'Hara, was shown in 1973. *Cannery Row* was adapted as a film starring Nick Nolte and Debra Winger by Metro-Goldwyn-Mayer, 1982. *Of Mice and Men* was adapted as CD-Rom by Byron Preiss Multimedia and Penguin USA (New York), 1995. It includes critical commentary by Steinbeck scholars, period music, video clips, scenes from the 1992 film version, and interviews with the author's widow.

SIDELIGHTS: Throughout his long and controversial career, John Steinbeck extolled the virtues of the American dream while he warned against what he believed to be the evils of an increasingly materialistic American society. Although his subject and style varied with each book, the themes of human dignity and compassion, and the sense of what a *Time* critic called "Steinbeck's vision of America," remained constant. Steinbeck was a uniquely American novelist, the critics contended, whose distrust and anger at society was offset by his faith and love for the land and its people. Of his seventeen novels, *The Grapes of Wrath* is perhaps the best example of Steinbeck's philosophy, perception, and impact. It is Steinbeck's "strongest and most durable novel," the *Time* reviewer commented, "a concentration of Steinbeck's artistic and moral vision."

Published in 1939, *The Grapes of Wrath* is a novel of social protest that caused a furor of both praise and denunciation. Although many protest novels appeared during the 1930s, none was as widely read nor as effective as Steinbeck's. According to Daniel Aaron, Steinbeck possessed a "special combination of marketable literary talent, sense of historical timing, eye for the significant subject, and power of identification," that made the book "the first of the Thirties protest novels to be read on a comparable scale with . . . best-selling novels." Peter Lisca recalled the impact of this combination: "*The Grapes of Wrath* was a phenomenon on the scale of a national event. It was publicly banned and burned by citizens; it was debated on national radio hook-ups; but above all it was read."

Written during the Depression, *The Grapes of Wrath* concerns the Joad family and their forced migration from the Dust Bowl of Oklahoma to what they had been told was "the land of promise," California. What they find, however, is a land of waste, corruption, and poverty. Expecting to find work, decent wages, and a chance to someday acquire their own land, they are instead introduced to a system of degrading migrant labor camps, menial wages, and near starvation. F. W. Watt commented: "The Paradise in front of them is a fallen world, . . . the place they have reached is as filled with suffering as the place from which they have fled. The subtle but relentless stages by which the realisation comes makes the irony all the more intense—to hear and gradually understand the term 'Okies' and to know that they are Okies; to realise that 'Hooverville'—any and every rough camp on a town's outskirts or garbage dump, named as an ironical tribute to the President who saw prosperity just around the corner—Hooverville was their home; to discover that the rich lands all around them are owned and controlled by large impersonal companies; to be hired for daily wages that barely cover the day's food, then to have those wages cut, and finally to be beaten and driven off at a sign of protest."

Shortly after the publication of his first major success, *Of Mice and Men,* and prior to penning *The Grapes of Wrath,* Steinbeck left for Oklahoma. There he joined a group of farmers embarking for California. For two years Steinbeck lived and worked with the migrants, seeking to lend authenticity to his account and to deepen his understanding of their plight. Steinbeck originally wrote about the plight of the migrant workers in a series of seven articles commissioned by *The San Francisco News* and published between October 5 and 12, 1936. These were brought together in an activist pamphlet, noted Jack Miles in the *Los Angeles Times Book Review,* published by the Simon J. Lubin Society of California in 1938 and republished more recently under Steinbeck's original title as *The Harvest Gypsies: On the Road to the Grapes of Wrath.*

According to Nicolaus Mills in his article for the *Nation,* in order to find material for his articles "Steinbeck traveled the California back roads in an old bakery truck." He was guided by the manager of a Federal Resettlement Administration's migrant labor camp whom he later used as the model for the manager of the Weedpatch camp in *The Grapes of Wrath.* Mills remarked that *The Harvest Gypsies* "contains some of Steinbeck's best journalism. . . . Unlike Agee and Orwell, Steinbeck did not make himself a central character in his writing. Rather. . .[he] was content to remain in the background and be a filter for his material. And what a filter! We may forget Steinbeck's presence. . .but we don't forget the sights the stark modesty of his prose conveys." William Kennedy, in his review for the *New York Times Book Review,* called the effort "a straightaway documentary: flat, narration of dismally depressing detail on the lives of immigrants, coupled to Steinbeck's informed and sensitive plea for change." "Even then," noted a *Bloomsbury Review* critic "it was evident that the last of these articles was only the beginning of a much larger battle."

At the end of 1937, Steinbeck first attempted to gain broader support and sympathy for the migrants' condition in a novel entitled *The Oklahomans,* which he abandoned early on. He followed that attempt with *L'Affaire Lettuceberg,* a satire that Steinbeck destroyed because he felt that it failed to promote understanding and came dangerously close to ridiculing the very people he wanted to help. "To make their story convincing, he had to report their lives with fidelity," Aaron explained, and Watt noted that Steinbeck's "personal involvement was intimate and his sympathies were strongly aroused by the suffering and injustice he saw at first hand." Critics contended that this combination of concern, first-hand knowledge, and commitment produced what a reviewer for the London *Times* termed "one of the most arresting [novels] of its time."

Steinbeck's journals, kept while maintaining the 2,000 words per day goal he had set for himself over the five month period in which he wrote *The Grapes of Wrath,* were published under the title *Working Days: The Journals of the Grapes of Wrath.* They "contain almost no meditations on the process of conceiving and embodying characters and themes but confine themselves largely to the actual working days and hours of a novel: what time [Steinbeck] sits down to write, how much he hopes to accomplish, and sometimes whether or not he did it," stated Robert Murray Davis in *World Literature Today.* "However, the journals do reveal a good deal about Steinbeck's cast of mind and working habits." In this sense, Davis commented, "*Working Days* should prove consoling to all writers who have similar problems and doubts." A reviewer for *Time* wrote, "the fascination of this document rests in its portrait of an artist at the peak of his skills."

Because he held a biological view of man, Steinbeck believed that the evolutionary concepts of adaption and "survival of the fittest" applied to men as well as animals. "The ability to adapt to new conditions is one of man's most valuable biological attributes, and the loss of it might well lead to man's extinction," is an important concept in Steinbeck's work, according to Frederick Bracher. Although Steinbeck is sympathetic toward the migrants in *The Grapes of Wrath,* "he is not blind to [their] defects," Warren French noted. "He shows clearly that he writes about a group of thoughtless, impetuous, suspicious, ignorant people." As such, French suggested, they too are bound by the laws of nature and "must also change if they are to survive." Thus, French described the book as "a dynamic novel about people who learn that survival depends upon their adaptability to new conditions." Jackson L.

Benson noticed an example of this evolutionary concept in *Of Mice and Men,* a short novel concerning two itinerant farm hands, George and Lennie. George, the "fittest" of the two, is compelled to shoot the strong but feeble-minded Lennie after the latter inadvertently kills their employer's daughter-in-law: "Lennie kills without malice—animals and people die simply because of his strength. Lennie himself must die simply because within the society of man he is an anomaly and weak."

The concept of "group-man" was another aspect of Steinbeck's biological view. This idea was later outlined in *Sea of Cortez,* Steinbeck's and marine biologist Ed Ricketts' account of their expedition to the Gulf of California. According to Peter Shaw: "The book took each day's observations of sea life as an occasion for the drawing of biological parallels with human society. The most striking parallel for Steinbeck was the seeming existence of a group instinct in man similar to that found in schools of fish and colonies of marine fauna. Man, Steinbeck suggested, . . . could be regarded as a group phenomenon as well as an individual one. Accordingly, it might be possible to discover more about an individual by studying his behavior as it related to the group than by studying him in isolation." Steinbeck took this premise one step further by suggesting that man as an individual has no identity and that mankind as a whole is the only reality. This idea is expressed by Doc Burton in Steinbeck's novel about a fruit picker's strike, *In Dubious Battle:* "I want to watch these group men, for they seem to me to be a new individual, not at all like single men. A man in a group isn't himself at all; he's a cell in an organism that isn't like him any more than the cells in your body are like you." Kennedy found the concept of group-man to be "the central point in Steinbeck's concept of life." He added: "Permeating his works is this idea, which is the very heart of his philosophy of life: that the concrete person is in himself virtually nothing, whereas the abstraction 'humanity' is all."

Critics have suggested that Steinbeck's best novels are those set in his birthplace, northern California's Salinas Valley. "He was a Californian," Nancy L. McWilliams and Wilson C. McWilliams remarked, "and his writings never succeeded very well when he tried to walk alien soil." They defined his California as "a very special one, . . . sleepy California that time passed by." Bruce Cook noted that while Steinbeck was "a writer of international reputation, he was almost a regionalist in his close concentration on the 50 miles or so of California that surrounded his birthplace. The farming towns up and down the Salinas Valley," Cook continued, "and the commercial fishing port of Monterey just a few miles across the mountains provided the settings for most of his best books."

Steinbeck often used this setting to stress his theme of the importance of the "relationship between man and his environment," Shaw claimed. "The features of the valley at once determined the physical fate of his characters and made symbolic comment on them." Moreover, while Steinbeck dwelled on the beauty and "fruitfulness" of the valley, he "did not make it a fanciful Eden," Shaw commented. "The river brought destructive floods as well as fertility, and the summer wind could blow hot for months without let-up." Thus, "Man struggled within a closed system that both formed and limited him; there he was responsible for his acts and yet unable to control the larger forces."

After *The Grapes of Wrath,* Steinbeck's reputation as a novelist began to decline. Although his later works, such as *The Moon Is Down, East of Eden,* and *The Winter of Our Discontent,* have been public favorites and best sellers, they have also been considered

critical disappointments. Too often, the reviewers contended, Steinbeck's later work is flawed by sentimentality, obvious symbolism, and the inability to achieve the power and statement of *The Grapes of Wrath.*

The first such novel to have provoked critical attack is *The Moon Is Down.* Published in 1942, it deals with a mythical European town and its invasion by what Watt described as a "totalitarian and inhumane power which arouses, instead of crushing, the desire of the conquered for freedom." The novel, most critics have agreed, is a thinly disguised account of Germany's occupation of Norway. It was written, according to Watt, "in the interest of the Office of Strategic Services in helping resistance movements in Occupied Europe. Steinbeck wrote the novel with the same sense of objectivity that had characterized his earlier work. He tried to present the Nazi-like characters as fully as possible; they are good as well as evil, strong as well as weak. In this instance, however, Steinbeck's objectivity worked against him. Kennedy explained: "His Nazi characters emerged as something like human beings, by no means admirable, but by no means demoniac either. For not making them intrinsically and uniformly monstrous, at a time when some of our most celebrated writers were trying to whip Americans up to a frenzy of indiscriminate hatred, Steinbeck was pilloried." Although at the novel's end the Europeans triumph over their enemy, Steinbeck was nevertheless accused, as French recalled, of being "soft toward the Nazis." Later critics, however, detached from the immediate tensions aroused by the war, found more serious fault with what French regarded as the novel's "artificiality."

East of Eden and *The Winter of Our Discontent* similarly fell short of critical expectations. The former, a biblical allegory of the Cain and Abel story, is considered Steinbeck's most ambitious novel. Yet the *Time* critic claimed that "the Biblical parallels of Cain and Abel are so relentlessly stenciled upon the plot that symbolized meaning threatens to overwhelm the narrative surface." *The Winter of Our Discontent,* Steinbeck's last novel, "is spoilt by sentimentality and the consequent evasion of the moral issues raised," the reviewer for the London *Times* remarked. "Steinbeck was unable in any of his later work to master the problems he seems to have set himself, and though several of his books were widely popular, they appeared too small an achievement to be worthy of the author of *The Grapes of Wrath.*" Max Westbrook echoed this claim when he wrote: "The general feeling is that novels like *East of Eden* . . . and *The Winter of Our Discontent* . . . ought to be like *The Grapes of Wrath* but are not. . . . Neither novel comes to grips with the problems handled so courageously in *The Grapes of Wrath.*"

French blamed these later failures on the popular and critical reaction to *Cannery Row.* Written after the war, the novel is a satire "on contemporary American life with its commercialised values, its ruthless creed of property and status, and its relentlessly accelerating pace," according to Watt. For the most part, however, the novel has been misread as lighthearted, escapist fare. French commented: "Another letter of advice to an erring world; but, as had happened before, the advice went not only unheeded but unperceived. After this, Steinbeck was to strain to make his points clear to the reader; and as he belabored his points, the quality of his fiction suffered."

In 1962, Steinbeck was awarded the Nobel Prize, an honor that many believed "had been earned by his early work," noted the London *Times* critic, rather than for his later efforts. Several reviewers, however, thought this attitude was unjust. Watt, for example, offered this assessment: "Like America itself, his work is a vast, fascinating, paradoxical universe: a brash experiment in democracy; a naive quest for understanding at the level of the common man; a celebration of goodness and innocence; a display of chaos, violence, corruption and decadence. It is no neatly-shaped and carefully-cultivated garden of artistic perfections, but a sprawling continent of discordant extremes." Shaw was seemingly in agreement when he wrote: "When one begins to talk about the shape of a career rather than about single books, one is talking about a major writer. Steinbeck used to complain that reviewers said each new book of his showed a falling-off from his previous one, yet they never specified the height from which his apparently steady decline had begun. What he was noticing was the special kind of concern for a grand design that readers feel when they pick up the book of a writer whose career seems in itself to be a comment on the times."

BIOGRAPHICAL/CRITICAL SOURCES:

BOOKS

Beegel, Susan F., et al, editors, *Steinbeck and the Environment,* University of Alabama Press, 1997.

Bloom, Harold, editor, *John Steinbeck's "Of Mice and Men,"* Chelsea House (New York), 1996.

Bloom, Harold, editor, *John Steinbeck's "The Grapes of Wrath,"* Chelsea House (New York), 1996.

Bryer, Jackson R., editor, *Sixteen Modern American Authors, Volume 2: A Survey of Research and Criticism since 1972,* Duke University Press, 1990, pp. 582-622.

Coers, Donald V., editor, *After the Grapes of Wrath: Essays on John Steinbeck in Honor of Tetsumaro Hayashi,* Ohio University Press (Athens), 1995.

Concise Dictionary of American Literary Biography: The Age of Maturity, 1929-1941, Gale (Detroit), 1989.

Contemporary Literary Criticism, Gale, Volume 1, 1973; Volume 5, 1976; Volume 9, 1978; Volume 13, 1980; Volume 21, 1982; Volume 34, *Yearbook, 1984,* 1985; Volume 45, 1987; Volume 59, 1990; Volume 75, 1993.

Cusick, Lee, *John Steinbeck's "The Grapes of Wrath,"* Research & Education Association (Piscataway, NJ), 1994.

Dictionary of Literary Biography, Gale, Volume 7: *Twentieth-Century American Dramatists,* 1981; Volume 9: *American Novelists, 1910-1945,* 1981.

Dictionary of Literary Biography Documentary Series, Volume 2, Gale, 1982.

Ditsky, John, editor, *Critical Essays on The Grapes of Wrath,* G. K. Hall, 1988.

Ferrell, Keith, *John Steinbeck: The Voice of the Land,* Evans, 1986.

French, Warren, *John Steinbeck's Fiction Revisited,* Twayne (New York), 1994.

French, Warren, *John Steinbeck's Nonfiction Revisited,* Twayne (New York), 1996.

Hadella, Charlotte, *Of Mice and Men: A Kinship of Power lessness,* Twayne (New York), 1995.

Harmon, Robert B., *Steinbeck Bibliographies: An Annotated Guide,* Scarecrow, 1987.

Harmon, Robert B., *John Steinbeck: An Annotated Guide to Biographical Sources,* Scarecrow, 1996.

Hayashi, Tetsumaro (with Beverly K. Simpson), *John Steinbeck: Dissertation Abstracts and Research Opportunities,* Scarecrow (Metuchen, NJ), 1994.

Hughes, R. S., *John Steinbeck: A Study of the Short Fiction,* Twayne, 1989.

Ito, Tom, *John Steinbeck,* Lucent Books (San Diego, CA), 1994.

Johnson, Claudia Durst, *Understanding Of Mice and Men, The Red Pony, and The Pearl: A Student Casebook to Issues, Sources, and Historical Documents,* Greenwood Press, 1997.

Karson, Jill, *Reading on Of Mice and Men,* Greenhaven Press, 1997.

Lisca, Peter, *The Grapes of Wrath: Text and Criticism,* 2nd edition, Penguin, 1996.

Loewen, Nancy, *John Steinbeck,* Creative Education (Mankato, MN), 1997.

McElrath, Joseph R., et al, editors, *John Steinbeck: The Contemporary Reviews,* Cambridge University Press (New York), 1996.

Owens, Louis, *John Steinbeck's Re-Vision of America,* University of Georgia Press, 1985.

Owens, Louis, *The Grapes of Wrath: Trouble in the Promised Land,* Twayne, 1989.

Parini, Jay, *John Steinbeck: A Biography,* Holt (New York), 1995.

Railsback, Brian E., *Parallel Expeditions: Charles Darwin and the Art of John Steinbeck,* University of Idaho Press (Moscow, ID), 1995.

Reef, Catherine, *John Steinbeck,* Clarion Books (New York), 1996.

Short Story Criticism, Gale, Volume 11, 1992.

Simmonds, Roy S., *John Steinbeck: The War Years, 1939-1945,* Bucknell University Press (Lewisburg, PA), 1996.

Swisher, Clarice, editor, *Readings on John Steinbeck,* Greenhaven Press (San Diego), 1996.

Timmerman, John H., *John Steinbeck's Fiction: The Aesthetics of the Road Taken,* University of Oklahoma Press, 1986.

Wilson, Edmund, *The Boys in the Back Room,* Colt Press, 1941.

PERIODICALS

American Literature, May, 1980, pp. 194-223.

Antioch Review, spring, 1967.

Bloomsbury Review, July/August, 1989, p. 13.

Chicago Tribune, April 21, 1989.

Choice, March, 1989, p. 1163.

Christian Science Monitor, September 25, 1952.

Commonweal, May 9, 1969.

Detroit Free Press, January 9, 1967.

Esquire, November, 1969.

Globe and Mail (Toronto), December 20, 1986; April 22, 1989.

Life, November 2, 1962.

Los Angeles Times, December 6, 1987; May 1, 1989.

Los Angeles Times Book Review, April 9, 1989, p. 15.

Modern Fiction Studies, summer, 1974, pp. 169-79.

Nation, March 20, 1989, p. 388.

National Observer, December 23, 1968.

New York Times, June 2, 1969; August 11, 1989.

New York Times Book Review, February 16, 1947; September 21, 1952; April 14, 1957; November 16, 1958; June 25, 1961; July 29, 1962; October 24, 1976; April 9, 1989, p. 1.

Publishers Weekly, October 14, 1988, p. 62.

Steinbeck Quarterly.

Studies in American Fiction, autumn, 1989, pp. 219-26.

Studies in Short Fiction, summer, 1971, winter, 1977.

Time, December 27, 1968; April 24, 1989, p. 87.

Times Literary Supplement, July 7, 1961.

Washington Post, December 21, 1968; December 23, 1969.

Washington Post Book World, April 16, 1989.

World Literature Today, winter, 1990, p. 120.

STEINEM, Gloria 1934-

PERSONAL: Born March 25, 1934, in Toledo, OH; daughter of Leo and Ruth (Nuneviller) Steinem. *Education:* Smith College, B.A. (magna cum laude), 1956; University of Delhi and University of Calcutta, India, graduate study, 1957-58.

ADDRESSES: Office—*Ms.* Magazine, 230 Park Ave. Fl. 7, New York, NY 10169-0799.

CAREER: Editor, writer, lecturer, activist. Independent Research Service, Cambridge, MA, and New York City, director, 1959-60; *Glamour* magazine, New York City, contributing editor, 1962-69; *New York* magazine, New York City, cofounder and contributing editor, 1968-72; *Ms.* magazine, New York City, cofounder and editor, 1972-87, columnist, 1980-87, consulting editor, 1987–. Contributing correspondent to NBC's "Today" show. Active in civil rights, feminist, and peace campaigns, including those of United Farm Workers, Vietnam War Tax Protest, and Committee for the Legal Defense of Angela Davis; active in political campaigns of Adlai Stevenson, Robert Kennedy, Eugene McCarthy, Shirley Chisholm, and George McGovern. Editorial consultant to Conde Nast Publications, 1962-69, Curtis Publishing, 1964-65, Random House Publishing, 1988–, and McCall Publishing.

MEMBER: PEN, National Press Club, Society of Magazine Writers, Authors Guild, Authors League of America, American Federation of Television and Radio Artists, National Organization for Women, Women's Action Alliance (cofounder; chairperson, 1970-), National Women's Political Caucus (founding member; member of national advisory committee, 1971-), Ms. Foundation for Women (cofounder; member of board, 1972-), Coalition of Labor Union Women (founding member, 1974), Voters for Choice (cofounder), Phi Beta Kappa.

AWARDS, HONORS: Chester Bowles Asian fellow in India, 1957-58; Penney-Missouri journalism award, 1970, for *New York* article "After Black Power, Women's Liberation"; Ohio Governor's journalism award, 1972; named Woman of the Year, *McCall's* magazine, 1972; Doctorate of Human Justice from Simmons College, 1973; Bill of Rights award, American Civil Liberties Union of Southern California, 1975; Woodrow Wilson International Center for Scholars fellow, 1977; Ceres Medal from United Nations; Front Page Award; Clarion Award; nine citations from *World Almanac* as one of the twenty-five most influential women in America; inducted into National Women's Hall of Fame, 1993.

WRITINGS:

The Thousand Indias, Government of India, 1957.
The Beach Book, Viking, 1963.
(Contributor) Peter Manso, editor, *Running against the Machine,* Doubleday, 1969.
(With G. Chester) *Wonder Woman,* Holt (New York), 1972.
(Author of introductory note) Marlo Thomas and others, *Free to Be . . . You and Me,* McGraw, 1974.
Outrageous Acts and Everyday Rebellions, Holt, 1983, 2nd edition with a new preface and notes by the author, Holt, 1995.
Marilyn: Norma Jeane, Holt, 1986.
Bedside Book of Self-Esteem, Little, Brown (Boston), 1989.
Revolution from Within: A Book of Self-Esteem, Little, Brown and Co., 1992.
Moving Beyond Words, Simon & Schuster (New York), 1994.

(Author of introduction) Andrea Johnston, *Girls Speak Out: Finding Your True Self,* Scholastic, 1997.

Writer for television, including series *That Was the Week that Was,* NBC, 1964-65. Author of films and political campaign material. Former author of column, "The City Politic," in *New York.* Contributor to periodicals, including *Esquire, Ms., Show, Vogue, Life,* and *Cosmopolitan.* Editorial consultant, *Seventeen,* 1969-70, and *Show.*

MEDIA ADAPTATIONS: "I Was a Playboy Bunny" was produced by Joan Marks as an ABC television movie, "A Bunny's Tale," starring Kirstie Alley, first broadcast February 25, 1985.

SIDELIGHTS: Gloria Steinem is recognized as one of the foremost organizers of the modern women's movement. Her grandmother, Pauline Steinem, was the president of a turn-of-the-century women's suffrage group and was a representative to the 1908 International Council of Women, but Gloria was not substantially influenced by her while growing up in Toledo, Ohio. Her parents divorced when she was young, and at the age of ten Gloria was left alone to care for herself and her mentally ill mother. She left home when she was seventeen to attend Smith College on a scholarship. Like most women in that era, she was engaged by her senior year; however, Steinem broke her engagement to continue her political science studies in India. She adjusted quickly to life there, adopting native dress and ways. Because English served as the common language, she was "able to really talk, and tell jokes, and understand political arguments," she told Miriam Berkley in *Publishers Weekly.* Steinem was also able to freelance for Indian newspapers. She supplemented her university studies by seeking out the company of the activists who were then working for an independent India. As a member of a group called the Radical Humanists, she traveled to southern India at the time of the terrible caste riots there, working as a member of a peacemaking team. Her experiences in India gave her a deep sympathy for the underclasses, as well as an enduring love of that country.

When the time came for her to return to the United States, Steinem did so filled with an "enormous sense of urgency about the contrast between wealth and poverty," she stated in her interview with Berkley. But because she "rarely met people who had shared this experience," it became "like a dream. It had no relation to my real, everyday life. . . . I couldn't write about it." Instead, she established a successful freelance career writing articles about celebrities, fashions, and tropical vacations, while devoting her spare time to work for the civil rights movement. Berkley describes Steinem's life in the early 1960s as "schizophrenically split between career and conscience." "I was . . . divided up into pieces as a person," the author told Elisabeth Bumiller in the *Washington Post.* "I was working on one thing, and caring about another, which I think is the way a lot of us have to live our lives. I'm lucky it came together."

Steinem's best-known article from her early career is "I Was a Playboy Bunny." Assigned to cover the 1963 opening of the New York City Playboy Club for *Show* magazine, she went undercover to work as a "Bunny," or waitress, for two weeks. The resulting article is an "excellent, ironic, illuminating bit of reporting," says Angela Carter in the *Washington Post Book World.* Steinem was instructed by the "Bunny Mother" in techniques for stuffing her bodice and bending over to serve drinks; she was cautioned against sneezing, which would split the seams of a Bunny costume; she was presented with a copy of the "Bunny Bible," the lengthy code of conduct for Playboy waitresses; and she was informed that all new Bunnies were required to have a pelvic examination performed by the club's specially appointed doctor. "I Was a Playboy Bunny" is "hysterically funny," according to Ann Marie Lapinski in the *Chicago Tribune,* but it is also "full of feminist consciousness as some of [Steinem's] later reportage," believes Carter, who comments, "If it is implicit rather than explicit, it is no less powerful for that." Of her experiences in the club, Steinem remarked to *Los Angeles Times* interviewer Elenita Ravicz, "Being a Bunny was more humiliating than I thought it would be. True, it was never the kind of job I would have considered under ordinary circumstances, but I expected it to be more glamorous and better paid than it was. . . . Customers there seemed to be there because they could be treated as superiors. . . . There is a real power difference when one group is semi-nude and the other is fully-clothed."

Her colleagues' reactions to a 1969 article she wrote about a New York abortion hearing shocked Steinem. She told Ravicz, "I went to that hearing and listened to women stand up and talk about how dangerous and difficult it was for them to get an illegal abortion. . . . They had tears running down their faces as they talked, many of them for the first time, about how they'd had to risk permanent injury and even give sexual favors to their abortionists. I wrote an article about the hearing and my male colleagues, really nice men I got along well with, took me aside one by one and said, 'don't get involved with these crazy women. You've taken so much trouble to establish your reputation as a serious journalist, don't throw it all away.' That was when I realized men valued me only to the extent I imitated them."

Instead of abandoning the subject, Steinem followed up her coverage of the abortion hearing with an extensively researched article on reproductive and other feminist issues. Her article "After Black Power, Women's Liberation" won her the Penney-Missouri journalism award, but it also "unleashed a storm of negative reactions . . . from male colleagues. The response from the publishing establishment, and its reluctance to publish other work on the subject, opened her eyes. She began to pursue not only writing but also speaking engagements and became an active part of the women's movement she had once only observed," relates Berkley. Steinem came to believe that a magazine controlled by women was necessary if a truly open forum on women's issues was to exist. Accordingly, she and others began working toward that goal. Clay Felker offered to subsidize a sample issue and to include a thirty-page excerpt of the new publication in *New York* magazine; Steinem and the rest of the staff worked without pay, and produced the first issue of *Ms.* in January of 1972. "We called it the spring issue," Steinem recalled to Berkley. "We were really afraid that if it didn't sell it would embarrass the women's movement. So we called it Spring so that it could lie there on the newsstands for a long time." Such worries were unfounded, for the entire 300,000-copy run of *Ms.* sold out in eight days.

As a spokesperson for the women's movement, Steinem has been criticized as subversive and strident by some and as overly tolerant and conservative by others. An overview of her opinions and her development as a feminist is provided by her 1983 publication *Outrageous Acts and Everyday Rebellions.* It is a collection representing twenty years of her writing on a variety of subjects, including politics, pornography, her mother, and Marilyn Monroe. Carter criticizes the book, complaining that Steinem presents only "the acceptable face of feminism" and that she is "straightjacketed by her own ideology." But Diane Johnson offers a more favorable appraisal in the *New York Times Book Review:*

"Reading Miss Steinem's essays . . . one is struck by their intelligence, restraint and common sense, as well as by the energetic and involved life they reflect. . . . This is a consciousness-raising book. . . . Her views, like her writing itself, are characterized by engaging qualities of unpretensious clarity and forceful expression." Douglas Hill concurs in the Toronto *Globe and Mail:* "Honesty, fairness and consistency gleam in these pages. And Steinem writes superbly. . . . It's her special strength to write as cleanly and affectingly about her mother's mental illness as about the practice of genital mutilation endured by 75 million women worldwide or the inadequacies of William Styron's fiction." *Detroit News* reviewer Fiona Lowther concludes, "Make no mistake: Whether you disagree with or espouse wholly or in part what Steinem stands for—or what you think she stands for—she is a worthy observer and reporter of the contemporary scene."

Steinem's next book grew from the essay in *Outrageous Acts* concerning Marilyn Monroe, the actress who became internationally famous for her "sex goddess" image in the 1950s and died by her own hand in 1962. When photojournalist George Barris decided to publish a series of photographs taken of Monroe shortly before her death, Steinem was asked to contribute the text. While researching *Marilyn: Norma Jeane,* she became aware that although over forty books had already been published about the late film star, only a few were written by women. Most of the biographies focused on the scandalous aspects of Monroe's death and personal relationships, or reinforced her image as the ultimate pin-up. Steinem explained to *Washington Post* interviewer Chip Brown, "I tried to take away the fantasy of Marilyn and replace it with reality. . . . The book doesn't have a thesis so much as an emphasis—an emphasis on Norma Jeane, on the private, real, internal person. I hadn't read a book about Marilyn that made me feel I knew her. My purpose was to try to get to know or to portray the real person inside the public image." Commenting on the ironic fact that Monroe derived little pleasure from her physical relationships, Steinem suggested to Brown, "It's hard for men to admit that a sex goddess didn't enjoy sex. . . . It's part of the desire to believe she was murdered—the same cultural impulse that says if she's a sex goddess she had to have enjoyed sex doesn't want to believe she killed herself, doesn't want to accept her unhappiness. . . . This country is media-sick. People who are seen in the media are considered to be more real, or different, or special or magic. . . . I tried to make Marilyn real."

"One aspect of writing about a woman like Marilyn is that you feel you're exploiting her all over again," Steinem disclosed to George James in the *New York Times Book Review.* That feeling led her to donate all her earnings from *Marilyn: Norma Jeane* to the establishment of the Marilyn Monroe Children's Fund. Under the auspices of Ms. Foundation for Women, which sponsors feminist causes, the Marilyn Monroe Children's Fund finances a variety of children's welfare projects. Steinem continues to work energetically for social change through her writing, fund-raising and speaking engagements. Bumiller asked the feminist leader about the state of the women's movement today: "She says it's not dead or even sick, but has instead spread out from the middle class to be integrated into issues like unemployment and the gender gap. Feminism, she says, has brought America closer to the democracy it ought to be, and has found words like sexual harrassment for events that '10 years ago were called life.' She sees four enormous goals ahead: 'reproductive freedom, democratic families, a depoliticized culture and work redefined. . . . Remember. We are talking about overthrowing, or humanizing—

pick your verb, depending on how patient you feel—the sex and race caste systems. Now that is a big job."

BIOGRAPHICAL/CRITICAL SOURCES:

BOOKS

Heilbrun, Carolyn G., *The Education of a Woman: The Life of Gloria Steinem,* Dial Press (New York), 1995.
Lazo, Caroline Evenson, *Gloria Steinem,* Lerner (Minneapolis), 1998.
Stern, Sidney Ladensohn, *Gloria Steinem: Her Passions, Politics, and Mystique,* Brich Lane/Carol Publishing, 1997.

PERIODICALS

Chicago Tribune, October 2, 1983; January 11, 1987.
Commentary, May, 1992, p. 54.
Cosmopolitan, July, 1990, p. 182.
Detroit News, August 28, 1983.
Esquire, June, 1984.
Globe and Mail (Toronto), February 8, 1986.
Interview, June, 1995, p. 98.
Los Angeles Times, December 11, 1984; December 10, 1986; May 6, 1987.
Mademoiselle, April, 1992, p. 68.
Mother Jones, November-December, 1995, p. 22.
National Review, March 2, 1992, p. 47.
New Republic, March 16, 1992, p. 30; August 10, 1992, p. 29; July 11, 1994, p. 32.
Newsweek, January 13, 1992, p. 64; June 20, 1994, p. 70.
New York Times, April 4, 1987; May 10, 1988.
New York Times Book Review, September 4, 1983; December 21, 1986; February 2, 1992, p. 13; May 22, 1994, p. 37.
People Weekly, June 11, 1984; February 25, 1985; February 10, 1992, p. 23.
Progressive, June, 1995, p. 34.
Publishers Weekly, August 12, 1983; November 23, 1990, p. 50.
Time, March 9, 1992, p. 55.
Times (London), February 19, 1987.
Washington Post, October 12, 1983; December 7, 1986.
Washington Post Book World, October 9, 1983.
Working Woman, January 1992, p. 66.

*   *   *

STEINER, George 1929-

PERSONAL: Born April 23, 1929, in Paris, France; came to the United States in 1940, naturalized citizen, 1944; son of Frederick George (a banker) and Elsie (Franzos) Steiner; married Zara Alice Shakow (a university professor), July 7, 1955; children: David Milton, Deborah Tarn. *Education:* University of Chicago, B.A., 1948; Harvard University, M.A., 1950; Oxford University, Ph.D., 1955. *Avocational interests:* Mountain walking, music, chess.

ADDRESSES: Home—32 Barrow Rd., Cambridge, CB2 2AS England. *Office*—Churchill College, Cambridge, England.

CAREER: Economist, London, England, member of editorial staff, 1952-56; Princeton University, Princeton, NJ, fellow of Institute for Advanced Study, 1956-58, Gauss Lecturer, 1959-60; Cambridge University, Cambridge, England, fellow of Churchill College, 1961-69, Extraordinary Fellow, 1969–; University of Geneva, Geneva, Switzerland, professor of English and comparative literature, 1974–. Visiting professor at New York University, 1966-67, University of California, 1973-74, and at Harvard University, Yale University, Princeton University, College of France, and Stanford University; University of London, Maurice lecturer, 1984; Cambridge University, Leslie Stephen lecturer, 1985; University of Glasgow, W. P. Ker lecturer, 1986; visiting professor College of France, 1992; Oxford University, First Lord Weidenfeld professor of comparative literature, 1994–.

MEMBER: English Association (president, 1975), Royal Society of Literature (fellow), German Academy of Literature (corresponding member), Athenaeum Club (London), Savile Club (London), Harvard Club (New York City), American Academy of Arts and Sciences (honorary member).

AWARDS, HONORS: Bell Prize, 1950; Rhodes scholar, 1955; Fulbright professorship, 1958-59; O. Henry Short Story Prize, 1959; Morton Dauwen Zabel Award from National Institute of Arts and Letters (United States), 1970; Guggenheim fellowship, 1971-72; Cortina Ulisse Prize, 1972; Remembrance Award, 1974, for *The Language of Silence;* PEN-Faulkner Award nomination, 1983, for *The Portage to San Cristobal of A. H.;* named Chevalier de la Legion d'Honneur, 1984; PEN Macmillan Fiction Prize, 1993. Macmillan Silver Pen Award for *Proofs and Three Parables,* 1992. Numerous honorary degrees from college and universities, including East Anglia, 1976, Lovain, 1980, Mount Holyoke, 1983, Bristol, 1989, Glasgow, 1990, Liege, 1990, Ulster, 1993, and Durham, 1995. Honorary Fellow, Baillol College, Oxford, 1995.

WRITINGS:

Tolstoy or Dostoevsky: An Essay in the Old Criticism, Penguin, 1958, Dutton, 1971.
The Death of Tragedy, Hill and Wang, 1960, Knopf, 1961.
(Editor with Robert Fagles) *Homer: A Collection of Critical Essays,* Prentice-Hall, 1962.
Anno Domini: Three Stories, Atheneum, 1964.
(Editor and author of introduction) *The Penguin Book of Modern Verse Translation,* Penguin, 1966, reprinted as *Poem into Poem: World Poetry in Modern Verse Translation,* 1970.
Language and Silence: Essays on Language, Literature, and the Inhuman, Atheneum, 1967.
Extraterritorial: Papers on Literature and the Language Revolution, Atheneum, 1971.
In Bluebeard's Castle: Some Notes toward the Redefinition of Culture, Yale University Press, 1971.
Fields of Force: Fischer and Spassky in Reykjavik, Viking, 1973 (published in England as *The Sporting Scene: White Knights in Reykjavik,* Faber, 1973).
Nostalgia for the Absolute, CBC Enterprises, 1974.
After Babel: Aspects of Language and Translation, Oxford University Press (New York City), 1975.
The Uncommon Reader, Bennington College Press, 1978.
On Difficulty and Other Essays, Oxford University Press, 1978.
Martin Heidegger, Viking, 1978 (published in England as *Heidegger,* Fontana, 1978).
The Portage to San Cristobal of A. H. (novel; also see below), Simon and Schuster, 1981.
George Steiner: A Reader, Oxford University Press, 1984.
Antigones: How the Antigone Legend Has Endured in Western Literature, Art, and Thought, Oxford University Press, 1984.
Real Presences: Is There Anything in What We Say? University of Chicago Press, 1989.
Proofs and Three Parables (fiction), Viking, 1992.
What Is Comparative Literature?: An Inaugural Lecture Delivered before the University of Oxford on 11 October, 1994, Oxford University Press, 1995.

No Passion Spent, Yale University Press, 1996.

The Deeps of the Sea (fiction; contains *The Portage to San Cristobal of A. H.*), Faber, 1996.

Errata: An Examined Life, Yale University Press, 1998.

Columnist and book reviewer for the *New Yorker;* contributor of essays, reviews, and articles to numerous periodicals, including *Commentary, Harper's,* and *Nation.*

RECORDINGS

A Necessary Treason: The Poet and the Translator (cassette), J. Norton, 1970.

The Poet as Translator: To Traduce or Transfigure, J. Norton, 1970.

MEDIA ADAPTATIONS: After Babel was adapted for television as *The Tongues of Men,* 1977. *The Portage to San Cristobal of A. H.* was adapted for the stage under the same title by Christopher Hampton, first produced in America at Hartford Stage, Hartford, Connecticut, January 7, 1983.

SIDELIGHTS: "George Steiner is the most brilliant cultural journalist at present writing in English, or perhaps in any language," a *Times Literary Supplement* reviewer writes. Steiner, who teaches at Cambridge University and the University of Geneva, is known on two continents for his literary criticism and far-ranging essays on linguistics, ethics, translation, the fine arts, and science. According to Pearl K. Bell in the *New Leader,* few present-day literary critics "can match George Steiner in erudition and sweep. Actually, he resists confinement within the fields of literature, preferring more venturesome forays into the history of ideas. . . . Steiner has proceeded on the confident assumption that no activity of the human mind is in any way alien or inaccessible to his own." Steiner writes for the educated general reader rather than for the academic specialist; London *Times* contributor Philip Howard calls the author "an intellectual who bestrides the boundaries of cultures and disciplines." In addition to his numerous books, including *Language and Silence: Essays on Language, Literature, and the Inhuman* and *After Babel: Aspects of Language and Translation,* Steiner produces regular columns for the *New Yorker* magazine, for which he serves primarily as a book reviewer. Almost always controversial for his bold assertions and assessments of highly specialized theories, Steiner "has been called both a mellifluous genius and an oversimplifying intellectual exhibitionist," to quote Curt Suplee in the *Washington Post. National Review* correspondent Scott Lahti claims, however, that most readers find Steiner's "provocative manner of expression . . . by turns richly allusive, metaphoric, intensely concerned, prophetic, apocalyptic—and almost always captivating."

Steiner was educated on two continents, having studied at the University of Chicago, Harvard, and Oxford University on a Rhodes scholarship. His first book, published the year he turned thirty, concerns not English literature but the works of two great Russian writers, Tolstoy and Dostoevsky. Entitled *Tolstoy or Dostoevsky: An Essay in the Old Criticism,* the book "announces the particular place Steiner has assigned himself," writes Bruce Robbins in the *Dictionary of Literary Biography.* "Neither Europe nor America, his Russia is a no-man's-land that permits him to remain, to use his term, unhoused." In addition to offering an analysis of the two writers' lives, thoughts, and historical milieux, the work challenges the *au courant* "New Criticism" by assigning moral, philosophical, and historical worth to the texts. A *Times Literary Supplement* correspondent observes that Steiner "is concerned not with a catalogue of casual, incidental parallels between life and fiction but with the overmastering ideas which so preoccupied the two men that they could not help finding parallel expression in their lives and their works." Another *Times Literary Supplement* reviewer likewise declares that Steiner "feels he is addressing not professional scholars merely, safely shut in the confines of one particular discipline, but all thinking men who are aware of the larger world of social and political realities about them. Dr. Steiner's style derives part of its force from his seeing intellectual questions against the background of historical crises and catastrophes."

In 1967 Steiner published *Language and Silence,* a collection of essays that establish the author's "philosophy of language." The book explores in depth the vision of the humanely educated Nazi and the diminution of the word's vitality in an audio-visual era. In the *New Republic,* Theodore Solotaroff maintains that *Language and Silence* "casts a bright and searching light into the murky disarray of current letters and literacy: it looks back to a darkness and disruption of Western culture that continues to plague and challenge the moral purpose of literature, among other fields, and it looks forward to possibilities of art and thought that may carry us beyond our broken heritage. It provides an articulate and comprehensive discussion of the impact of science and mass communications on the ability of language to describe the realities of the earth and the world." Steiner's conclusion—that silence and the refusal to write is the last-resort moral act in the face of bestiality—has aroused conflicting opinions among his reviewers. In the *New York Times Book Review,* Robert Gorham Davis suggests that the author "displaces onto language many of his feelings about history and religion. He makes it an independent living organism which can be poisoned or killed." The critic adds, however, that throughout the volume, "thoughts are expressed with such a fine and knowledgeable specificity that when we are forced to disagree with Steiner, we always know exactly upon what grounds. He teaches and enlightens even where he does not convince." *New York Times* contributor Eliot Fremont-Smith concludes that *Language and Silence* "will confirm, if confirmation is necessary, [Steiner's] reputation as one of the most erudite, resourceful and unrelentingly serious critics working today."

Most observers agree that *After Babel* is Steiner's monumental work, a "deeply ambivalent hymn to language," as Geoffrey H. Hartman puts it in the *New York Times Book Review.* The book offers a wide-ranging inquiry into the fields of linguistics and translation, with commentary on the vagaries of communication both inside and between languages. *Washington Post Book World* reviewer Peter Brunette explains that in *After Babel* Steiner proposes "the radical notion that the world's many diverse languages (4000 plus, at last count) were created to disguise and hide things from outsiders, rather than to assist communication, as we often assume. A corollary is that the vast majority of our day-to-day language production is internal, and is not meant to communicate at all." In *Listener,* Hyam Maccoby contends that Steiner's predilection is for a view "that a language is the soul of a particular culture, and affects by its very syntax what can be said or thought in that culture; and that the differences between languages are more important than their similarities (which he calls 'deep but trivial')." The book has brought Steiner into a debate with linguists such as Noam Chomsky who are searching for the key to a "universal grammar" that all human beings share. Many critics feel that in *After Babel* Steiner presents a forceful challenge to the notion of innate, universal grammar. According to Raymond Oliver in the *Southern Review,* the book "is dense but lucid and often graceful; its erudition is balanced by sharpness of insights, its theoretical intelligence by critical finesse; and it pleads the cause of poetry, language, and translation with impassioned eloquence. . . . We are ready to be sustained and delighted by the sumptuous literary feast [Steiner] has prepared us." *New Yorker* columnist Naomi Bliven likewise points out that Steiner's subject "is extravagantly rich, and he ponders it on the most generous scale, discussing how we use and misuse, understand and misunderstand words, and so, without always being aware of what we are doing, create art, history, nationality, and our sense of belonging to a civilization. . . . He is frequently ironic and witty, but for the most part his language and his ideas display even-handedness, seriousness without heaviness, learning without pedantry, and sober charm."

"Steiner's performance is mindful of a larger public," writes Robbins. Not surprisingly, therefore, the author does not shy from forceful communication or controversial conclusions. For instance, in his novel *The Portage to San Cristobal of A. H.,* Steiner gives readers an opportunity to ponder world history from Adolf Hitler's eloquent point of view. Some critics have found the novel morally outrageous, while others cite it for its stimulating—if not necessarily laudable—ideas. Steiner's essays also have their detractors. Writing in the London *Times,* Malcolm Bradbury suggests that his nonfiction has "a quality of onward-driving personal history, and it is not surprising that they have left many arguments in their wake." Bradbury adds that Steiner's impact "in provoking British scholars to a much more internationalist and comparative viewpoint has been great, but not always gratefully received." Lahti, for one, finds Steiner's conclusions "often fragmentary, and his frequent resort to extravagant assertions and perverse generalizations lessens the force of his arguments." Similarly, *New York Review of Books* essayist D. J. Enright faults Steiner for "a histrionic habit, an overheated tone, a melodramatization of what (God knows) is often dramatic enough, a proclivity to fly to extreme positions. The effect is to antagonize the reader on the brink of assent."

Steiner's *Proofs and Three Parables,* a slim collection of short fiction, received Britain's MacMillan Silver Pen Award. Reviewers praise the book, noting its function as an engagingly readable introduction to some of Steiner's philosophical ideas. The short story "Proofs," for example, features "a sustained and often hilarious debate between [a proofreader who is a former member of the Italian Communist party] and his old friend, Father Carlo Tessone, on the meaning of life in a post-communist world," summarizes David Lohrey in *Los Angeles Times Book Review.* Lohrey concludes that Steiner articulates "the superfluousness of the individual in our time and one's increasing belief that this world no longer cares for the distinction between things done well and those merely completed." The volume also contains three parables, "Desert Island Disks," "Noel, Noel," and "Conversation Piece," all of which use unusual symbolism and playful dialogue to articulate Steiner's philosophical ruminations concerning culture, history, and philosophy.

In *Real Presences,* Steiner "offers a dark picture of contemporary Western culture," according to Michael F. Suarez in *Review of English Studies.* Steiner argues in the volume for a return to the "transcendent" potential of art which, he believes, has been undermined by the post-modern concern with deconstruction of artistic "texts" and constant awareness of the "intertextuality" of all art forms. In other words, he deems the postmodern view of art as a series of "signs"—a destructive force that has contributed to the essential irrelevance of art in the modern world. "A [method of] criticism, then, that does not assume that it can transcend itself—let alone its object—is not real, and deconstruction is, *par*

excellence, such a criticism," comments Richard Cavell in *Canadian Literature.* "Only art, for Steiner, can answer to art."

With 1996's *No Passion Spent* Steiner presents a volume of essays on a variety of religious, philosophical, linguistic, and literary subjects. He explores the decline of literacy and serious reading in western civilization and searches for the source of philosophical divisions in human thought that contributed to destructive tendencies throughout history. Central to several of his essays is the history of Judaism and the adversarial relationship between Jewish faith and Christianity. "In *No Passion Spent,* Steiner faces his divine source and drinks from the Bible, Homer and Socrates, Jesus, Freud and Shakespeare, as well as Kafka, Kierkegaard, Husserl and Simone Weil," notes Guy Mannes-Abbott in *New Statesman & Society.* Commenting on Steiner's style and tone in *No Passion Spent* in the *Spectator,* Tony Connor finds Steiner's rhetoric "exhilarating," but complains that "too much of [Steiner's writing] is only interesting if one is interested in Steiner; too much of his commentary on writers serves only to direct the reader back to the authoritative and grandly dispensing figure of the critic."

Critics praise Steiner's collection of short fiction, *The Deeps of the Sea,* also published in 1996. The volume includes Steiner's acclaimed novel, *The Portage to San Cristobal of A. H.,* along with several shorter works. Connor finds Steiner's stories "better, on the whole, when they come closer to parables, and when they are interesting it is because of the ideas they contain."

Reviewers commonly suggest that Steiner intends to challenge his audience, deliberately provoking strong opinions. In the *New Republic,* Robert Boyers writes: "Readers will sense, on every page, an invitation to respond, to argue, to resist. But so nimble and alert to possibility is the critic's articulating voice that one will rather pay careful attention than resist. Ultimately, no doubt, 'collaborative disagreement' may seem possible, but few will feel dismissive or ungrateful. . . . No reader will fail to feel Steiner's encouragement as he moves out on his own." According to Edward W. Said in *Nation,* Steiner "is that rare thing, a critic propelled by diverse enthusiasms, a man able to understand the implications of trends in different fields, an autodidact for whom no subject is too arcane. Yet Steiner is to be read for his quirks, rather than in spite of them. He does not peddle a system nor a set of norms by which all things can be managed, every text decoded. He writes to be understood by nonspecialists, and his terms of reference come from his experience—which is trilingual, eccentric and highly urbane—not from something as stable as doctrine or authority."

BIOGRAPHICAL/CRITICAL SOURCES:

BOOKS

Contemporary Literary Criticism, Volume 24, Gale (Detroit), 1983.
Dictionary of Literary Biography, Volume 67: *American Critics since 1955,* Gale, 1988.
Scott, Nathan A., editor, *Reading George Steiner,* Johns Hopkins University (Baltimore), 1994.

PERIODICALS

Book World, January 2, 1972.
Canadian Literature, spring, 1995, p. 193.
Christian Science Monitor, May 25, 1975.
Commentary, October, 1968; November, 1975.
Commonweal, May 12, 1961; October 27, 1967.
Detroit News, April 25, 1982.

Listener, April 27, 1972; January 30, 1975; March 22, 1979; July 3, 1980.

London Magazine, December, 1967.

Los Angeles Times, October 23, 1980; June 6, 1993, p. 8.

Los Angeles Times Book Review, April 11, 1982; November 18, 1984.

Modern Language Review, January, 1987, p. 158.

Nation, March 2, 1985.

National Review, December 31, 1971; August 31, 1979; June 11, 1982; July 26, 1985.

New Leader, June 23, 1975.

New Republic, May 13, 1967; January 27, 1979; May 12, 1979; April 21, 1982; November 19, 1984.

New Statesman, November 17, 1961; October 20, 1967; October 22, 1971; January 31, 1975; December 1, 1978; June 27, 1980.

New Statesman & Society, January 5, 1996, p. 37; March 1, 1996, p. 36.

Newsweek, April 26, 1982; January 5, 1996, p. 37.

New Yorker, January 30, 1965; May 5, 1975.

New York Review of Books, October 12, 1967; November 18, 1971; October 30, 1975; April 19, 1979; August 12, 1982; December 6, 1984.

New York Times, March 20, 1967; June 22, 1971; July 1, 1974; May 7, 1975; April 16, 1982; January 7, 1983; April 1, 1993, p. C21; June 27, 1996, p. B5.

New York Times Book Review, May 28, 1967; August 1, 1971; October 13, 1974; June 8, 1975; January 21, 1979; May 2, 1982; December 16, 1984; June 30, 1996, p. 16.

Observer (London), December 17, 1978; March 28, 1993, p. 7; June 30, 1996, p. 16.

Southern Review, winter, 1978.

Spectator, April, 1960; December 2, 1978; July 19, 1980; January 13, 1996, p. 29.

Time, July 26, 1971; March 29, 1982.

Times (London), March 20, 1982; June 23, 1984; June 28, 1984.

Times Literary Supplement, March 11, 1960; September 28, 1967; December 17, 1971; May 19, 1972; May 18, 1973; January 31, 1975; November 17, 1978; June 12, 1981.

Theology Today, July, 1997.

Washington Post, May 13, 1982.

Washington Post Book World, January 14, 1979; May 2, 1982; December 30, 1984; January 19, 1986; June 23, 1996, p. 11.

World Literature Today, spring, 1997.

Yale Review, autumn, 1967.

*   *   *

STEINER, K. Leslie
See DELANY, Samuel R(ay Jr.)

*   *   *

STEPHEN, Virginia
See WOOLF, Virginia

*   *   *

STEPTOE, Lydia
See BARNES, Djuna

STERLING, Brett
See BRADBURY, Ray (Douglas)

*   *   *

STEVENS, Wallace 1879-1955
(Peter Parasol)

PERSONAL: Born October 2, 1879, in Reading, PA; died of cancer, August 2, 1955, in Hartford, CT; buried in Cedar Hills Cemetery, Hartford; son of Garrett Barcalow (a lawyer) and Margaretha Catharine (a schoolteacher; maiden name, Zeller) Stevens; married Elsie Viola Kachel, September 21, 1909; children: Holly Bright. *Education:* Attended Harvard University, 1897-1900; New York Law School, LL.B., 1903. *Avocational interests:* Collecting paintings, walking.

CAREER: Poet and insurance lawyer. *New York Tribune,* New York City, reporter, 1900-01; law clerk for W. G. Peckham in New York City, 1903-04; admitted to the Bar in New York State, 1904; law partner with Lyman Ward, c. 1904; worked in various law firms in New York City, 1904-08; American Bonding Co. (became Fidelity and Deposit Co.), New York City, lawyer, 1908-13; Equitable Surety Co. (became New England Equitable Insurance Co.), New York City, resident vice president, 1914-16; Hartford Accident and Indemnity Co., Hartford, CT, 1916-55, became vice president, 1934. Lecturer.

MEMBER: National Institute of Arts and Letters.

AWARDS, HONORS: Prize from Players Producing Co., c. 1916, for "Three Travelers Watch a Sunrise"; Levinson Prize from *Poetry,* 1920; poetry prize from *Nation,* 1936; Harriet Monroe Poetry Award, 1946; Bollingen Prize in Poetry, 1950; gold medal from Poetry Society of America, 1951; National Book Award for best poetry, 1951, for *The Auroras of Autumn;* National Book Award for best poetry and Pulitzer Prize for poetry, both 1955, both for *The Collected Poems of Wallace Stevens;* L.H.D., from Hartt College of Music, 1955; Litt.D., from Bard College, 1951, Harvard University, 1951, Mount Holyoke College, 1952, Columbia University, 1952, and Yale University, 1955.

WRITINGS:

Harmonium (poetry; includes "Le Monocle de Mon Oncle," "The Comedian as the Letter C," "The Emperor of Ice Cream," "Thirteen Ways of Looking at a Blackbird," "Peter Quince at the Clavier," "Sunday Morning," "Sea Surface Full of Clouds," and "In the Clear Season of Grapes"), Knopf, 1923, revised edition, 1931.

Ideas of Order (poetry; includes "Farewell to Florida," "The Idea of Order at Key West," "Academic Discourse at Havana," "Like Decorations in a Nigger Cemetery," and "A Postcard from the Volcano"), Alcestis Press, 1935, enlarged edition, Knopf, 1936.

Owl's Clover (poetry; also see below), Alcestis Press, 1936.

The Man with the Blue Guitar, and Other Poems (poetry; includes "The Man with the Blue Guitar," "A Thought Revolved," and "The Men That Are Falling"), Knopf, 1937.

Parts of a World (poetry; includes "The Poems of Our Climate," "The Well Dressed Man with a Beard," and "Examination of the Hero in a Time of War"), Knopf, 1942.

Notes Toward a Supreme Fiction (poetry; also see below), Cummington Press, 1942.

Esthetique du Mal (poetry; also see below), Cummington Press, 1945.

Transport to Summer (poetry; includes "The Pure Good of Theory," "A Word With Jose Rodriguez-Feo," "Description without Place," "The House Was Quiet and the World Was Calm," *Notes Toward a Supreme Fiction,* and *Esthetique du Mal*), Knopf, 1947.

Three Academic Pieces: The Realm of Resemblance, Someone Puts a Pineapple Together, Of Ideal Time and Choice (essays; also see below), Cummington Press, 1947.

A Primitive Like an Orb (poetry; also see below), Gotham Book Mart, 1948.

The Auroras of Autumn (poetry; includes "The Auroras of Autumn," "Large Red Man Reading," "In a Bad Time," "The Ultimate Poem Is Abstract," "Bouquet of Roses in Sunlight," "An Ordinary Evening in New Haven," and *A Primitive Like an Orb*), Knopf, 1950.

The Relations between Poetry and Painting (lecture), Museum of Modern Art, 1951.

Selected Poems, Fortune Press, 1952.

Selected Poems, Faber, 1953.

Raoul Duly: A Note (nonfiction), Pierre Beres, 1953.

The Collected Poems of Wallace Stevens (includes "The Rock," previously unpublished section featuring "The Poem That Took the Place of a Mountain," "A Quiet Normal Life," "Final Soliloquy of the Interior Paramour," "The Rock," "The Planet on the Table," and "Not Ideas about the Thing but the Thing Itself"), Knopf, 1954.

Opus Posthumous (includes "Owl's Clover" and essays "The Irrational Element in Poetry," "The Whole Man: Perspectives," "Horizons," "Preface to Time of Year," "John Crowe Ransom: Tennessean," and "Adagia"), edited by Samuel French Morse, Knopf, 1957.

Poems by Wallace Stevens, edited by Morse, Vintage Books, 1959.

The Necessary Angel: Essays on Reality and the Imagination (essays; includes "The Noble Rider and the Sound of Words," "The Figure of the Youth as Virile Poet," "Effects of Analogy," "The Realm of Resemblance," "Someone Puts a Pineapple Together," and "Of Ideal Time and Choice" from *Three Academic Pieces*), Faber, 1960.

Letters of Wallace Stevens, edited by daughter, Holly Stevens, Knopf, 1966.

The Palm at the End of the Mind: Selected Poems and a Play by Wallace Stevens, edited by Holly Stevens, Knopf, 1971.

Collected Poetry and Prose, Library of America (New York City), 1997.

Also author of preface to *William Carlos Williams's Collected Poems, 1921-1931,* Objectivist Press, 1934. Author of plays *Three Travelers Watch a Sunrise,* 1916, *Carlos among the Candles,* 1917, and *Bowl, Cat, and Broomstick,* c. 1917. Work represented in numerous anthologies, including *Modern American Poetry, The New Pocket Anthology of American Verse,* and *The Norton Anthology of Modern Poetry.* Contributor to periodicals, including *Accent, American Letters, Botteghe Oscure, Broom, Contact, Dial, Halcyon, Horizon, Hound and Horn, Kenyon Review, Life and Letters Today, Little Review, Measure, Modern School, Nation, New Republic, Others, Poetry* (some works published under pseudonym Peter Parasol, c. 1914), *Poetry London, Quarterly Review of Literature, Rogue, Secession, Soil, Southern Review, Voices,* and *Wake.*

MEDIA ADAPTATIONS: Poems from Harmonium were set to music by Vincent Persichetti to form a song cycle; "Thirteen Ways of Looking at a Blackbird" was set to music by John Gruen to form a song cycle and by J. Wisse to form a secular cantata; "Six Significant Landscapes" was set to music for voice and piano by Claire Brook.

SIDELIGHTS: Wallace Stevens is one of America's most respected poets. He was a master stylist, employing an extraordinary vocabulary and a rigorous precision in crafting his poems. But he was also a philosopher of aesthetics, vigorously exploring the notion of poetry as the supreme fusion of the creative imagination and objective reality. Because of the extreme technical and thematic complexity of his work, Stevens was sometimes considered a willfully difficult poet. But he was also acknowledged as an eminent abstractionist and a provocative thinker, and that reputation has continued since his death. In 1975, for instance, noted literary critic Harold Bloom, whose writings on Stevens include the imposing *Wallace Stevens: The Poems of Our Climate,* called him "the best and most representative American poet of our time."

Stevens was born in 1879 in Reading, Pennsylvania. His family belonged to the Dutch Reformed Church and when Stevens became eligible he enrolled in parochial schools. Stevens's father contributed substantially to his son's early education by providing their home with an extensive library and by encouraging reading. At age twelve Stevens entered public school for boys and began studying classics in Greek and Latin. In high school he became a prominent student, scoring high marks and distinguishing himself as a skillful orator. He also showed early promise as a writer by reporting for the school's newspaper, and after completing his studies in Reading he decided to continue his literary pursuits at Harvard University.

Encouraged by his father, Stevens devoted himself to the literary aspects of Harvard life. By his sophomore year he wrote regularly for the Harvard *Advocate,* and by the end of his third year, as biographer Samuel French Morse noted in *Wallace Stevens: Poetry as Life,* he had received all of the school's honors for writing. In 1899 Stevens joined the editorial board of the *Advocate*'s rival publication, the *Harvard Monthly,* and the following year he assumed the board's presidency and became editor. By that time Stevens had already published poems in both the *Advocate* and the *Monthly,* and as editor he additionally produced stories and literary sketches. Because there was a frequent shortage of manuscript during his tenure as editor, Stevens often published several of his own works in each issue of the *Monthly.* He thus gained further recognition on campus as a prolific and multi-talented writer. Unfortunately, his campus literary endeavors ended in 1900 when a shortage of family funds necessitated his withdrawal from the university.

By 1913 Stevens was enjoying great success in the field of insurance law. Unlike many aspiring artists, however, he was hardly stifled by steady employment. He soon resumed writing poetry, though in a letter to his wife he confided that writing was "absurd" as well as fulfilling. In 1914 he nonetheless published two poems in the modest periodical *Trend,* and later that year he produced four more verses for Harriet Monroe's publication, *Poetry.* None of these poems were included in Stevens's later volumes, but they are often considered his first mature writings.

After he began publishing his poems Stevens changed jobs again, becoming resident vice-president, in New York City, of the Equitable Surety Company (which, in turn, became the New England Equitable Company). He left that position in 1916 to work for the Hartford Accident and Indemnity Company, where he remained employed for the rest of his life, becoming vice-president in 1934.

This period of job changes was also one of impressive literary achievements for Stevens. In 1915 he produced his first important poems, "Peter Quince at the Clavier" and "Sunday Morning," and in 1916 he published his prize-winning play, *Three Travelers Watch a Sunrise.* Another play, *Carlos among the Candles,* followed in 1917, and the comic poem "Le Monocle de Mon Oncle" appeared in 1918. During the next few years Stevens began organizing his poems for publication in a single volume. For inclusion in that prospective volume he also produced several longer poems, including the masterful "Comedian as the Letter C." This poem, together with the early "Sunday Morning" and "Le Monocle de Mon Oncle," proved key to Stevens's volume *Harmonium* when it was published in 1923.

Harmonium bears ample evidence of Stevens's wide-ranging talents: an extraordinary vocabulary, a flair for memorable phrasing, an accomplished sense of imagery, and the ability to both lampoon and philosophize. "Peter Quince at the Clavier," among the earliest poems in *Harmonium,* contains aspects of all these skills. In this poem, a beautiful woman's humiliating encounter with lustful elders becomes a meditation on the nature of beauty (and the beauty of nature). Stevens vividly captures the woman's plight by dramatically contrasting the tranquility of her bath with a jarring interruption by several old folk. Consistent with the narrator's contention that "music is feeling," the woman's plight is emphasized by descriptions of sounds from nature and musical instruments. The poem culminates in a reflection on the permanence of the woman's physical beauty, which, it is declared, exists forever in memory and through death in the union of body and nature: "The body dies; the body's beauty lives. / So evenings die, in their green going, / A wave, interminably flowing."

"Peter Quince at the Clavier," with its notion of immortality as a natural cycle, serves as a prelude to the more ambitious "Sunday Morning," in which cyclical nature is proposed as the sole alternative to Christianity in the theologically bankrupt twentieth century. Here Stevens echoes the theme of "Peter Quince at the Clavier" by writing that "death is the mother of beauty," thus confirming that physical beauty is immortal through death and the consequent consummation with nature. Essentially an analysis of one woman's ennui, "Sunday Morning" ends by stripping the New Testament's Jesus Christ of transcendence and consigning him, too, to immortality void of an afterlife but part of "the heavenly fellowship / of men that perish." In this manner "Sunday Morning" shatters the tenets, or illusion, of Christianity essentially, the spiritual afterlife—and substantiates nature—the joining of corpse to earth as the only channel to immortality. In her volume *Wallace Stevens: An Introduction to the Poetry,* Susan B. Weston perceived the replacement of Christianity with nature as the essence of the poem, and she called "Sunday Morning" the "revelation of a secular religion."

In the mock epic "Comedian as the Letter C" Stevens presents a similarly introspective protagonist, Crispin, who is, or has been, a poet, handyman, musician, and rogue. The poem recounts Crispin's adventures from France to the jungle to a lush, Eden-like land where he establishes his own colony and devotes himself to contemplating his purpose in life. During the course of his adventures Crispin evolves from romantic to realist and from poet to parent, the latter two roles being, according to the poem, mutually antagonistic. The poem ends with Crispin dourly

viewing his six daughters as poems and questioning the validity of creating anything that must, eventually, become separate from him.

"The Comedian as the Letter C" is a fairly complex work, evincing Stevens's impressive, and occasionally intimidating, vocabulary and his penchant for obscure humor. Stevens later declared that his own motivations for writing the poem derived from his enthusiasm for "words and sounds." He stated: "I suppose that I ought to confess that by the letter C I meant the sound of the letter C; what was in my mind was to play on that sound throughout the poem. While the sound of that letter has more or less variety . . . all its shades may be said to have a comic aspect. Consequently, the letter C is a comedian."

Stevens more clearly explicated his notion of creative imagination in "The Idea of Order in Key West," among the few invigorating poems in *Ideas of Order* and one of the most important works in his entire canon. In this poem Stevens wrote of strolling along the beach with a friend and discovering a girl singing to the ocean. Stevens declares that the girl has created order out of chaos by fashioning a sensible song from her observations of the swirling sea. The concluding stanza extols the virtues of the singer's endeavor ("The maker's rage to order words of the sea") and declares that the resulting song is an actual aspect of the singer. In his book *Wallace Stevens: The Making of the Poem,* Frank Doggett called the concluding stanza Stevens's "hymn to the ardor of the poet to give order to the world by his command of language."

Following the publication of *Ideas of Order* Stevens began receiving increasing recognition as an important and unique poet. Not all of that recognition, however, was entirely positive. Some critics charged that the obscurity, abstraction, and self-contained, art-for-art's-sake tenor of his work were inappropriate and ineffective during a time of international strife that included widespread economic depression and increasing fascism in Europe. Stevens, comfortably ensconced in his half-acre home in Hartford, responded that the world was improving, not degenerating further. He held himself relatively detached from politics and world affairs, although he briefly championed leading Italian fascist Benito Mussolini, and contended that his art actually constituted the most substantial reality. "Life is not people and scene," he argued, "but thought and feeling. The world is myself. Life is myself."

Stevens contended that the poet's purpose was to interpret the external world of thought and feeling through the imagination. Like his alter-ego Crispin, Stevens became preoccupied with articulating his perception of the poet's purpose, and he sought to explore that theme in his 1936 book, *Owl's Clover.* But that book, comprised of five explications of various individuals' relations to art, proved verbose and thus uncharacteristically excessive. Immensely displeased, Stevens immediately dismantled the volume and reshaped portions of the work for inclusion in a forthcoming collection.

That volume, *The Man with the Blue Guitar,* succeeded where *Owl's Clover* failed, presenting a varied, eloquently articulated contention of the same theme the poet, and therefore the imagination, as the explicator of thought and feeling that had undone him earlier. In the title poem Stevens defends the poet's responsibility to shape and define perceived reality: "They said, 'You have a blue guitar, / You do not play things as they are.' / The man replied, 'Things as they are / Are changed upon the blue guitar.'" For Stevens, the blue guitar was the power of imagination, and the power of imagination, in turn, was "the power of the mind over the possibility of things" and "the power that enables us to perceive the normal in the abnormal."

The Man with the Blue Guitar, particularly the thirty-three-part title poem, constituted a breakthrough for Stevens by indicating a new direction: an inexhaustive articulation of the imagination as the supreme perception and of poetry as the supreme fiction. Bloom, in acknowledging Stevens's debacle *Owl's Clover,* described *The Man with the Blue Guitar* as the poet's "triumph over . . . literary anxieties" and added that with its completion Stevens renewed his poetic aspirations and vision. "The poet who had written *The Man with the Blue Guitar* had weathered his long crisis," Bloom wrote, "and at fifty-eight was ready to begin again."

Stevens followed *Parts of a World* with *Notes Toward a Supreme Fiction,* which is usually considered his greatest poem on the nature of poetry. This long poem, more an exploration of a definition than it is an actual definition, exemplifies the tenets of supreme fiction even as it articulates them. The poem is comprised of a prologue, three substantial sections, and a coda. The first main section, entitled "It Must Be Abstract," recalls *Harmonium*'s themes by hailing art as the new deity in a theologically deficient age. Abstraction is necessary, Stevens declares, because it fosters the sense of mystery necessary to provoke interest and worship from humanity. The second long portion, "It Must Change," recalls "Sunday Morning" in citing change as that which ever renews and sustains life: "Winter and spring, cold copulars, embrace / And for the particulars of rapture come." And in "It Must Give Pleasure," Stevens expresses his conviction that poetry must always be "a thing final in itself and, therefore, good: / One of the vast repetitions final in themselves and, therefore, good, the going round / And round and round, the merely going round, / Until merely going round is a final good, / The way wine comes at a table in a wood." *Notes Toward a Supreme Fiction* concludes with verses describing the poet's pursuit of supreme fiction as "a war that never ends." Stevens, directing these verses to an imaginary warrior, wrote: "Soldier, there is a war between the mind / And sky, between thought and day and night. It is / For that the poet is always in the sun, / Patches the moon together in his room / to his Virgilian cadences, up down, / Up down. It is a war that never ends." This is perhaps Stevens's most impressive description of his own sense of self, and in it he provides his most succinct appraisal of the poet's duty.

Although *Notes Toward a Supreme Fiction* elucidates Stevens's notions of poetry and poet, it was not intended by him to serve as a definitive testament. Rather, he considered the poem as a collection of ideas about the idea of supreme fiction. Writing to Henry Church, to whom the poem is dedicated, Stevens warned that it was not a systematized philosophy but mere notes—"the nucleus of the matter is contained in the title." He also reaffirmed his contention that poetry was the supreme fiction, explaining that poetry was supreme because "the essence of poetry is change and the essence of change is that it gives pleasure."

Notes Toward a Supreme Fiction was published as a small volume in 1942 and was subsequently included in the 1947 collection, *Transport to Summer.* Also featured in the collection is *Esthetique du Mal,* another long poem first published separately. In this poem Stevens explored the poetic imagination's response to specific provocations: pain and evil. Seconding philosopher Friedrich Nietzsche, Stevens asserted that evil was a necessary aspect of life, and he further declared that it was both inspirational and

profitable to the imagination. This notion is most clearly articulated in the poem's eighth section, which begins: "The death of Satan was a tragedy / For the imagination. A capital / Negation destroyed him in his tenement / And, with him, many blue phenomena." In a later stanza, one in which Bloom found the poem's "central polemic," Stevens emphasizes the positive aspect of evil: "The tragedy, however, may have begun, / Again, in the imagination's new beginning, / In the yes of the realist spoken because he must / Say yes, spoken because under every no / Lay a passion for yes that had never been broken." In *Wallace Stevens: The Poems of Our Climate,* Bloom called *Esthetique du Mal* Stevens's "major humanistic polemic" of the mid-1940s.

In 1950 Stevens published his last new poetry collection, *The Auroras of Autumn.* The poems in this volume show Stevens further refining and ordering his ideas about the imagination and poetry. Among the most prominent works in this volume is "An Ordinary Evening in New Haven," which constitutes still another set of notes toward a supreme fiction. Here Stevens finds the sublime in the seemingly mundane by recording his contemplations of a given evening. The style here is spare and abstract, resulting in a poem that revels in ambiguity and the elusiveness of definitions: "It is not the premise that reality / Is solid. It may be a shade that traverses / A dust, a force that traverses a shade." In this poem Stevens once again explicates as the supreme synthesis of perception and the imagination and produces a poem about poetry: "This endlessly elaborating poem / Displays the theory of poetry, / As the life of poetry." Other poems in *The Auroras of Autumn* are equally self-reflexive, but they are ultimately less ambitious and less provocative, concerned more with rendering the mundane through abstraction and thus prompting a sense of mystery and, simultaneously, order. As fellow poet Louise Bogan noted in a *New Yorker* review of the collection, only Stevens "can describe the simplicities of the natural world with more direct skill," though she added that his "is a natural world strangely empty of human beings."

By the early 1950s Stevens was regarded as one of America's greatest contemporary poets, an artist whose precise abstractions exerted substantial influence on other writers. Despite this widespread recognition, Stevens kept his position at the Hartford company, perhaps fearing that he would become isolated if he left his lucrative post. In his later years with the firm, Stevens amassed many writing awards, including the Bollingen Prize for Poetry, the National Book Award for *The Auroras of Autumn,* and several honorary doctorates. His greatest accolades, however, came with the 1955 publication of *The Collected Poems of Wallace Stevens,* which earned him the Pulitzer Prize for poetry and another National Book Award. In this volume Stevens gathered nearly all of his previously published verse, save *Owl's Clover,* and added another twenty-five poems under the title *The Rock.* Included in this section are some of Stevens's finest and most characteristically abstract poems. Appropriately, the final poem in *The Rock* is entitled "Not Ideas about the Thing but the Thing Itself," in which reality and the imagination are depicted as fusing at the instant of perception: "That scrawny cry—it was / A chorister whose *c* preceded the choir. / It was part of the colossal sun, / Surrounded by its choral rings, / Still far away. It was like / A new knowledge of reality."

BIOGRAPHICAL/CRITICAL SOURCES:

BOOKS

Bates, Milton J., *Wallace Stevens: A Mythology of Self,* University of California Press, 1985.

Berry, S. L., *Wallace Stevens,* Creative Education (Mankato, MN), 1997.

Bloom, Harold, *Figures of Capable Imagination,* Seabury, 1976.

Bloom, Harold, *Wallace Stevens: The Poems of Our Climate,* Cornell University Press, 1976.

Doggett, Frank, *Wallace Stevens: The Making of the Poem,* Johns Hopkins University Press, 1980.

Filreis, Alan, *Modernism from Right to Left: Wallace Stevens, the Thirties & Literary Radicalism,* Cambridge University Press (New York), 1994.

LaGuardia, David M., *Advance on Chaos: The Sanctifying Imagination of Wallace Stevens,* University Press of New England, 1983.

Lentricchia, Frank, *Modernist Quartet,* Cambridge University Press (New York), 1994.

Lombardi, Thomas F., *Wallace Stevens and the Pennsylvania Keystone: The Influence of Origins on his Life and Poetry,* Susquehanna University Press (Selinsgrove, PA), 1996.

McCann, Janet, *Wallace Stevens Revisited: "The Celestial Possible,"* Twayne (New York), 1995.

Morse, Samuel French, *Wallace Stevens: Poetry as Life,* Pegasus, 1970.

Murphy, Charles M., *Wallace Stevens: A Spiritual Poet in a Secular Age,* Paulist Press (New York City), 1997.

Richardson, Joan, *Wallace Stevens: The Early Years,* Morrow, 1986.

Rosu, Anca, *The Metaphysics of Sound in Wallace Stevens,* University of Alabama Press (Tuscaloosa), 1995.

Schulze, Robin G., *The Web of Friendship: Marianne Moore and Wallace Stevens,* University of Michigan Press (Ann Arbor), 1995.

Serio, John N., *Wallace Stevens: An Annotated Secondary Bibliography,* University of Pittsburgh Press, 1994.

Serio, John N., *Teaching Wallace Stevens: Practical Essays,* University of Tennessee Press (Knoxville), 1994.

Twentieth-Century Literary Criticism, Gale, Volume 3, 1980; Volume 12, 1984.

Vendler, Helen Hennessy, *On Extended Wings: Wallace Stevens' Longer Poems,* Harvard University Press, 1969.

Vendler, Helen Hennessy, *Wallace Stevens,* Harvard University Press, 1986.

Voros, Gyorgyi, *Notations of the Wild: Ecology in the Poetry of Wallace Stevens,* University of Iowa Press, 1997.

Whiting, Anthony, *The Never-Resting Mind: Wallace Stevens' Romantic Irony,* University of Michigan Press (Ann Arbor), 1996.

PERIODICALS

American Poetry Review, September-October, 1978.
Arizona Quarterly, autumn, 1955.
Catholic World, July-August, 1995, p. 154.
Contemporary Literature, autumn, 1975.
Critical Quarterly, autumn, 1960.
Criticism, winter, 1960; summer, 1965.
Encounter, November, 1979.
Hudson Review, autumn, 1957.
Journal of Modern Literature, May, 1982.
Kenyon Review, winter, 1957; winter, 1964.
Literary Review, autumn, 1963.
Modern Language Quarterly, September, 1969.
Nation, April 5, 1947.
New England Quarterly, December, 1971.
New York Times Magazine, August 28, 1994, p. 72.
New Yorker, October 28, 1950.
Poetry, March, 1924; December, 1931; February, 1937; January, 1956.
Sewanee Review, autumn, 1945; spring, 1952; winter, 1957.
Southern Review, July, 1971; July, 1976; October, 1979; January, 1982.
Western Review, autumn, 1955.
Yale Review, spring, 1955; spring, 1967; winter, 1982.

*   *   *

STEWART, J(ohn) I(nnes) M(ackintosh) 1906-1994 (Michael Innes)

PERSONAL: Born September 30, 1906, in Edinburgh, Scotland; died November 12, 1994, in Surrey, England; son of John (in education) and Eliza Jane (Clark) Stewart; married Margaret Hardwick (a physician), 1932 (died, 1979); children: three sons, two daughters. *Education:* Oriel College, Oxford, M.A., 1928.

ADDRESSES: Home—Lower Park House, Occupation Road, Lindley, Huddersfield HD3 3EE, England.

CAREER: Writer. University of Leeds, Yorkshire, England, lecturer in English, 1930-35; University of Adelaide, Adelaide, South Australia, jury professor of English, 1935-45; Queen's University, Belfast, Northern Ireland, lecturer, 1946-48; Oxford University, Oxford, England, reader in English literature, 1969-73. Student of Christ Church, Oxford, 1949-73, became emeritus; Walker Ames Professor at University of Washington, 1961.

AWARDS, HONORS: Matthew Arnold Memorial Prize, 1929; D.Litt., University of New Brunswick, 1962, University of Leicester, 1979, St. Andrews University, 1980; Honorary Fellow of the Royal Society, Edinburgh, 1990.

WRITINGS:

NOVELS

Mark Lambert's Supper, Gollancz (London), 1954.
The Guardians, Gollancz, 1955, Norton (New York City), 1957.
A Use of Riches, Norton, 1957.
The Man Who Won the Pools, Norton, 1961.
The Last Tresilians, Norton, 1963.
An Acre of Grass, Norton, 1965.
The Aylwins, Norton, 1966.
Vanderlyn's Kingdom, Norton, 1967.
Avery's Mission, Norton, 1971.
A Palace of Art, Norton, 1972.
Mungo's Dream, Norton, 1973.
The Gaudy (first book in "A Staircase in Surrey" quintet), Gollancz, 1974, Norton, 1975.
Young Pattullo (second book in "A Staircase in Surrey" quintet), Gollancz, 1975, Norton, 1976.
A Memorial Service (third book in "A Staircase in Surrey" quintet), Norton, 1976.
The Madonna of the Astrolabe (fourth book in "A Staircase in Surrey" quintet), Norton, 1977.
Full Term (fifth book in "A Staircase in Surrey" quintet), Norton, 1978.
Andrew and Tobias, Norton, 1980.
A Villa in France, Norton, 1982.
An Open Prison, Norton, 1984.
The Naylors, Norton, 1985.

NOVELS; UNDER PSEUDONYM MICHAEL INNES

Death at the President's Lodging, Gollancz, 1936, also published as *Seven Suspects,* Dodd (New York City), 1937.

Hamlet, Revenge! Dodd, 1937.

Lament for a Maker, Dodd, 1938.

The Spider Strikes Back, Dodd, 1939, published in England as *Stop Press,* Gollancz, 1939.

The Secret Vanguard (also see below), Gollancz, 1940, Dodd, 1941.

A Comedy of Terrors (also see below), Dodd, 1940, published in England as *There Came Both Mist and Snow,* Gollancz, 1940.

Appleby on Ararat, Dodd, 1941.

The Daffodil Affair, Dodd, 1942.

The Weight of the Evidence, Gollancz, 1943, Dodd, 1944.

What Happened at Hazelwood, Gollancz, 1944, Dodd, 1947.

Appleby's End, Dodd, 1945.

Unsuspected Chasm, Dodd, 1945, published in England as *From London Far,* Gollancz, 1946.

Night of Errors, Gollancz, 1947, Dodd, 1948.

The Case of the Journeying Boy, Dodd, 1949, published in England as *The Journeying Boy,* Gollancz, 1949.

Paper Thunderbolt, Dodd, 1951, published in England as *Operation Pax,* Gollancz, 1951.

One Man Show (also see below), Dodd, 1952, published in England as *A Private View,* Gollancz, 1952.

Christmas at Candleshoe, Dodd, 1953.

The Man from the Sea, Dodd, 1955.

A Question of Queens, Dodd, 1956, published in England as *Old Hall, New Hall,* Gollancz, 1956.

Death on a Quiet Day, Dodd, 1957, published in England as *Appleby Plays Chicken,* Gollancz, 1957.

The Long Farewell, Dodd, 1958.

Hare Sitting Up, Dodd, 1959.

The Case of Sonia Wayward, Dodd, 1960, published in England as *The New Sonia Wayward,* Gollancz, 1960.

Silence Observed, Dodd, 1961.

The Crabtree Affair, Dodd, 1962, published in England as *A Connoisseur's Case,* Gollancz, 1962.

Money from Holme, Gollancz, 1964, Dodd, 1965.

The Bloody Wood, Dodd, 1966.

A Change of Heir, Dodd, 1966.

Death by Water, Dodd, 1968.

Appleby at Allington, Dodd, 1968.

Picture of Guilt, Dodd, 1969, published in England as *A Family Affair,* Gollancz, 1969.

Death at the Chase, Dodd, 1970.

An Awkward Lie, Dodd, 1971.

The Open House, Dodd, 1972.

Appleby's Answer, Dodd, 1973.

Appleby's Other Story, Gollancz, 1973, Dodd, 1974.

The Mysterious Commission, Gollancz, 1974, Dodd, 1975.

The Gay Phoenix, Gollancz, 1976, Dodd, 1977.

Honeybath's Haven, Gollancz, 1977, Dodd, 1978.

The Ampersand Papers, Dodd, 1978.

Going It Alone, Dodd, 1980.

Lord Mullion's Secret, Dodd, 1981.

Sheiks and Adders, Dodd, 1982.

Appleby and Honeybath, Dodd, 1983.

Carson's Conspiracy, Dodd, 1984.

Appleby and the Ospreys, Dodd, 1986.

OTHER

(Editor) Michel Eyquen de Montaigne, *Montaigne's Essays: John Florio's Translation,* Random House (New York City), 1931.

Educating the Emotions, [Adelaide, Australia], 1944.

(Contributor) Raynor Heppenstall, editor, *Imaginary Conversations: Eight Radio Scripts,* Secker & Warburg (London), 1948.

Characters and Motive in Shakespeare: Some Recent Appraisals Examined, Longman, 1949.

(Under pseudonym Michael Innes; with Heppenstall) *Three Tales of Hamlet,* Gollancz, 1950.

(Under pseudonym Michael Innes) *Dead Man's Shoes,* Dodd, 1954, published in England as *Appleby Talking: Twenty-Three Detective Stories,* Gollancz, 1954.

(Under pseudonym Michael Innes) *Appleby Talks Again: Eighteen Detective Stories,* Gollancz, 1956, Dodd, 1957.

The Man Who Wrote Detective Stories and Other Stories, Norton, 1959.

Eight Modern Writers, Oxford University Press, 1963, published as *Writers of the Early Twentieth Century: Hardy to Lawrence,* 1990.

(Under pseudonym) *Appleby Intervenes: Three Tales from Scotland Yard* (contains *One Man Show, A Comedy of Terrors,* and *The Secret Vanguard*), Dodd, 1965.

Rudyard Kipling, Dodd, 1966.

(Author of introduction) J. B. Priestley, *Thomas Love Peacock,* Penguin, 1966.

(Editor) Wilkie Collins, *Moonstone,* Penguin, 1966.

(Editor and author of introduction) William Makepeace Thackeray, *Vanity Fair,* Penguin, 1968.

Joseph Conrad, Dodd, 1968.

Cucumber Sandwiches and Other Stories, Norton, 1969.

Thomas Hardy: A Critical Biography, Dodd, 1971.

Shakespeare's Lofty Scene, Oxford University Press for the British Academy, 1971.

(Under pseudonym Michael Innes) *The Appleby File: Detective Stories,* Gollancz, 1975, Dodd, 1976.

Our England Is a Garden (short stories), Norton, 1979.

The Bridge at Arta and Other Stories (short stories), Norton, 1981.

My Aunt Christina and Other Stories, Norton, 1983.

(Under pseudonym Michael Innes) *Parlour 4 and Other Stories,* Gollancz, 1986.

Myself and Michael Innes: A Memoir, Gollancz, 1987, Norton, 1988.

SIDELIGHTS: J. I. M. Stewart distinguished himself both as a novelist and as a literary scholar. Best known for his mysteries written under the pseudonym Michael Innes, Stewart was praised by critics for the mannered sophistication and erudition of his prose, which has drawn frequent comparisons with the nineteenth-century American novelist Henry James. Stewart also received acclaim as a literary biographer and historian, particularly for his biography of the early twentieth-century English poet and novelist Thomas Hardy and for his *Eight Modern Writers,* the fifteenth volume in the "Oxford History of English Literature" series.

Many of Stewart's novels are set in the privileged and eccentric milieu of Oxford University, where he himself spent a number of years as a professor of literature. In *The Gaudy,* the first of five volumes that make up the "Staircase in Surrey" quintet, Duncan Pattullo accepts a teaching fellowship at Oxford after a stint as a dramatist. The subsequent volumes in the series—*Young Pattullo,*

A Memorial Service, The Madonna of the Astrolabe, and *Full Term*—describe the humorous eccentricities and amorous misadventures of Pattullo and his colleagues. Stewart stated in his *Contemporary Authors Autobiography Series (CAAS)* entry that "in some regards these pages are closely autobiographical. . . . Duncan Pattullo . . . devotes several pages to describing his school-days at what is plainly the [Edinburgh] Academy," which Stewart himself attended for a little over eleven years.

Many critics enjoyed *The Gaudy* and its companion volumes. According to Reid Beddow in the *Washington Post Book World,* the series as a whole is "equal in entertainment to . . . Anthony Powell's *A Dance to the Music of Time* and within the genre of Oxford novels the funniest since Evelyn Waugh's *Brideshead Revisited.*" Melody Hardy, writing for *Best Sellers,* asserted that Stewart "captures the romance of an Oxford education and its impact on the men who experience it." A reviewer for the *Times Literary Supplement* was less impressed. "The present reviewer," it was noted, "hopes to be spared the next four installments." The writer added, "One feels that Mr. Stewart would have written better if he had known Christ Church, Oxford, less well." Susan Kennedy, reviewing *A Memorial Service* in the *Times Literary Supplement,* cited problems with Stewart's use of serial conventions. "One of the drawbacks of the serial novel is the need to remind the reader . . . of people and events introduced in earlier volumes," wrote Kennedy. "Mr. Stewart's way of handling this is to take up old threads in after-dinner conversations or on leisurely, companionable walks."

In spite of this mixed reception, many reviewers agreed that Stewart's autobiographical quintet presents a vivid and authentic portrait of life at Oxford. "Part of the fun in all this," wrote Beddow, "is in deciphering the true identity of some of the characters." Beddow sees many famous Oxford scholars, including J. R. R. Tolkien, Max Beerbohm, and Iris Murdoch, presented in various guises in Stewart's work. "When I look back on those years now," Stewart recollected in his *CAAS* entry, "they come to my [mind] as having been filled with frivolities—frivolities innocent enough for the most part, but compatible with our duty as students only because we found ourselves, for the time, within a highly privileged section of society. Everything of a workaday sort was done for us; we didn't even have to visit our tailor, since he came knocking at our door, smoothly anxious to know if he could be of service to us. We seemed to be—although we were not—young lords of unlimited leisure." The quintet itself, Beddow declared, presents "the graceful thanks of a man who knows he has been privileged to spend half a century in the most ivory of towers."

In addition to his scholarly works and novels, Stewart also penned several collections of short stories, including *Cucumber Sandwiches and Other Stories, Our England Is a Garden, The Bridge at Arta and Other Stories,* and *My Aunt Christina and Other Stories.* The tales in *Cucumber Sandwiches* were deemed "perfect" by a reviewer for the *New York Times Book Review,* and Stewart's short stories often remind critics of Henry James's shorter works—probably by design, for as Stewart himself stated in his *CAAS* entry, many of his early works "were made . . . distinctly under the pilotage of Henry James. I had spent the better part of a year in reading through almost everything that James wrote." Neil Millar noted in the *Christian Science Monitor* that *Cucumber Sandwiches* "exhales the drama of every battle between flesh and spirit. Its flesh never undresses in public, and nearly always dresses for dinner. Its spirit rarely raises—and never lowers—its kindly, cultured, understanding voice." The writer for

the *New York Times Book Review* also noted that Stewart "shapes and polishes each sentence with respectful craftsmanship." The same writer added, "Little enough is left us these days. Let us give deep thanks to J. I. M. Stewart for his intellect, his respect for undecayed English, and his preservative humor."

In addition to his high standing as a novelist, Stewart is well-regarded as a literary biographer. Orville Prescott, in his review of *Rudyard Kipling* in the *Saturday Review,* commented that "Mr. Stewart's most important achievement in this lucid and penetrating little book is to analyze the elements that make so many of Kipling's stories immortal. . . ." He added that "Mr. Stewart is adept in performing one of the critic's most useful tasks—pointing out the less obvious merits, the nuances, and the true significances which hasty readers easily overlook." Stewart's *Joseph Conrad* received mixed reviews, while his *Thomas Hardy: A Critical Biography* was more unanimously praised. Keith Cushman, writing in *Library Journal,* declared: "Students and teachers of Hardy will find [*Thomas Hardy*] to be one of the most useful and sensible studies available. . ."; and a reviewer for the *Virginia Quarterly Review* asserted that "[Stewart's] approach [in *Thomas Hardy*] is biographical, but biographical in an intelligent and flexible way that avoids the dogma implicit in the sets of consistent philosophy or structural criticism."

Stewart also wrote numerous mysteries under the pseudonym of Michael Innes. With his first mystery, *Death at the President's Lodging,* the author exhibited some of the characteristics that made him a popular success for more than fifty years. The novel "didn't go for length, or a large cast, or extended thoughts on man, nature, and society," Stewart commented. "But it did, although all-tentatively, try for a certain lightness of air and liveliness of talk side by side with the mysteriousness. This disposition, uncanonical from the 'classical' point of view, has remained with me, and turned me into one of the Farceurs (Julian Symons's excellent word for it) of the mystery story. . . . It has also delayed the point at which the aged jester will consent (Bernard Shaw's phrase, but directed elsewhere) to be led into the wings."

Many of the crime novels feature Inspector Sir John Appleby, a resourceful crime-solver who rises in rank to become chief police commissioner of London before retiring and who is probably the most popular of all of Stewart's characters. He "came into being," Stewart revealed in Otto Penzler's *The Great Detectives,* "during a sea voyage from Liverpool to Adelaide." By the time he arrived in Australia, Stewart "had completed a novel called *Death at the President's Lodging* . . . in which a youngish inspector from Scotland Yard solves the mystery of the murder of Dr. Umpleby, the president of one of the constituent colleges of Oxford University." Although the stories themselves exist in a timeless, literary realm, Stewart declared, "Appleby himself ages, and in some respects perhaps even matures. He ages along with his creator, and like his creator ends up as a retired man who still a little meddles with the concerns of his green unknowing youth."

Stewart commented further on Appleby's longevity in *The Great Detectives.* "Appleby," he stated, "is as much concerned to provide miscellaneous and unassuming 'civilized' entertainment as he is to hunt down baddies wherever they may lurk." In the many years of the character's existence, Stewart concluded, "I have never quite got tired of John Appleby as a pivot round which farce and mild comedy and parody and freakish fantasy revolve." Even in retirement, Appleby was present in Stewart's more recent mysteries, including *The Gay Phoenix* and *Appleby and the Ospreys.* Stewart also paired Appleby with another of his recurrent mystery solvers, the Royal Academy portrait painter Charles Honeybath, in *Appleby and Honeybath.*

BIOGRAPHICAL/CRITICAL SOURCES:

BOOKS

Contemporary Authors Autobiography Series, Volume 3, Gale (Detroit), 1986, pp. 343-60.
Contemporary Literary Criticism, Gale, Volume 7, 1977; Volume 14, 1980; Volume 32, 1985.
Penzler, Otto, *The Great Detectives,* Little, Brown (Boston), 1978.
Symons, Julian, *Mortal Consequences: A History—From the Detective Story to the Crime Novel,* Harper (New York City), 1972.

PERIODICALS

Armchair Detective, fall, 1991, p. 457; spring, 1992, p. 234.
Best Sellers, June, 1975.
Books and Bookmen, June, 1983.
Book World, November 28, 1971.
Chicago Tribune Book World, June 8, 1980, p. 15; March 28, 1982, p. 4; June 22, 1986, p. 33.
Christian Science Monitor, June 13, 1970.
Library Journal, March 1, 1972.
Listener, July 29, 1982.
London Review of Books, December 30, 1982.
Los Angeles Times Book Review, April 3, 1983, p. 9.
National Review, April 9, 1968.
New Leader, September 9, 1968.
New Statesman, December 20, 1968; September 24, 1971; February 9, 1973; June 13, 1975; April 30, 1976; July 7, 1978; August 10, 1979; November 12, 1982; May 20, 1983.
New York Times, December 11, 1982; December 2, 1983; June 19, 1987.
New York Times Book Review, April 7, 1968; June 19, 1970; May 29, 1977; June 11, 1978; April 29, 1979; February 14, 1982, p. 22; February 13, 1983, p. 31; January 1, 1984, p. 26; July 29, 1984, p. 20; September 15, 1985, p. 30; August 10, 1986, p. 19.
Observer, August 19, 1979.
Saturday Review, October 22, 1966, p. 58.
Southwest Review, autumn, 1977.
Spectator, September 22, 1967; October 31, 1981.
Times (London), April 18, 1987.
Times Literary Supplement, January 19, 1967; September 21, 1967; December 25, 1969; February 2, 1973; October 25, 1974; June 6, 1975; May 7, 1976; July 7, 1978, p. 757; January 16, 1981, p. 50; June 19, 1981, p. 690; July 2, 1982, p. 725; November 26, 1982, p. 1318; January 25, 1985, p. 86; January 31, 1986, p. 113; September 25, 1987, p. 1045.
Virginia Quarterly Review, winter, 1972.
Washington Post Book World, November 9, 1979; July 18, 1982, p. 16; October 30, 1988, p. 14.

*   *   *

STINE, Jovial Bob
See STINE, R(obert) L(awrence)

STINE, R(obert) L(awrence) 1943-
(Eric Affabee, Zachary Blue, Jovial Bob Stine)

PERSONAL: Born October 8, 1943, in Columbus, OH; son of Lewis (a shipping manager) and Anne (Feinstein) Stine; married Jane Waldhorn (owner/managing director of Parachute Press), June 22, 1969; children: Matthew Daniel. *Education:* Ohio State University, B.A., 1965; graduate study at New York University, 1966-67. *Religion:* Jewish. *Avocational interests:* Swimming, watching old movie classics from the 1930s and 1940s, reading (especially P. G. Wodehouse novels).

ADDRESSES: Office—c/o Parachute Press, 156 5th Avenue, New York, NY 10010.

CAREER: Writer. Social Studies teacher at junior high schools in Columbus, Ohio, 1967-68; *Junior Scholastic* (magazine), New York City, associate editor, 1969-71; *Search* (magazine), New York City, editor, 1972-75; *Bananas* (magazine), New York City, editor, 1972-83; *Maniac* (magazine), New York City, editor, 1984-85. Head writer for *Eureeka's Castle,* Nickelodeon cable television network.

MEMBER: Mystery Writers of America.

AWARDS, HONORS: Childrens' Choice Award, American Library Association, for several novels.

WRITINGS:

JUVENILE

The Time Raider, illustrations by David Febland, Scholastic Inc. (New York City), 1982.
The Golden Sword of Dragonwalk, illustrations by Febland, Scholastic Inc., 1983.
Horrors of the Haunted Museum, Scholastic Inc., 1984.
Instant Millionaire, illustrations by Jowill Woodman, Scholastic Inc., 1984.
Through the Forest of Twisted Dreams, Avon (New York City), 1984.
Indiana Jones and the Curse of Horror Island, Ballantine (New York City), 1984.
Indiana Jones and the Giants of the Silver Tower, Ballantine, 1984.
Indiana Jones and the Cult of the Mummy's Crypt, Ballantine, 1985.
The Badlands of Hark, illustrations by Bob Roper, Scholastic Inc., 1985.
The Invaders of Hark, Scholastic Inc., 1985.
Demons of the Deep, illustrations by Fred Carrillo, Golden Books, 1985.
Challenge of the Wolf Knight ("Wizards, Warriors and You" series), Avon, 1985.
James Bond in Win, Place, or Die, Ballantine, 1985.
Conquest of the Time Master, Avon, 1985.
Cavern of the Phantoms, Avon, 1986.
Operation: Deadly Decoy ("G.I. Joe" series), Ballantine, 1986.
Mystery of the Imposter, Avon, 1986.
Operation: Mindbender ("G.I. Joe" series), Ballantine, 1986.
Golden Girl and the Vanishing Unicorn ("Golden Girl" series), Ballantine, 1986.
Serpentor and the Mummy Warrior ("G.I. Joe" series), 1987.
Indiana Jones and the Ape Slaves of Howling Island, Ballantine, 1987.
Jungle Raid ("G.I. Joe" series), Ballantine, 1988.
Siege of Serpentor ("G.I. Joe" series), Ballantine, 1988.

The Beast, Minstrel, 1994.
I Saw You That Night! Scholastic Inc., 1994.
The Beast 2, Minstrel, 1995.
R. L. Stine's the Ghosts of Fear Street: Hide & Shriek, Minstrel, 1995.

JUVENILE; UNDER NAME JOVIAL BOB STINE

The Absurdly Silly Encyclopedia and Flyswatter, illustrations by Bob Taylor, Scholastic Inc., 1978.
How To Be Funny: An Extremely Silly Guidebook, illustrations by Carol Nicklaus, Dutton (New York City), 1978.
The Complete Book of Nerds, illustrations by Sam Viviano, Scholastic Inc., 1979.
The Dynamite Do-It-Yourself Pen Pal Kit, illustrations by Jared Lee, Scholastic Inc., 1980.
Dynamite's Funny Book of the Sad Facts of Life, illustrations by Lee, Scholastic Inc., 1980.
Going Out! Going Steady! Going Bananas! photographs by Dan Nelken, Scholastic Inc., 1980.
The Pigs' Book of World Records, illustrations by Peter Lippman, Random House (New York City), 1980.
(With wife, Jane Stine) *The Sick of Being Sick Book,* edited by Ann Durrell, illustrations by Nicklaus, Dutton, 1980.
Bananas Looks at TV, Scholastic Inc., 1981.
The Beast Handbook, illustrations by Taylor, Scholastic Inc., 1981.
(With Jane Stine) *The Cool Kids' Guide to Summer Camp,* illustrations by Jerry Zimmerman, Scholastic Inc., 1981.
Gnasty Gnomes, illustrations by Lippman, Random House, 1981.
Don't Stand in the Soup, illustrations by Nicklaus, Bantam (New York City), 1982.
(With Jane Stine) *Bored with Being Bored!: How to Beat the Boredom Blahs,* illustrations by Zimmerman, Four Winds (New York City), 1982.
Blips!: The First Book of Video Game Funnies, illustrations by Bryan Hendrix, Scholastic Inc., 1983.
(With Jane Stine) *Everything You Need to Survive: Brothers and Sisters,* illustrated by Sal Murdocca, Random House, 1983.
(With Jane Stine) *Everything You Need to Survive: First Dates,* illustrated by Murdocca, Random House, 1983.
(With Jane Stine) *Everything You Need to Survive: Homework,* illustrated by Murdocca, Random House, 1983.
(With Jane Stine) *Everything You Need to Survive: Money Problems,* illustrated by Murdocca, Random House, 1983.
Jovial Bob's Computer Joke Book, Scholastic Inc., 1985.
Miami Mice, illustrations by Eric Gurney, Scholastic Inc., 1986.
One Hundred and One Silly Monster Jokes, Scholastic Inc., 1986.
The Doggone Dog Joke Book, Parachute Press, 1986.
Spaceballs: The Book, Scholastic Inc., 1987.
One Hundred and One Wacky Kid Jokes, Turtleback, 1988.
Pork & Beans: Play Date, illustrations by Jose Aruego and Ariane Dewey, Scholastic Inc., 1989.
My Secret Identity: A Novelization, Scholastic Inc., 1989.
Ghostbusters 2 Storybook, Scholastic Inc., 1989.
One Hundred and One Vacation Jokes, illustrated by Rick Majica, Scholastic Inc., 1990.
One Hundred and One Creep Creature Jokes, Scholastic Inc., 1990.
One Hundred and One School Cafeteria Jokes, Scholastic Inc., 1990.
The Amazing Adventures of Me, Myself, and I, Bantam, 1991.

JUVENILE; UNDER PSEUDONYM ERIC AFFABEE

The Siege of the Dragonriders ("Wizards, Warriors and You" series), Avon, 1984.
G.I. Joe and the Everglades Swamp Terror ("G.I. Joe" Series), Ballantine, 1986.
Attack on the King, Avon, 1986.
G.I. Joe—Operation: Star Raider ("G.I. Joe" series), Ballantine, 1986.
The Dragon Queen's Revenge ("Wizards, Warriors and You" series), Avon, 1986.

JUVENILE; UNDER PSEUDONYM ZACHARY BLUE

The Protectors: The Petrova Twist, Scholastic Inc., 1987.
The Jet Fighter Trap, Scholastic Inc., 1987.

YOUNG ADULT NOVEL

Blind Date, Scholastic Inc., 1986.
Twisted, Scholastic Inc., 1986.
Broken Date ("Crosswinds" series), Simon & Schuster (New York City), 1988.
The Baby-Sitter, Scholastic Inc., 1989.
Phone Calls, Archway (New York City), 1990.
Curtains, Archway, 1990.
The Boyfriend, Scholastic Inc., 1990.
Beach Party ("Point Horror" series), Scholastic Inc., 1990.
How I Broke up with Ernie, Archway, 1990.
Snowman, Scholastic Inc., 1991.
The Girlfriend, Scholastic Inc., 1991.
Baby-Sitter 2, Scholastic Inc., 1991.
Beach House, Scholastic Inc., 1992.
Hit and Run, Scholastic Inc., 1992.
Hitchhiker, Scholastic Inc., 1993.
Baby-Sitter 3, Scholastic Inc., 1993.
The Dead Girlfriend, Scholastic Inc., 1993.
Halloween Night, Scholastic Inc., 1993.
Call Waiting, Scholastic Inc., 1994.
Halloween Night 2, Scholastic Inc., 1994.

"FEAR STREET" SERIES; PUBLISHED BY ARCHWAY

The New Girl, 1989.
The Surprise Party, 1990.
The Stepsister, 1990.
Missing, 1990.
Halloween Party, 1990.
The Wrong Number, 1990.
The Sleepwalker, 1991.
Ski Weekend, 1991.
The Secret Bedroom, 1991.
The Overnight, 1991.
Lights Out, 1991.
Haunted, 1991.
The Fire Game, 1991.
The Knife, 1992.
Prom Queen, 1992.
First Date, 1992.
The Best Friend, 1992.
Sunburn, 1993.
The Cheater, 1993.
The New Boy, 1994.
Bad Dreams, 1994.
The Dare, 1994.
Double Date, 1994.
The First Horror, 1994.
The Mind Reader, 1994.
One Evil Summer, 1994.

The Second Horror, 1994.
The Third Horror, 1994.
The Thrill Club, 1994.
College Weekend, 1995.
Final Grade, 1995.
The Stepsister 2, 1995.
Switched, 1995.
Truth or Dare, 1995.
Wrong Number 2, 1995.
Secret Admirer, 1996.
What Holly Heard, 1996.
The Perfect Date, 1996.
Night Game, 1996.
The Runaway, 1997.
Killer's Kiss, 1997.
All-Night Party, 1997.
The Rich Girl, 1997.
Cat, 1997.
Who Killed the Homecoming Queen?, 1997.
Into the Dark, 1997.
Trapped, 1997.
The Stepbrother, 1998.
Camp Out, 1998.

*"FEAR STREET: SUPER CHILLER" SERIES; PUBLISHED BY
     ARCHWAY*

Silent Night, 1991.
Party Summer, 1992.
Goodnight Kiss, 1992.
Silent Night 2, 1993.
Broken Hearts, 1993.
The Dead Lifeguard, 1994.
Bad Moonlight, 1995.
Dead End, 1995.
The New Year's Party, 1995.
Goodnight Kiss 2, 1996.
Silent Night 3, 1996.
High Tide, 1997.

*"FEAR STREET: CHEERLEADERS" SERIES; PUBLISHED BY
     ARCHWAY*

The First Evil, 1992.
The Second Evil, 1992.
The Third Evil, 1992.
The New Evil, 1994.
The Evil Lives, 1998.

"FEAR STREET SAGA" SERIES; PUBLISHED BY ARCHWAY

The Betrayal, 1993.
The Secret, 1993.
The Burning, 1993.
The Boy Next Door, 1996.
House of Whispers, 1996.
Forbidden Secrets, 1996.
A New Fear, 1996.

*"FEAR STREET: CATALUNA CHRONICLES" SERIES; PUBLISHED
     BY ARCHWAY*

The Evil Moon, 1995.
The Dark Secret, 1995.
The Deadly Fire, 1995.

*"FEAR STREET: FEAR PARK" SERIES; PUBLISHED BY
     ARCHWAY*

The First Scream, 1996.
The Loudest Scream, 1996.

The Last Scream, 1996.

*"FEAR STREET: FEAR HALL" SERIES; PUBLISHED BY
     ARCHWAY*

The Beginning, 1997.
The Conclusion, 1997.

*"GHOSTS OF FEAR STREET" SERIES; PUBLISHED BY
     MINSTREL BOOKS*

Hide and Shriek, 1995.
Who's Been Sleeping in My Grave?, 1995.
Attack of the Aqua Apes, 1995.
Nightmare in 3-D, 1996.
Stay Away from the Tree House, 1996.
Eye of the Fortuneteller, 1996.
Fright Knight, 1996.
The Ooze, 1996.
Revenge of the Shadow People, 1996.
The Bugman Lives!, 1996.
The Boy Who Ate Fear Street, 1996.
Night of the Werecat, 1996.
How to Be a Vampire, 1996.
Body Switchers from Outer Space, 1996.
Fright Christmas, 1996.
Don't Ever Get Sick at Granny's, 1997.
(With P. MacFearson) *House of a Thousand Screams,* 1997.
Camp Fear Ghouls, 1997.
Three Evil Wishes, 1997.
Spell of the Screaming Jokers, 1997.
The Creatures from the Club Lagoona, 1997.
(With P. MacFearson) *Field of Screams,* 1997.
Why I'm Not Afraid of Ghosts, 1997.
(With Rick Surmacz) *Monster Dog,* 1997.
Halloween Bugs Me!, 1997.
Go to Your Tomb—Right Now!, 1997.
Parents From the 13th Dimension, 1997.
Hide and Shriek 2, 1998.
Tale of the Blue Monkey, 1998.
I Was a Sixth Grade Zombie, 1998.
Escape of the He-Beast, 1998.

"GOOSEBUMPS" SERIES; PUBLISHED BY SCHOLASTIC INC.

Welcome to Dead House, 1992.
Stay Out of the Basement, 1992.
Monster Blood, 1992.
Say Cheese and Die, 1992.
The Curse of the Mummy's Tomb, 1993.
Let's Get Invisible, 1993.
Night of the Living Dummy, 1993.
The Girl Who Cried Monster, 1993.
Welcome to Camp Nightmare, 1993.
The Ghost Next Door, 1993.
The Haunted Mask, 1993.
Be Careful What You Wish For, 1993.
Piano Lessons Can Be Murder, 1993.
The Werewolf of Fever Swamp, 1993.
You Can't Scare Me, 1994.
One Day at Horrorland, 1994.
Why I'm Afraid of Bees, 1994.
Monster Blood 2, 1994.
Deep Trouble, 1994.
The Scarecrow Walks at Midnight, 1994.
Go Eat Worms!, 1994.
Ghost Beach, 1994.
Return of the Mummy, 1994.

Phantom of the Auditorium, 1994.
Attack of the Mutant, 1994.
My Hairiest Adventure, 1994.
A Night in Terror Tower, 1995.
The Cuckoo Clock of Doom, 1995.
Monster Blood 3, 1995.
It Came from Beneath the Sink, 1995.
The Night of the Living Dummy 2, 1995.
The Barking Ghost, 1995.
The Horror at Camp Jellyjam, 1995.
Revenge of the Lawn Gnomes, 1995.
A Shocker on Shock Street, 1995.
The Haunted Mask 2, 1995.
The Headless Ghost, 1995.
The Abominable Snowman of Pasadena, 1995.
How I Got My Shrunken Head, 1996.
Night of the Living Dummy 3, 1996.
Bad Hare Day, 1996.
Egg Monsters from Mars, 1996.
The Beast from the East, 1996.
Say Cheese and Die—Again!, 1996.
Ghost Camp, 1996.
How to Kill a Monster, 1996.
Legend of the Lost Legend, 1996.
Attack of the Jack-O'-Lanterns, 1996.
Vampire Breath, 1996.
Calling All Creeps!, 1996.
Beware, the Snowman, 1997.
How I Learned to Fly, 1997.
Chicken, Chicken, 1997.
Don't Go to Sleep, 1997.
The Blob That Ate Everyone, 1997.
The Curse of Camp Cold Lake, 1997.
My Best Friend is Invisible, 1997.
Deep Trouble 2, 1997.
The Haunted School, 1997.
Werewolf Skin, 1997.
I Live In Your Basement, 1997.
Monster Blood 4, 1997.

"GOOSEBUMPS 2000" SERIES; PUBLISHED BY SCHOLASTIC INC.

Cry of the Cat, 1998.
Bride of the Living Dummy, 1998.
Creature Teacher, 1998.
Invasion of the Body Squeezers, Part 1, 1998.
Invasion of the Body Squeezers, Part 2, 1998.

"GIVE YOURSELF GOOSEBUMPS" SERIES; PUBLISHED BY APPLE, EXCEPT AS NOTED

Escape from the Carnival of Horrors, 1995.
Tick Tock, You're Dead, 1995.
Trapped in Bat Wing Hell, 1995.
The Deadly Experiments of Dr. Eeek, 1996.
Night in Werewolf Woods, 1996.
Beware of the Purple Peanut Butter, 1996.
Under the Magician's Spell, 1996.
The Curse of the Creeping Coffin, 1996.
The Knight in Screaming Armor, 1996.
Diary of a Mad Mummy, Scholastic Inc., 1996.
Visita Aterradora, 1997.
Deep in the Jungle of Doom, 1996.
Welcome to the Wicked Wax Museum, 1997.
Scream of the Evil Genie, 1997.
The Creepy Creations of Professor Shock, 1997.

Please Don't Feed the Vampire!, 1997.
Secret Agent Grandma, 1997.
Little Comic Shop of Horrors, 1997.
Attack of the Beastly Baby-Sitter, 1997.
Escape from Camp Run-For-Your-Life, 1997.
Toy Terror: Batteries Included, 1997.
Return to the Carnival of Horrors, 1997.
Zapped in Space, 1997.
Lost in Stinkeye Swamp, 1997.
Shop Till You Drop. . .Dead, 1998.
Alone in Snakebite Canyon, Scholastic Inc., 1998.
Checkout Time at the Dead-End Hotel, 1998.
Night of a Thousand Claws, 1998.
Invaders from the Big Screen, 1998.
Into the Jaws of Doom, 1998.
Return to Terror Tower, Scholastic Inc., 1998.

Also author of *Tales to Give You Goosebumps,* and *More Tales to Give You Goosebumps.*

"SPACE CADETS" SERIES; PUBLISHED BY SCHOLASTIC INC.

Jerks-in-Training, 1991.
Losers in Space, 1991.
Bozos on Patrol, 1992.

ADULT NOVELS

Superstitious (horror), Warner Books (New York City), 1995.

MEDIA ADAPTATIONS: The "Goosebumps" series was produced by Scholastic Inc. as a live-action television series for the Fox Television Network beginning in 1995.

SIDELIGHTS: R. L. Stine has sold more than 90 million books, yet his name is unfamiliar to many adult readers. This best-selling author's success is based on his popularity among children and teens, who purchase the titles in his "Fear Street" and "Goosebumps" horror series at a rate of more than 1 million copies each month. A new book in each series is released every month, making Stine one of the most prolific authors of all time. To keep up with the demand for his frightening tales, Stine must turn out some twenty pages of manuscript six days a week. The result has not pleased all critics, some of whom dismiss his work as insignificant. But teachers, librarians, and parents report that many youngsters who were previously uninterested in books turned into avid readers after becoming hooked on Stine. The author himself once told *Contemporary Authors:* "I believe that kids as well as adults are entitled to books of no socially redeeming value."

Stine never wanted to be anything but a writer, and by the age of nine he was creating his own magazines filled with short stories and jokes. In college, he was editor of the campus humor magazine for three years. After graduation, he taught junior high school for one year, then set out for New York City in search of a job in magazine publishing. He paid his dues working for movie and fan magazines, and for a trade publication called *Soft Drink Industry,* then began a sixteen-year stint as an editor for Scholastic Inc., which publishes many classroom magazines and children's books. Stine worked on several titles before finally becoming editor of *Bananas,* a humor magazine for children aged twelve and older. He was thirty-two at the time and felt that he had achieved his life's ambition.

But greater success than he had ever dreamed of was still in store for him. For all his work in publishing, Stine had never published a book. His work on *Bananas* impressed an editor at Dutton, who asked him to create a humor book for children. *How To Be Funny:*

An Extremely Silly Guidebook was published in 1978 and led to a long string of funny books, many of which were published under the name "Jovial Bob Stine." When financial difficulties led to Stine being let go by Scholastic in 1985, he stepped up his career as a book author, turning out action-adventure and "twist-a-plot" stories (which allowed the readers to direct the action) in addition to his humorous story and joke books. In 1986, the editorial director at Scholastic asked him to try writing a horror novel for young adults. Stine obliged with *Blind Date,* and was pleasantly surprised at the book's success.

Young-adult horror was a fast-growing genre, and Stine proved he could duplicate the appeal of *Blind Date* with two subsequent scary tales, *Twisted* and *The Baby-Sitter.* Stine's wife Jane, who is also involved in the publishing industry, suggested that he try to come up with an idea for a series. Thus "Fear Street," a horror series designed for readers aged nine to fourteen, was born. Fear Street is a place where terrible things happen and where "your worst nightmares live," according to copy on the covers of the early titles. The main characters change from one book to the next, but all attend Shadyside High—a fictional school with an appalling frequency of murder. After "Fear Street" came the idea for "Goosebumps," a less gory but still spooky series for 8- to 11-year-old readers. Both "Fear Street" and "Goosebumps" rely on cliff-hanger endings in each chapter to keep readers turning the pages. Stine also works hard to make his fictional characters speak and act like real, modern kids, and he freely admits to using "cheap thrills" and "disgusting, gross things" to pump up the appeal of his stories, as he was quoted as saying in a *Time* article by Paul Gray.

In 1995, Stine took another big step in his career: publishing his first novel for adults, a horror story called *Superstitious.* Contrasting the book with Stine's young-adult offerings, a *Publishers Weekly* reviewer comments that in *Superstitious,* "several characters . . . curse, enjoy X-rated sex and die gruesomely detailed deaths." Characterizing Stine's writing as "crude yet functional," the reviewer concedes that "even those with minimal attention spans will keep turning pages," and concludes that the book is "about as sophisticated, though as effective, as jumping out from a dark corner and yelling 'boo!'"

BIOGRAPHICAL/CRITICAL SOURCES:

BOOKS

Contemporary Authors New Revision Series, Volume 53, Gale (Detroit), 1997.

PERIODICALS

Chicago Tribune, July 12, 1994, section 7, p. 1; December 6, 1994, section 7, p. 6.
English Journal, March, 1988, p. 86; April, 1989, p. 88.
Magazine of Fantasy and Science Fiction, August, 1995, p. 5.
New York Times, May 8, 1995, p. D8.
Publishers Weekly, August 22, 1986, p. 102; July 10, 1987, p. 71; June 9, 1989, p. 68; June 8, 1990, p. 56; September 19, 1994, p. 26; June 19, 1995, p. 47; July 17, 1995, pp. 208-9.
School Library Journal, November, 1986, pp. 108-9.
Time, August 2, 1993, p. 54.
USA Today, December 2, 1993, p. D6; October 27, 1994, p. D8; April 6, 1995, p. D4.
Voice of Youth Advocates, April, 1987, pp. 33, 34; December, 1987, p. 238; October, 1990, p. 220; February, 1991, p. 368; April, 1991, p. 9; June, 1991, p. 114; April, 1992, p. 36; August, 1992, p. 180; October, 1992, p. 232; December, 1992, p. 296; February, 1993, p. 360; April, 1993, pp. 20, 30,

47; June, 1993, p. 105; April, 1994, pp. 40, 41; August, 1994, p. 150; December, 1994, p. 290.
Washington Post, August 7, 1994, pp. B1, B4.

*   *   *

STONE, Irving 1903-1989

PERSONAL: Surname originally Tannenbaum; legally changed; born July 14, 1903, in San Francisco, CA; died of heart failure, August 26, 1989, in Los Angeles, CA; son of Charles Tannenbaum and Pauline (Rosenberg) Tannenbaum Stone; married Jean Factor (his editor since 1933), February 11, 1934; children: Paula Hubbell, Kenneth. *Education:* University of California, Berkeley, B.A., 1923, graduate study, 1924-26; University of Southern California, M.A., 1924. *Politics:* Independent. *Religion:* Jewish. *Avocational interests:* Collecting art.

CAREER: University of Southern California, Los Angeles, instructor in economics, 1923-24; University of California, Berkeley, instructor in economics, 1924-26; writer, 1926-89. Visiting professor of creative writing, University of Indiana, 1948, University of Washington, 1961, and Gustavus Adolphus College, 1982; lecturer, University of Southern California and California State Colleges, 1966, New York University and Johns Hopkins University, 1985. Specialist on cultural exchange for U.S. State Department to Soviet Union, Poland, and Yugoslavia, 1962; contributing member, American School of Classical Studies, Athens, Greece, 1965-89. Member of advisory board, University of California Institute for Creative Arts, 1963-89; founder, California State Colleges Committee for the Arts, 1967; member, Center for the Study of Evolution and the Origin of Life, University of California, Los Angeles, 1985. Member, U.S. delegation to Writers Conference, Kiev, Soviet Union, 1982; panelist, Nobel Conference on "Darwin's Legacy"; member, Soviet-American Writers Conference, Pepperdine University, 1984; Regents' professor, University of California, Los Angeles, 1984-89.

Member of California Civil War Centennial Commission, 1961-65, California Citizens' Committee for Higher Education, 1964, and California State Committee on Public Education, 1966-67. Member of Eleanor Roosevelt Memorial Foundation, 1963; vice-president, Eugene V. Debs Foundation, 1963-89; trustee, Douglass House Foundation, 1967-74; chairperson, Allan Nevins Memorial Fund, Huntington Library, 1972-89. Member of American Assembly, Columbia University, 1963-67; president, Beverly Hills Improvement Association, 1964-65. Founder with wife, Jean Stone, of two annual $1000 awards for the best biographical and historical novels published; founder, Jean and Irving Stone Honors Commons, University of California, Los Angeles, 1985.

MEMBER: Authors League of America, PEN, Society of American Historians, National Society of Arts and Letters (member of advisory council, 1976-89), Academy of American Motion Picture Arts and Sciences, Academy of Political Science, Academy of American Poets (founder), Western Writers of America, Renaissance Society of America, California Writers Guild (president, 1960-61), California Writers Club (honorary life member), Historical Society of Southern California, Fellows for Schweitzer (founder and president, 1955-89), Berkeley Fellows (charter member), Los Angeles Dante Alighieri Society (president, 1968-69).

AWARDS, HONORS: Christopher Award and Silver Spur Award from Western Writers of America, both 1957, for *Men to Match My Mountains;* Golden Lily of Florence, Rupert Hughes Award from Author's Club, Gold Medal from Council of American Artist Societies, and Gold Medal from Commonwealth Club of California, all for *The Agony and the Ecstasy;* named commendatore of Republic of Italy; American Revolution Round Table Award and Literary Father of the Year Award, both 1966, for *Those Who Love;* Gold Trophy from American Women in Radio and Television, 1968; Herbert Adams Memorial Medal from National Sculpture Society, 1970; Golden Plate Award from American Academy of Achievement, 1971; Alumnus of the Year from University of California, Berkeley, 1971; honorary citizen of Athens, Greece, 1972; Corpus Litterarum Award from Friends of the Libraries, University of California, Irvine, 1975; Distinguished Alumni Award from Los Angeles Unified School District, 1976; Author of the Year Award from Book Bank USA, 1976.

Distinguished body of work annual award, Los Angeles PEN Center, 1980; Rupert Hughes Award for excellence in writing from Author's Club, 1980; Call Achievement Award from University of Southern California, 1980; named Grand Ufficiale of the Italian Republic, 1982; Neil H. Jacoby Award from International Student Center, University of California at Los Angeles, 1983; honorary citation from Union of Soviet Writers, 1983; Commandeur dans l'Ordre des Arts et des Lettres from French Ministry of Culture, 1984; named Honorary Fellow of Southern California Historical Society, 1988. D.L. from University of Southern California, 1965; D.Litt. from Coe College, 1967, and California State Colleges, 1971; LL.D. from University of California, Berkeley, 1968; H.H.D. from Hebrew Union College, 1978.

WRITINGS:

Pageant of Youth, A. H. King, 1933.
Lust for Life (biographical novel about Vincent van Gogh; also see below), Longmans, Green, 1934, published with foreword by the author, Modern Library, 1939, published with reader's supplement, Washington Square Press, 1967, published as limited edition with portfolio of drawings by van Gogh, Franklin Library, 1980.
(Editor with wife, Jean Stone) *Dear Theo: The Autobiography of Vincent van Gogh,* Doubleday, 1937.
Sailor on Horseback (biographical novel about Jack London), Houghton, 1938, published as *Jack London, Sailor on Horseback,* Doubleday, 1947, published with twenty-eight stories by London as *Irving Stone's Jack London, His Life, Sailor on Horseback,* Doubleday, 1977.
False Witness (novel), Doubleday, 1940.
Clarence Darrow for the Defense (biography), Doubleday, 1941, abridged edition, Bantam, 1958.
Immortal Wife (biographical novel about Jessie Benton Fremont; also see below), Doubleday, 1944, condensed edition, 1954.
They Also Ran: The Story of the Men Who Were Defeated for the Presidency, Doubleday, 1945.
Adversary in the House (biographical novel about Eugene V. Debs), Doubleday, 1947.
Earl Warren: A Great American Story (biography), Prentice-Hall, 1948.
The Passionate Journey (biographical novel about John Noble), Doubleday, 1949.
We Speak for Ourselves: A Self-Portrait of America, Doubleday, 1950.

The President's Lady: A Biographical Novel of Rachel and Andrew Jackson (also see below), Doubleday, 1951.
Love Is Eternal: A Biographical Novel of Mary Todd and Abraham Lincoln, Doubleday, 1954, condensed large type edition, Ulverscroft, 1976.
Men to Match My Mountains: The Opening of the Far West, 1840-1900, Doubleday, 1956.
The Agony and the Ecstasy (biographical novel about Michelangelo Buonarroti; also see below), Doubleday, 1961, illustrated edition, 1963, published with illustrations by Bruce Waldman, Franklin Library, 1977, abridged juvenile edition with illustrations by Joseph Cellini published as *The Great Adventures of Michelangelo,* Doubleday, 1965.
(Editor with J. Stone) *I, Michelangelo, Sculptor: An Autobiography through Letters,* translated by Charles Speroni, Doubleday, 1962.
(Editor with Allan Nevins) *Lincoln: A Contemporary Portrait,* Doubleday, 1962.
Two Faces of Love: Lust for Life [and] *Immortal Wife,* Doubleday, 1962.
The Irving Stone Reader, Doubleday, 1963.
The Story of Michelangelo's Pieta, Doubleday, 1964.
Those Who Love (biographical novel about Abigail and John Adams), Doubleday, 1965.
(Editor and author of introduction) *There Was Light: Autobiography of a University; Berkeley,* Doubleday, 1970.
The Passions of the Mind (biographical novel about Sigmund Freud; Collectors Edition Club choice), Doubleday, 1971.
The Greek Treasure: A Biographical Novel of Henry and Sophia Schliemann, Doubleday, 1975.
The Origin (biographical novel about Charles Darwin), Doubleday, 1980.
Irving Stone: Three Complete Novels (includes *Lust for Life, The Agony and the Ecstasy,* and *The President's Lady*), Avenel Books, 1981.
Depths of Glory: A Biographical Novel of Camille Pissaro, Doubleday, 1985.
The Science, and the Art, of Biography (Naumburg Memorial lecture; monograph), Division of Honors, University of California, Los Angeles, 1986.
The Composition and Distribution of British Investment in Latin America, 1865-1913, Garland, 1987.
Keeping Spirit Journal, Doubleday, 1987.

OTHER

Magnificent Doll (screenplay), Universal, 1946.
(Editor, and author of introduction) *The Drawings of Michelangelo,* Borden Publishing, 1961.

Also author of *The Biographical Novel: A Lecture Presented at the Library of Congress,* 1957, *Evolution of an Idea,* 1965, and *Mary Todd Lincoln: A Final Judgment?,* 1973. Author of plays *The Dark Mirror,* 1928, *The White Life* (about Baruch Spinoza), 1929, and *Truly Valiant,* 1936, all produced in New York. Also contributor to *Fourteen Radio Plays,* edited by Arch Oboler, Random House. Art critic for the *Los Angeles Times Mirror,* 1959-60. Contributor to popular magazines, including *American Weekly, California Monthly, Catholic Digest, Coronet, Family Weekly, Good Housekeeping, Holiday, Horizon, Life, Saturday Evening Post, Saturday Review,* and *Suburbia Today.*

MEDIA ADAPTATIONS: Stone's novel *False Witness* was filmed by Republic in 1941 as *Arkansas Judge* and was released in Great Britain under its original title; *Immortal Wife* became a film by Twentieth Century-Fox in 1953 under the title *The President's*

Lady, starring Charlton Heston and Susan Hayward; *Lust for Life* was filmed by Metro-Goldwyn-Mayer in 1956 and starred Kirk Douglas and Anthony Quinn in an Academy Award-winning performance; *The Agony and the Ecstasy* was filmed by Twentieth Century-Fox in 1963 and starred Charlton Heston and Rex Harrison.

SIDELIGHTS: "Irving Stone is far and away the most magisterial of all the popular novelists working today," writes Peter Andrews in the *New York Times Book Review.* Although he has written both fiction and biography, Stone is considered the "undisputed king of the literary genre he terms 'biographical novel'" by critics such as Edwin McDowell of the *New York Times Book Review.* Ever since the publication more than fifty years ago of *Lust for Life,* his popular and enduring fictionalized biography of Vincent van Gogh, Stone has written best-selling biographical novels about such influential figures as Michelangelo in *The Agony and the Ecstasy,* Sigmund Freud in *The Passions of the Mind,* Charles Darwin in *The Origin,* and more recently, Camille Pissarro and the French impressionists in *The Depths of Glory.* While critics have been somewhat reluctant to appreciate the genre itself—considering it a mongrelized form that ultimately fails as biography as well as fiction—and have faulted Stone for what they perceive to be tedious, fact-laden tomes, they nonetheless commend his perseverance and meticulous research. "Searching relentlessly for evidence—letters, documents, records, scraps of paper—Stone has written a series of widely acclaimed books," says Marshall Berges in the *Los Angeles Times,* ". . . each time focusing on a long-departed giant and vividly restoring not only the era and the scene but most of all the person."

In the introduction to *The Irving Stone Reader,* Joseph Henry Jackson observes that working on his early detective stories taught Stone "the necessity of careful plotting, the trick of keeping a narrative on the move, the techniques of construction." Jackson suggests, however, that "the kind of spark that would fire his imagination . . . was character-ready-made, the story of someone who had lived, whose acts could be found in the record and whose motives might be traced by patient, careful, sympathetic investigation." What motivates Stone to bring a given character to life is "any suspicion that such a character had been misunderstood, perhaps even misrepresented through historical accident or through an early biographer's prejudice." While critical response to Stone's work has not paralleled his popularity, Peter Gorner maintains in the *Chicago Tribune* that most people are probably indebted to Stone for what they know about van Gogh, Freud, and Michelangelo, and that "Stone also has written about lesser-known folks he felt people should learn about. . . . And he has been quick to portray great lives he believes were unfairly wounded by cheap shots."

In *The Science, and the Art, of Biography* (his Naumburg Memorial Lecture at the University of California, Los Angeles), Stone presents his thoughts on the genre he has fostered and on the author's responsibility toward it: "The biographical novel is a true and documented story of one human being's journey across the face of the years, transmuted from the raw material of life into the delight and purity of an authentic art form. It is based on the conviction that the best of all plots lie in human character; and that human character is endlessly colorful and revealing. The biographical novel sets out to document this truth, for character is plot; character development is action; and character fulfillment is resolution." Stone also explains that while biography involves three persons—the subject, the reader, and the author as a mediator between them—the biographical novel involves but two,

since the author merges with his subject: "The author becomes the main character by years of intense study of his diaries, journals, correspondence, recorded dialogues, writings about him, his finished work, his character, personality, his manner of speaking, acting; geographic place in the world. The author slips slowly and authentically into his bloodstream, the millions of cells in his brain, the feelings in his gut and nervous system. A total portrait of this one human being's values, his beatings and failures, accomplishments and fulfillments."

Stone indicates to Grace Glueck in the *New York Times* that his preference for the biographical novel over nonfictionalized biography is partially due to the opportunity it affords him to use the "novelistic skills" he acquired during his early attempts at writing plays. But he also says: "I know from experience that biographies have a limited audience. We have thousands of readers who love [the biographical novel] and are thrilled by it, who'd never get near a conventional biography." In *The Science, and the Art, of Biography,* Stone asserts that "the research, dedication and techniques of the biographical novelist are identical to those of the biographer. The major difference is one of dramatization." Perhaps because of his efforts to champion the underdog or to set the historical record straight, Stone is aware of his responsibility for accurate representation in his work and has produced monumentally impressive research for each book. Moreover, Stone's patient and careful research has brought much previously unpublished and important information into print. In addition to the letters of Michelangelo, Stone has had access to van Gogh's letters and Freud's papers, as well as access to the friends and relatives of his more contemporary subjects.

Stone's research for *Lust for Life* included a stay not only in van Gogh's asylum cell but also, on the fortieth anniversary of his death, in the very room in which van Gogh died. As Stone recalls in *The Science, and the Art, of Biography:* "On the very night that Vincent died I went to bed about midnight, surrounded by colored reproductions of his canvases. I pored over them until one o'clock when I began to feel faint. I could not understand why until I realized that Vincent had died in that very bed at 1:20 in the morning. I grew fainter, until finally at 1:19 I threw off the covers, dashed to the back window, stuck my head out and took in deep lungsful of the night air."

Stone's intense identification with his subjects has prompted several critics to question the extent of his objectivity. In a review of *Lust for Life* in the *Nation,* for instance, Robert Morse suggests that "from a novelist one might have hoped for a dispassionate and honest attempt to clarify and explain the behavior of an extremely interesting human being. . . . I began to suspect that . . . Stone had fallen into the old attitude of unquestioning sentimental identification with his hero." However, a reviewer for the *Boston Transcript* notes in defense of this novel: "Stone did not need to call this fiction. Many biographers have taken more liberties with less results. There is reality here, pathos, humor, a knowledge of art and artists, and a delightful, nonchalant style which keeps us fascinated . . . to the end."

Decrying Stone's method of interpreting the life and motivation of his subject by "becoming" that character, some critics suggest that Stone tends toward idealization. R. J. Clements, for example, finds *The Agony and the Ecstasy* "an important and thoroughly enjoyable novel," but says in the *Saturday Review* that "Stone's Michelangelo is an idealized version, purged not only of ambisexuality, but of the egotism, faultfinding, harsh irony, and ill temper that we know were characteristic of Michelangelo." And although a *Kirkus Reviews* contributor calls *The Agony and the Ecstasy* "an enormous book, in scope, in historical background, in depth perception and characterization," others feel it is simply not a very good novel. Moreover, despite the enormous sales of his novels, many critics seem to agree that Stone is better suited to historical and biographical nonfiction. In the *New York Herald Tribune,* for example, Richard Winston distinguishes between Stone's weaknesses and his obvious talent: "How elegant and convincing some of . . . Stone's shrewd guesses and fictional insights might have been in a straight biography—whereas here they are so often embarrassing and give rise to uneasiness and dissatisfaction."

The critics' obvious admiration for Stone's impressive research does not prevent them from questioning his manipulation of the collected data. In the *Atlantic,* Steven Marcus praises Stone's fictionalized biography of Freud, *The Passions of the Mind,* for its bibliography, calling it "daunting in its compendiousness, impressive evidence of the earnestness with which [Stone] has taken this work to himself." However, he also believes that "the novel constitutes itself by an incessant, indiscriminate, and incontinent regurgitation of second-hand information." Similarly, Richard Locke refers to the book in the *New York Times* as "a 'massively researched' erector set of a novel crammed with biographical, architectural, gastronomical, geographical, medical, historical details." And while Edwin Fadiman, Jr. observes in *Saturday Review* that "the author's integrity is revealed in every line," he adds that "it is precisely this glacial earnestness, this obsession with detail that make *The Passions of the Mind* praiseworthy yet dull." In *Time,* Brad Darrach calls Stone "the taxidermist of biography" and suggests that he "seems more interested in the facts than he is in Freud." Several critics think that the accumulation of detail inhibits the reader's awareness of any inner evolution on the part of the subject. Marcus, for instance, writes: "There is suggested none of the pathological involvement without which a genius of Freud's magnitude is almost unthinkable. It is Freud without the warts." Yet Rosalind Wade calls the book "a magnificent memorial to Freud's achievement" in the *Contemporary Review.* "Apart from being an excellent narrative in its own right the book affords an illuminating blue-print of the means by which psychotherapy was belatedly accepted during the 'twenties and 'thirties in the London teaching hospitals,"

Some critics feel that because Stone's research is so thorough he may be overwhelmed by its sheer mass. Susan Isaacs, for example, finds that Stone's book about Camille Pissarro and the French impressionists, *The Depths of Glory,* "lacks the verve, narrative device and structure that made his earlier work so enjoyable." She adds in the *New York Times Book Review* that "this book is little more than mere data." Believing the purpose of detail should be "to flesh out character or add texture to the setting," Isaacs thinks "Stone seems overwhelmed by the piles of information he's gathered, and manages only the weakest narrative thread." However, Daniel Fuchs notes in the *Los Angeles Times Book Review* that Stone "willingly forgoes the useful devices of fiction—the suspense that comes from organized plot and drama, the winning, fictional characters, the manufactured pleasures and excitement and surprise of the actual event." Stone expressed to Glueck that he would like to see Camille Pissarro become as well-known as Vincent van Gogh, and Glueck remarks that "though as a subject, Pissarro lacks the glamour of Van Gogh and Michelangelo . . . Stone has spared no detail that might pique the reader's interest. He gives a full picture of Pissarro's travails as a painter and a family man . . . and conjures up a Paris art world where the schmaltz runs deep."

Stone admits that as a writer he may be verbose. His wife edits all his work and routinely cuts about ten percent of it before a finished product is achieved—a finished product which some reviewers may claim is still too long. Stone and his work, though, have prevailed over the critics, whom he refers to in *The Science, and the Art, of Biography* as "my sometimes critics—and how barren an author's life would be without critics!" The popularity of his work is certainly confirmed by the many languages into which it has been translated: French, German, Spanish, Italian, Greek, Swedish, Turkish, Arabic, Japanese, Russian, Finnish, Norwegian, Danish, Dutch, Portuguese, Polish, Hungarian, Rumanian, Czech, Slovene, Hebrew, Assamese, Hindu, Tamil, Gujarati, Kannada, Marathi, Kanarese, Bengali, Malayan, Latvian, Serbo-Croatian, Persian, Bratislavian, and Icelandic. Surmising that "the secret of the popularity of . . . Stone's novels may very well lie in their unreadability," Andrews remarks in the *New York Times Book Review* that getting through one of his books "gives one a sense of accomplishment." Perhaps, however, the secret rests in the formula Stone uses for his books. "The recurring theme," notes Gorner, "is one man (or woman) against the world, succeeding no matter what." Stone elaborated on this theme to Berges: "My goal always is to tell a universal story, meaning it's about a person who has an idea, a vision, a dream, an ambition to make the world somewhat less chaotic. He or she suffers hardships, defeats, miseries, illnesses, poverty, crushing blows. But ultimately that person accomplishes a big, beautiful, gorgeous job of work, leaving behind a testimonial that the human mind can grow and accomplish fantastic ends."

BIOGRAPHICAL/CRITICAL SOURCES:

BOOKS

Contemporary Authors Autobiography Series, Volume 3, Gale (Detroit), 1986.
Contemporary Literary Criticism, Volume 7, Gale, 1977.
Newquist, Roy, *Counterpoint,* Rand McNally, 1964.
Punchuk, Svetlana A., *Cross-Cultural Studies: American, Canadian and European Literatures: 1945-1985,* Filozofska Fakulteta, 1988.

PERIODICALS

Atlantic Monthly, May, 1961; November, 1965; April, 1971.
Boston Transcript, September 26, 1934.
British Book News, January, 1982, pp. 9-13.
Catholic World, August, 1961.
Chicago Sunday Tribune, March 26, 1961.
Chicago Tribune, August 26, 1980; August 28, 1989.
Christian Science Monitor, October 17, 1934; September 27, 1951; October 14, 1954; August 30, 1962; October 30, 1985, p. 20.
Contemporary Review, July, 1971.
English Journal, September, 1992, p. 97.
Journalism Quarterly, winter, 1977, pp. 804-5.
Kirkus Reviews, July 15, 1956; January 15, 1961.
Library Journal, October 15, 1991, p. 140.
Los Angeles Times, August 28, 1989.
Los Angeles Times Book Review, November 18, 1984; October 20, 1985.
Nation, November 7, 1934.
New Republic, September 21, 1938; June 5, 1971.
Newsweek, November 1, 1965.
New Yorker, June 26, 1995, p. 69.
New York Herald Tribune, September 26, 1934.
New York Herald Tribune Book Review, September 28, 1947; August 22, 1954; September 30, 1956.

New York Herald Tribune Lively Arts, March 19, 1961.
New York Times, September 30, 1934; September 18, 1938; April 14, 1940; November 9, 1941; October 1, 1944; March 27, 1971; August 7, 1980; October 16, 1985; August 28, 1989.
New York Times Book Review, March 19, 1961; August 26, 1962; March 14, 1965; November 7, 1965; March 14, 1971; August 20, 1972; October 12, 1975; September 14, 1980, pp. 12-13; August 9, 1981; September 16, 1984, p. 42; October 20, 1985, p. 16.
Publishers Weekly, December 6, 1991, p. 44.
Punch, July 5, 1993, p. 30.
Saturday Review, August 21, 1954; March 18, 1961; May 15, 1965; November 20, 1965; April 10, 1971, p. 26; May 27, 1972, p. 74; August, 1980, p. 66.
Saturday Review of Literature, September 30, 1944; September 29, 1951.
Science, January 16, 1981.
Spectator, May 29, 1971, pp. 739-41.
Time, September 19, 1938; November 5, 1965; April 5, 1971; September 15, 1975; October 10, 1977; November 11, 1985; September 11, 1989, p. 73.
Times (London), August 29, 1989.
Times Literary Supplement, July 13, 1967; April 6, 1971; January 2, 1976; June 19, 1981.
Variety, August 30, 1989, p. 97.
Washington Post, April 2, 1971; August 28, 1989.
Washington Post Book World, August 22, 1980.
World Literature Today, winter, 1980.

*   *   *

STONE, Rosetta
See GEISEL, Theodor Seuss

*   *   *

STOPPARD, Tom 1937-
(William Boot)

PERSONAL: Original name, Tomas Straussler; born July 3, 1937, in Zlin, Czechoslovakia; naturalized British citizen; son of Eugene Straussler (a physician) and Martha Stoppard; married Jose Ingle, 1965 (divorced, 1972); married Miriam Moore-Robinson (a physician), 1972 (divorced); children: (first marriage) Oliver, Barnaby; (second marriage) two sons. *Education:* Educated in England and Europe.

ADDRESSES: Home—Chelsea Harbor, London, England. *Agent*—Peters, Fraser & Dunlop, The Chambers, 5th Floor, Chelsea Harbor, Lots Road, London SW10 0XF, England.

CAREER: Playwright, novelist, and radio and television script writer. *Western Daily Press,* Bristol, England, reporter and critic, 1954-58; *Evening World,* Bristol, reporter, 1958-60; freelance reporter, 1960-63. Director of play *Born Yesterday,* London, England, 1973; director of film *Rosencrantz and Guildenstern Are Dead,* 1991. Member of Royal National Theatre Board, 1989–.

MEMBER: Royal Society of Literature (fellow).

AWARDS, HONORS: Ford Foundation grant to Berlin, 1964; John Whiting Award, Arts Council of Great Britain, 1967; *Evening Standard* Drama Awards, 1967, for most promising playwright, 1972, for best play *Jumpers,* 1974, for best comedy *Travesties,*

and 1983, for best play *The Real Thing; Plays and Players.* Awards for best new play, 1967, for *Rosencrantz and Guildenstern Are Dead,* and 1972, for *Jumpers;* Prix Italia, 1968, for *Albert's Bridge;* Antoinette Perry Awards for best play, 1968, for *Rosencrantz and Guildenstern Are Dead,* 1976, for *Travesties,* and 1984, for *The Real Thing;* New York Drama Critics Circle Awards, 1968, for best play *Rosencrantz and Guildenstern Are Dead,* 1976, for best play *Travesties,* and 1984, for best foreign play *The Real Thing;* M.Lit., University of Bristol, 1976, Brunel University, 1979, University of Sussex, 1980; Commander, Order of the British Empire, 1978; London *Evening Standard* Awards, 1978, for *Night and Day,* and 1982, for *The Real Thing;* Shakespeare Prize, Hamburg, 1979; Academy Award nomination, and Los Angeles Critics Circle Award for best original screenplay (with Terry Gilliam and Charles McKeown), both 1985, both for *Brazil;* Grand Prize, Venice Film Festival, 1990, for *Rosencrantz and Guildenstern Are Dead; Evening Standard* Best Play Award, 1993, for *Arcadia;* Oliver Award, 1994.

WRITINGS:

PLAYS

The Gamblers, produced in Bristol, England, 1965.
Tango (based on the play by Slawomir Mrozek; produced in London, 1966; produced on the West End, 1968), J. Cape, 1968.
Rosencrantz and Guildenstern Are Dead (three-act; also see below; first produced at Edinburgh Festival, 1966; produced on the West End, 1967; produced on Broadway, 1967), Samuel French, 1967.
Enter a Free Man (based on his teleplay *A Walk on the Water* [also see below]; first produced on the West End, 1968; produced off-Broadway, 1974), Faber, 1968, Grove, 1969.
The Real Inspector Hound (one-act; first produced on the West End, 1968; produced off-Broadway with *After Magritte,* 1972), Samuel French, 1968.
Albert's Bridge [and] *If You're Glad I'll Be Frank* (based on his radio plays [also see below]), produced in Edinburgh, 1969, produced in New York, 1987.
After Magritte (one-act; first produced in London, 1970; produced off-Broadway with *The Real Inspector Hound,* 1972), Faber, 1971, Grove, 1972.
Dogg's Our Pet (also see below; produced in London, 1971), published in *Six of the Best,* Inter-Action Imprint, 1976.
Jumpers (first produced on the West End, 1972; produced in Washington, DC, at the Kennedy Center, 1974; produced on Broadway, 1974), Grove, 1972, revised edition, Faber, 1986.
The House of Bernarda Alba (based on the play by Federico Garcia Lorca), produced in London, 1973.
Travesties (produced on the West End, 1974; produced on Broadway, 1974), Grove, 1975.
Dirty Linen and New-Found-Land (produced in London, 1976; produced on Broadway, 1977), Grove, 1976.
Every Good Boy Deserves Favor, music by Andre Previn, first produced in London, 1977, produced on the West End, 1978, produced at the Metropolitan Opera House, 1979.
Night and Day (produced on the West End, 1978; produced on Broadway, 1979), Grove, 1979, revised edition, Samuel French, 1980.
Dogg's Hamlet, Cahoot's Macbeth (double-bill of one-act plays; *Dogg's Hamlet* based on his play *Dogg's Our Pet;* produced in New York, 1979), Faber, 1979.
Undiscovered Country (adapted from Arthur Schnitzler's *Das Weite Land;* produced on the West End, 1979; produced in Hartford, CT, 1981), Faber, 1980, Samuel French, 1984.

On the Razzle (adapted from Johann Nestroy's *Einen Jux will er sich machen;* produced on the West End, 1981; produced in Los Angeles, CA, 1985), Faber, 1981.

The Real Thing (produced on the West End, 1982; produced on Broadway, 1984), Faber, 1982, revised edition, 1983.

Rough Crossing (adaptation of Ferenc Molnar's *The Play's the Thing;* produced in London, 1984; produced in New York, 1990), Faber, 1985.

Dalliance (adapted from Schnitzler's *Liebelei*), produced in London, 1986.

(Translator) Vaclav Havel, *Largo Desolato,* Faber, 1987.

Hapgood (produced in London and New York, 1988), Faber, 1988.

Artist Descending a Staircase (based on his radio play [also see below]; produced on the West End, 1988; produced on Broadway, 1989), Faber, 1990.

Arcadia, produced in London, 1994; produced on Broadway, 1995.

Also author of *Home and Dry* and *Riley.*

SCREENPLAYS

(With Thomas Wiseman) *The Romantic Englishwoman,* New World Pictures, 1975.

Despair (adapted from the novel by Vladimir Nabokov), New Line Cinema, 1978.

The Human Factor (adapted from the novel by Graham Greene), Metro-Goldwyn-Mayer (MGM), 1980.

(With Terry Gilliam and Charles McKeown) *Brazil,* Universal, 1985.

Empire of the Sun (adapted from the novel by J. G. Ballard), Warner Brothers, 1987.

The Russia House (adapted from the novel by John le Carre), MGM/United Artists, 1989.

(And director) *Rosencrantz and Guildenstern Are Dead* (adapted from his play), Cinecom, 1991, published as *Rosencrantz and Guildenstern Are Dead: The Film,* Faber, 1991.

Billy Bathgate (adapted from the novel by E. L. Doctorow), Touchstone, 1991.

FOR TELEVISION

A Walk on the Water, ITV Television, 1963, broadcast as *The Preservation of George Riley,* British Broadcasting Corporation (BBC-TV), 1964.

A Separate Peace, BBC-TV, 1966, published by Samuel French, 1977.

Teeth, BBC-TV, 1967.

Another Moon Called Earth, BBC-TV, 1967.

Neutral Ground, Thames Television, 1968.

The Engagement (based on his radio play *The Dissolution of Dominic Boot* [also see below]), *Experiment in Television,* NBC-TV, 1970.

One Pair of Eyes, BBC-TV, 1972.

(With Clive Exton) *Eleventh House,* BBC-TV, 1975.

(With Exton) *Boundaries,* BBC-TV, 1975.

Three Men in a Boat (based on the novel by Jerome K. Jerome), BBC-TV, 1975.

Professional Foul, BBC-TV, 1977, Public Broadcasting Service (PBS-TV), 1978.

Squaring the Circle: Poland, 1980-81, BBC-TV, 1985, published by Faber, 1985.

FOR RADIO

The Dissolution of Dominic Boot, BBC, 1964.

"M" Is for Moon among Other Things, BBC, 1964.

If You're Glad I'll Be Frank, BBC, 1966, published by Faber, 1969.

Albert's Bridge, BBC, 1967.

Where Are They Now? BBC, 1970.

Artist Descending a Staircase, BBC, 1972.

The Dog It Was That Died, BBC, 1982.

In the Native State, BBC, 1991, revised edition published as *Indian Ink,* Faber, 1995.

Indian Ink, Faber and Faber (Boston; London), 1995.

Also author of episodes of radio serials *The Dales,* 1964, and *A Student's Diary,* 1965.

OMNIBUS VOLUMES

Albert's Bridge [and] *If You're Glad I'll Be Frank: Two Plays for Radio,* Faber, 1969.

The Real Inspector Hound [and] *After Magritte,* Grove, 1970.

Artist Descending a Staircase and Where Are They Now?: Two Plays for Radio, Faber, 1973.

Albert's Bridge, and Other Plays, Grove, 1977.

Every Good Boy Deserves Favor [and] *Professional Foul,* Grove, 1978.

The Dog It Was That Died, and Other Plays (contains *Teeth Another Moon Called Earth, Neutral Ground, A Separate Peace, "M" Is for Moon among Other Things,* and *The Dissolution of Dominic Boot*), Faber, 1983.

Four Plays for Radio, Faber, 1984.

Dalliance [and] *Undiscovered Country,* Faber, 1986.

Stoppard: The Radio Plays 1964-1983, Faber, 1991.

OTHER

Lord Malquist and Mr. Moon (novel), Anthony Blond, 1966, Knopf, 1968.

(With Paul Delaney), *Tom Stoppard in Conversation,* University of Michigan Press (Ann Arbor), 1994.

(With Mel Gussow), *Conversations with Stoppard,* Limelight (New York City), 1995.

Conversations with Tom Stoppard, Grove (New York City), 1996.

Contributor of short stories to *Introduction 2,* 1964. Reviewer, sometimes under pseudonym William Boot, for *Scene,* 1962.

SIDELIGHTS: Tom Stoppard's plays have revolutionized modern theater with their uniquely comic combinations of verbal intricacy, complex structure, and philosophical themes. With such award-winning works as *Rosencrantz and Guildenstern Are Dead, Jumpers, Travesties,* and *The Real Thing* to his credit, Stoppard compares with "the masters of the comic tradition," Joan Fitzpatrick Dean writes in *Tom Stoppard: Comedy as a Moral Matrix.* "Like the best comic dramatists, his gift for language and physical comedy fuses with an active perception of the excesses, eccentricities, and foibles of man." "Stoppard is that peculiar anomaly—a serious comic writer born in an age of tragicomedy and a renewed interest in theatrical realism," Enoch Brater summarizes in *Essays on Contemporary British Drama.* "Such deviation from dramatic norms . . . marks his original signature on the contemporary English stage," the critic continues, for his "'high comedy of ideas' is a refreshing exception to the rule. Offering us 'a funny play,' Stoppard's world 'makes coherent, in terms of theatre, a fairly complicated intellectual argument.' That the argument is worth making, that it is constantly developing and sharpening its focus, and that it always seeks to engage an audience in a continuing dialogue, are the special characteristics of Stoppard's dramatic achievement. They are also the features which dignify and ultimately transform the comic tradition to which his work belongs."

"Tom Stoppard's virtuosity was immediately apparent" in his first major dramatic work *Rosencrantz and Guildenstern Are Dead,* Mel Gussow of the *New York Times* asserts. The play revisits Shakespeare's *Hamlet* through the eyes of the two players whose task of delivering Hamlet's death sentence prompts their own execution instead. Vaguely aware of the scheming at Elsinore and their own irrelevance to it, Rosencrantz and Guildenstern meander through the drama playing games of language and chance until, circumscribed by Shakespeare's script, they cease to exist. "In focusing on Shakespeare's minor characters Stoppard does not fill out their lives but rather extends their thinness," Anne Wright observes in her *Dictionary of Literary Biography* essay. By turning *Hamlet* "inside out" in this way, the play is able "to be simultaneously frivolous in conception but dead serious in execution," Brater states, and it addresses issues of existentialism reminiscent of Samuel Beckett's drama *Waiting for Godot.* The result, the critic adds, "is not only a relaxed view of *Hamlet,* but a new kind of comic writing halfway between parody and travesty."

Also notable is the play's innovative use of language and Shakespeare's actual text. *Rosencrantz and Guildenstern* is interwoven with references to *Hamlet* as well as actual lines of the bard's verse; in addition, Stoppard packs the drama with "intricate word plays, colliding contradictions and verbal and visual puns," as Gussow describes it. This "stylistic counterpoint of Shakespeare's poetry and rhetoric with the colloquial idiom of the linguistic games and music-hall patter" proves very effective, Wright comments. "Stoppard's lines pant with inner panic," a *Time* reviewer notes, as the title characters, according to *Village Voice*'s Michael Smith, ultimately "talk themselves out of existence." The play has become one of Stoppard's most popular and acclaimed works; twenty years after its premiere, Gussow concludes, *Rosencrantz and Guildenstern* "remains an acrobatic display of linguistic pyrotechnics as well as a provocative existential comedy about life in limbo."

"In *Jumpers,* much of the action and humor hinges on linguistic ambiguities and confusions," G. B. Crump writes in *Contemporary Literature.* "These confusions mirror larger ambiguities present in the reality represented in the drama." As Brater elaborates, the play "never fixes moral philosophy and musical comedy in any stable order, hierarchy, or progression." The consequence, C. W. E. Bigsby relates in *Contemporary Dramatists,* is that "the relativity of truth, man's apparent need to divert himself from painful realities, the failure of language to do more than parody conviction, the inability of the rational mind to adequately explain man to himself—all these coalesce in a play which unites the very best of Stoppard's characteristics as a playwright—a mastery of language, a clear sense of style and rhythm, and a wit which has both a verbal and visual dimension."

A *Times Literary Supplement* reviewer, however, believes that in *Jumpers* Stoppard's complex language overwhelms the drama: "Good intentions are swamped by words that get nowhere. No actor speaking this highly intellectual and convoluted jargon can talk and move at the same time. To be heard and understood, the actor must stand still and the stage around him must freeze." Thus, the critic continues, "the stage loses its scenic power, the word its resonance, and therefore, the playfulness of the 'play' is muted." In contrast, other critics find the playwright's linguistic intricacies suited to his sophisticated humor and ideas. Victor L. Cahn, for instance, states in his book *Beyond Absurdity: The Plays of Tom Stoppard* that Stoppard's "emphasis on variety of language" demonstrates his "belief in man's ability to communicate. He manages at the same time to make his language amusing, yet

richly woven with ideas." "Stoppard is one of those rare writers who can move easily between treating language as an object in itself and making it totally transparent to meaning," Jack Kroll of *Newsweek* likewise reports. In addition, this verbal ability allows Stoppard to successfully draw from and merge with the work of other writers; as Susan Rusinko claims in *World Literature Today,* "His inventive puns, parodies, and pastiches brilliantly serve the cause of theatricality to the point that the original disappears with the wave of the word magician's wand."

Stoppard makes use of another dramatic "adaptation" in his second Tony Award-winner, *Travesties.* The play takes as its starting point the historical fact that Zurich of 1917 was inhabited by three revolutionaries: the communist leader Lenin, modernist writer James Joyce, and dadaist poet-critic Tristan Tzara. Their interactions are related through the recollections of Henry Carr, a minor British official who meets Lenin at the local library and the others during a production of Oscar Wilde's *The Importance of Being Earnest.* In a manner similar to that of *Rosencrantz and Guildenstern,* Stoppard uses plot line and characterization from Wilde's play to parallel and emphasize events and characters in his own work; the play "races forward on Mr. Stoppard's verbal roller coaster, leaving one dizzy yet exhilarated by its sudden semantic twists, turns, dips, and loops," Wilborn Hampton remarks in the *New York Times.* The result, Wright asserts, is "a virtuoso piece, a 'travesty' of the style of each of its masters, including Joycean narrative and dadaist verse as well as Wildean wit. The parody extends to the discourse appropriate to Lenin, as the play incorporates lectures and polemical sequences."

Stoppard's political concerns come to the fore in *Every Good Boy Deserves Favor,* a piece for actors and orchestra set to the music of Andre Previn. Set in a prison hospital inhabited by lunatics and dissidents, *Every Good Boy* "has the witty dialogue and clever plot that we associate with Stoppard's plays, and a sense of social concern that we didn't," *Los Angeles Times* critic Dan Sullivan recounts. Stoppard brings the musicians into the action of the play through the character of a madman who believes he conducts an imaginary orchestra; not only does the group respond to his direction, but one of the violinists doubles as his psychiatrist. The play's use of "irony, mixed identities, outrageous conceits (not to mention a full-scale symphony orchestra)," observes *Washington Post* contributor Michael Billington, distinguishes it as "the work of a dazzling high-wire performer." In addition, the critic notes, *Every Good Boy* is "a profoundly moral play about the brainwashing of political dissidents in Soviet mental hospitals."

John Simon of *New York,* however, faults the play for being "too clever by half," and adds that the concept of a play for full orchestra seems forced and contrived. But Gussow, in his review of the Metropolitan Opera production, posits that "the full orchestra and the enormous stage give the play a richness and even an opulence that embellishes the author's comic point of view." He continues: "So much of the comedy comes from the contrast between the small reality—two men in a tiny cell—and the enormity of the delusion." "Nothing if not imaginative, Stoppard's plot makes the orchestra an active, provocative participant in the story," Richard Christiansen of the *Chicago Tribune* similarly avers. Nevertheless, the critic advises, the play also stands "on its own as a moving and eloquent work, an occasional piece of quick wit and deep thoughtfulness."

With *Night and Day* Stoppard broached another "public issue—the role of the press in what is commonly called the Western World," as James Lardner describes it in the *Washington Post.* Set in an African nation beset by revolution, *Night and Day* looks at issues of censorship, politics, colonialism, and journalistic ethics through the character of a young, idealistic reporter. "There are theatergoers who will not sit still for a play that encompasses an intellectual debate, no matter how gracefully rendered," Lardner theorizes. Indeed, some observers have criticized the play for emphasizing ideas over characters; *New York Times* reviewer Walter Kerr, for instance, says that "virtually no effort is made during the evening to link up thought and events, arguments and action. The debate really takes place in a void." In contrast, Judith Martin believes that in *Night and Day* "it even seems as if the good lines were written for the play, rather than the play's having been written to display unrelated good cracks," as she writes in the *Washington Post Weekend.* "This is a taut drama, dealing intelligently and with a degree of moral passion with a range of difficult issues," Wright concludes. "Moreover, despite its clear plea for freedom of speech and action, the play does not oversimplify the issues: *Night and Day* presents a genuine dramatic debate which confronts divergent and often contradictory attitudes."

In the double-bill *Dogg's Hamlet, Cahoot's Macbeth,* Stoppard "brilliantly harnesses his linguistic ingenuity to his passion for the cause of artistic freedom," Gerald M. Berkowitz notes in *Theatre Journal.* In the first half, *Dogg's Hamlet,* a group of schoolboys contort the English language by giving entirely new meanings to familiar words; their interactions with puzzled outsiders culminate in an abbreviated performance of *Hamlet.* The second play, *Cahoot's Macbeth,* presents an underground performance of Shakespeare which is interrupted by government censors; only by switching to "Dogg," the language of the first play, do the actors avoid arrest. Critics have split over the effectiveness of this double-bill; *Chicago Tribune* writer Sid Smith, for instance, finds that the second play "promises more than it delivers, certainly more than a rehash of the first play's comedy." Berkowitz, however, thinks that "Stoppard knows what he's doing," for instead of reducing "this serious play to the farcical level of the first" the switch to Dogg reinforces his message, which "strikes us with tremendous power: repressive societies fear artistic expression because it is a 'language' they don't share and thus can't control." As a result, the critic concludes, *Dogg's Hamlet, Cahoot's Macbeth* "may well be [Stoppard's] most important play so far, and a harbinger of major works to come."

Berkowitz's words were prophetic, for in 1982 Stoppard premiered one of his most highly acclaimed dramas, *The Real Thing.* While the playwright returned to a favorite form, that of the play-within-a-play, his subject—"an imaginatively and uniquely theatrical exploration of the pain and the power of love," as Christiansen characterizes it—surprised many critics. The opening reveals a man confronting his wife with evidence of her adultery; it soon becomes clear, however, that this encounter is only a scene in a play. "Reality" is much more complex, for the actors in the first scene are being betrayed by their spouses—the playwright and his mistress Annie, another actress. Henry is the successful author of witty, cerebral dramas of infidelity, but his own struggles with love, especially those in his sometimes-troubled marriage to Annie, prove more difficult and painful. Annie's romantic involvement with a young actor and professional involvement with the young revolutionary Brodie cause Henry to not only question his assumptions about love, but his opinions about the significance of writing. While the meaning of the "real thing" might seem a commonplace theme for Stoppard to examine, "home truths can be banal," Sullivan observes. "All that

an author can do is to write a non-banal play around them, and this Stoppard has done."

Stoppard's *Arcadia* juxtaposes three different time periods on one stage—the years 1809 and 1812 as well as present day—and combines such topics as mathematics and chaos theory, landscape gardening, and Lord Byron. In addition, notes Anne Barton in the *New York Review of Books,* "*Arcadia* constantly engages the imaginary in a dialogue with the historically true." Several reviewers noted the need for playgoers to review the printed text before seeing the play, seeing the play twice, or utilizing both methods to yield a better understanding of the complex story. In terms of staging and theatrics, however, "*Arcadia* is muted by comparison with most of Stoppard's previous work," finds Barton. Barton praises the effort, hailing it as "wonderfully inventive and funny, full of the epigrams, puns and verbal pyrotechnics characteristic of this dramatist." Joseph Hynes, commenting in the *Virginia Quarterly Review,* praises Stoppard's effort as "the wittiest, most movingly paradoxical, English dramatic language of this half-century."

Stoppard's personal insights into his work are captured in the book, *Conversations with Stoppard.* Spanning a twenty-year period, these conversations are the result of interviews Stoppard had with theater critic Mel Gussow and focus primarily on the development of and influences on his work. Bevya Rosten in *The New York Times Book Review* remarks, "Mr. Gussow offers a chance to engage with the witty and quirky mind of a unique artist." Susan Rushinko, writing in *World Literature Today,* comments that "Stoppard's remarks about his writing habits and sources of ideas for his plays are as freewheeling and as fascinating as the debates in his plays." Rushinko also notes Stoppard's confession of his "early admiration for Margaret Thatcher and Rupert Murdoch" as well as his sources of names for his characters. However, Jane Montgomery, writing for the *Times Literary Supplement,* finds Gussow to have been somewhat lax in his interviewing methods. "Gussow's interrogation is not probing . . . nor is his search for Stoppard's inner balance particularly contingent. His prepared questions often appear stilted in context, and he seems to rely chiefly on Stoppard's own graceful loquacity to steer the conversation." "On one level," Montgomery continues, "this is informative and interesting. . . . But just how many of [Stoppard's] 'apparent impromptus' were 'worked out beforehand' is the kind of interesting question Gussow will not, or cannot, address."

Stoppard's talents extend beyond writing for the stage; he is also noted for several highly literate screenplay adaptations, such as *Empire of the Sun, The Russia House,* and his own *Rosencrantz and Guildenstern Are Dead.* He has also distinguished himself as the creator of original works for radio, and he is "one of the writers who use the medium most imaginatively," Ronald Hayman states in the *Times Literary Supplement,* for Stoppard "enjoys doing what can't be done on any other medium." The playwright makes the most of the exclusively aural medium, for in works such as *Albert's Bridge* and *If You're Glad I'll Be Frank* "what is left to the imagination gives the comedy its impetus," Gussow observes. As Rollyson explains, this strategy works well because Stoppard "is under no constraint to hew to the facts or to balance his facility with words against the action or visualization for the stage and screen." In addition, Stoppard told Paul Donovan of the *Sunday Times Review,* "If you are dependent only on what people can hear, you can jerk things around in time and space, draw parallels and spin loops." The result, Rollyson concludes, is that "Stoppard has always worked well in radio and has produced for it some of his most innovative probings of human psychology."

Various reviewers have attempted to analyze and define Stoppard's thematic concerns as he presents them within his plays. His ideas are often considered from an existentialist perspective and encompass such concepts as "the nature of perception, art, illusion and reality, the relativity of meaning, and the problematic status of truth," Wright details. "Recurring themes include chance, choice, freedom, identity, memory, time, and death." Stoppard provided Tom Prideaux of *Look* with a simpler interpretation of his concerns: "One writes about human beings under stress—whether it is about losing one's trousers or being nailed to the cross." Cahn suggests, however, that Stoppard's works may contain a "unifying element" by consistently demonstrating Stoppard's "faith in man's mind." The critic elaborates: "He rejects the irrational, the reliance on emotion instead of intellect, the retreat from independent thought."

Because Stoppard's wit "can hold its own with Oscar Wilde, G. B. Shaw and Noel Coward," Edwin Wilson comments in the *Wall Street Journal,* he has been able to take his "fascination with ideas . . . and make them exciting." "Stoppard's special distinction is his linguistic and conceptual virtuosity," Gussow asserts in the *New York Times Magazine.* "One has to look back to Shaw and Wilde to find an English playwright who could so enlist the language as his companion in creativity. Others might finish ahead in terms of tragic vision or emotional commitment, but as a wordsmith Stoppard is supreme." Dean, who allies Stoppard with "the wittiest if not greatest writers of the English language," explains that "Stoppard indulges himself as well as his audience in the sheer pleasure of experiencing the density and richness of which the language is capable. Moreover, his attention to language results not only in humor but also in precision. As a means of considering the difficulty of communication as well as a comic vehicle, language is assiduously explored and exploited by Stoppard."

BIOGRAPHICAL/CRITICAL SOURCES:

BOOKS

Bock, Hedwig, and Albert Wetheim, editors, *Essays on Contemporary British Drama,* Hueber, 1981.

Cahn, Victor L., *Beyond Absurdity: The Plays of Tom Stoppard,* Associated University Presses, 1979.

Contemporary Dramatists, St. James Press, 1982.

Contemporary Literary Criticism, Gale (Detroit), Volume 1, 1973; Volume 3, 1975; Volume 4, 1975; Volume 5, 1976; Volume 8, 1978; Volume 15, 1980; Volume 29, 1984; Volume 34, 1985, Volume 63, 1991; Volume 91, 1996.

Dean, Joan Fitzpatrick, *Tom Stoppard: Comedy as a Moral Matrix,* University of Missouri Press, 1981.

Dictionary of Literary Biography, Volume 13: *British Dramatists since World War II,* Gale, 1982.

Dictionary of Literary Biography Yearbook: 1985, Gale, 1985.

Kelly, Katherine E., *Tom Stoppard and the Craft of Comedy: Medium and Genre at Play,* University of Michigan Press, 1991.

Schlueter, June, *Dramatic Closure: Reading the End,* Fairleigh Dickinson University Press (Madison, NJ), 1995.

PERIODICALS

America, February 18, 1984; January 29, 1994, p. 23.

Chicago Tribune, April 24, 1985; June 3, 1985; September 20, 1985; March 17, 1991.

Christian Science Monitor, April 25, 1974; November 6, 1975; December 6, 1982; January 11, 1984.

Classical and Modern Literature, winter, 1996.

Contemporary Literature, summer, 1979.

Harper's Bazaar, March, 1995, p. 126.

Life, February 9, 1968.

Look, December 26, 1967; February 9, 1968.

Los Angeles Times, June 6, 1986; December 20, 1986; February 20, 1991.

Nation, November 6, 1967; May 11, 1974; May 18, 1974.

National Review, December 12, 1967; Novemer 29, 1993, p. 71.

New Leader, September 21, 1992, p. 21.

New Republic, June 15, 1968; May 18, 1974; November 22, 1975; January 30, 1984.

Newsweek, August 7, 1967; August 31, 1970; March 4, 1974; January 8, 1975; November 10, 1975; January 16, 1984; April 3, 1995, p. 64.

New York, March 11, 1974; May 13, 1974; August 26, 1974; November 17, 1975; August 13-20, 1979; July 26, 1993, p. 51; January 9, 1995, p. 36.

New Yorker, May 6, 1967; October 28, 1967; May 4, 1968; May 6, 1972; March 4, 1974; May 6, 1974; January 6, 1975; January 24, 1977.

New York Review of Books, June 8, 1995, p. 28.

New York Times, October 18, 1967; October 29, 1967; March 24, 1968; May 8, 1968; June 19, 1968; July 8, 1968; October 15, 1968; April 23, 1974; July 29, 1979; August 1, 1979; October 4, 1979; November 25, 1979; November 28, 1979; June 23, 1983; November 22, 1983; January 6, 1984; January 15, 1984; February 20, 1984; August 1, 1984; May 17, 1987; May 18, 1987; November 22, 1987; November 3, 1989; November 26, 1989; December 26, 1989; February 8, 1991.

New York Times Book Review, August 25, 1968; March 3, 1996, p. 19.

New York Times Magazine, January 1, 1984.

Observer (London), August 1, 1993.

Publishers Weekly, February 12, 1996, p. 24.

Saturday Review, January 8, 1977.

Theatre Journal, March, 1980.

Time, October 27, 1967; August 9, 1968; March 11, 1974; May 6, 1974; June 20, 1983; August 24, 1992, p. 69; July 19, 1993, p. 60.

Times (London), November 18, 1982; April 3, 1985.

Times Literary Supplement, March 21, 1968; December 29, 1972; November 26, 1982; December 24, 1982; September 29, 1995, p. 23.

Times Saturday Review (London), June 29, 1991.

Village Voice, May 4, 1967; October 26, 1967; May 2, 1974.

Virginia Quarterly Review, autumn, 1995, p. 642.

Wall Street Journal, Mach 11, 1974; November 3, 1975; January 6, 1984.

Washington Post, May 11, 1969; June 25, 1969; July 9, 1969; August 29, 1978; November 26, 1978; January 12, 1984; May 23, 1985.

Washington Post Weekend, October 19, 1979.

World Literature Today, winter, 1978; summer, 1986; spring, 1995, p. 369; winter, 1996, p. 193.

STRACHEY, (Giles) Lytton 1880-1932
(Ignotus)

PERSONAL: Born March 1, 1880, in London, England; died of cancer, January 21, 1932, in Inkpen, Berkshire (some sources say Wiltshire), England; cremated; ashes placed in Strachey Chapel at Chew Magna Church, Somerset, England. *Education:* Trinity College, Cambridge, graduated 1903.

CAREER: Writer, biographer, essayist, and literary critic. Drama critic for *The Spectator,* c. 1905.

WRITINGS:

Euphrosyne: A Collection of Verse, Elijah Johnson, 1905.
Landmarks in French Literature, Henry Holt, 1912.
Eminent Victorians: Cardinal Manning, Florence Nightingale, Dr. Arnold, General Gordon (biography), Chatto & Windus, 1918.
Queen Victoria (biography), Chatto & Windus, 1921.
Books and Characters: French and English (criticism), Chatto & Windus, 1922.
Son of Heaven (play), produced in London at the Scala Theatre, July, 1925.
Pope, Cambridge University Press, 1925.
Elizabeth and Essex: A Tragic History (biography), Chatto & Windus, 1928.
Portraits in Miniature, and Other Essays (biography and essays), Chatto & Windus, 1931.
Characters and Commentaries, Chatto & Windus, 1933.
(Editor with Roger Fulford) *The Greville Memoirs,* 8 volumes, Macmillan, 1938.
The Collected Works of Lytton Strachey, 6 volumes, Chatto & Windus, 1948.
Virginia Woolf and Lytton Strachey: Letters, edited by Leonard Woolf and James Strachey, Hogarth Press/Chatto & Windus, 1956.
Spectatorial Essays, Chatto & Windus, 1964.
Ermyntrude and Esmerelda: An Entertainment (short story), Anthony Blond, 1969.
Lytton Strachey by Himself: A Self-Portrait (diary), Heinemann, 1971.
The Really Interesting Question and Other Papers, Weidenfeld & Nicolson, 1972.
The Shorter Strachey (biography, essays, criticism), Oxford University Press, 1980.

Also wrote under the pseudonym Ignotus.

Strachey's papers are located in several collections; his correspondence with Vanessa Bell and B. W. Swithinbank is at King's College, Cambridge; the manuscript of *Elizabeth and Essex* is at Duke University; the manuscript of *Queen Victoria* is at the University of Texas at Austin; and the manuscript of *Eminent Victorians* is in the British Library.

MEDIA ADAPTATIONS: The award-winning film *Carrington,* produced in 1995 and starring Jonathan Pryce as Lytton Strachey and Emma Thompson as Dora Carrington, was based on Michael Holroyd's biography *Lytton Strachey* and concerns the relationship between Carrington, her husband, and Strachey.

SIDELIGHTS: Lytton Strachey is best known as a biographer whose iconoclastic reexaminations of historical figures revolutionized the course of modern biographical writing. He conceived a type of biography that integrated established facts, speculative psychological interpretations, and imaginative recreations of his subjects' thoughts and actions which resulted in lively, perceptive, and above all human biographical portraits. In his major biographies—*Eminent Victorians, Queen Victoria,* and *Elizabeth and Essex: A Tragic History*—Strachey disclosed previously overlooked complexities of personality in some of the most prominent and revered figures of English history.

Born in London, Strachey was the eleventh child of a large, upperclass family. His father was a respected military general and an administrator to India. It was Strachey's mother, however, who was the major influence in his life, inspiring in him, through her teachings, an enthusiasm for the French language and literature. As early as age five he was encouraged to write verse, which was read aloud at family gatherings. His primary and secondary education was conducted at private schools and by private tutors until 1899, when he enrolled at Trinity College, Cambridge. There, Strachey formed important personal and literary relationships that endured throughout his life. Among his friends at Cambridge were Thoby Stephen, Leonard Woolf, Clive Bell, and John Maynard Keynes. With Strachey, they formed the nucleus of the coterie later known as the "Bloomsbury Group"—so-named after that section of London where members lived and met. The group also included Virginia Woolf; her sister, Vanessa Bell; Desmond MacCarthy, Roger Fry, and occasionally E. M. Forster. Bloomsbury's Thursday evening meetings were occasions for lively discussions of philosophy, literature, art, economics, politics, and life in general. Although the group observed no formal ideology, it was founded on philosopher G. E. Moore's *Principia Ethica,* the essence of which is summarized in Moore's statement that "one's prime objects in life were love, the creation and enjoyment of aesthetic experience, and the pursuit of knowledge." For Strachey, members of the Bloomsbury Group provided companionship and were his confederates in rejecting the remaining social conventions of the Victorian era.

In 1905 Strachey failed to obtain a fellowship at Trinity College, having submitted an unacceptable paper on the subject of the controversial English statesman Warren Hastings. Thwarted in his plans for an academic career, Strachey worked as a literary critic and essayist for several journals and became the drama critic for the *Spectator,* which was owned and edited by his cousin, St. Loe Strachey. During this time, Strachey polished his writing style and formulated his theories on the art of biography. His astute critiques of several French writers, and an essay on Jean Baptiste Racine, brought him to the attention of H. A. L. Fisher, a publishing representative. Commenting that Strachey was "one of those rare Englishmen who knew French from the inside," Fisher commissioned him to write a survey of French literature. The result was Strachey's first book, *Landmarks in French Literature.* Marked by his gift for incisive summary, the work was well received, but it did not bring him the fame he hoped to achieve. Despondent that he was not as artistically successful and productive as his friends among the Bloomsbury Group, Strachey decided that history might be his forte and turned his literary efforts to writing "silhouettes" of famous historical figures. Deploring the prevalent hagiographical bent of contemporary biographers and adhering to his dictum that "discretion is not the better part of biography," he wrote *Eminent Victorians.* Though Strachey's bold interpretation of the lives of Florence Nightingale, Cardinal Henry Edward Manning, Dr. Thomas Arnold, and General Charles George Gordon stirred controversies within the literary establishment, the work was a major success. Thus, having found his literary niche, he devoted his time to writing two other major biographies: *Queen Victoria,* a humanizing portrait of the queen and Prince Albert, and *Elizabeth and Essex,* an interesting, though artistically flawed, Freudian analysis of Queen Elizabeth I. In addition, Strachey wrote many biographical essays for periodicals, which were eventually collected in *Portraits in Miniature, and Other Essays,* and he became a respected literary critic of eighteenth- and nineteenth-century French and English literature. Suffering from ill health for most of his life, Strachey died at the age of fifty-two. His death prompted Dora Carrington, an artist with whom he lived, to commit suicide.

Eminent Victorians is Strachey's most critically discussed work. In his well-known preface to that work he expounded his theories of biography, maintaining that it should be more than a dull compilation of facts manipulated to venerate historical figures. Rather, Strachey believed that it is the biographer's business "to lay bare the facts of the case as he understands them . . . dispassionately, impartially, and without ulterior intention." His portraits of Nightingale, Manning, Arnold, and Gordon in *Eminent Victorians* combine literary artistry with selective biographical facts to produce new insights into personalities formerly assumed to be well understood. This biographical work is tightly written, colored by striking metaphors, and maintains Strachey's characteristically detached point of view. In addition, *Eminent Victorians* consistently employs an ironic tone which serves to deflate the reputations of his subjects. Michael Holroyd indicates that upon closer scrutiny Strachey's "detachment was part of a literary mannerism, skilfully employed so as to bring into sharper relief his irony and power of denigration." For all its success, however, *Eminent Victorians* was also harshly criticized by literary critics and historians who objected to Strachey's selective use of facts and his tendency to judge biographical subjects by modern standards, rather than in the context of their own era. Regardless of such criticism, *Eminent Victorians* became a model for a new kind of biography that was imitated throughout England and the United States.

Strachey's most popular biography, *Queen Victoria,* is often referred to as his most traditional work. Although he intended to reveal the mediocrity of Victoria's character, critics agree that Strachey became totally enraptured by his subject. In a series of vignettes, he depicted the Queen as a sympathetic figure administering to her advisors, to her public, and to her husband, Prince Albert. While Strachey's characteristic irony is less pervasive in *Queen Victoria,* he consistently raised rhetorical questions which allow readers to draw their own conclusions about the motivations behind Victoria's behavior, often interrupting his narrative to ask the reader such questions as "What was to be done?" or "What was going through her head?" Commentators remarked that, compared to *Eminent Victorians,* Strachey adhered more faithfully to historical fact in *Queen Victoria* and they have praised his psychological insight into the characters of Victoria and her courtiers. Strachey's next biography, *Elizabeth and Essex,* is often considered important for its innovative use of Freudian psychoanalysis. In his attempt to reveal the motives of Queen Elizabeth's behavior—from her political decisions to her choice of lovers—Strachey imaginatively reconstructed incidents of Elizabeth's early childhood. In a laudatory appraisal of *Elizabeth and Essex,* Sigmund Freud regarded Strachey's psychoanalysis of Queen Elizabeth to be correct.

Most critics agree that Strachey raised biography to an art form. While his use of historical facts was often contrived and unscholarly, he is generally praised for his artful and entertaining portraits. As a debunker, Strachey exposed the human frailties of prominent figures and maintained an irreverent stance toward the conventions of the past. According to Holroyd, "Strachey's

influence as a biographer has matched that of Plutarch and Boswell." Though his literary reputation has diminished somewhat in recent times, he is still considered a pioneer in the realm of modern biography.

BIOGRAPHICAL/CRITICAL SOURCES:

BOOKS

Beerbohm, Max, *Lytton Strachey,* Cambridge University Press, 1943.
Edmonds, Michael, *Lytton Strachey: A Bibliography,* Garland, 1981.
Ferns, John, *Lytton Strachey,* Twayne, 1988.
Holroyd, Michael, *Lytton Strachey,* Chatto & Windus, 1994.
Huxley, Aldus, *On the Margins,* 1923, pp. 141-57.
Strachey, Barbara, *The Strachey Line,* Gollancz, 1985.

PERIODICALS

English Literature in Transition, Volume 27, 1984, pp. 289-95; Volume 33, 1990, pp. 31-45.
Hudson Review, summer, 1989, pp. 201-21.
Prose Studies, September, 1981, pp. 146-52.
Victorian Institute Journal, Volume 18, 1990, pp. 1-15.

*   *   *

STRAUB, Peter (Francis) 1943-

PERSONAL: Born March 2, 1943, in Milwaukee, WI; son of Gordon Anthony and Elvena (Nilsestuen) Straub; married Susan Bitker (a counselor), August 22, 1966; children: Benjamin Bitker, Emma Sydney Valli. *Education:* University of Wisconsin—Madison, B.A., 1965; Columbia University, M.A., 1966; attended University College, Dublin, 1969-72. *Politics:* "Mainstream undecided." *Avocational interests:* Jazz, opera.

ADDRESSES: Home—53 W. 85th St., New York, NY 10024.

CAREER: University School, Milwaukee, WI, English teacher, 1966-69; writer, 1969–.

MEMBER: International PEN, Authors Guild, Authors League of America, Mystery Writers of America, Horror Writers Association, Writers Action Group.

AWARDS, HONORS: Nomination for best novel, World Fantasy Awards, 1981, for *Shadowland;* British Fantasy Award and August Derleth Award, both 1983, for *Floating Dragon;* Horror Writers Association Award, 1994; Grand Master Award, World Horror Convention, 1997.

WRITINGS:

Ishmael (poetry), Turret Books, 1972, Underwood/Miller, 1973.
Open Air (poetry), Irish University Press, 1972.
Marriages (novel), Coward, 1973.
Julia (novel), Coward, 1975 (published in England as *Full Circle,* Corgi, 1977).
If You Could See Me Now (novel), Coward, 1977.
Ghost Story (novel), Coward, 1979.
Shadowland (novel), Coward, 1980.
The General's Wife (story), D. M. Grant, 1982.
Floating Dragon (novel), Putnam, 1983.
Leeson Park and Belsize Square: Poems 1970-1975, Underwood/Miller, 1983.
(With Stephen King) *The Talisman* (novel), Viking, 1984.

Wild Animals: Three Novels (contains *Julia, If You Could See Me Now,* and *Under Venus*), Putnam, 1984.

Blue Rose (novella), Underwood/Miller, 1985.

Under Venus, Berkley, 1985.

Koko (novel; first installment of "Blue Rose" trilogy), Dutton, 1988.

Mystery (novel; second installment of "Blue Rose" trilogy), Dutton, 1991.

Mrs. God, Donald Grant, 1991.

Houses Without Doors (short stories), Dutton, 1991.

The Throat (novel; third installment of "Blue Rose" trilogy), Dutton, 1993.

The Hellfire Club (novel), Random House (New York City), 1996.

(Author of introduction) *Exorcisms and Ecstasies,* Fedogan and Bremer, 1997.

MEDIA ADAPTATIONS: Julia was adapted for the 1981 Peter Fetterman film, *The Haunting of Julia* (entitled *Full Circle* in England); *Ghost Story* was adapted for the 1981 Universal Pictures film of the same title. *Floating Dragon* was adapted for cassette by Listen for Pleasure Cassettes in 1987; *Koko* was adapted for cassette by Simon & Schuster Audioworks in 1989.

SIDELIGHTS: One of the most popular practitioners of horror and suspense fiction—more than 10 million copies of his novels have been sold—American writer Peter Straub is the author of such well-known titles as *Ghost Story, Shadowland, Floating Dragon, The Talisman* (with Stephen King), and *Koko.* Straub employs an array of ghastly elements—hauntings, vengeful agents of murder, gruesome deaths, fantastical happenings—and is especially good at, as *Maclean's* Barbara Matthews notes, "stark cold horror—the kind worshippers of the genre love to spirit away and read quickly, inhaling fright and holding it in their lungs until it becomes brittle enough to shatter if so much as a telephone rings." More than spine-tingling thrillers, however, Straub's novels are also imaginative explorations into the realistic, often personal, roots of the unreal. Patricia L. Skarda wrote in *Dictionary of Literary Biography Yearbook* that Straub's "best work . . . focuses on private experiences on the margin where nature and supernature meet, where reality converges with dream, where writing leaves off and the imagination takes over." Straub commented to Joseph Barbato in *Publishers Weekly* on the effects he wishes to elicit: "I want readers to feel as if they've left the real world behind just a little bit, but are still buoyed up and confident, as if dreaming. I want them left standing in midair with a lot of peculiar visions in their heads."

Straub's horror debut occurred in 1975 with *Julia,* the harrowing tale of an American woman in England haunted by the torturous ghost of a murdered child—and the emerging knowledge of responsibility in the death of her own daughter (the victim of an emergency tracheotomy). While some reviewers noted inconsistent plotting and characterization, many acknowledged Straub's flair for the gothic. "In the last resort, *Julia* . . . succeeds in the brutal business of delivering supernatural thrills," wrote Michael Mason in the *Times Literary Supplement;* Straub "has thought of a nasty kind of haunting, and he presses it upon the reader to a satisfying point of discomfort." Valentine Cunningham in *New Statesman* called the book "an extraordinarily gripping and tantalising read. . . . Every dubious solution and ambivalent pattern is possible, for almost anything becomes believable under the novelist's stunningly gothic manipulations."

After *Julia,* Straub wrote *If You Could See Me Now,* a tale set in the midwestern United States about the vengeful spirit of a murdered girl who returns to inflict horrors upon the community where she died. Critics particularly praised the novel's narrative timing, structure, and the authenticity of local settings. "Straub is good at slick manipulation of pace," wrote Jonathan Keates in *New Statesman,* "punctuating the story with chunks of police statement . . . , and he has an equally nifty way with rustic grotesques." Keates called the book "crisp, classy buggaboo . . . full of neatly managed understatements and chillingly calculated surprises." Peter Ackroyd in *Spectator* singled out the book's "filmic" qualities: "*If You Could See Me Now* makes great play, for example, with contrasts of speech and silence, of crowd scenes and empty landscapes, and of the ways in which a written 'close-up' can be employed to suggest deep 'emotion.' Some of the book's scenes, in fact, can only be understood in visual terms."

Following these ventures, Straub embarked upon the novel that would become his breakthrough, the 1979 bestselling *Ghost Story.* Drawing upon various horror story motifs and conventions, *Ghost Story* is the tale of a rural New England community terrorized when a young woman, killed years earlier, returns to exact retribution from four elderly townsmen (The Chowder Society) responsible for her death. The Chowder Society's members, who regularly meet to exchange ghost stories, become involved in a frantic race to save themselves and the town from the gruesome revenge of the "shapeshifter" Eva Galli. "What's interesting about '*Ghost Story*' is that Mr. Straub . . . seems to have decided to write a summarizing American tale of the supernatural, and to throw into it every scrap of horror-cliche and campfire trash that he can muster," commented Christopher Lehmann-Haupt in the *New York Times.* "Still, because Mr. Straub is so good at writing eerie set-pieces and because the very complexity of his story keeps it baffling to the end, I look back on the time spent reading '*Ghost Story*' as on an interval distorted by fever."

Straub's aim in *Ghost Story,* as Jennifer Dunning quoted the author in the *New York Times,* was to "take the genre and pull it upstairs a little bit. . . . Not exactly transcend the genre, but make a little more of the material than has been made of it in the recent past." *Ghost Story* draws from early masters in the field, including Nathaniel Hawthorne, Henry James, Edgar Allan Poe, and Sheridan Le Fanu. Some reviewers objected to the novel's overt deference to these influences. "Although Straub's 'affection' for the proven devices of his betters is estimable, many of these allusions seem rather pedantic and pointless," wrote Jack Sullivan in the *Washington Post Book World.* Douglas Hill commented in *Maclean's* that "at times the book stumbles over its structure: all the epigraphs and cute chapter titles are merely pretentious." "There was a certain amount of audacity in the overt references to the great writers," Straub admitted to Thomas Lask in the *New York Times,* "but today the form is debased, and it is a messianic thing to me to elevate it and make it honorable." A number of reviewers were, however, impressed with Straub's creation. Gene Lyons in the *New York Times Book Review* called *Ghost Story* "a quite sophisticated literary entertainment," while Valerie Lloyd remarked in *Newsweek* that "with considerable technical skill, Peter Straub has constructed an extravagant entertainment which, though flawed, achieves in its second half some awesome effects." She concluded: "It is, I think, the best thing of its kind since Shirley Jackson's 'The Haunting of Hill House.'"

Straub's 1983 bestselling novel, *Floating Dragon,* seemed to meet the expectations generated by *Ghost Story.* In a sweeping story of a malevolent spirit which periodically visits an affluent Connecticut suburb with death and destruction, Straub creates "a compendium of horrors designed to punish the shallow housewives, adulterers, corporate tycoons, and even the children in a commuter community," noted Skarda. "*Floating Dragon,* beneath its remarkable repertoire of horrific details, is a simple moral tale of the confrontation between good and evil," wrote Alan Bold in the *Times Literary Supplement.* "Nevertheless, it represents a new level of sophistication in the Gothic novel. Straub plays games with the structure, rapidly switching from third-person to first-person narrative, and teases the reader with biblical symbols and red herrings. The novel is sustained with great skill as the battle between good and evil is impressively, if agonizingly, stretched over the disturbingly supernatural plot." Alan Ryan commented in the *Washington Post Book World:* "If *Floating Dragon* is sometimes baffling, flawed in some structural elements, and perhaps a little too long for its own good, it is at the same time both ruthlessly contemporary and steeped in tradition, gruesomely chilling, and told with a narrative strength and a lively colloquial style that readers should welcome."

In his next novel, Straub teamed up with friend and fellow horror writer Stephen King—via networked word processors—to produce the 1984-85 blockbuster *The Talisman.* Drawing upon both writers' immense popularity, the book was an instant bestseller; critics, however, felt that it was a bit overstocked with mad capers and special effects. The fantasy/adventure story of a boy who goes in search of a magic object to cure his dying mother, *The Talisman* outlines a power struggle between good and evil in a strange world. "There's a dizzying amount of flipping in this book," noted Peter Gorner in the *Chicago Tribune,* "and often the point is elusive." Lehmann-Haupt wrote that *The Talisman* "suffers from a surfeit of monstrosity. It takes forever to develop its smallest plot complications. It telegraphs its clues with the subtlety of falling telephone poles. It stoops to outrageous sentimentality over its boy hero. . . . It repeats and repeats unto silliness." These elements, however, are also part of the book's appeal, according to Frank Herbert in the *Washington Post Book World:* "*The Talisman* is exactly what it sets out to be—a fine variation on suspense and horror filled with many surprises, a ground King and Straub have plowed before with great success, together and individually. Together, they demonstrate once more that they are the Minnesota Fats of the novel-into-film. When they say six ball in the side pocket, that's where the six ball goes."

Straub's 1988 bestseller, *Koko,* is a notable departure from his past supernatural novels, and the first in the loosely defined "Blue Rose" trilogy, which also consists of the subsequent novels *Mystery* and *The Throat.* A psychological suspense thriller, *Koko* is the story of four Vietnam War veterans who travel to the Far East to track down a former platoon member they believe has become a deranged killer. Straub remarked to *Bestsellers 89* on his change of direction: "By the time I began *Koko,* I had pretty much done everything I could think to do with supernatural fiction. . . . Whether I knew it or not, I was saying goodbye to imagery and situations involving hallucination versus reality with which I had been involved for years. . . . What I wanted to do next was to work with the set of feelings that lay behind horror—to move in closer to the world, to work more strictly within the realistic tradition." Straub's venture has been well-received. A reviewer for *Publishers Weekly* called *Koko* "a dizzying spin through those eerie psychic badlands where nightmare and insanity seem to fuse with reality." Emily Tennyson added in the *Detroit Free Press:* "Like the war that Straub seeks to analyze and explain, '*Koko*' wrenches the spirits of those who took part and

were taken apart by Vietnam. Much more than a tale of escape and murder, '*Koko*' is an examination of fear in the human soul."

Set in the mid-1950s and early 1960s, Straub's novel *Mystery* focuses on Tom Pasmore, who survives a near (or perhaps actual) death experience at age ten when he is hit by a car. As Tom recuperates from his trauma, he befriends a neighbor, Lamont von Heilitz, who gradually involves him in investigating two murders—one having occurred many years ago, the other being a recent event. "The story has more twists, turns, and blind alleys than most mysteries," commented Clarence Petersen in the Chicago *Tribune Books.* Also offering praise for the novel, Geoffrey Stokes of *Voice Literary Supplement* asserted that "it is the story of a secret that is trying to emerge."

The Throat is the concluding novel of Straub's trilogy of psychological horror fiction. Set in the town of Millhaven, the plot centers on the mysterious reemergence of the "Blue Rose" serial murders, which were thought to have been solved long ago. The main character, crime writer and sleuth Tim Underhill, "is forced to explore regions of his psyche and his past that are, to say the least, disturbing," observed Frank Wilson of the *New York Times Book Review.* Critics have emphasized the novel's defiance of many of the conventions of the genres it draws upon—horror and crime fiction being the most overt. Douglas E. Winter of *The Washington Post Book World,* for example, deemed the book "a masterpiece of concealment and revelation, the most intelligent novel of suspense to come along in years."

1996's *The Hellfire Club* portrays Dick Dart, a serial killer who has been preying upon women in a small Connecticut town. Much of the plot concerns the events that follow his kidnapping of Nora Chancel, who happens to be the publisher of a notoriously volatile and influential horror novel titled *Night Journey.* As the plot of *The Hellfire Club* progresses, Nora's experience begins to resemble that of the thriller her company published. Critics have emphasized the meta-fictional, multi-layered qualities of *The Hellfire Club,* admiring its complexity. "What remains impressive . . . is the way Mr. Straub has worked the fantastic elements of his story into a largely realistic plot, thereby allowing him to avoid a literal descent into the hellfire of his title," asserted Lehmann-Haupt of the *New York Times.* "This technique is promising, and one hopes he will exploit it even more successfully in future works."

BIOGRAPHICAL/CRITICAL SOURCES:

BOOKS

Bestsellers 89, Issue 1, Gale (Detroit), 1989.
Contemporary Literary Criticism, Volume 28, Gale, 1984.
Dictionary of Literary Biography Yearbook: 1984, Gale, 1985.

PERIODICALS

Chicago Tribune, May 16, 1979; December 16, 1981; November 8, 1984.
Detroit Free Press, November 13, 1988.
Entertainment Weekly, February 9, 1996, p. 46.
Kirkus Reviews, August 15, 1990, p. 1126.
Library Journal, November 15, 1995, p. 101.
Locus, September, 1991, p. 23.
Los Angeles Times Book Review, January 30, 1983; March 20, 1983; September 18, 1988; November 18, 1990.
Maclean's, May 21, 1979; January 12, 1981; March 14, 1983.
New Statesman, February 27, 1976; June 24, 1977.
Newsweek, March 26, 1979; December 24, 1984.

New York Times, April 3, 1979; April 27, 1979; May 20, 1979; October 24, 1980; December 16, 1981; January 26, 1983; November 8, 1984; February 1, 1996, p. B4.

New York Times Book Review, April 8, 1979; March 6, 1983; March 24, 1985; October 9, 1988; June 27, 1993, p. 24; February 25, 1996, p. 9.

People Weekly, January 28, 1985.

Publishers Weekly, January 28, 1983; May 11, 1984; August 12, 1988; April 10, 1995, p. 17; November 27, 1995, p. 49; June 23, 1997.

Spectator, July 9, 1977.

Times Literary Supplement, March 23, 1973; February 27, 1976; April 17, 1981; March 11, 1983.

Tribune Books (Chicago), October 2, 1988; January 20, 1991, p. 12; February 18, 1996, p. 6.

Voice Literary Supplement, May, 1993, p. 25.

Washington Post, October 31, 1980; February 6, 1981; February 16, 1981; November 27, 1984.

Washington Post Book World, April 8, 1979; October 14, 1984; August 21, 1988; April 28, 1991; May 16, 1993, p. 5.

*   *   *

STRINDBERG, (Johan) August 1849-1912

PERSONAL: Born January 22, 1849, in Riddarholm, Stockholm, Sweden; died of stomach cancer, May 14, 1912; buried in New Church Cemetery, Solna, Sweden; son of Carl Oscar (a grocer and shipping agent) and Ulrika Eleanora (a waitress) Strindberg; married Sigrid Sofia Matilda Elisabeth von Essen Wrangel (known as Siri von Essen), December 30, 1877 (divorced, 1892); married Maria Friederike Cornelia Uhl (a journalist; known as Frida Uhl), May 2, 1893 (divorced, 1897); married Harriet Bosse (an actress), May 6, 1901 (divorced, 1904); children: (first marriage) a daughter (died in infancy), Karin, Greta, Hans; (second marriage) Kerstin; (third marriage) Anne-Marie. *Education:* Attended University of Uppsala, 1867 and 1870-72. *Politics:* Social Democrat. *Religion:* Lutheran.

CAREER: Writer. Worked as telegraph clerk; journalist, 1872-74; assistant librarian at Royal Library, 1874. Founded Scandinavian Experimental Theatre in Copenhagen, Denmark, 1888; founded Intimate Theatre, 1907.

AWARDS, HONORS: Royal stipend for *Den fredloese,* c. 1871.

WRITINGS:

PLAYS

I Rom (one-act; title means "In Rome"; produced in Stockholm, 1870), [Stockholm, Sweden], 1880.

Hermione (five-act), [Stockholm], 1871.

Den fredloese (one-act; produced in Stockholm, 1871), [Stockholm], 1881, translation published as *The Outlaw* (also see below).

Maester Olof (five-act; written in 1872, revised version produced as *Mellanspelet,* 1875, verse version produced as *Maester Olof,* 1876, original prose version produced in 1881), [Stockholm], 1881, translation by Edwin Bjoerkman from original prose version published as *Master Olof,* American-Scandinavian Foundation, 1915.

Gillets hemlighet (four-act; title means "The Secret of the Guild"; produced in Stockholm, 1880), Seligmann (Stockholm), 1880.

Anno fyrtiaatta (four-act; title means "In the Year 1848"), [Stockholm], 1881.

Lycko-Pers resa (five-act; produced in 1883), [Stockholm], 1881, translation by Velma Swanston Howard published as *Lucky Pehr,* Stewart & Kidd, 1912.

Herr Bengt's hustru (five-act; title means "Sir Bengt's Wife"; produced in 1882), [Stockholm], 1882.

Fadren (three-act; produced in Copenhagen, Denmark, 1887; Oesterling (Helsingborg, Sweden), 1887, translation by N. Erichsen published as *The Father,* J. W. Luce, 1898.

Hemsoeborna (four-act; adapted from Strindberg's novel of the same title; produced in 1889), [Stockholm], 1887.

(With Axel Lundegard) *Kamraterna* (four-act; adapted from Strindberg's play *Marodoerer;* produced in Vienna, 1905), [Helsingborg], 1888, translation published as *Comrades* (also see below).

Froeken Julie (one-act; produced in Copenhagen in 1889), [Stockholm], 1888, translation by Charles Recht published as *Countess Julia,* Brown Bros., 1912, translation by C. D. Locock published as *Lady Julie,* International Modern Plays, 1950, translation by E. M. Sprinchorn published as *Miss Julie,* preface by Strindberg, Chandler, 1961.

Fordringsaegare (one-act; produced in Copenhagen, 1889), [Stockholm], 1888, translation by Francis J. Ziegler published as *The Creditor,* Brown Bros., 1910.

Den starkare (one-act; produced in Copenhagen, 1889), originally published in 1890, translation by Ziegler published as *The Stronger* in *Poet Lore,* Volume 17, number 1, 1906.

Paria (one-act; produced in Copenhagen, 1889), [Stockholm], 1890, translation by Bjoerkman published in *Plays by August Strindberg: Creditors, Pariah,* Scribner, 1912.

Samum (one-act; produced in 1890), originally published in 1890, translation by Horace B. Samuel published in *Paria* [and] *Simoon,* Hendersons, 1914.

Debit och kredit (one-act; produced in Berlin, Germany, 1900), originally published in 1892, translation published as *Debit and Credit* (also see below).

Himmelrikets nycklar; eller, Sankte Per vandrar pa jorden (five-act; title means "The Keys of the Kingdom of Heaven; or, St. Peter Wanders on Earth"; produced in 1929), originally published in 1892, translation published as *The Keys of Heaven* (also see below).

Infoer doeden (one-act; produced in Berlin, 1893), originally published in 1892, translation by Olive M. Johnson published as *Facing Death,* [Easton, PA], 1911.

Moderskaerlek (one-act; produced in Germany, 1894), originally published in 1893, translation by Ziegler published as *Motherlove,* Brown Bros., 1910.

Bandet (one-act; produced in Berlin, 1902), originally published in 1893, translations published as *The Bond* and *The Link* (also see below).

Loka med elden (one-act; produced in Berlin, 1893), originally published in 1893, translation by Michael Meyer published as *Playing with Fire,* French, 1963.

Foersta varningen (one-act; produced in Berlin, 1893), originally published in 1893, translation published as *The First Warning* (also see below).

Till Damaskus, foersta delen (seven scenes; title means "To Damascus, I"; produced in Stockholm, 1900), [Stockholm], 1898, translation published as *The Road to Damascus* (also see below).

Till Damaskus, andra delen (four-act; title means "To Damascus, II"; produced in Munich, Germany, 1916), [Stockholm], c.

1898, translation published as *The Road to Damascus* (also
see below).

Advent: Ett mysterium (five-act; produced in Munich, 1915; also
see below), [Stockholm], 1898, translation by Claud Field
published as *Advent,* Badger, 1914.

Vid hoegre raett (title means "At a Higher Court"; contains
Advent: Ett mysterium and *Brott och brott* [also see below]),
[Stockholm], 1899.

Gustaf Vasa (five-act; produced in Sweden, 1899), [Stockholm],
1899, translation published as *Gustavus Vasa* (also see
below).

Erik XIV (four-act; produced in Sweden, 1899), [Stockholm],
1899, translation by Joan Bulman published in *Master Olof
and Other Plays,* J. Cape/H. Smith, 1931.

Folkungasagan (five-act; produced in Sweden, 1901), [Stock-
holm], 1899, translation published as *The Saga of the
Folkungs* (also see below).

Gustaf Adolf (five-act; produced in Berlin, 1903), [Stockholm],
1900, translation by Walter Johnson published as *Gustav
Adolf,* University of Washington Press, 1957.

Paask (three-act; produced in Frankfurt am Main, Germany,
1901), [Stockholm], 1901, translation by Howard published
with stories as *Easter,* Stewart & Kidd, 1912, new translation
by Elizabeth Sprigge, Duckworth, 1949.

Engelbrekt (four-act; also see below), produced in Sweden, 1901.

Midsommar (six tableaux; title means "Midsummer"; produced in
Sweden, 1901), [Stockholm], 1901.

Kristina (four-act; produced in 1908), originally published in
1901, translation by W. Johnson published in *Queen Christina, Charles XII,* [and] *Gustav III,* University of Washington
Press, 1955.

Doedsdansen (two parts, each in two acts; produced in Cologne,
1905), [Stockholm], 1901, translation by Norman Ginsbury
published as *The Dance of Death,* Cornelius, 1966.

Kronbruden (six-part; produced in Sweden, 1906), [Stockholm],
1901, translation published as *The Bridal Crown* (also see
below).

Svanevit (three-act; produced in Helsingfors, 1908), [Stockholm],
1901, translation by Ziegler published as *Swanwhite,* Brown
Bros., 1909.

Ett droemspel (fourteen scenes: produced in Sweden, 1907),
[Stockholm], 1901, translation published as *The Dream Play*
(also see below).

Kaspers fet-tisdag (one-act; title means "Casper's Shrove Tuesday"), produced in Stockholm, 1901.

Carl XII (five-act; produced in Stockholm, 1902), [Stockholm],
1918, translation by W. Johnson published in *Queen Christina, Charles XII,* [and] *Gustav III,* University of Washington
Press, 1955.

Gustav III (four-act; produced in 1916), originally published in
1902, translation by W. Johnson published in *Queen Christina, Charles XII,* [and] *Gustav III,* University of Washington
Press, 1955.

Naektergalen i Wittenberg (five-act; produced in Berlin, 1914),
originally published in 1903, translation published as *The
Nightingale of Wittenberg* (also see below).

Till Damaskus, tredje delen (four-act; title means "To Damascus,
III"; produced in Munich, 1916), [Stockholm], 1904, translation published as *The Road to Damascus* (also see below).

Ovaeder (three scenes; produced in 1907), originally published in
1907, translations published as *The Thunderstorm* and *Storm
Weather* (also see below).

Braenda tomten (two scenes; produced in 1907), [Stockholm],
1907, translation published as *The Burned House* (also see
below).

Spoeksonaten (three scenes; produced in 1908), [Stockholm],
1907, translations published as *The Spook Sonata* and *The
Ghost Sonata* (also see below).

Pelikanen (three scenes; produced in 1907), [Stockholm], 1919,
translation published as *The Pelican* (also see below).

Abu Casems tofflor (title means "Abu Casem's Slippers"; produced in 1908), [Stockholm], 1908.

Sista riddaren (five-act; produced in Stockholm, 1909), [Stock-
holm], 1908, translations published as *The Last of the
Knights* (also see below).

Bjaelbo-Jarlen (five-act; produced in Sweden, 1909), [Stock-
holm], 1909, translation published as *Earl Birger of Bjalbo*
(also see below).

Riksfoerestaandaren (five-act; produced in Stockholm, 1911),
[Stockholm], 1909, translation published as *The Regents*
(also see below).

Stora landsvaegen (verse; produced in 1910), [Stockholm], 1909,
translation published as *The Great Highway* (also see below).

Brott och brott (four-act; produced in Munich, 1915), translation
by Bjoerkman published as *There Are Crimes and Crimes,*
Scribner, 1912.

Genom oeknar till arvland; eller, Moses (twenty-one tableaux;
title means "Through the Wilderness to the Promised Land;
or, Moses"; produced in Hanover, Germany, 1922), originally published in 1918, translation published as *Through
Deserts to Ancestral Lands* (also see below).

Hellas; eller, Sokrates (nineteen tableaux; title means "Hellas; or,
Socrates"; produced in Hanover, 1922), originally published
in 1918, translation published as *Hellas* (also see below).

Lammet och vilddjuret; eller, Kristus (fifteen tableaux; title means
"The Lamb and the Wild Beast; or, Christ"; produced in
Hanover, 1922), originally published in 1918, translation
published as *The Lamb and the Beast* (also see below).

Efterspelet (title means "Epilogue"), produced in Goeteborg,
Sweden, 1920.

Det sjunkande Hellas (three-act; verse; title means "Greece in
Decline"), Bokgillets foerlag (Uppsala, Sweden), 1960.

Also author of *En namnsdagsgaava* (title means "A Namesday
Gift") and *Fritaenkaren* (three-act; title means "The Free Thinker"), both 1869, *Marodoerer* (title means "Marauders"), 1886,
Svarta handsken (five-act; title means "The Black Glove"),
produced in 1909, and *Toten-Insel* (one scene; title means "Isle of
the Dead"), 1918. Plays also published in anthologies and multi-
title volumes.

PLAY COLLECTIONS IN ENGLISH TRANSLATION

Plays: Comrades, Facing Death, Pariah, Easter, translation by
Edith Oland and Waerner Oland, J. W. Luce, 1912.

Plays: The Father, Countess Julie, The Outlaw, The Stronger,
translation by E. Oland and W. Oland, J. W. Luce, 1912.

Plays by August Strindberg (four volumes; includes *The Dream
Play, The Link, The Thunderstorm, After the Fire, The Bridal
Crown, The Spook Sonata, Debit and Credit, The First
Warning,* and *Gustavus Vasa*), translation by Bjoerkman,
Scribner, 1912-16.

The Road to Damascus (includes parts 1-3), translation by
Graham Rawson, introduction by Gunnar Ollen, J. Cape,
1939, Grove, 1960.

Strindberg: Six Plays (includes *The Ghost Sonata*), translation by
Sprigge, Doubleday, 1955.

The Last of the Knights, The Regent, [and] *Earl Birger of Bjalbo,* translation by W. Johnson, University of Washington Press, 1956.

The Saga of the Folkungs [and] *Engelbrekt,* translation by W. Johnson, University of Washington Press, 1959.

Strindberg: Seven Plays (includes *The Bond*), translation by Arvid Paulson, Bantam, 1960.

The Chamber Plays (includes *Storm Weather, The Burned House,* and *The Pelican*), translation by Sprinchorn, Seabury Quinn, and Kenneth Petersen, Dutton, 1962.

Eight Expressionistic Plays (includes *The Keys of Heaven* and *The Great Highway*), translation by Paulson, Bantam, 1965.

World Historical Plays (includes *The Nightingale of Wittenberg, Through Deserts to Ancestral Lands, Hellas,* and *The Lamb and the Beast*), translation by Paulson, American-Scandinavian Foundation, 1970.

OTHER

Fraan Fjaerdingen och Svartbaecken (title means "From Town and Gown"), originally published in 1877, Askild & Kaernekull (Stockholm), 1971.

Roeda rummet (novel), [Stockholm], 1879, translation by Ellie Schleussner published as *The Red Room,* Putnam, 1913, translation by Sprigge published as *The Red Room: Scenes of Artistic and Literary Life,* Dutton, 1967.

Svenska folket i helg och soeken, i krig och i fred, hemma och ute; eller, Ett tusen aar af svenska bildningens och sedernas historia (title means "The Swedish People on Holy Day and Everyday, in War and Peace, at Home and Abroad; or, A Thousand Years of the History of Swedish Culture and Manners"), illustrations by Carl Larsson, C. E. Fritze, Volume 1, 1881, Volume 2, 1882.

I Vaarbrytningen: Ungdomsarbeten (for children), six volumes, [Stockholm], 1881.

Kulturhistoriska studier, Bonnier, 1881.

Det nya riket (essay; title means "The New Kingdom"), [Stockholm], 1882.

Svenska oeden och aefventyr (novel; title means "Swedish Destinies and Adventures"), [Stockholm], 1883, C. & E. Gernandt, 1899.

Dikter paa vers och prosa (title means "Poems in Verse and Prose"), [Stockholm], 1883.

I ikt och Olikt, [Stockholm], 1884.

Soemngaangarnaetter paa vakna dagar (verse), [Stockholm], 1884, translation by Paulson published in *"Sleepwalking Nights and Wide-Awake Days" and "Biographical,"* Law-Arts, 1978.

Utopier i verkligheten (title means "Utopias in Reality"), [Stockholm], 1885.

Giftas (stories), two volumes, [Stockholm], 1884-85, translation by Schleussner published as *Married,* J. W. Luce, 1913, translation by Mary Sandbach published as *Getting Married,* Viking, 1972.

Tjaenstekvinnans son (autobiographical novel), [Stockholm], 1886, translation by Field published as *The Son of a Servant,* introduction by Henry Vacher-Burch, Putnam, 1913, translation by Sprinchorn published as *The Son of a Servant: The Story of the Evolution of a Human Being (1849-1867),* Anchor, 1966.

Hemsoeborna (novel), Bonnier, 1887, translation by Elspeth Harley Schubert published as *The People of Hemso,* Bonnier, 1959, translation by Paulson published as *The Natives of Hemso,* Eriksson, 1965.

Vivisectioner (essays; title means "Vivisections"; includes "Om sjaelamord" ["On Psychic Murder"]), originally published in French, 1887-90, Bonnier, 1958.

Blomstermaalningar och djurstycken ungdomen tillaegnade (popular science; title means "Flowers and Animals"), [Stockholm], 1888.

Le Plaidoyer d'un fou (novel; in French), [Stockholm], 1888, translation by Schleussner published as *The Confession of a Fool,* Swift, 1912, Viking, 1925, translation by Sprinchorn published as *A Madman's Defense,* Anchor, 1967, translation by Anthony Swerling published as *A Madman's Manifesto,* Trinity Lane Press, 1968, University of Alabama Press, 1971.

Tschandala (novel), [Stockholm], 1888.

Skaerkarlslif: Beraettelser (title means "Life in the Skerries"), [Stockholm], 1888.

Bland franska boender (nonfiction; title means "Among French Peasants"), [Stockholm], 1889.

En haxa (novel), [Stockholm], 1890, translation by Mary Sandbach published as *A Witch,* Lapis Press, 1991.

I hafsbandet (novel), [Stockholm], 1890, translation by Elizabeth Clarke Westergren published as *On the Seaboard: A Novel of the Baltic Islands,* Stewart & Kidd, 1913, translation by Schleussner published as *By the Open Sea,* Palmer, 1913.

Tryckt och otryckt (plays, essays, and other writings), four parts, [Stockholm], 1890-97.

Les Relations de la France avec la Suede jusqu'a nos jours (in French), [Paris, France], 1891.

Antibarbarus (essays), [Stockholm], 1894.

Hortus Merlini: Lettres sur la chimie; Sylva sylvarum, Chamuel (Paris), 1897.

Inferno (autobiographical novel), [Stockholm], c. 1898, translation by Field published as *The Inferno,* Rider, 1912, Putnam, 1913, translation by Mary Sandbach published as *Inferno,* Hutchinson, 1962.

Legender, [Stockholm], 1898, translation published as *Legends: Autobiographical Sketches,* Melrose, 1912.

Klostret (novel), [Stockholm], 1898, translation by Mary Sandbach published as *The Cloister,* edited by C. G. Bjurstrom, Hill & Wang, 1969.

Typer och prototyper inom mineralkemien: Festskrift till firandet af Berzelii femtioaarsminne, [Stockholm], 1898.

Samvetsqval, [Stockholm], 1899.

Fagervik och Skamsund (fiction), [Stockholm], 1902, translation published as *Fair Haven and Foul Strand,* McBride, Nast, 1914.

Ensam (novella; title means "Alone"), [Stockholm], 1903, translation by Paulson published as *Days of Loneliness,* Phaedra, 1971.

Sagor (stories), [Stockholm], 1903, translation by L. J. Potts published as *Tales,* Chatto & Windus, 1930.

Oeppna brev till Intima Teatern (essay collection), 1903, translation by W. Johnson published as *Open Letters to the Intimate Theatre,* University of Washington Press, 1959.

Goetiska rummen (novel; title means "The Gothic Rooms"), [Stockholm], 1904.

Historiska miniatyrer (fiction), originally published in 1905, translation by Field originally published as *Historical Miniatures* in 1913.

Ordalek och smaakonst (poems; title means "Word Play and Miniature Art"), originally published in 1905, Bonnier, 1974.

Taklagsoel (novella), [Stockholm], 1907, translation by David Mel Paul and Margareta Paul published in *The Roofing Ceremony and The Silver Lake* (includes short story "The

Silver Lake," translated from the original Swedish manuscript, *Silvertrasket*), University of Nebraska Press, 1987.

Syndabocken (novella), [Stockholm], 1907, translation by Paulson published as *The Scapegoat,* Bantam, 1967.

Svarta fanor (novel; title means "Black Banners"), [Stockholm], 1907.

Kammarspel, [Stockholm], 1907.

En blaa bok (essays and journal entries; title means "A Blue Book"), four volumes, Bjoerck & Boerjesson (Stockholm), 1907-12, translation by Field published as *Zones of the Spirit: A Book of Thoughts,* introduction by Arthur Babillotte, Putnam, 1913.

Fabler och smaerre beraettelser, [Stockholm], 1909.

Shakespeares Macbeth, Othello, Romeo och Julia, Stormen, Kung Lear, Henrik VIII, En Midsommarnattsdroem, [Stockholm], 1909.

Tal till Svenska Nationen om olust i landet, levernet, litteraturen och laerdomen . . . Sjunde upplagan (title means "Speeches to the Swedish Nation"), [Stockholm], 1910.

Foerfattaren: En sjaels utvecklingshistoria, 1877-1887; Tredje upplagan (title means "The Author"), [Stockholm], 1910.

Folkstaten: Studier till en stundande foerfattningsrevision (title means "The People's State"), [Stockholm], 1910.

Kina och Japan: Studier, Bjoerck & Boerjesson, 1911.

Kinesiska spraekets haerkomst, Bjoerck & Boerjesson, 1912.

Samlade skrifter (collected works), fifty-five volumes, edited by John Landquist, Bonnier, 1912-20.

The Growth of a Soul, translation by Field, Rider, 1913.

The Martyr of Stockholm, translation by Field from the original Swedish manuscript, *Paa Godt och Ondt,* Thynne, 1914.

Han och hon: En sjaels utvecklingshistoria, 1875-76 (letters to Siri von Essen; title means "He and She"), Bonnier, 1919.

Strindbergs brev till Harriet Bosse: Natur och Kultur, Bokfoerlaget Natur och kultur (Stockholm), 1932, translation by Paulson published as *Letters of Strindberg to Harriet Bosse,* Grosset & Dunlap, 1959.

August Strindbergs och Ola Hanssons brevvaexling 1888-1892, Bonnier, 1938.

Aattio: Talsnoveller (title means "Eighty"), Bonnier, 1959.

Brev till min dotter Kerstin (letters), Bonnier, 1961.

Ur ockulta dagboken (journal), edited by Torsten Eklund, Bonnier, 1963, translation by Mary Sandbach published as *From an Occult Diary: Marriage with Harriet Bosse,* edited by Torsten Eklund, Hill & Wang, 1965.

Hoevdingaminnen, illustrations by Otte Skoeld, Bonnier, 1963.

Selected Essays by August Strindberg, edited by Michael Robinson, Cambridge University Press, 1996.

Also author of *Gamla Stockholm* (with Claes Lundin; cultural history; title means "Old Stockholm"), 1880; *Dikter och verkligheter* (verse and prose; title means "Poems and Realities"), 1881; *Kvarstadsresan* (autobiography; title means "Journey into Detention"), 1885; *Jaesningstiden* (autobiographical novel; title means "Time of Ferment"), 1886; *Jardin des plantes* (science; title means "Botanical Garden"), 1896; *Svensk natur* (title means "Swedish Nature"), c. 1897; *Jakob brottas* (journal; title means "Jacob Wrestling"), 1898; *Modersmaalets anor* (title means "The Origins of Our Mother Tongue"), *Vaerldspraakens roetter* (title means "The Roots of World Languages"), and *Religioes renaessans* (title means "Religious Renaissance"), all 1910. Author of essay "Vaerldshistoriens mystik" (title means "The Mysticism [or "Mystique" or "Hidden Meaning"] of World History"), 1901. Works also published in anthologies and multi-title volumes, including *In Midsummer Days, and Other Tales,* translation by

Schleussner, Latimer, 1913; and *The German Lieutenant, and Other Stories,* A. C. McClurg, 1915.

MEDIA ADAPTATIONS: Films of Strindberg's plays include *The Dance of Death,* featuring Laurence Olivier, Paramount, 1971, and *Miss Julie,* featuring Helen Mirren; televised productions include *Miss Julie* and *Creditors;* dramatic material was adapted by Charles Marowtiz in the volume *Sex Wars;* many of Strindberg's works have also been presented as radio productions, including Swedish presentations directed by Ingmar Bergman; *Miss Julie* has been staged as an opera.

SIDELIGHTS: Playwright, novelist, poet, amateur scientist, and painter, the Swedish writer August Strindberg was one of the most important figures in world literature during his time. A conflict-ridden and insecure man, he hesitated at first about his choice of profession. After two separate stays at the University of Uppsala, he left academia without a degree. University students were a privileged, romanticized group in Sweden at the time, but Strindberg, who years later was to refer to himself as "the son of a servant," did not feel at home among them. During his second sojourn in Uppsala he briefly joined the literary society Runa, whose members tried to revive the mythology, history, and civilization of Nordic antiquity and declared their support of pan-Scandinavianism, a topic of concern among many Northern intellectuals in the aftermath of Germany's attack on Denmark in 1864.

In the summer of 1872 Strindberg settled down on the small island of Kymmendo in the Stockholm archipelago, a place that would provide the setting for his most popular novel, *Hemsoeborna* (*The People of Hemso,* 1887). During his stay he finished *Maester Olof* (*Master Olof*), a five-act drama in prose about the Swedish sixteenth-century religious reformer Olaus Petri, a disciple of Martin Luther who helped free the Church of Sweden from Rome's domination. The play, which was rejected by the Royal Dramatic Theatre, was rewritten several times over the next decade. Deliberately choosing to seek recognition in the most popular dramatic genre of the day, the historical drama, Strindberg made himself an easy target for the conservative literary establishment by departing drastically from accepted dramatic norms. He boldly followed his main guide and master, William Shakespeare, in telescoping time and space, thus rearranging events and flouting historical accuracy; he also introduced realistic and colloquial speech, which violated the widely held belief that historical drama should be delivered in stately poetic language. But his critics' most serious accusations centered on Strindberg's inclusion of new moral and psychological principles based on his readings of British philosopher Thomas Buckle, Danish critic Georg Brandes, and American theologian Thomas Parker, readings that resulted in Strindberg's reevaluation of prominent personages in Swedish history.

Two crucial events occurred in Strindberg's life during the 1870s: he joined a coterie of young artists who gathered regularly in the Red Room at Berns' Restaurant in Stockholm, and he met Siri von Essen, a married baroness, who was to become his first wife in 1877. After his marriage Strindberg settled down to write *Roeda rummet* (*The Red Room*). Published in 1879, it marks the breakthrough of realism in modern Swedish literature. The novel, based on Strindberg's bohemian experiences prior to his marriage, revolves around an idealistic journalist, Arvid Falk, who is exposed to various levels of contemporary Swedish society, ranging from economic upstarts and swindlers to radical artists and revolutionaries. The late 1870s were a time of growing social and political unrest in Sweden, not unlike the atmosphere recreated in *The Red Room*. But the literary climate was still ultraconservative, with its proponents prescribing a purely aesthetic role for belles lettres, a romantically obsolete credo that Strindberg rejected in *The Red Room*. As in the case of *Master Olof*, he had produced a work that went against the mainstream of Swedish literary thinking.

One of the most hotly debated issues among the Scandinavian intelligentsia in the early 1880s was the role of women in contemporary society. Henrik Ibsen had fueled the debate with his play *Et dukkehjem* (*A Doll's House*, 1879), and Bjornstjerne Bjornson had expressed feminist views in his drama *En handske* (*A Glove*, 1883). Strindberg offered his thoughts on the matter in a collection of short stories titled *Giftas* (*Married*, 1884) in which he advocated an egalitarian relationship between men and women, though maintaining a traditional view of the sex roles. Emphasizing the sensual aspect of married life, he objected to the bourgeois custom of arranged marriages. *Married* caused a scandal and necessitated Strindberg's brief return to Sweden to stand trial on charges of blasphemy. Though acquitted, Strindberg suspected that he was being victimized by Swedish feminists, among them the queen herself. In bitterness he published in 1885 a second, less genial volume of *Married*, presenting marriage as a form of mental and emotional extortion in which women, by nature parasites, have the upper hand. Such a misogynist view was to color a great many of the male-female relationships depicted by Strindberg in a long series of dramas focusing on the battle of the sexes or on the theme of vampirism, among them: *Fadren* (*The Father*, 1887), *Froeken Julie* (*Miss Julie*, 1888), *Fordringsaegare* (*The Creditor*, 1888), *Doedsdansen* (*The Dance of Death*, 1901-05), *Spoeksonaten* (*The Ghost Sonata*, 1907), and *Pelikanen* (*The Pelican*, 1907).

The *Married* trial convinced Strindberg that he should pursue a scientific rather than literary career, and he began publishing articles on nonliterary subjects. In this scientific-oriented spirit he set out, in 1886, to write his autobiography, which he intended to be a social and psychological document. Strindberg was only thirty-seven when he began writing *Tjaenstekvinnans son* (*The Son of a Servant*), a book in four parts, of which the first ends in 1867, the year he left home for the University of Uppsala. The second part tells of his youth up to the year 1872. Part three, subtitled "In the Red Room," depicts him as a journalist and poet and ends with his meeting Siri von Essen. The fourth part, refused by his Swedish publishers, deals with the years 1877 to 1886 and did not appear until after his death. Omitted from the autobiography are the years from 1875 to 1877, during which time Strindberg wooed Siri von Essen and prepared for his marriage. Strindberg had planned to treat these years by printing letters exchanged between him and his future wife, but this correspondence, called *Han och Hon* ("He and She"), was not published until 1919.

The *Son of a Servant* is not a straightforward memoir but is instead an interpretation of the past in light of Strindberg's mood and philosophical stance in the 1880s. Though containing, in the tradition of the "confessions" of St. Augustine and Rousseau, passages of moral self-probing and histrionic self-exposure, *The Son of a Servant* is also a philosophical autobiography in the tradition of Johann Wolfgang von Goethe's writings. It has been argued by Eric O. Johanneson in *The Novels of August Strindberg: A Study in Theme and Structure* that because *The Son of a Servant* is told in the third person, the work might be considered a novel. Clearly, however, the book reflects Strindberg's personal position

in 1886 and 1887 as much as it depicts him as a child and young man; his growing anti-feminism, for example, tends to color his portrait of his parents. But his primary approach to his own background was through class-consciousness, as reflected in the book's title. To the end of his life he stressed this view of himself as a social outcast. Thus in his final play, *Stora landsvaegen* (*The Great Highway*, 1909), he identified his alter-ego, the Hunter, with the biblical Ishmael, who was driven into the desert by Sara, Abraham's wife.

When Strindberg sat down to write *The Father* he was experiencing doubts as to the paternity of his own children. His marriage was in crisis, and he also suspected that his arch-rival Ibsen had used him as a model for the pathetic, cuckolded husband Hjalmar Ekdal in the play *The Wild Duck*. Strindberg, however, transcended his own possible situation as a wronged and ridiculed husband by turning it into an archetypal vision of the irrevocable sexual warfare between man and woman. As Martin Lamm suggested in *August Strindberg*, the writer's intellectual springboard may have been an article about Euripides's play *The Oresteia* by French sociologist Paul Lafargue, who interpreted the classical Greek work as a dramatization of the birth of matriarchy and saw a similar struggle emerging in contemporary society. Matriarchy was not a benevolent concept to Strindberg, for to him it meant a world ruled by women who had abandoned their function as caring maternal beings in order to exercise power through the use of their irrational and possessive psyches. How this might be done and what the result could be is what Strindberg described in *The Father*.

Strindberg had set forth his ideas a year earlier in an important essay titled "Om sjaelamord" ("On Psychic Murder"), in which he referred to the psychological theories of the French School of Nancy, where doctors advocated the use of hypnosis. Strindberg became convinced that sexual warfare depended not on erotic power but on unmitigated will. The winning party was the person with the strongest and most unscrupulous mind, someone who like a hypnotist could drive a more sensitive psyche to its destruction. Remnants of this concept of psychological power struggles appear in such dramas as *The Creditor, Den starkare* (*The Stronger*, 1889), and *Pariah*. In *The Creditor*, a triangle play involving a man (Adolf), his wife (Tekla), and her former husband (Gustav), Strindberg presented the psychic murder concept in vampire or cannibalism motifs. Tekla is a devourer of souls; like Laura in *The Father* she has sucked the life force out of her husband. Gustav is depicted as a Nietzschean superman who controls others through his superior intellect. While Tekla instinctively feeds on people close to her, Gustav dissects them and sets the destructive interpersonal machinery in motion. In *Pariah*, another theatrical piece of human vivisection, the psychological power game takes place between an intellectual man and a subservient but ruthless criminal who is unmasked through a cunning strategy. In *The Stronger*, a one-act tour-de-force, Strindberg depicted the vampire or homunculus motif in the guise of a meeting between two women, one married, the other the former mistress of the first woman's husband.

Prior to writing *The Creditor* and his psychological one-act plays, Strindberg had completed *Miss Julie*, which was to become one of his best-known and most frequently produced dramas. The play was written with an avant-garde Parisian stage in mind, the Theatre Libre, started in 1887 by Andre Antoine, a former gas works clerk who produced naturalist one-act pieces called *quart d'heures*, using no curtain drops. *Miss Julie* is a full-length drama without act divisions; interludes such as a peasant dance and a pantomime replace conventional intermissions. Strindberg also attempted in this play to adhere to the naturalist dictum that a play demonstrate a law of nature, in this case the Darwinian concept of the survival of the fittest. The plot of *Miss Julie* depicts a twenty-five-year-old noblewoman who has a brief love affair with her father's valet, Jean, on the family estate. Hereditary and circumstantial elements determine the destinies of Jean and Julie. The former is a social climber portrayed by Strindberg as a man of the future to whom Julie, the degenerate aristocrat, must succumb. In his famous preface to the play, Strindberg attempted to disassociate himself from his characters and assume the analytical role of a naturalist playwright, but the play itself is vibrant with his emotional engagement in his dramatis personae. If the social situation in *Miss Julie* now seems somewhat obsolete, the play survives because of the psychological dynamics through which Jean and Julie transcend their roles as stereotypes in a social class struggle and become what Strindberg termed "characterless characters"—ambivalent and complex personages whose actions are based on a multitude of motives. Challenging earlier playwrights, Strindberg ultimately wished to avoid defining a character in terms of one dominant personality trait.

Strindberg, the "son of a servant," undoubtedly relied for his conception of *Miss Julie* on his own marriage to an aristocratic woman. By the time he composed the play, his family life had entered a tumultuous stage and his once passionate love for Siri von Essen had changed to jealousy and hatred. A divorce seemed inevitable. However, in 1888 a reconciliation of sorts occurred. Strindberg was now intent upon opening in Copenhagen, Denmark, a Scandinavian Experimental Theatre, whose manager was to be Siri von Essen. But both the new stage venture and the marital reconciliation were short-lived. Less than a year later Strindberg left Denmark and returned to Sweden, where he lived through the final phase of his divorce from Siri, who moved back to her native Finland with their children. Strindberg was later to make use of this unhappy phase in his life in *Bandet* (*The Bond*, 1893), a dramatized recollection of the divorce proceedings.

By September 1892 Strindberg found himself at an artistic dead end. Since he lived on his writing, his creative decline reduced his income, which in turn sent him into a depression for being unable to fulfill his financial obligations to his children and former wife. As his plight became known to his friends, a fund was established for him through an appeal in a German magazine. The money enabled him to leave Sweden and settle in artistic circles in Berlin, Germany. Here his spirits improved momentarily; his break with his past reminded him of his youthful bachelor days some twenty years earlier when he had broken with bourgeois society and joined the coterie of artists in the Red Room in Stockholm. Now his meeting place was a Berlin tavern that he named The Black Porker. There he made the acquaintance of a lively and diverse group of Scandinavian, Polish, and German artists. His attention soon began to focus on a young Austrian journalist by the name of Frida Uhl, who, twenty-three years his junior, became his wife in May 1893. The couple, to whom a daughter, Kerstin, was born a year later, soon separated, though their marriage was not formally dissolved until 1897. But Frida's family, especially her mother, was to have a crucial impact on Strindberg. A pious Catholic, Maria Uhl responded to her son-in-law's religious gropings, and in July 1894 the former atheist declared in a letter: "I feel the hand of our Lord resting over me."

However, Strindberg's religious conversion took place over a prolonged period of time and coincided with a series of psychic crises, the nature of which is still being debated. Some critics believe that he suffered throughout the mid-1890s from such severe paranoia that he became, at least temporarily, insane; others, most notably Evert Sprinchorn and Olof Lagercrantz, think he deliberately turned himself into his own guinea pig through psychological and drug-induced self-experimentation. What has not always been recognized is that the Inferno years, which were spent in Paris, France, were also productive years for Strindberg. They began in scientific or pseudo-scientific explorations of such fields as botany, chemistry, and optics and ended in Strindberg's return to literature with the publication of his edited journals, *Legender* and *Jakob brottas* (*Legends* and *Jacob Wrestling,* both 1898), in which he recorded the impact of his discovery of eighteenth-century mystic Emanuel Swedenborg. Strindberg continued to keep such diaries until 1908; parts of them were published in his so-called blue books, beginning with *En blaa bok* (*Zones of the Spirit,* 1907), and in the posthumously published *Ur ockulta dagboken* (*From an Occult Diary,* 1963).

The Inferno, Legends, Jacob Wrestling, and the *To Damascus* trilogy reveal a psychological rationalization process that ultimately undermines the artistic impact of these works. *The Inferno* and the first part of *To Damascus* are much more dynamic in their depiction of an inner agonizing conflict than their sequels, which reveal an intellectualized point of view. The same trend can be discerned in the drama *The Dance of Death* and in *Advent* and *Brott och brott* (*There Are Crimes and Crimes*), two plays that Strindberg wrote in the winter of 1898 and 1899 and published under the common title *Vid hoegre raett* ("At a Higher Court"). In *There Are Crimes and Crimes* the author's moralistic zeal fills the play with frequent undramatic lectures and cant. On the other hand, the ghoulish setting, macabre props, and abstract conception of character in *Advent* signal the beginnings of expressionist drama—a form of theater aiming at projecting the inner state of a single consciousness whose fears and aspirations materialize in visionary or hallucinatory scenes. Yet, although *Advent*'s projection of life as an evil dream foreshadows the structure of *Ett droemspel* (*The Dream Play,* 1901), its philosophical core, fusing Swedenborgian corrective spirits with New Testament Christian atonement, is closer to Strindberg's conventionally Christian dramas, *Paask* (*Easter,* 1901) and *Kronbruden* (*The Bridal Crown,* 1901).

In *Easter* the Christ figure expands beyond a stage metaphor and materializes in the main character, the "Easter Girl," Eleonora Heyst, who returns home to her family from an asylum. Being also a Swedenborgian angelic spirit, Eleonora is juxtaposed to another visitor to the Heyst family, the creditor Lindqvist, who is assigned the role of corrective spirit. Together these two bring about chastisement in Elis, Eleonora's proud brother, who has never accepted his father's imprisonment for embezzlement. Eleonora expresses Strindberg's belief that an individual can voluntarily atone for the sins of others by realizing that punishment is a sign of God's grace. Like *Easter, The Bridal Crown* dramatizes the redemptive power of a vicarious sufferer, this time through the destiny of young Kersti, whose atonement brings about a reconciliation of two farming families. But Kersti's fate is more personalized than Eleonora's, for she acts also on her own moral behalf: her acts are prompted by a sense of guilt for having murdered her illegitimate baby. In keeping with this internalization of the atonement theme, Strindberg returned in *The Bridal Crown* to the expressionist technique of *Advent* and projected Kersti's moral agony through materialized visions of specters and mythical figures from the stark world of folk legend.

In the famous note that precedes *The Dream Play* Strindberg drew attention to his former drama *To Damascus*. Both plays follow the pattern of the station drama with constantly shifting scenes and a thematic grouping of characters; both plays move between the sublime and the prosaic, between metaphysical concerns and marital squabbles. But the Stranger in *To Damascus* remains rooted in human predicaments, whereas Indra's daughter, the main character in *The Dream Play,* is of heavenly origin and has greater affinity to the esoteric Eleonora of *Easter*. The loosely constructed plot of *The Dream Play* tells of the descent of Indra's daughter to earth to learn of the plights of humanity. Her journey through life can be conceived of as a dream; hence Strindberg's attempt to present the events in the play in the associative pattern of the nocturnal psyche, where all time is a prolonged now and specific locations are transmutable because no spatial restrictions exist in a dream. During her kaleidoscopic travels Indra's daughter encounters an Officer imprisoned in a growing castle; she marries a Lawyer who takes upon himself the suffering of his clients; she sees social injustice and the sorrows of rejected lovers and outcasts; and she listens to the Poet's plaintive assessment of human life in Fingal's Cave. Carrying with her the lament of the people on earth—summed up in the line that echoes throughout the play, "Mankind is to be pitied"—she finally ascends to heaven through the Growing Castle that bursts into flames.

Beginning with *To Damascus* in 1898, a ruminating and meditative mood breaks into Strindberg's traditionally dynamic material, and lyrical passages interrupt the dramatic action. *The Great Highway,* often referred to as his literary testament, is a drama composed almost entirely of lyrical soliloquies spoken by the Hunter, a protagonist who functions both as Strindberg's alter ego and as an Everyman figure. Setting out on a circular journey designed as a *via dolorosa* ("road of sorrow"), the Hunter passes the seven stations of Golgotha, where Jesus Christ was crucified; yet because he functions not as a Christ figure but as a representative of humankind, his attained vision is a mixture of defiance and mellow resignation. *The Great Highway* is a stylized drama with highly abstracted characters, a further sign of Strindberg's continuous reaction against a realistic stagecraft. Shakespeare, for whom all is make-believe on the stage, rather than Zola, the advocate of a nineteenth-century form of kitchen-sink realism, remains his master, an influence that is also clear in the impressive cycle of historical dramas composed by Strindberg in the early 1900s.

Strindberg remained productive and active up to the last few months before his death of stomach cancer in May 1912. In addition to his plays, his work during the last decade of his life included short stories, fairy tales, novels, and novellas. He also participated vigorously in public debate, contributing a great number of polemical articles to the Swedish press (the so-called Strindberg feud). Though his later prose works never attained the popular status of earlier novels such as *The Red Room* and *The People of Hemso,* they are no longer looked upon as mere confessional tracts or revengeful diatribes on adversaries. In retrospect it is clear that novellas like *Ensam* (*Days of Loneliness,* 1903), *Taklagsoel* (*The Roofing Ceremony,* 1907), and *Syndabocken* (*The Scapegoat,* 1907), and novels like *Goetiska rummen* ("The Gothic Rooms," 1904) and *Svarta fanor* ("Black Banners," 1907), as well as the earlier novel written in French, *The Confession of a Fool,* advance the fiction genre in Swedish literature beyond the realistic trend of the nineteenth century and foreshadow the modernist fiction of Marcel Proust and Franz Kafka.

BIOGRAPHICAL/CRITICAL SOURCES:

BOOKS

Carlson, Harry G., *Strindberg and the Poetry of Myth,* University of California Press, 1982.

Dahlstroem, Carl Enoch William Leonard, *Strindberg's Dramatic Expressionism,* Blom, 1930.

Johanneson, Eric O., *The Novels of August Strindberg: A Study in Theme and Structure,* University of California Press, 1968.

Johnson, Walter, *August Strindberg,* Twayne, 1976.

Lagercrantz, Olof, *August Strindberg,* Faber & Faber, 1984.

Lamm, Martin, *August Strindberg,* translated and edited by Harry G. Carlson, Blom, 1971.

McGill, V. J., *August Strindberg: The Bedeviled Viking,* Russell & Russell, 1965.

Meyer, Michael, *Strindberg,* Random, 1985.

Mortensen, Brita M., and Brian W. Downs, *Strindberg: An Introduction to His Life and Work,* Cambridge University Press, 1965.

Ollen, Gunnar, *August Strindberg,* Ungar, 1972.

Smedmark, Carl Reinhold, editor, *Essays on Strindberg,* Beckmans, 1966.

Sprigge, Elizabeth, *The Strange Life of August Strindberg,* Macmillan, 1949.

Steene, Birgitta, *Greatest Fire: A Study of August Strindberg,* Southern Illinois University Press, 1973.

Twentieth-Century Literary Criticism, Gale (Detroit), Volume 1, 1978; Volume 8, 1982; Volume 21, 1986.

PERIODICALS

New Criterion, March, 1985.

*   *   *

STURGEON, Theodore (Hamilton) 1918-1985 (Frederick R. Ewing, E. Waldo Hunter, Ellery Queen, E. Hunter Waldo)

PERSONAL: Original name, Edward Hamilton Waldo; name legally changed upon adoption by stepfather; born February 26, 1918, in St. George, Staten Island, NY; died May 8, 1985, of pneumonia, in Eugene, OR; son of Edward (a retail paint businessman) and Christine (a teacher and writer; maiden name, Dicker) Waldo; married Dorothy Fillingame, 1940 (divorced, 1945); married Mary Mair (a singer), 1949 (divorced, 1951); married third wife, Marion, 1951; married Wina Bonnie Golden (a television personality), April 16, 1969 (divorced); married Jayne Enelhart; children: Colin, Patricia, Cynthia, Robin, Tandy, Noel, Timothy, Andros. *Education:* Attended Pennsylvania State Nautical School. *Religion:* Episcopal.

CAREER: Science fiction writer, 1938-85. Worked as an engine room wiper in the Merchant Marine, 1935-38; manager of a resort hotel in the West Indies, 1940-41; manager of a tractor lubrication center for the U.S. Army in Puerto Rico, 1941; bulldozer operator in Puerto Rico, 1942-43; copy editor for an advertising agency, 1944; literary agent in New York City, 1946-47; *Fortune* (magazine), New York City, circulation staff member, 1948-49; story editor for *Tales of Tomorrow* (magazine), 1950; *If* (magazine), New York City, feature editor, 1961-64, contributing editor, 1972-74. Teacher at workshops and writing conferences.

MEMBER: Writers Guild of America.

AWARDS, HONORS: Argosy magazine story award, 1947, for "Bianca's Hands"; International Fantasy Award, 1954, for *More Than Human;* guest of honor at Twentieth World Science Fiction Convention, 1962; Nebula Award, 1970, and Hugo Award, 1971, both for "Slow Sculpture"; World Fantasy Award for life achievement, World Fantasy Convention, 1986.

WRITINGS:

NOVELS

The Dreaming Jewels, Greenberg, 1950, published as *The Synthetic Man,* Pyramid, 1961.
More Than Human, Farrar, Straus, 1953.
The King and Four Queens (Western novel; based on a story by Margaret Fitts), Dell, 1956.
(Under pseudonym Frederick R. Ewing) *I, Libertine* (historical novel), Ballantine, 1956.
The Cosmic Rape, Dell, 1958.
Venus Plus X, Pyramid, 1960.
Some of Your Blood (also see below), Ballantine, 1961.
Voyage to the Bottom of the Sea (based on the screenplay by Irwin Allen and Charles Bennet), Pyramid, 1961.
(Under pseudonym Ellery Queen) *The Player on the Other Side,* Random House, 1963.
Two Complete Novels (contains *And My Fear Is Great* and *Baby Is Three*), Galaxy, 1965.
The Rare Breed, Fawcett, 1966.
Amok Time (based on one of his "Star Trek" television scripts), Bantam, 1978.
Godbody, limited edition, Donald I. Fine, 1986, New American Library, 1987.

STORY COLLECTIONS

"It" (single story), Prime Press, 1948.
Without Sorcery, with introduction by Ray Bradbury, Prime Press, 1948, revised edition published as *Not without Sorcery,* Ballantine, 1961.
E Pluribus Unicorn, Abelard, 1953.
Caviar, Ballantine, 1955.
A Way Home, Funk, 1955 (published in England as *Thunder and Roses,* M. Joseph, 1957).
A Touch of Strange, Doubleday, 1958.
Aliens 4, Avon, 1959.
Beyond, Avon, 1960.
The Unexpected, compiled by Leo Margulies, Pyramid, 1961.
Sturgeon in Orbit, Pyramid, 1964.
The Joyous Invasions, Gollancz, 1965.
Starshine, Pyramid, 1966.
(With Ray Bradbury and Oliver Chadwick Symmes) *One Foot and the Grave,* Avon, 1968.
Sturgeon Is Alive and Well, Putnam, 1971.
The Worlds of Theodore Sturgeon, Ace Books, 1972.
To Here and the Easel, Gollancz, 1973.
(With Don Ward) *Sturgeon's West,* Doubleday, 1973.
Case and the Dreamer, New American Library, 1974.
Visions and Venturers, Dell, 1978.
Maturity, Science Fiction Society (Minneapolis), 1979.
The Golden Helix, Doubleday, 1979.
The Stars Are the Styx, Dell, 1979.
Slow Sculpture, Pocket Books, 1982.
Alien Cargo, Bluejay, 1984.
To Marry Medusa, Baen Books, 1987.
A Touch of Sturgeon, Simon & Schuster, 1988.
The Omnibus of Modern Crime Stories, edited by Eleanor Sullivan, Robinson (London), 1991.

The Ultimate Egoist: The Complete Stories of Theodore Sturgeon, edited by Paul Williams, North Atlantic Books (Berkeley, CA), 1994.
Microcosmic God: The Complete Stories of Theodore Sturgeon, Volume 2, edited by Paul Williams, North Atlantic Books (Berkeley, CA), 1995.
Killdozer!: The Complete Stories of Theodore Sturgeon, Volume 3, edited by Paul Williams, North Atlantic Books (Berkeley, CA), 1996.
Thunder and Roses: The Complete Stories of Theodore Sturgeon, Volume 4, edited by Paul Williams, North Atlantic Books (Berkeley, CA), 1997.

RADIO AND TELEVISION SCRIPTS

Author of radio scripts, including "Incident at Switchpath," 1950; "The Stars Are the Styx," 1953; "Mr. Costello Here," 1956; "Saucer of Loneliness," 1957; "More Than Human," 1967; "The Girl Had Guts," "The Skills of Xanadu," and "Affair with a Green Monkey." Also author of television scripts for "Beyond Tomorrow," "Star Trek," "Playhouse 90," "CBS Stage 14," "Schlitz Playhouse," "Land of the Lost," "The Wild, Wild West," "The Invaders," and other television series. Also author, with Ed MacKillop, of television script "Killdozer!" (based on his short story), 1974.

OTHER

(Contributor) Leo Margulies and O. J. Friend, editors, *My Best Science Fiction Story,* Merlin Press, 1949.
It Should Be Beautiful (play), first produced in Woodstock, NY, c. 1963.
(Contributor) Reginald Bretnor, editor, *Science Fiction: Today and Tomorrow,* Harper, 1974.
(Contributor) Bretnor, editor, *The Craft of Science Fiction,* Harper, 1976.
Psychosis: Unclassified (play; based on his novel *Some of Your Blood*), first produced in 1977.
(Editor) *New Soviet Science Fiction,* Macmillan (London), 1980.

Work included in many anthologies. Also author of comic book scripts. Author of column, *National Review,* 1961-73. Contributor of short stories, sometimes under pseudonyms, to *Unknown, Astounding Science Fiction, Omni, Galaxy,* and other magazines. Book reviewer, *Venture,* 1957-58, *Galaxy,* 1972-74, *New York Times,* 1974-75, and *Hustler,* 1983.

SIDELIGHTS: The late Theodore Sturgeon was one of a handful of science fiction writers whose work revolutionized the genre. Beginning as a pulp writer in the late 1930s, Sturgeon became one of science fiction's Golden Age writers of the 1940s, a period when many of the genre's most popular writers came to prominence. Sturgeon published his stories in such influential magazines as *Astounding Science Fiction* and *Unknown.* His stream-of-consciousness technique, concern for humane values, and ability to create unlikely characters and situations, endeared him to readers and influenced a score of other writers. Kurt Vonnegut, Jr., is believed to have modeled his character Kilgore Trout, a prolific and inventive science fiction writer, on Sturgeon.

After dropping out of high school as a teenager, Sturgeon joined the Merchant Marine, worked in the West Indies and Puerto Rico, and finally found himself in the middle 1940s in New York City, working as a writer of science fiction and, for a time, as a literary agent for other writers in the field. His first widely acclaimed book, *More Than Human,* appeared in 1953; it won the International Fantasy Award. Later books, usually collections of short stories, established Sturgeon as one of science fiction's most accomplished and popular writers.

Among the subjects that Sturgeon made into legitimate science fiction was sex, particularly sex of an unusual or even aberrant nature. He was the first writer in science fiction to include homosexual characters in his work, and to portray them as being worthy of tolerance. His story "The World Well Lost" concerns a pair of homosexual lovers from another planet who are aided in their escape from outraged spacemen by an Earthman who empathizes with them. Sturgeon's early story "Bianca's Hands," first written in 1939 but considered too erotically daring by science fiction magazines of the 1940s, was finally published in the British adventure magazine *Argosy* in 1947. It won a $1,000 fiction prize, beating out entries by such writers as Graham Greene. The story tells of the deformed idiot Bianca, who possesses hands which "have a life and will of their own," as Donald L. Lawler explained in the *Dictionary of Literary Biography.* Bianca's friend Ran becomes obsessed with the hands, desiring nothing else but to be strangled by them. Sturgeon's novel *Venus Plus X* features a utopian society of the future whose citizens undergo surgery at birth to render themselves hermaphroditic. This sexual change allows them to transcend the normal conflicts between men and women. In many of Sturgeon's stories, love is seen as the surest method of overcoming the adversities of life. Sturgeon "never abandoned belief in the therapeutic power of love," Bob Collins noted in *Fantasy Review.*

An eccentric and outspoken man whose daring ideas made his fiction continually popular, Sturgeon was an iconoclast in his thinking. A long-time columnist for the conservative *National Review,* Sturgeon also wrote book reviews for the explicit pornography magazine *Hustler.* He was a nudist, a vegetarian, and a believer in herbal medicines and vitamin cures. "I have a right to my own life-style," he explained to Charles Platt in *Dream Makers, Volume II,* "and I don't like yahoos coming along to correct me. . . . I like to protect my own way of thinking." Speaking of his political persuasion, Sturgeon told Platt: "Libertarian, at the moment, feels more like home to me than anything else." In private life Sturgeon was also known for his unorthodox attitude toward finances. As Sam Moskowitz observed, "If ever an author epitomized the skittishness and sensitivity attributed to the 'artist,' it is Theodore Sturgeon. While he appreciated the need for money, his primary motivation was not the dollar. Despite the knowledge that he could sell *anything* of a fantastic nature he cared to write . . . , it was typical of him to take a couple of months off to write a three-act play *free* for a small-town theater, with the review in a local weekly his sole reward."

Sturgeon is credited with two observations that have become known not only in science fiction circles but among a wider audience as well. "Sturgeon's Law," so called because he claimed that it applied in every field of endeavor, is stated in polite terms as: "90 percent of everything is trash." His other abiding observation was the "concept of the 'Prime Directive'" created for the "Star Trek" television program, as Lawler noted. Sturgeon wrote two episodes for the popular series ("Amok Time" and "Shore Leave"). The "Prime Directive," or overriding law of the United Federation of Planets, "prohibits Federation interference with the normal development of alien life and societies," according to Bjo Trimble in *A Star Trek Concordance.*

In his fiction Sturgeon displayed a wide variety of styles, adapting his approach to the story he wanted to tell. Moskowitz, writing in *Seekers of Tomorrow: Masters of Modern Science Fiction,* stated

that Sturgeon "strives in *every* story to be as differently and bizarrely off-trail as he is able" and claimed that Sturgeon possessed an "adroitness at altering the rhythm of his writing to conform to the subject [which] gives him as many styles as stories." Lawler agreed. Sturgeon, he wrote, "uses a remarkable variety of styles, points of view, and narrative devices." Lawler also credited the author with having "pointed the way for new developments in the genre by combining the subject matter, themes, and formulas of science fiction with the ideas, modes of treatment, and stylistic features of mainstream literature."

Sturgeon's influence on other science fiction writers, and on the parameters of the genre as a whole, was impressive. Lawler explained that Sturgeon's influence was "great because it is so diffuse. It is not so much an acknowledged influence as it is pervasive, and it tends to be strongest in matters of tone, style, attitudes, and values." Among those writers influenced by Sturgeon were Ray Bradbury, Samuel R. Delaney, Philip K. Dick, Ursula K. LeGuin, and Kurt Vonnegut, Jr.

Vonnegut is believed to have modeled his character Kilgore Trout on Sturgeon. Trout is a science fiction writer who has authored hundreds of books filled with wildly inventive concepts. But Trout lives in poverty and obscurity because the ridiculous titles he gives his books, and the pornographic magazines in which his stories appear, severely limit his audience. Trout is both homage to Sturgeon for his inventiveness and his ability to confront major themes and a satire of Sturgeon's eccentricity.

Paul Anderson found Sturgeon's work to be among the best in science fiction. Writing in *National Review,* Anderson stated: "One can raise quibbles about Sturgeon, his touches of doctrinaire liberalism (though never, never collectivism), his ungrammatical treatment of 'thou,' his sometimes overly neat plots, nits like that. So what? It's as easy to pick them off Rembrandt and Beethoven, easier off Shakespeare, and none of these are lessened thereby, nor is Sturgeon. He is reliably a joy." In his tribute to Sturgeon for the *Washington Post Book World,* Stephen King noted that as a writer Sturgeon had "entertained, provoked thought, terrified, and occasionally ennobled. He fulfilled, in short, all the qualifications we use to measure artistry in prose."

BIOGRAPHICAL/CRITICAL SOURCES:

BOOKS

Contemporary Literary Criticism, Gale (Detroit), Volume 22, 1982; Volume 39, 1986.
Dictionary of Literary Biography, Volume 8: *Twentieth Century American Science Fiction Writers,* Gale, 1981.
Dictionary of Literary Biography Yearbook: 1985, Gale, 1986.
Ketterer, David, *New Worlds for Old: The Apocalyptic Imagination, Science Fiction, and American Literature,* Anchor Press, 1974.
Menger, Lucy, *Theodore Sturgeon,* Ungar Publications, 1981.
Moskowitz, Sam, *Seekers of Tomorrow: Masters of Modern Science Fiction,* World Publishing, 1965.
Platt, Charles, *Dream Makers, Volume II: The Uncommon Men and Women Who Write Science Fiction,* Berkley, 1983.
Trimble, Bjo, *A Star Trek Concordance,* Ballantine, 1976.

PERIODICALS

Bloomsbury Review, February, 1986.
Extrapolation, summer, 1979; fall, 1985.
Magazine of Fantasy and Science Fiction, December, 1971; February, 1994, p. 39.
National Review, May 4, 1971.

Publishers Weekly, November 20, 1995, p. 69.
Washington Post Book World, May 26, 1985.

*   *   *

STYRON, William 1925-

PERSONAL: Born June 11, 1925, in Newport News, VA; son of William Clark (a shipyard engineer) and Pauline (Abraham) Styron; married Rose Burgunder, May 4, 1953; children: Susanna, Paola, Thomas, Alexandra. *Education:* Attended Christchurch School, Middlesex County, VA, and Davidson College, NC, 1942-43; Duke University, B.A., 1947; studied writing at New School for Social Research, 1947. *Politics:* Democrat.

ADDRESSES: Home—12 Rucum Road, Roxbury, CT 06783; and Vineyard Haven, MA (summer).

CAREER: Writer. McGraw-Hill Book Co. (publishers), New York, NY, associate editor, 1947; *American Scholar,* member of editorial board, 1970-76. Fellow of Silliman College, Yale University, 1964–. Honorary consultant in American Letters to the Library of Congress. Cannes Film Festival jury president, 1983. Advisory editor of *Paris Review. Military service:* U.S. Marine Corps, World War II, 1944-45; became first lieutenant; recalled briefly in 1951.

MEMBER: National Institute of Arts and Letters, American Academy of Arts and Sciences, American Academy of Arts and Letters (inducted, 1988), Society of American Historians, Signet Society of Harvard (honorary), Phi Beta Kappa, Academie Goncourt.

AWARDS, HONORS: American Academy of Arts and Letters Prix de Rome, 1952, for *Lie Down in Darkness;* Litt.D., Duke University, 1968; Pulitzer Prize, 1968, and Howells Medal of the American Academy of Arts and Letters, 1970, both for *The Confessions of Nat Turner;* American Book Award, National Book Critics Circle Award nominee, both 1980, both for *Sophie's Choice;* Connecticut Arts Award, 1984; Cino del Duca prize, 1985; Litt.D., Davidson College (Davidson, North Carolina), 1986; Commandeur, Ordre des Arts et des Lettres (France), 1987; Edward MacDowell Medal, 1988; Bobst award, 1989; National Magazine award, 1990; National Medal of Arts, 1993; Medal of Honor, National Arts Club, 1995; Common Wealth Award, 1995.

WRITINGS:

Lie Down in Darkness, Bobbs-Merrill, 1951.
The Long March, Vintage, 1957.
Set This House on Fire, Random House, 1960.
The Confessions of Nat Turner, Random House, 1967.
In the Clap Shack (three-act play; first produced in New Haven at Yale Repertory Theatre, December 15, 1972), Random House, 1973.
Sophie's Choice, Random House, 1979.
This Quiet Dust & Other Writings (essays), Random House, 1982.
Darkness Visible: A Memoir of Madness, Random House, 1990.
(Author of introduction) Robert Satter, *Doing Justice: A Trial Judge at Work,* American Lawyer Books/Simon & Schuster, 1990.
A Tidewater Morning: Three Tales from Youth, Random House, 1993.
(With Mariana Ruth Cook) *Fathers and Daughters: In Their Own Words,* Chronicle Books (San Francisco), 1994.

Also author of *Inheritance of the Night: Early Drafts of "Lie Down in Darkness,"* 1993. Editor of *Paris Review: Best Short Stories,* Dutton, 1959. Contributor to *Esquire, New York Review of Books,* and other publications. Manuscript collections of Styron's work are held by the Library of Congress, Washington, DC, and Duke University, Durham, NC.

MEDIA ADAPTATIONS: Sophie's Choice was filmed for Universal Pictures in 1982; it featured Meryl Streep in the title role.

SIDELIGHTS: William Styron's novels have brought him major literary awards, broad critical notice, and a reputation for raising controversial issues. In *The Confessions of Nat Turner* and *Sophie's Choice,* Styron writes about two victims of oppression: a slave and a concentration camp survivor. Although some critics question his approach, most praise Styron for probing into difficult subjects. Reviewers consider Styron's timing a positive factor in the success of these two books; *Sophie's Choice,* published during renewed concern about the Holocaust, and *The Confessions of Nat Turner,* published during the racially explosive late Sixties, both found large audiences. George Steiner comments in the *New Yorker:* "The crisis of civil rights, the new relationships to each other and to their own individual sensibilities that this crisis has forced on both whites and Negroes . . . give Mr. Styron's fable [*The Confessions of Nat Turner*] a special relevance."

Styron based *The Confessions of Nat Turner* on the transcript of testimony given by a slave, Nat Turner, who had led a brief revolt against slave owners in Virginia's Tidewater district. Styron considers his book a "meditation on history" rather than a strict retelling of events. He explains in a letter to the *Nation* that "in writing *The Confessions of Nat Turner* I at no time pretended that my narrative was an exact transcription of historical events; had perfect accuracy been my aim I would have written a work of history rather than a novel." Philip Rahv asserts that Styron's viewpoint is more valuable than a historical perspective. He writes in the *New York Review of Books:* "This narrative is something more than a novelistic counterpart of scholarly studies of slavery in America; it incarnates its theme, bringing home to us the monstrous reality of slavery in a psychodynamic manner that at the same time does not in the least neglect social or economic aspects."

Styron's subjective approach draws ire from critics who feel that his portrait of Nat is based on white stereotypes. A *Negro Digest* critic takes particular issue with Styron's depiction of Nat's sexuality: "In the name of fiction, Mr. Styron can do whatever he likes with History. When his interpretation, however, duplicates what is white America's favorite fantasy (i.e., every black male—especially the leader—is motivated by a latent[?] desire to sleep with the Great White Woman), he is obligated to explain (in the structure of the novel, of course) this coincidental duplication—or to be criticized accordingly. Since there is no such explanation in the technique of the novel and since it offers no vision or new perspective, but rather reaffirms an old stale, shameful fantasy (which is still quite salable) it is at best a good commercial novel." Albert Murray concurs in the *New Leader:* "Alas, what Negroes will find in Styron's 'confessions' is much the same old failure of sensibility that plagues most other fiction about black people. That is to say, they will all find a Nat Turner whom many white people may accept at a safe distance, but hardly one with whom Negroes will easily identify."

Styron writes about human suffering in a more contemporary setting—post-World War II Brooklyn—in *Sophie's Choice.* Sophie is a beautiful Polish gentile who survived Auschwitz but lost two of her children and much of her self-esteem there. Her lover, Nathan (mad, brilliant, and Jewish) is haunted by the atrocities of the Holocaust, although he personally escaped them, and he torments Sophie with reminders. Stingo, a young writer who lives downstairs from Sophie and Nathan, narrates. According to Geoffrey Wolff of *Esquire*, "Stingo is in the tradition of *The Great Gatsby*'s Nick Carraway. Like Nick, he bears witness to the passion of characters he chances upon and tries modestly to judge and pardon. Like Nick, he is a refugee from settled values— Virginia's Tidewater country—back from a great war to make his way in the great world."

David Caute of the *New Statesman* hears additional voices. For him, the "neo-Biblical cadences of Southern prose, of Wolfe and Faulkner, jostle with the cosmopolitan sensibility of an F. Scott Fitzgerald." Other critics agree that the influence of other writers sometimes muffles Styron's own voice. Jack Beatty writes in the *New Republic* that *Sophie's Choice* "is written in an unvaryingly mannered style—High Southern—that draws constant spell-destroying attention to itself." The "Southern style" associated with Faulkner and Thomas Wolfe is characterized by elaborate, even Gothic descriptions, and although Styron is "a novelist hard to categorise," he shows his allegiance to that style here and "in all of [his] writing," according to Caute, with "a tendency towards post-Wolfian inflation, a reluctance to leave any noun uncaressed by an adjective." Paul Gray of *Time* agrees, noting that Styron "often lets Stingo pile up adjectives in the manner of Thomas Wolfe: 'Brooklyn's greenly beautiful, homely, teeming, begrimed and incomprehensible vastness'. . . . True, Stingo is pictured as a beginning writer, heavily in debt to Faulkner, Wolfe and the Southern literary tradition, but Styron may preserve more redundant oratory than the effect of Stingo's youth strictly requires."

Robert Towers, writing in the *New York Review of Books*, also faults Styron for verbosity. "'All my life, I have retained a strain of uncontrolled didacticism,' says Stingo at one point," Towers notes, "and *Sophie's Choice* bears him out. The novel is made to drag along an enormous burden of commentary, ranging all the way from the meaning of the Holocaust, the ineluctable nature of evil, the corrosive effects of guilt, the horrors of slavery, and the frailty of goodness and hope to such topics as the misunderstanding of the South by Northern liberals, Southern manners as opposed to those of New York taxi drivers, and the existence of prejudice and cruelty in even the best of us." But Wolff defends Styron, observing that "the book's narrative flow is suspenseful if languid, if sometimes even glacial," and that "*Sophie's Choice* achieves an almost palpable evocation of its place and time— Poland before and during the war, Brooklyn and Coney Island immediately after." And Caute, despite his criticisms, contends that Styron's prose is "marked also by clarity, honesty and accessibility."

In response to critics who question the validity of *Confessions* and *Sophie's Choice* on the grounds of Styron's personal background, Towers argues that "it should not be necessary to defend the right of Styron—a non-Jew, a Southern Protestant in background—to this subject matter—any more than his right to assume, in the first person, the 'identity' of the leader of a slave rebellion in Virginia in 1831." Gray agrees. "The question," he writes, "is not whether Styron has a right to use alien experiences but whether his novel proves that he knows what he is writing about. In this instance, the overriding answer is yes."

It cannot be said of Styron's 1990 work *Darkness Visible: A Memoir of Madness* that Styron was writing of "alien experiences" in his subject matter, as he had first-hand knowledge of it. *Darkness Visible* is Styron's account of his slow fall into depression in 1985. Leading up to his experience was the loss of his mother when he was thirteen, his father's own depression, and Styron's forty-year dependency on alcohol. According to an interview with Laurel Graeber in the *New York Times Book Review,* the catalyst for Styron's account of his depression was his defense of the writer, Primo Levi, who committed suicide in 1987. "Mr. Styron found himself defending Levi. . .from statements that seemed to attribute his action to moral weakness," writes Graeber. Following an essay he published on the subject, Styron spoke on it, wrote a longer article, and then produced *Darkness Visible.*

"[Styron] felt, in romantic confessional style, that he had to write it, and it is good to have it," states Karl Miller in the *London Review of Books*. "There is some tremendous writing in *Darkness Visible*. The rhythmic beat of some sentences demands that they be read aloud," writes Victoria Glendinning in the *New York Times Book Review*. Miller notes that "There are passages in the book which might have been written in the 19th century—some of them, give or take a word or two, by Poe. . . . Styron writes of the dungeons 'of his spirit,' of a 'long-beshrouded metaphysical truth'—language that belongs to the Gothic strain of certain of his fictions."

A Tidewater Morning: Three Tales from Youth was Styron's first work following his depression and recovery. The three stories are autobiographical in nature and are narrated by a man in his fifties. The title novella takes place in 1938, the year Styron's mother died, and focuses on a thirteen-year-old boy who watches his mother die of cancer. In the story "Love Day" the narrator recalls his experience in the Marines as a young man of twenty. The third story tells of a ten-year-old's friendship with neighbors who have descended from a prominent Southern family but have fallen onto harder times. The story "Shadrach" portrays a ninety-year-old former slave who returns to the family's land to die. James L. W. West III in *Sewanee Review* compares the collection to Faulkner's *Go Down, Moses* and Hemingway's *In Our Time,* due to the connectedness of the stories "in ways obvious and subtle: this arrangement gives them a cumulative weight and thematic resonance that they would not possess if read separately." According to West, "The strongest cords binding these stories together are thematic. Styron is working through familiar territory for him, contemplating the fearful mysteries of grief, remorse, memory, guilt, rebellion, warfare, and death. . . . At crucial points . . .[the narrator] lifts himself above his doubt or pain, and fashions an imaginative rendering of the moment. This, Styron seems to be telling us, is the only way finally to address some of the almost intolerable ambiguities and injustices of our time."

BIOGRAPHICAL/CRITICAL SOURCES:

BOOKS

Bryer, Jackson R., and Mary B. Hatem, *William Styron: A Reference Guide,* Hall, 1978.

Casciato, Arthur D., and James L. W. West III, editors, *Critical Essays on William Styron,* Hall, 1982.

Cologne-Brookes, Gavin, *The Novels of William Styron: From Harmony to History,* Louisiana State University (Baton Rouge), 1995.

Concise Dictionary of American Literary Biography: Broadening Views, 1968-1988, Gale, 1989.

Contemporary Literary Criticism, Gale (Detroit), Volume 1, 1973; Volume 3, 1975; Volume 11, 1979; Volume 15, 1980; Volume 60, 1990.

Cowley, Malcolm, *Writers at Work: The "Paris Review" Interviews,* First Series, Viking, 1958.

Crane, John K., *The Root of All Evil: The Thematic Unity of William Styron's Fiction,* University of South Carolina Press, 1985.

Dictionary of Literary Biography Yearbook: 1980, Gale, 1981.

Friedman, Melvin J., *William Styron,* Bowling Green University, 1974.

Geismar, Maxwell, *American Moderns,* Hill & Wang, 1958.

Hadaller, David, *Gynicide: Women in the Novels of William Styron,* Fairleigh Dickinson University Press (Madison, NJ), 1996.

Kostelanetz, Richard, editor, *On Contemporary Literature,* Avon, 1964.

Leon, Philip W., *William Styron: An Annotated bibliography of Criticism,* Greenwood Press, 1978.

Mackin, Cooper R., *William Styron,* Steck Vaughn, 1969.

Malin, Irving, and Robert K. Morris, editors, *The Achievement of William Styron,* University of Georgia Press, 1975, revised edition, 1981.

Pearce, Richard, *William Styron* (Pamphlets on American Writers Series, No. 98), University of Minnesota Press, 1971.

Ratner, Marc L., *William Styron,* Twayne, 1972.

Ross, Daniel William, *The Critical Response to William Styron,* Greenwood (Westport, CT), 1995.

Ross, Virginia, *William Styron's Darkness Visible,* 1991.

Ruderman, Judith, *William Styron,* Ungar, 1989.

Waldmeir, Joseph J., editor, *Recent American Fiction,* Michigan State University Press, 1963.

West, James L. W., III, *William Styron: A Descriptive Bibliography,* G. K. Hall, 1977.

West, James L. W., III, *William Styron: A Life,* Random House, 1998.

PERIODICALS

Chicago Tribune, July 3, 1989.

Chicago Tribune Book World, May 27, 1979; January 16, 1983.

College Literature, number 1, 1987, pp. 1-16.

Commonweal, December 22, 1967.

Critique: Studies in Modern Fiction, number 2, 1985, pp. 57-65.

Detroit News, June 24, 1979.

English Journal, April, 1996, p. 87.

Esquire, July 3, 1979; December 1, 1985.

Harper's, July, 1967.

JAMA: The Journal of the American Medical Association, Volume 265, number 9, March 6, 1991, pp. 1184-85.

London Review of Books, March 21, 1991, p. 6.

Los Angeles Times, December 14, 1983.

Los Angeles Times Book Review, January 16, 1983.

Mississippi Quarterly, number 2, 1989, pp. 129-45.

Nation, October 16, 1967; April 22, 1968; July 7, 1979.

New Leader, December 4, 1967.

New Republic, June 30, 1979.

New Statesman, May 7, 1979.

New Statesman & Society, March 8, 1991, pp. 37-38; November 19, 1993, pp. 47-48.

Newsweek, October 16, 1967; May 28, 1979.

New Yorker, November 25, 1967; June 18, 1979.

New York Review of Books, October 26, 1967; September 12, 1968; July 19, 1979.

New York Times, August 5, 1967; October 3, 1967; May 29, 1979; November 27, 1982.

New York Times Book Review, October 8, 1967; August 11, 1968; May 27, 1979; June 6, 1982; November 21, 1982; December 12, 1982; August 19, 1990.

Observer Review, May 5, 1968.

Partisan Review, winter, 1968; summer, 1968.

Sewanee Review, spring, 1994.

Spectator, October 13, 1979.

Time, October 13, 1967; June 11, 1979.

Times Literary Supplement, May 19, 1968; November 30, 1979; June 10, 1983; December 10, 1993, p. 19

Village Voice, December 14, 1967.

Voya, February, 1994, p. 374.

Washington Post, May 18, 1979; January 4, 1983.

Washington Post Book World, May 29, 1979; December 5, 1982.

Whole Earth Review, fall, 1995, p. 41.

Yale Review, winter, 1968.

*   *   *

SUAREZ LYNCH, B.
See BIOY CASARES, Adolfo
See BORGES, Jorge Luis

*   *   *

SULLIVAN, Vernon
See VIAN, Boris

*   *   *

SUSANN, Jacqueline 1921-1974

PERSONAL: Born August 20, 1921, in Philadelphia, PA; died of cancer, September 21, 1974, in New York, NY; daughter of Robert (a portrait artist) and Rose (a teacher; maiden name, Jans) Susann; married Irving Mansfield (a television and film producer); children: Guy. *Education:* Studied ballet and drama in New York, NY.

CAREER: Began as model, and later actress, appearing in more than twenty Broadway plays and road company productions, including *The Women,* 1937, *She Gave Him All She Had* and *When We Are Married,* 1939, *My Fair Ladies* and *Banjo Eyes,* 1941, *Jackpot* and *The Lady Says Yes,* 1944, and off-Broadway in *The Madwoman of Chaillot,* 1970; author and novelist, 1962-74. Made frequent appearances on television dramas, panels, and commercials.

AWARDS, HONORS: Valley of the Dolls has been cited in the *Guinness Book of World Records* as the best-selling novel of all time.

WRITINGS:

(With Beatrice Cole) *Lovely Me* (play), produced on Broadway, 1946.

Every Night, Josephine! (nonfiction), Geis, 1963.

Valley of the Dolls: A Novel, Geis, 1966.

The Love Machine (novel), Simon & Schuster, 1969.

Once Is Not Enough (novel), Morrow, 1973.

Dolores (novel), Morrow, 1976.

Yargo, Bantam, 1978.

WORK IN PROGRESS: At the time of her death, Susann was working on *Good Night, Sweet Princess,* and a sequel to *Every Night, Josephine!*

MEDIA ADAPTATIONS: Among Susann's best-sellers adapted as screenplays are *Valley of the Dolls,* released by Twentieth Century-Fox in 1967, *The Love Machine,* released by Columbia in 1971, and *Once Is Not Enough,* released by Paramount in 1975.

SIDELIGHTS: Jacqueline Susann was the first author to publish two number-one best-sellers back to back, and simultaneously to face the nearly unanimous outrage of critics. When asked if she read the reviews of her novels *Valley of the Dolls* and *The Love Machine,* the actress-turned-writer responded: "I'd like to have the critics like me, I'd like to have everybody like what I write. But when my book sells, I know people like the book. That's the most important thing, because writing is communication." Moreover Susann contended, "The day is over when the point of writing is just to turn a phrase that critics will quote, like Henry James. *I'm* not interested in turning a phrase; what matters to *me* is telling a *story* that *involves* people. The hell with what critics say. I've made characters live, so that people talk about them at cocktail parties, and that, to me, is what counts. You have to have a divine conceit in your judgment. I have it."

When the author of *Valley of the Dolls* was criticized as being a writer of pornography, she explained such was not her motivation: "I don't think it is a dirty book," she told Roy Newquist. "I do believe, however, that you cannot define characters without identifying them with the sexual acts they would commit and the language they would use. For example, it is one sort of person who would say, 'Oh, for goodness' sake!' when a rehearsal went wrong. You would know that woman has restraint, a basic dignity, and is likely to be in command of a given situation. But when a performer blows sky-high, loses control of herself and her tongue, and lashes out at everyone in sight, then you are aware of the deficiencies in personality and character that will play themselves out in later events in the novel. . . . If I didn't sometimes show these characters at their more bestial, weaker moments, I'd have written a dishonest book. Frankly, I'd rather risk being called the author of a dirty book than the author of a weak or inaccurate one."

As Nora Ephron noted, "If Jacqueline Susann is no literary figure, she is nevertheless an extraordinary publishing phenomenon. . . . With the possible exception of *Cosmopolitan* magazine, no one writes about sadism in modern man and masochism in modern woman quite as horribly and accurately as Jacqueline Susann." In addition, Ephron was able to identify the reason behind the incredible success of Susann's first best-seller: "*Valley* had a message that had a magnetic appeal for women readers: it described the standard female fantasy—of going to the big city, striking it rich, meeting fabulous men—and went on to show every reader that she was far better off than the heroines in the book—who took pills, killed themselves, and made general messes of their lives. It was, essentially, a morality tale. And despite its reputation, it was not really a dirty book. Most women, I think, do not want to read hard-core pornography. They do not even want to read anything terribly technical about the sex act. What they want to read about is lust. And Jacqueline Susann gave it to them."

Susann's second best-seller, *The Love Machine,* evoked another storm of criticism. Setting up the criterion for passing judgment on it, Christopher Lehmann-Haupt remarked that since it was going to "be devoured like popcorn at a Saturday matinee, . . .

it's irrelevant to judge it by any standard other than popcorn." He found it "salty (lots of four-letter words sprinkled into a morally square container). It dissolves in your mouth (the characters are so flat and interchangeable that at times I even forgot who Robin Stone was). It doesn't fill you up (I doubt if I've ever read a novel that made less of an impression). It goes down quickly and easily. It is the kernel of an idea, the seed of an inspiration, exploded into bite-sized nothingness."

To Jonathan Baumbach, "reading *The Love Machine* is a numbingly mindless experience. Its effect is narcotic. Miss Susann asks her readers not to think, not to feel, and, before all, not to see—nothing is asked and all is given. In a sense, the book is a collaboration—a shared inhuman cultural fantasy between author and readers, a reinforcement of culture-induced fantasies. Where real literature disturbs, books like *The Love Machine* comfort. It is only child's play to read but offers gratifyingly easy solutions. . . . The subliminal message of the novel is *stay as stupid as you are.*" He continued, "The main thrust of the novel is hedonistic—characters hop in and out of bed with one another in various combinations—but the novel opts finally for the middle-class puritan verities. . . . On the face of it, *The Love Machine* deplores the amoral world it describes. . . . Integrity and love triumph over hedonism and ambition. *The Love Machine* subscribes to cultural convention so successfully because it believes in it. There is no discernible vision in the novel outside popular culture's vision of itself, no higher intelligence, no other context." Baumbach concluded that "the novel is written in the very language of its world—a language wholly incapable of accounting for human experience, a language geared to genocide."

BIOGRAPHICAL/CRITICAL SOURCES:

BOOKS

Contemporary Literary Criticism, Volume 3, Gale (Detroit), 1975.
Seaman, Barbara, *Lovely Me: The City Life of Jacqueline Susann,* Seven Stories (New York City), 1996.

PERIODICALS

Chicago Tribune, February 17, 1983.
Cosmopolitan, January, 1967.
Harper's, October, 1969.
Life, May 30, 1969.
Nation, September 1, 1969.
New Statesman, March 8, 1968.
New Yorker, August 14, 1995, p. 66.
New York Times Book Review, May 11, 1969.
Punch, January 31, 1968.
Saturday Evening Post, February 24, 1968.
Village Voice, January 25, 1968.

* * *

SUZUKI, D. T.
See SUZUKI, Daisetz Teitaro

* * *

SUZUKI, Daisetz T.
See SUZUKI, Daisetz Teitaro

SUZUKI, Daisetz Teitaro 1870-1966
(D. T. Suzuki, Daisetz T. Suzuki, Teitaro Suzuki)

PERSONAL: Name originally Teitaro Suzuki; born October 18, 1870, in Kanazawa, Japan; died July 12, 1966, in Tokyo, Japan; son of Ryojun (a physician) and Masu (Kojima) Suzuki; married Beatrice Erskine Lane (a teacher and writer), 1911 (died, 1938). *Education:* Attended Imperial University.

CAREER: Zen scholar. Worked as English teacher in Japan, 1888; novice Zen monk in Kamakura, Japan, in 1890s; Open Court Publishing Co., La Salle, IL, proofreader, editor, and translator, 1897-1908; Imperial University, Tokyo, Japan, professor of English, 1909-14; professor of English at Gakushuin in early 1920s; Otani University, Kyoto, Japan, professor of English and of Buddhist philosophy, 1921-40; writer. Visiting professor at Columbia University, 1955-57; lecturer at numerous institutions, including Cornell University, Yale University, Harvard University, Cambridge University, and Oxford University. Participant at various conferences, including World Congress of Faith, 1936, East-West Philosophers' Conference, 1949, and World Congress of Buddhists, 1952. Founder and director of Matsuga-oka Bunko (library), 1946; president of Tibetan Tripitak Research Institute.

AWARDS, HONORS: D.Litt. from Otani University; named to Academy of Japan; medals from Japanese emperor, 1949, and from *Asahi,* 1955.

WRITINGS:

(Translator under name Teitaro Suzuki) *Acvaghosha's Discourse on the Awakening of Faith in the Mahayana,* Open Court, 1900.

(Translator under name Teitaro Suzuki, with Dr. Paul Carus) Lao Tze, *T'ai-shang kan-yang p'ien: Treatise of the Exalted One on Response and Retribution,* Open Court, 1906, later edition published as *Treatise on Response and Retribution,* with translators' names listed as D. T. Suzuki and Paul Carus, 1973.

Outlines of Mahayana Buddhism, Luzac, 1907.

A Brief History of Early Chinese Philosophy, Probsthain, 1914.

Essays in Zen Buddhism, Luzac, 1st series, 1927, 2nd series, 1933, 3rd series, 1934.

Studies in the Lankavatara Sutra, One of the Most Important Texts of Mahayana Buddhism, in Which Almost All Its Principal Tenets Are Presented, Including the Teachings of Zen, Routledge, 1932.

An Introduction to Zen Buddhism (also see below), Eastern Buddhist Society, 1934, edited by Christmas Humphreys, foreword by C. G. Jung, Philosophical Library, 1949.

The Training of the Zen Buddhist Monk, illustrations by Zenchu Sato, Eastern Buddhist Society, 1934, published as *The Zen Monk's Life,* Olympia Press, 1972, published under original title, Wingbow Press, 1974, Globe Press Books, 1991.

A Manual of Zen Buddhism, Eastern Buddhist Society, 1935.

Buddhist Philosophy and Its Effect on the Life and Thought of the Japanese People, Society for International Cultural Relations, 1936, published as *Buddhism in the Life and Thought of Japan,* Buddhist Lodge, 1937, published as *Zen Buddhism and Its Influence on Japanese Culture,* Eastern Buddhist Society, 1938, revised edition published as *Zen and Japanese Buddhism,* C. E. Tuttle, 1958, 2nd revised edition published as *Zen and Japanese Culture,* Pantheon Books, 1959, 3rd edition, Japan Travel Bureau, 1965.

Japanese Buddhism, Board of Tourist Industry, Japanese Government Railways, 1938.

The Essence of Buddhism (also see below), Buddhist Society, 1946, reprinted in *What Is Zen?* 2nd edition, 1947.

The Zen Doctrine of No-Mind: The Significance of the Sutra of Hui-neng, Rider, 1949.

Living by Zen, Rider, 1950.

Studies in Zen, edited by Humphreys, Philosophical Library, 1955.

(Under name D. T. Suzuki) *Zen Buddhism: Selected Writings of D. T. Suzuki,* edited by William Barrett, Doubleday, 1956.

(Translator) *The Lankavatara Sutra: A Mahayana Text,* Routledge & Kegan Paul, 1956.

Mysticism: Christian and Buddhist, the Eastern and Western Way, Harper, 1957.

(Contributor) Erich Fromm, editor, *Zen Buddhism and Psycho-analysis,* Harper, 1960.

(Under name Daisetz T. Suzuki) *The Essentials of Zen Buddhism: Selected From the Writings of Daisetz T. Suzuki,* edited by Bernard Philips, Dutton, 1962, published as *The Essentials of Zen Buddhism: An Anthology of the Writings of Daisetz T. Suzuki,* Rider, 1963.

On Indian Mahayana Buddhism, edited by Edward Conze, Harper, 1968.

The Field of Zen: Contributions to "The Middle Way," the Journal of the Buddhist Society, edited by Humphreys, Buddhist Society, 1969, Harper, 1970.

Shin Buddhism, Harper, 1970, revised and reprinted as *Buddha of Infinite Light,* Shambhala Publications (Boston), 1998.

What Is Zen? (includes *The Essence of Buddhism*), Buddhist Society, 1971, Harper, 1972.

(Translator) Soyen Shaku, *Sermons of a Buddhist Abbot: Addresses on Religious Subjects, Including the Sutra of Forty-two Chapters,* Weiser, 1971, published as *Zen for Americans: Including the Sutra of Forty-two Chapters,* Open Court, 1974.

(Under name Daisetz T. Suzuki) *Sengai, the Zen Master,* preface by Eva von Hoboken, New York Graphic Society, 1971.

Japanese Spirituality, ten volumes, Japan Society for the Promotion of Science, 1972.

Collected Writings on Shin Buddhism, edited by Eastern Buddhist Society, Shinashu Otaniha, 1973.

(Translator) Shinran, *The Kyogyoshin-sho,* Shinshu Otaniha, 1973.

An Introduction to Zen Buddhism (includes *An Introduction to Zen Buddhism* and *A Manual of Zen Buddhism*), introduction by Charles San, Causeway Books, 1974.

(Translator under name D. T. Suzuki, with Paul Carus) Lao-tze, *The Canon of Reason and Virtue,* Open Court, 1974.

The Awakening of Zen, edited by Humphreys, Prajna Press, 1980.

Swedenborg: Buddha of the North, translated and with an introduction by Andrew Bernstein, Swedenborg Foundation (West Chester, PA), 1996.

Also author and editor of works in Japanese; translator of works into Japanese, including *Self-Reliance of Noble Wisdom,* edited by Dwight Goddard, 1932.

SIDELIGHTS: During a career that spanned more than half of the twentieth century, Daisetz Teitaro Suzuki was probably the Western world's foremost authority on Zen Buddhism. His many writings influenced several leading thinkers—including writer Aldous Huxley, psychiatrist Carl Jung, and fellow Buddhists Christmas Humphreys and Alan Watts—and established Suzuki as an unrivaled exponent and interpreter of the Zen method and perspective. In a 1957 profile for *New Yorker,* Winthrop Sargeant asserted, "Dr. Suzuki is, in fact, merely the most celebrated and most eloquent international commentator on a branch of Buddhist thought that is followed, in a popular form, by millions of laymen in Japan . . . , and, in a more advanced form, is practiced with rigorous austerity by thousands of monks and acolytes in various secluded Japanese monasteries."

Suzuki's own acquaintance with Zen practices began after he had already worked as an English teacher in a small fishing village during the late 1880s. After leaving the village to study in Tokyo at the Imperial University, he became increasingly active in the Zen monastery in nearby Kamakura. Perhaps sensing his student's penchant for explication, Zen master Soyen Shaku eventually found a job for Suzuki as a translator for Open Court publishers in Illinois. Suzuki assumed the position in 1897, and for the next eleven years he worked at Open Court—primarily as a translator, but also as a proofreader and even an editor.

At Open Court, Suzuki translated Acvaghosha's *Discourse on the Awakening of Faith in the Mahayana,* a Chinese classic, and collaborated with Paul Carus on a translation of Lao Tze's *Treatise on Response and Retribution,* a noted volume in Chinese mysticism. In addition, Suzuki wrote *Outlines of Mahayana Buddhism,* in which he related the rituals and myths of the particularly mystical—and thus non-Zen—Mahayana faith.

After leaving Open Court in 1908, Suzuki worked in Europe translating works—including those of the Swedish mystic philosopher Emanuel Swedenborg—into Japanese. In 1909 Suzuki returned to Japan, and for the next thirty-one years he worked as a teacher of English and Buddhism. During this period he wrote his first important works on Zen, including the three-volume *Essays in Zen Buddhism* and *An Introduction to Zen Buddhism.* Many scholars consider these works most valuable to readers already familiar with Zen. Alan Watts, for instance, wrote in the introduction to his book *The Way of Zen* that Suzuki's Essays in Zen Buddhism were "an unsystematic collection of scholarly papers on various aspects of the subject, enormously useful for the advanced student but quite baffling to the general reader with an understanding of the general principles." Similarly, Watts referred to Suzuki's *Introduction to Zen* as a "delightful" but "narrow and specialized" volume.

During World War II Suzuki drew the ire of his countrymen for criticizing Japan's militaristic policies, and he even came under surveillance by Japanese police. After the war Suzuki moved back to the United States, where he lived in New York City and lectured at various institutions, including Columbia University in the mid-1950s. It was at this time that Suzuki gained prominence as an authority on Zen. His *Essays in Zen Buddhism* were reprinted to great acclaim, with Gerald, Heard countering Alan Watts in a *New York Times* article by contending that the volumes provide "a clear introduction to the subject."

As Suzuki's reputation grew in the West, so did the popularity of Zen. Its influence was evident in music, particularly jazz, and in literature, notably the fiction of J. D. Salinger. Watts, too, contributed to public interest in Zen through works such as *The Way of Liberation in Zen Buddhism* and *The Way of Zen.* But he acknowledged his debt to Suzuki, whose works Watts found especially important to his own *Spirit of Zen,* written in 1936 but reprinted in the mid-1950s. Watts also noted Suzuki's influence in the works of British Buddhist Humphreys, particularly his *Zen Buddhism.*

In the 1950s Suzuki enjoyed particular success with his volume *Mysticism: Christian and Buddhist,* in which he traced similarities between the two religions and supplemented his findings with translations of Japanese mystics. J. M. Kitigawa, reviewing the book in *Christian Century,* described it as "very rewarding" and cited Suzuki as "the most prominent authority on Zen Buddhism." Suzuki also reached readers through anthologies compiled from his previous works. His *Zen Buddhism,* edited by William Barrett, was even accessible to the general public, for Barrett had organized the volume into chapters exploring specific aspects of Zen. Noteworthy in the book are sections such as "The Meaning of Zen Buddhism" and "The Historical Background of Zen Buddhism," both of which feature provocative accounts of early Zen masters illustrating the elusive simplicity of the actual subject.

Suzuki devoted himself to more specialized subjects in other works. *Zen and Japanese Culture,* for instance, is concerned with detailing and analyzing the presence of Zen in Japan's art and social customs. This work earned more praise for Suzuki upon publication in the late 1950s. Christopher Logue called it "a good book" in *New Statesman* and added that it was "an amiable, intelligent account." N. W. Ross, writing in the *New York Times Book Review,* also complimented Suzuki, declaring that the scholar had produced "a rewarding volume." Ross added, "As one turns the pages of this delightful book one seems to catch intimations of how and why certain aspects of the 'spirit of Zen' are making themselves felt in America today."

Suzuki died in 1966 at age ninety-five. Since his death, however, several more of his writings have appeared, including translations of Buddhist texts. More anthologies have also been published, and his lectures have been collected in volumes such as *Shin Buddhism.* In addition, his earlier works are often reprinted, thus assuring his continued stature as Zen's most accomplished and articulate interpreter for Western readers.

BIOGRAPHICAL/CRITICAL SOURCES:

BOOKS

Switzer, A. Irwin III, *D. T. Suzuki: A Biography,* The Buddhist Society (London), 1985.
Watts, Alan Wilson, *The Way of Zen,* Pantheon, 1957.

PERIODICALS

Christian Century, December 28, 1949; June 8, 1955; April 10, 1957; March 18, 1970.
Guardian, November 4, 1960.
Nation, August 15, 1959.
New Statesman, August 29, 1959.
New Yorker, August 31, 1957.
New York Times, June 4, 1950.
New York Times Book Review, July 12, 1959; October 16, 1960.
Saturday Review, November 16, 1957.
Times Literary Supplement, May 13, 1955; April 15, 1960; February 17, 1961; July 7, 1972.

*   *   *

SUZUKI, Teitaro
See SUZUKI, Daisetz Teitaro

SWENSON, May 1919-1989

PERSONAL: Born May 28, 1919, in Logan, UT; died December 4, 1989, in Ocean View, DE (some sources say Bethany Beach, Delaware, or Salisbury, Maryland); daughter of Dan Arthur (a teacher) and Anna M. (Helberg) Swenson. *Education:* Utah State University, B.A., 1939.

CAREER: Poet, living in New York City, 1949-89. Formerly worked as an editor for New Directions, New York City; writer in residence at Purdue University, Lafayette, IN, 1966-67, University of North Carolina, 1968-69 and 1974, Lothbridge University, Alberta, Canada, 1970, and University of California, Riverside, 1976. Lectured and gave readings at more than fifty American universities and colleges, as well as at the New York YM-YWHA Poetry Center, and San Francisco Poetry Center. Conductor of workshops at University of Indiana Writers' Conference and Breadloaf, Vermont. Participant at the Yaddo and MacDowell colonies for writers.

MEMBER: Academy of American Poets (Chancellor, 1980), American Academy and Institute of Arts and Letters.

AWARDS, HONORS: Poetry Introductions Prize, 1955; Robert Frost Poetry Fellowship for Bread Loaf Writers' Conference, 1957; Guggenheim fellowship, 1959; William Rose Benet Prize of the Poetry Society of America, 1959; Longview Foundation award, 1959; National Institute of Arts and Letters award, 1960; Amy Lowell Travelling Scholarship, 1960; Ford Foundation grant, 1964; Brandeis University Creative Arts Award, 1967; Rockefeller Writing fellowship, 1967; Distinguished Service Medal of Utah State University, 1967; Lucy Martin Donnelly Award of Bryn Mawr College, 1968; Shelley Poetry Award, 1968; National Endowment for the Arts Grant, 1977; National Book Award nomination, 1978, for *New and Selected Things Taking Place;* Academy of American Poets fellowship, 1979; Bollingen Poetry Award, 1981; MacArthur Award, 1987; National Book Critics Circle award nomination (poetry), 1987, for *In Other Words.* Honorary degrees from Utah State University, 1987.

WRITINGS:

POETRY

Another Animal, Scribner (New York City), 1954.
A Cage of Spines, Rinehart (New York City), 1958.
To Mix With Time: New and Selected Poems, Scribner, 1963.
Poems to Solve (young adult), Scribner, 1966.
Half Sun Half Sleep (new poems and her translations of six Swedish poets), Scribner, 1967.
Iconographs (includes "Feel Me"), Scribner, 1970.
More Poems to Solve, Scribner, 1971.
(Translator with Leif Sjoberg) *Windows and Stones, Selected Poems of Tomas Transtromer* (translated from Swedish), University of Pittsburgh Press (Pittsburgh), 1972.
New and Selected Things Taking Place (includes "Ending"), Little, Brown (Boston), 1978.
In Other Words, Knopf (New York City), 1988.
The Love Poems of May Swenson, Houghton Mifflin (Boston), 1991.
The Centaur, illustrated by Barry Moser, Macmillan (New York City), 1994.
Nature: Poems Old And New, Houghton Mifflin, 1994.
May Out West, Utah State University Press (Logan), 1996.
Made with Words, edited by Gardner McFall, University of Michigan Press (Ann Arbor), 1997.

PLAYS

The Floor (one-act), first produced under the program title *Doubles and Opposites* in New York at American Place Theater, May 11, 1966, on a triple bill with *23 Pat O'Brien Movies,* by Bruce Jay Friedman, and *Miss Pete,* by Andrew Glaze.

CONTRIBUTOR

A Treasury of Great Poems, edited by Louis Untermeyer, Simon & Schuster, 1955.
New Poets 2, Ballantine, 1957.
New Poets of England & America, edited by Donald Hall, Robert Pack, and Louis Simpson, Meridian, 1957.
A Country in the Mind, edited by Ray B. West, Angel Island Publications, 1962.
Twentieth-Century American Poetry, edited by Conrad Aiken, Modern Library, 1963.
100 American Poems of the Twentieth Century, Harcourt, 1963.
The Modern Poets, edited by John Malcolm Brinnin and Bill Read, McGraw, 1963.
The New Modern Poetry, edited by M. L. Rosenthal, Macmillan, 1967.

OTHER

Works represented in other anthologies. Poems also included in translation in anthologies published in Italy and Germany. Contributor of poetry, stories, and criticism to *Poetry, Nation, Saturday Review, Atlantic, Harper's, New Yorker, Southern Review, Hudson Review,* and other periodicals. Swenson's work is included in the sound recording *Today's Poets: Their Poems, Their Voices,* Volume 2, Scholastic Records, 1968, and recordings for the Library of Congress, Spoken Arts Records, Folkways Records, and others. Her poems have been set to music by Otto Leuning, Howard Swanson, Emerson Meyers, Joyce McKeel, Claudio Spies, Lester Trimble, and Warren Benson.

SIDELIGHTS: During her prolific career, May Swenson received numerous literary-award prizes and nominations for her poetry. Often experimental in both form and appearance, her poems earned her widespread critical acclaim. As Priscilla Long comments in the *Women's Review of Books,* "Swenson was a visionary poet, a prodigious observer of the fragile and miraculous natural world."

Swenson's poetry has been praised for its imagery, which is alternately precise and beguiling, and for the quality of her personal and imaginative observations. In addition, her poetry "exhibits . . . her continuing alertness to the liveliness of nature. Correspondences among all life forms pour from her work, confirming that nothing is meaningless. The universe's basic beauty and balance is the stuff and soul of her poems," Eloise Klein Healy observes in the *Los Angeles Times.*

Richard Howard emphasizes in a *Tri-Quarterly* review that Swenson's enterprise is "to get out of herself and into those larger, warmer energies of earth, and to do so by liturgical means." Howard writes: "When May Swenson, speaking in her thauma-turgical fashion of poetry, says that 'attention to the silence in between is the amulet that makes it work,' we are reminded, while on other occasions in her work we are reassured, that there is a kind of poetry, as there used to be a kind of love, which dares not speak its name." Thus Swenson's "orphic cadences," her "siren-songs, with their obsessive reliance on the devices of incantation," are the means by which she seeks to "discover runes, the conjurations by which she can not only apostrophize the hand, the cat and the cloud in their innominate otherness, but by which she can, in some essential and relieving way, become them, leave her own impinging selfhood in the paralyzed region where names are assigned, and assume instead the energies of natural process."

Reviewing *Half Sun Half Sleep, New York Times Book Review* contributor Karl Shapiro writes: "[Swenson's] concentration on the verbal equivalent of experience is so true, so often brilliant, that one watches her with hope and pleasure, praying for victory all the way." In a *Poetry* review of *Half Sun Half Sleep,* William Stafford says of this collection: "No one today is more deft and lucky in discovering a poem than May Swenson. Her work often appears to be proceeding calmly, just descriptive and accurate; but then suddenly it opens into something that looms beyond the material, something that impends and implies. . . . So graceful is the progression in her poems that they launch confidently into any form, carrying through it to easy, apt variations. Often her way is to define things, but the definitions have a stealthy trend; what she chooses and the way she progresses heap upon the reader a consistent, incremental effect." And Shapiro offers this analysis of Swenson's achievement in this book: "The whole volume is an album of experiments . . . that pay off. It is strange to see the once-radical *carmen figuratum,* the calligraphic poem, spatial forms, imagist and surreal forms—all the heritage of the early years of the century—being used with such ease and unselfconsciousness."

Swenson herself wrote that the experience of poetry is "based in a craving to get through the curtains of things as they *appear,* to things as they are, and then into the larger, wilder space of things as they *are becoming.* This ambition involves a paradox: an instinctive belief in the senses as exquisite tools for this investigation and, at the same time, a suspicion about their crudeness." Swenson also noted: "The poet, tracing the edge of a great shadow whose outline shifts and varies, proving there is an invisible moving source of light behind, hopes (naively, in view of his ephemerality) to reach and touch the foot of that solid whatever-it-is that casts the shadow. If sometimes it seems he does touch it, it is only to be faced with a more distant, even less accessible mystery. Because all is movement—all is breathing change."

Among the "strategies and devices, the shamanism and sorcery this poet deploys," as Howard admiringly describes them, is Swenson's use of the riddle in *Poems to Solve.* The book may be enjoyed by both children and adults; the poems here are another serious attempt to accommodate "the mystery that only when a thing is apprehended as something else can it be known as itself." Swenson wrote of these poems: "It is essential, of course, with a device such as this to make not a riddle-pretending-to-be-a-poem but a poem that is also, and as if incidentally, a riddle—a solvable one. The aim is not to mystify or mislead but to clarify and make recognizable through the reader's own uncontaminated perceptions. By bringing into play the sensual apparatus of the reader, the poem causes him to realize the content eye-wise, ear-wise, taste, touch, and musclewise *before* beginning to cerebralize. The analyzing intellect ought not to be the first but the last tool that is applied to a poem, for applied alone, as it sometimes is, it can inhibit organic associative responses, can bypass initial curiosity and individual exploration, resulting in little more than a mechanistic contact with the poem."

Nature: Poems Old and New, published four years after Swenson's death, emphasizes Swenson's sympathy for and identification with the outdoors. "Swenson was an unrelentingly lyrical poet," writes Priscilla Long in the *Women's Review of Books,* "a master of the poetic line in which similar sounds accumulate and resonate so that the poem exists, beyond its meanings, as a rattle or a music box, or, in moments of greatness, a symphony." Her collection *Nature* is "so inward, independent, and intense, so intimate and impersonal at once," declares critic Langdon Hammer in the *Yale Review,* that "it has been difficult to place in the field of contemporary poetry." Several other critics, however, identify the work as an appreciation of Swenson's profound talent, collecting the best of her work between two covers. "The poetry tinks, feels, examines," asserts a *Publishers Weekly* contributor; "it's patiently, meticulously sensuous, and adventurously varied in form, much as nature is." "These poems, harvested from her life's work and arranged in this delightful format," states Rochelle Natt in the *American Book Review,* "promote a lasting vision of Swenson's valuable contribution to American poetry."

BIOGRAPHICAL/CRITICAL SOURCES:

BOOKS

Brinnin, John Malcolm, and Bill Read, editors, *The Modern Poets,* McGraw, 1963.
Contemporary Literary Criticism, Gale (Detroit), Volume 4, 1975; Volume 14, 1980.
Contemporary Poets, St. Martin's Press, 1980.
Deutsch, Babette, editor, *Poetry in Our Time,* 2nd edition, Doubleday, 1963.
Dictionary of Literary Biography, Volume 5: *American Poets since World War II,* Gale, 1980.
Hoffman, Daniel, editor, *The Harvard Guide to American Writing,* Belknap Press, 1977.
Nemerov, Howard, editor, *Poets on Poetry,* Basic Books, 1966.
Poems for Young Readers: Selections from Their Own Writing by Poets Attending the Houston Festival of Contemporary Poetry, National Council of Teachers of English, 1966.
Stepanchev, Stephen, *American Poetry Since 1945,* Harper, 1965.
Untermeyer, Louis, editor, *A Treasury of Great Poems, English and American,* Simon & Schuster, 1955.

PERIODICALS

American Book Review, September, 1995, p. 14.
Atlantic, February, 1968.
Booklist, June 1, 1993.
Book Week, June 4, 1967, Volume 4, number 30.
Chicago Tribune, December 10, 1989.
Christian Science Monitor, February 12, 1979.
Los Angeles Times, March 22, 1979; December 14, 1989.
New York Times, March 19, 1979; June 16, 1987; December 5, 1989.
New York Times Book Review, September 1, 1963; May 7, 1967; February 11, 1979; June 12, 1988; January 19, 1992.
Poetry, December, 1967; February, 1979; February, 1993.
Prairie Schooner, spring, 1968.
Publishers Weekly, May 30, 1994, pp. 46-47.
Tri-Quarterly, fall, 1966.
Washington Post, December 8, 1989.
Women's Review of Books, January, 1995, pp. 8-9.
Yale Review, January, 1995, pp. 121-41.

*   *   *

SWIFT, Augustus
  See LOVECRAFT, H(oward) P(hillips)

SWIFT, Graham (Colin) 1949-

PERSONAL: Born May 4, 1949, in London, England; son of Allan Stanley and Sheila Irene (Bourne) Swift. *Education:* Attended Dulwich College, 1960-67; Queens' College, Cambridge, B.A., 1970, M.A., 1975; attended York University, 1970-73.

ADDRESSES: Agent—A. P. Watt Ltd., 20 John St., London WC1N 2DR, England.

CAREER: Writer. Worked as part-time teacher of English at colleges in London, England, 1974-83.

MEMBER: PEN, Society of Authors, Royal Society of Literature (fellow).

AWARDS, HONORS: Geoffrey Faber Memorial Award, 1983, for *Shuttlecock; Guardian* Fiction Prize and nomination for Booker McConnell Prize, both 1983, Winifred Holtby Prize from Royal Society of Literature, 1984, and Italy's Premio Grinzane Cavour, 1987, all for *Waterland;* France's Prix du Meilleur Livre Etranger, 1994, for *Ever After;* Booker Prize, 1996, for *Last Orders.*

WRITINGS:

NOVELS

The Sweet-Shop Owner, Allen Lane (London, England), 1980, Washington Square Press (New York City), 1985.
Shuttlecock, Allen Lane, 1981, Washington Square Press, 1984.
Waterland, Heinemann (London), 1983, Poseidon Press (New York City), 1984.
Out of This World, Viking (London), 1988, Poseidon Press, 1988.
Ever After, Pan Books (London), 1992, Knopf (New York City), 1992.
Last Orders, Knopf, 1996.

OTHER

Learning to Swim and Other Stories, London Magazine Editions (London), 1982, Poseidon Press, 1985.
(Editor with David Profumo) *The Magic Wheel: An Anthology of Fishing in Literature,* Picador, 1986.

MEDIA ADAPTATIONS: Waterland was adapted for film by Peter Prince and released by Palace Pictures, 1992.

SIDELIGHTS: Graham Swift is among the most highly regarded British writers to appear in the 1980s. With the publication of his fourth book and third novel, *Waterland,* Swift established himself as one of Britain's leading writers. He is considered a master storyteller and an inquisitive, ceaselessly analytical artist—one whose works embrace both the dramatic and the enigmatic.

Swift's reputation—particularly in the United States—rests largely on the merits of *Waterland,* which was nominated for England's prestigious Booker McConnell Prize in 1983. This novel is a complex first-person account by history teacher Tom Crick, who relates his early romance, marital problems, and career difficulties all in obsessively analytical detail. *Waterland* begins with Crick recounting the discovery of a corpse in the Fens, a flat waterland where Crick's father works as a lock-keeper. After this episode, the narrative shifts to an apparent classroom, where Crick is discussing his dismissal from his teaching post. He reveals that his largely autobiographical lectures have prompted distress from school administrators, who thus urge him to resign. Crick also discloses that his life has been unsettled by his wife's arrest—and subsequent commitment in a mental institution—for having kidnapped a child.

Waterland shifts back and forth between Crick's recollection of discovering the corpse and his account of present private and professional difficulties. Interspersed among these autobiographical episodes are historical and philosophical analyses. Crick provides extensive background on the Fens and its inhabitants—past and present—while consistently debating the worth of this history. He acknowledges the possibly dubious nature of such history, yet he constantly returns to it as a means of explaining or understanding the present. The validity of history as a means of understanding the present is a major point of debate in *Waterland,* and one that provides much of its philosophical tension.

Upon its publication in 1983, *Waterland* was greeted enthusiastically by British critics and was considered among the year's finest novels. The following spring, when *Waterland* was published in the United States, reviewers hailed it as a wide-ranging, enlightening work. "Its textured descriptions of the English fens," explained fellow novelist Linda Gray Sexton in the *New York Times Book Review,* "invited comparisons with Thomas Hardy." Michiko Kakutani wrote in the *New York Times Book Review* that Swift's novel was "a highly ambitious book—a book that reads at once as a gothic family saga, a detective story and as a philosophical meditation on the nature and uses of history." Michael Wood noted in the *New York Review of Books* that *Waterland* was "formidably intelligent," and Charles Champlin declared in the *Los Angeles Times Book Review* that the novel "carries with all else a profound knowledge of a people, a place and their interweaving." Champlin called *Waterland* "a fine and original work."

Following the success of *Waterland,* Swift's previous two novels were published in the United States. His first work, *The Sweet-Shop Owner,* concerns the memories and opinions of an industrious shopkeeper named Willy Chapman as he lives his final hours. Victimized by his marriage to "an insistently assertive shrew, a frigid near-hysteric who retreats into illness and invalidism," according to Frank Rudman in the *Spectator,* and by an ungrateful daughter who refuses to visit him even long enough to collect her inheritance, Chapman finally closes his shop and heads home to die, reflecting on forty years of unhappiness and lack of fulfillment. Writing in the *New Statesman,* Alan Hollinghurst called *The Sweet-Shop Owner* a "marvelous first novel." American critics seconded that opinion. Michael Gorra, for instance, wrote in the *New York Times Book Review* that the work established Swift "as one of the brightest promises the English novel has now to offer." Like other reviewers, Gorra noted similarities between *The Sweet-Shop Owner* and writings of James Joyce. "There is a touch of Joyce," Gorra declared, "in . . . Swift's revelation of the hidden poetry of small men's lives."

Shuttlecock, Swift's second novel, is also an analytical tale about the past. The work's protagonist is a police department archivist who scans records to discover possible connections between various crimes. Like Swift's other protagonists, the archivist is obsessed with the past, particularly the life of his father, a former war hero in the French Resistance, once captured by the Gestapo, now confined in a mental hospital after a breakdown. Tension mounts when the archivist discovers evidence linking his father's past activities with information missing from police files—information that suggests, according to John Mellors in *London,* "that Dad's first breakdown had been in wartime, that he had betrayed other agents in the network, that his 'escape' had been set up for him by his captors as a quid pro quo." The narrator destroys the file that might have answered this question without reading it first, so the mystery remains unresolved at the novel's end. A reviewer for the *Washington Post Book World*, in assessing both *Shuttle-cock* and the earlier *Sweet-Shop Owner*, stated that "Swift's narratives twist and turn, knotting together inexorably the past with the present, sweeping us along steadily."

Swift's short story collection, *Learning to Swim and Other Stories*, was published in the United States in 1985, but its American reception failed to match that accorded *Waterland*, and more than one critic remarked that some of the tales seemed too studied and even uncompelling. But in Britain, where *Learning to Swim* had appeared in 1982, reviewers praised the stories as insightful and provocative. Hollinghurst, for instance, wrote in the *Times Literary Supplement*, "These concentrated, enigmatic stories address their subjects with such intelligent conviction and clarity that their ambiguities are . . . challengingly displayed." Hollinghurst was especially impressed with "The Watch," a tale about a family whose males are assured longevity by a magical watch, and "The Hypochondriac," the story of a patient's seemingly imagined—but ultimately real, and fatal—pains. "Swift's ideas are large," Hollinghurst observed, "but his manner is meticulous, orderly and attentive."

Out of This World, Swift's first novel after *Waterland*, again closely examines the interplay between history and the present. The book essentially consists of two interlocking monologues, those of former photojournalist Harry Beech and his estranged daughter, Sophie. Harry's dedication to photography—his photos of violence in war zones and elsewhere in the world were famous—contributed to the alienation of his daughter. At the beginning of the novel, explained *Times Literary Supplement* contributor Anne Duchene, "there has been no communication between them for ten years, since Harry's father was blown up by a car-bomb and Sophie saw Harry taking photographs a moment later." Now in his sixties, Harry works as an aerial photographer, trying to understand the acts of violence he has witnessed. Sophie, now married with two healthy children, lives in New York City, where she consults a psychiatrist in order to resolve her feelings about her father and herself. Eventually Harry writes to Sophie, asking her blessing on his remarriage, and she flies to England for a reunion with him.

The success of *Waterland* inevitably invited critics to compare *Out of This World* with it. J. L. Carr, writing in the *Spectator*, called *Waterland* "innovatory, moving, memorable"; but, the critic said, "although I read [*Out of This World*] with ringing ears, I was not unsettled by its protagonists' disasters. . . . Now and then, as the [father and daughter] pair tried to unload their little burdens of guilt upon me, I resentfully felt sorry for myself. What have they to complain about?" Duchene stated that "the writing . . . lacks the resonance of *Waterland* and the manic Kafkaesque energies of *Shuttlecock*." The reader, she continued, "might have wished to get more lift-off . . . from what we know to be the author's powerful, annealing imagination. We ask a great deal of him only because of his past flights." Sexton's *New York Times Book Review* article was more complimentary. "Swift's achievement is that the important story of [Harry's and Sophie's] self-education has been told with such simple, startling beauty," she declared. "Not a book the reader is likely to forget, *Out of This World* deserves to be ranked at the forefront of contemporary literature."

Ever After, Swift's 1992 novel, is reminiscent of its predecessors in its examination of the effects of history and ancestry on people living in modern times. It is the story of Bill Unwin, an erstwhile university professor who has just gone through a traumatic period:

within the past eighteen months he has lost his mother, his stepfather, and his beloved actress-wife. Seriously depressed, he attempts suicide, and it is while he convalesces that he begins to tell his tale. It turns out that Unwin's academic career was created for him—for many years he had been his wife's manager, and his seat at the university exists only because his rich American stepfather established it with the provision that Unwin was to have it. Unwin occupies his time at the university by editing the papers of a Victorian ancestor named Matthew Pearce, whose faith was shattered by the death of his son, his reading of Darwin's theories of natural selection, and his encounter with the fossil of an ichthyosaur on a beach in Dorset. Unwin is just as helpless to answer questions about Pearce's life as he is to answer questions about his own—why did his father, Colonel Unwin, commit suicide? Was Colonel Unwin really his father, and did news of his wife's supposed infidelity drive him to shoot himself? "A latter-day Hamlet," stated Pico Iyer in *Time* magazine, "Unwin is driven mad by the sense that all of us are playacting, adrift in a world of 'suppose's.'"

Like *Out of This World*, *Ever After* tempted critics to draw comparisons with *Waterland*. "It seems to be a convention that when you are writing about Graham Swift, somewhere in the first paragraph or two you refer to '*Waterland*, his best book,'" stated Hilary Mantel in the *New York Review of Books*. "It would be a great thing to kick over the traces and declare *Waterland* a mere bagatelle beside Swift's new novel; unfortunately, that is impossible." "How could any comment more sharply irritate Graham Swift," asked Michael Levenson in the *New Republic*, "than the cruelly recurrent, dully obvious opinion that neither his two novels written before *Waterland* nor the two written since even belong on the same shelf as that strong book?"

And, as was the case with *Out of This World*, reviews were mixed. Iyer, for instance, referred to the novel as "a dense, literary text that race[s] ahead with the compulsive fury of a page turner." Ursula K. Le Guin wrote in the *Washington Post Book World*, "The multiple plot covers 150 years in 276 pages quite effortlessly, and though full of references, characters, events and second thoughts, it turns and doubles without confusion in time and space. It is masterfully done. Only it all seems, despite its dense, charged texture, a bit thin and arbitrary." "The prose is rich, lush and unhurried," declared *New York Times Book Review* contributor MacDonald Harris; "this is a modern British novel for the reader who is getting bored with the contemporary American mode of fiction and turns back, now and then, to [Anthony] Trollope, Hardy or George Eliot." Lorna Sage, writing for the *Times Literary Supplement*, also compared Swift to Thomas Hardy "in his insistence that the naive questions about extinction matter." "*Ever After*," concluded Mantel, "may have deeply advanced Swift as a thinker, but sadly it has not advanced him as a novelist."

Swift attempted to capture the language and lore of working-class London in his 1996 novel *Last Orders*. The book was awarded the Booker Prize, Britain's highest literary honor. The action of the novel follows the death of Jack Dodds, a London butcher, when three of the dead man's drinking buddies gather together to scatter his ashes into the sea. The occasion provides the men, all World War II veterans, with an opportunity for reflection, remembrance, and revelation. Many readers saw similarities between Swift's book and William Faulkner's *As I Lay Dying*, which also uses the transport of a dead body as a jumping-off point for a sequence of monologues. But Swfit himself was quick to label the book an homage, not a copy.

Reviewing the novel for *Maclean's*, John Bemrose compared *Last Orders* favorably to *Waterland*, calling it "the finer achievement." Swift "has never before woven history so artfully into the texture of the present—the ghosts of the past taking their rightful, disturbing place in the minds of the living." James Bowman, writing in *National Review*, tweaked Swift for his employment of the "modish style," but conceded that "with discrete passages as fine as you could hope for, the book is undeniably affecting." The critic for the *Economist*, on the other hand, felt that Swift's use of monologues diminished the book's overall impact. "This technique reduces its potential imaginative scope, and makes it less multifarious, and more bitty and claustrophic, than it need have been."

Nonetheless, critics continue to respect Swift, and they expect great things from him in the future. "He is a figure to learn from," declared Levenson, "the professional in the imagination business who delivers his goods every few years, who raises no boasty thumbs in praise of his own talents but who doggedly composes 200 pages of serious story, without pandering either to those who write the reviews or to those who write the checks."

BIOGRAPHICAL/CRITICAL SOURCES:

BOOKS

Contemporary Literary Criticism, Volume 41, Gale (Detroit), 1987.

PERIODICALS

Books, January, 1993, p. 18.
Detroit News, May 19, 1985.
Economist, March 16, 1996.
Globe and Mail (Toronto), September 1, 1984; February 8, 1986.
Listener, January 6, 1983.
London, November, 1981, pp. 88-90.
Los Angeles Times Book Review, April 1, 1984.
Maclean's, May 6, 1996.
Nation, March 31, 1980.
National Review, March 10, 1997.
New Republic, June 22, 1992, pp. 38-40.
New Statesman, April 25, 1980; March 18, 1983; October 7, 1983.
Newsweek, April 30, 1984.
New York Review of Books, August 16, 1984; June 11, 1992, p. 23; April 4, 1996.
New York Times, March 20, 1984.
New York Times Book Review, March 25, 1984; June 23, 1985, pp. 11-12; September 11, 1988, p. 14; October 22, 1989, p. 38; March 29, 1992, p. 21; May 16, 1993, p. 40; May 5, 1996.
Publishers Weekly, February 22, 1993, p. 91.
Spectator, April 26, 1980, p. 23; October 8, 1983; March 12, 1988, p. 28; November 28, 1992, p. 40.
Time, April 13, 1992, p. 78.
Times Literary Supplement, July 27, 1982; October 7, 1983; March 11, 1988, p. 275; February 21, 1992, p. 6; April 16, 1993, p. 22.
Village Voice, July 2, 1985; September, 1993, p. 29.
Washington Post Book World, March 18, 1984; April 14, 1985; June 9, 1985; March 22, 1992, p. 6.
Writer, February, 1998.

*   *   *

SWITHEN, John
 See KING, Stephen (Edwin)

SYLVIA
 See ASHTON-WARNER, Sylvia (Constance)

*   *   *

SYMMES, Robert Edward
 See DUNCAN, Robert (Edward)

*   *   *

SYRUC, J.
 See MILOSZ, Czeslaw

*   *   *

SZYMBORSKA, Wislawa 1923-
 (Stancykowna)

PERSONAL: Born July 2, 1923, in Prowent-Bnin, near Poznan, Poland. *Education:* Attended Jagellonian University, 1945-48.

ADDRESSES: Home—Ul. Krolewska 82/89, 30-079, Cracow, Poland.

CAREER: Poet and critic. Poetry editor and columnist, *Zycie literackie* (literary weekly magazine), 1953-81.

MEMBER: Polish Writers' Association (member of general board, 1978-83).

AWARDS, HONORS: Cracow literary prize, 1954; Gold Cross of Merit, 1955; Ministry of Culture prize, 1963; Knight's Cross, Order of Polonia Resituta, 1974; Goethe Prize, 1991; Herder Prize, 1995; Polish PEN Club prize, 1996; Nobel Prize for Literature, 1996.

WRITINGS:

POETRY

Dlatego zyjemy (title means "That's Why We Are Alive"), [Warsaw], 1952.
Pytania zadawane sobie (title means "Questions Put to Myself"), [Warsaw], 1954.
Wolanie do Yeti (title means "Calling Out to Yeti"), [Warsaw], 1957.
Sol (title means "Salt"), Panstwowy Instytut Wydawniczy (Warsaw), 1962.
Wiersze wybrane (collection), Panstwowy Instytut Wydawniczy, 1964.
Sto pociech (title means "A Hundred Joys"), Panstwowy Instytut Wydawniczy, 1967.
Poezje wybrane (title means "Selected Poems"), Ludowa Spoldzielnia Wydawnicza (Warsaw), 1967.
Poezje (title means "Poems"), Przedmowa Jerzego Kwiatkowskiego (Warsaw), 1970.
Wybor poezje (collection), Czytelnik, 1970.
Wszelki wypadek (title means "There But for the Grace"), Czytelnik, 1972.
Wybor wierszy (collection), Panstwowy Instytut Wydawniczy, 1973.
Tarsjusz i inne wiersze (title means "Tarsius and Other Poems"), Krajowa Agencja Wydawnicza (Warsaw), 1976.
Wielka liczba (title means "A Great Number"), Czytelnik, 1976.

Sounds, Feelings, Thoughts: Seventy Poems, translated by Magnus J. Krynski and Robert A. Maguire, Princeton University Press (Princeton, NJ), 1981.

Poezje wybrane (II) (title means "Selected Poems II"), Ludowa Spoldzielnia Wydawnicza (Warsaw), 1983.

Ludzie na moscie, Czytelnik, 1986, translation by Adam Czerniawski published as *People on a Bridge: Poems,* Forest (London and Boston, MA), 1990.

Poezje = Poems (bilingual edition), translated by Krynski and Maguire, Wydawnictwo Literackie (Cracow), 1989.

Wieczor autorski: wiersze (title means "Authors' Evening: Poems"), Anagram, 1992.

Koniec i poczatek (title means "The End and the Beginning"), Wydawnictwo Literackie, 1993.

View with a Grain of Sand: Selected Poems, translated by Stanislaw Baranczak and Clare Cavanagh, Harcourt (New York City), 1995.

Also author of *Lektury nadobowiazkowe* (collection of book reviews; title means "Non-Compulsory Reading"), Wydawnictwo Literackie, 1973, and translator of French poetry. Work represented in anthologies, including *Polish Writing Today,* Penguin (New York City), 1967; *The New Polish Poetry,* University of Pittsburgh Press, 1978; and *Anthologie de la poesie polonaise: 1400-1980,* revised edition, Age d'homme, 1981. Also contributor, under pseudonym Stancykowna, to *Arka* (underground publication) and *Kultura* (exile magazine; published in Paris).

SIDELIGHTS: Wislawa Szymborska was thrust into the international spotlight in 1996 after receiving the Nobel Prize for literature. The reclusive and private Szymborska was cited by the Swedish Academy for "poetry that with ironic precision allows the historical and biological context to come to light in fragments of human reality." Her poetry, described by *Los Angeles Times* critic Dean E. Murphy, is "seductively simple verse . . . [which has] captured the wit and wisdom of everyday life for the past half century."

Though not widely known outside her native Poland, Szymborska received critical acclaim for the first collection of her work to appear in English translation, *Sounds, Feelings, Thoughts: Seventy Poems.* "Of the poetic voices to come out of Poland after 1945 Wislawa Szymborska's is probably the most elusive as well as the most distinctive," writes Jaroslaw Anders in the *New York Review of Books.* Anders comments: "*Sounds, Feelings, Thoughts* con-

tains poems from [Szymborska's] five books written since 1957, comprising more or less half of what the poet herself considers her canon. Its publication is of interest not only because of Szymborska's importance as a poet, but also because her work demonstrates that the diversity of poetic modes in Poland is much greater than is usually perceived." Alice-Catherine Carls, in a review of *Sounds, Feelings, Thoughts* in *Library Journal,* calls the work "one of those rare books which put one in a state of 'grace.'" Robert Hudzik, also in *Library Journal,* claims: "This volume reveals a poet of startling originality and deep sympathy."

The 1995 collection *Views with a Grain of Sand: Selected Poems* was also praised by many critics who laud Szymborska's directness and distinctive voice. Stephen Dobyns in the *Washington Post Book World* praises both the humor of Szymborska's work as well as the translation by Stanislaw Baranczak and Clare Cavanagh. Edward Hirsch in a *New York Review of Books* review concurs, arguing that the volume reveals "the full force of [Szymborska's] fierce and unexpected wit." Louis McKee, in a *Library Journal* review also praises the "wonderfully wicked" wit of Szymborska. Dobyns concludes: "The poems are surprising, funny and deeply moving. Szymborska is a world-class poet, and this book will go far to make her known in the United States."

BIOGRAPHICAL/CRITICAL SOURCES:

BOOKS

Contemporary Literary Criticism, Volume 99, Gale (Detroit), 1997.

Dictionary of Literary Biography Yearbook, 1996, Gale, 1997.

PERIODICALS

Antioch Review, March 22, 1997.

Humanities Review, spring, 1982, p. 141.

Library Journal, September 1, 1981, p. 1636; July, 1995, p. 85.

Los Angeles Times, October 4, 1996; October 13, 1996.

New Republic, January 1, 1996, p. 36.

New Yorker, December 14, 1992, p. 94; March 1, 1993, p. 86.

New York Review of Books, October 21, 1982, p. 47; October 21, 1993, p. 42; April 18, 1996, p. 35.

New York Times, October 4, 1996.

Observer (London), August 18, 1991, p. 51.

Wall Street Journal, October 4, 1996.

Washington Post Book World, July 30, 1995, p. 8.

Wilson Quarterly, March 22, 1997.

World Literature Today, spring, 1982, p. 368; January 1, 1997.

T

TAGORE, Rabindranath 1861-1941
(Ravindranatha Thakura)

PERSONAL: Some sources transliterate name as Ravindranatha Thakura; born May 7 (some sources say May 6), 1861, in Calcutta, Bengal, British India (now Calcutta, West Bengal, India); died August 7, 1941, in Calcutta, West Bengal, India; cremated; son of Debendranath (a philosopher, scholar, religious reformer, and writer) and Sarada Devi Tagore; married Mrinalini Devi Raichaudhuri, December 9, 1883; children: Madhurilata (daughter; also known as Bela), Rathindranath (son), Renuka (daughter), Mira (daughter), Samindranath (son). *Education:* Attended University College, London, 1879-1880.

CAREER: Poet, playwright, novelist, essayist, short story writer, musician, painter, actor, producer, director, political and social activist, and educator. Cofounder of Sarasvat Samaj (a literary organization), 1882; secretary of Adi Brahmo Samaj (a religious society), beginning in 1884; manager of Tagore family estates, beginning in 1890; vice-president of Academy of Bengali Letters, beginning in 1894; cofounder of businesses in Calcutta and Kushtia, 1895-1902; founder of and educator at school at Santiniketan (became Visva-Bharati University in 1918), 1901; founder of weaving school at Kushtia, 1905; founder of agricultural cooperative bank at Patisar, 1905; founder of Sriniketan (a rural reconstruction institute); founder of literary journals, including *Sadhana,* 1891, and *Santiniketan Patra,* 1919.

AWARDS, HONORS: Nobel Prize for literature, 1913, for *Gitanjali;* D.Litt. from University of Calcutta, 1913, University of Dacca, 1936, Osmania University, 1938, and Oxford University, 1940.

WRITINGS:

PUBLISHED IN INDIA IN BENGALI

Kavi-Kahini (poetry), 1878.
Bana-Phul (poetry), 1880.
Valmiki Pratibha (play), 1881.
Bhagnahriday (play), 1881.
Rudrachanda (play), 1881.
Europe-Pravasir Patra (letters), 1881.
Kal-Mrigaya (play), 1882.
Sandhya Sangit (poetry; title means "Evening Songs"), 1882.
Prabhat Sangit (poetry; title means "Morning Songs"), 1883.
Bau-Thakuranir Hat (novel), 1883.

Vividha Prasanga (essays), 1883.
Chhabi O Gan (poetry; title means "Pictures and Songs"), 1884.
Nalini (play), 1884.
Saisav Sangit (poetry), 1884.
Bhanusimha Thakurer Padavali (songs), 1884.
Alochana (essays), 1885.
Rabichchhaya (songs), 1885.
Kari O Kamal (poetry; title means "Sharps and Flats"), 1886.
Rajarshi (novel), 1887.
Chithipatra (essays), 1887.
Samalochana (essays), 1888.
Mayar Khela (play), 1888.
Manasi (poetry; title means "The Mind's Creation"), 1890.
Europe Yatrir Diary (travel), Part 1, 1891, Part 2, 1893.
Goday Galad (play), 1892, new edition published as *Sesh Raksha,* 1928.
Sonar Tari (poetry; title means "The Golden Boat"), 1894.
Chhota Galpa (short stories), 1894.
Vichitra Galpa (short stories), Parts 1 and 2, 1894.
Katha-Chatushtay (short stories), 1894.
Galpa-Dasak (short stories), 1895.
Nadi (poetry), 1896.
Chitra (poetry), 1896.
Chaitali (poetry), first published in *Kavya Granthavali,* 1896.
Vaikunther Khata (play), 1897.
Panchabhut (essays), 1897.
Kanika (poetry), 1899.
Katha (poetry), 1900.
Kalpana (poetry), 1900.
Kshanika (poetry), 1900.
Kahini (poetry and verse drama), 1900.
Naivedya (poetry; title means "Offerings"), 1901.
Smaran (poetry), first published in *Kavya-Grantha,* 1903.
Sisu (poetry), first published in *Kavya-Grantha,* 1903.
Karmaphal (story), 1903.
Atmasakti (essays), 1905.
Baul (songs), 1905.
Bharatvarsha (essays), 1906.
Kheya (poetry; title means "Ferrying Across"), 1906.
Vichitra Prabandha (essays), 1907.
Charitrapuja (essays), 1907.
Prachin Sahitya (essays), 1907.
Lokasahitya (essays), 1907.
Sahitya (essays), 1907.
Adhunik Sahitya (essays), 1907.

Hasya-Kautuk (plays), 1907.
Vyangakautuk (essays and plays), 1907.
Prajapatir Nirbandha (novel), 1908.
Raja Praja (essays), 1908.
Samuha (essays), 1908.
Svades (essays), 1908.
Samaj (essays), 1908.
Siksha (essays), 1908.
Mukut (play), 1908.
Sabdatattva (essays), 1909.
Dharma (sermons), 1909.
Santiniketan, Parts 1-8, 1909, Parts 9-11, 1910, Parts 12-13, 1911, Parts 14-15, 1915, Parts 15-16, 1916.
Prayaschitta (play; title means "Atonement"), 1909, new edition published as *Paritran,* 1929.
Vidyasagar-Charit (essays), c. 1909.
Galpa Chariti (short stories), 1912.
Achalayatan (play), 1912, new edition published as *Guru,* 1918.
Utsarga (poetry), 1914.
Gitali (title means "Songs"), 1914.
Atati Galpa (short stories), c. 1915.
Sanchay (essays), 1916.
Parichay (essays), 1916.
Galpasaptak (short stories), 1916.
Palataka (poetry), 1918.
Payla Nambar (short stories), 1920.
Sisu Bholanath (poetry), 1922.
Vasanta (play), 1923.
Puravi (poetry), 1925.
Grihapraves (play), 1925.
Pravahini (songs), 1925.
Chirakumar Sabha (play), 1926.
Sodhbodh (play), 1926.
Lekhan (epigrams), 1927.
Rituranga (plays), 1927.
Yatri (diary), 1929.
Yogayog (novel), 1929.
Tapati (play), 1929.
Bhanusimher Patravali (letters), 1930.
Navin (play), 1931.
Vanavani (poems and songs), 1931.
Sapmochan (play), 1931.
Punascha (poetry; title means "Postscript"), 1932.
Parisesh (poetry), 1932.
Kaler Yatra (play), 1932.
Manusher Dharma (lectures), 1933.
Vichitrita (poetry), 1933.
Taser Des (play), 1933.
Bharatpathik Rammohan Roy (essays and addresses), 1933.
Sravan-Gatha (play), 1934.
Shesh Saptak (poetry; title means "Last Octave"), 1935.
Sur O Sangati (letters), 1935.
Vithika (poetry), 1935.
Chhanda (essays), 1936.
Nrityanatya Chitrangada (play), 1936.
Japane-Parasye (travel), 1936.
Sahityer Pathe (essays), 1936.
Praktani (addresses), 1936.
Khapchhada (rhymes), 1937.
Kalantar (essays), 1937.
Sey (stories), 1937.
Chhadar Chhabi (poetry), 1937.
Pathe O Pather Prante (letters), 1938.
Banglabhasha Parichay (essays), 1938.

Semjuti (poetry; title means "Evening Lamp"), 1938.
Prahasini (poetry), 1939.
Akas-Pradip (poetry), 1939.
Pather Sanchay (essays and letters), 1939.
Nabajatak (poetry; title means "Newly Born"), 1940.
Sanai (poetry), 1940.
Tin Sangi (short stories), 1940.
Galpasalpa (stories and poetry), 1941.
Janmadine (poetry), 1941.
Asramer Rup O Vikas (essays), 1941.
Chhada (poetry), 1941.
Smriti (letters), 1941.
Chithipatra I (letters), 1942.
Chithipatra II (letters), 1942.
Chithipatra III (letters), 1942.
Atmaparichay (essays), 1943.
Sahiryer Svarup (essays), 1943.
Chithipatra IV (letters), 1943.
Sphulinga (poetry), 1945.
Chithipatra V (letters), 1945.
Muktir Upay (comedy), 1948.
Mahatma Gandhi (essays and addresses), 1948.
Visvabharati (addresses), 1951.
Baikali (songs and poetry), 1951.
Samavayaniti (essays), 1954.
Chitravichitra (poetry), 1954.
Itihas (essays), 1955.
Buddhadeva (essays and poetry), 1956.
Khrishta (essays and poems), 1959.
Chithipatra VI (letters), 1960.
Chithipatra VII (letters), 1960.
Chhinnapatravali (letters), 1960.

COLLECTED WORKS IN BENGALI

Kavya Granthavali, Satyaprasad Gangopadhyaya, 1896.
Galpaguchha, [India], Part 1, 1900, Part 2, 1901, enlarged edition in five parts, 1908-09, single volume edition, three parts, Visva-Bharati (Calcutta), 1960.
Kavya-Grantha, nine volumes, Majumdar Library, 1903-04, published in ten volumes, Indian Press, Volumes 1-6, 1915, Volumes 7-10, 1916.
Rabindra Granthavali, Hitavadi, 1904.
Gadya-Granthavali, sixteen volumes, [India], 1907-09.
Gitabitan (songs; title means "Song Collection"), [India], Part 1, 1914, Parts 1 and 2, 1931, Part 3, 1932, single volume edition, three parts, Visva-Bharati, 1960.
Ritu-Utsav, [India], 1926.
Patradhara (letters), [India], 1938.
Rabindra-Rachanavali, twenty-six volumes, Visva-Bharati, 1939-48.
Rabindra-Rachanavali Achalita Sangraha, two volumes, Visva-Bharati, 1940-41.
Rabindra-Rachanavali, Government of West Bengal, 1961.
Chelebhulano chaora (selection of Bengali rhymes, including essays and articles), edited by Biasvanatha Racya, Ananda Pabaliasarsa (Kalakata), 1995.

POETRY IN ENGLISH TRANSLATION

Gitanjali (title means "Song Offerings"), [India], 1910, translation by the author, introduction by W. B. Yeats, India Society (London), 1912, Macmillan (New York), 1913, Branden Press, 1978, translation by Brother James, University Press (Khaka, Bangladesh), 1983.

The Gardener, translation by the author, Macmillan (New York), 1913.

The Crescent Moon, translation by the author, Macmillan (London), 1913, Macmillan (New York), 1916.

Balaka, [India], 1916, translation by Aurobindo Bose published as *A Flight of Swans: Poems from Balaka,* foreword by S. Radhakrishnan, J. Murray, 1955.

Fruit-Gathering, Macmillan (New York), 1916.

Stray Birds, Macmillan (New York), 1916.

Lover's Gift and Crossing, Macmillan (New York), 1918.

The Fugitive and Other Poems, Santiniketan Press, 1919.

The Fugitive (poetry, songs, and plays), Macmillan (New York), 1921.

Lipika (poetry, allegories, and stories), [India], 1922, translation by A. Bose, Jaico Publishing House (Bombay), 1969.

Poems from Tagore, introduction by C. F. Andrews, Macmillan (Calcutta), 1923.

Rabindranath Tagore: Twenty-two Poems, translation by Edward J. Thompson, E. Benn, 1925.

Fireflies, Macmillan (New York), 1928, Collier Books, 1975.

Sheaves, Poems, and Songs by Rabindranath Tagore, compiled and translated by Nagendranath Gupta, Indian Press (Allahabad), 1929, 2nd edition, Greenwood Press, 1971.

The Child (originally published in English), Allen & Unwin, 1931.

Patraput (title means "Cupful of Leaves"), [India], 1935, translation by Sisir Chattopadhyaya, foreword by Kalidas Bhattacharya, Patrhikrit Prakashani (Calcutta), 1969.

Syamali, [India], 1936, translation by Sheila Chatterjee and the author, Visva-Bharati, 1955.

Prantik (title means "The Borderland"), [India], 1938 [and] *Rogashajyaya* (title means "From the Sickbed"), [India], 1940 [and] *Arogya* (title means "Recovery"), [India], 1940 [and] *Sesh Lekha* (title means "Last Writings"), [India], 1941, translated together by A. Bose as *Wings of Death: The Last Poems of Rabindranath Tagore,* foreword by Gilbert Murray, J. Murray, 1960.

The Herald of Spring: Poems from Mohua, translation by A. Bose, J. Murray, 1957.

Ode to a Parted Love, Jaico Publishing House (Bombay), 1959.

Shesh Lekha: The Last Poems of Rabindranath Tagore, translation by Pritish Nandy, Dialogue Publications (Calcutta), 1973.

Translated poetry collected in numerous omnibus volumes, including *Later Poems of Rabindranath Tagore,* translation and introduction by A. Bose, foreword by Yehudi Menuhin with assessment by Hermann Hesse, P. Owen, 1974, Funk, 1976, Minerva Press (New York), 1976; *Forty Poems of Rabindra Nath Tagore,* edited by Sisir Kumar Ghose, Arnold-Heinemann (New Delhi), 1984; *Some Songs and Poems from Rabindranath Tagore,* translation by Pratima Bowes, Allied, 1984; and *Selected Poems: Rabindranath Tagore,* translation by William Radice, Viking Penguin, 1985.

PLAYS IN ENGLISH TRANSLATION

Prakritir Pratisodh (verse drama), [India], 1884, translation by Edwin Lo-tien Fang published as *Sanyasi,* Commercial Press (Shanghai), 1936; also published as *Sanyasi; or, The Ascetic* in *Sacrifice and Other Plays,* Macmillan (New York), 1917.

Raja O Rani (verse drama), [India], 1889, translation published as *The King and Queen* in *Sacrifice and Other Plays,* Macmillan (New York), 1917; translation by Shakuntala Rao Sastri published as *Devouring Love,* East West Institute (New York), 1961.

Visarjan (verse drama), [India], 1890, translation published in *Sacrifice and Other Plays,* Macmillan (New York), 1917; new version edited and translated by R. K. Bamsal, published as *Sacrifice,* Uniteck Publications (Agra), 1971.

Chitrangada (verse drama), [India], 1892, translation by Birenda Nath Roy, Sribhumi Publishing Co., 1957; translation by the author published as *Chitra,* the India Society (London), 1913, Macmillan (New York), 1926.

Viday-Abhisap (verse drama), [India], 1894, translation by Thompson published as *The Curse at Farewell,* Harrap, 1924; also published as *Kach and Debjani* in *The Fugitive,* Macmillan (New York), 1921.

Malini, first published in *Kavya Granthavali,* Satyaprasad Gangopadhyaya, 1896, translation published in *Sacrifice and Other Plays,* Macmillan (New York), 1917.

Saradotsav (one act), [India], 1908 (new edition published as *Rinsodh,* 1921), translation published as *Autumn Festival,* Brahmo Mission Press (Calcutta), 1919.

Raja, [India], 1910 (new edition published as *Arup Ratan,* 1920), translation by the author published as *The King of the Dark Chamber,* Macmillan (New York), 1914.

Dak-Ghar, [India], 1912, translation by Devabrata Mukerjea published as *The Post Office,* preface by W. B. Yeats, Cuala Press (Ireland), 1914, T. M. MacGlinchey, 1971, new translation published as *The Post Office,* Macmillan (New York), 1914, Verry, 1978.

Phalguni, [India], 1916, translation by Andrews and Nishi-Kanta Sen with revision by the author published as *The Cycle of Spring,* Macmillan (New York), 1917.

Sacrifice and Other Plays, Macmillan (New York), 1917, Macmillan (London), 1963.

Mukta-dhara, [India], 1922, translation published as *The Waterfall* in *Modern Review,* 1922; translation by Marjorie Sykes published in *Three Plays,* Oxford University Press (Bombay), 1950.

Rakta-karavi, [India], 1924, translation published as *Red Oleanders,* illustrations by Gagendranath Tagore, in *Visva-Bharati Quarterly,* September, 1924, translation published as *Red Oleanders,* Macmillan (London), 1925, Macmillan (New York), 1926.

Natir Puja, [India], 1926 (first produced at Santiniketan, May 7, 1926), translation by Sykes published serially in *Visva-Bharati Quarterly,* February-October, 1945, published as *Dancing Girl's Worship* in *Three Plays,* Oxford University Press (Bombay), 1950.

Chandalika, [India], 1933 (first produced in Calcutta at Madan Theatre, September 12, 1933), translation and introduction by Kripalani published in *Visva-Bharati Quarterly,* February, 1938, translation by Sykes published in *Three Plays,* Oxford University Press (Bombay), 1950.

Chandalika Nrityanatya (dance drama), [India], 1938, translation by Shyamaree Devi published in *Orient Review,* January-February, 1956.

Syama, [India], 1939 (first produced in Calcutta, October 10, 1936), translation by Bharatendu Chakravarti published in *Eastern Post,* winter, 1955-56, translation by P. K. Saha published in *Thought,* July 31, 1971.

Bansari, Visva-Bharati, 1943.

Three Plays (contains *Mukta-dhara, Natir Puja,* and *Chandalika*), translation by Sykes, Oxford University Press (Bombay), 1950, Oxford University Press (New York), 1970.

Three Riddle Plays (contains *The Test, The Reception,* and *The Patron*), translation by Prithvindra Chakravarti, Ind-US, 1983.

NOVELS IN ENGLISH TRANSLATION

Nashtanir, [India], 1901, translation by Mary M. Lago and Supriya Sen published as *The Broken Nest,* introduction by Lago, University of Missouri Press, 1971.

Chokher Bali (first published serially in *Bangadarsan,* 1901), [India], 1903, translation by Surendranath Tagore published as *Eyesore* in *Modern Review,* January-December, 1914, translation by Kripalani published as *Binodini,* W. S. Heinman (New York), 1959, revised edition, Sahitya Akademi (New Delhi), 1968.

Nauka Dubi (first published serially in *Bangadarsan,* 1903), [India], 1906, translation by J. G. Drummond published as *The Wreck,* Macmillan (New York), 1921.

Gora (first published serially in *Pravasi,* 1907-10), [India], 1910, translation by W. W. Pearson published serially in *Modern Review,* January-December, 1923, translation by the author with revision by Surendranath Tagore, Macmillan (London), 1924, Macmillan (New York), 1925; abridged and simplified edition by E. F. Dodd, Macmillan (London), 1963.

Chaturanga, [India], 1916, translation published serially as *A Story in Four Chapters* in *Modern Review,* February-May, 1922, translation published as *Broken Ties,* Macmillan (London), 1925, translation by Asok Mitra published as *Chaturanga,* Sahitya Academi (New Delhi), 1963, Intercul-ture Associates, 1974.

Ghare-Baire, [India], 1916, translation by Surendranath Tagore published serially as *At Home and Outside* in *Modern Review,* January-December, 1918, translation with revision by the author published as *The Home and the World,* Macmillan (New York), 1919, Verry, 1978.

Sesher Kavita, [India], 1929, translation by Kripalani published as *Farewell My Friend,* New India Publishing Co. (London), 1946.

Dui Bon, [India], 1933, translation by Kripalani published as *Two Sisters,* Visva-Bharati, 1945.

Malancha, [India], 1934, translation by Kripalani published with *Sesher Kavita* as *Farewell My Friend* [and] *The Garden,* Jaico Publishing House (Bombay), 1956.

Char Adhyay, [India], 1934, translation published as *Novelette of Young India: Four Chapters in Asia,* December, 1936-April, 1937, translation by Surendranath Tagore published as *Four Chapters,* Visva-Bharati, c. 1950.

SHORT FICTION IN ENGLISH TRANSLATION

Glimpses of Bengal Life, translation and introduction by Rajani Ranjan Sen, G. A. Nateson & Co. (Madras), 1913.

The Hungry Stones and Other Stories, translation by the author, Andrews, Thompson, Panna Lal Basu, Prabhat Kumar Mukerji, and Sister Nivedita, Macmillan (New York), 1916, AMS Press, 1970.

Mashi and Other Stories, Macmillan (New York), 1918, Arno Press, 1978.

Tota-Kahini, translation published as *The Parrot's Training,* Thacker, Spink & Co., 1918, published in Bengali in *Lipika,* 1922.

The Trial of the Horse, Brahmo Mission Press (Calcutta), 1919, published in *The Parrot's Training and Other Stories.*

Broken Ties and Other Stories, Macmillan (London), 1925, Arno Press, 1978.

The Runaway and Other Stories, edited by Somnath Maitra, Visva-Bharati, 1958.

Translated short fiction collected in numerous omnibus volumes, including *Collected Stories from Rabindranath Tagore,* Macmil-lan (Calcutta), 1970, and *Collected Stories,* Macmillan (New Delhi), 1974.

NONFICTION IN ENGLISH TRANSLATION

Jivansmriti (autobiography; first published serially in *Pravasi,* 1911), [India], 1912, translation by Surendranath Tagore published serially in *Modern Review* as *My Reminiscences,* January-December, 1916, Macmillan (New York), 1917, Gordon Press, 1978, published as *Reminiscences,* Macmillan (London), 1946.

Sadhana: The Realisation of Life, Macmillan (New York), 1913, Omen Press (Tuscon, AZ), 1972.

Personality, Macmillan (New York), 1917, Macmillan (Madras), 1970.

Nationalism (lectures), Macmillan (New York), 1917, Greenwood Press, 1973.

Japan Yatri, [India], 1919, translation by Shakuntala Rao Sastri published as *A Visit to Japan,* edited by Walter Donald Kring, East West Institute, 1961.

Greater India, S. Ganesan (Madras), 1921.

Thought Relics, translation by the author, Macmillan (New York), 1921, enlarged edition published as *Thoughts from Rabindra-nath Tagore,* edited by Andrews, 1929.

Creative Unity, Macmillan (New York), 1922, Gordon Press, 1978.

Ethics of Destruction, Ganesh & Co. (Madras), 1923.

Talks in China: Lectures Delivered in April and May, 1924, Visva-Bharati, 1925.

The Religion of Man (lectures), Macmillan (New York), 1931, AMS Press, 1981.

India and the Pacific, Allen & Unwin, 1937.

The True India: A Plea for Understanding, Allen & Unwin, 1939.

Chhelebela, [India], 1940, translation by Sykes published as *My Boyhood Days,* Visva-Bharati (Santiniketan), 1940, 2nd edition, Visva-Bharati (Calcutta), 1941.

Man (lectures), Kitabistan (Allahabad), 1946, Andhra University Press (Waltair), 1965.

My Early Life, edited by Rajendra Verma, Macmillan (Madras), 1952, Macmillan (Bombay), 1955.

Visva-Bharati and Its Institutions, Pulinbihari Sen (Santiniketan), 1956.

Our Universe (first published as *Visva-Parichaya* 1937), transla-tion by Indu Dutt, foreword by Malcolm MacDonald, Meridian Books (London), 1958, Interculture Associates, 1969.

Towards Universal Man (essays), edited by Bhabani Bhattachar-ya, introduction by Humayan Kabir, Asia Publishing House (New York), 1961.

Pioneer in Education: Essays and Exchanges Between R. Tagore and L. K. Elmhirst, J. Murray, 1961.

Rabindranath Tagore on Rural Reconstruction, Publications Division, Ministry of Information and Broadcasting (New Delhi), 1962.

The Cooperative Principle (essays and addresses), edited by Pulinhihari Sen, translation by Surendranath Tagore, Apurva-kumar Chanda, Somnath Maitra, and Jitendranarayan Sen, Visva-Bharati, 1963.

Mahatma Gandhi, compiled by Pulinbihari Sen, Visva-Bharati, 1963.

Gagendranath Tagore (art criticism), edited by Pulinbihari Sen, Indian Society of Oriental Art (Calcutta), 1972.

Translated nonfiction collected in numerous omnibus volumes, including *Glorious Thoughts of Tagore,* compiled by N. B. Sen, New Book Society of India (New Delhi), 1965; *Upanishads in the*

Eyes of Rabindranath Tagore: An Anthology of the Poet Tagore's Writings, Interpretive of and Related to Upanishadic Verse, compiled by Anil Kumar Mukherji, foreword by Saroj Kumar Das, Dasgupta (Calcutta), 1975; and *Lectures and Addresses,* Asia Book Corporation of America, 1988.

LETTERS IN ENGLISH TRANSLATION

Chhinnapatra, [India], 1912, translation by Surendranath Tagore published as *Glimpses of Bengal,* Macmillan (London), 1911, Macmillan (New York), 1921.

Letters, Macmillan (New York), 1917.

Letters from Abroad (first published serially in *Modern Review,* October, 1921-December, 1922), S. Ganesan (Madras), 1924, enlarged edition published as *Letters to a Friend,* edited by Andrews, Allen & Unwin, 1928.

Paschim Yatrir Diary, [India], 1924, translation by Dutt published as *The Diary of a Westward Voyage,* Asia Publishing House (New York), 1962, Greenwood Press, 1975.

Russiar Chithi, [India], 1931, translation by Sasadhar Sinha published as *Letters from Russia,* Visva-Bharati, 1960.

(With Mohandas Gandhi) *Mahatmaji and the Depressed Humanity,* Visva-Bharati Book Shop (Calcutta), 1932.

(With Gilbert Murray) *East and West,* Allen & Unwin, 1935.

(With Yone Noguchi) *Poet to Poet,* Visva-Bharati, 1939.

Rolland and Tagore: Letters and Transcripts of Conversations, 1919-1930, translation by Indira Chaudhurani and Alex Aronson, edited by Aronson and Kripalani, Visva-Bharati, 1945.

Imperfect Encounter: Letters of William Rothenstein and Rabindranath Tagore, 1911-1941, edited with introduction and notes by Mary M. Lago, Harvard University Press, 1972.

Selected Letters of Rabindranath Tagore, edited by Andrew Robinson and Krishna Dutta, Cambridge University Press, 1997.

MEDIA ADAPTATIONS: Tagore's three short stories "Samapti" (title means "The Conclusion"), "Monihara" (title means "The Lost Jewels"), and "The Postmaster" were adapted for film by Satyajit Ray and released under the title *Teen Kanya* (title means "Three Daughters"), 1961; a version containing "The Postmaster" and "The Conclusion" was released in the United States as *Two Daughters,* 1963. The film *Charulata* (title means "The Lonely Wife") was adapted by Ray from a story by Tagore, R. D. Bansal, 1961. Tagore's novel *Ghare-Baire* (title means "The Home and the World") was adapted by Ray for film and released by European Classics, 1985.

SIDELIGHTS: On his seventieth birthday, in an address delivered at the university he founded in 1918, Rabindranath Tagore said: "I have, it is true, engaged myself in a series of activities. But the innermost me is not to be found in any of these. At the end of the journey I am able to see, a little more clearly, the orb of my life. Looking back, the only thing of which I feel certain is that I am a poet (*ami kavi*)."

Although Tagore thought of himself essentially as a poet, he also made notable contributions to literature as a dramatist, novelist, short story writer, and writer of nonfictional prose, especially essays, criticism, philosophical treatises, journals, memoirs, and letters. In addition, he expressed himself as musician, painter, actor-producer-director, educator, patriot, and social reformer. Referring to the variety and abundance of Tagore's creative output, Buddhadeva Bose declared in *An Acre of Green Grass:* "It would be trite to call him versatile; to call him prolific very nearly funny." Bose added, "The point is not that his writings run into a

hundred thousand pages of print, covering every form and aspect of literature, though this matters: he is a source, a waterfall, flowing out in a hundred streams, a hundred rhythms, incessantly."

A man of prodigious literary and artistic accomplishments, Tagore played a leading role in Indian cultural renaissance and came to be recognized, along with Mohandas Gandhi, as one of the architects of modern India. India's first Prime Minister, Jawaharlal Nehru, wrote in *Discovery of India:* "Tagore and Gandhi have undoubtedly been the two outstanding and dominating figures in the first half of the twentieth century. . . . [Tagore's] influence over the mind of India, and especially of successive rising generations has been tremendous. Not Bengali only, the language in which he himself wrote, but all the modern languages of India have been molded partly by his writings. More than any other Indian, he has helped to bring into harmony the ideals of the East and the West, and broadened the bases of Indian nationalism."

Tagore's career, extending over a period of more than sixty years, not only chronicled his personal growth and versatility but also reflected the artistic, cultural, and political vicissitudes of India in the late nineteenth and the first half of the twentieth century. Tagore wrote in "My Life," an essay collected in *Lectures and Addresses,* that he "was born and brought up in an atmosphere of the confluence of three movements, all of which were revolutionary": the religious reform movement started by Raja Rammohan Roy, the founder of the Bramo Samaj (Society of Worshipers of the One Supreme Being); the literary revolution pioneered by the Bengali novelist Bankim Chandra Chatterjee, who "lifted the dead weight of ponderous forms from our language and with a touch of his magic aroused our literature from her age-long sleep"; and the Indian National Movement, protesting the political and cultural dominance of the West. Members of the Tagore family had actively participated in all the three movements, and Tagore's own work, in a broad sense, represented the culmination of this three-pronged revolution.

His first notable book of lyrics, *Sandhya Sangit* (1882; "Evening Songs"), won the admiration of Bankim Chandra Chatterjee. Tagore later wrote in his *Reminiscences,* "the sadness and pain which sought expression in the *Evening Songs* had their roots in the depth of my being." The book was closely followed by *Prabhat Sangit* (1883; "Morning Songs"), in which he celebrated his joy at the discovery of the world around him. The new mood was the outcome of a mystical experience he had had while looking at the sunrise one day: "As I continued to gaze, all of a sudden a covering seemed to fall away from my eyes, and I found the world bathed in a wonderful radiance, with waves of beauty and joy swelling on every side. This radiance pierced in a moment through the folds of sadness and despondency which had accumulated over my heart, and flooded it with this universal light," he recalled in *Reminiscences.* He recounted this experience in greater detail in *The Religion of Man:* "I felt sure that some Being who comprehended me and my world was seeking his best expression in all my experiences, uniting them into an ever-widening individuality which is a spiritual work of art. To this Being I was responsible; for the creation in me is His as well as mine." He called this Being his *Jivan devata* ("The Lord of His Life"), a new conception of God as man's intimate friend, lover, and beloved that was to play an important role in his subsequent work.

His newly awakened sense of all-pervading joy in the universe expressed itself in *Chhabi O Gan* (1884; "Pictures and Songs") and *Kari O Kamal* (1886; "Sharps and Flats"), in which he boldly celebrated the human body in such poems as "Tanu" ("Body"), "Bahu" ("Arms"), "Chumban" ("The Kiss"), "Stan" ("Breasts"), "Deher Milan" ("Physical Union"), and "Vivasana" ("Undraped Beauty"). He described *Kari O Kamal* as "the Song of Humanity standing on the road in front of the gateway of the Palace of Life" and believed it to be an important landmark in the evolution of his poetic outlook. It was, however, his new contemplative, mystical, religious, and metaphysical tone dominating *Manasi* (1890; "The Mind's Creation"), *Sonar Tari* (1894; "The Golden Boat"), *Chitra* (1896), *Naivedya* (1901; "Offerings"), *Kheya* (1906; "Ferrying Across"), and *Gitanjali* (1910; *Song Offerings*) that gave his lyrical poetry depth, maturity, and serenity and that eventually brought him world renown with the publication of the English translations of *Gitanjali* in 1912.

The publication of *Gitanjali* was the most significant event in Tagore's writing career, for, following the volume's appearance, he won the Nobel Prize in literature in 1913—the first such recognition of an Eastern writer. And yet this slender volume of poems, which was "hailed by the literary public of England as the greatest literary event of the day" and which created "the literary sensation of the day" in America, according to the editors of the *Literary History of the United States,* reached English readers almost by chance. As Tagore explained in a letter to his niece Indira, he undertook the task of translating some of his poems into English during a March, 1912, illness that delayed his departure for England; he began his translations because he "simply felt an urge to recapture through the medium of another language the feelings and sentiments which had created such a feast of joy within me in the days gone by." And once on board the ship in May, 1912, he continued his translations to while away the time of travel.

Arriving in London in June, 1912, he gave these translations to English painter William Rothenstein, who had visited India in 1910 and had shown interest in the poet's work. Deeply impressed, Rothenstein had copies typed and sent to poet William Butler Yeats, poet and critic Stopford Brooke, and critic Andrew Bradley—all of whom enthusiastically received them. On June 30, Tagore gave a reading of his poems at Rothenstein's house to a distinguished group of fellow poets, including American poet Ezra Pound, who was at that time the foreign editor of *Poetry,* founded by Harriet Monroe. Pound wanted *Poetry* to be the first American magazine to print Tagore, and in a letter of December 24, 1912, he wrote to Harriet Monroe that Tagore's poems "are going to be THE sensation of the winter." In November, 1912, the India Society of London published a limited edition of 750 copies of *Gitanjali,* with an introduction by Yeats and a pencil-sketch of the author by Rothenstein as frontispiece. In December, 1912, *Poetry* included six poems from the book. And thus the *Gitanjali* poems reached both sides of the Atlantic to an ever-widening circle of appreciative readers.

In 1916 appeared *Balaka* (*A Flight of Swans*), which pointed to the new direction Tagore's poetry was to take. "The poems of *Balaka,*" wrote Mary M. Lago in *Rabindranath Tagore,* "reflect a time of account-taking and of Tagore's reactions to the turbulence of the past four years: the excitement surrounding the Nobel award and the knighthood that followed in 1915, the premonitions of political disaster, and the anxieties of the World War." The flying swans symbolized, for the poet, movement, restlessness, a longing for faraway sites, an eternal quest for the unknown. "I am like a migratory bird having two homes—and my home on the other side of the sea is calling me," he had written to William

Rothenstein in 1915. Between 1916 and 1934, Tagore made five visits to America and traveled to nearly every country in Europe and Asia, delivering lectures, promoting his educational ideas, and stressing the need for a meeting of the East and the West. And wherever he went he was greeted as a living symbol of India's cultural and spiritual heritage.

In the last decade of his life, as he became conscious of his approaching death, Tagore turned to radical experimentation in poetic techniques and to purely humanistic concepts dealing with the problems of life and death. This new trend was reflected especially in his later Bengali poems collected in *Punascha* (1932; *Postscript*), *Shesh Saptak* (1935; *Last Octave*), *Patraput* (1935; *Cupful of Leaves*), *Prantik* (1938; *The Borderland*), *Semjuti* (1938; *Evening Lamp*), *Nabajatak* (1940; *Newly Born*), *Rogashaj-yaya* (1940; *From the Sickbed*), *Arogya* (1941; *Recovery*), and *Sesh Lekha* (1941; *Last Writings*). These poems "became increasingly terse, luminous and precise in the use of imagery," wrote Amiya Chakravarty in *A Tagore Reader.* In *The Later Poems of Tagore,* Sisir Kumar Ghose said: "Full of dramatic discords, through alternate rhythms of intensity and exhaustion, the[se] poems unfold the history of a conflict, long and carefully concealed, at the heart of the Rabindrean imagination." He concluded, "To accept the best among the later poems is to alter our total conception of Tagore's poetry." "But," he added, "its hour is not yet. In order to do this as it should be done the ideal critic of Tagore needs to be as, if not more, sensitive than the poet himself. . . . Such a critic we do not have, unless he is in hiding."

Tagore also published more than forty plays, most of which were written for production in the open air for his students at Santiniketan. He himself took part in their performance as actor, producer, director, composer, and choreographer. He "mocked the commercial Bengali theater, burdened with heavy sets and realistic decor, and created a lyrical theater of the imagination," wrote Balwant Gargi in his *Folk Theater of India.* Though Tagore was influenced by Western dramatic techniques and his plays, as Mohan Lal Sharma pointed out in a *Modern Drama* essay, "have close affinity with the poetic or symbolist European drama of the present century typified in the works of such writers as Maurice Maeterlinck," he upheld the classical Indian tradition of drama as the depiction of emotion or *rasa* rather than of action. He blended this classical element with the folk tradition of Bengali *Jatra* performance—a combination of group singing, dancing, and acting induced by a trance-like state—to achieve a synthesis of music, poetry, dance, drama, and costume. Consequently, most of Tagore's plays are interspersed with songs and are either lyrical or symbolic with subtle emotional and metaphysical overtones. The main principle of his plays, as he said himself, was "the play of feeling and not of action." Judged by the standards of Western drama, therefore, they seem static, ill-constructed, and unsuitable for commercial production.

Among Tagore's allegorical-philosophical-symbolic plays, *Raja* (*The King of the Dark Chamber*) is the most complex, written in the vein of Maeterlinck. The story is taken from a Buddhist *Jataka,* or story of reincarnation, but it undergoes a spiritual transformation in Tagore's hands. The symbolic significance of the play has attracted the attention of many critics. In *An Introduction to Rabindranath Tagore,* Vishwarath S. Naravane wrote: "In this play, Queen Sudarshana represents the finite soul which longs for a vision of the Infinite" that is hidden in the dark, like "the true King, her real husband." Radhakrishnan, in *The Philosophy of Rabindranath Tagore,* gave the following interpretation of the play: "An individual cannot reach the ideal so long as fragments of finiteness stick to him, so long as intellect and will are bound to the realm of finite nature." As he explained in *The Bengali Drama,* P. Guha Thakurta regarded the theme of the play as the realization of truth through suffering and sorrow. Other critics have interpreted the play in terms of allegorical symbols: the real King is Truth or God or Life-Spirit; Queen Sudarshana is the individual soul; Suvama is Maya or illusion; Kanchi symbolizes the mind; and the maid Surangama represents self-surrender. Artistically, the play is a fine blending of the Jatra tradition and the classical form of Sanskrit drama.

Perhaps the most popular and the most frequently performed among Tagore's plays is *Dak-Ghar (The Post Office)*, which dramatizes the story of a lonely boy, Amal, confined to his sickroom, longing to be free. Day after day, he sits at the window, watching the colorful spectacle of life passing him by, until death brings him deliverance from earthly pain and confinement. The story presents Rabindranath's own childhood experience of bondage and loneliness in a house governed by "servocracy." As he wrote to Andrews, "I remember, at the time when I wrote it, my own feeling which inspired me to write it. Amal represents the man whose soul has received the call of the open road."

The play was produced in 1913 by the Abbey Theatre Company in Dublin and in London. Kripalani reported that after attending a performance of the play in London, William Butler Yeats testified: "On the stage the little play shows that it is very perfectly constructed, and conveys to the right audience an emotion of gentleness and peace." "Judged by a London standard," wrote Ernest Rhys in *Rabindranath Tagore: A Biographical Study,* "it may seem that all [Tagore's] dramatic work is lacking in ordinary stage effect, but to this criticism one can only reply that his plays were written to attain a naturalness of style and a simplicity of mode which only Irish players have so far realised for us." A London *Times* reviewer called the play "dreamy, symbolical, spiritual . . . a curious play, leaving to a certain extent a sense of incompleteness, since it ends before the climax, rich in poetical thought and imagery, as well as a kind of symbolism that must not be pressed too closely." Since *The Post Office* can be read on two levels, the naturalistic and the symbolic, it has remained a special favorite with Tagore readers. In his book *Rabindranath Tagore,* Thompson paid the play a high compliment: "*The Post Office* does what both Shakespeare and Kalidas failed to do. It succeeds in bringing on the stage a child who neither shows off nor is silly."

Following the public controversy that broke out between Mahatma Gandhi and Tagore in 1921 over the poet's opposition to Gandhi's noncooperation movement and his cult of the *charkha* (spinning wheel), Tagore's popularity suffered a steep decline and he found himself more and more publicly isolated. Gandhi, failing to enlist the poet's support, remarked: "Well, if you can do nothing else for me you can at least . . . lead the nation and spin." Tagore immediately replied: "Poems I can spin, songs I can spin, but what a mess I would make, Gandhiji, of your precious cotton!" There the controversy stopped. But the churnings in the poet's mind over the political situation in the country produced *Mukta-dhara* in January, 1922, a symbolic play with political overtones. A distant echo of *Prayaschitta* (1909; *Atonement*), the play has been regarded by several critics as a noble tribute to Mahatma Gandhi and his campaign of nonviolence. Kripalani called the ascetic central character Dhananjaya, who teaches the people of Shivtarai to defy the authority of their unjust ruler through nonviolent civil resistance, a "prototype of Mahatma Gandhi" and wrote: "Perhaps no other play of Tagore expresses

his political convictions with such directness and vigour. . . . His abhorrence of exploitation, whether by a foreign or a native tyrant, and his faith that tyranny can be effectively resisted by nonviolence and evil redeemed by voluntary sacrifice." Tagore was making preparations to stage the play, but when he heard the news of Gandhi's arrest in March, 1922, he abandoned the preparations and *Mukta-dhara* was never produced.

In *Gora* Tagore created a socio-political novel voicing the aspirations of the resurgent India. Published in 1910, the year of the *Gitanjali* series of poems, it represented the peak of his fictional career. "This work," wrote Naravane in *An Introduction to Rabindranath Tagore,* "has everything that one might expect from a masterpiece: brilliant delineation of characters; a story which offers surprises till the very end; a fluent, powerful style interspersed with bursts of poetic imagery, and absolute serenity." Though heavily filled with polemics reflecting the social, religious, and political issues of the time, the novel projected Tagore's concept of liberal nationalism based on the ideal of *vishwa-bandhutva* or international brotherhood. In a March 13, 1921, letter to Andrews, Tagore declared: "All humanity's greatest is mine. The infinite personality of man has come from the magnificent harmony of all races. My prayer is that India may represent the cooperation of all the people of the earth." In the extraordinary character and personality of the protagonist Gourmohan or Gora, Tagore tried to bring about the fusion of the East and the West to exemplify his ideal of the Universal Man. In *Rabindranath Tagore,* Mary M. Lago declared *Gora* "a study of the relation between Hindu orthodoxy and Indian nationalism." Gora's sudden discovery that he has no parents, no home, no country, no religion, brings him freedom from all barriers: "But today I am free—yes, am standing freely in the center of a vast truth. Only now do I have the right to serve India. Today I have truly become an Indian. For me there is no conflict between Hindu, Muslim and Christian."

The subject of *The Home and the World* is the political agitation resulting from the partition of Bengal in 1905. Tagore was at the time deeply involved in the Indian National Movement. But when militant Hindu nationalism began to turn to violence and terrorist methods, he took a public stand against this development and openly condemned the excesses of the Swadeshi (*swa,* self; *deshi,* national) movement, which advocated the use of goods made in India. This position made him so unpopular with the nationalist Hindu intelligentsia that, in utter disillusionment, he withdrew from active politics and retreated into what he called the "poet's corner." But to answer his critics who had accused him of desertion and to reaffirm his own faith in the principles of truth and nonviolence, he wrote *The Home and the World,* which, as Bhabani Bhattacharya noted in an article that appeared in *Rabindranath Tagore: A Centenary Volume,* "roused a storm of controversy when it first appeared in serial form in the literary magazine *Subui Patra* and harsh pens assailed it not only as 'unpatriotic' but 'immoral.'"

Tagore wrote about two hundred stories, the best of which appeared in English translation in four major collections during his lifetime: *The Glimpses of Bengal Life* (1913), *The Hungry Stones and Other Stories* (1916), *Mashi and Other Stories* (1918), and *Broken Ties and Other Stories* (1925). As a short story writer, Tagore was not only a pioneer in Bengali literature, but he also paved the way for modern writers like Premchand and such contemporary writers as Mulk Raj Anand, Raja Rao, and R. K. Narain. Bose acknowledged in *An Acre of Green Grass* that Rabindranath "brought us the short story when it was hardly known in England." Naravane wrote in *An Introduction to Rabindranath Tagore,* "The modern short story is Rabindranath Tagore's gift to Indian literature."

A substantial amount of Tagore's writing was in the form of nonfictional prose—essays and articles, religious and philosophical treatises, journals and memoirs, lectures and ·discourses, history and polemics, letters, and travel accounts. Of these, his philosophical writings—*Sadhana: The Realisation of Life* (1913), *Nationalism* (1917), *Personality* (1917), *Creative Unity* (1922), *The Religion of Man* (1931), and *Towards Universal Man* (1961)—were central to his thought. These writings were deeply influenced by the teachings of the Upanishads. In the preface to *Sadhana,* which was published in the Harvard lecture series, he confessed: "The writer has been brought up in a family where texts of the Upanishads are used in daily worship; and he has had before him the example of his father who lived his long life in the closest communion with God while not neglecting his duties to the world or allowing his keen interest in all human affairs to suffer any abatement." What appealed to Tagore the most in the teachings of the Upanishads was the concept of God as positive, personal, and realizable through love. He was also attracted to the Vaishnava ideal of love as the basis of man-God relationship. He believed that the love-drama between man and God was being enacted in the sensible world of color, sound, and touch. He was not only conscious of man's divinity but also of God's humanity. In *Sonar Tari* he wrote: "Whatever I can offer to God I offer to man and to God I give whatever can I give to man. I make God man and man God." Such philosophical wisdom was reflected in many of his lyrics and dramas.

BIOGRAPHICAL/CRITICAL SOURCES:

BOOKS

Acyuiba, Abu Sacyaida, *Modernism and Tagore,* Sahitya Akademi (New Delhi), 1995.

Basu, Sankar, *Chekov and Tagore: A Comparative Study of Their Short Stories,* Sterling Publishers, 1985.

Bhattacharya, Bhabani, *Rabindranath Tagore: A Centenary Volume, 1861-1961,* Sahitya Akademi (New Delhi), 1961.

Bose, Buddhadeva, *An Acre of Green Grass: A Review of Modern Bengali Literature,* Orient Longmans (Calcutta), 1948.

Chakrabarti, Mohit, *Rabindranath Tagore: A Quest,* Gyan (New Delhi), 1995.

Chatterjee, Bhabatosh, *Rabindranath Tagore and Modern Sensiblity,* Oxford University Press, 1996.

Dutta, Krishna, *Rabindranath Tagore: The Myriad-Minded Man,* St. Martin's (New York), 1995.

Dutta, Krishna, and Andrew Robinson, *Rabindranath Tagore: A Modern Reader,* St. Martin's Press, 1997.

Gargi, Balwant, *Folk Theater of India,* University of Washington Press, 1966.

Ghosha, aSacnkha, *The Poet's Intention: The Writer, the Writing, the Reader,* Papyrus (Calcutta), 1994.

Joshi, R. G., *Myth in Indian Drama,* B. R. Pub. Corp. (New Delhi), 1994.

Lago, Mary M., *Rabindranath Tagore,* Twayne, 1976.

Mathew, Mary Thundyil, *Female Development in the Novels of Rabindranath Tagore: A Cross-Cultural Analysis of Gender and Literature in British India,* Mellen University Press, 1995.

Mukherji, Bhabani Charan, *Vedanta and Tagore,* M. D. Publications (New Delhi), 1994.

Nagar, Anupam Ratan Shankar, *Mysticism in Tagore's Poetry,* Prakash Book Depot (Bareilly), 1995.

Nandy, Ashis, *The Illegitimacy of Nationalism,* Oxford University Press (New York), 1994.

Naravane, Vishwarath S., *An Introduction to Rabindranath Tagore,* Macmillan (Madras), 1977.

Nehru, Jawaharlal, *Discovery of India,* John Day, 1946.

Radhakrishman, Sarvepalli, *The Philosophy of Rabindranath Tagore,* Macmillan (London), 1918.

Raj, G. V., *Tagore: The Novelist,* South Asia Books, 1983.

Sheth, Nirumpama (with Ajita aSeotha), *Tagore, Indian Film & Film Music,* Pankaj Mullic Music Research Foundation (Bombay, India), 1994.

Spiller, Robert E., and others, editors, *Literary History of the United States,* Macmillan (New York), 1962, 4th Edition, revised, 1974.

Tagore, Rabindranath, *A Tagore Reader,* edited by Amiya Chakravarty, Macmillan (New York), 1961.

Thakurta, P. Guha, *The Bengali Drama: Its Origin and Development,* Routledge & Kegan Paul, 1930.

Twentieth Century Literary Criticism, Volume 3, Gale (Detroit), 1980.

Venma, Rajendra, *Man and Society in Tagore and Eliot,* Humanities, 1982.

PERIODICALS

American Quarterly, fall, 1962.

Booklist, July, 1992.

Books Abroad, Volume 46, number 3, 1972.

Encounter, January, 1974.

Indian Literature, Volume 9, number 5, 1976; September-October, 1980.

Journal of Asian Studies, November, 1959.

Journal of Commonwealth Literature, Volume 8, 1973.

Journal of Indian Writing in English, Volume 6, number 1, 1978.

Modern Drama, May, 1970.

New Statesman and Nation, August 16, 1941.

New Statesman and Society, June 14, 1991.

Saturday Review of Literature, August 16, 1941.

South Asian Review, Volume 5, number 2, 1981.

Studies in Romanticism, Volume 31, 1963-64.

Times (London), July 11, 1913.

Washington Post, August 8, 1941.

*   *   *

TALESE, Gay 1932-

PERSONAL: Given name originally Gaetano; born February 7, 1932, in Ocean City, NJ; son of Joseph Francis and Catherine (DePaulo) Talese; married Nan Ahearn (a vice president and executive editor at a publishing company), June 10, 1959; children: Pamela, Catherine. *Education:* University of Alabama, B.A., 1953.

ADDRESSES: Home—109 East 61st St., New York, NY 10021-8101; and 154 East Atlantic Blvd., Ocean City, NJ 08226-4511 (summer).

CAREER: New York Times, New York, NY, 1953-65, began as copy boy, became reporter; full-time writer, 1965–. *Military service:* U.S. Army, 1953-55; became first lieutenant.

MEMBER: PEN (vice president, 1984-87, board of directors, 1980-), Authors League of America, Sigma Delta Chi, Phi Sigma Kappa.

AWARDS, HONORS: Best Sports Stories Award-Magazine Story, E. P. Dutton & Co., 1967, for "The Silent Season of a Hero"; Christopher Book Award, 1970, for *The Kingdom and the Power.*

WRITINGS:

New York: A Serendipiter's Journey, Harper, 1961.
The Bridge, Harper, 1964.
The Overreachers, Harper, 1965.
The Kingdom and the Power (Book-of-the-Month Club alternate selection), World Publishing, 1969.
Fame and Obscurity, World Publishing, 1970.
Honor Thy Father (Literary Guild selection), World Publishing, 1971.
Thy Neighbor's Wife (Literary Guild special selection), Doubleday, 1980.
(Editor with Robert Atwan) *The Best American Essays 1987,* Ticknor & Fields, 1987.
Unto the Sons, Knopf (New York), 1992.
(With Barbara Lounsberry) *Writing Creative Nonfiction: The Literature of Reality,* HarperCollins (New York), 1995.

MEDIA ADAPTATIONS: Honor Thy Father was filmed as a made-for-television movie by Columbia Broadcasting System in 1973.

SIDELIGHTS: As a pioneer of the new journalism, Gay Talese was one of the first writers to apply the techniques of fiction to nonfiction. In a *Writer's Digest* interview with Leonard Wallace Robinson, Talese described how and why he began writing in this style while reporting for the *New York Times:* "I found I was leaving the assignment each day, unable with the techniques available to me or permissible to the *New York Times,* to really tell, to report, all that I saw, to communicate through the techniques that were permitted by the archaic copy desk. . . . [So] I started . . . to use the techniques of the short story writer in some of the *Esquire* pieces I did in the early Sixties. . . . It may read like fiction, it may give the impression that it was made up, over-dramatizing incidents for the effect those incidents may cause in the writing, but without question . . . there is reporting. There is reporting that fortifies the whole structure. Fact reporting, leg work."

Now considered classics of the genre, Talese's *Esquire* articles probed the private lives of celebrities such as Frank Sinatra, Joe DiMaggio, and Floyd Patterson. The success of these stories prompted Talese to apply this new technique to larger subjects, and, in 1969, he produced his first best-seller, *The Kingdom and the Power,* a nonfiction work about the *New York Times* written in novelistic style. Since then Talese has explored such controversial topics as the Mafia, in *Honor Thy Father* (1971), and sexuality in America, in *Thy Neighbor's Wife* (1980). Widely respected as a master of his craft, Talese has thought of writing fiction, but, as he explained to the *Los Angeles Times*'s Wayne Warga, nonfiction challenges him more: "I suggest there is art in journalism. I don't want to resort to changing names, to fictionalizing. The reality is more fascinating. My mission is to get deep into the heart and soul of the people in this country."

In 1961 Talese published his first book, *New York: A Serendipiter's Journey.* Composed largely of material from his *New York Times* articles, the book was a critical success and sold about 12,000 copies, mostly in New York. His next venture was *The Bridge,* a book in which, according to *Playboy* magazine, "he took the plunge into the book-length nonfiction novel style." To prepare for this story, Talese spent over a year observing the

workers who built the Verrazano-Narrows Bridge connecting Brooklyn and Staten Island. In the *New York Times Book Review,* Herbert Mitgang calls the book "a vivid document," noting that Talese "imparts drama and romance to this bridge-building story by concentrating on the boomers, the iron workers who stitch steel and live high in more ways than one." While the publication was not a best-seller, it was critically well received, and *Playboy* reports that "it was a minor classic in demonstrating how deeply—and subjectively—a reporter could involve himself in the lives of his subjects and bring the flesh and blood of real people to paper in a way that was usually expected only in novels." Furthermore, critics believe it set the scene for the three larger works which would follow in the next sixteen years.

In 1971, Talese produced what many consider to be another landmark—*Honor Thy Father,* an inside look at the life of mafioso Bill Bonanno and a book so popular that it sold more than 300,000 copies within four months of its publication. Like all of Talese's efforts, the story was extensively researched and written in the intimate style of the new journalism. Almost six years elapsed between the day in 1965 when Talese first met Bill Bonanno outside a New York courtroom and the publication of the book. During that time Talese actually lived with the Bonanno family and persuaded them to talk about their business and personal lives, becoming, to use his words, "a source of communication within a family that had long been repressed by a tradition of silence."

While the tone of the book is nonjudgmental, Talese's compassionate portrayal of underworld figures—including Bill and his father, New York boss Joseph Bonanno—incited charges that Talese was giving gangsters moral sanction. Writing in the *New York Times Book Review,* Colin McInnes says that "Gay Talese has become so seduced by his subject and its 'hero,' that he conveys the impression that being a mobster is much the same as being a sportsman, film star or any other kind of public personality." But others, such as the *Times Literary Supplement* critic, defend Talese's treatment, noting that "Mr. Talese's insight will do more to help us understand the criminal than any amount of moral recrimination." And writing in the *New York Review of Books,* Wilfrid Sheed expresses a similar view: "Gay Talese has been criticized for writing what amounts to promotional material for the Bonanno family, but his book is an invaluable document and I don't know how such books can be obtained without some compromise. It is a lot to ask of an author that he betray the confidence of a Mafia family. As with a tapped phone call, one must interpret the message. . . . Talese signals occasionally to his educated audience—dull, aren't they? Almost pathetic. But that's all he can do."

Furthermore, Sheed argues, the technique of new journalism, "an unfortunate strategy for most subjects, is weirdly right" here: "The prose matches the stiff watchful facade of the Mafia. One is reminded of a touched-up country wedding photo, with the cheeks identically rouged and the eyes glazed, of the kind the Bonanno family might have ordered for themselves back in Sicily."

After the success of *Honor Thy Father,* Doubleday offered Talese a $1.2 million contract for two books. "I was interested in sexual changes and how . . . morality was being defined," Talese told a *Media People* interviewer. To gather material for a chronicle of the American sexual revolution, Talese submerged himself in the subculture of massage parlors, pornographic publishing, blue movies, and, ultimately, Sandstone, the California sexual retreat. He also studied First Amendment decisions in the Supreme Court and law libraries, tracing the effect of Puritanism on Americans' rights. As his research stretched from months into years, however, Talese realized that what began as a professional exploration had become a personal odyssey. And because he was asking others to reveal their most intimate sexual proclivities, he felt it would be hypocritical not to reveal his own. Thus, before he had written a word of his book, Talese became the subject of two revealing profiles in *Esquire* and *New York* magazines, the latter entitled "An Evening in the Nude with Gay Talese." The public was titillated, and the resulting publicity virtually guaranteed the book's financial success (and "the critics' wrath," according to Nan, Talese's wife, in a letter to *Contemporary Authors*). In October, 1979, months before the publication reached bookstores, United Artists bid a record-breaking $2.5 million for film rights to the book Talese entitled *Thy Neighbor's Wife*. Published in 1980, the book became a best-seller and was number one on the *New York Times* best-seller list for three consecutive months.

In his *Playboy* review of the book, critic John Leonard articulates each of these objections: "Since Talese parajournalizes so promiscuously—reaching into [his subjects'] minds, reading their thoughts, scratching their itches—one would expect at the very least to emerge from his book, as if from a novel, with some improved comprehension of what they stand for and a different angle on the culture that produced them. One emerges instead, as if from a soft-porn movie in the middle of the afternoon, reproached by sunlight and feeling peripheral to the main business of the universe. If Talese expects us to take his revolutionaries as seriously as he himself takes them, he has to put them in a social context and make them sound interesting. He doesn't." Furthermore, Leonard continues, "Talese almost totally ignores feminism. Gay liberation doesn't interest him. Children, conveniently, do not exist; if they did exist, they would make group sex—Tinkertoys! Erector Sets!—an unseemly hassle. . . . Missing from *Thy Neighbor's Wife* are history and stamina and celebration and mystery, along with birth, blood, death and beauty, not to mention earth, fire, water, politics, and everything else that isn't our urgent plumbing, that refuses to swim in our libidinal pool." The book, responds Nan Talese, "is a sociological study of where we have been in regards to sex and how the sexual revolution changed us. It is fair to say that homosexuality is not represented and the women's movement not annotated, although there are many women in the book and quite a few of them are feminists. But one book cannot do everything and I think now it was a mistake for Doubleday to delete the subtitle *Lust and Longing in America* from the book. Gay had meant it to indicate, along with the title, that it was written very much about men from a man's point of view."

In *Unto the Sons* (1992), Talese's first large-scale work of nonfiction in over a decade, the author "recreates the transformation of hundreds of thousands of immigrants and their descendants from Italians into Americans by tracing his own family" history, explains Joseph A. Califano in the *Washington Post Book World*. The product of more than a decade of research in the small southern Italian town of Maida, the book, as Talese tells Jerry Adler in *Newsweek*, was a conscious change from writing about other famous figures. "After a lot of writing about people I didn't know," the author says, "I wanted to write about my private province." Califano compares *Unto the Sons* to Alex Haley's *Roots*, and declares that the author "has constructed from fact, scraps of memories and perceptive fancy a yeasty blend of public and family history that will ring true to anyone whose parents or grandparents migrated from Italy around the turn of the century." In some ways, the story that Talese presents is a metaphor for the

American immigrant experience. "In accepting and coming to terms with his own father," states William Broyles Jr. in the *Los Angeles Times Book Review*, Talese discovers how much of his father lives in him, and lets us see how much the Old World still lives in us."

BIOGRAPHICAL/CRITICAL SOURCES:

BOOKS

Contemporary Authors New Revision Series, Gale (Detroit), Volume 9, 1983; Volume 58, 1996.
Contemporary Issues Criticism, Volume 1, Gale, 1982.
Contemporary Literary Criticism, Volume 37, Gale, 1986.

PERIODICALS

Chicago Tribune, June 8, 1980; October 2, 1987.
Christian Century, October 8, 1969.
Commonweal, October 17, 1969.
Entertainment Weekly, April 3, 1992, p. 26; February 21, 1992, p. 46.
Life, June 27, 1969.
Los Angeles Times, May 23, 1980.
Los Angeles Times Book Review, April 27, 1980; February 23, 1992, pp. 2, 9.
Media People, May, 1980.
Nation, September 15, 1969.
National Review, August 12, 1969; March 6, 1981.
New Leader, May 26, 1969.
Newsweek, July 21, 1969; April 28, 1980; February 10, 1992, p. 62; February 10, 1992, p. 62.
New York Review of Books, July 20, 1972.
New York Times, May 21, 1969; October 5, 1971; April 30, 1980.
New York Times Book Review, January 17, 1965; June 8, 1969; August 2, 1970; October 31, 1971; May 4, 1980; February 9, 1992, p. 3; March 21, 1993, p. 32.
New York Times Magazine, April 20, 1980.
People Weekly, April 14, 1980.
Playboy, May, 1980.
Publishers Weekly, January 7, 1983.
San Francisco Review of Books, May-June, 1993, pp. 27-28.
Time, July 4, 1969; October 4, 1971; February 10, 1992, p. 72.
Times Literary Supplement, May 14, 1971; April 4, 1972; July 4, 1980.
Vogue, June, 1980; February, 1992, p. 120.
Washington Post, October 18, 1979; April 27, 1980; May 7, 1980; May 15, 1980.
Washington Post Book World, November 15, 1987; February 16, 1992, pp. 1-2.
Writer's Digest, January, 1970.

*   *   *

TAN, Amy (Ruth) 1952-

PERSONAL: Born February 19, 1952, in Oakland, CA; daughter of John Yuehhan (a minister and electrical engineer) and Daisy (a vocational nurse; maiden name, Tu Ching) Tan; married Louis M. DeMattei (a tax attorney), April 6, 1974. *Education:* San Jose State University, B.A., 1973, M.A., 1974; postgraduate study at University of California, Berkeley, 1974-76. *Avocational interests:* Billiards, skiing, drawing, piano playing.

ADDRESSES: Agent—Sandra Dijkstra, 1155 Camino del Mar, Del Mar, CA 92014.

CAREER: Writer. Alameda County Association for Mentally Retarded, Oakland, CA, language consultant to programs for disabled children, 1976-81; MORE Project, San Francisco, CA, project director, 1980-81; worked as reporter, managing editor, and associate publisher for *Emergency Room Reports* (now *Emergency Medicine Reports*), 1981-83; freelance technical writer, 1983-87.

AWARDS, HONORS: Commonwealth Club gold award for fiction, Bay Area Book Reviewers award for best fiction, American Library Association's best book for young adults award, nomination for National Book Critics Circle award for best novel, and nomination for *Los Angeles Times* book award, all 1989, all for *The Joy Luck Club; The Kitchen God's Wife* was a 1991 *Booklist* editor's choice and nominated for Bay Area Book Reviewers award; Best American Essays award, 1991; honorary LHD, Dominican College, 1991.

WRITINGS:

NOVELS

The Joy Luck Club, Putnam (New York City), 1989.
The Kitchen God's Wife, Putnam, 1991.
The Hundred Secret Senses, Putnam, 1995.

JUVENILE; ILLUSTRATED BY GRETCHEN SCHIELDS

The Moon Lady, Macmillan (New York City), 1992.
The Chinese Siamese Cat, Macmillan, 1994.

SCREENPLAY

(With Ronald Bass) *The Joy Luck Club,* Hollywood Pictures, 1993.

Also author of short stories, including "The Rules of the Game." Work represented in *State of the Language,* edited by Christopher Ricks and Leonard Michaels, second edition, University of California Press (Berkeley), 1989, and *Best American Essays, 1991* edited by Joyce Carol Oates, Ticknor & Fields (New York City), 1991. Contributor to periodicals, including *Atlantic Monthly, McCall's, Threepenny Review, Grand Street,* and *Seventeen.*

MEDIA ADAPTATIONS: *The Joy Luck Club* was released on audiocassette by Dove, as was *The Kitchen God's Wife,* 1991. *The Joy Luck Club* was adapted for the stage by Susan Kim and produced in China in 1993.

SIDELIGHTS: Amy Tan's novels, *The Joy Luck Club, The Kitchen God's Wife,* and *The Hundred Secret Senses,* have been enthusiastically received by critics as well as the book-buying public. Focusing on the lives of Chinese-American women, Tan's books introduce characters who are ambivalent, as she once was, about their Chinese background. Tan remarked in a *Bestsellers* interview that though she once tried to distance herself from her ethnicity, writing *The Joy Luck Club* helped her discover "how very Chinese I was. And how much had stayed with me that I had tried to deny." Upon *The Joy Luck Club's* release, Tan quickly became known as a gifted storyteller, a reputation she upheld with the publication of *The Kitchen God's Wife* and *The Hundred Secret Senses.* Impressed with *The Joy Luck Club,* Detroit News contributor Michael Dorris proclaimed Tan "a writer of dazzling talent."

Despite her achievements, Tan's literary career was not planned; in fact, she first began writing fiction as a form of therapy. Considered a workaholic by her friends, Tan had been working ninety hours per week as a freelance technical writer. She became dissatisfied with her work life, however, and hoped to eradicate

her workaholic tendencies through psychological counseling. But when her therapist fell asleep several times during her counseling sessions, Tan quit and decided to curb her working hours by delving into jazz piano lessons and writing fiction instead. Tan's first literary efforts were short stories, one of which secured her a position in the Squaw Valley Community of Writers, a fiction writers' workshop. Tan's hobby soon developed into a new career when her first novel, *The Joy Luck Club,* was published in 1989.

Set in the late 1980s, *The Joy Luck Club* details the generational and cultural differences between a young woman, June, and her late Chinese mother's three Chinese friends. June's mother and the three older women had formed the Joy Luck Club, a social group, in San Francisco in 1949. Nearly forty years later, June's mother has died. The surviving members, the "aunties," recruit June to replace her mother, then send her to China to meet her step-sisters and to inform them of the mother's death. When June expresses reservations about her ability to execute this assignment, the older women respond with disappointment. June then realizes that the women rightly suspect that she, and their own daughters, know little of the women's lives and the strength and hope they wished to give the next generation. Throughout the novel, the various mothers and daughters attempt to articulate their own concerns about the past and the present and about themselves and their relations.

The Joy Luck Club was praised as a thought-provoking, engaging novel. In *Quill and Quire,* Denise Chong assessed: "These moving and powerful stories share the irony, pain, and sorrow of the imperfect ways in which mothers and daughters love each other. Tan's vision is courageous and insightful." In her review for the Toronto *Globe and Mail,* Nancy Wigston declared that Tan's literary debut "is that rare find, a first novel that you keep thinking about, keep telling your friends about long after you've finished reading it." *Time* reviewer John Skow found the work "bright, sharp-flavored," adding that it "rings clearly, like a fine porcelain bowl." Some critics were particularly impressed with Tan's ear for authentic dialogue. Carolyn See, for instance, wrote in the *Los Angeles Times Book Review* that Tan ranks among the "magicians of language." Dorris placed the book within the realm of true literature, which "is writing that makes a difference, that alters the way we understand the world and ourselves, that transcends topicality, and by those criteria, *The Joy Luck Club* is the real thing."

Tan followed *The Joy Luck Club* with *The Kitchen God's Wife,* in which a young woman in California realizes a greater understanding of her mother's Chinese background. A generation gap exists between the two heroines: Mother Winnie has only awkwardly adapted to the relatively free-wheeling ways of American, particularly Californian, life; daughter Pearl, on the other hand, is more comfortable in a world of sports and fast food than she is when listening, at least initially, to her mother's recollections of her own arduous life in China. As Winnie recounts the secrets of her past, including her mother's mysterious disappearance, her marriage to a psychotic and brutal man, the deaths of her first three children, and her journey to America in 1949, Pearl is able to view her mother in a new light and gathers the courage to reveal a secret of her own.

Critics hailed *The Kitchen God's Wife,* admiring its poignancy and bittersweet humor. Sabine Durrant, writing in the London *Times,* called the book "gripping" and "enchanting," and Charles Foran, in his review for the Toronto *Globe and Mail,* proclaimed Tan's work "a fine novel" of "exuberant storytelling and rich drama." In a *Washington Post Book World* review, Wendy Law-Yone asserted that Tan exceeded the expectations raised by her first book, declaring that "*The Kitchen God's Wife* is bigger, bolder and, I have to say, better" than *The Joy Luck Club.* Referring to *The Kitchen God's Wife* in a *Time* review, Pico Iyer affirmed, "Tan has transcended herself again."

In her third novel, Tan shifted her focus from the mother-daughter bond to the relationship between sisters. The main characters in *The Hundred Secret Senses* are half-sisters Olivia and Kwan. Olivia is the daughter of an American mother and a Chinese father who died before her fourth birthday. In adulthood, she is a pragmatic, somewhat priggish yuppie. Kwan, her Chinese half-sister, arrives in her life when she is six. Twelve years older than Olivia, clumsy, and barely able to speak English, Kwan is an immediate source of resentment and embarrassment to Olivia. Kwan's belief that she can speak with spirits is another source of humiliation, one that leads her stepfather to commit her for electroshock therapy. Through the years, Olivia treats Kwan rudely and dismissively, yet her older sister remains devoted to her and is determined to awaken Olivia to the reality of the spirit world. To this end, the two travel to China, where Kwan believes they lived another life together in an earlier century.

For some reviewers, Tan's use of the supernatural posed a problem. Claire Messud, for example, wrote in the *New York Times Book Review* that Tan's evocation of the spirit world was unconvincing, and that "to accept the novel as anything more than a mildly entertaining and slightly ridiculous ghost story, the reader must also make [a] demanding leap of faith, turning a blind eye to rash improbabilities and a host of loose ends. For this reader, at least, that leap was not possible." She noted, however, that Kwan was "a memorable creation. . . . Kwan gently forces Olivia to face the worst in herself and, in so doing, to find her strengths. We could all do with such a sister."

New York Times reviewer Michiko Kakutani also expressed a mixed opinion of Tan's third novel. She praised it as "a contemporary tale of familial love and resentment, nimbly evoked in Ms. Tan's guileless prose," but qualified that it was "unfortunately overlaid by another, more sensational tale of reincarnation that undermines the reader's trust." She went on: "Of course, there's nothing inherently implausible about ghosts. Maxine Hong Kingston handled similar material with consummate ardor and grace in 'The Woman Warrior,' but Ms. Tan doesn't seem to know how to make Kwan's beliefs in the spirit world palpable or engaging." She affirmed, however, that "Ms. Tan is able to create enormously sympathetic people who inhabit some middle ground between real life and the more primary-colored world of fable. In doing so, she draws the reader into these characters' lives, and into the minutiae of their daily concerns."

Some other commentators were unreserved in their enthusiasm for *The Hundred Secret Senses.* Chicago *Tribune Books* contributor Penelope Mesic stated that the book contained "three qualities almost never found together: popularity, authenticity and excellence." Mesic concluded the work is an "effortless mix of invention and reliance on reality that makes Tan's fiction so engrossing—a kind of consistency of action that suggests one could ask anything about a character and Tan could answer. She provides what is most irresistible in popular fiction: a feeling of abundance, an account so circumstantial, powerful and ingenious that it seems the story could go on forever." Gail Caldwell of the *Boston Globe* declared that *The Hundred Secret Senses* is simply "the wisest and most captivating novel Tan has written."

BIOGRAPHICAL/CRITICAL SOURCES:

PERIODICALS

America, May 4, 1996, p. 27.
Boston Globe, November 10, 1992, p. 69; May 21, 1993, p. 23; September 19, 1993, p. 77; October 22, 1995, p. B37.
Canadian Literature, summer, 1992, p. 196.
Chicago Tribune, August 6, 1989; March 17, 1991; September 26, 1993, section 13, p. 20; November 9, 1995, section 2C, p. 16.
Christian Science Monitor, September 16, 1993, p. 11.
Critique, spring, 1993, p. 193.
Detroit News, March 26, 1989, p. 2D.
Economist, December 12, 1992, p. 101.
Fortune, August 26, 1991, p. 116; December 28, 1992, p. 105.
Globe and Mail (Toronto), April 29, 1989; June 29, 1991, p. C8.
Journal and Constitution (Atlanta), November 26, 1995, p. K11.
Kirkus, September 1, 1992, p. 1135.
Life, April, 1994, p. 108.
London Review of Books, July 11, 1991, p. 19.
Los Angeles Times, March 12, 1989; May 28, 1992, p. E7; September 5, 1993, "California" section, p. 8; September 8, 1993, p. F1; October 30, 1995, p. E4.
Los Angeles Times Book Review, March 12, 1989, p. 1; July 5, 1992, p. 10; December 6, 1992, p. 10.
Ms., November, 1991; November-December, 1995, p. 88.
New Statesman and Society, July 12, 1991, pp. 37-38; February 16, 1996, p. 38.
Newsweek, April 17, 1989, pp. 68-69; June 24, 1991, p. 63; November 6, 1995, p. 91.
New York, March 20, 1989, p. 82; June 17, 1991, p. 83.
New York Times, July 5, 1989; September 8, 1993, p. C15; November 17, 1995, p. C29.
New York Times Book Review, March 19, 1989, pp. 3, 28; June 16, 1991, p. 9; November 8, 1992, p. 31; October 29, 1995, p. 11.
People Weekly, April 10, 1989, pp. 149-50.
Publishers Weekly, July 7, 1989, pp. 24-26; April 5, 1991, pp. 4-7; July 20, 1992, pp. 249-50; August 9, 1993, pp. 32-34; July 11, 1994, p. 78; September 11, 1995, p. 73.
School Library Journal, September, 1992, p. 255.
Time, March 27, 1989, p. 98; June 3, 1991, p. 67.
Times (London), July 11, 1991, p. 16.
Times Educational Supplement (London), August 4, 1989, p. 19; August 2, 1991, p. 18; February 5, 1993, p. 10; January 16, 1995, p. 16.
Times Literary Supplement (London), December 29, 1989, p. 1447; July 5, 1991, p. 20.
Tribune Books (Chicago), March 12, 1989, pp. 1, 11; November 5, 1995, pp. 1, 11.
USA Today, October 5, 1993, p. D12.
Wall Street Journal, September 1, 1992, p. A12; August 19, 1993, p. A8; September 9, 1993, p. A18; December 6, 1994, p. B1.
Washington Post, October 8, 1989; May 21, 1993, p. WW16; May 27, 1993, p. D9; September 21, 1993, pp. D1, D10; September 24, 1993, p. WW47; October 23, 1995, p. D1.
Washington Post Book World, March 5, 1989, p. 7; June 16, 1991, pp. 1-2.

*   *   *

TANIZAKI, Jun'ichiro 1886-1965

PERSONAL: Born July 24, 1886, in Tokyo, Japan; died July 30, 1965, in Yugawara, Tokyo, Japan; son of Sogoro Tanizaki (a rice merchant); married Chiyoko Ishikawa, 1915 (divorced, 1930); married Furukawa Tomiko, April, 1931 (divorced). *Education:* Attended Tokyo Imperial University, 1908-10.

CAREER: Novelist, playwright, and short story writer.

MEMBER: American Academy (honorary member), National Institute of Arts and Letters (honorary member).

AWARDS, HONORS: Imperial Prize for Literature, 1949.

WRITINGS:

IN ENGLISH

A Spring-Time Case, translation by Zenchi Iwado from the original "*Otsuya koroshi,*" Japan Times, c. 1927.
Shunkin Sho, [Japan], 1933, translation by Howard S. Hibbett published as *A Portrait of Shunkin* (text in English and Japanese), Hara Shobo, 1965.
Ashikari [and] *Shunkin Sho,* Hokuseido Press, 1936, translation by Roy Humpherson and Hajime Okita published as *Ashikari* [and] *The Story of Shunkin: Two Japanese Novels,* Greenwood Press, 1970.
Tade kuu mushi, [Japan], 1936, translation by Edward G. Seidensticker published as *Some Prefer Nettles,* Knopf, 1955.
Sasame yuki, [Japan], 1949, translation by Seidensticker published as *The Makioka Sisters,* Knopf, 1957.
Kagi, [Japan], 1957, translation by Hibbett published as *The Key,* Knopf, 1960.
Futen Rojin, [Japan], 1962, translation by Hibett published as *Diary of an Old Man,* Knopf, 1965.
Seven Japanese Tales, translated by Hibbett, Knopf, 1963.

Also author of *Inei Raisan,* translation by Thomas J. Harper and Seidensticker published as *In Praise of Shadows,* Leetes Island Books, 1977. In Japanese; all published in Japan; fiction: *Kojin,* 1926; *Neko to Shozo to futari onna,* 1949; *Rangiku mongatari,* 1949; *Shoso Sigemoto no hahn,* 1950; *Shonen,* 1970; *Hagi no hana,* 1973. Collections of short stories: *Hyofu,* 1950; *Yume no ukihashi,* 1960; *Kokumin no bungaku,* 1964; *Shisei,* 1973; *Shisei, Shonen,* 1974. Collections of plays: *Alsureba koso,* 1923; *Shinzei,* 1949. Omnibus volumes: *Tanizaki Jun'ichiro zenshu,* twelve volumes, 1931, thirty volumes, 1958-59, twenty-eight volumes, 1966-70; *Tanizaki Jun'ichiro shu,* volume from "Gendai bungo meisaku zenshu" series, 1953, volume of short stories, 1970, two volumes of fiction, 1975, two volumes of short stories, 1975-77, volume of fiction, 1977; *Tanizaki Jun'ichiro bunko,* twelve volumes, 1973. Other: *Momoku mongatari,* 1932; *Banshu tokuhon,* 1936; *Sasameyuki,* 1949; *Kyo no yume: Osaka no yume,* 1950; *Toshei shika modoki,* 1961; *Setsugoan yawa,* 1968; *Kasai Zenzo to Hirotsu Kazuo,* 1972; *Adachi,* 1974. Also author with Jo Cem of film reproduction *Sumiko.*

SIDELIGHTS: Jun'ichiro Tanizaki was destined to live a life of extremes. Although his family had come into a substantial sum of money from his mother's wealthy relation, his father grossly mismanaged the funds, sending his rice business swinging like a pendulum back and forth, from success to failure and back again. Subsequently, when it came time for young Jun'ichiro to enter middle school, his family lacked the necessary tuition. Upon recommendation of his teachers, however, he was allowed to continue his education.

By the time Tanizaki enrolled at Tokyo University, he was already displaying a talent for writing, and five years later began his literary career in earnest. As the Russo-Japanese war had recently ended, influences from the West slowly started to seep into the East, freeing Japanese literature from centuries of binding conventions. Tanizaki revelled in Western thought and practices and advocated them in his early writings.

The turning point in Tanizaki's career came in 1923, the year of the great earthquake. He moved to Okamoto and enjoyed a simpler lifestyle, becoming increasingly interested in the traditional Japanese life, and critical of Western values and the modern industrialization of his homeland.

"In Praise of Shadows," an essay written early in the thirties, reflects this change of loyalties. The author discusses the opposing factions of East and West, and the dubious benefits derived from the juxtaposition of the two. According to D. J. Enright, the work is "a graceful, nostalgic piece," adding that "fanaticism and cultural chauvinism are calmly subverted by the humour that tinges Tanizaki's 'aesthetic' and the strong hints of earthly appetite which escape from it." While Tanizaki expresses gratitude for Western conveniences such as modern lavatories, he summons back the "shadows" of the past for the realm of art and culture.

Tanizaki's later works continued this apparent dichotomy of coexisting values, but presented it in an extremely different fashion. Condemned as indecent and pornographic by many reviewers, his works are praised by others as "excellent studies." *Diary of an Old Man,* for example, depicts an impotent elderly gentleman who receives erotic pleasures from a beautiful and sensual young girl in return for expensive trinkets. In *Some Prefer Nettles,* the conflict of East and West, of old and new, is also apparent. It is a story of a married couple, the wife very westernized and the husband firmly rooted in tradition, who have long since grown tired of one another, yet do not separate.

BIOGRAPHICAL/CRITICAL SOURCES:

BOOKS

Chambers, Anthony Hood, *The Secret Window: Ideal Worlds in Tanizaki's Fiction,* Harvard University Press, 1994.
Contemporary Literary Criticism, Volume 8, Gale (Detroit), 1978.
Ito, Ken K., *Visions of Desire: Tanizaki's Fictional Worlds,* Stanford University Press, 1991.

PERIODICALS

Atlantic Monthly, December 14, 1957.
Nation, May 22, 1972.
New Statesman, August 18, 1961.
New Yorker, December 14, 1957.
San Francisco Chronicle, November 17, 1957.
Saturday Review, August 21, 1965.
Time, August 20, 1965.
Times Literary Supplement, December 16, 1977.
World Literature Today, spring, 1978.

*   *   *

TANNER, William
See AMIS, Kingsley (William)

*   *   *

TARKINGTON, (Newton) Booth 1869-1946

PERSONAL: Born July 29, 1869, in Indianapolis, IN; died after a short illness, May 19, 1946, in Indianapolis, IN; son of John

Stevenson Tarkington (a lawyer) and Elizabeth (Booth) Tarkington; married Laurel Louisa Fletcher, June 18, 1902 (divorced, 1911); married Susanah Robinson, November 6, 1912; children: (first marriage) Laurel (deceased). *Education:* Attended business college and art school, 1889, Purdue University, 1890, and Princeton University, 1891-93. *Politics:* Republican.

ADDRESSES: Home—Indianapolis, IN; Kennebunkport, ME.

CAREER: Novelist, essayist, and playwright. Elected to the Indiana House of Representatives, 1902-03.

MEMBER: American Academy of Arts and Letters, Ivy Club, Players Club, University Club (Indianapolis), Century Club (New York), Nassau Club (Princeton), Triangle Club (president, 1892-93).

AWARDS, HONORS: Pulitzer Prizes for novel, Columbia University, 1919, for *The Magnificent Ambersons,* and 1922, for *Alice Adams;* Gold Medal, National Institute of Arts and Letters, 1933; Roosevelt Distinguished Service Medal, 1942; Howells Medal, American Academy of Arts and Letters, 1945; received honorary degrees from various institutions, including an M.A. from Princeton University, 1899, Litt.D. from Princeton University, 1918, De Pauw University, 1923, and Columbia University, 1924, and L.H.D. from Purdue University, 1939.

WRITINGS:

FICTION

The Gentleman from Indiana, Doubleday & McClure, 1899.
Monsieur Beaucaire (first serialized in *McClure's,* 1899), illustrated by C. D. Williams, McClure, Phillips, 1900, illustrated by T. M. Cleland, Limited Editions Club, 1961.
The Two Vanrevels, illustrated by Henry Hutt, McClure, Phillips, 1902.
Cherry, Harper & Brothers, 1903.
In the Arena: Stories of Political Life, illustrated by A. I. Keller, Power O'Malley, and J. J. Gould, McClure, Phillips, 1905.
The Conquest of Canaan: A Novel, illustrated by Lucius W. Hitchcock, Harper & Brothers, 1905.
The Beautiful Lady, McClure, Phillips, 1905.
His Own People, illustrated by Lawrence Mazzanovich and F. R. Gruger, Doubleday, Page, 1907.
The Guest of Quesnay, illustrated by W. J. Duncan, McClure, 1908.
Beasley's Christmas Party, illustrated by Ruth Sypherd Clements, Harper & Brothers, 1909.
The Spring Concert, Ridgeway, 1910.
The Flirt, illustrated by Clarence F. Underwood, Doubleday, Page, 1913.
The Turmoil: A Novel, illustrated by C. E. Chambers, Harper & Brothers, 1915.
Harlequin and Columbine, and Other Stories, Doubleday, Page, 1918.
Monsieur Beaucaire, The Beautiful Lady, His Own People, and Other Stories, Doubleday, Page, 1918.
The Magnificent Ambersons, illustrated by Arthur William Brown, Doubleday, Page, 1918, illustrated by Roy Andersen, Franklin Library, 1977.
Ramsey Milholland, illustrated by Gordon Grant, Doubleday, Page, 1919.
Alice Adams, illustrated by Brown, Doubleday, Page, 1921, illustrated by Jim Campbell, Franklin Library, 1979.
Gentle Julia, illustrated by C. Allan Gilbert and Worth Brehm, Doubleday, Page, 1922.

The Midlander, Doubleday, Page, 1923, published as *National Avenue* in *Growth.*
The Fascinating Stranger, and Other Stories, Doubleday, Page, 1923.
Women, Doubleday, Page, 1925.
Looking Forward, and Others, Doubleday, Page, 1926.
Growth (contains *The Turmoil, The Magnificent Ambersons,* and *National Avenue*), Doubleday, Page, 1927.
The Plutocrat: A Novel, Doubleday, Page, 1927.
Claire Ambler, Doubleday, Doran, 1928.
Young Mrs. Greeley, Doubleday, Doran, 1929.
Mirthful Haven, Doubleday, Doran, 1930.
Mary's Neck, Doubleday, Doran, 1932.
Wanton Mally, illustrated by Joseph Simont, Doubleday, Doran, 1932.
Presenting Lily Mars, Doubleday, Doran, 1933.
Little Orvie, illustrated by Brehm, Doubleday, Doran, 1934.
Mr. White, The Red Barn, Hell, and Bridewater (novelettes), Doubleday, Doran, 1935.
The Lorenzo Bunch, Doubleday, Doran, 1936.
Rumbin Galleries, illustrated by Ritchie Cooper, Doubleday, Doran, 1937.
The Fighting Littles, Doubleday, Doran, 1941.
The Heritage of Hatcher Ide (published serially as *The Man of the Family*), Doubleday, Doran, 1941.
Kate Fennigate, Doubleday, Doran, 1943.
Image of Josephine, Doubleday, Doran, 1945.
The Show Piece (unfinished novel), introduction by wife, Susanah Tarkington, Doubleday, 1947.
Three Selected Short Novels (contains *Walterson, Uncertain Molly Collicut,* and *Rennie Peddigoe*), Doubleday, 1947.

Also author of story "Old Fathers and Young Sons."

FOR CHILDREN AND YOUNG ADULTS

Penrod, illustrated by Gordon Grant, Doubleday, Page, 1914.
Penrod and Sam, illustrated by Worth Brehm, Doubleday, Page, 1916.
Seventeen: A Tale of Youth and Summer Time and the Baxter Family, Especially William, Harper & Brothers, 1916, illustrated by Arthur William Brown, Grosset & Dunlap, 1918, illustrated by Edwin Tunis, Harper & Brothers, 1932.
Penrod Jashber, illustrated by Grant, Doubleday, Doran, 1929.
Penrod: His Complete Story (contains *Penrod, Penrod and Sam,* and *Penrod Jashber*), illustrated by Grant, Doubleday, Doran, 1931.

PLAYS

(With Evelyn Greenleaf Sutherland) *Monsieur Beaucaire* (adapted from Tarkington's novel of the same title), produced as *Beaucaire* in New York City, 1901.
The Gentleman from Indiana, produced in Indianapolis, IN, 1905.
(With Harry Leon Wilson) *The Guardian,* privately printed, 1907, published as *The Man from Home* (produced in Chicago, IL, 1907, produced in New York City, 1908), Harper & Brothers, 1908, revised edition published as *The Man from Home: A Play in Four Acts,* S. French, 1934.
(With Wilson) *Cameo Kirby,* produced in New York City, c. 1907.
Springtime, produced in New York City, c. 1908.
(With Wilson) *Your Humble Servant* (produced in New York City, c. 1909), Rosenfield, 1908.
(With Wilson) *Foreign Exchange,* produced in New York City, 1909.

(With Wilson) *If I Had Money,* produced in New York City, 1909, produced as *Getting a Polish,* New York City, 1910.

Beauty and the Jacobin: An Interlude of the French Revolution (produced in New York City, 1912), illustrated by C. D. Williams, Harper & Brothers, 1912.

Mister Antonio: A Play in Four Acts (produced in New York City, 1916), S. French, 1935.

(With Julian Street) *The Ohio Lady* (four act; produced in New York City, 1916), Ebert Press, 1916, published as *The Country Cousin: A Comedy in Four Acts* (produced in New York City, 1917), S. French, 1921.

Clarence: A Comedy in Four Acts (four act; produced in New York City, 1919), S. French, 1921.

(With Wilson) *Up from Nowhere,* produced in New York City, 1919.

(With Wilson) *The Gibson Upright* (produced in Indianapolis, IN, 1919), Doubleday, Page, 1919.

Poldekin, produced in New York City, 1920.

The Intimate Strangers (three act; produced in New York City, 1921), S. French, c. 1922.

The Wren: A Comedy in Three Acts (produced in New York City, 1921), S. French, 1922.

The Ghost Story: A One-Act Play for Persons of No Great Age (produced in 1922), Stewart Kidd, 1922.

Rose Briar, produced in New York City, 1922.

The Magnolia, produced in New York City, 1923.

(With Wilson) *Tweedles: A Comedy* (produced in New York City, 1923, produced as *Bristol Glass* in Cleveland, OH, 1923), S. French, 1924.

The Trysting Place: A Farce in One Act (produced, 1923), Stewart Kidd, 1923.

Bimbo, the Pirate: A Comedy (produced in 1926), Appleton, 1926.

The Travelers (produced in 1927), Appleton, 1927.

Station YYYY (produced in 1927), Appleton, 1927.

(Under name N. Booth Tarkington; with Wilson) *How's Your Health? A Comedy in Three Acts* (produced in New York City, 1929), S. French, 1930.

Colonel Satan, produced in New York City, 1931.

The Help Each Other Club (produced in 1933), Appleton-Century, 1934.

Lady Hamilton and Her Nelson (produced in 1945), House of Books, 1945.

Also author of *The Man on Horseback,* produced c. 1911; seventy-five episodes of *Maud and Cousin Bill* (radio plays), 1932-33; and *Aromatic Aaron Burr,* 1938.

COLLECTIONS AND SELECTIONS

The Works of Booth Tarkington, fourteen volumes, Doubleday, Page, 1918-19.

Strack Selections from Booth Tarkington's Stories, arranged by Lilian Holmes Strack, Walter H. Baker, 1926.

The Gentleman from Indianapolis: A Treasury of Booth Tarkington, edited by John Beecroft, illustrated by John Alan Maxwell, Doubleday, 1957.

On Plays, Playwrights, and Playgoers: Selections from the Letters of Booth Tarkington to George C. Tyler and John Peter Toohey, 1918-1925, edited by Alan S. Downer, Princeton University Library, 1959.

Stories, illustrated by Peter Cox, Franklin Library, 1984.

OTHER

(Illustrator) James Whitcomb Riley, *The Boss Girl,* Bowen-Merrill, 1886.

(With Kenneth Lewis Roberts and Hugh MacNair Kahler) *The Collector's Whatnot: A Compendium, Manual, and Syllabus of Information and Advice on All Subjects Appertaining to the Collection of Antiques, Both Ancient and Not So Ancient, Compiled by Cornelius Obenchain Van Loot, Milton Kilgallen, and Murgatroyd Elphinstone,* Houghton, 1923.

Looking Forward, and Others (essays), Doubleday, Page, 1926.

(Illustrator) Kenneth Roberts, *Antiquamania,* Doubleday, Doran, 1928.

The World Does Move (semiautobiographical), Doubleday, Doran, 1928.

Some Old Portraits: A Book about Art and Human Beings, Doubleday, Doran, 1939.

Christmas This Year, Earle J. Bernheimer, 1945.

Your Amiable Uncle: Letters to His Nephews, self-illustrated, Bobbs-Merrill, 1949.

Also author of the following screenplays: *Edgar and the Teacher's Pet,* 1920; *Edgar's Hamlet,* 1920; *Edgar, The Explorer,* 1921; *Get Rich Quick Edgar,* 1921; (with Tom Geraghty) *Pied Piper Malone,* 1924; (with Geraghty) *The Man Who Found Himself,* 1925. Contributor to *Commemorative Tributes to Gillette and Howard and Others,* The Academy, 1940; *Commemorative Tributes of the Academy, 1905-41,* The Academy, 1942; and *There Were Giants in the Land,* Rinehart, 1942. Work represented in *The Collected Stories of the World's Greatest Writers,* Franklin Library, 1984.

MEDIA ADAPTATIONS: Cameo Kirby, Lasky Feature Play, 1914, Fox Film Corporation, 1923 and 1929. *Cherry,* Vitagraph, 1914. *The Two Vanrevels,* Thomas A. Edison, 1914. *Sophia's Imaginary Visitors* (adaptation of *Beasley's Christmas Party*), Thomas A. Edison, 1914. *The Man from Home,* Lasky Feature Play, 1914, Famous Players-Lasky Corporation, 1922. *The Gentleman from Indiana,* J. C. Ivers, 1915. *The Turmoil,* Columbia Pictures, 1916, Universal Pictures, 1924. *The Flirt,* Bluebird Photoplays, 1916, Universal Pictures, 1922. *Seventeen,* Famous Players Film Co., 1916, Paramount Pictures, 1940. *The Country Cousin,* Selznick Pictures, 1919. *The Adventures and Emotions of Edgar Pomeroy* (series of twelve films), Goldwyn Pictures, 1920-21. *The Conquest of Canaan,* Famous Players-Lasky Corporation, 1921. *Penrod,* Marshall Neilan Productions, 1922. *Boy of Mine,* Associated First National Pictures, 1923. *Penrod and Sam,* Associated First National Pictures, 1923, First National Pictures, 1931, Warner Brothers, 1937. *Gentle Julia,* Fox Film Corporation, 1923, Twentieth Century-Fox, 1936. *Monsieur Beaucaire,* Paramount Pictures, 1924 and 1946. *The Fighting Coward* (adaptation of *The Magnolia*), Paramount Pictures, 1924. *Pampered Youth* (adaptation of *The Magnificent Ambersons*), Vitagraph, 1925. *River of Romance* (adaptation of *The Magnolia*), Paramount Famous Lasky Corporation, 1929. *Geraldine,* Pathe Exchange, 1929. *Mister Antonio,* Tiffany-Stahl Productions, 1929. *Monte Carlo* (adaptation of *Monsieur Beaucaire*), Paramount Publix, 1930. *Father's Son* (adaptation of story "Old Fathers and Young Sons"), Warner Brothers/First National Pictures, 1931, Warner Brothers, 1941. *Bad Sister,* Universal Pictures, 1931. *Business and Pleasure* (adaptation of *The Plutocrat*), Fox Film, 1931. *Alice Adams,* RKO Radio Pictures, 1935. *Mississippi* (adaptation of *The Magnolia*), Paramount Pictures, 1935. *Clarence,* Paramount Pictures, 1937. *Penrod's Double Trouble,* Warner Brothers, 1938. *Penrod and His Twin Brother,* Warner Brothers, 1938. *Little Orvie,* RKO Radio Pictures, 1940. *The Magnificent Ambersons,* RKO Radio Pictures, 1942. *Presenting Lily Mars,* Metro-Goldwyn-Mayer, 1943. *On Moonlight Bay* (based on the "Penrod" stories), Warner Brothers, 1951. *By the Light of the Silvery Moon* (adaptation of *Penrod*), Warner Brothers, 1953. The plays *Monsieur Beaucaire,* by Ethel Hale Freeman, W. H. Baker, 1916, and *Booth Tarkington's Seventeen,* by Hugh S. Stange, Stannnard Mears, and Stuart Walker, S. French, 1924, were both adapted from Tarington's works.

SIDELIGHTS: Winner of two of the first four Pulitzer Prizes for literature, Booth Tarkington was best known for his narratives describing middle-class life in the American Midwest of the early twentieth century. He was a prolific writer as well. In a writing career that spanned more than five decades, Tarkington produced 171 stories, 9 novellas, 21 novels, and 19 plays, besides a number of movie scenarios, illustrations, and radio dramas. Many of his works were also adapted for film through the early part of the twentieth century. Although Tarkington was an extremely popular writer, his work did not receive overwhelming critical attention. Said James Woodress in a 1991 *Dictionary of Literary Biography* essay: "Although he had more talent than most of his contemporaries, his work never quite achieved major significance, and he had to be content with a large rather than a discriminating audience." However, Tarkington is still remembered for many of his writings, including chronicles of youth such as the "Penrod" series and *Seventeen* as well as his Pulitzer Prize-winning novels *The Magnificent Ambersons* and *Alice Adams.*

In 1895, Tarkington left for New York City to seek fame and fortune with, as related in his semiautobiographical book *The World Does Move,* a trunk full of "the manuscripts of two plays, of an unfinished novel, and of a now-forgotten number of short stories." It was here that he stumbled upon his first publishing venture after years of struggle, when one of his novels was accepted for publication in a magazine. He said in *The World Does Move:* "Five years of printed rejection slips had not prepared one to receive even an encouraging handmade letter of rejection from an editor, much less a letter of acceptance. Such a letter must be read several times to make certain that the reader's eye is not deceived, and then at intervals to be sure that his memory has not been tricky. But no; all these readings have confirmed the accuracy of the first, it became clear that the thin young man, however embarrassing he might be in his new capacity, was definitely no longer a loafer."

The publisher had, however, asked Tarkington to make changes in the manuscript, which he began immediately. In 1896, he returned to Indiana and continued working on what later became his first novel, *The Gentleman from Indiana.* The book was published in 1899, and Tarkington became an instant success in New York. In his essay, Tarkington explained that this book resulted from a decision to respond to the myth prevalent on the East Coast that Indiana was a "backwoods state." He said: "Sensitive and even resentful, I tried to make my novel answer all this nonsense. . . . A thing the novel tried to say was that in the matter of human character the people of such an out-of-the-way midland village were as estimable as any others anywhere. . . . This, in my sensitive young fervor, was my emotional tribute to the land of my birth." Although the book was a resounding commercial success, Tarkington was viewed differently by critics. An opinion expressed in the *Independent* in 1900 faulted the book for its lack of authenticity while admitting that it was "brim full of a certain boyish enthusiasm which is delightful."

For James Branch Cabell, writing in *Beyond Life: Dizain des demiurges,* Tarkington was a highly accomplished writer who had fallen short of realizing his potential. In Cabell's opinion, the commercial success of *The Gentleman from Indiana,* matched by

the similar triumph of *Monsieur Beaucaire,* "was one of the most dire calamities that ever befell American literature," and it resulted in Tarkington's concessions "to the necessity of being 'pleasant.'" *The Gentleman from Indiana* was perceived as a romance by most critics, and Tarkington was criticized for what reviewers called an optimistic and unrealistic portrayal of characters. Later, he was to receive similar criticism for another best-seller, *The Magnificent Ambersons,* for which he also won his first Pulitzer.

Tarkington followed *The Gentleman from Indiana* with *Monsieur Beaucaire,* which was serialized in *McClure's* in 1899 and published separately in 1900. The volume was written as a costume romance, which was a popular style at the time. The book was successful and was later adapted for the stage and as a feature film. Set in Bath, England, in the eighteenth century, the work describes the adventures of the Duke of Orleans as he masquerades as a barber amongst English nobility living at that popular resort. The plot revolves around the exposure of the duplicity and pretentiousness of some members of the nobility. Addressing the book in a 1937 *Indianapolis Star* article, Damon Runyon wrote that "*Monsieur Beaucaire* is ever green. It is a little literary cameo, and we read it over at least once a year."

In 1914, Tarkington began issuing the "Penrod" stories, which became instant successes. The stories describe the adventures of Penrod Schofield, a young boy growing up in late-nineteenth-century America. Penrod belongs to a middle-class family, and the character's childhood antics were popular with many readers from the time the tales first began appearing in *Everybody's Magazine.* The "Penrod" stories have been compared to Mark Twain's *Tom Sawyer* by many critics and recall many of Tarkington's own memories of a childhood spent in Indiana. Woodress called the works "everyday incidents in which style and arrangement of detail are everything" in the *Dictionary of Literary Biography.* The success of the first stories prompted Tarkington to write many more, and he eventually collected them into three books: *Penrod, Penrod and Sam,* and *Penrod Jashber.* In 1931 he collectively published all the books as *Penrod: His Complete Story.* The "Penrod" books sold a half-million copies while Tarkington was still alive. In *Booth Tarkington: Gentleman in Indiana,* Woodress cites Tarkington, who felt that "Penrod" was successful "because it has kept to *true* boy and avoided book-and-stage boy." And in a letter Tarkington wrote to a friend included in the same book, the author also said: "My prices astonish me . . . I'm rather sorry for the magazines that pay 'em." Assessing the *Penrod* tales in *Dictionary of Literary Biography,* Woodress said that "Tarkington was in full mastery of his craft when he wrote these stories. His style is supple, articulate, and witty, and the tales entertain children and delight adults."

While writing the "Penrod" stories, Tarkington also began work on *Seventeen: A Tale of Youth and Summer Time and the Baxter Family, Especially William,* another collection of stories about a young protagonist. He had worked on a similar theme in an earlier work, "Mary Smith," a short story dealing with young love, for which he had received favorable attention. *Seventeen* also proved very popular with Tarkington's readers. The stories deal with incidents in the life of Willie Baxter, a young man from the American Midwest, who is in love with a woman called Lola Pratt. Woodress said that although the stories seem dated today, *Seventeen* was a major success in Tarkington's own time, selling nearly eight hundred thousand copies as well as being adapted for a play, a musical comedy, and a feature film. This collection also provided Tarkington with a major character for another book,

Gentle Julia. The character of Florence Atwater, the protagonist of *Gentle Julia,* was inspired by the tomboyish character of Jane, Willie Baxter's sister in *Seventeen.* Woodress, in *Dictionary of Literary Biography,* said of *Gentle Julia:* "Tarkington understood girls as well as boys and, in depicting the activities of Florence, her cousin Herbert, and his buddy Henry, handles successfully the emotional and mental lag between the sexes at the age of thirteen."

By the 1920s Tarkington was living in the suburbs of Indianapolis, Indiana, and spending the summers in Kennebunkport, Maine. His observations of the life of suburban women in Indianapolis resulted in *Women,* stories of "daytime society made up of wives, teas, domestic servants, luncheons, children, literary clubs, and Amazon warfare of a highly sophisticated type," summarized Woodress in the *Dictionary of Literary Biography.* And his experiences in Kennebunkport, his summer home, directly impacted *Mirthful Haven,* published in 1930. Kennebunkport was a resort town, and in Woodress's opinion "it was inevitable that a novelist of manners would sooner or later make use of the clash in values and life-styles of the natives and the summer folk." Kennebunkport was also the inspiration for Tarkington's 1932 publication *Mary's Neck.*

According to Adam J. Sorkin, discussing Tarkington's work in a 1981 *Dictionary of Literary Biography* essay, although Tarkington was a popular and prolific writer throughout his literary career, the author "wrote his best works at the time of and just after World War I." It was in these years that Tarkington received two Pulitzer Prizes, one in 1919, for *The Magnificent Ambersons,* and the other in 1922, for *Alice Adams.* Although *The Magnificent Ambersons* was a very popular book with Tarkington's readers, reviewers criticized the author for romanticizing the story, thus reducing its elements of realism. *The Magnificent Ambersons* traces the fall and reclamation of the old and wealthy Amberson family through George Amberson Minafer, the spoiled heir. The Amberson family made its fortune because of the hard work of George's grandfather, Major Amberson. However, his daughter, who marries into an equally rich family, does not instill similar values in her son, George, who grows up to be a selfish, uncaring individual. Critics agreed that Tarkington successfully built up the list of George's follies, leading the reader to anticipate his fall from arrogant self-assurance. However, the direction of the story changes dramatically when in the end George, instead of receiving just punishment for his deeds, marries the wealthy daughter of his mother's rejected suitor and thus begins the reclamation of his family. George further enhances his return to material and moral success when he takes a job in a factory. Tarkington received criticism for this ending even though he was praised for his accurate description of middle-class life of the time.

Tarkington went on to write *The Midlander,* continuing the story of the economic and historical development of America. He later combined *The Magnificent Ambersons, The Midlander,* and *The Turmoil* to form the *Growth* trilogy, which, in Sorkin's words, "deals with the growing up of a nation," a subject of "potentially monumental proportions." *The Turmoil,* published in 1915, formed the second book of the trilogy. It drew favorable attention from critics at the time. According to Sorkin, in this book Tarkington explored the "raw ugliness and savagery" that characterized the growth of the nation. Although the book was written before *The Magnificent Ambersons,* it deals with a later period in history. In *The Turmoil* Tarkington dealt with the nouveau-riche Sheridan family, who, in Sorkin's words, "typify the new makers of material wealth and vulgar worshippers of

Bigness." The book relates the story of James Sheridan, an affluent man, and his son Bibbs, who wants no part of his father's vast empire. W. D. Howells, discussing the book in *Harper's,* expressed appreciation for the universality of the story of *The Turmoil.* Howells said that even though the book was particularly rooted in the American way of life, "the action of *The Turmoil* is possible everywhere that the human passions and volitions have play." William Lyon Phelps praised Tarkington in *The Advance of the English Novel* and expressed a hope that he would not surrender to the demands of the popular reading public, a criticism the author had faced in the past for the conclusion of *The Magnificent Ambersons.* However, Tarkington did receive similar censure for the ending of *The Turmoil.* Some critics found Bibbs Sheridan's sudden change from sensitive poet to successful capitalist at the end of the book contrived and unrealistic. Nevertheless Phelps called *The Turmoil* "the most ambitious and on the whole the best" novel Tarkington had written till that time, and he felt the book was proof that the author was "growing in spiritual grace."

Tarkington's other Pulitzer Prize-winning novel, *Alice Adams,* fared better with critics than *The Magnificent Ambersons.* In fact, some regarded *Alice Adams* as his best work. Sorkin lauded the book as "Tarkington's most admirable achievement, a neatly structured, deftly paced, validly observed social novel and ironic novel of manners that . . . illustrates its creator's many attributes." Carl Van Doren said in the *Nation* that in *Alice Adams* Tarkington had "produced a genuinely significant book." The work was originally conceived as the third part of the *Growth* trilogy but was not included because of its narrower focus on a single generation. Sorkin said *Alice Adams* is less idealistic than Tarkington's other work in its characterization of Alice Adams as a young American girl brought up by her socially aspiring mother to realize and achieve social and material prospects beyond her class. Alice is exhorted by her mother to marry Arthur Russell, an eligible, rich young man. The book follows Alice's attempts at snaring Russell, who eventually marries his wealthy cousin, Mildred Palmer, while Alice resigns herself to working as a typist and stenographer. Sorkin felt that in this volume "Tarkington achieves an accurate appraisal and sympathetic portrait of middle-class home life." *Alice Adams* received more favorable attention from critics than other novels Tarkington had written. In *Some Contemporary Americans: The Personal Equation in Literature* Percy H. Boynton expressed his appreciation of Tarkington's literary achievement: "In *Alice Adams* there are no eleventh-hour reprieves. Perhaps [Tarkington] has turned a corner."

Besides writing fiction, Tarkington also authored numerous plays. However, he was far less successful as a playwright than he was as a novelist. Critics like Barrett H. Clark in *A Study of Modern Drama* said that Tarkington was "an enormously successful novelist" who "never took playwriting seriously." But in an evaluation of Tarkington's plays in the *Princeton University Library Chronicle,* Albert Van Nostrand proposed that the subjects Tarkington explored in his plays were remarkably similar to the ones in his books. For example, said Van Nostrand, in many plays, including *Poldekin,* Tarkington presented his "thesis . . . about the ideology of capitalism," a subject the author also explored in his "economic novels." Produced in 1920, *Poldekin* relates the story of a revolutionary group of Russians who are sent on a mission to convert America into a communist state. The protagonist, Poldekin, is hesitant to believe the philosophy of his country unquestioningly, however, and he leaves the group to discover America for himself. Van Nostrand described the characters as symbolic representations of opposing points of view.

Tarkington's other plays included *Clarence,* which Clark also found noteworthy. The critic felt that in this play the author realized the promise he had displayed in his novels.

BIOGRAPHICAL/CRITICAL SOURCES:

BOOKS

Boynton, Percy H., *Some Contemporary Americans: The Personal Equation in Literature,* University of Chicago Press, 1924, pp. 108-25.

Cabell, James Branch, *Beyond Life: Dizain des demiurges,* R. M. McBride, 1919, pp. 277-322.

Clark, Barrett H., *A Study of the Modern Drama: A Handbook for the Study and Appreciation of Typical Plays, European, English, and American, of the Last Three-Quarters of a Century,* Appleton, 1938, pp. 359-410.

Dictionary of Literary Biography, Gale (Detroit), Volume 9: *American Novelists, 1910-1945,* 1981; Volume 102: *American Short-Story Writers, 1910-1945, Second Series,* 1991.

Fennimore, Keith J., *Booth Tarkington,* Twayne, 1974.

Mayberry, Susanah, *My Amiable Uncle: Recollections about Booth Tarkington,* Purdue University Press, 1983.

Phelps, William Lyon, *The Advance of the English Novel,* Dodd, Mead, 1916, pp. 267-301.

Twentieth-Century Children's Writers, 3rd edition, St. James Press, 1989, pp. 947-49.

Twentieth-Century Literary Criticism, Volume 9, Gale, 1983, pp. 451-75.

Woodress, James Leslie, *Booth Tarkington: Gentleman From Indiana,* Lippincott, 1955.

PERIODICALS

Bookman, December, 1921, pp. 394-95; March, 1927, pp. 12-21.

Harper's, May, 1915, pp. 958-61.

Indianapolis Star, August 7, 1937.

Nation, February 9, 1921.

Princeton University Library Chronicle, autumn, 1955, pp. 13-39.

Saturday Evening Post, August 23, 1941, pp. 27, 80-88.

*   *   *

TATE, (John Orley) Allen 1899-1979

PERSONAL: Born November 19, 1899, in Winchester, KY; died February 9, 1979, in Nashville, TN; son of John Orley and Eleanor (Varnell) Tate; married Caroline Gordon (a novelist), November 3, 1924 (divorced, 1959); married Isabella Stewart Gardner, August 27, 1959 (divorced, 1966); married Helen Heinz, July 30, 1966; children: (first marriage) Nancy Meriwether, (third marriage) John Allen, Michael Paul (deceased), Benjamin Lewis Bogan. *Education:* Vanderbilt University, B.A. (magna cum laude), 1922. *Politics:* Democrat. *Religion:* Roman Catholic convert, 1950.

ADDRESSES: Home—113 Groome Dr., Nashville, TN 37205. *Office*—Department of English, 127 Vincent Hall, University of Minnesota, Minneapolis, MN. *Agent*—Laurence Pollinger Ltd., 18 Maddox St., London W1, England.

CAREER: Writer, 1922-79. *Telling Tales,* New York, NY, assistant editor, 1924-25; Southwestern College, Memphis, TN, lecturer in English, 1934-36; University of North Carolina, Women's College, Greensboro, professor of English, 1938-39; Princeton University, Princeton, NJ, poet in residence, 1939-42; Library of Congress, Washington, D.C., chair of poetry, 1943-44,

fellow in American letters, 1944-50; *Sewanee Review,* Sewanee, TN, editor, 1944-46; New York University, New York, NY, lecturer, 1947-51; University of Chicago, Chicago, IL, visiting professor of humanities, 1949; University of Minnesota, Minneapolis, professor of English, 1951-66, Regents' Professor of English, 1966-68. Member of Columbia Broadcasting System (CBS) radio program "Invitation to Learning," 1940-41. Fulbright professor, University of Rome, 1953-54, Oxford University, 1958-59. Member of American delegation to UNESCO Conference on the Arts, and American representative to the International Exposition of the Arts (Congress for Cultural Freedom), both 1952. Lecturer for Department of State in England, France, Italy, and India, 1956. Senior fellow, Indiana School of Letters. Visiting lecturer and poet at numerous universities and public readings.

MEMBER: National Institute of Arts and Letters (president, 1968-69), American Academy of Arts and Letters, American Academy of Arts and Sciences, Society of American Historians, Southern Historical Association, Phi Beta Kappa (senate, 1952-53), Century Association, Princeton Club, Authors Club (London).

AWARDS, HONORS: Guggenheim fellowships, 1928 and 1929; National Institute of Arts and Letters award, 1948; Bollingen Prize for poetry, 1956; Brandeis University Medal for poetry, 1961; gold medal from Dante Society, Florence, Italy, 1962; Academy of American Poets award, 1963; Oscar Williams award, Mark Rothko award, Ingram Merrill award, and National Medal for Literature, all 1976. Numerous honorary degrees, including University of Louisville, 1948, Coe College, 1955, Colgate University, 1956, University of Kentucky, 1960, and Carleton College, 1963.

WRITINGS:

POETRY

(With Ridley Wills) *The Golden Mean, and Other Poems,* privately printed, 1923.

Mr. Pope, and Other Poems, Minton, 1928.

(Contributor) *Fugitives: An Anthology of Verse,* Harcourt, 1928.

Three Poems: Ode to the Confederate Dead, Message from Abroad, [and] *The Cross, Minton,* 1930.

Poems: 1928-1931, Scribner, 1932.

The Mediterranean and Other Poems, Alcestis, 1936.

Selected Poems, Scribner, 1937.

Sonnets at Christmas, Cummington, 1941.

(Translator) Pervigilium Veneris, *Vigil of Venus,* Cummington, 1943.

The Winter Sea, Cummington, 1944.

Fragment of a Meditation/MCMXXVIII, Cummington, 1947.

Poems, 1920-1945, Eyre, 1948.

Poems: 1922-1947, Scribner, 1948, enlarged edition, 1960.

Two Conceits for the Eye To Sing, If Possible, Cummington, 1950.

Poems, Scribner, 1960.

Christ and the Unicorn, Cummington, 1966.

The Swimmers and Other Selected Poems, Oxford University Press, 1970, Scribner, 1971.

Collected Poems, 1919-1976, Farrar, Straus, 1977.

PROSE

Stonewall Jackson: The Good Soldier, Minton, 1928.

Jefferson Davis: His Rise and Fall, Minton, 1929.

(Contributor) *I'll Take My Stand: The South and the Agrarian Tradition by Twelve Southerners,* Harper, 1930.

(With others) *The Critique of Humanism,* 1930.

(Contributor) *The Best Short Stories, 1934,* Houghton, 1934.

(Editor and contributor) *Who Owns America?: A New Declaration of Independence,* Houghton, 1936.

Reactionary Essays on Poetry and Ideas, Scribner, 1936.

(Contributor) *A Southern Harvest,* Houghton, 1937.

(With A. Theodore Johnson) *America through the Essay,* Oxford University Press, 1938.

The Fathers (novel; also see below), Putnam, 1938, revised edition, A. Swallow, 1960, 3rd edition (originally published by LSU press in 1977 as part of *The Fathers and Other Fiction*), Louisiana State University Press (Baton Rouge), 1996.

Reason in Madness: Critical Essays, Putnam, 1941.

(With Huntington Cairns and Mark Van Doren) *Invitation to Learning,* Random House, 1941.

On the Limits of Poetry: Selected Essays, 1928-1948, A. Swallow, 1948.

The Hovering Fly and Other Essays, Cummington, 1948.

The Forlorn Demon: Didactic and Critical Essays, Regnery, 1953.

The Man of Letters in the Modern World: Selected Essays, 1928-1955, Meridian, 1955.

Collected Essays, A. Swallow, 1959, revised and enlarged edition published as *Essays of Four Decades,* 1968.

Mere Literature and the Lost Traveller, George Peabody College for Teachers, 1969.

The Translation of Poetry, Gertrude Clark Whittall Poetry and Literature Fund, 1972.

John Tyree Fain and Thomas Daniel Young, editors, *The Literary Correspondence of Donald Davidson and Allen Tate,* University of Georgia Press, 1974.

Memoirs and Opinions, 1926-1974, Swallow, 1975 (published in England as *Memoirs & Essays Old and New, 1926-1974,* Carcanet, 1976).

The Fathers and Other Fiction, Louisiana State University Press, 1977.

Thomas Daniel Young and John J. Hindle, editors, *The Republic of Letters in America: The Correspondence of John Peale Bishop and Allen Tate,* University Press of Kentucky, 1981.

Ashley Brown and Frances Neel Cheney, editors, *The Poetry Reviews of Allen Tate,* Louisiana State University Press, 1983.

EDITOR

White Buildings: Poems by Hart Crane, Horace Liveright, 1926.

The Language of Poetry, Princeton University Press, 1942.

Princeton Verse between Two Wars: An Anthology, Princeton University Press, 1942.

(With John Peale Bishop) *American Harvest: Twenty Years of Creative Writing in the United States,* L. B. Fischer, 1942.

Recent American Poetry and Poetic Criticism: A Selected List of References, Library of Congress, 1943.

Sixty American Poets, 1896-1944, Library of Congress, 1945, revised edition, 1954.

A Southern Vanguard: The John Peale Bishop Memorial Volume, Prentice-Hall, 1947.

The Collected Poems of John Peale Bishop, Scribner, 1948.

(With wife, Caroline Gordon) *The House of Fiction: An Anthology of the Short Story, with Commentary,* Scribner, 1950, revised edition, 1960.

(With David Cecil) *Modern Verse in English,* Macmillan, 1958.

(With Ralph Ross and John Berryman) *The Arts of Reading,* Crowell, 1960.

(With Robert Penn Warren) *Selected Poems by Denis Devlin,* Delacorte, 1966.

T. S. Eliot, the Man and His Work: A Critical Evaluation by Twenty-six Distinguished Writers, Delacorte, 1967.

Complete Poetry and Selected Criticism of Edgar Allan Poe, New American Library, 1968.

Six American Poets from Emily Dickinson to the Present: An Introduction, University of Minnesota Press, 1971.

OTHER

Editor, *Kenyon Review,* 1938-42. Contributor of essays and poetry to numerous periodicals, including *Double-Dealer, Hound and Horn, The Fugitive, Literary Review, Nation, New Republic, Minnesota Review, Shenandoah, Kenyon Review, Partisan Review, Yale Review, Criterion, Le Figaro Litteraire,* and *Sewanee Review.* Tate's papers are collected at the Princeton University Library, the Columbia University Library, and the University of Victoria Library, British Columbia.

SIDELIGHTS: Allen Tate was a well-known man of letters from the American South, a central figure in the fields of poetry, criticism, and ideas. In the course of a career spanning the middle decades of the twentieth century, Tate authored poems, essays, translations, and fiction; *Dictionary of Literary Biography* contributor James T. Jones claimed that his "influence was prodigious, his circle of acquaintances immense." Tate relished his "man of letters" reputation—he consistently held for the highest standards of literature, feeling that the best creative writing offers the most cogent expressions of human experience. *Sewanee Review* correspondent J. A. Bryant, Jr. called Tate a "sage" who "kept bright the instrument of language in our time and . . . made it illuminate as well as shine."

Tate was born and raised in Kentucky, the youngest of three sons of John Orley and Eleanor Varnell Tate. His family moved frequently when he was young, so his elementary education was erratic. Influenced by his mother's love of literature, however, he did extensive reading on his own; he was admitted to Vanderbilt University in 1918. There Tate proved an excellent student, earning top honors and membership in Phi Beta Kappa. More importantly, while an undergraduate he became aware of the special circumstances of Southern culture and sensibility. *Dictionary of Literary Biography* essayist James A. Hart wrote: "With a Border background [Tate] had to face the question of whether he was a Southerner or an American. Affirming the first, he had to confront the dominant positivist and materialistic Yankee values which were supplanting the older values of the South." Under the influence of his teachers Walter Clyde Curry, Donald Davidson, and John Crowe Ransom, Tate began to analyze his inheritance from a critical, but respectful, perspective.

Tate was the only undergraduate to be admitted to membership in the Fugitives, an informal group of Southern intellectuals that included Ransom, Davidson, Merrill Moore, and Robert Penn Warren. The Fugitives met once a week to discuss poetry—their own and others'—and to mount a defense against the notion that the South did not possess a significant literature of its own. In the periodical *The Fugitive,* and later in an important anthology called *I'll Take My Stand,* Tate argued that the Southern agrarian way of life reflected the artistic beauty, intelligence, and wit of the ancient classic age. Hart explained that Tate and his fellow Fugitives "believed that industrialism had demeaned man and that there was a need to return to the humanism of the Old South." The Agrarian movement, Hart added, "would create or restore something in 'the moral and religious outlook of Western Man.'" Whatever its beliefs, the Fugitive group exerted an enormous influence on American letters in the 1920s and on into the

Depression era. A number of its members, including Tate, became the literary spokesmen for their generations.

Although Tate spent several years between 1928 and 1932 in France, he continued to write almost exclusively about the South. While he socialized with Ernest Hemingway, Gertrude Stein, and the other expatriate American writers in Paris, Tate still explored his own personal philosophical and moral ties to his homeland. He wrote two biographies of Southern Civil War heroes, *Stonewall Jackson: The Good Soldier* and *Jefferson Davis: His Rise and Fall,* he began his most important poem, "Ode to the Confederate Dead," and he worked on his only novel, *The Fathers. Southern Literary Journal* contributor George Core maintained that Tate was aware of the failings of the Old South, but it still remained "his chief model for his whole life. . . . Hence Tate's connections with the South—by inheritance, kinship, custom, and manner—have furnished him with . . . a central allegiance. Out of the tension between Tate's personal allegiance and his awareness of what he has called 'a deep illness of the modern mind' has come the enkindling subject of his work as a whole."

One of Tate's preoccupations was indeed "man suffering from unbelief." His modern Everyman, however, faced a more complex situation than the simple medieval morality tale hero. *Michigan Quarterly Review* contributor Cleanth Brooks explained: "In the old Christian synthesis, nature and history were related in a special way. With the break-up of that synthesis, man finds himself caught between a meaningless cycle on the one hand, and on the other, the more extravagant notions of progress—between a nature that is oblivious of man and a man-made 'unnatural' utopia." Even though he had periods of skepticism himself, Tate felt that art could not survive without religion. To quote Pier Francesco Listri in *Allen Tate and His Work: Critical Evaluations,* "In a rather leaden society governed by a myth of science, [Tate's] poetry conducts a fearless campaign against science, producing from that irony a measure both musical and fabulous. In an apathetic, agnostic period he [was] not ashamed to recommend a Christianity to be lived as intellectual anguish."

Having had a classical education himself, Tate employed numerous classical allusions in his work; he also often wrote intensely personal poetry that would not reveal itself instantly to a reader. In the *Sewanee Review,* Louise Cowan called Tate "the most difficult poet of the twentieth century," and other critics have offered similar assessments. Brooks, for one, noted: "Tate puts a great burden upon his reader. He insists that the reader himself, by an effort of his own imagination, cooperate with the poet to bring the violent metaphors and jarring rhythms into unity." *Georgia Review* contributor M. E. Bradford also contended that Tate, with "his preference for the lyric and for the agonized *persona* in that genre—along with the admiration which his ingenuities in the employment of all manner of strategies have together inspired—have confirmed his reputation for obscurity, allusive privacy, and consequent difficulty. Were it not for his politics, his poetics, and his honesty about them both, he could have become the object of coterie enthusiasms."

Monroe K. Spears offered some reasons why Tate never became merely the "object of coterie enthusiasms." In the *Sewanee Review,* Spears praised Tate for his "independence and common sense and avoidance of cant" as well as for "his stubborn honesty and candor; his ideal of poise, integrity, and intelligence." *New Republic* contributor James Dickey also found Tate to be more than a "Southern writer." Dickey wrote: "[Tate's] situation has certain perhaps profound implications for every man in every

place and every time. And they are more than implications; they are the basic questions, the possible solutions to the question of existence. How does each of us wish to live his only life?" Ferman Bishop concluded that Tate's place in American letters "is secure," adding: "He is one of a very small number of American writers who have had the ability to present the intellectual as well as the emotional side of the American experience. In a culture which has seemed so often to encourage and even depend on the anti-intellectual, he has emphasized the opposite. Ultimately, . . . he will be proved to have dealt with the truly significant elements in our experience."

BIOGRAPHICAL/CRITICAL SOURCES:

BOOKS

Bishop, Ferman, *Allen Tate,* Twayne, 1967.
Bradbury, John M., *The Fugitives: A Critical Account,* University of North Carolina Press, 1958.
Carrithers, Gale H., *Mumford, Tate, Eiseley: Watchers in the Night,* Louisiana State University Press (Baton Rouge), 1991.
Contemporary Literary Criticism, Gale (Detroit), Volume 2, 1974; Volume 4, 1975; Volume 6, 1976; Volume 9, 1978; Volume 11, 1979; Volume 14, 1980; Volume 24, 1983.
Dictionary of Literary Biography, Gale, Volume 4: *American Writers in Paris, 1920-1939,* 1980; Volume 45: *American Poets, 1880-1945, Third Series,* 1986; Volume 63: *Modern American Critics, 1920-1955,* 1988.
Doreski, William, *The Years of Our Friendship: Robert Lowell and Allen Tate,* University Press of Mississippi (Jackson), 1990.
Dupree, Robert S., *Allen Tate and the Augustinian Imagination: A Study of the Poetry,* Louisiana State University Press, 1983.
Exiles and Fugitives: The Letters of Jacques and Raeissa Maritain, Allen Tate, and Caroline Gordon, edited by John M. Dunaway, Louisiana State University Press (Baton Rouge), 1992.
Frye, Northrop, *Northrop Frye on Culture and Literature: A Collection of Review Essays,* University of Chicago Press, 1978.
Hammer, Langdon, *Hart Crane and Allen Tate: Janus-Faced Modernism,* Princeton University Press, 1993.
Huff, Peter A., *Allen Tate and the Catholic Revival: Trace of the Fugitive Gods,* Paulist Press (New York City), 1996.
Jancovich, Mark, *The Cultural Politics of the New Criticism,* Cambridge University Press (New York City), 1993.
Kazin, Alfred, *On Native Grounds: An Interpretation of Modern American Prose Literature,* Reynal & Hitchcock, 1942.
Malvasi, Mark G., *The Unregenerate South: The Agrarian Thought of John Crowe Ransom, Allen Tate, and Donald Davidson,* Louisiana State University Press, 1997.
Meiners, R. K., *The Last Alternatives: A Study of the Works of Allen Tate,* Swallow, 1963.
Pratt, William, editor, *The Fugitive Poets: Modern Southern Poetry in Perspective,* Dutton, 1965.
Purdy, Rob Roy, editor, *Fugitives Reunion: Conversations at Vanderbilt,* Vanderbilt University Press, 1959.
Ransom, John Crowe, editor, *The Kenyon Critics,* World, 1951.
Squires, Radcliffe, *Allen Tate: A Literary Biography,* Bobbs-Merrill, 1971.
Squires, Radcliffe, editor, *Allen Tate and His Work: Critical Evaluations,* University of Minnesota Press, 1972.
Stewart, John L., *The Burden of Time: The Fugitives and the Agrarians,* Princeton University Press, 1965.

Stineback, David C., *Shifting World: Social Change and Nostalgia in the American Novel,* Associated University Presses, 1976.

PERIODICALS

American Scholar, autumn, 1976.
Book World, March 2, 1969.
Commonweal, May 29, 1953.
Critique, spring, 1964.
Georgia Review, spring, 1968; spring, 1971.
Michigan Quarterly Review, fall, 1971.
New Republic, April 29, 1936; July 24, 1965; October 1, 1975.
New York Times Book Review, May 4, 1969; December 11, 1977; January 8, 1978; April 8, 1979.
Partisan Review, February, 1949; summer, 1968.
Poetry, May, 1968; April, 1970; January, 1972.
Publishers Weekly, November 2, 1992, p. 60.
Renascence, spring, 1971.
Sewanee Review, January, 1954; autumn, 1959; summer, 1968; spring, 1972; summer, 1974; spring, 1978; spring, 1979.
Shenandoah, spring, 1961; winter, 1968.
South Atlantic Quarterly, autumn, 1967.
Southern Literary Journal, autumn, 1969.
Southern Review, winter, 1936; winter, 1940; summer, 1971; autumn, 1972; autumn, 1976; April, 1978.
Virginia Quarterly Review, summer, 1969.
Washington Post, May 7, 1969.

*   *   *

TATE, Ellalice
See HIBBERT, Eleanor Alice Burford

*   *   *

TAYLOR, A(lan) J(ohn) P(ercivale) 1906-1990

PERSONAL: Born March 25, 1906, in Southport, Birkdale, Lancashire, England; died September 7, 1990, in London, England; son of Percy Lees and Constance (Thompson) Taylor; married third wife, Eva Haraszti (a historian), 1976; children: Giles, Sebastian, Amelia, Sophia, Crispin, Daniel. *Education:* Bootham School, student, 1919-24; Oriel College, Oxford, B.A., 1927, M.A., 1932. *Politics:* Labour Party.

CAREER: Rockefeller Fellow in social sciences, 1929-30; Manchester University, Manchester, England, lecturer in history, 1930-38; Oxford University, Oxford, England, fellow of Magdalen College, 1938-76, honorary fellow, 1976-90, tutor in modern history, 1938-63, university lecturer in international history, 1953-63, Ford's Lecturer in English History, 1955-56, honorary fellow of Oriel College, 1980-90. Leslie Stephen Lecturer, Cambridge University, 1961-62; Creighton Lecturer, London University, 1973; Benjamin Meaker Visiting Professor of History, University of Bristol, 1976-78. In charge of Beaverbrook Library.

MEMBER: British Academy (fellow), American Academy of Arts and Sciences (honorary member), Yugoslav Academy of Sciences (honorary member), Hungarian Academy of Sciences (honorary member), National Union of Journalists, City Music Society (London; president).

AWARDS, HONORS: Honorary degrees include D.C.L. from New Brunswick College, Oxford, 1961, D.Litt. from University of Bristol, 1978, University of Warwick, 1981, and University of Manchester, 1982.

WRITINGS:

The Italian Problem in European Diplomacy, 1847-1849, Manchester University Press, 1934, Barnes & Noble, 1970.
Germany's First Bid for Colonies, 1884-1885: A Move in Bismarck's European Policy, Macmillan, 1938, Archon, 1967.
The Habsburg Monarchy, 1815-1918, Macmillan, 1941, revised edition published as *The Habsburg Monarchy, 1809-1918: A History of the Austrian Empire and Austria-Hungary,* 1949, University of Chicago Press, 1976.
The Course of German History: A Survey of the Development of German History since 1815, Hamish Hamilton, 1945, revised edition, Coward-McCann, 1946.
From Napoleon to Stalin: Comments on European History, Hamish Hamilton, 1950.
Rumours of Wars, Hamish Hamilton, 1952.
The Struggle for Mastery in Europe, 1848-1918, Clarendon Press, 1954.
Bismarck: The Man and the Statesman, Knopf, 1955.
Englishmen and Others, Hamish Hamilton, 1956.
The Trouble Makers: Dissent over Foreign Policy, 1792-1939, Hamish Hamilton, 1957, Indiana University Press, 1958.
The Russian Revolution (television script), Associated Television, 1959.
Politics in the First World War, [London], 1959.
Lloyd George: Rise and Fall, Cambridge University Press, 1961.
The Origins of the Second World War, Hamish Hamilton, 1961, Atheneum, 1962, 2nd edition, Fawcett, 1966.
The First World War: An Illustrated History, Hamish Hamilton, 1963, published as *An Illustrated History of the First World War,* Putnam, 1964, published as *A History of the First World War,* Berkeley, 1966.
Politics in Wartime and Other Essays, Hamish Hamilton, 1964, Atheneum, 1965.
English History, 1914-1945 (Oxford History of England), Clarendon Press, 1965.
From Sarajevo to Potsdam, Thames & Hudson, 1966, Harcourt, 1967.
From Napoleon to Lenin: Historical Essays, Harper, 1966.
Europe: Grandeur and Decline, Penguin, 1967.
(With Robert Rhodes James, J. H. Plumb, Basil Liddell Hart, and Anthony Storr) *Churchill Revised: A Critical Assessment,* Dial, 1969.
War by Timetable: How the First World War Began, American Heritage Press, 1969.
Beaverbrook, Simon & Schuster, 1972.
(With others) *Churchill: Four Faces and the Man,* Penguin, 1973.
Essays in English History, Hamish Hamilton, 1976.
The Last of Old Europe: A Grand Tour with A. J. P. Taylor, Sidgwick & Jackson, 1976.
The War Lords, Hamish Hamilton, 1977, Atheneum, 1978.
The Russian War, 1941-1945, edited by Daniela Mrazkova and Vladimir Remes, J. Cape, 1978.
How Wars Begin, Atheneum, 1979.
Revolutions and Revolutionaries, Hamish Hamilton, 1980.
Politicians, Socialism and Historians, Hamish Hamilton, 1980, Stein & Day, 1982.
A Personal History (autobiography), Atheneum, 1983.
In Search of C. S. Lewis, Bridge Publications, 1983.
An Old Man's Diary, Hamish Hamilton, 1984.
How Wars End, Hamish Hamilton, 1985.

From Napoleon to the Second International: Essays on Nineteenth Century Europe (contains both essays selected from previous collections and pieces previously unpublished in volume form), edited by Chris Wrigley, Hamish Hamilton (London, UK), 1993, Allen Lane (New York), 1994.

EDITOR

(And cotranslator) Heinrich Friedjung, *The Struggle for Supremacy in Germany, 1859-1866,* Macmillan, 1935.

(With R. Reynolds) *British Pamphleteers,* Volume 2, Wingate, 1948-51.

(With Alan Louis Charles Bullock) *A Select List of Books on European History, 1815-1914,* Clarendon Press, 1949, 2nd edition, 1957.

(With Richard Pares) *Essays Presented to Sir Lewis Namier,* St. Martin's, 1956.

William Maxwell Aitken and Baron Beaverbrook, *The Abdication of King Edward VIII,* Atheneum, 1966.

(And author of introduction) K. Marx and F. Engels, *The Communist Manifesto,* Penguin, 1967.

(With Mortimer Wheeler and Hugh Trevor-Roper) Winston S. Churchill, *History of English-Speaking Peoples: Based on the Text of "A History of the English-Speaking Peoples,"* twelve volumes, New Caxton Library Service, 1969-74.

Lloyd George: Twelve Essays, Hamish Hamilton, 1971.

Frances Stevenson, *Lloyd George: A Diary,* Hutchinson, 1971.

W. P. Crozier, *Off the Record: Political Interviews, 1933-1943,* Hutchinson, 1973.

The Second World War: An Illustrated History, Putnam, 1975.

My Darling Pussy: The Letters of Lloyd George and Frances Stevenson, 1913-41, Weidenfeld & Nicolson, 1975.

The Illustrated History of the World Wars, Octopus, 1978.

(Coeditor) *Modern Perspectives on the Gold Standard,* Cambridge University Press (New York City), 1997.

(Coeditor) *Boundry-layer Meteriology—25th Anniversary Volume,* Kluwer Academic Publishers (Boston), 1997.

OTHER

(Author of introduction) F. Fertig, editor, *1848: The Opening of an Era,* Howard Fertig, 1967.

(Author of foreword) Arthur Schnitzler, *My Youth in Vienna,* Weidenfeld & Nicolson, 1971.

Also author of *The Russian Revolution of 1917,* 1958. Contributor to *Sunday Express, Observer, New Statesman,* and other publications. Editor in chief, "History of the Twentieth Century," for B.P.C. Publishing. A bibliography of Taylor's writings, articles, and lectures has been compiled by A. Wrigley.

SIDELIGHTS: A. J. P. Taylor "must be the most widely read English historian since G. M. Trevelyan, quite possibly since Lord Macaulay, and with good reason," stated John Goss in the *New York Times Book Review.* Taylor was familiar to many Britons through his long career as a television commentator, his columns in popular papers such as the *Sunday Express,* and through his television series. Woodrow Wyatt, writing in the London *Times,* called his television work "the best possible history lesson, combining entertainment with instruction," and added that "A. J. P. Taylor is the most gifted teacher on television." "My guess," Goss declared, "is that he is relatively better known in Britain than, say, John Kenneth Galbraith or Arthur Schlesinger Jr. is in America."

Piers Brendon in the *New Statesman & Society* noted that while in his professional career Taylor was "a dazzling amalgam of charm, fun and acuity," the "insufferable" Taylor was better displayed by his autobiography: "spiteful, vain, embittered, and self-pitying." Brendon commented that Taylor grew up as the son of "left-wing nonconformists permanently at odds with the political orthodoxies of their day." While he identified with proletariats, he was the only son of a wealthy manufacturer and was educated at Oxford. His marital relationships were less than conventional; after divorcing his first wife and marrying his second, he continued to live with the first for part of the week. And after marrying a third wife, Taylor continued his relationships with the first two. In his academic career, Taylor was again torn between his Northern privileged upbringing and his Southern identification as a "worker." He served as a history lecturer at Manchester University yet longed to become a professor at Oxford, an opportunity denied to him. He received a fellowship at Magdalen in 1938 and stayed to the end of his career. Though he was elected a Fellow of the British Academy, became vice-president of his college, and produced the final volume of the *Oxford History of England,* he failed to receive even a Regius Chair from Oxford due to his alienation of both conservatives and liberals at the college. David Cannadine, writing in the *Times Literary Supplement,* saw Taylor as a "victim of his own contrariness" and noted that "the only thing that was predictable about Taylor was his total unpredictability."

Taylor's books were widely acclaimed by critics. London *Times* contributor David Marquand declared that the historian is "capable of a sinewy, apparently effortless prose of bewitching grace." John Kenneth Galbraith, writing in the *Washington Post Book World,* asserted that "when [Taylor] turns to his historical writing, he has been as careful, even meticulous, as the better scholars in his areas of competence, and, in addition, he has shown a phenomenally greater capacity for continuous, committed labor." "He writes," Goss noted, "with a verve which will insure that books like his study of dissent in foreign policy, 'The Trouble Makers,' or 'English History 1914-1945' (in my opinion, his masterpiece) will survive on their literary merits even when they have been overtaken by subsequent research." "Where he excels most of all is in his ability to master a great mass of material, and to weave it into a continuous narrative, of which he is always in control," Marquand maintained. "In . . . *English History 1914-1945,* he did this better than anyone since Macaulay. It is hard to believe that anyone will do it as well again."

Many of Taylor's essays were collected in the volume *From Napolean to the Second International: Essays on Nineteenth Century Europe.* They include an autobiographical essay, subtitled "What happened next?" According to Peter Clarke in the *London Review of Books,* this was Taylor's favorite question, one he believed that historians had a "prime duty" to answer.

BIOGRAPHICAL/CRITICAL SOURCES:

BOOKS

Cole, Robert, *A. J. P. Taylor: The Traitor Within the Gates,* St. Martin's (New York), 1993.

Gilbert, Martin, editor, *A Century of Conflict, 1850-1950: Essays in Honour of A. J. P. Taylor,* Hamish Hamilton, 1966, Atheneum, 1967.

Sisman, Adam, *A. J. P. Taylor: A Biography,* Sinclair-Stevenson, 1994.

Sked, Alan, and Chris Cook, editors, *Crisis and Controversy: Essays in Honour of A. J. P. Taylor,* Macmillan, 1976.

Taylor, A. J. P., *A Personal History* (autobiography), Hamish Hamilton, 1983.

Taylor, A. J. P., *An Old Man's Diary,* Hamish Hamilton, 1984.

Wrigley, Chris, editor, *Warfare, Diplomacy and Politics: Essays in Honour of A. J. P. Taylor,* Hamish Hamilton, 1986.

PERIODICALS

Economist, July 13, 1991, p. 93.
Foreign Affairs, November-December, 1995, p. 128.
History Today, September, 1994, p. 58.
London Review of Books, January 27, 1994, p. 3.
Los Angeles Times Book Review, February 10, 1985.
New York Times Book Review, September 25, 1983; June 30, 1985.
Publishers Weekly, August 21, 1995, p. 55; September 19, 1994, p. 60.
New Statesman & Society, January 21, 1994, p. 37.
Times (London), April 11, 1983; June 2, 1983; April 19, 1984; April 4, 1985.
Times Literary Supplement, May 27, 1983; June 15, 1984; July 19, 1985; February 4, 1994, p. 3.
Washington Post Book World, September 4, 1983.

*   *   *

TAYLOR, Peter (Hillsman) 1917-1994

PERSONAL: Born January 8, 1917, in Trenton, TN; died of pneumonia, November 2, 1994, in Charlottesville, VA; son of Matthew Hillsman (a lawyer) and Katherine Taylor; married Eleanor Lilly Ross (a poet), June 4, 1943; children: Katherine Baird, Peter Ross. *Education:* Attended Vanderbilt University, 1936-37, and Southwestern at Memphis, 1937-38; Kenyon College, A.B., 1940.

CAREER: University of North Carolina at Greensboro, 1946-67, became professor of English; University of Virginia, Charlottesville, professor of English, 1967-94. Visiting lecturer, Indiana University, 1949, University of Chicago, 1951, Kenyon College, 1952-57, Oxford University, 1955, Ohio State University, 1957-63, Harvard University, 1964 and 1972-73, and University of Georgia, 1985. *Military service:* U. S. Army, 1941-45; served in England; became sergeant.

MEMBER: National Academy and Institute of Arts and Letters, American Academy of Arts and Sciences.

AWARDS, HONORS: Guggenheim fellowship in fiction, 1950; National Institute of Arts and Letters grant in literature, 1952; Fulbright fellowship to France, 1955; first prize, O. Henry Memorial Awards, 1959, for short story "Venus, Cupid, Folly and Time"; Ohioana Book Award, 1960, for *Happy Families Are All Alike;* Ford Foundation fellowship, to England, 1961; Rockefeller Foundation grant, 1964; second prize, *Partisan Review-Dial* for short story "The Scoutmaster"; National Academy and Institute of Arts and Letters gold medal for literature, 1979; Ritz Paris Hemingway Award and PEN/Faulkner Award for fiction, both 1986, and Pulitzer Prize for fiction, 1987, all for *A Summons to Memphis.*

WRITINGS:

NOVELS

A Woman of Means, Harcourt (New York City), 1950.
A Summons to Memphis, Knopf (New York City), 1986.
In the Tennessee Country, Knopf, 1994.

SHORT STORIES

A Long Fourth and Other Stories, introduction by Robert Penn Warren, Harcourt, 1948.
The Widows of Thornton (includes a play), Harcourt, 1954.
Happy Families Are All Alike: A Collection of Stories, Astor Honor (New York City), 1959.
Miss Leonora When Last Seen and Fifteen Other Stories, Astor Honor, 1963.
The Collected Stories of Peter Taylor, Farrar, Straus (New York City), 1969.
In the Miro District and Other Stories, Knopf, 1977.
The Old Forest and Other Stories, Dial (Garden City, NY), 1985.
The Oracle at Stoneleigh Court, Knopf, 1993.

Contributor of stories to numerous anthologies, including *The Best American Short Stories,* edited by Martha Foley, Houghton (Boston, MA), 1945-46, 1950, 1959, 1965, edited by Foley and David Burnett, 1960, 1961; *Prize Stories of 1950: The O. Henry Awards,* edited by Herschell Bricknell, Doubleday (New York City), 1950; *The Literature of the South,* edited by R. C. Beatty and others, Scott, Foresman (Glenview, IL), 1952; *Stories from the Southern Review,* edited by Cleanth Brooks and Robert Penn Warren, Louisiana State University Press (Baton Rouge, LA), 1953; *Prize Stories 1959: The O. Henry Awards,* edited by Paul Engle, Doubleday, 1959; *Prize Stories 1961: The O. Henry Awards,* edited by Richard Poirier, Doubleday, 1961; *Prize Stories 1965: The O. Henry Awards,* edited by Poirier and William Abrahams, Doubleday, 1965; and *The Sense of Fiction,* edited by Robert L. Welker and Herschel Gover, Prentice-Hall (Englewood Cliffs, NJ), 1966.

Contributor of short stories to *Sewanee Review, Virginia Quarterly Review, Kenyon Review, New Yorker,* and numerous other journals.

PLAYS

Tennessee Day in St. Louis, Random House (New York City), 1959.
A Stand in the Mountains (produced Abingdon, VA, 1971), published in *Kenyon Review,* 1965.
(Editor with Robert Lowell and Robert Penn Warren) *Randall Jarrell, 1914-1965,* Farrar, Straus, 1967.
Presences: Seven Dramatic Pieces (contains "Two Images," "A Father and a Son," "Missing Person," "The Whistler," "Arson," "A Voice through the Door," and "The Sweethearts"), Houghton, 1973.
(Editor) *The Road and Other Modern Stories,* Cambridge University Press, 1979.
Peter Taylor Reading and Commenting on His Fiction (audio tape), Archive of Recorded Poetry and Literature, 1987.

Contributor of an essay to *Tennessee: A Homecoming,* edited by John Netherton, Third National, 1985.

MEDIA ADAPTATIONS: "The Old Forest" was adapted into a short motion picture of the same name, directed by Steven John Ross, Pyramid Films, 1984.

SIDELIGHTS: Although author Peter Taylor received critical acclaim for his novels *A Woman of Means, In the Tennessee Country,* and the Pulitzer Prize-winning *A Summons to Memphis,* he is best known for his work in short fiction. He was called "one of the most accomplished short-story writers of our time" by Gene Baro in the *New York Herald Tribune Book Review,* and John Leonard of the *New York Times* praised Taylor by saying that he "makes stories the way Mercedes-Benz makes automobiles: to last."

Born in Trenton, Tennessee, the grandson of one of that state's former governors, Taylor is considered by many critics to be a Southern writer in the tradition of William Faulkner and Flannery O'Connor; as a *Village Voice* reviewer observed, he "often writes about the decay of the gentrified South (something he has observed firsthand)." In the *Times Literary Supplement*, Zachary Leader agreed, noting that Taylor's "roots in the Southern literary tradition are deep, . . . [and an understanding of his] complex relation to the tradition this background fostered is helpful to an appreciation of his stories."

Taylor was conscious of drawing his inspiration from the recollections of his childhood. As he once told *Contemporary Authors:* "My theory is that you listen to people talk when you're a child—a Southerner does especially—and they tell stories and stories and stories, and you feel those stories must mean something. So, really, writing becomes an effort to find out what these stories mean in the beginning, and then you want to find out what *all* the stories you hear or think of mean. The story you write is interpretation. People tell the same stories over and over, with the same vocabulary and the same important points, and I don't think it ever crosses their minds what they mean. But they do mean something, and I'm sure that is what influenced me. Then too, you just inherit a storytelling urge."

Out of Taylor's early exposure to the philosophy of the Agrarian movement through John Crowe Ransom, Randall Jarrell, and Robert Penn Warren "grew the dream of the 'Old South,' or what Taylor calls 'the old times,'" according to Leader. "These writings look past the South's supposedly aristocratic origins to the pre-settlement wilderness, an Eden whose native inhabitants were as unspoilt and unspoiling as the surroundings from which they drew their character." Yet, despite his grounding in the traditions of Southern culture and literature, Taylor is often praised for the universality of his short fiction. When his first collection, *A Long Fourth and Other Stories,* appeared in 1948, a *New Yorker* critic commented that the stories were "particularly notable for a vein of unobtrusive humor and for a complete lack of the regional chauvinism that Southern authors so frequently exhibit when writing about their own." Coleman Rosenberger, in the *New York Herald Tribune Book Review,* wrote: "These seven short stories by Peter Taylor are a little island of excellence in the flood of books from the South. They have the qualities of permanence: a fine craftsmanship, integrity, and the imprint of a subtle and original intelligence."

Critical response to Taylor's second collection of Southern-based short fiction, 1954's *The Widows of Thornton,* solidified his reputation as a master in his field. Mack Morriss, in a *Saturday Review* article, called the collection of nine stories "as free of ugliness as the lingering nutmeg and as unpretentious as coldwater cornbread. . . . [Taylor] has created a wistful, clinging, but utterly non-depraved image of the Deep South that some of us, his regional contemporaries, have been trying to recall from our childhood." F. H. Lyell of the *New York Times* commented that "The stories in [this book] are outwardly simple but psychologically complex and powerful, and under the surface of events in the regions he knows best the author discloses the universal longings of the human heart." And *Bloomsbury Review* critic Mimi MacFarland noted that "Wit, grace, and humor are abundant in the anachronistic possibilities created by Taylor's Southerners as they

are transported to faraway places, even into the future, dragging along their traditions like so much excess baggage."

Taylor continued to examine the lives and culture of the gentry of the "Upper South" in *In the Miro District and Other Stories,* and *The Old Forest and Other Stories,* each of which contain works of drama in addition to short fiction. The lives of his Southern nobility are drawn into a more ghostly milieu in Taylor's *The Oracle at Stoneleigh Court,* a collection of short stories published in 1993. "After 53 years of practicing his craft, [Taylor] has obviously chosen to keep growing, rather than to repeat elegant past triumphs," stated Gail Godwin in the *New York Times Book Review.* "In this volume he seems to have been seized by the necessity to refine out of existence some of his more rarefied specimens—specimens who were becoming ghosts in our society even as he precisely chronicled them—in order to make room for new characters and fresh perspectives that have emerged from their ruins and their genes." As in gothic-inspired stories like "Demons," in which a grown man looks back fondly on the inner voices he heard as a child, and "The Witch of Owl Mountain Springs," about a jilted bride who lives in eccentric seclusion until she dies in a fire of questionable origins, the ghosts inhabiting Taylor's fiction are not "floating wraiths and extraneous horrors," according to Godwin, but are "all those ghosts we have to face before we can rendezvous with the ghost of the person we can still become."

A Summons to Memphis was, according to Taylor, "a story that got out of hand." Scarcely more than novella-length, its two hundred pages are filled with what Jonathan Yardley described in the *Washington Post Book World* as "the sly depiction of contrasting folkways in Memphis and Nashville, the nostalgic yet unsentimental excursions into a lost way of life, the rich yet precise and unadorned prose. . . . Prose of such subtlety, taste and clarity—prose that so poignantly and exactly evokes a moment, and makes it real." In the genteel Upper South of Memphis, Phillip Carver and his sisters face their mother's death and the change of heart of a father who had undermined their youthful attempts at romance and marriage. With Phillip as narrator, Taylor's Pulitzer Prize-winning novel draws the reader into the many facets of revenge and family loyalties as the eighty-year-old father's attempts to both remarry and resolve a long-standing dispute with a former friend are thwarted by his frustrated, middle-aged offspring. "Mr. Taylor's sympathy for the chiaroscuro of familial emotion, combined with his command of naturalistic detail, remains so assured, so persuasive," stated *New York Times* critic Michiko Kakutani, "that we finish the novel feeling we've not only come to know his characters, but also come to share their inner truth."

Taylor's final novel, *In the Tennessee Country,* was published in 1994, the year of his death. Born into a Southern family that prides itself on roots buried deep in the milieu of the Civil War, Nathan Longfort maintains a lifelong obsession with his elusive cousin Aubrey, an illegitimate relative who had once courted Nathan's mother but for a reason Nathan is not privy to was shunned at family gatherings, a treatment that drove him away to make a life for himself independent of his family. Nathan's obsession with Aubrey and his whereabouts eventually destroys his relationship with his own son, a painter who ultimately seeks Aubrey out and joins him in isolation from his father. While Mary Flanagan stated in the *New York Times Book Review* that she "missed the delicious slyness of . . . *A Summons to Memphis,* its flash and bite, its malice," she goes on to say that *In the Tennessee Country* is, on the whole, "unnerving and, on reflection, closer to life. . . . Aubrey and [Nathan's son] fulfill the dream of transformation, of becoming better men. They escape history, Mr. Taylor sagely implies, because they understand that the pursuit of happiness involves a spell in the wilderness."

Praise for Taylor's fiction was sustained by critics throughout his long career: His natural ear for dialogue, his smooth, finely paced style, and especially his sensitive character portrayal have been consistently lauded. A *Times Literary Supplement* critic described him as "a cautious writer with an intellectual respect for his characters. Every change of mood and feeling is something he considers worth recording." And, in *Saturday Review*, William Peden wrote: "[Taylor's] stories succeed because his characters and their words are real, moving, and convincing. In each story there is always at least one character who becomes 'finely aware' (the phrase is Henry James's) of the situations in which they find themselves. It is this fine awareness that gives the 'maximum of sense' to what befalls them, which makes these quietly effective stories so meaningful to the reader." In a *Washington Post* remembrance of the author, Yardley described Taylor as a writer whose "world was not my own and whose narrative voice possessed an elegance to which I could never hope to aspire, yet who spoke to my innermost self with a depth of feeling and psychological insight that I had never before encountered. . . . [Taylor's] interest was kind rather than censorious; human faults were to be understood, even liked, rather than mocked or vilified. . . . Some of those to whom he was mentor went on to accomplished writing careers of their own, while others merely cherished the personal acquaintance they had been given with literary genius; but all are bound by their devotion and gratitude to this remarkable man."

BIOGRAPHICAL/CRITICAL SOURCES:

BOOKS

Contemporary Authors New Revision Series, Gale (Detroit), Volume 9, 1983; Volume 50, 1996.

Contemporary Literary Criticism, Gale, Volume 1, 1973; Volume 4, 1975; Volume 18, 1981; Volume 37, 1986; Volume 44, 1987; Volume 50, 1988; Volume 71, 1992.

Graham, Catherine Clark, *Southern Accents: The Fiction of Peter Taylor,* Lang (New York City), 1993.

Griffith, Albert, *Peter Taylor,* Twayne (Boston), 1970, revised, 1990.

Kramer, Victor A., *Andrew Lytle, Walker Percy, Peter Taylor: A Reference Guide,* G. K. Hall (Boston, MA), 1983.

McAlexander, Hubert H., *Conversations with Peter Taylor,* University Press of Mississippi (Jackson), 1987.

McAlexander, Hubert H., *Critical Essays on Peter Taylor,* G. K. Hall, 1993.

Robinson, David M., *World of Relations: The Achievement of Peter Taylor,* University Press of Kentucky, 1998.

Robinson, James Curry, *Peter Taylor: A Study of the Short Fiction,* Twayne, 1988.

Stephens, Ralph, and Linda B. Salamon, editors, *The Craft of Peter Taylor,* University of Alabama Press (Tuscaloosa), 1995.

Wright, Stuart T., *Peter Taylor: A Descriptive Bibliography, 1934-87,* University Press of Virginia (Charlottesville), 1988.

PERIODICALS

America, March 20, 1993, p. 19; March 11, 1995, p. 34.
Bloomsbury Review, July/August, 1994, p. 22.
Boston Globe, August 21, 1994, p. 61.

Chicago Tribune, May 14, 1950; December 6, 1959; October 26, 1986, sec. 14, p. 4; February 28, 1993, sec. 14, p. 6; September 11, 1994.
Christian Science Monitor, August 26, 1994, p. 13.
Hudson Review, winter, 1994, pp. 765-72.
Library Journal, July, 1994, p. 130.
Los Angeles Times, October 3, 1994, p. E4.
Los Angeles Times Book Review, February 21, 1993, p. 6.
New Republic, March 8, 1948; June 26, 1950; October 18, 1969; May 7, 1977; March 8, 1993, p. 40.
New Statesman, August 6, 1960; April 23, 1993, p. 39.
Newsweek, October 20, 1969.
New York, February 22, 1993, p. 65.
New Yorker, March 13, 1948.
New York Herald Tribune Book Review, March 14, 1948; May 2, 1950; May 2, 1954; December 6, 1959.
New York Review of Books, June 11, 1964; March 25, 1993, p. 43.
New York Times, March 21, 1948; June 11, 1950; May 2, 1954; October 11, 1969; April 7, 1977; September 24, 1986, p. C23; April 7, 1987, p. C15; November 2, 1994, p. C17.
New York Times Book Review, November 22, 1959; March 29, 1964; October 19, 1969; February 12, 1970; April 3, 1977; September 14, 1986, p. 3; February 21, 1993, p. 13; August 28, 1994, p. 6.
New York Times Magazine, January 1, 1995, p. 23.
Saturday Review, May 8, 1954; November 28, 1959; October 18, 1969; May 14, 1977; March 15, 1980.
Saturday Review of Literature, March 27, 1948.
Sewanee Review, autumn, 1962.
Shenandoah, winter, 1973; winter, 1977; summer, 1978.
Southern Review, winter, 1979; winter, 1994, pp. 156-64.
Spectator, September 3, 1994, pp. 35-36.
Time, May 15, 1950; August 22, 1994, p. 86.
Times Literary Supplement, August 19, 1960; September 30, 1977; January 22, 1982.
Village Voice, April 28, 1980.
Washington Post, March 15, 1980; May 9, 1993, p. 12; August 21, 1994, p. 3.
Washington Post Book World, September 14, 1986, p. 3.

*   *   *

TENNESHAW, S. M.
See SILVERBERG, Robert

*   *   *

TERKEL, Louis 1912-
(Studs Terkel)

PERSONAL: Born May 16, 1912, in New York, NY; son of Samuel and Anna (Finkel) Terkel; married Ida Goldberg, July 2, 1939; children: Paul. *Education:* University of Chicago, Ph.B., 1932, J.D., 1934.

ADDRESSES: Home—850 West Castlewood Terr., Chicago, IL 60640. *Office*—WFMT Radio, 5400 N. St. Louis Ave., Chicago, IL 60625.

CAREER: Worked as a civil service employee in Washington, DC, and as a stage actor and movie house manager during the 1930s and 1940s; host of interview show *Wax Museum* on radio station WFMT, Chicago, IL, 1945–. Moderator of television program *Studs' Place,* Chicago, 1950-53. Actor in stage plays, including *Detective Story,* 1950, *A View from the Bridge,* 1958, *Light Up the Sky,* 1959, and *The Cave Dwellers,* 1960. Master of ceremonies at Newport Folk Festival, 1959 and 1960, Ravina Music Festival, Ravina, IL, 1959, University of Chicago Folk Festival, 1961, and others. Also columnist and narrator of films.

AWARDS, HONORS: Ohio State University award, 1959, and UNESCO Prix Italia award, 1962, both for *Wax Museum;* University of Chicago Alumni Association Communicator of the Year award, 1969; National Book Award nominee, 1975; George Foster Peabody Broadcasting Award, 1980; Society of Midland Authors Award, 1982, for *American Dreams: Lost and Found,* and 1983, for best writer; Eugene V. Debs Award, 1983, for public service; Pulitzer Prize in nonfiction, 1985, for *"The Good War": An Oral History of World War II;* Hugh M. Hefner First Amendment Award for Lifetime Achievement, 1990.

WRITINGS:

UNDER NAME STUDS TERKEL

Giants of Jazz, Crowell, 1957, revised edition, Harper, 1975.
Division Street: America, Pantheon, 1967, 2nd edition, New Press, 1993.
Hard Times: An Oral History of the Great Depression, Pantheon, 1970.
Working: People Talk about What They Do All Day and How They Feel about What They Do, Pantheon, 1974.
Talking to Myself: A Memoir of My Times, Pantheon, 1977.
American Dreams: Lost and Found, Pantheon, 1980.
"The Good War": An Oral History of World War II, Pantheon, 1984.
(Author of foreword) Hollinger F. Barnard, editor, *Outside the Magic Circle: Autobiography of Virginia Foster Durr,* University of Alabama Press, 1985.
(With Ronald J. Grele and others) *Envelopes of Oral Sound: The Art of Oral History,* Precedent Publishing, 1985, 2nd edition, Praeger, 1990.
(With Nelson Algren) *The Neon Wilderness,* Writers and Readers, 1986.
Chicago, Pantheon, 1986.
The Great Divide: Second Thoughts on the American Dream, Pantheon, 1988.
Race: How Blacks and Whites Think and Feel about the American Obsession, New Press, 1992.
Coming of Age: The Story of Our Century by Those Who've Lived It, St. Martin's, 1995.
My American Century, New Press, 1997.

Also author of play "Amazing Grace," first produced in Ann Arbor, MI, by the University of Michigan's Professional Theater Program, 1967. Author of introduction, *The Grapes of Wrath,* by John Steinbeck, Viking, 1989. Featured on sound recordings, including *Television: The First Fifty Years,* Center for Cassette Studies, 1975.

MEDIA ADAPTATIONS: Working was adapted as a musical by Stephen Schwartz and first produced on Broadway, May 14, 1978, and later taped for a television broadcast; *American Dreams: Lost and Found* was adapted for the stage by Peter Frisch and published by Dramatists Play Service, 1987; *Talking to Myself* was adapted as a play by Paul Sills and first produced in Evanston, IL, at the Northlight Theater in 1988; *The American Clock: A Vaudeville,* a play by Arthur Miller, was based in part on *Hard Times* and published by Dramatists Play Service in 1992.

SIDELIGHTS: "Next to Richard Nixon, the person whose life has been most dramatically affected by the tape recorder is Studs Terkel," according to Paul Gray in *Time.* For some two decades, Terkel has been the sympathetic ear to the American people, devoting several of his books to their intimate, revealing, first-person narratives. Armed with his tape machine, Terkel travels cross-country to get his interviews. His subjects speak out on topics as distinct as the Great Depression, World War II, and their jobs and as nebulous as their definition of the American Dream. Some of Terkel's interviews are with celebrities, but his most remembered—and many say his best—are with "real people." "I celebrate the non-celebrated," the author once told *Philadelphia Bulletin* contributor Lewis Beale. "I've found that average people want to talk about themselves, their hopes, dreams, aspirations, provided they sense that you're interested in what they're saying." And, as Terkel explained in a 1985 talk to the Friends of Libraries U.S.A., he has also discovered that "the average American has an indigenous intelligence, a native wit. It's only a question of piquing that intelligence."

Born Louis Terkel in New York City, the writer is closely associated with his years living and working in Chicago; he adopted the name Studs from another colorful Chicago character, the fictional Studs Lonigan. Trained in law, Terkel became a successful actor and broadcaster. He was also an enthusiastic liberal whose fall from favor with the House Un-American Activities Committee during the 1950s led to the early cancellation of his television talk show, *Studs' Place.* As Terkel explained to Lee Michael Katz in a *Washington Post* interview, he was never a Communist, but he "belonged to a left-wing theater group. Basically my name appeared on many petitions. Rent control. Ending Jim Crow. Abolishing the poll tax. You know, as subversive issues as that. Coming out in favor of Social Security prematurely. You think I'm kidding? These were very controversial issues, considered commie issues." But the writer also feels that the blacklisting helped his career: "If it weren't for the blacklist I might have been emceeing [today] on these network TV shows and have been literally dead because . . . I'd have said something that would have knocked me off [the air], obviously. But I would never have done these books, I would never have gone on to the little FM station playing classical music. So, long live the blacklist!"

After his early successes *Division Street: America* and *Hard Times: An Oral History of the Great Depression,* Terkel produced possibly his best-known book of interviews, *Working: People Talk about What They Do All Day and How They Feel about What They Do.* It contains the recurring theme of disillusionment—many of his subjects told Terkel of the lack of emotional, spiritual, and, of course, monetary fulfillment in their jobs. A compendium of several dozen interviews from Americans in all walks of life, *Working* is described by *Washington Post Book World* reviewer Bernard Weisberger as "earthy, passionate, honest, sometimes tender, sometimes crisp, juicy as reality, seasoned with experience. It is tempting to say that people are naturally interesting talkers, but that would be untrue to our memories of boredom past and ungenerous to Terkel's skill. . . . He has a formidable gift for evoking and recognizing articulateness in a variety of people and coaxing it from private shelters." Although Anatole Broyard in the *New York Times* contends, "Most people gripe better than they sing, and 'Working' sometimes sounds like the Book of Job," Peter S. Prescott of *Newsweek* calls *Working* "an impressive achievement. . . . Terkel understands that what people need—more than sex, almost as much as food—and what they perhaps will never find, is a sympathetic ear. . . . This is, I think, a very valuable document, a book that would be of use to writers and sociologists if only for the vast amount of technical information it contains."

Following the success of *Working,* Terkel in 1977 turned his tape recorder on himself to create *Talking to Myself: A Memoir of My Times.* "This is not a personal book in the usual sense," warns Nora Ephron in the *New York Times Book Review.* "There is nothing about Terkel's father, next to nothing about his mother, a bare smidgen about his brother, a couple of stories about his wife. What you see is what you get: Terkel's voice. Talking to himself," Ephron writes. Indeed, the author acknowledges "an inhibition" in writing about his family; as Terkel told Katz in a *Washington Post* interview, "I shy away from personal stuff, I really do. In [*Talking to Myself*] there's stuff I haven't revealed, and it's not worth revealing." Terkel's autobiography is "a marvelous and maddening book," according to *New York Times* critic John Leonard. "Marvelous, because we get to know the stout-hearted Terkel; maddening, because having gotten to know him, we want more, and he won't give."

Terkel's next work, *American Dreams: Lost and Found,* used the same approach as *Working,* each book containing some one hundred interviews with an assortment of Americans. Michael Leapman in the London *Times* notes that Terkel "does not tell us the questions he used to provoke what streams of articulate observations from his one hundred subjects. The evidence suggests that one question to them all was 'What is the American Dream?'" In a *Newsweek* article, Prescott states, "Because it is not confined to a single city, or time, or particular part of the human condition, Terkel's *American Dreams: Lost and Found* is his most diverse." Robert Sherrill in the *New York Times Book Review* recounts the book's interviews with people such as the grandson of a slave remembering the day he registered to vote, and a former leader in the Ku Klux Klan who became a union organizer to consolidate workers of all colors. Sherrill concludes, "*American Dreams* offers us an apple on every one of these pages."

In the Pulitzer Prize-winning *"The Good War": An Oral History of World War II,* Terkel confines his interviews to those who experienced the war firsthand, providing a kind of informal history of that time. The author says that the quotation marks in the title are deliberate in order to drive home the irony of any war being "good." "As in Terkel's previous oral histories," Jonathan Yardley notes in the *Washington Post Book World,* "'The Good War' is a clangorous but carefully orchestrated jumble of voices." Loudon Wainwright in the *New York Times Book Review* finds that the book "gives the American experience in World War II great immediacy. Reading it, I felt a renewed connection with that slice of my own past and a surprisingly powerful kinship with the voices from it." Wainwright also comments, "It is hard to see how any reader now or then can fail to benefit from its 600 pages. For Mr. Terkel, who in six books over the past 15 years has turned an oral history into a popular literary form, has captured an especially broad and impressive chorus of voices on his tape recorder this time."

"The Good War" also drew much critical attention due to Terkel's interviews with African-American veterans of the era, who remember segregationist rules which applied on and off the base—one interviewee describes how African-American soldiers had to ride in the back of a streetcar while German prisoners of war rode up front. "Another explains why black pilots were so good," Prescott explains. "'We had extensive training,'" Prescott quotes a veteran as saying. "'In the beginning, they didn't know

what to do with us, so they just kept on training and training and training us. When we went overseas, most of our fliers had three times the flying training that white pilots had.'" On the other hand, as real-estate broker and writer Dempsey Travis recalled, the war for many African-Americans represented "a step on the first rung of the ladder." During the war, Travis was the manager of the first integrated post exchange (military store) in Maryland.

Terkel took a contemporary look at class inequity in *The Great Divide: Second Thoughts on the American Dream,* which follows his formula of interviewing and compiling anecdotes from some one hundred people. This work, however, deals with economics rather than ideology, commenting on standards of living and the way society's definitions of the poor have shifted. "Once, the poor were 'victims'; now, they are 'losers,'" related Richard Eder in the *Los Angeles Times Book Review.* "The dimensions of our social problems, the gulf between those who are making it and those who aren't, is as wide as ever, [Terkel] writes." However, "not everyone speaks of failed visions," such as the successful stockbroker Terkel interviews, Stefan Kanfer comments in *Time.* Yet, "Americans should weep, for this is a book about the moral effects of Reaganomics, the loss of memory and community, the dumbing and numbing of America," insists *Nation* contributor Bharati Mukherjee.

Harking back to the issue of race, which he had addressed in *"The Good War,"* Terkel compiled an entire work on the subject in 1992. *Race: How Blacks and Whites Think and Feel about the American Obsession* is, like his other volumes, a collection of voices from nearly 100 people of varying ethnicity, some famous, most not; this time they are speaking on the subject of racial relations in America. Juan Williams, writing for *Washington Post Book World,* asserts, "The strength of Terkel's book is its documentation of how race obsesses the national mind." In the *Village Voice,* Michael Tomasky observes, "Terkel reminds us that race is not just a debate about a set of policies, but a web of contradictory feelings and impulses inside all of us, and any mill worker or teacher or cop is capable of both meanness and generosity of spirit, often at the same time."

At the age of eighty-three, Terkel turned his interviewer's eye to a subject close to home. *Coming of Age: The Story of Our Century By Those Who've Lived It* is a compilation of Terkel's conversations with around seventy men and women, ages seventy and older. While he includes several famous seniors, such as John Kenneth Galbraith, Katherine Dunham, and Uta Hagen, the majority of his interviewees are plain folks. John Espey drily notes in the *Washington Post Book World,* "Most of them are unreconstructed Old Lefties, followed in number by enlightened moderates, the mix leavened with an occasional innocent." Espey continues, "What becomes clear as one reads on is the importance of the individual conviction of rightness, of carrying on." Rebecca Pepper Sinkler, writing for the *New York Times Book Review,* comments, "Studs Terkel aims higher than the old-codger interview . . . but . . . Mr. Terkel's interviews don't soar. He seems to have asked all his subjects a series of unimaginative questions . . . [which] elicit banal answers." However, ". . . the language and imagery in other interviews is inspired." Judith Dunford in Chicago *Tribune Books* reports, "For all its appeal, *Coming of Age* has real problems. One is the steady, nearly unvarying voice of the replies, which have been edited half to death." The other, she asserts is "the uneasy sense . . . that Terkel believes the '30s were the decade that matters, that . . . nothing else is." Dunford concludes that the book is "best read as a remarkable storybook. . . . It's like sitting at the feet of dozens of engaging elders."

Perhaps because of its nature, reviewers were somewhat kinder to Terkel's next book, *My American Century*. The book collects the most fascinating interviews from his earlier oral histories, including the former Klansman who became a civil rights activist and the housewife who went up against the mob and city hall to save her neighborhood. *Publishers Weekly* calls it "the best possible introduction to his splendid body of work" and finds that despite the work's realism, it is also "an antidote to despair." Robert Favini in the *Library Journal* recommends it for displaying "the human side of history," and Milton Garrison of the *New York Times Book Review* salutes Terkel's "compassion and loyalty to the radical populist tradition."

"Studs Terkel is an impassioned, humane, and remarkably energetic . . . Chicago broadcaster and writer who owes his status as a living legend and national treasure to his skill at what he calls 'prowling and stalking,'" lauds Jane Howard in the *Washington Post Book World*. "He prowls and stalks with a tape recorder, tracking down the ideas of his fellow Americans," she adds, "and he sure is good at what he does." "Terkel can be justly charged with employing a formula," according to Kanfer in *Time*. "Still, it is *his* formula, sedulously aped but never accurately reproduced." *Tribune Books* contributor Willie Morris asserts, "Terkel's books have touched profoundly upon our lives."

BIOGRAPHICAL/CRITICAL SOURCES:

BOOKS

Baker, James, *Studs Terkel*, Twayne, 1992.
Contemporary Literary Criticism, Volume 38, Gale (Detroit), 1986.
Parker, Tony, *Studs Terkel: A Life in Words*, Holt, 1996.

PERIODICALS

America, September 16, 1995, p. 31.
Atlantic Monthly, July, 1977; November, 1980; February, 1995, p. 99.
Chicago Tribune Book World, September 14, 1980.
Detroit News, September 21, 1980.
Detroit News Magazine, May 10, 1981.
Library Journal, March 15, 1993, p. 127; September 1, 1995, p. 190; July, 1997.
Los Angeles Times, December 12, 1980.
Los Angeles Times Book Review, September 28, 1980; October 14, 1984; October 10, 1988, p. 3; September 24, 1989, p. 14; May 3, 1992, p. 4.
Milwaukee Journal, April 23, 1974.
Modern Maturity, April-May, 1993, p. 72.
Mother Jones, September-October, 1995, p. 22.
Nation, March 30, 1970; April 6, 1974; June 4, 1977; December 8, 1984; December 5, 1988, p. 622; August 17, 1992, p. 178.
New Republic, April 6, 1974; November 15, 1980; November 28, 1988, p. 38; April 13, 1992, p. 30.
Newsweek, April 1, 1974; April 18, 1977; October 13, 1980; October 15, 1984.
New York, September 11, 1995, p. 88.
New York Review of Books, August 13, 1970.
New York Times, April 30, 1970; March 21, 1974; March 22, 1974; April 11, 1977; May 14, 1978; September 24, 1980; September 26, 1984.
New York Times Book Review, April 19, 1970; March 21, 1974; March 22, 1974; April 11, 1977; May 14, 1978; September 24, 1980; September 26, 1984; October 5, 1986, p. 58;

October 9, 1988, p. 10; May 3, 1992, p. 13; September 24, 1995, p. 7; December 19, 1996, p. 15; August 24, 1997.
People Weekly, December 4, 1995, p. 36.
Philadelphia Bulletin, April 17, 1974.
Progressive, November, 1995, p. 40.
Publishers Weekly, July 6, 1984; March 27, 1995, p. 23; July 14, 1997.
Saturday Review, April 18, 1970; April 20, 1974; April 30, 1977; September, 1980.
Scholastic Update, December 8, 1995, p. 8.
Spectator, March 15, 1986, p. 28.
Time, May 13, 1974; April 18, 1977; September 29, 1980; October 8, 1984; October 3, 1988, p. 88; March 30, 1992, p. 69.
Times (London), May 12, 1981; March 28, 1985.
Times Literary Supplement, December 16, 1977; June 26, 1981; March 7, 1986, p. 243; February 17, 1989, p. 157.
Tribune Books (Chicago), September 11, 1988, p. 1; September 10, 1995, p. 1.
Village Voice, May 23, 1977; October 2, 1984; March 31, 1992, p. 90.
Washington Post, May 5, 1974; April 24, 1977; October 5, 1980; September 30, 1984.
Washington Post Book World, May 5, 1974; April 24, 1977; October 5, 1980; September 30, 1984; December 22, 1985; September 11, 1988, p. 1; May 17, 1992, p. 1; August 27, 1995, p. 1.
Yale Review, January, 1993, p. 131.

* * *

TERKEL, Studs
  See TERKEL, Louis

* * *

THAKURA, Ravindranatha
  See TAGORE, Rabindranath

* * *

THEOBALD, Lewis Jr.
  See LOVECRAFT, H(oward) P(hillips)

* * *

THEROUX, Paul (Edward) 1941-

PERSONAL: Surname rhymes with "skiddoo"; born April 10, 1941, in Medford, MA; son of Albert Eugene (a salesman) and Anne (Dittami) Theroux; married Anne Castle (a broadcaster), December 4, 1967 (divorced 1993); married Sheila Donnely, November 18, 1995; children (first marriage): Marcel Raymond, Louis Sebastian. *Education:* Attended University of Maine, 1959-60; University of Massachusetts, B.A., 1963; Syracuse University, further study, 1963. *Avocational interests:* Rowing.

ADDRESSES: Home—35 Elsynge Rd., London SW18 2HR, England.

CAREER: Soche Hill College, Limbe, Malawi, lecturer in English, 1963-65; Makerere University, Kampala, Uganda, lecturer in English, 1965-68; University of Singapore, Singapore, lecturer in English, 1968-71; professional writer, 1971–. Visiting lecturer, University of Virginia, 1972-73. Has given numerous lectures on literature in the United States and abroad.

MEMBER: American Academy and Institute of Arts and Letters, Royal Geography Society, Royal Society of Literature.

AWARDS, HONORS: Robert Hamlet one-act play award, 1960; *Playboy* Editorial Award, 1971, 1976; *New York Times Book Review* "Editors' Choice" citation, 1975, for *The Great Railway Bazaar: By Train through Asia;* American Academy and Institute of Arts and Letters award for literature, 1977; American Book Award nominations, 1981, for *The Old Patagonian Express: By Train through the Americas,* and 1983, for *The Mosquito Coast;* Thomas Cook Travel Book Prize, 1989. Honorary degrees from Trinity College and Tufts University, both in 1980, and the University of Massachusetts—Amherst, 1988.

WRITINGS:

NOVELS

Waldo, Houghton (Boston), 1967.
Fong and the Indians, Houghton, 1968.
Girls at Play, Houghton, 1969.
Murder in Mount Holly, Alan Ross, 1969.
Jungle Lovers, Houghton, 1971.
Saint Jack (also see below), Houghton, 1973.
The Black House, Houghton, 1974.
The Family Arsenal, Houghton, 1976.
Picture Palace, Houghton, 1978.
The Mosquito Coast, with woodcuts by David Frampton, Houghton, 1982.
Doctor Slaughter (also see below), Hamish Hamilton, 1984.
Half Moon Street: Two Short Novels (contains *Doctor Slaughter* and *Doctor DeMarr*), Houghton, 1984.
O-Zone, Putnam, 1986.
My Secret History, Putnam, 1989.
Chicago Loop, Random House, 1991.
Millroy the Magician, Random House, 1994.
My Other Life, Houghton, 1996.
Kowloon Tong, G.K. Hall (Thorndike, ME), 1997.

SHORT STORIES

Sinning with Annie and Other Stories, Houghton, 1972.
The Consul's File, Houghton, 1977.
World's End and Other Stories, Houghton, 1980.
The London Embassy, Houghton, 1982.
The Collected Stories, Viking (New York City), 1997.

NONFICTION

V. S. Naipaul: An Introduction to His Works, Africana Publishing, 1972.
The Great Railway Bazaar: By Train through Asia, Houghton, 1975.
The Old Patagonian Express: By Train through the Americas, Houghton, 1979.
Sailing through China, illustrated by Patrick Procktor, Houghton, 1984.
The Kingdom by the Sea: A Journey around Great Britain, Houghton, 1985.
(With Steve McCurry) *The Imperial Way: By Rail from Peshawar to Chittagong,* Houghton, 1985.
Sunrise with Seamonsters: Travels and Discoveries 1964-1984, Houghton, 1985.
(With Bruce Chatwin) *Patagonia Revisited,* Houghton, 1986.

Riding the Iron Rooster: By Train through China, Ivy, 1989.
Travelling the World, Random House, 1990.
The Happy Isles of Oceania: Paddling the Pacific, Fawcett, 1992.
The Pillars of Hercules: A Grand Tour of the Mediterranean, Putnam, 1995.
(Author of introduction) Gerard D'Aboville, *Alone: The Man Who Braved the Vast Pacific & Won,* translated by Richard Seaver, Arcade Publishing, 1994.

PLAYS

(With Peter Bogdanovich and Howard Sackler) *Saint Jack* (screenplay), New World/Shoals Creek/Playboy/Copa de Oro, 1979.
White Man's Burden, 1987.

JUVENILES

A Christmas Card, illustrated by John Lawrence, Houghton, 1978.
London Snow: A Christmas Story, illustrated by Lawrence, Houghton, 1979.

MEDIA ADAPTATIONS: The Mosquito Coast was adapted as a motion picture in 1986, directed by Peter Weir, starring Harrison Ford; *Doctor Slaughter* was adapted as the motion picture *Half Moon Street* in 1986, directed by Bob Swaim, starring Sigourney Weaver and Michael Caine.

SIDELIGHTS: In a career spanning several decades, author Paul Theroux has established a reputation as one of modern literature's most respected chroniclers of the expatriate experience. His novels find themes in the anomalies of post-imperial life in such exotic locales as Malawi, Singapore, and Honduras, as well as in the economic and social decay besetting Great Britain in the late twentieth century. As Samuel Coale notes in *Critique:* "Drastic change indeed stalks the world of [Theroux's] fiction, that precisely rendered realm where cultures clash and characters encounter each other as society's pawns in a larger pattern." An American citizen who lives in London most of the year, Theroux has gained equal renown for his nonfiction travel books, some of which feature continent-crossing railway journeys of months' duration. By travelling, suggests *New Yorker* contributor Susan Lardner, "Theroux has tested a belief in the continuing strangeness of the world, and discovered openings for melodrama and romantic gestures that other writers have given up for lost." Helen Dudar writes in the *Chicago Tribune Book World* that Theroux has become "our foremost fictional specialist in the outsized outsider, the ravenous wanderer who sees or knows or wants more than most of us allow ourselves to hope for."

Theroux's family background and upbringing in the "prim suburbs of Boston" hardly seem adequate preparation for his adult role as an award-winning novelist, essayist, and world traveler. He was born in Medford, Massachusetts in 1941, to working-class parents who had, he claims in the *New York Times,* "no place, no influence, no money nor power." They did, however, have numerous children. In his essay collection *Sunrise with Seamonsters: Travels and Discoveries 1964-1984,* Theroux writes: "It was part of my luck to have been born in a populous family of nine unexampled wits." Included in this roster of six siblings are two elder brothers—Eugene, a Washington, D.C.-based lawyer and expert in Sino-American trade, and Alexander, a novelist whose critical reception has rivalled Paul's. *New York Times* contributor James Atlas characterizes the three oldest Theroux brothers as "collective tutors in the acquisition of culture" who "shared their various talents among themselves and passed them down to their younger brothers."

As a sophomore at the University of Massachusetts, he declared himself to be a pacifist and insisted on receiving an exemption from the mandatory R.O.T.C. program. Though "neither a brilliant nor inspired student," according to Atlas, Theroux called further attention to himself in 1962 by being arrested for leading an antiwar demonstration—"when demonstrations were rare and actually bothered people"—he notes in *Sunrise with Seamonsters.* Upon graduation from the University of Massachusetts in 1963, Theroux joined the Peace Corps, an organization he describes in *Sunrise with Seamonsters* as "a sort of Howard Johnson's on the main drag to maturity." He was sent to Limbe, Malawi, in South Central Africa to teach English.

For a time Theroux supplemented his Peace Corps stipend by writing articles for the *Christian Science Monitor* and several African periodicals. In the course of his stay in Malawi, he found himself on friendly terms with a group of political leaders who eventually fell from favor with the unstable Hastings Banda regime. This association, as well as a duplicitous use of some of Theroux's articles by the German equivalent of the C.I.A., led to Theroux's deportation from Malawi in 1965, under the charge of spying. Several years later, Theroux described the incident in an essay that has been reprinted in *Sunrise with Seamonsters.* "My readiness to say yes to favors may suggest a simplicity of mind, a fatal gullibility," he wrote, "but I was bored, and the daily annoyance of living in a dictatorship, which is like suffering an unhappy family in a locked house, had softened my temper to the point where anything different, lunch with a stranger, the request for an article, the challenge of a difficult task, changed that day and revived my mind. Theroux was expelled from the Peace Corps and fined for "six months' unsatisfactory service," but no further government action ensued based on the events in Malawi.

Immediately following his expulsion from the Peace Corps, Theroux returned to Africa, where he became a lecturer in English at Makerere University in Kampala, Uganda. He remained in Uganda until 1968, when he and his wife, Anne Castle, were attacked during a political demonstration against the policies of white-controlled Rhodesia. The violent end to his stay in Uganda notwithstanding, Theroux found much-needed intellectual stimulation at the university, as well as the time to work on his writing. In 1966, author V. S. Naipaul visited Makerere University and struck up an amiable but exacting working relationship with the young writer. Theroux remembers the period in *Sunrise with Seamonsters* : "It was like private tuition—as if, at this crucial time in my life, . . . he had come all the way to Africa to remind me of what writing really was and to make me aware of what a difficult path I was setting out on. . . . With me he was a generous, rational teacher." It was Naipaul, Theroux claims, who suggested that he write fiction about Africa, with attention to the comic and the tragic aspects of life there. Theroux, in turn, published a critical appraisal of Naipaul's work, titled *V. S. Naipaul: An Introduction to His Works,* in 1972.

Waldo, Theroux's first novel, was published in 1967, while the author was still living in Uganda. Timothy J. Evans notes in the *Dictionary of Literary Biography* that the work "deals with the theme of a man trying to find or create order in his life" and that the book is the first expression of themes that Theroux continues to use. "Order is not discovered by the characters" in *Waldo,* states Evans, "and it is not imposed by the writer on the novel." Evans claims that critical reaction to *Waldo* falls in extremes of praise and disparagement but that the book's quality falls rather midpoint between the two poles. "The novel does have a point," Evans concludes, "and it has some humorous, satiric passages which make it worth reading, but it is very episodic, with vignettes of uneven quality." A *Times Literary Supplement* reviewer offers a concurrent assessment: "Most of the time, *Waldo* seems to wander along, quite amiably and quite readably, but without much sense of direction."

In 1968 Theroux left Uganda and took a teaching position at the University of Singapore. While there he published three novels set in Africa: *Fong and the Indians, Girls at Play,* and *Jungle Lovers.* As a group, the works explore the frustrating and potentially tragic difficulties of social interaction in postcolonial Africa. Robert Towers in the *New York Review of Books* writes of Theroux: "Unafraid of ethnic generalizations, he spares no one—African, Englishman, Chinaman, Indian, American—in his wildly absurd confrontations between the old and the new exploiters and the poor bastards caught in the middle; recklessly he juxtaposes the crumbling institutions of colonialism with some of the more bizarre outgrowths of the Third World." In *Fong and the Indians,* for instance, Theroux describes the misadventures of a Chinese Catholic grocer in an imaginary African state. According to *Saturday Review* contributor Constance Wagner, the novel depicts "Africans, Asians, whites, cheating, despising, mistrusting one another. . . . With a smile Theroux lays bare the myopic self-serving not of Africa but of man. . . . Laugh as you will, you realize in the end that this short novel contains more of sanity and truth than a dozen fat morality plays on ugly Americanism."

Critics find elements of satire and hopelessness in Theroux's novels about Africa. In a *Times Literary Supplement* review of *Jungle Lovers,* a writer states: "Increasingly a more wryly observed Africa emerges from the condescension or primitivism of expatriate fiction. . . . [Theroux's] fable, with roots in satiric caricature and documentary terror, uses the linguistic complexity to underscore the wavering relationships between lingering British, Africans, and the two American protagonists." *Spectator* contributor Auberon Waugh calls *Jungle Lovers* "the most vivid account of the sheer hopelessness of independent Black Africa" and "a serious and excellent novel, welcome above all for its refreshing pessimism." Evans suggests that a "repeated assertion of empathy for the blacks does not convincingly cover an attitude of paternalism" on the author's part in *Jungle Lovers.* Evans nevertheless adds that in the book, "the British and American settlers are also viewed with ridicule, and Theroux seems content to leave the Americans' plans for change open to question." The destructive implications of one particularly naive American's plans for change form the violent climax of *Girls at Play,* a work one *Times Literary Supplement* critic characterizes as "unremittingly depressing." Lardner feels that Theroux's novels set in Africa reveal him to be "a connoisseur of the conflict of ideals and illusions with things as they turn out to be." Irony, she concludes, "is his natural style."

While teaching in Singapore, Theroux was made to promise that he would not write any fiction about that island. The informal constraint was removed when he relocated in London, and he published *Saint Jack,* a novel set in Singapore. *Atlantic* reviewer Edward Weeks calls the work "a highly professional, often amusing, withering account of prostitution in the once glamorous East." A low-key first person narrative by a middle-aged, expatriate American pimp, *Saint Jack* has received generous praise from critics. "There has never been any question about the quality of Theroux's prose or the bite of his satire," writes Jonathan Yardley in the *Washington Post Book World.* "In *Saint Jack,* more than in any of his previous fiction, the sardonic is balanced with compassion, and in Jack Flowers we are given a character whose yearnings touch upon our own." Evans feels that the protagonist "could never change, because he represents life in Singapore. . . . Jack may dream of an ideal existence and wish that he could write the novel which would depict it, but he cannot. . . . Life will be a treadmill for him." Though Weeks suggests that under the surface humor "one is aware of the author's scorn for this disheveled, corrupt memento of colonialism," other reviewers cite Theroux for a sympathetic portrayal of a quixotic hero. "Jack Flowers is funny, endearing, outrageous, poignant, noble—and utterly believable," contends Yardley. "He is Paul Theroux's finest accomplishment." In 1979, Peter Bogdanovich directed the movie version of "Saint Jack," based on a screenplay that Theroux helped to write.

Theroux's commercial and critical success was still to a certain extent dependent upon his British readership when he published *The Black House* in 1974. The novel, a gothic tale with psychological dimensions set in a rural part of England, has garnered mixed reviews. *New York Times Book Review* contributor Michael Mewshaw feels that while "it is a tribute to [Theroux's] integrity and ambition that he is not content to keep repeating himself," the work in question, "an abrupt departure from the comic vision of his earlier work, does a serious disservice to his talent." Claire Tomalin offers a different viewpoint in the *New Statesman*. "The book is about a man panicked by doubts about just where he and other creatures do belong," Tomalin writes. "The degree of skill with which Theroux handles these various themes, and the level of mastery of his writing, have produced a novel of unusual scope and promise still more for the future."

The Black House has gained added notoriety for being the manuscript Theroux dropped at the publishing house on his way to the train station for his now-famous transcontinental rail trip. In *Sunrise with Seamonsters* he writes: "Travel is a creative act—not simply loafing and inviting your soul, but feeding the imagination, accounting for each fresh wonder, memorizing and moving on. The discoveries the traveler makes in broad daylight—the curious problems of the eye he solves—resemble those that thrill and sustain a novelist in his solitude." Boarding a train at Victoria Station in London, Theroux set off on a four-month odyssey through Asia, the Far East, and the former Soviet Union, eventually returning to his point of departure with "four thick notebooks" on his lap. The edited notebooks became *The Great Railway Bazaar: By Train through Asia.*

Though travel accounts are not generally known for their commercial appeal, *The Great Railway Bazaar* was an enormous success. Writing for *Publishers Weekly,* John F. Baker calls Theroux's accomplishment an "amazing first." Baker notes: "He had made his way onto the best seller list . . . with nothing more than a travel book, . . . thereby becoming probably the first writer since Mark Twain whose travels made a more than fleeting impression in booksellers' accounts." Critics have lavished praise on the work. *Washington Post Book World* contributor David Roberts claims that the account "represents travel writing at its very best—almost the best, one is tempted to say, that it can attain. Paul Theroux . . . here transforms what was clearly a long, ultimately tedious journey by train . . . into a singularly entertaining book." "Though it is a travel book and not a novel," Towers comments, "it incorporates many of the qualities of Theroux's fiction: it is funny, sardonic, wonderfully sensuous and evocative in its descriptions, casually horrifying in its impact."

The success of *The Great Railway Bazaar,* combined with an admitted wanderlust, have led Theroux to pen several subsequent travel memoirs. Best known among these are *The Old Patagonian Express: By Train through the Americas, The Kingdom by the Sea: A Journey around Great Britain,* and *The Pillars of Herculese: A Grand Tour of the Mediterranean.* Employing the same techniques of rail travel, walking excursion, and personal rumination, these works explore Central and South America and the coastline regions of the British Isles, respectively. Neither volume has enjoyed the critical reception that attended publication of *The Great Railway Bazaar;* some reviewers find the works scornful and repetitive. As Patrick Breslin notes of *The Old Patagonian Express* in the *Washington Post Book World:* "Theroux so loses himself in the mechanics of how he got to Patagonia, and the people who irritated him along the way, that there is little room in the book for anything else. And since not very much out of the ordinary happened to him, one's interest flags." In the *New York Times,* John Leonard comments that Theroux's traveling style "tends to be contentious; at the drop of an offhand remark in a bar or a dining car, he will opinionize." Leonard adds, however: "One forgives him because one tends to agree with his opinions."

Reception to 1995's *The Pillars of Hercules* was similar. The account of Theroux's journey through the Mediterranean realm is typical of the author; "a marketing department's dream," notes Graham Coster in the *London Review of Books,* "designed with travel-brochure simplicity and accessibility." While questioning many of the author's references to location—"Clearly, he travels intuitively, disdaining maps and guidebooks. . . . I'm a little surprised he made it home"—*Washington Post Book World* reviewer John Ash felt that Theroux's contempt for his location was less than charming in its arrogance. Regarding the author's dismissal of Greece—"The whole of Greece seemed to me to be a cut-price theme park of broken marble, a place where you were harangued in a high-minded way about Ancient Greek culture, while some swarthy little person picked your pocket"—Ash responds that "Theroux is famous for his curmudgeonly verve, but this is not that. It is fatuous and ugly." Stephen Greenblatt excuses the author in the *New York Times Book Review,* saying that the many brief exchanges between Theroux and the people he meets on his journey "disclose a redeeming quality that lies behind Mr. Theroux's grumpiness and cynicism and helps to account for his improvisational energy: he is driven by an intense, insatiable curiosity."

The Mosquito Coast, a novel published in 1982, is among Theroux's best-known works of fiction. Told from the point of view of a thirteen-year-old narrator, the story explores a family's exodus from Massachusetts to the jungles of Honduras under the domination of a manic and eccentric father, Allie Fox. *Times Literary Supplement* contributor Valentine Cunningham comments on Theroux's characterization: "Allie Fox. . . [is] a truly amazing and unforgettable figure, an American titan whose actions unlock the essences of oppressive Americanism, revealing evils we're to take as intrinsic to the rationality and mechanization that helped make his country what it is." Towers likewise cites the theme of "Yankee-ingenuity-gone-berserk" in the *New York Review of Books,* adding that Theroux handles the concept "with commendable skill." "Though Allie Fox is an archetypal character whose career follows an emblematic line," Towers writes, "Theroux has avoided the sterility of much quasi-allegorical writing by endowing his main character with a lively and dense specificity." "In Allie Fox, Theroux has created his first epic hero," claims Jonathan Raban in the *Saturday Review.* "If one can imagine an American tradition that takes in Benjamin Franklin,

Captain Ahab, Huey Long, and the Reverend Jim Jones, then Allie Fox is its latest most complete incarnation."

The Mosquito Coast garnered an American Book Award nomination and numerous highly favorable reviews. Raban, for instance, terms the work "not just [Theroux's] finest novel so far. It is—in a characteristically hooded way—a novelist's act of self-definition, a midterm appraisal of his own resources. It is a wonderful book, with so many levels to it that it feels bottomless." The novel did not, however, meet with universal approval. *Los Angeles Times Book Review* contributor Edward M. White writes that *The Mosquito Coast* is "an abstract and witty book, embodying Theroux's usual themes about the conflict of cultures. The abstraction is particularly damaging, here, however, where it becomes authorial manipulation of characters and plotting in the interests of theoretical design." William Logan complains in the *Chicago Tribune Book World* that because Theroux "cannot create a human referent for his characters, the narrative is labored and overlong, the irony clumsy, and the end congested with symbolism." In his *New York Times Book Review* article, Thomas R. Edwards offers an opposite view. "Theroux's book. . . . is, characteristically, a fine entertainment, a gripping adventure story, a remarkable comic portrait of minds and cultures at cross-purposes. But under its unintimidating surface, . . . 'The Mosquito Coast' shows a cosmopolitan expatriate novelist pondering his imaginative sources as an American writer, and the relation of those sources to the world as it now seems to be. This excellent story . . . is also an impressively serious act of imagination."

Theroux extended his ruminations on America fifty years into the future in his next work, the lengthy *O-Zone*. The novel, writes Yardley in *Washington Post Book World*, "is on several counts a striking departure for its author. . . . It is his first genuinely 'American' novel . . . and it deals more directly with questions of American national identity and character than any of his other books, either fiction or nonfiction." The O-Zone of the title is a vast area of the U.S. heartland evacuated after a supposedly disastrous nuclear accident, and to the inhabitants of an overpopulated and overpoliced New York City, O-Zone represents both the terror of the unknown and a potential escape from a dreadful reality. O-Zone, notes Yardley, "is a foreign place within a nation that has become foreign to itself." Eight New Yorkers travel to O-Zone, and are surprised to find themselves in a paradise that allows them to reclaim their common humanity. Their leader is a fifteen-year-old math whiz named Fizzy who, in the words of *New York Times Book Review* contributor Susan Fromberg Schaeffer, is "the kind of man who can lead humanity out of the double wilderness of emotional alienation and dehumanizing science to achieve, in himself, a desperately needed symbiosis between the two."

Theroux's next effort, *My Secret History,* was immediately seized upon by reviewers as an account of the author's own life, for the story of Andre Parent bears close resemblance to that of his creator. Parent was born in Massachusetts, travels to Africa, marries a British woman, lives in London, and writes popular travel books. He is also a deeply troubled man leading a double life, and reviewers were quick to find in Parent's troubles clues to understanding Paul Theroux, despite Theroux's warning in a prefatory note: "Although some of the events and places depicted in the novel bear a similarity to those in my own life, the characters all strolled out of my imagination."

"*My Secret History,*" comments Yardley in the *Washington Post Book World*, "is the story of a man so haunted by guilt and so driven by sexual greed that he is capable only in rare moments of seeing women as anything except agents for the appeasement of his lust." Thus Parent's secret history consists of hidden sexual pleasures and lies and it is not surprising when that history blows up in the character's face, shaking his surface life to its very core. Parent survives the clash of his public and his secret life largely because his wife allows him to transcend it. Thus, writes *New York Times Book Review* contributor Wendy Lesser, *My Secret History* becomes a book "about the permanence of marriage in the face of mistrust and infidelity; it's about the wisdom of women and the foolishness of men; and it's about mature love as the necessary and sometimes successful antidote to youthful selfishness."

Theroux followed *My Secret History* with *My Other Life* in 1996. "This is a life I could have lived had things been different," concludes the author in prefacing the work, a similar disclaimer to that which appeared in the previous volume. Characterizing the work as a collection of short stories rather than a novel, Piers Paul Read notes in *Spectator* that "The Theroux of this fiction, if not the real-life Theroux, clearly dislikes his life in London. . . . in [some] stories there are . . . stinging comments on English life, accurate enough when it comes to the literary world but verging on the absurd when it comes, for example, to the royal family. A bitchiness creeps in." "Perhaps Theroux's travel writing habits affect his attitude here," Kate Kellaway speculates in the London *Observer*. "He makes a grand tour of himself observantly but uncritically as if looking through a train window." Much of the book revolves around its protagonist questioning what his life would have been like had it been of the traditional sort—at one point he visits the former husband of an ex-lover, "because whoever he might be he was the man I would have become." Noting particularly the author's "rendering of women as two-dimensional objects" and his "sourness about ex-wives," Rhoda Koenig maintains in the *Wall Street Journal* that "Theroux offhandedly tells us that things changed after he began spending so much time away writing his travel books. But isn't the real cause whatever it was that took him away?"

Parker Jagoda, the main character in Theroux's disturbing non-autobiographical novel *Chicago Loop,* finds his own "other" life encroaching on his public life, but here the results are disastrous, sending Jagoda spinning recklessly out of control. Jagoda is a wealthy and fastidious Chicago businessman who lives with his beautiful wife in a ritzy Northshore neighborhood. He has begun placing personal ads in the Chicago newspapers, and when a pathetic blonde named Sharon responds, Jagoda leads her back to her apartment and brutally kills her, all the while telling himself that she has made him do it. Though Jagoda tries to suppress the murder, the event keeps bubbling up in his consciousness and he decides that the only way to atone for his deed is to reenter Sharon's world—as Sharon. Thus begins an odyssey in which the successful urban professional dresses like the woman he has killed, seeks out situations where he will be sexually abused, and eventually commits spectacularly appropriate suicide.

Theroux's 1994 novel *Millroy the Magician* also deals with a dual life, but one with overtones far less dark. The satiric tale revolves around narrator Jilly Farina, a fourteen-year-old girl who runs away from an abusive alcoholic father and becomes enthralled by Millroy, a carnival magician who serves as the book's hero. Millroy eventually becomes widely hailed on supermarket tabloids and talk shows for his skills as an evangelist of the American diet; he stars on a children's television show and begins opening up a chain of restaurants run by his dietary converts and featuring his own biblically sanctioned recipes. Jilly, disguised as Millroy's son, Alex, handles the business side of Millroys' meteoric rise. Noting that the book depends on the technique of magic realism for its believability, Chicago *Tribune Books* critic Nicholas Delbanco contends that the development of the relationship between Jilly and Millroy "is never credible and takes too long. We feel as if we're getting every detail of Millroy's meteoric rise and fall, overhearing every conversation and meeting every visitor to trailer or diner or television studio or hut." Also noting that the novel loses its effect as a parable due to the same matter-of-factness, Sven Birkets writes in the *Washington Post Book World* that "The thing about Millroy and his narration through Jilly's eyes is that we are never, not even at the last, sure whether there is genuine goodness in him or whether he is but another power-seeker awed by his own self-myth." Calling the book an "unusual, often funny, dark satire of America's obsession with trim bodies and religious television," *New York Times Book Review* critic Charles Johnson adds that *Millroy the Magician* "may strike some readers as maddeningly predictable and aswim in stereotypes of Middle America, gay people, troubled children and people of color. . . . One can only hope that . . . those who reach the end of Mr. Theroux's three-ring circus of a novel see its final act as worth the price of admission."

Kowloon Tong is a timely political thriller in the Graham Greene vein: "Bunt" Mullard and his mother Betty, British expatriates in Hong Kong, live in a world of teas, horse races and Macao casinos, until the impending takeover by the People's Republic of China throws them into a world of dangerous intrigue. A Chinese gangster is determined to take over their textile factory, and he won't take no for an answer. Theroux wryly observes that Hong Kong, originally taken from the Chinese by military force, is on the way to being taken back in a similarly brutal way. Thomas Kenneally, writing in the *New York Times,* laments the passivity of Bunt's character, but "Mr. Theroux's astringent misanthropy and narrative momentum are powerful propellants." Richard Bernstein, writing in the *New York Times Book Review,* says *Kowloon Tong* is not one of Theroux's more ambitious works, "but one that is recognizably his, full of faulty, off-kilter characters and furnished with a graphic sense of place."

Theroux has long labored outside of the realm of academia, and he has occasionally expressed mild contempt for university creative writing programs and patronage in the form of fellowships, endowments, and grants. Succinctly stating his position in *Sunrise with Seamonsters,* he comments: "The writer doesn't want a patron half so badly as he wants a paying public." The takeover of creative writing by the universities in the United States has, he contends, "changed the profession out of all recognition. It has made it narrower, more rarified, more neurotic; it has altered the way literature is taught and it has diminished our pleasure in reading." Theroux's own writing, highly successful commercially, has not gained a great deal of attention within the academic community. As Theroux tells *Publishers Weekly,* however, "No serious writer writes for money alone, but it's equally a mistake to think that if your writing makes money you're not serious." He is more greatly concerned, he admits in a *Chicago Tribune Book World* interview, that his writing should continue to entertain readers. "My fear is that I'll be boring," he states. "You never actually run out of ideas, but you might run out of ideas that are intelligent, amusing, original. I don't want to be a bore. I would rather open a beauty parlor—I swear."

BIOGRAPHICAL/CRITICAL SOURCES:

BOOKS

Contemporary Literary Criticism, Gale (Detroit), Volume 5, 1976; Volume 8, 1978; Volume 11, 1979; Volume 15, 1980; Volume 28, 1984; Volume 46, 1988.
Dictionary of Literary Biography, Volume 2: *American Novelists Since World War II, First Series,* Gale, 1978.

PERIODICALS

Antioch Review, winter, 1977.
Atlantic Monthly, October, 1973; April, 1976; October, 1983.
Booklist, July 19, 1997.
Chicago Tribune Book World, September 16, 1979; February 21, 1982; August 15, 1982; March 27, 1983; November 13, 1983; June 30, 1985; February 9, 1986.
Critique, March, 1981.
Detroit News, June 4, 1978; September 9, 1979; November 13, 1983; February 16, 1986.
Economist, July 23, 1988, p. 77; October 24, 1992, p. 102; November 20, 1993, p. 111.
Esquire, December, 1971; April, 1983.
Globe and Mail (Toronto), October 19, 1985.
Kirkus Reviews, April 1, 1997.
Library Journal, March 1, 1994, p. 138; March 15, 1995, p. 102; April 1, 1995, p. 142; September 15, 1995, p. 85; February 1, 1996, p. 90.
London Review of Books, February 8, 1996, p. 18.
Los Angeles Times, November 13, 1983; October 25, 1984; September 26, 1986.
Los Angeles Times Book Review, October 7, 1979; September 21, 1980; April 18, 1982; March 13, 1983; September 21, 1986.
Maclean's, August 15, 1988, p. 50; August 14, 1989, p. 55.
National Review, June 29, 1971; November 10, 1972; June 2, 1989, p. 58.
New Republic, November 29, 1969; September 25, 1976; November 27, 1976; September 22, 1979; February 24, 1982; April 11, 1983; July 17, 1989, p. 40; March 2, 1992, p. 29.
New Statesman, June 11, 1971; October 4, 1974; October 17, 1975; March 26, 1976; September 1, 1978; October 24, 1980.
New Statesman & Society, September 16, 1988, p. 40; June 30, 1989, p. 33; April 6, 1990, p. 38; November 6, 1992, p. 49; October 8, 1993, p. 38.
Newsweek, September 24, 1973; November 11, 1974; September 8, 1975; June 19, 1976; August 15, 1977; September 10, 1979; March 1, 1982; April 25, 1983; October 24, 1983; October 22, 1984; August 12, 1985.
New York, February 28, 1994, p. 127.
New Yorker, November 11, 1967; November 8, 1969; December 29, 1975; January 7, 1985; February 16, 1987, p. 108; August 10, 1992, p. 80; March 14, 1994, p. 92; June 26, 1995, p. 144.
New York Review of Books, September 23, 1971; September 30, 1976; November 10, 1977; August 17, 1978; April 15, 1982; June 2, 1983.
New York Times, May 29, 1971; July 22, 1976; August 23, 1977; April 30, 1978; May 31, 1978; April 27, 1979; August 28, 1979; February 11, 1982; February 28, 1983; October 13, 1983; October 1, 1984; June 5, 1985; September 15, 1996; September 23, 1996, p. B2; June 8, 1997.
New York Times Book Review, November 3, 1968; September 28, 1969; August 8, 1971; November 5, 1972; September 9, 1973; September 8, 1974; August 24, 1975; December 28, 1975; July 11, 1976; August 21, 1977; June 18, 1978; July

22, 1979; August 26, 1979; August 24, 1980; February 14, 1982; March 20, 1983; October 23, 1983; April 22, 1984; October 28, 1984; June 2, 1985; November 10, 1985; September 14, 1986; May 10, 1987, p. 34; July 19, 1988, p. 17; June 4, 1989, p. 1; March 17, 1991, p. 7; December 1, 1991, p. 20; June 14, 1992, p. 7; December 6, 1992, p. 52; March 6, 1994, p. 9; November 5, 1995, p. 11; June, 1997.

Observer, June 30, 1996, p. 15.

Publishers Weekly, July 26, 1976; June 24, 1996, p. 43.

Saturday Review, September 28, 1968; July 24, 1976; September 3, 1977; July 8, 1978, October 27, 1979; February, 1982; November-December, 1983.

Spectator, June 12, 1971; October 12, 1974; March 15, 1975; October 18, 1975; March 27, 1976; June 4, 1977; September 16, 1978; October 17, 1981; June 30, 1984; June 29, 1985; July 6, 1996, p. 32.

Time, August 23, 1968; August 25, 1975; August 2, 1976; September 5, 1977; June 5, 1978; February 22, 1982; October 31, 1983; July 1, 1985; May 16, 1988, p. 95; May 22, 1989, p. 112; March 25, 1991, p. 71; June 15, 1992, p. 73; March 7, 1994, p. 69; November 6, 1995, p. 83.

Times Literary Supplement, April 11, 1968; June 12, 1969; June 25, 1971; November 17, 1972; April 27, 1973; October 4, 1974; March 14, 1975; March 26, 1976; June 3, 1977; October 31, 1980; November 21, 1980; October 16, 1981; October 8, 1982; October 28, 1983; June 8, 1984; August 2, 1985; October 31, 1986; July 5, 1996.

Tribune Books (Chicago), March 27, 1994, p. 4.

Wall Street Journal, September 13, 1996, p. A10.

Washington Post Book World, September 14, 1973; September 15, 1974; September 7, 1975; May 30, 1976; July 11, 1976; August 21, 1977; June 25, 1978; September 2, 1979; August 17, 1980; March 6, 1983; October 16, 1983; December 9, 1984; July 7, 1985; February 27, 1994, p. 2; October 8, 1995, p. 5.

Yale Review, spring, 1979.

*   *   *

THIBAULT, Jacques Anatole Francois 1844-1924
(Anatole France; Gerome, a house pseudonym)

PERSONAL: Born April 16, 1844, in Paris, France; died October 12, 1924, in Saint-Cyr-sur-Loire, Indre-et-Loire, France; buried in Neuilly, France; son of Francois-Noel (a bookseller) and Antoinette (Gallas) Thibault; married Marie-Valerie Guerin de Sauville, April 28, 1877 (divorced, August 12, 1893); married Emma Laprevotte (a housekeeper), 1920; children: Suzanne.

CAREER: Writer. Assistant at Librairie de France (father's bookstore), Paris, France, during 1860s; editorial assistant at Bachelin-Deflorenne publishing house, Paris, during mid-1860s; schoolteacher in Ivry-sur-Seine, France, 1869; Lemerre publishing house, Paris, reader and editor, c. 1869-75; Senate Library, Paris, assistant librarian, 1876-c. 1889.

MEMBER: French Academy, League of the Rights of Man.

AWARDS, HONORS: Award from French Academy, 1881, for *Le Crime de Sylvestre Bonnard;* French Legion of Honor, chevalier, 1884, officer, 1895; honorary doctorate from University of Athens, 1919; Nobel Prize in literature, 1921.

WRITINGS:

NOVELS; UNDER NAME ANATOLE FRANCE

Jocaste [and] *Le Chat maigre,* Calmann-Levy, 1879; translation by Agnes Farley published as *Jocasta* [and] *The Famished Cat,* John Lane, 1912.

Le Crime de Sylvestre Bonnard, membre de l'Institut, Calmann-Levy, 1881, revised, Calmann-Levy, 1902; translations published as *The Crime of Sylvestre Bonnard, Member of the Institute,* by Lafcadio Hearn, Harper, 1890, by Arabella Ward, T. Y. Crowell (Boston), 1897.

Les Desirs de Jean Servien, Lemerre, 1882; translation by Alfred Allinson published as *The Aspirations of Jean Servien,* John Lane, 1912.

Thais, Calmann-Levy, 1890; translations published as *Thais,* by A. D. Hall, N. C. Smith (Chicago), 1891, by Ernest Tristan, Lotus Library, 1902, Modern Library, 1925, by Robert B. Douglas, John Lane, 1909, by Basia Gulati, University of Chicago Press, 1976; translation by Ernest De Lancey Pierson published as *Thais; or, The Vengeance of Venus,* Minerva (New York), 1892.

La Rotisserie de la Reine Pedauque, Calmann-Levy, 1893; translation by Joseph A. V. Stritzko published as *The Queen Pedauque,* Gibbings, 1910, Boni & Liveright, 1923; translation by Mrs. Wilfrid Jackson published as *At the Sign of the Reine Pedauque,* John Lane, 1912; translation published as *The Romance of the Queen Pedauque,* Halcyon House, 1950.

Le Lys rouge, Calmann-Levy, 1894; translations published as *The Red Lily,* Brentano's (New York), 1898, by Winifred Stephens, John Lane, 1908.

L'Orme du mail (first in "Histoire contemporaine" series), Calmann-Levy, 1897; translation by M. P. Willcocks published as *The Elm-Tree on the Mall: A Chronicle of Our Own Times,* John Lane, 1910.

Le Mannequin d'osier (second in "Histoire contemporaine" series), Calmann-Levy, 1897; translation by M. P. Willcocks published as *The Wicker Work Woman: A Chronicle of Our Own Times,* John Lane, 1910.

L'Anneau d'amethyste (third in "Histoire contemporaine" series), Calmann-Levy, 1899; translation by B. Drillien published as *The Amethyst Ring,* John Lane, 1919.

Monsieur Bergeret a Paris (fourth in "Histoire contemporaine" series), Calmann-Levy, 1901; translation by B. Drillien published as *Monsieur Bergeret in Paris,* John Lane, 1921.

Histoire comique, Calmann-Levy, 1903; translation by Charles E. Roche published as *A Mummer's Tale,* John Lane, 1921.

L'Ile des pingouins, Calmann-Levy, 1908; translations published as *Penguin Island,* by A. W. Evans, John Lane, 1909, by Belle Notkin Burke, New American Library, 1968.

Les Dieux ont soif, Calmann-Levy, 1912; translations published as *The Gods Are Athirst,* by Alfred Allinson, John Lane, 1913, by Mrs. Wilfrid Jackson, Dodd, 1925, by Alec Brown, John Lane, 1951, Roy (New York), 1953, by Linda Frey, Marsha Frey, and Roman Zylawy, Norwood Editions, 1978; translation by Frederick Davies published as *The Gods Will Have Blood,* Penguin Books, 1979.

Les Anges, Editions de Gil Blas, 1913, revised edition published as *La Revolte des anges,* Calmann-Levy, 1914; translation by Mrs. Wilfrid Jackson published as *The Revolt of the Angels,* John Lane, 1914.

Les Autels de la peur (title means "The Altars of Fear"; first published serially in *Le Journal des debats,* March 2, 1884, to March 16, 1884), Joseph Place, 1926, Nizet, 1971.

Also author of the unfinished novel "Victor Mainvielle."

SHORT STORIES; UNDER NAME ANATOLE FRANCE

Abeille, Charavay freres, 1883, Bias, 1973; translation by Mrs. John Lane published as *Honey-bee,* John Lane, 1911; translation by Peter Wright published as *Bee, Princess of the Dwarfs,* Dutton, 1912.

Nos Enfants: Scenes de la ville et des champs, Hachette, 1887; translation by Alfred Allinson published as *Child Life in Town and Country* [bound with] *The Merrie Tales of Jacques Tournebroche,* John Lane, 1910 (see below); translation by A. G. Wippern published as *In All France: Children in Town and Country,* A. Whitman (Chicago), 1930; published in two volumes as *Nos Enfants: Scenes de la ville et des champs* and *Filles et Garcons: Scenes de la ville et des champs,* Hachette, 1900; translation published in two volumes as *Our Children: Scenes From the Country and the Town,* Duffield, 1917, and *Girls and Boys: Scenes From the Country and the Town,* Duffield, 1913.

Balthasar (includes "Abeille"), Calmann-Levy, 1889, published as *Balthasar et la reine Balkis,* Carteret, 1900; translation by Mrs. John Lane published as *Balthasar,* John Lane, 1909.

L'Etui de nacre (includes "Le Procurateur de Judee" and "Le Jongleur de Notre-Dame"), Calmann-Levy, 1892; translation by Henri Pene Du Bois published as *Tales From a Mother-of-Pearl Casket,* G. H. Richmond (New York), 1896; translation by Frederic Chapman published as *Mother of Pearl,* John Lane, 1908.

Le Puits de Sainte Claire, Calmann-Levy, 1895; translation by Alfred Allinson published as *The Well of Saint Claire,* John Lane, 1909.

Clio, Calmann-Levy, 1900; translation by Winifred Stephens, Dodd, 1922.

L'Affaire Crainquebille (includes "L'Affaire Crainquebille"), Pelletan, 1901, revised, Cahiers de la Quinzaine, 1902, revised edition published as *Crainquebille, Putois, Riquet, et plusieurs autres recits profitables,* Calmann-Levy, 1904; translation by Winifred Stephens published as *Crainquebille, Putois, Riquet, and Other Profitable Tales,* John Lane, 1915; translation by Jacques Le Clerq published as *Crainquebille,* Heritage Press (New York), 1949.

Les Contes de Jacques Tournebroche, Calmann-Levy, 1908, enlarged edition (includes *Clio*), 1921; translation by Alfred Allinson published as *The Merrie Tales of Jacques Tournebroche* [bound with] *Child Life in Town and Country,* John Lane, 1910.

Les Sept Femmes de la Barbe-Bleue et autres contes merveilleux, Calmann-Levy, 1909; translation by D. B. Stewart published as *The Seven Wives of Bluebeard and Other Marvellous Tales,* John Lane, 1920.

Marguerite (first published in *Les Lettres et les arts,* December 1, 1886), Coq, 1920; translation by J. Lewis May, John Lane, 1921.

Le Comte Morin, depute (first published in *La Revue Independante,* December, 1886), Mornav, 1921; translation by J. Lewis May published as *Count Morin, Deputy,* John Lane, 1921.

"PIERRE NOZIERE" SERIES OF AUTOBIOGRAPHICAL STORIES; UNDER NAME ANATOLE FRANCE

Le Livre de mon ami, Calmann-Levy, 1885; translations published as *My Friend's Book,* by J. Lewis May, John Lane, 1913, by Rosalie Feltenstein, Barron's Educational Series, 1950.

Pierre Noziere, Lemerre, 1899; translation by J. Lewis May, John Lane, 1916.

Le Petit Pierre, Calmann-Levy, 1918; translation by J. Lewis May published as *Little Pierre,* John Lane, 1920.

La Vie en fleur, Calmann-Levy, 1922; translation by J. Lewis May published as *The Bloom of Life,* Dodd, 1923.

PLAYS; UNDER NAME ANATOLE FRANCE

Au petit bonheur (one-act; first performed in Paris, France, June 1, 1898), Pour Pierre Dauze, 1898.

(With Gaston de Caillavet) *Le Lys rouge* (adapted from his novel of the same title; first performed at Vaudeville Theatre, February 25, 1899), published in the *Theatre* volume of *Oeuvres completes,* 1970 (see below).

Crainquebille (three-act; adapted from his short story "L'Affaire Crainquebille"; first performed at Theatre de la Renaissance, March 28, 1903), Calmann-Levy, 1903; translation by Barrett H. Clark published as *Crainquebille: A Comedy,* Samuel French, 1915.

Le Mannequin d'osier (adapted from his novel of the same title; first performed at Theatre de la Renaissance, 1904), published in Volume 14 of *Oeuvres completes illustres,* 1928 (see below).

La Comedie de celui qui epousa une femme muette (two-act; first published in *L'Illustration,* Christmas, 1908; first performed at Porte-Saint-Martin, May 30, 1912), Calmann-Levy, 1913; translation by Curtis Hidden Page published as *The Man Who Married a Dumb Wife,* John Lane, 1915.

POEMS; UNDER NAME ANATOLE FRANCE

Les Poemes dores (title means "Golden Poems"; includes groups of poems titled *Les Poemes dores* and *Idylles et legendes*), Lemerre, 1873.

Les Noces corinthiennes (dramatic poem), Lemerre, 1876, revised, Pelletan, 1902, revised, Lemerre, 1923; translation by Wilfrid Jackson and Emilie Jackson published as *The Bride of Corinth* in *The Bride of Corinth, and Other Poems and Plays,* John Lane, 1920.

Poesies (includes *Les Poemes dores* and *Les Noces Corinthiennes*), Lemerre, 1896.

COLLECTED ARTICLES AND SPEECHES; UNDER NAME ANATOLE FRANCE

La Vie litteraire (first published in *Le Temps*), four volumes, Calmann-Levy, 1888-92; published as *On Life and Letters,* Volume I: translation by A. W. Evans, John Lane, 1911, Volume II: translation by A. W. Evans, John Lane, 1914, Volume III: translation by D. B. Stewart, John Lane, 1922, Volume IV: translation by Bernard Miall, Dodd, 1924.

Les Opinions de Monsieur Jerome Coignard (first published in *L'Echo de Paris*), Calmann-Levy, 1893; translation by Mrs. Wilfrid Jackson published as *The Opinions of Jerome Coignard,* John Lane, 1913.

Le Jardin d'Epicure (first published in *Le Temps*), Calmann-Levy, 1895; translation by Alfred Allinson published as *The Garden of Epicurus,* John Lane, 1908.

Opinions sociales (title means "Social Opinions"), two volumes, Bellais, 1902.

Vers les temps meilleurs, Pelletan, 1906; translation by J. Lewis May published as *The Unrisen Dawn: Speeches and Addresses,* Dodd, 1928.

Le Genie latin (prefaces), Lemerre, 1913; translation by Wilfrid S. Jackson published as *The Latin Genius,* Dodd, 1924.

Sur la Voie Glorieuse, Champion, 1915; translation by Alfred Allinson published as *The Path of Glory,* John Lane, 1916.

Prefaces, Introductions, and Other Uncollected Papers, translation by J. Lewis May, John Lane, 1927, Dodd, 1928.

Les pensaees, edited by Eric Eugaene, Cherche-Midi (Paris), 1994.

LETTERS; UNDER NAME ANATOLE FRANCE

Lettres inedites d'Anatole France a Jacques Lion, edited by Marie-Claire Bancquart, Societe Anatole France, 1965.

Lettres inedites d'Anatole France a Paul-Louis Couchoud et sa femme, edited by Gerald Bloch, Societe Anatole France, 1968.

Lettres inedites d'Anatole France a Paul Grunebaum-Ballin, edited by Jean Diedisheim, Societe Anatole France, 1971.

Quelques lettres inedites d'Anatole France et de Madame Arman de Caillavet a Charles Maurras, edited by Max Philippe Delatte, Societe Anatole France, 1972.

Anatole France a l'Academie Francaise: lettres inedites, Societe Anatole France, 1975.

Le Secret du 'Lys rouge': Anatole France et Madame de Caillavet; Lettres intimes, 1888-1889, edited by Jacques Suffel, Nizet, 1984.

OTHER; UNDER NAME ANATOLE FRANCE, EXCEPT AS NOTED

Alfred de Vigny (biographical study), Bachelin-Deflorenne, 1868.

(Editor and author of introduction) *Oeuvres de Jean Racine* (anthology), Lemerre, five volumes, 1874-75.

Le Livre du bibliophile, Lemerre, 1874.

(Editor and author of introduction) *Lucile de Chateaubriand* (anthology), Charavay freres, 1879.

Le Chateau de Vaux-le-Vicomte (study), Lemercier, 1888, Calmann-Levy, 1933.

L'Elvire de Lamartine: Notes sur Monsieur et Madame Charles, Champion, 1893.

(With Octave Greard) *Discours prononces dans la seance publique tenue par l'Academie Francaise, pour la reception de Monsieur Anatole France, le 24 decembre 1896,* Firmin-Didot, 1896, published as *Seance de l'Academie Francaise du 24 decembre 1896: Discours de reception de Anatole France,* Calmann-Levy, 1897.

La Liberte par l'etude, Editions des Cahiers, 1902.

Discours prononce a l'inauguration de la statue d'Ernest Renan, Calmann-Levy, 1903.

L'Eglise et la Republique (essay; title means "The Church and the Republic"), Pelletan, 1904, Pauvert (Utrecht), 1964.

Sur la pierre blanche (philosophical dialogue), Calmann-Levy, 1905; translation by Charles E. Roche published as *The White Stone,* John Lane, 1910.

Vie de Jeanne d'Arc (biography), two volumes, Calmann-Levy, 1908; translation by Winifred Stephens published as *The Life of Joan of Arc,* John Lane, 1909.

(With others) *Aux etudiants,* Pelletan, 1910.

Les Poemes du Souvenir, Pelletan, 1910.

Dernieres pages inedites d'Anatole France, issued by Michel Corday, Calmann-Levy, 1925.

Under the Rose (philosophical dialogues), translation by J. Lewis May, Dodd, 1926.

Les Dieux asiatiques aux premiers siecles de l'ere chretienne, Imprimerie Ducros et Cloas, 1928.

Rabelais (biography), first published in Volume 17 of *Oeuvres completes illustres,* 1928 (see below); translation by Ernest Boyd, Holt, 1929.

Associated with *Histoire de France* (title means "History of France"), 1881. Author of introductions to numerous works, including Marquis de Sade, *Dorci; ou, La Bizarrerie du sort,* Charavay, 1881; Marcel Proust, *Les Plaisirs et les jours,* Calmann-Levy, 1896; Paul Grunebaum-Ballin, *La Separation des Eglises et de l'Etat,* Bellais, 1905; Michel Eyquem de Montiagne, *Essais,* J. Povolowsky, 1920; Jack London, *Le Talon de fer,* Cres, 1925.

Contributor to numerous periodicals, including *L'Amateur d'autographes, Le Bibliophile francais illustre, Le Chasseur bibliographe, L'Echo de Paris, Le Figaro, La Gazette rimee, Le Globe, La Guerre sociale, L'Humanite, La Jeune France, Parnasse contemporain, Le Rappel, La Revue bleue, Revue de Paris, Le Temps, L'Univers illustre* (sometimes under house pseudonym Gerome), *La Vogue parisienne.* Member of editorial board of *Le Bibliophile francais illustre* and *Parnasse contemporain;* literary adviser of *L'Humanite.*

COLLECTED WORKS; UNDER NAME ANATOLE FRANCE

Oeuvres completes illustres, edited by Leon Carias and Gerard Le Prat, Calmann-Levy, Volume 1: *Alfred de Vigny* [and] *Poesies* [and] *Les Noces Corinthiennes,* 1925; Volume 2: *Jocaste* [and] *Le Chat maigre* [and] *Le Crime de Sylvestre Bonnard,* 1925; Volume 3: *Les Desirs de Jean Servien* [and] *Le Livre de mon ami,* 1926; Volume 4: *Nos Enfants* [and] *Balthasar,* 1925; Volume 5: *Thais* [and] *L'Etui de nacre,* 1925; Volume 6: *La Vie litteraire,* parts 1 and 2, 1926; Volume 7: *La Vie litteraire,* parts 3 and 4, 1926; Volume 8: *La Rotisserie de la Reine Pedauque* [and] *Les Opinions de Monsieur Jerome Coignard,* 1926; Volume 9: *Le Lys rouge* [and] *Le Jardin d'Epicure,* 1927; Volume 10: *Le Puits de Sainte Claire* [and] *Pierre Noziere,* 1927; Volume 11: *L'Orme du Mail* [and] *Le Mannequin d'osier,* 1927; Volume 12: *L'Anneau d'amethyste* [and] *Monsieur Bergeret a Paris,* 1927; Volume 13: *Clio* [and] *Histoire comique* [and] *Sur la pierre blanche,* 1927; Volume 14: *Crainquebille, Putois, Riquet, et plusieurs autres recits profitables* [and the play] *Crainquebille* [and the play] *Le Mannequin d'osier* [and] *Au petit bonheur,* 1928; Volume 15: *Vie de Jeanne d'Arc,* part 1, 1929; Volume 16: *Vie de Jeanne d'Arc,* part 2, 1929; Volume 17: *Rabelais* [and] *Auguste Comte* [and] *Pierre Laffitte,* 1928; Volume 18: *L'Ile des pingouins* [and] *La Comedie de celui qui epousa une femme muette,* 1929; Volume 19: *Les Contes de Jacques de Tournebroche* [and] *Les Sept Femmes de la Barbe-Bleue,* 1930; Volume 20: *Les Dieux ont soif,* 1931; Volume 21: *Le Genie latin* [and] *Les Poemes du Souvenir,* 1931; Volume 22: *La Revolte des anges,* 1930; Volume 23: *Le Petit Pierre* [and] *La Vie en fleur,* 1932; Volume 24: *Pages d'histoire et de litterature,* part 1, 1934; Volume 25: *Pages d'histoire et de litterature,* part 2, 1935.

Oeuvres completes, Cercle du Bibliophile, several volumes: *Balthasar* [and] *Thais* [and] *L'Etui de nacre,* 1968; *Les Desirs de Jean Servien* [and] *Le Livre de mon ami* [and] *Nos Enfants,* 1968; *La Rotisserie de la Reine Pedauque* [and] *Les Opinions de Jerome Coignard,* 1968; *Le Lys rouge* [and] *Le Jardin d'Epicure,* 1968; *Le Puits de Sainte Claire* [and] *Pierre Noziere,* 1968; *Jocaste* [and] *Le Chat maigre* [and] *Le Crime de Sylvestre Bonnard,* 1969; *La Vie litteraire,* 1969; *L'Orme du mail* [and] *Le Mannequin d'osier,* 1969; *L'Anneau d'amethyste* [and] *Monsieur Bergeret a Paris,* 1969; *Crainquebille, Putois, Riquet, et plusieurs autres recits profitables* [and] *Histoire comique,* 1969; *Sur la pierre blanche* [and] *Les Contes de Jacques Tournebroche,* 1969; *Les Dieux ont soif,* 1969; *L'Ile des pingouins* [and] *Les Sept Femmes de la Barbe-Bleue,* 1969; *Vie de Jeanne d'Arc,* 1969; *La Revolte des Anges,* 1969; *Le Petit Pierre* [and] *La Vie en fleur,* 1969; *Alfred de Vigny* [and] *Poesies* (includes *Les Poemes dorees* and *Les Noces corinthiennes*), 1970; *Pages d'histoire et de litterature,* four volumes, 1970;

Theatre (plays; contains *Le Lys rouge, Crainquebille, Le Mannequin d'osier, Au petit bonheur,* and *La Comedie de celui qui epousa une femme muette*), 1970; *Vers les temps meilleurs,* 1970.

Oeuvres, edited by Marie-Claire Bancquart, four volumes, Gallimard, Volume I (includes early works), 1984; Volume II (contains *La Rotisserie de la Reine Pedauque, Les Opinions de Monsieur Jerome Coignard, Le Lys rouge, Le Puits de Sainte Claire, L'Orme du mail,* and *Le Mannequin d'osier*), 1987; Volume III (includes *L'Anneau d'amethyste* [1899] and *Les Contes de Jacques Tournebroche* [1908]), in press; Volume IV (includes *L'Ile des pingouins* [1908] and *La Vie en fleur* [1922]), in press.

The Works of Anatole France, 40 volumes, Gordon Press, 1975.

MEDIA ADAPTATIONS: Le Crime de Sylvestre Bonnard was adapted for a play of the same title by Pierre Frondaie, published in 1918, for a film of the same title, [France], 1929, and for the film *Chasing Yesterday,* RKO, 1935; *Thais* was adapted for an opera of the same title with music by Jules Massenet and libretto by Louis Gallet, Calmann-Levy, 1894, translated by Charles Alfred Byrne, Burden (New York), 1907, and for films of the same title, [France], 1911, Goldwyn, 1917; *La Rotisserie de la Reine Pedauque* was adapted for a play of the same title by Georges Ducqois, Calmann-Levy, 1920; "L'Affaire Crainquebille" was adapted for films of the same title, [France], 1922 and 1934, and for the film *Mort aux vaches,* [France], 1953.

SIDELIGHTS: Jacques Anatole Francois Thibault, who wrote under the name of Anatole France, was principally a lover of the written word whose childhood environment and education had conditioned him to critique the writings of others as well as to create his own pieces. The depth of knowledge and the critical sense he acquired gave him a decided advantage over other French intellectuals of his time. Until he was forty years old, he was a detached spectator, a humanist, a dilettante using several literary alter egos as his mouthpieces and leading an epicurean life. By the mid-1890s he had built a solid reputation as a novelist and short story writer, a literary critic, and a journalist. At the age of fifty-three, having won literary fame, he suddenly became politically and socially active by opting for the Dreyfusard position in the controversy surrounding the alleged spying by French Army Captain Alfred Dreyfus. Beginning in 1897, he produced his best prose works, which reflected in large part his new commitment to socialism and various left-wing causes. For a fleeting moment he shared the idealism of leftist philosophies, but generally his writings bore the stamp of skepticism that often became pessimism expressed with irony, scoring every French institution perceived as oppressive, especially the church. France was an inveterately subjective writer whose work was a sounding board for his ideas. In remarkably clear and elegant language, this turn-of-the-century Voltaire conveyed the message that humans should be free of all fetters; but he held out little hope for the future of mankind. As Jacques Suffel records in *Anatole France par lui-meme,* the writer once declared, "It is difficult for me to conceive that serious-minded and sensible men entertain the hope of one day making bearable the sojourn on this little sphere which, awkwardly circling the yellow and already half-obscured sun, supports us like a vermin on its decaying surface."

France considered and rejected several occupations before a friend steered him to his first real job, editorial assistant for the publisher Bachelin-Deflorenne. Encouraged by his success, he applied unsuccessfully for the post of assistant librarian at the Senate Library. A few months later in 1866, the sale of the family business made France's search for security more urgent, and he found the courage to approach the young publisher, Alphonse Lemerre, who promptly hired him as an editor and manuscript reader. In his new position, France came in contact with the Parnasse poets, who comprised an anti-Romantic, art-for-art's-sake literary movement during the mid-nineteenth century. Since most of the famous Parnasse poets, Catulle Mendes, Leconte de Lisle, Theophile Gautier, Theodore de Banville, and Sully Prud'homme contributed to Lemerre's new journal *Parnasse contemporain,* France found his way into a highly important segment of the literary world. Editing meant drudgery and boredom, but reviewing manuscripts was an invaluable experience for an aspiring writer. However, he was already looking beyond Lemerre's. France revived an almost defunct periodical, *Le Chasseur bibliographe,* and contributed to others such as *La Gazette rimee* and *L'Amateur d'autographes.* Still determined to earn a reputation as a poet, he used *Le Chasseur* to publish his first lengthy poem of any consequence, "La Legende de Sainte-Thais" ("The Legend of Saint Thais," 1867).

In 1868 two events impelled the Parnassians to acknowledge France as a bona fide member of their group: Bachelin-Deflorenne engaged his services as a contributor to a new periodical, *Le Bibliophile francais illustre,* appointing him to its editorial committee, and also agreed to publish his first book, a biographical study, *Alfred de Vigny.* As a member of the Parnasse circle, the twenty-eight-year-old France entered the social whirl of the Paris salons, especially those of the autocratic Leconte de Lisle and of the much less intimidating Nina de Villard (Anne-Marie Gaillard, Countess Hector de Callias). France edited Nina de Villard's contribution to the second *Parnasse contemporain* collection, which included two of his own poems, "Denys, tyran de Syracuse" ("Denys, Tyrant of Syracuse") and "Les Legions de Varus" ("The Legions of Varus"), both thinly-veiled jabs at Emperor Napoleon III; the young writer also engaged in a brief love affair with Nina, a relationship that was ended when he was physically attacked in a Left Bank cafe by Charles Cros, another Parnassian and a competitor for Nina's affections. In 1869 France's position as a part-time reader at Lemerre's also became permanent, and he began to display his talent as a journalist and literary critic by starting his first regular column in the newspaper *Le Rappel.*

Eighteen seventy-six marked France's logical transition from objective Parnasse poetry to subjective prose writing. It also saw substantial changes in his professional and personal life. In August of that year, nearly ten years after his first try, he was appointed assistant librarian at the Senate Library for an annual salary of 2,200 francs; the head librarian was his friend, Charles Edmond, who had helped found the daily newspaper *Le Temps* and had commissioned France to contribute a series of articles on contemporary authors. These often frank essays made their author friends and enemies (the latter including novelist Edmond de Goncourt) from among the French literati. No doubt the prestige of his new positions helped facilitate France's spring 1877 marriage to Marie-Valerie Guerin de Sauville, who brought with her a dowry of 50,000 francs.

France's career as a storyteller really began in 1878. From that time on much of his prose fiction appeared first in the pages of leading periodicals before being expanded and published as books. He was as much a subjective writer of prose fiction as he was a subjective critic, contended Suffel, who wrote in *Anatole France par lui-meme,* that France "romanticizes the story of his life and of his feelings, constantly mixing fiction with reality."

Short stories, novellas, and novels were the major thrust of his writing career.

In 1879 Calmann-Levy published *Jocaste* (*Jocasta*), which had appeared in a shorter form in *Le Temps* in 1878, adding *Le Chat maigre* (*The Famished Cat*) to create a book-length work. *Jocasta* bears to a degree the imprint of Zola's naturalism. It has all the elements of a great story never developed to its fullest, probably deliberately as an implicit protest against Zola's theories. *The Famished Cat,* a comic satire of the world of artists and writers, is entertaining but lacks substance. Though the two stories stirred little critical interest, a letter from Gustave Flaubert termed *Jocasta* excellent and *The Famished Cat* a masterpiece. As a second work for Calmann-Levy France reworked two more short stories which had already been serialized in Paris journals. He made them share a principal character, a type whose personal qualities were those of the old scholarly gentlemen who had been his father's customers, and thus created his first really successful novel, *Le Crime de Sylvestre Bonnard* (*The Crime of Sylvestre Bonnard;* 1881). A lyrical hymn to Paris, the book also conveys a message of moderation in living, of a Montaigne-like concept of human happiness, epicurean but reasonable. Although *Bonnard* was popular, it could not successfully challenge naturalism or survive the test of time. Yet it brought France recognition from colleagues such as Maurice Barres, Jules Lemaitre, Renan, and Taine; and it earned him an Academy prize.

The success of his early novels, especially *The Crime of Sylvestre Bonnard,* had a profound effect on France's personal and professional life, giving him full access to French cultural circles. Paris boasted several prominent literary salons at the time, one of the most influential being that of Madame Albert Arman de Caillavet (Leontine Lippmann) at 12 avenue Hoche. From the time he first visited her home in 1883, France was strongly attracted to the witty, charming Madame Arman, who had agreed with her husband, in the early 1870s, to live independent lives under the same roof. By 1888 France had become the central figure not only in Leontine's salon but also in her private life. His relationship with his pretentious and overbearing wife, Valerie, had been foundering in spite of his closeness to his frail and affectionate little daughter Suzanne. France finally left his wife in 1892, and when his 1893 divorce freed him of his domestic concerns, it also liberated his muse. The warmth and encouragement derived from a new openness in his affectionate but always complicated relationship with Leontine signaled the beginning of the most intense and creative years of his life.

France's next real success following *The Crime of Sylvestre Bonnard* was the first of four autobiographical stories. *Le Livre de mon ami* (*My Friend's Book*) painted scenes of childhood domestic bliss in Second Empire Paris. Parts of this work appeared in several important magazines before Calmann-Levy published it in book form in 1885. The publication in 1889 of *Balthasar,* a collection of strange tales, closed out France's fiction-writing activities in the 1880s. Although the decade had been dominated by gratifying events—an advantageous if stormy marriage, the birth of a daughter, contacts and close friendships with famous writers, access to prominent social circles, and the beginning of the lifelong relationship with Madame Arman de Caillavet—this period also saw the death of France's mother, with whom he had been very close, and his resignation, under rather complicated and embarrassing circumstances, from his position at the Senate library.

French politics in the 1890s witnessed a rise in anarchist, socialist, and other leftist activity. Anatole France's political and social opinions found their expression in several very successful books of the decade. In October of 1892 he contributed to *L'Echo de Paris* the first of fifty-four installments of *La Rotisserie de la Reine Pedauque* (*At the Sign of the Queen Pedauque*), which draws its title from the name of a small restaurant where the action takes place. Published in book form in March 1893, this widely acclaimed novel introduced the character of epicurean and scholar Jerome Coignard, a lecherous, drunken abbe reminiscent of the sixteenth-century French novelist Francois Rabelais. The cleric's bizarre eighteenth-century adventures, which combine comedy, mystery, philosophy, and the occult, provided a context for France's opinions on contemporary problems. A varied cast of supporting characters, an assortment of historical eighteen-century figures including Voltaire and Denis Diderot, and a rich style result in a masterpiece of wit and irony exposing France's humanistic and liberal attitudes. Like Sylvestre Bonnard and later Monsieur Bergeret, Coignard is his author's alter ego, whose adventures are told by the grill owner's son, protagonist Jacques Tournebroche. Suffel says in *Anatole France par lui-meme:* "Here finally is a broad narrative, rich in colors, full of variety and cheer, cast in magnificent language. And this book is something else: a sort of crucible into which all of the eighteenth-century . . . seems to have been melted and poured, to compose a porcelain of incomparable brilliance."

At the same time as he was composing *At the Sign of the Queen Pedauque,* France was rapidly writing a series of columns bearing the title *Les Opinions de Monsieur Jerome Coignard* (*The Opinions of Jerome Coignard*) for publication in *L'Echo de Paris* every two weeks. These essays attacked social and political policies of the Third Republic, especially the ascendancy of capitalism, by deploring the excesses of the Bourbon kings and of the French Revolution. Since the author blamed religious, political, military, and judicial authorities for his country's social ills, the essays revealed his increasing compassion for the common man and his struggle for freedom. *The Opinions,* collected in one volume and published by Calmann-Levy in the fall of 1893 as a sequel to *At the Sign of the Queen Pedauque,* fully established France's reputation as a social critic.

From a passive cynic, Anatole France had become an active liberal who would henceforth speak out publicly for a variety of socialist causes even though his stance cost him many friendships. The Dreyfus case and France's newly adopted militant attitude also affected his work in progress. The ecclesiastical intrigue of *The Amethyst Ring,* the third volume of *Contemporary History,* reflects the Dreyfus affair as Bergeret defends the cause with surprising vigor, and the fourth volume, *Monsieur Bergeret in Paris,* can be regarded as a pure socialist outcry. The stepped-up irony and political satire of the second half of *Contemporary History* overshadowed the charm and subtle wit that the novels still contained. Socialist leader Jean Jaures, who had also testified at the Zola trial, became France's close friend at the turn of the century and for several years personally supervised his conversion and activities on behalf of the socialist cause. His prestige generated many speaking invitations, and he actively supported the abortive 1905 Russian Revolution. In the summer of 1906, Anatole France witnessed with great emotion the results of his sustained support when Alfred Dreyfus, reinstated as an officer of the French Army, was admitted to the Legion of Honor.

France's writings for the remainder of the decade attempted to escape contemporary reality, to divorce his creative efforts from his political activism, often through a return to medieval subjects. His first project of this sort was a venture into historical writing with his *Vie de Jeanne d'Arc* (*The Life of Joan of Arc,* 1908). He had for twenty-five years been preparing the story of Joan, but the effort was doomed to failure. A critic who was proud of his subjective approach and a scholar who, despite his erudition, was always hard-pressed to organize his content could hardly be expected to produce an objective historical work. After four years and more than a thousand pages in two volumes, France's obvious anticlerical effort to remove the legendary halo and the supernatural aura from Joan of Arc foundered for many reasons. His attempt to humanize her displeased both the Catholics who considered her a saint and the free-thinkers who looked on her as a patriot; and historians rejected the account as valid biographical history because, though entertaining, it lacked focus, it drew few logical conclusions, and it contained many errors.

During the first decade of the twentieth century France's personal life was marked by difficulties. In 1899, to fulfill the still unresolved contract with Lemerre, he hurriedly collected scenes from his childhood that had appeared in magazines since 1890 and allowed Lemerre to publish them as *Pierre Noziere,* the second of his purely autobiographical works. The following year his ex-wife Valerie married a much younger man, and his daughter Suzanne made the first of two troubled marriages, the complications of which caused a schism between her and France that remained unresolved when Suzanne died in 1917. Moreover, by 1904 Madame Arman's health and youth were declining; France's dependency on her had been reduced by his association with Jaures, and he had transferred most of his professional activity, writing, and entertaining to the Villa Said from the avenue Hoche mansion where he now just took his meals. As time wore on, Madame Arman, whom Suffel calls in *Anatole France par lui-meme* "the secret potion, giving life its fullness," became increasingly suspicious and with good reason, for her lover was, in fact, beginning to stray. To escape the temper tantrums and violent arguments, he accepted an invitation to make an all-expenses-paid lecture tour in South America. From May to August 1909, enthusiastic but small audiences in Brazil, Argentina, and Uruguay heard his lectures on Rabelais and Auguste Comte, but the major excitement came from France's scandalous affair with a middle-aged actress, Jeanne Brindeau, a member of the touring Comedie Francaise troupe. The Brindeau affair ended as soon as the party returned home, and France spent many weeks trying to rekindle his relationship with Madame de Caillavet. When she died in January 1910, France's grief was deep and sincere; however, by December of that year, he felt free enough to invite Emma Laprevotte, one of Madame de Caillavet's maids, to live with him. The new arrangement was also not enough to keep him, at the age of sixty-seven, from other amorous adventures, notably an interlude in 1911 with a thirty-five-year-old American, Laura (MacAdoo) Gagey, who was distraught enough when it ended to commit suicide.

The years with Emma were extremely productive ones as France composed the most masterful works of his career. Though several chapters of two books, *Les Dieux ont soif* (*The Gods Are Athirst,* 1912) and *La Revolte des anges* (*The Revolt of the Angels,* 1913-14), had already been drafted before Leontine's death, they were essentially composed after 1910. *The Gods Are Athirst,* which borrowed its title from Camille Desmoulins, the famous journalist of the Revolution who was guillotined with Georges Jacques Danton, was the best structured and the most impressive of all France's fictional works. Its success derived in part from the youthful hours France had spent absorbing details of the French

Revolution as he worked the card file of the La Bedoyere collection in his father's bookstore. In *Anatole France, un sceptique passionne,* Bancquart declares the novel "a work which is scrupulously accurate even in its chronology and its locales . . . attempting to balance the fictitious subject matter with the cultural elements with which it is fraught." France also set aside his usual ironic tone and, combining clearly delineated characters with well-conducted intrigue, effectively told the tragic story of Evariste Gamelin. Where he had failed with legitimate history, he succeeded with the historical novel. Suffel announces in *Anatole France par lui-meme* that "the work is warm, sensitive, pulsating with life," calling it "a painting produced with incomparable vigor and richness of color." Most critics and the reading public have justifiably acclaimed *The Gods Are Athirst* as France's best effort and as one of the greatest French novels.

The Revolt of the Angels was to *The Gods Are Athirst* what *Penguin Island* had been to *The Life of Joan of Arc:* the recreation of a historical reality coincided with the invention of a fantasy tale of epic proportions. *The Revolt of the Angels* portrayed angels reduced to the human condition and plotting a second revolt where modern military methods would insure victory and avenge Lucifer's original defeat. French society and all its institutions were again fair game for the writer's satirical barbs, especially the church and its belief in the intervention of angels in the human existence. This new parody, an even greater commercial success than *The Gods Are Athirst,* showed once more that one of France's greatest strengths was his ability to spin an excellent, Voltaire-like philosophical tale, steeped in wit and irony. His books reflected a pervading pessimism that did not square with the idealism of his socialist colleagues; he found it hard to believe in the socialist recipe for a better world because of his conviction that man was essentially evil.

France's nonpolitical literary activities during his final years amounted to an essay on Stendhal in the *Revue de Paris* in 1920 and the fourth and last volume of the autobiographical Pierre Noziere series on his youth, *La Vie en fleur* (*The Bloom of Life*), published in 1922. Honors continued to come his way: an honorary doctorate from the University of Athens in 1919 and the prestigious Nobel Prize for literature in 1921. Although the Catholic church placed all his works on the Index of Forbidden Books in 1922, his personal life at last conformed to accepted social standards. He returned to the finally rebuilt Villa Said in 1920 and later in the year married Emma. His books were immensely popular; royalties and translation income and play and film rights insured a comfortable existence. His old age was made more tolerable by the presence of Suzanne's son and his only grandchild, Lucien Psichari, then in his teens. From 1922 on, France's health steadily declined. His eightieth birthday brought wishes from all over the world, but in August 1924 he became bedridden until his death on October 12. A national funeral in Paris was followed by burial at Neuilly. A suitable epitaph might be Suffel's comment in *Anatole France par lui-meme:* "Never was a Frenchman more French than this left-bank Parisian."

BIOGRAPHICAL/CRITICAL SOURCES:

BOOKS

Jefferson, Carter, *Anatole France: The Politics of Skepticism,* Rutgers University Press, 1965.
Levy, Diane Wolfe, *Techniques of Irony in Anatole France: Essay on "Les Sept Femmes de la Barbe-Bleue,"* University of North Carolina Press, 1978.

Sachs, Murray, *Anatole France: The Short Stories,* Edward Arnold, 1974.
Searle, William, *The Saint and the Skeptics: Joan of Arc in the Work of Mark Twain, Anatole France, and Bernard Shaw,* Wayne State University Press, 1976.
Suffel, Jacques, editor, *Anatole France par lui-meme,* Seuil, 1954.
Twentieth-Century Literary Criticism, Gale (Detroit), Volume 9, 1983.
Tylden-Wright, David, *Anatole France,* Walker, 1967.
Virtanen, Reino, *Anatole France,* Twayne, 1968.

PERIODICALS

Conradiana, summer, 1983.
History Today, November, 1975.
Journal of the History of Ideas, January, 1972.
Nation, November 5, 1924; April 22, 1944.
New Republic, September 7, 1932; December 7, 1932; October 24, 1934.
New York Times, April 23, 1944.
Nineteenth-Century French Studies, fall-winter, 1976-77.
PMLA, March, 1932.
Romanic Review, October, 1942; December, 1970.
Times Literary Supplement, September 29, 1966.

*   *   *

THOMAS, D(onald) M(ichael) 1935-

PERSONAL: Born January 27, 1935, in Redruth, Cornwall, England; son of Harold Redvers (a builder) and Amy (a homemaker; maiden name, Moyle) Thomas; children: Caitlin, Sean, Ross. *Education:* New College, Oxford, B.A. (with first-class honors), 1958, M.A., 1961. *Avocational interests:* "Besides sex and death, I am interested in Russian literature, music, most sports, and my Celtic homeland, Cornwall."

ADDRESSES: Home—The Coach House, Rashleigh Vale, Truro, Cornwall TR1 1TJ, England. *Agent*—John Johnson, Clerkenwell Green, London ECR 0HT, England.

CAREER: Poet, novelist, biographer, and translator. Grammar school English teacher in Teignmouth, Devonshire, England, 1960-64; Hereford College of Education, Hereford, England, lecturer, 1964-66, senior lecturer in English, 1966-79, head of department, 1977-79. Visiting lecturer in English, Hamline University, 1967; visiting professor of literature, American University, spring, 1982. *Military service:* British Army, two years.

MEMBER: Bard of the Cornish Gorseth.

AWARDS, HONORS: Richard Hilary Award, 1960; Translators Award from British Arts Council, 1975, for translations of works by Anna Akhmatova; Cholmondeley Award, 1978, for poetry; *Guardian*-Gollancz Fantasy Novel Award, 1979, for *The Flute-Player;* Cheltenham Prize, *Los Angeles Times* Book Award, and Booker McConnell Prize nomination, all 1981, all for *The White Hotel.*

WRITINGS:

POETRY

Personal and Possessive, Outposts, 1964.
(With Peter Redgrove and D. M. Black) *Modern Poets 11,* Penguin, 1968.
Two Voices, Grossman, 1968.

Lover's Horoscope: Kinetic Poet, Purple Sage, 1970.
Logan Stone, Grossman, 1971.
The Shaft, Arc, 1973.
Symphony in Moscow, Keepsake Press, 1974.
Lilith-Prints, Second Aeon Publications, 1974.
Love and Other Deaths, Merrimack Book Service, 1975.
The Honeymoon Voyage, Secker & Warburg, 1978.
Protest: A Poem after a Medieval Armenian Poem by Frik, privately printed, 1980.
Dreaming in Bronze, Secker & Warburg, 1981.
Selected Poems, Viking, 1983.
(With Sylvia Kantaris) *News from the Front,* Arc, 1983.
The Puberty Tree: New and Selected Poems, Bloodaxe, 1992.

FICTION; NOVELS, EXCEPT WHERE INDICATED

The Devil and the Floral Dance (juvenile), Robson, 1978.
The Flute-Player, Dutton, 1979.
Birthstone, Gollancz, 1980.
The White Hotel, Gollancz, 1980, Viking, 1981.
Flying in to Love, Bloomsbury, 1992.
Pictures at an Exhibition, Bloomsbury, 1993.
Eating Pavlova, Bloomsbury, 1994.
Lady with a Laptop (stories), Carroll & Graf (New York), 1996.

"RUSSIAN NIGHTS" SERIES; NOVELS

Ararat, Viking, 1983.
Swallow, Viking, 1984.
Sphinx, Gollancz, 1986, Viking, 1987.
Summit, Gollancz, 1987, Viking, 1988.
Lying Together, Viking, 1990.

EDITOR

The Granite Kingdom: Poems of Cornwall, Barton, 1970.
Poetry in Crosslight (textbook), Longman, 1975.
Songs from the Earth: Selected Poems of John Harris, Cornish Miner 1829-84, Lodenek Press, 1977.

TRANSLATOR

Anna Akhmatova, *Requiem and Poem without a Hero,* Ohio University Press, 1976.
Akhmatova, *Way of All the Earth,* Ohio University Press, 1979.
Yevgeny Yevtushenko, *Invisible Threads,* Macmillan, 1981.
Alexander Pushkin, *The Bronze Horseman,* Viking, 1982.
Yevtushenko, *A Dove in Santiago,* Viking, 1983.
Pushkin, *Boris Godunov,* Sixth Chamber Press, 1985.
Akhmatova, *You Will Hear Thunder: Poems,* Ohio University Press, 1985.
Akhmatova, *Selected Poems,* Penguin, 1989.

OTHER

Memories and Hallucinations: A Memoir, Viking, 1988.
Alexander Solzhenitsyn: A Century in His Life, St. Martin's, 1998.

Some of Thomas' translations have been performed as radio plays, including *You Will Hear Thunder,* 1981, and *Boris Godunov,* 1984. Work represented in anthologies, including *Best SF: 1969,* edited by Harry Harrison and Brian Aldiss, Putnam, 1970; *Inside Outer Space,* edited by Robert Vas Dias, Anchor Books, 1970; and *Twenty-Three Modern British Poets,* edited by John Matthias, Swallow Press, 1971. Contributor to literary journals in England and the United States.

SIDELIGHTS: In 1980, after spending nearly a year closeted in a small study at Oxford University, D. M. Thomas emerged with the manuscript for his third novel. Known until that time primarily as a poet and translator of Russian verse, Thomas had first branched out into adult fiction with the 1979 book *The Flute-Player,* a fantasy-like meditation on art and its struggle to endure and even flourish in a totalitarian regime. A second fantasy novel, *Birthstone,* followed soon after; it tells the story of a woman trying to create a single, stable identity out of the fragmented parts of her personality. Both works—especially *The Flute-Player,* which won a contest for best fantasy novel—received praise for their imaginative, poetic treatments of familiar themes. But neither work sold more than a few hundred copies.

Upon its publication in late 1980, Thomas's new novel, *The White Hotel,* seemed destined for the same fate. A complex blend of the real and the surreal and of the apparent dichotomy between the Freudian concepts of the pleasure instinct and the death instinct, the work generated relatively little interest among British critics and readers; what reaction there was, the author later recalled in a *New York Times Magazine* article, could best be summed up as "restrained approval." Within just a few months, however, it became clear that on the other side of the Atlantic, at least, that would not be the case. Appearing in the United States in the spring of 1981, *The White Hotel* met with what William Borders referred to in the *New York Times* as a "thunderclap of critical praise" that sparked sales and made Thomas an instant celebrity. Already into its second printing before the official publication date, *The White Hotel* eventually sold more than 95,000 copies in its hardcover edition and almost 1.5 million copies in the paperback reprint—making it without a doubt "the sleeper novel of the season," to quote a *Publishers Weekly* writer.

Divided into seven distinct sections, *The White Hotel* begins with a prologue that consists of a series of letters to, from, or about Freud and several of his colleagues in which the doctor discusses the case of one of his female patients, "Frau Anna G.," who is suffering from a severe hysterical illness. Her psychic distress manifests itself physically as asthma, anorexia, pains in the left breast and ovary, and a general feeling of anxiety that conventional treatments have not alleviated. In his letters, Freud speculates that the case of "Frau Anna G." will substantiate his theory of a death instinct that coexists with the erotic one.

Following the prologue are two sections devoted to writings by the mysterious "Frau Anna G." herself. The first sample is a long poem in which "Anna" describes an erotic fantasy she has concerning an affair with Freud's son. The affair begins in a train compartment and continues at a lakeside "white hotel," where a series of explicit and unusual love scenes is played out against a backdrop of horrible death and destruction involving other guests at the hotel; none of the violence, however, interferes with or diminishes the lovers' passion and self-absorbed pursuit of physical pleasure. The second writing sample, ostensibly written at Freud's request, is an expanded prose version of "Anna's" fantasy, "a wild, lyrical, irrational embroidery upon her original," remarked Thomas Flanagan in the *Nation.* According to *Village Voice* critic Laurie Stone, it is this prose version that serves as "a key to [Anna's] fears, imaginative transformations, and clairvoyant projections."

The fourth section of *The White Hotel* is comprised of Freud's long analysis of the case of "Frau Anna G.," now revealed to be Lisa Erdman, an opera singer of Russian-Jewish descent. A pastiche of actual case histories written by Freud, the section connects Lisa's fantasies to events in her real life and concludes with the doctor's observation that "she was cured of everything but life, so to speak. . . . She took away with her a reasonable

prospect of survival, in an existence that would doubtless never be less than difficult."

The fifth and sixth sections of the novel chronicle in detached prose the course of Lisa's life after she is treated and "cured" by Dr. Freud. The conventional narrative ends with a chilling account of her execution in 1941 at Babi Yar along with thousands of other Russian Jews; the reader then discovers what Lisa's fantasies have always meant in terms of her life and death and, in a broader sense, all of European history in the twentieth century.

The White Hotel's seventh and final section is a surreal epilogue in which Lisa, now in a purgatory-like land that is unmistakably Palestine, is reunited with people who had figured prominently in her life, including her mother and Freud. There, too, in this strange place are thousands of other souls awaiting forgiveness, love, and understanding; Lisa is last seen agreeing to help the latest wave of "immigrants" settle in: "No one could, or would, be turned away; for they had nowhere else to go."

The initial reaction to *The White Hotel* among British critics was "bafflingly contradictory," as Thomas himself reported in the *New York Times Magazine.* Among the few major periodicals that published reviews, the discussions often highlighted the novel's "pornographic" content, especially the two chapters containing Lisa's poetic and prose versions of her fantasy. *Punch* reviewers Mary Anne Bonney and Susan Jeffreys, for example, dismissed the entire book as "humorlessly insubstantial" and singled out Lisa's poem in particular as "a sexual fantasy of some crudity and little literary worth." Commenting in the *Times Literary Supplement,* Anne Duchene agreed that the early sections of the book "are not for the squeamish," but conceded that "they have to be undergone, by committed readers, as part of the raw material for the later, much more interesting sections."

Even the most gracious British reviews were, at best, reluctant in their praise. Though *London Review of Books* critic Robert Taubman also found the sexual scenes "not real or erotic," with an "unconvincing look of pornography," he nevertheless went on to declare: "The analysis that follows sounds an authentic note. . . . At the same time, it provides the reader with an absorbing Chinese box narrative of hidden memories, reversals of meaning and deceptions uncovered." A reviewer for *Encounter* compared reading *The White Hotel* to watching an Ingmar Bergman film: "You are battered with symbolism, in perpetual pursuit of images, of references, of bizarre surrealist objects. . . . I'm not sure that I enjoyed it, but I am certainly respectful."

As Thomas put it in the *New York Times Magazine,* "Any serious novel needs a miracle to bring it to the public's attention, and that miracle did not happen in Britain. It happened, instead, in the United States." By and large, American critics lauded *The White Hotel* as an ambitious, brilliant, and gripping tour de force. According to Thomas, their reviews were "individual, lengthy, well-considered, and concentrated within a short period of time; in Britain [*The White Hotel*] generally appeared among a miscellaneous bundle of three or four novels. . . . The British reviews stressed the book's complexity; the American reviews stressed its readability. The Americans seemed more open to largeness of theme and inventiveness of form. Their lips weren't so pursed."

The Americans, for example, were far less inclined than the British to make an issue out of *The White Hotel*'s "pornographic" content. The few who even raised the possibility described Thomas's poem and its prose rendition as highly erotic rather than pornographic; several reviewers mentioned that the decision to use such a technique was an unusual and very effective way of revealing the soul of Lisa Erdman. Though George Levine commented in the *New York Review of Books* that the author's language is occasionally "merely vulgar or banal," he went on to note that it often achieves "a lush, romantic intensity, with a remarkable precision of imagery. [The] writing is full of dislocation and surprise; it is seductive, frightening, and beautifully alive. . . . Such language immediately established the mysterious 'Anna G.' as a powerful presence." Leslie Epstein expressed a similar opinion, declaring in the *New York Times Book Review* that "the poem seems to speak directly from the unconscious." In short, wrote *Time*'s Paul Gray, *The White Hotel* "easily transcends titillation. Those who come to [Thomas's] novel with prurient interests alone will quickly grow baffled and bored."

Susan Fromberg Schaeffer, for instance, stated in the *Chicago Tribune Book World* that "the bones of a wonderful story are here [in *The White Hotel*], but Lisa Erdman and her world do not come alive. . . . Thomas loses sight of his own characters, his own obligation to breathe life and power into his fictional world." Epstein agreed, pointing out that Lisa "seems to float through the various crises that afflict her," and she has "no intellectual life" despite the complex political, social, and cultural forces that swirl around her. She is, in essence, no more that a "casualty at first of her psyche and then of history," in Taubman's opinion. In addition, Epstein contended, "the notion of the death instinct is shaky enough in Freud's own theory, and the application of a 'struggle between the life instinct and the death instinct' to this poor patient strikes me as nothing more that a bald assertion, unsupported by the evidence."

Next, Thomas turned his novelist's energies to *Ararat,* the first book in what became a trilogy and then stretched further into the "Russian Nights" quintet, dedicated to the Russian poet Alexander Pushkin. In *Ararat* the author sets up the beginning of an intricately woven mesh of deceptions that continues and grows through most of the quintet. As *Ararat* opens, the Russian poet Rozanov goes to Gorki to sleep with a blind woman who is writing a thesis on his poetry. Finding her unappealing as a sexual partner, he agrees to invent and tell a story on a subject she chooses, which turns out to be improvisation. In the story he improvises, there are three other storytellers—all writers attending a conference in Russian Armenia—who vie with each other in an improvisation contest. One of the tales offered in the contest includes a fragment of an unfinished Pushkin story that Thomas actually had translated and that is presented by the storyteller, the poet Surkov, as still being in progress, with himself as composer. In this story of Pushkin's (or Surkov's), there is an Italian storyteller who gives an inspired improvisation on a subject proposed for him by a St. Petersburg audience. Thus in Rozanov's telling, which involves on a second level the storytelling of the three others, stories and storytellers multiply within and around each other. As they do so, it becomes increasingly unclear who is the improviser and where the line is to be drawn between truth and fiction.

Ararat, like *The White Hotel* before it, met with a mixed critical reception (though not divided so dramatically along British and American lines as before). Galen Strawson, writing for the *Times Literary Supplement,* admired both the complexity and the disarray of the novel's construction and praised Thomas's portrayal of the "unwaveringly egotistical and calculatingly promiscuous" author. Strawson remarked, however, that "there are some very self-indulgent passages in this book . . . and some very slack ones too." He commented further that "a puzzle does

not make a work of literature; even if responses elicited by the former, as it works its illusion of depth and significance, can easily be mistaken for responses elicited by the latter." Isabel Raphael, reviewing *Ararat* for the London *Times,* found the structure "extraordinarily unpleasant . . . [like] one of those Russian dolls, with its tantalizingly identical layers leading to an ultimately impenetrable heart." Further, she noted, "Whereas *The White Hotel* was a triumphant hymn to the power of sexuality, here . . . every act of love [is] a violation couched in obscene language and calculated to sicken and revolt." Anthony Burgess expressed the view in *Punch* that Thomas "is to be watched, but with great suspicion."

Comparisons between *Ararat* and *The White Hotel* were inevitable, both because of the former's success and because of the unusual structures of each. In the *New Republic,* Ann Tyler pointed out that "*Ararat* takes its title from its preoccupation with the Armenian diaspora of 1915." The depiction of Nazi atrocities in *The White Hotel,* she recalled, "appeared to have some point; everything led up to it. . . . [The book] was disturbing to read, but one felt it was necessarily disturbing. *Ararat* disturbs without purpose. The Armenian tragedy is merely one more quirky scene in a book that's full of quirky scenes." She also reasoned, "Books are meant to carry us to other lives. . . . When a book drives its readers to diagramming the plot, you know it's not going to carry you very far." Diane Johnson made a more positive comparison in the *New York Times Book Review,* arguing that *Ararat,* like *The White Hotel,* "provides an abundant display of the author's astonishing virtuosity in poetry, in prose, in translating—a writer combining an impassioned European soul with the formal instincts of a spider weaving an immensely complex, elegant and sophisticated web."

In *Swallow* and *Sphinx,* Thomas carries his *Ararat* characters into more stories within stories and through narrative constructions that, like *Ararat* and *The White Hotel,* call into play not only prose but poetry and dreams. In *Swallow* Rozanov becomes a fiction, a creation of the Italian storyteller Corinna, introduced in *Ararat,* who is participating in an Olympiad, an international poetic improvisation contest. Corinna improvises not only Rozanov but also tells the story of *Ararat,* which elicits two opposite critical responses from the judges (as the actual book did from critics).

An insight provided by *Swallow,* as noted by Richard Eder in the *Los Angeles Times Book Review,* is that both the apparently "real" storytellers and the storytellers they create in their improvisations "are all variations of the same figure: the Soviet artist who navigates between libertarian impulses and the need to be officially supported. They travel, they prosper, they agonize and womanize and conduct a nicely calculated battle between speaking out and selling out." Eder found *Swallow* to be, "despite occasional indulgences, . . . an often-captivating book. Some flights are aborted, but most catch some flash of unsuspected light." John Leggett, on the other hand, felt that "while it is surely an unkindness to an author to give away the ending of his story, the resolution of Mr. Thomas's Olympiad strikes me as such a cop-out that I feel obliged to do just that"—whereupon he did, in the *New York Times Book Review.* Though he liked the "attractive architectural plan" of the book, Leggett believed that it raised expectations it failed to meet. "Alongside *The White Hotel,* which dealt so beguilingly with erotic fantasy and Freudian analysis," he concluded, "*Swallow* seems a bird of tawdry feather."

In a *New York Times* review of the third book of Thomas's quintet, Walter Goodman perceived that "the sphinx [of the title] may be Russia itself." *Sphinx* brings back some of the earlier characters and introduces two new ones: a Soviet Jewish storyteller, Shimon Barash, and a Welsh journalist named Lloyd George. Goodman dubbed *Sphinx* "a virtuoso performance," though he believed it did not "glisten quite as brightly as *Ararat* or provide the belly laughs of *Swallow.*" George Stade explained *Sphinx* in the *New York Times Book Review* as "a kind of trilogy" in itself, "a continuation that recapitulates the whole as we have it. Part One is an expressionist play, Part Two a prose narrative, Part Three a narrative poem." Though he acknowledged that each of the three books of the "Russian Nights" series written so far could be enjoyed on its own, he added that there was "no doubt that, from volume to volume, Mr. Thomas's meanings, especially those he grafts onto the concept of improvisation, sprout, grow, exfoliate in all directions."

"Thomas clearly had a lot of fun writing *Summit,*" surmised William French in the Toronto *Globe and Mail* of the quintet's fourth book. He wrote it in the tradition of following a trilogy of serious works with a light, farcical coda. "But beneath his japery," French continued, "we can glimpse several serious themes. Perhaps the strongest one is the difficulty of communicating, one human being to another, and being understood." This is part of what *Summit* demonstrates through its plot, involving a meeting in Geneva between superpower leaders Grobichov and "Tiger" O'Reilly, the U.S. president who was formerly a movie star and is accompanied by his vice-president, Shrub. Anthony Olcott in *Washington Post Book World* faulted *Summit's* attempt at farce and satire, citing Thomas's failure to "take the wholly unimaginable and persuade us that indeed, perhaps, these men, these leaders are capable of such grotesqueries" as they commit at the summit. On a more positive note, recalling that Thomas tells the reader that the entire story is "the dream of a woman about to die in an air crash," Olcott concluded that the series of "Russian Nights" books—four, at this juncture—"also slams into the ground with this final volume, but that only enhances Thomas' point in the whole quartet, that life's beauty lies in the dreaming, as his art so well conveys." Michiko Kakutani, writing in the *New York Times,* found it "a clever and often hilarious entertainment that opens a small window on the absurdities and perils of modern history."

The title of Thomas's 1992 novel, *Flying in to Love,* refers to the Dallas, Texas airfield that John F. Kennedy flew into in 1963 shortly before his assassination, and the book is about the president and the figures who were near him, both physically and professionally, at the time of his death. In the words of T. J. Binyon in the *Times Literary Supplement,* "The characters carom against each other like billiard balls, touching but not communicating, and each break takes us back to Kennedy himself to explore further aspects of his character." Binyon ultimately judged the novel to be, "despite its narrative pretensions . . . just another fictionalized investigation into the circumstances surrounding Kennedy's death."

In a *Concise Dictionary of British Literary Biography* essay, Karen Dorn quoted Thomas as reporting that, after he had finished the first draft of *Flying in to Love,* he had a dream that revealed a link between his compelling interest in Kennedy and his grief over his father's death, and that connected Kennedy's Camelot with the Cornish castle associated with the history and mythology of King Arthur. "Readers familiar with Thomas's interests," Dorn wrote in closing, "will remember the 1982 BBC radio talk in which he recalled Boris Pasternak's remark in *Doctor Zhivago* . . . that the artist is always meditating on death and thus always creating new life."

Thomas's 1993 novel, *Pictures at an Exhibition,* returns to the same territory of *The White Hotel. Pictures* shares many elements with Thomas's earlier novel: it comprises several distinct sections; it mixes actual historical events and persons with fictional ones; and it deals heavily with the Holocaust. In the novel's first section, a doctor working at the Auschwitz concentration camp seeks treatment for terrible headaches from a Jewish prisoner of the camp. The second section jumps to the present and is set in London, but it features many of the characters introduced in the first section. Later sections include a collection of Nazi documents, reproduced verbatim, describing the mass killing of ninety Jewish children. Thomas features several unsettling paintings by Norwegian artist Edvard Munch as a backdrop to his story.

Critics were mixed in their assessment of the novel. Frederick Busch, writing in the *New York Times Book Review,* praised the manner in which Thomas sets up the plot: "Thomas's construction of a narrative puzzle that we become eager to unlock is masterly." However, Busch concluded, Thomas fails to pull all of the novel's pieces together into an effective whole: "the book proves alternately horrifying and annoying. . . . its plot is tied together in an unconvincing Freudian bundle." Chicago *Tribune Books* contributor Andy Solomon, while admitting that Thomas's novel is disturbing, avers that "By the end, the plot has become a swirl of anguish, guilt and loss."

Eating Pavlova, Thomas's next novel, is a fictional account of Sigmund Freud's final days. Thomas features a Freud who has vivid sexual fantasies as he is dying of cancer and who struggles to define his relationship with his daughter, Anna. "This is a Freud designed to pep up any party," remarked David Buckley in the *Observer.* While noting the author's loose interpretation of the facts of Freud's life, *New Statesman & Society* reviewer David Cohen called the book "strange and often moving" and declared that "Thomas is so outrageous that no one should complain of his fact-mangling."

Thomas departed from the terrain of psychoanalysis and Holocaust themes in his 1996 novel, *Lady with a Laptop.* A meditation on the writer's life, the novel is set on the Greek island of Skagathos, where a mildly successful British author is teaching a creative writing class. The protagonist experiences bad luck and angst, but "as adventure becomes misadventure, the authorial tongue remains lodged in authorial cheek," commented Chicago *Tribune Books* reviewer Nicholas Delbanco. Delbanco concluded that the novel provides "a spicy slice of literary life."

Alexander Solzhenitsyn: A Century in His Life marks Thomas's first foray into biography. Solzhenitsyn, the uncompromising Russian writer and former political prisoner best known for *One Day in the Life of Ivan Denisovich, The Gulag Archipelago,* and *Oak and Calf,* is sympathetically portrayed by Thomas, who admires his subject's literary artistry, his adherence to principle, and his determination to be his own man. Solzhenitsyn himself is displeased with Thomas's speculative biography, which draws upon interviews with his first wife and, according to George Steiner, "dwells on intimacies for which there can be no direct evidence." Steiner explains, "It is often difficult to distinguish between conversations for which there is plausible testimony and those merely intuited by Thomas's busy imaginings. In compensation, there are numerous narrative brilliancies and the author's impassioned knowledge of Russian literature." Steiner praises Thomas's "insightful" account of the strains on the author's marriage created by his imprisonment. Lesley Chamberlain, writing in the *Los Angles Times Book Review,* says Thomas "deserves our thanks for writing a marvelously readable, indispensable book about an impossibly complex man."

BIOGRAPHICAL/CRITICAL SOURCES:

BOOKS

Concise Dictionary of British Literary Biography, Gale (Detroit), 1992.
Contemporary Authors Autobiography Series, Volume 11, Gale, 1990.
Contemporary Authors New Revision Series, Volume 45, Gale, 1995.
Contemporary Literary Criticism, Gale, Volume 13, 1980; Volume 22, 1982; Volume 31, 1985.
Dictionary of Literary Biography, Volume 40: *Poets of Great Britain and Ireland since 1960,* Gale, 1985.
Dictionary of Literary Biography Yearbook: 1982, Gale, 1983.

PERIODICALS

Chicago Tribune Book World, March 22, 1981; June 12, 1983.
Detroit News, March 22, 1981; November 17, 1982.
Encounter, August, 1981; July-August, 1983.
Globe and Mail (Toronto), March 10, 1984; July 21, 1984; February 27, 1988; August 4, 1990.
Library Journal, October 15, 1993, p. 91; September 1, 1994, p. 217.
London Review of Books, February 5, 1981; April 1, 1983.
Los Angeles Times, March 17, 1981; October 11, 1988.
Los Angeles Times Book Review, October 31, 1982; April 3, 1983; November 18, 1984; January 2, 1994, p. 6; February 15, 1998, p. 8.
Nation, May 2, 1981; April 23, 1983.
New Leader, April 20, 1981; May 30, 1983.
New Republic, March 28, 1981; April 4, 1983.
New Statesman, June 22, 1979; March 21, 1980; January 16, 1981; March 4, 1983; June 29, 1984.
New Statesman & Society, May 13, 1994, p. 40.
Newsweek, March 16, 1981; March 15, 1982; April 4, 1983.
New Yorker, March 30, 1981.
New York Review of Books, May 28, 1981; June 16, 1983; November 22, 1984.
New York Times, March 13, 1981; March 24, 1981; September 21, 1982; March 29, 1983; October 31, 1984; January 21, 1987; July 24, 1990.
New York Times Book Review, March 15, 1981; June 28, 1981; September 26, 1982; March 27, 1983; November 4, 1984; January 18, 1987; October 2, 1988; July 8, 1990; October 31, 1993, p. 13; October 23, 1994, p. 28; March 1, 1998, p. 9.
New York Times Magazine, June 13, 1982.
Observer, June 24, 1979; February 27, 1983; July 1, 1984; April 17, 1994, p. 22.
People Weekly, June 29, 1981.
Publishers Weekly, March 27, 1981; April 17, 1981; January 8, 1982; April 15, 1996, p. 48.
Punch, October 14, 1981; March 2, 1983.
School Library Journal, March, 1993, p. 236.
Time, March 16, 1981; April 25, 1983.
Times (London), January 15, 1981; March 3, 1983; June 9, 1983; March 10, 1984; June 28, 1984; October 15, 1988.
Times Literary Supplement, November 30, 1979; March 14, 1980; January 16, 1981; January 22, 1982; February 25, 1983; June 29, 1983; June 29, 1984; July 1-7, 1988; February 7, 1992.
Tribune Books (Chicago), November 7, 1993, p. 3; June 9, 1996, p. 9.
Voice Literary Supplement, October, 1982.
Wall Street Journal, May 20, 1996, p. A12.
Washington Post, December 15, 1979; January 27, 1982.
Washington Post Book World, March 15, 1981; May 16, 1982; March 27, 1983; September 9, 1984; January 24, 1988; October 2, 1988.

*   *   *

THOMAS, Dylan (Marlais) 1914-1953

PERSONAL: Born October 27, 1914, in Swansea, Carmarthenshire Wales (now Glamorganshire, Wales); died of pneumonia caused by acute alcoholism (some sources list cause of death as a cerebral ailment), November 9, 1953, in New York, NY; buried at St. Martin's Churchyard, Laugharne, Wales; son of D. J. (a grammar school master) and Florence (Williams) Thomas; married Caitlin Macnamara, July 11, 1937; children: Llewellyn (son), Colm (son), Aeron (daughter). *Education:* Completed grammar school in Swansea, Wales.

CAREER: Poet and prose writer. Reporter for the *South Wales Daily Post,* a reviewer for the *Herald of Wales,* and an actor; British Ministry of Information, scriptwriter during the mid-1930s; British Broadcasting Corporation (BBC), documentary scriptwriter and radio commentator on poetry during the 1940s; gave public poetry readings, including extensive lecture tours in the United States, 1950-53.

WRITINGS:

POETRY

Eighteen Poems, Sunday Referee and Parton Bookshop, 1934.
Twenty-five Poems, Dent, 1936.
New Poems, New Directions, 1943.
Deaths and Entrances, Dent, 1946, revised edition edited with notes by Walford Davies, illustrated by John Piper, Gwasg Gregynog, 1984.
Selected Writings of Dylan Thomas, New Directions, 1946, revised edition edited by J. P. Harries, Heinemann, 1970.
Twenty-six Poems, Dent, 1950.
In Country Sleep and Other Poems, Dent, 1952.
Collected Poems, 1934-1952, Dent, 1952, published as *The Collected Poems of Dylan Thomas,* New Directions, 1953, reprinted as *Collected Poems, 1934-1952,* Dent, 1984.
The Colour of Saying: An Anthology of Verse Spoken by Dylan Thomas, edited by Ralph Maud and Aneirin Talfan Davies, Dent, 1963, published as *Dylan Thomas's Choice,* New Directions, 1964.
Collected Poems, Dutton, 1966.
Poem in October, Coach House Press, 1970.
The Poems of Dylan Thomas, New Directions, 1971, revised edition, Dent, 1978.
Poems, edited by Daniel Jones, Dent, 1974.
Selected Poems of Dylan Thomas, Dent, 1975.

SHORT STORIES AND ESSAYS

Portrait of the Artist as a Young Dog (autobiographical short stories; includes "Peaches" and "One Warm Saturday"), New Directions, 1940.
Quite Early One Morning, preface and notes by Aneirin Talfan Davies, Dent, 1954, enlarged edition, New Directions, 1954.
A Child's Christmas in Wales, New Directions, 1955, new edition illustrated with woodcuts, 1959, Godine, 1984.
A Prospect of the Sea, and Other Stories and Prose Writings, edited by Daniel Jones, Dent, 1955.

Adventures in the Skin Trade, and Other Stories, New Directions, 1955 (published in England as *Adventures in the Skin Trade,* with a foreword by Vernon Watkins, Putnam [London], 1955, new edition with drawings by Ceri Richards, 1982).

The Collected Prose of Dylan Thomas, New Directions, 1969.

Early Prose Writings of Dylan Thomas, edited by Walford Davies, Dent, 1971.

The Collected Stories, Dent, 1983, New Directions, 1984.

Eight Stories, New Directions, 1993.

POETRY AND PROSE COLLECTIONS

The World I Breathe, New Directions, 1939.

The Map of Love, Dent, 1939.

Miscellany: Poems, Stories, Broadcasts, Dent 1963, reprinted as *Miscellany One: Poems, Stories, Broadcasts,* 1974.

Miscellany Two: A Visit to Grandpa's, and Other Stories and Poems, Dent, 1966.

Miscellany Three: Poems and Stories, Dent, 1978.

LETTERS AND NOTEBOOKS

Selected Letters of Dylan Thomas, edited by Constantine FitzGibbon, Dent, 1956, published as *Selected Letters,* New Directions, 1967.

Letters to Vernon Watkins, edited with introduction by Vernon Watkins, New Directions, 1957.

The Notebooks of Dylan Thomas, edited by Ralph Maud, New Directions, 1967 (published in England as *Poet in the Making: The Notebooks of Dylan Thomas,* Dent, 1968).

Twelve More Letters, Daedalus Press, 1969.

Collected Letters of Dylan Thomas, edited by Paul Ferris, Macmillan, 1985.

FILM SCRIPTS

The Doctor and the Devils (based on a short story by Donald Taylor), New Directions, 1953, published with an introduction by John Ormond, Time, 1964.

The Beach of Falesa (based on a short story by Robert Louis Stevenson), Stein & Day, 1963, 2nd edition, 1983.

Twenty Years A-Growing (based on a short story by Maurice O'Sullivan), Dent, 1964.

Me and My Bike (unfinished screenplay; introduction by Sydney Box, illustrations by Leonora Box), McGraw, 1965.

The Doctor and the Devils, and Other Scripts, New Directions, 1966.

Dylan Thomas: The Filmscripts, edited by John Ackerman, Dent (London), 1995.

Also author or coauthor of numerous educational film scripts for the British Ministry of Information.

SOUND RECORDINGS

Selections from the Writings of Dylan Thomas (five records), Caedmon, 1952-60.

Under Milk Wood: A Play for Voices (two records), Argo, 1954.

An Evening With Dylan Thomas Reading His Own And Other Poems, Caedmon, 1963.

Dylan Thomas Reading His Complete Recorded Poetry (two records), Caedmon, 1963.

Dylan Thomas Reading from His Own Work, Caedmon, 1971.

In Country Heaven: The Evolution of a Poem, Caedmon, 1971.

The Complete Recorded Stories and Humorous Essays, Caedmon, 1972.

Return Journey to Swansea (radio play; performed by Thomas and a supporting cast), Caedmon, 1972.

Dylan Thomas Reads from His Adventures in the Skin Trade and Two Poems, Caedmon, 1975.

OTHER

Under Milk Wood: A Play for Voices (first produced in New York City at the Young Men's/Young Women's Hebrew Association, May 14, 1953), New Directions, 1954, new edition, with preface and musical settings by Daniel Jones, published as *Under Milk Wood: A Play in Two Acts,* 1958, new edition, Dent, 1962.

Conversation about Christmas, privately printed, 1954.

Quite Early One Morning: Broadcasts by Dylan Thomas, with preface and notes by Ichiro Nishizaki and Nobutko Suto, Hokuseido Press (Tokyo), 1956.

Rebecca's Daughters, Little, Brown, 1965.

Two Tales: Me and My Bike [and] *Rebecca's Daughters,* illustrated by Leonora Box, Sphere, 1968.

(With John Davenport) *The Death of the King's Canary* (novel), introduction by Constantine FitzGibbon, Hutchinson, 1977.

On the Air with Dylan Thomas: The Broadcasts, edited by Ralph Maud, New Directions, 1992.

MEDIA ADAPTATIONS: The Doctor and the Devils was adapted for stage and performed at the Vanbrugh Theatre, Royal Academy of Dramatic Arts, 1961, and filmed by Ronald Harwood in 1985; the poem "The force that through the green fuse drives the flower" was adapted for soprano voice and orchestra by David Harden and released as a sound recording by University Microfilms, 1968; *Under Milk Wood* was performed and broadcast in Britain and the United States by the British Broadcasting Corporation (BBC), and filmed in 1971; several of Thomas's works were adapted into a play, *Dylan Thomas: Return Journey,* directed by Anthony Hopkins and produced at the Hudson Guild, New York City, 1990.

SIDELIGHTS: The work of Dylan Thomas has occasioned much critical commentary, although critics share no consensus on how bright his star shines in the galaxy of modern poetry. In fact, it is a curious phenomenon that so many critics seem obsessed with deciding once and for all whether Thomas's poems belong side by side with those of T. S. Eliot and W. H. Auden, or whether they are—in the words of a reputable critic quoted by Henry Treece in *Dylan Thomas: "Dog Among the Fairies"*—"intellectual fakes of the highest class." The latter is definitely a minority opinion; yet even Treece, an acquaintance of Thomas's, had to admit that the poet's work is "extremely ill-balanced."

The notebooks in which Thomas composed between 1930 and 1934, when he was sixteen to twenty years old, reveal the young poet's struggle with a number of personal crises, the origins of which are rather obscure. In his 1965 *Dylan Thomas,* Jacob Korg described them as "related to love affairs, to industrial civilization, and to the youthful problems of finding one's identity." Revised versions of some of the notebooks' poems became in 1934 his first published volume of poetry, *Eighteen Poems.*

Eighteen Poems was published in December, 1934, a short time after Thomas moved to London. The volume received little notice at first, but by the following spring some influential newspapers and journals had reviewed it favorably. Paul Ferris quoted from an anonymous review in the *Morning Post* that called the poems "individual but not private" and went on to strike a note that later became a frequent criticism: "a psychologist would observe Mr. Thomas's constant use of images and epithets which are secretory or glandular." Ferris also quoted a critic for *Time and Tide,* who wrote: "This is not merely a book of unusual promise; it is more probably the sort of bomb that bursts not more than once in three years." The book was also reviewed favorably by *Spectator, New Verse,* and the *Times Literary Supplement.*

This discussion of the difficulty of *Eighteen Poems* does not discount the fact that most of the poems have yielded their meanings to persistent readers—and books like William York Tindall's *A Reader's Guide to Dylan Thomas* and Clark Emery's *The World of Dylan Thomas* aid the reader's comprehension. Such poems as "I see the boys of summer," "A process in the weather of the heart," and the popular "The force that through the green fuse drives the flower" merit repeated readings, both for the artistic pleasure they give through their highly structured forms and for their embodiment of some of the key themes that run throughout the volume and, indeed, throughout much of Thomas's work. Among these themes are the unity of time, the similarity between creative and destructive forces in the universe, and the correspondence of all living things. This last theme was identified by Elder Olson in *The Poetry of Dylan Thomas* as part of the tradition of the microcosm-macrocosm: "He analogizes the anatomy of man to the structure of the universe . . . and sees the human microcosm as an image of the macrocosm, and conversely."

During the almost two years between the publication of *Eighteen Poems* in 1934 and *Twenty-five Poems* in 1936, Thomas moved back and forth between London and Wales a great deal. In London he began to meet influential people in the literary world: Herbert Read, Geoffrey Grigson, Norman Cameron, and Vernon Watkins, among others. He became particularly close to Watkins, an older man whose sedate lifestyle contrasted markedly with Thomas's. Watkins and Thomas would criticize each other's poetry, and Watkins became a frequent source of money for the continually destitute Thomas. At this time Thomas was carrying on a mostly long-distance relationship with the poet and novelist Pamela Hansford Johnson, later the wife of novelist C. P. Snow. While the affair lasted—it was finally torn asunder by Thomas's drinking—Thomas shared with her in letters his personal insecurities and his misgivings about his work. Ferris cited this letter written from Laugharne, Wales, circa May 21, 1934: "I am tortured today by every doubt and misgiving that an hereditarily twisted imagination, an hereditary thirst and a commercial quenching, a craving for a body not my own, a chequered education and too much egocentric poetry, and a wild, wet day in a tided town, are capable of conjuring up out of their helly deeps." During this period Thomas's drinking became a serious problem, and his friends would sometimes take him off to out-of-the-way places in Cornwall and Ireland to remove him from temptation with the hope that he would do more writing.

Thomas's second volume of poetry, *Twenty-five Poems,* was published in September, 1936. Most of the poems were revised from the notebooks; FitzGibbon reported in *The Life of Dylan Thomas* that "only six entirely new poems, that is to say poems written in the year and a half between the publication of [*Eighteen Poems*] and the despatch of the second volume to the printers, are to be found in that volume." Ferris noted that "the reviews were generally favourable, but with one exception they were not as enthusiastic as they were for [*Eighteen Poems*]." This exception, however, almost assured the volume's commercial success; it was a laudatory review by Dame Edith Sitwell in the *Sunday Times.* As cited by Ferris, the review proclaimed: "The work of this very young man (he is twenty-two years of age) is on a huge scale, both in theme and structurally. . . . I could not name one poet of this,

the youngest generation, who shows so great a promise, and even so great an achievement."

Some of the best poems in the book are rather straightforward pieces—"This bread break," "The hand that signed the paper," "And death shall have no dominion"—but others, such as "I, in my intricate image," are as involved and abstruse as the poems of the earlier volume. Derek Stanford, in *Dylan Thomas,* noted that still "there are traces of doubt, questioning, and despair in many of these pieces." Thomas, however, chose to place the optimistic "And death shall have no dominion" at the end of the volume. This poem has always been one of Thomas's most popular works, perhaps because, as Emery noted, it was "published in a time when notes of affirmation—philosophical, political, or otherwise—did not resound among intelligent liberal humanists, [and thus] it answered an emotional need. . . . It affirmed without sentimentalizing; it expressed a faith without theologizing."

The "Altarwise by owl-light" poems as well as "And death shall have no dominion" inevitably raise questions concerning the extent to which Dylan Thomas can be called a religious writer. In an essay for *A Casebook on Dylan Thomas* W. S. Merwin was one of the first to deal with this issue; he found Thomas to be a religious writer because he was a "celebrator in the ritual sense: a maker and performer of a rite. . . . That which he celebrates is creation, and more particularly the human condition." However, the positions on this issue can be—and have been—as various as the definitions of what constitutes a religious outlook. At one end of the scale, critics do not dispute that Thomas used religious imagery in his poetry; at the other end, critics generally agree that, at least during certain periods of his creative life, Thomas's vision was not that of any orthodox religious system. The range of interpretations was summarized by R. B. Kershner, Jr., in *Dylan Thomas: The Poet and His Critics:* "He has been called a pagan, a mystic, and a humanistic agnostic; his God has been identified with Nature, Sex, Love, Process, the Life Force, and with Thomas himself."

On July 11, 1937, Thomas married Caitlin Macnamara; they were penniless and lacked the blessings of their parents. After spending some time with each of their reluctant families, they moved to a borrowed house in Laugharne, Wales. This fishing village became their permanent address, though they lived in many temporary dwellings in England and Wales through the war years and after, until Thomas's death in 1953. The borrowing of houses and money became recurring events in their married life together. Korg associated these external circumstances in the poet's life with his artistic development: "Thomas's time of settling in Laugharne coincides roughly with the period when his poetry began to turn outward; his love for Caitlin, the birth of his first child, Llewellyn, responses to the Welsh countryside and its people, and ultimately events of the war began to enter his poetry as visible subjects."

Thomas's third book, *The Map of Love,* appeared in August, 1939, the year war broke out in Europe. It comprised a strange union of sixteen poems and seven stories, the stories having been previously published in periodicals. The volume was a commercial failure, perhaps because of the war. Ferris reported that "the book was respectfully and sometimes warmly reviewed, with a few dissenters"; yet these works of Thomas's middle period are his least successful. The short stories are inferior to those that appeared the next year in *Portrait of the Artist as a Young Dog.* They are mannered, misty, cumbersome—dealing often with dreams and vague imaginings. Some of these stories have been called surrealistic, opening up a vein of controversy, since Thomas often disavowed his use of surrealism. Annis Pratt, in *Dylan Thomas's Early Prose,* suggested that although surrealistic features exist in the stories, Thomas exercised careful control over his material. She quoted Thomas on this point: "I do not mind from where the images of a poem are dragged up; drag them up, if you like, from the nethermost sea of the hidden self; but, before they reach paper, they must go through all the rational processes of the intellect."

In sharp contrast to the stories in *The Map of Love* are those published the following year, 1940, in *Portrait of the Artist as a Young Dog.* Thomas claimed in a letter to Vernon Watkins that he "kept the flippant title for—as the publishers advise—money-making reasons." He also said that the title was not a parody of James Joyce's *A Portrait of the Artist as a Young Man*—a dubious proposition—though he did acknowledge the general influence of Joyce's *Dubliners.* These Thomas stories are different from the earlier ones in their particularity of character and place, their straightforward plot lines, and their relevance to Thomas's childhood in Wales. Thomas wrote to Watkins in August, 1939: "I've been busy over stories, pot-boiling stories for a book, semi-autobiographical, to be finished by Christmas."

Reviews of the book were mixed, and it didn't sell well at the time, though it later became enormously popular. According to Ferris, a reviewer for the *Times Literary Supplement* found that "the atmosphere of schoolboy smut and practical jokes and poetry is evoked with lingering accuracy but with nothing more." Subsequent critics have detected more in the stories, though most agree that Thomas is primarily a poet and only secondarily a writer of fiction. Korg commented that "taken as a group, [the stories] seem to trace the child's emergence from his domain of imagination and secret pleasures into an adult world where he observes suffering, pathos, and dignity." Two of the more successful stories in the collection are "The Peaches"—the first story—and "One Warm Saturday"—the last.

In 1940 Thomas began writing *Adventures in the Skin Trade,* a novel that he never completed, though its first section was subsequently published. It is essentially the time-honored story of a country boy in the big city. Pratt commented that Thomas intended the story to be "a series of 'adventures' in which the hero's 'skins' would be stripped off one by one like a snake's until he was left in a kind of quintessential nakedness to face the world."

Thomas's work next saw publication in a 1946 poetry collection, *Deaths and Entrances,* containing many of his most famous poems. This volume included such works as "A Refusal to Mourn the Death, by Fire, of a Child in London," "Poem in October," "The Hunchback in the Park," and "Fern Hill." *Deaths and Entrances* was an instant success. Ferris noted that three thousand copies sold in the first month after its publication and that the publisher, Dent, ordered a reprint of the same number. In *Vision and Rhetoric* G. S. Fraser said of the volume that "it increases the impression of variety and of steady development, which the earlier volumes, read in the order of their appearance, give." T. H. Jones, in his *Dylan Thomas,* declared the volume to be the core of Thomas's achievement. The poems of *Deaths and Entrances,* while still provoking arguments about interpretation, are less compressed and less obscure than the earlier works. Some, like "Fern Hill," illustrate an almost Wordsworthian harmony with nature and other human beings but not without the sense of the inexorability of time. As Korg said of these poems, "the figures and landscapes have a new solidity, a new self-sufficiency, and

the dialectic vision no longer penetrates them as though they were no more than windows opening on a timeless universe."

By the time of the publication of *Deaths and Entrances* Thomas had become a living legend. Through his very popular readings and recordings of his own work, this writer of sometimes obscure poetry gained mass appeal. For many, he came to represent the figure of the bard, the singer of songs to his people. Kershner asserted that Thomas "became the wild man from the West, the Celtic bard with the magical rant, a folk figure with racial access to roots of experience which more civilized Londoners lacked." His drinking, his democratic tendencies, and the frank sexual imagery of his poetry made him the focal point of an ill-defined artistic rebellion.

In 1949 Thomas and his family moved to the Boat House of Laugharne, Wales, a house provided for them by one of Thomas's benefactors, Mrs. Margaret Taylor. For the last four years of his life he moved between this dwelling and the United States, where he went on four separate tours to read his poetry and receive the adulation of the American public. The often sordid accounts of these tours are provided in John Malcolm Brinnin's *Dylan Thomas in America.* Thomas's last separate volume of poetry before the *Collected Poems, 1934-1952* (1952) was *Country Sleep,* published by New Directions in the United States in 1952. As originally published, this book contained six of the poet's most accomplished works: "Over Sir John's Hill," "Poem on his Birthday," "Do not go gentle into that good night," "Lament," "In the white giant's thigh," and "In country sleep." Concerning this volume, Rushworth M. Kidder commented in *Dylan Thomas: The Country of the Spirit* that "the fact of physical death seems to present itself to the poet as something more than distant event. . . . These poems come to terms with death through a form of worship: not propitiatory worship of Death as deity, but worship of a higher Deity by whose power all things, including death, are controlled." Tindall called these poems "Thomas at his mellowest." In "Do not go gentle into that good night," a poem written during his father's illness and in anticipation of his death, the son exhorts the father to affirm life in his dying. Similarly, though the women of "In the white giant's thigh" have died childless, the poet, as Korg pointed out, "memorializes their vitality by means of the paradox that their fertility survives through the memory of their many loves."

It has already been mentioned that Thomas began writing scripts during the war. Several of his film scripts have been published, including *The Doctor and the Devils* and *The Beach at Falesa.* Neither of these was produced, but they gave Thomas the opportunity to develop his dramatic skills. These skills culminated in his radio play, *Under Milk Wood,* written over a long period of time and frantically revised in America during the last months of his life. The play grew out of the story "Quite Early One Morning," which was broadcast by the BBC in 1945. *Under Milk Wood* is set in a small Welsh town called Llareggub and covers one day in the lives of its provincial characters. These characters are disembodied voices who reveal their nighttime dreams and their daily monotonous lives. Richard Morton, in *An Outline of the Works of Dylan Thomas,* commented that "the trivialities of small-town life are more than evocative, however; they are presented to us in ceremonial order, as though they have a kind of esoteric significance." The characters in the play are satisfied with their lives, and Thomas himself seems to accept and affirm their rural simplicity. Raymond Williams, in an essay for *Dylan Thomas: A Collection of Critical Essays,* said that *Under Milk Wood* is "not a mature work, but the retained extravagance of an adolescent's imaginings. Yet it moves, at its best, into a genuine involvement, an actual sharing of experience, which is not the least of its dramatic virtues." Thomas read the play as a solo performance in Cambridge, Massachusetts, on May 3, 1953; the first group reading was on May 14. In the following November, Dylan Thomas died in New York of ailments complicated by alcohol and drug abuse.

Publication of the rest of Thomas's BBC work occurred in 1992 with the release of *On The Air With Dylan Thomas: The Broadcasts.* This volume includes all of Thomas's radio work with the exception of *Under Milk Wood.* Peter Thorpe, writing for the *Bloomsbury Review* noted the immense power of Thomas's voice during these broadcasts, which "[tended] to overwhelm us with its incantational rhythms, its intoxicating iterations." Thorpe commented that the advantage of having these works in print "is that it allows his 'senior' followers . . . to assess a significant part of his work with the eye rather than the ear."

BIOGRAPHICAL/CRITICAL SOURCES:

BOOKS

Ackerman, John, *A Dylan Thomas Companion: Life, Poetry, And Prose,* Macmillan (Basingstoke, Hampshire), 1994.
Brinnin, John Malcolm, *Dylan Thomas in America,* Atlantic/ Little, Brown, 1955.
Brinnin, John Malcolm, editor, *A Casebook on Dylan Thomas,* Crowell, 1960.
Burdette, Robert K., *The Saga of Prayer: The Poetry of Dylan Thomas,* Crowell, 1960.
Cox, C. B., editor, *Dylan Thomas: A Collection of Critical Essays,* Prentice-Hall, 1966.
Dictionary of Literary Biography, Gale (Detroit), Volume 13: *British Dramatists since World War II,* 1982; Volume 20: *British Poets, 1914-1945,* 1983.
Emery, Clark, *The World of Dylan Thomas,* University of Miami Press, 1962.
Farringdon, J. M., and M. G., *A Concordance and Word Lists to the Poems of Dylan Thomas,* Ariel House, 1980.
Ferris, Paul, *Dylan Thomas,* Dial, 1977.
Ferris, Paul, *The Life of Caitlin Thomas,* Pimlico (London), 1995.
FitzGibbon, Constantine, *The Life of Dylan Thomas,* Little, Brown, 1965.
FitzGibbon, Constantine, editor, *Selected Letters of Dylan Thomas,* New Directions, 1967.
Fraser, G. S., *Vision and Rhetoric,* Faber, 1959.
Jones, T. H., *Dylan Thomas,* Barnes and Noble, 1963.
Kershner, R. B., Jr., *Dylan Thomas: The Poet and His Critics,* American Library Association, 1976.
Kidder, Rushworth M., *Dylan Thomas: The Country of the Spirit,* Princeton University Press, 1973.
Korg, Jacob, *Dylan Thomas,* Twayne, 1965.
Lane, Gary, *A Concordance to the Poems of Dylan Thomas,* Scarecrow Press, 1976.
Maud, Ralph, *Wales in His Arms: Dylan Thomas's Choice of Poetry,* University of Wales Press (Cardiff), 1994.
Morton, Richard, *An Outline of the Works of Dylan Thomas,* Forum House, 1970.
Olson, Elder, *The Poetry of Dylan Thomas,* University of Chicago Press, 1954.
Parekh, Pushpa Naidu, *Response to Failure: Poetry of Gerald Manley Hopkins, Francis Thompson, Lionel Johnson, and Dylan Thomas,* Lang (New York City), 1996.
Pratt, Annis, *Dylan Thomas's Early Prose: A Study in Creative Mythology,* University of Pittsburgh Press, 1970.
Stanford, Derek, *Dylan Thomas,* Neville Spearman, revised edition, 1964.
Tindall, William York, *A Reader's Guide to Dylan Thomas,* Farrar, Straus, 1962.
Treece, Henry, *Dylan Thomas: "Dog Among the Fairies,"* Benn, 1956.
Twentieth-Century Literary Criticism, Gale, Volume 1, 1978; Volume 8, 1982; Volume 45, 1992.

PERIODICALS

Bloomsbury Review, October/November, 1992, p. 16.
Booklist, April 1, 1992.
Library Journal, May 1, 1993, p. 118; November 15, 1995, p. 75.
Los Angeles Times, May 21, 1989.
New York Times, November 10, 1953; March 1, 1989; February 23, 1990; June 18, 1996, p. B3.
Observer (London), November 15, 1953.
People Weekly, December 19, 1994, p. 33.
Publishers Weekly, February 17, 1992, p. 56; March 15, 1993, p. 84.
Southern Review, October, 1967.
Spectator (London), November 13, 1953.
Studies in Short Fiction, fall, 1969; winter, 1969; spring, 1994, p. 265.
Time, November 16, 1953.
Times (London), November 10, 1953.
Wall Street Journal, June 8, 1967.
Washington Post Book World, April 18, 1993, p. 12.

*   *   *

THOMAS, Joyce Carol 1938-

PERSONAL: Born May 25, 1938, in Ponca City, OK; daughter of Floyd David (a bricklayer) and Leona (a housekeeper and hair stylist; maiden name, Thompson) Haynes; married Gettis L. Withers (a chemist), May 31, 1959 (divorced, 1968); married Roy T. Thomas, Jr. (a professor), September 7, 1968 (divorced, 1979); children: Monica Pecot, Gregory Withers, Michael Withers, Roy T. Thomas III. *Education:* Attended San Francisco City College, 1957-58, and University of San Francisco, 1957-58; College of San Mateo, A.A., 1964; San Jose State College (now University), B.A., 1966; Stanford University, M.A., 1967.

ADDRESSES: Home—Berkeley, CA. *Agent*—Jack Z. Tantleff, 375 Greenwich St., Suite 700, New York, NY 10013.

CAREER: Worked as a telephone operator in San Francisco, CA, 1957-58; Ravenwood School District, East Palo Alto, CA, teacher of French and Spanish, 1968-70; San Jose State College (now University), San Jose, CA, assistant professor of black studies, 1969-72, reading program director, 1979-82, professor of English, 1982-83; Contra Costa College, San Pablo, CA, teacher of drama and English, 1973-75; St. Mary's College, Moranga, CA, professor of English, 1975-77; full-time writer, 1982–. Visiting associate professor of English at Purdue University, spring, 1983; full professor of English, University of Tennessee, 1989–.

MEMBER: Dramatists Guild, Authors Guild, Authors League of America.

AWARDS, HONORS: Danforth Graduate Fellow, University of California at Berkeley, 1973-75; Stanford University scholar, 1979-80, and Djerassi Fellow, 1982 and 1983; *New York Times* outstanding book of the year citation, American Library Association (ALA) best book citation, and Before Columbus American Book Award, Before Columbus Foundation (Berkeley, CA), all 1982, and National Book Award for children's fiction, 1983, all for *Marked by Fire;* Coretta Scott King Honor Book Award, ALA, 1984, for *Bright Shadow;* named Outstanding Woman of the Twentieth Century, Sigma Gamma Rho, 1986; *A Gathering of Flowers: Stories about Being Young in America* was a National Conference of Christians and Jews recommended title for children and young adults, 1991; Coretta Scott King Honor Book Award, ALA, and Notable Children's Trade Book in the field of social studies, National Council for Social Studies and Children's Book Council, both 1994, for *Brown Honey in Broomwheat Tea.*

WRITINGS:

YOUNG ADULT NOVELS

Marked by Fire, Avon (New York City), 1982.
Bright Shadow (sequel to *Marked by Fire*), Avon, 1983.
Water Girl, Avon, 1986.
The Golden Pasture, Scholastic (New York City), 1986.
Journey, Scholastic, 1990.
When the Nightingale Sings, HarperCollins (New York City), 1992.
I Have Heard of a Land, illustrated by Floyd Cooper, HarperCollins Juvenile, 1998.
Cherish Me, HarperCollins, 1998.

POETRY

Bittersweet, Firesign Press, 1973.
Crystal Breezes, Firesign Press, 1974.
Blessing, Jocato Press, 1975.
Black Child, illustrated by Tom Feelings, Zamani Productions, 1981.
Inside the Rainbow, Zikawana Press, 1982.
Brown Honey in Broomwheat Tea, illustrated by Floyd Cooper, HarperCollins, 1993.
Gingerbread Days, illustrated by Cooper, HarperCollins, 1995.
The Blacker and the Berry: Poems, HarperCollins (New York City), 1997.
Crowning of Glory: Poems, HarperCollins, 1997.

PLAYS

(And producer) *A Song in the Sky* (two-act), produced in San Francisco at Montgomery Theater, 1976.
Look! What a Wonder! (two-act), produced in Berkeley at Berkeley Community Theatre, 1976.
(And producer) *Magnolia* (two-act), produced in San Francisco at Old San Francisco Opera House, 1977.
(And producer) *Ambrosia* (two-act), produced in San Francisco at Little Fox Theatre, 1978.
Gospel Roots (two-act), produced in Carson, CA, at California State University, 1981.
I Have Heard of a Land, produced in Oklahoma City, OK, at Claussen Theatre, 1989, published by HarperCollins (New York), 1997.
When the Nightingale Sings (musical; based on Thomas's novel of the same title), produced in Knoxville, TN, at Clarence Brown Theatre, 1991.

OTHER

(Editor) *A Gathering of Flowers: Stories about Being Young in America,* HarperCollins, 1990.

Contributor to periodicals, including *American Poetry Review, Black Scholar, Calafia, Drum Voices, Giant Talk,* and *Yardbird Reader.* Editor of *Ambrosia* (women's newsletter), 1980.

MEDIA ADAPTATIONS: Marked by Fire was adapted by James Racheff and Ted Kociolek for the stage musical *Abyssinia,* first produced in New York City at the C.S.C. Repertory Theatre in 1987.

SIDELIGHTS: Joyce Carol Thomas's background as a migrant farm worker in rural Oklahoma and California supplies her with the prolific stock of characters and situations that fill her novels. The author admittedly fell in love with words and with the songs she heard in church, and has spent much of her time as a writer trying to recreate the sounds of singing with her written language. She is well known for her book of poems *Brown Honey in Broomwheat Tea;* her ground-breaking anthology, *A Gathering of Flowers: Stories about Being Young in America;* and her young adult novels *Marked by Fire* and *Bright Shadow,* which are set in Thomas's hometown and focus on the indomitable spirit of Abyssinia Jackson and her people.

Thomas grew up in Ponca City, Oklahoma, a small, dusty town where she lived across from the school. "Although now I live half a continent away from my hometown," Thomas related in *Something about the Author Autobiography Series* (*SAAS*), "when it comes to my writing I find that I am still there." She has set three of her novels in her hometown: *Marked by Fire, Bright Shadow,* and *The Golden Pasture.*

When Thomas was ten years old, the family moved to rural Tracy, California. There Thomas learned to milk cows, fish for minnows, and harvest tomatoes and grapes. She also became intimately acquainted with black widow spiders—there was a nest of them under her bed. She was later to use this experience in her novel *Journey.* Likewise, she had a similar experience with wasps when her brother locked her in a closet containing a wasp nest; *Marked by Fire* contains some scary scenes with these insects.

In Tracy, California, Thomas continued her long summers harvesting crops. She worked beside many Mexicans and began a love affair with their language. "When the Spanish speakers talked they seemed to sing," Thomas remarked in *SAAS.* When she went to college—which she managed to do by working full-time as a telephone operator as well as raising her children—she majored in Spanish and French. "From this base of languages I taught myself all I know about writing," she related in *SAAS.* She went on to earn a master's degree from Stanford University, and then taught foreign languages in public school.

From 1973 to 1978, Thomas wrote poetry and plays for adults and became a celebrated author. She traveled to conferences and festivals all over the world, including Lagos, Nigeria. In 1982, Thomas's career took a turn when she published *Marked by Fire,* a novel for a young adult audience. Steeped in the setting and traditions of her hometown, the novel focuses on Abyssinia Jackson, a girl who was born in a cotton field during harvest time. The title refers to the fact that she received a burn on her face from a brush fire during her birth. This leaves her "marked for unbearable pain and unspeakable joy," according to the local healer.

The pain begins when Abyssinia is raped by an elder in the church when she is ten. Abby becomes mute after the violent act and is nursed back to health through the strength of the local women and her family. Abby's mother is named Patience in honor of Thomas's mother, who was a very patient parent. Strong, the father, has left the family in their time of need, but returns to them later—ironically—because he is not strong enough to face a crisis in his life. When Abby eventually regains her voice, she is able to tell her friend Lily Norene that after the rape she "felt dirty. Dirtier than playing in mud. The kind of dirt you can't ever wash off. . . . But the worst part was I felt like I was being spit on by God." It is the seeming abandonment by God that strikes Abby to the core—she must work through the horror before she can recover completely. Mother Barker, the town's midwife and healer, has a special role in the rehabilitation of Abby. In a more macabre way, so does Trembling Sally, a frightening, crazy woman who assaults the young girl with strange trials of fire, water, and insects. Eventually, Abby recovers with Mother Barker's help.

Marked by Fire has been well received by critics. Wendell Wray wrote in *Best Sellers* that Thomas "captures the flavor of black folk life in Oklahoma. . . . [She] has set for herself a very challenging task. . . . [But] Thomas' book works." Critic Dorothy Randall-Tsuruta commented in *Black Scholar* that Thomas's "poetic tone gives this work what scents give the roses already so pleasing in color. In fact often as not the lyrical here carries the reader beyond concerns for fast action. There too Thomas's short lived interest in writing plays figures in her fine regard and control of dialog." Hazel Rochman, writing in *School Library Journal,* admitted that "the lack of a fast-paced narrative line and the mythical overtones may present obstacles to some readers," but said that "many will be moved" by Abby's story.

The book was placed on required reading lists at many high schools and universities. Commenting on her stormy novel, Thomas once stated that "as a writer I work to create books filled with conflict. . . . I address this quest in part by matching the pitiful absurdities and heady contradictions of life itself, in part by leading the heroine to twin fountains of magic and the macabre, and evoking the holy and the horrible in the same breath. Nor is it ever enough to match these. Through the character of Abyssinia, I strive for what is beyond these, seeking, as do many writers, to find newer worlds."

Bright Shadow, a sequel to *Marked by Fire,* was published in 1983. In this work, Abyssinia goes to college and ends up falling in love with Carl Lee Jefferson. Abby is a young woman now, searching for what she wants as she completes her pre-medical studies. For reasons she can't figure out, Abby's father disapproves of Carl Lee. She suspects, however, that it is because of Carl Lee's alcoholic father. At the same time, the psychically sensitive Abby begins to have forebodings about her aunt's new husband. These feelings are validated when Aunt Serena is found brutally murdered.

Carl Lee begins to show his true colors when he is there to support Abby through her grief. Soon he has a revelation of his own when he finds out that the mysterious Cherokee woman that has been lurking around town is actually his mother. Despite these difficult hurdles, nothing is able to disrupt the young couple's love and support for one another. It is because of Carl Lee that Abby finds the light when all she can see are the dark shadows of her aunt's death. *Bright Shadow* concludes when Abby has a dream in which her aunt revisits her and gives her a lesson: "We are all taken from the same source: pain and beauty. One is the chrysalis that gives to the other some gift that even in death creates a new dimension in life."

Critical reaction to *Bright Shadow* was generally more mixed than for *Marked by Fire. School Library Journal* contributor Carolyn Caywood found the plot of *Bright Shadow* touched with melodrama and lacking in credibility, but admitted that Thomas's "story is readable and her sensuously descriptive passages celebrating the

physical beauty of the black characters are a nice touch." In the *Bulletin of the Center for Children's Books,* Zena Sutherland said that *Bright Shadow* as "a love story . . . is appealing, and the characterization is strong." However, she felt that "the often-ornate phraseology" sometimes weakens the story.

Several of Thomas's later books also feature the popular characters she created in *Marked by Fire* and *Bright Shadow,* including *The Golden Pasture,* which journeys back to Carl Lee's earlier life on his grandfather's ranch, and *Water Girl,* which tells the story of Abyssinia's teenage daughter Amber.

In 1990 Thomas edited the well-received anthology, *A Gathering of Flowers: Stories about Being Young in America.* The characters in these pieces represent various ethnic groups, including Native Americans, Asians, Hispanics, African Americans, and Anglos, and the authors include Gerald Vizenor, Jeanne Wakatsuki Houston, and Gary Soto. A critic noted in the *Bulletin of the Center for Children's Books* that "The collection is indeed rich and colorful, containing strong individual voices." *Voice of Youth Advocates* reviewer Judith A. Sheriff declared, "These stories will provide young adults with authentic glimpses of ethnic worlds they may seldom encounter personally."

In 1992 Thomas published *When the Nightingale Sings,* a young adult novel about the orphaned Marigold. The fourteen-year-old girl—a talented gospel singer—is living with a foster mother whose verbal abuse and bad temper make her less than an ideal parent. Although she is forced to spend her time cleaning and giving singing lessons to Ruby's unlikable children, Marigold resists believing in her foster mother's insults and instead concentrates on her singing. When the members of the Rose of Sharon Baptist Church hear her voice in the distance, their search for a new lead gospel singer just might be over. Although *Bulletin of the Center for Children's Books* contributor Betsy Hearne found the book's realistic plot to be at odds with its "fairy tale tone," Hazel S. Moore commented in *Voice of Youth Advocates,* "The element of suspension carries the story back to its roots—the African American family deeply involved with the African American Church."

Thomas's award-winning 1993 work, *Brown Honey in Broomwheat Tea,* is a collection of poetry illustrated by Floyd Cooper. *School Library Journal* reviewer Lyn Miller-Lachmann described it as "twelve short, interrelated poems about family, love, and African-American identity" which "are accessible, lyrical, and moving, with thought-provoking phrases and images." In the course of the book a family battles poverty and growing pains with love and pride. Cathy Collison, writing in the *Detroit Free Press,* commented on the recurring imagery that links the pieces: "The poems return often to tea, brewing the words into a blend as rich and seasoned as the warm Cooper portrait of a grandmother."

In 1995 Thomas and Cooper produced a companion volume to *Brown Honey in Broomwheat Tea* titled *Gingerbread Days.* Like its predecessor, *Gingerbread Days* contains twelve poems dealing with love and family in an African-American setting, but in this case the poems all relate to a month of the year. The narrator of the poems is a young boy, and as each month passes he learns valuable lessons about the love of his parents and grandparents, the independence of his sister, and the bonds of family. Critics praised Thomas for her restrained, inspirational verse and remarked that *Gingerbread Days* is a worthy successor to *Brown Honey in Broomwheat.*

With her imagination and ability to bring authenticity to her novels, Thomas has been highly praised and often compared to other successful African-American women authors, like Maya Angelou, Toni Morrison, and Alice Walker. Thomas takes scenes and characters from her youth and crafts them into powerful fiction. "If I had to give advice to young people," Thomas commented in her *SAAS* essay, "it would be that whatever your career choice, prepare yourself to do it well. Quality takes talent and time. Believe in your dreams. Have faith in yourself. Keep working and enjoying today even as you reach for tomorrow. If you choose to write, value your experiences. And color them in the indelible ink of your own background."

BIOGRAPHICAL/CRITICAL SOURCES:

BOOKS

Authors and Artists for Young Adults, Volume 12, Gale (Detroit), 1994.
Children's Literature Review, Volume 19, Gale, 1990.
Contemporary Literary Criticism, Volume 35, Gale, 1985.
Dictionary of Literary Biography, Volume 33: *Afro-American Fiction Writers after 1955,* Gale, 1984.
Pearlman, Mickey, and Katherine U. Henderson, editors, *Inter/view: Talks with America's Writing Women,* University Press of Kentucky, 1990.
Something about the Author Autobiography Series, Volume 7, Gale, 1989, pp. 299-311.
Yalom, Margaret, editor, *Women Writers of the West,* Capra Press, 1982.

PERIODICALS

Best Sellers, June, 1982, pp. 123-24.
Black Scholar, summer, 1982, p. 48.
Booklist, September 15, 1995, p. 176.
Bulletin of the Center for Children's Books, February, 1984, p. 119; January, 1991; February, 1993, p. 194.
Detroit Free Press, December 22, 1993.
Horn Book Magazine, March-April, 1996, p. 219.
New Directions, January/February, 1984.
Publishers Weekly, October 11, 1993, p. 87; September 25, 1995, p. 57.
San Francisco Chronicle, April 12, 1982.
School Library Journal, March, 1982, p. 162; January, 1984, pp. 89-90; November, 1993; January, 1996, p. 107.
Voice of Youth Advocates, December, 1990; June, 1993, p. 96.
Wilson Library Bulletin, June, 1994, p. 136.

*   *   *

THOMAS, Lewis 1913-1993

PERSONAL: Born November 25, 1913, in Flushing, NY; died December 3, 1993; son of Joseph S. (a surgeon) and Grace Emma (Peck) Thomas; married Beryl Dawson, January 1, 1941; children: Abigail, Judith, Eliza. *Education:* Princeton University, B.S., 1933; Harvard University, M.D., 1937.

CAREER: Boston City Hospital, Boston, MA, intern, 1937-39; Neurological Institute, New York City, resident in neurology, 1939-41; Boston City Hospital, Tilney Memorial Fellow at Thorndike Laboratory, 1941-42; Rockefeller Institute for Medical Research, New York City, visiting investigator, 1942-46; Johns Hopkins University, Baltimore, MD, assistant professor of pediatrics, 1946-48; Tulane University, New Orleans, LA, associate professor, 1948-50, professor of medicine, 1950, director of

Division of Infectious Disease, 1948-50; University of Minnesota, Minneapolis, professor of pediatrics and medicine and director of pediatric research laboratories at Heart Hospital, 1950-54; New York University, New York City, professor of pathology, 1954-69, head of department, 1954-58, director of University Hospital, 1959-66, dean of School of Medicine, 1966-69; Yale University, New Haven, CT, professor of pathology and head of department, 1969-72, dean of School of Medicine, 1971-73; Memorial Sloan-Kettering Cancer Center, New York City, president and chief executive officer, 1973-80, chancellor, 1980-83, emeritus president and member of Sloan-Kettering Institute, 1983-93.

Professor at Cornell University; adjunct professor at Rockefeller University (also member of board of trustees); member of board of overseers of Harvard University, 1976-82; member of scientific advisory board of C. V. Whitney Laboratory for Experimental Marine Biology and Medicine, at University of Florida, 1976-93; member of council of visitors of Bank Street College of Education, 1975-93; associate fellow of Ezra Stiles College, Yale University. Pediatrician at Harriet Lane Home for Invalid Children, of Johns Hopkins University, 1946-48; director of medical divisions at Bellevine Hospital, 1958-66, president of Medical Board, 1963-66; chief of pathology at Yale-New Haven Hospital, 1969-73; attending physician at Memorial Hospital; member of scientific advisory committee of Massachusetts General Hospital, 1969-72; member of scientific advisory board of Scripps Clinic and Research Foundation, 1973-78. Member of board of directors of New York City Public Health Research Institute, 1960-69; member of board of trustees of C. S. Draper Laboratory, 1974-81, Cold Spring Harbor Laboratory, 1974-93, and Hellenic Anticancer Institute (Athens), 1977-93; member of scientific advisory committee of Fox Chase Institute for Cancer Research, 1976-93; member of scientific council of International Institute of Cellular and Molecular Pathology (Brussels), 1977-93. Member of Commission on Streptococcal and Staphylococcal Diseases, of U.S. Department of Defense's Armed Forces Epidemiological Board, 1950-62; member of New York City Board of Health, 1955-60, and Health Research Council, 1974-75 (head of narcotics advisory committee, 1961-63); member of National Advisory Health Council, 1958-62, and National Advisory Child Health and Human Development Council, 1963-67; member of President's Science Advisory Committee, 1967-70; head of National Academy of Sciences committee to review national cancer plan, 1972; member of special medical advisory group to U.S. Veterans Administration. Member of board of trustees of Guggenheim Foundation, 1975-85, and board of directors of Squibb Corp., 1969-93, and Josiah Macy, Jr. Foundation, 1975-84. *Military service:* U.S. Naval Reserve, Medical Corps, active duty, 1941-46; became lieutenant commander.

MEMBER: International Academy of Pathology, Association of American Physicians, American Academy and Institute of Arts and Letters (inducted, 1984), American Pediatric Society, American Association of Immunologists, Society for Experimental Biology and Medicine, American Academy of Microbiology (charter member), American Rheumatism Association, American Society for Clinical Investigation, National Academy of Sciences Institute of Medicine (member of council, 1973-76), American Philosophical Society, American Academy of Arts and Sciences, American Association of University Professors, Peripatetic Clinical Society, Practitioners Society, Harvey Society, Interurban Clinical Club, Phi Beta Kappa, Alpha Omega Alpha, Century Association, Harvard Club.

AWARDS, HONORS: Honorary degrees include M.A. from Yale University, 1969, Sc.D. from University of Rochester, 1974, Princeton University, 1976, Medical College of Ohio, 1976, Columbia University, 1978, Williams College, 1982, and University of Illinois, 1989, LL.D. from Johns Hopkins University, 1976, L.H.D. from Duke University, 1976, Reed College, 1977, and Mt. Sinai School of Medicine, 1990; National Book Award in Arts and Letters, 1974, for *The Lives of a Cell;* distinguished achievement award from *Modern Medicine,* 1975; visiting scholar of Phi Beta Kappa, 1977-78; American Academy and Institute of Arts and Letters award, 1980; American Book Award for science, 1981, for *The Medusa and the Snail;* Richard Hopper Day Award, Philadelphia Academy of Natural Sciences, 1985; Milton Helpern Memorial Award, 1986; Alfred P. Sloan, Jr. Memorial Award, 1987; William B. Coley Award, Cancer Research Institute, 1987; Public Service Award, American Society for Experiential Biology, 1988; Honor Award for Science and Technology, Mayor of New York City, 1989; Loren Eiseley Award, 1990; John Stearns Award, New York Academy of Medicine, 1991; Lewis Thomas Prize, Rockefeller University, 1993.

WRITINGS:

The Lives of a Cell: Notes of a Biology Watcher, Viking, 1974.
The Medusa and the Snail: More Notes of a Biology Watcher, Viking, 1979.
The Youngest Science: Notes of a Medicine-Watcher, Viking, 1983.
Late Night Thoughts on Listening to Mahler's Ninth Symphony, Viking, 1984.
Et Cetera, Et Cetera: Notes of a Word-Watcher, Little, Brown, 1990.
The Fragile Species, Scribner's, 1992.

CONTRIBUTOR

Rheumatic Fever: A Symposium, University of Minnesota Press, 1952.
Gregory Schwartzman, editor, *The Effects of ACTH and Cortisone Upon Infection and Resistance,* Columbia University Press, 1953.
Russell Cecil and R. F. Loeb, editors, *A Textbook of Medicine,* Saunders, 1953.
H. S. Lawrence, editor, *Cellular and Humoral Aspects of the Hypersensitive States,* Paul B. Hoeber, 1959.
Biological Problems of Grafting, Les Congres et Colloques de L'Universite de Liege, 1959.
Streptococcus, Rheumatic Fever, and Glomerulonephritis, Williams & Wilkins, 1964.
W. Braun and M. Landy, editors, *Bacterial Endotoxins,* Rutgers University, Institute of Microbiology, 1964.
The Inflammatory Process, Academic Press, 1965.
The Modern Hospital, McGraw, 1967.
P. A. Miescher, C. Henze, and R. Schett, editors, *The Modern University: Structure, Functions, and Its Role in the New Industrial State,* Georg Thieme Verlag, 1969.
Microbial Toxins, Volume 3, Academic Press, 1970.
G. I. Gallagher, editor, *Immunological Disorders of the Nervous System,* Williams & Wilkins, 1971.
I. Z. Bowers and E. F. Purcell, editors, *Advances in American Medicine: Essays at the Bicentennial,* Josiah Macy, Jr. Foundation, 1976.

Author of column, "Notes of a Biology Watcher," in *New England Journal of Medicine,* 1971-93. Member of editorial board of *Human Pathology, Journal of Immunology, American Journal of Pathology, Cellular Immunology, Journal of Medicine and Philosophy, Inflammation, Perspectives in Biology and Medicine, Human Nature, Journal of Developmental and Comparative Immunology,* and *Daedalus.*

SIDELIGHTS: The observation of the natural world was Lewis Thomas's vocation and avocation. Although his medical specialty was pathology, Thomas's interest was captured by the range of natural phenomena from the unit of the cell to human social patterns. In 1971 he began contributing a popular column, "Notes of a Biology Watcher," to the prestigious *New England Journal of Medicine.* Some of these essays were collected and published in 1974 as *The Lives of a Cell: Notes of a Biology Watcher.* The book, which according to a *Time* reviewer combined wit and "imagination" with a "bold, encouraging vision of both man and nature," received a National Book Award the same year. Critics were dazzled with Thomas's accomplishment, but he was somewhat embarrassed by his newfound status as a book author. "I mean it's not really fair to have a book with a cover and everything when you never wrote a book, except in such little tiny bits," he told Barbara Yuncker. "I love having it, but it doesn't seem as though I'd earned it."

Symbiosis—the mutually beneficial relationship between organisms—is the main theme of *The Lives of a Cell.* "There is a tendency for living things to join up," explains Thomas in the book, "establish linkages, live inside each other, return to earlier arrangements, get along whenever possible. This is the way of the world." He decries man's attempt to remove himself from nature, and concludes that "the whole dear notion of one's own self— marvelous old free-willed, free-enterprising, autonomous, independent, isolated island of a Self—is a myth."

New Yorker reviewer John Updike noted that Thomas's "absorption in the marvels of symbiotic interconnection intoxicates this scientist, and leads him into flights of what must be fantasy." Some of his ideas, Updike commented, seem "more mystical than demonstrable." He continued: "Dr. Thomas has the mystic's urge toward total unity. He views the earth as a single cell in its membrane of atmosphere. . . . Not that he professes any use for old-fashioned supernaturalist religion. Yet his doctrine of universal symbiosis soars with an evangelical exultation, and it is interesting that even his careful prose lapses into the grammar of teleology."

In the *New York Times Book Review,* Joyce Carol Oates pondered how best to praise Thomas's work. She remarked: "A reviewer who concentrates upon Dr. Thomas's effortless, beautifully-toned style, even to the point of claiming that many of the twenty-nine essays in this book are masterpieces of the 'art of the essay,' would direct attention away from the sheer amount of scientific information these slender essays contain. A reviewer who deals with the book as 'science' would be forced, by Dr. Thomas's marvelous use of paradox, to admit that the book might not yield its wisdom at a single reading." She continued: "One might as well rise to the higher speculation that [this book] anticipates the kind of writing that will appear more and more frequently, as scientists take on the language of poetry in order to communicate human truths too mysterious for old-fashioned common sense."

After the publication of *The Lives of a Cell,* more of Thomas's essays were collected in *The Medusa and the Snail: More Notes of a Biology Watcher, The Youngest Science: Notes of a Medicine-Watcher,* and *Late Night Thoughts on Listening to Mahler's Ninth Symphony.* Barbara Brotman wrote in the *Chicago Tribune* of *The Medusa and the Snail,* "Despite all his intense concentration through powerful microscopes at minute particles of life, Thomas never has stopped marveling at the Big Picture, how well everything on this Earth works: the civility of the symbiotic relationship between the sea slug and the jellyfish or medusa, the subject of the title essay, the mysterious way warts can actually be *thought* away, the almost always accurate pinpointing and destruction by our antibodies of foreign cells."

The Fragile Species, published only a year before Thomas's death in 1993, takes a much less optimistic look at some of the problems facing humanity—the "fragile species" of the title. *"The Fragile Species* is striking for the distance its author has traveled from *The Lives of a Cell* and the book that followed it, *The Medusa and the Snail,"* declared Michael Skube in the *Washington Post Book World.* Mass extinction of species, the explosion of the human population—4.5 billion individuals at the time Thomas was writing—and the AIDS epidemic all contributed to the author's anxiety. The volume, concluded Skube, "bespeaks eloquently the interrelatedness of earthly life in all its forms. That some species perish guarantees nothing to the survivors. Dynasties or dinosaurs, we are all guests of the Earth." "But our lives are full of ameliorating circumstances," explains George Klein in a *Nature* review of the work. "The sun is always breaking through the clouds in Thomas's sky."

BIOGRAPHICAL/CRITICAL SOURCES:

BOOKS

Contemporary Literary Criticism, Volume 35, Gale (Detroit), 1985.

PERIODICALS

Booklist, March 15, 1993, p. 1369.
Chicago Tribune, July 11, 1979.
Detroit News, May 27, 1979.
Kliatt, July, 1993, p. 37.
Library Journal, February 1, 1993, p. 134; March 15, 1993, p. 127.
Nature, July 9, 1992, pp. 115-16.
Newsweek, June 24, 1974.
New Yorker, July 15, 1974.
New York Post, June 29, 1974.
New York Review of Books, November 28, 1974.
New York Times, April 27, 1979; February 9, 1983; November 5, 1983.
New York Times Book Review, May 26, 1974.
New York Times Magazine, November 21, 1993, p. 50.
Time, July 22, 1974; May 14, 1979.
Village Voice, June 27, 1974.
Washington Post, August 28, 1979; September 1, 1979.
Washington Post Book World, May 31, 1992, p. 9.

      ✝   ❊   ❊

THOMAS, Paul
See MANN, (Paul) Thomas

      *   *   *

THOMPSON, Francis Clegg
See MENCKEN, H(enry) L(ouis)

THOMPSON, Hunter S(tockton) 1939-

PERSONAL: Born July 18, 1939, in Louisville, KY; son of Jack R. (an insurance agent) and Virginia (Ray) Thompson; married Sandra Dawn, May 19, 1963 (divorced); children: Juan. *Education:* Attended public schools in Louisville, KY; studied journalism at Columbia University. *Politics:* Anarchist. *Religion:* None. *Avocational interests:* Collecting guns.

ADDRESSES: Home—P.O. Box 220, Owl Farm, Woody Creek, CO 81656. *Office*—c/o Janklow & Nesbit, 598 Madison Ave., New York, NY 10022.

CAREER: Writer and journalist. Began as a sports writer in Florida; *Time,* Caribbean correspondent, 1959; *New York Herald Tribune,* Caribbean correspondent, 1959-60; *National Observer,* South American correspondent, 1961-63; *Nation,* West Coast correspondent, 1964-66; *Ramparts,* columnist, 1967-68; *Scanlan's Monthly,* columnist, 1969-70; *Rolling Stone,* national affairs editor, 1970-84; *High Times,* global affairs correspondent, 1977-82; *San Francisco Examiner,* media critic, 1985-90; *Smart,* editor at large, 1988–. Political analyst for various European magazines (including *London Observer, Tempo, Time Out, Das Magazine, Nieuwe Revu,* and *Die Woche*), 1988–. Candidate for sheriff of Pitkin County, CO, 1968; member, Sheriff's Advisory Committee, Pitkin County, 1976-81; executive director, Woody Creek Rod and Gun Club. *Military service:* U.S. Air Force, 1956-58; wrote for base magazine.

MEMBER: Overseas Press Club (executive director), National Press Club, American Civil Liberties Union, Fourth Amendment Foundation (founder), National Rifle Association (executive director), U.S. Naval Institute (executive director), Air Force Association (executive director), National Organization for the Reform of Marijuana Laws (NORML; member of national advisory board, 1976-), Hong Kong Foreign Correspondents Club, Kona Coast Marlin Fisherman's Association, Vincent Black Shadow Society, Key West Mako Club.

WRITINGS:

Hell's Angels: A Strange and Terrible Saga, Random House, 1966.
Fear and Loathing in Las Vegas: A Savage Journey to the Heart of the American Dream, illustrated by Ralph Steadman, Random House, 1972, published with an introduction by P. J. O'Rourke as *Fear and Loathing in Las Vegas and Other American Stories,* Modern Library, 1996.
Fear and Loathing on the Campaign Trail '72, illustrated by Steadman, Straight Arrow Books, 1973.
The Great Shark Hunt: Strange Tales from a Strange Time; Gonzo Papers, Volume One, Summit Books, 1979.
The Curse of Lono, illustrated by Steadman, Bantam, 1983.
(Contributor) Etel Adnan, *Russell Chatham,* Winn Books, 1984.
Generation of Swine: Tales of Shame and Degradation in the '80s; Gonzo Papers, Volume Two, Summit Books, 1988.
(Author of introduction) Steadman, *America,* Fantagraphics Books, 1989.
Songs of the Doomed: More Notes on the Death of the American Dream; Gonzo Papers, Volume Three, Summit Books, 1990.
Silk Road: Thirty-three Years in the Passing Lane, Simon & Schuster, 1990.
Untitled Novel, David McKay, 1992.
Better than Sex: Confessions of a Political Junkie; Gonzo Papers, Volume Four, Random House, 1993.

The Proud Highway: The Saga of a Desperate Southern Gentleman, 1995-1967, Villard (New York City), 1997.
Polo Is My Life, Random House, 1998.

Also author of *Screwjack,* 1991, and novels *Prince Jellyfish,* 1960, and *The Rum Diary,* 1967, excerpts from which appear in *Songs of the Doomed.* Contributor of articles and essays to *Esquire, London Observer, New York Times Magazine, Reporter, Harper's,* and other publications.

MEDIA ADAPTATIONS: Where the Buffalo Roam, filmed in 1980 by Universal and starring Bill Murray, was based on a Thompson character. *Fear and Loathing in Las Vegas* was adapted as a film by Terry Gilliam in 1998, starring Johnny Depp.

SIDELIGHTS: Hunter S. Thompson ranks among the first and foremost practitioners of New Journalism, a genre that evolved in the 1960s to reflect the particular mood of those times. Thompson, who has called his brand of reporting "Gonzo Journalism," was perhaps the most visible—and most vituperative—of the New Journalism correspondents, a group whose ranks included Tom Wolfe and Gay Talese, among others. As national affairs editor for *Rolling Stone,* freelance writer, and author of such widely read books as *Hell's Angels, Fear and Loathing in Las Vegas,* and *Fear and Loathing on the Campaign Trail '72,* Thompson recorded both the disillusionment and the delirium of a volatile era. According to Morris Dickstein in *Gates of Eden: American Culture in the Sixties,* Thompson "paraded one of the few original prose styles of recent years," a style that indulged in insult and stream-of-invective to an unparalleled degree. He pioneered a new approach to reporting, allowing the story of covering an event to become the central story itself, while never disguising the fact that he was "a half-cranked geek journalist caught in the center of the action," to quote Jerome Klinkowitz in *The Life of Fiction.*

Thompson was considered a seasoned journalist while still in his twenties. Between 1959 and 1965 he served as a Caribbean correspondent for *Time* and the *New York Herald Tribune,* as South American correspondent for the *National Observer,* and as contributor to magazines such as the *Nation, Harper's, Reporter* and *Scanlan's Monthly.* His early works were conventional, but as the tenor of the nation began to change (and as his own experiments with drugs increased), he embraced the nascent New Journalism style. *New York Times Book Review* contributor Crawford Woods explains that New Journalism's roots lay in "the particular sense of the nineteen-sixties that a new voice was demanded by the way people's public and private lives were coming together in a sensual panic stew, with murder its meat and potatoes, grass and acid its spice. How to tell the story of a time when all fiction was science fiction, all facts lies? The New Journalism was born." It was a style that "put the pseudo-objective soporifics of the broadsheets to shame by applying to journalism the techniques of the realistic novel," explains Richard Vigilante in *National Review.* "But, at the same time, it required a romance with reality that undermined the ideologues' lust for self-deceit. For all the literary liberties of the most famous New Journalists, their stories, when done right, were more true than traditional journalism."

Riding and drinking with the Hell's Angels motorcycle gang, taking massive quantities of hallucinogenic drugs, and careening to assignments on little food and less sleep, Thompson became the "professional wildman" of the New Journalists, to quote *Village Voice* contributor Vivian Gornick. He also became a nationally known figure whose work "in particular caused currents of envy in the world of the straight journalists, who coveted his freedom

from restraint," according to an *Atlantic* essayist. "He became a cult figure," Peter O. Whitmer writes in *Saturday Review:* "the outlaw who could drink excessively, drug indulgently, shout abusively, *and* write insightfully."

In *Critique,* John Hellmann writes: "By conceiving his journalism as a form of fiction, Thompson has been able to shape actual events into meaningful works of literary art." Thompson's "Gonzo Journalism" narratives are first-person accounts in which the author appears as a persona—sometimes Raoul Duke, but more commonly Dr. Hunter S. Thompson, a specialist variously in divinity, pharmaceuticals, or reporting. Hellmann describes this self-caricature in his book *Fables of Fact: The New Journalism as New Fiction.* It is "a paradox of compulsive violence and outraged innocence, an emblem of the author's schizophrenic view of America. . . . But the persona also has a determined belief in the power of good intentions and right methods which runs counter to his violent impulses. Despite the psychotic threatening, his artistic aims include the corrective impulse of satire."

To research *Hell's Angels: A Strange and Terrible Saga,* Thompson's 1966 account of the infamous California motorcycle gang, the young author rode with the Angels for almost a year, recording their road rallies, their home lives, and their sexual adventures. The book strives to present the gang objectively while exposing the fact that its brutal reputation was primarily the creation of the scandal-mongering media. *New Republic* contributor Richard M. Elman observes that in *Hell's Angels* Thompson has "managed to correct many popular misconceptions about [the Angels], and in the process, provided his readers with a tendentious but informative participant-observer study of those who are doomed to lose." In the *Nation,* Elmer Bendiner likewise notes that throughout the book "Thompson's point of view remains eminently sane and honest. He does not weep for the Angels or romanticize them or glorify them. Neither does he despise them. Instead, he views them as creatures of an irresponsible society, given their image by an irresponsible press, embodying the nation's puerile fantasy life. He sees the menace not so much in the Hell's Angels themselves, as in the poverty of spirit and perennial adolescence that spawned them." *Hell's Angels* has garnered a mixture of critical reactions. *Atlantic* correspondent Oscar Handlin contends that Thompson's "lurid narrative, despite its sympathy for his subjects, reveals the threat they pose." Conversely, William Hogan in *Saturday Review* calls the work "a jarring piece of contemporary Californiana, as well as an examination of a weird branch of present-day show business." According to Elman, Thompson's "fascinating invocation to, evocation *of,* and reportage *about* the Hell's Angels . . . is certainly the most informative, thorough, and vividly written account of this phenomenon yet to appear."

In 1972 Thompson published *Fear and Loathing in Las Vegas,* an all-out display of Gonzo that remains his best-known work. Hellmann describes the book in *Fables of Fact:* "*Fear and Loathing in Las Vegas* is, in barest outline, the author's purported autobiographical confession of his failure to fulfill the magazine's assignment to 'cover' two events in Las Vegas, the Fourth Annual 'Mint 400' motorcycle desert race and the National Conference of District Attorneys Seminar on Narcotics and Dangerous Drugs. It is more exactly the author's (or 'Raoul Duke's') tale of his hallucinations and adventures. . . . The book is, then, even in its most general subject and presentation, either a report of an actual experience which was largely fantasy or an actual fantasy which is disguised as report."

In the guise of Raoul Duke, Thompson relates a series of episodic adventures revolving around drug use and *carte blanche* access to Las Vegas's finest hotels, accompanied by a three-hundred-pound Samoan attorney called Dr. Gonzo (based on Thompson's friend Oscar Zeta Acosta) who "serves as a parody of noble savage 'sidekicks' from Chingachgook to Tonto," according to Hellmann. *National Observer* contributor Michael Putney calls the book "a trip, literally and figuratively, all the way to bad craziness and back again. It is also the most brilliant piece of writing about the dope subculture since Tom Wolfe's *Electric Kool-Aid Acid Test* and, at the same time, an acid, wrenchingly funny portrait of straight America's most celebrated and mean-spirited pleasure-dome, Las Vegas."

Thompson continues to explore "the politics of unreason" in his 1973 book, *Fear and Loathing on the Campaign Trail '72,* a collection of articles that first appeared in *Rolling Stone* magazine. *Nation* correspondent Steven d'Arazien calls the work "a New Journalism account of the [1972 presidential] campaign from before New Hampshire to Miami and beyond. . . . It will be regarded as a classic in the genre." As national affairs editor for *Rolling Stone,* Thompson travelled with the press corps that followed George McGovern; Dickstein notes that the author "recorded the nuts and bolts of a presidential campaign with all the contempt and incredulity that other reporters must feel but censor out." According to Jules Witcover in *Progressive* magazine, the book's "heavily personalized writing-on-the-run, riddled here and there by the clear eye of hindsight, does convey an honest picture of a political writer picking his way through all the hoopla, propaganda, tedium, and exhaustion of a campaign." Critics' opinions of the book depend on their assessment of Thompson's reporting style. *Columbia Journalism Review* essayist Wayne C. Booth characterizes the work as "an inflated footnote on how [Thompson] used the campaign to achieve a 'very special kind of High.'" He concludes: "Cleverness, energy and brashness cannot, finally, make up for ignorance and lack of critical training." On the other hand, *Saturday Review* contributor Joseph Kanon finds *Fear and Loathing on the Campaign Trail '72* "the best political reporting in some time—it manages to give politics, after years of televised lobotomy, some flesh." *New York Times* columnist Christopher Lehmann-Haupt admits that while Thompson "doesn't exactly see America as Grandma Moses depicted it, or the way they painted it for us in civics class, he does in his own mad way betray a profound democratic concern for the polity. And in its own mad way, it's damned refreshing."

Thompson's subsequent books, *The Great Shark Hunt: Strange Tales from a Strange Time* (in which many of his essays on Watergate are collected), *The Curse of Lono, Generation of Swine: Tales of Shame and Degradation in the '80s,* and *Songs of the Doomed: More Notes on the Death of the American Dream* continue to mine his vein of personal, high-energy reporting. *Los Angeles Times Book Review* correspondent Peter S. Greenburg notes that *The Great Shark Hunt* "is not so much an attack on America as it is a frightfully perceptive autopsy of our culture. . . . In each story—or rather adventure—he leads us on a scattered but very personal journey of experience. The bottom line is that he's really a Charles Kuralt for crazy people, but Thompson's version of 'On the Road' is filled with so many detours that ultimately there isn't just one fork in the road but a complete service for eight. Nevertheless, there seems to be method in his madness. He is the master of the cosmic metaphor and combines this talent with all the subtlety of a run at someone's jugular with a red-hot rail spike." In *The Curse of Lono* Thompson recounts his antics during a visit to Hawaii with his longtime friend and illustrator, Ralph Steadman. Once again the author demonstrates his "very nearly unrelieved distemper," an attribute William F. Buckley describes as "the Sign of Thompson" in the *New York Times Book Review. Washington Post Book World* reviewer Michael Dirda claims of the work, "No one writes like Hunter Thompson, though many have tried, and *The Curse of Lono* dispenses pages rabid with his hilarious, frenzied rantings, gusts of '60s madness for the stuffy '80s."

In February, 1990, Thompson became the subject of media attention when a woman (described variously as an actress, a reporter, and an ex-pornographic film producer) accused the writer of sexual assault, claiming that Thompson had grabbed her left breast when she refused his invitation to join him in his hot tub. Local police conducted an eleven-hour search of Thompson's home, uncovering small quantities of marijuana and cocaine, a number of Valium-like pills, thirty-nine hits of LSD, an antique Gatling gun, and four sticks of dynamite. Thompson was charged with five felonies and three misdemeanors and faced up to fifty years in prison if found guilty on all counts. Soon, however, the case against Thompson began to erode and, after a preliminary hearing, the charges were dismissed. A number of people suggested that the entire case had simply been an attempt to rid the exclusive Aspen community of what many of its newer residents considered a nuisance.

These events, and others, are described in Thompson's 1990 collection *Songs of the Doomed: More Notes on the Death of the American Dream.* Though *Tribune Books'* Clarence Petersen calls the collection "vintage Thompson" in which the author "covers old ground, and some new, by no means on retread tires," a *Washington Post Book World* contributor suspects at times "that 'Dr.' Thompson has, after years of pursuing the complete derangement of his senses, finally made the journey to real madness—to a place where the parameters of truth and fantasy have blended into each other—and the result of this loss of perspective is often more disconcerting than it is enlightening."

More critics praise Thompson than disparage him, however. Klinkowitz writes: "For all of the charges against him, Hunter S. Thompson is an amazingly insightful writer. His 'journalism' is not in the least irresponsible. On the contrary, in each of his books he's pointed out the lies and gross distortions of conventional journalism. . . . Moreover, his books are richly intelligent." According to Gornick, Thompson's talent "lies in his ability to describe his own manic plunge into drink, drugs, and madness through a use of controlled exaggeration that is truly marvelous. There are many moments in his stories—all having to do with paranoia finally induced after hours and days of swallowing, snorting, slugging down amounts of pills, powders, and alcohol that would long ago have killed an army of Berbers—that are so wonderfully funny you are left shaking with laughter and the happiness of literary creation." John Leonard expresses a similar opinion in the *New York Times.* Thompson "became, in the late 1960's, our point guard, our official crazy, patrolling the edge," Leonard writes. "He reported back that the paranoids were right, and they were. The cool inwardness . . . the hugging of the self to keep from cracking up, is not for him. He inhabits his nerve endings; they are on the outside, like the skin of a baby. . . . He is also, as if this needs to be said, hilarious."

BIOGRAPHICAL/CRITICAL SOURCES:

BOOKS

Adnan, Etel, *Russell Chatham,* Winn Books, 1984.

Carroll, E. Jean, *Hunter: The Strange and Savage Life of Hunter S. Thompson*, Plume, 1993.

Contemporary Literary Criticism, Gale (Detroit), Volume 9, 1978; Volume 17, 1981; Volume 40, 1986.

Dickstein, Morris, *Gates of Eden: American Culture in the Sixties*, Basic Books, 1977.

Hellman, John, *Fables of Fact: The New Journalism as New Fiction*, University of Illinois Press, 1981.

Klinkowitz, Jerome, *The Life of Fiction*, University of Illinois Press, 1977.

Vonnegut, Kurt, Jr., *Wampeters Foma & Granfalloons*, Delacorte, 1974.

Whitmer, Peter, *When the Going Gets Weird: The Twisted Life and Times of Hunter S. Thompson: A Very Unauthorized Biography*, Hyperion, 1993.

PERIODICALS

American Spectator, December, 1990, p. 42.

Atlantic Monthly, February, 1967; July, 1973.

Booklist, October 1, 1994, p. 187.

Columbia Journalism Review, November-December, 1973; September-October, 1979.

Commonweal, April 7, 1967.

Critique: Studies in Modern Fiction, Volume XXI, number 1, 1979.

Detroit News, August 26, 1979; November 27, 1983.

Entertainment Weekly, September 9, 1994, p. 73.

Esquire, April, 1991, p. 152; February, 1993, p. 61.

Harper's, July, 1973.

London Magazine, June-July, 1973.

Los Angeles Times Book Review, August 12, 1979.

Nation, April 3, 1967; August 13, 1973; October 13, 1979; June 4, 1990, p. 765.

National Observer, August 5, 1972.

National Review, September 16, 1988, p. 52.

New Leader, November 28, 1988, p. 21.

New Republic, February 25, 1967; October 14, 1972; October 13, 1973; August 25, 1979; January 7, 1991, p. 38.

New Statesman and Society, November 11, 1988, p. 33.

Newsweek, March 6, 1987.

New York, September 26, 1994, p. 102.

New Yorker, March 4, 1967.

New York Review of Books, October 4, 1973.

New York Times, February 23, 1967; June 22, 1972; May 18, 1973; August 10, 1979.

New York Times Book Review, January 29, 1967; March 5, 1967; July 23, 1972; July 15, 1973; December 2, 1973; August 5, 1979; October 14, 1979; January 15, 1984; August 14, 1988, p. 17; November 25, 1990, pp. 7-8; October 23, 1994, p. 18.

Progressive, July, 1973.

Rolling Stone, June 28, 1990, pp. 64-68; July 12, 1990, pp. 21-22; May 30, 1991, pp. 38-39; January 23, 1992, pp. 22-32; June 16, 1994, pp. 42-44.

Saturday Night, March, 1991, pp. 62-63.

Saturday Review, February 18, 1967; April 21, 1973.

Times (London), May 12, 1982.

Times Literary Supplement, January 11, 1968; November 3, 1972.

Village Voice, November 19, 1979.

Washington Monthly, April, 1981.

Washington Post Book World, August 19, 1979; December 18, 1983.

THORNTON, Hall
See SILVERBERG, Robert

*   *   *

THURBER, James (Grover) 1894-1961

PERSONAL: Born December 8, 1894, in Columbus, OH; died November 2, 1961, in New York, NY, of pneumonia following a stroke; buried in Columbus, OH; son of Charles Leander (name later changed to Lincoln; a politician) and Mary Agnes (Fisher) Thurber; married Althea Adams, May 20, 1922 (divorced, May 24, 1935); married Helen Muriel Wismer, June 25, 1935; children: (first marriage) Rosemary. *Education:* Graduated from Ohio State University, 1919.

CAREER: Humorist, cartoonist, illustrator, and playwright. *Columbus Dispatch*, Columbus, OH, reporter, 1921-24; *Chicago Tribune*, Chicago, IL, reporter for Paris edition, 1925-26; *New York Evening Post*, New York City, reporter, 1926; *New Yorker*, New York City, managing editor, 1927, staff writer, chiefly for "Talk of the Town" column, 1927-33, regular contributor, 1933-61. Artwork was exhibited in several one-man shows, including shows at the Valentine Gallery, New York City, 1933, and the Storran Gallery, London, England, 1937. *Military service:* Code clerk at the Department of State, Washington, DC, and at the American Embassy, Paris, France, 1918-20.

MEMBER: Authors League of America, Dramatists Guild, Phi Kappa Psi, Sigma Delta Chi.

AWARDS, HONORS: Ohioana Book Award second place, Martha Kinney Cooper Ohioana Library Association, 1944, for *The Great Quillow;* Caldecott Honor Book, 1944, for *Many Moons;* Ohioana Book Award, Martha Kinney Cooper Ohioana Library Association, 1946, for *The White Deer;* Laughing Lions of Columbia University Award, 1949; Sesquicentennial Career Medal, Martha Kinney Cooper Ohioana Library Association, 1953; T-Square Award, American Cartoonists Society, 1956; Library and Justice Award, American Library Association, 1957, for *Further Fables for Our Time;* Antoinette Perry ("Tony") Special Award, 1960, for *A Thurber Carnival;* Certificate of Award, Ohio State University Class of 1916, for "Meritorious Service to Humanity and to Our Alma Mater," 1961.

WRITINGS:

ESSAYS AND STORIES

(With E. B. White) *Is Sex Necessary?; or, Why You Feel the Way You Do*, Harper, 1929.

The Owl in the Attic and Other Perplexities, Harper, 1931.

The Seal in the Bedroom and Other Predicaments, introduction by Dorothy Parker, Harper, 1932.

My Life and Hard Times (includes "The Night the Bed Fell," "The Day the Dam Broke," and "More Alarms at Night"; also see below), Harper, 1933.

The Middle-Aged Man on the Flying Trapeze: A Collection of Short Pieces (includes "One Is a Wanderer" and "Mr. Preble Gets Rid of His Wife"), Harper, 1935.

Let Your Mind Alone!, and Other More or Less Inspirational Pieces, Harper, 1937.

The Last Flower: A Parable in Pictures (also see below), Harper, 1939.

Cream of Thurber, Hamish Hamilton, 1939.

Fables for Our Time and Famous Poems Illustrated (includes "Little Red Riding Hood" and "The Green Isle in the Sea"), Harper, 1940.

My World—and Welcome to It (includes "The Secret Life of Walter Mitty"; also see below), Harcourt, 1942.

Thurber's Men, Women, and Dogs, Harcourt, 1943.

The Thurber Carnival, Harper, 1945, abridged edition published as *Selected Humorous Stories from "The Thurber Carnival,"* edited by Karl Botzenmayer, F. Shoeningh, 1958.

The Beast in Me and Other Animals: A Collection of Pieces and Drawings about Human Beings and Less Alarming Creatures, Harcourt, 1948.

The Thurber Album: A New Collection of Pieces about People, Simon & Schuster, 1952.

Thurber Country: A New Collection of Pieces about People, Simon & Schuster, 1953.

Thurber's Dogs: A Collection of the Master's Dogs, Simon & Schuster, 1955.

A Thurber Garland, Hamish Hamilton, 1955.

Further Fables for Our Time, Simon & Schuster, 1956.

Alarms and Diversions, Harper, 1957.

The Years with Ross (Book-of-the-Month Club selection), Little, Brown, 1959.

Lanterns and Lances, Harper, 1961.

Credos and Curios, Harper, 1962.

Vintage Thurber, two volumes, Hamish Hamilton, 1963.

Thurber & Company, introduction by Helen Thurber, Harper, 1966.

Snapshot of a Dog, Associated Educational Services, 1966.

The Secret Life of Walter Mitty (also see below), Associated Educational Services, 1967.

The Catbird Seat, Associated Educational Services, 1967.

Selected Letters of James Thurber, edited by his wife, Helen Thurber, and Edward Weeks, Little Brown, 1981.

The Night the Ghost Got In, Creative Education, Inc., 1983.

In a Word, Harper, 1989.

Collecting Himself: James Thurber On Writing and Writers, Humor and Himself, Harper, 1990.

PLAYS

(With Elliott Nugent) *The Male Animal* (three-act; first produced on Broadway at the Cort Theatre, 1940; also see below), Random House, 1940.

Many Moons (also see below), produced in New York City, 1947.

A Thurber Carnival (produced in Columbus, OH, at the Hartman Theatre, 1960; later produced on Broadway at the ANTA Theatre, 1960; also see below), Samuel French, 1962.

Also author of librettos for *Oh My, Omar,* and other musicals produced by the Scarlet Mask Club, Columbus, OH, and of the two-act musical *Nightingale.*

CHILDREN'S FICTION

Many Moons (also see below), illustrations by Louis Slobodkin, Harcourt, 1943.

The Great Quillow (also see below), illustrations by Doris Lee, Harcourt, 1944.

The White Deer, illustrations by Don Freeman, Harcourt, 1945.

The Thirteen Clocks (also see below), illustrations by Marc Simont, Simon & Schuster, 1950.

The Wonderful O (also see below), illustrations by M. Simont, Simon & Schuster, 1957.

The Thirteen Clocks [and] *The Wonderful O,* illustrations by Ronald Searle, Penguin, 1962.

ILLUSTRATOR

Margaret Samuels Ernst, *The Executive's in a Word Book,* Knopf, 1939.

Elizabeth Howes, *Men Can Take It,* Random House, 1939.

James R. Kinney, *How to Raise a Dog,* Simon & Schuster, 1953 (published in England as *The Town Dog,* Harvill, 1954).

OTHER

People Have More Fun Than Anybody: A Centennial Celebration of Drawings and Writings by James Thurber: Being a Hundred Or So. . . , edited by Michael J. Rosen, Harcourt Brace (New York), 1994.

Writings and Drawings, Library of America (New York), 1996.

Most of Thurber's papers are in the Thurber Collection at the Ohio State University Library in Columbus, Ohio.

MEDIA ADAPTATIONS: My Life and Hard Times was filmed as *Rise and Shine* by Twentieth Century-Fox in 1941; *The Male Animal* was filmed by Warner Brothers in 1942, and again in 1952 as *She's Working Her Way through College; The Secret Life of Walter Mitty* was filmed by Samuel Goldwyn Productions in 1947; *A Unicorn in the Garden* was adapted as an animated film by Learning Corporation of America in 1952, and by Columbia Pictures in 1953; *The Thirteen Clocks* was adapted as an opera and as a television special in 1954; several of Thurber's stories were adapted as the play *Three by Thurber,* written by Paul Ellwood and St. John Terrell, first produced in New York City at the Theatre de Lys in 1955; some of Thurber's work was adapted for the film *Fireside Book of Dog Stories* by State University of Iowa in 1957; *The Last Flower* was adapted as a dance by a French ballet company, 1959; "The Catbird Seat" was filmed as *The Battle of the Sexes* by Continental Distributing in 1960; *Many Moons* was filmed by Rembrandt Films, c. 1960, was adapted as a filmstrip by H. M. Stone Productions in 1972, and as an animated film by Contemporary Films/McGraw in 1975; *My World—and Welcome to It* was adapted as a television series in 1969; several of Thurber's stories were adapted as *The War between Men and Women* by National General Pictures Corporation in 1972.

SIDELIGHTS: Called "one of the world's greatest humorists" by Alistair Cooke in the *Atlantic,* James Thurber was one of the mainstays of the *New Yorker* magazine, where his short stories, essays, and numerous cartoons were published for over thirty years. "Comedy is his chosen field," wrote Malcolm Cowley in *Thurber: A Collection of Critical Essays,* "and his range of effects is deliberately limited, but within that range there is nobody who writes better than Thurber, that is, more clearly and flexibly, with a deeper feeling for the genius of the language and the value of words."

Although Thurber's writings cover a wide range of genres, including essays, short stories, fables, and children's books, it is his stories concerned with middle-class domestic situations, often based on actual events in Thurber's own life, that made his reputation. In these stories, timid and befuddled men are overwhelmed by capable and resourceful women or by the mechanical contraptions of modern life. The conflict between the sexes—inspired in part by Thurber's troubled first marriage—and the dangerously precarious nature of everyday life are the recurring subjects in all of his work.

Thurber wrote for the *New Yorker* full time until 1933 and was a regular contributor to the magazine until his death in 1961. "Between 1927 and 1935," wrote Judith S. Baughman in the *Dictionary of Literary Biography,* "Thurber became one of the most prolific and best known of the *New Yorker* writers." He always credited E. B. White with having helped him fine tune his writing style for the magazine. "I came to the *New Yorker*," Peter A. Scholl quoted Thurber in the *Dictionary of Literary Biography*, explaining, "a writer of journalese and it was my study of White's writing, I think, that helped me to straighten out my prose so that people could see what I meant." This style, described by Thurber as "played-down," was economical, lean, and conversational. Because many of his humorous subjects bordered on the bizarre, Thurber deliberately chose a writing style that was calm and precise. Thurber understood, Scholl argued, "that the comedy is heightened by the contrast between the unexcitable delivery and the frenetic events described." Michael Burnett, in his contribution to *Thurber: A Collection of Critical Essays,* also noted the unobtrusive nature of Thurber's style. "It is a style," Burnett observed, "which does its best not to call attention to itself through any deviations from the norm." Louis Hasley, writing in the *South Atlantic Quarterly,* found that Thurber "was, it must be conceded, a fastidious stylist with psychological depth, subtlety and complexity; with a keen sense of pace, tone, ease, and climax; and with imagination that often wandered into surrealism."

Because he had no formal art training, Thurber's cartoons were simple and rudimentary. Dorothy Parker, in her foreword to *The Seal in the Bedroom and Other Predicaments,* fondly described all of Thurber's characters as having "the outer semblance of unbaked cookies." *The Seal in the Bedroom and Other Predicaments,* a collection of Thurber's drawings, takes its title from one of his most famous cartoons. Like other of his works, this cartoon evolved by accident. The original cartoon—drawn in pencil while Thurber doodled at the office—showed a seal on a rock in the Arctic waste. In the distance are two specks. "Hmmm, explorers," says the seal. The published version of the cartoon is quite different. After drawing the seal on the rock, this time in ink, Thurber decided that his rock looked less like a rock and more like a headboard for a bed. So he added a couple lying in the bed. The wife is saying, "All right, have it your way—you heard a seal bark!"

Thurber's writing career, Richard C. Tobias noted in *The Art of James Thurber,* falls into three loosely defined periods. The first, from 1929 until about 1937, "develops the comedy of the little man menaced by civilization." The second period is a time of exploration for Thurber, when he published fables like *The Last Flower: A Parable in Pictures* and *Fables for Our Time and Famous Poems Illustrated,* had his play *The Male Animal* successfully produced, and wrote the first of his children's books. The last period, the 1950s, saw Thurber return to the subject matter of his early work but with a deeper understanding. The books of Thurber's first period, collections of short pieces and drawings first published in the *New Yorker,* are generally considered to contain most of his best work. Many later titles reprint pieces from these books, sometimes including other Thurber material not previously reprinted from the *New Yorker.*

In 1929 Thurber teamed with White to produce a spoof of the sex manual genre entitled *Is Sex Necessary?; or, Why You Feel the Way You Do.* As Edward C. Simpson reported in the *Dictionary of Literary Biography,* the two authors "parody the serious writers on the subject, making light of complexities, taking a mock-serious attitude toward the obvious, delighting in reducing the case-history technique to an absurdity, and making fun of those writers who proceeded by definition." The two men wrote alternate chapters of the manual, while Thurber provided the illustrations. The artwork—some forty drawings—took Thurber

only one night to produce. "The next morning," Thurber told Cooke, "we took them down to the publishers, and when we got there, we put them down on the floor. Three bewildered and frightened publishers looked at them, and one man, the head publisher, said, 'These I suppose are rough sketches for the guidance of some professional artist who is going to do the illustrations?' and Andy [E. B. White] said, 'Those are the actual drawings that go in the book.'" The drawings were included. In his foreword to the manual, White found in Thurber's artwork "a strong undercurrent of grief" and described Thurber's men as "frustrated, fugitive beings." White went on to speak of "the fierce sweep, the economy, and the magnificent obscurity of Thurber's work. . . . All I, all anybody, can do is to hint at the uncanny faithfulness with which he has caught—caught and thrown to the floor—the daily, indeed the almost momently, severity of life's mystery, as well as the charming doubtfulness of its purpose." *Is Sex Necessary?* has gone through dozens of printings since its initial publication.

The Owl in the Attic and Other Perplexities, Thurber's second book and first collection of *New Yorker* pieces, includes eight stories, a selection of drawings and short writings about pets and the "Ladies' and Gentlemen's Guide to Modern English." Most of the stories are taken from Thurber's own life and feature the character of John Monroe in domestic battles with his wife and with uncooperative household products. Some of the marital battles are based on Thurber's own stormy first marriage. The Monroe stories, Tobias believes, combined the comic with the tragic. John Monroe "has more potential for pathos than comedy," Tobias wrote, "but his frightening and agonizing situations are more extreme than that and thus comic. Further, the situations also suggest that behind the comic mask is a raw human experience which the writer, by his craft, has subdued for our pleasure. What is painful in life is transformed into a finer tone by the comic vision." Scholl reported that with the publication of *The Owl in the Attic,* "Thurber's reputation as a writer and an artist was firmly established." And Tobias found *Is Sex Necessary?* and *The Owl in the Attic* to be "astonishing performances for the beginning of a career."

Perhaps the most important of Thurber's early books is the story collection *My Life and Hard Times,* which recounts some outlandish events and disastrous misunderstandings from Thurber's childhood. Calling it the "peak achievement of Thurber's early career," Charles S. Holmes added in *The Clocks of Columbus: The Literary Career of James Thurber,* "For many readers it is his one unquestioned masterpiece." One of the chief virtues of the collection is the distance that Thurber maintained between himself and his past experiences, allowing him to use his own life to comic effect. As he wrote in the afterword to collection, "The confusion and the panics of last year and the year before are too close for contentment. Until a man can quit talking loudly to himself in order shout down the memories of blunderings and gropings, he is in no shape for the painstaking examination of distress and the careful ordering of event so necessary to a calm and balanced exposition of what, exactly, was the matter."

My Life and Hard Times, stated Scholl, "is Thurber's best single collection of integrated stories, a series that can be read as a well-wrought and unified work of art." Hasley found that "despite its autobiographical basis," the book represents "the most consistently creative and humorous of all his books," and displays "Thurber's eminence in the portrayal of actual people." Holmes analyzed the stories in this collection and believed that throughout the book Thurber had celebrated "what might be called the Principle of Confusion. . . . Nearly every episode shows the disruption of the orderly pattern of everyday life by the idiosyncratic, the bizarre, the irrational." With *My Life and Hard Times,* concluded Holmes, Thurber "arrived at full artistic maturity."

In *The Middle-Aged Man on the Flying Trapeze,* a book described by Baughman as a "generally darker-toned miscellany," there is one curiously unfunny piece that sheds light on Thurber's personal life. The story "One Is a Wanderer" portrays a lonely middle-aged man in New York City who lives alone, drinks too much, and has alienated most of his friends. Taken from Thurber's situation during his first marriage, when he lived alone in New York City while his wife and daughter lived in the country, the story ends with the revelation, "Two is company, four is a part, three is a quarrel. One is a wanderer." In the humorous stories, too, there are depictions of Thurber's troubled life. "The quarrels, the fights, the infidelities, and the loneliness of these years are animated in the humorous pieces," Scholl commented. In "Mr. Preble Gets Rid of His Wife," for example, Thurber successfully blends the absurdly comic with the tragic. Mr. Preble wants his wife to go into the cellar with him; she knows he wants to kill her there but, because she is tired of arguing about it and is as dissatisfied with their marriage as he is, she accompanies him. Another argument develops in the cellar over Mr. Preble's choice of murder weapon—Mrs. Preble does not wish to be hit on the head with a shovel—and the story ends with the husband leaving for the store to buy a more suitable weapon. His wife waits patiently in the cellar for his return.

In his second period Thurber explored new types of writing, while continuing to write the essays and short stories that had made his reputation. During the 1940s he wrote fables, a play, and children's books in addition to several collections of *New Yorker* pieces. In *The Last Flower,* published in 1940, Thurber created a picture book fable for adults that tells the story of World War XII and what survived: a man, a woman, and a single flower. From these three items, love emerges in the waste land. But love leads to family, to tribe, to civilization, and inevitably and sadly, to another war. Inspired by the Spanish Civil War of the 1930s and the joint Soviet and Nazi invasion of Poland in 1939, the book was published shortly before America's entry into World War II. The book "is not funny," wrote a *Boston Transcript* reviewer. "It isn't meant to be funny. *The Last Flower* is magnificent satire." As E. Charles Vousden stated in the *Dictionary of Literary Biography,* "The message of the work . . . is . . . one of despair—humanity will never learn to avoid war."

Thurber returned to the allegorical fable in his *Fables for Our Time,* a collection of Aesop parodies that Fred Schwed Jr., of the *Saturday Review of Literature* thought showed "rather conclusively, I'm afraid, that at its worst the human race is viciously silly, while at its best it is just as silly." Containing what Vousden called "astute observations on the human condition," *Fables for Our Time* commented on such contemporary figures as Adolf Hitler and had fun with some of the more familiar fairy tale situations. Thurber's version of "Little Red Riding Hood," for instance, ended with Little Red shooting the wolf with a pistol. "You can read as much or as little as you please into these light and perfectly written little tales," G. W. Stoner wrote in the *New Statesman and Nation.*

The Male Animal, Thurber's first produced play, was written with his old friend Elliott Nugent and staged in 1940. It is set at a Midwestern college where an English professor finds himself at odds with a university trustee who is more interested in football and alumni support than with academic values. "For the first time," Tobias remarked, "the tart, astringent Thurber dialogue gets a larger framework." Thurber learned about some important differences between writing a play and having it produced. He told *New Yorker* colleague Wolcott Gibbs: "During rehearsal you discover that your prettiest lines do not cross the footlights, because they are too pretty, or an actor can't say them, or an actress doesn't know what they mean. . . . On the thirteenth day of rehearsal, the play suddenly makes no sense to you and does not seem to be written in English." *The Male Animal* was a huge success for Thurber, though, running for 243 performances in New York City and adapted as a film starring Henry Fonda.

Included in *My World—and Welcome to It* is one of Thurber's most famous short stories, "The Secret Life of Walter Mitty." The story concerns a man who daydreams heroic adventures to escape from a domineering wife and a boring job. "The story is a masterpiece of associational psychology," wrote Hasley, "in its shuttling between the petty, humiliating details of his outer life and the flaming heroism of his self-glorifying reveries." In this story, according to Carl M. Lindner in the *Georgia Review,* Thurber "touched upon one of the major themes in American literature—the conflict between individual and society."

Although he was barely able to see after several major operations on his eye in one year, Thurber began to write books for children during this second period. According to David McCord in *Twentieth-Century Children's Writers,* "The anatomy of these . . . books is interchangeable: impossible tasks, indomitable courage, improbable solutions, appropriate wizardry, and nothing so serious or warped as not to be funny." Each of these books is a fairy tale, subtly modernized by Thurber's perspective. Comparing Thurber's children's books to the works of Frank Stockton, Edmund Wilson stated in his review for the *New Yorker* that like Stockton, Thurber took traditional fairy tale situations and made "them produce unexpected results."

Thurber wrote *Many Moons,* his first book for children, on Martha's Vineyard while recuperating from eye surgery. In the story, an indulged royal child becomes sick from eating too many raspberry tarts and refuses to get better unless she can have the moon. Although her father promises her the moon, none of his court but the jester is able to resolve the dilemma and save the princess. "Written with aptness and felicity of phrase," stated Joan Vatsek in the *Saturday Review of Literature,* "the story has a very special quality of lightness." Describing the book in a *New York Times* review, E. L. Buell commented, "Brief, unpretentious, but sound and right of its sort, his fable is one which adults and children both will enjoy for its skillful nonsense and for a kind of humane wisdom which is not always a property of his *New Yorker* stories."

According to Vousden, "Marc Simont, illustrator of two of Thurber's later books, said that Thurber told him 'he wanted to write something lasting about McCarthyism.'" As a result, Thurber wrote *The Wonderful O,* his last fairy tale. The book is about a pirate named Black who lands on the Island of Ooroo in search of jewels; finding none, he takes control of the island. Because he hates the letter "O" and all words that contain it, he banishes them from use. When, however, a poet calls upon love and memory to overthrow the pirate, he returns freedom to the island. Calling it "witty" and "extremely clever," E. W. Foell also noted in the *Christian Science Monitor* that "it has a moral." But critics were most impressed by the book's style, which Dan Wickenden described in the *New York Herald Tribune Book Review* as "a strongly rhythmic, alliterative style that is full of echoes, assonances, outright rhymes and meters." And in the *Library Journal,* E. F. Walbridge called it "a dazzling feat of verbal virtuosity, with frequent lapses into interior rhyme." However, as Fanny Butcher pointed out in the *Chicago Sunday Tribune,* "Like all good fables, it is told in simple language and in a manner children can delight in."

Perhaps Thurber's most important book of the 1950s is *The Years with Ross.* An informal biography of Harold Ross, founder and editor of the *New Yorker,* the book is also a history of the magazine and a recounting of Thurber's friendship with Ross. Told in a rambling and anecdotal style, the book is divided into sections dealing with various aspects of Ross' life and career, treating each one "as an entity in itself," as Thurber explained in the book's foreword. "The unity I have striven for. . . .," wrote Thurber, "is one of effect." Thurber relied on his own memories of Ross, the memories of other *New Yorker* staff members, and on letters and published articles to trace Ross' career. The book fared well with the critics, although several reviewers found Thurber's portrait of Ross a bit unclear. Finding the book "often fascinating," Gerald Weales of *Commonweal,* for example, said that he "came out with the feeling that Thurber must still know something that he has failed to tell me." Peter Salmon of the *New Republic* called it "a great book"; and writing in the *San Francisco Chronicle,* Mark Schorer commented: "This is a book to savor, and to treasure. It has two heroes: The first, obviously, is Harold Ross himself, a flashing and fascinating man; the second is James Thurber, a retiring and a great one." The criticism that especially hurt Thurber, though, came from his friends. E. B. White and his wife Katharine, friends of both Thurber and Ross for many years, did not like the book. Scholl noted, however, that *The Years with Ross* "has a lasting power to entertain and move the reader."

Thurber's last major work, *A Thurber Carnival,* is a series of skits, some of which are adapted from earlier stories and some of which are new material. In one skit a woman reads from *The Last Flower* and displays the book's illustrations on an easel. Some of Thurber's cartoons were enlarged and used as backdrops for the New York City production of the play. After premiering in Thurber's hometown of Columbus, the play opened on Broadway on February 26, 1960, and enjoyed a national road tour as well. When ticket sales for the Broadway production slowed, Thurber himself joined the cast, playing himself in one of the skits for some 88 performances. Ticket sales increased. A critical and popular success, *A Thurber Carnival* won a special Tony Award in 1960.

On October 3, 1961, Thurber suffered a stroke at his home in New York City. While in the hospital he developed pneumonia and on November 2, 1961, he passed away. Toward the end of his life it seemed to many observers that Thurber's work had become pessimistic. "During the last ten years of his life," Hasley noted, "Thurber turned more and more to serious treatments of literary subjects and people. . . . While he never yielded wholly to despair, the note of gloom is unmistakable." Holmes, too, found this bleak outlook. "The theme of all of Thurber's late work is decline—of form, style, good sense, 'human stature, hope, humor,'" he wrote. This outlook is reflected in his personal life, too. Scholl quoted Thurber as saying to Nugent shortly before his death, "I can't hide anymore behind the mask of comedy. . . . People are not funny; they are vicious and horrible—and so is life!"

BIOGRAPHICAL/CRITICAL SOURCES:

BOOKS

Atteberry, Brian, *The Fantasy Tradition in American Literature,* Indiana University Press, 1980.
Bernstein, Burton, *Thurber,* Dodd, 1975, published as *Thurber: A Biography,* Ballantine, 1976.
Blair, Walter, and Hamlin Hill, *America's Humor: From Poor Richard to Doonesbury,* Oxford University Press, 1978.
Contemporary Literary Criticism, Gale (Detroit), Volume 5, 1976; Volume 11, 1979; Volume 25, 1983.
Conversations with James Thurber, edited by Thomas French, University Press of Mississippi, 1989.
Cowley, Malcolm, *Writers at Work: The Paris Review Interviews,* Viking, 1959.
Dictionary of Literary Biography, Gale, Volume 4: *American Writers in Paris, 1920-1939,* 1980; Volume 11: *American Humorists, 1800-1950,* 1982; Volume 22: *American Writers for Children, 1900-1960,* 1983.
Gill, Brendan, *Here at the New Yorker,* Random House, 1975.
Grauer, Neil, *Remember Laughter: A Life of James Thurber,* University of Nebraska Press, 1994.
Holmes, Charles S., *The Clocks of Columbus: The Literary Career of James Thurber,* Atheneum, 1972.
Kenney, Catherine M., *Thurber's Anatomy of Confusion,* Shoe-String Press, 1984.
Kinney, Harrison, *James Thurber: His Life And Times,* Holt (New York), 1995.
Kramer, Dale, *Ross and the "New Yorker,"* Doubleday, 1951.
Long, Robert E., *James Thurber,* Twayne, 1988.
Thurber: A Collection of Critical Essays, edited by Charles S. Holmes, Prentice-Hall, 1974.
Tobias, Richard C., *The Art of James Thurber,* Ohio State University Press, 1969.
Toombs, Sara E., *James Thurber: An Annotated Bibliography of Criticism,* Garland, 1987.
Twentieth-Century Children's Writers, 3rd edition, St. James Press, 1989.

PERIODICALS

Atlantic, August, 1956, pp. 36-40.
Boston Transcript, December 9, 1939.
Chicago Sunday Tribune, June 9, 1957, p. 6.
Children's Literature in Education, autumn, 1984, pp. 147-56.
Choice, December, 1986, p. 599.
Christian Science Monitor, October 13, 1945, p. 14; May 29, 1957, p. 5; May 28, 1959; December 14, 1981.
Commonweal, July 17, 1959.
Economist, February 13, 1982.
Esquire, August, 1975.
Georgia Review, summer, 1974.
Horn Book Magazine, November-December, 1994, p. 727.
Library Journal, July, 1957, p. 1780.
Listener, January 28, 1982.
Los Angeles Times Book Review, May 6, 1984, p. 4; November 26, 1989, p. 33; October 21, 1990, p. 10; November 25, 1990, p. 25; July 24, 1994, p. 3.
Lost Generation Journal, winter (special Thurber issue), 1975.
Maclean's, January 18, 1982.
Nation, June 13, 1959; November 21, 1981.
National Review, April 2, 1982; August 9, 1985, p. 53.
New Republic, September 20, 1940; June 29, 1959.
New Statesman, December 14, 1962; November 28, 1986, p. 26.

New Statesman and Nation, December 23, 1939; December 14, 1940; December 19, 1942.
Newsweek, March 24, 1975; December 10, 1990, p. 80.
New Yorker, October 27, 1945; December 9, 1950, p. 166; November 11, 1961, p. 247; December 3, 1973, p. 198; June 23, 1975; December 1, 1975, p. 178; January 4, 1982, p. 90; June 27, 1994, p. 168.
New York Herald Tribune Book Review, December 3, 1950, p. 7; May 26, 1957, p. 5.
New York Times, February 22, 1931; September 12, 1937; September 19, 1943, p. 6; February 4, 1945; September 30, 1945, p. 5; May 31, 1959.
New York Times Book Review, March 25, 1973; May 6, 1973, p. 26; July 14, 1974, p. 30; October 30, 1977, p. 57; November 8, 1981, p. 3; January 10, 1982, p. 35; December 12, 1982, p. 35; March 13, 1983, p. 27; May 13, 1984, p. 38; November 5, 1989, p. 36.
New York Times Magazine, December 4, 1949, p. 17.
Observer, February 15, 1987, p. 25.
Reader's Digest, September, 1972.
Saturday Review of Literature, December 2, 1939; November 23, 1940; November 13, p. 25; November 11, 1944, p. 29; February 3, 1945.
School Library Journal, November, 1994, p. 91; February, 1996, p. 62.
South Atlantic Quarterly, autumn, 1974.
Time, July 9, 1951, pp. 88-94; March 31, 1975.
Times Literary Supplement, January 29, 1982, p. 101; November 16, 1984, p. 1323; December 29, 1989, p. 1437.
Tribune Books (Chicago), January 27, 1991, p. 8; July 10, 1994, p. 5.
Washington Post Book World, November 8, 1981; August 5, 1990, p. 15; September 23, 1990, p. 15; July 31, 1994, p. 13.
Village Voice, December 15, 1975, p. 72.
Virginia Quarterly Review, spring, 1990, p. 50.
Voice Literary Supplement, September, 1990, p. 24.
Yale Review, autumn, 1965.

*   *   *

TIGER, Derry
See ELLISON, Harlan (Jay)

*   *   *

TILLICH, Paul (Johannes) 1886-1965

PERSONAL: Surname pronounced *Till*-ik; born August 20, 1886, in Starzeddel, Kreis Guben, Prussia; died October 22, 1965, in the United States; came to America in 1933, naturalized in 1940; son of Johannes (a Lutheran pastor) and Mathilde (Duraelen) Tillich; married Hannah Werner, 1924; children: Erdmuthe Tillich Farris, Rene Descartes. *Education:* Studied at University of Berlin, 1904-05, 1908, University of Tuebingen, 1905, University of Halle, 1905-07; University of Breslau, Ph.D., 1911; University of Halle, Licentiat of Theology, 1912.

ADDRESSES: Home—84 Woodlane, Easthampton, Long Island, NY. *Office*—Divinity School, University of Chicago, 5801 South Ellis, Chicago, IL.

CAREER: Ordained minister of Evangelical Lutheran Church, 1912. University of Berlin, Berlin, Germany, privat-dozent, 1919-

24; University of Marburg, Marburg, Germany, professor of theology, 1924-25; University of Dresden, Dresden, Germany, professor of theology, 1925-29; University of Leipzig, Leipzig, Germany, professor of theology, 1928-29; University of Frankfurt-am-Main, Frankfurt, Germany, professor of philosophy, 1929-33; Union Theological Seminary, New York, NY, professor of theology and philosophy, 1933-54; Harvard University, Cambridge, MA, University Professor, 1955-62; University of Chicago, Divinity School, Chicago, IL, John Nuven Professor of Theology, 1962-65. Visiting lecturer at numerous universities in the United States, Europe, and Japan, including Tailor Lecturer, Yale University, 1935, Terry Lecturer, Yale, 1950, and Gifford Lecturer, University of Edinburgh, 1953. Cofounder of Self-Help for Emigres from Central Europe, Inc.; member of executive committee of American Committee for Christian Refugees; vice-chairman of Center for German and Austrian Art and Handicraft; provisional chairman of Council for a Democratic Germany. *Military service:* German Army, chaplain, 1914-18; awarded Iron Cross, First Class.

MEMBER: American Philosophical Association, American Theological Association, American Academy of Arts and Sciences, Philosophy Club, Academy of Religion and Mental Health.

AWARDS, HONORS: Grosse Verdienstkreuz from West German Republic, 1956; Goethe Medal from City of Frankfurt, 1956; Hanseatic Goethe Prize from City of Hamburg, 1958; Stern zum Grossen Verdienstkreuz from West German Republic, 1961; Academy of Religion and Mental Health Award, 1962; Paul Tillich Chair created at Union Theological Seminary, 1971. Numerous honorary degrees, including University of Halle, 1926, Yale University, 1940, University of Glasgow, 1951, Princeton University, 1953, Harvard University, 1954, University of Chicago, 1955, New School for Social Research, 1955, Brandeis University, 1955, Free University of Berlin, 1956, Franklin and Marshall College, 1960, and Bucknell College, 1960.

WRITINGS:

Die religiose Lage der Gegenwart, Ullstein, 1926, translation by H. Richard Niebuhr published in America as *The Religious Situation,* Henry Holt, 1932.
Religiose Verwirklichung, Furche, 1929.
Die sozialistische Entscheidung, A. Protte, 1933, 2nd edition, Bollwerk, 1948.
The Interpretation of History, Scribner, 1936.
Christian Answers by Paul J. Tillich and Others, Scribner, 1945.
The Shaking of the Foundations (sermons), Scribner, 1948.
The Protestant Era, University of Chicago Press, 1948, abridged edition, 1957.
Systematic Theology, University of Chicago Press, Volume 1, 1951, Volume 2, 1959, Volume 3, 1963.
Christianity and the Problem of Existence, Henderson, 1951.
Politische Bedeutung der Utopie im Leben der Voelker, Gebr. Weiss, 1951.
The Courage to Be (Terry Lectures), Yale University Press, 1952.
Die Judenfrage: Ein christliches und ein deutsches Problem, Gebr. Weiss, 1953.
Love, Power, and Justice, Oxford University Press, 1954.
The New Being (sermons), Scribner, 1955.
Biblical Religion and the Search for Ultimate Reality, University of Chicago Press, 1955, 2nd edition, 1964.
Dynamics of Faith, Harper, 1956.
Die Philosophie der Macht, Colloquium, 1956.
(Contributor) *Religion and Health: A Symposium,* Association Press, 1958.

Theology of Culture, Oxford University Press, 1959.

Gesammelte Werke, Evangelisches Verlagswerk, 1959.

Fruhe Hauptwerke, Evangelisches Verlagswerk, 1959.

Wesen und Wandel des Glaubens, Ullstein, 1961.

Philosophie und Schicksal, Evangelisches Verlagswerk, 1961.

Auf der Grenze: Aus dem Lebenswerk Paul Tillichs, Evangelisches Verlagswerk, 1962.

Der Protestantismus als Kritik und Gestaltung, Evangelisches Verlagswerk, 1962.

(Contributor) Reinhold Niebuhr, *A Prophetic Voice in Our Time: Essays in Tribute,* Seabury, 1962.

Christianity and the Encounter of the World Religions, Columbia University Press, 1963.

Morality and Beyond, Harper, 1963.

The Eternal Now, Scribner, 1963.

Das religiose Fundament des moralischen Handelns, Verlagswerk, 1965.

The World Situation, Fortress Press, 1965 (first published as a chapter in the symposium *The Christian Answer*).

Ultimate Concern: Tillich in Dialogue, Harper, 1965.

The Future of Religions, Harper, 1966.

On the Boundary (revision and new translation of part one of *The Interpretation of History*), Scribner, 1966.

My Search for Absolutes, with illustrations by Saul Steinberg, Simon & Schuster, 1967.

Perspectives on 19th and 20th Century Protestant Theology, Harper, 1967.

A History of Christian Thought, Harper, 1968.

My Travel Diary, 1936: Between Two Worlds, with illustrations by Alfonso Ossorio, Harper, 1970.

Political Expectation, Harper, 1971.

Begegnungen (collected works), Evangelisches Verlagswerk, 1972.

E. J. Tinsley, editor, *Paul Tillich 1886-1965* (collected works), Epworth, 1973.

Mysticism and Guilt-Consciousness in Schelling's Philosophical Development, English translation by Victor Nuovo, Bucknell University Press, 1974.

The Construction of the History of Religion in Schelling's Positive Philosophy: Its Presuppositions and Principles, English translation by Nuovo, Bucknell University Press, 1975.

Philosophical Development, English translation by Nuovo, Bucknell University Press, 1975.

Perry LeFevre, editor, *The Meaning of Health: The Relation of Religion and Health,* North Atlantic, 1981.

James L. Adams, editor, *Political Expectation,* Mercer University Press, 1981.

Das System der Wissenschaften nach Gegenstanden und Methoden, published in America as *The System of the Sciences According to Objects and Methods,* Bucknell University Press, 1981.

The Socialist Decision, English translation by Franklin Sherman, University Press of America, 1983.

John Dillenberger and Jane Dillenberger, editors, *Paul Tillich on Art and Architecture,* Crossroad, 1987.

F. Forrester Church, editor, *The Essential Tillich: An Anthology of the Writings of Paul Tillich,* Macmillan, 1987.

Religiose Reden, De Gruyter, 1987.

J. Mark Thomas, editor, *The Spiritual Situation in Our Technical Society,* Mercer University Press, 1988.

Palmer, Michael F., editor, *Writings in the Philosophy of Culture,* Walter de Gruyter (New York), 1990.

Stone, Robert, editor, *Theology of Peace* (in the original English and German), Westminster/John Knox (Louisville, KY), 1990.

Gert Hummel, editor, *Theological Writings* (English and German), Walter de Gruyter (New York), 1992.

Paul Tillich, First-Hand: A Memoir of the Harvard Years, Exploration Press (Chicago), 1996.

The Irrelevance and Relevance of the Christion Message, edited by Durwood Foster, Pilgrim Press, 1996.

Against the Third Reich: Paul Tillich's Wartime Addresses to Nazi Germany, Westminster John Knox Press, 1998.

Contributor to journals, including *Christian Century, History of Ideas,* and *Social Research.* Member of editorial board, *Daedalus, Pastoral Psychology, Aufbau,* and *Journal of Religion and Mental Health.*

SIDELIGHTS: Paul Tillich was perhaps the best known Protestant theologian in America from 1933 until his death in 1965. One of the first non-Jewish academicians to be expelled from Nazi Germany for his opposition to Hitler, Tillich spent the most productive years of his life at the Union Theological Seminary in New York City. From his base there he wrote numerous works in both English and German and delivered innumerable sermons and lectures on the meaning of the Christian faith for twentieth-century man. "Paul Tillich was a giant among us," wrote colleague Reinhold Niebuhr in the *New York Times Book Review.* "His influence extended beyond theological students and circles to include many from other disciplines. . . . He combined theological with philosophical and psychological learning, and also, he combined religious insights with an understanding and appreciation of the arts. Thus he displayed to the American communities of learning and culture, the wholeness of religious philosophy and of the political and social dimensions of human existence."

From his earliest years Tillich was passionate about both Christianity and scholarship. He was born in Prussia in 1886, the son of a Lutheran pastor of high standing. Tillich attended school in Brandenburg and later in Berlin, earning sufficient grades to qualify for university training. This he took at colleges in Halle, Breslau, Tuebingen, and Berlin, eventually earning a Ph.D. and a Licentiate of Theology. He was ordained as a minister of Germany's Evangelical Lutheran Church in 1912. During World War I, Tillich served as a chaplain to the German ground forces, earning decoration for his work among the troops. At the war's conclusion he accepted the post of *privat-dozent* of theology at the University of Berlin, the first of several prestigious universities on whose faculties he would serve.

Tillich quickly established a reputation as one of Germany's most important philosopher/theologians, whose "influence on . . . religious life was maximal," to quote Niebuhr. Throughout the 1920s he authored a number of important works, including *Die religiose Lage der Gegenwart,* translated into English as *The Religious Situation.* In this and other books, Tillich proposed his central theme, namely that religion is the ultimate concern overriding all human activities, and that only by discerning God could modern man discover the courage to be. Tillich expanded on these notions in his English-language books after the Nazi regime dismissed him from his post and more or less forced him to emigrate.

It was Niebuhr, in fact, who helped Tillich secure a position at Union Theological Seminary in 1933. Tillich stayed at the seminary for more than twenty years, during which he wrote a number of books, lectures, and sermons aimed primarily at the lonely and alienated "contemporary" man. The author often said that he considered himself an explorer "on the boundary" between religion, philosophy, and psychology. In books such as *The Shaking of the Foundation* and *The Courage to Be* he was able to integrate existential philosophy with the religious basis of human life, suggesting that religion could be a "unifying center" for existence. Tillich's scholarly yet humanistic works provided a welcome alternative for American Protestants who were not comfortable with fundamentalist interpretations of the Bible. To quote Niebuhr, he "emancipated the intellectually questioning in the churches from literalistic dogma."

By the time of his death in 1965 Tillich had written more than forty full-length works, some in German and some in English. During the 1950s and the 1960s he was given prizes and honorary doctorates in America and in his native land for his memorable contributions to Protestant theology. In the *New Republic,* Roger Hazelton contended that Tillich's greatness as a thinker lay "in the fact that he [knew] what man is made of, what he suffers from, and what he can hope for." A *Times Literary Supplement* reviewer likewise found Tillich "a great constructive thinker" who "was a very human and humane personality." The reviewer added: "His remarkable ability to identify himself with others in their happiness and in their anguish is reflected again and again."

Not surprisingly, Tillich's influence has survived his passing, especially in academic circles. No less than fifteen works have been published posthumously, including collections in both German and English, and Union Theological Seminary has honored the professor by creating a chair in his name. As John K. Roth put it in the *Los Angeles Times Book Review,* Tillich's philosophical theology "decisively influenced mainline American Protestantism during its heyday in the middle third of this century. . . . Tillich explored the uncertainties of human existence and, in spite of those conditions, helped people to discern the God who provides the courage to be."

BIOGRAPHICAL/CRITICAL SOURCES:

BOOKS

Barron, Robert E., *A Study of the De Potentia of Thomas Aquinas in Light of the Dogmatik of Paul Tillich: Creation of Discipleship,* Mellen Research University Press (San Francisco), 1993.

Baumgarten, Barbara Dee Bennett, *Visual Art As Theology,* Lang (New York), 1994.

Bulman, Raymond F., and Frederick J. Parrella, editors, *Paul Tillich: A New Catholic Assessment,* Liturgical Press (Collegeville, MN), 1994.

Bush, Randall B., *Recent Ideas of Divine Conflict: The Influences of Psychological And Sociological Theories of Conflict Upon the Trinitarian Theology of Paul Tillich and Juergen Moltmann,* Mellen Research University Press (San Francisco), 1991.

Cali, Grace (introduction by Jerald C. Brauer), *Paul Tillich, First-Hand: A Memoir of the Harvard Years,* Exploration (Chicago), 1996.

Cooper, John Charles, *The Significance of the Pauline Spirit-Christology for the Theology of Paul Tillich,* Mercer University Press, 1997.

Dreisbach, Donald F., *Symbols and Salvation: Paul Tillich's Doctrine of Religious Symbols and His Interpretation of the Symbols of the Christian Tradition,* University Press of America (Lanham, MD), 1993.

Ferrell, Donald R., *Logos And Existence: The Relationship of Philosophy And Theology in the Thought of Paul Tillich,* Lang (New York), 1992.

Losee, John, *Religious Language and Complementarity,* University Press of America, 1992.

Morrison, Roy Dennis, *Science, Theology, and the Transcendental Horizon: Einstein, Kant, and Tillich,* Scholars Press (Atlanta, GA), 1994.

Natural Theology Versus Theology of Nature?: Tillich's Thinking As Impetus for a Discourse Among Theology, Philosophy, and Natural Sciences: The IVth International Paul Tillich Symposium, Held in Frankfurt/Main, 1992, edited by Gert Hummel, Walter de Gruyter (New York), 1992.

New Creation Or Eternal Now: Is There an Eschatology in Paul Tillich's Work?: Contributions Made to the III. International Paul Tillich Symposium Held in Frankfurt/Main, 1990, edited by Gert Hummel, Walter de Gruyter (New York), 1991.

Nikkel, David H., *Panentheism in Hartshorne and Tillich: A Creative Synthesis,* Lang (New York), 1995.

Park, Jong-Chun, *Paul Tillich's Categories for the Interpretation of History: An Application to the Encounter of Eastern and Western Cultures,* P. Lang (New York), 1996.

Pomeroy, Richard M., *In Search of Meaning,* Glen-Berkeley Press (Berkeley, CA), 1991.

Pongo, Kodzo Tita, *Expectation As Fulfillment: A Study in Paul Tillich's Theory of Justice,* University Press of America (Lanham, MD), 1996.

Ring, Nancy, *Doctrine Within the Dialectic of Subjectivity and Objectivity: A Critical Study on the Positions of Paul Tillich and Bernard Lonergan,* Mellen Research University Press (San Francisco), 1991.

Taylor, Mark Kline, *Paul Tillich: Theologian of the Boundaries,* Collins (San Francisco), 1987.

The Theological Paradox: Interdisciplinary Reflections on the Centre of Paul Tillich's Thought: Proceedings of the V. International Paul Tillich Symposium Held in Frankfurt/Main, 1994, edited by Gert Hummel, Walter de Gruyter (New York), 1995.

Thomas, J. Heyward, *Paul Tillich: An Appraisal,* Westminster, 1963.

PERIODICALS

Commentary, April, 1967.
Encounter, winter, 1967; summer, 1967.
Library Journal, October 1, 1990, p. 93.
Los Angeles Times Book Review, November 22, 1987.
New Republic, January 6, 1968.
Newsweek, May 17, 1954.
New York Herald Tribune Book Review, March 8, 1953.
New York Times, June 4, 1950.
New York Times Book Review, June 27, 1948; October 24, 1965; October 15, 1967; May 10, 1970.
Time, October 20, 1952; March 16, 1959.
Times Literary Supplement, December 4, 1970; January 28, 1972.

*   *   *

TOFFLER, Alvin 1928-

PERSONAL: Born October 28, 1928, in New York, NY; married Adelaide (Heidi) Farrell, April 29, 1950; children: Karen. *Education:* New York University, B.A., 1949.

ADDRESSES: *Agent*—c/o Bantam Books, 666 Fifth Ave., New York, NY 10103

CAREER: Washington correspondent for various newspapers and magazines, 1957-59; *Fortune* magazine, New York, NY, associate editor, 1959-61; freelance writer, 1961–. Member of faculty, New School for Social Research, 1965-67; visiting professor, Cornell University, 1969; visiting scholar, Russell Sage Foundation, 1969-70. Member of board of trustees, Antioch University. Consultant to organizations, including Rockefeller Brothers Fund, American Telephone & Telegraph Co., Institute for the Future, and Educational Facilities Laboratories, Inc.

MEMBER: American Society of Journalists and Authors, Society for the History of Technology (member of advisory council).

AWARDS, HONORS: Award from National Council for the Advancement of Educational Writing, 1969, for *The Schoolhouse in the City;* McKinsey Foundation Book Award, 1970, and Prix du Meilleur Livre Etranger (France), 1972, both for *Future Shock; Playboy* magazine best article award, 1970; Doctor of Laws from University of Western Ontario, D.Litt. from University of Cincinnati, D.Sc. from Rensselaer Polytechnic Institute, and D.Litt. from Miami University, all 1972; Doctor of Letters, Ripon College, 1975; Author of the Year Award, American Society of Journalists and Authors, 1983; American Association for the Advancement of Science fellow, 1984; Centennial Award, Institute of Electrical and Electronics Engineers, 1984; Officier de l'Ordre des Arts et des Lettres, 1984; Doctor of Laws, Manhattan College, 1984.

WRITINGS:

The Culture Consumers: A Study of Art and Affluence in America (Literary Guild selection), St. Martin's, 1964.
(Editor) *The Schoolhouse in the City,* Praeger, 1968.
Future Shock, Random House, 1970.
(Editor) *The Futurists,* Random House, 1972.
(Editor) *Learning for Tomorrow: The Role of the Future in Education,* Random House, 1974.
The Eco-Spasm Report, Bantam, 1975.
The Third Wave, Morrow, 1980.
Previews and Premises, Morrow, 1983.
The Adaptive Corporation, McGraw, 1984.
Order Out of Chaos: Man's New Dialogue with Nature, Bantam, 1984.
Powershift: Knowledge, Wealth, and Violence at the Edge of the 21st Century, Bantam, 1991.
(With wife, Heidi Toffler) *War and Anti-War: Survival at the Dawn of the Twenty-First Century,* Little, Brown, 1993.
(With Heidi Toffler) *Creating a New Civilization: The Politics of the Third Wave,* Progress and Freedom Foundation, 1994.

CONTRIBUTOR

Bricks and Mortarboards, Educational Facilities Laboratories, Inc., 1966.
B. M. Gross, editor, *A Great Society?* Basic Books, 1968.
K. Baier and N. Rescher, editors, *Values and the Future,* Free Press, 1969.
Gross, editor, *Social Intelligence for America's Future,* Allyn & Bacon, 1969.
Cultures beyond the Earth, Vintage, 1975.
Anticipatory Democracy, Vintage, 1975.
Science Fiction at Large, Gollancz, 1976.
Order out of Chaos, Bantam, 1984.

WORK APPEARING IN ANTHOLOGIES

Politics, U.S.A., edited by A. M. Scott and E. Wallace, 2nd edition, Macmillan, 1965.
Essays Today, edited by William Moynihan, Harcourt, 1968.
The Sociology of Art and Literature, edited by M. C. Albrecht and others, Praeger, 1970.

Contributor to *Fortune, Life, Reader's Digest, Horizon, New York Times Magazine, Saturday Review, Playboy, New Republic, Nation,* and other publications.

SIDELIGHTS: Alvin Toffler is a journalist and intellectual who has written several bestselling books about how changing societal dynamics will impact future generations. In *Future Shock* and *The Third Wave,* Toffler presents his speculations about future developments in our society and his recommendations for adapting to the problems and opportunities these changes will create. "I'm no prophet," Toffler tells Edwin McDowell of the *New York Times Book Review.* "I don't believe anybody knows the future. . . . What I do is throw out large-scale hypotheses, new ideas, in hopes of stimulating fresh thinking." In the 1970s and 1980s, Toffler became an international celebrity as a result of his books. In the 1990s, Toffler's wife, Heidi, began accepting byline credit for collaborating with her husband on their books.

In the best-selling *Future Shock,* Toffler indeed stimulated some fresh thinking. He argues in this book that the rate of change in contemporary society is now so fast that many people are being overwhelmed by it. The term "future shock," explains Arnold A. Rogow in the *Saturday Review,* refers to "a condition of confusion and dislocation" brought on by sudden, massive societal change. Toffler bases his concept on the anthropological idea of "culture shock," the inability of some primitive cultures to adapt when first coming into contact with a highly advanced culture. Applying this idea to our own constantly-changing society, Toffler argues that members of our society are experiencing a clash between the culture they grew up in and the emerging technological culture around them, which is replacing and destroying their familiar world. "Future shock is a time phenomenon," Toffler writes in his book, "a product of the greatly accelerated rate of change in society. It arises from the superimposition of a new culture on an old one. It is culture shock in one's own society."

Toffler believes there is a limit to the amount of change that human beings can readily accept, and that we may be reaching that limit. "We have," Elting E. Morison states in the *New York Times Book Review,* ". . . discoverable limits, physiological and emotional, to the numbers of signals we can take in from the world to come." The rising rates for divorce, drug use, and crime all point, Toffler states, to the disastrous effects that future shock is having on Western society. But, writes John Greenway in the *American Journal of Sociology,* the "limits of change the human organism can absorb are discoverable and are therefore controllable." Toffler suggests several ways to control the ill effects of future shock. Children should read more science fiction, he believes, contemporary rituals should be developed to celebrate technological progress, and the study of the future should be given a more prominent place in our society.

Although he finds *Future Shock* "monstrous, mind-coshing, premeditatedly inexact, over-and-overstated and, above all, over-long," P. M. Grady of *Book World* nonetheless believes the book "might assist us not only in preparing for a softer landing into the future, but also in diagnosing more keenly some of today's social puzzles." Calling *Future Shock* "the most prophetic, disturbing, and stimulating social study of this year," Edward Weeks of the

Atlantic goes on to agree with Toffler's argument that "we have it in our power to shape change; we may choose one future over another." Neil Millar of the *Christian Science Monitor* also sees an optimism in *Future Shock*. "It over-simplifies some issues . . . ," he writes, "[but] it also opens bright vistas of hope."

This hope is also found in *The Third Wave*, a book which extends and develops the ideas first presented in *Future Shock*. The great changes Toffler warns about in *Future Shock* are presented in *Third Wave* as the harbingers of a new and potentially liberating form of civilization. "This new civilization," Toffler writes, "brings with it new family styles; changed ways of working, loving, and living; a new economy; new political conflicts; and beyond all this an altered consciousness as well."

The first two "waves" of history, Toffler explains, were the invention of agriculture ten thousand years ago and the industrial revolution of a few centuries ago. The "third wave" involves the restructuring of industrial civilization along more humane lines. Decentralization, renewable energy sources, high technology, and new forms of participatory democracy are all features of this coming civilization.

Several critics disparage Toffler's writing style in *Third Wave* but believe he does raise some important questions for further discussion. "Toffler's style suffers from evangelism: sonorous, incremental cascades, prose panoramas," Anatole Broyard writes in the *New York Times*. "While he is often right, he has the hortatory tone we associate with being wrong. . . . Even so, *The Third Wave* has many virtues. In his hectic way, Mr. Toffler raises all sorts of good questions." Similarly, Langdon Winner of the *New York Times Book Review* believes Toffler "offers many provocative observations about contemporary social trends, especially on patterns evolving in work and family life. But he's in such a hurry to package his ideas in flashy conceptual wrappers that he seldom completes a thought."

Rosalind H. Williams, reviewing *Third Wave* for *Technology Review,* disagrees with some of Toffler's interpretations of present-day trends. Toffler sees, for example, current high technology industries as harbingers of his "third wave" civilization. Williams, however, believes "these developments would prolong the present order, not alter it radically. New markets do not make a new civilization. . . . Toffler's problem is not that he dares to predict, but that his prophecies overlook possible extensions of the community-and energy-intensive civilization of today." But Williams still finds much value in *Third Wave* as "a manual of survival strategies" and as a "stimulus to the imagination." Reviewing the book for *American Anthropologist,* Magorah Maruyama writes that "overall, the shortcomings of the book are very minor compared to its contribution in encouraging readers to revise many of their assumptions and patterns of thinking about cultural processes."

Toffler stresses to Charles Platt in *Dream Makers, Volume II: The Uncommon Men and Women Who Write Science Fiction* that in all his work he has promoted the idea of citizen participation in the decisions regarding future technological developments. "These decisions," he explains, "can no longer be left to scientific, business, or political elites. . . . If you do not give people that voice, you are not giving them a voice in the selection of their own future." He believes his own role is "to open up the reader's mind to other ways of conceptualizing our political and social structures. I think that that helps people adapt; and to have a repertoire of alternatives is necessary."

In the 1990s, Toffler and his wife have continued to write about the future. In *War and Anti-War: Survival at the Dawn of the 21st Century,* the Tofflers warn about the new kinds of weaponry and strategy that will become evident in the future. And in *Creating a New Civilization,* the pair update their classic *Third Wave* by discussing how corporations and governments continue to be stuck in Second Wave habits.

BIOGRAPHICAL/CRITICAL SOURCES:

BOOKS

Platt, Charles, *Dream Makers,* Volume II: *The Uncommon Men and Women Who Write Science Fiction,* Berkley Publishing, 1983.

PERIODICALS

American Anthropologist, Volume LXXXIII, number 2, 1981.
American Journal of Sociology, July, 1971.
Atlantic Monthly, August, 1970.
Book World, September 6, 1970.
Chicago Tribune Book World, March 23, 1980.
Christian Science Monitor, August 6, 1970.
Commentary, October, 1971; July, 1995, p. 32.
Economist, June 21, 1980.
Fortune, November, 1970.
Los Angeles Times, April 4, 1980.
Los Angeles Times Book Review, March 23, 1980; October 17, 1993, p. 12.
Maclean's, April 14, 1980.
Nation, January 25, 1971.
New Republic, January 9, 1995, p. 19; February 27, 1995, p. 6; October 9, 1995, p. 16.
New Society, October 1, 1970.
New Statesman, October 2, 1970.
New Statesman & Society, January 28, 1994.
Newsweek, August 24, 1970.
New York Times, March 22, 1980; July 13, 1980.
New York Times Book Review, July 26, 1970; March 30, 1980; May 7, 1995, p. 9.
New York Times Magazine, June 11, 1995, p. 46.
Observer, January 23, 1994.
Psychology Today, April, 1980.
Saturday Review, December 12, 1970; March 29, 1980.
Technology Review, October, 1980.
Time, March 24, 1980; January 23, 1995, p. 20.
Times Literary Supplement, August 8, 1975; October 31, 1980.
Washington Post Book World, May 4, 1980; June 12, 1983; December 11, 1994, p. 3.

*   *   *

TOLAND, John (Willard) 1912-

PERSONAL: Born June 29, 1912, in La Crosse, WI; son of Ralph (a concert singer) and Helen (Snow) Toland; married present wife, Toshiko Matsumura, March 12, 1960; children: (previous marriage) Diana, Marcia; (present marriage) Tamiko (daughter). *Education:* Williams College, B.A., 1936; attended Yale Drama School, 1937.

ADDRESSES: Home—101 Long Ridge Rd., Danbury, CT 06810. *Agent*—Carl D. Brandt, Brandt & Brandt Literary Agents Inc., 1501 Broadway, New York, NY 10036.

CAREER: Writer. Advisor to the National Archives. *Military service:* U.S. Air Force, six years; became captain.

MEMBER: Overseas Press Club, Authors Guild, PEN, Accademia del Mediterraneo, Western Front Association (honorary vice president).

AWARDS, HONORS: Overseas Press Club award, 1961, for *But Not in Shame,* 1967, for *The Last 100 Days,* 1970, for *The Rising Sun: The Decline and Fall of the Japanese Empire, 1936-1945,* and 1976, for *Adolf Hitler;* L.H.D., Williams College, 1968; Van Wyck Brooks Award for nonfiction, 1970, and Pulitzer Prize for nonfiction, 1970, both for *The Rising Sun: The Decline and Fall of the Japanese Empire, 1936-1945;* L.H.D., University of Alaska, 1977; National Society of Arts and Letters gold medal, 1977, for *Adolf Hitler;* Accademia del Mediterrano, 1978; L.H.D., University of Connecticut, 1986.

WRITINGS:

Ships in the Sky, Holt, 1957.
Battle: The Story of the Bulge, Random House, 1959.
But Not in Shame, Random House, 1961.
The Dillinger Days, Random House, 1963.
The Flying Tigers (juvenile), Random House, 1963.
The Last 100 Days, Random House, 1966.
The Battle of the Bulge (juvenile), Random House, 1966.
The Rising Sun: The Decline and Fall of the Japanese Empire, 1936-1945, Random House, 1970.
Adolf Hitler, Doubleday, 1976.
Hitler: The Pictorial Documentary of His Life, Doubleday, 1978.
No Man's Land: 1918, The Last Year of the Great War, Doubleday, 1980.
Infamy: Pearl Harbor and Its Aftermath, Doubleday, 1982.
Gods of War (novel), Doubleday, 1985.
Occupation (novel), Doubleday, 1987.
In Mortal Combat, Morrow, 1991.
Captured by History: One Man's Vision of Our Tumultuous Century, St. Martin's Press, 1997.

SIDELIGHTS: John Toland's "approach to history," Diana Loercher writes in the *Christian Science Monitor,* "is that of an investigative reporter." For each of his books Toland interviews the participants in a historic event, sometimes several hundred of them, in order to get all sides of a story from those people who know it best. He then presents these interviews as objectively as is possible. "I believe it's my duty," Toland explains, "to tell you everything and let you draw your own conclusions. I keep my opinions to a minimum."

Among Toland's more popular books are the Pulitzer Prize-winning *The Rising Sun: The Decline and Fall of the Japanese Empire, 1936-1945;* his *Adolf Hitler,* a biography; *No Man's Land: 1918, The Last Year of the Great War; Infamy: Pearl Harbor and Its Aftermath;* and the novel *Gods of War.* Many of these titles have been best-sellers and have helped to establish Toland as "a superb popular historian of World War II," as Jack Lessenberry states in the *Detroit News.*

Toland's most successful book is *The Rising Sun,* which traces the collapse of the Japanese Empire after its fatal decision to wage war during the 1930s. It is a "big, absorbing and finally very moving history of the Pacific war, told primarily from the Japanese viewpoint," as Walter Clemons explains in the *New York Times.* William Craig of the *Washington Post Book World* believes that "nowhere in American literature has the Japanese side of the war in the jungles been so well told."

To uncover the Japanese version of the Second World War, Toland interviewed hundreds of participants, "ranging from former generals and admirals to former first-class privates of the Imperial Army and housewives who somehow lived through Hiroshima," the *Times Literary Supplement* critic states. He interweaves this material with relevant written documents to produce a narrative history of Imperial Japan. "Although in the main a narrative account," the *Times Literary Supplement* critic writes, "[*The Rising Sun*] is not devoid of passages of shrewd analytical insight." Craig believes that "*The Rising Sun* makes a significant contribution to our knowledge of the recent past. . . . Toland has fashioned a compelling portrait of Japan at the brink of national suicide."

The extensive research for *The Rising Sun* resulted in the clearing up of historical inaccuracies and the unearthing of new information. Toland found, for example, that a simple misunderstanding during Japanese-American negotiations prior to World War II was one of the reasons Japan went to war. During these negotiations, the United States had demanded that the Japanese remove their troops from China. Although agreeable to a withdrawal from China, the Japanese assumed that this demand included Manchuria, an area of China they wished to keep, and so refused to withdraw. In fact, the United States had not meant to include Manchuria in its demand. If this point had been clarified, Japanese-American relations may have been normalized and the subsequent war averted. "In showing how just about all of the Japanese leaders in 1941 sincerely hoped to avoid war," notes F. X. J. Homer in *Best Sellers,* "Toland makes it possible for us to recognize that Pearl Harbor was the result of failings on the part of American diplomacy as well as of Japanese aggression. . . . Toland adds a new dimension to orthodox military history in going beyond grand strategy to portray the human side of the conflict."

In *Adolf Hitler,* a study of the National Socialist leader of World War II Germany, Toland's research again uncovered new facts and dispelled some widely believed misinformation. As with Toland's previous books, *Adolf Hitler* relies on extensive interviews. Toland spoke to almost two hundred people who knew or worked with Hitler. Piecing together their accounts, he constructs a multi-faceted portrait of one of the pivotal figures of the war. Because this portrait presents observations from "generals and diplomats [and] some of Hitler's closest friends and attendants," as W. Warren Wagar notes in the *Saturday Review, Adolf Hitler* contains "hundreds of chatty anecdotes and odd glimpses into Hitler's life that help to give him a human, if often unpleasing, face."

Toland's book reveals that until the Second World War began, Hitler was overwhelmingly popular in Germany. He had brought his country out of a depression, instituted a series of massive building programs that provided much-needed jobs, established sweeping social reforms, and given the German people a sense of common purpose. Internationally, Hitler enjoyed an equally favorable reputation. Gertrude Stein believed he deserved a Nobel Peace Prize. George Bernard Shaw praised him in newspaper articles. The Vatican cooperated with him. Toland states that "if Hitler had died in 1937 . . . he would undoubtedly have gone down as one of the greatest figures in German history."

Critical reaction to *Adolf Hitler* particularly praised the sheer mass of information that Toland gathers into one book. "Put simply," Peter S. Prescott comments in *Newsweek,* "Toland tells us more about Hitler than anyone knew before." And because of the vast amount of information provided in the book, *Adolf Hitler* is one of the most comprehensive studies of its subject available. "Not only is 'Adolf Hitler' marvelously absorbing popular history," Christopher Lehmann-Haupt writes in the *New York Times,* "it also must be ranked as one of the most complete pictures of Hitler we have yet had." "Toland's book," Eliot Freemont-Smith claims in the *Village Voice,* "is very good, in most ways the best Hitler biography so far. . . . What makes it 'best' is Toland's superb command of an enormous amount of detail, of where to place emphasis in order to increase our understanding and of tone."

In *No Man's Land: 1918, The Last Year of the Great War,* Toland turned from his studies of the Second World War to look at how the First World War had ended. The last year of that conflict saw stunning military reversals and massive casualties. It began with a stalemate on the Western Front, where soldiers on both sides endured a stagnant and bloody trench warfare. But in the spring of 1918 the Kaiser completed a peace treaty with Russia and was able to move troops from the Russian front to the Western Front. With some 600,000 men, far more than the French and British armies could muster, the Germans launched "the greatest military assault in history," as Timothy Foote writes in *Time.* It appeared as if the Germans would soon capture Paris.

But in July the Allies counterattacked, driving the German army back some twenty miles. The French and British armies then captured some 50,000 German soldiers in one battle near Amiens and put an end to the Kaiser's hopes of victory. When American troops began to arrive shortly thereafter, at the rate of some 250,000 a month, the German high command realized that the war was lost. Toland's account of the dramatic finish of the First World War is "scrupulously accurate while at the same time absorbing and dramatic," according to Richard M. Watt of the *New York Times Book Review.*

Some reviewers were critical of Toland's approach. Brian Bond of the *Times Literary Supplement* calls *No Man's Land* "essentially a story without any real attempt to analyse issues, reappraise evidence or reach conclusions." In the *Detroit News,* Bernard A. Weisberger complains that Toland "seems to have relied on first-hand accounts by soldiers who still had some notion of the war as an adventure." But the London *Times'* Laurence Cotterell praises Toland's objectivity. "While describing in exhaustive detail the direction and course of battle," writes Cotterell, "Toland displays remarkably little partisanship [and] yet evokes all the intrinsic colour and passion of the situation, enabling the reader to form his or her own conclusions."

With *Infamy: Pearl Harbor and Its Aftermath,* Toland examined the tragic attack which brought the United States into the Second World War. Some 2,400 American servicemen died when the Japanese fleet staged a surprise attack on the naval base at Pearl Harbor, Hawaii, on December 7, 1941. Toland had written about this event in his *The Rising Sun* in 1970. But, he tells Andrew R. McGill of the *Detroit News,* "I made a mistake in *The Rising Sun* by saying the attack was a total surprise. . . . Subsequently, enough people came to me with contrary information that I learned I had fallen into a trap."

Toland argues in *Infamy* that President Franklin D. Roosevelt and a handful of top government officials wanted to provoke a war with Japan but were held back by the isolationism of the American people. Their provocations finally drove the Japanese to plan an attack on Pearl Harbor, America's largest naval base in the Pacific. When Roosevelt learned of the upcoming attack, he and his aides deliberately kept the information from the Naval commanders at Pearl Harbor. Roosevelt's purpose was to make the Japanese fire the first shot and "make Americans so mad they'd abandon their isolationism and plunge into the confrontation with fascism," as Jeff Lyon explains in the *Chicago Tribune Book World.*

Reaction to Toland's assertion that Roosevelt knew of the coming Pearl Harbor attack and did nothing to stop it drew some harsh criticism. "I'm getting the greatest hatred on this," Toland told Lyon. And yet, his conclusions are based on what D. J. R. Bruckner of the *New York Times Book Review* calls "tons of documents unsealed by the Freedom of Information Act." Among the evidence are reports that radio messages from the Japanese naval force were intercepted days before the attack; that a Dutch diplomat who visited the navy's Washington command center in early December of 1941 watched as intelligence officers tracked the Japanese fleet on its way to Hawaii; and that a British double agent alerted the United States that a Pearl Harbor attack was planned. "The evidence [Toland] has gathered . . . ," Lyon writes, "is fresh and compelling." Bill Stout of the *Los Angeles Times Book Review* finds that *Infamy*'s evidence amounts to "a strong indictment of Franklin D. Roosevelt and most of his wartime inner circle."

After writing for more than twenty years about recent history, particularly about the Second World War, Toland decided in 1985 to transform historical fact into fiction. *Gods of War,* his first novel, traces the experiences of two families during World War II: the McGlynns are an American family; the Todas, a Japanese family. Together, their stories provide a panoramic look at the entire war in the Pacific. "Toland makes a majestic sweep of conditions, events and personalities," Webster Schott explains in the *New York Times Book Review.*

Although Lessenberry believes that *Gods of War* "is a ponderous, 598-page pedestrian work in which the substance of characters range from cardboard to knotty pine," other critics find much to praise. While admitting that "Toland is an analyst of history, not personality," and that "his characters act rather than struggle," Schott concludes that *Gods of War* "is compelling as information and impressive as performance. It's history dressed as fiction. Very well dressed." Noel Barber of the *Washington Post Book World* maintains that, "small faults aside, this is a massive novel, broad in its scope and fascinating in its detail. Like all good sagas based on recent war history, it cannot fail."

In *Captured by History,* Toland tells the stories behind the writing of his histories, of meeting with disgraced Japanese generals and members of Adolf Hitler's inner circle, of penetrating the wall of silence around Emperor Hirohito, of wheedling secret Korean War documents out of the Chinese government. "[A] mix of recollections and reflections as well as anecdotes," Boyd Childress reports in the *Library Journal,* the work is aptly subtitled "one man's vision of our tumultuous century." Childress calls it an "engrossing, extremely readable autobiography" and a "remarkable reflection on 20th-century history." Similarly, Mary Carroll, writing in *Booklist,* concludes that "Toland has produced a shelf of classic studies of war and peace in the twentieth century, and this fascinating memoir will rest very comfortably on that shelf." In a review of *Captured by History* in the *New York Times Book Review,* David Greenberg concludes that Toland's "fortitude led him to triumph over adversity, and to unearth information that might otherwise have been lost."

BIOGRAPHICAL/CRITICAL SOURCES:

PERIODICALS

American Historical Review, February, 1972.
Best Sellers, February 1, 1971.
Booklist, May 1, 1997.
Books and Bookmen, July, 1977.
Book World, January 3, 1971.
Chicago Tribune Book World, September 28, 1980; May 15, 1982; April 14, 1985.
Christian Science Monitor, March 3, 1966; October 27, 1976.
Detroit News, October 19, 1980; June 13, 1982; March 10, 1985.
Library Journal, July, 1997.
Los Angeles Times, December 28, 1980.
Los Angeles Times Book Review, May 9, 1982; March 3, 1985.
Nation, January 22, 1977.
National Review, April 29, 1977.
New Republic, November 20, 1976; June 16, 1979.
Newsweek, March 7, 1966; December 28, 1970; September 20, 1976.
New York Review of Books, May 26, 1977; December 18, 1980; May 27, 1982.
New York Times, December 7, 1970; October 12, 1976.
New York Times Book Review, November 29, 1970; September 26, 1976; November 12, 1980; August 22, 1982; April 21, 1985; October 13, 1991, p. 7; October 19, 1997.
Progressive, February, 1977.
Saturday Review, March 12, 1966; January 2, 1971; September 18, 1976; September, 1980.
Time, December 7, 1970; December 6, 1976; September 22, 1980.
Times (London), December 11, 1980.
Times Literary Supplement, September 1, 1972, p. 1029; February 6, 1981, p. 144.
Village Voice, November 15, 1976.
Virginia Quarterly Review, summer, 1977.
Wall Street Journal, February 28, 1966.
Washington Post, October 27, 1980; May 3, 1982; October 29, 1987.
Washington Post Book World, January 3, 1971; September 5, 1976; April 23, 1985.
Yale Review, June, 1971.

* * *

TOLKIEN, J(ohn) R(onald) R(euel) 1892-1973

PERSONAL: Surname is pronounced *"tohl*-keen"; born January 3, 1892, in Bloemfontein, South Africa, brought to England in April, 1895; died of complications resulting from a bleeding gastric ulcer and a chest infection, September 2, 1973, in Bournemouth, England; buried in Wolvercote Cemetery, Oxford; son of Arthur Reuel (a bank manager) and Mabel (Suffield) Tolkien; married Edith Mary Bratt (a pianist), March 22, 1916 (died November 29, 1971); children: John, Michael, Christopher, Priscilla. *Education:* Exeter College, Oxford, B.A., 1915, M.A., 1919. *Religion:* Roman Catholic.

CAREER: Author and scholar. Assistant on *Oxford English Dictionary,* 1918-20; University of Leeds, Leeds, England, reader in English, 1920-24, professor of English language, 1924-25: Oxford University, Oxford, England, Rawlinson and Bosworth Professor of Anglo-Saxon, 1925-45, Merton Professor of English Language and Literature, 1945-59, fellow of Pembroke College, 1926-45, honorary resident fellow of Merton College, 1972-73.

Freelance tutor, 1919; Leverhulme research fellow, 1934-36; Sir Israel Gollancz Memorial Lecturer, British Academy, 1936; Andrew Lang Lecturer, St. Andrews University, 1939; W. P. Ker Lecturer, University of Glasgow, 1953; O'Donnell Lecturer, Oxford University, 1955. *Military service:* Lancashire Fusiliers, 1915-18.

MEMBER: Royal Society of Literature (fellow), Philological Society (vice president), Science Fiction Writers of America (honorary), Hid Islenzka Bokmenntafelag (honorary).

AWARDS, HONORS: New York Herald Tribune Children's Spring Book Festival award, 1938, for *The Hobbit;* Dr. en Phil. et Lettres, Liege, 1954; D.Litt., University College, Dublin, 1954, and Oxford University, 1972; International Fantasy Award, 1957, for *The Lord of the Rings;* Benson Medal, 1966; Commander, Order of the British Empire, 1972; *Locus* Award for best fantasy novel, 1978, for *The Silmarillion.*

WRITINGS:

(Editor with C. L. Wiseman, and author of introductory note) Geoffrey Bache Smith, *A Spring Harvest* (poems), Erskine Macdonald, 1918.
A Middle English Vocabulary, Clarendon Press, 1922.
(Editor with Eric V. Gordon) *Sir Gawain and the Green Knight,* Clarendon Press, 1925, 2nd edition, revised by Norman Davis, 1967.
(With Gordon and others) *Songs for the Philologists* (verse), Department of English, University College, Oxford, 1936.
Beowulf: The Monsters and the Critics (originally published in *Proceedings of the British Academy,* 1936; also see below), Oxford University Press, 1937.
(Self-illustrated) *The Hobbit; or, There and Back Again,* Allen & Unwin, 1937, Houghton, 1938, 2nd edition, 1951, 3rd edition, 1966, 4th edition, 1978.
Chaucer as a Philologist, Oxford University Press, 1943.
Farmer Giles of Ham (also see below), Allen & Unwin, 1949, Houghton, 1950, 2nd edition, Allen & Unwin, 1975, Houghton, 1978.
The Lord of the Rings, Houghton, Volume 1: *The Fellowship of the Ring,* 1954, Volume 2: *The Two Towers,* 1954, Volume 3: *The Return of the King,* 1955, with new foreword by the author, Ballantine, 1966, 2nd edition, Allen & Unwin, 1966, Houghton, 1967.
The Adventures of Tom Bombadil and Other Verses from the Red Book (also see below), Allen & Unwin, 1962, Houghton, 1963, 2nd edition, Houghton, 1978.
(Editor) *Ancrene Wisse: The English Text of the Ancrene Riwle,* Oxford University Press, 1962.
Tree and Leaf (includes "On Fairy-Stories" and "Leaf By Niggle" [originally published in *Dublin Review,* 1945]; also see below), Allen & Unwin, 1964, Houghton, 1965, 2nd edition, Allen & Unwin, 1975.
The Tolkien Reader (includes "The Homecoming of Beorhtnoth" [originally published in *Essays and Studies,* English Association, 1953; also see below], *Tree and Leaf, Farmer Giles of Ham,* and *The Adventures of Tom Bombadil*), introduction by Peter S. Beagle, Ballantine, 1966.
The Road Goes Ever On: A Song Cycle, music by Donald Swann, Houghton, 1967.
Smith of Wootton Major (also see below), Houghton, 1967, 2nd edition, Allen & Unwin, 1975, Houghton, 1978.
Smith of Wootton Major [and] *Farmer Giles of Ham,* Ballantine, 1969.

(Translator) *Sir Gawain and the Green Knight, Pearl,* [and] *Sir Orfeo,* edited by Christopher Tolkien, Houghton, 1975.

Tree and Leaf, Smith of Wootton Major, The Homecoming of Beorhtnoth, Unwin Books, 1975.

Farmer Giles of Ham, The Adventures of Tom Bombadil, Unwin Books, 1975.

The Father Christmas Letters, edited by Baillie Tolkien, Houghton, 1976.

The Silmarillion, edited by Christopher Tolkien, Houghton, 1977.

Pictures by J. R. R. Tolkien, foreword and notes by Christopher Tolkien, Houghton, 1979.

Unfinished Tales of Numenor and Middle-Earth, edited by Christopher Tolkien, Houghton, 1980.

Poems and Stories, Allen & Unwin, 1980.

The Letters of J. R. R. Tolkien, selected and edited by Humphrey Carpenter and Christopher Tolkien, Houghton, 1981.

(Author of text and commentary, and translator) *The Old English Exodus,* edited by Joan Turville-Petre, Oxford University Press, 1981.

Mr. Bliss (reproduced from Tolkien's illustrated manuscript), Allen & Unwin, 1982, Houghton, 1983.

Finn and Hengest: The Fragment and the Episode, edited by Alan Bliss, Allen & Unwin, 1982, Houghton, 1983.

The Monsters and the Critics and Other Essays, edited by Christopher Tolkien, Allen & Unwin, 1983, Houghton, 1984.

Bilbo's Last Song (verse), illustrated by Pauline Baynes, Riverwood Publishers, 1990.

"HISTORY OF MIDDLE EARTH" SERIES; EDITED BY CHRISTOPHER TOLKIEN

The Book of Lost Tales, Part 1, Allen & Unwin, 1983, Houghton, 1984.

The Book of Lost Tales, Part 2, Houghton, 1984.

The Lays of Beleriand, Houghton, 1985.

The Shaping of Middle-Earth: The Quenta, the Ambarkanta, and the Annals, Houghton, 1986.

The Lost Road and Other Writings: Language and Legend before The Lord of the Rings, Houghton, 1987.

The Return of the Shadow: The History of The Lord of the Rings, Part 1, Houghton, 1988.

The Treason of Isengard: The History of The Lord of the Rings, Part 2, Houghton, 1989.

The War of the Ring: The History of The Lord of the Rings, Part 3, Houghton, 1990.

Sauron Defeated: The History of The Lord of the Rings, Part 4, Houghton, 1992.

The War of the Jewels: The Later Silmarillion, Part Two, The Legends of Beleriland, Houghton (Boston), 1994.

The Peoples of Middle-Earth, Houghton Mifflin (Boston), 1996.

Roverandom, Houghton Mifflin (Boston), 1998.

OTHER

(Contributor) G. D. H. Cole and T. W. Earp, editors, *Oxford Poetry, 1915,* B. H. Blackwell, 1915.

(Contributor) *A Northern Venture: Verses by Members of the Leeds University English School Association,* Swan Press, 1923.

(Contributor) G. S. Tancred, editor, *Realities: An Anthology of Verse,* Gay & Hancock, 1927.

(Contributor) *Report on the Excavation of the Prehistoric, Roman, and Post-Roman Sites in Lydney Park,* Gloucestershire, Reports of the Research Committee of the Society of Antiquaries of London, Oxford University Press, 1932.

(Author of foreword) Walter E. Haigh, *A New Glossary of the Dialect of the Huddersfield District,* Oxford University Press, 1928.

(Author of preface) John R. Clark Hall, *Beowulf and the Finnesburg Fragment: A Translation into Modern English Prose,* edited by C. L. Wrenn, Allen & Unwin, 1940.

(Contributor) *Essays Presented to Charles Williams,* Oxford University Press, 1947.

(Author of preface) *The Ancrene Riwle,* translated by M. Salu, Burns & Oates, 1955.

(Contributor) *Angles and Britons: O'Donnell Lectures,* University of Wales Press, 1963.

(Contributor) Caroline Hillier, editor, *Winter's Tales for Children: 1,* St. Martin's, 1965.

(Contributor) William Luther White, *The Image of Man in C. S. Lewis,* Abingdon Press, 1969.

(Contributor) Roger Lancelyn Green, *The Hamish Hamilton Book of Dragons,* Hamish Hamilton, 1970.

(Contributor) Jared Lobdell, editor, *A Tolkien Compass,* Open Court, 1975.

(Contributor) Mary Salu and Robert T. Farrell, *J. R. R. Tolkien: Scholar and Storyteller,* Cornell University Press, 1979.

Contributor of translations to *The Jerusalem Bible,* Doubleday, 1966. Contributor to *The Year's Work in English Studies,* 1924 and 1925, *Transactions of the Philological Society,* 1934, *English Studies,* 1947, *Studia Neophilologica,* 1948, and *Essais de philologie moderne,* 1951. Contributor to periodicals, including *The King Edward's School Chronicle, Oxford Magazine, Medium Aevum, Dublin Review, Welsh Review,* and *Shenandoah: The Washington and Lee University Review.*

The greater part of the manuscripts of *The Hobbit, The Lord of the Rings, Farmer Giles of Ham,* and *Mr. Bliss* are in the collection of Marquette University, Milwaukee, WI. Various of Tolkien's letters are in the collections of the BBC Written Archives, the Bodleian Library of Oxford University, the Oxford University Press and its Dictionary Department, the Humanities Research Center of the University of Texas at Austin, and the Wade Collection of Wheaton College, Wheaton, IL.

MEDIA ADAPTATIONS: Recordings of J. R. R. Tolkien reading from his own works include *Poems and Songs of Middle-earth, The Hobbit and The Fellowship of the Ring* and *The Lord of the Ring,* have all been released by Caedmon. Christopher Tolkien reads *The Silmarillion: Of Beren and Luthien,* also for Caedmon. Tolkien's illustrations from *Pictures by J. R. R. Tolkien* have been published in various editions of his books, and have appeared on calendars, posters, and postcards. Rankin-Bass animated a version of *The Hobbit* for television, which aired in 1977. Ralph Bakshi directed a theater film based on *The Fellowship of the Ring* and bits and pieces of *The Two Towers,* which was released as "The Lord of the Rings" in 1978. A Bunraku-style puppet version of *The Hobbit* was produced in Los Angeles in 1984 by Theatre Sans Fil of Montreal.

SIDELIGHTS: J. R. R. Tolkien is best known to most readers as the author of *The Hobbit* and *The Lord of the Rings,* regarded by Charles Moorman in *Tolkien and the Critics* as "unique in modern fiction," and by Augustus M. Kolich in the *Dictionary of Literary Biography* as "the most important fantasy stories of the modern period." From 1914 until his death in 1973, Tolkien drew on his familiarity with Northern and other ancient literatures and his own invented languages to create not just his own story, but his own world: Middle-earth, complete with its own history, myths, legends, epics and heroes. "His life's work," Kolich continues, ". . . encompasses a reality that rivals Western man's own attempt at recording the composite, knowable history of his species. Not since Milton has any Englishman worked so successfully at creating a secondary world, derived from our own, yet complete in its own terms with encyclopedic mythology; an imagined world that includes a vast gallery of strange beings: hobbits, elves, dwarfs, orcs, and, finally, the men of Westernesse." His works—especially *The Lord of the Rings*—have pleased countless readers and fascinated critics who recognize their literary depth.

Tolkien began to create his secondary world while still in school, shortly before enlisting to fight in World War I. In 1914, Humphrey Carpenter states in *J. R. R. Tolkien: A Biography,* Tolkien wrote a poem based on a line from the works of an Old English religious poet. Entitled "The Voyage of Earendel, the Evening Star," the poem marked the first appearance in his work of the mariner who sails across the heavens through the night, and was "the beginning of Tolkien's own mythology"—the stories that, edited by Christopher Tolkien, appeared after the author's death in "The History of Middle Earth" and *The Silmarillion.* Nearly all of Tolkien's fiction drew on these stories for their background. *The Hobbit* had at first no connection with Tolkien's legendary histories; he wrote it to please his own children and later remarked that "Mr. Baggins got dragged against my original will" into his imagined mythos. *The Lord of the Rings* also moved into the realm of legend until it became the chronicle of the last days of the Third Age of Middle-earth. After *The Lord of the Rings,* Tolkien published a sequence of related poems, *The Adventures of Tom Bombadil,* but the other fiction he published during his lifetime, including the satirical *Farmer Giles of Ham,* the allegorical *Leaf by Niggle,* and *Smith of Wootton Major,* one of his last works, drew on other sources.

However, Tolkien held another reputation not as well known to readers of his fantasies: he "was in fact one of the leading philologists of his day," Kolich reports. His essay "Beowulf: The Monsters and the Critics"—a plea to study the Old English poem "Beowulf" as a poem, and not just as a historical curiosity—is regarded as a classic critical statement on the subject, and his renditions of the Middle English poems "Sir Orfeo," "Sir Gawain and the Green Knight," and "Pearl" into Modern English are used as texts in some literature classes. His academic work, teaching English language and literature at Leeds and later at Oxford, heavily influenced his fiction; Tolkien himself wrote that "a primary 'fact' about my work [is] that it is all of a piece, and *fundamentally linguistic* in inspiration." "Philology," says T. A. Shippey in *The Road to Middle-Earth,* quoting Tolkien, "is indeed the only proper guide to a view of Middle-earth 'of the sort which its author may be supposed to have desired.'" Carpenter declares, "There were not two Tolkiens, one an academic and the other a writer. They were the same man, and the two sides of him overlapped so that they were indistinguishable—or rather they were not two sides at all, but different expressions of the same mind, the same imagination."

Throughout his fiction, from the early tales of *The Silmarillion* to *The Hobbit* and *The Lord of the Rings,* Tolkien exercised his philological talents and training to create an "asterisk-epic"—an inferred history—that revealed elements of the Northern (and especially the English) literature he loved, and of which so little remains. "The dwarf-names of 'Thorin and Company,' as well as Gandalf's," declares Shippey, "come from a section of the Eddic poem *Voluspa,* often known as the *Dvergatal* or 'Dwarves'

Roster.'" "In the case of the 'ents,'" states A. N. Wilson in the *Spectator,* quoting Tolkien, ". . . as usual with me they grew rather out of their name than the other way about. I always felt that something ought to be done about the peculiar Anglo-Saxon word *ent* for a "giant" or a mighty person of long ago—to whom all old works are ascribed.' He was not content to leave the ents as they appear on the page of *Beowulf,* shadowy, unknown figures of an almost forgotten past." "That is lovely," writes Ursula Le Guin in *The Language of the Night: Essays on Fantasy and Science Fiction;* "that is the Creator Spirit working absolutely unhindered—making the word flesh."

The value of linguistics, or comparative philology, lies in its applicability. Knowing the history of the words forgotten people used can reveal something about the way those people thought and about the modern languages descended from their tongues. Once philologists recognized the relationship between English and Gothic (the oldest recorded Germanic language), for instance, they proved able to explain why certain English words are pronounced and spelled the way they are: "a whole series of things which people said, and still *say,* without in the least knowing why, turn out to have one very old but clear, 100 per cent predictable reason. It's almost like genetics," declares Shippey. Historians frequently use linguistic principles to trace patterns of settlement through place names. In England, for example, towns whose names end in the element-*caster* or-*chester* (from the Latin *castrum,* a fort) mark sites where Roman legions built fortifications, according to the *Oxford English Dictionary.* Towns whose names end in-*ham* or-*wich* were once inhabited by speakers of Old English; in that language, *wic* is an encampment or village, while *hamme* can mean a meadow or a manor-house. Towns whose names end in-*by,* however, were settled by invading Vikings; *byr* is an Old Norse term for a dwelling-place. Tolkien, Shippey points out, uses place names in a "Celtic 'style,'" to make subliminally the point that hobbits were immigrants too, that their land had a history before them." The Carrock, the rocky island in the middle of the river of Wilderland in *The Hobbit,* is derived from the Welsh *carrecc,* a rock, while the town of Bree in *The Lord of the Rings* comes from a Welsh word for a hill.

Tolkien used the evocative power of language to create his English legend. Names in Tolkien's fiction are not merely identifying sounds, Shippey points out; they are also descriptions of the people, places and creatures that bear them. The name Gandalf, for instance, is made up of two Norse words: *gandr,* a magical implement (probably a staff), and *alfr,* an elf. Tolkien's Gandalf, therefore, is an elf with a staff, or a wizard. Shippey explains, "Accordingly when Gandalf first appears [in *The Hobbit*], 'All that the unsuspecting Bilbo saw that morning *was an old man with a staff.'*. . . He turns out not to be an elf, but by the end of *The Lord of the Rings* it is clear he comes from Elvenhome." The character Gollum continually refers to himself and to the Ring throughout *The Hobbit* and *The Lord of the Ring* as "my precious"; Douglas A. Anderson, in his notes to *The Annotated Hobbit,* cites Constance B. Hieatt, who declares that "Old Norse gull/goll, of which one inflected form would be *gollum,* means 'gold, treasure, something precious' and can also mean 'ring,' a point which may have occurred to Tolkien." In the last appendix to *The Lord of the Rings,* Shippey points out, Tolkien derives the word *hobbit* itself from an Old English asterisk-word—*hol-bytla,* meaning "hole-dweller" or "-builder"—although he worked out the meaning long after he first used the word.

Tolkien also drew on ancient words for inspiration. Shippey traces the origins of the Balrog—the evil creature Gandalf faces on the bridge in Moria—to an article Tolkien published in two parts in the journal *Medium Aevum* on the Anglo-Saxon word *Sigelhearwan,* used to translate Latin biblical references to natives of Ethiopia. Tolkien suggested that the element *sigel* meant both 'sun' and 'jewel,' and that the element *hearwa* was related to the Latin *carbo,* meaning soot. He further conjectured that when an Anglo-Saxon used the word, he did not picture a dark-skinned man but a creature like the fire-giants of Northern myth. "What was the point of the speculation," asks Shippey, "admittedly 'guess-work,' admittedly 'inconclusive'? It offers some glimpses of a lost mythology, suggested Tolkien with academic caution, something 'which has coloured the verse-treatment of Scripture and determined the diction of poems.' A good deal less boringly, one might say, it had helped to naturalise the 'Balrog' in the traditions of the North, and it had helped to create (or corroborate) the image of the *silmaril,* that fusion of 'sun' and 'jewel' in physical form." "Tolkien's attitude to language," writes Janet Adam Smith in the *New York Review of Books,* "is part of his attitude to history . . . to recapture and reanimate the words of the past is to recapture something of ourselves; for we carry the past in us, and our existence, like Frodo's quest, is only an episode in an age-long and continuing drama."

Although many readers have viewed *The Lord of the Rings* as an allegory of modern history (especially of the Second World War), Tolkien explicitly rejected such an interpretation; in the foreword to the Ballantine edition of *The Lord of the Rings,* he stated, "As for any inner meaning or 'message,' it has in the intention of the author none. It is neither allegorical nor topical." "I cordially dislike allegory in all its manifestations," he continued, "and have always done so since I grew old and wary enough to detect its presence. I much prefer history, true or feigned, with its varied applicability to the thought and experience of readers. I think that many confuse 'applicability' with 'allegory'; but the one resides in the freedom of the reader, and the other in the purposed dominations of the author." He expanded on these comments in a letter to his publisher Stanley Unwin in *The Letters of J. R. R. Tolkien:* "There is a 'moral,' I suppose, in any tale worth telling. But that is not the same thing. Even the struggle between light and darkness (as [Rayner Unwin] calls it, not me) is for me just a particular phase of history, one example of its pattern, perhaps, but not The Pattern; and the actors are individuals—they each, of course, contain universals or they would not live at all, but they never represent them as such." "You can make the Ring into an allegory of our own time, if you like," he concluded: "an allegory of the inevitable fate that waits for all attempts to defeat evil power by power. But that is only because all power magical or mechanical does always so work. You cannot write a story about an apparently simple magic ring without that bursting in, if you really take the ring seriously, and make things happen that would happen, if such a thing existed."

Tolkien did, however, suggest that his work had an underlying theme. "*The Lord of the Rings,*" he wrote in a letter to the Jesuit Father Robert Murray published in *The Letters of J. R. R. Tolkien,* "is of course a fundamentally religious and Catholic work; unconsciously so at first, but consciously in the revision." Shippey points out that the rejoicing of the forces of the West after the downfall of Sauron in *The Return of the King* is an example of what Tolkien called a "eucatastrophe." Tolkien wrote to his son Christopher that in his essay "On Fairy Stories" "I coined the word 'eucatastrophe': the sudden happy turn in a story which pierces you with a joy that brings tears (which I argued it is the highest function of fairy-stories to produce). And I was there led to the view that it produces its peculiar effects because it is a sudden glimpse of Truth." "It perceives," he explained, ". . . that this is indeed how things really do work in the Great World for which our nature is made. And I concluded by saying that the Resurrection was the greatest 'eucatastrophe' possible in the greatest Fairy Story—and produces that essential emotion: Christian joy which produces tears because it is qualitatively so like sorrow, because it comes from those places where Joy and Sorrow are at one." "Of course," he added, "I do not mean that the Gospels tell what is *only* a fairy-story; but I do mean very strongly that they do tell a fairy-story: the greatest. Man the story-teller would have to be redeemed in a manner consonant with his nature: by a moving story."

Tolkien implies that to take *The Lord of the Rings* too seriously might be a mistake. "I think that a fairy story has its own mode of reflecting 'truth,' different from allegory or (sustained) satire, or 'realism,' and in some ways more powerful," he stated. "But first of all it must succeed just as a tale, excite, please, and even on occasion move, and within its own imagined world be accorded literary belief. To succeed in that was my primary object." "The tale is after all in the ultimate analysis a tale," Tolkien wrote, "a piece of literature, intended to have literary effect, and not real history. That the device adopted, that of giving its setting an historical air or feeling, and (an illusion of ?) three dimensions, is successful, seems shown by the fact that several correspondents have treated it in the same way . . . as if it were a report of 'real' times and places, which my ignorance or carelessness had misrepresented in places or failed to describe properly in others." "Having set myself a task," he concluded, "the arrogance of which I fully recognized and trembled at: being precisely to restore to the English an epic tradition and present them with a mythology of their own: it is a wonderful thing to be told that I have succeeded, at least with those who have still the undarkened heart and mind."

BIOGRAPHICAL/CRITICAL SOURCES:

BOOKS

Anderson, Douglas A., author of introduction and notes, *The Annotated Hobbit,* Houghton, 1988.
Carpenter, Humphrey, *J. R. R. Tolkien: A Biography,* Allen & Unwin, 1977, published as *Tolkien: A Biography,* Houghton, 1978.
Carpenter, Humphrey, *The Inklings: C. S. Lewis, J. R. R. Tolkien, Charles Williams and Their Friends,* Allen & Unwin, 1978, Houghton, 1979.
Contemporary Literary Criticism, Gale (Detroit), Volume 1, 1973; Volume 2, 1974; Volume 3, 1975; Volume 8, 1978; Volume 12, 1980; Volume 38, 1986.
Curry, Patrick, *Defending Middle-Earth: Tolkien, Myth and Modernity,* St. Martin's Press, 1997.
Day, David, *Tolkien's Ring,* HarperCollins (London), 1994.
Dictionary of Literary Biography, Volume 15: *British Novelists, 1930-1959,* Gale, 1983.
Flieger, Verlyn, *Splintered Light: Logos and Language in Tolkien's World,* Eerdmans, 1983.
Flieger, Verlyn, *A Question of Time: J. R. R. Tolkien's Road to Faerie,* Kent State University, 1997.
Green, William, *The Hobbit: A Journey into Maturity,* Twayne (New York), 1995.
Grotta, Daniel, *The Biography of J. R. R. Tolkien: Architect of Middle Earth,* Courage Books, 1996.
Hammond, Wayne G. (with Christina Scull), *J. R. R. Tolkien: Artist & Illustrator,* Houghton (Boston), 1995.

Harvey, David, *Song of Middle Earth,* Allen & Unwin, 1985.

Helms, Paul (with Paul S. Ritz), *Tolkien's Peaceful War: A History and Explanation of Tolkien Fandom and War,* American Tolkien Society (Highland, MI), 1994.

√ Isaacs, Neil D., and Rose A. Zimbardo, editors, *Tolkien and the Critics,* University of Notre Dame Press, 1968.

√ Johnson, Judith A., *J. R. R. Tolkien: Six Decades of Criticism,* Greenwood Press, 1986.

√ Le Guin, Ursula K., *The Language of the Night: Essays on Fantasy and Science Fiction,* edited and with an introduction by Susan Wood, Putnam, 1979.

√ Neimark, Anne E., *Myth Maker: J. R. R. Tolkien,* illustrated by Brad Weinman, Harcourt Brace (San Diego), 1996.

Shippey, T. A., *The Road to Middle-Earth,* Allen & Unwin, 1982, Houghton, 1983.

Strachey, Barbara, *Journeys of Frodo: An Atlas of J. R. R. Tolkien's The Lord of the Rings,* Ballantine, 1981.

√ Tyler, J. E. A., *The Tolkien Companion,* Houghton Mifflin, 1982.

PERIODICALS

Atlantic Monthly, March, 1965.
Book Week, February 26, 1967.
British Book News, December, 1984.
Chicago Tribune Book World, March 22, 1981.
Christian Century, February 24, 1993, p. 208.
Chronicles of Culture, April, 1985.
Commentary, February, 1967.
Commonweal, December 3, 1965.
Criticism, winter, 1971.
Esquire, September, 1966.
Hudson Review, number 9, 1956-57.
Kenyon Review, summer, 1965.
Los Angeles Times Book Review, January 4, 1981; February 10, 1985.
Nation, April 14, 1956.
New Republic, January 16, 1956.
New Statesman and Society, December 20, 1991, p. 47.
New York Review of Books, December 14, 1972.
New York Times Book Review, March 14, 1965; October 31, 1965; November 16, 1980; May 27, 1984; June 17, 1984.
New York Times Magazine, January 15, 1967.
Saturday Evening Post, July 2, 1966.
Sewanee Review, fall, 1961.
South Atlantic Quarterly, summer, 1959; spring, 1970.
Spectator, November, 1954.
Sunday Times (London), September 19, 1982.
Times Literary Supplement, July 8, 1983; July 19, 1985; December 23, 1988.
Washington Post Book World, September 4, 1977; December 9, 1980; February 13, 1983.

*　　　*　　　*

TONSON, Jacob
See BENNETT, (Enoch) Arnold

*　　　*　　　*

TOOLE, John Kennedy 1937-1969

PERSONAL: Born in 1937 in New Orleans, LA; committed suicide, March 26, 1969, in Biloxi, MS; son of John (a car salesman) and Thelma (a teacher; maiden name, Ducoing) Toole.

Education: Received degree from Tulane University, 1958; Columbia University, M.A., 1959; graduate studies at Tulane University, mid-1960s.

CAREER: Teacher at colleges in New York and Louisiana, including University of Southwestern Louisiana, Lafayette, and St. Mary's Dominican College, New Orleans, LA, 1959-68. *Military service:* U.S. Army, 1962-63.

AWARDS, HONORS: Pulitzer Prize in fiction and Faulkner Award nomination from PEN, both 1981, both for *A Confederacy of Dunces.*

WRITINGS:

A Confederacy of Dunces, foreword by Walker Percy, Louisiana State University Press, 1980.
The Neon Bible, Grove, 1989.

SIDELIGHTS: John Kennedy Toole wrote *A Confederacy of Dunces* in the early 1960s, when he was a soldier stationed in Puerto Rico. It was rejected by Simon & Schuster in 1966 and remained unpublished when Toole committed suicide in 1969. During the next seven years, his mother submitted the novel to eight more publishers, all of whom rejected it. In 1976 she took the manuscript to novelist Walker Percy, who agreed, reluctantly, to read it. He perused the opening pages of the smudged carbon copy, "first with the sinking feeling that it was not bad enough to quit, then with a prickle of interest, then a growing excitement, and finally an incredulity: surely it was not possible it was so good."

Percy recommended *A Confederacy of Dunces* to Louisiana State University Press, a scholarly publisher that had accepted only a few novels in the past. The book was published in the spring of 1980, and by summer Toole was, posthumously, a successful author, critically and commercially. *Confederacy* went through five printings, a total of 45,000 hardcover copies—an amazing number for an academic press. The novel was selected by the Book-of-the-Month Club, Grove Press bought the paperback rights, and Twentieth Century-Fox bought the movie rights. The hardcover edition made local best-seller lists in several cities, and the Grove edition was number one on the *New York Times* trade paperback best-seller list for over a month.

The critics' response was also enthusiastic. Jean Strouse of *Newsweek* called *A Confederacy of Dunces* "an astonishingly good novel, radiant with intelligence and artful high comedy." Richard Brown of the *Times Literary Supplement* praised "the clarity of its episodic architecture, its ability to rely effectively on dialogue for the evocation of scene and character, and . . . some splendid close observation, which arises mainly from a determination to work with the peculiarities of a New Orleans setting and language." The book was commended for being highly accessible and entertaining as well as a serious literary work, "a great rumbling farce of Falstaffian dimensions," as Percy called it.

A Confederacy of Dunces is the story of Ignatius J. Reilly, who is "a misfit, an iconoclast, a liar, a virgin, a raconteur, and, above all, a grossly overweight mamma's boy," in the words of *Detroit New* reviewer Charles J. Larson. Ignatius is devoted to medieval philosophy and spends much of his time in bed, writing indictments of the modern world and its trespasses against "theology and geometry." His outrage is directed at diverse targets, including Greyhound Scenicruisers, Doris Day, fashion, ambition, and sex. His mother thinks he should get a job, his girlfriend thinks he needs sex, and several people think he should be locked up in a jail or an asylum. Ignatius, however, considers himself a genius and aspires to be a reformer; when he has to take a job in a pants factory he organizes the black workers in a "Crusade for Moorish Dignity." When the crusade and the job end in chaos, he becomes a hot dog vendor in the French Quarter, selling few hot dogs but sowing a good deal of confusion when he tries to organize homosexuals as "sodomites for peace." Finally he is caught up in the exposure of a pornography ring that operates out of the Night of Joy nightclub, and he has to flee to New York to escape his mother's plan to commit him to a mental hospital. "The form of the novel represents a triumph all its own," wrote Phelps Gay in the *New Republic.* "Characters run into each other with an excess of coincidence rather like a Hardy novel, but every thread of the tale is followed and resolved with clarity and comedy."

Called "one of the funniest books ever written" by Gay and "a masterwork of comedy" by *New York Times Book Review* critic Alan Friedman, *A Confederacy of Dunces* has been compared favorably with such comic novels as John Irving's *The World According to Garp,* Joseph Heller's *Catch-22,* and Miguel Cervantes's *Don Quixote.* Much of the humor arises from the bizarre characters who populate the book: Ignatius's vapid, alcoholic mother; Patrolman Mancuso, who dons grotesque disguises to entice suspicious characters and is repeatedly arrested; Miss Trixie, the senile secretary of Levy Pants, who occasionally becomes lucid enough to look about her and ask, "am I retired?"; and Burma Jones, the black janitor at the Night of Joy, "a superb comic character of immense wit and resourcefulness," who plots sabotage in his perpetual cloud of cigarette smoke. "Caricature . . . is an art that Toole handles at his best with a nearly Dickensian skill." Friedman pointed out.

A Confederacy of Dunces also won praise from several critics, including Andrew Sinclair of the *Times Literary Supplement,* for its vivid depiction of "the gingerbread squalor and raffish charm of the delta city" of New Orleans. Gay wrote that Toole is "uncannily accurate in portraying the sights and sounds of New Orleans." Several reviewers applauded the authenticity of Toole's rendering of New Orleans speech, particularly in the character of Jones, "whose comedy," Brown noted, "comes from his language as much as from his situation: 'Hey! I'm working in modren slavery. If I quit, I get report for bein vagran. If I stay, I'm gainfully employ on a salary ain ever startin to be a minimal wage.'"

Even the book's defenders acknowledged its imperfections. Friedman conceded that it is "flawed in places by its very virtues. Characters are overdone; caricatures are done to death; there are swatches of repetition . . . . Toward the end especially, there are doldrums and crudities." But Friedman, like others, found the flaws minor: "No attack can seriously damage a text as energetic, resourceful and supple as this one. It resists the corrosion of our criticism . . . . The novel astonishes with its inventiveness, it lives in the play of its voices. *A Confederacy of Dunces* is nothing less than a grand comic fugue."

BIOGRAPHICAL/CRITICAL SOURCES:

BOOKS

Contemporary Literary Criticism, Volume 19, Gale (Detroit), 1981.

PERIODICALS

Chicago Tribune Book World, June 29, 1980.
Detroit News, June 17, 1980.
Horizon, September, 1980.

New Republic, July 19, 1980.
Newsweek, May 26, 1980.
New York Times Book Review, June 22, 1980.
People Weekly, September 22, 1980.
Publishers Weekly, June 12, 1981.
Time, June 2, 1980.
Times Literary Supplement, July 18, 1980; June 12, 1981.

*   *   *

TOOMER, Jean 1894-1967
(Nathan Eugene Toomer)

PERSONAL: Born December 26, 1894, in Washington, DC; died March 30, 1967; in Doylestown, PA; married Marjory Latimer, 1931 (deceased); married Marjorie Content, 1934. *Education:* Attended University of Wisconsin, 1914, and City College of New York of the City University of New York), 1917-18; also attended Gurdjieff Institute (France). *Religion:* Quaker.

CAREER: Writer. Taught physical education in a school near Milwaukee, 1918; clerk, Acker Merrall and Condit Grocery Company, New York, 1918; shipyard worker, New York; worked at Howard Theatre, Washington, DC, 1920; worked as teacher in Georgia, 1920-21; studied at Gurdjieff Institute in Fontainebleau, France, 1924; led Gurdjieff groups in Harlem, 1925, and Chicago, 1926-33; lived in Pennsylvania after 1934.

WRITINGS:

Cane (novel comprised of poems and short stories), Boni & Liveright, 1923.
Essentials (aphorisms and apothegms), Lakeside Press, 1931.
The Flavor of Man (lecture), Young Friends Movement of the Philadelphia Yearly Meetings, 1949.
The Wayward and the Seeking: A Miscellany of Writings, edited by Darwin Turner, Howard University Press, 1978.
Jean Toomer: Selected Essays And Literary Criticism, edited by Robert B. Jones, University of Tennessee Press (Knoxville), 1996.

Author of plays, including *Natalie Mann.* Author of unpublished works, including "Portage Potential," 1931, "Eight-Day World," 1932, and an autobiography, "Outline of Autobiography," 1934. Novella *York Beach* included in anthology *The New American Caravan,* Macaulay, 1929; short stories and poetry included in numerous anthologies.

SIDELIGHTS: Jean Toomer's major contribution to literature is *Cane,* a novel comprised of poetry and prose which Robert Bone hailed as the product of a "universal vision." Upon the publication of *Cane* in 1923, Toomer was ranked with Ralph Ellison and Richard Wright as a leading figure in the Harlem Renaissance. In his introduction to *Cane,* Waldo Frank wrote that "a poet has arisen among our American youth who has known how to turn the essences and material of his Southland into the essences and materials of literature."

Cane's structure is of three parts. The first third of the book is devoted to the black experience in the Southern farmland. As Bernard W. Bell noted, "Part One, with its focus on the Southern past and the libido, presents the rural thesis." Houston A. Baker, Jr., called Toomer's style "Southern psychological realism." The characters inhabiting this portion of the book are faced with an inability to succeed. Citing the story "Fern" as an example, Baker wrote: "The temptations and promises presented by Fern's body are symbolic of the temptations and promises held out by the road of life. . . which stretches before the rural black American, and the frustration experienced by men in their affairs with Fern is symbolic of the frustration of the life journey. Men are willing to give their all, but the result is simply frustration, haunting memory, and hysteria." Toomer infused much of the first part with poetry. "In the sketches, the poet is uppermost," wrote Robert Littell. "Many of them begin with three of four lines of verse, and end with the same lines, slightly changed. The construction here is musical."

The second part of *Cane* is more urban oriented and concerned with Northern life. The writing style throughout is much the same as the initial section with poetry interspersed with stories. Charles W. Scruggs noted that Toomer revealed the importance of the second section in a letter to the author's brother shortly before the publication of *Cane*. "From three angles, Cane's design is a circle," Scruggs quoted Toomer as writing. "Aesthetically, from simple forms to complex ones, and back to simple forms. Regionally, from the South up into the North, and back into the South again." But Toomer, in the same letter, also cited the completion of the "circle" as the story "Harvest Song," which is contained in the second section. As Scruggs explained, "Toomer is describing *Cane* in organic terms, and therefore it never really ends." Scrugg noticed the acceleration of the narrative as the novel's focus moved from South to North. "The spiritual quest which gains momentum in the agrarian South 'swings upward' in the electric beehive of Washington," he declared. "The 'cane-fluted' world does not die in the North. It continues to haunt the dreams and lives of those who have strayed far from their roots to dwell in the cities."

The concluding third of the novel is a prose piece entitled "Kabnis." Bell called this final part "a synthesis of the earlier sections." The character of Kabnis, Bell claimed, represented "the Black writer whose difficulty in reconciling himself to the dilemma of being an Afro-American prevents him from tapping the creative reservoir of the soul." Littell, as opposed to seeing "Kabnis" as a "synthesis" of the earlier portions, called it a "strange contrast to the lyric expressionism of the shorter pieces." Earlier he'd written that of the three sections, "Kabnis" was by "far the most direct and most living, perhaps because it seems to have grown so much more than been consciously made. There is no pattern in it, and very little effort at poetry."

Many critics have offered interpretations of the title *Cane*. "Toomer uses Cain as a symbol of the African in a hostile land," wrote Scruggs, "tilling the soil of the earth, a slave, without enjoying her fruits. Yet strangely enough, this Cain receives another kind of nourishment from the soil, spiritual nourishment, which the owners of it are denied." Bell owned a slightly different perspective regarding the title. He wrote: "Equally important as a symbol of the rural life is sugar cane itself. Purple in color, pungently sweet in odor, mysteriously musical in sound, and deep-rooted in growth, cane represents the beauty and pain of living close to nature. It also represents the Gothic qualities of the Black American's African and southern past, especially his ambivalent attitude toward this heritage." Baker acknowledged the validity of the *Cane* image in the Northern portion of the novel. He contended that "even when Toomer deals with the life of the urban black American . . . , he still presents the rhythms and psychological factors that condition life in the land of sugar cane, a land populated by the 'sons of Cane.'"

Praise for Toomer's writing is extensive. Baker cited his "mysterious brand of Southern psychological realism that has been matched only in the best work of William Faulkner." Kenneth Rexroth, writing in *American Poetry in the Twentieth Century,* was no less impressed. "Toomer is the first poet to unite folk culture and the elite culture of the white avant-garde," he contended, "and he accomplishes this difficult task with considerable success. He is without doubt the most important Black poet." Critics such as Bell and Gorham Munson preferred to dwell on Toomer's use of language. "There can be no question of Jean Toomer's skill as a literary craftsman," asserted Munson. "Toomer has founded his own speech, now swift and clipped for violent narrative action, now languorous and dragging for specific characterizing purposes, and now lean and sinuous for the exposition of ideas, but always cadenced to accord with an unusually sensitive ear." Bell attributed *Cane*'s "haunting, illusive beauty" to "Toomer's fascinating way with words." He wrote, "The meaning of the book is implicit in the arabesque pattern of imagery, the subtle movement of symbolic actions and objects, the shifting rhythm of syntax and diction, and the infrastructure of a cosmic consciousness."

After the publication of *Cane,* Toomer continued writing prodigiously. However, most of his work was rejected by publishers. He became increasingly interested in the teachings of George I. Gurdjieff, a Greek spiritual philosopher, and turned to teaching Gurdjieff's beliefs in America. Finally, Toomer embraced the Quaker religion and lived his last decade as a recluse. S. P. Fullwinder summed up Toomer's life as "a story of tragedy." He wrote: "As long as he was searching he was a fine creative artist; when the search ended, so did his creative powers. So long as he was searching his work was the cry of one caught in the modern human condition; it expressed modern man's lostness, his isolation. Once Toomer found an identity-giving absolute, his voice ceased to be the cry of modern man and became the voice of the schoolmaster complacently pointing out the way—his way."

BIOGRAPHICAL/CRITICAL SOURCES:

BOOKS

Baker, Howard A. Jr., *Black Literature in America,* McGraw, 1971.

Benson, Brian Joseph, and Mabel Mayle Dillard, *Jean Toomer,* Twayne Publishers, 1980.

Black Literature Criticism, Gale (Detroit), Volume 3, 1992.

Bone, Robert A., *The Negro Novel in America,* Yale University Press, 1965.

Bontemps, Arna, editor, *The Harlem Renaissance Remembered,* Dodd, 1972, pp. 51-62.

Contemporary Literary Criticism, Gale, Volume 1, 1973; Volume 4, 1975; Volume 13, 1980; Volume 22, 1982.

Durham, Frank, editor, *The Merrill Studies in "Cane,"* Charles E. Merrill Publishing, 1971.

Jones, Robert B., *Jean Toomer: Selected Essays and Literary Criticism,* University of Tennessee Press, 1996.

Kerman, Cynthia Earl, and Richard Eldridge, *The Lives of Jean Toomer: A Hunger for Wholeness,* Louisiana State University Press, 1987.

McKay, Nellie Y., *Jean Toomer, Artist: A Study of His Literary Life and Work, 1894-1936,* University of North Carolina Press, 1984.

Poetry Criticism, Gale, Volume 7, 1994.

Rexroth, Kenneth, *American Poetry in the Twentieth Century,* Herder, 1971.

Short Story Criticism, Gale, Volume 1, 1988.

Rusch, Frederik L., editor, *A Jean Toomer Reader: Selected Unpublished Writings*, Oxford University Press, 1993.

PERIODICALS

American Literature, May, 1972; March, 1975, pp. 84-96.
Black American Literature Forum, fall, 1987, pp. 275-87; fall, 1989, pp. 593-99.
Black World, September, 1974.
Negro American Literature Forum, July, 1970, pp. 61-63.
South Carolina Review, April, 1975, pp. 61-64.
Southern Humanities Review, winter, 1971, pp. 76-80.
Southern Quarterly, fall, 1981, pp. 75-84.

*   *   *

TORNIMPARTE, Alessandra
See GINZBURG, Natalia

*   *   *

TORRE, Raoul della
See MENCKEN, H(enry) L(ouis)

*   *   *

TOURNIER, Michel (Edouard) 1924-

PERSONAL: Born December 19, 1924, in Paris, France; son of Alphonse (a records rights dealer) and Marie-Madeleine (Fournier) Tournier. *Education:* Attended University of Paris and University of Tuebingen. *Avocational interests:* Photography.

ADDRESSES: Home—Le Presbytere, Choisel, 78460 Chevreuse, France. *Office*—c/o Beverly Gordey, Collins Publishers, 16 rue de Savoie, 75006 Paris, France.

CAREER: Writer. Producer and director, R.T.F., 1949-54; newspaper work, 1955-58; Editions Plon, Paris, France, director of literary services, 1958-68; host of television series *Le Chambre noire* (title means "The Black Box"), 1960-65; radio announcer, Europe Numero Un; translator. Founder of Recontres Internationales de Photographie, an annual festival held in Arles, France. Frequent guest on television talk shows. Guest lecturer in France, Germany, and Africa.

MEMBER: Academie Goncourt (1972-).

AWARDS, HONORS: Grand Prix du Roman from Academie Francaise, 1967, for *Vendredi; ou, Les Limbes du Pacifique;* Prix Goncourt, 1970, for *Le Roi des Aulnes;* Officier de la Legion d'Honneur.

WRITINGS:

NOVELS

Vendredi; ou, Les Limbes du Pacifique (title means "Friday; or, The Limbo of the Pacific"), Gallimard, 1967, revised edition, 1978, translation by Norman Denny published as *Friday,* Doubleday, 1969 (published in England as *Friday; or, The Other Island,* Collins, 1969).
Le Roi des Aulnes, Gallimard, 1970, translation by Barbara Bray published as *The Ogre,* Doubleday, 1972 (published in England as *The Erl King,* Collins, 1972).

Vendredi; ou, La Vie sauvage (juvenile), Flammarion, 1971, translation by Ralph Manheim published as *Friday and Robinson: Life on Esperanza Island,* Knopf, 1972.
Les Meteores, Gallimard, 1975, translation by Anne Carter published as *Gemini,* Doubleday, 1981.
Gaspard, Melchior et Balthazar, Gallimard, 1980, translation by Manheim published as *The Four Wise Men,* Doubleday, 1982.
Gilles et Jeanne, Gallimard, 1983, translation by Alan Sheridan published as *Gilles and Jeanne,* Methuen, 1987.
A Garden at Hammamet, translation by Barbara Wright of *Un Jardin a Hammamet,* Lord John, 1985.
La Goutte d'or, Gallimard, 1986, translation by Wright published as *The Golden Droplet,* Doubleday, 1987.
Angus, illustrations by Pierre Joubert, Piste, 1988.
Le Medianoche Amoureux, Gallimard, 1989, translation by Barbara Wright published as *The Midnight Love Feast,* Collins, 1991.
The Mirror of Ideas, translation by Jonathan Krell, University of Nebraska Press, 1998.

OTHER

(Author of introduction) Laurent Gouvion Saint-Cyr, *Aventures et secrets du collectionneur,* Stock, 1971.
(Author of introduction) *Venise, hier et demain,* photographs by Fulvia Roiter, Editions du Chene, 1973.
(Author of introduction) Lucien Clergue, *Mers, plages, sources et torrents, arbres,* Editions Perceval, 1974.
Arroyo (portraits), K. Flinker, 1974.
Le Vent paraclet (literary autobiography), Gallimard, 1977, translation by Arthur Goldhammer published as *The Wind Spirit: An Autobiography,* Beacon Press, 1988.
(With Edouard Boubat) *Canada: Journal de voyage* (nonfiction), photographs by Edouard Boubat, La Press, 1977, republished as *Journal de voyage au Canada,* Robert Laffont, 1984.
(With Joseph Goebbels) *Derniers carnets,* Flammarion, 1977.
Amandine ou Les Deux Jardins (title means "Amandine, or the Two Gardens"; juvenile; also see below), Rouge et Or, 1977.
La Famille des enfants (short prose and photos), Flammarion, 1977.
Le Coq de bruyere (collection; title means "The Woodcock"; includes the play *Le Fetischiste: Un Acte por un homme seul,* first produced in 1974; produced Off Broadway in 1984), Gallimard, 1978, translation by Wright published as *The Fetishist and Other Stories,* Doubleday, 1984.
(With Georges Lemoine) *Des clefs et des serrures* (short prose and photos; title means "Of Keys and Locks"), Editions du Chene/Hachette, 1979.
Le Fugue du Petit Poucet (title means "Tom Thumb Ran Away"; a Christmas story), Rouge et Or, 1979.
Pierrot et les secrets de la nuit, Gallimard, 1979.
Barbedor (short prose and photos), Gallimard, 1980.
Vues de dos (short prose and photos; title means "Views of Blacks"), Gallimard, 1981.
Le Vol du Vampire (essays; title means "The Flight of the Vampire"), Mercure de France, 1981.
(Author of introduction) *Morts et resurrections de Dieter Appelt,* photographs by Dieter Appelt, Herscher, 1981.
L'Aire du muguet (title means "The Lily of the Valley Rest Area"), Gallimard, 1982.
(With Konrad R. Mueller) *Francois Mitterand* (biography), Flammarion, 1983.
Les Rois Mages, Gallimard, 1983.

(With Jean-Max Toubeau) *Le Vagabond immobile,* Gallimard, 1984.

Sept contes, Gallimard, 1984.

(Author of introduction) Marrianne Fulton, *Lucien Clergue,* New York Graphic Society/Little, Brown, 1985.

Marseille, ou Le Present incertain (short prose and photos), P.U.F., 1985.

Le Tabor et le Sinai: Essais sur l'art contemporain, Belfond, 1989.

Le Crepuscule Des Masques (prose and photos), Hobeke (Paris), 1992.

(Author of essay) Arno Rafael Minkkinen, *Waterline,* photographs by Minkkinen, Aperture, 1994.

(Author of essay) Alaia Azzedine, *Alaia,* photographs by Azzedine, Distributed Art Publishers, 1998.

Also translator of many German novels, including the works of Erich Maria Remarque.

MEDIA ADAPTATIONS: Several stories published in the collection *Le Coq de bruyere,* have been adapted for and broadcast on French television.

SIDELIGHTS: Winner of two prestigious French literary prizes, Michel Tournier, as *Times Literary Supplement* critic John Sturrock observes, "has no rival among French novelists of his generation for writing books that are at once vivid and intellectually provocative." Tournier is a radical social critic, challenging cultural notions of the social contract handed down through myth and showing characters who select alternative modes of relating to their environment. The products of a highly imaginative mind, his novels—consisting primarily of philosophical speculation—are not for the casual reader. Like the works of Thomas Pynchon, John Barth, and Vladimir Nabokov, Tournier's tales are densely packed with a complex network of symbols and allusions. They have been criticized for their pretentiousness and, on occasion, for their somewhat disturbing and even frightening themes. Narrators of his tales include a pederast and a fetishist who is obsessed with lingerie. The controversial nature of his subjects has brought him much critical attention. Bob Halliday comments in the *Washington Post Book World,* "In Europe, where Tournier is recognized as the major French novelist of the past 20 years . . ., his morally often uncomfortable works have aroused hot controversy and sold in the millions."

Born in Paris in 1924 to parents with an interest in Germany, Tournier learned to speak German and developed a critical view of Parisian life. After spending most of his college years in Tuebingen following the Second World War, he scored poorly on the French philosophy exam, and began working as a literary translator. In *La Vent paraclet* (*The Wind Spirit: An Autobiography*), he explains that his understanding of literary style allowed him to produce French translations that were also translations into the style of French novelists such as Emile Zola, Gustave Flaubert, and Guy de Maupassant. When he recognized that his education in philosophy was excellent preparation for writing novels, he spent fifteen years figuring out how to combine myth, philosophy, and fiction. After completing three original novels he judged unworthy of publication, Tournier wrote *Vendredi; ou, Les Limbes du Pacifique* (*Friday*) and *Les Roi des Aulnes* (*The Ogre*), which quickly established him as one of the most remarkable writers to appear on the postwar French literary scene. Tournier's first published original novel, *Friday,* came out in print when he was forty-three.

Beginning with the traditional Robinson Crusoe formula (which views man as a rational, tool-using creature who seeks to control his world through the imposition of physical and social order), Tournier deviates from the Daniel Defoe version somewhat to stress the existence of other alternatives—mainly non-rational and non-technical ones—that man has at his disposal to deal with the environment. While both Defoe and Tournier's castaways at first strive to "civilize" life on their little island, Tournier has his Crusoe gradually become less and less interested in imposing his will on nature as he grows mystically closer to his surroundings. By the time his would-be savior Friday arrives, Crusoe is ready to go completely "native." In a reversal of the roles found in the original Crusoe story, with Friday as his teacher, Crusoe learns to abandon the old European conventions as he sheds his clothes, worships the sun, and eats, sleeps, and works only when he feels like it. Tournier has Friday, not Crusoe, join the crew of a rescue ship headed for Europe; Crusoe remains on the island. Thus, as opposed to the rationalism espoused by the eighteenth-century Defoe, Tournier, using the same basic material, suggests another, more "modern" approach to determining one's place in the natural world—an approach that is more sensual and spontaneous, and largely independent of culturally transmitted values.

T. J. Fleming of the *New York Times Book Review* reports that Tournier "has attempted nothing less than an exploration of the soul of modern man [in *Friday*]. . . . Again and again, he finds fresh and original ways of viewing primary experiences such as time and work and religious faith, the relationship of men to animals and trees and their own shadowy selves, to civilization and the essential earth. The telling is intensely French. The focus is on thinking, and thinking about feeling. . . . [*Friday*] works, because the framework of the classic makes this abracadabra of believability convincing." At first glance, a *New Yorker* critic found all of this philosophizing to be "not a particularly attractive prospect" for a novel. Yet, he concludes, "Tournier is a cultivated and disciplined writer, and his Robinson . . . is most likable."

With the publication of *The Ogre,* Tournier received world-wide attention. Based in part on Johann Goethe's poem "The Erl King," *The Ogre* is set in Germany between 1938 and 1945, where an imprisoned giant of a Frenchman, Abel Tiffauges, serves his Nazi captors as a procurer of young boys for an elite Hitler youth camp. Tiffauges, who fears chaos, is happy to be a member of a group where his values and function are so clearly defined. The brooding Tiffauges views his role in life as that of a "beast of burden," a man who will save himself by saving others, yet he is haunted by the symbolic nature of his own actions and of the destructive actions of mankind in general. Readers find his role difficult to determine, for while Tiffauges seems, in the end, to be a somewhat shadowy symbol of resistance (he dies after marching into a bog while carrying a Jewish child he rescued from a concentration camp), he can also—as the author suggests when someone attempts to assassinate him on July 20, 1944—be regarded as an embodiment of Hitler as well. As the *Times Literary Supplement* reviewer explains: "The book as a whole is a journey from a contrived surrealism to, as it were, the real thing. The novel is so charged with symbols that it is hard to tell . . . just how menacing an ogre Tiffauges is. . . . He is no simple monster."

Many critics, including Jean Amery in *Merkur,* gave the book a hostile reception, calling it a glorification of neo-Nazi ideals. However, William Cloonan argues in the *Dictionary of Literary Biography* that this reading results from mistaking Tiffauges as a spokesman for Tournier, who has deliberately presented his character in a negative light. It also ignores the fact that Tournier depicts Tiffauges as a man separated from recognizing the ultimate evil of his actions by elaborate self-delusions. Cloonan relates that "Tournier is depicting a deeply confused person whose personality is at once a portrait and parody of the Nazi psyche," and an illustration of how important it is for individuals and nations to distinguish between fantasy and reality.

Other critics, too, have been baffled by the multiplicity of ideas and interpretations present in the story, yet they still regard reading it as a worthwhile literary experience. *Newsweek*'s Peter Prescott calls it a "fine novel" that is "more likely to be praised than read. . . . *The Ogre* is built in the way Bach built his fugues; themes and statements are introduced, inverted, tangled and marched past each other, all to be resolved in loud, majestic chords. . . . And yet the symbols and correspondences of this story, which are far more complex than I have been able to indicate, would be insufficient to sustain it as fiction. Tournier's achievement rests in his remarkable blend of myth with realism. . . . [He] offers a succession of scenes . . . which, as Abel says, not only decipher the essence of existence, but exalt it."

As he reveals in *Le Vent paraclet*, Tournier makes a conscious effort to include "eternal and disturbing" elements in novels that are otherwise conventional (as opposed to experimental) in form. For example, in the novel *Gaspard, Melchior et Balthazar* (*The Four Wise Men*), a retelling of the Biblical story of the Magi, the three Wise Men come to Bethlehem to see the Messiah, and resolve some personal problems when they find him. Cloonan relates, "Gaspard is black and ashamed of his skin color. Balthazar's love of art puts him at odds with the religious bigots who control his court, and Melchior is the victim of a palace revolt that has cost him his throne. . . . [In Bethlehem,] Gaspard sees that the infant in the manger is black; Balthazar's conscience is eased by the discovery that any depiction of the world is a tribute to the Creator; and Melchior . . . realizes that the kingdom he has really been seeking is not of this world."

In the novel, a fourth seeker of the Christ Child misses the birth of the Messiah, spends the next thirty-three years in prison in another man's place, misses the crucifixion, eats the leftovers from the Last Supper, and is welcomed into heaven. Meanwhile the other kings, moved by their encounter with the Christ Child, become "nurturing" men, capable of sheltering children with a care usually associated with maternal instincts. Critics applaud Tournier for accomplishing a unique blend of religious and secular elements. Robert Taylor comments in the *Boston Globe*, "*The Four Wise Men* is a miracle of a novel, a successful devotional work by an author thoroughly conversant with modernism. . . . Indeed, contemporary literature, dominated by secular values, has few works to compare with this, in which imaginary characters mingle authoritatively with historical figures."

Cloonan sees in *The Four Wise Men* an important development in Tournier's work. "In the earlier novels his characters feared complexity and sought elaborate, albeit simplistic ways of clarifying experience. This novel champions the complex and appreciates disorder as a part of life. . . . Tournier's earlier heroes might have opted for one pole of [a dichotomy] over the other: blackness rather than kingship, power over poverty, or flesh instead of spirit. Such simplifications do not occur in *Gaspard, Melchior et Balthazar,* and in fact there are numerous parodies of what earlier had appeared to be insoluble dichotomies." At the manger, they discover that in godhead incarnate the opposite poles of many dichotomies are resolved in paradox. As Tournier writes,

"Cet Heritier du Royaume mele des attributs incompatibles, la grandeur et la petitesse, la puissance et l'innocence, la plenitude et la pauvrete" (This Heir to the Kingdom mingles incomparable attributes, greatness and smallness, power and innocence, plenitude and poverty).

Tournier's novel *La Goutte d'or* treats the theme of the quest for identity in a world where images are valued more than realities, where the primary force of culture seems to be its ability to construct convincing illusions. Idriss, a young Berber shepherd, for example, leaves Northern Africa to discover that "the Sahara desert, a subject of study and romanticization among the French and for many other Westerners as well, it is a concept unknown to its inhabitants," Cloonan explains. "The Sahara is as much an intellectual structure as a geographical location for those who live far from it. . . . For Idriss the Sahara is . . . a constantly shifting series of designs in the sand, a world alien to permanence of any sort. The Sahara is a fixed entity only when its ambiguous, transitory qualities are denied by an act tantamount to fictionalization." The Africa perceived in the Western world bears no resemblance to the continent as Idriss knows it, demonstrating the power of images to supercede realities.

Idriss is warned that he will lose his identity if he is photographed or becomes a model for a clothing store. Eventually he does lose the golden nugget of the title—a mark of citizenship once worn by Romans—which is a symbol of his identity. Tracing this loss and the boy's attempts to regain his *goutte d'or*, Tournier also writes a revealing depiction of Arab and Western traditional world views in conflict. He also explores the differences between film and written fiction as media having different possibilities, different limitations, and differing impacts on people through culture. Idriss begins to regain his identity when he studies Arab calligraphy, though his later act—an attempt to steal what he thinks is his lost *goutte d'or* from a storefront window display—reinforces Tournier's message about the power of visual images.

Tournier weaves his unique tales on the frames of conventional forms of fiction. According to a *Times Literary Supplement* reviewer, Tournier confesses to adhering to an orthodox structure "partly as bait, in order to get people to read what they might otherwise refuse. Deception is needed because he is a metaphysical novelist, more likely to find charm and inspiration in [the philosophers] Leibniz or Spinoza than in the work of other novelists. . . . He adapts the supposedly safe conventions of realism to fantastic, transcendent ends." This strategy makes Tournier's novels more accessible than the works of other fabulists, and partly accounts for their popularity among less sophisticated readers as well as those who take an interest in Tournier's philosophical concerns. Roger Shattuck explains in the *New York Review of Books*, "Insofar as they adapt existing legends and celebrate earlier forms of wisdom, his works leave behind the preoccupation with originality that has propelled the arts for the last two centuries. . . . By sparing himself the need to innovate in form, he has been able to direct his inventive powers simultaneously toward elaborating a story line and toward marshalling a powerful style."

Though a *French Review* critic has said that Tournier's novels are too playful to be "taken very seriously," *World Literature Today* reviewer Daniele McDowell insists that they are worthy of serious attention. "Tournier's tales in their symbolic significance are more convincing than realistic fiction," she declares. "They represent a poetic rendering of his relationship to the world. Concretizing arcane reality through delusion or enchantment, Tournier is a magician who gives us the reassurance that there is a secret garden next to our backyard, that there is another world behind the mirror and that there is a small island in the Pacific Ocean where we lived happily once upon a time." Cloonan adds that readers appreciate Tournier's pessimistic yet "smiling" view of the human condition. He explains, "Tournier's work displays few illusions about human goodness, and even less confidence in the collective progress of mankind. His books do, however, reflect a continuous amazement before the wonder of life, before the incredible privilege of being alive."

BIOGRAPHICAL/CRITICAL SOURCES:

BOOKS

Anderson, Christopher, *Michel Tournier's Children: Myth, Intertext, Initiation,* Lang (New York), 1996.
Cloonan, William, *Michel Tournier,* Twayne, 1985.
Colin, Davis, *Michel Tournier: Philosophy and Fiction,* Clarendon Press, 1988.
Contemporary Literary Criticism, Gale (Detroit), Volume 6, 1976; Volume 23, 1983; Volume 36, 1986.
Dictionary of Literary Biography, Volume 83: *French Novelists since 1960,* Gale, 1989.
Gascoigne, David, *Michel Tournier,* Berg (Washington, D.C.), 1996.
Guichard, Nicole, *Michel Tournier Autrui et la quete du double,* Diffusion Didier Erudition (Paris), 1990.
Kochhar-Lindgren, Gray, *Narcissus Transformed: The Textual Subject in Psychoanalysis and Literature,* Pennsylvania State University Press, 1993.
Petit, Susan, *Michel Tournier's Metaphysical Fictions,* Benjamins (Philadelphia), 1991.
Roberts, Martin, *Michel Tournier: Bricolage and Cultural Mythology,* ANMA Libri (Saratoga, CA), 1994.
Worton, Michael, editor, *Michel Tournier,* Longman (New York), 1995.

PERIODICALS

Atlantic Monthly, October, 1982.
Boston Globe, November 23, 1988.
Chicago Tribune Book World, September 6, 1981; October 25, 1987.
French Review, May, 1978; April, 1979; December, 1981; February, 1994; December, 1994.
Los Angeles Times Book Review, September 16, 1984; May 19, 1985; December 27, 1987.
Merkur, number 28, 1973.
New Republic, February 11, 1985; February 21, 1985.
New Statesman, February 7, 1969.
Newsweek, October 4, 1972.
New Yorker, June 14, 1969.
New York Review of Books, November 30, 1972; December 14, 1972; April 28, 1983; November 8, 1984.
New York Times, October 24, 1987.
New York Times Book Review, April 13, 1969; October 3, 1972; October 4, 1981; October 24, 1982; September 9, 1984; November 1, 1987.
Observer, January 30, 1983; November 1, 1987.
Publishers Weekly, September 14, 1984 (interview).
Time, August 21, 1972; November 18, 1982.
Times Literary Supplement, October 23, 1970; October 7, 1977; October 13, 1978; February 13, 1981; October 16, 1981; November 5, 1987; August 11, 1989; February 15, 1991.
Washington Post Book World, November 21, 1982; October 28, 1984; December 27, 1987; December 11, 1988.

World Literature Today, spring, 1979; summer, 1981.

*   *   *

TOURNIMPARTE, Alessandra
See GINZBURG, Natalia

*   *   *

TRAKL, Georg 1887-1914

PERSONAL: Born February 3, 1887, in Salzburg, Austria; died November 3, 1914, in Krakow, Poland. *Education:* Attended University of Vienna.

CAREER: Austrian Army medical corps; writer, 1900(?)-1914.

WRITINGS

Gedichte, 1913.
Sebastian im traum, 1915.
Die dichtungen, 1918.
Aus goldenem kelch: Die Jugenddichtungen, edited by Erhard Buschbeck, Muller (Salzburg), 1939.
Gesamtausgabe (collected works), edited by Wolfgang Schneditz, 3 volumes, Salzburg, 1938-49.
Decline: Twelve Poems, translation by Michael Hamburger, Latin Press (St. Ives), 1952.
Twenty Poems, translation by James Wright and Robert Bly, Sixties Press (Madison), 1961.
Selected Poems, edited by Christopher, translation by Robert Grenier and others, Cape (London), 1968.
Dichtungen und briefe, Muller, 1969.
In the Red Forest, 1973.
Poems, translation by Lucia Getsi, Mundus Artium Press (Athens), 1973.
Winter Night: Four Prose Poems, translation by David J. Black, Thunder City Press (Birmingham), 1979.
Georg Trakl: A Profile, edited by Frank Graziano, Logbridge-Rhodes (Durango), 1983.
Song of the West: Selected Poems of Georg Trakl, translation by Robert Firmage, North Point Press (San Francisco), 1988.
Autumn Sonata: Selected Poems of Georg Trakl, translation by Daniel Simko, Moyer Bell (Mt. Kisco), 1989.

Contributor of poetry to *Der Brenner.*

MEDIA ADAPTATIONS: Paul Hindemith's *Die junge Magd, sechs Gedichte von George Trakl, fur eine Altstimme, mit Flote, Klarinette, und Streichquartett, Opus 23, Nr. 2,* Schott (Mainz), 1949, was adapted from Trakl's poetry. Camillo Togni's *Helian, de Trakl: Cinque lieder per soprano e orchestra da camera,* Edizioni Suvini Zerboni (Milan), 1962, was adapted from Trakl's poetry. Peter Maxwell Davies's *Revelation and Fall: Offenbarung und Untergang, for Soprano and Sixteen Instruments,* Boosey & Hawkes, 1971, was adapted from Trakl's poetry. Egon Wellesz's *Vision: Sopran and Orchester, Opus 99,* Doblinger (Wien), 1982, was adapted from Trakl's poetry. Oliver Knutson's *Symphony No. 2 for High Soprano and Chamber Orchestra, Op. 7 (1970-71),* Faber Music (London), Schirmer (New York City), 1984, was adapted from the poetry of Trakl and Sylvia Plath. Larry Sitsky's *Music in the Mirabell Garden: A Song Cycle for Soprano and 8 Players,* translation by James McAuley, Seesay Music (New York City), 1996, text adapted from Trakl's poetry.

SIDELIGHTS: Georg Trakl is an important lyric poet in German literature of the early twentieth century. Critics associate his work with various modern artistic movements, and he is viewed as one of the principal writers to set the dark, introspective tone that later influenced the course of German expressionism. Affinities with imagism have also been noted in Trakl's strikingly visual style. In addition, the dreamlike flow of images in his poems has indicated to some commentators a compositional method similar to the automatic writing of the surrealists, with whom Trakl also shared a preoccupation with violence, perversity, and death. Trakl's strongest literary affiliation, however, is with the French symbolists of the nineteenth century, primarily Arthur Rimbaud, whose disordered and conflict-ridden genius is said to be incarnated in the Austrian poet.

Of great significance in Trakl's early home life in Salzburg was his close, possibly incestuous, relations with his sister Grete. Critics frequently identify her as the inspiration for "the sister," a multifaceted symbolic figure in the poems. Trakl attended a Catholic elementary school, while receiving Protestant religious instruction; he was an unsuccessful student and eventually dropped out of school. Later, however, he entered the University of Vienna for training as a pharmacist, a vocation which facilitated his lifelong use of drugs. Soon after leaving the university he was drafted into the Austrian army and assigned to the medical corps. Returning to civilian life, Trakl found a job in a pharmacy, failed to adjust to the routine of working life, and reenlisted in the army. In 1912, while stationed in Innsbruck, he met Ludwig von Ficker, editor of *Der Brenner.* Ficker became friend and mentor to Trakl for the remaining years of his short life, publishing the poet's work regularly in his literary journal. Trakl died of a self-administered, though perhaps accidental, drug overdose in a Polish hospital while recovering from his battle experience during World War I.

Critics agree that, though Trakl had been writing poetry from an early age, his best work dates from the final two years of his life, displaying a noticeable development from his efforts prior to 1912. Personal torment and unrelieved sense of horror and disintegration dominated the earlier poems. The tone of Trakl's later poems is more impersonal and ambiguous. In these works Trakl transcends the extreme subjectivity of his former poetic self to universalize his existential vision. Some critics describe this new quality in Trakl's mature poems as a mythic objectivity, while confronting the paradox that this poet's world is essentially private, resembling that of a schizophrenic. Critical analysis of Trakl's work has revealed its disjointed, fragmentary nature, summarizing it as a collection of often-repeated symbols and motifs without consistent meaning. these poems, however, are credited with a consistency of mood and attitude which unifies them into a cohesive, though nonrational, statement. In essence they form the poet's protest against the corrupt, fallen condition of humankind.

In just two years, Trakl managed to produce the poems that place him among the most important and original poets of the German language. His language was simple and clear, even in translation, resembling the work of Hoelderlin, with strong and precise imagery, darkly brooding sensitivity, and an adept feeling for color. He wrote about death, decay, and doom, hiding himself in lyrical metaphor and the ambiguity of his images. Trakl saw the world collapsing around him and taking him with it; and while his poetry is overwhelmingly negative, critics find in it a gesture of affirmation. Internal evidence of the poems and statements made by Trakl have indicated to many commentators that he was a Christian or at least gave voice to Christian doctrine, and thus balanced his visions of damnation with the possibility of ultimate redemption. He described poetry as "imperfect penance" for "unabsolved guilt." Other critics see in this more positive side to his work the influence of pantheistic views acquired from Hoelderlin. Herbert Lindenberger wrote, "The lofty stance, the cosmic range, and the haunting music of Trakl's poetry now mark him, with Rilke, as perhaps the last great representative of what could be called the sublime tradition in German."

BIOGRAPHICAL/CRITICAL SOURCES:

BOOKS

Cagey, T. J., *Manshape That Shone: An Interpretation of Trakl,* Blackwell, 1964.

Cohen, J. M., *Poetry of This Age: 1908-1965,* Hutchinson University Library, 1966.

Detsch, Richard, *Georg Trakl's Poetry: Toward a Union of Opposites,* Pennsylvania State University Press, 1983.

Hamburger, Michael, *Reason and Energy: Studies in German Literature,* Grove Press, 1957.

Heidegger, Martin, *On the Way to Language,* translated by Peter Hertz, Harper, 1971.

Kurrik, Maire Jaanus, *Georg Trakl,* Columbia University Press, 1974.

Leiva-Merikakis, Erasmo, *The Blossoming Thorn: Georg Trakl's Poetry of Atonement,* Bucknell University Press, 1987.

Lindenberger, Herbert, *George Trakl,* Twayne, 1971.

Sokel, Walter H., *The Writer in Extremis: Expressionism in Twentieth-Century German Literature,* Stanford University Press, 1959.

Williams, Eric B., editor, *The Dark Flutes of Fall: Critical Essays on Georg Trakl,* Camden House (Columbia), 1991.

Williams, Eric B., *The Mirror and the Word: Modernism, Literary Theory, and Georg Trakl,* University of Nebraska Press, 1993.

PERIODICALS

German Life & Letters, January, 1949, pp. 122-37.
Listener, October 24, 1968, p. 542.
Times Literary Supplement, September 7, 1970, p. 752.

*   *   *

TREMBLAY, Michel 1942-

PERSONAL: Born June 25, 1942, in Montreal, Quebec, Canada; son of Armand (a linotype operator) and Rheauna Tremblay. *Education:* Attended Institut des Arts Graphiques.

ADDRESSES: Agent—Agence Goodwin, 839 Sherbrooke E., Suite 2, Montreal, Quebec H2L 1K6, Canada.

CAREER: Writer, Radio-Canada television, linotype operator, costume department, 1963-66.

MEMBER: Union of Quebec Writers, CEAD, Playwrights Union.

AWARDS, HONORS: First prize in Radio Canada's Young Author's Competition, 1964, for unpublished play *Le Train;* Meritas Trophy, 1970, 1972; Canada Council Award, 1971; Floyd S. Chalmers Canadian Play awards, Ontario Arts Council, 1972-75, 1978, 1986, and 1989, for *Le Vrai Monde?;* Prix Victor-Morin, Societe Saint-Jean-Baptiste de Montreal, 1974; Canadian Film Festival Award for best scenario, 1975, for *Francoise Durocher, Waitress;* Ontario Lieutenant-Governor's Medal, 1976 and 1977; Prix France-Quebec, Quebec Ministere des Relations Internationales, 1981, for novel *Therese et Pierrette a l'ecole des Saints-Anges,* and 1985, for novel *La Duchesse et le Roturier;* Premiere Selection, Prix Medicis, 1983; L'Ordre des arts et des lettres (France), Chevalier, 1984, Officier, 1991; *Albertine, en cinq temps* was named best play at Le Festival du theatre des Ameriques, 1985; Montreal's Prix de la Critique, 1986, for *Albertine, en cinq temps;* Athanase-David, 1988; Prix du public au Festival de Bruxelles, 1990, for *Le Coeur decouvert: Roman d'amours;* Grand Prix du Public, 1990; Doctorat Honoris Causa from Concordia University, 1990, McGill University, 1991, Stirling University, Scotland, 1992, and Windsor University, Ontario, 1993; Prix Jacques-Cartier Lyon, 1991; Banff National Center Award, 1993; received six grants from the Canadian Arts Council.

WRITINGS:

PLAYS

Le Train (originally broadcast by Radio Canada, 1964; first produced in Montreal, 1965), Lemeac, 1990.

Cinq (one-act plays; includes *Berthe, Johnny Mangano and His Astonishing Dogs,* and *Gloria Star*), first produced in Montreal, 1966, revised version published as *En pieces detachees* (first produced in Montreal, 1969), Lemeac, 1972, translation by Allan Van Meer published as *Like Death Warmed Over* (produced in Winnipeg, 1973), Playwrights Co-op (Toronto), 1973, translation published as *Montreal Smoked Meat* (produced in Toronto, 1974), Talon Books, 1975, translation also produced as *Broken Pieces,* Vancouver, 1974.

Les Belles-Soeurs (title means "The Sisters-In-Law"; two-act; first produced in Montreal, 1968), Holt (Montreal), 1968, translation by John Van Burek and Bill Glassco, Talon Books, 1974, published as *The Guid Sisters* (first produced in Toronto and Glasgow, 1987), Exile (Toronto), 1988.

La Duchesse de Langeais (two-act), first produced in Montreal, 1970.

En pieces detachees [and] *La Duchesse de Langeais,* Lemeac, 1970.

Les Paons (one-act fantasy; first produced in Ottawa, 1971), CEAD, 1969.

Trois Petit Tours (television adaptations of *Berthe, Johnny Mangano and His Astonishing Dogs,* and *Gloria Star;* broadcast in 1969), Lemeac, 1971.

A toi, pour toujours, ta Marie-Lou (one-act; first produced in Montreal, 1971), introduction by Michel Belair, Lemeac, 1971, translation by Van Burek and Glassco published as *Forever Yours, Marie-Lou,* Talon Books, 1975.

Demain matin, Montreal m'attend (title means "Tomorrow Morning, Montreal Wait for Me"; first produced in Montreal, 1972), Lemeac, 1972.

Hosanna (two-act; first produced in Montreal, 1973, produced on Broadway, 1981), translation by Van Burek and Glassco, Talon Books, 1974.

Hosanna [and] *La Duchesse de Langeais,* Lemeac, 1973.

Bonjour, la, bonjour (title means "Hello, There, Hello"; first produced in Ottawa, 1974), Lemeac, 1974, translation by Van Burek and Glassco published as *Bonjour, la, bonjour* (produced in 1975), Talon Books, 1975.

Les Heros de mon enfance (musical comedy; title means "My Childhood Heroes"; first produced in Eastman, Quebec, 1975), Lemeac, 1976.

Surprise! Surprise! (one-act), first produced in Montreal, 1975.

Sainte-Carmen de la Main (two-act; first produced in Montreal, 1976), Lemeac, 1976, translation by Van Burek published at *Sainte-Carmen of the Main* (broadcast on BBC-Radio, 1987), Talon Books, 1981.

La Duchesse de Langeais and Other Plays (includes *La Duchesse de Langeais, Trois Petit Tours,* and *Surprise! Surprise!*), translations by Van Burek, Talon Books, 1976.

Damnee Manon, sacree Sandra (one-act; first produced in Montreal, 1977; produced as *Sandra/Manon* in Edinburgh and London, 1984), translation by Van Burek published as *Damnee Manon, sacree Sandra* (produced in United States, 1981), Talon Books, 1981.

Damnee Manon, sacree Sandra [and] *Surprise! Surprise!* Lemeac, 1977.

L'Impromptu d'Outremont (two-act; first produced in Montreal, 1980), Lemeac, 1980, translation by Van Burek published as *The Impromptu of Outremont* (produced, 1981), Talon Books, 1981.

Les Anciennes Odeurs (first produced in Montreal, 1981), Lemeac, 1981, translation by John Stowe published as *Remember Me,* Talon Books, 1984.

Les Grandes Vacances, first produced in Montreal, 1981.

Albertine, en cinq temps (first produced in Ottawa, 1984), Lemeac, 1984, translation by Van Burek and Glassco published as *Albertine in Five Times* (produced in Toronto, Edinburgh, and London, 1986), Talon Books, 1987.

Le Vrai Monde? (first produced concurrently in Ottawa and Montreal, 1987), Lemeac, 1987, translation published as *The Real World?* (produced in London, 1990), Talon Books, 1988.

La Maison suspendue (first produced in Montreal and Toronto, 1990), Lemeac, 1990, translation by Van Burek, Talonbooks, 1991.

Marcel poursuivi par les chiens (first produced in Montreal, 1992), Lemeac, 1992, translation by Van Burek and Glassco.

Theatre I (includes ten plays), Actes Sud, 1991.

En circuit ferme, Lemeac, 1994.

RADIO PLAYS

Six heures au plus tard, Lemeac, 1986.

FICTION

Contes pour buveurs attardes (stories), Editions du Jour, 1966, translation by Michael Bullock published as *Stories for Late Night Drinkers,* Intermedia Press, 1977.

La Cite dans l'oeuf (fantasy novel; title means "The City Inside the Egg"), Editions du Jour, 1969.

C't'a ton tour, Laura Cadieux (title means "It's Your Turn, Laura Cadieux"), Editions du Jour, 1973.

La Grosse Femme d'a cote est enceinte (first novel in "Chroniques du plateau Mont-Royal" tetralogy), Lemeac, 1978, translation by Sheila Fischman published as *The Fat Woman Next Door Is Pregnant,* Talon Books, 1981.

Therese et Pierrette a l'ecole des Saints-Anges (second in tetralogy), Lemeac, 1980, translation by Fischman published as *Therese and Pierrette and the Little Hanging Angel,* McClelland & Stewart, 1984.

La Duchesse et le roturier (third in tetralogy), Lemeac, 1982.

Des Nouvelles d'Edouard (fourth in tetralogy), Lemeac, 1984.

Le Coeur decouvert: Roman d'amours, Lemeac, 1986, translation by Fischman published as *The Heart Laid Bare,* McClelland & Stewart, 1989, published as *Making Room,* Serpent's Tail, 1990.

Le Premier quartier de la lune, Lemeac, 1989.

Douze coups de theatre, Lemeac, 1992.

Le Coeur eclate, Lemeac, 1993.

Quarante-quatre minutes, quarante-quatre secondes, Lemeac, 1997.

FILMS

(Author of screenplay and dialogue, with Andre Brassard) *Francoise Durocher, Waitress,* National Film Board of Canada, 1972.

(Author of screenplay and dialogue, with Brassard) *Il etait une fois dans l'est* (title means "Once Upon a Time in the East"), Cine Art, 1974.

(Author of scenario and dialogue) *Parlez-nous d'amour* (title means "Speak to Us of Love"), Films 16, 1976.

(Author of scenario and dialogue) *Le Soleil se leve en retard,* Films 16, 1977.

Also author of *Le Coeur decouvert,* 1986, *Le Grand Jour,* 1988, and *Le Vrai Monde?* 1991.

DRAMATIC ADAPTATIONS

Messe noir (adapted from selected stories in *Contes pour buveurs attardes*), first produced in Montreal, 1965.

(With Andre Brassard) *Lysistrata* (translated and adapted from Aristophanes's play of the same title; first produced in Ottawa, 1969), Lemeac, 1969.

L'Effet des rayons gamma sur les vieux-garcons (translated and adapted from Paul Zindel's *The Effect of Gamma Rays on Man-in-the-Moon Marigolds;* first produced in Montreal, 1970), Lemeac, 1970.

". . . Et Mademoiselle Roberge boit un peu . . ." (three-act; translated and adapted from Zindel's *And Miss Reardon Drinks a Little;* first produced in Montreal, 1972), Lemeac, 1971.

Le Pays du Dragon (translated and adapted from four of Tennessee Williams's one-act plays), first produced in Montreal, 1971.

Mistero buffo (translated and adapted from Dario Fo's play of the same name), first produced in Montreal, 1973.

Mademoiselle Marguerite (translated and adapted from Roberto Athayde's *Aparaceu a Margarida;* first produced in Ottawa, 1976), Lemeac, 1975.

(With Kim Yaroshevskaya) *Oncle Vania* (translated and adapted from Anton Chekhov's play of the same name), Lemeac, 1983.

Le Gars de Quebec (adapted from Nikolay Gogol's *Le Revizov;* first produced in Montreal, 1985), Lemeac, 1985.

Six heures au plus tard (adapted from a work by Marc Perrier; first produced in Montreal, 1986), Lemeac, 1986.

Que a peur de Virginia Woolf (translated and adapted from Edward Albee's *Who's Afraid of Virginia Woolf*), first produced in Montreal, 1988.

Les Trompettes de la Mort (adapted from a work by Tilly), first produced in Montreal, 1991.

Premiere de classe (adapted from a work by Casey Kurtl), first produced in Montreal, 1992.

OTHER

(With Claude Paulette and Luc Noppen) *Quebec, trois siecles d'architecture,* Libre Expression, 1979.

Nelligan (opera libretto; produced in Montreal, 1990), Lemeac, 1990.

Les Vues animees (title means "The Movies"), Lemeac, 1990.

Also author of *Bonheur d'occasion,* an adaptation of a novel by Gabrielle Roy, 1977. Contributor to anthologies, including *Hero-ines,* edited by Joyce Doolittle, Players Press, 1992. Also contributor to periodicals, including *La Barre de Jour.* A collection of Tremblay's manuscripts is held at the Bibliotheque National du Canada, Ottawa.

MEDIA ADAPTATIONS: Sainte-Carmen of the Main was adapted as a two-act opera with music by Sydney Hodkinson, libretto by Lee Devin, and published by Associated Music Publishers, 1986.

SIDELIGHTS: Michel Tremblay is "the most important Quebecois artist of his generation," declared Salem Alaton in a 1986 Toronto *Globe and Mail* review. Beginning his career in the mid-1960s, the French-Canadian playwright, fiction writer, and screenwriter has become best known for dramatic works that challenge traditional myths of French-Canadian life. Indeed, for years critics contended that Tremblay's concentration on the social and cultural problems of Quebec earned him local acclaim at the expense of more universal recognition. In the 1980s, however, Tremblay began to command an international audience. Alaton theorized that it is the "edgy, Quebecois specificity" of Tremblay's work, once considered a liability, that is responsible for the playwright's success. With his work widely translated and produced, Tremblay is now regarded as a world-class dramatist who, in the words of *Quill and Quire* reviewer Mark Czarnecki, provides a persuasive example "of the much-debated cultural proposition that the more local the reference, the more universal the truth."

Tremblay grew up in the east end of Montreal, in the working-class neighborhood of the rue Fabre. The oppressive conditions of life in this impoverished area, along with the glitzy nightlife of the Main district, later provided the backdrop for much of Tremblay's work. Despite the inauspicious environment of his youth, Tremblay began writing when quite young and was a promising student who at thirteen received a scholarship to a classical college. Unable to endure the elitist attitudes fostered at the school, however, Tremblay left after several months to study graphic arts and become a linotype operator. He nevertheless continued to write during those years and by the time he was eighteen had completed his first play, *Le Train.* Several years later, in 1964, it won first prize in Radio Canada's Young Author Competition.

Shortly thereafter, Tremblay made Quebec theater history. Eschewing the classical French typically used in works for the stage, Tremblay wrote a play, *Les Belles-Soeurs,* in *joual,* the language of the people. Though Tremblay had not intended to create a political work, his use of *joual*—regarded by many as a debased form of the French language—signaled to his detractors and supporters alike the desire to supplant the province's traditional French culture with an independent Quebec culture. His critics decried the play while his admirers lauded it as a contribution to what is known in Quebec as the "theatre of liberation."

Written in 1965 but denied production until 1968, *Les Belles-Soeurs* catapulted the young dramatist to fame. The play was not radical, however, for its language alone. *Les Belles-Soeurs* was also controversial for its naturalistic view of French-Canadian life. Its plot is straightforward: after winning one million trading stamps, Gabriel Lauzon, an average east-end Montreal housewife, invites her women friends to a stamp-pasting gathering; by play's end, the women have turned on one another in a battle for the stamps. *Les Belles-Soeurs,* averred John Ripley in a critique for *Canadian Literature,* "explodes two centuries of popular belief, ecclesiastical teaching, and literary myth about Quebecois women. Far from being the traditional guardians of religious and moral values, happy progenitors of large families, and good-humored housekeepers, they stand revealed as malevolent misfits, consumed with hatred of life and of themselves."

Les Belles-Soeurs is the first in what became an eleven-play cycle which, in its entirety, many critics regarded as Tremblay's finest achievement. Ripley suggested that Quebec's "recent past, characterized by a desperate struggle to replace authoritarianism, negative identity, and destructiveness with self-respect, love, and transcendence, is nowhere better encapsulated than in the *Les Belles-Soeurs* cycle." Ripley's sentiments were echoed by critic Renate Usmiani, who in his *Studies in Canadian Literature: Michel Tremblay* stated: "The most general underlying theme of all [Tremblay's] works is the universal desire of the human being to transcend his finite condition." More specifically, Usmiani proposed that the typical Tremblay character is either trying to escape from family life as represented by the rue Fabre, from the false world of the Main, or from the limitations of self into a transcendent ecstasy.

One picture of life along the rue Fabre is offered by *A toi, pour toujours, ta Marie-Lou.* Deemed "a devastating psycho-social analysis of the traditional working-class Quebecois family" by Ripley, the play presents four characters juxtaposed in two different time periods. Marie-Louise is a housewife whose problems manifest themselves as sexual frigidity and religious fanaticism; Leopold, her husband, is a factory worker who becomes an alcoholic. Their marriage, according to Ripley, "is a sado-masochistic battle with no prospect of victory for either side," and thus Leopold ends their lives in a suicidal car crash. The drama progresses as, ten years later, their daughters discuss the tragedy and its impact on their lives. Manon, still living in the family home, has remained loyal to her mother and taken refuge in a similar fanaticism, seemingly unable to save herself. For Carmen, who has managed to make a life for herself as a singer in the Main district, there appears to be some hope. Both characters return in subsequent plays.

In *Damnee Manon, sacree Sandra,* the final play of the cycle, Tremblay moves away from the nightmare of family life and illusions of the Main to explore the possibility of fulfillment through mysticism. The drama unfolds through the monologues of two characters. Manon, from the earlier *A toi, pour toujours, ta Marie-Lou,* represents an attempt at transcendence through religious mysticism. Sandra, who also appeared previously in Tremblay's work, is a transvestite who seeks transcendence through sex. Both now live on the rue Fabre, as they did in childhood, and during the course of the play each comes to appreciate that the other has chosen a different path toward the same goal. Usmiani described the two characters as "physical incarnations, exteriorizations, of the two paths toward ecstasy conceived by the author," adding that on one level their world "is not a physical reality on the rue Fabre, but the psychological reality of the poet's own mind." The critic concluded that in Tremblay's work "there is no transcendence beyond that which the self can provide."

By the time Tremblay finished the *Belles-Soeurs* cycle in 1977, the political climate in Quebec had improved, and he gave permission, previously withheld, for his plays to be produced in English in Quebec. At this juncture he also switched genres, beginning work on a series of semi-autobiographical novels. The playwright's venture into fiction has been successful, and thus far, at least two of the volumes in his "Chroniques du plateau Mont-Royal" tetralogy have been translated into English. The first volume in the series, *La Grosse Femme d'a cote est enceinte,* was translated as *The Fat Woman Next Door is Pregnant.* Not only are the characters of this novel residents of the rue Fabre, as in so many of Tremblay's dramas, but the fat woman of the title is Tremblay's mother, and the story is based on the author's recollections of life in the apartment of his birth. *Quill and Quire* reviewer Czarnecki contended that *The Fat Woman*'s one-day time frame achieves "a similar effect" to that of James Joyce's famed *Ulysses.* Reviewing for the same publication, Philip Stratford called *The Fat Woman* "a generous, good-natured fresco teeming with life and invention." Regarded as both funny and sentimental, the book became a best-seller in Quebec.

Its sequel, *Therese et Pierrette a l'ecole des Saints-Anges,* translated as *Therese and Pierrette and the Little Hanging Angel,* also fared well, winning the prestigious Prix France-Quebec in 1981. Set during a four-day time period, the volume concentrates on three eleven-year-old students at the Ecole des Saints-Anges, a Roman Catholic girls' school. In this novel censuring the religious education system, Tremblay exhibits "epic gifts," in Czarnecki's opinion, that "extend to capturing life in its smallest details, creating an imaginative world complete in itself, ready to immerse and rebaptize the reader."

Tremblay concluded his tetralogy with *La Duchesse et le Roturier* in 1982 and *Des Nouvelles d'Edouard* in 1984. During the 1980s, however, Tremblay also returned to writing plays. Although some critics regard his dramas of the eighties as unequal to his earlier work, many of them appraise the 1987 *Le Vrai Monde?* as his best. In this play Tremblay looks back to 1965, to his own beginning as an artist, and questions what right he had to use the lives of family and friends in service to his art. Calling it both "an expression of guilt" and "an eloquent statement about the relationship between art and life," *Globe and Mail* critic Matthew Fraser found *Le Vrai Monde?* "a masterful piece of drama." Another reviewer for the *Globe and Mail,* Ray Conlogue, contended that it is "a formidable play" in which Tremblay tries "to defend his art." In his interview for the Toronto paper with Alaton, Tremblay offered a slightly different perspective, telling the critic: "It is almost a condemnation of what an artist does to real life." And when Alaton asked him why he wrote, the dramatist responded: "Maybe I am an artist because artists give purpose to a thing which has not purpose, which is life. . . . You put [a play] before 500 people every night and you say, 'Sometimes, this is what life might mean.' And people who live the same nonsense life as you understand this."

Tremblay's 1990 play *La Maison Suspendue* departs from other Tremblay plays in that it is set in rural Quebec rather than in Montreal. In the play, three generations of a family endure life in a big house in the country. The generations are bound together by an eleven-year-old boy, who appears as the same person in each generation. "*La Maison Suspendue* is about the ways in which a family creates and recreates itself through stories," remarked *Books in Canada* contributor Ann Jansen. Writing in *Canadian Literature,* Neal Carson noted, "The play can be read as a story of family conflict and reconciliation, or even as an expression of the author's own regrets and apprehensions as he reaches late middle age."

In *Les Vues animees,* Tremblay presents a dozen autobiographical narratives, each centered around a particular movie. "With this charming collection of short, autobiographical narratives, Tremblay affirms his double debt to the cinema as spiritual mother of his creative awakening and catalyst of the initiatory phases of his early years," commented Constantina Mitchell in *Canadian*

Literature. Discussing the work with David Homel of *Books in Canada,* Tremblay explained, "I wanted to write a coming-of-age book using the movies. Each chapter was like a step forward for the character, a discovery—of fear, of sexuality, of art—and that thematic aspect saved me from nostalgia."

BIOGRAPHICAL/CRITICAL SOURCES:

BOOKS

Contemporary Literary Criticism, Volume 29, Gale (Detroit), 1984.
Contemporary World Writers, 2nd edition, St. James Press, 1993.
Coyle, William, editor, *Aspects of Fantasy,* Greenwood, 1986.
Dictionary of Literary Biography, Volume 60: *Canadian Writers since 1960, Second Series,* Gale, 1987.
Gay and Lesbian Literature, St. James Press, 1994.
International Dictionary of Theatre, Volume 2: *Playwrights,* St. James Press, 1994.
Massey, Irving, *Identity And Community: Reflections on English, Yiddish, and French Literature in Canada,* Wayne State University Press, 1994.
Usmiani, Renate, *Michel Tremblay: A Critical Study,* Douglas & McIntyre, 1981.
Usmiani, *Studies in Canadian Literature: Michel Tremblay,* Douglas & McIntyre, 1982.
Usmiani, *The Theatre of Frustration: Super Realism in the Dramatic Work of F. X. Kroetz and Michel Tremblay,* Garland, 1990.

PERIODICALS

Books in Canada, January/February, 1986; February, 1992, pp. 16, 28; March, 1995, p. 38.
Canadian Book Review Annual, 1996.
Canadian Drama, number 2, 1976, pp. 206-18.
Canadian Literature, summer, 1980; autumn, 1992, p. 171; spring, 1993, p. 134.
Canadian Theatre Review, fall, 1979, pp. 12-37.
Chicago Tribune, March 8, 1980.
Essays on Canadian Writing, number 11, 1978.
French Review, May, 1997.
Globe and Mail (Toronto), November 16, 1986; April 25, 1987; October 3, 1987.
Maclean's, April 30, 1984; April 22, 1985; December 30, 1991, pp. 36-37.
New York Times, December 11, 1983.
Perspectives, February 17, 1973, pp. 6-9.
Quebec Studies, number 4, 1986.
Quill and Quire, February, 1982; April, 1982; June, 1984; January, 1995, p. 38.
Studies in Canadian Literature, Volume 14, number 2, 1989.
Variety, January 24, 1994, p. 76.
Washington Post, June 22, 1978.

*   *   *

TREVOR, William
  See COX, William Trevor

*   *   *

TRILLIN, Calvin (Marshall) 1935-

PERSONAL: Born December 5, 1935, in Kansas City, MO; son of Abe and Edyth (Weitzman) Trillin; married Alice Stewart, August

13, 1965; children: Abigail, Sarah. *Education:* Yale University, B.A., 1957.

ADDRESSES: Office—c/o New Yorker, 25 West 43rd St., New York, NY 10036.

CAREER: Time magazine, New York City, 1960-63, began as reporter in Atlanta and New York City, became writer in New York City; *New Yorker,* New York City, staff writer, 1963–; *Nation,* columnist, 1978-85; syndicated columnist, 1986–.

AWARDS, HONORS: National Book Award nomination (paperback), 1980, for *Alice, Let's Eat: Further Adventures of a Happy Eater;* Books-across-the-Sea Ambassador of Honor citation, English-Speaking Union, 1985, for *Third Helpings.* Honorary degrees from Beloit College, 1987, and Albertus Magnus College, 1990.

WRITINGS:

NONFICTION

An Education in Georgia: Charlayne Hunter, Hamilton Holmes, and the Integration of the University of Georgia, Viking, 1964.
U.S. Journal, Dutton, 1971.
American Fried: Adventures of a Happy Eater, Doubleday, 1974.
Alice, Let's Eat: Further Adventures of a Happy Eater, Random House, 1978.
Uncivil Liberties (collected columns), Ticknor & Fields, 1982.
Third Helpings, Ticknor & Fields, 1983.
Killings, Ticknor & Fields, 1984.
With All Disrespect: More Uncivil Liberties (collected columns), Ticknor & Fields, 1985.
If You Can't Say Something Nice (collected columns), Ticknor & Fields, 1987.
Travels with Alice, Ticknor & Fields, 1989.
Enough's Enough (And Other Rules of Life) (collected columns), Ticknor & Fields, 1990.
(With Wolfgang Puck) *Adventures in the Kitchen,* Random House, 1991.
Remembering Denny, Farrar, Straus, 1993.
The Tummy Trilogy (contains *American Fried, Alice, Let's Eat,* and *Third Helpings*), Farrar, Straus, 1994.
(Author of introduction) Richard Rovere, *Howe & Hummel: Their True and Scandalous History,* Syracuse University Press, 1996.
Family Man, Farrar, Straus, 1998.

FICTION

Barnett Frummer Is an Unbloomed Flower and Other Adventures of Barnett Frummer, Rosalie Mondle, Roland Magruder, and Their Friends (short stories), Viking, 1969.
Runestruck (novel), Little, Brown, 1977.
Floater (novel), Ticknor & Fields, 1980.
American Stories (short stories), Ticknor & Fields, 1991.

OTHER

(And performer) *Calvin Trillin's Uncle Sam* (one-man show), produced at American Place Theatre, New York City, 1988.
(And performer) *Calvin Trillin's Words, No Music* (one-man show), produced at American Place Theatre, New York City, 1990.
Deadline Poet, or, My Life as a Doggerelist, Farrar, Straus, 1994.
Too Soon to Tell, Farrar, Straus, 1995.
Messages from My Father, Farrar, Straus, 1996.
Calvin Trillin, Piece by Piece (audiocassette), HighBridge, 1996.

Author of the column "Uncivil Liberties," *Nation*, 1978-85, King Features Syndicate, 1986–. Contributor to periodicals, including *Atlantic, Harper's, Life, Esquire,* and *New York Times Magazine.*

SIDELIGHTS: Calvin Trillin is a journalist, critic, and novelist who has won acclaim "partly because of his wayward scrambles across [America] in search of regional food . . . and partly because he has mastered a television manner that communicates his understated, tongue-in-cheek humor," according to Barry Siegel in a *Los Angeles Times* article. But in some ways, continues Siegel, "it is regrettable that Trillin is so funny, because this quality tends to obscure the fact that in his "U.S. Journal" [a continuing series in the *New Yorker*] he may be offering some of the most valuable and unique reporting in the country today."

Trillin's early career saw him working at *Time,* where as a journalistic "floater" he migrated from one department to the next. As the author told *Publishers Weekly* interviewer John F. Baker, he spent some time in the "Medicine" section: "I didn't care for that—it seemed to tend toward the intestinal whenever I was there, with weekly breakthroughs in spleen research"; and also in the "Religion" section, which ill-suited Trillin. "I finally got out of that by prefacing everything with 'alleged'; I'd write about 'the alleged parting of the Red Sea,' even 'the alleged Crucifixion,' and eventually they let me go."

Apparently, Trillin gained enough insight from his career at *Time* to produce, years later, a comic novel titled *Floater.* The fictional newsweekly through which protagonist Fred Becker floats is populated with trend-obsessed editors, egomaniacal writers, and eccentrics of every description. Becker enjoys his unfettered career until a rumor provided to him by a remarkably unreliable source threatens his future. The rumor—that the President's wife is pregnant—could cause Becker to be promoted to an odious bureau chief position if he is the first to report it truthfully. While Becker ponders what to do with his scoop, he accidentally leaks the rumor, only to find that the scoop is phony, "part of an elaborate, internecine power struggle at the magazine that is as unlikely as it is hilarious," according to Dan Wakefield in *Nation.*

Trillin's nonfiction, gleaned from his magazine pieces, covers a wide range. There are humor collections—*Uncivil Liberties* and *With All Disrespect: More Uncivil Liberties*—political and social commentary—*U.S. Journal* and *Too Soon to Tell*—a study of homicide—*Killings*—and a book devoted to his father, the subject of several of Trillin's columns over the years, titled *Messages from My Father.*

With *U.S. Journal* the author recalls his travels across America, finding stories in everyday events in which there may be no apparent "news value." These subjects befit Trillin, who grew up in Kansas City, Missouri, and has always considered himself a Midwesterner, despite his years of living in New York City. He sees his subjects as worthy of examination, even if they are not famous or important.

Writing about *U.S. Journal* in the *New York Times Book Review,* Evan S. Connell states: "Trillin's scales usually are balanced; he is a judicious journalist and has presented an agreeable collection. More important, several passages show compelling depth. As cautious as he is, he can create a wave of emotion in the reader—usually a wave of rage at the bigots, paralytic bureaucrats and myopic hucksters who infest [the book]. His account of desperate people in South Carolina is guaranteed to spoil your lunch."

In 1978, Trillin began to write "Uncivil Liberties," a humor column for the *Nation.* More recently published in syndication throughout the country, the column has been both a popular and critical success. *Uncivil Liberties* and *With All Disrespect: More Uncivil Liberties,* which present that work in collected form, are likewise praised for the author's slightly skewed views of today's culture. "At the outset, Trillin defined the column as 'a thousand words every three weeks for saying whatever's on my mind, particularly if what's on my mind is marginally ignoble,'" as Jonathan Yardley reports in a *Washington Post* review. "Even in his less-inspired efforts," says Yardley, "he is perceptive, funny and iconoclastic." Trillin is "consistently sharp and imaginative" in *Uncivil Liberties,* according to a *Detroit News* critic, "but don't expect a banquet of belly laughs from these fifty easy pieces. They're more likely to elicit appreciative smiles at the author's capacity for setting up and delivering clever dissections of his chosen prey."

More of Trillin's columns appear in the collections *If You Can't Say Something Nice, Enough's Enough (And Other Rules of Life),* and *Too Soon to Tell.* The columnist even conformed his comic view of U.S. politics to tropes and iambs in *Deadline Poet; or, My Life as a Doggerelist.* In this collection, which contains three years' worth of verse Trillin penned with regularity for the *Nation,* readers will enjoy one of the few known versifications of U.S. economic fluctuations: "Statistics now show where the boom dough went. / The middle classes hardly gained a nickel. / Two-thirds went to the richest one percent. / A breakthrough: we produced an upward trickle." As political satirist Mark Russell writes in the *New York Times Book Review:* "Calvin Trillin is the name to lob into those fashionable hand-wringing laments about what has happened to the state of American humor and how the schlock is the message. Mark Twain, Robert Benchley and [S. J.] Perelman are dead, but Calvin Trillin is right there with the post-funeral cocktail to assure us that life goes on."

In 1990's *Too Soon to Tell,* ninety columns mix the author's characteristic humor with pointed commentary on modern culture. From monkfish to the poseur lip-synching rock duo Milli Vanilli, Trillin uses newsworthy events as stepping stones toward each of his well-reasoned and pointed observations, opinions, or recollections. Noting that the author's "deadpan timing" keeps his essays from becoming dated, Michael Dirda comments in the *Washington Post Book World* that "Trillin can write well about anything: murder, Washington politics, Kansas City barbecue, the death of a gay friend, out-of-the-way places, growing up. What seems common to his diverse productiveness," the critic continues, "is a kind of old-fashioned patriotism: Trillin loves and celebrates American life even as he grouses about it."

More focused in subject matter was Trillin's 1984 collection, *Killings.* Based on several *New Yorker* articles, the book examines the kinds of murder that don't ordinarily make national headlines—those occurring in small towns, their victims uncelebrated individuals. "Trillin's interest—and ours—lies not in how some of us die but in how we live," notes *Nation* reviewer Ann Jones. The author, continues Jones, finds that the motivation for some of the murders should be viewed within the context of the social tensions in the cities and towns where the killings took place. "He describes what sociologists would call a conflict of cultures," says Jones. "A hillbilly guns down a trespassing filmmaker. A frustrated Navajo abducts a New Mexico mayor. . . . Sometimes the conflict is more intimate [as in the case of] Lawrence Hartman, an exemplary Iowa farmer who in middle age, bedazzled by the big city and a young cocktail waitress, beat his wife to death." "In several cases the killing seems inadvertent, as if the killer didn't actually want to do it, but couldn't think of any other way to pass through the situation. Lack of imagination may be a motive," Anatole Broyard points out in a *New York Times* piece.

If empathy and intelligence characterize Trillin's attitude toward people, most critics agree that passion and poignancy describe his attitude toward food. The author has made his true love known in three volumes, each celebrating the variety of American cuisine. Indeed, Trillin's eloquence on such matters as fried chicken and Chicago-style pizza has caused him to be labeled "the Walt Whitman of American eats" by Craig Claiborne in the *New York Times Book Review* and a "food pornographer" by Nelson W. Polsby in *Harper's*. *American Fried: Adventures of a Happy Eater* is the first of Trillin's books on food and travel, and is "composed of a blend of waspish sociology and a sensuality so explicit as to border on the prurient," warns a *Saturday Review* critic. In his review, Polsby appreciates the author's dilemma as a roving gourmand. When Trillin arrives in town, explains Polsby, the gentry "refuse to tell him where [the good] restaurants are. Instead, they are forever touting him into big-priced fake 'Continental' eateries, places with lots of decor, long-winded menus, revolving views of the surrounding wasteland, and terrible food. When hunger strikes in a strange town, he despairs of interviewing local informants, and he has taken to rummaging through the restaurant section of the Yellow Pages, looking for restaurants having no display ads or those called by only the first name of the proprietor." "Some will say [that, in *American Fried*, Trillin] has written a nasty satire on gourmets, but they err who think so," claims *Washington Post Book World* writer Henry Mitchell. "Trillin genuinely loves all the stuff he writes about, no doubt of that. Love transforms all. As Proust took the simple madeline and with genius made it a glory of his book, so Trillin takes the hamburger, takes the chili-dog, takes the pizza, and does as much or more."

An entreaty to his wife comprises the title of Trillin's second food-appreciation book, *Alice, Let's Eat: Further Adventures of a Happy Eater*. Alice, it seems, does not quite share her husband's enthusiasm for barbecue and burgers, and the couple's conflicts figure as a dramatic element in the volume. While Trillin has some fun at his wife's expense in *Alice, Let's Eat,* Alice told her side of the story in a *Nation* review of her husband's book. "I am not against quests for the perfect ham hock or the perfect barbecue or even, for that matter, for the perfect roast polecat haunch," Alice Trillin explained. "But I think that anyone starting out on such a quest should be aware that his guide is someone who will travel all the way to a place called Horse Cave, Kentucky, because he likes the way the name Horse Cave, Kentucky, sounds when he drops it to me over the phone."

Third Helpings differs from Trillin's first two food books because it contains a campaign "to have the national Thanksgiving dish changed from turkey to spaghetti carbonara." The author defends his stance with a retelling of the First Thanksgiving legend. In Trillin's version the Indians joined the Pilgrims for a Thanksgiving feast, taking the precaution "of [bringing] along one dish of their own. They brought a dish their ancestors had been taught earlier by Christopher Columbus, discoverer of the New World. The dish was spaghetti carbonara." As in the earlier works, American patriotism figures into *Third Helpings*. After sampling the food at a Mediterranean resort, Trillin declares that the fancy fare is no better "than the Italian sausage sandwiches he dotes upon on Mulberry Street in lower Manhattan," as *Newsweek's* Gene Lyons relates. "Neither, for that matter, does the Italian cuisine surpass the roast duck and dirty rice at Didee's in Baton Rouge or Opelousas, Louisiana." In pieces such as the account of

the Crawford County, Kansas, fried chicken war between Chicken Annie and Chicken Mary, Trillin proves to Beryl Lieff Benderly that "under cover of a mania for dim sum, spaghetti carbonara, and pit barbecue, [the author] is actually a superlative prose stylist, an inimitable humorist, and an absolutely first-rate people writer."

Trillin's fourth contribution to his ongoing saga of food and travel is *Travels with Alice*. In this volume, Trillin wanders through France, Italy, and other places around the globe, ostensibly to take in the culture, but really to take in the native eatables. "Even when the itinerary is the standard tour of museums, monuments and monasteries," states *Chicago Tribune* contributor James Idems, "his nose is atwitch and his eye peeled for the out-of-the-way market or cafe that specializes in the local cuisine." "This late-20th-century autocrat of the breakfast table takes these setbacks in stride, ever confident that if he just keeps hanging around, keeping one eye on the scenery and the other on the menu, sooner or later a meal worth eating will make its presence known," declares Yardley in the *Washington Post*. "So far he's been right, with the happy result that he's well-fed and his readers are well-read."

From love of food and all things American, Trillin turned to love of family in 1996's *Messages from My Father: A Memoir*. Writing about his father—a dreamer who wanted greatness for his children, a proud American, and a loving, idealistic man with a subtle sense of humor—Trillin recalls his own childhood memories of his Russian-born father Abe Trillin, a grocery store owner who was determined that Calvin graduate from Yale and become president of the United States. "I don't think it ever occurred to my father that it might not work out," the son affectionately adds. "In *Messages from My Father*, Mr. Trillin reveals the elusive source of his gifts . . . ," maintains Christopher Lehmann-Haupt in his *New York Times* review, "and he demonstrates how well he learned the subtle lessons conveyed to him." On a more somber note, Trillin recounts the death of a homosexual friend he had known since his days at Yale in the best-selling 1993 work *Remembering Denny*, which Michael Dorris lauds as "an eloquent, heartfelt protest against disappointment and stunted opportunity" in the *New York Times Book Review*.

In 1988, following in the footsteps of Mark Twain, Trillin took his humor on the stage—he had previously performed on the Johnny Carson show and on radio—with the opening of his one-man show *Calvin Trillin's Uncle Sam*, which featured geography. He succeeded it in 1990 with another, *Calvin Trillin's Words, No Music*, which featured "language . . . politics, certainly some mention of a few presidents," he told fellow humorist Jackie Mason in a conversation published in the *New York Times*. "Calvin Trillin is the Buster Keaton of performance humorists," declares Mel Gussow in a *New York Times* review of the second show. "As droll as he is deadpan, he never once suggests that he thinks he is as funny as we know he is. He lets the audience do the laughing. . . . His ease and professionalism in facing his public should be an inspiration to writers who hide behind hard covers."

BIOGRAPHICAL/CRITICAL SOURCES:

PERIODICALS

America, April 16, 1994, p. 2.
Chicago Tribune, February 26, 1984; December 15, 1988; November 23, 1989.
Chicago Tribune Book World, November 30, 1980; March 18, 1984.
Commentary, August, 1971.
Detroit News, May 30, 1982.

Entertainment Weekly, June 2, 1995, p. 53.
Harper's, August, 1974.
Kansas City Magazine, November, 1974.
Library Journal; April 15, 1994, p. 82; May 1, 1995, p. 97; April 15, 1996, p. 144; May 1, 1996, p. 104.
Life, November 7, 1969.
Los Angeles Times, November 18, 1980; March 11, 1984; March 23, 1984.
Los Angeles Times Book Review, December 7, 1980; April 24, 1984; November 11, 1990, p. 9; March 8, 1992, p. 10; April 19, 1994, p. 6; June 16, 1996.
Nation, October 21, 1978; October 11, 1980; March 3, 1984; December 22, 1984.
New Republic, April 17, 1971; October 7, 1978.
Newsweek, October 27, 1980; April 4, 1983; February 13, 1984.
New York Times, November 7, 1969; July 2, 1971; May 12, 1977; October 14, 1980; May 26, 1982; April 14, 1983; January 28, 1984; October 7, 1990; October 15, 1990; June 6, 1996, p. C17.
New York Times Book Review, November 8, 1987, p. 11; October 22, 1989, p. 10; October 28, 1990, p. 9; December 9, 1990, p. 38; October 13, 1991, p. 22; January 12, 1992, p. 24; April 24, 1994, p. 16; June 25, 1995, p. 20; June 30, 1996, p. 15.
People Weekly, November 2, 1987.
Publishers Weekly, November 21, 1980; April 3, 1995, p. 50; March 25, 1996, p. 70.
Saturday Review, May 8, 1971; May 18, 1974.
Time, March 22, 1971; December 22, 1980; July 5, 1982; March 5, 1984; February 12, 1996, p. 17.
Times Literary Supplement, January 17, 1992, p. 24.
Tribune Books (Chicago), October 21, 1990, p. 8; October 13, 1991, p. 6; February 9, 1992, p. 8; February 23, 1992, p. 8.
Village Voice, September 25, 1978.
Voice Literary Supplement, October, 1989.
Washington Post, October 23, 1980; December 4, 1980; May 19, 1982; February 8, 1984; April 16, 1985; October 11, 1989.
Washington Post Book World, October 26, 1969; June 2, 1974; April 10, 1983; April 10, 1987; October 18, 1987; March 29, 1992, p. 12.

*   *   *

TRILLING, Diana (Rubin) 1905-1996

PERSONAL: Born July 21, 1905, in New York, NY; died October 23, 1996; daughter of Joseph (a businessman) and Sadie Helene (Forbert) Rubin; married Lionel Trilling (a critic and professor of English), June 12, 1929 (died November 5, 1975); children: James Lionel. *Education:* Radcliffe College, A.B., 1925.

ADDRESSES: Home—35 Claremont Ave., New York, NY 10027.

CAREER: Nation, New York City, fiction critic and author of column "Fiction in Review," 1941-49; freelance writer and critic, 1949-96.

MEMBER: American Academy of Arts and Sciences, Phi Beta Kappa (honorary member of Radcliffe chapter).

AWARDS, HONORS: Guggenheim fellowships, 1950-51, 1991-92; joint grant from National Endowment for the Humanities and Rockefeller Foundation, 1977-79; Pulitzer Prize nomination, 1982, for *Mrs. Harris: The Death of the Scarsdale Diet Doctor;* fellow of American Academy of Arts and Sciences.

WRITINGS:

Claremont Essays, Harcourt (New York City), 1964.
We Must March My Darlings: A Critical Decade (essays), Harcourt, 1977.
Reviewing the Forties (fiction criticism), introduction by Paul Fussell, Harcourt, 1978.
Mrs. Harris: The Death of the Scarsdale Diet Doctor, Harcourt, 1982.
The Beginning of the Journey: The Marriage of Diana and Lionel Trilling, Harcourt, 1993.

EDITOR

(And author of introduction) *The Viking Portable D. H. Lawrence,* Viking (New York City), 1947.
(And author of introduction) *Selected Letters of D. H. Lawrence,* Farrar, Straus (New York City), 1958.
The Uniform Edition of the Works of Lionel Trilling, Harcourt, 1979.

OTHER

(Author of introduction) Mark Twain, *Tom Sawyer,* Crowell-Collins (New York City), 1962.

Editor of *Uniform Edition of the Works of Lionel Trilling,* 1978-80. Contributor to volume on D. H. Lawrence published by Weidenfeld & Nicolson (London). Author of column "Here and Now," for *New Leader,* 1957-59. Contributor of essays and reviews on literary, sociological, and political subjects to numerous periodicals, including *Partisan Review, New York Times, Harper's, Vogue, Esquire, Commentary, Newsweek,* and *Times Literary Supplement.* Member of editorial board, *American Scholar.*

SIDELIGHTS: "To the extent that America has an intellectual conscience," Elizabeth Janeway wrote in the *Los Angeles Times Book Review,* "Diana Trilling is part of it, a literary critic who knows that literature can't be understood apart from its context in social, cultural, and political life. She has been disagreed with, but no one has ever thought her opinions shabby, easily come by or uninteresting." Despite her success as a critic, however, Diana Trilling did not set out to become a writer. She initially trained for a career in opera, but her aspirations as a singer were thwarted by a serious thyroid condition that left her unable to perform. In attempting to refocus her life, she began writing stories to pass the time. In 1941, the literary editor of the *Nation* asked her husband, the well-respected educator and literary critic Lionel Trilling, if he could recommend someone to write brief, unsigned fiction notes for the magazine; Diana suggested he recommend her. Within a year, she was given her own column, "Fiction in Review," in which she covered all novels that came in for review. According to Nathan A. Scott, Jr., in *Commonweal,* Trilling soon earned the respect of her peers "by virtue of the wit and intelligence and courtesy with which she scrutinized and evaluated the current fiction that came across her desk week after week."

A selection of the reviews Trilling wrote during her years as the *Nation's* fiction critic was published in 1978 under the title *Reviewing the Forties.* About this collection, a reviewer for *Publishers Weekly* remarked: "Reading her reviews is a stimulating experience. Even when the books are now forgotten, her pungent comments are still provocative. And her literary judgments are always clear-cut and candid." In the *Nation,* Emile Capouya observed: "What appears to be characteristic and characterological is her delight in the real thing, which, when she comes upon it in a writer, lifts her own writing to an intensity of praise which is ravishing in its music, its clarity and its subtle discriminations. . . . At such moments she is herself wonderfully moving and infects the reader with a sympathy that seems less an emotion than a form of knowledge. That is a great gift. It transforms good literary journalism into art."

In 1971 Trilling returned to her alma mater, Radcliffe College, more than forty years after her graduation, to interview some of its current students and to see, in her words, "what similarities and differences I might find between the present-day undergraduate and my own college generation." Trilling and her husband, Lionel, spent nearly nine weeks on the campus, living in the same hall in which she had lived as an undergraduate at Radcliffe. The experience resulted in several chapters in her volume *We Must March My Darlings: A Critical Decade.*

Even before publication, *We Must March My Darlings* stirred up considerable controversy in the literary world. Consistent with the book's purpose, to examine past and present social issues and concerns, Trilling reprinted in the volume an essay she had published entitled "Liberal Anti-Communism Revisited." Michiko Kakutani explained in the *Chicago Tribune* that Trilling "raised questions about *Scoundrel Time,* Lillian Hellman's account of the McCarthy years, and re-examined the rift that has existed for decades between intellectuals who remained vaguely sympathetic with communism and those who broke openly with the party." Little, Brown & Co. had originally contracted with Trilling to publish the book but refused to do so unless she deleted the references to Hellman. The firm had earlier published *Scoundrel Time* and Hellman was also one of its more popular and commercially successful authors. Trilling refused to alter the few sentences which spoke of Hellman, so the publisher opted to void the contract. Trilling then submitted the manuscript to William Jovanovich of Harcourt Brace Jovanovich, Inc., who published it in 1977.

Regarding the controversial material, a writer for *Newsweek* remarks that "when one of the passages was made public, it seemed so esoteric and ideological that it was hard to imagine anyone being upset. Indeed, the big surprise was that there was a brouhaha at all. Trilling had said that disagreements originating at an anti-Communist symposium in 1967 still divided the intellectual community, but with 'always diminishing intellectual force.' She used Hellman's . . . best seller, *Scoundrel Time,* as an example of the division." In *Esquire,* Alfred Kazin reflected, "the imbroglio is funny enough in its way," and commented that after examining *We Must March My Darlings* he found "no hysterical personal attack on Lillian Hellman. There is a stiffly courteous, reasoned and documented critique of Hellman's longstanding inability to understand the nature of Soviet society."

Although author of several volumes of literary and social criticism, Trilling achieved her greatest public recognition with her account of the trial of Jean Harris, the former girls' school headmistress convicted of murdering her lover, the famous diet doctor Herman Tarnower. "What makes *Mrs. Harris: The Death of the Scarsdale Diet Doctor* different from Trilling's previous work is its promise to reach a popular audience and become a financial success," states Kakutani in a *New York Times* interview. Bruce Cook elaborated in the *Saturday Review:* "Although her work has appeared over a period of four decades, Diana Trilling is hardly a writer with a large public. To a certain readership, so loyal and intense one is almost tempted to call it a constituency, she is very well known indeed. These readers are the survivors and enthusiasts of the late great literary wars of New York."

According to a *New York Times* reporter, Trilling decided to write about the Harris case just two days after the shooting. "Six months later, before the trial, I had completed a first draft, and thought I had only to add a summary of the trial and the verdict," Trilling told the reporter. "I couldn't have been more wrong. Things were not as cut and dried as they seemed, and I wound up tossing the whole thing out and starting over again." Trilling explained in more detail to Jean W. Ross in a *Contemporary Authors* interview: "I was still trying to save some of the things I had written before the trial. It presented structural problems which I finally realized I could not overcome; that's when I decided I had to throw the book out and start again. . . . I had to figure out how to structure the book not only in relation to what I'd written in the summer [before the trial] but in relation to the chronicle [that she'd written of daily courtroom happenings]. . . . I finally realized it was a question of either giving up the whole project or starting from the beginning again, and I decided, fortunately, to do the second. That is, I retained only my daily chronicle, threw out everything else."

Before her death, Trilling undertook the editing duties of several collections of her late husband's work. As she told John Firth of the *Saturday Review,* "There's such an enormous amount to do after Lionel's death—putting his papers in order, looking at the unpublished material." In a review of her volume of Lionel Trilling's previously uncollected reviews and essays, *Speaking of Literature and Society,* Robert Alter declared in the *New York Times Book Review* that "the appearance of this selection . . . is a rare homage to pay to a recent American writer, especially to a literary critic, and it obviously reflects a confidence that [Lionel] Trilling now deserves a place both on the library shelves and in the minds of the literate public as a major American author. . . . Mrs. Trilling's selection of these miscellaneous publications, most of them reviews, is both generous and intelligent."

About *The Beginning of the Journey: The Marriage of Diana and Lionel Trilling,* Trilling explained to John F. Baker in a *Publishers Weekly* interview that her decision to record the story of her life with Lionel stemmed in part from wanting to publish a true account before another biographer saw them as likely subjects. *The Beginning of the Journey* was written by dictation, since Trilling had by then lost most of her sight.

Baker described *The Beginning of the Journey: The Marriage of Diana and Lionel Trilling* as "partly an account of his life, partly of hers, but mostly of their life together; it is a riveting story of a marriage at the heart of New York literary and intellectual life, a relationship that also had extraordinary personal and financial strains." Trilling commented to Baker: "It's a real story of two people and their struggles with family, with money, with career. It's the story of how Lionel was fired [as a young Columbia instructor] but then fought back to become a famous Columbia professor. It is also cultural and social history."

BIOGRAPHICAL/CRITICAL SOURCES:

BOOKS

Contemporary Authors New Revision Series, Volume 46, Gale (Detroit), 1995.

PERIODICALS

Chicago Tribune, November 29, 1981.
Chicago Tribune Book World, November 1, 1981; November 14, 1982.
Christian Science Monitor, August 5, 1977.

Commentary, July, 1977; January, 1979; March, 1979; January, 1994, p. 59.
Commonweal, September 28, 1979; March 25, 1994, p. 21.
Detroit News, November 24, 1981.
Esquire, August, 1977.
Harper's, April, 1977.
Los Angeles Times Book Review, November 1, 1981.
Nation, October 21, 1978; November 21, 1981.
National Review, November 25, 1996.
New Republic, October 28, 1978; November 4, 1981.
Newsweek, October 11, 1976; October 19, 1981.
New York, October 26, 1981; January 30, 1995; p. 54.
New York Times, May 19, 1977; October 10, 1981; October 13, 1981; November 16, 1981; October 25, 1996.
New York Times Book Review, May 28, 1977; May 29, 1977; May 14, 1978; June 3, 1979; May 25, 1980; October 12, 1980; October 25, 1981; November 14, 1982; October 24, 1993.
Observer (London), September 25, 1983, p. 31.
Publishers Weekly, April 25, 1977; July 31, 1978; July 30, 1979; August 13, 1982; November 1, 1993, pp. 54-55.
Saturday Review, May 28, 1977; November, 1981.
Time, June 13, 1977; October 19, 1981; January 4, 1982.
Times Literary Supplement, May 14, 1982.
Washington Post Book World, October 25, 1981.

*   *   *

TRILLING, Lionel 1905-1975

PERSONAL: Born July 4, 1905, in New York, NY; died November 5, 1975; son of David W. (a businessman) and Fannie (Cohen) Trilling; married Diana Rubin (a writer and critic), June 12, 1929; children: James Lionel. *Education:* Columbia University, B.A., 1925, M.A., 1926, Ph.D., 1938.

ADDRESSES: Home—35 Claremont Ave., New York, NY 10027. *Office*—Hamilton Hall, Columbia University, New York, NY 10027.

CAREER: Literary and social critic, educator, editor, essayist, and author. University of Wisconsin, Madison (now University of Wisconsin—Madison), instructor in English, 1926-27; Hunter College (now Hunter College of the City University of New York), New York City, instructor in English, 1927-30; Columbia University, New York City instructor, 1931-39, assistant professor, 1939-45, associate professor, 1945-48, professor of English, 1948-65, George Edward Woodberry Professor of Literature and Criticism, 1965-70, university professor, 1970-74, professor emeritus and special lecturer, 1974-75. George Eastman Visiting Professor, Oxford University, 1964-65; Charles Eliot Norton Professor of Poetry, Harvard University, 1969-70. Visiting fellow, All Souls College, Oxford University, 1972-73. Organizer with John Crowe Ransom and F. O. Mattheissen and senior fellow, Kenyon School of Letters, Kenyon College.

MEMBER: American Academy of Arts and Sciences, National Institute of Arts and Letters, Phi Beta Kappa, Athenaeum Club (London), Century Club (New York).

AWARDS, HONORS: D.Litt. from Trinity College (Hartford, CT), 1955, Harvard University, 1962, Case Western Reserve University, 1968, University of Durham, 1973, and University of Leicester, 1973; L.H.D. from Northwestern University, 1964, Brandeis University, 1974, and Yale University, 1974; Mark Van Doren Award from the student body of Columbia College, 1966;

Brandeis University Creative Arts Award, 1967-68; Thomas Jefferson Award from National Endowment for the Humanities, 1972.

WRITINGS:

Matthew Arnold, Norton, 1939, 2nd edition, Columbia University Press, 1949.
E. M. Forster, New Directions, 1943, revised edition, 1965, published in England as *E. M. Forster: A Study,* Hogarth, 1944.
The Middle of the Journey (novel), Viking, 1947, reprinted with new introduction by Trilling, Scribner, 1975.
The Liberal Imagination: Essays on Literature and Society, Viking, 1950.
(Author of introduction) Leo Tolstoy, *Anna Karenina,* Cambridge University Press, 1951.
The Opposing Self: Nine Essays in Criticism, Viking, 1955.
Freud and the Crisis of Our Culture, Beacon Press, 1955.
A Gathering of Fugitives (essays), Beacon Press, 1956.
(Author of introduction) Isaak Babel, *The Collected Stories,* Criterion, 1957.
(Author of introduction) Saul Bellow, *The Adventures of Augie March,* Modern Library, 1965.
Beyond Culture: Essays on Literature and Learning, Viking, 1965.
Sincerity and Authenticity (lectures), Harvard University Press, 1972.
Mind in the Modern World (Thomas Jefferson Lectures in the Humanities), Viking, 1973.
The Last Decade: Essays and Reviews, 1965-1975, edited by Diana Trilling, Harcourt, 1979.
Prefaces to the Experience of Literature, edited by D. Trilling, Harcourt, 1979.
Of This Time, Of That Place, and Other Stories, edited by D. Trilling, Harcourt, 1979.
Speaking of Literature and Society, edited by D. Trilling, Harcourt, 1980.

EDITOR

(And author of introduction) Mark Twain, *Adventures of Huckleberry Finn,* Holt, 1948.
(And author of introduction) *The Portable Matthew Arnold,* Viking, 1949, published in England as *The Essential Matthew Arnold,* Chatto & Windus, 1969.
(And author of introduction) John Keats, *Selected Letters of John Keats,* Farrar, Straus, 1951.
(And author of introduction) John O'Hara, *Selected Short Stories of John O'Hara,* Modern Library, 1956.
(And author of introduction) Jane Austen, *Emma,* Houghton, 1957.
(With Steven Marcus) Ernest Jones, *The Life and Work of Sigmund Freud,* Basic Books, 1961.
(With Charles Kaplan and author of critical commentary) *The Experience of Literature: A Reader with Commentaries,* Holt, 1967, revised edition, 1969.
(And author of introduction) *Literary Criticism: An Introductory Reader,* Holt, 1970.
(Coeditor) *The Oxford Anthology of English Literature,* Oxford University Press, 1972.
(With Harold Bloom) *Victorian Prose and Poetry,* Oxford University Press, 1973.

CONTRIBUTOR

Malcolm Cowley, editor, *After the Genteel Tradition: American Writers, 1910-1930,* Norton, 1937, revised edition, Southern Illinois University Press, 1964.

Morton Dauwen Zabel, editor, *Literary Opinion in America,* Harper, 1937, 3rd revised edition, 1962.

Margaret Denny and William H. Gilman, editors, *The American Writer and the European Tradition,* University of Minnesota Press, 1950.

Chandler Brossard, editor, *The Scene Before You: A New Approach to American Culture,* Rinehart, 1955.

Irving Howe, editor, *Modern Literary Criticism,* Beacon Press, 1958.

Harold Beaver, editor, *American Critical Essays: Twentieth Century,* Oxford University Press, 1959.

Meyer Howard Abrams, editor, *English Romantic Poets: Modern Essays in Criticism,* Oxford University Press, 1960.

Sylvan Barnet, Morton Berman, and William Burto, editors, *The Study of Literature: A Handbook of Critical Essays and Terms,* Little, Brown, 1960.

Alfred Kazin, editor, *The Open Form: Essays for Our Time,* Harcourt, 1961.

Frederick J. Hoffman, editor, *The Great Gatsby: A Study,* Scribner, 1962.

Northrup Frye, editor, *Romanticism Reconsidered· Selected Papers from the English Institute,* Columbia University Press, 1963.

Carroll Camden, editor, *Literary Views: Critical and Historical Essays,* University of Chicago Press, 1964.

Norman Podhoretz, editor, *The Commentary Reader: Two Decades of Articles and Stories,* Atheneum, 1966.

Work represented in many anthologies, including *The Stature of Theodore Dreiser: A Critical Survey of His Life and His Work,* edited by Alfred Kazin and Charles Shapiro, Indiana University Press, 1955, *Literature in America,* edited by Philip Rahv, Meridian Books, 1957, *The Art of the Essay,* edited by Leslie Fiedler, Crowell, 1958, 2nd edition, 1969, *Hemingway and His Critics: An International Anthology,* edited by Carlos Baker, Hill & Wang, 1961, and *Modern British Fiction: Essays in Criticism,* edited by Mark Schorer, Oxford University Press, 1961. Contributor to *Menorah Journal, Partisan Review, New York Evening Post, Nation, New Republic, New York Times Book Review, New Yorker, Commentary, Poetry,* and numerous other periodicals. Member of editorial board of *Partisan Review* and *Kenyon Review.*

SIDELIGHTS: "In the hands of Lionel Trilling, criticism became not merely a consideration of a work of literature but also of the ideas it embodied and what these ideas said of the society that gave them birth," Thomas Lask stated in the *New York Times.* "Criticism was a moral function, a search for those qualities by which every age in its turn measured the virtuous man and the virtuous society."

Generally considered to be a major force in the world of literary criticism, Trilling was also a well-respected educator (his students included Allen Ginsberg, John Hollander, and Norman Podhoretz) and author of a novel and several short stories. He was once described by Steven Marcus in the *New York Times Book Review* as being the rather unlikely combination of "an American academic who was also a genuine intellectual in the non-academic sense [and] a professor of English who could really think, whose writing—elegant and elaborate as it often was—moved to the movement of ideas. And these ideas, one felt, were important."

With the publication of *Matthew Arnold,* Trilling's criticism was almost immediately recognized for its unique contribution to the literary world. Because of his incomparable method of examining his subjects, Trilling revealed to his readers fresh insights into the work of the nineteenth-century English poet and critic. He not only studied Arnold's writing but also examined his thoughts as they related to his role in society. As Trilling explained in the preface: "I have undertaken in this book to show the thought of Matthew Arnold in its complex unity and to relate it to the historical and intellectual events of his time. . . . However, because I have treated Arnold's ideas in their development, this study may be thought of as a biography of Arnold's mind." James Orrick commented in the *Saturday Review of Literature* that "the importance of the book is that it is a comprehensive study of the whole man. For Matthew Arnold was not primarily a literary critic; the clue to his enigma is that he was really a social critic. . . . With learning, penetration, and common sense Mr. Trilling analyzes Arnold's career from lyric poetry, through literary and political criticism, to the religious writings which his contemporaries found so baffling." H. F. Lowry remarked in the *New York Times:* "Because he is concerned with Arnold's organic unity and not merely with a catalogue of his manoeuvres, Mr. Trilling has given us a valuable book. With intelligence and artistry and a sincerity that ennobles every chapter, he well advances his appointed task. . . . The most interesting part of the book is its psychological criticism, its account of the organic unity behind Arnold's multifold activity."

A number of critics have written at length of the similarities between Trilling and Matthew Arnold. John Henry Raleigh compared the two in his book *Matthew Arnold and American Culture* and pointed out that some readers believed Arnold was an unconscious model for Trilling. Raleigh explained that Trilling's "particular blend of literary sensibility, learning, historical orientation and a civilized, urbane and ironical prose style is all too rare, and getting rarer. What he has tried to do in his career as a whole, as I understand it, is to perform in twentieth-century America the two roles that Matthew Arnold performed in nineteenth-century England: the conserver of what was valuable from the past and the proponent of the free play of the critical intelligence on the present." And John Wain comments in *Spectator* that in his criticism Trilling's "tone is not conversational or intimate, but rather Arnoldian, without sharing Arnold's tendency to nag or preach. And, far more than Arnold, he had the true critic's gift of describing exactly the thing he is talking about. His criticism is not technical, nor aesthetic, but moral. What makes a great book great, for him, is the spiritual and moral health it embodies."

Trilling's philosophy of looking at each person as an individual separate from society carried over to his method of reviewing literature. He ignored the established rules of criticism and chose to regard each piece of writing apart from its larger context or place in literature as a whole. A writer for *Time* explained that in *Beyond Culture,* Trilling argued that "the primary function of art and thought is to liberate the individual from the tyranny of his culture in the environmental sense and to permit him to stand beyond it in an autonomy of perception and judgment." As G. F. Whicher noted in the *New York Herald Tribune,* this approach manifested itself in Trilling's reluctance "to commit himself to any single critical attitude. He cherished a freedom to experiment, to use a combination of methods and a diversity of standards as tools at his disposal."

Trilling's contemporaries were generally impressed with this distinctive method of viewing the subjects or issues in his works of literary and social criticism. "Each of Trilling's books represents a determination to redeem and enforce the values consecrated in such words as reason, mind, sincerity, pleasure, society, self, and criticism," remarked Denis Donoghue in *Sewanee Review*. "Witness the attempt to speak up for mind in *Beyond Culture*, self in *The Opposing Self*, idea in *The Liberal Imagination*, virtue in *The Middle of the Journey*. A classic occasion was Trilling's defense of reason, maintained in *Sincerity and Authenticity*."

A number of critics agreed that it was just this defense of a particular way of thinking that was revealed in Trilling's second published critical study. Whicher stated in a review of *E. M. Forster* published in the *New York Herald Tribune Weekly Book Review* that "this mature and vibrant book is more important than its status in a series of critical studies might seem to imply. It is far from being a merely perfunctory contribution: it is a manifesto. . . . Those who are reluctant to accept the sad spiritual fascism of T. S. Eliot as the characteristic voice of our epoch will do well to ponder Mr. Trilling's pages. They will find there a notable study of a culture in disintegration, along with exciting premonitions of a new faith about to rise from the ashes of the old." And Clifton Fadiman explained in the *New Yorker* that *E. M. Forster* "is a model of the kind of criticism not too easily discoverable among us today—restrained, balanced, unashamed of its roots in a long intellectual tradition, academic in the finest sense. It is an admirable introduction to and summation of a novelist whose work, still largely unappreciated in America, quietly refuses to die."

E. M. Forster was followed five years later by Trilling's first and only novel, *The Middle of the Journey*. As is true of Trilling's other books, *The Middle of the Journey* requires the reader to look within himself for the answers to the questions subtly proposed by Trilling. As Lloyd Morris observed in the *New York Herald Tribune Weekly Book Review*: "*The Middle of the Journey* is both moving and intellectually provocative, but readers, like this reviewer, may find that its strongest effects lie in what is implied and suggested rather than in what is directly represented. It is a book so sensitively written, so deliberately loaded with implications of a larger significance than that actually expressed that its excellences may in part be revealed only by means of what readers bring to it."

"This mature and intelligent novel will be welcomed by those readers of the best contemporary American fiction who are growing weary of historical tales, group narratives in the Grand Hotel pattern, and the wistful, nostalgic family sagas of a lost generation," stated R. A. Cordell in *Saturday Review of Literature*. "*The Middle of the Journey* is a novel of ideas, objective, subtle, teasing in a sort of incompleteness as though the fastidious novelist would avoid the banality of telling too much. There are paragraphs that require rereading before they yield full meaning, not because they are vague or ambiguous, for the writing is of such a consistent excellence that one is tempted to fall back on some such cliche as 'classic style' to describe it, but because the thought is subtle."

Although Mark Shechner wrote in *Salmagundi* that to his mind *The Middle of the Journey* "is more a document than a realized piece of fiction," he concluded that "its values lie in its grasp of an historical moment and of a generation's disillusionment and conversion, out of which came not only a revised and subdued politics but a reconstituted aesthetics as well." Finally, Morton Dauwen Zabel stated in *Nation* that Trilling's novel is "a brilliant

example of a new mode of fiction, one whose function in the moral dilemmas of our age his acute critical sense has seen, and whose claims on the imaginative resources of his generation the finely controlled, humanly faithful art of this novel demonstrates. It is a book that brings the best critical intelligence now discernible in America into play with an absolutely honest creative talent."

In 1950 Trilling's first collection of critical essays was published. A number of critics agreed with E. J. Shoben's statement in his book *Lionel Trilling* that *The Liberal Imagination: Essays on Literature and Society* brought Trilling "immediate and widespread recognition. Established as a literary critic of the first rank and of distinctive range in the kinds of topics to which he addressed himself, and in the nature of his insights into human condition, he found his career assured. For the next twenty-five years with grace and an unassuming confidence, he walked the critic's path of his own choosing, a deeply respected and frequently honored figure in the intellectual world." Marcus agreed that it was after the publication of this book that "Trilling began to acquire the wide recognition he would subsequently enjoy." Marcus went on to remark in the *New York Times* that "*The Liberal Imagination* was much more than a book of essays with an intermittently overt political interest. To those of us who read it at the time, it was unmistakable that a major figure in modern literary criticism had put in his appearance. Trilling at once took his place beside F. R. Leavis and Edmund Wilson as one of the three or four dominating and decisive presences in 20th-century critical discourse—that discourse in which literature, culture, history, ideas and values freely and richly mingle."

The Opposing Self: Nine Essays in Criticism was released five years after *The Liberal Imagination*. "Only Trilling, in *The Opposing Self*, could have caught so eloquently the modern self's 'intense and adverse imagination of the culture in which it has its being,' an imagination 'characterized by certain powers of indignant perception,'" stated Anatole Broyard in the *New York Times*. A critic for *Kirkus Reviews* commented that "this is as distinguished and richly rewarding a book of criticism as has appeared in America in many years." However, David Daiches commented in the *Manchester Guardian* that "Mr. Trilling has led us to expect so much more from him than from other critics that we are disappointed in not finding in this collection of essays— perceptive and illuminating though they often are—both the larger illumination and the careful assessment of the individual work."

In 1955 Trilling's *Freud and the Crisis of Our Culture* was published. Since his student days Trilling had spent much time reading and writing about the man he once described as "one of the few great Plutarchian characters of our time." In fact, many reviewers feel that Sigmund Freud was as great an influence on Trilling as Matthew Arnold had been. Shoben remarked in his critical study that "no set of ideas so consistently, so dominantly, preoccupied Lionel Trilling throughout his career as those formulated by Sigmund Freud in *Civilization and Its Discontents*. . . . In a number of ways, his familiarity with Freud increasingly shaped and gave a language to some of Trilling's most intimate experiences and lent a distinctive color to some of his central values."

Two additional collections of critical essays, *A Gathering of Fugitives* and *Beyond Culture: Essays on Literature and Learning*, followed Trilling's book on Freud. After reading *A Gathering of Fugitives*, Leon Edel remarked in the *New Republic* that Trilling "is perhaps at his best in his literary essays. . . . There are . . . a number of evocative autobiographical passages in the essays, a conscious effort at measurement of the Trilling self." And R. G. Davis wrote in the *New York Times* that "few contemporary critics demonstrate so consistently as Lionel Trilling the art of right thinking."

In 1972 the text from six lectures Trilling gave at Harvard University was published under the title *Sincerity and Authenticity.* Laurence Lerner suggested in a review of this book published in *New Statesman* that "like all good critics, Trilling is both predictable and unpredictable. All his criticism bears the stamp of contemporary concern and of a gifted, individual mind." Writing in *National Review,* D. Keith Mano commented that *Sincerity and Authenticity* "flashes brilliance—better than brilliance, wisdom." Anatole Broyard agreed, writing in the *New York Times* that "it would be difficult to imagine anyone else writing Trilling's *Sincerity and Authenticity,* a brilliant study of our 'moral life in process of revising itself.'"

In *Mind in the Modern World,* the last book Trilling published before his death, the general theme of the place of the "mind" in culture still was present. Trilling urged the adoption of objectivity and the separation of an individual's intellect from common functional matters. In a review of *Mind in the Modern World,* a critic for *Virginia Quarterly Review* stated that "Trilling is a great critic in the tradition of Matthew Arnold. Like Arnold, Professor Trilling instructs and persuades through the example of his style, learning, and insight. He upholds the ideals of dispassionate objectivity, order, and urbanity."

Since Trilling's death several collections of his writings (containing some previously unpublished work) have been compiled, edited, and published. Trilling's wife, the highly-respected literary and social critic Diana Trilling, took on the editing duties for several of these collections, including *Prefaces to the Experience of Literature, The Last Decade, Of This Time, Of That Place, and Other Stories,* and *Speaking of Literature and Society.*

BIOGRAPHICAL/CRITICAL SOURCES:

BOOKS

Anderson, Quentin, Stephen Donadio, and Steven Marcus, editors, *Art, Politics, and Will: Essays in Honor of Lionel Trilling,* Basic Books, 1977.
Chace, W. M., editor, *Lionel Trilling: Criticism and Politics,* Stanford University Press, 1980.
Contemporary Literary Criticism, Gale (Detroit), Volume 9, 1978; Volume 11, 1979; Volume 24, 1983.
Dictionary of Literary Biography, Gale, Volume 28: *Twentieth-Century American-Jewish Fiction Writers,* 1984; Volume 63: *Modern American Critics, 1920-1955,* 1988.
Leitch, Thomas M., *Lionel Trilling: An Annotated Bibliography,* Garland, 1993.
O'Hara, Daniel T., *Lionel Trilling: The Work of Liberation,* University of Wisconsin Press, 1988.
Raleigh, John Henry, *Matthew Arnold and American Culture,* University of California Press, 1957.
Scott, Nathan A., Jr., *Three American Moralists: Mailer, Bellow, Trilling,* University of Notre Dame Press, 1973.
Shoben, Edward Joseph, *Lionel Trilling,* Ungar, 1981.
Tanner, Stephen L., *Lionel Trilling,* Twayne, 1988.
Trilling, Diana, *The Beginning of the Journey: The Marriage of Diana and Lionel Trilling,* Harcourt Brace, 1993.

PERIODICALS

American Scholar, winter, 1978; autumn, 1990, p. 587; summer, 1992, p. 337.
Best Sellers, September 1, 1967.
Book World, September 24, 1964.
Canadian Forum, October 5, 1950.
Christian Science Monitor, May 20, 1939.
Commentary, April, 1968; March, 1979.
Commonweal, September 24, 1943; November 14, 1947; March 9, 1956.
Detroit News, November 25, 1977.
Encounter, August, 1966.
Library Journal, February 1, 1955.
Manchester Guardian, March 21, 1939; August 23, 1955.
Nation, March 11, 1939; August 7, 1943; October 18, 1947; March 5, 1955; August 13, 1955; October 19, 1970; September 17, 1977.
New Republic, March 22, 1939; September 6, 1943; November 19, 1956; March 13, 1976; March 13, 1979; November 1, 1993, p. 30.
New Statesman, March 11, 1939; August 13, 1955; April 11, 1975.
New Yorker, August 14, 1943; October 12, 1947; January 21, 1956; September 13, 1993, p. 90.
New York Herald Tribune, April 9, 1950; April 3, 1955.
New York Herald Tribune Weekly Book Review, September 5, 1943; October 12, 1947.
New York Review of Books, December 9, 1965; February 2, 1989, p. 16.
New York Times, January 29, 1939; August 15, 1943; October 12, 1947; April 9, 1950; February 13, 1955; November 4, 1956; October 26, 1965; April 11, 1968; July 9, 1979; October 26, 1979.
New York Times Book Review, February 13, 1955; November 14, 1965; December 31, 1967; January 20, 1980; October 12, 1980; October 3, 1993, p. 15.
Partisan Review, summer, 1966.
Poetry, December, 1968.
Salmagundi, spring, 1978.
Saturday Review, February 12, 1955; February 14, 1958; November 6, 1965.
Saturday Review of Literature, January 28, 1939; August 28, 1943; October 11, 1947; February 14, 1948; April 15, 1950.
Sewanee Review, spring, 1976; spring, 1978.
Spectator, April 28, 1939; July 29, 1955.
Studies in Short Fiction, winter, 1976.
Time, October 20, 1947.
Times Literary Supplement, March 11, 1939; August 26, 1955; August 21, 1981.

* * *

TRIMBALL, W. H.
See MENCKEN, H(enry) L(ouis)

* * *

TRISTRAM
See HOUSMAN, A(lfred) E(dward)

TRUNDLETT, Helen B.
See ELIOT, T(homas) S(tearns)

*   *   *

TSVETAEVA (EFRON), Marina (Ivanovna) 1892-1941
(Marina Ivanovna Tsvetaeva Efron)

PERSONAL: Given name also transliterated as Maryna and Mariny; surname also transliterated as Tsvetayeva, Cvetaeva, Zwetajewa, Zvetaieva, Cvetajevova, Tzvetaeva, Tzvetayeva, Cwietajewa, and Tsvetaevoi; born in 1892 in Moscow, Russia; committed suicide, August 31, 1941, in Elabuga, Tatar Republic; daughter of an art history professor and a homemaker; married Sergej Efron (a soldier); children: Ariadna, another daughter (deceased), Georgij. *Education:* Attended University of Paris (Sorbonne).

CAREER: Poet, essayist, critic, translator.

WRITINGS:

Vechernii al'bom: Stikhi (poetry; title means "Evening Album"), A. N. Mamonmova, 1910.
Volshebnyi fonar': Vtoraia kniga stikhov (poetry; title means "The Magic Lantern"), Ole-Lukoie, 1912, YMCA-Press (Paris), 1979.
Iz dvukh knig (poetry; title means "From Two Books"), Ole-Lukoie, 1913.
Versty II (poetry; title means "Mileposts II"), Kostry, 1921.
Versty I (poetry; title means "Mileposts I"; includes "Poema gory"), Gosudarstevnnoe Izdatel'stvo, 1922, facsimile edition, Ardis, 1972, Prideaux Press (Letchworth, England), 1979.
Stikhi k Bloku (poetry; title means "Poems to Blok"), Ogon'ki (Berlin), 1922, Prideaux Press, 1978.
Tsar'-Devitsa (epic poem; title means "The King-Maiden"), Epokha, 1922, published as *Tsar'-Devitsa: The King Maiden,* Prideaux Press, 1971.
Razluka (poetry; title means "Parting"; includes "Na krasnom kone"), Gelikon, 1922.
Psikheia (poetry; title means) "Psyche"), Z. I. Grzhebina, 1923.
Remeslo (poetry; title means "Craft"), Gelikon, 1923, reprinted with introduction and notes by Efim Etkind, W. A. Meeuws, 1981.
Molodets (poems; title means "The Swain"), Plamia, 1924, published as *Molodets: Poems,* Prideaux Press, 1971.
Posle Rossii, 1922-1925 (poetry; title means "After Russia"), Parizh, 1928.
Proza (essays; title means "Prose"), Chekhov Publishing House, 1953, published with introduction by Valentina S. Coe as *Proza: Prose [of] Marina Tsvetaeva,* Bradda, 1969.
Izbrannoe (title means "Selected Works"), Goslitizdat, 1961.
Izbrannye proizvedeniia (title means "Selected Works"), Sovetskii Pisatel', 1965.
Moi Pushkin (title means "My Pushkin"), Sovetskii Pisatel', 1967, published as *Moi Pushkin: My Pushkin,* Prideaux Press, 1977.
(Translator) *Prosto serdtse: Stikhi zarubezhnykh poetov v perevode Mariny Tsvetaevoi* (title means "Simply the Heart: Poems of Foreign Poets in Marina Tsvetaeva's Translations"), Progress, 1967.

Pis'ma k A. Teskovoi (title means "Letters to Teskova"), Academia, 1969, reprinted with introductory articles by Zdenek Mathauser and Vadim Morkovin as *Pis'ma k Anne Teskovoi,* Versty, 1982.
Stikhotvoreniia (poetry), reprint of original edition, introduction by J. Norbury, Bradda, 1969.
Nesobrannye proizvedeniia (title means "Uncollected Works"), W. Fink, 1971.
Neizdannye pis'ma (title means "Unpublished Letters"; includes April, 1925 letter to Ariadna Kolbasina), edited by Gleb Struve and Nikita Struve, YMCA-Press, 1972.
Neizdannoe: Stikhi, teatr, proza (title means "Unpublished Works: Poetry, Drama, Prose"), YMCA-Press, 1976.
Metel' (verse play; title means "The Snowstorm") [and] *Prikliuchenie* (verse play; title means "An Adventure") [and] *Ariadna,* Prideaux Press, 1978.
Izbrannaia v dvukh tomakh: 1917-1937 (title means "Selected Prose in Two Volumes"; includes essays "Geroj truda," "Zhivoe o zhivom," "Mat' i muzyka," "Poet o kritike," "Natalia Goncharova," and "Zemnye primety," "Epos i lirika sovremennoj Rossii," and "Iskusstvo pri svete Sovesti"), two volumes, Russica (New York), 1979.
Stikhotvoreniia i poemy (title means "Lyric Poems and Longer Poems"; includes collection *Junosheskie stikhi*), Sovetskii Pisatel', 1979, Russica, 1980.
Sochinenia v dvukh tomakh (title means "Selected Prose in Two Volumes"), two volumes, Russica, 1979, Khudozhestvennaya Literatura, 1980.
Stikhotvoreniia i poemy v piati tomakh (selected poems; title means "Lyric Poems and Longer Poems in Five Volumes"), five volumes, Russica, 1980–.
Stikhi i poemy (selected poems), Vaga, 1988.

Also author of unpublished manuscript titled "Tvoia smcrt'"; author of unproduced verse plays "Chervonnij valet" (title means "Jack of Hearts"), 1918, "Kamennyj angel" (title means "The Stone Angel"), 1919, *Fortuna* (title means "Fortune") 1919, and *Konets Kazanovy* (title means "Casanova's End"), 1919, revised and expanded version published as *Feniks* (title means "Phoenix"), 1924.

Contributor of "Krysolov" (title means "The Rat Catcher"), "Poema kontsa" (title means "Poem of the End"), "Poema gory" (title means "Poem of the Hill"), and other poems to Russian journals, including *Sovremennye zapiski, Volja Rossii, Novyj mir,* and *Novyj zhurnal;* correspondence published in Russian journals. Editor of *Kovcheg,* 1926.

IN ENGLISH TRANSLATION

Lebedinyi stan (poetry; includes "Oh, My Little Mushroom"), originally published in 1957, bilingual English and Russian edition with translation, introduction, notes, and commentaries by Robin Kemball published as *The Demesne of the Swans,* Ardis, 1980.
Selected Poems of Marina Tsvetayeva, translated by Elaine Feinstein, foreword by Max Hayward, Oxford University Press, 1971, revised and enlarged edition with literal versions by Angela Livingstone and others, 1981, Dutton, 1987.
A Captive Spirit: Selected Prose, edited and translated by J. Marin King, Ardis, 1980, reprinted with introduction by Susan Sontag, Virago, 1983.
Three Russian Women Poets: Anna Akhmatova, Marina Tsvetayeva, Bella Akhmadulina (poetry), translated by Mary Maddock, introduction by Edward J. Brown, Crossing Press, 1983.

Letters, Summer 1926: Boris Pasternak, Marina Tsvetayeva, Rainer Maria Rilke, edited by Yevgeny Pasternak, Yelena Pasternak, and Konstantin M. Azadovsky, translated by Margaret Wettlin and Walter Arndt, Harcourt, 1985.

Selected Poems, translated by David McDuff, Bloodaxe Books, 1987.

Art in the Light of Conscience: Eight Essays on Poetry, translated by Angela Livingstone, Harvard University Press (Cambridge, MA), 1992.

Poem of the End: Selected Lyrical and Narrative Poetry, translated by Nina Kossman, Ardis (Ann Arbor), 1995.

Contributor to *The Diary of Valery Bryusov (1893-1905),* edited and translated with an introduction by Joan Delaney Grossman, University of California Press.

SIDELIGHTS: Marina Tsvetaeva was an important Russian poet whose career spanned several decades. Although the auspicious beginning of her literary career was borne out artistically in numerous volumes of poetry and essays, her early success belied the immense hardships that she would face during the rest of her life. Many of these hardships were occasioned by historical events; revolution and civil war led to emigration, political troubles, and ill-advised repatriation leading to personal deprivation and poverty. Yet the major difficulties Tsvetaeva encountered were in the realm of her art; dictated by integrity and a strong sense of responsibility, she voluntarily assumed to carry out her poetic task. Despite the personal and professional adversity out of which her work arose, Tsvetaeva's poetry and essays now enjoy widespread critical respect and receive increasing Western attention and admiration.

In October, 1910, Tsvetaeva began her literary career with a book of verse titled *Vechernii al'bom* ("Evening Album"), which appeared in Moscow in a private printing of five hundred copies. An unknown eighteen-year-old schoolgirl at the time, Tsvetaeva had the volume published at her own expense "for reasons," as she declared in her 1925 essay "Geroj truda" ("A Hero of Labor"), "extraneous to literature, but related to poetry—in place of a letter to a person with whom I was deprived of the possibility of communicating in any other way." No announcements or advertisements heralded the appearance of the book; even the young poet's family remained unaware of its existence for some time.

Given *Vechernii al'bom*'s highly personal nature and its modest publication, critical response was astonishing. No fewer than four prominent writers took notice of the book and published highly laudatory reviews praising the poet's talent, originality, and artistic independence. They noted the remarkable intimacy achieved in the verse, responded with interest to the poetic themes that appeared in it, and spoke highly of the intuitive grasp of the laws of poetry evident in the collection.

It was at least in part due to the success of *Vechernii al'bom* that Tsvetaeva became acquainted with the poet Maksimilian Voloshin, who became her personal friend and literary mentor. Voloshin, whose spirit Tsvetaeva later captured in her 1933 essay "Zhivoe o zhivom" ("A Living Word About a Living Man"), broadened the young poet's literary tastes by supplying her with reading material and by introducing her at Musaget, the editorial office of a prominent publishing house and a site of literary gatherings. There Tsvetaeva had the opportunity to meet with some of the principal writers of her time and to be accepted as a fellow poet. In an anthology of contemporary Russian verse Musaget published in 1911, two of her poems appeared beside works by the major poets of the time.

In 1912 Tsvetaeva published her second book of verse, *Volshebnyi fonar'* ("The Magic Lantern"), and in 1913 her third, *Iz dvukh knig* ("From Two Books"), a selection of poems from the first two collections. The thematically naive poems of *Volshebnyi fonar'*, like those of *Vechernii al'bom,* revealed a remarkably mature mastery of poetic idiom, but the concerns they expressed were still adolescent ones. A prevalent theme, for example, was the writer's reluctance to leave the magical realm of childhood to enter the mundane adult world. Tsvetaeva's second and third books did not meet with the same enthusiasm that *Vechernii Al'bom* had generated, since they were essentially a continuation of the first collection and thus a part of the initial manifestation of Tsvetaeva's artistic potential but not the further development that the critics expected and that was, in fact, to come.

The widening scope of Tsvetaeva's personal experiences and literary schooling is reflected in each of her subsequent collections. The title *Junosheskie stikhi* ("Juvenilia"), for a fourth volume of poems—written between 1913 and 1915 but not published during Tsvetaeva's lifetime—would have been more appropriate for the earlier collections, since the poems appearing in this book show a distinct transition from the romantic youthfulness of Tsvetaeva's first three volumes to the more fully developed outlook found in the subsequent collection, *Versty I* ("Mileposts I"). Written in 1916, the poems of *Versty I* must be counted among Tsvetaeva's mature works and demonstrate the rapid development of her talent. "Stylistically and technically," Simon Karlinsky wrote in *Marina Tsvetaeva: The Woman, Her World and Her Poetry, Versty I* "was the most daringly experimental of Tsvetaeva's collections and it constituted a watershed in her poetic evolution. In it, she not only learned whatever the great age of Russian poetry in which she lived had to teach her, but she also became a major innovator in her own right."

The next stage in Tsvetaeva's artistic development coincided with the period of Russian history that included the February and October revolutions of 1917 and the civil war that followed them. During this time, generally known as the War Communism period, Tsvetaeva experienced extreme hardships. Her husband, Sergej Efron, traveled to southern Russia, where he joined the anti-Bolshevik White Army. Tsvetaeva, as helpless in daily life as she was masterful in her poetry, was stranded in Moscow for the next five years with her two daughters, the younger of whom died of malnutrition.

As was to happen again later, after Tsvetaeva left Russia, the years of greatest physical deprivation became the most fruitful artistically. Tsvetaeva recorded the period 1917 to 1922 in poems that were included in the collections *Lebedinyi stan (The Demesne of the Swans),* which was not published in its entirety until 1957, *Versty II* ("Mileposts II"), comprised of poems dating from 1917 to 1921, and *Remeslo* ("Craft"), a volume of poems from the years 1921 and 1922.

In *The Demesne of the Swans* Tsvetaeva identified with a legendary medieval Russian chronicler who had recorded troubled times in the history of his country. In this collection, as always in her art and life, Tsvetaeva's sympathy was with the underdog— the White Army that her husband had joined and that was then fighting a losing battle against the Bolsheviks. The stance Tsvetaeva adopted was politically untenable and contributed to the steadily increasing hardships she endured during this time. Her adamant refusal to compromise her views in the face of public, political, and social pressures was characteristic of her insistence on a larger, truer perspective untrammeled by temporary animosities and prejudices. In 1914, when war had broken out with Germany and anti-German sentiment raged in Russia, Tsvetaeva had recited verse in which she praised German culture. Similarly, in Bolshevik-controlled Moscow she recited verses praising the White resistance before an audience comprised largely of Red soldiers. This gesture was not political—Tsvetaeva abhorred politics—but human. With it she protested the narrow designations, whether religious, national, or political, that are applied to people or movements and that limit perception and understanding. Tsvetaeva insisted that in the context of a higher reality such divisions are meaningless. In the poem "Oh, My Little Mushroom," for example, she wrote of the dead on a battlefield: "One was White but turned red: Blood made him crimson. / Another was Red but turned white: Death whitened him."

Although not all of Tsvetaeva's works found immediate publication, her reputation as a writer gradually grew. Fortunately, these productive years in the late 1910s and early 1920s coincided with a period when Soviet cultural policy did not yet place the severe restrictions on artistic method that were soon to follow. These restrictions were imposed, however, just as Tsvetaeva received word that her husband, from whom she had not heard since he had entered the White Army in 1917, was in Prague, Czechoslovakia, and left Russia to join him. In May of 1922 she was granted an exit visa and traveled to Berlin with her surviving daughter, Ariadna. There she was greeted by a thriving, appreciative Russian emigre literary community and had the opportunity to meet a number of fellow writers. After a brief stay during which she continued to write lyric poetry, Tsvetaeva traveled on to Czechoslovakia, where she remained for the next three years.

During her Czech years, Tsvetaeva assembled the collection *Psikheia* ("Psyche"), which consists of both new poems and some that had already appeared elsewhere. She also wrote the poems that, along with the twenty-one she had written in Berlin, comprise *Posle Rossii* ("After Russia"). *Posle Rossii* holds a special place among Tsvetaeva's works, for it represents both the pinnacle of her development as a lyric poet and her final collection of lyric verse. This collection provides a synthesis of the diction, metrical forms, and themes with which Tsvetaeva had experimented in her earlier works. In *Posle Rossii* Tsvetaeva retained her dynamic and often passionate tone, and at the same time achieved a detached, philosophical outlook. Shakespeare's *Hamlet,* Racine's *Phedre,* the myths of Ariadne, of Orpheus and Eurydice, and of the Cumaean Sibyl, all, in Tsvetaeva's interpretation, became a means of conveying the increasingly focused poetic philosophy that she continued to develop in her prose. The indivisibility of form and content on which Tsvetaeva insisted is demonstrated in the verse of *Posle Rossii* in which she united exquisite use of language with profoundly innovative rhythmic structures. Like all of Tsvetaeva's verse, the poems in this collection are based on her personal experience of life and of literature, experience that played a vital role in her maturity as an artist. Tsvetaeva directed many of the poems to Boris Pasternak, whose work she had discovered in the early 1920s and whom she had come to regard as a kindred spirit in the realm of poetry.

In November of 1925 Tsvetaeva, her daughter Ariadna, and her son Georgij, who had been born in Czechoslovakia, moved to Paris, where Efron later joined them. The large Russian emigre community in Paris greeted Tsvetaeva as a celebrity. She found, at once, a sizeable reading public, received considerable praise, and was published in a variety of Russian literary journals. The public reading she gave in February 1926 in Paris was hailed as a major literary event. Tsvetaeva was pleased by this reception, but it did not weaken her deep mistrust of fame, which, she believed, almost inevitably resulted from the wrong (that is, extra-literary) reasons and had the dangerous potential of diverting the artist from the solitary path of his art.

At the same time, Tsvetaeva's poetry was becoming more difficult, placing considerable demands on her readers. Tsvetaeva was conscious of the difficulty of her works, but this difficulty was not, as some hostile critics suggested, the poet's intentional posturing. It was rather the inevitable result of her poetic evolution. Tsvetaeva answered not to the demands of her reader but to the higher demands of her art. As she declared in "Poet o kritike": "To please the reader with beautifully plashing words is not the goal of creation. My goal, when I sit down to work is not to make anyone happy, neither myself nor anyone else, but to give a work as perfect as possible." From her reader Tsvetaeva expected active participation in the creative process, as she also made clear in "Poet o kritike": "And what is reading but deciphering, interpretation, the extraction of the secrets that remain beyond the lines, beyond the limits of words. . . . Reading is—above all—co-creation. If a reader is lacking in imagination no book will survive." The reader, in Tsvetaeva's view, bore considerable responsibility toward the work of art, and in "A Poet on Criticism" Tsvetaeva recognized the extent of her demand without mitigating it: "The reader's exhaustion is not devastating but creative. Co-creative. It does honor both to the reader and to me."

During her final years outside Russia, Tsvetaeva commenced her third prose period. From 1917 to 1920 she had produced memoirs and diary entries, and from 1922 to 1931 she had written essays in criticism, tributes inspired by the deaths of poets Tsvetaeva admired, and a piece about the painter Natalia Goncharova. The third and final period of Tsvetaeva's prose was dominated by her interest in her past in relation to far broader artistic concerns. As J. Marin King observed—in an essay published in *A Handbook of Russian Literature,* edited by Victor Terras—"In 1933 Tsvetaeva's prose began to draw heavily on her past, although few of the some twenty prose pieces of this period can be called 'autobiographical' in the usual sense of that word. Rather, the prose begins from Tsvetaeva's strongly-sensed duty to preserve a vanished past and then plunges beyond autobiography into a mythic recreation of her childhood that serves, in turn, as a metaphor for the genesis and destiny of the poet." To a significant extent all of Tsvetaeva's writing—poetry, prose, and the several volumes of personal letters that exist—are about poetry and the poet, and nearly everything Tsvetaeva wrote can be regarded as a "mythic recreation" of the world.

Tsvetaeva pursues those themes in the collection edited by Angela Livingstone, *Art in the Light of Conscience: Eight Essays on Poetry.* Written between 1922 and 1934, the "essays range widely, from a response to a hostile critic, to a discussion of the meaning of contemporaneity in literature, to a defense of the moral independence of the poet," noted Patricia Pollock Brodsky in *World Literature Today.* In the *New Republic,* Tomas Venclova applauded the selections for focusing on "Tsvetaeva's meditations on literary art." "Whatever her subject, [Tsvetaeva] is finally always speaking about poetry, which is, for her, coterminous with risk, with a courage oblivious to self, with intensity of feeling," Venclova noted.

In the late 1930s it became known that Tsvetaeva's husband had become an agent for the Soviet secret police and had participated in a political murder—a fact Tsvetaeva refused to believe. She was shunned by most of the Russian emigre community, which could not find her professed ignorance of her husband's activities credible. In mid-1939 Tsvetaeva made the difficult and dangerous decision to return to the Soviet Union, prompted not so much by the awkwardness of her situation in France as by the demands of her family, especially her son, whom she adored. The full extent of the Stalinist terror was not known at this time in the West, and Efron and Ariadna, who had become increasingly pro-Soviet during their years in France, were the first of her family to decide to repatriate. Georgij insisted that he had no future in France and wanted to do the same.

On June 18, 1939, shortly after Tsvetaeva and Georgij arrived in Moscow, Ariadna and Efron (who was later shot) were arrested. Tsvetaeva's sister, Anastasija Tsvetaeva, she learned, had been imprisoned two years earlier. Most of Tsvetaeva's former friends, including several prominent writers, were afraid to associate with her. Politically, Tsvetaeva's situation was precarious; artistically, it was impossible. The proclamation in the 1930s of Socialist Realism as the only acceptable form for Soviet arts precluded publication of any of Tsvetaeva's highly original works in the Soviet Union.

Shortly after Germany invaded Russia in the summer of 1941, Tsvetaeva became concerned for her son's safety and joined a group of writers being evacuated from Moscow to the Tatar Republic. More privileged authors in the politically determined hierarchy were given accommodation in the town of Chistopol, but Tsvetaeva and Georgij found themselves in Elabuga, a small, provincial village where there was neither a literary community nor the prospect of work. They rented a room in the hut of a local couple; here Tsvetaeva hanged herself on August 31, 1941. No one attended her funeral, and she was buried in an unmarked common grave.

"The age for my poems—as for precious wines—will come," Tsvetaeva wrote in a 1913 poem that was included in the collection "Juvenilia." This orientation towards the future was characteristic of Tsvetaeva; as in much of her poetry and prose, she insisted on the timelessness of her art. Her youthful prophecy revealed both the profundity of her faith in her poetry and her artistic clairvoyance, for the prophecy is in fact being fulfilled. In the 1950s the publication of Tsvetaeva's poetry, prose, and letters began growing steadily, as did her readership. Largely through the efforts of Ariadna, who survived imprisonment and exile and devoted the remainder of her life to getting her mother's poetry into print, selected works of Tsvetaeva's have appeared in Russia. Memoirs and biographies of Tsvetaeva have also appeared there, including one by Anastasija that discusses her sister's life and poetry with new frankness. More accurate accounts of Tsvetaeva's life and work and the most complete collections of her poetry, prose, and letters have appeared in the West, and, together with a rapidly expanding body of Russian and Western scholarship, they have increased readers' understanding and appreciation of this remarkable poet.

BIOGRAPHICAL/CRITICAL SOURCES:

BOOKS

Efron, Ariadna, *Straniitsy vospominanii* (title means "Pages of Reminiscences"), Lev, 1979.
Feiler, Lily, *Marina Tsvetaeva: The Double Beat of Heaven and Hell,* Duke University Press, 1994.
Feinstein, Elaine, *A Captive Lion: The Life of Marina Tsvetayeva,* Dutton, 1987.

Hasty, Olga Peters, *Tsvetaeva's Orphic Journeys in the Worlds of the Word,* Northwestern University Press, 1996.
Karlinsky, Simon, *Marina Tsvetaeva: The Woman, Her World and Her Poetry,* Cambridge University Press, 1985.
Proffer, Ellendea, editor, *Tsvetaeva: A Pictorial Biography,* translation by J. Marin King, Ardis, 1980.
Razumovsky, Maria, *Marina Tsvetayeva: A Critical Biography,* Bloodaxe Books (Newcastle upon Tyne), 1994.
Schweitzer, Viktoria, *Tsvetsaeva,* Farrar, Straus and Giroux, 1993.
Smith, Alexandra, *The Song of the Mocking Bird: Pushkin in the Works of Marina Tsvetaeva,* P. Lang, 1994.
Tsvetaeva, Anastasija, *Vospominanija* (title means "Memoirs"), Sovetskii Pisatel', 2nd edition, 1974.

PERIODICALS

Iowa Review, Volume 9, number 4, 1978.
Los Angeles Times Book Review, January 4, 1981.
Modern Language Review, October, 1993, p. 1053.
New Republic, April 5, 1993, p. 38.
New Yorker, February 7, 1994, p. 90.
New York Times Book Review, October 12, 1980.
Poetry, November, 1993, p. 97.
Times Literary Supplement, March 6, 1981; January 8, 1982.
Virginia Quarterly Review, autumn, 1992, p. 122.
Weiner Sluwistischer Alumanach, Sonderband 3, 1981.
World Literature Today, summer, 1992, p. 542.

* * *

TUCHMAN, Barbara W(ertheim) 1912-1989

PERSONAL: Born January 30, 1912, in New York, NY; died from complications resulting from a stroke, February 6, 1989, in Greenwich, CT; daughter of Maurice (a banker) and Alma (Morgenthau) Wertheim; married Lester R. Tuchman (a physician), 1940; children: Lucy, Jessica, Alma. *Education:* Radcliffe College, B.A., 1933.

CAREER: Institute of Pacific Relations, New York City, research and editorial assistant, 1933, Tokyo, 1934-35; *Nation,* New York City, staff writer and foreign correspondent, 1935-37, correspondent in Madrid, 1937-38; *The War with Spain* (magazine), London, England, staff writer, 1937-38; *New Statesman and Nation,* London, U.S. correspondent, 1939; Office of War Information, New York City, editor for Far Eastern Affairs, 1943-45. Trustee, Radcliffe College, 1960-72, New York Public Library, 1980-89. Appointed Jefferson Lecturer for the National Endowment for the Humanities, 1980. Lecturer at Harvard University, University of California, U.S. Naval War College, and other institutions.

MEMBER: Society of American Historians (president, 1970-73), Authors Guild (treasurer), Authors League of America (member of council), American Academy of Arts and Letters (president, 1979), American Academy of Arts and Sciences, Cosmopolitan Club.

AWARDS, HONORS: Pulitzer Prize, 1963, for *The Guns of August,* and 1972, for *Stilwell and the American Experience in China, 1911-1945;* gold medal for history, American Academy of Arts and Sciences, 1978; Regent Medal of Excellence, University of the State of New York, 1984; Sarah Josepha Hale Award, 1985; Abraham Lincoln Literary Award, Union League Club, 1985; received Order of Leopold from the Kingdom of Belgium; D.Litt. from Yale University, Columbia University, New York University, Williams College, University of Massachusetts, Smith College, Hamilton College, Mount Holyoke College, Boston University, Harvard University, and other schools.

WRITINGS:

The Lost British Policy: Britain and Spain since 1700, United Editorial, 1938.

Bible and Sword: England and Palestine from the Bronze Age to Balfour, New York University Press, 1956.

The Zimmermann Telegram, Viking, 1958, revised edition, Macmillan, 1966.

The Guns of August (Book-of-the-Month Club selection), Macmillan, 1962, published in England as *August, 1914,* Constable, 1962.

The Proud Tower: A Portrait of the World before the War, 1890-1914 (Book-of-the-Month Club selection), Macmillan, 1966.

Stilwell and the American Experience in China, 1911-1945 (Book-of-the-Month Club selection), Macmillan, 1971 (published in England as *Sand against the Wind: Stilwell and the American Experience in China, 1911-1945,* Macmillan [London], 1971).

Notes from China, Collier Books, 1972.

A Distant Mirror: The Calamitous Fourteenth Century, Knopf, 1978.

Practicing History: Selected Essays, Knopf, 1981.

The March of Folly: From Troy to Vietnam, Knopf, 1984.

The First Salute: A View of the American Revolution, Knopf, 1988.

(Author of preface) O'Brian, John, *Degas to Matisse: The Maurice Wertheim Collection,* Harry N. Abrams, 1988.

The Book: A Lecture Sponsored by the Center for the Book in the Library of Congress and the Authors League of America, Presented at the Library of Congress, October 17, 1979, Library of Congress, 1988.

Also author of *The Alternative to Arms Control,* Center for International Relations, and *The Palestine Question in American History,* Ayer. Contributor to *Harper's, Atlantic, New York Times, American Scholar, Foreign Affairs,* and other publications.

SIDELIGHTS: Barbara W. Tuchman wrote narrative histories that are strongly literary in nature, believing that the work of most historians is often too obscure for the average reader. "Historians who stuff in every item of research they have found, every shoelace and telephone call of a biographical subject, are not doing the hard work of selecting and shaping a readable story," she commented. Her approach to history has won her two Pulitzer Prizes.

Tuchman was also "a bestselling author and America's foremost popular historian," as Wendy Smith writes in *Publishers Weekly.* Although not trained as a historian, Tuchman did not see that as a disadvantage. "I never took a Ph.D.," she admitted. "It's what saved me, I think. If I had taken a doctoral degree, it would have stifled any writing capacity." To prepare for her books, Tuchman first researched the available information and then visited the appropriate historical sites. For *The Guns of August,* she walked the battlefields of World War I; for *A Distant Mirror: The Calamitous Fourteenth Century,* she crossed the same mountains the Crusaders of the fourteenth century crossed.

It wasn't until her third book, *The Zimmermann Telegram,* that Tuchman achieved success as a writer. A best-seller, the book concerns the infamous German telegram to Mexico during World War I which promised the Mexican government portions of the

American Southwest if it would enter the war on Germany's behalf. The exposure of the telegram was instrumental in bringing the United States into the war against Germany. As Ferdinand Kuhn explains in *Saturday Review,* "the blundering telegram was important in history, and for this reason the story is worth telling." Tuchman's account of the pivotal affair is singled out for its remarkable detail. "There can only be praise," writes a *Times Literary Supplement* critic, "for the writer's mastery of a mass of documents treating all sides of this amazing affair." Ernest S. Pisko of the *Christian Science Monitor* notes Tuchman's "stupendous knowledge of all the facts and all the persona even remotely involved in the dramatic story."

The Guns of August, a look at the opening days of World War I, was Tuchman's next best-seller and winner of her first Pulitzer Prize. It is, Bruce Blivenn, Jr. writes in the *New Yorker,* a "neatly perfect literary triumph." Focusing on the opening strategies and battles of the war, Tuchman argues that errors on all sides in the conflict led to the stalemate of trench warfare—a four-year period of enormous and largely pointless casualties. "There is much of battle orders, of tactical, strategic, and logistical problems in the pages of 'The Guns of August,'" Pisko writes. "But such is the skill of the author that these technical issues become organic parts of an epic never flagging in suspense." Although Cyril Falls of the *New York Times Book Review* finds that "the errors and omissions of 'The Guns of August' mount to a formidable total," he judges the book to be "a lucid, fair, critical and witty account." Blivenn claims that "Tuchman leans toward seeing issues as black and white, but her control of her material is so certain and her opinions are so passionate that it would be risky to argue with her."

With *The Proud Tower: A Portrait of the World before the War, 1890-1914,* Tuchman turned to an examination of society before the First World War and of the events and forces which led to the war. World War I, she writes in the book, "lies like a band of scorched earth dividing that time from ours. In wiping out so many lives which would have been operative on the years that followed, in destroying beliefs, changing ideas, and leaving incurable wounds of disillusion, it created a physical as well as psychological gulf between two epochs." In eight chapters, each covering a different topic, Tuchman provides varied glimpses of pre-war society. "*The Proud Tower,*" Oscar Handlin comments in the *Atlantic,* "is consistently interesting. [Tuchman] is a skillful and imaginative writer. She has the storyteller's knack for getting the maximum dramatic effect out of the events which crowd her pages."

Tuchman won her second Pulitzer Prize for the 1971 book *Stilwell and the American Experience in China, 1911-1945.* It follows the career of Joseph Warren Stilwell, an American military officer who served in China in various capacities from 1911 to 1944. Stilwell's years in China saw that country's transformation from a feudal society to a communist state. The book is, Anthony Grey writes in the *Washington Post Book World,* "an extremely creditable compendium of the mightiness, the miseries, the personalities, the perversities, the facts and frustrations of China in the past half-century seen through unhappy American eyes." O. Edmund Clubb, writing in the *Saturday Review,* finds *Stilwell and the American Experience in China* to be "an admirably structured work that is excellent as narrative and fascinating as history," while Allen S. Whiting, in a review for the *Nation,* calls it "the most interesting and informative book on U.S.-China relations to appear since World War II."

Although Tuchman's most popular books had dealt with twentieth-century history, in 1978 she published a book about the Middle Ages, *A Distant Mirror: The Calamitous Fourteenth Century.* Her interest in the period stemmed from what she saw as similarities between the fourteenth century and our own time; the book's title refers to this similarity. David Benson, writing in the *Spectator,* lists the "resemblances between that period and our own" as "almost continual warfare, both civil and international, widespread political instability and popular uprisings, a crisis of confidence in almost all institutions, especially the Church, and a rise of individualism combined with a general decline in authority." The central event of the fourteenth century was the bubonic plague, which swept across Europe and Asia, killing nearly a third of the population. Tuchman compares the plague to the possible devastation a nuclear war might cause in our own century.

Following the career of Enguerrand de Coucy VII, a French knight and nobleman, *A Distant Mirror* becomes an "ambitious, absorbing historical panorama," as Naomi Bliven writes in the *New Yorker.* De Coucy was related to both the French and English royal families and owned land near the troublesome Flemish border, so his life touched upon many key events and personalities of the time. Tuchman's narrative brings these events and personalities to vivid life. Despite the book's several drawbacks, Laurence Stone of the *New York Review of Books* finds it "beautifully written, careful and thorough in its scholarship, extensive in the range of topics peripherally touched upon, and enlivened by consistently intelligent comment. What Mrs. Tuchman does superbly is to tell *how* it was, to convey a sense of time and place." This ability to recreate the texture of fourteenth-century life is also noted by Brian Tierney of the *Washington Post Book World.* Tuchman's "special gift," Tierney writes, "is to bring a past age to life by the accumulation of countless concrete details, lovingly collected and deftly presented. . . . The result is a kind of brilliant, dazzling, impressionistic picture of the surface of medieval life."

In *The March of Folly: From Troy to Vietnam,* Tuchman ranges over Western history from the mythical Trojan horse of ancient Greece to the Vietnam War, examining in depth four episodes where governmental "folly" is most evident: the Trojans' decision to bring the wooden horse into their city; the corruption of the Renaissance popes, which helped to provoke the Protestant Reformation; the English policy towards the rebellious American colonies; and the American involvement in the Vietnam War. These episodes were similar, Michael Howard explains in the *Washington Post Book World,* in that "the actors involved pursued a course of action which was not only foolish but seen at the time to be foolish; which was the responsibility of an entire group or class rather than a single misguided individual, and to which a sensible and feasible alternative was quite obviously available." *The March of Folly* was a change in approach for Tuchman. "I've done what I always said I would never do," she told Smith, "and that is to take a theory before I wrote a book. My other books were narrative, and I tried not to adopt a thesis except what emerged from the material. It's what I don't believe in when writing history, actually."

Some critics took exception to the thesis of *The March of Folly.* Jack Lessenberry of the *Detroit News,* speaking of the four historic events that Tuchman discusses, asks: "What common thread links these events? I can't tell, and I read the book." Christopher Lehmann-Haupt of the *New York Times* believes that much of what Tuchman discusses in the book has been better handled by other writers: "Any way one approaches 'The March

of Folly,' it is unsatisfying. . . . Better books have been written about Vietnam, the American Revolution, the Renaissance Popes and the Trojan Horse. Better things have been said about human folly."

In her collection, *Practicing History: Selected Essays,* Tuchman presented her own ideas on how history should best be written. Divided into three parts—"The Craft," "The Practice," and "Learning from History"—the book reveals many of the assumptions and concerns which have made Tuchman one of the most popular historians in the country. She particularly emphasized the importance of narrative writing. "The historian's basic mode," Marcus Cunliffe explains in his review of the book for the *Washington Post Book World,* "is that of narration: movement through time, so as to disclose to the reader in a clear, compelling sequence a set of significant events."

Despite some criticism of her work by the academic world—Walter Kendrick of the *Village Voice* reports that "academic historians disdain her work now and always will"—few observers doubt the sheer power of Tuchman's writing. "Tuchman may not be a historian's historian," Laurence Freedman admits in the *Times Literary Supplement,* "but she is a pleasure for the layman to read." "Whatever her subject," Smith writes, "Tuchman brings to it a flair for the dramatic, a striking ability to combine narrative sweep with individual character analysis, and a vividly entertaining prose style." Because of her ability to turn "complex historical muddles into narrative that preserves an air of complexity but can be simply read . . . ," Kendrick argues, Tuchman will be remembered "as an entertainer, one who made the past palatable to millions of readers."

BIOGRAPHICAL/CRITICAL SOURCES:

BOOKS

Bowman, Kathleen, *New Women in Social Sciences,* Creative Education Press, 1976.
Contemporary Issues Criticism, Volume 1, Gale (Detroit), 1982.

PERIODICALS

Atlantic Monthly, February, 1966; October, 1978; April, 1984; December, 1988.
Books and Bookmen, May, 1979.
Book World, February 28, 1971.
Boston Globe, March 4, 1984.
Chicago Tribune Book World, March 4, 1984.
Christian Century, May 14, 1975.
Christian Science Monitor, October 2, 1958; February 1, 1962; March 24, 1971; September 18, 1978.
Chronicle Review, October 2, 1978.
Commentary, December, 1978.
Contemporary Review, April, 1982.
Cosmopolitan, January, 1967.
Detroit News, March 25, 1984.
Economist, February 26, 1966.
Esquire, June, 1971.
Globe and Mail (Toronto), April 21, 1984.
Harper's, February, 1966.
History Today, April, 1989; October, 1989.
Journal of American History, September, 1966; December, 1971.
Life, February 19, 1971.
Listener, January 6, 1972; March 29, 1979.
Los Angeles Times Book Review, March 18, 1984.
Ms., July, 1979.
Nation, February 14, 1966; April 26, 1971.
National Review, February 8, 1966; December 8, 1978.

New Leader, October 9, 1978; November 14, 1988.
New Republic, March 27, 1971; October 28, 1978; October 21, 1981; March 26, 1984; November 28, 1988.
New Statesman, June 22, 1962.
Newsweek, February 15, 1971; September 25, 1978; March 12, 1984; October 10, 1988.
New Yorker, April 14, 1962; February 5, 1966; November 13, 1978.
New York Review of Books, February 3, 1966; July 22, 1971; August 9, 1973; September 28, 1978; March 29, 1984; December 22, 1988.
New York Times, February 15, 1971; February 27, 1979; September 29, 1981; September 7, 1982; March 7, 1984.
New York Times Book Review, January 28, 1962; January 9, 1966; February 7, 1971; April 22, 1973; November 12, 1978; September 27, 1981; March 11, 1984; March 24, 1985; October 16, 1988.
Publishers Weekly, March 2, 1984.
Saturday Review, October 18, 1958; January 27, 1962; January 15, 1966; February 20, 1971; October 28, 1978.
Spectator, March 31, 1979; July 21, 1984.
Time, February 9, 1962; January 14, 1966; February 15, 1971; March 26, 1984; October 3, 1988.
Times (London), May 17, 1984.
Times Literary Supplement, March 20, 1959; June 8, 1962; December 10, 1971; June 22, 1984.
Village Voice, June 19, 1978; September 30, 1981.
Virginia Quarterly Review, summer, 1966.
Wall Street Journal, January 14, 1966.
Washington Post, October 5, 1978.
Washington Post Book World, February 13, 1972; October 8, 1978; September 27, 1981; February 2, 1984.

*		*		*

TUROW, Scott 1949-

PERSONAL: Born April 12, 1949, in Chicago, IL; son of David D. (a physician) and Rita (a writer; maiden name, Pastron) Turow; married Annette Weisberg (an artist), April 4, 1971; children: Rachel, Gabriel, Eve. *Education:* Amherst College, B.A., 1970; Stanford University, M.A., 1974; Harvard University, J.D., 1978. *Religion:* Jewish.

ADDRESSES: Office—Sonnenschein, Carlin, Nath and Rosenthal, Sears Tower, Suite 8000, Chicago, IL 60606.

CAREER: Stanford University, Stanford, CA, E. H. Jones Lecturer in Creative Writing, 1972-75; Suffolk County District Attorney's Office, Boston, MA, clerk; United States Court of Appeals (7th District), Chicago, IL, assistant United States attorney, 1978-86; Sonnenschein, Carlin, Nath, & Rosenthal (law firm), Chicago, IL, partner, 1986–. Writer, 1972–.

AWARDS, HONORS: Writing award, College English Association and Book-of-the-Month Club, 1970; Edith Mirrielees fellow, 1972; Silver Dagger Award, Crime Writers Association, 1988, for *Presumed Innocent.*

WRITINGS:

One L: An Inside Account of Life in the First Year at Harvard Law School (nonfiction), Putnam, 1977.
Presumed Innocent (novel), Farrar, Straus, 1987.
The Burden of Proof (novel), Farrar, Straus, 1990.
Pleading Guilty (novel), Farrar, Straus, 1993.

The Laws of Our Fathers (novel), Farrar, Straus, 1996.

Also author of *The Way Things Are,* unpublished novel. Work anthologized in *Best American Short Stories,* 1971, 1972. Contributor of stories, articles, and reviews to literary journals, including *Transatlantic Review, Ploughshares, Harvard, New England,* and *Place,* and to newspapers.

MEDIA ADAPTATIONS: Presumed Innocent, a film based on Turow's novel of the same name, was released by Warner Brothers in 1990 and starred Harrison Ford.

SIDELIGHTS: Scott Turow uses his insider's knowledge of the American legal system to form the basis for bestselling suspense novels. A practicing attorney who has also studied creative writing, Turow is the author of *Presumed Innocent* and *The Burden of Proof,* both of which explore the murky terrain of urban justice through highly plotted fiction. "No one on the contemporary scene writes better mystery-suspense novels than Chicago attorney Scott Turow," notes Bill Blum in the *Los Angeles Times Book Review.* "In a genre overcrowded with transparent plots and one-dimensional super-sleuths, Turow's first novel, *Presumed Innocent,* was a work of serious fiction as well as a gripping tale of murder and courtroom drama." *New York Times Magazine* correspondent Jeff Shear praises Turow for the "brash, backroom sensibility that informs his work as a novelist."

It is a rare writer indeed who collects millions of dollars from a first novel. Even more rare is the author who crafts a novel while holding a full-time, high-profile job. Turow did both, writing drafts of *Presumed Innocent* in his spare moments on the commuter train while working as an assistant United States attorney in Chicago. *Washington Post* contributor Steve Coll claims that through his determination to write fiction without sacrificing his profession, Turow "has fulfilled every literate working stiff's fantasy."

At Amherst College in Massachusetts, Turow began to write short stories and novels. A few of his short pieces were printed in literary magazines such as the *Transatlantic Review,* a rare feat for an undergraduate. After earning his bachelor's degree in 1970, Turow won a fellowship to the Stanford University creative writing program. There he taught while working on a novel about Chicago called *The Way Things Are.* He began to question the direction of his career when he received twenty-five rejections for *The Way Things Are.* Only one publisher, Farrar, Straus & Giroux, offered even the slightest encouragement. Turow told the *New York Times Magazine* that the cool reception his novel earned "made me realize that I wasn't one-tenth the writer I hoped to be. . . . I could not sustain the vision of myself as a writer only." In a *Los Angeles Times* interview he said: "I became convinced that one could not make a living in the U.S. writing serious fiction. I was never terribly bitter about that. I didn't see why the world had an obligation to support novelists."

Even while writing *The Way Things Are* Turow realized that he was becoming very interested in the law. In 1975, he entered Harvard Law School. Even then he put his writing talents to work. His literary agent was able to secure him a contract for a personal, nonfiction account of the first year in the fabled law school. He took notes during his hectic class schedule and finished the book during the summer recess. In 1977, Putnam published Turow's *One L: An Inside Account of Life in the First Year at Harvard Law School.* The work sold modestly at first, but it has since become "required reading for anyone contemplating a career in law," to quote Justin Blewitt in *Best Sellers. New York Times* correspondent P. M. Stern calls *One L* "a compelling and important book. It is compelling in its vivid portrayal of the high-tension competitiveness of Harvard Law School and of the group madness it seems to induce in the student body. It is important because it offers an inside look at what law students do and don't learn and who they are and are not equipped to represent when they graduate."

After receiving his law degree in 1978, Turow returned to Chicago to work with the United States Attorney's office. As a prosecutor, he was assigned to the infamous "Operation Greylord," a series of trials that exposed judicial corruption in the city's courts. Turow was a member of the team that prosecuted Circuit Court Judge Reginald Holzer and former Illinois Attorney General William J. Scott. Little by little, the intrigues of corruption and legal wrangling began to work their way into the notebooks Turow kept for his fiction. He set aside a novel he was drafting and began to tinker with a story about an attorney. "I was learning a lot about bribery and I wanted to write about that," he told the *Washington Post.*

For several years Turow did his writing in the little spare time left him after meeting the demands of Operation Greylord and his growing family in the suburbs. He edited chapters of his new novel during his commute to and from work on the train, and he rose early in the morning to work on his fiction before he left for the office. Finally his wife convinced him to quit his job and finish the novel. He accepted a partnership at the downtown Chicago firm of Sonnenschein, Carlin, Nath and Rosenthal and then took a three-month hiatus from the law in order to write. His finished manuscript was mailed to a New York agent just two weeks before he was due to start his new job.

Turow was confident that his novel would be published, but he was astonished by the level of interest shown by New York's biggest publishing houses. A bidding war ensued over the rights to publish the work, and the sums soon exceeded $200,000. Ultimately Turow did not choose the high bidder but instead took an offer from Farrar, Straus because of its literary reputation—and because of the encouragement he had received from its editors during his student days. The $200,000 payment Farrar, Straus offered Turow was the largest sum that company had ever paid for a first novel.

Presumed Innocent tells the story of a troubled deputy prosecutor in a big city who is assigned to investigate the murder of a female colleague. As the nightmare case unfolds, the prosecutor—Rusty Sabich—finds himself on trial for murdering the woman, with whom he once had an adulterous affair. *Time* magazine reviewer Paul Gray writes that in *Presumed Innocent* Turow "uses [a] grotesque death as a means of exposing the trail of municipal corruption that has spread through [fictitious] Kindle County. The issue is not merely whether a murderer will be brought to justice but whether public institutions and their guardians are any longer capable of finding the truth." Turow told *Publishers Weekly* that his book is "a comment on the different kinds of truth we recognize. If the criminal-justice system is supposed to be a truth-finding device, it's an awkward one at best. There are all kinds of playing around in the book that illuminate that, and yet by the same token, the results in the end are just. And that's not accidental. . . . Absolutely everybody in the novel is guilty of something. That's a truth of life that I learned as a prosecutor. We all do things we wish we hadn't done and that we're not necessarily proud of."

Fellow attorney-turned-author George V. Higgins notes in the *Chicago Tribune* that *Presumed Innocent* is a "beautifully crafted tale. . . . Packed with data, rich in incident, painstakingly imagined, it snags both of your lapels and presses you down in your chair until you've finished it." Likewise, Toronto *Globe & Mail* correspondent H. J. Kirchhoff contends that the novel is "surprisingly assured," adding: "The prose is crisp and polished, every character is distinct and fully realized, and the dialogue is authentic. Turow has blended his experience in the rough-and-tumble of the criminal courts with a sympathetic eye for the vagaries of the human condition and an intimate understanding of the dark side of the human soul." Shear concludes that the criminal-justice system *Presumed Innocent* portrays, "without tears or pretense, has seldom appeared in literature quite like this."

"*Presumed Innocent* won the literary lottery," observes Mei-Mei Chan in *USA Weekend.* The novel spent more than forty-three weeks on the bestseller lists, went through sixteen hard cover printings, and sold 4 million paperback copies. Turow reaped 3 million dollars for the paperback rights and another 1 million for the movie rights. A film adaptation of the work, released in 1990, was one of the ten top-grossing movies of that year. When Turow published his second novel—almost simultaneously with the debut of the movie version of *Presumed Innocent*—he joined the ranks of Ernest Hemingway, J. D. Salinger, and Alex Haley by becoming the 92nd writer to appear on the cover of *Time* magazine.

By the time *The Burden of Proof* appeared in the summer of 1990, Turow had established a routine that included several hours a day for his writing. He still practices law, but he spends his mornings at home, in contact with the downtown firm by telephone and fax machine. His schedule is still daunting, however, as his celebrity status has made him a sought-after interview subject in the various media. Turow told *New York Times Magazine* that he does his best work under such pressure. "I run on a combination of fear, anxiety, and compulsion," he said. "I have to control my habit to work all the time."

The Burden of Proof takes its hero from among the characters in *Presumed Innocent.* Sandy Stern is a middle-aged defense attorney who returns home from a business trip to find his wife dead, a suicide. As he confronts the loss—and the circumstances behind it—he becomes enmeshed in a web of family intrigues, insider stock trading schemes, and unanswered questions about his wife's private life. Toronto *Globe & Mail* reviewer Margaret Cannon maintains that in *The Burden of Proof* Turow "has let his imagination loose and, while courtroom derring-do is still a hefty part of the plot, it doesn't subsume the tragic story about some very damaged people." In the *Washington Post Book World,* Jonathan Yardley writes: "Scott Turow's second novel proves beyond any reasonable doubt that his hugely successful first was no fluke. . . . It's that rare book, a popular novel that is also serious, if not 'literary' fiction. *The Burden of Proof* means to entertain, and does so with immense skill, so if all you want is intelligent amusement it will serve you handily: but it is also a complex, multi-layered meditation on 'the heartsore arithmetic of human events,' and as such rises far above the norm of what is generally categorized as 'commercial' fiction."

Turow's third novel, *Pleading Guilty,* broke new ground for the author. "Although fully peopled with lawyers," explains Charles Champlin in the *Los Angeles Times Book Review,* "the story hardly peeps into a courtroom." A high-placed partner in a prestigious midwestern law firm has suddenly gone missing, along with about five and a half million dollars of the firm's funds. Instead of calling in the police (which would raise a scandal and cost the firm business), the partners turn to one of their employees, Mack Malloy, a former policeman, to find the missing partner and the missing money. In the process, Malloy encounters a body in a refrigerator, an old nemesis, and, eventually, the missing man and money. "*Pleading Guilty,* written as Mack's diary of the . . . events, demonstrates that Mr. Turow, at his best descriptive form, is worthy to be ranked with Dashiell Hammett or Raymond Chandler." "Scott Turow writes as well as ever," declares *Washington Post Book World* contributor Ross Thomas, "and is skilled enough not only to entertain his readers but also convince them they are acquiring vital inside stuff about the legal profession."

Although *The Laws of Our Fathers* reintroduces Turow's famous court scenes, it also moves in different directions compared to the author's previous work. The shooting death of the wife of a state senator reunites a group of 1960s radicals who had been friends but had gone their own ways at the end of the decade. "The novel is less a legal thriller than a meditative examination of the hold that time past exerts over time present," says Michiko Kakutani in the *New York Times.* "Beneath the layers of deep legal deviousness," states a *Kirkus Reviews* contributor, "Turow never lets you forget that his characters lived and loved before they ever got dragged into court." "The resulting story is by turns moving and manipulative, compelling and contrived," Kakutani concludes. "Though deeply flawed, it stands as Mr. Turow's most ambitious novel yet."

BIOGRAPHICAL/CRITICAL SOURCES:

BOOKS

Lundy, Derek, *Scott Turow: Meeting the Enemy,* ECW Press, 1995.

PERIODICALS

Best Sellers, November, 1977.
Chicago Tribune, June 7, 1987; June 10, 1987; February 16, 1990; August 17, 1997.
Detroit News, May 1, 1988; June 1, 1990.
Globe & Mail (Toronto), July 11, 1987; August 8, 1987; June 16, 1990.
Harper's Bazaar, June, 1990.
Interview, June, 1990, p. 170.
Kirkus Reviews, August 1, 1996, p. 1090.
Ladies Home Journal, July, 1996, p. 124.
Library Journal, August, 1996, p. 115.
Los Angeles Times, July 24, 1987; October 12, 1989; June 3, 1990; June 11, 1990; July 27, 1990; September 9, 1990.
Los Angeles Times Book Review, June 3, 1990; June 13, 1993, p. 11.
Maclean's, July 9, 1990, p. 43.
New Republic, March 14, 1994, pp. 32-38.
New Statesman, January 22, 1988, p. 33.
Newsweek, October 17, 1977; June 29, 1987; June 4, 1990; July 5, 1993; July 26, 1993.
New York, June 27, 1988, p. 94
New York Review of Books, November 19, 1987, p. 21.
New York Times, September 15, 1977; February 8, 1987; June 15, 1987; August 6, 1987; December 1, 1987; April 19, 1988; May 31, 1990; October 8, 1996, p. B4; January 28, 1998.
New York Times Book Review, September 25, 1977; June 28, 1987, pp. 1, 29; June 3, 1990; June 6, 1993, p. 7.
New York Times Magazine, June 7, 1987.

Publishers Weekly, July 10, 1987; September 15, 1989; April 1, 1996, p. 22.
Time, July 20, 1987; June 11, 1990.
Times (London), October 8, 1987; October 22, 1987.
USA Weekend, June 1-3, 1990.
Washington Post, October 2, 1977; August 30, 1987; June 9, 1990; June 12, 1990; July 27, 1990.
Washington Post Book World, June 3, 1990; December 2, 1990; June 27, 1993, pp. 1, 8.

*   *   *

TUTUOLA, Amos 1920-1997

PERSONAL: Born 1920, in Abeokuta, Nigeria; died June 8, 1997; son of Charles (a cocoa farmer) and Esther (Aina) Tutuola; married Alake Victoria, 1947; children: Olubunmi, Oluyinka, Erinola, five others. *Education:* Attended schools in Nigeria. *Religion:* Christian.

ADDRESSES: Home—P.O. Box 2251, Ibadan, Nigeria. *Office*—c/o Federal Radio Corp., Broadcasting House, New Court Rd., Ibadan, Nigeria, West Africa.

CAREER: Worked on father's farm; trained as a coppersmith; employed by Nigerian Government Labor Department, Lagos, and by Nigerian Broadcasting Corp., Ibadan, Nigeria. Freelance writer. Visiting research fellow, University of Ife, 1979; associate, international writing program at University of Iowa, 1983. *Military service:* Royal Air Force, 1943-45; served as metal worker in Nigeria.

MEMBER: Modern Language Association of America, Mbari Club (Nigerian authors; founder).

AWARDS, HONORS: Named honorary citizen of New Orleans, 1983; *The Palm-Wine Drinkard and His Dead Palm-Wine Tapster in the Dead's Town* and *My Life in the Bush of Ghosts* received second place awards in a contest held in Turin, Italy, 1985; Noble Patron of Arts, Pan African Writers Association, 1992.

WRITINGS:

The Palm-Wine Drinkard and His Dead Palm-Wine Tapster in the Dead's Town, Faber, 1952, Grove, 1953.
My Life in the Bush of Ghosts, Grove, 1954.
Simbi and the Satyr of the Dark Jungle, Faber, 1955.
The Brave African Huntress, illustrated by Ben Enwonwu, Grove, 1958.
The Feather Woman of the Jungle, Faber, 1962.
Ajaiyi and His Inherited Poverty, Faber, 1967.
(Contributor) *Winds of Change: Modern Short Stories from Black Africa,* Longman, 1977.
The Witch-Herbalist of the Remote Town, Faber, 1981.
The Wild Hunter in the Bush of the Ghosts (facsimile of manuscript), edited with an introduction and a postscript by Bernth Lindfors, Three Continents Press, 1982, 2nd edition, 1989.
Pauper, Brawler, and Slanderer, Faber, 1987.
Yoruba Folktales, Ibadan University Press (Nigeria), 1986.
The Village Witch Doctor and Other Stories, Faber, 1990.
The Palm-Wine Drinkard [and] *My Life in the Bush of Ghosts,* Grove Press, 1994.

WORK REPRESENTED IN ANTHOLOGIES

Rutherford, Peggy, editor, *Darkness and Light: An Anthology of African Writing,* Drum Publications, 1958.

Hughes, Langston, editor, *An African Treasury: Articles, Essays, Stories, Poems by Black Africans,* Crown, 1960.

Hughes, Langston, and Christiane Reynault, editors, *Anthologie africaine et malgache,* Seghers, 1962.

Ademola, Frances, editor, *Reflections,* African Universities Press, 1962, new edition, 1965.

Sainville, Leonard, editor, *Anthologie de la litterature negroafricaine: Romanciers et conteurs negro africains,* two volumes, Presence Africaine, 1963.

Whiteley, W. H., compiler, *A Selection of African Prose,* two volumes, Oxford University Press, 1964.

Rive, Richard, editor, *Modern African Prose,* Heinemann Educational, 1964.

Komey, Ellis Ayitey and Ezekiel Mphahlele, editors, *Modern African Stories,* Faber, 1964.

Tibble, Anne, editor, *African-English Literature: A Survey and Anthology,* Peter Owen, 1965.

Edwards, Paul, compiler, *Through African Eyes,* two volumes, Cambridge University Press, 1966.

Mphahlele, Ezekiel, editor, *African Writing Today,* Penguin, 1967.

Beier, Ulli, editor, *Political Spider: An Anthology of Stories from "Black Orpheus,"* Heinemann Educational, 1969.

Larson, Charles, editor, *African Short Stories: A Collection of Contemporary African Writing,* Macmillan, 1970.

MEDIA ADAPTATIONS: Kola Ogunmola has written a play in Yoruba entitled *Omuti,* based on *The Palm-Wine Drinkard,* published by West African Book Publishers.

SIDELIGHTS: With the publication of his novel *The Palm-Wine Drinkard and His Dead Palm-Wine Tapster in the Dead's Town* in 1952, Amos Tutuola became the first internationally recognized Nigerian writer. Since that time, Tutuola's works, in particular *The Palm-Wine Drinkard,* have been the subject of much critical debate. *The Palm-Wine Drinkard* was praised by critics outside of Nigeria for its unconventional use of the English language, its adherence to the oral tradition, and its unique, fantastical characters and plot. Nigerian critics, on the other hand, described the work as ungrammatical and unoriginal. Discussing the first criticism in the book *The Growth of the African Novel,* Eustace Palmer writes: "Tutuola's English is demonstrably poor; this is due partly to his ignorance of the more complicated rules of English syntax and partly to interference from Yoruba." The second criticism, concerning Tutuola's lack of originality, is based on similarities between Tutuola's works and those of his predecessor, O. B. Fagunwa, who writes in the Yoruba language.

The influence of Fagunwa's writings on Tutuola's work has been noted by several critics, including Abiola Irele, who writes in *The African Experience in Literature and Ideology:* "It is clear that much of the praise and acclaim that have been lavished upon Tutuola belong more properly to Fagunwa who provided not only the original inspiration but indeed a good measure of material for Tutuola's novels. The echoes of Fagunwa in Tutuola's works are numerous enough to indicate that the latter was consciously creating from a model provided by the former." Irele adds, however, "that despite its derivation from the work of Fagunwa, Tutuola's work achieves an independent status that it owes essentially to the force of his individual genius."

Tutuola's genius is described by reviewers as an ability to refashion the traditional Yoruba myths and folktales that are the foundation of his work. Palmer notes, for instance, in *The Growth of the African Novel:* "Taking his stories direct from his people's traditional lore, he uses his inexhaustible imagination and inventive power to embellish them, to add to them or alter them, and generally transform them into his own stories conveying his own message." O. R. Dathorne comments in an essay published in *Introduction to Nigerian Literature:* "Tutuola is a literary paradox; he is completely part of the folklore traditions of the Yorubas and yet he is able to modernize these traditions in an imaginative way. It is on this level that his books can best be approached. . . . Tutuola deserves to be considered seriously because his work represents an intentional attempt to fuse folklore with modern life."

In *The Palm-Wine Drinkard,* for example, the Drinkard's quest for his tapster leads him into many perilous situations, including an encounter with the Red Fish, a monster Tutuola describes as having thirty horns "spread out as an umbrella," and numerous eyes that "were closing and opening at the same time as if a man was pressing a switch on and off." Tutuola also amends a traditional tale concerning a Skull who borrows appendages belonging to other persons in order to look like a "complete gentleman" to include references to modern warfare. Tutuola writes: "If this gentleman went to the battlefield, surely, enemy would not kill him or capture him and if bombers saw him in a town which was to be bombed, they would not throw bombs on his presence, and if they did throw it, the bomb itself would not explode until this gentleman would leave that town, because of his beauty." Gerald Moore observes in *Seven African Writers* that these descriptions are evidence "of Tutuola's easy use of the paraphernalia of modern life to give sharpness and immediacy to his imagery."

Despite the reservations of critics like West, Tutuola went on to publish several additional works, and while critics are, as Charles R. Larson observes in *The Emergence of African Fiction,* "a little less awed now than they were in the early 1950's," Tutuola's works continue to merit critical attention. Among the more widely reviewed of these books is *The Witch-Herbalist of the Remote Town.* Published thirty years after *The Palm-Wine Drinkard,* this book involves a quest initiated by the protagonist, a hunter, to find a cure for his wife's barrenness. The journey to the Remote Town takes six years; along the way the hunter encounters bizarre and sometimes frightening places and people, including the Town of the Born-and-Die Baby and the Abnormal Squatting Man of the Jungle, who can paralyze opponents with a gust of frigid air by piercing his abdomen. The hunter eventually reaches the Remote Town, and the witch-herbalist gives him a broth guaranteed to make his wife fertile. The plot is complicated though, when the hunter, weak from hunger, sips some of the broth.

As with *The Palm-Wine Drinkard,* critical commentary of *The Witch-Herbalist of the Remote Town* focuses in particular on Tutuola's use of the English language. Edward Blishen, for instance, comments in the *Times Educational Supplement:* "The language is wonderfully stirring and odd: a mixture of straight translation from Yoruba, and everyday modern Nigerian idiom, and grand epical English. The imagination at work is always astonishing. . . . And this, not the bargain, is folklore not resurrected, but being created fresh and true in the white heat of a tradition still undestroyed." *Voice Literary Supplement* critic Jon Parales writes: "His direct, apparently simple language creates an anything-can-happen universe, more whacky and amoral than the most determinedly modern lit." *Washington Post Book World* contributor Judith Chettle offers this view: "Tutuola writes with an appealing vigor and his idiosyncratic use of the English idiom gives the story a fresh and African perspective, though at times the clumsiness of some phrasing does detract from the thrust of the narrative. No eye-dabbing sentimentalist, Tutuola's commentary is clear-eyed if not acerbic, but underlying the tale is a quiet and persistent lament for the simpler, unsophisticated and happier past of his people."

An *Africa Today* contributor, Nancy J. Schmidt, observes that Tutuola's language has become increasingly more like that of standard English over the years. She cites other differences between this work and earlier ones as well. "Tutuola's presence is very evident in *Witch-Herbalist,* but the strength of his presence and his imagination are not as strong as they once were," writes Schmidt, who adds that "neither Tutuola nor his hero seem to be able to take a consistent moral stand, a characteristic that is distinctly different from Tutuola's other narratives." Commenting on the reasons for these differences, Schmidt writes: "They may reflect contemporary Yoruba culture, Tutuola's changing attitude toward Yoruba and Nigerian cultures as well as his changing position in Yoruba and Nigerian cultures, the difficulties of writing an oral narrative for an audience to whom oral narratives are becoming less familiar and less related to daily behavior, and the editorial policies for publishing African fictional narratives in the 1980s."

Tutuola's 1990 story collection, *The Village Witch Doctor and Other Stories,* contains eighteen stories based on traditional Yoruba fables. Like most of his previous work, the stories in this collection deal with greed, betrayal, and tricksterism. In the title story, for instance, a village witch doctor tricks others again and again before getting a dose of his own medicine. *Dictionary of Literary Biography* reviewer Bernth Lindfors remarks that "the same buoyant imagination [found in his earlier work] is in evidence, the same fascination with comically grotesque fantasy worlds. Tutuola, after more than forty years of writing, remains a very resourceful raconteur."

BIOGRAPHICAL/CRITICAL SOURCES:

BOOKS

Black Literature Criticism, Gale (Detroit), 1992.
Collins, Harold R., *Amos Tutuola,* Twayne, 1969.
Contemporary Literary Criticism, Gale, Volume 5, 1976; Volume 14, 1980; Volume 29, 1984.
Dictionary of Literary Biography, Volume 125: *Twentieth-Century Caribbean and Black African Writers, Second Series,* Gale, 1993.
Herskovits, Melville J., and Francis S. Herskovits, *Dahomean Narrative: A Cross-Cultural Analysis,* Northwestern University Press, 1958.
Irele, Abiola, *The African Experience in Literature and Ideology,* Heinemann, 1981.
King, Bruce, editor, *Introduction to Nigerian Literature,* Evans Brothers, 1971.
Larson, Charles R., *The Emergence of African Fiction,* revised edition, Indiana University Press, 1972.
Laurence, Margaret, *Long Drums and Cannons: Nigerian Dramatists,* Praeger, 1969.
Lindfors, Bernth, editor, *Critical Perspectives on Amos Tutuola,* Three Continents Press, 1975.
Lindfors, Bernth, *Early Nigerian Literature,* Africana Publishing, 1982.
Moore, Gerald, *Seven African Writers,* Oxford University Press, 1962.

O'Mos, Ikushasa, *Aspects of Yoruba Cosmology in Tutuola's Novels,* Centre de Recherches Pedagogiques (Kinshasa, Nigeria), 1990.
Palmer, Eustace, *The Growth of the African Novel,* Heinemann, 1979.
Quayson, J. Currey, *Strategic Transformations in Nigerian Writing,* Indiana Universtiy Press (Bloomington), 1997.
Tucker, Martin, *Africa in Modern Literature: A Survey of Contemporary Writing in English,* Ungar, 1967.

PERIODICALS

Africa Today, Volume 29, number 3, 1982.
Ariel, April, 1977.
Books Abroad, summer, 1968.
Critique, fall/winter, 1960-61; fall/winter, 1967-68.
Journal of Canadian Fiction, Volume 3, number 4, 1975.
Journal of Commonwealth Literature, August, 1974; August, 1981; Volume 17, number 1, 1982.
Listener, December 14, 1967.
London Review of Books, April 2, 1987.
Los Angeles Times Book Review, August 15, 1982.
Nation, September 25, 1954.
New Statesman, December 8, 1967.
New Yorker, April 23, 1984.
New York Times Book Review, July 4, 1982.
Observer, July 6, 1952; November 22, 1981.
Spectator, October 24, 1981.
Times Educational Supplement, February 26, 1982.
Times Literary Supplement, January 18, 1968; February 26, 1982; August 28, 1987; May 18, 1990, p. 534.
Voice Literary Supplement, June, 1982.
Washington Post, July 13, 1987.
Washington Post Book World, August 15, 1982.
World Literature Today, summer, 1991, p. 539.

*   *   *

TYLER, Anne 1941-

PERSONAL: Born October 25, 1941, in Minneapolis, MN; daughter of Lloyd Parry (a chemist) and Phyllis (Mahon) Tyler; married Taghi Modarressi (a psychiatrist and writer), May 3, 1963 (died, 1997); children: Tezh, Mitra. *Education:* Duke University, B.A., 1961; graduate study at Columbia University, 1961-62. *Religion:* Quaker.

ADDRESSES: Home—222 Tunbridge Rd., Baltimore, MD, 21212-3422. *Agent*—Russell & Volkening, 50 West 29th St., New York, NY 10001.

CAREER: Writer. Duke University Library, Durham, NC, Russian bibliographer, 1962-63; McGill University Law Library, Montreal, Quebec, Canada, assistant to the librarian, 1964-65.

MEMBER: PEN, American Academy and Institute of Arts and Letters, Authors Guild, Phi Beta Kappa.

AWARDS, HONORS: Mademoiselle award for writing, 1966; Award for Literature, American Academy and Institute of Arts and Letters, 1977; National Book Critics Circle fiction award nomination, 1980, Janet Heidinger Kafka prize, 1981, and American Book Award nomination in paperback fiction, 1982, all for *Morgan's Passing;* National Book Critics Circle fiction award nomination, 1982, and American Book Award nomination in fiction, PEN/Faulkner Award for fiction, and Pulitzer Prize nomination for fiction, all 1983, all for *Dinner at the Homesick Restaurant;* National Book Critics Circle fiction award and Pulitzer Prize nomination for fiction, both 1985, both for *The Accidental Tourist;* Pulitzer Prize, 1988, for *Breathing Lessons.*

WRITINGS:

NOVELS

If Morning Ever Comes, Knopf (New York City), 1964.
The Tin Can Tree, Knopf, 1965.
A Slipping-Down Life, Knopf, 1970.
The Clock Winder, Knopf, 1972.
Celestial Navigation, Knopf, 1974.
Searching for Caleb, Knopf, 1976.
Earthly Possessions, Knopf, 1977.
Morgan's Passing, Knopf, 1980.
Dinner at the Homesick Restaurant, Knopf, 1982.
The Accidental Tourist, Knopf, 1985.
Breathing Lessons (also see below), Knopf, 1988.
Saint Maybe, Knopf, 1991.
Ladder of Years, Knopf, 1995.
A Patchwork Planet, Random House, 1998.

OTHER

(Editor with Shannon Ravenel, and author of introduction) *Best American Short Stories 1983,* Houghton (Boston, MA), 1983.
Anne Tyler: Four Complete Novels (omnibus volume; contains *Dinner at the Homesick Restaurant, Morgan's Passing, The Tin Can Tree,* and *If Morning Ever Comes*), Avenel Books (New York City), 1990.
Anne Tyler: A New Collection (omnibus volume; contains *The Accidental Tourist, Breathing Lessons,* and *Searching for Caleb*), Wings Books (New York City), 1991.
Tumble Tower, illustrated by daughter Mitra Modarressi, Orchard Books (New York City), 1993.
(With Robert W. Lenski) *Breathing Lessons* (screenplay based on her novel), Republic Pictures, 1994.
(Editor with Shannon Ravenel) *Best of the South: From Ten Years of New Stories from the South,* Algonquin Books (Chapel Hill, NC), 1996.

Contributor of short stories to *Saturday Evening Post, New Yorker, Seventeen, Critic, Antioch Review,* and *Southern Review.*

MEDIA ADAPTATIONS: The Accidental Tourist, starring Kathleen Turner and William Hurt, was released by Warner Brothers in 1988.

SIDELIGHTS: Anne Tyler's work has always been critically well received, but reviews of her early novels were generally relegated to the back pages of the book sections. Not until the publication of *Celestial Navigation* (1974), when she captured the attention of novelist Gail Godwin, and *Searching for Caleb* (1976), when John Updike recommended her to readers, did she gain widespread acclaim. "Now," says *Detroit News* reporter Bruce Cook, "her books are reviewed in the front of the literary journals and that means she is somebody to reckon with. No longer one of America's best unknown writers, she is now recognized as one of America's best writers. Period."

Writing in the *New Yorker,* John Updike compares her to Flannery O'Connor, Carson McCullers, and Eudora Welty, noting: "Anne Tyler, in her gifts both of dreaming and of realizing, evokes comparison with these writers, and in her tone and subject matter seems deliberately to seek association with the Southern ambience that, in less cosmopolitan times, they naturally and inevitably breathed. Even their aura of regional isolation is imitated by Miss

Tyler as she holds fast, in her imagination and in her person, to a Baltimore with only Southern exits; her characters when they flee, never flee north. Yet she is a citizen of the world, born in Minneapolis, a graduate student of Russian at Columbia, and now married to a psychiatrist from Iran. The brand names, the fads, the bastardized vistas of our great homogenized nation glint out at us from her fiction with a cheerful authority."

Other reviewers, such as Katha Pollitt, find Tyler's novels more difficult to classify. "They are Southern in their sure sense of family and place," she writes in the *New York Times Book Review,* "but [they] lack the taste for violence and the Gothic that often characterizes self-consciously Southern literature. They are modern in their fictional techniques, yet utterly unconcerned with the contemporary moment as a subject, so that, with only minor dislocations, her stories could just as well have taken place in the twenties or thirties. The current school of feminist-influenced novels seems to have passed her by completely: her women are strong, often stronger than the men in their lives, but solidly grounded in traditional roles."

The key to Tyler's writing may well lie in the homage she pays to Eudora Welty, her favorite writer and one to whom she is repeatedly compared. "Reading her taught me there were stories to be written about the mundane life around me," she told Cook. Or as Tyler phrased it to Marguerite Michaels in the *New York Times Book Review,* "Reading Eudora Welty when I was growing up showed me that very small things are often really larger than the large things." Thomas M. Disch is one of several critics who believes that Tyler's insight into the lives of ordinary people is her special gift. Writing in the *Washington Post Book World,* he calls it an "uncommon accomplishment that she can make such characters interesting and amusing without violating their limitations."

Because the action of her novels is so often circular—ending exactly where it begins—Tyler's fiction has been criticized for lack of development. This is especially true of her early novels where the narratives are straightforward and the pacing slow. In fact, what impressed reviewers most about Tyler's first book, *If Morning Ever Comes,* was not the story itself but the promise it seemed to hold for future works of fiction. "The trouble with this competently put-together book is that the hero is hardly better defined at the end than he is at the beginning," observes Julian Gloag in the *Saturday Review.* "Writing about a dull and totally humorless character, Miss Tyler has inevitably produced a totally humorless and mainly dull novel. Anne Tyler is only twenty-two, and in the light of this her refusal to take risks is a bit puzzling. I'd like to see what she could do if she stopped narrowing her own eyes and let herself go. It might be very good." The *Times Literary Supplement* reviewer echoes these sentiments: "It will be surprising if a writer so young does not outgrow her hesitant efforts to produce big answers to emotional muddles and her sometimes over-literary sentences, and let her considerable gift for dialogue and comedy produce a very good novel indeed."

For her part, Tyler reportedly now dislikes her first book as well as her second, which received similar criticism. Written largely to pass the time while she was looking for a job, *The Tin Can Tree* concerns the inhabitants of a three-family house on the edge of a North Carolina tobacco field and their reactions to the accidental death of the six-year-old girl who lives there. Though the family is initially devastated by the tragedy, their emotional balance is restored in the end, and, for this reason, some critics find the novel static. Millicent Bell, for example, writes in the *New York Times*

Book Review: "Life, this young writer seems to be saying, achieves its once-and-for-all shape and then the camera clicks. This view, which brings her characters back on the last page to where they started, does not make for that sense of development which is the true novel's motive force. Because of it, I think, her book remains a sketch, a description, a snapshot. But as such, it still has a certain dry clarity. And the hand that has clicked its shutter has selected a moment of truth."

Tyler's fifth novel is *Celestial Navigation,* a book that the author wrote while "fighting the urge to remain in retreat even though the children had started school." In the character of Jeremy Paulding, an agoraphobic artist who is afraid to leave his Baltimore block, Tyler sees much of herself. While her characters are not usually autobiographical, Tyler told Mary Ellen Brooks, in the *Dictionary of Literary Biography,* that creating Jeremy was a way of investigating her own "tendency to turn more and more inward." The story opens with the death of Jeremy's mother and moves quickly to an exploration of the relationship he establishes with the woman who will take her place—a self-sufficient boarder named Mary Tell. Attracted by her sunny self-confidence, Jeremy proposes marriage and soon Mary has stepped in as Jeremy's intermediary to the outside world. As years pass, he comes to feel dwarfed by Mary's competence—she does not even alert him when she leaves for the hospital to have her fifth child because she knows he dreads the trip. Suffocated by her over-protectiveness, the disoriented artist withdraws even further into the private world of his studio where he fashions collages from scraps of other people's lives. Eventually Mary and the children abandon him, and Jeremy does venture out to find them. But the price he pays for conquering his fear is that he loses them for good. At the novel's end, Mary and Jeremy each remain in a separate existence, each still dominated by what Brooks calls "his innate driving characteristic. Jeremy returns to his life as a reclusive artist in a crumbling dark house while Mary prepares for winter in a rundown shack, knowing that another man will eventually provide for her."

Told from the viewpoints of six different characters, *Celestial Navigation* is far more intricate than Tyler's earlier novels, and most critics consider it a breakthrough. Katha Pollitt finds the work "extraordinarily moving and beautiful," while Doris Grumbach proclaims Tyler's "ability to enmesh the reader in what is a simple, uneventful story a notable achievement." In her *New York Times Book Review* article, Gail Godwin explains how "Tyler is especially gifted at the art of freeing her characters and then keeping track of them as they move in their unique and often solitary orbits. Her fiction is filled with displaced persons who persist stubbornly in their own destinies. They are 'oddballs,' visionaries, lonely souls, but she has a way of transcribing their peculiarities with such loving wholeness that when we examine them we keep finding more and more pieces of ourselves."

In her eighth novel, *Morgan's Passing,* Tyler turns from an exploration of the "oddball" as introvert to the "oddball" as extrovert in the creation of Morgan Gower—a 42-year-old hardware store manager with a knack for assuming other roles. Simply put, Morgan is an imposter, a man who changes identities every time he changes clothes. "You're walking down the street with him and this total stranger asks him when the International Brotherhood of Magicians is meeting next," his wife Bonny explains. "You're listening to a politician's speech and suddenly you notice Morgan on the platform, sitting beside a senator's wife with a carnation in his buttonhole. You're waiting for your crabs at Lexington Market and who's behind the counter but Morgan in

a rubber apron, telling the other customers where he caught such fine oysters." These fantasies contrast sharply with the dullness of Morgan's actual life. At home, in the brick colonial house acquired with his wife's money, he feels overwhelmed by the clutter of his wife, their seven daughters, his adult sister, and his feeble-minded mother.

Though *Morgan's Passing* was nominated for a National Book Critics Circle Award in hardback and an American Book Award in paperback fiction, critics are sharply divided in their assessment of the work. Those who like it praise Tyler's handling of character and her artful mingling of comedy and seriousness. "Though she allows her tale to veer toward farce, Tyler always checks it in time with the tug of an emotion, a twitch of regret," writes *Time*'s Paul Gray. He concludes: "*Morgan's Passing* is not another novel about a mid-life crisis, it is a buoyant story about a struggle unto death." Tyler acknowledged in her *Detroit News* interview with Bruce Cook that her "big worry in doing the book was that people would be morally offended by [Morgan]." But critic Marilyn Murray Willison sings his praises. "In spite of his inability to restore order to his life, his nicotine-stained hands and teeth, his silly wardrobe, his refusal to accept reality, Morgan emerges from Tyler's book a true hero," she writes in the *Los Angeles Times Book Review.*

With *Dinner at the Homesick Restaurant,* her ninth and, some say, finest novel, Tyler redeems herself in many critics' eyes. Updike, for instance, maintains that this book achieves "a new level of power and gives us a lucid and delightful yet complex and sombre improvisation on her favorite theme, family life." Writing in the *Chicago Tribune Book World,* Larry McMurtry echoes these sentiments: "She recognizes and conveys beautifully the alternations of tragedy and farce in family life, and never more beautifully than in *Dinner at the Homesick Restaurant.*" Benjamin Demott is even more impressed. "Funny, heart-hammering, wise, [the novel] edges deep into truth that's simultaneously (and interdependently) psychological, moral and formal—deeper than many living novelists of serious reputation have penetrated, deeper than Miss Tyler herself has gone before. It is a border crossing," he writes in the *New York Times Book Review.*

The story's plot is a simple one—"deceptively simple," Sarah English notes in the *Dictionary of Literary Biography Yearbook.* Eighty-five-year-old Pearl Tull—who married late in life and bore three children before her traveling salesman husband deserted her—recalls her past from her deathbed. She reconstructs the moment, thirty-five years before, when Beck Tull announced he was leaving, the years of struggle that ensued as she singlehandedly (and sometimes heartlessly) raised her children, and the scars which Cody, Jenny, and Ezra still bear.

The novel unfolds in a series of self-contained chapters, each, in Updike's words, "rounded like a short story," and each reflecting a different family member's point of view. This narrative technique, as English notes, "allows [Tyler] to juxtapose past and present and thus to convey the vision—that she has always had—of the past not as a continuum but as layers of still, vivid memories. The wealth of points of view also allows Tyler to show more fully than ever the essential subjectivity of the past. Cody and Jenny remember Pearl as a witch; Ezra remembers her as a source of strength and security. Every character's vision of the past is different."

This portrait of family entanglements is too somber for some critics' tastes, including Cynthia Propper Seton's. "What may be the trouble with *Dinner at the Homesick Restaurant,*" she writes in the *Washington Post Book World*, "is that the Tull family is not marginal enough, its members are too grave a proposition for a mind so full of mischief as Anne Tyler's. They depressed her." In her *Detroit News* review, however, Cynthia King maintains that "despite the joyless atmosphere, the author's humor bubbles through in Pearl's tackiness, in Jenny's self-protective flippancy. And more than a few times—awful as Pearl is, warped and doomed as her children are—what keeps us turning pages is the suspicion that there may be a bit of each of them in each of us." "What one wants to do on finishing such a work as *Dinner at the Homesick Restaurant*," concludes Benjamin Demott, "is maintain balance, keep things intact for a stretch, stay under the spell as long as possible. The before and after are immaterial; nothing counts except the knowledge, solid and serene, that's all at once breathing in the room. We're speaking obviously, about an extremely beautiful book."

The Accidental Tourist, Tyler's tenth novel, again combines the author's subtle, understated probing into human nature and her eye for comic detail. The title serves both as a reference to the protagonist's occupation and as a metaphor for his life. Macon Leary writes travel guides for people who dislike traveling and who would prefer to stay in the comfort and familiarity of their own homes. The guide books—the series is titled *The Accidental Tourist*—advise reluctant travelers on how to visit foreign places without experiencing the annoyances and jarring peculiarities that each new city offers. Thus, Macon counsels his readers on where they can find American-style hamburgers in Amsterdam, for instance, or on the type of reading material to carry on the plane so as to ward off chatty passengers.

Macon's suggestions are indicative of his own nature. Insular and wary of anything foreign or unexpected, Macon surrounds himself with rituals in an attempt to make his life ordered and safe. When his twelve-year-old son is murdered in a restaurant, he retreats even further into his cocoon, driving away his wife in the process. His son's dog, Edward, though, does not respond well to the changes in his environment. As Macon fills his life with more elaborate rituals, Edward develops a mean streak and begins to terrorize Macon's friends and relatives. Eventually, Edward requires a trainer, and it is this trainer that shocks Macon into reassessing his life. Muriel Pritchett is everything that Macon is not: impetuous, carefree, and disordered. Macon becomes attracted to Muriel and her odd lifestyle, seeing in it all the vitality and passion that his life lacks. When his wife changes her mind and asks Macon to resume their marriage, Macon is forced to choose between the two women. He opts for Muriel, recognizing the exuberance for life that she has awakened in him.

As with her previous novels, reviewers praised the gently ironic humor and sympathetic, likable characters that Tyler creates in *The Accidental Tourist*. Richard Eder of the *Los Angeles Times Book Review* notes that the character of Macon Leary "is an oddity of the first water, and yet we grow so close to him that there is not the slightest warp in the lucid, touching and very funny story of an inhibited man moving out into life." Other critics observe that in this book Tyler fuses the mix of tragedy and comedy that appears in most of her previous books. McMurtry, writing in the *New York Times Book Review* about "the mingling of misery and contentment in the daily lives of her families" that Tyler constructs, comments that "these themes, some of which she has been sifting for more than twenty years, cohere with high definition in the muted . . . personality of Macon Leary." Some reviewers criticize Tyler for her tendency to draw sympathetic characters and to infuse humor into so many of her scenes.

Chicago Tribune Book World critic John Blades wonders whether "Tyler, with her sedative resolutions to life's most grievous and perplexing problems, can be taken seriously as a writer." Most reviewers, though, praise the book and its author. As Eder notes, "I don't know if there is a better American writer going."

In her Pulitzer Prize-winning eleventh novel, *Breathing Lessons*, Tyler examines the themes of marriage, love, and regret. The story concerns Maggie and Ira Moran, married for twenty-eight years, and a journey they make to the funeral of an old friend. During the trip they both reflect on their years together—some happy, some sad. Maggie is gregarious and curious, while Ira is practical and withdrawn. Both at times regret their decision to marry, but they also recognize the strength of the bond between them. Critics still remark on Tyler's ability to evoke sympathy for her characters and her talent for constructing humorous scenes. Eder, again writing in the *Los Angeles Times Book Review*, sums up critical reaction by noting that "there are moments when the struggle among Maggie, Ira, and the melancholy of time passing forms a fiery triangle more powerful and moving . . . than anything she has done."

"Tyler's twelfth novel, *Saint Maybe*," writes *Dictionary of Literary Biography* contributor Caren J. Town, "addresses most directly another important Tyler concern: religion." The protagonist of *Saint Maybe* is Ian Bedloe, a well-adjusted teenager. Ian's family life changes drastically when his older brother Danny marries a divorcee named Lucy, who has two children of her own. Danny commits suicide after the birth of his daughter Daphne and Lucy dies of an overdose of sleeping pills soon after. Ian is overcome with guilt; he seeks guidance from a fundamentalist sect known as the Church of the Second Chance, led by the charismatic Brother Emmett. Emmett charges Ian to care for his brother's children as a penance for his connection with Danny's death. "Tyler has a well-known skepticism about the premise of most religions," declares Town: "'It's not that I have anything against ministers,' she . . . [said] in a discussion about *Earthly Possessions*, 'but that I'm particularly concerned with how much right anyone has to change someone, and ministers are people who feel they have that right.'" "*Saint Maybe*," remarks Brad Leithauser in the *New York Review of Books*, "winds up being something of a curious creation: a secular tale of holy redemption."

Tyler moved in quite a different direction with her next book, *Tumble Tower*—which features illustrations by her daughter Mitra Modarressi—"a kid-pleasing story about Princess Molly the Messy and her royal family of neatniks," according to *Christian Science Monitor* contributor and children's literature specialist Karen Williams. Unlike her obsessed parents and siblings, including Prince Thomas the Tidy, Molly lives a comfortably unkempt life. "The moral of Tyler's tale," declares Suzanne Curley in the *Los Angeles Times Book Review*, "is that a princess unfazed by half-eaten candy bars left under her chair cushions, kittens nesting among fluffy slippers on the closet floor or a bed 'all lumpy and knobby with half-finished books' probably has her priorities straight, and may have much to teach about the way clutter often goes hand-in-hand with coziness."

"In *Ladder of Years*, Ms. Tyler's 13th novel," states *New York Times Book Review* contributor Cathleen Schine, "the story that appears to unfold of its own accord is a fairy tale of sorts, a fairy tale with echoes of both the tragedy of *King Lear* and the absurdity of the modern romance novel." "*Ladder of Years*," writes Suzanne L. MacLachlan in the *Christian Science Monitor*,

". . . is written from the viewpoint of a woman approaching middle age who feels she is losing her family." One day Delia Grinstead simply walks out on her obnoxious husband and her uncaring teenaged children and starts a new life in a Maryland town some miles away. She becomes self-supporting, taking a job as a lawyer's secretary. "Just as she subverts the domestic with fantasy—her situations are earthbound until you notice that they are gliding along two inches above the earth—she subverts fantasy with the domestic," explains a *Los Angeles Times Book Review* contributor. Delia's old patterns of behavior begin to reassert themselves and she returns home for her oldest daughter's wedding. "Her eventual journey back to her home and family are, in many ways," MacLachlan states, "the universal search for self. She finds, in the end, that the people she has left behind have traveled further than she." "As always," declares *New York Times* reviewer Christopher Lehmann-Haupt, "Ms. Tyler writes with a clarity that makes the commonplace seem fresh and the pathetic touching."

BIOGRAPHICAL/CRITICAL SOURCES:

BOOKS

Dictionary of Literary Biography, Volume 6: *American Novelists Since World War II, Second Series,* Gale (Detroit), 1980.
Dictionary of Literary Biography Yearbook: 1982, Gale, 1982.
Evans, Elizabeth, *Anne Tyler,* Twayne, 1993.
Petry, Alice Hall, *Understanding Anne Tyler,* University of South Carolina Press, 1990.
Petry, Alice Hall, editor, *Critical Essays on Anne Tyler,* G. K. Hall, 1992.

PERIODICALS

Atlantic Monthly, March, 1976.
Chicago Tribune Book World, March 23, 1980; March 21, 1982; July 20, 1986.
Christian Science Monitor, September 25, 1991, p. 13; December 17, 1993, p. 12; May 18, 1995, p. 13.
Commonweal, November 8, 1991, pp. 656-58; June 16, 1995, pp. 21-22.
Detroit News, April 6, 1980; April 18, 1982.
Globe and Mail (Toronto), September 21, 1985; October 8, 1988.
Kirkus Reviews, February 15, 1995, p. 180.
Library Journal, April 1, 1995, p. 127.
London Review of Books, March 12, 1992, pp. 23-24.
Los Angeles Times, March 30, 1982; September 14, 1983.
Los Angeles Times Book Review, March 30, 1980; September 15, 1985; September 11, 1988; September 5, 1993, p. 9; May 7, 1995, p. 3.
Ms., August, 1977.
National Catholic Reporter, May 24, 1996, p. 25.
National Observer, May 30, 1977.
National Review, June 26, 1995, pp. 59-60.
Newsweek, April 5, 1982; September 9, 1985.
New Yorker, March 29, 1976; June 6, 1977; June 23, 1980; April 5, 1982; May 8, 1995, pp. 89-90.
New York Review of Books, April 3, 1980; January 16, 1992, pp. 53-55.
New York Times, May 3, 1977; March 17, 1980; March 22, 1982; September 30, 1983; September 3, 1988; April 27, 1995, p. B2.
New York Times Book Review, November 22, 1964; November 21, 1965; March 15, 1970; May 21, 1972; April 28, 1974; January 18, 1976; May 8, 1977; March 14, 1982; September 8, 1985; August 25, 1991, pp. 1, 26; May 7, 1995, p. 12.

Saturday Review, December 26, 1964; November 20, 1965; June 17, 1972; March 6, 1976; September 4, 1976; March 15, 1980.
Time, May 9, 1977; March 17, 1980; April 5, 1982; September 16, 1985.
Times (London), January 12, 1989.
Times Literary Supplement, July 15, 1965; May 23, 1975; December 9, 1977; October 31, 1980; October 29, 1982; October 4, 1985; January 20, 1989.
Tribune Books (Chicago), August 28, 1988.
Washington Post Book World, March 16, 1980; April 4, 1982; September 4, 1988.

*   *   *

TYNAN, Kenneth (Peacock) 1927-1980

PERSONAL: Born April 2, 1927, in Birmingham, England; died of emphysema, July 26, 1980, in Santa Monica, CA; buried in England; son of Sir Peter Peacock and Letitia Rose Tynan; married Elaine Bundy (an American writer), January 25, 1951 (divorced, 1964); married Kathleen Halton (a writer), June, 1967; children: (first marriage) Tracy; (second marriage) Roxanna Nell, Matthew. *Education:* Magdalen College, Oxford, B.A., 1948. *Politics:* Socialist. *Religion:* None.

CAREER: Drama critic and writer. Director of weekly repertory company, Lichfield, Staffordshire, England, 1949; director of *Man of the World,* Lyric Theatre, London, England, 1950, and *Othello,* for the Arts Council Tour, 1950; drama critic, *Spectator,* London, 1950-51, *Evening Standard,* London, 1952-53, and *Daily Sketch,* London, 1953-54; *Observer,* London, drama critic, 1954-58 and 1960-63, film critic, 1964-66, arts columnist, 1968-69; *New Yorker,* New York City, drama critic, 1958-60; British National Theatre, literary manager, 1963-69, literary consultant, 1969-73; *New Yorker,* feature writer, 1976-80. Actor in Alec Guinness's *Hamlet,* New Theatre, London, 1951; coproducer of Rolf Hochhuth's *Soldiers,* New Theatre, 1968. Head of script department, Ealing Films, 1954-56; creator of British television feature "We Dissent," 1960; editor of British television program "Tempo," 1961; television producer, 1961-62. Former member of British Council drama panel.

MEMBER: Royal Society of Literature (fellow).

WRITINGS:

He That Plays the King, Longmans, Green, 1950.
Persona Grata, photographs by Cecil Beaton, Wingate, 1953, Putnam, 1954.
Alec Guinness: An Illustrated Study of His Work for Stage and Screen, with a List of His Appearances, Rockliff, 1953, Macmillan, 1955, 3rd edition, Macmillan, 1961.
Bull Fever, Harper, 1955, enlarged edition, Atheneum, 1966.
Nowhere to Go (screenplay), Metro-Goldwyn-Mayer, 1958.
(Contributor) Tom Maschler, editor, *Declaration,* MacGibbon & Kee, 1959.
(With Harold Lang) *The Quest for Corbett* (radio play; first produced by British Broadcasting Corp.-Radio, 1956), Gabberbocchus, 1960.
Curtains, Atheneum, 1961.
Tynan on Theatre, Penguin, 1964.
(Editor) George Farquhar, *The Recruiting Officer* (National Theatre production), Hart-Davis, 1965.

(Editor) William Shakespeare, *Othello* (National Theatre production), Hart-Davis, 1966, Stein & Day, 1967.

(Author of introduction) Lenny Bruce, *How to Talk Dirty and Influence People,* P. Owen, 1966.

Tynan Right and Left: Plays, Films, People, Places and Events, Atheneum, 1967.

The Actors (television documentary script), Independent Television (ITV), 1968.

(Deviser and contributor) *Oh! Calcutta! An Entertainment with Music* (first produced off-Broadway at Eden Theatre, June 17, 1969; produced in London at The Roundhouse, July 27, 1970), Grove, 1969.

(Contributor) Douglas A. Hughes, editor, *Perspectives on Pornography,* St. Martin's, 1970.

(With Roman Polanski) *Macbeth* (screenplay; based on Shakespeare's play of the same title), Columbia, 1971.

The Sound of Two Hands Clapping, Holt, 1975.

A View of the English Stage, 1944-1963, Methuen, 1975.

Show People: Profiles in Entertainment, Simon & Schuster, 1980.

Profiles, selected and edited by Kathleen Tynan and Ernie Eban, preface by Simon Callow, HarperPerennial, 1990, with new introduction by Kathleen Tynan, Random House, 1995.

Kenneth Tynan: Letters, edited by Kathleen Tynan, Random House, 1995.

SIDELIGHTS: "A critic," as Kenneth Tynan was once quoted by Richard West in the *Los Angeles Times,* "is a man who knows the way but can't drive the car." For three decades this critic expressed his views in books and in such periodicals as the *Spectator,* the *Observer,* and the *New Yorker.* "Regarded by many in England as 'the greatest theater critic since Shaw,'" notes Michiko Kakutani in the *New York Times,* "Mr. Tynan exerted a lasting influence on the stage." Harold Clurman, reviewing Tynan's 1961 book *Curtains,* drew this profile of the author/critic: "What makes Tynan that rare phenomenon, a genuine theatre critic, is that he is disposed toward the theatre in the sense that we speak of certain people being naturally musical." Clurman added, "[He] experiences the theatre with his nerves, body, mind and spirit. He possesses in regard to the theatre something like absolute pitch." Tynan was also a noted writer of celebrity profiles and the creator of *Oh! Calcutta!,* a theater piece which, because of its countercultural tone and its onstage nudity, became one of the most notorious successes of the 1960s.

Tynan's contributions to the lively arts were remembered by *New York Times* contributor Robert Cushman, who on the occasion of Tynan's death recalled the critic's emergence onto the 1950s theater scene: "He was dissatisfied with the state of contemporary English drama; . . . he was uncertain what should be put in its place. All he knew is that he wanted a break from plays set in Mayfair flats or swank country houses." Cushman explained that John Osborne's play "'Look Back in Anger,' with its articulate, poverty-stricken and discontented hero struck a chord, this, [Tynan] proclaimed, was what he'd waited for. He became the critical spokesman for what soon proved to be a new generation of socially aware left-wing playwrights."

Show People: Profiles in Entertainment, published just months before its author's death, is a compendium of several *New Yorker* sketches that Tynan wrote during the 1970s. As Jack Richardson noted in a *New York Times Book Review* article, "Mr. Tynan concedes in his foreword there is no theme or overview connecting these portraits except the admiration he feels for his subjects and the wish to include them all in an ideal dinner party." The five subjects are British actor Sir Ralph Richardson, playwright Tom Stoppard, writer/comic Mel Brooks, silent-screen star Louise Brooks, and television personality Johnny Carson. About these subjects, Tynan revealed, in the words of *Saturday Review* contributor Stephen Harvey, "minute biographical trivia, painstakingly analyzing the themes and techniques that have marked these figures' professional achievements, watching and describing them at work when possible, interviewing his subjects and their friends and colleagues at length."

"Tynan's elegant, lean essays cruise along smoothly at top speed," commented Jean Strouse in *Newsweek,* "and he uses the English language with all the grace and precision of a well-muscled athlete exercising his body." And according to Richardson, "As any good host should, Mr. Tynan tries to treat all his guests with equal interest and courtesy. However, being human, he does betray a greater affection for certain members of the gathering and, as an unregenerate critic, he is from time to time compelled to lecture them on their shortcomings." Strouse characterized Tynan's collection as a blend of "companionable chat with delightful anecdote and shrewd surmise." Concluded Michael Dirda in a *Washington Post Book Review* article, "Kenneth Tynan once described himself as 'a student of craftsmanship, with a special passion for imaginative craftsmen.' These pieces allow one to share his passion, and to admire—as people have for 30 years—the gifts of a splendid writer, still our finest connoisseur of the performing arts."

A larger collection of Tynan's celebrity sketches was published after his death as *Profiles.* The book contains fifty biographical profiles in chronological order, beginning with Tynan's student days at the age of sixteen (1943) and ending with pieces written shortly before his death in 1980. Among those profiled are Noel Coward, Marlene Dietrich, Laurence Olivier, Orson Welles, and Tennessee Williams. Critics commented on Tynan's star-struck interest in the famous actors, directors, and producers he profiled—many of whom became his friends. Reviewers also noted Tynan's penchant for writing colorful, expressive prose. Reviewing the collection in the *Observer,* Peter Conrad remarked, "The most impressive thing about this book is its revelation that the precocious, dandified schoolboy did outgrow the excesses of his early manner. . . . He begins by mythologising his idols, and ends by analysing them."

Another posthumous collection of Tynan's work to be published were his private letters, gathered and edited by his wife, Kathleen, and published as *Kenneth Tynan: Letters.* The letters show Tynan offering advice to writers and directors; bickering with theater management; and musing on women to friends. Writing in the *Spectator,* William Gaskell noted, "Ken was a lover of stars just as he was a lover of women—a lover with a voracious appetite." *New Statesman & Society* reviewer Aleks Sierz commented that "Tynan loved to make a crisis out of drama. His best letters are those aimed at the stuffed shirts of the establishment."

BIOGRAPHICAL/CRITICAL SOURCES:

BOOKS

Tynan, Kathleen, *The Life of Kenneth Tynan,* Quill, 1989.

PERIODICALS

American Spectator, June, 1991, p. 39.
Detroit News, August 10, 1980.
Library Journal, September 1, 1990, p. 222.
Los Angeles Times, July 29, 1980.
New Republic, August 23, 1980.
New Statesman & Society, November 25, 1994, p. 38.

Newsweek, February 11, 1980.
New York Review of Books, March 6, 1980.
New York Times, January 22, 1980; August 17, 1980.
New York Times Book Review, March 19, 1961; January 20, 1980;
    October 21, 1990, p. 25.
Observer, October 1, 1989, p. 48.
Publishers Weekly, August 3, 1990, p. 70.
Saturday Review, February 2, 1980.
Spectator, January 31, 1981; November 12, 1994, p. 45.
Time, January 21, 1980.
Times Literary Supplement, January 2, 1981.
Tribune Books (Chicago), October 7, 1990, p. 8.
Variety, November 19, 1990, p. 96.
Washington Post Book World, February 17, 1980.

*   *   *

TZARA, Tristan 1896-1963

PERSONAL: Surname is pronounced "*tsa*-ra"; born Samuel Rosenfeld; name legally changed, 1925; born April 4, 1896 (some sources say April 16, 1896), in Moinesti, Bacu, Romania; immigrated to Switzerland, 1916; immigrated to France, 1919, naturalized citizen at the end of World War II; died December 24, 1963, in Paris, France. *Education:* Bucharist University, 1914-15. *Politics:* Member of Communist Party, 1935-63. *Religion:* Jewish.

CAREER: Poet, dramatist, essayist, and critic. Founder, with Ion Vinea, of journal *Simbolul,* 1912; founder, with Ion Vinea, of journal *Chemarea,* 1915; founder, with Hugo Ball, Emmy Hennings, Marcel Janco, Richard Huelsenbeck, and Hans Arp, of Dadaist movement, Zurich, 1916. Member of Surrealist group of writers in Paris, 1929-34. Cultural ambassador to the Spanish Republic for the Writers' Association for the Defense of Culture; lecture tour through Central and Eastern Europe for French Ministry of Foreign Affairs, 1946. *Military service:* Served with Loyalists during the Spanish Civil War; directed the cultural broadcast of the French Resistance in the south of France, 1943-44, and wrote for Resistance magazines.

MEMBER: Writers' Association for the Defense of Culture.

AWARDS, HONORS: Taormina International Grand Prize for Poetry, 1961.

WRITINGS:

La premiere aventure celeste de Monsieur Antipyrine (poetry), [Paris], 1916.
Vingt-cinq poemes (poetry), Fontaine, 1918.
Anthologie Dada, Mouvement Dada, 1919.
Cinema calendrier du coeur abstrait maisons (poetry), [Paris], 1920.
La coeur a gaz (drama), [Paris], 1920, translation by Michael Benedikt published as *The Gas Heart,* 1964.
(With Hans Arp and Max Ernst) *Dada au grand air,* [Paris], 1921.
Faites vos jeux (unfinished autobiographical novel), [Paris], 1923.
De nos oiseaux (poetry), [Paris], 1923, translation by Lee Harwood published as *Cosmic Realities Vanilla Tobacco Dawnings,* Arc Publications, 1975.
Sept manifestes dada (essays), [Paris], 1924, translation by Barbara Wright published as *Seven Dada Manifestos and Lampisteries,* Calder, 1977.
Mouchoir de nuages (drama), Editions de la Galerie Simon, 1925.
Indicateur des chemins de coeur (poetry), [Paris], 1928.
L'arbre des voyageurs (poetry), [Paris], 1930.

Essai sur la situation de la poesie (essay), [Paris], 1931.
L'homme approximatif (poetry), Fourcade, 1931, translation by Mary Ann Caws published as *Approximate Man, and Other Writings,* Wayne State University Press, 1973.
Ou boivent les loups (poetry), [Paris], 1932.
L'antitete (prose poems), Editions des Cahiers libres, 1933.
Parler seul (poetry), Caracteres, 1933.
Abrege de la nuit (poetry and prose), [Paris], 1934.
Grains et issues (essay), Les Editions Denoel et Steele, 1935.
La main passe (poetry), [Paris], 1935.
Sur le champ, [Paris], 1937.
Vigies, [Paris], 1937, Alexandre Loewy, 1963.
La deuxieme aventure celeste de Monsieur Antipyrine (poetry), [Paris], 1938.
Midis gagnes (poetry), [Paris], 1939.
Ca va, [Paris], 1944.
Une route seul soleil, [Paris], 1944.
Entre-temps (poetry), [Paris], 1946.
Le signe de vie (poetry), Bordas, 1946.
Terre sur terre (poetry), Editions des Trois collines, 1946.
La fuite (drama), Gallimard, 1947.
Morceaux choisis, Bordas, 1947.
Le surrealisme et l'apres-guerre (essay), Nagel, 1947.
Picasso et les chemins de la connaissance, A. Skira, 1948.
Phases, P. Seghers, 1949.
Sans coup ferir (prose poem), [Paris], 1949.
De memoire d'homme (poetry), [Paris], 1950.
L'art oceanien, [Paris], 1951.
La premiere main, [Paris], 1952.
La face interieure (poetry), [Paris], 1953.
Picasso et la poesie (essay), [Paris], 1953.
L'Egypte face a face, Guilde du livre, 1954.
La bonne heure (poetry), [Paris], 1955.
A haute flamme (poetry), [Paris], 1955.
Le temps naissant, [Paris], 1955.
Le fruit permis (poetry), Caracteres, 1956.
(With Philippe Bonnet) *Peintures,* Berggruem and Cie, 1956.
(With Hans Arp and Richard Huelsenbeck) *Dada: Die Geburt des Dada,* Im Verlag der Arche, 1957.
Frere bois (poetry), PAB, 1957.
La rose et le chien (poetry), [Paris], 1958.
Juste present, [Paris], 1961.
De la coupe aux levres, Edizioni Rapporti europei, 1961.
Les premiers poemes (poetry), translation from Romanian into French by Claude Sernet (Mihail Cosma), Seghers, 1965, translation into English by Michael Impey and Brian Swann published as *Primele poeme/First Poems,* New Rivers Press, 1976.
Thirteen Poems (poetry), [Paris], 1969.
Destroyed Days, [Paris], 1971.
Oeuvres completes (poetry, dramas, essays, and criticism), 6 vols., edited by Henri Behar, Flammarion, 1975-91.
Selected Poems (poetry), translation by Lee Harwood, Trigram Press, 1975.

Selections of Tzara's works in English translation appear in *Axel's Castle,* by Edmund Wilson, 1932; *Surrealism,* by J. Levy, 1936; and *The Dada Painters and Poets,* by R. Motherwell, 1951.

SIDELIGHTS: Tristan Tzara is remembered as a proponent and theoretician for Dadaism, an intellectual movement of the World War I era whose adherents espoused intentional irrationality and urged individuals to repudiate traditional artistic, historical, and religious values. In response to the alienation and absurdity of World War I and the staid, unimaginative art forms predominant in Europe during that era, Tzara and other European artists sought to establish a new style in which random associations would serve to evoke a vitality free from the restraints of logic and grammar. Tzara articulated the aesthetic theories of Dadaism in his seminal collection of essays, *Sept manifestes dada* (1924; "Seven Dada Manifestos"). This volume, in which Tzara advocates "absolute faith in every god that is the immediate product of spontaneity," represents a chaotic assault on reason and convention. Although his work often defies standard classification and is regarded by most contemporary English-speaking scholars as little more than a literary curiosity, Tzara is esteemed in France for his large and diverse body of poetry, which is unified by his critique of and search for a universal language and cosmic wisdom.

Tzara's first published poetry appeared in a literary review in 1912. Many of these poems, written in Rumanian and influenced by French symbolist writers, appear in *Les premiers poemes* (1965; "Primele poemes: First Poems"). Tzara immigrated to Switzerland from Rumania in 1916. Together with Jean Arp, Hugo Ball, and others, Tzara founded Dadaism and staged Dadaist performances at the Cabaret Voltaire in Zurich. Tzara left Switzerland in 1919 and settled in Paris, where he engaged in Dadaist experiments with such literary figures as Andre Breton and Louis Aragon. Serious philosophical differences caused a split between Tzara and Breton in 1921; soon after, Breton founded Surrealism, and by 1922, the Dada movement had dissolved. Tzara's early Dadaist verse, written between 1916 and 1924, utilizes agglomerations of obscure images, nonsense syllables, outrageous juxtapositions, ellipses, and inscrutable maxims to perplex readers and to illustrate the limitations of language. Volumes such as *Vingt-cinq poemes* (1918) and *De nos oiseaux* (1923) display the propositions outlined in Tzara's manifestos and critical essays, often blending criticism and poetry to create hybrid literary forms.

From 1929 to 1934, Tzara participated in the activities of the Surrealist group in Paris. In this environment, he created a more sustained and coherent poetry that places less emphasis on the ridiculous than his Dadaist verse. Tzara's works published during this period include *L'homme approximatif* (1931; "Approximate Man and Other Writings"), an epic poem that is widely considered a landmark of twentieth-century French literature. This work portrays an unfulfilled wayfarer's search for a universal knowledge and language. Roger Cardinal asserted: "[In] this apocalyptic explosion of language, Tzara finally approaches the primal seat of creativity, the point where the naked word reveals the naked truth about the world." This and Tzara's later Surrealist volumes—*L'arbre des voyageurs* (1930), *Ou boivent les loups* (1932), *L'antitete* (1933), and *Grains et issues* (1935)—reveal his obsession with language, his vision of humanity's destiny of

tedium and alienation, and his concern with the struggle to achieve completeness and enlightenment.

In 1934, Tzara left the Surrealists to join France's communist party. As his commitment to left-wing politics increased, his poetry included greater political content and stressed revolutionary and humanistic values while maintaining his lifelong interest in free imagery and linguistic experiments. *Midis gagnes* (1939) focuses on Tzara's impressions of Spain during the country's Civil War, while *La fuite* (1947) depicts the frantic German evacuation of Nazi-occupied France during World War II. The prose poems *Sans coup ferir* (1949) and *A haute flamme* (1955) also address political topics related to the Second World War. Critics generally regard such later works as *Terre sur terre* (1946), *Parler seul* (1950), and *Le fruit permis* (1956) as less vigorous and inventive but more controlled than his earlier poetry.

Tzara's dramas have received less critical attention than his manifestos and poetry. Written during his Dadaist phase, Tzara's best-known plays, *La coeur a gaz* (1920; "The Gas Heart") and *Mouchoir de nuages* (1925), rely on absurdity and wordplay, parodying such literary forms as classical Greek and Shakespearean theater and French symbolist poetry. In *Essai sur la situation de la poesie* (1931), a collection of critical essays, Tzara celebrates poetry as a liberating force from conventional modes of expression.

BIOGRAPHICAL/CRITICAL SOURCES:

BOOKS

Ball, Hugo, *Flight Out of Time: A Dada Diary,* Viking Press, 1974.

Browning, Gordon Frederick, *Tristan Tzara: The Genesis of the Dada Poem or from Dada to Aa,* Akademischer Verlag Heinz, 1979.

Erickson, John D., *Dada: Performance, Poetry, and Art,* Twayne Publishers, 1984.

Harwood, Lee, *Tristan Tzara: A Bibliography,* Aloes Books, 1974.

Janco, Marcel, *Dada: Monograph of a Movement,* St. Martin's Press, 1975.

Ko, Won, *Buddhist Elements in Dada: A Comparison of Tristan Tzara, Takahashi Shinkichi, and Their Fellow Poets,* New York University Press, 1977.

Lewis, Helena, *The Politics of Surrealism,* Paragon House Publishers, 1988.

PERIODICALS

Architectural Digest, Volume 48, April, 1991, pp. 104-9.

Miorita: A Journal of Romanian Studies, Volume 9, numbers 1-2, 1985, pp. 1-18.

U

UCHIDA, Yoshiko 1921-1992

PERSONAL: Surname is pronounced "Oo-*chee*-dah"; born November 24, 1921, in Alameda, CA; died after a stroke, June 21, 1992, in Berkeley, CA; daughter of Dwight Takashi (a businessman) and Iku (Umegaki) Uchida. *Education:* University of California, Berkeley, A.B. (cum laude), 1942; Smith College, M.Ed., 1944. *Politics:* Democrat. *Religion:* Protestant. *Avocational interests:* Fine arts, folk crafts.

CAREER: Elementary school teacher in Japanese relocation center in Utah, 1942-43; Frankford Friends' School, Philadelphia, PA, teacher, 1944-45; membership secretary, Institute of Pacific Relations, 1946-47; secretary, United Student Christian Council, 1947-52; full-time writer, 1952-57; University of California, Berkeley, secretary, 1957-62; full-time writer, 1962-92.

AWARDS, HONORS: Ford Foundation research fellow in Japan, 1952; Children's Spring Book Festival honor award, *New York Herald Tribune,* 1955, for *The Magic Listening Cap;* Notable Book citation, American Library Association, 1972, for *Journey to Topaz;* medal for best juvenile book by a California author, Commonwealth Club of California, 1972, for *Samurai of Gold Hill;* Award of Merit, California Association of Teachers of English, 1973; citation, Contra Costa chapter of Japanese American Citizens League, 1976, for outstanding contribution to the cultural development of society; Morris S. Rosenblatt Award, Utah State Historical Society, 1981, for article, "Topaz, City of Dust"; Distinguished Service Award, University of Oregon, 1981; Commonwealth Club of California medal, 1982, for *A Jar of Dreams;* award from Berkeley Chapter of Japanese American Citizens League, 1983, *School Library Journal,* Best Book of the Year citation, 1983, for *The Best Bad Thing;* New York Public Library, Best Book of the Year citation, 1983, for *The Best Bad Thing;* Best Book of 1985 citation, Bay Area Book Reviewers, 1985, for *The Happiest Ending;* Child Study Association of America, Children's Book of the Year citation, 1985, for *The Happiest Ending;* San Mateo and San Francisco Reading Associations, Young Authors' Hall of Fame award, 1985, for *The Happiest Ending;* Friends of Children and Literature award, 1987, for *A Jar of Dreams;* Japanese American of the Biennium award, Japanese American Citizens Leagues, 1988, for outstanding achievement.

WRITINGS:

JUVENILE

The Dancing Kettle and Other Japanese Folk Tales, illustrations by Richard C. Jones, Harcourt, 1949.

New Friends for Susan, illustrations by Henry Sugimoto, Scribner, 1951.

(Self-illustrated) *The Magic Listening Cap—More Folk Tales from Japan,* Harcourt, 1955.

(Self-illustrated) *The Full Circle* (junior high school study book), Friendship, 1957.

Takao and Grandfather's Sword, illustrations by William M. Hutchinson, Harcourt, 1958.

The Promised Year, illustrations by Hutchinson, Harcourt, 1959.

Mik and the Prowler, illustrations by Hutchinson, Harcourt, 1960.

Rokubei and the Thousand Rice Bowls, illustrations by Kazue Mizumura, Scribner, 1962.

The Forever Christmas Tree, illustrations by Mizumura, Scribner, 1963.

Sumi's Prize, illustrations by Mizumura, Scribner, 1964.

The Sea of Gold, and Other Tales from Japan, illustrations by Marianne Yamaguchi, Scribner, 1965.

Sumi's Special Happening, illustrations by Mizumura, Scribner, 1966.

In-Between Miya, illustrations by Susan Bennett, Scribner, 1967.

Hisako's Mysteries, illustrations by Bennett, Scribner, 1969.

Sumi and the Goat and the Tokyo Express, illustrations by Mizumura, Scribner, 1969.

Makoto, the Smallest Boy: A Story of Japan, illustrations by Akihito Shirawaka, Crowell, 1970.

Journey to Topaz: A Story of the Japanese-American Evacuation, illustrations by Donald Carrick, Scribner, 1971,

Samurai of Gold Hill, illustrations by Ati Forberg, Scribner, 1972.

The Old Man with the Bump (cassette based on story from *The Dancing Kettle*), Houghton, 1973.

The Birthday Visitor, illustrations by Charles Robinson, Scribner, 1975.

The Rooster Who Understood Japanese, illustrations by Robinson, Scribner, 1976.

The Two Foolish Cats (filmstrip with cassette based on a story from *The Sea of Gold*), Encyclopaedia Britannica Educational, 1977.

Journey Home (sequel to *Journey to Topaz*), illustrations by Robinson, McElderry Books, 1978.

The Fox and the Bear (cassette based on a story from *The Magic Listening Cap*), Science Research Associates, 1979.

A Jar of Dreams, McElderry Books, 1981.

The Best Bad Thing (sequel to *A Jar of Dreams*), McElderry Books, 1983.

Tabi: Journey through Time, Stories of the Japanese in America, United Methodist Publishing House, 1984.

The Happiest Ending (sequel to *The Best Bad Thing*), McElderry Books, 1985.

The Two Foolish Cats, illustrations by Margot Zemach, McElderry Books, 1987.

The Terrible Leak, Creative Education, 1990.

The Magic Purse, illustrations by Keiko Narahashi, McElderry Books, 1993.

The Bracelet, illustrations by Joanna Yardley, Philomel, 1993.

The Wise Old Woman, illustrations by Martin Springett, McElderry Books, 1994.

FOR ADULTS

We Do Not Work Alone: The Thoughts of Kanjiro Kawai, Folk Art Society (Japan), 1953.

(Translator of English portions) Soetsu Yanagi, editor, *Shoji Hamada,* Asahi Shimbun Publishing, 1961.

The History of Sycamore Church, Sycamore Congregational Church, 1974.

Desert Exile: The Uprooting of a Japanese-American Family, University of Washington Press, 1982.

Picture Bride (novel), Northland Press, 1987.

The Invisible Thread (an autobiography for young adults), J. Messner, 1991.

OTHER

Contributor to many books, including *Flight Near and Far,* Holt, 1970; *Scribner Anthology for Young People,* Scribner, 1976; *Literature and Life,* Scott, Foresman, 1979; *Fairy Tales of the Sea,* Harper, 1981; *Anthology of Children's Literature,* Scott, Foresman, 1984; and *Explorations,* Houghton, 1986. Author of regular column, "Letter from San Francisco," in *Craft Horizons,* 1958-61. Contributor to exhibit catalogue of Oakland Museum, 1976. Contributor of adult stories and articles to newspapers and periodicals, including *Woman's Day, Gourmet, Utah Historical Quarterly, Far East,* and *California Monthly.* The Kerlan Collection holds Uchida's manuscripts for *In-Between Miya* and *Mik and the Prowler.* Other manuscript collections are at the University of Oregon Library, Eugene, and the Bancroft Library, University of California, Berkeley.

SIDELIGHTS: Yoshiko Uchida's appreciation for her Japanese heritage inspired her to become the author of many books on Japanese culture for readers of all ages. "In fiction, the graceful and lively books of Yoshiko Uchida have drawn upon the author's own childhood to document the Japanese-American experience for middle-grade readers," Patty Campbell commented in the *New York Times Book Review.* And among her non-fiction works for adults are studies of Japanese folk artists such as *We Do Not Work Alone: The Thoughts of Kanjiro Kawai,* as well as a memoir of wartime imprisonment, *Desert Exile: The Uprooting of a Japanese-American Family.*

After the bombing of Pearl Harbor, Americans of Japanese descent were incarcerated by order of the government. Uchida was a senior at the University of California, Berkeley, when her family was sent to Tanforan Racetrack, where thousands of Japanese-Americans lived in stables and barracks. After five months at Tanforan, they were moved to Topaz, a guarded camp in the Utah desert. Uchida taught in the elementary schools there until the spring of 1943, when she was released to accept a fellowship for graduate study at Smith College. Her parents were also released that year.

Uchida earned a Master's Degree in education; but because teaching limited her time for writing, she found a secretarial job that allowed her to write in the evenings. As she explained in her contribution to *Something about the Author Autobiography Series,* "I was writing short stories at the time, sending them to the *New Yorker, Atlantic Monthly* and *Harper's*—and routinely receiving printed rejection slips. After a time, however, the slips contained encouraging penciled notes and a *New Yorker* editor even met with me to suggest that I write about my concentration camp experiences. . . . And many of the short stories I wrote during those days were published eventually in literature anthologies for young people."

By the time *Woman's Day* accepted one of her stories, Uchida found that writing for children promised more success. Her first book, *The Dancing Kettle and Other Japanese Folk Tales,* was well-received, and when a Ford Foundation grant enabled Uchida to visit Japan, she collected more traditional tales. In addition, she became fascinated with Japanese arts and crafts, and learned more about them from Soetsu Yanagi, the philosopher, and other founders of the Folk Art Movement in Japan. But her most important gain from the visit, she wrote, was the awareness "of a new dimension of myself as a Japanese-American and [a] deepened . . . respect and admiration for the culture that had made my parents what they were."

The death of the author's mother in 1966 prompted Uchida to write a book for her parents "and the other first-generation Japanese (the Issei), who had endured so much." The result was the book *Journey to Topaz: A Story of the Japanese-American Evacuation.* Based on her own experiences in the camps during the war, it marked a shift in emphasis from Japanese culture to the Japanese-American experience in the United States. Every book Uchida wrote after *Journey to Topaz* responded to the growing need for identity among third generation Japanese-Americans. Uchida once explained to *Contemporary Authors:* "Through my books I hope to give young Asian-Americans a sense of their past and to reinforce their self-esteem and self-knowledge. At the same time, I want to dispel the stereotypic image still held by many non-Asians about the Japanese and write about them as real people. I hope to convey the strength of spirit and the sense of hope and purpose I have observed in many first-generation Japanese. Beyond that, I write to celebrate our common humanity, for the basic elements of humanity are present in all our strivings."

BIOGRAPHICAL/CRITICAL SOURCES:

BOOKS

Children's Literature Review, Volume 6, Gale (Detroit), 1984.

Contemporary Authors New Revision Series, Volume 47, Gale, 1995.

Something about the Author Autobiography Series, Volume 1, Gale, 1986.

Twentieth-Century Children's Writers, 3rd edition, St. James Press, 1989.

PERIODICALS

Children's Book World, November 5, 1967.

New York Times Book Review, February 9, 1986.

Young Readers' Review, January, 1967.

UNAMUNO (Y JUGO), Miguel de 1864-1936

PERSONAL: Born September 29, 1864, in Bilbao, Spain; died December 31, 1936, in Salamanca, Spain; married Concepcion Lizarraga Ecenarro, 1891; children: ten. *Education:* Attended Colegio de San Nicolas and Instituto Vizacaino, Bilbao, Spain; University of Madrid, Ph.D., 1884.

CAREER: Educator, poet, novelist, and playwright. University of Salamanca, Salamanca, Spain, professor of Greek, 1891-1924, 1930-34, and rector, 1901-1914, 1934-36; exiled to Canary Islands, 1924, and lived and wrote in France, 1924-30; placed under house arrest for criticism of Franco government, 1936. Cortes (Spanish parliament) deputy from Salamanca; president, Council for Public Education. Taylor lecturer, Oxford University.

AWARDS, HONORS: Cross of the Order of Alfonso XII, 1905; honorary doctorate, University of Grenoble, 1934.

WRITINGS:

FICTION

Paz en la guerra, F. Fe, 1897, translation by Allen Lacy and Martin Nozick with Anthony Kerrigan published as *Peace in War* (Volume 1 of *Obras selectas* [*Selected Works,*]), edited by Kerrigan, Princeton University Press, 1983.
Amor y pedogogia, 1902, Espasa-Calpe, 1934, translation by Michael Vande Berg published as *Love and Pedagogy,* P. Lang, 1996.
El espejo de la muerte (also see below), 1913, Compania Ibero-americana de Publicaciones, 1930.
Niebla, 1914, Renacimiento, 1928, translation by Warner Fite published as *Mist,* Knopf, 1928.
Abel Sanchez: Una historia de pasion, Renacimiento, 1917, translation published as *Abel Sanchez,* edited by Angel del Rio and Amelia de del Rio, Holt, 1947.
Tres novelas ejemplares y un prologo, Espasa-Calpe, 1920, translation by Angel Flores published as *Three Exemplary Novels and a Prologue,* A. & C. Boni, 1930.
La tia Tula (also see below), Renacimiento, 1921.
San Manuel Bueno, martir, y tres historias mas (also see below), Espasa-Calpe, 1933, translation by Francisco de Segovia and Jean Perez published in bilingual edition as *San Manuel Bueno, martir,* Harrap, 1957.
Cuentos (stories), edited by Eleanor Krane Paucker, Minotauro, 1961.
Ver con los ojos y otros relatos novelescos (stories), Espasa-Calpe, 1973.
San Manuel Bueno, martir [and] *La novela de don Sandalio, jugador de ajedrez* (title means "The Novel of Don Sandalio, Chessplayer"; also see below), edited with introduction and notes by C. A. Longhurst, Manchester University Press, 1984.

Also author of *Tulio Montalban y Julio Macedo,* 1920.

PLAYS

El otro, misterio en tres jornadas y un epilogo (title means "The Other"; also see below), Espasa-Calpe, 1932.
El hermano Juan; o, El mundo es teatro, Espasa-Calpe, 1934.
La esfinge (also see below), 1934, Alfil, 1960.
Soledad (also see below), Espasa-Calpe, 1957.
El pasado que vuelve, edited by Manuel Garcia Blanco, Alfil, 1960.

Also author of *La venda* (also see below), *La princesa,* [and] *Dona Lambra,* 1913, *Fedra* (also see below), 1924, *Sombras de sueno,* 1931, *Raquel encadenada* (also see below), 1933, *La difunta,* 1959, and *Medea* (also see below).

POETRY

Poesias, J. Rojas, 1907.
Rosario de sonetos liricos, Imprenta Espanola, 1911.
El Cristo de Velazquez, Calpe, 1920, translation by Eleanor L. Turnbull published as *The Christ of Velazquez,* Johns Hopkins Press, 1951.
Teresa: Rimas de un poeta desconocido presentadas y presentado por Miguel de Unamuno (also known as *Teresa: Rhymes of an Unknown Poet Presented by Miguel de Unamuno*), Renacimiento, 1923.
De Fuerteventura a Paris: Diario intimo de confinamiento y destierro vertido en sonetas (verse and prose), Excelsior, 1925.
Poems, translation by Turnbull, Johns Hopkins Press, 1952.
Cancionero: Diario poetico, edited by Federico de Onis, Losada, 1953.
Cincuenta poesias ineditas (previously unpublished work), edited by Garcia Blanco, Papeles de Son Armadans, 1958.
Poemas de los pueblos de Espana, selected by Garcia Blanco, Anaya, 1961.
Poesias escogidas, selected by Guillermo de Torre, Losada, 1965.
The Last Poems of Miguel de Unamuno, translation by Edita Mas-Lopez, Fairleigh Dickinson University Press, 1974.

Also author of *Rimas de dentro,* 1923.

ESSAYS

En torno al casticismo, F. Fe, 1902.
Vida de Don Quijote y Sancho, F. Fe, 1905, translation by Homer P. Earle published as *The Life of Don Quixote and Sancho,* Knopf, 1927.
Mi religion y otros ensayos breves, 1910, Espasa-Calpe, 1942, translation by Stuart Gross published as *Perplexities and Paradoxes,* Philosophical Library, 1945.
Soliloquios y conversaciones, 1911, Espasa-Calpe, 1942.
Del sentimiento tragico de la vida en los hombres y en los pueblos, 1913, Renacimiento, 1928, translation by J. E. Crawford Flitch published as *The Tragic Sense of Life in Men and in Peoples,* Macmillan, 1926.
La agonia del cristianismo, 1925, Renacimiento, 1931, translation by Pierre Loving published as *The Agony of Christianity,* Payson & Clark, 1928, translation by Kurt F. Reinhardt published as *The Agony of Christianity,* Ungar, 1960.
Essays and Soliloquies, translation and introduction by Flitch, Knopf, 1925.
Como se hace una novela (title means "How to Make a Novel"; also see below), Alba, 1927.
Dos articulos y dos discursos, Historia Nueva, 1930.
Algunas consideraciones sobre la literatura hispano-americana, Espasa-Calpe, 1947.
Visiones y comentarios, Espasa-Calpe, 1949.
Espana y los espanoles (also see below), edited with notes by Garcia Blanco, Aguado, 1955.
Inquietudes y meditaciones, prologue and notes by Garcia Blanco, Aguado, 1957.
La vida literaria, Espasa-Calpe, 1967.
El gaucho Martin Fierro, Americalee, 1967.

Also author of *Tres ensayos,* 1900, and *El porvenir de Espana,* with Angel Ganivet, 1912 (also see below).

JOURNALISTIC PIECES

Pensamiento politico, edited by Elias Diaz, Tecnos, 1965.

Desde el mirador de la guerra, edited by Louis Urrutia, Centre de Recherches Hispaniques (Paris), 1970.

Discursos y articulos, Escelicer, 1971.

En torno a las artes: Del teatro, el cine, las bellas artes, la politica y las letras, Espasa-Calpe, 1976.

Escritos socialistas: Articulos ineditos sobre el socialismo, 1894-1922, edited by Pedro Ribas, Ayuso, 1976.

Articulos olvidados sobre Espana y la primera guerra mundial, edited by Christopher Cobb, Tamesis, 1976.

Cronica politica espanola (1915-1923), edited by Vicente Gonzalez Martin, Almar, 1977.

Republica espanola y Espana republicana, edited by Gonzalez Martin, Almar, 1979.

Unamuno: Articulos y discursos sobre Canarias, edited by Francisco Navarro Artiles, Cabildo Insular de Fuerteventura, 1980.

Ensueno de una patria: Periodismo republicano, 1931-36 (political), Pre-Textos, 1984.

Articulos en "La Nacion" de Buenos Aires, 1919-1924, Ediciones Universidad de Salamanca, 1994.

LETTERS

(With Juan Maragall) *Epistolario,* Edimar, 1951, revised edition, Distribuidora Catalonia, 1976.

(With Juan Zorrilla de San Martin) *Correspondencia,* [Montevideo], 1955.

Trece cartas ineditas de Miguel de Unamuno a Alberto Nin Frias, La Mandragora, 1962.

Cartas ineditas, compiled by Sergio Fernandez Larrain, Zig-Zag, 1965.

(With Alonso Quesada) *Epistolario,* edited by Lazaro Santana, Museo Canario, 1970.

Cartas 1903-1933, compiled by Carmen de Zulueta, Aguilar, 1972.

Unamuno "agitador de espiritus" y Giner: Correspondencia inedita, edited by D. Gomez Molleda, Narcea, 1976.

(With Leopoldo Gutierrez Abascal and Juan de la Encina) *Cartas intimas: Epistolario entre Miguel de Unamuno y los hermanos Gutierrez Abascal,* edited with notes by Javier Gonzalez de Durana, Equzki, 1986.

(With Jose Ortega y Gasset) *Epistolario completo Ortega-Unamuno,* edited by Laureano Robles Carcedo with Antonio Ramos Gascon, El Arquero, 1987.

AUTOBIOGRAPHY

Recuerdos de ninez y de mocedad, V. Suarez, 1908, selected and edited by William Atkinson, Longmans, Green, 1929.

En el destierro (recuerdos y esperanzas), selected and annotated by Garcia Blanco, Pegaso, 1957.

Mi vida y otros recuerdos personales, complied by Garcia Blanco, Losada, 1959.

Diario intimo (also see below), edited by P. Felix Garcia, Escelicer, 1970.

De mi vida, Espasa-Calpe, 1979.

OMNIBUS VOLUMES IN ENGLISH

Abel Sanchez and Other Stories, translated by Kerrigan, Regnery, 1956, revised edition, with an introduction by Mario J. Valdes, Regnery (Washington, DC), 1996.

Our Lord Don Quixote and Sancho with Related Essays (Volume 3 of *Obras selectas* [*Selected Works*]), translated and edited by Kerrigan, Princeton University Press, 1967.

The Tragic Sense of Life in Men and Nations (Volume 4 of *Obras selectas* [*Selected Works*]), translated and edited by Kerrigan, Princeton University Press, 1972.

The Agony of Christianity and Essays on Faith (Volume 5 of *Obras selectas* [*Selected Works*]), translated and edited by Kerrigan, Princeton University Press, 1974.

Novela/Nivola (Volume 6 of *Obras selectas* [*Selected Works*]; includes "How to Make a Novel"), translated and edited by Kerrigan, Princeton University Press, 1976.

Ficciones: Four Stories and a Play (Volume 7 of *Obras selectas* [*Selected Works*]; includes *The Other, Tia Tula,* and *The Novel of Don Sandalio, Chessplayer*), translated and edited by Kerrigan, Princeton University Press, 1976.

The Private World: Selections from the Diario Intimo and Selected Letters (Volume 2 of *Obras selectas* [*Selected Works*]), translated by Kerrigan, Lacy, and Nozick, edited by Kerrigan, Princeton University Press, 1984.

Miguel de Unamuno's Political Writings, 1918-1924, edited by G. D. Robertson, E. Mellen Press, 1996.

ANTHOLOGIES AND OMNIBUS VOLUMES IN SPANISH

Ensayos (essays), seven volumes, Fortanet, 1916-18, revised edition, two volumes, Aguilar, 1942.

Ensayos y sentencias de Unamuno, edited with introduction and notes by Wilfred A. Beardsley, Macmillan, 1932.

Prosa diversa, selected by J. L. Gili, Oxford University Press, 1939.

Antologia poetica (poetry), edited by Luis Felipe Vivanco, Escorial, 1942.

Antologia poetica (poetry), edited by Jose Maria de Cossio, Espasa-Calpe, 1946.

Obras selectas (selected works), Pleyade, 1946.

De esto y de aquello, edited by Garcia Blanco, Sudamericana, 1950.

Obras completas (collected works), Aguado, 1950-51.

Teatro: Fedra. Soledad. Raquel encadenada. Medea. (plays), edited by Garcia Blanco, Juventud, 1954.

Obras completas (collected works), ten volumes, edited by Garcia Blanco, Aguado, 1958-61.

Teatro completo, edited by Garcia Blanco, Aguilar, 1959.

Antologia, edited by Luis Gonzalez Seara, Doncel, 1960.

Antologia, Fondo de Cultura Economica, 1964.

El espejo de la muerte, y otros relatos novelescos, Juventud, 1965.

Cancionero: Antologia (poetry), selected by Ramos Gascon, Taurus, 1966.

Unamuno: Sus mejores paginas, edited by Philip Metzidakis, Prentice-Hall, 1966.

Obras completas, Las Americas, Volume 1: *Paisajes y ensayos,* Volume 2: *Novelas,* Volume 3: *Nuevos ensayos,* Volume 4: *La raza y la lengua,* Volume 5: *Teatro completo y monodialogos,* Volume 6: *Poesia,* Volume 7: *Meditaciones y ensayos espirituales,* 1966-69.

La agonia del cristianismo, Mi religion, y otros ensayos (collected essays), Las Americas, 1967.

Tres nivolas de Unamuno (novels), edited by Demetrios Basdekis, Prentice-Hall, 1971.

El porvenir de Espana y los espanoles (contains *El porvenir de Espana* and *Espana y los espanoles*), Espasa-Calpe, 1972.

Novela (novels), edited by Eugenio de Bustos Tovar, Noguer, 1976.

Antologia poetica (poetry), edited by Jose Maria Valverde, Alianza, 1977.

Antologia poetica (poetry), edited by Mercedes Santos Moray, Editorial Arte y Literatura, 1979.

Jubilacion de don Miguel de Unamuno: Cuaderno de la Magdalena y otros papeles (papers), Libreria Estudio, 1980.

Unamuno multiple: Antologia, edited by Amelia de del Rio, University of Puerto Rico, 1981.

La esfinge; La venda; Fedra (plays), edited by Jose Paulino, Castalia, 1987.

Poesia completa, Alianza, 1987–.

Nuevo Mundo, Editorial Trotta, 1994.

Works also published in multiple editions.

OTHER

Paisajes (travel), 1902, Aguado, 1950.

De mi pais (travel), F. Fe, 1903.

Por tierras de Portugal y de Espana (travel), V. Prieto, 1911.

Contra esto y aquello, Renacimiento, 1912.

(Editor) *Simon Bolivar, libertador de la America del Sur, por los mas grandes escritores americanos,* Renacimiento, 1914, reprinted with prologue by Manuel Trujillo as *Bolivar,* Biblioteca Ayacucho, 1983.

Andanzas y visiones espanolas (travel), Renacimiento, 1922.

Romancero del destierro, Alba, 1928.

La ciudad de Henoc: Comentario 1933, Seneca, 1941.

Cuenca iberica (lenguaje y paisaje), Seneca, 1943.

El caballero de la triste figura, Espasa-Calpe, 1944.

Almas de jovenes, Espasa-Calpe, 1944.

La dignidad humana, Espasa-Calpe, 1944.

Paisajes del alma, Revista de Occidente, 1944.

La enormidad de Espana, Seneca, 1945.

Madrid, Aguado, 1950.

Mi Salamanca, selected by Mario Grande Ramos, Escuelas Graficas de la Santa Casa de Misericordia, 1950.

(With Ruben Dario) *Don Jose Lazaro, 1862-1947,* edited by Antonio R. Rodriguez Monino, Castalia, 1951.

Viejos y jovenes, Espasa-Calpe, 1956.

Autodialogos, Aguilar, 1959.

Escritos de toros, Union de Bibliofilos Taurinos, 1964.

Mi bochito, selected by Garcia Blanco, Libreria Arturo, 1965.

La raza vasca y el vascuence: En torno a la lengua espanola, Espasa-Calpe, 1968.

(Translator) Arthur Schopenhauer, *Sobre la voluntad en la naturaleza,* Alianza, 1970.

Solitana (bilingual edition), edited by Pablo Bilbao and Emilia Doyaga, Washington Irving, 1970.

Libros y autores espanoles contemporaneos, Espasa-Calpe, 1972.

Monodialogos, Espasa-Calpe, 1972.

Gramatica y glosario del Poema del Cid, edited by Barbara D. Huntley and Pilar Liria, Espasa-Calpe, 1977.

La muerte de Ramirez y las olvidadas memorias del general Anacleto Medina, A. Pena Lillo, 1980.

Also translator of *Etica de las prisiones, Exceso de legislacion, De las leyes en general,* by Herbert Spencer, three volumes, 1895, *Historia de la economica politica,* by J. K. Ingram, c. 1895, and *Historia de las literaturas castellana y portuguesa,* by Ferdinand J. Wolf, two volumes, 1895 96.

MEDIA ADAPTATIONS: Julio de Hoyos adapted one of the novellas from *Tres novelas ejemplares, Nada menos que todo un hombre,* into a drama titled *Todo un hombre.*

SIDELIGHTS: "At his death in 1936," Arthur A. Cohen claimed in the *New York Times Book Review,* "Miguel de Unamuno was the most influential thinker in Spain, more renowned than his younger contemporary [Jose] Ortega y Gasset and regarded by his own aficionados as the greatest stylist in the Spanish language since Cervantes." Author of fiction, drama, poetry, philosophical essays, and a variety of nonfiction, Unamuno "dug deeper into the national spirit than any of his contemporaries, a generation whose collective project was the exploration of Spanishness," Enrique Fernandez proposed in the *Voice Literary Supplement.* "Quixote incarnate, he lived out his nationality to its logical philosophical conclusions. . . . The soul-searching of the first Spanish moderns, who would be called the generation of 1898, found its fullest expression in Unamuno. In poems, plays, novels, and essays," the critic continued, Unamuno questioned "Spanishness, modernity, science, politics, philosophy, faith, God, everything."

"The evolution of [Unamuno's] thought was marked by three books or great essays, more professions of faith than philosophical treatises:" *The Life of Don Quixote and Sancho, The Tragic Sense of Life in Men and Peoples,* and *The Agony of Christianity,* as Arturo and Ilsa Barea catalogued in their book *Unamuno.* In these works, Unamuno fought what *Nation* contributor Mark Van Doren referred to as "the windmills of despair," an emotion inspired by his knowledge of his own mortality. Nevertheless, the critic added, "Unamuno fights because he knows there is not a chance in the world to win. He has tasted the glory of absurdity. He has decided to hope what he cannot believe. He has discovered grounds for faith in the very fact that there are no grounds." Thus it was this "continuous struggle with death," according to Cohen, that for Unamuno "makes [life] worth living. . . . Any means by which a man subverts the kingdom of death is a triumph for life and, in Unamuno's clever logic, for eternity."

This conflict between faith and reason, between "the truth thought and the truth felt," Salvador de Madariaga remarked in *The Genius of Spain,* became the primary focus of Unamuno's meditations. "It is because *The Tragic Sense of Life* is the most direct expression of [Unamuno's conflict] that this book is his masterpiece." In this essay, Angel and Amelia de del Rio recounted in the introduction to *Abel Sanchez,* "Unamuno analyzes what he calls the tragic essence of modern civilization, resulting from the longing for knowledge which, guided by reason, has destroyed man's faith in God and in immortality, a faith necessary for his emotional life. Hence, modern humanity, incapable of solving the problem, is forced to struggle in uncertainty, and at the same time to strive after truth, a struggle and agony inherently tragic." In a style that would characterize all Unamuno's essays, the Bareas asserted, *The Tragic Sense of Life* "was not meant as an orderly philosophical treatise on the human condition, but as one man's record of his thoughts on life and death, confessed before his fellow-mortals with all the passionate sincerity of which that man was capable." The work "is the greatest of the many monologues Unamuno wrote," the critics continued. "Every bit of reasoning in it springs from his intimate spiritual needs; nothing is 'objective.' This is as he meant it to be, and he argues at the very beginning of the book that this subjectivity is the only truthful approach possible." The result, as Van Doren described it, was "modern Catholicism's richest, most passionate, most brilliant statement of the grounds that exist for faith in immortality, now that reason and science have done their worst."

In *The Life of Don Quixote and Sancho,* Unamuno brought a new approach to the literary essay. As Demetrios Basdekis summarized in his *Miguel de Unamuno,* "it is literary criticism which is not quite a critical essay; it is a novelizing of a particular novel and a theory of the novel in general; it is creative prose which is not quite prose fiction, although it sometimes borders on this." In arguing that the character of Don Quixote surpassed his creator— that Cervantes was unaware of his own work's implications— Unamuno "set forth the essential premise of all his intellectual criticism: madness is reality, and historical objectivity is madness," Cohen stated. Thus, "the chivalric vocation and undertakings of Don Quixote, continuously pragmatized by his sympathetic squire [Sancho Panza], are treated by Unamuno as the ultimate pilgrimage." "Don Quixote became in the eyes of Unamuno a prophet, a divinely inspired figure preaching the doctrine of quixotism, which is the doctrine of immortality through mundane glory, salvation through high-minded battle against the mean reality of the world," Howard T. Young postulated in *The Victorious Expression: A Study of Four Contemporary Spanish Poets.* "Turning Cervantine irony into the tragic irony of life, Unamuno exalted Don Quixote as a stirring figure struggling against human fate." "Unamuno's *The Life of Don Quixote and Sancho,*" concluded Basdekis, "is a major theoretical doctrine; in turn it is a huge step toward his 'novel of extreme situations' entitled *Mist.*"

Despite his success as an essayist and novelist, Unamuno "maintained that he would be best remembered by his poetry," the Bareas reported. "His rough-tongued poems with their blend of fervour and contemplation brought indeed a new note into Spanish lyrical poetry at the turn of the century, but their poetic form was never strong enough to absorb the sentiments and thoughts that inspired them." As Young outlined, Unamuno believed that "ideas—and, consequently, feelings, for in Unamuno the two could never be separated—take precedence over all other considerations. What the poet says is more important than how he says it; meter, rhyme, and pattern are secondary to content and emotion."

The intense emotions Unamuno brought to *The Christ of Velazquez* and his other works have led critics to observe a poetic sense in all his writing. "For Unamuno, a poem or novel (and he holds that a novel is but a poem) is the outpouring of a man's passion, the overflow of the heart which cannot help itself and lets go," Madariaga proposed. The Bareas similarly commented that "Unamuno's true poetic creation was the personality he projected into all his work; his 'agony,' his ceaseless struggle with himself and the universe, was the core of every one of his novels and stories, poems and essays." "His style, rather than the clear, orderly style of a philosopher, is always that of a poet, impassioned, full of images, sometimes difficult because of the abundance of allusions, paradoxes, digressions, parentheses, exclamations, and ingenious plays upon words and ideas," the del Rios wrote. Jose Ferrater Mora, in *Unamuno: A Philosophy of Tragedy,* similarly declared that in analyzing Unamuno's work, "it must always be kept in mind that a poetic *elan* breathes within it, that the written word is meant to be only a shadow of the creative voice. . . . Unamuno wanted to dissolve all 'genres,' all classifications, to fuse all 'genres' together in the deathless fountain of poetry. For Unamuno the only 'literary form' was the poem, and the numerous, perhaps infinite, forms that the poem adopts."

The author's poetic emphasis and concern with human mortality have led many critics to characterize his work as distinctively Spanish. Calling Unamuno "the greatest literary figure of Spain [of his time]," Madariaga asserted that the author "is head and shoulders above [his contemporaries] in the highness of his purpose and in the earnestness and loyalty with which, Quixote-like, he has served all through his life. . . . Unamuno, by the cross which he has chosen to bear, incarnates the spirit of modern Spain," the critic continued. "His eternal conflict between faith and reason, between life and thought, between spirit and intellect, between heaven and civilization, is the conflict of Spain herself." Cohen likewise noted a unique Spanish temperament in the

author's work; "the principal debate, the argument that undergirds all of Unamuno's life and thought and gives to it a power most peculiarly Spanish and most thoroughly universal . . . is Unamuno's contest with death." The critic elaborated, stating that "Spain, a culture which has stylized violence, is overwhelmed with death and committed to resurrection."

BIOGRAPHICAL/CRITICAL SOURCES:

BOOKS

Barea, Arturo, and Ilsa Barea, *Unamuno,* translated by I. Barea, Bowes & Bowes, 1952.

Basdekis, Demetrios, *Miguel de Unamuno,* Columbia University Press, 1969.

Ferrater Mora, Jose, *Unamuno: A Philosophy of Tragedy,* translated by Philip Silver, University of California Press, 1962.

Ilie, Paul, *Unamuno: An Existential View of Self and Society,* University of Wisconsin Press, 1967.

Jurkevich, Gayana, *The Elusive Self: Archetypal Approaches to the Novels of Miguel de Unamuno,* University of Missouri Press, 1991.

Lacy, Allen, *Miguel de Unamuno: The Rhetoric of Existence,* Mouton & Co., 1967.

Lopez, Julio, *Unamuno,* Jucar, 1985.

Madariaga, Salvador de, *The Genius of Spain, and Other Essays on Spanish Contemporary Literature,* Oxford University Press, 1923.

Marias, Julian, *Miguel de Unamuno,* translated by Frances M. Lopez-Morillas, Harvard University Press, 1966.

Nozick, Martin, *Miguel de Unamuno,* Twayne, 1971.

Rubia Barcia, Jose, and M. A. Zeitlin, editors, *Unamuno: Creator and Creation,* University of California Press, 1967.

Rudd, Margaret Thomas, *The Lone Heretic: A Biography of Miguel de Unamuno y Jugo,* University of Texas Press, 1963.

Tibbetts, Orlando L., *The Man of Salamanca,* Rutledge Books, 1996.

Twentieth-Century Literary Criticism, Gale, Volume 2, 1979; Volume 9, 1983.

Watson, Peggy W., *Intra-Historia in Miguel de Unamuno's Novels: A Continual Presence,* Scripta Humanistica, 1993.

Wyers, Frances, *Miguel de Unamuno: The Contrary Self,* Tamesis, 1976.

Young, Howard T., *The Victorious Expression: A Study of Four Contemporary Spanish Poets,* University of Wisconsin Press, 1964.

PERIODICALS

Hispania, December, 1941.
Humanities Association Bulletin, winter, 1970.
Modern Language Notes, Volume 79, number 2, 1964.
Modern Languages, June, 1973.
Nation, May 17, 1922; June 24, 1968.
New York Times Book Review, December 16, 1973.
Voice Literary Supplement, May, 1987.

*   *   *

UNCLE SHELBY
See SILVERSTEIN, Shel(by)

UNDSET, Sigrid 1882-1949

PERSONAL: Born May 20, 1882, in Kalundborg, Denmark; died after a stroke, June 10, 1949, in Lillehammer, Norway; daughter of Ingvald Martin (an archeologist) and Anna Charlotte Undset; married Anders C. Svarstad (an artist), 1912 (marriage annulled, 1924); children: Anders, Maren Charlotte, Hans. *Education:* Received secretarial certificate from Christiania Commercial College, c. 1898. *Religion:* Roman Catholic.

CAREER: German Electric Company, Christiania (now Oslo), Norway, secretary, c. 1898-1908. Full-time writer, 1908-49.

AWARDS, HONORS: Nobel Prize for literature from the Swedish Academy, 1928; Grand Cross of the Order of Saint Olav from King Haakon VII, 1947.

WRITINGS:

CONTEMPORARY NOVELS

Fru Marta Oulie (title means "Mrs. Marta Oulie"), Aschehoug, 1907.
Jenny, Aschehoug, 1911, translation by W. Emme published under the same title, Knopf, 1921.
Vaaren (title means "Spring"), Aschehoug, 1914.
Gymnadenia, Aschehoug, 1929, translation by Arthur G. Chater published as *The Wild Orchid,* Knopf, 1931.
Den brennende busk, Aschehoug, 1930, translation by Chater published as *The Burning Bush,* Knopf, 1932.
Ida Elisabeth, Aschehoug, 1932, translation by Chater published under the same title, Knopf, 1933.
Den trofaste hustru, Aschehoug, 1936, translation by Chater published as *The Faithful Wife,* Knopf, 1937.

HISTORICAL NOVELS

Fortellingen om Viga-Ljot og Vigdis [and] *Sankt Halvards liv, dod og jaertgen,* Aschehoug, 1909, translation of the former by Chater published as *Gunnar's Daughter,* Knopf, 1936.
Kristin Lavransdatter, three volumes, Aschehoug, Volume I: *Kransen,* 1920, translation by Charles Archer and J. S. Scott published as *The Bridal Wreath,* Knopf, 1923 (published in England as *The Garland,* Knopf, 1930), translated by Tiina Nunnally and published as *The Wreath,* Penguin, 1997; Volume II: *Husfrue,* 1921, translation by Archer published as *The Mistress of Husaby,* Knopf, 1925; Volume III: *Korset,* 1922, translation by Archer published as *The Cross,* Knopf, 1927; single volume Nobel Prize edition translated by Archer and Scott published as *Kristin Lavransdatter,* Knopf, 1929.
Olav Audunsson i Hestviken, two volumes, Aschehoug, 1925, two-volume translation by Chater published as *The Axe,* Knopf, 1928, and *The Snake Pit,* Knopf, 1929 (both volumes included in *The Master of Hestviken;* also see below).
Olav Audunsson og hans born, two volumes, Aschehoug, 1927, two-volume translation by Chater published as *In the Wilderness,* Knopf, 1929, and *The Son Avenger,* Knopf, 1930 (both volumes included in *The Master of Hestviken;* also see below).
The Master of Hestviken (contains novels *The Axe, The Snake Pit, In the Wilderness,* and *The Son Avenger*), translated by Chater, Nobel Prize edition, Knopf, 1934.
Madame Dorthea, Aschehoug, 1939, translation by Chater published under the same title, Knopf, 1940.
The Axe (originally published in Norwegian as part 1 of *Olav Audunsson i Hestviken*), Vintage Books, 1994.
The Snake Pit (originally published in Norwegian as part 2 of *Olav Audunsson i Hestviken*), Vintage Books, 1994.

The Son Avenger (originally published in Norwegian as part 2 of *Olav Audunsson og Hans Born*), Vintage Books, 1995.
In the Wilderness (originally published in Norwegian as part 1 of *Olav Audunsson og Hans Born*), Vintage Books, 1995.

OTHER

Den lykkelige alder (stories; title means "The Happy Age"), Aschehoug, 1908.
Fattige skjebner (stories; title means "Poor Fortunes"); contains "Forste mote," "Simonsen," "Selma Broter," "Omkring sedelighetaballet," "Froken Smith Tellefsen," and "Nikkedukken"), Aschehoug, 1912, translations of "Simonsen," "Selma Broter," and "Froken Smith Tellefsen" by Naomi Walford published in *Four Stories,* Knopf, 1959 (also see below).
Fortellinger om Kong Artur og ridderne av det Runde bord (adapted from Thomas Mallory's tales of King Arthur), Aschehoug, 1915.
Splinten av troldspeilet (contains *Fru Hjeld* and *Fru Waage*), Aschehoug, 1917, translation of *Fru Hjeld* by Chater published as *Images in a Mirror,* Knopf, 1938.
De kloge jomfruer (stories; title means "The Wise Virgins"; contains "Smaspiker," "Thjodolf," and "Gunvald og Emma"), Aschehoug, 1918, translation of "Thjodolf" by Walford published in *Four Stories,* Knopf, 1959 (also see below).
Et kvindesynspunkt (essays), Aschehoug, 1919.
Die saga von Vilmund Vidutan und seinen Gefaehrten (children's story), Hausen Verlagagesellschaft, 1931, translation published as *Sigurd and His Brave Companions: A Tale of Medieval Norway,* illustrations by Gunvor Bull Teilman, Knopf, 1943.
Etapper: Ny rakke (essays), Aschehoug, 1933, translation by Chater published as *Stages on the Road,* Knopf, 1934.
Elleve aar (autobiography; title means "Eleven Years"), Aschehoug, 1934, translation by Chater published as *The Longest Years,* Knopf, 1935.
Norske helgener (essays), Aschehoug, 1937, translation by E. C. Ramsden published as *Saga of Saints,* Longmans, Green, 1934.
Selvportretter og landskapsbilleder (essays), Aschehoug, 1938, translation by Chater published as *Men, Women, and Places,* Knopf, 1939.
Return to the Future (autobiography), translated by Henrietta C. K. Naeseth, Knopf, 1942.
(Editor) *True and Untrue, and Other Norse Tales* (based on original stories from Asbjoernsen and Moe's *Folkeeventyr*), illustrations by Frederick T. Chapman, Knopf, 1945.
Lykkelige dager (reminiscences), [Oslo], 1947, translation by Joran Birkeland published as *Happy Times in Norway,* Knopf, 1948.
Caterina av Siena (biography), Aschehoug, 1951, translation by Kate Austin-Lund published as *Catherine of Siena,* Sheed & Ward (New York), 1954.
Artikler og taler fra krigstiden, edited by A. H. Winsnes, Aschehoug, 1952.
Four Stories (contains "Thjodolf," "Selma Broter," "Simonsen," "Miss Smith-Tellefsen"), translated by Naomi Walford, Knopf, 1959.
Kirke og klosterliv: Tre essays fro norsk middelalder, Cappelen, 1963.
Djaere dea (letters), edited with foreword by Christianne Undset Svarstad, Cappelen, 1979.

Kritikk og tro: Tekster (essays), edited by Liv Bliksrud, St. Olav, 1982.

Sigrid Undset skriver hjem: En vandring gjennom enigrantarene i Amerika (letters), edited by Arne Skouen, Aschehoug, 1982.

Also author of a play titled *In the Gray Light of Dawn* and a verse collection; translator of various Icelandic tales. Work represented in anthologies, including *A Woman's Point of View,* 1919. Contributor to periodicals.

COLLECTED WORKS

Middelalder-romaner (medieval novels), ten volumes, Aschehoug, 1949.

Romaner og fortellinger fra nutiden (contemporary works), ten volumes, Aschehoug, 1964-65, reprinted as *Natidsverker,* twelve volumes, 1983.

Middelalder-verker (medieval works), eight volumes, Aschehoug, 1982.

SIDELIGHTS: Sigrid Undset won a secure place in literary history as one of the foremost authors of historical novels and as the most prominent Catholic author Scandinavia has produced. Carl F. Bayerschmidt, in his critical study *Sigrid Undset,* labeled the Norwegian novelist "one of the greatest realistic writers of the first half of the twentieth century." A. H. Winsnes, in *Sigrid Undset: A Study in Christian Realism,* called the author "the Christian realist *par excellence.*" Undset's works are powerful not only because of their moral message but also because of her mastery of technique: few other novelists have so accurately painted background and setting or so completely banned romanticism from their works. As Winsnes pointed out, Undset has been called "the [Emile] Zola of the Middle Ages." Very few other writers have understood so fully the past and its connection with the present. Winsnes noted that "history is Sigrid Undset's muse. No one since [thirteenth-century poet and historian] Snorri Sturluson has presented medieval Norway with such power."

The story of Unset's life is one of self-sacrifice and responsibility. Born in Kalundborg, Denmark, she was the eldest of three daughters of Anna Charlotte Undset and the renowned Norwegian archeologist Ingvald Undset. Ingvald Undset had come from Trondelag, an area of Norway accurately described in his daughter's masterpiece, *Kristin Lavransdatter* (1920-22). Anna Charlotte Undset, who was a reserved and proud woman, inspired respect in her daughter but not the deep affection that the child felt for her father—in the portrayal of Kristin's father Lavrans in *Kristin Lavransdatter,* Undset paid tribute to her own father. At the age of two, she moved with her family to the city of Christiania (now Oslo), where her father was associated with the archeological section of the University Museum. As Ingvald Undset's health declined (he had caught malaria on an expedition to the Mediterranean), the family moved frequently, and Undset became intimately acquainted with many areas of the city of Oslo. As the daughter of an archeologist, she acquired an acute sense of history; the Undset home was filled with books, and the child was encouraged by her father to read extensively, especially works of history and Old Norse sagas. When Undset was eleven years old, her father died, and the family experienced genuine poverty. Her autobiographical memoir, *Elleve aar* (*The Longest Years,* 1934), records memories of the first eleven years of her life. That she gave herself the name "Ingvild" in these memoirs suggests the strength of her attachment to and identification with her father.

Although Undset attended the liberal school of Ragna Nielsen and had the opportunity to enroll in the university, she chose at the age of fifteen to prepare for a secretarial career at the Christiania

Commercial College. Her certificate from this school a year later helped her to obtain a position in the local office of the German Electric Company, where she worked for ten years. Undset's intimate acquaintance with young working girls provided the material for many of her earliest works. In her free time from her secretarial job, Undset turned her hand to writing. She submitted a historical novel to the Gyldendal publishing house in Copenhagen only to be told that she should turn to modern themes that seemed more suited to her talents. Undset followed this advice, and her first contemporary social novel, *Fru Marta Oulie* (title means "Mrs. Marta Oulie"), appeared in the fall of 1907. After the publication of three additional works of moderate success, Undset felt secure enough to quit her job for a full-time career as a writer. In 1909 she received a travel grant from the Norwegian government and went to Rome, where she met her future husband, the painter Anders Svarstad. Married in 1912, the couple lived first in London and later in Norway, where Undset continued to produce fiction, nonfiction, and translations. After the births of three children—Anders, Maren Charlotte, and Hans—Svarstad and Undset eventually became estranged, and their marriage was annulled when she accepted the Catholic faith on All Saints' Day, November 24, 1924.

Remaining in Lillehammer, Norway, until 1940, Undset devoted herself both to her work, for which she received the Nobel Prize for literature in 1928, and to her children. Maren Charlotte, who was born retarded, lived only to the age of twenty-three; Anders, Undset's eldest son, was killed in 1940 when German armies invaded Norway. With Hans, her only surviving child, Undset then made the long journey through Sweden to Russia, from there to Japan, and from there to San Francisco. During the war, she channeled her considerable energies into the war effort, giving lectures, writing propaganda, and calling attention to the plight of occupied Norway. In August, 1945, she returned to her homeland, and in 1947 King Haakon VII conferred upon her the Grand Cross of the Order of Saint Olav for service to her country. On June 10, 1949, Undset died in Lillehammer. Her life provided the impetus for her works: her religious faith, her pride in the past of her people, and her assessment of motherhood as woman's most important calling are all mirrored in her imaginative works and clearly stated in her nonfiction.

The novel *Jenny* (1912), which caused a sensation in Scandinavian feminist circles, is the story of a promising young artist who commits suicide. Jenny has, along the way, had an affair with her fiance's father, borne a child out of wedlock, suffered through the death of that child, and experienced frustration as a creative artist. Whether Jenny's suicide is caused by her failure as an artist or by her failure in erotic and maternal relationships is open to interpretation. In any case, the work is the most successful of all of Undset's social novels with contemporary settings.

Several later works also treat realistically problems of sexual fidelity and parenthood, stressing the importance of forgiveness and presenting the child as the element that can weld the most disparate parents together. *Vaaren* (title means "Spring," 1914) describes the marriage of a young couple; *Splinten av troldspeilet* (half of which was later translated as *Images in a Mirror,* 1917) contains two short stories that deal with infidelity and a young wife's conflict between family and career; *De kloge jomfruer* (title means "The Wise Virgins," 1918) emphasizes the importance of motherhood. Written towards the end of Undset's career, *Ida Elisabeth* (1932) presents a wife who sacrifices her personal happiness to remain faithful to her marriage vows, and *Den trofaste hustru* (*The Faithful Wife,* 1936) records the disintegration of a childless marriage, though in the latter work a religious element new to the social novels is introduced. Through these novels Undset was placed squarely at the head of the women's movement in Scandinavia, whether she wished to be in that position or not. An intelligent, creative working woman who also experienced marriage and motherhood, she could write eloquently of the problems that beset such women.

As controversial as some of her novels of contemporary life may have been, none of them could compare with Undset's masterpieces of medieval life. Critics agree that it is the multi-volume *Kristin Lavransdatter* and the *Olav Audunsson* series (*The Master of Hestviken,* 1925-27), that have secured her place in literary history. Showing a mastery of style lacking in the novels of contemporary life, these works also reveal the understanding of vanished cultures and love of the past instilled in the writer by her father. Her intimate knowledge of the laws, culture, and history of earlier ages had given her a sense of the continuity of life. Despite the copious and meticulously accurate historical details that embellish these novels, there is nothing strange about the people who inhabit that distant world.

Kristin Lavransdatter consists of three volumes: *Kransen* (*The Bridal Wreath,* 1920), *Husfrue* (*The Mistress of Husaby,* 1921), and *Korset* (*The Cross,* 1922). In the first volume, the affectionate relationship between the upright Lavrans Bjørgulfsson and his beloved daughter Kristin is vividly portrayed; however, when Kristin defies her father to marry the man whom she loves and her father deems unworthy, the relationship is strained. The novel ends with a pregnant Kristin finally joined in wedlock with Erlend Nikulausson, the man of her choice. She has forced her father to acquiesce to her will, but she has used deception and is unaffected by the worst sin: she and Erlend have forced the suicide of Eline Ormsdatter, Erlend's former mistress and mother of his two illegitimate children. The Norwegian title *Kransen* is significant in more than one way. As a child Kristin had been frightened in the woods by an elf-maiden, who beckoned to her with a garland of flowers; according to Bayerschmidt, the elf-maiden "is a symbol of the beautiful but dangerous world of the senses which makes use of all its snares and temptations to entice people who would put their own desires and gratifications above the higher order of a supernatural will." Furthermore, in the second novel, Kristin must make a pilgrimage to the shrine of St. Olav and offer her golden "krans," symbol of her virginity, to the priests. The meaning in the garland and virginal golden ornament is thus twofold.

The second and third volumes of *Kristin Lavransdatter* detail further hardships. *The Mistress of Husaby* documents the unhappy marriage of Erlend and Kristin, whose selfish passion has brought unhappiness to many. Kristin must suffer the infidelity of her husband, his seeming indifference to their seven sons, and the loss of his estate because of his attempted coup against King Magnus. Kristin herself has been petty and vindictive; the thoughtless Erlend is never allowed to forget all the wrongs he has done her, and finally he leaves her to retire to a shack in the mountains—the last bit of property he owns. The third volume, *The Cross,* relates Kristin's disappointment in her sons after the violent death of Erlend—the oldest two join a monastery (the second of the youths has been afflicted with blindness), the youngest dies of illness, her twins move away to serve Knights in other parts of the country, another of the young men travels to Iceland, and the son who takes over the estate of Kristin's father is revealed as a weakling. In despair, Kristin joins a convent, where she is stricken with the Black Death and dies. In the course of the trilogy Kristin Lavransdatter has to learn to accept whatever destiny God inflicts

on her; she has to learn to subjugate her own will to the supernatural will, embodied in the figure of a holy monk, Brother Edvin. Here the work stresses the Medieval belief that the spiritual world has primacy over the material one, a belief with which Undset herself concurred but found lacking in most of her twentieth-century contemporaries.

The Master of Hestviken, which stretches from the second half of the thirteenth century to the early part of the fourteenth century, also pivots around guilt and unconfessed sin. In this work, as in *Kristin Lavransdatter,* two young people who love each other are separated by circumstances. When the young woman Ingunn becomes pregnant by the Icelander Teit, the protagonist Olav kills his rival and disposes of the body. He marries Ingunn and claims the child as his own. Throughout his life he bears the burden of his secret guilt. The book presents a gloomy picture: Olav, who has been moved by love for Ingunn and who cared for her tenderly throughout an extended illness, is unable to win the affection of Ingunn's child and of the daughter they have together. Eventually Olav is wounded and deformed in battle and at the end of the novel is prevented from confessing his crime by a stroke which deprives him of the power of speech. While Winsnes saw the novel's conclusion as pessimistic, Margaret Mary Dunn, in her two *Scandinavian Studies* articles, disagreed, contending that Olav eventually comes to realize that the greatest sin "is to despair of God's mercy." Chosen by God to bear much, the Job-like Olav thus becomes the man who "does full penance." "Throughout a lifetime of purgation," Dunn asserted, "Olav's spirit has been purified like gold in a furnace, and it is thus exultant at the end of the novel."

Undset's descriptions of nature in *Kristin Lavransdatter* and *The Master of Hestviken* reveal her appreciation of the land. Moreover, nature is used to suggest the medieval consciousness of the continuity of life. Characters feel themselves links in a chain tied to a single location: ancestors and coming generations thus take precedence over individuals. The emphasis on genealogy, on the extended family, and on topography is reminiscent of the old Icelandic family sagas, by which Undset was heavily influenced. In *The Longest Years,* for instance, she recorded the thematic and stylistic importance of Norse sagas—especially *Nal's Saga*—on her own work.

Undset's last historical novel is *Madame Dorthea,* published in incomplete form in 1939. The writer abandoned the work when she fled Norway at the onset of World War II, and after 1939 she turned her energies to the war effort and to nonfiction. Set in the eighteenth century, the Age of Enlightenment, *Madame Dorthea* charts the title figure's efforts to solve the mystery of her husband's unexplained disappearance. An intelligent and rational woman, she seeks logical explanations to an enigma. Much of the almost plotless novel concerns the contrast between Madame Dorthea's intellectualism and the fervent belief of the Catholic, Scharlach.

Madame Dorthea, the medieval historical novels, and some of the social novels of contemporary times clearly contain religious themes. At least two of the later novels with modern settings may be regarded primarily as Catholic propaganda. *Gymnadenia* (*The Wild Orchid,* 1929) and its sequel, *Den Brennende busk* (*The Burning Bush,* 1930), chart the conversion to Catholicism of Paul Selmer. Bayerschmidt stated that Paul's long struggle for truth "reflects Sigrid Undset's own development from an agnostic or freethinker to a believing Christian, so that the novel [cycle] may be considered the most autobiographical of all her works." Once again in these works the theme of the renunciation of selfish passion in favor of familial responsibility is explored.

Whether they are set in modern times or in the Middle Ages, Undset's works explore both the importance of the family and the dangers inherent in selfish physical passion. Undset had an understanding of sensuality and a dislike of prudishness, but she also realized the risks to the psyche passion poses. As Bayerschmidt explained, "Physical love has no rights of its own when it comes into conflict with moral and ethical laws. This is a thought which finds a constant echo in [Undset's] entire literary production." Although an emancipated woman herself, the novelist considered the natural desire of women to be for home and children and felt that a career should not be pursued instead of motherhood but only in addition to it. In "Some Observations on the Emancipation of Women," the writer claimed that "the loneliest and most worn-out worker at a typewriter, in office, shop or factory, or at a sewing machine has the right to hope and wait and dream of a happiness as a lover and wife and mother." The heroine of the early novel *Jenny* longs for family and despairs over the death of her child; art cannot fill the void for her. She realizes, according to Bayerschmidt, that "women can never reach the point where their work means everything to them." Motherhood is, in Undset's view, woman's inescapable destiny.

The question of whether Undset was a feminist or an antifeminist is a thorny one; selective quoting can produce arguments for either side. Bayerschmidt maintained that "Sigrid Undset was not a militant feminist, but neither was she an antifeminist. She believed that every woman should be free to practice an art or a profession or occupy herself in any form of work without losing the right to love and to establish a family." It was after the children were in bed that the author worked on her novels. In her portrait of Kristin Lavransdatter, Undset presents in a negative light Kristin's defiance of her father. On the other hand, Undset shows us a Kristen who lives for her seven sons and who, as mistress of Husaby, efficiently manages an estate and a family. Thus, if Undset's message is conservative in essence, it is also liberal in the respect that it confirms a woman's right to excel in whatever field she might choose.

BIOGRAPHICAL/CRITICAL SOURCES:

BOOKS

Bayerschmidt, Carl F., *Sigrid Undset*, Twayne, 1970.
Beach, Joseph Warren, *The Twentieth Century Novel: Studies in Technique*, Appleton-Century-Crofts, 1932.
Dunn, Margaret, Sister, *Paradigms and Paradoxes in the Life and Letters of Sigrid Undset*, University Press of America, 1994.
Hudson, Deal W., editor, *Sigrid Undset: On Saints and Sinners*, Ignatius Press, 1994.
McFarlane, James Walter, *Ibsen and the Temper of Norwegian Literature*, Oxford University Press, 1960.
Twentieth-Century Literary Criticism, Volume 3, Gale (Detroit), 1980.
Vinde, Victor, *Sigrid Undset: A Nordic Moralist*, translated by Babette Hughes and Glenn Hughes, University of Washington Book Store, 1930.
Winsnes, A. H., *Sigrid Undset: A Study in Christian Realism*, translated by P. G. Foote, Sheed & Ward, 1953.

PERIODICALS

American-Scandinavian Review, June, 1929; July, 1929.
Books Abroad, winter, 1950.
Critic, January-February, 1974.
Library Journal, March 15, 1995, p. 102.

Literary Review, April, 1923.
Ms., January, 1981.
New Republic, October 5, 1921.
Saturday Review of Literature, June 2, 1928.
Scandinavian Studies, November, 1966; August, 1968.
Thought, spring, 1965.

*   *   *

UPDIKE, John (Hoyer) 1932-

PERSONAL: Born March 18, 1932, in Shillington, PA; son of Wesley Russell (a teacher) and Linda Grace (an author; maiden name, Hoyer) Updike; married Mary Entwistle Pennington, June 26, 1953 (divorced, 1977); married Martha Ruggles Bernhard, September 30, 1977; children: (first marriage) Elizabeth Pennington, David Hoyer, Michael John, Miranda; (second marriage) three stepchildren. *Education:* Harvard University, A.B. (summa cum laude), 1954; attended Ruskin School of Drawing and Fine Art, Oxford, 1954-55. *Politics:* Democrat. *Religion:* Christian.

ADDRESSES: Home—Beverly Farms, MA 01915.

CAREER: Novelist, critic, short story writer, poet, essayist, and dramatist. *The New Yorker*, reporter for the "Talk of the Town" column, 1955-57. Visited the U.S.S.R. as part of a cultural exchange program of U.S. Department of State, 1964.

MEMBER: American Academy and Institute of Arts and Letters (chancellor).

AWARDS, HONORS: Guggenheim fellowship in poetry, 1959; American Academy and National Institute of Arts and Letters Richard and Hinda Rosenthal Foundation Award, 1960, for *The Poorhouse Fair*; National Book Award in fiction, 1963, for *The Centaur*; Prix Medicis Etranger, 1966, for *The Centaur*; O. Henry Award for fiction, 1966, for short story, "The Bulgarian Poetess"; Fulbright fellow in Africa, 1972; American Book Award nomination, 1980, for *Too Far to Go*; Edward MacDowell Medal for Literature, MacDowell Colony, 1981; Pulitzer Prize for fiction, American Book Award, and National Book Critics Circle award for fiction, all 1982, all for *Rabbit Is Rich*; National Book Critics Circle award for criticism, 1984, for *Hugging the Shore: Essays in Criticism*; Medal of Honor for Literature, National Arts Club (New York City), 1984; National Book Critics Circle award in fiction nomination, 1986, for *Roger's Version*; PEN/Malamud Memorial Prize, PEN/Faulkner Award Foundation, 1988, for "excellence in short story writing"; National Book Critics Circle Award and Pulitzer Prize, both 1991, both for *Rabbit at Rest*.

WRITINGS:

NOVELS

The Poorhouse Fair (also see below), Knopf, 1959.
Rabbit, Run (also see below), Knopf, 1960.
Centaur, Knopf, 1963.
Of the Farm, Knopf, 1965.
The Poorhouse Fair [and] *Rabbit, Run*, Modern Library, 1965.
Couples, Knopf, 1968.
Rabbit Redux (also see below), Knopf, 1971.
A Month of Sundays, Knopf, 1975.
Marry Me: A Romance, Knopf, 1976.
The Coup, Knopf, 1978.
Rabbit Is Rich (also see below), Knopf, 1981.
Rabbit Is Rich/Rabbit Redux/Rabbit, Run, Quality Paperback Book Club, 1981.

The Witches of Eastwick, Knopf, 1984.
Roger's Version, Knopf, 1986.
S., Knopf, 1988.
Rabbit at Rest, Fawcett, 1990.
Memories of the Ford Administration, Knopf, 1992.
Brazil, Knopf, 1994, limited signed edition, Franklin Library, 1994.
Rabbit Angstrom: A Tetralogy (contains *Rabbit, Run; Rabbit Redux; Rabbit Is Rich;* and *Rabbit at Rest*), Knopf, 1995.
In the Beauty of the Lilies, Knopf, 1996.
Toward the End of Time, Knopf, 1997.

POETRY

The Carpentered Hen and Other Tame Creatures (also see below), Harper, 1958, published as *Hoping for a Hoopoe,* Gollancz, 1959.
Telephone Poles and Other Poems (also see below), Knopf, 1963.
Verse: The Carpentered Hen and Other Tame Creatures/Telephone Poles and Other Poems, Fawcett, 1965.
The Angels (poem; limited edition), King and Queen Press (Pensacola, FL), 1968.
Bath after Sailing (poem; limited edition), Pendulum Press (Monroe, CT), 1968.
Midpoint and Other Poems, Knopf, 1969.
Seventy Poems, Penguin, 1972.
Six Poems (limited edition), Oliphant Press, 1973.
Cunts (poem; limited edition), Frank Hallman, 1974.
Tossing and Turning, Knopf, 1977.
Sixteen Sonnets (limited edition), Halty Ferguson (Cambridge, MA), 1979.
Five Poems (limited edition), Bits Press, 1980.
Spring Trio (limited edition), Palaemon Press (Winston-Salem, NC), 1982.
Jester's Dozen (limited edition), Lord John (Northridge, CA), 1984.
Facing Nature: Poems, Knopf, 1985.
A Soft Spring Night in Shillington (limited edition), Lord John, 1986.
Collected Poems: 1953-1993, Knopf, 1993.

SHORT STORIES

The Same Door, Knopf, 1959.
Pigeon Feathers and Other Stories, Knopf, 1962.
Olinger Stories: A Selection, Vintage, 1964.
The Music School, Knopf, 1966.
Bech: A Book, Knopf, 1970.
Museums and Women and Other Stories, Knopf, 1972.
Warm Wine: An Idyll (short story; limited edition), Albondocani Press (New York), 1973.
Couples: A Short Story (limited edition), Halty Ferguson, 1976.
From the Journal of a Leper (short story; limited edition), Lord John, 1978.
Too Far to Go: The Maples Stories, Fawcett, 1979.
Three Illuminations in the Life of an American Author (short story; limited edition), Targ (New York), 1979.
Problems and Other Stories, Knopf, 1979.
Your Lover Just Called: Stories of Joan and Richard Maple, Penguin Books, 1980.
The Chaste Planet (short story; limited edition), Metacom (Worcester, MA), 1980.
People One Knows: Interviews with Insufficiently Famous Americans (limited edition), Lord John, 1980.
Invasion of the Book Envelopes (short story; limited edition), Ewert (Concord, MA), 1981.

Bech Is Back, Knopf, 1982.
The Beloved (short story; limited edition), Lord John, 1982.
Confessions of a Wild Bore (short story; limited edition), Tamazunchale Press, 1984.
A & P (short story; limited edition), Redpath Press, 1986.
More Stately Mansions: A Story (short story; limited edition), Nouveau Press (Jackson, MS), 1987.
Trust Me: Short Stories, Knopf, 1987.
Brother Grasshopper (short story; limited edition), Metacom Press, 1990.
The Afterlife and Other Stories, Knopf, 1994.
Golf Dreams: Writings on Golf, Knopf, 1996.
Bech at Bay, Knopf, 1998.

ESSAYS

Assorted Prose, Knopf, 1965.
On Meeting Authors (essay; limited edition), Wickford (Newburyport, MA), 1968.
A Good Place (essay; limited edition), Aloe, 1973.
Picked-Up Pieces, Knopf, 1975.
Hub Fans Bid Kid Adieu (essay; limited edition), Lord John, 1977.
Talk from the Fifties (limited edition), Lord John, 1979.
Ego and Art in Walt Whitman (essay; limited edition), Targ, 1980.
Hawthorne's Creed (essay; limited edition), Targ, 1981.
Hugging the Shore: Essays and Criticism, Knopf, 1983.
Emersonianism (essay; limited edition), Bits Press, 1984.
Just Looking: Essays on Art, Knopf, 1989.
Odd Jobs: Essays and Criticism, Knopf, 1991.
Concert at Castle Hill, Lord John, 1992.

OTHER

(Contributor of short story) Martin Levin, editor, *Five Boyhoods,* Doubleday, 1962.
(Adapter with Warren Chappell of libretto of Mozart's opera) *The Magic Flute* (juvenile fiction), Knopf, 1962.
(Adapter with Chappell of libretto of Wagner's opera) *The Ring* (juvenile fiction), Knopf, 1964.
A Child's Calendar (juvenile poetry), Knopf, 1965.
Three Texts from Early Ipswich (historical pageant; produced in Ipswich, MA, 1968), 17th Century Day Committee of the Town of Ipswich, 1968.
(Adapter) *Bottom's Dream* (from William Shakespeare's *A Midsummer Night's Dream;* juvenile fiction), Knopf, 1969.
(Editor) David Levine, *Pens and Needles: Literary Caricatures,* Gambit, 1970.
(Contributor of translations) Norman Thomas di Giovanni, editor, Jorge Luis Borges, *Selected Poems: 1923-1967,* Delacorte, 1972.
A Good Place: Being a Personal Account of Ipswich, Massachusetts, Aloe Editions (New York), 1973.
Buchanan Dying (play; produced in Lancaster, MA, 1976), Knopf, 1974.
(Author of introduction) Henry Green, *Loving, Living, Party Going,* Penguin Books, 1978.
(Author of introduction) Bruno Schulz, *Sanatorium under the Sign of the Hourglass,* Penguin Books, 1979.
(Author of afterword) Edmund Wilson, *Memoirs of Hecate County,* Nonpareil, 1980.
(Editor with Shannon Ravenel and author of introduction) *The Best American Short Stories: 1984,* Houghton, 1984.
(Contributor of translations) William Meredith, editor, *Poets of Bulgaria,* Unicorn Press, 1985.
Self-Consciousness: Memoirs, Knopf, 1989.
The Alligators (for children), Creative Education, 1989.

Conversations with John Updike, University Press of Mississippi, 1994.

A Helpful Alphabet of Friendly Objects (children's poems), illustrated by David Updike, Knopf, 1995.

Also author with Gunther Schuller of words and music for "The Fisherman and His Wife," performed at Savoy Theatre in Boston, MA, by the Opera Company of Boston, May, 1970. "Talk of the Town" reporter, *New Yorker,* 1955-57. Contributor of short stories, book reviews, and poems to the *New Yorker,* and to numerous other periodicals. A collection of Updike's papers are found in the Houghton Library, Harvard University.

MEDIA ADAPTATIONS: Couples was purchased by United Artists in 1969; *Rabbit, Run* was filmed by Warner Bros. in 1970; *Bech: A Book* was adapted for a play entitled, *Bech Takes Pot Luck,* produced in New York at Theatre Guild, 1970; *The Music School* was networked by Public Broadcasting System, 1976; *Too Far to Go* was made into a television movie by National Broadcasting Co. in March, 1979, later revised and released for theater distribution by Sea Cliff Productions, 1982; director George Miller's movie *The Witches of Eastwick,* 1987, was loosely based on Updike's novel of the same title; "The Christian Roommates," a short story, was made into a ninety-minute movie for television.

SIDELIGHTS: John Updike "has earned an . . . imposing stance on the literary landscape," writes *Los Angeles Times* contributor Katherine Stephen, "earning virtually every American literary award, repeated best-sellerdom and the near-royal status of the American author-celebrity." However hailed by critics and readers as one of America's great novelists, John Updike has also acquired his share of detractors. As Joseph Kanon explains in *Saturday Review:* "The debate over John Updike's work has long since divided itself into two pretty firmly entrenched camps: those who admire the work consider him one of the keepers of the language; those who don't say he writes beautifully about nothing very much."

Updike acknowledges this charge but believes the complaint lacks validity. "There is a great deal to be said about almost anything," Updike explained to Jane Howard in a *Life* magazine interview. "Everything can be as interesting as every other thing. An old milk carton is worth a rose. . . . The idea of a hero is aristocratic. Now either nobody is a hero or everyone is. I vote for everyone. My subject is the American Protestant small town middle class. I like middles. It is in middles that extremes clash, where ambiguity restlessly rules. . . . There's a 'yes-but' quality about my writing that evades entirely pleasing anybody. It seems to me that critics get increasingly querulous and impatient for madder music and stronger wine, when what we need is a greater respect for reality, its secrecy, its music."

Debate about the effectiveness of Updike's writing began in 1957 with publication of *The Poorhouse Fair,* his first novel. As Curt Suplee notes in his *Washington Post* profile of the author: "Updike's fiction is not overburdened by action, and his spare story lines are embellished with a lush and elegantly wrought style that some readers find majestic (John Barth calls him the Andrew Wyeth of American writers) and others intolerable. Norman Podhoretz described his prose in 'The Poorhouse Fair' as 'overly lyrical, bloated like a child who has eaten too much candy.'" Other critics saw the novel differently than Podhoretz; in the *New York Times,* for example, Donald Barr called the book "a work of art." And, in the *Chicago Sunday Tribune* Fanny Butcher referred

to "the author's brilliant use of words and . . . his subtle observations."

"There is one point on which his critics all agree," observes Rachael C. Burchard in *John Updike: Yea Sayings.* "His style is superb. His work is worth reading if for no reason other than to enjoy the piquant phrase, the lyric vision, the fluent rhetoric." In a cover story on the author *Time* magazine's Paul Gray claimed: "No one else using the English language over the past two and a half decades has written so well in so many ways as he." And, a reviewer for *Books Abroad* noted, "Critics continually comment on the technical virtuosity of Updike," while in *John Updike* Suzanne Henning Uphaus declared, "In the midst of diversity there are certain elements common to all of Updike's writing. Most important, there is Updike's remarkable mastery of language."

However, in direct contrast to the glowing evaluations of Burchard, Gray, and others that might agree with them, are the opinions of still other commentators who fail to see Updike's work in such a favorable light. For example, in her *Partisan Review* commentary on *Couples,* Elizabeth Dalton asserts, "In its delicacy and fullness Updike's style seems to register a flow of fragments almost perfectly toned. And yet, after pages and pages of his minutely detailed impressions, the accumulated effect is one of waste." John W. Aldridge writes in *Time to Murder and Create: The Contemporary Novel in Crisis* that the novelist "has none of the attributes we conventionally associate with major literary talent. He does not have an interesting mind. He does not possess remarkable narrative gifts or a distinguished style. He does not create dynamic or colorful or deeply meaningful characters. . . . In fact, one of the problems he poses for the critic is that he engages the imagination so little that one has real difficulty remembering his work long enough to think clearly about it." "Updike has difficulty in reining in his superfluous facility with words," Edward Hoagland complains in the *New York Times Book Review.* "He is too fluent."

"Much criticism of John Updike's fiction derives from the same middle-class repressions he writes about," Robert Detweiler notes in *Twentieth Century Literature.* Thus, many of the most disparaging reviews of Updike's work have come from critics that object not only to his writing style, but also to the author's subject matter. Commenting on the frenzy of criticism from reviewers that met the 1968 publication of *Couples,* Updike's explicit look at sexual freedom in a small New England town, Detweiler notes in *John Updike,* "As frequently happens, the furor accompanying the depiction of sexual amorality increased the difficulty of judging the novel's artistic quality. Most of the reviews appeared to be impulsive reactions to the subject matter rather than measured assessments." In the case of this novel, negative critical response did nothing to tone down public enthusiasm for the work: it appeared on the *Publishers Weekly* best-seller list for thirty-six weeks.

Couples wasn't the first Updike novel to deal with the sexual habits of middle-class America or to receive disapproving reviews from commentators upset by the author's frank language. "Looking back," writes Eliot Fremont-Smith in the *Village Voice,* "it must have been the sexuality that so upset the respectable critics of *Rabbit, Run* in 1960. Their consternation had to do with what seemed a great divide between John Updike's exquisite command of prose . . . and the apparent no-good vulgar nothing he expended it on." *Rabbit, Run* was the first installment in Updike's continuing saga of Harry "Rabbit" Angstrom which would later include *Rabbit Redux* and, the highly celebrated *Rabbit Is Rich.* Published at ten-year intervals, the novels follow the life of "Rabbit" as he first tries to leave his marriage, later, as he discovers his wife has been unfaithful and finds himself laid off from his blue-collar job, and, later yet, as he confronts middle age.

Although the third volume in Updike's series of Rabbit novels received the Pulitzer Prize, the National Book Critics Circle award, and the American Book Award, some critics found its sexual focus offensive. While claiming the book "reeks of vulgarity," in his *Washington Post* review of *Rabbit Is Rich,* for example, Jonathan Yardley writes, "Updike fancies himself the chronicler of the common man, and he fills page after page with the most clinical evidence of that fellow's gaucherie." Others viewed the sexual content of the book (and the other two volumes in the planned tetralogy) as merely a part of what they considered to be Updike's accurate depictions of U.S. society. Anthony Quinton's London *Times* review seems to summarize the feeling of many critics when he observes, "The Rabbit novels are John Updike's best since they give the fullest scope to his remarkable gifts as observer and describer. What they amount to is a social and, so to speak, emotional history of the United States over the last twenty years or more, the period of Rabbit's and his creator's conscious life."

America's sexual mores have continued to be a dominant subject in Updike's fiction along with the additional theme of religion. In his *John Updike and the Three Great Secret Things,* George Hunt suggests that sex and religion along with art "characterize the predominant subject matter, thematic concerns, and central questions found throughout [Updike's] adult fiction." According to *Contemporary Authors Bibliographical Series* contributor Donald J. Greiner, Updike criticism has in fact shifted since the 1960s from a consideration of the novelist's style to a focus on his themes and how they interrelate. "Later commentators," Greiner asserts, "are concerned with his intellectually rigorous union of theology and fiction and with his suggestion that sex is a kind of emerging religion in the suburban enclaves of the middle class."

Exploring the interrelatedness of sex and religion in Updike's fiction, Jean Strouse observes in a *Newsweek* review of Updike's *Bech Is Back,* "Readers and critics have accused Updike of being obsessed with sex. Maybe—but I think he is using Harry Angstrom [from his 'Rabbit' novels], and Piet Hanema in 'Couples,' and Richard Maple in 'Too Far to Go,' to explore that modern search for 'something behind all this . . . that wants me to find it.' Melville—and many others—may have announced the demise of God, but nobody has managed to excise the desire for something beyond death and daily life, a desire that has in the 20th century shifted its focus from God to sex." The *New York Times*'s Michiko Kakutani offers a similar explanation of the development of what he calls Updike's "favorite preoccupations" in his review of *Roger's Version.* "His heroes, over the years, have all suffered from 'the tension and guilt of being human.' Torn between vestigial spiritual yearnings and the new imperatives of self-fulfillment, they hunger for salvation even as they submit to the importunate demands of the flesh."

In *Toward the End of Time,* Updike, in the tradition of Kurt Vonnegut, spins the tale of Ben Turnbull, a retired financier stricken with prostate cancer in the dystopic near future. The dying protagonist may be losing his mind, or he may be hitting tripwires in time that send him spiralling into past lives, including those of the Apostle Mark, a medieval monk, and a Nazi camp guard. Turnbull's inner life—his bouts with panic, nostalgia, and

sexual obsession—forms the core of the novel, which unfolds in fragments and through journal passages.

Many critics failed to appreciate Updike's experiment. Robert Boyers, writing in the *New Republic,* claims that the novel's chief fault is that it ascribes a universal significance to Turnbull's plight that it did not merit. "To mistake one's own spiritual condition for the final measure of reality." Boyers wrote, "to confuse one's own aggrieved, attenuated shadow on the wall with being itself in all its variety, is to offer a terribly impoverished version of experience." Other critics found fault with the novel's structure. A reviewer for the *Economist* calls *Toward the End of Time* "an absurdly ambitious novel in which a writer who has scarcely written a bad sentence in his previous 46 books finally over-reaches himself."

Still, Updike's skill in portraying the anxieties and frustrations of middle-America seems to be the feature most mentioned by approving critics. "He is our unchallenged master at evoking the heroic void of ordinary life," Suplee maintains, "where small braveries contend in vain against the nagging entropy of things, where the fear of death drips from a faulty faucet and supermarket daydreams turn to God. With heart-clutching clarity, he transmutes the stubborn banality of middle-class existence into tableaux that shiver with the hint of spiritual meaning." "His work has not only lyrically defined the joys and sorrows of the American middle class," Kakutani concludes, "but also gives—as he once wrote of another author—'the happy impression of an oeuvre, of a continuous task carried forward variously, of a solid personality, of a plenitude of gifts explored, knowingly.'"

BIOGRAPHICAL/CRITICAL SOURCES:

BOOKS

Aldridge, John W., *Time to Murder and Create: The Contemporary Novel in Crisis,* McKay, 1966.

Bloom, Harold, *John Updike: Modern Critical Views,* Chelsea House, 1987.

Burchard, Rachel C., *John Updike: Yea Sayings,* Southern Illinois University Press, 1971.

Campbell, Jeff H., *Updike's Novels: Thorns Spell a Word,* Midwestern State University Press, 1987.

Concise Dictionary of American Literary Biography, 1968-1987, Gale (Detroit), 1989.

Contemporary Authors Bibliographical Series, Volume 1, Gale, 1986.

Contemporary Literary Criticism, Gale, Volume 1, 1973; Volume 2, 1974; Volume 3, 1975; Volume 5, 1976; Volume 7, 1977; Volume 9, 78; Volume 13, 1980; Volume 15, 1980; Volume 23, 1983; Volume 34, 1985; Volume 43, 1987; Volume 70, 1992.

De Bellis, Jack, editor, *John Updike: A Bio-Bibliography, 1967-1993,* Greenwood Publishing, 1994.

Detweiler, Robert C., *John Updike,* Twayne, 1972, revised edition, 1984.

Detweiler, Robert C., *John Updike,* Twayne, 1984.

Dictionary of Literary Biography, Gale, Volume 2: *American Novelists since World War II,* 1978; Volume 5: *American Poets since World War II,* 1980; Volume 143: *American Novelists since World War II,* 1994.

Dictionary of Literary Biography Documentary Series, Volume 3, Gale, 1983.

Dictionary of Literary Biography Yearbook, Gale, *1980,* 1981, *1982,* 1983.

Greiner, Donald J., *Adultery in the American Novel: Updike, James, and Hawthorne,* University of South Carolina Press, 1985.

Greiner, Donald J., *John Updike's Novels,* Ohio University Press, 1984.

Greiner, Donald J., *The Other John Updike: Poems/Short Stories/ Prose/Play,* Ohio University Press, 1981.

Hunt, George, *John Updike and the Three Great Secret Things,* Eerdmans, 1980.

Macnaughton, William R., editor, *Critical Essays on John Updike,* G. K. Hall, 1982.

Newman, Judie, *John Updike,* St. Martin's, 1988.

O'Connell, Mary, *Updike and the Patriarchal Dilemma: Masculinity in the Rabbit Novels,* Southern Illionis University Press, 1996.

Ristoff, Dilvo I., *Updike's America: The Presence of Contemporary American History in John Updike's Rabbit Trilogy,* Peter Lang, 1988.

Schiff, James A., *Updike's Version: Rewriting "The Scarlet Letter,"* University of Missouri Press, 1992.

Searles, George J., *The Fiction of Philip Roth and John Updike,* Southern Illinois University Press, 1985.

Short Story Criticism, Gale, Volume 13, 1993.

Tallent, Elizabeth, *Married Men and Magic Tricks: John Updike's Erotic Heroes,* Creative Arts, 1981.

Thorburn, David, and Howard Eiland, editors, *John Updike: A Collection of Critical Essays,* G. K. Hall, 1982.

Uphaus, Suzanne Henning, *John Updike,* Ungar, 1980.

Wood, Ralph C., *The Comedy of Redemption: Christian Faith and Comic Vision in Four American Novelists,* University of Notre Dame Press, 1988.

PERIODICALS

America, February 24, 1990, p. 179; November 13, 1993, p. 22; August 13, 1994, p. 20.

Atlantic Monthly, April, 1988, p. 78; January, 1993, p. 125; November, 1997.

Books Abroad, winter, 1967.

Chicago Sunday Tribune, January 11, 1959.

Commonweal, May 17, 1991, p. 315; April 8, 1994.

Economist, January 29, 1994, p. 92; February 24, 1996, p. 89; November 15, 1997.

Library Journal, October 15, 1994, p. 89; December, 1995, p. 160.

Life, November 4, 1966.

Los Angeles Times, January 4, 1987.

Maclean's, May 29, 1989, p. 60; December 7, 1992, p. 59; April 11, 1994, p. 65A; February 26, 1996, p. 70; November 3, 1997.

Modern Fiction Studies (special issue on Updike), spring, 1974; autumn, 1975; (special issue on Updike) spring, 1991.

Nation, July 10, 1989, p. 59; December 3, 1990, p. 688; February 12, 1996, p. 25; November 3, 1997.

New Leader, April 18, 1988, p. 20; December 27, 1993, p. 28; December 18, 1995, p. 27; December 1, 1997.

New Republic, February 2, 1987, p. 41; June 20, 1988, p. 39; March 21, 1994, p. 40; May 27, 1996, p. 29; November 17, 1997.

New Statesman, September 18, 1987, p. 31; September 25, 1987, p. 31; April 8, 1994, p. 41; February 10, 1995, p. 44; May 3, 1996, p. 37.

Newsweek, November 15, 1971; September 28, 1981; October 18, 1982; November 9, 1992, p. 68; November 14, 1994, p. 96; October 13, 1997.

New Yorker, November 23, 1993, p. 145; January 18, 1993, p. 104; February 14, 1994, p. 101; March 11, 1996, p. 105; December 8, 1997.

New York Review of Books, April 11, 1968; August 8, 1974; April 3, 1975; November 19, 1981; November 18, 1982; November 24, 1983; June 14, 1984; December 4, 1986; May 12, 1988, p. 3; May 18, 1989, p. 3; October 25, 1990, p. 11; December 17, 1992, p. 45; May 12, 1994, p. 23; June 23, 1994, p. 21; December 4, 1997.

New York Times, January 11, 1959; October 7, 1982; August 27, 1986; September 19, 1996, p. B5.

New York Times Book Review, March 18, 1962; April 7, 1963; April 7, 1968; June 21, 1970; November 14, 1971; September 27, 1981; October 17, 1982; September 18, 1983; May 13, 1984; August 31, 1986; April 26, 1987, p. 1; March 13, 1988, p. 7; March 5, 1989, p. 7; October 15, 1989, p. 12; September 30, 1990, p. 1; November 10, 1991, p. 12; November 1, 1992, p. 11; February 6, 1994, pp. 1, 27; November 6, 1994, p. 7; January 28, 1996, p. 96; December 7, 1997.

New York Times Sunday Magazine, December 10, 1978.

Partisan Review, winter, 1969.

People Weekly, March 21, 1994, p. 30; February 5, 1996, p. 34.

Poetry, February, 1994, p. 285.

Saturday Review, March 17, 1962; September 30, 1972.

School Library Journal, November, 1995, p. 94.

Time, April 26, 1968; October 18, 1982; August 25, 1986; November 9, 1992, p. 80; November 14, 1994, p. 96; January 29, 1996, p. 78.

Times (London), January 14, 1982.

Times Literary Supplement, January 15, 1982; January 20, 1984; September 28, 1984; October 24, 1986.

Twentieth Century Literature, April, 1966; July, 1967; October, 1971; winter, 1978.

Village Voice, September 30, 1981.

Washington Post, September 27, 1981; April 26, 1982.

Yale Review, July, 1994, p. 165.

*   *   *

UPSHAW, Margaret Mitchell
See MITCHELL, Margaret (Munnerlyn)

*   *   *

URIS, Leon (Marcus) 1924-

PERSONAL: Born August 3, 1924, in Baltimore, MD; son of Wolf William (a shopkeeper) and Anna (Blumberg) Uris; married Betty Katherine Beck, 1945 (divorced January, 1968); married Margery Edwards, September 8, 1968 (died February 20, 1969); married Jill Peabody (a photographer), February 15, 1970; children: (first marriage) Karen Lynn, Mark Jay, Michael Cady; (third marriage) Rachael Jackson, one other child. *Education:* Attended public schools in Baltimore, MD. *Avocational interests:* Skiing, bowling, trail-biking, and tennis.

ADDRESSES: Home—Aspen, CO. *Office*—c/o Doubleday & Co. Inc., 1540 Broadway, New York, NY 10036-4039.

CAREER: Writer. Worked previously as a circulation district manager for the *San Francisco Call-Bulletin. Military service:*

U.S. Marine Corps, 1942-45; served in the Pacific at Guadalcanal and Tarawa.

MEMBER: Writers League, Screenwriters Guild.

AWARDS, HONORS: Daroff Memorial Award, 1959; National Institute of Arts and Letters grant, 1959; California Literature Silver Medal award, 1962, for *Mila 18,* and Gold Medal award, 1965, for *Armageddon;* honorary doctorates, University of Colorado, 1976, Santa Clara University, 1977, Wittenberg University, 1980, and Lincoln College, 1985; John F. Kennedy Medal, Irish/American Society of New York, 1977; gold medal, Eire Society of Boston, 1978; Jobotinsky Medal, State of Israel, 1980; Hall Fellowship (with wife, Jill Uris), Concord Academy, 1980; Scopus Award, Hebrew University of Jerusalem, 1981; Books for the Teen Age designation, New York Public Library, 1980-82, for *Exodus.*

WRITINGS:

NOVELS

Battle Cry (also see below), Putnam, 1953 (bound with *Tales of the South Pacific,* by James A. Michener, and *Mister Roberts,* by Thomas Heggen, Wings Books, 1996.)
The Angry Hills, Random House, 1955.
Exodus (also see below) Doubleday, 1957.
Mila 18, Doubleday, 1960.
Armageddon: A Novel of Berlin, Doubleday, 1964.
Topaz, McGraw, 1967.
QB VII, Doubleday, 1970.
Trinity, Doubleday, 1976.
The Haj, Doubleday, 1984.
Mitla Pass (Literary Guild main selection), Doubleday, 1988.
Redemption (sequel to *Trinity*), HarperCollins, 1995, large print edition, G. K. Hall, 1995.

SCREENPLAYS

Battle Cry, Warner Brothers, 1954.
Gunfight at the O.K. Corral (also see below), Paramount, 1957.

OTHER

(Author of commentary) *Exodus Revisited,* photographs by Dimitrios Harissiadis, Doubleday, 1959, published in England as *In the Steps of Exodus,* Heinemann, 1962.
The Third Temple (essay), bound with William Stevenson's *Strike Zion,* Bantam, 1967.
Ari (book and lyrics based on his novel, *Exodus;* also known as *Exodus, the Musical*), music by Walt Smith, produced on Broadway, 1971.
(Author of commentary) *Ireland: A Terrible Beauty: The Story of Ireland Today,* photographs by wife, Jill Uris, Doubleday, 1975.
(With J. Uris) *Jerusalem, Song of Songs,* photographs by J. Uris, Doubleday, 1981.

Contributor to several anthologies, including *Fabulous Yester days,* Harper, 1961; *American Men at Arms,* compiled by F. Van Wyck Mason, Little, Brown, 1965; *A Treasury of Jewish Sea Stories,* edited by Samuel Sobel, Jonathan David, 1965; and *Great Spy Stories from Fiction,* by Allan Dulles, Harper, 1969. Also contributor to periodicals, including *Esquire, Coronet, Ladies' Home Journal,* and *TWA Ambassador.* Author's work has been translated into other languages, including Spanish, Italian, and Portuguese.

MEDIA ADAPTATIONS: Gunfight at the O.K. Corral was novelized by Nelson C. Nye, Norden Publications, 1956; *The*

Angry Hills was adapted for film and released by Metro-Goldwyn-Mayer, 1959; *Exodus* was adapted for a film directed by Otto Preminger, United Artists (UA), 1960; *Topaz* was adapted for a film directed by Alfred Hitchcock, UA, 1969; *QB VII* was adapted into a television movie, ABC-TV, 1974.

SIDELIGHTS: American writer Leon Uris is the author of several best-selling novels based upon details and events drawn from contemporary history. He received acclaim early in his career as the author of such popular books as *Exodus,* a landmark novelization of the history of the Jewish settlement of modern Israel, and the espionage thriller *Topaz.* Uris's later works include *QB VII,* a semi-autobiographical account of the trial of an author charged with libel by a German physician and former Nazi, and *Trinity,* a novel set amid Ireland's political and religious turmoil. Panoramic historical fiction that has proved to be commercially successful, Uris's fast-paced novels have earned him a dedicated readership. Yet, throughout his career, critical opinion on his work has been mixed. While critics praise his storytelling abilities—the appeal of his novels has been described as cinematic in nature—Uris is sometimes cited for problems with grammatical technique, for his occasionally cardboard characters and stiff dialogue, and for taking liberties with historical facts. Sharon D. Downey and Richard A. Kallan, noting both Uris's immense popular appeal and what they perceive as flaws in regards to traditional literary standards, assert in *Communication Monographs,* "in short, Uris remains a reader's writer and a critic's nightmare."

Uris began writing in the early 1950s, inspired by his four-year tour of duty with the U.S. Marine Corps during World War II. His first novel, *Battle Cry,* was published by G. P. Putnam in 1953 after making the rounds of several publishing houses. "There were those who thought I was crazy, others who gave me encouragement," Uris told Bernard Kalb in *Saturday Review.* "My guiding thought throughout was that the real Marine story had not been told. We were a different breed of men who looked at war in a different way." The book was praised by reviewers for its realistic depiction of the dedicated men who risked their lives in the front lines of battle. Commenting on the unique approach to the subject of war in *Battle Cry,* critic Merle Miller notes in the *Saturday Review* that the novel "may have started a whole new and healthy trend in war literature." The book proved to be as popular with readers as it was with critics, and Uris went on to write the screenplay for the film version of his novel, which was released by Warner Brothers in 1954.

The success of *Battle Cry* encouraged Uris to continue writing and he was soon at work on his second novel, *The Angry Hills.* Loosely based on the diary of an uncle who had fought in Greece with a Jewish unit of the British armed forces, the work was published in 1955. Although the response from critics was that as an adventure story, the book was too fast-paced, *The Angry Hills* is significant in that it focused Uris's interest in the Middle East, the Palestinian issue, and the history of Israel, home to many of his relatives. Although his preoccupation with these subjects would stay out of his major work for the next few years—after publication of his second novel, Uris was soon at work on a screenplay for the classic western drama, *Gunfight at the O.K. Corral*—it would figure prominently in several of his later novels, most notably *Exodus,* which would become one of the largest-selling books in publishing history.

Exodus is the history of European Jews and their efforts to establish the state of Israel as a Jewish homeland. Although faulting Uris for what they perceive to be a tendency towards lengthy and partisan passages, critics have hailed *Exodus* as a gripping human drama and a novel of heroic proportions. A descriptive account of the Warsaw Ghetto included in this novel provided the seed for Uris's next book, *Mila 18,* which continued his fascination with the predicament of Jews in the twentieth century. From there, he worked with noted Greek photographer Dimitrios Harissiadis on the photo-essay *Exodus Revisited,* a complement to the research he did for *Mila 18.* The author's lifelong passion for the Jewish people and for Israel would be the motivation behind several other books, including *The Haj,* an account of the birth of Israel told from the point of view of a Palestinian Arab, and *Mitla Pass,* a novel about an Israeli soldier during the Sinai War that was published in 1988 to mixed reviews but immediate best-seller status.

Some critics have viewed flaws of a technical nature as an acceptable trade-off for a well-wrought story when reviewing Uris's novels. Pete Hamill writes in the *New York Times Book Review:* "Leon Uris is a storyteller, in a direct line from those men who sat around fires in the days before history and made the tribe more human. The subject is man, not words; story is all, the form it takes is secondary." Although not unaware of the problematic aspects of the novel genre, Hamill states: "It is a simple thing to point out that Uris often writes crudely, that his dialogue can be wooden, that his structure occasionally groans under the excess baggage of exposition and information. Simple, but irrelevant. None of that matters as you are swept along in the narrative." Critic Dan Wakefield agrees, noting in a review of *Exodus* for the *Nation:* "The plot is so exciting that the characters become exciting too; not because of their individuality or depth, but because of the historic drama they are involved in." Wakefield goes on to add, "The real achievement . . . lies not so much in its virtues as a novel as in its skillful rendering of the furiously complex history of modern Israel in a palatable, popular form that is usually faithful to the spirit of the complicated realities."

In order to write *Exodus,* Uris read almost 300 books, traveled 12,000 miles within Israel's boundaries, and interviewed more than 1,200 individuals. Similar efforts went into his other books, including *Trinity,* which arose out of the people and places Uris and his third wife, photographer Jill Peabody Uris, encountered on a trip to document modern Ireland. The wealth of historical background in his novels has caused Uris's books to be alternately called "non-fiction" novels, "propaganda" novels, or just plain "journalism" by critics. A reviewer for the *Christian Science Monitor* addresses the danger in mixing fact and fiction: "Few readers are expert enough to be 100 percent certain where Mr. Uris's imagination has taken over the record." Nevertheless, as Maxwell Geismar points out in the *Saturday Review:* "If Mr. Uris sometimes lacks tone as a novelist, if his central figures are social types rather than individual portraits, there is also a kind of 'underground power' in his writing. No other novel I have read recently has had the same capacity [as *Exodus*] to refresh our memory, inform our intelligence, and to stir the heart." In the same vein, Hamill writes of *Trinity:* "The novel sprawls, occasionally bores, meanders like a river. . . . But when the story is finished the reader has been to places where he or she has never been before. The news items . . . will never seem quite the same again."

Uris revisits the Ireland of *Trinity* after almost twenty years in *Redemption.* The earlier volume looked at the 19th-century Irish struggle for independence; *Redemption* takes the story through the years of World War I. "The conflict between two of the three dominant families of *Trinity,* the tempestuous Larkins and their staid British counterparts, the Hubbles, is the focus here," explains a *Publishers Weekly* reviewer. The story, in which young Rory Larkin makes an attempt to assist Irish rebels in the Catholic Easter Uprising of 1916, describes how Rory's commanding officer is assassinated and how Rory himself is implicated. "With its contrivances, digressions and shifting time lines," Malachy Duffy states in the *New York Times Book Review,* "the novel often resembles the Irish countryside—full of twists and turns, replete with bogs and quagmires."

Webster Scott offers his assessment of the author's work in the *Washington Post Book World.* Novelists with mass audience appeal such as Uris, in which group Scott includes noted authors James A. Michener and James Clavell, "may tell us relatively little about our inner weather, but they report on storms and setting suns outside. They read the environment we must function in. Occasionally they replicate our social structures. They sift the history that brought us to the present. They give us the briefing papers necessary to convert news stories into human stories. All of which serve our emotional need to make order out of confusion," concludes Scott, "to explain the inexplicable."

BIOGRAPHICAL/CRITICAL SOURCES:

BOOKS

Cain, Kathleen Shine, *Leon Uris: A Critical Companion,* Greenwood, 1998.
Contemporary Literary Criticism, Gale (Detroit), Volume 7, 1977; Volume 32, 1985.
Contemporary Novelists, 4th edition, St. James Press/St. Martin's, 1986.
Something about the Author, Gale, Volume 49, 1987.

PERIODICALS

Atlantic Monthly, July, 1964.
Booklist, April 15, 1995, p. 1453.
Chicago Tribune, November 24, 1988.
Chicago Tribune Book World, April 29, 1984, p. 33.
Christian Science Monitor, December 4, 1958; November 16, 1967.
Commentary, October, 1961.
Communication Monographs, September, 1982.
Globe and Mail (Toronto), January 7, 1989.
Inside Books, November, 1988, pp. 25-26.
Kirkus Reviews, April 1, 1995, p. 422-23.
Los Angeles Times Book Review, September 27, 1984, p. 8; October 30, 1988, p. 12.
Nation, April 11, 1959.
Newsweek, May 21, 1984, p. 84.
New York Herald Tribune Book Review, September 28, 1958.
New York Review of Books, April 16, 1964.
New York Times, October 12, 1958; April 27, 1984.
New York Times Book Review, June 4, 1961; June 28, 1964; October 15, 1967; March 14, 1976, p. 5; April 22, 1984, p. 7; January 1, 1989, p. 14; July 2, 1995, p. 11.
Philadelphia Bulletin, March 31, 1976.
Publishers Weekly, March 29, 1976, pp. 6-7; September 23, 1988, p. 59; April 24, 1993, p. 58.
Saturday Review, April 25, 1953, pp. 16-17; September 27, 1958.
Time, December 8, 1958; June 2, 1961.
Times Literary Supplement, October 27, 1961.
Washington Post Book World, April 1, 1984, pp. 1-2; October 30, 1988.

URMUZ
See CODRESCU, Andrei

*   *   *

USTINOV, Peter (Alexander) 1921-

PERSONAL: Born April 16, 1921, in London, England; son of Iona (a journalist; professional name, Klop) and Nadia (a painter and scenic designer; maiden name, Benois) Ustinov; married Isolde Delham, 1940 (divorced, 1950); married Suzanne Cloutier (an actress), 1953 (marriage ended, 1971); married Helen du Lau d'Allemans, June 17, 1972; children: (first marriage) Tamara; (second marriage) Pavla, Igor, Andrea. *Education:* Attended Westminster School, London, England, 1934-37, Mr. Gibbs Preparatory School, London, and London Theatre Studio, 1937-39. *Avocational interests:* Reading voluminously, cars, music, collecting old masters' drawings, lawn tennis, and squash.

ADDRESSES: Office—11 rue de Silly, 92100 Boulogne, France. *Agent*—Margaret Gardner, 17 Onslow Sq., London SW7 3NJ England.

CAREER: Actor and director in theater, films, and television; playwright, film writer, and author. Joint Director, Nottingham Playhouse, 1963–. First rector, University of Dundee, 1968-74. Chancellor, University of Durham, 1971-73. Goodwill ambassador for UNICEF, 1969–. Director of stage productions, including *The Man in the Raincoat, No Sign of the Dove, Photo Finish* (in Paris), and *King Lear* (in Ontario, Canada); director of films, including *The Spies, An Angel Flew over Brooklyn, Schools for Secrets, Vice Versa, Private Angelo, Billy Budd, Lady L, Hammersmith Is Out,* and *Memed My Hawk.*

Director of operas with the Royal Opera at Covent Garden, 1962, the Hamburg Opera, 1968, 1985, and 1987, the Edinburgh Festival, 1973, the Paris Opera, 1973, the Berlin Opera, 1978, the Piccola Scala Milan, 1981 and 1982, the Mozarteum, 1987, and the Dresden Opera, 1993. *Military service:* British Army, Royal Sussex Regiment, 1942-46; also served with Royal Army Ordnance Corps and Kinematograph Service.

MEMBER: Royal Society of Arts (fellow), Royal Society of Literature, British Actors' Equity, British League of Dramatists, London Society of Authors, British Film Academy, British Screen Writers' Society, Societe des Auteurs (France), New York Dramatists Guild, Hollywood Screen Actors' Guild, Garrick Club, Savage Club, Royal Automobile Club, Queen's Club.

AWARDS, HONORS: Golden Globe Award for best actor in a supporting role, Hollywood Foreign Press Association, 1952, for *Quo Vadis;* New York Drama Critics Circle Award, 1953, for *The Love of Four Colonels; Evening Standard* Drama Award for best new play, 1956, for *Romanoff and Juliet;* Benjamin Franklin Medal, Royal Society of Arts, 1957; Academy Awards for best supporting actor, Academy of Motion Picture Arts and Sciences, 1960, for *Spartacus,* and 1964, for *Topkapi;* Emmy Award, Academy of Television Arts and Sciences, for best actor in a comedy or drama special, 1958, for *The Life of Samuel Johnson,* 1966, for *Barefoot in Athens,* and 1970, for *Storm in Summer;* Grammy Award for best children's recording, National Academy of Recording Arts and Sciences, 1959, for *Peter and the Wolf;* First prize of Syndicat des journalistes et ecrivains (France), 1964, for *Photo Finish;* Academy Award nomination for best story and screenplay, and British comedy screenplay award from Writers

Guild, both 1969, for *Hot Millions;* Doctor of Law, University of Dundee, 1969; Mus.D., Cleveland Conservatory of Music, 1967; D.F.A., La Salle College, 1971; D.Litt., University of Lancaster, 1972; Order of the Smile (for dedication to the idea of international assistance to children), Warsaw, 1974; Commander of British Empire, 1975; Jordanian Independence Medal and UNICEF Award for Distinguished Services, both 1978; Prix de la Butte and Variety Club of Great Britain Award for Best Actor, both 1979; honorary doctorate, University of Toronto, 1984, 1995; Commandeur des Arts et des Lettres (France), 1985; elected to Academy of Fine Arts, Institut de France, Paris, 1988; Banff Television Festival Award of Excellence (Canada), 1988; D.H.L., Georgetown University, 1988; Gold Medal of the City of Athens, 1990; Knight of the Realm, 1990; Medal of the Greek Red Cross, 1990; D.H.L, University of Ottawa, 1991; Medal of Honour, Charles University (Prague), 1991; D.H.L., University of Durham, 1992; Chancellor, University of Durham, 1992; President, World Federalist Movement, 1992; Britannia Award, British Academy of Film and Television Arts, 1992; Critics' Circle Award, 1993; Ordern Nacional do Cruzerio do Sul (Brazil), 1994; German Cultural Award, 1994; German Bambi, 1994; International Child Survival Award, UNICEF, 1995; honorary doctorate, Pontifical Institute of Medieval Studies, St. Michael's College, University of Toronto, 1995; Ruldolph Valentino Award for Lifetime Achievement in Motion Pictures, 1995; Doctorate Honoris Causa, Free Flemish University of Brussels, 1995; Norman Cousins Global Governance Award, World Federalist Movement, 1995; also awarded Order of Istiglal of the Hashemite Kingdom of Jordan and the Order of the Yugoslav Flag.

WRITINGS:

Add a Dash of Pity (short stories), Little, Brown (Boston), 1959.
Ustinov's Diplomats (photographs and commentary), Bernard Geis Associates, 1960.
The Loser (novel), Little, Brown, 1960.
We Were Only Human (caricatures), Little, Brown, 1961.
(Illustrator) Paul Marc Henry, *Poodlestan: A Poodle's Eye View of History,* Reynal, 1965.
The Frontiers of the Sea (short stories), Little, Brown, 1966, published as *God and the State Railways,* O'Mara (London), 1993.
The Wit of Peter Ustinov, compiled by Dick Richards, Frewin, 1969.
Krumnagel (novel), Little, Brown, 1971.
Dear Me (autobiography), Little, Brown, 1977.
(Author of introduction) Gordon Forbes, *A Handful of Summers,* Paddington, 1979.
My Russia, Macmillan (London), 1983.
(Author of introduction) Tom Hutchinson, *Niven's Hollywood,* Salem House, 1984.
Peter Ustinov in Russia, Summit Books (New York City), 1988.
The Disinformer: Two Novellas, Arcade (New York City), 1989.
The Old Man and Mr. Smith (novel), O'Mara, 1990, Arcade, 1991.
Ustinov at Large (collected articles), O'Mara, 1991.
Ustinov Still at Large (collected articles), O'Mara, 1993, Prometheus (Buffalo, NY), 1994.
The Quotable Ustinov (compilation), Prometheus, 1995.
Brewer's Theater, HarperCollins, 1995.
Life Is an Operetta and Other Short Stories, Prometheus, 1997.

PUBLISHED PLAYS

House of Regrets (three-act tragi-comedy; first produced in London at Arts Theatre, 1942), J. Cape (London), 1943.

Beyond (one act; first produced at Arts Theatre, 1943; also see below), English Theatre Guild (London), 1944.

The Banbury Nose (four acts; first produced in London at Wyndham's Theatre, 1944), J. Cape, 1945.

Plays about People (includes *Blow Your Own Trumpet,* first produced in London at Old Vic Theatre, 1943; *The Tragedy of Good Intentions,* first produced in Liverpool at Old Vic Theatre, 1945; *The Indifferent Shepherd,* first produced in London at Criterion Theatre, 1948), J. Cape, 1950.

The Love of Four Colonels (three acts; first produced at Wyndham's Theatre, 1951; also see below), English Theatre Guild, 1951, Dramatists Play Service (New York City), 1953.

The Moment of Truth (four acts; first produced in London at Adelphi Theatre, 1951; also see below), English Theatre Guild, 1953.

Romanoff and Juliet (three-act comedy; first produced in London at Piccadilly Theatre, 1956; produced in New York at Plymouth Theatre, 1957; also see below), English Theatre Guild, 1957, Random House (New York City), 1958, musical version, with libretto by Ustinov, produced as *R Loves J,* at Chichester Festival Theatre, 1973.

Photo Finish: An Adventure in Biography in Three Acts (first produced in London at Saville Theatre, 1962), Heinemann (London), 1962, Little, Brown, 1963, revised acting edition, Dramatists Play Service, 1964.

Five Plays (includes *Romanoff and Juliet, The Moment of Truth, Beyond, The Love of Four Colonels,* and *No Sign of the Dove,* produced in London at Savoy Theatre, 1953), Little, Brown, 1965.

The Unknown Soldier and His Wife (two acts; first produced in New York at Vivian Beaumont Theatre, July 6, 1967), Random House, 1967, published in England as *The Unknown Soldier and His Wife: Two Acts of War Separated by a Trace,* Heinemann, 1968.

Halfway up the Tree (three-act comedy; first produced in New York at Brooks Atkinson Theatre, November 7, 1967), Random House, 1968.

UNPUBLISHED PLAYS

The Bishop of Limpopoland (sketch), produced in London, 1939.

(Translator and adapter from the French) Jean Sarment, *Fishing for Shadows,* produced in London, 1940.

Frenzy (adapted from the Swedish of Ingmar Bergman), produced in London at St. Martin's Theatre, 1948.

The Man in the Raincoat, produced at Edinburgh Festival, 1949.

High Balcony, produced in 1952.

The Empty Chair, produced in Bristol at Old Vic Theatre, 1956.

Paris Not So Gay, produced in Oxford, England, 1958.

The Life in My Hands, produced at Nottingham Playhouse, 1963.

Who's Who in Hell, first produced in New York at Lunt-Fontanne Theatre, December 9, 1974.

Overheard, first produced in London at Haymarket Theatre, May 17, 1981.

The Marriage, produced at Edinburgh Festival, 1982.

Beethoven's Tenth (two-act comedy), first produced in New York at Nederlander Theatre, April 22, 1984.

SCREENPLAYS

(With Eric Ambler) *The Way Ahead,* Twentieth Century-Fox, 1946, also released as *Immortal Battalion.*

School for Secrets, Two Cities, 1946, released as *Secret Flight,* 1951.

Vice Versa, Rank/Two Cities, 1947.

Private Angelo, Pilgrim/ABF-Pathe, 1949.

(With Patricia Chester Moyes) *School for Scoundrels,* Guardsman, 1960.

Romanoff and Juliet, Universal, 1961.

(With Robert Rossen) *Billy Budd,* Allied Artists, 1962.

Lady L, Champion-Concordia/Metro-Goldwyn-Mayer (MGM), 1965.

(With Ira Wallach) *Hot Millions,* Milberg/MGM, 1968.

Hammersmith Is Out, Cinerama, 1972.

Memed My Hawk, Peter Ustinov-Jadran/Focus, 1984.

SIDELIGHTS: Peter Ustinov, once described in the *New Statesman and Nation* as "a tubby character with the affable, slouchy, sulky exterior of a Giant Panda," has enjoyed a remarkable career in show business. Best known as the rotund character actor whose portrayals have earned two Academy Awards, three Emmy Awards, and even a Grammy Award for narration, Ustinov is also esteemed as a playwright, director, and producer. *New York Times* correspondent Leslie Bennets calls Ustinov a "one-man creative industry" who has "won enough honors to furnish a house." John Lahr offers a similar assessment of Ustinov in the *New York Times Book Review,* noting that as "playwright, novelist, short story writer, actor, film director, raconteur, Ustinov has turned his urbane intelligence to all facets of public entertainment and made a good show of it." Indeed, Ustinov's writing and acting careers are often inseparable; for many years he has accomplished the rare feat of performing in plays and films of his own authorship, usually to critical acclaim. A long list of such dual credits includes the movies *Billy Budd,* and *Hot Millions,* and the plays *Romanoff and Juliet, The Unknown Soldier and His Wife,* and *Beethoven's Tenth,* to name only a few. In a *Maclean's* profile, Lawrence O'Toole accords Ustinov a lofty status befitting his vast achievements: "By pluralizing the very concept of career in the way he has, Ustinov qualifies for admission to that august company which avails itself of the royal 'we.'"

Ustinov was born and raised in Great Britain, but his heritage is French and Russian through his widely travelled, artistic parents. "His father," writes a *Forbes* magazine contributor, "was a well-known journalist in London with a gift for storytelling. Smiling, Ustinov recalls Rebecca West's observation 'that I was very good—but not up to my father.'" According to *Dictionary of Literary Biography* contributor Audrey Williamson, this fusion of cultural influences "explains the volatility and range of [Ustinov's] dramatic writings: his multitudinous relatives were concerned both with the arts and diplomacy, and a liberal-minded and at times highly satiric view of politics and international attitudes is evident in his best plays."

From an early age, Ustinov wrote; he was serving in the Royal Sussex Regiment when his first play, *House of Regrets,* was produced in London in 1942. A study of aging White Russians in exile, the work was well-received by both critics and audiences. Two years later Ustinov scored an even bigger success with *The Banbury Nose,* an examination of generational conflict that Williamson contends is his "most original and effective exercise in dramatic craftsmanship." Thereafter, the ambitious and indefatigable Ustinov acted, wrote, and directed scores of dramas and comedies in England and the United States. His authored works such as *The Love of Four Colonels, Romanoff and Juliet, Photo Finish: An Adventure in Biography in Three Acts,* and *Beethoven's Tenth* found audiences on both sides of the Atlantic.

Ustinov's plays generally explore some political or cultural characteristic in juxtaposition to its polar opposite. In *Romanoff and Juliet,* for instance, a Russian boy and an American girl fall in love while their parents are serving as diplomats in a small neutral nation. *The Unknown Soldier and His Wife* explores soldiering in successive historical periods, and *Beethoven's Tenth* pits the famous composer, returned from the dead, against a stuffy modern music critic. In her essay on his works, Williamson notes that Ustinov, "with a heredity ensuring the overstepping of nationalistic barriers, has always refused to play the power game in politics or to concede either right-wing or left-wing assumptions in his works. Like W. S. Gilbert in another age, his mockery is of all sides and without allegiance, if one excepts allegiance to humanity as a whole." Williamson concludes: "In a world at best maintaining a precarious peace, Ustinov, the traditional serious clown, is a valuable reminder of civilization's most conspicuous and recurring follies. . . . His dramatic career . . . appears remarkable when one assesses it as only one part of a theatrical life which continues to encompass acting and directing for both film and television as well as the stage."

In addition to his numerous plays and screenplays, Ustinov has written short stories, novels, nonfiction collections, and several volumes of memoirs. Critics do not always appreciate Ustinov's efforts in these genres—a *Kirkus Reviews* critic, writing about *Ustinov Still at Large,* calls it "a fine friendship garland of civilized, perishable memories, but nothing worth saving," while a *Publishers Weekly* critic complains that Ustinov's stance in his articles "doesn't always work." Reviewers, however, generally acknowledge Ustinov's skill at storytelling. "It is easy to argue that Ustinov is the world's finest living raconteur," asserts a *Forbes* magazine contributor. "Along with a lethal gift for mimicry, he is a linguist who lifts accents from everywhere. . . . Talking with Ustinov is like being with a clever friend as he wanders through a costume shop, trying on the masks."

"The trick has always been to write as easily as you talk," notes William Cole in the *Saturday Review.* "Peter Ustinov does just that, and he's the grandest monopolistic talker I've ever stood in a circle around, spellbound." Writing about Ustinov's fable *The Old Man and Mr. Smith,* a *Publishers Weekly* reviewer declares that "within this loquacious novel's cosmic banter, Ustinov offers priceless philosophical nuggets, as well as scathing satirical barbs." His one-man show *An Evening with Peter Ustinov* is described by *Chicago Tribune* writer Sid Smith as "talk-show anecdote raised to art, tripping its way through light-hearted, possibly spurious tattletales" to a broad range of imitations, including a barking dog, crying cat, a flamenco guitar, and "an infant's gastric disturbances." Ustinov is also a gifted musician and historical commentator: his narration of the PBS television special *Inside the Vatican* is, according to Walter Goodman in the *New York Times,* delivered "in orotund tones. . . . It's the classiest interview show of the week." In the two-hour television special *The Mozart Mystique with Peter Ustinov,* a tribute to the Austrian composer, Ustinov "has a kind of avuncular self-awareness that allows you to enjoy his beneficent pomposity as much as he does," declares Daniel B. Wood in the *Christian Science Monitor.* "He can begin one sentence as a raving twit and finish it off with a scowl of unquestionable authority, all in character."

Reflecting on the various facets of his career, Ustinov told the *New York Times:* "Acting is probably much safer than directing or writing. . . . Acting is intrinsically easy. But I've always thought my chief work is what I write. It's much more difficult, and writing for theater is the most difficult of all. In a novel it's enough to know what to write; in theater it's essential to know what not to write." "As an actor you're not dealing entirely with the unknown," Ustinov continued. "Writing is much more mysterious, and more personal. Sitting in front of a white piece of paper and filling it, and then doing that four or five hundred times—it's like a miracle. When writing comes off, it's absolutely thrilling."

Although he is well into his seventh decade, Ustinov expresses no interest in lightening his workload. On the occasion of his seventieth birthday, he tells Douglas J. Rowe of the *Chicago Tribune,* he gathered his family together and said to them, "'I've reached an age that I must, sooner or later, decide what I'm going to do with my life.' And there was a pause and my son said, 'Don't hurry.'" "I like that very much," the author confided to Rowe. "One of the functions of life is that throughout it you discover, sometimes painfully, your limitations." "I have no feeling of achievement at all," he told the *New York Times.* "Every time you do something it's the first time, in a way. . . . I've never got out of the habit of being surprised."

BIOGRAPHICAL/CRITICAL SOURCES:

BOOKS

Cohn, Ruby, *Modern Shakespeare Offshoots,* Princeton University Press (Princeton, NJ), 1976.
Contemporary Literary Criticism, Volume 1, Gale (Detroit), 1973.
Dictionary of Literary Biography, Volume 13: *British Dramatists since World War II,* Gale, 1982.
Thomas, Tony, *Ustinov in Focus,* A. S. Barnes (San Diego), 1971.
Trewin, J. C., *A Play Tonight,* Elek (London), 1952.
Warwick, Christopher, *The Universal Ustinov,* Sidgwick & Jackson (London), 1990.
Williams, Geoffrey, *Peter Ustinov,* Copp, 1957, Transatlantic, 1958.

PERIODICALS

Atlantic Monthly, July, 1964.
Book World, January 2, 1972.
Chicago Tribune, May 10, 1992, pp. 12-13; May 14, 1992, p. 28; January 15, 1993, p. 7.
Christian Science Monitor, May 17, 1990, p. 11.
Daily Telegraph (London), August 23, 1952.
Drama, summer, 1958.
Forbes, November 22, 1993, pp. 77-78.
Kirkus Reviews, July 1, 1989, p. 951; February 1, 1995, p. 153.
Life, April 14, 1958; April 19, 1963.
Listener, February 17, 1966; February 24, 1966.
Look, April 29, 1958.
Los Angeles Times, October 8, 1983.
Maclean's, October 1, 1979.
National Review, January 18, 1993.
New Statesman and Nation, December 1, 1951; March 27, 1954.
Newsweek, March 10, 1958; September 19, 1977.
New Yorker, July 15, 1967.
New York Herald Tribune, December 10, 1953; July 10, 1955.
New York Times, January 24, 1965; October 15, 1977; July 30, 1979; March 7, 1982; April 22, 1984; April 23, 1984; May 4, 1987; October 24, 1994, p. C16.
New York Times Book Review, November 28, 1971; September 25, 1977; December 23, 1984; September 17, 1989, p. 30; May 21, 1995, p. 32.
New York Times Magazine, January 29, 1961.
Publishers Weekly, April 19, 1991, pp. 58-59; February 6, 1995, p. 82.
Punch, October 6, 1989, p. 45.

Saturday Review, November 13, 1971; September 3, 1977.
Spectator, August 7, 1971.
Time, March 10, 1958.
Times (London), May 21, 1983; September 15, 1987.
Times Literary Supplement, December 1, 1966; January 9, 1969;
     July 1, 1983.
Variety, March 13-9, 1995, p. 37.

V

VALERY, (Ambroise) Paul (Toussaint Jules) 1871-1945

PERSONAL: Born October 30, 1871, in Cette (now Sete), France; died of a heart ailment, July (some sources say August) 20, 1945, in Paris, France; buried in Cimetiere Marin, Sete, France; son of Barthelemy (a customs officer) and Fanny (Grassi) Valery; married Jeannie (some sources spell given name Jeanne) Gobillard, 1900; children: Francois, Agathe (some sources say three). *Education:* University of Montpellier, licence en droit, 1892.

CAREER: Poet, philosopher, essayist, critic, and dramatist. Ministry of War, Artillery Munitions Bureau, Paris, France, clerk, 1897-1900; Havas News Agency, Paris, private secretary to agency director, 1900-22; coeditor of literary review *Commerce,* 1924-32; Centre Universitaire Mediterraneen, Nice, France, administrator, beginning in 1933; College de France, Paris, professor of poetry, 1937-45. President of League of Nations Committee for Intellectual Cooperation, 1936. *Military service:* French Army, 1889-90; stationed in Montpellier.

AWARDS, HONORS: Legion of Honor (France), Chevalier, 1923, Officer, 1926, Commander, 1931; elected to the French Academy, 1925; numerous honorary doctorates, including Oxford University, 1931, and foreign decorations; street where Valery lived was renamed rue de Paul Valery; at his death Valery was given a full state funeral.

WRITINGS:

POETRY

La Jeune Parque (title means "The Young Fate"), Editions de la Nouvelle Revue Francaise, 1917, with commentary by Alain, Gallimard, 1936, enlarged edition with critical document study by Octave Nadal published as *La Jeune Parque: Manuscrit autographe, texte de l'edition 1942, etats successifs et brouillons inedits du poem* (includes unpublished drafts), Club du Meilleur Livre, 1957.

Album de vers anciens, 1890-1900 (collection; title means "Album of Old Verse"; includes "La Fileuse," "Helene," "Naissance de Venus," "Feerie," "Baignee," "Au Bois dormant," "Le Bois amical," "Un Feu distinct . . . ," "Narcisse parle," "Episode," "Vue," "Valvins," "Ete," "Anne," "Orphee," "Semiramis," "L'Amateur de poemes"), A. Monnier, 1920, Editions de la Nouvelle Revue Francaise, 1927.

Charmes; ou, Poemes (collection; title means "Songs; or, Poems"; contains "L'Abeille," "Au Plantane," "Aurore," "Le Cantique des colonnes," "La Ceinture," "Le Cimetiere marin," "Dormeuse," "La Fausse Morte," "Les Grenades," "L'Insinuant," "Interieur," "Fragments du Narcisse," "Ode secrete," "La Pythie Les Pas," "Poesie," "Air de Semiramis," "Le Vin perdu," "Le Sylphe," "Ebauche d'un serpent," "Le Rameur," "Palme"), Editions de la Nouvelle Revue Francaise, 1922, French text edited by Charles G. Whiting with English introduction and notes, Athlone Press, 1973, translation by James L. Brown published as *Charms,* Forsan Books, 1983.

Melange (collection; contains "Melange," "Petites Etudes," "Poesie brute," "Colloques," "Instants," "Cantate du Narcisse"), Gallimard, 1941.

L'Ange, Gallimard, 1946.

Le Cimetiere marin (first published in *Nouvelle Revue Francaise,* June 1, 1920), preface by Henri Mondor, Roissard, 1954, introduction by Sylvio Samama, illustrations by Abram Krol, A. Krol (Paris), 1964; dual-language edition translated by C. Day Lewis as *Le Cimetiere marin/The Graveyard by the Sea,* Secker & Warburg, 1946; dual-language edition edited and translated by Graham Dunstan Martin as *Le Cimetiere marin/ The Graveyard by the Sea,* University of Texas Press, 1971.

Abeille spirituelle (previously unpublished poem), privately printed, 1968.

First drafts of Valery's poem *La Jeune Parque* are included in *Rompre le silence: Les Premiers Etats de La Jeune Parque* by Bruce Pratt, J. Corti (Paris), 1976, and in *Chant du cygne: Edition critique des premiers etats de La Jeune Parque,* by Pratt, J. Corti, 1979.

PROSE

La Conquete allemande (first published in *New Review* [London], January 1, 1897), Extrait du Mercure de France, 1915, revised edition published as *Une Conquete methodique,* Champion, 1924.

Introduction a la methode de Leonard de Vinci (first published in *Nouvelle Revue,* August 15, 1894 [some sources say 1895]), Editions de la Nouvelle Revue Francaise, 1919, Gallimard, 1964, translation by Thomas McGreevy published as *Introduction to the Method of Leonardo da Vinci,* J. Rodker, 1929.

La Soiree avec M. Teste (short story; first published in *Centaure,* September, 1896), Editions de la Nouvelle Revue Francaise,

1919, translation by Ronald Davis published as *An Evening With Mr. Teste,* R. Davis (Paris), 1925; new and enlarged edition published as *Monsieur Teste* (contains Preface, "La Soiree avec M. Teste," "Lettre de Mme. Emilie Teste," "Extraits du logbook de monsieur Teste," "Lettre d'un ami," "La Promenade avec monsieur Teste," "Pour un portrait de monsieur Teste," "Quelques pensees de monsieur Teste," "Fin de monsieur Teste"), Gallimard, 1946, revised, 1969, translation with notes by Jackson Mathews published as *Monsieur Teste* (contains Preface, "An Evening with Mr. Teste," "Letter from Mme. Emilie Teste," "Excerpts from M. Teste's Logbook," "Letter from a Friend," "A Walk with M. Teste," "Dialogue, For a Portrait of M. Teste," "More Excerpts From the Logbook," "End of M. Teste"), Knopf, 1947, McGraw, 1964.

Eupalinos; ou, L'Architecte, precede de L'Ame et la danse (two dialogues; *Eupalinos* first published as *Paradoxe sur l'architecte* in *Ermitage,* March, 1891, translation by William McCausland Stewart published as *Eupalinos; or, The Architect,* Oxford University Press/H. Milford, 1932; *L'Ame et la danse* first published in *Revue Musicale,* December, 1920, translation by Dorothy Busay published as *Dance and the Soul,* John Lehmann, 1951), Gallimard, 1923, translated and edited with introduction and notes by Vera J. Daniel as *Eupalinos, and, L'Ame et la danse,* Oxford University Press, 1967.

Fragments sur Mallarme, R. Davis (Paris), 1924.

Situation de Baudelaire, Madame Lesafe (Paris), 1924.

Variete (essays; includes "Fragment d'un Descartes Le Retour de Hollande," "Sur Bossuet," "Oraison funebre d'une fable," "Preface aux lettres persanes, Stendhal, Situation de Baudelaire, Passage de Verlaine, Stephane Mallarme," "Le Coup de des," "Derniere visite a Mallarme," "Lettre sur Mallarme," "Souvenir de J. K. Huysmans," "Petite lettre sur les mythes," "Etudes," "Je disais quelquefois a Stephane Mallarme," "Questions de poesie," "Au sujet du 'Cimetiere marin,'" "Commentaires de 'Charmes,'" "Amphion [melodrame]," *Semiramis [melodrame],* "Leonard et les philosophes," "La 'Peur des morts,'" "La Politique de l'esprit," "Inspirations mediterraneennes," "Le Bilan de l'intelligence," "Remerciement a l'Academie francaise," "Reponse au remerciement du Marechal Petain a l'Academie francaise," "Discours en l'honneur de Goethe," "Discours de l'histoire prononce a la distribution solennelle des prix du Lycee Janson-de-Sailly, le 13 juillet 1892," "Discours de la Maison d'education de la Legion d'honneur de Saint-Denis, le 11 juillet 1892," "Rapport sur les prix de vertu Discours prononce a l'occasion de la distribution des prix du College de Sete," "Descartes, Discours prononce du deuxieme Congres international d'esthetique et de science de l'art," "L'Homme et la coquille," "Discours aux chirurgiens," "Reflexions simples sur le corps," "Fragments des memoires d'un poeme," "Le Prince et la jeune parque," "Poesie et pensee abstraite," "Cantiques spirituels," "Sur Phedre femme," "La Tentation de [saint] Flaubert," "Une Vue de Descartes," "Seconde Vue de Descartes," "Svedenborg," "Enseignement de la poetique," "Lecon inaugurale de cours de poetique du College de France"), five volumes, Gallimard, 1924-44, translation by Malcolm Cowley, William Aspenwall Bradley, and others published as *Variety* (includes Introduction, "The Intellectual Crisis," "Note," "Adonis," "A Foreword," "On Poe's 'Eureka,'" "Variations on a Theme from Pascal," "A Tribute," "An Introduction to the Method of Leonardo da Vinci,"

"Villon and Verlaine," "Concerning Carot," "The Position of Baudelaire"), Harcourt, 1927-38.

Durtal, Champion, 1925.

Etudes et fragments sur le reve, Claude Aveline (Paris), 1925.

Petit recueil de paroles de circonstance, Plaisir de Bibliophile, 1926.

Discours de la diction des vers, Le Livre, 1926, revised edition published as *De la diction des vers,* Emile Chamontin (Paris), 1933.

Durtal; ou, Les Points d'une conversion (criticism), M. Senac (Paris), 1927.

Maitres et amis (title means "Masters and Friends"), Beltrand, 1927.

Discours sur Emile Verhaeren (lecture), Champion, 1927.

Discours de reception a l'Academie francaise, Gallimard, 1927.

Odes: Compositions de D. Galanis (criticism), Aux Aldes, 1927.

Poesie: Essais sur la poetique et le poete (essays), Bertrand Guegan (Paris), 1928.

Remarques exterieures, illustrations by L. J. Soulas, Editions des Cahiers Libres, 1929.

Variation sur une "Pensee," annotee par l'auteur, Balancier, 1930.

Litterature (notes; first published in *Commerce,* 1929), Gallimard, 1930.

Regards sur le monde actuel (essays), Stock (Paris), 1931, introduction by Jean Danielou, Vlaletay, 1973; revised and enlarged edition published as *Regards sur le monde actuel et autres essais* (contains "Avantpropos," "Grandeur et decadence de l'Europe," "De l'histoire," "Fluctuations sur la liberte," "L'Idee de dictature," "Au sujet de la dictature," "Souvenir actuel," "L'Amerique, projection de l'esprit europeen," "Images de la France," "Fonction de Paris," "Presence de Paris," "Le Yalou," "Propos sur le progres Pensee et art francais," "Notre destin et les lettres," "La Liberte de l'esprit," "La France travaille," "Metier d'homme," "Coup d'oeil sur les lettres francaises," "Economie de guerre de l'esprit," "Fonction et mystere de l'academie," "Le Centre Universitaire mediterraneen"), Gallimard, 1945, translation by Francis Scarfe published as *Reflections on the World Today,* Pantheon, 1948, Thames & Hudson, 1951.

L'Idee fixe (dialogue), Les Laboratories Martinet (Paris), 1932, new revised and corrected edition published as *L'Idee fixe; ou, Deux Hommes a la mer,* Gallimard, 1933.

Choses tues, Gallimard, 1932.

Moralites, Gallimard, 1932.

Suite, Gallimard, 1934.

Etat de la vertu: Rapport a l'academie, L. Pichon (Paris), 1935.

Analecta (extracts from "Notebooks" and other personal records), Gallimard, 1935.

L'Homme et la coquille, illustrations by Henri Mondor, Gallimard, 1937.

Discours aux chirurgiens (lecture), Gallimard, 1938.

Introduction a la poetique, Gallimard, 1938.

Degas, danse, dessin (fragments first published in *Nouvelle Revue Francaise,* October, 1935, April, 1938), Gallimard, 1938, translation by Helen Burlin published as *Degas, Dance, Drawing,* Lear (New York), 1948.

Poesie et pensee abstraite (lecture), Clarendon Press (Oxford), 1939.

Tel quel (extracts), two volumes, Gallimard, 1941-43.

La Politique de l'esprit, notre souverain bien (address), introduction by Lucy Leveaux, Editions de l'Universite de Manchester, 1941.

Mauvaises pensees et autres (extracts), Gallimard, 1942.

Dialogues de l'arbre, Firmin-Didot (Paris), 1943.

Au sujet de Nerval, Textes Pretextes (Paris), 1944.

Un Poete inconnu (contains two interviews with Valery), Lettres Francaises, 1944.

(With Paul Eluard, Renee Moutard-Uldry, Georges Blaizot, and Louis-Marie Michon) *Paul Bonet,* A. Blaizot (Paris), 1945.

Discours sur Voltaire (lecture), Domat-Montchrestien (Paris), 1945.

Henri Bergson, Domat-Montchrestien (Paris), 1945.

Souvenirs poetiques, Le Prat (Paris), 1947.

Vues, illustrations by Gilbert Poilliot, Table Ronde, 1948.

Histoires brisees, Gallimard, 1950.

Ecrits divers sur Stephane Mallarme, Editions de la Nouvelle Revue Francaise, 1950.

Propos sur le livre, Bibliophiles Francais, 1956.

The Outlook for Intelligence, edited by Jackson Mathews, translation from original French manuscript by Denise Folliot and Mathews, preface by Francois Valery, Harper, 1963.

Reflexions simples sur le corps, de Paul Valery, ayant inspire des lithographies originales a Hans Erni, E. A. D. (Paris), 1967.

(With Francois Valery) *Les Principes d'anarchie pure et appliquee* [and] *Paul Valery et la politique* (the former by P. Valery, the latter by F. Valery), Gallimard, 1984.

NOTEBOOKS

Rhumbs (notes et autres) par Paul Valery (extracts), Divan, 1926.

Autres rhumbs de Paul Valery (extracts), Editions de France, 1927.

Cahier B 1910 (extracts), Gallimard, 1930.

Autres rhumbs (extracts), Gallimard, 1934.

Cahiers (title means "Notebooks"), twenty-nine volumes, Centre National de Recherche Scientifique, 1957-61, definitive edition presented and annotated by Judith Robinson, Gallimard, 1973-74.

CORRESPONDENCE

Lettres a quelques-uns, Gallimard, 1952.

Gaston Poulain, *Paul Valery, tel quel* (includes unpublished letters), illustrations by P. Valery, Licorne, 1955.

(With Andre Gide) *Andre Gide—Paul Valery: Correspondance, 1890-1942,* preface and notes by Robert Mallet, Gallimard, 1955, reprinted as *Correspondance Andre Gide—Paul Valery, 1890-1942,* 1973, abridged and translated edition by June Guicharnaud published as *Self-Portraits: The Gide/Valery Letters, 1890-1942,* edited by Mallet, University of Chicago Press, 1966.

(With Gustave Fourment) *Paul Valery—Gustave Fourment: Correspondance, 1887-1933,* introduction, notes, and documents by Octave Nadal, Gallimard, 1957.

(With Frandcois Valery) *L'Entre-Trois-Guerres de Paul Valery,* Diffusion, Harmonia Mundi, 1994.

COLLECTIONS

Morceaux choisis: Prose et poesie (anthology; contains "Poemes," "Ecrits en prose," "Sur la poesie," "Sur l'architecte," "Sur la danse," "Essais divers," "Cycle Teste"), Gallimard, 1930, abridged translation published as *Selected Writings,* New Directions, 1950.

Poesies, Gallimard, 1931, 2nd edition, 1942, reprinted as *Poesies: Album de vers anciens, La Jeune Parque, Charmes, Pieces diverses, Cantate du Narcisse, Amphion, Semiramis,* Gallimard, 1966, Bibliotheque des Chefs-d'Oeuvre, 1979.

Les Divers Essais sur Leonard de Vinci (contains "Introduction a la methode de Leonard de Vinci," "Note et digression," "Leonard et les philosophes"), Editions du Sagittaire, 1931.

Eupalinos, L'Ame et la Danse, Dialogue de l'arbre, Gallimard, 1944.

Oeuvres choisis (includes "Reconnaissance a Valery," "La Crise de l'esprit," "L'Europeen"), introduction by Daniel Simond, Abbaye du Livre, 1947.

Paul Valery: Prose et vers, compiled by Henri Payre, Blaisdell (Paris), 1968.

La Jeune Parque; L'Ange; Agathe; Histoires brisees, edited with preface and notes by Jean Levaillant, Gallimard, 1974.

Paul Valery: An Anthology (excerpts from *Collected Works*), selected with introduction by James R. Lawler, Princeton University Press, 1976.

Une Chambre conjecturale: Poemes ou proses de jeunesse (juvenalia), Bibliotheque Artistique & Litterature, 1981.

Paul Valery secret, 1937-1945: Lettres intimes, poemes inedits, Ader, Picard, Tajan Commissaires-priseurs Associes (Monaco), 1982.

COMPLETE WORKS

Oeuvres de Paul Valery, twelve volumes, Volumes 1-2, Sagittaire, 1931; Volumes 3-12, Gallimard, 1933-50.

The Collected Works of Paul Valery (fifteen-part collection), edited by Jackson Mathews, Pantheon/Princeton University Press; Part I: *Poems,* translation by David Paul, [and] *On Poets and Poetry,* selected with translation from the *Notebooks* (see above) by James R. Lawler, 1971; Part II: *Poems in the Rough,* translation by Hilary Corke, introduction by Octave Nadal, 1969; Part III: *Plays* (some text in French and English), translation by D. Paul and Robert Fitzgerald, introduction by Francis Fergusson, memoir by Igor Stravinsky, 1960; Part IV: *Dialogues,* translation by W. M. Stewart, prefaces by W. Stevens, 1956; Part V: *Idee fixe,* translation by D. Paul, preface by J. Mathews, introduction by Philip Wheelwright, 1965; Part VI: *Monsieur Teste,* translation and introduction by J. Mathews, 1973; Part VII: *The Art of Poetry,* translation by Denise Folliot, introduction by T. S. Eliot, 1958, Random House, 1961; Part VIII: *Leonardo, Poe, Mallarme,* translation by Malcolm Cowley and Lawler, 1972; Part IX: *Masters and Friends,* translation by Martin Turnell, introduction by Joseph Frank, 1968; Part X: *History and Politics,* translation by Folliot and J. Mathews, preface by Francois Valery, introduction by Salvador de Madariaga, 1962; Part XI: *Occasions,* translation by Roger Shattuck and Frederick Brown, introduction by Shattuck, 1970; Part XII: *Degas, Manet, Morisont,* translation by D. Paul, introduction by D. Cooper, 1960; Part XIII: *Aesthetics,* translation by Ralph Manheim, introduction by Herbert Read, 1964; Part XIV: *Analecta,* translation by Stuart Gilbert, introduction by W. H. Auden, 1970; Part XV: *Moi,* translation by Marthiel Mathews and J. Mathews, 1975.

Oeuvres, two volumes, edited and annotated by Jean Hytier, Gallimard, 1957-60.

OTHER

(Contributor to text) *Tableaux de Paris* (volume of illustrations), Editions Emile-Paul Freres (Paris), 1927.

Amphion (ballet; first produced at The Opera, Paris, France, 1931; music by Arthur Honegger), Rouart Lerolle (Paris), 1931.

Semiramis (three-act ballet; first produced at The Opera, 1934; music by Honegger), Gallimard, 1934.

(Editor and contributor) *Problemes nationaux vus par des francaises* (includes *Avantpropos*), Editions du Sagittaire, 1934.

(Author of text) *Paraboles* (collection of twelve watercolors), Editions du Raisin, 1935.

(Contributor) *Maillol,* Publications Techniques, 1943.

(Author of preface) E. A. van Moe, *Les Fouquet de la Bibliotheque nationale,* Editions de la Revue Verve, 1943.

(Librettist) Germaine Tailleferre, *Cantate du Narcisse* (opera; first produced in 1939), Gallimard, 1944, Centraux Bibliophiles, 1956.

Mon Faust (unfinished play), Gallimard, 1946.

(Author of prefaces with Stephane Mallarme) *Seize Aquarelles* (title means "Sixteen Watercolors"), Editions des Quatres Chemins, 1946.

(Illustrator) Paul de Man, *Les Dessins de Paul Valery* (anthology of drawings), Editions Universelles, 1948.

(Contributor) *Leonardo da Vinci, 1452-1519* (collection of paintings; includes *Introduction a la methode de Leonard de Vinci*), Nouvelle Revue Francaise, 1950.

(Author of introduction) Martin Huerlimann, photographer, *La France* (photographs), Braun (Paris), 1951, translation published with historical notes by Valery as *Eternal France: 216 Pictures in Photogravure,* Thames & Hudson (New York), 1952, revised and enlarged edition published as *France: 217 Pictures in Photogravure,* Studio Publications, 1957, new and enlarged edition published as *France,* Studio Publications, 1968.

(Translator) Publius Vergilius Maro, *Les Bucoliques de Virgile* (verse), illustrations by Jacques Villon, Scripta & Pica (Paris), 1953, enlarged edition published as *Bucoliques de Virgile,* Gallimard, 1956.

(Author of preface) *Anthologie des poetes de la Nouvelle revue francaise,* 3rd edition, Gallimard, 1958.

(Compiler and author of explanatory notes) Rene Descartes, *Les Pages immortelles de Descartes,* Buchet/Chastel, 1961.

(Translator and author of commentary) *Fragments des Marginalia* (selections from *Marginalia* by Edgar Allan Poe), Fata Morgana (France), 1980.

MEDIA ADAPTATIONS: Valery's short story *Monsieur Teste* was adapted as *Monsieur Teste,* a play by Pierre Franck, L'Avantscene (Paris), 1975.

SIDELIGHTS: Paul Valery occupies a position in the history of French letters that is at once strategic and highly problematic. Critics have affixed to him various labels, all of them partially correct. He has been called the last French symbolist, the first post-symbolist, a masterful classical prosodist, an advocate of logical positivism, and a cerebral narcissist. Clearly, Valery was heir to the symbolist tradition of another French poet, Stephane Mallarme, whom he knew and venerated, who encouraged his early work, and whose other young disciples—Pierre Louis in particular—got Valery's work published. On the other hand, he is understood as having broken away from symbolism, as having rejected the cult of poetry for its own sake in favor of a cult of the mind. These views need not be contradictory.

A brief comparison of Valery's famous poem "The Young Fate" ("La Jeune Parque") to Mallarme's "Herodiade" concretely illustrates the nature of the older writer's influence on the young one. Both poems depict a young woman engaged in narcissistic introspection, both embody a severely formal, musical prosody, and both deliberately reject any identifiable "content," or theme. Valery's poem is, in fact, more obscure and less musical than Mallarme's simply because it is more purely metaphysical (one is compelled to use the term despite Valery's abhorrence of it as connoting a certain intellectual frivolity).

Valery's passion for "scientific speculation," which is how he preferred to label his metaphysical writing and that of others, was the reason for his lifelong fascination with American writer Edgar Allan Poe. In *The Tell-Tale Heart: The Life and Works of Edgar Allan Poe,* Julian Symons has described Poe as divided between two obsessive tendencies in his writings, a visionary one and a logical one. Although Mallarme and French poet Charles Baudelaire had celebrated the visionary qualities in Poe, Valery most fully admired his powers of reason, as revealed through Poe's pseudo-scientific meditation on the nature of human knowledge, "Eureka," and through his brilliant practical logician, Auguste Dupin, the detective of "The Murders in the Rue Morgue" and "The Purloined Letter." Valery's unyielding positivism (rationalism) is thus another characteristic setting him apart from other French writers. In an early letter to Andre Gide, Valery wrote: "Poe, and I shouldn't talk about it for I promised myself I wouldn't, is the only writer—with no sins. Never was he mistaken—not led instinctively—but lucidly and successfully, he made a synthesis of all the vertigoes."

Valery conceived himself as an anti-philosopher, and he despised the new discipline of psychology as it was emerging in the work of neurologist and psychoanalytical pioneer Sigmund Freud, because both philosophy and psychology sought to do precisely what he wished to avoid: to *interpret,* to *reduce,* the form of thought, event, and act to a content. He criticized French novelist Marcel Proust for this very tendency, though in doing so he misread Proust. Valery, it must be admitted, was blinded to a great deal in literature by his obsessive commitment to purity of thought. In *Margins of Philosophy* Jacques Derrida has discussed Valery's aversion to Freud: "We will not ask what the meaning of this resistance is before pointing out that what Valery intends to resist is meaning itself. What he reproaches psychoanalysis for is not that it interprets in such or such a fashion, but quite simply that it interprets at all, that it is an interpretation, that it is interested above all in signification, in meaning, and in some principal unity—here, a sexual unity—of meaning."

Perhaps the most salient characteristic of Valery's work and person, and certainly the one to which he himself would have attached greatest importance, was his cult of the intellectual self. His fascination and personal identification with the Narcissus myth is well documented. Of an early poem on this subject, "Narcissus Speaks" ("Narcisse Parle"), he wrote (quoted in volume I of *Oeuvres [Works]*): "The theme of Narcissus, which I have chosen, is a sort of poetic autobiography which requires a few explanations and indications. There exists in Montpellier a botanical garden where I used to go very often when I was nineteen. In a rather secluded corner of this garden, which formerly was much wilder and prettier, there is an arch and in it a kind of crevice containing a slab of marble, which bears three words: PLACANDIS NARCISSAE MANIBUS (to placate the spirit of Narcissa). That inscription had brought on reveries in me, and here, in two words, is its story. In 1820, at this place, a skeleton was discovered, and according to local traditions, it was thought to be the tomb of the poet [Edward] Young. This girl, who died in Montpellier toward the end of the eighteenth century, couldn't be buried in the cemetery, since she was a Protestant. Her father is supposed to have buried her, on a moonlit night. The dead girl's name was Narcissa. The remains that had been found were identified as hers. For me the name Narcissa suggested Narcissus. Then I developed the idea of the myth of this young man, perfectly handsome or who found himself so in his reflection. I wrote at the time the very first *Narcissus,* an irregular sonnet. . . ."

In 1892, Valery completed work on his law degree and embarked upon an unrequited and, by his own admission, "ludicrous" love affair. Similar more or less debilitating infatuations symptomatic of Valery's extreme but repressed emotionalism and sensitivity occurred throughout his life. This first love probably had something to do with the intellectual and spiritual crisis of 1892 that caused him to renounce poetry for twenty years. He took up poetry again, of course, but even as an old man he would continue to be profoundly troubled by what he regarded as the unsolvable equation of love.

One of his last works, a two-part dramatic work called *My Faust (Mon Faust)*, attempted to deal with the issue and was never completed. As Charles G. Whiting has written in *Paul Valery,* "The unfinished play 'Lust' . . . remains as a testimony of his longing for a perfect communion he never found." In "Lust" and "The Solitary" ("Le Solitaire"), which together comprise *My Faust,* one finds the most frank treatment by Valery of his profound fear of sensuality. This fear probably accounts more than any other factor for his emotional crisis and twenty-year renunciation of poetry, since poetry, despite his attempts to purify or sterilize it, emblemized for Valery a certain sensuality of mind. His fear of sensuality may also explain his violent intellectual prejudices—against Freud, for instance, or against philosophy. According to Derrida, Valery rejected psychoanalysis and metaphysics because they focused upon meaning, and for Valery meaning was associated with the elevation of the physical, the sensual, over the formal properties of 'pure' intellect. Furthermore, Freud offered the obvious explanation of why Valery might so vociferously vilify a belief in and search for meaning: the mind's repressed contents are always sexual. "Lust" allegorizes this profound conflict, never resolved by Valery.

Valery himself wrote in his *Notebooks* that "Lust and Faust are *me*—and nothing but me. Experience has shown me that what I wanted most is not to be found in another—and cannot find the *other* capable of trying without reserve to go to the end of the will to . . . *take love where it has never been*." Neither the period of relative silence from 1892 to 1912 nor the resumption of a poetic vocation resolved this crisis, the dilemma of all Valery's life and work: he was never able to bring himself to embrace Lust, though at the end of his life he admitted that she was as integral to him as was the austere, argumentative, and intellectually prudish Faust.

During the years from 1892 to 1922, Valery first worked as a bureaucrat in the French War Office and then as secretary to Edouard Lebey, director of the French Press Association; he attended the Tuesday evening gatherings of artists, writers, and intellectuals at the home of Mallarme, and he married Jeannie Gobillard, a friend of Mallarme's daughter. He continued writing his *Notebooks* and began to publish essays—"Introduction to the Method of Leonardo da Vinci" ("Introduction a la methode de Leonard de Vinci"), and his inquiry into dreams, "Studies" ("Etudes"). He also wrote and published "The Evening With Monsieur Teste" ("La Soiree avec Monsieur Teste"), in which he created the fictional character of Edouard Teste, a paragon of intellectual austerity and self-absorption, an "ideal" thinker, and therefore a role model for Valery himself. Teste might be thought of as a precursor of the figure Faust, but without the opposing figure of Lust. What Valery admired so much in Teste was that, as "The Evening With Monsieur Teste" reveals, he had "*killed his puppet.*" That is, he did nothing conventional, "never smiled, nor said good morning or good night, . . . seemed not to hear a 'How are you?'" In "Letter From Madame Emilie Teste" ("Lettre de Madame Emilie Teste"), Valery's narrator imagined in him

"incomparable intellectual gymnastics. This was not, in him, an excessive trait but rather a trained and transformed faculty. Here are his own words: 'I gave up books twenty years ago. I have burned my papers also. I scrape the quick. . . . I keep what I want.'"

In 1912, Valery was persuaded to break his poetical fast by undertaking a major revision of his earlier poems, which would be published under the title *Album of Old Verses (Album de vers anciens)* in 1920. Suzanne Nash, in the introduction to *Paul Valery's Album de vers anciens: A Past Transfigured,* writes, "Valery seems to have understood that any reconsideration of his own work would perforce lead him to a deeper understanding of problems fundamental to the creative process itself. . . . This potentially self-constitutive dimension of the *Album* was certainly for Valery its ultimate justification. . . . [Its somewhat dated tone is] the result of his intention to mount a critical engagement with his heritage, to offer a portrait gallery of predecessors whose faces emerge transfigured and transvalued according to the exigencies of a new poetics." Thus, Nash continues, "The *Album de vers anciens* . . . is a particularly precious and innovative poetic document, one which holds, inscribed within its structure, the poet's interpretation of his creative confrontation with his past. It represents a kind of chronicle in which the older poet seeks to recreate the intellectual crisis which led him to reject a nineteenth-century concept of poetry founded on an ethics of Symbolist idealism in favor of a poetry which claims autonomy through critical self-reference."

By 1920, Valery had already published *The Young Fate,* a long, very difficult poem, to great critical and popular acclaim. He followed the *Album of Old Verses* with *Charms* ("songs" or "incantations") in 1922, and had written his first quasi-Platonic dialogues, *Eupalinos; or, The Architect (Eupalinos; ou, L'architecte)* and *The Soul and the Dance (L'Ame et la danse)* in 1921. The former dialogue treats much the same topics as "The Seaside Cemetery" ("Le Cimetiere marin"), probably Valery's best-known poem: the relationships of life and death, light and darkness, movement and stasis, which compose life itself. Phaedrus proclaims in this dialogue that "nothing beautiful can be separated from life, and life is that which dies." *The Soul and the Dance* deals with the power of art to transcend individuality and the body and to reach toward the Absolute.

In 1922, Edouard Lebey, Valery's employer at the French Press Association, died, and the necessity of finding a new source of income further confirmed his revived sense of a literary—a publicly literary—vocation. From this point until the end of his life, Valery was known as *the* French poet. In 1924, *Variety (Variete),* a collection of his essays, appeared. It contained the essay on Leonardo first published in 1895, the important article on Poe's "Eureka," and "Variations on a Thought" ("Variations sur une pensee"), in which he attacked Pascal as a thinker. Valery would publish four more volumes of *Variety* in his lifetime. In 1925, he was elected to the French Academy, and in his 1927 inaugural speech he made the unprecedented gesture of attacking his predecessor, novelist Anatole France, probably because France, as coeditor of a literary magazine, had rejected the poetry of Mallarme. In 1937 Valery was appointed to the new chair in poetry at the College de France, a position he held until his death in 1945.

BIOGRAPHICAL/CRITICAL SOURCES:

BOOKS

Carlson, Eric W., editor, *The Recognition of Edgar Allan Poe: Selected Criticism Since 1829,* University of Michigan Press, 1966.
Derrida, Jacques, *Margins of Philosophy,* translated with notes by Alan Bass, University of Chicago Press, 1982.
Grubbs, Henry A., *Paul Valery,* Twayne (New York), 1968.
Harari, Josue V., editor, *Textual Strategies,* Cornell University Press, 1979.
Ince, W. N., *The Poetic Theory of Valery,* University Press, 1961.
Kluback, William, *Paul Valery: Illusions of Civilization,* P. Lang, 1996.
Kluback, William, *Paul Valery: The Continuous Search for Reality,* P. Lang, 1996.
Kluback, William, *Paul Valery: The Realms of the Analecta,* Peter Lang Publishing, 1998.
Lawler, James, *The Poet as Analyst: Essays on Paul Valery,* University of California Press, 1974.
Mackay, Agnes E., *The Universal Self: A Study of Paul Valery,* University of Toronto Press, 1961.
Mallet, Robert, editor, *Self-Portraits: The Gide/Valery Letters, 1890-1942,* abridged and translated by June Guicharnaud, University of Chicago Press, 1966.
Putnam, Walter C., *Paul Valery Revisited,* Twayne, 1995.
Rouart-Valery, Agathe, editor, *Paul Valery,* Gallimard, 1966.
Symons, Julian, *The Tell-Tale Heart: The Life and Works of Edgar Allan Poe,* Harper, 1978.
Taylor, Benjamin, *Into the Open: Reflections on Genius and Modernity,* New York University Press, 1995.
Whiting, Charles G. *Paul Valery,* Athlone Press/University of London, 1978.

*   *   *

VALLEJO, Antonio Buero
See BUERO VALLEJO, Antonio

*   *   *

VANCE, Gerald
See SILVERBERG, Robert

*   *   *

VAN DOREN, Mark 1894-1972

PERSONAL: Born June 13, 1894, in Hope, IL; died December 10, 1972, in Torrington, CT; buried in Cornwall Hollow, CT; son of Charles Lucius (a physician) and Dora (Butz) Van Doren; married Dorothy Graffe (a writer), September 1, 1922; children: Charles, John. *Education:* University of Illinois at Urbana-Champaign, A.B., 1914, A.M., 1915; Columbia University, Ph.D., 1920.

ADDRESSES: Home—Falls Village, CT 06031.

CAREER: Columbia University, New York, NY, instructor, 1920-24, assistant professor, 1924-35, associate professor, 1935-42, professor of English, 1942-59. Lecturer at St. John's College (Maryland), 1937-57; visiting professor of English at Harvard University, 1963. Participant in "Invitation to Learning," CBS

radio talk show, 1940-42. *Military service:* Served in U.S. Army, Infantry, during World War I.

MEMBER: National Institute of Arts and Letters, American Academy of Arts and Letters.

AWARDS, HONORS: Pulitzer Prize for poetry, 1940, for *Collected Poems;* Litt.D. from Bowdoin College, 1944, University of Illinois, 1958, Columbia University, 1960, Knox College, 1966, Harvard University, 1966, and Jewish Theological Seminary of America, 1970; L.H.D. from Adelphi University, 1957, and Mount Mary College, 1965; St. John's College fellowship, 1959; Alexander Hamilton Medal, Columbia College, 1959; Sarah Josepha Hale Award, Richards Free Library (Newport, New Hampshire), 1960; Golden Rose Award, New England Poetry Society, 1960; brotherhood award, National Conference of Christians and Jews, 1960; creativity award, Huntington Hartford Foundation, 1962; Emerson-Thoreau Award, American Academy of Arts and Sciences, 1963; M.D., Connecticut State Medical Society, 1966; Academy of American Poets fellowship, 1967.

WRITINGS:

POEMS

Spring Thunder and Other Poems, Seltzer, 1924.
7 P.M. and Other Poems, Boni, 1926.
Now the Sky and Other Poems, Boni, 1928.
Jonathan Gentry, Boni, 1931.
A Winter Diary and Other Poems, Macmillan, 1935.
The Last Look and Other Poems, Holt, 1937.
Collected Poems, 1922-1928, Holt, 1939.
The Mayfield Deer, Holt, 1941.
Our Lady Peace and Other War Poems, New Directions, 1942.
The Seven Sleepers and Other Poems, Holt, 1942.
The Country Year, Morrow, 1946.
The Careless Clock: Poems about Children in the Family, Sloane, 1947.
New Poems, Sloane, 1948.
Humanity Unlimited: Twelve Sonnets, College of William and Mary Press, 1950.
In That Far Land, Prairie Press, 1951.
Mortal Summer, Prairie Press, 1953.
Spring Birth and Other Poems, Holt, 1953.
Selected Poems, Holt, 1954.
Morning Worship and Other Poems, Harcourt, 1960.
Collected and New Poems, 1924-1963, Hill & Wang, 1963.
(With Archibald MacLeish) *Narrative Poems,* Hill & Wang, 1964.
John Bradford, Hayloft Press, 1966.
100 Poems, Hill & Wang, 1967.
The Stove I Worship, Hayloft Press, 1967.
Winter Calligraphy, Hill & Wang, 1968.
That Shining Place, Hill & Wang, 1969.
In Winter Sing Summer, Bridge & Bryon, Inc., 1970.
Good Morning: Last Poems, Hill & Wang, 1973.

Also author of *Parents' Recompense,* 1965.

FICTION

Dick and Tom: Tales of Two Ponies (juvenile), Macmillan, 1931.
Dick and Tom in Town (juvenile), Macmillan, 1932.
The Transients, Morrow, 1935.
Windless Cabins, Holt, 1940.
The Transparent Tree (juvenile), Holt, 1940.
Tilda, Holt, 1943.
The Witch of Ramoth and Other Tales, Maple Press, 1950.
The Short Stories of Mark Van Doren, Abelard, 1950.

Nobody Say a Word and Other Stories, Holt, 1953.
Home with Hazel and Other Stories, Harcourt, 1957.
Collected Stories, Hill & Wang, Volume I, 1962, Volume II, 1965, Volume III, 1968.
(Author of introduction) Richard Henry Dana, *Two Years before the Mast,* Bantam, 1963.
Somebody Came (juvenile), Quist, 1966.

NONFICTION

Henry David Thoreau, Houghton, 1916.
The Poetry of John Dryden, Harcourt, 1920, revised edition, Minority Press, 1931, published as *John Dryden: A Study of His Poetry,* Holt, 1946.
(With brother, Carl Van Doren) *American and British Literature since 1890,* Century Co., 1925, 2nd revised edition, Appleton, 1967.
Edwin Arlington Robinson, Literary Guild, 1927.
Shakespeare, Holt, 1939.
(With Theodore Spencer) *Studies in Metaphysical Poetry,* Columbia University Press, 1939.
(With Huntington Cairns and Allen Tate) *Invitation to Learning,* Random House, 1941.
(With others) *The New Invitation to Learning,* Random House, 1942.
The Private Reader, Holt, 1942.
Liberal Education, Holt, 1943, published with new introduction, Beacon Press, 1959.
The Noble Voice: A Study of Ten Great Poems, Holt, 1946, published as *Great Poems of Western Literature,* Collier Books, 1962.
Nathaniel Hawthorne, Sloane, 1949.
Man's Right to Knowledge and the Free Use Thereof, Columbia University Press, 1954.
The Autobiography of Mark Van Doren, Harcourt, 1958.
Don Quixote's Profession, Columbia University Press, 1958.
(Author of introduction) Francis Parkman, *The Oregon Trail,* Holt, 1959.
The Happy Critic, Hill & Wang, 1961.
The Dialogues of Archibald MacLeish and Mark Van Doren, edited by Warren V. Bush, Dutton, 1964.
(With others) *Insights into Literature,* Houghton, 1965.
Carl Sandburg, U.S. Government Printing Office, 1969.
(With Maurice Samuel) *In the Beginning, Love: Dialogues on the Bible,* edited by Edith Samuel, John Day, 1973.

Also contributor to *The Letters of Robinson Jeffers,* Ann N. Ridgeway, editor, 1966.

EDITOR

An American Bookshelf, five volumes, Macy Masius, 1927-28.
Samuel Sewell's Diary, Macy Masius, 1927.
Mason Locke Weems, *A History of Life and Death, Virtues and Exploits of General George Washington,* Macy Masius, 1927.
The Travels of William Bartram, Macy Masius, 1928.
Robert Montgomery Bird, *Nick of the Woods, or, Jibbenainosay: A Tale of Kentucky,* Macy Masius, 1928.
William Byrd, *A Journey to the Land of Eden and Other Papers,* Macy Masius, 1928.
An Anthology of World Poetry, Boni, 1928, 2nd revised edition, Harcourt, 1963.
(With Garibaldi M. Lapolla) *A Junior Anthology of World Poetry,* Boni, 1929.
An Autobiography of America, Boni, 1929.

Correspondence of Aaron Burr and His Daughter Theodosia, Covici-Friede, 1929.
Cotton Mather, *The Life of Sir William Phips,* Covici-Friede, 1930.
American Poets, 1630-1930, Little, Brown, 1932.
The Oxford Book of American Prose, Oxford University Press, 1932.
(With Lapolla) *The World's Best Poems,* Boni, 1932.
(With John W. Cunliffe and Karl Young) *Century Readings in English Literature,* 5th edition (Van Doren was not associated with earlier editions), Appleton-Century-Crofts, 1940.
A Listener's Guide to "Invitation to Learning," Columbia Broadcasting System, Volume I: *1940-41,* 1940, Volume II: *1941-42,* 1942.
The Night of the Summer Solstice and Other Stories of the Russian War, Holt, 1943.
Walt Whitman, Viking, 1945, revised edition by Malcolm Cowley, 1973.
The Portable Emerson, Viking, 1946.
William Wordsworth, Selected Poetry, Random House, 1950.
The Best of Hawthorne, Ronald, 1951.
Introduction to Poetry, Sloane, 1951, also published as *Enjoying Poetry,* Sloane, 1951.
Selected Letters of William Cowper, Farrar, Straus, 1951.
(With others) *Riverside Poetry: 48 New Poems by 27 Poets,* Twayne, 1956.

PLAYS

The Last Days of Lincoln (produced in Tallahassee at Florida State University, October 18, 1961), Hill & Wang, 1959.
Never, Never Ask His Name (also see below), produced in Tallahassee at Florida State University, 1965.
Three Plays (contains *Never, Never Ask His Name, A Little Night Music,* and *The Weekend That Was*), Hill & Wang, 1966.

SIDELIGHTS: Mark Van Doren's interest in poetry began with his introduction to Wordsworth. "No poetry had made any great difference to me," he told Archibald MacLeish, "until suddenly I found myself reading Wordsworth. . . . It was music."

During his 39 years of teaching at Columbia University, Van Doren had many opportunities to advise students interested in becoming writers. "My advice to an ambitious young writer," he told Roy Newquist in *Counterpoint,* "is to get the best education he can. . . . And never should he get too far from the soul of man, which is the basic concern of all art." He considered the question of a student's eventual success as a writer to be an impossible one to answer and recalled: "One day when I was talking to such a student, I said, 'Oh dear, let's see. Do you like coffee?' And he said, 'I'm crazy about coffee.' Well, he got the point right away. That's all the point I had." Included among Van Doren's former students are Thomas Merton, Lionel Trilling, Louis Zukofsky, Whittaker Chambers, Jack Kerouac, and Allen Ginsberg.

Van Doren's work is a studied application of his theories of knowledge, poetry, and teaching. He told MacLeish: "The subject [of a poem] is something that has struck you very deeply just because it's there, and because it's beautiful and important." Philip Booth found that "Van Doren's poems are seemingly simply talk made music; he deals with universal themes in the most specific terms, but he risks abstractions where nothing else will reach, and love is a word he is unafraid to write out." Although Paul Engle thought that "now and then one wishes that [Van Doren] would commit some wildness to the page," Theodore

Roethke saw him as "a careful craftsman with a sharp eye for the homely and a mind aware of the profound implications of the casual."

Van Doren never considered himself a part of New York's literary world, nor did he establish friendships with writers simply because they were such. As Van Doren himself remained outside of literary circles, so his work stands apart from the mainstream of contemporary American letters. *Poetry* editors commented: "Van Doren has not received, nor will he evoke, applause from the avant garde; he is solidly entrenched in the tradition of definite purpose framed in strict patterns. There is nothing spectacular about his style. . . . He avoids either extreme of the obsessively confessional and the unemotionally unaffected. . . . Van Doren has never been a slave to a vogue, and never having been in fashion will never be out of it."

Van Doren's place among the critics is also characterized by non-extremism. "Among good critics," wrote Alfred Kazin, "Mr. Van Doren has always stood out as The Great Neutral, and that neutrality is the secret and condition of his quality. For if he has an ardent mind, it is also a tidy one; and if it is never aloof, it always lives on its own track; a mind exact and generous and often piercing in its intuitions, but very careful never to overreach, to say too much; ambitious only to stop on the necessary point made, the observation perfectly seen."

In an interview with Melvin Maddocks, Van Doren stated: "The job of the poet is to render the world—to see it and report it without loss, without perversion. No poet ever talks about feelings. Only sentimental people do. Feelings aren't pleasant. No one ever enjoyed real feelings—fear, pity, jealousy, all the feelings connected with love. Feelings mean suffering. Writing poems is a way of getting rid of feelings. You have to think to do anything well. . . . You finally express what you have to express in cold blood."

Van Doren did not turn his talents to writing plays until the middle 1950's, when he composed *The Last Days of Lincoln.* Of this work he told MacLeish: "Having become utterly enthralled by this person, I just had to do something about it. I had to get him talking." The play is wholly in verse except for Lincoln's speeches. "This play scores high as poetic drama," noted critic John Holmes, "and as a distinguished addition to Civil War literature."

BIOGRAPHICAL/CRITICAL SOURCES:

BOOKS

Bush, Warren V., editor, *The Dialogues of Archibald MacLeish and Mark Van Doren,* Dutton, 1964.
Contemporary Literary Criticism, Gale (Detroit), Volume 6, 1976; Volume 10, 1979.
Kreymbourg, Alfred, *Our Singing Strength,* Coward, 1924.
Ledbetter, J. T., *Mark Van Doren,* P. Lang, 1997.
Newquist, Roy, *Counterpoint,* Rand McNally, 1964.
Nyren, Dorothy, editor, *Library of Literary Criticism,* 2nd edition, Ungar, 1961.
Van Doren, Dorothy, *The Professor and I,* Appleton, 1959.
Van Doren, Dorothy, *The Country Wife,* Morrow, 1950.

PERIODICALS

Christian Science Monitor, February 25, 1960.
Library Journal, October 15, 1958.
Life, June 30, 1969.
National Review, November 7, 1994, p. 78.
Newsweek, February 23, 1959.

New York Herald Tribune, March 29, 1942.
New York Herald Tribune Book Review, February 15, 1959.
New York Times, October 26, 1958, January 31, 1965, January 11, 1969, June 13, 1969.
New York Times Book Review, November 10, 1968.
New York Times Magazine, October 9, 1994, p. 32.
Poetry, November, 1960, March, 1964.
Saturday Review, November 17, 1937.
Washington Post, June 11, 1969.

*   *   *

VAN DYNE, Edith
See BAUM, L(yman) Frank

*   *   *

VARGAS LLOSA, (Jorge) Mario (Pedro) 1936-

PERSONAL: Born March 28, 1936, in Arequipa, Peru; son of Ernesto Vargas Maldonaldo and Dora Llosa Ureta; married Julia Urquidi, 1955 (divorced); married Patricia Llosa, 1965; children: (second marriage) Alvaro, Gonzalo, Morgana. *Education:* Attended University of San Marcos; University of Madrid, Ph.D., 1959. *Politics:* Liberal. *Religion:* Agnostic. *Avocational interests:* Movies, jogging, football.

ADDRESSES: Home—Las Magnolias 295-6 Piso, Barranco, Lima, 04, Peru. *Office*—Agencia Carmen Balcells, Diagonal 580, 08021 Barcelona, Spain. *Agent*—c/o PEN, 7 Duke Street, London, SW3, England or c/o Faber and Faber Ltd, 3 Queen Square, WC1N 3AU..

CAREER: Writer. Journalist with *La Industria,* Piura, Peru, and with Radio Panamericana and *La Cronica,* both in Lima, Peru, during 1950s; worked in Paris, France, as a journalist with Agence France-Presse, as a broadcaster with the radio-television network ORTF, and as a language teacher; University of London, Queen Mary College and Kings College, London, England, faculty member, 1966-68; Washington State University, Seattle, writer in residence, 1968; University of Puerto Rico, Puerto Rico, visiting professor, 1969; *Libre,* Paris, cofounder, 1971; Columbia University, New York City, Edward Laroque Tinker Visiting Professor, 1975; former fellow, Woodrow Wilson Center, Washington, DC; former host of Peruvian television program "The Tower of Babel"; Peruvian presidential candidate, Liberty Movement, 1990.

MEMBER: PEN (president 1976-79), Academy Peruana de la Lengua.

AWARDS, HONORS: Premio Leopoldo Alas, 1959, for *Los jefes;* Premio Biblioteca Breve, 1962, for *La ciudad y los perros;* Premio de la Critica Espanola, 1963, for *La ciudad y los perros,* and 1967, for *La casa verde;* Premio Nacional de la Novela, 1967, for *La casa verde;* Premio Internacional Literatura Romulo Gallegos, 1967, for *La casa verde;* Ritz Paris Hemingway Award, 1985, for *The War of the End of the World;* Principe de Asturias Prize for Letters, 1986; Cervantes Prize for literature, 1994; Jerusalem prize, 1995.

WRITINGS:

FICTION

Los jefes (story collection; title means "The Leaders"), Rocas (Barcelona), 1959, translation by Ronald Christ and Gregory

Kolovakos published in *The Cubs and Other Stories* (also see below).

La ciudad y los perros (novel), Seix Barral (Barcelona), 1963, translation by Lysander Kemp published as *The Time of the Hero,* Grove (New York City), 1966.

La casa verde (novel), Seix Barral, 1966, translation by Gregory Rabassa published as *The Green House,* Harper (New York City), 1968.

Los cachorros (novella; title means "The Cubs"), Lumen (Barcelona), 1967, translation by Christ and Kolovakos published, with six short stories, in *The Cubs and Other Stories* (also see below).

Conversacion en la catedral (novel), two volumes, Seix Barral, 1969, translation by Rabassa published as *Conversation in the Cathedral,* Harper, 1975.

Los cachorros; Los jefes, Peisa (Lima), 1973.

Pantaleon y las visitadoras (novel), Seix Barral, 1973, translation by Christ and Kolovakos published as *Captain Pantoja and the Special Service,* Harper, 1978.

La tia Julia y el escribidor (novel), Seix Barral, 1977, translation by Lane published as *Aunt Julia and the Scriptwriter,* Farrar, Straus (New York City), 1982.

The Cubs and Other Stories (includes *The Leaders* and *The Cubs*), translations by Ronald Christ and Gregory Kolovakos, Harper, 1979.

La guerra del fin del mundo (novel), Seix Barral, 1981, translation by Lane published as *The War of the End of the World,* Farrar, Straus, 1984.

Historia de Mayta (novel), Seix Barral, 1985, translation by Alfred MacAdam published as *The Real Life of Alejandro Mayta,* Farrar, Straus, 1986.

Quien mato a Palomino Molero? (novel), Seix Barral, 1986, translation by MacAdam published as *Who Killed Palomino Molero?,* Farrar, Straus, 1987.

El hablador (novel), Seix Barral, 1987, translation by Lane published as *The Storyteller,* Farrar, Straus, 1989.

Elogio de la madrastra (novel), Tusquets (Barcelona), 1988, translation by Lane published as *In Praise of the Stepmother,* Farrar, Straus, 1990.

Lituma en los Andes (novel), Planeta (Barcelona), 1993, translation by Edith Grossman published as *Death in the Andes,* Farrar, Straus, 1996.

PLAYS

La senorita de Tacna (first produced as *Senorita from Tacna* in New York City, 1983; produced as *The Young Lady from Tacna* in Los Angeles, 1985), Seix Barral, 1981, translation by David Graham-Young published as *The Young Lady from Tacna* in *Mario Vargas Llosa: Three Plays* (also see below).

Kathie y el hipopotamo: Comedia en dos actos (play; translation by Kerry McKenny and Anthony Oliver-Smith produced as *Kathie and the Hippopotamus* in Edinburgh, Scotland, 1986), Seix Barral, 1983, translation by Graham-Young published in *Mario Vargas Llosa: Three Plays* (also see below).

La chunga (play; translation by Joanne Pottlitzer first produced in New York City, 1986), Seix Barral, 1986, translation by Graham-Young published in *Mario Vargas Llosa: Three Plays* (also see below).

Mario Vargas Llosa: Three Plays (contains *The Young Lady from Tacna, Kathie and the Hippopotamus,* and *La chunga*), Hill & Wang (New York City), 1990.

El senor de los balcones (play; title means "Lord of the Balconies"), Seix Barral, 1993.

Also author of *Le Huida* (title means "The Escape"), produced in Piura, Peru.

OTHER

La novela, Fundacion de Cultura Universitaria (Montevideo), 1968.

(With Gabriel Garcia Marquez) *La novela en America Latina,* Milla Batres (Lima), 1968.

(Editor with G. Brotherston) *Seven Stories from Spanish America,* Elsevier Science, 1968.

Antologia minima de M. Vargas Llosa, Tiempo Contemporaneo (Buenos Aires), 1969.

Letra de batalla per "Tirant lo Blanc," Edicions 62, 1969, published as *Carta de batalla por Tirant lo Blanc,* Seix Barral, 1991.

(With Oscar Collazos and Julio Cortazar) *Literatura en la revolucion y revolucion en la literatura,* Siglo Veintiuno (Mexico City), 1970.

Los cachorros; El desafio; Dia domingo, Salvat (Barcelona), 1970.

Dia domingo, Amadis (Buenos Aires), 1971.

Garcia Marquez: Historia de un deicidio (title means "Garcia Marquez: The Story of a Deicide"), Seix Barral, 1971), Seix Barral, 1971.

La historia secreta de una novela, Tusquets, 1971.

(With Martin de Riquer) *El combate imaginario: Las cartas de batalla de Joanot Martorell,* Seix Barral, 1972.

(With Angel Rama) *Garcia Marquez y la problematica de la novela,* Corregidor-Marcha (Buenos Aires), 1973.

Obras escogidas: Novelas y cuentos, Aguilar (Madrid), 1973.

La orgia perpetua: Flaubert y "Madame Bovary," Seix Barral, 1975, translation by Helen Lane published as *The Perpetual Orgy: Flaubert and "Madame Bovary,"* Farrar, Straus, 1986.

Conversacion en la catedral; La orgia perpetua; Pantaleon y las visitadoras, Aguilar, 1978.

Jose Maria Arguedas, entre sapos y halcones, Ediciones Cultura Hispanica del Centro Iberoamericano de Cooperacion (Madrid), 1978.

La utopia arcaica, Centre of Latin American Studies, University of Cambridge (Cambridge, England), 1978.

The Genesis and Evolution of "Pantaleon y las visitadoras," City College (New York City), 1979.

Art, Authenticity and Latin American Culture, Wilson Center (Washington, DC), 1981.

Entre Sartre y Camus, Huracan (Rio Piedras, Puerto Rico), 1981.

Contra viento y marea (journalism; title means "Against All Odds"), three volumes, Seix Barral, 1983-90.

La cultura de la libertad, la libertad de la cultura, Fundacion Eduardo Frei (Santiago, Chile), 1985.

El debate, Universidad del Pacifico, Centro de Investigacion (Lima), 1990.

La verdad de las mentiras (essays; title means "The Truth of Lies"), Seix Barral, 1990.

A Writer's Reality, Syracuse University Press (Syracuse, NY), 1991.

El pez en el agua: Memorias, Seix Barral, 1993, translated by Lane as *A Fish in the Water: A Memoir,* Farrar, Straus, 1994.

Desafios a la Libertad, Aguilar, 1994.

Contributor to *The Eye of the Heart,* 1973; contributor to periodicals, including *Commentary, Harper's, National Review, New Perspectives Quarterly, New York Times Book Review, New York Times Magazine, UNESCO Courier,* and *World Press Review.* Selected works have been recorded by the Library of Congress Archive of Recorded Poetry and Literature.

MEDIA ADAPTATIONS: "The Cubs" was filmed in 1971; *Captain Pantoja and the Special Service* was filmed in 1976 (Vargas Llosa directed the film, which was banned in Peru); *Aunt Julia and the Scriptwriter* was adapted as a television series in Peru, as a screenplay written by William Boyd and directed by Jon Amiel in 1989, and as a motion picture titled *Tune in Tomorrow,* c. 1990.

SIDELIGHTS: Peruvian writer Mario Vargas Llosa often draws from his personal experiences to write of the injustices and corruption of contemporary Latin America. At one time an admirer of communist Cuba, since the early 1970s Vargas Llosa has been opposed to tyrannies of both the political left and right. He now advocates democracy, a free market, and individual liberty, and he cautions against extreme or violent political action, instead calling for peaceful democratic reforms. In 1989 he was chosen to be the presidential candidate of Fredemo, a political coalition in Peru; though at one point he held a large lead in election polls, in the end he lost the election to Alberto Fujimori. Through his novels—marked by complex structures and an innovative merging of dialogue and description in an attempt to recreate the actual feeling of life—Vargas Llosa has established himself as one of the most important of contemporary writers in the Spanish language. His novels, a London *Times* writer comments, "are among the finest coming out of Latin America."

Vargas Llosa wrote *The Time of the Hero* after leaving Peru for Europe in 1958, when he was twenty-two. In embracing Europe and entering into self-imposed exile from his native land, Vargas Llosa was following in the footsteps of numerous Latin American writers, including Jorge Luis Borges, Julio Cortazar, and Carlos Fuentes. Vargas Llosa was to stay in Europe for thirty years, returning to Peru in the late 1980s after the country had slipped into political chaos and economic impoverishment-conditions that prompted Vargas Llosa's decision to seek the presidency of Peru. During his three decades in Europe, Vargas Llosa became an internationally celebrated author.

Though Vargas Llosa had attracted widespread attention with his first novel, it was his second novel that cemented his status as a major novelist. In the award-winning *The Green House* (*La casa verde* in the Spanish edition), Vargas Llosa draws upon another period from his childhood for inspiration. For several years his family lived in the Peruvian jungle town of Piura, and his memories of the gaudy local brothel, known to everyone as the Green House, form the basis of his novel. The book's several stories are interwoven in a nonlinear narrative revolving around the brothel and the family that owns it, the military that runs the town, a dealer in stolen rubber in the nearby jungle, and a prostitute who was raised in a convent. "Scenes overlap, different times and places overrun each other . . . echoes precede voices, and disembodied consciences dissolve almost before they can be identified," Luis Harss and Barbara Dohmann write in *Into the Mainstream: Conversations with Latin-American Writers.* Gregory Rabassa, writing in *World Literature Today,* notes that the novel's title "is the connective theme that links the primitive world of the jungle to the primal lusts of 'civilization' which are enclosed by the green walls of the whorehouse." Rabassa sees, too, that Vargas Llosa's narrative style "has not reduced time to a device of measurement or location, a practical tool, but has conjoined it with space, so that the characters carry their space with them too . . . inseparable from their time." Harss and Dohmann find that *The Green House* "is probably the most accomplished work of fiction ever to come out of Latin America. It has sweep, beauty, imaginative scope, and a sustained eruptive power that carries the reader from first page to last like a fish in a bloodstream."

With *Conversation in the Cathedral* (first published in Spanish as *Conversacion en la catedral*) Vargas Llosa widened his scope. Whereas in previous novels he had sought to recreate the repression and corruption of a particular place, in *Conversation in the Cathedral* he attempts to provide a panoramic view of his native country. As John M. Kirk states in *International Fiction Review,* this novel "presents a wider, more encompassing view of Peruvian society. [Vargas Llosa's] gaze extends further afield in a determined effort to incorporate as many representative regions of Peru as possible." Set during the dictatorship of Manuel Odria in the late 1940s and 1950s, the society depicted in the novel "is one of corruption in virtually all the shapes and spheres you can imagine," Wolfgang A. Luchting writes in the *Review of the Center for Inter-American Relations.* Penny Leroux, in a review of the book for *Nation,* calls it "one of the most scathing denunciations ever written on the corruption and immorality of Latin America's ruling classes."

The nonlinear writing of *Conversation in the Cathedral* is seen by several critics to be the culmination of Vargas Llosa's narrative experimentation. Writing in the *Review of the Center for Inter-American Relations,* Ronald Christ calls the novel "a masterpiece of montage" and "a massive assault on simultaneity." Christ argues that Vargas Llosa links fragments of prose together to achieve a montage effect that "promotes a linking of actions and words, speech and description, image and image, point of view and point of view." Kirk explains that in *Conversation in the Cathedral,* Vargas Llosa is "attempting the ambitious and obviously impossible plan of conveying to the reader all aspects of the reality of [Peruvian] society, of writing the 'total' novel." By interweaving five different narratives, Vargas Llosa forces the reader to study the text closely, making the reader an "accomplice of the writer [which] undoubtedly helps the reader to a more profound understanding of the work." Kirk concludes that *Conversation in the Cathedral* is "both a perfect showcase for all the structural techniques and thematic obsessions found in [Vargas Llosa's] other work, as well as being the true culmination of his personal anguish for Peru."

A farcical novel involving a military officer's assignment to provide prostitutes for troops in the Peruvian jungle, *Captain Pantoja and the Special Service* is "told through an artful combination of dry military dispatches, juicy personal letters, verbose radio rhetoric, and lurid sensationalist news reports," Gene Bell-Villada writes in *Commonweal.* Vargas Llosa also mixes conversations from different places and times, as he did in previous novels. And like these earlier works, *Captain Pantoja and the Special Service* "sniffs out corruption in high places, but it also presents something of a break, Vargas Llosa here shedding his high seriousness and adopting a humorous ribald tone," Bell-Villada concludes. The novel's satirical attack is aimed not at the military, a *Times Literary Supplement* reviewer writes, but at "any institution which channels instincts into a socially acceptable ritual. The humor of the narrative derives less from this serious underlying motive, however, than from the various linguistic codes into which people channel the darker forces."

The humorous tone of *Captain Pantoja and the Special Service* is also found in *Aunt Julia and the Scriptwriter* (*La tia Julia y el escribidor* in the original Spanish edition). The novel concerns two characters based on people in Vargas Llosa's own life: his first wife, Julia, who was his aunt by marriage, and a writer of radio soap opera who Vargas Llosa names Pedro Camacho in the novel. The 18-year-old narrator, Mario, has a love affair with the 32-year-old Julia. Their story is interrupted in alternate chapters by Camacho's wildly complicated soap opera scripts. As Camacho goes mad, his daily scripts for ten different soap operas become more and more entangled, with characters from one serial appearing in others and all of his plots converging into a single unlikely story. The scripts display "fissures through which are revealed secret obsessions, aversions and perversions that allow us to view his soap operas as the story of his disturbed mind," Jose Miguel Oviedo writes in *World Literature Today.* "The result," explains Nicholas Shakespeare in the *Times Literary Supplement,* "is that Camacho ends up in an asylum, while Mario concludes his real-life soap opera by running off to marry Aunt Julia."

In *The War of the End of the World,* Vargas Llosa for the first time sets his story outside of his native Peru. He turns instead to Brazil of the 19th century and bases his story on an apocalyptic religious movement that gained momentum towards the end of the century. Convinced that the year 1900 marked the end of the world, these zealots, led by a man named the Counselor, set up the community of Canudos. Because of the Counselor's continued denunciations of the Brazilian government, which he called the "antichrist" for its legal separation of church and state, the national government sent in troops to break up this religious community. The first military assault was repulsed, as were the second and third, but the fourth expedition involved a force of some 4,000 soldiers. They laid waste to the entire area and killed nearly 40,000 people.

Vargas Llosa tells Wendy Smith in *Publishers Weekly* that he was drawn to write of this bloody episode because he felt the fanaticism of both sides in this conflict was exemplary of present-day Latin America. "Fanaticism is the root of violence in Latin America," he explains. In the Brazilian war, he believes, is a microcosm of Latin America. "Canudos presents a limited situation in which you can see clearly. Everything is there: a society in which on the one hand people are living a very old-fashioned life and have an archaic way of thinking, and on the other hand progressives want to impose modernism on society with guns. This creates a total lack of communication, of dialogue, and when there is no communication, war or repression or upheaval comes immediately," he tells Smith. In an article for the *Washington Post,* Vargas Llosa explains to Curt Suplee that "in the history of the Canudos war you could really see something that has been happening in Latin American history over the 19th and 20th centuries—the total lack of communication between two sections of a society which kill each other fighting *ghosts,* no? Fighting fictional enemies who are invented out of fanaticism. This kind of reciprocal incapacity of understanding is probably the main problem we have to overcome in Latin America."

Although his political views have changed during the course of his career, taking him from a leftist supporter of communist Cuba to a strong advocate of democracy, Vargas Llosa's abhorrence of dictatorship, violence, and corruption has remained constant. And he sees Latin American intellectuals as part of a continuing cycle of "repression, chaos, and subversion," he tells Philip Bennett in the *Washington Post.* Many of these intellectuals, Vargas Llosa explains further, "are seduced by rigidly dogmatic stands. Although they are not accustomed to pick up a rifle or throw bombs from their studies, they foment and defend the violence." Speaking of the ongoing conflict in Peru between the government and a Maoist guerrilla movement, the Shining Path, Vargas Llosa clarifies to Suplee that "the struggle between the guerrillas and the

armed forces is really a settling of accounts between privileged sectors of society, and the peasant masses are used cynically and brutally by those who say they want to 'liberate' them."

Vargas Llosa believes that a Latin American writer is obligated to speak out on political matters. "If you're a writer in a country like Peru," he tells Suplee, "you're a privileged person because you know how to read and write, you have an audience, you are respected. It is a moral obligation of a writer in Latin America to be involved in civic activities." This belief led Vargas Llosa in 1987 to speak out when the Peruvian government proposed to nationalize the country's banks. His protest quickly led to a mass movement in opposition to the plan, and the government was forced to back down. Vargas Llosa's supporters went on to create Fredemo, a political party calling for democracy, a free market, and individual liberty. Together with two other political parties, Fredemo established a coalition group called the Liberty Movement. In June of 1989, Vargas Llosa was chosen to be the coalition's presidential candidate for Peru's 1990 elections.

Vargas Llosa chronicles his experience as a presidential candidate in *A Fish in the Water.* In addition to discussing the campaign, however, the author also offers a memoir of his early years in Peru. Notes Rockwell Gray in the Chicago *Tribune Books,* "One string of alternating chapters in the book ends with the young writer's departure for France in 1958; the other recreates the exhausting and dangerous [presidential] campaign that carried him to every corner of Peru." Alan Riding in the *New York Times Book Review* adds that the book "serves as [Vargas Llosa's] mea culpa: he explains why the aspiring writer of the 1950's became a politician in the late 1980's and why, in the end, this was a terrible mistake." Vargas Llosa's account of his childhood and young adulthood includes his ambivalent relationship with his father, whom he met for the first time at age eleven and toward whom he had an intense dislike. Mark Falcoff, writing in the *Times Literary Supplement,* declares, "The pages of this book dealing with the father-son relationship are among the most violent and passionate Vargas Llosa has ever written." The author also covers his years at a military prep school and his university years in Lima.

After losing the campaign, Vargas Llosa returned to Europe—this time to Spain, where he assumed Spanish citizenship. However, his first novel after running for president, *Death in the Andes,* is set in his homeland amid the modern political and social strife evidenced by the rebellion of the Shining Path guerilla movement. In part a murder mystery, the novel follows Corporal Lituma as he ventures from his home in Peru's coastal region to a mountain village to investigate the disappearance of three men. In addition to the story line of the missing men, Vargas Llosa intersperses tales of violence committed by the Shining Path as well as a romantic story involving Tomas Carreno, Lituma's guide and partner. Critics praised Vargas Llosa's skill in creating a technically ambitious novel, although some reviewers remarked that the author failed to integrate the various plot lines into a coherent story line.

The relationship of politics and literature once again commands Vargas Llosa's attention in his 1997 essay collection, *Making Waves.* The pieces included here, written over three decades, address two of the author's principal concerns: his contention that writers serve their homelands best as voices of "protest, disagreement, and criticism" and the more radical notion that a country is itself a kind of living text. "A nation," he writes, "is a political fiction imposed on a social geographic reality almost always by force for the benefit of a political minority." Authors and their works, including William Faulkner and Vaclav Havel, often provide the point of departure for Vargas Llosa's political contemplations. "Ever tantalized by an insatiable hunger for beauty and justice, Vargas Llosa is a writer of great integrity and humor," writes the reviewer for *Publishers Weekly,* adding that "his new volume will be treasured by those who relish the brilliance and clarity of his prose." Writing in *Booklist,* Brad Hooper finds Vargas Llosa's polemics persuasive, saying he "employs his consummate articulateness to coax the reader into seeing things his way."

"A major figure in contemporary Latin American letters," as Richard Locke of the *Washington Post Book World* explains, and "the man whom many describe as the national conscience of his native Peru," as George de Lama writes in the *Chicago Tribune,* Vargas Llosa is usually ranked with Jorge Luis Borges, Gabriel Garcia Marquez, and other writers of what has been called the Latin American "Boom" of the 1960s. His body of work set in his native Peru, Suzanne Jill Levine writes in the *New York Times Book Review,* is "one of the largest narrative efforts in contemporary Latin American letters. . . . [He] has begun a complete inventory of the political, social, economic and cultural reality of Peru. . . . Very deliberately, Vargas Llosa has chosen to be his country's conscience."

BIOGRAPHICAL/CRITICAL SOURCES:

BOOKS

Booker, M. Keith, *Vargas Llosa among the Postmodernists,* University Press of Florida, 1994.
Contemporary Literary Criticism, Gale (Detroit), Volume 3, 1975; Volume 6, 1976; Volume 9, 1978; Volume 10, 1979; Volume 15, 1980; Volume 31, 1985; Volume 42, 1987; Volume 85, 1995.
Dictionary of Literary Biography, Volume 145: *Modern Latin-American Fiction Writers, Second Series,* Gale, 1994.
Feal, Rosemary Geisdorfer, *Novel Lives: The Fictional Autobiographies of Guillermo Cabrera Infante and Mario Vargas Llosa,* University of North Carolina Press, 1986.
Gerdes, Dick, *Mario Vargas Llosa,* Twayne (Boston), 1985.
Harss, Luis, and Barbara Dohmann, *Into the Mainstream: Conversations with Latin-American Writers,* Harper, 1967.
Hispanic Literature Criticism, Gale, 1994.
Lewis, Marvin A., *From Lime to Leticia: The Peruvian Novels of Mario Vargas Llosa,* University Press of America (Lanham, MD), 1983.
A Marxist Reading of Fuentes, Vargas Llosa, and Puig, University Press of America, 1994.
Moses, Michael Valdez, *The Novel and the Globalization of Culture,* Oxford University Press, 1995.
Rossmann, Charles, and Alan Warren Friedman, editors, *Mario Vargas Llosa: A Collection of Critical Essays,* University of Texas Press, 1978.
Williams, Raymond Leslie, *Mario Vargas Llosa,* Ungar, 1986.

PERIODICALS

Booklist, May 15, 1997.
Chicago Tribune, January 3, 1989; June 23, 1989; August 3, 1989.
Chicago Tribune Book World, October 7, 1979; January 12, 1986.
Commonweal, June 8, 1979.
Esquire, April, 1990, p. 103.
Harper's, June, 1987, p. 15.
Hispamerica, Volume 63, 1992, pp. 33-41.
Hispania, March, 1976.
Hudson Review, winter, 1976.

International Fiction Review, January, 1977.
Interview, September, 1988, p. 86.
Latin American Literary Review, Volume 11, number 22, 1983, p. 15-25; January-June, 1987, pp. 121-31, 201-6.
Library Journal, March 15, 1994, p. 116; May 1, 1994, p. 114.
Los Angeles Times, May 20, 1985; December 18, 1988.
Los Angeles Times Book Review, February 2, 1986.
Maclean's, April 9, 1990, p. 32.
Modern Language Notes, March, 1990, pp. 351-66.
Mother Jones, January, 1989, p. 22.
Nation, November 22, 1975; February 12, 1996, p. 28.
National Review, December 10, 1982; May 16, 1994, p. 65; April 17, 1995, p. 53.
New Leader, March 17, 1975; November 15, 1982.
New Republic, August 16-23, 1982; October 8, 1984, pp. 25-27; June 8, 1987, p. 54; February 12, 1990, p. 20.
Newsweek, February 10, 1986; April 9, 1990, p. 33; October 1, 1990, p. 67.
New York, August 23, 1982.
New Yorker, February 24, 1986, pp. 98, 101-4; August 24, 1987, p. 83; December 25, 1989, p. 103; October 1, 1990, pp. 107-10; April 15, 1996, p. 84.
New York Review of Books, March 20, 1975; January 24, 1980; July 16, 1987, p. 35; October 11, 1990, p. 17; May 26, 1994, p. 19; May 9, 1996, p. 16.
New York Times, March 30, 1985; January 8, 1986; February 9, 1986; February 12, 1986; September 10, 1989.
New York Times Book Review, March 23, 1975; April 9, 1978; September 23, 1979; August 1, 1982; December 2, 1984; February 2, 1986; May 31, 1987, p. 13; October 29, 1989, p. 1; October 14, 1990, p. 11; March 10, 1991, p. 13; May 15, 1994, p. 10; February 18, 1996, p. 7.
New York Times Magazine, November 20, 1983; November 5, 1989, p. 44.
Paris Review, fall, 1990, pp. 47-72.
Partisan Review, Volume 46, number 4, 1979.
PMLA, Volume 106, number 1, 1991, pp. 46-59.
Publishers Weekly, October 5, 1984; November 20, 1995, p. 65; April 21, 1997.
Review of the Center for Inter-American Relations, spring, 1975.
Time, February 17, 1975; August 9, 1982; January 27, 1986; March 10, 1986; July 27, 1987 p. 64; September 7, 1987; November 13, 1989, p. 110; April 9, 1990, p. 56; October 22, 1990, p. 89; June 13, 1994, p. 75; February 12, 1996, p. 75.
Times (London); May 13, 1985; August 5, 1986.
Times Literary Supplement, October 12, 1973; May 20, 1983; March 8, 1985; May 17, 1985; July 1, 1988; June 17, 1994, p. 11.
Tribune Books (Chicago), October 29, 1989; September 11, 1994, p. 7; March 3, 1996, p. 6.
Washington Post, August 29, 1983; October 1, 1984; March 26, 1989.
Washington Post Book World, August 26, 1984; February 9, 1986; May 22, 1994, p. 5; February 25, 1996, p. 1.
World Literature Today, winter, 1978 (special issue on Vargas Llosa); spring, 1978.

OTHER

Sklodowska, Elzbieta, *An Interview with Mario Vargas Llosa,* American Audio Prose Library, 1994.

VENDLER, Helen (Hennessy) 1933-

PERSONAL: Born April 30, 1933, in Boston, MA.; daughter of George (a teacher) and Helen (a teacher; maiden name, Conway) Hennessy; divorced; children: David. *Education:* Emmanuel College, A.B. (summa cum laude), 1954; attended University of Louvain, 1954-55, and Boston University, 1955-56; Harvard University, Ph.D., 1960.

ADDRESSES: Home—54 Trowbridge St. # 2, Cambridge, MA 02138-4113. *Office*—Department of English, 8 Prescott St., Harvard University, Cambridge, MA 02138-3929.

CAREER: Cornell University, Ithaca, NY, instructor in English, 1960-63; Haverford College, Haverford, PA, lecturer in English, and Swarthmore College, Swarthmore, PA, lecturer in English, both 1963-64; Smith College, Northampton, MA, assistant professor of English, 1964-66; Boston University, Boston, MA., associate professor, 1966-68, professor of English, 1968-85, director of graduate studies, department of English, 1970-75 and 1978-79; Harvard University, Cambridge, MA., visiting professor, 1981-85, professor of English, 1985–, William R. Kenan Professor of English and American Literature and Language, 1986–, associate dean of arts and sciences, 1987-92; Porter University, professor, 1990–; Fulbright lecturer in American literature, University of Bordeaux, 1968-69; Fanny Hurst Visiting Professor, Washington University, St. Louis, MO, fall, 1975. Judge for National Book Award in poetry, 1972, and Pulitzer Prize in poetry, 1974, 1976, 1978, and 1986. Member of subcommittee on literary criticism awards, Guggenheim Foundation, 1974, 1976, 1977, and 1978; jury member for Mellon fellowships and Rockefeller fellowships, both 1979. Member, Rockefeller Commission on the Humanities, 1978-79, and Board of Educational Consultants, National Endowment for the Humanities; Pulitzer Prize Board, 1991–; senior fellow Harvard Society Fellows, 1981-93; member of the educational advisory board, Guggenheim Foundation, 1991–.

MEMBER: Modern Language Association of America (member of executive council, 1971-75; second vice-president, 1978; first vice-president, 1979; president, 1980), American Academy of Arts and Sciences (councillor, 1976-80), English Institute (member of supervisory board, 1970-73; trustee, 1977-86), American Philosophical Society, Norwegian Academy of Letters and Sciences; PEN Society of Fellows—Harvard University, Phi Beta Kappa.

AWARDS, HONORS: Fulbright fellowship, 1954-55; American Association of University Women fellowship, 1959-60; American Council of Learned Societies, grant-in-aid, 1963, fellowship, 1971; James Russell Lowell Prize, Modern Language Association, and *Explicator* Literary Foundation Award, 1969, both for *On Extended Wings: Wallace Stevens' Longer Poems;* Guggenheim fellowship, 1971; National Institute of Arts and Letters Award, 1975; Metcalf Teaching Award, Boston University, 1975; National Endowment for the Humanities fellowship, 1977-78, 1986-87 and 1994; Graduate Society Medal, Radcliffe College, 1978; National Book Critics Circle Award in criticism, and "Notable Book" citation from American Library Association, 1980, both for *Part of Nature, Part of Us: Modern American Poets;* nomination for National Book Critics Circle Award in criticism, 1983, for *The Odes of John Keats;* Keats-Shelley Association Award, 1994; Charles Stewart Parnell fellow, Magdalene College, 1995; many honorary degrees, among others from Smith College, University of Oslo, Kenyon College, University of Hartford, Union College, and Columbia University.

WRITINGS:

Yeats's Vision and the Later Plays, Harvard University Press, 1963.
On Extended Wings: Wallace Stevens' Longer Poems, Harvard University Press, 1969.
(Editor with Reuben Brower and John Hollander; also contributor) *I. A. Richards: Essays in His Honor,* Oxford University Press, 1973.
The Poetry of George Herbert, Harvard University Press, 1975.
Part of Nature, Part of Us: Modern American Poets, Harvard University Press, 1980.
The Odes of John Keats, Harvard University Press, 1983.
Wallace Stevens: Words Chosen Out of Desire, University of Tennessee Press, 1984.
(Editor and author of introduction) *The Harvard Book of Contemporary American Poetry,* Harvard University Press, 1985 (published in England as *The Faber Book of Contemporary American Poetry,* Faber, 1987).
(Contributing editor and author of introduction to contemporary poetry section) Donald McQuade, general editor, *The Harper American Literature,* two volumes, Harper, 1987.
(Editor, author of introduction, and contributor) *Voices and Vision: The Poet in America* (companion to "Voices and Vision," broadcast on PBS-TV, January 26 April 19, 1988), Random House, 1987.
The Music of What Happens: Poems, Poets, Critics, Harvard University Press, 1988.
The Given and the Made: Strategies of Poetic Redefinition, Harvard University Press, 1995.
Soul Says: On Recent Poetry, Belknap Press (Cambridge), 1995.
The Breaking of Style: Hopkins, Heaney, Graham, Harvard University Press, 1995.
The Art of Shakespeare's Sonnets, Harvard University Press (Cambridge, MA), 1997.
Peoms, Poets, Poetry: An Introduction and Anthology, Bedford Books of St. Martin's Press (Boston), 1997.

CONTRIBUTOR

Roy Harvey Pearce and Hillis Miller, editors, *The Act of the Mind,* Johns Hopkins Press, 1964.
Reuben Brower, editor, *Forms of Lyric,* Columbia University Press, 1970.
Irvin Ehrenpreis, editor, *Wallace Stevens,* Penguin, 1972.
William H. Pritchard, editor, *William Butler Yeats,* Penguin, 1972.
W. K. Wimsatt, editor, *Literary Criticism: Idea and Act,* University of California Press, 1974.
Frank Doggett and Robert Buttel, editors, *Wallace Stevens: A Celebration,* Princeton University Press, 1980.
Lloyd Schwartz and Sybil P. Estess, editors, *Elizabeth Bishop and Her Art,* University of Michigan Press, 1983.
Keats, John, *Poetry Manuscripts at Harvard,* edited by Jack Stillinger, Belknap Press (Cambridge), 1990.
Stevens, Wallace, *Poems,* selected by Vendler, Knopf, 1993.

Also contributor to "Modern Critical Views" series, edited by Harold Bloom, Chelsea House. Contributor of numerous articles to periodicals, including *Atlantic Monthly, Mademoiselle, Massachusetts Review, New Republic, New Yorker, New York Times Book Review, Parnassus: Poetry in Review, Salmagundi,* and *Southern Review;* contributor of numerous reviews to periodicals, including *American Scholar, Nation,* and *Yale Review.*

OTHER

Member of advisory board, *Studies in Romanticism;* consulting poetry editor, *New York Times Book Review,* 1971-74; member of editorial board, *American Scholar,* 1978-81; poetry critic, *New Yorker,* 1978.

SIDELIGHTS: Helen Vendler is regarded by many as one of America's foremost critics of poetry. Since the mid-1960s, she has contributed numerous reviews and articles on poetry to prominent literary publications, in particular the *New York Times Book Review,* and since 1978 has served as poetry critic for the *New Yorker.* In addition to her reviews and articles, Vendler is the author of acclaimed book-length studies of poets W. B. Yeats, George Herbert, Wallace Stevens, and John Keats. Her most noted work, the award-winning collection of criticism *Part of Nature, Part of Us: Modern American Poets,* is recognized as an extensive and informed view of contemporary American poetry. A second collection, *The Music of What Happens: Poems, Poets, Critics,* further explores the diversities and issues that surround contemporary British and American poetry. Regarding Vendler's accomplishments, William H. Pritchard once remarked in the *New Republic:* "To begin with a judgment widely shared, if not a truth universally acknowledged: Helen Vendler is the best poetry reviewer in America."

Vendler is often cited as one of poetry's best "close readers," her criticism frequently praised for its insightful explication of individual poems and its comprehension of individual aesthetic principles. Furthermore, she is known as a devout disciple of poetry, the literary art which, she states in the foreword to *Part of Nature, Part of Us,* is "the one form of writing that is to me the most immediate, natural, and accessible." "Poetry, clearly, is Vendler's passion," writes Phoebe Pettingell in the *New Leader.* "She directs her observations straight at the heart of the matter, so that her readers may recognize at once what she finds so marvelous in a poem." Vendler's critical writings have been recognized as assured and illuminating discussions of poetry. Pritchard cites "the pressure of an appetite" and an "unreticent forcefulness" at work in Vendler's poetry criticism, adding that "her virtues are a rigorous attending to verbal structure and texture; the ability to quote appositely and economically; a sure though not a too-exclusive taste; above all, the ability to do the poem one better by putting into words the relevant responses we might have had if we'd been smarter and more feeling." In a review of *Part of Nature, Part of Us* for the *New York Times,* Anatole Broyard describes a respect for poetry that becomes apparent in Vendler's criticism: "Unlike some critics, Helen Vendler puts herself entirely at the service of the poets she is talking about. Although she writes too well to be invisible, she does not compete or pontificate either. . . . What she does is to offer the poetry to you and somehow push and pull you into shape until you can accept it."

Part of Nature, Part of Us was a resounding accomplishment for Vendler, a collection of her reviews and essays published between 1966 and 1979 which "provides a sweeping overview of contemporary American poetry," writes John C. Hawley in *America.* During the time span that these reviews and essays appeared, Vendler's reputation as a formidable literary critic was also bolstered by her extended studies of Stevens and Herbert. *On Extended Wings: Wallace Stevens' Longer Poems* "ought to be read, with care and gratitude, by every reader of Stevens, for no critic before her has understood so well his major poems," says Harold Bloom in the *New York Times Book Review,* adding: "Helen Vendler . . . has written a superb and badly needed book,

giving us readings unlikely to be surpassed of Stevens's longer poems, which tend to be his best." Likewise, Vendler's *The Poetry of George Herbert* was praised as an in-depth study of the early seventeenth-century English metaphysical poet. "Vendler is undoubtedly a finely trained and extraordinarily resourceful reader, and I cannot imagine that anybody who cares for Herbert, or more generally for poetry, will fail to learn something from this book," comments Frank Kermode in the *New York Times Book Review.* Kermode adds that although Vendler displays a "willfulness" by examining those of Herbert's poems which most closely "fit her model," she lays the foundations of her study in the works themselves: "Her meditations are nearly always faithful to their texts—she very rarely succumbs to the vice of the 'close reader,' which is to speak more wonders than the poem he is considering; and she has brought off a quite notable feat of construction in making a collection of disparate commentaries stand up as a book."

Vendler's critical perspective and writing style are central to the impact of *Part of Nature, Part of Us* and emerge as overall strengths of her literary criticism. Irvin Ehrenpreis writes in the *New York Review of Books* that Vendler's critical stance is distinguished in that it does not start with the "poem as a completed object"; rather, "Vendler starts with the act of creation. She stands beside the poet and watches him compose. Reading her essays, one acquires a sense of works of art not laid out in an operating theater but just coming into being." Similarly, Harold Beaver notes in *Parnassus: Poetry in Review* that Vendler's "strategy is not so much to center on the poem, or on the poet, but on the problem of writing such and such a poem." Thus, he explains, "the act of writing is itself treated as a critical act: the critic's role is to ponder and assess that act." John Bayley, in *Times Literary Supplement,* contends that Vendler "is certainly the most thoughtful and humane, as she is the least system-bound, critic of poetry now writing. . . . Her examination of a poet is always as absolutely business-like and thorough as it is sympathetic, like that of a really good doctor."

Vendler attracted much attention with her next book of criticism, *The Odes of John Keats,* a groundbreaking—in some circles, controversial—study of the nineteenth-century English Romantic poet. In the book, Vendler examines several of Keats's most famous odes, not only in regards to their often praised rich language, but, as Ehrenpreis notes, "find[ing] . . . a special relation, dealing progressively with a common theme, the creative imagination." Pettingell explains that "Vendler presents the sequential progression of the odes as a series of tentative solutions, proposed, rejected, then used as building blocks toward the next." A number of reviewers, although impressed with Vendler's reading of the individual odes, point out problems in organizing them as a progressive larger structure. Ehrenpreis writes that "Vendler takes for granted both an order and a progression, with each principle supporting the other. To some readers, therefore, her demonstrations will appear circular." *New Republic* contributor David Bromwich claims that by examining the odes as a progressive development, Vendler "is obliged to discover a fair amount of shortcomings in the earlier odes which readers not attuned to her story have either passed over or refused to consider as faults." And, Frank Kermode comments in the *New York Times Book Review* that Vendler's "overriding need to show development from ode to ode imposes some constraints, perhaps exquisite, on the expositor. It imposes orders, and these orders replace what might be rewarding in a different way, an acceptance of fortuity." Vendler's approach, however, also bears witness to a respect for the strength of Keats's writing, contends Maureen

Corrigan in the *Voice Literary Supplement:* "By adopting close reading as her critical technique, she pays Keats the highest compliment of viewing his work as a crystallization of language and culture that anticipates, within its own structures, all the myriad 'outside' frameworks that could be imposed upon it."

While some reviewers take issue with Vendler's thesis in *The Odes of John Keats,* many are quick to point out typical strengths of her literary criticism. "She is a materialist—and in a noble sense of the word," writes Nicholas Bromell in the *Boston Review.* "Vendler roots her discussion of the odes in her deeply felt response to Keats's language. Her ability to *present* what Keats is doing and to describe the effects, registered in our minds, of Keats's verbal facility, is breathtaking." Ehrenpreis concurs, commenting that although "reading the odes as a group is less likely to be successful than individual readings[,] . . . the most appealing feature of Vendler's work remains; and that is her desire to follow the poet in his labor of creation."

In *The Music of What Happens: Poems, Poets, Critics,* Vendler returns to her study of contemporary poetry and, in addition to presenting new studies of poets such as Seamus Heaney, John Ashbery, and A. R. Ammons, offers further insight into the foundations of her critical work. Aligning her methods with what she terms "aesthetic criticism," Vendler is first concerned with approaching a particular poem as a distinct artistic expression, understandable within its own context. She writes in the book's introduction that her aim "is to describe the art work in such a way that it cannot be confused with any other art work (not an easy task), and to infer from its elements the aesthetic that might generate this unique configuration." Vendler distinguishes her approach from "both ideological and hermeneutic (or interpretation-centered) critics [who] want to place the literary work principally within the sphere of history and philosophy." An "aesthetic critic," she explains, "would rather place it in the mimetic, expressive, and constructivist sphere of the fine arts— theater, painting, music, sculpture, dance—where it may more properly belong." Outside of such theoretical bearings, however, *The Music of What Happens* is primarily devoted to offering new insights into a range of contemporary poetry. "These essays confirm Vendler's authority as a subtle, shrewd and demanding critic of recent American poetry," writes James E. B. Breslin in the *Los Angeles Times Book Review,* while Anthony Thwaite comments in the *Washington Post Book World* that "some of Vendler's most incisive, balanced, and sometimes astringent pieces are on poets who are not Americans: Ted Hughes, Stephen Spender, [Donald] Davie." The essays in *The Music of What Happens,* according to Breslin, "aim not to display the cleverness of the critic but to make poetry a habitable place."

BIOGRAPHICAL/CRITICAL SOURCES:

PERIODICALS

America, July 25, 1981.
Book World, February 25, 1996, p. 4.
Boston Review, April, 1984.
Chicago Tribune, May 18, 1988.
English Journal, October, 1984.
Globe and Mail (Toronto), December 14, 1985.
Hudson Review, winter, 1980.
Library Journal, April 15, 1995, p. 78.
London Review of Books, June 21-July 4, 1984.
Los Angeles Times Book Review, December 22, 1985; February 7, 1988; February 21, 1988; September 17, 1995, p. 2.
Nation, March 9, 1970; December 25, 1995, p. 841.

New Leader, June 2, 1980; January 9, 1984; December 18, 1995, p. 22.
New Republic, March 29, 1980; December 5, 1983.
New York Review of Books, May 29, 1980; April 12, 1984.
New York Times, March 29, 1980.
New York Times Book Review, October 5, 1969; July 6, 1975; March 23, 1980; November 27, 1983.
Parnassus: Poetry in Review, Volume 8, number 2, 1980.
South Atlantic Quarterly, summer, 1976.
Times (London), January 29, 1987.
Times Literary Supplement, August 22, 1980; March 2, 1984; May 24, 1985; May 1, 1987; May 22, 1987.
Virginia Quarterly Review, summer, 1976; autumn, 1980; spring, 1985.
Voice Literary Supplement, December, 1983.
Washington Post Book World, April 6, 1980; January 31, 1988.
World Literature Today, spring, 1981.
Yale Review, summer, 1984.

*   *   *

VENISON, Alfred
See POUND, Ezra

*   *   *

VERDI, Marie de
See MENCKEN, H(enry) L(ouis)

*   *   *

VERDU, Matilde
See CELA, Camilo Jose

*   *   *

VIALIS, Gaston
See SIMENON, Georges (Jacques Christian)

*   *   *

VIAN, Boris 1920-1959
(Vernon Sullivan, Baron Visi, Adolph Schmurz, Bison Ravi)

PERSONAL: Born March 10, 1920, in Ville d'Avray, a suburb of Paris, France; died of a heart attack, June 23, 1959; son of Paul and Yvonne Ravenez Vian; married Michelle Leglise, 1941 (divorced 1952), married Ursula Kubler, 1954; children: two from first marriage. *Education:* Lycee de Sevres, Lycee Condorcet, Lycee Hoche, baccalaureats, 1935, 1937; L'ecole Central des Arts et Manufactures, Angouleme, 1942, diploma in engineering.

CAREER: Engineer, novelist, playwright, poet, journalist, essayist, translator, critic, reviewer, jazz musician and singer, composer, librettist.

MEMBER: College of Pataphysicians.

WRITINGS:

COLLECTIONS

Theatre, 2 volumes, Union General d'Editions (Paris) 1965, 1971.

Textes et chansons, Union General d'Editions, 1966; Christian Bourgois (Paris), 1984.

Chroniques de jazz, edited by Lucien Malson, Editions de la Jeune Parque (Paris), 1967.

Chansons et poemes, Tchou (Paris), 1967.

Theatre inedit, Bourgois, 1970.

Cantilenes en Gelee; (precede de) Barnum's Digest; (et suivi de) Vingt poemes inedits; Je voudrais pas crever; (suivi de) Lettres au College de pataphysique; (et) Textes sur la litterature (collection), Bourgois, 1976.

Cantilenes en Gelee; Barnum's Digest; Vingt poemes inedits (collection), Union generale d'editions, 1978.

Romans, poemes, novelles et theatre, J.-J Pauvert (Paris), 1978.

Operas (includes *Les marquis de lejanes; Fiesta; Lily Strasa; Arne sakmussem; Le mercenaire*), edited by Noel Arnaud, Bourgois, 1982.

Romains, nouvelles, ourvres diverses, edited by Gilbert Pestureau, Le Livre de Poche (Paris), 1991.

FICTION

Vercoquin et le plancton, Gallimard (Paris), 1946.

(Under pseudonym Vernon Sullivan) *J'irai cracher sur vos tombes,* 1946; Bourgois, 1973; as *I Shall Spit on Your Graves,* translation by Vian and Milton Rosenthal, 1948.

L'ecume de jours, 1947, Rombaldi (Paris), 1972, Bourgois, 1994; translation by Stanley Chapman, published as *Froth on the Daydream,* 1967; translation by John Sturrock, published as *Mood Indigo,* Grove Press (New York), 1968.

L'automne a Pekin, 1947, Bourgois, 1983.

(Under pseudonym Vernon Sullivan) *Les morts ont tous la meme peau,* 1947, Bourgois, 1976.

Le loup-garou (stories), 1947, Bourgois, 1970.

(Under pseudonym Vernon Sullivan) *Et on tuera tous les affreux,* Bourgois, 1948.

Les fourmis (stories), 1949; translation by Julia Older, published as *Blues for a Black Cat and Other Stories,* University of Nebraska Press (Lincoln), 1992.

Les poissons morts, 1949.

L'herbe rouge (stories), 1950.

L'arrache-coeur, 1953, Union Generale d'Editions, 1974; Pauvert, 1980, Rombaldi, 1977; translation by Stanley Chapman, published as *Heartsnatcher,* Rapp & Whiting (London), 1968.

(Under pseudonym Vernon Sullivan) *Elles se rendent pas Compte,* E. Losfeld, 1953, Bourgois, 1976.

Les lourettes fourrees (stories), 1962.

Trouble dans les andians, Bourgois, 1966.

Le ratichon baigneur et autres novelles inedites (stories), Bourgois, 1981.

L'herbe rouge; les lurettes fourrees (stories), Bourgois, 1975.

POETRY

Barnum's Digest, 1948.

Cantilenes en Gelee, 1949.

Je voudrais pas crever, J.-J. Pauvert, 1962.

Cent sonnets, edited by Noel Arnaud, Bourgois, 1984.

PLAYS

L'equarrissage pour tous, 1948, translation by Marc Estrin, published as *Nackery for All,* translation by Simon Watson Taylor, published as *The Knacker's ABC: A Paramilitary Vaudeville in One Long Act,* Grove, 1968.

Le Chevalier de Neige, Bourgois, 1953.

Les Batisseurs d'Empire, L'Arche, 1959, translation by Simon Watson Taylor, published as *The Empire Builders,* Methuen (London), 1971.

Fiesta (opera libretto), music by Darius Milhard, Huegel (Paris), 1958.

Le govter des generaux, 1962, translation by Simon Watson Taylor, published as *The Generals' Tea Party,* Grove, 1967.

Petits spectacles (nightclub skits), Bourgois, 1977.

SCREENPLAYS

Rue des ravissantes, et dix-huit autres scenarios cinematographiques, Bourgois, 1957.

OTHER

Livre d'or, 1940.

Les adventures de A., 1957.

En avant la zizique . . . et par ici les gros sous, 1958.

En verve (selection), 1970.

Chroniques de jazz, La Jeune Parque, 1967; revised, 1986.

Chroniques du menteur, Bourgois, 1974.

Manuel de Saint-Germain-des Pres, Chane, 1974.

Derriere la zizique (articles), Bourgois, 1976.

Cinema science-fiction, Bourgois, 1978.

Memoire concernant le calcul numerique de dieu par les methodes simples et fausses, Cymbalum pataphysicum, 1979.

Traite de civisme, Bourgois, 1979.

Ecrits pornographiques, edited by Noel Arnaud, Bourgois, 1980.

Ecrits sur jazz, 1981; translation by Mike Zwerin, published as *Roundabout Close to Midnight: The Jazz Writings of Boris Vian,* Quartet Books (London) 1988.

Autres ecrits sur le jazz, 2 vols., Bourgois, 1981-82.

La belle epoque (articles), Bourgois, 1982.

Chansons, Bourgois, 1984.

Autres Ecrits sur le Jazz, 2 vols., ed. Claude Raueil, Bourgois, 1981-82.

TRANSLATIONS

August Strindberg, *Mademoiselle Julie,* 1982.

A. E. van Vogt, *Le Monde des A,* 1953.

Richard Wright, *La-bas Pres de la Riviere,* 1957.

Nelson Algren, *L'Homme au Bras d'Or,* 1957.

Peter Cheyney, *Les Femmes s'En Balancent,* 1949.

SIDELIGHTS: Boris Vian's notoriety as a writer began when he was 26, with the publication of *J'irai Cracher sur Vos Tombes;* he died 13 years later of a heart attack while watching a preview of a film made from the same novel. A prolific writer, he left behind some 20 volumes of published work, with many others published posthumously. He wrote novels, short stories, plays, essays, reviews, screenplays, and libretti for several operas. While Vian lived, his novels were more controversial than successful, and he supported himself by writing magazine articles and translating books into French, notably works by August Strindberg, A. E. van Vogt, and Nelson Algren. He was also a jazz trumpeter and singer who performed at numerous Parisian cabarets and wrote over 400 songs. Since his death, popular and critical respect for his works has increased, and several have been translated into English.

Vian's work reflects his preoccupation with death, but he appears to have embraced life fully. He developed an interest in jazz when he was 18, after hearing Duke Ellington's orchestra in Paris, and learned to play the trumpet. By age 22, he was performing with the Claude Abadie orchestra, and he later became a songwriter and composer. His schooling pointed him toward engineering, a profession which he practiced for five years during his early 20s. At the same time, he began writing articles. His friendship with Jean Paul Sartre and Simone de Bouvoir, among others, provided him with the influence to publish short stories in the important periodical *Temps Moderne*. After the appearance of his *Froth on the Pudding,* at age 27, he abandoned engineering and turned to writing full time.

Vian wrote two novels in the early 1940s, but his first published novel was *J'irai cracher sur vos tombes* (1946; *I Shall Spit on Your Graves*). He wrote it in response to an editor friend's request for advice on an American author he might publish in order to improve his business. Instead of advice, Vian wrote a book for him in 10 days, while on vacation. Vian pretended that he had merely translated the novel of one "Vernon Sullivan," an "American novelist." The narrator is a mulatto who passes easily as a white person; to avenge his lynched brother, he sleeps with two beautiful sisters, both rich and white, then kills them brutally. (Vian's knowledge of race relations in the United States was based on what he had learned from black American jazz musicians.) The book was an instant success, selling over 100,000 copies and earning Vian a great deal of money.

Sales were further enhanced in 1947 when a salesman in Paris strangled a woman and left a copy of the book next to her body, opened to the page describing the death of one of the sisters. The book was banned in 1949 as "objectionable foreign literature" and Vian was brought to trial, accused by the press of having inspired the murder. In the meantime, he and an American writer produced an English translation of the work, presenting it as the original, "American version." Nevertheless, in 1951, Vian was fined 100,000 francs. Although he wrote four other novels under the name Vernon Sullivan and five novels under his own name, *J'irai cracher sur vos tombes* was his only important publishing success to appear during his lifetime.

Vian contracted rheumatic fever when he was 12, which left him with a heart condition; he expected to die at any time and certainly not to live past the age of 40. The major themes in his fiction and plays were freedom and spontaneity, humor, nonsense and absurdity, anti-clericalism, hatred of bureaucracy, sexual situations, violence, pacifism, and death. His titles often bore little relation to the content; for example, *L'automne a Pekin (Autumn in Peking)* has nothing to do with either; its characters construct a railroad in a desert, and route it through a hotel. *Les batisserurs d'empire (The Empire Builders)* depicts a family of three moving to progressively smaller apartments, hounded by "the Noise." *L'herbe rouge (Red Grass)* is about a man who travels endlessly through his own past after building a time machine that was supposed to take him to the future. In the words of critic Zvjezdana Rudelic, Vian consistently "rejected boundaries, classifications, and traditions in favor of spontaneous and apparently illogical thought."

According to critic Jennifer Walters, Vian presents death as violent, sudden, unexpected, and unimportant. It happens at any time to anybody. *The General's Tea Party* ends with the protagonists, one by one, losing at Russian roulette; their deaths are accompanied by the joyous laughter of the survivors. At the end of the surprise party in *Vercoquin et le plancton,* a protagonist machine guns every fourth guest, then ravages the entire block. In the play *Knackery for All (L'equarrissage pour tous),* a Boy Scout shows up at a farmhouse with a box of dynamite; only one person survives the resulting explosion. In Vian's work, the behavior of

the living is unaltered by the large number of fatalities around them.

In contrast to the violence and death in his work, Vian's language is inventive, fresh, and fluid; according to critic Walters, this shows his love of life and active awareness of it. But, she continues, the way in which he destroys expected forms "shows his uncertainty, and the mental shock thus produced creates an impression of an absurd world over which man has no control."

In *L'ecume des jours* (1947; *Froth on the Dream or Mood Indigo*), for example, Vian tells a tragic love story set in a world where figures of speech assume literal reality, and familiar objects fight back surrealistically. Streets are named after jazz figures Sidney Bichet and Louis Armstrong; Colin, the hero, has a "100,000 doublezoons;" before dinner, Colin and Chloe drink "piano cocktails" created by a machine which mixes exotic drinks according to the music of Duke Ellington; Chloe becomes fatally stricken when a water-lily grows on her lung. There being no money for a funeral, the undertaker throws her coffin out the window, where it strikes an innocent child and breaks her leg. According to critic Robert Phelps's summary of the novel in the *New York Times Book Review,* "The world is a lousy place." Readers of absurdist literature, writes Alfred Cismaru, find Vian "a writer in whose prolific work they could recognize a heretofore unknown pertinence: for his preoccupations and obsessions are indeed those of today."

BIOGRAPHICAL/CRITICAL SOURCES:

BOOKS

Cismaru, Alfred, *Boris Vian,* Twayne Publishers (Boston), 1974.
Dictionary of Literary Biography, Volume 72: *French Novelists, 1930-1960,* Gale (Detroit), 1988.
Encyclopedia of World Literature in the 20th Century, revised edition, Continuum.
Reference Guide to World Literature, second edition, St. James Press (Detroit), 1995.
Twentieth-Century Literary Criticism, Volume 9, Gale, 1983.

PERIODICALS

New York Times Book Review, January 26, 1969, p. 5.

*   *   *

VIDAL, Gore 1925-
(Edgar Box)

PERSONAL: Original name Eugene Luther Gore Vidal; born October 3, 1925, at the U.S. Military Academy, West Point, NY; son of Eugene Luther (Director of Air Commerce under President Franklin Roosevelt) and Nina (Gore) Vidal. *Education:* Graduate of Phillips Exeter Academy, 1943. *Politics:* Democrat.

ADDRESSES: Office—c/o Random House, 201 E. 50th St., New York, NY, 10022. *Agent*—Owen Laster, William Morris Agency, 1350 Avenue of the Americas, New York, NY 10019.

CAREER: Writer. E. P. Dutton, New York City, editor, 1946; lived in Antigua, Guatemala, 1947-49; Democratic Party candidate for Congress in the Twenty-ninth District of New York, 1960; member of President's Advisory Committee on the Arts, 1961-63; host of *Hot Line* television program, 1964; lived in Italy, 1967-76; cofounder of New Party, 1968-71; cochairman of People's Party, 1970-72; ran for nomination as Democratic Party senatorial candidate in California, 1982. Lecturer; appears frequently on television and radio talk shows. *Military service:* U.S. Army, Army Transportation Corps, 1943-46; became First Mate; served in Pacific Theater during World War II.

AWARDS, HONORS: Edgar Allan Poe Award, Mystery Writers of America, 1955, for television drama; Screen Writers Annual Award nomination and Cannes Critics Prize, both 1964, both for screenplay *The Best Man;* National Book Critics Circle Award for criticism, 1982, for *The Second American Revolution and Other Essays;* named honorary citizen, Ravello, Italy, 1983; Prix Deauville, 1983, for *Creation;* National Book Award for nonfiction, 1993, for *United States: Essays, 1952-1992.*

WRITINGS:

NOVELS

Williwaw (also see below; published in paperback as *Dangerous Voyage,* Amereon, Ltd.), Dutton, 1946.
In a Yellow Wood, Dutton, 1947.
The City and the Pillar, Dutton, 1948, revised edition published as *The City and the Pillar Revised,* 1965.
The Season of Comfort, Dutton, 1949.
A Search for the King: A Twelfth-Century Legend, Dutton, 1950.
Dark Green, Bright Red, Dutton, 1950.
The Judgment of Paris, Dutton, 1952, revised edition, Little, Brown, 1965.
Messiah, Dutton, 1954, revised edition, Little, Brown, 1965.
Julian (also see below; two chapters first printed as *Julian the Apostate*), Little, Brown, 1964.
Washington, D.C., Little, Brown, 1967.
Myra Breckinridge (also see below), Little, Brown, 1968.
Two Sisters: A Novel in the Form of a Memoir, Little, Brown, 1970.
Burr (also see below), Random House, 1973.
Myron (also see below), Random House, 1974.
1876, Random House, 1976.
Kalki (also see below), Random House, 1978.
Creation, Random House, 1981.
Duluth, Random House, 1983.
Lincoln, Random House, 1984.
Myra Breckinridge [and] *Myron,* Random House, 1986.
Empire, Random House, 1987.
Hollywood: A Novel of America in the 1920s, Random House, 1990.
Live from Golgotha: The Gospel According to Gore Vidal, Random House, 1992.
The Smithsonian Institution: A Novel, Random House, 1998.

UNDER PSEUDONYM EDGAR BOX; MYSTERIES

Death in the Fifth Position (also see below), Dutton, 1952.
Death before Bedtime . . . (also see below), Dutton, 1953.
Death Likes It Hot (also see below), Dutton, 1954.
Three by Box: The Complete Mysteries of Edgar Box (contains *Death in the Fifth Position, Death before Bedtime . . . ,* and *Death Likes It Hot*), Random House, 1978.

TELEPLAYS

Visit to a Small Planet and Other Television Plays (contains *Visit to a Small Planet* [also see below; aired on *Goodyear Playhouse,* 1955], *Barn Burning* [1954], *Dark Possession* [1954], *The Death of Billy the Kid* [1955], *A Sense of Justice* [1955], *Smoke* [1954], *Summer Pavilion* [1955], and *The Turn of the Screw* [1955]), Little, Brown, 1956.
Dress Gray (also see below; based on the novel by Lucien Truscott), National Broadcasting Corporation (NBC-TV), 1986.

Also author or adaptor of *Dr. Jekyll and Mr. Hyde,* 1955, *Stage Door,* 1955, *A Farewell to Arms,* 1955, *Honor* (also see below), 1956, *Portrait of a Ballerina,* 1956, *The Indestructible Mr. Gore,* 1959, and *Dear Arthur,* 1960. Author of teleplays for series *Philco-Goodyear Playhouse, Studio One,* and *Omnibus Theater.*

SCREENPLAYS

The Catered Affair, Metro-Goldwyn-Mayer (MGM), 1956.
I Accuse, MGM, 1958.
(With Robert Hamer) *The Scapegoat,* MGM, 1959.
(With Tennessee Williams) *Suddenly Last Summer,* Columbia, 1959.
The Best Man (adapted from the play; produced by United Artists, 1964), edited by George P. Garrett, Irvington, 1989.
(With Francis Ford Coppola) *Is Paris Burning?* (based on the novel by Dominique Lapierre), Paramount, 1966.
The Last of the Mobile Hotshots, Warner Bros., 1970.
(With others) *Caligula,* Analysis Film, 1980.

Also author of screenplay adaptations of his novels *Kalki* and *Burr;* also author of screenplay adaptation of Lucien Truscott's *Dress Gray.*

STAGE PLAYS

Visit to a Small Planet: A Comedy Akin to a Vaudeville (also see below; adapted from his television play; produced on Broadway, 1957), Little, Brown, 1957, revised edition, Dramatists Play Service, 1959.
The Best Man: A Play of Politics (also see below; produced on Broadway, 1960), Little, Brown, 1960, revised edition, Dramatists Play Service, 1977.
On the March to the Sea: A Southron Comedy (also see below; adapted from the teleplay *Honor*), produced in Bonn, West Germany (now Germany), 1961.
Three Plays (contains *Visit to a Small Planet, The Best Man: A Play of Politics,* and *On the March to the Sea: A Southron Comedy*), Heinemann, 1962.
(Translator and editor of English translation) Freidrich Duerrenmatt, *Romulus: A New Comedy* (produced on Broadway, 1962), Dramatists Play Service, 1962.
Weekend (produced in New Haven, CT, 1968; produced on Broadway, 1968), Dramatists Play Service, 1968.
An Evening with Richard Nixon (produced in New York City, 1972), Random House, 1972.

Vidal's *Romulus: The Broadway Adaptation* was performed with Friedreich Durrenmatt's *Romulus the Great* (translated by Gerhard Nelhaus), 1966.

ESSAYS

Rocking the Boat, Little, Brown, 1962.
Sex, Death, and Money, Bantam, 1968.
Reflections upon a Sinking Ship, Little, Brown, 1969.
Homage to Daniel Shays: Collected Essays, 1952-1972, Random House, 1972, published as *Collected Essays, 1952-1972,* Heinemann (London), 1974, published as *On Our Own Now,* Panther, 1976).
Matters of Fact and of Fiction: Essays, 1973-1976, Random House, 1977.
The Second American Revolution and Other Essays (published in England as *Pink Triangle and Yellow Star and Other Essays*), Random House, 1982.
Armageddon? Essays, 1983-1987, Deutsch, 1987.
At Home: Essays, Random House, 1989.
A View from the Diner's Club: Essays, 1987-1991, Deutsch, 1991.
Screening History, Harvard University Press, 1992.

The Decline and Fall of the American Empire, Odonian Press, 1992.

United States: Essays, 1952-1992, Random House, 1992.

OTHER

A Thirsty Evil: Seven Short Stories (also see below), Zero Press, 1956.

Three: Williwaw [and] *A Thirsty Evil: Seven Short Stories* [and] *Julian the Apostate,* New American Library, 1962.

(Editor) *Best Television Plays,* Ballantine, 1965.

An Evening with Richard (recording; based on the play *An Evening with Richard Nixon*), Ode Records, 1973.

(With others) *Great American Families,* Norton, 1977.

(Author of introduction) *Edith Wharton Omnibus,* Doubleday, 1978.

(With Robert J. Stanton) *Views from a Window: Conversations with Gore Vidal,* Lyle Stuart, 1980.

(Author of introduction) *The Collected Stories of Paul Bowles,* Black Sparrow Press, 1983.

(Author of foreword) Logan Pearsall Smith, *All Trivia,* Ticknor & Fields, 1984.

(Author of introduction) Tennessee Williams, *The Collected Stories,* New Directions, 1985.

(Author of introduction) Fritz Peters, *Finistere,* Seeker Press, 1985.

(Editor) Henry James, *The Golden Bowl,* Penguin, 1985.

Vidal in Venice, Summit Books, 1987.

(Author of introduction) *Dawn Powell,* QPB, 1989.

(Author of foreword) Alfred Chester, *Head of a Sad Angel: Stories, 1953-1966,* edited by Edward Field, Black Sparrow Press, 1990.

(Author of foreword) Marion E. Rodgers, editor, *Impossible H. L. Mencken: A Selection of His Best Newspaper Stories,* Doubleday, 1991.

(Author of introduction) Don Bachardy and James P. White, editors, *Where Joy Resides: A Christopher Isherwood Reader,* Farrar, Straus, 1991.

(Author of foreword) Robert McAlmon, *Miss Knight and Others,* edited by Edward N. Lorusso, University of New Mexico Press, 1992.

Palimpsest: A Memoir, Random House, 1995.

The Essential Vidal, Random House, 1998.

Contributor to periodicals, including *New York Review of Books, Times Literary Supplement,* and *Nation.* Member of advisory board, *Partisan Review,* 1960-71.

MEDIA ADAPTATIONS: The Death of Billy the Kid was the basis for the film *The Left-Handed Gun,* filmed by Warner Bros., 1958, and for the made-for-cable movie *Gore Vidal's Billy the Kid,* broadcast on Turner Network Television, May 10, 1989. *Visit to a Small Planet* was filmed by Paramount in 1960; *Myra Breckinridge* was filmed by Twentieth Century-Fox in 1970.

SIDELIGHTS: Gore Vidal is one of the best known literary figures in America. Familiar to millions as a witty and wicked talk show guest, two-time political candidate, and the creator of the outrageous Myra Breckinridge, Vidal has written numerous novels, plays, screenplays, essays, and reviews. Called "one of the more alert and favoured writers of our time" by a critic in the *Observer* and "the Gentleman Bitch of American Letters" by the *New Republic*'s Stefan Kanfer, Vidal has been the subject of critical and media attention for four decades. His work is noted for its eloquence, intelligence, urbane humor, and biting satire, as well as for its attacks on cultural and political sacred cows. "Gore

Vidal's novels, plays, and essays can be divided roughly into three areas of animosity," remarks *Time*'s R. Z. Sheppard. "The first is the author's belief that Western civilization erred, when it abandoned pagan humanism for the stern, heterosexual authority of the Judaeo-Christian patriarchy. . . . The second area that draws Vidal's scorn is American politics, which he dramatizes as a circus of opportunism and hypocrisy. . . . The most freewheeling disdain is directed at popular culture, macho sexuality and social pretensions."

Vidal's genres run the gamut from historical fiction to autobiographical essays to political commentary, his styles from witty and cultured to sarcastic and acidic. "Vidal is a difficult writer to categorize because he is a man of several voices," writes Robert F. Kiernan in the book *Gore Vidal.* "He has brooded over ancient empires in several novels, as though he were possessed by the spirit of Gibbon, yet he has also written about the American *crise de virilite* and managed to sound a good deal like Hemingway. He has sent young Americans in search of old Europe, as a dutiful son of Henry James, but he has also written novels about the American political system and acknowledged a debt to Henry Adams. In his essays he often seems like Lord Macaulay, magisterial and urbane, while in the Breckinridge novels he evokes Ronald Firbank, irrepressible and playful."

Greatly influenced by his maternal grandfather, Oklahoma senator Thomas P. Gore, Vidal developed a lifelong passion for politics. "I do nothing but think about my country," he said in a *Time* article. "The United States is my theme, and all that dwell in it." His interest has taken a variety of forms outside his writing: he has twice run for political office (for the U.S. House of Representatives in 1960 and the U.S. Senate in 1982), originated the idea of the Peace Corps, campaigned for presidential candidate Eugene McCarthy in 1968, and served as an organizer and secretary-of-state designate for the ultra-liberal People's party and as political commentator and journalist. "The only thing I've ever really wanted in my life was to be President," he told the *Time* writer. His interest in the U.S. political system, as well as his intimate knowledge of politicians and powerbrokers, has informed much of Vidal's work, such as his political plays, *The Best Man, Weekend,* and *An Evening with Richard Nixon,* and his novels, *Washington, D.C., Burr, 1876, Lincoln,* and *Empire.*

With the publication of *Williwaw* in 1946, Vidal joined the ranks of the literary *enfants terribles* who dominated the American cultural scene just after World War II. His name was often linked with other post-War prodigies such as Truman Capote, John Horn Burns, James Jones, and—several years later—Norman Mailer. Begun while Vidal was recuperating from a bout of rheumatoid arthritis he contracted during his Army Transportation Corps service in the Bering Sea during World War II, *Williwaw* describes the effect of an Arctic squall (called a "williwaw") on the crew members of an Army transport ship. The plotting is simple, the language concise—traits for which the book has been cited by a number of critics, who applaud Vidal's self-restraint. Aldridge, writing in *After the Lost Generation,* calls it "a slight and unpretentious book," and Kiernan proclaims, "that nineteen-year-old Gore Vidal should have been capable of writing *Williwaw* is astonishing."

Vidal quickly followed up the success of *Williwaw* with another novel, *In a Yellow Wood,* published barely a year later. The book, which takes its title from the Robert Frost poem "The Road Not Taken" ("Two roads diverged in a yellow wood / . . . I took the one less travelled by / And that has made all the difference"), recounts a day in the life of Robert Holton, a rather dull young clerk at a brokerage house. Holton is a determinedly conventional man and when he again meets his exotic Italian wartime mistress and his happy-go-lucky army buddy, he is disturbed rather than excited by their invitations to experiment with a more fascinating life. He turns down their offers, choosing to continue his boring but safe existence.

The novel shows "a psychological astuteness," notes *New York Herald Tribune Weekly Book Review*'s Stephan Stepanchev, who admires the way Vidal structures the book by reflecting Holton through the eyes of the various people with whom he comes in contact. *In a Yellow Wood*, Stepanchev continues, demonstrates "that the author has a good eye for metropolitan surfaces and an accurate ear for ordinary speech." Some critics, such as N. L. Rothman in the *Saturday Review of Literature*, praise *In a Yellow Wood* for its "controlled naturalism, . . . concentrated workmanship, . . . rigid and painstaking selection of details, plus . . . [a] delicacy of understatement that reaps its delicacy of overtone." Though the book received many favorable reviews at the time of its publication, Vidal himself considers it a failure. Twenty-seven years after its release in 1947, Vidal told a *Paris Review* interviewer that it is doomed to remain "in limbo forever. I can't rewrite it because it's so bad that I can't reread it."

With two fairly successful novels to his credit, Vidal wanted to try something different. "I was bored with playing it safe," he recalled in the foreword to the 1965 revision of his 1948 novel *The City and the Pillar.* "I wanted to take risks, to try something no American had done before." *The City and the Pillar* immediately appeared on bestseller lists and raised conflicts in the New York publishing world that would reverberate for years. The subject of *The City and the Pillar*—homosexuality—was not a topic new to American literature; what was new, however, was the way in which Vidal treated his subject: the novel's young homosexual protagonist was presented as a perfectly average, athletic, handsome boy-next-door type. "[Vidal] wrote what had never been published by a reputable American writer: an unreserved novel about the homosexual demimonde and the 'naturalness' of homosexual relations," writes Kiernan.

While an inquisitive public put *The City and the Pillar* on the bestseller lists, the more conservative press helped dampen the career of its author. The *New York Times* gave the book a very negative review, refused to accept any advertising for it, and then either did not review or published extremely harsh reviews of Vidal's next five novels and books of short stories. (At one point Vidal resorted to publishing a series of mystery novels under the pseudonym Edgar Box in order to get them reviewed.) According to Vidal in his annotation to the revised version of *The City and the Pillar*, the *New York Times*'s judgment continued "to haunt that book, and all my writing ever since."

Television was in its heyday in the mid-1950s when Vidal was writing scripts for such highly acclaimed programs as *Philco-Goodyear Playhouse, Studio One,* and *Omnibus Theater.* As a screenwriter for the movies he made contributions to the scripts of *Ben Hur, I Accuse, Suddenly Last Summer, The Catered Affair, The Scapegoat,* and *The Left-Handed Gun,* among others. A self-proclaimed "writer for hire," Vidal eventually met his goal of financial independence, although it took him closer to ten years than five.

During his Hollywood years Vidal also began to write plays. His first theater script, *Visit to a Small Planet,* grew out of a television play of the same title. The story of a visitor from another planet

who comes to Earth to watch the Civil War battle at Manassas but instead ends up in present-day Virginia, *Visit to a Small Planet* had a Broadway run of 338 performances and an extended national and international tour, and was later produced as a motion picture starring Jerry Lewis.

With the success of *Visit to a Small Planet,* Vidal continued to write plays. "As a playwright, I am a sport, whose only serious interest is the subversion of a society which bores and appalls me," Vidal writes in an essay about this vocation, and the rest of his plays have indeed been attacks on politics, politicians, and what he views as middle class hypocrisy. A typical example is *The Best Man,* a political drama concerning two contenders for the presidential nomination and one of Vidal's most successful plays. Produced in 1959 in order to take advantage of the 1960 election fever, *The Best Man* had a respectable Broadway run and was later adapted into an award-winning film, which is still often shown on television.

In 1964 Vidal published *Julian,* his first novel in ten years and his first historical novel written in the style that has become his trademark. Presented as the journal of the eccentric fourth-century Roman emperor Julian and framed by a commentary in the form of margin notes and letters by two of Julian's aging contemporaries, the novel is full of cutting remarks, catty asides, ribald jokes, fourth-century gossip, and references to the state of the commentators' health, careers, and sexual performance. It is this humorous interjection of the trivial and the personal into an impeccably researched historical novel for which Vidal has become famous.

In writing historical fiction, "the interpreter is everything," says Dudley Fitts in the *New York Times Book Review,* and "if, like Gore Vidal in this evocation of Julian the Apostate, he is able to penetrate to depths of human meaning . . . his vision may create a design not wholly remote from parable or allegory." Like Fitts, a number of other reviewers also appreciate that Vidal "is attempting something other than the recreation of the past for its own sake," as Walter Allen puts it in the *New York Review of Books.* "While it would be absurd to see the novel as a parable for our time or to look for any close parallels between Julian's situation and our own, it is impossible to escape the conclusion that Vidal intends the book to have some direct relevance to the world today. The brilliance of his portrayal of Julian persuades us that it has." Still, other critics find Vidal's Julian a less compelling figure; *Saturday Review*'s Granville Hicks, for instance, insists that he "doesn't . . . really grasp the imagination. Looking at him simply as a character in a novel, one wonders whether he is worth writing about at such great length."

The *New York Times*'s John Leonard points out that Vidal has a tendency to "twin" his novels, following one book sometime later with another one using either the same characters, subject, or milieu. Kiernan observes that *"Messiah* and *Kalki* are twin novels about the coming apocalypse, whereas *Burr* and *1876* are paired novels about American history. *Myra Breckinridge* and *Myron* are unmistakable twins, enjoying virtually Siamese attachment. The second novels in these pairs never seem to represent a rethinking or reworking of the material in the first."

Julian's twin is *Creation,* an epic of the ancient world as told by Cyrus Spitama. Contemptuous of the Greeks and their philosophical concepts, Cyrus is an avid defender of the Zoroastrian doctrine of dualism. Yet he also seeks to confirm his understanding of the world, and in his travels he speaks with the great prophets and philosophers of the East. "As a grandson and the last descendant in the male line of the prophet Zoroaster, Cyrus feels obliged to argue theology, to devise an acceptable theory for the creation of the universe and to account for the existence of evil within it," explains *Time*'s Paul Gray. Though Cyrus often strays from this narrative path, Kanfer considers Cyrus's message about creation to be best revealed through the telling of his life's story, rather than stated explicitly. *"Julian* was wonderful," says Leonard; *"Creation,* I am happy to report, is even better."

Burr is told as the memoirs of American founding father-turned-renegade Aaron Burr, and *1876* is an account of the United States's centennial year. Both are narrated by the character Charles Schemerhorn Schuyler, who first appears as the young, opportunistic illegitimate son of Aaron Burr, and in the second novel is seen forty years later, a jaded expatriate come home to recoup his lost fortunes. These novels are told in the style familiar to readers of *Julian* and *Creation;* as Gray remarks, "[Vidal] can make old facts look like contemporary gossip. And he takes wicked pleasure in turning accepted notions about the past upside down." Reviewing *Burr,* Christopher Lehmann-Haupt of the *New York Times* concurs: "Mr. Vidal gives us an interpretation of our early history that says in effect that all the old verities were never much to begin with. . . . And how thoroughly enjoyable is the entire process of disillusionment!"

1876 also takes demythologizing the American past as its task and, as many critics point out, the events recounted in the novel are startlingly similar to those taking place near the time of the book's publication in 1976. Parallels abound: the corrupt Ulysses S. Grant with Richard Nixon, the Whiskey Ring scandal with Watergate, the Hayes-Tilden presidential race with the election of 1972 and the administration of Gerald Ford. *1876* is, according to Paul Levy in *Books and Bookmen,* "an historical contribution of large importance. . . . What Vidal has done by investigating the scandals leading up to the 1876 election and the election itself is to show that nothing much has changed in America's last hundred years."

Lincoln is also concerned with the history of the United States. Released in 1984 with an extraordinary 200,000-copy first printing and preview excerpts in the *Atlantic* and *Gentleman's Quarterly, Lincoln* is called "a momentous fictional biography" and a "masterpiece" by Stephen Rubin in the *Chicago Tribune Book World.* "The intelligence, the wit, the humor, the outrageousness are omnipresent," says the critic. "If Vidal is impatient with novelistic techniques such as transitions, he allows himself the luxury to marvelously plot a true political novel of breadth and rich texture. The pace he sets for himself is a noble andante that gives him the time for a spectacular array of detail work, the element that ultimately makes *Lincoln* unforgettable."

Vidal subsequently published two additional installments in his American history series, 1987's *Empire* and 1990's *Hollywood: A Novel of America in the 1920s.* Set in the late 1890s to early 1900s, *Empire,* according to *Newsweek*'s David Gates, "reanimates the moribund genre of historical fiction with a few modernist jots—and still stays within the conventions of the Good Read," adding that even critics of the novel "won't be able to deny that they've been elegantly entertained." And Lehmann-Haupt considers *Empire* the best of Vidal's series, stating that Vidal tells "a dramatically compelling story without sacrificing either his complex view of American history or his unusual ability to caricature its major players."

Popular as Vidal's historical novels have been, the author's greatest coup, say critics, is *Myra Breckinridge,* a campy, satiric look at modern America. An instant smash, *Myra Breckinridge*

takes shots at almost everything, from uptight heterosexuality to the burgeoning population, the New American Novel to 1940s movie stars, American youth to the American dream. Above all, *Myra Breckinridge* is about breaking the barriers of sexuality.

"To say Mr. Vidal's new novel is queer would be an understatement; it is a queer, queer book, a virtuoso exercise in kinkiness, a draught of fizzy hemlock, a strikingly intelligent attempt to go as far as possible in outrageousness," declares John Weightman in *Observer Review.* "Literature about sex is so often soggy and embarrassing or clinical and sick-making. Mr. Vidal pitches his narrative in a key of slightly demented funniness, and sustains this note right to the end." Indeed, the irrepressible Myra is an odd character: a homosexual male turned female by a sex change operation, she goes to California to claim her share in a drama academy and to write a book about the films of the 1940s. Teaching Empathy and Posture at the academy, Myra expounds her views on every possible subject—yet in the end, according to her logic, it all leads back to sex and power. "Myra Breckinridge herself sees all life as a naming of parts, an equating of groins, a pleasing and/or painful forcing of orifices. Which is the essence, after all, of pornography," observes a *Times Literary Supplement* critic.

The book is sexually graphic, and most reviewers at the time recognized it as a satire on pornography that had at the same time become what it was satirizing. Hentoff notes that Vidal, "walking on the waters of polymorphous perversity and sexual revolution, . . . has written the first popular book of perverse pornography—a book for which one does not need even the slightest special taste." *Newsweek*'s Joseph Morgenstern refers to it as "gleefully dirty, wittily dirty, gracefully and intricately dirty in its creation and development of a genuine film freak." *Myron,* a sequel to the *Breckenridge* novel in which Myra returns to her male form and is transported to the set of a 1940s B-movie, is described as "surprisingly colorless and lumpish" by James Boatright in the *New Republic.*

In 1992 Vidal penned the much-hyped novel *Live from Golgotha: The Gospel According to Gore Vidal,* a scathingly irreverent examination of the origins and subsequent perversion of Christianity. The novel's protagonist is Timothy, the confidant of Saint Paul who will become Saint Timothy. Some sixty years after the crucifixion of Jesus Christ, Timothy is visited by the ghost of Saint Paul, who warns him that, in the distant future, a super-sophisticated computer hacker is deleting the Gospels from the files of Heaven and Earth alike, thereby erasing the memories of the faithful. Timothy's task, Paul explains, is to write the last, definitive account of the Gospels and hide it, so that it can be discovered by theologians two thousand years hence.

The problem, we soon discover, is that Timothy's recollections are vastly different from those of the New Testament's Matthew, Mark, Luke, and John: Saint Paul, for example, is depicted as an evangelical huckster and a pederast, and Jesus is a buffoon with a glandular problem. History is further obfuscated by the visitations, in the form of visions, of celebrities and network executives from the twentieth century; having perfected the technology to both travel and broadcast through time, they plan to broadcast the crucifixion "live" on television, and they ask Timothy to act as emcee. When introduced to television—and, in particular, to CNN—Timothy's memories and accounts become increasingly unreliable, and he calls into question whether it was actually Jesus who died on the cross.

There is no question that, with *Live from Golgotha,* Vidal intended to offend a number of readers. "Very early on," observes *New Statesman*'s Douglas Kennedy, "Vidal lets it be known that he is gunning for the Rushdie prize for droll blasphemy," and Andrew Greeley, writing in the *Washington Post Book World,* warns that "if Christians viewed blasphemy the way orthodox Moslems do, some Christian version of the Ayatollah might have put out a contract on Vidal." *Los Angeles Times Book Review*'s John Rechy, moreover, proclaims: "If God exists and Jesus is His son, then Gore Vidal is going to hell."

Perhaps in anticipation of negative press surrounding the 1992 publication of *Live from Golgotha,* Vidal coincided his release of that controversial novel with publication of a collection of lectures titled *Screening History.* In these lectures, originally given to audiences at Harvard, Vidal identifies the rise of the American film industry as the cause for the decline of American literature. "To speak today of a famous novelist is like speaking of a famous cabinetmaker or speedboat designer," he writes. "Adjective is inappropriate to noun." He continues to accuse the film industry of ignoring the largely untapped resource of American history, choosing instead to depict the histories of England, France, and other countries. Throughout the lectures Vidal intersperses anecdotes from his own history—from his earliest memories in Washington movie houses to his years as a screenwriter in Hollywood. "Despite his bleak thoughts about present-day America, Vidal has a Puckish faith, and these essays are never dreary," comments Jane Mendelsohn in the *Voice Literary Supplement,* and Sheed recommends: "*Screening History* could profitably be reread with each of Vidal's books.

Throughout most of his fifty-odd-year career as a writer and public personality, Vidal vowed that he would never write an autobiography. However, the 1995 publication of *Palimpsest: A Memoir* would prove him wrong. Covering the first thirty-nine years of his life, the book focuses on what *Washington Post Book World* critic Jonathan Yardley terms "the most public period of his life," in which Vidal worked as a Hollywood scriptwriter, playwright, and sometime political candidate. "Vidal knows . . . ," adds Yardley, "that private turmoil and public provocation make splendid stories, while laboring away in his office, [as Vidal did after age forty,] makes no story at all. Thus craftsmanship far more than reticence or coyness is surely the explanation for his decision to cut things off where he does." Feasting on the tumultuous saga of his dysfunctional family, high-profile friendships, numerous homosexual liaisons but only one great love, various forays into the political arena, and writings, *Palimpsest,* with its perspective of its author's seventy years, is, "for all its tilts and malice and wonderful jokes, an oddly disinterested work," according to Michael Wood in the *New York Times Book Review.* "As I am supposed to be remembering myself, I am central to these memories," Vidal writes; "I am, however, happier to be at the edge, as one is in an essay, studying someone else or what someone else has made art of." Widely praised by reviewers, *Palimpsest* would prompt Karl Miller to write in the *Times Literary Supplement:* "[Vidal's] essays, and this memoir, with its repertoire of stories and sayings, are a dimension of his elegant and pointed speech, and there are admirers of his who think that he speaks better than he writes, and that his essays are better than his fictions."

BIOGRAPHICAL/CRITICAL SOURCES:

BOOKS

Aldridge, John W., *After the Lost Generation: A Critical Study of the Writers of Two Wars,* McGraw, 1951.
Contemporary Literary Criticism, Gale (Detroit), Volume 2, 1974; Volume 4, 1975; Volume 6, 1976; Volume 8, 1978; Volume 10, 1979; Volume 22, 1982; Volume 33, 1985; Volume 72, 1992.
Dick, Bernard F., *The Apostate Angel: A Critical Study of Gore Vidal,* Random House, 1974.
Dictionary of Literary Biography, Volume 6: *American Novelists since World War II,* Gale, 1980; Volume 152: *American Novelists since World War II, Fourth Series,* Gale, 1995.
Kiernan, Robert F., *Gore Vidal,* Ungar, 1982.
Parini, Jay, editor, *Gore Vidal: Writer against the Grain,* Columbia University Press, 1992.
Stanton, Robert J., and Gore Vidal, editors, *Views from a Window: Conversations with Gore Vidal,* Lyle Stuart, 1980.
Weightman, John, *The Concept of the Avant Garde: Explorations in Modernism,* Alcove, 1973.
White, Ray Lewis, *Gore Vidal,* Twayne, 1968.

PERIODICALS

America, September 5, 1970; May 20, 1978; January 16, 1993.
American Film, November, 1987.
Atlantic Monthly, February, 1949; March, 1972; December, 1973; April, 1976; April, 1981; October, 1992.
Books and Bookmen, August, 1967; May, 1974; June, 1976; October, 1977; October, 1982.
Chicago Tribune, November 20, 1985; June 22, 1987; February 18, 1990.
Christian Science Monitor, June 18, 1964; May 11, 1967.
Commentary, March, 1974; June, 1977.
Commonweal, January 7, 1977; November 6, 1992.
Detroit News, May 31, 1981; June 19, 1983; June 17, 1984; January 24, 1990.
Economist, November 6, 1993.
Esquire, August, 1977; April, 1981.
Film Quarterly, fall, 1993.
Gentlemen's Quarterly, November, 1995, p. 72.
Globe and Mail (Toronto), June 20, 1987; February 24, 1990.
Interview, June, 1987; June, 1988; January, 1996, p. 22.
Journal of American History, September, 1994, p. 806.
Library Journal, December 1, 1947; January, 1994, p. 186; November 1, 1995, p. 76.
Los Angeles Times, March 24, 1981; July 15, 1984; February 14, 1987; October 7, 1987; November 12, 1987; December 5, 1988; August 4, 1989.
Los Angeles Times Book Review, July 3, 1983; June 24, 1984; January 12, 1986; February 18, 1990; September 13, 1992; October 11, 1992.
Los Angeles Times Magazine, January 28, 1990.
Nation, April 1, 1968; May 25, 1974; April 17, 1976; March 21, 1981; June 16, 1984; November 16, 1992; July 5, 1993.
National Review, May 20, 1969; March 1, 1974; May 12, 1978; September 18, 1981; August 20, 1982; November 30, 1992; December 31, 1995, p. 41.
New Republic, February 25, 1957; July 18, 1970; May 27, 1972; April 24, 1976; May 12, 1978; April 25, 1981; October 5, 1992; August 1, 1994, p. 8.
New Statesman, July 14, 1967; September 20, 1968; March 22, 1974; March 19, 1976; August 19, 1977; April 14, 1978; April 6, 1979; May 8, 1981; August 20, 1982; May 6, 1983;

November 3, 1989, p. 38; November 15, 1991; November 6, 1992; October 27, 1995, p. 44.

Newsweek, June 15, 1964; February 26, 1968; March 31, 1969; July 6, 1970; November 5, 1973; November 18, 1974; March 8, 1976; May 9, 1977; April 20, 1981; June 11, 1984; June 15, 1987, p. 70; October 9, 1995, p. 82.

New Yorker, March 22, 1947; January 10, 1948; February 16, 1957; April 23, 1960; May 6, 1972; April 5, 1976; April 17, 1978; October 26, 1992.

New York Herald Tribune Weekly Book Review, March 16, 1947; January 18, 1949.

New York Review of Books, July 30, 1964; June 15, 1967; May 9, 1968; June 19, 1969; March 22, 1973; November 15, 1973; November 14, 1974; April 29, 1976; May 26, 1977; April 20, 1978; May 14, 1981; April 8, 1993.

New York Times, June 23, 1946; March 16, 1947; June 11, 1948; February 6, 1949; January 27, 1957; February 8, 1957; February 3, 1968; March 25, 1969; July 7, 1970; April 28, 1972; May 1, 1972; October 25, 1973; March 2, 1976; April 20, 1977; March 30, 1978; March 10, 1981; April 27, 1982; May 30, 1984; March 23, 1986; May 22, 1987; June 11, 1987; November 14, 1988; May 10, 1989; January 18, 1990; September 9, 1990; September 23, 1992; May 7, 1996, p. A17.

New York Times Book Review, August 12, 1962; May 31, 1964; April 30, 1967; January 28, 1968; February 1, 1968; February 15, 1968; September 1, 1968; April 6, 1969; July 12, 1970; December 31, 1972; October 28, 1973; March 7, 1976; April 17, 1977; April 2, 1978; December 21, 1980; March 29, 1981; May 2, 1982; June 5, 1983; June 3, 1984; June 14, 1987; January 21, 1990; August 30, 1992; October 4, 1992; November 29, 1992; June 20, 1993; October 8, 1995, p. 7.

Observer Review, September 15, 1968; July 6, 1969; February 7, 1971.

People Weekly, September 12, 1988; November 2, 1992.

Saturday Review, February 23, 1957; August 4, 1962; June 6, 1964; June 24, 1967; May 20, 1972; December 16, 1972; February 8, 1975; March 6, 1976; April 29, 1978; March, 1981; May, 1982.

Saturday Review of Literature, July 6, 1946; May 31, 1947; January 10, 1948; January 15, 1949; October 14, 1950.

Time, July 27, 1962; June 12, 1964; March 28, 1969; August 22, 1969; July 13, 1970; December 11, 1972; October 21, 1974; March 1, 1976; March 27, 1978; March 30, 1981; June 13, 1983; June 22, 1987; September 28, 1992; November 29, 1993, p. 23; October 9, 1995, p. 76.

Times (London), April 30, 1981; September 28, 1983; June 19, 1987; November 16, 1991.

Times Literary Supplement, November 12, 1964; July 27, 1967; October 10, 1968; July 24, 1969; September 18, 1970; February 21, 1975; March 26, 1976; September 30, 1977; April 14, 1978; May 29, 1981; August 27, 1982; May 13, 1983; November 10-16, 1989; December 6, 1991; October 2, 1992; October 20, 1995, p. 7.

Tribune Books (Chicago), April 26, 1981; April 22, 1984; June 3, 1984; June 22, 1987; January 28, 1990; September 6, 1992; September 20, 1992.

Vanity Fair, November, 1995, p. 60.

Variety, December 15, 1971; May 3, 1972; October 16, 1995, p. 8.

Voice Literary Supplement, September, 1992.

Washington Post, July 4, 1984; June 21, 1987; October 24, 1987; November 3, 1987; January 14, 1990.

Washington Post Book World, October 28, 1973; May 1, 1977; April 16, 1978; January 18, 1981; March 22, 1981; April 25, 1982; May 15, 1983; June 10, 1984; January 14, 1990; September 20, 1992; October 8, 1995, p. 3.

*   *   *

VINE, Barbara
See RENDELL, Ruth

*   *   *

VIOLIS, G.
See SIMENON, Georges (Jacques Christian)

*   *   *

VISI, Baron
See VIAN, Boris

*   *   *

VIZENOR, Gerald (Robert) 1934-

PERSONAL: Born October 22, 1934, in Minneapolis, MN; son of Clement William and LaVerne Lydia (Peterson) Vizenor; married Judith Helen Horns, 1959 (some sources say September, 1960; divorced, 1968); married Laura Jane Hall, May, 1981; children: (first marriage) Robert Thomas. *Education:* Attended New York University, 1955-56; University of Minnesota, B.A., 1960, graduate study, 1962-65; additional graduate study at Harvard University.

ADDRESSES: Office—Native American Studies, 522 Barrows Hall, University of California, Berkeley, CA 94720.

CAREER: Ramsey County Corrections Authority, St. Paul, MN, group worker, 1957-58; Capital Community Center, St. Paul, roving group worker, 1958; Minnesota Department of Corrections, Minnesota State Reformatory, St. Cloud, corrections agent, 1960-61; *Minneapolis Tribune,* Minneapolis, MN, staff writer, 1968-70; Park Rapids Public Schools, Park Rapids, MN, teacher trainer, 1971; instructor at Lake Forest College, Lake Forest, IL, and Bemidji State University, Bemidji, MN, 1971-73; University of California, Berkeley, lecturer, 1976-80, professor of Native American Studies, 1991–; University of Minnesota, Minneapolis, professor of American Indian studies, 1980-87; University of California, Santa Cruz, professor of literature, 1987-90; University of California, Berkeley, professor of Native American studies. Kresge College, acting provost, 1990; University of Oklahoma, David Burke Chair of Letters, 1991. *Military service:* Minnesota National Guard, 1950-51; U.S. Army, 1952-55, served in Japan.

AWARDS, HONORS: Research grants for writing from University of Minnesota Graduate School; Fiction Collective prize, 1986, and American Book Award, 1988, for *Griever: An American Monkey King in China;* Josephine Miles Award, PEN Oakland, 1990, for *Interior Landscapes: Autobiographical Myths and Metaphors.*

WRITINGS:

POETRY

Born in the Wind, privately printed, 1960.

The Old Park Sleepers, Obercraft, 1961.

Two Wings the Butterfly (haiku), privately printed, 1962.

South of the Painted Stone, Obercraft, 1963.

Raising the Moon Vines (haiku), Callimachus, 1964.

Seventeen Chirps (haiku), Nodin, 1964.

Empty Swings (haiku), Nodin, 1967.

(Contributor) Kenneth Rosen, editor, *Voices of the Rainbow,* Viking, 1975.

Matsushima: Pine Islands (haiku), Nodin, 1984.

NOVELS

Darkness in Saint Louis Bearheart, Truck Press, 1973.

Griever: An American Monkey King in China, Fiction Collective, 1987.

The Heirs of Columbus, Wesleyan University Press, 1992.

Dead Voices: Natural Agonies in the New World, University of Oklahoma Press, 1992.

Hotline Healers, Wesleyan University Press, 1997.

OTHER

Thomas James White Hawk, Four Winds, 1968.

(Editor) *Escorts to White Earth, 1868-1968: 100 Year Reservation,* Four Winds, 1968.

The Everlasting Sky, Crowell, 1972.

Anishinabe Nagomon: Songs of the Ojibwa, Nodin, 1974.

Anishinabe Adisokan: Stories of the Ojibwa, Nodin, 1974.

Tribal Scenes and Ceremonies (editorial articles), Nodin, 1976.

(Contributor) Chester Anderson, editor, *Growing up in Minnesota* (autobiographical stories), University of Minnesota Press, 1976.

Wordarrows: Indians and Whites in the New Fur Trade (stories), University of Minnesota Press, 1978.

(Contributor) Jane Katz, editor, *This Song Remembers* (autobiographical stories), Houghton, 1980.

Summer in the Spring: Ojibwa Songs and Stories, Nodin, 1981, new edition, University of Oklahoma Press, 1993.

Earthdivers: Tribal Narratives on Mixed Descent (stories), University of Minnesota Press, 1981.

The People Named the Chippewa: Narrative Histories, University of Minnesota Press, 1984.

(Editor) *Narrative Chance: Postmodern Discourse on Native American Literatures,* University of Oklahoma Press (Norman), 1989.

Crossbloods: Bone Courts, Bingo, and Other Reports (essays), University of Minnesota Press, 1990.

Interior Landscapes: Autobiographical Myths and Metaphors, University of Minnesota Press, 1990.

Landfill Meditation (short stories), Wesleyan University Press, 1991.

Manifest Manners: Postindian Warriors of Survivance (essays), Wesleyan University Press, 1994.

Shadow Distance: Gerald Vizenor Reader (selected fiction and essays), Wesleyan University Press, 1994.

(Editor) *Native American Literature: A Brief Introduction and Anthology,* HarperCollins, 1995.

SIDELIGHTS: A multifaceted writer, Gerald Vizenor is an acclaimed novelist, poet, and teacher. The themes and content of his works have arisen not only from his personal and cultural experiences, but also from the strong oral traditions of his Native American ancestors.

Born on October 22, 1934, in Minneapolis, Minnesota, Vizenor is of mixed-blood descent. His father, Clement William, was an Ojibwa Indian, originally from the White Earth Reservation in

Minnesota, and his mother, LaVerne Peterson, lived in the city of Minneapolis; the two met when Vizenor's father first came to the city. In 1950 Vizenor joined the Minnesota National Guard and from 1952 to 1955, he served with the U.S. Army in Japan. Vizenor attended New York University from 1955 to 1956 and acquired his bachelor of arts degree from the University of Minnesota in 1960. He also did some graduate study there from 1962 through 1965 and later studied at Harvard University. Since then, he has been a social worker, civil rights activist, journalist, and community advocate for Native people living in urban centers. Vizenor organized the Indian Studies program at the Bemidji State University and has taught literature and tribal history at Lake Forest College, the University of Minnesota, the University of California at Berkeley, and Macalester College.

While serving in Japan, Vizenor became familiar with haiku, an unrhymed, seventeen syllable Japanese poetic form in which nature and human nature are linked in the poet's perception and representation of a single moment. "The Japanese and their literature were my liberation," he later wrote in the *Chicago Review.* "That presence of haiku, more than other literature, touched my imagination and brought me closer to a sense of tribal consciousness. . . . I would have to leave the nation of my birth to understand the wisdom and survivance of tribal literature." During the following decade, he produced several volumes of haiku, including *Raising the Moon Vines* and *Seventeen Chirps,* both published in 1964, and *Empty Swings,* published in 1967.

In the years following, Vizenor explored many different genres. In 1973 he published his first novel, *Darkness in Saint Louis Bearheart,* in which he explores his own Native American experience, particularly the impoverished circumstances of his youth. He has also published several translations of collected Ojibwa songs and prose and in 1978, Vizenor published *Wordarrows: Indians and Whites in the New Fur Trade,* his first of many short story collections. In 1984 Vizenor wrote an historical account of his tribe, *The People Named Chippewa: Narrative Histories.*

In the 1980s Vizenor forewent a tenured position at the University of Minnesota to explore a teaching opportunity in China. Originally planning on writing essays during his stay, Vizenor's poetic outlook underwent a radical transformation after attending a theatrical production which included scenes from the Monkey King opera. The Monkey King is a mischievous figure from Chinese myth similar to the "trickster" character found in Native American legend. In an interview with Larry McCaffery and Tom Marshall for *Chicago Review,* Vizenor confided this to be a significant if not pivotal experience that altered his perspective and "changed everything" for him. Seeing a dynamic Chinese audience "so completely engaged in the production," led Vizenor to rethink his original, graduate school reading of the Monkey King. Experiencing the performance transformed the material from mere cultural documentation to a work beyond sociopolitical ramifications, encompassing the consciousness of the Chinese people as folk literature. Sensing he had a "powerful theme" for a book born of this experience, Vizenor then developed Griever, a trickster main character, for his award-winning novel *Griever: An American Monkey King in China,* published in 1987. *The Trickster of Liberty: Tribal Heirs to a Wild Baronage,* published in 1988, also explores the trickster theme and imagery.

In 1990 Vizenor published an autobiographical volume, *Interior Landscapes: Autobiographical Myths and Metaphors.* He has also written several Native American novels and a number of works concerning the economic, social, and political plight of American Indians, specifically his own Ojibwa tribe. "George Raft was an inspiration to my mother and, in a sense, he was responsible for my conception," Gerald Robert Vizenor wrote in *Interior Landscapes.* "She saw the thirties screen star, a dark social hero with moral courage, in the spirited manner of my father, a newcomer from the White Earth Reservation.'"The first time I saw your father he looked like George Raft, not the gangster but the dancer. He was handsome and he had nerve,' my mother told me. 'The first thing he said to me was, "I got lots of girls but I always like new ones." He came by in a car with one of his friends. Nobody would talk like that now, but that's how we got together.' "I was conceived on a cold night in a kerosene heated tenement near downtown Minneapolis. President Franklin Delano Roosevelt had been inaugurated the year before, at the depth of the Great Depression. He told the nation, 'The only thing we have to fear is fear itself.' My mother, and millions of other women stranded in cold rooms, heard the new president, listened to their new men, and were roused to remember the movies; elected politicians turned economies, but the bright lights in the depression came from the romantic and glamorous screen stars."

Vizenor's *Landfall Meditation* is a collection of short fiction that demonstrates the author's concern with the theme of mixed racial heritage and his familiar narrative technique of combining autobiographical elements with fiction. The opening story, "Almost Browne," for example, is a semi-autobiographical story of a pregnant white woman and her Chippewa partner who run out of gas on their way to a reservation hospital. Commented Robert L. Berner in *World Literature Today,* Vizenor's "fictions are almost stories, almost fictional, almost real."

In *Dead Voices: Natural Agonies in the New World,* Vizenor explores the Native American myth of the trickster figure in the context of the modern world. Using the motif of a Native American card game called "wanaki" as the narrative structure, the novel's chapters each begin with the turn of a playing card accompanied by a different animal. Ritual, symbol, magic, transformation, and jokes all play a role in the narrative, which reviewers have alternately found highly inventive and confusing. "The attempt to resurrect traditional myths and set them loose in the modern world is a creditable one," observed Robert Crum in *The New York Times Book Review.* "Unfortunately, the characters in this book are less animals than puppets." Articulating the challenge Vizenor presents to readers of *Dead Voices,* David Mogen of *Western American Literature* asserted: "Because the very voice of the novel embodies a paradox of articulation, this is a difficult book to read, one in which meaning and narrative alike seem to hover just beyond the reach of written language."

Vizenor's novel *Hotline Healers* follows trickster Almost Browne on a series of loosely connected adventures; indeed, the book started as a collection of short stories. The centerpiece of this wry, self-referential work is a commencement address at the University of California, where Browne—a lecturer in the school's mythical Transethic Situations Department—scandalizes the assembled graduates and faculty. In other comic episodes, Browne receives a commission from President Richard Nixon to launch an Indian invasion of Cuba. Later he starts his very own native healers telephone service, modeled after the Psychic Friends Network. Critics found the caustic work to their liking, though some found Vizenor's idiosyncratic style potentially off-putting for first-time readers. "Some loose ends and a fondness for narrative loops are drawbacks," commented the critic for *Kirkus Reviews,* "but the

novel also draws real strength from its style and wit; those acclimated to Vizenor's eclecticism will find much here to enjoy."

As editor of *Narrative Chance: Postmodern Discourse on Native American Indian Literatures,* Vizenor selected diverse essays exploring the role of Native American writers in the context of the European literary tradition. "[*Narrative Chance* challenges] the reader to consider what it means when Native peoples apart from a European critical tradition must write within that tradition to preserve and maintain distinctly different world views," according to Alanna Kathleen Brown in *Modern Fiction Studies.* Among the noted essays included in the collection are Elaine Jahner's "Metalanguages," Louis Owens's "Gerald Vizenor's *Darkness in Saint Louis Bearheart,*" and Vizenor's introductory essay, "Trickster Discourse: Comic Holotropes and Languages Games."

BIOGRAPHICAL/CRITICAL SOURCES:

BOOKS

Blaeser, Kimberly M., *Gerald Vizenor: Writing in Oral Tradition,* University of Oklahoma Press, 1996.
Bruchac, Joseph, *Survival This Way: Interviews with American Indian Poets,* Sun Tracks and The University of Arizona Press, 1987, pp. 287-310.
Contemporary Literary Criticism, Volume 103, Gale (Detroit), 1998.
Dictionary of Literary Biography, Volume 175: *Native American Writers of the United States,* Gale, 1997.
Krupat, Arnold, *The Turn to the Native: Studies in Criticism and Culture,* University of Nebraska Press, 1996.
Swann, Brian, and Arnold Krupat, *I Tell You Now: Autobiographical Essays by Native American Writers,* University of Nebraska Press, 1987, pp. 100-283.
Velie, Alan R., *Four American Indian Literary Masters: N. Scott Momaday, James Welch, Leslie Marmon Silko, and Gerald Vizenor,* University of Oklahoma Press, 1982, pp. 123-48.

PERIODICALS

American Book Review, January-February, 1988, pp. 12-13, 20.
American Indian Quarterly, Special Issue, winter, 1985, pp. 1-78.
Bloomsbury Review, April-May, 1991, p. 5.
Chronicle of Higher Education, July 13, 1994, pp. A8, A12.
Kirkus Reviews, March 15, 1997.
Library Journal, October 15, 1994, p. 73; January, 1995, p. 103.
Los Angeles Times Book Review, September 8, 1991; October 11, 1992, p. 6.
MELUS, spring, 1991-92, pp. 75-85.
Modern Fiction Studies, summer, 1994, p. 362.
Nation, October 21, 1991, pp. 465, 486-90.
New York Times Book Review, January 10, 1988, p. 18; November 8, 1992, p. 18.
Voice Literary Supplement, November, 1991, p. 29.
Western American Literature, August, 1988, p. 160; August, 1992, pp. 180-81; winter, 1994, p. 361.
Wilson Library Bulletin, December, 1992, p. 33.
World Literature Today, summer, 1992, p. 561; spring, 1993, pp. 423-24.

*   *   *

VOLLMANN, William T. 1959-

PERSONAL: Born July 28, 1959, in Santa Monica, CA; son of Thomas E. (a professor) and Tanis (a homemaker) Vollmann. *Education:* Attended Deep Springs College, 1977-79; Cornell

University, B.A. (summa cum laude), 1981; graduate study at University of California, Berkeley, 1982-83. *Politics:* "Environmentalist egalitarian." *Religion:* "Agnostic plus." *Avocational interests:* Bookmaking, sketching, wilderness travel, ladies, exotic weapons.

ADDRESSES: Office—c/o Viking-Penguin, 375 Hudson St., New York, NY 10014.

CAREER: Writer. CoTangent Press, founder.

MEMBER: Center for Book Arts.

AWARDS, HONORS: Ella Lyman Cabot Trust fellowship grant, 1982; regent's fellow, University of California, Berkeley, 1982-83; Aid for Afghan Refugees grant-in-aid, 1983; Ludwig Vogelstein Award, 1987; corecipient of Maine Photographic Workshops grant, 1987; Whiting Writers' Award, 1988, for *You Bright and Risen Angels: A Cartoon;* Shiva Naipaul Memorial Prize, 1989, for an excerpt from *Seven Dreams: A Book of North American Landscapes.*

WRITINGS:

You Bright and Risen Angels: A Cartoon (novel), Atheneum, 1987.
The Rainbow Stories, Atheneum, 1989.
Seven Dreams: A Book of North American Landscapes, Viking, Volume 1: *The Ice-Shirt,* 1990, Volume 2: *Fathers and Crows,* 1992, Volume 6: *The Rifles,* 1994.
Whores for Gloria; or, Everything Was Beautiful until the Girls Got Anxious (documentary novel), Pan-Picador, 1991, Pantheon, 1992.
Thirteen Stories and Thirteen Epitaphs, Deutsch, 1991.
An Afghanistan Picture Show: Or, How I Saved the World (memoir), Farrar, Straus, 1992.
Butterfly Stories: A Novel, Grove/Atlantic, 1993.
The Atlas: People, Places, and Visions, Viking, 1996.

SIDELIGHTS: The literary imagination manifested in William T. Vollmann's first three books prompted critics to compare the author to the innovative American novelist Thomas Pynchon. In his novels and short stories, which contain complicated plots and numerous character types, Vollmann critiques past and present human behavior. *You Bright and Risen Angels: A Cartoon* examines the nature of political power struggles through the depiction of an inane war between insects and the inventors of electricity. At the beginning of the story the godlike narrator, referred to as "the author," creates each of the characters by means of a computer. The individuals are divided into ideological sects such as reactionaries and revolutionaries that, along with the insects, wage constant battles against one another in order to obtain dominion over all. The presence in the novel of a vast number of characters and geographic locations drew criticism from *New York Times Book Review* contributor Gail Pool, who termed *You Bright and Risen Angels* "a large, sprawling, disorderly book. . . that operates on many levels and suggests many interpretations." Pool, however, concluded her review by praising the novel's "ingenious creation of a universe whose bizarre characters and events illuminate our own."

Vollmann's second book, a collection of short narratives entitled *The Rainbow Stories,* was proclaimed a "domineering display of a rare talent" by John Calvin Batchelor in the *Chicago Tribune.* Set mainly in the slums of San Francisco, California, the tales offer a candid and often disturbing insight into the lives of prostitutes, derelicts, and criminals. Each story's tone is to some extent

determined by the color of the spectrum included in its title; the theme of death, for example, pervades "The Blue Yonder," an unsettling account of the death and autopsy of a bag lady. Abundant in detailed description, the narration of the stories often takes a journalistic approach; Vollmann acknowledges in footnotes and in a section at the end of the book the information he obtained from people he met in San Francisco's Tenderloin district. Although the book's authentic accounts were described by Caryn James in the *New York Times Book Review* as "amazing in their power to attract and repel at once," the reviewer said that Vollmann "merely hides behind the reporter's adherence to facts" and neglects to adequately develop his characters. James noticed, however, "touches of hard brilliance" in the work and recognized in Vollmann "huge ambition and talent." And Batchelor, in his review, lauded *The Rainbow Stories* as "playful, wildly energetic low-life visions."

With *The Ice-Shirt,* the first volume of *Seven Dreams: A Book of North American Landscapes,* Vollmann begins what he terms a "symbolic history" of North America, as quoted by James Wood in the London *Times.* Drawing on a significant number of historical and mythological sources, listed at the end of the novel, Vollmann recounts the brief colonization of a portion of North America by Vikings, an event that is believed to have occurred long before Christopher Columbus's voyage to the West. The author's symbolic interpretation of the event asserts, in part, that winter was brought to the previously temperate environment of North America by the power-hungry Norse people who waged destructive wars against the natives before leaving a few years later. David Sacks in the *New York Times Book Review* noticed that "without apparent strain, the story interweaves numerous characters, sea voyages, murders and supernatural horrors." Wood called *The Ice-Shirt* a "seriously adventurous modernist book" but complained that "it is impossible to recount the plot, . . . because it is impossible to follow it." Although he also acknowledged some weaknesses in the novel with regard to plot, Sacks contended that "*The Ice-Shirt* impresses mightily in its scope, its scene-painting and its enciphered social message."

Fathers and Crows, the second volume in Vollmann's metahistorical *Seven Dreams* series, is an epic hybrid of history and fiction that recounts the missionary endeavors of French Jesuit priests in seventeenth century Canada. Continuing some 500 years after the conclusion of *The Ice-Shirt,* Vollmann assumes the fictional identity of William the Blind to recreate the complex and brutal conflict between the French and native people, supported by numerous historical sources, maps, chronologies, and glossaries. In an interview quoted in *Publishers Weekly,* Vollmann commented on *Fathers and Crows:* "In many ways I think this book is comparable to *War and Peace.* I'd like to see these books taught in history classes." David Ulin wrote in the *Los Angeles Times Book Review,* "*Fathers and Crows* is a difficult book, minutely detailed and densely written, flowing lush and heavy. . . . But it is a . . . work of such elegant structure and uncompromising intelligence that it will change the way you think about the opening of the New World—indeed, the way you think about all of history, and what it means." Citing Vollmann's obvious sympathy with the Native Americans, Steven Moore observed in a *Washington Post Book World* review, "*Fathers and Crows* is neither a romantic evocation of the Noble Savage nor a politically correct idealization. The Native Americans could be as racist, sexist, and brutal as any European imperialist." Madison Smartt Bell commended Vollmann's effective juxtaposition of time in the novel and balanced treatment of the vastly complicated series of relationships. He wrote in a *Chicago Tribune* review, "Dozens of individual stories unfold in this book, and Vollmann has blended them so skillfully into his Stream of Time that the great flood of history itself is imbued with a human poignancy."

The Rifles, the third installment (numbered volume six) in the *Seven Dreams* series, centers on the tragic adventures of the British explorer Sir John Franklin, who perished on a naval expedition to discover a Northwest passage in the Canadian Arctic. Franklin's mid-nineteenth century exploits are mirrored in a parallel plot involving a modern day affair between a Native American woman and an American novelist who bears resemblance to Vollmann, though he claims to be the reincarnation of John Franklin. As in previous volumes of the series, Vollmann draws heavily on historical sources to reinterpret the European domination of North American. However, his proclivity for elaborate historical commentary and narrative digression has received criticism. James McManus wrote in the *New York Times Book Review,* "*The Rifles* often has the feel of unrevised field notes hastily shuffled with printed source material—as though the moral urgency of the subject precluded much fuss about narrative integrity." Summarizing Vollmann's recurring preoccupation in the *Seven Dreams* series, John Skow wrote in a *Time* review of *The Rifles,* "Corruption of native inhabitants by Europeans is the broad theme of this enormously ambitious project." He added that Vollmann conjures "a vision of absolute evil: civilization, native cultures not excepted, is a pestilence, and mankind is a monstrous curse laid upon nature."

In *Whores for Gloria,* Vollmann returns to the locale of *The Rainbow Stories* to recount the hardships of Jimmy, an alcoholic Vietnam veteran who wanders among the derelicts of San Francisco's Tenderloin district in search of a beloved prostitute named Gloria. Unable to locate the elusive or illusory Gloria, Jimmy reconstructs her through conversation with other prostitutes. Eli Gottlieb wrote in a *Voice Literary Supplement* review, "Vollmann deftly strews the path of his narrative with vignettes, offering us sharp verite glances into the lives of the half-dozen hookers, bums, and pimps who cross Jimmy's path." Gottlieb added, "The time [Vollmann] doubtless spent among his subjects, and the intricate sympathy he established with them as a result, are an essential part of his achievement." According to a *Kirkus Reviews* commentator, "Vollmann's fierce writing seems often more designed to shock than to elucidate, but poor Jimmy does have some credibility, even if at times strained."

Thirteen Stories and Thirteen Epitaphs chronicles a series of fictitious travels and vignettes in the United States and abroad. Catherine Bush wrote in the *New York Times Book Review* that the collection "can be read as a feverish contemporary travelogue— and as a tour of Mr. Vollmann's brain." She observed, "It's a frontline bulletin from the world of those whom . . . Pico Iyer has called 'the Transit Loungers,' the new rootless wanderers who speed through cities and continents as if through revolving doors, torn between global familiarity and the loss of home." Jumping from San Francisco to Afghanistan, Thailand, Guatemala, the American Southwest, and an allegorical New York called Gun City, Vollmann portrays idiosyncratic extremity and depravity through the experiences of prostitutes, junkies, hobos, skinheads, and other marginalized people. Mary Hawthorne wrote in *The Times Literary Supplement,* "The fragmentary, sometimes chaotic nature of most of these stories, however—their illogic, their clutter of styles and digressions—renders them, like life, like dreams, elusive in the end." Sven Birkerts wrote in a *New Republic* review, "Reading Vollmann's stories, we feel that the

lower depths may be stranger and more disturbingly various than we had allowed."

An Afghanistan Picture Show: Or, How I Saved the World recounts Vollmann's post-college excursion to Pakistan to aid the Afghan guerrillas against Soviet invaders in the early 1980s. At age twenty-two, driven by a youthful and naive humanitarian desire to support the cause of freedom against oppression, Vollmann spent several months along the border of Afghanistan, interviewing refugees and recording their experiences. However, Vollmann's weakened physical health and inexperience with weapons rendered him ineffective when finally summoned to accompany the guerrillas on a raid. Annette Kobak noted in the *New York Times Book Review,* "[Vollmann] tells us. . . that he wanted to be the man personally to give the guerrillas both nickels and shells: he would take photographs to exhibit back home to raise cash for the cause (the literal meaning of his 'Picture Show'); and he would go into Afghanistan with the mujahedeen and sock the Soviets." Steven Moore commented on *An Afghanistan Picture Show* in *Washington Post Book World,* "The book succeeds not only in achieving its original goal—to bring attention to the plight of Afghan refugees . . . but also in dramatizing the limitations of altruism and activism, the difficulty of understanding the context of any culture other than your own." Writing in the *Los Angeles Times Book Review,* William McGowan commented, "Despite its unevenness and unexplained assumptions, however, *An Afghanistan Picture Show* is a bold and original accomplishment, hardly the 'Failed Pilgrim's Progress' that Vollmann dejectedly calls it. . . . [I]n his honest accounts of [the Afghanis'] plight, and his morally and emotionally complicated reactions to it, Vollmann. . . has written a powerful, searching addition to the literature of personal witness."

In *Butterfly Stories,* Vollman chronicles the peregrinations of an unnamed narrator, variously referred to as "the butterfly boy," "the journalist," and "the husband," who survives schoolyard bullying to travel about North America, Europe, and Asia in search of love. Vollmann describes extensive indulgence in Far Eastern brothels; the protagonist eventually contracts AIDS, then falls in love with a Cambodian prostitute. As described in the *Review of Contemporary Fiction,* "The narrator flits like a butterfly: not a symbol of lighthearted caprice but of ceaseless wandering and searching. . . . The narrator's lack of shame and pride is almost ascetic in its self-abnegation, giving him a pure quality despite his incessant whoring." In a *New York Times Magazine* review, Madison Smartt Bell termed the work a "parable of suicide through sexual intercourse; the purpose of the act is to unite the journalist with his dead prostitute lover, but the story is still terrifying to read." Critical of Vollmann's sensationalism and perceived "artificial compassion," Gary Krist commented in the *Hudson Review,* "In Vollmann's eyes, the world is teeming with prostitutes and consumers of prostitution, buying and selling, degrading and being degraded   as they look for a satisfaction they'll never find."

More overtly autobiographical than his other volumes of short stories, *The Atlas* relates Vollmann's far-flung travels in the United States, Canada, India, and Europe, including experiences in war-ravaged Bosnia. A *Publishers Weekly* reviewer observed, "Although Vollmann's style is to play it coy with respect to what is fact and what is fiction, there is no mystery as to who is doing the talking here." Vollmann's assemblage of sketches and vignettes takes the form of a palindrome, with twenty-six numbered pieces followed by another twenty-six reverse numbered pieces, complemented by a prologue, title piece, and epilogue. Describing the book as somewhat fragmented and redundant, a *Library Journal* reviewer noted that Vollmann's essays vacillate between "stark reportage" and surreal depiction of "violence, lust, greed, and alienation." As in his many other writings, the central characters are prostitutes and various social misfits connected by their existential loneliness.

BIOGRAPHICAL/CRITICAL SOURCES:

BOOKS

Contemporary Literary Criticism, Volume 89, Gale (Detroit), 1996.

PERIODICALS

Booklist, March 15, 1993, p. 1299; January 1, 1994, p. 808; February 1, 1996, p. 899.
Chicago Tribune, July 26, 1992, p. 3.
Entertainment Weekly, March 29, 1996, p. 59.
Hudson Review, summer 1994, pp. 299-305.
Kirkus Reviews, November 15, 1991; March 1, 1993; September 1, 1993.
Library Journal, March 1, 1996, p. 95.
Los Angeles Times Book Review, July 19, 1992, p. 3; August 23, 1992, p. 2.
Nation, March 21, 1994, p. 384; May 6, 1996, pp. 72, 74-5.
New Republic, April 11, 1994, p. 40.
New York, September 11, 1995, p. 86; April 8, 1996, p. 58.
New York Times Book Review, April 21, 1987, p. 10; August 13, 1989, p. 6; October 14, 1990, p. 13; July 26, 1992, p. 10; September 6, 1992, p. 14; February 27, 1994, p. 6; October 23, 1994, p. 12.
New York Times Magazine, February 6, 1994, p. 18.
Publishers Weekly, May 18, 1992, pp. 51-52; July 13, 1992, pp. 36-37; January 15, 1996, p. 441.
Review of Contemporary Fiction, spring 1994, pp. 212-13.
Time, March 28, 1994, p. 68.
Times (London), May 31, 1990.
Times Literary Supplement, November 29, 1991.
Tribune Books (Chicago), June 25, 1989; November 4, 1990, p. 5.
Voice Literary Supplement, February 1992, p. 6.
Washington Post Book World, August 2, 1992, p. 1; February 13, 1994, p. 11.
Yale Review, April, 1994, p. 152.

* * *

VON HAYEK, Friedrich August
See HAYEK, F(riedrich) A(ugust von)

* * *

VONNEGUT, Kurt 1922-

PERSONAL: Born November 11, 1922, in Indianapolis, IN; son of Kurt (an architect) and Edith Sophia (Lieber) Vonnegut; married Jane Marie Cox, September 1, 1945 (divorced, 1979); married Jill Krementz (a photographer), November, 1979; children: (first marriage) Mark, Edith, Nanette; (adopted deceased sister's children) James, Steven, and Kurt Adams; (second marriage) Lili (adopted). *Education:* Attended Cornell University, 1940-42, and Carnegie Institute of Technology (now Carnegie-Mellon University), 1943; attended University of Chicago, 1945-47, M.A., 1971. *Avocational interests:* Painting, wood carving, welded sculpture.

ADDRESSES: Home—New York, NY. *Attorney/Agent*—Donald C. Farber, esq., Farber & Rich LLP, 1370 Avenue of the Americas, 32nd Floor, New York, NY, 10019-4602.

CAREER: Editor, *Cornell Daily Sun,* 1941-42; Chicago City News Bureau, Chicago, IL, police reporter, 1947; General Electric Co., Schenectady, NY, employed in public relations, 1947-50; freelance writer, 1950–. Teacher at Hopefield School, Sandwich, MA, 1965–; lecturer at University of Iowa Writers Workshop, 1965-67, and at Harvard University, 1970-71; Distinguished Professor of English Prose, City College of the City University of New York, 1973-74. Speaker, National Coalition against Censorship briefing for the Attorney General's Commission on Pornography hearing, 1986. *Military service:* U.S. Army, Infantry, 1942-45; was POW; received Purple Heart.

MEMBER: Authors League of America, PEN (American Center; vice-president, 1974-), National Institute of Arts and Letters, Delta Upsilon, Barnstable Yacht Club, Barnstable Comedy Club.

AWARDS, HONORS: Guggenheim fellow, Germany, 1967; National Institute of Arts and Letters grant, 1970; Litt.D., Hobart and William Smith Colleges, 1974; Literary Lion award, New York Public Library, 1981; Eugene V. Debs Award, Eugene V. Debs Foundation, 1981, for public service; Emmy Award for Outstanding Children's Program, National Academy of Television Arts and Sciences, 1985, for *Displaced Person;* Bronze Medallion, Guild Hall, 1986.

WRITINGS:

NOVELS

Player Piano, Scribner (New York City), 1952, published as *Utopia 14,* Bantam (New York City), 1954, published under original title with new preface, Holt (New York City), 1966.
The Sirens of Titan, Dell (New York City), 1959.
Mother Night, Gold Medal Books (New York City), 1961; hardcover edition, Harper (New York City), 1966.
Cat's Cradle, Holt, 1963.
God Bless You, Mr. Rosewater; or, Pearls before Swine, Holt, 1965.
Slaughterhouse Five; or, The Children's Crusade: A Duty-Dance with Death, by Kurt Vonnegut, Jr., a Fourth-Generation German-American Now Living in Easy Circumstances on Cape Cod (and Smoking Too Much) Who, as an American Infantry Scout Hors de Combat, as a Prisoner of War, Witnessed the Fire-Bombing of Dresden, Germany, the Florence of the Elbe, a Long Time Ago, and Survived to Tell the Tale: This Is a Novel Somewhat in the Telegraphic Schizophrenic Manner of Tales of the Planet Tralfamadore, Where the Flying Saucers Come From, Seymour Lawrence/Delacorte (New York City), 1969, twenty-fifth anniversary edition, 1994.
Breakfast of Champions; or, Goodbye Blue Monday, Seymour Lawrence/Delacorte, 1973.
Slapstick; or, Lonesome No More, Seymour Lawrence/Delacorte, 1976.
Jailbird, Seymour Lawrence/Delacorte, 1979.
Deadeye Dick, Seymour Lawrence/Delacorte, 1982.
Galapagos: A Novel, Seymour Lawrence/Delacorte, 1985.
Bluebeard, Delacorte (New York City), 1987.
Hocus Pocus, Putnam (New York City), 1990.
Three Complete Novels (contains *Breakfast of Champions, God Bless You, Mr. Rosewater,* and *Cat's Cradle*), Wings, 1995.
Timequake, Putnam (New York City), 1997.

SHORT FICTION

Canary in a Cathouse, Fawcett (New York City), 1961.

Welcome to the Monkey House: A Collection of Short Works, Seymour Lawrence/Delacorte, 1968.

PLAYS

Penelope (produced on Cape Cod, MA, 1960), revised version published as *Happy Birthday, Wanda June* (produced off-Broadway, 1970), Seymour Lawrence/Delacorte, 1971, revised edition, Samuel French (New York City), 1971.

Between Time and Timbuktu; or, Prometheus Five: A Space Fantasy (television play; produced on National Educational Television Network, 1972), Seymour Lawrence/Delacorte, 1972.

Miss Temptation, edited by David Coperman, Dramatic Publishing Company, 1993.

Also author of *Something Borrowed,* 1958; *The Very First Christmas Morning,* 1962; *EPICAC,* 1963; *My Name Is Everyone,* 1964; and *Fortitude,* 1968.

OTHER

Wampeters, Foma, and Grandfalloons: (Opinions) (essays), Seymour Lawrence/Delacorte, 1974.

(With Ivan Chermayeff) *Sun, Moon, Star* (juvenile), Harper, 1980.

Palm Sunday: An Autobiographical Collage, Seymour Lawrence/Delacorte, 1981.

(Contributor) *Bob and Ray. A Retrospective, June 15-July 10, 1982,* Museum of Broadcasting, 1982.

(Contributor) Block, W. E., and M. A. Walker, editors, *Discrimination, Affirmative Action, and Equal Opportunity: An Economic and Social Perspective,* Fraser Institute, 1982.

Nothing Is Lost Save Honor: Two Essays (contains "The Worst Addiction of Them All" and "Fates Worth Than Death: Lecture at St. John the Divine, New York City, May 23, 1982"), Toothpaste Press (West Branch, IA), 1984.

Fates Worse than Death: An Autobiographical Collage of the 1980s (autobiography), Putnam, 1991.

(Author of foreword) Leeds, Marc, *The Vonnegut Encyclopedia: An Authorized Compendium,* Greenwood Press (Westport, CT), 1995.

Contributor of fiction to numerous publications, including *Cornell Daily Sun, Cosmopolitan, Ladies' Home Journal, McCall's, Playboy,* and *Saturday Evening Post.*

MEDIA ADAPTATIONS: Happy Birthday, Wanda June was adapted for film, Red Lion, 1971; *Slaughterhouse Five* was adapted for film, Universal, 1972; "Who Am I This Time" (short story) was adapted for film, Rubicon Films, 1982; *God Bless You, Mr. Rosewater* was adapted for the stage by Howard Ashman and produced by Vonnegut's daughter, Edith, 1979; *Slapstick* was adapted for film as *Slapstick of Another Kind,* Paul-Serendipity, 1984; "D. P." (short story) was adapted for television as *Displaced Person,* Hemisphere, 1985.

SIDELIGHTS: Now lauded as one of America's most respected novelists, Kurt Vonnegut was virtually ignored by critics at the beginning of his writing career. In *Literary Disruptions: The Making of a Post-Contemporary Fiction,* Jerome Klinkowitz observes that "Vonnegut's rise to eminence coincides precisely with the shift in taste which brought a whole new reading public—and eventually critical appreciation—to the works of Richard Brautigan, Donald Barthelme, Jerzy Kosinski, and others. Ten years and several books their elder, Vonnegut by his long exile underground was well prepared to be the senior member of the new disruptive group, and the first of its numbers to be seriously considered for the Nobel Prize. By 1973, when *Breakfast of Champions* appeared, . . . there was little doubt that a fiction widely scorned only six years before was now a dominant mode in serious contemporary literature."

While such early works as *Piano Player* and *The Sirens of Titan* were at first categorized as science fiction, Vonnegut's books go far beyond the realm of most pure SF. Ernest W. Ranly explains in *Commonweal:* "Vonnegut at times adds fantasy to his stories, whereas pure sci-fi permits only what is possible within a given scientific hypothesis. Vonnegut adds humor, a wild black humor, while most sci-fi is serious to the point of boredom. Vonnegut, generally, adds a distinctive sense and literary class. And, finally, Vonnegut seems pre-occupied with genuine human questions, about war, peace, technology, human happiness. He is even bitterly anti-machine, anti-technology, anti-science."

Mother Night, Vonnegut's third novel, is the story of an American playwright living in Germany at the outbreak of World War II, who is persuaded by the Allies to remain in Germany as a spy while posing as a radio propagandist. After the war he fades into obscurity in the United States until, with his wartime cover still intact, he is kidnapped by Israeli agents to stand trial for his crime. Michael Wood remarks in the *New York Review of Books,* "What is impressive about *Mother Night* is its extraordinary tone which allows Vonnegut to be very funny without being crass or unfeeling. . . . [*Mother Night*] is not an attempt to defeat an enemy by ridicule, but an attempt to contemplate horror by means of laughter, because laughter, of all our inappropriate responses to total, terminal horror, seems the least inappropriate, the least inhuman."

Mother Night is Vonnegut's first novel to be written with a first-person narrator, and is also the first in which technology and the future play no significant part. For this reason it is seen by many as a "transitional" novel between Vonnegut's early and later work. Perhaps most obvious, in comparison with the first two novels, *Mother Night* relies very little on time shifts, resulting in a more unified or "conventional" book. *Kurt Vonnegut, Jr.* author Peter J. Reed describes it as "Vonnegut's most traditional novel in form. Paradoxically, perhaps, that also accounts for the relative weaknesses of the book. For *Mother Night* lacks some of the excitement and verve of *The Sirens of Titan,* for example, and it is sometimes less likely to carry its reader along than that earlier, more wandering fantasy."

If one single point must be chosen for the transition of Vonnegut from "cult figure" to "popular author" it would most probably be a statement by Graham Greene calling the author's 1963 novel *Cat's Cradle* "one of the three best novels of the year by one of the most able living writers." *Cat's Cradle* is as autobiographical as any of Vonnegut's work up to that point. The Hoenikker family of the novel closely parallels Vonnegut's own family, consisting of an elder son who is a scientist, a tall middle daughter, and a younger son who joins Delta Upsilon. The narrator is again a writer who, in this case, is working on a book called *The Day the World Ended,* about the bombing of Hiroshima. Since its publication, *Cat's Cradle* has consistently appeared on high school and college reading lists; Reed says that it might be the most widely-read of Vonnegut's novels among young people. He explains that "to 'the counter-culture' it should appeal as a book which counters almost every aspect of the culture of our society. To a generation which delights in the 'put on,' parody and artifice, often as the most meaningful expressions of deeply held convictions in a world which they see as prone to distortion, *Cat's Cradle*'s play with language, symbol and artifice should find accord."

God Bless You, Mr. Rosewater; or, Pearls before Swine introduces a theme that crops up repeatedly in the later novels and which is often considered to be the essence of all of Vonnegut's writing. It is expressed by the main character, Eliot Rosewater, in the motto "Goddamn it, you've got to be kind." John R. May comments in a *Twentieth Century Literature* review that it is the author's "most positive and humane work. . . . We may not be able, Vonnegut is saying, to undo the harm that has been done, but we can certainly love, simply because there are people, those who have been made useless by our past stupidity and greed, our previous crimes against our brothers. And if that seems insane, then the better the world for such folly." *Book Week* contributor Daniel Talbot writes: "It's a tribute to Kurt Vonnegut Jr. that he has covered such a large territory of human follies in so short a book. . . . The net effect is at once explosively funny and agonizing."

In *Slaughterhouse Five; Or, the Children's Crusade,* Vonnegut finally delivers a complete treatise on the World War II bombing of Dresden. The main character, Billy Pilgrim, is a very young infantry scout who is captured in the Battle of the Bulge and quartered in a Dresden slaughterhouse where he and other prisoners are employed in the production of a vitamin supplement for pregnant women. During the February 13, 1945, firebombing by Allied aircraft, the prisoners take shelter in an underground meat locker. When they emerge, the city has been levelled and they are forced to dig corpses out of the rubble. The story of Billy Pilgrim is the story of Kurt Vonnegut who was captured and survived the firestorm in which 135,000 German civilians perished, more than the number of deaths in the bombings of Hiroshima and Nagasaki combined. Robert Scholes sums up the theme of *Slaughterhouse Five* in the *New York Times Book Review,* writing: "Be kind. Don't hurt. Death is coming for all of us anyway, and it is better to be Lot's wife looking back through salty eyes at the Deity that destroyed those cities of the plain in order to save them." The reviewer concludes that "*Slaughterhouse Five* is an extraordinary success. It is a book we need to read, and to reread."

The popularity of *Slaughterhouse Five* is due, in part, to its timeliness; it deals with many issues that were vital to the late sixties: war, ecology, overpopulation, and consumerism. Klinkowitz, writing in *Literary Subversions: New American Fiction and the Practice of Criticism,* sees larger reasons for the book's success: "Kurt Vonnegut's fiction of the 1960s is the popular artifact which may be the fairest example of American cultural change. . . . Shunned as distastefully low-brow . . . and insufficiently commercial to suit the exploitative tastes of high-power publishers, Vonnegut's fiction limped along for years on the genuinely democratic basis of family magazine and pulp paperback circulation. Then in the late 1960s, as the culture as a whole exploded, Vonnegut was able to write and publish a novel, *Slaughterhouse Five,* which so perfectly caught America's transformative mood that its story and structure became best-selling metaphors for the new age."

Writing in *Critique,* Wayne D. McGinnis comments that in *Slaughterhouse Five,* Vonnegut "avoids framing his story in linear narration, choosing a circular structure. Such a view of the art of the novel has much to do with the protagonist . . . Billy Pilgrim, an optometrist who provides corrective lenses for Earthlings. For Pilgrim, who learns of a new view of life as he becomes 'unstuck in time,' the lenses are corrective metaphorically as well as physically. Quite early in the exploration of Billy's life the reader learns that 'frames are where the money is.' . . . Historical events like the bombing of Dresden are usually 'read' in the framework of moral and historical interpretation." McGinnis feels that the novel's cyclical nature is inextricably bound up with the themes of "time, death, and renewal," and goes on to say that "the most important function of 'so it goes' [a phrase that recurs at each death in the book], . . . is its imparting a cyclical quality to the novel, both in form and content. Paradoxically, the expression of fatalism serves as a source of renewal, a situation typical of Vonnegut's works, for it enables the novel to go on despite—even because of—the proliferation of deaths."

After the publication of *Slaughterhouse Five,* Vonnegut entered a period of depression during which he vowed, at one point, never to write another novel. He concentrated, instead, on lecturing, teaching, and finishing a play, *Happy Birthday, Wanda June,* that he had begun several years earlier. The play, which ran off-Broadway from October, 1970 to March, 1971, received mixed reviews. *Newsweek*'s Jack Kroll wrote that "almost every time an American novelist writes a play he shows up most of our thumb-tongued playwrights, who lack the melody of mind, the wit, dash and accuracy of Saul Bellow and Bruce Jay Friedman. And the same thing must be said of the writing in *Happy Birthday, Wanda June* . . . Vonnegut's dialogue is not only fast and funny, with a palpable taste and crackle, but it also means something. And his comic sense is a superior one; *Wanda June* has as many laughs as anything by Neil Simon." On the other hand, in the *New Republic* Stanley Kauffmann called it "a disaster, full of callow wit, rheumatic invention, and dormitory profundity. . . . The height of its imagination is exemplified by a scene in Heaven between a golden-haired little girl and a Nazi Gauleiter in which they discuss the way Jesus plays shuffleboard."

Breakfast of Champions marked the end of Vonnegut's depression and a return to the novel; in honor of this event, Vonnegut subtitled the work, *Goodbye Blue Monday.* Nora Sayre writes in the *New York Times Book Review* that "in this novel Vonnegut is treating himself to a giant brain-flush, clearing his head by throwing out acquired ideas, and also liberating some of the characters from his previous books. Thus, he has celebrated his fiftieth birthday in the same spirit that made Tolstoy release his serfs and Thomas Jefferson free his slaves. Once again, we're back on the people-grid; major and minor personae from other novels resurface in this one, their lives ridiculously entangled. . . . This explosive meditation ranks with Vonnegut's best."

In *Breakfast of Champions,* as in most of Vonnegut's work, there are very clear autobiographical tendencies. In this novel, however, the author seems to be even more wrapped up in his characters than usual. He appears as Philboyd Sludge, the writer of a book which stars Dwayne Hoover, a Pontiac dealer (Vonnegut once ran a Saab dealership) who goes berserk after reading a novel by Kilgore Trout, who also represents Vonnegut. Toward the end of the book, Vonnegut arranges a meeting between himself and Trout, whom Robert Merrill calls his "most famous creation," in which he casts the character loose forever; by this time the previously unsuccessful Trout has become rich and famous and is finally able to stand on his own.

Catastrophe comes easily in 1982's *Deadeye Dick.* The title character's father saves the life of a starving artist, the young

Hitler, when they are in school together; the narrator, Rudy Waltz, gains his cruel nickname at age twelve when a shot he fires from his father's rifle accidentally kills a pregnant woman; and later, a neutron bomb detonates, either by accident, or by the government's covert design, in Waltz's home town, killing everyone, but leaving the machines and buildings unharmed. Interspersed with these horrors are recipes, provided by Rudy, who has become a chef and copartner with his brother in a restaurant in Haiti. Throughout, "the grand old Vonnegutian comedy of causelessness still holds center stage. . . . Why does the child of a gun safety specialist, using a rifle from his father's collection, emerge as a double murderer? A tough question. Why do human beings take satisfaction in creating a neutron bomb that destroys 'only' human beings, not their accoutrements? Another toughie. Why should grief-struck Rudy Waltz, headed for a presumably moving moment at his parents' graveside, allow his train of thought to light on a certain cookie, whereupon . . . instead of grief we're provided with a recipe for almond macaroons?," Benjamin De Mott asks in *New York Times Book Review.*

If catastrophe comes more easily to man than courtesy and decency, man's large brain is to blame, Vonnegut asserts in his next novel. "*Galapagos* brings Vonnegut's lifelong belief in the imperfectibility of human nature to its logical conclusion," observes a London *Times* reviewer. The novel recounts the evolution of man over thousands of years. Narrated by the spectral remains of Vietnam vet Leon Trout, the story tells how a group of tourists are shipwrecked in the islands where Darwin formulated the notion of progressive adaptation; over time, their oversized brains diminish, sexual interests atrophy, and their hands become flippers, all to the benefit of the race and the ecosystem. "This will eliminate war, starvation, and nuclear terror—that is, many of the things Mr. Vonnegut likes to complain about in his novels," remarks *New York Times* reviewer Michiko Kakutani. But for all the seriousness of its message, the book contains sufficient humor to make it satisfying as "a well-crafted comic strip," Kakutani adds.

Though some reviewers find Vonnegut's jokes an easy target for criticism, Thomas M. Disch, writing in the *Times Literary Supplement,* sees in the humor a secondary purpose, "which is moral instruction. Indeed, the interest of the Vonnegut voice is not in what it reveals of the author but in the audience that it hypothesizes, an audience that must have the most basic facts of life explained to it in the simplest terms, an audience that will crack up at the sound of a fart, an audience that has the best of intentions even as it paves the road to hell, an audience of children who know they need to be scolded. Vonnegut is unusual among novelists who dramatize the conflict (ever recurring in his work) between fathers and sons in that his sympathies always lie on the sadder-but-wiser side of the generation gap. In an era that has institutionalized adolescent rebellion, here is a father for foundlings of all ages. Small wonder that he is so popular."

Although it takes place in the near future, the text of 1990's *Hocus Pocus,* like many Vonnegut novels, ranges freely through the much of the twentieth century. As Vonnegut's protagonist Eugene Debs Hartke describes it, America in 2001 is "a thoroughly looted bankrupt nation whose assets had been sold off to foreigners, a nation swamped by unchecked plagues and superstition and illiteracy and hypnotic TV." Like the central characters in *Mother Night* and *Slaughterhouse-Five,* Hartke is a man incarcerated. His story ranges from West Point to Vietnam (he is the last American soldier to leave), from his job as physics instructor at a college for dyslexics (he is dismissed for his pessimism) to his job at a prison

run for profit by the Japanese. Hartke is unjustly accused of masterminding a prison break and ends up in jail himself. Along the way some familiar Vonnegut standbys—the Tralfamadorians from *Sirens of Titan,* the SF writer Kilgore Trout from *Breakfast of Champions*—turn up, and as in other novels, Vonnegut freely peppers the text with quotes from Bartlett's *Familiar Quotations.*

The novel *Timequake* appeared in 1997, though Vonnegut had completed the novel several years earlier. At that earlier date, having found his novel "pointless," he had reworked its best parts into a digressive stew which he then declared as his final literary utterance. The germ of a plot remains: At the turn of the millennium, the world falls victim to a wrinkle in space-time which forces everyone on earth to relive the 1990s. This provides jumping-off point for Vonnegut's ruminations about moral decay, mortality, and the state of Western culture at the close of the twentieth century. A few familiar devices do remain, such as the presence of Kilgore Trout and the employment of a Zen-like repetitive phrase. "Hi ho" and "So it goes" had been refrains in earlier novels; this time the refrain is "tingaling." Reviews split on *Timequake*'s significance, though few reserved comment on Vonnegut's claim that he was washed up. R. Z. Sheppard of *Time* derided Vonnegut for "seeking sympathy" from book reviewers by announcing *Timequake* as his final novel. "Having a novelist's free hand to write what you will does not mean you are entitled to a free ride," he observed. He was also annoyed by the novel's lack of story and Vonnegut's "familiar tone of weary bemusement." In *Newsweek,* Brad Stone called the author "notoriously skilled in this business of lowering reader expectations" but then went on to praise the novel lavishly. *Timequake,* he wrote, was Vonnegut's "funniest book since *Breakfast of Champions.*"

While Vonnegut's fiction is couchedly candid in its reflection of his personal views on many subjects, his essays and other works of nonfiction are even more so. He has published several collections of essays, interviews, and speeches, including *Palm Sunday: An Autobiographical Collage* in 1981 and *Fates Worse than Death: An Autobiographical Collage of the 1980s,* a similar mix to *Palm Sunday,* published a decade later. In *Fates Worse than Death,* collected essays and speeches are interwoven with memoir and parenthetical commentary written especially for the volume. Subject matter ranges from the broadly political—Western imperialism and America's war-greed—to the painfully personal—Vonnegut's own prisoner-of-war experiences and bouts with mental illness. Douglas Anderson describes the collection in the *New York Times Book Review* as "scarily funny" and feels that "it offers a rare insight into an author who has customarily hidden his heart." In the *Times Literary Supplement,* James Woods concludes that the "more Vonnegut writes the more American he seems—a kind of de-solemnized Emerson, at once arguer, doubter, sermonizer and gossip."

Vonnegut's status as a master of contemporary fiction is built only partly on the strength of his themes. Concludes Robert Group in the *Dictionary of Literary Biography,* "The contribution of Kurt Vonnegut Jr. to American literature is twofold: through his artistry (and persistence) he has helped to elevate the pulp genre of science fiction to the level of critical recognition; and through his philosophy he offers a mixture of wistful humanism and cynical existentialism that implies a way of dealing with modern realities completely different from that of most American writers. In the tradition of [Laurence] Sterne and [Henry] Fielding, he uses wit and wisdom to show that though man may live in a purposeless universe full of self-seeking manipulations, there is hope for something better. . . . Like Trout or Vonnegut one must cry out against absurdity, even if one is ignored. Vonnegut creates a vision so preposterous that indignation might provide the basis for change—while laughter allows one to cope with the moment."

BIOGRAPHICAL/CRITICAL SOURCES:

BOOKS

Broer, Lawrence R., editor, *Sanity Plea: Schizophrenia in the Novels of Kurt Vonnegut* (revised edition), University of Alabama Press (Tuscaloosa), 1994.
Chernuchin, Michael, editor, *Vonnegut Talks!*, Pylon Press (Forest Hills, NY), 1977.
Contemporary Literary Criticism, Gale (Detroit), Volume 1, 1973; Volume 2, 1974; Volume 3, 1975; Volume 4, 1975; Volume 5, 1976; Volume 8, 1978; Volume 12, 1980; Volume 22, 1982; Volume 60, 1986.
Dictionary of Literary Biography, Gale, Volume 2: *American Novelists since World War II*, 1978; Volume 8: *Twentieth-Century American Science Fiction Writers, Part 2*, 1981.
Dictionary of Literary Biography Documentary Series, Volume 3, Gale, 1983.
Dictionary of Literary Biography Yearbook 1980, Gale, 1981.
Giannone, Richard, *Vonnegut: A Preface to His Novels*, Kennikat, 1977.
Kazin, Alfred, *Bright Book of Life: American Novelists and Storytellers from Hemingway to Mailer*, Little, Brown (Boston), 1973.
Klinkowitz, Jerome, and John Somer, editors, *The Vonnegut Statement: Original Essays on the Life and Work of Kurt Vonnegut*, Delacorte (New York City), 1973.
Klinkowitz, Jerome, *Literary Disruptions: The Making of a Post-Contemporary American Fiction*, University of Illinois Press, 1975.
Klinkowitz, Jerome, and Donald L. Lawler, editors, *Vonnegut in America: An Introduction to the Life and Work of Kurt Vonnegut*, Delacorte, 1977.
Klinkowitz, Jerome, *The American 1960s: Imaginative Acts in a Decade of Change*, Iowa State University Press (Ames), 1980.
Klinkowitz, Jerome, *Kurt Vonnegut*, Methuen (New York City), 1982.
Klinkowitz, Jerome, *Literary Subversions: New American Fiction and the Practice of Criticism*, Southern Illinois University Press (Carbondale), 1985.
Krementz, Jill, editor, *Happy Birthday, Kurt Vonnegut: A Festschrift for Kurt Vonnegut on His Sixtieth Birthday*, Delacorte, 1982.
Leeds, Marc, *The Vonnegut Encyclopedia: An Authorized Compendium*, Greenwood Press, 1995.
Lundquist, James, *Kurt Vonnegut*, Ungar, 1977.
Mustazza, Leonard, editor, *The Critical Response to Kurt Vonnegut*, Greenwood Press, 1994.
Plimpton, George, editor, *Writers at Work: The "Paris Review" Interviews*, sixth series, Penguin (New York City), 1984.
Reed, Peter J., *Kurt Vonnegut, Jr.*, Warner Books, 1972.
Reed, Peter J., and Marc Leeds, editors, *The Vonnegut Chronicles: Interviews and Essays*, Greenwood Press, 1996.
Schatt, Stanley, *Kurt Vonnegut, Jr.*, Twayne (Boston), 1976.

PERIODICALS

Book Week, April 11, 1965.
Commonweal, September 16, 1966; June 6, 1969; November 27, 1970; May 7, 1971; December 7, 1973.
Critique: Studies in Modern Fiction, Volume 12, number 3, 1971; Volume 14, number 3, 1973; Volume 15, number 2, 1973; Volume 17, number 1, 1975; Volume 18, number 3, 1977; Volume 26, number 2, 1985.
Detroit News, June 18, 1972; September 16, 1979; October 3, 1982; November 10, 1985; January 5, 1986.
Film Comment, November/December, 1985.
Globe and Mail (Toronto), March 17, 1984; February 8, 1986; October 17, 1987.
International Fiction Review, summer, 1980.
Life, April 9, 1965; August 16, 1968; September 12, 1969; November 20, 1970.
Los Angeles Times, February 7, 1983.
Los Angeles Times Book Review, September 23, 1979; October 31, 1982; March 3, 1984; April 18, 1984; September 29, 1985; September 2, 1990, pp. 1, 10.
Modern Fiction Studies, spring, 1973; summer, 1975; winter, 1980-81.
Nation, September 23, 1968; June 9, 1969; September 15, 1979; March 21, 1981; November 13, 1982.
National Review, September 28, 1973; November 26, 1976; November 23, 1979; December 10, 1982.
New Republic, August 18, 1952; October 8, 1966; April 26, 1969; November 7, 1970; June 12, 1971; May 12, 1973; September 28, 1973; June 1, 1974; July 5, 1974; September 25, 1976; November 26, 1976.
Newsweek, August 19, 1968; March 3, 1969; April 14, 1969; October 19, 1970; December 20, 1971; May 14, 1973; October 1, 1979; September 29, 1997.
New Yorker, August 16, 1952; May 15, 1965; May 17, 1969; October 17, 1970; October 25, 1976; November 8, 1982.
New York Review of Books, July 2, 1970; May 31, 1973; November 25, 1976; November 22, 1979.
New York Times, August 19, 1968; September 13, 1969; October 6, 1970; October 18, 1970; May 27, 1971; May 13, 1973; October 3, 1975; September 7, 1979; September 24, 1979; October 15, 1979; March 27, 1981; November 5, 1982; February 4, 1983; February 17, 1983; September 25, 1985; January 27, 1987; April 4, 1987.
New York Times Book Review, June 2, 1963; April 25, 1965; August 6, 1967; September 1, 1968; April 6, 1969; February 4, 1973; May 13, 1973; October 3, 1976; September 9, 1979; March 15, 1981; October 17, 1982; October 6, 1985; October 18, 1987, p. 12; September 9, 1990, p. 12; September 15, 1991, p. 26; November 1, 1992, p. 32.
New York Times Magazine, January 24, 1971.
People Weekly, October 19, 1987.
Progressive, August, 1981.
Publishers Weekly, October 25, 1985; January 31, 1986.
South Atlantic Quarterly, winter, 1979.
Time, August 30, 1968; April 11, 1969; June 29, 1970; June 3, 1974; October 25, 1976; September 10, 1979; October 25, 1982; October 21, 1985; September 28, 1987, p. 68; September 3, 1990, p. 73; September 29, 1997.
Times (London), July 8, 1981; February 17, 1983; May 17, 1986; May 30, 1987.
Times Literary Supplement, November 11, 1965; December 12, 1968; July 17, 1969; November 5, 1976; December 7, 1979; June 19, 1981; September 26, 1980; February 25, 1983; November 8, 1985; October 26, 1990, p. 1146; November 15, 1991, p. 8.
Tribune Books (Chicago), September 27, 1987, p. 1; August 19, 1990, p. 6; September 1, 1991, p. 4; November 24, 1991, p. 8; September 6, 1992, p. 2.
Twentieth Century Literature, January, 1972.
Village Voice, February 22, 1983.

Virginia Quarterly Review, summer, 1981.
Washington Post, October 12, 1970; May 13, 1973; May 15, 1981; February 2, 1982.
Washington Post Book World, March 8, 1981; October 17, 1982; September 22, 1985; October 4, 1987; August 19, 1990, pp. 1-2; October 21, 1990, p. 15.
Western Humanities Review, summer, 1974.
World Literature Today, winter, 1981.

*   *   *

VON RACHEN, Kurt
   See HUBBARD, L(afayette) Ron(ald)

*   *   *

VOSCE, Trudie
   See OZICK, Cynthia

W

WAIN, John (Barrington) 1925-1994

PERSONAL: Born March 14, 1925, in Stoke-on-Trent, Staffordshire, England; died of a stroke, May 24, 1994, in Oxford, England; son of Arnold A. (a dentist) and Anne Wain; married Marianne Urmston, 1947 (divorced, 1956); married Eirian James, 1960 (died, 1988); married Patricia Dunn, 1989; children: (second marriage) William, Ianto, Tobias. *Education:* St. John's College, Oxford, B.A., 1946, M.A., 1950. *Avocational interests:* Walking, canoeing.

CAREER: St. John's College, Oxford University, Oxford, England, Fereday Fellow, 1946-47; University of Reading, Reading, England, lecturer in English literature, 1947-55; writer and critic, 1955-94. Churchill Visiting Professor at University of Bristol, 1967; visiting professor at Centre Experimental de Vincennes, University of Paris, 1969; George Elliston Lecturer on Poetry at University of Cincinnati; Professor of Poetry at Oxford University, 1973-78. Director of Poetry Book Society's festival, London, 1961.

MEMBER: Oxford Union Society.

AWARDS, HONORS: Somerset Maugham Award, 1958, for *Preliminary Essays;* Royal Society of Literature fellow, 1960; Brasenose College creative arts fellowship from Oxford University, 1971-72; James Tait Black Memorial Prize and Heinemann Award from Royal Society of Literature, both 1975, both for *Samuel Johnson;* Whitbread Literary Award, 1985, for *The Free Zone Starts Here;* honorary degrees from the University of Keele and the University of Loughborough, both 1985; honorary fellow, St. John's College, Oxford, 1985-94.

WRITINGS:

FICTION

Hurry on Down (novel), Secker & Warburg (London), 1953, published as *Born in Captivity,* Knopf (New York City), 1954, published as *Hurry on Down,* Viking (New York City), 1965.
Living in the Present (novel), Secker & Warburg, 1955, Putnam (New York City), 1960.
The Contenders (novel), St. Martin's (New York City), 1958.
A Travelling Woman (novel), St. Martin's, 1959.
Nuncle and Other Stories (short stories), Macmillan (London), 1960, St. Martin's, 1961.
Strike the Father Dead (novel), St. Martin's, 1962.

The Young Visitors (novel), Viking, 1965.
Death of the Hind Legs and Other Stories (short stories), Viking, 1966.
The Smaller Sky (novel), Macmillan, 1967.
A Winter in the Hills (novel; also see below), Viking, 1970.
The Life Guard (short stories), Macmillan, 1971, Viking, 1972.
King Caliban and Other Stories (short stories), Macmillan, 1978.
The Pardoner's Tale (novel), Macmillan, 1978, Viking, 1979.
Lizzie's Floating Shop (juvenile), Bodley Head (London), 1981.
Young Shoulders (juvenile), Macmillan, 1982, published as *The Free Zone Starts Here,* Delacorte (New York City), 1982.
Where the Rivers Meet (novel), Hutchinson (London), 1988.
Comedies (novel; sequel to *Where the Rivers Meet*), Hutchinson, 1990.
Hungry Generations (novel; sequel to *Comedies*), Hutchinson, 1994.

POETRY

Mixed Feelings, University of Reading (Berkshire), 1951.
(Contributor) D. J. Enright, editor, *Poets of the Fifties,* [London], 1955.
A Word Carved on a Sill, St. Martin's, 1956.
(Contributor) Robert Conquest, editor, *New Lines,* [London], 1956.
Weep before God, St. Martin's, 1961.
A Song about Major Eatherly, Qara Press (Iowa City), 1961.
(Contributor) Chad Walsh, editor, *Today's Poets,* Scribner (New York City), 1964.
Wildtrack, Macmillan, 1965, Viking, 1966.
Letters to Five Artists, Macmillan, 1969, Viking, 1970.
The Shape of Feng, Covent Garden Press (London), 1972.
Feng, Viking, 1975.
Poems for the Zodiac (limited edition), Pisces (London), 1980.
Thinking about Mr. Person, Chimaera Press (Kent), 1980.
Poems, 1949-1979, Macmillan, 1981.
The Twofold, Hunting Raven Press (Somerset), 1981.
Mid-week Period Return: Home Thoughts of a Native, Celandine Press (Stratford-upon-Avon), 1982.

PLAYS

Harry in the Night, first produced in Stoke-on-Trent, England, 1975.
You Wouldn't Remember (radio play), first produced by British Broadcasting Corporation (BBC), 1978.

A Winter in the Hills (radio play; adapted from the author's novel), 1981.
Frank (radio play; first produced by BBC), Amber Lane Press (Oxford), 1984.
Good Morning Blues (radio play), first produced by BBC, 1986.
Johnson Is Leaving: A Monodrama, Pisces, 1994.

NONFICTION

Preliminary Essays, St. Martin's, 1957.
Gerard Manley Hopkins: An Idiom of Desperation, Oxford University Press (London), 1959.
(Contributor) Tom Maschler, editor, *Declaration*, MacGibbon & Kee, 1959.
Sprightly Running: Part of an Autobiography, Macmillan, 1962, St. Martin's, 1963.
Essays on Literature and Ideas, St. Martin's, 1963.
The Living World of Shakespeare: A Playgoer's Guide, St. Martin's, 1964.
Arnold Bennett, Columbia University Press (New York City), 1967.
A House for the Truth: Critical Essays, Macmillan, 1972, Viking, 1973.
Samuel Johnson (biography; Book-of-the-Month Club selection), Macmillan, 1974, Viking, 1975.
Professing Poetry, Macmillan, 1977, Viking, 1978.
Dear Shadows: Portraits from Memory, J. Murray (London), 1986.

EDITOR

Contemporary Reviews of Romantic Poetry, Barnes & Noble (New York City), 1953.
Interpretations: Essays on Twelve English Poems, Routledge & Kegan Paul (London), 1955, Hillary (New York City), 1957, 2nd edition, Routledge & Kegan Paul, 1972.
International Literary Annual, two volumes, J. Calder, 1958, 1959, Criterion, 1959, 1960.
Frances Burney d'Arblay, *Fanny Burney's Diary*, Folio Society (London), 1961.
Anthology of Modern Poetry, Hutchinson, 1963.
(Author of introduction and notes) *Pope*, Dell (New York City), 1963.
(Author of introduction) Thomas Hardy, *The Dynasts*, St. Martin's, 1966.
Selected Shorter Poems of Thomas Hardy, Macmillan, 1966.
Selected Stories of Thomas Hardy, St. Martin's, 1966.
Shakespeare: Macbeth; a Casebook, Macmillan, 1968, Aurora Publications (Nashville, TN), 1970.
Shakespeare: Othello; a Casebook, Macmillan, 1971.
Johnson as Critic, Routledge & Kegan Paul, 1973.
Samuel Johnson, *Lives of the English Poets*, Dent (London), 1975, Dutton, 1976.
Johnson on Johnson: A Selection of the Personal and Autobiographical Writings of Samuel Johnson, Dutton, 1976.
Edmund Wilson: The Man and His Work, New York University Press (New York City), 1978 (published in England as *An Edmund Wilson Celebration*, Phaidon Press [Oxford], 1978).
Personal Choice: A Poetry Anthology, David & Charles (North Pomfret, VT), 1978.
(With wife, Eirian Wain) *The New Wessex Selection of Thomas Hardy's Poetry*, Macmillan, 1978.
Anthology of Contemporary Poetry: Post-War to the Present, Hutchinson, 1979.
Everyman's Book of English Verse, Dent, 1981.
Arnold Bennett, *The Old Wives' Tale*, Penguin, 1983.

James Hogg, *The Private Memoirs and Confessions of a Justified Sinner*, Penguin, 1983.
Oxford Anthology of English Poetry, Oxford University Press, 1990.
(And author of introduction) *The Journals of James Boswell, 1762-1795*, Yale University Press (New Haven, CT), 1991.
(With Ted Walker) *Modern Poetry* (sound recording), BFA Educational Media, 1972.
The Poetry of John Wain (sound recording), Jeffrey Norton, 1976.
Geoffrey Halson, editor, *A John Wain Selection*, Longman, 1977.
(Translator from Anglo-Saxon) *The Seafarer*, Grenville Press, 1982.
Open Country, Hutchinson, 1987.

Contributor to numerous periodicals, including *New Republic, Observer, New Yorker, Times Literary Supplement, Saturday Evening Post, Harper's Bazaar*, and *Ladies' Home Journal*. Founding editor of *Mandrake*, 1944.

SIDELIGHTS: For more than forty years, John Wain, a British man of letters, devoted his energies primarily to writing. The diversity of his output demonstrated his commitment to his craft—from 1951 until his death in 1994, he penned novels, short stories, poetry, critical essays, and a highly acclaimed biography, *Samuel Johnson*. According to *Dictionary of Literary Biography* contributor A. T. Tolley, Wain's novels and stories "make up one of the more substantial bodies of contemporary fiction in English," while his poetry "stands as an important contribution to his total achievement and displays that concern with the life of literature in our day that has permeated his work." Wain was likewise commended for his critical judgments that proved him "adamantly committed to the mystery of literary truths that can advance the universal human experience," in the words of *Dictionary of Literary Biography* essayist Augustus M. Kolich. Kolich called Wain "an iconoclast who is uncompromising in his dedication to the belief that in a world where 'destruction and disintegration' are the norm, only the artist's creative language can clear the ruins and establish a foundation for heroic individualism." Wain's writings pursued this high ideal in an unpretentious and readable style; Susan Wood noted in the *Washington Post Book World* that the author, while an Oxford graduate, "is no dour Oxford don. . . . Instead, he typifies the very best of what one might call 'Englishness'—good sense, moderation, a feeling for language, erudition without pretension, and wit."

Addressing Wain's fiction specifically, *Esquire* critic Geoffrey Wolff commented: "From his first novel, *Hurry on Down* (1953), Wain has concerned himself with contemporary English manners, with the small choices that comprise a program of values. . . . Wain writes about boredom, the killing regularity of diminished, stunted lives; because he is so skilled a writer, he creates an accurate evocation of the awful coziness and regularity of English conventions." Wain was also preoccupied, in much of his work, with the survival of individual dignity and purpose in a world where bullying and domination often prevail. Kolich stated: "In Wain's criticism of contemporary English society, his target is clearly the totalitarian consciousness which has as its object the manipulation and domination of the small child in all of us—that part of our self-concept that naturally sees through folly and pretense and always expects to be left uncontrolled and free. Hence, Wain's fiction is above all morally pledged to a set of values that aim at offending the status quo, when it seems either silly, absurd, or oppressive, and championing commonsense individualism, whenever it can be championed in a world of antiheroes."

Disillusioned Englishmen figure in many of Wain's subsequent novels, including *Strike the Father Dead, The Contenders,* and *The Smaller Sky.* Kolich wrote: "In the process of breaking away from the confines of economic and social success and the seductive powers of competitive capitalism, Wain's heroes still must face the unsettling business of reordering their lives outside the conventional set plans that either religion or business might offer. . . . Very often, . . . they seem lost and unable to cope with the shifting emotional currents generated by those toward whom they feel drawn." In general, critics found Wain's novels of the late 1950s and 1960s less successful than his debut fiction work. As *South Atlantic Quarterly* contributor Elgin W. Mellown described it, Wain "commands an almost flawless technique and can write in a truthful, accurate, and revealing way about human beings interacting on the personal level; but when he looks beyond these individuals and attempts to put them into a larger focus or to give them a wider significance, their thoughts and beliefs condemn them as second-rate." In his book entitled *Postwar British Fiction: New Accents and Attitudes,* James Gindin contended: "For the kind of point Wain is making about the contemporary world that he depicts with such specificity, force, and intelligence, he does require some tangible expression of the value of the personal and the humane. But the form of expression often lacks a comic richness that would avoid both the brittle gimmick and the heavy sediment of emotion." Undaunted by the sometimes harsh criticism, Wain continued to produce fiction. His later works found favor with reviewers, and, in retrospect, his seriousness of purpose and sheer productivity led Mellown to suggest that "these [early] novels are the most impressive output of any of the postwar British writers."

Kolich described *A Winter in the Hills,* Wain's 1970 novel, as "perhaps the most typical . . . in terms of themes and characters." The story concerns a philologist who moves to North Wales and becomes involved in a local bus driver's efforts to thwart a business takeover. *Newsweek* contributor Raymond A. Sokolov found the work "an unashamedly romantic, heroic, plot-heavy, character-ridden, warm piece of narration with a beginning, a middle and an end. . . . Wain proves there is still much life in the old tricks." A *Times Literary Supplement* reviewer asserted that *A Winter in the Hills* "goes farther, perhaps, in defining and developing Mr. Wain's basic concerns as a writer than most of his earlier works; and does it with a growing maturity and conviction." The reviewer noted Wain's continuing interest in the quality of individual living, and added, "Observing social situations, catching hints of character and motive in conversational habits, contriving elaborate and efficient plots—these continue to be [Wain's] strengths."

The Pardoner's Tale, published in 1978, proved even more popular than *A Winter in the Hills.* In *Time,* R. Z. Sheppard called the work a "thoughtful treatment of two middle-aged men joyfully making fools of themselves over younger women." The book is a novel-within-a-novel; an author, Giles Hermitage, seeks to resolve his own romantic misadventures by writing about a fictitious businessman and *his* encounter with a woman. The resulting pastiche of stories evokes "a steady sensuous glow that warms the brain," according to Sheppard. *Saturday Review* correspondent Carole Cook contended that it is Wain himself who "shines as the hero" in *The Pardoner's Tale.* "He has beaten the clock," Cook wrote, "enticed us into the game, and held us so captivated by his voice of a man desperate for a second chance at life that it becomes, word by word, our own." Amy Wilentz argued a different viewpoint in the *Nation.* She found *The Pardoner's Tale* a "well-intentioned book," but subsequently declared that there is

"so little true atmosphere in Wain's book that his characters, who are sporadically well drawn, also seem shadowy and displaced." Conversely, D. A. N. Jones praised the novel in the *Times Literary Supplement.* "The lineaments of gratified desire are persuasively drawn," Jones asserted. "Precise details of plot and character dissolve into an amorous haze, spreading delight. . . . John Wain's novel is written in a warmly forgiving spirit; and this, together with its engaging riggishness, contributes to the reader's delight."

In an essay for the *Contemporary Authors Autobiography Series,* Wain claimed that his book about Samuel Johnson was "the most successful work of my middle life." *Samuel Johnson* provided a comprehensive biography of one of England's leading literary figures, written expressly for the general reader. Many critics praised the account not only for its accessibility to the non-academic public, but also for its subtle reflections on the literary life in any age. *Harper's* reviewer Jack Richardson wrote: "To John Wain, Johnson is not only a great figure in literature, he is also a magnificent companion, someone who brings with him a feeling of good company when met for the first time or recalled for the hundredth; and it is this feeling which Wain wishes to celebrate, and which makes *Samuel Johnson* more than anything else a narrative of friendship." In the *Nation,* Robert L. Chapman stated: "John Wain's own stature as a literary-academic person assures us a voice both authoritative and eloquent" in *Samuel Johnson,* but the author is still "less interested in the precise delineation of a dead man than in the appraisal of an immortal colleague. . . . I cherish the lively, novelistic quality of [Wain's] book, where I can see an idea being born, growing, and at last enforcing itself as the prime focus of meaning."

Wain's poetry is also seen as a significant contribution to the body of English letters since 1945. Tolley explained that, in his early poems, Wain is "affronting the whole modernist poetic, where the emphasis had been on the image, on the maximization of sensory impact, and where generalizations had been seen as the enemies of the poetic. Wain . . . is comfortable with a poetry of statement. However, these [early] poems are far from being doctrinaire literary stunts. Many stand out as simple and passionate state-ments on what have proved to be some of Wain's abiding themes: love, isolation, honesty, and sympathy for the deprived. . . . Poems . . . seemingly artificial . . . survive as expressions of tenderness." Wain is perhaps better known for his long poems such as *Wildtrack, Feng,* and *Letters to Five Artists.* "Wain's devotion to the long poem," wrote Tolley, "is at once courageous and surprising in view of his steady adherence to the realistic tradition in his novels. Whatever may be said about his attainment in his longer poems, he has not been content with the diminished ambitions that have often led to diminished poetry in Britain the last quarter of a century." According to Philip Gardner in the *Times Literary Supplement,* Wain, "concerned with the communi-cation both of humane values and of an imaginative response to experience, . . . sometimes errs on the side of too much clarity: over-insistent, he button-holes the reader or goes on too long." Derek Stanford expressed a different opinion in *Books:* "Wain's unitary theme is the relationship between art and life—particularly that between the individual work and the individual produc-er. . . . All in all, *Letters to Five Artists* is full of vigorous poetry, written in sinewy masculine language but without any of that paraded toughness sometimes indulged in by the New Move-ment." A *Times Literary Supplement* reviewer concluded that there is "no deliberate order or consistency in Mr. Wain's reflections, except for the unity given by an underlying compas-sion."

In 1973 Wain was elected to the prestigious Professor of Poetry chair at Oxford. He held the chair for five years, giving lectures on subjects that reflected his critical concerns. These lectures are collected in *Professing Poetry.* Kolich contends that, as a literary critic, Wain projects an iconoclasm "derived from a privately felt moral sense of self-determination, a concept that he hopes can be shared by a community of equals, scholars and artists, working toward 'the establishment of a hierarchy of quality.'" According to Herbert Leibowitz in the *New York Times Book Review,* Wain "detests the art chatter and sensationalism of the modern age, with its denial of complexity and the rich diapason of language. For Wain, the imagination is under siege by an 'insistence on explicitness,' 'intellectual slapstick' replaces thought, and our art 'abandons the search for standards' by stupidly rejecting the past." As might be expected of one educated at and honored by Oxford, Wain's critical judgments reside "in his devotion to the idea that the study of the best literature that has been written can provide the criteria for the best judgments," Kolich concluded.

For many years before his death, Wain experienced deteriorating health and increasing blindness due to diabetes. Despite his disabilities, he worked diligently to complete his last major literary achievement—a trilogy of novels based on his life at Oxford. *Where the Rivers Meet* was the first in the trio, followed by *Comedies* and *Hungry Generations.* Their protagonist was Peter Leonard, a lower-middle-class youth who attends Oxford on a scholarship. The widening gap between Peter and his family and the young man's struggle to adapt to his new environment are convincingly portrayed. *Spectator* reviewer Raymond Carr singled out a wedding episode as "a superb set piece," and called Peter's relationship with his family "subtly and movingly done." Carr and other commentators pointed out, however, that Peter's insatiable sexual appetite dominated the book inappropriately. "At times Wain appears to have a bet on with himself to see how many different ways he can find of describing erectile tissue," complained Hugh Barnes in the *Observer.* John Melmoth concluded in *Times Literary Supplement* that *Where the Rivers Meet* is "sprawling, randy, over-long, self-indulgent and disingenuously plain-blokeish. True to a certain type of English fiction, it is too relaxed about its own limitations, and the narrator is content to describe himself as 'a philistine.'"

"As a writer I have regarded my basic material as the word rather than as this or that literary form," Wain stated in the *Contemporary Authors Autobiography Series.* Wain refused to be classified as "primarily" one specific sort of writer—novelist, poet, or essayist. "I am always primarily what I am doing at the moment," he explained. The author also claimed that he knew from an early age that he intended to write, the career being "not a profession but a condition." He offered these thoughts on literature: "The books I most admire are those that take human life as I know it and live it from day to day and describe it honestly and lovingly, and illuminate it fearlessly. As a novelist I have always seen myself as contributing to the central tradition of the novel, the tradition that grew up in the eighteenth century, which means recognisable human beings in familiar settings, doing the kind of things that you and I do, with all the usual consequences. . . . Everything important, everything lyrical and tragic and horrifying and uplifting and miraculous, is there in our ordinary lives if we can open our eyes and see it."

BIOGRAPHICAL/CRITICAL SOURCES:

BOOKS

Contemporary Authors Autobiography Series, Volume 4, Gale (Detroit), 1986.
Dictionary of Literary Biography, Volume 27: *Poets of Great Britain and Ireland, 1945-1960,* Gale, 1984.
Gindin, James J., *Postwar British Fiction: New Accents and Attitudes,* University of California (Berkeley and Los Angeles), 1962.

PERIODICALS

Atlantic Monthly, May, 1979.
Books, February, 1970; June, 1970;
Books Abroad, summer, 1967.
Contemporary Review, October, 1978; January, 1979.
Esquire, April 10, 1979.
Globe and Mail (Toronto), June 16, 1984.
Harper's, July, 1975; July, 1979.
Listener, October 12, 1967; October 26, 1978.
London Magazine, November, 1956; October, 1967.
London Review of Books, September 1, 1988, pp. 24-25; June 5, 1986, p. 10.
Los Angeles Times Book Review, August 6, 1978.
Nation, October 5, 1970; April 19, 1975; April 7, 1979.
New Leader, July 3, 1978.
New Republic, March 15, 1975.
New Statesman, October 6, 1967; May 19, 1978.
Newsweek, September 14, 1970; February 17, 1975.
New Yorker, April 28, 1975; May 7, 1979.
New York Review of Books, April 14, 1966; March 23, 1967; February 20, 1975.
New York Times, February 13, 1975; December 26, 1978; April 6, 1979.
New York Times Book Review, January 25, 1959; October 24, 1965; December 18, 1966; September 13, 1970; March 19, 1972; July 29, 1973; March 16, 1975; March 25, 1979.
Observer, October 8, 1967; May 3, 1970; December 20, 1970; May 4, 1986, p. 23; June 26, 1988, p. 42; July 3, 1994, p. 20; November 13, 1994, p. 22.
Poetry, February, 1978.
Saturday Review, May 7, 1955; July 27, 1957; October 16, 1965; December 3, 1966; February 8, 1975; April 28, 1979.
South Atlantic Quarterly, summer, 1969; autumn, 1979.
Spectator, May 16, 1970; November 30, 1974; May 3, 1986, p. 26; July 30, 1988, pp. 26-27; October 8, 1988, p. 38.
Time, April 2, 1979.
Times (London), January 7, 1984; April 24, 1986.
Times Educational Supplement, July 20, 1956; June 20, 1986, p. 25.
Times Literary Supplement, July 26, 1963; July 29, 1965; September 30, 1965; October 3, 1966; October 5, 1967; July 3, 1969; February 12, 1970; April 30, 1971; November 19, 1971; March 8, 1974; November 22, 1974; September 26, 1975; February 24, 1978; May 19, 1978; October 13, 1978; November 17, 1978; February 27, 1981; July 10, 1981; October 15, 1982; April 25, 1986, p. 445; July 8, 1988, p. 758; August 12, 1994, p. 23.
Wall Street Journal, December 21, 1992, p. A7.
Washington Post Book World, February 23, 1975; October 8, 1978; April 22, 1979; May 13, 1984.
World Literature Today, spring, 1979.

WAKOSKI, Diane 1937-

PERSONAL: Born August 3, 1937, in Whittier, CA; daughter of John Joseph and Marie (Mengel) Wakoski; married S. Shepard Sherbell (a magazine editor), October 22, 1965 (divorced); married Michael Watterlond, February 22, 1973 (divorced, 1975); married Robert J. Turney, February 14, 1982. *Education:* University of California, Berkeley, B.A., 1960. *Avocational interests:* Astrology, detective fiction, cooking, collecting American Art pottery, growing orchids.

ADDRESSES: Home—607 Division, East Lansing, MI 48823.ne (517) 332-3385. *Office*—Michigan State University, 207 Morrill Hall, East Lansing, MI 48824-1036.

CAREER: Poet, *Writer's Digest* Advisory Board member. Clerk at British Book Centre, New York City, 1960-63; teacher at Junior High School 22, New York City, 1963-66; lecturer at New School for Social Research, 1969; visiting writer, Lake Forest College, 1974, Colorado College, 1974, Macalester College, 1975; writer-in-residence at California Institute of Technology, 1972, University of Virginia, 1972-73, Williamette University, 1974, University of California, Irvine, 1974, University of Wisconsin, Madison, 1975, Michigan State University, 1975, Whitman College, 1976, University of Washington, 1977, University of Hawaii, 1978, and Emory University, 1980, 1981; member of faculty at Michigan State University, 1976–.

MEMBER: PEN, Authors Guild, Authors League of America, Poetry Society of America (PSA).

AWARDS, HONORS: Robert Frost fellowship, Bread Loaf Writers Conference, 1966; Cassandra Foundation award, 1970; New York State Council on the Arts grant, 1971; Guggenheim Foundation grant, 1972; National Endowment for the Arts grant, 1973; Fulbright grant, 1984; Michigan Arts Council grant, 1988; Michigan Arts Foundation award recipient, 1989; distinguished faculty award, Michigan State University, 1989; William Carlos Williams Prize, 1989, for *Selected Poems, 1962-1987;* university distinguished professor award, Michigan State University, 1990.

WRITINGS:

POETRY, EXCEPT AS INDICATED

Coins and Coffins (also see below), Hawk's Well Press, 1962.
(With Rochelle Owens, Barbara Moraff, and Carol Berge) *Four Young Lady Poets,* edited by LeRoi Jones, Totem-Corinth, 1962.
Discrepancies and Apparitions (also see below), Doubleday (New York City), 1966.
The George Washington Poems (also see below), Riverrun Press (New York City), 1967.
The Diamond Merchant, Sans Souci Press, 1968.
Inside the Blood Factory, Doubleday, 1968.
The Lament of the Lady Bank Dick, Sans Souci Press, 1969.
The Moon Has a Complicated Geography, Odda Tala, 1969.
Poems, Key Printing Co., 1969.
Some Black Poems for the Buddha's Birthday, Pierripont Press, 1969.
Thanking My Mother for Piano Lessons, Perishable Press, 1969.
Love, You Big Fat Snail, Tenth Muse, 1970.
The Motorcycle Betrayal Poems, Simon & Schuster (New York City), 1971.
This Water Baby, for Tony, Unicorn Press (Greensboro, NC), 1971.
Exorcism, My Dukes, 1971.
The Purple Finch Song, Perishable Press, 1972.

Sometimes a Poet Will Hijack the Moon, Burning Deck (Providence, RI), 1972.
Stillife: Michael, Silver Flute and Violets, University of Connecticut Library, 1973.
The Owl and the Snake: A Fable, Perishable Press, 1973.
Dancing on the Grave of a Son of a Bitch, 1973.
(Contributor) Karl Malkoff, editor, *Crowell's Handbook of Contemporary American Poetry,* Crowell (New York City), 1973.
The Wandering Tatler, Perishable Press, 1974.
Trilogy (includes *Coins and Coffins, Discrepancies and Apparitions,* and *The George Washington Poems*), Doubleday, 1974.
Virtuoso Literature for Two and Four Hands, Doubleday, 1975.
The Fable of the Lion and the Scorpion, Pentagram Press (Markesan, WI), 1975.
The Laguna Contract of Diane Wakoski, Crepuscular Press, 1976.
George Washington's Camp Cups, Red Ozier Press, 1976.
The Man Who Shook Hands, Doubleday, 1978.
(Author of introduction) Barbara Drake, *Love at the Egyptian Theatre,* Red Cedar Press (East Lansing, MI), 1978.
Toward a New Poetry (essays), University of Michigan Press (Ann Arbor), 1979.
(Author of introduction) Lynne Savitt, *Lust in Twenty-Eight Flavors,* Second Coming Press (San Francisco), 1979.
Saturn's Rings, Targ Editions, 1982.
Divers, Barbarian Press, 1982.
The Lady Who Drove Me to the Airport, Metacom (Worcester, MA), 1982.
Making a Sacher Torte, Perishable Press, 1982.
Why My Mother Likes Liberace: A Musical Selection, SUN/ Gemini Press, 1985.
Roses, Caliban (Dover, NH), 1987.
Husks of Wheat, California State University, Northridge Library (Northridge), 1987.

ALL PUBLISHED BY BLACK SPARROW PRESS (SANTA BARBARA, CA)

(With Robert Kelly and Ron Loewinsohn) *A Play and Two Poems,* 1968.
Greed, Parts 1 and 2, 1968, Parts 3 and 4, 1969, Parts 5-7, 1971, Parts 8, 9, 11, 1973.
Black Dream Ditty for Billy "the Kid" M Seen in Dr. Generosity's Bar Recruiting for Hell's Angels the Black Mafia, 1970.
The Magellanic Clouds, 1970.
On Barbara's Shore: A Poem, 1971.
(Contributor) *The Nest,* 1971.
Smudging, 1972.
The Pumpkin Pie; or, Reassurances Are Always False, Tho We Love Them, Only Physics Counts, 1972.
Form Is an Extension of Content (essay), 1972.
Winter Sequences, 1973.
Looking for the King of Spain (also see below), 1974.
Abalone, 1974.
Creating a Personal Mythology (essays), 1975.
Waiting for the King of Spain, 1976.
The Last Poem, 1976.
Variations on a Theme (essay), 1976.
The Ring, 1977.
Spending Christmas with the Man from Receiving at Sears, 1977.
Pachelbel's Canon (also see below), 1978.
Trophies, 1979.
Cap of Darkness (includes *Looking for the King of Spain* and *Pachelbel's Canon*), 1980.

The Magician's Feastletters, 1982.
The Collected Greed, Parts 1-13, 1984.
Emerald Ice: Selected Poems 1962-1987, 1990.
Medea the Sorceress, 1991.
Jason the Sailor, 1993.
The Emerald City of Las Vegas, 1995.
Argonaut Rose: The Archaeology of Movies and Books, 1997.

Author of "Dream Sheet," 1965. Contributor to "Burning Deck Post Cards: The Third Ten," Burning Deck. Regular columnist for *American Poetry Review,* 1972-74; contributor to numerous periodicals. Editor of *Software.*

SIDELIGHTS: Diane Wakoski, described as an "important and moving poet" by Paul Zweig in the *New York Times Book Review,* is frequently named among the foremost contemporary poets by virtue of her experiential vision and her unique voice. Wakoski's poems focus on intensely personal experiences—on her unhappy childhood, on the painful relationships she has had with men, and, perhaps most frequently, on the subject of being Diane Wakoski.

A few critics find her thematic concerns difficult to appreciate, especially the recurring "anti-male rage" theme noted by Peter Schjeldahl in the *New York Times Book Review.* Wakoski's poems, according to Schjeldahl, "are professionally supple and clear . . . but their pervasive unpleasantness makes her popularity rather surprising. One can only conclude that a number of people are angry enough at life to enjoy the sentimental and desolating resentment with which she writes about it."

Many other critics, however, believe that it is through this very rage and resentment that Wakoski makes a significant statement in her work. James F. Mersmann, for example, comments in *Margins* on the body of Wakoski's poetry: "It gives us a moving vision of the terrible last stages of a disintegrating personality and a disintegrating society, and it painfully embodies the schizophrenia, alienation, and lovelessness of our time." Douglas Blazek concludes in *Poetry* that Wakoski's poems have the "substance necessary to qualify them notches above the works of creative 'geniuses', 'stylists', and 'cultural avatars' who have little to say."

In *Poetry,* Sandra M. Gilbert describes Wakoski as "a fabulist, a weaver of gorgeous webs of imagery and a teller of archetypically glamorous tales [who has] always attempted self-definition through self-mythologizing. 'The poems are a way of inventing myself into a new life,' she has said." "The myth of herself," says H. Zinnes in *World Literature Today,* is of "one 'clothed in fat,' with an ugly face, without wit, brilliance or elegance, but having some 'obsession for truth and history.' This plain seeker after love. . . is of course a poet with a great deal of wit. . . , a poet who in her work and life is not merely searching for a lover," although many of her poems touch on this theme.

Wakoski's personal mythology embraces many other archetypal figures as well, including George Washington, the King of Spain, the motorcycle mechanic, the "man in Receiving at Sears," Beethoven, the "man with the gold tooth," and the "man who shook hands." These characters, most of whom appear more than once in Wakoski's canon, serve as symbols, emblematic of emotional states, past experiences, fantasies, and, sometimes, of real people in the poet's life.

George Washington, for example, appears in *The George Washington Poems,* a collection that Sheila Weller in *Ms.* calls "witty, caustic takes on the male mystique. In a voice by turns consciously absurdist and tremulously earnest, she takes the first President as her 'mythical father-lover,' romanticizes and barbs

'the militaristic, penalizing, fact-over-feeling male mind that I've always been afraid of and fascinated by.'" Wakoski speaks to George Washington in the poems with various voices—as Martha Washington, as a bitter child whose father has left home, as a lover left behind in the Revolutionary War. As Norman Martien explains in *Partisan Review,* "the George Washington myths serve to express the failure of a woman's relations to her men, but the myths also give her a means of talking about it. Partly *because* 'George' is so distant, he can be a safe listener . . . [and] he can allow her a voice that can reaffirm human connection, impossible at closer ranges." This theme of the failure of relationships, of betrayal by others (especially men), is a central concern of Wakoski's, and many of her mythological figures embody one or more of the facets of human relations in which she sees the possibility of betrayal or loss.

The figure of the motorcycle mechanic in *The Motorcycle Betrayal Poems* symbolizes, as Wakoski says in her dedicatory statement, "all those men who betrayed me at one time or another." According to Zweig, the book is "haunted by a curious mythology composed of mustached lovers, 'mechanics' who do not understand the engine humming under [the narrator's] skin, the great-grandfatherly warmth of Beethoven and George Washington, to whom she turns with humor but also with a sort of desperation." In this book, says Eric Mottram in *Parnassus,* Wakoski "operates in a world of women as adjuncts to men and the erotics of bikes; the poems are survival gestures." According to Weller, the book "made . . . women start at [Wakoski's] power to personalize the paradox" of male-female relationships—"their anger at the rejecting male archetype . . . yet their willing glorification of it. . . . The book's theme is the mythology and confusions of. . . love, and the fury at betrayal by symbols, envy, lovers, and self."

The theme of betrayal, and its resulting pain, also appears in *Inside the Blood Factory.* Here, as Zweig observes, Wakoski writes "poems of loss. The loss of childhood; the loss of lovers and family; the perpetual loss a woman lives with when she thinks she is not beautiful. These losses [create] a scorched earth of isolation around her, which she [describes] harshly and precisely. . . . From this vulnerable retreat, a stream of liberating images [emerges] to grapple with the world and mythify it." Peter D. Zivkovic, writing in *Southwest Review,* believes that *Inside the Blood Factory* is "significantly more than a memorable reading experience. Perhaps the most remarkable thing about. . . [the book] is the consistent strength of the individual poems. There is not," Zivkovic concludes, "a single weak poem in the volume—an achievement worthy of Frost and other American giants."

Fourteen years after *Inside the Blood Factory* Wakoski produced both *Saturn's Rings* and *The Magician's Feastletters. Saturn's Rings* is a collection of surrealist poems loosely connected by the metaphorical theme of self-banishment and characteristic self-scrutiny. Holly Prado notes in the *Los Angeles Times Book Review,* "Fearing decay, ignorance, and the inevitability of death, Wakoski writes with the intensity of someone fiercely alive, who still wants to unscramble failures, loneliness, the image of herself as the homely girl who was never acceptable." Noting the limitations of her shorter pieces in the collection, Paul Oppenheimer comments in *American Book Review* on the concluding series of eleven poems from which the title of the collection derives: "'Saturn's Rings'. . . is an often captivating, often self-pitying cry from the depths. . . . The cry is especially moving when uttered in the bright, chromic voice of Wakoski's most surrealistic lines. She is fine at depicting the possibility that 'the world / is flying out of control,' and that we may be living in 'a disintegrating time.' " In *The Magician's Feastletters*, arranged in four sections after the seasons, Wakoski uses food as a metaphor for love and deprivation. Though tending toward abstraction, Clayton Eshleman notes the concreteness of Wakoski's imagery and description of everyday items. He writes in the *Los Angeles Times Book Review*, "Wakoski [begins] to reverse a whole system of frozen values geared to affirm youth/sexuality/summer/product and to denigrate aging/impotence/winter/soul. Especially in the light of current fashions in American poetry (where empty description is as touted as pretentious nonsense), Wakoski's poetry is extremely valuable."

The Collected Greed, Parts 1-13 and *Emerald Ice: Selected Poems 1962-1987* bring together examples of Wakoski's finest writing over a twenty-five year period. *The Collected Greed* is an assemblage of poetry from previous installments of *Greed* between 1968 and 1973, with the addition of two previously unpublished parts. In the *Los Angeles Times Book Review*, Kenneth Funsten offers high praise for "The Greed To Be Fulfilled," one of the new sections. Here Wakoski traces her personal quest for purpose and completion in a surreal glass house where she revisits George Washington and representations of Charles Bukowski and the King of Spain. Funsten writes, "The confessional voice of the self-centered ego, reaches a new plane of maturity when it decides that intellectual things, not emotional ones, are what matter." Throughout the collection Wakoski explores various manifestations of greed, defined by her as "an unwillingness to give up one thing / for another," as quoted in Funsten's review.

In the 1990s Wakoski produced *Jason the Sailor* and *The Emerald City of Las Vegas*, both belonging to "The Archaeology of Movies and Books" series that began with *Medea the Sorceress* in 1991. In *Jason the Sailor*, consisting of poems, letters to men, and excerpted texts by Camille Paglia, Nick Herbert, and Jeremy Bernstein, Wakoski explores archetypal love, betrayal, and the dynamics of male-female relationships, surmising, as quoted in a *Kliatt* review of the work, "Women need men, the other halves of ourselves." *The Emerald City of Las Vegas* similarly examines the mythology of modern America in casinos and through excerpts from Frank Baum's *The Wizard of Oz*. A *Publishers Weekly* reviewer concludes that the book represents Wakoski's "inner conversation about what it means to be a woman, to be no longer young, to be a poet."

BIOGRAPHICAL/CRITICAL SOURCES:

BOOKS

Contemporary Literary Criticism, Gale (Detroit), Volume 2, 1974; Volume 4, 1975; Volume 7, 1977; Volume 9, 1978; Volume 11, 1979; Volume 40, 1986.
Dictionary of Literary Biography, Volume 5: *American Poets after World War II*, Part 2, edited by Donald J. Greiner, Gale, 1980.

PERIODICALS

American Book Review, September/October, 1987.
Contemporary Literature, winter, 1975.
Hudson Review, summer, 1974.
Kliatt, September, 1993, p. 26.
Library Journal, June 1, 1982, p. 1100; November 15, 1986, p. 100; December, 1988; February 1, 1991; August, 1993, p. 109; August, 1995, p. 80.
Los Angeles Times Book Review, July 18, 1982, p. 11; November 4, 1984, p. 4; October 26, 1986, p. 14

Margins, January/February/March, 1976.
Mediterranean Review, spring, 1972.
Ms., March, 1976.
New York Times Book Review, December 12, 1971; August 13, 1978.
Parnassus, fall/winter, 1972; spring/summer, 1973.
Partisan Review, winter, 1971.
Poetry, June, 1974; August, 1976.
Prairie Schooner, spring, 1973.
Publishers Weekly, July 31, 1995, p. 74.
Southwest Review, spring, 1975.
Virginia Quarterly Review, autumn, 1972.
World Literature Today, autumn, 1978.
Writer's Digest, November, 1991; November, 1994; February, 1995.

*   *   *

WALCOTT, Derek (Alton) 1930-

PERSONAL: Born January 23, 1930, in Castries, St. Lucia; son of Warwick (a civil servant) and Alix (a teacher) Walcott; married Fay Moston, 1954 (divorced, 1959); married Margaret Ruth Maillard, 1962 (divorced); married Norline Metivier (an actress and dancer; divorced); children: one son (first marriage), two daughters (second marriage). *Education:* Attended St. Mary's College (St. Lucia); University of the West Indies (Kingston, Jamaica), B.A. 1953, D.Litt, 1972.

ADDRESSES: Home—165 Duke of Edinburgh Ave., Diego Martin, Trinidad and Tobago (summer); 71 St. Mary's, Boston, MA 02215 (winter). *Office*—Creative Writing Department, Boston University, 236 Bay State Rd., Boston, MA 02215. *Agent*—c/o Farrar, Straus & Giroux, 19 Union Square W., New York, NY 10003-3307 or Faber and Faber, 3 Queen Square, London, WC1N 3AU, England.

CAREER: Poet and playwright. Teacher at St. Mary's College, St. Lucia, Boys' Secondary School, Grenada, and at Kingston College, Jamaica. Founding director of Trinidad Theatre Workshop, 1959–. Visiting professor at Columbia University, 1981, and Harvard University, 1982; visiting professor in Creative Writing Department of Boston University, 1985–. Also lecturer at Rutgers University and Yale University.

AWARDS, HONORS: Rockefeller fellowship, 1957; Jamaica Drama Festival prize, 1958, for *Drums and Colours: An Epic Drama;* Guinness Award, 1961, for "A Sea-Chantey"; Borestone Mountain poetry awards, 1963, for "Tarpon," and 1976, for "Midsummer, England"; named fellow of the Royal Society of Literature, 1966; Heinemann Award, Royal Society of Literature, 1966, for *The Castaway*, and 1983, for *The Fortunate Traveller;* Cholmondeley Award, 1969, for *The Gulf;* Eugene O'Neill Foundation-Wesleyan University fellowship, 1969; Order of the Humming Bird, Trinidad and Tobago, 1969 (one source says 1979); Obie Award, 1971, for *Dream on Monkey Mountain;* honorary doctorate of letters, University of the West Indies, 1972; Officer of British Empire, 1972; Jock Campbell/*New Statesman* Prize, 1974, for *Another Life;* Guggenheim fellowship, 1977; named honorary member of the American Academy and Institute of Arts and Letters, 1979; *American Poetry Review* Award, 1979; National Writer's Prize, Welsh Arts Council, 1979; John D. and Catherine T. MacArthur Foundation grant, 1981; *Los Angeles Times Book Review* Prize in poetry, 1986, for *Collected Poems,*

1948-1984; Queen Elizabeth II Gold Medal for Poetry, 1988; Nobel Prize for literature, 1992; St. Lucia Cross, 1993.

WRITINGS:

POETRY

Twenty-Five Poems, Guardian Commercial Printery, 1948.
Epitaph for the Young: A Poem in XII Cantos, Advocate (Bridgetown, Barbados), 1949.
Poems, Kingston City Printery (Jamaica), 1953.
In a Green Night: Poems, 1948-1960, J. Cape (London), 1962.
Selected Poems (includes poems from *In a Green Night: Poems, 1948-1960*), Farrar, Straus (New York City), 1964.
The Castaway and Other Poems, J. Cape, 1965.
The Gulf and Other Poems, J. Cape, 1969, published with selections from *The Castaway and Other Poems* as *The Gulf: Poems,* Farrar, Straus, 1970.
Another Life (long poem), Farrar, Straus, 1973, second edition published with introduction, chronology and selected bibliography by Robert D. Hammer, Three Continents (Washington, DC), 1982.
Sea Grapes, J. Cape, 1976, slightly revised edition, Farrar, Straus, 1976.
Selected Verse, Heinemann (London), 1976.
The Star-Apple Kingdom, Farrar, Straus, 1979.
The Fortunate Traveller, Farrar, Straus, 1981.
Selected Poetry, selected, annotated, and introduced by Wayne Brown, Heinemann, 1981, revised edition, 1993.
The Caribbean Poetry of Derek Walcott, and the Art of Romare Beardon, Limited Editions Club (New York City), 1983.
Midsummer, Farrar, Straus, 1984.
Collected Poems, 1948-1984, Farrar, Straus, 1986.
The Arkansas Testament, Farrar, Straus, 1987.
Omeros, Farrar, Straus, 1989.
The Bounty, Farrar, Straus, 1997.

Contributor of poems to numerous periodicals, including *New Statesman, London Magazine, Encounter, Evergreen Review, Caribbean Quarterly, Tamarack Review,* and *Bim.*

PLAYS

Henri Christophe: A Chronicle in Seven Scenes (first produced in Castries, St. Lucia, 1950, produced in London, England, 1951), Advocate, 1950.
Harry Dernier: A Play for Radio Production, Advocate, 1951.
Wine of the Country, University College of the West Indies (Mona, Jamaica), 1953.
The Sea at Dauphin: A Play in One Act (first produced in Mona, Jamaica, 1953, produced in London, 1960), Extra-Mural Department, University College of the West Indies, 1954.
Ione: A Play with Music (first produced in Port of Spain, Trinidad, 1957), Extra-Mural Department, University College of the West Indies, 1957.
Drums and Colours: An Epic Drama (first produced in Kingston, Trinidad, 1958), published in *Caribbean Quarterly,* March-June, 1961.
Ti-Jean and His Brothers, first produced in Port of Spain, Trinidad, 1958, produced off-Broadway at Delacorte Theatre, 1972.
Malcochon; or, Six in the Rain (one-act; first produced as *Malcochon* in Castries, St. Lucia, 1959, produced in London under title *Six in the Rain,* 1960, produced off-Broadway at St. Mark's Playhouse, 1969), Extra-Mural Department, University of West Indies, 1966.

Dream on Monkey Mountain, first produced in Toronto, 1967, produced off-Broadway at St. Mark's Playhouse, 1971.
Dream on Monkey Mountain and Other Plays (contains *Dream on Monkey Mountain, Sea at Dauphin, Malcochon; or, Six in the Rain, Ti-Jean and His Brothers,* and the essay "What the Twilight Says: An Overture"), Farrar, Straus, 1970.
In a Fine Castle, first produced in Jamaica, 1970, produced in Los Angeles, CA, 1972.
The Joker of Seville (musical), first produced in Port of Spain, Trinidad, 1974.
The Charlatan, first produced in Los Angeles, 1974.
O Babylon!, first produced in Port of Spain, Trinidad, 1976.
Remembrance (three-act), first produced in St. Croix, Virgin Islands, December, 1977, produced off-Broadway at The Other Stage, 1979.
Pantomime, Port of Spain, Trinidad, 1978, produced off-Broadway at the Hudson Guild Theater, 1986.
The Joker of Seville and O Babylon!: Two Plays, Farrar, Straus, 1978.
Remembrance & Pantomime: Two Plays, Farrar, Straus, 1980.
The Isle Is Full of Noises, first produced at the John W. Huntington Theater, Hartford, CT, 1982.
Three Plays (contains *The Last Carnival, Beef, No Chicken,* and *A Branch of the Blue Nile*), Farrar, Straus, 1986.
Steel, first produced at the American Repertory Theatre, Cambridge, MA, 1991.
Odyssey: A Stage Version, Farrar, Straus, 1993.
(With Paul Simon) *The Capeman: A Musical,* Farrar, Straus, 1998.

Also author of *Franklin, a Tale of the Islands, Jourmard,* and *To Die for Grenada.*

CONTRIBUTOR

John Figueroa, editor, *Caribbean Voices,* Evans, 1966.
Barbara Howes, editor, *From the Green Antilles,* Macmillan (New York City), 1966.
Howard Sergeant, editor, *Commonwealth Poems of Today,* Murray (London), 1967.
O. R. Dathorne, editor, *Caribbean Verse,* Heinemann, 1968.
Anne Walmsley, compiler, *The Sun's Eye: West Indian Writing for Young Readers,* Longmans, Green (London) 1968.
Orde Coombs, editor, *Is Massa Day Dead?,* Doubleday (New York City), 1974.
D. J. Enright, editor, *Oxford Book of Contemporary Verse, 1945-1980,* Oxford University Press, 1980.
Errol Hill, editor, *Plays for Today,* Longman, 1985.

OTHER

The Poet in the Theatre, Poetry Book Society (London), 1990.
Antilles: Fragments of Epic Memory, Farrar, Straus, 1993.
Conversations with Derek Walcott, edited by William Baer, University of Mississippi, 1996.
(With Seamus Heaney and Joseph Brodsky) *Homage to Frost,* Farrar, Straus, 1996.

Art and literature critic for *Trinidad Guardian;* feature writer for *Public Opinion* (Jamaica).

SIDELIGHTS: Although born of mixed racial and ethnic heritage on St. Lucia, a West Indian island where a French/English patois is spoken, poet and playwright Derek Walcott was educated as a British subject. Taught to speak English as a second language, he grew to be skilled in his adopted tongue. His use of the language has drawn praise from critics, including British poet and novelist Robert Graves who, according to *Times Literary Supplement* contributor Vicki Feaver, "has gone as far to state that [Walcott] handles English with a closer understanding of its inner magic than most (if not all) of his English-born contemporaries." In their statement upon awarding Walcott the Nobel Prize for Literature in 1992, the Swedish Academy, as quoted in the *Detroit Free Press,* declared: "In him, West Indian culture has found its great poet." Walcott is the first native Caribbean writer to win the prize. In its citation, the Academy noted that "in his literary works, Walcott has laid a course for his own cultural environment, but through them he speaks to each and every one of us."

The major theme of Walcott's writing is the dichotomy between black and white, subject and ruler, and the elements of both Caribbean and Western civilization present in his culture and ancestry. In "What the Twilight Says," the introduction to *Dream on Monkey Mountain and Other Plays,* Walcott refers to his "schizophrenic boyhood," in which he led "two lives: the interior life of poetry [and] the outward life of action and dialect." In his study *Derek Walcott,* Robert D. Hamner notes that this "schizophrenia" is common among West Indians and comments further that "since [Walcott] is descended from a white grandfather and a black grandmother on both paternal and maternal sides, he is living example of the divided loyalties and hatreds that keep his society suspended between two worlds."

One often-quoted poem, "A Far Cry from Africa," from *In a Green Night: Poems, 1948-1960,* deals directly with Walcott's sense of cultural confusion. "Where shall I turn, divided to the vein? / I who have cursed / The drunken officer of British rule, how choose / Between this Africa and the English tongue I love? / Betray them both, or give back what they give?" In another poem, "The Schooner Flight," from his collection *The Star-Apple Kingdom,* the poet uses a Trinidadian sailor named Shabine to appraise his own place as a person of mixed blood in a world divided into whites and blacks. According to the mariner: "The first chain my hands and apologize, 'History'; / the next said I wasn't black enough for their pride." Not white enough for whites, not black enough for blacks, Shabine sums up the complexity of his situation near the beginning of the poem, saying: "I had a sound colonial education, / I have Dutch, nigger and English in me, / and either I'm nobody or I'm a nation."

Although pained by the contrasts in his background, Walcott has chosen to embrace both his island and his colonial heritage. His love of both sides of his psyche is apparent in his work. As Hamner notes: "Nurtured on oral tales of gods, devils, and cunning tricksters passed down by generations of slaves, Walcott should retell folk stories; and he does. On the other hand, since he has an affinity for and is educated in Western classics, he should retell the traditional themes of European experience; and he does. As inheritor of two vitally rich cultures, he utilizes one, then the other, and finally creates out of the two his own personalized style."

Walcott's 1997 volume, *The Bounty,* is a collection of lyrics, many written in the terza rima scheme favored by Dante Alighieri. The poems address many of Walcott's chief concerns, including the problems of language colonialism, and history. But a more pronounced fixation on aging, death, and loss emerges as well. The eponymous opening poem eulogizes both his late mother and the deranged English Romantic John Clare, while in several others the (as of 1997) 67-year-old poet confronts his own mortality. Writing in the *New Leader,* Phoebe Pettingell sees echoes of Dante in Walcott's content as well as his form. "Like Dante," she writes, "Walcott fashions a mystical journey through the near and

distant past as he tries to envision the lives and deaths of people close to him in context that will reveal some ultimate meaning to salve his loss." Other critics have praised Walcott for his mastery of language and poetic technique. "Images keep recurring, crisscrossing, gaining new associations in verses that have the noble radiance of stained glass, grave but full of light," observed Pico Iyer in *Time* magazine. Adam Kirsch, writing in the *New Republic,* perceives *The Bounty* as the consummation of Walcott's poetic efforts to that point. "Only a few poets at any given time are capable of a distinctive style, much less a distinctive mature style; and Walcott's mature style, as evolved in *Midsummer* and further perfected here, is his best."

Walcott seems closest to his island roots in his plays. For the most part, he has reserved his native language—patois or creole—to them. They also feature Caribbean settings and themes. According to *Literary Review* contributor David Mason, through his plays Walcott hopes to create a "catalytic theater responsible for social change or at least social identity."

Although a volume of poems was his first published work, Walcott originally concentrated his efforts on the theater. In the fifties, he wrote a series of plays in verse, including *Henri Christophe: A Chronicle in Seven Scenes, The Sea at Dauphin: A Play in One Act,* and *Ione: A Play with Music.* The first play deals with an episode in Caribbean history: ex-slave Henri Christophe's rise to kingship of Haiti in the early 1800s. The second marks Walcott's first use of the mixed French/English language of his native island in a play. Dennis Jones notes in *Dictionary of Literary Biography Yearbook: 1981* that while Walcott uses the folk idiom of the islands in the play, the speech of the characters is not strictly imitative. It is instead "made eloquent, as the common folk represented in the work are made noble, by the magic of the artist."

In "What the Twilight Says" Walcott describes his use of language in his plays. In particular, he expresses a desire to mold "a language that went beyond mimicry, . . . one which finally settled on its own mode of inflection, and which begins to create an oral culture, of chants, jokes, folk-songs, and fables." The presence of "chants, jokes, and fables" in Walcott's plays causes critics such as Jones and the *Los Angeles Times*'s Juana Duty Kennedy to use the term "folk dramas" to describe the playwright's best pieces for theater. In *Books and Bookmen* Romilly Cavan observes the numerous folk elements in Walcott's plays: "The laments of superstitious fishermen, charcoal-burners and prisoners are quickly counter-pointed by talking crickets, frogs, and birds. Demons are raised, dreams take actual shape, [and] supernatural voices mingle with the natural lilting elliptical speech rhythms of downtrodden natives." Animals who speak and a folk-representation of the devil, for example, are characters in the play *Ti-Jean and His Brothers.*

Walcott's most highly praised play, *Dream on Monkey Mountain,* is also a folk drama. It was awarded a 1971 Obie Award and deemed "a poem in dramatic form" by Edith Oliver in the *New Yorker.* The play's title is itself enough to immediately transport the viewer into the superstitious, legend-filled world of the Caribbean back country. In the play, Walcott draws a parallel between the hallucinations of an old charcoal vendor and the colonial reality of the Caribbean. Islanders subjected to the imposition of a colonial culture on their own eventually question the validity of both cultures. Ultimately, they may determine that their island culture—because it has no official status other than as an enticement for tourists—is nothing but a sterile hallucination.

Conversely, as Jones notes, they may reach the conclusion at which Walcott wishes his audience to arrive: the charcoal vendor's "dreams connect to the past, and that it is in that past kept alive in the dreams of the folk that an element of freedom is maintained in the colonized world."

Perhaps because of critics' unfamiliarity with the Caribbean reality which Walcott describes in his plays, the author's work for theater has received only mixed reviews in this country. For example, while Walter Goodman writes in the *New York Times* that Walcott's *Pantomime* "stays with you as a fresh and funny work filled with thoughtful insights and illuminated by bright performances," Frank Rich's comments on the play in the same newspaper are not as favorable. "Walcott's best writing has always been as a poet. . . ," Rich observes, "and that judgment remains unaltered by *Pantomime.* For some reason, [Walcott] refuses to bring the same esthetic rigor to his playwriting that he does to his powerfully dense verse."

In James Atlas's *New York Times Magazine* essay on Walcott, the critic confronts Rich's remarks head on, asserting that the poet would respond to Rich by commenting "that he doesn't conceive of his plays as finished works but as provisional effects to address his own people. 'The great challenge to me,' he says, 'was to write as powerfully as I could without writing down to the audience, so that the large emotions could be taken in by a fisherman or a guy on the street, even if he didn't understand every line.'"

If Walcott's plays reveal what is most Caribbean about him, his poetry reveals what is most English. If he hopes to reach the common person in his plays, the same cannot be said of his poetry. His poems are based on the traditional forms of English poetry, filled with classical allusions, elaborate metaphors, complex rhyme schemes, and other sophisticated poetic devices. In the *New York Times Book Review,* Selden Rodman calls Walcott's poems "almost Elizabethan in their richness." The *New York Times*'s Michiko Kakutani also recognizes British influences in Walcott's poetry, noting that "from England, [Walcott] appropriated an old-fashioned love of eloquence, an Elizabethan richness of words and a penchant for complicated, formal rhymes. In fact, in a day when more and more poets have adopted a grudging, minimalist style, [his] verse remains dense and elaborate, filled with dazzling complexities of style."

Some critics object that Walcott's attention to style sometimes detracts from his poetry, either by being unsuitable for his Caribbean themes or by becoming more important than the poems' content. Denis Donoghue, for example, remarks in the *New York Times Book Review,* "It is my impression that his standard English style [is] dangerously high for nearly every purpose except that of Jacobean tragedy." In Steve Ratiner's *Christian Science Monitor* review of *Midsummer,* the critic observes that "after a time, we are so awash in sparkling language and intricate metaphor, the subject of the poem is all but obscured." Helen Vendler, in the *New York Review of Books,* finds an "unhappy disjunction between [Walcott's] explosive subject . . . and his harmonious pentameters, his lyrical allusions, his stately rhymes, [and] his Yeatsian meditations."

More criticism comes from those who maintain that the influence of other poets on Walcott's work has drowned out his authentic voice. While Vendler, for instance, describes Walcott as a "man of great sensibility and talent," she dismisses much of his poetry as "ventriloquism" and maintains that in Walcott's collection *The Fortunate Traveller* he seems "at the mercy of influence, this time

the influence of Robert Lowell." Poet J. D. McClatchy also notices Lowell's influence in *The Fortunate Traveller* as well as two other Walcott poetry collections: *The Star-Apple Kingdom* and *Midsummer.* In his *New Republic* review, McClatchy not only finds similarities in the two men's styles but also a similar pattern of development in their poetry. "Like Lowell," the critic notes, "Walcott's mode has . . . shifted from the mythological to the historical, from fictions to facts, and his voice has gotten more clipped and severe. There are times when the influence is almost too direct, as in 'Old New England,' [a poem from *The Fortunate Traveller*] where he paces off Lowell's own territory."

In *Omeros,* whose title is the contemporary Greek word for Homer, Walcott pays homage to the ancient poet in an epic poem that replaces the Homeric Cyclades with the Antilles. Two of the main characters, the West Indian fishermen Achille and Philoctete, set out on a journey to the land of their ancestors on the West African coast. The characters are concerned not with the events of the Trojan War, but rather with the array of civilization, from African antiquity to frontier America and present-day Boston and London. Halfway through the book, the poet himself enters the narrative. Nick Owchar remarks in the *Los Angeles Times Book Review* that "the message of *Omeros* grows with the poet's entrance." He notes that "Walcott's philosophical intentions never come closer to being realized than when he turns . . . criticism on himself. Divestiture, as an artist, is Walcott's forte. He considers his own dangerous use of metaphors: 'When would I not hear the Trojan War / in two fishermen cursing?' he asks near the end. The poet's danger, like every person's, is to distance himself from human suffering by reinterpreting it."

Michael Heyward observes in the *Washington Post Book World:* "*Omeros* is not a translation or even a re-creation of either of Homer's great epics. . . . The ancient work it resembles most . . . is Ovid's *Metamorphoses,* with its panoply of characters, its seamless episodic structure, and its panoramic treatment of a mythic world both actual and legendary." He concludes, "We are used to encountering the dynamic exploration of politics and history and folk legend in the contemporary novel, the domain—thanks to Rushdie, Marquez, Gaddis, and others—of modern epic. . . . *Omeros* is not a novel and it does not approximate the form of a novel, but it does rival the novel's mastery of a mythic, multi-dimensional narrative. Strenuous and thrilling, it swims against the tide."

BIOGRAPHICAL/CRITICAL SOURCES:

BOOKS

Brown, Stewart, editor, *The Art of Derek Walcott,* Dufour (Chester Springs, PA), 1991.
Contemporary Literary Criticism, Gale (Detroit), Volume 2, 1974; Volume 4, 1975; Volume 9, 1978; Volume 14, 1980; Volume 25, 1983; Volume 42, 1987; Volume 67, 1992; Volume 76, 1993.
Dictionary of Literary Biography, Volume 117, Gale, 1992.
Dictionary of Literary Biography Yearbook, 1981, Gale, 1982.
Dictionary of Literary Biography Yearbook, 1992, Gale, 1993.
Goldstraw, Irma, *Derek Walcott: An Annotated Bibliography of His Works,* Garland Publishing (New York City), 1984.
Hamner, Robert D., *Derek Walcott,* Twayne (Boston), 1981.
Hamner, Robert D., *Epic of the Dispossessed: Derek Walcott's Omeros,* University of Missouri Press, 1997.
King, Bruce Alvin, *Derek Walcott and West Indian Drama,* Oxford University, 1995.

Olaniyan, Tejumola, *Scars of Conquest/Masks of Resistance: The Invention of Cultural Identities in African, African-American, and Caribbean Drama,* Oxford University Press, 1995.

Parker, Michael, and Roger Starkey, *Postcolonial Literatures: Achebe, Ngugi, Desai, Walcott,* St. Martin's Press, 1995.

Terada, Rei, *Derek Walcott's Poetry: American Mimicry,* Northeastern University Press (Boston), 1992.

PERIODICALS

America, February 10, 1996, p. 25.

Books and Bookmen, April, 1972.

Chicago Tribune Book World, May 2, 1982; September 9, 1984; March 9, 1986.

Christian Science Monitor, March 19, 1982; April 6, 1984.

Detroit Free Press, October 9, 1992.

English Journal, March, 1994, p. 94.

Georgia Review, summer, 1984.

Hudson Review, summer, 1984.

Library Journal, November 1, 1994, p. 127.

Literary Review, spring, 1986.

London Magazine, December, 1973-January, 1974; February-March, 1977.

Los Angeles Times, November 12, 1986.

Los Angeles Times Book Review, April 4, 1982; May 21, 1985; April 6, 1986; October 26, 1986; September 6, 1987; January 20, 1991.

Nation, February 12, 1977; May 19, 1979; February 27, 1982.

National Review, November 3, 1970; June 20, 1986.

New Leader, September 8, 1997.

New Republic, November 20, 1976; March 17, 1982; January 23, 1984; March 24, 1986; December 15, 1997.

New Statesman, March 19, 1982; July 21, 1995, p. 30.

New Yorker, March 27, 1971; June 26, 1971.

New York Review of Books, December 31, 1964; May 6, 1971; June 13, 1974; October 14, 1976; May 31, 1979; March 4, 1982.

New York Times, March 21, 1979; August 21, 1979; May 30, 1981; May 2, 1982; January 15, 1986; December 17, 1986.

New York Times Book Review, September 13, 1964; October 11, 1970; May 6, 1973; October 31, 1976; May 13, 1979; January 3, 1982; April 8, 1984; February 2, 1986; December 20, 1987.

New York Times Magazine, May 23, 1982.

Poetry, February, 1972; December, 1973; July, 1977; December, 1984; June, 1986.

Time, March 15, 1982; October 19, 1992; October 31, 1994, p. 78; July 14, 1997.

Times Literary Supplement, December 25, 1969; August 3, 1973; July 23, 1976; August 8, 1980; September 8, 1980; September 24, 1982; November 9, 1984; October 24, 1986.

Tribune Books (Chicago), November 8, 1987.

TriQuarterly, winter, 1986.

Village Voice, April 11, 1974.

Virginia Quarterly Review, winter, 1974; summer, 1984.

Washington Post Book World, February 21, 1982; April 13, 1986; November 11, 1990.

Western Humanities Review, spring, 1977.

World Literature Today, spring, 1977; summer, 1979; summer, 1981; winter, 1985; summer, 1986; winter, 1987.

Yale Review, October, 1973.

WALDO, E. Hunter
See STURGEON, Theodore (Hamilton)

*   *   *

WALDO, Edward Hamilton
See STURGEON, Theodore (Hamilton)

*   *   *

WALKER, Alice (Malsenior) 1944-

PERSONAL: Born February 9, 1944, in Eatonton, GA; daughter of Willie Lee and Minnie Tallulah (Grant) Walker; married Melvyn Rosenman Leventhal (a civil rights lawyer), March 17, 1967 (divorced, 1976); children: Rebecca. *Education:* Attended Spelman College, 1961-63; Sarah Lawrence College, B.A., 1965.

ADDRESSES: Home—San Francisco, CA. *Office*—Harcourt Brace Jovanovich, 111 5th Ave., New York, NY 10003-1005.

CAREER: Writer. Wild Trees Press, Navarro, CA, cofounder and publisher, 1984-88. Has been a voter registration worker in Georgia, a worker in Head Start program in Mississippi, and on staff of New York City welfare department. Writer in residence and teacher of black studies at Jackson State College, 1968-69, and Tougaloo College, 1970-71; lecturer in literature, Wellesley College and University of Massachusetts—Boston, both 1972-73; distinguished writer in Afro-American studies department, University of California, Berkeley, spring, 1982; Fannie Hurst Professor of Literature, Brandeis University, Waltham, MA, fall, 1982. Lecturer and reader of own poetry at universities and conferences. Member of board of trustees of Sarah Lawrence College. Consultant on black history to Friends of the Children of Mississippi, 1967. Coproducer of film documentary, *Warrior Marks,* directed by Pratibha Parmar with script and narration by Walker, 1993.

AWARDS, HONORS: Bread Loaf Writer's Conference scholar, 1966; first prize, *American Scholar* essay contest, 1967; Merrill writing fellowship, 1967; McDowell Colony fellowship, 1967, 1977-78; National Endowment for the Arts grant, 1969, 1977; Radcliffe Institute fellowship, 1971-73; Ph.D., Russell Sage College, 1972; National Book Award nomination and Lillian Smith Award from the Southern Regional Council, both 1973, both for *Revolutionary Petunias and Other Poems;* Richard and Hinda Rosenthal Foundation Award, American Academy and Institute of Arts and Letters, 1974, for *In Love and Trouble: Stories of Black Women;* Guggenheim fellowship, 1977-78; National Book Critics Circle Award nomination, 1982, and Pulitzer Prize and American Book Award, both 1983, all for *The Color Purple;* Best Books for Young Adults citation, American Library Association, 1984, for *In Search of Our Mother's Gardens: Womanist Prose;* D.H.L., University of Massachusetts, 1983; O. Henry Award, 1986, for "Kindred Spirits"; Langston Hughes Award, New York City College, 1989; Nora Astorga Leadership award, 1989; Fred Cody award for lifetime achievement, Bay Area Book Reviewers Association, 1990; Freedom to Write award, PEN West, 1990; California Governor's Arts Award, 1994.

WRITINGS:

POETRY

Once: Poems (also see below), Harcourt (New York City), 1968.

Five Poems, Broadside Press (Highland Park, MI), 1972.

Revolutionary Petunias and Other Poems (also see below), Harcourt, 1973.

Goodnight, Willie Lee, I'll See You in the Morning (also see below), Dial (New York City), 1979.

Horses Make a Landscape Look More Beautiful, Harcourt, 1984.

Alice Walker Boxed Set—Poetry: Good Night, Willie Lee, I'll See You in the Morning; Revolutionary Petunias and Other Poems; Once, Poems, Harcourt, 1985.

Her Blue Body Everything We Know: Earthling Poems, 1965-1990 Complete, Harcourt, 1991.

FICTION; NOVELS EXCEPT AS INDICATED

The Third Life of Grange Copeland, Harcourt, 1970.

In Love and Trouble: Stories of Black Women, Harcourt, 1973.

Meridian, Harcourt, 1976.

You Can't Keep a Good Woman Down (short stories), Harcourt, 1981.

The Color Purple, Harcourt, 1982.

Alice Walker Boxed Set—Fiction: The Third Life of Grange Copeland, You Can't Keep a Good Woman Down, and In Love and Trouble, Harcourt, 1985.

The Temple of My Familiar, Harcourt, 1989.

Possessing the Secret of Joy, Harcourt, 1992.

Everyday Use, edited by Barbara Christian, Rutgers University Press (New Brunswick, NJ), 1994.

FOR CHILDREN

Langston Hughes: American Poet (biography), Crowell (New York City), 1974.

To Hell with Dying, illustrations by Catherine Deeter, Harcourt, 1988.

Finding the Green Stone, Harcourt, 1991.

NONFICTION

In Search of Our Mothers' Gardens: Womanist Prose, Harcourt, 1983.

Living by the Word: Selected Writings, 1973-1987, Harcourt, 1988.

(With Pratibha Parmar) *Warrior Marks: Female Genital Mutilation and the Sexual Blinding of Women,* Harcourt, 1993.

Alice Walker Banned, with introduction by Patricia Holt, Aunt Lute Books (San Francisco), 1996.

Anything We Love Can Be Saved: A Writer's Activism, Random House (New York City), 1997.

OTHER

(Editor) *I Love Myself When I'm Laughing . . . and Then Again When I Am Looking Mean and Impressive: A Zora Neale Hurston Reader,* introduction by Mary Helen Washington, Feminist Press, 1979.

The Same River Twice: Honoring the Difficult: A Meditation of Life, Spirit, Art, and the Making of the Film "The Color Purple," Ten Years Later, Scribner, 1996, large print edition, Wheeler, 1996.

Contributor to anthologies, including *Voices of the Revolution,* edited by Helen Haynes, E. & J. Kaplan (Philadelphia), 1967; *The Best Short Stories by Negro Writers from 1899 to the Present: An Anthology,* edited by Langston Hughes, Little, Brown (Boston), 1967; *Afro-American Literature: An Introduction,* Harcourt, 1971; *Tales and Stories for Black Folks,* compiled by Toni Cade

Bambara, Zenith Books (New York City), 1971; *Black Short Story Anthology,* compiled by Woodie King, New American Library (New York City), 1972; *The Poetry of Black America: An Anthology of the Twentieth Century,* compiled by Arnold Adoff, Harper (New York City), 1973; *A Rock against the Wind: Black Love Poems,* edited by Lindsay Patterson, Dodd (New York City), 1973; *We Be Word Sorcerers: Twenty-five Stories by Black Americans,* edited by Sonia Sanchez, Bantam (New York City), 1973; *Images of Women in Literature,* compiled by Mary Anne Ferguson, Houghton (Boston), 1973; *Best American Short Stories: 1973,* edited by Margaret Foley, Hart-Davis, 1973; *Best American Short Stories, 1974,* edited by M. Foley, Houghton, 1974; *Chants of Saints: A Gathering of Afro-American Literature, Art and Scholarship,* edited by Michael S. Harper and Robert B. Stepto, University of Illinois Press (Chicago), 1980; *Midnight Birds: Stories of Contemporary Black Women Authors,* edited by Mary Helen Washington, Anchor Press (New York City), 1980; and *Double Stitch: Black Women Write about Mothers and Daughters,* edited by Maya Angelou, HarperCollins (New York City), 1993.

MEDIA ADAPTATIONS: The Color Purple was made into a feature film directed by Steven Spielberg, Warner Bros., 1985.

SIDELIGHTS: Alice Walker has earned critical and popular acclaim as a major American novelist and intellectual. Her literary repuatation was secured with her Pulitzer Prize-winning third novel, *The Color Purple,* which was transformed into a popular film by Steven Speilberg. Upon the release of the novel in 1982, critics sensed that Walker had created something special. "*The Color Purple . . .* could be the kind of popular and literary event that transforms an intense reputation into a national one," according to Gloria Steinem of *Ms.* Judging from the critical enthusiasm for *The Color Purple,* Steinem's words have proved prophetic. Walker "has succeeded," as Andrea Ford notes in the *Detroit Free Press,* "in creating a jewel of a novel." Peter S. Prescott presents a similar opinion in a *Newsweek* review. "I want to say," he comments, "that *The Color Purple* is an American novel of permanent importance, that rare sort of book which (in Norman Mailer's felicitous phrase) amounts to 'a diversion in the fields of dread.'"

Jeanne Fox-Alston and Mel Watkins both feel that the appeal of *The Color Purple* is that the novel, as a synthesis of characters and themes found in Walker's earlier works, brings together the best of the author's literary production in one volume. Fox-Alston, in the *Chicago Tribune Book World,* remarks: "Celie, the main character in Walker's third . . . novel, *The Color Purple,* is an amalgam of all those women [characters in Walker's previous books]; she embodies both their desperation and, later, their faith." Watkins states in the *New York Times Book Review:* "Her previous books . . . have elicited praise for Miss Walker as a lavishly gifted writer. *The Color Purple,* while easily satisfying that claim, brings into sharper focus many of the diverse themes that threaded their way through her past work."

Walker was born in Eatonton, Georgia, a southern town where most African-American people toiled at the difficult job of tenant farming. Her writing reflects these roots, where black vernacular was prominent and the stamp of slavery and oppression were still present. When she was eight, Walker was accidentally shot in the eye by a brother playing with his BB gun. Her parents, who were too poor to afford a car, could not take her to a doctor for several days. By that time, her wound was so bad that she had lost the use of her right eye. This handicap eventually aided her writer's voice, because she withdrew from others and became a meticulous observer of human relationships and interaction.

An excellent student, Walker was awarded a scholarship to Spelman College in 1961. The civil rights movement attracted her, and she became an activist. In 1963, she decided to continue her education at Sarah Lawrence College in New York, where she began to work seriously on writing poems, publishing several in a college journal. After graduation, she moved to Mississippi to teach and continue her social activism, and she met and married Melvyn Leventhal, a Jewish civil rights lawyer. The two became the only legally married interracial couple living in Jackson, Mississippi. After their divorce in 1976, Walker's literary output increased.

Walker coined the term "Womanist," to describe her philosophical stance on the issue of gender. As a Womanist, which is different from a feminist, she sees herself as someone who appreciates women's culture, emotions, and character. Her work often reflects this stance, and, paradoxically, the universality of human experience. Walker's central characters are almost always black women; Walker, according to Steinem, "comes at universality through the path of an American black woman's experience. . . . She speaks the female experience more powerfully for being able to pursue it across boundaries of race and class." This universality is also noted by Fox-Alston, who remarks that Walker has a "reputation as a provocative writer who writes about blacks in particular, but all humanity in general."

Walker's earlier books—novels, volumes of short stories, and poems—have not received the same degree of attention, but neither have they been ignored. Gloria Steinem points out that *Meridian,* Walker's second novel, "is often cited as the best novel of the civil rights movement, and is taught as part of some American history as well as literature courses." In *Everyday Use,* Barbara Christian finds the story "Everyday Use," first published in Walker's collection *In Love and Trouble: Stories of Black Women,* to be "pivotal" to all of Walker's work in its evocation of black sisterhood and black women's heritage of quilting. William Peden, writing in *The American Short Story: Continuity and Change, 1940-1975,* calls this same collection "a remarkable book," and Barbara Smith observes in *Ms.* that "this collection would be an extraordinary literary work, if its only virtue were the fact that the author sets out consciously to explore with honesty the texture and terror of black women's lives . . . the fact that Walker's perceptions, style, and artistry are also consistently high makes her work a treasure." Similarly, Mary Helen Washington remarks in a *Black World* review that "the stories in *In Love and Trouble* . . . constitute a painfully honest, searching examination of the experiences of thirteen black women."

Some reviewers criticize Walker's fiction for portraying an overly negative view of black men. Katha Pollitt, for example, in the *New York Times Book Review,* calls the stories in *You Can't Keep a Good Woman Down* "too partisan." The critic adds: "The black woman is always the most sympathetic character." Guy notes: "Some readers . . . will object to her overall perspective. Men in [*The Color Purple*] are generally pathetic, weak and stupid, when they are not heartlessly cruel, and the white race is universally bumbling and inept." Charles Larson, in his *Detroit News* review of *The Color Purple,* points out: "I wouldn't go as far as to say that all the male characters [in the novel] are villains, but the truth is fairly close to that." However, neither Guy nor Larson feel that this emphasis on women is a major fault in the novel. Guy, for example, while conceding that "white men . . . are invisible in

Celie's world," observes: "This really is Celie's perspective, however—it is psychologically accurate to her—and Alice Walker might argue that it is only a neat inversion of the view that has prevailed in western culture for centuries." Larson also notes that by the end of the novel, "several of [Walker's] masculine characters have reformed."

This idea of reformation, this sense of hope even in despair, is at the core of Walker's vision, even though, as John F. Callahan states in *New Republic,* "There is often nothing but pain, violence, and death for black women [in her fiction]." In spite of the brutal effects of sexism and racism suffered by the characters of her short stories and novels, critics note what Art Seidenbaum of the *Los Angeles Times* calls Walker's sense of "affirmation . . . [that] overcomes her anger." This is particularly evident in *The Color Purple,* according to several reviewers. Ford, for example, asserts that the author's "polemics on . . . political and economic issues finally give way to what can only be described as a joyful celebration of human spirit—exulting, uplifting and eminently universal." Prescott discovers a similar progression in the novel. He writes: "[Walker's] story begins at about the point that most Greek tragedies reserve for the climax, then . . . by immeasurable small steps . . . works its way toward acceptance, serenity and joy." Walker, according to Ray Anello, who quotes the author in *Newsweek,* agrees with this evaluation. Questioned about the novel's importance, Walker explains: "Let's hope people can hear Celie's voice. There are so many people like Celie who make it, who come out of nothing. People who triumph."

Harsh criticisms of Walker's work crested with the 1989 publication of her fourth novel, *The Temple of My Familiar.* The novel, featuring several of the characters of *The Color Purple,* reflects concerns hinted at in that novel: racism, a reverence for nature, and a search for spiritual truths. But according to David Gates in his *Newsweek* review, the novel "is fatally ambitious. It encompasses 500,000 years, rewrites Genesis and the Beatitudes and weighs in with mini-lectures on everything from Elvis (for) to nuclear waste (against)." David Nicholson of the *Washington Post Book World* feels that *The Temple of My Familiar* "is not a novel so much as it is an ill-fitting collection of speeches . . . a manifesto for the Fascism of the New Age. . . . There are no characters, only types representative of the world Walker lives in or wishes could be." In a similar vein, *Time*'s Paul Grey notes that "Walker's relentless adherence to her own sociopolitical agenda makes for frequently striking propaganda," but not for good fiction. Though generally disliked even by sympathetic critics, the novel has its defenders. Novelist J. M. Coetzee, writing in the *New York Times Book Review,* implores the reader to look upon the novel as a "fable of recovered origins, as an exploration of the inner lives of contemporary black Americans as these are penetrated by fabulous stories," and Bernard W. Bell, writing in the *Chicago Tribune,* feels that the novel is a "colorful quilt of many patches," and that its "stylized lovers, remembrances of things past, bold flights of fantasy and vision of a brave new world of cultural diversity and cosmic harmony challenge the reader's willingness to suspend disbelief."

Critics are nearly unanimous in their praise of Walker's controversial fifth novel, *Possessing the Secret of Joy,* about the practice of female genital mutilation in certain African, Asian and Middle Eastern cultures. Writing in the *Los Angeles Times Book Review,* Tina McElroy Ansa says that taking on such a taboo subject shows Walker's depth and range and feels that her portrait of the suffering of Tashi—a character from *The Color Purple*—is "stunning." "The description of the excision itself and its after effect is graphic enough to make one gag," but is the work of a thoughtful, impassioned artist, rather than a sensationalist, notes Charles R. Larson in the *Washington Post Book World.* And Donna Haisty Winchell writes in her *Dictionary of Literary Biography* essay that *Possessing the Secret of Joy* is "much more concise, more controlled, and more successful as art" than *The Temple of My Familiar* and demonstrates an effective blend of "art and activism."

Walker's concerns about the international issue of female genital mutilation prompted her to further explore the issue, both on film and in the book *Warrior Marks: Female Genital Mutilation and the Sexual Blinding of Women,* coauthored with documentary film director Pratibha Parmar. According to *Publishers Weekly, Warrior Marks* is a "forceful account" of how the two filmed a documentary on the ritual circumcision of African women.

In 1995, Walker produced *The Same River Twice: Honoring the Difficult.* The book focuses mainly on Walker's feelings about, and struggles with, the filming of her novel *The Color Purple.* While having the book transformed into a film by Steven Spielberg was a high point in her life, it was also riddled with difficulties. First, Spielberg rejected Walker's screenplay of the book and implemented one with which Walker was not happy. In addition, the film itself was met with controversy and attacks on Walker's ideas—some people thought she had attacked the character of black people in general and black men specifically. Also at the time, Walker's mother was critically ill, while Walker herself was suffering from a debilitating illness that turned out to be Lyme Disease. Included in the book are fan letters, reviews, and Walker's original version of the script. Francine Prose in *Chicago Tribune Book World* finds fault with the book, feeling that Walker's protests about how things did not go her way ring of artistic posturing: "Walker seems to have so lost touch with the lives and sensibilities of ordinary humans that she apparently cannot hear how her complaints . . . might sound to the less fortunate, who have been less generously favored by greatness."

Regardless of such criticism, however, Walker's literary reputation is secure. Among her recent works, which are mostly nonfiction, is 1997's *Anything We Love Can Be Saved: A Writer's Activism.* Here, Walker turns her talents to a spirited defense of political activism. The essays address such subjects as female genital mutilation (which she abhors), Cuban communism (which she is for), and the murder trial of Winnie Mandela (about which she is outraged). There are also tributes—to her mother, to the poet Audre Lord, and to others in whom Walker detects the strain of leftist/progressivist activism. Some critics found the essays in *Anything We Love Can Be Saved* tendentious, dogmatic, and full of sanctimony. "For all her apparent impartiality," Charles Cumming charged in his review for the *New Statesman & Society,* "Walker is a biased (and occasionally hot-headed) observer of the political scene, prone to preach from the moral high ground with little or no regard for facts or opinions that might undermine her point of view." Other critics found Walker's ruminations on politics inspiring. At the center of each narrative," wrote Donna Seaman in *Booklist,* "is Walker's belief that every attempt to change the world for the better, no matter how modest, is transcendent."

BIOGRAPHICAL/CRITICAL SOURCES:

BOOKS

Allan, Tuzyline Jita, *Womanist and Feminist Aesthetics: A Comparative Review,* Ohio University Press, 1995.
Black Literature Criticism, Volume 1, Gale, 1992, pp. 1808-829.
Christian, Barbara, editor, *Everyday Use,* Rutgers University Press (New Brunswick, NJ), 1994.
Contemporary Literary Criticism, Gale, Volume 5, 1976; Volume 6, 1976; Volume 9, 1978; Volume 19, 1981; Volume 27, 1984; Volume 46, 1988; Volume 58, 1990; Volume 103, 1998.
Dictionary of Literary Biography, Gale, Volume 6: *American Novelists since World War II, Second Series,* 1980; Volume 33: *Afro-American Fiction Writers after 1955,* 1984; Volume 143: *American Novelists since World War II, Third Series,* 1994, pp. 277-93.
Evans, Mari, editor, *Black Women Writers (1950-1980): A Critical Evaluation,* Anchor (New York City), 1984.
Johnson, Yvonne, *The Voices of African American Women: The Use of Narrative and Authorial Voice in the Works of Harriet Jacobs, Zora Neale Hurston, and Alice Walker,* P. Lang, 1995.
Kaplan, Carla, *The Erotics of Talk: Women's Writing and Feminist Paradigms,* Oxford University Press, 1996.
Kramer, Barbara, *Alice Walker: Author of "The Color Purple,"* Enslow, 1995.
O'Brien, John, *Interviews with Black Writers,* Liveright (New York City), 1973.
Peden, William, *The American Short Story: Continuity and Change, 1940-1975,* 2nd revised and enlarged edition, Houghton, 1975.
Prenshaw, Peggy W., editor, *Women Writers of the Contemporary South,* University Press of Mississippi (Jackson), 1984.
Short Story Criticism, Volume 5, Gale, 1990, pp. 400-24.

PERIODICALS

African American Review, spring, 1995, p. 67.
Black Scholar, April, 1976.
Black World, September, 1973; October, 1974.
Booklist, November 15, 1995, p. 514; March 1, 1997.
Chicago Tribune, December 20, 1985; April 23, 1989.
Chicago Tribune Book World, August 1, 1982; September 15, 1985.
Commonweal, April 29, 1977.
Critique, summer, 1994.
Detroit Free Press, August 8, 1982; July 10, 1988; January 4, 1989.
Detroit News, September 15, 1982; October 23, 1983; March 31, 1985.
Entertainment Weekly, December 30, 1994, p. 64.
Essence, February, 1996, p. 84.
Globe and Mail (Toronto), December 21, 1985.
Library Journal, November 15, 1994, p. 103; December, 1995, p. 110.
Los Angeles Times, April 29, 1981; June 8, 1983.
Los Angeles Times Book Review, August 8, 1982; May 29, 1988; May 21, 1989, p. 1; July 5, 1992, p. 4.
Ms., February, 1974; July, 1977; July, 1978; June, 1982; September, 1986.
Nation, November 12, 1973; December 17, 1983.
Negro Digest, September/October, 1968.
New Republic, September 14, 1974; December 21, 1974; May 29, 1989, pp. 28-29.
New Statesman & Society, August 15, 1997.
Newsweek, May 31, 1976; June 21, 1982; April 24, 1989, p. 74; June 8, 1992, pp. 56-57.
New York Times, December 18, 1985; January 5, 1986.
New York Times Book Review, March 17, 1974; May 23, 1976; May 29, 1977; December 30, 1979; May 24, 1981; July 25,

1982; April 7, 1985; June 5, 1988; April 30, 1989, p. 7; June 28, 1992, p. 11; January 14, 1996, p. 18.
New York Times Magazine, January 8, 1984.
People Weekly, April 29, 1996, p. 36.
Poetry, February, 1971; March, 1980.
Publishers Weekly, August 31, 1970; February 26, 1988; March 1, 1991, p. 64; October 25, 1991, p. 66; October 25, 1993, p. 49; February 24, 1997, p. 77.
Time, May 1, 1989, p. 69.
Times Literary Supplement, August 19, 1977; June 18, 1982; July 20, 1984; September 27, 1985; April 15, 1988; September 22, 1989, p. 1023; October 9, 1992, p. 22.
Tribune Books (Chicago), July 17, 1988; April 23, 1989, p. 5; June 21, 1992, p. 3; January 21, 1996, p. 5.
Washington Post, October 15, 1982; April 15, 1983; October 17, 1983.
Washington Post Book World, November 18, 1973; October 30, 1979; December 30, 1979; May 31, 1981; July 25, 1982; December 30, 1984; May 29, 1988; May 7, 1989, p. 3; July 5, 1992, p. 1; January 16, 1994, pp. 4-5.
World Literature Today, winter, 1985; winter, 1986.

*   *   *

WALKER, Margaret (Abigail) 1915-

PERSONAL: Born July 7, 1915, in Birmingham, AL; daughter of Sigismund C. (a Methodist minister) and Marion (Dozier) Walker (a music teacher); married Firnist James Alexander, June 13, 1943 (deceased); children: Marion Elizabeth, Firnist James, Sigismund Walker, Margaret Elvira. *Education:* Northwestern University, B.A., 1935; University of Iowa, M.A., 1940, Ph.D., 1965. *Religion:* Methodist.

ADDRESSES: Home—2205 Guynes Street, Jackson, MS 39213. *Office*—Department of English, Jackson State College, Jackson, MS 39217.

CAREER: Worked as a social worker, newspaper reporter, and magazine editor; Livingstone College, Salisbury, NC, member of faculty, 1941-42; West Virginia State College, Institute, WV, instructor in English, 1942-43; Livingstone College, professor of English, 1945-46; Jackson State College, Jackson, MS, professor emeritus of English (professor since 1949), director of Institute for the Study of the History, Life, and Culture of Black Peoples, 1968-. Lecturer, National Concert and Artists Corp. Lecture Bureau, 1943-48. Visiting professor in creative writing, Northwestern University, Spring, 1969. Staff member, Cape Cod Writers Conference, Craigville, Massachusetts, 1967 and 1969. Participant, Library of Congress Conference on the Teaching of Creative Writing, 1973.

MEMBER: National Council of Teachers of English, Modern Language Association, Poetry Society of America, American Association of University Professors, National Education Association, Alpha Kappa Alpha.

AWARDS, HONORS: Yale Series of Younger Poets Award, 1942, for *For My People;* named to Honor Roll of Race Relations, a national poll conducted by the New York Public Library, 1942; Rosenthal fellowship, 1944; Ford fellowship for study at Yale University, 1954; Houghton Mifflin Literary fellowship, 1966; Fulbright fellowship, 1971; National Endowment for the Humanities, 1972; Doctor of Literature, Northwestern University, 1974; Doctor of Letters, Rust College, 1974; Doctor of Fine Arts,

Dennison University, 1974; Doctor of Humane Letters, Morgan State University, 1976.

WRITINGS:

POETRY

For My People, Yale University Press, 1942.
Ballad of the Free, Broadside Press, 1966.
Prophets for a New Day, Broadside Press, 1970.
October Journey, Broadside Press, 1973.
This Is My Century, University of Georgia Press, 1989.

PROSE

Jubilee (novel), Houghton, 1965, Bantam, 1981.
How I Wrote "Jubilee," Third World Press, 1972.
(With Nikki Giovanni) *A Poetic Equation: Conversations between Nikki Giovanni and Margaret Walker,* Howard University Press, 1974.
Richard Wright: Daemonic Genius, Dodd, 1987.
On Being Female, Black, and Free: Essays by Margaret Walker, 1932-1992, University of Tennessee Press (Knoxville, TN), 1997.

CONTRIBUTOR

Addison Gayle, editor, *Black Expression,* Weybright & Tally, 1969.
Stanton L. Wormley and Lewis H. Fenderson, editors, *Many Shades of Black,* Morrow, 1969.
Henderson, Stephen, *Understanding the New Black Poetry: Black Speech and Black Music as Poetic References,* Morrow, 1973.

Also contributor to numerous anthologies, including Adoff's *Black Out Loud,* Weisman and Wright's *Black Poetry for All Americans,* and Williams's *Beyond the Angry Black.*

SIDELIGHTS: When *For My People* by Margaret Walker won the Yale Younger Poets Series Award in 1942, "she became one of the youngest Black writers ever to have published a volume of poetry in this century," as well as "the first Black woman in American literary history to be so honored in a prestigious national competition," notes Richard K. Barksdale in *Black American Poets between Worlds, 1940-1960.* Walker's first novel, *Jubilee,* is notable for being "the first truly historical black American novel," according to University of Maryland professor Joyce Anne Joyce, reports Washington Post contributor Crispin Y. Campbell. It was also the first work by a black writer to speak out for the liberation of the black woman. The cornerstones of a literature that affirms the African folk roots of black American life, these two books have also been called visionary for looking toward a new cultural unity for black Americans that will be built on that foundation.

The title of Walker's first book, *For My People,* denotes the subject matter of "poems in which the body and spirit of a great group of people are revealed with vigor and undeviating integrity," says Louis Untermeyer in the *Yale Review.* Here, in long ballads, Walker draws sympathetic portraits of characters such as the New Orleans sorceress Molly Means; Kissie Lee, a tough young woman who dies "with her boots on switching blades;" and Poppa Chicken, an urban drug dealer and pimp. Other ballads give a new dignity to John Henry, killed by a ten-pound hammer, and Stagolee, who kills a white officer but eludes a lynch mob. In an essay for *Black Women Writers (1950-1980): A Critical Evaluation,* Eugenia Collier notes, "Using . . . the language of the grass-roots people, Walker spins yarns of folk heroes and heroines: those who, faced with the terrible obstacles which haunt Black people's very existence, not only survive but prevail—with style." Soon after it appeared, the book of ballads, sonnets and free verse found a surprisingly large number of readers, requiring publishers to authorize three printings to satisfy popular demand.

"If the test of a great poem is the universality of statement, then 'For My People' is a great poem," remarks Barksdale. The critic explains in Donald B. Gibson's *Modern Black Poets: A Collection of Critical Essays* that the poem was written when "world-wide pain, sorrow, and affliction were tangibly evident, and few could isolate the Black man's dilemma from humanity's dilemma during the depression years or during the war years." Thus, the power of resilience presented in the poem is a hope Walker holds out not only to black people, but to all people, to "all the adams and eves." As she once remarked, "Writers should not write exclusively for black or white audiences, but most inclusively. After all, it is the business of all writers to write about the human condition, and all humanity must be involved in both the writing and in the reading."

Jubilee, a historical novel, is the second book on which Walker's literary reputation rests. It is the story of a slave family during and after the Civil War, and took her thirty years to write. During these years, she married a disabled veteran, raised four children, taught full time at Jackson State College in Mississippi, and earned a Ph.D. from the University of Iowa. The lengthy gestation, she believes, partly accounts for the book's quality. As she told Claudia Tate in *Black Women Writers at Work,* "Living with the book over a long period of time was agonizing. Despite all of that, *Jubilee* is the product of a mature person," one whose own difficult pregnancies and economic struggles could lend authenticity to the lives of her characters. "There's a difference between writing about something and living through it," she said in the interview; "I did both."

The story of *Jubilee*'s main characters Vyry and Randall Ware was an important part of Walker's life even before she began to write it down. As she explains in *How I Wrote "Jubilee,"* she first heard about the "slavery time" in bedtime stories told by her maternal grandmother. When old enough to recognize the value of her family history, Walker took initiative, "prodding" her grandmother for more details, and promising to set down on paper the story that had taken shape in her mind. Later on, she completed extensive research on every aspect of the black experience touching the Civil War, from obscure birth records to information on the history of tin cans. "Most of my life I have been involved with writing this story about my great-grandmother, and even if *Jubilee* were never considered an artistic or commercial success I would still be happy just to have finished it," she claims.

Soon after *Jubilee* was published in 1966, Walker was given a Fellowship award from Houghton-Mifflin, and a mixed reception from critics. Granting that the novel is "ambitious," *New York Times Book Review* contributor Wilma Dykeman deemed it "uneven." Arthur P. Davis, writing in *From the Dark Tower: Afro-American Writers, 1900-1960,* suggests that the author "has crowded too much into her novel." Even so, say reviewers, the novel merits praise. Abraham Chapman of the *Saturday Review* appreciates the author's "fidelity to fact and detail" as she "presents the little-known everyday life of the slaves," their music, and their folkways. In the *Christian Science Monitor,* Henrietta Buckmaster comments, "In Vyry, Miss Walker has found a remarkable woman who suffered one outrage after the other and yet emerged with a humility and a mortal fortitude that

reflected a spiritual wholeness." Dykeman concurs, "In its best episodes, and in Vyry, 'Jubilee' chronicles the triumph of a free spirit over many kinds of bondages." Later critical studies of the book emphasize the importance of its themes and its position as the prototype for novels that present black history from a black perspective. Claims Roger Whitlow in *Black American Literature: A Critical History,* "It serves especially well as a response to white 'nostalgia' fiction about the antebellum and Reconstruction South."

Walker's next book to be highly acclaimed was *Prophets for a New Day,* a slim volume of poems. Unlike the poems in *For My People,* which, in a Marxist fashion, names religion an enemy of revolution, says Collier, *Prophets for a New Day* "reflects a profound religious faith. The heroes of the sixties are named for the prophets of the Bible: Martin Luther King is Amos, Medgar Evars is Micah, and so on. The people and events of the sixties are paralleled with Biblical characters and occurrences. . . . The religious references are important. Whether one espouses the Christianity in which they are couched is not the issue. For the fact is that Black people from ancient Africa to now have always been a spiritual people, believing in an existence beyond the flesh." One poem in *Prophets* that harks back to African spiritism is "Ballad of Hoppy Toad" with its hexes that turn a murderous conjurer into a toad. Though Collier feels that Walker's "vision of the African past is fairly dim and romantic," the critic goes on to say that this poetry "emanates from a deeper area of the psyche, one which touches the mythic area of a collective being and reenacts the rituals which define a Black collective self." Perhaps more importantly, in all the poems, says Collier, Walker depicts "a people striking back at oppression and emerging triumphant."

Much of Walker's responsiveness to the black experience, communicated through the realism of her work, can be attributed to her growing up in a southern home environment which emphasized the rich heritage of black culture. Margaret Abigail Walker was born 7 July 1915 in Birmingham, Alabama, to the Reverend Sigismund C. Walker and Marion Dozier Walker. The family moved to New Orleans when Walker was a young child. A Methodist minister who had been born near Buff Bay, Jamaica, Walker's father was a scholar who bequeathed to his daughter his love of literature—the classics, the Bible, Benedict de Spinoza, Arthur Schopenhauer, the English classics, and poetry. Similarly, Walker's musician mother played ragtime and read poetry to her, choosing among such varied authors and works as Paul Laurence Dunbar, John Greenleaf Whittier's "Snowbound," the Bible, and Shakespeare. At age eleven Walker began reading the poetry of Langston Hughes and Countee Cullen. Elvira Ware Dozier, her maternal grandmother, who lived with her family, told Walker stories, including the story of her own mother, a former slave in Georgia. Before she finished college, at Northwestern University in Evanston, Illinois, in the early 1930s, Walker had heard James Weldon Johnson read from *God's Trombones* (1927), listened to Marian Anderson and Roland Hayes sing in New Orleans, and, in 1932, heard Hughes read his poetry in a lecture recital at New Orleans University, where her parents then taught. She met Hughes in 1932, and he encouraged her to continue writing poetry. Her first poem was published in *Crisis* in 1934.

As a senior at Northwestern in 1934, Walker began a fruitful association with the Works Progress Administration. She lived on Chicago's North Side and worked as a volunteer on the WPA recreation project. The project directors assigned her to associate with so-called delinquent girls, mainly shoplifters and prostitutes, in order to determine if Walker's different background and training might have a positive influence on them. She became so fascinated by an Italian-Black neighborhood that she eventually chose it as the setting and title for an unpublished novel that she began writing, *Goose Island*. On Friday, 13 March 1936, Walker received notice to report to the WPA Writer's Project in Chicago as a full-time employee. Classified as a junior writer—her salary was eighty-five dollars a month—her work assignment was the Illinois Guide Book. Other writers on the project were Nelson Algren, Jacob Scher, James Phelan, Sam Ross, Katherine Dunham, Willard Motley, Frank Yerby, Fenton Johnson, and Richard Wright. In 1937 the WPA office allowed her to come into the downtown quarters only twice weekly so that she might remain at home working on her novel.

Perhaps her most rewarding interaction with a writer at the project was Walker's friendship with Wright, a liaison that, while it lasted, proved practical and beneficial to both fledgling writers. Before she joined the project, Walker had met Wright in Chicago in February 1936, when he had presided at the writer's section of the first National Negro Congress. Walker had attended solely to meet Hughes again, to show him the poetry she had written since their first meeting four years earlier. Hughes refused to take her only copy of the poems, but he introduced her to Wright and insisted that he include Walker if a writer's group organized. Wright then introduced her to Arna Bontemps and Sterling A. Brown, also writers with the WPA.

Although Wright left Chicago for New York on 28 May 1937, neither his friendship with Walker nor their literary interdependence ended immediately. Walker provided him, in fact, with important help on *Native Son* (1940), mailing him (as he requested) newspaper clippings about Robert Nixon, a young black man accused of rape in Chicago, and assisting Wright in locating a vacant lot to use as the Dalton house address when Wright returned to Chicago briefly the next year. Furthermore, Walker was instrumental in acquiring for him a copy of the brief of Nixon's case from attorney Ulysses S. Keyes, the first black lawyer hired for the case. (He was later replaced by an NAACP attorney.) Together, Wright and Walker visited Cook County jail, where Nixon was incarcerated, and the library, where on her library card they checked out a book on Clarence Darrow and two books on the Loeb-Leopold case, from which, in part, Wright modeled Bigger's defense when he completed his novel in the spring of 1939.

Walker began teaching in the 1940s. She taught at North Carolina's Livingstone College in 1941 and West Virginia State College in 1942. On 13 June 1943 she married Firnist James Alexander. In that year, too, she began to read her poetry publicly when she was invited by Arthur P. Davis to read "For My People" at Richmond's Virginia Union University, where he was then teaching. After the birth of the first of her four children in 1944 Walker returned to teach at Livingstone for a year. She also resumed the research on her Civil War novel in the 1940s. She began with a trip to the Schomburg Center in 1942. In 1944 she received a Rosenwald Fellowship to further her research. In 1948 Walker was unemployed, living in High Point, North Carolina, and working on the novel. By then she clearly envisioned the development of *Jubilee* as a folk novel and prepared an outline of incidents and chapter headings. (Almost all the chapter headings were supplied by the stories of her grandmother.) In 1949 Walker moved to Jackson, Mississippi, and began her long teaching career at Jackson State College (now Jackson State University).

The fictional history of Walker's great-grandmother, here called Vyry, *Jubilee* is divided into three sections: the antebellum years in Georgia on John Dutton's plantation, the Civil War years, and the Reconstruction era. Against a panoramic view of history Walker focuses the plot specifically on Vyry's life as she grows from a little girl to adulthood. In the first section Vyry, the slave, matures, marries and separates from Randall Ware, attempts to escape from slavery with her two children, and is flogged. The second section emphasizes the destruction of war and the upheaval for slaveowner and slaves, while the last section focuses on Vyry as a displaced former slave, searching for a home.

Walker said her research was done "to undergird the oral tradition" and *Jubilee* is primarily known for its realistic depiction of the daily life and folklore of the black slave community. Although there are also quotes from Whittier and the English romantic poets, she emphasizes the importance of the folk structure of her novel by prefacing each of the fifty-eight chapters with proverbial folk sayings or lines excerpted from spirituals. The narrative is laced with verses of songs sung by Vyry, her guardian, or other slaves. A portion from a sermon is included. The rhymes of slave children are also a part of the narrative. A conjuring episode is told involving the overseer Grimes, suggesting how some folk beliefs were used for protection. Vyry provides a catalogue of herbs and discusses their medicinal and culinary purposes.

Responses to Walker's Civil War story were mixed. Guy Davenport in *National Review* (4 October 1966) said that "the novel from end to end [is] about a place and a people who never existed." For him Walker had merely recalled all the elements of the southern myth, writing a lot of "tushery that comes out of books, out of Yerby and Margaret Mitchell." He further found "something deeply ironic in a Negro's underwriting the made-up South of the romances, agreeing to every convention of the trade." More justly, Abraham Chapman in the *Saturday Review* (24 September 1966) found "a fidelity to fact and detail" in the depictions of slave life that was better than anything done before. Lester Davis in *Freedomways* (Summer 1967) decided that one could overlook the "sometimes trite and often stilted prose style" because the novel is "a good forthright treatment of a segment of American history about which there has been much hypocrisy and deliberate distortion." He found the "flavor of authenticity . . . convincing and refreshing." Walker's *How I Wrote Jubilee* (1972), a history of the novel's development from her grandmother's oral history, is an indirect response to those critics who compared *Jubilee* with books like Mitchell's *Gone with the Wind* (1936) and who accused Walker of sustaining the southern myth from the black perspective. She answers her detractors by citing the references and historical documents she perused over several years in order to gird her oral story with historical fact.

Walker's second volume of poetry, *Prophets for a New Day,* was published in 1970. She has called *Prophets for a New Day* her civil rights poems, and only two poems in the volume, "Elegy" and "Ballad of the Hoppy Toad," are not about the civil rights movement. Walker begins the volume with two poems in which the speakers are young children; one eight-year-old demonstrator eagerly waits to be arrested with her group in the fight for equality, and a second one is already jailed and wants no bail. Her point is that these young girls are just as much prophets for a new day as were Nat Turner, Gabriel Prosser, Denmark Vesey, Toussaint L'Ouverture, and John Brown. In "The Ballad of the Free" Walker establishes a biblical allusion and association as an integral part of the fight to end racism: "The serpent is loosed and the hour is come / The last shall be first and the first shall be none / The serpent is loosed and the hour is come."

The title poem, "Prophets for a New Day," and the seven poems which follow it invite obvious comparisons between the biblical prophets and the black leaders who denounced racial injustice and prophesied change during the civil rights struggle of the 1960s. For example, several prophets are linked to specific southern cities marked by racial turmoil: in "Jeremiah," the first poem of the series, Jeremiah "is now a man whose names is Benjamin / Brooding over a city called Atlanta / Preaching the doom of a curse upon the land." Among the poems other prophets mentioned are "Isaiah," "Amos," and "Micah," a poem subtitled "To the memory of Medgar Evers of Mississippi."

In *For My People* Walker urged that activity replace complacency, but in *Prophets for a New Day* she applauds the new day of freedom for black people, focusing on the events, sites, and people of the struggle. Among the poems that recognize southern cities associated with racial turbulence are "Oxford Is A Legend," "Birmingham," "Jackson, Mississippi," and "Sit-Ins." Of these, the latter two are the most accomplished pieces. "Sit-Ins" (Greensboro, North Carolina, in the spring of 1960) is a recognition of "those first bright young to fling [their] . . . names across pages / Of new Southern history / With courage and faith, convictions, and intelligence."

BIOGRAPHICAL/CRITICAL SOURCES:

BOOKS

Bankier, Joanna, and Dierdre Lashgari, editors, *Women Poets of the World,* Macmillan, 1983.

Baraka, Amiri, *The Black Nation,* Getting Together Publications, 1982.

Bigsby, C. W. E., editor, *The Second Black Renaissance: Essays in Black Literature,* Greenwood Press, 1980.

Contemporary Literary Criticism, Gale (Detroit), Volume 1, 1973; Volume 2, 1976.

Davis, Arthur P., *From the Dark Tower: Afro-American Writers, 1900 to 1960,* Howard University Press, 1974.

Emanuel, James A., and Theodore L. Gross, editors, *Dark Symphony: Negro Literature in America,* Free Press, 1968.

Evans, Mari, editor, *Black Women Writers (1950-1980): A Critical Evaluation,* Anchor/Doubleday, 1982.

Gayle, Addison, editor, *The Black Aesthetic,* Doubleday, 1971.

Gibson, Donald B., editor, *Modern Black Poets: A Collection of Critical Essays,* Prentice-Hall, 1983.

Jackson, Blyden, and Louis D. Rubin, Jr., *Black Poetry in America: Two Essays in Historical Interpretation,* Louisiana State University Press, 1974.

Jones, John Griffith, in *Mississippi Writers Talking,* Volume II, University of Mississippi Press, 1983.

Kent, George E., *Blackness and the Adventure of Western Culture,* Third World Press, 1972.

Lee, Don L., *Dynamite Voices I: Black Poets of the 1960s,* Broadside Press, 1971.

Miller, R. Baxter, editor, *Black American Poets between Worlds, 1940-1960,* University of Tennessee Press, 1986.

Pryse, Marjorie, and Hortense J. Spillers, editors, *Conjuring: Black Women, Fiction, and Literary Tradition,* Indiana University Press, 1985.

Redmond, Eugene B., *Drumvoices: The Mission of Afro-American Poetry—A Critical Evaluation,* Doubleday, 1976.

Tate, Claudia, editor, *Black Women Writers at Work,* Continuum, 1983.

Whitlow, Roger, *Black American Literature: A Critical History,* Nelson Hall, 1973.

PERIODICALS

Atlantic Monthly, December, 1942.
Black World, December, 1971; December, 1975.
Book Week, October 2, 1966.
Callaloo, May, 1979.
Christian Science Monitor, November 14, 1942; September 29, 1966; June 19, 1974.
CLA Journal, December 1977.
Ebony, February, 1949.
Freedomways, summer, 1967.
Mississippi Quarterly, fall, 1988; fall 1989.
National Review, October 4, 1966.
Negro Digest, February, 1967; January, 1968.
New Republic, November 23, 1942.
New York Times, November 4, 1942.
New York Times Book Review, August 2, 1942; September 25, 1966.
Publishers Weekly, April 15, 1944; March 24, 1945.
Saturday Review, September 24, 1966.
Times Literary Supplement, June 29, 1967.
Washington Post, February 9, 1983.
Yale Review, winter, 1943.

*   *   *

WALLACE, David Foster 1962-

PERSONAL: Born February 21, 1962, in Ithaca, NY; son of James Donald (a teacher) and Sally (a teacher; maiden name, Foster) Wallace. *Education:* Amherst College, A.B. (summa cum laude), 1985; University of Arizona, M.F.A., 1987. *Politics:* "Independent." *Religion:* "No affiliation."

ADDRESSES: Agent—Frederick Hill Associates, 1842 Union St., San Francisco, CA 94123.

CAREER: Writer. Associate professor of English, 1993–.

AWARDS, HONORS: Whiting Writers' Award, Mrs. Giles Whiting Foundation, 1987; Residency Fellowship to the corporation of Yaddo, Saratoga Springs, NY, 1987, 1989; John Traine Humor Prize, *The Paris Review,* for "Little Expressionless Animals," 1988; inclusion of "Here and There" in *Prize Stories 1989: The O. Henry Awards,* edited by William Abrahams, 1988; National Endowment for the Arts Writer's Fellowship, 1989; Illinois Arts Council Award for Non-Fiction for "Fictional Futures and the Conspicuously Young," 1989; Quality Paperback Book Club's New Voices Award in Fiction for *Girl with Curious Hair,* 1991; nomination of *Signifying Rappers* for Pulitzer Prize in nonfiction, 1991; inclusion of "Forever Overhead" in *Best American Short Stories of 1992,* edited by Robert Stone, 1993; inclusion of "Three Protrusions" in *The Pushcart Prize XVIII,* edited by Bill Henderson, 1993; "Ticket to the Fair" named a Finalist for National Magazine Award, 1995; named Contributing Editor of *Harper's,* 1995; Lannan Foundation Award for Literature, 1996; selected as Judge for 1997 O. Henry Awards, 1997; "David Lynch Keeps his Head" named a finalist for National Magazine Award, 1997; "The String Theory" selected for *Best American Sportswriting 1997,* Houghton Mifflin, 1997; MacArthur Foundation Fellowship, 1997.

WRITINGS:

The Broom of the System, Viking, 1987.
Girl with Curious Hair (short stories and novellas; includes "Girl with Curious Hair," "Little Expressionless Animals," "My Appearance," "Westward the Course of Empire Takes Its Way," "Lyndon," "John Billy," and "Everything Is Green"), Penguin, 1988, hardcover edition, Norton, 1989.
(With Mark Costello) *Signifying Rappers: Rap and Race in the Urban Present* (nonfiction), Ecco Press (New York City), 1990.
Infinite Jest, Little, Brown (Boston), 1996.
A Supposedly Fun Thing I'll Never Do Again: Essays and Arguments, Little, Brown, 1997.

Contributor of short fiction and nonfiction to numerous periodicals, including *Contemporary Fiction, Harper's,* and *The New Yorker.*

SIDELIGHTS: David Foster Wallace is the kind of writer whose talent leaves critics groping for the proper artistic comparison. Thomas Pynchon, John Irving, filmmaker David Lynch, and even comic David Letterman have all been invoked as readers tackle the sardonic humor and complicated style that have led Wallace to be cited as Generation X's first literary hero. Wallace, according to Frank Bruni in his *New York Times Magazine* profile, "is to literature what Robin Williams or perhaps Jim Carrey is to live comedy: a creator so maniacally energetic and amused with himself that he often follows his riffs out into the stratosphere, where he orbits all alone."

In his debut novel, *The Broom of the System,* Wallace uses a variety of writing techniques and points of view to create a bizarre, stylized world which, despite its strangeness, resonates with contemporary American images. Set in Cleveland on the edge of the state-constructed Great Ohio Desert (also known as G.O.D.), the story follows Lenore Beadsman's search for her ninety-two-year-old great-grandmother, also named Lenore Beadsman, who has disappeared from her nursing home. In attempting to find her childhood mentor, the younger Lenore encounters a bewildering assemblage of characters with names such as Rick Vigorous, Biff Diggerence, Candy Mandible, and Sigurd Foamwhistle. It is significant that the elder Lenore was a student of language philosopher Ludwig Wittgenstein, since *The Broom of the System* has been viewed as an elaborate exploration of the relationship between language and reality. Wallace orchestrates Lenore's coming of age through the use of innovative plotting and language. The character's search for her great-grandmother becomes the search for her own identity.

Critics praised the skill and creativity evident in Wallace's experimental bildungsroman. Rudy Rucker, writing in the *Washington Post Book World,* judged *The Broom of the System* to be a "wonderful book" and compared Wallace to novelist Thomas Pynchon. Despite finding the novel to be "unwieldy" and "uneven" in parts, *New York Times* reviewer Michiko Kakutani commended Wallace's "rich reserves of ambition and imagination" and was impressed by his "wealth of talents." *New York Times Book Review* critic Caryn James liked the novel's "exuberance" and maintained that it "succeeds as a manic, human, flawed extravaganza."

In Wallace's second work, a collection of short stories titled *Girl with Curious Hair,* the author employs a mix of facts, fiction, and his own distinctive use of language to make observations about American culture. "Little Expressionless Animals," one of several

stories that deals with American television, reveals a plan by the producers of the game show *Jeopardy!* to oust a long-time champion because of their sensitivity to her continuing lesbian love affair. The difference between appearance and reality is the subject of "My Appearance," the story of an actress's tranquilizer-induced nervous ramblings while she is waiting to do a guest appearance on the David Letterman show. In the title story, "Girl with Curious Hair," a young, Ivy League-trained corporate lawyer reveals the roots of his sadistic sexual impulses when he reflects on a Keith Jarrett concert he once attended with a group of violent punk rockers.

To reviewers, Wallace's imagination and energy are enticing. "David Foster Wallace . . . proves himself a dynamic writer of extraordinary talent," asserted Jenifer Levin in the *New York Times Book Review,* commenting that "he succeeds in restoring grandeur to modern fiction." Writing in Chicago's *Tribune Books,* Douglas Seibold commended Wallace's "irrepressible narrative energy and invention" claiming that, "as good a writer as he is now, he is getting better."

The buildup given to Wallace through his first books served as an appetizer to the hype that surrounded his 1996 novel, *Infinite Jest*—a work that, in the words of *Chicago Tribune* writer Bruce Allen, could "confirm the hopes of those who called Wallace a genius and, to a lesser extent, the fears of those who think he's just an overeducated wiseacre with a lively prose style." The book as released was massive—over 1,000 pages—and the publicity was no less so. The marketing unit of publishers Little, Brown piqued prepublication interest by sending 4,000 influential booksellers and media outlets a series of six postcards. Each card "cryptically heralded the release of an at-first-unspecified book that gives 'infinite pleasure' with 'infinite style,'" writes Bruni. "And when blurbs to that effect became available from other authors and critics, Little, Brown put them on postcards and dispatched another series of three."

On the heels of that publicity, *Infinite Jest* became *de rigueur* as a book that literary fans bought and displayed, but would not—or could not—spend much time reading. Some of the reason lies in the volume's heft and some in Wallace's dense prose style, peppered for the occasion with numerous pharmacological references that are partly responsible for the novel's 900 footnotes.

Infinite Jest is set in the not-too-distant future, in a date unspecified except as "the Year of the Depend Adult Undergarment," corporate sponsors having taken over the calendar. The United States is now part of the Organization of North American Nations (read ONAN) and has sold off New England to Canada to be used as a toxic waste dump. Legless Quebecoise separatists have taken to terrorism in protest; what's more, President Limbaugh has just been assassinated. The book's title refers to a lethal movie—a film so entertaining that those who see it may be doomed to die of pleasure.

Into this fray steps the Incandenza brothers: tennis ace Hal, football punter Orin, and the less-gifted Mario. The boys have endured a tough childhood—their father "having committed suicide by hacking open a hole in a microwave door, sealing it around his head with duct tape and making like a bag of Orville Redenbacher," as *Nation* reviewer Rick Perlstein noted. The brothers's adventures in this bizarre society fuel the novel's thick and overlapping storylines. Readers looking for a traditional linear ending, however, are in for a surprise: Those who manage to "stay with the novel until the pages thin will come to realize that Wallace has no intention of revealing whether *les Assassins des*

Fauteuils Rollents succeed or fail in their quest," Perlstein continued. "Nor whether . . . Orin will master his awful desires . . . or whether Hal Incandenza will sacrifice himself to the Oedipal grail. Readers will turn the last page, in other words, without learning anything they need to know to secure narrative succor."

For the most part, critical reaction to *Infinite Jest* mixed admiration with consternation. "There is generous intelligence and authentic passion on every page, even the overwritten ones in which the author seems to have had a fit of graphomania," said *Time*'s R. Z. Sheppard. Paul West, writing in the *Washington Post Book World,* came prepared for Pynchon but came away with the opinion that "there is nothing epic or infinite about [the novel], although much that's repetitious or long." As West saw it, "the slow incessant advance of Wallace's prose is winningly physical, solid and even, more personable actually than the crowd of goons, ditzes, inverts, junkies, fatheads and doodlers he populates his novel with."

Indeed, said Michiko Kakutani, "the whole novel often seems like an excuse for [the author] to simply show off his remarkable skills as a writer and empty the contents of his restless mind." Kakutani's *New York Times* review went on to laud "some frighteningly vivid accounts of what it feels like to be a drug addict, what it feels like to detox and what it feels like to suffer a panic attack." In the crowd of ideas and characters, the critic concluded, "somewhere in the mess, . . . are the outlines of a splendid novel, but as it stands the book feels like one of those unfinished Michelangelo sculptures: you can see a godly creature trying to fight its way out, but it's stuck there, half excavated, unable to break completely free."

Kakutani had more encouraging words for Wallace's 1997 release, *A Supposedly Fun Thing I'll Never Do Again: Essays and Arguments.* This nonfiction collection "is animated by [the author's] wonderfully exuberant prose, a zingy, elastic gift for metaphor and imaginative sleight of hand, combined with a taste for amphetaminelike stream-of-consciousness riffs." *Supposedly Fun Thing* covers Wallace's observations on cultural themes, such as the influence television has on new fiction. It also contains recollections of the author's childhood in the Midwest, thoughts on tennis (Wallace was a highly ranked player in his youth) and even a tour of the Illinois State Fair. While finding some aspects of the collection flawed, Kakutani ultimately praised *Supposedly Fun Thing* as a work that "not only reconfirms Mr. Wallace's stature as one of his generation's pre-eminent talents, but it also attests to his virtuosity, an aptitude for the essay, profile and travelogue, equal to the gifts he has already begun to demonstrate in the realm of fiction."

BIOGRAPHICAL/CRITICAL SOURCES:

BOOKS

Contemporary Literary Criticism, Volume 50, Gale (Detroit), 1988.

PERIODICALS

Chicago Tribune, March 24, 1996.
Los Angeles Times, February 11, 1996; March 18, 1996.
Los Angeles Times Book Review, February 1, 1987.
Nation, March 4, 1996.
National Review, June 17, 1996, p. 54.
New York Times, December 27, 1986; February 13, 1996; February 4, 1997; January 1, 1998, p. F2.

New York Times Book Review, March 1, 1987; November 5, 1989; March 3, 1996.
New York Times Magazine, March 24, 1996.
Time, February 19, 1996.
Tribune Books (Chicago), January 21, 1990.
Washington Post Book World, January 11, 1987; August 6, 1989; March 24, 1996.

*   *   *

WALLACE, Dexter
See MASTERS, Edgar Lee

*   *   *

WALLACE, Irving 1916-1990

PERSONAL: Born March 19, 1916, in Chicago, IL; died June 29, 1990; son of Alexander and Bessie (Liss) Wallace; married Sylvia Kahn (a writer), June 3, 1941; children: David Wallechinsky, Amy Wallace. *Education:* Attended Williams Institute, Berkeley, California, and Los Angeles City College. *Avocational interests:* Travel; collecting autographed letters, inscribed first-edition books, and impressionist paintings.

CAREER: Freelance magazine writer and interviewer, 1931-53; screenwriter, 1949-58, for Columbia, Warner Bros., Twentieth Century-Fox, Universal, RKO, Metro-Goldwyn-Mayer, and Paramount. Reporter for the Chicago Daily News/Sun Times Wire Service at the Democratic and Republican national conventions, 1972. *Military service:* U.S. Army Air Forces, writer in the First Motion Picture Unit and Signal Corps Photographic Center, 1942-46; became staff sergeant.

MEMBER: Authors Guild, Authors League of America, PEN, Writers Guild of America, Manuscript Society, Society of Authors (London).

AWARDS, HONORS: Supreme Award of Merit and honorary fellowship from George Washington Carver Memorial Institute, 1964, for writing *The Man* and for contributing "to the betterment of race relations and human welfare"; Commonwealth Club silver medal, 1965; Bestsellers magazine award, 1965, for *The Man;* Paperback of the Year citation, National Bestsellers Institute, 1970, for *The Seven Minutes;* Popular Culture Association award of excellence, 1974, for distinguished achievements in the popular arts; Venice Rosa d'Oro Award, 1975, for contributions to American letters.

WRITINGS:

The Fabulous Originals: Lives of Extraordinary People Who Inspired Memorable Characters in Fiction, Knopf, 1955.
The Square Pegs, Knopf, 1957.
The Fabulous Showman: The Life and Times of P. T. Barnum, Knopf, 1959.
The Sins of Philip Flemming (novel), Fell, 1959.
The Chapman Report (novel), Simon & Schuster, 1960.
The Twenty-Seventh Wife (biography), Simon & Schuster, 1960.
The Prize (novel), Simon & Schuster, 1962.
The Three Sirens (novel), Simon & Schuster, 1963.
The Man (novel), Simon & Schuster, 1964.
The Sunday Gentleman (collected writings), Simon & Schuster, 1965.
The Plot (novel), Simon & Schuster, 1967.

The Writing of One Novel (nonfiction), Simon & Schuster, 1968.
The Seven Minutes (novel), Simon & Schuster, 1969.
The Nympho and Other Maniacs, Simon & Schuster, 1971.
The Word (novel), Simon & Schuster, 1972.
The Fan Club (novel), Simon & Schuster, 1974.
(Editor with son, David Wallechinsky) *The People's Almanac,* Doubleday, 1975.
The R Document (novel), Simon & Schuster, 1976.
(Editor with D. Wallechinsky and daughter, Amy Wallace) *The People's Almanac Presents the Book of Lists,* Morrow, 1977.
(Editor with D. Wallechinsky) *The People's Almanac #2,* Morrow, 1978.
(With A. Wallace) *The Two: A Biography,* Simon & Schuster, 1978.
The Pigeon Project (novel), Simon & Schuster, 1979.
(Editor with wife, Sylvia Wallace, A. Wallace, and D. Wallechinsky) *The People's Almanac Presents the Books of Lists #2,* Morrow, 1980.
The Second Lady (novel), New American Library, 1980.
(Editor with A. Wallace and D. Wallechinsky) *The People's Almanac Presents the Book of Predictions,* Morrow, 1980.
(Editor with A. Wallace, S. Wallace, and D. Wallechinsky) *The Intimate Sex Lives of Famous People,* Delacorte, 1981.
(Editor with D. Wallechinsky) *The People's Almanac #3,* Morrow, 1981.
The Almighty (novel), Doubleday, 1982.
(Editor with A. Wallace and D. Wallechinsky) *The People's Almanac Presents the Book of Lists #3,* Morrow, 1983.
(Editor with A. Wallace and D. Wallechinsky) *Significa,* Dutton, 1983.
The Miracle (novel), Dutton, 1984.
The Seventh Secret (novel), Dutton, 1986.
The Celestial Bed (novel), Delacorte, 1987.
The Guest of Honor (novel), Delacorte, 1989.
The Sins of Philip Fleming: A Compelling Novel of a Man's Intimate Problems, Fell Publishers, 1993.

SCREENPLAYS

(With John Monks, Jr., and Charles Hoffman) *The West Point Story,* Warner Bros., 1950.
Meet Me at the Fair, Universal, 1953.
(With Lewis Meltzer) *Desert Legion,* Universal, 1953.
(With William Bowers) *Split Second,* RKO, 1953.
(With Roy Huggins) *Gun Fury,* Columbia, 1953.
(With Horace McCoy) *Bad for Each Other,* Columbia, 1954.
(With Gerald Adams) *The Gambler from Natchez,* Twentieth Century-Fox, 1954.
Jump into Hell, Warner Bros., 1955.
Sincerely Yours, Warner Bros., 1955.
The Burning Hills, United Artists, 1956.
Bombers B-52, Warner Bros., 1957.
(With Irwin Allen and Charles Bennett) *The Big Circus,* Allied Artists, 1959.

OTHER

Author of plays *And Then Goodnight, Because of Sex, Hotel Behemoth, Speak of the Devil, Murder by Morning,* and, with Jerome Weidman, *Pantheon.* Also author of biographies for *Collier's Encyclopedia,* 1960, *American Oxford Encyclopedia,* and *Encyclopedia Britannica.* Contributor of over 500 articles and short stories to magazines, including *Saturday Evening Post, Reader's Digest, Esquire, Parade,* and *Cosmopolitan.*

MEDIA ADAPTATIONS: Columbia Pictures bought *The Fabulous Showman* and *The Fan Club;* Warner Bros. filmed *The Chapman Report* in 1962; Metro-Goldwyn-Mayer filmed *The Prize* in 1963; Brenco Pictures and Stanley Meyer bought *The Three Sirens;* ABC Circle Films bought and filmed *The Man,* which was released by Paramount in 1972; Twentieth Century-Fox bought *The Plot,* and filmed *The Seven Minutes* in 1971, then bought film rights to *The Intimate Sex Lives of Famous People;* United Artists bought *The R Document.* Television productions—Columbia Broadcasting System (CBS) bought *The Word* and broadcast an eight-hour miniseries in 1978; Lindsay Wagner's independent production company bought rights to *The Second Lady.*

SIDELIGHTS: One of America's most popular writers (and one of its chief literary exports with volumes printed in 31 languages worldwide), Irving Wallace began his career while still in his teens, contributing stories and articles to magazines. He reports that he was amazed when, at that young age, he discovered that the periodicals actually paid people to write for them, and from that moment on, he knew how he would spend his life. Romance combined with career when Wallace married fellow writer Sylvia Kahn in 1941; they would collaborate on two books and two children. The Wallaces saw their writing dynasty continue when their offspring, Amy Wallace and David Wallechinsky (the latter having adopted his paternal grandfather's original surname) became successful authors on their own.

Best known for his novels, Wallace has through the years developed an unusual forte in his fiction. He takes a highly complicated subject—a Kinsey-type survey or the Nobel Prize selection, for instance—and weaves it into a plot designed to hook readers with characters who have much at stake. In this way, Wallace's novels are notable for the amount of research that goes into them. As the author elaborates in John Leverence's study *Irving Wallace: A Writer's Profile,* when he begins a book he's "always curious to investigate what psychological motives bring a certain person into his field or profession. Why is a surgeon a surgeon? Why does he enjoy cutting flesh? Why does he like to tune in on patients' private lives? Why does that woman like to teach, and why does this man like to dig into the earth?"

Among Wallace's early fiction, *The Chapman Report* and *The Prize* (all of the author's novels begin with "The," a trait he attributes to superstition), dealing respectively with the Kinsey plot and the Nobel Prize story, are the most popular. Both works, according to *New York Times Book Review* critic Lawrence Lafore, "skillfully combine the most alluring features of the headline, the expose, the editorial and the mystery story." *The Chapman Report* in particular proved a highly controversial book when it first appeared in 1960, mainly because its sexual *roman a clef* elements were based on discussions Wallace had conducted with his actual neighbors at the time.

Controversy and its ensuing publicity combined to help make *The Chapman Report* a bestseller, and such fictions are rarely greeted with critical hosannas. But no one could deny that the author could reach an audience that might not otherwise investigate such subject matter. In Lafore's article, the critic remarks that a reader might learn almost nothing about the novel's main characters "except their sexual maladjustments. While a unique fascination with mass rape may create problems, it does not in itself create a personality." Yet at the same time, notes Lafore, Wallace "is refreshingly free of the pedantries and complexities to which novelists are too often prey. He uses few words (aside from anatomical ones), and introduces few ideas, that would be unfamiliar to a high-school sophomore."

On the heels of *The Chapman Report* came *The Prize,* a novel born of the fact that no fictional work had ever been published about the Nobel Prize. After extensive research that included trips to Stockholm and unprecedented interviews with subjects involved in the Nobel selection committee, Wallace released the book to praise for its unique theme and pans for what some saw as stylistic faults. In the Leverence work, Ray B. Browne includes *The Prize* in his critique of Wallace's sense of continuity. While the author's plots "are rich and complex, and each contains an important message," writes Browne, "once this message has been developed, . . . and after the puzzle has been solved, Wallace seems to lose most of his interest in the book. [He] is actually mostly gripped by the themes themselves. Little wonder then that after the questions and answers have been demonstrated and worked out, the author rushes to close the book, apparently content to erase the characters once they have illustrated his point." Still, finds Brown, Wallace, with his "direct, carefully chosen and clear" style, has produced in *The Prize* "a kind of high-water mark in subject and accomplishment. Since that novel Wallace has continued to explore new areas of investigation and to provide rich entertainment."

Such rich entertainment came in the form of two subsequent novels, *The Man* and *The Word,* another pair of bestsellers. Each contains a provocative theme. In *The Man,* the author speculates on what might happen should a black man, alone in the white bastion of American politics, suddenly find himself appointed president. Protagonist Douglass Dilman, a midlevel congressman who becomes chief of state when circumstances eliminate those ahead of him, came about as a Wallace-style reaction to the controversy then brewing over the integration of public schools. As the author himself reveals in his *Contemporary Authors Autobiography Series* article, *The Man* "was an immediate success, . . . [drawing] heavy mail, much of it from readers who admitted it had changed their attitude toward blacks completely."

In a *Best Sellers* review, Eugene J. Linehan sees merit in Wallace's presentation of an emotional theme: "The test of a novel is its people. You will find the men and women of these event singularly real. It is not easy to write well of current events; to walk us around the White House and maintain balance and sense. The danger is that such a choice of subject may lead the author into gross sentimentality or sensationalism. It seems to me that Irving Wallace has succeeded [in *The Man*] in bringing a thrilling story to the end of his book and kept his people alive and real."

Wallace tackled no less a subject than the Bible in *The Word.* Fabricating the discovery of a new set of New Testaments written by James, brother of Jesus, was challenging scholarship, the author acknowledges. But the sense of realism he developed in *The Word* resulted in "endless letters . . . asking me if The Gospel According to James, which I had invented, really had been dug up by archeologists, translated, and where copies might be purchased," as Wallace notes in the Leverence book. "While creating my gospel," he adds, "I drew upon the best research, archeological discoveries, theories and speculations of the finest Biblical scholars."

The Word, published in 1972, quickly attained international bestseller status. Its commercial acceptance, however, didn't stop some reviewers from accusing the author of concocting a potboiler. "The Irving Wallace formula for a best seller seems to be: put everything in, make a goulash," as a *New Republic* critic states, adding that besides the Biblical plot, the novel traffics in "spies, international police, two miracles (one gets tentatively canceled out) and a proposed Protestant Vatican. . . . It also has doses of sex, drugs, tragic irony, [and] scholarly hokum."

To Steven Kroll, in a *New York Times Book Review* piece, *The Word* presents an uncomfortable attitude toward women. "Even well-educated women end up as assistants and secretaries," he says. "If they're not capable of real love, they tend to go in for 'geisha acrobatics.' No doubt about it. Wallace women serve." But Kroll further goes on to say that whatever reservations he has about the author's tone, Wallace does have "a flair for controversial, topical subjects and a good liberal's serious respect for honesty, justice and nonconformity. He's also very adept at those unlikely coincidences that keep a reader wondering. But when you've been made to wonder, you feel cheated if you don't get answers, and 'The Word' bypasses those answers for a sweeping message of faith."

Not all Wallace novels center on lofty themes of sexual research, Nobel Prizes, integration, or religion. Many of his other fictional works fall into the category of hard-driving entertainments. Chief among them is *The Fan Club,* a suspense tale in which a Marilyn Monroe-type movie star is kidnapped by a group of men who had made her the object of their long-running fantasies. "The group hassles about how they deserve the actress, since 'the fat cats' get everything in life, including tax write-offs," *New York Times Book Review* writer Joe Flaherty finds. Flaherty, while pointing out that *The Fan Club*'s implicit appeal "is not sexual but [in] our passion to consummate with consumerism," sees in this point that Wallace's "genius comes to the fore. Every brand name is right; and the jet set life style, as decadent as it may be, is the stuff that makes a closet queen of every straphanger."

The 1980s brought a steady stream of fiction from Wallace, including *The Almighty, The Miracle, The Seventh Secret,* and *The Celestial Bed.* None of these novels was hailed as a masterpiece, though in Anatole Broyard's opinion, "a novel like 'The Miracle' is beyond criticism because it has no literary pretensions." As Broyard continues in a *New York Times* feature, this tale of a purported series of healing miracles in Lourdes, where the Virgin Mary was said to have appeared on several occasions in the past, employs "a timely theme that will interest a wide readership." Further, "There is a kind of crossword-puzzle suspense in reading 'The Miracle,' what might be called a mechanical curiosity. The main trouble with the book is not that it has renounced literary ambition in favor of a more ordinary appeal, but that it doesn't do justice to the ordinary. The language, for example, is not conversational, but a strange dialect of pidgin English used by some popular novelists."

Nonfiction readers can find the Wallace name on a number of volumes he characterizes in *Contemporary Authors Autobiography Series* as "our family books." These include *The People's Almanac* series and its popular spinoff, *The People's Almanac Presents the Book of Lists.* "It all began with my son," Wallace remarks in the autobiographical essay. "From the age of eight, David had always been an almanac buff. . . . Then, one day in 1971, he began to question the infallibility of the almanacs and other reference books he had been reading. He began to see that a good deal of history and current events was distorted by reference books—not necessarily deliberately, but for various reasons." And worst of all, adds Wallace, "most [almanacs] were unforgivably dull."

And so it was David Wallechinsky who embarked on a new sort of reference work, with the enthusiastic input of his father and the assistance of 169 freelance writers, among them Charles Schulz, "who wrote the definitive biography of Snoopy for us," continues Wallace. As for working alongside his son, the author finds that "David's ego was strong enough to accept me, and we became collaborators—and before it was over we became friends."

The People's Almanac debuted in 1975 to warm reviews and high-ranking bestseller status. Critics and public alike seemed to respond to a reference work that covered topics of history and trivia that no one had ever studied. When research showed that readers especially enjoyed the various lists contained within the series, the result was *The People's Almanac Presents the Book of Lists* (known popularly as just *The Book of Lists*), which would join its predecessor in multiple volumes throughout the 1970s and 1980s. Eventually, each member of the Wallace family would have a hand in the browser's delights. "We aren't a conglomerate," the patriarch tells Joseph McLellan in a *Washington Post* interview. "We're four very autonomous individuals having fun together. We enjoy sitting around and talking about book ideas and it's good for me. Writing fiction is a lonely kind of work. These [nonfictions] are more relaxing than a novel, and your research isn't far from your writing."

BIOGRAPHICAL/CRITICAL SOURCES:

BOOKS

Cawelti, John G., *Adventure, Mystery, and Romance,* University of Chicago Press, 1976.
Contemporary Authors Autobiography Series, Volume 1, Gale, 1984.
Contemporary Literary Criticism, Gale, Volume 7, 1977; Volume 13, 1980.
Leverence, John, *Irving Wallace: A Writer's Profile,* Popular Press, 1974.
Newquist, Roy, *Conversations,* Rand McNally, 1967.

PERIODICALS

Best Sellers, September 15, 1964.
Chicago Tribune, January 17, 1988.
Chicago Tribune Book World, April 29, 1977.
Detroit News, September 23, 1984.
Journal of Popular Culture, summer, 1973.
Los Angeles Times, June 4, 1981; December 19, 1982; January 27, 1985; April 27, 1987.
Los Angeles Times Book Review, May 15, 1977; September 23, 1984; March 2, 1986.
New Republic, March 25, 1972.
Newsweek, November 1, 1982.
New York, April 1, 1974.
New York Times, August 31, 1984; June 30, 1990.
New York Times Book Review, September 22, 1963; December 12, 1965; May 28, 1967; October 2, 1969; October 12, 1969; March 21, 1971; March 19, 1972; June 16, 1974; March 14, 1976; March 19, 1978; October 12, 1980; October 31, 1982; September 13, 1984; September 19, 1984; July 16, 1989.
Publishers Weekly, February 27, 1987.
Saturday Review, March 18, 1978.
Time, April 15, 1974.
Times (London), August 23, 1974; April 30, 1987.
Times Literary Supplement, May 13, 1965; September 10, 1971; October 25, 1974.
Washington Post, April 11, 1976; February 28, 1980; September 23, 1980; October 22, 1980; November 17, 1982.
Washington Post Book World, March 19, 1978; August 12, 1984.

WALLANT, Edward Lewis 1926-1962

PERSONAL: Born October 19, 1926, in New Haven, CT; died December 5, 1962, in Norwalk, CT; son of Sol Ellis and Ann (Mendel) Wallant; married Joyce Fromkin, 1948; children: Scott Ellis, Leslie Ann, Kim Robin. *Education:* Attended Pratt Institute, 1947-50, and New School for Social Research, 1954-55.

CAREER: Worked as a graphic artist for various advertising agencies, 1950-62. *Military service:* U.S. Navy, 1944-46; gunner's mate on U.S.S. *Glennon.*

AWARDS, HONORS: Bread Loaf Writers' Conference fellow, 1960; Harry and Ethel Daroff Memorial Fiction Award, Jewish Book Council of America, 1961, for *The Human Season;* Guggenheim fellow, 1962; National Book Award nomination, 1962, for *The Pawnbroker.*

WRITINGS:

NOVELS

The Human Scene, Harcourt, 1960.
The Pawnbroker, Harcourt, 1961.
The Tenants of Moonbloom, Harcourt, 1963.
The Children at the Gate, Harcourt, 1964.

CONTRIBUTOR

Don M. Wolfe, editor, *New Voices 2: American Writing Today,* Hendricks House, 1955.
Charles I. Glicksberg, editor, *New Voices 3: American Writing Today,* Hendricks House, 1958.
D. M. Wolfe, editor, *American Scene: New Voices,* Lyle Stuart, 1963.

MEDIA ADAPTATIONS: The Pawnbroker was filmed by Paramount in 1964.

SIDELIGHTS: Although Edward Lewis Wallant published only two novels during his life, and two more appeared posthumously, he achieved a reputation as "one of the most important figures among postwar Jewish writers in the United States," as David R. Mesher wrote in the *Dictionary of Literary Biography.* "Despite his small output," Thomas M. Lorch stated in the *Chicago Review,* "Wallant merits recognition as one of our outstanding contemporary novelists."

After working for several years as an advertising artist, Wallant turned to writing seriously at the age of thirty. From that time until his death at the age of thirty-six, Wallant produced the small body of work for which he is remembered. Speaking to *Library Journal* of his turn to literature, Wallant explained: "To say I *enjoy* writing would be less a mistake of degree than of species. I sweat and ache and writhe in my chair; it is decidedly *not* in the nature of a relaxing hobby. . . . I do not write to entertain myself or others (although there may sometimes happily *be* entertainment in my writing). I write to share my views and feelings of the lives of human beings. . . . However a writer can illuminate the human condition, so must he do it."

Wallant's first novel, *The Human Season,* appeared in 1960 and won the Harry and Ethel Daroff Memorial Fiction Award, an award since renamed in honor of Wallant himself. Telling the story of middle-aged plumber Joe Berman as he seeks to recover from his wife's recent death, *The Human Season* presents Berman's transition from bitterness and apathy to a renewed faith in God and humanity. Berman begins the novel cut off from the rest of the world and questioning God, but he ends the book by rejoining society and regaining his faith. Lorch found the book a suitable showcase for Wallant's abilities. "Wallant," he wrote, "immediately reveals himself as a highly skilled craftsman in *The Human Season*. He brings his characters alive, and by his selection of the most ordinary concrete details, gestures and actions he evokes a deeply moving human situation."

Several critics noted the similarity between Berman's story and that of the biblical tale of Job, who also doubted God's wisdom. The *Kirkus* reviewer called the novel "an absorbing portrait of a modern man and a compelling, compassionate retelling of the story of Job." Mesher saw the story of Job as "a parallel which Wallant skillfully develops into an underlying resonance, at times specifically referring to the biblical book." "Wallant's book," the *Time* critic believed, "is a tour de force: what might seem a hopeless tale impresses by the clarity of its compassion." Lorch concluded that "Wallant's fusion of memory, imagery and style renders *The Human Season* a beautifully poetic yet richly human novel."

It was with his second novel, *The Pawnbroker,* that Wallant established himself as a major new writer. The novel is set in a pawnshop in Harlem owned by Sol Nazerman, a concentration camp survivor. Nazerman survived the camp by suppressing his emotions and cutting himself off from others as much as possible. "The figure of the Pawnbroker looms through the work, a colossus of despair," Jonathan Baumbach stated in his *The Landscape of Nightmare: Studies in the Contemporary American Novel,* "carrying the burden of the world's horror in the dull pain of his spirit. He is an amazing characterization, one of the memorably dark heroes of our fiction."

Nazerman undergoes an emotional reawakening when his young assistant is accidentally killed during a robbery attempt. "In crying for his assistant," Baumbach wrote, "[Nazerman] is able at last to mourn for the death of his family, for all his losses, for all his dead. In discovering the shock of loss, he discovers the redemptive and agonizing wonder of love." David Boroff of the *Saturday Review* found that "the pawnbroker's return to the emotionally-living is not entirely convincing, nor is the somewhat ambiguous sacrifice of his assistant. But there can be no gainsaying the power of this remorselessly honest book. . . . Wallant is a gifted writer who probes with a kind of troubled tenderness into pools of human darkness."

Critical praise for *The Pawnbroker* often spoke of its great emotional power and stirring testimony to the importance and dignity of human life. "Nazerman's emotional resurrection, limited as it seems to be, is a powerful expression of the author's ultimate faith in humanity," Mesher maintained. Boroff described *The Pawnbroker* as "an ambitious, unparochial novel that says something about man's responsibility to man. . . . It is consistently absorbing, highly serious, and often moving." The *Kirkus* reviewer found it "an unforgettable, raw, horrifying portrait of man's inhumanity to man." The *Time* critic was especially drawn to Nazerman, "a creature of fascinating complexity. As the centerpiece of a flawed book, he is that literary rarity—the character whose sorrows seem as real as the reader's own."

With the success of *The Pawnbroker,* Wallant was able to leave his position at an advertising agency. He and his family spent most of 1962 traveling in Europe, where Wallant worked on his two final novels, *The Tenants of Moonbloom* and *The Children at the Gate.* Upon his return to the United States in the fall of 1962, Wallant submitted *The Tenants of Moonbloom* to his publisher and was working on the last rewrite of *The Children at the Gate.*

This planned revision was never completed. On December 5, 1962, Wallant died of a ruptured aneurysm at the age of thirty-six.

The Tenants of Moonbloom was published in 1963. Described as a "comic masterpiece" by Leo Gurko in *Twentieth Century Literature,* the novel revolves around landlord Norman Moonbloom and his quixotic attempts to make the necessary repairs to the tenement buildings he manages. Moonbloom imagines that these repairs will somehow change the lives of his poor tenants as well. As do the characters in Wallant's previous novels, Moonbloom undergoes an emotional transformation. "In the tenements," Lorch explained, "Moonbloom is brought face to face with humanity. His awakening develops almost naturally, even inevitably, from this confrontation." Moonbloom's moment of revelation leads him to embrace "Love, Courage and Delusion." S. P. Ryan of *Best Sellers* called *The Tenants of Moonbloom* "a novel of power and strength" which displays "a genuine respect for the human condition." The *Time* critic believed that "no one since Nathanael West has written better of the rootlessness of metropolitan life."

Wallant's final novel, *The Children at the Gate,* appeared in 1964. It tells the story of nineteen-year-old Angelo De Marco, who works at his uncle's drugstore and makes the deliveries to a local hospital. At the hospital he meets Sammy, an orderly whose ultimate suicide leads Angelo to break out of his emotional isolation. The book is, R. K. Burns wrote in *Library Journal,* "a fine story, unpretentious and courageous, a small masterpiece." Baumbach, writing for the *Saturday Review,* called it "a beautifully written short novel of almost unbearable impact." But not all critics were so generous in their appraisal. Mesher believed that *The Children at the Gate* was "Wallant's weakest" novel, while Lorch thought it "an interesting but inferior reworking of *The Pawnbroker.*"

"Each of Wallant's novels," Lorch explained, "describes a form of rebirth, the process of returning to or achieving an affirmation of life." Joe Berman of *The Human Season* regains his faith; Sol Nazerman in *The Pawnbroker* undergoes a rebirth of his emotions; Norman Moonbloom in *The Tenants of Moonbloom* experiences a revelation about humanity; and Angelo De Marco of *The Children at the Gate* breaks out of his isolation. "All of Wallant's novels," Baumbach stated, "have a similar, ritual structure: a man cut off from the source of himself, in a delicate truce with the nightmare of survival, slowly, terrifyingly, at the risk of everything, rediscovers the possibility of feeling." Charles Alva Hoyt, in his study *Minor American Novelists,* concluded that all of Wallant's characters "initiate or take part in certain symbolic acts which eventually result in freeing them for the kind of deep human relationship which their author demands for all men."

This recurring portrayal of an emotional resurrection amid a usually squalid urban landscape makes Wallant's novels important, David W. Pitre wrote in the *Dictionary of Literary Biography,* "because they defiantly affirm that modern man need not and must not despair, for life, with all its vicissitudes, offers so much." Similarly, Gurko found that "dominating the field of [Wallant's] art is his vision of the great city, at once sickeningly ugly and disintegrative, yet in its swarming vitality holding forth the promise of some soul-stirring, spellbinding rejuvenation." M. F. Schulz of *Critique* claimed that "in all four of Wallant's novels, the dead are resurrected, the sleeping awakened, the unborn born. . . . [Wallant's novels] are *bildungsroman* of a special sort. Wallant deals with the coming of age, not in years, not in conventional education and acceptance of society's manners and rules, but in sensibility. It is the terrors of growth and change in the human heart . . . that are all important to him."

BIOGRAPHICAL/CRITICAL SOURCES:

BOOKS

Baumbach, Jonathan, *The Landscape of Nightmare: Studies in the Contemporary American Novel,* New York University Press, 1965.

Contemporary Literary Criticism, Gale (Detroit), Volume 5, 1976; Volume 10, 1979.

Dictionary of Literary Biography, Gale, Volume 2: *American Novelists since World War II,* 1978; Volume 28: *Twentieth Century American-Jewish Fiction Writers,* 1984.

Galloway, David, *Edward Lewis Wallant,* Twayne, 1979.

Hoyt, Charles Alva, *Minor American Novelists,* Southern Illinois University Press, 1970.

Malin, Max F., editor, *Radical Sophistication: Studies in Contemporary Jewish American Novelists,* Ohio University Press, 1969.

PERIODICALS

America, September 14, 1963.

Best Sellers, August 15, 1963; March 15, 1964.

Chicago Review, Volume 19, number 2, 1967.

Critique, Volume X, number 3, 1968; Volume XII, number 2, 1970.

Kirkus, June 15, 1960; June 1, 1961.

Library Journal, June 1, 1960; August, 1960; February 15, 1964.

Literary Review, winter, 1974.

New York Times Book Review, September 11, 1960; September 3, 1961; August 18, 1963; March 8, 1964.

Renascence, winter, 1972.

Saturday Review, August 26, 1961; February 29, 1964.

Time, September 5, 1960; August 18, 1961; August 16, 1963.

Twentieth Century Literature, October, 1974.

Yale University Library Gazette, Volume 56, numbers 1-2, 1981.

*　　*　　*

WALLEY, Byron
See CARD, Orson Scott

*　　*　　*

WALPOLE, Hugh (Seymour) 1884-1941

PERSONAL: Born March 13, 1884, in Auckland, New Zealand; died June 1, 1941, in Cumberland, England; son of George Henry Somerset (a clergyman) and Mildred Barham Walpole. *Education:* King's School, Canterbury; Emmanuel College, Cambridge University.

ADDRESSES: Agent—c/o Macmillan and Co. Ltd., London.

CAREER: Lay missioner on the staff of Mersey Mission to Seamen and teacher, 1906-09; writer, 1909-1941; Russian Red Cross, 1914-16.

AWARDS, HONORS: Georgian Medal for service with Russian Red Cross, 1918; Commander of the British Empire, 1918; knighted, 1937.

WRITINGS:

Maradick at Forty: A Transition, Smith, Elder, 1910.

(Editor) *Essays and Studies,* English Association (London), 1910.

Mr. Perrin and Mr. Traill: A Tragi-Comedy, Mills & Boon (London), 1911; published as *The Gods and Mr. Perrin: A Tragi-Comedy,* Century (New York City), 1911.

The Prelude to Adventure, Mills & Boon, 1912, Century, 1912.

Fortitude, Being a True and Faithful Account of the Education of an Explorer, Secker (London), 1913, Doran, 1913.

The Duchess of Wrexe, Her Decline and Death: A Romantic Commentary, Secker, 1914, Doran, 1914.

The Wooden Horse, Smith, Elder (London), 1915, Doran (New York City), 1915.

The Golden Scarecrow, Cassell (London), 1915, Doran, 1915.

The Dark Forest, Secker, 1916, Doran, 1916.

Joseph Conrad, Nisbet (London), 1916, Holt (New York City), 1917, revised edition published by Nisbet, 1924.

The Green Mirror: A Quiet Story, Doran, 1917, Macmillan (London), 1918.

(Author of preface) Denis Norman Garstin, *The Shilling Soldiers,* Hodder and Stoughton (London), 1918.

The Secret City, Macmillan, 1919, Doran, 1919.

Jeremy, Cassell, 1919, Doran, 1919.

The Art of James Branch Cabell, McBride (New York City), 1920.

The Captives, Macmillan, 1920, Doran, 1920.

The Thirteen Travellers, Hutchinson (London), 1921, Doran, 1920.

The Young Enchanted: A Romantic Story, Macmillan, 1921, Doran, 1921.

A Hugh Walpole Anthology, London and Toronto, 1921.

(Author of introduction) *The Plays of Hubert Henry Davies,* Chatto & Windus (London), 1921.

(Author of introduction) Sinclair Lewis, *Babbitt,* 1922.

The Cathedral, Macmillan, 1922, Doran, 1922.

Jeremy and Hamlet: A Chronicle of Certain Incidents in the Lives of a Boy, a Dog, and a Country Town, Cassell, 1923, Doran, 1923.

(Author of introduction) Hugh Lofting, *The Story of Doctor Dolittle,* 1923.

The Crystal Box, R. Maclehose (Glasgow), 1924.

The Old Ladies, Macmillan, 1924, Doran, 1924.

The English Novel: Some Notes on Its Evolution, Cambridge University Press (Cambridge), 1924.

Portrait of a Man with Red Hair: A Romantic Macabre, Macmillan, 1925, Doran, 1925.

Harmer John: An Unworldly Story, Macmillan, 1926, Doran, 1926.

Reading: An Essay, Jarrolds (London), 1926, Doran, 1926.

(Author of introduction) Boufflers, Stanislas Jean de, *The Queen of Golconda, and Other Tales,* translated by Eric Sutton, Chapman & Hall (London), 1926, McBride, 1926.

Jeremy at Crale: His Friends, His Ambitions and His One Great Enemy, Cassell, 1927, Doran, 1927.

Anthony Trollope, Macmillan, 1928, Macmillan (New York City), 1928.

My Religious Experience, Benn (London), 1928.

The Silver Thorn: A Book of Stories, London, 1928, Doubleday (New York City), 1928.

Wintersmoon: Passages in the Lives of Two Sisters, Janet and Rosalind Grandison, Macmillan, 1928, Doubleday, 1928.

(With J. B. Priestley) *Farthing Hall,* Macmillan, 1929, Doubleday, 1929.

Hans Frost, Macmillan, 1929.

Rogue Herries, Macmillan, 1930, Doubleday, 1930.

Above the Dark Circus: An Adventure, Macmillan, 1931, published as *Above the Dark Tumult: An Adventure,* Doubleday, 1931.

Judith Paris, Macmillan, 1931, Doubleday, 1931.

(Author of introduction) A. M. M. Douton, *A Book with Seven Seals,* 1931.

The Apple Trees: Four Reminiscences, Golden Cockerel Press (Waltham, Saint Lawrence), 1932.

The Fortress, Macmillan, 1932, Doubleday, 1932.

A Letter to a Modern Novelist, Hogarth (London), 1932.

(Editor) *The Waverley Pageant: Best Passages from the Novels of Sir Walter Scott,* Eyre & Spottiswoode (London), 1932.

All Souls' Night: A Book of Stories, Macmillan, 1933, Doubleday, 1933.

Vanessa, Macmillan, 1933, Doubleday, 1933.

The Young Huntress (drama), produced 1933.

Extracts from a Diary, Maclehose, 1934.

Captain Nicholas: A Modern Comedy, Macmillan, 1934, Doubleday, 1934.

(Editor, with Wilfred Partington, and author of introduction) *The Gateway of Literature: Five Centuries of Great Tales of Youth,* Daily Express Publications (London), 1934.

Cathedral Carol Service, Faber and Faber (London), 1934.

The Cumberland Edition (collected works), 20 vols., Macmillan, 1934-40.

The Inquisitor, Macmillan, 1935, Doubleday, 1935.

(Contributor, with Clemence Dane and others) *Claude Houghton: Appreciations,* Heinemann (London), 1935.

A Prayer for My Son, Macmillan, 1936, Doubleday, 1936.

(Author of introduction) George H. Borrow, *Lavengro,* 1936.

The Cathedral: A Play in Three Acts, Macmillan, 1937.

John Cornelius: His Life and Adventures, Macmillan, 1937, Doubleday, 1937.

(Editor) *A Second Century of Creepy Stories,* Hutchinson, 1937.

(Editor, with Alec Waugh and others) *The Nonesuch Dickens,* 1937.

Head in Green Bronze, and Other Stories, Macmillan, 1938, Doubleday, 1938.

The Joyful Delaneys, Macmillan, 1938, Doubleday, 1938.

(Author of introduction) Thomas Gray, *Elegy Written in a Country Church-Yard,* 1938.

The Haxtons: A Play in Three Acts, Deane (London), Baker International Play Bureau (Boston), 1939.

The Sea Tower, Macmillan, 1939, Doubleday, 1939.

The Herries Chronicle (includes *Rogue Herries, Judith Paris, the Fortress,* and *Vanessa*), Macmillan, 1939.

Roman Fountain, Macmillan, 1940, Doubleday, 1940.

The Bright Pavilions, Macmillan, 1940, Doubleday, 1940.

A Note by Hugh Walpole on the Origins of the Herries Chronicle; Together with a Bibliography, Notes on "The Bright Pavilions" and the First Four volumes of The Herries Chronicle, and Photographic Views of the Author's Cumberland Home, Doubleday, 1940.

The Blind Man's House, Macmillan, 1941, Doubleday, 1941.

Open Letter of an Optimist, Macmillan, 1941.

The Jeremy Stories: Jeremy, Jeremy and Hamlet, Jeremy at Crale, Macmillan, 1941.

The Killer and the Slain: A Strange Story, Macmillan, 1942, Doubleday, 1942.

Katherine Christian, Doubleday, 1943, Macmillan, 1944.

Mr. Huffam and Other Stories, Macmillan, 1948.

Contributor of reviews and fiction to the *Criterion, London Standard, Colophon, Bookman, English Review,* and other periodicals.

SIDELIGHTS: Hugh Walpole was among England's most popular novelists writing just before World War II. His skill at painting the settings of his works, his gift for interesting plots, and his accessibility as a lecturer and public figure contributed to his wide readership in the United Kingdom and North America. Many readers preferred the familiarity of Walpole's traditional style to the literary experiments of Virginia Woolf, James Joyce, and other modernist writers.

The son of a cleric, Walpole was born in Auckland, New Zealand, moved to England at an early age, and attended school in several towns that provided scenes for his books. After studying for the clergy, he rejected his father's vocation, feeling drawn to writing. However, Walpole examined the nature of God and humanity throughout his work, most notably in a story collection, *The Golden Scarecrow,* which presents a Wordsworthian vision of humankind as being born "trailing clouds of glory" but losing the memory of God ("who is our home") with the passing of years and the attainment of jaded experience.

Walpole's first novel, *The Wooden Horse* (1909) barely repaid the cost of having it typed. His first success was *Mr. Perrin and Mr. Traill,* published in 1911. From then on his works were consistently popular. Henry James provided Walpole with guidance and encouragement during the younger writer's early years of literary effort. *The Duchess of Wrexe* (1914) and *The Green Mirror* (1917), of all Walpole's books, most clearly demonstrate James's influence, which was to some extent sensed by Virginia Woolf in her review of *The Green Mirror.* In an unsigned notice published in the *Times Literary Supplement,* Woolf praised the author's skill at apprehending the small, mundane details of everyday life amid an English culture fast vanishing in the cataclysm of World War I: "We have seldom met a better account of a long Sunday in the country and the cold supper with which it ends. On this occasion the servants were out, and there was no soup. These are the small things in which Mr. Walpole is invariably happy, and in our view it is no disparagement to a writer to say that his gift is for the small things rather than for the large. . . . If you are faithful with the details the large effects will grow inevitably out of those very details."

The elements of several nineteenth-century styles appear in Walpole's work; Dostoevsky, Trollope, Dickens, and Hardy all influenced him. Most important, however, is the romanticism of Sir Walter Scott, which pervades Walpole's entire canon, except for his earliest efforts. Of his more than three dozen novels, *Mr. Perrin and Mr. Traill, The Cathedral* (1922), *Rogue Herries* (1930), and *Judith Paris* (1931) are considered among his best books, while *Fortitude* (1913), *The Old Ladies* (1924), and the three *Jeremy* books have been among his most popular.

Although Walpole's works were hugely popular, major critics of the day, many of them proponents of modernism, disliked Walpole's works, objecting primarily to the author's traditional style and themes. Furthermore, they criticized the vagueness of his philosophical passages and the carelessness of his writing. Walpole's reputation with critics suffered throughout the 1930s especially, after Somerset Maugham, in his *Cakes and Ale,* created a mocking portrait of Walpole in the character Alroy Kear, a romantic literary lightweight and opportunist. It is true that through his frequent lectures and autograph sessions Walpole sought to increase his popularity and prestige as a writer, and succeeded. But however much his reputation may have been inflated, his possessed strong talents nonetheless, as James, Woolf, and Joseph Conrad, among many others recognized. Among them were his versatility in describing varied settings and characters and an ability to unobtrusively give eternal and spiritual import to commonplace scenes. An additional strength was his proficiency in using disparate novel forms. *The Herries Chronicle* (1939)—comprising *Rogue Herries, Judith Paris, The Fortress,* and *Vanessa* (1933)—which sparked a resurgence of interest in historical novels during the 1930s, displays Walpole's boldest use of a neglected form.

Interest in Walpole's books, intimately tied to the author himself, dropped off sharply after his death in 1941. The advent of World War II and subsequent changes in literary styles also contributed to a decline in critical and popular attention. Those who venture to read his books today may well find truth in his friend Joseph Conrad's assessment: "We see Mr. Walpole grappling with the truth of things spiritual and material with his characteristic earnestness, and we can discern the characteristics of this acute and sympathetic explorer of human nature: His love of adventure and the serious audacity he brings to the task of recording the changes of human fate and the movements of human emotion, in the quiet backwaters or in the tumultuous open streams of existence."

BIOGRAPHICAL/CRITICAL SOURCES:

BOOKS

Beach, Joseph Warren, *The Twentieth Century Novel: Studies in Technique,* Appleton-Century-Crofts, 1932.
Braybrooke, Patrick, *Philosophies in Modern Fiction,* Daniel, 1929.
Chesterton, G. K., *The Collected Works of G. K. Chesterton, Vol. 34: The Illustrated London News, 1926-1928,* Ignatius Press, 1991.
Conrad, Joseph, Arnold Bennett, and Joseph Hergesheimer, *Hugh Walpole: Appreciations,* edited by Grant Overton, Doran, 1923.
Dane, Clemence, *Tradition and Hugh Walpole,* Doubleday, 1929.
Hart-Davis, Rupert, *Hugh Walpole: A Biography,* Macmillan, 1952.
James, Henry, *Notes on Novelists with Some Other Notes,* Scribner, 1914.
Steele, Elizabeth, *Hugh Walpole,* Twayne, 1972.
Steen, Marguerite, *Hugh Walpole: A Study,* Doubleday, 1933.
Strong, L. A. G., *Personal Remarks,* Liveright, 1953.

PERIODICALS

Athenaeum, June 12, 1909, p. 697; October 15, 1920, pp. 519-20.
Bookman (New York City), January, 1923, pp. 625-28.
English Journal, September, 1928, pp. 529-36.
Nation & The Athenaeum, July 16, 1921, pp. 584-85.
Spectator, September 22, 1939, p. 420.
Times Literary Supplement, January 24, 1918, p. 43.

* * *

WAMBAUGH, Joseph (Aloysius, Jr.) 1937-

PERSONAL: Born January 22, 1937, in East Pittsburgh, PA; son of Joseph A. (a police officer) and Anne (Malloy) Wambaugh; married Dee Allsup, November 26, 1955; children: Mark (deceased), David, Jeannette. *Education:* Chaffey College, A.A., 1958; California State College (now University), Los Angeles, B.A., 1960, M.A., 1968. *Religion:* Roman Catholic.

ADDRESSES: Home—70-555 Thunderbird Mesa, Rancho Mirage, CA 92270.

CAREER: Los Angeles Police Department, Los Angeles, CA, 1960-74, began as patrolman, became detective sergeant; writer, 1971-. Creator and consultant, *The Blue Knight,* Columbia Broadcasting Company (CBS-TV), and *Police Story,* National Broadcasting Company (NBC-TV), 1973-77. *Military service:* U.S. Marine Corps, 1954-57.

AWARDS, HONORS: Edgar Allan Poe Award, special award for nonfiction, Mystery Writers of America, 1974, for *The Onion Field;* Edgar Allan Poe Award, best motion picture, 1981, for *The Black Marble;* Rodolfo Walsh Prize for investigative journalism, International Association of Crime Writers, 1989, for *Lines and Shadows.*

WRITINGS:

NOVELS

The New Centurions, Atlantic-Little Brown, 1971.
The Blue Knight, Atlantic-Little Brown, 1972.
The Choirboys, Delacorte, 1975.
The Black Marble (also see below), Delacorte, 1978.
The Glitter Dome (also see below), Morrow, 1981.
The Delta Star, Morrow, 1983.
The Secrets of Harry Bright, Morrow, 1985.
The Golden Orange, Morrow, 1990.
Fugitive Nights (also see below), Morrow, 1992.
Finnegan's Week, Morrow, 1993, large print edition, Thorndike, 1994.
Floaters, Bantam, 1996.

NONFICTION

The Onion Field (also see below), Delacorte, 1973.
Lines and Shadows, Morrow, 1984.
Echoes in the Darkness (also see below), edited by Jeanne Bernkopf, Morrow, 1987.
The Blooding, edited by Bernkopf, Morrow, 1989.

OTHER

The Onion Field (screenplay), Avco Embassy, 1979.
The Black Marble (screenplay), Avco Embassy, 1980.
The Glitter Dome (teleplay), Home Box Office, 1984.
Echoes in the Darkness (miniseries teleplay), CBS-TV, 1987.
Fugitive Knights (teleplay; based on the novel *Fugitive Nights*), NBC-TV, 1993.

MEDIA ADAPTATIONS: The New Centurions was directed by Richard Fleischer and released by Columbia Pictures, 1972; *The Choirboys* was directed by Robert Aldrich and released by Universal Studios, 1977; *The Blue Knight* was produced by NBC-TV as a television miniseries starring William Holden, and then by CBS-TV as a regular series with George Kennedy in the title role, both 1973.

SIDELIGHTS: Though Joseph Wambaugh spent ten years with the Los Angeles Police Department before publishing his first novel, *The New Centurions,* he is more than just a cop-turned-writer, and his novels are much more than just "cop stories": they have effectively redefined the genre of police drama and the way police officers are depicted therein. Wambaugh's cops are frightened, profane, violent, and fallible, forced to protect citizens who resent them. His writing—both fiction and non-fiction—

"takes us into the minds and hearts, into the nerves and (sometimes literally) into the guts of other human beings," claims Thomas Fleming in the *New York Times Book Review.* "It achieves a mixture of empathy and objectivity that creates genuine understanding." His ability to evoke sympathy for crude and often distasteful characters has made Wambaugh popular with both readers and critics. "Let us dispel forever the notion that Mr. Wambaugh is only a former cop who happens to write books," comments Evan Hunter in the *New York Times Book Review.* "This would be tantamount to saying that Jack London was first and foremost a sailor. Mr. Wambaugh is, in fact, a writer of genuine power, style, wit and originality, who has chosen to write about the police in particular as a means of expressing his views on society in general."

Wambaugh's reputation as a powerful writer was established with his first four books: *The New Centurions, The Blue Knight, The Onion Field,* and *The Choirboys.* The first two were penned while Wambaugh was still a full-time police officer, and while in retrospect he often dismisses them as his "moonlighting" novels, they instantly shattered the preconceptions many readers had of cops. Published in 1971, *The New Centurions* follows four young men through the Police Academy, onto the streets of Los Angeles, and ultimately to the battlefield of the 1965 riots in Watts. Along the way, the reader witnesses how idealistic cadets become callous and distant, feeling that they have been cast—against their wills— in the role of civilization's front line. John Greenway, writing in *National Review,* hails Wambaugh's first novel as "incomparably the best revelation of the lives and souls of policemen ever written."

Whereas *The New Centurions* depicts the beginnings of a police officer's career, 1972's *The Blue Knight* depicts the end. The protagonist, Officer Bumper Morgan, spends his last three days on the force in much the same way he had spent the previous twenty years: accepting free meals, leaning on "stoolies," taking liberties with certain obliging females, and occasionally making an arrest. David K. Jeffrey, writing in the *Dictionary of Literary Biography,* describes Morgan as "a fallible human being, fat, crude, and stubborn, [who] has been a cop for so long he now believes he *is* the law. He believes, too, that the legal system often corrupts and thwarts justice; he therefore 'bends the law' to ensure that criminals do not go unpunished." In the end, Morgan perjures himself during a trial to obtain a conviction. *The Blue Knight* "is an effective study of the ways in which police work can corrupt and change policemen," Jeffrey continues. The *New York Times's* Eric Pace writes that, despite some flaws, "*The Blue Knight* abounds in vivid vignettes of police life and the Los Angeles streets. It effectively conveys the loneliness of an aging man who puts too much of himself into his work." Pace goes on to predict: "Its warty portrayal of the police will make it controversial in some quarters."

Wambaugh's "moonlighting" novels did, in fact, create something of a stir, particularly in the offices of the Los Angeles Police Department (L.A.P.D.). Wambaugh's superiors were not pleased that the young officer had written an inside view of their department, let alone one that featured officers who accepted gratuities and committed perjury. Wambaugh recalls in a *Publishers Weekly* interview the reaction of his superior officers: "The problem arose because [my novels] depicted cops as human beings, complete with rotten moods and frailties, and not as the robots people are accustomed to seeing on television shows about policemen. . . . I could see the administration being mad if I were giving away secrets, but I'm not: there are no secrets to

reveal." Still, pressure from superiors and his increasing celebrity forced Wambaugh to take an extended leave from the L.A.P.D., during which time he researched and wrote what would become his most important work.

In 1963 two young Los Angeles policemen, officers Ian Campbell and Karl Hettinger, pulled over a suspicious-looking car; the men inside, a pair of small-time criminals who had spent the evening robbing liquor stores, overpowered the policemen and drove them, at gunpoint, to a remote onion field, where Campbell was executed. Hettinger escaped, and the two men were apprehended the next day. Though they were soon brought to trial and convicted of murder, the introduction of the Escobedo and Miranda laws (designed to protect the rights of criminals) delayed their executions; the ensuing appeals and retrials dragged on for seven years, making theirs the longest criminal proceeding in California history. In the meantime, Hettinger suffered a nervous breakdown, became suicidal, and was thrown off the force for shoplifting. He finally became a farmer, working just a few miles from that same onion field.

Wambaugh transformed the story of officers Campbell and Hettinger into his 1974 book *The Onion Field.* It was his first work of nonfiction, based entirely upon interviews, case records, and some 45,000 pages of court transcriptions. An officer during the time of the murder, Wambaugh often cites the Hettinger case as his motivation for becoming a writer. He explains in *Playboy:* "I feel I was put on earth to write this story, and I've never had that feeling before or since. Nothing could ever stop me from writing *The Onion Field.* I felt it was my sole reason for living, and that no one else understood or knew the ramifications of the onion-field murder."

James Lardner of the *New York Times Book Review* calls *The Onion Field* "a perfect double helix of a narrative in which the harrowing stories of two policemen and two criminals wound around each other, replicating what is laughably called the criminal justice system." The novel's principle theme is guilt and punishment: for the murderers, who feel no guilt at all, punishment is slow in coming; however, for Hettinger, who has assumed the blame for his partner's death, punishment in the form of ostracization is swift. Jeffrey, quoting Wambaugh, explains: "Policemen believe that 'no man-caused calamity happens by chance, that there is always a step that should have been taken, would have been taken if the [officer] had been alert, cautious, brave, aggressive—in short, if he'd been like a prototype policeman. . . .' By this measure, Hettinger was a failure who shared responsibility for the murder of Campbell just as surely as did [the murderers]."

"Very little in Wambaugh's first two novels prepares one for the scabrous humor and ferocity of *The Choirboys,*" notes John Leonard of Wambaugh's third novel in the *New York Times Book Review.* According to a reviewer for *Atlantic Monthly,* "Mr. Wambaugh appears to have thrown into this novel everything that loyalty and discretion deleted from his work while he remained a member of the Los Angeles Police Department. The action is constant and the dialogue is tough. The writing has a careless barbarity that may be deliberate, for Mr. Wambaugh is explaining that police work is a one-way ticket to hell."

The Choirboys is the story of ten Los Angeles cops who alleviate the pain and stress of their job through a ritual called "choir practice"—debaucherous after-hours meetings in MacArthur Park, filled with aimless violence and alcoholic howling. Jeffrey explains: "The manic hilarity and drunkenness at their meetings serve the choirboys as defense mechanism against full consciousness of the fact that the ordinary people they protect are, by and large, barbaric savages, capable of any horror." The tone of *The Choirboys* is dark and satiric, told in a series of comic, yet ominous, vignettes. In this way, Wambaugh's novel has been compared to Joseph Heller's *Catch-22*—a work Wambaugh cites as a major influence. He recalls in the *Chicago Tribune:* "After [*The Onion Field*] I decided to try something very different, to use black comedy to deal with serious themes. And Heller enabled me to find my voice."

In retrospect, Wambaugh often describes the writing of *The Choirboys* as the turning point in his career, the place where he "found his voice." The novels that followed—among them *The Black Marble, The Glitter Dome,* and *The Golden Orange*—have maintained the gallows humor established in *The Choirboys.* Richard Eder observes in the *Los Angeles Times Book Review:* "Wambaugh's cops, like the soldiers in *Catch-22,* are men and women in a frenzy, zany grotesques made that way by the outrageous nature of the things they deal with," while the *New York Times*'s John Leonard proclaims: "There is more absurd action in a chapter of Wambaugh than there is in the entire collected works of George V. Higgins." Digby Diehl, looking back on Wambaugh's career in the *Detroit News,* calls the ex-cop "a good writer who becomes better with each successive book."

In 1993's *Finnegan's Week* Wambaugh portrays two main characters: Finbar Finnegan, a San Diego detective who is in pursuit of a stolen fifty-five-gallon container of a lethal substance called guthion, and "Bad Dog," a female police detective who is attempting to solve the theft of 2,000 pairs of shoes from a Navy warehouse. Noting that the two unusual crimes are found to be interrelated, Cassandra Smith of *Los Angeles Times Book Review* observes that "Wambaugh uses his talent to entangle his characters in a farcical web of circumstances." Reviewers also emphasize Wambaugh's explosive style in the novel. Jack Olsen of the *New York Times Book Review,* for example, comments: "[Wambaugh] punches up his text with italics, exclamation points and other typographic firecrackers. . . . And yet it works."

Wambaugh's subsequent novel, *Floaters,* depicts the attempt of San Diego police detectives to solve a murder that takes place against the backdrop of the America's Cup sailing competition. Reviewers note that two plots are interwoven to heighten the novel's suspense, the first being the scheme of Ambrose Lutterworth, Jr., the keeper of the cup, to sabotage New Zealand's entry in the race. Lutterworth solicits the help of a prostitute, Blaze Duvall, in carrying out his plan, but Blaze mysteriously disappears after her call-girl friend Dawn Coyote turns up dead. Critics emphasized Wambaugh's characteristically raw language and energetic style in portraying the efforts of two cops, Fortney and Leeds, to solve the double mystery.

Reviewers also continue to praise Wambaugh's nonfiction works, which include *Lines and Shadows, Echoes in the Darkness,* and *The Blooding.* Whether examining the chaotic relations between the police and illegal aliens along the California-Mexico border, as he does in *Lines and Shadows,* or tracing the search for a brutal English killer, as in *The Blooding,* Wambaugh has proven his ability to create suspense and drama with accounts of actual events. While some critics suggest that Wambaugh excels in writing fiction rather than nonfiction, most agree that Wambaugh's books make for absorbing reading. Writing in the *New York Times Book Review,* Walter Walker called *The Blooding* "a well-written, meticulously researched, nontechnical tour de

force," and the *Washington Post Book World*'s Douglas E. Winter hails it as "a blessed respite from the lubricious leers of the tabloid school of crime journalism."

Before *The New Centurions, The Blue Knight* and the highly praised television series *Police Story* (for which Wambaugh wrote and consulted), law enforcement officers were usually presented as cool and cerebral, like *Dragnet*'s Joe Friday, or as fearless superhero-detectives, like *The Untouchables*'s Elliot Ness, who crash into a villain's hideout with both guns blaring. "Generally the cops in my books don't perform heroic acts the likes of which will earn them a Medal of Valor," Wambaugh explains in the *Los Angeles Times.* "No, the heroic acts they perform are just coping with their character disorders or neuroses or whatever, and continuing to do the job with the worst of people. They don't all make it. . . . But while they cope, they're heroic to me."

BIOGRAPHICAL/CRITICAL SOURCES:

BOOKS

Contemporary Literary Criticism, Gale (Detroit), Volume 3, 1975; Volume 18, 1981.
Dictionary of Literary Biography, Volume 6: *American Novelists Since World War II, Second Series,* Gale, 1980.
Van Dover, J. Kenneth, *Centurions, Knights, and Other Cops: The Police Novels of Joseph Wambaugh,* Brownstone Books, 1995.

PERIODICALS

America, January 19, 1974, p. 38; May 22, 1981, p. 549; May 19, 1984, p. 386.
Atlantic Monthly, October, 1973, p. 129; November, 1975, p. 124; August, 1981, p. 88; April, 1984, p. 149.
Best Sellers, January 15, 1971, p. 438; February 15, 1972, p. 518; October 15, 1973, p. 323; February, 1976, p. 334.
Chicago Tribune, September 28, 1979, p. 15; March 10, 1980; June 17, 1981; February 8, 1987, p. 3; February 5, 1989, p. 3.
Detroit Free Press, March 29, 1989.
Detroit News, July 12, 1981, p. E2; October 20, 1985.
Globe and Mail (Toronto), March 10, 1984; February 14, 1987; March 4, 1989.
Insight, June 4, 1990, p. 63.
Kirkus Reviews, March 1, 1996, p. 330.
Los Angeles Times, March 9, 1983, p. 12; August 5, 1987; May 4, 1990, p. E1.
Los Angeles Times Book Review, March 6, 1983; February 19, 1984, p. 3; November 10, 1985, p. 2; March 1, 1987, p. 3; February 5, 1989, p. 2; April 29, 1990, p. 4; June 9, 1991, p. 14; January 5, 1992, p. 1; December 26, 1993, p. 7.
Maclean's, July 8, 1996, p. 46.
National Review, March 9, 1971, p. 271; April 2, 1976, pp. 343-44.
Newsweek, May 2, 1983, p. 78; February 6, 1984, p. 80; March 2, 1987, p. 76; January 20, 1992, p. 61.
New Yorker, April 1, 1972, p. 105; August 31, 1981, p. 108; May 9, 1983, p. 136; November 18, 1985, p. 177.
New York Times, January 22, 1971, p. 37; September 7, 1973, p. 33; January 8, 1978; January 12, 1978, p. 25; September 19, 1979; September 24, 1979, p. C14; October 9, 1979; March 7, 1980; June 22, 1981; February 23, 1987, p. 15; June 13, 1996, p. B2.
New York Times Book Review, January 31, 1971, p. 34; February 13, 1972, p. 4; September 2, 1973, p. 5; December 2, 1973, p. 74; November 2, 1975, p. 6; January 8, 1978, p. 11; June 28, 1981, p. 3; March 20, 1983, p. 12; January 8, 1984, p. 34;

February 5, 1984, p. 12; October 6, 1985, p. 11; March 1, 1987, p. 12; February 19, 1989; May 6, 1990, pp. 7-9; May 19, 1991, p. 42; February 2, 1992, p. 12; October 17, 1993, p. 38; June 9, 1996, p. 29.

People Weekly, January 17, 1994, p. 31; May 20, 1996, p. 40.

Playboy, July, 1979, p. 69; May, 1996, p. 28.

Publishers Weekly, August 23, 1971, pp. 33-35; January 3, 1972; July 23, 1973; September 1, 1975; July 12, 1976; April 22, 1996, p. 60.

Time, February 15, 1971, p. 82; February 28, 1972, p. 83; September 24, 1973, p. 126; June 8, 1981, p. 76; March 5, 1984, p. 84; October 28, 1985, p. 96; February 23, 1987, p. 75.

Times (London), June 6, 1987; February 18, 1989.

Times Literary Supplement, March 16, 1973, p. 303; November 1, 1974, p. 1220; April 9, 1976, p. 413.

Tribune Books (Chicago), June 13, 1982; March 27, 1983, p. 2; October 6, 1985; February 8, 1987, p. 3; February 5, 1989, p. 3; May 15, 1990, p. 6; May 26, 1991, p. 8; December 29, 1991, p. 6.

Wall Street Journal, February 16, 1984, p. 32; November 22, 1985, p. 28; March 19, 1987, p. 32; January 24, 1992, p. A12.

Washington Post, February 19, 1979; October 19, 1979, p. B1, B3, 31; June 30, 1981; April 1, 1983; March 6, 1984; September 30, 1985; February 12, 1987; April 17, 1990; December 31, 1991, p. C3.

Washington Post Book World, March 5, 1972, p. 6; September 2, 1973, p. 15; October 20, 1974, p. 4; October 3, 1976, p. F4; January 24, 1978; March 22, 1987, p. 8; March 19, 1989; December 29, 1991, p. 12.

West Coast Review of Books, March, 1978, p. 31; March, 1983, p. 41; March, 1984, p. 34; November, 1985, p. 23; number 2, 1987, p. 31.

*   *   *

WARNER, Sylvia (Constance) Ashton
See ASHTON-WARNER, Sylvia (Constance)

*   *   *

WARNER, Sylvia Townsend 1893-1978

PERSONAL: Born December 6, 1893, in Harrow, Middlesex, England; died May 1, 1978, in Maiden Newton, Dorsetshire, England; daughter of George Townsend (a schoolmaster) and Eleanor Mary (Hudleston) Warner. *Education:* Privately educated in England.

CAREER: Writer.

MEMBER: Royal Society of Literature (fellow), American Academy of Arts and Letters (honorary member), Rachel Carson Trust (sponsor).

AWARDS, HONORS: Prix Menton, 1968.

WRITINGS:

NOVELS

Lolly Willowes; or, The Loving Huntsman (Book-of-the-Month Club selection; also see below), Viking, 1926.

Mr. Fortune's Maggot (Literary Guild selection; also see below), Viking, 1927.

The True Heart, Viking, 1929.

Summer Will Show, Viking, 1936.

The Corner That Held Them, Viking, 1948.

The Flint Anchor, Viking, 1954.

Lolly Willowes, and Mr. Fortune's Maggot, Viking, 1966.

After the Death of Don Juan, introduction by Wendy Mulford, Virago, 1989.

STORY COLLECTIONS

Some World Far from Ours [and] *Stay, Corydon, Thou Swain,* Mathews, 1929.

Elinor Barley, Cresset Press, 1930.

A Moral Ending and Other Stories, Joiner & Steele, 1931.

The Salutation, Viking, 1932.

More Joy in Heaven and Other Stories, Cresset Press, 1935.

(With Graham Greene and James Laver) *Twenty-four Stories,* Cresset Press, 1939.

The Cat's Cradle Book, Viking, 1940.

A Garland of Straw: Twenty-eight Stories, Viking, 1943 (published in England as *A Garland of Straw and Other Stories,* Chatto & Windus, 1943).

The Museum of Cheats: Stories, Viking, 1947.

Winter in the Air and Other Stories, Chatto & Windus, 1955, Viking, 1956.

A Spirit Rises: Short Stories, Viking, 1962.

Swans on an Autumn River: Stories, Viking, 1966 (published in England as *A Stranger with a Bag and Other Stories,* Chatto & Windus, 1966).

The Innocent and the Guilty, Viking, 1971.

Kingdoms of Elfin, Viking, 1977.

One Thing Leading to Another: And Other Stories, edited by Susanna Pinney, Viking, 1984.

Selected Stories of Sylvia Townsend Warner, Viking, 1988.

POEMS

The Espalier, Viking, 1925.

Time Importuned, Viking, 1928.

Opus 7: A Poem, Viking, 1931.

Rainbow, Knopf, 1932.

(With Valentine Ackland) *Whether a Dove or Seagull,* Viking, 1933.

(With Reynolds Stone) *Boxwood,* Monotype Corp., 1958, edition, Chatto & Windus, 1960.

King Duffus and Other Poems, Clare, 1968.

Twelve Poems, Chatto & Windus, 1980.

Collected Poems, edited by Claire Harman, Viking, 1983.

NONFICTION

The Portrait of a Tortoise: Extracted from the Journals of Gilbert White, Chatto & Windus, 1946.

Somerset, Elek, 1949.

Jane Austen: 1775-1817, Longmans, Green, 1951, revised edition, 1957.

Sketches from Nature, Clare, 1963.

T. H. White: A Biography, J. Cape, 1967, Viking, 1968, Oxford University Press, 1989.

Scenes of Childhood, Viking, 1982.

Letters, edited by William Maxwell, Viking, 1983.

Sylvia and David: The Townsend Warner/Garnett Letters, selected and edited by Richard Garnett, Sinclair-Stevenson (London), 1994.

The Diaries of Sylvia Townsend Warner, edited by Claire Harman, Chatto & Windus, 1994.

TRANSLATOR

Marcel Proust, *By Way of Saint-Beuve,* Chatto & Windus, 1958, published as *On Art and Literature: 1896-1917,* Dell, 1964, published as *Marcel Proust on Art and Literature, 1896-1919,* Carroll & Graf, 1984.

Jeane Rene Huguenin, *A Place of Shipwreck,* Chatto & Windus, 1963.

EDITOR

(With others) *Tudor Church Music,* ten volumes, Oxford University Press, c. 1925-30.

The Weekend Dickens, MacLehose, 1932.

SIDELIGHTS: Sylvia Townsend Warner had what she once described as an "accidental career" as a writer. She began writing poetry, *Publishers Weekly* quoted her as claiming, because she was given some paper with a "particularly tempting surface," and only wrote her first novel, *Lolly Willowes; or, The Loving Huntsman,* because she "happened to find some very agreeable thin lined paper in a job lot." However she came by her career, once embarked on it Warner was quite prolific. She published some thirty-five books of fiction, nonfiction, and poetry.

Lolly Willowes, Mr. Fortune's Maggot, and *The True Heart*—Warner's first three novels—established her reputation as a fine prose stylist. "These three short novels, taken together," J. I. M. Stewart wrote in the *Times Literary Supplement,* "surely constitute one of the most notable achievements of English fiction in the 1920s." *Lolly Willowes,* a novel W. J. Strachan of *London Magazine* called Warner's "first masterpiece," has particularly garnered critical attention. It is the story of Laura Willowes, an English spinster who is unable to accept the conventional demands of her life and so makes a pact with the devil and becomes a witch. Willowes explained her unusual decision as a way "to have a life of one's own, not an existence doled out to you by others." This wish for independence stems from her awareness that "women have such vivid imaginations, and lead such dull lives." John Updike, writing in the *New Yorker,* maintained that the novel is "witty, eerie, tender but firm." Stewart found it "a moral fable, fully realized but sparely told." Warner's "sly and almost subdued comedy" reminded Edwin Clark of the *New York Times* of Jane Austen, while L. P. Hartley of *Saturday Review* thought the book "owes something to [David] Garnett in its conception and to [Daniel] Defoe in its execution." "It is quite simply and charmingly written," the *New Republic* critic believed, "with here and there stabs of genuine beauty and happy phrase." *Lolly Willowes* was the first selection of the newly formed Book-of-the-Month Club in 1926.

In her next two novels, Warner "moved from fantasy to realism," Thomas Lask of the *New York Times* noted, "and subtle social criticism could be found between the lines." This trend can be seen in *Mr. Fortune's Maggot,* the story of a homosexual relationship between an English missionary and a South Seas native. During his attempts to convert the humorous and naive people of a remote island, Reverend Timothy Fortune becomes more heathen himself. In the end, he decides to forego the chance to convert his lover and instead leaves the island. "When Mr. Fortune returns to 'the real world,'" Judith Gies wrote in the *New York Times Book Review,* "we grieve for him." The *Spectator* reviewer saw the possibility for a "good many interpretations of this book; one reader will say that it is an attack on foreign missions and conventional religion, another that it is a skit on the church's methods of salvation, a third that it is pure nonsense and a fourth that it is a sad story of man's disillusionment." Critics

generally praised the book, however they interpreted it. "The story," Christopher Morley commented in the *Saturday Review of Literature,* "is written with tranquil grace and a most dainty humor." Naomi Royde-Smith of *New Statesman* judged it a "witty, penetrating little tragedy."

In *The True Heart,* an orphan girl is put to work as a farmer's drudge. She falls in love with an idiot and, when he is taken away, goes in search for him. Her faithfulness is eventually rewarded when she is reunited with her love. Although the story has a rustic, fairy tale quality, it is essentially realistic. Katherine Anne Porter described the book for the *New York Herald Tribune* as "not whimsical . . . not fantastic. . . . It might be called fantasy [because it is set] in a world of symbolic truths. . . . [The novel] is like the changing landscape of a dream where figures move on some ageless errand." The *Times Literary Supplement* critic saw the novel in similar terms. "Though the author," the critic wrote, "does not shrink from the ugly and the violent this very charming tale does not belong to the actual world at all, but to the ever-imagined youth of the world when a true and innocent heart could go unscathed through every danger, unspoiled by any contact, to find its love at the last." The book has a "nameless and unusual combination of imp and cherub," Grace Frank wrote in the *Saturday Review of Literature,* "of humor and a lyric tenderness, that makes the story so delectable." Similarly, the *Outlook* reviewer believed *The True Heart* to be "more ambitious" than Warner's previous novels "but no less delicate in its blend of humor and pathos."

Subsequent Warner novels were based on historical events. *Summer Will Show,* set at the time of the French Revolution, was described by L. A. MacKay of *Canadian Forum* as "an excellent novel. The delicate and distinctive style of Miss Warner's earlier work, the deft irony and subtle characterization, reappear in a work of broader scope and more serious feeling." Written during Warner's brief involvement with the British Communist Party, the novel has serious political undertones. Mary McCarthy, in her review for the *Nation,* called *Summer Will Show* "the most skilful, the most sure-footed, sensitive, witty piece of prose yet to have been colored by left-wing ideology." Writing in the *Spectator,* William Plomer praised Warner's style. The book, he said, was "written with great care, it is well constructed and with rare skill—particularly in the choice and arrangement of descriptive detail—it builds up a picture in the reader's mind so that afterwards it seems almost like some old memory revived, some personal experience recalled."

In *The Corner That Held Them* Warner again writes an historical novel, setting her story in a fourteenth-century English convent. Surveying a thirty-three-year period in the convent's history, from the Black Death to the Peasant Uprising, the book focuses on the daily life of the cloistered nuns and not on the historical events of the time. It has been cited for its vivid recreation of medieval life. R. G. Davis of the *New York Times* believed the novel to be "a remarkable feat of living into another period, of making it immediately present to all the physical senses and to common sense as well." This authenticity was also noted by Richard McLaughlin in the *Saturday Review of Literature.* "Much of the appeal of the novel," McLaughlin asserted, "may be traced to Miss Warner's masterful resuscitation of medieval times, for she has not only recaptured the gusty full-bloodedness of that age but has positively drawn life-size figures which might have sprung from the pages of [Honore de] Balzac's 'Droll Stories.'"

The Flint Anchor, a chronicle of family life over a fifty-year period, distinguishes itself from other historical novels, Anthony West wrote in the *New Yorker,* "by being both beautifully written and psychologically profound about family relationships." Dealing with the life story of a family tyrant in nineteenth-century England, the novel unfolds in a deceptive manner, "as a piece of newsy family gossip," according to West. But at book's end a larger theme becomes apparent, "the idea that much more suffering and pain come from blind good will than from wickedness." While complimenting Warner's "witty, precise, unhurried" style, Paul Pickrel of the *Yale Review* nonetheless believed that "the waste of love, the unfulfilled capacity for affection, might have been treated with less sprightliness and more sympathy." Pickrel concluded that *The Flint Anchor* was not among the best of family chronicles, but "it is nevertheless the best example of that kind of fiction in some time."

Although her early reputation was made as a novelist, Warner also published many short stories—144 of them in the *New Yorker* alone—and these stories constitute an important part of her life's work. Warner's stories examine, with wit and charm, the motives and actions of often-eccentric characters. She wrote of a debutante who became a looter during World War II, of a brother and sister who cultivated their dullness to divert attention from their incestuous relationship, and of a clergyman stung to death by insects. "The knowledge that human beings are dangerous, incalculable, and extraordinary," Gies maintained, "is the animating spark at the center of her work." Warner's fiction, Michiko Kakutani wrote in the *New York Times Book Review,* is "peopled by eccentrics, and it is often animated by a gift for mischievous irony that lends the stories a charming, fable-like quality." Benedict Kiely, also writing in the *New York Times Book Review,* believed that whatever her subject matter, Warner "displays always that irony, that ruthless coolness, that clear sight, that style."

Although many of her stories are of a fantastic or whimsical nature, it is only in *Kingdoms of Elfin* that Warner crosses the line into pure fantasy. Set in a fairyland of elf kingdoms, these sixteen stories form an imaginary saga, which, in occasional asides, offers ironic observations on the world of men. "It has," William Jay Smith observed in the *New York Times Book Review,* "all the freshness, wit, originality of perception and clarity of insight that have won for [Warner's] rhythmical prose so many admirers. . . . It offers us an unforgettable journey through time and space, a cast of truly fantastic characters and an impressive and seemingly unending display of verbal fireworks." Gabriele Annan pointed out in the *Times Literary Supplement* that Warner's humor in this book is aimed "against religion, against superstition, gullibility, clericalism and priggishness." She also judged the collection to be "poetic, and the poetry comes not only from the fastidious elfin magic of [Warner's] prose, but also from a feeling for nature which could, perhaps, be called mystical."

When writing of her own life in *Scenes of Childhood,* Warner mixed reminiscence with fiction to create a series of sketches loosely based on the characters and events of her turn-of-the-century childhood. Many of the sketches provide autobiographical insights into Warner's early life. Her schoolmaster father, for example, doubted the value of literacy because it encouraged children not to observe, remember, and think for themselves, and so Warner learned to read much later than did her contemporaries. "Warner airs the glamorous and charming eccentricities of her upper middle-class background with a telling irony," Carol Rumens reported in the *Times Literary Supplement.* "With wit and

an elegant exactitude of language," Peter S. Prescott wrote in *Newsweek,* "[Warner] develops a garden, a few rooms in a house, a church interior; she then populates her small spaces with amiable eccentrics and leaves to those who will the impulse to infer the larger society. Beside her gentle stories, a tempest in a teapot would appear a life-threatening event." These sketches, however, moved Melvin Maddocks to warn in *Time* that "the too-casual reader . . . who thinks he is strolling down the garden path of English whimsy will soon find his heels being nipped by demons. . . . The Warner world is haunted."

More details of Warner's life can be found in *Letters,* a collection of her correspondence. Although the collection does not include her love letters to Valentine Ackland, the woman with whom she lived for many years, it does provide an insight into Warner's domestic routine. "The two women," Kakutani stated, "led an essentially quiet, bourgeois life, deep in the countryside of England. What Miss Warner's letters do best is convey, with lots of chatty facts, the texture of that life." Visiting friends, gardening, travel abroad, cooking, her own thoughts on other authors—these are the subjects of Warner's correspondence. The letters, Vicki Feaver wrote in the *Times Literary Supplement,* "form the record of what was ostensibly a retired and uneventful life in the country. . . . What really makes these letters come alive is Warner's capacity to turn the stuff of ordinary existence into a stream of perceptive, witty, compassionate, and sometimes tart observation."

Warner's diaries, edited and published in 1994 as *The Diaries of Sylvia Townsend Warner,* provide a more substantial view of Warner's relationship with Valentine Ackland. Warner began keeping a diary when her friend David Garnett gave her a notebook in 1927. Although she sometimes ignored her diaries for years, she kept writing in them until her death in 1978. Reviewing the edited diaries in the *Observer,* Anne Chisholm noted that Warner's infatuation with Ackland, and their long, turbulent relationship, forms "the heart of the diaries." While Warner remained obsessed with her younger companion throughout their relationship, Ackland often reacted to Warner's love with disdain, professional jealousy, infidelity, and emotional cruelty. Claire Tomalin, writing in the *New York Times Book Review,* contended that Warner "was not an exuberant or even a natural diarist. She rarely cut a dash in her own eyes, and she did not want her diaries published. They were too sad, she said."

BIOGRAPHICAL/CRITICAL SOURCES:

BOOKS

Contemporary Literary Criticism, Gale (Detroit), Volume 7, 1977; Volume 19, 1981.

Dictionary of Literary Biography, Gale, Volume 34: *British Novelists, 1890-1929: Traditionalists,* 1985; Volume 139: *British Short-Fiction Writers, 1945-1980,* 1994.

Harman, Claire, *Sylvia Townsend Warner: A Biography,* New Amsterdam, 1993.

Mulford, Wendy, *This Narrow Place: Sylvia Townsend Warner and Valentine Ackland: Life, Letters and Politics 1930-1951,* Pandora (London), 1988.

Updike, John, *Picked-Up Pieces,* Knopf, 1976.

PERIODICALS

British Book News, June, 1980.

Canadian Forum, November, 1936; March, 1948.

Chicago Tribune Book World, February 7, 1982.

Christian Science Monitor, December 31, 1932.

Library Journal, January 5, 1966; December, 1988, p. 135.

London Magazine, November, 1979.
Los Angeles Times, April 7, 1989.
Nation, May 25, 1927; November 9, 1932; August 15, 1936; April 11, 1966.
New Republic, February 17, 1926; March 5, 1966.
New Statesman, May 21, 1927.
Newsweek, January 11, 1982; January 9, 1989, p. 57.
New Yorker, August 28, 1943; October 9, 1954; August 20, 1979.
New York Herald Tribune, February 17, 1929.
New York Times, February 7, 1926; February 17, 1929; September 5, 1943; October 31, 1948; December 30, 1981.
New York Times Book Review, February 6, 1966; March 27, 1977; January 17, 1982; April 17, 1983; November 11, 1984; February 18, 1996, p. 6.
Observer (London), June 19, 1994, p. 18; June 26, 1994, p . 15.
Outlook, February 27, 1929.
Publishers Weekly, October 7, 1988, p. 105.
Saturday Review, February 6, 1926.
Saturday Review of Literature, April 16, 1927; March 9, 1929; June 27, 1936; December 4, 1948.
School Library Journal, May, 1992, p. 74.
Spectator, April 30, 1927; September 25, 1936; December 3, 1948; December 23, 1955.
Studies in Short Fiction, winter, 1973.
Time, February 4, 1966; February 21, 1977; February 1, 1982.
Times Literary Supplement, February 28, 1929; September 22, 1932; July 31, 1943; January 14, 1977; March 10, 1978; May 23, 1980; November 6, 1981; March 18, 1983.
Washington Post, February 6, 1982.
Washington Post Book World, December 18, 1988, p. 3.
Yale Review, autumn, 1954.

*   *   *

WARREN, Robert Penn 1905-1989

PERSONAL: Born April 24, 1905, in Guthrie, KY; died of cancer September 15, 1989, in Stratton, VT; son of Robert Franklin (a businessman) and Anna Ruth (Penn) Warren; married Emma Brescia, September 12, 1930 (divorced, 1950); married Eleanor Clark (a writer), December 7, 1952; children: (second marriage) Rosanna Phelps, Gabriel Penn. *Education:* Vanderbilt University, B.A. (summa cum laude), 1925; University of California, Berkeley, M.A., 1927; Yale University, graduate study, 1927-28; Oxford University, B.Litt., 1930. *Politics:* Democrat.

CAREER: Poet, novelist, essayist, playwright, educator, literary critic, and editor. Southwestern Presbyterian University (now Southwestern at Memphis), Memphis, TN, assistant professor of English, 1930-31; Vanderbilt University, Nashville, TN, acting assistant professor, 1931-34; Louisiana State University, Baton Rouge, assistant professor, 1934-36, associate professor, 1936-42; University of Minnesota, Minneapolis, professor of English, 1942-50; Yale University, New Haven, CT, professor of playwrighting in School of Drama, 1950-56, professor of English, 1961-73, professor emeritus, 1973-89. Visiting lecturer, State University of Iowa, 1941; Jefferson Lecturer, National Endowment for the Humanities, 1974. Staff member of writers conferences, University of Colorado, 1936, 1937, and 1940, and Olivet College, 1940. Consultant in poetry, Library of Congress, 1944-45.

MEMBER: American Academy of Arts and Letters (member of board), Academy of American Poets (chancellor), American Academy of Arts and Sciences, American Philosophical Society, Modern Language Association (honorary fellow), Century Club (New York).

AWARDS, HONORS: Rhodes Scholar, Oxford University, 1928-30; Caroline Sinkler Prize, Poetry Society of South Carolina, 1936, 1937, and 1938; Levinson Prize, *Poetry* magazine, 1936; Houghton Mifflin literary fellowship, 1936; Guggenheim fellowship, 1939-40 and 1947-48; Shelley Memorial Prize, 1942, for *Eleven Poems on the Same Theme;* Pulitzer Prize for fiction, 1947, for *All the King's Men;* Southern Prize, 1947; Robert Meltzer Award, Screen Writers Guild, 1949; Union League Civic and Arts Foundation Prize, *Poetry* magazine, 1953; Sidney Hillman Award, 1957, Edna St. Vincent Millay Memorial Award, American Poetry Society, 1958, National Book Award, 1958, and Pulitzer Prize for poetry, 1958, all for *Promises: Poems, 1954-1956;* Irita Van Doren Award, *New York Herald Tribune,* 1965, for *Who Speaks for the Negro?;* Bollingen Prize in poetry, Yale University, 1967, for *Selected Poems: New and Old, 1923-1966;* National Endowment for the Arts grant, 1968.

Van Wyck Brooks Award for poetry, National Medal for Literature, and Henry A. Bellaman Prize, all 1970, all for *Audubon: A Vision;* award for literature, University of Southern California, 1973; Golden Rose Trophy, New England Poetry Club, 1975; Emerson-Thoreau Medal, American Academy of Arts and Sciences, 1975; Copernicus Prize, American Academy of Poets, 1976; Wilma and Robert Messing Award, 1977; Pulitzer Prize for poetry, 1979, for *Now and Then: Poems, 1976-1978;* Harriet Monroe Award for poetry, 1979, for *Selected Poems: 1923-1975;* MacArthur Foundation fellowship, 1980; Commonwealth Award for Literature, 1980; Hubbell Memorial Award, Modern Language Association, 1980; Connecticut Arts Council award, 1980; Presidential Medal of Freedom, 1980; National Book Critics Circle Award nomination, 1980, and American Book Award nomination, 1981, both for *Being Here: Poetry, 1977-1980;* poetry prize nomination, *Los Angeles Times,* 1982, for *Rumor Verified: Poems, 1979-1980;* creative arts award, Brandeis University, 1984; named first Poet Laureate of the United States, 1986; National Medal of Arts, 1987; honorary degrees from many universities.

WRITINGS:

POETRY

Thirty-Six Poems, Alcestis Press, 1935.
Eleven Poems on the Same Theme, New Directions, 1942.
Selected Poems: 1923-1943, Harcourt, 1944.
Brother to Dragons: A Tale in Verse and Voices, Random House, 1953, revised edition published as *Brother to Dragons: A Tale in Verse and Voices—A New Version,* 1979.
Promises: Poems, 1954-1956, Random House, 1957.
You, Emperors and Others: Poems, 1957-1960, Random House, 1960.
Selected Poems: New and Old, 1923-1966, Random House, 1966.
Incarnations: Poems, 1966-1968, Random House, 1968.
Audubon: A Vision, Random House, 1969.
Or Else: Poems, 1968-1974, Random House, 1974.
Selected Poems, 1923-1975, Random House, 1976.
Now and Then: Poems, 1976-1978, Random House, 1978.
Being Here: Poetry, 1977-1980, Random House, 1980.
Rumor Verified: Poems, 1979-1980, Random House, 1981.
Chief Joseph of the Nez Perce, Random House, 1983.
New and Selected Poems, 1923-1985, Random House, 1985.

(Author of introduction and contributor), *Sixty Years of American Poetry: Celebrating the Anniversary of the Academy of American Poets,* preface by Richard Wilbur, wood engravings by Barry Moser, revised edition of *Fifty Years of American Poetry,* Harry N. Abrams (New York City), 1996.

FICTION

Night Rider (novel), Houghton, 1939, abridged edition, edited and introduced by George Mayberry, New American Library, 1950.

At Heaven's Gate (novel), Harcourt, 1943, abridged edition, edited and introduced by Mayberry, New American Library, 1949.

All the King's Men (also see below; novel), Harcourt, 1946.

Blackberry Winter (novelette), Cummington Press, 1946.

The Circus in the Attic, and Other Stories (short stories), Harcourt, 1947.

World Enough and Time (novel), Random House, 1950.

Band of Angels (novel), Random House, 1955.

The Cave (novel), Random House, 1959.

The Gods of Mount Olympus (adaptations of Greek myths for young readers), Random House, 1959.

Wilderness: A Tale of the Civil War (novel), Random House, 1961.

Flood: A Romance of Our Time (novel), Random House, 1964.

Meet Me in the Green Glen (novel), Random House, 1971.

A Place to Come To (novel), Random House, 1977.

NONFICTION

John Brown: The Making of a Martyr, Payson & Clarke, 1929.

(With others) *I'll Take My Stand: The South and the Agrarian Tradition,* Harper, 1930.

(Contributor) Herbert Agar and Allen Tate, editors, *Who Owns America?: A New Declaration of Independence,* Houghton, 1936.

(Author of critical essay) Samuel Taylor Coleridge, *The Rime of the Ancient Mariner,* illustrated by Alexander Calder, Reynal & Hitchcock, 1946.

Segregation: The Inner Conflict in the South, Random House, 1956.

Remember the Alamo!, Random House, 1958.

Selected Essays, Random House, 1958.

How Texas Won Her Freedom: The Story of Sam Houston and the Battle of San Jacinto (booklet), San Jacinto Museum of History, 1959.

The Legacy of the Civil War: Meditations on the Centennial, Random House, 1961.

Who Speaks for the Negro?, Random House, 1965.

A Plea in Mitigation: Modern Poetry and the End of an Era (lecture), Wesleyan College, 1966.

Homage to Theodore Dreiser (criticism), Random House, 1971.

Democracy and Poetry, Harvard University Press, 1975.

(Contributor) *A Time to Hear and Answer: Essays for the Bicentennial Season,* University of Alabama Press, 1977.

Jefferson Davis Gets His Citizenship Back (essay), University of Kentucky Press, 1980.

New and Selected Essays, Random House, 1989.

WITH CLEANTH BROOKS

(Editors with John T. Purser) *An Approach to Literature,* Louisiana State University Press, 1936, 5th edition, Prentice-Hall, 1975.

(Editors) *Understanding Poetry: An Anthology for College Students,* Holt, 1938, 4th edition, 1976.

(Editors) *Understanding Fiction,* Crofts, 1943, 2nd edition, Appleton-Century-Crofts, 1959, shortened version of 2nd edition published as *Scope of Fiction,* 1960, 3rd edition published under original title, Prentice-Hall, 1979.

Modern Rhetoric, Harcourt, 1949, published as *Fundamentals of Good Writing: A Handbook of Modern Rhetoric,* 1950, 2nd edition published under original title, 1958, 4th edition, 1979.

(Editors) *An Anthology of Stories from the Southern Review,* Louisiana State University Press, 1953.

(And R. W. B. Lewis) *American Literature: The Makers and the Making* (criticism), two volumes, St. Martin's, 1974.

Cleanth Brooks and Robert Penn Warren: A Literary Correspondence, edited by James A. Grimshaw, Jr., University of Missouri Press, 1998.

EDITOR

A Southern Harvest: Short Stories by Southern Writers, Houghton, 1937.

(With Albert Erskine) *Short Story Masterpieces,* Dell, 1954, 2nd edition, 1958.

(With Erskine) *Six Centuries of Great Poetry,* Dell, 1955.

(With Erskine) *A New Southern Harvest,* Bantam, 1957.

(With Allen Tate) Denis Devlin, *Selected Poems,* Holt, 1963.

Faulkner: A Collection of Critical Essays, Prentice-Hall, 1966.

Randall Jarrell, 1914-1965, Farrar, Straus, 1967.

John Greenleaf Whittier's Poetry: An Appraisal and a Selection, University of Minnesota Press, 1971.

Selected Poems of Herman Melville, Random House, 1971.

Katherine Anne Porter: A Collection of Critical Essays, Prentice-Hall, 1979.

The Essential Melville, Ecco Press, 1987.

PLAYS

Proud Flesh (in verse), produced in Minneapolis, MN, 1947, revised prose version produced in New York City, 1948.

(With Erwin Piscator) *Blut auf dem Mond: Ein Schauspiel in drei Akten* (adaptation of Warren's novel *All the King's Men;* produced in 1947; produced in Dallas, TX, as Willie Stark: His Rise and Fall, 1958; produced on Broadway, 1959), Lechte, 1956.

All the King's Men (adaptation of Warren's novel of same title; produced off-Broadway at East 74th St. Theatre), Random House, 1960.

Ballad of a Sweet Dream of Peace: An Easter Charade (produced in New York City at Cathedral of St. John the Divine), music by Alexei Haieff, Pressworks, 1981.

(Contributor of a play) *The Grotesque in Art and Literature: Theological Reflections,* edited by J. L. Adams and W. Yates, W. B. Eerdmans (Grand Rapids, MI), 1997.

OTHER

A Robert Penn Warren Reader, Random House, 1987.

Portrait of a Father, University Press of Kentucky, 1988.

Cofounding editor, *Fugitive,* 1922-25; founder and editor, with Cleanth Brooks, *Southern Review,* 1935-42; advisory editor, *Kenyon Review,* 1938-61.

The complete papers of Robert Penn Warren are collected at Yale University's Beinecke Rare Book and Manuscript Library.

MEDIA ADAPTATIONS: Two of Robert Penn Warren's novels have been made into films: *All the King's Men* (winner of an Academy Award for "Best Picture"), released by Columbia Pictures, 1949, and *Band of Angels,* released by Warner Brothers, 1956. *All the King's Men* also served as the basis for an opera by

Carlisle Floyd, *Willie Stark,* broadcast on television, and was adapted as a play by Adrian Hall, *All the King's Men,* presented by Trinity Repertory Company, Providence, RI, April, 1987.

SIDELIGHTS: Described by *Newsweek* reviewer Annalyn Swan as "America's dean of letters and, in all but name, poet laureate," Robert Penn Warren was among the last surviving members of a major literary movement that emerged in the South shortly after World War I. A distinguished poet, novelist, critic, and teacher, he won virtually every major award given to writers in the United States and was the only person to receive a Pulitzer Prize in both fiction (once) and poetry (twice). He also achieved a measure of commercial success that eludes many other serious artists. In short, as Hilton Kramer once observed in the *New York Times Book Review,* Warren "has enjoyed the best of both worlds. . . . Few other writers in our history have labored with such consistent distinction and such unflagging energy in so many separate branches of the literary profession. He is a man of letters on the old-fashioned, outsize scale, and everything he writes is stamped with the passion and the embattled intelligence of a man for whom the art of literature is inseparable from the most fundamental imperatives of life."

Literature did not always play a central role in Warren's life, however. In an interview with John Baker published in *Conversations with Writers,* Warren revealed that he did not expect to become a writer. He originally planned to be a naval officer, but an accident prevented him from accepting an appointment to Annapolis. Instead, he went to Vanderbilt University, intending to study chemical engineering, but soon found the English courses much more interesting.

The freshman English teacher Warren found so fascinating was fellow Southerner John Crowe Ransom, "a real, live poet, in pants and vest, who had published a book and also fought in the war. . . . As a man, he made no effort to charm his students, but everything he said was interesting." Ransom, recognizing that Warren was no ordinary English student, encouraged the young man to enroll in one of his more advanced courses. He also invited Warren to join the "Fugitives," a group of Vanderbilt teachers and students as well as several local businessmen who had been meeting informally since around 1915 to discuss trends in American life and literature. By 1922, the year Warren joined, many of the Fugitives' discussions focused on poetry and critical theory, Warren's favorite subjects at the time. "In a very important way," says Warren in retrospect, "that group was my education."

The Fugitives drifted apart in the mid-1920s, about the same time Warren graduated from Vanderbilt and headed west to continue his education at the University of California in Berkeley. After receiving his M.A. from there in 1927, Warren attended Yale University and then England's Oxford University where, as he described, he "stumbled on" writing fiction. Homesick and weary of devoting his days and nights to working on his dissertation, Warren, at the request of one of the editors of the literary annual *American Caravan,* agreed to compose a novelette based on the folk tales he had heard as a boy in Kentucky. As he later remarked to Baker, his contribution to the annual received "some pleasant notices in the press," and soon publishers were asking him to write novels.

Though Warren did indeed write several novels during the next decade (only one of which, *Night Rider,* was published), most of his time and effort was spent trying to earn a living. Returning to Tennessee in 1930 after completing his studies at Oxford, he briefly served on the faculty of Southwestern Presbyterian

University (now Southwestern at Memphis) before obtaining a teaching position at Vanderbilt. From there Warren went to Louisiana State University in 1934, teaming up with friend and fellow faculty member Cleanth Brooks to write a series of immensely successful and influential textbooks, including *An Approach to Literature and Understanding Poetry.* Based on the authors' class notes and conversations, these books have been largely responsible for disseminating the theories of the New Criticism to several generations of college students and teachers. According to Helen McNeil in the *Times Literary Supplement,* Warren and Brooks helped to establish the New Criticism as "an orthodoxy so powerful that contemporary American fiction and poetry are most easily defined by their rebellion against it."

The New Criticism—a method of analyzing a work of art that focuses attention on the work's intrinsic value as an object in and of itself, more or less independent of outside influences (such as the circumstances of its composition, the reality it creates, the effect it has on readers, and the author's intention) grew out of discussions Warren had participated in first as a member of the Fugitives, then as an Agrarian. (The Agrarians were former Fugitives who banded together again in the late 1920s to extol the virtues of the rural South and to promote an agrarian as opposed to an industrial economy). Despite his close association with the Agrarians and his key role in publicizing their theories, Warren did not consider himself to be a professional critic. As he explained to Baker: "I have only two roles, essentially: poetry and fiction—and only a certain kind of fiction. . . . A real critic, like Cleanth Brooks or I. A. Richards, has a system. . . . He's concerned with that, primarily. I'm not. I'm interested in trying to understand this poem or that poem, but I'm not interested in trying to create a system. I'm interested in a different kind of understanding, you might say, a more limited kind of understanding. I'm interested in my enjoyment, put it that way, more than anything else. I've certainly written some criticism, but I usually take it from my class notes. I'm just not a professional critic. That business is just something that happens. . . . But writing fiction, poetry, that's serious—that's for keeps."

Poetry and fiction were thus Warren's main concerns throughout his long career, with poetry having edged out fiction as the author's preferred genre since the mid-1950s. He saw nothing unusual in the fact that he made notable contributions to both, remarking to Baker that "a poem for me and a novel are not so different. They start much the same way, on the same emotional journey, and can go either way. . . . At a certain level an idea takes hold. Now it doesn't necessarily come with a form; it comes as an idea or an impulse. . . . I've started many things in one form and shifted to another. . . . The interesting topics, the basic ideas in the poems and the basic ideas in the novels are the same."

Despite his reliance on history for material, Warren balked at being labeled a "historical novelist." "I just happened to encounter stories that had the right germ of an idea for a novel," he once stated in a *Saturday Review* article. "I should hope that the historical novel would be a way of saying something about the present." To this end, he often changes the actual historical focus of a story to concentrate on peripheral characters whose behavior reveals more about the ethical or dramatic issues *behind* the facts. Therefore, maintain Everett Wilkie and Josephine Helterman in the *Dictionary of Literary Biography,* Warren's "main obsession is knowledge," not history. Explain the critics: "His works reflect the many forms in which he himself has found knowledge. . . . [His] wisdom is the wisdom of interpretation; his main question, 'How is one to look at life?' From an elaboration of the complex forces which shape both our lives and our perceptions, he shows us history as a living force which can yet tell us something about ourselves."

The "action" in most of Warren's work thus consists primarily of an idealistic narrator's search for his or her identity in an atmosphere of confusion and/or corruption. This search eventually leads to recognition of the world's fallen state and, consequently, of the self's "innate depravity," to use Strandberg's phrase. In an attempt to overcome the sense of alienation caused by these "warring parts of the psyche," a typical Warren character undergoes a period of intense self-examination that ideally results in a near-religious experience of conversion, rebirth, and a mystical feeling of oneness with God. This in turn opens the door to further knowledge, not only about the self but about the world as well. Though the search for identity may not always end in success, notes Strandberg, "the craving to recreate that original felicity [that existed before the Fall] is one of mankind's deepest obsessions, in Warren's judgment."

Most observers find Warren's language, style, and tone to be perfectly suited to his subject matter. His language, for example, is a lyrical mixture of earthiness and elegance, of the folk speech of Kentucky and Tennessee and what James Dickey refers to in the *Saturday Review* as a "rather quaintly old-fangled scholastic vocabulary." Richard Jackson offers a similar description in the *Michigan Quarterly Review:* "[Warren's] idiom . . . is at once conversational and lyric, contemporary and historic, profane and sacred. It is a language in which he can slip easily from necessary precept to casual observation, cosmic vision to particular sighting." According to a *Sewanee Review* article by Calvin Bedient, Warren's poetry is written "in a genuinely expansive, passionate style. Look at its prose ease and rapidity oddly qualified by log-piling compounds, alliteration, successive stresses, and an occasional inversion something rough and serviceable as a horse-blanket yet fancy to—and you wonder how he ever came up with it. It is excitingly massive and moulded and full of momentum. Echoes of Yeats and Auden still persist, but it is wonderfully peculiar, homemade."

After emerging from a ten-year-long period of "poet's block" in 1954, Warren devoted most of his creative energies to writing verse. Unlike his early (pre-1944) poetry, which sprang from either the contemplation of complex metaphysical concepts or the ballads and narratives native to his region, Warren's later poetry was inspired by a mood, a natural event, or a memory that often takes shape as "a moralized anecdote," to use Warren's own words. It is a highly personal and often autobiographical (but by no means confessional) form of poetry. In fact, maintains Kramer, "[Warren's] poetry is so unlike that of most other poets claiming our attention . . . that it requires a certain adjustment of the eye and the ear, and of that other faculty—call it the moral imagination—to which Mr. Warren's verse speaks with so much urgency and that of so many other poets nowadays does not. We are a long way, in this poetry, from the verse snapshot and the campy valentine—a long way, too, from the verse diaries, confessions and dirty laundry lists that have come to occupy such a large place in our poetic literature. . . . [His] is a poetry haunted by the lusts and loves of the flesh, filled with dramatic incident, vivid landscapes and philosophical reflection—a poetry of passion recollected in the tragic mode. It teems with experience, and with the lessons and losses of experience."

Warren's later poetry is noted for its rambling conversational rhythm, due in part to what Edward L. Stewart refers to in the

Washington Post Book World as its "wide range of conventional but loose-limbed, free but masterfully controlled verse patterns." Warren favored very long and very short lines, the use of which creates an irregular meter and sentences that seem to wind down the page, "run[ning] forward, as it were, into experience," says Bedient in *Parnassus.* The overall tone is one of reflection and meditation, though not in a passive sense, writes Alan Williamson, another *Washington Post Book World* critic. "In the whiplash of [Warren's] long line, the most ordinary syntax becomes tense, muscular, searching," comments Williamson. "His ear is formidable, though given to strong effects rather than graceful ones." The *Times Literary Supplement*'s Jay Parini also finds that "power is the word that comes to mind" when reading Warren's work—power that is expressed in the "raw-boned, jagged quality" of his verse.

According to John Rees Moore of the *Sewanee Review,* these are the same features that make Warren's poetry stand out "in sharp contrast to the jittery rhythms and fragmented images—the reaching out for a style—that are characteristic of much recent poetry. Not that wit, boldness, and even a certain nervous energy are missing but that Warren's poetic quest for identity has reached a stage where he is freer to disregard whatever is not of central interest to him and mull over with increased concentration whatever is." In short, notes Peter Clothier in the *Los Angeles Times Book Review,* "in an age when the quick gratification of surface glitter often replaces slower pleasures of craft and care, Robert Penn Warren's poetry reminds us that the work of a master craftsman is literally irreplaceable. . . . [His] is work of absolute formal and intellectual integrity."

In his book *Contemporaries,* Alfred Kazin points out that "all [of Warren's] work seems to deal with the Fall of Man. And if in reading [him] I have come to be more wary of his handling of this theme, it is because of the nostalgia it conveys, the strident impatient language with which it is expressed, the abstract use to which it is put. . . . Warren tends to make rhetoric of his philosophy." Bedient expresses a similar thought in the *Sewanee Review,* commenting that Warren "seems bitten by the Enormity of it all. He *will* have mystery." As a result, concludes Bedient, his philosophical musings are "sometimes truly awkward and sometimes pseudo-profound."

A few reviewers attribute Warren's occasional awkwardness to the very quality that has made him such a noteworthy figure in American literature: his versatility. Eric Bentley, for one, speculates that Warren's dual role as both artist *and* critic hinders his ability to "submerge himself in the artist." Continues Bentley in a *Kenyon Review* article: "Trite as it is nowadays to stigmatize an author as a dual personality, I cannot help pointing to a duality in Warren that may well constitute his major problem: it is his combination of critical and creative power. I am far from suggesting that the critical and the creative are of their nature antithetic and I am fully ready to grant that what makes Warren remarkable among American writers is his double endowment. The problem lies precisely in his being so two-sidedly gifted; he evidently finds it endlessly difficult to combine his two sorts of awareness."

Many critics, of course, disagree with these evaluations of Warren's poetry. In another *Parnassus* article, for instance, Paul Mariani writes: "I could quarrel with certain things in Warren I find alien to my own sense of poetics: a sometimes loose, rambling line, a nostalgia verging on obsession, a veering towards philosophical attitudinizing, the mask of the redneck that out-rednecks the redneck. But I would rather leave such critical caveats for others. There is enough [in his poetry] to praise, and I am thankful to have been given to drink, if not out of those too rare 'great depths,' then at least from a spring sufficiently deep, sufficiently clear."

Monroe K. Spears reports in the *Sewanee Review* that Warren's failings "are hard for me to specify; I find his attitudes and themes—moral, psychological, and religious—so congenial that it is difficult for me to regard the poetry with proper detachment. Sometimes the themes are perhaps a little too explicit, not very fully dramatized; and there is a danger in the fact that they are basically few, though combined and varied in many ways." Nevertheless, continues Spears, "Warren's later poetry seems to me to embody most of the special virtues of 'open' poetry—accessibility, immediate emotional involvement, wide appeal—and to resist the temptations to formlessness and to moral exhibitionism, self-absorption, and sentimentality that are the chief liabilities of that school."

One point critics do agree on, however, is the extraordinary nature of Warren's contribution to literature. In his critical study of the author, *Robert Penn Warren*, Charles H. Bohner declares that "no other American literary figure of the twentieth century has exhibited greater versatility than Robert Penn Warren. . . . While arguments about his preeminence in any one field would be ultimately inconclusive, his total accomplishment . . . surpasses that of any other living writer." Marshall Walker has similar words of praise for Warren in the *London Magazine*, calling him "America's most distinguished man of letters in the European sense of a writer involved with books and human kind and at ease in a variety of *genres*. . . . The range of his achievement testifies to the scope and commitment of Warren's human sympathies. Each intellectual act, whether formally poem, novel, or one of the interviews with black leaders in *Who Speaks for the Negro?* is of the nature of a poem, according to his own definition of the poem as 'a way of getting your reality shaped a little better'. . . . Underlying the energy, even the violence that is part of Warren's metaphor of the world as well as of the world itself, is a concern to visualize the meaning of common experience and, without artistic concessions, to make this meaning available in a body of work which, with astonishing success, unites metaphysical and social themes in a single vision."

Writing in the *Saturday Review*, Dickey suggests Warren's depth rather than his range should be celebrated. "[Warren] is direct, scathingly honest, and totally serious about what he feels," Dickey begins. "He plunges as though compulsively into the largest of subjects: those that seem to cry out for capitalization and afflatus and, more often than not in the work of many poets, achieve only the former. . . . He is a poet of enormous courage, with a highly individual intelligence." But above all, concludes Dickey, Robert Penn Warren "looks, and refuses to look away   [He] wounds deeply; he strikes in at blood-level and gut-level, with all the force and authority of time, darkness, and distance themselves, and of the Nothingness beyond nothingness, which may even be God."

BIOGRAPHICAL/CRITICAL SOURCES:

BOOKS

Berger, Walter, *A Southern Renascence Man: Views of Robert Penn Warren*, Louisiana State University Press, 1984.

Blotner, Joseph Leo, *Robert Penn Warren: A Biography*, Random House, 1997.

Bohner, Charles H., *Robert Penn Warren*, Twayne, 1964.

Bradbury, John, *The Fugitives*, University of North Carolina Press, 1958, pp. 172-255.

Burt, John, *Robert Penn Warren and American Idealism*, Yale University Press, 1988.

Casper, Leonard, *Robert Penn Warren: The Dark and Bloody Ground*, University of Washington Press, 1960.

Casper, Leonard, *The Blood-Marriage of Earth and Sky: Robert Penn Warren's Later Novels*, Louisiana State University Press, 1997.

Clark, William Bedford, editor, *Critical Essays on Robert Penn Warren*, Twayne, 1981.

Concise Dictionary of American Literary Biography: Broadening Views, 1968-88, Gale (Detroit), 1989.

Contemporary Literary Criticism, Gale, Volume 1, 1973; Volume 4, 1975; Volume 6, 1976; Volume 8, 1978; Volume 10, 1979; Volume 13, 1980; Volume 18, 1981; Volume 39, 1986; Volume 53, 1989; Volume 59, 1990.

Conversations with Writers, Gale, 1977.

Cowley, Malcolm, editor, *Writers at Work: The Paris Review Interviews*, Viking, 1959.

Dictionary of Literary Biography, Gale, Volume 2: *American Novelists since World War II*, 1978; Volume 48: *American Poets, 1880-1945, Second Series*, 1986.

Dictionary of Literary Biography Yearbook: 1980, Gale, 1981.

Dictionary of Literary Biography Yearbook: 1989, Gale, 1990.

Donohue, Cecilia, *Robert Penn Warren's Novels: Feminine and Feminist Discourse*, P. Lang, 1997.

Ferriss, Lucy, *Sleeping with the Boss: Female Subjectivity and Narrative Pattern in the Fiction of Robert Penn Warren*, Louisiana State University Press (Baton Rouge), 1997.

Gray, Richard, editor, *Robert Penn Warren: A Collection of Critical Essays*, Prentice-Hall, 1980.

Grimshaw, James A., Jr., *Robert Penn Warren: A Descriptive Bibliography 1922-1979*, University Press of Virginia, 1981.

Grimshaw, James A., Jr., *Time's Glory: Original Essays on Robert Penn Warren*, University of Central Arkansas Press, 1986.

Kazin, Alfred, *Contemporaries*, Atlantic-Little, Brown, 1962.

Koppelman, Robert S., *Robert Penn Warren's Modernist Spirituality*, University of Missouri Press, 1995.

Nakadate, Neil, editor, *Robert Penn Warren: Critical Perspectives*, University Press of Kentucky, 1981.

Newquist, Roy, editor, *Conversations*, Rand McNally, 1967.

Short Story Criticism, Gale, Volume 4, 1990.

Snipes, Katherine, *Robert Penn Warren*, Ungar, 1983.

Strandberg, Victor H., *The Poetic Vision of Robert Penn Warren*, University Press of Kentucky, 1977.

Watkins, Floyd C., and John T. Hiers, editors, *Robert Penn Warren Talking: Interviews 1950-1978*, Random House, 1980.

Watkins, Floyd C., *Then & Now: The Personal Past in the Poetry of Robert Penn Warren*, University Press of Kentucky, 1982.

PERIODICALS

America, November 14, 1987, p. 359.

Chicago Tribune, September 10, 1978; April 7, 1985; June 1, 1987.

Chicago Tribune Book Review, October 14, 1979; September 7, 1980; February 28, 1982.

Detroit News, February 15, 1981.

Kenyon Review, summer, 1948.

London Magazine, December, 1975/January, 1976.

Los Angeles Times, March 19, 1981.

Los Angeles Times Book Review, September 7, 1980; October 19, 1980; January 17, 1982; July 30, 1986.
Michigan Quarterly Review, fall, 1978.
Mississippi Quarterly, winter, 1958, pp. 19-28; winter, 1970-71, pp. 47-56; winter, 1971-72, pp. 19-30.
Nation, August 24, 1946.
Newsweek, August 25, 1980; March 10, 1986.
New Yorker, August 24, 1946; December 29, 1980.
New York Times, August 18, 1946; December 16, 1969; March 2, 1977; June 2, 1981; March 27, 1983; April 24, 1985; October 6, 1986.
New York Times Book Review, June 25, 1950; January 9, 1977; November 2, 1980; May 12, 1985.
Parnassus: Poetry in Review, fall/winter, 1975; summer, 1977; spring/summer, 1979.
People Weekly, March 17, 1986.
Saturday Review, June 24, 1950; August 20, 1955; August, 1980.
Sewanee Review, spring, 1970; spring, 1974; spring, 1975; summer, 1977; spring, 1979; summer, 1980.
Time, August 18, 1975.
Times Literary Supplement, November 28, 1980; January 29, 1982; February 17-23, 1989.
Virginia Quarterly Review, summer, 1977.
Washington Post, May 2, 1980; September 23, 1989.
Washington Post Book World, March 6, 1977; October 22, 1978; September 30, 1979; August 31, 1980; October 4, 1981; June 26, 1983; April 30, 1989.
Yale Review, autumn, 1946.

*   *   *

WARSHOFSKY, Isaac
   See SINGER, Isaac Bashevis

*   *   *

WASSERSTEIN, Wendy 1950-

PERSONAL: Born October 18, 1950, in Brooklyn, NY; daughter of Morris W. (a textile manufacturer) and Lola (a dancer; maiden name, Schleifer) Wasserstein. *Education:* Mount Holyoke College, B.A., 1971; City College of the City University of New York, M.A., 1973; Yale University Drama School, M.F.A., 1976.

ADDRESSES: Agent—Royce Carlton Inc., 866 United Nations Plaza, Suite 4030, New York, NY 10017. *Office*—c/o ICM, 40 W. 57th St., New York, NY 10019.

CAREER: Dramatist and screenwriter. Teacher at Columbia University and New York University, New York City. Actress in plays, including *The Hotel Play,* 1981. Member of artistic board of Playwrights Horizons.

MEMBER: Dramatists Guild (member of steering committee and women's committee), British American Arts Association (board member), Dramatists Guild for Young Playwrights; WNET (board member), McDowell Colony (board member).

AWARDS, HONORS: Joseph Jefferson Award, Dramalogue Award, and Inner Boston Critics Award, all for *Uncommon Women and Others;* grant for playwriting from Playwrights Commissioning Program of Phoenix Theater, c. 1970s; Hale Mathews Foundation Award; Guggenheim fellowship, 1983; grant for writing and for studying theater in England from British-

American Arts Association; grant for playwriting from American Playwrights Project, 1988; Pulitzer Prize for drama, Antoinette Perry Award (Tony) for best play from League of American Theatres and Producers, Drama Desk Award, Outer Critics Circle Award, Susan Smith Blackburn Prize, and award for best new play from New York Drama Critics' Circle, all 1989, all for *The Heidi Chronicles;* Outer Critics Circle Award, 1993, for *The Sisters Rosensweig.*

WRITINGS:

PLAYS

Any Woman Can't, produced off-Broadway at Playwrights Horizons, 1973.
Happy Birthday, Montpelier Pizz-zazz, produced in New Haven, CT, 1974.
(With Christopher Durang) *When Dinah Shore Ruled the Earth,* first produced in New Haven, CT, at Yale Cabaret Theater, 1975.
Uncommon Women and Others (also see below; first produced as a one-act in New Haven, CT, 1975; revised and enlarged two-act version produced off-Broadway by Phoenix Theater at Marymount Manhattan Theater, November 21, 1977), Avon (New York City), 1978.
Isn't It Romantic (also see below; first produced off-Broadway by Phoenix Theater at Marymount Manhattan Theater, June 13, 1981; revised version first produced off-Broadway at Playwrights Horizons, December 15, 1983), Nelson Doubleday, 1984.
Tender Offer (one-act), first produced off-off Broadway at Ensemble Studio Theatre, 1983.
The Man in a Case (one-act; adapted from the short story of the same title by Anton Chekhov), written as part of *Orchards* (anthology of seven one-act plays, all adapted from short stories by Chekhov; produced off-Broadway by the Acting Company at Lucille Lortel Theater, April 22, 1986), Knopf (New York City), 1986.
Miami (musical), first produced off-Broadway at Playwrights Horizons, January, 1986.
The Heidi Chronicles (also see below; produced off-Broadway at Playwrights Horizons, December 11, 1988, produced on Broadway at Plymouth Theatre, March 9, 1989), Dramatists Play Service (New York City), 1990.
The Heidi Chronicles and Other Plays (contains *Uncommon Women and Others, Isn't It Romanic,* and *The Heidi Chronicles*), Harcourt (San Diego), 1990.
The Sisters Rosensweig (produced at Mitzi E. Newhouse Theater, Lincoln Center, October 22, 1992), Harcourt (New York City), 1993.
An American Daughter, Harcourt, 1997.

SCREENPLAYS; FOR TELEVISION

Uncommon Women and Others (adapted from Wasserstein's play of the same title; also see above), Public Broadcasting Service (PBS), 1978.
The Sorrows of Gin (adapted from the short story of the same title by John Cheever), PBS, 1979.

Also author of *'Drive,' She Said,* PBS, and of sketches for the series *Comedy Zone,* CBS-TV, 1984.

OTHER

Bachelor Girls (comic essays), Knopf, 1990.
Pamela's First Musical (children's picture book), illustrated by Andrew Jackness, Hyperion (New York City), 1996.

Author of unproduced film scripts, including (with Christopher Durang) "House of Husbands," adapted from the short story "Husbands"; and a script adapted from the novel *The Object of My Affection* by Stephen McCauley. Contributor of articles to periodicals, including *Esquire, New York Times,* and *New York Woman.* Contributing editor, *New York Woman.*

SIDELIGHTS: "Serious issues and serious people can be quite funny," said dramatist Wendy Wasserstein in the *New York Times.* In her best-known plays—*Uncommon Women and Others, Isn't It Romantic,* and *The Heidi Chronicles*—Wasserstein spotlights college-educated women of the postwar baby boom, who came of age in the late 1960s as feminism was redefining American society. Such women, she suggests, have been torn between a newfound spirit of independence and the traditional values of marriage and motherhood that they were taught as children. While portraying the struggles of her characters with deep sympathy, Wasserstein imbues her plays with a comic tone. "On some level, I'm terribly earnest," she told Sylvie Drake of the *Los Angeles Times.* "I almost have to look at problems with a sense of humor." Wasserstein has held the attention of theater critics since the late 1970s, when *Uncommon Women* opened to favorable reviews in New York City; a few years later, according to the *New York Times*'s Michiko Kakutani, she had "won recognition as one of this country's most talented young playwrights." In 1989, Wasserstein received the Pulitzer Prize in drama for *The Heidi Chronicles.*

Born into a New York City family in 1950, Wasserstein attended a series of young women's schools, including the elite Mount Holyoke College, that were marked by social conservatism. She rebelled against the schools' traditions of propriety, preferring to cultivate a lively sense of humor—"I always thought in terms of getting by on being funny," she said in the *New York Times.* She did graduate work at New York's City University, studying creative writing under playwright Israel Horovitz and novelist Joseph Heller before gaining a master's degree in 1973. That year saw Wasserstein's first professional production: *Any Woman Can't,* a bitter farce about a woman's efforts to dance her way to success in a male-dominated environment. The show was presented by a small experimental theater group, Playwrights Horizons, that would later prosper and play a major role in Wasserstein's career.

When Wasserstein graduated from City University, she was unsure of her future. The emergent women's movement brought the prospect of a career in law or business, but Wasserstein was not enthusiastic about these professions. She was drawn to a career as a playwright, a tenuous life made ever more so by the growing popularity of television and film. She applied to two prestigious graduate programs—Columbia Business School and Yale Drama School—was accepted by both, and opted for Yale. The leader of Yale's drama program was Robert Brustein, renowned in the American theater community as an advocate of professional discipline and artistic creativity. Under his auspices, according to *Horizon*'s Steve Lawson, Yale became "the foremost theatrical training ground in the country." Brustein "felt that theater was as important as law or medicine," Wasserstein later told the *New York Times.* "It gave you high standards to maintain." Her classmates at Yale included Christopher Durang and Albert Innaurato, later to become award-winning playwrights, and Meryl Streep, an actress who later earned acclaim in films.

Wasserstein's work at Yale evolved from broad mockery to more subtle portrayals of character. Of her student plays, two are

forthright satires: *Happy Birthday, Montpelier Pizz-zazz* shows the social maneuvers at a college party, and *When Dinah Shore Ruled the Earth,* written with Durang, mocks a beauty pageant. But in *Uncommon Women and Others*—which Wasserstein began as her Yale master's thesis—the characters are more complex; and the humor, more low-keyed, is underlain with tension.

Uncommon Women is about a fictional group of Mount Holyoke students who trade quips about men and sex while wondering about their own futures with a mixture of hope and apprehension. As the play makes clear, when feminism reached college campuses in the late 1960s it expanded women's horizons but filled them with uncertainty. The character Rita dominates the play as an outspoken aspiring novelist. As a student she tells her friends that "when we're thirty we're going to be pretty amazing," but she eventually hopes for a "Leonard Woolf" who will, like Virginia Woolf's husband, support her while she perfects her writing. Holly, dubbed "imaginative" and "witty" by *Nation*'s Harold Clurman, makes a pathetic effort to find a husband on the eve of graduation by phoning a young doctor she once met. He has since married and has forgotten all about her. Surrounding the central characters, each of whom struggles to define herself, are other young women whose self-assurance seems vaguely unsettling by contrast. Leilah, self-contained and inscrutable, makes a cold peace with the world, deciding to become an anthropologist and marry a man from the Middle East. Susie is a booster for outmoded college traditions; Carter, a stereotypical genius who seems guaranteed of success. The play's opening and closing scenes show the central characters at a reunion luncheon a few years after college. Most seem confused and unfulfilled. Rita now asserts that by the age of forty-five they will all be "amazing." Chekhov, Wasserstein later revealed, inspired Rita's funny-sad refrain.

Uncommon Women was first presented at Yale in 1975 as a one-act play. Then Wasserstein rewrote the play in a two-act version and prepared it for the professional stage, receiving encouragement along the way from both Playwrights Horizons and the Eugene O'Neill Playwrights Conference. The finished work received widespread attention from reviewers when it premiered in 1977 under the auspices of Phoenix Theater, a troupe that spotlighted new American plays. While *Time*'s T. E. Kalem found Wasserstein's characters "stereotypical," Richard Eder of the *New York Times* wrote that "if the characters . . . represent familiar alternatives and contradictions, Miss Wasserstein has made each of them most real." *New Yorker*'s Edith Oliver said the work was "a collage of small scenes" rather than a "play." Nonetheless, she found the result a "wonderful, original comedy" in which "every moment is theatrical," adding that "for all [the characters'] funny talk and behavior, they are sympathetically drawn." In conclusion, Oliver declared Wasserstein "an uncommon young woman if ever there was one." *Uncommon Women* soon reached national television as part of the Public Broadcasting Service's *Theatre in America* series.

Wasserstein began her next major work, *Isn't It Romantic,* as she approached the age of thirty in the late 1970s. Observing that many women her own age were suddenly planning to marry, she pondered the reasons for such a choice, including the possibility that women might marry simply because it was expected of them. "Biological time bombs were going off all over Manhattan," she told the *Washington Post.* "It was like, it's not wild and passionate, but it's *time.*" *Isn't It Romantic,* observed *Nation*'s Elliott Sirkin, "has the kind of heroine the whole world thinks of as a New Yorker: Janie [Blumberg], a bright, plump, emotionally agitated young Jewish woman, who insults herself with sophisticated quips" while resisting the entreaties of an earnest but boring young doctor. Janie's mother, outgoing and energetic, urges her daughter to get married. In contrast to the Blumbergs are Janie's best friend Harriet—an emotionally restrained Anglo-Saxon, more attractive and successful than Janie—and Harriet's mother, cooler and more successful yet. The play consists of many short scenes, abundant with comic one-liners, that explore how and why women choose a husband, a career, or a way of life. As the play ends, Janie, shocked to realize that Harriet is about to marry a man she does not love, pointedly refuses to move in with her own boyfriend.

When the original version of *Romantic* was premiered by the Phoenix Theater in 1981, a number of reviewers found that the play's episodic structure and Wasserstein's flair for jokes distracted from the issues that had inspired the work. Wasserstein is "better at parts than at wholes, more gag- than goal-oriented," wrote *New York*'s John Simon. He suggested that the first draft was encumbered by "Yale Drama School or Christopher Durang humor, which consists of scrumptious, scattershot bitchiness that . . . refus[es] to solidify into shapeliness." However, he concluded, Wasserstein "has a lovely forte: the comic-wistful line. . . . This could be a vein of gold, and needs only proper engineering to be efficiently mined."

As Wasserstein established her theater career, she became clearly identified with Playwrights Horizons, which also attracted Durang, Innaurato, and several other well-educated writers of about the same age. Under the growing influence of Andre Bishop, who joined as an administrator in 1975, Playwrights became "the most critically acclaimed off-off-Broadway group since Joseph Papp's Public Theater began in 1967," according to John Lombardi in the *New York Times*. "What [the dramatists at Playwrights Horizons] really have in common," Bishop told Lombardi, "is that they are all extremely literate and extremely intelligent, two qualities that don't necessarily go together." He continued: "They come at the world from a humorous angle that is rooted in an angry desire for truth." Bishop wanted the organization and its writers to have lasting professional ties, and it developed such a relationship with Wasserstein. After producing the revised *Romantic*, Playwrights Horizons commissioned Wasserstein's next full-length work, *Miami*, a musical comedy about a teenage boy on vacation with his family in the late 1950s. The show received a limited run at the group's theater in early 1986. More successful was Wasserstein's subsequent full-length play, *The Heidi Chronicles*, which received its New York debut at Playwrights in late 1988.

The Heidi Chronicles was inspired by a single image in Wasserstein's mind: a woman speaking to an assembly of other women, confessing her growing sense of unhappiness. The speaker evolved into Dr. Heidi Holland, an art history professor who finds that her successful, independent life has left her alienated from men and women alike. Most of the play consists of flashbacks that capture Heidi's increasing disillusionment. Starting as a high-school girl, she experiences in turn the student activism of the late 1960s, feminist consciousness-raising of the early 1970s, and the tough-minded careerism of the 1980s. Friends disappoint her: a feminist activist becomes an entertainment promoter, valuing the women's audience for its market potential; a boyfriend becomes a manipulative and selfish magazine editor; a gay male friend tells her that in the 1980s, when gays are dying of AIDS, her unhappiness is a mere luxury. Heidi remains subdued until the play's climactic scene, when she addresses fellow alumnae from a private school for girls. "We're

all concerned, intelligent, good women," she tells her old classmates, as quoted in the *New York Times*. "It's just that I feel stranded. And I thought the whole point was that we wouldn't feel stranded. I thought the point was we were all in this together." At the end of the play Heidi adopts a baby and poses happily with the child in front of an exhibition of works by Georgia O'Keefe, an acclaimed woman artist.

Reviewers debated how well the play reflected the reality of Heidi's, and Wasserstein's, generation. In *Village Voice*, Alisa Solomon suggested that the playwright lacked sympathy with the aspirations of feminism. *New York*'s John Simon felt the characters were oversimplified, averring that "Heidi's problem as stated—that she is too intellectual, witty, and successful for a mere hausfrau—just won't wash." Mimi Kramer, however, told readers of *New Yorker* that "Wasserstein's portrait of womanhood always remains complex." The reviewer found "generosity in the writing," contending that no character in the play "is made to seem ludicrous or dismissible." Praising Wasserstein's skill as a dramatist, Kramer declared that the playwright "never states anything that can be inferred. . . . She condemns these young men and women simply by capturing them in all their charm and complexity, without rhetoric or exaggeration." *The Heidi Chronicles* soon became Wasserstein's first show to move to a Broadway theater; soon afterwards, the play brought its author the Pulitzer Prize.

In 1990, Wasserstein published *Bachelor Girls*, a collection of humorous essays from *New York Woman* magazine. *Booklist* reviewer Ilene Cooper compared Wasserstein to Fran Lebowitz, whose humor also turns on the trials of being a single, Jewish woman in New York City. According to Cooper, the great difference is that Wasserstein's "wit is gently filtered rather than raw and rough." She noted, however, that "that doesn't mean she pulls her punches." *Time* contributor Margaret Carlson was less generous in her assessment of *Bachelor Girls*, stating that "the territory Wasserstein covers has been strip-mined by those who preceded her. . . . A piece about the split between women who shave their legs and those who don't would have to come up with some dazzling insights to merit another look." Carlson believed that Wasserstein's best work is most evident in the last piece in the book, a one-act play. A *Publishers Weekly* reviewer was also lukewarm, terming the collection only "semi-humorous," but a *Los Angeles Times Book Review* writer deemed it a "very funny blend of self-deprecation, pride and bemusement."

In her next play, Wasserstein again demonstrated humor underlaid with seriousness. *The Sisters Rosensweig* "looks at the lives of women who are weighing priorities and deciding which doors to open and deciding which gently to close," reported Linda Simon in the *Atlanta Journal-Constitution*. The play is set in London, where fifty-four-year-old Sara is celebrating her birthday with her two younger sisters. Twice divorced and having long abandoned any hope of real romance in life, she is surprised when love suddenly seems possible after all. "With her focus on the hidden yearnings and emotional resistance of the women, . . . [Wasserstein's] obvious debt is to Noel Coward. . . . *The Sisters Rosensweig* is very much a drawing room comedy." Mel Gussow, theater reviewer for the *New York Times*, found echoes of Chekhov in Wasserstein's work: "Overlooking the play is the symbolic figure of Anton Chekhov, smiling. Although the characters do not directly parallel those in *The Three Sisters*, the comparison is intentional. . . . Ms. Wasserstein does not overstate the connection but uses it like background music while diverting her attention to other cultural matters."

Wasserstein's much-anticipated play *An American Daughter* debuted in 1997. A satire on the manners and mores of "official" Washington, it is peopled by a host of recognizable political animals, from a crusty Southern Senate baron to a closeted gay conservative. At the center of the storm of comings and goings is Dr. Lyssa Dent Hughes, an upright feminist physician nominated to become the next Surgeon General. Confirmation problems ensue when it is revealed that she forgot to show up for jury duty some years before. Many reviewers found the play muddled, the comedy weighed down by political pretension. "Wasserstein has little to say, and that little is false," wrote Stefan Kanfer in the *New Leader,* deriding the play for its shallow characters and "sitcom soul." The play's "brisk satire gives way to whiny venting and windy summations that have marred earlier Wasserstein plays," wrote Misa Berson in the *Seattle Times,* though she found some of Wasserstein's political quipping trenchant and breezy.

In earlier plays, Wasserstein frequently presented remarkable women who, despite their gifts, felt their options closing down with the passing of the years. In *The Sisters Rosensweig,* the playwright presented images of strong, intelligent, middle-aged women whose lives are still full of possibilities. Several reviewers characterized it as Wasserstein's most hopeful play. Discussing the process of aging with Claire Carter for *Parade,* Wasserstein noted that she found turning forty to be a liberating experience. "Before turning 40, I got very depressed," she mused. "I kept making lists of things I had to do before 40. I drove myself crazy. Then after I turned 40, I thought, 'I don't have to do these things.' I was much happier after that."

BIOGRAPHICAL/CRITICAL SOURCES:

PERIODICALS

American Book Review, November-December, 1989, p. 4.
Atlantic Journal-Constitution, May 23, 1993, p. N10.
Booklist, March 15, 1990, p. 1413.
Boston Globe, February 1, 1990, p. 69; March 3, 1991, p. B1; March 8, 1991, p. 25; March 22, 1991, p. 78; April 1, 1993, p. 61; January 27, 1994, p. 45; October 9, 1994, section 13, p. 7.
Chicago Tribune, October 12, 1985; November 10, 1985; April 24, 1990, section 5, p. 3; October 21, 1990, section 6, p. 1; March 15, 1992, section 13, p. 22; November 30, 1992, section 5, p. 1; October 9, 1994, section 13, p. 7.
Christian Science Monitor, April 30, 1986; April 30, 1991, p. 12; November 5, 1992, p. 13; November 15, 1994, p. 14.
Harper's Bazaar, April, 1994, p. 120.
Horizon, February, 1978.
Los Angeles Magazine, September, 1994, p. 140.
Los Angeles Times, January 31, 1984; October 28, 1984; October 30, 1984; December 17, 1988; October 15, 1990, p. F1; September 20, 1991, p. F20; July 31, 1994, section CAL, p. 45; December 29, 1994, p. F1.
Los Angeles Times Book Review, August 25, 1991, p. 10; May 30, 1993, p. 6.
Nation, December 17, 1977; February 18, 1984; May 1, 1989, pp. 605-6; October 16, 1995, p. 443.
New Leader, December 7, 1994, p. 22.
Newsweek, March 20, 1989, pp. 76-77.
New York, June 29, 1981; January 2, 1989, pp. 48-49; March 27, 1989, pp. 66, 68; June 13, 1994, p. 72; November 7, 1994, p. 102.
New Yorker, December 5, 1977; June 22, 1981; June 13, 1983; December 26, 1983; December 26, 1988, pp. 81-82; November 14, 1994, p. 130; March 6, 1995, p. 132.

New York Post, November 22, 1977; December 16, 1983; April 23, 1986; December 12, 1988.
New York Times, November 22, 1977; May 24, 1978; June 23, 1978; December 27, 1978; June 8, 1979; February 15, 1981; May 24, 1981; June 15, 1981; June 28, 1981; July 17, 1983; December 16, 1983; January 1, 1984; January 3, 1984; February 26, 1984; June 13, 1984; January 3, 1986; March 28, 1986; April 23, 1986; January 11, 1987; August 30, 1987; January 24, 1988; June 8, 1988; December 11, 1988; December 12, 1988, p. C13; February 19, 1989; March 12, 1989; October 9, 1989, pp. C13, 16; January 24, 1991, p. C15; October 18, 1992, section 2, pp. 1, 24; October 23, 1992, p. C3; November 1, 1992, section 2, p. 5; December 6, 1992, section 9, p. 12; February 13, 1994, section 2, p. 5; May 23, 1994, p. C14; October 16, 1994, section 2, p. 5; October 27, 1994, p. C15; May 2, 1995, section 1, p. 37.
Parade, September 5, 1993, p. 24.
People Weekly, March 26, 1984.
Publishers Weekly, March 2, 1990, p. 68.
Seattle Times, May 1, 1997.
Time, December 5, 1977; December 26, 1983; March 27, 1989, pp. 90-92; April 16, 1990, p. 83.
Village Voice, December 20, 1988.
Wall Street Journal, December 16, 1988.
Washington Post, May 3, 1985; May 6, 1985; March 22, 1991, p. F3; November 12, 1991, p. D4; March 13, 1994, pp. G1, 6-7.

*   *   *

WATERHOUSE, Keith (Spencer) 1929-
(Lee Gibb, a joint pseudonym)

PERSONAL: Born February 6, 1929, in Leeds, England; son of Ernest and Elsie Waterhouse; married Joan Foster, October 21, 1950 (divorced, 1968); children: Penelope, Sarah, Robert. *Education:* Attended Osmondthorpe Council School, Leeds.

ADDRESSES: Home—29 Kenway Rd., London SW5 0RP, England. *Agent*—London Management, 2-4 Noel St., London, W1V 3RB, England.

CAREER: Journalist, screenwriter, playwright, novelist.

WRITINGS:

(With Guy Deghy) *Cafe Royal: Ninety Years of Bohemia,* Hutchinson, 1955.
There Is a Happy Land (novel), M. Joseph, 1957.
(With Paul Cave) *Britain's Voice Abroad,* Daily Mirror Newspapers (London), 1957.
The Future of Television, Daily Mirror Newspapers, 1958.
(With Herald Froy [pseudonym of Guy Deghy]) *How to Avoid Matrimony,* Muller, 1958, Day, 1959.
(With Deghy, under joint pseudonym Lee Gibb) *The Joneses: How to Keep Up with Them,* Muller, 1959.
Billy Liar (novel), M. Joseph, 1959, Norton, 1960.
(With Willis Hall) *Billy Liar: A Play in Three Acts* (based on the novel; first produced in London at the Cambridge Theatre, September 13, 1960; first produced in Los Angeles at the Stage Society Theatre, January, 1963), M. Joseph, 1960, Norton, 1961.
(With Deghy, under joint pseudonym Lee Gibb) *The Higher Jones,* Muller, 1961.
(With Hall) *Celebration* (play; first produced in Nottingham, England, at the Nottingham Playhouse, March, 1961; first

produced in London at the Duchess Theatre, June 8, 1961), M. Joseph, 1961.

(With Hall) *England, Our England* (play, first produced in London at the Green Hippodrome, April 9, 1962; produced in London at the Prince's Theatre, May 7, 1962), Evans Brothers, 1964.

(With Hall) *All Things Bright and Beautiful* (play; first produced in Bristol, England, at the Bristol Old Vic, October 23, 1962; first produced in London at the Phoenix Theatre, December 13, 1962), M. Joseph, 1963.

(With Hall) *The Sponge Room* and *Squat Betty* (plays; first produced in Nottingham, England, at the Nottingham Playhouse, November 13, 1962; first produced in London at the Royal Court Theatre, December 18, 1962), Evans Brothers, 1963.

(With Hall) *Joey, Joey* (play), first produced in Bristol, England, at the Bristol Old Vic, December 26, 1962; first produced in London at the Saville Theatre, November, 1966.

Jubb (novel), M. Joseph, 1963, Putnam, 1964.

(With Hall) *They Called the Bastard Stephen* (play; first produced in Bristol at the Bristol Old Vic, 1964; first produced in London at the Wimbledon Theatre as *Come Laughing Home*, March 29, 1965), published as *Come Laughing Home*, Evans Brothers, 1966.

(With Hall) *Say Who You Are* (play; first produced in Guildford, England, at the Yvonne Arnaud Theatre, August 3, 1965; first produced in London at the Haymarket Theatre, October 14, 1965; first produced on Broadway at the Booth Theatre as *Help Stamp Out Marriage*, September 29, 1966), Evans Brothers, 1966.

(Editor with Hall) *Writers' Theatre*, Heinemann, 1967.

(With Hall) *Whoops-a-Daisy* (play; first produced in Nottingham at the Nottingham Playhouse, December, 1968), Evans Brothers, 1978.

The Bucket Shop (novel), M. Joseph, 1968, published in America as *Everything Must Go*, Putnam, 1969.

(With Hall) *Children's Day* (play; first produced in Nottingham at the Nottingham Playhouse, July, 1969), Samuel French, 1975.

The Warmongers (television script), British Broadcasting Corp., 1970.

(With Hall) *Who's Who* (play; first produced in Coventry, England, at the Belgrade Theatre, July 6, 1971; first produced in London at the Fortune Theatre, June 27, 1973), Samuel French, 1974.

(With Hall) *The Card* (play; adaptation of novel by Arnold Bennett), first produced in Bristol at the Bristol Old Vic, 1973; first produced in London at the Queen's Theatre, July 23, 1973.

(With Hall) *Saturday, Sunday, Monday* (play; adaptation of play by Eduardo de Filippo; first produced in London at the National Theatre, October 31, 1973), Heinemann, 1974.

The Passing of the Third Floor Buck, M. Joseph, 1974.

Billy Liar on the Moon, M. Joseph, 1975, Putnam, 1976.

Mondays, Thursdays, M. Joseph, 1976.

Office Life, M. Joseph, 1978.

(With Hall) *Filumena* (adaptation of the play by Filippo), Samuel French, 1978.

The Upchat Line (television script), Thames Television, 1978.

The Upchat Connection (television script), Thames Television, 1979.

(With Hall) *The Television Adventures of Worzel Gummidge*, Penguin, 1979.

Rhubarb, Rhubarb, and Other Noises, M. Joseph, 1979.

(With Hall) *Worzel Gummidge* (play), first produced in Birmingham, England, at the Birmingham Repertory Theatre, December 12, 1980.

(With Hall) *More Television Adventures of Worzel Gummidge*, Penguin, 1980.

(With Hall) *Worzel Gummidge at the Fair*, Penguin, 1980.

(With Hall) *Worzel Gummidge Goes to the Seaside*, Penguin, 1980.

(With Hall) *The Trials of Worzel Gummidge*, Penguin, 1981.

Maggie Muggins; or, Spring in Earl's Court, M. Joseph, 1981.

"Daily Mirror" Style, Mirror Books, 1981.

West End Tales (television script), Thames Television, 1981.

In the Mood, M. Joseph, 1983.

Mrs. Pooter's Diary, Corgi, 1984.

Thinks, M. Joseph, 1984.

(With Hall) *Irish Adventures of Worzel Gummidge*, Severn House Publishers, 1984.

Theory and Practice of Lunch, M. Joseph, 1986.

The Collected Letters of a Nobody, M. Joseph, 1986.

(With Hall) *Worzel Gummidge Down Under*, Grafton Books, 1987.

Waterhouse at Large, Grafton Books, 1987.

Our Song, Hodder, 1988.

Jeffrey Bernard Is Unwell (play), first produced in London at the Apollo Theatre, October, 1989.

Bookends (based on Craig Brown's *The Marsh Marlowe Letters*), first produced in London at the Apollo Theatre, November, 1990.

Bimbo, Hodder & Stoughton, 1990.

English, Our English (and How to Sing It), Viking, 1991.

Unsweet Charity, Hodder & Stoughton, 1992.

City Lights: A Street Life, Hodder & Stoughton, 1994.

Streets Ahead: Life After City Lights, Hodder & Stoughton, 1995.

SCREENPLAYS; WITH WILLIS HALL

Whistle Down the Wind (adaptation of novel by Mary Hayley Bell), AFM-Beaver, 1961.

A Kind of Loving (adaptation of novel by Stan Barstow), BHP-Euro-International, 1962.

The Valiant, BHP-Euro-International, 1963.

Billy Liar, Vic-Waterhall, 1963.

West Eleven (adaptation of novel by Laura del Rivo), Dial Films, 1963.

Man in the Middle (adaptation of novel by Howard Fast), Pennebaker-Belmont, 1964.

Pretty Polly (adaptation of story by Noel Coward), George-Granat-Universal, 1967.

Lock Up Your Daughters (adaptation of play by Bernard Miles), Domino, 1969.

TELEVISION SCRIPTS; WITH WILLIS HALL

Inside George Webley (series), Yorkshire Television, 1968.

Queenie's Castle (series), Yorkshire Television, 1970.

Budgie (series), Weekend Television, 1971-72.

The Upper Crusts (series), London Weekend Television, 1973.

Three's Company (series), BBC, 1973.

Billy Liar (series), London Weekend Television, 1973-74.

RADIO SCRIPTS

The Town That Wouldn't Vote, BBC, 1951.

There Is a Happy Land, BBC, 1962.

The Woollen Bank Forgeries, BBC, 1964.

The Last Phone-In, BBC, 1976.

The Big Broadcast of 1922, BBC, 1979.

SIDELIGHTS: Keith Waterhouse's satire and caricatures have been cited in discussions of the "Angry Young Men" school of writing, while his heroes have been compared with those of Alan Sillitoe and John Osborne. But he defies classification. Burling Lowrey in the *Saturday Review* writes: "He is not visibly anti-Establishmentarian, nor pro-Red Brick, nor a prole. He is himself an original with a talent for exposing hypocrisy, stupidity, and corruption with comic detachment." Waterhouse's novels and plays are marked by what Paul Schlueter in the *Dictionary of Literary Biography* calls "a sardonic, even cynical perspective, in which seemingly doomed characters flounder as they attempt to discover who they are and what they have to offer the world. Waterhouse uses humor, especially exaggeration and wit, as a calculated, objective means of showing his characters to be both psychically and ethically empty."

Billy Liar, a novel about a daydreaming undertaker's assistant who has trouble distinguishing his fantasies from reality, established Waterhouse as a novelist of distinction, and most critics agree with Hubert Saal of *Saturday Review,* who called the book "a brilliant novel, in language fresh and sweet, with characters vivid and singular in an inventive and dynamic story. It teems, it bursts with originality." Judith Thompson notes in the *Dictionary of Literary Biography* that "the combination of humor and pathos in Billy's adolescent fantasies about life in London and his absurd and painful relationship with his social and domestic context was readily translatable onto the stage." The stage version of the story ran for 600 performances in London; a television series based on the book ran on London Weekend Television in 1973-74.

The play *Jeffrey Bernard Is Unwell* is based on the life and writings of *Spectator* writer Jeffrey Bernard, whose column, "Low Life," chronicles his life at the Coach and Horses pub in London's Soho district. The title comes from the euphemistic explanation the *Spectator* runs on those weeks when Bernard is not sober enough to write his column. The play begins with the columnist crawling out from under a table to find himself locked in the Coach and Horses for the night. Once he realizes his predicament, he settles down with a drink and begins to look back over his life, his three marriages, and his many visits to the dog and horse tracks. Bernard is a pub philosopher whose anecdotes, regrets, reminiscences, and observations form the core of the play. *Jeffrey Bernard Is Unwell* ran for nearly two years, first at the Apollo Theatre and then at the larger Shaftesbury Theatre.

Other Waterhouse works range from the North Country realism of *All Things Bright and Beautiful* to the black comedy of *Jubb.* In his best work, he manages to present characters "on the fringes of society, finely drawing out the pathos and dignity," as Carol Rumens observes in the *Times Literary Supplement.* Alan Hollinghurst, writing in *New Statesman,* finds that Waterhouse "has compacted two kinds of comedy: a relentlessly observant ridicule of the world, and a private systematisation of things carried out by the characters to protect themselves from their uncharitable and ridiculous circumstances." Thompson believes that Waterhouse's versatility may have "denied him some rightful acclaim," but concludes: "He is a man of exceptionally varied talents: his wit, intelligence, and capacity to entertain are fired by an acute and compassionate observation of society and human behavior, a modest humanitarianism which cares deeply that people should have access to beauty—and to laughter."

Our Song, published a year before *Jeffrey Bernard Is Unwell* debuted, recounts a failed love affair between a married advertising executive and a much younger office worker. In the form of unsent letters to the young woman, the jilted older man chronicles their romance involving champagne lunches, lost jobs, financial woes, and his relentless fascination with her alluring, though dangerously unpredictable, behavior. Drawing thematic comparisons to earlier works such as *Jubb* and *Thinks,* D. A. N. Jones writes in a *Times Literary Supplement* review of *Our Song,* "It deals ruthlessly with the steady disintegration of a middle-aged 'no hoper' who surrenders to his lusts, passions, obsessions: the victim has set up a mechanism that entraps him, leading him toward madness." While noting similarities between *Our Song* and Vladimir Nabokov's *Lolita,* some critics cite overly sentimental and sexist elements in the novel. However, as John Naughton concludes in an *Observer* review, Waterhouse "has the knack of making you feel for his characters even as you laugh at them."

Unsweet Charity, published in 1992, is a satire on large scale modern fund-raising campaigns and involves a newspaper editor and reporter, bankers, and a nymphomaniac widow. The novel received unfavorable reviews on account of perceived tabloid superficiality and hackneyed writing. Critical of Waterhouse's underdeveloped and unoriginal message, Tom Shone writes in the *Spectator,* "Charity, [Waterhouse] concludes, with that authority which comes from thousands having said the same thing before, is a selfish thing, a balm to the conscience."

In 1994 Waterhouse produced *City Lights: A Street Life,* a memoir of his formative years in Leeds between 1936 and 1953 in which he recounts early experiences as the fifth child of a widow, wanderings and life in the commercial town, initial experiments with writing, and his rise as a journalist. Praising Waterhouse's unsentimental portrayal of working class culture, Michael Ratcliffe writes in the *Observer,* "Keith Waterhouse writes so well about the fabled country of childhood that I cannot imagine anyone reading this seductive, loving, and very funny memoir without being stirred into making comparisons with their own lives." Another *Observer* reviewer describes *City Lights* as "one of the best English autobiographies of recent years." *Streets Ahead: Life After City Lights,* published the next year and a sequel to *City Lights,* continues Waterhouse's autobiographical story to the present. Reflecting on his long career as a professional writer, Waterhouse chronicles his multifarious experiences as a reporter, novelist, scriptwriter, and playwright. Though some reviewers criticize Waterhouse for revealing little of his personal life or private motivations, a sentiment also directed at *City Lights,* others note that Waterhouse offers an engaging description of Fleet Street writers and his own accomplishments. As Richard Ingrams avers in the *Observer,* "the generally self-congratulatory tone of the book may be too much of a good thing, but unlike many who blow their own trumpet, Waterhouse has a good deal of which he can feel justly proud."

Speaking to Candida Crewe in the London *Times,* Waterhouse remarks: "I'm a journeyman writer. There were lots in the pre-war days. Shaw used to write magazine articles about how ladies shouldn't wear hats in the cinema. There are a lot of snoots about but, me, I'm ever-grateful to be earning a living from writing."

BIOGRAPHICAL/CRITICAL SOURCES:

BOOKS

Armstrong, W. A., and others, *Experimental Drama,* G. Bell, 1963.
Contemporary Fiction in America and England, 1950-1970, Gale (Detroit), 1976.
Contemporary Literary Criticism, Volume 47, Gale, 1988.

Dictionary of Literary Biography, Gale, Volume 13: *British Dramatists since World War II,* 1982; Volume 15: *British Novelists, 1930-1959,* 1983.

Gindin, James, *Postwar British Fiction: New Accents and Attitudes,* University of California Press, 1962.

Gray, Nigel, *The Silent Majority: A Study of the Working Class in Post-War British Fiction,* Barnes & Noble, 1973.

Handley, Graham, *Brodie's Notes on Billy Liar,* Pan Books, 1977.

Karl, Frederick R., *The Contemporary English Novel,* Farrar, Straus, 1962.

O'Connor, William Van, *The New University Wits,* Southern Illinois University Press, 1963.

PERIODICALS

Books, August, 1988.

Books and Bookmen, January, 1979; July, 1983.

British Book News, December, 1983; October, 1984.

Chicago Sunday Tribune, June 10, 1960.

Critique, Volume 10, number 3, 1968.

Drama, summer, 1966.

Hudson Review, spring, 1961.

Illustrated London News, December 29, 1962.

Listener, November 6, 1975; June 30, 1983; September 6, 1984.

New Statesman, September 12, 1959; September 17, 1960; December 28, 1962; October 4, 1968; June 12, 1981; March 16, 1990, p. 35; March 29, 1991, p. 34.

Newsweek, April 6, 1964.

New Yorker, March 7, 1964.

New York Times, September 30, 1966; December 13, 1968; December 1, 1989; December 3, 1989.

New York Times Book Review, January 3, 1960; April 5, 1964; January 26, 1969; February 8, 1976.

Observer, November 5, 1978; October 2, 1983; April 13, 1986; July 10, 1988; March 21, 1994; March 5, 1995; October 22, 1995.

Saturday Review, February 27, 1960; April 4, 1964.

Spectator, September 11, 1959; December 28, 1962; October 25, 1975; July 16, 1988; October 21, 1989; April 4, 1992; April 30, 1994; September 23, 1995; November 25, 1995.

Times (London), February 21, 1961; May 8, 1962; October 15, 1965; September 4, 1969; September 6, 1984; April 17, 1986; March 15, 1990; October 20, 1990; March 16, 1991; March 27, 1991.

Times Literary Supplement, September 4, 1959; September 27, 1963; October 25, 1974; May 29, 1981; May 13, 1983; April 18, 1986; August 12-18, 1988; March 22, 1990; March 27, 1992.

Yale Review, March, 1960.

*   *   *

WATKINS, Gloria 1952-
(bell hooks)

PERSONAL: Born September 25, 1952, in Hopkinsville, KY; daughter of Veodis and Rosa Bell Watkins. *Education:* B.A., Stanford University, 1973; M.A., University of Wisconsin, 1976; Ph.D. in English, University of California, Santa Cruz, 1987.

ADDRESSES: Home—291 W. 12th St., New York, NY 10031. *Office*—Department of Afro-American Studies, Yale University, New Haven, CT 06520.

CAREER: Social critic, educator, and writer. Yale University, New Haven, CT, assistant professor of Afro-American studies and English, 1980-85; Oberlin College, OH, associate professor, 1985-94; City College of New York, professor of English, 1994–.

AWARDS, HONORS: Writer's award, Lila Wallace-Reader's Digest Fund, 1994.

WRITINGS:

UNDER NAME BELL HOOKS

Ain't I a Woman: Black Women and Feminism, South End Press, 1981.

Feminist Theory: From Margin to Center, South End Press, 1984.

Talking Back: Thinking Feminist, Thinking Black, Between-the-Lines, 1988.

Yearning: Race, Gender, and Cultural Politics, Between-the-Lines, 1990.

(With Cornell West) *Breaking Bread: Insurgent Black Intellectual Life,* South End Press, 1991.

A Woman's Mourning Song, Writers and Readers, 1992.

Black Looks: Race and Representation, South End Press, 1992.

Sisters of the Yam: Black Women and Self Recovery, South End Press, 1993.

Outlaw Culture: Resisting Representations, Routledge, 1994.

Teaching to Transgress: Education as the Practice of Freedom, Routledge, 1994.

Changing the Subject: Painting and Prints, Art In General, 1994.

Art on My Mind: Visual Politics, New Press, 1995.

Killing Rage: Ending Racism, Holt, 1995.

Reel to Real: Race, Sex and Class at the Movies, Routledge, 1996.

Bone Black: Memories of Girlhood, Holt, 1996.

Wounds of Passion: A Writing Life, Holt, 1997.

Happy to be Nappy (children's book), Hyperion, 1998.

Also contributor to *Double Stitch: Black Women Write about Mothers and Daughters,* 1992.

SIDELIGHTS: Gloria Watkins takes an analytical yet impassioned look at how certain factors—black womanhood, feminism, the civil rights movement, critical theory—cooperate and clash in the world at large and within herself. "At her best she exhibits a command of various voices that range from subtle overlays of the personal and historical to a refreshing public forthrightness that stings," writes P. Gabrielle Foreman in the *Women's Review of Books.* "Inevitably, a reader will cheer through one essay and scowl through another."

Born Gloria Watkins, the author writes under the name of bell hooks, the name of her great-grandmother, in order, according to Paula Giddings in *Ms.,* to "honor the unlettered wisdom of her foremothers." Indeed, it is the unheard voice of black women in general which drives her overall work.

Black women finding their voices within mainstream feminism is the focus of hooks's first three works: *Ain't I a Woman: Black Women and Feminism, Feminist Theory: From Margin to Center,* and *Talking Back: Thinking Feminist, Thinking Black. Ain't I a Woman* is her formative work in this regard. She develops her black feminism through an examination of the special oppression under which African American women suffered and still suffer, from slavery until the time of her writing. She finds, in the web of racism, sexism, and classism that make up that oppression, that black and white women are sometimes allies and sometimes at odds. Generally, competitiveness and the white woman's vested interest in classism often drives the wedge of racism between her and her black sisters.

This thesis is further systematized in *Feminist Theory,* in which she clearly states the basic ills of the three "isms": racism, classism, and sexism have at their root the notion of domination, which is the basis of the hierarchical—or "authoritarian/bureaucratic" organization—of (at least American) society. This kind of organization is opposed to a consensual/collectivist model which would eradicate the existing forces of control, manipulation, and domination, and thus redefine power throughout society. Being at the bottom of the power structure as it now stands, black women are naturally in the vanguard of liberation from the existing structure, by their very efforts at individual self-determination. They are not, however, recognized as such by mainstream feminist organizations, who see the world with the same hierarchical eyes as do white males, wanting merely to be in their positions. Real feminism, says hooks, should attack the whole hierarchical system.

Hooks's first three works have sometimes been seen as taking on too many voices to deal with their complex, inflammatory issues. A reviewer for *Publishers Weekly,* for example, notes that "although the author makes perceptive and provocative observations, they are diminished by redundancy and weakened by her doctrinaire Marxist rhetoric." In her review of *Feminist Theory,* Giddings wonders why black women and other women from the margins, since they *are* the vanguard, need to lobby at all to be included in other segments of the feminist movement, appearing to assign "proprietary rights to the same 'privileged' women she criticizes for their narrow perspective." And Patricia Bell-Scott, in the *Women's Review of Books,* admits to reacting defensively to some arguments that run against the feminist grain, and again points to the Marxist flavor as possibly irritating. "However," Bell-Scott continues, "we must keep in mind the author's goal, to enrich feminist discourse and 'to share in the work of making a liberatory ideology,' as we struggle with the uncomfortable issues she raises."

Though all of hooks's work contains self-examination, her fourth book, *Yearning: Race, Gender, and Cultural Politics,* seems to reassess all her efforts, as well as her various voices. In it she continues to broaden her cultural criticism, using more and more of the theoretical tools available to (and expected from) a cutting-edge, post-modern academic. Critics like P. Gabrielle Foreman find that central to this effort is an essay, "Homeplace: A Site of Resistance," in which hooks once more returns home to find her "location" of strength, a sense of community in the households set up by black women. This "location" helps her to solidify her base point of view, even as she sets out to examine more of her overall culture, and a black woman's part in it, from more varied and theoretical perspectives. This might be the reason that critics, among them Foreman, see her often contradicting herself and taking on the white feminists' point of view. For Foreman, though, it is her "'intervention' into the politics of post-modern theory and practice that makes *Yearning* so timely and valuable." She tries, for example, to untangle the theories of "Otherness"— the position of outsiders within a culture—that have been primarily produced by insiders or white scholars. This includes their theorizing on "essentialism"—in this case the reality of racial groupings, and the politics of identity based on those groupings. This is a complicated question for hooks, since blacks can be affected by both sides of this dilemma.

Teaching to Transgress: Education as the Practice of Freedom, hooks's 1994 collection of essays about teaching, was described by a *Publishers Weekly* reviewer as "full of hope and excitement for the possibility of education to liberate and include." While some of hooks's essays are critical of the established teaching community, the reviewer concluded that "while some will find her rejection of certain difficult theory narrow-minded, it is a small flaw in an inspired and thought-provoking collection."

Outlaw Culture: Resisting Representations is a collection of twenty-one essays that, as a *Publishers Weekly* reviewer said, "will enhance . . . hooks' reputation as an astute, vigorous and freewheeling critic on matters of race, class and gender." hooks again focuses on women of color in these essays, expounding on questions of censorship, black feminist perspectives on people like Malcolm X, and the impact of mainstream gender theorists. The reviewer concluded by stating that "though formulaic at times, hooks' critical style is refreshingly brash and accessible and often inflected by personal experience." Sharon Firestone, writing for *Library Journal,* said that the collection "does not make for comfortable reading—and is not meant to." Firestone referred to hooks's essays as "cogent" and necessitating "the reader reexamine familiar assumptions." The book is highly recommended for all, but especially as an addition to collections on feminism, gender, and race.

In *Art on My Mind: Visual Politics,* hooks continues to explore the place of African-American women through a collection of eighteen essays. Commenting on contemporary art, hooks describes the relationship between the dominant white, male art and the creativity of African-American artists, particularly black women. Relating her own personal experiences, hooks looks at her artistic background as both creator and observer of art. A writer for *Kirkus Reviews* described the book as "an odd creature." The book is divided into two parts, and the *Kirkus* reviewer wrote, "The first half is a rocky road full of academic artcrit jargon . . . the second half . . . a return to form for one of the most astute cultural and political writers in the country today." The reviewer concluded that "it is impossible to imagine hooks writing a book devoid of interest." Hooks's essays portray her frustration with the lack of black critics writing on contemporary art. A *Publishers Weekly* reviewer described her "knack for balancing flat academic jargon with vivid language, illuminating the historical and psychoanalytic underpinnings of her topics while anticipating the visceral responses of a lay audience." Her approach to the subject of art and the part black women take in it "transforms academic abstractions into recognizable human patterns linking the everyday lives of Americans, black or white." Donna Seaman, a critic for *Booklist,* summarized the valuable contribution hooks makes with her essays in *Art on My Mind* when she wrote that hooks "hones her aesthetic in her adept interpretations of the work and impact of black artists. . . . As erudite and sophisticated as hooks is, she is also eminently readable, even exhilarating."

Killing Rage: Ending Racism is hooks' 1995 collection of essays which address the continuing debate of the lasting psychological effects of white oppression on black society. Robert Fleming in *The Quarterly Black Review* wrote about these essays, saying that they "exemplify the power of positive thinking, humanist thought, and a deep-seated belief that fundamental change is possible in this society despite the cabal of old white men at the helm, dedicated to its denial." The sections on rage are a highlight, illustrating how white bigotry breeds frustration and pain. She explains how the "black elite" have taught themselves to suppress the existence of black rage and how, traditionally, blacks have ignored it or taken their anger and frustrations out on others— never on white society. Fleming encourages everyone to read hooks. She "is a pleasure to read because she possesses one of our most synthetic minds, usually accessible and highly capable in forging information from several sources into a cohesive whole." He went on to describe *Killing Rage* as having a "complex, savvy approach to the issues . . . not the type of book to be skimmed."

In *Reel to Real: Race, Sex and Class at the Movies,* hooks shares her essays on film. Although not reviews of movies, per se, her essays discuss culture as viewed through certain movies. The position of black women in culture, a theme so often addressed by hooks, surfaces again in this collection of essays. She discusses the differences between movies and books, as in her essay on *Waiting to Exhale.* A *Publishers Weekly* reviewer wrote: "This mix of theory, reality, popular art and popular criticism . . . is effective in forcing a rethinking of the films in question." Hooks extends her essays to also discuss "the black female gaze" as well as black male masculinity and how it is treated in the movies. The only criticism raised by the reviewer was that "the essays could have benefited from more thoughtful organization."

In hooks's 1996 memoir, *Bone Black: Memories of Girlhood* the author avoids convention in order to enlighten her readers about the lives of black girls in society. A *Publishers Weekly* reviewer declared that "her effort deserves close reading." Reviewing her own life, hooks recalls finding support in her black community, religion, and the library. She openly discusses finding sexuality and dealing with crushes, parental fighting, and white teachers in the black community. Overall, the reviewer described the book as "leav[ing] us with a familiar but not unsatisfying image, that of a sensitive youth finding in books deliverance from 'the wilderness of spirit,'" A writer for *Kirkus Reviews* saw the narrative employed by hooks as "oddly disembodied, somehow disturbingly disengaged [where] . . . moments of real force and pain are not sustained." Conversely, Seaman of *Booklist* expressed enthusiasm for hooks' writing, describing her as "ardent, questioning and rigorous." Seaman called *Bone Black* a "lyrical, deeply moving, and brilliantly structured autobiography of 'perceptions and ideas.'"

In a follow-up to *Bone Black,* hooks continued her memoir with *Wounds of Passion: A Writing Life,* taking the reader on a journey through a fifteen-year bittersweet relationship with a man, her return to her roots in the South, and into a relationship with someone who shares her passions for writing and sexual enjoyment. A *Publishers Weekly* reviewer complimented hooks, saying that she "straddles two worlds admirably, writing with great insight about both academia and the world beyond . . . [asking] the open-ended question of whether it is possible to live what we believe." *Library Journal* reviewer Ann Burns followed suit with her comments, describing the book as "exceptionally written, strongly recommended for poetry aficionados and feminist collections." Seaman of *Booklist* wrote that "hooks uses both direct first person narrator and a more distanced, pseudo-objective third-person persona, thus enriching the resonance of her personal and cultural reflection and realizations." But *Kirkus Reviews* took a less compliemtary view of hooks's writing, speaking of her shift from first to third person as resulting in "an ungainly and repetitive hodgepodge of tones that's most effective when it's most conventional."

BIOGRAPHICAL/CRITICAL SOURCES:

PERIODICALS

Atlanta Journal and Constitution, November 14, 1996.
Black Enterprise, June, 1992, p. 23.
Black Scholar, January, 1983, pp. 38, 46.
Booklist, June 1, 1995; September 15, 1996; September 15, 1997.
Choice, April, 1982, p. 1141; July, 1985, p. 1703; March, 1996.

Essence, July, 1989, p. 20; July, 1992, p. 124; July, 1993, p. 60; November, 1993, p. 81; September, 1994, p. 148; May, 1995, p. 187; August, 1995, p. 69; October, 1997, p. 44.
Kirkus Reviews, April 15, 1995; June 15, 1995; August 15, 1996; September 1, 1997.
Library Journal, December, 1981, p. 178; March 15, 1985, p. 68; December, 1988, p. 126; July, 1992, p. 109.
Los Angeles Times, April 9, 1995; February 2, 1996.
Ms., July, 1983, p. 24; October, 1985 p. 25; November/December, 1995, p. 85; September/October, 1994, p. 82.
Multicultural Review, April, 1992.
New Directions for Women, January, 1992, p. 22.
New Statesman & Society, October 22, 1982, p. 31; November 30, 1990, p. 39.
New York Times, June 21, 1997, p. 19; November 13, 1997, p. F1.
New York Times Book Review, September 17, 1995, p. 25; December 15, 1996, p. 32.
Phylon, March, 1983, p.85.
Political Science Quarterly, spring, 1983, p. 84.
Progressive, March, 1991, p. 42; October 1, 1997.
Publishers Weekly, November 18, 1988, p.72; November 22, 1991, p.49; June 15, 1992, p. 95; November 7, 1994; March 27, 1995; September 3, 1996; September 2, 1997.
Quarterly Black Review, 1995.
Queen's Quarterly, summer, 1990, p. 318.
Sight and Sound, June, 1991, p. 36.
Voice Literary Supplement, June, 1982, p. 10; November 7, 1995, p. 19.
West Coast Review of Books, April, 1982, p. 51.
Women's Review of Books, February, 1985, p. 3; September, 1991, p. 12; March 1, 1995.

*   *   *

WATSON, Irving S.
See MENCKEN, H(enry) L(ouis)

*   *   *

WATSON, Richard F.
See SILVERBERG, Robert

*   *   *

WAUGH, Evelyn 1903-1966

PERSONAL: Born October 28, 1903, in Hampstead, London, England; died April 10, 1966, in Combe Florey, Somerset, England; son of Arthur (an editor and publisher) and Catherine Charlotte (Raban) Waugh; married Evelyn Gardner, 1928 (divorced, 1930; marriage annulled, 1936); married Laura Herbert, 1937; children: (second marriage) Auberon, Margaret, Teresa, Harriet, James, Septimus. *Education:* Attended Hertford College, Oxford, 1921-24, and Heatherley's Art School, 1924. *Religion:* Roman Catholic.

CAREER: Writer. Worked as a school teacher, a journalist for the London *Daily Express,* and as war correspondent in Abyssinia (now Ethiopia). *Military service:* Royal Marines, 1939-40, Commandos, 1940-43, and the Royal Horse Guards, 1943-45; served in Crete, North Africa, and Yugoslavia; earned rank of major.

AWARDS, HONORS: Hawthornden Prize, 1936, for *Edmund Campion: Scholar, Priest, Hero, and Martyr;* James Tait Black Memorial Prize, 1953; Royal Society of Literature fellow and companion of literature, 1963; honorary degree from Loyola College; refused to accept Commander of the British Empire award.

WRITINGS:

NOVELS

Decline and Fall, Chapman & Hall, 1928, Doran, 1929.
Vile Bodies, J. Cape & H. Smith, 1930.
Black Mischief, Farrar & Rinehart, 1932.
A Handful of Dust, Farrar & Rinehart, 1934.
Scoop, Little, Brown, 1938, published in England as *Scoop: A Novel About Journalists,* Chapman Hall, 1938.
Put Out More Flags, Little, Brown, 1942.
Brideshead Revisited: The Sacred and Profane Memories of Captain Charles Ryder, Little, Brown, 1945, revised edition, Chapman & Hall, 1960.
Scott-King's Modern Europe, Chapman & Hall, 1947, Little, Brown, 1949.
The Loved One: An Anglo-American Tragedy, Little, Brown, 1948.
Helena, Little, Brown, 1950.
Men at Arms (also see below), Little, Brown, 1952.
Love among the Ruins: A Romance of the Near Future, Chapman & Hall, 1953.
Officers and Gentlemen (also see below), Little, Brown, 1955.
The Ordeal of Gilbert Pinfold: A Conversation Piece, Little, Brown, 1957.
Unconditional Surrender (also see below), Chapman & Hall, 1961, published as *The End of the Battle,* Little, Brown, 1962.
Basil Seal Rides Again; or, The Rake's Regress, Little, Brown, 1963.
Sword of Honour (contains *Men at Arms, Officers and Gentlemen,* and *Unconditional Surrender*), Chapman & Hall, 1965, Little, Brown, 1966.

STORY COLLECTIONS

Mr. Loveday's Little Outing and Other Sad Stories, Little, Brown, 1936, expanded edition published as *Charles Ryder's Schooldays and Other Stories,* 1982.
Work Suspended: Two Chapters of an Unfinished Novel, Chapman & Hall, 1942, expanded edition published as *Work Suspended and Other Stories Written before the Second World War,* Chapman & Hall, 1949.
Tactical Exercise, Little, Brown, 1954.

OTHER

The World to Come (poems), Westminster Press, 1916.
P.R.B.: An Essay on the Pre-Raphaelite Brotherhood, 1847-1854, Graham, 1926.
Rosetti: His Life and Works, Dodd, 1928.
A Bachelor Abroad, J. Cape & H. Smith, 1930 (published in England as *Labels: A Mediterranean Journal,* Duckworth, 1930).
Remote People, Duckworth, 1931, published as *They Were Still Dancing,* Farrar & Rinehart, 1932.
An Open Letter to His Eminence, the Cardinal Archbishop of Westminster, Whitefriars, 1933.
Ninety-Two Days: The Account of a Tropical Journey through British Guinea and Part of Brazil, Farrar & Rinehart, 1934 (published in England as *Ninety-Two Days: A Journey in Guinea and Brazil,* Duckworth, 1986).
Edmund Campion: Scholar, Priest, Hero, and Martyr, Sheed, 1935.
Waugh in Abyssinia, Longmans, 1936.
Mexico: An Object Lesson, Little, Brown, 1939 (published in England as *Robbery Under Law: The Mexican Object Lesson,* Chapman & Hall, 1939).
When the Going Was Good, Little, Brown, 1946.
Wine in Peace and War, Saccone & Speed, 1947.
The Holy Places (essays), Queen Anne, 1952, Queen Anne British Book Centre, 1953.
The World of Evelyn Waugh, edited by Charles J. Rolo, Little, Brown, 1958.
Monsignor Ronald Knox, Fellow of Trinity College, Oxford, and Protonotary Apostolic to His Holiness Pope Pius XII, Little, Brown, 1959 (published in England as *The Life of the Right Reverend Ronald Knox, Fellow of Trinity College, Oxford, and Protonotary Apostolic to His Holiness Pope Pius XII,* Chapman & Hall, 1959).
Tourist in Africa, Little, Brown, 1960.
A Little Learning: An Autobiography, the Early Years, Little, Brown, 1964, published in England as *A Little Learning: The First Volume of an Autobiography,* Chapman & Hall, 1964.
The Diaries of Evelyn Waugh, edited by Michael Davie, Weidenfeld & Nicolson, 1976, Little, Brown, 1977.
A Little Order: A Selection from the Journalism of Evelyn Waugh, edited by Donat Gallagher, Eyre Methuen, 1977.
The Letters of Evelyn Waugh, edited by Mark Amory, Ticknor & Fields, 1980.
The Essays, Articles and Reviews of Evelyn Waugh, edited by Donat Gallagher, Little, Brown, 1984.
Evelyn Waugh, Apprentice: The Early Writings, 1910-1927, edited and with an introduction by Robert Murray Davis, Pilgrim Books (Norman, OK), 1985.
Saint Edmund Campion: Priest and Marter, Sophia Institute Press (Manchester, NH), 1996.
The Letters of Nancy Mitford and Evelyn Waugh, Houghton Mifflin Co. (Boston), 1997.

MEDIA ADAPTATIONS: The Loved One was filmed by Metro-Goldwyn-Mayer in 1965; *Decline and Fall* was filmed as "Decline and Fall of a Bird Watcher" by Twentieth Century-Fox in 1969; film rights to *Brideshead Revisited* were sold in the late 1940s, but Waugh did not give final approval to the script and the film was never made; *Brideshead Revisited* was filmed for television as an eleven-and-one-half hour series by Granada Television in 1981 and adapted for a play by Roger Parsley in 1994; *A Handful of Dust* was adapted into a 1988 film by screenwriters Tim Sullivan and Derek Granger and director Charles Sturridge.

SIDELIGHTS. During a career lasting four decades, Evelyn Waugh was considered to be England's most prominent man of letters. He published highly regarded travel books, short stories, essays, and literary criticism. But it is as a novelist that Waugh is most remembered. Such early novels as *Decline and Fall, Vile Bodies,* and *Black Mischief* established his literary reputation as a fine satirist, while such later works as *Brideshead Revisited* brought him popular acclaim from an international audience. He was "one of the most devastating and effective satirists in the history of English letters," Paul A. Doyle of the *Dictionary of Literary Biography* declared, "and one of its greatest stylists." In an article for the *American Spectator,* George McCartney described Waugh as a "superbly gifted entertainer [who] was also one of our century's most important novelists."

Decline and Fall, written by Waugh at the age of twenty-five, is a satiric novel in which young Paul Pennyfeather is dismissed from Oxford and must make his own way in the world. Pennyfeather is a Candide-like innocent who passively watches the disturbing and corrupt events he finds himself in. The evil prosper, the good are punished, and no standards of behavior are operable. Pennyfeather lives in "a world as remote from moral considerations as a fairy story or a Marx Brothers film," Walter Allen wrote in *The Modern Novel.* Like many of Waugh's narrators, Pennyfeather "stands at the centre of [Waugh's] comedy, omniscient yet evasively neutral, surrounded by outrage and absurdity," as Malcolm Bradbury stated in *Possibilities: Essays on the State of the Novel.*

Because of the scandalous nature of *Decline and Fall,* Waugh was forced by his publisher to remove certain scenes from the novel and to preface the book with a disclaimer. On a first reading, it may seem as if Waugh were "allowing all seven deadly sins to hold sway and was enjoying the triumph of evil and decadence . . . with the most carefree insouciance possible," as Doyle stated. But a more careful examination of the text, Doyle continued, showed that "underneath the surface of absurdity and seeming indifference, there lies a basic standard of decency and fair play against which human aberrations are sharply contrasted." Anthony Burgess argued in his *Urgent Copy: Literary Studies* that the novel's continuing power is due to its underlying moral purpose. "Waugh's humour," Burgess wrote, "is never flippant. *Decline and Fall* would not have maintained its freshness for nearly forty years if it had not been based on one of the big themes of our Western literature—the right of the decent man to find decency in the world."

Black Mischief, Waugh's third novel, is set in Africa and concerns the attempted modernization of the country of Azania. "The abortive attempt to modernize Azania," Stephen Jay Greenblatt explained in *Three Modern Satirists: Waugh, Orwell, and Huxley,* "is not a statement of the African nation's inability to share in the glories of civilization but a sly and satiric examination of modernity itself." The Emperor Seth of Azania enlists the aid of the Englishman Basil Seal to bring his backward country into the twentieth century. But Seal's understanding of modern civilization is sadly shallow, and Seth's fervent efforts to follow Seal's guidelines result in tragedy for his people. Doyle called *Black Mischief* a "wild, rollicking comedy . . . with a more savage note of satire" than was found in Waugh's earlier books. Greenblatt saw *Black Mischief* as being concerned with the same themes as Waugh's earlier novels: "the shabbiness of Western culture, the decline and fall of institutions, the savagery underlying society."

Waugh's early novels established his reputation as a satirist of the first order. But Edmund Wilson, in his *Classics and Commercials: A Literary Chronicle of the Forties,* believed these books to be more than good satire. Wilson ranked them among the best novels written during the 1920s. Waugh's novels are, he wrote, "the only things written in England that are comparable to Fitzgerald and Hemingway. They are not so poetic; they are perhaps less intense; they belong to a more classical tradition. But I think that they are likely to last and that Waugh, in fact, is likely to figure as the only first-rate comic genius that has appeared in England since Bernard Shaw." *Gene Kellogg, writing in The Vital Tradition: The Catholic Novel in a Period of Convergence,* also praised Waugh's early novels. "The books which assure Waugh his place in literature," Kellogg wrote, "are his satires. Their vitality is such

that when one reads them the 'lost generation' and all the tragic emptiness that beset England after the First World War live again in startling immediacy."

Waugh's disenchantment with modern society led in 1930 to his conversion to Catholicism, an act which Rita Dallas of the *Washington Post* called "the most important event in his life." The conversion was spurred by the breakup of Waugh's first marriage. As Doyle explained it, "he was searching for a focus of order and stability where marriage vows were taken seriously and moral values were constantly emphasized."

This newfound religious purpose is first reflected in *A Handful of Dust,* published in 1934. Here, Waugh presents three-dimensional characters in "a seemingly simple story of the failure of a marriage," Greenblatt stated. But the novel, Greenblatt continued, becomes "a terrifying and bitter examination of humanism and modern society." Gone is the wild satire of Waugh's previous novels. "Waugh turned with this novel to more subtle satire and biting irony," Doyle wrote. "His comic satire [became] more embittered."

Largely autobiographical, the novel traces the collapse of Tony and Brenda Last's marriage after Brenda has an affair with John Beaver. Brenda's affair is encouraged by her sophisticated London friends. "The adultery of Lady Brenda Last and her parasite John Beaver," Brigid Brophy wrote in *Don't Never Forget: Collected Views and Reviews,* "catches a particular cold lust in action—in the very action of cold-sweating; theirs is a sado-masochistic relation which is expressed and enjoyed in social terms, in the actual mental vocabulary of snobbism." The novel ends in tragicomedy. A despairing Tony travels to the Brazilian jungle to forget his troubles but is taken prisoner by a Mr. Todd. Todd, a devotee of Charles Dickens, forces Tony into reading to him from Dickens' novels, presumably for the rest of his life.

The title of the novel is taken from a line in "The Waste Land" by T. S. Eliot, "I will show you fear in a handful of dust." The novel does convey, according to Wilson, "the impression of a terror, of a feeling that the bottom is just about to drop out of things." Doyle also saw this horrific element in *A Handful of Dust,* commenting that the novel was concerned with "the horror of twentieth-century amorality" and calling it "a classic portrayal of contemporary savagery." Robert Murray Davis, in *Papers on Literature and Language,* argued that *Decline and Fall, Black Mischief,* and *A Handful of Dust* were Waugh's "most successful novels." In each, Davis wrote, Waugh "presents the madness of the outer world as inevitable and therefore beyond judgment and the refuge as desirable and necessary but not fully secure or satisfying." Speaking of *A Handful of Dust* in relation to other Waugh novels, Davis found that "because it confronts directly the ills of modern civilization and embodies them in characters rather than in a series of intellectual fads and because it traces more vividly and uncompromisingly the effects of seeking refuge from the world without adequate resources for the retreat or an ordered, enduring place of withdrawal, *A Handful of Dust* is the most penetrating of Waugh's novels."

Brideshead Revisited chronicles twenty years in the lives of the Marchmains, a wealthy English Catholic family. It is narrated by Charles Ryder, who befriends Sebastian Marchmain while attending Oxford in the 1920s and is later engaged to Sebastian's sister, Julia. Sebastian is an alcoholic; Julia has her first marriage annulled; and their father, long separated from his wife, returns to the Church only on his deathbed. "The lives of the Marchmains and of Charles Ryder are not pretty ones," James F. Carens admitted in *The Satiric Art of Evelyn Waugh,* "and their Catholicism is no easy consolation." Despite their trials, the "Marchmain family, in their various fashions, all yield, ultimately, to the promptings of their faith and bear witness to its enduring virtue," Wilson noted. Upon witnessing Lord Marchmain's deathbed return to the Church, Charles, too, accepts Catholicism as his faith.

Because of its essentially Catholic message and its alleged idealizing of the English upper classes, *Brideshead Revisited* proved to be the most controversial of Waugh's novels. "Its sentimentality and its apparent obeisance to the old siren attractions of both the English gentry and the Church," L. E. Sissman wrote in the *New Yorker,* "made [*Brideshead Revisited*] unswallowable to critics." One such critic is Bernard Bergonzi. Writing in *Critical Quarterly,* Bergonzi maintained that in *Brideshead Revisited,* "the aristocracy—particularly the Catholic aristocracy—were seen as the unique custodians of the traditional values in a world increasingly threatened by the barbarians." Wilson claimed that "Waugh's snobbery, hitherto held in check by his satirical point of view, has here emerged shameless and rampant."

Steven Marcus in his *Representations: Essays on Literature and Society* thought that the novel's religious ambitions were undermined by Waugh's inherent class bias. "Waugh's snobbery and growing biliousness," Marcus wrote, "could not accommodate themselves to humane, religious impulses. . . . Even Catholicism, most hierarchic of religious dispensations, is too democratic for Waugh. . . . The unpleasant atmosphere of *Brideshead Revisited* was directly a result of the far-reaching disagreement between Waugh and his religion." But Brad Leithauser of the *New Republic* argued that Waugh's Catholicism "gives *Brideshead Revisited,* the most unfairly denigrated of his novels, its submerged power. *Brideshead* was . . . the book in which Waugh invested the most of himself: in some ways, it was the book of his life."

Other critics noted a lush romanticism in Waugh's prose. Carens complained that Waugh tended in *Brideshead Revisited* "so to romanticize experience that his tone degenerates into sentimentality" and found the section of the book dealing with the affair between Julia and Charles to be filled with "one purple passage after another." Doyle explained in his book *Evelyn Waugh* that "the only serious mistake for which Waugh blamed himself was to write *Brideshead Revisited* in a romantic style, which has been called lush and lavish by several critics. . . . Waugh had committed an offense against his own canons of stylistic purity and restraint." In 1960 Waugh revised *Brideshead Revisited* in an attempt to curb the lush excesses of the original edition.

In the trilogy composed of *Men at Arms, Officers and Gentlemen,* and *The End of the Battle*—later published in a single volume as *Sword of Honour*—Waugh wrote of another religious conversion, that of Guy Crouchback, who is transformed "from an unloving 'loner' to a man of compassion," as Doyle explained in the *Dictionary of Literary Biography.* Tracing Crouchback's military career during the Second World War, the trilogy combines Waugh's usual satire with an emotional depth not found in his previous works. The success of the trilogy moved Patrick O'Donovan of the *New Republic* to call it "the one genuine masterpiece to come out of the war."

The first novel of the trilogy, *Men at Arms,* relates Crouchback's attempts to join the British war effort, his acceptance by the Royal

Corps of Halberdiers, and his military career until 1940. Crouchback is one of the last remaining members of an old and distinguished English family. Because he has been deserted by his wife, and his Catholic religious convictions do not permit him to remarry, Crouchback is a lonely and emotionally distant man. He sees the outbreak of the war, with its clear-cut moral distinctions, as a way to give his life meaning and purpose. But few of the other soldiers share his conviction. As Waugh explained to Jebb, "*Men at Arms* was a kind of uncelebration, a history of Guy Crouchback's disillusion with the army. Guy has old-fashioned ideas of honor and illusions of chivalry; we see these being used up and destroyed by his encounters with the realities of army life." Most of the novel's satire is directed at the cynicism and inefficiency of the military. The novel ends with Crouchback facing a court-martial for his role in a successful but unauthorized raid on enemy territory.

Reviewers especially praised *Men at War* for its satire of British military life. Edward Weeks of the *Atlantic* called it "a highly entertaining novel about some of the 'preposterous' experiences of the Second World War. . . . Waugh's sharp wit and sure touch of satire are always at work." James Hilton of the *New York Herald Tribune Book Review* judged *Men at War* to be "the wittiest of the war novels." And the *Times Literary Supplement* critic thought that "the novel contains comic passages as funny as anything since [*Decline and Fall*]."

In the next novel of the trilogy, *Officers and Gentlemen,* the satire is again dominant, although combined with more serious overtones. "The book," Christopher Hollis explained in his *Evelyn Waugh,* "is mainly concerned, as the title implies, with a study of how gentlemen behave before the challenge of modern war." "Because it verifies a deepening seriousness and charity in Mr. Waugh's art," R. T. Horchler said of the novel in *Commonweal,* "it extends and renews the promise of his brilliant talent." Speaking of the "blend of unlike ingredients" to be found in *Officers and Gentlemen,* James Gray of *Saturday Review* thought that the book "stimulates laughter again and again but its aftertaste is as bitter as the author meant it to be. . . . With it Waugh takes a higher place than he seemed previously to occupy."

The pivotal scene of *Officers and Gentlemen* is set on the Mediterranean island of Crete. Crouchback's unit is called upon to assist the beleaguered English forces fighting on the island. But the battle ends in total defeat as the Germans drive the English troops into the sea. The English officer Ivor Claire, "in whom Guy had thought that he recognized the perfect example of the type," Hollis wrote, "behaves badly at the evacuation, deserting his men in order to save himself."

Officers and Gentlemen is "satire, surely," Richard Sullivan wrote in the *New York Herald Tribune Book Review.* "But behind the mockery there is insight, sympathy and understanding that goes deep." Although disapproving of Waugh's political and social values as expressed in this novel, C. J. Rolo of the *Atlantic* admitted that *Officers and Gentlemen* "is a highly polished piece of work." Similarly, Maurice Richardson of the *New Statesman and Nation* marveled at "how consistently well [Waugh] writes, how much more conscientious he is about his words than most established novelists." Speaking of *Officers and Gentlemen* in the *New York Times,* Anatole Broyard called it "undoubtedly the best novel by an Englishman about [World War II]."

In the final volume of the trilogy, *The End of the Battle,* Crouchback is given a leave from the army to attend his father's funeral. The event serves to reacquaint him with the family religion, and he comes to embrace Catholicism with renewed vigor. His newfound sense of purpose contrasts sharply with his directionless companions. Crouchback "finds himself everywhere in the company of people with no roots, no understanding of what life is about, no sense of the dignity of its purpose," Hollis wrote. Because of his own moral stance, however, Crouchback can now take selfless actions on behalf of others. When his wife returns to him pregnant by a man she no longer loves, Crouchback takes her in to give the child a name and family, explaining that the war has created enough abandoned children. Sent to Yugoslavia to assist the underground, Crouchback helps a group of Jewish refugees to leave the country, despite efforts by the communist partisans to prevent it.

Shortly before his death Waugh published *A Little Learning: An Autobiography, the Early Years,* the first volume in a projected multi-volume autobiography. Because this projected work was never completed, and because Waugh's carefully nurtured public persona as an irascible reactionary distorted his true character, the public knew little about Waugh's actual life. This lack of knowledge was remedied with the posthumous publication of several volumes, including *The Diaries of Evelyn Waugh, The Letters of Evelyn Waugh,* and *The Essays, Articles and Reviews of Evelyn Waugh.* Waugh's diaries, letters, and collected articles revealed three levels of his character, as Paul Gray argued in *Time.* "First came the *Diaries,*" Gray wrote, "a revealing look at Waugh's private, sometimes drunken and usually unflattering thoughts about his contemporaries. Next arrived the *Letters . . . ,* in which the writer appeared in the less scathing demeanor he put on for his correspondents. Now this massive selection of Waugh's journalism [*The Essays, Articles and Reviews of Evelyn Waugh*] displays him fully dressed for his reading public."

The Diaries of Evelyn Waugh cover the years from 1911, when he was a young boy, to 1965, the year before his death. Omitted from the collection are Waugh's diaries for his years at Oxford, those written during his first marriage, and those from the period of his nervous breakdown in the 1950s. "The whole Oxford period was destroyed by Waugh," Nigel Dennis revealed in the *New York Review of Books.* During his college years Waugh had gone through a homosexual phase, later renounced, and did not want the record of that period preserved. Similarly, his first marriage and his breakdown were painful memories that Waugh preferred to omit.

A more favorable side of Waugh's personality is revealed in *The Letters of Evelyn Waugh.* "This is a far more amusing book than the hefty selection from Waugh's 'Diaries,'" Walter Clemons wrote in *Newsweek.* "Waugh reveals unexpected capacities for friendship: generosity, loyalty, delicacy and concern." Brad Leithauser of the *New Republic* thought that "the Evelyn Waugh who emerges [in the letters] is far more humane and interesting than the man who was presented a few years ago with the publication of his diaries." Waugh's letters to his family were especially revealing. "The letters to his children," Geoffrey Wheatcroft wrote in the *Spectator,* "are delightful and if he describes them to others with ironic resignation there is also a gleaming humorous affection." "His love letters to his second wife during their courtship," Michael Howard of the *Times Literary Supplement* commented, "are as tender and moving as any in the English language."

Evaluations of Waugh's career often focus on the reactionary persona which he enjoyed presenting to the world. "Waugh was The Great Literary Snob," Karl Keller maintained in the *Los Angeles Times Book Review.* "Most of the time this was natural enough, for he was high-bred, smart-setted and sharp-eyed. At other times it was a grand pose, for he found the world a great bore and himself a needed performer in it. . . . He gained his notoriety from his snobbery and so he played it to the hilt." Marcus observed that Waugh has been called "nasty, hateful, snobbish, trivial, reactionary, vindictive, fawning, immature, pompous, and rude, ascriptions which are substantially true yet somehow beside the point." McCartney found that Waugh's critics could not agree on a label that properly described him. "In their frustration," McCartney commented, "their labels anxiously proliferate: dandy, curmudgeon, wit, moralist, conservative, anarchist, Tory satirist, Catholic romancer, gentleman, snob, loyal friend, and, off the record, one mean son of a bitch. Well, which is it?" Because of Waugh's "contradictions, paradoxes, biases, and unpredictability," Doyle allowed in the *Dictionary of Literary Biography* that "in the notable history of British character oddities and great eccentrics, he must occupy a prominent place."

BIOGRAPHICAL/CRITICAL SOURCES:

BOOKS

Acton, Harold, *Memories of an Aesthete, 1934-1968,* Viking, 1970 (published in England as *More Memoirs of an Aesthete,* Methuen, 1970).

Allen, Walter, *The Modern Novel,* Dutton, 1964.

Bradbury, Malcolm, *Evelyn Waugh,* Oliver & Boyd, 1964.

Bradbury, Malcolm, *Possibilities: Essays on the State of the Novel,* Oxford University Press, 1973.

Brophy, Brigid, *Don't Never Forget: Collected Views and Reviews,* Holt, 1966.

Burgess, Anthony, *The Novel Now: A Guide to Contemporary Fiction,* Norton, 1967.

Burgess, Anthony, *Urgent Copy: Literary Studies,* Norton, 1969.

Carens, James F., *The Satiric Art of Evelyn Waugh,* University of Washington Press, 1966.

Clement, A., *The Novels of Evelyn Waugh: A Study in the Quest-Motif,* Prestige Books, 1994.

Contemporary Literary Criticism, Gale (Detroit), Volume 1, 1973; Volume 3, 1975; Volume 8, 1978; Volume 13, 1980; Volume 19, 1981; Volume 27, 1984; Volume 44, 1987.

Davis, Robert Murray, *Evelyn Waugh, Writer,* Pilgrim Books (Norman, OK), 1981.

Davis, Robert Murray, *A Catalogue of the Evelyn Waugh Collection at the Humanities Research Center,* The University of Texas at Austin, Whitston, 1981.

Dictionary of Literary Biography, Volume 15: *British Novelists, 1930-1959,* Gale, 1983.

Doyle, Paul A. and others, editors, *A Bibliography of Evelyn Waugh,* Whitston, 1986.

Greenblatt, Stephen Jay, *Three Modern Satirists: Waugh, Orwell, and Huxley,* Yale University Press, 1965.

Hastings, Selina, *Evelyn Waugh: A Biography,* Houghton Mifflin, 1994.

Heath, Jeffrey, *The Picturesque Prison: Evelyn Waugh and His Writing,* McGill-Queens University Press, 1982.

Hollis, Christopher, *Evelyn Waugh,* Longmans, Green, 1954.

Kellogg, Gene, *The Vital Tradition: The Catholic Novel in a Period of Convergence,* Loyola University Press, 1970.

Littlewood, Ian, *The Writings of Evelyn Waugh,* Basil Blackwell, 1983.

Mack, Maynard, and Ian Gregor, editors, *Imagined Worlds: Essays on Some English Novels and Novelists in Honour of John Butt,* Methuen, 1968.

Marcus, Steven, *Representations: Essays on Literature and Society,* Random House, 1975.

Morriss, Margaret, and D. J. Dooley, *Evelyn Waugh: A Reference Guide,* G. K. Hall, 1984.

Page, Norman, *An Evelyn Waugh Chronology,* St. Martin's Press, 1997.

Patey, Douglas Lane, *The Life of Evelyn Waugh: A Critical Biography,* Blackwell Publishers (Cambridge, MA), 1998.

Plimpton, George, editor, *Writers at Work: The "Paris Review" Interviews,* third series, Viking, 1967.

Stannard, Martin, editor, *Evelyn Waugh: The Critical Heritage,* Routledge & Kegan Paul, 1984.

Ward, A. C., *Twentieth-Century English Literature, 1901-1960,* Methuen, 1960.

Waugh, Alec, *My Brother Evelyn and Other Profiles,* Farrar, Straus, 1967.

Wilson, Edmund, *Classics and Commercials,* Farrar, Straus, 1950.

Wilson, John Howard, *Evelyn Waugh: A Literary Biography, 1903-1924,* Fairleigh Dickinson University Press, 1996.

PERIODICALS

American Spectator, January, 1985.

Atlantic Monthly, December, 1952; August, 1955; November, 1980.

Commonweal, October 24, 1952; August 12, 1955; February 2, 1962; January 26, 1996, p. 6.

Critical Quarterly, spring, 1963.

Esquire, September, 1973.

Essays in Criticism, October, 1978.

Evelyn Waugh Newsletter, 1967.

Georgia Review, summer, 1973.

Journal of Modern Literature, April, 1976.

Library Journal, October 1, 1977; March 1, 1995, p. 118.

London Magazine, August/September, 1973.

Los Angeles Times, July 14, 1988.

Los Angeles Times Book Review, February 15, 1981; October 3, 1982.

Midwest Quarterly, winter, 1977.

Modern Fiction Studies, summer, 1965.

Nation, January 20, 1962.

National Review, May 3, 1966; June 10, 1983; December 28, 1984; December 11, 1995, p. 128.

New Republic, July 11, 1955; February 12, 1962; May 12, 1979; October 18, 1980; December 6, 1982.

New Statesmen and Nation, July 9, 1955.

Newsweek, April 25, 1966; January 22, 1968; May 7, 1973; November 24, 1975; October 27, 1980.

New Yorker, February 4, 1974; January 16, 1978; December 22, 1980.

New York Herald Tribune Book Review, October 19, 1952; July 10,, 1955; January 7, 1962.

New York Review of Books, December 8, 1977; December 4, 1980.

New York Times, July 10, 1955; December 28, 1977; March 23, 1979; April 7, 1984; August 15, 1984.

New York Times, April 11, 1966.

New York Times Book Review, January 7, 1962; July 1, 1973; February 10, 1974; October 16, 1977; November 2, 1980; January 25, 1981.

Papers on Literature and Language, summer, 1967; spring, 1976.

Publishers Weekly, April 18, 1966.

Saturday Review, July 9, 1955; January 6, 1962; November 12, 1977.

Spectator, May 5, 1959; October 11, 1980; February 4, 1984.

Time, July 11, 1955; January 19, 1962; April 25, 1966; December 8, 1975; October 17, 1977; February 12, 1979; November 12, 1984.

Times Literary Supplement, May 16, 1960; October 27, 1961; September 3, 1976; February 3, 1978; October 17, 1980; October 5, 1984.

Washington Post, January 27, 1981.

Washington Post Book World, December 5, 1982; September 23, 1984.

*   *   *

WAYS, C. R.
See BLOUNT, Roy (Alton), Jr.

*   *   *

WEIL, Simone (Adolphine) 1909-1943
(Emile Novis)

PERSONAL: Born February 3, 1909, in Paris, France; died of starvation and pulmonary tuberculosis, August 24, 1943, in Ashford, England; daughter of Bernard (a physician) and Salomea (also known as Selma) Weil. *Education:* Studied under Alain at Henri IV Lycee, Paris, 1925-28; graduated from Ecole Normale Superieure, agregation (diploma), 1931. *Religion:* Jewish, converted to Christianity, c. late 1930s.

CAREER: French religious philosopher, essayist, dramatist, and poet. Taught philosophy at five girls' lycees, 1931-38; worked as a machine operator in three Paris factories for one year, c. 1930s; briefly worked in fall grape harvest near Marseilles, 1941. *Military service:* Volunteer for Republican forces during Spanish Civil War and for Free French forces in London during World War II.

WRITINGS:

(As Emile Novis) "L'Iliade, ou, Le Poeme de La Force" (essay), *Cahiers du Sud* (journal), 1940, published in the U.S. as "The Iliad, or The Poem of Force," translated by Mary McCarthy, in *Politics* (journal), November, 1945, reprinted as a pamphlet by Pendle Hill Publications (Wallingford, PA), 1956; 150 copies republished with preface by George P. Elliott, Stone Wall Press (Iowa City, IA), 1973.

La Pesanteur et La Grace (essays), introduction by Gustave Thibon, Librairie Plon (Paris), 1947, published as *Gravity and Grace,* translated by Arthur Wills, Putnam (New York City), 1952, Ark Paperbacks (London), 1987.

L'Enracinement: Prelude a une Declaration des Devoirs Envers L'Etre Humain (essay), Gallimard (Paris), 1949, published in U.S. as *The Need for Roots: Prelude to a Declaration of Duties toward Mankind,* translated by Arthur Wills, preface by T. S. Eliot, Putnam, 1952, Octagon Books, 1979, Ark Paperbacks, 1987.

L'Attente de Dieu (letters and essays), preface and notes by Joseph-Marie Perrin, La Colombe (Paris), 1950, published as *Waiting on God,* foreword by Malcolm Muggeridge, Routledge (London), 1951, published as *Waiting for God,* translated by Emma Craufurd, introduction by Leslie A. Fiedler, Putnam, 1951, Harper (New York), 1985.

La Connaissance Surnaturelle (title means "Supernatural Knowledge," also known as *Cahiers d'Amerique;* notebooks), Gallimard, 1950, published as *First and Last Notebooks* (containing *New York Notebook* and *London Notebook*), translated by Richard Rees, Oxford University Press (London), 1970.

La Condition Ouvriere (title means "The Workers' Condition," essays), Gallimard, 1951.

Les Intuitions Pre-chretiennes (essays), La Colombe, 1951.

Lettres a un Religieux (letters), Gallimard, 1951, also published as *Letters to a Priest,* translated by Arthur Wills, Routledge, 1953, Putnam, 1954.

Cahiers (notebooks), three volumes, Librairie Plon, 1951-56, portions published as *The Notebooks of Simone Weil,* two volumes, translated by Arthur Wills, Routledge, 1956, Putnam, 1956.

La Source Grecque (essays), Gallimard, 1953.

Oppression et Liberte (essays), Gallimard, 1955, published as *Oppression and Liberty,* translated by Arthur Wills and John Petrie, introduction by F. C. Ellert, University of Massachusetts Press (Amherst, MA), 1958.

Venise Sauvee: Tragedie en Trois Actes (play), Gallimard, 1955, revised with an introduction and notes by Jean-Marie Lhote, Theater Universitaire (Marseilles, France), 1965.

Ecrits de Londres et Dernieres Lettres (essays and letters), Gallimard, 1957.

Intimations of Christianity among the Ancient Greeks (contains translated selections from *La Source Grecque* and *Les Intuitions Pre-chretiennes*), edited and translated by Elisabeth Chase Geissbuhler, Routledge, also published in U.S. by Beacon Press (Boston), 1958.

Lecons de Philosophie de Simone Weil (Roanne 1933-1934) (lectures), edited by Anne Reynaud, Librairie Plon, 1959, published as *Lectures on Philosophy,* translated by Hugh Price, introduction by Peter Winch, Cambridge University Press (Cambridge), 1978.

Ecrits Historiques et Politiques (title means "Historical and Political Writings"; essays), Gallimard, 1960.

Selected Essays: 1934-1943, translated and arranged by Richard Rees, Oxford University Press (London), 1962.

Pensees sans Ordre Concernant L'Amour de Dieu (aphorisms), Gallimard, 1962.

Sur La Science (essays), Gallimard, 1965.

Seventy Letters, translated and arranged by Richard Rees, Oxford University Press, 1965.

Poemes, Suivis de "Venise Sauvee" (poetry and drama), 1968.

On Science, Necessity, and the Love of God, collected, translated, and edited by Richard Rees, Oxford University Press, 1968.

Gateway to God, edited by David Raper with collaborations by Malcolm Muggeridge and Vernon Sproxton, Fontana (London), 1974, Crossroad (New York City), 1982.

The Simone Weil Reader, edited by George A. Panichas, McKay (New York City), 1977.

Reflexions sur Les Causes de La Liberte et de L'Oppression Social (title means "Reflections on the Causes of Liberty and Social Oppression"), Gallimard, 1980.

Two Moral Essays: Draft for a Statement of Human Obligations and Human Personality, edited by Ronald Hathaway, Pendle Hill, 1981.

Simone Weil, an Anthology, edited and introduced by Sian Miles, Virago (London), 1986, Weidenfeld & Nicholson (New York City), 1986.

Formative Writings, 1929-1941, edited and translated by Dorothy Tuck McFarland and Wilhelmina Van Ness, University of Massachusetts Press, 1987.

COLLECTED WORKS

Oeuvres Completes, Edition Publiee sous La Direction d'Andre A. Devaux et de Florence de Lussy (title means "Complete Works, Edition Published under the Direction of Andre A. Devaux and Florence de Lussy"), six volumes, Gallimard, 1989-94.

SIDELIGHTS: During her lifetime, Simone Weil published only a few poems and articles in obscure left-wing journals. Since her death by starvation and pulmonary tuberculosis in a British sanitorium in 1943, however, Weil's essays, notebooks, and letters have been widely published, with the result that she has become one of the influential—and also one of the more controversial—religious thinkers of the twentieth century. Born in 1909 in Paris, the daughter of an Alsatian physician and his Austrian-Galician wife, Weil was doubly an outsider in French culture by virtue of her immigrant background and of being Jewish. Intelligent and sensitive, she refused to eat sugar at age five because no sugar was rationed to French soldiers who currently were fighting World War I. She graduated at age fifteen from a prestigious lycee, or high school, where she studied under the philosopher Alain (Emile Chartier). Her adolescence was marked by near-breakdowns and thoughts of suicide. She suffered from a lifelong feeling of inferiority to her older brother Andre, who had been considered a math prodigy from his earliest years. Anne Fremantle in *Saturday Review* physically described Simone Weil as "clumsy and unattractive" and that "she purposely wore dowdy clothes." After graduating from the Ecole Normale Superieure in 1931 (another excellent French school), Weil taught philosophy at girls' schools, but was unpopular with students and employers, and went through five jobs in seven years. According to a 1979 article by Jean Amery, Weil's students were bored by her, so much so that most failed the final exam.

For one year during the 1930s, Weil took a self-assigned furlough by working in factories. Amery described her as a "hopelessly inept worker." Weil, in the 1930s, was a leftist activist who participated in picket lines, published articles on the workers, and gave most of her salary to the poor, leaving herself only with the amount given to the unemployed as relief. Nevertheless, she expressed contempt for the revolutionary rhetoric of Lenin and others, which she considered unauthentic. She served briefly with an anarchist group during the Spanish Civil War, but left the experience feeling disenchanted by the brutality on both sides. The years 1936 through 1938 marked the crucial spiritual change in Weil's life. She began to study Christianity, which she considered the "religion of slaves"—a compliment in her view, since she identified with the oppressed. Afflicted with severe migraine headaches (which she suffered from all her life) and possibly malnourished, Weil experienced several mystical episodes. At the chapel of St. Francis of Assisi, in Assisi, Italy, in 1937, she felt pulled to her knees by an overpowering force. Other pivotal experiences occurred in 1938 while listening to Gregorian chants at an Easter mass, and while reciting British metaphysical poet George Herbert's "Love." During the latter experience, as she later wrote, "Christ Himself came down and took possession of me." In 1940, with the fall of France to the Nazis, her life changed of necessity. She moved to Marseilles and came under the influence of a Catholic priest, Jean-Marie Perrin, who in turn introduced her to Gustave Thibon, a farmer who was also a Catholic philosopher, and who hired Weil to work in the grape harvest. Weil left Thibon her notebooks for use in his own writing.

Weil then went to London to work with the Free French. She pleaded to be allowed to parachute into France, an action that would probably have been suicidal if permitted, since she was both Jewish and in frail physical health. In England she contracted tuberculosis and refused treatment, insisting that her food be limited to the rations given to French civilians. She died in a sanitorium at Ashford, Kent. The coroner's diagnosis, according to Amery, was "heart failure due to myocardial insufficiency caused by hunger and pulmonary tuberculosis," but Amery rephrased this as "suicide resulting from a religious compulsion neurosis." According to a *Twentieth-Century Literary Criticism* contributor, the cause of death was "voluntary starvation," although "it is still a matter for debate whether her death was a result of anorexia, actual suicide, mental illness, or a self-imposed martyrdom due to her unbending asceticism." In any event, the manner of Weil's death contributed greatly to her posthumous mystique, which in turn contributed to a welcome reception to the first publications of her works in the late 1940s and 1950s.

Weil's theology was highly personal and unorthodox, and has received both praise and criticism from all sides of the philosophical spectrum. She felt drawn to the Roman Catholic Church, but criticized it sharply for its rejection of other religions (although she criticized it equally for its absorption of Jewish influences), and refused to be baptized. The true Christian, she felt, did not consider herself worthy of baptism. Commentators have at times sought among the Christian heresies of the past for labels to apply to Weil. Eliot claimed that Weil fell into "something very like the Marcionite heresy" while Nobel Prize-winning poet Czeslaw Milosz called Weil, "at least by temperament, an Albigensian, a Cathar." Others have found Manichean dualistic elements in her writings. Weil's thought also was inspired by elements of Platonic philosophy, Greek tragedy, Hindu Upanishads, and ancient Egyptian and Chaldean worldviews.

In the first two decades after her death, Weil's work was variously edited and brought out in individual volumes. Her first title available in English was *Waiting for God* (1951), which was a collection of letters and essays from the early 1940s, all but one to the Dominican Father Jean-Marie Perrin. Anne Fremantle in *Saturday Review* commented that Weil's intelligence displayed in *Waiting for God* was "high." "So sharp are her analyses of ordinary human situations that these situations seem clearly visible for the first time," noted Fremantle. A reviewer for the *Times Literary Supplement* described Weil's attraction to Roman Catholicism and her refusal of complete attachment to it: "like the beggar at the gate of heaven, she lived on the threshold of the Roman Church, refusing to come in but ever gazing through the open door at the distant altar." The reviewer for *Times Literary Supplement* felt that the reader was "likely to feel well rewarded with the many things, unexpected, profound, and true which he will find her uttering."

The second volume available in English was *The Need for Roots: Prelude to a Declaration of Duties toward Mankind* (1952). Arthur Wills (a prominent translator of Weil's writings) translated the work and T. S. Eliot wrote the introduction. The subject of *The Need for Roots*, according to a reviewer for *Times Literary Supplement*, was "politics in the widest Aristotelian understanding of the term, and the treatment is of exceptional originality and breadth of human sympathy." Weil wrote the volume at the request of the French in London, who were curious about her thoughts on the potential of France's reconstruction after World War II, but as the *Times Literary Supplement* critic reported, "the [book] is of equal interest and appeal . . . no matter what

country." Jenny Turner in *New Statesmen* stated that Weil specifically wrote the piece for General de Gaulle for "it was intended to provide a philosophical foundation for the Fifth Republic." The reviewer for *Times Literary Supplement* also related that the reaction of feeling "provocation to agree with her, and more often to disagree, is . . . strong." S. M. Fitzgerald in *New Republic* observed: "[Weil's] thinking is sometimes idiosyncratic in the extreme, displaying a lack of objectivity that seems almost willful, and some of her outbursts are so emotional as to be almost altogether untrustworthy."

In *Letters to a Priest*, 1953, Weil related thirty-five of her essential beliefs to Father Perrin to see if they violated any of the doctrines of the Roman Catholic faith. A reviewer in *New Yorker* called Weil's writing "an interesting work, but chiefly" it was a "picture of a brilliant mind caught in the web of comparative religions." The *Times Literary Supplement* noted that "so far as is known the letter went unanswered." The reviewer further describes the thirty-five beliefs as "a series of philosophic queries which go to the very roots of religion." The essays contained in another work, *Oppression and Liberty*, 1958, related, according to a reviewer for *New York Times Book Review*, "discerning appraisals of Marxism." This work is the only one to outline Weil's responses to Marxism and her personal reactions to the political ideology. A young student of Weil's at the girls' lycee in Roanne, Anne Reynaud, kept thorough notes in class and the notes were eventually translated and gathered into a book, *Lectures on Philosophy*, which was first published in French in 1951. The lectures, according to a reviewer for *Choice*, "systematically explore" many of Weil's prevalent issues, including ethics, moral psychology, and theories of knowledge. The *Lectures* shed light on the events leading up to Weil's final embrace of Christianity.

Two volumes of *The Notebooks of Simone Weil* were released in 1956. A reviewer for the *Times Literary Supplement* observed that "it is a great pity that the *Notebooks* have not been more imaginatively edited. There is no introduction . . . the footnotes . . . are totally inadequate. At best the *Notebooks* will send the reader back to other works." Anne Fremantle in the *New York Times Book Review* stated: "It is unfortunate that these volumes lack an editor. The reader longs for some signposts." A reviewer for the *Times Literary Supplement*, impressed by Weil's mind, made this observation: "The kind of all-around scholar who could grasp Simone Weil's every thought in its 'incandescent stage' hardly exists today: [the scholar] would have to be familiar with theology, ancient and modern literature, comparative religion, folklore, geometry, algebra, physics, mechanics, astrology, the history of science, sociology, economics, and of course, philosophy."

A translation by Richard Rees, *Selected Essays, 1934-1943* (1962), contained a variety of essays on several subjects, aiding in the illumination of Weil's thought. "By nature Weil seems to have thought in aphorisms rather than in sequences of ideas," noted a reviewer for *Times Literary Supplement*. John Ratte, in *Commonweal*, attempted to define Weil's thoughts: "In its ranging, her mind draws parallels, suggests analogies and makes connections (both safe and wild) in a tireless effort to increase man's understanding of his own nature and of his society in order to create new possibilities for action." The reviewer for the *Times Literary Supplement* set forth the attraction of Weil: "The fact remains that we value her not because she supplies us with a coherent philosophy but because she sets our minds working."

In 1965 Richard Rees translated and arranged another compilation of Weil's writings, titled *Seventy Letters.* A *Times Literary Supplement* reviewer decided that "these letters, though they cannot be compared for depth with other works by Simone Weil . . . will serve as an introduction to her thoughts and life and tempt readers to ask more." Rees also translated *On Science, Necessity, and the Love of God* (1968). This book, according to a reviewer for the *Times Literary Supplement,* relates that "what obsessed Simone Weil here, as always, was the problem of God: God as conceived by Plato, God as revealed by Jesus Christ." The reviewer added, "we might reach the conclusion that Simone Weil is a far more profound philosopher of the absurd than Camus." Rees translated *First and Last Notebooks* (1970), which received favorable reviews. Weil's writings here were described by a reviewer for *Times Literary Supplement:* "Simone Weil not only makes hard reading, which is doubtless why she has been passed by in superficial sociology or journalistic theology, but she also took a poor view of our technological civilization and of our ecclesiastical Establishments."

Another compendium, *Formative Writings, 1929-1941* (1987), was translated by Dorothy Tuck McFarland and Wilhelmina Van Ness. Kate Soper in *New Statesmen* felt this volume was to "direct attention to the 'other Weils'—to Weil the political activist and Weil the philosopher-teacher." Soper also commented on Weil's "intellect almost stumbling over itself" attempting "to gain a grip on historical momentum rapidly about to escape from all rational control." "[The writings] reveal an intelligent and sensitive woman deeply engaged in the travails of the world, one whose commitment is to the underdog, the exploited and destitute," wrote George L. Farre in *America.* Farre found the book "well worth reading and pondering," but was taken by Weil's inconsistency, which he felt "was rooted in a naive conception of a brotherhood of men." Elizabeth Kamarck Minnich in *Women's Review of Books* found *Formative Writings* rewarding: "I was left once again stunned by Weil's brilliance, troubled—almost repelled—by her passion for suffering, awed by her extreme independence, and then troubled again by some of her views." Minnich noted that "as the agonies of Weil's world increased, so did her need to participate in them."

Simone Weil: An Anthology, edited by Sian Miles, was another volume of arranged writings, but a reviewer for *Observer* decided that the *Notebooks* contained "the best of Weil's work." French publishing company Gallimard began publishing a uniform edition of her complete works in 1988. With voluminous writings by Weil in print, in so many arrangements, compiled from such diverse sources, and with an industry of commentary arising, perhaps the most conclusive statement that could be made about her came from Elisabeth Young-Bruehl, reviewing *Formative Writings, 1929-1941* in the *New York Times Book Review:* "Simone Weil can no longer be reduced to a noun's worth, or even two, of doctrinal type or ideology. She has become again the puzzle she was while she lived."

BIOGRAPHICAL/CRITICAL SOURCES:

BOOKS

Amery, Jean, "Simone Weil: 'Beyond the Legend,'" in *Radical Humanism: Selected Essays,* edited and translated by Sidney Rosenfeld and Stella P. Rosenfeld, Indiana University Press, 1984.

Dictionary of Twentieth-Century Culture, Volume 2, Gale (Detroit), 1995.

Meyerhoff, Hans, "Contra Simone Weil: 'The Voices of Demons for the Silence of God,'" in *Arguments and Doctrines: A Reader of Jewish Thinking in the Aftermath of the Holocaust,* edited by Arthur A. Cohen, Harper, 1970.

Milosz, Czeslaw, "The Importance of Simone Weil," in *Emperor of the Earth: Modes of Eccentric Vision,* University of California Press, 1977.

Twentieth-Century Literary Criticism, Volume 23, Gale, 1987.

PERIODICALS

America, September 19, 1987, p. 139.

Choice, April, 1974, p. 274; May, 1979, p. 405.

Commonweal, March 22, 1963, pp. 669-70; November 6, 1987, pp. 638-39.

Library Journal, January 15, 1979, pp. 195-96.

Ms., December, 1985.

New Republic, August 18, 1952, p. 18; July 2, 1977, p. 33-37.

New Statesman, August 28, 1987, p. 24; September 4, 1987.

New Yorker, April 3, 1954, p. 133.

New York Times Book Review, March 14, 1954, p. 7; December 16, 1956, p. 6; September 11, 1977, pp. 16, 20; June 25, 1978; August 2, 1987, p. 19.

Observer (London), February 16, 1986.

Saturday Review, March 8, 1952, p. 26; May 10, 1952, pp. 20-21.

Times Literary Supplement, October 26, 1951, p. 681; May 30, 1952, p. 365; March 20, 1953, p. 192; November 16, 1956, p. 685; December 28, 1962, p. 1003; October 17, 1968, p. 1174; August 14, 1970, p. 904; January 4, 1980, p. 19; July 28, 1989, p. 821; July 13, 1990, p. 747; August 23, 1991, p. 7.

Washington Post Book World, October 2, 1977, p. E5; January 24, 1993, p. 15.

Women's Review of Books, October, 1987, pp. 13-14.

*   *   *

WEINSTEIN, Nathan
See WEST, Nathanael

*   *   *

WEINSTEIN, Nathan von Wallenstein
See WEST, Nathanael

*   *   *

WELDON, Fay 1931-

PERSONAL: Born September 22, 1931, in Alvechurch, Worcestershire, England; daughter of Frank Thornton (a physician) and Margaret (a writer; maiden name Jepson) Birkinshaw; married Ronald Weldon (an antique dealer), 1960 (divorced, 1994); children: Nicholas, Daniel, Thomas, Samuel. *Education:* University of St. Andrews, M.A., 1954.

ADDRESSES: Agent—Giles Gordon, 3 Ann St., Edinburgh, Scotland.

CAREER: Novelist, playwright, television and radio scriptwriter. Worked as a propaganda writer for the British Foreign Office and as a market researcher for the *Daily Mirror,* London, England. Advertising copywriter for various firms in London; creator of the slogan "Go to work on an egg." Former member of the Art Council of Great Britain's literary panel and of the GLA's film and video panel; chairperson of the judges' panel for the Booker McConnell Prize, 1983.

AWARDS, HONORS: Society of Film and Television Arts award for best series, 1971, for "On Trial" episode of *Upstairs, Downstairs* television series; Writer's Guild award for best radio play, 1973, for *Spider;* Giles Cooper Award for best radio play, 1978, for *Polaris;* Booker McConnell Prize nomination, National Book League, 1979, for *Praxis;* Society of Authors' travelling scholarship, 1981; D.Litt., University of St. Andrew's, 1989.

WRITINGS:

NOVELS

The Fat Woman's Joke (also see below), MacGibbon & Kee, 1967, published as *. . . And the Wife Ran Away,* McKay, 1968.
Down among the Women, Heinemann, 1971, St. Martin's, 1972.
Female Friends, St. Martin's, 1974.
Remember Me, Random House, 1976.
Words of Advice, Random House, 1977, published as *Little Sisters,* Hodder & Stoughton, 1978.
Praxis, Summit Books, 1978.
Puffball, Hodder & Stoughton, 1979, Summit Books, 1980.
The President's Child, Hodder & Stoughton, 1982, Doubleday, 1983.
The Life and Loves of a She-Devil, Hodder & Stoughton, 1983, Pantheon, 1984.
The Shrapnel Academy, Viking, 1986.
The Hearts and Lives of Men, Viking, 1987.
The Rules of Life, HarperCollins, 1987.
Leader of the Band, Viking, 1988.
The Heart of the Country, 1988.
The Cloning of Joanna May, Viking, 1990.
Darcy's Utopia, Viking, 1991.
Life Force, Viking, 1992.
Trouble, Viking, published as *Affliction,* HarperCollins (London), 1993.
Splitting, Atlantic Monthly Press, 1995.
Worst Fears, Atlantic Monthly Press, 1996.
Growing Rich, Penguin, 1998.

PLAYS

Permanence (produced in the West End at Comedy Theatre, 1969), published in *Mixed Blessings: An Entertainment on Marriage,* Methuen, 1970.
Time Hurries On, published in *Scene Scripts,* edited by Michael Marland, Longman, 1972.
Words of Advice (one-act; produced in Richmond, England, at Orange Tree Theatre, 1974), Samuel French, 1974.
Friends, produced in Richmond at Orange Tree Theatre, 1975.
Moving House, produced in Farnham, England, at Redgrave Theatre, 1976.
Mr. Director, produced at Orange Tree Theatre, 1978.
Action Replay (produced in Birmingham, England, at Birmingham Repertory Studio Theatre, 1979; produced as *Love among the Women* in Vancouver, British Columbia, at City Stage, 1982), Samuel French, 1980.
I Love My Love, produced in Exeter, England, at Northcott Theatre, 1981.
Woodworm, first produced as *After the Prize,* off-Broadway at Phoenix Theatre, 1981; produced in Melbourne, Australia, at Playbox Theatre, 1983.

Also author of *Watching Me, Watching You,* a stage adaptation of four of her short stories; *Jane Eyre,* a stage adaptation of the novel by Charlotte Bronte, 1986; and *The Hole in the Top of the World,* 1987.

TELEVISION PLAYS

The Fat Woman's Tale, Granada Television, 1966.
Wife in a Blond Wig, British Broadcasting Corp. (BBC-TV), 1966.
Office Party, Thames Television, 1970.
"On Trial" (episode in *Upstairs, Downstairs* series), London Weekend Television, 1971.
Hands, BBC-TV, 1972.
Poor Baby, ATV Network, 1975.
The Terrible Tale of Timothy Bagshott, BBC-TV, 1975.
Aunt Tatty (dramatization based on an Elizabeth Bowen short story), BBC-TV, 1975.
Married Love (film on the Marie Stopes *Six Women* series), BBC-TV, 1977.
Pride and Prejudice (five-part dramatization based on the novel by Jane Austen), BBC-TV, 1980.
"Watching Me, Watching You" (episode in *Leap in the Dark* series), BBC-TV, 1980.
Life for Christine, Granada Television, 1980.
Little Miss Perkins, London Weekend Television, 1982.
Loving Women, Granada Television, 1983.
The Wife's Revenge, BBC-TV, 1983.

Also author of *Big Women,* a four-part series, for Channel 4 television, and over twenty-five other teleplays for BBC-TV and independent television networks.

RADIO PLAYS

Housebreaker, BBC Radio 3, 1973.
Mr. Fox and Mr. First, BBC Radio 3, 1974.
The Doctor's Wife, BBC Radio 4, 1975.
"Weekend" (episode in *Just before Midnight* series), BBC Radio 4, 1979.
All the Bells of Paradise, BBC Radio 4, 1979.
Polaris, American Broadcasting Co. (ABC Radio), 1980, published in *Best Radio Plays of 1978: The Giles Cooper Award Winners,* Eyre Methuen, 1979.
The Hearts and Lives of Men, BBC Radio 4, 1996.

Also author of *Spider,* 1972, and *If Only I Could Find the Words,* BBC.

OTHER

(Editor with Elaine Feinstein) *New Stories 4: An Arts Council Anthology,* Hutchinson, 1979.
Watching Me, Watching You (short stories; also includes the novel *The Fat Woman's Joke*), Summit Books, 1981.
Letters to Alice on First Reading Jane Austen (nonfiction), Michael Joseph, 1984.
Polaris and Other Stories, Hodder & Stoughton, 1985.
Moon over Minneapolis: or, Why She Couldn't Stay (short stories), Viking, 1992.
So Very English, Serpent's Tail, 1992.
Wicked Women: A Collection of Short Stories, Flamingo (London), 1995.

Also author of children's books, including *Wolf the Mechanical Dog,* 1988, *Party Puddle,* 1989, and *Nobody Likes Me,* 1997.

MEDIA ADAPTATIONS: The Life and Loves of a She-Devil was adapted into the film *She-Devil* in 1989, written by Barry Strugatz and Mark R. Burns, directed by Susan Seidelman, starring Roseanne Barr and Meryl Streep.

SIDELIGHTS: In her novels, short stories, and plays for the theater, television, and radio, Fay Weldon's "major subject is the experience of women," writes Agate Nesaule Krouse in *Critique.* "Sexual initiation, marriage, infidelity, divorce, contraception, abortion, motherhood, housework, and thwarted careers . . . all receive attention." Products of a keen mind concerned with women's issues, Weldon's novels have been labeled "feminist" by many reviewers. Yet, Weldon's views are her own and are not easily classified. In fact, feminists have at times taken exception to her portrayal of women, accusing the author of perpetuating traditional stereotypes.

Fay Weldon's fiction fosters disparate interpretations because its author sees the complexity of the woman's experience. As Susan Hill notes in *Books and Bookmen,* Weldon has "the sharpest eyes for revealing details which, appearing like bubbles on the surface, are clues to the state of things lying far, far below." Weldon accepts feminist ideology as a liberating force, but she also understands its limitations. Thus, what emerges from Weldon's writing is more than an understanding of women's issues; she appreciates the plight of the individual woman. She told Sybil Steinberg in an interview in *Publishers Weekly,* "Women must ask themselves: What is it that will give me fulfillment? That's the serious question I'm attempting to answer."

Weldon's early novels, especially *Down among the Women, Female Friends,* and *Remember Me,* gained recognition both for their artistry and their social concerns. "Vivid imagery, a strong sense of time and place, memorable dialogue, complex events, and multiple characters that are neither confusing nor superficially observed," characterize these novels according to Krouse, making them "a rich rendering of life with brevity and wit." In her writing, John Braine adds in *Books and Bookmen,* Fay Weldon "is never vague. . . . She understands what few novelists understand, that physical details are not embellishments on the story, but the bricks from which the story is made." And, like few other novelists, especially those that deal with women's issues, observes Braine, "She possesses that very rare quality, a sardonic, earthy, disenchanted, slightly bitter but never cruel sense of humour."

Although each of these books possesses elements typical of a Weldon novel, they focus on different aspects of the female experience and the forces that influence them. *Down among the Women* reflects how three generations of women, each the product of a different social climate, react to the same dilemma. Krouse finds that in this book Weldon creates "a work whose very structure is feminist." She adds in her *Critique* review, "The whole novel could profitably be analyzed as a definition of womanhood: passages describing how one has to live 'down among the women' contrast with anecdotes of male behavior." The image of womanhood offered here is not ideal, but as Krouse comments, Weldon's ability to blend "the terrible and the ridiculous is one of the major reasons why a novel filled with the pain endured by women . . . is neither painfully depressing nor cheerfully sentimental."

As its title suggests, *Female Friends* examines relationships among women, how the companionship of other women can be comforting to a woman wearied by the battle of the sexes. "The most radical feminist could not possibly equal the picture of injustice [Weldon] paints with wry, cool, concise words," writes L. E. Sissman in the *New Yorker.* Sissman finds that "the real triumph of *Female Friends* is the gritty replication of the gross texture of everyday life, placed in perspective and made universal; the perfectly recorded dialogue, precisely differentiated for each

character; the shocking progression of events that, however rude, seem real." Weldon does not overlook the injustices committed by women in this day-to-day struggle, however. Ultimately, her characters suggest, women are responsible for their own lives. As Arthur Cooper concludes in *Newsweek,* Weldon "has penetrated the semidarkness of the semiliberated and shown that only truth and self-awareness can set them free."

Remember Me is the story of one man's impact on the lives of three women and how the resentment of one of those women becomes a disruptive force even after her death. This novel suggests that elements beyond the control of the individual often dictate her actions. "Scores of . . . coincidences . . . emphasize the theme that chance, misunderstanding, and necessarily limited knowledge play a significant part in human life," observes Krouse. Human frailties, Krouse adds, body functions, pain, sickness "and death are recurrent images underscoring human mortality." Phyllis Birnbaum, writing in the *Saturday Review,* states, "Precise satire, impassioned monologue, and a sense of limited human possibility make this novel a daring examination of twentieth-century discontent."

By the time she had written her sixth novel, *Praxis* (the fifth, *Words of Advice,* appeared in 1977), Fay Weldon was considered, as Susan Hill puts it, "an expert chronicler of the minutiae of women's lives, good at putting their case and pleading their cause." Kelley Cherry points out in the *Chicago Tribune Book World* that *Praxis* is a novel about endurance. The central character, Praxis Duveen, must endure in a world filled with "just about every kind of manipulation and aggression that men use to get women where they want them," observes Katha Pollitt in the *New York Times Book Review,* "and just about every nuance of guilt and passivity that keeps women there." Struggling against most of the catastrophes that can befall a woman, Praxis does emerge, revealing according to Hill, that even though "Weldon's women are victims, they do have many compensatory qualities—toughness, resilience, flexibility, inventiveness, patience, nerve."

A novel in which so many misfortunes plague one character runs the risk of becoming unbelievable. Yet, Kelley Cherry writes, "The writing throughout is brisk and ever so slightly off the wall—sufficiently askew to convey the oddness of events, sufficiently no-nonsense to make that oddness credible." And, concludes Katha Pollitt, "As a narrative it is perhaps too ambitious, but as a collection of vignettes, polemics, epigrams, it is often dazzling, pointing up the mad underside of our sexual politics with a venomous accuracy for which wit is far too mild a word."

In her next novel, *Puffball,* "Weldon mixes gynecology and witchcraft to concoct an unusual brew," Joan Reardon notes in the *Los Angeles Times Book Review.* Here, more than before, Weldon confronts the woman's condition on a physical level, focusing on pregnancy. "Weldon has the audacity to include technical information on fertility, conception, and fetal development as an integral part of the story," comments Lorallee MacPike in *Best Sellers.* "She makes the physical process preceding and during pregnancy not only interesting but essential to the development of both story and character."

In the eyes of some reviewers such as Joan Reardon, however, the technical information weakens the novel. She writes that in *Puffball,* "perspicacity has given way to whimsy and 'the pain in my soul, my heart, and my mind' has become a detailed analysis of the pituitary system." Moreover, some feminists fault this book for its old-fashioned images of women; as Anita Brookner points out in the *Times Literary Supplement,* "superficially, it is a great leap backwards for the stereotype feminist. It argues in favour of the old myths of earth and motherhood and universal harmony: a fantasy for the tired businesswoman." Yet a reviewer for the *Atlantic* finds that "the assertion of the primacy of physical destiny that lies at the center of *Puffball* gives the book a surprising seriousness and an impressive optimism."

In *The President's Child,* Weldon breaks new ground, exploring the impact of political intrigue on individual lives. Her next novel, however, is reminiscent of *Praxis.* Like Praxis, the protagonist of Fay Weldon's ninth novel, *The Life and Loves of a She-Devil,* is buffeted by the injustice of her world. Yet, whereas Praxis endures, Ruth gets revenge. Losing her husband to a beautiful romance novelist, tall, unattractive Ruth turns against husband, novelist, and anyone else who gets in her way. Unleashing the vengeance of a she-devil, she ruins them all; the novelist dies and the husband becomes a broken man. In the end, having undergone extensive surgery to make her the very image of her former competitor, she begins a new life with her former husband. "What makes this a powerfully funny and oddly powerful book is the energy that vibrates off the pages," writes Carol E. Rinzler in the *Washington Post Book World.* Weldon has created in *She-Devil,* Sybil Steinberg notes in *Publishers Weekly,* a "biting satire of the war between the sexes, indicting not only the male establishment's standards of beauty and feminine worthiness, but also women's own willingness . . . to subscribe to these standards."

Seeing Ruth's revenge as a positive response to the injustice of the male establishment, some reviewers are disappointed by her turnaround at the novel's end. As Michiko Kakutani points out in the *New York Times,* "Her final act—having extensive plastic surgery that makes her irresistible to men—actually seems like a capitulation to the male values she says she despises." Weldon is aware of the contradictions suggested by her story; she discussed this issue in her interview with Sybil Steinberg: "The first half of the book is an exercise in feminist thought. . . . It's the feminist manifesto really: a woman must be free, independent and rich. But I found myself asking, what then?. . . . I think women are discovering that liberation isn't enough. The companionship of women is not enough. The other side of their nature is unfulfilled."

"Central to many of [Weldon's] plots is the rise of the Nietzschean superwoman," contends Daniel Harris in prefacing his review of the author's 1993 novel *Trouble* in the *Los Angeles Times Book Review.* Paralleling Weldon's own rise to literary acceptance from her former career as a lowly advertising copywriter, Harris characterizes such women as emerging "out of the seething multitudes of hungry romantic careerists just waiting for their chance to advance up a hierarchical power structure that Weldon describes as the equivalent among women of a food chain." Annette Horrocks, the pregnant protagonist of *Trouble* is just such a woman, the second wife of a chauvinistic businessman who becomes threatened when his wife publishes a novel. In a twist, the husband runs, not into the arms of yet another manipulative woman, but into the clutches of a pair of pseudo-therapists, who convince him that Annette is his enemy. Meeting with a mixed critical reception, the novel was faulted for being uncharacteristic Weldon. "The characters are thin, the plot maniacally unreal, the dialogue brisk and bleak," notes *Observer* critic Nicci Gerrard, maintaining that *Trouble* contains too large a dose of its author's personal anger.

Weldon's twentieth novel, *Splitting,* finds the author returned to form, according to Bertha Harris in the *New York Times Book Review.* Seventeen-year-old former rock star Angelica White is determined to become the perfect female companion in order to endear herself to dissolute but wealthy Sir Edwin Rice and obtain a marriage commitment. She discards her image as the rock queen Kinky Virgin, doffs the nose rings and the spectacularly colored hair, and becomes overweight, drug-abusing Edwin's helpmate. "In effect, Angelica's troubles begin when she resolves that it's 'time to give up and grow up,'" according to Harris. Soon the typical flock of avaricious females descend on Angelica, breaking up her home and causing her to fracture into four separate personalities. Ultimately banished from the Rice estate, her money having long since been usurped by her husband, Angelica ultimately avenges herself through the savvy, recklessness, and sense of fun created by her multiple selves. "The splitting device works shamelessly well," explains Kate Kellaway in the *Observer.* "Weldon uses it as a way of exploring and rejoicing in the theatricality of women, their volatility, their love of disguise, of fancy dress, of playing different parts." As the author has one of Angelica's new selves say, "Women tend to be more than one person at the best of times. Men just get to be the one."

Weldon has since continued her pace, not only with novels such as 1996's *Worst Fears,* but also with a short story collection, appropriately titled *Wicked Women,* which she published in 1995. In *Worst Fears,* a widowed woman suddenly realizes that her life has not in fact been the rosy picture she imagined it. Snubbed by her friends, and lacking sympathy in favor of her husband's mistress, Alexandra soon finds that such deception by the living is nothing compared to the deceptions practiced on her by her now dead husband. Left with nothing, she plans her revenge in true Weldon fashion in a novel in which the author "has filed down a few sharp edges. . .," according to *New York Times Book Review* critic Karen Karbo, "and that makes it one of her best novels yet." Variations on this traditional Weldon theme are also played out in the sixteen short stories in *Wicked Women.* While noting that the collection is somewhat uneven in effectiveness, *Spectator* reviewer Susan Crosland hastens to add that "When the seesaw swings up, Fay Weldon is on form: sparkling, sharply observing, insights delivered with a light touch that puts us in a good mood, however dark the comedy. And one of the great things about short stories is that you can pick and chose."

Fay Weldon's understanding of the individual woman, living in a world somewhere between the nightmare of male chauvinism and the feminist ideal, has allowed her to achieve a balance in her writing. "She has succeeded in uniting the negative feminism, necessarily evident in novels portraying the problems of women, with a positive feminism, evident in the belief that change or equilibrium is possible," writes Agate Nesaule Krouse. For this reason, "[Weldon] speaks for the female experience without becoming doctrinaire," notes *New York Times Book Review* contributor Mary Cantwell, "and without the dogged humorlessness that has characterized so much feminist writing." Having found an audience for her writing—insights into the condition of woman, shaped by her intelligence and humor—Fay Weldon has risen to prominence in literary circles. Writing in the *Times Literary Supplement,* Anita Brookner calls Weldon "one of the most astute and distinctive women writing fiction today."

BIOGRAPHICAL/CRITICAL SOURCES:

BOOKS

Barreca, Regina, *Fay Weldon's Wicked Fictions,* University Press of New England, 1994.

PERIODICALS

Atlantic, August, 1980.
Best Sellers, October, 1980.
Booklist, May 1, 1995, p. 1554; June 1, 1995, p. 1804; May 1, 1996, p. 1470.
Books and Bookmen, January, 1977; March, 1979; May, 1979.
Chicago Tribune Book World, November 12, 1978; September 28, 1980; February 14, 1982.
Critique, December, 1978.
Entertainment Weekly, June 16, 1995, p. 57.
Library Journal, February 15, 1995, p. 198; April 15, 1995, p. 117; March 15, 1996, p. 110; May 15, 1996, p. 85.
Los Angeles Times Book Review, September 7, 1980; April 19, 1987; April 10, 1988; December 18, 1988; June 4, 1989; June 25, 1995, pp. 3, 9.
Newsweek, November, 1974; December 4, 1978.
New Statesman and Society, February 11, 1994, p. 40; January 5, 1996, p. 39.
New Yorker, March 3, 1975; November, 1978.
New York Times, November 24, 1981; December 21, 1981; August 21, 1984; October 29, 1988; May 31, 1989; March 16, 1990.
New York Times Book Review, June 11, 1995, p. 48; June 9, 1996, p. 19.
Observer (London), February 13, 1994; May 7, 1995.
Publishers Weekly, January 13, 1984; August 24, 1984.
Saturday Review, December, 1976.
Spectator, March 1, 1980; July 1, 1981; October 2, 1982; February 12, 1994, pp. 29-30; May 13, 1995, pp. 39-40.
Times Literary Supplement, September 10, 1971; February 22, 1980; May 22, 1981; September 24, 1982; January 20, 1984; July 6, 1984; August 9, 1985; February 13, 1987; July 15, 1988; February 18, 1994.
Tribune Books, March 13, 1988; November 20, 1988; June 18, 1989; March 18, 1990.
Washington Post Book World, November 3, 1974; September 30, 1984; July 14, 1985; May 10, 1987; April 24, 1988; November 13, 1988; April 1, 1990.

*   *   *

WELLS, H(erbert) G(eorge) 1866-1946
(Reginald Bliss)

PERSONAL: Born September 21, 1866, in Bromley, England; died August 13, 1946, in London, England; cremated and ashes scattered over English Channel; son of Joseph (a gardener, cricket player, and shopkeeper) and Sarah (a housekeeper; maiden name, Neal) Wells; married Isabel Mary Wells, October 31, 1891 (divorced January, 1895); married Amy Catherine Robbins (a writer), October 27, 1895 (died, 1927); children: (second marriage) George Philip, Frank Richard; (with Amber Reeves) Anna-Jane White; (with Rebecca West) Anthony West. *Education:* Attended Normal School of Science (now Imperial College of Science and Technology), 1884-87; University of London, B.S. (with honors), c. 1889, D.Sc., 1943. *Politics:* Liberal democrat.

CAREER: Rodgers & Denyer, Windsor, England, apprentice draper, 1880; pupil-teacher at school in Wookey, England, 1880; apprentice pharmacist in Midhurst, England, 1880-81; Hyde's Southsea Drapery Emporium, Hampshire, England, apprentice draper, 1881-83; student-assistant at grammar school in Midhurst, 1883-84; teacher at schools in Wrexham, Wales, 1887-88, and London, England, 1889; University Correspondence College, London, tutor, 1890-93; writer, 1893-1946. Member of Research Committee for the League of Nations, 1917; affiliated with British Ministry of Information, 1918; director of Policy Committee for Propaganda in Enemy Countries, 1918.

MEMBER: International PEN (international president, 1934-46), British Association for the Advancement of Science (president of educational science section, 1937), British Diabetic Association (founding president), Abortion Law Reform Society (vice-president, 1936), Film Society (cofounder), Savile Club.

AWARDS, HONORS: D.Litt. from University of London, 1936; honorary fellow of Imperial College of Science and Technology.

WRITINGS:

NOVELS

The Time Machine: An Invention (science fiction; first published in *Science Schools Journal* as *The Chronic Argonauts,* 1888), Holt, 1895, expanded, introduction and appendices by Leon E. Stover, McFarland, 1995.
The Wonderful Visit (science fiction), Macmillan, 1895.
The Wheels of Chance: A Bicycling Idyll (first published serially in *Today,* 1896), illustrations by J. Ayton Symington, Macmillan, 1896, published as *The Wheels of Chance: A Holiday Adventure,* Dent, 1896.
The Island of Doctor Moreau: A Possibility (science fiction), Stone & Kimball, 1896, expanded, with notes by Leon E. Stover, McFarland, 1996.
The Invisible Man: A Grotesque Romance (science fiction; first published serially in *Pearson's Weekly,* June-July, 1897), Arnold, 1897, published as *The Invisible Man: A Fantastic Sensation,* Robert Bentley, 1981, edited by David Lake, with an introduction by John Sutherland, Oxford University Press, 1996.
The War of the Worlds (science fiction; first published serially in *Pearson's Magazine,* April-December, 1897), Harper & Brothers, 1898.
When the Sleeper Wakes (science fiction; first published serially in *The Graphic,* 1898-99), Harper & Brothers, 1899, revised as *The Sleeper Awakes,* Thomas Nelson, 1910.
Love and Mr. Lewisham: The Story of a Very Young Couple, George H. Doran, 1899.
The First Men in the Moon (science fiction; first published serially in *Strand Magazine,* December, 1900-August, 1901), Bowen-Merrill, 1901.
The Sea Lady (first published serially in *Pearson's Magazine,* July-December, 1901), D. Appleton, 1902 (published in England as *The Sea Lady: A Tissue of Moonshine,* Methuen, 1902).
The Food of the Gods, and How It Came to Earth (science fiction; first published serially in *Pearson's Magazine,* December, 1903-June, 1904), Scribner, 1904.
A Modern Utopia (first published serially in *Fortnightly Review,* October, 1904-April, 1905), illustrations by E. J. Sullivan, Scribner, 1905.

Kipps: A Monograph (first published serially in *Pall Mall,* 1905), Scribner, 1905, published as *Kipps: The Story of a Simple Soul,* 1905.

In the Days of the Comet (science fiction; first published serially in *Daily Chronicle,* 1905-06), Century, 1906.

The War in the Air, and Particularly How Mr. Bert Smallways Fared While It Lasted (first published serially in *Pall Mall*), Macmillan, 1908.

Tono-Bungay, Duffield, 1908.

Ann Veronica: A Modern Love Story, Harper & Brothers, 1909.

The History of Mr. Polly, Duffield, 1909.

The New Machiavelli (first published serially in *English Review,* May-October, 1910), Duffield, 1910.

Marriage, Duffield, 1912.

The Passionate Friends: A Novel (first published serially in *Grand Magazine,* March-November, 1913), Harper & Brothers, 1913.

The Wife of Sir Isaac Harman, Macmillan, 1914.

The World Set Free: A Story of Mankind (science fiction; first published serially in *English Review,* December, 1913-May, 1914), E. P. Dutton, 1914.

Bealby: A Holiday (first published serially in *Grand Magazine,* August, 1914-March, 1915), Macmillan, 1915.

(Under name Reginald Bliss) *Boon, The Mind of the Race, The Wild Asses of the Devil, and The Last Trump: Being a First Selection From the Literary Remains of George Boon, Appropriate to the Times, Prepared for Publication by Reginald Bliss With an Ambiguous Introduction by H. G. Wells,* George H. Doran, 1915, published under name H. G. Wells, Unwin, 1920.

The Research Magnificent, Macmillan, 1915.

Mr. Britling Sees It Through (first published serially in *Nation,* May-October, 1916), Macmillan, 1916.

The Soul of a Bishop (first published serially in *Collier's Weekly,* 1917), Macmillan, 1917 (published in England as *The Soul of a Bishop: A Novel—With Just a Little Love in It—About Conscience and Religion and the Real Troubles of Life,* Cassell, 1917).

Joan and Peter: The Story of an Education, Macmillan, 1918.

The Undying Fire: A Contemporary Novel (first published serially in *International Review,* March-June, 1919), Macmillan, 1919.

The Secret Places of the Heart (first published serially in *Nash's* and *Pall Mall,* December, 1921-July, 1922), Macmillan, 1922.

Men Like Gods: A Novel (science fiction; first published serially in *Westminster Gazette,* December, 1922-February, 1923), Macmillan, 1923.

The Dream: A Novel (first published serially in *Nash's* and *Pall Mall,* October, 1923-May, 1924), Macmillan, 1924.

Christina Alberta's Father, Macmillan, 1925.

The World of William Clissold: A Novel at a New Angle, George H. Doran, 1926.

Meanwhile: The Picture of a Lady, George H. Doran, 1927.

Mr. Blettsworthy on Rampole Island, Doubleday, Doran, 1928.

The King Who Was a King: An Unconventional Novel, Doubleday, Doran, 1929 (published in England as *The King Who Was a King: The Book of a Film,* E. Benn, 1929).

The Autocracy of Mr. Parham: His Remarkable Adventures in This Changing World, Doubleday, Doran, 1930.

The Bulpington of Blup: Adventures, Poses, Stresses, Conflicts, and Disaster in a Contemporary Brain, Hutchinson, 1932, Macmillan, 1933.

The Shape of Things to Come: The Ultimate Revolution, Macmillan, 1933.

The Croquet Player, Chatto & Windus, 1936, Viking, 1937.

Star-Begotten: A Biological Fantasia (science fiction), Viking, 1937.

Brynhild; or, The Show of Things, Scribner, 1937 (published in England as *Brynhild,* Methuen, 1937).

The Camford Visitation, Methuen, 1937.

Apropos of Dolores, Scribner, 1938.

The Brothers: A Story, Viking, 1938.

The Holy Terror, Simon & Schuster, 1939.

Babes in the Darkling Wood, Alliance Book, 1940.

All Aboard for Ararat (science fiction), Secker & Warburg, 1940, Alliance Book, 1941.

You Can't Be Too Careful: A Sample of Life, 1901-1951, Secker & Warburg, 1941, G. P. Putnam's Sons, 1942.

The Wealth of Mr. Waddy: A Novel (early draft of *Kipps*), edited with introduction by Harris Wilson, preface by Harry T. Moore, Southern Illinois University Press, 1969.

A Story of the Days to Come (science fiction), Corgi, 1976.

The Works of H. G. Wells (contains *The Time Machine, The Island of Dr. Moreau, The Invisible Man,* and *The War of the Worlds*), Longmeadow Press, 1994.

Four Complete Novels (contains *The Time Machine, The Island of Dr. Moreau, The Invisible Man,* and *The War of the Worlds*), Barnes & Noble, 1994.

The Time Machine [and] *The Island of Doctor Moreau,* edited with an introduction by Patrick Parrinder, Oxford University Press, 1996.

SHORT STORIES

Select Conversations With an Uncle, Now Extinct, and Two Other Reminiscences, Merriam, 1895.

The Stolen Bacillus and Other Incidents (science fiction), Methuen, 1895.

The Red Room, Stone & Kimball, 1896.

A Perfect Gentleman on Wheels (first published as *A Perfect Gentleman on Wheels; or, The Humours of Cycling* in *Woman at Home,* April, 1897), published in *The Humours of Cycling,* James Bowden, 1897.

Thirty Strange Stories (science fiction), Arnold, 1897.

The Plattner Story, and Others (science fiction), Methuen, 1897.

A Cure for Love, E. Scott, 1899.

Tales of Space and Time (science fiction), Doubleday & McClure, 1899.

The Vacant Country, A. E. Kent, 1899.

Twelve Stories and a Dream (science fiction), Macmillan, 1903.

The Door in the Wall, and Other Stories (science fiction), M. Kennerley, 1911, reprinted with photographs by Alvin Langdon Coburn and afterword by Jeffrey A. Wolin, Godine, 1996.

The Country of the Blind, and Other Stories (science fiction), Thomas Nelson, 1911, reprinted with an introduction by Michael Sherborne, Oxford University Press, 1996.

The Star (in simplified spelling), Sir Isaac Pitman & Sons, 1913.

The Country of the Blind (science fiction), privately printed, 1915, Golden Cockerel Press, 1939.

The Short Stories of H. G. Wells (science fiction), E. Benn, 1927, Doubleday, Doran, 1929, published as *The Complete Short Stories of H. G. Wells,* E. Benn, 1966, St. Martin's, 1970.

The Adventures of Tommy (for children), self-illustrated, Frederick A. Stokes, 1929.

The Valley of Spiders, London Book, 1930.

The Stolen Body, and Other Tales of the Unexpected, London Book, 1931.

The Favorite Short Stories of H. G. Wells, Doubleday, Doran, 1937, published as *The Famous Short Stories of H. G. Wells,* Garden City Publishing, 1938.

Short Stories by H. G. Wells, notes and questions by A. J. J. Ratcliff, T. Nelson, 1940.

The Land Ironclads, Todd Publishing, 1943.

The New Accelerator (science fiction), Todd Publishing, 1943.

The Empire of the Ants, Todd Publishing, 1943.

The Inexperienced Ghost, Todd Publishing, 1943.

The Truth About Pyecraft, and Other Short Stories, Todd Publishing, 1943.

The Inexperienced Ghost and The New Accelerator, Vallancey Press, 1944.

Twenty-eight Science Fiction Stories, Dover, 1952.

Seven Stories, Oxford University Press, 1953.

Tales of Life and Adventure, introduction by Frank Wells, Collins, 1953.

Tales of the Unexpected, introduction by Frank Wells, Collins, 1954.

Tales of Wonder, introduction by Frank Wells, Collins, 1954.

The Desert Daisy (for children), introduction by Gordon N. Ray, Beta Phi Mu, 1957.

Selected Short Stories, Penguin Books, 1958.

The Inexperienced Ghost, and Nine Other Stories, Bantam, 1965.

Best Science Fiction Stories of H. G. Wells, Dover, 1966.

The Man With a Nose: And the Other Uncollected Short Stories of H. G. Wells, edited with an introduction by J. R. Hammond, Athlone Press, 1984.

The H.G. Wells Reader, Courage Books (Philadelphia, PA), 1996.

NONFICTION

Text-Book of Biology, two volumes, introduction by G. B. Howes, W. B. Clive, Volume I, 1892, Volume II, 1893, revision by A. M. Davies published as *Text-Book of Zoology,* 1898, 7th edition, revised and rewritten by J. T. Cunningham and W. H. Leigh-Sharpe, 1929.

(With R. A. Gregory) *Honours Physiography,* Joseph Hughes, 1893.

Certain Personal Matters: A Collection of Material, Mainly Autobiographical, Lawrence & Bullen, 1898.

Anticipations of the Reaction of Mechanical and Scientific Progress Upon Human Life and Thought (first published serially as *Anticipations: An Experiment in Prophecy* in *Fortnightly Review,* April-December, 1901), Harper & Brothers, 1902, with new introduction, Chapman & Hall, 1914.

Mankind in the Making (first published serially in *Fortnightly Review,* September, 1902-September, 1903), Chapman & Hall, 1903, Scribner, 1904, with new introduction, Chapman & Hall, 1914.

The Future in America: A Search After Realities (first published serially in *Harper's Weekly,* July 14-October 6, 1906), Harper & Brothers, 1906.

First and Last Things: A Confession of Faith and a Rule of Life, G. P. Putnam's Sons, 1908, definitive edition, Watts, 1929.

New Worlds for Old, Macmillan, 1908, revised edition, Constable, 1914.

Floor Games (for children; first published in *Strand Magazine,* December, 1911), self-illustrated, Frank Palmer, 1911, Small, Maynard, 1912.

(Editor with G. R. Taylor and Frances Evelyn Warwick, and contributor) *The Great State: Essays in Construction* (first published as *Socialism and the Great State* in *Harper's,* 1911), Harper & Brothers, 1912, published as *Socialism and the Great State: Essays in Construction,* 1914.

Little Wars: A Game for Boys From Twelve Years of Age to One Hundred and Fifty and for That More Intelligent Sort of Girls Who Like Boys' Games and Books With an Appendix on Kriegspiel (first published serially in *Windsor Magazine,* December, 1912, and January, 1913), Small, Maynard, 1913.

Social Forces in England and America (essays), Harper & Brothers, 1914 (published in England as *An Englishman Looks at the World: Being a Series of Unrestrained Remarks Upon Contemporary Matters,* Cassell, 1914).

The War That Will End War (essays), Duffield, 1914.

The War and Socialism, Clarion Press, 1915.

What Is Coming? A European Forecast, Macmillan, 1916 (published in England as *What Is Coming? A Forecast of Things After the War,* Cassell, 1916).

Introduction to Nocturne, G. H. Doran, 1917.

God, the Invisible King, Macmillan, 1917.

Italy, France, and Britain at War, Macmillan, 1917 (published in England as *War and the Future: Italy, France, and Britain at War,* Cassell, 1917).

In the Fourth Year: Anticipations of a World Peace, Macmillan, 1918 (abridged edition published in England as *Anticipations of a World Peace,* Chatto & Windus, 1918).

(With Viscount Grey, Lionel Curtis, William Archer, H. Wickham Steed, A. E. Zimmern, J. A. Spender, Viscount Bryce, and Gilbert Murray) *The Idea of a League of Nations: Prolegomena to the Study of World-Organisation,* Atlantic Monthly Press, 1919.

(With Viscount Grey, Gilbert Murray, J. A. Spender, A. E. Zimmern, H. Wickham Steed, Lionel Curtis, William Archer, Ernest Barker, G. Lowes Dickinson, John Hilton, and L. S. Woolf) *The Way to the League of Nations: A Brief Sketch of the Practical Steps Needed for the Formation of a League,* Oxford University Press, 1919.

(With Arnold Bennett and Grant Overton) *Frank Swinnerton: Personal Sketches; Together With Notes and Comments on the Novels of Frank Swinnerton,* G. H. Doran, 1920.

(With advice and editorial help of Ernest Barker, H. H. Johnston, E. Ray Lankester, and Gilbert Murray) *The Outline of History: Being a Plain History of Life and Mankind,* illustrations by J. F. Horrabin, Macmillan, 1920, published as *The New and Revised Outline of History: Being a Plain History of Life and Mankind,* Garden City Publishing, 1931, published as *The Enlarged and Revised Outline of History: Being a Plain History of Life and Mankind,* Triangle Books, 1940, under original title revised and brought up to the end of World War II by Raymond Postgate, Garden City Publishing, 1949, published as *The Outline of History: Being a Plain History of Life and Mankind From Primordial Life to Nineteen-sixty,* Cassell, 1961, under original title revised and brought up to date by Postgate and G. P. Wells, Doubleday, 1971.

Russia in the Shadows (first published serially in *Sunday Express,* October 31-November 28, 1920), Hodder & Stoughton, 1920, George H. Doran, 1921.

The Salvaging of Civilization: The Probable Future of Mankind, Macmillan, 1921.

A Short History of the World, Macmillan, 1922.

Washington and the Riddle of Peace (first published in *New York World,* November-December, 1921), Macmillan, 1922 (published in England as *Washington and the Hope of Peace,* Collins, 1922).

The Story of a Great Schoolmaster: Being a Plain Account of the Life and Ideas of Sanderson of Oundle (biography; first published serially in *New Leader,* September 14-October 26, 1923), Macmillan, 1924.

A Year of Prophesying (articles), Unwin, 1924, Macmillan, 1925.

A Short History of Mankind, adapted from *A Short History of the World* by E. H. Carter, Macmillan, 1925.

Mr. Belloc Objects to "The Outline of History," George H. Doran, 1926.

Wells' Social Anticipations, edited with introduction by Harry W. Laidler, Vanguard Press, 1927.

(Editor and author of introduction) *The Book of Catherine Wells,* Chatto & Windus, 1928.

The Way the World Is Going: Guesses and Forecasts of the Years Ahead; Twenty-six Articles and a Lecture, E. Benn, 1928, Doubleday, Doran, 1929.

The Open Conspiracy: Blue Prints for a World Revolution, Doubleday, Doran, 1928, published as *The Open Conspiracy: Blue Prints for a World Revolution; a Second Version of This Faith of a Modern Man Made More Explicit and Plain,* Hogarth Press, 1930, revised edition published as *What Are We to Do With Our Lives?* Doubleday, Doran, 1931, published as *The Open Conspiracy,* Gordon Press, 1979.

(With Bertrand Russell, Fannie Hurst, Theodore Dreiser, Warwick Deeping, Rebecca West, Andre Maurois, and Lionel Feuchtwanger) *Divorce as I See It,* Douglas, 1930.

(With G. Lowes Dickinson, Dean Inge, J. B. S. Haldane, Sir Oliver Lodge, and Sir Walford Davis) *Points of View: A Series of Broadcast Addresses,* Allen & Unwin, 1930.

(With H. R. Knickerbocker, Sir John Russell, Sir Bernard Pares, Margaret S. Miller, B. Mouat-Jones, Stafford Talbot, and Frank Owen) *The New Russia: Eight Talks Broadcast,* Faber & Faber, 1931.

(With Julian S. Huxley and G. P. Wells) *The Science of Life: A Summary of Contemporary Knowledge About Life and Its Possibilities,* Amalgamated Press, 1930, Doubleday, Doran, 1931 (portions published severally as The Science of Life series, Doubleday, Doran, 1932; various volumes published in England by Cassell, 1937).

Selections From the Early Prose Works of H. G. Wells, University of London Press, 1931.

The Work, Wealth, and Happiness of Mankind, Doubleday, Doran, 1931, published as *The Outline of Man's Work and Wealth,* Garden City Publishing, 1936.

After Democracy: Addresses and Papers on the Present World Situation, Watts, 1932.

Experiment in Autobiography: Discoveries and Conclusions of a Very Ordinary Brain (Since 1866), self-illustrated, Macmillan, 1934.

The New America: The New World, Macmillan, 1935.

The Anatomy of Frustration: A Modern Synthesis, Macmillan, 1936.

World Brain (essays and addresses), Doubleday, Doran, 1938.

The Fate of Man: An Unemotional Statement of the Things That Are Happening to Him Now, and of the Immediate Possibilities Confronting Him, Longmans, Green, 1939 (published in England as *The Fate of Homo Sapiens: An Unemotional Statement of the Things That Are Happening to Him Now, and of the Immediate Possibilities Confronting Him,* Secker & Warburg, 1939).

Travels of a Republican Radical in Search of Hot Water, Penguin Books, 1939.

The Common Sense of War and Peace: World Revolution or War Unending, Penguin Books, 1940.

H. G. Wells, S. de Madariaga, J. Middleton Murry, C. E. M. Joad on the New World Order, National Peace Council, 1940.

The New World Order: Whether It Is Attainable, How It Can Be Attained, and What Sort of World a World at Peace Will Have to Be, Secker & Warburg, 1939, Knopf, 1940.

The Rights of Man; or, What Are We Fighting For? Penguin Books, 1940.

Guide to the New World: A Handbook of Constructive World Revolution, Gollancz, 1941.

The Pocket History of the World, Pocket Books, 1941.

Modern Russian and English Revolutionaries: A Frank Exchange of Ideas Between Commander Lev Uspensky, Soviet Writer, and H. G. Wells, privately printed, 1942.

The Conquest of Time (written to replace his *First and Last Things*), Watts, 1942.

The Outlook for Homo Sapiens: An Unemotional Statement of the Things That Are Happening to Him Now, and of the Immediate Possibilities Confronting Him (an amalgamation and modernization of *The Fate of Homo Sapiens* and *The New World Order*), Secker & Warburg, 1942.

Phoenix: A Summary of the Inescapable Conditions of World Reorganisation, Secker & Warburg, 1942.

Crux Ansata: An Indictment of the Roman Catholic Church, Penguin Books, 1943.

'42 to '44: A Contemporary Memoir Upon Human Behaviour During the Crisis of the World Revolution, Secker & Warburg, 1944.

(With J. S. Huxley and J. B. S. Haldane) *Reshaping Man's Heritage: Biology in the Service of Man,* Allen & Unwin, 1944.

The Happy Turning: A Dream of Life, Heinemann, 1945.

(With Joseph Stalin) *Marxism vs. Liberalism: An Interview,* New Century, 1945, published as *H. G. Wells' Interview With J. V. Stalin (Marxism v. Liberalism),* Current Book Distributors (Sydney), 1950.

Mind at the End of Its Tether (first published in *Sunday Express*), Heinemann, 1945.

Henry James and H. G. Wells: A Record of Their Friendship, Their Debate on the Art of Fiction, and Their Quarrel (correspondence), edited with introduction by Leon Edel and Gordon N. Ray, University of Illinois Press, 1958.

Arnold Bennett and H. G. Wells: A Record of a Personal and a Literary Friendship (correspondence), edited with introduction by Harris Wilson, University of Illinois Press, 1960.

George Gissing and H. G. Wells: Their Friendship and Correspondence, edited with introduction by Royal A. Gettmann, University of Illinois Press, 1961.

Journalism and Prophecy, 1893-1946: An Anthology (addresses, essays, and lectures), compiled and edited by W. Warren Wagar, Houghton, 1964.

H. G. Wells's Literary Criticism, edited by Patrick Parrinder and Robert M. Philmus, Harvester Press, 1980.

H. G. Wells In Love: Postscript to an Experiment in Autobiography, edited by G. P. Wells, Little, Brown, 1984.

Treasury of H. G. Wells, Octopus Books, 1985.

Bernard Shaw and H. G. Wells (correspondence), University of Toronto Press, 1995.

OTHER

Socialism and the Family (pamphlet; contains "Socialism and the Middle Classes" and "Modern Socialism and the Family"), A. C. Fifield, 1906.

This Misery of Boots (pamphlet; first published in *Independent Review,* December, 1905), Fabian Society, 1907, Ball Publishing, 1908.

The H. G. Wells Calendar: A Quotation From the Works of H. G. Wells for Every Day in the Year, selected by Rosamund Marriott Watson, Frank Palmer, 1911.

Great Thoughts From H. G. Wells, selected by Rosamund Marriott Watson, Dodge, 1912.

Thoughts From H. G. Wells, selected by Elsie E. Morton, Harrap, 1913.

The Works of H. G. Wells: Atlantic Edition, 28 volumes, Scribner, 1924-27.

The Essex Thin-Paper Edition of the Works of H. G. Wells, 24 volumes, E. Benn, 1926-27.

Democracy Under Revision: A Lecture Delivered at the Sorbonne, March 15th, 1927 (pamphlet), George H. Doran, 1927.

Things to Come: A Film Story Based on the Material Contained in His History of the Future "The Shape of Things to Come" (science fiction), Macmillan, 1935.

Man Who Could Work Miracles: A Film by H. G. Wells, Based on the Short Story Entitled "The Man Who Could Work Miracles," Macmillan, 1936 (published in England as *Man Who Could Work Miracles: A Film Story Based on the Material Contained in His Short Story "Man Who Could Work Miracles,"* Cresset Press, 1936).

The H. G. Wells Papers at the University of Illinois, edited by Gordon N. Ray, University of Illinois Press, 1958.

Hoopdriver's Holiday (dramatization of his novel *The Wheels of Chance*), edited with notes and introduction by Michael Timko, English Department, Purdue University, 1964.

H. G. Wells: Early Writings in Science and Science Fiction, edited with critical commentary and notes by Robert M. Philmus and David Y. Hughes, University of California Press, 1975.

H. G. Wells Science Fiction Treasury, Crown, 1987.

The Correspondence of H. G. Wells, edited by David Clayton Smith, Pickering & Chatto (Brookfield, VT), 1996.

Also author of *Two Hemispheres or One World?* 1940, and many pamphlets. Author of film scripts, including "Bluebottles," "Daydreams," and "The Tonic." Contributor of introductions and prefaces to numerous books.

Work represented in anthologies, including *Thirty-one Stories by Thirty and One Authors,* edited by Ernest Rhys and C. A. Dawson Scott, Butterworth, 1923, and *Masterpieces of Science Fiction,* edited by Sam Moskowitz, World Publishing, 1967.

Contributor of reviews, letters, essays, and stories to periodicals, including *Clarion, English Review, Fortnightly Review, Independent Review, Labour Leader,* London *Daily Mail,* London *Times, Nation, New Age, Times Literary Supplement,* and *Saturday Review.*

MEDIA ADAPTATIONS: Numerous works by Wells have been adapted as comic books, films, plays, sound recordings, and radio and television productions, including *The Shape of Things to Come,* adapted as the film *Things to Come,* 1936, and *The War of the Worlds,* adapted by Orson Welles and broadcast by Columbia Broadcasting System (CBS-Radio) on October 30, 1938.

SIDELIGHTS: H. G. Wells, best remembered for imaginative novels such as *The Invisible Man* and *The War of the Worlds,* prototypes for modern science fiction, was a prolific writer and one of the most versatile in the history of English letters. He produced an average of nearly three books a year for more than fifty years, in addition to hundreds of newspaper and magazine articles. His works ranged from fiction to history, science, social activism, literary criticism, biography, and film. Altogether, Wells penned more words than William Shakespeare and Charles Dickens combined.

Born of lower-middle-class parents—they were, in fact, servants to the gentry—he escaped a servile life by winning a scholarship to the Normal School of Science at South Kensington, a London parliamentary borough, in 1884. Britain's first college to offer a science education for teachers, the Normal School of Science was founded by T. H. Huxley, who also served as its first dean. Wells regarded Huxley as the greatest man he ever met (although they never engaged in actual conversation). Recalling studying biology under Huxley, Wells in *The Fate of Man: An Unemotional Statement of the Things That Are Happening to Him Now, and of the Immediate Possibilities Confronting Him* (1939) declared he had then come to see the world "as I see it today. . . . There has been a lot of expansion and supplementing since, but nothing like fundamental reconstruction." He later summed up his life's work in *'42 to '44: A Contemporary Memoir Upon Human Behaviour During the Crisis of the World Revolution* (1944) by saying, "My role has always been that of a propagandist, direct or indirect, for world socialism." He labeled this ideology "Wellsism," a kind of "political religion," as he described it in *God, the Invisible King* (1917), that informs everything from his novels of social criticism to his utopian pictures of the world as it might be.

The connection between Wellsism and the writer's worship of Huxley may be explained as follows. Before founding the school, Huxley became famous for defending naturalist Charles Darwin in the great Oxford Debate of 1860, doing battle with the Church over the issue of evolution raised in Darwin's *Origin of Species by Means of Natural Selection* (1859). Huxley's merciless victory over Bishop Wilberforce at Oxford, at a time when one did not lightly insult leaders of the established religion, impressed on science students that theirs was more than a harmless academic discipline. With Huxley, science, especially biology, was radical, even revolutionary—at the expense of theology. It inspired Wells from the start, as he said in *The Anatomy of Frustration: A Modern Synthesis* (1936), to cast himself as "a sort of one-man Royal Commission of enquiry into the significance of the universe, as it had been understood and stated heretofore."

As it happened Wells lost his scholarship after his third year. Only Huxley, who taught Wells his first year, interested him. Thereafter he failed to keep up with his studies, preoccupied with activities such as debating and the college magazine, which he founded and edited. Wells had no intention of becoming a man of letters, though he showed an early interest in writing, as revealed by *The Desert Daisy,* a narrative written when he was about twelve years old. He began as a professional by producing journalistic sketches, some of which were collected in *Select Conversations With an Uncle, Now Extinct, and Two Other Reminiscences* (1895) and *Certain Personal Matters: A Collection of Material, Mainly Autobiographical* (1898). These essays were bright and informed enough to win the attention of the English *Saturday Review,* which then assigned him to carry the main burden of its fiction reviewing. From 1895 to 1897 he passed judgment on almost every new novel published in English. Sifting out those books deserving of review, as exemplars either of artistic excellence or of instructive failure, he made a distinguished career of producing thoughtful and intelligent literary criticism on a weekly basis.

Wells's term as a book reviewer set new standards of precision in literary criticism, especially with his careful distinction between novels of romance and of realism. He helped define these categories to the benefit of both writers and critics. In addition, he brought public attention to authors Joseph Conrad and James Joyce, writing for their first novels the perceptive review articles that helped launch their distinguished careers.

He would not limit himself to reviewing, however. All along, Wells had nurtured a single promising idea, first introduced in "The Chronic Argonauts," published in his college magazine two years after he dropped out of school—an idea that he hoped would establish him as a novelist in his own right. Developed after many false starts, it finally appeared as *The Time Machine* in 1895. This first novel was hailed as a work of genius, and it is regarded by today's critics as the one great Victorian epic dramatizing the Darwinian vision of cosmic time outside historical time. Wells was on his way to winning fame with a series of similar novels, the scientific romances, as he called them. These are Wells's only works to have remained continuously in print since his death. The best of them are *The Time Machine, The Island of Doctor Moreau* (1896), *The Invisible Man* (1897), *The War of the Worlds* (1898), and *The First Men in the Moon* (1901).

With the scientific romances, Wells defined a new department of twentieth-century literature, not only for science fiction authors but for a number of great mainstream writers who lent their talents to the genre. Notables who have acknowledged this debt include Evgeny Zamyatin, Aldous Huxley, C. S. Lewis, George Orwell, William Golding, Vladimir Nabokov, and Jorge Luis Borges. Wells's scientific romances were accepted by Victorian critics as masterful works of art. But later critics took a different view. When the scientific romances were reprinted in the first issues of *Amazing Stories,* which from 1926 established science fiction as a publisher's category among the many other forms of topical fiction dominating the American pulp magazine industry, Wells was proclaimed "the father of modern science fiction." Critics of the day associated Wells's scientific romances with lowbrow literature belonging to popular culture. Eventually the science fiction genre won critical attention, while Bernard Bergonzi rediscovered Wells's scientific romances for quality literature.

Between 1903 and 1908, Wells was a member of the Fabian Society, a group of upper-middle-class intellectuals that promoted socialism. Wells wrote a number of attention-getting Fabian pamphlets, most notably *Socialism and the Family* (1906) and *This Misery of Boots* (1907). Some of the ideas advanced in the pamphlets were later adopted by British Parliament, measures now basic to the British welfare state.

Shortly after leaving the Fabian Society, Wells in 1909 wrote the novel *Ann Veronica,* considered scandalous in its time for presenting the theme of woman's emancipation. That movement traces its ideological ancestry in large part to the transatlantic influence of this novel, together with other Wells books like it, such as *Marriage* (1912), *The Passionate Friends* (1913), *The Wife of Sir Isaac Harman* (1914), and *Christina Alberta's Father* (1925). Wells was also an outspoken advocate of sexual liberation, and his testimony in another author's obscenity trial helped establish the freedom in England to publish explicit books about contraception. Earlier, Wells had lent his name to Margaret Sanger's crusade for family planning in the United States by writing the introduction to her *Pivot of Civilization* (1923).

At the same time, Wells influenced the course of the novel itself. As he says in his autobiography, "After *Ann Veronica,* things were never quite the same again in the world of English fiction." Within a few years other novelists followed the example of this *succes de*

scandale, which sold out in a number of editions despite the abuse heaped upon it by press and pulpit. The marketplace became more open to a new kind of fiction, free to explore all aspects of morality. Wells's boldness helped clear the way for such writers as D. H. Lawrence and the mature James Joyce.

Furthermore, the commercial success of packaged war games owes directly to Wells's invention in this field, with his publication of *Little Wars* (1913). Based on a floor game he devised for his children, this book also led to the improvement of the war games played by the military staff colleges of the British Army. Even here, Wells could not resist scoring a political point. He observed that real war was so childish and yet so horrible that the only proper place for uniformed patriots was in the Little Wars toybox; or else the militarism of independent sovereign nation-states would lead, sooner or later, to a ruinous world conflict. If man doesn't end war, war will end man was the message added to this not-so-playful children's book, published just before the onset of World War I.

This idea, in fact, was the central one of his most successful book, *The Outline of History,* which sold more than two million copies during his lifetime. In it Wells wrote, "History is more and more a race between education and catastrophe." The book was intended to help avert that catastrophe, forming as it did the first title of his educational trilogy, which also included *The Science of Life: A Summary of Contemporary Knowledge About Life and Its Possibilities* (1930) and *The Work, Wealth, and Happiness of Mankind* (1931), called by Wells his Bible of World Civilization. Wells believed that if only this new and secular Bible were taught in schools worldwide, mankind would learn the survival values of world citizenship and socialism and unlearn the doom-laden falsities of nationalism and patriotic schooling. With *The Outline of History,* Wells was the first to write the planetary story of mankind, using the insights of the Darwinian biologists and of the early anthropologists in the field of sociocultural evolution.

History for Wells was not only a story about the past. He presumed to write a history of the future as well, as in *The Shape of Things to Come.* A motion picture based on this book was made in 1936. Wells was then seventy years old but still influential enough to stimulate the most expensive production ever mounted by a British studio to that date. One of the first science fiction films, it was the direct ancestor of such big-budget cinematic space operas as "2001: A Space Odyssey" and "Star Wars." But "Things to Come" was no mere entertainment. He meant it to be a "propagandist film" for Wellsism, a plug for the world socialist state. As such it was yet another statement, looking ahead to the coming of World War II, of his war-to-end-war theme. But the audience of the time found his fears concerning yet another world war unconvincing (this only three short years before war actually broke out), and the film was a box office failure. As a result its message was lost, and the movie circulates today among science fiction film clubs only as a nostalgic predecessor to the big blockbusters.

During the actual course of the war he so accurately predicted, Wells published *The Rights of Man; or, What Are We Fighting For?* (1940). Based on the work of the Sankey Commission, on which he was invited to serve, it declared a list of about a dozen human rights, proposed as the basis for a lasting world peace should the Germans be defeated. As the subtitle indicates, Wells believed that these human rights were what the Allies should be fighting for. He later enlarged the scope of the commission's work, in *Phoenix* and in *'42 to '44,* to read as a declaration of the rights of the world citizen. In this form, it was intended to serve as the legal charter for the world state of his dream. His tireless efforts on its behalf did have one important practical effect. As James Dilloway documents in *Human Rights and World Order* (1983), Wells's contribution to the Sankey Commission directly shaped the language of the charter of the United Nations Organization in its Declaration of Human Rights, adopted December 10, 1948.

This contribution may turn out to be Wells's most important service to humanity, a service he was always ambitious to provide in some way. Yet Wells himself, it seems, thought of human rights not as individual but as collective rights, to be defined to the benefit of socialist planning under his idealized world state. The direction the world will take in the future depends entirely upon which definition prevails. In any event, perhaps no man of letters had more influence than did H. G. Wells in shaping the world's agenda for the days to come.

BIOGRAPHICAL/CRITICAL SOURCES:

BOOKS

Bergonzi, Bernard, *The Early H. G. Wells: A Study of the Scientific Romances,* Manchester University Press, 1961.
Bergonzi, Bernard, editor, *H. G. Wells: A Collection of Critical Essays,* Prentice-Hall, 1976.
Concise Dictionary of British Literary Biography, Volume 6: *Modern Writers, 1914-1945,* Gale (Detroit), 1991.
Costa, Richard Hauer, *H. G. Wells,* Twayne, 1966, revised edition, 1985.
Dictionary of Literary Biography, Gale, Volume 34: *British Novelists, 1890-1929: Traditionalists,* 1985; Volume 70: *British Mystery Writers, 1860-1919,* 1988.
Dilloway, James, *Human Rights and World Order,* H. G. Wells Society, 1983.
Foot, Michael, *H. G.: The History of Mr. Wells,* Counterpoint (Washington DC), 1995.
Huntington, John, editor, *Critical Essays on H. G. Wells,* G. K. Hall, 1991.
Kemp, Peter, *H. G. Wells and the Culminating Ape: Biological Imperatives and Imaginative Obsessions,* St. Martin's (New York), 1982.
MacKenzie, Norman, and Jeanne MacKenzie, *H. G. Wells: A Biography,* Simon & Schuster, 1973.
MacKenzie, Norman, and Jeanne MacKenzie, *The Time Traveller: The Life of H. G. Wells,* Simon & Schuster, 1973.
McConnell, Frank, *The Science Fiction of H. G. Wells,* Oxford University Press, 1981.
Parrinder, Patrick, *Shadows of the Future: H. G. Wells, Science Fiction, and Prophecy,* Syracuse University Press, 1995.
Scheick, William J., *The Critical Response to H. G. Wells,* Greenwood Press, 1995.
Short Story Criticism, Volume 6, Gale, 1990.
Suvin, Darko, and Robert M. Philmus, editors, *H. G. Wells and Modern Science Fiction,* Bucknell University Press, 1977.
Twentieth-Century Literary Criticism, Gale, Volume 6, 1982; Volume 12, 1984; Volume 19, 1986.
West, Anthony, *H. G. Wells: Aspects of a Life,* Random House, 1984.

PERIODICALS

American Heritage, September-October, 1989, pp. 42-54.
American History Illustrated, October, 1988, pp. 14-22.
Booklist, April 15, 1994, p. 1547.
Entertainment Weekly, February 17, 1995, p. 67.
Interview, January, 1989, p. 80-3.
Library Journal, September 1, 1987, p. 183; March 15, 1993, pp. 78-79; August, 1995, p. 125.
Los Angeles Times Book Review, December 9, 1984.
Magazine of Fantasy and Science Fiction, March, 1996, p. 6.
New Republic, November 6, 1989, p. 68-74.
New Statesman, December 15, 1995, p. 14.
Newsweek, May 28, 1984.
New York, May 30, 1994, pp. 69-70.
New York Times Book Review, March 3, 1985; September 21, 1986; October 30, 1988, p. 1.
Omni, February, 1992, p. 6.
Saturday Night, April, 1993, pp. 24-27.
School Library Journal, May, 1988, p. 73; April, 1991, p. 124.
Times (London), October 4, 1984.
Times Literary Supplement, January 25, 1985; February 7, 1986; September 18-24, 1987, p. 1020.
USA Today Magazine, May, 1990, p. 52-4.
Variety, May 30, 1994, p. 56; September 18, 1995, p. 105.
Washington Post Book World, January 6, 1985.

*   *   *

WELTY, Eudora 1909-
(Michael Ravenna)

PERSONAL: Born April 13, 1909, in Jackson, MS; daughter of Christian Webb (an insurance company president) and Chestina (Andrews) Welty. *Education:* Attended Mississippi State College for Women (now Mississippi University for Women), 1926-27; University of Wisconsin, B.A., 1929; attended Columbia University Graduate School of Business, 1930-31.

ADDRESSES: Home—1119 Pinehurst St., Jackson, MS 39202.

CAREER: Worked for newspapers and radio stations in Mississippi during early Depression years, and as a publicity agent for the state office of the Works Progress Administration (WPA). Was briefly a member of the *New York Times Book Review* staff, in New York City. Honorary consultant in American letters, Library of Congress, 1958–.

MEMBER: American Academy and Institute of Arts and Letters.

AWARDS, HONORS: Guggenheim fellowship, 1942; O. Henry Award, 1942, 1943, 1968; National Institute of Arts and Letters, 1944, grant in literature, 1972, Gold Medal for fiction writing; William Dean Howells Medal from American Academy of Arts and Letters, 1955, for *The Ponder Heart;* Creative Arts Medal for fiction, Brandeis University, 1966; Edward McDowell Medal, 1970; National Book Award nomination in fiction, 1971, for *Losing Battles;* Christopher Book Award, 1972, for *One Time, One Place: Mississippi in the Depression; A Snapshot;* National Institute of Arts and Letters Gold Medal, 1972; Pulitzer Prize in fiction, 1973, for *The Optimist's Daughter;* National Medal for Literature, 1980; *The Collected Stories of Eudora Welty* was named an American Library Association notable book for 1980; Presidential Medal of Freedom, 1980; American Book Award, 1981, for *The Collected Stories of Eudora Welty,* 1984, for *One Writer's Beginnings;* Common Wealth Award for Distinguished Service in Literature from Modern Language Association of America, 1984; National Book Critics Circle Award and *Los Angeles Times* Book Prize nominations, both 1984, for *One Writer's Beginnings;* Reader of the Year Award from Mystery

Writers of America, 1985; National Medal of Arts, 1987; Chevalier de l'order des Arts et Lettres, 1987.

WRITINGS:

A Curtain of Green (short stories; also see below) with a preface by Katherine Anne Porter, Doubleday, 1941, published as *A Curtain of Green, and Other Stories,* Harcourt, 1964.

The Robber Bridegroom (novella), Doubleday, 1942.

The Wide Net, and Other Stories (also see below), Harcourt, 1943.

Delta Wedding (novel), Harcourt, 1946.

Music from Spain, Levee Press, 1948.

Short Stories (address delivered at University of Washington), Harcourt, 1949.

The Golden Apples (connected stories; also see below), Harcourt, 1949.

Selected Stories (contains all of the short stories in *A Curtain of Green,* and *The Wide Net, and Other Stories*) introduction by Porter, Modern Library, 1953.

The Ponder Heart (novel), Harcourt, 1954.

The Bride of Innisfallen, and Other Stories, Harcourt, 1955.

Place in Fiction (lectures for Conference on American Studies in Cambridge, England), House of Books, 1957.

John Rood (catalog of sculpture exhibition), [New York], 1958.

Three Papers on Fiction (addresses), Smith College, 1962.

The Shoe Bird (juvenile), Harcourt, 1964.

Thirteen Stories, edited and introduction by Ruth M. Vande Kieft, Harcourt, 1965.

A Sweet Devouring (nonfiction), Albondocani Press, 1969.

Losing Battles (novel), Random House, 1970.

A Flock of Guinea Hens Seen from a Car (poem), Albondocani Press, 1970.

One Time, One Place: Mississippi in the Depression; A Snapshot Album, illustrated with photographs by Welty, Random House, 1971, revised edition, University Press of Mississippi, 1996.

The Optimist's Daughter (novelette), Random House, 1972.

The Eye of the Story (selected essays and reviews), Random House, 1978.

Miracles of Perception, The Library (Charlottesville), 1980.

The Collected Stories of Eudora Welty, Harcourt, 1980.

One Writer's Beginnings (lectures; includes *Beginnings*), Harvard University Press, 1984.

Morgana: Two Stories from "The Golden Apples," University Press of Mississippi, 1988.

Photographs, University Press of Mississippi, 1989.

Eudora Welty's The Hitch-Hikers, edited by Larry Ketron, Dramatists Play Service, 1990.

(Editor with Ronald A. Sharp) *The Norton Book of Friendship,* Norton, 1991.

A Worn Path, Creative Edcation, 1991.

A Writer's Eye: Collected Book Reviews, edited by Pearl A. McHaney, University Press of Mississippi, 1994.

Contributor to *Southern Review, Atlantic, Harper's Bazaar, Manuscript, New Yorker,* and other periodicals. Also contributor of articles under pseudonym, Michael Ravenna, to *New York Times Book Review.* Author of introduction of *Novel-Writing in an Apocalyptic Time,* by Walker Percy, Faust, 1986, *The Democratic Forest,* by William Eggleston, Doubleday, 1989, and *The Capers Papers,* by Charlotte Capers, University Press of Mississippi, 1992.

MEDIA ADAPTATIONS: The Ponder House was adapted for the stage and first produced on Broadway in 1956, and was adapted as an *opera bouffe* and produced in 1982; *The Robber Bridegroom* was adapted for the stage as a musical and first produced in 1978; "The Hitch-hikers" was adapted for the stage in 1986; "Lily Daw and the Three Ladies" was adapted for the stage and produced.

SIDELIGHTS: With the publication of *The Eye of the Story* and *The Collected Stories,* Eudora Welty achieved the recognition she has long deserved as an important contemporary American fiction writer. Her position was confirmed in 1984 when her autobiographical *One Writer's Beginnings* made the best-seller lists with sales exceeding 100,000 copies. During the early decades of her career, she was respected by fellow writers but often dismissed by critics as a regionalist, a miniaturist, or an oversensitive "feminine" writer. The late 1970s and 1980s, however, saw a critical reevaluation of her work. Michael Kreyling declared in *Eudora Welty's Achievement of Order* that the value of her work is not that it is "primarily regional writing, or even excellent regional writing, but [that it conveys] the vision of a certain artist who must be considered with her peers—[Virginia] Woolf, [Elizabeth] Bowen, and [E. M.] Forster."

Although Welty has always distanced herself from the women's movement, feminist critical interest in the works of women writers also stimulated renewed attention to her fiction in the 1970s and 1980s. In an article collected in *Eudora Welty: Critical Essays,* Margaret Jones Bolsterli expressed some of the major assumptions of the feminist approach when she argues that "Understanding women's views of themselves and of men is necessary if we are ever going to get at the truth, and the vision Eudora Welty presents of the women's worlds in [her] novels illuminates not only half of the great world which we do not often see, but also touches gently sometimes on the terrible state of affairs on this darkling plain when men and women do not see each other clearly at all." The reading public and the scholarly establishment began to realize that a major body of American fiction had been produced by Southern women writers, as Anne Goodwyn Jones has documented in *Tomorrow Is Another Day: The Woman Writer in the South, 1859-1936.* Moreover, critics perceived that Welty, the most prolific and versatile of these writers, was producing works of an astonishing range: from folktale to historical romance, grotesque farce to novel of manners; from dramatizations of lives consumed by sharecropping in the Depression to portraits of relationships in Delta plantations and upper-middle-class suburbs. And all these modes of fiction and varieties of subject matter are complemented by her distinguished essays, reviews—many of which were published in *A Writer's Eye: Collected Book Reviews*—and reminiscences, notably those collected in *The Eye of the Story* and *One Writer's Beginnings.*

The oldest of her family's three children and the only girl, Welty grew up in Jackson, Mississippi. That neither of her parents came from the Deep South may have given her some detachment from her culture and helped her become an astute observer of its manners. Her father, Christian Welty, had been raised on a farm in Ohio and had become a country school teacher in West Virginia. Marrying a fellow teacher, Chestina Andrews, he had moved to Jackson to improve his fortunes by entering business. Starting as a bookkeeper in an insurance company, he eventually advanced to become the company's president.

Chestina Andrews, the daughter of transplanted Virginians, had grown up on a mountain in West Virginia. At fifteen, she had taken her critically ill father down an icy river on a raft to the railroad and then to a hospital in Baltimore where he died on the operating table of a ruptured appendix. In later years she took her young daughter on memorable summer visits "up home"; Welty's formidable grandmother and five bachelor uncles make a poignant fictional appearance in their mountaintop world as Laurel Hand's grandmother and uncles in *The Optimist's Daughter.*

Welty's education in the Jackson schools was followed by two years at Mississippi State College for Women between 1925 and 1927, and then by two more years at the University of Wisconsin and a B.A. in 1929. Her father, who believed that she could never earn a living by writing stories, encouraged her to study advertising at the Columbia University Graduate School of Business in New York during 1930-1931. The years in Wisconsin and New York broadened Welty's horizons, and the time she spent in New York City was especially meaningful. The Harlem Renaissance was at its height, and Welty and her friends went to dances in Harlem clubs and to musical and theatrical performances all over the city. "Everybody that was wonderful was then at their peak," the writer told Jan Norby Gretlund in an interview collected in *Conversations with Eudora Welty.* "For somebody who had never, in a sustained manner, been to the theater or to the Metropolitan Museum, where I went every Sunday, it was just a cornucopia."

Her father's sudden death in 1931 brought an end to Welty's northern sojourn. She went home to help her mother and brothers, and she has essentially remained in Jackson ever since. To support herself, Welty first tried various small jobs with local newspapers and with radio station WJDX, which her father had started in the tower of his insurance building. Then, in 1933, she was offered a position as a publicity agent for the Works Progress Administration (WPA). "I did reporting, interviewing," she explained to Jean Todd Freeman in an interview collected in *Conversations with Eudora Welty.* "It took me all over Mississippi, which is the most important thing to me, because I'd never seen it. . . . [The experience] was the real germ of my wanting to become a real writer, a true writer."

Welty's WPA work of the mid-1930s provided her with far more than visual training. Seeing at first hand the Depression-struck lives of rural and small-town people in a state that had always been the poorest in the nation, she was stimulated to capture their struggles and triumphs in stories, beginning with "Death of a Traveling Salesman," which was published in the literary magazine *Manuscript* in 1936. Other stories followed during the next five years, including some of her most famous—"Why I Live at the P.O.," "Powerhouse," "A Worn Path," "Petrified Man," "Lily Daw and the Three Ladies." Six stories were accepted by *Southern Review* between 1937 and 1939 and earned her the friendship and admiration of writers Albert Erskine, Robert Penn Warren, Katherine Anne Porter, and Ford Madox Ford. In his 1944 *Kenyon Review* essay, "The Love and Separateness in Miss Welty," Warren commented on the contrast between "the said, or violent, or warped" subjects of the stories and a tone that is "exhilarating, even gay, as though the author were innocently delighted . . . with the variety of things that stories could be and still be stories." These early works established Welty's characteristic comic genius with dialogue and with recording the incongruous developments of everyday life. Here she also developed a way of treating poverty, loss, and pain with a lightness that amounts to exquisite respect and discretion. In 1941 a collection of these stories was published as *A Curtain of Green* with a preface by Katherine Anne Porter. As Ruth Vande Kieft explains in *Eudora Welty,* the stories "are largely concerned with the mysteries of the inner life," "the enigma of man's being—his relation to the universe; what is secret, concealed, inviolable in any human

being, resulting in distance or separation between human beings; the puzzles and difficulties we have about our own feelings, our meaning and our identity."

Welty's first sustained experiment with folk materials appeared in 1942 as *The Robber Bridegroom,* a bold fusing of Mississippi history, tall tale, and fairytales of mysterious seducers drawn from British and Germanic sources as well as from the Greek story of Cupid and Psyche. Here, as Carol Manning explains in *With Ears Opening Like Morning Glories: Eudora Welty and the Love of Storytelling,* the innocent tone of the narrative counteracts the dire stuff of robberies, murders, and the depredations of a cruel stepmother. To many early reviewers the result seemed pure magic. Alfred Kazin claimed in a review for the *New York Herald Tribune Books* that Welty had captured "the lost fabulous innocence of our departed frontier, the easy carelessness, the fond bragging and colossal buckskin strut." In the *New York Times Book Review,* Marianne Hauser called it "a modern fairy tale, where irony and humor, outright nonsense, deep wisdom and surrealistic extravaganzas become a poetic unity through the power of a pure, exquisite style." Although some other commentators found it lacking in substance, Kreyling has defended *The Robber Bridegroom* as a valuable addition to the pastoral tradition in American literature: "Welty seems to be saying that the dream of a pastoral paradise on earth is always one step ahead of the dreamers; it is, sadly, only possible in a dream world removed from contact with human flesh and imperfections. But still worth dreaming."

Welty continued to experiment with such materials in her next collection, *The Wide Net, and Other Stories.* Here she explored the interrelationships of everyday Mississippi life with the timeless themes and patterns of myth, creating for her apparently ordinary characters a universality that links them with all times and cultures. The title story, for instance, places a domestic quarrel within the context of fertility tales; the work climaxes with a descent into a watery underworld where the hero encounters "the King of the Snakes" and proves worthy to return to his pregnant wife. In an essay appearing in *Eudora Welty: Critical Essays,* Garvin Davenport sees each of the stories in *The Wide Net* as presenting "at least one character who confronts or encounters a situation which is in some way dark, mysterious or dreamlike. Each such encounter contributes to an awakening or renewal—sometimes only temporarily—of that character's potential for emotional enrichment and experiential meaning. If the nature of the encounter often suggests a kind of regression to a more primitive or fundamental level of consciousness, the overall structures of the stories make clear that it is regression as a phase in problem-solving."

Welty's first novel, *Delta Wedding,* marks a significant change in her focus. Fertility myth still runs as an undercurrent through the daily affairs described in the book, but Welty has shifted from the dreamlike atmosphere of *The Wide Net* to the ordinary milieu of family life in the Mississippi Delta. Many of the circumstances of the Fairchild family in *Delta Wedding* recall those of the Ramsay family in Woolf's *To the Lighthouse.* The center of the Fairchild family is a mother of eight who continually ministers to her husband, her children, and a wider circle of relatives and friends. The novel is organized around domestic imagery of cooking and eating, wedding preparations, and diplomatic maneuvers to avert conflicts and soothe hurt feelings so that the wedding, on which the work centers, can occur. Both Woolf's and Welty's novels admiringly explore the experience and values of women characters and celebrate the community, harmony, and renewal created by mothers for their families.

The narrative technique is similar to Woolf's in its use of multiple perspectives. In Welty's case the observers are all female, from nine-year-old Laura McRaven, a visiting cousin, to the mother, Ellen Fairchild, and her many daughters. In an interview collected in *Conversations with Eudora Welty,* the writer told Jo Brans that the world of *Delta Wedding* is a matriarchy but that it is not at all hostile to men. Men, instead, are the objects of loving attention and perform the occasional acts of heroism that are necessary to protect the charmed and fertile pastoral world of the plantation. Chief among these men is Uncle George Fairchild, who reenacts in modern form the mythic rescue of a maiden from a dragon by St. George. In this case, the dragon is an approaching train, and George Fairchild's rush to pull his niece from the track symbolically expresses his function for the whole Fairchild family.

Delta Wedding was followed in 1949 by *The Golden Apples,* a closely related group of stories that functions almost as a novel. *The Golden Apples* depicts several families in the little town of Morgana, Mississippi, during the 1930s or early 1940s, focusing particularly on the defiant and talented Virgie Rainey, who rejects the conventional life of a Southern lady and creates an independent existence for herself while helping her widowed mother run her dairy farm. Fertility myths weave through these stories with particular attention given to the Pan-like figure of King Maclain, who wanders in and out of town seducing maidens like a mythical satyr and then disappearing in almost a twinkling of cloven hooves. But the main emphasis remains on the lives of the townspeople—the growing pains of children, the tragicomic disappointment of the fierce German music teacher Miss Eckhart, the near-drowning of an orphan girl at summer camp, and then the aging of the community and blighting of the lives of many characters who began as children full of possibility in the early stories.

Welty's next book, *The Ponder Heart,* is a comic tour de force that concentrates many of her favorite themes in the dramatic events of an eccentric Southern gentleman's life. Set in the small town of Clay, Mississippi, *The Ponder Heart* is ostensibly an examination of the "heart" or character of Uncle Daniel Ponder, narrated by his spinster niece Edna Earle. Uncle Daniel is one of Welty's typical male heroes who unaccountably marries a selfish and brassy lower-class girl. (George Fairchild of *Delta Wedding* and Judge McKelva of *The Optimist's Daughter* are two more serious versions of the type.) In a tone combining sympathy and outrage, Edna Earle describes her uncle's wooing of seventeen-year-old Bonnie Dee Peacock in a dime store, their elopement, her desertion, return, death and burial, and Uncle Daniel's trial for murder.

Playful use of cliche, giddy inversion of social conventions, and the juxtaposition of kindly motives and silly disasters prevent the story from ever moving outside the realm of farce. When Uncle Daniel literally tickles his wife to death in an attempt to distract her from her fear of a thunderstorm, readers can only laugh and recognize the ridiculous dimensions of the most painful human experiences. *The Ponder Heart* can also be seen as a satire on the ideal of the Southern gentleman, a satire which is quite horrifying beneath its humor. The old husband does in fact murder his estranged wife during an attempted reconciliation; family and friends side with him, as does the tone of the novella, so that the death of the young wife is a joke at best and only an inconvenience at worst. Welty received the William Dean

Howells Medal of the American Academy of Arts and Letters for *The Ponder Heart* in 1955; and the work was successfully translated into a Broadway play in 1956 and adapted as an *opera bouffe* in 1982.

In 1955, Welty published another collected of short stories, *The Bride of Innisfallen, and Other Stories,* experimenting with a more allusive style. Three of the stories—"Circe," "Going to Naples," and "The Bride of Innisfallen"—are set in Europe and lack the vivid sense of place that gives solidity to most of Welty's fiction. The other four stories operate in familiar Mississippi settings. With the exception of "The Burning," a cryptic account of the burning of a plantation by Yankee soldiers during the Civil War, most continue Welty's comedy of small-town manners: adulterous trysts are foiled by rain and curious children ("Ladies in Spring") or by heat and spiritual fatigue ("No Place for You, My Love") and a visiting niece offers bemused observations on and childhood memories of her Mississippi relatives' social milieu ("Kin").

One Time, One Place, the collection of photographs from Welty's 1930s WPA travels, appeared in 1971, followed in 1972 by Pulitzer Prize-winning novel, *The Optimist's Daughter.* The sparest of her novels, it recounts an adult daughter's return to Mississippi to be with her elderly father during an eye operation and then to preside over his funeral a few weeks later. As Laurel Hand confronts her memories of both parents, she comes to understand the pain of her mother's dying years and their effect on her father. Laurel is reconciled to her father's unwise second marriage to a ruthless young woman, and at the same time finally recognizes her own grief for the husband she has lost many years before. Welty's exploration of grief in *The Optimist's Daughter* which was in part a working-out of her own losses during the 1960s, contains many autobiographical elements, particularly in the portrait of Laurel's mother. But the novel is also a close fictional examination of the interdependence of child and parents. In an interview collected in *Conversations with Eudora Welty,* Welty told Martha van Noppen that she "tried to give that feeling of support and dependence that just ran in an endless line among the three of them [mother, father, and daughter]." Finally, Laurel Hand works through her grief to achieve a calmer and more practical accommodation with the past.

Losing Battles and *The Optimist's Daughter* brought renewed attention to Welty's writing and consequently an increasingly heavy burden of requests for interviews and speaking engagements. She continued to protect the essential privacy of her daily life, however, by discouraging biographic inquiries, carefully screening interviews, and devoting most of her energies to her work. During the later 1970s this work consisted largely of collecting her nonfiction writings for publication as *The Eye of the Story* and of assembling her short stories as *The Collected Stories of Eudora Welty.* With these two important collections she rounded out the shape of her life's work in literary commentary and fiction.

An invitation to give a series of lectures at Harvard in 1983 resulted in the three autobiographical pieces published as *One Writer's Beginnings* the next year. Perhaps because she wished to forestall potential biographers or because she came to accept public interest in a writer's early experiences in shaping her vision, Welty provided in *One Writer's Beginnings* a re-creation of the world that nourished her own imagination. Characteristically, however, she omitted family difficulties and intimate matters, focusing instead on the family love of books and storytelling, the values and examples her parents provided, and the physical sensations of life in Jackson that influenced her literary sensitivities.

Meanwhile, the tide of critical comment about and interest in Welty's work has not diminished, with scholars analyzing all elements of her various writings. 1994, for instance, saw the publication of *A Writer's Eye,* a complete collection of Welty's book reviews written between 1942 and 1984. Carol Shields, commenting in the *Times Literary Supplement,* calls the collection "graceful" and adds, "[Welty's] strength lies in identifying—sharply, wittily, often metaphorically—the centre of a writer's power, or else a debilitating weakness."

Welty's fictional chronicle of Mississippi life adds a major comic vision to American literature, a vision that affirms the sustaining power of community and family life and at the same time explores the need for solitude. In his 1944 essay, Robert Penn Warren aptly identifies these twin themes in Welty's work as love and separateness. While much of modern American fiction has emphasized alienation and the failure of love, Welty's stories show how tolerance and generosity allow people to adapt to each other's foibles and to painful change. Welty's fiction particularly celebrates the love of men and women, the fleeting joys of childhood, and the many dimensions and stages of women's lives.

BIOGRAPHICAL/CRITICAL SOURCES:

BOOKS

Abadie, Ann J., and Louis D. Dollarhide, editors, *Eudora Welty: A Form of Thanks,* University Press of Mississippi, 1979.
Aevlin, Albert J., *Welty: A Life in Literature,* 1987.
Bloom, Harold, editor, *Welty,* Chelsea House, 1986.
Bryant, Joseph A., Jr., *Eudora Welty,* University of Minnesota Press, 1968.
Carson, Barbara Harrell, *Eudora Welty: Two Pictures at Once in Her Frame,* Whitston, 1992.
Champion, Laurie, *The Critical Response to Eudora Welty's Fiction,* Greenwood Press, 1994.
Concise Dictionary of American Literary Biography, Volume 5: *The New Consciousness, 1941-1968,* Gale (Detroit), 1987.
Contemporary Authors Bibliographical Series, Volume 1, Gale, 1986.
Contemporary Literary Criticism, Gale, Volume 1, 1973; Volume 2, 1974; Volume 5, 1976; Volume 14, 1980; Volume 22, 1982; Volume 33, 1985.
Devlin, Albert J., *Welty's Chronicle: A Story of Mississippi,* University Press of Mississippi, 1983.
Dictionary of Literary Biography, Gale, Volume 2: *American Novelists since World War II,* 1978; Volume 102: *American Short Story Writers, 1910-1945, Second Series,* 1991; Volume 143: *American Novelists since World War II, Third Series,* 1994.
Dictionary of Literary Biography Yearbook: 1987, Gale, 1988.
Evans, Elizabeth, *Eudora Welty,* Ungar, 1981.
Gretlund, Jan Norby, *Eudora Welty's Aesthetics of Place,* Associated University Presses, 1994.
Gygax, Franziska, *Serious Daring from Within: Female Narrative Strategies in Eudora Welty's Novels,* Greenwood Press, 1990.
Harrison, Suzan, *Eudora Welty and Virginia Woolf: Gender, Genre, and Influence,* Louisiana State University Press, 1996.
Jones, Anne Goodwyn, *Tomorrow Is Another Day: the Woman Writer in the South, 1859-1936,* Louisiana State University Press, 1981.

Kreyling, Michael, *Eudora Welty's Achievement of Order,* Louisiana State University Press, 1980.
Manning, Carol, *With Ears Opening Like Morning Glories: Eudora Welty and the Love of Storytelling,* Greenwood Press, 1985.
Mark, Rebecca, *The Dragon's Blood: Feminist Intertextuality in Eudora Welty's "The Golden Apples,"* University Press of Mississippi, 1994.
Mortimer, Gail L., *Daughter of the Swan: Love and Knowledge in Eudora Welty's Fiction,* University of Georgia Press, 1994.
Pingatore, Diana R., *A Reader's Guide to the Short Stories of Eudora Welty,* Prentice Hall, 1996.
Polk, Noel, *Eudora Welty—A Bibliography of Her Work,* University Press of Mississippi, 1994.
Prenshaw, Peggy Whitman, editor, *Eudora Welty: Critical Essays,* University Press of Mississippi, 1979.
Prenshaw, Peggy Whitman, editor, *Conversations with Eudora Welty,* University Press of Mississippi, 1984.
Prenshaw, Peggy Whitman, editor, *More Conversations with Eudora Welty,* University Press of Mississippi, 1996.
Schmidt, Peter, *The Heart of the Story: Welty's Short Fiction,* University Press of Mississippi, 1991.
Short Story Criticism, Volume 1, Gale, 1988.
Trouard, Dawn, editor, *Eudora Welty: Eye of the Storyteller,* Kent State University Press, 1990.
Vande Kieft, Ruth, *Eudora Welty,* Twayne, 1962.

PERIODICALS

American Book Collector, January/February, 1981.
Booklist, June 1, 1994, p. 1775; November 1, 1994, p. 530; April 15, 1996, p. 1409.
Chicago Tribune, December 20, 1984.
Chicago Tribune Book World, April 1, 1982.
English Journal, January, 1990.
Globe and Mail (Toronto), March 24, 1984.
Harper's Magazine, February, 1990.
Kenyon Review, spring, 1944.
Library Journal, March 1, 1994, p. 89; September 1, 1994, p. 230; April 1, 1995, p. 142.
Los Angeles Times, November 13, 1987.
Mississippi Quarterly, fall, 1973; fall, 1984.
New Yorker, February 19, 1996, p. 36.
New York Herald Tribune, October 25, 1942.
New York Times, February 18, 1984; March 1, 1985; April 22, 1990.
New York Times Book Review, November 1, 1942; April 12, 1970; February 19, 1984.
PMLA, October, 1984.
Sewanee Review, July-September, 1952; summer, 1990.
Shenandoah, spring, 1969.
Times Literary Supplement, August 12, 1994.
Twentieth Century Literature, winter, 1982.
World & I, October, 1997.
Yale Review, April, 1996.

* * *

WEST, (Mary) Jessamyn 1902-1984

PERSONAL: Born July 18, 1902, in Jennings County, IN; died of a stroke February 23 (some sources say February 22), 1984 in Napa, CA; daughter of Eldo Ray (a citrus farmer) and Grace Anna (Milhous) West; married Harry Maxwell McPherson (a school superintendent) August 16, 1923; children: Ann Cash (adopted daughter). *Education:* Whittier College, A.B., 1923; attended University of California at Berkeley; studied at Oxford University, 1929. *Religion:* Society of Friends (Quaker).

ADDRESSES: Home and office—2480 3rd Ave., Napa, CA 94558.

CAREER: Writer, 1935-84. Taught at writers' conferences at Breadloaf, Indiana University, University of Notre Dame, University of Colorado, Squaw Valley University of Utah, University of Washington, Stanford University, University of Montana, Portland University, University of Kentucky, and Loyola Marymount University. Visiting professor at Wellesley College, University of California at Irvine, Mills College, and Whittier College. Visiting lecturer at numerous colleges.

MEMBER: American Civil Liberties Union, National Association for the Advancement of Colored People.

AWARDS, HONORS: Indiana Authors' Day Award, 1956, for *Love, Death, and the Ladies' Drill Team;* Thermod Monsen Award, 1958, for *To See the Dream;* California Commonwealth Club award, 1970, and California Literature Medal, 1971, both for *Crimson Ramblers of the World, Farewell;* Janet Kafke Prize for fiction, 1976; Indiana Arts Commission Award for Literature, 1977, for body of work. Honorary doctorates from Whittier College, Mills College, Swarthmore College, Indiana University, University of Indiana-Terre Haute, Western College for Women, Wheaton College, Juniata College, and Wilmington College.

WRITINGS:

FICTION

The Friendly Persuasion (short stories), Harcourt, 1945.
The Witch Diggers (novel), Harcourt, 1951.
Cress Delahanty (short stories; Book-of-the-Month Club selection), Harcourt, 1953.
Little Men (novel), Ballantine, 1954, republished as *The Chile Kings,* 1967.
Love, Death, and the Ladies' Drill Team (short stories), Harcourt, 1955 (published in England as *Learn To Say Goodbye,* Hodder & Stoughton, 1960).
South of the Angels (novel), Harcourt, 1960.
A Matter of Time (novel), Harcourt, 1966.
Leafy Rivers (novel), Harcourt, 1967.
Except for Me and Thee: A Companion to "The Friendly Persuasion" (short stories), Harcourt, 1969.
Crimson Ramblers of the World, Farewell (short stories), Harcourt, 1970.
The Massacre at Fall Creek (novel; Literary Guild main selection), Harcourt, 1975.
The Life I Really Lived (novel), Harcourt, 1979.
The State of Stony Lonesome (novel), Harcourt, 1984.
The Collected Stories of Jessamyn West, Harcourt, 1986.

NONFICTION

To See the Dream, Harcourt, 1957.
Love Is Not What You Think, Harcourt, 1959 (published in England as *A Woman's Love,* Hodder & Stoughton, 1960).
Hide and Seek: A Continuing Journey, Harcourt, 1973.
The Woman Said Yes: Encounters with Death and Life (Book-of-the-Month Club alternate selection), Harcourt, 1976 (published in England as *Encounters with Death and Life: Memoirs,* Gollancz, 1978).
Double Discovery: A Journey, Harcourt, 1980.

PLAYS

A Mirror for the Sky (opera libretto; first performed at the University of Oregon at Eugene, May 24, 1957), Harcourt, 1948.
The Friendly Persuasion (screenplay; based on story collection of same title), produced by Allied Artists, 1956.
The Big Country (screenplay), produced by United Artists, 1958.
Stolen Hours (screenplay), produced by United Artists, 1963.

OTHER

(Contributor) *Cross Section 1948: A Collection of New American Writing,* Simon & Schuster, 1948.
(Editor) *A Quaker Reader,* Viking, 1962, with introduction, Pendle Hill, 1992.
The Secret Look: Poems, Harcourt, 1974.

Contributor to *O. Henry Memorial Award Prize Stories of 1946,* and to *The Living Novel,* 1957. Also contributor of fiction and nonfiction articles to numerous periodicals, including *Town and Country, Mademoiselle, Collier's, Ladies' Home Journal, New Mexico Quarterly, Yale Review, Kenyon Review, Good Housekeeping, McCall's, Harper's, New Yorker, Redbook,* and *Saturday Evening Post.* West's collected papers are stored at Whittier College.

SIDELIGHTS: Jessamyn West was a prolific and varied writer whose works include fiction, nonfiction, poetry, screenplays, and even an opera libretto. She is remembered, however, for her numerous short stories that plumb rural American life without sentiment or oversimplicity. Much of West's fiction reflects her involvement with the Society of Friends (Quakers), the religion of her ancestors who farmed in southern Indiana. Her popular story collections *The Friendly Persuasion* and *Except for Me and Thee: A Companion to "The Friendly Persuasion"* recreate Quaker lives in a nineteenth century farming community; these and her tales of adolescence, *Cress Delahanty* and *The State of Stony Lonesome,* remain her best known works. *New York Times Book Review* contributor Nancy Hale called West's stories "homespun but with an exceedingly subtle warp and woof," and explained that West used "small-town life to convey human events that warm the heart and evoke instant sympathy." According to Bill Crider in the *Dictionary of Literary Biography,* West's many volumes were "well-received, even acclaimed, by reviewers" for their "vivid, vigorous, and eloquent style and the compassion and humanity with which she treats . . . serious themes." In his book-length study entitled *Jessamyn West,* Alfred S. Shivers concluded that the author's work retains its "high merit with respect to sensitivity of characterizations, restraint, genuineness of feeling, psychology, and delightful humor."

West's chronicles of rural life are hardly mere idyllic tales of simpler times, however. She strove to create realistic characters, especially teenagers and women, with personalities well-grounded in human nature. Writing in the *Indiana Magazine of History,* John T. Flanagan found West's people "a constant delight, freshly conceived, individual, even a bit eccentric. . . . Generally commonsensical but often endowed with a quirky humor or an ironical point of view, her characters enter the reader's presence in full stature and linger there like old acquaintances." Her Quaker background notwithstanding, West tackled the subject of sexual passion, generally but not always celebrating the stability of marriage over the momentary attraction of a liaison. According to *New York Times Book Review* contributor Webster Schott, West dominated among women novelists as "an advocate of human respect, reason over emotions, and a tough, all-purpose femininity that can face and solve most situations on its own terms." Shivers similarly observed that the author made "no claim that fiction should be morally improving" even though many of her books "exude a subtle moral atmosphere." Within the parameters of domestic drama, West explored universal themes such as values, sexuality, and maturity; to quote *Dictionary of Literary Biography Yearbook* essayist Ann Dahlstrom Farmer, her characters "are complex, not because they represent several ideas but because they are realistic, many-faceted individuals."

West was born in Indiana on July 18, 1902, to a farming family of modest circumstances. She was related to Richard Nixon through her mother's family, and she became a close and lifelong friend of his, sometimes even travelling with the presidential entourage. When West was still young, her father decided to seek his fortune in California. Eventually the family moved to an undeveloped wilderness area near Yorba Linda, where they began a successful citrus orchard. West and her brother and sister were allowed to roam freely through the arid Orange County lands, and the young girl was able to cultivate her solitary, observant nature. Adolescence brought an interest in reading as well as a fascination with the life and work of Thoreau. Dahlstrom Farmer observed that Thoreau's writings prized two things that West herself prized, namely "solitude and journal-keeping as enhancers of observation and introspection." Although she admired many writers, West quelled her own authorial ambitions and studied to become a school teacher. After graduating from Whittier College, she married Harry Maxwell McPherson and set to work in a one-room school. She soon discovered a great desire to further her education, however, and in 1929 she embarked for a summer session at Oxford University. Upon her return to the United States, she enrolled in a graduate program at the University of California at Berkeley.

Just before taking her doctoral orals, West suffered a severe lung hemorrhage and was diagnosed as having an advanced case of tuberculosis. She was placed in the terminal ward of a Los Angeles sanitorium, and her doctors gave her little hope of survival. After two years in the hospital, West was sent home so that she could "die amongst her loved ones." West's mother refused to accept the inevitability of her daughter's untimely death, however. She went to great lengths to provide favorite foods, and just as important for the depressed patient, entertainment. Reaching into her own past, West's mother recalled her Quaker forebears and told West about them. According to Angela Wigan in *Time* magazine, the elder West recounted "stories about courtship and farming, blizzards and Quaker meetings." As West slowly recovered, she "turned her mother's gift into her own response to extinction—her writing." While still an invalid she began to create sketches about an Indiana Quaker farm couple raising a family during the civil War era. Her husband encouraged her to submit the stories to magazines, and by the time she had regained her health—early in 1940—her work was being accepted by such publications as the *Atlantic Monthly, Harper's,* and the *Ladies' Home Journal.* In retrospect, West was quoted in *Women Writers of the West Coast* as crediting her near-fatal illness with giving her the courage to begin writing. "I thought my life was over," she said of those hopeless days. "Instead, for me, it was the beginning of my life."

The Friendly Persuasion, published in 1945, collects a number of West's stories about Jess and Eliza Birdwell, the Quaker farmers in rural Indiana. Crider described the book thus: "The stories carry the family from the ten years preceding the Civil War to Jess's old age, around the turn of the century. A remarkable feeling of

familial love and understanding permeates the book, which is also notable for its warmth and humor." Crider added that the collection "was an immediate success," with critics and general readers alike. *Saturday Review* commentator William Hogan called *The Friendly Persuasion* "a warm, winning tale" that established West's reputation for "style, characterization, humor, and impetuosity." In *Book Week,* Flora Henderson wrote that the work "makes a delightful addition to American literature. There is poetry here, but so subtly woven into the fabric of story and character that it never intrudes." Ernestine Evans made similar observations in the *New York Herald Tribune Book Review.* "Miss West's style is full of surprises, vivid metaphors, odd turns of plot, yet she is never disconcerting, over-ingenious or repetitive," Evans contended. "Though distilled from family legends of the Irish Quaker community into which she was born, the tales are less nostalgic than provocative. One feels not that loveliness used to be and is no more but that life could be. . . . even quieter and funnier than currently advertised."

According to Shivers, West was able to reconcile her religious tradition with the demands of artistic truth in *The Friendly Persuasion* and its sequel, *Except for Me and Thee.* West "resisted the moralizing impulse," Shivers noted, even though her stories revolve around characters with traditional values. In the *Saturday Review,* Nathan L. Rothman commented: "If we do not get any definitive sense of the world outside [West's Quaker community,] we do get something at least as precious, an intimate knowledge of their inner life. . . . While the tales are slight . . . each of them permits Miss West the full expression of her central theme, the lovely, gentle, ethical essence of the . . . Quaker. The mood is nostalgic, primitive, like a dream of vanished innocence." Another *Saturday Review* critic pointed out that although West was writing of a pioneer family, she depicted them "with loving sympathy rather than sentimentality." Flanagan concluded in the *Great Lakes Review* that both story collections reveal "a fine understanding of the operations of the folk mind." West wrote a screenplay based on *The Friendly Persuasion,* and it was produced as a feature film in 1956. The movie won the Golden Palm Award at the Cannes Film Festival and was nominated for an Academy Award for best picture of the year.

Some of West's early short stories explore the life of a young girl growing up on the California desert. These were collected in a volume entitled *Cress Delahanty,* published in 1953. Acclaimed as a work for teens and adults alike, *Cress Delahanty* follows the heroine of the title through the years of her adolescence, showing moments that advance her maturity. *English Journal* essayist Frederic I. Carpenter called Cress "the typical adolescent American girl," portrayed with "complete success." *New York Times* reviewer Frances Gaither likewise described the character as "no guileless sprite, but a warm-blooded morsel of humanity." In a *Commonweal* review, T. E. Cassidy wrote: "Anyone who knows adolescence, and especially that of young girls, will love [*Cress Delahanty.*] It is beautifully written, with the most extraordinary insight and delicacy." West continued to be fascinated by the transitional years between youth and womanhood; her books *The Witch Diggers, Leafy Rivers, Crimson Ramblers of the World, Farewell,* and *The State of Stony Lonesome* all contain one or more young characters who are determined to establish their identities through a positive affirmation of maturity. Flanagan noted: "Miss West's most engaging portraits . . . are the adolescent girls, the young women reaching out for emotional and economic security, whose lives are strange juxtapositions of embarrassment, humiliation, surprise, and minor triumph." Addressing his comments to the adult audience, Shivers concluded:

"In Miss West's detailed sketches of pert, intelligent, and nearly always engaging little people, she attains a success enviable in any literature and in any period."

West was always conscious of death due to her own ill health, but her involvement with the theme of mortality intensified when her sister was stricken with a painful—and fatal—form of cancer. West wrote about her sister's ordeal in two controversial books, the novel *A Matter of Time* and the nonfiction memoir *The Woman Said Yes: Encounters with Death and Life.* The latter volume revealed that West cooperated with her sister and helped her commit suicide when her pain became unendurable. Some reviewers objected to both works on ethical grounds; others, including Crider, saw a deeper point to the author's confession. In his assessment of *The Woman Said Yes,* Crider wrote: "Though for many readers West's complicity in her sister's suicide will seem the center of the story, the life enhancement theme should not be ignored; and though many readers may doubt the morality of the sister's final decision for euthanasia, it is an unforgettable statement." Dahlstrom Farmer also observed that, true to West's belief in the individual, "she considered both the fictional and the factual accounting [of her sister's death] to be about personal choice, not about a general recommendation." Dahlstrom Farmer further explained that West felt "the most important search anyone could make is the search for self, to learn what 'feelings, beliefs, and convictions' he holds, and once having found them, to have the courage and integrity to be true to them." This, Dahlstrom Farmer concluded, is the abiding message of West's writings on euthanasia—the individual's prerogative to act on conviction.

In 1975 West published *The Massacre at Fall Creek,* a historical novel based on the first American trial of white men for the slaying of Indians. Most critics praised the work for its sensitive delineation of complex issues such as the difference between murder and an act of war and the definition of basic humanity. *Newsweek* reviewer Peter S. Prescott called *The Massacre at Fall Creek* "an honorable, affecting piece of work that grapples plainly with what I take to be the principal concerns of good fiction: who we are and why, how we live and what we think of our condition." Elizabeth Fisher offered even more favorable comments in the *New York Times Book Review,* writing that West took "a little-known incident . . . and fashioned from it a rousing adventure story solidly informed with philosophical and moral content. . . . Working at the height of her powers, with wisdom and maturity, ofttimes a quiet irony, close observation and well-researched detail, West has written a novel of character and incident. Believable women and men are caught in a train of events that make the reader turn the pages. . . . This is a fine piece of work, effective fiction and entertainment, and more besides."

Jessamyn West died in 1984, the same year her final novel, *The State of Stony Lonesome,* was published. By the time she died, West had documented her long life in several nonfiction memoirs, spanning all her years save her infancy. The earliest of these biographies is *To See the Dream,* the 1957 chronicle of her adventures during the filming of "The Friendly Persuasion" in Hollywood. The 1973 title *Hide and Seek: A Continuing Journey* contains reminiscences about her childhood in California as well as some philosophical reflections that form the basis for her fiction. *The Woman Said Yes* explores her mother's courageous decision to nurse her back to health when she was tubercular and then details West's decision to aid her sister in suicide. *Double Discovery,* released in 1980, is composed of both her youthful letters and journals from her first trip abroad in 1929 and her mature reflections on the rediscovery of that long-lost youthful

self. In a *Dictionary of Literary Biography Yearbook* eulogy, Jacqueline Koenig concluded that West "accomplished things when she'd never actually known anyone else who did them. She must have been fearless. In her life and her work, she perfected a combination of intelligence, toughness, determination, compassion, talent, beauty, kindness, and love that is inspirational. She truly lived the life she really wanted." That life ended suddenly, in a massive stroke.

"The works of Jessamyn West provide the literary record of a remarkable career," Crider maintained in his essay. Indeed, West's reputation for realistic character studies and careful use of local detail has attracted the attention of regional scholars in the Midwest as well as in California. Crider noted, however, that West's "talents as a storyteller" have accounted for her "large popular success." Shivers also observed that West wove "some stories of incomparable beauty; and she has made richer the imagination of millions of now loyal readers throughout the world." Flanagan offered the most cogent praise of West's contribution to national letters in his *Indiana Magazine of History* retrospective on her work. "Certainly few contemporary writers evince the ability to create people with the idiosyncrasies, homeliness, honesty, wit and simple humanity of those in whose portraiture Jessamyn West [excelled]," Flanagan wrote. "A reader must be grateful for her precision, her authenticity, and her charm. She is a writer to be treasured."

BIOGRAPHICAL/CRITICAL SOURCES:

BOOKS

Contemporary Literary Criticism, Gale (Detroit), Volume 7, 1977; Volume 17, 1981.
Dictionary of Literary Biography, Volume 6: *American Novelists since World War II, Second Series,* Gale, 1980.
Dictionary of Literary Biography Yearbook 1984, Gale, 1985.
Shivers, Alfred S., *Jessamyn West,* Twayne, 1972, revised edition, 1992.
Women Writers of the West Coast, Capra, 1983.

PERIODICALS

Atlantic Monthly, January, 1954; December, 1955; May, 1975.
Book Week, November 18, 1945.
Chicago Sun Tribune, January 14, 1951; January 3, 1954.
Chicago Tribune Book Week, November 6, 1966.
Christian Science Monitor, January 13, 1951.
Commonweal, February 16, 1951; January 15, 1954; March 8, 1957.
English Journal, September, 1957.
Explicator, December, 1964.
Great Lakes Review, winter, 1975.
Harper's, July, 1969.
Indiana Magazine of History, December, 1971.
Los Angeles Times, July 24, 1983; February 26, 1987.
Los Angeles Times Book Review, December 23, 1984.
Nation, March, 1957.
Newsweek, April 14, 1975; November 12, 1979.
New York Herald Tribune Book Review, November 25, 1945; January 14, 1951; January 3, 1954; October 16, 1955; February 10, 1957; April 24, 1960.
New York Post, October 5, 1970.
New York Times, November 25, 1945; January 14, 1951; October 17, 1963; October 27, 1966; October 5, 1967; November 2, 1980.
New York Times Book Review, January 14, 1951; January 3, 1954; October 16, 1955; February 10, 1957; April 24, 1960;

October 1, 1967; May 11, 1969; January 10, 1971; May 13, 1973; April 27, 1975; May 2, 1976; December 16, 1979; October 19, 1980; January 6, 1985.

Publishers Weekly, April 28, 1969.

San Francisco Chronicle, January 15, 1951; January 10, 1954; April 28, 1960.

Saturday Review, November 17, 1945; January 9, 1954; December 3, 1955; February 23, 1957; September 21, 1957; April 23, 1960; October 7, 1967; May 10, 1969; September 26, 1980.

Time, May 24, 1976.

Times Literary Supplement, April 8, 1977.

Washington Post, January 5, 1980.

Washington Post Book World, April 1, 1973; May 18, 1975; January 6, 1985.

Writer's Digest, May, 1967; January, 1976.

*   *   *

WEST, Morris L(anglo) 1916-
(Michael East, Julian Morris)

PERSONAL: Born April 26, 1916, in Melbourne, Australia; son of Charles Langlo and Florence Guilfoyle (Hanlon) West; married Joyce Lawford, August 14, 1952; children: Christopher, Paul, Melanie, Michael. *Education:* Studied with Christian Brothers Order, 1933; University of Melbourne, Australia, B.A., 1937.

ADDRESSES: Home—P. O. Box 102, Avalon, New South Wales 2107, Australia.

CAREER: Teacher of modern languages and mathematics in New South Wales, Australia, and Tasmania, 1933-39; secretary to William Morris Hughes, former prime minister of Australia, 1943; managing director, Australasian Radio Productions, 1943-53; film and drama writer for Shell Co. and Australian Broadcasting Network, 1954–; commentator and writer, 1954–. Publicity manager in Melbourne, 1945-46; chairperson, National Book Council; chairperson, Council of the National Library of Australia. *Military service:* Australian Imperial Forces, 1939-43; became lieutenant.

MEMBER: Royal Society of Literature (fellow), World Academy of Arts and Sciences, Royal Prince Alfred Yacht Club (Sydney).

AWARDS, HONORS: William Heinemann Award of the Royal Society, 1959, National Brotherhood Award of the National Council of Christians and Jews, 1960, and James Tait Black Memorial Award, 1960, both for *The Devil's Advocate;* Bestsellers Paperback of the Year Award, 1965, for *The Shoes of the Fisherman;* Dag Hammarskjoeld International Prize; Pax Mundi, Diplomatic Academy of Peace, 1978; Universe Literary Prize, 1981, for *The Clowns of God;* D.Litt., University of Santa Clara, Mercy College (Dobbs Ferry, NY), University of Western Sydney, 1993, and Austalian National University Canberra, 1995; invested as member of Order of Australia, 1985 Honours List; fellow, World Academy of Arts and Sciences; Award in the Order of Australia, 1997; Lloyd O'Neill Award (Australian publishing industry accolade), 1997.

WRITINGS:

(Under pseudonym Julian Morris) *Moon in My Pocket,* Australasian Publishing, 1945.

Gallows on the Sand (also see below), Angus & Robertson (London), 1956.

Kundu (also see below), Dell (New York City), 1956.

The Crooked Road, Morrow (New York City), 1957, published in England as *The Big Story,* Heinemann (London), 1957.

Children of the Shadows: The True Story of the Street Urchins of Naples, Doubleday (New York City), 1957, published in England as *Children of the Sun,* Heinemann, 1957.

Backlash, Morrow, 1958, published in England as *The Second Victory* (also see below), Heinemann, 1958, second edition, Hodder & Stoughton (London), 1985.

(Under pseudonym Michael East) *McCreary Moves In,* Heinemann, 1958, published as *The Concubine* (also see below), New English Library (London), 1967, reprinted under name Morris L. West under original title, Coronet Books, 1983.

The Devil's Advocate (also see below), Morrow, 1959.

(Under pseudonym Michael East) *The Naked Country* (also see below), Heinemann, 1960.

Daughter of Silence (novel; also see below), Morrow, 1961.

Daughter of Silence: A Dramatization of the Novel (play; produced on Broadway by Richard Halliday, 1961), Morrow, 1962.

The Shoes of the Fisherman (novel; also see below), Morrow, 1963, limited edition, Franklin Library, 1980.

The Ambassador, Morrow, 1965.

The Tower of Babel (Book-of-the-Month Club selection), Morrow, 1967.

The Heretic: A Play in Three Acts, Morrow, 1969.

(With Robert Francis) *Scandal in the Assembly: The Matrimonial Laws and Tribunals of the Roman Catholic Church, 1970,* Morrow, 1970.

Summer of the Red Wolf, Morrow, 1971.

The Salamander (also see below), Morrow, 1973.

Harlequin, Morrow, 1974.

The Navigator, Morrow, 1976.

Selected Works, Heinemann Octopus (London), 1977.

The Devil's Advocate [and] *The Second Victory* [and] *Daughter of Silence* [and] *The Salamander* [and] *The Shoes of the Fisherman,* Heinemann, 1977.

Proteus, limited first edition, Franklin Library, 1979, Morrow, 1979.

The Clowns of God (novel; also see below), Morrow, 1981.

A West Quartet: Four Novels of Intrigue and High Adventure (contains *The Naked Country, Gallows on the Sand, The Concubine,* and *Kundu*), Morrow, 1981.

The World Is Made of Glass (novel), Avon (New York City), 1983.

Cassidy, Doubleday, 1986.

Masterclass (novel), St. Martin's (New York City), 1988.

Lazarus (novel; also see below), Heinemann Octopus, 1990.

The Ringmaster, Heinemann Octopus, 1991.

The Lovers (novel), D. I. Fine (New York City), 1993, large print edition, Thorndike Press, 1994.

Three Complete Novels (contains *The Shoes of the Fisherman, The Clowns of God,* and *Lazarus*), Wings Books (New York City), 1993.

Vanishing Point (novel), HarperCollins, 1996.

A View from the Ridge: The Testimony of a Twentieth-Century Christian, HarperCollins (San Francisco), 1996.

Images and Inscriptions (anthology of writings, illustrations, and decorative elements), HarperCollins Australia, 1997.

Also author of play *The World Is Made of Glass,* 1984, adapted from his novel of the same title.

MEDIA ADAPTATIONS: The Devil's Advocate, dramatized by Dore Schary, was produced by the Theatre Guild at the Billy Rose

Theatre in 1961; *The Shoes of the Fisherman* was filmed by Metro-Goldwyn-Mayer (MGM) in 1968.

SIDELIGHTS: Since the mid-1950s, Australian novelist Morris L. West has written suspense novels that plunge the reader into political turmoil, world-wide governmental corruption, and the internal workings of the Catholic Church. West spent several years in a Roman Catholic monastery and worked for six months as the Vatican correspondent for the *London Daily Mail.* These experiences have contributed to a moral and ethical outlook on current events that permeates all his work. According to *New York Times Book Review* contributor Herbert Mitgang, "West is known for his theological thrillers that pose hard, frequently unanswerable questions about today's turbulent world—including the constraints on liberty imposed by democratic societies." Claims Diane Casselberry Manuel in the *Christian Science Monitor,* "At his best, author West is a skillful storyteller who knows how to build suspense into every twist of the plot." Having written over twenty novels, "Morris West invents stories as though the world were running out of them," comments Webster Schott in the *New York Times Book Review.*

Three of West's better known works—*The Devil's Advocate, The Shoes of the Fisherman,* and *The Clowns of God*—feature protagonists who are representatives of the Church. *The Devil's Advocate* concerns a dying Catholic priest who is sent to an Italian village to investigate the life of a proposed saint and who ends up learning an important lesson for his own life. According to *Renascence* contributor Arnold L. Goldsmith, *The Devil's Advocate* is "a richly textured, finely constructed story with all of the ingredients of a literary classic. . . . West is able to blend the personal with the local and the universal, giving us not only the memorable portrait of a deeply disturbed theologian, but also a wider view of the troubled soul of a church, a country, and the world."

In *The Shoes of the Fisherman,* a humble Ukrainian pope finds himself the central negotiator in an attempt to prevent the United States and the Soviet Union from starting World War III. During the negotiations, the pope must confront the Russian who once tortured him. The work, a popular and critical success, demonstrates West's concern with modern man's inability to communicate. "We're not using the same words. We don't understand each other. We are not selecting, we aren't balancing . . . simply because life is too risky, too tormenting. . . . I've been trying, therefore, to use what is a very old manner of story telling. To make this conflict of legitimate points of view clear, through the medium of the novel," West told Shari Steiner in a *Writer's Digest* interview. "In *The Shoes of the Fisherman,* the idea of the central character was a man who believed that he was—and publicly claimed to be—the Vicar of Christ," West continued. "Now, theoretically, this is the man who must look at the world through the eye of God, and try to make some sense out of its complexity. He was therefore a natural character medium through which this hopeless attempt had to be made."

Eighteen years later, West again used a pope as a central character, this time in *The Clowns of God.* Pope Gregory is forced by the Church to abdicate his seat when he receives a vision of the Second Coming of Christ and decides to communicate this apocalyptic message to the rest of the world. *The Clowns of God* shows the Church in a harsher light than did West's previous theological novels and reflects West's ambivalence with the institution as a governing unit. "West has great faith in the power of faith, but little tolerance for the bureaucratic wranglings that

often seem to accompany organized religion," declares the *Christian Science Monitor*'s Manuel. The ambivalence may have originated in West's experiences with the Christian Brothers monastery where he studied and taught for ten years. Intending to become a priest, he left before taking his final vows. "My education with the Christian Brothers . . . was very strongly tinged with Jansenism, a restrictive, puritanical attitude to religion," West explained to Steiner in *Writer's Digest.* "This has probably produced in me an attitude of extreme tolerance and the desire to find out what the other man thinks first before we make any judgments."

The Clowns of God received mixed reviews. Walter Shapiro in the *Washington Post* dislikes West's description of Christ, who appears at the book's conclusion. Robert Kaftan writes in the *Christian Century* that "the characters become so many pieces to be manipulated to propel the story forward." He applauds the novel's setting, however, saying that West's "portrait of the world at the edge is chilling and disquieting." The *Wall Street Journal*'s Edmund Fuller admires West's premise: "As a melodrama it is tautly absorbing in its doomthreat genre. Yet the book far transcends that aspect, for Mr. West is an intelligent, thoughtful writer with knowledge of the ecclesiastical and theological issues that are the essence of his tale." And Richard A. Blake maintains in *America* that "West has succeeded . . . in raising the most significant questions of human survival in a very human and religious context."

West's third theological papal thriller, *Lazarus,* was published in 1990. A fictitious cleric, Ludovico Gadda, has schemed and manipulated his way into becoming Pope Leo XIV. As pontiff, however, Leo—committed to remorselessly eliminating any religious opposition—lacks the compassion and understanding characteristic of earlier popes; rather, his vision of the papacy encompasses strict observance of Catholic doctrine and inflexible interpretation of holy teachings. As his health deteriorates due to heart disease, he faces coronary bypass surgery and realizes he must modify his uncompromising ambition. Like the biblical Lazarus raised from the dead by Jesus, so Leo attains a measure of resurrection in both mind and body through his fight for his life, promising to restore the Church to its congregants and members. Complicating Leo's convalescence and execution of his papal responsibilities is the discovery of an assassination plot against him by a mid-Eastern terrorist organization, the Sword of Islam. The novel explores in depth Leo's private demons in addition to offering political and religious intrigue.

Don G. Campbell hails *Lazarus* in the *Los Angeles Times Book Review* as "an absorbing novel of a complex man," further remarking that "West's knowledge of the inner working of the Catholic Church is encyclopedic—the political infighting, the jealousies, the stresses and strains that abound in the Vatican." Campbell concludes that the book presents "an agonizing story of a man in torment, impossible to forget." Hans Knight notes in the *New York Times Book Review* that "the last of the Australian novelist's papal trilogy might be the most potent yet," adding that West "has once more proved himself a masterly mixer of homily and horror."

In an exception from his mystery thrillers, *The World Is Made of Glass* treats a psychological relationship rooted in pseudo-fact. Andrew Greeley comments in the *Detroit News* that "so sharp is the departure from earlier stories that one wonders if West . . . has not reached an important and extremely fruitful turning point in his career as a storyteller." The basis of this book is West's imaginative expansion of a brief entry in Carl Jung's diary in which he records meeting with a woman who, after refusing to give her name, asked him to hear a confession. The lady, according to West, is Magda Liliane Kardoss von Gamsfeld, a horse breeder, physician, and the illegitimate daughter of an English Duchess and a Hungarian nobleman. Raised by her father, Magda was seduced by him at sixteen, which started her on a path of lesbianism, sadomasochism, and finally, murder. She comes to Jung in a state of suicidal depression.

The story deviates from West's usual fare in that it contains only two characters, Jung and Magda, who relate the plot in monologue form. "Within the course of a single day Jung has become the recipient of confessions that it would probably take the average psychoanalyst weeks, months or even years to elicit from a patient," writes Francis King in the *Spectator*. But Magda's confessions produce an unexpected reaction in the psychiatrist. "Jung himself is constantly and disturbingly aware of the parallel between his own situation, in which he is poised to attempt the symbolic murder of his beloved father-figure Freud, and that of this siren, who is guilty of real murder," King continues. Magda's honesty also leads Jung to more closely examine his broken marriage and affair with a former student, plus his suddenly remembered, unsavory memories from childhood. The impact of these memories and realizations forces him to acknowledge similarities in their perceptions of reality. Jung's disclosures and behaviors prompt Magda finally to question his sanity.

Detroit News contributor Greeley believes *The World Is Made of Glass* to be one of West's finest works. "Morris West has done for Carl Gustav Jung what D. M. Thomas did for Sigmund Freud—written a novel which brings Jung and his milieu alive. In the process he has produced a story which is very unlike most of his previous work. . . . Jung's chaotic personal life is vividly portrayed." *New York Times Book Review* contributor Philippe Van Rjndt says "Magda von Gamsfeld is Mr. West's most impressive creation." Patricia Olson comments in the *Christian Century* that while West is generally "known for his realistic narration, his sensitive character portrayal and his concern for modern religion, [he] has never before presented such melodrama, such passionate characters, or such a critique of conventional Christianity as he does here."

Some reviewers criticized the book's conclusion, in which the physician who initially sent Magda to Jung provides her with a solution by giving her a job as director of a refuge for fallen women. Mayo Mohs notes in *Time* that "the author kisses off this denouement in a scant few pages, barely hinting at the thoughts and feelings of the new Magda. Having built the novel on the spectacle of her corruption, West might have reflected a bit more on the drama of her return to grace." Beryl Lieff Benderly indicates in the *Washington Post* that "Magda functions not as a person but as a plot device to permit West's exploration of certain themes—the line between good and evil, the nature of guilt and obsession, the curative power of redemption. . . . But to touch deeply, a story about sin and redemption or madness and cure must involve real people in a palpable world, not made-to-order abstractions in a universe of concepts." Van Rjndt, however, finds Magda's new life believable: "For all the cruelty Magda inflicts and receives, her struggle towards redemption demands our respect and compels our fascination."

In 1993's *The Lovers*, Mike Cuthbert observes in the *Washington Post Book World*, West "returns to some of his favorite themes: power politics of the Roman Catholic Church, the complexities of international politics and the successes and failures of powerful men." The novel chronicles the experiences of Irish-Australian Bryan de Courcy Cavanagh and Giulia Farnese, who first meet aboard the yacht of Giulia's American fiancee, where Giulia is a guest and Bryan a crew member. Giulia is promised to the wealthy Lou Molloy; the Farnese-Molloy marriage has been arranged by both Giulia's family and Molloy, with each seeking to solidify political, religious, and financial ambitions. Cavanagh and Giulia fall in love on board the yacht, but are inevitably parted and do not meet again until forty years later. The action of the novel is "woven through a rich tapestry of intrigue, betrayal, suspense and murder," remarks Sybil Steinberg in *Publishers Weekly*. Cuthbert further describes the book as "a novel of sexual passion, Cold War politics, murder, betrayal and morals."

Vanishing Point, published in 1996, features international settings, West's usual action-packed drama, and an exploration of manic depression in one of the novel's key characters. Protagonist Carl Strassberger, the only son of a wealthy banking family, has left behind the family business for a life of painting in the south of France. However, Strassberger is called away from his French hideaway when his brother-in-law-Larry Lucas, now the heir-apparent to run the banking business-mysteriously vanishes, leaving behind not only the business but a wife and two children. In journeying throughout Europe in search of his brother-in-law, Strassberger discovers that Lucas suffered from manic depression and may have given his entire fortune away to a dubious financier who helps people disappear. Strassberger must dodge attempts on his life by the clever villain to find Lucas and salvage the family fortune. Critics praised the novel's detail-filled plot, glamorous settings, and fast-moving narrative.

Subtitled "The Testimony of a Twentieth-Century Christian," *A View from the Ridge* was the eighty-year-old West's attempt to record a memoir of faith in place of conventional autobiography. The book charts his progress from his earliest days in an Irish monastery, through his service in World War II, to his days at the summit of the Australian literary world. Along the way there are conflicts involving family and church, a pilgrim's progress that sees West ask and answer the basic questions of life as a Catholic. While commending the book to West's fans, *Publishers Weekly* acknowledged its universal appeal: "No prior acquaintance with his work is required to appreciate the magnificent concluding chapter in which he faces death, proclaims his hard-won faith and affirms his optimism." Lawrence S. Cunningham, writing in *Commonweal*, called the memoir "a worthy testimony to the life of an eighty-year-old writer who now stands looking at his past and our future 'from the ridge.'"

BIOGRAPHICAL/CRITICAL SOURCES:

BOOKS

Contemporary Literary Criticism, Gale (Detroit), Volume 6, 1976; Volume 33, 1985.

PERIODICALS

America, August 29, 1981.
Best Sellers, March 1, 1968; April 1, 1970; June 1, 1970.
Booklist, May 1, 1996, p. 1470.
Books and Bookmen, April, 1968; April, 1979; August, 1983.
Catholic World, September, 1961; February, 1962.
Chicago Tribune Book World, December 25, 1983.
Christian Century, May 20, 1981; October 12, 1983.
Christian Science Monitor, August 10, 1981.
Commonweal, April 11, 1997.
Detroit News, July 10, 1983.

Kirkus Reviews, April 15, 1996, p. 559.
Library Journal, June 1, 1996, p. 153.
Life, February 23, 1968.
Los Angeles Times Book Review, February 18, 1979; July 17, 1983; October 19, 1986; April 15, 1990, p. 15.
Nation, December 16, 1961; May 17, 1965.
National Observer, March 11, 1968.
National Review, February 14, 1975.
Newsweek, December 11, 1961.
New Yorker, December 9, 1961.
New York Times, May 27, 1987.
New York Times Book Review, April 25, 1965; February 22, 1968; April 7, 1968; September 19, 1971; October 21, 1973; October 27, 1974; August 29, 1976; March 4, 1979; March 11, 1979; August 9, 1981; November 26, 1981; July 3, 1983; November 9, 1986; May 27, 1987; April 15, 1990, p. 14; March 31, 1991, p. 28; June 9, 1991, p. 12.
Observer (London), March 25, 1990, p. 66.
Observer Review, March 3, 1968.
Publishers Weekly, July 5, 1993, p. 60; December 11, 1995, p. 23; May 13, 1996, p. 54; September 30, 1996.
Renascence, summer, 1962.
Saturday Review, April 24, 1965; February 24, 1968.
Spectator, March 8, 1968; October 5, 1974; July 23, 1983.
Time, December 8, 1961; July 6, 1970; November 4, 1974; October 4, 1976; January 22, 1979; July 25, 1983; July 1, 1991, p. 71.
Times (London), May 6, 1965; July 14, 1983; February 5, 1987.
Times Literary Supplement, May 6, 1965; July 16, 1970; August 3, 1973.
Tribune Books (Chicago), June 16, 1991, p. 8.
Wall Street Journal, August 24, 1981.
Washington Post, June 8, 1981; July 8, 1983; November 15, 1986.
Washington Post Book World, October 3, 1993, p. 11.
Writer's Digest, February, 1971.

*   *   *

WEST, Nathanael 1903-1940
(Nathan Weinstein, Nathan von Wallenstein Weinstein)

PERSONAL: Name originally Nathan Weinstein; name legally changed, August 16, 1926; born October 17, 1903, in New York, NY; died following an automobile accident, December 22, 1940, near El Centro, CA; buried in Mount Zion Cemetery, Queens, NY; son of Max (a building contractor) and Anna (Wallenstein) Weinstein; married Eileen McKenney, April 19, 1940. *Education:* Attended Tufts College (now University), 1921; Brown University, Ph.B., 1924.

CAREER. Writer. Worked for father's construction firm during early 1920s; Kenmore Hall (residence hotel), New York City, assistant manager, 1927-1930; Sutton Club Hotel, New York City, manager, 1930-1933; screenwriter for film studios in California, including Columbia, 1933 and 1938, Republic, 1936-38, RKO, 1938 and 1939-40, and Universal, 1938-39.

MEMBER: League of American Writers (member of Hollywood committee), Screen Writers Guild (member of executive board, beginning 1939), Motion Picture Guild (member of executive board), Motion Picture Artists Committee (member of executive board), Motion Picture Democratic Committee, Hollywood Anti-Nazi League.

WRITINGS:

NOVELS

The Dream Life of Balso Snell, Contact Editions, 1931.
Miss Lonelyhearts, Liveright, 1933.
A Cool Million: The Dismantling of Lemuel Pitkin, Covici, Friede, 1934.
The Day of the Locust, Random House, 1939, recent edition, Buccaneer, 1981.
The Complete Works of Nathanael West (omnibus volume of four novels), introduction by Alan Ross, Farrar, Straus, 1957.

SCREENPLAYS

(With Jack Natteford) *Ticket to Paradise,* Republic, 1936.
(With Lester Cole) *The President's Mystery,* Republic, 1936.
(With Cole and Samuel Ornitz) *Follow Your Heart,* Republic, 1936.
Rhythm in the Clouds, Republic, 1937.
(With Ornitz) *It Could Happen to You,* Republic, 1937.
Born to Be Wild, Republic, 1938.
I Stole a Million, Universal, 1939.
(With Jerry Cady and Dalton Trumbo) *Five Came Back,* RKO, 1939.
(With Whitney Bolton) *The Spirit of Culver,* Universal, 1939.
Men Against the Sky, RKO, 1940.
Let's Make Music, RKO, 1940.

OTHER

(With Joseph Schrank) *Good Hunting* (play), first produced on Broadway, 1938.
(Under name Nathan Weinstein) *My Island Of Sonnets* (poems), Exposition, 1974.

Also author, with S. J. Perelman, of the unproduced play "Even Stephen." Contributor of articles, short stories, and poems to periodicals, including *Casements* (under name Nathan von Wallenstein Weinstein), *Americana, Contact, Contempo,* and *Pacific Weekly.* Associate editor of *Contact,* 1931-32, and *Americana,* 1933.

MEDIA ADAPTATIONS: Miss Lonelyhearts was adapted by Leonard Praskins for the film *Advice to the Lovelorn,* Fox/United Artists, 1933; by Howard Teichmann for a play of the original title, 1957; by Dore Schary for the film *Lonelyhearts,* United Artists, 1958; and by Michael Dinner and others for a television play of the original title, Public Broadcasting Service, 1983. *The Day of the Locust* was adapted by Waldo Salt for a film of the same title, Paramount, 1975.

SIDELIGHTS: An American novelist who wrote primarily during the Great Depression of the 1930s, Nathanael West was called "the chief neglected talent of [his] age" by Leslie Fiedler in *Love and Death in the American Novel.* While many of his contemporaries composed straightforward novels about social and economic injustice, West produced an idiosyncratic blend of pathos and comedy, realism and wild unreality. "He too deplored the emptiness of twentieth-century life in the United States," declared Richard B. Gehman in *Atlantic Monthly,* "but he chose to depict that life in terms not of people who were consciously involved in a struggle, but of those who were unconsciously trapped—people who were, in their blindness, so tragic as to be comic figures." Little-known to the American public for years after his death, West's work maintained a select following in literary circles. As popular tastes in the novel changed, West's fiction gained a broader audience, and he was widely hailed as a precursor of the "black humor" novelists who wrote in the 1950s, 1960s, and beyond.

Born in 1903 in New York City, West was the son of Jewish immigrants Max Weinstein, a prosperous building contractor, and Anna Wallenstein, who fancied herself a descendant of a German nobleman of the same last name. West's parents were more concerned with status and money than art. His father expected him to enter the family business, and he gave West several Horatio Alger novels—highly popular tales in which honest young men work their way to financial success. But West was a high-school dropout whose friends called him "Pep" because he showed so little energy.

To enroll in Tufts College, West lied about his grades, and when Tufts asked him to leave because of laziness, another student's transcript gained him admission to Brown. There West read widely, but he was better known for his enthusiastic socializing and a biting intellectual wit. When classmate and future journalist Quentin Reynolds pressed him for a graduation speech, West created the story of St. Puce, a flea who lives in the armpit of Christ. During the 1920s West wove St. Puce and similar anecdotes into *The Dream Life of Balso Snell,* a broad parody of the ideals of Western civilization that became his first published novel.

By providing rent-free lodgings to struggling writers, West remained close to the New York literary world. His charity aided the literary critic Edmund Wilson; novelists Robert M. Coates, Erskine Caldwell, and Dashiell Hammett; and playwright Lillian Hellman. West also housed his newlywed sister and her husband, S. J. Perelman, a renowned satirist and a lifelong friend. West became fascinated with the desperate lives of his other tenants: a onetime actress worked as a prostitute; young men headed for work at businesses failing under the impact of the Depression; lonely residents killed time in the lobby reading magazines. At the Sutton Club Hotel six people committed suicide by jumping from the same terrace. When West was especially curious about a lodger, he would steam open the person's mail, sometimes with Hellman's assistance.

One evening Perelman introduced West to an advice columnist for the *Brooklyn Eagle.* She showed the two men a sample of her mail, wondering if it might inspire Perelman to write a comedy. West was deeply moved by the pain and helplessness the letters displayed, and he soon began work on *Miss Lonelyhearts,* the tale of a young advice columnist who destroys himself by becoming personally involved in the miserable lives of his readers. Considered a major advance over *Balso Snell, Miss Lonelyhearts* was lauded in the *New Yorker* and the *New York Times Book Review* when it was published in 1933. But sales of the book faltered when its publisher, Liveright, declared bankruptcy.

As the 1930s wore on West became increasingly concerned about his failure to gain either artistic recognition or a steady income from his writing. He joined the staffs of two literary magazines—including *Contact,* where he joined poet William Carlos Williams—but the journals soon folded. When Columbia Pictures offered West a screenwriting job, he eagerly accepted, only to be laid off within a year. Supported by friends he wrote a third novel, *A Cool Million,* which vented his bitterness about the Great Depression by satirizing the myth of success portrayed in Horatio Alger novels. Commentators have since contended that the strength of West's anger damaged the book, which received largely unenthusiastic reviews and sold poorly.

A major Hollywood studio bought the rights to *A Cool Million,* however, and the sale encouraged West to move to California in 1935 for a second try at screenwriting. Several months passed and he was unable to find work, even with the aid of an agent. Hammett had become successful in the movie business, and West repeatedly approached him for help with a job but was greeted with taunts. Moreover, at a time when the major studios were trying to keep unions out of the film industry, West's membership in the Screen Writers Guild hurt his prospects. Depressed and poor, West became desperately afraid that he would always be a failure. Money from Perelman sustained him.

Immersed in the unglamorous side of Hollywood, West wrote *The Day of the Locust,* his fourth and final book. Unusual among Hollywood novels, it ignores film stars and financiers to concentrate on the obscure, disheartened people who inhabit the town's social fringes. Like *Miss Lonelyhearts, Day of the Locust* was praised in literary circles but ignored by the larger public. Over the course of his lifetime, West earned less than thirteen hundred dollars from his books.

By contrast, the commercial film industry that West scorned in *Day of the Locust* began to appreciate his screenwriting. He continued to write undistinguished films, but now he worked for the higher-paying major studios, particularly Universal and RKO. While his friend F. Scott Fitzgerald, a highly popular novelist during the 1920s, struggled to survive as a screenwriter, West earned a comfortable income for the first time in his life. He bought a pleasant house in the Hollywood hills and married Eileen McKenney, immortalized as the vivacious title character of Ruth McKenney's book *My Sister Eileen.* Eight months later the couple died in a traffic accident when West ran a stop sign.

As James F. Light noted in *Nathanael West: An Interpretative Study,* if "there is any constant pattern in the novels of West, it is the pilgrimage around which each novel centers." He continued: "In each the hero is in search of something in which he can believe and to which he can belong . . . but the result is always the same: tragic disillusionment." In *The Dream Life of Balso Snell,* the title character pursues cultural enlightenment by journeying to the site of ancient Troy, where Trojans and Greeks had clashed thousands of years earlier in a war that inspired the earliest classic of Western literature, Homer's *Iliad.* Snell finds the wooden horse that the Greeks used to invade and conquer Troy. Entering the horse through its anus, he begins a dreamlike journey through Western culture. The artists and philosophers Snell meets, however, are frauds and fools—one is the devoted chronicler of St. Puce. West derides the characters by making them blatantly repulsive, often associating them with excrement.

Commentators have generally agreed that West has a serious point to make in *Balso Snell*—that art and ideas have become too removed from human reality—but they disagreed substantially about the merits of his technique. Admirers observed that West's vivid imagery and his concern with human dreams and delusions anticipate his later works. Detractors, however, said that *Balso Snell* is overstated and contains too many scholarly allusions—mistakes, some suggested, that a recent college graduate might make. In the *New York Times Book Review,* Malcolm Cowley called the book "an elaborate joke . . . that doesn't quite come off."

Miss Lonelyhearts has repeatedly garnered praise for its adept language and its tight dramatic focus. In fifteen short chapters, West chronicles progressive stages of the columnist's emotional disintegration. Pritchett called the book "a selection of hard, diamond-fine miniatures" and noted the "precision" of the author's "poetic images." As Brad Darrach noted in *Time,* "Nothing else in American fiction radiates the compacted fury of this little parable."

West's third novel, *A Cool Million,* is a political satire directed against America's image as a land of prosperity—a predictable target during the Great Depression. Subtitled *The Dismantling of Lemuel Pitkin,* the book chronicles the misadventures of a well-intentioned fool who is physically torn apart as he quests for financial success. As the novel opens, Pitkin gets a loan from Shagpoke Whipple, a dishonest banker who advises him to venture forth from their small town to pursue his fortune. After Pitkin loses his teeth, an eye, his leg, a thumb, and his scalp, he becomes a performing freak in a vaudeville show, entertaining the audience by being beaten on stage. Shot dead by a Communist agent, Pitkin is turned into a martyr by Whipple's Fascist party. Though *A Cool Million* displays West's gift for a colorful plot, most commentators agree that the book is hampered by a heavy-handed use of mock-heroic prose. West seems uninvolved with his characters, biographer Robert Emmet Long averred, and the book "seems surprisingly crude and rambling," especially "in comparison with *Miss Lonelyhearts.*"

The Day of the Locust has repeatedly been called the best Hollywood novel ever written. "Mr. West has caught the emptiness of Hollywood," wrote Edmund Wilson in *New Republic,* "and he is, as far as I know, the first writer to make this emptiness horrible." And in *Hudson Review,* Daniel Aaron praised West for turning the movie capital into a powerful symbol. "Not an isolated piece of dreamland or a national joke," Aaron wrote, West's Hollywood "is America carried out to its logical conclusion."

Literary critics have generally agreed that West's work is difficult to categorize. Many have linked him to surrealism, a French aesthetic movement of the 1920s and 1930s that stressed the imagery of dreams; others, citing his interest in America's downtrodden, have linked him to naturalism, a more political movement that stressed an individual's helplessness in a hostile society. In an article titled "West's Disease," which appeared in *The Dyer's Hand and Other Essays,* poet W. H. Auden declared that West "is not, strictly speaking, a novelist" because he portrays neither dreams nor society in an accurate fashion. Fiedler praised this characteristic of West's work, calling the author "the inventor of a peculiar kind of book . . . the neo-gothic novel," which derived from West's understanding that "literary truth is not synonymous with fact." Fiedler wrote that such a style, unburdened by the minutiae of factual and psychological detail, "opened up possibilities . . . of capturing the quality of experience in a mass society." He concluded: "Putting down a book by West, a reader is not sure whether he has been presented with a nightmare endowed with the conviction of actuality or with actuality distorted into the semblance of a nightmare; but in either case, he has the sense that he has been presented with a view of a world in which, incredibly, he lives."

As West himself observed, the world he presents is unrelieved by hope. "There is nothing to root for in my books," Martin quotes him. Reviewers have been particularly troubled by West's portrayal of human relationships. In his books friendship and sexual love appear repulsive, inadequate, or ridiculous, for such ideals are overwhelmed by loneliness, despair, and brutality. Some critics call West's world-view a sign of his limitations as a writer, and some suggest that it reflects deep-seated psychological

problems. In West's books, wrote biographer Kingsley Widmer, "Female sexuality tends to be fascinatingly horrific, women destructive powers demanding hostile responses. . . . West's sex-violence obsessions in his fiction may suggest erotic difficulties in [his] life."

As many commentators have observed, West's vivid, brooding humor, so unusual in his own time, became a widespread trend in American literature after World War II. By "the middle decades of the twentieth century," Widmer averred, West had become "one of *the* authors to read." West's followers included Flannery O'Connor, whose novel *Wise Blood* centers on a tormented young Southerner who preaches a new religion called "The First Church Without God." Literary critics found echoes of West in the works of many postwar American novelists, whose writings often blend comedy, chaos, and pessimism. As Stanley Edgar Hyman wrote in his book *Nathanael West,* the author "was a true pioneer and culture hero, making it possible for the younger symbolists and fantasists who came after him, and who include our best writers, to do with relative ease what he did in defiance of the temper of his time, for so little reward, in isolation and in pain."

BIOGRAPHICAL/CRITICAL SOURCES:

BOOKS

Auden, W. H., *The Dyer's Hand and Other Essays,* Random House, 1962.

Barnard, Rita, *The Great Depression and the Culture of Abundance: Kenneth Fearing, Nathanael West, and Mass Culture in the 1930s,* Cambridge University Press, 1995.

Bloom, Harold, editor, *Nathanael West: Modern Critical Views,* Chelsea House, 1986.

Concise Dictionary of Literary Biography: The Age of Maturity, 1929-1941, Gale (Detroit), 1989.

Dictionary of Literary Biography, Gale, Volume 4: *American Writers in Paris, 1920-1939,* 1980; Volume 9: *American Novelists, 1910-1945,* 1981; Volume 28: *Twentieth-Century American Jewish Fiction Writers,* 1984.

Fiedler, Leslie A., *Love and Death in the American Novel,* revised edition, Stein & Day, 1966.

Hyman, Stanley Edgar, *Nathanael West,* University of Minnesota Press, 1962.

Light, James F., *Nathanael West: An Interpretive Study,* second edition, Northwestern University Press, 1971.

Long, Robert Emmet, *Nathanael West,* Ungar, 1985.

Madden, David, editor, *Nathanael West; The Cheaters and the Cheated: A Collection of Critical Essays,* Everett/Edwards, 1973.

Siegel, Ben, editor, *Critical Essays on Nathanael West,* G. K. Hall (New York), 1994.

Twentieth-Century Literary Criticism, Gale, Volume 1, 1978; Volume 14, 1984.

Veitch, Jonathan, *American Superrealism: Nathanael West and the Politics of Representation in the 1930s,* University of Wisconson Press, 1997.

White, William, *Nathanael West: A Comprehensive Bibliography,* Kent State University Press, 1975.

Widmer, Kinglsey, *Nathanael West,* Twayne, 1982.

Wisker, Alistair, *The Writing of Nathanael West,* St. Martin's Press, 1990.

PERIODICALS

Atlantic Monthly, September, 1950; October, 1970.

Commonweal, May 10, 1957; October 23, 1970.

Entertainment Weekly, December 23, 1994, p. 84.

Hudson Review, winter, 1951.

Nation, July 25, 1934; July 15, 1939; May 4, 1957; August 17, 1970.

New Republic, July 26, 1939; May 23, 1970.

New Statesman, December 7, 1957; October 11, 1968.

Newsweek, September 4, 1950; May 13, 1957; June 29, 1970.

New York, April 17, 1995, p. 111.

New Yorker, April 15, 1933; May 18, 1957; October 10, 1970.

New York Times, June 2, 1974; February 2, 1987; February 8, 1987.

New York Times Book Review, April 23, 1933; July 1, 1934; May 21, 1939; May 12, 1957; December 23, 1990, p. 3.

Saturday Review, May 13, 1933; May 20, 1939; May 11, 1957; June 27, 1970.

Spectator, July 19, 1968.

Time, June 17, 1957; August 17, 1970.

Times Literary Supplement, January 24, 1958; April 11, 1958.

Washington Post, January 25, 1983.

*   *   *

WEST, Paul 1930-

PERSONAL: Born February 23, 1930, in Eckington, Derbyshire, England; son of Alfred Massick and Mildred (Noden) West; children: Amanda Klare. *Education:* University of Birmingham, B.A. (with first honors), 1950; Oxford University, graduate study, 1950-53; Columbia University, M.A., 1953. *Avocational interests:* Music, swimming, travel, and astronomy.

ADDRESSES: Office—c/o Elaine Markson, 44 Greenwich Avenue, New York, NY 10011.

CAREER: Memorial University of Newfoundland, St. John's, Newfoundland, began as assistant professor, associate professor of English, 1957-62; Pennsylvania State University, University Park, associate professor, 1963-69, professor of English and comparative literature, 1969-95, senior fellow of Institute for Arts and Humanistic Studies, 1969-95, professor emeritus, 1995–. Visiting professor, University of Wisconsin, 1956-66; Pratt Lecturer, Memorial universitiy of Newfoundland, 1970; Crawshaw Professor of English, Colgate University, 1972; Virginia Woolf Lecturer, University of Tulsa, 1972; Melvin Hill Distinguished Visiting Professor of Humanities, Hobart and William Smith Colleges, 1974; distinguished writer in residence, Wichita State University, 1982; writer in residence, University of Arizona, 1984; visiting professor of English, Cornell University, 1987–; visiting professor and novelist in residence, Brown University, 1992. Judge, CAPS fiction panel, 1975, Heinz fiction prize, 1980 and 1986, National Book Award, 1990. *Military service:* Royal Air Force, 1954-57; became flight lieutenant.

MEMBER: Authors League of America, Authors Guild.

AWARDS, HONORS: Canada Council senior fellowship, 1959; Guggenheim fellowship, 1962-63; listed in "Books of the Year" by *New York Times,* 1969, for *Words for a Deaf Daughter,* 1970, for *I'm Expecting to Live Quite Soon,* 1971, for *Caliban's Filibuster,* and 1986, for *Rat Man of Paris; Words for a Deaf Daughter* included in "Best Books of the Year" list by *Time,* 1969; *Paris Review* Aga Khan Prize for fiction, 1974; National Endowment for the Humanities fellowship, 1975; National Endowment for the Arts fellowship, 1980, 1985; Hazlitt Memorial Award for Excellence in Arts (Literature), 1981; Governor of Pennsylvania's award for excellence in the arts, 1981; American Academy and Institute of Arts and Letters award in literature, 1985, 1986; Pushcart Prize, 1987; named Literary Lion by New York Public Library, 1987; Best American Essays award, 1990; nominated for Medicis, Femina, and Meilleur Livre prizes, and Grand Prix Halperine-Kaminsky (France), 1993; Lannan Prize for Fiction, 1993, for *Love's Mansion;* Distinguished Teaching Award, Graduate Schools of the North-East, 1995; Chevalier de l'ordre des arts et des lettres, France, 1996; National Book Critics Circle Award nomination for fiction, 1996, for *The Tent of Orange Mist.*

WRITINGS:

The Fantasy Poets: Number Seven, Fantasy Press, 1952.

The Growth of the Novel, Canadian Broadcasting Corp., 1959.

The Fossils of Piety: Literary Humanism in Decline, Vantage Press (New York), 1959.

The Spellbound Horses (poems), Ryerson, 1960.

Byron and the Spoiler's Art, St. Martin's (New York City), 1960.

A Quality of Mercy, Chatto & Windus (London), 1961.

I, Said the Sparrow (memoirs), Hutchinson, 1963.

(Editor) *Byron: A Collection of Critical Essays,* Prentice-Hall (Englewood Cliffs, NJ), 1963.

The Modern Novel (two volumes), Hillary, 1963, 2nd edition, 1965.

Robert Penn Warren, University of Minnesota Press (Minneapolis), 1964.

The Snow Leopard (poems), Hutchinson, 1964, Harcourt, 1965.

Tenement of Clay, Hutchinson (London), 1965, McPherson & Co. (Kingston, NY), 1993.

Alley Jaggers (first novel in trilogy), Harper (New York City), 1966.

The Wine of Absurdity: Essays on Literature and Consolation, Pennsylvania State University Press (University Park), 1966.

Words for a Deaf Daughter (biography), Harper, 1969, expanded edition with new preface by West published as *Words for a Deaf Daughter* [and] *Gala,* Dalkey Archive (Normal, IL), 1993.

I'm Expecting to Live Quite Soon (second novel in trilogy), Harper, 1970.

Caliban's Filibuster, Doubleday (New York City), 1971.

Bela Lugosi's White Christmas (third novel in trilogy), Harper, 1972.

Colonel Mint, Dutton (New York City), 1973.

Gala (see also below), Harper, 1976.

The Very Rich Hours of Count von Stauffenberg (historical novel), Harper, 1980.

Out of My Depths: A Swimmer in the Universe (nonfiction), Anchor Press, 1983.

Rat Man of Paris, Doubleday, 1986.

Sheer Fiction (essays), McPherson, 1987, Volume 2, 1991, Volume 3, 1994.

The Universe, and Other Fictions (short fiction), Overlook Press (Woodstock, NY), 1988.

The Place in Flowers Where Pollen Rests, Doubleday, 1988.

Lord Byron's Doctor (biographical novel), Doubleday, 1989.

Portable People (character sketches), drawings by Joe Servello, British American Publishers (Latham, NY), 1990.

The Women of Whitechapel and Jack the Ripper (historical novel), Random House (New York City), 1991.

Love's Mansion, Random House, 1992.

Duets, photographs by James Kiernan, Random House, 1994.

The Tent of Orange Mist, Scribner (New York City), 1995.

A Stroke of Genius: Illness and Self-Discovery (autobiographical memoir), Viking, 1995.

My Mother's Music (memoir), Viking, 1996.
Sporting with Amaryllis, Overlook (New York City), 1997.
Terrestrials: A Novel, Scribner (New York City), 1997.

Regular contributor to *Washington Post Book World, Boston Phoenix,* and *New York Times Book Review.* Also contributor of essays, poems, and reviews to periodicals, including *TriQuarterly, New Statesman, Iowa Review, Parnassus, Conjunctions, Quimera* (Barcelona), *Nation, Kenyon Review, Sinn und Form, Partisan Review, Washington Post, New York Times, Harper's, GQ Magazine, Paris Review,. New Directions Literary Anthology, Paris Review, Yale Review, Chelsea,* and *Harper's.* Fiction critic, *New Statesman,* 1959-60.

SIDELIGHTS: Paul West's writings span the genres of poetry, essay, criticism, biography, and the novel. Although his work in each genre has received critical praise, West favors the novel form for expression and experimentation. As *Dictionary of Literary Biography* contributor Brian McLaughlin notes, "It is as a fiction writer that he seems most happy, for there he can demonstrate at one and the same time the strength of the critic and the grace of the poet." *Book World* contributor Diane Johnson likewise comments that one of the most positive aspects of West's work "is his faith in the novel as an art form, as a dignified production of the human mind, capable of rendering, in its infinite variety, social comment, philosophic statement, comedy, pain, all of which West can do—impressively." Within West's novels, the author takes the guise of a variety of characters, including Jack the Ripper, the Rat Man of Paris, and his deaf daughter. West even reflects upon his parents' courtship and love life before he was born.

In his historical novel *The Very Rich Hours of Count von Stauffenberg,* for example, West portrays Count von Stauffenberg, a key figure in the anti-Nazi movement who orchestrated an unsuccessful plot to bomb Hitler's office in 1944. Von Stauffenberg was executed, and many of his conspirators were tortured and killed. "On these bones," writes Frederick Busch in the *New York Times Book Review,* "Mr. West lays a flesh of living words: Dead dreams—of self, love, nobility, military service—are the stuff of his narrative." Written as a fictional memoir, the novel reveals the various facets of von Stauffenberg's character and chronicles his transformation from a moderate supporter of Hitler to an activist against him. In a preface to the novel, West explains the genesis of *The Very Rich Hours of Count von Stauffenberg:* "I was devouring books about the bomb plot against Hitler, some grand, some shoddy, many of them giving details the others omitted, and almost all of them contradicting one another until I felt that some of what I was reading was fiction already and that a fictional attempt of my own—say an historical impersonation—might go."

The novel was indeed a critical success. *Partisan Review* contributor Ronald Christ comments: "Having resisted the temptation to write an account, or indictment, Paul West has written instead a novel . . . that never forgets language and the sensibility it issues from as the real protagonist. The richness of West's prose is the real wealth here, and it is, like Stauffenberg's hours, loaded with all the treasures of a 'truant mind.'" *Washington Post Book World* contributor Joe David Bellamy similarly observes, "There is little attention to conventional plotting and suspense, to the aspects that could have made the novel 'a thriller.' But a rich, textured style and metaphorical inventiveness are the dividends."

West's novel *Rat Man of Paris,* like *The Very Rich Hours of Count von Stauffenberg,* is based on a historical figure. Inspired by stories of a man who haunted the boulevards of Paris at the end

of World War II, flashing a rat at passersby, West began to "[fill] in the blanks" of Rat Man's life, as he explains to *Publishers Weekly* interviewer Amanda Smith. West's Rat Man is Etienne Poulsifer, and he carries a fox stole, not a rat. The stole is one of the few belongings Rat Man was able to take with him after his family and their entire village were burned alive by Nazis. This event, reminiscent of the actual German extermination of the French village Oradour, has shaped Rat Man's existence. Observes *New York Times Book Review* contributor Lore Segal: "[*Rat Man of Paris*] addresses the large question of our time: How does one live one's daily life in the span between past atrocity and atrocity to come? What happens to the wound that does not heal, that will not scar over?" Despite Rat Man's various eccentricities—he also bathes with his clothes on and hangs his soiled sheets out his window in the hope that the police will, according to *Los Angeles Times* critic Richard Eder, "arrest and launder them"—Rat Man attracts a lonely high school teacher, Sharli, who views him as "another of her pupils: bigger, heavier, and more of a liability, to be sure, yet a fount of promise so long as he is able to take his time." West describes Rat Man in *Publishers Weekly* as "a parallel man, a man of distance who has a very uncertain relationship with civilization. He doesn't quite know what it is and where he belongs in it, and he's amazed that people think he *does* belong in it."

When Rat Man discovers that a Nazi war criminal has been extradited to France, he wrongly assumes that the convict is responsible for murdering the villagers. As an attempt at vengeance, Rat Man outfits himself like a Nazi and walks the streets of Paris carrying a sign with the Nazi's picture on it and wheeling the "rat" about in a pram. Rat Man becomes, like his real-life counterpart, a local celebrity, but his renown ends when he is injured by a sniper's bullet. Eder writes: "Up until the shooting, West's fable is compassionate and chilling. His Poulsifer, victim and avenger, has a questioning and original humanity. And then it all fogs over." Expressing a similar opinion, *Newsweek* reviewer Peter S. Prescott argues that "*Rat Man of Paris* achieves its quite dazzling effects early on and then settles down to work variations on them. The effect isn't one of motion or of answers obtained, but of a faint glow."

West's 1988 novel, *The Place in Flowers Where Pollen Rests,* is set in a Hopi settlement in northeastern Arizona, and is told in various narrative voices, including those of George, Oswald, their deceased relatives, and Sotuqnangu, a mythical Hopi spirit. George The Place In Flowers Where Pollen Rests is a doll carver; his nephew Oswald Beautiful Badger Going Over The Hill wants to be a Hollywood actor. When Oswald leaves the community, he ends up as a pornographic movie star, and enlists for a tour of duty in Vietnam. Oswald, as Thomas R. Edwards reveals in a *New York Times Book Review* article on *The Place in Flowers,* "tries to live up to his name by deserting his birthplace" and his people in favor of the White occidental world. But for Oswald, the "Anglo world . . . both attracts and nauseates," and he returns to his Hopi people when "the horrors of White America come closer to destroying him."

Much critical attention focused on the textual complexity of *The Place in Flowers.* For John Calvin Batchelor, writing in the *Washington Post Book World,* West is "a writer's writer who aggressively goes too far, thinks too much, turns too many metaphors and explores too much strangeness for the casual reader." Steven Moore agrees that the novel is challenging, but finds that the textual intricacy conveys "not only the Hopi culture but its linguistic structure as well." In his review of the novel in the *Review of Contemporary Fiction,* Moore argues that the novel requires careful, slow reading, in order that "the reader can better appreciate the detailed, visceral texture of the places West describes."

In the 1989 biographical novel *Lord Byron's Doctor,* West focuses on the small group of people who spent the summer of 1816 with the exiled George Gordon, Lord Byron, focusing specifically on John William Polidori. Polidori, the least famous member of the group which included Mary Wollstonecraft Godwin, Percy Bysshe Shelley and, Byron's mistress and Mary Godwin's step-sister, Claire Clairmont, was a "young physician traveling as the club-footed Byron's secretary and medical adviser. He also had a five hundred pound commission from a London publisher to report on the poet's adventures," notes R. Z. Sheppard in a *Time* review of the novel. *Lord Byron's Doctor* is West's version of the events written about in Polidori's diary, including the love/hate relationship between the doctor and Byron, the sexual exploits of Byron and Shelley, and Polidori's suicide. Noting that the author is himself a Byron scholar, Steven Moore in the *Review of Contemporary Fiction* explains that West has fleshed out "Polidori's skeletal diary in a robust early-nineteenth-century style . . . [creating] a penetrating psychological portrait of Lord Byron's Doctor."

"Through Polidori, West compiles a lurid case history on the cruelty of genius," finds Sheppard, who sees the author as "one of the most vigorous and inviting literary talents still punching away in semiobscurity." Moore concludes that *Lord Byron's Doctor* is a "stylistic tour de force of nineteenth-century eloquence, slang and technical jargon; and a wholly successful recreation of that crucial year in literary history when Romantic yearnings confronted the darker recesses of the unconscious, wreaking havoc in the personal lives of their creators, but also giving birth to poetry and monsters that haunt us still."

West chose another infamous historical figure for the focus of his 1991 novel. In *The Women of Whitechapel and Jack the Ripper,* West revisits the fall of 1888 to explain the murders of five London prostitutes. The story begins some years prior, when Queen Victoria's grandson, Prince Eddy, and the painter and Prince Eddy's chaperon, Walter Richard Sickert, are spending much of their time at London brothels. Sickert introduces Prince Eddy to the poor, young Annie Crook, the two fall in love, and soon after, Annie becomes pregnant. The pregnancy becomes the precipitating event to a savage conspiracy involving the royal family.

When the Queen learns of the affair, she and the Prime Minister, Lord Salisbury, arrange to have Annie kidnapped and taken to the royal family's personal physician, Sir William Gull, who lobotomizes and permanently hospitalizes her. One of Annie's friends, Marie Kelly, and a few of her fellow prostitutes at Whitechapel, sends a blackmail letter to the Queen, demanding Annie's release and a sum of money to keep the matter quiet. The Queen then sets Gull loose to hunt the prostitutes down and silence them, and Sickert is taken along to identify the women who signed the letter. Gull is eventually held in a private psychiatric hospital, and Sickert, who became increasingly entranced by the murders, takes into his own care Alice Margaret, the daughter of Prince Eddy and Annie.

The Women of Whitechapel is "superbly written and intricately choreographed, a work both sensational and serious," writes Sven Birkerts in a review of the novel in the *New Republic.* "But what finally remains vivid, long after the novel has shrunk down to its

afterimage in the mind, is the feverish abandon of Gull and the descriptions of his myriad mutilations," continues Birkerts. "The passages are raw and uninhibited; they transmit perfectly Sickert's fascinated repulsion. The visual precision is a triumph of artistic detachment, even as it horrifies." West's "prose glistens with bright ideas and boldly inventive turns of phrase," comments Dan Cryer in *Newsday.* Josh Rubins in the *New York Times Book Review* concurs, finding that West's "specialty is filling in the missing details—psychological and otherwise—through verbally exquisite interior monologues or provocatively vivid evocations of unfamiliar milieus." Vance Bourjaily, in *Chicago Tribune Books,* calls West "possibly our finest living stylist in English."

In the Lannan prize-winning *Love's Mansion,* West's 1992 semi-autobiographical novel, the author explores the life of his own parents before his conception. Albert Mobilio argues in the *Voice Literary Supplement* that only an author like West, who "dotes on the minds of assassins, madmen, and murderers . . . might be . . . adequately girded to peer under the sheets on his parents' wedding night. In *Love's Mansion* . . . he does just that, pulling back the covers on both how he came to be, and how memory comes to life." *Love's Mansion* is the story of Clive Moxon, a novelist in his mid-fifties who asks his 94-year-old Mother Hilly about her relationship with his father. The novel recounts Clive's father Harry's adventure in World War I, from which he returns blind. Despite this handicap, upon his return, he and Hilly get married. Joseph Coates notes in *Chicago Tribune Books:* "Both of them know it's a misalliance, each having 'made a new demand on life' that excludes the other without having the resources to enforce it. Harry is an existentialist before his time, wanting nothing better than a life of continental vagrancy and sensuality; Hilly wanting a life in art." Over time, as Jonathan Yardley comments in the *Washington Post Book World,* their "marriage seems 'an enormous barrier to what used to be their affection.'" Yardley summarizes: "Hilly, determined over Harry's objections to have a child, at last becomes pregnant with Clive and then with a daughter, Kotch. However improbable a family they may be, a family is what they are: a small mansion with four rooms, but a mansion all the same."

With *The Tent of Orange Mist,* notes a *Publishers Weekly* reviewer, West's "versatility and imagination are again evident." Scald Ibis, a 16-year-old, becomes the property of Colonel Hayashi as her home is turned into a brothel for Japanese soldiers during the assault and occupation of Nanking, China. West's story of severe and unspeakable violence becoming commonplace, which was nominated for the National Book Critics Circle fiction award, comes highly recommended by Robert E. Brown, who calls the work in a *Library Journal* review, "both moving and intriguing. . . . An affecting novel." Commenting that West explores and "illuminates the consciousness of each of his . . . characters—especially Scald Ibis' struggle to come to terms with her pillaged youth," Donna Seaman in a *Booklist* review lauds West's "scorching insights into the consequences of evil." John David Morley in the *New York Times Book Review,* however, disagrees. Despite calling *Orange Mist* a "most arresting thesis," and West a "gifted writer," Morley faults the novel on credibility: ". . . that Scald Ibis should become reconciled to her fate with such savvy and bounce—is so far removed from experience that it is impossible to participate in the book's jollity. Victims of rape under the threat of imminent murder simply do not behave like this." Though arguing that West's narrative does wear "thin in spots," Seaman nonetheless concludes that West writes with "mind-stopping clarity and power." Richard Eder, in the *Los Angeles Times Book Review,* calls the novel "a small masterpiece," and argues that "West has never written anything so risky and triumphant."

One of West's most eloquently written and widely read books is *Words for a Deaf Daughter,* a biography of his daughter Mandy, born deaf and suffering from a brain dysfunction. Like the characters in some of West's novels, Mandy is an outsider. People turn away from her in the street because, according to West, "they don't like a universe that's absurd," relates Claire Tomalin in the *New Statesman.* Mandy is destructive yet obsessed with order and symmetry. She will fly into a rage because of a missing button or crooked barrette, for example, yet she will happily paint her face green, chew cigarettes, and cut her hair at random. The Wests' hope that Mandy will, with encouragement, develop fully, and the book is written in anticipation that she will one day be able to read about the early years of her life.

Novelist Chaim Potok observes in the *New York Times Book Review:* "Trapped, by whatever it is that traps people, into a potential horror and hell, West converted the trap into a doorway to a world filled with the strange fruit of nonverbal communication and creative silence." *Time* critic R. Z. Sheppard argues that "West writes joyfully for a can-be Mandy, but obviously adores Mandy as is. . . . A lifelong slave of words and reasons, [West] envies the intensity with which Mandy perceives the world nonverbally through her four acute senses." *Commentary* contributor Johanna Kaplan, however, finds West's optimistic, celebratory portrait of Mandy disturbing. She disputes West's description of Mandy's handicaps as a special gift. "For whom is it a gift?" she asks. "Not Mandy, clearly, for so cut off is she from the ordinary and essential means of human interchange that to try to understand the function of everyday objects, to give them some kind of place in what is for her an especially confusing world, she must 'smell at a pencil newly sharpened, inhaling from the beechwood its own sour-soot bouquet, or trace with addicted fingers the corrugations on the flat of a halved cabbage before eating it raw.'"

Words for a Deaf Daughter was reprinted with a new introduction by West in 1993. West comments to Amanda Smith in *Publishers Weekly:* "*Words for a Deaf Daughter* was written a long time ago, and it's a sort of hard and fast and settled book. Maybe the sense of the outsider, the dispossessed prince or princess, the pariah, the person who is shunned or spurned for whatever unjust reason—maybe this is a gathering pattern in one's work over twenty years. I'm sure one could make a good case, but I don't think in those terms. If I did, I wouldn't be able to write."

West's autobiographical work, *A Stroke of Genius: Illness and Self-Discovery,* explores the author's experience with several diseases, including migraine headaches, heart disease and diabetes, and his stroke, which forced him to accept a pacemaker implant to regulate his heartbeat. D. T. Max in the *Los Angeles Times Book Review* comments: "[West] must have been, without doubt, a nightmarish patient. As feckless as any autodidact, he reads and rereads the diagnostic manual with a fervor born of terror." Max praises *Stroke of Genius* despite finding that West buries disease itself under an "avalanche of prose." In West's book, the reader is allowed closer to the trauma of disease than in other memoirs of a similar nature, "not because West is braver—he is a complete chicken—but because he is franker," concludes Max. Dwight Garner notes in a *Nation* review that West focuses on his "generation's ingrained existentialism," which argues against passivity and leads "happily" to "a simple dignity in being a 'critic, fighter, and perfectionist to the end.'" Alexander

Theroux, in a *Chicago Tribune* review of *Stroke of Genius,* quotes West's explanation for his preoccupation with his illness: "I ponder such matters in much the same spirit as I memorize the names of all the actors when a movie's final credits roll—not because I care who they are, but because I want to show myself I am still competent."

BIOGRAPHICAL/CRITICAL SOURCES:

BOOKS

Dictionary of Literary Biography, Volume 14: *British Novelists since 1960,* Gale (Detroit), 1983.
Madden, David, *Understanding Paul West,* University of South Carolina Press, 1994.

PERIODICALS

Booklist, August, 1994, p. 2017; August, 1995, p. 1929; November 1, 1996.
Book World, May 28, 1972.
Chicago Tribune Books, April 14, 1991, p. 1; October 18, 1992, p. 5; February 19, 1995, p. 13.
Commentary, January, 1971.
Commonweal, September 30, 1966; December 9, 1977.
Harper's, October, 1970.
Kirkus Reviews, December 15, 1992, p. 1534; October 1, 1996.
Library Journal, September 15, 1988, p. 95; May 1, 1993, p. 119; August, 1995, p. 121.
Los Angeles Times, March 21, 1983; February 12, 1986.
Los Angeles Times Book Review, October 9, 1988, p. 2; September 10, 1989, p. 3; September 6, 1992, p. 3; May 7, 1995, p. 1; September 10, 1995, p. 3.
Nation, January 8, 1977; March 20, 1995, pp. 391-94.
New Republic, August 19, 1972; May 6, 1991, p. 37.
Newsday, April 21, 1991.
New Statesman, August 29, 1969.
Newsweek, August 31, 1970; March 10, 1986.
New Yorker, October 24, 1970; August 25, 1980.
New York Times Book Review, May 3, 1970; September 27, 1970; September 10, 1972; July 3, 1977; November 9, 1980; February 16, 1986; September 11, 1988, p. 7; May 12, 1991, p. 11; October 18, 1992; July 11, 1993, p. 20; September 20, 1993, p. 16; September 3, 1995, p. 17; October 19, 1997.
Partisan Review, summer, 1982.
Publishers Weekly, February 28, 1986; July 29, 1988, p. 219; July 21, 1989, p. 50; January 18, 1993, p. 464; July 11, 1994, p. 72; July 3, 1995, p. 48.
Review of Contemporary Fiction, fall, 1988, p. 156; fall, 1989, p. 215; spring, 1991 (special Paul West issue).
Sewanee Review, spring, 1993, p. 300.
Southern Review, winter, 1979.
Time, September 7, 1970; September 11, 1989, p. 82.
Times Literary Supplement, January 21, 1965; October 16, 1969; April 23, 1971; January 28, 1972; June 8, 1973; February 6, 1981; November 8, 1991, p. 31.
Voice Literary Supplement, September, 1992, p. 15.
Washington Post Book World, April 26, 1970; August 23, 1970; January 2, 1977; August 3, 1980; February 2, 1986; September 18, 1988, p. 3; September 27, 1992, p. 3.

WEST, Rebecca 1892-1983
(Lynx)

PERSONAL: Name originally Cicily Isabel Fairfield; adopted name Rebecca West c. 1911; born December 21, 1892, in County Kerry, Ireland; died March 15, 1983 of pneumonia in London, England; daughter of Charles (an army officer, editor, and writer) and Isabella (a musician; maiden name, Mackenzie) Fairfield; married Henry Maxwell Andrews (a banker and investment counselor), November 1, 1930 (died, 1968); children: (with H. G. Wells) Anthony (Panther) West. *Education:* George Watson's Ladies' College, Edinburgh, Scotland, graduate; attended Royal Academy of Dramatic Art, London.

CAREER: Journalist, novelist, biographer, and critic. Began journalist career in 1911 as reviewer for *Freewoman,* a feminist magazine; joined *Clarion* as a political writer in 1912, contributing from then on to British, and later American, newspapers and magazines; during the years following World War I she was the book critic of the *New Statesman and Nation* and regularly contributed to the *New Republic.* Became an advocate of Socialism and was active, for a while, in the Fabian Society. During World War II, supervised British Broadcasting Corp. talks to Yugoslavia; covered postwar treason trials of William Joyce (Lord Haw-Haw) and others, for the *New Yorker.* Fellow of Saybrook College, Yale University. Made cameo appearance in film "Reds," 1981.

MEMBER: Royal Society of Literature (fellow), American Academy of Arts and Sciences (honorary member), Oxford and Cambridge Club, Lansdowne Club.

AWARDS, HONORS: Order of St. Sava, 1937; Women's Press Club Award for Journalism, 1948; named Commander of the British Empire, 1949; Chevalier of the Legion of Honor, 1957; named Dame Commander of the British Empire, 1959; D.Litt. from New York University, 1965, and Edinburgh University, 1980; Benson Medal from Royal Society of Literature, 1966; Book of the Year Award from *Yorkshire Post,* 1966, for *The Birds Fall Down.*

WRITINGS:

Henry James, Holt, 1916.
The Return of the Soldier (novel), Century, 1918.
The Judge (novel), Doran, 1922.
(Editor) Carl Sandburg, *Selected Poems,* Harcourt, 1926.
The Strange Necessity (literary essays), Doubleday, 1928.
(Author of text under pseudonym Lynx) *Lions and Lambs,* illustrated by David Low, Harcourt, 1929.
Harriet Hume: A London Fantasy (novel), Doubleday, 1929.
D. H. Lawrence, Martin Secker, 1930, limited autographed edition published as *Elegy,* Phoenix Book Shop, 1930.
Arnold Bennett Himself (monograph), John Day, 1931.
Ending in Earnest: A Literary Log (collection of essays), Doubleday, 1931.
St. Augustine (biography), Appleton, 1933.
A Letter to a Grandfather (monograph), Hogarth, 1933.
The Modern "Rake's Progress," illustrated by Low, Hutchinson, 1934.
The Harsh Voice: Four Short Novels (includes "Life Sentence," "There Is No Conversation," "The Salt of the Earth," and "The Abiding Vision"), Doubleday, 1935.
The Thinking Reed (novel), Viking, 1936.
Black Lamb and Grey Falcon: The Record of a Journey through Yugoslavia, two volumes, Macmillan, 1937, published as

Black Lamb and Grey Falcon: A Journey through Yugoslavia, Viking, 1941, revised edition, 1977.
The Meaning of Treason (Book-of-the-Month Club selection), Viking, 1947, also published as *The New Meaning of Treason,* 1964.
A Train of Powder (political and social essays), Viking, 1955.
The Fountain Overflows (first novel in a trilogy; Literary Guild selection; Book Club choice in England), Viking, 1956.
The Court and the Castle: Some Treatments of a Recurrent Theme, Yale University Press, 1957 (published in England as *The Court and the Castle: A Study of the Interactions of Political and Religious Ideas in Imaginative Literature,* Macmillan, 1957).
The Vassall Affair, Sunday Telegraph (London), 1963.
The Birds Fall Down (novel; Book-of-the-Month Club selection), Viking, 1966.
McLuhan and the Future of Literature, Oxford University Press, 1969.
Rebecca West: A Celebration, introduction by Samuel Hynes, Viking, 1977.
The Young Rebecca: Writings of Rebecca West, 1911-1917, edited by Jane Marcus, Viking, 1982.
1900, Viking, 1982.
This Real Night (second novel in a trilogy), Viking, 1984.
Cousin Rosamund (third novel in a trilogy), Viking, 1986.
Sunflower, Viking, 1987, with afterword by Vicoria Glendinning, Penguin, 1988.
Family Memories: An Autobiographical Journey, Viking, 1988.
The Only Poet & Short Stories, edited with introduction by Antonia Till, Virago Press (London), 1992.

MEDIA ADAPTATIONS: The Return of the Soldier was produced as a motion picture starring Alan Bates, Julie Christie, Glenda Jackson, and Ann-Margaret by Brent Walker-Barry R. Cooper Productions in association with Skreba Films and released in 1985; an adaptation of West's *The Birds Fall Down* was broadcast on the BBC.

SIDELIGHTS: Rebecca West was best known as a journalist, but to designate her so is both to diminish and to distort her achievement as a writer. She was a great journalist; she was also a feminist, a book reviewer and literary critic, a novelist, a biographer, a social satirist, and a travel writer. She was eclectic in her interests, and her writing reflects this eclecticism. Though varied, her work is characterized by a literary style of remarkable clarity and vigor, a constant interest in what it means to be a woman, and, as Samuel Hynes quotes in his introduction to *Rebecca West: A Celebration,* a desire to "celebrate communion with reality," whether that reality is the immediate physicality of existence or the more difficult problem of the human continuum and how one fits into it.

Christened Cicily Fairfield, the youngest of three daughters born to Charles and Isabella Fairfield, she had a childhood filled with intellectual stimulation but marred by poverty and instability, the death of her father, and her own attacks of tuberculosis. Both her parents were gifted, her father with words and ideas, particularly those relating to politics, and her mother with music. Cicily was born and spent her early childhood in London, then accompanied her mother and sisters to Edinburgh where Cicily finished her education. Her father died alone in Liverpool, and a few years later the family moved back to London. There Cicily entered the Royal Academy of Dramatic Art. Her talents proved ill suited to acting, but she stayed long enough to play the part of Rebecca West in Ibsen's *Rosmersholm,* a play she later characterized as "the 'Hamlet' of the revolutionary intellectual movement," in a 1919 London *Daily News* article. Thus she found the name she made her own.

West began her career as an author very much in the spirit of the name she had adopted. She joined the staff of the *Freewoman,* a militantly feminist publication, as a reviewer of books. This was not a matter of happenstance. She was committed already to the Suffragist movement, and she was aware of her talent with language. As she stated in a 1955 *Saturday Review* interview with Bernard Kalb, "I write because all my family do, it is in the blood." The books she reviewed were heterogeneous, but she tested whatever came to hand both as a literary statement and as a comment about women. Since she held strong opinions on both topics and had no fear of expressing them in often witty and memorable language, she quickly was recognized as a new literary personality. Mrs. Humphrey Ward, a formidable member of the literary establishment and a foe of the Suffragists, was one of her first targets. H. G. Wells was another, but he was so intrigued by her clever audacity that he sought her out. Thus began the liaison that resulted in the birth of their son Anthony West in August 1914.

In 1912, West moved to the *Clarion,* a popular socialist newspaper that she found compatible to her feminist interests. There she published essays that rank "among the finest" produced by anyone in this turbulent period of the British feminist movement, according to Jane Marcus in *The Young Rebecca.* These essays are graphic, filled with urgency and brash frankness. Many recount West's reactions to the sometimes violent strategies of the Suffragists and the even more violent reactions of the government. Others contain her equally sharp reactions to publications on topics West thought had feminist significance: women's suffrage foremost, but also economic, legal, professional, and social equality for women. Her ideas were often unorthodox, but they were always rational and cogent.

It was not long before West's name became known in the United States, her first essay there appearing in the premier issue of the *New Republic.* Later in that same journal, she published a series of essays with the composite title "World's Worst Failure," in which she attacked the timidity and incompetence of British women; she soon followed this series with "Women in England" in the *Atlantic Monthly.* In 1923 and 1924 West made a lecture tour to the United States, speaking on the topic "Woman's View of Life's Problems." That tour was almost aborted before it began because she heard that her relationship with Wells had activated an effort to hold her at Ellis Island. Her tour, however, was a success, resulting in more opportunities for publication in the United States.

In this period when West was most active as a reviewer (1916-1931), she also produced three books and a monograph of criticism, three novels, and, in collaboration with David Low, a volume of satiric portrayals of contemporary personalities. The first of the critical studies, *Henry James* (1916), was West's first book. Published in the year of James's death, it is unusual for several reasons. In her work for the *Freewoman* and the *Clarion,* West had not indicated any strong interest in the fiction of James; for her to choose his work for her first book thus seems a departure from her primary interests. Also, in 1915 H. G. Wells's *Boon* had featured a violent attack on James and his concept of art. For West to have published in the following year a study basically supportive of James suggested an anomaly in her relationship with Wells. Whatever its purpose, the book contrasted

with the generally indifferent temper of Jamesian criticism of that period and still remains a study scholars consider. In *1900,* West reaffirmed her respect for James as an artist, and those, like Peter Wolfe, who have studied her fiction have found there evidence of James's influence, both in theme and technique.

The first of West's novels, *The Return of the Soldier* (1916), employs what for the time was an original device, amnesia from shellshock, and an unusual perspective on the war, that of those who waited at home. These elements permit West to explore the reactions of three women to a returning soldier who, though married, remembers only an earlier, idyllic love for another woman. The novel describes the women's efforts to bring him back to reality, an act which would mean his return to war and possible death. This is the shortest of West's novels, and although it may be "composed entirely of the fictional cliches of its time," as Martin Green declared in a 1977 *Saturday Review* essay, it remains her most frequently reprinted novel.

The Judge (1922) is a much larger, more ambitious work. Kobler labels it "a long, untidy novel raw with power and pain" and compares it with Hardy's fiction. Its epigraph—"Every mother is a judge who sentences the children for the sins of the father"— expresses the dour theme of the novel and provides evidence of West's conviction that women may nurture love and life but that the nature of men is to frustrate both. Committed to her theme, West permits no happy outcome for her central character, Ellen Melville, who, though more confident of the value of reason than of feeling, is drawn into the destructive vortex created by the man she loves. In *The Novels of Rebecca West: A Complex Unity,* Sister Mary Orlich found the novel flawed by a melodramatic murder and lapses in dialogue, but offered a generally favorable estimate. Patrick Braybrooke's judgment in *Novelists We Are Seven* was less favorable. He disliked "the solid blocks of very close print in which Miss West indulges," which he thought were "not only extremely irritating but tend to obscure the meaning." A strength of West's essays, her ability to explain and comment, becomes a fault in most of her fiction.

Harriet Hume: A London Fantasy (1929) represents a radical departure for West. In this narrative she tries to move away from the somber realism of her first two novels toward a more fanciful, more imaginative embodiment of idea. As in her previous fiction, however, the female and male principles are pitted in contest against each other. The female is allied with music, the male with politics. The female can love with a single-minded, direct purpose that the male, caught between his personal love and his public commitment, lacks; he thus can betray his personal avowal. H. G. Wells's praise of this novel, in a letter to West, seems extravagant. Although she often pursued the intricacies of abstraction as well as anyone, West failed to breathe fictive life into these abstractions in *Harriet Hume.*

In David Low, her collaborator on *Lions and Lambs* (1929), West found someone with a mischievous impiety that she, who tended to look more soberly at the world, was hard pressed to match, sharp-tongued as she may have been. Low makes one laugh; West is more apt to wound. The book is a series of pictorial and verbal portraits of contemporaries, some important, some less important, but all recognizable. For what the book reveals about West, the most important item is probably her comment on Clemence Dane, who to West characterized that fault in female novelists she considered most common and deadly—their tendency to be what the public thinks they should be instead of being true to themselves. Looking at Low's sketch of Clemence Dane, one may read West's comment as satiric, but it is too basic to West's fundamental feminist convictions to be dismissed so lightly. Yet, on the whole, West and Low worked so well together they later created a second book, *The Modern "Rake's Progress"* (1934).

During the early 1930s West was active preparing a series of book reviews for the London *Daily Telegraph* and a series of anecdotal essays for Hearst's New York *American*. The fact that she was hired by the Hearst newspaper to boost its sagging subscription list is evidence of her growing fame as a journalist. By early 1934 she had completed both of these projects, and from then until the end of World War II she published fewer periodical pieces than in any previous period of her career. When she did publish it was mostly in *Time and Tide*. For that journal she prepared in 1935 a short series of articles on political life in Washington, one of which contains a memorable sketch of Huey Long that catches his feral energy.

She began her exploration of history with a short, popular biography, *St. Augustine* (1933), which only begins to suggest the absorbing interest this fourth-century bishop held for her. "Every phrase I read of his," she wrote in *Black Lamb and Grey Falcon,* "sounds in my ears like the sentence of my doom and the doom of my age." West saw Augustine's perception of human nature as still alive in her world, even in herself. It was something primitive, an element in man that had, as she wrote in her comment on Kipling's work, "crawled out of the dark uncharted sea of our common humanity." Or stated differently in one of her comments on St. Augustine, "It seemed to him as if humanity was saturated with the obscene, not by reason of what it did but of what it was." Such a view of human nature provides nothing secure on which to build; whatever man's achievements, they are realized in defiance of rather than as a result of his nature. West also saw historical parallels between Augustine's age and her own; both were sliding into chaos. History was pointed towards disaster. It is doubtful that many readers of *St. Augustine* would have seen West's larger purpose in writing it, but when read in the context of *A Letter to a Grandfather* (1933), *The Thinking Reed* (1936), and that hard-to-characterize masterwork *Black Lamb and Grey Falcon* (1941), the darker theme running through it emerges more clearly.

Near the end of *Black Lamb and Grey Falcon,* West stated her reasons for writing this work, the last of her efforts to understand pre-World-War-II Europe: "I resolved to put on paper what a typical Englishwoman felt and thought in the late nineteen-thirties when, already convinced of the inevitability of the second Anglo-German war, she had been able to follow the dark waters of that event back to its source." For this most ambitious effort, two volumes in length, West chose as her subject Yugoslavia, a country she found one of the most diverse and culturally complex in Europe. It brought together the two Catholic traditions St. Augustine had seen falling into chaos. It was European, yet not a part of the advanced industrial development that West believed had spawned many of Europe's problems. In Yugoslavia she found history with continuity. However, she also found a study in contradictions. And to readers in Western Europe, Yugoslavia was largely unknown, a backwash of old empires. Here West could try to weave together all those threads she saw running in a crazy pattern through the rest of Europe.

This insight from *Black Lamb and Grey Falcon* is central to West's next book, *The Meaning of Treason* (1947). Six years intervened between the two books. At the end of the war, when British courts began to bring to trial those men who had betrayed their country, West realized that they exemplified the opposite

side of what she had admired in Yugoslavia. She drew the title of her book from her earlier *Harper's* essay of the same name, in which she defined her own understanding of treason. Using this essay as the prefatory statement for her book, she then presented the case histories of the traitors she had observed in the courts. West realized that allegiance—what it is and how and to what or whom it is given—is a topic of particular significance in the twentieth century. She sat through the trials and wrote her book because she feared that otherwise these court cases would not get the attention they deserved. Her studies concentrated on the psychological characteristics of the traitors; she asked herself what caused these people to do what they did. Her long examination of William Joyce, better known as Lord Haw Haw, is an example of her method at its best. When the book was published, it became a Book-of-the-Month Club selection. In his *Saturday Review of Literature* assessment, Struthers Burt described it as "the most admirable and important book Miss West has written."

However, soon after this first version of *The Meaning of Treason* appeared, its author realized that all the facts were not in. New traitors were uncovered, but this time they were not making propaganda for an alien Nazi Germany, they were spying for an alien Communist Soviet Union. So West revised her book, deleting old material and adding new, until finally it emerged in 1964 as *The New Meaning of Treason*. Since the end of World War II the scandal of Communist spies in high places has caused recurrent shocks in the British government, and the literature written about it is extensive. It is a tribute to West's acumen that she recognized the importance of the topic so early.

West wrote much more on treason and related topics in various periodicals. Some of this material she collected in two books, *A Train of Powder* (1955) and *The Vassall Affair* (1963). The courtroom atmosphere of *The Meaning of Treason* is present again in *A Train of Powder*. Although it contains two essays on the development of political awareness in postwar Germany, the book focuses primarily on trials: for war crimes at Nuremberg, for a racially motivated murder in South Carolina, for a greed-inspired killing in London, and—again—for treason of various kinds. West's ability to bring these courtroom dramas to life, to make their participants live on the page, enhanced her reputation as one of the greatest journalists of her period. Telford Taylor, U.S. Chief Counsel at the Nuremberg trials, began his *Saturday Review* appraisal of this book with the statement, "If words can paint, Rebecca West's do." As a lawyer, he paid her as well a professional compliment: "With all her literary attainments Miss West is also an exceedingly good lawyer." *The Vassall Affair,* her report of a young Englishman who spied for the Soviets, can be read as an addendum to *The New Meaning of Treason*. The report primarily illustrates how demoralizing the discovery of these spies was to the British government's confidence in its own integrity and its ability to function in the country's best interests.

During the 1950s and 1960s West was not entirely absorbed, however, in the topic of treason. When asked to present the Terry Lectures at Yale University, she returned to an earlier interest, literary criticism. For her topic she took as her cue a statement by Paul Valery: "Our greatest authors have nearly always written only about the court." Her lectures were later amplified and published as *The Court and the Castle* (1957). As West used the term *court,* in its narrowest sense it is the seat of government, more broadly it is society. The castle is the castle of God. Beginning with Shakespeare and ending with Kafka, she traced the evolving relationship of the courtier, the individual, to these external forces.

Another of West's uncompleted fictionalized family accounts, *Family Memories: An Autobiographical Journey,* was published in 1988. "In *Family Memories,* Rebecca West presents her 'creative' account of events in which she was involved and 'recreates' settings, stories, scenes outside her direct experience," explained Dale Spender in the *Women's Review of Books.* The stories are about her mother's and father's lives and her husband's mixed ancestry. A *Publishers Weekly* reviewer commented: "The novelist embellishes her delightful accounts of these remarkable men and women with imagination and wit but also with dislike, sarcasm and vitriol."

For West the postwar years were as professionally fruitful as one could expect, considering that during the whole period, her husband suffered from a painful disease that required their remaining at Ibstone House until his death in 1968. The marriage was a happy one, full of mutual affection, and West did what she could to comfort her husband and alleviate his suffering. After Henry Maxwell Andrews's death she moved back to London.

Back in London, West remained busy, but her interests became increasingly retrospective. She oversaw the preparation of *H. G. Wells and Rebecca West* (1974) by Gordon N. Ray. She helped select the work included in *Rebecca West: a Celebration* (1977). She worked closely with Jane Marcus in the preparation of *The Young Rebecca* (1982). She tried also to bring her fictional trilogy to completion, and, moving further back in memory, prepared a memoir of her mother and father. Her last book published while she was still living, *1900* (1982), appeared when she was ninety years old. It is a miscellany of topics pertinent to the year 1900, with pictures and a text by her. Some of her comments are personal reminiscences, but most of them fully reflect the strengths of her best writing: a sharp wit, striking images, an ability to reduce complexities to a comprehensible form.

Published in celebration of West's centenary, *The Only Poet & Short Stories* "serves as a sampling of West's very varied output as a novelist and story-writer, varied both in manner and quality," Claire Harman wrote in the *Times Literary Supplement.* Harman noted that "drama, melodrama, speech-making and the spotlight all feature in the collection of stories and fragments." In the London *Observer,* Jane Dunn characterized the pieces as having "a rawness and energy." Dunn concluded: "This collection . . . makes one grateful that [West] was unsuited to the stage and could turn her fiery energies instead to pursuit of . . . ideas and experiences."

West's literary production was so varied and at times so unorthodox that attempting to restrain her within any conventional category would do her an injustice. It would be better to ask such questions as "Was she widely read in her lifetime?" and "Did her writing influence significantly those who read it?" and "Will her books continue to be read?" She did have a large reading audience, though its composition shifted from book to book. The readers attracted to *The Fountain Overflows* were not the same as those who sought out *The Meaning of Treason.* As a consequence, she might be thought of by most readers as a one or possibly two-book author. As a novelist she was popular, but her influence was minimal, if for no other reason than that she was not technically innovative. As a book reviewer West had great impact. Since her major targets were shoddy writing and sloppy thinking, her influence was generally beneficial, as painful as it may have been for her victims. Her unorthodoxy, her unwillingness to work

within any particular critical method, and her failure to attract imitators makes her criticism singular. She thus will be read for her evaluations of particular authors, not for any critical theory she advanced.

The ability to recognize what is important at the moment is a characteristic of a great journalist, which is a reason why the term *journalist* so often is attached to West. Victoria Glendinning noted this quality when she wrote in the *New Republic:* "Rebecca West's vision, as it always has, picks out the facts that are really important." But the term *journalist* also has an ephemeral quality that West often transcends. Thus William Shawn could comment in the *New York Times:* "No one in this century . . . looked at the intricacies of human character and the ways of the world more intelligently." She may be remembered, like Robert Burton and T. E. Lawrence, as a writer of eminence *sui generis,* but she also may serve as that "ideal model for any study of twentieth-century woman" Glendinning considered her to be.

BIOGRAPHICAL/CRITICAL SOURCES:

BOOKS

Beaton, Cecil, and Kenneth Tynan, *Persona Grata,* Putnam, 1954.
Braybrooke, Patrick, *Novelists We Are Seven,* C. E. Daniel, 1926.
Contemporary Literary Criticism, Gale (Detroit), Volume 7, 1977; Volume 9, 1978; Volume 31, 1985; Volume 50, 1988.
Cowan, *Rebecca West Revisited,* Twayne, 1998.
Deakin, Motley F., *Rebecca West,* Twayne, 1980.
Dictionary of Literary Biography, Volume 36: *British Novelists, 1890-1929: Modernists,* Gale, 1985.
Dictionary of Literary Biography Yearbook: 1983, Gale, 1984.
Glendinning, Victoria, *Rebecca West; A Life,* Fawcett Columbine, 1998.
Hammond, J. R., *H. G. Wells and Rebecca West,* St. Martin's Press (New York), 1991.
Hutchinson, G. Evelyn, *A Preliminary List of the Writings of Rebecca West, 1912-1951,* Yale University Press, 1957.
Marcus, Jane, *The Young Rebecca,* Viking, 1982.
Orlich, Sister Mary Margarita, *The Novels of Rebecca West: A Complex Unity,* University Microfilms, 1967.
Packer, Jean Garrett, *Rebecca West: An Annotated Bibliography,* Garland (New York), 1991.
Rollyson, Carl E., *Rebecca West: A Life,* Scribner (New York), 1996.
Rollyson, Carl E., *The Literary Legacy of Rebecca West,* International Scholars Publications (San Francisco, CA), 1998.
Scott, Bonnie Kime, *Refiguring Modernism,* Indiana University Press, 1995.
West, Anthony, *H. G. Wells: Aspects of a Life,* Random House, 1984.
Williams, William Carlos, *Selected Essays of William Carlos Williams,* Random House, 1954.
Wolfe, Peter, *Rebecca West: Artist and Thinker,* Southern Illinois University Press, 1971.

PERIODICALS

Antioch Review, summer, 1986, p. 380.
Atlantic Monthly, December, 1966.
Book Week, October 2, 1966.
Bulletin of Bibliography, June, 1982.
Chicago Tribune, April 21, 1985.
Chicago Tribune Book World, May 23, 1982; April 20, 1986.
Encounter, March, 1961.

London Review of Books, November 21, 1985, p. 16; August 7, 1986, p. 22.
Los Angeles Times, July 24, 1986; April 3, 1987.
Los Angeles Times Book Review, May 2, 1982; April 14, 1985.
Nation, January 4, 1958.
New Republic, November 18, 1916; September 13, 1922; December 10, 1924; June 8, 1953; November 25, 1957; April 22, 1985.
Newsweek, May 17, 1982.
New York, April 3, 1982.
New Yorker, October 25, 1941; October 3, 1977; April 15, 1996, p. 74.
New York Herald Tribune Weekly Book Review, April 22, 1956.
New York Review of Books, August 12, 1982.
New York Times, July 8, 1981; May 28, 1982; March 16, 1983; February 15, 1985; March 23, 1985.
New York Times Book Review, August 20, 1922; November 3, 1929; December 14, 1947; December 9, 1956; October 2, 1977; August 18, 1985; February 15, 1987, p. 26; July 31, 1988; May 7, 1989, p. 42; February 10, 1991, p. 1.
Observer (London), June 29, 1986, p. 2; November 8, 1992, p. 59.
Publishers Weekly, February 12, 1988, p. 76.
Saturday Review, March 19, 1955; December 8, 1956; November 12, 1966; October 15, 1977.
Saturday Review of Literature, April 29, 1933; December 7, 1947.
Time, December 8, 1947.
Times (London), September 1, 1975; February 18, 1982; March 4, 1982; December 6, 1982; October 3, 1985.
Times Literary Supplement, February 8, 1957; December 21, 1973; November 22, 1974; October 18, 1985; July 25, 1986; November 20, 1987; December 25, 1992.
Tribune Books (Chicago), February 8, 1987; April 10, 1988.
Washington Post, March 31, 1987.
Washington Post Book World, May 2, 1982; April 7, 1985; June 7, 1987, p. 12.
Women's Review of Books, December, 1988, p. 4.

*   *   *

WEST, V(ictoria Mary) Sackville
See SACKVILLE-WEST, V(ictoria Mary)

*   *   *

WESTLAKE, Donald E(dwin) 1933-
(John B. Allan, Curt Clark, Tucker Coe, Richard Stark)

PERSONAL: Born July 12, 1933, in New York, NY; son of Albert Joseph (a salesman) and Lillian Marguerite (Bounds) Westlake; married Nedra Henderson, August 10, 1957 (divorced, 1966); married Sandra Foley, April 9, 1967 (divorced, 1975); married Abigail Adams, May 18, 1979; children: Sean Alan, Steven Albert, Tod, Paul Edwin; stepchildren: Adrienne Adams, Patrick Adams, Katharine Adams. *Education:* Attended Champlain College and State University of New York at Binghamton.

ADDRESSES: Home—409 Bleecker St., New York, NY 10014. *Agent*—Knox Burger, 39 AB Washington Square South, New York, NY 10012.

CAREER: Worked at odd jobs prior to 1958 ("the same list as every other writer, except that I was never a short-order cook");

associate editor at literary agency, 1958-59; writer, 1959–. *Military service:* U.S. Air Force, 1954-56 ("no awards, by mutual agreement").

AWARDS, HONORS: Edgar Allan Poe Award from Mystery Writers of America, 1967, for *God Save the Mark;* Edgar Allan Poe Grand Master Award from Mystery Writers of America, 1992; Lifetime Achievement Award, Mystery Awards at Bouchercon.

WRITINGS:

The Mercenaries, Random House, 1960.
Killing Time, Random House, 1961.
361, Random House, 1962.
Killy, Random House, 1963.
Pity Him Afterwards, Random House, 1964.
The Fugitive Pigeon, Random House, 1965.
The Busy Body, Random House, 1966.
The Spy in the Ointment, Random House, 1966.
God Save the Mark, Random House, 1967.
Philip, Crowell, 1967.
(Compiler with Philip Klass) *Once against the Law,* Macmillan, 1968.
The Curious Facts Preceding My Execution, and Other Fictions, Random House, 1968.
Who Stole Sassi Manoon? Random House, 1968.
Somebody Owes Me Money, Random House, 1969.
Up Your Banners, Macmillan, 1969.
Adios, Scheherezade, Simon & Schuster, 1970.
I Gave at the Office, Simon & Schuster, 1971.
Under an English Heaven, Simon & Schuster, 1971.
Cops and Robbers (see also below), M. Evans, 1972.
(With Brian Garfield) *Gangway,* M. Evans, 1972.
Help I Am Being Held Prisoner, M. Evans, 1974.
Two Much, M. Evans, 1975.
A Travesty, M. Evans, 1975.
Brothers Keepers, M. Evans, 1975.
Dancing Aztecs, M. Evans, 1976 (published in England as *A New York Dance,* Hodder & Stoughton, 1979).
Enough!, M. Evans, 1977.
Nobody's Perfect, M. Evans, 1977.
Castle in the Air, M. Evans, 1980.
Kahawa, Viking, 1982.
Levine, Mysterious Press, 1984.
A Likely Story, Penzler Books, 1984.
High Adventure, Mysterious Press, 1985.
Another Circus, Mysterious Press, 1985.
(With Abby Westlake) *High Jinx,* MacMillan, 1987.
(With A. Westlake) *Transylvania Station,* MacMillan, 1987.
Trust Me on This, Mysterious Press, 1988.
Tomorrow's Crimes (includes *Anarchaos,* a novel, and other stories published between 1961-84), Mysterious Press, 1989.
Sacred Monster, Mysterious Press, 1989.
Humans, Mysterious Press, 1992.
Give Till It Hurts: A Christmas Story, Mysterious Bookshop, 1993.
Baby, Would I Lie? A Romance of the Ozarks, Mysterious Press, 1994.
Smoke, Mysterious Press, 1995.
What's the Worst that Could Happen?, Mysterious Press, 1996.
The Ax, Mysterious Press, 1997.

"JOHN A. DORTMUNDER" CRIME SERIES

The Hot Rock, Simon & Schuster, 1970.
Bank Shot, Simon & Schuster, 1972.

Jimmy the Kid, M. Evans, 1974.

Why Me? (also see below), Viking, 1983.

Good Behavior, Mysterious Press, 1986.

Drowned Hopes (also see below), Mysterious Press, 1990.

Don't Ask, Mysterious Press, 1993.

UNDER PSEUDONYM JOHN B. ALLAN

Elizabeth Taylor: A Fascinating Story of America's Most Talented Actress and the World's Most Beautiful Woman, Monarch, 1961.

UNDER PSEUDONYM TUCKER COE

Kinds of Love, Kinds of Death, Random House, 1966.

Murder among Children, Random House, 1968.

Wax Apple, Random House, 1970.

A Jade in Aries, Random House, 1971.

Don't Lie to Me, Random House, 1972.

UNDER PSEUDONYM RICHARD STARK

The Hunter (also see below), Pocket Books, 1963, published as *Point Blank,* Berkley, 1973, reprinted under original title with a new introduction by the author, Gregg Press, 1981.

The Man with the Getaway Face (also see below), Pocket Books, 1963, published as *The Steel Hit,* Coronet (London), 1971, Berkley, 1975, published under original title, Allison & Busby, 1985.

The Outfit (also see below), Pocket Books, 1963.

The Mourner (also see below), Pocket Books, 1963.

The Score (also see below), Pocket Books, 1964.

The Jugger, Pocket Books, 1965.

The Seventh (also see below), Pocket Books, 1966, published in England as *The Split,* Allison & Busby, 1984.

The Handle, Pocket Books, 1966, published as *Run Lethal,* Berkley, 1966.

The Damsel, Macmillan, 1967.

The Dame, Macmillan, 1967.

The Rare Coin Score, Fawcett, 1967.

The Green Eagle Score, Fawcett, 1967.

The Black Ice Score, Fawcett, 1968.

The Sour Lemon Score, Fawcett, 1969.

The Blackbird, Macmillan, 1969.

Deadly Edge, Random House, 1971.

Slayground, Random House, 1971.

Lemons Never Lie, World Publishing Co., 1971.

Plunder Squad, Random House, 1972.

Butcher's Moon, Random House, 1974.

Stark Mysteries (contains *The Hunter, The Man with the Getaway Face, The Outfit, The Mourner, The Score,* and *The Seventh*), G. K. Hall, 1981.

Comeback, Mysterious Press, 1997.

SCREENPLAYS

(With Michael Kane) *Hot Stuff,* Columbia, 1979.

The Stepfather, New Century/Vista, 1986.

The Grifters, Miramax, 1990.

Also author of screenplays *Cops and Robbers,* upon which Westlake based the novel, and *Why Me?,* based on the novel.

OTHER

(Editor) *Murderous Schemes: An Anthology of Classic Detective Stories,* Oxford University Press, 1996.

Contributor to anthologies. Author of science fiction, sometimes under the pseudonym Curt Clark.

MEDIA ADAPTATIONS: Eleven other novels written by the author, either under the name Donald E. Westlake or pseudonym Richard Stark, have been made into films: *The Jugger,* adaptation produced in France as *Made in the USA,* 1966; *The Busy Body,* film produced by Paramount, 1967; *The Hunter,* adaptation produced as *Point Blank,* Metro-Goldwyn-Mayer, 1967; *The Score,* adaptation produced in France as *Mise en Sac,* 1967; *The Seventh,* adaptation produced as *The Split,* Metro-Goldwyn-Mayer, 1968; *The Hot Rock,* film released by Twentieth Century-Fox, 1972; *Bank Shot,* film produced by United Artists, 1974; *The Outfit,* film produced by Metro-Goldwyn-Mayer, 1974; *Jimmy the Kid,* film produced by New World, 1982; *Slayground,* film produced by Universal, 1984; *Two Much,* adaptation produced in France as *Le Jumeau.*

SIDELIGHTS: "The Neil Simon of the crime novel" is the way Donald E. Westlake is described by *New York Times Book Review* critic Newgate Callendar. It is a title Westlake earned through such popular books as *The Hot Rock, Bank Shot,* and *Two Much,* all characteristic of the author's talent for combining laughs with thrills in his fiction. In a Westlake tale, criminals and law enforcement officers are equally incompetent, and daring felonies fall prey to bad timing, bad weather, and bad luck. The author's plots revolve around the offbeat: "Who else could write a book about a man who pretends to be twins in order to marry a pair of identical heiresses?" asks Sheldon Bart in another *New York Times Book Review* article.

Westlake's first published books were more conventional crime novels; funny cops-and-robbers stories were not considered marketable. He had been working on a running character named Parker, a thief who "handles frustration very badly—he gets annoyed and kills everybody," according to Westlake in Bart's article. When the author realized the comic potential in a no-win criminal, Westlake created another character, named John Dortmunder, and starred him in a gem-stealing caper, *The Hot Rock.* So successful was this character, who, notes *Newsweek* writer David Lehman, "makes burglar seem synonymous with bungler," that Westlake continued Dortmunder's adventures in several subsequent novels, including *Bank Shot* and *Jimmy the Kid.*

Westlake departed from the crime novel format with his works *A Likely Story* and *Trust Me on This.* A farce about the world of publishing and one writer's attempt to market his Christmas book, *A Likely Story* almost never got published. *Washington Post* critic Alan Ryan finds no small irony in the fact that "all the big-time New York publishers turned this book down. Why? Because it wasn't a crime novel, because it was different from Westlake's previous books, and—one assumes—because they didn't think it was funny and/or didn't think it would sell." But even writing out of his usual genre, "Westlake knows what he's doing," continues Ryan. "[His] comic eye is hilariously perceptive and ruthlessly unsparing. The result is likely the funniest book of the year."

In *Trust Me on This,* aspiring journalist Sara Joslyn lands a job with *The Weekly Galaxy* tabloid and is soon immersed in the world of madcap reportage. The bulk of the book involves the *Galaxy* crew invading Martha's Vineyard to cover a movie star's wedding. William A. Henry III, writing in *Time,* states: "Rather than mock the already preposterous, Westlake explores the mentality that capable, rational people would need in order to crank out such stuff." Henry describes *Trust Me* as "perhaps the most beguiling beheading of journalists since Evelyn Waugh's *Scoop,*" and calls the work "a frantic, inventive story with lots of good dialogue." In *Newsweek,* reviewer Peter S. Prescott proclaims: "Donald E. Westlake writes a comic novel so well it's a wonder he bothers with crime at all."

Westlake returned to his Dortmunder series with the publication of *Good Behavior.* In this novel, the clever thief crash-lands in a Manhattan convent, the sanctuary of a sisterhood of nuns vowed to silence. They persuade Dortmunder to rescue Sister Mary Grace, a tycoon's daughter who has been spirited away by her father and held prisoner in a high-security skyscraper's penthouse. Dortmunder and crew attempt to save the girl, but, in typical fashion, their plans go haywire when they confront mercenaries training for the overthrow of a South American dictatorship. Writing in the *Washington Post Book World,* Jean M. White emphasizes: "In the midst of these antics, Westlake never allows his comedy to slide into silly farce or buffoonery," and Callendar remarks in the *New York Times Book Review:* "He has a wonderful feeling for the absurd, revels in farce and slapstick, [and] piles complication upon complication" on the hapless burglars.

Drowned Hopes, yet another Dortmunder caper, pits the ill-fated crook against ex-cellmate Tom Jimson, who plans to blow up a dam, endangering thousands of lives, to retrieve his hidden loot, now buried under fifty feet of water. In the Chicago *Tribune-Books,* Kevin Moore observes that "Westlake, the Mel Brooks of mayhem, has great fun making it all much more complicated than that." About the Dortmunder novels, Katherine Dunn comments in the *New York Times Book Review,* "These are hard-nosed but never hard-boiled romps, with a hero you could trust to babysit but wouldn't ask to polish the silver." Dunn gave high marks to *Drowned Hopes,* judging: "Westlake's lean prose and deadpan delivery are engaging, as always. His psychology is sharp and his characters colorful."

A later work, *Sacred Monster,* unfolds as a lengthy interview with a drunken, drug-using Hollywood superstar. Charles Champlin, in the *Los Angeles Times Book Review,* terms the book "a sparkling little set-piece," and comments that "Westlake's ingenuity in spinning out his tale and working his sleight-of-hand finale is an audacious treat." *Tomorrow's Crimes* gathers Westlake's previously unpublished 1967 novel, *Anarchaos,* and nine shorter science fiction-mystery stories. Gary Dretzka, in the Chicago *Tribune Books,* calls the stories "fast, thought-provoking studies" of humankind in a universe disrupted by the inherited evils of corporate and individual greed and a deteriorating environment. Despite minor reservations, Randall Short, in the *New York Times Book Review,* determines that "devotees of either genre can look forward to a smooth, satisfying read."

In *Humans,* God orders the angel Ananayel to bring about the Apocalypse. Ananayel enlists five human agents to assist him, but the bringer of doom is drawn off course by a growing concern for humanity, as well as his battle with X, the force who wishes to perpetuate humanity's suffering for his own demonic pleasure. Garry Abrams, in the *Los Angeles Times Book Review,* suggests that "a major purpose of the book" may be "to satirize the cleverness and conventions of the typical thriller through the stereotypes of an earlier, more faithful era," but he points out: "in [its] final section, *Humans* becomes more and more like the standard thriller it parodies. . . . The climax also is something of a whimper, considering the buildup." The *New York Times Book Review's* Michael Upchurch opines that Westlake's "narrative building blocks include . . . a labyrinthine plot and an unnerving insight into the depths of human behavior. The writing isn't as crisp as it could be, however, and the author has a persistently

hokey side to him that may seem simply sophomoric to some readers." Upchurch did note that the human agents "with their sense of rage and helplessness . . . give *Humans* a compelling urgency that, in its best passages, outweighs its obvious gimmicks" and found that "in bringing his characters to the brink of oblivion, Donald Westlake zeroes in on what is most precious about life. The ride may be bumpy in terms of technique but the view is, in unexpected ways, divine."

Westlake returns to the character of Sara Joslyn and the seamy world of tabloid journalism with his novel *Baby, Would I Lie?* Sara is now working for a weekly newsmagazine, *Trend: The Magazine for the Way We Live This Instant,* and is sent to Branson, Missouri, to cover the trial of Ray Hanson, a country-western star accused of murder. Ronald C. Miller, writing for *The Armchair Detective* calls *Baby, Would I Lie?* "a comedic cornucopia . . . [that] lampoons journalists, contemporary music, entrepreneurs, and the IRS, among others." Charles Champlin in the *Los Angeles Times Book Review* terms it "a deliciously nutty sequel" to *Trust Me on This* and "the funniest mystery of the year." Michael Lewis, reviewer for the *New York Times Book Review* is less complimentary. Although praising "Mr. Westlake's usually fine work," he feels that the novel's "humor . . . seems more like an excuse for the absence of any real mystery and its mystery an apology for the fact that it isn't very funny." He concludes, "in the end, the book's real satire is of itself."

Smoke lampoons the tobacco industry and resurrects the concept of the Invisible Man, but as Don Sandstrom points out in *The Armchair Detective,* "Do not dismiss [Westlake's protagonist] Freddie Noon as another invisible man like H. G. Wells's Doctor Griffin, Thorne Smith's George Kirby, or . . . H. F. Saint's Nick Holloway. This is a Westlake production." Gary Dretzka, writing for Chicago's *Tribune Books,* calls *Smoke* "the kind of novel mystery fans will pass along to the unconverted as an example of just how enjoyable genre writing can be." In the *Washington Post Book World,* Kathi Malo terms it "one of his best books in years." And Terry Teachout, writing for the *New York Times Book Review,* compares Westlake to P. G. Wodehouse and says of *Smoke,* "Squirrel it away for emergency use the next time you find yourself stuck in an airport lounge with a departure time of maybe. The bartender may resent the fact that you're too busy laughing to order another drink, but you'll definitely feel better in the morning."

John Dortmunder finds new ways to bungle old tricks in *What's the Worst That Could Happen?* The hapless but obliviously confident burglar decides unburdening a media magnate's empty mansion of its riches will be a piece of cake. Inconveniently, but perhaps not surprisingly, the owner, Max Fairbanks, is at home at the time of the robbery. Dortmunder is captured by Fairbanks, who informs the police that their new prisoner's own lucky ring is really his own. Eventually Dortmunder, outraged at having his own ring taken from him, sets out for revenge. *Booklist's* Thomas Gaughan states that this novel shows why "Westlake's Dortmunder stories are among the best comic crime novels in existence," adding that *What's the Worst That Could Happen?* should be recommended to anyone "with a sense of humor or who looks like she/he can use a laugh."

Westlake's *The Ax* is a dark situational-ethics-driven novel. It is nearly 180 degrees in tone from the almost light-hearted Dortmunder tales. In it, middle manager Burke Devore is downsized and quickly knocked out of the middle class. Devore decides it is worth anything to keep himself and his family from living below the standard to which they had been accustomed. Finding the perfect position for himself, he learns who currently holds the job and then retires him permanently. To fail-safe his coup, he learns who his most able competition will be and begins to systematically eliminate them. According to D. Keith Mano, writing in the *New York Times Book Review,* in *The Ax* "Donald Westlake has caught and logged our unspoken fiscal dread in a novel of excruciating brilliance," going on to describe the book as "pretty much flawless. . . . Burke Devore is American Man at the millennium—as emblematic of his time as George F. Babbitt and Holden Caufield and Capt. John Yossarian were of theirs."

In *Comeback,* Westlake resurrects Parker, the incorrigible anti-hero he created 23 years earlier under the alias Richard Stark. This time the anti-social master thief is intent on preying on a mercenary televangelist, figuring that the ill-gotten gains of the phony man of God would be better off in his own pocket. The scheme to "transfer" these funds proceeds like clockwork until some disloyal confederates put their interests above Parker's. In the *New York Times Book Review,* Marilyn Stasio writes that she appreciates "the author's biting irony toward characters who talk the big talk about love and trust and loyalty but ditch their Christian values for a hot babe or a cool buck. In a world of warped values an honest crook like Parker is a true treasure."

BIOGRAPHICAL/CRITICAL SOURCES:

BOOKS

Contemporary Literary Criticism, Gale (Detroit), Volume 7, 1977; Volume 33, 1985.

PERIODICALS

Armchair Detective, spring, 1995, p. 206; winter, 1996, p. 106.
Booklist, August, 1995, p. 1911; August, 1996, p. 1857.
Chicago Tribune Book World, April 25, 1982.
Entertainment Weekly, February 28, 1992; April 2, 1993; May 12, 1995, p. 59.
Film Quarterly, winter, 1987.
Harper's, September, 1988.
Library Journal, July, 1994, p. 130; November 1, 1994, p. 126; January, 1995, p. 158.
Los Angeles Times, February 28, 1983; August 7, 1985.
Los Angeles Times Book Review, April 25, 1981; July 13, 1986; May 8, 1988; June 4, 1989; April 15, 1990; March 1, 1992; September 11, 1994, p. 18.
Ms., June, 1986.
National Review, February 16, 1973.
New Republic, December 13, 1975.
New Statesman, January 10, 1986.
Newsweek, February 21, 1983; April 22, 1985; July 18, 1988; September 5, 1994.
New York, July 3 1989.
New Yorker, August 15, 1988.
New York Times, March 5, 1982.
New York Times Book Review, November 19, 1972; June 3, 1973; July 14, 1974; May 18, 1975; October 31, 1976; October 2, 1977; April 13, 1980; May 16, 1982; January 9, 1983; June 22, 1986; July 10, 1988; July 30, 1989; October 15, 1989; April 8, 1990; April 14, 1991; June 28, 1992; September 11, 1994, p. 20; October 8, 1995, p. 3; June 29, 1997; October 19, 1997.
Observer, February 9, 1986.
People Weekly, November 6, 1989; October 24, 1994.
Saturday Review, May 29, 1971; September 25, 1971.
Spectator, January 29, 1977.

Time, July 22, 1974; August 8, 1988.
Times Literary Supplement, September 24, 1971; December 7, 1979.
Tribune Books (Chicago), November 9, 1986; October 1, 1989; April 1, 1990; October 1, 1995, p. 4.
Wall Street Journal, September 30, 1994.
Washington Post, December 24, 1984; July 23, 1985.
Washington Post Book World, May 18, 1986; March 22, 1992; March 29, 1992; December 17, 1995, p. 11.
West Coast Review of Books, September 1986; Volume 13, number 6, 1988.

* * *

WESTMACOTT, Mary
See CHRISTIE, Agatha (Mary Clarissa)

* * *

WHARTON, Edith (Newbold Jones) 1862-1937

PERSONAL: Born January 24 (some sources say 23), 1862 (some sources say 1861), in New York, NY; died of a heart attack, August 11, 1937, in St. Brice-sous-Foret, France; buried in Versailles, France, next to Walter Berry; daughter of George Frederic (heir to merchant-ship fortune) and Lucretia Stevens (Rhinelander) Jones; married Edward Robbins Wharton (a banker), 1885 (divorced, 1912). *Education:* Educated privately in New York and Europe.

CAREER: American novelist, poet, and short story writer. *Military service:* Organized American committee of Red Cross in Paris, France, and worked on behalf of Belgian refugees during World War I.

MEMBER: National Institute of Arts and Letters, 1930-37; American Academy of Arts and Letters, 1934-37.

AWARDS, HONORS: Pulitzer Prize, 1921, for *The Age of Innocence;* D. Litt., Yale University, 1923; Nobel Prize nomination, 1927; Gold Medal, National Institute of Arts and Letters; Cross of the Legion of Honor (France); Chevalier of the Order of Leopold (Belgium); Montyon Prize, French Academy.

WRITINGS:

NOVELS

The Valley of Decision, Scribner, 1902.
Sanctuary, Scribner, 1903.
The House of Mirth (also see below), Scribner, 1905, new edition with forward by Marcia Davenport, 1951.
Madame de Treymes, Scribner, 1907.
The Fruit of the Tree, Scribner, 1907.
Ethan Frome (also see below), Scribner, 1911, new edition, 1938, reprinted with author's introduction, 1960, with an introduction by Elaine Showalter, Oxford University Press, 1996.
The Custom of the Country, Scribner, 1913.
The Reef, Scribner, 1913, reprinted with an introduction by Louis Auchincloss, 1996.
Summer (also see below), Scribner, 1917.
The Marne, Appleton, 1918.
The Age of Innocence, Meredith, 1920; with an introduction by Regina Barecca, Signet Classic (New York City), 1996, edited with an introduction by Cynthia Griffin Wolff and

notes by Laura Dluzynski Quinn, Penguin (New York City), 1996.

The Glimpses of the Moon, Appleton, 1922.

A Son at the Front, Scribner, 1923.

Old New York: False Dawn (The 'Forties), The Old Maid (The 'Fifties), The Spark (The 'Sixties), New Year's Day (The 'Seventies) (four short novels), Scribner, 1924, reprinted as *Old New York: Four Novellas,* Scribner Paperback, 1995.

The Mother's Recompense, Appleton, 1925.

Twilight Sleep, Appleton, 1927.

The Children, Meredith, 1928, published as *The Marriage Playground,* 1930.

Hudson River Bracketed, Meredith, 1929.

The Gods Arrive (sequel to *Hudson River Bracketed*), Meredith, 1932.

The Buccaneers (unfinished), Appleton-Century, 1938.

Ethan Frome [and] *Summer,* with introduction by Michael Millgate, Constable, 1965.

The Edith Wharton Omnibus (includes *The Age of Innocence, Ethan Frome,* and *Old New York*), Scribners, 1978.

Madame de Treymes and Three Novelists, Macmillan, 1987.

The House of Mirth; The Reef; The Custom of the Country; The Age of Innocence, edited by R. W. B. Lewis, Cambridge University Press, 1988.

Madame de Treymes and Others, Virago, 1988, reprinted as *Madame de Treymes and Three Novellas,* Scribner, 1995.

Two Novels by Edith Wharton: Ethan Frome and Summer, North, 1993.

Edith Wharton: Three Complete Novels (contains *The House of Mirth, Ethan Frome,* and *The Custom of the Country*), Gramercy Books (New York), 1994.

Edith Wharton: The Age of Innocence and Two Other Complete Works of Love, Morals, and Manners (also contains *Summer,* and *Madame De Treymes*), Gramercy Books, 1996.

Four Novels (contains *The House of Mirth, Ethan Frome, The Custom of the Country,* and *The Age of Innocence*), Library of America (New York), 1996.

SHORT STORIES

The Greater Inclination (includes "The Muse's Tragedy," "A Journey," "The Pelican," "Souls Belated," "A Coward," "The Twilight of the God," "A Cup of Cold Water," and "The Portrait"), Scribner, 1899.

Crucial Instances (includes "The Duchess at Prayer," "The Angel at the Grave," "The Recovery," "'Copy': A Dialogue," "The Rembrandt," "The Moving Finger," and "The Confessional"), Scribner, 1901.

The Descent of Man, and Other Stories (includes "The Mission of Jane," "The Other Two," "The Quicksand," "The Dilettante," "The Reckoning," "Expiation," "The Lady's Maid's Bell," and "A Venetian Lady's Entertainment"), Scribner, 1904.

The Hermit and the Wild Woman and Other Stories (includes "The Last Asset," "In Trust," "The Pretext," "The Verdict," "The Potboiler," and "The Best Man"), Scribner, 1908.

Xingu and Other Stories (includes "Xingu," "Coming Home," "Autres temps . . . ," "Kerfol," "The Long Run," "The Triumph of Night," "The Choice," and "The Bunner Sisters"), Scribner, 1916.

Here and Beyond (includes "Miss Mary Pask," "The Young Gentleman," "Bewitched," "The Seed of the Faith," "The Temperate Zone," and "Velvet Ear-Pads"), Appleton, 1926.

Certain People (includes "Atrophy," "A Bottle of Perrier," "After Holbein," "Dieu d'Amour," "The Refugees," and "Mr. Jones"), Appleton, 1930.

Human Nature (includes "Her Son," "The Day of the Funeral," "A Glimpse," "Joy in the House," and "Diagnosis"), Appleton, 1933.

The World Over (includes "Charm Incorporated," "Pomegranate Seed," "Permanent Wave," "Confession," "Roman Fever," "The Looking-Glass," and "Duration"), Appleton-Century, 1936.

Ghosts (includes "All Souls," "The Eyes," "Afterward," "The Lady's Maid's Bell," "Reform," "The Triumph of Night," "Mrs. Mary Pask," "Bewitched," "Mr. Jones," "Pomegranate Seed," and "A Bottle of Perrier"), Appleton-Century, 1937.

An Edith Wharton Treasury (includes *The Age of Innocence, The Old Maid,* "After Holbein," "A Bottle of Perrier," "The Lady's Maid's Bell," "Roman Fever," "The Other Two," *Madame de Treymes,* "The Moving Finger," "Xingu," "Autres temps . . . ," and "The Bunner Sisters"), edited by A. H. Quinn, Appleton-Century-Crofts, 1950.

The Best Short Stories of Edith Wharton, edited by Wayne Andrews, 1958.

Stories (includes "The Other Two," "The Lady's Maid's Bell," and "The View"), adapted with notes and exercises by Kenneth Croft and E. F. Croft, Prentice-Hall International, 1962.

Roman Fever and Other Stories (includes "Roman Fever," "Xingu," "The Other Two," "Souls Belated," "The Angel at the Grave," "The Last Asset," "After Holbein," and "Autres temps . . ."), Scribner, 1964.

The Edith Wharton Reader (includes *Ethan Frome, The Bunner Sisters,* selections from *The House of Mirth* and *The Age of Innocence,* and short stories), compiled by Louis Auchincloss, Scribner, 1965.

Collected Short Stories (two volumes; includes stories from the ten volume edition and thirteen additional stories), edited by R. W. B. Lewis, Scribner, 1967.

The Ghost Stories of Edith Wharton (includes "The Lady's Maid's Bell," "The Eyes," "Afterward," "Kerfol," "The Triumph of Night," "Miss Mary Pask," "Bewitched," "Mr. Jones," "Pomegranate Seed," "The Looking-Glass," and "All Souls"), New York, 1973.

Quartet: Four Stories (includes "Roman Fever," "The Other Two," "The Last Asset," and "Afterward"), Allen Press, 1975.

The Stories of Edith Wharton, edited by Anita Brookner, Simon & Schuster, 1988.

Short Stories, Dover, 1994.

Edith Wharton's New England: Seven Stories and Ethan Frome, edited by Barbara Anne White, University Press of New England, 1995.

Afterward, Modern Library, 1996.

The Collected Stories of Edith Wharton, edited by Anita Brookner, Carroll & Graf, 1998.

OTHER

Verses, C. E. Hammett, Jr. (Rhode Island), 1878.

(With Ogden Codman) *The Decoration of Houses* (nonfiction), Scribner, 1897, revised and expanded edition, Norton, 1995.

The Touchstone (novelette), Scribner, 1900 (published in England as *A Gift from the Grave: A Tale*).

(Translator) Hermann Sudermann, *The Joy of Living,* Scribner, 1902.

Italian Villas and their Gardens (nonfiction), Century, 1904.

Italian Backgrounds (memoirs), Scribner, 1905.

A Motor-Flight through France (nonfiction), Scribner, 1908.

Artemis to Actaeon and Other Verse, Scribner, 1909.

Tales of Men and Ghosts, Scribner, 1910.

Fighting France, from Dunkerque to Belfort (nonfiction), Scribner, 1915.

(Compiler) *The Book of the Homeless,* Scribner, 1916.

French Ways and Their Meaning (essays), Appleton, 1919.

In Morocco, Scribner, 1920.

The Writing of Fiction (criticism), 1925.

Twelve Poems, The Medici Society (London), 1926.

A Backward Glance (autobiography), Appleton-Century, 1934.

(Compiler with Robert Norton and Gaillard Lapsley) *Eternal Passion in English Poetry,* Appleton-Century, 1939.

The Old Maid (play based on the novel of the same title), French (New York), 1951.

(Under name David Olivieri) *Fast and Loose: A Novelette by David Olivieri,* edited by Viola Hopkins Winner, University Press of Virginia, 1977.

Ethan Frome: Authoritative Text, Backgrounds and Contexts, Criticism, edited by Kristin O. Lauer and Cynthia G. Wolff, Norton, 1994.

Edith Wharton Abroad: Selected Travel Writings, 1888-1920, edited by Sarah Bird Wright, St. Martin's Press, 1995, large print edition, Thorndike, 1996.

Edith Wharton: Uncollected Critical Writings, Princeton University Press, 1997.

Also adaptor, with Clyde Fitch, of a play version of *The House of Mirth.* Contributor of poems and stories to literary journals and women's magazines, including *Scribner's, Harper's,* and *Century.*

MEDIA ADAPTATIONS: A play based on *The Old Maid* adapted by Zoe Akins won a Pulitzer Prize for drama in 1935; a dramatization of *Ethan Frome* by Owen and Donald Davis was produced in New York in 1936; a stage version of *The Custom of the Country* by Jane Stanton Hitchcock was produced On Broadway at McGinn/Cazale Theater, in 1985; "Old New York," adapted from Wharton's story by Donald Sanders, was produced in the parlor of the Old Merchant's House Museum in New York in 1987; *Two By Wharton,* a play based on the stories "The Other Two" and "Autres temps . . ." adapted by Dennis Krausnick was produced at The Mount (Wharton's restored estate) in Lenox, MA, in 1987; a film version of *The Age of Innocence* starring Daniel Day-Lewis, Winona Ryder, and Michelle Pfeiffer was produced for Columbia Pictures by Martin Scorsese in 1993.

SIDELIGHTS: American novelist Edith Wharton was the first woman to receive some of the country's most distinguished literary awards—the Gold Medal of the National Institute of Arts and Letters and an honorary degree from Yale—and the most celebrated American female author of her times. The friend of novelist and fellow American expatriate Henry James, Wharton shared with him many of the same themes and values. Wharton is generally perceived as preserving more of the details of her character's lives and less of the Jamesian analysis of their personalities, yet her works show a concentrated interest in personality; her first book, *The Decoration of Houses,* introduced the notion that furnishings should express the homeowner's personal tastes; her novels show the conflict between her characters' individual values and social expectations. Though her characters seek to escape from the pressure to conform, they often find themselves bound by it. Wharton experienced this conflict first-hand, sometimes as the defender of the social establishment, and sometimes as an individualist who paid a high price for her personal freedom. Best known for her novels *The House of Mirth, Ethan Frome,* and *The Age of Innocence,* she also published poetry, criticism, nonfiction about the First World War, travel

writing, and several collections of short stories. Her books suffered a period of critical neglect because of their similarity to the works of James. But a revived interest in what they reveal about women's roles in society brought them back into discussion. Her books have been translated into Italian, German, and French.

Wharton was the daughter of George Frederic Jones, a descendent of the merchant ship-owners the Schermerhorns and the Rhinelanders. Her mother descended from Gen. Ebenezer Stevens, who took part in the Boston tea party, the expedition against Quebec, and the battle at Yorktown. Their sensibility, in part determined by their Dutch Reformed and Episcopalian beliefs, did not include a high regard for the world of art. Thus, when the teenager began to write verse and short stories, her family did not encourage it, and later seldom mentioned her literary success. The New York social circuit was also increasingly made up of the *nouveaux riches,* whose appreciation for culture lagged somewhat behind their knack for gaining wealth. Understandably shy in this environment, Edith happily traveled Europe with her parents. There she met Henry James, who became her mentor and admiring critic. When not traveling, she spent most of her time in her father's library, only entering the social milieu when her parents insisted.

In 1885, Edith married Boston banker Edward Robbins Wharton, known to the family because of his membership in her mother's social circle. He was more than ten years older than Edith and suffered ill health, which, combined with Edith's dissatisfactions with their social life, encouraged her to devote more of her time to writing. They owned a house in Newport, Rhode Island, which she redecorated with the help of the architect Ogden Codman. The book they wrote about the project, *The Decoration of Houses,* explained that a house's decor ought to express the owners' personalities instead of merely aping aristocratic tastes. The book sold well, to the dismay of her family; confirmed in her pursuit of a writing career by its success, she moved to Lenox, Massachusetts and enjoyed her association with other writers who lived nearby. Her next book was a volume of short stories, *The Greater Inclination,* published in 1899, followed by another collection and a novelette, *The Touchstone,* published in 1901 and 1902, respectively. She published, on the average, a book each year for the rest of her life.

These first stories were praised for their cleverness, Henry Dwight Sedgwick noted in an *Atlantic* piece on the novelist's work. "To most people," Sedgwick summarized, "the point she plays most brilliantly is the episode. . . . In Mrs. Wharton, this aptitude is not single, but a combination. It includes the sense of proportion, and markedly that elementary proportion of allotting the proper space for the introduction of the story,—so much to bring the *dramatis personae* into the ring, so much for the preliminary bouts, so much for the climax, and, finally, the proper length for the recessional. It includes the subordination of one character to another, of one picture to another, the arrangement of details in proper hierarchy to produce the desired effect." John Bayley wrote in the *Times Literary Supplement* that "her fiction, like her life, was built on rules and concealments. Neither, she must have felt, was worth much without them." *Bookman* critic Harry Thurston Peck commented in 1899, "In the way of fiction we have seen nothing this year that has impressed us so much as [*The Greater Inclination*]. . . . There is a finish, an assurance, and a tenacity of grasp about her work that show her to be already an accomplished literary artist."

The Writing of Fiction explained what Wharton had learned about the craft from her fellow novelist Henry James. Noticeable similarities in their works are based on a common interest in the rules of society as they encroach upon the freedom of individuals from several social strata, in particular the wealthy and the American abroad. Like characters drawn by James, Wharton's characters met with two kinds of tragedy, Calvin Winter explained in a *Bookman* review. Their problems were due "on the one hand, to the complications arising from not understanding, from the impossibility of ever wholly getting inside another person's mind; and on the other, from the realisation that one cannot escape from one's environment, that one's whole family and race have for generations been relentlessly weaving a network of custom and precedent too strong for the individual to break."

Wharton was sometimes harshly critical of society. Irving Howe commented in *Encounter*, "In *The Custom of the Country* . . . she turned to—I think it fair to say, she was largely the innovator of—a tough-spirited, fierce and abrasive satire of the barbaric philistinism she felt to be settling upon American society and the source of which she was inclined to locate, not with complete accuracy, in the new raw towns of the Midwest." A member of New York's elite having "old money," Wharton was keenly aware of the relative lack of gentility among those whose fortunes were gained in industry instead of real estate. The corrupting power of wealth was particularly evident among the *nouveaux riches* and the rising middle class. Howe added, "Endless numbers of American novels would later be written on this theme, and Sinclair Lewis would commonly be mentioned as a writer particularly indebted to *The Custom of the Country;* but the truth is that no American novelist of our time—with the single exception of Nathaniel West—has been so ruthless, so bitingly cold as Mrs. Wharton in assaulting the vulgarities and failures of our society."

Wharton was especially effective at piercing the veil of moral respectability that sometimes masked a lack of integrity among the rich. In *House of Mirth,* for example, an intelligent and lovely girl must lose her status as a member of the leisure class if she is to avoid moral ruin. Lily Bart rebels against the standards of her social group enough to smoke, gamble, and be seen in public with married men; however, her sense of decency keeps her from marrying a wealthy but vulgar suitor merely to secure her fortunes. Her other opportunity consists of a young lawyer who makes fun of the "high society" his modest but adequate means entitle him to observe. When the first proposes, she turns him down; when the second proposes, it is too late—he finds the distraught Lily dead of an overdose of sleeping pills. Publication of this best seller in 1905 provoked much discussion in the United States, where it was hailed as one of the best novels the country had ever produced.

Wharton believed that good faith among the rich was not to be taken for granted, since it was grounded not in conformity to social standards but in an individual's commitment to respond to the needs of the less fortunate. She also understood that social pressure among the poor could be just as confining. In her novel *Ethan Frome,* she shows how the title character suffers when he is caught between two women—his wife, on whom he depends for economic survival, and his true love, a younger relative of his wife's who has come to the farm to help with the work. Ethan and his love see no way out except suicide, but their attempt fails, and they become invalids waited on by Zeena. Edwin Bjoerkman commented in *Voices of Tomorrow: Critical Studies of the New Spirit in Literature* that Ethan lives "between those two spectres of his lost hopes: the woman he needed and the woman he loved. All other tragedies that I can think of seem mild and bearable beside this one." Though often regarded by reviewers as a departure from Wharton's usual subject matter, Bjoerkman suggested, "after all, the tragedy unveiled to us is social rather than personal. . . . 'Ethan Frome' is to me above all else a judgment on that system which fails to redeem such villages as Mrs. Wharton's Starkfield. Those who dwell in our thousand and one Starkfields are [as] wrecked mariners, fallen into their hapless positions through no fault of their own. And though helpless now, they need by no means prove useless under different conditions."

Some critics felt that Wharton's portraits of men were unfairly negative. "Men especially have a hard time of it in Mrs. Wharton's novels," Howe commented in *Encounter*. He continued, "In their notorious vanity and faithlessness, they seldom 'come through'; they fail Mrs. Wharton's heroines less from bad faith than weak imagination, a laziness of spirit that keeps them from a true grasp of suffering; and in a number of her novels one finds a suppressed feminine bitterness, a profound impatience with the claims of the ruling sex." *New York Times Book Review* contributor Janet Malcolm, however, looking back on *The House of Mirth, The Reef, The Custom of the Country,* and *The Age of Innocence,* remarked that in Wharton's fiction, "the callousness and heartlessness by which this universe is ruled is the callousness and heartlessness of women. There are no bad men in Wharton's fiction. There are weak men and there are foolish men and there are vulgar New Rich men, but no man ever deliberately causes harm to another person; that role is exclusively reserved for women." While not accusing Wharton of misanthropy or misogyny, other critics have spoken of her pervasive pessimism. Howe related Wharton's "feminist resentment" to "a more radical and galling inequity at the heart of the human scheme. The inability of human beings to achieve self-sufficiency drives them to seek relationships with other people, and these relationships necessarily compromise their freedom by subjecting them to the pain of a desire either too great or too small. Things, in Mrs. Wharton's world, do not work out."

Wharton produced a body of work that affirmed the need to conserve certain fundamental values that were quickly losing ground in the twentieth century. *The Valley of Decision,* her first long novel, depicted the moral decline in Italy during the eighteenth century, and was deemed a successful work of history recreated in exquisitely-crafted fiction. James W. Tuttleton explained in the *Yale Review,* "She continually argued the necessity of the individual's commitment to the cultural tradition; . . . the catastrophe which ensues when social upheavals like revolution, anarchy, and war destroy the slowly and delicately spun web of that tradition; and the necessity of imaginatively preserving . . . the precious values of the past." By showing in her fiction what becomes of people when culture ceases to be a moral force, and by recording her memories of a time when it was, Wharton "hoped to revive the memory of a set of slowly evolved cultural values suddenly wiped out by a succession of destructive changes in American life beginning in the 1880's—including the rise of the industrial plutocracy ('the lords of Pittsburgh,' as she called them); massive immigration which totally altered the ethnic character of New York City; the First World War, the depression, and the New Deal; and the nationalistic hatreds, at the close of her life in 1937, building toward the Second World War." Wharton seems to have "felt that the universe—which for her is virtually to say, organised society—was profoundly inhospitable to human need and desire," Howe commented in *Encounter*.

In addition to writing about the importance of values, Wharton validated them in her service to the less fortunate during and after the First World War. An energetic fund-raiser, she was aided by "Edith Wharton" committees in New York, Boston, Philadelphia, Washington, and Providence. With her financial support, an ambulance unit, a workroom for female garment workers, and a sanatorium for women and children with tuberculosis were established in France. She also compiled *Le livre des sans-foyer* (*The Book of the Homeless*), sold to raise money for American hostels for refugees and the Children of Flanders rescue committee. France recognized her philanthropy by awarding her the Cross of the Legion of Honor; she also was made Chevalier of the Order of Leopold in Belgium.

Books informed by her war experience, however, were not regarded as her best. Louis Auchincloss explained that she saw the war "from a simple but consistent point of view: France, virtually singlehanded, was fighting the battle of civilization against the powers of darkness. It was the spirit that made men fight and die, but it has never, unfortunately, been the spirit of fiction. Reading *The Marne . . .* and *A Son at the Front . . .* today gives one the feeling of taking an old enlistment poster out of an attic trunk. . . . Mrs. Wharton knew that the war was terrible; she had visited hospitals and even the front itself. But the exhilaration of the noncombatant, no matter how dedicated and useful her services, has a shrill sound to postwar ears."

After the First World War, *The Age of Innocence,* another novel about Old New York society, again showed passionate characters hemmed in by their desire to keep their membership in a dispassionate social group. Newland Archer is engaged to marry an acceptable and attractive girl, but falls in love with Ellen Olenska, a European divorcee. Olenska had married a Polish Count, a villain from whom she escaped with the eager aid of his secretary. Equally passionate but seeking to reestablish her honor in New York society (which is not sure she is acceptable), Olenska encourages Archer to keep his commitment. To make it easier for him, she returns to Europe. Thirty years later Archer's son is free to live the life of feeling Archer could not bring himself to embrace. "Archer, with his insecurity, his sensitivity, and his passion has obeyed the moral imperatives of his class and time and has given up Ellen and love for the furtherance of the shallow-seeming aims, all amorphous as they are, of his [New York] world," observed Louis O. Coxe in *New Republic.* Wharton allowed Archer to confess that a life of duty had its rewards—and yet it was a lonely life, since the next generation, represented by Archer's son, enjoyed a freedom from social pressure that made them unable to understand this kind of sacrifice, Coxe added. The novel was highly acclaimed as one of Wharton's best novels, and, according to *New York Times* writer W. L. Phelps, as "one of the best novels of the twentieth century" in 1920, and "a permanent addition to literature." *The Age of Innocence* won the Pulitzer Prize in 1921. Wharton believed the honor should have gone to Sinclair Lewis, who dedicated his next novel, *Babbitt,* to her in 1922.

Commenting on Wharton's place in literary history, Louise Bogan wrote in *Selected Criticism,* "Mrs. Wharton's work formed a bridge from the nineteenth-century novel to the magazine fiction of the present. . . . She contained in herself, as it were, the whole transitional period of American fiction, beginning in the bibelot and imported-European-culture era of the late nineties, and ending in the woman's-magazine dream of suburban smartness." Malcolm suggested, "Her strongest work . . . has a stylization and abstraction, a quality of 'madeness,' that propels it out of the sphere of 19th-century realism and nudges it toward the self-reflexive literary experimentation of [the 20th] century." In addition, Alfred Kazan noted in the *Virginia Quarterly Review,* Wharton "could speak out plainly with a force [James] never could muster; and her own alienation and loneliness gave her a sympathy for erratic spirits and illicit emotions that was unique in its time. It has been forgotten how much Edith Wharton contributed to the plain-speaking traditions of American realism." Ten years before her death in 1937, Wharton was nominated to receive the Nobel Prize in recognition that she had become the most distinguished American writer of her generation. That she did not receive the award does not diminish either her achievement in letters or the high esteem granted to her by her contemporaries in both America and Europe. Percy Lubbock maintained in *Portrait of Edith Wharton* in 1947, "The sagest and sternest of the craftsmen must admit that she meets them on their ground."

BIOGRAPHICAL/CRITICAL SOURCES:

BOOKS

Auchincloss, Louis, *Edith Wharton,* University of Minnesota Press, 1961.

Bauer, Dale M., *Edith Wharton's Brave New Politics,* University of Wisconsin Press, 1994.

Beer, Janet, *Kate Chopin, Edith Wharton, and Charolotte Perkins Gilman: Studies in Short Fiction,* St. Martin's Press, 1997.

Bell, Millicent, *The Cambridge Companion to Edith Wharton,* Cambridge University Press, 1995.

Benstock, Shari, *No Gifts from Chance: A Biography of Edith Wharton,* Macmillian (New York), 1994.

Bentley, Nancy, *The Ethnography of Manners: Hawthorne, James, Wharton,* Cambridge University Press, 1995.

Bjoerkman, Edwin, *Voices of Tomorrow: Critical Studies of the New Spirit in Literature,* Kennerly, 1913.

Bogan, Louise, *Selected Criticism,* Noonday, 1955.

Craig, Theresa (photography by John Bessler), *Edith Wharton: A House Full of Rooms, Architecture, Interiors, and Gardens,* Monacelli (New York), 1996.

Dictionary of Literary Biography, Gale (Detroit), Volume 4: *American Writers in Paris,* 1980; Volume 9: *American Novelists, 1910-1945,* 1981; Volume 12: *American Realists and Naturalists,* 1982.

Dwight, Eleanor, *Edith Wharton: An Extraordinary Life,* Abrams, 1994.

Dyman, Jenni, *Lurking Feminism: The Ghost Stories of Edith Wharton,* P. Lang, 1995.

Fedorko, Kathy A., *Gender and the Gothic in the Fiction of Edith Wharton,* University of Alabama Press, 1995.

Fracasso, Evelyn E., *Edith Wharton's Prisoners of Consciousness: A Study of Theme and Technique in the Tales,* Greenwood Press, 1994.

Gentry, Deborah S., *The Art of Dying: Suicide in the Works of Kate Chopin, Edith Wharton, and Sylvia Plath,* P. Lang, 1998.

Goodman, Susan, *Edith Wharton's Inner Circle,* University of Texas Press, 1994.

Killoran, Helen, *Edith Wharton: Art and Allusion,* University of Alabama Press, 1996.

Lubbock, Percy, *Portrait of Edith Wharton,* Appleton-Century, 1947.

McDowell, Margaret B., *Edith Wharton,* Twayne, 1976.

Nettles, Elsa, *Language and Gender in American Fiction: Howells, James, Wharton, and Cather,* University Press of Virginia, 1997.

Price, Alan, *The End of the Age of Innocence: Edith Wharton and the First World War,* St. Martin's Press, 1996.

Singley, Carol J., *Edith Wharton: Matters of Mind and Spirit,* Cambridge University Press, 1995.

Turk, Ruth, *Edith Wharton: Beyond the Age of Innocence,* Tudor (Greensboro, NC), 1997.

Twentieth-Century Literary Criticism, Gale, Volume 3, 1980; Volume 9, 1982.

Wagner-Martin, Linda, *The Age of Innocence: A Novel of Ironic Nostaglia,* Twayne Publishers, 1996.

White, Barbara A., *Edith Wharton: A Study of the Short Fiction,*

Worth, Richard, *Edith Wharton,* Messner (New York), 1994.

Wright, Sarah Bird, *Edith Wharton's Travel Writing: The Making of a Connoisseur,* St. Martin's Press, 1997.

Wright, Sarah Bird, *Edith Wharton A-Z: The Essential Guide to the Life and Work,* Facts on File, 1998.

PERIODICALS

American Literature, March, 1972.
Architectural Digest, March, 1994, p. 84.
Atlantic Monthly, August, 1906; February, 1978.
Bookman, volume 9, June, 1899; volume 33, 1911.
Encounter, July, 1962.
Films in Review, February, 1977.
Library Journal, July, 1994, p. 146; August, 1994, p. 154; October 15, 1994, p. 103; February 1, 1995, p. 112; July, 1995, p. 109; November 15, 1995, p. 116.
Life, April, 1994, p. 78.
London Review of Books, March 7, 1996. p. 21.
Nation, November 3, 1920.
New Republic, June 27, 1955.
Newsweek, September 22, 1975; October 9, 1995, p. 68.
New York, November 21, 1994, p. 70.
New Yorker, September 4, 1978.
New York Review of Books, February 23, 1978; November 30, 1995, p. 16.
New York Times, October 17, 1920; October 25, 1986.
New York Times Book Review, November 16, 1986; January 2, 1994, p. 7.
Publishers Weekly, November 6, 1995, p. 87.
Saturday Review, August 9, 1975.
School Library Journal, May, 1994, p. 73.
Sewanee Review, autumn, 1932.
Times (London), July 13, 1984.
Times Literary Supplement, April 1, 1988.
Twentieth Century Literature, January, 1973.
Variety, January 24, 1994, p. 68.
Virginia Quarterly Review, winter, 1941.
Yale Review, summer, 1972.

*   *   *

WHARTON, James
See MENCKEN, H(enry) L(ouis)

*   *   *

WHITE, E(lwyn) B(rooks) 1899-1985

PERSONAL: Born July 11, 1899, in Mount Vernon, NY; died after suffering from Alzheimer's disease, October 1, 1985, in North Brookline, ME; son of Samuel Tilly (a piano manufacturer) and Jessie (Hart) White; married Katharine Sergeant Angell (a *New Yorker* editor), November 13, 1929 (died, July 20, 1977); children: Joel McCoun; stepchildren: Nancy Angell Stableford, Roger Angell. *Education:* Cornell University, A.B., 1921.

CAREER: Reporter with United Press and the American Legion News Service, 1921; *Seattle Times,* Seattle, WA, reporter, 1922-23; copywriter with Frank Seaman, Inc., and Newmark, Inc., New York City, 1924-25; *New Yorker,* New York City, writer and contributing editor, beginning 1926. *Military service:* U.S. Army, 1918.

MEMBER: National Institute of Arts and Letters, American Academy of Arts and Sciences (fellow), American Academy of Arts and Letters, Phi Beta Kappa, Phi Gamma Delta.

AWARDS, HONORS: Limited Editions Club gold medal, 1945, for "a work most likely to attain the stature of a classic," for *One Man's Meat;* Litt.D., Dartmouth College, University of Maine, and Yale University, all 1948, Bowdoin College, 1950, Hamilton College, 1952, and Harvard University, 1954; Newbery Honor Book, 1953, Lewis Carroll Shelf Award, 1958, George C. Stone Center for Children's Books Recognition of Merit Award, 1970, and the New England Round Table of Children's Libraries Award, 1973, all for *Charlotte's Web;* Page One Award, New York Newspaper Guild, 1954, and National Association of Independent Schools Award, 1955, both for *The Second Tree from the Corner;* L.H.D., Colby College, 1954. National Institute of Arts and Letters gold medal, 1960, for his contribution to literature; Presidential Medal of Freedom, 1963; Laura Ingalls Wilder Award, American Library Association, 1970, for "a lasting contribution to children's literature"; National Medal for Literature, National Institute of Arts and Letters, 1971; *The Trumpet of the Swan* was nominated for a National Book Award, 1971, was included on the International Board on Books for Young People Honor List, 1972, and received the Children's Book Award from the William Allen White Library at Emporia State University, 1973, the Sequoyah Children's Book Award from the Oklahoma Library Association, 1973, the Sue Hefley Award from the Louisiana Association of School Librarians, 1974, and the Young Hoosier Award from the Indiana School Librarians Association, 1975; Pulitzer Prize special citation, 1978, for the body of his work.

WRITINGS:

The Lady Is Cold (poems), Harper, 1929.
(With James Thurber) *Is Sex Necessary?; or, Why You Feel the Way You Do,* Harper, 1929.
(Author of introduction) James Thurber, *The Owl in the Attic,* Harper, 1931.
(Editor) *Ho-Hum: Newsbreaks from the "New Yorker,"* Farrar & Rinehart, 1931.
(Editor) *Another Ho-Hum: More Newsbreaks from the "New Yorker,"* Farrar & Rinehart, 1932.
Alice through the Cellophane (pamphlet), John Day, 1933.
Every Day Is Saturday, Harper, 1934.
Farewell to Model T, Putnam, 1936.
The Fox of Peapack and Other Poems, Harper, 1938.
Quo Vadimus?; or, The Case for the Bicycle, Harper, 1939.
(Editor with wife, Katharine Sergeant White, and author of introduction) *A Subtreasury of American Humor,* Coward, 1941.
One Man's Meat (also see below; essays previously published in *Harper's*), Harper, 1942.
(Author of introduction) Roy E. Jones, *A Basic Chicken Guide for the Small Flock Owner,* Morrow, 1944.

World Government and Peace: Selected Notes and Comment, 1943-1945, F. R. Publishing, 1945.

Stuart Little (also see below; juvenile), Harper, 1945.

The Wild Flag: Editorials from the "New Yorker" on Federal World Government and Other Matters, Houghton, 1946.

Here Is New York, Harper, 1949.

(Author of introduction) Don Marquis, *the lives and times of archy and mehitabel,* Doubleday, 1950.

Charlotte's Web (also see below; juvenile), Harper, 1952.

The Second Tree from the Corner, Harper, 1954, new edition, with new introduction, 1984.

(Editorial supervisor and contributor) William Strunk, Jr., *The Elements of Style,* Macmillan, 2nd edition (White not associated with previous edition), 1959, 3rd edition, 1979.

The Points of My Compass: Letters from the East, the West, the North, the South, Harper, 1962.

An E. B. White Reader, edited by William W. Watt and Robert W. Bradford, Harper, 1966.

Topics: Our New Countryman at the U.N. (pamphlet), Congressional Press, 1968.

The Trumpet of the Swan (also see below; juvenile), Harper, 1970.

E. B. White Boxed Set (contains *Charlotte's Web, Stuart Little,* and *The Trumpet of the Swan*), Harper, 1975.

Letters of E. B. White, edited by Dorothy Lobrano Guth, Harper, 1976.

Essays of E. B. White, Harper, 1977.

(Editor) K. S. White, *Onward and Upward in the Garden,* Farrar, Straus, 1979.

Poems and Sketches of E. B. White, Harper, 1981.

(With others) *A Gift from Maine,* Guy Gannett, 1984.

Writings from the New Yorker, 1925-1976, edited by Rebecca M. Dale, Harper, 1990.

Author of column, "One Man's Meat," *Harper's,* 1938-43.

RECORDINGS

Stuart Little, Dell, 1973.

Charlotte's Web (narrated by White), RCA, 1976.

MEDIA ADAPTATIONS: Stuart Little was filmed for television by the National Broadcasting Company in 1966; *Charlotte's Web* was adapted as an animated film by Paramount in 1972. The short story "The Family That Dwelt Apart" was adapted as an animated film by Learning Corporation of America in 1974.

SIDELIGHTS: Few writers have achieved recognition in as many fields as did E. B. White. He was regarded as one of the finest essayists of the twentieth century; he was the author of two classics of children's literature, *Charlotte's Web* and *Stuart Little;* and his extensive contributions to the *New Yorker* were instrumental in making that magazine a success.

White began his writing career in 1921 after graduating from Cornell University, where he served as editor of the school newspaper. He worked for a time as a reporter with two news services in New York City, then drove a Model T cross country with his friend Howard Cushman. "When they ran out of money," the late James Thurber recounted in an article for the *Saturday Review of Literature,* "they played for their supper—and their gasoline—on a fascinating musical instrument that White had made out of some pieces of wire and an old shoe or something." Ending up in Seattle, White took a job as a reporter for the *Seattle Times.* He lasted less than a year. White explained in *The Points of My Compass: Letters from the East, the West, the North, the South:* "As a newspaper reporter I was almost useless." He worked for a short time as a mess boy on a ship bound for Alaska

but soon returned to New York, where he spent two years as an advertising copywriter.

It was while working as a copywriter that White began to submit short pieces to the fledgling *New Yorker* magazine, barely a few months old at the time. Editor Harold Ross "was so taken by the pieces White submitted to *The New Yorker,*" John Ciardi wrote in the *Washington Post Book World,* "that he hired White to write the 'Talk of the Town' section with which the magazine still opens." Both Ross and Katharine Angell, the magazine's literary editor who later became White's wife, found White's style ideal for the *New Yorker.* They "were not slow to perceive that here were the perfect eye and ear, the authentic voice and accent for their struggling magazine," Thurber stated. Over the next forty years, White contributed poems, essays, sketches, stories, and even photo captions to the *New Yorker.* He wrote the "Talk of the Town" section for eleven years. For many years, too, he wrote the "Newsbreak" fillers, short items taken from magazines and newspapers and reprinted with a humorous comment. White, Thurber explained, "had a hand in everything: he even painted a cover and wrote a few advertisements."

In 1929 White collaborated with Thurber on *Is Sex Necessary?; or, Why You Feel the Way You Do,* a spoof of sex manuals. The book made "both White and Thurber well known," according to Edward C. Sampson in the *Dictionary of Literary Biography.* The two authors, Sampson explained, "parody the serious writers on the subject, making light of complexities, taking a mock-serious attitude toward the obvious, delighting in reducing the case-history technique to an absurdity, and making fun of those writers who proceeded by definition." They expound on such crucial topics as "Osculatory Justification," "Schmalhausen Trouble" (when couples live in small apartments), and "The Nature of the American Male: A Study of Pedestalism." Will Cuppy of the *New York Herald Tribune Book Review* called *Is Sex Necessary?* "a minor classic—and one uses the term 'minor' only because it is gorgeously funny and not quite ponderous enough to be major. Let's compromise and just call it a classic." Thurber's drawings, turned out in a few hours, illustrate the book, which has gone through more than twenty-five printings since it first appeared. White's share of the royalties enabled him to marry Katharine Angell on November 13, 1929.

Over the years, it has been White's essays for the *New Yorker*—many of which are collected in 1977's *Essays of E. B. White*—that have done the most to build his literary reputation. White's essays are personal and informal, seem to happen upon their subject as they ramble along, and have a gentle humor about them. New York City, where the *New Yorker* has its offices, and the Maine countryside, where White owned a farm, are the two most common settings. White often began with a small incident in his own life and then extrapolated larger implications from it. One of his first pieces for the *New Yorker,* for example, was a recounting of an accident at a Manhattan restaurant in which a glass of buttermilk was spilled on his suit. The waitress, White related, "was a little girl, so I let her blot me. In my ear she whispered a million apologies, hopelessly garbled, infinitely forlorn. And I whispered that the suit was four years old, and that I hated dark clothes anyway. One has, in life, so few chances to lie heroically." In other pieces, Christopher Lehmann-Haupt of the *New York Times* noted, White has arrived "at the subject of disarmament by way of Mary Martin's furniture, or at the prospects of American democracy by the route of a dachshund named Fred." This idea is echoed by the late Joseph Wood Krutch, writing in the *Saturday Review,* who maintained that White is "generally concerned less with the Queen than with the little mouse under her chair." William Howarth of the *Washington Post Book World* argued that, for White, "connecting small moments to big issues is a literary impulse." Howarth went on to say that White "can capture moments of rare evanescence—a small tree, second from the corner and backlit by the sun, 'each gilt-edged leaf perfectly drunk with excellence and delicacy.'"

When White turned his attention to political matters, he often focused on the arms race and the tensions between the world's nations. His approach to politics was typically oblique. In one essay published in *The Second Tree from the Corner,* for example, White tells of participating in a routine air raid drill in his office building. As his elevator passes the thirteenth floor on its way to the basement, he notices that it is numbered "14." Nuclear scientists had successfully looked "into the core of the sun," White observed, "but it might have been a good idea if they had waited to do that until the rest of us could look the number 13 square in the face. Such is the true nature of our peculiar dilemma." White was known as a forceful advocate of world government, which he recommended for democratic nations only, and as a defender of individual privacy.

A concern for the environment, inspired by Henry David Thoreau's *Walden,* was also evident in White's life and work. White described Thoreau, in one of the essays collected in *The Points of My Compass,* as being the companion and chider for the "fellows who hate compromise and have compromised, fellows who love wildness and have lived tamely," and as the man "who long ago gave corroboration to impulses they perceived were right and issued warnings against things they instinctively knew to be their enemies." In common with Thoreau, White was skeptical about the benefits of material progress and suspected that perhaps what has been left behind is more valuable than what has replaced it. He is, Louis Hasley commented in the *Connecticut Review,* "a cautious critic of progress, fearing the loss of the precious sense for basic things." Following the example of Thoreau, who lived close to the land, White in 1934 bought a salt water farm in North Brookline, Maine. He and his wife moved there permanently in 1938 and took to raising geese, chickens, and sheep. The essays collected in *One Man's Meat,* originally written as monthly columns for *Harper's* magazine, are set on White's farm and chronicle his daily life in the country.

Although White's essays have won him overwhelming critical acclaim, he was more popularly known as the author of *Charlotte's Web* and *Stuart Little,* two classics of American children's literature. White wrote only three books for children in all, but many observers rank him with such notables in the field of children's literature as Lewis Carroll, the author of *Alice in Wonderland.* Sampson acknowledged that *Charlotte's Web* "may well turn out to be the longest remembered of his works." "What makes White's three books outstanding," Sampson continued, "is that he has written them in the classical tradition of children's stories. . . . What the child [learns from White's books]—and what children learn from the other fine children's books—is a great deal about loyalty, honesty, love, sadness, and happiness."

Inspired by a vivid dream, White began in 1939 to write a children's story about a small, mouse-like character. Whenever one of his eighteen nieces and nephews wanted to be told a story, White improvised new adventures for his hero, whom he named Stuart Little. In 1945, he gathered these adventures together into a book-length manuscript which he sent to Harper & Row for consideration. Children's book editor Ursula Nordstrom found it

"marvelously well-written, and funny, and touching," she recalled in an article for the *New York Times Book Review,* and accepted *Stuart Little* for publication.

The book tells the story of the Little family's second child, Stuart, who happens to be two inches tall and looks like a mouse, although the Littles themselves are normal-sized and human. Because of his modest stature and adventurous nature, Stuart finds himself in a series of wild situations: he is hoisted aloft by a window shade, attacked by a housecat, dropped into a bathtub drain to retrieve a lost ring, and even put into a piano to free some stuck keys. Stuart's "somewhat random adventures show him to be brave, ingenious, enterprising, and of romantic inclination," Peter M. Neumeyer wrote in the *Dictionary of Literary Biography.* Neumeyer also believed that White "has imaginatively extrapolated [Stuart's adventures] with all the ingenuity of Jonathan Swift plotting Gulliver's stay in Lilliput."

When Stuart's newfound love Margalo, a bird, flies away to escape the Littles' housecat, Stuart follows. The remainder of the book concerns his unsuccessful quest for her. "Like any knight errant," Neumeyer wrote, "Stuart is tempted and distracted during this pursuit." These distractions include wooing a girl during a canoe ride and teaching a class of fifth-graders when their regular teacher is sick. But the book ends with Stuart driving away in his toy car, continuing his search for Margalo. Calling *Stuart Little* "a lively and, at times, tender book that is a delight to both the imagination and the emotions," John Gillespie and Diana Lembo nevertheless found that "the rather inconclusive ending has somewhat marred its appeal for a few readers." Speaking of the book's ending in his *Letters of E. B. White,* White revealed: "Quite a number of children have written me to ask about Stuart. They want to know whether he got back home and whether he found Margalo. They are good questions, but I did not answer them in the book because, in a way, Stuart's journey symbolizes the continuing journey that everybody takes—in search of what is perfect and unattainable. This is perhaps too elusive an idea to put into a book for children, but I put it in anyway." John Rowe Townsend, in his *Written for Children: An Outline of English Language Children's Literature,* mused that "perhaps the ending is right; Stuart's is a quest for freedom and beauty, and such a quest is never completed."

Several reviewers believed that *Stuart Little* has the same wide appeal as do the classics of children's literature. Writing in the *Saturday Review of Literature,* R. C. Benet believed that readers of all ages will enjoy the book. "The exact number of years of the reader," he stated, "won't matter here any more than it does with 'Alice,' 'The Wind in the Willows,' some of [A. A.] Milne, or indeed the work of Walt Disney, who created that other popular mouse." The *Springfield Republican* critic agreed, finding that "readers of [Ernest] Hemingway as well as six-year-olds will find the book worth their while, much as grown-up readers of 'Alice in Wonderland' . . . find that classic. 'Stuart Little,' indeed, is in the school of 'Alice,' though by no means an imitation." It is a "memorable *Wanderjahr* for children," Timothy Foote wrote in *Time,* "loaded with longing and nostalgia." Foote went on to note that *Stuart Little* "still sells and sells." On its way to becoming "one of the classics of American children's literature," as Neumeyer described it, *Stuart Little* has sold more than two million copies in English and has been translated into twenty other languages.

White's next children's book, *Charlotte's Web,* was published in 1952. Without fanfare, or even a previous mention that he was working on another children's book, White dropped by his publisher's office with the manuscript. He took Nordstrom by surprise. "He gave me the only copy in existence of 'Charlotte's Web,'" she remembered, "got back on the elevator and left." Nordstrom read only a few chapters before deciding to publish the book. "I couldn't believe that it was so good!" she commented.

Called by Roger Sale in his *Fairy Tales and After: From Snow White to E. B. White* "probably *the* classic American children's book of the last thirty years," *Charlotte's Web* is set on a farm much like the one White owned in Maine. The story "seems to have developed," Neumeyer observed, "directly and exclusively out of White's joy in his own rural existence." White explained to Lee Bennett Hopkins in *More Books by More People:* "I like animals and my barn is a very pleasant place to be. . . . One day when I was on my way to feed the pig, I began feeling sorry for the pig because, like most pigs, he was doomed to die. This made me sad. So I started thinking of ways to save a pig's life. I had been watching a big, gray spider at her work and was impressed by how clever she was at weaving. Gradually I worked the spider into the story, . . . a story of friendship and salvation on a farm." Sale noted that White has referred to *Charlotte's Web* as a "hymn to the barn." "It is the word 'hymn,'" Sale wrote, "and the sense of celebration and praise, that is important here. . . . The essential celebration is of the beautiful things change brings or can bring."

Charlotte's Web tells the story of Wilbur, a small pig destined for slaughter, who is saved by his friend Charlotte, a spider, when she weaves the words "Some Pig" into a web above Wilbur's pen. People who see this miraculous message are so impressed by it that Wilbur is spared and even put on display at the local fair. But during their stay at the fair, Charlotte dies. In the final lines of the book, Wilbur remembers her as being "in a class by herself. It is not often that someone comes along who is a true friend and a good writer. Charlotte was both." David Rees, writing in *The Marble in the Water: Essays on Contemporary Writers of Fiction for Children and Young Adults,* called *Charlotte's Web* "the one great modern classic about death." Speaking of the book's closing lines, Rees believed them to be "comforting, not depressing. White is telling the child that he is allowed to mourn; that he is allowed to remember with a certain sadness." "The profound themes of selfless love and acceptance of death are found in this story," Gillespie and Lembo wrote, "and are significantly although delicately explored."

Charlotte's death is shown to be a natural part of the cycle of existence. It is "made bearable," Townsend believed, "by the continuance of life through her offspring." Rees pointed out that immediately following the passage about Charlotte's death comes another passage about the birth of her children and of small animals on the farm. White's idea "that death is an inevitable and necessary part of the whole scheme of things," Rees stated, "is made acceptable by the emphasis he puts, after Charlotte dies, on the joy and happiness of birth." Townsend, too, saw that "the passage of seasons, the round of nature, are unobtrusively indicated" throughout the story.

Charlotte's Web is written in a style that reminded Neumeyer of "an eighteenth-century definition of poetry: 'proper words in proper places'—the *mot juste.*" This quality is also noted by Eleanor Cameron in her study *The Green and Burning Bush: On the Writing and Enjoyment of Children's Books.* "The artistry of [*Charlotte's Web*]," Cameron wrote, "lies not at all in the use of unusual words but, as in all of Mr. White's prose for adults and

children alike, in the way he combines words, creates intimations." In *A Critical History of Children's Literature,* contributor Ruth Hill Viguers argued that the story of *Charlotte's Web* is thin and nonsensical, but that White, partly through his style, manages to overcome this weakness. "Mr. White has triumphed," Viguers stated. "The style and wit of his writing, his wisdom and his remembrance of a child's rapt concern with the things he loves strengthened the slender thread of story."

Critical evaluation of *Charlotte's Web* places it among the very best of its genre. It is "outstanding among post-war American children's fiction," Townsend believed. "As a piece of work," Eudora Welty wrote in the *New York Times,* "[*Charlotte's Web*] is just about perfect, and just about magical in the way it is done." The reviewer for the *Chicago Sunday Tribune* judged *Charlotte's Web* to be a "rare story of a beautiful friendship," as well as "witty and wise, lively and tender." Since its initial publication in 1952, *Charlotte's Web* has become a classic of American children's literature and has sold well over three million copies. Among books for children, Neumeyer summed up, *Charlotte's Web* "must surely be one of the most widely read and best beloved of this century."

Not until 1970 did White published his next children's book, *The Trumpet of the Swan.* It has much in common with his earlier efforts. As in *Stuart Little* and *Charlotte's Web,* the characters in *The Trumpet of the Swan* are animals who participate in the human world and overcome great obstacles to achieve their desires. And like the previous two books, *The Trumpet of the Swan* grew out of an experience in White's own life. His fascination with the trumpeter swans at the Philadelphia Zoo, initiated by a story in the *New York Times,* led White to tell the story of Louis, a voiceless trumpeter swan. Because he cannot speak, his human friend Sam Beaver takes Louis to school with him to learn to read and write. Thereafter, Louis carries a chalkboard and chalk with him to write out his messages. His father, wanting him to be able to communicate with other swans as well, steals a trumpet for him to play. Soon Louis's trumpet playing leads to nightclub work and to a meeting with Serena, a female swan with whom he falls in love.

Writing in the *New York Times Book Review,* John Updike expressed his opinion that *The Trumpet of the Swan* joins *Stuart Little* and *Charlotte's Web* "on the shelf of classics." Although it differs from the previous books, Updike found that *Trumpet* "has superior qualities of its own; it is the most spacious and serene of the three, the one most imbued with the author's sense of the precious instinctual heritage represented by wild nature, . . . yet [the book] does not lack the inimitable tone of the two earlier works—the simplicity that never condescends, the straight and earnest telling that happens upon, rather than veers into, comedy." Neumeyer believed that although it does not compare favorably with *Stuart Little* and *Charlotte's Web, The Trumpet of the Swan* "is adventurous, imaginative, and it has some touching moments."

Upon receiving the National Medal for Literature in 1971, White wrote an article for *Publishers Weekly* in which he thanked the National Institute of Arts and Letters for the award. In this article he defines the role of the writer. "I have always felt," White stated, "that the first duty of a writer was to ascend—to make flights, carrying others along if he could manage it. To do this takes courage. . . . Today, with so much of earth damaged and endangered, with so much of life dispiriting or joyless, a writer's courage can easily fail him. I feel this daily. . . . But despair is not good—for the writer, for anyone. Only hope can carry us aloft. . . . Only hope, and a certain faith. . . . This faith is a writer's faith, for writing itself is an act of faith, nothing else. And it must be the writer, above all others, who keeps it alive—choked with laughter, or with pain."

BIOGRAPHICAL/CRITICAL SOURCES:

BOOKS

Agosta, Lucien L., *E. B. White: The Children's Books,* Twayne (New York), 1995.

Berg, Julie, *E. B. White,* Abdo & Daughters, 1994.

Cameron, Eleanor, *The Green and Burning Bush: On the Writing and Enjoyment of Children's Books,* Atlantic-Little, Brown, 1969.

Children's Literature Review, Volume 1, Gale (Detroit), 1976.

Contemporary Literary Criticism, Gale, Volume 10, 1979; Volume 34, 1985; Volume 39, 1986.

Dictionary of Literary Biography, Gale, Volume 11: *American Humorists, 1800-1950,* Part 2, 1982; Volume 22: *American Writers for Children, 1900-1960,* 1983.

Elledge, Scott, *E. B. White: A Biography,* Norton, 1984.

Fadiman, Clifton, *Party of One,* World Publishing, 1955.

Gherman, Beverly, *E. B. White, Some Writer!* (biography), Beech Tree Books, 1994.

Gillespie, John, and Diana Lembo, *Introducing Books: A Guide for the Middle Grades,* Bowker, 1970.

Gillespie, John, and Diana Lembo, *Juniorplots: A Book Talk Manual for Teachers and Librarians,* Bowker, 1967.

Hopkins, Lee Bennett, *More Books by More People,* Citation, 1974.

Neumeyer, Peter F., *The Annotated Charlotte's Web,* HarperCollins, 1994.

Rees, David, *The Marble in the Water: Essays on Contemporary Writers of Fiction for Children and Young Adults,* Horn Book, 1980.

Rogers, Barbara J., *E. B. White,* Scribner, 1979.

Root, Robert L., *Critical Essays on E. B. White,* G. K. Hall, 1994.

Sale, Roger, *Fairy Tales and After: From Snow White to E. B. White,* Harvard University Press, 1978.

Sampson, Edward C., *E. B. White,* Twayne, 1974.

Tingum Janice, *E. B. White: The Elements of a Writer,* Lerner (Minneapolis), 1995.

Townsend, John Rowe, *Written for Children: An Outline of English Language Children's Literature,* revised edition, Lippincott, 1974.

PERIODICALS

Chicago Tribune, November 2, 1990.

Los Angeles Times Book Review, August 22, 1982.

Nation, August 14, 1929.

National Review, June 10, 1977.

New Republic, February 15, 1954; November 24, 1962.

New York Herald Tribune Book Review, May 26, 1929; December 28, 1929; January 17, 1954; October 21, 1962.

New York Review of Books, October 27, 1977.

New York Times, October 7, 1934; October 28, 1945; October 19, 1952; January 17, 1954; July 11, 1969; January 23, 1970; November 17, 1976; September 19, 1977; November 20, 1981; October 27, 1985; February 11, 1986; December 19, 1990.

New York Times Book Review, October 28, 1962; May 24, 1970; June 28, 1970; May 12, 1974; November 8, 1981.

Publishers Weekly, December 6, 1971; December 13, 1976.

Saturday Review, January 30, 1954; November 24, 1962; June 27, 1970.

Saturday Review of Literature, December 7, 1929; October 27, 1934; October 15, 1938; December 8, 1945; August 30, 1947.

Springfield Republican, October 21, 1945.

Time, December 20, 1976; January 25, 1982.

Washington Post, December 1, 1982.

Washington Post Book World, November 8, 1981; October 14, 1984.

Wilson Library Bulletin, February, 1972.

*   *   *

WHITE, Edmund (Valentine III) 1940-

PERSONAL: Born January 13, 1940, in Cincinnati, OH; son of Edmund Valentine II (an engineer) and Delilah (a psychologist; maiden name, Teddlie) White. *Education:* University of Michigan, B.A., 1962.

ADDRESSES: Agent—Maxine Groffsky, Maxine Groffsky Literary Agency, 2 Fifth Ave., New York, NY 10011.

CAREER: Time, Inc., Book Division, New York City, writer, 1962-70; Saturday Review, New York City, senior editor, 1972-73; Johns Hopkins University, Baltimore, MD, assistant professor of writing seminars, 1977-79; Columbia University School of the Arts, New York City, adjunct professor of creative writing, 1981-83; Brown University, Providence, RI, professor, 1990-92; writer. Instructor in creative writing at Yale University, New York University, and George Mason University, Fairfax, VA. Executive director of New York Institute for the Humanities, 1982-83.

AWARDS, HONORS: Hopwood Awards, University of Michigan, 1961 and 1962, for fiction and drama; Ingram Merrill grants, 1973 and 1978; Guggenheim fellow, 1983; American Academy and Institute of Arts and Letters award for fiction, 1983; citation for appeal and value to youth from Enoch Pratt Free Library's Young Adult Advisory Board, 1988, for *The Beautiful Room Is Empty;* Chevalier de l'ordre des arts et lettres, 1993; National Book Critics Circle award for biography, 1994, for *Genet: A Biography.*

WRITINGS:

NONFICTION

(With Peter Wood) *When Zeppelins Flew,* Time-Life (Alexandria, VA), 1969.

(With Dale Browne) *The First Men,* Time-Life, 1973.

(With Charles Silverstein) *The Joy of Gay Sex: An Intimate Guide for Gay Men to the Pleasures of a Gay Lifestyle,* Crown (New York City), 1977.

States of Desire: Travels in Gay America, Dutton (New York City), 1980.

Genet: A Biography, Knopf (New York City), 1993.

NOVELS

Forgetting Elena, Random House (New York City), 1973.

Nocturnes for the King of Naples, St. Martin's (New York City), 1978.

A Boy's Own Story, Dutton, 1982, reprinted with new introduction by White, 1994.

Caracole, Dutton, 1985.

The Beautiful Room Is Empty, Knopf (New York City), 1988.

OTHER

Blue Boy in Black (play), produced off-Broadway, 1963.

(With others) *Aphrodisiac* (short stories), Chatto (London), 1984.

(With Adam Mars-Jones) *The Darker Proof: Stories from a Crisis,* New American Library/Plume, 1988.

(Editor) *The Faber Book of Gay Short Fiction,* Faber & Faber (Winchester, MA), 1991.

(Compiler) *The Selected Writings of Jean Genet,* Ecco Press (New York City), 1993.

The Burning Library: Essays, Knopf, 1994.

Skinned Alive: Stories, Knopf, 1995.

Our Paris: Sketches from Memory, Knopf, 1995.

Also author of *Argument for Myth.* Contributor to anthologies, including *The Fabric of Memory: Ewa Kuryluk: Cloth Works, 1978-1987,* Northwestern University Press, 1987. Contributor of articles and reviews to *Architectural Digest, Artforum International, Home and Garden, Mother Jones, New York Times Book Review, Savvy Woman, Southwest Review,* and other periodicals. Editor, *Saturday Review* and *Horizon;* contributing editor, *Vogue.*

SIDELIGHTS: Edmund White is a master stylist who has produced acclaimed novels, intrepid and insightful nonfiction on gay society, and semi-autobiographical novels that combine the best features of fiction and nonfiction. Known as a "gay writer," White also belongs among those writers whose literary reputations transcend simplistic labels. William Goldstein explains in *Publishers Weekly,* "To call Edmund White merely a gay writer is to oversimplify his work and his intentions. Although that two-word label . . . aptly sums up White's status, the first word no doubt helps obscure the fact that the second applies just as fittingly." White's fiction in particular has garnered critical acclaim; the author has received grants from the Ingram Merrill Foundation, the Guggenheim Foundation, and the American Academy and Institute of Arts and Letters. White's studies of the gay lifestyle and changing attitudes about homosexuality in America, including the impact of AIDS on the gay community, are important contributions to contemporary social history. Though male homosexuality is the subject of his nonfiction, White offers insights into human behavior in general, according to reviewers. *Nation* contributor Carter Wilson comments, "Edmund White is to be envied not only for his productivity, . . . but because he is a gifted writer who has staked himself a distinguished claim in the rocky territory called desire."

White's wish to have his works appreciated as serious literature seems to have been granted from the outset of his fiction-writing career. Critics praised his first novel, *Forgetting Elena,* for its satiric and insightful look at social interaction as well as for its elegant prose. A first-person narrative of an amnesia victim struggling to determine his identity and the identities of those around him, *Forgetting Elena* exposes the subtle entrapments of social hierarchy and etiquette. White told *Library Journal* that the novel's premise illustrates the "sinister" aspects of life in an artistically obsessed society. In such a culture, he explained, "Every word and gesture would . . . convey a symbolic meaning. Ordinary morality would be obscured or forgotten. People would seek the beautiful and not the good—and, perhaps, cut free from the ethics, the beautiful would turn out to be merely pretty." Setting the novel's action at a fictitious resort reminiscent of New York's Fire Island, White creates, in the words of *Nation* contributor Simon Karlinsky, "a semiology of snobbery, its complete sign system." Karlinsky feels that "what might at first seem to be merely a witty parody of a particular subculture's foibles and vagaries actually turns out to be something far more serious and profound. . . . He has produced a parable about the nature of social interaction that transcends any given period and applies to the human predicament at large."

Most critics consider *Forgetting Elena* a highly accomplished first novel. Karlinsky calls the work "an astounding piece of writing—profound, totally convincing and memorable." Alan Friedman likewise praises the book in the *New York Times Book Review,* though not without qualifications. Friedman writes, "There is something so unfailingly petty about the narrator's apprehensions . . . and something so oppressive about his preoccupations . . . that it is often difficult to be receptive to the book's genuine wonders." Friedman nevertheless concludes that this "tale of a sleuth who strives to detect the mystery of the self" is "an astonishing first novel, obsessively fussy, yet uncannily beautiful."

Nocturnes for the King of Naples, White's second novel, won acclaim for its discerning treatment of human values and relationships. As John Yohalem explains in the *New York Times Book Review,* "*Nocturnes* is a series of apostrophes to a nameless, evidently famous dead lover, a man who awakened the much younger, also nameless narrator . . . to the possibility of sexual friendship. It was an experience that the narrator feels he did not justly appreciate," Yohalem continues, "and that he has long and passionately—and fruitlessly—sought to replace on his own terms." David Shields of the *Chicago Tribune* offers this assessment of the novel's impact: "Because of the speaker's final realization of the impossibility of ever finding a ground for satisfaction, a home, this book is more than a chronicle of sorrow and regret. It becomes, rather, a true elegy in which sorrow and self-knowledge combine and transform into a higher form of insight. This higher insight is the artistic intuition of the mortality of human things and ways."

According to J. D. McClatchy in *Shenandoah,* White's "special gift is his ability to empty out our stale expectations from genres . . . and types . . . and to reimagine them in a wholly intriguing and convincing manner." While Doris Grumbach suggests in the *Washington Post Book World* that White "will seem to the careful reader to be the poet of the burgeoning homosexual literature," she also notes, "The music of White's prose is seductive. It is of course possible that a tone-deaf, a melody-indifferent reader might turn his back on White's homo-erotic narrative." However, she adds, White's prose in *Nocturnes* promises satisfaction to "the lover of good fictional writing who is open to this most subtle exploration of the many ways of love, desertion, loss, and regret."

Caracole, White's 1985 novel, goes back to an earlier century and retrieves a more elaborate fictional form. Christopher Lehmann-Haupt observes in his *New York Times* column that White has "certainly conceived a 19th century plot steeped in the conventions of romanticism" when he writes of two country lovers forcibly separated who turn to sexual escapades in a large city. The resulting story is a "puzzling melange of comic opera and sleek sensuality," says the reviewer. *New York Times Book Review* contributor David R. Slavitt describes *Caracole* as "a grand fantasy. . . . Shrewdness and self-awareness ooze from every intricate sentence, every linguistic arabesque and hothouse epigram." Slavitt concludes that *Caracole* "is, provokingly, a challenge to taste, which is likely to vary from one reader to another or even from moment to moment in the same reader."

White's nonfiction on the gay life in America is as compelling as his fiction. *The Joy of Gay Sex: An Intimate Guide for Gay Men to the Pleasures of a Gay Lifestyle,* published in the late 1970s, attempted to make the topic less mysterious for curious heterosexuals and to provide useful information for gay men. In 1980, White published *States of Desire: Travels in Gay America.* A documentary on segments of homosexual life in fifteen major American cities, *States of Desire* contains interviews, autobiographical reminiscences, and accounts of cultural and entertainment centers for gays. According to Ned Rorem in the *Washington Post Book World*, *States of Desire* "poses as a documentary . . . on our national gay bourgeoisie. Actually it's an artist's selective vision . . . of human comportment which is and is not his own, mulled over, distilled, then spilled onto the page with a melancholy joy."

Some critics feel White's scope and objectivity are limited in *States of Desire*. Goldstein points out, "Nowhere in [the book] is there any sense of how different life is for a working-class homosexual, for a lesbian, or for a black." *New York Times Book Review* contributor Paul Cowan comments that White does not make "the promiscuous America he portrays . . . even remotely attractive to an outsider." Despite these qualifications, critics find much to applaud in *States of Desire*. John Leonard concludes in the *New York Times*, "Simply as anthropology, *States of Desire* commands attention and respect."

The Joy of Gay Sex and *States of Desire* qualified White as one of the most prominent spokespersons for gay men in America. He knew that publishing these works would engage him in politics to some extent. He explained in a *Paris Review* interview, "It was a political act for me to sign the *The Joy of Sex* at the time. The publisher could not have cared less, but for me it was a big act of coming out. Charles Silverstein, my co-author, and I were both aware that we would be addressing a lot of people and so in that sense we were spokesmen. We always pictured our ideal reader as someone who thought he was the only homosexual in the world. *States of Desire* was an attempt to see the varieties of gay experience and also to suggest the enormous range of gay life to straight and gay people—to show that gays aren't just hairdressers, they're also petroleum engineers and ranchers and short-order cooks. Once I'd written *States of Desire* I felt it was important to show one gay life in particular depth, rather than all of these lives in a shorthand version. *A Boy's Own Story* and its sequel, *The Beautiful Room Is Empty,* grew out of that."

In addition to his accomplished fiction and nonfiction, White has produced several semi-autobiographical novels that bring together the best features of both kinds of writing, beginning with *A Boy's Own Story,* a first-person narrative of a homosexual boy's adolescence during the 1950s. As a *Harper's* reviewer describes it, *A Boy's Own Story* "is a poignant combination of the two genres . . . written with the flourish of a master stylist." The main conflict in this psychological novel is the narrator's battle against negative judgments from society and from within. Emotional turmoil related to homosexuality, though prominent in the novel, is only one difficulty among many related to coming of age, the *Harper's* reviewer observes. "[*A Boy's Own Story*] is an endearing portrait of a child's longing to be charming, popular, powerful, and loved, and of his struggles with adults, . . . told with . . . sensitivity and elegance."

More than one reviewer has called *A Boy's Own Story* a "classic" work. Comparing White to James Baldwin, Herman Wouk, and Mary McCarthy, Thomas M. Disch writes in the *Washington Post Book World* that the novel "represents the strongest bid to date by a gay writer to do for his minority experience what the writers above did for theirs—offer it as a representative, all-American instance." *New York Times Book Review* contributor Catharine R. Stimpson finds the book "as artful as [White's] earlier novels but more explicit and grounded in detail, far less fanciful and

elusive. . . . Balancing the banal and the savage, the funny and the lovely, he achieves a wonderfully poised fiction." *Voice Literary Supplement* columnist Eliot Fremont-Smith concludes: "*A Boy's Own Story* seems intended to be liberating, as well as touching and clever and smart. It is something else as well: unsettling to the willing heart. This makes it a problem, with no happy solution guaranteed, which defines what's wrong with the book. But also what's right, what intrigues." Lehmann-Haupt calls the work "superior fiction," adding: "Somehow . . . Mr. White does succeed in almost simultaneously elevating and demeaning his self-history. And these extremes of epiphany and emptiness are what is most universal about this haunting Bildungsroman."

In *The Beautiful Room Is Empty,* the sequel to *A Boy's Own Story,* the narrator alternately revels in his homosexuality and rejects himself for it. Psychoanalysis and increasing surrender to sensual activity escalate the young man's battle for self-acceptance. Though his sexuality troubles him, the excitement and audacity of his experiences with gay men in public restrooms seems a needed respite from the blandness of his suburban life. While recreating these scenes, White evokes both humor and terror. The gay characters easily upstage the others in the book with their outspoken opinions, witty banter, and daring sexual exploits, while "White takes us through [the narrator's] unsentimental education like an indulgent pal, making graceful introductions, filling in with pungent details, saving his harshest judgments for himself," Vince Aletti comments in the *Voice Literary Supplement.* Sometimes the adolescent makes bold moves—as when he shouts "Gay is good!" in a Greenwich Village demonstration. At other times, he acts out his self-loathing, as when he seduces his music teacher and betrays him to the authorities. By depicting both kinds of behavior, the narrator helps White to evoke "the cautious emergence of a gay consciousness" taking place in the surrounding culture, Aletti remarks.

White's interest and familiarity with French culture are evident in *Genet: A Biography,* White's study of the acclaimed French writer, Jean Genet. White spent seven years researching and writing the biography, interviewing those who knew Genet and examining Genet's literary output. He chronicles Genet's early hardships (being abandoned by his parents and becoming a ward of the state); his adolescent initiation into stealing, which became a lifelong addiction; his first burst of literary creativity during the 1940s, which resulted in five novels and secured his fame; and his turbulent personal life, marked by his homosexuality and his apparent brutish ways towards friends and lovers alike. Noting Genet's legendary habit of falsifying the events of his life, *New York Review of Books* reviewer Tony Judt commends White for attempting "to unravel the threads that Genet so assiduously knotted and crossed in his various writings and interviews."

Critical reaction to *Genet* was mostly positive, with several reviewers calling the biography a "definitive" work, in the words of *New York Times Book Review* contributor Margo Jefferson. Writing in the Chicago *Tribune Books,* Thomas McGonigle avers that "White has written a wonderfully readable account of a thoroughly repulsive individual," adding that "White brings to bear on the life of Genet a grand literary sensibility." Similarly, *Los Angeles Times Book Review* contributor Daniel Harris calls the work "an extraordinarily lucid biography" and notes that "White delights in ferreting out Genet's most compromising secrets." Some reviewers criticized White for focusing too heavily on Genet's homosexuality as a means of interpreting his life and literary output. Judt, for instance, states that occasionally White falls "victim to his own anachronistic concern with sexual preference as a key to aesthetic appreciation." Writing in the *New York Times Book Review,* Isabelle de Courtivron concurs, noting that "at times White comes perilously close to reducing his subject's complex works to an overinterpretation in light of" Genet's homosexuality. Nevertheless, comments de Courtivron, White's work "is so meticulously researched and detailed, his understanding and illumination of the works is so rich, that the book ultimately succeeds in resisting the nagging temptation of reductionism." Jefferson concludes, White "presents the life meticulously, reads Genet's work intelligently and writes beautifully." Reflecting the positive critical opinion of the book, *Genet* was awarded the National Book Critics Circle award for biography in 1994.

In *Artforum,* White observes that gay writers have a further task ahead: "Art must compete with (rectify, purge) the media, which have thoroughly politicized AIDS in a process that is the subject of a book to be published shortly in England. It is *Policing Desire: Pornography, AIDS and the Media,* by Simon Watney. . . . To confront AIDS more honestly than the media have done, it must begin in tact, avoid humor, and end in anger." Tact is important, he says, "because we must not reduce individuals to their deaths," and "because we must not let the disease stand for other things." Humor is "grotesquely inappropriate to the occasion," since it "puts the public (indifferent when not uneasy) on cozy terms with what is an unspeakable scandal: death." He continues, "End in anger, I say, because it is only sane to rage against the dying of the light, because strategically anger is a political response, because psychologically anger replaces despondency, and because essentially anger lightens the solitude of frightened individuals."

Many of the essays in which White explores the intersection of homosexuality, culture, and AIDS are collected in *The Burning Library: Essays.* Consisting of forty pieces, many of them previously published, the collection aptly chronicles White's literary and personal odyssey from the pre-Stonewall period to the sexually liberating 1970s and into the devastation wrought by AIDS in the 1980s and 1990s. Noting the "unparalleled stylistic elegance deployed" by White in these essays, *Observer* reviewer Jonathan Keates characterizes White as being "armed with [a] . . . deep moral awareness and the . . . ability to charm the socks of the reader even while retailing unpalatable truths." Writing in the *Los Angeles Times,* Chris Goodrich calls *The Burning Library* "strikingly traditional, a writer's attempt to fathom his own identity and that of the subculture in which he works and lives."

Times Literary Supplement contributor Neil Powell claims that *The Burning Library*'s more personal essays are stronger than those in which White discusses other writers and their works. "Often in the book," comments Powell, "White's admirable capacity for sympathetic understanding not only inhibits his critical judgment but actually weakens the case being argued." Goodrich, focusing on the more personal essays, notes that White's "reflections on AIDS are uncommonly thoughtful. Keates concurs, writing that White's "own HIV-positive status might have fuelled him with accusatory hysteria and recrimination. Instead, . . . he has challenged mortality with these noble fragments."

White's concern about AIDS has also left its mark on his writing. White's stories in *The Darker Proof* zero in on the experience of AIDS in order to make use of the way fiction can minister to deep emotional needs. He told Walter Kendrick of the *Village Voice,* "AIDS is a very isolating and frightening situation. . . . To show that someone else has the same thoughts, fears, hopes—the same

daily anxiety—is one of the main things fiction does." White also told Stewart Kellerman in the *New York Times Book Review* that because of the AIDS epidemic, he sees "everything as a potential last work." Now that nearly forty of his friends and former students have died from AIDS, he feels "the urge to memorialize the dead, to honor their lives," he wrote in *Artforum.* He added, "There is an equally strong urge to record one's own past—one's own *life*—before it vanishes."

White answered that urge in *Skinned Alive: Stories,* a collection of eight short stories published in 1995. Several of the stories feature "gay love and loss in the shadow of AIDS" as a central motif, comments Maxine Chernoff in a review of the work in the Chicago *Tribune Books.* In "Running on Empty," a man returns to his hometown in Texas after traveling in Europe and confronts his worsening illness. "Palace Days" offers a love triangle in which one character is dying of AIDS while another, though healthy, is coping with the recent discovery that he is HIV-positive. And in "An Oracle," a man grieving for his dead lover falls in love with a young man while traveling in Greece.

"What Edmund White conjures here is a serious, sustained look at how AIDS measures and shapes the meaning of our existence," notes *Los Angeles Times Book Review* contributor Michael Bronski. While noting that the stories dealing with AIDS are "rarely somber," *New York Times Book Review* commentator Morris Dickstein avers that "in the best stories, . . . the author sometimes gives way to a sadness that reverberates more deeply than in anything else he has written." "White is never ponderous but vastly compassionate, and has the grace to be humorous in his compassion," remarks Alberto Manguel in the *Observer.* Reviewing the work in *London Review of Books,* James Woods criticizes the parts of these stories in which White writes about sex as repetitious and unoriginal: "All one needs to do, to verify that such passages are weak stylistically, is compare them with the brilliance of White's non-sexual portraiture." Nevertheless, Woods commends "the scattered gorgeousness" in White's writing and concludes that "*Skinned Alive* shows us that for all his confusions, White has lost none of his artistry." As Chernoff observes, White's "subject is the human condition, no matter our sexual practices, and our final estrangement from each other, despite our efforts to hold on."

BIOGRAPHICAL/CRITICAL SOURCES:

BOOKS

Contemporary Literary Criticism, Volume 27, Gale (Detroit), 1984.
McCaffery, Larry, *Alive and Writing: Interviews,* University Press of Illinois, 1987.

PERIODICALS

Advocate, October 5, 1993.
American Book Review, May, 1989.
Artforum, January, 1987.
Booklist, October 1, 1994; June 1, 1995, p. 732; November 1, 1995, p. 453.
Chicago Tribune, December 10, 1978; April 6, 1980; February 14, 1994.
Harper's, March, 1979; October, 1982; May, 1987.
Library Journal, February 15, 1973; October 1, 1994, p. 82; June 15, 1995, p. 95; November 15, 1995, p. 92; February 1, 1996, p. 75.
Life, fall, 1989.
London Review of Books, April 17, 1986; March 3, 1988; June 10, 1993, p. 3; August 24, 1995, p. 12.

Los Angeles Times, January 12, 1994, p. C7.
Los Angeles Times Book Review, May 4, 1980; April 3, 1982; November 21, 1993, p. 1; July 16, 1995, p. 4.
Mother Jones, June, 1983.
Nation, January 5, 1974; March 1, 1980; November 13, 1982; November 16, 1985; April 9, 1988; January 3, 1994; August 28, 1995, p. 214.
New Republic, February 21, 1994.
New Statesman, March 14, 1986; January 29, 1988; June 17, 1994, p. 38.
Newsweek, April 30, 1973; February 11, 1980; January 17, 1983; November 29, 1993.
New York Review of Books, October 21, 1993, p. 15.
New York Times, January 21, 1980; December 17, 1982; September 8, 1985; March 17, 1988; December 8, 1993, p. C23.
New York Times Book Review, March 25, 1973; December 10, 1978; February 3, 1980; October 10, 1982; September 15, 1985; March 20, 1988; November 7, 1993; October 23, 1994, p. 18; July 23, 1995, p. 6; December 3, 1995, p. 50.
New York Times Magazine, June 16, 1991.
Observer, March 16, 1986; December 14, 1986; January 24, 1988; November 13, 1988; June 20, 1993; June 19, 1994; June 14, 1995.
Paris Review, fall, 1988 (interview).
Playboy, November, 1993.
Publishers Weekly, September 24, 1982 (interview); March 21, 1994, p. 8.
Punch, March 19, 1986; January 8, 1988.
Rolling Stone, December 19, 1985.
Shenandoah, Volume 30, number 1, fall, 1978.
Time, April 11, 1988; July 30, 1990; December 27, 1993.
Times Literary Supplement, September 5, 1980; August 19, 1983; January 22, 1988; July 1, 1994, p. 13; March 17, 1995, p. 20.
Tribune Books (Chicago), October 24, 1993, p. 3; August 13, 1995, p. 4.
Village Voice, January 28, 1980; June 28, 1988 (interview).
Vogue, February, 1984; November, 1984; May, 1985; January, 1986; July, 1986; July, 1987.
Voice Literary Supplement, December, 1982; April, 1988; June, 1988.
Washington Post Book World, November 12, 1978; December 10, 1978; January 27, 1980; October 17, 1982; October 6, 1985; April 3, 1988.

*   *   *

WHITE, Phyllis Dorothy James 1920-
(P. D. James)

PERSONAL: Born August 3, 1920, in Oxford, England; daughter of Sidney Victor (a tax officer) and Dorothy May Amelia (Hone) James; married Ernest Conner Bantry White (a medical practitioner), August 8, 1941 (died, 1964); children: Clare, Jane. *Education:* Attended Cambridge High School for Girls, 1931-37. *Politics:* "I belong to no political party." *Religion:* Church of England. *Avocational interests:* Exploring churches, walking by the sea.

ADDRESSES: Agent—Greene & Heaton Ltd., 37 Goldhawk Rd., London, W12 8QQ, England.

CAREER: Festival Theatre, Cambridge, England, assistant stage manager prior to World War II; worked as a Red Cross nurse and at the Ministry of Food during World War II; North West Regional Hospital Board, London, England, became principal administrative assistant, 1949-68; Department of Home Affairs, London, principal administrative assistant in Police Department, 1968-72, and in Criminal Policy Department, 1972-79; full-time writer, 1979—. Associate fellow, Downing College, Cambridge, 1986; British Broadcasting Corp. (BBC) General Advisory Council, 1987-88, member of Arts Council of Great Britain, 1988-92, and of British Council, 1988-93; governor, BBC, 1988-93. Magistrate, 1979-84.

MEMBER: Royal Society of Literature (fellow), Royal Society of Arts (fellow), Society of Authors (chair, 1985-87), Crime Writers Association, Detection Club, Institute of Hospital Administration (fellow).

AWARDS, HONORS: First prize, Crime Writers Association contest, 1967, for short story, "Moment of Power"; Order of the British Empire, 1983; created Life Peer of United Kingdom (Baroness James of Holland Park), 1991; Diamond Dagger Award, Crime Writers Association for services to crime writing; Silver Dagger Awards, Crime Writers Association, for *Shroud for a Nightingale* and *The Black Tower;* Edgar Award, Mystery Writers of America, for *Shroud for a Nightingale;* Scroll Award, Mystery Writers of America, for *An Unsuitable Job for a Woman;* Litt. D., University of Buckingham, 1992; Doctor of Literature, University of London, 1993.

WRITINGS:

MYSTERY NOVELS, UNDER NAME P. D. JAMES

Cover Her Face, Faber, 1962, Scribner, 1966.
A Mind to Murder, Faber, 1963, Scribner, 1967, large print edition, G. K. Hall, 1994.
Unnatural Causes, Scribner, 1967.
Shroud for a Nightingale, Scribner, 1971.
An Unsuitable Job for a Woman, Faber, 1972, Scribner, 1973.
The Black Tower, Scribner, 1975.
Death of an Expert Witness, Scribner, 1977.
Innocent Blood (Book-of-the-Month Club selection), Scribner, 1980.
The Skull beneath the Skin, Scribner, 1982.
A Taste for Death, Faber, 1985, Knopf, 1986.
Devices and Desires, Faber, 1989, Random House, 1990.
The Children of Men, Faber, 1992, Knopf, 1993.
Original Sin, signed 1st edition, Franklin Library, 1995, Knopf, 1995, large print edition, Random House, 1995.
A Certain Justice, Knopf, 1997.

OMNIBUS VOLUMES, UNDER NAME P. D. JAMES

Crime Times Three (includes *Cover Her Face, A Mind to Murder, and Shroud for a Nightingale*) Scribner, 1979.
Murder in Triplicate (includes *Unnatural Causes, An Unsuitable Job for a Woman,* and *The Black Tower*), Scribner, 1982.
Trilogy of Death, Scribner, 1984.
P. D. James: Three Complete Novels, Crown, 1987.
An Omnibus P. D. James (includes *Death of an Expert Witness, Innocent Blood,* and *An Unsuitable Job for a Woman*), Faber, 1990.
A Dalgliesh Trilogy (includes *The Black Tower, Death of an Expert Witness,* and *Shroud for a Nightingale*), Penguin/ Faber, 1991.

CONTRIBUTOR, UNDER NAME P. D. JAMES

Ellery Queen's Murder Menu, World Publishing, 1969.
Virginian Whitaker, editor, *Winter's Crimes 5,* Macmillan (London), 1973.

Ellery Queen's Masters of Mystery, Davis Publications, 1975.

Hilary Watson, editor, *Winter's Crimes 8,* Macmillan (London), 1976.

Dilys Wynn, editor, *Murder Ink: The Mystery Reader's Companion,* Workman Publishing, 1977.

Crime Writers, BBC Publications, 1978.

Julian Symons, editor, *Verdict of Thirteen,* Harper, 1979.

George Hardinge, *Winter's Crimes 15,* St. Martin's Press, 1983.

OTHER, UNDER NAME P. D. JAMES

(With Thomas A. Critchley) *The Maul and the Pear Tree: The Ratcliffe Highway Murders, 1811,* Constable, 1971.

A Private Treason (play), first produced in the West End at the Palace Theatre, March 12, 1985.

MEDIA ADAPTATIONS: Cover Her Face, Unnatural Causes, The Black Tower, A Taste for Death, Devices and Desires, Death of an Expert Witness (1985) and *Shroud for a Nightingale* (1986) have been adapted as television miniseries and broadcast by the Public Broadcasting System (PBS).

SIDELIGHTS: As P. D. James, a name she chose because it is short and gender-neutral, Phyllis Dorothy James White has established herself as one of England's most prominent mystery writers. Often ranked with such masters of the genre as Agatha Christie, Dorothy L. Sayers, and Margery Allingham, James is critically acclaimed for her ability to combine complex and puzzling plots with psychologically believable characters, particularly in her novels featuring Commander Adam Dalgliesh of Scotland Yard. Her "keen, cunning mind and a positively bloody imagination" make her "one of the finest and most successful mystery writers in the world," Peter Gorner writes in the *Chicago Tribune.*

James began her writing career relatively late in life. When her husband returned from World War II suffering from mental illness, James needed to support her family on her own. For nineteen years she worked as a hospital administrator and then, following her husband's death, entered the British Department of Home Affairs as a civil servant in the criminal department. Although she had wanted to write for many years, James was not able to devote time to this pursuit until the late 1950s. Then, as she tells David Lehman and Tony Clifton in *Newsweek,* "I realized that if I didn't make the effort and settle down to begin that first book, eventually I would be saying to my grandchildren, 'Of course I really wanted to be a novelist.' There never was going to be a convenient time." While working in a hospital she began her first novel, *Cover Her Face.* Over a three-year period James wrote for two hours every morning before going to work, composing her story in longhand on notepaper, a method she still prefers. Once completed, the novel was accepted by the first publisher to whom it was sent and James's career as a mystery writer was launched. Since then she has published ten more mystery novels in addition to a novel about a twenty-first century dystopia, *The Children of Men,* and a work of non-fiction, *The Maul and the Pear Tree.* The latter book, written with Thomas A. Critchley, investigates a particularly gruesome murder committed in London in 1811. James has been a full-time writer since her retirement from government service in 1979.

There is an old-fashioned quality to James's mystery novels that puts them squarely in the tradition of classic English detective fiction as practiced by Agatha Christie and similar writers. The character of Adam Dalgliesh, Scotland Yard detective and published poet, for example, follows the familiar pattern of the gentleman detective popularized by such earlier writers as Dorothy L. Sayers and Ngaio Marsh. James's plots are puzzles which, she tells Wayne Warga of the *Los Angeles Times,* follow the traditional formula. "You have a murder, which is a mystery," she explains. "There is a closed circle of suspects. . . . You have, in my case, a professional detective. He finds clues and information which, as he discovers them, are also available to the reader. And at the end of the story there is a credible and satisfactory resolution that the reader could have arrived at as well." James's style, too, writes Thomas Lask in the *New York Times,* "is what we think of as typically British. Her writing is ample, leisurely, and full of loving description of house and countryside." And like that of a number of other mystery writers, states Norma Siebenheller in her study *P. D. James,* James's "work is literate, tightly constructed, and civilized. Her people are genteel and polite."

James's concern for realism is reflected in her creation of Adam Dalgliesh, a complex character who is, Siebenheller believes, "a far cry from the almost comical characters who served Christie and Sayers as sleuths." Dalgliesh is an introspective, serious figure—intensely devoted to solving the case at hand—who suppresses his personal feelings. His personality has been shaped by one tragic event many years before: the death of his wife and son during childbirth. It is this painful memory, and the essential chaos it implies, that has formed Dalgliesh's "vision of the world," as Erlene Hubly states in *Clues: A Journal of Detection.* Because of this memory, Dalgliesh is a "Byronic hero," Hubly argues, unable "to adjust to or accept society." Yet, because of his fear of chaos and death, he enforces the rules of society, convinced that they are all humanity has with which to create order. Dalgliesh tries, writes Hubly, "to bring order out of chaos: if he cannot stop death he can at least catch and punish those who inflict it on others."

While Dalgliesh is her most popular character, James's secondary characters are equally realistic. All of her books, Julian Symons notes in the *New York Times Book Review,* "are marked by powerful and sympathetic characterizations." Perhaps her most fully realized character after Dalgliesh is Cordelia Gray, a female private detective who appears in *An Unsuitable Job for a Woman* and *The Skull beneath the Skin.* As James relates in the first of these two novels, Gray was raised in a series of foster homes she found "very interesting." Despite her past misfortunes, Gray is "a totally positive person," Siebenheller relates. "Not only is she optimistic, capable, and clever, she is good-natured as well. . . . This is not to say Cordelia is a Pollyanna. She fully acknowledges the rougher edges of life." She and Dalgliesh enjoy a cordial rivalry whenever they meet on a murder case.

Moved by a deep moral concern, James sees mystery writing as an important expression of basic human values. Mystery novels, she tells Carla Heffner in the *Washington Post,* "are like twentieth-century morality plays; the values are basic and unambiguous. Murder is wrong. In an age in which gratuitous violence and arbitrary death have become common, these values need no apology." The "corrosive, destructive aspect of crime," Siebenheller maintains, is one of James's major themes. She traces the effects of crime not only on the victim and criminal, but on their family and friends as well. James's concern is obvious, too, in the values she gives her characters. Comparing Adam Dalgliesh to James herself, Warga describes him as "a man who is a realistic moralist much like his creator."

James moved away from her signature genre to a futuristic tale with *The Children of Men,* published in 1992. The story is set in the year 2021, after twenty-five years have passed during which humans have stopped bearing children as the result of a global disease. James examines the outcome through the eyes of Dr. Theodore Faron, an Oxford professor. Walter Wangerin, Jr., writing for the *New York Times Book Review,* compares the effort to James's crime novels and finds that "In her other novels, the author's attention is upon the plot and these concerns [about the nature of humankind] appear only indirectly. But here Miss James makes these contemplations the very business of her book, and her view is Olympian." James Sallis, in the *Los Angeles Times Book Review,* views the novel "from first to last exceedingly well-wrought" but believes it falls short by making it a eulogy for a British culture that is long past. "James set out to provide a cosmic poem; considered for a while folding in the makings of a political novel; decided somewhere along the way to interpolate a religious fable; and ended up with a book that's none of these, but a kind of sympathy card for her own time and class." Peter Reading, writing for the *Times Literary Supplement,* notes that "if this departure from James's usual genre is intended as a fable, its meaning is not readily communicated. However . . . her ability to create a well-paced plot ensures that her audience will find *The Children of Men* as exciting as her crime stories."

James "triumphantly [reverts] to original form," as Kate Kellaway notes in the *Observer,* with her novel *Original Sin.* The story is set in a publishing company, where an elderly employee and part-time crime novelist, Esme Carling, is fired after thirty years at Peverell Press. Carling is later strangled with her most recent manuscript and her body dumped in the Thames. In an interview with James, Kellaway asks her what she would do upon meeting the detective Dalgliesh, who returns here too in fine form. "If I met him I would say 'I did enjoy your last book of verse' and I wonder if he would then look at me very coolly." Susannah Clapp, writing for the *Times Literary Supplement,* remarks that both James's moral "finger-wagging" as well as Dalgliesh's old-fashioned "rectitude and solemnity" extend the story unnecessarily. "By making Dalgliesh such a beacon not just of the law but of morality, spirituality and aesthetics, and by constantly hinting at the darkness of the age which laps him, she risks making her own criminal world seem cosily dated." Clapp concludes, "There is never any danger of drivel, or difficulty with continuing to read P. D. James's novels—she always makes you want to go on—but they are least lively when most anxious to instruct."

A Certain Justice is James's thirteenth novel, an Adam Dalgliesh mystery in which the sometimes bard/fulltime pillar of British justice must solve the murder of a highly ambitious and successful defense lawyer named Venetia Aldridge. Aldridge is depicted as a person with the quality many men and some women call arrogance when it is found in a woman, but healthy assertiveness when it inheres in men. Hence there are many among her colleagues who would not be expected to mourn her passing; this complicates the mission of Dalgliesh and his team. Of *A Certain Justice, Library Journal* opines, "The incomparable James is at the top of her form," calling it "brilliantly plotted" and adding that it "depicts the many faces of the human psyche and contemplates the question, 'What is Justice?'"

The success of James's novels can be attributed to their popularity among two different audiences, Heffner argues, "the lovers of a good 'whodunit' who read her novels for their action and intricate plots; and the literary world that admires the books for their character and motivation." In the words of Christopher Lehmann-Haupt, writing in the *New York Times,* this wide acceptance has made James "one of the most esteemed practitioners of the [mystery] genre in the English-speaking world."

BIOGRAPHICAL/CRITICAL SOURCES:

BOOKS

Contemporary Literary Criticism, Gale (Detroit), Volume 18, 1981, pp. 272-77; Volume 46, 1988, pp. 204-11.
Siebenheller, Norma, *P. D. James,* Ungar, 1981.
Wynn, Dilys, editor, *Murder Ink,* Workman Publishing, 1977.
Wynn, Dilys, editor, *Murderess Ink,* Workman Publishing, 1977.

PERIODICALS

Chicago Tribune, June 10, 1980; November 6, 1986; November 16, 1986; February 4, 1990, pp. 1, 4.
Chicago Tribune Book World, May 18, 1980; September 19, 1982.
Christian Century, May 19, 1993, p. 561.
Christian Science Monitor, June 25, 1980.
Clues: A Journal of Detection, fall/winter, 1982; spring/summer, 1985.
Commonweal, April 23, 1993, p. 26.
Globe and Mail (Toronto), May 10, 1986; November 8, 1986; February 3, 1990, p. C8.
Library Journal, January, 1994, p. 184; September 1, 1995, p. 226; November 1, 1997, p. 120.
Los Angeles Times, June 6, 1980; November 6, 1986; January 21, 1987.
Los Angeles Times Book Review, June 22, 1980; November 30, 1986, p. 6; February 25, 1990, pp. 1, 11; April 4, 1993, p. 12.
Ms., April, 1974; August, 1979.
National Catholic Reporter, May 28, 1993, p. 23.
New Republic, July 31, 1976; November 26, 1977.
New Statesman & Society, September 25, 1992, p. 55; November 11, 1994, p. 37.
Newsweek, January 23, 1978; May 12, 1980; September 13, 1982; October 20, 1986, pp. 81-83; February 19, 1990, p. 66.
New Yorker, March 11, 1976; March 6, 1978; June 23, 1980; March 22, 1993, p. 111.
New York Review of Books, July 17, 1980; April 26, 1990, p. 35.
New York Times, December 11, 1977; July 18, 1979; February 8, 1980; April 27, 1980; May 7, 1980; March 11, 1986; October 5, 1986; October 23, 1986; January 25, 1990, p. C22; May 9, 1996, p. C20.
New York Times Book Review, July 24, 1966; January 16, 1972; April 22, 1973; November 23, 1975; April 27, 1980; September 12, 1982; April 6, 1986; November 2, 1986, p. 9; January 28, 1990, pp. 1, 31; April 26, 1990, p. 35; March 28, 1993, p. 23; April 2, 1995, p. 11.
New York Times Magazine, October 5, 1986.
Observer, October 16, 1994, p. 19.
People Weekly, December 8, 1986; March 29, 1993, p. 23; February 13, 1995, p. 41.
Publishers Weekly, January 5, 1976, pp. 8-9; October 25, 1985; December 1, 1989, p. 48.
Time, April 17, 1978; May 26, 1980; March 31, 1986; October 27, 1986, p. 98; March 1, 1993, p. 69.
Times Literary Supplement, October 22, 1971; December 13, 1974; March 21, 1980; October 29, 1982; June 27, 1986, p. 711; September 25, 1992, p. 26; October 21, 1994.
Tribune Books (Chicago), February 4, 1990.
Village Voice, December 15, 1975; December 18, 1978.
Voice Literary Supplement, October, 1982; April, 1990, p. 10.
Washington Post, April 30, 1980; November 10, 1986.

Washington Post Book World, April 15, 1977; April 27, 1980; September 19, 1982; April 20, 1986; November 9, 1986, pp. 5-6; January 21, 1990, p. 7.

*   *   *

WHITE, Theodore H(arold) 1915-1986

PERSONAL: Born May 6, 1915, in Boston, MA; died after a stroke, May 9, 1986; son of David and Mary (Winkeller) White; married Nancy Ariana Van Der Heyden Bean, March 29, 1947 (divorced, 1971); married Beatrice Kevitt Hofstadter, March, 1974; children: (first marriage) Ariana Van Der Heyden, David Fairbank. *Education:* Harvard University, A.B. (summa cum laude), 1938. *Avocational interests:* Woodworking, gardening, and painting.

CAREER: Time magazine, New York City, Far East correspondent and chief of China bureau, 1939-45; *New Republic* magazine, New York City, editor, 1947; Overseas News Agency, New York City, chief European correspondent, 1948-50; *Reporter* magazine, New York City, chief European correspondent, 1950-53; *Collier's* magazine, national correspondent, 1955-56; freelance writer and correspondent, 1956-86. Covered China war front, Indian uprising, and Honan famine during World War II; present at Japanese surrender aboard U.S.S. *Missouri,* 1945; covered post-World War II European events, including administration of Marshall Plan and North Atlantic Treaty Organization. Member of board of overseers, Harvard University, 1968-74.

MEMBER: Council on Foreign Relations, Foreign Correspondents Club (president, 1944-45), Phi Beta Kappa, Century Club, Harvard Club.

AWARDS, HONORS: Sidney Hillman Foundation Award, 1954, and National Association of Independent Schools Award, 1954, both for *Fire in the Ashes;* Benjamin Franklin Magazine Award, 1956, for article in *Collier's,* "Germany—Friend or Foe?"; Ted V. Rodgers Award, 1956; Pulitzer Prize for general nonfiction, 1962, and National Association of Independent Schools Award, 1962, both for *The Making of the President: 1960;* Emmy Awards, National Academy of Television Arts and Sciences, 1964, for best television film in all categories, for *The Making of the President: 1960,* 1967, for best documentary television writing, for *China: The Roots of Madness,* and 1985, for best documentary television writing, for *Television and the Presidency;* Fourth Estate Award, National Press Club; Journalist of the Year Award, Columbia School of Journalism; English-Speaking Union Books-Across-the-Sea Ambassador of Honor Books, 1984, for *America in Search of Itself;* honorary doctor of humane letters, Hebrew Union College, 1985.

WRITINGS:

(With Annalee Jacoby) *Thunder Out of China* (Book-of-the-Month Club selection), Sloane, 1946.
(Editor) Joseph Warren Stilwell, *The Stilwell Papers,* Sloane, 1948.
Fire in the Ashes (Book-of-the-Month Club selection), Sloane, 1953.
The Mountain Road (Book-of-the-Month Club selection), Sloane, 1958.
The View from the Fortieth Floor (Literary Guild selection), Sloane, 1960.

The Making of the President: 1960, Atheneum, 1961, reprinted as *The Making of the President, 1960: A Narrative History of American Politics in Action,* Macmillan, 1988.
The Making of the President: 1964, Atheneum, 1965.
Caesar at the Rubicon: A Play about Politics, Atheneum, 1968, published as *Caesar at the Rubicon: A Play in Three Acts,* Samuel French, 1971.
China: The Roots of Madness (also see below; revision of television documentary script), Norton, 1968.
The Making of the President: 1968, Atheneum, 1969.
The Making of the President: 1972 (Literary Guild selection), Atheneum, 1973.
Breach of Faith: The Fall of Richard Nixon (Book-of-the-Month Club selection), Atheneum, 1975.
In Search of History: A Personal Adventure (autobiography), Harper, 1978.
America in Search of Itself: The Making of the President 1956-1980, Harper, 1982.
(With Marvin W. Peterson and Ellem Earle Chaffee) *Organization and Governance in Higher Education: An ASHE Reader,* Ginn (Massachusetts), 1991.
(With John W. and Jane R. Mosser) *New Perspectives on Marketing Cooperative Education,* Collegiate Career Planning Foundation, 1991.
Theodore II. White at Large: The Best of His Magazine Writing, 1939-1986, edited by Edward T. Thompson, Pantheon, 1992.

Also author of television documentaries, including *The Making of the President: 1960, China: The Roots of Madness, The Making of the President: 1968,* and *Television and the Presidency,* 1985. Contributor to *Life, Time, Fortune, Reporter, Holiday, Harper's, Saturday Review, Collier's, New York, New York Times Magazine,* and other magazines and newspapers.

SIDELIGHTS: With the publication of *The Making of the President: 1960,* his Pulitzer Prize-winning report on the 1960 presidential campaign and election, Theodore White established a tradition of excellence that not only he but also others have found difficult to live up to. Considered by many to be a classic in political journalism, it was, as a *National Observer* critic noted, "a ground-breaking achievement," for "no one before had thought to bring a whole presidential campaign together in a single, lucid, anecdotal, and timely volume." A *San Francisco Chronicle* reviewer called it "the most exhilarating non-fiction of the season. . . . It is both exciting and revealing Americana. . . . A familiar story . . . appears to be new and fresh as White reconstructs it. He does so with brilliance, intelligence and for the most part scrupulous objectivity."

James MacGregor Burns, writing in the *New York Times Book Review,* stated: "No book that I know of has caught the heartbeat of a campaign as strikingly as Theodore White has done in *The Making of the President: 1960.* . . . By artistic rearrangement of his materials he has gained space for long, hard appraisals of American politics. . . . If this book were merely a campaign report, it could be recommended glowingly on its own terms. But it is more than this." A *Saturday Review* critic saw it as "an extraordinary performance by a shrewd interpreter of the American scene. . . . It launches what I hope will be a new genre in American political literature. It is sensitive and brilliant reporting, and an invaluable document for history."

The Making of the President: 1964 was not as successful as its predecessor, perhaps, as a *National Observer* critic pointed out, "because the campaign itself was less interesting. . . . [White] found no heroes in 1964; like so many others, he saw no romance in Lyndon Johnson or Barry Goldwater." In the *New York Review of Books,* I. F. Stone admitted that "Theodore H. White has become the poet laureate of American presidential campaigns." Nevertheless, he concluded, *The Making of the President: 1964* "is on a lower level" than its predecessor. "The wonder and zest of the first often decline into a schoolgirlish gushiness in the second. The first is muscular, the second mawkish. . . . [Yet] no one could feel a candidate's pulse more sympathetically [than White]." The *New Yorker* noted that "[Mr. White] does quite a good job of it. . . . His method is a compound of diary-keeping, daily journalism, weekly journalism, editorial writing, and extra-sensory perception. It is an entertaining mixture, and some of the microscopic details are priceless, but on the whole, it is more White than history." A *Times Literary Supplement* reviewer wrote: "Alas, the 1964 version has all and much more than all the faults of the first book and hardly any of its merits. It is a depressing failure. . . . The *aficionados* of American politics will find a little new information here, some, if too infrequent, patches of Mr. White at his brilliant reporter's best . . . and a good deal of unimpressive political cogitation."

On the other hand, an *Atlantic* reviewer noted: "In *The Making of the President: 1960* Theodore H. White had almost a classical plot with a single action and a single hero. . . . By comparison, 1964 presented a more diffuse and less focused drama. Yet *The Making of the President: 1964* is in many ways a more exciting book, if only because his earlier triumph has sharpened Mr. White's skill at a style of reporting that he seems to have made all his own. . . . His politicians . . . emerge as three-dimensional characters in a way not usual in political reporting."

It was not, however, until the appearance of *The Making of the President: 1968* that critics began to take a long, hard look at White's approach. What had only been mentioned more or less in passing by a few reviewers in 1960 and 1964—namely, White's occasional lack of objectivity as well as his patriotic sentimentality about America and the American political system—became a major problem in the eyes of the 1968 reviewers. A *Commonweal* critic wrote: "Like Harold Stassen, T. H. White is ruining a good thing with his quadrennial lustings after the presidency. . . . This third *Making* book is the plain *reductio ad absurdum* of the first, which—for all its fascination and birth of genre—was conspicuously sanguine on issues and soft on politicians. . . . While White's coziness with the candidates may not have hurt his books all that much in 1960 and 1964 when the old politics still had some kick, he is terribly guilty by his associations in *Making 1968*. . . . The unhappiest feature of *Making 1968* is the reporter's undisguised sympathy for the establishment. . . . Except for the Wallace campaign and the peace movement, basely equated in their extremism, White is all heroes and worship. . . . [But] apart from internal criticism, *Making 1968* fails for large reasons. A single reporter is simply incommensurate with a presidential campaign. . . . 'This is the most dramatic confrontation of America and its problems in over 100 years,' White mused in *Newsweek* before publication. 'It's just a question of whether I'm good enough to write the story for what it's really worth.' He wasn't."

Bill Moyers, writing in *Saturday Review,* noted: "If Theodore White did not exist, the Ford Foundation would have to award Harvard University a grant to create him. How else would the Establishment tell its story? *The Making of the President: 1968* is essentially that: the authorized version, the view through the official keyhole. For Teddy White, the most successful entrepren-

eur of political detail and perception in American journalism today, tells the story of 1968 as he did four and eight years. . . . But times have changed. . . . 1968 was the Year of Decay. . . . Under such circumstances no single author, not even a Teddy White, could chart the shifting boundaries of our political terrain. That he has tried, against impossible odds, is a tribute to the man's intrepid will. Certainly his is the most coherent and the most eloquent account we are likely to get from any reporter's notes. . . . But there is a tone in it that we are not accustomed to hearing in Teddy White."

White's *The Making of the President: 1972* was criticized for virtually the same excesses and deficiencies as the 1968 version. "The rambling chronicle offers few new insights into either the Nixon victory or the McGovern defeat," wrote a *New Republic* reviewer. "Watergate aside, White willingly accepts most of the Nixon rationale—even on the war. . . . But if the analysis is disappointing, the level of characterization is more gratifying, reflecting the legwork, extensive interviews and careful research involved." Garry Wills of the *New York Review of Books,* noting the author's "indiscriminate celebration of the ruler" (Nixon), concluded that "the 'Whitiad,' now in its second decade, gets worse stanza by stanza. . . . White conducts his old civics lesson without having learned a thing." Finally, Anthony Lewis of the *New York Times* commented: "Theodore H. White is so awesomely diligent a reporter, so accomplished a political analyst, so engaging a person that criticizing him seems like sacrilege. . . . But . . . it is time for someone to say that White has written a bad book. *The Making of the President: 1972* is as impressive as its predecessors in its eye for both the revealing detail and the sweep of events. But White naturally does more than describe. He gives his own judgment on larger historical issues, and there I think he has gone profoundly wrong. . . . Alas, one [also] detects in Theodore White some of that unfortunate pleasure in curling up with the powerful. . . . [As a result,] winners take all in the White universe; and losers get no mercy."

In 1976, restless and unable to apply himself to the task of preparing for and writing *The Making of the President: 1976,* White broke with tradition and turned to writing about himself instead. The result, *In Search of History,* was called "a minor classic of American biography" by the *New Leader.* "It vibrates with the themes most characteristic of national self-discovery," continued the reviewer, "recording the passage from obscurity and poverty to the close observation of power; from facts to ideas, from promise to fulfillment and then to perplexity." But even in his autobiography White came under fire for his lack of objectivity. "The special insignia of White's writing has long been the evocation of sympathy," reported the *New Leader.* "The autobiography is similarly free of rancor. Almost everyone . . . is washed in authorial good will." Furthermore, the reviewer wrote, White's "own sense of politics remains rooted in camaraderie rather than causes, and in attributing to politicians ideas that are really only mental gestures, White once again exaggerates the importance of the men he has covered."

Richard Rovere of the *New York Times Book Review* called *In Search of History* "by far [White's] finest, most affecting work. . . . It has all the pace and energy of the earlier work and more of many other things; more insight, more reflection, more candor, more intimacy, more humor, more humility, surer and sharper judgments of those he writes about, including himself." On the other hand, Christopher Lehmann-Haupt of the *New York Times* felt that "somewhere in this public autobiography Mr. White seems to lose his way. The first half is extremely strong—

the sections covering his youth, his education, and his adventures in China. Here personal experience very nearly equals history. . . . But somehow in the second half, the momentum of White's narrative falters. This isn't to say that vivid close-up portraits of historical figures don't continue to appear. . . . It is simply that when White moves on from China to Europe to witness that continent's post-war recovery, and then back to the United States to report on domestic politics, the center of the action moves away from him. He is no longer really part of the story he is covering, as he was in China. So when he writes about himself he neglects history, and vice versa." Lehmann-Haupt, in addition to several other reviewers, found White's occasional use of the third person when referring to himself to be somewhat distracting. "Nowhere do these passages stop reminding us by their lack of irony and humor how much more successfully this device fares in the hands of Norman Mailer," he concluded.

William Greider of *Book World* stated that, as a reflective memoir, *In Search of History* simply "doesn't work. [White] begins bravely, announcing self-doubts and confusion, but after traveling through many continents and interesting events, glimpsing famous men from Mao to Eisenhower, one is left at the conclusion with the same questions. Readers who loved the powerful narrative line of White's other books will find this one strangely disjointed and unthematic. . . . The memoir ends lamely, acknowledging that he has not really sorted out the fundamental confusions about politics and the nation." Unlike other reviewers, however, Greider did not particularly find the first part of the book to be much better than the last half, noting that "even [White's] memories of wartime China and *Time* are seen through a murky lens," as if he is "unable to address them directly."

White's last book, *America in Search of Itself: The Making of the President, 1956-1980*, examines the administrations of Eisenhower through Jimmy Carter, up to the election of Ronald Reagan as president in 1980. The book received comments similar to those for White's other books on presidential elections. "This is a somewhat disjointed volume, because of its dual purpose—to philosophize over recent history and to map a particular moment. White is a better mapmaker than philosopher," noted Paul Barker in the London *Times*. "Mr. White demurs, 'I could not present myself as a historian,' but from the start his tone is something other than reportorial," commented Susan Bolotin in the *New York Times*, adding that White "tends to speak in aphorisms . . . , to categorize in terms of big themes . . . , [and] to look back from a vantage point more opinionated than analytic." Despite these criticisms, Bolotin conceded that White "deserves full credit for his talent as a storyteller" and that "his campaign remembrances are winning."

In 1992 a collection of White's periodical journalism was published. *Theodore H. White at Large: The Best of His Magazine Writing, 1939-1986* collects fifty-five articles on topics ranging from domestic political and social affairs to the most significant events in Asia and Europe in the twentieth century. Herbert Mitgang wrote in the *New York Times* that "White was a reporter with a sense of history, which is why the articles [published here] . . . hold up so beautifully." In *The Los Angeles Times Book Review*, Chris Goodrich averred that White's "vivid writing style" and moral expounding, once assets, eventually weakened his writing. Nevertheless, concluded Goodrich, "Skip the last 200-odd pages in this book and you'll likely agree White was one of the best reporters of the last 50 years."

BIOGRAPHICAL/CRITICAL SOURCES:

BOOKS

Griffith, Thomas, *Harry and Teddy: The Turbulent Friendship of Press Lord Henry R. Luce and His Favorite Reporter, Theodore H. White,* Random House, 1995.
Hoffmann, Joyce, *Theodore H. White and Journalism as Illusion,* University of Missouri Press, 1995.

PERIODICALS

American Heritage, April/May, 1982.
Atlantic Monthly, June, 1958; August, 1961; August, 1965; May, 1968.
Booklist, November 15, 1992, p. 578.
Book Week, July 11, 1965.
Book World, July 14, 1968; July 27, 1969; October 12, 1969; August 27, 1978.
Chicago Tribune Book World, May 16, 1982.
Commentary, September, 1982.
Commonweal, December 8, 1961; August 22, 1969.
Harper's, August, 1965.
Library Journal, December, 1992, p. 152.
Life, June 18, 1965.
Los Angeles Times Book Review, October 15, 1978; May 30, 1982; December 29, 1985.
Maclean's, October 24, 1983.
Nation, October 14, 1978.
National Observer, July 12, 1965; August 18, 1969.
New Leader, October 23, 1978.
New Republic, July 10, 1961; July 10, 1965; August 16, 1969; August 11, 1973; September 9, 1978.
Newsweek, January 13, 1969; July 28, 1969; August 13, 1973; August 14, 1978.
New York, September 8, 1969.
New Yorker, June 4, 1960; July 22, 1961; August 7, 1965; September 20, 1969.
New York Post, July 22, 1969.
New York Review of Books, August 5, 1965; October 4, 1973; November 9, 1978.
New York Times, January 2, 1969; July 9, 1969; July 23, 1969; February 21, 1971; August 30, 1973; June 1, 1982; January 4, 1993.
New York Times Book Review, May 11, 1958; May 22, 1960; July 9, 1961; July 11, 1965; April 14, 1968; September 22, 1968; August 6, 1978; December 24, 1978; May 9, 1982.
Observer (London), November 23, 1969.
People Weekly, July 31, 1978.
Playboy, May, 1968.
San Francisco Chronicle, July 5, 1961; July 6, 1961.
Saturday Review, May 10, 1958; May 21, 1960; July 8, 1961; July 10, 1965; August 9, 1969; October 9, 1973; September 2, 1978.
Time, May 23, 1960; July 21, 1961; March 29, 1968; August 1, 1969; July 3, 1978; May 17, 1982.
Times (London), May 19, 1983.
Times Literary Supplement, December 2, 1960; November 4, 1965; June 10, 1983.
Washington Post Book World, May 9, 1982; January 5, 1986.

WHITNEY, Phyllis A(yame) 1903-

PERSONAL: Born September 9, 1903, in Yokohama, Japan; daughter of U.S. citizens, Charles Joseph and Lillian (Mandeville) Whitney; married George A. Garner, July 2, 1925 (divorced, 1945); married Lovell F. Jahnke (in business), 1950 (died, 1973); children: (first marriage) Georgia. *Education:* Attended public schools in Chicago, IL. *Avocational interests:* "My only hobby is collecting backgrounds for new books, and that takes most of my time, since I visit these places and do a great deal of research."

ADDRESSES: Agent—McIntosh and Otis Inc., 310 Madison Ave., New York, NY 10017-6009.

CAREER: Writer, 1941–. Children's book editor with the *Chicago Sun* (now *Chicago Sun Times*), 1942-46, and *Philadelphia Inquirer,* 1946-48. Teacher of juvenile writing at Northwestern University, Evanston, IL, 1945-46, New York University, New York City, 1947-58, and at writers' conferences.

MEMBER: Authors Roundtable (president, 1943); Executive Board, Fifth Annual Writers Conference, Northwestern University (president, 1944); Authors League of America; Mystery Writers of America (member of board of directors, 1959-62; president, 1975); Malice Domestic; Sisters in Crime; American Crime Writers League; Society of Children's Book Writers; Children's Reading Round Table; Midland Authors.

AWARDS, HONORS: Youth Today contest winner, and *Book World*'s Spring Book Festival Award, both 1947, both for *Willow Hill;* Edgar Allan Poe Award for best juvenile mystery, Mystery Writers of America, 1961, for *Mystery of the Haunted Pool,* and 1964, for *Mystery of the Hidden Hand;* Edgar Allan Poe nominations, 1962, for *The Secret of the Tiger Eyes,* 1971, for *Mystery of the Scowling Boy,* and 1974, for *The Secret of the Missing Footprint;* Sequoyah Children's Book Award, 1963, for *Mystery of the Haunted Pool;* Friends of Literature Award for Contribution to Children's Literature, 1974; "Today's Woman" citation, Council of Cerebral Palsy Auxiliaries of Nassau County, 1983; Grandmaster Award, Mystery Writers of America, 1988, for lifetime achievement; Malice Domestic Award, 1989, for lifetime achievement; Romance Writers of America Award, 1990, for lifetime achievement; Agatha Award, 1990, for lifetime achievement.

WRITINGS:

JUVENILE NOVELS

A Place for Ann, illustrated by Helen Blair, Houghton (Boston), 1941.
A Star for Ginny, illustrated by Hilda Frommholz, Houghton, 1942.
A Window for Julie, illustrated by Jean Anderson, Houghton, 1943.
The Silver Inkwell, illustrated by Frommholz, Houghton, 1945.
Willow Hill, McKay (New York City), 1947.
Ever After, Houghton, 1948.
Linda's Homecoming, McKay, 1950.
Love Me, Love Me Not, Houghton, 1952.
Step to the Music, Crowell (New York City), 1953.
A Long Time Coming, McKay, 1954.
The Fire and the Gold, Crowell, 1956.
The Highest Dream, McKay, 1956.
Creole Holiday, Westminster (Philadelphia), 1959.
Nobody Likes Trina, Westminster, 1972.

JUVENILE MYSTERIES

Mystery of the Gulls, illustrated by Janet Smalley, Westminster, 1949.
The Island of Dark Woods, illustrated by Philip Wishnefsky, Westminster, 1951, published as *Mystery of the Strange Traveller,* 1967.
Mystery of the Black Diamonds, illustrated by John Gretzer, Westminster, 1954 (published in England as *Black Diamonds,* Brockhampton, 1957).
Mystery on the Isle of Skye, illustrated by Ezra Jack Keats, Westminster, 1955.
Mystery of the Green Cat, illustrated by Richard Horwitz, Westminster, 1957.
Secret of the Samurai Sword, Westminster, 1958.
Mystery of the Haunted Pool, illustrated by H. Tom Hall, Westminster, 1960.
Secret of the Tiger's Eye, illustrated by Horwitz, Westminster, 1961.
Mystery of the Golden Horn, illustrated by Georgeann Helmes, Westminster, 1962.
Mystery of the Hidden Hand, illustrated by Hall, Westminster, 1963.
Secret of the Emerald Star, illustrated by Alex Stein, Westminster, 1964.
Mystery of the Angry Idol, illustrated by Al Fiorentino, Westminster, 1965.
Secret of the Spotted Shell, illustrated by John Mecray, Westminster, 1967.
Secret of Goblin Glen, illustrated by Fiorentino, Westminster, 1968.
Mystery of the Crimson Ghost, Westminster, 1969.
Secret of the Missing Footprint, illustrated by Stein, Westminster, 1970.
The Vanishing Scarecrow, Westminster, 1971.
Mystery of the Scowling Boy, illustrated by Gretzer, Westminster, 1973.
Secret of Haunted Mesa, Westminster, 1975.
Secret of the Stone Face, Westminster, 1977.

ADULT NOVELS

Red Is for Murder, Ziff-Davis, 1943, published as *The Red Carnelian,* Paperback Library, 1965.
The Quicksilver Pool, Appleton, 1955.
The Trembling Hills, Appleton, 1956.
Skye Cameron, Appleton, 1957.
The Moonflower, Appleton, 1958 (published in England as *The Mask and the Moonflower,* Hurst & Blackett, 1960).
Thunder Heights, Appleton, 1960.
Blue Fire, Appleton, 1961.
Window on the Square, Appleton, 1962.
Seven Tears for Apollo, Appleton, 1963.
Black Amber, Appleton, 1964.
Sea Jade, Appleton, 1965.
Columbella, Doubleday (New York City), 1966.
Silverhill, Doubleday, 1967.
Hunter's Green, Doubleday, 1968.
The Winter People, Doubleday, 1969.
Lost Island, Doubleday, 1970.
Listen for the Whisperer, Doubleday, 1972.
Snowfire, Doubleday, 1973.
The Turquoise Mask, Doubleday, 1974.
Spindrift, Doubleday, 1975.
The Golden Unicorn, Doubleday, 1976.
The Stone Bull, Doubleday, 1977.

The Glass Flame, Doubleday, 1978.
Domino, Doubleday, 1979.
Poinciana, Doubleday, 1980.
Vermilion, Doubleday, 1981.
Emerald, Doubleday, 1982.
Rainsong, Doubleday, 1984.
Dream of Orchids, Doubleday, 1985.
Flaming Tree, Doubleday, 1986.
Silversword, Doubleday, 1987.
Feather on the Moon, Doubleday, 1988.
Rainbow in the Mist, Doubleday, 1989.
The Singing Stones, Doubleday, 1990.
Woman without a Past, Doubleday, 1991.
The Ebony Swan, Doubleday, 1992.
Star Flight, Crown (New York City), 1993.
Daughter of the Stars, Crown, 1994.
Amethyst Dreams, Crown, 1997.

OTHER

Writing Juvenile Fiction (also see below), Writer, Inc. (Boston), 1947, revised edition, 1960.
Writing Juvenile Stories and Novels: How to Write and Sell Fiction for Young People (contains portions of *Writing Juvenile Fiction*), Writer, Inc., 1976.
Guide to Writing Fiction, Writer, Inc., 1982, second edition, 1988.

SIDELIGHTS: Since the publication of her first novel in 1941, Phyllis A. Whitney has published over seventy-five mysteries for readers of all ages, giving her the reputation of "America's queen of romantic suspense" and the title of "Grandmaster." Her work is very popular, with over 40 million copies of her novels still in print in paperback. With a scenic detail sustained by her extensive travels, Whitney brings to life stories of young women whose attempts to unlock secrets and solve puzzles often put them in danger.

Like the plots in some of her books, Whitney's early life also featured exotic places and frequent travel. Born in Yokohama, Japan, to American parents, Whitney lived in Japan, China, and the Philippines until the death of her father when she was fifteen. She then came to the United States with her mother, who passed away two years later. Settling in Chicago with an aunt, Whitney finished high school and got married a year after graduation. Already she was writing stories, even though sales to magazines were few and far between. But in 1941 she published *A Place for Ann,* a young adult novel that brought her a measure of success and self-sufficiency.

In 1945 Whitney approached her editor about writing a book involving racial issues. "My editor objected to the story idea," Whitney related in *Library Journal.* "She didn't think I could do it. She doubted that it would sell, and she didn't want to publish it anyway." Whitney went ahead with the project nonetheless, and another publisher brought out *Willow Hill* in 1947. Presenting the story of how a young white girl and her high school friends deal with the integration of a housing project into their community, *Willow Hill* won the Youth Today contest and became one of Whitney's most popular children's books.

Critics have also admired the novel. "For all the problems involved," M. C. Scoggin comments in the *New York Times,* *Willow Hill* "is not a thesis hung on a clothes-horse of a plot. It is full of flesh-and-blood boys and girls." A *Saturday Review of Literature* critic agrees, noting that "this is a story that comes completely and excitingly to life. . . . A book with a message, it gains rather than loses by its preoccupation." As a result, Bobbie

Ann Mason notes in *Twentieth-Century Children's Writers,* "the book seems daringly ahead of its time in its sympathy and in its honest portrayal of race relations."

Soon after *Willow Hill,* the author turned to writing stories of mystery and intrigue because, as she told Diana Gleasner in *Breakthrough: Women in Writing,* "I like mystery novels. It's a difficult form to master because the plotting is so complicated; you have to juggle so many balls at the same time." Whitney's young adult suspense novels "are lively, light mysteries," as Mason describes them, with young female protagonists "who tend to be normal kids with shortcomings and frustrations, rather than sophisticated, independent, idealized heroines. Thus Whitney has been praised for her honesty, realism, and intellectually stimulating themes." As G. P. Lancaster remarks in a *Christian Science Monitor* review of the Edgar-winning *Mystery of the Haunted Pool,* "The author has a fine flair for making her characters likable, lively, and natural."

More recently, Whitney has focused on adult novels of "psychological" or "romantic suspense," stories of young women who must unravel puzzles that often involve mysterious family relationships. But while Whitney's heroines often find romance along the way, they are also "liberated women," according to Barbara Mertz in the *Washington Post Book World.* "They may—and do—end up in the arms of the hero, but they have to solve their own problems before they get there." As Allen J. Hubin similarly notes in the *New York Times Book Review,* "Whitney seeks to create that mood of impending doom . . . without much recourse to the idiotic behavior common to heroines of the genre." The author explained in a *Parade* interview with Pam Proctor: "The girls in my books are out solving their own problems. They've always been women's libbers because I've always been a liberated woman. I've always done whatever I've wanted to do."

Another distinguishing feature of Whitney's mysteries is her striking use of unique settings. *The Stone Bull,* for instance, uses a Catskills setting that combines "mythology, drama, and botany," Irene M. Pompea remarks in *Best Sellers;* with this novel, "Phyllis Whitney has given her public an experience of genuine suspense." More recent offerings eschew exotic locations and time periods for modern situations such as child-custody disputes and kidnappings, a popular singer's widow coping with the press, and psychic phenomena. *Feather on the Moon,* besides including British Columbia's "lush scenery," is "a smoothly written tale," Sherman W. Smith states in *West Coast Review of Books.* "It is indeed an art to glue readers to the pages and Whitney has honed that art to its peak," another *West Coast Review of Books* writer similarly concludes of *Rainsong.*

In her most recent adult novels, Whitney has produced plot lines that feature rediscovered family secrets and murder. *Woman without A Past,* described as a "good modern gothic novel" by Claudia Moore in *School Library Journal* follows a woman's search to uncover events surrounding her childhood after learning that she may have been kidnapped as an infant before arriving to her adoptive parents. Setting the novel in Charleston, South Carolina, Whitney evokes the atmosphere of the historic city and its old, traditional families to heighten the intrigue. In *The Ebony Swan,* Whitney crafts a suspenseful, psychological drama set in the scenic tidewater region of northern Virginia. The story centers on a woman's return to her childhood home, where twenty-five years earlier she witnessed her mother's murder. The woman encounters troubling mysteries surrounding the tragedy, including the implication of her maternal grandmother, a former ballerina.

The novel is described by a *Kirkus Reviews* commentator as "tighter, neater, better than ever" and by a *Publishers Weekly* reviewer as "one of her best efforts."

Star Flight describes a woman's quest to uncover the truth behind two family deaths. Set in a resort town in western North Carolina, the complex plot links the protagonist's grandmother's suicide decades ago with her husband's recent accidental death while filming a documentary about a film star. As it turns out, an adulterous affair between the film star and her grandmother in the 1930s produced her own mother. Her husband's death arouses suspicion when she learns that he may have discovered new information suggesting that her distraught grandmother's death was not self-inflicted. The story is further complicated by the introduction of many characters and sub-plots, including UFOs and government conspiracies, drawing criticism from several reviewers on the grounds of excessive dialogue and an implausible plot. *Daughter of the Stars* similarly involves childhood revelations and domestic intrigue in historic Harpers Ferry, West Virginia. In this story, a children's book author revisits her birth place to investigate unresolved speculation surrounding the circumstances of her father's murder thirty years earlier. Whitney weaves an intricate plot involving Civil War ancestors, daunting matriarchs, and eccentric half-siblings which, according to a *Publishers Weekly* reviewer, "culminates in a gratifying surprise ending."

In *Amethyst Dreams,* Whitney offers another novel of romantic suspense tinged with family intrigue. Hallie Knight's former college roommate, Susan, has disappeared without a reason or evidence of where she has gone. Called to Susan's grandfather's island home to help find her, Hallie is relieved to have something other than her own marital problems to focus upon. While working to resolve the mystery of Susan's disappearance, Hallie bravely begins to sort out her own troubled situation, working to untangle this other source of frustrated puzzlement. In *Booklist,* Stephanie Zvirin states that *Amethyst Dreams* is "somewhat shy on thrills, but the author hasn't forgotten the fine nuances and descriptive prose that her devoted fans have come to expect." Zvirin also advises that the books's "languid pace is perfect for cozy, rainy-day reading" and offers her general approval by judging the novel a "[p]redictably solid performance from an old hand with name-brand appeal." M. E. Chitty, in *Library Journal,* is more effusive about this volume, noting that Whitney "has a magical way with words, whether with a book's title, location, or character names." Chitty avers that what is most important about the novel "are the characters' wonderfully wrought temperaments—no sinners, no saints, but ultimately lots of forgiveness" and the captivating suspense which will "keep readers looking for answers right up to the satisfying conclusion."

Whitney once commented: "I have always written because I couldn't help it. From the age of twelve on I loved to make up stories, and I've been doing it ever since. I believe in entertaining my readers, and I also hope to make them think and feel. I have great respect and admiration for fellow writers in the mystery-suspense field, and I read both to enjoy and to learn. I seem to have been born with a hunger for stories." Although she has been publishing for over fifty years, Whitney shows no signs of slowing down. As she told Sarah Booth Conroy of the *Washington Post:* "These are my happiest years. I always want to live long enough to finish the book I'm working on and see it published. But then I start another book before the previous one is in the stores, so I always have a reason to go on."

BIOGRAPHICAL/CRITICAL SOURCES:

BOOKS

Budd, Elaine, *Thirteen Mistresses of Murder,* Ungar (New York City), 1986, pp. 125-35.
Contemporary Literary Criticism, Volume 42, Gale (Detroit), 1987, pp. 431-38.
Gleasner, Diana, *Breakthrough: Women in Writing,* Walker, 1980, pp. 126-45.
Twentieth-Century Children's Writers, third edition, St. James Press (Detroit), 1989, pp. 1037-39.

PERIODICALS

Best Sellers, September, 1977, pp. 173-74.
Booklist, June 1, 1992, p. 1748; September 1, 1993, p. 38; September 15, 1994, p. 115; October 15, 1995, p. 421; May 1, 1997, p. 1462.
Chicago Tribune, June 16, 1991, section 14, p. 8; July 26, 1992, section 14, p. 4.
Christian Science Monitor, May 26, 1960, p. 17; November 23, 1960, p. 11.
Cosmopolitan, May, 1989, p. 13.
Kirkus Reviews, April 15, 1992, p. 498; July 1, 1993, p. 817; July 1, 1994, p. 884.
Library Journal, October 15, 1963; November 1, 1989, p. 128; August, 1991, p. 161; May 15, 1997, p. 105.
New York Times, April 6, 1947, p. 27.
New York Times Book Review, September 29, 1957, p. 41; May 18, 1969, p. 31; November 22, 1970, p. 61; February 20, 1972, p. 27; February 5, 1984, pp. 18-19; May 27, 1990.
Parade, November 2, 1975.
Publishers Weekly, May 4, 1992, p. 42; August 16, 1993, p. 88; August 8, 1994, p. 378.
Saturday Review, September 29, 1956.
Saturday Review of Literature, September 6, 1947, p. 34.
School Library Journal, August, 1990, p. 177; December, 1991, p. 150; March, 1995, p. 236.
Washington Post, September 2, 1991, pp. D1, D9.
Washington Post Book World, January 2, 1983, p. 4; January 6. 1985, p. 11.
West Coast Review of Books, number 1, 1985, p. 54; number 6, 1988, p. 27.
Writer, February, 1980, pp. 11-14, 46; June, 1985, pp. 9-12; July, 1987, p. 7; August, 1988, p. 9; December, 1989, p. 13; May, 1991, p. 11; August, 1992, p. 29.

* * *

WHITTLEBOT, Hernia
See COWARD, Noel (Peirce)

* * *

WIDEMAN, John Edgar 1941-

PERSONAL: Born June 14, 1941, in Washington, DC; son of Edgar and Betty (French) Wideman; married Judith Ann Goldman, 1965; children: Daniel Jerome, Jacob Edgar, Jamila Ann. *Education:* University of Pennsylvania, B.A., 1963; New College, Oxford, B.Phil., 1966.

ADDRESSES: Office—Department of English, University of Massachusetts-Amherst, Amherst, MA 01003.

CAREER: Howard University, Washington, DC, teacher of American literature, summer, 1965; University of Pennsylvania, Philadelphia, 1966-74, began as instructor, professor of English, 1974, director of Afro-American studies program, 1971-73; University of Wyoming, Laramie, professor of English, 1974-1985; University of Massachusetts-Amherst, professor of English, 1986–. Made U.S. Department of State lecture tour of Europe and the Near East, 1976; Phi Beta Kappa lecturer, 1976; visiting writer and lecturer at numerous colleges and universities; has also served as administrator/teacher in a curriculum planning, teacher-training institute sponsored by National Defense Education Act. Assistant basketball coach, University of Pennsylvania, 1968-72. National Humanities Faculty consultant in numerous states; consultant to secondary schools across the country, 1968–.

MEMBER: Association of American Rhodes Scholars (member of board of directors and of state and national selection committees), American Studies Association (council, 1980-81), Modern Language Association, American Academy of Arts and Sciences, Phi Beta Kappa.

AWARDS, HONORS: Received creative writing prize, University of Pennsylvania; Rhodes Scholar, Oxford University, 1963; Thouron fellow, Oxford University, 1963-66; Kent fellow, University of Iowa, 1966, to attend creative writing workshop; named member of Philadelphia Big Five Basketball Hall of Fame, 1974; Young Humanist fellow, 1975; PEN/Faulkner Award for fiction, 1984, for *Sent for You Yesterday;* National Book Award nomination, 1984, for *Brothers and Keepers;* John Dos Passos Prize for Literature from Longwood College, 1986; Lannan award, 1991; MacArthur fellow, 1993; honorary doctorate, University of Pennsylvania.

WRITINGS:

A Glance Away (novel), Harcourt, 1967.
Hurry Home (novel), Harcourt, 1970.
The Lynchers (novel), Harcourt, 1973.
Damballah (short stories), Avon, 1981.
Hiding Place (novel), Avon, 1981.
Sent for You Yesterday (novel), Avon, 1983.
Brothers and Keepers (memoirs), H. Holt, 1984.
The Homewood Trilogy (includes *Damballah, Hiding Place,* and *Sent For You Yesterday*), Avon, 1985.
Reuben (novel), H. Holt, 1987.
Fever (short stories), H. Holt, 1989.
Philadelphia Fire (novel), H. Holt, 1990.
All Stories Are True, Vintage Books, 1992.
The Stories of John Edgar Wideman, Pantheon Books, 1992.
A Glance Away, Hurry Home, and The Lynchers: Three Early Novels by John Edgar Wideman, Holt, Henry, and Co., 1994.
Fatheralong, Pantheon, 1994.
The Cattle Killing, Houghton Mifflin, 1996.

Contributor of articles, short stories, book reviews, and poetry to periodicals, including *American Poetry Review, Negro Digest, Black American Literature Forum, Black World, American Scholar, Gentleman's Quarterly, New York Times Book Review, North American Review,* and *Washington Post Book World.*

SIDELIGHTS: John Edgar Wideman has been hailed by Don Strachen in the *Los Angeles Times Book Review* as "the black Faulkner, the softcover Shakespeare." Such praise is not uncommon for this author, whose novel *Sent for You Yesterday* was selected as the 1984 PEN/Faulkner Award winner over works by Bernard Malamud, Cynthia Ozick, and William Kennedy. Wide-

man attended Oxford University in 1963 on a Rhodes scholarship, earned a degree in eighteenth-century literature, and later accepted a fellowship at the prestigious University of Iowa Writers' Workshop. Yet this "artist with whom any reader who admires ambitious fiction must sooner or later reckon," as the *New York Times* called him, began his college career not as a writer, but as a basketball star. "I always wanted to play pro basketball—ever since I saw a ball and learned you could make money at it," he told Curt Suplee in the *Washington Post.* Recruited by the University of Pennsylvania, Wideman first studied psychology, attracted by the "mystical insight" he told Suplee that he thought this major would yield. When his subjects of study instead "turned out to be rats" and clinical experiments, Wideman changed his major to English, while continuing to be mainly concerned with basketball. He played well enough to earn a place in the Philadelphia Big Five Basketball Hall of Fame, but, he told Suplee, as his time at the university drew to a close, "I knew I wasn't going to be able to get into the NBA [National Basketball Association]. What was left?" The Rhodes scholarship answered that question. Wideman began to concentrate on his writing rather than sports and did so with such success that his first novel, *A Glance Away,* was published just a year after he earned his degree from Oxford.

The story of a day in the life of a drug addict, *A Glance Away* reflects the harsh realities that Wideman saw and experienced during his youth in Pittsburgh's ghetto, Homewood. And, though the author later resided in other locales, including Wyoming, his novels continued to describe black urban experiences. He explained to Suplee, "My particular imagination has always worked well in a kind of exile. It fits the insider-outside view I've always had. It helps to write away from the center of the action."

Wideman's highly literate style is in sharp contrast to his gritty subject matter, and while reviews of his books have been generally favorable from the start of his writing career, some critics initially expressed the opinion that such a formal style was not appropriate for his stories of street life. For example, Anatole Broyard praised *The Lynchers* in his *New York Times* review, stating: "Though we have heard the themes and variations of violence before in black writing, *The Lynchers* touches us in a more personal way, for John Edgar Wideman has a weapon more powerful than any knife or gun. His weapon is art. Eloquence is his arsenal, his arms cache. His prose, at its best, is a black panther, coiled to spring." But Broyard went on to say that the book is not flawless: "Far from it. Mr. Wideman ripples too many muscles in his writing, often cannot seem to decide whether to show or snow us. . . . [He] is wordy, and *The Lynchers* is as shaky in its structure as some of the buildings his characters inhabit. But he can *write,* and you come away from his book with the feeling that he is, as they say, very close to getting it all together." In the *New York Times,* John Leonard commented on the extensive use of literary devices in *The Lynchers:* "Flashback, flashforward, first person, third person, journals, identity or change, interior monologue, dreams (historical and personal), puns, epiphanies. At times the devices seem a thicket through which one must hack one's weary way toward meanings arbitrarily obscure, a vegetable indulgence. But John Edgar Wideman is up to much more than storytelling. . . . He is capable of moving from ghetto language to [Irish writer James] Joyce with a flip of the page."

Saturday Review critic David Littlejohn agreed that Wideman's novels are very complex, and in his review of *Hurry Home* he criticized those who would judge this author as a storyteller:

"Reviewers . . . are probably more responsible than anyone else for the common delusion that a novel is somehow contained in its discernible, realistic plot. . . . *Hurry Home* is primarily an experience, not a plot: an experience of words, dense, private, exploratory, and non-progressive." Littlejohn described *Hurry Home* as a retelling of an American myth, that of "the lonely search through the Old World" for a sense of cultural heritage, which "has been the pattern of a hundred thousand young Americans' lives and novels." According to Littlejohn, Wideman's version is "spare and eccentric, highly stylized, circling, allusive, antichronological, far more consciously symbolic than most versions, than the usual self-indulgent and romantic works of this genre—and hence both more rewarding and more difficult of access." Reviewing the same book in the *New York Times Book Review,* Joseph Goodman stated: "Many of its pages are packed with psychological insight, and nearly all reveal Mr. Wideman's formidable command of the techniques of fiction. Moreover, the theme is a profound one—the quest for a substantive sense of self. . . . The prose, paratactic and rich with puns, flows as freely as thought itself, giving us . . . Joycean echoes. . . . It is a dazzling display. . . . We can have nothing but admiration for Mr. Wideman's talent."

Enthusiastic reviews such as these established Wideman's reputation in the literary world as a major talent. When his fourth and fifth books—*Damballah,* a collection of short stories, and *Hiding Place,* a novel—were issued originally as paperbacks, some critics, such as John Leonard and Mel Watkins, reacted with indignation. Leonard's *New York Times* review used extensive quotes from the books to demonstrate Wideman's virtuosity, and stated, "That [these] two new books will fall apart after a second reading is a scandal." Watkins's *New York Times Book Review* article on the two books, which were published simultaneously, had special praise for the short-story volume, and ended with a sentiment much like Leonard's on the books' binding. "In freeing his voice from the confines of the novel form," Watkins wrote, "[Wideman] has written what is possibly his most impressive work. . . . Each story moves far beyond the primary event on which it is focused. . . . Like [Jean] Toomer, Mr. Wideman has used a narrative laced with myth, superstition and dream sequences to create an elaborate poetic portrait of the lives of ordinary black people. . . . These books once again demonstrate that John Wideman is one of America's premier writers of fiction. That they were published originally in paperback perhaps suggests that he is also one of our most underrated writers." Actually, it was the author himself who had decided to bring the books out as original paperbacks. His reasons were philosophical and pragmatic. "I spend an enormous amount of time and energy writing and I want to write good books, but I also want people to read them," he explained to Edwin McDowell in the *New York Times.* Wideman's first three novels had been slow sellers "in spite of enormously positive reviews," he told Suplee, and it was his hope that the affordability of paperbacks would help give him a wider readership, particularly among "the people and the world I was writing about. A $15.95 novel had nothing to do with that world."

Damballah and *Hiding Place* had both been set in Homewood, Wideman's early home, and in 1983 he published a third book with the same setting, *Sent for You Yesterday.* Critics were enthusiastic. "In this hypnotic and deeply lyrical novel, Mr. Wideman again returns to the ghetto where he was raised and transforms it into a magical location infused with poetry and pathos," wrote Alan Cheuse in the *New York Times Book Review.* "The narration here makes it clear that both as a molder of language and a builder of plots, Mr. Wideman has come into his full powers. He has the gift of making 'ordinary' folks memorable." Stated Garett Epps in the *Washington Post Book World,* "Wideman has a fluent command of the American language, written and spoken, and a fierce, loving vision of the people he writes about. Like the writing of William Faulkner, Wideman's prose fiction is vivid and demanding—shuttling unpredictably between places, narrators and times, dwelling for a paragraph on the surface of things, then sneaking a key event into a clause that springs on the reader like a booby trap. . . . *Sent for You Yesterday* is a book to be savored, read slowly again and again."

When he ventured into nonfiction for the first time with his book *Brothers and Keepers,* Wideman continued to draw inspiration from the same source, Homewood. In this book, Wideman comes to terms with his brother Robby, younger by ten years, whose life was influenced by the street, its drugs, and its crime. The author writes, "Even as I manufactured fiction from the events of my brother's life, from the history of the family that had nurtured us both, I knew something of a different order remained to be extricated. The fiction writer was a man with a real brother behind real bars [serving a life sentence in a Pennsylvania penitentiary]." In his review in the *Washington Post Book World,* Jonathan Yardley called *Brothers and Keepers* "the elder Wideman's effort to understand what happened, to confess and examine his own sense of guilt about his brother's fate (and his own)." The result, according to the reviewer, is "a depiction of the inexorably widening chasm that divides middle-class black Americans from the black underclass." Wideman's personal experience, added Yardley, also reveals that for the black person "moving out of the ghetto into the white world is a process that requires excruciating compromises, sacrifices and denials, that leaves the person who makes the journey truly at home in neither the world he has entered nor the world he has left."

Wideman has, however, made a home for himself in literary circles, and at the same time has learned from his experience how to handle his success. When *Sent for You Yesterday* won the PEN/Faulkner Award—the only major literary award in the United States to be judged, administered, and largely funded by writers—Wideman told Suplee he felt "warmth. That's what I felt. Starting at the toes and filling up. A gradual recognition that it could be real." Still, the author maintained that if such an honor "doesn't happen again for a long time—or never happens again—it really doesn't matter," because he "learned more and more that the process itself was important, learned to take my satisfaction from the writing" during the years of comparative obscurity. "I'm an old jock," he explained. "So I've kind of trained myself to be low-key. Sometimes the crowd screams, sometimes the crowd doesn't scream."

The narrator of Wideman's 1987 novel, *Reuben,* provides inexpensive legal aid to residents of Homewood. One of his clients is Kwansa, a young black prostitute whose husband, a recovering drug addict, kidnaps and seeks legal custody of their illegitimate child as revenge against her. Another customer is Wally, an assistant basketball coach at a local white university who seeks Reuben's counsel for two reasons, one being the killing of a white man in Chicago and the other being his fear that he will be blamed for the illegal recruiting practices of his department. Reviewing the book in *Washington Post Book World,* Noel Perrin characterized Wideman's novels as myths. "In the end," Perrin wrote, "one sees that all the shocks—the murders, the fantasies, burnings, strong words—all of them amount to a kind of metaphor for the psychic damage that human beings do to each other and that is no less hurtful than spread-eagled beating, just less visible to the outer eye."

In *Philadelphia Fire,* Wideman brings together two stories, combining fact in fiction. In the first, he describes the events in Philadelphia when the police, under the direction of black mayor Wilson Goode, bombed the headquarters of an organization known as Move, a group that had defied city eviction notices and was armed with weapons. The police bombing killed six adults and five children, destroyed fifty three homes, and left 262 people homeless. Wideman's novel begins with a quote by William Penn, the founder of Pennsylvania, stating his dream that the town would "never be burnt, and always be wholesome." As Chicago *Tribune Books* reviewer Paul Skenazy pointed out, *Philadelphia Fire* tries to make sense of the changes that have occurred since Penn's statement, changes that include poverty and racism and that result in the burning of the Philadelphia neighborhood. The other story being told in the book is that of Wideman's relationship with his son who has received a life sentence for murder. "Few pages of prose," Skenazy said, "carry as much pain as do Wideman's thoughts on his son, his words to him in prison, his feelings of confusion as a father." Skenazy concluded that *Philadelphia Fire* is "about a person, and a nation, losing its grip, destroying the very differences and dissonance that provide spirit, beauty, life." Rosemary L. Bray in the *New York Times Book Review* concurred; "the author takes his readers on a tour of urban America perched on the precipice of hell," Bray wrote, "a tour in which even his own personal tragedy is part of the view."

In 1992, Wideman published *The Stories of John Edgar Wideman,* a volume that combined several earlier story collections, including *Damballah,* originally published in 1981, 1989's *Fever,* and *All Stories Are True* from 1992. Michael Harris wrote in the *Los Angeles Times Book Review* that a comparison between Wideman and Faulkner makes sense "because of the scope of Wideman's project, his ear for voices, . . . and the way he shows the present as perpetually haunted by the past." *New York Times Book Review* contributor Michael Gorra also believed the Faulkner comparison is apt. "It is appropriate," Gorra wrote, "because both are concerned with the life of a community over time. It is appropriate because they both have a feel for the anecdotal folklore through which a community defines itself, because they both often choose to present their characters in the act of telling stories, and because in drawing on oral tradition they both write as their characters speak, in a language whose pith and vigor has not yet been worn into cliche." It is Gorra's conclusion that "the more you read John Edgar Wideman, the more impressive he seems."

Wideman's 1994 book, *Fatheralong,* like *Philadelphia Fire* and the Homewood stories, juxtaposes Wideman's personal life with larger issues. Mel Watkins in the *New York Times Book Review* referred to it as a hybrid of memoir and "a meditation on fatherhood, race, metaphysics, time and the afterlife." Wideman explores his strained relationship with his father and his troubles with his own son, and then frames them in the context of all father-son relationships as well as America's racist legacy. A *Village Voice* critic found the sections on Wideman's son, Jacob, to be his "most artful work. The Jacob sections overshadow simply because they're so much better written, their subject more emotionally grasped than any other." Mitchell Duneier in the *Los Angeles Times Book Review* called *Fatheralong* "a masterpiece of sociological speculation, constructed with such an abundance of wisdom as to compensate for its lack of evidence regarding questions to which there are no easy answers." In the Chicago *Tribune Books,* Michael Boynton, calling the work "part memoir,

part manifesto," concluded "*Fatheralong* is an odd, sad book. Filled with flashes of insight told in Wideman's distinctive prose-poetry, it is at once personal and essentially opaque. . . . It leaves the reader wanting to know more, hoping that its author will one day find the key he has been looking for."

Wideman returned to fiction with his 1996 novel, *The Cattle Killing.* In it, he weaves together memories from his narrator's childhood in Philadelphia with the plight of blacks in the city in the late-eighteenth century and the story of the South African Xhosa tribe, pulling threads of history, religion, and race to form his story. The complex story was met with mostly positive reviews, with critics finding flaws in the novel's coherence but praising Wideman's imaginative storytelling powers.

BIOGRAPHICAL/CRITICAL SOURCES:

BOOKS

Black Literature Criticism, Gale (Detroit), 1992.
Black Writers, Gale, 1989.
Byerman, Keith Eldon, *John Edgar Wideman: A Study of the Short Fiction,* Twayne, 1998.
Contemporary Literary Criticism, Gale, Volume 5, 1976; Volume 34, 1985; Volume 36, 1986; Volume 67, 1992.
Dictionary of Literary Biography, Volume 33: *Afro-American Fiction Writers after 1955,* Gale, 1984; Volume 143: *American Novelists since World War II, Third Series,* Gale, 1994.
Mbalia, Doreatha D., *John Edgar Wideman: Reclaiming the African Personality,* Associated University Presses (London), 1995.
O'Brien, John, editor, *Interviews with Black Writers,* Liveright, 1973.
Tusmith, Bonnie, editor, *Conversations with John Edgar Wideman,* University Press of Mississippi, 1998.

PERIODICALS

Booklist, August, 1994, p. 1987; September 15, 1994, p. 153.
Christian Science Monitor, July 10, 1992.
Journal of Negro History, January, 1963.
Kirkus Reviews, August 1, 1996, p. 1092.
Library Journal, March 1, 1994, p. 134; September 15, 1994, p. 85; July, 1996, p. 164.
Los Angeles Times, November 11, 1987.
Los Angeles Times Book Review, April 17, 1983; December 23, 1984; December 29, 1985; September 30, 1990; September 13, 1992; December 25, 1994, p. 2.
Negro Digest, May, 1963.
New Republic, July 13, 1992.
New Statesman, September 1, 1995, p. 34.
Newsweek, May 7, 1970.
New York Magazine, October 1, 1990.
New York Review of Books, May 11, 1995, p. 27.
New York Times, April 2, 1970; May 15, 1973, November 27, 1981; May 16, 1984; October 29, 1984; September 4, 1986; July 21, 1992.
New York Times Book Review, September 10, 1967; April 19, 1970; April 29, 1973; April 11, 1982; May 15, 1983; November 4, 1984; January 13, 1985; December 15, 1985; May 11, 1986; November 30, 1986; November 8, 1987; October 16, 1988; December 10, 1989; September 30, 1990; October 14, 1990; November 17, 1991; June 14, 1992; November 13, 1994, p. 11.
Publishers Weekly, August 12, 1996, p. 63.
Saturday Review, October 21, 1967; May 2, 1970.

Shenandoah, winter, 1974.

Tikkun, March-April, 1995, p. 80.

Time, October 1, 1990.

Times (London), December 6, 1984.

Times Literary Supplement, December 21, 1984; January 16, 1987; August 5, 1988; August 23, 1991.

Tribune Books (Chicago), December 23, 1984; November 29, 1987; October 28, 1990; November 24, 1991; October 23, 1994, p. 8.

Village Voice, October 25, 1994.

Washington Post, May 10, 1984; May 12, 1984.

Washington Post Book World, July 3, 1983; October 21, 1984; November 15, 1987; October 16, 1988; October 21, 1990.

Whole Earth Review, summer, 1995, p. 78.

*   *   *

WIESEL, Elie(zer) 1928-

PERSONAL: Born September 30, 1928, in Sighet, Romania; came to the United States, 1956, naturalized U.S. citizen, 1963; son of Shlomo (a grocer) and Sarah (Feig) Wiesel; married Marion Erster Rose, 1969; children: Shlomo Elisha. *Education:* Attended Sorbonne, University of Paris, 1948-51. *Religion:* Jewish.

ADDRESSES: Office—University Professors, Boston University, 745 Commonwealth Ave., Boston, MA 02215-1401. *Agent*—Georges Borchardt, 136 East 57th St., New York, NY 10022.

CAREER: Foreign correspondent at various times for *Yedioth Ahronoth,* Tel Aviv, Israel, *L'Arche,* Paris, France, and *Jewish Daily Forward,* New York City, 1949–; City College of the City University of New York, New York City, distinguished professor, 1972-76; Boston University, Boston, MA, Andrew Mellon professor in the humanities, 1976–, professor of Philosophy, 1988–; Whitney Humanities Center, Yale University, New Haven, CT, Henry Luce visiting scholar in Humanities and Social Thought, 1982-83; Florida International University, Miami, distinguished visiting professor of literature and philosophy, 1982. Chairman, United States President's Commission on the Holocaust, 1979-80, U.S. Holocaust Memorial Council, 1980-86.

MEMBER: Amnesty International, PEN, Writers Guild of America, Author's Guild, American Academy of Arts and Sciences, Jewish Academy of Arts and Sciences, European Academy of Arts and Sciences, Foreign Press Association (honorary lifetime member), Writers and Artists for Peace in the Middle East, Royal Norwegian Society of Sciences and Letters, Phi Beta Kappa, Societe des autheurs.

AWARDS, HONORS: Prix Rivarol, 1963; Remembrance Award, 1965, for *The Town beyond the Wall* and all other writings; William and Janice Epstein Fiction Award, Jewish Book Council, 1965, for *The Town beyond the Wall;* Jewish Heritage Award, 1966, for excellence in literature; Prix Medicis, 1969, for *Le Mendiant de Jerusalem;* Prix Bordin, French Academy, 1972; Eleanor Roosevelt Memorial Award, 1972; American Liberties Medallion, American Jewish Committee, 1972; Frank and Ethel S. Cohen Award, Jewish Book Council, 1973, for *Souls on Fire;* Martin Luther King, Jr., Award, City College of the City University of New York, 1973; Faculty Distinguished Scholar Award, Hofstra University, 1973-74; Joseph Prize for Human Rights, Anti-Defamation League of B'nai B'rith, 1978; Zalman Shazar Award, State of Israel, 1979; Jabotinsky Medal, State of

Israel, 1980; Prix Livre-International, 1980, and Prix des Bibliothecaires, 1981, both for *Le Testament d'un poete juif assassine;* Anatoly Scharansky Humanitarian Award, 1983; Congressional Gold Medal, 1984; humanitarian award, International League for Human Rights, 1985; Freedom Cup award, Women's League of Israel, 1986; Nobel peace prize, 1986; Special Christopher Book Award, 1987; achievement award, Artists and Writers for Peace in the Middle East, 1987; Profiles of Courage award, B'nai B'rith, 1987; Human Rights Law Award, International Human Rights Law Group, 1988; Presidential medal, Hofstra University, 1988; Human Rights Law award, International Human Rights Law Group, 1988; Bicentennial medal, Georgetown University, 1988; Janus Korczak Humanitarian award, NAHE, Kent State University, 1989; Count Sforza award in Philanthropy Interphil, 1989; Lily Edelman award for Excellence in Continuing Jewish Education, B'nai B'rith International, 1989; George Washington award, American Hungarian Foundation, 1989; Bicentennial medal, New York University, 1989; Humanitarian award Human Rights Campaign Fund, 1989; International Brotherhood award, C.O.R.E., 1990; Frank Weil award for distinguished contribution to the advancement of North American Jewish culture, Jewish Community Centers Association of North America, 1990; 1st Raoul Wallenberg medal, University of Michigan, 1990; Award of Highest Honor, Soka University, 1991; Facing History and Ourselves Humanity award, 1991; La Medaille de la Ville de Toulouse, 1991; 5th Centennial Christopher Columbus medal, City of Genoa, 1992; 1st Primo Levi award, 1992; Literature Arts award, National Foundation for Jewish Culture, 1992; Ellis Island Medal of Honor, 1992; Guardian of the Children award, AKIM USA, 1992; Bishop Francis J. Mugavero award for religious and racial harmony, Queens College, 1994; Golden Slipper Humanitarian award, 1994; Interfaith Council on the Holocaust Humanitarian award, 1994; Crystal award, Davos World Economic Forum, 1995; First Niebuhr award, Elmhurst College, 1995; named Humanitarian of the Century, Council of Jewish Organizations; recipient of numerous honorary degrees; honors established in his name: Elie Wiesel award for Holocaust Research, University of Haifa; Elie Wiesel Chair in Holocaust Studies, Bar-Ilan University; Elie Wiesel Endowment Fund for Jewish Culture, University of Denver; Elie Wiesel Distinguished Service award, University of Florida; Elie Wiesel awards for Jewish Arts and Culture, B'nai B'rith Hillel Foundations; Elie Wiesel Chair in Judaic Studies, Connecticut College

WRITINGS:

Un Di Velt Hot Geshvign (title means "And the World Has Remained Silent"), [Buenos Aires], 1956, abridged French translation published as *La Nuit* (also see below), foreword by Francois Mauriac, Editions de Minuit, 1958, translation by Stella Rodway published as *Night* (also see below), Hill & Wang, 1960.

L'Aube (also see below), Editions du Seuil, 1961, translation by Frances Frenaye published as *Dawn* (also see below), Hill & Wang, 1961.

Le Jour (also see below), Editions du Seuil, 1961, translation by Anne Borchardt published as *The Accident* (also see below), Hill & Wang, 1962.

La Ville de la chance, Editions du Seuil, 1962, translation by Stephen Becker published as *The Town beyond the Wall,* Atheneum, 1964, new edition, Holt, 1967.

Les Portes de la foret, Editions du Seuil, 1964, translation by Frenaye published as *The Gates of the Forest,* Holt, 1966.

Le Chant des morts, Editions de Seuil, 1966, translation published as *Legends of Our Time,* Holt, 1968.

The Jews of Silence: A Personal Report on Soviet Jewry (originally published in Hebrew as a series of articles for newspaper *Yedioth Ahronoth*), translation and afterword by Neal Kozodoy, Holt, 1966, 2nd edition, Vallentine, Mitchell, 1973.

Zalmen; ou, la Folie de Dieu (play), 1966, translation by Lily and Nathan Edelman published as *Zalmen; or, The Madness of God,* Holt, 1968.

Le Mendiant de Jerusalem, 1968, translation by the author and L. Edelman published as *A Beggar in Jerusalem,* Random House, 1970.

La Nuit, L'Aube, [and] *Le Jour,* Editions du Seuil, 1969, translation published as *Night, Dawn,* [and] *The Accident: Three Tales,* Hill & Wang, 1972, reprinted as *The Night Trilogy: Night, Dawn, The Accident,* Farrar, Straus, 1987, translation by Rodway published as *Night, Dawn, Day,* Aronson, 1985.

Entre deux soleils, Editions du Seuil, 1970, translation by the author and L. Edelman published as *One Generation After,* Random House, 1970.

Celebration Hassidique: Portraits et legendes, Editions du Seuil, 1972, translation by wife, Marion Wiesel, published as *Souls on Fire: Portraits and Legends of Hasidic Masters,* Random House, 1972.

Le Serment de Kolvillag, Editions du Seuil, 1973, translation by M. Wiesel published as *The Oath,* Random House, 1973.

Ani maamin: A Song Lost and Found Again (cantata), music composed by Darius Milhaud, Random House, 1974.

Celebration Biblique: Portraits et legendes, Editions du Seuil, 1975, translation by M. Wiesel published as *Messengers of God: Biblical Portraits and Legends,* Random House, 1976.

Un Juif aujourd'hui: Recits, essais, dialogues, Editions du Seuil, 1977, translation by M. Wiesel published as *A Jew Today,* Random House, 1978.

(With others) *Dimensions of the Holocaust,* Indiana University Press, 1977.

Four Hasidic Masters and Their Struggle against Melancholy, University of Notre Dame Press, 1978.

Le Proces de Shamgorod tel qu'il se deroula le 25 fevrier 1649: Piece en trois actes, Editions du Seuil, 1979, translation by M. Wiesel published as *The Trial of God (as It Was Held on February 25, 1649, in Shamgorod): A Play in Three Acts,* Random House, 1979.

Images from the Bible, illustrated with paintings by Shalom of Safed, Overlook Press, 1980.

Le Testament d'un poete Juif assassine, Edition du Seuil, 1980, translation by M. Wiesel published as *The Testament,* Simon & Schuster, 1981.

Five Biblical Portraits, University of Notre Dame Press, 1981.

Somewhere a Master, Simon & Schuster, 1982, reprinted as *Somewhere a Master: Further Tales of the Hasidic Masters,* Summit Books, 1984.

Paroles d'etranger, Editions du Seuil, 1982.

The Golem: The Story of a Legend as Told by Elie Wiesel (fiction), illustrated by Mark Podwal, Summit Books, 1983.

Le Cinquieme Fils, Grasset (Paris), 1983, translation by M. Wiesel published as *The Fifth Son,* Summit Books, 1985.

Against Silence: The Voice and Vision of Elie Wiesel, three volumes, edited by Irving Abrahamson, Holocaust Library, 1985.

Signes d'exode, Grasset & Fasquelle (Paris), 1985.

Job ou Dieu dans la tempete, Grasset & Fasquelle, 1986.

Le Crepuscule au loin, Grasset & Fasquelle, 1987, translation by M. Wiesel published as *Twilight,* Summit Books, 1988.

(With Albert H. Friedlander) *The Six Days of Destruction,* Paulist Press, 1989.

L'Oublie: Roman, Seuil, 1989.

(With Philippe-Michael de Saint-Cheron) *Evil and Exile,* translated by Jon Rothschild, University of Notre Dame Press, 1990.

(With John Cardinal O'Connor) *A Journey of Faith,* Donald I. Fine, foreword by Gabe Pressman, 1990.

Sages and Dreamers: Biblical, Talmudic, and Hasidic Portraits and Legends, Summit, 1991.

The Forgotten (novel), translated by Stephen Becker, Summit, 1992, paperback edition, Schocken Books, 1995.

(With Salomon Malka) *Monsieur Chouchani: L'enigme d'un Maitre du XX Siecle: Entretiens Avec Elie Wiesel, Suivis d'une Enquete,* J. C. Lattes (Paris), 1994.

Tous les Fleuves Vont a la Mer: Memoires, Editions du Seuil (Paris), 1994, published as *All Rivers Run to the Sea: Memoirs,* Knopf, 1995.

(With Francois Mitterrand) *Memoire a Deux Voix,* Jacob (Paris), 1995, published as *Memoir in Two Voices,* Arcade (New York City), 1996.

Also author of *A Song for Hope,* 1987, *The Nobel Speech,* 1987, and *From the Kingdom of Memory* (essays), 1990.

SIDELIGHTS: In the spring of 1944, the Nazis entered the Transylvanian village of Sighet, Romania, until then a relatively safe and peaceful enclave in the middle of a war-torn continent. Arriving with orders to exterminate an estimated 600,000 Jews in six weeks or less, Adolf Eichmann, chief of the Gestapo's Jewish section, began making arrangements for a mass deportation program. Among those forced to leave their homes was fifteen-year-old Elie Wiesel, the only son of a grocer and his wife. A serious and devoted student of the Talmud and the mystical teachings of Hasidism and the Cabala, the young man had always assumed he would spend his entire life in Sighet, quietly contemplating the religious texts and helping out in the family's store from time to time. Instead, along with his father, mother, and three sisters, Wiesel was herded onto a train bound for Birkenau, the reception center for the infamous death camp Auschwitz.

For reasons he still finds impossible to comprehend, Wiesel survived Birkenau and later Auschwitz and Buna and Buchenwald; his father, mother, and youngest sister did not (he did not learn until after the war that his older sisters also survived). With nothing and no one in Sighet for him to go back to, Wiesel boarded a train for Belgium with four hundred other orphans who, like him, had no reason or desire to return to their former homes. On orders of General Charles de Gaulle, head of the French provisional government after World War II, the train was diverted to France, where border officials asked the children to raise their hands if they wanted to become French citizens. As Wiesel (who at that time neither spoke nor understood French) recalls in the *Washington Post,* "A lot of them did. They thought they were going to get bread or something; they would reach out for anything. I didn't, so I remained stateless."

Wiesel chose to stay in France for a while, settling first in Normandy and later in Paris, doing whatever he could to earn a living: tutoring, directing a choir, translating. Eventually he began working as a reporter for various French and Jewish publications. But he could not quite bring himself to write about what he had seen and felt at Auschwitz and Buchenwald. Doubtful of his—or of anyone's—ability to convey the horrible truth without diminishing it, Wiesel vowed never to make the attempt.

The young journalist's self-imposed silence came to an end in the mid-1950s, however, after he met and interviewed the Nobel Prize-winning novelist Francois Mauriac. Deeply moved upon learning of Wiesel's tragic youth, Mauriac urged him to speak out and tell the world of his experiences, to "bear witness" for the millions of men, women, and children whom death, and not despair, had silenced. The result was *Night*, the story of a teen-age boy plagued with guilt for having survived the camps and devastated by the realization that the God he had once worshipped so devoutly allowed his people to be destroyed. For the most part autobiographical, it was, says Richard M. Elman in the *New Republic*, "a document as well as a work of literature—journalism which emerged, coincidentally, as a work of art."

Described by the *Nation*'s Daniel Stern as "undoubtedly the single most powerful literary relic of the holocaust," *Night* is the first in a series of nonfiction books and autobiographical novels this "lyricist of lamentation" has written that deal, either directly or indirectly, with the Holocaust. "He sees the present always refracted through the prism of these earlier days," comments James Finn in the *New Republic*. The *New York Times*'s Thomas Lask agrees, stating: "For [more than] twenty-five years, Elie Wiesel has been in one form or another a witness to the range, bestiality, and completeness of the destruction of European Jewry by the Germans. . . . Auschwitz informs everything he writes—novels, legends, dialogues. He is not belligerent about it, only unyielding. Nothing he can say measures up to the enormity of what he saw, what others endured. The implications these experiences have for mankind terrify him. . . . He is part conscience, part quivering needle of response and part warning signal. His writing is singular in the disparate elements it has unified, in the peculiar effect of remoteness and immediacy it conveys. He is his own mold."

Other novels by Wiesel about the Jewish experience during and after the Holocaust include *Dawn* and *The Accident*, which were later published together with *Night* in *The Night Trilogy: Night, Dawn, The Accident*. Like *Night*, the other two books in the trilogy have concentration camp survivors as their central characters. *Dawn* concerns the experiences of one survivor just after World War II who joins the Jewish underground efforts to form an independent Israeli state; and *The Accident* is about a man who discovers that his collision with an automobile was actually caused by his subconscious, guilt-ridden desire to commit suicide.

In two of Wiesel's later novels, *The Testament* and *The Fifth Son*, the author also explores the effects of the Holocaust on the next generation of Jews. Some critics such as *Globe and Mail* contributor Bronwyn Drainie have questioned the validity of the author's belief that children of Holocaust survivors would be "as morally galvanized by the Nazi nightmare as the survivors themselves." But, asserts Richard F. Shepard in the *New York Times*, even if the feelings of these children cannot be generalized, "the author does make all of us 'children' of that generation, all of us who were not there, in the sense that he outlines for us the burdens of guilt, of revenge, of despair."

In addition to his intense preoccupation with ancient Jewish philosophy, mythology, and history, Wiesel displays a certain affinity with modern French existentialists, an affinity Josephine Knopp believes is a direct consequence of the Holocaust. Writes Knopp in *Contemporary Literature*: "To the young Wiesel the notion of an 'absurd' universe would have been a completely alien one. . . . The traditional Jewish view holds that life's structure and meaning are fully explained and indeed derive from the divinely granted Torah. . . . Against this background the reality of Auschwitz confronts the Jew with a dilemma, an 'absurdity' which cannot be dismissed easily and which stubbornly refuses to dissipate of its own accord. . . . The only possible response that remains within the framework of Judaism is denunciation of God and a demand that He fulfill His contractual obligation [to protect those who worship Him]. This is the religious and moral context within which Wiesel attempts to apprehend and assimilate the events of the Holocaust. [He seeks] to reconcile Auschwitz with Judaism, to confront and perhaps wring meaning from the absurd." In a more recent novel, *Twilight*, Wiesel explores this absurdity—in this case, he goes so far as to call it madness—of the universe. Again, the protagonist is a Jew, who begins to wonder, as *New York Times* reviewer John Gross explains, whether "it is mad to go on believing in God. Or perhaps . . . it is God who is mad: who else but a mad God could have created such a world?"

The strong emphasis on Jewish tradition and Jewish suffering in Wiesel's works does not mean that he speaks only to and for Jews. In fact, maintains Robert McAfee Brown in *Christian Century*, "writing out of the particularity of his own Jewishness . . . is how [Wiesel] touches universal chords. He does not write about 'the human condition,' but about 'the Jewish condition.' Correction: in writing about the Jewish condition, he thereby writes about the human condition. For the human condition is not generalized existence; it is a huge, crazy-quilt sum of particularized existences all woven together."

To Stern, this time commenting in the *Washington Post Book World*, it seems that "Wiesel has taken the Jew as his metaphor—and his reality—in order to unite a moral and aesthetic vision in terms of all men." Manes Sperber of the *New York Times Book Review* expresses a similar view, stating that "Wiesel is one of the few writers who, without any plaintiveness, has succeeded in revealing in the Jewish tragedy those features by which it has become again and again a paradigm of the human condition."

According to Michael J. Bandler in the *Christian Science Monitor*, Wiesel conveys his angry message to God "with a force and stylistic drive that leaves the reader stunned." Concise and uncluttered, yet infused with a highly emotional biblical mysticism, the author's prose "gleams again and again with the metaphor of the poet," writes Clifford A. Ridley in the *National Observer*. Though it "never abandons its tender intimacy," reports Sperber, "[Wiesel's] voice comes from far away in space and time. It is the voice of the Talmudic teachers of Jerusalem and Babylon; of medieval mystics; of Rabbi Nachman of Bratzlav whose tales have inspired generations of Hasidim and so many writers." As Lask observes, "[Wiesel] has made the form of the telling his own. The surreal and the supernatural combine abrasively with the harsh fact; the parable, the rabbinic tale support and sometimes substitute for narrative. The written law and oral tradition support, explain and expand the twentieth-century event." In the *Nation*, Laurence Goldstein, noting the author's "remarkably compassionate tone," declares that "he writes with that possessive reverence for language that celebrates, as much as describes, experience. The written word becomes a powerful assertion, the triumph of life over death and indifference. . . . Words carved on gravestones, legend torn from the pit where millions of broken bodies lie. This is the inheritance which Elie Wiesel brings to us. His voice claims us with its urgency. His vision lights the mystery of human endurance."

Wiesel expresses what *Commonweal*'s Irving Halpern calls "the anguish of a survivor who is unable to exorcise the past or to live with lucidity and grace in the present" in the book *Night*, his first attempt to bear witness for the dead. Wiesel writes: "Never shall I forget that night, the first night in camp, which has turned my life into one long night, seven times cursed and seven times sealed. Never shall I forget that smoke. Never shall I forget the little faces of the children, whose bodies I saw turned into wreaths of smoke beneath a silent blue sky. Never shall I forget those flames which consumed my Faith forever. Never shall I forget that nocturnal silence which deprived me, for all eternity, of the desire to live. Never shall I forget those moments which murdered my God and my soul and turned my dreams to dust. Never shall I forget these things, even if I am condemned to live as long as God Himself. Never."

Concern that the truths of the Holocaust, and memories in general, might in time be forgotten has often fueled Wiesel's writing. In comparing his many works, Wiesel remarked to *Publishers Weekly* interviewer Elizabeth Devereaux, "What do they have in common? Their commitment to memory. What is the opposite of memory? Alzheimer's disease. I began to research this topic and I discovered that this is the worst disease, that every intellectual is afraid of this disease, not just because it is incurable, which is true of other diseases, too. But here the identity is being abolished." From this realization Wiesel created *The Forgotten*, a novel in which a Holocaust survivor fears he is losing his memories to an unnamed ailment. He beseeches his son to listen and remember as he recounts the events of his life. The dutiful son embarks for Romania to recover the details of his father's experience, including the death of his family at the hands of the Nazis and his role as an Eastern European partisan and freedom fighter for the establishment of Israel. Though Wiesel told Devereaux that this novel is "less autobiographical" than his others, *The Forgotten* contains recognizable allusions to his own life and work in references to the one-word titles of his first three novels and similarities between the father's childhood village and Wiesel's own. As Frederick Busch observes in the *New York Times Book Review*, Wiesel "intends to warn us that many of the survivors of the Holocaust are dying, that the cruel truth of the war against the Jews might one day be lost or clouded." Citing the author's "characteristic blend of petition, contemplative discourse, and devotion to Jewish tradition," Jonathan Dorfman writes in a *Chicago Tribune* review, "*The Forgotten* is ample proof that . . . Wiesel remains a writer of significance and high merit."

Wiesel produced the first volume of his projected two-volume personal memoirs with *All Rivers Run to the Sea*, spanning the years from his childhood to the 1960s. He begins by recollecting the haunting premonition of a well-known rabbi which foretold the young Wiesel's future greatness, though it predicted that neither Wiesel nor his mother would live to know of his acclaim. In the reminiscence and anecdote that follows, Wiesel revisits his early village life, post-war orphanage and education in France, initiation as a professional journalist, and involvement in events surrounding the birth of Israel. As James E. Young notes in the *New Leader*, Wiesel devotes only twenty pages of the book to his concentration camp experiences. "Wiesel's memoir is not about what happened during those eleven months," Young writes, "but about how they shaped his life afterward, how they have been remembered, how he has lived in their shadow." Despite Wiesel's confessed over-sensitivity to criticism and painful episodes of self-doubt, critics note that his memoir reveals little about the author's personal life that is not evident in his previous works. Daphne Merkin writes in the *New York Times Book Review*, "If

the reader finishes this book with an impression that the public and private Elie Wiesel seem to dance around each other without every really connecting, the author has foreseen this: 'Some see their work as a commentary on their life; for others it is the other way around. I count myself among the latter. Consider this account, then, as a kind of commentary.'" Wiesel concludes, as quoted by Vivian Gornick in the *Nation*, by writing, "The aim of the literature I call testimony is to disturb. I disturb the believer because I dare to put questions to God. I disturb the miscreant because I refuse to break with the religious and mystical universe that has shaped my own. Most of all, I disturb those who are comfortably settled within a system—be it political, psychological, or theological."

Memoir in Two Voices is a record of years of conversations between Elie Wiesel and Francois Mitterand. In it, they discuss history, war, especially World War II and the Holocaust, religious faith, literature, and personal topics. Writing in *Booklist*, Bonnie Smothers calls *Memoir in Two Voices* "a very special book, powerful at times, always provoking the reader's inner thoughts."

Many years after *Night*, Wiesel is still torn between words and silence. "You must speak," he told a *People* magazine interviewer, "but how can you, when the full story is beyond language?" Furthermore, he once remarked in the *Washington Post*, "there is the fear of not being believed . . . the fear that the experience will be reduced, made into something acceptable, perhaps forgotten." But as he went on to explain in *People*: "We [survivors] believe that if we survived, we must do something with our lives. The first task is to tell the tale." In short, concluded Wiesel, "The only way to stop the next holocaust—the nuclear holocaust—is to remember the last one. If the Jews were singled out then, in the next one we are all victims." For his enduring efforts to keep the memory of the Holocaust alive so that such a tragedy would not repeat itself ever again, Wiesel was awarded the Nobel peace prize in 1986. In a *New York Times* article on the event, James M. Markham quotes Egil Aarvik, chairman of the Norwegian Nobel Committee: "Wiesel is a messenger to mankind. . . . His message is one of peace, atonement and human dignity. His belief that the forces fighting evil in the world can be victorious is a hard-won belief . . . repeated and deepened through the works of a great author."

BIOGRAPHICAL/CRITICAL SOURCES:

BOOKS

Authors and Artists for Young Adults, Volume 7, Gale (Detroit), 1991.

Berenbaum, Michael, *Elie Wiesel: God, the Holocaust, and the Children of Israel*, Behrman House, 1994.

Cohen, Myriam B., *Elie Wiesel: Variations sur le Silence*, Rumeur des ages, 1988.

Contemporary Authors Autobiography Series, Volume 4, Gale, 1986.

Contemporary Issues Criticism, Volume 1, Gale, 1982.

Contemporary Literary Criticism, Gale, Volume 3, 1975; Volume 5, 1976; Volume 11, 1979; Volume 37, 1986.

Davis, Colin, *Elie Wiesel's Secretive Texts*, University Press of Florida, 1994.

Dictionary of Literary Biography, Volume 83: *French Novelists since 1960*, Gale, 1989.

Dictionary of Literary Biography Yearbook: 1987, Gale, 1988.

Lazo, Caroline Evensen, *Elie Wiesel*, Macmillian (New York City), 1994.

Pariser, Michael, *Elie Wiesel: Bearing Witness,* Millbrook Press, 1994.

Rosenfeld, Alvin, *Confronting the Holocaust,* Indiana University Press, 1978.

Schuman, Michael, *Elie Wiesel: Voice from the Holocaust,* Enslow, 1994.

Sibelman, Simon P., *Silence in the Novels of Elie Wiesel,* St. Martin's Press, 1995.

Stern, Ellen Norman, *Elie Wiesel: A Voice for Humanity,* Jewish Publication Society, 1996.

PERIODICALS

America, November 19, 1988.

Best Sellers, March 15, 1970; May, 1981.

Booklist, February 15, 1994, p. 1100; September 1, 1995, p. 96; July, 1996, p. 1798.

Book Week, May 29, 1966.

Chicago Tribune Book World, October 29, 1978; March 29, 1981; May 3, 1992.

Christian Century, January 18, 1961; June 17, 1970; June 3, 1981.

Christian Science Monitor, November 21, 1968; February 19, 1970; November 22, 1978.

Commentary, June, 1996, p. 64.

Commonweal, December 9, 1960; January 6, 1961; March 13, 1964; October 14, 1966.

Contemporary Literature, spring, 1974.

Detroit Free Press, April 12, 1992.

Detroit News, April 4, 1992.

Globe and Mail (Toronto), April 20, 1985; August 6, 1988.

Library Journal, February 15, 1994, p. 202; December, 1995, p. 120.

London Times, September 3, 1981.

Los Angeles Times Book Review, June 19, 1988.

Nation, October 17, 1966; February 24, 1969; March 16, 1970; January 5, 1974; December 25, 1995, p. 839.

National Observer, February 2, 1970.

National Review, June 12, 1981.

New Choices, December-January, 1993, p. 64.

New Leader, December 30, 1968; June 15, 1981; December 18, 1995, p. 17.

New Republic, July 5, 1964; December 14, 1968.

Newsweek, May 25, 1964; February 9, 1970.

New York, December 11, 1995, p. 72.

New Yorker, March 18, 1961; January 9, 1965; August 20, 1966; July 6, 1970; July 12, 1976.

New York Review of Books, July 28, 1966; January 2, 1969; May 7, 1970.

New York Times, December 15, 1970; March 10, 1972; April 3, 1981; April 16, 1984; March 21, 1985; October 15, 1986; June 10, 1988; December 5, 1995, p. B2.

New York Times Book Review, July 16, 1961; April 15, 1962; July 5, 1964; January 21, 1979; April 12, 1981; August 15, 1982; April 30, 1989; April 19, 1992, p. 8; December 17, 1995, p. 7.

People Weekly, October 22, 1979.

Publishers Weekly, April 6, 1992; October 16, 1995, p. 49; October 23, 1995, p. 33; January 15, 1996, p. 320; May 20, 1996, p. 245.

Saturday Review, December 17, 1960; July 8, 1961; July 25, 1964; May 28, 1966; October 19, 1968; January 31, 1970; November 21, 1970.

Time, March 16, 1970; May 8, 1972; July 12, 1976; December 25, 1978; April 20, 1981.

Times Literary Supplement, August 19, 1960; November 20, 1981; June 6, 1986.

Washington Post, October 26, 1968; February 6, 1970; November 15, 1986; November 4, 1989.

Washington Post Book World, October 20, 1968; January 18, 1970; August 8, 1976; October 29, 1978; April 12, 1981; May 29, 1988.

*   *   *

WILBUR, Richard (Purdy) 1921-

PERSONAL: Born March 1, 1921, in New York, NY; son of Lawrence Lazear (a portrait artist) and Helen Ruth (Purdy) Wilbur; married Mary Charlotte Hayes Ward, June 20, 1942; children: Ellen Dickinson, Christopher Hayes, Nathan Lord, Aaron Hammond. *Education:* Amherst College, A.B., 1942; Harvard University, A.M., 1947. *Politics:* Independent. *Religion:* Episcopal. *Avocational interests:* Tennis, herb gardening, walking.

ADDRESSES: Home—R.R.1, Box 82, Dodwells Rd., Cummington, MA 01026; 715R Windsor Ln., Key West, FL 33040. *Office*—Department of English, Smith College, Northampton, MA 01063 *Agent*—(Theatrical) Gilbert Parker, William Morris Agency, 1350 Avenue of the Americas, New York, NY 10019.

CAREER: Harvard University, Cambridge, MA, Society of Fellows, junior fellow, 1947-50, assistant professor of English, 1950-54; Wellesley College, Wellesley, MA, associate professor of English, 1955-57; Wesleyan University, Middletown, CT, professor of English, 1957-77; Smith College, Northampton, MA, writer in residence, 1977-86; Library of Congress, Washington, DC, Poet Laureate of the United States, 1987-88. Lecturer at colleges, universities, and Library of Congress. U.S. State Department cultural exchange representative to the U.S.S.R., 1961. *Military service:* U.S. Army, Infantry, 1943-45; became staff sergeant.

MEMBER: American Academy and Institute of Arts and Letters (president, 1974-76; chancellor, 1976-78), American Academy of Arts and Sciences, PEN, Academy of American Poets (chancellor), Dramatists' Guild, Modern Language Association (honorary fellow), ASCAP, Authors League of America, Century Club, Chi Psi.

AWARDS, HONORS: Harriet Monroe Memorial Prize, *Poetry* magazine, 1948, 1978; Oscar Blumenthal Prize, *Poetry* magazine, 1950; M.A., Amherst College, 1952; Guggenheim fellowships, 1952-53, 1963; Prix de Roma fellowship, American Academy of Arts and Letters, 1954; Edna St. Vincent Millay Memorial Award, 1957; Pulitzer Prize for poetry and National Book Award for poetry, both 1957, for *Things of This World;* Boston Festival Award, 1959; Ford Foundation fellowship for drama, 1960; Melville Cane Award, 1962; corecipient, Bollingen Prize for translation, Yale University Library, 1963, for *Tartuffe,* and for poetry, 1971, for *Walking to Sleep;* Sarah Josepha Hale Award, 1968; Creative Arts Award, Brandeis University, 1971; Prix Henri Desfueilles, 1971; Shelley Memorial Award, 1973; *Book World's* Children's Spring Book Festival award, 1973, for *Opposites: Poems and Drawings;* PEN translation prize, 1983, for *Moliere: Four Comedies;* St. Botolph's Club Foundation Award, 1983; Drama Desk Award, 1983; Chevalier, Ordre des Palmes Academiques, 1983; named Poet Laureate of the United States, Library of Congress, 1987-88; Taylor Poetry Award, *Sewanee Review* and

University of the South, 1988; Bunn Award, 1988; Washington College Literature Award, 1988; National Book Critics Circle Award nomination, 1988, *Los Angeles Times* Book Prize, 1988, and Pulitzer Prize for poetry, 1989, all for *New and Collected Poems;* St. Louis Literature Award, 1988; Gold Medal for Poetry, American Academy and Institute of Arts and Letters, 1991; Edward MacDowell medal, 1992; National Arts Club Medal of Honor for Literature, 1994; PEN/Manheim Medal for Translation, 1994; Milton Center prize, 1995; Academy American Achievement award, 1995; recipient of numerous honorary degrees, including L.H.D., Lawrence College (now Lawrence University of Wisconsin), 1960, Washington University, 1964, Williams College, 1975, University of Rochester, 1976, and Carnegie-Mellon University, 1980, State University of New York, Potsdam, 1986, Skidmore College, 1987, University of Lowell, 1990; Litt.D., Amherst College, 1967, Clark University, 1970, American International College, 1974, Marquette University, 1977, Wesleyan University, 1977, and Lake Forest College, 1982.

WRITINGS:

The Beautiful Changes and Other Poems, Reynal, 1947.
Ceremony and Other Poems, Harcourt, 1950.
Things of This World: Poems (also see below), Harcourt, 1956.
Poems, 1943-1956, Faber, 1957.
(With Robert Hillyer and Cleanth Brooks) *Anniversary Lectures,* U.S. Government Printing Office, 1959.
(With Louise Bogan and Archibald MacLeish) *Emily Dickinson: Three Views* (criticism), Amherst College Press, 1960.
Advice to a Prophet, and Other Poems, Harcourt, 1961.
Loudmouse (juvenile), illustrated by Don Almquist, Collier, 1963, Harcourt, 1982.
The Poems of Richard Wilbur, Harcourt, 1963.
(Translator) Philippe de Thaun, *The Pelican from a Bestiary of 1120* (poem), privately printed, 1963.
Prince Souvanna Phouma: An Exchange between Richard Wilbur and William Jay Smith (poem), limited edition, Phoenix Book Shop, 1968.
Walking to Sleep: New Poems and Translations, Harcourt, 1969.
Digging to China: Poem (Child Study Association book list; first published in *Things of This World*), Doubleday, 1970.
(Self-illustrated) *Opposites: Poems and Drawings* (children's poems), Harcourt, 1973, illustrated by Henrik Drescher, Harcourt Brace, 1994.
Seed Leaves: Homage to R. F. (poem), limited edition, David R. Godine, 1974.
Responses: Prose Pieces, 1953-1976, Harcourt, 1976.
The Mind-Reader: New Poems, Harcourt, 1976.
Seven Poems, Abbatoir Editions, 1981.
(Translator) *The Whale and Other Uncollected Translations,* Boa Editions, 1982.
Richard Wilbur's Creation, University of Michigan Press, 1983.
New and Collected Poems, Harcourt, 1988.
More Opposites (children's poems), Harcourt, 1991.
The School for Husbands by Moliere, Harcourt, 1992.
(Translator) *The Imaginary Cuckold,* Dramatists Play Service, 1993.
(Translator) Moliere, *The School for Husbands & Sganarelle, or the Imaginary Cuckold,* Harcourt, 1994.
A Game of Catch, illustrations by Barry Moser, Harcourt, 1994.
Runaway Opposites, Harcourt, 1995, illustrated by Henrik Drescher, Harcourt, 1995.

PLAYS

(Translator) Moliere, *The Misanthrope: Comedy in Five Acts, 1666* (also see below; first produced in Cambridge, MA, by the Poet's Theatre, October 25, 1955; produced off-Broadway at Theatre East, November 12, 1956), Harcourt, 1955.
(Lyricist with John Latouche, Dorothy Parker, Lillian Hellman, and Leonard Bernstein) Voltaire, *Candide: A Comic Operetta Based on Voltaire's Satire* (musical; based on adaptation by Lillian Hellman; music by Leonard Bernstein; first produced on Broadway at Martin Beck Theatre, December 1, 1956; produced on the West End at Saville Theatre, April 30, 1959), Random House, 1957.
(Translator) Moliere, *Tartuffe: Comedy in Five Acts, 1669* (also see below; first produced in Milwaukee, WI, at Fred Miller Theatre, January, 1964; produced on Broadway at ANTA Theatre, January 14, 1965), Harcourt, 1963.
(Translator) Moliere, *The Misanthrope* [and] *Tartuffe,* Harcourt, 1965.
(Translator) Moliere, *The School for Wives: Comedy in Five Acts, 1662* (first produced on Broadway at Lyceum Theatre, February 16, 1971), Harcourt, 1971.
(Translator) Moliere, *The Learned Ladies: Comedy in Five Acts, 1672* (first produced in Williamstown, MA, at the Williamstown Festival Theatre, 1977), Harcourt, 1978.
(Translator) Jean Racine, *Andromanche: Tragedy in Five Acts, 1667,* Harcourt, 1982.
(Translator) *Moliere: Four Comedies,* Harcourt, 1982.
(Translator) Racine, *Phaedra,* Harcourt, 1986.
(Translator) Moliere, *Amphitryon,* Dramatists Play Service, 1995, Harcourt, 1995.

EDITOR

(With Louis Untermeyer and Karl Shapiro) *Modern American and Modern British Poetry,* revised abridged edition, Harcourt, 1955.
A Bestiary (anthology), Pantheon, 1955.
(And author of introduction and notes) Edgar Allan Poe, *Poe: Complete Poems,* Dell, 1959.
(Editor of section on Poe) *Major Writers of America,* Harcourt, 1962.
(With Alfred Harbage, and author of introduction) William Shakespeare, *Poems,* Penguin, 1966, revised edition published as *Shakespeare, the Narrative Poems and Poems of Doubtful Authenticity,* 1974.
(And author of introduction) Poe, *The Narrative of Arthur Gordon Pym,* David R. Godine, 1974.
(And author of introduction) Witter Bynner, *Selected Poems,* Farrar, Straus, 1978.

OTHER

(Contributor) Gygory Kepes, editor, *The New Landscape in Art and Science,* Paul Theobald, 1955.
Poems (recording), Spoken Arts, 1959.
(Contributor) Don C. Allen, editor, *The Moment of Poetry,* Johns Hopkins Press, 1962.
(Lyricist) *On Freedom's Ground* (cantata; music by William Schuman), first produced in New York City at the Lincoln Center for the Statue of Liberty Centennial, October, 1986.
(Author of foreword) Rollie McKenna, *A Life in Photography,* Knopf, 1991.
The Catbird's Song: Prose Pieces, 1963-1995, Harcourt Brace, 1997.

Also recorded "Richard Wilbur Reading His Own Poems," for Caedmon, and additional readings for the Archive of Recorded

Poetry and Literature, Library of Congress. Translator of *The Funeral of Bobo,* by Joseph Brodsky, for Ardis. Work represented in anthologies. Contributor of critical reviews to periodicals. General editor, "Laurel Poets" series, for Dell; former member of poetry board, Wesleyan University Press.

SIDELIGHTS: Richard Wilbur "is a poet for all of us, whose elegant words brim with wit and paradox," announced Librarian of Congress Daniel J. Boorstin when the poet succeeded Robert Penn Warren to become the second Poet Laureate of the United States. Elizabeth Kastor further quotes Boorstin in her *Washington Post* article: "He is also a poet's poet, at home in the long tradition of the traveled ways of the great poets of our language. . . . His poems are among the best our country has to offer." The second poet laureate has won the Pulitzer Prize and National Book Award for his collection *Things of This World: Poems* and a second Pulitzer for *New and Collected Poems,* among other numerous awards for his poetry. His translations of French verse, especially Voltaire's *Candide* and the plays of Moliere and Jean Racine, are also highly regarded by critics; his translation of Moliere's *Tartuffe* won the 1971 Bollingen Prize. But because of Wilbur's dedication to the traditional forms of rhyme and meter, and his unwillingness to compose experimental poetry, his work has in the past stirred controversy among critics.

The son of a commercial artist, Wilbur was interested in painting as a youth; but he eventually opted to pursue writing as his avocation, a decision he attributes to the influence of his mother's father and grandfather, both of whom were editors. As a student, Wilbur wrote stories, editorials, and poems for his college newspaper and magazine, but, as the poet comments in *Twentieth Century Authors: A Biographical Dictionary of Modern Literature:* "It was not until World War II took me to Cassino, Anzio, and the Siegfried Line that I began to versify in earnest. One does not use poetry for its major purposes, as a means to organize oneself and the world, until one's world somehow gets out of hand." Witnessing war firsthand has had a major effect on Wilbur's poetry. "Many of his first poems had a common motive," writes Richard L. Calhoun in the *Dictionary of Literary Biography,* "the desire to stress the importance of finding order in a world where war had served as a reminder of disorder and destruction."

Because of this motivation, Wilbur's first collection, *The Beautiful Changes and Other Poems,* contains "more poetic exercises on how to face the problems of disorder and destruction than laments over the losses occasioned by the war," notes Calhoun. The poems in this book, according to Donald L. Hill in his *Richard Wilbur,* also demonstrate "a pervasive good humor, a sweetness of spirit, unusual among the major poets of the century." This generally light-hearted approach that Wilbur uses in his poetry has caused some critics of his early work to charge the poet with avoiding tragic themes by covering them with purely aesthetic verse. James Dickey, for example, writes in his book, *Babel to Byzantium,* that one has "the feeling that the cleverness of phrase and the delicious aptness of Wilbur's poems sometimes mask an unwillingness or inability to think or feel deeply; that the poems tend to lapse toward highly sophisticated play." John Reibetanz speculates in *Modern Poetry Studies* that this is because "for Richard Wilbur, the sights offered by World War II contradict and threaten his most basic beliefs, as we can infer them from his writings: that love is more powerful than hatred; that nature is a source of values and of reassurance; and that there is a strong creative urge in both man and nature which constantly seeks and finds expression in images of graceful plenitude." "But in the 1940's," Reibetanz

concludes, "the utter disparity between what he saw and what he wished to see made him run for cover."

The explanation for his choice of subjects and preference for a light-hearted tone in his poetry is, in Wilbur's view, not so much a matter of running from reality as it is a matter of affirming a philosophical conviction. "I feel that the universe is full of glorious energy," he explains in an interview with Peter Stitt in the *Paris Review,* "that the energy tends to take pattern and shape, and that the ultimate character of things is comely and good. I am perfectly aware that I say this in the teeth of all sorts of contrary evidence, and that I must be basing it partly on temperament and partly on faith, but that's my attitude." Still, the poet does not completely refuse to address serious issues. Robert B. Shaw comments in *Parnassus: Poetry in Review* that while "it is true that some of Wilbur's earlier poems veer with disconcerting abruptness from the naturalistic to the esthetic. . . . He has never, in fact, avoided negative subject matter as completely as some critics have charged." The critic later asserts that several poems in his third collection, *Things of This World,* deal directly with humane and political issues.

While Wilbur obdurately composed reflective, optimistic poetry, using traditional patterns of rhyme and meter, the changing poetic movements that flowed by him caused his image to change over the years. "His poetry was judged too impersonal for the early 1960s," testifies Calhoun; "it was not politically involved enough during the literary protests against the war in Vietnam in the later 1960s, and, in the 1970s, not sufficiently postmodernist." Calhoun does note that Wilbur's poems of the 1960s show some experimentation, "but in comparison with what other poets, Robert Lowell and John Berryman for example, were doing by 1961, the experimentation is comparatively minor." His skill at using rhyme and meter, however, is generally acknowledged among critics like *London Magazine* reviewer Roy Fuller, who believes that "Wilbur is excellent at inventing stanza forms, and his stanzas rhyming in pairs are particularly effective." "His intricately patterned poems reflect the discovery of patterns of natural beauty," adds Shaw.

Wilbur's insistence on formalism, critics soon found, was naturally suited to his work in translating French poetry and plays. Speaking of his "tactful, metrical and speakable translation of verse drama," *Hudson Review* critic Alan Shaw comments: "Wilbur's [translations] are almost the solitary example of this kind in English. And it is precisely, I think, because he has stood somewhat apart from the tradition on English-language poetry in this century . . . that he has been able to achieve this." He concludes that "Richard Wilbur's translations of classic French drama are among the undiscovered treasure of our recent literature." The expertise and importance of the poet's translations of plays by Moliere, Voltaire, and Racine has been little questioned by reviewers. "The rendition [of Moliere's *The Misanthrope*], delightful and literate, made Moliere accessible for the first time to a wide American audience and was the start of a lucrative sideline for the poet," writes David H. Van Biema in *People.* Compared to other translators, *Saturday Review* contributor John Ciardi believes that "instead of cognate-snapping, as the academic dullards invariably do, [in his translation of *The Misanthrope*] Wilbur has found English equivalents for the turn and nuance of the French, and the fact that he has managed to do so in rhymed couplets that not only respect themselves as English poetry but allow the play to be staged . . . with great success is testament enough."

Analyzing the laureate's book *New and Collected Poems, Los Angeles Times Book Review* contributor Joshua Odell believes these newer poems "clearly show a continued evolution in style from an ornate elegance found particularly in Wilbur's first collection, *The Beautiful Changes,* toward a simple, direct and crisp verse." Still, poems like those in *The Mind Reader* manage "to stand up against every kind of poetic chic," according to Bruce Michelson in *Southern Review.* And as some critics have noted, the changes in Wilbur's poetry have not affected the basic philosophy his verses have always shown. "He seems to be seeking even firmer and more affirmative statements of the need for order and responsibility; and his tone in the later poems is more confident, more self-assured," asserts Calhoun. This is a need that Wilbur feels all poets should attempt to meet in their work. In his book, *Responses: Prose Pieces, 1953-1976,* the laureate declares: "Every poet is impelled to utter the whole of the world that is real to him, to respond to that world in some spirit, and to draw all its parts toward some *coherence.*"

In addition to his adult-oriented poetry, Wilbur has also published a number of works for children. These include a trio of word-play books devoted to synonyms and antonyms: 1973's *Opposites,* 1991's *More Opposites,* and 1995's *Runaway Opposites.* Featuring illustrations by Henrik Drescher, these books offer amusing poems devoted to words with opposite meanings. Another of Wilbur's works for children is *A Game of Catch,* first published in the *New Yorker* in 1953 and reprinted as a separate volume in 1994. The story revolves around three boys and a seemingly innocuous game of catch. When two of the boys refuse to let the third boy play, the outsider climbs a tree and turns the tables on his adversaries using mind games.

BIOGRAPHICAL/CRITICAL SOURCES:

BOOKS

Contemporary Literary Criticism, Gale (Detroit), Volume 3, 1975; Volume 6, 1976; Volume 9, 1978; Volume 14, 1980; Volume 53, 1989.
Dickey, James, *Babel to Byzantium,* Farrar, Straus, 1968.
Dictionary of Literary Biography, Volume 5: *American Poets since World War II,* Gale, 1980.
Edgecombe, Rodney Stenning, *A Reader's Guide to the Poetry of Richard Wilbur,* University of Alabama Press, 1995.
Hill, Donald L., *Richard Wilbur,* Twayne, 1967.
Hougen, John B., *Ecstasy within Discipline: The Poetry of Richard Wilbur,* Scholars Press, 1995.
Hungerford, Edward, editor, *Poets in Progress,* Northwestern University Press, 1962, new edition, 1967.
Jarrell, Randall, *Poetry and the Age,* Knopf, 1953.
Jarrell, Randall, *The Third Book of Criticism,* Farrar, Straus, 1969.
Kunitz, Stanley, and Vineta Colby, *Twentieth Century Authors: A Biographical Dictionary of Modern Literature,* H. W. Wilson, 1955.
Nemerov, Howard, editor, *Poets on Poetry,* Basic Books, 1966.
Rosenthal, M. L., *The Modern Poets,* Oxford University Press, 1965.

PERIODICALS

America, October 15, 1994, p. 18.
Hollins Critic, April, 1977.
Hudson Review, summer, 1969; summer, 1987.
London Magazine, July, 1957.
Los Angeles Times, March 17, 1983; April 18, 1987; October 13, 1987.
Los Angeles Times Book Review, July 31, 1988; October 9, 1988.

Modern Poetry Studies, Volume 2, numbers 1 and 2, 1982.
Nation, November 3, 1956.
National Review, September 2, 1988.
New Republic, June 5, 1976.
New York, February 13, 1995, p. 102.
New Yorker, December 12, 1994, p. 122.
New York Times, January 28, 1983.
New York Times Book Review, December 14, 1969; December 26, 1982; April 18, 1987; May 29, 1988; August 27, 1995, p. 27.
Paris Review, winter, 1977.
Parnassus: Poetry in Review, spring/summer, 1977.
People Weekly, October 5, 1987.
Publishers Weekly, August 2, 1991, p. 60; March 13, 1995, p. 68.
Saturday Review, August 18, 1956.
School Library Journal, September, 1992, p. 272; April, 1994, p. 132; May, 1995, p. 117.
Sewanee Review, spring, 1978.
Shenandoah, fall, 1965.
Southern Review, summer, 1973; July, 1979.
Southwest Review, summer, 1973.
Time, November 19, 1984.
Times (London), July 15, 1989.
Times Literary Supplement, May 20, 1977; September 15-21, 1989, p. 999.
Tribune Books (Chicago), July 24, 1988.
Variety, January 3, 1994, p. 58; May 30, 1994, p. 58; February 16, 1995, p. 82.
Washington Post, July 25, 1976; October 6, 1987.

*   *   *

WILDER, Laura (Elizabeth) Ingalls 1867-1957

PERSONAL: Born February 7, 1867, in Pepin, WI; died February 10, 1957, in Mansfield, MO; buried in Mansfield Cemetery; daughter of Charles Philip and Caroline Lake (Quiner) Ingalls; married Almanzo James Wilder, August 25, 1885 (died October 23, 1949); children: Rose (Mrs. Gillette Lane), a son. *Education:* Attended schools in Wisconsin, Iowa, Minnesota, and the Dakota Territory.

ADDRESSES: Home—Rocky Ridge Farm, Mansfield, MO.

CAREER: Teacher in schools near De Smet, Dakota Territory (now South Dakota), 1882-85; farmer in De Smet, 1885-94, and Mansfield, MO, beginning in 1894; worked with Missouri Home Development Association, beginning in 1910; *Missouri Ruralist,* household editor and contributing editor, 1911-24; Mansfield Farm Loan Association, secretary-treasurer, 1919-27; writer, 1932-43.

MEMBER: Athenian Club, Justamere Club, Interesting Hour Club, Wednesday Study Club, and Eastern Star.

AWARDS, HONORS: Newbery Honor Book, 1938, for *On the Banks of Plum Creek,* 1940, for *By the Shores of Silver Lake,* 1941, for *The Long Winter,* 1942, for *Little Town on the Prairie,* and 1944, for *These Happy Golden Years;* Pacific Northwest Library Association Young Readers' Choice Award, 1942, for *By the Shores of Silver Lake; Book World* Children's Spring Book Festival Award, 1943, for *These Happy Golden Years;* Laura Ingalls Wilder Award, American Library Association, 1954, for her autobiographical novels (since 1960 this award in her honor is made every five years to an outstanding author or illustrator of children's books); elected to Ozark Hall of Fame, 1977; inducted into South Dakota Cowboy and Western Hall of Fame, 1978.

WRITINGS:

AUTOBIOGRAPHICAL NOVELS; PUBLISHED BY HARPER, EXCEPT AS NOTED

Little House in the Big Woods, illustrated by Helen Sewell, 1932, new edition, illustrated by Garth Williams, 1953.

Farmer Boy, illustrated by Sewell, 1933, new edition, illustrated by Williams, 1953.

Little House on the Prairie, illustrated by Sewell, 1935, new edition, illustrated by Williams, 1953.

On the Banks of Plum Creek, illustrated by Sewell and Mildred Boyle, 1937, new edition, illustrated by Williams, 1953.

By the Shores of Silver Lake, illustrated by Sewell and Boyle, 1939, new edition, illustrated by Williams, 1953, special edition, E. M. Hale, 1956.

The Long Winter, illustrated by Sewell and Boyle, 1940, new edition, illustrated by Williams, 1953.

Little Town on the Prairie, illustrated by Sewell and Boyle, 1941, new edition, illustrated by Williams, 1953.

These Happy Golden Years, illustrated by Sewell and Boyle, 1943, new edition, illustrated by Williams, 1953.

The First Four Years, edited by Roger Lea MacBride, illustrated by Williams, Harper, 1971.

ADAPTED FROM THE LITTLE HOUSE BOOKS; PUBLISHED BY HARPERCOLLINS EXCEPT AS NOTED

A Little House Christmas: Holiday Stories from the Little House Books, illustrated by Garth Williams, 1994.

Winter Days in the Big Woods, illustrated by Williams, 1994.

Dance at Grandpa's, illustrated by Renee Graef, 1994.

Going to Town, illustrated by Graef, 1994.

The Deer in the Wood, illustrated by Graef, 1995.

Christmas in the Big Woods, illustrated by Graef, 1995.

Merry Christmas, Laura, illustrated by Graef, 1995.

Summertime in the Big Woods, illustrated by Graef, 1996.

Going West, illustrated by Graef, 1996.

Winter on the Farm, illustrated by Jody Wheeler and Graef, 1996.

Animal Adventures, illustrated by Graef, 1997.

Prairie Days, illustrated by Graef, 1997.

A Little House Birthday, illustrated by Doris Ettlinger, 1997.

The Adventures of Laura and Jack, illustrated by Graef, 1997.

My Little House ABC, illustrated by Graef, 1997.

County Fair, illustrated by Jody Wheeler, 1997.

Pioneer Sisters, illustrated by Graef, 1997.

School Days, illustrated by Graef, 1997.

My Little House 1-2-3, illustrated by Graef, 1997.

Little House Farm Days, illustratee by Graef, 1998.

A Little House Reader: A Collection of Writings, edited by William Anderson, 1998.

OTHER

On the Way Home: The Diary of a Trip from South Dakota to Mansfield, Missouri, in 1894, edited by daughter, Rose Wilder Lane, Harper, 1962.

West from Home: Letters of Laura Ingalls Wilder, San Francisco, 1915, edited by MacBride, Harper, 1974.

(With Rose Wilder Lane) *A Little House Sampler,* edited by William T. Anderson, University of Nebraska Press, 1988.

Little House in the Ozarks (nonfiction), edited by Stephen W. Hines, Nelson, 1991.

Words from a Fearless Heart: A Collection of Wit, Wisdom, and Whimsy, edited by Stephen W. Hines, T. Nelson Publishers (Nashville, TN), 1995.

The Laura Ingalls Wilder Country Cookbook, commentary by William Anderson, photographs by Leslie A. Kelly, Harper-Collins, 1995.

Dear Laura: Letters from Children to Laura Ingalls Wilder, HarperCollins, 1996.

Little House Sisters: Collected Stories from the Little House Books, illustrated by Garth Williams, Harper, 1997.

Saving Graces: The Inspirational Writings of Laura Ingalls Wilder, edited by Stephen Hines, Broadman & Holman (Nashville, TN), 1997.

Contributor of articles and poetry to magazines and newspapers, including *Country Gentleman, McCall's Youth's Companion, St. Nicholas, Child Life, San Francisco Bulletin, St. Louis Star, Missouri Ruralist, De Smet News,* and *Christian Science Monitor.*

Manuscripts and letters by Wilder are housed at the Laura Ingalls Wilder Home and Museum, Mansfield, MO, the Detroit Public Library, Detroit, MI, and the Pomona Public Library, Pomona, CA.

MEDIA ADAPTATIONS: Wilder's novels were adapted for the television series *Little House on the Prairie,* NBC, 1974-82, and *Little House: A New Beginning,* NBC, 1982-83; the sound recording *Little House in the Big Woods,* Pathways of Sound, 1976; and the musical *Prairie,* produced on Broadway, 1982.

SIDELIGHTS: Recounting her girlhood experiences on the American frontier in her autobiographical novels, Laura Ingalls Wilder became one of the most loved and respected children's writers of the twentieth century. Her homely tales of pioneer life sold millions of copies, remaining continuously in print after the first of them appeared in the 1930s. To the Depression era they offered reminders of another time, when people enduring hardship found joy in simple things like the sound of a fiddle and warm family relationships. Decades later Wilder's characters and settings won over another generation in a long-running television series. An honest, unsentimental, and vivid combination of storytelling, history, and autobiography, Wilder's books captured the maturing both of an individual and of a country.

Like the Laura of her novels, Wilder spent her early childhood in a house built by her father, Charles Ingalls, in a Wisconsin forest. Her first novel, *Little House in the Big Woods,* draws on Wilder's actual experiences in Wisconsin, but like the series as a whole it does not follow her life exactly. As Janet Spaeth noted in her book *Laura Ingalls Wilder,* Wilder's intention in writing the books "demanded a refashioning of the events of her life to retain the larger truth that she wanted to convey—the pioneer experience in America." *Little House in the Big Woods* depicts this in detail.

In *Little House in the Big Woods* the Ingallses are isolated from most other people, so they do many things for themselves. They smoke their own meat, raise their own vegetables, and make almost everything else they need, from butter to bullets. On rare trips to town they trade for other supplies, such as cloth, gunpowder, salt, tea, tobacco, and "store sugar," which they use for special occasions instead of their homemade maple sugar. Formal schooling is not available. Laura and her older sister, Mary, learn only what their parents can teach them, which includes reading, housekeeping chores and other farm tasks, and good manners. Pa entertains the family with stories and his fiddle playing. In the pioneer setting, the family serves as its own small community, and good family relations and Christian values are very important. Wilder's first book conveys a child's perspective on such a world, and "the routine of life in the Big Woods assumes a certain timelessness," observed Kathy Piehl, writing in the *Dictionary of Literary Biography.* Commented Eileen H. Colwell in *Junior Bookshelf,* "Here are real people sharing joys and sorrows within an atmosphere of emotional security."

In *Little House on the Prairie* Wilder chronicled the family's move from the Big Woods to the Great Plains, which the government has promised will soon be open to settlement. Traveling in a covered wagon, they cross the frozen Mississippi River and make their way to the grassy prairie. A new house goes up, with shingled roof, stone fireplace and chimney, and a door assembled with pegs instead of nails. Wilder describes each bit of construction step by step, "in such detail that a careful reader could probably accomplish such feats" just from reading about them, remarked Piehl. In this book the Ingallses also encounter Indians—a friendly one who comes into their house and eats and smokes with them, and several less friendly who demand or simply take food and other goods. After noticing increasing unrest at distant Indian camps, the family learns that U.S. soldiers are coming to remove the settlers from what is now labeled "Indian territory," and once again they must pack up their wagon.

After a brief return to Wisconsin, the Ingallses soon moved west again. This time they settled in a dugout house near the Minnesota town of Walnut Grove, where *On the Banks of Plum Creek* begins. This book shows a changing and challenging frontier, where Pa must build a house with purchased lumber instead of logs he has felled himself, the girls attend school and church for the first time, and grasshopper plagues devastate the family's cash crops. Over these years Laura becomes more aware of her parents' concerns and her own growing responsibilities. *By the Shores of Silver Lake* presents further evidence of her growth and the spread of civilization. Two years of disastrous farming and dwindling game have taxed the family's resources, and Mary has lost her sight to illness. Pa accepts an offer to go west to work for the railroad, and the story follows the Ingallses into the Dakota Territories—an area that later became the states of Wyoming, Montana, and North and South Dakota. Ma and the girls come after Pa on a train, and Wilder's account of this trip suggests some of the origins of her later storytelling ability. When Mary went blind, Pa had told Laura to serve as her eyes, and throughout the train ride young Laura describes for Mary everything about the train and the passing landscape in great detail—much the way she later described everything in her books for her reading audience. Laura's increasing maturity shows in her decision to work toward a teaching certificate—even though she does not really want to teach—so that she can help the family send Mary to a school for the blind.

In *The Long Winter* the Ingallses settle into a little shanty on the new homestead in De Smet, in what became South Dakota. Laura takes an ever more active part in adult work. Watching Pa trying to cut and stack his hay by himself, she offers to help, and the two of them together do the work in half the time it would have taken Pa alone. Later, Laura recognizes her more adult role, reflecting that she is "old enough now to stand beside [Pa] and Ma in hard times." *The Long Winter* recounts some very hard times. An early frost comes, and after a brief Indian summer the blizzards begin. Trusting an old Indian who warns the town of a seven-month winter, Pa moves the family from the half-built shanty to the sturdier town buildings until spring. Wilder's account of the long snowbound months with meager rations prompted some critics to

call the book one of the most impressive of the series. Wrote Piehl, "The creation of mood and the study of how people react to an increasingly perilous situation is masterful."

Wilder depicted the maturation of both Laura and De Smet in *Little Town on the Prairie* and *These Happy Golden Years.* The community grows rapidly, with new settlers arriving constantly and new buildings going up in the area, including two new schools and a new church. Losing some of the independence that made them pioneers, the townsfolk come to depend more and more on others for entertainment and for goods and services they once could have provided for themselves. Laura earns her first wages by sewing in town, and soon she leaves home to teach for a two-month term. As she becomes more independent, she attends social functions both with and without her family and begins to go on outings with homesteader and horse-trainer Almanzo Wilder. The author had described Almanzo's childhood in *Farmer Boy,* and in her last two books she developed his relationship with Laura from their first casual drives together to their marriage. By the end of the series the town is well established and Laura has grown up to be a housewife.

Combining gifts of observation, memory, and storytelling, Wilder created a legacy in children's literature. More than just the account of one life, her books became a record of a dynamic period of American history and a testament to the courage, resourcefulness, family values, and optimism that shaped a young nation. Wilder's saga has pleased generations of readers and critics alike. Writing in *Junior Bookshelf,* Colwell marveled at "the seeing eye of the poet" revealed in the "Little House" books, and others hailed Wilder for depicting well-rounded characters who grow and mature over the course of the series. Her simple yet detailed, direct, and honest prose also won praise; several writers remarked on how the increasing complexity of the prose parallels Laura's own development. Summarizing the quality of the books in *Atlantic Monthly,* Susan Bagg commented, "You are reading something that promised to be entertainment and that turns out to be art."

BIOGRAPHICAL/CRITICAL SOURCES:

BOOKS

Anderson, William T., *The Plum Creek Story of Laura Ingalls Wilder,* Anderson, 1987.

Anderson, William T., editor, *The Horn Book's Laura Ingalls Wilder,* Anderson, 1987.

Anderson, William T., *Pioneer Girl: The Story of Laura Ingalls Wilder,* HarperCollins, 1998.

Bingham, Jane M., editor, *Writers for Children,* Scribner, 1988, pp. 617-23.

Black, Sheila, *Laura Ingalls Wilder: American Authoress,* Kipling Press, 1987.

Children's Literature Review, Volume 2, Gale (Detroit), 1976.

Dictionary of Literary Biography, Volume 22: *American Writers for Children, 1900-1960,* Gale, 1983.

Glasscock, Sarah, *Laura Ingalls Wilder: An Author's Story,* Steck-Vaughn (Austin, TX), 1998.

MacBride, Roger Lea, *New Dawn on Rocky Ridge,* illustrated by David Gilleece, HarperCollins, 1997.

Marshall, Richard, editor, *Laura Ingalls Wilder: A Family Collection,* illustrated by Susan Sternau, Barnes and Noble Books (New York City), 1993.

Romines, Ann, *Constructing the Little House: Gender, Culture, and Laura Ingalls Wilder,* University of Massachusetts Press, 1997.

Spaeth, Janet, *Laura Ingalls Wilder,* Twayne, 1987.
Subramanian, Jane M., *Laura Ingalls Wilder: An Annotated Bibliography of Critical, Biogrpahical, and Teaching Studies,* Greenwood Press, 1997.
Treasures from Laura Wilder, Sherwood Publishing, 1982.
Twentieth-Century Children's Writers, 3rd edition, St. James Press, 1989.
Wadsworth, Ginger, *Laura Ingalls Wilder: Storyteller of the Prairie,* Lerner Publications (Minneapolis), 1997.
Walner, Alexandra, *Laura Ingalls Wilder,* Holiday House (New York City), 1997.
Wilkes, Maria D., *Little Town at the Crossroads,* illustrations by Dan Andersen, HarperCollins, 1997.

PERIODICALS

American West, Volume 21, 1984, pp. 35-42.
Atlantic Monthly, February, 1975, pp. 117-18.
Children's Literature, Number 4, 1975, pp. 105-19; Number 7, 1978, pp. 7-16; Number 11, 1983, pp. 49-63.
Children's Literature Association Quarterly, Volume 9, 1984-1985, pp. 168-70.
Christian Science Monitor, June 23, 1981.
Horn Book, December, 1953, pp. 411-39; October, 1965, pp. 465-73.
Jack and Jill, March, 1981.
Junior Bookshelf, November, 1962, pp. 237-43.
Lion and the Unicorn, spring, 1979, pp. 74-88.
Modern Maturity, April, 1982.
Peabody Journal of Education, September, 1966.
Time, March 15, 1971.
Wilson Library Bulletin, April, 1948.

*   *   *

WILDER, Thornton (Niven) 1897-1975

PERSONAL: Born April 17, 1897, in Madison, WI; died of a heart attack, December 7, 1975, in Hamden, CT; son of Amos Parker (a newspaper editor and U.S. Consul to China) and Isabella Thornton (Niven) Wilder. *Education:* Attended public and private schools in the United States and in Chefoo, China; attended Oberlin College, 1915-17; Yale University, A.B., 1920; attended American Academy in Rome 1920-21; Princeton University, A.M., 1926. *Politics:* Democrat. *Religion:* Congregationalist.

CAREER: Lawrenceville School, Lawrenceville, NJ, French teacher and assistant master of Davis House, 1921-25; tutor and writer in the United States and abroad, 1925-27; Davis House, master, 1927-28; writer and cross-country lecturer, 1928-29; University of Chicago, Chicago, IL, lecturer in comparative literature, 1930-36; writer for several motion picture studios, 1930-36; University of Hawaii, Honolulu, visiting professor, 1935; American delegate to Institut de Cooperation Intellectuelle, Paris, France, 1937; goodwill representative to Latin America for U.S. Department of State, 1941; International PEN Club Congress delegate with John Dos Passos, 1941; Harvard University, Cambridge, MA, Charles Eliot Norton Professor of poetry, 1950-51; chief of U.S. delegation to UNESCO Conference of Arts, Venice, 1952. Actor in *Our Town,* New York City and summer stock, beginning 1939, in *The Skin of Our Teeth,* stock and summer theaters. *Military service:* Coast Artillery Corps, Fort Adams, RI, 1918; became corporal; commissioned captain in U.S. Army Air Intelligence, and served 1942-45, advancing to lieutenant colonel; awarded Legion of Merit, Bronze Star; Legion d'Honneur, Honorary Member of the Order of the British Empire (M.B.E.).

MEMBER: American Academy of Arts and Letters, Modern Language Association of America (honorary member), Authors Guild, Actors Equity Association, Hispanic Society of America, Bayerische Akademie (corresponding member), Akademie der Wissenschaften und der Literatur (Mainz, West Germany), Bavarian Academy of Fine Arts (honorary member), Century Association (New York), Players (honorary member), Graduate Club, Elizabethan Club, Alpha Delta Phi.

AWARDS, HONORS: Pulitzer Prize, 1928, for *The Bridge of San Luis Rey,* 1938, for *Our Town,* and 1943, for *The Skin of Our Teeth;* Chevalier, Legion of Honor, 1951; Gold Medal for Fiction, American Academy of Arts and Letters, 1952; Friedenspreis des Deutschen Buchhandels (Frankfurt on the Main, West Germany), 1957; Sonderpreis des Oesterreichischen Staatspreises, 1959, Goethe-Plakette, 1959; Brandeis University Creative Arts Award, 1959-60, for theater and film; Edward MacDowell Medal (first time presented), 1960; Century Association Art Medal; Medal of the Order of Merit (Peru); Order Pour le Merite (Bonn, West Germany); invited by President Kennedy's cabinet to present reading, 1962; Presidential Medal of Freedom, 1963; National Book Committee's National Medal for Literature (first time presented), 1965; National Book Award, 1968, for *The Eighth Day;* honorary degrees from New York University, Yale University, Kenyon College, College of Wooster, Harvard University, Northeastern University, Oberlin College, University of New Hampshire, University of Zurich.

WRITINGS:

NOVELS

The Cabala (excerpt published in *Double Dealer,* September, 1922; also see below), Boni, 1926, Avon, 1975.
The Bridge of San Luis Rey (also see below), Boni, 1927, limited edition with illustrations by William Kaughan, Franklin Library, 1976.
The Woman of Andros (based on *Andria* by Terence; also see below), Boni, 1930.
Heaven's My Destination (Book-of-the-Month Club selection), Longmans, Green, 1934, Harper, 1935.
The Ides of March (Book-of-the-Month Club selection), Harper, 1948.
The Eighth Day, Harper, 1967.
Theophilus North, Harper, 1973.

Adapter, with Jerome Kilty, of stage version of *The Ides of March.*

PLAYS

The Trumpet Shall Sound (first published in *Yale Literary Magazine,* 1919-20), produced by the American Laboratory Theater, December 10, 1926.
(Adapter and translator) *Lucrece* (based on *The Rape of Lucrece* by Andre Obey; first produced on Broadway at the Belasco Theatre, December 20, 1932), Houghton, 1933.
Our Town (three-act play; first produced in Princeton, NJ, January 22, 1938; produced in New York at the Henry Miller Theatre, February 4, 1938; produced on Broadway at the Lyceum Theater, December 5, 1988; also see below), Coward, 1938, acting edition, Coward, 1965, limited edition with introduction by Brooks Atkinson and illustrations by Robert J. Lee, Limited Editions Club, 1974.

(Adapter and translator) Henrik Ibsen, *A Doll's House,* first produced on Broadway at the Morosco Theatre, December 27, 1938.

The Merchant of Yonkers: A Farce in Four Acts (based on *Einen Jux will er sich Machen* by Johann Nestroy; first produced on Broadway December 28, 1938), Harper, 1939; revised version renamed *The Matchmaker* (first produced in 1954 for Edinburgh Festival; produced on Broadway at the Royale Theatre, December 5, 1955; also see below), Samuel French, 1957.

The Skin of Our Teeth (three-act play; first produced in New Haven, CT, October 15, 1942; produced on Broadway at the Plymouth Theatre, November 18, 1942; produced in New York City by Classic Stage Company, November 24, 1986; also see below), Harper, 1942, Longmans, Green, 1958.

Our Century (three-scene burlesque; first produced April 26, 1947, in New York City at the Century Association), Century Association, 1947.

The Happy Journey to Trenton and Camden, produced with *The Respectful Prostitute* by Jean Paul Sartre, on Broadway at the Cort Theatre, February 9, 1948.

(Translator) Jean-Paul Sartre, *The Victors,* produced off-Broadway, 1949.

The Alcestiad (based on *Alcestis* by Euripides), first produced as *A Life in the Sun,* at Assembly Hall, Edinburgh, Scotland, August 25, 1955.

The Wreck of the 5:25 and *Bernice,* first performed at Congresshalle Theater in West Berlin, West Germany, September 20, 1957.

The Drunken Sisters (satyr play; first appeared in centennial issue of *Atlantic Monthly,* 1957; first produced as fourth act of *Die Alkestiade* [also see below], produced in Brooklyn Heights, NY, at Spencer Memorial Church, June 28, 1970), Samuel French, 1957.

Childhood (one-act; first appeared in *Atlantic Monthly,* November, 1960; also see below), Samuel French, 1960.

The Long Christmas Dinner (also see below), revised edition, Samuel French, 1960.

(Author of libretto) *Das Lange Weihnachtsmal* (opera; adapted from play *The Long Christmas Dinner;* first produced at National Theatre in Mannheim, Germany, December 17, 1961), music by Paul Hindemith, translated into German by Hindemith, libretto published by Schott Music, 1961.

Infancy, A Comedy in One Act (also see below), Samuel French, 1961.

Plays for Bleecker Street (three volumes; includes *Infancy, Childhood,* and *Someone from Assisi;* first produced off-Broadway at Circle in the Square, January 11, 1962), Samuel French, 1960-61.

(Author of libretto) *Die Alkestiade* (opera; adaptation of *A Life in the Sun*), music by Louise Talma, first produced at Stadische Dulmen in Frankfurt, West Germany, March 1, 1962.

Pullman Car Hiawatha (also see below), produced off-Broadway at Circle in the Square, December 3, 1964.

Thornton Wilder's Triple Bill (includes *The Long Christmas Dinner, The Queens of France* [also see below], and *The Happy Journey to Trenton and Camden* [also see below]), produced off-Broadway at Cherry Lane Theatre, September 6, 1966.

OMNIBUS VOLUMES

The Angel That Troubled the Waters, and Other Plays (includes *Nascunter Poetae, Proserpina and the Devil, Fanny Otcott, Brother Fire, The Penny That Beauty Spent, The Angel on the Ship, The Message and Jehanne, Childe Roland to the Dark Tower Came, Centaurs, Leviathan, And the Sea Shall Give Up Its Dead, Now the Servant's Name Was Malchus, Mozart and the Gray Steward, Hast Thou Considered My Servant Job?, The Flight into Egypt,* and *The Angel That Troubled the Waters*), Coward, 1928.

The Long Christmas Dinner and Other Plays in One Act (includes *The Long Christmas Dinner, Pullman Car Hiawatha, Such Things Only Happen in Books, The Happy Journey to Trenton and Camden, Love and How to Cure It,* and *The Queens of France*), Yale University Press, 1931.

(Author of preface) *Three Plays: Our Town, The Skin of Our Teeth, The Matchmaker,* Harper, 1938, published as *Our Town; The Skin of Our Teeth; The Matchmaker,* Penguin Books, 1962, limited edition with illustrations by Dick Brown, Franklin Library, 1979.

A Thornton Wilder Trio: The Cabala, The Bridge of San Luis Rey, The Woman of Andros, Criterion, 1956.

The Cabala and The Woman of Andros, Harper, 1968.

The Alcestiad; or, A Life in the Sun: A Play in Three Acts, with a Satyr Play, The Drunken Sisters, Harper, 1977, limited edition published as *The Alcestiad; or, A Life in the Sun; The Drunken Sisters,* illustrations by Daniel Maffia, Franklin Library, 1977.

The Collected Short Plays of Thornton Wilder, edited by Donald Gallup and A. Tappan Wilder, Theatre Communications Group, 1998.

The Thornton Wilder Reader, Modern Library, 1998.

OTHER

We Live Again (screenplay; based on *Resurrection* by Leo Tolstoy), Metro-Goldwyn-Mayer, 1936.

An Evening with Thornton Wilder, April Thirtieth, 1962, Washington, D.C. (consists of third act of *Our Town*), Harper, 1962.

American Characteristics and Other Essays, edited by Donald Gallup, foreword by Isabel Wilder, Harper, 1979.

The Journals of Thornton Wilder: With Two Scenes of an Uncompleted Play, "The Emporium," Yale University Press, 1985.

Mirrors of Friendship: The Letters of Gertrude Stein and Thornton Wilder, edited by Edward M. Burns, Yale University Press, 1996.

Author of screenplay, *Shadow of a Doubt,* 1942. Contributor to periodicals, including *Harper's, Hudson Review, Poetry, Atlantic,* and *Yale Review.* Theater reviewer for *Theatre Arts Monthly,* 1925.

The autograph of *The Bridge of San Luis Rey* is held in Yale University's American Literature Collection of the Beinecke Rare Book and Manuscript Library.

MEDIA ADAPTATIONS: The Bridge of San Luis Rey was filmed three times, initially in 1929; also filmed were *Our Town,* 1940, and *The Matchmaker,* 1958. *The Matchmaker* was adapted by Michael Stewart made into a musical, *Hello, Dolly!,* with words and music by Jerry Herman, and opened in 1964. *Our Town* was made into the musical *Grover's Corners,* by Harvey Schmidt and Tom Jones, in 1987. *Theophilus North* was made into the movie *Mr. North* by John Huston, starring Danny Huston, Anjelica Huston, and Robert Mitchum. There have also been radio and television versions of many of Wilder's works.

SIDELIGHTS: Thornton Wilder occupied, wrote Edmund Wilson, "a unique position, between the Great Books and Parisian sophistication one way, and the entertainment industry the other way, and in our culture this region, though central, is a dark and almost uninhabited no man's land." Louis Broussard noted that "In such company as O'Neill, Eliot, Anouilh, and many other post-war pessimists, Wilder emerges as a lone dissenter. Not because he was an optimist . . . but because his optimism grows out of an indifference to his own period. . . . No other writer begins with so hopeful a premise: that this age is essentially no different from any other, that its problems, whatever they may be . . . will resolve themselves in change which can only be better than the past. His is not the search for an exit from dilemma; there is no dilemma."

Wilder himself believed the theater consists of presenting experience for its own sake. "I regard the theater as the greatest of all art forms," he told the *Paris Review,* "the most immediate way in which a human being can share with another the sense of what it is to be a human being. This supremacy of the theater derives from the fact that it is always 'now' on the stage." Ignoring conflict, preferring comedy to tragedy, extolling traditional ideas, Wilder was the artist of the anachronism," wrote Malcolm Cowley. In commenting on *Our Town,* Broussard said Wilder could "present the cycle of life without conflict because the foundations upon which his ideals rest have not yet been shaken. Romantic love, marriage, the concept of the 'Mind of God'. . . . These remain safe behind the barrier of isolated time." *The Skin of Our Teeth,* which portrays a five thousand-year history of man which some critics think has some basis in James Joyce's *Finnegans Wake,* "is really a way of trying to make sense out of the multiplicity of the human race and its affections," remarked Wilder.

Harold Clurman found Wilder's plays particularly American in "their benign humor, their old-fashioned optimism, their use of the charmingly homely detail, the sophisticated employment of the commonplace, their avuncular celebration of the humdrum, their common sense, popular moralism, and the simplicity—one might almost say simplemindedness—behind a shrewdly captivating manipulation of a large selection of classic elements." Edmund Wilson believed "all of this works very well in the theater. . . . But if one happens to be feeling a little morose . . . or if one tries the experiment of reading [*The Skin of Our Teeth*] in cold blood, the marriage of Plato and Groucho Marx may fail to appeal." Wilder, however, concluded that the theater addresses itself to the group and "partakes of the nature of festival." A play "presupposes a crowd." He once said: "I would love to be the poet laureate of Coney Island."

Originally, Wilder had been somewhat ignored by serious critics. In fact, *Our Town* closed after one week in Boston in 1938, because of bad notices. But in time, Wilder was praised for his experimentation and innovation, and *The Skin of Our Teeth* has become a modern classic. Travis Bogard called Wilder "a man who, along with O'Neill, freed the American theater from its traditional forms through his experiments in *Our Town* and *The Skin of Our Teeth.* . . . In a sense, perhaps, all of Wilder's plays are about the Day of Judgment, imaging human character as a bubble rising to burst on the surface of eternity. There undoubtedly were influences on his experimental style, but, in the last analysis, Wilder's innovations are important consequences of his point of view and of his way of commenting on experience." Wilder may have taken himself less seriously; as he once told the *Paris Review:* "I'm the kind of man whom timid old ladies stop on the street to ask about the nearest subway station."

BIOGRAPHICAL/CRITICAL SOURCES:

BOOKS

Blank, Martin, *Critical Essays on Thornton Wilder,* Prentice Hall, 1996.
Bogard, Travis, and William I. Oliver, editors, *Modern Drama: Essays in Criticism,* Oxford University Press, 1965.
Broussard, Louis, *American Drama,* University of Oklahoma Press, 1962.
Bryer, Jackson R., editor, *Conversations with Thornton Wilder,* University Press of Mississippi, 1992.
Burbank, R., *Thornton Wilder,* Twayne, 1961.
Cohn, Ruby, *Dialogue in American Drama,* Indiana University Press, 1971.
Contemporary Literary Criticism, Gale (Detroit), Volume 1, 1973; Volume 5, 1976; Volume 6, 1976; Volume 10, 1979; Volume 15, 1980; Volume 35, 1985; Volume 82, 1994.
Cowley, Malcolm, editor, *Writers at Work: The Paris Review Interviews,* Viking, 1957.
Dictionary of Literary Biography, Gale, Volume 4: *American Writers in Paris, 1920-1939,* 1980.
Drama Criticism, Volume 1, Gale, 1991.
Goldstone, Richard H., *Thornton Wilder, An Intimate Portrait,* Dutton, 1975.
Grebanier, Bernard, *Thornton Wilder,* University of Minnesota Press, 1965.
Haberman, Donald, *The Plays of Thornton Wilder,* Wesleyan University Press, 1967.
Lifton, Paul, *Vast Encyclopedia: The Theatre of Thornton Wilder,* Greenwood, 1995.
Schroeder, Patricia R., *The Presence of the Past in Modern American Drama,* Fairleigh Dickinson University Press, 1989, pp. 53-75.
Simon, Linda, *Thornton Wilder: His Work,* Doubleday, 1979.
Walsh, Claudette, *Thornton Wilder: A Reference Guide, 1926-1990,* G. K. Hall, 1993.
Wilder, Amos Niven, *Thornton Wilder and His Public,* Fortress Press, 1980.
Wilson, Edmund, *A Literary Chronicle: 1926-1950,* Anchor Books, 1956.

PERIODICALS

AB Bookman's Weekly, January 5, 1976.
Antioch Review, summer, 1967, pp. 264-69.
Classical and Modern Literature, fall, 1991.
Kenyon Review, spring, 1986, pp. 126-30.
Modern Drama, September, 1972.
Nation, September 3, 1955.
New Republic, August 8, 1928.
New York Review of Books, November 21, 1985, pp. 31-34.
New York Times, November 24, 1986; December 20, 1987; December 5, 1988; December 11, 1988.
New York Times Book Review, December 30, 1979.
Paris Review, winter, 1957, pp. 36-57.
Philadelphia Inquirer, December 14, 1975.
Saturday Review, October 6, 1956.
School Library Journal, December, 1995, p. 56.
Sewanee Review, winter, 1987, pp. 162-68.
Times Literary Supplement, March 14, 1986, p. 281.
Twentieth Century Literature, No. 9, 1963, pp. 93-100.
Variety, April 29, 1996, p. 149.
Virginia Quarterly Review, winter, 1953, pp. 103-17.
Yale Review, October, 1994, p. 17.
Yankee, March, 1994, p. 98.

WILLIAMS, Tennessee 1911-1983

PERSONAL: Name originally Thomas Lanier Williams; born March 26, 1911, in Columbus, MS; choked to death February 24, 1983, in his suite at Hotel Elysee, New York, NY; buried in St. Louis, MO; son of Cornelius Coffin (a traveling salesperson) and Edwina (Dakin) Williams. *Education:* Attended University of Missouri, 1931-33, and Washington University, St. Louis, MO, 1936-37; University of Iowa, A.B., 1938. *Religion:* Originally Episcopalian; converted to Roman Catholicism, 1969.

CAREER: Playwright, novelist, short story writer, and poet; full-time writer, 1944-83; first published in 1927, winning third prize in an essay contest sponsored by *Smart Set* magazine; first published story in *Weird Tales,* August, 1928; first published under name Tennessee Williams in *Story,* summer, 1939. International Shoe Co., St. Louis, MO, clerical worker and manual laborer, 1934-36; worked various jobs, including waiter and hotel elevator operator, New Orleans, LA, 1939; worked as teletype operator, Jacksonville, FL, 1940; worked various jobs, including waiter and theater usher, New York, NY, 1942; worked as screenwriter for Metro-Goldwyn-Mayer, 1943.

MEMBER: Dramatists Guild, National Institute of Arts and Letters, American Society of Composers, Authors, and Publishers (ASCAP), American Automatic Control Council (president, 1965-67), Alpha Tau Omega.

AWARDS, HONORS: Group Theatre Award, 1939, for *American Blues;* Rockefeller Foundation fellowship, 1940; grant, American Academy and National Institute of Arts and Letters, 1943; New York Drama Critics Circle Award, Donaldson Award, and Sidney Howard Memorial Award, 1945, all for *The Glass Menagerie;* New York Drama Critics Circle Award, Pulitzer Prize, and Donaldson Award, 1948, all for *A Streetcar Named Desire;* elected to National Institute of Arts and Letters, 1952; New York Drama Critics Circle Award and Pulitzer Prize, 1955, both for *Cat on a Hot Tin Roof;* London Evening Standard Award, 1958, for *Cat on a Hot Tin Roof;* New York Drama Critics Circle Award, 1962, for *The Night of the Iguana;* first place for best new foreign play, London Critics' Poll, 1964-65, for *The Night of the Iguana;* creative arts medal, Brandeis University, 1964-65; National Institute of Arts and Letters Gold Medal, 1969; received first centennial medal of Cathedral of St. John the Divine, 1973; elected to Theatre Hall of Fame, 1979; Kennedy Honors Award, 1979; Common Wealth Award for Distinguished Service in Dramatic Arts, 1981.

WRITINGS:

PLAYS

Cairo, Shanghai, Bombay! (comedy), produced in Memphis, TN, by Memphis Garden Players, 1935.

Headlines, produced in St. Louis, MO, at Wednesday Club Auditorium, 1936.

Candles to the Sun, produced in St. Louis at Wednesday Club Auditorium, 1936.

The Magic Tower, produced in St. Louis, 1936.

The Fugitive Kind (also see below), produced in St. Louis at Wednesday Club Auditorium, 1937.

Spring Song, produced in Iowa City, IA, at the University of Iowa, 1938.

The Long Goodbye (also see below), produced in New York City at New School for Social Research, 1940.

Battle of Angels (also see below; produced in Boston, MA, at Wilbur Theatre, 1940), New Directions, 1945.

Stairs to the Roof, produced in Pasadena, CA, at Playbox, 1944.

The Glass Menagerie (also see below; first produced in Chicago, IL, at Civic Theatre, 1944; produced on Broadway at Playhouse, 1945), Random House, 1945, published as *The Glass Menagerie: Play in Two Acts,* Dramatists Play Service, 1948.

(With Donald Windham) *You Touched Me!: A Romantic Comedy in Three Acts* (produced on Broadway at Booth Theatre, 1945), Samuel French, 1947.

27 Wagons Full of Cotton (also see below; part of triple bill entitled "All in One"; produced on Broadway at Playhouse, 1955), published in *The Best One-Act Plays of 1944,* Dodd, 1945.

This Property Is Condemned (also see below), produced off-Broadway at Hudson Park Theatre, 1946.

Moony's Kids Don't Cry (also see below), produced in Los Angeles, CA, at Actor's Laboratory Theatre, 1946, published in *The Best One-Act Plays of 1940,* edited by Margaret Mayorga, Dodd, 1940.

Portrait of a Madonna (also see below), produced in Los Angeles at Actor's Laboratory Theatre, 1946, produced in New York City as part of "Triple Play," 1959.

The Last of My Solid Gold Watches (also see below), produced in Los Angeles at Actor's Laboratory Theatre, 1946.

27 Wagons Full of Cotton, and Other One-Act Plays by Tennessee Williams (includes *The Long Goodbye, This Property Is Condemned, Portrait of a Madonna, The Last of My Solid Gold Watches, Auto-da-Fe, The Lady of Larkspur Lotion, The Purification, Hello from Bertha, The Strangest Kind of Romance,* and *Lord Byron's Love Letter* [also see below]), New Directions, 1946, 3rd edition with preface by Williams (contains two new plays, *Talk to Me Like the Rain and Let Me Listen* and *Something Unspoken* [also see below]), 1953.

Lord Byron's Love Letter (also see below), produced in New York City, 1947, revised version produced in London, England, 1964.

Auto-da-Fe, produced in New York City, 1947, produced in Bromley, Kent, England, 1961.

The Lady of Larkspur Lotion, produced in New York City, 1947, produced in London, 1968.

Summer and Smoke (first produced in Dallas, TX, at Theatre '47, 1947; produced on Broadway at Music Box, 1948; revised as Eccentricities of a Nightingale, produced in Washington, DC, 1966, at Washington Theatre Club), New Directions, 1948, published as *Summer and Smoke: Play in Two Acts,* Dramatists Play Service, 1950, published as *The Eccentricities of a Nightingale, and Summer and Smoke: Two Plays,* New Directions, 1964.

A Streetcar Named Desire (also see below; first produced on Broadway at Ethel Barrymore Theatre, 1947), New Directions, 1947, edition with preface by Williams, 1951, revised edition published as *A Streetcar Named Desire: A Play in Three Acts,* Dramatists Play Service, 1953, edition with foreword by Jessica Tandy and introduction by Williams, Limited Editions Club, 1982, edition with introduction by Williams, New American Library, 1984.

American Blues: Five Short Plays (contains *Moony's Kids Don't Cry, The Dark Room, The Case of the Crushed Petunias, The Long Stay Cut Short; or, the Unsatisfactory Supper,* and *Ten Blocks on the Camino Real;* also see below), Dramatists Play Service, 1948.

The Rose Tattoo (also see below; produced in New York City at Martin Beck Theatre, 1951), edition with preface by Williams, New Directions, 1951.

Camino Real: A Play (also see below; expanded version of *Ten Blocks on the Camino Real;* produced in New York City at National Theatre, 1953), edition with foreword and afterword by Williams, New Directions, 1953.

Cat on a Hot Tin Roof (also see below; first produced on Broadway at Morosco Theatre, 1955), edition with preface by Williams, New Directions, 1955, published as *Cat on a Hot Tin Roof: A Play in Three Acts,* Dramatists Play Service, 1958.

Three Players of a Summer Game (first produced in Westport, CT, at White Barn Theatre, 1955), Secker & Warburg, 1960.

(Librettist) Raffaello de Banfield, *Lord Byron's Love Letter: Opera in One Act,* Ricordi, 1955.

The Case of the Crushed Petunias, produced in Cleveland, OH, 1957, produced in New York City, 1958.

Orpheus Descending: A Play in Three Acts (also see below; revision of *Battle of Angels;* produced in New York City at Martin Beck Theatre, 1957; produced off-Broadway, 1959), New Directions, 1959.

Orpheus Descending, with Battle of Angels: Two Plays, with preface by Williams, New Directions, 1958.

A Perfect Analysis Given by a Parrot: A Comedy in One Act (also see below), Dramatists Play Service, 1958.

The Rose Tattoo, and, Camino Real, introduced and edited by E. Martin Browne, Penguin, 1958.

Garden District: Two Plays; Something Unspoken and Suddenly Last Summer (also see below; produced off-Broadway at York Playhouse, 1958), Secker & Warburg, 1959.

Suddenly Last Summer, New Directions, 1958.

Talk to Me Like the Rain and Let Me Listen, first produced in Westport, CT, at White Barn Theatre, 1958, produced in New York City at West Side Actors Workshop, 1967.

I Rise in Flame, Cried the Phoenix: A Play about D. H. Lawrence (first produced off-Broadway, 1958-59, produced off-Broadway at Theatre de Lys, 1959), with a note by Frieda Lawrence, New Directions, 1951.

Sweet Bird of Youth (first produced at Martin Beck Theatre, 1959), edition with foreword by Williams, New Directions, 1959, revised edition, Dramatists Play Service, 1962.

Period of Adjustment; High Point Over a Cavern: A Serious Comedy (first produced in Miami, FL, at Coconut Grove Playhouse, 1959 [codirected by Williams], produced on Broadway at Helen Hayes Theatre, 1960, simultaneously published in *Esquire*), New Directions, 1960, reprinted as *Period of Adjustment; or, High Point is Built on a Cavern: A Serious Comedy,* Dramatists Play Service, 1961.

The Purification, produced off-Broadway at Theatre de Lys, 1959.

The Night of the Iguana (also see below; from Williams's short story of the same title; short version first produced in Spoleto, Italy, 1960, expanded version produced on Broadway at Royale Theatre, 1961), New Directions, 1961.

Hello from Bertha, produced in Bromley, 1961.

To Heaven in a Golden Coach, produced in Bromley, 1961.

The Milk Train Doesn't Stop Here Anymore (also see below; produced as one-act in Spoleto at Festival of Two Worlds, 1962, expanded version produced on Broadway at Morosco Theatre, 1963, revision produced on Broadway at Brooks Atkinson Theatre, 1964), New Directions, 1964.

Slapstick Tragedy (contains *The Mutilated* and *The Gnaediges Fraulein;* also see below), first produced on Broadway at Longacre Theatre, 1966.

The Dark Room, produced in London, 1966.

The Mutilated: A Play in One Act, Dramatists Play Service, 1967.

The Gnaediges Fraulein: A Play in One Act, Dramatists Play Service, 1967, revised as *The Latter Days of a Celebrated Soubrette,* produced in New York City at Central Arts Theatre, 1974.

Kingdom of Earth: The Seven Descents of Myrtle (first published in *Esquire* as one-act Kingdom of Earth, 1967, expanded as *The Seven Descents of Myrtle,* produced on Broadway at Ethel Barrymore Theatre, 1968, revised as *Kingdom of Earth,* produced in Princeton, NJ, at McCarter Theatre, 1975), New Directions, 1968, published as *The Kingdom of Earth (The Seven Descents of Myrtle): A Play in Seven Scenes,* Dramatists Play Service, 1969.

The Two-Character Play (first produced in London, at Hampstead Theatre Club, 1967), revised as *Out Cry* (produced in Chicago at Ivanhoe Theatre, 1971, produced on Broadway at Lyceum Theatre, 1973), New Directions, 1969.

In the Bar of a Tokyo Hotel (first produced off-Broadway at Eastside Playhouse, 1969), Dramatists Play Service, 1969.

The Strangest Kind of Romance, produced in London, 1969.

(Contributor) *Oh! Calcutta!* produced off-Broadway at Eden Theatre, 1969.

The Frosted Glass Coffin [and] *A Perfect Analysis Given by a Parrot,* produced in Key West, FL, at Waterfront Playhouse, 1970.

The Long Stay Cut Short; or, The Unsatisfactory Supper (also see below), produced in London, 1971.

I Can't Imagine Tomorrow [and] *Confessional,* produced in Bar Harbor, ME, at Maine Theatre Arts Festival, 1971.

Small Craft Warnings (produced off-Broadway at Truck and Warehouse Theatre, 1972), New Directions, 1972.

The Red Devil Battery Sign (produced in Boston, 1975, revised version produced in Vienna, Austria, at English Theatre, 1976), New Directions, 1988.

Demolition Downtown: Count Ten in Arabic, produced in London, 1976.

This Is (An Entertainment), produced in San Francisco at American Conservatory Theatre, 1976.

Vieux Carre (produced on Broadway at St. James Theatre, 1977), New Directions, 1979.

A Lovely Sunday for Creve Coeur (first produced under title Creve Coeur in Charleston, SC, at Spoleto Festival, 1978, produced off-Broadway at Hudson Guild Theatre, 1979), New Directions, 1980.

Clothes for a Summer Hotel: A Ghost Play (produced on Broadway at Cort Theatre, 1980), Dramatists Play Service, 1981.

Steps Must Be Gentle: A Dramatic Reading for Two Performers, Targ Editions, 1980.

It Happened the Day the Sun Rose, Sylvester & Orphanos, 1981.

The Remarkable Rooming-House of Mme. Le Monde: A Play, Albondocani Press, 1984.

Something Cloudy, Something Clear (first produced off-off Broadway at Bouwerie Lane Theatre, 1981), introduction by Eve Adamson, New Directions, 1995.

The Notebook of Trigorin: A Free Adaptation of Anton Chekhov's The Sea Gull, New Directions, 1997.

Not about Nightingales, originally written in 1939, first scheduled for production at the Royal National Theatre in London, February 1998.

Also author of "Me, Vashya," "Kirche, Kutchen und Kinder," "Life Boat Drill," "Will Mr. Merriwether Return from Memphis?," "Of Masks Outrageous and Austere," and "A House Not Meant to Stand." Also author of television play, "I Can't Imagine

Tomorrow." Contributor to anthologies. Contributor to periodicals, including *Esquire.*

COLLECTIONS

Four Plays (contains *The Glass Menagerie, A Streetcar Named Desire, Summer and Smoke,* and *Camino Real*), Secker & Warburg, 1956.

Five Plays (contains *Cat on a Hot Tin Roof, The Rose Tattoo, Something Unspoken, Suddenly Last Summer,* and *Orpheus Descending*), Secker & Warburg, 1962.

Three Plays: The Rose Tattoo, Camino Real, Sweet Bird of Youth, New Directions, 1964.

Baby Doll: The Script for the Film [and] *Something Unspoken* [and] *Suddenly Last Summer,* Penguin, 1968.

The Night of the Iguana [and] *Orpheus Descending,* Penguin, 1968.

The Milk Train Doesn't Stop Here Anymore [and] *Cat on a Hot Tin Roof,* Penguin, 1969.

Dragon Country: A Book of Plays, New Directions, 1970.

Battle of Angels [and] *The Glass Menagerie* [and] *A Streetcar Named Desire,* New Directions, 1971.

Cat on a Hot Tin Roof [and] *Orpheus Descending* [and] *Suddenly Last Summer,* New Directions, 1971.

The Eccentricities of a Nightingale [and] *Summer and Smoke* [and] *The Rose Tattoo* [and] *Camino Real,* New Directions, 1971.

The Theatre of Tennessee Williams, New Directions, Volume 1, 1971; Volume 2, 1971; Volume 3, 1971; Volume 4, 1972; Volume 5, 1976; Volume 6, 1981; Volume 7, 1981.

Three by Tennessee Williams, New American Library, 1976.

Cat on a Hot Tin Roof [and] *The Milk Train Doesn't Stop Here Anymore* [and] *The Night of the Iguana,* Penguin, 1976.

Selected Plays, illustrations by Jerry Pinkney, Franklin Library, 1977.

Tennessee Williams: Eight Plays, introduction by Harold Clurman, Doubleday, 1979.

Selected Plays, illustrations by Herbert Tauss, Franklin Library, 1980.

Ten by Tennessee (one-act plays), produced in New York City at Lucille Lortel Theatre, May, 1986.

SCREENPLAYS

(With Gore Vidal) *Senso,* Luchino Visconti, c. 1949.

(With Oscar Saul) *The Glass Menagerie,* Warner Bros., 1950.

A Streetcar Named Desire, 20th Century-Fox, 1951.

(With Hal Kanter) *The Rose Tattoo,* Paramount, 1955.

Baby Doll, Warner Bros., 1956, published as *Baby Doll: The Script for the Film,* New American Library, 1956, published as *Baby Doll; the Script for the Film, Incorporating the Two One-Act Plays which Suggested It: 27 Wagons Full of Cotton* [and] *The Long Stay Cut Short; or, The Unsatisfactory Supper,* New Directions, 1956.

(With Vidal) *Suddenly Last Summer,* Columbia, 1959.

(With Meade Roberts) *The Fugitive Kind* (based on *Orpheus Descending*), United Artists, 1959, published as *The Fugitive Kind,* Signet, 1960.

Boom (based on *The Milk Train Doesn't Stop Here Anymore*), Universal, 1968.

Stopped Rocking and Other Screenplays (contains *All Gaul Is Divided, The Loss of a Teardrop Diamond, One Arm,* and *Stopped Rocking*), introduced by Richard Gilman, New Directions, 1984.

A Streetcar Named Desire: A Screen Adaptation Directed by Elia Kazan, Irvington, 1989.

Baby Doll and Tiger Tail, New Directions, 1991.

Also author, with Paul Bowles, of "The Wanton Countess" (English-language version), filmed in 1954.

STORIES

One Arm, and Other Stories (includes The Night of the Iguana), New Directions, 1948.

Hard Candy: A Book of Stories, New Directions, 1954.

Man Brings This Up Road: A Short Story, Street & Smith, 1959.

Three Players of a Summer Game, and Other Stories, Secker & Warburg, 1960.

Grand, House of Books, 1964.

The Knightly Quest: A Novella and Four Short Stories, New Directions, 1967.

Eight Mortal Ladies Possessed: A Book of Stories, New Directions, 1974.

Collected Stories, introduction by Gore Vidal, New Directions, 1985.

OTHER

The Roman Spring of Mrs. Stone (novel), New Directions, 1950.

In the Winter of Cities: Poems, New Directions, 1956.

(Author of introduction) Carson McCullers, *Reflections in a Golden Eye,* Bantam, 1961.

Glass Menagerie and The Street Car Named Desire Notes, Cliffs Notes, 1965.

Memoirs, Doubleday, 1975.

Moise and the World of Reason (novel), Simon & Schuster, 1975.

Tennessee Williams's Letters to Donald Windham, 1940-65, edited with commentary by Windham, [Verona], 1976, Holt, 1977.

Androgyne, Mon Amour: Poems, New Directions, 1977.

Where I Live: Selected Essays, edited by Christine R. Day and Bob Woods, introduction by Day, New Directions, 1978.

Conversations with Tennessee Williams, edited by Albert J. Devlin, University Press of Mississippi, 1986.

Five O'Clock Angel: Letters of Tennessee Williams to Maria St. Just, 1948-1982 Knopf, 1990.

A collection of Williams's manuscripts and letters is located at the Humanities Research Center of the University of Texas at Austin.

MEDIA ADAPTATIONS: The Roman Spring of Mrs. Stone was filmed by Warner Bros. in 1961; *Sweet Bird of Youth* was filmed in 1962; *Period of Adjustment* was filmed in 1962; *This Property Is Condemned* was filmed by Paramount in 1966; *I Can't Imagine Tomorrow* and *Talk to Me Like the Rain and Let Me Listen* were televised together under the title "Dragon Country," December 3, 1970, by New York Television Theatre; an adaptation of *The Seven Descents of Myrtle* was filmed by Warner Bros. in 1970 under the title, *The Last of the Mobile Hot-Shots; Summer and Smoke: Opera in Two Acts,* Belwin-Mills, 1972, was adapted from Williams's play, with music by Lee Hoiby and libretto by Lanford Wilson; *The Glass Menagerie* was filmed by Burt Harris for Cineplex Odeon in 1987; *A Streetcar Named Desire* was filmed for television in 1984 and broadcast on ABC-TV; *Cat on a Hot Tin Roof* was filmed for television in 1984 by International TV Group; *Summer and Smoke* was filmed for television in 1989 and broadcast on NBC-TV.

SIDELIGHTS: The production of his first two Broadway plays, *The Glass Menagerie* (1945) and *A Streetcar Named Desire* (1947), secured Tennessee Williams's place, with Eugene O'Neill and Arthur Miller, as one of America's major playwrights of the twentieth century. Critics, playgoers, and fellow dramatists recognized in him a poetic innovator who, refusing to be confined in what Stark Young in the *New Republic* called "the usual sterilities of our playwriting patterns," pushed drama into new fields, stretched the limits of the individual play, and became one of the founders of the so-called "New Drama." Praising *The Glass Menagerie* "as a revelation of what superb theater could be," Brooks Atkinson in *Broadway* asserted that "Williams's remembrance of things past gave the theater distinction as a literary medium." Twenty years later, Joanne Stang wrote in the *New York Times* that "the American theater, indeed theater everywhere, has never been the same" since the premier of *The Glass Menagerie.* Four decades after that first play, C. W. E. Bigsby in *A Critical Introduction to Twentieth-Century American Drama* termed it "one of the best works to have come out of the American theater." *A Streetcar Named Desire* became only the second play in history to win both the Pulitzer Prize and the New York Drama Critics Circle Award. Eric Bentley, in *What Is Theatre?,* called it the "master-drama of the generation." "The inevitability of a great work of art," T. E. Kalem stated in Albert J. Devlin's *Conversations with Tennessee Williams,* "is that you cannot imagine the time when it didn't exist. You can't imagine a time when *Streetcar* didn't exist."

More clearly than with most authors, the facts of Williams's life reveal the origins of the material he crafted into his best works. The Mississippi in which Thomas Lanier Williams was born March 26, 1911, was in many ways a world that no longer exists, "a dark, wide, open world that you can breathe in," as Williams nostalgically described it in Harry Rasky's *Tennessee Williams: A Portrait in Laughter and Lamentation.* The predominantly rural state was dotted with towns such as Columbus, Canton, and Clarksdale, in which he spent his first seven years with his mother, his sister Rose, and his maternal grandmother and grandfather, an Episcopal rector. A sickly child, Tom was pampered by doting elders. In 1918, his father, a traveling salesman who had often been absent—perhaps, like his stage counterpart in *The Glass Menagerie,* "in love with long distances"—moved the family to St. Louis. Something of the trauma they experienced is dramatized in the 1945 play. The contrast between leisurely small-town past and northern big-city present, between protective grandparents and the hard-drinking, gambling father with little patience for the sensitive son he saw as a "sissy," seriously affected both children. While Rose retreated into her own mind until finally beyond the reach even of her loving brother, Tom made use of that adversity. St. Louis remained for him "a city I loathe," but the South, despite his portrayal of its grotesque aspects, proved a rich source to which he returned literally and imaginatively for comfort and inspiration. That background, his homosexuality, and his relationships, painful and joyous, with members of his family were the strongest personal factors shaping Williams's dramas.

Plays, stories, poems, and personal essays were all drawn from the experiences of his persona. Williams saw himself as a shy, sensitive, gifted man trapped in a world where "mendacity" replaced communication, brute violence replaced love, and loneliness was, all too often, the standard human condition. These tensions "at the core of his creation" were identified by Harold Clurman in his introduction to *Tennessee Williams: Eight Plays* as a terror at what Williams saw in himself and in America, a terror that he must "exorcise" with "his poetic vision." In the preface to *The Rose Tattoo,* the playwright declared that "snatching the eternal out of the desperately fleeting" was "the great magic trick of human existence." In an interview collected in *Conversations with Tennessee Williams,* Williams identified his main theme as a

defense of the Old South attitude—"elegance, a love of the beautiful, a romantic attitude toward life"—and "a violent protest against those things that defeat it." An idealist aware of what he called in a *Conversations* interview "the merciless harshness of America's success-oriented society," he was ironically, naturalistic as well, conscious of the inaccessibility of that for which he yearned. He early developed, according to John Gassner in *Theatre at the Crossroads: Plays and Playwrights of the Mid-Century American Stage,* "a precise naturalism" and continued to work toward a "fusion of naturalistic detail with symbolism and poetic sensibility rare in American playwriting." The result was a unique romanticism, as Kenneth Tynan observed in *Curtains,* "which is not pale or scented but earthy and robust, the product of a mind vitally infected with the rhythms of human speech."

Williams's South provided not only settings but other characteristics of his work: the romanticism that tinges almost every play; a myth of an Arcadian existence now disappeared; a distinctive way of looking at life, including both an inbred Calvinistic belief in the reality of evil eternally at war with good and what Bentley called a "peculiar combination of the comic and the pathetic." The South also inspired Williams's fascination with violence, his drawing upon regional character types, and his skill in recording Southern language—eloquent, flowery, sometimes bombastic. Moreover, Southern history, particularly the lost cause of the Civil War and the devastating Reconstruction period, imprinted on Williams, as on such major Southern fiction writers as William Faulkner, Flannery O'Connor, and Walker Percy, a profound sense of separation and alienation. Williams, as Thomas E. Porter declared in *Myth and Modern American Drama,* explored "the mind of the Southerner caught between an idyllic past and an undesirable present," commemorating the death of a myth even as he continued to examine it. "His broken figures appeal," Bigsby asserted, "because they are victims of history—the lies of the old South no longer being able to sustain the individual in a world whose pragmatics have no place for the fragile spirit." In a *Conversations* interview the playwright commented that "the South once had a way of life that I am just old enough to remember—a culture that had grace, elegance. . . . I write out of regret for that."

Beginning with *Battle of Angels,* two opposing camps have existed among Williams's critics, and his detractors sometimes have objected most strenuously to the innovations his supporters deemed virtues. His strongest advocates among established drama critics, notably Stark Young, Brooks Atkinson, John Gassner, and Walter Kerr, praised him for realistic clarity; compassion and a strong moral sense; unforgettable characters, especially women, based on his keen perception of human nature; dialogue at once credible and poetic; and a pervasive sense of humor that distinguished him from O'Neill and Miller. Young commended his revolt against archaic dramatic conventions and his "true realism" with all its "variety, suddenness, passion and freedom"; he applauded Williams's relation to a tradition and his "free and true" language and motifs. In 1968, Bentley, commenting on Williams's influence on American drama, suggested that he "bids fair to become, theatrically speaking, the father of his country: the new playwrights derive from him, not from O'Neill, [Clifford] Odets, [Thornton] Wilder or Miller, . . . his only conceivable rivals." Crediting Williams with overcoming "resistance to emotional improvisations that dispensed with the conventional dramatic forms," Atkinson termed Williams and Miller "two natural theater men" who resuscitated a failing art and dominated it in the years after World War II. In them, Frederick Lumley stated in *New Trends in Twentieth Century Drama: A Survey since*

Ibsen and Shaw, "the immigrant strain is less conscious," because they learned from the European masters without becoming mere disciples. Miller identified Williams's "greatest value" as "his aesthetic valor," that is, "his very evident determination to unveil and engage the widest range of causation conceivable to him." Even in 1979, when Williams's career, near its end, had survived years of failed productions and bad reviews, Kerr would pronounce him "our finest living playwright."

Not surprisingly, it was from the conservative establishment that most of the adverse criticism came. Obviously appalled by this "upstart crow," George Jean Nathan, dean of theater commentators when Williams made his revolutionary entrance onto the scene, sounded notes often to be repeated. In *The Theatre Book of the Year, 1947-1948,* he faulted Williams's early triumphs for "mistiness of ideology," "questionable symbolism," "debatable character drawing," "adolescent point of view," "theatrical fabrication," and obsession with sex, fallen women, and "the deranged Dixie damsel." In short, Nathan saw Williams as a melodramatist whose attempts at tragedy were as ludicrous as "a threnody on a zither." Subsequent detractors—notably Richard Gilman, Robert Brustein, Clive Barnes, and John Simon—taxed the playwright for theatricality, repetition, lack of judgment and control, excessive moralizing and philosophizing, and conformity to the demands of the ticket-buying public. His plays, they variously argued, lacked unity of effect, clarity of intention, social content, and variety; these critics saw the plays as burdened with excessive symbolism, violence, sexuality, and attention to the sordid, grotesque elements of life. Additionally, certain commentators charged that Elia Kazan, the director of the early masterpieces, virtually rewrote *A Streetcar Named Desire* and *Cat on a Hot Tin Roof.* A particular kind of negative criticism, often intensely emotional, seemed to dominate evaluations of the plays produced in the last twenty years of Williams's life.

But most critics, even his detractors, have praised the dramatist's skillful creation of dialogue. "What we need in the theater is a sense of language, a sense of texture in speech," Young wrote of *The Glass Menagerie,* in which he heard "the echo of great literature, or at least a respect for it." Twenty years later Bentley asserted that "no one in the English-speaking theater" created better dialogue, that Williams's plays were really "*written*—that is to say, set down in living language." Ruby Cohn stated in *Dialogue in American Drama* that Williams gave to American theater "a new vocabulary and rhythm" by expanding dialogue in range and content to embrace "nostalgia, frustration, sadness, gaiety, cruelty, and compassion." Praising Williams's "uncanny ear" for dialogue that was "effortlessly euphonious, rich in subtle gradations of the vernacular," Clurman concluded, "No one in the theater has written more melodiously. Without the least artificial flourish, his writing takes flight from the naturalistic to the poetic." Even Mary McCarthy, no ardent fan, stated in *Theatre Chronicles: 1937-1962* that Williams was the only American realist other than Paddy Chayevsky with an ear for dialogue and that although he sometimes abandoned real speech for "his special poetic long-play prose," he knew speech patterns and really heard his characters. There were, of course, objections to Williams's lyrical dialogue, different as it is from the dialogue of O'Neill, Miller, or any other major American playwright. Bentley admitted to finding his "fake poeticizing" troublesome at times, while Bigsby insisted that Williams was at his best only when he restrained "over-poetic language" and symbolism with "an imagination which if melodramatic is also capable of fine control." However, those long poetic speeches or "arias" in plays of the first

twenty-five years of his career became a hallmark of the dramatist's work.

Critics favorable to Williams have agreed that one of his virtues lay in his characterization. Those "superbly actable parts," Atkinson stated, derived from his ability to find "extraordinary spiritual significance in ordinary people." Cohn admired Williams's "Southern grotesques" and his knack for giving them "dignity," although some critics have been put off by the excessive number of such grotesques, which contributed, they argued, to a distorted view of reality. Commentators generally concurred in their praise of Williams's talent in creating credible female roles. "No one in American drama has written more intuitively of women," Clurman asserted; Gassner spoke of Williams's "uncanny familiarity with the flutterings of the female heart." Walter Kerr in *The Theatre in Spite of Itself* expressed wonder at such roles as that of Hannah in *The Night of the Iguana,* "a portrait which owes nothing to calipers, or to any kind of tooling; it is all surprise and presence, anticipated intimacy. It is found gold, not a borrowing against known reserves." Surveying the "steamy zoo" of Williams's characters with their violence, despair, and aberrations, Stang commended the author for the "poetry and compassion that comprise his great gift." *Compassion* is the key word in all tributes to Williams's characterization. It is an acknowledgment of the playwright's uncanny talent for making audiences and readers empathize with his people, however grotesque, bizarre, or even sordid they may seem on the surface.

Although they granted him compassion, some of his detractors felt Williams did not exhibit a clear philosophy of life, and they found unacceptable the ambiguity in judging human flaws and frailties that was one of his most distinctive qualities. Bentley chided Williams for his "besetting sin" of "fake philosophizing, a straining after big statements." Noting that Williams had "said that he only feels and does not think," the critic stated that perhaps "he only thinks he feels," since the "Serenity and Truth, of which he *speaks* and *thinks,* tend to remain in the head too—mere abstractions." On the other hand, Arthur Ganz in *Realms of the Self: Variations on a Theme in Modern Drama,* insisted that Williams's best work "derives its force from the strength of his moral temper, which leads him to censure even what he most wishes to exalt." One difficulty (for those concerned about his seeming lack of judgments on characters and their actions), stemmed from the playwright's recognition of and insistence on portraying the ambiguity of human activities and relationships. Moral, even puritanical, though he might be, Williams never seemed ready to condemn any action other than "deliberate cruelty," and even that was sometimes portrayed as resulting from extenuating circumstances.

In terms of dramatic technique, those who acknowledged his genius disagreed as to where it was best expressed. For Jerold Phillips, writing in *Dictionary of Literary Biography Documentary Series,* Williams's major contribution lay in turning from the Ibsenesque social problem plays to "Strindberg-like explorations of what goes on underneath the skin," thereby freeing American theater from "the hold of the so-called well-made play." For Allan Lewis in *American Plays and Playwrights of the Contemporary Theatre* he was a "brilliant inventor of emotionally intense scenes" whose "greatest gift [lay] in suggesting ideas through emotional relations." His preeminence among dramatists in the United States, Jean Gould wrote in *Modern American Playwrights,* resulted from a combination of poetic sensitivity, theatricality, and "the dedication of the artist." If, from the beginning of his career, there were detractors who charged

Williams with overuse of melodramatic, grotesque, and violent elements that produced a distorted view of reality, Kerr, in *The Theatre in Spite of Itself,* termed him "a man unafraid of melodrama, and a man who handles it with extraordinary candor and deftness." Agreeing that Williams's endings were melodramatic, Lewis compared them to Jacobean drama, powerful in that "they reach beyond the immediate locale to wherever brutality and ugliness suppress the cry for beauty." Robert Heilman believed, however, that like O'Neill, Williams himself despaired and thus did not develop "the authentic note of tragic completeness."

Late in his career, Williams was increasingly subject to charges that he had outlived his talent. Beginning with *Period of Adjustment,* a comedy generally disliked by critics, there were years of rejection of play after play: *The Milk Train Doesn't Stop Here Any More, Kingdom of Earth, Small Craft Warnings, Out Cry, Vieux Carre, Clothes for a Summer Hotel, The Red Devil Battery Sign.* By the late 1960s, even the longtime advocate Brooks Atkinson observed that in "a melancholy resolution of an illustrious career" the dramatist was producing plays "with a kind of desperation" in which he lost control of content and style. Lewis, accusing Williams of repeating motifs, themes, and characters in play after play, asserted that in failing "to expand and enrich" his theme, he had "dissipated a rare talent." Berating him for "heavy-handed gongorism," John Simon said that Williams's style was becoming as "baroque" as his subject matter; Richard Gilman, in a particularly vituperative review entitled "Mr. Williams, He Dead," included in his *Common and Uncommon Masks: Writings on Theatre, 1961-1970,* charged that the "moralist," subtly present in earlier plays, was "increasingly on stage." Citing the dramatist's growing concern with his own unconscious, Brustein accused him of hypocritically pandering to "the very groups he assaults." Even if one granted a diminution of creative powers, however, the decline in Williams's popularity and position as major playwright in the 1960s and 1970s can be attributed in large part to a marked change in the theater itself. Audiences constantly demanded variety, and although the early creations of the playwright remained popular, theatergoers wanted something different, strange, exotic. One problem, Kerr pointed out, was that Williams was so good, people expected him to continue to get better; judging each play against those which had gone before denied a fair hearing to the new creations. Sadly, the playwright's accidental death came when his career, after almost two decades of bad reviews and of dismissals of his "dwindling talents," was at its lowest ebb since the abortive 1940 production of *Battle of Angels.* Since his death, however, an inevitable reevaluation has begun. Bigsby, for example, has found in a reanalysis of the late plays more than mere vestiges of the strengths of earlier years, especially in *Out Cry,* an experimental drama toward which Williams felt a particular affection.

Following Williams's death, some of those who had been his severest critics during his last years acknowledged the greatness of his achievement. Even John Simon, who had dismissed play after play as valueless repetitions created by an author who had outlived his talent, acknowledged in a 1983 *New York* essay that he had underestimated the playwright's genius and significance. Tennessee Williams was, finally, a rebel who broke with the rigid conventions of drama that had preceded him, explored new territory in his quest for a distinctive form and style, created characters as unforgettable as those of Charles Dickens, Nathaniel Hawthorne, or William Faulkner, and lifted the language of the modern stage to a poetic level unmatched in his time.

Posthumous publications of Williams's writings—correspondence and plays among them—show the many sides of this complex literary legend. *Five O'Clock Angel: Letters of Tennessee Williams to Maria St. Just, 1948-1982* takes its title from the name the author gave to Russian-born actress and socialite Maria Britneva, later Maria St. Just, "the confidante Williams wrote to in the evening after his day's work—his 'Five O'Clock Angel,' as he called her in a typically genteel, poetic periphrasis," noted Edmund White in a piece for the *New York Times Book Review.* These letters allow "us to see the source of everything in his work that was lyrical, innocent, loving, and filled with laughter." It was St. Just's control over Williams's estate, however, that made publication of a two-volume biography of the author so difficult to publish. Lyle Leverich, Williams's authorized biographer, reportedly began work on the project in 1979 but was stymied again and again, mainly by St. Just's tight hold over the playwright's works. She "guarded her power fiercely," explained Gayle Feldman in a *Publishers Weekly* account of the publication struggle. Upon St. Just's death, though, Leverich obtained the backing he needed to release the long-awaited biography.

Among the other Williams publications of the mid-1990s was *Something Cloudy, Something Clear.* A play first produced in 1981 and published in 1995, it recounts the author's homosexual relationship with a doomed dancer in Provincetown. Homosexuality—this time in a violent context—also takes center stage in *Not about Nightingales,* a tale of terror in a men's prison. Actress Vanessa Redgrave reportedly played a key role in bringing this early play—circa 1939—to the London stage in 1998.

BIOGRAPHICAL/CRITICAL SOURCES:

BOOKS

Atkinson, Brooks, *Broadway,* revised edition, Macmillan, 1974.
Bentley, Eric, *What Is Theatre?* Atheneum, 1968.
Bernstein, Samuel J., *The Strands Entwined: A New Direction in American Drama,* Northeastern University Press, 1980.
Bigsby, C. W. E., *Confrontation and Commitment: A Study of Contemporary American Drama 1959-66,* University of Missouri Press, 1968.
Bigsby, C. W. E., *A Critical Introduction to Twentieth-Century American Drama,* three volumes, Cambridge University Press, 1985.
Cohn, Ruby, *Dialogue in America Drama,* Indiana University Press, 1971.
Concise Dictionary of American Literary Biography: The New Consciousness, 1941-1968, Gale (Detroit), 1987.
Contemporary Literary Criticism, Gale, Volume 1, 1973; Volume 2, 1974; Volume 5, 1976; Volume 7, 1977; Volume 8, 1978; Volume 11, 1979; Volume 15, 1980; Volume 19, 1981; Volume 30, 1984; Volume 39, 1986; Volume 45, 1987.
Crandell, George W., *Tennessee Williams: A Descriptive Bibliography,* University of Pittsburgh Press, 1995.
Crandell, George W., *The Critical Response to Tennessee Williams,* Greenwood Press, 1996.
Devlin, Albert J., *Conversations with Tennessee Williams,* University Press of Mississippi, 1986.
Dictionary of Literary Biography, Volume 7: *Twentieth-Century American Dramatists,* Gale, 1981.
Dictionary of Literary Biography Documentary Series, Volume 4, Gale, 1984.
Dictionary of Literary Biography Yearbook: 1983, Gale, 1984.
Fleche, Anne, *Mimetic Disillusion: Eugene O'Neill, Tennessee Williams, and U.S. Dramatic Realism,* University of Alabama Press, 1997.

Ganz, Arthur, *Realms of the Self: Variations on a Theme in Modern Drama,* New York University Press, 1980.

Gassner, John, *Theatre at the Crossroads: Plays and Playwrights of the Mid-Century American Stage,* Holt, 1960.

Gilman, Richard, *Common and Uncommon Masks: Writing on Theatre, 1961-1970,* Random House, 1971.

Gould, Jean, *Modern American Playwrights,* Dodd, 1966.

Heilman, Robert Bechtold, *Tragedy and Melodrama: Versions of Experience,* University of Washington Press, 1968.

Kerr, Walter, *The Theatre in Spite of Itself,* Simon & Schuster, 1963.

Leverich, Lyle, *Tom: The Unknown Tennessee Williams,* Crown Publishers, 1995.

Lewis, Allen, *American Plays and Playwrights of the Contemporary Theatre,* Crown, 1965.

Martin, Robert A., editor, *Critical Essays on Tennessee Williams,* Prentice Hall International, 1997.

McCarthy, Mary, *Theatre Chronicles: 1937-1962,* Farrar, Straus, 1963.

O'Connor, Jacqueline, *Dramatizing Dementia: Madness in the Plays of Tennessee Williams,* Bowling Green State University Popular Press, 1997.

Porter, Thomas E., *Myth and Modern American Drama,* Wayne State University Press, 1969.

Rasky, Harry, *Tennessee Williams: A Portrait in Laughter and Lamentations,* Dodd, 1986.

Roudane, Matthew C., editor, *The Cambridge Companion to Tennessee Williams,* Cambridge University Press, 1997.

Schlueter, June, *Dramatic Closure: Reading the End,* Associated University Presses, 1995.

Tynan, Kenneth, *Curtains,* Atheneum, 1961.

Windham, Donald, *Lost Friendships: A Memoir of Truman Capote, Tennessee Williams, and Others,* Morrow, 1987.

Yacowar, Maurice, *Tennessee Williams and Film,* Ungar, 1977.

PERIODICALS

Atlantic Monthly, November, 1970; July, 1994, p. 91.
Booklist, September 15, 1995, p. 131.
Choice, February 1996, p. 954.
Detroit News, June 11, 1997.
Esquire, November, 1969; September, 1971.
Library Journal, September 1, 1995, p. 178; October 15, 1995, p. 100.
Modern Drama, Volume 2, 1959; Volume 15, 1972.
Nation, Volume 165, 1947.
New Republic, Volume 112, 1945; June 17, 1996, p. 26.
New York, March 14, 1983; November 28, 1994, p. 75; May 15, 1995, p. 59; October 23, 1995, p. 60; October 30, 1995, p. 137; April 1, 1996, p. 62.
New Yorker, July 18, 1994, p. 68; November 21, 1994, p. 124; December 19, 1994, p. 76; May 15, 1995, p. 100; April 8, 1996, p. 103.
New York Review of Books, July 19, 1990, p. 12
New York Times, May 1, 1960; March 28, 1965; November 3, 1975.
New York Times Book Review, May 27, 1990, p. 1.
Observer (London), May 5, 1991, p. 60.
Playboy, April, 1973.
Publishers Weekly, January 16, 1995, p. 320; August 7, 1995, p. 447.
Southern Living, March, 1996, p. 26.
Southern Review, summer, 1979.
Tennessee Studies in Literature, Volume 10, 1965.
Theatre Arts, January, 1962.
Time, December 5, 1994, p. 94.
Times Literary Supplement, April 19, 1991, p. 8.
Variety, November 21, 1994, p. 43; November 28, 1994, p. 103; May 15, 1995, p. 234; October 16, 1995, p. 105; March 25, 1996, p. 77.
Washington Post, April 4, 1979.
Western Humanities Review, Volume 18, 1964.
World Literature Today, winter, 1992, p. 133.

*　　*　　*

WILLIAMS, William C.
See WILLIAMS, William Carlos

*　　*　　*

WILLIAMS, William Carlos 1883-1963
(William C. Williams)

PERSONAL: Born September 17, 1883, in Rutherford, NJ; died March 4, 1963, in Rutherford, NJ; son of William George (in business) and Raquel Helene (Hoheb) Williams; married Florence Herman, December 12, 1912; children: William, Eric, Paul Herman. *Education:* University of Pennsylvania, M.D., 1906; postgraduate study at University of Leipzig, 1909-10.

CAREER: Poet, playwright, novelist, essayist, and physician. French Hospital and Nursery and Child's Hospital, New York City, intern, 1906-09; private medical practice in Rutherford, New Jersey, 1910-51. University of Washington, Seattle, visiting professor of English, 1948.

MEMBER: American Academy of Arts and Letters, National Institute of Arts and Letters, Academy of American Poets, Bergen County (New Jersey) Medical Association.

AWARDS, HONORS: Dial Award, 1926, for distinguished service to American literature; Guarantors Prize from *Poetry,* 1931; LL.D. from University of Buffalo, 1946, and Fairleigh Dickinson University, 1959; Russell Loines Memorial Award for poetry from National Institute of Arts and Letters, 1948; Litt.D. from Rutgers University, 1948, Bard College, 1948, and University of Pennsylvania, 1952; appointed to chair of poetry at Library of Congress, 1949 (appointment withdrawn, but subsequently renewed); National Book Award for poetry, 1950, for *Selected Poems* and *Paterson,* Book III; Bollingen Prize in poetry from Yale University Library, 1952; Levinson Prize, 1954, and Oscar Blumenthal Prize, 1955, both for poems published in *Poetry;* Academy of American Poets fellowship, 1956; Brandeis University creative arts medal in poetry-fiction-nonfiction, 1957-58, in recognition of a lifetime of distinguished achievement; Pulitzer Prize in poetry for *Pictures From Brueghel* and American Academy of Arts and Letters gold medal for poetry from National Institute of Arts and Letters, both 1963.

WRITINGS:

POEMS

(Under name William C. Williams) *Poems,* privately printed, 1909.
The Tempers, Elkin Matthews, 1913.
Al Que Quiere! Four Seas, 1917.
Kora in Hell: Improvisations, Four Seas, 1920 (also see below).
Sour Grapes, Four Seas, 1921.
Go Go, Monroe Wheeler, 1923.

Spring and All, Contact Publishing, 1923 (also see below).

The Cod Head, Harvest Press, 1932.

Collected Poems, 1921-1931, preface by Wallace Stevens, Objectivist Press, 1934.

An Early Martyr and Other Poems, Alcestis Press, 1935.

Adam & Eve & The City, Alcestis Press, 1936.

The Complete Collected Poems of William Carlos Williams, 1906-1938, New Directions, 1938.

The Broken Span, New Directions, 1941.

The Wedge, Cummington Press (Cummington, Massachusetts), 1944.

Paterson, New Directions, Book I, 1946, Book II, 1948, Book III, 1949, Book IV, 1951, Book V, 1958, Books I-V published in one volume, 1963.

The Clouds, Wells College Press and Cummington Press, 1948.

Selected Poems, introduction by Randall Jarrell, New Directions, 1949, revised edition, 1968.

The Pink Church, Golden Goose Press, 1949.

The Collected Later Poems, New Directions, 1950, revised edition, 1963.

Collected Earlier Poems, New Directions, 1951, revised edition, 1966.

The Desert Music and Other Poems, Random House, 1954 (also see below).

Journey to Love (includes "Asphodel, That Greeny Flower"), Random House, 1955 (also see below).

The Lost Poems of William Carlos Williams; or, The Past Recaptured, collected by John C. Thirlwall, published in *New Directions 16,* New Directions, 1957.

Pictures From Brueghel and Other Poems (includes "The Desert Music" and "Journey to Love"), New Directions, 1962.

Selected Poems, introduction by Charles Tomlinson, Penguin, 1976.

Collected Poems: Volume 1, 1909-1939, edited by A. Walton Litz and Christopher MacGowan, Carcanet, 1988, *Volume 2, 1939-1962,* edited by MacGowan, 1989.

Asphodel, That Greeny Flower & Other Love Poems, new Directions, 1994.

OTHER

The Great American Novel, Three Mountains Press, 1923 (also see below).

In the American Grain (essays), A. & C. Boni, 1925, reprinted with introduction by Horace Gregory, New Directions, 1967.

A Voyage to Pagany (novel), Macaulay, 1928.

(Translator) Philippe Soupault, *Last Nights of Paris,* Macaulay, 1929.

The Knife of the Times, and Other Stories (short stories), Dragon Press, 1932.

A Novelette and Other Prose, TO Publishers, 1932 (also see below).

The First President (three-act libretto for an opera), published in *American Caravan,* 1936.

White Mule (novel; part I of trilogy), New Directions, 1937.

Life along the Passaic River (short stories), New Directions, 1938.

In the Money (novel; part II of *White Mule* trilogy), New Directions, 1940.

A Dream of Love (three-act play), New Directions, 1948.

A Beginning on the Short Story: Notes, Alicat Bookshop Press, 1950.

Make Light of It: Collected Stories, Random House, 1950.

Autobiography, Random House, 1951, published as *The Autobiography of William Carlos Williams,* New Directions, 1967.

The Build-Up (novel; part III of *White Mule* trilogy), Random House, 1952.

(Translator with mother, Raquel Helene Williams) Pedro Espinosa, *A Dog and the Fever* (novella), Shoe String Press, 1954.

Selected Essays, Random House, 1954.

The Selected Letters of William Carlos Williams, edited by John C. Thirlwall, McDowell, Obolensky, 1957.

I Wanted to Write a Poem: The Autobiography of the Works of a Poet, edited by Edith Heal, Beacon Press, 1958.

Yes, Mrs. Williams: A Personal Record of My Mother, McDowell, Obolensky, 1959.

Many Loves and Other Plays: The Collected Plays of William Carlos Williams, New Directions, 1961.

The Farmers' Daughters: Collected Stories, introduction by Van Wyck Brooks, New Directions, 1961.

The William Carlos Williams Reader, edited and introduced by M. L. Rosenthal, New Directions, 1966.

Imaginations (contains *Kora in Hell, Spring and All, The Great American Novel, The Descent of Winter,* and *A Novelette and Other Prose*), edited by Webster Schott, New Directions, 1970.

The Embodiment of Knowledge (philosophy), edited by Ron Loewinsohn, New Directions, 1974.

Interviews With William Carlos Williams: "Speaking Straight Ahead," edited and introduced by Linda Welshimer Wagner, New Directions, 1976.

A Recognizable Image: William Carlos Williams on Art and Artists, edited by Bram Dijkstra, New Directions, 1978.

William Carlos Williams: The Doctor Stories, compiled with an introduction by Robert Coles, New Directions, 1984.

The Collected Stories of William Carlos Williams, New Directions, 1996.

Pound/Williams: Selected Letters of Ezra Pound and William Carlos Williams, edited by Hugh Witemeyer, New Directions, 1996.

The Letters of William Carlos Williams and Charles Tomlinson, edited by Barry Magid and Hugh Witemeyer, Dim Gray Bar Press, 1998.

Contributor to numerous literary magazines and journals, including *Poetry, The Dial, Origin, Blast, Pagany, Little Review, New Masses, Partisan Review,* and *Glebe.* Contributing editor of literary magazines and journals, including *Contact I,* 1920-23, and *Contact II,* 1932.

SIDELIGHTS: William Carlos Williams has always been known as an experimenter, an innovator, a revolutionary figure in American poetry. Yet in comparison to artists of his own time who sought a new environment for creativity as expatriates in Europe, Williams lived a remarkably conventional life. A doctor for more than forty years serving the New Jersey town of Rutherford, he relied on his patients, the America around him, and his own ebullient imagination to create a distinctively American verse. Often domestic in focus and "remarkable for its empathy, sympathy, its muscular and emotional identification with its subjects," Williams's poetry is also characteristically honest: "There is no optimistic blindness in Williams," wrote Randall Jarrell, "though there is a fresh gaiety, a stubborn or invincible joyousness."

The conflict Williams felt between his parents' hopes for their son's success in medicine and his own less conventional impulses is mirrored in his poetic heroes of the time—John Keats and Walt Whitman. Keats's traditionally rhymed and metered verse impressed the young poet tremendously. "Keats was my God,"

Williams later revealed; and his first major poetic work was a model of Keats's "Endymion." In contrast, Whitman's free verse offered "an impulse toward freedom and release of the self," said Donald Barlow Stauffer. Williams explained how he came to associate Whitman with this impulse toward freedom when he said, "I reserved my 'Whitmanesque' thoughts, a sort of purgation and confessional, to clear my head and heart from turgid obsessions." Yet, by his first year at Pennsylvania Williams had found a considerably more vivid mentor than Whitman in a friend, Ezra Pound.

Williams's friendship with Pound marked a watershed in the young poet's life: he later insisted, "before meeting Pound is like B.C. and A.D." "Under Pound's influence and other stimuli," reported John Malcolm Brinnin, "Williams was soon ready to close the door on the 'studied elegance of Keats on one hand and the raw vigor of Whitman on the other.'" Aside from the poetic influences, Pound introduced Williams to a group of friends, including poet Hilda Doolittle (H.D.) and painter Charles Demuth, "who shared the kinds of feelings that in Rutherford had made him frightened and isolated," James E. Breslin declared. H.D., for example, with her arty dress and her peculiarities—sometimes she'd splash ink onto her clothes "to give her a feeling of freedom and indifference towards the mere means of writing"—fascinated Williams with a "provocative indifference to rule and order which I liked."

In a similar way, it was a reaction against the rigid and ordered poetry of the time that led Williams to join Pound, H.D., and others as the core of what became known as the Imagist movement. While correlative revolutionary movements had begun in painting (Cezanne), music (Stravinsky), and fiction (Stein), poetry was still bogged down by "the inversions and redundancies imposed by the effort 'to fill out a standard form,'" explained David Perkins. The Imagists broke from this formulaic poetry by stressing a verse of "swift, uncluttered, functional phrasing." Williams's first book, *Poems* (1909), a "conventional" work, "correct in sentiment and diction," preceded the Imagist influence. But in *The Tempers* (1913), as Bernard Duffey realized, Williams's "style was directed by an Imagist feeling, though it still depended on romantic and poeticized allusiveness." And while Pound drifted towards increased allusiveness in his work, Williams stuck with Pound's tenet to "make it new." By 1917 and the publication of his third book, *Al Que Quiere!*, "Williams began to apply the Imagist principle of 'direct treatment of the thing' fairly rigorously," declared James Guimond. Also at this time, as Perkins demonstrated, Williams was "beginning to stress that poetry must find its 'primary impetus'. . . in 'local conditions.'" "I was determined to use the material I knew," Williams later reflected; and as a doctor, Williams knew intimately the people of Rutherford.

Beginning with his internship in the decrepit "Hell's Kitchen" area of New York City and throughout his forty years of private practice in Rutherford, Williams heard the "inarticulate poems" of his patients. As a doctor, his "medical badge," as he called it, permitted him "to follow the poor defeated body into those gulfs and grottos. . . , to be present at deaths and births, at the tormented battles between daughter and diabolic mother." From these moments, poetry developed: "it has fluttered before me for a moment, a phrase which I quickly write down on anything at hand, any piece of paper I can grab." Some of his poems were born on prescription blanks, others typed in a few spare minutes between patient visits. Williams's work, however, did more than fuel his poetry: it allowed him "to write what he chose, free from

any kind of financial or political pressure. From the beginning," disclosed Linda Wagner, "he understood the tradeoffs: he would have less time to write; he would need more physical stamina than people with only one occupation. . . . [He] was willing to live the kind of rushed existence that would be necessary, crowding two full lifetimes into one, . . . learning from the first and then understanding through the second." There is little doubt that he succeeded in both: Richard Ellman and Robert O'Clair called him "the most important literary doctor since Chekov."

While Williams continued with his innovations in the American idiom and his experiments in form, he fell out of favor with some of his own contemporaries. *Kora in Hell: Improvisations,* for example, suffered some stinging attacks. For a year Williams had made a habit of recording something—anything—in his notebooks every night, and followed these jottings with a comment. One of "Williams's own favorite books. . . , the prose poetry of *Kora* is an extraordinary combination of aphorism, romanticism, philosophizing, obscurity, obsession, exhortation, reverie, beautiful lines and scary paragraphs," wrote Webster Schott. Yet, as Hugh Fox reported, few peers shared Williams's enthusiasm for the book. Pound called it "incoherent" and "un-American"; H.D. objected to its "flippancies," its "self-mockery," its "un-seriousness"; and Wallace Stevens complained about Williams's "tantrums." Fox defended the avant-garde Williams against his critics by saying, "Anything hitherto undone is tantrums, flippancy, opacity. . . they don't see (as Williams does) that they are confronting a new language and they have to learn how to decipher it before they can savor it."

According to Breslin, T. S. Eliot's *The Waste Land* was a major influence on Williams's next book, *Spring and All*. The last in a decade of experimental poetry, *Spring and All* viewed the same American landscape as did Eliot but interpreted it differently. Williams "saw his poetic task was to affirm the self-reliant, sympathetic consciousness of Whitman in a broken industrialized world," Stauffer noted. "But unlike Eliot, who responded negatively to the harsh realities of this world, Williams saw his task as breaking through restrictions and generating new growth."

Fox explained how Williams used the imagination to do just that: "Williams . . . sees the real function of the imagination as breaking through the alienation of the near at hand and reviving its wonder." Williams himself explained in one of *Spring and All*'s prose passages that "Imagination is not to avoid reality, nor is it a description nor an evocation of objects or situations, it is to say that poetry does not tamper with the world but moves it—It affirms reality most powerfully and therefore, since reality needs no personal support but exists free from human action, as proven by science in the indestructibility of matter and of force, it creates a new object, a play, a dance which is not a mirror up to nature but—."

In *In the American Grain*, Williams tried "to find out for myself what the land of my more or less accidental birth might signify" by examining the "original records" of "some of the American founders." In its treatment of the makers of American history, ranging from Columbus to Lincoln, *In the American Grain* has impressed many as Williams's most succinct definition of America and its people. D. H. Lawrence, for example, learned from Williams that "there are two ways of being American, and the chief . . . is by recoiling into individual smallness and insentience, and gutting the great continent in frenzies of mean fear. It is the Puritan way. The other is by touch; touch America as she is; dare to touch her! And this is the heroic way." Another prose book of the period, *A Voyage to Pagany,* was a type of travel book based on the author's 1924 trip to Europe. "While its subject matter is essentially Europe," informed Vivienne Koch, "it is, in reality, an assessment of that world through the eyes of America too." Williams focused directly on America and the Depression in his aptly titled short story collection, *The Knife of the Times.* In these stories and in other similar works of the thirties, "Williams blamed the inadequacies of American culture for both the emotional and economic plight of many of his subjects," declared James Guimond.

Williams's novel trilogy, *White Mule, In the Money,* and *The Build-Up,* also focused on America, and on one family in particular—his wife's. He first conceived the idea for *White Mule* because he wanted to write about a baby—he delivered more than two thousand in his career—and had heard stories of Floss's babyhood. But beyond the story of the infant Floss Stecher is the story of her infant American family, immigrants growing toward success in America. Philip Rahv gave this description of Joe and Gurlie Stecher: "Gurlie is so rife with the natural humors of a wife that she emerges as a veritable goddess of the home, but since it is an American home she is constantly urging her husband to get into the game, beat the other fellow, and make money. Joe's principal motivation, however, is his pride of workmanship; he is the pure artisan, the man who has not yet been alienated from the product of his labor and who thinks of money as the reward of labor and nothing else." In *In the Money* Williams follows Joe as he establishes his own printing business and moves to the suburbs, making way for the picture of middle-class life he presents in *The Build-Up.* W. T. Schott gave these examples of Williams's focus: "The stolid admirable Joe, the arrogant Gurlie on her upward march in society, a neighbor woman ranting her spitefulness, . . . Flossie and her sister at their little-girl wrangling over bathroom privileges." Reed Whittemore felt that such moments reveal Williams's fond tolerance of middle-class life. *The Build-Up* does have its "tough sections," Whittemore admitted, but "its placidness is striking for a book written by a long-time literary dissenter. What it is is a book of complacent reflection written from inside apple-pie America. It has not the flavor of the letters of the real young doctor-poet sitting in his emptiness forty years earlier in Leipzig. . . . Between 1909, then, and the time of the writing of *The Build-Up* WCW was *taken* inside, and found that with reservations he liked it there."

While the many years of writing may have gone largely unnoticed, they were hardly spent in vain: Breslin revealed that "Williams spent some thirty years of living and writing in preparation for *Paterson.*" And though some dismiss the "epic" label often attached to the five-book poem, Williams's intentions were certainly beyond the ordinary. His devotion to understanding his country, its people, its language—"the whole knowable world about me"—found expression in the poem's central image, defined by Whittemore as "the image of the city as a man, a man lying on his side peopling the place with his thoughts." With roots in his 1926 poem "Paterson," Williams took the city as "my 'case' to work up. It called for a poetry such as I did not know, it was my duty to discover or make such a context on the 'thought.'"

In his prefatory notes to the original four-book *Paterson,* Williams explained "that a man himself is a city, beginning, seeking, achieving and concluding his life in ways which the various aspects of a city may embody—if imaginatively conceived—any city, all the details of which may be made to voice his most intimate convictions." A. M. Sullivan outlined why Williams chose Paterson, New Jersey: It was once "the prototype of the American industrial community. . . the self-sustaining city of skills with the competitive energy and moral stamina to lift the burdens of the citizen and raise the livelihood with social and cultural benefits." One hundred years later, continued Sullivan, "Williams saw the Hamilton concept [of 'The Society of Useful Manufacturers'] realized, but with mixed results of success and misery. The poet of Paterson understood the validity of the hopes of Hamilton but also recognized that the city slum could be the price of progress in a mechanized society." The world Williams chose to explore in this poem about "the myth of American power," added James Guimond, was one where "this power is almost entirely evil, the destructive producer of an America grown pathetic and tragic, brutalized by inequality, disorganized by industrial chaos, and faced with annihilation."

Williams revealed "the elemental character of the place" in Book I. The time is spring, the season of creativity, and Paterson is struck by the desire to express his "immediate locality" clearly, observed Guimond. The process is a struggle: to know the world about him Paterson must face both the beauty of the Passaic Falls and the poverty of the region. In Book II, said Williams, Paterson moves from a description of "the elemental character" of the city to its "modern replicas." Or, as Guimond pointed out, from the "aesthetic world" to the "real material world where he must accomplish the poet's task as defined in Book I—the invention of a language for his locality. . . . The breakdown of the poet's communication with his world is a disaster," both for himself and for others. Williams himself, on the other hand, made his own advance in communication in Book II, a "milestone" in his development as a poet. A passage in Section 3, beginning "The descent beckons. . . ," "brought about—without realizing it at the time—my final conception of what my own poetry should be." The segment is one of the earliest examples of Williams's innovative method of line division, the "variable foot."

To invent the new language, Paterson must first "descend from the erudition and fastidiousness that made him impotent in Book II," summarized Guimond. As Paterson reads—and reflects—in a library, he accepts the destruction in Book II, rejects his learning, and realizes "a winter of 'death' must come before spring." Williams believed that "if you are going to write realistically of the concept of filth in the world it can't be pretty." And so, Book IV is the dead season, symbolized by the "river below the falls," the polluted Passaic. But in this destruction, the poet plants some seeds of renewal: a young virtuous nurse; a Paterson poet, Allen Ginsburg, who has promised to give the local new meaning; Madame Curie, "divorced from neither the male nor knowledge." At the conclusion of Book IV, a man, after a long swim, dresses on shore and heads inland—"toward Camden," Williams said, "where Walt Whitman, much traduced, lived the later years of his life and died." These seeds of hope led Breslin to perceive the basic difference between *Paterson* and Williams's long-time nemesis, Eliot's *Waste Land.* "'The Waste Land' is a kind of anti-epic," Breslin said, "a poem in which the quest for meaning is entirely thwarted and we are left, at the end, waiting for the collapse of Western civilization. *Paterson* is a pre-epic, showing that the process of disintegration releases forces that can build a new world. It confronts, again and, again, the savagery of contemporary society, but still affirms a creative seed. Eliot's end is Williams's beginning."

Paterson did help bring Williams some of the attention he had been missing for many years. One honor came in 1949 when he was invited to become consultant to the Library of Congress. Whittemore reported that Williams first refused the appointment because of poor health, but decided in 1952 that he was ready to assume the post. Unfortunately for Williams, the editor and publisher of the poetry magazine *Lyric* got word of Williams's appointment and subsequently announced Williams's "Communist" affiliations. Williams's poem "Russia," she insisted, spoke in "the very voice of Communism." Though few newspapers brought the charges to light, the Library of Congress suddenly backed off from the appointment. After several excuses and postponements, some made, ostensibly, out of a concern for Williams's health, Librarian Luther Evans wrote, "I accordingly hereby revoke the offer of appointment heretofore made to you." A few months before the term was to have ended, Williams learned that the appointment had been renewed. The Library of Congress, however, made no offer to extend the appointment through the following year.

Williams's health accounts for a major change in mood in his later poetry. In the late 1940s he suffered the first of several heart attacks and strokes which would plague him for the rest of his life. And though Williams later complained of the effects of a particularly serious stroke (1952)—"That was the end. I was through with life"—his devotion to poetry did not suffer. Breslin reported that after retiring from medicine in 1951, and after recuperating from a stroke, Williams spoke "optimistically of the 'opportunity for thought' and reading afforded by his new idleness." Marc Hofstadter pointed out that "death was a major focus of this reflectiveness," and explained how Williams reflected his concerns in his poetry: "In the face of death what Williams seeks is renewal—not a liberation toward another world but an intensified return to this one. Revitalization both of one's inner energies and of one's contact with the outside world, renewal is the product of two forces: love and the imagination. . . . Love and imagination are the essence of life. He who loses them is as good as dead."

Williams explored the theme of renewed love in two particular later works, the play *A Dream of Love* and the poem "Asphodel, That Greeny Flower." In *A Dream of Love* the protagonist has an affair with his secretary and confesses to his wife that he did it only to "renew our love." The explanation fails to convince her. Thus, Williams dramatizes his belief in the "conflict between the male's need for emotional renewal in love and the female's need for constancy in love," explained Guimond. According to Thomas Whitaker, "'A Dream of Love' points to an actuality that Williams at this time could not fully face but that he would learn to face—most noticeably in 'Asphodel, That Greeny Flower.'" In this "elegiac epithalamian," Williams confesses his infidelities to his wife and asks for her forgiveness; "he seeks new life on the very edge of death," said Whitaker. While Williams proclaimed his life as a husband in his love poem, his strength as a poet was evident, too: "Asphodel" received some very complimentary reviews, including W. H. Auden's praise as "one of the most beautiful poems in the language."

But Williams's weakened physical powers, apparently, strengthened his creative ones. "I think he did much better work after the stroke slowed him down," reflected Flossie. Stanley Koehler agreed. *The Desert Music* and *Journey to Love*, he said, "were written in an unusual period of recovery of creative power after Dr. Williams's first serious illness in 1952." Aside from featuring the variable foot and such outstanding poems as "Asphodel," these two books impressed readers as the mature work of a poet very much in control of his life and craft. Reviewing *Desert Music*, Kenneth Rexroth called the title poem "an explicit statement of the irreducible humaneness of the human being." The

book's ideas are "simple, indisputable, presented with calm maturity," continued Rexroth. "I prophesy that from now on, as Williams grows older, he will rise far above his contemporaries as Yeats did in his later years." The love poems of *Journey to Love* were no less impressive to Babette Deutsch. "The poet gives us vignettes of the daily scene, notations on the arts, affirmations of a faith no less sublime for being secular, in the language, the rhythms, that he has made his own," reported Deutsch. "The pages bear the indelible signature of his honesty, his compassion, his courage." Finally, to highlight a decade of productivity, Williams's last book, *Pictures From Brueghel,* won a Pulitzer Prize in 1963.

Despite his failing health, Williams lived as productively as possible throughout his later years. He traveled, gave lectures, and entertained writers in the same home that had been visited by members of the Imagist movement more than forty years earlier. Williams wrote, too—poetry, of course, as well as essays and short stories. He continued to cooperate with writers interested in him and his work: John Thirlwall worked with him in the publication of *Selected Letters* and a series of discussions with Edith Heal became the "autobiography" of his works, *I Wanted to Write a Poem.* A partially paralyzing stroke in 1958 and a 1959 cancer operation, however, stole much of his remaining energy and capabilities. No longer able to read, by the end of the decade he depended on Floss to read to him, often as long as four hours a day. A particularly painful view of the aging Williams appeared in his 1962 interview with Stanley Koehler for the *Paris Review.* "The effort it took the poet to find and pronounce words can hardly be indicated here," reported Koehler. Continued failing health further slowed Williams until, on March 4, 1963, he died in his sleep.

BIOGRAPHICAL/CRITICAL SOURCES:

BOOKS

Ahearn, Barry, *William Carlos Williams and Alterity: The Early Poetry,* Cambridge University Press, 1994.

Axelrod, Steven Gould, and Helen Deese, *Critical Essays on William Carlos Williams,* MacMillan, 1994.

Breslin, James E., *William Carlos Williams: An American Artist,* Oxford University Press, 1970.

Brinnin, John Malcolm, *William Carlos Williams,* University of Minnesota Press, 1963.

Cirasa, Robert J., *The Lost Works of William Carlos Williams: The Volumes of Collected Poerty as Lyrical Sequences,* Associated University Presses, 1995.

Comens, Bruce, *Apocalypse and After: Modern Strategy and Postmodern Tactics in Pound, Williams, and Zukofsky,* University of Alabama Press, 1995.

Concise Dictionary of American Literary Biography: The Twenties, 1917-1929, Gale (Detroit), 1989.

Contemporary Literary Criticism, Gale, Volume 1, 1973; Volume 2, 1974; Volume 5, 1976; Volume 9, 1978; Volume 13, 1980; Volume 22, 1982; Volume 42, 1987; Volume 67, 1991.

Deutsch, Babette, *Poetry in Out Time,* Holt, 1952.

Dictionary of Literary Biography, Gale, Volume 4: *American Writers in Paris, 1920-1939,* 1980; Volume 16: *The Beats: Literary Bohemians in Postwar America,* 1983; Volume 54: *American Poets, 1880-1945, Third Series,* 1987; Volume 86: *American Short Story Writers, 1910-1945, First Series,* Gale, 1989.

Duffy, Bernard, *Poetry in America: Expression and Its Values in the Times of Bryant, Whitman, and Pound,* Duke University Press, 1978.

Gregory, Elizabeth, *Quotation and Modern American Poetry: Imaginary Gardens with Real Toads,* Rice University Press, 1995.

Guimond, James, *The Art of William Carlos Williams: A Discovery and Possession of America,* University of Illinois Press, 1968.

Halter, Peter, *The Revolution in the Visual Arts and the Poetry of William Carlos Williams,* Cambridge University Press, 1994.

Hartman, Charles, *Free Verse: An Essay on Prosody,* Northwestern University Press (Evanston, IL), 1996.

Jarrell, Randall, *Poetry and the Age,* Knopf-Vintage, 1953.

Jarrell, Randall, *The Third Book of Criticism,* Farrar, Straus, 1969.

Kinnahan, Linda A., *Poetics of Feminine: Authority and Literary Tradition in William Carlos Williams, Mina Loy, Denise Levertov, and Kathleen Fraser,* Cambridge University Press, 1994.

Koch, Vivienne, *William Carlos Williams,* New Directions, 1950.

Koehler, Stanley, *Countries of the Mind: The Poetry of William Carlos Williams,* Bucknell University Press, 1999.

Larson, Kelli A., *Guide to the Poetry of William Carlos Williams,* Prentice-Hall, 1995.

Laughlin, James, *Remembering William Carlos Williams,* New Directions, 1995.

Lowney, John, *The American Avant-Garde Tradition: William Carlos Williams, Postmodern Poetry, and the Politics of Cultural Memory,* Bucknell University Press, 1996.

Markos, Donald W., *Ideas in Things: The Poems of William Carlos Williams,* Associated University Presses (London), 1994.

Marzan, Julio, *The Spanish American Roots of William Carlos Williams,* University of Texas Press, 1994.

Morris, Daniel, *The Writings of William Carlos Williams: Publicity for the Self,* University of Missouri Press, 1995.

Nardi, Marcia, *The Last Word: Letters Between Marcia Nardi and William Carlos Williams,* University of Iowa Press, 1994.

Perkins, David, *A History of Modern Poetry: From the 1890's to the High Modernist Mode,* Harvard University Press, 1976.

Poetry Criticism, Volume 7, Gale, 1994, pp. 343-413.

Qian, Zhaoming, *Orientalism and Modernisn: The Legacy of China in Pound and Williams,* Duke University Press, 1995.

Rexroth, Kenneth, *American Poetry in the Twentieth Century,* Herder, 1971.

Stauffer, Donald Barlow, *A Short History of American Poetry,* Dutton, 1974.

Wagner, Linda Welshimer, *The Poems of William Carlos Williams,* Wesleyan University Press, 1964.

Whitaker, Thomas R., *William Carlos Williams,* Twayne, 1968.

Whittemore, Reed, *William Carlos Williams: Poet From New Jersey,* Houghton, 1975.

Writers at Work: The Paris Review Interviews, third series, introduction by Alfred Kazin, Viking, 1967.

PERIODICALS

American Poetry Review, September-October, 1985.

Atlantic Monthly, October, 1951; September, 1957; May, 1958; July, 1959.

Commonweal, October 4, 1946; November 7, 1952; December 10, 1954.

Criticism, winter, 1972.

Dial, November, 1928.

English Journal, November, 1987.

English Literary History, winter, 1986.

Explicator, fall, 1976.

Hudson Review, winter, 1961-62.

Lancet, July 10, 1993.

Library Journal, February 1, 1994, p. 77; March 15, 1996, p. 71.

London Magazine, June/July, 1974.

Los Angeles Times Book Review, October 17, 1982.

Mosiac, winter, 1987.

Nation, April 4, 1926; March 28, 1934; June 26, 1937; November 19, 1938; November 23, 1940; April 14, 1945; August 24, 1946; June 19, 1948; July 9, 1949; April 8, 1950; March 3, 1951; August 25, 1951; November 8, 1952; April 24, 1954; January 22, 1955; October 5, 1957; May 31, 1958; November 23, 1970; December 14, 1970; December 11, 1976.

National Review, March 26, 1963.

New Criterion, September, 1988.

New Leader, June 9, 1975.

New Statesman and Society, March 6, 1992.

Newsweek, March 16, 1963.

New York Review of Books, November 13, 1975.

New York Times, February 7, 1926; September 30, 1928; February 18, 1934; November 15, 1936; June 20, 1937; July 23, 1939; November 7, 1954; December 18, 1955; September 1, 1957; April 13, 1958; September 14, 1958; October 25, 1966; October 20, 1984.

New York Times Book Review, June 28, 1959; December 26, 1971; October 5, 1975; September 18, 1983; January 4, 1987; April 3, 1994.

Partisan Review, November-December, 1951.

Poetry, May, 1934; May, 1936; November, 1936; September, 1939; April, 1945; February, 1947; April, 1949; May, 1952; April, 1954; March, 1955; March, 1956; June, 1958; May, 1959; February, 1964; October, 1967.

Raritan, winter, 1987.

Southern Review, November, 1987.

Southwest Review, summer, 1974.

Time, December 4, 1950; March 15, 1963; September 21, 1970.

Times Literary Supplement, November 29, 1928; March 23, 1951; February 1, 1952; January 29, 1954; July 29, 1965; February 10, 1966; April 13, 1967; June 22, 1967; April 27, 1984; May 22, 1987; February 19, 1988; May 19, 1989.

Twentieth Century Literature, October, 1975; December, 1977; fall, 1989.

Voice Literary Supplement, September, 1982.

William Carlos Williams Review.

Yale Review, spring, 1939; autumn, 1948; spring, 1950; autumn, 1951; winter, 1952; winter, 1955; December, 1957; December, 1958; May, 1959; December, 1961; June, 1970.

*   *   *

WILLIE, Frederick
See LOVECRAFT, H(oward) P(hillips)

*   *   *

WILLIS, Charles
See CLARKE, Arthur C(harles)

WILLY
   See COLETTE, (Sidonie-Gabrielle)

*   *   *

WILLY, Colette
   See COLETTE, (Sidonie-Gabrielle)

*   *   *

WILSON, A(ndrew) N(orman) 1950-

PERSONAL: Born October 27, 1950, in Stone, Staffordshire, England; son of Norman (a business director) and Jean Dorothy (Crowder) Wilson; married Katherine Duncan-Jones (an academic), 1971; children: two daughters. *Education:* New College, Oxford, M.A., c. 1976.

ADDRESSES: Home—91 Albert St., London, NW1 7LX, England. *Agent*—c/o A.D. Peters Ltd., 10 Buckingham St., London WC2N 6BU, England.

CAREER: Writer. Teacher at Oxford University and a tutorial agency, 1975; Merchant Taylor's School, Northwood, Middlesex, England, schoolmaster, 1975-80; lecturer in English at Oxford University, 1977-80; teacher at Stanford University, 1978-80.

MEMBER: Royal Society of Literature (fellow).

AWARDS, HONORS: Chancellor's Essay Prize from Oxford University, 1971; Ellerton Theological Prize from Oxford University, 1975; John Llewelyn Rhys Memorial Prize, 1978, for *The Sweets of Pimlico;* Somerset Maugham Award, Southern Arts Prize, and Arts Council National Book Award, all 1981, all for *The Healing Art;* John Llewelyn Rhys Memorial Prize, 1981, for *The Laird of Abbotsford: A View of Sir Walter Scott;* W. H. Smith Literary Award, 1983, for *Wise Virgin.*

WRITINGS:

NOVELS

The Sweets of Pimlico, Secker & Warburg, 1977.
Unguarded Hours, Secker & Warburg, 1978.
Kindly Light, Secker & Warburg, 1979.
The Healing Art, Secker & Warburg, 1980.
Who Was Oswald Fish?, Secker & Warburg, 1981, David & Charles, 1983.
Wise Virgin, Secker & Warburg, 1982, Viking, 1983.
Scandal; or, Priscilla's Kindness, Hamish Hamilton, 1983, Viking, 1984.
Gentlemen in England: A Vision, Viking, 1985.
Love Unknown, Hamish Hamilton, 1986, Viking, 1987.
Incline Our Hearts, H. Hamilton, 1988.
Pen Friends from Porlock, H. Hamilton, 1988.
A Bottle in the Smoke, Viking, 1990.
How Can We Know?, Doubleday (New York City), 1991.
Daughters of Albion, Sinclair-Stevenson (London), 1991.
The Vicar of Sorrows, Sinclair-Stevenson, 1993.
Hearing Voices, Sinclair-Stevenson, 1995.
A Watch in the Night, Norton, 1996.

NONFICTION

The Laird of Abbotsford: A View of Sir Walter Scott, Oxford University Press, 1980.
The Life of John Milton, Oxford University Press, 1983.

Hilaire Belloc, Hamish Hamilton, 1984, Atheneum, 1984.
How Can We Know? An Essay on the Christian Religion, Atheneum, 1985.
(With Charles Moore and Gavin Stamp) *The Church in Crisis,* Hodder & Stoughton, 1986.
Tolstoy, Norton (New York City), 1988.
Eminent Victorians, BBC Books (London), 1989.
C.S. Lewis: A Biography, Norton, 1990.
Against Religion, Chatto & Windus (London), 1991.
Jesus, Norton, 1992.
The Rise and Fall of the House of Windsor, Norton, 1993.
Paul: The Mind of the Apostle, Norton, 1997.

OTHER

(Editor) Bram Stoker, *Dracula* (novel), Oxford University Press, 1983.
(Editor) Walter Scott, *Ivanhoe* (novel), Penguin, 1984.
Stray (for children), Walker, 1987.
(Editor) *The Lion and the Honeycomb: The Religious Writings of Tolstoy,* translated by Robert Chandler, Harper and Row (San Francisco), 1987.
Tabitha, illustrated by Sarah Fox-Davies, Orchid Books (New York City), 1989.
(Editor and author of introduction) *Prayers, Poems, Meditations,* Crossroad (New York City), 1990.
Hazel the Guinea Pig, illustrated by Jonathan Heale, Candlewick Press (Cambridge, MA), 1992.
(Author of introduction) Leo Tolstoy, *How Much Does a Man Need?: And Other Short Stories,* Penguin Books (New York City), 1993.
(Editor) *The Norton Book of London,* Norton, 1994.
The Tabitha Stories, illustrated by Sarah Fox-Davies, Candlewick Press, 1997.

Literary editor of *Spectator,* 1980-83.

SIDELIGHTS: A. N. Wilson is probably best known for his wide-ranging farcical novels mocking British life. He began his writing career in the late 1970s with several intricately plotted works exploiting the absurdities of Britain's social institutions. In more recent years he has also produced more somber works delineating the shallowness of the British bourgeoisie. But these novels are also valued for their satirical perspectives. In addition to his fiction, Wilson has written highly regarded biographies of John Milton, Walter Scott, and Hilaire Belloc and has published works on Christianity and Britain's religious climate. His success in both fiction and nonfiction has earned him praise as both a major novelist and an important, provocative critic-historian.

In his first novel, *The Sweets of Pimlico,* Wilson revealed a marked penchant for mining both the eccentric and the banal to comic advantage. The work concerns a young woman, Evelyn Tradescant, whose main interests are Charles Darwin's evolution theory, gardens, and beetles. Her sheltered life is irrevocably altered, however, when she befriends a mysterious German aristocrat, Theo Gormann, who shows extreme interest in Evelyn's mundane existence. Through her involvement with the self-consciously enigmatic baron, Evelyn finds herself in increasingly unusual predicaments: she commits incest with her supposedly homosexual brother, witnesses a museum bombing, and acquires a great deal of money. She also adopts the baron's own secretive behavior and ultimately finds herself in social intrigue with both him and his acquaintances. Paul Ableman, in a brief review for *Spectator,* called *The Sweets of Pimlico* "an enchanting first novel" and commended Wilson's skill in producing a work of "intrinsic elegance as well as great charm and wit."

Wilson next wrote *Unguarded Hours,* a 1978 novel relating the misadventures of innocent protagonist Norman Shotover in the often ludicrous worlds of academia and organized religion. The novel begins, "Had the Dean's daughter worn a bra that afternoon, Norman Shotover might never have found out about the Church of England; still less about how to fly." From that intriguing opening sentence, Norman is portrayed as a good-natured fellow who pursues a clerical career for lack of an alternative and courts the college dean's daughter for want of true love. Much of the humor in *Unguarded Hours* derives from Norman's encounters with several outrageous characters, including Mr. Skeggs, an alcoholic self-proclaimed bishop—formerly an electrician—who haphazardly ordains Norman; Mungo, the aristocratic Dundee of Caik, given to impulsive comments such as "I don't hold with the Lake District"; and the dean, a rabble-rousing clergyman whose incendiary books include *Chuck It, God.* Wandering among these eccentrics is Shotover, who stumbles upon various lovers-in-action and ultimately finds his own sexual solace with the dean's compliant daughter, Cleopatra.

Unguarded Hours met with praise in Britain. Jeremy Treglown wrote in *New Statesman* that, like *The Sweets of Pimlico,* Wilson's second novel possesses "a simple but impelling narrative movement . . . supported by a comic touch." Michael Neve also compared *Unguarded Hours* favorably with its predecessor. He wrote in the *Times Literary Supplement* that Wilson's first two novels were both "well observed" and concluded that "*Unguarded Hours* shows A. N. Wilson continuing to write acute and funny novels, small vignettes from a gentle Anglican moralist."

Wilson continued his chronicle of the hapless Shotover in *Kindly Light,* where the hero is first depicted as an unwilling member of the Catholic Institute of Alfonso (CIA). Norman is now disillusioned with religion, but various attempts to provoke excommunication backfire and result in his continued good standing with church authorities. Among his few enemies is prominent CIA figure Father Cassidy, who suspects Norman of anti-church treachery. Cassidy eventually causes Norman's transfer to South America. But en route Norman becomes separated from his traveling companion—an alcoholic priest—and ultimately drifts through a series of occupations, including grapefruit picker and movie extra. Years after leaving the CIA, Norman falls in love with the daughter of a popular novelist. He also reunites with the drunkard priest, and the novel ends after several principals have convened in Israel for further escapades.

Wilson followed *Kindly Light* with *The Healing Art,* a more sentimental comedy about a middle-aged woman, Pamela Cowper, who learns that she is dying of cancer. Pamela is informed that she can significantly lengthen her lifespan by agreeing to chemotherapy. She refuses the treatment but finds that her health remains adequate. Her ward mate, however, degenerates noticeably, whereupon Pamela suspects that their physician, Doctor Tulloch, may have accidentally switched the two patients' x-rays. From this premise Wilson launches his familiar expose on bungling bureaucracy, concentrating on that of the medical world but also mining academia for comedic value.

Like Wilson's preceding novels, *The Healing Art* earned generally favorable appraisals. In the *Times Literary Supplement,* William Boyd called Wilson's novel "a stimulating and thoughtful book." Boyd was most impressed with those aspects of the novel exploring Pamela's despair and subsequent hope for life. "*The Healing Art* is to be applauded for confronting such a painful and moving subject," Boyd commented. Simon Blow, who reviewed *The Healing Art* in *New Statesman,* was more impressed with Wilson's comic achievement. Blow declared that though the novel's theme was "deeply tragic," Wilson was still successful "at playing black comedy that can make us laugh just when we should cry." Blow added that "Wilson has created a holocaust of avoidable errors where few remain standing" and that his "triumph is to make his devastating and truthful material so instantly acceptable."

Who Was Oswald Fish?, Wilson's fifth novel, concerns eccentric celebrity Fanny Williams and her efforts to restore a Gothic Victorian church designed by Oswald Fish. During the characteristic mayhem, Fish's memoirs are discovered, and these largely sexual accounts afford Wilson ample opportunity to contrast Victorian and contemporary British society. Tim Heald, writing in the London *Times,* called *Who Was Oswald Fish?* "an enjoyable, clever piece of black comedy."

Wilson derived humor from gloom in *Wise Virgin,* his 1981 novel about Giles Fox, a blind scholar obsessed with editing a medieval text advocating virginity. Fox's life has been one of emotional hardship: his first wife died in childbirth; he subsequently suffered blindness; and his second wife died in an automobile mishap. Hardened by tragedy, Fox devotes himself to his literary work and tolerates only the company of his daughter and his secretary, both of whom are virgins. Fox invests all his hopes in the book and his daughter, but upon publication his edition is dismissed in academia as inaccurate and untimely, and his daughter, whose virginity he so prized, falls in love with a manipulative fellow who actually prefers men.

Wise Virgin served to indicate Wilson's sense of compassion and his concern with life's crushing disappointments. In a review for the *New York Times,* Michiko Kakutani contended that Wilson had seemed rather detached in his previous works, but that in *Wise Virgin* he had "successfully balanced his gift for wicked comedy with caring and compassion." Likewise, *Newsweek*'s Martha Duffy found *Wise Virgin* "deeper and more compassionate than Wilson's earlier novels," and she praised him for finding "his own balance between light and dark comedy." Pat Rogers also expressed these observations, writing in the *Times Literary Supplement* that Wilson's work was "groping towards a more tolerant version of contemporaneity." Rogers called *Wise Virgin* "an accomplished novel."

In 1983 Wilson published *Scandal; or, Priscilla's Kindness,* a comedy about sexual hijinks and British politics. The novel's protagonist is Derek Blore, a promising Parliament member whose social sophistication belies his preference for sadomasochistic sex. As often happens in Wilson's novels, however, a cast of secondary eccentrics rival the hero for outrageousness and thus earn the reader's interest. Among the more offbeat characters in *Scandal* are Blore's wife, Priscilla, who commits adultery out of kindness; Feathers, an amusingly despicable journalist who craves alcohol; and Bernadette, a dull prostitute who blandly ministers to Blore's need for a regular flogging. It is, of course, Blore's private practices that spark the criminal intrigue upon which the novel is structured.

Scandal earned Wilson further praise as a comic master. Writing in the *Washington Post,* Jonathan Yardley described the novel as "deliciously witty" and deemed Wilson's prose "mercilessly tart." Yardley called *Scandal* "an exceedingly funny novel." Similarly, Stuart Evans wrote in the London *Times* that Wilson writes "with fastidious humour" and that "*Scandal* is a sinister novel." In a laudatory review for the *Los Angeles Times,* Elaine Kendall accorded particular acclaim to Wilson's skills at characterization. "Where else," Kendall asked, "will you find a hoodlum who changes his name from Costigan to Costigano for professional reasons?" She called *Scandal* a "comic novel in the classic English tradition."

Wilson turned to the Victorian period for his next novel, *Gentlemen in England.* In this work he lampooned that repressive period and exposed the often turbulent emotions inhibited in the English of that time. The novel centers on the Nettleship family, whose patriarch is an arrogant geologist. His wife is a woman of great self-control, but her formal demeanor yields to rampant passion when she meets an attractive painter. Other characters include Severus Egg, who laments the passing of the Romantic age and rues the Victorian period, and Timothy Lupton, the virile painter who wins Mrs. Nettleship's affections but is actually in love with her daughter, Maudie. Among the most enthusiastic reviewers of *Gentlemen in England* was Michiko Kakutani, who wrote in the *New York Times* that the novel marked Wilson's continued development as a comic writer. Kakutani noted that Wilson's most recent fiction—including the earlier *Wise Virgin* and *Scandal*—"attested to both a widening canvas and a growing sense of compassion." The reviewer contended that *Gentlemen in England* was Wilson's "most ambitious work yet."

In his next novel, *Love Unknown,* Wilson focused on another key period in British history: the 1960's. Here Wilson tells of adulterous lovers, Simon and Monica, who frequent museums and indulge in artfully deliberate conversations about life, love, and art. Like his previous novels, *Love Unknown* contains a coterie of typically eccentric characters, and like the preceding works it too offers pointed barbs at institutions such as organized religion and social subjects such as feminism and infidelity.

Aside from his fiction, Wilson has produced noteworthy biographies. *The Laird of Abbotsford: A View of Sir Walter Scott* was his first work in the genre, and its success encouraged critical re-evaluation of Scott's writings. Some critics complained that the book's seeming lack of critical insights undermined Wilson's contention that Scott was a great writer, but other reviewers commended Wilson's unabashed appreciation of Scott as a profound, prolific writer. A critic for *Economist* acknowledged Wilson's reverence for Scott's works and stated, "Few books of literary criticism in this disillusioned age have been so full of infectious enthusiasm."

For his next biography Wilson turned to John Milton, arguably England's finest poet, whose *Paradise Lost* is generally considered the greatest epic in English verse. Wilson's work, *The Life of John Milton,* was cited as an engaging and incisive work on an artist who would seem to have already been chronicled excessively. The biography nonetheless earned praise from critical quarters such as the *Los Angeles Times Book Review,* where it was described as "scholarly and entertaining," and the *Times Literary Supplement,* where reviewer D. J. Enright deemed it "concise" and "trimly organized." Enright also applauded Wilson's skills as a researcher and added that his "interpretation of events is humane and level-headed."

Wilson's third biography is *Hilaire Belloc,* an account of the complex, wide-ranging British writer whose career stretched from the late nineteenth to mid-twentieth centuries. Belloc's canon includes light verse, children's stories, and many volumes on English history, but his often controversial opinions have rendered him notorious as an anti-Semite and idiosyncratic Catholic. Noel Annan wrote in the *Times Literary Supplement* that Wilson makes Belloc's onetime popularity seem credible. Annan considered *Hilaire Belloc* "an outstanding biography."

In addition to his novels and biographies, Wilson has also written several works on religion. In *How Can We Know?* he explicates his own relation to Christianity, and in *The Church in Crisis,* which he wrote with Charles Moore and Gavin Stamp, he contributes to an analysis of the Church of England's seeming decline. "The Clergy," Wilson's contribution to *The Church in Crisis,* was appraised by George Steiner as "elegantly and wittily couched." Steiner, writing in the *Times Literary Supplement,* added that Wilson's essay was "informed with theological awareness and with a genuine perception of the relevant dimensions."

In 1990 Wilson published an acclaimed if controversial biography of C. S. Lewis, the writer and theologian. Ironically, at about this time Wilson, a longtime Christian, publicly rejected Christianity. This act colored the critical reception of his subsequent biographies *Jesus* (1992) and *Paul: The Mind of the Apostle* (1997). In the former, Wilson reaches some provocative conclusions about Jesus' life and ministry. Among the revelations he espouses are that Jesus never set out to establish a church, that he was probably married, and that there was no resurrection. In the latter, Wilson used psychological interpretation to divine the motives behind Paul's actions, purporting to show how the Apostle to the Gentiles "invented" Christianity through his teaching and proselytizing. Focus was also given to Paul's skillful navigation through the perilous labyrinth of Roman politics. Not surprisingly, critical response to both volumes was mixed and divided along fairly predictable lines. Reviewing *Paul* in *National Review,* Luke Timothy Johnson excoriated Wilson for his "pedantic and slightly patronizing manner," going on to cite the author for sanctimony and sloppy research. "Wilson has no consistent basis for his historical judgments," Johnson wrote, "and provides no evidence or argument to support them." On the other hand, writing in the *National Catholic Reporter,* Stephen Binns praised Wilson for his literary historian's appreciation of Paul's writing. "The Christian believer who cannot for a moment go along with Wilson's theses may still find entertainment in this spectacle of a synthesis, and may even find somewhere in the book enrichment of his or her belief."

More recently, Wilson has published a children's book, *Stray,* which concerns a seven-year-old cat and his recollections of life on the road and in a pet shop, a convent, and an animal experimentation laboratory. "Grim as it is in places," reported David Profumo in the *Times Literary Supplement,* "the overall impression that the book creates is one of proper affection." In his review Profumo praised Wilson's "imaginative sympathy."

BIOGRAPHICAL/CRITICAL SOURCES:

BOOKS

Contemporary Literary Criticism, Volume 33, Gale (Detroit), 1985.
Dictionary of Literary Biography, Volume 14: *British Novelists Since 1960,* Gale, 1983.

PERIODICALS

Christian Science Monitor, November 29, 1983.
Economist, June 28, 1980; February 5, 1983.
Encounter, July-August, 1983.
Globe and Mail (Toronto), March 31, 1984.

Listener, May 11, 1978; July 24, 1980; November 12, 1981; January 27, 1983; April 26, 1984.
Los Angeles Times, November 22, 1984.
Los Angeles Times Book Review, April 10, 1983.
National Catholic Reporter, September 5, 1997.
National Review, June 16, 1997.
New Republic, May 23, 1983.
New Statesman, May 27, 1977; April 28, 1978; May 25, 1979; June 6, 1980; August 22, 1980; October 23, 1981; October 29, 1982; January 21, 1983.
Newsweek, October 31, 1983.
New York Times, October 27, 1983; July 24, 1984; March 12, 1986; May 16, 1987.
New York Times Book Review, November 27, 1983; September 2, 1984; February 17, 1985.
Observer (London), April 22, 1984.
Publishers Weekly, May 15, 1987.
Spectator, November 25, 1978; June 2, 1979; May 24, 1980; November 21, 1981; January 22, 1983; September 10, 1983; January 31, 1985.
Time, December 5, 1983; November 5, 1984.
Times (London), June 10, 1980; October 22, 1981; November 4, 1982; January 20, 1983; September 8, 1983; June 5, 1985.
Times Literary Supplement, April 28, 1978; November 30, 1979; June 6, 1980; October 3, 1980; October 23, 1981; November 5, 1982; February 4, 1983; September 9, 1983; April 27, 1984; February 1, 1985; August 29, 1986; November 7, 1986; April 3, 1987.
Tribune Books, July 5, 1987.
Washington Post, October 24, 1984.
Washington Post Book World, March 30, 1986.

*   *   *

WILSON, Angus (Frank Johnstone) 1913-1991

PERSONAL: Surname originally Johnstone-Wilson; born August 11, 1913, in Bexhill, Sussex, England; died May 31, 1991; son of William and Maude (Caney) Johnstone-Wilson. *Education:* Merton College, Oxford, B.A. (with honors), 1936. *Avocational interests:* Gardening, travel, medieval history.

CAREER: Writer. British Museum, London, England, member of staff of department of printed books, 1936-42, 1946-49, deputy superintendent of the Reading Room, 1949-55; University of East Anglia, Norwich, England, lecturer, 1963-66, professor of English literature, 1966-78, professor emeritus, beginning 1978. Ewing Lecturer, University of California, Los Angeles, 1960; Bergen Lecturer, Yale University, 1960; William Vaughan Moody Lecturer, University of Chicago, 1960; Northcliffe Lecturer, University College, London, 1961; Leslie Stephen Lecturer, Cambridge University, 1962-63; Beckman Professor, University of California, Berkeley, 1967; John Hinkley Visiting Professor, Johns Hopkins University, 1974; Ida Beam Professor, University of Iowa, 1978 and 1986. *Military service:* Foreign Office, intelligence officer, 1942-46.

MEMBER: Society of Authors, PEN, Royal Society of Literature (president, 1982-91), Powys Society (president, 1970-91), Dickens Fellowship (president, 1974-75), Kipling Society (president, 1980-88), American Academy and Institute of Arts and Letters (honorary member), Athenaeum Club.

AWARDS, HONORS: Royal Society of Literature, fellow, 1958, companion of literature, 1972; James Tait Black Memorial Prize,

1959, for *The Middle Age of Mrs. Eliot;* Prix de Meilleur Roman Etranger, 1960; Commander, Order of the British Empire, 1968, knighted, 1980; honorary fellow, Cowell College, University of California, Santa Cruz, 1968; *Yorkshire Post* Book of the Year Award, 1970, for *The World of Charles Dickens;* Chevalier de l'Ordre des Arts et des Lettres, 1972; D.Litt., University of Leicester, 1978, University of East Anglia, 1979, University of Liverpool, 1979, and University of Sussex, 1981; honorary doctoral degree, the Sorbonne, 1983; Focus Award, 1985.

WRITINGS:

NOVELS

Hemlock and After, Viking, 1952.
Anglo-Saxon Attitudes (Book Society choice), Viking, 1956.
The Middle Age of Mrs. Eliot, Secker & Warburg, 1958, Viking, 1959.
The Old Men at the Zoo, Viking, 1961.
Late Call, Secker & Warburg, 1964, Viking, 1965.
No Laughing Matter, Viking, 1967.
As If by Magic, Viking, 1973.
Setting the World on Fire, Viking, 1980.

STORY COLLECTIONS

The Wrong Set and Other Stories (Book Society choice), Secker & Warburg, 1949, Morrow, 1950.
Such Darling Dodos and Other Stories (Book Society choice), Secker & Warburg, 1950, Morrow, 1951.
A Bit Off the Map and Other Stories, Viking, 1957.
Death Dance: Twenty-Five Stories, Viking, 1969.
The Collected Stories of Angus Wilson, Secker & Warburg, 1987.

NONFICTION

Emile Zola: An Introductory Study of His Novels, Morrow, 1952, 2nd edition, Secker & Warburg, 1964.
(With Phillippe Jullian) *For Whom the Cloche Tolls: A Scrapbook of the Twenties,* Methuen, 1953.
The Wild Garden; or, Speaking of Writing (lectures), University of California Press, 1963.
Tempo: The Impact of Television on the Arts, Studio Vista, 1964, Dufour, 1966.
The World of Charles Dickens, Viking, 1970.
(With Kathleen Tillotson and Sylvere Monad) *Dickens Memorial Lecture, 1970,* Viking, 1970.
The Naughty Nineties, Methuen, 1976.
The Strange Ride of Rudyard Kipling: His Life and Works, Secker & Warburg, 1977, Viking, 1978.
Diversity and Depth in Fiction: Selected Critical Writings of Angus Wilson, Secker & Warburg, 1983, Viking, 1984.
Reflections in a Writer's Eye: Writings on Travel, Secker & Warburg, 1986.

EDITOR

(And author of introduction) W. Somerset Maugham, *A Maugham Twelve,* Heinemann, 1966, expanded edition published as *Cakes and Ale, and Twelve Stories,* Doubleday, 1967.
(With Peter Fairclough) Charles Dickens, *Oliver Twist,* Penguin, 1967.
Writers of East Anglia, Secker & Warburg, 1977.
East Anglia in Verse and Prose, Secker & Warburg, 1982.
(And author of introduction) *The Portable Dickens,* Penguin, 1983.
Essays by Divers Hands, Boydell & Brewer, 1984, Longwood, 1985.

PLAYS

The Mulberry Bush (three-act; first produced in Bristol, England, at the Bristol Old Vic, September 27, 1955), Secker & Warburg, 1956.

TELEVISION PLAYS

After the Show, British Broadcasting Corporation (BBC), 1959.
The Stranger, BBC, 1960.
The Invasion, BBC, 1963.

RADIO PLAYS

Skeletons and Assegais, BBC.

Television critic, *Queen Magazine,* 1962-63. Contributor of short stories, essays, reviews, and articles to *Observer, Sunday Times, Sunday Telegraph, Encounter, New York Times, New Statesman, Atlantic, Holiday, New Yorker, Partisan Review,* and other publications.

SIDELIGHTS: Although British author Angus Wilson earned an esteemed reputation for his literary criticism, short stories, and biographies, and for editing the works of Charles Dickens, he is best remembered and most widely acclaimed for his novels. He was, Jay L. Halio maintains in the *Dictionary of Literary Biography,* "one of the leading novelists of the post-World War II period and the only one of his generation . . . to be knighted by Queen Elizabeth II for his services to literature and the arts." His ability to successfully combine the techniques of modernist fiction with the traditional novel moves Michael Moorcock, writing in *Books and Bookmen,* to argue that "Wilson better than any novelist of his generation . . . confront[ed] the problems of writing a fiction which is not stifled by the conventions of the past hundred years, yet avoid[ed] obscurity and retain[ed] the dramatic elements which, to my mind, are necessary if a book is justifiably to be called a novel." Julian Symons, in a review for the *Washington Post Book World,* describes Wilson as "the most finely and directly ambitious of contemporary British novelists [and] one of the few . . . who confront[ed] the modern world head-on, making no attempt to take refuge in rediscovery of their own childhood, or in minute examination of a single class or group." Peter Faulkner, in his book *Angus Wilson: Mimic and Moralist,* finds that "Wilson has established himself as one of the half-dozen most distinguished English writers."

Wilson began his writing career relatively late in life. He spent nearly fifteen years on the staff of the British Museum and served as deputy superintendent of its renowned Reading Room for six of those years. It was only while undergoing psychotherapy during World War II that Wilson, following the advice of his doctor, began to write for therapeutic reasons. These efforts did not lead to any serious work at the time, but after the war Wilson began to write short stories on weekends as a way to divert himself from his work at the museum. He showed some of these stories to his friend Robin Ironside, who passed them along to the editor of *Horizon* magazine, Cyril Connolly. Connolly published two of the stories; an editor at the publishing house of Secker & Warburg saw them, and Wilson was asked to do a collection. The resulting volume *The Wrong Set and Other Stories,* appeared in 1949. It was followed in 1950 by *Such Darling Dodos and Other Stories* and by *A Bit Off the Map and Other Stories* in 1957. *Death Dance: Twenty-Five Stories* is a selection of stories from the earlier collections.

These early short stories are noted for their incisive wit and satire and for their accurate portraits of postwar English society. James Gindin writes in *Postwar British Fiction: New Accents and*

Attitudes that Wilson's stories "depict, with precision and detachment, the delusions and the pretense under which people operate." As Faulkner explains, the stories in *The Wrong Set and Other Stories* are concerned with the question, "can there be relationships . . . which allow and help all concerned to grow and develop, or are they necessarily props for some and prisons for others? The sombreness which underlies the wit comes from the fact that the answer suggested is negative." Writing in the *Saturday Review,* Joyce Carol Oates describes Wilson's short stories as "masterful, concise, rather macabre tales of post-war England," and judges Wilson to be "a master of what we now call the Chekhovian short story." These early collections helped to bring Wilson recognition as what Richard Boston of the *New York Times Book Review* calls "one of the most brilliant short-story writers of the century."

But despite this immediate success, Wilson was dissatisfied with the short story, wishing to express his ideas in a longer and more developed form. Before trying his hand at a novel, however, he wrote a study of the great French novelist of the nineteenth century, Emile Zola. In this book, *Emile Zola: An Introductory Study of His Novels,* Wilson examined the relationship between the author's personal life and his fiction. More importantly, as Halio points out, the study of Zola's writing methods confirmed Wilson's own ideas about how to write a novel: "writing copious notes and sketches until one is ready to draft the entire novel," as Halio states. The critical study received generally favorable reviews, with V. S. Pritchett of the *New Statesman and Nation* calling it "pithy, searching and decided," and Henri Peyre of the *New York Times* finding it "intelligent and lively."

During his annual four-week vacation from the British Museum in 1951, Wilson wrote his first novel, *Hemlock and After,* which appeared in 1952. It tells the story of famous novelist Bernard Sands, who establishes an anarchistic writer's colony. Sands considers this colony a great success but soon comes to doubt the wisdom of what he has done. He wonders if his administration of authority in the writer's colony runs contrary to his humanistic beliefs. In his personal life, Sands finds that he has not fulfilled his ideals about marriage and parenthood. His wife suffers from a neurotic illness, his children are unhappy, and Sands has begun to have homosexual affairs. The realization of his own fallibility— what he considers to be the aspect of evil in every man—brings Sands to a nervous breakdown and a fatal heart attack.

Faulkner sees the novel questioning "the adequacy of liberalism . . . on both the public and the private planes," citing the failure of Sands's beliefs in his professional and personal life. But Halio argues that "if Bernard's humanism finally fails him because it screens off the uglier aspects of human motive and behavior and pretends to qualify acts of altruism with only the most enlightened or innocuous self-interest, it nevertheless contains something of positive value." *Hemlock and After* met with a favorable critical reception and sold well enough for Wilson to leave his British Museum post and become a full-time writer.

It was with his second novel, *Anglo-Saxon Attitudes,* that Wilson established himself among the most important new British writers of the 1950s. While similar to *Hemlock and After* in that the protagonist comes to a self-realization after examining the course of his life, in *Anglo-Saxon Attitudes* "the lines . . . have become firmer than in [the earlier novel], and the mature wit gives tone and shape to the material," Frederick R. Karl writes in *A Reader's Guide to the Contemporary British Novel.* The book revolves around Gerald Middleton, a professor of history who is alienated from his family and friends. The story delineates the course of events that have led to this impasse. Around this central narrative are a cluster of related stories "and a vast company of characters representing all phases of contemporary life," James Gray recounts in the *Saturday Review.*

Several critics comment on the enormous range of the novel. Bernard Bergonzi notes in *The Situation of the Novel* that *Anglo-Saxon Attitudes* possesses a "crowded canvas and broad temporal sweep." Karl admits that "the characters of the novel are varied, the range of comment wide, the point of view . . . sophisticated, and the verbal gifts . . . abundant," although he finds that it "fails for several reasons to realize its potential." Gray believes that "covering four decades of English social life, touching every level from those of political and spiritual leader to that of the criminal, exploring every mood from that of high comedy to that of bitter melodrama, Wilson's book seems to be as boldly conceived and as deftly executed as any novel of the great tradition."

With *The Middle Age of Mrs. Eliot,* Wilson wrote a different kind of novel than he had previously attempted. "Whereas *Anglo-Saxon Attitudes* flashed words, events, and thoughts against one another in a complicated pattern," Gindin explains, "*The Middle Age of Mrs. Eliot* unfolds slowly." Faulkner calls it "the most relaxed of Wilson's early novels." The book also narrows its focus to a single character, Meg Eliot, and explores in depth her thoughts and emotions. Meg is an upper-middle-class English woman whose husband is killed in the Far East. His death destroys her stable world, resulting in her nervous breakdown. But Meg eventually recovers and is able to go on with her life. "Her heroism," Halio writes, "consists of an ability to look deeply within herself and, seeing what is there, to accept what she finds and, properly disciplined, move on."

The Middle Age of Mrs. Eliot has been critically well-received and won the James Tait Black Memorial Prize and the Prix du Meilleur Roman Etranger. Gindin judges the book to be "as complete and as totally satisfying as is *Anglo-Saxon Attitudes.*" Robert Kiely of the *New York Times Book Review* finds *Anglo-Saxon Attitudes* and *The Middle Age of Mrs. Eliot* "Wilson's two most acclaimed and best-known works of the 1950's. . . . Both novels contain whole sections of glittering dialogue, wonderfully satiric imitations of academics, politicians, diplomats, artists, [and] scientists. [Wilson] probes the inner lives and especially the disappointments of the 'unheroic' figures who are the central characters in his fiction."

This focus on individual crisis was abandoned with *No Laughing Matter,* a generations-spanning novel with a host of characters. "Hundreds of characters and incidents crowd the canvas," Liam Lenihan writes in the *Nation,* "yet Wilson manages to juggle them all with consummate skill, and the relationships are all sharply drawn." Wilson follows the eight members of the Matthews family—mother, father, and six children—from 1912 to 1967. The Matthews are an eccentric family, no longer wealthy, whose experiences echo those of twentieth-century British society at large. Wilson tells their story through their dreams, the play-acting of the children, and selected scenes spanning five decades. As a family chronicle, writes Marilyn Gardner in the *Christian Science Monitor,* it is "a *magnum opus* in every sense of the term, a complex, intricate work spanning half a century and crisscrossing nearly a dozen lives. Mr. Wilson's scope is simultaneously intimate and global, his technique varied and highly unconventional." But it is more than a family chronicle, Gardner observes; it is also "a fascinating compendium of recent history." Lenihan

describes the book as "a shrewd and compassionate appraisal of social and political England from its sunny, easy days of greatness to its twilight hours." Richard Mayne, writing in the *Reporter,* goes beyond the categories of family chronicle and historical novel to describe the book. *No Laughing Matter,* he maintains, "is in many respects an experimental novel that uses dazzling free-hand technique to enter deeply into the nature of personality and perception, revealing more thoroughly than any of Angus Wilson's previous work the complex responses, the image-making, mimesis, parody, and unconscious feedback that inform a family entity."

Wilson's next novel, *As If by Magic,* presents Hamo, a scientist who has developed a hybrid rice to feed the Third World, and his goddaughter Alexandra, a hippie who travels with her two lovers and young child. The two characters leave England and journey to the Far East, Hamo to see the effects of his rice, which he calls "magic" rice, and Alexandra to find spiritual enlightenment in first a Moroccan commune and then an Indian ashram. Both are seeking a quick answer to life's major problems. But Hamo finds that his new rice does not solve the Third World's hunger problem. It causes new problems instead. Alexandra discovers that the Indian swami she turns to for guidance is a sham. Both Hamo's rationalism and Alexandra's spiritualism fail.

"None of these 'magics,' or any of the sorts that people put their faith in, can truly solve the problems of human society or human predicaments," Halio explains. ". . . At the same time, Wilson is also concerned with the magic of art—literature—and the ways it can touch our lives, not transform us or solve our problems, but awaken in us something other than what we have previously known or felt or otherwise experienced." Though acknowledging the novel's humor, Phoebe Adams of the *Atlantic* states that Wilson's "underlying purpose is serious. He is quite savagely out of patience with the fashion for magic shortcuts to Utopia and Nirvana." Discussing the wide range of characters, classes, and locales found in *No Laughing Matter* and *As If by Magic,* Jonathan Raban writes in the *New Review* that "the two novels form something very close to an encyclopedia of life in society in the 20th century, an inventory of roles and stages."

Although not trained as a literary critic—he studied medieval history while attending Oxford—Wilson provides insights into the works of others by using a biographical approach. He was, Alice Green Fredman writes in *Twentieth Century Literature,* "a critic who scrutinizes the relationship between a writer's life and art in the belief that what transpires in the work of art is illuminated and elucidated by what has been lived in the life." Perhaps his most successful use of this approach occurs in *The World of Charles Dickens* and *The Strange Ride of Rudyard Kipling,* both of which are critical biographies. *The World of Charles Dickens* compares events in Dickens's life to incidents found in his fiction and is illustrated with engravings and paintings of places and people of the time. It is, Geoffrey Wolff summarizes for *Newsweek,* "at once a biography, a splendidly condensed critical examination by one writer of another's work and a re-creation—through portraits, plates and photographs of artifacts—of the externals of Charles Dickens's mid-nineteenth-century world." K. J. Fielding says in the *New York Times Book Review* that the book's illustrations link "Dickens's life, his writings and the world that lay about him."

Wolff sees a strong similarity between Wilson and Dickens, describing Wilson as "a fellow novelist, whose own fiction, in its attention to social details and the mesh between imagination and active life, moves in the wide groove Dickens cut." Calling

Wilson "the most outstanding British novelist today," Fielding also compares him with Dickens, finding that both men "share certain gifts and obsessions: the deepening concern with self-discovery . . . , an understanding of their characters' life-styles and their relation to society, and the power of mimicry aided by a sharp eye and sensitive ear." Because of these similarities Fielding believes that "there has never been a comparable study of how Dickens's imagination fed on his vision of the world about him." And Virginia Tiger of the *Washington Post* judges *The World of Charles Dickens* to be "a beautifully measured, gentle study, yet critical and tough about the faults of the man and the flaws in the books."

Wilson's affinity for Dickens led him to edit an edition of *Oliver Twist,* to deliver the Dickens Memorial Lecture, to contribute to *Dickens and the Twentieth Century,* a collection of essays, and to compile *The Portable Dickens,* a book of selections from Dickens's oeuvre. In his essay "Charles Dickens: A Haunting," published in *Diversity and Depth in Fiction,* Wilson admitted to a "constant and haunting pressure of Dickens's created world upon my imagination." In an interview with Frederick P. W. McDowell in the *Iowa Review,* the author commented on the similarities between his work and the work of Dickens. "Apart from the humour of Dickens which lies very close to a good deal of my humour," Wilson stated, "what is vital to his approach and to mine is that he sees his central figures always in relation to, first of all, a group and then in relation to the whole of society. Frequently with him the direction in his novels is, rather, outward from society and inwards toward the group and the central figure but always in connection with a great number of other people; he sees the central figures internally and the others are presented externally. On the whole, this has been my method. It has been the only way, I think, in which I can present my sense of man's total isolation, his working out of his problems within himself but also in terms of the other human beings whom he comes across."

Diversity and Depth in Fiction: Selected Critical Writings of Angus Wilson is a collection of essays, reviews, introductions, and lectures that Wilson wrote on novelists of the last three centuries. The authors covered range from Dostoevsky to Proust and from Zola to Grass. "It's as a novelist—on the job, as it were—that [Wilson] has analyzed the forms of fiction," Lorna Sage comments in the *Observer.* This approach allows Wilson to present his personal reactions to books and authors. "He seems to have deliberately displayed a most unprofessional capacity for flexibility, tolerance, and changing his mind," Sage remarks. James Atlas of the *New York Times Book Review* agrees with this assessment, saying that "there *is* something amateurish about Mr. Wilson's criticism—amateurish in the good sense. Unimpaired by professional envy or ideological bias, he writes about literature with a student's pure enthusiasm. . . . Wilson ranges effortlessly among the whole of English literature, rattling off subplots and minor characters. . . . For all his reiterated insistence on his amateur status, Mr. Wilson is clearly up on contemporary criticism and unafraid to challenge the big boys in the field."

Wilson's standing in contemporary British letters is unique because of the range of his writings and his iconoclastic stance. He was, as Frederick Busch writes in the *New York Times Book Review,* "a superior novelist, dramatist, storywriter, and critic." Sage, writing in *Twentieth Century Literature,* states that "Wilson . . . always combined two roles—novelist and man of letters (bohemian and literary statesman, iconoclast and professional, risk-taker and representative)—that are traditionally, tactfully assumed to follow one after the other. It's not particularly surprising, in retrospect, that the authority and vitality of his early fiction 'established' him so quickly. What *is* extraordinary and distinctive is his having gone on taking risks." Malcolm Bradbury calls Wilson "unquestionably a leading novelist of his generation and one of Britain's most important literary figures, but there is something in his career and character which is fierily resistant to all such formulae. He began as a comic writer, a maverick and mimic, and he has continued to be so. He has always written with a strong sense of a tradition, yet in urgent dispute with it. [Critics] have sensed something elusive about him, and often seem unsure in what mode of definition to cast their commentary. This is, I believe, the spirit of a virtuous career, but it is a spirit not always understood."

BIOGRAPHICAL/CRITICAL SOURCES:

BOOKS

Bergonzi, Bernard, *The Situation of the Novel,* University of Pittsburgh Press, 1970.

Bradbury, Malcolm, *Possibilities: Essays on the State of the Novel,* Oxford University Press, 1973.

Bradbury, Malcolm, editor, *The Novel Today: Contemporary Writers on Modern Fiction,* Manchester University Press, 1977.

Burgess, Anthony, *The Novel Now: A Guide to Contemporary Fiction,* Norton, 1976.

Contemporary Literary Criticism, Gale (Detroit), Volume 2, 1974; Volume 3, 1975; Volume 5, 1976; Volume 25, 1983; Volume 34, 1985.

Cowley, Malcolm, editor, *Writers at Work: The 'Paris Review' Interviews,* Viking, 1959.

Cox, C. B., *The Free Spirit,* Oxford University Press, 1963.

Dictionary of Literary Biography, Gale, Volume 15, 1983; Volume 155, Gale, 1995.

Drabble, Margaret, *Angus Wilson: A Biography,* St. Martin's, 1996.

Faulkner, Peter, *Angus Wilson: Mimic and Moralist,* Viking, 1980.

Gardner, Averil, *Angus Wilson,* Twayne, 1985.

Gindin, James, *Postwar British Fiction: New Accents and Attitudes,* University of California Press, 1962.

Halio, Jay L., editor, *Critical Essays on Angus Wilson,* G. K. Hall, 1985.

Karl, Frederick R., *A Reader's Guide to the Contemporary English Novel,* Farrar, Straus, 1962.

Rabinovitz, Rubin, *The Reaction against Experiment in the English Novel, 1950-1960,* Columbia University Press, 1967.

Shapiro, Charles, editor, *Contemporary British Novelists,* Southern Illinois University Press, 1965.

Wilson, Edmund, *The Bit between My Teeth: A Literary Chronicle, 1950-1965,* Farrar, Straus, 1965.

The Writer's Place: Interviews on the Literary Situation in Contemporary Britain, University of Minnesota Press, 1974.

PERIODICALS

Atlantic Monthly, November, 1973; May, 1978; October, 1980; May, 1984.

Books and Bookmen, May, 1973; July, 1973; July, 1980.

Christian Science Monitor, December 7, 1967; October 1, 1970.

Commentary, January, 1968.

Commonweal, March 26, 1965; March 8, 1968.

Contemporary Literature, Number 21, 1980.

Critical Quarterly, autumn, 1961; spring, 1970.

Detroit News, November 30, 1981.

Encounter, November, 1980.

Essays in Criticism, Number 9, 1959.
Guardian, June 2, 1973.
Harper's Bazaar, May, 1970.
Hudson Review, spring, 1968; winter, 1974.
Iowa Review, fall, 1972.
Kenyon Review, March, 1967.
Listener, October 5, 1967; July 10, 1980; November 16, 1989, p. 30.
Literary Review, November, 1980.
London Magazine, November, 1967.
London Review of Books, December 1-21, 1983, January 7, 1988, p. 16.
Nation, April 15, 1968; November 23, 1970.
National Review, September 13, 1974.
New Leader, January 25, 1971; November 17, 1980.
New Republic, November 8, 1980.
New Review, April, 1974.
New Statesman, October 6, 1967; November 11, 1977; July 18, 1980; September 9, 1983; June 14, 1991, p. 39.
New Statesman and Nation, March 29, 1952.
Newsweek, August 31, 1970; December 21, 1970; November 26, 1973.
New Yorker, August 23, 1952; October 6, 1956; January 16, 1965; April 3, 1978.
New York Review of Books, February 25, 1965; January 18, 1968; October 8, 1970; November 1, 1973; March 9, 1978; November 20, 1980.
New York Times, May 18, 1952; November 23, 1967; October 14, 1973; March 16, 1978; October 17, 1980.
New York Times Book Review, November 26, 1967; September 13, 1970; March 12, 1978; November 16, 1980; August 19, 1984; September 7, 1986, p. 23; January 29, 1995, p. 3.
Observer, May 24, 1970; July 6, 1980; August 28, 1983.
Publishers Weekly, March 9, 1984; August 8, 1986, p. 61.
Reporter, February 8, 1968.
Saturday Review, January 16, 1965; November 18, 1967; July 5, 1969; March 4, 1978; October, 1980.
Spectator, February 29, 1952; September 17, 1954; October 6, 1967; July 12, 1980.
Studies in the Novel, spring, 1970.
Time, December 1, 1967; December 3, 1973; March 13, 1978.
Times (London), July 7, 1980; September 1, 1983.
Times Literary Supplement, April 6, 1967; October 5, 1967; December 23, 1977; July 11, 1980; September 16, 1983; February 7, 1986, p. 147; November 6, 1987, p. 1226.
Twentieth Century Literature, summer, 1983.
Washington Post, December 30, 1970.
Washington Post Book World, November 11, 1973; November 2, 1980; July 3, 1983.
Yale Review, spring, 1968; summer, 1974.

*   *   *

WILSON, August 1945-

PERSONAL: Born Frederick August Kittel in 1945, in Pittsburgh, PA; son of Frederick August (a baker) and Daisy (a cleaning woman; maiden name, Wilson) Kittel; stepfather, David Bedford; married second wife, Judy Oliver (a social worker), 1981 (marriage ended); married Constanza Romero (a costume designer); children: (first marriage) Sakina Ansari.

ADDRESSES: Office—c/o John Breglio, Paul Weiss Rifkind Wharton & Garrison, 1285 Avenue of the Americas, New York, NY 10019.

CAREER: Writer. Cofounder (with Rob Penny), scriptwriter, and director of Black Horizons on the Hill (theater company) Pittsburgh, PA, 1968-78; scriptwriter for Science Museum of Minnesota, St. Paul, MN, 1979.

AWARDS, HONORS: Award for best play of 1984-85 from New York Drama Critics Circle, 1985, Antoinette Perry ("Tony") Award nomination from League of New York Theatres and Producers, 1985, and Whiting Writers' Award from the Whiting Foundation, 1986, all for *Ma Rainey's Black Bottom;* Outstanding Play Award from American Theatre Critics, 1986, Drama Desk Outstanding New Play Award, 1986, New York Drama Critics Circle Best Play Award, 1986, Pulitzer Prize for drama, Antoinette Perry Award for best play, and award for best Broadway play from Outer Critics Circle, all 1987, all for *Fences;* John Gassner Award for best American playwright from Outer Critics Circle, 1987; named Artist of the Year by *Chicago Tribune,* 1987; Literary Lion Award from New York Public Library, 1988; New York Drama Critics Circle Best Play award, and Antoinette Perry Award nomination for best play, both 1988, both for *Joe Turner's Come and Gone;* Drama Desk Outstanding New Play Award, New York Drama Critics Circle Best Play Award, Antoinette Perry Award for Best Play, American Theatre Critics Outstanding Play Award, and Pulitzer Prize for drama, all 1990, all for *The Piano Lesson;* Black Filmmakers Hall of Fame Award, 1991; Antoinette Perry Award nomination for best play, and American Theatre Critics' Association Award, both 1992, both for *Two Trains Running;* Clarence Muse Award, 1992; New York Drama Critics Circle Award, 1996, for *Seven Guitars;* recipient of Bush and Guggenheim Foundation fellowships.

WRITINGS:

Jitney (two-act play), first produced in Pittsburgh, PA, at the Allegheny Repertory Theatre, 1982.
Ma Rainey's Black Bottom (play; first produced in New Haven, CT, at the Yale Repertory Theatre, 1984; produced on Broadway at the Cort Theatre, October, 1984; also see below), New American Library (New York City), 1985.
Fences (play; first produced at Yale Repertory Theatre, 1985; produced on Broadway at 46th Street Theatre, March, 1987; also see below), New American Library, 1986.
Joe Turner's Come and Gone (play; first produced at Yale Repertory Theatre, 1986; produced on Broadway at Barrymore Theatre, March, 1988; also see below), New American Library, 1988.
The Piano Lesson (play; first produced in New Haven at the Yale Repertory Theatre, 1987; produced on Broadway at Walter Kerr Theatre, 1990; also see below), New American Library, 1990.
(And author of preface) *August Wilson: Three Plays* (contains *Ma Rainey's Black Bottom, Fences,* and *Joe Turner's Come and Gone*), afterword by Paul C. Harrison, University of Pittsburgh Press (Pittsburgh), 1991.
Two Trains Running (first produced at Yale Repertory Theatre, 1990, produced at Walter Kerr Theatre, 1992), New American Library/Dutton, 1993.
Seven Guitars (first produced in Chicago at Goodman Theatre, 1995), Dutton, 1996.
The Piano Lesson (teleplay; adapted from his play), "Hallmark Hall of Fame," CBS-TV, 1995.

Also author of the plays *The Homecoming,* 1979, *The Coldest Day of the Year,* 1979, *Fullerton Street,* 1980, *Black Bart and the Sacred Hills,* 1981, and *The Mill Hand's Lunch Bucket,* 1983. Author of the book for a stage musical about jazz musician Jelly Roll Morton. Work represented in *A Game of Passion: The NFL Literary Companion,* Turner, 1994, *Selected from Contemporary American Plays,* 1990, and *The Poetry of Blackamerica,* Adoff. Contributor to periodicals, including *Black Lines* and *Connection.*

SIDELIGHTS: August Wilson has been hailed since the mid-1980s as an important talent in the American theater. He spent his childhood in poverty in Pittsburgh, Pennsylvania, where he lived with his parents and five siblings. Though he grew up in a poor family, Wilson felt that his parents withheld knowledge of even greater hardships they had endured. "My generation of blacks knew very little about the past of our parents," he told the *New York Times* in 1984. "They shielded us from the indignities they suffered." Wilson's goal is to illuminate that shadowy past with a series of plays, each set in a different decade, that focus on black issues. *Ma Rainey's Black Bottom, Fences, Joe Turner's Come and Gone, The Piano Lesson, Two Trains Running,* and *Seven Guitars* are part of this ambitious project.

Wilson has noted that his real education began when he was sixteen years old. Disgusted by the racist treatment he endured in the various schools he had attended until that time, he dropped out and began educating himself in the local library. Working at menial jobs, he also pursued a literary career and successfully submitted poems to black publications at the University of Pittsburgh. In 1968 he became active in the theater by founding—despite lacking prior experience—Black Horizons on the Hill, a theater company in Pittsburgh. Recalling his early theater involvement, Wilson described himself to the *New York Times* as "a cultural nationalist . . . trying to raise consciousness through theater."

According to several observers, however, Wilson found his artistic voice—and began to appreciate the black voices of Pittsburgh—after he moved to St. Paul, Minnesota, in 1978. In St. Paul, Wilson wrote his first play, *Jitney,* a realistic drama set in a Pittsburgh taxi station. *Jitney,* noted for the fidelity with which it portrayed black urban speech and life, had a successful engagement at a small theater in Pittsburgh. Wilson followed *Jitney* with another play, *Fullerton Street,* but this work failed to strengthen his reputation.

Wilson then resumed work on an earlier unfinished project, *Ma Rainey's Black Bottom,* a play about a black blues singer's exploitation of her fellow musicians. This work, whose title role is named after an actual blues singer from the 1920s, is set in a recording studio in 1927. In the studio, temperamental Ma Rainey verbally abuses the other musicians and presents herself—without justification—as an important musical figure. But much of the play is also set in a rehearsal room, where Ma Rainey's musicians discuss their abusive employer and the hardships of life in racist America.

Ma Rainey's Black Bottom earned Wilson a trip to the O'Neill Theatre Center's National Playwrights Conference. There Wilson's play impressed director Lloyd Richards from the Yale Repertory Theatre. Richards worked with Wilson to refine the play, and when it was presented at Yale in 1984 it was hailed as the work of an important new playwright. Frank Rich, who reviewed the Yale production in the *New York Times,* acclaimed Wilson as "a major find for the American theater" and cited

Wilson's ability to write "with compassion, raucous humor and penetrating wisdom."

Wilson enjoyed further success with *Ma Rainey's Black Bottom* after the play came to Broadway later in 1984. The *Chicago Tribune*'s Richard Christiansen reviewed the Broadway production as "a work of intermittent but immense power" and commended the "striking beauty" of the play's "literary and theatrical poetry." Christiansen added that "Wilson's power of language is sensational" and that *Ma Rainey's Black Bottom* was "the work of an impressive writer." The London *Times*'s Holly Hill agreed, calling Wilson "a promising new playwright" and hailing his work as "a remarkable first play."

Wilson's subsequent plays include the Pulitzer Prize-winning *Fences,* which is about a former athlete who forbids his son to accept an athletic scholarship, and *Joe Turner's Come and Gone,* which concerns an ex-convict's efforts to find his wife. Like *Ma Rainey's Black Bottom,* these plays underwent extensive rewriting. Guiding Wilson in this process was Lloyd Richards, dean of Yale's drama school and director of the school's productions of Wilson's plays. "August is a wonderful poet," Richards told the *New York Times* in 1986. "A wonderful poet turning into a playwright." Richards added that his work with Wilson involved "clarifying" each work's main theme and "arranging the material in a dynamic way."

Both *Fences* and *Joe Turner's Come and Gone* were praised when they played on American stages. The *New York Times*'s Frank Rich, in his review of *Fences,* wrote that the play "leaves no doubt that Mr. Wilson is a major writer, combining a poet's ear for vernacular with a robust sense of humor (political and sexual), a sure instinct for cracking dramatic incident and passionate commitment to a great subject." And in his critique of *Joe Turner's Come and Gone,* Rich speculated that the play "will give a lasting voice to a generation of uprooted black Americans." Rich contended that the work was "potentially its author's finest achievement yet" and described it as "a teeming canvas of black America . . . and a spiritual allegory."

In 1990, Wilson claimed his second Pulitzer Prize, this time for *The Piano Lesson.* Set during the Great Depression of the 1930s, this drama pits brother against sister in a contest to decide the future of a treasured heirloom—a piano, carved with African-style portraits by their grandfather, an enslaved plantation carpenter. The brother wants to sell it to buy land, while the sister adamantly insists that the instrument carries too much family history to part with. Acclaim for the play was widespread, although some commentators were put off by the supernatural elements that came to play in the climax of this otherwise realistic piece. "When ghosts begin resolving realistic plays, you can be sure the playwright has failed to master his material," wrote Robert Brustein in the *New Republic.* Brustein also found the play overlong and repetitious, and asserted that Wilson's focus on the effects of racism was limiting him artistically. Others praised the work unreservedly, however, including Clive Barnes of the *New York Post.* He declared: "This is a play in which to lose yourself—to give yourself up . . . to August Wilson's thoughts, humors and thrills, all caught in a microcosm largely remote for many of us from our own little worlds, yet always talking the same language of humanity." Frank Rich of the *New York Times* wrote that Wilson has given "miraculous voice" to the black experience, and William A. Henry III of *Time* dubbed the play's piano "the most potent symbol in American drama since Laura Wingfield's glass menagerie" in the Tennessee Williams classic. Barnes concluded:

"This is a wonderful play that lights up man. See it, wonder at it, and recognize it." Wilson later adapted *The Piano Lesson* for a "Hallmark Hall of Fame" television production. It was judged a success by John J. O'Connor, who wrote in the *New York Times:* "If anything, *The Piano Lesson* is even more effective in this shortened version."

Two Trains Running continued Wilson's projected ten-play cycle about black American history. The play, which came to Broadway in 1992, is set in a run-down diner on the verge of being sold. Reactions by the diner's regular patrons to the pending sale make up the body of the drama. Some critics, such as the *New Yorker's* Mimi Kramer, found the play less subtle and dramatic than its predecessors, but *Newsweek's* David Ansen praised the "musical eloquence" of Wilson's language, which he felt enhanced a "thematically rich" work. And Henry wrote in *Time* that *Two Trains Running* is a "delicate and mature" play that shows Wilson "at his lyrical best."

Two Trains Running was followed in 1995 by *Seven Guitars.* Set in the 1940s, it recounts the tragic story of blues guitarist Floyd Barton, whose funeral opens the play. Action then flashes back to recreate the events of Floyd's last week of life. *Seven Guitars* was the first major production of a Wilson play without the direction of Richards, who was forced to abandon the project due to illness. The task of directing fell to Walter Dallas, whose staging at the Goodman Theatre in Chicago William Tynan characterized as "skillful" in a *Time* review. Yet the critic's overall assessment was mixed. "Part bawdy comedy, part dark elegy, part mystery," he wrote, "August Wilson's rich new play, *Seven Guitars,* nicely eludes categorization. . . . But though full and strong in its buildup, the play loses its potency as it reaches its climax. . . . Though Floyd is as charming and sympathetic a protagonist as we could want, the surprising truth is that his death has little effect on us. We leave the theater entertained and admiring but not truly moved." Vincent Canby differed markedly in his judgment, writing in the *New York Times:* "Though the frame of 'Seven Guitars' is limited and employs only seven characters, Mr. Wilson writes so vividly that the play seems to have the narrative scope and depth of a novel. When the curtain comes down, it's difficult to remember which characters you've actually seen and which you have come to know only through stories recollected on stage. . . . 'Seven Guitars' plays with such speed that you begin the journey one minute, and the next thing you know, you're leaving the theater on a high."

Further praise came from *Newsweek* reviewer Jack Kroll, who called *Seven Guitars* "a kind of jazz cantata for actors," with "a gritty, lyrical polyphony of voices that evokes the character and destiny of these men and women who can't help singing the blues even when they're just talking." The play, he continued, "bristles with symbolism" and with "anguished eloquence." Kroll found the protagonist's death "shocking, unexpected, yet inevitable" and the characters overall "not victims, wallowing in voluptuous resentment," but "tragic figures, bursting with the balked music of life."

Discussing Wilson's body of work, Lawrence Bommer stated in the *Chicago Tribune,* "August Wilson has created the most complete cultural chronicle since Balzac wrote his vast 'Human Comedy,' an artistic whole that has grown even greater than its prize-winning parts." As for the playwright, he has repeatedly stressed that his first objective is simply getting his work produced. "All I want is for the most people to get to see this play," he told the *New York Times* while discussing *Joe Turner's*

Come and Gone. Wilson added, however, that he was not opposed to having his works performed on Broadway. He told the *New York Times* that Broadway "still has the connotation of Mecca" and asked, "Who doesn't want to go to Mecca?"

BIOGRAPHICAL/CRITICAL SOURCES:

BOOKS

Elkins, Marilyn, editor, *August Wilson: A Casebook,* Garland, 1994.
Nadel, Alan, editor, *May All Your Fences Have Gates: Essays on the Drama of August Wilson,* University of Iowa Press, 1994.
Pereira, Kim, *August Wilson and the African-American Odyssey,* University of Illinois Press, 1995.
Shannon, Sandra Garrett, *The Dramatic Vision of August Wilson,* Howard University Press, 1995.

PERIODICALS

African American Review, spring, 1996, p. 99.
Chicago Tribune, October 15, 1984; June 8, 1987; December 17, 1987; December 27, 1987, pp. 4-5; January 20, 1993, p. section 1, p. 20; January 24, 1993, section 13, pp. 8-9; January 26, 1993, section 1, p. 16; January 15, 1995, section 13, pp. 16-17, 21.
Chicago Tribune Book World, February 9, 1986, pp. 12-13.
Christian Science Monitor, October 16, 1984, pp. 29-30; March 27, 1987, pp. 1, 8; March 30, 1988, p. 21.
Ebony, January, 1985; November, 1987, pp. 68, 70, 72, 74.
Esquire, April, 1989, pp. 116, 118, 120, 122-27.
Essence, August, 1987, pp. 51, 111, 113.
Los Angeles Times, November 24, 1984; November 7, 1986; April 17, 1987; June 7, 1987; June 8, 1987; June 9, 1987; February 6, 1988.
Maclean's, May 28, 1990, p. 62; May 18, 1992, pp. 56-57.
Massachusetts Review, spring, 1988, pp. 87-97.
Nation, April 18, 1987, p. 518; June 1, 1990, pp. 832-33; June 8, 1992, pp. 799-800.
New Republic, May 21, 1990, pp. 28-30.
Newsweek, April 6, 1987; April 11, 1988, p. 82; April 27, 1992, p. 70; February 6, 1995, p. 60.
New York, April 6, 1987, pp. 92-94; May 7, 1990, pp. 82-83.
New Yorker, April 6, 1987, p. 81; April 11, 1988, p. 107; April 30, 1990, p. 85; April 27, 1992, p. 85.
New York Post, March 28, 1988; April 17, 1990.
New York Times, April 11, 1984; April 13, 1984; October 12, 1984; October 22, 1984, p. C15; May 5, 1985, p. 80; May 6, 1986; May 14, 1986; May 19, 1986, p. C11; June 20, 1986; March 27, 1987, p. C3; April 5, 1987, II, pp. 1, 39; April 9, 1987; April 17, 1987; May 7, 1987; December 10, 1987; December 11, 1987; March 27, 1988, pp. 1, 34; March 28, 1988, p. C15; January 30, 1989, p. 69; April 17, 1990, p. C13; March 10, 1991, section 2, pp. 5, 17; January 25, 1995, pp. C13-C14; February 3, 1995, p. D26; February 5, 1995, section 2, pp. 1, 5.
New York Times Book Review, March 3, 1996, p. 22.
New York Times Magazine, June 10, 1987, pp. 36, 40, 49, 70.
People Weekly, May 13, 1996, p. 63.
Theater, fall-winter, 1984, pp. 50-55; summer-fall, 1986, pp. 64; summer-fall, 1988, pp. 69-71.
Theatre Journal, December, 1994, pp. 468-76.
Time, April 6, 1987, p. 81; April 27, 1987; April 11, 1988, pp. 77-78; January 30, 1989, p. 69; April 27, 1992, pp. 65-6; February 6, 1995, p. 71.
Times (London), November 6, 1984; April 18, 1987; April 24, 1987.

Variety, February 26, 1996, p. 175.
Vogue, August, 1988, pp. 200, 204.
Washington Post, May 20, 1986; April 15, 1987; June 9, 1987; October 4, 1987; October 9, 1987.

* * *

WILSON, Dirk
See POHL, Frederik

* * *

WILSON, Edmund 1895-1972

PERSONAL: Born May 8, 1895, in Red Bank, NJ; died June 12, 1972; buried in Wellfleet, MA; son of Edmund (a lawyer) and Helen Mather (maiden name, Kimball) Wilson; married Mary Blair (an actress), 1923 (divorced, 1929); married Margaret Canby, 1930 (deceased, 1932); married Mary McCarthy (a writer and critic), 1938 (divorced, 1946); married Elena Thornton Mumm, 1946; children: Rosalind (first marriage), Reuel (third marriage), Helen (fourth marriage). *Education:* Princeton University, A.B., 1916.

CAREER: Writer. *New York Evening Sun,* New York City, reporter, 1916-17; managing editor, *Vanity Fair* magazine, 1920-21; associate editor, *New Republic* magazine, 1926-31; *New Yorker* magazine, New York City, book reviewer, 1944-48. *Military service:* U.S. Army, 1917-19; served as enlisted man at Base Hospital 36, in France, and in the Intelligence Corps.

MEMBER: Charter Club (Princeton), Princeton Club (New York).

AWARDS, HONORS: Guggenheim fellowship, 1935; National Institute of Arts and Letters Gold Medal Award, 1955, for essays and criticism; Presidential Medal of Freedom, 1963; Edward MacDowell Medal, 1964; Emerson-Thoreau Medal, 1966; National Medal for Literature, National Book Committee, 1966; Aspen Award, 1968; Golden Eagle Award, Nice Book Festival, Nice, France, 1971.

WRITINGS:

I Thought of Daisy (novel; also see below), Scribner, 1929.
The American Jitters: A Year of the Slump (essay collection), Scribner, 1932, published in England as *Devil Take the Hindmost,* Scribner, 1932.
Travels in Two Democracies (essays and story collection), Harcourt, 1936.
To the Finland Station: A Study in the Writing and Acting of History, Harcourt, 1940, revised edition, Farrar, Straus, 1972.
Memoirs of Hecate County (story collection), Doubleday, 1946, revised edition, W H Allen, 1958, Farrar, Straus, 1959, reprinted with an afterword by John Updike, David R. Godine, 1980.
Europe without Baedeker: Sketches among the Ruins of Italy, Greece, and England, Doubleday, 1947, revised edition published as *Europe without Baedeker: Sketches among the Ruins of Italy, Greece, and England, Together with Notes from a European Diary: 1963-64,* Farrar, Straus, 1966.
The Scrolls from the Dead Sea, Oxford University Press, 1955, revised edition published as *The Dead Sea Scrolls: 1947-1969,* 1969.
Red, Black, Blond, and Olive: Studies in Four Civilizations; Zuni, Haiti, Soviet Russia, Israel, Oxford University Press, 1956.

A Piece of My Mind: Reflections at Sixty, Farrar, Straus, 1957.
The American Earthquake: A Documentary of the Twenties and Thirties, Doubleday, 1958.
Apologies to the Iroquois, Farrar, Straus, 1960, revised edition, Syracuse University Press, 1992.
(Contributor) Donald Alfred Stauffer, editor, *The Intent of the Critic,* Peter Smith, 1963.
The Cold War and the Income Tax: A Protest, Farrar, Straus, 1963.
O Canada: An American's Notes on Canadian Culture, Farrar, Straus, 1965.
A Prelude: Landscapes, Characters, and Conversations from the Earlier Years of My Life, Farrar, Straus, 1967.
Galahad [and] *I Thought of Daisy* (novels), Farrar, Straus, 1967.
(With Marianne Moore) *Homage to Henry James,* Appel, 1971.
Upstate: Records and Recollections of Northern New York, Farrar, Straus, 1971.
The Twenties: From Notebooks and Diaries of the Period, edited by Leon Edel, Farrar, Straus, 1975.
Letters on Literature and Politics, 1912-1972, edited by wife, Elena Wilson, Farrar, Straus, 1977.
The Nabokov-Wilson Letters: Correspondence between Vladimir Nabokov and Edmund Wilson, 1940-1971, edited by Simon Karlinsky, Harper, 1979.
The Thirties: From Notebooks and Diaries of the Period, edited by Edel, Farrar, Straus, 1980.
The Forties: From Notebooks and Diaries of the Period, edited by Edel, Farrar, Straus, 1983.
The Portable Edmund Wilson, edited by Lewis M. Dabney, Viking, 1983.
The Fifties: From Notebooks and Diaries of the Period, edited by Edel, Farrar, Straus, 1986.
The Sixties: The Last Journal, 1960-1972, edited by Lewis M. Dabney, Farrar, Straus, 1993.
From the Uncollected Edmund Wilson, edited by Janet Groth and David Castronovo, Ohio University Press, 1995.

LITERARY CRITICISM

Axel's Castle: A Study in the Imaginative Literature of 1870-1930, Scribner, 1931, with an introduction by Hugh Kenner, Modern Library (New York), 1996.
The Triple Thinkers: Ten Essays on Literature, Harcourt, 1938, revised edition published as *The Triple Thinkers: Twelve Essays on Literary Subjects,* Oxford University Press, 1948, published as *The Triple Thinkers & The Wound and the Bow: A Combined Volume,* Northeastern University Press, 1984.
The Boys in the Back Room: Notes on California Novelists, Colt Press, 1941.
The Wound and the Bow: Seven Studies in Literature, Houghton, 1941, revised edition, Oxford University Press, 1965.
Classics and Commercials: A Literary Chronicle of the Forties, Farrar, Straus, 1950.
The Shores of Light: A Literary Chronicle of the Twenties and Thirties, Farrar, Straus, 1952.
Patriotic Gore: Studies in the Literature of the American Civil War, Oxford University Press, 1962.
The Bit between My Teeth: A Literary Chronicle of 1950-1965, Farrar, Straus, 1965.
A Window on Russia for the Use of Foreign Readers, Farrar, Straus, 1972.
The Devils and Canon Barham: Ten Essays on Poets, Novelists, and Monsters, Farrar, Straus, 1973.

POETRY

(With John Peale Bishop) *The Undertaker's Garland,* Knopf, 1922.
Poets, Farewell! Scribner, 1929.
Note-Books of Night, Colt Press, 1942.
Night Thoughts, Farrar, Straus, 1961.

PLAYS

The Crime in the Whistler Room (also see below), produced in New York City, 1924.
Discordant Encounters: Plays and Dialogues, Boni, 1926.
This Room and This Gin and These Sandwiches: Three Plays (contains *The Crime in the Whistler Room, Beppo and Beth,* and *A Winter in Beech Street*), New Republic, 1937.
The Little Blue Light (produced in Cambridge, MA, 1950), Farrar, Straus, 1950.
Five Plays: Cyprian's Prayer, The Crime in the Whistler Room, This Room and This Gin and These Sandwiches, Beppo and Beth, The Little Blue Light, Farrar, Straus, 1954.
The Duke of Palermo and Other Plays, with an Open Letter to Mike Nichols (includes *The Duke of Palermo, Dr. McGrath,* and *Osbert's Career; or, The Poet's Progress*), Farrar, Straus, 1969.

Also author of *The Evil Eye* (lyrics by F. Scott Fitzgerald, music by P. B. Dickey and F. Warburton Guilbert), produced in 1915.

EDITOR

F. Scott Fitzgerald, *The Last Tycoon: An Unfinished Novel by F. Scott Fitzgerald, Together with The Great Gatsby and Selected Stories,* Scribner, 1941.
The Shock of Recognition: The Development of Literature in the United States Recorded by the Men Who Made It, Doubleday, 1943, revised edition, Farrar, Straus, 1955.
Fitzgerald, *The Crack-Up: With Other Uncollected Pieces, Note-Books, and Unpublished Letters,* New Directions, 1945, reissued, 1993.
John Peale Bishop, *The Collected Essays of John Peale Bishop,* Scribner, 1948.
Anton Chekhov, *Peasants and Other Stories,* Doubleday, 1956.
(With Malcolm Cowley) Fitzgerald, *Three Novels* (contains *The Great Gatsby, Tender Is the Night,* and *The Last Tycoon*), Scribner, 1970.

OTHER

The Edmund Wilson Reader, edited by Lewis M. Dabney, Da Capo Press (New York), 1997.

Wilson's papers are collected at the Beinecke Rare Book and Manuscript Library, Yale University.

SIDELIGHTS: As one of the nation's foremost literary critics, Edmund Wilson enjoyed a high position in American letters. L. E. Sissman called him "the greatest of our critics of this century, and among the three or four greatest—along with T. S. Eliot, Wallace Stevens, and F. Scott Fitzgerald—of our literary men." Wilson, according to T. S. Matthews, was "the foremost American man of letters of the twentieth century." Norman Podhoretz judged Wilson as "one of the greatest men of letters this country has ever produced."

Wilson's influence upon American literature was substantial. Warner Berthoff said that "for nearly every important development in contemporary writing Edmund Wilson was in some way a spokesman—an arbiter of taste, a supplier of perspective, at the least (to adapt his own phrase for Hemingway) a gauge of intellectual morale." Leonard Kriegel described Wilson's writing as "one of the standards of sanity in this culture." Despite misgivings about some of Wilson's strongly held opinions, Berthoff believed that "all who have to do with literature have played parasite to his writings, his discoveries and revaluations, and are too much in his debt to allow much complaining. He has been one of his time's indispensable teachers and transmitters of important news."

One of Wilson's most important contributions was his role in giving an international perspective to American literature. Speaking of this, Sissman praised Wilson for his "destruction of the literary isolationism of this continent." "No man," Anthony Burgess wrote, "has had a profounder influence on the capacity of a couple of generations (including my own) to form its own judgements on a very large and important sector of European literature." A *Times Literary Supplement* reviewer cited Wilson's "incontestably important task" as "explaining the world to America and explaining America to itself."

Axel's Castle, Wilson's first book of literary criticism, established his reputation as a critic and still stands as one of his most important works. Sherman Paul explained that the book, a study of the Symbolist literary movement, "established the writers of the *avant garde* in the consciousness of the general reader: not only did it place them in a significant historical development, it taught the uninitiated how to read them." Pointing out the book's lasting value, Kriegel wrote that "the book remains one of the truly seminal works of literary criticism published in our century."

Wilson's strongly held opinions were expressed in a manner that drew respect from even those readers who did not agree with him. When reading Wilson, Burgess claimed, one was "enlightened with conclusions that, so well are they stated and so logically arrived at, appear inevitable and hence obvious." George H. Douglas believed that "even when we find [Wilson's] ideas eccentric, perverse, and opinionated, as at times all of his readers must, we cannot but admire his ability to think through all of his problems for himself, his ceaseless endeavor to understand the world that confronts him and bring some order to it." Alfred Kazin wrote that Wilson "fascinates even when he is wrong." Joseph Epstein complained that "the stamp of Wilson's personality was on every sentence he wrote, yet nothing he wrote could by any stretch of the imagination be called 'personable.'" Nevertheless, he admired Wilson as "a living embodiment of the belief in literature . . . as a guide to life, and a weapon . . . with which to bring some sort of order to an otherwise possibly quite senseless world."

Wilson's concern with literary values was reflected in his concern for political values as well. "He always retained his strong faith in our American democratic traditions," Douglas wrote, "even though he found the original dream of the founding fathers foundering in a sea of commercial ethics and impersonal, insensate government." After a brief interest in socialism, culminating in *To the Finland Station,* a study of the subject, Wilson grew disillusioned with politics. His writings after the Second World War ignored the contemporary scene. "Having lived through two World Wars in which he did not believe," Robert Emmet Long wrote, "[Wilson could] no longer believe in the power of rationality to create a humane and meaningful world." Despite his disillusionment with politics, Wilson protested the Cold War of the 1950s by not paying his income taxes for nine years on the grounds that the money was used to purchase nuclear and bacteriological weapons.

Wilson's substantive contribution has continued even after his death, in the form of the many volumes of his writings that have been published in the ensuing decades. Among these are Wilson's journals from the 1920s to 1960s. According to Lewis M. Dabney, editor of *The Sixties: The Last Journal, 1960-1972,* the final volume in the series, "the strength of Wilson's criticism and histories is his mastery of concrete details, and the journals illustrate his ability to catch the essence of a time and situation."

Carol Brightman commented on the unaffected style of Wilson's journals. His wry and earthy candor when writing on issues ranging from sex to incontinence in old age are undeniably shocking. "It's time for a closer look" at Wilson and his works, noted Brightman in a 1994 *Nation* review of *The Sixties.* "This [is] flat uninflected reporting of the facts of life at the end of the road. Old age is stripped of the glossy patina of New Beginnings it has acquired in recent years, with the result that its burdens are actually lightened, often by the humor Wilson invariably finds in the worst circumstances." "The primary impression left by any of these volumes covering the decades," Julian Symons argued in the *Times Literary Supplement,* "is of admiration for the power of Wilson's mind, and astonishment at the variety of his interests and the voracious curiosity with which he informs himself about them."

Among the other notable posthumous publications of Wilson's writings, in the opinion of David Castronovo, is *Letters on Literature and Politics 1912-1972.* In an essay for the *Dictionary of Literary Biography,* Castronovo wrote that "this collection shows the range of Wilson's informal interests as well as a partial record of his varied and often hectic life. Many of the letters also reveal him in the role of friend and encourager—a guider and nurturer of talent and relentless battler with circumstances, both personal and social, that keep writers from working."

The Portable Edmund Wilson, also edited by Lewis Dabney, gathered work representative of Wilson's remarkable career. Of its selections, Saul Goodwin proposed in *National Review* "that Wilson, himself a pretty fair anthologist, would have been satisfied with the results." R. W. B. Lewis, disappointed by the absence of representative fiction and poetry in the collection, nevertheless remarked in the *New York Times Book Review* that the anthology does reveal Wilson in the role of "critic of history." "To suggest the extraordinary reach of the man," Lewis wrote, "one need only list the most powerful and comprehensive essays in [*The Portable Edmund Wilson,*] those on Marx and Engels, Dickens, the Supreme Court's Oliver Wendell Holmes, and the Philoctetes myth." Christopher Hawtree asserted in *Spectator:* "A hod or a trolley would be necessary for the amount of Edmund Wilson's writing one would wish to be in print." With the publication of *From the Uncollected Edmund Wilson* in 1995, however, some critics admitted that there really *do* exist some writings by Wilson that should remain "uncollected."

Speaking of Wilson's standing in literature today, Castronovo commented: "Wilson's name still stands for tireless dedication to literature, relentless pursuit of libertarian and progressive ideas, and yearning to transcend the limits of class, critical category, and fashion. His reputation, as well as threats to it, rests on his identity as a professor without a university, a critic without a field, a historian without a period, a thinker without a school."

BIOGRAPHICAL/CRITICAL SOURCES:

BOOKS

Berthoff, Warner, *Fiction and Events: Essays in Criticism and Literary History,* Dutton, 1971.
Burgess, Anthony, *Urgent Copy: Literary Studies,* Norton, 1968.
Castronovo, David, *Edmund Wilson,* Frederick Ungar, 1984.
Castronovo, David, *Edmund Wilson Revisited,* Twayne, 1998.
Contemporary Literary Criticism, Gale (Detroit), Volume 1, 1973; Volume 2, 1974; Volume 3, 1975; Volume 8, 1978; Volume 24, 1983.
Costa, Richard Hauer, *Edmund Wilson: Our Neighbor from Talcottville,* Syracuse University Press, 1980.
Dabney, Lewis M., *Edmund Wilson: Centennial Reflections,* Princeton University Press, 1997.
Dictionary of Literary Biography, Volume 63: *Modern American Critics, 1920-1955,* Gale, 1988.
Douglas, George, *Edmund Wilson's America,* University of Kentucky Press, 1983.
Frank, Charles P., *Edmund Wilson,* Twayne, 1970.
Kazin, Alfred, *On Native Grounds,* Reynal, 1942.
Kazin, Alfred, *The Inmost Leaf: A Selection of Essays,* Harcourt, 1955.
Kazin, Alfred, *Contemporaries,* Little, Brown, 1962.
Kriegel, Leonard, *Edmund Wilson,* Southern Illinois Press, 1971.
Meyers, Jeffrey, *Edmund Wilson: A Biography,* Houghton Mifflin, 1995.
Paul, Sherman, *Edmund Wilson: A Study of Literary Vocation in Our Time,* University of Illinois Press, 1965.
Podhoretz, Norman, *Doings and Undoings,* Farrar, Straus, 1964.
Stoll, Elmer Edgar, *From Shakespeare to Joyce: Authors and Critics, Literature and Life,* Doubleday, 1944.
Trilling, Diana, *Reviewing the Forties,* Harcourt, 1978, pp. 150-54.
Wain, John, editor, *Edmund Wilson: The Man and His Work,* New York University Press, 1978.

PERIODICALS

America, June 24, 1972; December 13, 1980, p. 393; June 8, 1987, p. 468.
American Scholar, summer, 1984, p. 422; spring, 1988, p. 263; summer, 1994, p. 379.
Chicago Tribune Book World, August 21, 1986, p. 4.
Christian Science Monitor, April 26, 1962; September 8, 1980, p. 16; August 31, 1983, p. 11; May 6, 1985, p. 32.
Commentary, August, 1962; August, 1980, p. 38.
Detroit News, July 24, 1983.
Economist, December 6, 1980, p. 103.
Esquire, July, 1963; May, 1972.
Hudson Review, spring, 1981, p. 117.
Library Journal, September 1, 1995, p. 178.
Los Angeles Times Book Review, May 1, 1983, p. 1; September 21, 1986, p. 3.
Modern Fiction Studies, winter, 1981, p. 732; winter, 1985, p. 751.
Modern Language Review, January, 1980, p. 180.
Nation, October 16, 1948; December 8, 1956; June 26, 1972; August 7, 1972; October 2, 1972; October 4, 1980, p. 317; January 17, 1994, p. 62.
National Review, September 12, 1975; July 13, 1984, p. 53.
New Statesman, April 26, 1958; May 21, 1960; June 22, 1962; February 21, 1986, p. 27; April 18, 1986, p. 27.
Newsweek, March 11, 1946; November 12, 1956; August 30, 1971; August 18, 1980, p. 80.

New Yorker, July 5, 1958; June 24, 1972; January 5, 1987, p. 83.

New York Review of Books, October 7, 1971; September 25, 1980, p. 4; November 10, 1983, p. 22; October 9, 1986, p. 7; June 8, 1995, p. 4.

New York Times, June 13, 1972; October 6, 1977; August 18, 1980; April 13, 1983; August 26, 1986.

New York Times Book Review, February 9, 1958; March 20, 1960; December 10, 1961; July 2, 1972; July 29, 1973; June 5, 1975; June 8, 1980, p. 11; August 31, 1980, p. 1; May 22, 1983, p. 1; May 6, 1984, p. 42; November 18, 1984, p. 54; August 31, 1986, p. 3; November 29, 1987, p. 34; December 31, 1995, p. 17.

Progressive, August, 1973; December, 1977; January, 1984, p. 36; February, 1987, p. 45.

Publishers Weekly, July 10, 1995, p. 17.

Sewanee Review, April, 1948; January, 1986, p. 160.

Spectator, April 25, 1958; May 27, 1960; November 17, 1973; June 25, 1983, p. 26; October 4, 1986, p. 26; March 16, 1996, p. 34.

Time, November 13, 1939; May 4, 1962; September 13, 1971; May 2, 1983, p. 73; September 8, 1986, p. 77.

Times Literary Supplement, April 25, 1958; June 3, 1960; May 19, 1972; November 7, 1980, p. 1249; December 26, 1986, p. 1442; October 27, 1995, p. 4.

Tribune Books (Chicago), September 21, 1986, p. 4.

Wall Street Journal, September 16, 1971; October 16, 1986, p. 30.

Washington Post Book World, March 9, 1980, p. 10; August 24, 1980, p. 5; May 2, 1982, p. 12; April 17, 1983, p. 3; September 14, 1986, p. 5; September 29, 1991, p. 12.

World Literature Today, summer, 1981, p. 479; winter, 1984, p. 107; spring, 1987, p. 293; winter, 1994, p. 138.

*   *   *

WILSON, Edward O(sborne, Jr.) 1929-

PERSONAL: Born June 10, 1929, in Birmingham, AL; son of Edward O., Sr. (an accountant) and Inez (Freeman) Wilson; married Irene Kelley, October 30, 1955; children: Catherine Irene. *Education:* University of Alabama, B.S., 1949, M.S., 1950; Harvard University, Ph.D., 1955.

ADDRESSES: Home—9 Foster Rd., Lexington, MA 02173-5505. *Office*—Museum of Comparative Zoology, Harvard University, Cambridge, MA 02138.

CAREER: Harvard University, Cambridge, MA, assistant professor of biology, 1956-58, associate professor of zoology, 1958-64, professor of zoology, 1964-76, Frank B. Baird Jr. Professor of Science, 1976-94, Pellegrino Professor, 1994–, Curator of Entomology at Museum of Comparative Zoology, 1972–; writer. Member of selection committee, J. S. Guggenheim Foundation. Trustee of Marine Biological Laboratory (Woods Hole). Member of board of directors, World Wildlife Fund, 1983-94, Organization for Tropical Studies, 1984–, New York Botanical Gardens, 1991–, American Museum of Natural History, 1992–, American Academy of Liberal Education, 1993–, Shubert Prize, Germany, 1996, Washburn Award, 1996, Hutchinson medal, Garden Club of America, 1997, and Conservation International, 1997.

MEMBER: World Wildlife Fund (member of advisory council, 1977-), Deutsche Akademie Naturforsch (fellow), Society for the Study of Evolution, British Ecological Society (honorary life member), Royal Society (London), Finnish Academy of Science and Letters, Russian Academy of Natural Science, Royal Society of Science (Uppsala), American Philosophical Society (fellow), American Genetics Association (honorary life member), National Academy of Sciences, American Academy of Arts and Sciences (fellow), Entomological Society of America (honorary life member), Zoological Society of London (honorary life member), Netherlands Society of Entomology (honorary life member), American Humanist Society, Academy of Humanism (honorary life member).

AWARDS, HONORS: Cleveland Award, American Association for the Advancement of Science, 1969; Mercer Award, Ecological Society of America, 1971; Founders Memorial Award, Entomological Society of America, 1972; Distinguished Service Award, American Institute of Biological Sciences, 1976; National Medal of Science, 1977; Leidy Medal, Academy of Natural Sciences, 1979; Pulitzer Prize in general nonfiction, 1979, for *On Human Nature,* and 1990 (with Bert Holldobler), for *The Ants;* Sesquicentennial Medal, University of Alabama, 1981; Distinguished Humanist Award, American Humanist Association, 1982; Tyler Ecology Prize, 1984; Richard M. Weaver Award for Scholarly Letters, Ingersoll Foundation, 1989; Crafoord Prize, Royal Swedish Academy, 1990; Prix d'Institute de la Vie (Paris), 1990; Revelle Medal, 1990; Gold Medal, Worldwide Fund for Nature, 1990; National Wildlife Association Award and Sir Peter Kent Conservation Prize, both 1991, both for *The Diversity of Life;* National Wildlife Federation Achievement award, 1992; Shaw Medal, Missouri Botanical Garden, 1993; International Prize in biology, Japanese government, 1993; Audubon Medal, Audubon Society, 1995; John Hay Award, Orion Society, 1995; *Los Angeles Times* Book Prize for science and technology, 1995, for *Naturalist;* recipient of numerous honorary degrees.

WRITINGS:

(With R. H. MacArthur) *The Theory of Island Biogeography,* Princeton University Press (Princeton, NJ), 1967.

The Insect Societies, Belknap Press (Cambridge, MA), 1971.

(With W. H. Bossert) *A Primer of Population Biology,* Sinauer Associates, 1971.

(Coauthor) *Life on Earth,* Sinauer Associates, 1973.

(Editor) *Ecology, Evolution and Population Biology: Readings from Scientific American,* W. H. Freeman (San Francisco), 1974.

Sociobiology: The New Synthesis, Belknap Press, 1975.

(Author of introduction with Thomas Eisner) *The Insects: Readings from Scientific American,* Freeman, 1977.

(With George F. Oster) *Caste and Ecology in Social Insects,* Princeton University Press, 1978.

On Human Nature, Harvard University Press (Cambridge, MA), 1978.

(With Charles J. Lumsden) *Genes, Mind, and Culture: The Coevolutionary Process,* Harvard University Press, 1981.

(With Lumsden) *Promethean Fire: Reflections on the Origin of the Mind,* Harvard University Press, 1983.

Biophilia: The Human Bond to Other Species, Harvard University Press, 1984.

(Editor) *Biodiversity,* National Academy Press (Washington, DC), 1988.

(With Bert Holldobler) *The Ants,* Belknap Press, 1990.

Success and Dominance in Ecosystems: The Case of the Social Insects, Ecology Institute (Luhe, Germany), 1990.

The Diversity of Life, Belknap Press, 1992.

(Editor, with Stephen R. Kellert) *The Biophilia Hypothesis,* Island Press (Washington, DC), 1993.

(With Holldobler) *Journey to the Ants: A Story of Scientific Exploration,* Belknap Press, 1994.
Naturalist (autobiography), Island Press, 1994, illustrated by Laura Simonds Southworth, Warner Books (New York City), 1995.
In Search of Nature, Island Press, 1996.
(Editor with others) *Biodiversity II: Understanding and Protecting Our Biological Resources,* Joseph Henry (Washington, DC), 1997.
Consilience, Knopf (New York City), 1998.

Contributor of over three hundred articles to scientific and popular journals. Coeditor, *Theoretical Population Biology,* 1971-74, *Behavioral Ecology and Sociobiology,* 1975–, and *Psyche.*

MEDIA ADAPTATIONS: The Ants was adapted as the model for *SimAnt,* a computer game created by Maxis Company, 1991.

SIDELIGHTS: Prior to 1975, Edward O. Wilson was primarily known as one of America's foremost experts on the insect world, with his specialty being the study of ants and their social behavior. As a noted professor of entomology at Harvard University, he produced several books on insect culture and physiology before becoming, as Peter Gwynne describes in *Newsweek,* "one of the most visible and articulate spokesmen for sociobiology, the controversial scientific discipline whose purpose is to examine the biological bases of behavior." The author of two Pulitzer Prize-winning works of nonfiction and the recipient of the National Medal of Science, Wilson has become, in the words of *Los Angeles Times Book Review* critic Jonathan Weiner, "one of the preeminent evolutionary biologists of our time." In 1996 *Time* magazine named him one of the twenty-five most influential contemporary Americans, and John Simmons, in *The Scientific 100,* ranked him among the one hundred most influential scientists of all time.

Sociobiology: The New Synthesis, which Wilson published in 1975, is considered groundbreaking. The first detailed study of the emerging science of sociobiology, it catapulted its author to both fame and controversy in the field of human behavior. The most debated tenet of sociobiology is that all human behavior is genetically based, or, as Wilson once put it, that "genes hold culture on a leash." A *Time* writer elaborates upon the theory: "All forms of life exist solely to serve the purposes of DNA, the coded master molecule that determines the nature of all organisms and is the stuff of genes." Sociobiologists, the journalist continues, "argue that without consideration of biology, the study of human culture makes no sense." This position has continued to arouse heated debate in both scientific and cultural communities since its inception. While some of its critics have merely dismissed it as "so-so biology," others have gone as far as labeling sociobiology "dangerously racist," according to *Time,* because "the new science would give comfort to the supporters of psychologist Arthur Jensen, a leading proponent of another controversial theory that racial differences in IQs have a genetic basis." Still others have accused Wilson and other sociobiologists of advocating the idea of eugenics, the so-called "purifying" of races by genetic control of breeding.

Sociobiology's explanation of altruism is equally controversial: *Time* notes that some twenty years prior to the science's formal inception, British biologist J. B. S. Haldane "anticipated the gene-based view of sociobiology when, tongue in cheek, he announced that he would lay down his life for two brothers or eight cousins. His reasoning: the survival of two full siblings (each with about half of his genes identical to Haldane's) or the group of cousins

(each with about one-eighth of his genes the same as Haldane's) made the decision genetically acceptable." "According to sociobiologists," *Time* continues, "evolution produces organisms that automatically follow this mathematical logic, as if they were computers, totting up the genetic costs or benefits of helping out relatives who bear many of the same genes." This theory, which seems to undermine the concepts of culture and conscience, angers some sociologists. There is even a sociobiological exegesis for religion, adding further fuel to the controversy.

Wilson describes *On Human Nature,* which he published in 1978, as "not a work *of* science," but rather "a work *about* science, and about how far the natural sciences can penetrate into human behavior before they will be transformed into something new." *On Human Nature* "takes up in a philosophical way where *Sociobiology* left off," observes William McPherson in a *Washington Post Book World* review. "It is a vastly ambitious attempt to bring the 'two cultures' of science and the humanities together." As with the earlier book, some of Wilson's hypotheses in *On Human Nature* met with skepticism from the scientific community. For instance, a passage from the work reveals Wilson's prediction that a "durable foundation for peace" might be found by creating "a confusion of cross-finding loyalties," according to the *New York Times Book Review,* "to prevent the formation of the kinds of group loyalties that give rise to aggressive behavior," as reviewer Colin Beer, a professor of psychology, describes it. But Beer responds that "it is doubtful whether this solution, in itself, would be sufficient to make human aggression, in all its forms, a thing of the past. But the argument that [the author] uses here is typical of his tactics throughout most of the book: it is quietly persuasive rather than belligerently coercive, and it appeals to plausible possibility rather than logical necessity. At least to readers of good will, most of the conclusions will seem reasonable interpretations of the evidence—so much so that many may be left wondering what all the fuss has been about."

Wilson's "most grandiose and least appealing scheme is to replace conventional religion with a mythology based on scientific materialism and incorporating a more objectively chosen value system," notes Nicholas Wade in *New Republic.* "Gee-whiz wonders from the scientific textbooks—evolution, the Big Bang and so forth—would replace religious awe and the sense of the sacred. This false touch makes the reader wonder if Wilson here hasn't slipped too far afield." However, Wade concludes that *On Human Nature* "is a splendid departure from the dead-hand canons of the scientific 'literature.' Clarity, precision and boldness distinguish Wilson's attempt to complete the Darwinian revolution. He is dealing with matters that lie mostly beyond the reach of present scientific methods, and perhaps for that reason has chosen to present his ideas in a way that makes them accessible to the public at large as well as to his scientific peers." And despite the controversy surrounding its subject matter, *On Human Nature* was awarded the 1979 Pulitzer Prize in general nonfiction, an honor that its author told the *Washington Post's* Megan Rosenfeld was "an affirmation that this is an important new area of thought. It's not necessarily a certification that I'm right, but an affirmation that this is an important thing we should be talking about."

In 1981 Wilson and theoretical physicist Charles J. Lumsden collaborated on *Genes, Mind, and Culture: The Coevolutionary Process.* Extending the theory of sociobiology, the two scientists described what they labeled the "gene-culture coevolution," a process by which human genetic makeup "helps guide and create culture, while culture in turn operates directly on the genes," according to *Harper's* reviewers James L. Gould and Carol Grant

Gould. Two years later Wilson and Lumsden produced *Promethean Fire: Reflections on the Origin of the Mind,* a layperson's book on the subject.

One example of the authors' gene-culture theory can be seen in their detailed study of the incest taboo included in *Promethean Fire.* Historically considered a cultural phenomenon, the incest taboo, Wilson and Lumsden propose, has actually been programmed genetically into humans as a reaction against the mentally and physically deformed offspring that incestuous unions can produce. Thus, the cultural taboo of familial sexual relations is an outgrowth of the genetic rule. "The authors also point out how easily (and in some cases even spontaneously) certain deep, long-lasting phobias appear [to such ancient terrors as snakes, spiders, and thunderstorms, for instance], while determined attempts on the part of parents to instill fear of the real threats of modern-day life (electrical outlets, knives, and busy streets) rarely succeed, at least at the phobia level," note the *Harper's* critics. "Surely this argues for a type of genetic programming that could have a role in culture."

In 1992's *The Diversity of Life* Wilson explores the meaning of an offshoot of ecology known as *biodiversity*—the underlying relationships existing between all life forms that result in the creation and perpetuation of healthy virgin ecosystems. Praising Wilson for his "elegant and ingratiating literary style," *Washington Post Book World* critic T. H. Watkins hails *The Diversity of Life* as "a book that will enlighten the uninformed, correct the misinformed and serve as a beacon of lucidity in the wilderness." Beginning with the discussion of what he terms the "fundamental unit" species—or, in reference to its unique DNA code, a "living genetic library"—Wilson goes on to discuss the elaborate system of checks and balances that functions within the processes of evolution, adaptation, colonization, reproduction, migration, and transmogrification. Cautioning readers as to the devastating ecological consequences of humankind's continued destruction of such sensitive ecosystems, Wilson devotes the second section of his book to conservation: humans' moral dilemma as it relates to the stewardship of life on earth. "If there is danger in the human trajectory," he warns, "it is not so much in the survival of our own species as in the fulfillment of the ultimate irony of organic evolution: that in the instant of achieving self-understanding through the mind of man, life has doomed its most beautiful creations. And thus humanity closes its door on its past."

Wilson considers 1990's *The Ants* to be his *magnum opus,* not only because the book itself weighed seven and a half pounds, but because the work brings together for the first time all the knowledge and widely scattered information now known about ants. Working with fellow myrmecologist and Harvard faculty member Bert Holldobler, Wilson organizes a monumental amount of information about everything from ant evolution and history to modern ant communication and social structures. *Journey to the Ants: A Story of Scientific Exploration,* published four years later, once again united Wilson and Holldobler. A layperson's introduction to the same amazing variation existing within the ant kingdom, *Journey* also provides a revealing look at the motivations of those who have devoted their lives to the study of these surprisingly social creatures.

Wilson's attraction to biology, evolution, and ecology grew from his fascination, as a young boy, with the natural wonders surrounding the many places were he and his family lived: from the rural Alabama countryside to Washington, DC, where Wilson discovered the treasures contained in both the National Zoo and

the Smithsonian Institution. The scientist's *biophilia*—what he describes as "the innate tendency to focus on life and lifelike processes"—is the subject of several books, including *Biophilia: The Human Bond to Other Species* and *Naturalist.*

"No one can doubt [that Wilson] is powerfully drawn to other creatures, but he wants to make some larger points: human attraction to other living things is innate, and this natural affinity should serve as the philosophical basis for a new conservation ethic," suggests *New York Times Book Review* critic Sarah Boxer in her review of *Biophilia.* While Wilson's "attempt to promote conservation is noble and appealing," Boxer contends that he "loses the thread of his main argument" when he "flits from a reverie about time scales to a reminiscence about his work in biogeography."

"What happened, what we *think* happened in distant memory, is built around a small collection of dominating images," Wilson wrote in *Naturalist,* a personal memoir of his own evolution from young boy to biologist. From an unstable childhood as the son of an alcoholic father, the biologist eventually attended military school, channelling his developing intellect, self-discipline, reverence for single-mindedness of purpose, and interest in nature into a passion for the study of insects. "Wilson emerges not only as a gifted scientist, but also as a likable, passionate, eloquent person," notes Jared Diamond, reviewing *Naturalist* in the *New York Review of Books.* William Howarth has equal praise for the work in the *Washington Post Book World:* "What distinguishes Wilson's story is its handsome prose, honed by years of practice into a concise and sly discourse. Among literary scientists, no one since Rachel Carson has more effectively joined humble detail to a grand vision of life processes and structures." Unlike Wilson's previous works, *Naturalist* is illuminating on a personal as well as an instructional level. "It is still possible to realize the romantic ideal of exploration that many of us harbor in childhood, and then abandon as impractical," Diamond adds. "By explaining how Wilson realized that ideal, his book helps us to understand one of the brighter trajectories in twentieth-century intellectual life."

In Search of Nature incorporates into one volume a dozen writings which Wilson published between 1975 and 1993. These articles and book chapters address three seminal themes of Wilson's work: the genetic basis of human behavior, the deep-rooted interrelation of animal nature and human nature, and the relevance of maintaining biodiversity in relation to human welfare. *In Search of Nature* is "nature writing at its best," claims Lynne C. Badger in *Library Journal,* adding that Wilson's writing is "exquisite, crystalline, precise and eminently readable." In the *Los Angeles Times Book Review,* Edward Hoagland avers that Wilson "is a writer of enthralling importance for our place in time" because works like *In Search of Nature* advocate reverence for all forms of life, no matter how simple. To illustrate, he quotes Wilson's answer to people who ask him what to do about ants in the kitchen: "Watch where you step. Be careful of little lives. . . . [Get] a magnifying glass and you will be as near as any person may ever come to seeing social life as it may evolve on another planet."

In *Consilience,* Wilson advocates with urgency the major project for which classical philosophy was created: a unified scientific theory which is internally consistent for every object and phenomenon in the cosmos and affirms the harmony and logic of creation. In *Booklist,* Ray Olson calls *Consilience* "a book that is truly a magnum opus." He also avers that Wilson conveniently reinterprets the Enlightenment, a period in which Wilson's concept of consilience was passionately sought, arguing that it would be remembered in a more sympathetic light were it not for the Reign of Terror amid the French Revolution. Nonetheless Olson states, "As human population burgeons and its environment deteriorates, continued human success depends on making the wise choices that sound knowledge makes possible. Wilson dazzlingly reaffirms the cogency and the power of scientific materialism."

BIOGRAPHICAL/CRITICAL SOURCES:

BOOKS

Simmons, John, *The Scientific 100: A Ranking of the Most Influential Scientists, Past and Present,* Citadel Press, 1996.
Something about the Author Autobiography Series, Volume 16, Gale (Detroit), 1985.
Wright, Robert, *Three Scientists and Their Gods: Looking for Meaning in an Age of Information,* Times Books, 1988.

PERIODICALS

Booklist, February 1, 1998.
Boston Globe, April 11, 1991, p. 29; September 15, 1992, p. 1; October 9, 1994; November 6, 1994, p. B20.
Chicago Tribune Book World, November 5, 1978; March 16, 1990.
Christian Science Monitor, May 29, 1990, p. 13; October 22, 1992, p. 11; December 5, 1994, p. 13.
Commentary, October, 1983.
Harper's, June, 1983.
Humanist, July/August, 1981; September/October, 1982.
Library Journal, September 1, 1996, p. 206.
London Review of Books, April 22, 1993, p. 20; July 20, 1995, pp. 26-27.
Los Angeles Times, August 12, 1988, p. V4; October 16, 1994, p. E2; December 29, 1996.
Los Angeles Times Book Review, December 17, 1984; September 5, 1993, p. 7; October 23, 1994, p. 4; December 10, 1995.
New Republic, November 11, 1983.
Newsweek, October 16, 1978.
New York Review of Books, August 7, 1975; October 12, 1978; November 5, 1992, pp. 3-6; January 12, 1995, pp. 16-19.
New York Times, December 18, 1978; September 21, 1989; August 20, 1991, p. C1; September 22, 1992, p. C4; October 1, 1992, p. C17.
New York Times Book Review, July 27, 1975; October 18, 1981; November 26, 1981; April 24, 1983; October 7, 1984; July 29, 1990, p. 6; October 4, 1992, p. 1, October 16, 1994, pp. 15-17; April 26, 1998, p. 11.
New York Times Magazine, May 30, 1993, p. 24.
Omni, February, 1979.
Time, August 1, 1977; June 17, 1996.
Times Literary Supplement, August 13, 1993, pp. 5-6.
Tribune Books (Chicago), November 25, 1992, p. 3; December 18, 1994, p. 6.
Washington Post, May 4, 1979; April 10, 1991, p. B1.
Washington Post Book World, October 8, 1978; October 15, 1978; March 25, 1990, p. 4; September 27, 1992, pp. 1, 13; December 12, 1993, p. 8; October 16, 1994, p. 4.

WILSON, John (Anthony) Burgess 1917-1993
(Anthony Burgess, Joseph Kell)

PERSONAL: Born February 25, 1917, in Manchester, England; died of cancer, November 25, 1993, in London, England; son of Joseph and Elizabeth (Burgess) Wilson; married Llewela (Lynn) Isherwood Jones, January 23, 1942 (died, 1968); married Lilliana Macellari (a translator), 1968; children: (second marriage) Andreas. *Education:* Attended Bishop Bilsborrow School, Xaverian College; Manchester University, B.A. (honors), 1940.

CAREER: Writer. Lecturer, Central Advisory Council for Adult Education in the Forces, 1946-48; lecturer in phonetics, Ministry of Education, 1948-50; Banbury Grammar School, Oxfordshire, England, master, 1950-54; Colonial Service, education officer in Malaya and Brunei, 1954-59. Visiting professor, Columbia University, 1970-71, and City University of New York, 1972-73. Visiting fellow, Princeton University, 1970-71. Literary adviser, Guthrie Theater, 1972-93. Composer. *Military service:* British Army, Education Corps, 1940-46; became sergeant-major.

MEMBER: Royal Society of Literature (fellow).

AWARDS, HONORS: Prix du Meilleur Livre Etranger, 1981, for *Earthly Powers.* Honorary degrees from Manchester University and Birmingham University.

WRITINGS:

FICTION; UNDER PSEUDONYM ANTHONY BURGESS, EXCEPT AS INDICATED

The Right to an Answer, Norton, 1960.
The Doctor Is Sick, Heinemann, 1960, Norton, 1966.
The Worm and the Ring, Heinemann, 1961, revised edition, 1970.
Devil of a State, Heinemann, 1961, Norton, 1962.
(Under pseudonym Joseph Kell) *One Hand Clapping,* P. Davies, 1961, published under pseudonym Anthony Burgess, Knopf, 1972.
A Clockwork Orange (also see below), Heinemann, 1962, published in the United States with last chapter omitted, Norton, 1963.
The Wanting Seed, Heinemann, 1962, Norton, 1963.
Honey for the Bears (also see below), Heinemann, 1963, Norton, 1964.
Nothing Like the Sun: A Story of Shakespeare's Love Life, Norton, 1964.
The Eve of Saint Venus, Sidgwick & Jackson, 1964, Norton, 1970.
A Vision of Battlements, Sidgwick & Jackson, 1965, Norton, 1966.
A Clockwork Orange [and] *Honey for the Bears,* Modern Library, 1968.
MF, Knopf, 1971.
Tremor of Intent, Penguin, 1972.
Napoleon Symphony, Knopf, 1974.
Beard's Roman Women, McGraw, 1976.
A Long Trip to Tea Time, Stonehill Publishing, 1976.
Moses the Lawgiver (based on Burgess' screenplay of the same title; also see below), Stonehill Publishing, 1976.
Abba, Abba, Faber, 1977.
Nineteen Eighty-Five, Little, Brown, 1978.
Man of Nazareth (based on Burgess' teleplay *Jesus of Nazareth;* also see below), McGraw, 1979.
The Land Where the Ice Cream Grows, Doubleday, 1979.
Earthly Powers, Simon & Schuster, 1980.
On Going to Bed, Abbeville Press, 1982.

The End of the World News: An Entertainment, Hutchinson, 1982, McGraw, 1983.

This Man and Music, McGraw, 1983.

The Kingdom of the Wicked (also see below), Arbor House, 1985.

The Pianoplayers, Arbor House, 1986.

The Devil's Mode (short stories), Random House, 1989.

Any Old Iron, Random House, 1989.

A Dead Man in Deptford, Hutchinson (London), 1993.

Byrne: A Novel, Hutchison, 1995.

THE MALAYAN TRILOGY; UNDER PSEUDONYM ANTHONY BURGESS

Time for a Tiger (also see below), Heinemann, 1956.

The Enemy in the Blanket (also see below), Heinemann, 1958.

Beds in the East (also see below), Heinemann, 1959.

The Long Day Wanes: A Malayan Trilogy (includes *Time for a Tiger, The Enemy in the Blanket,* and *Beds in the East;* published in England as *Malayan Trilogy,* Penguin, 1972), Norton, 1965.

THE "ENDERBY" SERIES; UNDER PSEUDONYM ANTHONY BURGESS, EXCEPT AS INDICATED

(Under pseudonym Joseph Kell) *Inside Mr. Enderby* (also see below), Heinemann, 1963.

Enderby Outside (also see below), Heinemann, 1968.

Enderby (includes *Inside Mr. Enderby* and *Enderby Outside*), Norton, 1968.

The Clockwork Testament, or Enderby's End, Hart-Davis, 1974, Knopf, 1975.

Enderby's Dark Lady, or No End to Enderby, McGraw, 1984.

NONFICTION; UNDER PSEUDONYM ANTHONY BURGESS, EXCEPT AS INDICATED

(Under name John Burgess Wilson) *English Literature: A Survey for Students,* Longmans, 1958, revised edition published under pseudonym Anthony Burgess, 1974.

The Novel Today, British Council, 1963.

Language Made Plain, English Universities Press, 1964, Crowell, 1965, revised edition, Fontana, 1975.

Re Joyce (published in England as *Here Comes Everybody,* Faber, 1965), Norton, 1965.

The Novel Now: A Guide to Contemporary Fiction (published in England as *The Novel Now: A Student's Guide to Contemporary Fiction,* Faber, 1967, revised edition, 1971), Norton, 1967.

Urgent Copy: Literary Studies (essays), J. Cape, 1968, Norton, 1969.

Shakespeare, J. Cape, 1970, Knopf, 1971, I. R. Dee, 1994.

Joysprick: An Introduction to the Language of James Joyce, Deutsch, 1973, Harcourt, 1975.

Ernest Hemingway and His World, Scribner, 1978.

Ninety-Nine Novels: The Best in English since 1939, Summit, 1984.

D. H. Lawrence in Italy, Penguin, 1985.

Flame into Being: The Life and Work of D. H. Lawrence, Arbor House, 1985.

But Do Blondes Prefer Gentlemen? Homage to QWERTYUIOP: Selected Journalism, 1978-1985, McGraw, 1986.

Little Wilson and Big God (autobiography), Weidenfeld & Nicolson, 1987.

You've Had Your Time: Being the Second Part of the Confessions of Anthony Burgess (autobiography), Heinemann, 1990, Grove Weidenfeld, 1991.

On Mozart: A Paean for Wolfgang, Ticknor and Fields, 1991, published as *Mozart and the Wolf Gang,* Hutchinson, 1991.

A Mouthful of Air: Languages, Languages—Especially English, Morrow, 1993.

Contributor to *Partisan Review, Hudson Review, Times Literary Supplement, New York Times Book Review,* and other periodicals.

TRANSLATOR; UNDER PSEUDONYM ANTHONY BURGESS

(With first wife, Lynne Burgess) Michel de Saint-Pierre, *The New Aristocrats,* Gollancz, 1962.

(With L. Burgess) Jean Pelegri, *The Olive Trees of Justice,* Sidgwick & Jackson, 1962.

Jean Sewin, *The Man Who Robbed Poor Boxes,* Gollancz, 1965.

(And adaptor) Edmond de Rostand, *Cyrano de Bergerac* (play; produced on Broadway as *Cyrano,* 1973), Knopf, 1971, Applause, 1996.

(And adaptor) Sophocles, *Oedipus the King* (play; produced in Minneapolis, MN, 1972), University of Minnesota Press, 1972.

OTHER; UNDER PSEUDONYM ANTHONY BURGESS

(Editor) Daniel Defoe, *A Journal of the Plague Year,* Penguin, 1966.

(Editor) James Joyce, *A Shorter Finnegan's Wake,* Faber, 1966, Viking, 1967.

Moses the Lawgiver (screenplay), ITC/RAI, 1976.

Jesus of Nazareth (teleplay), National Broadcasting Company, 1977.

(Editor) *New York,* Time-Life, 1977.

The Rage of D. H. Lawrence (teleplay), TVOntario, 1986.

A Clockwork Orange 2004 (stage play; adapted from Burgess' novel *A Clockwork Orange*), produced at Barbican Theater, London, 1990.

Also author of the stage play *Morning in His Eyes,* 1968, and of the television miniseries *A.D.,* based on Burgess' novel *The Kingdom of the Wicked.*

MEDIA ADAPTATIONS: A Clockwork Orange was adapted for film and directed by Stanley Kubrick, Warner Bros., 1971.

SIDELIGHTS: John Burgess Wilson, better known to the reading public as Anthony Burgess, was regularly lauded by critics and peers for his imagination, his humor, his varied knowledge, and his sheer productivity. He was once described by *Washington Post Book World* reviewer Michael Dirda as "the most consummate professional writer now alive. His knowledge of literary, linguistic and musical arcana rivals that of any Oxford don; he writes with a lyrical verve; and he seems willing to turn his hand to anything whatever." Though he was most often known as the author of *A Clockwork Orange* (a work from whose shadow, he often lamented, he could not seem to escape), Burgess' output also included textbooks; essays; scripts for stage, screen and television; translations of dramatic and literary masterpieces; and numerous reviews of books, plays, and music. "Burgess, one would swear, has it all," proclaimed *American Spectator'*s Reid Buckley. "He is fecund and prolific (dear God, *is* he!) and a master of language. There seems to be almost nothing that he cannot *say,* and so say it that it sticks to the tastebuds deliciously long after." Gore Vidal, writing in the *New York Review of Books,* concurred: "He is easily the most interesting English writer of the last half century."

It was not until 1959, when he and his wife were living in Borneo, that Burgess was forced to begin writing full-time—though the circumstances surrounding that decision are somewhat bizarre. While giving a lecture to a classroom of students, Burgess abruptly collapsed on the floor. Though he later considered his seizure to have been "a willed collapse out of sheer boredom and frustration," doctors at the time attributed it to an inoperable brain tumor, giving Burgess a year to live at best. Concerned for his wife's financial security, Burgess devoted his "terminal year" to writing, hoping that the profits from his writings would be enough to support his soon-to-be widow. He completed five novels: *The Doctor Is Sick, One Hand Clapping, The Worm and the Ring, The Wanting Seed,* and *Inside Mr. Enderby.* The doctors' diagnosis proved, of course, to be overly pessimistic; looking back, Burgess suggested that his "brain tumor" had been merely a political decision, a device for sending an occasional public embarrassment back to England.

Of these five novels, the one that enjoyed the greatest critical and financial success was 1963's *Inside Mr. Enderby.* It introduces F. X. Enderby, a middle-aged but largely immature poet who can only compose while sitting in his bathroom; the poetry he produces is quite good, though, and he is regarded highly by those few people who still read poetry. Burgess "intended for *Inside Mr. Enderby* to be 'a kind of trumpet blast on behalf of the besieged poet of today—the man who tries to be independent, tries to write his poetry not on the campus, but in the smallest room in the house,' where he can have some privacy," wrote Geoffrey Aggeler in the *Dictionary of Literary Biography.* The poet once again appeared in 1968's *Enderby Outside,* which Aggeler, writing in *Anthony Burgess: The Artist as Novelist,* dismissed as "an overall assessment of the condition of modern poetry—a pessimistic assessment, to be sure." When the two books were released in America as simply *Enderby,* Burgess considered it "the book in which I say most, mean most to myself about the situation of the artist."

When *The Clockwork Testament, or Enderby's End* was released in 1974, it was clear to critics that this somewhat frumpy poet was becoming a mouthpiece for Burgess himself. "His comic escapades palliate for Burgess his own unhappy ventures," observed Roger Lewis in *Punch.* "Being a receptacle for incidents in his creator's life, when Burgess had a malady of the brain, Enderby followed suit by going completely mad. He lost his memory and appropriated the name Piggy Hogg." In *The Clockwork Testament,* Enderby travels to California to work as a Hollywood screenwriter; not coincidentally, Burgess penned this novel shortly after his own book, *A Clockwork Orange,* was made into a movie. As the title implies, Enderby dies at the conclusion of *The Clockwork Testament,* killed by a heart attack "induced by seeing his screenplay of Hopkins' *The Wreck of the Deutschland* altered by moguls into a pornographic movie about Nazis and raped nuns," according to Lewis. Aggeler wrote: "Burgess' impulse to write *The Clockwork Testament* came presumably from the experience of being 'demoted' as an artist by the filming of *A Clockwork Orange.* It is his answer to those who would so demote him and the art of fiction itself."

The death of F. X. Enderby evoked such a clamor among Burgess' readers that the author was ultimately forced to resurrect the poet. *Enderby's Dark Lady, or No End to Enderby,* published in 1984, is supposedly a "lost chapter" in the life of Enderby, a chapter in which he travels to Indiana to author and eventually star in a play based on the life of Shakespeare. Along the way, Burgess (via Enderby) makes a number of observations concerning the "heartland" of America—a country the author has berated on many occasions. Though Walter Kerr, writing in the *New York Times Book Review,* considered this latest Enderby novel "more patchwork than clockwork," he admitted that it will be "welcomed

by all those Burgess fans who simply cannot conceive of a world without Enderby."

Burgess indicated several events that led to his writing *A Clockwork Orange.* First was a report he'd read about American prisons using "behaviorist methods of reforming criminals . . . with the avowed purpose of limiting the subjects' freedom of choice to what society called 'goodness,'" according to Aggeler. Second was a trip Burgess and his wife had taken to the Soviet Union, during which they had encountered a group of rogues called *stilyagi*—marauding thugs who, strangely, maintained a kind of honor code. Lastly was the 1943 attack on Burgess' then-pregnant wife by a group of AWOL American GIs—an attack that sent Lynne to the hospital and caused her to abort her child; this scene was mirrored in the novel when Alex enters the home of the writer F. Alexander, beating him and raping his wife.

In addition to its protagonist's celebration of violence—a "guiltless joy" that, Aggeler noted, "suggests, however incongruously, innocence to the reader"—*A Clockwork Orange* garnered immediate attention for its use of the language *nadsat,* a construction in which Burgess combined Cockney slang and Russian. John W. Tilton, writing in *Cosmic Satire in the Contemporary Novel,* explained Burgess' three main reasons for creating *nadsat:* "To assure the survival of the novel by creating a slang idiom for Alex that would not grow stale or outmoded as real slang does; to brainwash the reader so that he emerges from the novel with a minimal knowledge of Russian; and . . . 'to cushion the reader from the violence . . . [presenting it] through a filmy curtain of an alien language that the reader would have to fight through before he could get to the violence.'" Though the American edition of the novel included a glossary to assist in the translation of *nadsat,* Aggeler asserted that, "after a few pages of the novel, a reader of even moderate sensitivity should not need a glossary and will do well to refrain from consulting this one, whose translations, even when they are accurate, may substitute terms which lack the rich onomatopoeic suggestiveness of Burgess' language."

When *A Clockwork Orange* was brought to America, it underwent a now-famous transformation. In its original form, the book's final chapter shows Alex, grown bored with mindless violence, considering a more "adult" life in which he settles down with a family. The American publisher, W. W. Norton, chose to omit this final chapter, concluding instead with Alex unreformed, free to resume his life of wanton destruction. Because he needed the money, Burgess supported Norton's decision, telling interviewers that he found the novel to be better without the last chapter. "Much of my later life has been expended on Xeroxing statements of intention and the frustration of intention," Burgess said in the *New York Times* in 1986, "while both Kubrick and my New York publisher coolly bask in the rewards of their misdemeanor."

The Kubrick to whom Burgess referred is celebrated film director Stanley Kubrick who, in 1971, filmed *A Clockwork Orange* from a screenplay he had adapted himself. The film was a stylish and deeply disturbing depiction of gang violence and moral depravity that quickly overshadowed Burgess' novel. Like the American text, Kubrick's film omitted Alex's ultimate maturation, forever twisting Burgess' message of freedom of choice for all—even the amoral—into a celebration of violence. This further raised the author's ire toward America, where he felt he was known only "as Stanley Kubrick's underpaid assistant," according to John Sutherland of the *Times Literary Supplement.* The film's graphic violence caused it to be withdrawn from British theaters, and even today it is illegal to show *A Clockwork Orange* anywhere in Britain, whether on film or videotape.

In the years after *A Clockwork Orange* was published, Burgess continued to reside in the shadow of that work and its film adaptation. His output did not decrease, though. He produced several screenplays for film and television, including Franco Zefferelli's *Jesus of Nazareth;* he composed the scores to operas, musicals, and concerts; and he continued to turn out works of fiction and nonfiction. But it was not until 1980 that he completed what many critics consider his masterpiece, *Earthly Powers.*

The novel centers on playwright and novelist Kenneth M. Toomey, a famous homosexual who, at the age of eighty-one, decides it is time to record his memoirs. Toomey—an amalgam of novelists Graham Greene, Evelyn Waugh, Burgess himself, and especially W. Somerset Maugham—relates the story of his life, describing with equal passion scenes of tremendous joy and despair. During the course of his autobiography Toomey recalls his meeting one Don Carlo Campanatti, an Italian priest who goes on to become Pope; Don Carlo is, according to Aggeler, "a Faustian figure who made a bargain with the devil in return for the earthly powers of the papacy." The two men hold vastly different views on the nature of man: Toomey, the empiricist, believes that evil is endemic to mankind, while Don Carlo sees man as inherently pure and evil as a kind of coat that can be easily removed. "Burgess effectively juxtaposes Carlo's and Toomey's views and explanations of various evils in the twentieth century," observed Aggeler, "and he suggests that both views are to some extent partially correct, but [that] both are also significantly limited."

In 1987, in the week that he turned 70 years old, Burgess released the first volume of his memoirs, *Little Wilson and Big God.* Beginning with his birth and childhood in northern England, Burgess relates the often bizarre details of his life in England, Malaya, Borneo and elsewhere, giving us a close-up look at not only himself but his surroundings. "His memory is as richly stocked with details as his fictions," wrote Peter Ackroyd in the London *Times.* "Like his literary hero, James Joyce, he has a proper respect for what the world calls trivia; and these fragments of memory are like small windows opening on a lost time. You need not read this book as autobiography at all, but simply as social history of a superior sort." The volume is subtitled "the confessions of Anthony Burgess," and many of those confessions concern the author's first wife, Lynne, an abusive and paranoid alcoholic. "Lynne . . . dominates the book," observed Phil Kloer in the *Atlanta Journal and Constitution.* "She gave Burgess great joy and unimaginable pain."

With *Little Wilson and Big God* concluding with Burgess' "death sentence" in 1959, it was clear that a second autobiographical volume was to come; that volume, *You've Had Your Time,* was published in 1990. It chronicled Burgess' new life as a professional writer, as well as his rapidly deteriorating marriage to Lynne, her death from cirrhosis in 1968, and the author's marriage to the Italian student Lilliana Macellari with whom he had conceived a child out of wedlock. As in *Little Wilson and Big God,* these introspective details are inserted between long passages relating Burgess' many authorial duties, from novels to plays to drama and music criticism. "His polymathic pursuits, which as they come in at us, chapter after chapter, sometimes page after page, yield up finally a pointillist portrait of [Burgess]," wrote William F. Buckley, Jr., in the *New York Times Book Review.* "The reader is, however, entitled to ask: is there a human narrative under this

truckload of cultural petit point? Not a whole lot, to tell the truth, but some." Burgess instead entertains the reader with numerous seemingly-apocryphal anecdotes, including the famous story of how he reviewed one of his own books (*Inside Mr. Enderby,* originally published under the pseudonym Joseph Kell) in a literary supplement.

Though shortly after the publication of *Little Wilson and Big God* Burgess predicted in the *Atlanta Journal and Constitution,* "Unless some miracle of renewed inspiration occurs, the second volume of my memoirs [*You've Had Your Time*] will bring my writing career to an end," he did produce one last work of fiction, *Dead Man in Deptford,* and one last work of nonfiction, *A Mouthful of Air: Languages, Languages—Especially English,* both published in 1993. *A Mouthful of Air* is something of an extension of Burgess' 1964 text *Languages Made Plain,* a forum for the author to share with his readers his life-long love of languages, both foreign and domestic. "If Anthony Burgess were turned upside down and briskly shaken, the heap of objects that fell out of his pockets would much resemble this book," wrote Richard Eder in the *Los Angeles Times Book Review.* "In no particular order, it is just about everything he has to say about words, and that is a great deal." Not only does Burgess explore English—its mutations through history, for example, or the lip and tongue movements required to speak it—but other languages as well. "He thinks that even a smattering of the sounds of alien tongues does wonders for ones sense of the rich relativity of one's own," noted *Observer* contributor Lorna Sage, who pronounced *A Mouthful of Air* "provocative, full of life, of odd snippets of information, boasts and confessions, hates and loves."

In his final book, *A Dead Man in Deptford,* Burgess further revels in the joys of language. A mystery novel focussing on the murder of sixteenth-century dramatist Christopher Marlowe (who wrote *Doctor Faustus* and *Edward II*), it is told in a mixture of Elizabethan prose and Cockney—a combination that "is very, very difficult to get right," according to Robert Carver in the *New Statesman and Society,* but "Burgess gives the impression he speaks it like a native. . . . [He] is the last of our great, unreconstructed, Joyce-influenced modernist writers. While steeped in the old . . . he resolutely makes it new as wordsmith and coiner—and so, paradoxically, achieves the right timeless-historical note." The *Observer*'s John Banville also praised Burgess' prose, calling it "adventurous and demanding, a wonderfully dense and inventive mock-Elizabethan that bobs along on a ceaseless ripple of wordplay." "*A Dead Man in Deptford* is not just a very good novel; it may well be Burgess' masterpiece," summarized Carver. "His grasp of the age and its angsts is profound, and his portrait of Marlowe sympathetic, critical and brilliantly imagined all at once."

Burgess died of cancer on November 22, 1993, after a long illness. A London *Times* obituarist commented upon his literary impact: "When some future Burgess a century from now comes to write the cultural history of the second half of the 20th century, Burgess will be recognised as a giant in his tattered humanity and his intolerable wrestle with words and meanings. . . . He enriched his generation more than most, and left a body of work to keep readers arguing and delighted as long as reading survives, and civilisation does not fall into one of his own nightmare visions."

BIOGRAPHICAL/CRITICAL SOURCES:

BOOKS

Aggeler, Geoffrey, *Anthony Burgess: The Artist as Novelist,* University of Alabama Press, 1979.

Concise Dictionary of British Literary Biography, Volume 8: *Contemporary Writers, 1960 to the Present,* Gale (Detroit), 1992.

Contemporary Literary Criticism, Gale, Volume 1, 1973; Volume 2, 1974; Volume 4, 1975; Volume 5, 1976; Volume 8, 1978; Volume 10, 1979; Volume 13, 1980; Volume 15, 1982; Volume 40, 1986; Volume 62, 1991.

DeVitis, A. A., *Anthony Burgess,* Twayne, 1972.

Dictionary of Literary Biography, Volume 14: *British Novelists since 1960,* Gale, 1982.

Dix, Carol M., *Anthony Burgess,* Longman, 1971.

Mathews, Richard, *The Clockwork Universe of Anthony Burgess,* Borgo Press, 1978.

Solotaroff, Theodore, *The Red Hot Vacuum,* Atheneum, 1970.

Tilton, John W., *Cosmic Satire in the Contemporary Novel,* Bucknell University Press, 1977.

PERIODICALS

American Spectator, August, 1983, pp. 38-40.

Atlanta Journal and Constitution, March 1, 1987.

Atlantic Monthly, February, 1975; January, 1990; June, 1991; June, 1995, p. 120.

Chicago Tribune, October 29, 1978; April 15, 1979; January 12, 1987; May 19, 1991.

Chicago Tribune Book World, November 23, 1980; March 27, 1983; September 8, 1985; October 13, 1985; May 4, 1986.

Commonweal, May 28, 1971; December 6, 1974; February 11, 1994, p. 9, 12.

Globe and Mail (Toronto), July 7, 1984; November 16, 1985; November 23, 1985; April 5, 1986; May 24, 1986; November 29, 1986; February 28, 1987; July 11, 1987; April 29, 1989; December 14, 1991, p. C12.

Los Angles Times, November 7, 1985; March 27, 1986.

Los Angeles Times Book Review, December 14, 1980; May 30, 1982; May 1, 1983; March 16, 1986; May 10, 1987; December 31, 1989; October 21, 1990; December 8, 1991; August 15, 1993, p. 3.

National Review, May 9, 1975; December 27, 1993, p. 18.

New Statesman and Society, April 23, 1993, p. 36; October 20, 1995, p. 41.

Newsweek, February 21, 1966; June 4, 1974; October 25, 1976; October 24, 1994, p. 82.

New Yorker, May 7, 1966; May 20, 1991; August 7, 1995, p. 64.

New York Review of Books, September 30, 1976; May 7, 1987, pp. 3, 6, 8; October 5, 1995, p. 47.

New York Times, December 1, 1965; November 18, 1980; March 12, 1983; August 8, 1983; April 14, 1984; September 11, 1985; December 31, 1986; February 14, 1987; February 14, 1990.

New York Times Book Review, May 1, 1966; December 4, 1966; November 29, 1970; November 19, 1978; April 15, 1979; December 7, 1980; March 6, 1983; April 22, 1984, p. 10; September 22, 1985; March 30, 1986; June 1, 1986; November 2, 1986; February 22, 1987; February 26, 1989, p. 12; December 10, 1989; October 21, 1990; April 28, 1991; May 5, 1991; June 9, 1991; June 16, 1991; May 31, 1992; May 28, 1995, p. 12.

New York Times Magazine, April 2, 1967.

Observer, November 1, 1992, p. 62.

Punch, June 12, 1968; March 28, 1984, p. 59.

Time, March 21, 1983, p. 76; October 17, 1983; April 23, 1984; November 17, 1986; February 16, 1987.

Times (London), January 16, 1964; October 20, 1980; April 4, 1982; October 28, 1982; March 29, 1984; May 16, 1985; August 12, 1985; March 6, 1986; May 17, 1986; August 28, 1986; February 27, 1987; October 10, 1987; March 2, 1989; October 10, 1991.

Times Literary Supplement, November 4, 1965; October 24, 1980; October 8, 1982; November 5, 1982; December 10, 1982; December 24, 1982; March 30, 1984; May 31, 1985; October 18, 1985; November 16, 1985; April 4, 1986; August 29, 1986; February 27, 1987; April 7, 1989; October 26, 1990; October 11, 1991; April 30, 1993, p. 21.

Tribune Books (Chicago), January 12, 1987; February 15, 1987; January 29, 1989; May 19, 1991, p. 4.

Washington Post Book World, March 31, 1968; November 23, 1980; June 13, 1982; March 13, 1983; January 1, 1984; April 8, 1984; March 17, 1985; May 12, 1985; October 6, 1985; January 19, 1986; March 9, 1986; November 16, 1986; March 1, 1987; February 12, 1989; May 12, 1991, p. 1; December 22, 1991; August 15, 1993, p. 3.

*　　　*　　　*

WINTERSON, Jeanette 1959-

PERSONAL: Born August 27, 1959, in Manchester, England. *Education:* St. Catherine's College, Oxford, M.A., 1981. *Avocational interests:* Opera, ballet, champagne.

ADDRESSES: Agent—International Creative Management, 40 West 57th St., New York, NY 10019.

CAREER: Writer.

AWARDS, HONORS: Publishing for People Award, and Whitbread Award for best first novel from Booksellers Association of Great Britain and Ireland, both 1985, for *Oranges Are Not the Only Fruit;* John Llewellyn Rhys Memorial Prize, Book Trust, 1987, for *The Passion;* E. M. Forster Award, American Academy of Arts and Letters, 1989, for *Sexing the Cherry.*

WRITINGS:

NOVELS

Oranges Are Not the Only Fruit, Pandora, 1985, Atlantic Monthly Press, 1987.

The Passion, Bloomsbury, 1987, Atlantic Monthly Press, 1988.

Sexing the Cherry, Bloomsbury, 1989, Atlantic Monthly Press, 1990.

Written on the Body, J. Cape, 1992, Knopf, 1993, Vintage, 1994.

Art & Lies: A Piece for Three Voices and a Bawd, J. Cape, 1994, Knopf, 1995.

Gut Symmetries, Knopf, 1997.

OTHER

(Editor) *Passionfruit* (stories), Pandora, 1986.

Fit for the Future (health), Pandora, 1986.

Art Objects. Essays on Ecstasy and Effrontery, J. Cape, 1995, Knopf, 1996.

Also author of *Oranges Are Not the Only Fruit,* a television screenplay adapted from Winterson's novel of the same title, 1991; and a screenplay titled *Great Moments in Aviation,* directed by Beeban Kidron, 1993.

SIDELIGHTS: Jeanette Winterson is among England's most acclaimed novelists to have gained publication in the 1980s. Provocative and outspoken, she has garnered significant media attention as "one of England's hottest young writers and London's most celebrated literary lesbian," noted Kelleher Jewett in a

Nation review of Winterson's essay collection, *Art Objects.* She began her career as a novelist with *Oranges Are Not the Only Fruit,* a first-person narrative about an adopted daughter's ties to her mother, a religious fanatic. The heroine, Jeanette, is raised to perceive sin as ever present, and she blindly adheres to her mother's plans for her to become a missionary. A social outsider, Jeanette serves her mother's organization, Society for the Lost, and regularly participates in church functions and activities, including prayer meetings and the dispensation of materials at street corners. Jeanette eventually falls in love with another church member, Melanie, with whom she enjoys sexual relations. Jeanette's mother, however, discovers the affair and openly humiliates the lovers at a church service. Jeanette then enters into another lesbian love affair, and when this too ends disturbingly, she makes some difficult personal decisions.

Oranges Are Not the Only Fruit, which won England's Whitbread Prize for best first novel in 1985, earned Winterson substantial acclaim as a bold and refreshing novelist. Joseph Olshan, in his review for the *Chicago Tribune,* began by hailing Winterson's work as a "daring, unconventionally comic novel" and ended by deeming it "penetrating." And Sarah Gold, in her review for the *Washington Post,* hailed *Oranges Are Not the Only Fruit* as "a strikingly quirky, delicate and intricate work." Roz Kaveney, writing in the *Times Literary Supplement,* simply termed the novel "excellent."

The Passion, Winterson's next work, won the John Llewellyn Rhys Memorial Prize in 1987. Here Henri, a cook from Napoleon's army, befriends Villanelle, who had loved another woman in her native Venice only to be brought by her abusive husband to Russia, where she was eventually sold to a similarly cruel French soldier. Together, Henri and Villanelle trek across the wintry Russian landscape in an effort to reach Venice, where Villanelle hopes to recover her own sense of self. *Chicago Tribune* reviewer Alan Cheuse found *The Passion* a compelling, powerful work. "If you require strong medicine for your heart before bedtime," Cheuse advised, "take this novel in a few large doses."

Winterson's popular novel, *Sexing the Cherry,* is a fantastical historical work—set in the early seventeenth century—about a young man's magical adventures. Found floating down the Thames River as a newborn, the hero—Jordan—is raised by Dog-Woman, a foul-smelling, pock-marked giantess. Jordan eventually leaves his squalid home, which is inhabited by more than two dozen dogs, and sets sail with a botanist determined to bring rare plants back to England. Jordan travels to magical realms, including a land where princesses fly to a floating city. He falls in love with the youngest of these princesses after spying her from an open window, and he expends considerable energy, and imagination, trying to meet her. Dog-Woman, meanwhile, affords a second narration, fighting in military conflicts and opposing religious injustices. Her path eventually crosses with that of the wandering Jordan, and the novel culminates in some surprising, and timely, revelations.

Sexing the Cherry is celebrated as a provocative, entertaining, even experimental novel. *Los Angeles Times* reviewer Richard Eder contrasted Winterson's novel with James Joyce's *Finnegan's Wake,* and *New York Times* critic Michiko Kakutani deemed the novel "wonderfully inventive." Kakutani added that Winterson "possesses the ability to combine the biting satire of [Jonathan] Swift with the ethereal magic of [Gabriel] Garcia Marquez, the ability to reinvent old myths even as she creates new ones of her

own." And Toronto *Globe and Mail* reviewer Nancy Wigston, who likened *Sexing the Cherry* to works of Swift and Italo Calvino (author of one Winterson's favorite novels, *Invisible Cities*), claimed that the novel "shows an astonishing imagination at work." Wigston contended that "Winterson combines the outlook of a philosopher with the energy of a catapult." The result, Wigston observed, is a novel that "sparkles with youthful virtuosity."

Winterson's more recent novels have received more negative criticism than her earlier works, although she still garners praise for her experimental writing style. In *Written on the Body,* Winterson tells the story of an unnamed narrator's love affair with a married woman, Louise. The novel focuses on the nature of physical passion and the meaning of desire, and it includes both a straightforward narrative as well as a number of prose love poems written by the narrator in honor of Louise. Andree Pages, writing in *American Book Review,* criticized the novel as "overly dramatic and unconvincing at times" and commented that "the plot is often unnecessarily baroque." However, Pages also called Winterson "an amazing writer" and noted that the author "achieves a real depth of feeling, a savoring of sex and the body and life itself."

In *Art and Lies: A Piece for Three Voices & a Bawd,* Winterson offers three loosely connected plot lines centering around Sappho, Picasso, and Handel. "This is *not* beautiful writing, despite its frantic claims to the title," stated Julie Burchill in the *Spectator.* "It is a garish, artificial, bejewelled mechanical nightingale of a prose style." However, *Times Literary Supplement* contributor Lorna Sage characterized the novel as "safely good." She noted, "Winterson writes beautifully about the value of *lightness,* about the thrills you can engineer for yourself if you stop trying to represent the world, or describe it like a drudge."

Gut Symmetries depicts the progress of a shipboard love triangle between Stella, a poet, Alice, a physicist, and her colleague Jove. This three-way relationship begins quite innocuously aboard the Queen Elizabeth II, and ends dramatically on a yacht. *Gut Symmetries* has invoked divergent reviews. Writing in the *Times Literary Supplement,* Katy Emck issued the equivocal statement, "This is a beautiful, stirring and brilliant story but it does not make sense," in part because "it is hard to care what happens to Alice, Stella and Jove." Robert Alter, in the *New Republic,* went further, stating, "Jeanette Winterson does not always write such hackneyed stuff: but her worst writing is a symptom of why she is not better than she is." *Booklist*'s Donna Seaman, on the other hand, finds *Gut Symmetries* "masterfully written, highly suspenseful and penetrating."

In addition to her novels, Winterson has also written screenplays as well as a collection of essays, *Art Objects: Essays on Ecstasy and Effrontery.* A *Kirkus Reviews* contributor denigrated the collection as "self-important." Michael Dirda, writing in the *Washington Post Book World,* acknowledged that Winterson has come under fire for her provocative public persona. Winterson, Dirda commented, has been criticized "for being lesbian, shamelessly self-promoting, and more than a little abrasive." But in his review of *Art Objects,* Dirda averred that "anyone who values literature will want to keep these essays around, to argue with, marvel at, find consolation in."

BIOGRAPHICAL/CRITICAL SOURCES:

BOOKS

Allen, Carolyn, *Following Djuna: Women Lovers and the Erotics of Loss,* Indiana University Press, 1996.

PERIODICALS

American Book Review, March, 1995, p. 19.
Atlantic Monthly, February, 1993, p. 112.
Booklist, April 1, 1997, p. 1283.
Chicago Tribune, July 5, 1988; November 8, 1987, section 14, p. 8.
Entertainment Weekly, April 14, 1995, p. 61.
Globe and Mail (Toronto), March 31, 1990.
Kirkus Reviews, December 15, 1995, p. 1761.
Library Journal, March 1, 1995, p. 104; February 15, 1996, p. 153.
Los Angeles Times, May 3, 1990.
Mademoiselle, February, 1993, p. 52.
Magazine of Fantasy and Science Fiction, April, 1995, p. 34.
Nation, July 9, 1990, p. 64; February 12, 1996, p. 30.
New Republic, April 7, 1997, p. 36.
New Statesman & Society, October 12, 1990, p. 44; September 18, 1992, p. 37; July 1, 1994, p. 38.
New York, January 25, 1993, p. 61.
New York Review of Books, March 4, 1993, p. 22.
New York Times, April 27, 1990.
New York Times Book Review, November 8, 1987, p. 26; February 14, 1993, p. 10; March 26, 1995, p. 14; February 25, 1996, p. 20.
People Weekly, March 8, 1993, p. 27.
Publishers Weekly, March 20, 1995, p. 38.
Spectator, June 25, 1994, p. 26.
Times Literary Supplement, March 22, 1985, p. 326; November 1, 1985, p. 1228; June 17, 1994, p. 22; January 3, 1997, p. 21.
Vanity Fair, February, 1995, p. 112.
Vogue, February, 1993, p. 128.
Washington Post, October 1, 1987.
Washington Post Book World, May 13, 1990, p. 9; March 24, 1996, p. 3.
Wilson Library Bulletin, May, 1991, p. 37.
Yale Review, October, 1993, p. 124.

*   *   *

WITTGENSTEIN, Ludwig (Josef Johann) 1889-1951

PERSONAL: Born April 26, 1889, in Vienna, Austria-Hungary (now Austria); died, April 29, 1951, in Cambridge, England; son of Karl (an engineer and industrialist) and Leopoldine (maiden name, Kalmus) Wittgenstein; immigrated to England; became naturalized British citizen, 1938. *Education:* Technische Hochschule in Berlin, University of Manchester, Oxford University.

CAREER: Philosopher, architect, educator, and author.

WRITINGS:

Tractatus Logico-Philosophicus, introduction by Bertrand Russell, Harcourt, Brace (New York City), 1922.
Philosophical Investigations, translated by G. E. M. Anscombe, MacMillan (New York City), 1953.
Remarks on the Foundations of Mathematics, edited by G. H. von Wright, R. Rhees, and G. E. M. Anscombe, translated by Anscombe, Blackwell (Oxford), 1956.
The Blue and Brown Books: Preliminary Studies for the Philosophical Investigations, 1958.
Notebooks 1914-1916, edited by G. H. von Wright and G. E. M. Anscombe, translated by Anscombe, Blackwell (Oxford), 1961.

On Certainty, edited by G. E. M. Anscombe and G. H. von Wright, translated by Denis Paul and Anscombe, Harper (New York City), 1969.

SIDELIGHTS: From the publication in 1922 of his *Tractatus Logico-Philosophicus,* his first and most famous book (and the only one published during his lifetime), Ludwig Wittgenstein's stature has grown considerably: hailed by his colleagues as a genius, he is widely regarded, by experts in various fields of science and the humanities, as one of the seminal thinkers of the twentieth century. According to scholars, works have inspired much original thought in a variety of fields of inquiry, including the foundations of mathematics, philosophy of science, linguistics, logic, even metaphysics, ethics, esthetics, and theology. The University of Oxford's Peter Hacker wrote in the *Oxford Companion to Philosophy,* "Although [Wittgenstein] did not, nor indeed wished to, found a philosophical school of thinkers, the evolution of philosophy this century would be unintelligible without his work as would that of twentieth-century art without Picasso." Although Wittgenstein did not found a school or formulate a complete philosophical system, his investigations of the nature of language, initially presented in the *Tractatus,* considerably widened the intellectual horizons of philosophers who were struggling to elucidate the foundations of logic and mathematics. Wittgenstein, who started his work as a philosopher by investigating the foundations of logic and mathematics, clearly understood, as David Pears pointed out in *Oxford Companion to the Mind,* that "anyone who wants to understand how logical formulae work achieve necessary truth must first understand how ordinary statements achieve contingent truth." Indeed, as commentators have observed, the connection between logic and natural language was not a revolutionary idea when Wittgenstein started writing; however, starting from this idea, Wittgenstein developed original, even revolutionary, theories of language. Explaining that "it was Wittgenstein who converted Bertrand Russell that the propositions of logic and pure mathematics were 'tautologies,'"—a tautology being a true proposition which introduces no new knowledge—Frederick Copleston pointed out that Wittgenstein provided a clear, and original, distinction between tautologies and propositions. According to Copleston, a proposition, as Wittgenstein defines it, distinguishing it from a tautology, "is a picture or representation of a possible fact or state of affairs in the world. A proposition in this sense is either true or false; but we cannot know by inspecting its meaning (*Sinn*) whether it is true or false. To know this we have to compare it, as it were, with reality, with the empirical facts."

Wittgenstein was born in 1889—the youngest of eight children-to an Austrian iron and steel magnate. His mother, devoted much of time to music, while his father was a connoisseur of art. In fact, Wittgenstein's father financially supported his favorite artists—for example, Gustav Klimt. The Wittgenstein home thus cultivated a refined atmosphere in which artists and intellectuals often met and conversed, and this is the atmosphere in which Wittgenstein and his siblings grew up. Unlike his siblings, however, Wittgenstein did not play a musical instrument as a child; however, his knowledge of music was profound, and music, as his biographers have noted, played a very important role in his life. His brother Paul, an accomplished concert pianist, lost an arm during World War I, and Maurice Ravel wrote the *Concerto for the Left Hand* for him. Home-schooled until the age of 14, the Wittgenstein enrolled in the Realschule at Linz (Adolf Hitler was a contemporary there), where he studied mathematics and physics. At 17, he matriculated at the Technische Hochschule in Berlin, bent on a career in mechanical engineering. Two years later,

Wittgenstein moved to England in order to study aeronautics at the University of Manchester, where he experimented with kites and also designed a jet reaction propeller. However, Wittgenstein's interest shifted from engineering to mathematics; this in turn led to a preoccupation with the foundations of mathematics. He read, with great enthusiasm, Bertrand Russell's *Principles of Mathematics* and also the works of the prominent logician and philosopher Gottlob Frege, particularly his *Fundamental Laws of Arithmetic.* The course of his life had unalterably changed. Early in 1912 he was accepted into the philosophy program at Cambridge University, where Russell taught. He spent the better part of two years there as Russell's star pupil, then abruptly moved to Skjolden in Sogn, Norway, where he lived in near seclusion. The move may have precipitated by the death of his father in 1912. Wittgenstein was plagued by intermittent bouts of depression throughout his life: three of his four brothers had committed suicide, and he also entertained suicidal thoughts from time to time. However, he was able to find solace in his work. In order to concentrate on work, he sought remote rural areas. However, he kept up his correspondence with friends and colleagues, particularly with Russell.

When World War I broke out in 1914, Wittgenstein returned to Vienna and enlisted as an artillery officer in the Austrian Army. He was consigned to a ship on the Vistula River in Poland for much of the war, but in February of 1918 he was transferred to the Italian front. Under the chaotic circumstances of his military service, apparently able to concentrate amidst the havoc of war, Wittgenstein worked on the manuscript of the of *Tractatus.* Captured by Italian forces in October of 1918, Wittgenstein spent the next ten months as a prisoner of war. He finished the work in the prison camp and had it smuggled out to Bertrand Russell.

The *Tractatus* was first published in 1921, in Wilhelm Osterwald's journal *Annalen der Naturphilosophie;* the following year, Wittgenstein's work appeared as a book, in a bilingual edition: C. K. Ogden provided the translation into English, and Russell wrote the introduction. Russell and his followers hailed Wittgenstein's short, terse, aphoristic book as an instant classic. Indeed, in the opening paragraph of his introduction to the *Tractatus,* Russell wrote that Wittgenstein's work, "whether or not it proves to give the ultimate truth on the matters with which it deals, certainly deserves, by its breadth and scope and profundity, to be considered an important event in the philosophical world." Wittgenstein's goal, however, was to give the ultimate truth on the philosophy of language. For Wittgenstein, as David Pears explained in *The Oxford Companion to the Mind,* "factual discourse" represents the fundamental type of discourse. As Pears remarked, according to the *Tractatus,* factual discourse, "mirrors the actual world by presenting it as it is." In other words, a proposition exemplifying factual discourse, as opposed to a tautology, constitutes a picture of the world. According to Pears, the "words the make up the statement are correlated with things in the worlds, just as the points on a map are correlated with points on the ground." While Russell accepts Wittgenstein's that a statement can be related to projection in geometry, particularly to the fact that a geometrical figure's projective properties remain unchange regardless of the way in which the figure is projected, other commentators have insisted that Wittgenstein's pictorial theory of meaning implies a high level of logical abstraction, and cannot be understood literally. In her discussion of Wittgenstein's pictorial theory, Hannah Arendt questioned the originality of Wittgenstein's idea, stating "that Wittgenstein's early language theory is solidly rooted in the old metaphysical axiom of truth as *adequation rei et intellectus.*" According to Arendt, the equation

of objects and thoughts "is possible only as an intuition, namely as an internal image that copies the sensorially given object." In Arendt's view, a relation between language and the world, which certainly exist, cannot be pictorial. "If it were a pictorial relation," Arendt declared, "every proposition, unless it repeats an accidental error in sensory perception (something looks like a tree but turns out to be a man on closer inspection), would be true."

The critical response to the *Tractatus* was tremendous; both philosophers and non-philosophers read it; logical positivists embraced it, despite their misgivings about the author's purported mysticism. Indeed, it was a book that in many ways embodies the spirit of twentieth-century philosophy. Writing from a cosmological perspective, Stephen Hawking lamented the fact that philosophy had reduced its scope of inquiry from the universe to language, citing Wittgenstein, "the most famous philosopher of this century," as one of the forces behind this paradigm shift.

After completing the *Tractatus,* Wittgenstein concluded that his work as a philosopher was finished. After being released from the Italian prison camp in 1919, he started searching for a new direction in life. A multi-talented person, Wittgenstein never defined himself as a professional philosopher. In addition, not having gone through the traditional philosophical curriculum, and never feeling compelled to read widely in the field of philosophy, Wittgenstein freely pursued various interests, such as music and literature. He was particularly attached to the Russian writers Leo Tolstoy and F. M. Dostoyevsky. Apparently influenced by Tolstoy's *Gospel in Brief,* a re-telling of the New Testament, which he read and re-read during the war, Wittgenstein sought to simplify in his life, so he could devote his great energy to useful work. He gave away the family fortune he had inherited and, beginning in 1920, he took a series of jobs teaching in elementary schools in remote Austrian villages. Ever restless, Wittgenstein quit teaching in 1926 and was employed briefly as a gardener for a monastery. He moved back to Vienna and reconnected with his family whom he had been estranged from for more than a decade. During this period, he worked as an architect, designing and building an austere mansion for his sister Gretl. Essentially dissatisfied with his life, he returned to philosophy, eventually moving to England, accepting a position at Trinity College, Cambridge, in 1930. A Fellow of Trinity College from 1930 to 1936, he worked as professor from 1939 to 1947. In 1938, when Austria was incorporated into the Third Reich, Wittgenstein, refusing to be a citizen of Hitler's Germany, became a British subject. During World War II, he performed war services, working as a porter in Guy's Hospital, in London.

At Cambridge, Wittgenstein led an austere life. His sparsely furnished rooms had deck-chairs, for his students, a fireproof safe for his manuscripts, and little else. A magnetic and charismatic personality, Wittgenstein was an extraordinary teacher, sharing his enormous intellectual struggles with his students in the classroom, transforming the entire lecture format into a dramatic, tense, at times silent, quest for truth. One of the results of Wittgenstein's quest during his Cambridge period was his second great work, the posthumously published *Philosophical Investigations.*

In his *Philosophical Investigations,* Wittgenstein proposes a new philosophy of language. In fact, the foundation of his new orientation is a radical re-definition of language. In essence, Wittgenstein now instructs philosophers to accept language as it is, without trying to purify it, or make it more precise. What philosophy can do, however, is to describe language. Having lost the power to prescribe rules of discourse, philosophy has no other choice, according to Wittgenstein, but to face the bewildering richness of different types of discourse. While is used to explicate the world of scientific fact, it serves a variety of other of purposes, i.e. there are many different ways of speaking (e.g. praying, questioning, commanding, imploring, etc.). In other words, words are like tools that can serve a variety of functions.

In addition to metaphysical subjects, Wittgenstein was, throughout life, often preoccupied by questions pertaining to the arts, noting his reflections, all of which were published posthumously in various volumes, including *The Blue and Brown Books.* While flatly rejecting the idea that a particular work of art, or a certain aspect thereof, necessarily causes a particular aesthetic response, Wittgenstein insists on the intelligibility of art. In fact, intelligibility, according to Wittgenstein, is what language and the arts have in common. Commentators, however, have noted Wittgenstein's parallels between language and the arts remain general, and allow no unjustified equations. "Obviously," affirmed Ian MacKenzie in an article in *Philosophy and Literature,* "visual perception *per se* is not linguistic, but evaluating a painting, making an interpretation of form, a comparison, or an attribution, quite apart from communicating any of this to anyone else, is a linguistic process. Wittgenstein writes, 'we say we understand' a genre of painting, for example, 'if we recognise what is happening in it, what the people are doing. Here the criterion for this recognition is perhaps that if asked what they are doing we explain it in words.'" For Wittgenstein, language remains a tool; however, while allowing the use of language in the process of formulating an aesthetic response, Wittgenstein rejects the idea of translating non-verbal "text" into discursive utterances. However, Wittgenstein also opposes the notion of aesthetic sensation that by their nature cannot be expressed verbally. Essentially, for Wittgenstein, aesthetic sensations are neither ineffable nor easily translated into verbal discourse. "Although Wittgenstein," MacKenzie observed, "disdains the notion of private sensations that cannot be put into word, he allows the aesthetic responses may be such that they can only be 'explained' by citing other objects which elicit similar responses. Such comparisons are idiosyncratic, unempirical, and shamelessly impressionistic—the kind of responses despised by linguists who wish to come to the aid of literary studies." Indeed, Wittgenstein's comparisons between literature and music may appear impressionistic and idiosyncratic, particularly the statement that the music of Johannes Brahms reminded him of the writing of Gottfried Keller. However, Wittgenstein is careful to point out that the seemingly familiar connection, in the mind of perceiving subject, between a musical composition and a literary work, stems not from any kind of parallelism, but from perceived, but not easily explained, similarities. In fact, MacKenzie may be offering a succinct summary of Wittgenstein's aesthetics when he says that art, "music or literary criticism attempts to bring about a community of perception rather than to demonstrate the validity of particular responses." However, despite his efforts to keep his comparisons between language and art, or language and music, at a level of abstraction which precludes unjustifiable parallels, Wittgenstein never hesitated to explore the area where, for instance, music and language intersect. However, even when he speaks of the musicality of language, Wittgenstein limits his discussion to elements which can be empirically verified. As Ben-Ami Scharfstein explained, to Wittgenstein, understanding a sentence "is akin to understanding a theme in music, because the sentence has its individual patterns of variation in loudness and tempo; and, in the sense that musical themes cannot replace one another, neither can sentences."

In 1947, Wittgenstein, realizing that teaching and writing was too much of a burden for him, decided to give up his professorship at Cambridge. He subsequently traveled, staying in remote places in Ireland, where he focused on his writing, addressing various philosophical problems, particularly questions pertaining to the philosophy of mind. Always restless, Wittgenstein traveled to North America in 1949, where he fell ill. Upon his return in England, he was diagnosed with prostate cancer. Nevertheless, he continued working and travelling as much as he could, visiting Vienna and Norway in 1950. Wittgenstein, who passionately sought solitude throughout his life, died in Cambridge surrounded by caring friends.

Wittgenstein has been described as a great twentieth-century philosopher; some critics even view him as the most eminent representative of twentieth-century thought, an embodiment of the human ability to continue a dialogue with the world in spite of the world's apparent indifference, even animosity, to philosophical concerns. As the emblematic philosopher of the twentieth century, Wittgenstein is also known as a seminal thinker, whose truly multidisciplinary work has left profound traces in a wide variety of fields, including, in addition to philosophy, psychology, linguistics, aesthetics, and literary criticism. Yet, for all of its apparent rootedness in twentieth-century modernism, Wittgenstein's writings possesses timeless quality of seminal philosophical works. Not surprisingly, Wittgenstein's early champion and interpreter in France was Pierre Hadot, the eminent historian of ancient philosophy. Everything, according to Hadot, "that touches the domain of the existential—which is most important for human beings—for instance, our feeling of existence, our impressions when faced by death, our perception of nature, our sensations, and a fortiori the mystical experience, is not directly communicable. The phrases we use to describe them are conventional and banal; we realize this when we try to console one over the loss of a loved one. That's why it often happens that a poem or a biography are more philosophical than a philosophical treatise, simply because they allow us to glimpse this unsayable in an indirect way. Here again, we find the kind of mysticism evoked in Wittgenstein's *Tractatus:* 'There is indeed the inexpressible. This shows itself; it is the mystical.'"

BIOGRAPHICAL/CRITICAL SOURCES:

BOOKS

Arendt, Hannah, *The Life of the Mind,* Volume 1: *Thinking,* Harcourt Brace Jovanovich (New York City), 1978, 243-45.

Bohlin, Henrik, *Groundless Knowledge,* Almqvist & Wiksell (Stockholm), 1997.

Brill, Susan B., *Wittgenstein and Critical Theory,* Ohio University Press (Athens), 1995.

Cioffi, Frank, *Essays on Wittgenstein,* Cambridge University Press (Cambridge), 1998.

Copleston, Frederick, *A History of Philosophy,* Volume 9: *Bentham to Russell,* Image Books (Garden City, NY), 1966, pp. 495-504.

Dale, Jacquette, *Wittgenstein's Thought in Transition,* Purdue University Press (West Lafayette, IN), 1997.

Edwards, J. C., *Ethics Without Philosophy: Wittgenstein and the Moral Life,* University of Southern Florida Press (Gainesville), 1982.

Gregory, Richard L., editor, *The Oxford Companion to the Mind,* Oxford University Press, 1987, pp. 811-16.

Hadot, Pierre, *Philosophy as a Way of Life: Spiritual Exercises from Socrates to Foucault,* translated by Michael Chase, Blackwell (Oxford), 1995, pp. 17-18, 280-85.

Hark, Michel Ter, *Beyond The Inner and The Outer: Wittgenstein's Philosophy of Psychology,* Kluwer (Dordrecht), 1990.

Hawking, Stephen W., *A Brief History of Time: From the Big Bang to Black Holes,* Bantam Books (Toronto), 1988, pp. 171-75.

Hilmy, S. S., *The Later Wittgenstein: The Emergence of a New Philosophical Methods,* Blackwell (Oxford), 1987.

Honderich, Ted, editor, *The Oxford Companion to Philosophy,* Oxford University Press (Oxford), 1995.

Huitfeldt, Claus, and Viggo Rossvaer, *The Norwegian Wittgenstein Project Report 1988,* Norwegian Computing Center for the Humanities (Bergen), 1989.

Kenny, Anthony, *The Legacy of Wittgenstein,* Blackwell (Oxford), 1984.

Kripke, Saul, *Wittgenstein on Rules and Private Language,* Harvard University Press (Cambridge), 1982.

Malcolm, Norman, *Nothing Is Hidden: Wittgenstein Criticism of His Early Thought,* Blackwell (Oxford), 1986.

Mathieu, Marion, *Wittgenstein, Finitism, and the Foundation of Mathematics,* Clarendon Press (New York City), 1998.

McDonough, Richard, *The Argument of the Tractatus,* State University of New York Press (Buffalo), 1986.

Midgley, Mary, *Wisdom, Information, and Wonder: What Is Knowledge For?* Routledge (London), 1989.

Palmer, Donald, *Looking at Philosophy: The Unbearable Heaviness of Philosophy Made Lighter,* Mayfield (Mountain View, CA), 1988, pp. 344-60.

Park, Byong-Chal, *Phenomenological Aspects of Wittgenstein's Philosophy,* Kluwer (Dordrecht), 1998.

Pears, David Francis, *Ludwig Wittgenstein,* Harvard University Press (Cambridge, MA), 1986.

Scharfstein, Ben-Ami, *The Philosophers: Their Lives and the Nature of Their Thought,* Oxford University Press (New York City), 1980, pp. 318-34.

Schulte, Joachim, *Wittgenstein: An Introduction,* State University of New York Press (Albany), 1992.

Sluga, Hans, and David G. Stern, editors, *The Cambridge Companion to Wittgenstein,* Cambridge University Press (Cambridge), 1996.

Steiner, George, *Real Presences,* University of Chicago Press (Chicago), 1989, pp. 101-4.

Stern, David G., *Wittgenstein on Mind and Language,* Oxford University Press (New York City), 1995.

Twentieth Century Literary Criticism, Volume 59, Gale (Detroit), 1995.

PERIODICALS

Economist, Volume 327, number 7807, 1993, p. 88.
Inquiry, Volume 31, 1981, pp. 357-69.
Mind, Volume 32, 1923, pp. 465-78.
Monist, Volume 74, 1991, pp. 579-604.
New Republic, Volume 210, number 25, 1994, p. 34.
Philosophy and Literature, Volume 10, number 2, 1986, pp. 263-70; Volume 11, number 1, 1987, pp. 92-103.
Synthese, Volume 87, 1991, pp. 183-202.

*   *   *

WODEHOUSE, P(elham) G(renville) 1881-1975

PERSONAL: Surname is pronounced "*wood*-house"; born October 15, 1881, in Guildford, Surrey, England; naturalized U.S. citizen, 1955; died of a heart attack, February 14, 1975, in Southampton, New York; son of Henry Ernest (a civil servant and judge) and Eleanor (Deane) Wodehouse; married Ethel Rowley, September 30, 1914; children: Leonora (stepdaughter). *Education:* Attended Dulwich College, 1894-1900.

CAREER: Novelist, short story writer, and playwright. Hong Kong & Shanghai Bank, London, England, clerk, 1901-03; *London Globe,* London, assistant on "By the Way" column, 1902-03, writer of column, 1903-09; writer, under various pseudonyms, and drama critic for *Vanity Fair,* 1915-19.

MEMBER: Dramatists Guild, Authors League of America, Old Alleynian Association (New York; president), Coffee House (New York).

AWARDS, HONORS: Litt.D., Oxford University, 1939; named Knight Commander, Order of the British Empire, 1975.

WRITINGS:

NOVELS

A Prefect's Uncle, A & C Black, 1903, Macmillan, 1924.

The Head of Kay's, A & C Black, 1905, Macmillan, 1922.

Love among the Chickens, George Newnes, 1906, Circle Publishing, 1909, revised edition, Jenkins, 1921, autograph edition, 1963.

The White Feather, A & C Black, 1907, Macmillan, 1922.

(With A. W. Westbrook) *Not George Washington,* Cassell, 1907.

The Swoop!; or, How Clarence Saved England: A Tale of the Great Invasion, Alston Rivers, 1909.

Mike: A Public School Story, two parts, A & C Black, 1909, Macmillan, 1924, revised edition of second part published as *Enter Psmith,* Macmillan, 1935, entire book published in two volumes as *Mike at Wrykyn* and *Mike and Psmith,* both Jenkins, 1953.

The Intrusion of Jimmy, W. J. Watt, 1910 (published in England as *A Gentleman of Leisure,* Alston Rivers, 1910, abridged edition, George Newnes, 1920, autograph edition, Jenkins, 1962).

Psmith in the City, A & C Black, 1910.

The Prince and Betty, W. J. Watt, 1912 (published in England as *Psmith, Journalist,* A & C Black, 1915).

The Little Nugget, Methuen, 1913, W. J. Watt, 1914, reprinted with a new preface by the author, Barrie & Jenkins, 1972, Viking, 1991.

Something New, Appleton, 1915 (published in England as *Something Fresh,* Methuen, 1915).

Uneasy Money, Appleton, 1916.

Piccadilly Jim, Dodd, 1917, revised edition, 1931, autograph edition, Jenkins, 1966.

A Damsel in Distress, Doran, 1919, autograph edition, Jenkins, 1956.

Their Mutual Child, Boni & Liveright, 1919 (published in England as *The Coming of Bill,* Jenkins, 1920, autograph edition, 1966).

The Little Warrior, Doran, 1920 (published in England as *Jill the Reckless,* Jenkins, 1921, autograph edition, 1958).

Three Men and a Maid, Doran, 1922 (published in England as *The Girl on the Boat,* Jenkins, 1922, autograph edition, 1956).

The Adventures of Sally, Jenkins, 1922, published as *Mostly Sally,* Doran, 1923.

Leave It to Psmith, Jenkins, 1923, Doran, 1924, autograph edition, 1961.

Bill the Conqueror: His Invasion of England in the Springtime, Methuen, 1924, Doran, 1925.

Sam in the Suburbs, Doran, 1925 (published in England as *Sam the Sudden,* Methuen, 1925, reprinted with a new preface by the author, Barrie & Jenkins, 1972, Penguin, 1978).

The Small Bachelor (based on his play *Oh! Lady, Lady!* [also see below]), Doran, 1927.

Money for Nothing, Doubleday, Doran, 1928, autograph edition, Jenkins, 1959.

Fish Preferred, Doubleday, Doran, 1929 (published in England as *Summer Lightning,* Jenkins, 1929, autograph edition, 1964).

Big Money, Doubleday, Doran, 1931, autograph edition, Jenkins, 1965.

If I Were You, Doubleday, Doran, 1931, autograph edition, Jenkins, 1958.

Doctor Sally, Methuen, 1932.

Hot Water, Doubleday, Doran, 1932, autograph edition, Jenkins, 1956.

Heavy Weather, Little, Brown, 1933, autograph edition, Jenkins, 1960.

Thank You, Jeeves, Little, Brown, 1934, autograph edition, Jenkins, 1956.

Brinkley Manor, Little, Brown, 1934 (published in England as *Right Ho, Jeeves,* Jenkins, 1934, autograph edition, 1957).

Trouble Down at Tudsleigh, International Magazine Co., 1935.

The Luck of the Bodkins, Jenkins, 1935, Little, Brown, 1936, autograph edition, Jenkins, 1956.

Laughing Gas, Doubleday, Doran, 1936, autograph edition, Jenkins, 1959.

Summer Moonshine, Doubleday, Doran, 1937, autograph edition, Jenkins, 1956.

The Code of the Woosters, Doubleday, Doran, 1938, autograph edition, Jenkins, 1962.

Uncle Fred in the Springtime, Doubleday, Doran, 1939, autograph edition, Jenkins, 1962.

Quick Service, Doubleday, Doran, 1940, autograph edition, Jenkins, 1960.

Money in the Bank, Doubleday, Doran, 1942.

Joy in the Morning, Doubleday, 1946, reprinted with a new preface by the author, Jenkins, 1974, published as *Jeeves in the Morning,* HarperCollins, 1983.

Full Moon, Doubleday, 1947.

Spring Fever, Doubleday, 1948.

Uncle Dynamite, Jenkins, 1948.

The Mating Season, Didier, 1949.

The Old Reliable, Doubleday, 1951.

Angel Cake (based on the play *The Butter and Egg Man* by George F. Kaufman), Doubleday, 1952 (published in England as *Barmy in Wonderland,* Jenkins, 1952, autograph edition, 1958).

Pigs Have Wings, Doubleday, 1952, reprinted with a new preface by the author, Barrie & Jenkins, 1974.

Ring for Jeeves, Jenkins, 1953, autograph edition, 1963, published as *The Return of Jeeves,* Simon & Schuster, 1954

Jeeves and the Feudal Spirit, Jenkins, 1954, published as *Bertie Wooster Sees It Through,* Simon & Schuster, 1955.

French Leave, Jenkins, 1956, Simon & Schuster, 1959, reprinted with a new preface by the author, Barrie & Jenkins, 1974.

The Butler Did It, Simon & Schuster, 1957 (published in England as *Something Fishy,* Jenkins, 1957).

Cocktail Time, Simon & Schuster, 1958.

How Right You Are, Jeeves, Simon & Schuster, 1960 (published in England as *Jeeves in the Offing,* Jenkins, 1960).

Ice in the Bedroom, Simon & Schuster, 1961.

Service with a Smile, Simon & Schuster, 1961.

Stiff Upper Lip, Jeeves, Simon & Schuster, 1963.

Biffen's Millions, Simon & Schuster, 1964 (published in England as *Frozen Assets,* Jenkins, 1964).

The Brinkmanship of Galahad Threepwood: A Blandings Castle Novel, Simon & Schuster, 1965 (published in England as *Galahad at Blandings,* Jenkins, 1965).

The Purloined Paperweight, Simon & Schuster, 1967 (published in England as *Company for Henry,* Jenkins, 1967).

Do Butlers Burgle Banks? Simon & Schuster, 1968.

A Pelican at Blandings, Jenkins, 1969, published as *No Nudes Is Good Nudes,* Simon & Schuster, 1970.

The Girl in Blue, Barrie & Jenkins, 1970, Simon & Schuster, 1971.

Jeeves and the Tie That Binds, Simon & Schuster, 1971 (published in England as *Much Obliged, Jeeves,* autograph edition, Barrie & Jenkins, 1971).

Pearls, Girls, and Monty Bodkins, Barrie & Jenkins, 1972, published as *The Plot That Thickened,* Simon & Schuster, 1973.

Bachelors Anonymous, Barrie & Jenkins, 1973, Simon & Schuster, 1974.

The Cat-Nappers: A Jeeves and Bertie Story, Simon & Schuster, 1974 (published in England as *Aunts Aren't Gentlemen: A Jeeves and Bertie Story,* Barrie & Jenkins, 1974).

Sunset at Blandings, Chatto & Windus, 1977, Simon & Schuster, 1978.

Life with Jeeves, Viking, 1983.

The World of Jeeves, HarperCollins, 1988.

P. G. Wodehouse: Five Complete Novels, Grammercy, 1996.

STORIES

The Pothunters and Other School Stories, A & C Black, 1902, Macmillan, 1924.

Tales of St. Austin's, A & C Black, 1903, Macmillan, 1923.

The Gold Bat and Other School Stories, A & C Black, 1904, Macmillan, 1923.

The Man Upstairs and Other Stories, Methuen, 1914, reprinted with a new preface by the author, Barrie & Jenkins, 1971.

The Man with Two Left Feet and Other Stories, Methuen, 1917, A. L. Burt, 1933.

My Man Jeeves, George Newnes, 1919, published as *Carry On, Jeeves,* Jenkins, 1925, autograph edition, 1960.

The Indiscretions of Archie, Doran, 1921.

The Clicking of Cuthbert, Jenkins, 1922, autograph edition, 1956, published as *Golf without Tears,* Doran, 1924.

Jeeves, Doran, 1923 (published in England as *The Inimitable Jeeves,* Jenkins, 1923, autograph edition, 1956).

Ukridge, Jenkins, 1924, autograph edition, 1960, published as *He Rather Enjoyed It,* Doran, 1926.

The Heart of a Goof, Jenkins, 1926, autograph edition, 1956, revised edition, Classics of Golf, 1990, published as *Divots,* Doran, 1927.

Meet Mr. Mulliner, Jenkins, 1927, Doubleday, Doran, 1928, autograph edition, Jenkins, 1956.

Mr. Mulliner Speaking, Jenkins, 1929, Doubleday, Doran, 1930, autograph edition, Jenkins, 1961.

Very Good, Jeeves, Doubleday, Doran, 1930, autograph edition, Jenkins, 1958.

Mulliner Nights, Doubleday, Doran, 1933, autograph edition, Jenkins, 1966.

Blandings Castle, Doubleday, Doran, 1935 (published in England as *Blandings Castle and Elsewhere,* Jenkins, 1935, autograph edition, 1957).

Young Men in Spats, Doubleday, Doran, 1936, autograph edition, Jenkins, 1957.

The Crime Wave at Blandings, Doubleday, Doran, 1937 (published in England as *Lord Emsworth and Others,* Jenkins, 1937, autograph edition, 1956).

Eggs, Beans and Crumpets, Doubleday, Doran, 1940, autograph edition, Jenkins, 1963.

Dudley Is Back to Normal, Doubleday, Doran, 1940.

Nothing Serious, Jenkins, 1950, Doubleday, 1951, autograph edition, Jenkins, 1964.

Selected Stories, introduction by John W. Aldridge, Modern Library, 1958.

A Few Quick Ones, Simon & Schuster, 1959.

Plum Pie, Jenkins, 1966, Simon & Schuster, 1967.

Jeeves, Jeeves, Jeeves, Avon, 1976.

The Swoop and Other Stories, edited by David A. Jasen, foreword by Malcolm Muggeridge, Seabury, 1979.

The World of Mr. Mulliner, Taplinger, 1985.

Tales from the Drones Club, International Polygonics, 1991.

The Golf Omnibus, Outlet Book, 1991.

The Uncollected Wodehouse, edited by D. A. Jasen, foreword by M. Muggeridge, International Polygonics, 1992.

Enter Jeeves: 15 Early Stories, Dover Publications (Mineola, NY), 1997.

PLAYS

(With John Stapleton) *A Gentleman of Leisure* (comedy; based on Wodehouse's novel of the same name), first produced on Broadway at Playhouse Theatre, August 24, 1911.

(With Stapleton) *A Thief for the Night,* first produced on Broadway at Playhouse Theatre, 1913.

(With H. W. Westbrook) *Brother Alfred,* first produced on West End at Savoy Theatre, 1913.

The Play's the Thing (three-act drama; based on *Spiel in Schloss* by Ferenc Molnar; first produced on Broadway at Henry Miller's Theatre, November 3, 1926), Brentano's, 1927.

(With Valerie Wyngate) *Her Cardboard Lover* (based on a play by Jacques Deval), first produced in New York at Empire Theatre, March 21, 1927.

Good Morning, Bill (three-act comedy; based on a play by Ladislaus Fodor; first produced on West End at Duke of York's Theatre, November 28, 1927), Methuen, 1928.

(With Ian Hay) *A Damsel in Distress* (three-act comedy; based on Wodehouse's novel of the same name; first produced off-Broadway at New Theatre, August 13, 1928), Samuel French, 1930.

(With Hay) *Baa, Baa, Black Sheep* (three-act comedy; first produced off-Broadway at New Theatre, April 22, 1929), Samuel French, 1930.

Candlelight (three-act drama; based on "Kleine Komodie" by Siegfried Geyer; first produced in New York at Empire Theatre, September 30, 1929), Samuel French, 1934.

(With Hay) *Leave It to Psmith* (three-act comedy; based on Wodehouse's novel of the same name; first produced in London at Shaftesbury Theatre, September 29, 1930), Samuel French, 1932.

(With Guy Bolton) *Who's Who* (three-act comedy), first produced on West End at Duke of York's Theatre, September 20, 1934.

The Inside Stand (three-act farce), first produced in London at Saville Theatre, November 20, 1935.

(With Bolton) *Don't Listen, Ladies* (two-act comedy; based on the play *N'ecoutez pas, mesdames,* by Sacha Guitry), first produced on Broadway at Booth Theatre, December 28, 1948.

(With Bolton) *Carry On, Jeeves* (three-act comedy; based on Wodehouse's novel of the same title), Evans Brothers, 1956.

MUSICALS

(Author of lyrics with others) *The Gay Gordons,* book by Seymour Hicks, music by Guy Jones, first produced in London at Aldwych Theatre, 1913.

(With C. H. Bovill and F. Tours) *Nuts and Wine,* first produced in London at Empire Theatre, 1914.

(With Guy Bolton and H. Reynolds) *Miss Springtime,* music by Emmerich Kalman and Jerome Kern, first produced in New York at New Amsterdam Theatre, September 25, 1916.

(With Bolton) *Ringtime,* first produced in New York, 1917.

(Author of book and lyrics with Bolton) *Have a Heart,* music by Kern, first produced in New York at Liberty Theatre, January 11, 1917.

(Author of book and lyrics with Bolton) *Oh, Boy,* first produced in New York at Princess Theatre, February 20, 1917, produced in London as Oh, Joy, 1919.

(Author of book and lyrics with Bolton) *Leave It to Jane* (musical version of *The College Widow* by George Ade) music by Kern, first produced in Albany, NY, July, 1917, produced on Broadway at Longacre Theatre, August 28, 1917.

(Author of book and lyrics with Bolton) *The Riviera Girl,* music by Kalman, first produced in New York at New Amsterdam Theatre, September 24, 1917.

(Author of book and lyrics with Bolton) *Miss 1917,* music by Victor Herbert and Kern, first produced off-Broadway at Century Theatre, November 5, 1917.

(With Bolton) *The Second Century Show,* first produced in New York, 1917.

(Author of book and lyrics with Bolton) *Oh! Lady, Lady!,* music by Kern, first produced in New York at Princess Theatre, February 1, 1918.

(With Bolton) *See You Later,* music by J. Szule, first produced in Baltimore at Academy of Music, April 15, 1918.

(Author of book and lyrics with Bolton) *The Girl behind the Gun* (based on play *Madame et son filleul,* by Hennequin and Weber), music by Ivan Caryll, first produced in New York at New Amsterdam Theatre, September 16, 1918, produced in London as *Kissing Time* at Winter Garden Theatre, 1918.

(Author of book and lyrics with Bolton) *Oh My Dear,* music by Louis Hirsch, first produced in New York at Princess Theatre, November 27, 1918, produced in Toronto as *Ask Dad,* 1918.

(With Bolton) *The Rose of China,* music by Armand Vecsey, first produced in New York at Lyric Theatre, November 25, 1919.

(Author of lyrics with Clifford Grey) *Sally,* music by Kern, first produced in New York by Flo Ziegfeld, 1920.

(Author of book and lyrics with Fred Thompson) *The Golden Moth,* music by Ivor Novello, first produced in London at Adelphi Theatre, October 5, 1921.

(Author of book and lyrics with George Grossmith) *The Cabaret Girl,* music by Kern, first produced in London at Winter Garden Theatre, 1922.

(Author of book and lyrics with Grossmith) *The Beauty Prize,* music by Kern, first produced in London at Aldwych Theatre, September 5, 1923.

(Author of book and lyrics with Bolton) *Sitting Pretty,* music by Kern, first produced in New York at Fulton Theatre, April 8, 1924.

(Adapter with Laurie Wylie) *Hearts and Diamonds* (light opera; based on *The Orlov* by Biuno Granichstaedten and Ernest Marischka; first produced in London at Strand Theatre, June

1, 1926), English lyrics by Graham John, Keith Prowse & Co., 1926.

(With others) *Showboat,* music by Oscar Hammerstein, first produced on Broadway at Ziegfeld Theatre, December 27, 1927.

(Author of book with Bolton) *Oh Kay!,* lyrics by Ira Gershwin, music by George Gershwin, first produced on Broadway at Imperial Theatre, November 8, 1926.

(Author of book and lyrics with Bolton) *The Nightingale,* music by Vecsey, first produced on Broadway at Al Jolson's Theatre, January 3, 1927.

(Author of lyrics with Ira Gershwin) *Rosalie,* book by Bolton and Bill McGuire, music by George Gershwin and Sigmund Romberg, first produced in New York at New Amsterdam Theatre, January 10, 1928.

(Author of book with Grossmith; author of lyrics with Grey) *The Three Musketeers* (based on the novel by Alexandre Dumas; first produced in New York at Lyric Theatre, March 13, 1928), music by Rudolph Frinil, Harms Inc., 1937.

(Author of book with Bolton, Howard Lindsay, and Russel Crouse) *Anything Goes* (first produced on Broadway at Alvin Theatre, November 21, 1934), music and lyrics by Cole Porter, Samuel French, 1936.

FILMS

Coauthor of *A Damsel in Distress,* based on his novel of the same title, released by RKO General, Inc., 1920; author of *Rosalie,* based on his play of the same title, released by Metro-Goldwyn-Mayer, Inc., 1930. Also author of *Summer Lightning,* based on his novel of the same title, and *Three French Girls.*

OTHER

(Adapter) *William Tell Told Again* (based on the classic tale), A & C Black, 1904.

(With H. W. Westbrook) *The Globe "By the Way" Book: A Literary Quick-Lunch for People Who Have Only Got Five Minutes to Spare,* Globe, 1908, edited by W. K. Haselden, Heineman, 1985.

Louder and Funnier (essays), Faber, 1932, autograph edition, Jenkins, 1963.

(Editor) *A Century of Humour,* Hutchinson, 1934.

(Editor with Scott Meredith and author of introduction) *The Week-End Book of Humour,* Washburn, 1952, published as *P. G. Wodehouse Selects the Best of Humor,* Grosset, 1965.

(Editor with Meredith and author of introduction) *The Best of Modern Humour,* Metcalf, 1952.

Performing Flea: A Self-Portrait in Letters (letters written by Wodehouse to William Townsend), introduction by Townsend, Jenkins, 1953, published as *Author! Author!* Simon & Schuster, 1962.

(With Guy Bolton) *Bring on the Girls!: The Improbable Story of Our Life In Musical Comedy with Pictures to Prove It,* Simon & Schuster, 1953.

America, I Like You, Simon & Schuster, 1956, revised edition published as *Over Seventy: An Autobiography with Digressions,* Jenkins, 1957.

(Editor with Meredith and author of introduction) *A Carnival of Modern Humor,* Delacorte, 1967.

Most of P. G. Wodehouse, Simon & Schuster, 1969.

Wodehouse on Wodehouse (contains *Performing Flea, Bring On the Girls!* and *Over Seventy*), Hutchinson, 1980.

The Great Sermon Handicap, photographs by William Hewison, James H. Heineman, 1983, published as *The Great Sermon Handicap,* Volume 1: *Rendered in English, Phonetic English, Latin, French, Spanish, Italian, Catalan, Portuguese, Rumanian, and Rhaetomansch,* 1989; Volume 2: *Rendered in English, Phonetic English, Chaucerian English, Dutch, Flemish, Afrikaans, Frisian, German Mittelhochdeutsch, Plattdeutsch, Luxemburgian, Yiddish, Schiwzerdeutsch,* 1990; Volume 3: *Rendered in English, Phonetic English, Danish, Swedish, Old Norse, Icelandic, Faroese, Norwegian,* 1991; Volume 4: *Rendered in English, Phonetic English, Esperanto, Pidgin English, French Creole, Papiamento, Finnish, Hungarian, Basque, Romany, Welsh, Breton, Irish, Gaelic,* 1992; Volume 4: *Rendered in English, Phonetic English, Russian, Ukrainian, Belorussian, Polish, Czech, Slovak, Bulgarian, Serbo-Croatian, Macedonian,* 1993; Volume 5: *Afro-Asiatic or Hamito-Semitic Languages,* 1993.

Nuggets, edited by Richard Osborne, Heineman, 1983.

Fore! The Best of Wodehouse on Golf, edited by D. R. Bensen, Ticknor & Fields, 1985.

A Wodehouse Bestiary, edited by D. R. Bensen, Houghton, 1985.

Life at Blandings, Viking, 1988.

What's in Wodehouse? or, Jeeves Has Gone-a-Shrimping and Bertie Is in the Soup: A Quiz Book, edited by Charles E. Gould, Heineman, 1989.

Yours, Plum (letters), Heineman, 1990.

Wodehouse on Crime, International Polygonics, 1990.

Wodehouse Is the Best Medicine, International Polygonics, 1992.

Week-End Wodehouse, Trafalgar Square, 1993.

MEDIA ADAPTATIONS: Several of Wodehouse's novels were adapted by Edward Duke into a play, *Jeeves Takes Charge,* c. 1984. Some of Wodehouse's short stories were produced by the BBC under the title *Wodehouse Playhouse.*

SIDELIGHTS: P. G. Wodehouse long entertained thoughts of becoming a writer—he told interviewer Gerald Clarke of the *Paris Review:* "I was writing stories when I was five. I don't remember what I did before that. Just loafed, I suppose." Best known for his stories concerning the young Bertram Wilberforce Wooster ("Bertie") and his valet Jeeves, Wodehouse is considered a master of English humor and a powerful influence on many later writers.

The characters in Wodehouse's world are thoroughly unique. Easily his most famous characters are Bertram Wilberforce Wooster and his incredible valet Jeeves. They first appeared in a story entitled "Extricating Young Gussie" which Wodehouse wrote for the *Saturday Evening Post.* While Bertie was a main character in the story, Jeeves was relegated to a minor part. As Wodehouse explained to Clarke: "I only intended to use him once. His first entrance was: 'Mrs. Gregson to see you, Sir'. . . . He only had one other line: 'Very good, Sir. Which suit will you wear?' But then I was writing a story, 'The Artistic Career of Corky,' about two young men, Bertie Wooster and his friend Corky, getting into a lot of trouble. I thought: Well, how can I get them out? And I thought: 'Suppose one of them had an omniscient valet?' I wrote a short story about him, then another short story, then several more short stories and novels." In the introduction to his *Jeeves Omnibus,* Wodehouse wrote, "I still blush to think of the off-hand way I treated him at our first encounter."

Contrary to the assumptions of many readers and critics, Jeeves is no mere butler; he is a valet or, as he puts it, a gentleman's personal gentleman. In addition to the duties normally performed by a butler, a gentleman's gentleman is responsible for the running of the entire household as well as such things as his employer's dress and daily schedule. Jeeves, unlike most valets, is also entrusted with the task of saving the lives of Bertie and his numerous scheming accomplices from time to time.

Bertie, for his part, may be seen as the most outstanding example of a long line of irresponsible young gentlemen characterized by Wodehouse, or, as Richard Voorhees phrases it, the "crowning achievement in the creation of the silly young ass," and "one of literature's idiots." While there can be little doubt as to Bertie's lack of intelligence (he readily admits it; in one of the stories in *My Man Jeeves,* when Jeeves says, "We must think, sir," Bertie replies, "You do it. I don't have the equipment."), he remains one of Wodehouse's most personable and engaging characters. He is extremely good natured and gregarious, always ready for a dinner party or a weekend at one of his aunts' country houses. Although he is presumably in his late twenties, he persists in childish schemes that invariably backfire leaving his salvation, time and again, in the hands of Jeeves. Bertie lives by the strict "Code of the Woosters" which compels him never to let a pal down. As a result he is at the mercy of an endless supply of old school chums and girl friends who entreat him to rescue them from a variety of sticky situations. R. B. D. French surmises that "if the Duke of Wellington had asked the Wooster of that day to charge the Old Guard, you would not have heard that Wooster saying that he had to run into Brussels for a moment and was afraid he would not be able to manage it. He would have been where Bertie is to be found—in the thick of the grape-shot, or purloining a policeman's helmet to get young Stephanie Byng out of a jam, as the case may be."

As a result of his distinctive writing style—a style that has served as the inspiration for a number of contemporary humorists—many critics have labeled Wodehouse the dominant force in the establishment of modern humorous fiction technique. But Robert A. Hall, who notes that the author has been hailed as "the greatest master of twentieth-century prose," says that "despite general recognition of Wodehouse's merits as a stylist . . . there has been relatively little detailed analysis of the features that have contributed to his almost unparalleled success in humorous writing." Hall's book *The Comic Style of P. G. Wodehouse* is a thorough study of the stylistic devices Wodehouse used for comic effect. "Humor," says Hall, "has two essential ingredients. For us to laugh at something, it must contain some kind of incongruity, and we must be emotionally neutral, without our personal feelings being involved." He finds that "Wodehouse makes use of just about every resource available in standard English plus a few from non-standard English, to obtain his effects."

Another good example of Wodehouse's unique use of language to evoke humor can be found running throughout the Jeeves and Bertie stories. Even though Bertie is supposedly a graduate of Eton and Oxford, his vocabulary is extremely limited, and he spends a good deal of time groping for the right word, or, as Wodehouse so often says, the *mot juste.* In *Stiff Upper Lip, Jeeves* he says, "I suppose Stiffy's sore about this . . . what's the word? . . . Not vaseline . . . Vacillation, that's it." In *Jeeves and the Feudal Spirit* Hall finds one of the many instances in which Bertie depends on Jeeves to fill in the blank: "Let a plugugly like young Thos loose in the community with a cosh, and you are inviting disaster and . . . what's the word? Something about cats." Jeeves replies, "Cataclysms, sir?"

Jeeves's vocabulary is, in fact, so broad that Bertie, who is at least somewhat accustomed to it, is often forced to translate for his friends. Hall refers to a scene in "The Artistic Career of Corky" as an example; Jeeves says, "The scheme I would suggest cannot fail

of success, but it has what may seem to you a drawback, sir, in that it requires a certain financial outlay." "He means," Bertie explains to Corky, "that he has got a pippin of an idea but it's going to cost a lot."

But Hall identifies Wodehouse's best-known stylistic device as "his imagery involving similes, metaphors, and other types of comparison. The chief characteristic of his imagery is the wide range from which he draws his comparisons, using them in every instance to emphasize resemblances which at first glance seem highly incongruous (and hence provide the reader's laughter), but which at the same time are highly appropriate to the particular person or situation described. His imagery—carefully planned, of course, like all the rest of his writing—is therefore particularly vivid and apposite." An example from *Leave It to Psmith:* "A sound like two or three pigs feeding rather noisily in the middle of a thunderstorm interrupted his meditation." In *The Mating Season* Wodehouse used, "That 'ha, ha,' so like the expiring quack of a duck dying of a broken heart." And finally in *The Code of the Woosters* we find: "Have you ever heard Sir Watkyn Bassett dealing with a bowl of soup? It's not unlike the Scottish express going through a tunnel." As Hall says, "such a list could be continued almost indefinitely; a whole volume could be compiled simply by excerpting all the imagery which Wodehouse uses in his stories."

Wodehouse's brilliance in utilizing these various stylistic devices, his deft handling of the English language, and his humorous observations on human nature combined to make him one of the most popular writers of the twentieth century. David A. Jasen, who calls Wodehouse the "funniest writer in the world," believes that the author built up a large following through the use of repetition. "It is always a delight to welcome an old friend," he writes, "for old friends recall happily shared experiences, and this is the sense of intimacy gotten when reading the works of Wodehouse." Jasen says that Wodehouse "took pieces of his childhood, blended with snatches of the quickly altering world of the Edwardians and the early Georgians, and added his own abundantly creative imagination. His plots fit his people, who are consistent not with reality but with themselves and the world of his conception. He attempted to be realistic only in this way and achieved a timelessness in his world which makes his writings universally appealing. His humor depends mainly on exaggeration and understatement, the incongruous, the inappropriate phrase, and the use of the literal interpretation of an idiomatic expression out of context for effect. He developed a new vocabulary, mixing slang along with classical phrases, and fashioning supremely inventive as well as highly diverting hyperboles. He is extremely serious about his work and took tremendous trouble with its construction. He polished his sentences as meticulously as one of his Drones would choose a tie. His only object in writing was purely and simply to amuse." Wodehouse confirmed this in his autobiographical *Over Seventy* when he wrote: "My books may not be the sort of books the cognoscenti feel justified in blowing the twelve and a half shillings on, but I do work at them. When in due course Charon ferries me across the Styx and everyone is telling everyone else what a rotten writer I was, I hope at least one voice will be heard piping up: 'But he did take trouble.'"

BIOGRAPHICAL/CRITICAL SOURCES:

BOOKS

Concise Dictionary of British Literary Biography, Volume 6: *Modern Writers, 1914-1945,* Gale (Detroit), 1991.

Contemporary Literary Criticism, Gale, Volume 1, 1973; Volume 2, 1974; Volume 5, 1976; Volume 10, 1979; Volume 22, 1982.

D'Auzac, Evelyn, *The Lyrics of P. G. Wodehouse,* P. Lang, 1998.

Dictionary of Literary Biography, Volume 34: *British Novelists, 1890-1929: Traditionalists,* Gale, 1985.

French, R. B. D., *P. G. Wodehouse,* Oliver & Boyd, 1966, Barnes & Noble, 1967.

Green, Benny, *P. G. Wodehouse: A Literary Biography,* Rutledge Press, 1981.

Hall, Robert A., Jr., *The Comic Style of P. G. Wodehouse,* Archon, 1974.

Heineman, James H., and Donald R. Benson, editors, *P. G. Wodehouse: A Centenary Celebration, 1881-1981,* Pierpoint Morgan Library, 1981.

Jasen, David A., *P. G. Wodehouse: A Portrait of A Master,* Mason & Lipscomb, 1974.

Short Story Criticism, Volume 2, Gale, 1989.

Sproat, Iain, *Wodehouse at War,* Ticknor & Fields, 1981.

Usborne, *Wodehouse Nuggets,* Hutchinson, 1983.

Voorhees, Richard, *P. G. Wodehouse,* Twayne, 1966.

PERIODICALS

Chicago Tribune, October 15, 1981.

Economist, September 22, 1990, p. 100.

Library Journal, February 1, 1994, p. 128; June 1, 1994, p. 188; December, 1994, p. 155; January, 1995, p. 162; April 15, 1995, p. 120; May 1, 1995, p. 150; November 1, 1995, p. 126; November 15, 1995, p. 119; December, 1995, p. 182; March 15, 1996, p. 112.

National Review, December 11, 1995, p. 132.

Newsweek, December 5, 1988, p. 57.

New York, July 24, 1995, p. 43.

New Yorker, May 22, 1948; May 22, 1989, p. 94.

New York Times, February 15, 1975; October 18, 1981; November 12, 1984; November 7, 1985; October 20, 1987; March 23, 1989.

New York Times Book Review, April 28, 1991, p. 17.

Paris Review, winter, 1975.

Times (London), November 24, 1983; June 21, 1984; June 29, 1985; July 9, 1987.

Wall Street Journal, May 2, 1996, p. A13.

Washington Post, February 3, 1984.

Washington Post Book World, November 29, 1981.

*   *   *

WOLFE, Gene (Rodman) 1931-

PERSONAL: Born May 7, 1931, in Brooklyn, NY; son of Roy Emerson (in sales) and Mary Olivia (Ayers) Wolfe; married Rosemary Frances Dietsch, November 3, 1956; children: Roy II, Madeleine, Therese, Matthew. *Education:* Attended Texas A & M University, 1949-52; University of Houston, B.S.M.E., 1956. *Religion:* Roman Catholic.

ADDRESSES: Home—P.O. Box 69, Barrington, IL 60011. *Agent*—Virginia Kidd, Box 278, Milford, PA 18337.

CAREER: Project engineer with Procter & Gamble, 1956-72; *Plant Engineering Magazine,* Barrington, IL, senior editor, 1972-84; writer. *Military service:* U.S. Army, 1952-54; received Combat Infantry badge.

MEMBER: Science Fiction Writers of America.

AWARDS, HONORS: Nebula Award, Science Fiction Writers of America, 1973, for novella *The Death of Doctor Island;* Chicago Foundation for Literature Award, 1977, for *Peace;* Rhysling Award, 1978, for poem "The Computer Iterates the Greater Trumps"; Nebula Award nomination, 1979, for novella *Seven American Nights;* Illinois Arts Council award, 1981, for short story "In Looking-Glass Castle"; World Fantasy Award, 1981, for *The Shadow of the Torturer,* 1996, for life achievement; Nebula Award, and *Locus* Award, both 1982, both for *The Claw of the Conciliator;* British Science Fiction Award, 1982; British Fantasy Award, 1983; *Locus* Award, 1983, for *The Sword of the Lictor;* John W. Campbell Memorial Award, Science Fiction Research Association, 1984, for *The Citadel of the Autarch;* World Fantasy Award, 1989, for collection *Storeys from the Old Hotel;* nominated for Nebula Award, 1993, for *Nightside the Long Sun.*

WRITINGS:

SCIENCE FICTION/FANTASY

Operation ARES, Berkley Publishing (New York City), 1970.

The Fifth Head of Cerberus (three novellas), Scribner (New York City), 1972.

(With Ursula K. LeGuin and James Tiptree, Jr.) *The New Atlantis, and Other Novellas of Science Fiction,* edited by Robert Silverberg, Hawthorn (New York City), 1975.

The Devil in a Forest (juvenile), Follett, 1976.

The Island of Doctor Death and Other Stories and Other Stories, Pocket Books (New York City), 1980.

The Shadow of the Torturer (first book in "The Book of the New Sun" tetralogy), Simon & Schuster (New York City), 1980.

Gene Wolfe's Book of Days (short stories), Doubleday (New York City), 1981.

The Claw of the Conciliator (second book in "The Book of the New Sun" tetralogy), Simon & Schuster, 1981.

The Sword of the Lictor (third book in "The Book of the New Sun" tetralogy), Simon & Schuster, 1982.

The Citadel of the Autarch (fourth book in "The Book of the New Sun" tetralogy), Simon & Schuster, 1983.

The Wolfe Archipelago (short stories), Ziesing Bros. (Willimantic, CT), 1983.

Plan(e)t Engineering, New England Science Fiction Association, 1984.

Free Live Free, Ziesing Bros., 1984, new edition, Tor Books (New York City), 1985.

Soldier of the Mist, Tor Books, 1986.

The Urth of the New Sun (sequel to "The Book of the New Sun" tetralogy), Tor Books, 1987.

There Are Doors, Tor Books, 1988.

Storeys from the Old Hotel (short stories), Kerosina, 1988.

Endangered Species (short stories), Tor Books, 1989.

Seven American Nights (bound with *Sailing to Byzantium,* by Silverberg), Tor Books, 1989.

Soldier of Arete (sequel to *Soldier of the Mist*), St. Martin's (New York City), 1989.

Pandora by Holly Hollander, Tor Books, 1990.

Castleview, Tor Books, 1991.

Castle of Days, Tor Books, 1992.

Nightside the Long Sun, Tor Books, 1993.

Lake of the Long Sun, Tor Books, 1993.

Sword and Citadel, Orb, 1994.

Calde of the Long Sun, Tor Books, 1994.

Shadow & Claw (contains *The Shadow of the Torturer,* and *The Claw of the Conciliator*), Orb, 1994.

Exodus from the Long Sun, Tor Books, 1995.

OTHER

Peace (novel), Harper (New York City), 1975.
The Castle of the Otter (essays), Ziesing Bros., 1982.
Bibliomen, Cheap Street (New Castle, VA), 1984.
Empires of Foliage and Flower, Cheap Street, 1987.
For Rosemary (poetry), Kerosina, 1988.

SIDELIGHTS: "With the publication of his tetralogy *The Book of the New Sun,* Gene Wolfe has entered the ranks of the major contemporary writers of science fiction," Pamela Sargent asserts in *Twentieth-Century Science Fiction Writers.* The series is set on Earth and takes place far in the future in a society reminiscent of medieval Europe in its social structure where long-forgotten technologies appear magical. When Severian, an apprentice torturer, is exiled from his guild for aiding the suicide of a prisoner he loves, a journey of discovery is inaugurated that culminates in Severian's elevation to Autarch, ruler of Urth. "The far-future world of Urth through which Wolfe's characters move is a world of beauty and horror, one in which humanity's great accomplishments are not only past, but also nearly forgotten, and in which the lack of resources makes the knowledge that remains nearly useless," notes Sargent. Severian, however, possesses perfect recall, making his retrospective narration fecund with detail and meaning. As Thomas D. Clareson says in his *Dictionary of Literary Biography* essay, Severian's account is "a rich tapestry rivaling any imaginary world portrayed in contemporary science fiction"; he calls the series of books "one of the high accomplishments of modern science fiction."

While *The Book of the New Sun* series has been celebrated for the vividness of its descriptions, reviewers also commend Wolfe's intricate imagery. "In fact, there are two 'Books of the New Sun,'" Nicholls argues. "Out in the open is the wonderfully vivid and inventive story of a brave and lonely hero; below is the sea of allusion and juxtaposition . . . [and] a pungent debate on ontology, eschatology and the metaphysics of time." Contributing to the series' profundity, C. N. Manlove suggests in *Kansas Quarterly,* is Wolfe's literary skill: "The author creates his images with such apparent effortlessness that they seem to have been come upon, to have been always there, rather than to have been invented. Every stage of Severian's journey is accompanied by a startling new image or landscape." "With great urgency, layer after layer," John Clute similarly maintains in the *Washington Post Book World,* Wolfe "has created a world radiant with meaning, a novel that makes sense in the end only if it is read as an attempt to represent the Word of God."

It is this layering of image and meaning that has led critics such as Algis Budrys to praise the overall literary quality of Wolfe's series: "As a piece of literature, the work is simply overwhelming," Budrys relates in the *Magazine of Fantasy and Science Fiction.* "Severian is a character realized in a depth and to a breadth we have never seen in SF before," the critic explains, adding that "as craftsmanship and as literature, what we're talking about are attributes that are world-class as *prose,* not 'just' as SF." As Thomas M. Disch elaborates in the *Washington Post Book World:* "Gene Wolfe has managed to do what no science fantasy author has done heretofore—he's produced a work of art that can satisfy adult appetites and in which even the most fantastical elements register as poetry rather than as penny-whistle whimsy. Furthermore, he's done this without in any way sacrificing the showmanship and splashy colors that auger a popular success." "In a triumph of imagination, [Wolfe] creates a truly alien social order that the reader comes to experience from within," concludes *New York Times Book Review* critic Gerald Jonas. "The result

does not make for easy reading. But once into it, there is no stopping—and you will not quickly forget Severian or his world." Although the author leaves room for future volumes, a *Booklist* reviewer proposes that "it is not necessary that we see any more for this series to loom as a major landmark of contemporary American literature. . . . Wolfe has wrought a genuine marvel here."

While *The Urth of the New Sun* continues Severian's story, it is "neither afterthought nor reprise," *Times Literary Supplement* reviewer Colin Greenland remarks. Nevertheless, Roz Kaveney writes in the *Washington Post Book World,* "this volume makes of the whole work a palimpsest, in which moments from an underlay of earlier versions of reality crop up suddenly, producing seeming inconsistencies. . . . *The Urth of the New Sun* makes of the whole sequence a more perfect work by showing us [these] inconsistencies before ironing them out." The novel traces the journey of Severian, now Autarch, as he travels to a high galactic court to petition for the "new sun" that will renew Urth. While the concept of one person representing his race to a higher authority is a common science fiction convention, a *Washington Post Book World* critic notes that "as usual, Wolfe takes this old chestnut and makes it into something very rich and very strange."

Kaveney likewise claims that "Gene Wolfe's career has thus far been dedicated to making us see in a new light some of what we had thought of as the stock habits of science fiction and fantasy." In *Free Live Free,* for example, "Wolfe extends his freedom in another direction, embracing for his own purposes that problematic mix of nonscientific lore and dreams of power known as the occult," comments Jonas. The result, says the critic, is a series of "character studies," something "rare in science fiction." *Soldier of the Mist* is also innovative in its account of Latro, a soldier of ancient Greece whose memory is wiped clean every time he sleeps—payment for having seen the gods; Latro's condition necessitates the keeping of a journal in which he records each day's events—with each new day he must read the journal and relearn his life. Guided by his text and various gods, Latro journeys to regain his memory. Wolfe continues Latro's story in *Soldier of Arete,* in which Latro becomes embroiled in the political and military rivalry between Greece and Sparta. John Calvin Batchelor observes in the *Washington Post Book World* that *Soldier of the Mist,* while difficult reading, is "a work of consequence." The author "is a master of science fiction," Batchelor concludes, "and for the best of all reasons, vaulting ambition."

Some of Wolfe's novels are set in contemporary American society and present the intrusion of fantastic elements into mundane reality. A subtle example of this is *Pandora by Holly Hollander,* a murder mystery narrated by a teenage girl named Pandora. The investigation focuses on the contents of a mysterious box, and, as Faren Miller observes in *Locus,* while everything in the novel "has an explanation in human fear, curiosity, passion, or greed. . . , the little things, the offbeat details, manage to give a sparkle of fairytale to the book." In contrast, *Castleview* is an out-and-out fantasy in which the long-time residents of Castleview, Illinois, have all seen visions of a medieval castle floating in air. In the course of the novel, in which the reader follows the arrival to town of Will E. Shields, new owner of the local auto dealership, figures from Arthurian legend appear along with the fictional feline Puss-in-Boots and increasing numbers of dead bodies from bizarre accidents.

Although Wolfe became famous for his novels, the "Urth" series in particular, his literary reputation is also bolstered by his short fiction, notably the collections *Storeys from the Old Hotel*—a highly accessible gathering of imaginative fiction—and *Endangered Species*—a somewhat more challenging volume of philosophically inclined tales. As Clareson asserts in an *Extrapolation* review of *Gene Wolfe's Book of Days,* the collection "is another cornerstone in emphasizing how important a writer Gene Wolfe has been throughout his surprising brief career. His stature becomes apparent by reading a number of his works. Only in that way does one realize the skill and subtlety with which he brings a fresh perspective to established themes and situations." *Gene Wolfe's Book of Days* was recently republished in a volume entitled *Castle of Days* that also includes the essay collection *The Castle of the Otter* as well as previously unpublished fiction and nonfiction. Clareson contends in his *Dictionary of Literary Biography* essay that Wolfe is "a major figure whose stories and novels must be considered among the most important science fiction published in the 1970s. He will undoubtedly become increasingly significant in the 1980s because he skillfully uses the materials of science fiction and fantasy to explore the themes which dominate contemporary fiction." "Gene Wolfe is a writer for the thinking reader," Sargent similarly states; "he will reward anyone searching for intelligence, crafted prose, involving stories, and atmospheric detail. He is the heir of many literary traditions—pulp stories, fantasy, adventure stories of all kinds, and serious literature—and he makes use of all of them," she continues. "His work can be read with pleasure many times; new discoveries are made with each reading, and the stories linger in one's mind."

In the early 1990s, Wolfe started a new multivolume series to rival "The Book of the New Sun." Occasionally referred to as the "Starcrosser's Planetfall" series, the series includes the novels *Nightside the Long Sun, Lake of the Long Sun, Calde of the Long Sun,* and *Exodus from the Long Sun.* The main character of the series is a cleric named Patera Silk whose universe comprises the vast interior of the cylindrical starship Whorl, an environment lighted by a "long sun" that runs the length of the cylinder. The society inside the Whorl is roughly medieval, but there are numerous elements of high—albeit decaying—technology. Silk's adventure begins when he prophesies the existence of a god, the Outsider, who is not one of the nine who rule the Whorl.

Tom Easton, reviewing *Nightside the Long Sun* in *Analog Science Fiction and Fact,* comments that "Wolfe is a master of style and texture." Similarly, Gerald Jonas of the *New York Times Book Review* notes, "Sentence by sentence, Mr. Wolfe writes as well as anyone in science fiction today." "His writing is stamped by extraordinary grace," adds Easton in a review of the series' second volume, *Lake of the Long Sun.* "It flows so smoothly and clearly and evocatively that one is hardly aware that one is reading and not living."

Wolfe wrote in *Contemporary Authors Autobiography Series:* "The books and stories I write are what are usually called escapist, in the pejorative sense. They do not teach the reader how to build a barbecue, or get a better job, or even how to murder his mother and escape detection. I have never understood what was wrong with escape. If I were in prison, or aboard a sinking vessel, I would escape if I could. I would try to escape from East Germany or the U.S.S.R., if I were unfortunate enough to find myself in one of those places. My work is intended to make life—however briefly—more tolerable for my readers, and to give them the feeling that change is possible, that the world need not always be as it is now, that their circumstances may be radically changed at any time, by their own act or God's."

BIOGRAPHICAL/CRITICAL SOURCES:

BOOKS

Andre-Driussi, Michael, *Lexicon Urthus: A Dictionary for the Urth Cycle,* Sirius Fiction (San Francisco), 1994.
Contemporary Authors Autobiography Series, Volume 9, Gale (Detroit), 1989.
Contemporary Literary Criticism, Volume 25, Gale, 1983.
Dictionary of Literary Biography, Volume 8: *Twentieth Century American Science Fiction Writers,* Gale, 1981.
Gordon, Joan, *Gene Wolfe,* Borgo (San Bernardino, CA), 1986.
Lane, Daryl, William Vernon, and David Carson, editors, *The Sound of Wonder: Interviews from "The Science Fiction Radio Show,"* Volume 2, Oryx (Phoenix, AZ), 1985.
Twentieth-Century Science Fiction Writers, St. James Press (Detroit), 1986.

PERIODICALS

Analog Science Fiction & Fact, August, 1990, p. 143; June, 1991, p. 178; April, 1993, p. 160; June, 1994, p. 161; February, 1995, p. 159; March, 1997.
Booklist, July 1, 1975; November 1, 1982; August, 1989; November 15, 1992; September 15, 1994, p. 118; October 1, 1996.
Chicago Tribune Book World, June 8, 1980; June 14, 1981.
Extrapolation, summer, 1981; fall, 1982.
Kansas Quarterly, summer, 1984.
Library Journal, November 15, 1990, p. 95; December, 1992, p. 191; August, 1994, p. 139; September 15, 1994, p. 94; October 15, 1996.
Locus, March, 1989; February, 1990; November, 1990; January, 1993; December, 1993; August, 1994.
Los Angeles Times Book Review, April 3, 1983; July 29, 1990.
Magazine of Fantasy and Science Fiction, April, 1971; May, 1978; June, 1981; September, 1994, p. 16.
New York Times Book Review, July 13, 1975; September 12, 1976; May 22, 1983; November 24, 1985; July 2, 1989; May 13, 1990; May 9, 1993, p. 20; January 2, 1994, p. 22; September 11, 1994, p. 46; November 3, 1996.
Publishers Weekly, September 8, 1989; November 9, 1992; October 7, 1996.
Times Literary Supplement, May 18, 1973; January 15, 1988.
Washington Post Book World, May 25, 1980; March 22, 1981; July 26, 1981; January 24, 1982; January 30, 1983; November 24, 1985; October 26, 1986; October 27, 1987; August 28, 1988; April 30, 1989; January 31, 1993; December 26, 1993; October 23, 1994.

*   *   *

WOLFE, Thomas (Clayton) 1900-1938

PERSONAL: Born October 3, 1900, in Asheville, NC; died of miliary tuberculosis of the brain, September 15, 1938, in Baltimore, Maryland; buried in Riverside Cemetery, Asheville, NC; son of William Oliver (a stonecutter) and Julia Elizabeth (a boardinghouse proprietor; maiden name, Westall) Wolfe. *Education:* University of North Carolina, Chapel Hill, B.A., 1920; Harvard University, M.A., 1922, graduate study, 1923.

CAREER: Writer. New York University, New York City, instructor in English at Washington Square College, intermittently, 1924-30. Worked in naval shipyards, Newport News, VA, 1918.

MEMBER: National Institute of Arts and Letters.

AWARDS, HONORS: Worth Prize, 1919, for essay *The Crisis in Industry;* Guggenheim Fellowship, 1930; *Scribner's Magazine* Prize, 1932, for *A Portrait of Bascom Hawke.*

WRITINGS:

The Crisis in Industry (essay), University of North Carolina, 1919.

The Return of Buck Gavin: The Tragedy of a Mountain Outlaw (play; first produced by Carolina Playmakers, March, 1919), published in *Carolina Folk-Plays, Second Series,* edited by Frederick H. Koch, Holt, 1924.

Third Night (play), first produced by Carolina Playmakers, December, 1919.

The Mountains: A Play in One Act (produced by 47 Workshop at Harvard University, Boston, MA, 1921), edited with an introduction by Pat M. Ryan, University of North Carolina Press, 1970.

Welcome to Our City (play; first produced in 1923), abridged version published in *Esquire,* October, 1957, published as *Welcome to Our City: A Play in Ten Scenes,* edited with an introduction by Richard S. Kennedy, Louisiana State University Press, 1983.

Look Homeward, Angel: A Story of the Buried Life (novel), Scribner, 1929 (published in England under same title with textual variations, Heinemann, 1930), published with introduction by Maxwell E. Perkins, illustrations by Douglas W. Gorsline, Scribner, 1952.

A Portrait of Bascom Hawke (novella), published in *Scribner's Magazine,* 1932.

Of Time and the River: A Legend of Man's Hunger in His Youth (novel), Scribner, 1935, recent edition, 1971.

From Death to Morning (short stories), Scribner, 1935, recent edition, 1970.

The Story of a Novel (essay), serialized in *Saturday Review of Literature,* December, 1935, published in one volume with certain modifications, Scribner, 1936, published with *Writing and Living* as *The Autobiography of an American Novelist,* edited by Leslie Field, Harvard University Press, 1983 (also see below).

A Note on Experts: Dexter Vespasian Joyner (fragment), House of Books (New York), 1939.

The Web and the Rock (novel), Harper, 1939, recent edition, Perennial Library, 1986.

You Can't Go Home Again (novel), Harper, 1940, recent edition, Perennial Library, 1973.

The Hills Beyond (contains a novel fragment, the play *Gentleman of the Press,* and short stories, including "The Lost Boy" and "The Web of Earth"), biographical note by Edward C. Aswell, Harper, 1941, recent edition, New American Library, 1968 (also see below).

Mannerhouse: A Play in a Prologue and Three Acts (produced by the Yale University dramatic association, 1949), Harper, 1948, recent edition, edited by Louis D. Rubin, Jr., and John L. Idol, Jr., Louisiana State University Press, 1985.

A Western Journal: A Daily Log of the Great Parks Trip, June 20-July 2, 1938, University of Pittsburgh Press, 1951, recent edition, 1967.

Thomas Wolfe's Purdue Speech: Writing and Living, edited with an introduction and notes by William Braswell and Field, Purdue University Studies, 1964, published as *Writing and Living* with *The Story of a Novel* as *The Autobiography of an American Novelist,* edited by Field, Harvard University Press, 1983 (also see below).

The Notebooks of Thomas Wolfe, edited by Kennedy and Paschal Reeves, two volumes, University of North Carolina Press, 1970.

The Streets of Durham (play), introduction by Richard Walser, Wolf's Head Press, 1982.

The Autobiography of an American Novelist: The Story of a Novel [and] *Writing and Living,* edited by Field, Harvard University Press, 1983.

The Hound of Darkness (play), edited with foreword by Idol, Thomas Wolfe Society (Akron, Ohio), 1986.

The Starwick Episodes, edited by Richard S. Kennedy, Louisiana State University Press, 1994.

The Party at Jack's (novella), edited by Suzanne Stutman and John L. Idol, Jr., University of North Carolina Press, 1995.

CORRESPONDENCE

Thomas Wolfe's Letters to His Mother, Julia Elizabeth Wolfe (facsimile edition), edited with an introduction by John Skally Terry, Scribner, 1943, revised edition newly edited from the original manuscript by C. Hugh Holman and Sue Fields Ross published as *The Letters of Thomas Wolfe to His Mother,* University of North Carolina Press, 1968.

The Correspondence of Thomas Wolfe and Homer Andrew Watt, edited by Oscar Cargill and Thomas Clark Pollock, New York University Press, 1954.

Letters, collected and edited with introduction and explanatory text by Elizabeth Nowell, Scribner, 1956 (abridged version with selection by Daniel George published in England as *Selected Letters of Thomas Wolfe,* Heinemann, 1958).

"Dear Mabel": Letters of Thomas Wolfe to His Sister, Mabel Wolfe Wheaton, edited by Mary Lindsay Thornton, published in *South Atlantic Quarterly,* autumn, 1961 (Durham, NC), 1961.

Beyond Love and Loyalty: The Letters of Thomas Wolfe and Elizabeth Nowell; Together With "No More Rivers," a Story, edited by Kennedy, University of North Carolina Press, 1983.

My Other Loneliness: Letters of Thomas Wolfe and Aline Bernstein, edited by Suzanne Stutman, University of North Carolina Press, 1983.

Holding On For Heaven: The Cables and Postcards of Thomas Wolfe and Aline Bernstein, edited by Stutman, Thomas Wolfe Society, 1985.

SELECTED WRITINGS

The Face of a Nation: Poetical Passages From the Writings of Thomas Wolfe, selected and edited with introduction by John Hall Wheelock, Scribner, 1939.

A Stone, A Leaf, A Door: Poems by Thomas Wolfe, selected and arranged in verse by John S. Barnes, foreword by Louis Untermeyer, Scribner, 1945, recent edition, 1961.

The Portable Thomas Wolfe, edited by Maxwell Geismar, Viking, 1946 (published in England as *The Portable Thomas Wolfe: Selections From the Works of Thomas Wolfe,* Heinemann, 1952).

Short Novels, edited with an introduction and notes by Holman, Scribner, 1961.

The Thomas Wolfe Reader, edited with an introduction and notes by Holman, Scribner, 1962.

K-19: Salvaged Pieces, edited with an introduction by Idol, Thomas Wolfe Society, 1983.

The Complete Short Stories of Thomas Wolfe, edited by Francis E. Skipp, foreword by James Dickey, Scribner, 1987.

OTHER

The William B. Wisdom collection of Wolfe's letters, manuscripts, inscribed works, galley and page proofs, notebooks, and school papers is gathered at the Houghton Library at Harvard University. A smaller collection of both printed and manuscript materials is housed at the Library of the University of North Carolina and a collection of printed materials and some letters is gathered at the Pack Memorial Public Library in Asheville, NC.

MEDIA ADAPTATIONS: Look Homeward, Angel was adapted as a three-act comedy-drama by Ketti Frings, first produced in New York at the Ethel Barrymore Theater in 1957, and published by Scribner in 1958; it won the Pulitzer Prize, was made into a motion picture, and was adapted by Frings and Peter Udell as the musical comedy *Angel,* published by S. French in 1979. *Mannerhouse* was translated into French and adapted for the stage by Georges Sion and first produced as *Le Manoir* at the Theatre National de Belgique in 1957.

SIDELIGHTS: Thomas Wolfe was an important twentieth-century American writer who will be remembered for his four sprawling novels, *Look Homeward, Angel, Of Time and the River, The Web and the Rock,* and *You Can't Go Home Again,* all of which burst with youthful exuberance and reveal an unquenchable thirst for experience. "I will go everywhere and see everything," Wolfe wrote early in his career to his mother, as cited in the *Dictionary of Literary Biography.* "I will meet all the people I can. I will think all the thoughts, feel all the emotions I am able, and I will write, write, write." Though Wolfe was popular with the reading public during his lifetime, critical reaction to his works was mixed. None, however, could dismiss his contribution to the American literary tradition: two American Nobel laureates, William Faulkner and Sinclair Lewis, even commended him in their acceptance speeches. Yet controversy followed Wolfe all his life. His disclosure that he freely collaborated with his editors cast doubt upon his literary abilities, while his highly autobiographical novels—*Look Homeward, Angel* in particular—angered the residents of his small southern hometown, who saw themselves in its pages. Shaken but undaunted by adverse criticism, Wolfe declared in a 1935 essay titled *The Story of a Novel:* "A man must use the material and experience of his own life if he is to create anything that has substantial value."

Wolfe's novels read as a fictional chronicle of his life. He was born October 3, 1900, in the Blue Ridge Mountain resort town of Asheville, North Carolina, which he would romanticize as Altamont in *Look Homeward, Angel* and *Of Time and the River* and as Old Catawba in *The Web and the Rock* and *You Can't Go Home Again.* He was the youngest of six surviving children born to Julia Elizabeth Westall, a cold, overprotective, and parsimonious native who avidly purchased property but forced her children to wear shoes they long outgrew, and William Oliver Wolfe, an uproarious Pennsylvania tombstone cutter who recited Shakespeare. From 1906 the couple lived apart, with W. O. and one daughter sharing the apartment behind his shop and Julia and the rest of the children residing at the boardinghouse she owned and operated.

Wolfe portrays himself through *Look Homeward, Angel*'s Eugene Gant as a child who identified with the heroes of his adventure stories and history books. He attended public elementary school in Asheville, but, a promising student, he entered a private school there in 1912 at the request of its supervisors, Mr. and Mrs. J. M.

Roberts (the Leonards in *Look Homeward, Angel*). Though basically uninspiring teachers, the Robertses introduced him to the arts and classical literature and encouraged him to write. At his mother's urging—she grudgingly paid his private-school tuition but willingly financed college—Wolfe entered the University of North Carolina at Chapel Hill at age fifteen, intending to pursue a career as a dramatist. As a freshman, while overwrought with anxiety about contracting venereal disease, Wolfe lost his virginity in a brothel, and the next year he had an affair with one of his mother's boarders, who was five years his senior. He would later write about their bittersweet romance in the Laura James episodes in *Look Homeward, Angel,* which critics claimed capture perfectly the passion and angst of adolescent love.

In March, 1919, Wolfe's first play, the melodrama *The Return of Buck Gavin: The Tragedy of a Mountain Outlaw,* was staged by the university's Carolina Playmakers. Encouraged by its success, Wolfe entered Harvard University as a graduate student in 1920 to study playwriting under George Pierce Baker at his famous 47 Workshop. The Workshop performed two of Wolfe's plays, *The Mountains* and *Welcome to Our City,* but attempts to secure New York producers for the verbose dramas were unsuccessful. Needing money after graduating with his master's degree, Wolfe taught English at Washington Square College of New York University intermittently between 1924 and 1930.

Look Homeward, Angel, which tells the story of Wolfe's coming of age through the character of Eugene Gant, is primarily concerned with Eugene's turbulent relationships with his family during his childhood and later with society in general as a college student at North Carolina. The episodic novel climaxes with his beloved brother's death and Eugene's vowing to seek artistic and spiritual fulfillment within himself. The novel met with an enthusiastic reception and many hailed Wolfe as a writer of great promise. " 'Look Homeward, Angel' is as interesting and powerful a book as has ever been made out of the drab circumstances of provincial American life," Margaret Wallace opined in the *New York Times Book Review.* "It is at once enormously sensuous, full of the joy and gusto of life, and shrinkingly sensitive, torn with revulsion and disgust. Mr. Wolfe's style is sprawling, fecund, subtly rhythmic and amazingly vital." Some detractors, though, complained that the novel lacked structure and was self-indulgent and unabashedly lyric. "Whenever Mr. Wolfe feels like it, which is fairly often, he launches into episodes, descriptions and proclamations of his own that could be cut out without impairing the architectural unity of his book," Geoffrey T. Hellman revealed in a *New Republic* review. "Such deletions, however, would rob it of its gusto, and anyone in favor of making them is the sort of person who thinks that 'Moby Dick' would be a good book if it weren't for Mr. Melville's digressions."

Look Homeward, Angel's autobiographical content angered residents of Asheville. They were provoked by its thinly disguised and often unflattering characterizations, and many Southerners were appalled by passages that indicted Southern society in general. "Years later," Wolfe wrote of Eugene in one such passage, "when he could no longer think of the barren spiritual wilderness, the hostile and murderous entrenchment against all new life—when their cheap mythology, their legend of the charm of their manner, the aristocratic culture of their lives, the quaint sweetness of their drawl, made him writhe—when he could think of no return to their life and its swarming superstition without weariness and horror, so great was his fear of the legend, his fear of their antagonism, that he still pretended the most fantastic devotion to them, excusing his Northern residence on grounds of necessity rather than desire." Shaken by their hostility—one indignant local wrote the author that she longed to see his "big overgoan karkus" dragged across the public square—Wolfe did not return to Asheville for seven years.

Of Time and the River continues the story of Eugene's growth and development. Covering the years 1920 to 1925 in the author's life, the novel opens with Eugene, now an aspiring novelist, on a northbound train anticipating life in Boston. The book follows him to England, France, and Germany, where his homesickness is apparent in his vivid memories and idyllic descriptions of American life. *Of Time and the River* ends with Eugene returning home on an ocean liner and falling in love with Esther Jack, a stage designer based on Wolfe's former mistress Aline Bernstein.

Again, critical reaction was mixed. *Of Time and the River* was faulted for its episodic nature—whole segments of the story seemed disconnected—and its apparent "formlessness." Some reviewers, however, maintain that the "formlessness" was intentional and that Wolfe, instead of ordering the novel around a sequence of events, unified it around a series of sense impressions, thereby capturing the diversity of the American experience and of life itself. Although various reviewers condemned the book for its lyricism and excessive emotion, others claimed that the rhapsodic, elegiac style complemented the book's loose structure.

Malcolm Cowley's *New Republic* assessment of *Of Time and the River* was representative of general critical opinion. "Thomas Wolfe at his best is the only contemporary American writer who can be mentioned in the same breath with [Charles] Dickens and [Fyodor] Dostoevsky," he wrote. "But the trouble is that the best passages are scattered, that they occur without logic or pattern, except the biographical pattern of the hero's life, and they lack the cumulative effect, the slow tightening of emotions to an intolerable pitch, that one finds in great novels." Cowley also pointed out that "the author's style goes flabby as soon as attention is taken away from the outside world and concentrated on the hero's yearning and hungering soul." William Styron's impressions were similar. He wrote in his *Harper's* assessment of the novel: "That furrow-browed, earnest sense of discovery in which the reader participates willingly in *Look Homeward, Angel* loses a great deal of its vivacity when the same protagonist has begun to pass into adulthood." Thomas C. Moser simply stated in *The American Novel:* "The older [Eugene] becomes, the less interesting the central character. When Wolfe writes badly, the subject is almost always Eugene."

Many critics were deeply moved by Wolfe's energy, however. *New York Post* contributor Herschel Brickell, for one, announced in his review of *Of Time and the River:* "You can't, if you are of ordinary stature and vitality, believe completely in [Wolfe's] gigantic world of shadow shapes, where everything is magnified and intensified, but you will be fascinated just the same, swept along on the tides of his passions, carried away with the gargantuan appetite of a man who wishes to swallow life whole when most of us are content to chew a tiny fragment in our frightened and dyspeptic way." Bernard DeVoto was less impressed with Wolfe's passion than exasperated by the author's lack of rhetorical restraint. He complained in his notorious *Saturday Review of Literature* critique "Genius Is Not Enough" that all of Eugene's experiences are portrayed with equal intensity: "If the death of one's father comes out emotionally even with a ham-on-rye, then the art of fiction is cockeyed." *Of Time and the River* nonetheless was a best-selling novel, and Wolfe cemented his literary reputation later in 1935 with the publication

of his short story volume *From Death to Morning,* which Maxwell Perkins culled from manuscript discarded from *Look Homeward, Angel* and *Of Time and the River.*

In 1936 Wolfe took his seventh and last trip to Europe. He spent much of his time in Germany, where he was celebrated, his success due in part to fine translations of his works by German writer Hermann Hesse. Wolfe was dismayed, however, at the changes in Germany that had taken place since Adolf Hitler's rise to power. Upon returning to the United States Wolfe discussed the new Germany in the *New Republic* essay "I Have a Thing to Tell You." He wrote that the dark forests, with "their legendary sense of magic and time," were replaced by the "dark Messiah" Hitler and his Nazi followers who beat Jews in the streets. The following year Wolfe, no longer vilified, visited his native Asheville. Though he was also disheartened by changes he encountered there—a land boom brought industry and commerce and corruption to the town—he rented a cottage nearby and wrote there during the summer of 1937.

During the first part of 1938 Wolfe wrote in seclusion in Brooklyn before he accepted an invitation to tour the national parks in the West. En route he stopped at Purdue University, where he delivered a speech that would later be published as *Writing and Living.* In this essay he admitted that as a youthful writer he was too egocentric and that he had only recently realized his responsibility to society. In his new novels he planned to address problems common to all men and to integrate his growing knowledge of worldwide political and socioeconomic situations. To symbolize his new literary direction, he changed his protagonist from recognizable alter-ego Eugene Gant to George "Monk" Webber.

Wolfe resumed his trip across America but while in Seattle in July he caught pneumonia. When his condition worsened he was taken back east to Baltimore, where doctors diagnosed tuberculosis of the brain. Wolfe unknowingly contracted tuberculosis in his youth, the pneumonia activated old tubercular scars in his lungs, and the tuberculosis found its way to his brain through his bloodstream. After a series of operations Wolfe died on September 15, 1938, only a few weeks before his thirty-eighth birthday.

Before Wolfe traveled out west he had entrusted Edward C. Aswell with a packing crate of manuscript eight feet high, containing thirty-five notebooks and other papers recording his impressions of America and Europe. He had also provided Aswell with extensive outlines and summaries for his works, and within three years Aswell edited—many say overedited—much of the manuscript, extracting from it the novels *The Web and the Rock* (1939) and *You Can't Go Home Again* (1940) and the volume *The Hills Beyond* (1941), a collection of short stories, a play, and a novel fragment.

The Web and the Rock carries forward Wolfe's story through protagonist George Webber, a successful novelist whose works resemble Wolfe's own. The first half of *The Web and the Rock* parallels *Look Homeward, Angel*—although it is written in a more detached tone than *Angel*—as the story of a small-town southern boy arriving in the North eager to experience life. The book's second half, which stands as a sequel to *Of Time and the River,* is devoted to George's affair with his muse, the sophisticated Esther Jack, and features luxuriant passages describing their lovemaking, feasts, and quarrels and reconciliations.

But George and Esther's love affair ultimately collapses, precipitated by events surrounding a swank dinner party the Jacks host for the New York literati and various socialites at their Park Avenue apartment. Elsewhere in the building a fire breaks out, and as the guests evacuate, the superficial sophisticates mix with elevator operators, fire fighters, and street people in a sharp commentary on the gap between the rich and poor in Depression-era America. Rejecting Esther and the privileged life she represents, George flees to Europe. But he cannot find solace there, for in Germany Hitler had risen to power, dashing Wolfe's romantic image of the nation. Thus at the end of *The Web and the Rock* George learns that time and change can only corrupt.

George is also disappointed when he returns to his native North Carolina in Wolfe's next novel, *You Can't Go Home Again.* Having avoided his hometown throughout much of the burgeoning 1920s, George discovers that newfound wealth has debased many of its natives, including a once-respected judge who has degenerated into a syphilitic loan shark. Regardless of the present corruption, *You Can't Go Home Again* ends with an optimistic cry of faith for all Americans: "I believe that we are lost here in America but I believe we shall be found." Although the Americans cannot recapture the innocence lost during the 1920s, Wolfe maintains, they must have faith in the future, when all Americans will be able to fulfill their potential through honest work, to live—as he professed to be doing—the American dream. "Though he used his life and art interchangeably," wrote Alfred Kazin in *On Native Grounds,* "they were, taken together, a reflection of Wolfe's conviction that he himself was a prime symbol of American experience and of a perpetual American ambition."

The Web and Rock and *You Can't Go Home Again* received mixed reviews. While critics commended the author for passages revealing his heightened sensitivity to the plight of the oppressed, many noticed that Wolfe's more restrained style often fell flat. Most were struck by the disconcerting mixture of brilliant and poor writing in the novels (recent studies of the original texts show that Aswell amalgamated early and late writing in these works). Stephen Vincent Benet, nevertheless, acknowledged Wolfe's growth as a writer and as a social being in his *Saturday Review of Literature* critique of *You Can't Go Home Again:* "There is . . . a mature line. George Webber does grow up."

Aswell also edited Wolfe's posthumous collection *The Hills Beyond,* which contains some of Wolfe's finest short stories, including "The Lost Boy," a moving account of his brother's death, and "The Web of Earth," a monologue in which Wolfe's mother relates her life story. Also collected is a 150-page novel fragment—from which the work takes its title—which was to be a history of George Webber's maternal ancestors. Wolfe planned to tell the story of America through the descendants of one man and his twenty children, including a lawyer, politician, teacher, and businessman. Although Wolfe asked his mother to send him their family tree as a basis, none of the characters were derived from people he knew. Some critics maintained that *The Hills Beyond* features some of Wolfe's most restrained and controlled writing, as well as some of his least exciting. Others, such as J. Donald Adams, admired Wolfe's more objective, dispassionate style. Critiquing the volume in the *New York Times Book Review,* Adams noted: "It contains some of his best, and certainly his most mature, work. The unfinished novel from which the book takes its title would, I think, have surpassed in creative power those other four on which his reputation must rest."

Fifty years after Wolfe's death critics still debate his merits as a novelist. Although many decry his craftsmanship, none can dismiss his epic, exuberant, and unaffected celebration of American and European life. "[I intend] to use myself to the top of my bent," Wolfe wrote in *You Can't Go Home Again.* "To use everything I have. To milk the udder dry, squeeze out the last drop, until there is nothing left." "My admiration for Wolfe is that he tried his best to get it all said," William Faulkner wrote to Richard Walser, editor of *The Enigma of Thomas Wolfe.* "He was willing to throw away style, coherence, all the rules of preciseness, to try to put all the experience of the human heart on the head of a pin."

BIOGRAPHICAL/CRITICAL SOURCES:

BOOKS

Bassett, John Earl, *Thomas Wolfe: An Annotated Critical Bibliography,* Scarecrow, 1996.

Berger, Brian F., *Thomas Wolfe: The Final Journey,* Willamette River Press, 1984.

Bloom, Harold, editor, *Thomas Wolfe,* Chelsea House, 1987.

Boyd, Madeleine, *Thomas Wolfe: The Discovery of a Genius,* edited by Aldo P. Magi, Thomas Wolfe Society, 1981.

Concise Dictionary of American Literary Biography: The Age of Maturity, 1929-1941, Gale (Detroit), 1989.

Dictionary of Literary Biography, Volume 9: *American Novelists, 1910-1945,* Gale, 1982; Volume 102: *American Short Story Writers, 1910-1945, Second Series,* Gale, 1991.

Dictionary of Literary Biography Documentary Series, Volume 2, Gale, 1982.

Dictionary of Literary Biography Yearbook: 1985, Gale, 1986.

Griffin, John Chandler, *Memories of Thomas Wolfe: A Pictorial Companion to "Look Homeward, Angel,"* Summerhouse Press (Columbia, SC), 1996.

Johnston, Carol, *Of Time and the Artist: Thomas Wolfe, His Novels, and the Critics,* Camden House, 1995.

Kazin, Alfred, *On Native Grounds: An Interpretation of Modern American Prose Literature,* Harcourt, 1970.

Magi, Aldo P., and Richard Walser, editors, *Thomas Wolfe Interviewed: 1929-1938,* Louisiana State University Press, 1985.

Twentieth-Century Literary Criticism, Gale, Volume 4, 1981; Volume 13, 1984; Volume 29, 1988.

PERIODICALS

American Review, April, 1935.

American Scholar, autumn, 1995, p. 624.

Atlantic Monthly, January, 1940.

Harper's, April, 1968.

Harvard Library Bulletin, autumn, 1947.

Harvard Magazine, September-October, 1981, pp. 48-53, 62.

Library Journal, April 1, 1995, p. 127.

Modern Fiction Studies, autumn, 1965.

New Republic, December 18, 1929; March 20, 1935, September 28, 1938.

New York Post, March 8, 1935; June 22, 1939.

New York Times, September 16, 1938.

New York Times Book Review, October 27, 1929; October 26, 1941; October 29, 1995.

Publishers Weekly, December 24, 1938; August 22, 1994, p. 43.

Saturday Review of Literature, April 25, 1936; September 21, 1940.

Times Literary Supplement, January 2, 1969.

Tribune Books (Chicago), May 21, 1995, p. 6.

World Literature Today, autumn, 1995, p. 805.

Yale Review, October, 1980, pp. 79-84.

WOLFE, Thomas Kennerly Jr. 1930-
(Tom Wolfe)

PERSONAL: Born March 2, 1931, in Richmond, VA; son of Thomas Kennerly (a scientist and business executive) and Helen (Hughes) Wolfe; married Sheila Berger (art director of *Harper's* magazine), 1978; children: Alexandra, Thomas. *Education:* Washington and Lee University, B.A. (cum laude), 1951; Yale University, Ph.D., 1957. *Avocational interests:* Window shopping.

ADDRESSES: Home—New York, NY. *Office*—Farrar Straus & Giroux, Inc., 19 Union Sq. W, New York, NY 10003-3007. *Agent*—International Creative Management, 40 West 57th St., New York, NY 10019.

CAREER: Writer, journalist, social commentator, and artist. *Springfield Union,* Springfield, MA, reporter, 1956-59; *Washington Post,* Washington, DC, reporter and Latin American correspondent, 1959-62; *New York Herald Tribune,* New York City, reporter and writer for *New York* Sunday magazine (now *New York* magazine), 1962-66; *New York World Journal Tribune,* New York City, writer, 1966-67; *New York* magazine, New York City, contributing editor, 1968-76; *Esquire* magazine, New York City, contributing editor, 1977–; *Harper's* magazine, New York City, contributing artist, 1978-81. Has exhibited drawings in one-man shows at Maynard Walker Gallery, 1965, and Tunnel Gallery, 1974.

AWARDS, HONORS: Washington Newspaper Guild awards for foreign news reporting and for humor, both 1961; Society of Magazine Writers award for excellence, 1970; D.F.A., Minneapolis College of Art, 1971; Frank Luther Mott research award, 1973; D.Litt., Washington and Lee University, 1974; named Virginia Laureate for literature, 1977; American Book Award and National Book Critics Circle Award, both 1980, for *The Right Stuff;* Harold D. Vursell Memorial Award for excellence in literature, American Institute of Arts and Letters, 1980; Columbia Journalism Award, 1980; citation for art history from National Sculpture Society, 1980; L.H.D. from Virginia Commonwealth University, 1983, and Southampton College, 1984; John Dos Passos Award, 1984; Gari Melchers Medal, 1986; Benjamin Pierce Cheney Medal from Eastern Washington University, 1986; Washington Irving Medal for literary excellence from Nicholas Society, 1986; D.F.A., School of Visual Arts, 1987; L.H.D, Randolph-Macon College, and L.H.D., Manhattanville College, 1988; L.H.D., Longwood College, 1989; D.Litt, St. Andrews Presbyterian College, and John Hopkins University, 1990; St. Louis Literary award, Quinnipiac College, 1990, presidential award, 1993; D.Litt., University Richmond, 1993.

WRITINGS:

UNDER NAME TOM WOLFE

(Self-illustrated) *The Kandy-Kolored Tangerine-Flake Streamline Baby* (essays), Farrar, Straus, 1965.
(Contributor) Alan Rinzler, editor, *The New York Spy,* David White, 1967.
The Electric Kool-Aid Acid Test, Farrar, Straus, 1968.
The Pump House Gang (essays), Farrar, Straus, 1968 (published in England as *The Mid-Atlantic Man and Other New Breeds in England and America,* Weidenfeld & Nicolson, 1969).
Radical Chic and Mau Mauing the Flak Catchers (two essays), Farrar, Straus, 1970.
(Editor with E. W. Johnson and contributor) *The New Journalism* (anthology), Harper, 1973.
(Self-illustrated) *The Painted Word,* Farrar, Straus, 1975.

(Self-illustrated) *Mauve Gloves & Madmen, Clutter & Vine, and Other Short Stories* (essays), Farrar, Straus, 1976.
(Contributor) Susan Feldman, editor, *Marie Cosindas, Color Photographs,* New York Graphic Society, 1978.
The Right Stuff (Book-of-the-Month-Club selection), Farrar, Straus, 1979.
(Self-illustrated) *In Our Time* (essays), Farrar, Straus, 1980.
From Bauhaus to Our House, Farrar, Straus, 1981.
(Self-illustrated) *The Purple Decades: A Reader* (collection), Farrar, Straus, 1982.
The Bonfire of the Vanities (novel), Farrar, Straus, 1987.
Two Complete Books (contains *The Right Stuff* and *The Bonfire of the Vanities*), Wings, 1994.

MEDIA ADAPTATIONS: The Right Stuff was adapted for a film of the same title, Warner Bros., 1983; *Bonfire of the Vanities,* directed by Brian DePalma and starring Tom Hanks, Melanie Griffith, and Bruce Willis, was filmed and released in 1990.

SIDELIGHTS: Satirist, caricaturist, social critic, coiner of phrases ("Radical Chic," "The Me Decade"), Thomas Kennerly Wolfe, Jr. has become known as a leading chronicler of American trends. "Those of you who are not aware of Tom Wolfe should—really—do your best to acquaint yourselves with him," writes William F. Buckley in *National Review.* "He is probably the most skillful writer in America. I mean by that he can do more things with words than anyone else." Wolfe's painstaking research and detailed accounts have made him a widely respected reporter; at the same time, his unorthodox style and frequently unpopular opinions have resulted in a great deal of controversy. Leslie Bennetts of the *Philadelphia Bulletin* calls him "a professional rogue," who has "needled and knifed at the mighty of every description, exposing in print the follies and foibles of superstars from Leonard Bernstein to the Hell's Angels. Gleefully ripping off every shred of disguise from anyone's pretensions, Wolfe has performed his dissections in *New York* Magazine, *Esquire,* and *Rolling Stone,* not to mention his earlier years on the *New York Herald Tribune* and the *Washington Post.*"

Wolfe's association with New Journalism began in 1963, when he wrote his first magazine article, a piece on custom automobiles. He had become intrigued with the strange subculture of West Coast car customizers and was beginning to see these individuals as folk artists worthy of serious study. He convinced *Esquire* magazine to send him to California, where he researched the story, interviewed a number of subjects, and, says Margo Harakas in the *Fort Lauderdale Sun-Sentinel,* "racked up a $750 tab at the Beverly Wilshire Hotel (picked up by *Esquire,* of course)." Then, having returned to New York to write the article, he found that standard journalistic techniques, those he had employed so successfully during his years of newspaper work, could not adequately describe the bizarre people and machines he had encountered in California.

Stymied, he put off writing the story until, finally, he called Byron Dobell, his editor at *Esquire,* and admitted that he was unable to finish the project. Dobell told him to type up his notes so that the magazine could get another writer to do the job. In the introduction to *The Kandy-Kolored Tangerine-Flake Streamline Baby,* Wolfe writes: "About 8 o'clock that night I started typing the notes out in the form of a memorandum that began, 'Dear Byron.' I started typing away, starting right with the first time I saw any custom cars in California." In an attempt to provide every possible detail for the writer who was to finish the piece, he wrote in a stream-of-consciousness style, including even some of his most garbled notes and random thoughts. "I wrapped up the memorandum about 6:15 A.M., and by this time it was 49 pages long. I took it over to *Esquire* as soon as they opened up, about 9:30 A.M. About 4 P.M. I got a call from Byron Dobell. He told me they were striking out the 'Dear Byron' at the top of the memorandum and running the rest of it in the magazine."

It is the style developed during the writing of the custom car article—his unique blend of "pop" language and creative punctuation—that for many years remained Wolfe's trademark. He was a pioneer in the use of what several reviewers refer to as an "aural" style of writing, a technique intended to make the reader come as close as possible to experiencing an event first-hand. Wilfrid Sheed, in the *New York Times Book Review,* says that Wolfe tries to find "a language proper to each subject, a special sound to convey its uniqueness"; and *Newsweek*'s Jack Kroll feels that Wolfe is "a genuine poet" among journalists, who is able "to get under the skin of a phenomenon and transmit its metabolic rhythm. . . . He creates the most vivid, most pertinent possible dimension of his subject." F. N. Jones, in a *Library Journal* article, describes Wolfe's prose as "free-flowing colorful Joycean, quote-slang, repetitive, cult or class jargon with literary and other reverberations."

Wolfe's style, combined with solid reporting and a highly critical eye, quickly gained a large audience for his magazine pieces. When his first book, *The Kandy-Kolored Tangerine-Flake Streamline Baby,* a collection of twenty-two of his best essays, was published in 1965, William James Smith wrote in *Commonweal:* "Two years ago [Tom Wolfe] was unknown and today those who are not mocking him are doing their level best to emulate him. Magazine editors are currently flooded with Zonk! articles written, putatively, in the manner of Wolfe and, by common account, uniformly impossible. . . . None of his parodists—and even fewer of his emulators—has successfully captured much of the flavor of Wolfe. . . . They miss the spark of personality that is more arresting than the funny punctuation. Wolfe has it, that magical quality that marks prose as distinctively one's own."

In *The Electric Kool-Aid Acid Test,* Wolfe applies his distinctive brand of journalism to novelist Ken Kesey and his "Merry Pranksters," a West Coast group dedicated to LSD and the pursuit of the psychedelic experience. Joel Lieber of the *Nation* says that in this book Wolfe "has come as close as seems possible, with words, at re-creating the entire mental atmosphere of a scene in which one's understanding is based on feeling rather than verbalization. . . . [The book] is nonfiction told as experimental fiction; it is a genuine feat and a landmark in reporting style." Lawrence Dietz, in a *National Review* article, calls *The Electric Kool-Aid Acid Test* "the best work Wolfe has done, and certainly the most profound and insightful book that has been written about the psychedelic life. . . . [He] has elicited a history of the spread of LSD from 1960 (when Kesey and others got their first jolts in lab experiments) to 1967, when practically any kid with five dollars could buy some kind of trip or other." Dietz feels that Wolfe displays "a willingness to let accuracy take the place of the hysterical imprecations that have passed for reportage in most magazine articles and books" on this subject.

Wolfe's 1970 book, *Radical Chic and Mau Mauing the Flak Catchers,* was made up of two lengthy essays. The first, "Radical Chic," elicited by far the most critical commentary; it deals with a fund-raising party given by Leonard Bernstein in his Park Avenue apartment on January 14, 1970, to raise money for the Black Panthers. Wolfe was at the party, and he became aware of the incongruity of the scene, distinguished, according to Melvin Maddocks of the *Christian Science Monitor,* by "white liberals nibbling caviar while signing checks for the revolution with their free hand." Thomas R. Edwards writes in the *New York Times Book Review:* "For Wolfe, the scene in the Bernsteins' living room demonstrates his pet sociological thesis, here called *nostalgie de la boue,* the aristocrat's hankering for a proletarian primitivism. He shows us cultivated parvenu Jews, torn between cherished new 'right wing' lifestyles and the 'left wing' politics of their own oppressive history, ludicrously confused about how to take the black revolution. Though there's a touch of ugliness in his determination to let us know, without seeming to do so, that certain socialites with gentile names weren't born that way, 'Radical Chic' is sometimes brilliant and telling in its dramatization of this case."

In *From Bauhaus to Our House,* published in 1981, Wolfe does to modern architecture what he did to modern art in *The Painted Word,* and the response has been similar: Readers close to the subject tend to resent the intrusion by an "outsider," while those with a more detached point of view often appreciate the author's fresh perspective. *New York Times* architecture critic Paul Goldberger, in a *New York Times Book Review* article, writes: "Mr. Wolfe wants to argue that ideology has gotten in the way of common sense. Beginning half a century ago with the origins of the International Style in Europe, he attempts to trace the development of that style, which for many, including Mr. Wolfe, is a virtual synonym for modern architecture. . . . We are told how the International Style became a 'compound'—a select, private, cult-like group of ideologues [including Walter Gropius, Mies van der Rohe, Marcel Breuer, and Josef Albers] whose great mission, as Mr. Wolfe sees it, was to foist modern design upon an unwilling world. . . . The problem, I think . . . is that Tom Wolfe has no eye. He has a wonderful ear, and he listens hard and long, but he does not seem to see. . . . He does precisely what he warns us against; he has listened to the words, not looked at the architecture."

And in a *Washington Post Book World* review, *Post* architecture critic Benjamin Forgey says that "the book is a case of crying Wolfe for one more time. *Bauhaus* is distinguished by the same total loathing of modern culture that motivated *The Painted Word.* . . . Wolfe's explanation is that modernism has been a conspiracy. In place of the New York critics who foisted abstract art upon us, we have the European giants of architecture . . . and their abject American followers. In Wolfe's view the motivation was pretty much the same, too. They were all playing the hypocritical bohemian game of spitting on the bourgeois." Forgey feels that "there is some truth in this, but it makes for a thin book and a narrow, limited history of architecture in the 20th century."

On the other hand, *New York Times* literary critic Christopher Lehmann-Haupt makes the point that even many architects have been unhappy with the structures created by proponents of the Bauhaus school. This style of architecture (distinguished by what is often referred to as a "glass box" appearance) was, for instance, denigrated by architect Peter Blake in his 1977 book, *Form Follows Fiasco.* According to Lehmann-Haupt, Blake "anathematized modern architecture for being sterile, functionless and ugly"; thus Wolfe "has not really come up with anything very startling when he laments the irony that four-fifths of the way into the American Century, when what we ought to be expressing with our building is 'exuberance, power, empire, grandeur, or even high spirits and playfulness,' what we still see inflicted upon us is the anti-bourgeois, socialist, pro-worker ideas that arose from 'the smoking rubble of Europe after the Great War.'"

In 1979 Wolfe published the book that many critics consider his finest: *The Right Stuff,* an award-winning study of the early years of the American space program. At one point in the book Wolfe attempts to define the "ineffable quality" from which the title is taken: "It obviously involved bravery. But it was not bravery in the simple sense of being willing to risk your life . . . any fool could do that. . . . No, the idea . . . seemed to be that a man should have the ability to go up in a hurtling piece of machinery and put his hide on the line and then have the moxie, the reflexes, the experience, the coolness, to pull it back in the last yawning moment—and then to go up again *the next day,* and the next day, and every next day."

The main characters in the book are, of course, the first U.S. astronaut team: Scott Carpenter, Gordon Cooper, John Glenn, Gus Grissom, Wally Schirra, Alan Shepard, and Deke Slayton. Wolfe assiduously chronicles their early careers as test pilots, their private lives, their selection for the astronaut program and the subsequent medical processing and training. But, as *Commonweal*'s Thomas Powers points out, *The Right Stuff* "is not a history; it is far too thin in dates, facts and source citations to serve any such pulse. It is a work of literature which must stand or fall as a coherent text, and its subject is not the Mercury program itself but the impulse behind it, the unreflecting competitiveness which drove the original astronauts to the quite extraordinary lengths Wolfe describes so vividly." That the author goes beyond mere reportage of historical fact is confirmed by Mort Sheinman in a *Chicago Tribune* article: "Wolfe tells us what it's like to go 'shooting straight through the top of the sky,' to be 'in a king's solitude, unique and inviolate, above the dome of the world.' He describes what happens when someone is immolated by airplane fuel, and he talks about the nightmares and hallucinations experienced by the wives. . . . [*The Right Stuff*] is a dazzling piece of work, something that reveals much about the nature of bravery and celebrity and—yes—patriotism."

Time writer R. Z. Sheppard says that the book "is crammed with inside poop and racy incident that 19 years ago was ignored by what [Wolfe] terms the 'proper Victorian gents' of the press. The fast cars, booze, astro groupies, the envies and injuries of the military caste system were not part of what Americans would have considered the right stuff. Wolfe lays it all out in brilliantly stated Op Lit scenes: the tacky cocktail lounges of Cocoa Beach where one could hear the *Horst Wessel Song* sung by ex-rocket scientists of the Third Reich; Vice President Lyndon Johnson furiously cooling his heels outside the Glenn house because Annie Glenn would not let him in during her husband's countdown; Alan Shepard losing a struggle with his full bladder moments before lift-off; the overeager press terrifying Ham the chimp after his proficient flight; the astronauts surrounded by thousands of cheering Texans waving hunks of raw meat during an honorary barbecue in the Houston Coliseum."

Former test pilot and astronaut Michael Collins (a member of the Gemini 10 flight and command module pilot on the Apollo 11 moon flight), writes in a *Washington Post Book World* review: "I lived at Edwards [Air Force Base, site of the Air Force Flight Test Center,] for four years, and, improbable as some of Tom's tales seem, I know he's telling it like it was. He is the first gifted writer to explore the relationship between test pilots and astronauts—the obvious similarities and the subtle differences. He's obviously done a lot of homework—too much in some cases. Some of this stuff could only be interesting to Al Shepard's mother. While the first part of the book is a paean to guts, to the 'right stuff,' it is followed by a chronology—but one that might have profited from a little tighter editing. But it's still light-years ahead of the endless drivel [Norman] Mailer has put out about the Apollo program, and in places the Wolfe genius really shines." Collins feels that at times Wolfe allows himself to get too close to his subject: "He's almost one of the boys—and there's too much to admire and not enough to eviscerate." As a result *The Right Stuff* is not vintage, psychedelic Tom Wolfe, but if you . . . have ever been curious about what the space program was really all about in those halcyon Kennedy and Mercury years, then this is your book."

By the mid-1980s Wolfe had a new ambition for his writing. As he told the *New York Times:* "I was curious, having spouted off so much about fiction and nonfiction, and having said that the novelists weren't doing a good job, to see what would happen if I tried it. Also, I guess I subconsciously had the suspicion that maybe, what if all this to-do I've made about nonfiction is because I really, secretly think I can't do a novel? So I said, well, I've got to prove this to myself." The result was *The Bonfire of the Vanities,* a novel that exposes the greed and hate seething in modern New York City. In the book, a smug Wall Streeter named Sherman McCoy is reduced to a political pawn when he is implicated in the hit-and-run traffic death of a young black man. *Washington Post Book World*'s Jonathan Yardley called *Bonfire* "a superb human comedy and the first novel ever to get contemporary New York, in all its arrogance and shame and heterogeneity and insularity, exactly right." After his novel became a major bestseller, Wolfe issued what he called a "literary manifesto" in *Harper's* magazine. He urged fellow novelists to abandon the esoteric literary experiments that have characterized fiction for much of the twentieth century and use realism to chronicle the bizarre and astounding world around them. The author's peers reacted with both praise and condemnation. "Ever the provocateur," reported *Time,* "Wolfe is enjoying the controversy."

Although there can be no question that Tom Wolfe has achieved a reputation as a superb stylist and skillful reporter, no discussion of Wolfe would be complete without some mention of his famous wardrobe. *Philadelphia Bulletin* writer Leslie Bennetts tells of an encounter with the author when he lectured at Villanova University: "The legendary sartorial splendors were there, of course: the gorgeous three-piece creamy white suit he has been renowned for . . . (how many must he have, do you suppose, to appear in spotless vanilla every day: rows upon rows of them hanging in shadowed closets, a veritable army of Gatsby ghosts waiting to emerge?). Not to mention the navy suede shoes, dark as midnight, or the jaunty matching suede hat, or the sweeping midnight cashmere coat of the exact same hue, or the crisp matching tie on which perched a golden half-moon pin to complement the glittering gold watch chain that swung gracefully from the milky vest. Or the navy silk handkerchief peeking out from the white suit pocket, or the white silk handkerchief peeking out from the navy coat pocket."

BIOGRAPHICAL/CRITICAL SOURCES:

BOOKS

Bellamy, Joe David, editor, *The New Fiction: Interviews With Innovative American Writers,* University of Illinois Press, 1974.

Contemporary Literary Criticism, Gale (Detroit), Volume 1, 1973; Volume 2, 1974; Volume 9, 1978; Volume 15, 1980; Volume 35, 1985; Volume 51, 1989.

McKeen, William, *Tom Wolfe,* Prentice Hall, 1995.

Shomette, Doug, editor, *The Critical Response to Tom Wolfe,* Greenwood Press, 1992.

PERIODICALS

Atlantic Monthly, October, 1979; December, 1987.

Chicago Tribune, September 9, 1979; September 15, 1979; January 16, 1983; November 4, 1987; February 17, 1995.

Chicago Tribune Book World, December 7, 1980; October 25, 1981; January 16, 1983.

Christian Science Monitor, November 17, 1970; November 3, 1987.

Commonweal, September 17, 1965; December 20, 1968; March 3, 1978; October 12, 1979; February 26, 1988.

Detroit News, October 14, 1979; November 9, 1980.

Economist, December 22, 1990, p. 120.

Fort Lauderdale Sun-Sentinel, April 22, 1975.

Globe and Mail (Toronto), December 5, 1987.

Guardian Weekly, February 21, 1988.

Harper's, February, 1971; November, 1989; January, 1990.

Library Journal, August, 1968; February 15, 1995, p. 199.

Listener, February 11, 1988.

London Review of Books, February 18, 1988.

Los Angeles Times, October 19, 1979; November 22, 1987; October 12, 1989.

Los Angeles Times Book Review, November 2, 1980; October 25, 1981; October 17, 1982; January 23, 1983; October 25, 1987.

Nation, March 5, 1977; November 3, 1977; January 28, 1991, p. 100.

National Review, August 27, 1968; January 26, 1971; August 1, 1975; February 19, 1977; December 18, 1987.

New Republic, July 14, 1965; December 19, 1970; November 23, 1987.

New Statesman, February 12, 1988.

Newsweek, June 28, 1965; August 26, 1968; June 9, 1975; September 17, 1979; October 26, 1987.

New York, September 21, 1981; March 21, 1988; January 7, 1991, p. 64.

New Yorker, February 1, 1988.

New York Review of Books, August 26, 1965; December 17, 1970; June 26, 1975; January 20, 1977; October 28, 1979; November 4, 1982; February 4, 1988.

New York Times, November 25, 1970; May 27, 1975; November 26, 1976; September 14, 1979; October 9, 1981; December 20, 1981; October 13, 1987; October 22, 1987; November 21, 1987; December 31, 1987; January 3, 1988; March 11, 1988.

New York Times Book Review, June 27, 1965; August 18, 1968; November 29, 1970; December 3, 1972; June 15, 1975; December 26, 1976; October 28, 1979; October 11, 1981; October 10, 1982; November 1, 1987.

People Weekly, December 24, 1979; November 23, 1987; October 13, 1997.

Philadelphia Bulletin, February 10, 1975.

Rolling Stone, August 21, 1980; November 5-December 10, 1987.

Time, September 6, 1968; December 21, 1970; June 23, 1975; December 27, 1976; September 29, 1979; November 9, 1987; February 13, 1989; November 27, 1989.

Wall Street Journal, October 29, 1987; December 31, 1996.

Washington Post, September 4, 1979; October 23, 1980; March 27, 1988; October 17, 1989; August 29, 1997.

Washington Post Book World, September 9, 1979; November 23, 1980; November 15, 1981; November 7, 1982; October 25, 1987.

*　　　*　　　*

WOLFE, Tom
See WOLFE, Thomas Kennerly Jr.

*　　　*　　　*

WOLFF, Tobias (Jonathan Ansell) 1945-

PERSONAL: Born June 19, 1945, in Birmingham, AL; son of Arthur Saunders (an aeronautical engineer) and Rosemary (Loftus) Wolff; married Catherine Dolores Spohn (a clinical social worker), 1975; children: Michael, Patrick, Mary Elizabeth. *Education:* Oxford University, B.A. (with first class honors), 1972, M.A., 1975; Stanford University, M.A., 1978.

ADDRESSES: Agent—Amanda Urban, International Creative Management, 40 West 57th St., New York, NY 10019.

CAREER: Stanford University, Stanford, CA, Jones Lecturer in Creative Writing, 1975-78; Syracuse University, Syracuse, NY, Peck Professor of English, 1980–. Member of faculty at Goddard College, Plainfield, VT, and Arizona State University, Tempe. Former reporter for *Washington Post. Military service:* U.S. Army, 1964-68 (Special Forces, 1964-67); served in Vietnam; became first lieutenant.

MEMBER: PEN, Associated Writing Programs.

AWARDS, HONORS: Wallace Stegner fellowship in creative writing, 1975-76; National Endowment for the Arts fellowship in creative writing, 1978 and 1985; Mary Roberts Rinehart grant, 1979; Arizona Council on the Arts and Humanities fellowship in creative writing, 1980; Guggenheim fellowship, 1982; St. Lawrence Award for Fiction, 1982, for *In the Garden of the North American Martyrs;* PEN/Faulkner Award for Fiction, 1985, for *The Barracks Thief;* Rea Award for short story, 1989; *Los Angeles Times* Book Prize for biography, and National Book Critics Circle Award finalist, both 1989, and Ambassador Book Award of the English Speaking Union, all for *This Boy's Life: A Memoir;* Whiting Foundation Award, 1990; Lila Wallace-*Reader's Digest* Award, 1993; Lyndhurst Foundation Award, 1994; National Book Award finalist, and Esquire-Volvo-Waterstone's Prize for Nonfiction (England), both 1994, and *Los Angeles Times* Book Award for biography finalist, 1995, all for *In Pharaoh's Army: Memories of the Lost War.*

WRITINGS:

Ugly Rumours, Allen & Unwin (London), 1975.

In the Garden of the North American Martyrs (short stories), Ecco Press (New York City), 1981, published in England as *Hunters in the Snow* (also see below), J. Cape (London), 1982.

(Editor) *Matters of Life and Death: New American Stories,* Wampeter (Green Harbor, ME), 1982, hardcover edition, 1983.

The Barracks Thief (novella; also see below), Ecco Press, 1984, published as *The Barracks Thief and Other Stories,* Bantam (New York City), 1984.

Back in the World (short stories; also see below), Houghton (Boston, MA), 1985.

(Editor) *A Doctor's Visit: The Short Stories of Anton Chekhov*, Bantam, 1987.

The Stories of Tobias Wolff (contains *Hunters in the Snow, Back in the World,* and *The Barracks Thief*), Picador (London), 1988.

This Boy's Life: A Memoir, Atlantic Monthly Press (New York City), 1989.

(Editor) *The Picador Book of Contemporary American Stories,* Picador, 1993.

(Editor and author of introduction) *The Vintage Book of Contemporary American Short Stories,* Random House (New York City), 1994.

In Pharaoh's Army: Memories of the Lost War (memoir), Knopf (New York City), 1994.

(Editor) *Best American Short Stories,* Houghton, 1994.

The Night in Question: Stories, Knopf, 1996.

MEDIA ADAPTATIONS: This Boy's Life: A Memoir was made into the movie *This Boy's Life,* 1993, produced by Art Linson, directed by Michael Caton-Jones, starring Robert De Niro as Wolff's stepfather, Ellen Barkin as Wolff's mother, and Leonardo DiCaprio playing Wolff as a teenager.

SIDELIGHTS: Tobias Wolff, short story writer, novelist, memoirist, editor and journalist, has received critical acclaim since the publication of his first collection of short stories in 1981. Both *Los Angeles Times* book reviewer James Kaufman and *New Statesman* contributor Bill Greenwell label the stories of *In the Garden of the North American Martyrs* "impressive," and the *Chicago Tribune*'s Bruce Allen deems it "one of the most acclaimed short-story collections within memory." In the twelve tales which comprise *In the Garden of the North American Martyrs,* according to *Nation* reviewer Brina Caplan, Wolff "scrutinizes the disorders of daily living to find significant order; in the best of [these] stories . . . he informs us not only of what happened but of why it had to happen as it did. . . . Distant in age, class and geography, [his characters] have in common lives crowded with the results of previous choices." *Best Sellers* reviewer James C. Dolan advises: "relax and enter into the sometimes comic, always compassionate world of ordinary people who suffer twentieth-century martyrdoms of growing up, growing old, loving and lacking love, living with parents and lovers and wives and their own weaknesses."

Among the characters of *In the Garden of the North American Martyrs*—all of whom, claims Alane Rollings of the *Chicago Tribune,* readers can "care for"—are a teenage boy who tells morbid lies about his home life, a timid professor who, in the first genuine outburst of her life, pours out her opinions in spite of a protesting audience, a prudish loner who gives an obnoxious hitchhiker a ride, and an elderly couple on a golden anniversary cruise who endure the offensive conviviality of the ship's social director. Rollings concludes that "Wolff's ironic dialog, misfit heroes, and haphazard events play beautifully off the undercurrent drift of the searching inner mood which wins over in the end." *New York Times Book Review* critic Le Ann Schreiber admires Wolff's avoidance of "the emotional and stylistic monotone that constricts so many collections of contemporary short stories," pointing out that "his range, sometimes within the same story, extends from fastidious realism to the grotesque and the lyrical. . . . He allows [his] characters scenes of flamboyant madness as well as quiet desperation, moments of slap-happiness as well as muted contentment." In addition, observing that the time covered by the collection's stories varies from a few hours to

two decades, Schreiber declares Wolff's vision "so acute" and his talent "so refined" that "none of them seems sketchy" and that in fact, they evoke our "amazed appreciation."

Wolff's novella *The Barracks Thief* won the prestigious PEN/Faulkner Award as the best work of fiction of 1984. Linda Taylor writes in the *Times Literary Supplement* that "*The Barracks Thief* is a book to be taken in all at once: the ingenuousness of the narration and the vulnerability of the characters are disarmingly seductive." Narrated retrospectively by one of three paratroopers stationed at Fort Bragg, North Carolina, during the Vietnam years, the story focuses on an event that leaves a lasting impression on the trio. Assigned to guard a nearby ammunition dump on a steamy Fourth of July evening in 1967, they face the threat of an approaching forest fire. The temptation to allow the dump to ignite and explode proves exhilarating and unites them in a bond of friendship. "The world of *The Barracks Thief* contains no answers," observes *New York Times* reviewer Walter Kendricks. "We are left to make up our own minds whether it is better to die spectacularly or to dribble on for decades in safe conventionality." Kendricks also hails Wolff's "boundless tolerance for the stupid sorrow of ordinary human entanglements" and his "command of eloquent detail." *America* critic Andre Dubus concludes, "If words on paper could make sounds, you would hear me shouting now, urging you to read this book."

Wolff's 1985 short story collection, *Back in the World,* derives its title from the expression used by servicemen during the Vietnam War to refer to post-war life at home in the United States. The experience of returning home, however, proves more disillusioning than hopeful to the veterans in Wolff's stories. Feeling alienated from society and powerless to change their circumstances, his characters capitulate to whatever life deals them, only briefly—if at all—challenging fate. They seek relief from their cheerless, detached existence in drugs, casual sex, and, as the *Chicago Tribune*'s Allen observes, "contriving falsely romantic or interesting versions of themselves and their experiences." Yet, *New York Times* reviewer Michiko Kakutani notes that Wolff suggests for these people "the power of some kind of redemption in their fumbling efforts to connect with one another, and even in their sad attempts to shore up their dignity with their pipe dreams and clumsy fictions." This "power of . . . redemption," according to Kakutani, "enables these characters to go on, and it is also what invests these stories with the burnished glow of compassion."

Wolff's next work, *This Boy's Life: A Memoir,* "is about growing up, as inevitably any such memoir must be," comments Jonathan Yardley in the *Washington Post Book World.* The book addresses Wolff's teenage years, when he and his mother moved from Florida to Utah to Washington State to escape her abusive boyfriend. Wolff had lost contact with his father and brother (writer Geoffrey Wolff, author of *The Duke of Deception: Memories of My Father,* an autobiography about his youth spent with their father) following his parents' divorce. In Washington his mother remarried, and Wolff experienced difficulties with his new stepfather. Yardley remarks that, in part, *This Boy's Life* "is the story of what happens to a child when the peculiarities of a mother's romance place him at the mercy of a man who is neither his father nor his protector, but it is not a self-pitying lament and it is not really a tale of abuse and neglect."

New York Times Book Review's Joel Conarroe notes the literary quality of the book: "*This Boy's Life* is apparently straight autobiography—the facts, attired in their exotic garments. The book, however, reads very much like a collection of short stories, each with its own beginning, middle and end. Lifted from their context, the individual chapters would be at home in the fiction pages of any good magazine." Francine Prose makes a similar observation in the *New York Times Magazine:* "*This Boy's Life* reads like the work of a writer who has long understood himself to be 'surrounded by stories.' Its strategy is novelistic; details have been altered, events ordered and edited, to give Wolff's memoir the shape of fiction." Prose adds that "Tobias Wolff admits to having omitted things from *This Boy's Life*—real events he chose to leave out lest the true account of his life seem too markedly patterned and shaped. 'It would have seemed too contrived,' he says. 'Too much like a novel.'"

Some critics consider Wolff's acclaimed memoir *In Pharaoh's Army: Memories of the Lost War,* to be a logical continuation of *This Boy's Life.* Yet, the author tells Nicholas A. Basbanes in a *Publishers Weekly* interview that the book is not a sequel: "I'm a really different person in the new book. I see it as a story about a young man going off to war, and the kind of moral transformations that take place." The book, which was nominated for the National Book Award in 1994 and received England's Esquire-Volvo-Waterstone's Prize for Nonfiction, recounts the author's one-year Vietnam tour of duty in the Mekong Delta village of My Tho in thirteen chapters, or "episodes." Paul Gray comments in *Time,* that each "of Wolff's thirteen chapters reads like a rigorously boiled-down short story, but the effects never seem artificial or contrived," and calls the book a "terse, mesmerizing memoir."

In Pharaoh's Army focuses on events which took place during the Vietnam War. But as Basbanes notes in *Publishers Weekly,* readers who are "in search of riveting battle scenes will have to look elsewhere; of far greater moment is the maturation of Tobias Wolff. The immature lieutenant who arrives in the war zone returns home as a man ready to spend four years at Oxford University (1968-72) and to begin his life as a writer." Judith Coburn observes in *Washington Post Book World* that "Mostly [Wolff] tells stories, awful, hilarious stories, often at his own expense, of what it was like day-to-day, trying to get by." Similarly, an *American Heritage* reviewer describes the writing as "relaxed, utterly lucid prose" and characterized the book as "melancholy and hilarious by turns." A reviewer for *Publishers Weekly* calls the book an "intense, precisely observed memoir," while the *New York Times Book Review*'s Bruce Bawer finds that the book "in style and tone has much in common with the low-key domestic minimalism of Raymond Carver and Ann Beattie."

The memoir treats aspects of the Vietnam War through the use of spare, uncomplicated prose. Although Wolff does not write specifically of atrocity and carnage, critics infer abominations from the very simplicity of his stories. Richard Eder suggests in the *Los Angeles Times Book Review,* that "because there was no actual horror, we see more clearly what underlay the horror." Coburn comments in the *Washington Post Book World* that "Wolff's strategy is to tell his story in an elegantly simple style and with a deceptively casual voice. The tension between this form and the horror of the war's content made this reader, anyway, feel by the book's end as if somehow I had gone out of my mind without noticing." While Bawer, in the *New York Times Book Review,* questions the "limitations" of Wolff's literary style applied to the horrors and intensity of war, he nonetheless declares: "There is a great deal of precise, evocative writing here." Gray comments in *Time* that the war taught Wolff "how to portray life as both desperately serious and perfectly absurd."

BIOGRAPHICAL/CRITICAL SOURCES:

BOOKS

Hannah, James, *Tobias Wolff: A Study of the Short Fiction,* Twayne Publishers, 1996.

PERIODICALS

America, September 8, 1984.
American Heritage, November, 1994, p. 120.
Best Sellers, November, 1981.
Bloomsbury Review, March/April, 1995, p. 13.
Booklist, September 1, 1994, p. 2.
Boston Review, December, 1985.
Chicago Tribune Books, January 22, 1989.
Chicago Tribune Book World, October 18, 1981; December 8, 1985.
Esquire, October, 1994, p. 133.
Globe and Mail (Toronto), February 8, 1986.
Hudson Review, summer, 1982; autumn, 1986.
Life, September, 1990, p. 95.
Los Angeles Times Book Review, January 3, 1982; November 17, 1985; January 8, 1989, p. 3; November 5, 1989, p. 12; June 6, 1993, p. 15; October 16, 1994, pp. 3, 10.
Nation, February 6, 1982, p. 152.
New Statesman, July 23, 1982, p. 22; August 12, 1983, p. 27.
Newsweek, January 23, 1989, p. 64; October 24, 1994, p. 78.
New York, April 12, 1993, p. 58.
New York Times, November 25, 1981; October 2, 1985, p. 27; October 28, 1985; October 30, 1985; January 12, 1989.
New York Times Book Review, November 15, 1981, p. 11; June 2, 1982; October 17, 1982, p. 45; October 20, 1985, p. 9; October 5, 1986, p. 58; January 15, 1989, p. 1; November 27, 1994, p. 10.
New York Times Magazine, February 5, 1989, p. 22.
People Weekly, October 7, 1985.
Publishers Weekly, August 29, 1994, p. 55; October 24, 1994, pp. 45-46; August 5, 1996.
Time, December 2, 1985, p. 99; February 6, 1989, p. 70; October 31, 1994, p. 81.
Times (London), May 4, 1989; May 11, 1989.
Times Literary Supplement, March 14, 1975, p. 269; July 30, 1982, p. 815; January 24, 1986; November 6, 1987, p. 1227; May 13, 1988, p. 532; May 12, 1989.
Village Voice, January 31, 1989.
Virginia Quarterly Review, spring, 1982.
Wall Street Journal, January 3, 1989.
Washington Post Book World, December 26, 1982, p. 12; November 3, 1985, p. 5; January 22, 1989, p. 3; November 6, 1994, pp. 3, 12.
Writer's Digest, August, 1989, p. 52.

*   *   *

WOODCOTT, Keith
See BRUNNER, John (Kilian Houston)

*   *   *

WOODIWISS, Kathleen E(rin) 1939-

PERSONAL: Born June 3, 1939, in Alexandria, LA; daughter of Charles Wingrove, Sr., and Gladys (Coker) Hogg; married Ross Eugene Woodiwiss (a U.S. Air Force major), July 20, 1956 (divorced); children: Sean Alan, Dorren James, Heath Alexander. *Education:* Attended schools in Alexandria, LA. *Politics:* Republican.

ADDRESSES: *Home*—Princeton, MN. *Office*—c/o Avon Books, 1350 Avenue of the Americas, New York, NY 10019.

CAREER: Writer. Worked as a model in fashion shows in Tokyo, Japan.

WRITINGS:

The Flame and the Flower, Avon, 1972.
The Wolf and the Dove, Avon, 1974.
Shanna, Avon, 1977.
Ashes in the Wind, Avon, 1979.
A Rose in Winter, Avon, 1982.
Come Love a Stranger, Avon, 1984.
So Worthy My Love, Avon, 1989.
Forever in Your Embrace, Avon, 1992.
(With others) *Three Weddings and a Kiss* (anthology), Avon, 1995.
(Editor and contributor) *Married at Midnight,* Avon, 1996.
Petals on the River, Avon, 1997.

SIDELIGHTS: A pioneering writer of romance fiction, Kathleen E. Woodiwiss's first novel is generally credited with creating the subgenre known as "erotic historical" romance. When *The Flame and the Flower* was published in 1972 the field of romance writing was dominated by "contemporary gothics" produced by writers such as Mary Stewart, Victoria Holt, and Phyllis Whitney. *The Flame and the Flower* differed from its predecessors in that it was substantially longer, but also because it contained lengthy, often detailed passages describing the sexual encounters of the hero and heroine. The immediate success of *The Flame and the Flower* cleared the way for writers like Rosemary Rogers and Laura McBain, authors who, along with Woodiwiss, have helped make the historical romance an enormously popular form.

The novels following *The Flame and the Flower* continued to be ground-breakers and assured Woodiwiss a large and loyal readership. *Shanna,* Woodiwiss's third book, made publishing history by becoming the first historical romance released in a trade paperback edition, and went on to sell over three million copies and spend a full year on the *New York Times* bestseller list. And in 1979 Avon published *Ashes in the Wind* with a first printing of 1.5 million copies and backed the book with a huge promotional campaign, including full-page advertisements in national women's magazines and commercials on network television. The publicity paid off almost immediately as *Ashes in the Wind* sold over two million copies and went into a third printing within a month of its release. All told, Woodiwiss's books have sold over ten million copies.

Historical romances vary in some respects but share fundamental similarities. Settings are typically exotic and frequently change from continent to continent. Heroes are characteristically handsome and commanding while heroines are beautiful and sensitive. Often innocent, the heroine is usually introduced to the hero with whom she falls in love, only to be parted from him for much of the story. The book inevitably ends with the heroine being united with her true love. *The Flame and the Flower* clearly embodies the traditions of its genre. The heroine, Heather, is a teenager throughout the narrative, which begins in England around 1800 and eventually moves to the American Carolinas. A beautiful and decorous girl who becomes the ward of a cruel aunt, Heather is raped by an attractive Yankee who in turn is forced to marry her.

After many adventures, the pair reunite and their initial hatred for each other turns to love. *The Flame and the Flower* also maintains the traditional structural relationship of males as dominant to and protective of females.

Where *The Flame and the Flower* and other Woodiwiss novels break with tradition is in their frank depiction of the sexual relationship between the hero and the heroine. While her books contain occasional sexual passages, Woodiwiss objects to charges that her books are "erotic." "I'm insulted when my books are called erotic," she maintains in a *Cosmopolitan* interview. "I don't think people who say that have read my books. I believe I write love stories. With a little spice. Some of the other current romances are a bit savage, though. They make sex dirty. It's embarrassing to read them. But women are looking for the love story. I get a lot of fan mail, and they tell me that." Janice Radway, writing in *Twentieth-Century Romance and Historical Writers,* sees the erotic passages in Woodiwiss's novels as being integral parts of "complex plots which all focus on the *gradual* development of love between the two principal characters. Unlike many writers of this subgenre who keep the heroine and the hero apart until the final pages of the novel, Woodiwiss brings them into contact early in the tale. Having established their initial attraction for each other, she then shows how love develops between two extraordinary individuals, emphasizes that the relationship must be cultivated carefully, and demonstrates that compromise, tenderness, and generosity are necessary to maintain it."

Just such a relationship is presented in Woodiwiss's 1979 novel *Ashes in the Wind.* This tale features the heroine Alaina MacGaren, a seventeen-year-old orphan who must leave her home in Virginia for New Orleans when a rumor is started that she is a traitor. In order to keep her identity a secret, Alaina assumes a number of disguises, including that of a street urchin, a penniless widow, and a hospital volunteer. In the midst of these many identities, the life of surgeon Captain Cole Lattimer becomes entangled with Alaina's, and the two overcome adversity to find a deep and lasting love. Although *Washington Post Book World* contributor Maude McDaniel finds *Ashes in the Wind* to be filled with silly characters, a formulaic plot, and awful writing, she goes on to conclude: "Actually, I rather enjoyed." And a *Publishers Weekly* contributor maintains that Woodiwiss "has fashioned her heroine in a picaresque tradition. Readers will find Alaina's spunky ingenuity refreshing."

In Woodiwiss's 1989 romance *So Worthy My Love,* Maxim Seymour, another alleged traitor, this time to Queen Elizabeth, is thought to be dead. The young man, hated by the noble Radborne family, is actually hiding in Germany, desperately wanting his beloved, Arabella Radborne, to be with him. Sending his men to kidnap her, Maxim is surprised when they bring back Arabella's beautiful cousin Elise by mistake. Unable to let Elise go, the two battle each other defiantly until they realize that they are actually in love. Woodiwiss "provides ripe descriptions" in *So Worthy My Love,* states a *Publishers Weekly* contributor, adding: "This long romance by a veteran of the genre delivers well-paced, well-structured diversion."

Although *So Worthy My Love,* and most of Woodiwiss's other novels, are enormously successful with the public, they are generally ignored by "serious" reviewers. This situation does not seem to bother Woodiwiss, however, nor does it make her wish to change her approach to writing. "I never started out to win any prizes for my writing," she relates in her interview with Judy

Klemesrud in the *New York Times Book Review.* "I wanted to appease a hunger for romantic novels, and that is what I shall continue to do." Woodiwiss similarly points out in an interview with Jean W. Ross for *Contemporary Authors* that her books are only an attempt to give readers "enjoyment. Escape. I would like to be able to give the reader a time period of relaxation and pleasure, a time of being able to put the worries and everything aside and just enjoy and relax."

BIOGRAPHICAL/CRITICAL SOURCES:

BOOKS

Falk, Kathryn, *Love's Leading Ladies,* Pinnacle Books, 1982.
Henderson, Lesley, editor, *Twentieth-Century Romance and Historical Writers,* 2nd edition, St. James Press, 1990.
Woodiwiss, Kathleen, in an interview with Jean W. Ross for *Contemporary Authors New Revisions Series,* Volume 23, Gale (Detroit), 1988, pp. 461-63.

PERIODICALS

Cosmopolitan, February, 1978.
Library Journal, May 15, 1974, p. 1410; February 15, 1995, p. 198.
New York Times Book Review, November 4, 1979.
Publishers Weekly, January 21, 1974, p. 88; January 31, 1977; May 30, 1977; September 3, 1979, p. 94; October 22, 1982, p. 51; August 25, 1989, p. 57.
Village Voice, May 9, 1977.
Washington Post Book World, April 9, 1972, p. 9; October 7, 1979, pp. 9, 14.
West Coast Review of Books, January, 1983, p. 42.

*   *   *

WOODRUFF, Robert W.
See MENCKEN, H(enry) L(ouis)

*   *   *

WOOLF, (Adeline) Virginia 1882-1941
(Virginia Stephen)

PERSONAL: Born January 25, 1882, in London, England; committed suicide by drowning, March 28, 1941, in Lewes, Sussex, England; daughter of Sir Leslie (a biographer, critic, and scholar) and Julia Prinsep Jackson Stephen; married Leonard Woolf (an economist, publisher, critic, and writer), August 10, 1912 (died, 1969). *Education:* Self-educated.

CAREER: Writer. Morley College, London, England, instructor in English, c. 1905-1907; founder and operator of Hogarth Press, with husband, Leonard Woolf, beginning in 1917.

AWARDS, HONORS: Prix *Femina* from *Femina* and *Vie Heureuse* reviews, 1928.

WRITINGS:

The Voyage Out (novel; also see below), Duckworth, 1915, revised, Doran, 1920.
Two Stories Written and Printed by Virginia Woolf and L. S. Woolf, Hogarth, 1917, story by Virginia Woolf published separately as *The Mark on the Wall* (also see below), Hogarth, 1919.
Kew Gardens (short stories; also see below), Hogarth, 1919.

Night and Day (novel), Duckworth, 1919, Doran, 1920.
Monday or Tuesday (short stories; includes "The Mark on the Wall" and "Kew Gardens"), Harcourt, 1921.
Jacob's Room (novel), Hogarth, 1922, Harcourt, 1923.
Mr. Bennett and Mrs. Brown (criticism), Hogarth, 1924.
The Common Reader (criticism), Harcourt, 1925.
Mrs. Dalloway (novel; also see below), Harcourt, 1925, reprinted with introduction by Woolf, Modern Library, 1928.
To the Lighthouse (novel), Harcourt, 1927.
Orlando (novel), Crosby Gaige, 1928.
A Room of One's Own (essays), Harcourt, 1929.
The Waves (novel), Harcourt, 1931.
The Second Common Reader (criticism), Harcourt, 1932, published in England as *The Common Reader, Second Series,* Hogarth, 1932.
Flush: A Biography, Harcourt, 1933.
The Years (novel; also see below), Harcourt, 1937.
Three Guineas (essays), Harcourt, 1938.
Roger Fry (biography), Harcourt, 1940.
Between the Acts (novel), Harcourt, 1941.
The Death of the Moth, and Other Essays, Harcourt, 1942.
A Haunted House, and Other Short Stories, Hogarth, 1943, Harcourt, 1944.
The Moment, and Other Essays, Hogarth, 1947, Harcourt, 1948.
The Captain's Death Bed, and Other Essays, Harcourt, 1950.
Granite and Rainbow (essays), Harcourt, 1958.
Contemporary Writers (essays), preface by Jean Guiguet, Hogarth, 1965, Harcourt, 1966.
Nurse Lugton's Golden Thimble (juvenile), 1966, published as *Nurse Lugton's Curtain,* illustrated by Julie Vivas, Harcourt, 1991.
Collected Essays, four volumes, Hogarth, 1966-67, Harcourt, 1967.
Mrs. Dalloway's Party: A Short Sequence, edited with an introduction by Stella McNichol, Hogarth, 1973, Harcourt, 1975.
Moments of Being (autobiographical essays), edited by Jeanne Schulkind, Chatto & Windus, 1976, Harcourt, 1977.
Freshwater (comedy), edited with a preface by Lucio P. Ruotolo, illustrated by Loretta Trezzo, Harcourt, 1976.
Books and Portraits: Some Further Selections from the Literary and Biographical Writings of Virginia Woolf, edited by Mary Lyon, Hogarth, 1977, Harcourt, 1978.
The Pargiters: The Novel-Essay Portion of "The Years," edited with an introduction by Mitchell A. Leaska, New York Public Library, 1977.
Melymbrosia: An Early Version of "The Voyage Out," edited with an introduction by Louise A. DeSalvo, New York Public Library, 1982.
The Complete Shorter Fiction of Virginia Woolf, edited by Susan Dick, Harcourt, 1985.
The Essays of Virginia Woolf, edited by Andrew McNeillie, Harcourt, 1986.
Woolf Omnibus (contains *Jacob's Room, Mrs. Dalloway, To the Lighthouse,* and *The Waves*), Oxford University Press, 1994.

Also author of essays under maiden name, Virginia Stephen. Essays, novels, and short stories published in numerous other collections; short stories also published separately.

JOURNALS

A Writer's Diary: Being Extracts from the Diary of Virginia Woolf, edited by husband, Leonard Woolf, Hogarth, 1953, Harcourt, 1954.

The Diary of Virginia Woolf, five volumes, edited by Anne Olivier Bell, introductory notes by Quentin Bell, Volume 1: *1915-1919,* Hogarth, 1977, Harcourt, 1979; Volume 2: *1920-1924,* Harcourt, 1978; Volume 3: *1925-1930,* Harcourt, 1980; Volume 4: *1931-1935,* Harcourt, 1982; Volume 5: *1936-1941,* Hogarth, 1984.

A Passionate Apprentice: The Early Journals, 1897-1909, edited by Mitchell A. Leaska, Harcourt, 1990.

A Moment's Liberty: The Shorter Diary of Virginia Woolf, abridged and edited by Anne Olivier Bell, Harcourt, 1990.

CORRESPONDENCE

Letters: Virginia Woolf and Lytton Strachey, edited by Leonard Woolf and James Strachey, Harcourt, 1956.

The Letters of Virginia Woolf, six volumes, edited by Nigel Nicolson and Joanne Trautmann, Volume 1: *The Flight of the Mind, 1888-1912,* Hogarth, 1975, published as *1888-1912,* Harcourt, 1975; Volume 2: *The Question of Things Happening, 1912-1922,* Hogarth, 1976, published as *1912-1922,* Harcourt, 1976; Volume 3: *A Change of Perspective, 1923-1928,* Hogarth, 1977, published as *1923-1928,* Harcourt, 1978; Volume 4: *A Reflection of the Other Person, 1929-1931,* Hogarth, 1978, published as *1929-1931,* Harcourt, 1979; Volume 5: *The Sickle Side of the Moon, 1932-1935,* Hogarth, 1979, published as *1932-1935,* Harcourt, 1979; Volume 6: *Leave the Letters Till We're Dead, 1936-1941,* Hogarth, 1980, published as *1936-1941,* Harcourt, 1980.

OTHER

Virginia Woolf "The Hours": The British Museum Manuscript of Mrs. Dalloway, transcribed and edited by Helen M. Wussow, University Press of America (Lanham, MD), 1996.

Translator, with S. S. Koteliansky, of works by Fedor Dostoevsky and Leo Tolstoy.

MEDIA ADAPTATIONS: To the Lighthouse was adapted as a film by the British Broadcasting Company (BBC-TV), written by Hugh Stoddart, directed by Colin Gregg, 1983; *The Waves* was adapted into a musical play by David Bucknam and Lisa Peterson, produced at the Perry Street Theater, 1990; *Orlando* was adapted as a film by Sony Pictures, written and directed by Sally Potter, 1993; *Mrs. Dalloway* was adapted as a film by Mrs. D. Productions/Bergen Films, written by Eileen Atkins, directed by Marleen Gorris, 1997.

SIDELIGHTS: English writer Virginia Woolf was one of the most innovative and influential literary figures of the twentieth century. A prolific author of essays, journals, letters, and long and short fiction, she is probably best remembered for her provocative experimental novels. As an early practitioner of stream-of-consciousness writing, Woolf subordinated dramatic action and plot development in her novels, exploring instead the inner thoughts and feelings of her characters. Through her revolutionary writings, she questioned both the nature of reality and the significance of the individual human being in an alienating and dehumanizing world. Her works offer a unique perspective on such topics as sexuality, feminism, life and death, madness and sanity, and the disintegration of society. Deeming Woolf "one of the half-dozen novelists of the present century whom the world will not easily let die," David Daiches, writing in *Virginia Woolf,* asserted: "There can be little question that she was the greatest woman novelist of her time, though she herself would have objected to the separation of her sex implied in such a judgment."

Throughout her early years, Woolf saw several members of her family fall victim to insanity and illness. Her half sister's mental illness and her cousin's madness from an accidental head injury both exerted a profound effect on her. And in his 1972 study, *Virginia Woolf: A Biography,* Quentin Bell alleged that Woolf's endurance of sexual abuse as a young girl by her older half brother permanently altered her attitude toward sex. In addition to the psychological strain brought on by the abuse, the perverted relationship, according to Bell, may have contributed to Woolf's frigidity as a married woman. Critics have indicated that the combined effect of these childhood experiences drained Woolf of her delicate emotional reserves, heightened her sensitivity to the harsh realities of life, and seriously damaged her ability to cope.

Woolf's first mental breakdown was precipitated by the 1895 death of her mother, Julia Stephen, a warm and loving individual who had worked to achieve an atmosphere of harmony in the Stephen household. Slowly recovering from the trauma after a prolonged period of rest and introspection, Woolf suffered additional trials in rapid succession. Her half sister Stella Duckworth, who had taken over some of the homemaking responsibilities after Julia Stephen's death, became ill and died in 1902. Two years later, Woolf's father also died. Woolf experienced another mental collapse in the months following her father's death, and she attempted suicide that same year. Upon her recovery, she moved with her sister Vanessa and brothers Thoby and Adrian from the family home at Hyde Park Gate to Bloomsbury, a London district with relatively inexpensive housing.

In 1906, Thoby Stephen was taken ill with typhoid and died. His death—at the age of twenty-six—devastated Woolf, and her sister Vanessa's marriage to Clive Bell intensified that sense of loss. She moved with her younger brother Adrian to a smaller house in Bloomsbury, maintained her ties with the Bloomsbury group, and concentrated on writing. Although annoyed by suggestions that she should find a husband, Woolf harbored thoughts—revealed in her letters—that she would never marry. Lytton Strachey, a known homosexual, proposed to Woolf, but after due consideration they both thought better of such an arrangement. Woolf soon experienced another mental breakdown, and Strachey, still concerned about the author, encouraged Leonard Woolf, a friend from Cambridge, to pursue her. The Woolfs were married in 1912, and for the next three decades, Leonard sought to instill in her a sense of stability, confidence, and worthiness.

Several years after their marriage, the Woolfs founded the Hogarth Press. Leonard engineered the couple's foray into publishing, hoping that the experience of setting type and operating the press might relieve his wife of some of the tension brought on by her writing. The Hogarth Press became an important publisher of experimental and alternative literature, including works by Woolf, W. H. Auden, E. M. Forster, Sigmund Freud, Robert Graves, Katherine Mansfield, H. G. Wells, and many others then perceived as radical.

Woolf became gravely ill in 1913 after finishing the manuscript for her debut novel, *The Voyage Out,* about a young woman coming of age while traveling in South America. This tragic tale, which offered radical new views on women and education, was generally viewed as the work of a promising author. But according to Bell, Woolf's fears of a negative critical reception had already driven her to despair, causing severe headaches, a profound state of melancholia, and both visual and audio hallucinations, including one in which she was taunted by a mocking crowd. A brief stay at a nursing home proved ineffective therapy, and Woolf returned home anorectic, insomniac, and suicidal. Under her husband's nurturing care, she slowly improved, but, as Bell theorized, "After two years of intermittent lunacy it appeared [thereafter] that her mind and her character were permanently affected."

Woolf wrote her second novel, *Night and Day,* while recuperating from the mental breakdown brought on by the completion of *The Voyage Out.* Published in 1919, the work revolves around a group of poorly matched young couples and the events that lead to their recombining as more suitable duos. Woolf viewed *Night and Day* as a safe project, one less demanding psychologically than its predecessor. But while critics generally commended Woolf for her writing style in *Night and Day,* many—including Mansfield—found the book's subject matter trite and its treatment predictable. Although the book received only mixed reviews, Woolf herself was more satisfied with it than with *The Voyage Out.*

Woolf was less confident in withstanding the critical ambivalence accorded her next book, the 1921 short fiction collection *Monday or Tuesday,* which contains stories usually regarded as precursors to her best experimental long works. Though hailed for their stunning imagery and evocations of characters' inner lives, the stories in *Monday or Tuesday,* according to some critics, are obscured by indirectness. "The reader is left with nothing definite in his mind," a *Springfield Republican* reviewer noted, "no real idea or purpose, no clear-cut thought." Perhaps as a consequence of the book's reception, Woolf underwent another period of extreme self-doubt: "I'm a failure as a writer. I'm out of fashion," she proclaimed in an entry from *A Writer's Diary,* ever sensitive to critical commentary. But at this time Woolf was already writing the experimental *Jacob's Room*—the book that marked a turning point in her career.

The idea for *Jacob's Room* reportedly came to Woolf as she stared into the fireplace at Hogarth House. A powerful depiction of the effects of a harsh world on an individual human being, the novel chronicles the life and wartime death of young Jacob Flanders, who is revealed indirectly through brief glimpses of the contents of his room and scattered impressions from others. Reviewers generally considered *Jacob's Room* a stunning progression that demonstrated a technical mastery lacking in both *The Voyage Out* and *Night and Day.* "For the first time Virginia Woolf caught both her society and her sense of the soul in a unified vision," asserted A. D. Moody in *Virginia Woolf. Jacob's Room* remains a testament to Woolf's achievements as a writer, containing some of her most vivid imagery and polished lyrical prose. As a *Spectator* reviewer commented, "There is no writer who can give the illusion of reality with more certainty and with so complete a concealment of illusionary devices behind a perfection of style which is at once solid and ethereal."

Already known for rendering with precision the thoughts and feelings of her characters, Woolf gained recognition with her next novel, *Mrs. Dalloway,* for evoking the actual thought process. Commenting on the work in an essay included in *Abinger Harvest,* Forster wrote: "It is easy for a novelist to describe what a character thinks of. . . . But to convey the actual process of thinking is a creative feat, and I know of no one except Virginia Woolf who has accomplished it."

Favorably compared to James Joyce's classic *Ulysses, Mrs. Dalloway* ranks among Woolf's greatest triumphs. Following the events of a single day in the life of Clarissa Dalloway, an upper-class English woman, the work is regarded as a stunning

document of the state of post-World War I society. The story opens with Mrs. Dalloway making last minute preparations for a party to be held at her home that evening. Utilizing the stream-of-consciousness technique, Woolf exposes Mrs. Dalloway's inner thoughts as the heroine reviews the course her life has taken. Prior to marrying the respectable but passionless Parliament member Richard Dalloway, Mrs. Dalloway had been pursued by sprightly suitor Peter Walsh. But after an emotionally fulfilling encounter with another woman, Mrs. Dalloway rejected Walsh in favor of Mr. Dalloway, thus insulating herself from the true nature of her sexuality. On the day of her party, Walsh reenters Mrs. Dalloway's life.

Mrs. Dalloway never meets the novel's other significant character, World War I veteran Septimus Smith. His sensitive temperament destroyed, Smith leaps to his death from a balcony at the prospect of commitment to a sanatorium. More than merely the culmination of his madness, Septimus's suicide is generally viewed as an expression of freedom, his ultimate assertion of independence at a time when he had lost control over his own future. During her party, Mrs. Dalloway learns of Septimus's suicide. Commenting on the evolution of the story line in her introduction to the 1928 edition of *Mrs. Dalloway,* Woolf noted some of the revisions she had made to the text: "In the first version Septimus, who later is intended to be [Mrs. Dalloway's] double, had no existence; and . . . Mrs. Dalloway was originally to kill herself, or perhaps merely to die at the end of the party."

With the publication of her 1927 novel *To the Lighthouse,* Woolf established herself as a leading writer of the twentieth century. Divided into three sections, the lush, poetic narrative offers insights into the processes of decay and renewal and the enduring influence of the past on the present. The story revolves around the Ramsays—a family that occupies a summer house off the coast of Scotland—and several of their guests, including a painter named Lily Briscoe. Mrs. Ramsay functions as a link between the members of the household. In the first of the book's sections, young James Ramsay's hopes of trekking to the island's lighthouse are frustrated by the pessimistic and preoccupied Mr. Ramsay's prediction of rain. Part two of the book begins with the storm's onset. In this section ten years elapse, during which Mrs. Ramsay and two of the Ramsay children die and the summer house falls to ruin. Even after her death, though, Mrs. Ramsay's memory lives on, and in part three the remaining Ramsays return to the house, James and Mr. Ramsay complete the journey to the lighthouse, and Lily Briscoe—also back at the house—finally completes a painting she had begun a decade earlier.

To the Lighthouse has been judged a profound and moving portrait of the human spirit. As Conrad Aiken wrote in a piece from his *Collected Criticism,* "Nothing happens, in this houseful of odd nice people, and yet all of life happens. The tragic futility, the absurdity, the pathetic beauty of life—we experience all of this." Speculating on the symbolism intended in *To the Lighthouse,* James Ginden wrote in his *Harvest of a Quiet Eye:* "The lighthouse itself, distant and ambiguous across the water, stands as the central symbol of meaning and achievement in the novel. . . . Mrs. Woolf's symbolic searcher must suffer, must pass through the tumult of destruction and war, before he can reach the lighthouse." In a diary entry for November 28, 1928, Woolf admitted: "I used to think of [father] and mother daily; but writing the *Lighthouse* laid them in my mind. . . . I was obsessed by them both, unhealthily; and writing of them was a necessary act." But, as quoted by Bell, the author disclaimed any single critical interpretation of the novel: "I meant *nothing* by *The Light-*

house. . . . [I] trusted that people would make it the deposit for their own emotions—which they have done, one thinking it means one thing another another. I can't manage Symbolism except in this vague, generalised way. . . . [When] directly I'm told what a thing means, it becomes hateful to me."

Woolf's next novel, the thinner *Orlando*, is a mock biography that transcends the limits of time, mortality, and sexuality. Published in 1928, this fantastic work traces the adventures of young Orlando, a sixteenth-century poet born to a wealthy English family. Having taken Queen Elizabeth as a lover and engaged in a steamy affair with a Russian princess, the charming Orlando falls into a series of deep sleeps, awakening in the eighteenth century as a thirty-six-year-old woman who maintains her youth throughout the twentieth century. Woolf based the character of Orlando on Vita Sackville-West, an English writer and Bloomsbury member with whom Woolf shared an intimate friendship. The book is said to be a mythic reconciliation of Woolf's sexual duality. Critics heralded *Orlando* as a clever and substantial literary document that catalogs English manners and sensibilities over various generations and examines human history from multiple perspectives through the androgynous Orlando.

Woolf reaffirmed her place in contemporary literature with her 1931 publication *The Waves*, a highly experimental novel without dialogue. Widely regarded as the most difficult of Woolf's books, *The Waves* focuses on three men and three women, all of whom reveal themselves through soliloquies and interior monologue. As the characters eulogize their heroic friend Percival, they progress in their understanding of life's mutability. Some reviewers objected to the novel's radical structure and found its premise overly obscure. Others lauded Woolf's revolutionary vision and technical acumen. Alluding to the sense of mystery inherent in *The Waves*, Gerald Bullett, in a review for *New Statesman and Nation*, asserted, "It is impossible to describe, impossible to do more than salute, the richness, the strangeness, the poetic illumination of this book. The characters are not analysed, . . . they are entered into, intuited."

In her 1937 novel *The Years* Woolf again addresses life's mysteries and tragedies, offering insights into the effects of war, the aging process, and modernization on both the individual and society as a whole. Chronicling three generations of the mundane Pargiter family, the novel presents an overview of England's upper middle class from the end of the nineteenth through the beginning of the twentieth century. True to Woolf's style, *The Years* lacks substantial action, but several critics applauded the book as a valuable exploration of both the evolution of modern society and the inner resources of the human personality. "Many people will wonder what on earth Mrs. Woolf is trying to say in so many uneventful pages. [But] the long last chapter plainly tells," surmised Olga Owens in the *Boston Transcript*. George Stevens, writing in *Saturday Review*, commented: "An expression of abstract experience, *The Years* is one of Mrs. Woolf's most brilliant achievements, written with imagination that is luminous and evocative."

But Woolf's feelings of anguish eventually returned. In an entry for January of 1941, as documented in *A Writer's Diary*, she resolved, "This trough of despair shall not, I swear, engulf me." Two months later, however, fearing that she lacked the stamina needed to recover from any further bouts of depression, Woolf filled her pockets with rocks and waded into the Ouse River. In her last note to Leonard, excerpted in *Virginia Woolf: A Biography*, she explained: "I am doing what seems the best thing

to do. . . . If anybody could have saved me it would have been you. Everything has gone from me but the certainty of your goodness. I can't go on spoiling your life any longer. I don't think two people could have been happier than we have been."

Woolf's final novel, *Between the Acts*, was published in 1941, shortly after her death. The slim volume concerns an English family and their guests, all of whom gather one summer day in the country to watch a village pageant. The audience, however, lacks a commonality of spirit: the failure of the viewers to unite symbolizes the fragmentation of society. At the end of the pageant, the members of the audience go their own separate ways, absorbed by their own personal obsessions. *Between the Acts* received mixed reviews, and critics differed in their assessments of its meaning. Though not generally regarded as one of Woolf's major works, the posthumous novel is said to contain several unforgettably disturbing passages. David Cecil's *Spectator* review captured the critical consensus: "Perhaps had she lived to revise [*Between the Acts*], Mrs. Woolf would have brought it into clear pattern and harmony. As it is, it must be counted as in part a failure. But Mrs. Woolf's failures are more precious than most writers' successes."

In addition to her status as a novelist and short story writer, Woolf distinguished herself as both a critic and essayist with several impressive works of nonfiction, including *Mr. Bennett and Mrs. Brown*, *A Room of One's Own*, and *Three Guineas*. In *Mr. Bennett and Mrs. Brown*, Woolf attacks John Galsworthy, Arnold Bennett, and H. G. Wells—leading writers of the day—for their inability to capture a character's individuality in their works. *A Room of One's Own*—which Rebecca West in *Ending in Earnest: A Literary Log* deemed "an uncompromising piece of feminist propaganda: . . . the ablest yet written"—offers witty commentary on women and literature, and *Three Guineas* provides insightful political discourse on women and society. The keenness and precision with which Woolf articulates her opinions has made her nonfiction as valuable and enduring as her fiction.

Since Woolf's death in 1941, critics and biographers have produced a voluminous body of books and articles about the author's life and work. In addition, Woolf's own substantial private writings—her journals and letters—have been edited and published. *A Passionate Apprentice: The Early Journals, 1897-1909* contains the entirety of seven notebooks that Woolf kept between the ages of fifteen and twenty-seven. Although Woolf's life during this period was filled with major events, including a nervous breakdown and the deaths of her father, her half-sister, Stella, and her beloved brother, Thoby, she does not expound on these experiences in much detail. The early notebooks of this volume record mostly matter-of-fact items from Woolf's daily existence: shopping trips, minor illnesses, visits by friends and relatives, and other routine activities. Critics reviewing the journals note the gap in the journals between 1897 and 1899, after which Woolf's daily comments take on a different character: "Now we can see that there is some point in speaking of these journals as recording an apprenticeship. . . . [T]he entries are longer, things happen and get conscientiously described. . . . There are also serious exercises in the description of character," explained *London Review of Books* critic Frank Kermode. Added *Bloomsbury Review* contributor Robin Lippincott on the change in Woolf's entries after 1899: "She is teaching herself to write. Many of these early attempts are stiff and stilted, but subsequent notebooks record her improvement, growing success, and confidence." At the close of these diaries in 1909, Woolf had begun work on her first published novel, *The Voyage Out*.

Woolf's remaining diaries, written between 1915 and 1941 and comprising thirty manuscript volumes, were condensed by Anne Olivier Bell and published in five volumes between 1977 and 1984. In 1990 Bell produced *A Moment's Liberty: The Shorter Diary of Virginia Woolf,* a one-volume edition of these diaries that focused on the major events in Woolf's personal life. In this way, the volume stands as a companion to Leonard Woolf's *A Writer's Diary,* which focused more heavily on Virginia Woolf's working life. Numerous collections of Woolf's letters have also been published, most notably in a six-volume work edited by Nigel Nicolson and Joanne Trautmann published between 1975 and 1980.

BIOGRAPHICAL/CRITICAL SOURCES:

BOOKS

Aiken, Conrad, *Collected Criticism,* Oxford University Press, 1968.

Allan, Tuzyline Jita, *Womanist and Feminist Aesthetics: A Comparative Review,* Ohio University Press, 1995.

Anderson, Linda, *Women and Autobiography in the Twentieth Century,* Prentice Hall, 1996.

Barrett, Eileen, and Patricia Cramer, editors, *Re: Reading, Re: Writing, Re: Teaching Virginia Woolf: Selected Papers from the Fourth Annual Conference on Virginia Woolf,* Pace University Press, 1995.

Bell, Quentin, *Virginia Woolf: A Biography,* Harcourt, 1972.

Daiches, David, *Virginia Woolf,* New Directions, 1963.

Dictionary of Literary Biography, Gale (Detroit), Volume 36: *British Novelists, 1890-1929: Traditionalists,* 1985; Volume 100: *Modern British Essayists, Second Series,* 1990; Volume 162: *British Short-Fiction Writers, 1915-1945,* 1996.

Diment, Galya, *The Autobiographical Novel of Co-Consciousness: Goncharov, Woolf, and Joyce,* University of Florida Press, 1994.

Forster, E. M., *Abinger Harvest,* Harcourt, 1936.

Forster, E. M., *Virginia Woolf,* Harcourt, 1942.

Gindin, James, *Harvest of a Quiet Eye: The Novel of Compassion,* Indiana University Press, 1971.

Gordon, Lyndall, *Virginia Woolf: A Writer's Life,* Norton, 1984.

Hanson, Clare, *Virginia Woolf,* St. Martin's, 1994.

Hussey, Mark, *Virginia Woolf A to Z: A Comprehensive Reference for Students, Teachers, and Common Readers to Her Life, Work, and Critical Reception,* Facts on File, 1995.

Jackson, Tony E., *The Subject of Modernism: Narrative Alterations in the Fiction of Eliot, Conrad, Woolf, and Joyce,* University of Michigan Press, 1994.

King, James, *Virginia Woolf,* Hamish Hamilton, 1994.

Lee, Hermione, *Virginia Woolf,* Chatto and Windus, 1996.

Little, Judy, *The Experimental Self: Dialogic Subjectivity in Woolf, Pym, and Brooke-Rose,* Southern Illinois University Press, 1996.

McNees, Eleanor Jane, *Virginia Woolf: Critical Assessments,* Helm Information, 1994.

Moody, A. D., *Virginia Woolf,* Oliver & Boyd, 1963.

Noble, Joan Russell, *Recollections of Virginia Woolf,* Ohio University Press, 1994.

Phillips, Kathy J., *Virginia Woolf against Empire,* University of Tennessee Press, 1994.

Poole, Roger, *The Unknown Virginia Woolf,* Cambridge University Press, 1996.

Ratcliffe, Krista, *Anglo-American Feminist Challenges to the Rhetorical Traditions: Virginia Woolf, Mary Daly, and Adrienne Rich,* Southern Illinois University Press, 1996.

Reese, Judy S., *Recasting Social Values in the Work of Virginia Woolf,* Associated University Presses, 1996.

Reid, Panthea, *Art and Affection: A Life of Virginia Woolf,* Oxford University Press, 1996.

Rosenberg, Beth Carole, *Virginia Woolf and Samuel Johnson: Common Readers,* St. Martin's, 1995.

Rosenman, Ellen Bayuk, *A Room of One's Own: Women Writers and the Politics of Creativity,* Twayne, 1995.

Saxton, Ruth, and Jean Tobin, *Woolf and Lessing: Breaking the Mold,* St. Martin's Press, 1994.

Schroeder, Steven H., *Virginia Woolf's Subject and the Subject of Ethics: Notes Toward a Poetics of Persons,* Mellen, 1996.

Stansky, Peter, *On or about December 10: Early Bloomsbury and Its Intimate World,* Harvard University Press, 1996.

Stape, J. H., *Virginia Woolf: Interviews and Recollections,* University of Iowa Press, 1995.

Tratner, Michael, *Modernism and Mass Politics: Joyce, Woolf, Eliot, Yeats,* Stanford University Press, 1995.

Twentieth-Century Literary Criticism, Gale, Volume 1, 1978; Volume 5, 1981; Volume 20, 1986; Volume 43, 1992; Volume 56, 1995.

West, Rebecca, *Ending in Earnest: A Literary Log,* Doubleday, 1931.

Whittier-Ferguson, John, *Framing Pieces: Designs of the Gloss in Joyce, Woolf, and Pound,* Oxford University Press, 1996.

Woolf, Leonard, *Downhill All the Way: An Autobiography of the Years 1919-1939,* Harcourt, 1967.

Woolf, Leonard, *The Journey Not the Arrival That Matters: An Autobiography of the Years 1939-1969,* Harcourt, 1970.

Wussow, Helen, editor, *New Essays on Virginia Woolf,* Contemporary Research Press, 1994.

PERIODICALS

Bloomsbury Review, October/November, 1991, p. 21.

Boston Transcript, April 10, 1937.

English Studies, June, 1960.

Library Journal, August, 1995, p. 136.

London Review of Books, April 25, 1991, p. 17.

Modern Fiction Studies, autumn, 1972; summer, 1979.

New Republic, January 3, 1981.

New Statesman and Nation, October 10, 1931.

New Yorker, June 5, 1995, p. 58.

New York Review of Books, April 20, 1978.

New York Times, May 10, 1990.

New York Times Book Review, February 17, 1991; May 19, 1991; July 5, 1992, p. 20.

Observer (London), October 21, 1990, p. 58.

Publishers Weekly, April 6, 1990, p. 105.

Saturday Review, April 10, 1937; February, 1982.

School Library Journal, June, 1995, p. 71.

Spectator, November 11, 1922; July 18, 1941.

Springfield Republican, December 25, 1921.

Times (London), August 16, 1990; April 25, 1991.

Times Literary Supplement, July 20, 1990, p. 770; December 14, 1990.

Wilson Library Bulletin, May, 1994, p. 103.

*   *   *

WOOLRICH, Cornell
  See HOPLEY-WOOLRICH, Cornell George

WOUK, Herman 1915-

PERSONAL: Surname is pronounced "Woke"; born May 27, 1915, in New York, NY; son of Abraham Isaac (an industrialist) Esther (Levine) Wouk; married Betty Sarah Brown, December 9, 1945; children: Abraham Isaac (deceased), Nathaniel, Joseph. *Education:* Columbia University, B.A. (with honors), 1934. *Religion:* Jewish. *Avocational interests:* Judaic scholarship, Zionist studies, travel (especially in Israel).

ADDRESSES: Agent—BSW Literary Agency, 3255 N St. N.W., Washington, DC 20007-2845.

CAREER: Gag writer for radio comedians, New York City, 1934-35; scriptwriter for Fred Allen, 1936-41; U.S. Treasury Department, "dollar-a-year-man," writing and producing radio plays to promote war bond sales, 1941; self-employed writer, 1946-. Visiting professor, Yeshiva University, 1953-57; scholar in residence, Aspen Institute of Humanistic Studies, 1973-74; lectured in China, 1982. Trustee, College of the Virgin Islands, 1962-69; member of board of directors, Washington National Symphony, 1969-71, and Kennedy Center Productions, 1974-75; member of advisory council, Center for U.S.-China Arts Exchange, 1981-87. *Military service:* U.S. Navy, 1942-46; served on Pacific Ocean aboard two destroyer-minesweepers, U.S.S. *Zane* and U.S.S. *Southard;* became lieutenant; received four campaign stars and Presidential Unit Citation.

MEMBER: Authors Guild, PEN, Dramatists Guild, Reserve Officers Association of the United States, Writers Guild of America East, Century Club (New York City), Bohemian Club (San Francisco); Cosmos Club, Metropolitan Club (both Washington, DC).

AWARDS, HONORS: Richard H. Fox Prize, 1934; Pulitzer Prize in fiction, 1952, for *The Caine Mutiny: A Novel of World War II;* Columbia University Medal of Excellence, 1952; L.H.D., Yeshiva University, 1955; LL.D., Clark University, 1960; Litt.D., American International University, 1979; PhD., Bar-Ilan University, 1990; Alexander Hamilton Medal, Columbia College Alumni Association, 1980; American Book Award nomination, 1981, for *War and Remembrance;* Ralph Waldo Emerson Award, International Platform Association, 1981; University of California—Berkeley Medal, 1984; Golden Plate Award, American Academy of Achievement, 1986; *Washingtonian* Book Award, 1986, for *Inside, Outside;* USN Memorial Foundation "Lone Sailor" Award, 1987; Yad Vashem KaZetnik award, 1990.

WRITINGS:

Aurora Dawn; or, The True History of Andrew Reale, Containing a Faithful Account of the Great Riot, Together With the Complete Texts of Michael Wilde's Oration and Father Stanfield's Sermon (novel; Book-of-the-Month Club selection), Simon & Schuster, 1947.
The City Boy: The Adventures of Herbie Bookbinder and His Cousin, Cliff (novel; Reader's Digest Condensed Book Club selection; Family Book Club selection; Book-of-the-Month Club alternate selection), Simon & Schuster, 1948, published as *The City Boy,* Doubleday, 1952, published as *City Boy: The Adventures of Herbie Bookbinder,* Doubleday, 1969.
The Caine Mutiny: A Novel of World War II (Reader's Digest Condensed Book Club selection; Literary Guild alternate selection), Doubleday, 1951, published as *The Caine Mutiny,* Dell, 1966.

Marjorie Morningstar (novel; Reader's Digest Condensed Book Club selection; Book-of-the-Month Club selection), Doubleday, 1955.
This Is My God (nonfiction; Reader's Digest Condensed Book Club selection; Book-of-the-Month Club alternate selection), Doubleday, 1959, published as *This Is My God: The Jewish Way of Life,* 1970, revised edition, Collins, 1973.
Youngblood Hawke (novel; Reader's Digest Condensed Book Club selection; Book-of-the-Month Club selection), Doubleday, 1962.
Don't Stop the Carnival (novel; Book-of-the-Month Club selection), Doubleday, 1965.
The "Lomokome" Papers, Pocket Books, 1968.
The Winds of War (novel; Literary Guild selection; Reader's Digest Condensed Book Club selection), Little, Brown, 1971.
War and Remembrance (novel; sequel to *The Winds of War;* Literary Guild selection; Reader's Digest Condensed Book Club selection), Little, Brown, 1978.
Inside, Outside (novel; Book-of-the-Month Club selection), Little, Brown, 1985.
The Hope, Little, Brown, 1994.
The Glory, Little, Brown, 1994.

PLAYS

The Traitor (two-act; first produced on Broadway at Forty-Eighth Street Theater, April 4, 1949), Samuel French, 1949.
The Caine Mutiny Court-Martial (two-act; based on his novel *The Caine Mutiny;* first produced in Santa Barbara, CA, 1953; produced on Broadway at Plymouth Theater, January 20, 1954), Doubleday, 1954.
Slattery's Hurricane (screenplay; produced by Twentieth Century-Fox, 1949), Permabooks, 1956.
Nature's Way (two-act comedy; first produced on Broadway at Coronet Theater, October 15, 1957), Doubleday, 1958.

Also author of screenplay *The Winds of War,* ABC-TV, 1983, and coauthor of screenplay *War and Remembrance,* ABC-TV, 1988.

MEDIA ADAPTATIONS: The Caine Mutiny was filmed by Columbia in 1954, starring Humphrey Bogart as Captain Queeg; *The City Boy* was made into a motion picture by Columbia in 1950; Warner Bros. filmed *Marjorie Morningstar* and *Youngblood Hawke* in 1958 and 1964, respectively. A television adaptation of "The Caine Mutiny Court Martial," with Barry Sullivan, Lloyd Nolan, and Frank Lovejoy, aired on "Ford Star Jubilee" in 1955; *The Winds of War* and *War and Remembrance* were adapted as television miniseries airing on ABC-TV in 1983 and 1988, respectively.

SIDELIGHTS: An American novelist and playwright of Russian-Jewish heritage, Herman Wouk received the 1952 Pulitzer Prize in fiction for *The Caine Mutiny: A Novel of World War II* and has since published several other best-sellers, including *The Winds of War* and *War and Remembrance.* The *Atlantic*'s Edward Weeks calls him a compelling narrator "who uses large canvases and who, without much fuss for style or symbolism, drives his story ahead with an infectious belief in the people he is writing about." According to a reviewer for *Time,* Wouk's chief significance is that "he spearheads a mutiny against the literary stereotypes of rebellion—against three decades of U.S. fiction dominated by skeptical criticism, sexual emancipation, social protest, and psychoanalytic sermonizing." He remains, writes Pearl K. Bell in *Commentary,* "an unembarrassed believer in such 'discredited' forms of commitment as valor, gallantry, leadership, patriotism." Because of the reaffirmation of traditional values in his works,

Wouk has enjoyed wide readership but has also been accused by some critics of pandering to popular prejudice.

Wouk began writing fiction in 1943 while on sea duty on the Pacific Ocean, and he later used his Navy experience aboard the U.S.S. *Zane* and U.S.S. *Southard* as background for his third novel, *The Caine Mutiny* (which is not autobiographical). The book is not concerned with battles at sea but with adherence to appointive authority. The conflict centers around Lieutenant Commander Philip Francis Queeg, who, according to W. J. Stuckey in *The Pulitzer Prize Novels,* "manifests a professional incompetence that will probably remain unparalleled in or out of fiction." When it appears that Queeg is too terrified to issue the necessary orders to save the ship during a typhoon, Lieutenant Maryk, the ship's executive officer, is persuaded by Lieutenant Keefer and his followers to seize control. Maryk is subsequently tried for making a mutiny but is acquitted through the efforts of Lieutenant Barney Greenwald, an adept trial lawyer. Ironically, at a party celebrating Maryk's acquittal, Greenwald tells Maryk that it is he, Maryk (and not Queeg), who is morally guilty, for he deserted a military system that had, despite its flaws, protected America from foreign fascists.

Several critics consider Wouk's treatment of the military affair insightful and carefully constructed. Harry Gilroy, for example, writes in the *New York Times* that Wouk "has a profound understanding of what Navy men should be, and against some who fell short of the mark he has fired a deadly broadside." Edmund Fuller points out in his *Man in Modern Fiction* that the book's ability "to view the problem within the inescapable military premise without oversimplifying it" distinguishes *The Caine Mutiny* from other World War II novels. Discussing the justification of the mutiny in his *In My Opinion,* Orville Prescott says that it is "the crux of [the novel, and] Mr. Wouk develops it extremely well, with racy wit and genial humor, with lively pace and much ingenuity of incident and with unexpected subtlety." Similarly, a reviewer for the *Times Literary Supplement* concludes: "So convincingly has Mr. Wouk created his officers, so subtly has he contrived the series of incidents that culminate in the final drama, that, given both the characters and the situations, the climax is perfectly acceptable."

Marjorie Morningstar, Wouk's fourth novel, also focuses on rebellion but in a civilian context. The book traces the life of a beautiful, intelligent girl who renounces the values and authority of her hard-working Jewish parents only to end up, years later, affirming them as a suburban matron and community servant. E. W. Foell notes in the *Christian Science Monitor* that Wouk "has not flinched at what he sees in his characters' thoughts, [but] many of his readers are likely to." A *Time* critic writes that, indeed, "Wouk [sets] teeth on edge by advocating chastity before marriage, suggesting that real happiness for a woman is found in a home and children, cheering loud and long for the American middle class and blasting Bohemia and Bohemians. Wouk is a Sinclair Lewis in reverse." Reviewing the book in the *New York Times,* Maxwell Geismar believes that "here as in *The Caine Mutiny* [the conflict] is settled by a final bow to the red-tape of a bureaucracy or to the properties of a social class, under the impression that these are among the eternal verities. *Marjorie Morningstar* is very good reading indeed. But to this reviewer at least the values of true culture are as remote from its polished orbit as are, at base, the impulses of real life."

After *Marjorie Morningstar,* Wouk interrupted his career as a novelist to write a short, clear account of the Jewish faith from a personal viewpoint—something he had been thinking of doing for years. Dedicated to the memory of his grandfather, Mendel Leib Levine, a rabbi from Minsk, *This Is My God* was published in 1959 and became a best-seller. Then, with *Youngblood Hawke* and *Don't Stop the Carnival,* Wouk returned to writing fiction, but he also began work on a second ambition: a panoramic novel of World War II.

Wouk first considered doing a global war novel in 1944, according to *Time*'s Timothy Foote. Later, *The Caine Mutiny* "threatened to sprawl in that direction," notes Foote, "with more home-front material and a subplot in Europe. Wisely, Wouk cut it back and waited." Having begun reading standard histories in 1962, Wouk moved to Washington two years later to utilize the National Archives and Library of Congress, as well as to interview surviving military leaders. His quest for information also led him to England, France, Italy, Germany, Poland, Czechoslovakia, Israel, Iran, and the Soviet Union. Due to the scope of his task, Wouk ended up writing not one but two novels: *The Winds of War* and a sequel, *War and Remembrance.* "Since both have been best sellers, it is likely that more Americans have learned about, or remembered, the war through Wouk's account than from any other single source in the last decade," claims Michael Mandelbaum in *Political Science Quarterly.*

Generally praised by critics for their depth and accuracy of detail, the two books may be described as the history of the Second World War seen through the eyes of an American family and their immediate friends and contacts. *The Winds of War* takes Commander Victor "Pug" Henry and his family from the invasion of Poland to the attack on Pearl Harbor, Hawaii, and *War and Remembrance* details their experiences from Pearl Harbor to the dropping of the atomic bomb on Hiroshima, Japan. Over the course of the war, Henry serves as a special presidential envoy; meets Hitler, Stalin, Churchill, and Mussolini; is in Hawaii the day after the attack on Pearl Harbor; is present at the summit meetings off Nova Scotia in 1940 and in Tehran in 1943; is in London during the Battle of Britain; accompanies the Harriman-Beaverbrook mission to Moscow in 1941; participates in the battles of Midway, Guadalcanal, and Leyte Gulf; tours the Russian front in 1944; and even comes in contact with people working on the Manhattan Project. What he fails to witness, members of his family see: the invasion of Poland, the war in North Africa, the fall of Singapore, and the horrors of Auschwitz.

In reviewing the two books, critics often point out that this technique of depicting the effects of war on ordinary people (some of whom rub shoulders with the high and mighty) is a familiar one. Timothy Foote, among others, suggests that Wouk's opus is reminiscent of *War and Peace*—though not of the same quality—and that Wouk's aim is "nothing less than to do for the middle-class American vision of World War II pretty much what [Leo] Tolstoy did for the Battle of Borodino." More often, however, reviewers like Granville Hicks of the *New York Times Book Review* cite the resemblance between "Pug" Henry and Upton Sinclair's Lanny Budd: "Like Lanny, Pug becomes a kind of secret Presidential agent. In this role, he turns up at most of the places where history is being made."

Several critics charge that the technique results in characterization that is purely functional. Though Hicks admits that Wouk has "the gift of compelling narrative," he feels that the characters in *The Winds of War,* "even Pug Henry, are never living human beings. Although [Wouk] tries to give these men and women some semblance of reality by involving them in more or less complicated love affairs, they remain essentially observers and reporters." Similarly, Pearl K. Bell, reviewing *War and Remembrance* in *Commentary,* describes the characters as "not merely trivial but offensively so. Time and again, Wouk the student of history writes a brilliantly evocative account of battle—he has mastered every maneuver, knows exactly how submarines, aircraft carriers, battleships, destroyers, dive bombers work, how the vast machinery of war was deployed during a particular operation—only to return with a dismaying thump to his super-Lanny Budd hero, Captain (eventually Admiral) Victor (Pug) Henry." Foote is willing "to forgive Henry, and the author, the narrative necessities that shoot [Henry] hither and yon and miraculously equip him with the Russian and German necessary to do his work for Wouk, F.D.R., and the reader. [But] not so the other Henrys. The wife who would worry about getting her hair done on the day of Armageddon, a wayward daughter caught up in the sleazy radio industry in New York, two naval-officer sons, all are conventional appurtenances, without the emotional or dynastic depth to support a drama on the scale of World War II."

Wouk widens the scope of the story by presenting a German perspective on the war through excerpts of General Armin von Roon's *World Empire Lost,* an imaginary treatise based on actual writings of German generals. Richard R. Bolton claims in *Midwest Quarterly* that von Roon's views, "and (in places) Henry's 'later' comments on them, jolt the reader out of enough preconceptions to make him more receptive to Wouk's own explanations of why things turned out as they did, or (more important) *how* they might have been made to turn out better." Bolton surmises that, according to Wouk, World War II was a "natural" disaster in that it arose from fallible human nature: "Human cruelty, of which war is the most massive and spectacular manifestation, occurs not because most people are cruel, but because most people are weak or lazy, or too wishful to perceive in time what truly cruel people like the Nazis are about. . . . Given that fallibility, World War II, and possibly other wars since, probably could not have been avoided." But, he continues, "given also the availability of enough men with the training and virtues of Victor Henry—the truly 'best' in Wouk's view, those who do not lack conviction—that war, and possibly others since, could have been ameliorated, at least. It was not ameliorated, because democratic societies, notably ours, have little stomach for the unpleasant facts that are a military professional's daily fare."

Wouk's 1985 novel, *Inside, Outside,* "comes as close to being an outright autobiography as he is likely to write," declares John Eisenhower in the *Chicago Tribune Book World.* It tells of a Jewish man who, like Wouk, was born in New York City in 1915, the son of immigrant parents who established a commercial laundry business. Like Wouk, protagonist Israel David Goodkind—"Yisroelke" to his friends and family on the "inside"—worked as a gag writer, although Goodkind becomes a lawyer rather than a novelist. Goodkind is, however, writing his memoirs, which transforms Wouk's novel into "a paean to the American Jewish experience," according to *Diversion* contributor Sybil S. Steinberg. Unifying the novel, which deals by turns with Goodkind's present reality as a speech writer for U.S. President Richard Nixon and with Goodkind's childhood and relatives, is the tension between the "inside" (which includes Jewish religious life, values, and heritage as well as the search for identity for Jew or gentile) and the "outside" (secular American life).

The novel—Wouk's first in seven years—received mixed reviews. Critics such as Steinberg praise the "breezy, humorous style" in which it is written and cite its compassion and wisdom.

Writes Eisenhower, it is "an easy-to-read, informative tale that . . . provides an enlightening perspective on Jewish attitudes." He singles out one scene in which "Jews of varying persuasions . . . exchange views and insults" and concludes that "that scene alone, which illuminates so much of the current Jewish dilemma, gives this novel the right to be regarded as Wouk's most significant work since 'The Caine Mutiny.'" In contrast, Christopher Lehmann-Haupt of the *New York Times* finds the novel "remarkably predictable" and, "worst of all, . . . smug."

Nearly a decade later Wouk produced two expansive historical novels on the founding of the modern state of Israel. *The Hope* picks up at the end of the Second World War and recounts the creation and early development of Israel through the lives of several military men and their families. The central character is Zev Barak, an Israeli officer who participates in the 1948 War of Independence, the 1956 Suez Campaign, and the Six Day War of 1967, and who is privy to political and diplomatic intrigue involving David Ben-Gurion, Yitzhak Rabin, and Menachem Begin. In *The Glory,* the sequel, Wouk continues his story of Israel's struggle for nationhood through the experiences of the Barak family, covering the period from 1967 to the early 1980s.

Though finding weakness in Wouk's characterizations and obtuse rendering of military action in *The Hope, People* reviewer Sara Nelson notes that "Wouk has invented plenty of behind-the-scenes machinations that make for frequent page turning—as well as educational reading." *Washington Post Book World* contributor Webster Schott similarly finds the narrative of *The Hope* compelling despite "literary lapses." According to Schott, "burning Jewish pride or chauvinism . . . animates Wouk's novel. It is not an emotion likely to lead to epiphany in fiction but it makes for heroic storytelling, especially when all the wars are for survival and all the military odds are unfavorable." Irving Abrahamson writes of *The Hope* in Chicago *Tribune Books,* "Though Wouk serves up a full cast of characters and keeps the pot constantly boiling with their largely unfulfilled love affairs, his primary aim is to describe the heroic aspects of Israel's rebirth and to trace Israel's part in the game of power politics played out by Britain, France, Russia and America in the Middle East."

Despite noting melodramatic elements in both novels, *Booklist* reviewer Gilbert Taylor praises *The Glory* for Wouk's ability to "humanize these intense events" while incorporating major historical figures. Relying on authentic sources for his material, Wouk provides several pages of historical notes in *The Hope* and claims to have quoted Arab leaders directly from historical records and contemporary journalism. "Though underappreciated by literary types," writes Arnold Beichman in *National Review,* "Herman Wouk is one of our outstanding historical novelists."

BIOGRAPHICAL/CRITICAL SOURCES:

BOOKS

Beichman, Arnold C., *Herman Wouk: The Novelist as Social Historian,* Transaction Books, 1984.
Contemporary Literary Criticism, Gale (Detroit), Volume 1, 1973; Volume 9, 1978; Volume 38, 1986.
Dictionary of Literary Biography Yearbook: 1982, Gale, 1983.
Fiedler, Leslie A., *Love and Death in the American Novel,* Stein & Day, 1966.
Fuller, Edmund, *Man in Modern Fiction: Some Minority Opinions on Contemporary American Writing,* Random House, 1958.
Hyman, Stanley Edgar, *Standards: A Chronicle of Books for Our Time,* Horizon Press, 1966.
Mazzeno, Laurence W., *Herman Wouk,* Macmillian, 1994.

Prescott, Orville, *In My Opinion,* Bobbs-Merrill, 1952.
Sarner, Harvey, *A Checklist of the Works of Herman Work,* Brunswick Press, 1995.
Stuckey, W. J., *The Pulitzer Prize Novels,* University of Oklahoma Press, 1966.

PERIODICALS

Atlantic, August, 1951; October, 1955; December, 1971.
Booklist, December 15, 1994, p. 715.
Boston Sunday Globe, March 24, 1985.
Chicago Tribune, February 6, 1983; September 12, 1988.
Chicago Tribune Book World, November 14, 1971; March 24, 1985.
Christian Science Monitor, September 1, 1955; September 24, 1959; May 24, 1962; October 23, 1978.
Commentary, December, 1978.
Detroit Free Press, February 6, 1983; April 7, 1985.
Detroit News, January 24, 1985.
Diversion, May, 1985.
Economist, November 20, 1971.
Entertainment Weekly, January 14, 1994, p. 49.
Globe and Mail (Toronto), June 15, 1985.
Library Journal, February 15, 1994, p. 204; June 15, 1995, p. 110.
Life, June, 1962; November 19, 1971.
Los Angeles Times Book Review, March 3, 1985; May 8, 1986; December 12, 1993, p. 3.
Midwest Quarterly, July, 1975.
National Review, January 23, 1995, p. 72.
New Republic, February 15, 1954; September 3, 1955; June 11, 1962; October 14, 1978.
Newsweek, March 9, 1965; November 29, 1971; October 9, 1978; February 7, 1983.
New York Times, April 20, 1947; August 29, 1948; March 18, 1951; September 4, 1955; September 27, 1959; January 2, 1983; January 21, 1983; January 30, 1983; February 5, 1983; February 6, 1983; March 7, 1985.
New York Times Book Review, September 16, 1951; May 20, 1962; November 14, 1971; November 12, 1978; March 10, 1985; January 9, 1994, p. 10.
People Weekly, January 24, 1994, p. 27.
Publishers Weekly, February 7, 1972; June 10, 1996, p. 47.
Time, April 9, 1951; September 5, 1955; May 18, 1962; March 5, 1965; November 22, 1971; October 16, 1978; February 7, 1983; February 28, 1983; April 1, 1985.
Times (London), March 2, 1985.
Times Literary Supplement, November 9, 1951.
Tribune Books (Chicago), December 26, 1993, p. 5.
Washington Post, April 29, 1985; May 31, 1986.
Washington Post Book World, October 8, 1978; March 10, 1985; December 12, 1993, p. 3.

*   *   *

WRIGHT, Charles (Penzel, Jr.) 1935-

PERSONAL: Born August 25, 1935, in Pickwick Dam, Hardin County, TN; son of Charles Penzel and Mary Castleman (Winter) Wright; married Holly McIntire, April 6, 1969; children: Luke Savin Herrick. *Education:* Davidson College, B.A., 1957; University of Iowa, M.F.A., 1963; graduate study, University of Rome, 1963-64.

ADDRESSES: Home—940 Locust Ave., Charlottesville, VA 22901-4030 *Office*—Department of English, Bryan Hall, University of Virginia, Charlottesville, VA 22903.

CAREER: University of California, Irvine, 1966-83, began as assistant professor, became professor of English; University of Virginia, Charlottesville, Souder Family Professor of English, 1983–. Fulbright lecturer in Venice, Italy, 1968-69, distinguished visiting professor, Universita Degli Studi, Florence, Italy, 1992. *Military service:* U.S. Army, Intelligence Corps, 1957-61.

MEMBER: PEN American Center, American Academy of Arts and Letters, Fellowship of Southern Writers.

AWARDS, HONORS: Fulbright scholar at University of Rome, 1963-65; Eunice Tietjens Award, *Poetry* magazine, 1969; Guggenheim fellow, 1975; Melville Cane Award, Poetry Society of America, and Edgar Allan Poe Award, Academy of American Poets, both 1976, both for *Bloodlines;* Academy-Institute Award, American Academy and Institute of the Arts, 1977; PEN translation award, 1979; Ingram Merrill fellow, 1980 and 1993; National Book Award in poetry (cowinner), 1983, for *Country Music: Selected Early Poems;* National Book Critics Circle Award nomination in poetry, 1984, for *The Other Side of the River;* Brandeis Creative Arts Citation for poetry, 1987; Merit Medal, American Academy and Institute Arts and Letters, 1992; Ruth Lilly Poetry Prize, 1993; Lenore Marshall Poetry Prize, Academy of American Poets, 1996; Wood Prize, *Poetry* magazine, 1996.

WRITINGS:

POETRY

Six Poems, David Freed, 1965.
The Dream Animal (chapbook), House of Anansi (Toronto), 1968.
Private Madrigals, limited edition, Abraxas Press (Madison, WI), 1969.
The Grave of the Right Hand, Wesleyan University Press (Middletown, CT), 1970.
The Venice Notebook, Barn Dream Press, 1971.
Hard Freight, Wesleyan University Press, 1973.
Bloodlines, Wesleyan University Press, 1975.
China Trace, Wesleyan University Press, 1977.
Colophons, limited edition, Windhover (New York City), 1977.
Wright: A Profile, with interview and critical essay by David St. John, Grilled Flowers Press, 1979.
Dead Color, limited edition, Meadow Press, 1980.
The Southern Cross, Random House (New York City), 1981.
Country Music: Selected Early Poems, Wesleyan University Press, 1982.
Four Poems of Departure, limited edition, Trace Editions, 1983.
The Other Side of the River, Random House, 1984.
Five Journals (also see below), limited edition, Red Ozier Press, 1986.
Zone Journals (includes *Five Journals*), Farrar, Straus (New York City), 1988.
The World of the Ten Thousand Things: Poems, 1980-1990, Farrar, Straus, 1990.
Chickamauga, Farrar, Straus, 1995.
Black Zodiac, Farrar, Straus, 1997.

OTHER

The Voyage, Patrician Press, 1963.
Backwater, Golem Press, 1973.
(Translator) Eugenio Montale, *The Storm,* Field Editions, 1978.
(Translator) Montale, *Motets,* Windhover, 1981.

(Translator) Dino Campana, *Orphic Songs,* Field Editions, 1984.
Halflife: Improvisations and Interviews, 1977-1987, University of Michigan Press (Ann Arbor), 1988.
Quarter Notes: Improvisations and Interviews, University of Michigan Press, 1995.

SIDELIGHTS: Charles Wright's reputation has increased steadily with each poetry collection he has published. From his early collection *The Grave of the Right Hand* to more recent books, such as *The Other Side of the River* and *Zone Journals,* Wright has worked in a style which creates a feeling of immediacy and concreteness by emphasizing objects and personal perspective. Many critics believe that Wright's childhood in rural Tennessee remains a vital force in his writing, for he shows a typically Southern concern for the past and its power. He began writing poetry while serving in Italy with the U.S. Army. While there, he "began using Ezra Pound's Italian Cantos first as a guide book to out-of-the-way places, then as a reference book and finally as a 'copy' book," *Dictionary of Literary Biography Yearbook: 1982* essayist George F. Butterick quotes the author as saying.

Ezra Pound's influence is evident in *The Grave of the Right Hand,* Wright's first major collection. These poems "have the polished clarity one would expect from a master of the plain style," *Georgia Review* contributor Peter Stitt observes. "They are obviously meant to speak to the reader, to communicate something he can share." At the same time, *The Grave of the Right Hand* is the most symbolic of all Wright's works, with images of gloves, shoes, hands, and hats recurring throughout. Through these images, the poet introduces themes that recur in all his later work: "mortality, the uses of memory, the irrepressible past, states of being, personal salvation, the correspondence between nature and the spiritual work, and, most broadly, the human condition," as Butterick describes.

Wright is credited with finding his own voice in *Hard Freight,* which Peter Meinke calls in a *New Republic* review "less Poundian, less hard-edged, than his first book, *The Grave of the Right Hand.*" John L. Carpenter likewise applauds Wright for reaching for his own style in a *Poetry* review of *Hard Freight:* "It is less incisive and less deliberate than the first book, but it is more experimental, less ironclad and defensive." It is in this volume that the poet first exhibits his technique of creating poetry by compiling catalogs of fragmented images. It is a device which requires "that the reader assist in the creative activity," finds *Washington Post Book World* contributor Edward Kessler. "[Wright's] almost spastic writing can at times be enlivening and fascinating, like watching the changing fragments of a kaleidoscope."

This technique is not praised by all critics, however; some find it excessive. As Sally M. Gall declares in *Shenandoah:* "He frantically piles up details, images, similes, and metaphors as if sheer quantity can replace quality of perception. His catalogues can be perniciously boring rather than enlightening." But Kessler disagrees with this assessment, stating that Wright's "senses are awake, and even when he cannot quite bring his *things* of the world into a satisfying shape, his fragments are rife with suggestions. This man is feeling his way toward a personal definition."

Bloodlines continues in the same vein as *Hard Freight,* but many reviewers feel that Wright's voice is even stronger in this volume. *Yale Review* contributor J. D. McClatchy, for instance, believes that "Charles Wright has come completely home in *Bloodlines,* a book that confirms and emphasizes his reputation." Carol Muske

also notes the power of this collection in *Parnassus: Poetry in Review:* "[Wright] is on the move. His poems fairly explode from the page in hurly-burly refrain, elliptical syntax, and giddy shifts that recall Hopkins." McClatchy adds that Wright "recreates not aspects but images of his past experiences—prayer meetings, sexual encounters, dreams—mingling memory and fantasy. The poems are suffused with remembered light."

Hard Freight, Bloodlines, and *China Trace* comprise what Wright thinks of as a trilogy of poetry collections. Explains Kathleen Agena in *Partisan Review,* "Like Wallace Stevens, Wright has conceived of his work as a whole. Individual poems are arresting but none of them quite has its meaning alone. The poems elucidate and comment on each other, extending and developing certain key metaphors and images." In *China Trace,* Wright again considers universal connections to the past. According to Butterick, the poet describes this collection as "a book of Chinese poems that don't sound like Chinese poems and aren't Chinese poems but are *like* Chinese poems in the sense that they give you an idea of one man's relationship to the endlessness, the ongoingness, the everlastingness of what's around him, and his relationship to it as he stands in the natural world."

Works such as *Zone Journals* and the collection *The World of the Ten Thousand Things* reflect Wright's "departure from his earlier crystalline short lyrics that aimed for inevitability of effect," Helen Vendler observes in *New Republic.* These journal poems "weave diverse thematic threads into a single autobiographical fabric" which can be read as a single work, Richard Tillinghast writes in the *New York Times Book Review.* "Freed from the stringencies of unity and closure demanded by the sort of poem most readers are used to, Mr. Wright is at liberty to spin out extended meditations that pick up, work with, lay aside and return again to landscapes, historical events and ideas." With his "subtle cadences" and "famously 'good ear,'" the critic adds, Wright "continues to reveal himself as a poet of great purity and originality."

Writing in *Poetry* about *Chickamauga,* David Baker observes that Wright uses abstractions to sustain the oblique. Of Wright's style he comments, "Almost nothing ever happens in a Charles Wright poem. This is his central act of restraint, a spiritualist's abstinence, where meditation is not absence but an alternative to action and to linear, dramatic finality." David Mason admits in the *Hudson Review* that Wright's poetry disappoints him. Mason finds that Wright's "ideas are uninteresting, his poems undramatic; his language is only intermittently charged or lyrical." He remarks, "There is plenty of meditative near-spirituality in *Chickamauga,* but it's all air and light, history without the details." According to James Longenbach in the *Yale Review,* Wright's career seems to change with *Chickamauga,* as he tries to constrain his writing. "Wright seems to feel that all he can do is spin new variations on a limited number of subjects and scenes" in *Chickamauga,* writes the critic, although the work is "a beautiful book, bearably human yet in touch with the sublime."

BIOGRAPHICAL/CRITICAL SOURCES:

BOOKS

Andrews, Tom, *The Point Where All Things Meet: Essays on Charles Wright,* Oberlin College Press (Oberlin, OH), 1995.
Contemporary Authors Autobiography Series, Volume 7, Gale (Detroit), 1988.
Contemporary Literary Criticism, Gale, Volume 6, 1976; Volume 13, 1980; Volume 28, 1984.

Dictionary of Literary Biography, Volume 165: *American Poets since World War II, Fourth Series,* Gale, 1996.

Dictionary of Literary Biography Yearbook: 1982, Gale, 1983.

Friebert, Stuart, and David Young, editors, *A Field Guide to Contemporary Poetry and Poetics,* Longman, 1980.

Ingersoll, Earl W., and others, editors, *Post-Confessionals: Conversations with American Poets of the Eighties,* Fairleigh Dickinson University Press, 1989.

Perkins, David, *A History of Modern Poetry,* Harvard University Press, 1987.

Vendler, Helen, *The Music of What Happens,* Harvard University Press, 1988.

PERIODICALS

America, April 25, 1992, p. 361.

American Poetry Review, September/October, 1982.

Antioch Review, spring, 1982; summer, 1989.

Georgia Review, summer, 1978; spring, 1982.

Hudson Review, spring, 1974; autumn, 1975; spring, 1996, p. 166.

Library Journal, April 1, 1995, p. 99.

Los Angeles Times Book Review, February 7, 1982.

Michigan Quarterly Review, fall, 1978.

New Republic, November 24, 1973; November 26, 1977; January 18, 1988; August 7, 1995, p. 42.

New Yorker, October 29, 1979.

New York Times Book Review, February 17, 1974; September 7, 1975; December 12, 1982; July 1, 1984; September 4, 1988; February 24, 1991, p.18.

Parnassus: Poetry in Review, spring-summer, 1976; spring-summer, 1982.

Partisan Review, Volume 43, number 4, 1976.

Poetry, December, 1974; December, 1978; December, 1989; August, 1991, p. 280; April, 1996, p. 33.

Publishers Weekly, February 27, 1995, p. 97.

Sewanee Review, spring, 1974.

Shenandoah, fall, 1974.

Times Literary Supplement, March 1, 1985.

Washington Post Book World, May 5, 1974.

Yale Review, autumn, 1975; October, 1995, p. 144.

*   *   *

WRIGHT, James (Arlington) 1927-1980

PERSONAL: Born December 13, 1927, in Martins Ferry, OH; died of cancer, March 25, 1980, in New York, NY; married second wife, Edith Anne Runk, 1967; children: (first marriage) Franz Paul, Marshall John. *Education:* Kenyon College, B.A., 1952; University of Washington, M.A., 1954, Ph.D., 1959; also studied with John Crowe Ransom and Theodore Roethke.

CAREER: Poet and translator; instructor in English at University of Minnesota, Minneapolis, 1957-64, and Macalester College, St. Paul, MN, 1963-65; Hunter College of the City University of New York, New York City, professor of English, 1966-80. Visiting lecturer, State University of New York at Buffalo, 1974. *Military service:* U.S. Army, during World War II.

MEMBER: Academy of American Poets (fellow).

AWARDS, HONORS: Fulbright fellow in Austria, 1952-53; Eunice Tietjens Memorial Prize, 1955, and Oscar Blumenthal Award, 1968, both from *Poetry;* Yale Series of Younger Poets award, 1957, for *The Green Wall; Kenyon Review* fellowship in poetry, 1958; National Institute of Arts and Letters grant in literature, 1959; Ohiona Book Award, 1960, for *Saint Judas;* Guggenheim fellowship, 1964 and 1978; Creative Arts Award, Brandeis University, 1970; Academy of American Poets fellowship, 1971; Melville Cane Award, Poetry Society of America, 1972; Pulitzer Prize in poetry, 1972, for *Collected Poems.*

WRITINGS:

POETRY

The Green Wall, Yale University Press, 1957.

Saint Judas, Wesleyan University Press, 1959.

(With William Duffy and Robert Bly) *The Lion's Tail and Eyes: Poems Written Out of Laziness and Silence,* Sixties Press, 1962.

The Branch Will Not Break, Wesleyan University Press, 1963.

Shall We Gather at the River, Wesleyan University Press, 1968.

Collected Poems, Wesleyan University Press, 1971.

Two Citizens, Farrar, Straus, 1973.

I See the Wind, Brandea, 1974.

Old Booksellers and Other Poems, Cotswold Press, 1976.

Moments of the Italian Summer, Dryad, 1976.

To a Blossoming Pear Tree, Farrar, Straus, 1978.

This Journey, Random House, 1982.

The Temple in Nimes, Metacom Press, 1982.

Above the River: The Complete Poems, Farrar, Straus, & Giroux, 1992.

Also author of *Salt Mines and Such,* 1971, and *The Shape of Light: Prose Poems,* White Pine. Work represented in anthologies, including *Poems on Poetry,* edited by Robert Wallace and J. G. Taaffe, Dutton, 1965; *An Introduction to Poetry,* edited by Louis Simpson, St. Martin's, 1967; *Heartland,* edited by Lucien Stryk, Northern Illinois University Press, 1967; and *Poems of Our Moment,* edited by John Hollander, Pegasus, 1968.

TRANSLATOR

(With Bly) *Twenty Poems of Georg Trakl,* Sixties Press, 1961.

(With Bly and John Knoepfle) *Twenty Poems of Cesar Vallejo,* Sixties Press, 1962.

Theodor Storm, *The Rider on the White Horse,* New American Library, 1964.

(With Bly) *Twenty Poems of Pablo Neruda,* Sixties Press, 1968.

(And editor) Hermann Hesse, *Poems,* Farrar, Straus, 1970.

(With Bly and Knoepfle) *Neruda and Vallejo: Selected Poems,* Beacon Press, 1971.

Hesse, *Wandering: Notes and Sketches,* Farrar, Straus, 1972.

OTHER

The Poetry and Voice of James Wright (recording), Caedmon, 1977.

(Editor) *Winter's Tales Twenty-Two,* St. Martin's, 1977.

Collected Prose, edited by Anne Wright, University of Michigan Press, 1982.

A Secret Field, edited by Anne Wright, Logbridge-Rhodes, 1985.

Town of Moravia, Higginson Book Company, 1993.

Also author of *The Summers of James and Annie Wright,* 1980, and *With the Delicacy and Strength of Lace: Letters between Leslie Marmon Silko and Wright,* edited by Wright, 1986. Also recorded, with others, *Today's Poets Three,* for Folkways. Contributor to *Hudson Review, Kenyon Review, Sewanee Review, Western Review, Yale Review, Harper's, Poetry, Frescoe, New Poets of England and America, Paris Review, London Magazine, Botteghe Obscure, New Yorker, Minnesota Review, Big Table, Audience, Nation,* and other publications.

SIDELIGHTS: James Wright was frequently referred to as one of America's finest contemporary poets. He was admired by critics and fellow poets alike for his willingness and ability to experiment with language and style, as well as for his thematic concerns. In the *Minnesota Review,* Peter A. Stitt wrote that Wright's work both represents and parallels the development of the best modern American poets: "Reading the *Collected Poems* of James Wright from the point of view of style is like reading a history of the best contemporary American poetry. One discovers a development which could be said to parallel the development generally of our finest recent poets. . . . [This development shows] a movement generally away from rhetoric, regular meter and rhyme, towards plainer speech, looser rhythms and few rhymes."

Although Wright experimented with style and language, his themes—loneliness and alienation—remained constant. "Perhaps the most pervasive general theme in Wright's poetry . . . is that of separation," Stitt suggested. "Separation appears in two guises—as the result of death and as the result of being at odds with one's society." James Seay, writing in the *Georgia Review,* agreed and elaborated: "His most abiding concern has been loneliness. It is the one abstract word that recurs most frequently in his work. In a sense the theme of loneliness gives rise to, or is somehow connected with, most of Wright's other thematic concerns." The critic named death and "Wright's compassion for what Auden . . . called 'social outsiders'—criminals, prostitutes, drunks, and social outcasts in general" as the poet's other concerns. Seay continued, "In Wright's poems these people are almost always lonely and damned."

Eric Pace of the *New York Times* noted that while "the mood of the poet was sometimes very dark, . . . one of his great strengths . . . was the life-affirming quality of his work." Edward Butscher of the *Georgia Review* contended that a "pattern" of despair followed by celebration ran throughout Wright's work: "Despair and celebration, ritual damnation and ritual salvation, . . . the agony of human existence miraculously made bearable by nature's . . . eloquence." In a *Washington Post Book World* review of *Two Citizens,* Marjorie Perloff further explained Wright's view of nature and salvation, stating that "his poems . . . usually present the poet in a specific midwestern locale, contemplating a landscape which seems wholly alien until a sudden gesture or change in perspective momentarily unites poet and nature, self and other, in a muted epiphany."

For the most part, *The Branch Will Not Break* is considered the watershed of Wright's career. Stitt called it "Wright's happiest book" and noted that "the book's title indicates its major affirmation—the faith that nature will endure and continue to sustain man." Moreover, Cor van den Heuvel in *MOSAIC* praised the "great advance in technical proficiency [and the] dazzling blossoming of images." Paul Zweig of the *Partisan Review* termed it "one of the key books of the 1960s." Seay offered a similar appraisal: "I cannot recall experiencing anything like that keen sense of discovery which I felt in reading *The Branch Will Not Break.* . . . What Wright offered in [that book], as far as I could tell, was unlike anything being written in America at the time."

Above the River: The Complete Poems appeared more than a decade after Wright's death. William Pratt noted in *World Literature Today,* "Wright's complete poems brings together nearly four hundred pages of strongly carved words, the lifework of a much-admired, imitated, and lamented American poet, one of the most clearly recognizable voices of his generation." *New York*

Times Book Review contributor J. D. McClatchy wrote, "Lucidity, precision, rhythmical poise, sentiment, intelligence and the rigors of a conscious craft that liberated the imagination—these were the poetic values [Wright] cherished, and they remain the keynotes of *Above the River.*" Samuel Maio also praised Wright and his collected poetry in the *Bloomsbury Review:* "James Wright wasn't afraid to find out who he really was, no matter how frightening that self may have been. This is the essence of the pure, clear voice we encounter in his poems, and this is why James Wright endures."

One criticism aimed at Wright's poetry was that it lacks discipline. Roger Hecht of *Nation* identified Wright's "weaknesses" as "self-pity" and "talkiness." And a *Sewanee Review* critic found *Two Citizens* "badly marred by personal indulgence and conversationality." The poet himself seemed aware of these shortcomings. "My chief enemy in poetry is glibness," he told Stitt in an interview published in the *Paris Review.* He continued: "My family background is partly Irish, and this means many things, but linguistically it means that it is too easy for me to talk sometimes. I keep thinking of Horace's idea which Byron so very accurately expressed in a letter . . . 'Easy writing is damned hard reading.' I suffer from glibness. . . . I have [to struggle] to strip my poems down."

Finally, in discussing Wright's work, critics spoke of the evident craftsmanship, of his skill and gift as a poet. Van den Heuvel found that "there is a universality in Wright's work not only in subject matter but in form and technique as well." The reviewer added that "[he is] a craftsman who can put to use the traditional elements of his art while at the same time exploring new means of expression." Seay voiced a like assessment, stating that "what makes Wright's poetry special is not that he has any new philosophical insights into the problems of existence but that he has the gift of using language in a way that the human spirit is awakened and alerted to its own possibilities."

BIOGRAPHICAL/CRITICAL SOURCES:

BOOKS

Carroll, Paul, *The Poem in Its Skin,* Follett, 1968.
Contemporary Literary Criticism, Gale (Detroit), Volume 3, 1975; Volume 5, 1976; Volume 10, 1979; Volume 28, 1984.
Dictionary of Literary Biography, Volume 5: *American Poets since World War II,* Gale, 1980.
Graziano, Frank, *James Wright: A Profile,* Logbridge-Rhodes, 1988.
Maley, Saundra R., *Solitary Apprenticeship: James Wright and German Poetry,* Mellen University Press (Lewiston, NY), 1996.
Roberson, William H., *James Wright: An Annotated Bibliography,* Scarecrow Press, 1995.
Stepanchev, Stephen, *American Poetry since 1945,* Harper, 1965.

PERIODICALS

Bloomsbury Review, March, 1992, p. 7.
Contemporary Literature, winter, 1973.
Georgia Review, spring, 1973; summer, 1974.
Library Journal, May 1, 1995, p. 152.
Los Angeles Times Book Review, May 16, 1982.
Michigan Quarterly Review, summer, 1972.
Minnesota Review, spring, 1972.
MOSAIC, spring, 1974.
Nation, August, 1971.
New Republic, September 3, 1990, p. 38.
New York Times, March 27, 1980.

New York Times Book Review, February 12, 1978; March 18, 1984; June 17, 1990, p. 22.
Paris Review, summer, 1975.
Partisan Review, Volume 15, number 2, 1973.
Poetry, March, 1991, p. 343.
Saturday Review, January 21, 1978.
Sewanee Review, spring, 1974.
Shenandoah, winter, 1974.
Tribune Books (Chicago), August 5, 1990, p. 3.
Washington Post Book World, September 16, 1973; June 27, 1982.
World Literature Today, winter, 1991, p. 117.

*   *   *

WRIGHT, Judith (Arandell) 1915-

PERSONAL: Born May 31, 1915, in Armidale, New South Wales, Australia; daughter of Phillip Arundell and Ethel Mabel (Bigg) Wright; married Jack Philip McKinney (a philosophical writer; died, 1966); children: Meredith Anne. *Education:* Attended New South Wales Correspondence School, New England Girls' School, and University of Sydney. *Politics:* "Swing voter." *Avocational interests:* Gardening.

ADDRESSES: Home—1/17 Devonport St., Lyon, ACT, 2606, Australia. *Office*—Box 93, Braidwood, New South Wales 2622, Australia.

CAREER: J. Walter Thompson (advertising agency), Sydney, Australia, secretary, 1938-39; University of Sydney, Sydney, Australia, secretary, 1940-42; Australian Universities Commission, Brisbane, Australia, clerk, 1943-46; University of Queensland, Brisbane, statistician, 1946-49. Part-time lecturer in Australian literature at various Australian universities. President, Wildlife Preservation Society of Queensland, 1962-74; member, Committee of Inquiry into the National Estate, Australia, 1973-74; member, Aboriginal Treaty Committee, 1978-83.

MEMBER: Society of Authors (Australia; council member), Australian Academy of the Humanities (fellow).

AWARDS, HONORS: Grace Leven Prize, 1953; D.Litt., University of New England, Armidale, Australia, 1963, Monash University, 1977, University of Sydney, 1977, Australian National University, 1980, University of New South Wales, 1985, Griffith University, 1988, University of Melbourne, 1988; *Encyclopedia Britannica* Award, 1964; Robert Frost Medallion, Fellowship of Australian Writers, 1975; Asan World Prize, Asan Memorial Association, 1984; New South Wales Premier's Special Prize for Poetry, 1991; Queen's Gold Medal for Poetry, 1992; Human Rights Poetry Award, 1994.

WRITINGS:

Kings of the Dingoes (juvenile), illustrated by Barbara Albiston, Oxford University Press, 1958.
The Generations of Men, illustrated by Alison Forbes, Oxford University Press, 1959, revised edition, Harper, 1995.
The Day the Mountains Played (juvenile), Jacaranda, 1960, Boolarong, 1988.
Range the Mountains High (juvenile), Lansdowne Press, 1962, 3rd edition, 1971.
Charles Harpur (biography and criticism), Lansdowne Press, 1963.
Country Towns (juvenile), Oxford University Press, 1963.

Preoccupations in Australian Poetry (history and criticism), Oxford University Press, 1965, new edition, 1966.
The Nature of Love (short stories), Sun Books (Melbourne, Australia), 1966.
The River and the Road (juvenile), Lansdowne Press, 1966, revised edition, 1971.
Henry Lawson, Oxford University Press, 1967.
Because I Was Invited, Oxford University Press, 1975.
The Coral Battleground (documentary), Thomas Nelson (Australia), 1977.
The Cry for the Dead, Oxford University Press, 1981.
We Call for a Treaty, William Collins/John M. Fontana, 1985.
Born of the Conquerors: Selected Essays, Aboriginal Studies Press, 1991.
Going on Talking, Butterfly Books, 1992.

POETRY

The Moving Image, Meanjin, 1946, revised edition, 1953.
Woman to Man, Angus & Robertson, 1949, 2nd edition, 1955.
The Gateway, Angus & Robertson, 1953.
The Two Fires, Angus & Robertson, 1955.
Birds, Angus & Robertson, 1962, 3rd edition, 1978.
Five Senses: Selected Poems, Angus & Robertson, 1963, revised edition, 1972.
City Sunrise, limited edition, Shapcott Press, 1964.
The Other Half, Angus & Robertson, 1966.
Collected Poems, Angus & Robertson, 1971, 2nd edition, 1975.
Alive: Poems 1971-1972, Angus & Robertson, 1973.
Fourth Quarter, and Other Poems, Angus & Robertson, 1976.
The Double Tree: Selected Poems, Houghton, 1978.
(Contributor) Fay Zwicky, editor, *Journeys: Poems,* Sisters (Carleton South, Australia), 1982.
Phantom Dwelling, Angus & Robertson, 1985.
A Human Pattern: Selected Poems, Angus & Robertson, 1990.
Collected Poems, 1942-1985, Angus & Robertson, 1994.

EDITOR

Australian Poetry, Angus & Robertson, 1948.
(And author of introduction) *A Book of Australian Verse,* Oxford University Press, 1956, 2nd revised edition, 1968.
(And author of introduction) *New Land, New Language: An Anthology of Australian Verse,* Oxford University Press, 1957.
Judith Wright (selected poetry), Angus & Robertson, 1963.
Shaw Neilson (biography and selected poetry), Angus & Robertson, 1963.
(With Andrew Thomson) *The Poet's Pen,* Jacaranda, 1965.
John Shaw Neilson, *Witnesses of Spring: Unpublished Poems of Shaw Neilson,* Angus & Robertson, 1970.

SIDELIGHTS: A well-known author and poet in Australia, Judith Wright has been "outrageously neglected" outside of her native land, according to *London Magazine* critic D. M. Thomas. After years of publishing her verses in Australian periodicals, as well as in books in her homeland and abroad, Wright has accumulated much critical attention in Australia for her distinctly endemic poetry. One Australian reviewer, *Meanjin* contributor Elizabeth Vassilieff, considers Wright to be "the most interesting of Australian poets, with no exceptions." "Her poetry has the touch and feel of [Australia]," notes another *Meanjin* reviewer, S. Musgrove, "for she knows that man . . . must not lose that immediate contact" with the land. But although her poetry has gained her the most attention, Ken Goodwin writes in his *A History of Australian Literature,* "Judith Wright, in both poetry and prose, presents a wide panorama of the interests of the socially conscious present-day Australian."

Wright's prose writing includes children's stories, which she originally composed for her daughter, criticism, a biographical novel, *The Generations of Men,* and a historical work, *The Cry for the Dead.* The latter two books concern the author's own ancestors; Wright's grandfather, Albert Wright, figures prominently in both books, and the author takes much of her material for these books from her grandfather's diary. Next to other comparable novels, critics have viewed these retrospects on life in nineteenth-century Australia favorably. One "never has the feeling . . . that he is watching an artificial period-piece or costume melodrama," remarks *Meanjin* contributor Russel Ward. *New Statesman* critic V. S. Pritchett observes, too, that in *The Generations of Men* Wright "is also free of that family complacency which affects so many writers when they are describing their pioneer forebears." In another review of this book, Leonie Kramer writes in *Southerly:* "Judith Wright has shown herself to be a biographer of rare sensitivity." Kramer later concludes that the author's "prose transmits particularly well the atmosphere of the times, and the arid beauty of the country."

Both books not only tell the story of the author's family, but also that of the land itself. Albert Wright's diary becomes a helpful source in this regard, for, as Goodwin describes, "his book tells less of the official story than of the disastrous neglect of proper land-management procedures and the story of the brutal extermination of Aborigines." The tragic waste which these practices have brought to Australia is a concern in much of Wright's poetry as well. As a result, several of the author's poems are meditations "on the problem of how to give meaning to, or discover meaning in, this 'flowing and furious world,'" says *Australian Quarterly* critic R. F. Brissenden, quoting a poem from Wright's *Five Senses: Selected Poems.*

Maintaining a respect for the timelessness of the land throughout her work, Wright expresses in such poetry collections as *Alive: Poems 1971-1972* and *Fourth Quarter, and Other Poems* a horror "at the efficiency with which her fellow countrymen are raping their country," writes Peter Porter in the *London Observer.* Having been raised on a "station," or ranch, as a child, and being active as an adult in the conservation movement in Australia, Wright maintains a strong bond with her surroundings, which is evident in her poetry. She has, asserts Arthur Murphy in *Southerly,* an ability "to merge herself with all natural forces, delving deep into the almost inexpressible in verse of highly wrought formation and full content." But although several critics, such as one *Times Literary Supplement* reviewer, feel that her poems "about people, landscapes, and animals are good when she describes her subjects directly," Val Vallis remarks in the *Times Literary Supplement* that "the most commonly heard objection to her poetry as it progressed was that its author 'had gone too philosophical.'" *Carleton Miscellany* critic Keith Harrison, however, notes that even though one might see some "occasional vagueness" in her sometimes metaphysical poems, "the strengths of her work far outweigh the faults."

Some of these strengths, declares Elyne Mitchell in *Southerly,* include "vivid imagery, lovely songs of creation and of a creator, poems of philosophic journey, of the integration of dark and light, [and] of rebirth." Wright is a poet, who, as S. E. Lee characterizes her in *Southerly,* is "a rare combination of metaphysical thinker . . . and down-to-earth realist." Her "best poems then," concludes Lee, "integrate the intellect, passion, imagination and common

sense of the thinker-mystic-poet-country wife." What is evident in both Wright's prose and poetry is "her bond to her native land and its once pastoral wilderness," asserts Margaret Gibson in the *Library Journal.* Goodwin summarizes the author's career this way: "Her lifelong quest [has been] to define Australia as a land, a nation and a metaphysical entity, in language that [shows] awareness of contemporary overseas writing in English but also [recognizes] the unique environment and society of Australia."

BIOGRAPHICAL/CRITICAL SOURCES:

BOOKS

Contemporary Literary Criticism, Gale (Detroit), Volume 11, 1979; Volume 53, 1989.
Goodwin, Ken, *A History of Australian Literature,* St. Martin's, 1986.
Hope, A. D., *Judith Wright,* Oxford University Press (Melbourne), 1975.
Kramer, L., editor, *The Oxford History of Australian Literature,* Oxford University Press, 1982.
Strauss, Jennifer, *Judith Wright,* Oxford University Press, 1995.
Walker, Shirley, *The Poetry of Judith Wright,* Edward Arnold, 1980.
Walker, Shirley, *Judith Wright,* Oxford University Press, 1981.
Walker, Shirley, *Flame and Shadow: A Study of Judith Wright's Poetry,* University of Queensland Press, 1991.
Walker, Shirley, *Vanishing Edens: Responses to Australia in the Works of Mary Gilmore, Judith Wright, and Dorothy Hewett,* Foundation for Australian Literary Studies, 1992.

PERIODICALS

American Poetry Review, September/October, 1980.
Australian Quarterly, March, 1964.
Carleton Miscellany, summer, 1980.
Library Journal, June 15, 1978.
London Magazine, May, 1967.
London Observer, May 7, 1978.
Meanjin, September, 1946; March, 1950; June, 1960; December, 1962.
New Statesman, September 5, 1959.
Southerly, Volume 11, number 3, 1950; Volume 16, number 1, 1955; Volume 17, number 2, 1956; Volume 20, number 9, 1959; Volume 23, number 2, 1963; Volume 27, number 1, 1967.
Times Literary Supplement, September 10, 1964; April 9, 1976; October 15, 1982; November 27, 1987.

*   *   *

WRIGHT, Richard (Nathaniel) 1908-1960

PERSONAL: Born September 4, 1908, near Natchez, MS; died of a heart attack, November 28, 1960, in Paris, France; buried in Pere Lachaise, Paris, France; son of Nathan (a mill worker) and Ellen (a teacher) Wright; married Rose Dhima Meadman, 1938 (marriage ended); married Ellen Poplar, 1941; children: two daughters. *Education:* Attended school in Jackson, MS.

CAREER: Novelist, short story writer, poet, and essayist. Worked at odd jobs in Memphis, TN, and other cities; clerk at U.S. Post Office in Chicago, IL, during 1920s; associated with Works Progress Administration Federal Writers' Project, Chicago, and New York City, 1935-37.

AWARDS, HONORS: Prize from *Story* magazine, 1938, for *Uncle Tom's Children;* Guggenheim fellowship, 1939; Spingarn Medal from National Association for the Advancement of Colored People, 1940, for *Native Son.*

WRITINGS:

Uncle Tom's Children: Four Novellas, Harper, 1938, expanded edition published as *Uncle Tom's Children: Five Long Stories,* 1938.

Native Son (novel; also see below), Harper, 1940, new edition with text by Richard Bucci, illustrations by Arnold Turovskiy Research and Education Association (Piscataway, NJ), 1996.

Twelve Million Black Voices: A Folk History of the Negro in the U.S., Viking, 1941.

(With Paul Green) *Native Son* (play; adapted from own novel; first produced on Broadway at the St. James Theatre, March 24, 1941), Harper, 1941, revised edition, Samuel French, 1980.

Black Boy: A Record of Childhood and Youth (autobiography), Harper, 1945.

Native Son (screenplay; adapted from own novel), Classic Films, 1951.

The Outsider (novel), Harper, 1953.

Savage Holiday (novel), Avon, 1954.

Black Power: A Record of Reactions in a Land of Pathos, Harper, 1954.

The Color Curtain: A Report on the Bandung Conference (nonfiction), World, 1956.

Pagan Spain: A Report of a Journey into the Past (nonfiction), Harper, 1957.

White Man, Listen! (nonfiction), Doubleday, 1957.

The Long Dream (novel), Doubleday, 1958.

(Editor and contributor) *Quintet* (short stories), Pyramid Books, 1961.

Eight Men (short stories), World, 1961.

Lawd Today (novel), Avon, 1963.

(With Louis Sapin) *Daddy Goodness* (play), first produced off-Broadway at St. Mark's Playhouse, June 4, 1968.

The Man Who Lived Underground (novella), Aubier-Flammarion, 1971.

(Contributor) Hiroshi Nagase and Tsutomu Kanashiki, editors, *What the Negro Wants,* Kaitakusha, 1972.

Farthing's Fortunes, Atheneum, 1976.

American Hunger (autobiography), Harper, 1977.

The Richard Wright Reader, edited by Ellen Wright and Michel Fabre, Harper, 1978.

Rite of Passage, HarperCollins, 1994.

MEDIA ADAPTATIONS: Native Son was adapted for a film of the same title by the author, Classic Films, 1951; and by Richard Wesley, Cinecom, 1986.

SIDELIGHTS: One of the most influential black American authors of the twentieth century, Richard Wright was "the first American Negro writer of large ambitions to win a major reputation in [American] literary life." The southern-born Wright was the first black novelist to write of life in the ghettos of northern cities and of the rage felt by blacks at the white society that excluded them. As James A. Page observed in *English Journal,* Wright was "powerful enough to break out of the narrow compartment previously occupied by Black writers. . . . He made sense, he handled his themes with authority, expressed himself with power and eloquence, and was entitled to the place he had won in the literary firmament of the Depression years. . . . That Wright was the most impressive literary talent yet produced by negro America was rarely disputed in his

time. . . . His name was bracketed with the small handful of America's foremost writers."

Wright's concern with the social roots of racial oppression led Wright to join the Communist party in 1932. He was a party activist in Chicago and New York, and worked at developing a Marxist perspective in the poems and short stories he was writing at that time. But his individualism brought him into conflict with other party members, who labeled him an intellectual and regarded his writing with suspicion. Wright, in turn, found himself repelled by the narrowness and rigidity of his fellow Communists, whose minds he found "sealed against new ideas, new facts, new feelings, new attitudes, new hints at ways to live. They denounced books they could never understand, and doctrines they could not pronounce." In 1944, after witnessing the trial of a party member for ideological "deviationism," Wright resigned from the party.

Until 1938, Wright's work appeared only in left-wing publications such as *New Masses* and *Left Front.* In that year, *Story* magazine offered a $500 prize for the best book-length manuscript by a writer connected with the Federal Writers' Project. Wright's collection of four long stories inspired by the life of a black communist he had known in Chicago won the contest and was published as *Uncle Tom's Children.* Malcolm Cowley, in the *New Republic,* found the book "heartening, as evidence of a vigorous new talent, and terrifying as the expression of a racial hatred that has never ceased to grow and gets no chance to die." All of the stories (a fifth, "Bright and Morning Star," was added to subsequent editions) deal with the oppression of black people in the South, of the violence of whites against blacks, and the violence to which the black characters are driven by their victimization. Some critics have found the stories in *Uncle Tom's Children* too melodramatic and marred by the infusion of communist ideology. But Houston A. Baker, in his *Black Literature in America,* wrote: "Wright showed a mastery of style and a dramatic sense far superior to that of most of black contemporaries and predecessors and on a par with that of his most talented white contemporaries. The violence and the terrible effects of prejudice are perhaps nowhere more skillfully set forth."

Though *Uncle Tom's Children* was well received, Wright was dissatisfied with the response to it. He realized, he wrote later, "that I had written a book which even bankers' daughters could read and weep over and feel good. I swore to myself that if I ever wrote another book, no one would weep over it; that it would be so hard and deep that they would have to face it without the consolation of tears." The book he wrote was *Native Son,* the story of Bigger Thomas, a young black man in Chicago who murders two women and is condemned to death. To depict the dehumanization of blacks in the "hard and deep" manner he wished, Wright avoided making his protagonist a sympathetic character. As reviewer Margaret Marshall wrote in the *Nation,* "Mr. Wright has chosen for his 'hero,' not a sophisticated Negro who at least understands his predicament and can adapt himself to it, but a 'bad nigger,' a 'black ape,' who is only dimly aware of his extra-human status and therefore completely at the mercy of the impulses it generates. . . . One gets a picture of a dark world enclosed by a living white wall. . . . Bigger and his friends are resentful; all feel powerless and afraid of the white world, which exploits, condescends to, and in turn fears the race it has segregated. . . . Mr. Wright has laid bare, with a ruthlessness that spares neither race, the lower depths of the human and social relationship of blacks and whites; and his ruthlessness. . . . clearly springs not from a vindictive desire to shock but from a passionate—and compassionate—concern with a problem obviously lying at the core of his own personal reality. . . . It is not pleasant to feel at the end that one is an accessory to the crimes of Bigger Thomas; but that feeling is impressive evidence of the power of Mr. Wright's indictment with its cutting and accurate title of 'Native Son.'"

Bigger Thomas is a young tough and a petty thief who is hired as a chauffeur by a rich white man. He drives his employer's daughter, Mary, to a political lecture, where he is confused and frightened by the white communists' insistence on treating him as an equal, something he can only interpret as mockery. Mary gets drunk, and Bigger, after driving her home, carries her to her room. When Mary's mother, who is blind, enters the room, Bigger accidentally smothers Mary while trying to keep her from speaking and revealing his presence. He burns Mary's body in a furnace, then conceives a scheme to extort money from her parents by pretending to have kidnapped her and demanding ransom. When Mary's charred bones are discovered, Bigger kills his girlfriend, Bessie, who was his accomplice in the kidnap plot. He is captured by the police and, despite an eloquent defense by his communist lawyer, convicted and condemned. The lawyer, Max, argues that Bigger cannot be held responsible for his crimes, that the greater guilt lies with the society that would not accept him as a full human being, and so drove him to his brutal acts. Bigger feels that he has found a measure of freedom in the act of murder—the only act in his life that seems to him to have been truly creative, to have involved genuine self-assertion.

Some critics have seen in the ending of *Native Son* a clash between two literary and philosophical visions. Much of the book is in the tradition of naturalism, especially of Theodore Dreiser's novel *An American Tragedy.* This deterministic philosophy is made explicit when Max argues, in Marxist terms, that Bigger, as a product of his environment, is not truly guilty of the murders he committed. But Bigger's final sense of violence as a vital act of self-definition is drawn from Fedor Dostoevski's *Crime and Punishment,* and prefigures the existentialist position Wright adopted in his later work. In his book, *The Art of Richard Wright,* Edward Margolies found the two attitudes incompatible, and their conflict a weakness in the novel: "Wright was probing larger issues than racial injustice and social inequality. He was asking questions regarding the ultimate nature of man. What indeed are man's responsibilities in a world devoid of meaning and purpose? . . . The contradiction is never resolved, and it is precisely for this reason that the novel fails to fulfill itself. For the plot, the structure, even the portrayal of Bigger himself are often at odds with Wright's official determinism. . . . The chief philosophical weakness of *Native Son* is not that Bigger does not surrender his freedom to Max's determinism or that Bigger's Zarathustrian principles do not jibe with Max's socialist visions; it is that Wright himself does not seem able to make up his mind. . . . Wright, though intellectually committed to Max's views, is more emotionally akin to Bigger's. . . . There is an inconsistency of ideologies, an irresolution of philosophical attitudes which prevent Bigger and the other characters from developing properly, which adulterate the structure of the novel, and which occasionally cloud up an otherwise lucid prose style."

James Baldwin, who began his writing career as Wright's protege, called *Native Son* "the most powerful and celebrated statement we have yet had of what it means to be a Negro in America." But for Baldwin, the novel is marred by Wright's use of Bigger as a social symbol. Baldwin noted: "Bigger has no discernible relationship to himself, to his own life, to his own people, nor to any other people—in this respect, perhaps, he is most American—and his

force comes not from his significance as a social (or anti-social) unit, but from his significance as the incarnation of a myth. It is remarkable that, though we follow him step by step from the tenement room to the death cells, we know as little about him when this journey is ended as we did when it began; and, what is even more remarkable, we know almost as little about the social dynamic which we are to believe created him. . . . What is missing in this situation and in the representation of his psychology—which makes his situation false and his psychology incapable of development—is any revelatory apprehension of Bigger as one of the Negro's realities or as one of the Negro's roles. This failure is part of the . . . failure to convey any sense of Negro life as a continuing and complex group reality."

Wright's autobiography, *Black Boy,* published in 1945, is considered by many critics to be his most important work. In it he told of his southern childhood, up to the time when he left Memphis for Chicago. Ralph Ellison, in his essay "Richard Wright's Blues," wrote: "In *Black Boy* Wright has used his own life to probe what qualities of will, imagination, and intellect are required of a Southern Negro in order to possess the meaning of his life in the United States. . . . Imagine Bigger Thomas projecting his own life in lucid prose, guided, say, by the insights of Marx and Freud, and you have an idea of this autobiography. . . . Along with the themes, equivalent descriptions of milieu and the perspectives to be found in Joyce, Nehru, Dostoevski, George Moore and Rousseau, *Black Boy* is filled with blues-tempered echoes of railroad trains, the names of Southern towns and cities, estrangements, fights and flights, deaths and disappointments, charged with physical and spiritual hungers and pain. And like a blues song by such an artist as Bessie Smith, its lyrical prose evokes the paradoxical, almost surreal image of a black boy singing lustily as he probes his own grievous wound. . . . And while it is true that *Black Boy* presents an almost unrelieved picture of a personality corrupted by brutal environment, it also presents those fresh, human responses brought to its world by the sensitive child."

Along with his accounts of mistreatment by whites, Wright describes the complicity of southern blacks in their own oppression. Wright's family strove to make him conform to the submissive, servile behavior expected of black people, often beating him when he asserted himself too strongly. "In scene after scene," noted Morris Dickstein in *Gates of Eden,* "Wright represents his younger self as a rebellious misfit, incapable of adapting to . . . modes of deference. . . . He makes an intense effort of self-restraint, but try as he will there is always a provocative hint of pride and self-respect, a touch of the uppity nigger about him. A latecomer to the white world, he is unable to quite master the shuffling, degraded, but apparently contented manner that will tell whites he not only knows his place but loves it." Christianity is portrayed as an instrument of white oppression, by which blacks are convinced of their inferiority and convinced to passively accept their position; Wright, like many of his fictional characters, bitterly rejects the black church. *Black Boy* was attacked by some for its one-sided picture of southern life, but David Littlejohn, in *Black on White: A Critical Survey of Writing by American Negroes,* praised it for revealing "the inside dimension of the Negro's experience of prejudice in America: what it feels like to live in the mad prison house of sadistic white obsessions."

Howard Mumford Jones, writing in the *Saturday Review of Literature,* found *Black Boy* a powerful social document and indictment of racism, but a weak literary work. "The total effect of the volume is an effect of passive suffering, punctuated by outbursts of blind emotional rebellion. . . . [Wright] emphasizes an endless array of wrongs, but he minimizes the development of his own personality. . . . In contrast to the passivity of virtue in these pages, the acts of the boy's persecutors, white and black, are presented in dramatic scenes of vivid and even violent writing. . . . In some degree this verbal violence may conceal the central failure of the story, which is the failure to chronicle the growth of a personality under suffering. . . . This either-or formula of passive virtue . . . and active evil is the formula of melodrama; and just as an easy recourse to melodrama was the structural weakness of 'Native Son,' so it is the structural weakness of 'Black Boy.'"

American Hunger, unpublished for more than thirty years until 1977, continues Wright's autobiography as he arrives in Chicago in 1927 from Mississippi. Although free for the first time of the pervasive threat of physical violence he knew in the South, Wright finds that northern racism, though subtler than its southern form at the time, still wounds. The author describes working at a series of menial jobs, including washing dishes and mopping floors, and he relates being inspired to write after reading Marcel Proust's *Remembrance of Things Past.* "For all its gaps and awkwardnesses," wrote Irving Howe in the *New York Times Book Review,* "this is an enormously moving book-moving as the story of an ill-educated young black man who grapples for his personal existence and is a fitful picture of the Depression years in Chicago, a city that could frighten anyone." Howe in particular praised Wright's handling of his fleeting association with the American communist movement, noting that this part of the book represents its "most striking pages."

In 1946, the government of France invited Wright to visit that country. He spent six months in Paris and returned to France in 1947, to live there until his death. In Paris, Wright became acquainted with the circle of existentialist writers of whom the most prominent were Jean-Paul Sartre and Simone de Beauvoir. Existentialism appealed to Wright's deeply felt sense of alienation and rootlessness, and his later work combined racial themes with existentialist metaphysics. Wright's existentialism was as much instinctive as adopted, and similar ideas inform his work as early as *Native Son,* but the first novel he wrote after moving to France, *The Outsider,* was more overtly motivated by philosophical concerns. Granville Hicks, in the *New York Times Book Review,* noted that *The Outsider* was "one of the first consciously existentialist novels to be written by an American."

Cross Damon, the hero of *The Outsider,* is black, but his central problems have nothing to do with race. Harassed by his wife, his mother, and his mistress, he finds an escape from his encumbered life when he is believed killed in a subway accident. Seeking a new identity, Damon joins the Communist party, not out of sympathy with its political goals but out of a fascination with the party's "conviction that it had mastered the art of living, its will that it could define the ends of existence." Damon kills two communists and a fascist, but the district attorney who solves the crimes understands Damon's nihilistic creed and chooses to let him go free: "You are your own law, so you'll be your own judge," the lawyer tells him. Left alone, more an outsider than ever, Damon is executed by the Communist party's hired gunmen.

Hicks concluded: "'The Outsider' is both melodrama and novel of ideas. . . . If the ideas are sometimes incoherent, that does not detract from the substance and power of the book. . . . [*The Outsider*] is only incidentally a book about Negroes. Being a Negro helps Cross Damon to understand that he is an outsider,

. . . but there are . . . many outsiders. 'The Outsider' is, as it was intended to be, a book about modern man, and, because of Mr. Wright's driving force, it challenges the modern mind as it has rarely been challenged in fiction." But *The Outsider* was not generally well received; a number of critics found the melodramatic aspects of the plot too lurid, the philosophy poorly integrated with the story (especially a fourteen-page speech in which Cross Damon explains his philosophy of history), and the style clumsy. Phoebe Adams of the *Atlantic Monthly* called *The Outsider* "a very disappointing novel, for the qualities of sympathy, directness, effective detail, and mordant humor which distinguished Mr. Wright's earlier books seem to operate at cross-purposes in *The Outsider.* . . . Whether Mr. Wright nailed his grim thesis to a plot already in his mind, or concocted his plot, which is full of coincidence, accident, and blind luck, to fit his thesis, the book shows a hiatus between means and ends."

Many critics have felt that Wright made more effective use of existentialist ideas in his novella *The Man Who Lived Underground,* a surreal fable about a black man named Fred Daniels, a fugitive who takes refuge from the police in a sewer system. From his underground hiding place he spies on and robs the society from which he is excluded; he comes to understand the absurdity of that society and finds a new identity in his very anonymity and invisibility. When he emerges from his sewer, even though he has been cleared of the crime for which he was originally wanted, he is shot in cold blood by the police. Edward Margolies wrote: "Fred Daniels . . . is not merely the victim of a racist society, . . . he has become by the very nature of his experiences a symbol of all men in that society. . . . The underground man is the essential nature of all men—and is composed of dread, terror, and guilt. . . . Fred Daniels is then Everyman, and his story is very nearly a perfect modern allegory. The Negro who lives in the underground of the city amidst its sewage and slime is not unlike the creature who dwells amidst the sewage and slime of the human heart. And Fred Daniels knows that all of the ways men attempt to persuade themselves that their lives are meaningful and rational are delusions." Stanley Edgar Hyman declared, "'The Man Who Lived Underground' is a pioneering work in going beyond realism and naturalism to symbolism and fantasy, and is thus perhaps the single most revolutionary work in American Negro literature."

Much of Wright's energy during his years in Paris was devoted to writing nonfiction and to supporting national independence movements in Africa. In 1953 he traveled to the Gold Coast (now Ghana), one of the first British colonies in Africa to be granted self-government. In *Black Power* Wright describes his experiences in Africa and sets forth his ideas for the political future of the continent under black rule. While critics praised Wright's reporting, his political recommendations sparked controversy, especially his advocacy of a militarized and regimented social structure to provide the coherence that tribal traditions, he believed, could not. Joyce Cary, in the *Nation,* remarked: "The author has rejected the party, but his political thinking still belongs to communism. He imagines that violence, cruelty, injustice, and some clever lying can achieve a new civilization. But this is false. They can only produce new forms of oppression." But Cary found that *Black Power,* as reporting, "is a first-class job and gives the best picture I've seen of an extraordinary situation. . . . Wright . . . writes so honestly, so directly as he feels, that he gives material for another book contradicting his own arguments. . . . There are no easy answers in politics. . . . We are still groping our way, and need, above all, the facts. . . . That is why books like this of Wright's are so valuable—so far, that is, as they give facts, and so far as the facts can be distinguished from the bias. Wright is so honest a reporter, so vivid a writer, that this is easily done."

Wright's reputation ebbed during the 1950s as younger black writers such as James Baldwin and Ralph Ellison rejected his naturalistic approach and the ideological preoccupations of his fiction. But in the 1960s, with the growth of the militant black consciousness movement, there was a resurgence of interest in Wright's work. Wright's place in American literature remains controversial: some contend that his writing is of sociological and historical, rather than literary interest; his defenders believe that his books of the early 1940s are as important in the American naturalist tradition as they are in the history of black literature, and that Wright is properly ranked with such writers as Dreiser, James T. Farrell, and John Steinbeck. Warren French wrote that Wright was "a man praised too soon for the wrong reasons and too soon dismissed for more wrong reasons. . . . In death as in life, Wright has been forced to win as a Negro who happened to be a writer the recognition that he desired as a *writer* who happened to be a Negro."

BIOGRAPHICAL/CRITICAL SOURCES:

BOOKS

Baker, Houston A., Jr., *Black Literature in America,* McGraw, 1971.

Baldwin, James, *Notes of a Native Son,* Beacon Press, 1955.

Baldwin, James, *Nobody Knows My Name,* Dial, 1961.

Bigsby, C. W. E., editor, *The Black American Writer: Fiction, Volume One,* Everett/Edwards, 1969.

Black Literature Criticism, Volume 3, Gale (Detroit), 1992.

Bloom, Harold, editor, *Richard Wright's Native Son,* Chelsea House, 1995.

Butler, Robert, *The Critical Response to Richard Wright,* Greenwood Press, 1995.

Campbell, James, *Exiled in Paris: Richard Wright, James Baldwin, Samuel Beckett and Others on the Left Bank,* Scribner, 1995.

Concise Dictionary of American Literary Biography: The Age of Maturity, 1929-1941, Gale, 1989.

Contemporary Literary Criticism, Gale, Volume 1, 1973; Volume 3, 1975; Volume 4, 1975; Volume 9, 1978; Volume 14, 1980; Volume 21, 1982; Volume 48, 1988; Volume 74, 1993.

Dickstein, Morris, *Gates of Eden,* Basic Books, 1977.

Dictionary of Literary Biography, Gale, Volume 76: *Afro-American Writers, 1940-1955,* 1988; Volume 102, *American Short-Story Writers, 1910-1945, Second Series,* 1991.

Dictionary of Literary Biography Documentary Series, Volume 2, Gale, 1982.

Ellison, Ralph, *Shadow and Act,* Random House, 1945.

Guest, David, *Sentenced to Death: The American Novel and Capital Punishment,* University Press of Mississippi (Jackson, MS), 1997.

Hakutani, Yoshinobu, *Richard Wright and Racial Discourse,* University of Missouri Press, 1996.

Haynes, Elizabeth Ross, *Unsung Heroes: The Black Boy of Atlanta: Negroes in Domestic Service,* introduction by Francille Rusan Wilson, G.K. Hall (New York City), 1997.

Kinnamon, Keneth, editor, *Critical Essays on Richard Wright's Native Son,* Twayne Publishers (New York City), 1997.

Littlejohn, David, *Black on White: A Critical Survey of Writing by American Negroes,* Viking, 1966.

Margolies, Edward, *The Art of Richard Wright,* Southern Illinois University Press, 1969.

Miller, James A., *Approaches to Teaching Wright's Native Son,* Modern Language Association of America (New York City), 1997.

Rampersad, Arnold, editor, *Richard Wright: A Collection of Critical Essays,* Prentice Hall, 1995.

Ray, David, and Robert M. Farnsworth, editors, *The Life and Works of Richard Wright,* University of Missouri, 1979.

Short Story Criticism, Volume 2, Gale, 1989.

PERIODICALS

African American Review, fall, 1994, p. 375.

Atlantic Monthly, May, 1940; June, 1940; March, 1945; May, 1953; March, 1970.

Ebony, March, 1987; February, 1989.

English Journal, May, 1973.

KLIATT, March, 1996, p. 12.

Library Journal, May 1, 1995, p. 138.

Los Angeles Times, December 24, 1986.

Nation, March 16, 1940; April 5, 1941; April 7, 1945; October 16, 1954; October 25, 1958.

National Review, February 3, 1978.

New Republic, April 6, 1938; April 7, 1941; March 12, 1945; February 18, 1957; November 24, 1958; February 13, 1961.

New York Times, December 23, 1986; December 24, 1986; December 26, 1986.

New York Times Book Review, March 3, 1940; March 4, 1945; March 22, 1953; September 26, 1954; March 18, 1956; February 24, 1957; October 26, 1958; June 26, 1977, p. 1, 34; February 11, 1979, p. 37.

Publishers Weekly, January 3, 1994, p. 82.

Saturday Review, March 2, 1940; March 3, 1945; March 28, 1953; October 23, 1954; October 18, 1958; March 30, 1963; January 21, 1978.

School Library Journal, February, 1994, p. 123; June, 1996, p. 80.

Time, May 30, 1977, p. 74.

Village Voice, July 4, 1977.

Washington Post, January 16, 1987; November 20, 1988.

Y

YANEZ, Jose Donoso
  See DONOSO, Jose

*   *   *

YEATS, W. B.
  See YEATS, William Butler

*   *   *

YEATS, William Butler 1865-1939
(W. B. Yeats)

PERSONAL: Born June 13, 1865, in Sandymount, Ireland; died January 28, 1939, in Roquebrune, France; buried in Drumcliffe, Sligo, Ireland; son of John Butler (a lawyer and an artist) and Susan Mary (Pollexfen) Yeats; married Georgiana Hyde-Lees, October 20, 1917; children: Anne Butler, William Michael Butler. *Education:* Attended Metropolitan School of Art, Dublin, 1884-86.

CAREER: Writer. Cofounder of the Irish Literary Theatre. Senator of the Irish Free State, 1923-29.

AWARDS, HONORS: D. Litt., Queen's University, Belfast, and Trinity College, Dublin, both 1922, Oxford University, 1931, and Cambridge University, 1933; Nobel Prize for literature, 1923.

WRITINGS:

Mosada: A Dramatic Poem (first published in *Dublin University Review,* March, 1885), Sealy, Bryers & Walker, 1886.

The Wanderings of Oisin and Other Poems, Kegan Paul Trench & Company, 1889.

John Sherman [and] *Dhoya* (fiction), Cassell Publishing Company, 1891.

The Countess Kathleen and Various Legends and Lyrics (poetry and plays; includes *The Countess Kathleen,* play first produced in Dublin at Antient Concert Rooms, May 8, 1899), Roberts Brothers, 1892, title play revised and published separately as *The Countess Kathleen,* T. Fischer Unwin, 1912.

The Celtic Twilight (nonfiction), Lawrence & Bullen, 1893, Macmillan, 1894, revised and enlarged edition, A. H. Bullen, 1902.

The Land of Heart's Desire (play; first produced in London at Avenue Theatre, March 29, 1894), Stone & Kimball, 1894.

Poems, T. Fisher Unwin, 1895, revised editions, 1899, 1901, 1912, 1927.

The Table of the Law [and] *The Adoration of the Magi* (fiction), privately printed, 1897, Elkin Mathews, 1904.

The Secret Rose (short stories), illustrations by father, John Butler Yeats, Dodd, Mead, 1897.

The Wind among the Reeds (poetry), John Lane/Bodley Head, 1899.

The Shadowy Waters (play; first produced in Dublin at Molesworth Hall, January 14, 1904), Hodder & Stoughton, 1900, Dodd, Mead, 1901.

1899 to 1900, first edition, 1900.

1901 to 1908, seven volumes, first edition, 1901.

Cathleen ni Houlihan (one-act play; first produced in Dublin at St. Teresa's Hall April 2, 1902), A. H. Bullen, 1902.

Where There Is Nothing (five-act play; first produced in London at Royal Court Theatre, June 26, 1904), John Lane, 1902, revised (with Lady Gregory) as *The Unicorn from the Stars* (first produced in Dublin at Abbey Theatre, November 21, 1907) in *The Unicorn from the Stars and Other Plays,* Macmillan, 1908, new edition published as *Where There Is Nothing* [and] *The Unicorn from the Stars,* Catholic University Press, 1987.

On Baile's Strand (play; first produced in Dublin at Abbey Theatre, December 27, 1904), Dun Emer Press, 1903.

In the Seven Woods: Being Poems Chiefly of the Irish Heroic Age, Macmillan, 1903.

The Hour Glass: A Morality (play; first produced in Dublin at Molesworth Hall, March 14, 1903, revised version produced in Dublin at Abbey Theatre, November 21, 1912), Heinemann, 1903, expanded editon, edited by Catherine Phillips, Cornell University Press, 1994.

Ideas of Good and Evil (nonfiction), Macmillan, 1903.

The Hour Glass and Other Plays (includes *The Hour Glass: A Morality* and *The Pot of Broth,* first produced in Dublin at Antient Concert Rooms, October 30, 1902), Macmillan, 1904.

The King's Threshold (play; first produced in Dublin at Molesworth Hall, October 8, 1903, revised version produced in Dublin at Abbey Theatre, October 13, 1913), John Quinn, 1904.

The King's Threshold [and] *On Baile's Strand* (plays), A. H. Bullen, 1904.

The Hour-Glass and Other Plays, first edition, 1904.

Stories of Red Hanrahan (short stories), Dun Emer Press, 1905.

Poems, 1899-1905, A. H. Bullen (London), 1906.

The Poetical Works of William B. Yeats, two volumes, Macmillan, 1906, revised edition, 1912.

Deirdre (play; first produced in Dublin at Abbey Theatre, November 24, 1906), A. H. Bullen, 1907.

Discoveries: A Volume of Essays, Dun Emer Press, 1907.

The Golden Helmet (play; first produced in Dublin at Abbey Theatre, March 19, 1908), John Quinn, 1908, revised as The Green Helmet (produced in Dublin at Abbey Theatre, February 10, 1910), published in *The Green Helmet and Other Poems* (also see below).

(With Lionel Johnson) *Poetry and Ireland,* first edition, 1908.

Poems: Second Series, A. H. Bullen, 1910.

(With Lady Gregory) *The Travelling Man* (play), first produced in Dublin at Abbey Theatre, March 2, 1910.

The Green Helmet and Other Poems (includes poems "Words, Against Unworthy Praise," and "The Mask"), Cuala Press, 1910, R. Harold Paget, 1911, enlarged edition, Macmillan, 1912.

Synge and the Ireland of His Time (nonfiction), Cuala Press, 1911.

The Cutting of an Agate (nonfiction), Macmillan, 1912, enlarged edition, 1919.

Poems Written in Discouragement, 1912-1913, Cuala Press, 1913.

Stories of Red Hanrahan, The Secret Rose, Rosa Alchemica (fiction), A. H. Bullen, 1913, Macmillan, 1914.

A Selection from the Poetry of W. B. Yeats, Bernard Tauchnitz, 1913.

A Selection from the Love Poetry of W. B. Yeats, Cuala Press, 1913.

Responsibilities (poetry; includes "To a Shade," "The Magi," and "A Coat"), Cuala Press, 1914, enlarged edition, Macmillan, 1916.

The Wild Swans at Coole (poetry and plays; includes play *At the Hawk's Well,* first performed privately in London, April 2, 1916, produced in Dublin at Abbey Theatre, July 25, 1933), Cuala Press, 1917, enlarged edition, Macmillan, 1919, expanded edition, Cornell University Press, 1994.

Per Amica Silentia Lunae (nonfiction), Macmillan, 1918.

Two Plays for Dancers (includes *The Only Jealousy of Emer,* first produced in foreign language in Amsterdam at Hollandsche Schouwburg, April 2, 1922, produced in English in Dublin at Abbey Theatre, May 9, 1926, revised as *Fighting the Waves* [also see below]; and *The Dreaming of the Bones,* first produced in Dublin at Abbey Theatre, December 6, 1931), Cuala Press, 1919.

Four Plays for Dancers (includes *The Only Jealousy of Emer* and *At the Hawk's Well*), Macmillan, 1921.

Selected Poems, Macmillan, 1921.

Michael Robartes and the Dancer (poetry), Cuala Press, 1921, expanded edition, edited by Thomas Francis Parkinson and Anne Brannen, Cornell University Press, 1994.

Plays in Prose and Verse, Written for an Irish Theatre (includes *The Player Queen,* first produced in London at King's Hall, May 25, 1919), Macmillan, 1922.

Later Poems, Macmillan (London), 1922, Macmillan (New York), 1924.

Seven Poems and a Fragment, first edition, 1922.

Plays and Controversies, Macmillan (London), 1923, Macmillan (New York), 1924.

Essays, Macmillan, 1924.

"*The Cat and the Moon*" *and Certain Poems* (includes play *The Cat and the Moon,* first produced in Dublin at Abbey Theatre, May 9, 1926), Cuala Press, 1924.

The Bounty of Sweden (nonfiction), Cuala Press, 1925.

A Vision: An Explanation of Life Founded upon the Writings of Giraldus and upon Certain Doctrine Attributed to Kusta Ben Luka, T. Werner Laurie, 1925, revised edition published as *A Vision,* Macmillan (London), 1937, Macmillan (New York), 1938, published as *A Critical Edition of "Yeats's A Vision" (1925),* edited by George Mills Harper and Walter Kelly Hood, Macmillan, 1978.

October Blast (poetry), Cuala Press, 1927.

(Translator) *Sophocles' "Oedipus at Colonus"* (also see below), first produced in Dublin at Abbey Theatre, September 12, 1927.

(Translator) *Sophocles' "King Oedipus"* (play; first produced in Dublin at Abbey Theatre, December 7, 1926), Macmillan, 1928.

The Tower (poetry; includes "The Tower," "Sailing to Byzantium," "Leda and the Swan," "Nineteen Hundred Nineteen," and "Among School Children"), Macmillan, 1928.

A Packet for Ezra Pound (nonfiction), Cuala Press, 1929.

The Winding Stair (poetry), Fountain Press, 1929, enlarged edition, Macmillan, 1933, expanded edition, Cornell University Press, 1995.

Words for Music Perhaps and Other Poems, Cuala Press, 1932.

Stories of Michael Robartes and His Friends (plays and fiction; includes play *The Resurrection,* first produced in Dublin at Abbey Theatre, July 30, 1934), Cuala Press, 1932.

Letters to the New Island (essays and reviews), edited by Horace Reynolds, Harvard University Press, 1934.

Wheels and Butterflies (plays), Macmillan (London), 1934, Macmillan (New York), 1935.

The King of the Great Clock Tower (play; first produced in Dublin at Abbey Theatre, July 30, 1934), Cuala Press, 1934, Macmillan, 1935.

The Words upon the Window Pane (play; first produced in Dublin at Abbey Theatre, November 17, 1930), Cuala Press, 1934.

Wheels and Butterflies (includes *Fighting the Waves* [revision of *The Only Jealousy of Emer;* also see above]), Macmillan, 1934.

A Full Moon in March, Macmillan, 1935.

Poems, Cuala Press, 1935.

New Poems, Cuala Press, 1938.

The Herne's Egg and Other Plays (includes *The Herne's Egg,* first produced in 1950), Macmillan, 1938.

Purgatory (first produced in Dublin at Abbey Theatre, August 10, 1938), critical edition, Cornell University Press, 1985.

Last Poems and Two Plays (includes play *The Death of Cuchulain;* and poems "The Gyres," "Lapis Lazuli," "The Wicked Old Man," "Crazy Jane on the Mountain," "The Man and the Echo," "Politics," and "Under Ben Bulben"), Cuala Press, 1939.

On the Boiler (nonfiction), Cuala Press, 1939.

Two Plays, Cuala Press, 1939.

Last Poems and Plays, Macmillan, 1940.

If I Were Four-and-Twenty (nonfiction), Cuala Press, 1940.

The Death of Cuchulain (first produced in 1949), critical edition edited by Phillip L. Marcus, Cornell University Press, 1981.

(With George Moore) *Diarmuid and Grania* (play; first produced in Dublin at Gaiety Theatre, October 21, 1901), Becker, 1951.

The Variorum Edition of the Poems of W. B. Yeats, edited by Peter Allt and Russell K. Alspach, Macmillan (New York), 1957.

Mythologies (stories and essays), Macmillan, 1959.

The Senate Speeches of W. B. Yeats, edited by Donald R. Pearce, Indiana University Press, 1960.

Essays and Introductions, Macmillan, 1961.

Explorations (nonfiction), Macmillan, 1962.

The Variorum Edition of the Plays of W. B. Yeats, edited by Russell K. Alspach, Macmillan, 1966.

Uncollected Prose by W. B. Yeats, two volumes, edited by John P. Frayne and Colton Johnson, Columbia University Press, 1970.

(With Thomas Kinsella) *Davis, Mangan, Ferguson* (critical study), Dufour, 1971.

The Speckled Bird (unfinished novel), edited by William H. O'Donnell, Cuala Press, 1974, annotated edition, McClelland & Stewart, 1977.

(With Swami Shree) *The Ten Principal Upanishads,* Macmillan, 1975.

The Secret Rose: Stories by W. B. Yeats: A Variorum Edition, edited by Phillip L. Marcus, Warwick Gould, and Michael J. Sidnell, Cornell University Press, 1981.

Byzantium, Black Swan, 1983.

The Poems: A New Edition, edited by Richard J. Finneran, Macmillan, 1983.

Poems of W. B. Yeats: A New Selection, with an introduction and notes by A. Norman Jeffares, Macmillan, 1984.

A Poet to His Beloved: The Early Love Poems of W. B. Yeats, St. Martin's, 1985.

Treasury of Irish Myth, Legend, and Folklore, Crown, 1986.

Mosada [and] *The Island of Statues: Manuscript Materials,* edited by George Bornstein, Cornell University Press, 1987.

The Early Poems: Manuscript Materials, edited by George Bornstein, Cornell University Press, 1987.

(With others) *The Second Book of the Rhymers Club,* British American Books, 1987.

(With Lady Gregory) *Complete Irish Mythology,* Slaney Press (London), 1994.

The Wanderings of Oisin, and Other Early Poems, Cornell University Press, 1994.

Under the Moon: The Unpublished Early Poetry, edited by George Bornstein, Scribner, 1995.

Also author of *Irish Fairy and Folk Tales,* 1918. Contributor to periodicals. *A Poet to His Beloved* has been published with musical score by Lowell Liebermann, T. Presser, 1994.

AUTOBIOGRAPHIES AND DIARIES

Reveries Over Childhood and Youth, Cuala Press, 1915, Macmillan, 1916.

Four Years, Cuala Press, 1921.

The Trembling of the Veil, T. Werner Laurie, 1922.

Autobiographies: "Reveries Over Childhood and Youth" and "The Trembling of the Veil," Macmillan (London), 1926, Macmillan (New York), 1927.

The Death of Synge and Other Passages from an Old Diary, Cuala Press, 1928.

Dramatis Personae, Cuala Press, 1935.

"Dramatis Personae," "Estrangement," "The Death of Synge," "The Bounty of Sweden," Macmillan (London and New York), 1936.

The Autobiography of William Butler Yeats, Consisting of "Reveries Over Childhood and Youth," "The Trembling of the Veil," and "Dramatis Personae," Macmillan, 1938, published with *Estrangement, The Death of Synge,* and *The Bounty of Sweden,* as *Autobiographies,* Macmillan, 1955.

Pages from a Diary Written in Nineteen Hundred and Thirty, Cuala Press, 1944.

Memoirs: Autobiography, edited by Denis Donoghue, Macmillan, 1972.

LETTERS

Letters on Poetry from W. B. Yeats to Dorothy Wellesley, Oxford University Press, 1940.

W. B. Yeats and T. Sturge Moore: Their Correspondence: 1901-1937, edited by Ursula Bridge, Routledge & Kegan Paul, 1953.

Some Letters from W. B. Yeats to John O'Leary and His Sister, edited by Allan Wade, New York Public Library, 1953.

Letters of W. B. Yeats to Katharine Tynan, edited by Roger McHugh, Macmillan, 1953.

The Letters of W. B. Yeats, edited by Allan Wade, Macmillan, 1954.

Ah, Sweet Dancer: W. B. Yeats and Margot Ruddock, a Correspondence, edited by Roger McHugh, Macmillan, 1970.

The Correspondence of Robert Bridges and W. B. Yeats, edited by Richard J. Finneran, Macmillan, 1977.

Theatre Business: The Correspondence of the First Abbey Theatre Directors: William Butler Yeats, Lady Gregory and J. M. Synge, edited by Ann Saddlemyer, Colin Smythe, 1982.

The Collected Letters of W. B. Yeats, Volume 1: *1865-1895,* edited by John Kelly and Eric Domville, Oxford University Press, 1986.

The Gonne-Yeats Letters, 1893-1938, edited by Anna Macbride White and Norman A. Jeffares, Syracuse University Press, 1994.

EDITOR

(With Edwin John Ellis) *The Works of William Blake, Poetic, Symbolic, and Critical,* Quaritch, 1893.

The Oxford Book of Modern Verse: 1892-1935, Clarendon Press, 1936.

(And translator, with Shri Purohit Swami) *The Ten Principal Upanishads,* Macmillan, 1937.

Fairy and Folk Tales of Ireland, Colin Smythe, 1973.

Representative Irish Tales, Dufour, 1979.

Also editor of *A Book of Irish Verse,* 1900.

COLLECTED WORKS

The Collected Works in Verse and Prose of William Butler Yeats, eight volumes, Shakespeare Head Press, 1908.

The Collected Poems, Macmillan (London and New York), 1933.

The Collected Plays (includes Sophocles' "Oedipus at Colonus"), Macmillan, 1934.

Nine One-Act Plays, Macmillan, 1937.

The Poems of W. B. Yeats, two volumes, Macmillan, 1949.

The Collected Poems of W. B. Yeats, Macmillan, 1950.

The Collected Plays of W. B. Yeats, Macmillan (London), 1952, Macmillan (New York), 1953.

Eleven Plays of William Butler Yeats, Macmillan, 1967.

Selected Poems and Three Plays, 3rd revised edition edited by M. L. Rosenthal, Macmillan, 1987.

Collected works also published in fourteen volumes by Macmillan, 1989–.

SIDELIGHTS: William Butler Yeats is widely acknowledged as the greatest Irish poet of the twentieth century. He belonged to the Protestant, Anglo-Irish minority that had controlled the economic, political, social, and cultural life of Ireland since at least the end of the seventeenth century. Most members of this minority considered themselves English people who merely happened to have been born in Ireland, but Yeats was staunch in affirming his Irish nationality. Although he lived in London for fourteen years of his childhood (and kept a permanent home there during the first half of his adult life), Yeats maintained his cultural roots, featuring Irish legends and heroes in many of his poems and plays. He was equally firm in adhering to his self-image as an artist. This conviction led many to accuse him of elitism, but it also unquestionably contributed to his greatness. As fellow poet W. H. Auden noted in a 1948 *Kenyon Review* essay entitled "Yeats as an Example," Yeats accepted the modern necessity of having to make a lonely and deliberate "choice of the principles and presuppositions in terms of which [made] sense of his experience." Auden assigned Yeats the high praise of having written "some of the most beautiful poetry" of modern times.

Eighteen eighty-five was an important year in Yeats's early adult life, marking the first publication, in the *Dublin University Review,* of his poetry and the beginning of his important interest in occultism. It was also the year that he met John O'Leary, a famous patriot who had returned to Ireland after totaling twenty years of imprisonment and exile for revolutionary nationalistic activities. O'Leary had a keen enthusiasm for Irish books, music, and ballads, and he encouraged young writers to adopt Irish subjects. Yeats, who had preferred more romantic settings and themes, soon took O'Leary's advice, producing many poems based on Irish legends, Irish folklore, and Irish ballads and songs. As he explained in a note included in the 1908 volume *Collected Works in Verse and Prose of William Butler Yeats:* "When I first wrote I went here and there for my subjects as my reading led me, and preferred to all other countries Arcadia and the India of romance, but presently I convinced myself . . . that I should never go for the scenery of a poem to any country but my own, and I think that I shall hold to that conviction to the end."

As Yeats began concentrating his poetry on Irish subjects, he was compelled to accompany his family in moving to London at the end of 1886. There he continued to devote himself to Irish subjects, writing poems, plays, novels, and short stories—all with Irish characters and scenes. In addition, he produced book reviews, usually on Irish topics. The most important event in Yeats's life during these London years, however, was his acquaintance with Maud Gonne, a tall, beautiful, prominent young woman passionately devoted to Irish nationalism. Yeats soon fell in love with Gonne, and for nearly three decades he courted her; although he eventually learned that she had already borne two children from a long affair, with Gonne's encouragement Yeats redoubled his dedication to Irish nationalism and produced such nationalistic plays as *The Countess Kathleen* (1892), which he dedicated to her, and *Cathleen ni Houlihan* (1902), which featured her as the personification of Ireland in the title role.

Gonne also shared Yeats's interest in occultism and spiritualism. Yeats had been a theosophist, but in 1890 he turned from its sweeping mystical insights and joined the Golden Dawn, a secret society that practiced ritual magic. The society offered instruction and initiation in a series of ten levels, the three highest of which were unattainable except by magi (who were thought to possess the secrets of supernatural wisdom and enjoy magically extended lives). Yeats was fascinated by the possibility of becoming a magi, and he became convinced that the mind was capable of perceiving past the limits of materialistic rationalism. Yeats remained an active member of the Golden Dawn for thirty-two years, becoming involved in its direction at the turn of the century and

achieving the coveted sixth grade of membership in 1914, the same year that his future wife, Georgiana Hyde-Lees, also joined the society.

Most of Yeats's poetry used symbols from ordinary life and from familiar traditions, and much of his poetry in the 1890s continued to reflect his interest in Irish subjects. During this decade he also became increasingly interested in poetic techniques. He befriended English decadent poet Lionel Johnson, and in 1890 they helped found the Rhymers' Club, a group of London poets who met to read and discuss their poems. The Rhymers placed a very high value on subjectivity and craftsmanship and preferred sophisticated aestheticism to nationalism. The club's influence is reflected in the lush density of Yeats's poetry of the times, culminating in *The Wind among the Reeds* (1899). Although Yeats was soon to abandon that lush density, he remained permanently committed to the Rhymers' insistence that a poet should labor "at rhythm and cadence, at form and style"—as he reportedly told a Dublin audience in 1893.

The turn of the century marked Yeats's increased interest in theater, an interest influenced by his father, a famed artist and orator whose love of highly dramatic moments in literature certainly contributed to Yeats's lifelong interest in drama. In the summer of 1897 the author enjoyed his first stay at Coole Park, the County Galway estate of Lady Augusta Gregory. There he devised, with Lady Gregory and her neighbor Edward Martyn, plans for promoting an innovative, native Irish drama. In 1899 they staged the first of three annual productions in Dublin, including Yeats's *The Countess Kathleen,* and in 1902 they supported a company of amateur Irish actors in staging both George Russell's Irish legend "Deirdre" and Yeats's *Cathleen ni Houlihan.* The success of these productions led to the founding of the Irish National Theatre Society with Yeats as president. With a wealthy sponsor volunteering to pay for the renovation of Dublin's Abbey Theatre as a permanent home for the company, the theater opened on December 27, 1904, and included plays by the company's three directors: Lady Gregory, John M. Synge (whose 1907 production "The Playboy of the Western World" would spark controversy with its savage comic depiction of Irish rural life), and Yeats, who was represented that night with *On Baile's Strand,* the first of his several plays featuring heroic ancient Irish warrior Cuchulain.

During the entire first decade of the twentieth century Yeats was extremely active in the management of the Abbey Theatre company, choosing plays, hiring and firing actors and managers, and arranging tours for the company. At this time he also wrote ten plays, and the simple, direct style of dialogue required for the stage became an important consideration in his poems as well. He abandoned the heavily elaborated style of *The Wind among the Reeds* in favor of conversational rhythms and radically simpler diction. This transformation in his poetic style can be traced in his first three collections of the twentieth century: *In the Seven Woods* (1903), *The Green Helmet and Other Poems* (1910), and *Responsibilities* (1914). Several poems in those collections use style as their subject. For example, in "A Coat," written in 1912, Yeats derided his 1890s poetic style, saying that he had once adorned his poems with a coat "covered with embroideries / Out of old mythologies." The poem concludes with a brash announcement: "There's more enterprise / In walking naked." This departure from a conventional nineteenth-century manner disappointed his contemporary readers, who preferred the pleasant musicality of such familiar poems as "The Lake Isle of Innisfree," which he wrote in 1890.

Eventually, Yeats began experimenting as a playwright; in 1916, for instance, he adopted a deliberately esoteric, nonrealistic dramatic style based on Japanese Noh plays, a theatrical form to which he had been introduced by poet Ezra Pound. These plays were described by Yeats as "plays for dancers."

While Yeats fulfilled his duties as president of the Abbey Theatre group for the first fifteen years of the twentieth century, his nationalistic fervor, however, was less evident. Maud Gonne, with whom he had shared his Irish enthusiasms, had moved to Paris with her husband, exiled Irish revolutionary John MacBride, and the author was left without her important encouragement. But in 1916 he once again became a staunch exponent of the nationalist cause, inspired by the Easter Rising, an unsuccessful, six-day armed rebellion of Irish republicans against the British in Dublin. MacBride, who was now separated from Gonne, participated in the rebellion and was executed afterward. Yeats reacted by writing "Easter, 1916," an eloquent expression of his complex feelings of shock, romantic admiration, and a more realistic appraisal.

The Easter Rising contributed to Yeats's eventual decision to reside in Ireland rather than England, and his marriage to Georgie Hyde-Lees in 1917 further strengthened that resolve. Earlier, in an introductory verse to *Responsibilities,* he had asked his ancestors' pardon for not yet having married to continue his Irish lineage: "Although I have come close on forty-nine, / I have no child, I have nothing but a book." Once married, however, Yeats traveled with his bride to Thoor Ballylee, a medieval stone tower where the couple periodically resided. With marriage came another period of exploration into complex and esoteric subjects for Yeats. He had long been fascinated by the contrast between a person's internal and external selves—between the true person and those aspects that the person chooses to present as a representation of the self. Yeats had first mentioned the value of masks in 1910 in a simple poem, "The Mask," where a woman reminds her lover that his interest in her depends on her guise and not on her hidden, inner self. Yeats gave eloquent expression to this idea of the mask in a group of essays, *Per Amica Silentia Lunae* (1918): "I think all happiness depends on the energy to assume the mask of some other life, on a re-birth as something not one's self." This notion can be found in a wide variety of Yeats's poems.

Yeats also continued to explored mysticism. Only four days after the wedding, his bride began what would be a lengthy experiment with the psychic phenomenon called automatic writing, in which her hand and pen presumably served as unconscious instruments for the spirit world to send information. Yeats and his wife held more than four hundred sessions of automatic writing, producing nearly four thousand pages that Yeats avidly and patiently studied and organized. From these sessions Yeats formulated theories about life and history. He believed that certain patterns existed, the most important being what he called *gyres,* interpenetrating cones representing mixtures of opposites of both a personal and historical nature. He contended that gyres were initiated by the divine impregnation of a mortal woman—first, the rape of Leda by Zeus; later, the immaculate conception of Mary. Yeats found that within each two-thousand-year era, emblematic moments occurred at the midpoints of the thousand-year halves. At these moments of balance, he believed, a civilization could achieve special excellence, and Yeats cited as examples the splendor of Athens at 500 B.C., Byzantium at A.D. 500, and the Italian Renaissance at A.D. 1500.

During these years of Yeats's esoterica Ireland was rife with internal strife. In 1921 bitter controversies erupted within the new

Irish Free State over the partition of Northern Ireland and over the wording of a formal oath of allegiance to the British Crown. These issues led to an Irish civil war, which lasted from June, 1922, to May, 1923. In this conflict Yeats emphatically sided with the new Irish government. He accepted a six-year appointment to the senate of the Irish Free State in December, 1922, a time when rebels were kidnapping government figures and burning their homes. In Dublin, where Yeats had assumed permanent residence in 1922 (after maintaining a home for thirty years in London), the government even posted armed sentries at his door. As senator, Yeats considered himself a representative of order amid the chaotic new nation's slow progress toward stability. He was now the "sixty-year-old smiling public man" of his poem "Among School Children," which he wrote after touring an Irish elementary school. But he was also a world renowned artist of impressive stature, having received the Nobel Prize for literature in 1923.

Yeats's poems and plays produced during his senate term and beyond are, at once, local and general, personal and public, Irish and universal. At night the poet could "sweat with terror" (a phrase in his poem "Nineteen Hundred and Nineteen") because of the surrounding violence, but he could also generalize those terrifying realities by linking them with events in the rest of the world and with all of history. The energy of the poems written in response to these disturbing times gave astonishing power to his collection *The Tower* (1928), which is often considered his best single book, though *The Wild Swans at Coole* (1917; enlarged edition, 1919), *Michael Robartes and the Dancer* (1921), *The Tower, The Winding Stair* (1929); enlarged edition, 1933), and *Words for Music Perhaps and Other Poems* (1932), also possess considerable merit.

As Yeats aged, he saw Ireland change in ways that angered him. The Anglo-Irish Protestant minority no longer controlled Irish society and culture, and with Lady Gregory's death in 1932 and the consequent abandonment of the Coole Park estate, Yeats felt detached from the brilliant achievements of the eighteenth-century Anglo-Irish tradition. According to Yeats's unblushingly antidemocratic view, the greatness of Anglo-Irishmen such as Jonathan Swift, philosopher George Berkeley, and statesman Edmund Burke, contrasted sharply with the undistinguished commonness of contemporary Irish society, which seemed preoccupied with the interests of merchants and peasants. He stated his unpopular opinions in late plays such as *Purgatory* (1938) and the essays of *On the Boiler* (1939).

But Yeats offset his frequently brazen manner with the personal conflicts expressed in his last poems. He faced death with a courage that was founded partly on his vague hope for reincarnation and partly on his admiration for the bold heroism that he perceived in Ireland in both ancient times and the eighteenth century. In proud moods he could speak in the stern voice of his famous epitaph, written within six months of his death, which concludes his poem "Under Ben Bulben": "Cast a cold eye / On life, on death. / Horseman, pass by!" But the bold sureness of those lines is complicated by the error-stricken cry that "distracts my thought" at the end of another late poem, "The Man and the Echo," and also by the poignantly frivolous lust for life in the last lines of "Politics," the poem that he wanted to close *Last Poems:* "But O that I were young again / And held her in my arms."

Throughout his last years, Yeats's creative imagination remained very much his own, isolated to a remarkable degree from the successive fashions of modern poetry despite his extensive contacts with other poets. Literary modernism held no inherent attraction for him except perhaps in its general association with youthful vigor. He admired a wide range of traditional English poetry and drama, and he simply was unconcerned that, during the last two decades of his life, his preference for using rhyme and strict stanza forms would set him apart from the vogue of modern poetry. Yeats's allegiance to poetic tradition did not extend, however, to what he considered an often obscure, overly learned use of literary and cultural traditions by T. S. Eliot and Pound. Yeats deplored the tremendous enthusiasm among younger poets for Eliot's *The Waste Land,* published in 1922. Disdaining Eliot's flat rhythms and cold, dry mood, Yeats wanted all art to be full of energy. He felt that the literary traditions furnishing Eliot with so many allusions and quotations should only be included in a poem if those traditions had so excited the individual poet's imagination that they could become poetic ingredients of the sort Yeats described in "The Tower": "Poet's imaginings / And memories of love, / Memories of the words of women, / All those things whereof / Man makes a superhuman / Mirror-resembling dream."

BIOGRAPHICAL/CRITICAL SOURCES:

BOOKS

Adams, Hazard, *The Book of Yeat's Vision: Romantic Modernism and Antithetical Tradition,* University of Michigan Press, 1995.

Albright, Daniel, *Quantum Poetics: Yeats, Pound, Eliot, and the Science of Modernism,* Cambridge University Press, 1997.

Allison, Jonathan, *Yeat's Political Identities,* University of Michigan Press, 1996.

Blake, James J., *Yeats, "The Wanderings of Oisin," and Irish Gaelic Literature,* P. Lang, 1996.

Bloom, Harold, *Yeats,* Oxford University Press, 1970.

Concise Dictionary of British Literary Biography, Volume 5: *Late Victorian and Edwardian Writers, 1890-1914,* Gale (Detroit), 1991.

Connor, Lester I., *A Yeats Dictionary: Persons and Places in the Poetry of William Butler Yeats,* Syracuse University Press, 1998.

Dictionary of Literary Biography, Gale, Volume 10: *Modern British Dramatists, 1940-1945,* 1982; Volume 19: *British Poets, 1840-1914,* 1983; Volume 98: *Modern British Essayists, First Series,* Gale, 1990.

Ellis, Sylvia C., *The Plays of W. B. Yeats: Yeats and the Dancer,* St. Martin's Press, 1994.

Ellmann, Richard, *The Identity of Yeats,* 2nd edition, Faber, 1964.

Ellmann, Richard, *Yeats: The Man and the Masks,* 2nd edition, Faber, 1961.

Fleming, Deborah, *A Man Who Does Not Exist: The Irish Peasant in the Work of W. B. Yeats and J. M. Synge,* University of Michigan Press, 1995.

Gorski, William T., *Yeats and Alchemy,* State University of New York Press, 1996.

Howes, Marjorie Elizabeth, *Yeat's Nations: Gender, Class, and Irishness,* Cambridge University Press, 1997.

Larrissy, Edward, *William Butler Yeats,* Oxford University Press, 1997.

Macrae, Alasdair D. F., *W. B. Yeats: A Literary Life,* St. Martin's, 1995.

Maddox, Brenda, *The Secret Life of William Butler Yeats,* Harpercollins, 1998.

Malins, Edward Greenway, and John Arthur Purkis, *A Preface to Yeats,* Longman, 1994.

McCready, Sam, *A William Butler Yeats Encyclopedia,* Greenwood Press, 1997.

Murphy, William Michael, *Family Secrets: William Butler Yeats and His Relatives,* Syracuse University Press, 1995.

Peterson, Richard, *William Butler Yeats,* Twayne, 1982.

Pierce, David, *Yeat's Worlds: Ireland, England, and the Poetic Imagination,* Yale University Press, 1995.

Purdy, Dwight H., *Biblical Echo and Allusion in the Poetry of W. B. Yeats: Poetics and the Art of God,* Associated University Presses, 1994.

Rosenthal, M. L., *Running to Paradise: Yeat's Poetic Art,* Oxford University Press, 1994.

Sidnell, Michael J., *Yeat's Poetry and Poetics,* St. Martin's, 1996.

Stanley, Michael, *Famous Dubliners: W. B. Yeats, James Joyce, Jonathan Swift, Wolfe Tone, Oscar Wilde, Edward Carson,* Wolfhound Press (Dublin, Ireland), 1996.

Tratner, Michael, *Modernism and Mass Politics: Joyce, Woolf, Eliot, Yeats,* Stanford University Press, 1995.

Twentieth-Century Literary Criticism, Gale, Volume 1, 1978; Volume 11, 1983; Volume 18, 1985; Volume 31, 1989.

Unterecker, John Eugene, *A Reader's Guide to William Butler Yeats,* Syracuse University Press, 1996.

Vendler, Helen, *Yeats's "Vision" and the Later Plays,* Harvard University Press, 1963.

Watanabe, Nancy Ann, *Beloved Image: The Drama of W. B. Yeats, 1865-1939,* University Press of America, 1995.

Watson, George J., *Irish Identity and the Literary Revival: Synge, Yeats, Joyce, and O'Casey,* Catholic University of America Press, 1994.

Yeats Annual, Macmillan (London), 1982–.

Yeats: An Annual of Critical and Textual Studies, Cornell University Press, 1983–.

PERIODICALS

Booklist, August, 1995, p. 1925.

Commentary, November, 1995, p. 76.

New York Review of Books, April 21, 1994, p. 49.

Poetry, October-November, 1995, p. 94.

Publishers Weekly, November 13, 1995, p. 53.

School Library Journal, April, 1996, p. 90.

Times (London), January 28, 1989; May 6, 1989.

Tri-Quarterly, winter, 1965.

*   *   *

YORK, Simon
   See HEINLEIN, Robert A(nson)

*   *   *

YOUNG, Collier
   See BLOCH, Robert (Albert)

*   *   *

YOURCENAR, Marguerite 1903-1987

PERSONAL: Born June 8, 1903, in Brussels, Belgium; originally French citizen; naturalized U.S. citizen, 1947; died December 18, 1987 (some sources say December 17), in Mount Desert Island, ME; daughter of Michel and Fernande (de Cartier de Marchienne) de Crayencour. *Education:* Educated privately.

CAREER: Writer, 1921-87. Professor of comparative literature at Sarah Lawrence College, 1940-50; lecturer at universities in the United States and Europe, 1940-1987.

MEMBER: Academie Francaise (first female member), Academie Royale de langue et de litterature francaises de Belgique, American Academy and Institute of Arts and Letters, American Civil Rights Association.

AWARDS, HONORS: Prix Femina-Vacaresco, 1951, for *Memoires d'Hadrien;* Page One Award from Newspaper Guild of New York, 1955; L.T.D. from Smith College, 1961; Prix Combat, 1963, for ensemble of work; Prix Femina, 1968, for *L'Oeuvre au noir;* L.T.D. from Bowdoin College, 1968; L.T.D. from Colby College, 1972; Prix Monaco, 1973, for ensemble of work; Grand Prix National des Lettres from French Ministry of Culture, 1975; Grand Prix de La Litterature from Academie Francaise, 1980; L.T.D. from Harvard University, 1981; National Arts Club Medal of Honor for Literature, 1985; commander of Legion of Honor (France) officer Order of Leopold (Belgium).

WRITINGS:

IN ENGLISH TRANSLATION

Alexis; ou, Le Traite du vain combat (novel), [Paris], 1929, revised edition, Plon, 1965, translation by Walter Kaiser published as *Alexis,* Farrar, Straus, 1984.

Dernier du reve (novel), Grasset, 1934, revised edition, 1959, translation by Dori Katz published as *A Coin in Nine Hands,* Farrar, Straus, 1982.

Feux (poems), [Paris], 1936, revised edition, Gallimard, 1974, translation by Katz published as *Fires,* Farrar, Straus, 1981.

Nouvelles Orientales (short stories), Gallimard, 1938, translation by Alberto Manguel published as *Oriental Tales,* Farrar, Straus, 1985.

Le Coup de grace (novel), Gallimard, 1939, translation by Grace Frick published as *Coup de Grace,* Farrar, Straus, 1957.

Memoires d'Hadrien (novel), Plon, 1951, translation by Frick published as *Memoirs of Hadrian,* Farrar, Straus, 1954.

Les Charites d'Alcippe (poems), [Brussels], 1956, translation published as *The Alms of Alcippe,* Targ Editions, 1982.

Sous benefice d'inventaire (essays), Gallimard, 1962, revised edition, 1978, translation by Richard Howard published as *The Dark Brain of Piranesi and Other Essays,* Farrar, Straus, 1984.

L'Oeuvre au noir (novel), Gallimard, 1968, translation by Frick published as *The Abyss,* Farrar, Straus, 1976.

Theatre (plays), two volumes, Gallimard, 1971, translation by Katz published as *Plays,* Performing Arts Journal Publications, 1985.

Les Yeux ouverts: Entretiens avec Matthieu Galey, Centurion, 1980, translation by Arthur Goldhammer published as *With Open Eyes: Conversations with Matthieu Galey,* Beacon Press, 1986.

Mishima; ou, La Vision du vide (biography), Gallimard, 1981, translation by Manguel published as *Mishima: A Vision of the Void,* Farrar, Straus, 1986.

Comme L'eau qui coule (short stories), Gallimard, 1982, translation by Kaiser published as *Two Lives and a Dream,* Farrar, Straus, 1987.

Le temps, ce Grand Sculpteur: Essais (essays), Gallimard, 1983, translation by Kaiser published as *That Mighty Sculptor, Time,* Farrar, Straus, 1989.

Memoirs of Hadrian [and] *Reflections on the Composition of Memoirs of Hadrian,* Modern Library, 1995.

A Blue Tale and Other Stories (also contains *The First Evening* and *An Evil Spell*), translation by Alberto Manguel, University of Chicago Press, 1995.

IN FRENCH

Le Jardin des chimeres (poetry; title means "The Garden of Chimeras"), Librairie Academique, 1921.

Les Dieux ne sont pas morts (poetry: title means "The Gods Are Not Dead"), Editions Sansot, 1922.

La Nouvelle Eurydice (novel; title means "The New Eurydice"), Grasset, 1931.

Pindare, Grasset, 1932.

Les Dieux ne sont pas morts (short stories; title means "The Gods Are Not Dead"), Grasset, 1934.

Les Songes et les sorts, Grasset, 1938.

Electra; ou, La Chute des masques, Plon, 1954.

(Author of critique and translator from the Greek with Constantin Dimaras) *Presentation critique de Constantin Cavafy, 1863-1933,* Gallimard, 1958.

Le Mystere d'Alceste [and] *Qui n'a pas son minotaure?* Plon, 1963.

(Translator from the English) *Fleuve profond, sombre riviere: Les Negro spirituals,* Gallimard, 1964.

(Author of critique and translator from the English) *Presentation critique d'Hortense Flexner,* Gallimard, 1969.

Suite d'estampes pour Kou-Kou-Hai, High Loft, 1980.

Discours de reception de Mme Marguerite Yourcenar a L'Academie Francaise et reponse de M. Jean d'Ormesson, Gallimard, 1981.

Oeuvres romanesques, Gallimard, 1982.

Blues et gospels, Gallimard, 1984.

La Couranne et le lyre (title means "The Crown and the Lyre"), French and European Publications, 1984.

Le Cheval noir a tete blanche: Contes enfants Indiens, French and European Publications, 1985.

La Voix des choses (title means "The Voices of Things"), French and European Publications, 1987.

Dialogue dans le marecage (title means "Dialogue in the Swamp"), French and European Publications, 1988.

En pelerin et en etranger (essays), Gallimard, 1990.

Le Tour de la Prison, French and European Publications, 1991.

Lettres a ses Amis et Quelques Autres, Gallimard, 1995.

Also author of *Anna Sonor,* 1979, and *Un Homme obscur,* 1982.

LE LABYRINTHE DU MONDE SERIES

Souvenirs pieux, Gallimard, 1974, translation published as *Dear Departed,* Farrar, Straus & Giroux, 1992.

Archives du nord, Gallimard, 1977, translation by Maria Louise Ascher published as *How Many Years,* Farrar, Straus & Giroux, 1995.

Quoi? L'Enternite, Gallimard, 1990.

OTHER

Translator of works by Henry James, Virginia Woolf, and ancient Greek poets.

SIDELIGHTS: When author Marguerite Yourcenar was elected to the Academie Francaise in 1981, she became the first woman to receive the French state's highest literary honor. Throughout its three hundred fifty years of existence, the Academie Francaise had elected only men until the octogenarian novelist was asked to join its ranks. The honor was formidable, and most critics agree that Yourcenar, long a resident of Mount Desert Island off the coast of Maine, deserves such unprecedented acclaim. She wrote fiction, essays, poetry, and a biography, but remains best known for two thought-provoking historical novels, *Memoires of Hadrian* and *The Abyss,* first published in France as *Memoires d'Hadrien* and *L'Oeuvre au noir.* According to Moses Hadas in the *Saturday Review,* Yourcenar's "highest usefulness and greatest success is in a field beyond the range of the orthodox historian, a field to which only the imaginative writer can be adequate." Her example, Hadas adds, "is to be commended to all writers of historical fiction." *Los Angeles Times Book Review* contributor Frances McConnel offers a similar appraisal of the Belgian-born writer: "Whatever magic she is about, Yourcenar crosses barriers of century, discipline, language, myth and history with no sense of impropriety or danger. The path her mind takes through these landscapes is always stepping-stone easy to follow, yet everywhere full of bold jumps and staggering views." In *World Literature Today,* Alexander Coleman concludes that an open-minded reader "will discover in all Yourcenar's writings a luminous and keenly magisterial intelligence."

Commentary essayist Joseph Epstein discusses the theme that arises from much of Yourcenar's fiction. "Intricate moral questions are usually not at the center of Marguerite Yourcenar's work," Epstein writes. "Human destiny, its meaning and even more its mysteries, are. She has a clearer sense than anyone now writing of the tragedy yet also the hope inherent in human lives. . . . The effect of reading her novels is to be reminded of the difficulty of life and of its heroic possibilities—hardly a thing that contemporary literature does best, if at all. Most of us are undone by life. Ours is but to do, then die. Marguerite Yourcenar's novels make us question why. This is what major writers have always done. This is why she is among their number." In the *Times Literary Supplement,* George Steiner reflects on the notion that through strong central characters, Yourcenar "argues her vision of essential human solitude, of the radical incapacity of human beings, particularly and paradoxically when they are most self-conscious and articulate, to communicate to others, even to those they love best, the final quality or truth of their convictions. This, indeed, is the Yourcenar leitmotif." The vision is sometimes bleak; *New York Times Book Review* contributor Michael Wood feels that Yourcenar's characters "make tremendous demands of themselves and generally despair of others," but erudition and estimations of human potential for intellectual and spiritual sovereignty alleviate the solemnity. In a *New York Times Book Review* piece, Stephen Koch calls Yourcenar "one of the great scholar-artists," who provides ". . . riches for anyone interested in history, humanism or the psychology of power."

Yourcenar "had an ideally vagrant and unsettling youth for a writer of historical fiction," according to John Sturrock in the *New York Times Book Review.* She was born in Brussels in 1903; her father was French and her mother Belgian. Yourcenar lost her mother to a fever shortly after her birth, so her father undertook sole responsibility for her care. Together they traveled extensively in England, France, Italy and Switzerland, using the family name of de Crayencour that Yourcenar later scrambled to form her unusual nom de plume. As a youngster, Marguerite de Crayencour was educated privately, largely by her father. In the *Times Literary Supplement,* John Weightman writes of him: "M. de Crayencour must have been a curious mixture of playboy and free-thinking, gentleman-scholar, because it was he who gave [Yourcenar] a grounding in Latin and Greek and read many of the French classics with her; nor does he seem to have imposed on her any of the conventional restraints of the time. Father and daughter were fairly constant companions until his death in 1929, after which she continued the nomadic life, in undefined circumstances but with apparently adequate financial resources, sharing her time

between France, Italy, Greece and other countries." Yourcenar began writing while still in her teens, and she was twenty-six when her first novel, *Alexis; ou, Le Traite du vain combat,* was published. *New Republic* contributor Anne Tyler reflects on how Yourcenar's unsettled youth—interrupted by both World Wars—influences her writings: "Her physical distance from her Belgian homeland and her psychological distance from the country she has adopted [the United States] combine to give a picture of someone watching the world at one remove—as Marguerite Yourcenar most certainly does. Her concern is man's relationship with history. Her characters are most often tiny, lonely figures in a vortex of political events."

Her book *Memoirs of Hadrian* is hailed in France and America as a classic achievement in postwar fiction. In the *Spectator,* Miranda Seymour calls the work "arguably the finest historical novel of this century." Likewise, *New York Herald Tribune Book Review* contributor Geoffrey Bruun notes that *Memoirs of Hadrian* "is an extraordinarily expert performance. . . . It has a quality of authenticity, of verisimilitude, that delights and fascinates." Drawing on her vast knowledge of ancient Rome, Yourcenar has recreated the world of the Emperor Hadrian, who, in a series of first-person letters to his nephew Marcus Aurelius, reminisces about his life and times. James Boatwright describes the work in the *Washington Post Book World:* "In a prose of exquisite clarity and grace, the Emperor Hadrian . . . reveals himself as both a creator and worshiper of beauty, a man of keen intelligence and strong passion, powerful and magnanimous, a poet, a lover, a prince 'who was *almost* wise.'" According to Epstein, the novel's outlook "is worldly; its tone philosophical; its feeling completely Roman. The book is a triumph of historical ventriloquism; it is impossible to read it and not think that, had Hadrian left memoirs, this is how they would have read. . . . To bring off such a book requires not only artistry and scholarship but intelligence of a very high order."

Other critics are similarly impressed with *Memoirs of Hadrian.* In the *Nation,* Stanley Cooperman calls it "historical fiction at its best" and adds that Yourcenar "has avoided the usual hack plot and romantic baubles and produced a moving and scholarly recreation of a fascinating scene and epoch—Hadrian's Rome." Cooperman further comments that *Memoirs of Hadrian* reaches "deeply into the blend of humanism and cruelty, decadence and power, art and economics referred to in adequately as 'pagan Rome.'" Hadas writes: "Even a reader indifferent to history and historical personages must find the Hadrian here presented a full and sensitive man well worth knowing. . . . Miss Yourcenar breathes life into the enigmatic data concerning the man and communicates a vivid sense of the multifarious empire he ruled." *Washington Post* correspondent Michael Kernan expresses the opinion that it "is hard to find a reader who refuses to love 'Hadrian.' The man comes through so clearly, in the loneliness of his intelligence, in his practiced but wary handling of his own immense power, in his grief over the death of his young lover Antinous, that we feel this is what greatness must be like." *New Yorker* columnist George Steiner goes so far as to suggest that *Memoirs of Hadrian* earned Yourcenar her invitation to join the Academie Francaise. "It is in [Hadrian's] eminent glow," Steiner concludes, "that the new Academician took her historic seat."

The Abyss, published in France as *L'Oeuvre au noir,* first appeared in English translation in 1976. Another historical/philosophical novel, the work follows the life of a fictitious Renaissance physician, Zeno of Bruges. In a *New York Times Book Review* assessment of the French edition, Marc Slonim calls the book "at the same time a study of the Renaissance and a picture of that turbulent era as seen through the eyes of a poet. . . . What gives this fateful story a singular dimension is its high intellectual content. . . . 'L'Oeuvre au noir,' written in the compact, poetic language so typical of Mme. Yourcenar, is a stirring, unusual and often disturbing experience for the contemporary reader." Once again critics have praised *The Abyss* for its authenticity and intellectual content. As Muriel Haynes notes in *Ms.* magazine, Yourcenar's "immense erudition and meticulous scholarship recreate this period of dissolution. . . . Beneath this richly textured surface, the book is a compendium of ideas, a philosophical examination of the abyss in which humankind is plunged still. . . . Like *Memoirs of Hadrian* it is a meditation on history in which the past is seen as both present and eternal." Kernan likewise feels that the work "is a brilliant tapestry of western Europe in the Middle Ages, . . . so rich in smells and sounds and scenes that it seems like superb reporting." Haynes suggests that although Zeno is a fictitious character, "his cast of mind, his convictions and experiences, are a kind of collage of those of actual personages who shared his century," and a *Times Literary Supplement* reviewer offers the compliment that the novel "will delight historians of this period."

In addition to her novels, Yourcenar has published poetry, essays, and stories, and many of these have also been made available in English translation. *Fires* is a collection of poetic monologues based on classical Greek and Judeo-Christian stories; Boatwright contends that the pieces "are variations on the theme of absolute love, its terrible price and transcendent rewards, whatever its form." *Times Literary Supplement* contributor Oswyn Murray feels that the poems in *Fires* demonstrate "those qualities which were to make [Yourcenar] a great novelist—empathy, a sense of individuality, and wisdom." *Oriental Tales* offers a series of folktales from various European and Far Eastern cultures. In the *New York Times Book Review*, Koch states that the stories "are wonderful. . . . [Each] of them seems a small window opened, magically, on some quite real but lost world. For Miss Yourcenar, scholarship is the entryway to the imagination, and, like all her work, these borrowed stories are simultaneously efforts at reconstruction and new creation. . . . At once immemorial and new, they show us the fabulist as mythographer and sage." Yourcenar's first essay collection, *Sous benefice d'inventaire*, published in the United States as *The Dark Brain of Piranesi and Other Essays*, has also garnered critical praise. Assessing the work in the *New York Times*, John Gross concludes that Yourcenar's essays "make it clear that she is . . . an outstanding critic. They are forceful, deeply pondered, the record of a full imaginative response."

In *That Mighty Sculptor Time*, a collection of Yourcenar's essays published in 1989, "Yourcenar displays all the breadth of understanding and range of knowledge one would expect from this most intellectual of writers," notes Stephen Galloway in the *Los Angeles Times Book Review*. Unfortunately, Galloway continues, "cerebralism never rises above petty scholarship here." D.A.N. Jones, commenting in the *London Review of Books* on Yourcenar's essay subjects, remarks: "Many good points are made about her own time (and ours), about feminism and the environment, but more pleasing and eerie is her account of the coincidences' that have attended her writing of historical fiction." P. N. Furbank in the *New York Review of Books* concludes: "There is a place in the world for belle-lettrism, and this is an appealing example."

Yourcenar's *En Pelerin et en etranger* includes not only Yourcenar's essays but also previously unpublished extracts from Yourcenar's diaries from 1942 to 1948. John Taylor, writing for the *Times Literary Supplement*, finds the collection "disappointing" despite its broad range of topics. John L. Brown in *World Literature Today* is also less than satisfied with the collection. Commenting on the publishing industry's penchant for capitalizing on deceased authors, he writes, "Despite certain pages which have the flavor of vintage Yourcenar, the literary journalism collected in *En Pelerin et en etranger*, much of it already published elsewhere, does little to enhance the reputation of one of the outstanding women of letters of our time."

Yourcenar was an intensely private person who preferred to avoid the literary circles in both New York and Paris. For half the year she lived in the cottage on Mount Desert Island that she and the late Grace Frick purchased together; Yourcenar told the *New York Times* that she stayed there both to avoid autograph-seekers and because she liked the "village rhythm" and the beautiful scenery. Although Gross, among others, notes that the author "is reticent about her private life, and . . . more preoccupied with long perspectives than with the fashion of the hour," Yourcenar has published some books about herself. One project was *Le Labyrinthe du monde*; its completed components, *Souvenirs pieux* and *Archives du nord* describe her parents' families in the century before she was born. She has also released a series of interviews the English translation of which is entitled *With Open Eyes: Conversations with Matthieu Galey*. Gross claims that the views expressed in that book "are all of a piece—those of a liberal and a humanitarian who believes that 'the social problem is more important than the political problem,' and whose deepest public concerns tend to be cultural and ecological."

Mavis Gallant, in the *New York Review of Books*, feels that Yourcenar "stands among a litter of flashier reputations as testimony to the substance and clarity of the French language and the purpose and meaning of a writer's life." The author continued to write, travel, and contemplate historical and philosophical issues central to the human condition into her eighties. "Some novelists pull us more deeply into our own time," Epstein observes, "she pulls us away from it—or rather above it. Marguerite Yourcenar's subject is human destiny. It was the only serious subject for the Greeks, whom she so much admires. It has always been the great subject of the novel, and always will be, even though few writers in our day have been able to find the means to take it on, let alone so directly as Marguerite Yourcenar has done." In his *Saturday Review* essay, Koch concludes: "As an artist and thinker—for Yourcenar's novels must be regarded as simultaneously art, scholarship, and profound philosophical meditation—Marguerite Yourcenar writes squarely in defense of the very highest standards and traditions of that enlightened humanism which Hadrian promulgated for an empire and to the agonized rebirth of which her Zeno dies a martyr. It is, to say the least, heartening to find a writer so deeply committed to that humanism who is producing major art at this moment in our own history. It is, in fact, inspiring."

BIOGRAPHICAL/CRITICAL SOURCES:

BOOKS

Contemporary Literary Criticism, Gale (Detroit), Volume 19, 1981; Volume 38, 1986; Volume 87, 1995.
Dictionary of Literary Biography, Volume 72: *French Novelists, 1900-1930*, Gale, 1988.

Frederick, Particia E., *Mythic Symbolism and Cultural Anthropology in Three Early Works of Marguerite Yourcenar: Nouvelles Orientales, Le Coup de Grace, Comme L'eau qui Coule,* Mellen University Press, 1995.

Majer O'Sickey, Ingeborg, *A Case of Betrayal?: Women in Marguerite Yourcenar's Early Work,* P. Lang, 1996.

Shurr, Georgia H., *Marguerite Yourcenar: A Reader's Guide,* University Press of America, 1987, 150 p.

PERIODICALS

Booklist, June 1, 1995, p. 1721; October 1, 1995, p. 253.

Classical and Modern Literature, winter, 1984, pp. 87-99.

Commentary, Vol. 74, No. 2, August, 1982, pp. 60-65.

Commonweal, August, 1982.

Essays in French Literature, Number 23, November, 1986, pp. 60-70.

Globe & Mail (Toronto), November 16, 1985; November 15, 1986; January 24, 1987.

Harper's, October, 1984.

Hudson Review, winter, 1976-77.

Library Journal, May 15, 1995, p. 70; September 15, 1995, p. 96.

London Review of Books, August 20, 1992, p. 22.

Los Angeles Times, November 28, 1986; June 26, 1987.

Los Angeles Times Book Review, October 3, 1982; February 3, 1985; November 3, 1985; June 21, 1992, p. 11.

Ms., August, 1976.

Nation, December 25, 1954; October 30, 1976.

New Republic, January 10-17, 1983.

New Yorker, June 14, 1976; August 17, 1981, pp. 104-6; February 11, 1985; July 13, 1992.

New York Herald Tribune Book Review, November 21, 1954.

New York Review of Books, October 14, 1976; October 10, 1985; December 5, 1985; January 16, 1992, pp. 30-33; October 19, 1995, p. 49.

New York Times, December 3, 1979; March 7, 1980; December 27, 1984; April 10, 1987.

New York Times Book Review, August 25, 1968; July 11, 1976; October 4, 1981; January 30, 1983; September 16, 1984; February 24, 1985; September 22, 1985; December 5, 1985, p. 19; December 14, 1986; April 19, 1987; January 10, 1988; March 1, 1992, p. 13.

Partisan Review, summer, 1989, pp. 370-73.

Saturday Review, November 27, 1954; July 20, 1957; June 12, 1976; June, 1981.

Spectator, June 19, 1982; February 19, 1983; November 12, 1983.

Times Literary Supplement, October 3, 1968; August 6, 1971; August 23, 1974; March 3, 1978; April 4, 1980; May 29, 1981; August 13, 1982; October 8, 1982; April 1, 1983; July 22, 1983; February 17, 1984; November 30, 1984; November 8, 1985; February 2, 1990, p. 108; September 25, 1992, p. 36.

Washington Post, August 8, 1983.

Washington Post Book World, July 11, 1976; December 19, 1982; September 2, 1984; September 22, 1985; September 6, 1986; December 28, 1986; June 14, 1987; September 3, 1995, p.4.

Women's Review of Books, March, 1992, pp. 12-13.

World Literature Today, autumn, 1978; autumn, 1979; autumn, 1981; spring, 1982; autumn, 1984; summer, 1985; summer, 1986; winter, 1991, pp. 78-79; winter, 1992, p. 89.

Z

ZELAZNY, Roger (Joseph) 1937-1995
(Harrison Denmark)

PERSONAL: Born May 13, 1937, in Cleveland, OH; died June 14, 1995; son of Joseph Frank and Josephine (Sweet) Zelazny; married Sharon Steberl, December 5, 1964 (divorced, June 27, 1966); married Judith Alene Callahan, August 20, 1966; children: (second marriage) Devin, Trent (sons), Shannon (daughter). *Education:* Western Reserve University (now Case Western Reserve University), B.A., 1959; Columbia University, M.A., 1962.

CAREER: Writer, 1969-95. U.S. Social Security Administration, claims representative in Cleveland, OH, 1962-65, claims policy specialist in Baltimore, MD, 1965-69. Lecturer at colleges, universities, and at writing workshops and conferences. *Military service:* U.S. Army Reserve, 1960-66.

MEMBER: Authors Guild, Authors League of America, School of American Research, Science Fiction Oral History Association, Science Fiction Research Association, Science Fiction Writers of America (secretary-treasurer, 1967-68), Ohioana Library Association, Santa Fe Chamber of Commerce.

AWARDS, HONORS: Nebula Award, Science Fiction Writers of America, 1965, for best novella, "He Who Shapes," 1965, for best novelette, "The Doors of His Face, the Lamps of His Mouth," and 1975, for best novella, "Home Is the Hangman"; Hugo Award, World Science Fiction Convention, 1966, for best novel, *This Immortal,* 1968, for best novel, *Lord of Light,* 1975, for best novella, "Home Is the Hangman," 1983, for best novelette, "Unicorn Variations," 1986, for best novella, "Twenty-Four Views of Mount Fuji by Hokusai," and 1987, for best novelette, "Permafrost"; Prix Apollo, 1972, for French edition of *Isle of the Dead;* Guest of Honor, World Science Fiction Convention, 1974, Australian National Science Fiction Convention, 1978, and at numerous regional and local science fiction conventions; *Doorways in the Sand* named one of the best young adult books of the year, 1976, American Library Association; Balrog Award, 1980, for best story, "The Last Defender of Camelot," and 1984, for best collection, *Unicorn Variations; Locus* Award, 1984, for collection *Unicorn Variations,* and 1986, for novel *Trumps of Doom;* nominated for Nebula Award, 1994, for *A Night in the Lonesome October.*

WRITINGS:

SCIENCE FICTION NOVELS

This Immortal, Ace Books, 1966.
The Dream Master, Ace Books, 1966.
Lord of Light, Doubleday, 1967.
Isle of the Dead, Ace Books, 1969.
Creatures of Light and Darkness, Doubleday, 1969.
Damnation Alley, Putnam, 1969.
Jack of Shadows, Walker & Co., 1971.
Today We Choose Faces, Signet, 1973.
To Die in Italbar, Doubleday, 1973.
Doorways in the Sand, Harper, 1976.
Bridge of Ashes, New American Library, 1976.
(With Philip K. Dick) *Deus Irae,* Doubleday, 1976.
Roadmarks, Ballantine, 1979.
Changeling, Ace Books, 1980.
The Changing Land, Ballantine, 1981.
Madwand, Ace Books, 1981.
(With Fred Saberhagen) *Coils,* Simon & Schuster, 1982.
Eye of Cat, Ultramarine, 1982.
Dilvish, the Damned, Ballantine, 1983.
(With others) *Berserker Base,* Tor Books, 1985.
A Dark Traveling, Walker & Co., 1987.
(With Robert Sheckley) *Bring Me the Head of Prince Charming,* Bantam Books, 1991.
(With Robert Sheckley) *If at Faust You Don't Succeed,* Bantam Books, 1993.
(With Robert Sheckley) *A Farce to Be Reckoned With,* Bantam Books, 1995.
Card Sharks, edited by George R. R. Martin and Melinda M. Snograss, Baen (Riverdale, NY), 1996.
(With Jane Lindskold), *Donnerjack,* Avon Books, 1997.

"AMBER" SERIES

Nine Princes in Amber (also see below), Doubleday, 1970.
The Guns of Avalon (also see below), Doubleday, 1972.
Sign of the Unicorn (also see below), Doubleday, 1975.
The Hand of Oberon (also see below), Doubleday, 1976.
The Courts of Chaos (also see below), Doubleday, 1978.
The Chronicles of Amber (contains *Nine Princes in Amber, The Guns of Avalon, Sign of the Unicorn, The Hand of Oberon,* and *The Courts of Chaos*), Doubleday, 1979.
A Rhapsody in Amber (chapbook), Cheap Street, 1981.
Trumps of Doom, Arbor House, 1985.

Blood of Amber, Arbor House, 1986.

Sign of Chaos, Arbor House, 1987.

(With Neil Randell) *Roger Zelazny's Visual Guide to Castle Amber,* Avon, 1988.

Knight of Shadows, Morrow, 1989.

Prince of Chaos, Morrow, 1991.

STORY COLLECTIONS

Four for Tomorrow, Ace Books, 1967 (published in England as *A Rose for Ecclesiastes,* Hart Davis, 1969).

The Doors of His Face, The Lamps of His Mouth, and Other Stories, Doubleday, 1971.

My Name Is Legion, Ballantine, 1976.

The Last Defender of Camelot, Pocket Books, 1980.

Unicorn Variations, Pocket Books, 1983.

Frost and Fire: Fantasy and Science Fiction Stories, Morrow, 1989.

OTHER

(Author of introduction) Harlan Ellison, *From the Land of Fear,* Belmont/Tower, 1967.

(Author of introduction) Philip Jose Farmer, *A Private Cosmos,* Ace Books, 1968.

(Editor) *Nebula Award Stories 3,* Doubleday, 1968.

Poems, Discon, 1974.

(Author of introduction) Bruce Gillespie, editor, *Philip K. Dick: Electric Shepherd,* Norstrilia Press, 1975.

(With Gray Morrow) *The Illustrated Roger Zelazny,* Baronet, 1978.

The Bells of Shoredan (booklet), Underwood/Miller, 1979.

When Pussywillows Last in the Catyard Bloomed (poems), Norstrilia Press, 1980.

For a Breath I Tarry, Underwood/Miller, 1980.

To Spin Is Miracle Cat (poems), Underwood/Miller, 1982.

He Who Shapes: The Infinity Box (novella), Tor Books, 1989.

Wizard World, Baen Books, 1989.

A Night in the Lonesome October (novel), illustrated by Gahan Wilson, Morrow, 1993.

(Author of introduction) Neil Gaiman, *The Books of Magic,* DC Comics (New York City), 1993.

(With Gerald Hausman) *Wilderness,* Forge, 1994.

(Editor) *The Williamson Effect,* Tor, 1996.

Contributor of more than one hundred stories, sometimes under pseudonym Harrison Denmark, to *New Worlds, Omni, Magazine of Fantasy and Science Fiction, Fantastic Stories, Amazing Stories,* and *Galaxy.*

SIDELIGHTS: Known for his colorful prose style and innovative adaptations of ancient myth, Roger Zelazny was a popular science fiction writer. His early works, first published in the 1960s, feature characters derived from Egyptian and Hindu mythology, while his more recent "Amber" series concerns a world existing in all times and places at once, and of which the Earth and other worlds are mere reflections. Speaking of the wide range of interests and approaches found in his work, Michael Vance of *Fantasy Newsletter* claims that Zelazny is "not easily categorized. He seems at home swimming with or against the main currents of science fiction. . . . [But] Zelazny wins awards and sells books because he weaves wordspells that transport readers into the farthest reaches of space or the darkest mysteries of magic with equal ease."

Zelazny's most important writings from his early period are novellas between 20,000 and 40,000 words in length. "A Rose for Ecclesiastes" and "The Doors of His Face, the Lamps of His

Mouth" have been cited by critics as among the best of his early work. Zelazny's novellas, George Warren writes in the *Los Angeles Times Book Review,* are "full of fantastic imagery and soaring, even overblown, poetry." Writing in *Voices for the Future: Essays on Major Science Fiction Writers,* Thomas D. Clareson claims that "A Rose for Ecclesiastes" "revitalized science fiction. . . . Zelazny introduced color, poetry, metaphor, and a deeper psychological dimension into science fiction." The story concerns an Earth man, Gallinger, who works on Mars as a translator of ancient religious texts. The Martian race is sterile and dying out. When Gallinger impregnates Braxa, a Martian woman with whom he has fallen in love, it promises a continuance of the Martian race. But Gallinger soon realizes that Braxa has never loved him, has only had his child to fulfill an old religious prophecy, and his ego is shattered. Gallinger attempts suicide. This painful episode leads him to undergo a dramatic personality change. Carl B. Yoke remarks that "in 'A Rose for Ecclesiastes' Zelazny brilliantly explores man's capability to grow from his experience."

Zelazny again borrowed from biblical precedents for the title of "The Doors of His Face, the Lamps of His Mouth," which is taken from the Book of Job. The protagonist of this story, Carlton Davits, is similar to the biblical Job as well. Both are wealthy, self-centered men. Davits is undone when he travels to Venus in quest of a giant sea creature never before caught by Earthlings. The creature wrecks his ship and kills six of his crew, and Davits is reduced to bankruptcy and alcoholism. But during a later trip in search of the creature, this time with his ex-wife, Davits succeeds in capturing and killing the monster. This triumph brings him to a new maturity. Like Gallinger in "A Rose for Ecclesiastes," Davits undergoes a personality change. In an article for *Extrapolation,* Yoke notes that "in the pattern of his development, Davits mirrors the psychological evolution of many Zelazny protagonists." Acknowledging the story's popularity among science fiction readers, Douglas Barbour of *Riverside Quarterly* refers to "The Doors of His Face, the Lamps of His Mouth" as "the now famous" story. Zelazny won a Nebula Award for the work.

By 1969, having established himself in the science fiction field, Zelazny left his job with the Social Security Administration to become a full-time writer. The career move entailed one major change in his writing. While employed with the government, Zelazny had been obliged to write relatively short works, stories he could finish in his spare time. But once he relied on science fiction for his livelihood, he relegated the shorter, less profitable works to secondary status and focused his attention on the writing of novels. As George R. R. Martin explains in the *Washington Post Book World,* "it was in the shorter forms that he first made a name for himself. Like many other writers, however, Zelazny was soon seduced away from his first love by the greater glory and riches of the novel."

Zelazny's first novel, *This Immortal,* was inspired in part by the author's experiences while serving in the Army's Arts, Monuments, and Archives unit, a department which preserves important historical and cultural landmarks in occupied foreign countries. In the novel, the alien Myshtigo is on a tour of Earth's cultural monuments, guided by the immortal Earthling Conrad. Myshtigo has bought the planet, long before devastated by nuclear war and conquered by the Vegans, and is now interested in learning something about his property. His unspoken desire is to determine whether Conrad is fit to lead the massive restoration effort Myshtigo plans for the ruined Earth.

The novel's focus is on Conrad's ability to overcome his long-standing antagonism to the aliens and see where both he and Myshtigo share common goals and concerns. His immortality has enabled Conrad to experience widely divergent aspects of life. Through this process he has learned that "things, places, people are real; judgments that might have applied to reality in the past, though, cannot be trusted," as contributor Joseph L. Sanders remarks in *Death and the Serpent: Immortality in Science Fiction and Fantasy.* By suppressing his strong aversion to the aliens and allowing himself to learn about Myshtigo, Conrad is eventually given leadership of the effort to restore the Earth, an effort that even the most persistent opponents of the Vegans support. "Conrad," Joseph V. Francavilla writes in *Extrapolation,* "passes from being a destroyer, disrupter, and fighter to being a creator, restorer, and peacemaker." "The main thing Zelazny shows about immortality in *This Immortal,*" Sanders writes, "is that the successful immortal, such as Conrad, who not only stays alive but does something satisfying with his life, does so by avoiding confinement within a set of rules or preconceptions." Writing in the *Dictionary of Literary Biography,* Yoke maintains that "the striking originality of the story and its characterization make [*This Immortal*] well worth reading." *This Immortal* won a Hugo Award in 1966.

Lord of Light is concerned with many of the same themes introduced in *This Immortal,* including personality growth, immortality, and the renewal of a planet. It is set on a far future world where technologically advanced human beings have set themselves up as gods over the less advanced populace. Taking the Hindu deities as their models, they have enhanced their mental powers through neurosurgery, hypnosis, and drugs to achieve a semblance of actual godlike ability. One of their number has succeeded in reaching inner perfection. When it becomes clear to him that his companions have become tyrants, he overthrows their system and frees the native population. *Lord of Light,* Yoke explains in the *Dictionary of Literary Biography,* "was hailed as a science-fiction classic" when it first appeared, and won Zelazny a Hugo Award.

Perhaps Zelazny's most ambitious project is the series of books set in the imaginary world of Amber; the series consists of a five-novel sequence, additional novels in a new, ongoing sequence, and a chapbook. The world of Amber transcends normal time and space limitations. It exists in all times at once, and its inhabitants are immortals who can time travel as they please between an endless multitude of alternate worlds. These alternate worlds, one of which is the Earth, are mere reflections of the one true world of Amber. As Edwin Morgan of the *Times Literary Supplement* maintains, "Amber is a place, a city, a state, a 'world'. . . . Amber is the perfect place, the Substance to which everything else is Shadow. It is not in our space and time, and its inhabitants, although they talk and act for the most part in human ways, are not human. Since they have enormous powers, they appear at times like gods."

The series follows the machinations among Amber's ruling family as they vie for power over multiple worlds. The first five novels form one complete story in which Corwin seeks the throne during a demonic invasion that threatens to reduce Amber and her shadow worlds to chaos. He begins the first novel with amnesia, his memory wiped clean by his rivals, and ends the fifth book as the ruler of Amber. "In the Amber series, as Corwin finally comes to understand," Sanders writes in his Zelazny bibliography, "life exists between two poles, Pattern and Chaos. Neither 'wins'. The difficult, creative tension between them continues, just as life

continues." Lester Del Rey, writing in *Analog: Science Fiction/ Science Fact,* warns that the Amber "books have to be read from first to last. They form a single novel, not a series of novels." He concludes with the comment that the five novels would have been a better story if written as a single book. "Had that been done," Del Rey writes, "this could well have been a genuinely superb piece of fantasy. As it is, it's a good story—no more." But Marshall B. Tymm, Kenneth J. Zoharski, and Robert H. Boyer have a more positive reaction to the five-novel Amber sequence in their *Fantasy Literature: A Core Collection and Reference Guide.* These books are, they claim, "on the whole excellent, both for their unusually original fantasy elements and for their literary qualities," and they judge Amber to be "one of the more ingeniously conceived secondary worlds in fantasy literature."

Later Amber novels concern the adventures of Corwin's son, Merlin, who is stalked through alternate worlds by an unknown group of assassins. Speaking of *Blood of Amber,* H. J. Kirchhoff of the Toronto *Globe and Mail* states: "As usual in the Amber books, Zelazny parlays hip dialogue, quirky characters and an anything-is-possible multiple universe into a winning swords-and-sorcery adventure." *Trumps of Doom,* the first in the new Amber series won a Locus Award in 1986. In the installments that followed, *Knight of Shadows* and *Prince of Chaos,* Merlin remains at the center of political intrigue involving the courts of Amber and Chaos against the descriptive background of cyberspace and computers. Critics generally regard these later volumes as an overextension of the series with diminishing results, described by *Kirkus Reviews* as "increasingly detached and irrelevant." A *Publishers Weekly* review of *Prince of Chaos* notes that the novel "fails to capture the spirit that rendered the five original Amber novels so enjoyable."

Zelazny received better reviews with his novel *A Night in the Lonesome October.* The work consists of thirty-one chapters, one for each day of October, and involves a large cast of literary and film legends, including Jack the Ripper, Sherlock Holmes, and Count Dracula. Narrated by Snuff, Jack the Ripper's dog, the macabre story records the alignment of various personages for and against the Earth-bound malevolent Elder Gods. *Wilson Library Bulletin* contributor Gene LaFaille praises the endearing Snuff character and Zelazny's fusion of "classical horror references" and "very offbeat fantasy that rambles tongue-in-cheek through our subconscious." Carolyn Cushman concludes in *Locus,* "All in all, this look at the lighter side of the dark is definitely amusing." According to a *Publishers Weekly* review, "its deft, understated good humor and spare, poetic prose reaffirm Zelazny as one of fantasy's most skilled practitioners."

Zelazny's work has explored a range of genre types during his career, moving from strict science fiction based on mythological models to an alternate world fantasy of castles, kings, and sword-wielding heroes. Charles Platt of the *Washington Post Book World* notes that "in his early work, . . . closely observed characters interacted with advanced technology; today, Zelazny deals more with sorcery than science, in fanciful mythic landscapes, laconically described. He still writes more fluently and with more authority than nine-tenths of his contemporaries." Lew Wolkoff of *Best Sellers* believes that Zelazny could handle both types of fiction well. "He can take a reader," Wolkoff writes, "on tour across a radiation-scarred America in one story and show him/her a wizards' duel in the next, swinging easily from hard science to dark fantasy."

Zelazny maintains a prominent position in contemporary science fiction. Martin places the book *The Doors of His Face, the Lamps of His Mouth, and Other Stories* "among the three best story collections of the last decade," and calls Zelazny "one of the most important contemporary science-fiction writers." "There is no question of his stature," Yoke writes in the *Dictionary of Literary Biography*. "He has contributed major works to the field, and perhaps more than any other writer has brought the techniques, style, and language of serious literature to science fiction. His greatest contribution, however, may be that he has brought to a literature famous for its cardboard figures, characters who are psychologically credible, who are sympathetic, who have scope and dimension." Clareson concludes that "Zelazny has dealt intelligently, lightly, and good-humoredly with a number of serious questions about the ways in which our fantasies mesh with our realities." Although holding some reservations about Zelazny's work, Clareson nevertheless believes he was "a story teller, an entertainer in the best sense," and praises his "exemplary craftsmanship, which . . . continued with few hiatuses throughout his career."

BIOGRAPHICAL/CRITICAL SOURCES:

BOOKS

Clareson, Thomas D., *Voices for the Future: Essays on Major Science Fiction Writers,* Bowling Green State University, 1979.
Collins, R. A., editor, *Scope of the Fantastic: Culture, Biography, Themes in Children's Literature,* Greenwood Press, 1985.
Contemporary Literary Criticism, Volume 21, Gale (Detroit), 1982.
Dictionary of Literary Biography, Volume 8: *Twentieth-Century American Science Fiction Writers,* Gale, 1981.
Krulik, Theodore, *The Complete Amber Sourcebook,* Avonva, 1996.
Krulik, Theodore, *Roger Zelazny,* Ungar, 1986.
Lindskold, Jane M., *Roger Zelazny,* Twayne, 1993.
Reilly, Robert, editor, *The Transcendent Adventure,* Greenwood Press, 1984.
Sanders, Joseph L., *Roger Zelazny: A Primary and Secondary Bibliography,* G. K. Hall, 1980.
Tymm, Marshall B., Kenneth J. Zoharski, and Robert H. Boyer, *Fantasy Literature: A Core Collection and Reference Guide,* Bowker, 1979.
Yoke, Carl B., *Roger Zelazny and Andre Norton: Proponents of Individualism,* State Library of Ohio, 1979.
Yoke, Carl B., *A Reader's Guide to Roger Zelazny,* Starmont, 1979.
Yoke, Carl B., and Donald M. Hassler, editors, *Death and the Serpent: Immortality in Science Fiction and Fantasy,* Greenwood Press, 1985.

PERIODICALS

Analog: Science Fiction & Fact, February, 1979; March 2, 1981; March, 1983; April, 1992, p. 166; August, 1993, p. 166.
Best Sellers, September, 1976; June, 1978.
Extrapolation, December, 1973; summer, 1980; spring, 1984.
Fantasy Newsletter, October, 1980; January, 1983; September, 1983.
Globe and Mail (Toronto), February 14, 1987; November 14, 1987.
Kirkus Reviews, October 1, 1989, p. 1438; September 15, 1991, p. 1190; October 1, 1991, p. 1250; February 1, 1995, p. 114.
Library Journal, September 15, 1969; June 15, 1989, p. 84; October 15, 1989, p. 105; October 15, 1991, p. 127;

November 15, 1991, p. 111; November 15, 1992, p. 122; July, 1993, p. 146; August, 1993, p. 160; February 1, 1994, p. 114; April 15, 1995, p. 119; April 15, 1996, pp. 72, 125.
Locus, October, 1983; July, 1993, p. 32.
Los Angeles Times Book Review, January 11, 1981.
Magazine of Fantasy and Science Fiction, May, 1971; August, 1974; February, 1982.
New York Review of Books, October 2, 1975.
New York Times Book Review, May 23, 1976; December 19, 1982; August 20, 1989, p. 24.
Observer, June 24, 1979.
People Weekly, September 4, 1989, p. 27.
Publishers Weekly, June 16, 1989, p. 60; October 6, 1989, p. 84; October 11, 1991, p. 52; July 26, 1993, p. 61; January 3, 1994, p. 71; April 22, 1996, p. 64.
Riverside Quarterly, June, 1970; August, 1973.
Science Fiction: A Review of Speculative Literature, June, 1978; December, 1979.
Science Fiction Chronicle, January, 1985.
Science Fiction Review, May, 1980; August, 1980.
Times Literary Supplement, February 29, 1968; March 28, 1968; February 13, 1981.
Washington Post Book World, December 23, 1979; January 25, 1981; December 25, 1983.
Wilson Library Bulletin, April, 1993, p. 107; September, 1993, p. 102.

*   *   *

ZINDEL, Paul 1936-

PERSONAL: Born May 15, 1936, in Staten Island, NY; son of Paul (a police officer) and Betty (a practical nurse; maiden name, Frank) Zindel; married Bonnie Hildebrand (a novelist), October 25, 1973; children: David Jack, Elizabeth Claire. *Education:* Wagner College, B.S., 1958, M.Sc., 1959.

ADDRESSES: Office—c/o Harper & Row Inc., 10 East 53rd St., New York, NY 10022-5244.

CAREER: Allied Chemical, New York City, technical writer, 1958-59; Tottenville High School, Staten Island, NY, chemistry teacher, 1959-69; playwright and author of children's books, 1969–. Alley Theatre, Houston, TX, playwright in residence, 1967.

MEMBER: Actors Studio.

AWARDS, HONORS: Ford Foundation grant, 1967, for drama; *The Pigman* was selected one of Child Study Association of America's Children's Books of the Year, 1968, and received the *Boston Globe-Horn Book* Award for Text, 1969; Outstanding Children's Book of the Year citations from *New York Times,* 1969, for *My Darling, My Hamburger,* 1970, for *I Never Loved Your Mind,* 1976, for *Pardon Me, You're Stepping on My Eyeball!* 1978, for *The Undertaker's Gone Bananas,* and 1980, for *The Pigman's Legacy;* Obie Award for the Best American Play from the *Village Voice,* Vernon Rice Drama Desk Award from the New York Drama Critics for the Most Promising Playwright, and New York Drama Critics Circle Award for Best American Play of the Year, all 1970, Pulitzer Prize in drama and New York Critics Award, both 1971, all for *The Effect of Gamma Rays on Man-in-the-Moon Marigolds;* Honorary Doctorate of Humanities from Wagner College, 1971; American Library Association's Best Young Adult Books citations, 1971, for *The Effect of Gamma*

Rays on Man-in-the-Moon Marigolds, 1975, for *Pigman,* 1976, for *Pardon Me, You're Stepping on My Eyeball!* 1977, for *Confessions of a Teenage Baboon,* 1980, for *The Pigman's Legacy,* and 1982, for *To Take a Dare; Media & Methods* Maxi Award, 1973, for *The Pigman;* New York Public Library "books for the teen age" citations, 1980, for *Confessions of a Teenage Baboon,* 1980, 1981, and 1982, for *The Effect of Gamma Rays on Man-in-the-Moon Marigolds,* 1981, for *A Star for the Latecomer,* and 1981 and 1982, for *The Pigman's Legacy;* New Jersey Library Association's Garden State Teen Book Award, 1997.

WRITINGS:

FOR YOUNG ADULTS, EXCEPT AS NOTED

The Pigman, Harper, 1968.
My Darling, My Hamburger, Harper, 1969.
I Never Loved Your Mind, Harper, 1970.
The Effect of Gamma Rays on Man-in-the-Moon Marigolds, Harper, 1971.
I Love My Mother (juvenile), illustrated by John Melo, Harper, 1975.
Pardon Me, You're Stepping on My Eyeball! Harper, 1976.
Confessions of a Teenage Baboon, Harper, 1977.
The Undertaker's Gone Bananas, Harper, 1978.
(With wife, Bonnie Zindel) *A Star for the Latecomer,* Harper, 1980.
The Pigman's Legacy, Harper, 1980.
The Girl Who Wanted a Boy, Harper, 1981.
(With Crescent Dragonwagon) *To Take a Dare,* Harper, 1982.
Harry and Hortense at Hormone High, Harper, 1984.
The Amazing and Death-Defying Diary of Eugene Dingman, Harper, 1987.
A Begonia for Miss Applebaum, Harper, 1989.
Attack of the Killer Fishsticks (juvenile), Bantam, 1993.
The Fifth-Grade Safari (Bantam), 1993.
Fright Party (juvenile), Bantam, 1993.
David & Della (juvenile), HarperCollins, 1993.
100% Laugh Riot (juvenile), Bantam, 1994.
Loch, HarperCollins, 1994, paperback edition, Hyperion, 1996.
The Doom Stone, HarperCollins, 1995, paperback edition, Hyperion, 1996.
Reef of Death, HarperCollins, 1998.

FOR ADULTS

When Darkness Falls, Bantam, 1984.
The Pigman and Me (autobiography) HarperCollins, 1992.

PLAYS

Dimensions of Peacocks, first produced in New York, 1959.
Euthanasia and the Endless Hearts, first produced in New York at Take 3, 1960.
A Dream of Swallows, first produced off-Broadway, April, 1962.
The Effect of Gamma Rays on Man-in-the-Moon Marigolds (first produced in Houston, TX, at Alley Theatre, May, 1964; produced off-Broadway at Mercer-O'Casey Theatre, April 7, 1970), illustrated by Dong Kingman, Harper, 1971.
And Miss Reardon Drinks a Little (first produced in Los Angeles at Mark Taper Forum, 1967, produced on Broadway at Morosco Theatre, February 25, 1971), Dramatists Play Service, 1971.
The Secret Affairs of Mildred Wild (first produced in New York City at Ambassador Theatre, November 14, 1972), Dramatists Play Service, 1973.
Let Me Hear You Whisper [and] *The Ladies Should Be in Bed* (*Let Me Hear You Whisper* was televised on NET-TV, 1966; *The Ladies Should Be in Bed* was first produced in New York, 1978), Dramatists Play Service, 1973, *Let Me Hear You Whisper* published separately, illustrated by Stephen Gammell, Harper, 1974.
Ladies at the Alamo (first produced at Actors Studio, May 29, 1975, produced on Broadway at Martin Beck Theatre, April 7, 1977, produced as *Ladies on the Midnight Planet,* in Hollywood at Marilyn Monroe Theatre, 1982), Dramatists Play Service, 1977.
A Destiny on Half Moon Street, first produced in Florida at Coconut Grove, 1985.
Amulets against the Dragon Forces (first performed by the Circle Repertory Company, New York, 1989), Dramatists Play Service, 1990.

SCREEN AND TELEVISION PLAYS

The Effect of Gamma Rays on Man-in-the-Moon Marigolds National Educational Television (NET), October 3, 1966.
Let Me Hear You Whisper, NET, 1966.
Up the Sandbox (based on Anne Roiphe's novel), National, 1972.
Mame (based on Patrick Dennis's novel *Auntie Mame*), Warner Bros., 1974.
Maria's Lovers, Cannon Films, 1984.
Alice in Wonderland, CBS-TV, December 9, 1985.
(With Djordje Milicevic and Edward Bunker) *Runaway Train* (based on a screenplay by Akira Kurosawa), Cannon Films, 1985.
(With Leslie Bricusse) *Babes in Toyland,* NBC-TV, 1986.

SIDELIGHTS: Paul Zindel is a best-selling author of young adult works who has pioneered the genre's break with romanticism toward a more realistic mode. Zindel's characters are often desperately unhappy. His stories do not have tidy endings or shallow platitudes about a perfect world. Quite the contrary: Zindel deals honestly with loneliness, eccentricity, escapism, sexual tension, and drug and alcohol abuse. As Theodore W. Hipple puts it in the *Dictionary of Literary Biography,* the author has produced "a steady stream of novels that explore teenagers' lives in realistic ways."

Zindel was a successful playwright before he began writing fiction. His theatrical experience has helped him to create teenaged characters who tell their life experiences in their own words. In *Elementary English,* Beverly A. Haley and Kenneth L. Donelson note that Zindel "looks at the world through the eyes of adolescents, many kinds of adolescents, all trying to find some meaning in a world apparently gone mad, all concerned with man's cruelty and 'matters of consequence.' By selecting an adolescent point of view, Zindel forces the reader to look at the world as if he were awakening to it for the first time, a kind of rebirth." *Dictionary of Literary Biography* contributor Ruth L. Strickland feels that much of the author's best material is autobiographical, "a working out and blending of his own past and his grotesque sense of humor." Strickland concludes of Zindel: "At his best he is sensitive, funny, warm, and perceptive, usually presenting an affirmation of life emerging even from the most desperate circumstances."

In 1951, at the age of fifteen, Zindel contracted tuberculosis. He spent eighteen months in a sanatorium where he was the only teenager. "Once again the world became something I could look at only through a frame," he said in the *New York Times.* "Big deal, Paul Zindel—fifteen years old, tubercular, loveless and desperate." After his cure, Zindel returned to Staten Island to finish his public education. By the time he graduated, he had attended four different high schools.

Zindel attended Wagner College on Staten Island, where he majored in chemistry and education. For a change of pace, he took a play writing course with noted author Edward Albee, and he found both course and teacher highly inspiring. Although he earned a master's degree in science—and taught high school chemistry for a decade—Zindel became passionately involved with the theater, writing plays in his spare time and attending professional productions. Some of his early plays, such as *Dimensions of Peacocks* and *A Dream of Swallows,* were staged in New York City in the early 1960s.

In 1964, Zindel's play *The Effect of Gamma Rays on Man-in-the-Moon Marigolds* had its premier at the Alley Theater in Houston. The play offers a piercing glimpse at the life of Tillie, a teenager who lives with her abusive mother and epileptic sister in conditions that threaten her sanity. For a school science project, Tillie raises marigolds that have been exposed to radiation, discovering that while some form only stunted flowers and leaves, others bloom wildly. The project echoes Tillie's dreary life and provides some hope that she will find fulfillment despite her mad family.

The Effect of Gamma Rays on Man-in-the-Moon Marigolds opened off-Broadway in 1970 and moved to Broadway the following year. It ran for 819 performances and won numerous prestigious theatrical awards, including the Obie Award, the New York Drama Critics Circle Award, and the Pulitzer Prize. Reflecting on his play in the foreword to the Bantam edition, Zindel says: "I suspect it is autobiographical, because whenever I see a production of it I laugh and cry harder than anyone else in the audience."

An early televised version of the play brought Zindel to the attention of Charlotte Zolotow, an editor at Harper and Row. Zolotow proposed that Zindel write a novel for teenagers. In 1968, Zindel published *The Pigman,* his first young adult book. Considered rather revolutionary in its time, *The Pigman* realistically documents the lives of two teens from dysfunctional families and their friendship with the elderly—and fragile—Mr. Pignati. The teens take turns narrating the story of their betrayal of Mr. Pignati's trust and his fatal reaction to their callousness. *Horn Book* reviewer Diane Farrell writes of the work: "Few books that have been written for young people are as cruelly truthful about the human condition. Fewer still accord the elderly such serious consideration or perceive that what we term senility may be a symbolic return to youthful honesty and idealism."

Zindel followed *The Pigman* with a number of controversial books about and for teens: *My Darling, My Hamburger,* about teenage pregnancy, *The Girl Who Wanted a Boy,* about a teen goaded into an improper love relationship, and *Harry and Hortense at Hormone High,* about two misfits and their eccentric classmates. Many of Zindel's stories are concerned with teenagers who are alienated from their parents and teachers, young people who struggle to find meaning and self-worth in a society that batters them. Zindel told the *English Journal* that sympathy for teenage readers serves two functions in his work: "Through pathos I can see the world as one of the most hilarious and comic places that there can be to live," he said. "Then, by use of pathos again, I can look at another element and see the world as quite ghastly, see it through very morbid eyes and find everything threatening and dangerous."

Zindel's message is not hopelessly grim, however. His young heroes and heroines discover their worth, connect with one another, and learn important lessons about life—sometimes the hard way. In facing ugly reality, they see beyond the ugliness to something better, and they strive for that better vision. "Teenagers *have* to rebel," the author told *Publishers Weekly.* "It's part of the growing process. In effect, I try to show them they aren't alone in condemning parents and teachers as enemies or ciphers. I believe I must convince my readers that I am on their side; I know it's a continuing battle to get through the years between twelve and twenty—an abrasive time. And so I write always from their own point of view."

Zindel continues to examine adolescents' relationships with adults through a variety of realistic characters. Michael J. Meyer points out in *Children's Literature Association Quarterly* that "Zindel's sympathetic portraits of abused male adolescents are especially valuable because he offers not only a picture of why such abuse occurs but also provides hope that the situation can be resolved positively." In *The Amazing and Death-Defying Diary of Eugene Dingman* Zindel's protagonist is more or less ignored by his dysfunctional parents. But during his summer as a waiter at an Adirondack resort, he finds surrogate mentors to learn from. In *David and Della* David Maholy's parents fax him messages from throughout the world but have a difficult time conversing with him in person. Stephen Mannes in *Washington Post Book World* says of the book, "Zindel hasn't lost a step in his ability to create snappy dialogue and . . . goofy but believable and endearing characters." However, Ruth E. Dishnow notes in *School Librarian* that "a reader may. . . . come off of Zindel's roller coaster feeling like he/she just ate too much cotton candy." The adults in *A Begonia for Miss Applebaum* and *Loch* are more loving, but their experiences directly impact the adolescent protagonists. Miss Applebaum is the favorite teacher of Henry and Zelda. When she is forced to retire due to her poor health (cancer), the two friends learn "important lessons about living life to the fullest, and about dying with dignity" from their former teacher, according to Linda Halpern in *Voice of Youth Advocates.* In *Loch* it is the children themselves who "help their father regain his self-respect," writes Connie Tyrrell Burns in *School Library Journal.*

More than twenty years ago Zindel quit teaching to become a full-time writer. "What I think of the world really is reflected in my books," he told the *English Journal.* "I see the world as a problem solving situation, and the solution of those problems through fiction seems to be the adventure that I've chosen for myself."

BIOGRAPHICAL/CRITICAL SOURCES:

BOOKS

Authors and Artists for Young Adults, Volume 2, Gale (Detroit), 1989.

Children's Literature Review, Volume 3, Gale, 1978.

Contemporary Authors New Revision Series, Volume 31, Gale, 1991.

Contemporary Literary Criticism, Gale, Volume 6, 1976; Volume 26, 1983.

Dictionary of Literary Biography, Volume 7: *Twentieth-Century American Dramatists,* Gale, 1981, pp. 368-73; Volume 52: *American Writers for Children since 1960: Fiction,* Gale, 1986, pp. 405-10.

Rees, David, *The Marble in the Water: Essays on Contemporary Writers of Fiction for Children and Young Adults,* Horn Book, 1980.

PERIODICALS

Booklist, October 1, 1993, p. 347; November 15, 1994, p. 591; September 15, 1995, p. 184; December 15, 1995, p. 698.
Children's Literature Association Quarterly, fall, 1992, p. 11.
Elementary English, October, 1974, pp. 941-45.
English Journal, October, 1977.
Horn Book, February, 1969; March-April, 1994, p. 209; May-June, 1995, p. 318.
Junior Bookshelf, June, 1994, p. 116.
Kirkus Reviews, April 1, 1989, p. 556.
Kliatt, January, 1991, p. 17.
New York Post, May 8, 1971; March 6, 1978.
New York Times, April 8, 1970; April 19, 1970; July 26, 1970; November 22, 1970; February 26, 1971; March 2, 1971; March 7, 1971; April 9, 1971; April 2, 1989; April 6, 1989.

Publishers Weekly, December 5, 1977; October 25, 1993, p. 64; October 17, 1994, p. 82; December 4, 1995, p. 63.
School Librarian, May, 1994, p. 63.
School Library Journal, March, 1992, p. 164; October, 1993, p. 136; January, 1995, p. 138; April, 1995, p. 37; December, 1995, p. 132; January, 1998, p. 43.
Voice of Youth Advocates, June, 1989, p. 109; February, 1994, p. 375; April, 1995.
Washington Post Book World, May 8, 1994, p. 20.

*   *   *

ZOILUS
See LOVECRAFT, H(oward) P(hillips)

Nationality/Ethnicity Index

This index lists writers alphabetically under their country of origin and/or their country of citizenship.
In some cases, an author's ethnic heritage is also indexed.

AFRICAN
ABRAHAMS, Peter (Henry)
ACHEBE, (Albert) Chinua(lumogu)
BETI, Mongo
BRINK, Andre (Philippus)
CAMPBELL, Roy
CLARK, John Pepper
COETZEE, J(ohn) M(ichael)
EKWENSI, Cyprian (Odiatu Duaka)
EMECHETA, Buchi
GORDIMER, Nadine
HEAD, Bessie
La GUMA, (Justin) Alex(ander)
LAYE, Camara
MAHFOUZ, Naguib
MATHABANE, Mark
MOFOLO, Thomas (Mokopu)
MPHAHLELE, Ezekiel
NGUGI WA THIONG'O
OKIGBO, Christopher
OKRI, Ben
PATON, Alan (Stewart)
p'BITEK, Okot
SENGHOR, Leopold Sedar
SMITH, Wilbur (Addison)
SOYINKA, Wole
TUTUOLA, Amos

AFRICAN AMERICAN
AMMONS, A(rchie) R(andolph)
ANGELOU, Maya
BALDWIN, James (Arthur)
BAMBARA, Toni Cade
BARAKA, Amiri
BONTEMPS, Arna(ud Wendell)
BROOKS, Gwendolyn
BROWN, Sterling Allen
BULLINS, Ed
BUTLER, Octavia E(stelle)
CAMPBELL, Bebe Moore
CHASE-RIBOUD, Barbara

CHESNUTT, Charles W(addell)
CHILDRESS, Alic
CLEAVER, (Leroy) Eldridge
CLIFTON, (Thelma) Lucille
CULLEN, Countee
DAVIS, Ossie
DELANEY, Samuel R(ay)
DOVE, Rita
Du BOIS, W. E. B.
ELLISON, Ralph (Waldo)
GAINES, Ernest J(ames)
GATES, Henry Louis, Jr.
GIOVANNI, Nikki
HALEY, Alex(ander Murray Palmer)
HAMILTON, Virginia
HANSBERRY, Lorraine (Vivian)
HAYDEN, Robert E(arl)
HIMES, Chester (Bomar)
HOOKS, bell
HUGHES, (James) Langston
HURSTON, Zora Neale
JOHNSON, Charles (Richard)
JOHNSON, James Weldon
JONES, Gayl
KINCAID, Jamaica
KING, Martin Luther, Jr.
KNIGHT, Etheridge
LITTLE, Malcolm
LORDE, Audre (Geraldine)
MADHUBUTI, Haki R.
MARSHALL, Paule
McMILLAN, Terry (L.)
McPHERSON, James Alan
MORRISON, Toni
MOSLEY, Walter
MYERS, Walter Dean
NAYLOR, Gloria
PARKS, Gordon
REED, Ishmael
SANCHEZ, Sonia
SHANGE, Ntozake

THOMAS, Joyce Carol
TOOMER, Jean
WALKER, Alice (Malsenior)
WALKER, Margaret (Abigail)
WIDEMAN, John Edgar
WILSON, August
WRIGHT, Richard (Nathaniel)

ALGERIAN
CAMUS, Albert
CIXOUS, Helene

AMERICAN
ABBEY, Edward
ADAMS, Alice (Boyd)
ADAMS, Henry (Brooks)
ADLER, Mortimer J(erome)
AGEE, James (Rufus)
AIKEN, Conrad (Potter)
ALBEE, Edward (Franklin III)
ALEXIE, Sherman (Joseph)
ALGREN, Nelson
ALLEN, Paula Gunn
ALLISON, Dorothy
ALVAREZ, Julia
AMMONS, A(rchie) R(andolph)
ANAYA, Rudolfo A(lfonso)
ANDERSON, Maxwell
ANDERSON, Poul (William)
ANDERSON, Sherwood
ANGELOU, Maya
ANTHONY, Piers
ARENDT, Hannah
ARIAS, Ron(ald Francis)
ARNOW, Harriette
ASHBERY, John (Lawrence)
ASIMOV, Isaac
AUDEN, W(ystan) H(ugh)
AUSTER, Paul
BAKER, Nicholson
BAKER, Russell (Wayne)

BALDWIN, James (Arthur)
BAMBARA, Toni Cade
BANKS, Russell (Earl)
BARAKA, Amiri
BARNES, Djuna
BARTH, John (Simmons)
BARTHELME, Donald
BAUM, L(yman) Frank
BAXTER, Charles
BEAGLE, Peter S(oyer)
BEATTIE, Ann
BELL, Madison Smartt
BELLOW, Saul
BENCHLEY, Peter (Bradford)
BENET, Stephen Vincent
BERENDT, John (Lawrence)
BERGER, Thomas (Louis)
BERRY, Wendell (Erdman)
BERRYMAN, John
BETTELHEIM, Bruno
BISHOP, Elizabeth
BLACK ELK
BLOCH, Robert (Albert)
BLOCK, Lawrence
BLOOM, Harold
BLOUNT, Roy (Alton), Jr.
BLUME, Judy (Sussman)
BLY, Robert (Elwood)
BOGAN, Louise
BONTEMPS, Arna(ud Wendell)
BOWLES, Paul (Frederick)
BOYLE, Kay
BOYLE, T(homas) Coraghessan
BRADBURY, Ray (Douglas)
BRADLEY, Marion Zimmer
BRESLIN, James
BRODSKY, Joseph
BROOKS, Cleanth
BROOKS, Gwendolyn
BROWN, Dee (Alexander)
BROWN, Rita Mae
BROWN, Sterling Allen
BROWNMILLER, Susan
BRUCHAC, Joseph, III
BUCHWALD, Art(hur)
BUCK, Pearl S(ydenstricker)
BUCKLEY, William F(rank) Jr.
BUECHNER, (Carl) Frederick
BUKOWSKI, Charles
BULLINS, Ed
BURKE, Kenneth (Duva)
BURROUGHS, Edgar Rice
BURROUGHS, William S(eward)
BUTLER, Octavia E(stelle)
BUTLER, Robert Olen (Jr.)
CABELL, James Branch
CALDWELL, Erskine (Preston)
CALDWELL, Taylor
CALISHER, Hortense
CAMPBELL, Bebe Moore

CAMPBELL, Joseph
CAMPBELL, Roy
CAPOTE, Truman
CARD, Orson Scott
CARR, John Dickson
CARROLL, James P.
CARRUTH, Hayden
CARSON, Rachel (Louise)
CARVER, Raymond
CATHER, Willa Sibert
CATTON, (Charles) Bruce
CHANDLER, Raymond (Thornton)
CHASE-RIBOUD, Barbara
CHAVEZ, Denise (Elia)
CHEEVER, John
CHESNUTT, Charles W(addell)
CHILDRESS, Alice
CHOMSKY, (Avram) Noam
CIARDI, John (Anthony)
CISNEROS, Sandra
CLANCY, Thomas L.
CLARK, Mary Higgins
CLAVELL, James (duMaresq)
CLEARY, Beverly (Atlee Bunn)
CLEAVER, (Leroy) Eldridge
CLIFTON, (Thelma) Lucille
CODRESCU, Andrei
COMMAGER, Henry Steele
COMMONER, Barry
CONDON, Richard (Thomas)
CONNELL, Evan S(helby), Jr.
CONROY, (Donald) Pat(rick)
COOVER, Robert (Lowell)
CORMIER, Robert (Edmund)
CORNWELL, Patricia Daniels
CORSO, (Nunzio) Gregory
COUSINS, Norman
COWLEY, Malcolm
COZZENS, James Gould
CRANE, (Harold) Hart
CREELEY, Robert (White)
CREWS, Harry (Eugene)
CRICHTON, (John) Michael
CULLEN, Countee
CUMMINGS, E(dward) E(stlin)
DANTICAT, Edwidge
DAVIS, Ossie
DeLILLO, Don
de MAN, Paul (Adolph Michel)
De VRIES, Peter
DELANY, Samuel R(ay, Jr.)
DICK, Philip K(indred)
DICKEY, James (Lafayette)
DIDION, Joan
DILLARD, Annie
DISCH, Thomas M(ichael)
DOCTOROW, E(dgar) L(aurence)
DONLEAVY, J(ames) P(atrick)
DOOLITTLE, Hilda
DORRIS, Michael (Anthony)

DOS PASSOS, John (Roderigo)
DOVE, Rita (Frances)
DREISER, Theodore
D'SOUZA, Dinesh
Du BOIS, W. E. B.
DUNCAN, Robert (Edward)
DUNN, Katherine (Karen)
DURANG, Christopher (Ferdinand)
DURANT, Will(iam James)
DWORKIN, Andrea
EHRENREICH, Barbara
EINSTEIN, Albert
ELIOT, T(homas) S(tearns)
ELKIN, Stanley L(awrence)
ELLIS, Alice Thomas
ELLIS, Bret Easton
ELLISON, Harlan (Jay)
ELLISON, Ralph (Waldo)
ELLMANN, Richard (David)
ELLROY, James
ERDRICH, Louise
ERIKSON, Erik H(omburger)
ESTLEMAN, Loren D.
FALUDI, Susan
FARRELL, James T(homas)
FAST, Howard (Melvin)
FAULKNER, William (Cuthbert)
FERBER, Edna
FERLINGHETTI, Lawrence
FIEDLER, Leslie A(aron)
FISHER, M(ary) F(rances) K(ennedy)
FITZGERALD, F(rancis) Scott (Key)
FOOTE, Shelby
FORCHE, Carolyn (Louise)
FORD, Richard
FRENCH, Marilyn
FRIEDAN, Betty (Naomi)
FRIEDMAN, Milton
FROST, Robert (Lee)
FULLER, R(ichard) Buckminster (Jr.)
FUSSELL, Paul
GADDIS, William
GAINES, Ernest J(ames)
GALBRAITH, John Kenneth
GARDNER, Erle Stanley
GARDNER, John (Champlin), Jr.
GASS, William H(oward)
GATES, Henry Louis, Jr.
GEISEL, Theodor Seuss
GIBBONS, Kaye
GIBSON, William
GIBSON, William (Ford)
GILCHRIST, Ellen
GILL, Brendan
GILMAN, Charlotte Perkins
GINSBERG, Allen
GIOVANNI, Nikki
GLASGOW, Ellen
GLUCK, Louise (Elisabeth)
GODWIN, Gail (Kathleen)

GORDON, Caroline
GOULD, Stephen Jay
GRAY, Francine du Plessix
GRAY, Spalding
GREELEY, Andrew M(oran)
GREEN, Julian (Hartridge)
GREY, Zane
GRISHAM, John
GRUMBACH, Doris (Isaac)
GUARE, John
GUEST, Judith (Ann)
GUTERSON, David
HALBERSTAM, David
HALE, Janet Campbell
HALEY, Alex(ander Murray Palmer)
HALL, Donald (Andrew Jr.)
HAMILTON, Virginia
HAMMETT, (Samuel) Dashiell
HANSBERRY, Lorraine (Vivian)
HARDWICK, Elizabeth
HARJO, Joy
HAWKES, John
HAYCRAFT, Anna
HAYDEN, Robert E(arl)
HEINLEIN, Robert A(nson)
HELLER, Joseph
HELLMAN, Lillian (Florence)
HELPRIN, Mark
HEMINGWAY, Ernest (Miller)
HEMPEL, Amy
HENLEY, Elizabeth Becker
HERBERT, Frank (Patrick)
HERSEY, John (Richard)
HIAASEN, Carl
HIGHSMITH, (Mary) Patricia
HIJUELOS, Oscar
HILLERMAN, Tony
HIMES, Chester (Bomar)
HINOJOSA(-SMITH), Rolando (R.)
HINTON, S(usan) E(loise)
HOBAN, Russell (Conwell)
HOFFMAN, Alice
HOOKS, bell
HOPLEY-WOOLRICH, Cornell
HORGAN, Paul
HOWARD, Maureen
HOWE, Irving
HOWELLS, William Dean
HUBBARD, L(afayette) Ron(ald)
HUGHES, (James) Langston
HURSTON, Zora Neale
HWANG, David Henry
INGE, William Motter
IRVING, John (Winslow)
ISAACS, Susan
JACKSON, Shirley
JAKES, John (William)
JAMES, Henry
JARRELL, Randall
JEFFERS, (John) Robinson

JHABVALA, Ruth Prawer
JOHNSON, Charles (Richard)
JOHNSON, James Weldon
JONES, Gayl
JONG, Erica
JUSTICE, Donald (Rodney)
KAEL, Pauline
KANTOR, MacKinlay
KAUFMAN, George S.
KEILLOR, Garrison
KENNEDY, William
KEROUAC, Jack
KESEY, Ken (Elton)
KEYES, Daniel
KIENZLE, William X(avier)
KINCAID, Jamaica
KING, Martin Luther, Jr.
KING, Stephen (Edwin)
KINGSOLVER, Barbara
KINGSTON, Maxine Hong
KINNELL, Galway
KINSEY, Alfred C(harles)
KIRK, Russell (Amos)
KIZER, Carolyn (Ashley)
KNIGHT, Etheridge
KNOWLES, John
KOCH, Kenneth
KOSINSKI, Jerzy (Nikodem)
KUMIN, Maxine (Winokur)
KUNITZ, Stanley (Jasspon)
KUSHNER, Tony
L'AMOUR, Louis (Dearborn)
LARDNER, Ring(gold) W(ilmer)
LASCH, Christopher
LEAVITT, David
LEE, (Nelle) Harper
Le GUIN, Ursula K(roeber)
LEIBER, Fritz (Reuter, Jr.)
L'ENGLE, Madeleine
LEONARD, Elmore (John, Jr.)
LEVERTOV, Denise
LEVIN, Ira
LEWIS, (Harry) Sinclair
LEYNER, Mark
LIEBLING, A(bbott) J(oseph)
LINDBERGH, Anne Morrow
LIPPMANN, Walter
LITTLE, Malcolm
LONDON, John Griffith
LOOS, Anita
LORDE, Audre (Geraldine)
LOVECRAFT, H(oward) P(hillips)
LOWELL, Amy
LOWELL, Robert (Traill Spence, Jr.)
LOWRY, Lois
LUDLUM, Robert
LUSTBADER, Eric Van
MAAS, Peter
MacDONALD, John D(ann)
MacINNES, Helen (Clark)

MacKINNON, Catharine A.
MacLEISH, Archibald
MADHUBUTI, Haki R.
MAILER, Norman
MALAMUD, Bernard
MAMET, David (Alan)
MANCHESTER, William
MANN, (Paul) Thomas
MARQUAND, John P(hillips)
MARSHALL, Paule
MASLOW, Abraham H.
MASON, Bobbie Ann
MASTERS, Edgar Lee
MATTHIESSEN, Peter
MAUPIN, Armistead (Jones, Jr.)
McCAFFREY, Anne (Inez)
McCARTHY, Charles, Jr.
McCARTHY, Mary (Therese)
McCULLERS, (Lula) Carson (Smith)
McKAY, Festus Claudius
McINERNEY, Jay
McMILLAN, Terry (L.)
McMURTRY, Larry (Jeff)
McNALLY, Terrence
McPHEE, John (Angus)
McPHERSON, James Alan
MEAD, Margaret
MENCKEN, H(enry) L(ouis)
MENDEZ, Miguel
MENNINGER, Karl (Augustus)
MERRILL, James (Ingram)
MERTON, Thomas
MERWIN, W(illiam) S(tanley)
METALIOUS, Grace
MICHENER, James A(lbert)
MILLAR, Kenneth
MILLAY, Edna St. Vincent
MILLER, Arthur
MILLER, Henry (Valentine)
MILLETT, Kate
MILLHAUSER, Steven
MILOSZ, Czeslaw
MITCHELL, Margaret
MOMADAY, N(avarre) Scott
MOORE, Marianne
MORRIS, Wright
MORRISON, Toni
MORROW, James (Kenneth)
MOSLEY, Walter
MUKHERJEE, Bharati
MYERS, Walter Dean
NABOKOV, Vladimir (Vladimirovich)
NASH, (Fredric) Ogden
NAYLOR, Gloria
NEMEROV, Howard (Stanley)
NIN, Anais
NIVEN, Laurence Van Cott
OATES, Joyce Carol
OATES, Stephen B(aery)
O'BRIAN, Patrick

O'BRIEN, (William) Tim(othy)
O'CONNOR, (Mary) Flannery
ODETS, Clifford
O'HARA, Frank
O'HARA, John (Henry)
OLDS, Sharon
OLSEN, Tillie
OLSON, Charles (John)
O'NEILL, Eugene (Gladstone)
OZICK, Cynthia
PAGLIA, Camille (Anna)
PALEY, Grace
PARKER, Dorothy (Rothschild)
PARKS, Gordon
PAULING, Linus (Carl)
PERCY, Walker
PERCY, William Alexander
PERELMAN, S(idney) J(oseph)
PHILLIPS, Jayne Anne
PIERCY, Marge
PINSKY, Robert
PIRSIG, Robert M(aynard)
PLATH, Sylvia
PLIMPTON, George (Ames)
POHL, Frederik
POLLITT, Katha
PORTER, Katherine Anne
PORTER, William Sydney
POTOK, Chaim
POUND, Ezra
PROKOSCH, Frederic
PROULX, E(dna) Annie
PUZO, Mario
PYLE, Ernest Taylor
PYNCHON, Thomas (Ruggles, Jr.)
QUINDLEN, Anna
RAND, Ayn
RANSOM, John Crowe
RAWLINGS, Marjorie Kinnan
REED, Ishmael
REMARQUE, Erich Maria
REXROTH, Kenneth
RICE, Anne
RICE, Elmer (Leopold)
RICH, Adrienne (Cecile)
RICHTER, Conrad (Michael)
ROBBINS, Harold
ROBBINS, Thomas Eugene
ROBINSON, Edwin Arlington
ROETHKE, Theodore (Huebner)
ROGERS, Will(iam Penn Adair)
ROSSNER, Judith (Perelman)
ROTH, Henry
ROTH, Philip (Milton)
RUKEYSER, Muriel
RULE, Ann
RUNYON, (Alfred) Damon
SAGAN, Carl (Edward)
SAID, Edward W.
SALAS, Floyd Francis

SALINGER, J(erome) D(avid)
SANCHEZ, Sonia
SANDBURG, Carl
SANDOZ, Mari(e Susette)
SAROYAN, William
SARTON, (Eleanor) May
SCHAEFFER, Susan Fromberg
SCHLESINGER, Arthur M(eier), Jr.
SCHWARTZ, Delmore (David)
SCHWARTZ, Lynne Sharon
SENDAK, Maurice (Bernard)
SEXTON, Anne (Harvey)
SHANGE, Ntozake
SHAPIRO, Karl (Jay)
SHAW, Irwin
SHEED, Wilfred
SHELDON, Sidney
SHEPARD, Sam
SHIELDS, Carol
SHILTS, Randy
SHIRER, William L(awrence)
SIDDONS, (Sybil) Anne Rivers
SILKO, Leslie Marmon
SILVERBERG, Robert
SILVERSTEIN, Shel(by)
SIMIC, Charles
SIMON, (Marvin) Neil
SIMPSON, Louis (Aston Marantz)
SINCLAIR, Upton (Beall)
SINGER, Isaac Bashevis
SKINNER, B(urrhus) F(rederic)
SMILEY, Jane (Graves)
SMITH, Clark Ashton
SMITH, Martin Cruz
SNODGRASS, W(illiam) D(e Witt)
SNYDER, Gary (Sherman)
SONTAG, Susan
SOTO, Gary
SPIEGELMAN, Art
SPILLANE, Mickey
SPOCK, Benjamin (McLane)
STAFFORD, Jean
STEEL, Danielle (Fernande)
STEGNER, Wallace (Earle)
STEIN, Gertrude
STEINBECK, John (Ernst)
STEINEM, Gloria
STEINER, George
STEVENS, Wallace
STINE, R(obert) L(awrence)
STONE, Irving
STRAUB, Peter (Francis)
STURGEON, Theodore (Hamilton)
STYRON, William
SUSANN, Jacqueline
SWENSON, May
TALESE, Gay
TAN, Amy (Ruth)
TARKINGTON, (Newton) Booth
TATE, (John Orley) Allen

TAYLOR, Peter (Hillsman)
TERKEL, Studs
THEROUX, Paul (Edward)
THOMAS, Joyce Carol
THOMAS, Lewis
THOMPSON, Hunter S(tockton)
THURBER, James (Grover)
TOFFLER, Alvin
TOLAND, John (Willard)
TOOLE, John Kennedy
TOOMER, Jean
TRILLIN, Calvin (Marshall)
TRILLING, Diana (Rubin)
TRILLING, Lionel
TUCHMAN, Barbara W(ertheim)
TUROW, Scott
TYLER, Anne
UCHIDA, Yoshiko
UPDIKE, John (Hoyer)
URIS, Leon (Marcus)
VAN DOREN, Mark
VENDLER, Helen (Hennessy)
VIDAL, Gore
VIZENOR, Gerald
VOLLMANN, William T.
VONNEGUT, Kurt, Jr.
WAKOSKI, Diane
WALKER, Alice (Malsenior)
WALKER, Margaret (Abigail)
WALLACE, David Foster
WALLACE, Irving
WALLANT, Edward Lewis
WAMBAUGH, Joseph (Aloysius, Jr.)
WARREN, Robert Penn
WASSERSTEIN, Wendy
WATKINS, Gloria
WELTY, Eudora
WEST, (Mary) Jessamyn
WEST, Nathanael
WEST, Paul
WESTLAKE, Donald E(dwin)
WHARTON, Edith
WHITE, E(lwyn) B(rooks)
WHITE, Edmund (Valentine III)
WHITNEY, Phyllis A(yame)
WIDEMAN, John Edgar
WIESEL, Elie(zer)
WILBUR, Richard (Purdy)
WILDER, Laura (Elizabeth) Ingalls
WILDER, Thornton (Niven)
WILLIAMS, Tennessee
WILLIAMS, William Carlos
WILSON, August
WILSON, Edmund
WILSON, Edward O(sborne, Jr.)
WODEHOUSE, P(elham) G(renville)
WOLFE, Gene (Rodman)
WOLFE, Thomas (Clayton)
WOLFE, Thomas Kennerly, Jr.
WOLFF, Tobias (Jonathan Ansell)

WOODIWISS, Kathleen E(rin)
WOUK, Herman
WRIGHT, Charles (Penzel, Jr.)
WRIGHT, James (Arlington)
WRIGHT, Richard (Nathaniel)
YOURCENAR, Marguerite
ZELAZNY, Roger (Joseph)
ZINDEL, Paul

ANTIGUAN
KINCAID, Jamaica

ARGENTINIAN
BIOY CASARES, Adolfo
BORGES, Jorge Luis
CORTAZAR, Julio
PUIG, Manuel
SABATO, Ernesto (R.)

ASIAN-AMERICAN
HWANG, David Henry
KINGSTON, Maxine Hong
TAN, Amy (Ruth)
UCHIDA, Yoshiko

AUSTRALIAN
CALDICOTT, Helen (Mary)
CAREY, Peter
CLAVELL, James (duMaresq)
FRANKLIN, Miles
GREER, Germaine
HOPE, A(lec) D(erwent)
KENEALLY, Thomas (Michael)
MALOUF, (George Joseph) David
McCULLOUGH, Colleen
STEAD, Christina (Ellen)
WEST, Morris L(anglo)
WRIGHT, Judith (Arandell)

AUSTRIAN
BETTELHEIM, Bruno
BUBER, Martin
FREUD, Sigmund
HANDKE, Peter
HAYEK, F(riedrich) A(ugust von)
KAFKA, Franz
LORENZ, Konrad Zacharias
MUSIL, Robert (Edler von)
POPPER, Karl R(aimund)
RILKE, Rainer Maria
WITTGENSTEIN, Ludwig

BARBADIAN
CLARKE, Austin C(hesterfield)
LAMMING, George (William)

BELGIAN
de MAN, Paul (Adolph Michel)
LEVI-STRAUSS, Claude
SARTON, (Eleanor) May
SIMENON, Georges

BOTSWANAN
HEAD, Bessie

BRAZILIAN
AMADO, Jorge

BULGARIAN
CANETTI, Elias

CAMEROONIAN
BETI, Mongo

CANADIAN
ATWOOD, Margaret (Eleanor)
BELLOW, Saul
BLAIS, Marie-Claire
CALLAGHAN, Morley Edward
CLARKE, Austin C(hesterfield)
DAVIES, (William) Robertson
FRYE, (Herman) Northrop
GALBRAITH, John Kenneth
GALLANT, Mavis
HAILEY, Arthur
HEBERT, Anne
HIGHWAY, Tomson
KINSELLA, W(illiam) P(atrick)
KOGAWA, Joy Nozomi
LAURENCE, Margaret
LAYTON, Irving (Peter)
LEACOCK, Stephen (Butler)
MacLENNAN, (John) Hugh
MacLEOD, Alistair
MAILLET, Antonine
McLUHAN, (Herbert) Marshall
MONTGOMERY, L(ucy) M(aud)
MOORE, Brian
MOWAT, Farley (McGill)
MUNRO, Alice
MUKHERJEE, Bharati
ONDAATJE, (Philip) Michael
PERETTI, Frank E.
RICHLER, Mordecai
SHIELDS, Carol
SKVORECKY, Joseph (Vaclav)
TREMBLAY, Michel

CHILEAN
ALLENDE, Isabel
DONOSO, Jose
MISTRAL, Gabriela
NERUDA, Pablo

CHINESE
CH'IEN, Chung-shu
MAO, Tse-tung

COLOMBIAN
GARCIA MARQUEZ, Gabriel

CUBAN
ARENAS, Reinaldo
CABRERA INFANTE, G(uillermo)

CZECH
CAPEK, Karel
HASEK, Jaroslav (Matej Frantisek)
HAVEL, Vaclav
KAFKA, Franz
KUNDERA, Milan
SEIFERT, Jaroslav
SKVORECKY, Josef (Vaclav)
STOPPARD, Tom

DANISH
BLIXEN, Karen
HOEG, Peter

EGYPTIAN
MAHFOUZ, Naguib

ENGLISH
ACKROYD, Peter
ADAMS, Douglas (Noel)
ADAMS, Richard (George)
ALDISS, Brian W(ilson)
ALLINGHAM, Margery (Louise)
AMBLER, Eric
AMIS, Kingsley (William)
AMIS, Martin (Louis)
ANTHONY, Piers
AUDEN, W(ystan) H(ugh)
AYCKBOURN, Alan
AYER, A(lfred) J(ules)
BAINBRIDGE, Beryl (Margaret)
BALLARD, J(ames) G(raham)
BARFIELD, (Arthur) Owen
BARKER, Clive
BARNES, Julian (Patrick)
BARRIE, J(ames) M(atthew)
BATES, H(erbert) E(rnest)
BEERBOHM, (Henry) Max(imilian)
BELLOC, Hilaire
BENNETT, Alan
BENNETT, (Enoch) Arnold
BETJEMAN, John
BLAIR, Eric (Arthur)
BOWEN, Elizabeth (
BRADBURY, Malcolm (Stanley)
BRITTAIN, Vera (Mary)
BROOKE, Rupert (Chawner)
BROOKNER, Anita
BROPHY, Brigid (Antonia)
BRUNNER, John (Kilian Houston)
BYATT, A(ntonia) S(usan Drabble)
CALDWELL, Taylor
CARTER, Angela (Olive)
CARTLAND, Barbara (Hamilton)
CHALLANS, Mary
CHESTERTON, G(ilbert) K(eith)
CHRISTIE, Agatha (Mary Clarissa)
CHURCHILL, Winston
CLARK, Kenneth (Mackenzie)
CLARKE, Arthur C(harles)

COMFORT, Alex(ander)
COMPTON-BURNETT, I(vy)
CONNOLLY, Cyril (Vernon)
CONRAD, Joseph
COOKSON, Catherine (McMullen)
COOPER, Susan (Mary)
CORNWELL, David (John Moore)
COWARD, Noel (Peirce)
DAHL, Roald
DAY LEWIS, C(ecil)
DEIGHTON, Leonard Cyril
de la MARE, Walter (John)
DEXTER, (Norman) Colin
DOYLE, Arthur Conan
DRABBLE, Margaret
du MAURIER, Daphne
DURRELL, Lawrence (George)
EAGLETON, Terence (Francis)
ELIOT, T(homas) S(tearns)
ELLERMAN, Annie Winifred
ESSLIN, Martin (Julius)
EMPSON, William
FITZGERALD, Penelope
FLEMING, Ian (Lancaster)
FORD, Ford Madox
FORSTER, E(dward) M(organ)
FORSYTH, Frederick
FOWLES, John (Robert)
FRASER, George MacDonald
FRAYN, Michael
FRY, Christopher
GALSWORTHY, John
GARNER, Alan
GARNETT, David
GOLDING, William (Gerald)
GRAHAME, Kenneth
GRAVES, Robert (von Ranke)
GREENE, Graham Henry
GRIGSON, Geoffrey
HAGGARD, H(enry) Rider
HAILEY, Arthur
HALL, (Marguerite) Radclyffe
HARDY, Thomas
HARTLEY, L(eslie) P(oles)
HAWKING, Stephen W(illiam)
HERRIOT, James
HEYER, Georgette
HIBBERT, Eleanor Alice Burford
HODGSON, William Hope
HOLROYD, Michael
HOLT, Victoria
HOUSMAN, A(lfred) E(dward)
HOYLE, Fred
HUGHES, Ted
HUXLEY, Aldous (Leonard)
ISHERWOOD, Christopher
ISHIGURO, Kazuo
JHABVALA, Ruth Prawer
JOHNSON, Pamela Hansford
KAYE, M(ary) M(argaret)

KEYNES, John Maynard
KIPLING, (Joseph) Rudyard
KOESTLER, Arthur
LARKIN, Philip (Arthur)
LAWRENCE, D(avid) H(erbert)
LEAVIS, F(rank) R(aymond)
Le CARRE, John
LEHMANN, Rosamond (Nina)
LESSING, Doris (May)
LEVERTOV, Denise
LEWIS, (Percy) Wyndham
LEWIS, C(live) S(taples)
LIVELY, Penelope (Margaret)
LODGE, David (John)
LOWRY, (Clarence) Malcolm
MacINNES, Colin
MASEFIELD, John (Edward)
MAUGHAM, W(illiam) Somerset
McEWAN, Ian (Russell)
MILNE, A(lan) A(lexander)
MOORCOCK, Michael (John)
MORTIMER, John (Clifford)
MUGGERIDGE, Malcolm (Thomas)
MUNRO, H(ector) H(ugh)
MURDOCH, (Jean) Iris
NAIPAUL, V. S.
NESBIT, E(dith)
NORWAY, Nevil Shute
ORTON, John Kingsley
ORWELL, George
OSBORNE, John (James)
OWEN, Wilfred (Edward Salter)
PHILLIPS, Caryl
PINTER, Harold
POTTER, (Helen) Beatrix
POWELL, Anthony (Dymoke)
POWYS, John Cowper
PRIESTLEY, J(ohn) B(oynton)
PRITCHETT, V(ictor) S(awdon)
PYM, Barbara (Mary Crampton)
RATTIGAN, Terence (Mervyn)
RENDELL, Ruth (Barbara)
RHYS, Jean
RICHARDS, I(vor) A(rmstrong)
RUSHDIE, (Ahmed) Salman
RUSSELL, Bertrand
SACKS, Oliver (Wolf)
SACKVILLE-WEST, V(ictoria Mary)
SASSOON, Siegfried (Lorraine)
SAYERS, Dorothy L(eigh)
SHAFFER, Peter (Levin)
SHIEL, M(atthew) P(hipps)
SILLITOE, Alan
SITWELL, Dame Edith (Louisa)
SMITH, Florence Margaret
SNOW, C(harles) P(ercy)
SPENDER, Stephen (Harold)
STEWART, J. I. M.
STOPPARD, Tom
STRACHEY, (Giles) Lytton

SWIFT, Graham (Colin)
TAYLOR, A(lan) J(ohn) P(ercivale)
THOMAS, D(onald) M(ichael)
TOLKIEN, J(ohn) R(onald) R(euel)
TYNAN, Kenneth (Peacock)
USTINOV, Peter (Alexander)
WAIN, John (Barrington)
WARNER, Sylvia Townsend
WATERHOUSE, Keith (Spencer)
WAUGH, Evelyn (Arthur St. John)
WELDON, Fay
WELLS, H(erbert) G(eorge)
WEST, Paul
WEST, Rebecca
WHITE, Phyllis Dorothy James
WHITE, Theodore H(arold)
WILSON, A(ndrew) N(orman)
WILSON, Angus (Frank Johnstone)
WILSON, John (Anthony) Burgess
WINTERSON, Jeanette
WITTGENSTEIN, Ludwig
WODEHOUSE, P(elham) G(renville)
WOOLF, (Adeline) Virginia

FRENCH
ANOUILH, Jean (Marie Lucien Pierre)
APOLLINAIRE, Guillaume
ARAGON, Louis
ARTAUD, Antonin (Marie Joseph)
BARTHES, Roland (Gerard)
BEAUVOIR, Simone de
BECKETT, Samuel (Barclay)
BONNEFOY, Yves
BRETON, Andre
BUTOR, Michel (Marie Francois)
CAMUS, Albert
CHAR, Rene (-Emile)
CIXOUS, Helene
COCTEAU, Jean
COLETTE, (Sidonie-Gabrielle)
DERRIDA, Jacques
DURAS, Marguerite
FOUCAULT, Michel
GENET, Jean
GIDE, Andre (Paul Guillaume)
GOURMONT, Remy de
GRAY, Francine du Plessix
GREEN, Julian (Hartridge)
IONESCO, Eugene
LEVI-STRAUSS, Claude
MALRAUX, (Georges-)Andre
MARCEL, Gabriel Honore
MAURIAC, Francois (Charles)
MAUROIS, Andre
MERTON, Thomas
NIN, Anais
PROUST, Marcel
QUENEAU, Raymond
QUOIREZ, Francoise
ROBBE-GRILLET, Alain

SAINT-EXUPERY, Antoine de
SARRAUTE, Nathalie
SARTRE, Jean-Paul
SIMENON, Georges
THIBAULT, Jacques Anatole Francois
TOURNIER, Michel (Edouard)
TZARA, Tristan
VALERY, Paul
VIAN, Boris
YOURCENAR, Marguerite

GERMAN
AMICHAI, Yehuda
ARENDT, Hannah
BOELL, Heinrich (Theodor)
BRECHT, Bertolt
BUKOWSKI, Charles
EINSTEIN, Albert
ERIKSON, Erik H(omburger)
FRANK, Anne(lies Marie)
GRASS, Guenter (Wilhelm)
HEIDEGGER, Martin
HESSE, Hermann
HOCHHUTH, Rolf
JHABVALA, Ruth Prawer
MANN, (Paul) Thomas
REMARQUE, Erich Maria
RILKE, Rainer Maria
SACHS, Nelly
TILLICH, Paul (Johannes)

GREEK
CAVAFY, C(onstantine) P(eter)
ELYTIS, Odysseus
KAZANTZAKIS, Nikos

GUADELOUPEAN
CONDE, Maryse

GUATEMALAN
ASTURIAS, Miguel Angel

GUINEAN
LAYE, Camara

HAITIAN
DANTICAT, Edwidge

HISPANIC AMERICAN
ALVAREZ, Julia
ANAYA, Rudolfo A(lfonso)
ARENAS, Reinaldo
ARIAS, Ron(ald Francis)
CHAVEZ, Denise (Elia)
CISNEROS, Sandra
HIJUELOS, Oscar
HINOJOSA(-SMITH), Rolando (R.)
MENDEZ M., Miguel
SOTO, Gary

HUNGARIAN
ESSLIN, Martin (Julius)
KOESTLER, Arthur
LUKACS, Gyorgy (Szegedy von)

INDIAN
ANAND, Mulk Raj
DESAI, Anita
D'SOUZA, Dinesh
GANDHI, Mohandas Karamchand
MUKHERJEE, Bharati
NAIPAUL, V. S.
NAIPAUL, Shiva(dhar Srinivasa)
NARAYAN, R. K.
RAO, Raja
RUSHDIE, (Ahmed) Salman
SETH, Vikram
TAGORE, Rabindranath

IRISH
BECKETT, Samuel (Barclay)
BEHAN, Brendan (Francis)
BINCHY, Maeve
BOLAND, Eavan (Aisling)
BOWEN, Elizabeth
CARY, (Arthur) Joyce (Lunel)
COX, William Trevor
DAY LEWIS, C(ecil)
DONLEAVY, J(ames) P(atrick)
DOYLE, Roddy
DUNSANY, Lord
HEANEY, Seamus (Justin)
JOYCE, James (Augustine Aloysius)
KINSELLA, Thomas
MacNEICE, (Frederick) Louis
MOORE, Brian
O'BRIAN, Patrick
O'BRIEN, Edna
O'CASEY, Sean
O'FAOLAIN, Sean
O'FLAHERTY, Liam
SHAW, George Bernard
YEATS, William Butler

ISRAELI
AGNON, S(hmuel) Y(osef Halevi)
AMICHAI, Yehuda
OZ, Amos

ITALIAN
CALVINO, Italo
ECO, Umberto
FO, Dario
GINZBURG, Natalia
LAMPEDUSA, Giuseppi
LEVI, Primo
MORANTE, Elsa
MORAVIA, Alberto
PIRANDELLO, Luigi

JAMAICAN
McKAY, Festus Claudius
SIMPSON, Louis (Aston Marantz)

JAPANESE
ABE, Kobo
ENDO, Shusaku
ISHIGURO, Kazuo
KAWABATA, Yasunari
MISHIMA, Yukio
OE, Kenzaburo
SUZUKI, Daisetz Teitaro
TANIZAKI, Jun'ichiro

KENYAN
NGUGI WA THIONG'O

LEBANESE
GIBRAN, Kahlil

LESOTHAN
MOFOLO, Thomas (Mokopu)

MARTINICAN
CESAIRE, Aime (Fernand)

MEXICAN
AZUELA, Mariano
CASTELLANOS, Rosario
ESQUIVEL, Laura
FUENTES, Carlos
PAZ, Octavio
RULFO, Juan

NATIVE AMERICAN
ALEXIE, Sherman (Joseph)
ALLEN, Paula Gunn
BLACK ELK
BRUCHAC, Joseph III
DORRIS, Michael (Anthony)
ERDRICH, Louise
HALE, Janet Campbell
HARJO, Joy
HIGHWAY, Tomson
MOMADAY, N(avarre) Scott
SILKO, Leslie (Marmon)
VIZENOR, Gerald Robert

NEW ZEALANDER
ASHTON-WARNER, Sylvia
BEAUCHAMP, Kathleen Mansfield
CLUTHA, Janet Paterson Frame
MARSH, (Edith) Ngaio

NICARAGUAN
ALEGRIA, Claribel
CARDENAL, Ernesto
DARIO, Ruben

NIGERIAN
ACHEBE, (Albert) Chinua(lumogu)
CLARK, J(ohn) P(epper)
EKWENSI, Cyprian (Odiatu Duaka)
EMECHETA, (Florence Onye) Buchi
OKIGBO, Christopher
OKRI, Ben
SOYINKA, Wole
TUTUOLA, Amos

NORWEGIAN
HAMSUN, Knut
HEYERDAHL, Thor
UNDSET, Sigrid

PALESTINIAN
DARWISH, Mahmud
SAID, Edward W.

PERUVIAN
ALLENDE, Isabel
VARGAS LLOSA, Mario (Pedro)

POLISH
AGNON, S(hmuel) Y(osef Halevi)
CONRAD, Joseph
KOSINSKI, Jerzy (Nikodem)
MANDELSTAM, Osip (Emilievich)
MILOSZ, Czeslaw
ROSEWICZ, Tadeusz
SCHULZ, Bruno
SINGER, Isaac Bashevis
SZYMBORSKA, Wislawa

PUERTO RICAN
CRUZ, Victor Hernandez
FERRE, Rosario
SALAS, Floyd Francis

ROMANIAN
CODRESCU, Andrei
IONESCO, Eugene
TZARA, Tristan
WIESEL, Elie(zer)

RUSSIAN
AKHMATOVA, Anna
ASIMOV, Isaac
BABEL, Isaak (Emmanuilovich)
BRODSKY, Joseph
BUGAYEV, Boris Nikolayevich
BULGAKOV, Mikhail (Afanasevich)
GORKY, Maxim
LEONOV, Leonid (Maximovich)
MANDELSTAM, Osip (Emilievich)
MAYAKOVSKY, Vladimir
NABOKOV, Vladimir (Vladimirovich)
PASTERNAK, Boris (Leonidovich)
RAND, Ayn
SARRAUTE, Nathalie

SHOLOKHOV, Mikhail
SOLZHENITSYN, Aleksandr
TSVETAEVA (EFRON), Marina

SALVADORAN
ALEGRIA, Claribel

SCOTTISH
BARRIE, J(ames) M(atthew)
BUCHAN, John
GRAY, Alasdair (James)
LEIGH, Stephen (W.)
MacINNES, Helen (Clark)
SPARK, Muriel (Sarah)

SENEGALESE
SENGHOR, Leopold Sedar

SOUTH AFRICAN
ABRAHAMS, Peter (Henry)
BRINK, Andre (Philippus)
CAMPBELL, Roy
COETZEE, J(ohn) M(ichael)
GORDIMER, Nadine
HEAD, Bessie
La GUMA, (Justin) Alex(ander)
MATHABANE, Mark
MPHAHLELE, Ezekiel
PATON, Alan (Stewart)
SMITH, Wilbur (Addison)
TOLKIEN, J(ohn) R(onald) R(euel)

SPANISH
ALEIXANDRE, Vicente
BENAVENTE (y Martinez), Jacinto
BUERO VALLEJO, Antonio
CELA, Camilo Jose
GARCIA LORCA, Federico
GOYTISOLO, Juan
JIMENEZ, Juan Ramon
ORTEGA y GASSET, Jose
UNAMUNO (Y JUGO), Miguel de

ST. LUCIAN
WALCOTT, Derek (Alton)

SWEDISH
BERGMAN, (Ernst) Ingmar
LAGERLOEF, Selma
LAGERKVIST, Paer (Fabian)
SACHS, Nelly
SPIEGELMAN, Art
STRINDBERG, (Johan) August

SWISS
CANETTI, Elias
DUERRENMATT, Friedrich
FRISCH, Max (Rudolf)
HESSE, Hermann
JUNG, C(arl) G(ustav)

KUENG, Hans
PIAGET, Jean

SYRIAN
GIBRAN, Kahlil

TRINIDADIAN
NAIPAUL, Shiva(dhar Srinivasa)
NAIPAUL, V. S.

UGANDAN
p'BITEK, Okot

UKRAINIAN
AKHMATOVA, Anna

URUGUAYAN
ONETTI, Juan Carlos

WELSH
ABSE, Dannie
DAHL, Roald
FRANCIS, Dick
THOMAS, Dylan (Marlais)

WEST INDIAN
PHILLIPS, Caryl
RHYS, Jean
WALCOTT, Derek (Alton)

YUGOSLAVIAN
SIMIC, Charles

Genre/Subject Index

This index lists writers alphabetically under the genres for which they are most well known and under the principal subjects reflected in their work.

ADVENTURE FICTION
BURROUGHS, Edgar Rice
CONDON, Richard (Thomas)
CONRAD, Joseph
HAGGARD, H(enry) Rider
KIPLING, (Joseph) Rudyard
LONDON, Jack
SMITH, Wilbur (Addison)

ART
CLARK, Kenneth (Mackenzie)
LEWIS, (Percy) Wyndham
MALRAUX, (Georges-)Andre
PAGLIA, Camille (Anna)

ASTRONOMY
EINSTEIN, Albert
HAWKING, Stephen W(illiam)
HOYLE, Fred
SAGAN, Carl (Edward)

AUTOBIOGRAPHY/MEMOIR
ANDERSON, Sherwood
ANGELOU, Maya
ASHTON-WARNER, Sylvia
BEAUVOIR, Simone de
BLACK ELK
CHURCHILL, Winston
COUSINS, Norman
DINESEN, Isak
DURRELL, Lawrence (George)
FISHER, M(ary) F(rances) K(ennedy)
FRANK, Anne(lies Marie)
FRANKLIN, Miles
HALEY, Alex(ander Murray Palmer)
HERRIOT, James
LEVI, Primo
LEVI-STRAUSS, Claude
LINDBERGH, Anne Morrow
MAILER, Norman
MALCOLM X

MALRAUX, (Georges-)Andre
McCARTHY, Mary (Therese)
MERTON, Thomas
MILLER, Henry (Valentine)
NIN, Anais
O'CASEY, Sean
PERCY, William Alexander
PIRSIG, Robert M(aynard)
PROUST, Marcel
SARTON, May (Eleanor)
STEIN, Gertrude
THOMPSON, Hunter S(tockton)
TRILLIN, Calvin (Marshall)
WIESEL, Elie(zer)
WILDER, Laura Ingalls
WILSON, Edmund
WRIGHT, Richard (Nathaniel)

BIOGRAPHY
ACKROYD, Peter
ELLMANN, Richard (David)
HOLROYD, Michael
MAAS, Peter
MAILER, Norman
MANCHESTER, William (Raymond)
MAUROIS, Andre
OATES, Stephen B(aery)
RUSSELL, Bertrand
SACKVILLE-WEST, V(ictoria Mary)
SANDBURG, Carl
STONE, Irving
STRACHEY, (Giles) Lytton

CARTOONS/ILLUSTRATION
GEISEL, Theodore Seuss
PERELMAN, S(idney) J(oseph)
SENDAK, Maurice (Bernard)
SILVERSTEIN, Shel(by)
SPIEGELMAN, Art
THURBER, James (Grover)

CHILDREN'S/YOUNG ADULT FICTION
ADAMS, Richard (George)
BARRIE, J(ames) M(atthew)
BAUM, L(yman) Frank
BLUME, Judy (Sussman)
CLEARY, Beverly (Atlee Bunn)
COOPER, Susan (Mary)
CORMIER, Robert (Edmund)
DAHL, Roald
de la MARE, Walter (John)
FLEMING, Ian
GARNER, Alan
GEISEL, Theodor Seuss
GRAHAME, Kenneth
HAMILTON, Virginia
HINTON, S(usan) E(loise)
HOBAN, Russell (Conwell)
KAYE, M(ary) M(argaret)
KEENE, Carolyn
KIPLING, (Joseph) Rudyard
KONIGSBURG, E(laine) L(obl)
L'ENGLE, Madeleine
LEWIS, C(live) S(taples)
LIVELY, Penelope (Margaret)
LOWRY, Lois
MILNE, A(lan) A(lexander)
MONTGOMERY, L(ucy) M(aud)
MYERS, Walter Dean
NESBIT, E(dith)
POTTER, (Helen) Beatrix
SAINT EXUPERY, Antoine de
SENDAK, Maurice (Bernard)
STINE, R(obert) L(awrence)
THOMAS, Joyce Carol
THURBER, James (Grover)
UCHIDA, Yoshiko
WHITE, E(lwyn) B(rooks)
WILDER, Laura Ingalls
ZINDEL, Paul

CIVIL/HUMAN RIGHTS
ACHEBE, (Albert) Chinua(lumogu)

ALEGRIA, Claribel
ARENAS, Reinaldo
CALDICOTT, Helen (Mary)
COUSINS, Norman
EHRENREICH, Barbara
GANDHI, Mohandas Karamchand
KING, Martin Luther, Jr.
MALCOLM X
MOWAT, Farley (McGill)
NERUDA, Pablo
NGUGI WA THIONG'O
OLSEN, Tillie
ORWELL, George
OZ, Amos
PALEY, Grace
PATON, Alan (Stewart)
PAULING, Linus (Carl)
RICE, Elmer (Leopold)
RUKEYSER, Muriel
SINCLAIR, Upton
SPOCK, Benjamin (McLane)

EARTH SCIENCES
COMMONER, Barry
EINSTEIN, Albert
GOULD, Stephen Jay
HAWKING, Stephen
PAULING, Linus (Carl)
SAGAN, Carl (Edward)
THOMAS, Lewis
WILSON, Edward O(sborne)

ECONOMICS
FRIEDMAN, Milton
GALBRAITH, John Kenneth
HAYEK, F(riedrich) A(ugust von)
KEYNES, John Maynard
POUND, Ezra (Weston Loomis)

ENVIRONMENTAL ISSUES
ABBEY, Edward
BERRY, Wendell (Erdman)
CALDICOTT, Helen (Mary)
CARSON, Rachel (Louise)
COMMONER, Barry
DILLARD, Annie
FULLER, R(ichard) Buckminster, Jr.
LINDBERGH, Anne Morrow
LORENZ, Konrad Zacharias
MOWAT, Farley (McGill)

ESSAYS/SPEECHES
ADAMS, Henry (Brooks)
CHURCHILL, Winston
HIRAOKA, Kimitake
KING, Martin Luther, Jr.
LEVI, Primo
MILNE, A(lan) A(lexander)
PAGLIA, Camille (Anna)
PAZ, Octavio

POUND, Ezra (Weston Loomis)
SABATO, Ernesto (R.)
SAID, Edward W.
SHEED, Wilfrid (John Joseph)
SONTAG, Susan
STEINER, George
THURBER, James (Grover)
WHITE, E(lwyn) B(rooks)
WOOLF, (Adeline) Virginia

FEMINISM/WOMEN'S STUDIES
ATWOOD, Margaret (Eleanor)
BEAUVOIR, Simone de
BRITTAIN, Vera (Mary)
BROPHY, Brigid (Antonia)
BROWNMILLER, Susan
CARTER, Angela (Olive)
CATHER, Willa (Sibert)
DWORKIN, Andrea
EHRENREICH, Barbara
FALUDI, Susan
FRENCH, Marilyn
FRIEDAN, Betty (Naomi)
GILMAN, Charlotte Perkins
GREER, Germaine
HALL, (Marguerite) Radclyffe
LESSING, Doris (May)
MacKINNON, Catharine A.
MARSHALL, Paule
MILLETT, Kate
PIERCY, Marge
POLLITT, Katha
RICH, Adrienne (Cecile)
SARTON, (Eleanor) May
STEINEM, Gloria
WALKER, Alice (Malsenior)
WEST, Rebecca
WOOLF, (Adeline) Virginia

FILM/SCREENPLAYS
AGEE, James (Rufus)
AMBLER, Eric
ANDERSON, Maxwell
BENNETT, Alan
BERGMAN, (Ernst) Ingmar
COCTEAU, Jean
DAVIS, Ossie
HIRAOKA, Kimitake
JHABVALA, Ruth Prawer
LEONARD, Elmore (John, Jr.)
LOOS, Anita
MAMET, David (Alan)
PARKER, Dorothy (Rothschild)
PARKS, Gordon
PERELMAN, S(idney) J(oseph)
PUZO, Mario
RATTIGAN, Terence (Mervyn)
SHELDON, Sidney
SIMON, (Marvin) Neil
USTINOV, Peter (Alexander)

WALLACE, Irving
WATERHOUSE, Keith (Spencer)
WEST, Nathaniel
ZINDEL, Paul

GAY AND LESBIAN STUDIES
ARENAS, Reinaldo
BARNES, Djuna
BROWN, Rita Mae
DELANY, Samuel R(ay, Jr.)
DOOLITTLE, Hilda
DUNCAN, Robert (Edward)
DURRELL, Lawrence (George)
ELLERMAN, Annie Winifred
GENET, Jean
GIDE, Andre
GINSBERG, Allen
HALL, (Marguerite) Radclyffe
ISHERWOOD, Christopher
KUSHNER, Tony
LEAVITT, David
LORDE, Audre (Geraldine)
MANN, (Paul) Thomas
MAUPIN, Armistead
PAGLIA, Camille (Anna)
PROUST, Marcel
RICH, Adrienne (Cecile)
SACKVILLE-WEST, V(ictoria Mary)
SARTON, May (Eleanor)
SHILTS, Randy
STEIN, Gertrude
WHITE, Edmund (Valentine, III)
WINTERSON, Jeanette
WOOLF, (Adeline) Virginia

HISTORICAL FICTION
ACKROYD, Peter
BROWN, Dee (Alexander)
CHALLANS, Mary
CHASE-RIBOUD, Barbara
CLAVELL, James (duMaresq)
FAST, Howard (Melvin)
FRASER, George MacDonald
JAKES, John (William)
JHABVALA, Ruth Prawer
KANTOR, MacKinlay
KENEALLY, Thomas (Michael)
McCULLOUGH, Colleen
MICHENER, James A(lbert)
MITCHELL, Margaret (Munnerlyn)
OATES, Joyce Carol
O'BRIAN, Patrick
PASTERNAK, Boris (Leonidovich)
RICHTER, Conrad
STONE, Irving
UNDSET, Sigrid
URIS, Leon (Marcus)
VIDAL, Gore
WEST, Paul
YOURCENAR, Marguerite

HISTORY
ADAMS, Henry (Brooks)
ADLER, Mortimer J(erome)
BROWN, Dee (Alexander)
CATTON, Bruce
CHURCHILL, Winston
CLARK, Kenneth (Mackenzie)
COMMAGER, Henry Steele
CONNELL, Evan S(helby)
DURANT, Will(iam James)
FOOTE, Shelby
FRASER, (Lady) Antonia (Pakenham)
FUSSELL, Paul
HALBERSTAM, David
HALEY, Alex(ander Murray Palmer)
HORGAN, Paul
KIRK, Russell (Amos)
MAILLET, Antonine
OATES, Stephen B(aery)
SANDOZ, Mari(e Susette)
SCHLESINGER, Arthur M(eier), Jr.
SHIRER, William L(awrence)
TAYLOR, A(lan) J(ohn) P(ercivale)
TOLAND, John (Willard)
TUCHMAN, Barbara W(ertheim)
WHITE, Theodore H(arold)
YOURCENAR, Marguerite

HOLOCAUST LITERATURE
FRANK, Anne(lies Marie)
KENEALLY, Thomas (Michael)
KOSINSKI, Jerzy
OZICK, Cynthia
SPIEGELMAN, Art
STYRON, William
WIESEL, Elie(zer)

HORROR, SUPERNATURAL, AND GOTHIC FICTION
BARKER, Clive
BLOCH, Robert (Albert)
BRADBURY, Ray (Douglas)
HODGSON, William Hope
JACKSON, Shirley
KING, Stephen (Edwin)
KIRK, Russell (Amos)
LEVIN, Ira
LOVECRAFT, H(oward) P(hillips)
OATES, Joyce Carol
RICE, Anne
SMITH, Clark Ashton
STINE, R(obert) L(awrence)
STRAUB, Peter (Francis)

HUMOR/SATIRE
BAKER, Russell (Wayne)
BEERBOHM, (Henry) Max(imilian)
BLOUNT, Roy (Alton), Jr.
BRADBURY, Malcolm (Stanley)
BUCHWALD, Art(hur)
de VRIES, Peter

ELKIN, Stanley L(awrence)
KEILLOR, Garrison
LARDNER, Ring(gold) W(ilmer)
LEACOCK, Stephen (Butler)
LEWIS, (Harry) Sinclair
LEWIS, (Percy) Wyndham
LEYNER, Mark
MENCKEN, H(enry) L(ouis)
MUGGERIDGE, Malcolm (Thomas)
MUNRO, H(ector) H(ugh)
NASH, (Frederic) Ogden
PARKER, Dorothy (Rothschild)
PERELMAN, S(idney) J(oseph)
PORTER, William Sydney
ROGERS, Will(iam Penn Adair)
RUNYON, (Alfred) Damon
TRILLIN, Calvin (Marshall)
WHITE, E(lwyn) B(rooks)

INTERNATIONAL POLITICS
ALEGRIA, Claribel
BIYIDI, Alexandre
CALDICOTT, Helen (Mary)
CHOMSKY, (Avram) Noam
CHURCHILL, Winston
HAVEL, Vaclav
MALRAUX, (Georges-)Andre
MAO Tse-Tung
MPHAHLELE, Ezekiel
NERUDA, Pablo
RUSHDIE, (Ahmed) Salman
SAID, Edward W.
SOYINKA, Wole
VARGAS LLOSA, (Jorge) Mario
WELLS, H(erbert) G(eorge)

JEWISH LITERATURE
FRANK, Anne(lies Marie)
KOSINSKI, Jerzy (Nikodem)
MALAMUD, Bernard
MANDELSTAM, Osip (Emilievich)
OZ, Amos
OZICK, Cynthia
POTOK, Chaim
RICHLER, Mordecai
ROTH, Philip (Milton)
SACHS, Nelly
SIMON, (Marvin) Neil
SINGER, Isaac Bashevis
WALLANT, Edward Lewis
WIESEL, Elie(zer)
WOUK, Herman

JOURNALISM/WRITING
ABRAHAMS, Peter
BAKER, Russell (Wayne)
BUCKLEY, William F(rank), Jr.
BRESLIN, Jimmy
GILL, Brendan
HALBERSTAM, David

HERSEY, John (Richard)
KENNEDY, William
LIEBLING, A(bbott) J(oseph)
LIPPMANN, Walter
MENCKEN, H(enry) L(ouis)
MUGGERIDGE, Malcolm (Thomas)
ORWELL, George
PYLE, Ernest Taylor
QUINDLEN, Anna
RUNYON, (Alfred) Damon
THOMPSON, Hunter S(tockton)
TRILLIN, Calvin (Marshall)
WEST, Rebecca
WOLFE, Thomas Kennerly

LAW
MacKINNON, Catharine A.
MacLEISH, Archibald
MASTERS, Edgar Lee
MORTIMER, John (Clifford)
SARRAUTE, Nathalie
TUROW, Scott

LETTERS/CORRESPONDENCE
DURRELL, Lawrence (George)
GANDHI, Mohandas Karamchand
JAMES, Henry
MANN, (Paul) Thomas
MERTON, Thomas
MILLER, Henry (Valentine)
POUND, Ezra (Weston Loomis)
PROUST, Marcel
RILKE, Rainer Maria
WAUGH, Evelyn

LITERARY CRITICISM AND HISTORY
AIKEN, Conrad (Potter)
AUDEN, W(ystan) H(ugh)
BARTHES, Roland (Gerard)
BLOOM, Harold
BROOKS, Cleanth
BURKE, Kenneth (Duva)
CONNOLLY, Cyril (Vernon)
COWLEY, Malcolm
de MAN, Paul (Adolph Michel)
DERRIDA, Jacques
DIDION, Joan
EAGLETON, Terrence
ELIOT, T(homas) S(tearns)
EMPSON, William
ESSLIN, Martin (Julius)
FIEDLER, Leslie A(aron)
FORD, Ford Madox
FRYE, (Herman) Northrop
GASS, William H(oward)
GATES, Henry Louis, Jr.
GRIGSON, Geoffrey
HARDWICK, Elizabeth
HOWE, Irving

HOWELLS, William Dean
JAMES, Henry
KAEL, Pauline
LEAVIS, F(rank) R(aymond)
LEWIS, C(live) S(taples)
LODGE, David (John)
LUKACS, Gyorgy (Szegeny von)
MAUROIS, Andre
MENCKEN, H(enry) L(ouis)
NABOKOV, Vladimir (Vladimirovich)
NEMEROV, Howard (Stanley)
PINSKY, Robert
POUND, Ezra (Weston Loomis)
PRIESTLEY, J(ohn) B(oynton)
PRITCHETT, V(ictor) S(awdon)
RANSOM, John Crowe
REXROTH, Kenneth
RICHARDS, I(vor) A(rmstrong)
STEINER, George
TATE, (John Orley) Allen
TOLKIEN, J(ohn) R(onald) R(euel)
TRILLING, Diana (Rubin)
TRILLING, Lionel
TYNAN, Kenneth (Peacock)
UPDIKE, John (Hoyer)
VAN DOREN, Mark
VENDLER, Helen (Hennessy)
WARREN, Robert Penn
WILSON, Edmund

MAGIC REALISM
ALEGRIA, Claribel
ALLENDE, Isabel
ARIAS, Ron(ald Francis)
CORTAZAR, Julio
ESQUIVEL, Laura
FERRE, Rosario
GARCIA MARQUEZ, Gabriel
OKRI, Ben
RULFO, Juan

MODERNISM
ANDERSON, Sherwood
DOOLITTLE, Hilda
DOS PASSOS, John (Roderigo)
ELIOT, T(homas) S(tearns)
FAULKNER, William (Cuthbert)
FITZGERALD, F(rancis) Scott (Key)
HEMINGWAY, Ernest (Miller)
JOYCE, James (Augustine Aloysius)
LEWIS, (Percy) Wyndham
POUND, Ezra (Weston Loomis)
STEIN, Gertrude
WOOLF, (Adeline) Virginia

MUSIC
COWARD, Noel (Peirce)
MILLAY, Edna St. Vincent
MOORCOCK, Michael (John)

MYSTERY, CRIME, AND SUSPENSE FICTION
ALLINGHAM, Margery (Louise)
AMBLER, Eric
AUSTER, Paul
BARKER, Clive
BARNES, Julian (Patrick)
BLOCK, Lawrence
BUCHAN, John
BUCKLEY, William F(rank), Jr.
CARR, John Dickson
CHANDLER, Raymond (Thornton)
CHESTERTON, G(ilbert) K(eith)
CHRISTIE, Agatha (Mary Clarissa)
CLANCY, Thomas L.
CLARK, Mary Higgins
CORNWELL, Patricia Daniels
DEIGHTON, Leonard Cyril
DEXTER, (Norman) Colin
DOYLE, Arthur Conan
ELLROY, James
ESTLEMAN, Loren D.
FLEMING, Ian (Lancaster)
FORSYTH, Frederick
FRANCIS, Dick
FRASER, (Lady) Antonia (Pakenham)
GARDNER, Erle Stanley
GREELEY, Andrew M(oran)
GRISHAM, John
HAMMETT, (Samuel) Dashiell
HEYER, Georgette
HIAASEN, Carl
HIBBERT, Eleanor Alice Burford
HIGHSMITH, (Mary) Patricia
HILLERMAN, Tony
HOPLEY-WOOLRICH, Cornell
ISAACS, Susan
JAMES, P(hyllis) D(orothy)
KAYE, M(ary) M(argaret)
KEENE, Carolyn
KIENZLE, William X(avier)
Le CARRE, John
LEONARD, Elmore (John, Jr.)
LEVIN, Ira
LUDLUM, Robert
MacDONALD, John D(ann)
MacINNES, Helen (Clark)
MARSH, (Edith) Ngaio
MILLAR, Kenneth
MOSLEY, Walter
RENDELL, Ruth (Barbara)
SAYERS, Dorothy L(eigh)
SHIEL, M(atthew) P(hipps)
SIMENON, Georges
SMITH, Martin Cruz
SPILLANE, Frank Morrison
WAMBAUGH, Joseph (Aloysius, Jr.)
WEST, Morris L(anglo)
WESTLAKE, Donald E(dwin)
WHITNEY, Phyllis A(yame)

MYTHOLOGY AND FOLKLORE
AGNON, S(hmuel) Y(osef Halevi)
BRUCHAC, Joseph, III
CAMPBELL, Joseph
CARTER, Angela (Olive)
GARCIA MARQUEZ, Gabriel
GARNER, Alan
GRAVES, Robert (von Ranke)
HURSTON, Zora Neale
SINGER, Isaac Bashevis
YEATS, William Butler

PHILOSOPHY
ADLER, Mortimer J(erome)
ARENDT, Hannah
AYER, A(lfred) J(ules)
BUBER, Martin
BURKE, Kenneth (Duva)
CANETTI, Elias
de MAN, Paul
FOUCAULT, Michel
FULLER, R(ichard) Buckminster, Jr.
GANDHI, Mohandas Karamchand
GIBRAN, Kahlil
HEIDEGGER, Martin
LUKACS, Gyorgy (Szegeny von)
MARCEL, Gabriel Honore
MURDOCH, (Jean) Iris
MUSIL, Robert (Edler von)
ORTEGA y GASSET, Jose
POPPER, Karl R(aimund)
RAND, Ayn
RUSSELL, Bertrand (Arthur William)
SARTRE, Jean-Paul
SUZUKI, Daisetz Teitaro
TILLICH, Paul
WITTGENSTEIN, Ludwig

PLAYS
ABE, Kobo
ABSE, Dannie
ALBEE, Edward (Franklin III)
ANOUILH, Jean
ARTAUD, Antonin (Marie Joseph)
AYCKBOURN, Alan
BARAKA, Amiri
BECKETT, Samuel (Barclay)
BELY, Andrey
BENAVENTE (y Martinez), Jacinto
BRECHT, Bertolt
BUERO VALLEJO, Antonio
BULGAKOV, Mikhail (Afanas'evich)
BULLINS, Ed
CLARK, John Pepper
COCTEAU, Jean
COWARD, Noel (Peirce)
DUERRENMATT, Friedrich
DURANG, Christopher
FERBER, Edna
FO, Dario

FRAYN, Michael
FRISCH, Max (Rudolf)
FRY, Christopher
GARCIA LORCA, Federico
GIBSON, William
GRAY, Spalding
GUARE, John
HANDKE, Peter
HANSBERRY, Lorraine (Vivian)
HAVEL, Vaclav
HELLMAN, Lillian (Florence)
HIGHWAY, Tomson
HOCHHUTH, Rolf
HWANG, David Henry
INGE, William Motter
IONESCO, Eugene
KAUFMAN, George S.
KOCH, Kenneth
KUSHNER, Tony
LEVIN, Ira
MAILLET, Antonine
MAMET, David (Alan)
MARCEL, Gabriel Honore
MAUGHAM, W(illiam) Somerset
McNALLY, Terrence
MILLER, Arthur
MISHIMA, Yukio
MORTIMER, John (Clifford)
O'CASEY, Sean
ODETS, Clifford
O'NEILL, Eugene (Gladstone)
ORTON, John Kingsley
OSBORNE, John (James)
PINTER, Harold
PIRANDELLO, Luigi
PRIESTLEY, J(ohn) B(oynton)
RATTIGAN, Terence (Mervyn)
RICE, Elmer (Leopold)
SHAFFER, Peter (Levin)
SHANGE, Ntozake
SHAW, George Bernard
SHEPARD, Sam(uel)
SIMON, (Marvin) Neil
SOYINKA, Wole
STOPPARD, Tom
STRINDBERG, (Johan) August
USTINOV, Peter (Alexander)
WASSERSTEIN, Wendy
WATERHOUSE, Keith (Spencer)
WILDER, Thornton (Niven)
WILLIAMS, Tennessee
WILSON, August
YEATS, William Butler
ZINDEL, Paul

POETRY
ABSE, Dannie
ACKROYD, Peter
AIKEN, Conrad (Potter)
AKHMATOVA, Anna

ALEIXANDRE, Vicente
ALEXIE, Sherman (Joseph)
AMICHAI, Yehuda
AMMONS, A(rchie) R(andolph)
ANGELOU, Maya
APOLLINAIRE, Guillaume
ARAGON, Louis
ASHBERY, John (Lawrence)
AUDEN, W(ystan) H(ugh)
BARAKA, Amiri
BELLOC, Hilaire
BENET, Stephen Vincent
BERRYMAN, John
BETJEMAN, John
BISHOP, Elizabeth
BLY, Robert (Elwood)
BOGAN, Louise
BOLAND, Eavan (Aisling)
BONNEFOY, Yves
BRETON, Andre
BRODSKY, Joseph
BROOKE, Rupert (Chawner)
BROOKS, Gwendolyn
BROWN, Sterling Allen
BRUCHAC, Joseph, III
BUKOWSKI, Charles
CAMPBELL, Roy
CARDENAL, Ernesto
CARROLL, James P.
CARRUTH, Hayden
CAVAFY, C(onstantine) P(eter)
CESAIRE, Aime (Fernand)
CHAR, Rene(-Emile)
CHESTERTON, G(ilbert) K(eith)
CIARDI, John (Anthony)
CLARK, John Pepper
CLIFTON, (Thelma) Lucille
COCTEAU, Jean
CORSO, (Nunzio) Gregory
CRANE, (Harold) Hart
CREELEY, Robert (White)
CRUZ, Victor Hernandez
CULLEN, Countee
CUMMINGS, E(dward) E(stlin)
DARIO, Ruben
DARWISH, Mahmud
DAY LEWIS, C(ecil)
de la MARE, Walter
DICKEY, James (Lafayette)
DOOLITTLE, Hilda
DOVE, Rita (Frances)
DUNCAN, Robert (Edward)
DURRELL, Lawrence (George)
ELIOT, T(homas) S(tearns)
ELYTIS, Odysseus
FERLINGHETTI, Lawrence
FORCHE, Carolyn (Louise)
FROST, Robert (Lee)
GARCIA LORCA, Federico
GIBRAN, Kahlil

GINSBERG, Allen
GIOVANNI, Nikki
GLUCK, Louise (Elisabeth)
GORKY, Maxim
GOURMONT, Remy de
GRAVES, Robert (von Ranke)
GRIGSON, Geoffrey
HALL, Donald (Andrew, Jr.)
HARJO, Joy
HAYDEN, Robert E(arl)
HEANEY, Seamus (Justin)
HEBERT, Anne
HOPE, A(lec) D(erwent)
HOUSMAN, A(lfred) E(dward)
HUGHES, Ted
JARRELL, Randall
JEFFERS, (John) Robinson
JIMENEZ (Mantecon), Juan Ramon
JUSTICE, Donald (Rodney)
KEROUAC, Jack
KINNELL, Galway
KINSELLA, Thomas
KIPLING, (Joseph) Rudyard
KIZER, Carolyn (Ashley)
KNIGHT, Etheridge
KOCH, Kenneth
KUMIN, Maxine (Winokur)
KUNITZ, Stanley (Jasspon)
LARKIN, Philip (Arthur)
LAYTON, Irving (Peter)
LEVERTOV, Denise
LORDE, Audre (Geraldine)
LOWELL, Amy
LOWELL, Robert (Traill Spence, Jr.)
MacLEISH, Archibald
MacNEICE, (Frederick) Louis
MADHUBUTI, Haki R.
MALOUF, (George Joseph) David
MANDELSTAM, Osip (Emilievich)
MASEFIELD, John (Edward)
MASTERS, Edgar Lee
MAYAKOVSKY, Vladimir
MERRILL, James (Ingram)
MERTON, Thomas
MILLAY, Edna St. Vincent
MILOSZ, Czeslaw
MISTRAL, Gabriela
MOORE, Marianne
NASH, (Frederic) Ogden
NEMEROV, Howard (Stanley)
NERUDA, Pablo
O'HARA, Frank
OKIGBO, Christopher
OLDS, Sharon
OLSON, Charles (John)
ONDAATJE, (Philip) Michael
OWEN, Wilfred (Edward Salter)
PASTERNAK, Boris (Leonidovich)
PAZ, Octavio
P'BITEK, Okot

PIERCY, Marge
PINSKY, Robert
PLATH, Sylvia
POLLITT, Katha
POUND, Ezra (Weston Loomis)
QUENEAU, Raymond
RANSOM, John Crowe
REED, Ishmael
REXROTH, Kenneth
RICH, Adrienne (Cecile)
RILKE, Rainer Maria
ROBINSON, Edwin Arlington
ROETHKE, Theodore
ROZEWICZ, Tadeusz
RUKEYSER, Muriel
SACHS, Nelly
SACKVILLE-WEST, V(ictoria Mary)
SANCHEZ, Sonia
SANDBURG, Carl
SARTON, (Eleanor) May
SASSOON, Siegfried (Lorraine)
SCHWARTZ, Delmore (David)
SEIFERT, Jaroslav
SETH, Vikram
SEXTON, Anne (Harvey)
SHAPIRO, Karl (Jay)
SIMIC, Charles
SIMPSON, Louis (Aston Marantz)
SITWELL, (Dame) Edith
SMITH, Stevie
SNODGRASS, W(illiam) D(e Witt)
SNYDER, Gary (Sherman)
SOTO, Gary
SPENDER, Stephen (Harold)
STEVENS, Wallace
SWENSON, May
SZYMBORSKA, Wislawa
TAGORE, Rabindranath
TATE, (John Orley) Allen
THOMAS, Dylan (Marlais)
TSVETAEVA, Marina (Ivanovna)
TZARA, Tristan
VALERY, Paul
VAN DOREN, Mark
WAKOSKI, Diane
WALCOTT, Derek (Alton)
WALKER, Margaret (Abigail)
WARREN, Robert Penn
WILBUR, Richard
WILLIAMS, William Carlos
WRIGHT, James (Arlington)
WRIGHT, Judith (Arandell)
WRIGHT, Charles (Penzel, Jr.)
YEATS, William Butler

POLITICS/GOVERNMENT
ALEGRIA, Claribel
ALLENDE, Isabel
ARENDT, Hannah
AZUELA, Mariano

BEHAN, Brendan
BIYIDI, Alexandre
BUCKLEY, William F(rank), Jr.
CESAIRE, Aime
CHURCHILL, Winston
COMMONER, Barry
FAST, Howard (Melvin)
GALBRAITH, John Kenneth
GANDHI, Mohandas Karamchand
KING, Martin Luther, Jr.
KIRK, Russell (Amos)
KOESTLER, Arthur
KUENG, Hans
LEONOV, Leonid (Maximovich)
LEVERTOV, Denise
LIPPMANN, Walter
LUKACS, Gyorgy (Szegeny von)
MALRAUX, (Georges-)Andre
MAO Tse-tung
MISTRAL, Gabriela
NGUGI WA THIONG'O
OKRI, Ben
ORTEGA y GASSET, Jose
PALEY, Grace
PAULING, Linus (Carl)
RICE, Elmer (Leopold)
SENGHOR, Leopold Sedar
SKVORECKY, Josef (Vaclav)
SNOW, C(harles) P(ercy)
THOMPSON, Hunter S(tockton)
TRILLIN, Calvin (Marshall)
VARGAS LLOSA, Mario
WHITE, Theodore H(arold)

POSTMODERNISM
AUSTER, Paul
BARTHELME, Donald
COOVER, Robert (Lowell)
DeLILLO, Don
FUENTES, Carlos

PSYCHOLOGY
BETTELHEIM, Bruno
ERIKSON, Erik H(omburger)
FREUD, Sigmund
JUNG, C(arl) G(ustav)
MASLOW, Abraham H.
MENNINGER, Karl (Augustus)
PIAGET, Jean
SACKS, Oliver (Wolf)
SKINNER, B(urrhus) F(rederic)
SPOCK, Benjamin (McLane)

RACE/CULTURAL ISSUES
ABRAHAMS, Peter (Henry)
ACHEBE, (Albert) Chinua(lumogu)
ALEXIE, Sherman (Joseph)
ALLEN, Paula Gunn
ALVAREZ, Julia

ANAND, Mulk Raj
ANAYA, Rudolfo A(lfonso)
ASHTON-WARNER, Sylvia
BALDWIN, James (Arthur)
BETI, Mongo
BLACK ELK
BONTEMPS, Arna(ud Wendell)
BRINK, Andre (Philippus)
BUCK, Pearl S(ydenstricker)
BUTLER, Octavia E(stelle)
CESAIRE, Aime (Fernand)
CHAVEZ, Denise (Elia)
CHESNUTT, Charles W(addell)
CHILDRESS, Alice
CLARKE, Austin C(hesterfield)
CLEAVER, (Leroy) Eldridge
CLIFTON, (Thelma) Lucille
COETZEE, J(ohn) M(ichael)
DESAI, Anita
D'SOUZA, Dinesh
Du BOIS, W. E. B.
ELLISON, Ralph (Waldo)
EMECHETA, (Florence Onye) Buchi
FAULKNER, William (Cuthbert)
GAINES, Ernest J(ames)
GATES, Henry Louis, Jr.
GORDIMER, Nadine
HALEY, Alex(ander Murray Palmer)
HEAD, Bessie
HIJUELOS, Oscar
HIMES, Chester (Bomar)
HOOKS, bell
HUGHES, (James) Langston
JHABVALA, Ruth Prawer
JOHNSON, Charles (Richard)
JOHNSON, James Weldon
JONES, Gayl
KING, Martin Luther, Jr.
KINGSTON, Maxine Hong
KOGAWA, Joy Nozomi
LAMMING, George (William)
LAYE, Camara
LEE, (Nelle) Harper
LESSING, Doris (May)
MADHUBUTI, Haki R.
MALCOLM X
MATHABANE, Mark
McKAY, Festus Claudius
McLUHAN, (Herbert) Marshall
MEAD, Margaret
MENDEZ M., Miguel
MOFOLO, Thomas (Mokopu)
MOMADAY, N(avarre) Scott
MORRISON, Toni
MPHAHLELE, Ezekiel
MUKHERJEE, Bharati
NAIPAUL, V(idiadhar) S(urajprasad)
NARAYAN, R. K.
NAYLOR, Gloria
NGUGI WA THIONG'O

PARKS, Gordon
PATON, Alan (Stewart)
P'BITEK, Okot
PHILLIPS, Caryl
REED, Ishmael
SANCHEZ, Sonia
SANDOZ, Mari(e Susette)
SHANGE, Ntozake
SILKO, Leslie Marmon
SOYINKA, Wole
STYRON, William
TAN, Amy
TOOMER, Jean
TUTU, Desmond M(pilo)
UCHIDA, Yoshiko
VIZENOR, Gerald Robert
WALKER, Alice (Malsenior)
WIDEMAN, John Edgar
WILSON, August
WRIGHT, Richard (Nathaniel)

RELIGION/THEOLOGY
ADLER, Mortimer J(erome)
AGNON, S(hmuel) Y(osef Halevi)
BELLOC, Hilaire
BOELL, Heinrich (Theodor)
BUBER, Martin
BUECHNER, (Carl) Frederick
CARROLL, James P.
CHESTERTON, G(ilbert) K(eith)
ENDO, Shusaku
GREENE, Grahame
HUBBARD, L(afayette) Ron(ald)
KAZANTZAKIS, Nikos
KING, Martin Luther, Jr.
KUENG, Hans
L'ENGLE, Madeleine
LEWIS, C(live) S(taples)
MERTON, Thomas
MORROW, James (Kenneth)
MUGGERIDGE, Malcolm (Thomas)
O'CONNOR, (Mary) Flannery
PERETTI, Frank
SAYERS, Dorothy L(eigh)
SUZUKI, Daisetz Teitaro
TILLICH, Paul (Johannes)
TUTU, Desmond M(pilo)
UNDSET, Sigrid

ROMANCE FICTION
CALDWELL, (Janet Miriam) Taylor
CARTLAND, Barbara (Hamilton)
COOKSON, Catherine (McMullen)
Du MAURIER, Daphne
HEYER, Georgette
HIBBERT, Eleanor Alice Burford
HOLT, Victoria
KAYE, M(ary) M(argaret)
SIDDONS, (Sybil) Anne Rivers
STEEL, Danielle (Fernande)

SUSANN, Jacqueline
WOODIWISS, Kathleen E(rin)

SCIENCE
See ASTRONOMY
EARTH SCIENCES
ENVIRONMENTAL ISSUES
PSYCHOLOGY
SOCIAL SCIENCES

SCIENCE FICTION AND FANTASY FICTION
ADAMS, Douglas (Noel)
ALDISS, Brian W(ilson)
ANDERSON, Poul (William)
ANTHONY, Piers
ASIMOV, Isaac
BALLARD, J(ames) G(raham)
BAUM, L(yman) Frank
BEAGLE, Peter S(oyer)
BRADBURY, Ray (Douglas)
BRADLEY, Marion Zimmer
BRUNNER, John (Kilian Houston)
BURGESS, Anthony
BUTLER, Octavia E(stelle)
CABELL, James Branch
CALVINO, Italo
CAPEK, Karel
CARD, Orson Scott
CARTER, Angela (Olive)
CLARKE, Arthur C(harles)
COOPER, Susan (Mary)
DELANY, Samuel R(ay, Jr.)
DICK, Philip K(indred)
DISCH, Thomas M(ichael)
DUNSANY, Lord
ELLISON, Harlan (Jay)
GIBSON, William (Ford)
HEINLEIN, Robert A(nson)
HERBERT, Frank (Patrick)
HUXLEY, Aldous (Leonard)
Le GUIN, Ursula K(roeber)
LEIBER, Fritz (Reuter, Jr.)
L'ENGLE, Madeleine
LESSING, Doris (May)
McCAFFREY, Anne (Inez)
MOORCOCK, Michael (John)
MORROW, James (Kenneth)
NIVEN, Laurence Van Cott
POHL, Frederik
SILVERBERG, Robert
STURGEON, Theodore (Hamilton)
TOLKIEN, J(ohn) R(onald) R(euel)
VONNEGUT, Kurt, Jr.
WELLS, H(erbert) G(eorge)
WOLFE, Gene (Rodman)
ZELAZNY, Roger (Joseph)

SHORT STORIES
ACHEBE, (Albert) Chinua(lumogu)
AGNON, S(hmuel) Y(osef Halevi)

ALEXIE, Sherman (Joseph)
ALGREN, Nelson
ALLENDE, Isabel
ALLINGHAM, Margery (Louise)
ANDERSON, Sherwood
BABEL, Isaak (Emmanuilovich)
BAMBARA, Toni Cade
BARNES, Djuna
BARTH, John
BARTHELME, Donald
BATES, H(erbert) E(rnest)
BAXTER, Charles
BEATTIE, Ann
BERRY, Wendell (Erdman)
BIOY CASARES, Adolfo
BORGES, Jorge Luis
BOWEN, Elizabeth (Dorothea Cole)
BOYLE, Kay
BOYLE, T(homas) Coraghessan
BUKOWSKI, Charles
CALISHER, Hortense
CALLAGHAN, Morley Edward
CAREY, Peter
CARVER, Raymond
CHEEVER, John
CORTAZAR, Julio
COX, William Trevor
COZZENS, James Gould
DANTICAT, Edwidge
DINESEN, Isak
FAULKNER, William (Cuthbert)
FITZGERALD, F(rancis) Scott (Key)
FRANCE, Anatole
GALLANT, Mavis
GARCIA MARQUEZ, Gabriel (Jose)
GILCHRIST, Ellen
GORDON, Caroline
GUTERSON, David
HEMINGWAY, Ernest (Miller)
HEMPEL, Amy
HIRAOKA, Kimitake
HURSTON, Zora Neale
JACKSON, Shirley
JAMES, Henry
JOYCE, James (Augustine Aloysius)
KINCAID, Jamaica
LARDNER, Ring(gold) W(ilmer)
LAURENCE, Margaret
LAWRENCE, D(avid) H(erbert)
MAHFOUZ, Naguib
MALAMUD, Bernard
MANN, (Paul) Thomas
MANSFIELD, Katherine
MASON, Bobbie Ann
MAUGHAM, W(illiam) Somerset
McPHERSON, James Alan
MISHIMA, Yukio
MUNRO, Alice
MUNRO, H(ector) H(ugh)
OATES, Joyce Carol

O'CONNOR, (Mary) Flannery
O'FAOLAIN, Sean
O'FLAHERTY, Liam
O'HARA, John (Henry)
OLSEN, Tillie
OZICK, Cynthia
PALEY, Grace
PARKER, Dorothy (Rothschild)
PHILLIPS, Jayne Anne
PORTER, Katherine Anne
PORTER, William Sydney
PRITCHETT, V(ictor) S(awdon)
SAROYAN, William
SHAW, Irwin
SILKO, Leslie Marmon
SINGER, Isaac Bashevis
STAFFORD, Jean
TAYLOR, Peter (Hillsman)
UPDIKE, John (Hoyer)
VONNEGUT, Kurt, (Jr.)
WELTY, Eudora
WEST, (Mary) Jessamyn
WIDEMAN, John Edgar
WILSON, Angus (Frank Johnstone)
WOLFF, Tobias (Jonathan Ansell)

SOCIAL COMMENTARY

ABE, Kobo
ADAMS, Henry (Brooks)
AGEE, James (Rufus)
ALGREN, Nelson
AMADO, Jorge
ANAND, Mulk Raj
ANDERSON, Sherwood
ASTURIAS, Miguel Angel
BALDWIN, James (Arthur)
CANETTI, Elias
CLEAVER, (Leroy) Eldridge
DONOSO, Jose
DOS PASSOS, John (Roderigo)
D'SOUZA, Dinesh
ELLISON, Ralph (Waldo)
HAMSUN, Knut
HUXLEY, Aldous (Leonard)
JAMES, Henry
La GUMA, (Justin) Alex(ander)
LASCH, Christopher
LEONOV, Leonid (Maximovich)
LESSING, Doris (May)
LEVERTOV, Denise
LEWIS, (Harry) Sinclair
MATABANE, Mark
McLUHAN, (Herbert) Marshall
ODETS, Clifford
OE, Kenzaburo
O'FAOLAIN, Sean
O'FLAHERTY, Liam
OLSEN, Tillie
ORTEGA y GASSET, Jose
ORWELL, George

SINCLAIR, Upton (Beall)
SOLZHENITSYN, Aleksandr
STEINBECK, John (Ernst)
STEINEM, Gloria
TERKEL, Louis
THOMPSON, Hunter S(tockton)
TOFFLER, Alvin
TOURNIER, Michel (Edouard)
VIDAL, Gore
WHARTON, Edith (Newbold Jones)

SOCIAL SCIENCES

See also PSYCHOLOGY
BERRY, Wendell
CAMPBELL, Joseph
CANETTI, Elias
CHOMSKY, (Avram) Noam
COMFORT, Alex(ander)
HEYERDAHL, Thor
KINSEY, Alfred C(harles)
MEAD, Margaret
POPPER, Karl R(aimund)
RUSSELL, Bertrand
SPOCK, Benjamin (McLane)
TERKEL, Louis

SOUTHERN AMERICAN LITERATURE

CALDWELL, Erskine
CAPOTE, Truman
CREWS, Harry (Eugene)
FAULKNER, William (Cuthbert)
GAINES, Ernest J(ames)
GIBBONS, Kaye
GLASGOW, Ellen
GORDON, Caroline
HENLEY, Elizabeth Becker
LEE, (Nelle) Harper
MASON, Bobbie Ann
McCARTHY, Cormac
McCULLERS, (Lula) Carson (Smith)
O'CONNOR, (Mary) Flannery
PERCY, Walker
PERCY, William Alexander
TATE, (John Orley) Allen
TAYLOR, Peter (Hillsman)
WELTY, Eudora
WOLFE, Thomas (Clayton)

SURREALISM

ARTAUD, Antonin
BOWLES, Paul (Frederick)
COCTEAU, Jean
GENET, Jean
HAWKES, John
KOCH, Kenneth
NIN, Anais
QUENEAU, Raymond
SCHULZ, Bruno

TRAVEL/EXPLORATION

BUCK, Pearl S(ydenstricker)
DURRELL, Lawrence
FORSTER, E(dward) M(organ)
JAMES, Henry
KAZANTZAKIS, Nikos
LAWRENCE, D(avid) H(erbert)
LONDON, Jack
MATTHIESSEN, Peter
THEROUX, Paul (Edward)
WAUGH, Evelyn

TRUE CRIME

BERENDT, John (Lawrence)
CAPOTE, Truman
ELLROY, James
MAAS, Peter
RULE, Ann

WAR AND MILITARY

BROWN, Dee (Alexander)
BUTLER, Robert Olen, (Jr.)
HASEK, Jaroslav (Matej Frantisek)
HELLER, Joseph
HEMINGWAY, Ernest (Miller)
MAILER, Norman
O'BRIEN, (William) Tim(othy)
OWEN, Wilfred (Edward Salter)
PYLE, Ernie
REMARQUE, Erich Maria
ROZEWICZ, Tadeusz
SASSOON, Siegfried (Lorraine)
SHUTE, Nevil
STYRON, William
TOLAND, John (Willard)
VONNEGUT, Kurt, (Jr.)
WOUK, Herman

WESTERNS

BROWN, Dee (Alexander)
CATHER, Willa (Sibert)
ESTLEMAN, Loren D.
GREY, Zane
JAKES, John (William)
L'AMOUR, Louis (Dearborn)
LEONARD, Elmore (John, Jr.)
McMURTRY, Larry (Jeff)
RICHTER, Conrad (Michael)
ROGERS, Will(iam Penn Adair)
SANDOZ, Mari(e Susette)
WEST, (Mary) Jessamyn
WILDER, Laura Ingalls